The
World Book
Encyclopedia

M   Volume 13

World Book–Childcraft International, Inc.

A subsidiary of The Scott & Fetzer Company

Chicago London Paris Sydney Tokyo Toronto

The World Book Encyclopedia

Copyright © 1981, U.S.A.
by
World Book–Childcraft International, Inc.

Printed in the United States of America

ISBN 0-7166-0081-1

Library of Congress Catalog Card Number 80-50324

Mm

M is the 13th letter of our alphabet. It was also the 13th letter in the alphabet used by the Semites, who once lived in Syria and Palestine. They named it *mem*, their word for *water*, and adapted an Egyptian *hieroglyphic*, or picture symbol, for water. The Greeks called it *mu*. See ALPHABET.

Uses. *M* or *m* ranks as the 14th most frequently used letter in books, newspapers, and other printed material in English. It stands for *mile* or *meter* in measurements of distance. In chemistry, *m* is the short form for *metal*. *M* in the Roman numeral system stands for 1,000, while $\overline{M}$ stands for 1,000,000. *M* is also the abbreviation for *Master* in college degrees, and *m* stands for *milli*, as in *millimeter*. In Germany, people use *M* to stand for the *mark*, the basic unit of their money. In French, *M* stands for *monsieur*, equal to our *mister*. It is the seventh letter of the Hawaiian alphabet.

Pronunciation. In English, a person pronounces *m* by closing both lips and making the sound through his nose. Double *m* usually has the same sound, as in *stammer*. But there are some words, like *immobile*, in which each *m* is often pronounced. These words come from a Latin prefix ending in *m* and a Latin stem beginning with *m*. The letter has almost exactly the same sound in French, German, Italian, and Spanish as it has in English. The Romans also gave it the same sound. The Portuguese nasalize the sound when it follows a vowel. See PRONUNCIATION.　I. J. GELB and JAMES M. WELLS

Development of the Letter M

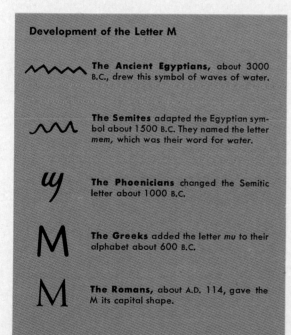

The Ancient Egyptians, about 3000 B.C., drew this symbol of waves of water.

The Semites adapted the Egyptian symbol about 1500 B.C. They named the letter *mem,* which was their word for *water.*

The Phoenicians changed the Semitic letter about 1000 B.C.

The Greeks added the letter *mu* to their alphabet about 600 B.C.

The Romans, about A.D. 114, gave the M its capital shape.

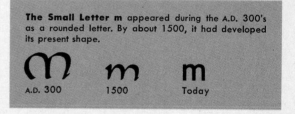

The Small Letter m appeared during the A.D. 300's as a rounded letter. By about 1500, it had developed its present shape.

A.D. 300　　1500　　Today

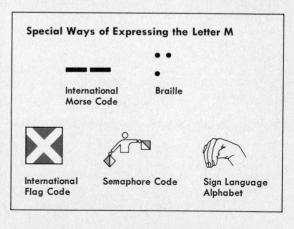

Special Ways of Expressing the Letter M

International Morse Code

Braille

International Flag Code

Semaphore Code

Sign Language Alphabet

Common Forms of the Letter M

Handwritten Letters vary from person to person. Manuscript (printed) letters, *left,* have simple curves and straight lines. Cursive letters, *right,* have flowing lines.

Roman Letters have small finishing strokes called *serifs* that extend from the main strokes. The type face shown above is Baskerville. The italic form appears at the right.

Sans-Serif Letters are also called *gothic letters.* They have no serifs. The type face shown above is called Futura. The italic form of Futura appears at the right.

Computer Letters have special shapes. Computers can "read" these letters either optically or by means of the magnetic ink with which the letters may be printed.

1

M14, M16. See RIFLE (Automatic and Semiautomatic Rifles).

MA YÜAN, *mah you ON,* was the most famous member of an honored family of painters. With his fellow painter Hsia Kuei, Ma Yüan produced some of the greatest landscape paintings in ink during the early 1200's in the Southern Sung period in China.

Ma Yüan's typical compositions are severely simple, with a framework of strong diagonal lines usually developed in one corner. His foregrounds may contain a few boldly silhouetted forms—rocks, a mountain path, a dramatically angular pine tree. The rest of the scene is largely mist, through which river banks or silhouetted faraway peaks can be seen.

Ma Yüan was born in Ho-Chung in Shansi province. His birth and death dates are unknown.   ALEXANDER SOPER

MAAS RIVER. See MEUSE RIVER.

MAB, QUEEN. See FAIRY.

MABINOGION. See MYTHOLOGY (Celtic Mythology); WALES (The Arts).

MAC, Mc. Biographies of persons whose names begin with *Mac,* such as *MacDonald,* are listed alphabetically under *Mac.* Names which begin with *Mc,* such as *McKinley,* are listed alphabetically under *Mc,* following all names beginning *Ma* and *Mb.*

MACADAM. See ROADS AND HIGHWAYS (Paving).

MACADAMIA NUT is a large, round seed that grows on the macadamia tree, a tropical Australian evergreen. Macadamia trees were brought to Hawaii in the late 1800's, and today the nuts rank as an important crop there. In the late 1970's, Hawaii's annual macadamia nut crop had a value of about $7½ million.

Macadamia nuts have a hard, smooth shell that is cracked by a special machine. The white kernels are roasted in oil. The roasted nuts, which taste somewhat like Brazil nuts, are salted and canned. They also may be used in cakes, candy, and ice cream. The macadamia tree grows more than 40 feet (12 meters) tall and has dark green, leathery leaves and creamy-white flowers. Macadamia nuts are also called *Australian nuts, bopple nuts, bush nuts,* and *Queensland nuts.*

Scientific Classification. The macadamia tree belongs to the protea family, *Proteaceae.* It is genus *Macadamia,* species *M. integrifolia.*   HENRY Y. NAKASONE

Rick Golt, Rapho Guillumette

Macadamia Nuts have a large white kernel surrounded by a shell. The roasted kernels taste somewhat like Brazil nuts.

MACAO, *muh KOW,* or MACAU, is a Portuguese territory on the southeast coast of China. It consists of the city of Macao, which occupies a peninsula, and three small islands. The territory has a population of 286,000 and covers about 6 square miles (16 square kilometers). It lies at the mouth of the Pearl River, about 40 miles (64 kilometers) west of Hong Kong. For location, see ASIA (political map).

Some areas of Macao have old, pastel-colored houses that line cobblestone streets and provide a European atmosphere. Other sections include modern high-rise hotels and apartment buildings. More than 90 per cent of the people of Macao are Chinese, and most of the rest are Portuguese.

Macao's economy is based on tourism and light industry, chiefly the manufacture of fireworks and textiles. Gambling casinos in Macao attract many tourists, mainly from Hong Kong.

A governor appointed by the president of Portugal heads the government of Macao. A legislative assembly of both appointed and elected members makes laws for the territory. In practice, however, China dominates the political life of Macao. The Chinese government may veto any government policies or laws concerning the territory.

The Portuguese settled Macao in 1557. China has allowed them to remain because Macao contributes to China's economy. Macao buys almost all its food and drinking water from China. These purchases provide China with foreign currency, which it uses in international trade.   DONALD W. KLEIN

MACAQUE, *muh KAHK,* is the name of several species of large, powerful monkeys. Some macaques weigh more than 30 pounds (14 kilograms). Most live in warm areas of southern Asia. One species, the Barbary ape, lives in northern Africa (see BARBARY APE). Another, the Japanese macaque, lives as far north as Honshu Island, where snow falls in winter.

Most macaques have gray or brown fur, with pink or red skin on the face and rump. Some have long tails, others have short tails, or no tails at all. Males have long, sharp teeth which they use in fighting. Strong males rule most groups of macaques.

Many macaques live both in trees and on the ground. Most species eat fruits, grains, insects, and vegetables, but the crab-eating monkey eats crabs and clams.

Arthur W. Ambler, NAS

The Japanese Macaque is often used for scientific research because of its ability to learn quickly.

The rhesus monkey, a macaque of India, is used in medical research and may be seen on many "monkey islands" in zoos. People of Malaysia train the pig-tailed macaque to pick coconuts from trees. At least one species of macaque, the lion-tailed macaque of India, is classified as an endangered species.

Scientific Classification. Macaques belong to the Old World monkey family, *Cercopithecidae.* They are genus *Macaca.* The rhesus monkey is *M. mulatta.*   NEIL C. TAPPEN

National Macaroni Institute

Macaroni Shapes vary from long solid rods to tiny egg rings. The United States has the largest macaroni industry in the world. It produces macaroni in more than 100 different shapes and sizes.

MACARONI, MACK uh RO nee, is a popular food made from *durum* (hard wheat) flour mixed with water. Macaroni products come in many shapes and kinds. The best known are long, hollow tubes of dough, about $\frac{1}{10}$ to $\frac{1}{4}$ inch (3 to 6 millimeters) in diameter. *Elbow* macaroni is formed into short, curved tubes. *Shell* macaroni has the shape of tiny sea shells. *Spaghetti* is made from the same kind of dough as macaroni, but it is thinner and has solid tubes. *Vermicelli*, another macaroni product, consists of tiny strings. Manufacturers add 5 per cent or more of egg solids to macaroni dough to make *egg* macaroni or *egg noodles*. Other ingredients in macaroni may include milk, whole wheat, soy flour, vegetables, seasonings, and salt.

Macaroni contains about three-fourths carbohydrates. Manufacturers enrich most macaroni to supply from one-fourth to one-half of a person's daily requirements of the B vitamins. Macaroni is easily digested.

To make ordinary macaroni, the flour and water are thoroughly mixed and formed into dough. After the dough has been kneaded, it goes to a press where it is forced through holes. Steel pins in the center of the holes go through the dough and form it into hollow tubes. Forced air dries the dough in heated drying rooms. Other macaroni products are made in a similar way.

Macaroni has been a staple food in many European countries for hundreds of years. Because of macaroni's bland taste, it can be served with many types of food.

The invention of macaroni occurred long ago. Historians believe the Chinese probably developed the food, and they generally credit the Germans and Italians with introducing it into Europe.   ROBERT M. GREEN

MACARTHUR, DOUGLAS (1880-1964), was one of the leading American generals of World War II. He gallantly defended Bataan Peninsula in the Philippine Islands in the early days of the war, and later led the Allied forces to victory in the Southwest Pacific. After the war, he proved his ability as a statesman in his administration of American-occupied Japan. He directed the changeover of Japan from dictatorship to democracy.

MacArthur became United Nations commander in Korea at the outbreak of the Korean War in 1950. He directed the invasion at Inchon, and the attack that carried UN troops to the northern border of North Korea. But he disagreed with President Harry S. Truman over the conduct of the war. When MacArthur defied Truman's orders in 1951, Truman recalled him from Korea.

Early Career. MacArthur was born in Little Rock, Ark., on Jan. 26, 1880. He was greatly influenced by his father, Arthur MacArthur, also a famous general. Arthur MacArthur joined the Union Army when he was 17 and fought in the Civil War. He won the Congressional Medal of Honor for heroism at Missionary Ridge in the Battle of Chattanooga. Douglas MacArthur was awarded the medal in 1942. This marked the only time the son of a Medal of Honor winner also won the medal.

In 1898, the elder MacArthur was ordered to the Philippines. Douglas remained in the United States with his mother, the former Mary Pinkney Hardy of Norfolk, Va., to prepare for his entrance to the U.S. Military Academy.

Douglas MacArthur was graduated from the U.S. Military Academy in 1903 as the leading man in his class. He spent his first year after graduation as an engineer helping to map the Philippines. MacArthur served at various U.S. Army posts from 1904 until 1914. In 1914, he performed a daring mission in Mexico under secret orders from the Army Chief of Staff. Relations between the U.S. and Mexico were strained at this time. MacArthur was sent there to find locomotives that could move U.S. troops in Mexico in case of war.

MacArthur held the rank of colonel when the United States entered World War I in 1917. He became chief of staff of the famous 42nd (Rainbow) Division. MacArthur rose to the rank of brigadier general in 1918. He won fame as a front-line general during the war in France in the battles of the Meuse-Argonne and Saint Mihiel. He was wounded 3 times, decorated 13 times, and cited for bravery in action 7 times.

MacArthur became Superintendent of the U.S. Military Academy in 1919. He is credited with broadening the academy's curriculum and raising its academic standards. MacArthur was transferred to the Philippines in 1922. In 1925, he returned to the United States as a major general. In 1930, he became a four-star general and was named Army Chief of Staff, the youngest in U.S. history.

At the height of the Great Depression, in 1932, several thousand unemployed World War I veterans gathered in Washington, D.C. The veterans, called the *Bonus Army*, demanded immediate payment of war bonuses. On orders from President Herbert Hoover, MacArthur and his troops drove the veterans from Washington. This action brought MacArthur severe criticism.

United Press Int.

Douglas MacArthur

From 1935 to 1941, MacArthur worked as military adviser to the Philippine government. He helped prepare the Philippines for an expected Japanese attack. MacArthur was named Grand Field Marshal of the Philippines.

Defense of the Philippines. President Franklin D. Roosevelt named MacArthur commander of all U.S. Army forces in the Far East in July, 1941. MacArthur held this position when the Japanese attacked the Philippines on Dec. 8, 1941. His forces were isolated, but they fought desperately. MacArthur withdrew his troops to Bataan Peninsula, where they resisted courageously for four months.

In March, 1942, President Roosevelt ordered MacArthur to Australia to become commander of the Allied forces in the Southwest Pacific. By night, a Navy torpedo boat took MacArthur, his wife, and son from Corregidor to the southern Philippines. From there they flew to Australia, where he spoke of his reluctance to leave his men in the Philippines and made his famous promise, "I shall return." See BATAAN PENINSULA.

The Road Back. MacArthur spent several months assembling men and supplies. Late in 1942, he opened a three-year offensive against the Japanese. By early 1944, his troops had freed most of New Guinea, New Britain, the Solomons, and the Admiralty Islands. By autumn 1944, MacArthur was ready to make good his promise to return to the Philippines. On Oct. 20, 1944, his forces invaded Leyte Island, and six months later most of the Philippine Islands were free. During this period, MacArthur showed great military genius and personal bravery. His haughty manner aroused some resentment. But his heroism was seldom questioned.

MacArthur became a five-star general of the Army in December, 1944. He took command of all American Army forces in the Pacific in April, 1945. President Truman announced the Japanese acceptance of Allied surrender terms on Aug. 14, 1945. Truman made MacArthur supreme commander for the Allied Powers. As supreme commander, it was MacArthur's job to receive the surrender and to rule Japan. He accepted the Japanese surrender aboard the battleship *Missouri* on Sept. 2 (Sept. 1 in the United States), 1945.

He set up headquarters in Tokyo and became the sole administrator of the military government in Japan. His firm, but fair, methods soon won him the respect of the Japanese, who had feared a harsh occupation. In keeping with Allied plans, MacArthur introduced reforms in government, education, and industry. These reforms were designed to turn Japan into a democracy.

War in Korea. In 1950, North Korean Communists invaded South Korea, and the United Nations authorized the United States to organize armed forces to fight the Communists. MacArthur, in addition to his occupation duties, became UN commander in Korea. After the Chinese Communists entered the war on the side of the North Koreans, MacArthur wanted to attack the Chinese mainland. But his superiors forbade this action, feeling it would increase the risk of a world war.

MacArthur made several public statements that did not agree with UN policies and those of the U.S. State and Defense departments. He also violated an order of public silence imposed on him by President Truman. In April, 1951, Truman relieved MacArthur of his Far Eastern commands, causing a nationwide controversy.

MacArthur returned home, received a hero's welcome, and defended his policies in a memorable address before a joint meeting of Congress. The speech included the famous reference to a line from a military ballad: "Old soldiers never die, they just fade away." In 1952, he became board chairman of Remington Rand, Inc. (now the Sperry Rand Corp.). He received many honors later in life. In 1962, he received a unanimous joint resolution of tribute from the U.S. Congress. In 1963, at the request of President John F. Kennedy, he helped settle a dispute between the National Collegiate Athletic Association and the Amateur Athletic Union that endangered the U.S. Olympic team.

MacArthur died on April 5, 1964, at the age of 84. President Lyndon B. Johnson called MacArthur "one of America's greatest heroes," and proclaimed a week of public mourning. MacArthur was buried in a crypt of the MacArthur Memorial in Norfolk, Va.   JULES ARCHER

See also TRUMAN, HARRY S. (The Korean War); JAPAN (Allied Military Occupation); KOREAN WAR; WORLD WAR II.

MACAU. See MACAO.

MACAULAY, THOMAS BABINGTON (1800-1859), was the most widely read English historian of the 1800's. He also achieved fame for his essays and for his poems based on ancient legends. However, his writings—especially his poetry—have declined in popularity during the 1900's.

Macaulay was born in Leicestershire. His father, Zachary Macaulay, was a leading religious reformer. In 1825, Macaulay published his first article, an essay on the English poet John Milton, in the famous literary magazine *The Edinburgh Review*. The *Review* continued to publish many of Macaulay's scholarly but popular essays on historical and literary topics.

While Macaulay was gaining a reputation as an author, he was also pursuing a political career. He was elected to Parliament in 1830 and helped lead a movement to reform Great Britain's voting laws. His speeches in Parliament were so brilliant that he became a famous public figure. In 1833, the English East India Company appointed Macaulay to the Supreme Council, which governed the British colony of India. He served on the council until 1838. During this period, he lived in India and helped lay the foundations for English—in place of Oriental—systems of criminal law and education in the colony.

After Macaulay returned to England, he began his greatest work—*History of England from the Accession of James II*. Macaulay published two volumes in 1848 and two more in 1855, but he died before finishing the work. The *History* became a best seller in England and the United States because of its vivid descriptions and powerful prose style. Macaulay made some factual errors in the work, and scholars have challenged his slanted political views. But Macaulay's *History* remains a highly readable introduction to a period of English history.

While working on his *History*, Macaulay remained a leading orator in Parliament and held several government positions. At the same time, he also wrote *Lays of Ancient Rome* (1842). This collection of poems about ancient Roman heroes became very popular and is still read by young people. The best-known poem in the collection is "Horatius."　　　AVROM FLEISHMAN

See also HORATIUS; FOURTH ESTATE.

MACAW, *muh KAW*, is a long-tailed parrot that lives in South America and northwestern Mexico. It has long, pointed wings and a short, arched bill. Beautifully colored feathers of blue, red, yellow, and green cover the macaw's body. Macaws fly swiftly in pairs. They eat nuts, seeds, and fruit. Macaws can be easily tamed, but do not readily learn to talk. Their loud screams and the danger of their biting make them undesirable pets.

Scientific Classification. Typical macaws are members of the parrot family, *Psittacidae*. They make up the genus *Ara*.　　　RODOLPHE MEYER DE SCHAUENSEE

See also PARROT (picture: Scarlet Macaw).

MACBETH, *muk BETH* (? -1057), seized the throne of Scotland in 1040 after defeating and killing Duncan I. He based his claim to the crown on his wife's royal descent. Malcolm III, son of Duncan I, and Earl Siward of Northumberland defeated Macbeth at Dunsinane in 1054, but they did not dethrone him. Three years later, Malcolm III killed Macbeth at Lumphanan. Macbeth's stepson Lulach reigned for a few months, and then Malcolm III succeeded him as king.

William Shakespeare based his play, *Macbeth*, upon a distorted version of these events which he found in Raphael Holinshed's *Chronicles of England, Scotlande, and Irelande*. The only kernel of historical truth in the play is Duncan's death at the hand of Macbeth. From this fact, Shakespeare drew his portrait of ambition leading to a violent and tragic end.　ROBERT S. HOYT

See also SHAKESPEARE, WILLIAM (*Macbeth*).

MACCABEE, JUDAH. See JUDAH MACCABEE.

MACCABEES is the name of a line of Jewish rulers. The name probably comes from a Hebrew or Aramaic word meaning *the hammerer*, a title given to Judah, son of Mattathias. Judah led the Jews in their great revolt against the Syrians. It began in 168 or 167 B.C. The Syrian king, Antiochus IV (called Epiphanes), wanted to stamp out the Jewish religion and make the Jews worship Greek gods. The old Jewish priest Mattathias killed a renegade Jew and a Syrian who were leading a pagan celebration. Mattathias and his sons then fled to the Judean hills. Other Jews joined them. Judah led them to a series of victories against much larger forces. He had won back most of Jerusalem by the end of 164 B.C., but he was killed in 160 B.C. The leadership went to his brother Jonathan, and then to another brother, Simon, who, with his descendants, ruled for more than 100 years. See also HASMONEANS.　　BRUCE M. METZGER

MACCABEES, *MAK uh beez*, is the name of a fraternal and benevolent legal reserve society (see FRATERNAL SOCIETY). Families of deceased members receive benefits in the form of legal-reserve insurance. The name comes from the Biblical Maccabees. The order was founded in London, Ont., in 1878, and reorganized in 1883. Before 1914, it was known as The Knights of the Maccabees. The headquarters of the order is at 25800 Northwestern Highway, Southfield, Mich. 48075.　　D. A. TALUCCI

MACCOOL, FINN. See FINN MACCOOL.

MACCORMICK, AUSTIN H. (1893-1979), was an American expert on prison reform. He became known for his surveys of prisons and juvenile institutions. From 1940 to 1976, he served as executive director of The Osborne Association, Inc., a group that works to aid former prisoners and bring about prison reforms.

MacCormick was born in Georgetown, Ont. From 1934 to 1940, he served as New York City's commissioner of correction. He was a consultant on correctional problems for the United States Army from 1942 to 1965. MacCormick was also a professor of criminology at the University of California from 1951 to 1960.　O. W. WILSON

MACDONALD, JAMES E. H. (1874-1932), was a Canadian painter. He was an original member of the Group of Seven, an influential group of Toronto painters. His works stressed subjects of local interest such as farm pumps, picket fences, sunflowers, and apple trees.

MacDonald was born in Durham, England, and came to Canada in 1887. He studied at the Hamilton Art School and the Ontario School of Art in Toronto. He was elected a member of the Ontario Society of Artists in 1909 and of the Royal Canadian Academy of Arts in 1929. MacDonald wrote a volume of poems, *West By East*, published in 1933.　WILLIAM R. WILLOUGHBY

MACDONALD, JAMES RAMSAY (1866-1937), led Great Britain's first Labour Party government. He served as the first Labour Party prime minister of Britain in 1924, and from 1929 to 1935. He was secretary of Britain's Labour Party from the party's origin in 1900 until 1911.

He entered Parliament in 1906. As Labour Party leader in 1914, he opposed England's entrance into World War I. His stand met considerable opposition within his own party. His pacifism resulted in his defeat for re-election to Parliament in 1918. However, he was elected in 1922, and became prime minister in 1924, with Liberal Party support. MacDonald remained in office for a period of only 10 months. He was defeated, in part, because his government was considered too friendly toward Russia. He accepted, but did not wholeheartedly support, the 1926 general strike on behalf of coal miners faced with reduced wages and longer working hours.

The Labour Party won the general election of 1929, and MacDonald formed his second government as prime minister. It achieved considerable success in international affairs. Diplomatic relations with Russia were resumed. MacDonald visited the United States to discuss with President Herbert Hoover proposals for naval reduction. He became chairman of the London arms conference in 1930. But MacDonald was unable to deal effectively with rapidly rising unemployment and his government resigned in August, 1931. MacDonald continued as prime minister, heading a national coalition government of Labour, Conservative, and Liberal Party members. A large majority of the Labourites in Parliament disapproved of his move. The Conservatives held an overwhelming majority in the government. They overshadowed MacDonald. Stanley Baldwin replaced him as prime minister in 1935.

MacDonald was born of farmer parents in the Scottish seaside village of Lossiemouth. He left school at the age of 13, to help support the family. Six years later, he went to London and worked as a clerk, accountant, and newspaper writer. He read widely in the fields of science, history, and economics. He became interested in socialism, joined the Fabian Society, and became one of its speakers.　　ALFRED F. HAVIGHURST

See also FABIAN SOCIETY.

SIR JOHN A. MACDONALD

Prime Minister of Canada
1867-1873
1878-1891

| MACDONALD | MACKENZIE | MACDONALD | ABBOTT |
| 1867-1873 | 1873-1878 | 1878-1891 | 1891-1892 |

Detail of a portrait by Frederick Arthur Verner;
National Gallery of Canada, Ottawa (John Evans)

MACDONALD, SIR JOHN ALEXANDER (1815-1891), was the first Prime Minister of the Dominion of Canada. He is often called the father of present-day Canada because he played the leading role in establishing the dominion in 1867. Macdonald served as Prime Minister from 1867 until 1873, and from 1878 until his death in 1891. He held the office for nearly 19 years, longer than any other Canadian Prime Minister except W. L. Mackenzie King, who served for 21 years.

Macdonald, a Conservative, entered politics when he was only 28 years old. During his long public career, Canada grew from a group of colonies into a self-governing, united dominion extending across North America. Macdonald stood out as the greatest political figure of Canada's early years. He helped strengthen the new nation by promoting western expansion, railway construction, and economic development.

A man of great personal charm, Macdonald knew how to make people like him. He was naturally sociable, with a quick wit and a remarkable ability to remember faces. Macdonald was not a flowery-speaking orator as were most politicians of his day. He kept his speeches short and filled with funny stories. People preferred his talks to the long, dull speeches of others.

Early Life

Boyhood and Education. John Alexander Macdonald was born on Jan. 11, 1815, in Glasgow, Scotland. He was the son of Helen Shaw Macdonald and Hugh Macdonald, an easy-going and usually unsuccessful businessman. John had an older sister, Margaret, and a younger sister, Louisa. He was 5 years old when the family moved to Canada in 1820.

The Macdonalds settled in Kingston, Upper Canada (present-day Ontario). Hugh opened a small shop, and the family lived above it. The business did not prosper, so Hugh decided he would be more successful elsewhere. In 1824, the family moved westward to Hay Bay. They moved to Glenora in Prince Edward county in 1825, then back to Kingston. Hugh tried one business after another, but none brought him success.

As a boy, John developed an interest in books and was a bright student. He finished his formal schooling in 1829 when he was 14. The next year, John began to study law with George Mackenzie, a prominent Kingston lawyer.

Macdonald lived with the Mackenzie family and worked in the law office. In 1832, Mackenzie opened a branch office in nearby Napanee, and 17-year-old John became its manager. In 1833, John learned that a relative, a lawyer in Hallowell, Prince Edward county, was seriously ill. John agreed to take over his practice.

Lawyer. Macdonald returned to Kingston in 1835. He was admitted to the bar of Upper Canada in 1836. That same year, he took on his first apprentice-lawyer, Oliver Mowat, who became prime minister of Ontario.

During the Rebellion of 1837-1838, Macdonald served in the Frontenac county militia. In 1838, some of William Lyon Mackenzie's American supporters staged a raid into Canada. About 150 raiders were captured, and Macdonald defended some of them in court. Several Americans were hanged, but the case

6

helped establish Macdonald's legal reputation. See RE-
BELLION OF 1837-1838; MACKENZIE, WILLIAM LYON.

In 1841, Upper Canada (part of present-day Ontario) and Lower Canada (part of present-day Quebec)
united to form the Province of Canada. The Province
of Canada, sometimes called United Canada, had one
legislative assembly, with an equal number of members
from Upper and Lower Canada.

Kingston, in Upper Canada, became the capital of
the Province of Canada. Both the city and Macdonald's
law practice grew prosperous. In 1843, Macdonald began a law partnership with Alexander Campbell, who
had been his second apprentice-lawyer.

Marriages. On the same day that he set up his law
partnership, Macdonald married his cousin, Isabella
Clark. The Macdonalds had two sons, John Jr., who
died at the age of 1, and Hugh John, who became prime
minister of Manitoba.

In 1845, Isabella was stricken by tuberculosis.
Macdonald tried everything to cure her. He and his
wife were separated for long periods while Isabella
tried to restore her health in the southern United States
or sought medical care in New Haven, Conn. But she
died in 1857.

The years of his wife's illness were a strain on John
Macdonald, both physically and financially. He remained at Isabella's bedside as much as possible. But
he was also building a law practice and a political
career. He often felt he was not giving enough attention
to his wife, to his practice, or to politics.

Ten years after the death of Isabella, in 1867, Macdonald married Susan Agnes Bernard, a widow. The
couple had a daughter, Mary.

Early Public Career

In 1843, at the age of 28, Macdonald was elected an
alderman in Kingston. In 1844, he accepted the Conservative nomination in Kingston for the legislative assembly of the Province of Canada. He easily won election.

Macdonald took his seat in the assembly on Nov. 28,
1844. His associates soon recognized his abilities. In
1847, he was appointed receiver-general in the Conservative administration of William Henry Draper. But
Draper's government was defeated later that year.

For the next few years, Macdonald helped rebuild
the Conservative party. He wanted the party to include
men of liberal and conservative views, French-Canadians and English-Canadians, Roman Catholics and
Protestants, and rich and poor. A Liberal-Conservative
coalition party was formed. It came to power in 1854
under Conservative leader Sir Allan McNab. Macdonald served as attorney general in this administration.

Associate Provincial Prime Minister. In 1856, Macdonald and Sir Étienne P. Taché became associate
prime ministers of the Province of Canada. Taché was
the senior prime minister in what was called the Taché-
Macdonald government. The next year, Taché retired.
Macdonald became senior prime minister with Georges
É. Cartier as his associate prime minister. The Conservatives adopted a policy favoring confederation of
all the British provinces in North America.

In 1858, the Macdonald-Cartier government was defeated. But Macdonald returned to power a week later
when the governor-general asked Cartier to become
senior prime minister and form a government. Cartier

needed Macdonald's help in the task, and the new government became the Cartier-Macdonald government.

The formation of the Cartier-Macdonald government
became known as the "double shuffle." The action
was legal, but the opposition charged it was dishonest.
Macdonald and Cartier simply took advantage of a
provision in the law. This provision permitted a cabinet
minister to resign and accept another cabinet position
within a month without running for re-election. All the
government ministers resigned. A few days later, they
all returned to office with new titles. Then they quickly
dropped the new titles and resumed their former offices.

The Conservative government was defeated in 1862,
although Macdonald won re-election to the assembly
from Kingston. Macdonald served as leader of the opposition party until 1864. The Conservatives won the
election that year. Taché came out of retirement, and
the second Taché-Macdonald government was formed.

Forming the Dominion. In the early 1860's, the
northern half of North America was called British North
America. It consisted of only a few provinces. Most of
the people lived in the east. The Maritime Provinces—
New Brunswick, Newfoundland, Nova Scotia, and
Prince Edward Island—lay along the Atlantic coast.
The Province of Canada was next to them on the west.
Of these five provinces, Nova Scotia and the Province of
Canada were older and more developed. The other
three had only begun to govern themselves in the 1840's
and 1850's. Farther west was an expanse of mainly un-
settled territory owned by the Hudson's Bay Company
(see HUDSON'S BAY COMPANY). On the west coast lay
British Columbia, then a British colony.

For several years, the British provinces in North
America had considered the idea of confederation. Several factors gave force to this idea. They included the
frequent changes of provincial governments, the desire
to expand to the west, and fear of U.S. expansion.

Nova Scotia and the Province of Canada took the
lead in the confederation movement. In the Province of
Canada, Macdonald joined forces with his opponent,
Liberal leader George Brown, to achieve confederation.

From 1864 to 1867, Macdonald led in planning confederation. In September, 1864, he attended a conference in Charlottetown, P.E.I., to present the confederation plan to the Maritime Provinces. In October,
delegates from all the provinces gathered at a second
conference in Quebec. At this meeting, Macdonald was
largely responsible for drawing up the Quebec Resolutions, the plan for confederation.

New Brunswick, Nova Scotia, and the Province of
Canada approved the idea, but Newfoundland and
Prince Edward Island rejected it. Final details were
agreed upon at a conference in London, England, in
1866. In 1867, the British parliament passed the British
North America Act, which brought the Dominion of
Canada into being (see BRITISH NORTH AMERICA ACT).
The new nation had four provinces: Ontario (previ-
ously Upper Canada), Quebec (previously Lower
Canada), New Brunswick, and Nova Scotia. Governor-
General Charles S. Monck asked Macdonald to lead the
first dominion government as Prime Minister.

Confederation was largely Macdonald's achievement
and Queen Victoria knighted him for it. The announce-

MACDONALD, SIR JOHN A.

ment of his knighthood came on July 1, 1867, the first day of the dominion's existence. A general election was held in August, and the new parliament assembled on Nov. 6, 1867.

First Term As Prime Minister (1867-1873)

Completing the Dominion. Sir John A. Macdonald took office as Prime Minister of the Dominion of Canada on July 1, 1867. His goal was to enlarge the dominion into a unified nation extending across the continent.

In 1869, the Canadian and British governments agreed with the Hudson's Bay Company to purchase the company's lands. The company was paid 300,000 pounds (about $1½ million) and 5 per cent of the land south of the North Saskatchewan River. But the *métis* (persons of mixed European and Indian descent) in the territory rebelled. They were led by Louis Riel. They feared that an onrush of settlers would deprive them of their lands. Many Canadians also thought the United States might annex this land. Parliament passed the Manitoba Act in 1870, and in July, 1870, the lands became the fifth Canadian province (see RED RIVER RE-

BELLION). British Columbia became the sixth province in 1871, and Prince Edward Island the seventh in 1873.

In 1871, delegates from Great Britain and the United States held a conference in Washington, D.C. Mac-

IMPORTANT DATES IN MACDONALD'S LIFE

1815 (Jan. 11) Born in Glasgow, Scotland.
1820 Macdonald family moved to Kingston, Upper Canada.
1836 Admitted to the bar of Upper Canada.
1843 (Sept. 1) Married Isabella Clark.
1844 (Oct. 14) Elected to legislative assembly of the Province of Canada.
1856 Became associate prime minister of Province of Canada.
1857 (Dec. 28) Mrs. Isabella Macdonald died.
1867 British parliament passed the British North America Act.
(Feb. 16) Married Susan Agnes Bernard.
(July 1) Macdonald became the first Prime Minister of the Dominion of Canada and was knighted.
1869-1870 Louis Riel led the Red River Rebellion.
1870 Manitoba became the fifth Canadian province.
1871 British Columbia became the sixth province.
1873 Prince Edward Island became the seventh province.
1878 (Oct. 17) Became Prime Minister for second time.
1885 Riel led the Saskatchewan Rebellion.
The Canadian Pacific Railway was completed.
1891 Macdonald and the Conservatives won re-election.
(June 6) Died in Ottawa, Ont.

IMPORTANT EVENTS DURING MACDONALD'S ADMINISTRATIONS

National Film Board, Toronto, Canada

Fathers of Confederation, a painting by J. D. Kelly, represents the scene at the Quebec Conference of 1864. Macdonald is shown standing in the center of this group.

Houses of Parliament, *left,* looked like this in 1867 when Macdonald first became Prime Minister. The buildings were constructed in the early 1860's.

6b

donald attended the meeting as the Canadian member of the British delegation. He tried to obtain a trade agreement with the United States, but failed. Nevertheless, Macdonald signed the Treaty of Washington. Among other points, this treaty granted the United States extensive fishing rights in Canadian waters. Macdonald felt that refusal to sign the treaty might encourage the United States to back its demands with force. He was always careful to do nothing that might endanger the young Canadian nation. See WASHINGTON, TREATY OF.

The Pacific Scandal. Next, Macdonald turned to the goal of building a transcontinental railroad to unify Canada. The completion of such a railroad had been one of the terms of British Columbia's entry into the confederation.

Two financial groups competed with each other to build the line. Then, in 1873, it was learned that Sir Hugh Allan, head of one of the groups, had contributed a large sum of money to help re-elect Macdonald's government in the 1872 election. Some Liberal members of parliament charged there had been an "understanding" between Allan and the government. They accused the government of giving Allan a charter to build the railroad because he had contributed to the Conservatives' election fund.

The incident became known as the Pacific Scandal. Macdonald was innocent, but some of his associates had received money from Allan. Macdonald resigned as Prime Minister. He offered to resign as head of the Conservative party, but his supporters persuaded him to remain in that post. The Conservatives lost the 1874 election, although Macdonald won re-election to parliament from Kingston. Alexander Mackenzie, the leader of the Liberal party, became Prime Minister of Canada.

The National Policy. For the next four years, Macdonald led the opposition party in the house of commons. During this period, he worked to rebuild the Conservative party. Macdonald formed a program of economic nationalism that he called the National Policy. This program called for developing Canada by protecting its industries against those of other countries.

The idea appealed to Canadians, especially because a depression had begun in 1873. On the strength of the National Policy, the Conservatives defeated the Liberals

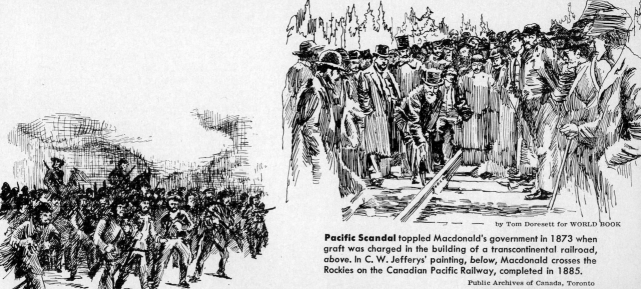

by Tom Doresett for WORLD BOOK

Pacific Scandal toppled Macdonald's government in 1873 when graft was charged in the building of a transcontinental railroad, *above.* In C. W. Jefferys' painting, *below,* Macdonald crosses the Rockies on the Canadian Pacific Railway, completed in 1885.

Public Archives of Canada, Toronto

Louis Riel led revolts against the Canadian government in 1869 and 1885. English-Canadians called him a traitor. But French-Canadians hailed Riel as a hero.

Ottawa, Canada. National Film Board

Macdonald Memorial stands on Parliament Hill in Ottawa, Ont. A memorial tablet in St. Paul's Cathedral in London, England, also honors the first Prime Minister of Canada.

ernment. In 1888, the prime ministers met at a conference in Quebec. They proposed changes in the British North America Act that would decentralize the government. Great Britain rejected their demands. But the conference showed the growing strength of provincial opinion against federal centralization.

Still another blow to Macdonald was the depression of 1883. The National Policy had not produced all the expected results. In 1886 and 1887, a demand arose for a change in Canada's financial policy. Some persons favored political federation with Great Britain. Others spoke of a commercial union with the United States. Macdonald opposed both proposals.

In the 1891 election, the Liberals adopted a party platform calling for unrestricted reciprocal trade with the United States (see RECIPROCAL TRADE AGREEMENT). The 75-year-old Macdonald fought this proposal with all the strength he could muster.

"Shall we endanger our possession of the great heritage bequeathed to us by our fathers," he asked the Canadian people, "and submit ourselves to direct taxation for the privilege of having our tariffs fixed at Washington, with the prospect of ultimately becoming a portion of the American Union? . . . As for myself, my course is clear. A British subject I was born, a British subject I will die." With this appeal, Macdonald won his last election.

Death. The strain of campaigning proved severe for Macdonald. He caught cold after a long day of speaking, and suffered a stroke on May 29, 1891. He died on June 6 in Ottawa. Macdonald was buried near his mother in Kingston, Ont.   G. F. G. STANLEY

Related Articles in WORLD BOOK include:

Brown, George
Canada, Government of
Canada, History of
Cartier, Sir Georges-É.
Mackenzie, Alexander

Monck, Baron
Political Party (Political
  Parties in Canada)
Riel, Louis
Taché, Sir Étienne-Paschal

in the 1878 election. They returned to power with an election victory in almost every province.

Second Term As Prime Minister (1878-1891)

National Prosperity. Macdonald began his second term as Prime Minister on Oct. 17, 1878. The government immediately put tariffs on a variety of goods to protect the manufacturing and mining industries. Macdonald again began to push for construction of a transcontinental railroad. With government support, a new company was formed. By November, 1885, the Canadian Pacific Railway had been completed to the Pacific Ocean. Macdonald had achieved his program of western expansion, railway construction, and economic nationalism. Canada was riding a wave of prosperity.

Threats to Canadian Unity. Macdonald had worked long and hard to build a unified Canadian nation. But beginning in 1885, a number of political developments seriously threatened this unity.

In 1885, the métis of northwest Canada rebelled for the second time. They were again led by Louis Riel. When Riel finally surrendered, the government found him guilty of treason and sentenced him to hang. The sentence caused severe bad feeling between French-Canadians and English-Canadians. For a time, the issue threatened to split the confederation. But Macdonald refused to give in to Riel's supporters. "He shall die though every dog in Quebec bark in his favour," Macdonald declared. Riel was hanged in November, 1885. See SASKATCHEWAN REBELLION.

Macdonald next faced an attack by the provincial prime ministers on his program for a strong central gov-

MACDONALD, JOHN SANDFIELD (1812-1872), served as joint Prime Minister of the Province of Canada from 1862 to 1864, before the formation of the Canadian federation. He also served as first premier of Ontario from 1867 to 1871. He held office in both Liberal and Conservative governments. On most public issues, he voted as a member of the Reform, or Liberal, Party. But he differed, on occasion, with the party leader, George Brown (see BROWN, GEORGE). Macdonald voted against the Liberal aim of "representation by population."

He opposed provincial union at first, but finally accepted it. He agreed in 1867 to Sir John A. Macdonald's request that he form a Liberal-Conservative coalition government for Ontario (see MACDONALD, SIR JOHN A.). The noncoalition Liberals defeated him in 1871, and he retired from public life.

Macdonald was born in St. Raphael, Ont. He became a lawyer in 1840, and a member of the legislature

John S. Macdonald, portrait by Samuel B. Waugh, Public Archives of Canada, Toronto

John S. Macdonald

for Glengarry County in 1841. Macdonald represented Cornwall County in the legislature from 1857 to 1867. In 1840, he married a daughter of George Waggaman, a U.S. Senator from Louisiana. Macdonald and his wife had three sons and four daughters. He died in Cornwall on June 1, 1872.   G. F. G. STANLEY

MACDONALD, ROSS (1915-   ), is the pen name of Kenneth Millar, an American writer of detective novels. Macdonald's best-known books feature Lew Archer, a private detective. The Archer novels are "hard-boiled" detective fiction, which emphasizes realism and violence. But Macdonald also explores the psychological and social forces that lead to crime.

Much of Macdonald's work features the theme of a family broken by the loss of the father. Many of his characters seek close personal relationships and the meaning of life in a world that seems impersonal. The action takes place amid southern California's landscapes and changing life styles, which Macdonald portrays vividly. The Archer novels include *The Moving Target* (1949), *The Chill* (1964), *The Far Side of the Dollar* (1965), *The Goodbye Look* (1969), *The Underground Man* (1971), and *The Blue Hammer* (1976).

Macdonald was born in Los Gatos, Calif., and grew up in Canada. His Canadian-born wife, Margaret Millar, also writes detective novels. The couple live in southern California.   HERBERT BREAN

MACDONOUGH, *muhk DAHN uh*, **THOMAS** (1783-1825), an American naval officer, became a hero of the War of 1812. In 1814, he defeated the British on Lake Champlain at Plattsburgh, N.Y., in one of the most decisive battles ever fought by the U.S. Navy.

When Macdonough took command of the Lake Champlain naval squadron in 1812, he found small, poorly armed vessels that lacked supplies and had untrained crews. After two years of preparations, he entered the harbor at Plattsburgh, carefully stationed his ships, and awaited the British. His victory there destroyed the British plan of invading New York state, and forced the British Army to retreat into Canada.

Macdonough was born in New Castle County, Delaware, on Dec. 31, 1783. He became a midshipman at 16. In 1804, he helped Stephen Decatur destroy the *Philadelphia*, which had been taken by Tripoli pirates. Macdonough became commander of the Mediterranean Squadron in 1824.   RICHARD S. WEST, JR.

See also WAR OF 1812 (The War at Sea; Lake Champlain).

MACDOWELL, EDWARD ALEXANDER (1861-1908), was an American composer and pianist. He is best remembered for such short, descriptive piano pieces as "To a Wild Rose" and "To a Water Lily." Many of these pieces are grouped in sets, which the composer called *Fireside Tales*, *New England Idyls*, *Sea Pieces*, and *Woodland Sketches*. He also wrote concertos, sonatas, symphonic poems, and songs.

MacDowell was born in New York City, where he studied piano under Teresa Carreño, a brilliant Venezuelan pianist. He also studied in France and Germany. He married his former pupil, Marian Nevins, in 1884. MacDowell headed the music department at Columbia University from 1896 to 1904. He was elected to the Hall of Fame in 1960.   GILBERT CHASE

MACE is a liquid tear gas that can be sprayed from a pressurized container. It causes a burning sensation and makes the eyes fill with tears. Mace disables a person temporarily but causes no lasting effects. *Chemical Mace* is a trade name, but the term *Mace* is used for all hand-controlled liquid chemical irritants.

Many police departments in the United States use Mace to help control riots and violent demonstrations. It can be used on individual targets without affecting people nearby.

Some persons claim that Mace permanently harms the eyes or nervous system. But the U.S. Public Health Service reported in 1968 that its tests of Chemical Mace indicated no permanent effects. Nevertheless, all such substances should be used only by trained officers under careful control and regulation.   MARVIN E. WOLFGANG

MACE is a club-shaped staff used as a symbol of authority. It is most often seen in legislative assemblies where it is used chiefly to restore order. The mace originally was a weapon of the Middle Ages. It was a club with a long handle, heavily weighted at one end. As the science of war developed, the weighted end became a heavy iron ball. Archers and other unmounted warriors used the mace as a hand arm. Some church officials also used it. Sergeants at arms, who were guards of kings and other high officials, carried maces. Gradually the mace gained a ceremonial character. The mace used in the U.S. House of Representatives is about 3 feet (91 centimeters) long. It is made up of ebony rods bound with a band of silver. A longer ebony rod in the center of the bundle has a silver globe mounted on it. A silver eagle is on top of the globe.   WILLIAM C. BARK

Mace of U.S. House of Representatives   Mace of the British House of Commons

MACE is a highly flavored spice used on foods. It comes from the red covering of the nutmeg (see NUTMEG). Fresh mace is fleshy, and smells and tastes like nutmeg. Before it is sold, it is dried in the sun. When dry, it becomes orange-yellow and transparent. Then it is ground or used in its whole form.

See also SPICE (with picture).

MACEDONIA is a mountainous region in the Balkan Peninsula in southeastern Europe. It covers 25,636 square miles (66,397 square kilometers) and has a population of about 4 million. Most of the people are farmers. They raise barley, corn, rice, rye, tobacco, wheat, and a variety of fruits and vegetables. They also raise sheep and goats.

Macedonia is inhabited chiefly by Slavs in the north and Greeks in the south. The Balkan Wars in 1912-1913 divided Macedonia between Serbia (now Yugoslavia), Greece, and Bulgaria.

Greek Macedonia covers 13,206 square miles (34,203 square kilometers) and has a population of about 1,890,000. Much of Greek Macedonia is a plain, watered by the Nestos, Struma, and Vardar rivers. Its capital is Salonika.

Yugoslavian Macedonia is one of Yugoslavia's six "republics." It covers 9,928 square miles (25,713 square kilometers) and has about 1,784,000 people. Skopje is the capital.

Bulgarian Macedonia covers 2,502 square miles (6,480 square kilometers) and has a population of about 303,000. Its capital is Blagoevgrad.

WORLD BOOK map
Macedonia

History. A savage European people called the Thracians moved into the region about 2000 B.C. After 1100 B.C., the Macedonians came under the influence of the Greeks. King Philip II of Macedonia unified the Greeks in 338 B.C., and prepared an expedition against the Persians. His son Alexander the Great founded a vast new empire on ruins of the Persian Empire. After his death in 323 B.C., his generals divided his empire.

Macedonia became a Roman province in 148 B.C. It was made part of the Byzantine Empire when the Roman Empire was divided in A.D. 395. Macedonia was included in the first Bulgarian empire in the 800's and in the Serbian empire in the 1300's. From 1389 until 1912, the Turks had possession of Macedonia.

The Bulgarian, Greek, and Serb inhabitants of Macedonia struggled against Turkey from the 1890's to 1912. The Balkan allies defeated Turkey in the First Balkan War in 1912, and Macedonia was divided among Greece, Serbia (Yugoslavia), and Bulgaria. Bulgaria started the Second Balkan War in 1913 to get more land but was defeated by the other Balkan countries. In attempts to gain more of Macedonia, Bulgaria invaded the region during both World Wars. Both times, the Greeks and Serbs fought on the victorious side and drove the Bulgarians from Macedonia.   G. G. ARNAKIS

See also ALEXANDER THE GREAT; ANTIGONID DYNASTY; BALKANS; GREECE, ANCIENT (The End of the Classical Period); PHILIP II; SALONIKA.

MACGREGOR, ROBERT. See ROB ROY.

MACH, *makh,* **ERNST** (1838-1916), was an Austrian physicist and psychologist. He studied the action of bodies moving at high speeds through gases, and developed an accurate method for measuring their speeds in terms of the speed of sound. This method is important in problems of supersonic flight.

Mach's work remained obscure until the speed of aircraft began to approach the speed of sound. Then the term *Mach number* came to be used as a measure of speed. *Mach 0.5* is half the speed of sound, or *subsonic*. *Mach 1* is the speed of sound, or *transonic*. *Mach 2* is twice the speed of sound, or *supersonic*, and so on (see AERODYNAMICS [Shock Waves and Sonic Booms]).

Mach was deeply interested in the historical development of the ideas on which the science of mechanics is based. He taught that all knowledge of the physical world comes to us by the five senses—sight, hearing, smell, taste, and feeling. He also taught that a scientific law was a correlation between observed data.

Mach was born at Turas, Moravia. He was graduated from the University of Vienna.   R. T. ELLICKSON

MACH NUMBER. See AERODYNAMICS (Shock Waves and Sonic Booms); MACH, ERNST.

MACHADO, ANTONIO. See SPANISH LITERATURE (The 1900's).

MACHETE, *muh SHEHT ee,* or *muh SHEHT,* is a large heavy knife with a blade shaped like a broadsword. It is used chiefly in South America and the West Indies. Machetes used as weapons have narrow blades often 2 to 3 feet (61 to 91 centimeters) long. Short-bladed machetes are used to cut sugar cane and to clear brush. See also KNIFE.

MACHIAVELLI, *MAH kyah VEL lee,* **NICCOLÒ** (1469-1527), was an Italian statesman and student of politics. His name has long stood for all that is deep, dark, and treacherous in political leadership. In Elizabethan literature, for example, there are hundreds of references that connect him with the Evil One or the Devil.

He is best known for his book *The Prince*, written in 1513 and published in 1532. This book established Machiavelli as the father of the modern science of politics. It skillfully sets forth the idea that rulers need not trouble themselves about the means they use to accomplish a purpose. They must use any means, no matter how wicked, to strike down enemies and make people obey. Machiavelli set down rules to be followed to keep power. The book also sets forth the idea of a united Italy. He also wrote a *History of Florence*, *The Art of War*, and *Discourses Upon the First Ten Books of Livy*, expressing his favor for a republican form of government.

Machiavelli was born in Florence. The son of a jurist, and a member of an old Tuscan family, Machiavelli was educated chiefly through private study. He became a leading figure in the Republic of Florence after the Medici family was driven out in 1498 (see MEDICI). For 14 years, he served as first secretary of the council of the republic. His duties brought him in contact with the notorious Cesare Borgia (see BORGIA). He also became interested in reorganizing the militia.

The Medici family returned to power in 1512, and dismissed Machiavelli from his office. They arrested, tortured, and imprisoned him. They finally released him on order of Pope Leo X. He spent the last 14 years of his life in retirement near Florence. There he wrote his books on history and politics. He also wrote poetry and comedies. He became a leading literary figure of the Renaissance.   R. JOHN RATH

See also ITALIAN LITERATURE (The 1500's and 1600's).

Sculpture by Lorenzo Bartolini, Uffizi, Florence (Alinari from Art Reference Bureau)
Niccolò Machiavelli

MACHINE is a device that does work. Industries use giant drill presses, lathes, and presses to make the products we use. Businesses depend on typewriters, computers, and other office machines. Automobiles, buses, and airplanes transport people swiftly over great distances. Trucks, railroads, and ships are machines used to haul goods to and from markets. Without machines, the residents of our cities would find it more difficult to live, and farmers could not raise enough food to feed us. Almost every activity of our daily life depends in some way on machines.

Man has constructed a wide variety of machines to satisfy his needs. Early man made stone axes that served as weapons and tools. The machines that man gradually developed gave him great control over his *environment* (physical surroundings). To operate his improved machines, he harnessed the energy of falling water and of such fuels as coal, oil, and the atom. Today, we use so many machines that the age we live in is often called the *machine age*.

Principles of Machines

A machine produces force and controls the direction and the motion of force. But it cannot create energy. A machine can never do more work than the energy put into it. It only transforms one kind of energy, such as electrical energy, and passes it along as mechanical energy. Some machines, such as diesel engines or steam turbines, are called *prime movers*, because they change energy directly into mechanical motion. For example, the energy of falling water rushing through the wheel of a turbine produces rotary motion. This direct motion of the wheel can be used to turn a generator that produces electricity. Other machines, such as a generator, a water pump, or a harvesting machine, are run by prime movers. These machines only control or produce certain forces and motions.

The ability of a machine to do work is measured by two factors. These factors are known as *efficiency* and *mechanical advantage*.

Efficiency. The efficiency of a machine is the ratio between the energy it supplies and the energy put into it. Machines that transmit only mechanical energy may have an efficiency of nearly 100 per cent. But some machines have an efficiency as low as 5 per cent. No machine can operate with 100 per cent efficiency, because the friction of its parts always uses up some of the energy that is supplied to the machine. All machines produce some friction. For this reason, a perpetual-motion machine is impossible (see PERPETUAL MOTION MACHINE).

A simple lever is a good example of a machine that has a high efficiency (see LEVER). The work it puts out is almost equal to the energy it receives, because the energy used up by friction is quite small. On the other hand, an automobile engine has an efficiency of only about 25 per cent, because much of the energy supplied by the fuel is lost in the form of heat that escapes into the surrounding air. See EFFICIENCY.

Mechanical Advantage. In machines that transmit only mechanical energy, the ratio of the force exerted by the machine to the force applied to the machine is known as *mechanical advantage*. Mechanical advantage can be demonstrated with a crowbar, which is a type of lever. When one end of the crowbar is directly under the weight, a part of the crowbar must rest on a *fulcrum* (support). The closer the fulcrum is to the load, the less the effort required to raise the load by pushing down on the handle of the crowbar, and the greater the mechanical advantage of the crowbar. For example, if the load is 200 kilograms, and the distance from the load to the fulcrum is one fourth of the distance from the handle to the fulcrum, it will take 50 kilograms of effort to raise the load. Therefore, the mechanical advantage

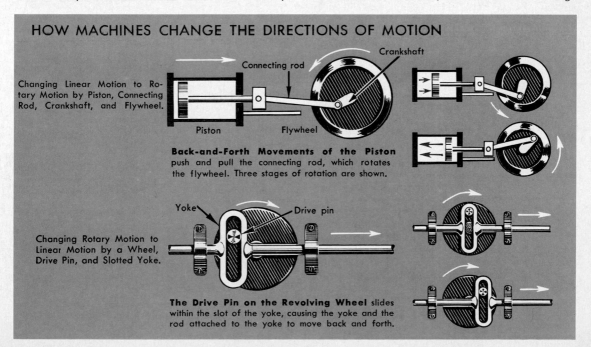

HOW MACHINES CHANGE THE DIRECTIONS OF MOTION

Changing Linear Motion to Rotary Motion by Piston, Connecting Rod, Crankshaft, and Flywheel.

Connecting rod

Crankshaft

Piston   Flywheel

Back-and-Forth Movements of the Piston push and pull the connecting rod, which rotates the flywheel. Three stages of rotation are shown.

Changing Rotary Motion to Linear Motion by a Wheel, Drive Pin, and Slotted Yoke.

Yoke   Drive pin

The Drive Pin on the Revolving Wheel slides within the slot of the yoke, causing the yoke and the rod attached to the yoke to move back and forth.

will be four to one. But the distance the load will be moved will be only one-fourth of the distance through which the effort is applied.

Six Simple Machines

Most machines consist of a number of elements, such as gears and ball bearings, that work together in a complex way. But no matter how complex they are, all machines are based in some way on six types of simple machines: the lever, the wheel and axle, the pulley, the inclined plane, the wedge, and the screw.

Lever. There are three basic types of levers, depending on where the effort is applied, on the position of the load, and on the position of the fulcrum. In a first-class lever, such as a crowbar, the fulcrum is between the load and the applied force. In a second-class lever, such as a wheelbarrow, the load lies between the fulcrum and the applied force. In a third-class lever, the effort is applied between the load and the fulcrum. For example, when a person lifts a ball in the palm of the hand, the load is at the hand and the fulcrum is at the elbow. The forearm supplies the upward force that lifts the ball. See LEVER.

Wheel and Axle. The wheel and axle is essentially a modified lever, but it can move a load farther than a lever can. In a windlass used to raise water from a well, the rope that carries the load is wrapped around the axle of the wheel. The effort is applied to a crank handle on the side of the wheel. The center of the axle serves as a fulcrum. The mechanical advantage depends upon the ratio between the radius of the axle and the distance traveled by the crank handle. The wheel-and-axle machine has important applications when it is used to transport heavy goods by rolling rather than by sliding. The wheel itself is regarded as one of the most important inventions of all time. It is widely used in all types of machinery and motor vehicles. See WHEEL; WHEEL AND AXLE.

Pulley. A pulley is a wheel over which a rope or belt is passed. It is a form of the wheel and axle. The mechanical advantage of a single pulley is one, because the downward force exerted on the rope equals the weight lifted by the other end of the rope that passes over the pulley. The main advantage of the single pulley is that it changes the direction of the force. For example, to lift a load, a person can more conveniently pull down on a rope and also use the weight of the body. When one pulley is attached to a support and another is attached to the load and allowed to move freely, a definite mechanical advantage is obtained. See PULLEY.

Inclined Plane. The inclined plane is such a simple device that it scarcely looks like a machine at all. The average person cannot raise a 200-pound box up 2 feet into the rear of a truck. But by placing a 10-foot plank from the truck to the ground, a person could raise the load easily. If there were no friction, the force required to move the box would be exactly 40 pounds. The mechanical advantage of an inclined plane is the length of the incline divided by the vertical rise. The mechanical advantage increases as the slope of the incline decreases. But the load will then have to be moved a greater distance. By adding rollers, it is pos-

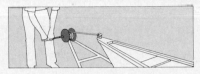

The Lever is one of the earliest and simplest machines. Its advantage lies in the short distance between the fulcrum (pivotal point) and load, and in the long distance between the fulcrum and the point where effort is applied.

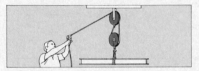

The Wheel and Axle has a rope attached to the axle to lift the load. The crank handle is the point where effort is applied. The effort is smaller than the load because it is at a greater distance from the axle which is the fulcrum.

The Pulley consists of a wheel with a grooved rim over which a rope is passed. It is used to change the direction of the effort applied to the rope. A block and tackle uses two or more pulleys to reduce the amount of effort needed to lift a load.

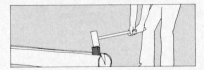

The Inclined Plane makes it easier to slide or skid a load upward than to lift it directly. The longer the slope, the smaller the effort required. The amount of work, however, is no less than if the load were lifted directly upward.

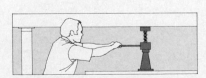

The Wedge, when struck with a mallet or sledge, exerts a large force on its sides. A gently tapering, or thin, wedge is more effective than a thick one. The mechanical advantage of the wedge is of great importance.

The Screw is a spiral inclined plane. The jackscrew is a combination of the lever and the screw. It can lift a heavy load with relatively small effort. Therefore, it has a very high mechanical advantage for practical purposes.

sible to make a roller conveyor that will reduce friction and have great efficiency. See INCLINED PLANE.

Wedge. The wedge is an adaptation of the inclined plane. It can be used to raise a heavy load over a short distance or to split a log. The wedge is driven by blows from a mallet or sledge hammer. The effectiveness of the wedge depends on the angle of the thin end. The smaller the angle, the less the force required to raise a given load. See WEDGE.

Screw. The screw is actually an inclined plane cut in a spiral around a shaft. The mechanical advantage of a screw is approximately the ratio of the circumference of the screw to the distance the screw advances during each revolution.

A *jackscrew*, such as those sometimes used to raise homes and other structures, combines the usefulness of both the screw and the lever. The lever is used to turn the screw. The mechanical advantage of a jackscrew is quite high, and only a small effort will raise a heavy load. See SCREW.

Designing Machines

By combining the principles of simple machines, engineers develop new and specialized machines. The parts for many of these machines are often standardized so they can be used in a variety of machines that perform entirely different tasks. Some of the more common parts found in machines include ball bearings, gears, pistons, V-belt pulleys, connecting rods, valves, universal joints, and flexible shafts. There is an increasing demand in industry today for new machines to perform new tasks and for improvements that will increase the value of old machines.   ALLEN S. HALL, JR.

Related Articles in WORLD BOOK include:

MACHINE AGE. See MACHINE; INDUSTRIAL REVOLUTION.

MACHINE GUN is an automatic weapon that can fire from 400 to 1,600 rounds of ammunition each minute. Machine gun barrels range in size from .22 caliber to 30 millimeters. Ammunition is fed into the gun from a cloth or metal belt, or from a cartridge holder called a *magazine*. Because machine guns fire so rapidly, they must be cooled by water or air. Machine guns are heavy weapons and are usually mounted on a support.

Operation. In all machine guns, extremely high gas pressure provides the operating energy for the firing cycle. The cycle begins when the propellant charge in the cartridge case burns. This combustion creates the gas pressure that is used in the *blowback*, *gas*, and *recoil* operating systems. All three systems fire the projectile through the *bore* of the barrel, eject the cartridge case, place a new cartridge in the firing chamber, and ready the mechanism to repeat the cycle.

In the *blowback system*, the operating energy comes from the cartridge case as the case is forced to the rear by the gas pressure. The case moves against the bolt, driving the bolt backward against a spring. The case is ejected, and the compressed spring drives the bolt forward. As the bolt moves forward, it cocks the firing mechanism, picks up a new cartridge, carries it into the chamber, and the cycle begins again.

In the *gas system*, the gas pressure drives a piston against the bolt. The bolt is driven to the rear, providing energy for a cycle similar to the blowback system.

In the *recoil system*, the bolt locks to the barrel when the gun is fired. These parts remain locked together as they are forced to the rear by the gas pressure. This movement provides energy to operate the gun.

Ground Weapons. The 7.62-millimeter M60 machine gun is a major infantry weapon. It is air-cooled, gas operated, and fires about 600 rounds a minute. The M60 replaced the Browning machine gun, an important weapon in World Wars I and II. The standard U.S.

U.S. Army

The M60 Machine Gun, a major infantry weapon, may be fired on a support, *above*, or from the hip or shoulder.

Machine Guns of World Wars I and II. The heavy machine gun, *far left,* was the most destructive weapon of World War I. Machine guns used during World War II included light machine guns, *right,* and the submachine gun M3, carried by the standing soldier.

Army submachine gun is the .45-caliber M3, a short-range weapon weighing 9 pounds (4 kilograms).

Aircraft Weapons. By the close of World War I, several types of machine guns were mounted on airplanes. These types included the Vickers, Maxim, Hotchkiss, Colt-Martin, and Lewis. Some of these guns were synchronized to fire in between the blades of propellers.

During World War II, fighters and bombers carried machine guns as armament. They also carried automatic cannon up to 20 millimeters in size. Today, most fighter planes carry rockets for air-to-air and air-to-ground use. Bombers use machine guns mounted in groups of two or four in power-driven turrets. The Vulcan 20-millimeter aircraft cannon has six rotating barrels. It can fire more than a ton of metal and explosives each minute.

Antiaircraft Weapons. The .50-caliber Browning machine gun was used as an antiaircraft weapon during World War II. It was used alone, or in groups of two or four. Large-caliber automatic cannon that fired explosive shells were also developed as antiaircraft weapons. The 20-millimeter Oerlikon gun was used on U.S. Navy ships. It was a self-fed, self-firing cannon that could fire 600 rounds a minute.

History. A type of machine gun appeared as early as the 1500's. It consisted of several guns bound together in a bundle or spread out in a row. A device that was fitted to the gun barrels caused them to fire simultaneously or in series. But little success was achieved until the Civil War, when many quick-fire guns appeared. Practical, rapid-fire, mechanical guns were used in the Franco-Prussian War, when soldiers operated them with a crank or lever. The French *Montigny mitrailleuse* and the American *Gatling* were among the more successful of these guns. In 1889, Hiram Maxim, an American-born inventor, developed the first entirely automatic weapon to gain wide acceptance. By the time of World War I, many different types of machine guns had come into use.　　　　　　　　JOHN D. BILLINGSLEY

See also ANTIAIRCRAFT DEFENSE; GATLING, RICHARD JORDAN; LEWIS, ISAAC NEWTON; MAXIM (Sir Hiram Stevens).

14

EARLY MACHINE GUNS

Maxim Gun

Hiram Maxim invented the first fully automatic machine gun.

Gatling Gun

Richard Gatling produced a hand-cranked machine gun in 1862.

Montigny Mitrailleuse

The Montigny mitrailleuse was a quick-firing gun with 37 barrels.

MACHINE TOOL is a power-driven machine used to shape metal. Machine tools bend, cut, drill, grind, hammer, plane, and squeeze metal into any desired shape. More advanced machine tool operations involve the use of such forces as electrical or chemical energy, heat, magnetism, or ultrasound.

Machine tools play an important part in the manufacture of almost all metal products. Machinists use them in making parts for such products as automobiles, radios, refrigerators, and television sets. Many other products, including books, furniture, and textiles, are made by machines that were manufactured by machine tools.

There are about 500 kinds of machine tools, and each performs one or more metalworking operations. Machines called *single-function machine tools* perform only one operation. Others, known as *multifunction machine tools*, perform two or more tasks.

Machines called *transfer machines* consist of a series of machine tools linked together. The metal being machined, called the *workpiece*, moves automatically from one tool to the next. Transfer machines perform every machine operation necessary for the mass production of a complex part, such as an automobile cylinder block. Machines can also be automated by a system called *numerical control*.

Machine tools vary greatly in size. A transfer machine may measure several hundred feet long, but a machine that produces parts for clocks and watches can be mounted on a workbench.

Basic Machine Tool Operations

There are seven basic machine tool operations: (1) drilling and boring, which include reaming and tapping; (2) forming, which includes bending, forging, pressing, and shearing; (3) grinding, which includes lapping and honing; (4) milling; (5) planing and shaping, which include broaching; (6) sawing; and (7) turning.

Drilling and Boring. Drilling involves cutting round holes up to 3 inches (7.5 centimeters) in diameter in a piece of metal. These holes, cut by a rotating *twist drill*, may be as small as a few thousandths of an inch in diameter.

In most machine shops, twist drills are mounted on large machines called *drill presses*. The machinist places the workpiece on a table beneath the drill and lowers the drill into the metal. The bit of the drill has several sharp cutting edges. Two or more spiral grooves along the bit help remove metal shavings from the hole.

Boring is a process used to cut round holes greater than 3 inches in diameter. Boring is also used to enlarge and *finish* (smooth) holes that have already been drilled.

Metal is bored on machines that have a cutting tool with only one sharp edge. On small boring machines, the tool revolves and the workpiece remains stationary. On large machines, the tool is stationary and the workpiece revolves.

Drilling and boring include two other operations, *reaming* and *tapping*. Reaming consists of smoothing the inside of a hole. Tapping is the process of cutting a screw thread inside a hole (see SCREW).

Forming is the manufacture of metal parts from sheet metal. There are four main types of forming machines: (1) forging machines, (2) presses, (3) press brakes, and (4) shears.

Forging Machines form metal by hammering and squeezing it. Some of these machines hammer hot metal into any shape. Others squeeze hot metal in a *die* (mold) under great pressure. The metal flows to every part of the die and takes the desired shape. Forging machines produce extremely tough and durable metal parts.

Presses stamp a metal sheet into a certain shape. Then they use a die to squeeze this piece of metal, called a *blank*, into the final shape. *Punch presses* punch holes in metal sheets.

Press Brakes bend sheets of metal for use as parts of various products, including the sides of cabinets and refrigerators. Large press brakes have special dies that form metal into complex shapes for the manufacture of such parts as automobile fenders, hoods, and roofs.

Shears cut large sheets of metal much as scissors cut sheets of paper. Machinists then work the metal into finished parts of the desired shape and size.

Grinding involves removing metal from the surface of a workpiece to make it smooth. A grinding machine has a *grinding wheel* that spins at high speed against the workpiece. This wheel is made of an abrasive material similar to that on sandpaper (see ABRASIVE). Early grinding wheels were made from blocks of sandstone or some other type of natural abrasive. Today, grinding

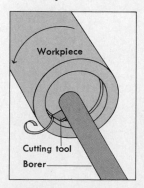

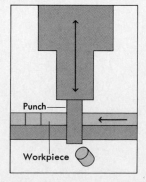

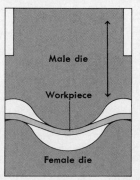

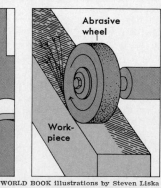

WORLD BOOK illustrations by Steven Liska

A Borer cuts and smooths round holes. Its cutting tool has a single sharp edge.

A Punch Press is a forming machine that stamps holes into sheet metal.

Press Brakes form metal into a desired shape by pressing it between two dies.

A Grinding Wheel rubs against the surface of a workpiece to make it smooth.

wheels are made of artificial as well as natural abrasives.

Two of the main types of grinding operations are *cylindrical grinding* and *surface grinding*. In cylindrical grinding, a round workpiece rotates against the grinding wheel. In surface grinding, the wheel rotates and a flat workpiece moves back and forth against it. In both processes, the surface of the workpiece is finished by the friction created by the wheel rubbing against the metal.

Grinding includes two other operations, *lapping* and *honing*. Lapping uses an abrasive paste or other substance to remove metal. It provides an extremely smooth surface when only a small amount of metal must be removed. A lapping machine has a metal plate covered with an abrasive. *Honing* assures maximum accuracy in finishing holes to precise dimensions. In this process, an abrasive paste is applied to cylindrical parts called *heads*, which are inserted into the hole. The heads rotate while moving up and down.

Milling. In this operation, a round tool with several cutting edges rotates against a workpiece. The cutting tool of most milling machines looks like a wheel with teeth sticking out of it. This tool makes flat surfaces on metal. Machinists use special milling tools to cut such shapes as those of bevels, gear teeth, straight slots, and T-shaped slots.

Some milling machines manufacture metal parts small enough to fit in a person's hand. Others, such as *special contour milling machines*, produce airplane wing sections as long as 80 feet (24 meters).

Planing and Shaping. Planing smooths flat surfaces of large pieces of metal. The process resembles smoothing wood with a hand plane. However, the cutting tool of a planing machine remains stationary while the metal moves back and forth beneath it. Shaping smooths flat surfaces of small pieces of metal. The cutting tool moves back and forth over a stationary workpiece.

Planing and shaping include another technique, called *broaching*, which shapes holes in a piece of metal. For example, broaching can change round holes to square ones. A broach is a machine that looks like a long metal bar with rows of teeth on it. Each tooth cuts a little deeper than the one before. A broach is pulled or pushed through a hole, and the teeth cut the metal to the desired shape.

Milling has replaced planing and shaping almost entirely. The cutting tools of milling machines can smooth metal surfaces faster than those of planers or shapers.

Sawing consists of machining a piece of metal with a cutting tool that has sharp teeth along one edge. There are two types of machine-tool sawing, *cutoff sawing* and *contour sawing*. Machinists use cutoff sawing to cut metal bars to a certain length. Contour sawing cuts flat pieces of metal into the desired shape.

Turning is used chiefly to cut metal into round or cylindrical shapes. Turning machines are the most common machine tools in the United States. They manufacture gear blanks, shafts, wheels, and many other metal parts.

The *lathe* is the basic turning machine. On a lathe, the workpiece is fastened to a rotating spindle, and the cutting tool is mounted at the side of the workpiece. The tool moves against the rotating workpiece, peeling metal until the workpiece has the desired shape. A *turret lathe* has several kinds of cutting tools mounted on a revolving toolholder called a *turret*. This type of lathe can perform various cutting operations, one after the other.

Some turning machines have several spindles and cutting tools that operate at the same time. Such a *multispindle machine* performs various operations at once on several workpieces. The machine moves each workpiece from one cutting tool to the next until all the operations have been performed.

Advanced Machine Tool Operations

Many new kinds of machine tools have been developed since the late 1950's. These machines cut extremely hard metals into complex shapes by means of electrical or chemical energy, heat, magnetism, ultrasound, or other forces. Many kinds of advanced machine tool operations were first used to make extremely precise, intricately shaped parts for spacecraft and jet airplanes. Today, the automobile industry and a number of other industries depend on them to produce parts quickly and efficiently. These methods include (1) electrical discharge machining, (2) electrochemical machining, (3) chemical machining, and (4) high-energy rate forming.

Electrical Discharge Machining (EDM) cuts holes in extremely hard metals, including steel alloys that cannot be cut by traditional machining methods. EDM produces smooth, accurate holes, many of which have

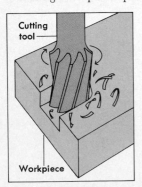

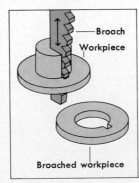

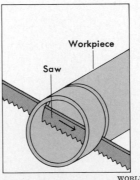

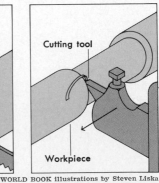

WORLD BOOK illustrations by Steven Liska

A Milling Tool cuts flat surfaces or special shapes as it rotates against a workpiece.

A Broach changes the shape of a hole. The tool is pushed or pulled through a workpiece.

A Saw cuts a piece of metal to a certain length or into a desired shape.

A Turning Machine has a cutting tool that peels metal from a rotating workpiece.

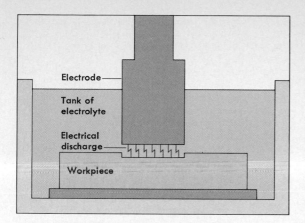

Electrical Discharge Machining (EDM) produces smooth, accurate holes in metal by means of an electric current.

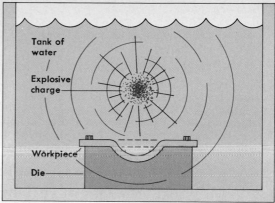

High-Energy Rate Forming (HERF) uses an explosive charge to force sheet metal into the contours of a die.

extremely complex shapes. It is the most widely used advanced machine tooling process.

EDM involves an *electrode* made of brass, copper, or a similar material that conducts electricity (see ELECTRODE). The electrode is cut to the shape of the hole to be made in the workpiece. The electrode and the workpiece are dipped into an *electrolyte*, a liquid that conducts electricity. An electric current is then directed between the electrode and the workpiece, producing a discharge of sparks. This discharge has the shape of the electrode. The sparks thus erode a hole of the same shape in the workpiece.

Electrochemical Machining (ECM) uses electricity to create a chemical reaction that erodes metal from a workpiece. Electricity flows from a positively charged workpiece to a negatively charged cutting tool. An electrolyte is pumped at high pressure into the space between the workpiece and the tool. The electrolyte conducts current between them, causing an electrochemical reaction that erodes metal from the surface of the workpiece. The finished workpiece takes the shape of the face of the cutting tool.

Chemical Machining. In this operation, the workpiece is covered by a chemically resistant mask. The mask has holes cut in it of the shape of those to be cut in the workpiece. The workpiece is dipped into a strong chemical solution, which dissolves the metal from the sections of the workpiece that are not covered by the mask. Chemical machining cuts holes from $\frac{1}{4}$ inch (0.64 centimeter) to $\frac{1}{2}$ inch (1.27 centimeters) deep in metal.

High-Energy Rate Forming (HERF) involves transmitting pressure through a liquid, usually water, to force sheet metal into the contours of a die. In most cases, the pressure is created by setting off an explosive in the liquid or by discharging an electric spark in it. HERF is used chiefly to make large metal parts that have an unusual shape, such as a radar antenna shaped like a disk.

Other Advanced Machining Operations. In *laser cutting*, machinists aim a thin beam of concentrated light at the workpiece. This light is created by a device called a *laser*. When a laser beam is aimed at an extremely small area, it may produce temperatures higher than 10,000° F. (5538° C). Machinists use laser beams to make small, precise cuts or holes by melting through metal or other materials. See LASER.

In an operation called *magnetic forming*, an electromagnet is created when an electric current is directed through a coil. If the coil surrounds the workpiece, the electromagnetic force shapes the workpiece by pushing the metal in. If the coil is placed within the workpiece, the force pushes the metal out.

In *plasma spraying and cutting*, machinists use a heated stream of ionized gas, called *plasma*, to melt holes in extremely hard metals and other materials. The plasma is sprayed at a high speed from an instrument called a *plasma torch* onto the workpiece. A similar process, called *electron beam machining*, cuts holes in a workpiece by means of a stream of electrons traveling at a high rate of speed.

Another operation, called *ultrasonic machining*, cuts holes in extremely hard metal. The cutting tool of an ultrasonic cutter vibrates into the workpiece at a speed higher than the frequency of sound. The workpiece is immersed in an abrasive fluid. Friction created by the tool vibrating against the abrasive grinds the metal into shape.

Numerical Control of Machine Tools

Numerical control, a system for automating machine tools, gives a machine its instructions by means of a *control tape*. This tape, which is made of paper or plastic, contains the instructions in the form of a number code. The numbers are represented on the tape by a series of holes or by magnetized spots. The information on the tape comes from design drawings of the part to be produced. The tape is fed into the machine, which has a control unit that reads the code. This process creates electric signals that correspond to the code. The signals control the direction and speed of the machine as it moves across the workpiece.

A *machining center* is a multipurpose machine programmed by numerical control. It can perform several machining tasks in one operation and produce a finished product. A machining center does the work of several machines without moving the workpiece.

In some machining systems, computers have replaced control tapes. A system called *direct numerical control* has a computer that directs the operations of more than 100 machines. The computer sends instructions to each machine in the system.

History

The basic machine tool operations developed from processes originally used with hand tools, which cut and shaped wood. The first modern machine tool was invented in 1775 by John Wilkinson, an English iron-maker. Wilkinson's invention, a boring machine, enabled precise holes to be drilled in metal. As a result, James Watt, a Scottish engineer and inventor, was able to develop a steam engine that did not leak steam. A number of other machine tools, including the planer, the shaper, and the first successful screw-cutting lathe, were also invented in England during the 1800's.

In the United States, the machine tool industry began about 1800. Machine tools were used principally to make guns and cannons for the armed forces. In 1873, C. M. Spencer of the United States developed a completely automatic lathe. Transfer machines were developed during the 1920's. The number of machine tools in the United States more than doubled during World War II (1939-1945).

Since the 1950's, the development of spacecraft and other types of modern aircraft has resulted in the advanced machining operations. The use of numerical control, machining centers, and computers brought new speed and efficiency to the industry. In the United States, the machine tool industry consists of about 400 companies. EDWARD J. LOEFFLER

Related Articles in WORLD BOOK include:

Drilling Tools	Sound (picture:
Forging	Ultrasound)
Grinding and Polishing	Steam Hammer
Nasmyth, James	

MACHINIST. See MACHINE TOOL; MACHINISTS AND AEROSPACE WORKERS, INTERNATIONAL ASSOCIATION OF.

MACHINISTS AND AEROSPACE WORKERS, INTERNATIONAL ASSOCIATION OF, formerly the INTERNATIONAL ASSOCIATION OF MACHINISTS, is a labor union affiliated with the American Federation of Labor and Congress of Industrial Organizations. It has locals in the United States and its territories and in Canada.

Membership is open to men and women who work in the metalworking industries, on production lines, in machine shops, garages, toolrooms, and everywhere that machinery and equipment are manufactured, installed, repaired, or operated.

Founded in Atlanta, Ga., in 1888, the International Association of Machinists and Aerospace Workers is one of the largest unions in the aircraft and guided-missile industry, as well as one of the largest among the railroad, automobile mechanics, airlines, machine tool, and business machine industry unions. Services include a research and statistical department, an educational department, and a department of health and welfare. The union publishes a weekly newspaper, *The Machinist*. Headquarters are at 1300 Connecticut Ave. NW, Washington, D.C. 20036. For membership, see LABOR MOVEMENT (table). GORDON H. COLE

MACHU PICCHU, *MAH choo PEEK choo*, is the site of an ancient Inca city about 50 miles (80 kilometers) northwest of Cusco, Peru. The stone structures which are the ruins of Machu Picchu stand on a mountain about 8,000 feet (2,400 meters) high. In 1911, Hiram Bingham discovered the ruins. See also SOUTH AMERICA (color picture); INCA.

MACINTOSH, CHARLES (1766-1843), a British chemist and inventor, is best known as the inventor of waterproof fabrics. The *mackintosh*, a waterproof outer garment, is named after him. He also made many significant contributions to chemical technology. He opened a factory to manufacture alum and sal ammoniac before he was 20. He also introduced into Great Britain the manufacture of lead and aluminum acetates and contributed to the technology of dyeing. He was born in Glasgow. ROBERT E. SCHOFIELD

MACK, ALEXANDER. See BRETHREN, CHURCH OF THE.

MACK, CONNIE (1862-1956), became one of the greatest managers in baseball history. He helped organize the American League, and served as owner-manager of the Philadelphia Athletics from 1901 until he retired in 1950. Mack spent more than 60 years in baseball, and led the Athletics in nine World Series. They won five of them. His sons later sold the team, and it was moved to Kansas City, Mo. Mack was born Cornelius McGillicuddy in East Brookfield, Mass. He was elected to the National Baseball Hall of Fame in 1937. ED FITZGERALD

MACKAY was the family name of two American businessmen, father and son.

John William Mackay (1831-1902) and James Gordon Bennett, Jr., organized the Commercial Cable Company and the Postal Telegraph Company in 1883. They laid two cables under the Atlantic Ocean, and were beginning one under the Pacific when Mackay died.

Mackay was born in Ireland, but came to New York City with his parents as a boy. In 1851 he went to California to seek gold. Mackay made his fortune as one of the owners of the "Big Bonanza" gold and silver mine. This mine, discovered in 1873 at Virginia City, Nev., was the richest deposit of gold and silver ore ever found. The value of a share in it shot up from 15 cents to $1,850.

Clarence Hungerford Mackay (1874-1938) succeeded his father as a director of the telegraph and cable companies. He became vice-president of the Postal Telegraph Company at 23. Congress combined his cable and telegraph companies with the Western Union Telegraph Company in 1943. Mackay was born in San Francisco. DONALD L. KEMMERER

MACKENZIE (pop. 29,299) is a district of the Northwest Territories of Canada. It lies east of the Yukon Territory and west of the District of Keewatin. Mackenzie covers an area of 527,490 square miles (1,366,193 square kilometers), including 34,265 square miles (88,746 square kilometers) of inland water. Fur trade opened the district to settlement. But today, minerals, notably gold, are more important. There also are rich deposits of tungsten, base metals, and petroleum. Fisheries operate on Great Slave Lake.

Mackenzie was made a district in 1895. It elects four members to the Council of the Northwest Territories, and one to the federal House of Commons. The federal and territorial governments provide civil administration. All the Indians of the Northwest Territories live in Mackenzie. R. A. J. PHILLIPS

See also NORTHWEST TERRITORIES.

ALEXANDER MACKENZIE

Prime Minister of Canada
1873-1878

MACDONALD 1867-1873   MACKENZIE 1873-1878   MACDONALD 1878-1891

Detail of a portrait by J. W. L. Forster; Parliament Buildings, Ottawa (John Evans)

MACKENZIE, ALEXANDER (1822-1892), served as prime minister of Canada from 1873 to 1878. He was the second person, and the first Liberal, to hold that office.

Mackenzie faced many national economic problems as prime minister, chiefly because he served during a worldwide depression. But he strengthened the new nation by promoting honest, democratic government and greater independence from Great Britain. He won respect for his determination, hard work, and honesty.

Mackenzie, a Scottish immigrant, had little formal education. He worked as a stonemason before entering politics, and his appearance reflected his humble background. He had the muscular body and strong hands of a laborer. A reddish beard emphasized his strong chin. Mackenzie spoke with a Scottish accent.

Early Life

Childhood and Education. Alexander Mackenzie was born on Jan. 28, 1822, in the village of Logierait, Scotland, about 50 miles (80 kilometers) north of Edinburgh. He was the third of the 10 children—all sons—of Alexander Mackenzie, a carpenter, and Mary Fleming Mackenzie. When Alexander was 10, he began to herd

IMPORTANT DATES IN MACKENZIE'S LIFE

1822 (Jan. 28) Born in Logierait, Scotland.
1842 (May) Settled in Kingston, Upper Canada.
1845 (March 28) Married Helen Neil.
1852 (Jan. 4) Helen Neil Mackenzie died.
1853 (June 17) Married Jane Sym.
1861 Elected to the Legislative Assembly of the Province of Canada.
1873 (Nov. 7) Became prime minister of Canada.
1878 (Oct. 17) Resigned as prime minister.
1892 (April 17) Died in Toronto.

sheep to help support the family. His father, whose health had been poor, died three years later. Alexander then left school to train as a stonemason.

Alexander continued to read on his own and, in time, gave himself a good education. He finished his training as a stonemason when he was about 20 and got a job on a railroad construction project near Irvine, Scotland.

Emigration to Canada. In Irvine, Mackenzie fell in love with Helen Neil, the daughter of a stonemason. Her family emigrated to Canada in 1842, and Mackenzie went along. They settled in Kingston, the capital of the Province of Canada. The province consisted of Upper Canada (present-day Ontario) and Lower Canada (present-day Quebec). Mackenzie became a builder and contractor, and he and Helen were married in 1845.

In 1847, the young couple moved to what was then the Far West of Canada. They settled in Sarnia, Upper Canada. Helen and Alexander had three children, but only one, their daughter Mary, survived. Helen died in 1852. The next year, Mackenzie married Jane Sym, whose father was a Sarnia farmer.

Entry into Political Life

Member of the Reformers. Soon after settling in Canada, Mackenzie joined the Reform Party, a liberal political party. He became a follower of George Brown, a Reform leader and the publisher of the *Globe* in Toronto. In 1851, Mackenzie helped Brown win election to the Legislative Assembly of the Province of Canada. Brown in time became the leader of the Reform Party. From 1852 to 1854, Mackenzie edited the *Lambton Shield*, a newspaper that supported the Reformers. In 1861, he won election to the Legislative Assembly from Lambton County, Upper Canada.

In 1867, several British colonies in North America united and formed the Dominion of Canada. Sir John A. Macdonald, the leader of the Conservative Party, became the first prime minister after Confederation. The Dominion's first elections took place in 1867. Mackenzie won election to the House of Commons, but Brown was defeated. Mackenzie then replaced Brown as head of the Reform Party. He united Reformers and liberals throughout Canada into a new Liberal Party.

Leader of the Opposition. The Conservatives won a majority in Parliament in the 1872 elections, and Macdonald remained prime minister. Mackenzie had unofficially led the Liberal Party since Confederation. In 1873, the party appointed him to the official position of *leader of the Opposition*. This office is held by the head of the second largest party in the House.

Later in 1873, a scandal disgraced the Macdonald administration. Two financial groups had competed for a government contract to build the Canadian Pacific Railway between eastern Canada and the Pacific Coast. The government gave the contract to the group headed by Sir Hugh Allan, the owner of a shipping line. But then it was learned that Allan had contributed $300,000 to the Conservative election campaign of 1872. Mackenzie and other Liberals attacked the Macdonald Government about the so-called Pacific Scandal, and Macdonald resigned. On Nov. 7, 1873, Mackenzie became Canada's second prime minister.

Prime Minister

Reforms. Mackenzie called for new elections to be held in January, 1874. The Liberal Party won a large majority in the House. Under Mackenzie's leadership, Parliament took many steps to promote honest, democratic government. For example, it passed laws to prevent dishonest election practices and allow more citizens to vote. It also introduced the secret ballot, which was first used in 1878.

To guarantee honesty in his administration, Mackenzie himself took charge of the Department of Public Works. This department controlled the construction of such projects as railroads and public buildings. It spent more money than any other government department—and thus offered the greatest possibilities for dishonesty.

Strengthening the New Nation. Mackenzie's administration strengthened Canadian independence in international relations by dealing directly with the United States. Previously, British diplomats had met with representatives of other nations in Canada's behalf. Mackenzie also established the Royal Military College in 1874 and the Supreme Court of Canada in 1875. These institutions enabled Canada to handle more of its own military and legal affairs.

The Pacific Railway Dispute occurred when the government ran short of time and money in building the Canadian Pacific Railway. In 1871, British Columbia had become part of Canada on the condition that the transcontinental railroad be completed by 1880. Mackenzie asked for more time, and the province threatened to secede.

The dispute between British Columbia and the Canadian government led to one of Mackenzie's most important achievements as prime minister. At that time,

the British statesman Frederick T. Blackwood, Marquis of Dufferin and Ava, was governor general—the British monarch's representative in Canada. Lord Dufferin proposed that an official in London settle the dispute. But Mackenzie protested against such British interference in Canadian affairs. He insisted that the governor general respect decisions made by Canadian officials. As a result, the British government revised the governor general's powers and allowed Canada to handle its own internal affairs. The railroad was completed in 1885.

Economic Difficulties and Defeat. Mackenzie served as prime minister during a worldwide depression. With the Canadian economy in a slump, taxes did not provide enough income to pay the government's expenses. Mackenzie, following the economic beliefs of his time, reduced government spending and increased taxes. But these steps failed to lift Canada out of the depression.

Hoping to win a vote of confidence, Mackenzie called for new elections to be held in September, 1878. In the election campaign, the Conservatives attacked Mackenzie's leadership during the depression. Macdonald called for a "National Policy" that included tariff protection for Canadian industries. This idea appealed to many voters because of the nation's economic difficulties. The Conservatives won a large majority in Parliament, and Macdonald replaced Mackenzie as prime minister on Oct. 17, 1878.

Later Years

Mackenzie was re-elected to the House of Commons from Lambton County and again became leader of the Opposition. But the strain of office had damaged his health, and he resigned as Opposition leader in 1880. Mackenzie won re-election to the House three more times. He was still a Member of Parliament when he died in Toronto on April 17, 1892.　　Dale C. Thomson

See also Brown, George; Canada, History of; Dufferin and Ava, Marquis of; Macdonald, Sir John A.

MACKENZIE, SIR ALEXANDER (1763 or 1764-1820), was a Canadian trader and explorer. He was the first white man to reach the Mackenzie River and to cross the northern part of the North American continent to the Pacific Ocean.

In 1789, Mackenzie left Fort Chipewyan on Lake Athabasca with a small party of Canadians and Indian guides. He pushed his way north to Great Slave Lake, and then followed the river that now bears his name. It took him to the Arctic Ocean. He had hoped that the river would lead him to the Pacific Ocean, and was keenly disappointed. Because of this, Mackenzie called it the *River of Disappointment*.

Three years later, Mackenzie started on his trip to the west coast. He followed the Peace River, crossed the Rocky Mountains, and reached the Pacific Ocean in 1793. This trip convinced him that a search for a Northwest Passage to the Orient would be useless.

He wrote *Voyages on the River Saint Lawrence and Through the Continent of North America to the Frozen and Pacific Oceans in the Years 1789 and 1793* (1801). This book contains much valuable information on Indian tribes and Canadian history.

Mackenzie was born on the island of Lewis with Harris. He went to Canada in 1778. There, he entered the countinghouse of a Montreal fur-trading firm. After his last trip, he made a large fortune as a fur trader. He spent his last years in Scotland.　　WILLIAM R. WILLOUGHBY

MACKENZIE, RODERICK (1760?-1844), was a Canadian frontiersman and fur trader. He accompanied his cousin, Sir Alexander Mackenzie, on a trip to western Canada in 1786, and built Fort Chipewyan in northeastern Alberta in 1788. He commanded the fort from 1789 to 1793. He was a capable administrator rather than a trailbreaker. He returned to eastern Canada in 1797, and became a partner in the North West Company in 1799. Later, he served in the Legislative Council of Lower Canada. He was born in Scotland, and lived at Terrebonne, Canada.　　THOMAS D. CLARK

MACKENZIE, WILLIAM LYON (1795-1861), a Canadian politician, led the unsuccessful December Rebellion of 1837 in Upper Canada. As a member of the Reform party, Mackenzie was elected to the Legislative Assembly in 1828. He was a busy agitator from the start. Although he was not an original thinker, he succeeded in popularizing the ideas of others. Mackenzie insisted that Canada have more self-government than Britain allowed, and urged more democratic govern-

Sir Alexander Mackenzie
Portrait by Sir Thomas Lawrence.
The National Gallery of Canada,
Canadian War Memorials
Collection, Ottawa

William L. Mackenzie
Portrait by J. W. L. Forster.
Public Archives of Canada, Ottawa

ment within Canada itself. He wanted an independent judiciary, responsible government like that in Britain, less power for the governor-general, and more power for the legislature, especially control over taxation.

In 1837 the British Parliament rejected the demands of the Reform party, and Mackenzie and the party were defeated in the elections. Mackenzie, angry and bitter after his defeat, decided to revolt. But his plans were badly organized, and only about 800 of his followers gathered to march on Toronto. The Loyalist militia quickly defeated them.

Mackenzie escaped to the United States and established a temporary government on Navy Island in the Niagara River. After a month's stay, United States officials arrested him for breaking the neutrality laws. In 1849 he was permitted to return to Canada, where he was re-elected to the Legislative Assembly in 1851.

Mackenzie was born near Dundee, Scotland, and moved to Canada in 1820.　　WILLARD M. WALLACE

See also CANADA, HISTORY OF (Struggle for Responsible Government); KING, WILLIAM LYON MACKENZIE.

MACKENZIE RIVER, in the Northwest Territories, is the longest river in Canada. It flows north and west for about 1,000 miles (1,600 kilometers) from Great Slave

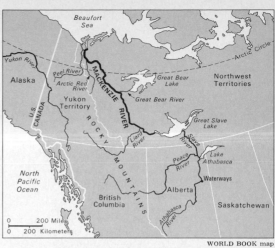

Location of the Mackenzie River

Lake to the Beaufort Sea. Much of the river is more than 1 mile (1.6 kilometers) wide. Every second, an average of about 500,000 cubic feet (1,400 cubic meters) of water flows from its mouth. Water flows into the Mackenzie from many tributaries, including the Liard, Great Bear, Arctic Red, and Peel rivers. Water also enters from Great Slave Lake. It reaches the lake through the Slave River, which collects water from the Peace and Athabasca rivers. The Mackenzie was named for the Canadian explorer Sir Alexander Mackenzie (see MACKENZIE, SIR ALEXANDER).

All the rivers mentioned above are part of the *Mackenzie River System,* Canada's largest river system. This vast system drains water from about 682,000 square miles (1,766,000 square kilometers), an area larger than Alaska. Its most distant water source is high in Alberta's Rocky Mountains, 2,635 miles (4,241 kilometers) from the Arctic mouth of the Mackenzie. In North America, only the Mississippi-Missouri system is longer than the Mackenzie system.

A 1,700-mile (2,740-kilometer) stretch of the Mackenzie system, from Waterways, Alberta, to the Beaufort Sea, is navigable. Only a 7-mile (11-kilometer) rapids on the Slave River interferes with shipping.

The Mackenzie River basin is rich in natural resources. The Peace River area of Alberta and British Columbia includes abundant farmland. It also has petroleum and natural gas deposits and water for hydroelectric power. In the northern part of the basin, the delta at the mouth of the Mackenzie is a muskrat-trapping area. It has little agriculture but has petroleum, radium, and uranium deposits.　　D. F. PUTNAM

See also NORTHWEST TERRITORIES; RIVER (chart: Longest Rivers).

MACKEREL, *MACK er ul,* is one of the most valuable food fishes. It lives in the North Atlantic Ocean. On the American side, it lives in waters from Cape Hatteras to the Strait of Belle Isle between Newfoundland and Labrador. In European waters, it can be found from Norway to the Mediterranean and Adriatic seas.

The mackerel is related to the tuna. Its shape and beautiful colors make it outstanding. Its body is of vari-

The Frigate Mackerel Lives in Most Warm Seas.

ous shades of blue and green. The mackerel is silvery-white below, and has wavy black stripes on its back. *Mackerel*, or *mackerel-back*, clouds are so named because they resemble the markings on the back of this fish.

The mackerel has two large fins on its back and two smaller ones beneath. Its large tail is shaped like a fork. Five tiny fins are on each side just in front of the tail. Mackerel grow 10 to 18 inches (25 to 46 centimeters) long, and weigh $\frac{1}{2}$ to 3 pounds (0.2 to 1.4 kilograms).

In spring, schools of mackerel appear near Cape Hatteras and swim north into Canadian waters. In autumn, they return to deeper seas. Their spawning season on the North American coast is from May to July. June is the most active spawning month. Mackerel breed chiefly in shallow waters of New England and the Gulf of St. Lawrence. Mackerel flesh tastes best when the fish is caught just after the spawning period.

Sharks, bluefish, porpoises, and whales attack and eat mackerel. A sea bird, the gannet, eats small mackerel. Mackerel themselves eat crustaceans, herring, anchovies, menhaden, and other small fish.

The mackerel fisheries of Great Britain, Ireland, Norway, Canada, and the United States provide most of the world's supply of this fish.

Scientific Classification. Mackerel belong to three families, the *Scombridae, Cybiidae,* and *Katsuworidae.* The common mackerel is in the family *Scombridae.* It is genus *Scomber,* species *S. scombrus.*   LEONARD P. SCHULTZ

See also FISH (picture: Fish of Coastal Waters and the Open Ocean); FISHING INDUSTRY (table: Chief Kinds of Ocean Fish); KINGFISH; TUNA.

MACKINAC, *MACK ih naw,* **STRAITS OF,** is an important link in the water route between Lake Michigan and the Atlantic Ocean. The straits connect Lake Michigan and Lake Huron. They are at the northern end of the Lower Peninsula of Michigan (see MICHIGAN [physical map]). Mackinac Island lies in the straits. The straits are about 40 miles (64 kilometers) long, and about 5 miles (8 kilometers) wide at the narrowest point. The Mackinac Bridge across the straits is one of the world's longest suspension bridges. Its center span is 3,800 feet (1,160 meters) long. The bridge links Mackinaw City in the Lower Peninsula with the city of St. Ignace in the Upper Peninsula.   WILLIS F. DUNBAR

MACKINAC ISLAND, *MACK ih naw,* or *MACH ih nack,* is a north Michigan island summer resort in the Straits of Mackinac (see MICHIGAN [political map]). It covers an area of about 4 square miles (10 square kilometers). The Chippewa Indians called the island *Michilimackinac,* usually defined as *Great Spirits* or *Great*

Turtle. The city of Mackinac Island lies on the southeastern end of the island. No passenger cars are permitted on Mackinac. Ferries link the island with the mainland. The world's longest fresh-water yachting event is the Chicago-to-Mackinac Island race, held each July.

In 1671, Father Jacques Marquette established a mission at nearby Point St. Ignace. The French built forts at St. Ignace and Mackinaw City, on the Michigan mainland. In 1761, the French surrendered the area to the British. The British built Fort Mackinac on the island in 1780. In 1796, the United States gained the island, but the British recaptured it in 1812. In 1815, the British returned it to the United States. The island became the headquarters of John Jacob Astor's American Fur Company. After the fort was abandoned in 1894, the federal government transferred much of the island to the state of Michigan. Most of this land became Mackinac Island State Park.   WILLIS F. DUNBAR

See also HENRY, ALEXANDER.

MACKINDER, SIR HALFORD. See GEOPOLITICS.

MACLEISH, ARCHIBALD (1892-   ), is an American poet, dramatist, and critic. He also served as librarian of Congress from 1939 to 1944 and assistant secretary of state in 1944 and 1945.

MacLeish's early work is lyrical and thoughtful, using free verse and other technical methods of such older poets as Ezra Pound and T. S. Eliot. *Conquistador* (1932) is a strong, individual achievement, describing in epic terms the Spanish exploration of the New World. The work gained MacLeish the first of his three Pulitzer prizes. With social unrest in America and the rise of fascism abroad, MacLeish turned to more direct expression of the issues of his day. He particularly explored these issues in *Public Speech* (1936) and his two radio dramas, *The Fall of the City* (1937) and *Air Raid* (1938).

MacLeish's later work became less topical and more philosophic in tone. His verse drama *J.B.* raises the eternal problem of humanity's suffering, treating the Biblical story of Job in terms of modern American life. The play won the 1959 Pulitzer prize for drama. His *Collected Poems, 1917-1952* won the 1953 Pulitzer prize.

MacLeish's most mature reflections on the value of poetry as a means of knowledge are developed in *Poetry and Experience* (1961). He concludes, "To face the truth of the passing away of the world, and make song of it, make beauty of it, is not to solve the riddle of our mortal lives but perhaps to accomplish something more."

MacLeish was born in Glencoe, Ill. He earned a law degree, but gave up practice to devote himself to literature. He taught at Harvard from 1949 to 1962, and at Amherst from 1963 to 1967.   ELMER W. BORKLUND

MACLENNAN, HUGH (1907-   ), is a Canadian author known for his novels about historic events and public issues in Canada. These events and issues have a strong impact on the lives of the characters in MacLennan's books.

MacLennan based his first novel, *Barometer Rising* (1941), on an explosion that destroyed much of the city of Halifax, N.S., in 1917. *Two Solitudes* (1945) and *Return of the Sphinx* (1967) deal with conflicts between English Canadians and French Canadians. *The Watch That Ends the Night* (1959) tells how a group of characters were affected by the Great Depression of the 1930's and by World War II (1939-1945).

MacLennan also wrote several volumes of essays. The

essays include comments on Canadian life, and sensitive descriptions of nature. Three of the essay collections are *Cross Country* (1949), *Thirty and Three* (1954), and *Rivers of Canada* (1974). John Hugh MacLennan was born in Glace Bay, N.S.   CLAUDE T. BISSELL

See also CANADIAN LITERATURE (picture).

MACLEOD, *muh KLOUD,* **JOHN JAMES RICKARD** (1876-1935), was a Scottish physiologist. He and Sir Frederick Banting won the 1923 Nobel prize for physiology or medicine for their discovery of insulin in 1921 (see BANTING, SIR FREDERICK G.). Macleod was born near Dunkeld, Scotland. He taught physiology In Cleveland, Toronto, and Aberdeen.   A. M. WINCHESTER

MACLURE, WILLIAM. See NEW HARMONY.

MACMANUS, *muhk MAN uhs,* **SEUMAS,** *SHAY muhs* (1869-1960), was an Irish writer of stories, poems, and plays. He was born in County Donegal, and worked as a shepherd and farm hand. He listened to old Irish tales, and later retold them in his stories. MacManus' first book of poems was *Shuilers* (Vagrants) (1893). He described his childhood and youth in *The Rocky Road to Dublin* (1938). He also wrote *Top o' the Mornin'* (1920), *Well of the World's End* (1939), and *The Bold Heroes of Hungry Hill* (1951). He taught in a mountain school until he came to the United States in the 1890's to sell many of his stories.   JOSEPH E. BAKER

MACMECHAN, ARCHIBALD McKELLAR (1862-1933), was a Canadian essayist, critic, and educator. He published about fifteen books, including such essays as *The Life of a Little College* (1914) and *The Book of Ultima Thule* (1927); such historical works as *The Winning of Responsible Government* (1915); such literary history and criticism as *Headwaters of Canadian Literature* (1924); and one book of poems, *Late Harvest* (1934). He was born in Berlin (now Kitchener), Ont., and graduated from the University of Toronto. He received his Ph.D. degree from Johns Hopkins University. He served as a professor of English at Dalhousie University in Halifax, N.S., from 1889 to 1933.   DESMOND PACEY

MACMILLAN, DONALD BAXTER (1874-1970), an American polar explorer, added much to our knowledge of Greenland and the Canadian Arctic. He advanced the belief that the glacier fields are pushing southward. He discovered coal deposits 9 degrees from the North Pole. These contained remains of 36 kinds of trees, showing that the climate there had once been milder.

MacMillan's 1924 Arctic expedition used radio extensively. He established winter quarters in Etah, Greenland. MacMillan's 1925 expedition was one of the first to use airplanes in the Far North. His men made many special aerial photographs.

He received the Special Congressional Medal for surveying and charting Greenland and the Canadian Arctic for the United States Army during World War II.

In 1957, at the age of 82, MacMillan went on his 31st trip to the Arctic. He wrote several books about his experiences, including *Four Years in the White*

United Press Int.

MacMillan's Ship was often greeted by crowds as he returned from exploring Arctic waters. The explorer and a team of scientists studied the movements of glaciers, and discovered coal deposits only 9 degrees from the North Pole.

North (1918), *Etah and Beyond* (1927), and *How Peary Reached the Pole* (1932).

MacMillan was born in Provincetown, Mass. He studied at Bowdoin College and Harvard University. He taught school until 1908, when he made his first polar expedition as assistant to Commander Robert Peary. MacMillan helped train many younger explorers including Richard E. Byrd. MacMillan served in the U.S. Navy during World War II, and retired as a rear admiral in the naval reserve.   JOHN EDWARDS CASWELL

MACMILLAN, SIR ERNEST CAMPBELL (1893-1973), a Canadian musician, began his career as a concert organist at the age of 10. From 1926 to 1942, he served as principal of the Toronto Conservatory of Music. He was dean of music at the University of Toronto from 1927 to 1952. Macmillan served as conductor of the Toronto Symphony Orchestra from 1931 to 1956. He was born in Mimico, Ontario, and was graduated from the University of Toronto.   WILLIAM R. WILLOUGHBY

MACMILLAN, HAROLD (1894-   ), served as prime minister of Great Britain from January, 1957, until October, 1963. He was forced to resign because of illness. Macmillan succeeded Anthony Eden. Eden resigned after the failure of the attack on Egypt by Great Britain and France in October, 1956.

Macmillan was elected to the House of Commons in 1924, as a Conservative. In the 1930's, he was a progressive back-bench member. He criticized Prime Minister Neville Chamberlain and the Munich settle-

Brown Bros.

Donald B. MacMillan

United Press Int.

Harold Macmillan

23

ment with Nazi Germany in 1938 (see MUNICH AGREEMENT). He also urged action to combat the depression.

He served in Winston Churchill's wartime coalition government as British resident minister at Allied Headquarters in Northwest Africa, from 1942 to 1945. Macmillan served as Churchill's minister of housing and local government from 1951 to 1954, and as minister of defense in 1954. He became foreign secretary under Eden in April, 1955, and was named chancellor of the exchequer in December, 1955.

Maurice Harold Macmillan was born in London. He attended Eton College and was graduated from Balliol College, Oxford. CHARLES LOCH MOWAT

MACMURRAY COLLEGE. See UNIVERSITIES AND COLLEGES (table).

MACMURROUGH, DERMOT. See IRELAND (The Norman Invaders).

MACON, *MAY kuhn,* Ga. (pop. 122,423; met. area 226,782), is a center of manufacturing and trade and the third largest city in the state. Among Georgia's cities, only Atlanta and Columbus are larger. Macon lies on the Ocmulgee River in central Georgia and is called the *Heart of Georgia.* Its location helped Macon become a convention center for state and regional meetings. For location, see GEORGIA (political map).

Macon is the home of Wesleyan College and Mercer University. The Georgia Academy for the Blind is also in Macon. Poet Sidney Lanier was born in Macon.

Macon serves as the trading center for the famous peach region of Georgia, and produces a large part of Georgia's lumber output. Peanuts, pecans, watermelons, and other crops are marketed or processed in Macon. One of the world's largest kaolin deposits lies near Macon. It provides about 80 per cent of the country's kaolin and clay. Macon has over 170 manufacturing and processing plants. Cotton textile manufacturing is the most important of these. Other products include farm machinery, fertilizer, and fruits. Macon also has railroad shops, paper mills, and canned-food plants.

Four railroads provide freight service. Trucks, airlines, and bus lines also serve the city, but no intercity passenger trains stop there.

Creek Indians first settled the Macon area. Thomas Jefferson established Fort Hawkins there in 1806. The city was chartered in 1823 and named for Nathaniel Macon, a North Carolina congressman. During the 1840's and 1850's, Macon became an important railroad center. Confederates repulsed a Union attack on Macon in 1864.

Macon Mall, a $100-million shopping mall, opened in downtown Macon in 1975. Macon has a mayor-council form of government. It is the county seat of Bibb County. ALBERT B. SAYE

MACON ACT. See WAR OF 1812 (American Reaction).

MACPHAIL, AGNES CAMPBELL (1890-1954), was the first woman ever elected to the Canadian House of Commons. She served in the federal Parliament from 1921 to 1940, and in the Ontario Legislature from 1943 to 1945 and from 1948 to 1951. She represented Canada in the Assembly of the League of Nations. MacPhail was elected to Parliament as a United Farmers of Ontario candidate. She later supported the Cooperative Commonwealth Federation (C.C.F.). She was born in Grey County, Ont., and taught in Canadian schools before she entered politics. JOHN T. SAYWELL

MACPHERSON, JAMES. See GAELIC LITERATURE.

MACQUARIE ISLAND is a Tasmanian dependency in the South Pacific. The island lies about 800 miles (1,300 kilometers) southeast of Tasmania. It is about 21 miles (34 kilometers) long and 2 miles (3 kilometers) wide. The island is a breeding ground for penguins, albatrosses, and fur seals. Macquarie Island is uninhabited, but the Australian National Antarctic Research Expeditions has a permanent research station there.

MACRAMÉ, *MAK ruh may,* is the art of creating practical and decorative articles by knotting cord, rope, or string. It can be used to make clothing and such accessories as belts and purses, as well as sculptures, wall-hangings, and other ornamental items.

Many individual cords are knotted together to make a macramé article. The two basic knots used are the clove hitch and the square knot (see KNOTS, HITCHES, AND SPLICES [illustrations: The Clove Hitch; The Square Knot]). These knots may be combined with each

Joe De Grandis

Macon Mall, *above,* is a shopping center in Macon. The city, known as the *Heart of Georgia,* lies in the center of the state.

WORLD BOOK photo

A Macramé Purse is a decorative and inexpensive accessory. It was created by knotting pieces of string together.

other or with different knots in an unlimited number of arrangements. Beads, bells, feathers, and other small objects can be tied into the work for variety.

Arabian weavers probably developed knotting during the 1200's. But the word *macramé* was not used until about the 1400's. The word comes from an Arabic or Turkish word for *fringe*. During the 1800's, sailors knotted such items as bottle covers and nets.　DONA Z. MEILACH

MACREADY, WILLIAM CHARLES. See SHAKE-SPEARE, WILLIAM (The 1800's).

MACROPHAGE. See LYMPHATIC SYSTEM; IMMUNITY.

MAD ANTHONY WAYNE. See WAYNE, ANTHONY.

MADAGASCAR is an African country made up of one large island and many tiny nearby islands. It lies in the Indian Ocean, about 240 miles (386 kilometers) southeast of the African mainland. The large island, also called Madagascar, is the fourth largest island in the world. The country is about twice as big as the state of Arizona. Most of its people are farmers or herders of either black African or Indonesian descent. Antananarivo is Madagascar's capital and largest city.

Madagascar was a favorite base for sea pirates in the 1600's and 1700's, including the famous Captain William Kidd. The pirates founded a republic called *Libertalia* there, but it lasted only a short time.

France took control of Madagascar in 1896. Madagascar gained independence from France in 1960. The country was called the Malagasy Republic until 1975, when its name was changed to Madagascar (officially the *Democratic Republic of Madagascar*).

Government. Officially, the country is a republic. It has a parliament whose members are elected by the people. But since 1972, military rulers have controlled the government. A government body called a military directory makes the country's laws and runs the government. The leader of the directory serves as chief of government and chief of state of Madagascar.

The central government closely controls all local governments. The country is divided into six provinces which are divided into prefectures and subprefectures.

────── **FACTS IN BRIEF** ──────

Capital: Antananarivo.

Official Languages: Malagasy and French.

Form of Government: Republic.

Area: 226,658 sq. mi. (587,041 km²). *Greatest Distances*—north-south, 980 mi. (1,580 km); east-west, 360 mi. (579 km). *Coastline*—2,600 mi. (4,180 km).

Population: *Estimated 1981 Population*—9,589,000; distribution, 83 per cent rural, 17 per cent urban; density, 41 persons per sq. mi. (16 persons per km²). *1966 Census*—6,200,000. *Estimated 1986 Population*—11,117,000.

Chief Products: *Agriculture*—cattle, coffee, rice, vanilla. *Mining*—graphite, mica, semi-precious stones. *Manufacturing*—chemicals, cigarettes, sisal, sugar, textiles.

Flag: A white vertical stripe appears at the left, with a red horizontal stripe over a green one at the right. White is for purity, red for sovereignty, and green for hope. See FLAG (color picture: Flags of Africa).

Money: *Basic Unit*—franc. See MONEY (table: Exchange Rates).

───────────────

Richard Adloff, contributor of this article, is Research Associate at The Hoover Institution on War, Revolution, and Peace, and coauthor of several books on Africa.

Madagascar

● Capital
• Other City or Town
── Road
↦ Rail Line
▲ MOUNTAIN
〜 River
〜 Canal

WORLD BOOK map

People. The people belong to two major groups—those of black African descent and those of Indonesian descent. The blacks live in the coastal regions, and make up the larger group. The people of Indonesian descent live in the central and south-central highlands.

Political rivalries have developed between the two groups. The coastal people of African descent control the government. The Merina, who are of Indonesian descent, are better educated than the coastal people and resent being governed by them. But the Merina are in the minority, and have little chance of coming to power.

Malagasy is the language spoken throughout the country. It resembles Malay and Indonesian. French and Malagasy are the official languages. Almost one-third of the people are Christians. The rest—especially those living along the coasts—practice tribal religions.

24a

Irrigation in Dry Southern Madagascar has helped the people develop plantations. Most of the farmers also raise cattle.

The Narrow Streets of Antananarivo, the capital of Madagascar, are crowded on market day.

They worship ancestors and spirits, and perform cattle sacrifices and other ceremonies at family tombs.

Many people of Madagascar wear European-style clothing. However, people of isolated southern tribes often wear little clothing. Most houses are built of brick and many are several stories high. They have tile or thatched roofs. The people eat rice, vegetables, fruit, and sometimes meat and fish.

About 45 per cent of the people can read and write. Almost 50 per cent of the school age children attend primary schools and about 4 per cent attend secondary schools. The University of Madagascar, founded in 1961, has about 4,000 students. About 6,000 students attend teachers colleges and technical schools.

Land. Northern Madagascar has fertile soil. Mountains separate it from the rest of the island. Western Madagascar has wide plains, some fertile river valleys, and a fairly sheltered coast. A narrow plain lies along the east coast, but reefs and storms make the east coast dangerous for ships. Some coastal shipping uses the Pangalanes Canal, which runs along the east coast between Foulpointe and Farafangana. The climate is warm and humid on the coast. The southern end of the island is mainly desert, and has a hot, dry climate.

Central Madagascar consists of highlands with altitudes of 2,000 to 4,000 feet (610 to 1,200 meters) and some higher mountains. The soil is *eroded* (worn away) and the region is *deforested* (cleared of trees), but it has the densest population. The highlands are cool and temperatures at Antananarivo range between 55° F. (13° C) and 67° F. (19° C).

Economy. Four-fifths of the people are farmers and herders. Rice is their chief food crop, but cassava, corn, and potatoes are also grown. Coffee is the most valuable export, and Madagascar is the world's greatest vanilla producer. Other exports include sisal, which is used to make binding twine, and sugar. The country has more cattle (about 10 million) than people.

Most of the country's few industries process hides, meat, ores, sisal, and sugar for export. Most of the foreign trade is with France. But the United States buys coffee, cloves, and vanilla from the country.

Madagascar has about 1,300 miles (2,090 kilometers) of paved roads, 3,900 miles (6,280 kilometers) of unpaved roads, and 535 miles (861 kilometers) of railroads. Tamatave and Majunga are the leading seaports.

History. Immigrants from Indonesia came to the island in successive waves starting long before the time of Christ and lasting until the A.D. 1400's. They settled in the central highlands. Immigrants from Africa and the Arabian peninsula settled on the coasts. A number of kingdoms developed on the island, but by about 1800 the Merina kingdom ruled most of the island.

Radama I welcomed English and French traders and missionaries to the island after he became king in 1810. The missionaries opened churches and schools and persuaded the king to end the slave trade. In the 1840's, Queen Ranavalona I tried to end European influence and expelled Europeans from the island. Europeans returned after she died in 1861. French influence increased after 1869. Merina resentment against the French led to the Franco-Malagasy wars of the 1880's and 1890's. Madagascar became a French colony in 1896.

During World War I, Merina leaders began to demand independence. France gave the colony's people some control of financial matters and the right to elect an assembly in 1945. It also allowed them to elect representatives to the French parliament. But this did not satisfy the people. An armed revolt that lasted almost two years broke out in 1947.

Madagascar moved toward self-government in peaceful stages in the late 1950's. A government council with some power to administer laws was elected in 1956. In 1958, Madagascar became a self-governing republic in the French Community. Called the Malagasy Republic, it became fully independent on June 26, 1960. Philibert Tsiranana became the country's first president in 1959. He was re-elected in 1965 and 1972.

In May 1972, antigovernment demonstrations caused Tsiranana to resign. Army officers then took control of the government and set up a system of military rule. In June 1975, Didier Ratsiraka became the fourth in a series of military rulers to head the government. Under Ratsiraka and the earlier military leaders, the government took control of important parts of the country's economic activity, including many businesses owned by the French and other foreigners.

In late 1975, the country changed its name from Malagasy Republic to Madagascar. In 1977, a parliament was established, but the military directory still controls the government. RICHARD ADLOFF

See also ANTANANARIVO; LEMUR; ROSEWOOD; VANILLA.

MADAMA BUTTERFLY. See OPERA (Opera Repertoire).

MADAME BOVARY. See FLAUBERT, GUSTAVE; NOVEL (France).

MADDEN DAM. See PANAMA CANAL (The Canal Since 1920).

MADDER is a plant which is grown in Europe and Asia for use in making dyes. The madder has rough, prickly leaves and small greenish-yellow flowers. The fruit is black. The roots of the madder produce the coloring matter which manufacturers use to make dyes. A madder which grows in Levant and Italy produces Turkey-red dye. Many other colors can be obtained by chemical treatment. These colors vary from pink and red to yellow, purple, and brown. Madder also produces coloring extracts such as alizarin and purpurin. A closely related plant, called *white bedstraw*, grows in Europe and eastern North America.

Scientific Classification. Madder belongs to the family Rubiaceae. The madder used by dyers is classified *Rubia tinctorum*. White bedstraw is *Galium mollugo*. FRED FORTESS

MADEIRA ISLANDS, *muh DEER uh*, are a group of islands that belong to Portugal. The islands, of volcanic origin, lie in the Atlantic Ocean off the northwest coast of Africa. For location, see ATLANTIC OCEAN (map).

The islands cover 308 square miles (797 square kilometers). Most of the 245,000 residents live on Madeira, the larger of the two inhabited islands. The other inhabited island is Porto Santo. Noted for its sandy beaches, it lies about 26 miles (42 kilometers) northeast of Madeira. About 3,900 persons live there. The Desertas and Selvagens are groups of tiny, uninhabited isles.

The Island of Madeira, largest and most important of the group, is a great ocean mountain range rising to a height of 6,104 feet (1,860 meters) above sea level in the Pico Ruivo. Madeira is known as the *Rock Garden of the Atlantic* because its settlements and farms rise in terraces, covered with exotic flowers and trees. There are lush growths of orchids, bougainvillaea, bignonia, hibiscus, camellias, hydrangeas, wisteria, and jacaranda. Trees include the mimosa, eucalyptus, Brazilian auracarian, Indian fig, West Indies coral, and Japanese camphor, bamboo, laurel, and palm.

The richness of the vegetation is remarkable because rain falls only in the winter months. In order to grow crops, water has to be rationed and distributed by stone aqueducts, called *levadas*. Water retained from the rainy season flows down the levadas from the mountains to the farms and villages.

Chief crops include sugar cane, corn and other vegetables, bananas, oranges, mangoes, pomegranates, and the grapes that have made Madeira famous for wine.

Wine production is the principal industry of Madeira. Next in importance are the making of willow wicker furniture and baskets, and embroidering. Most women embroider at home. Fishing also contributes to the economy. Britons handle much of Madeira's trade.

Funchal is the capital of Funchal district, which includes the Madeira Islands. It ranks as the largest city and chief resort center of the group. Funchal has ship connections with Lisbon, Portugal, and English ports, and air links with European and North African cities. See FUNCHAL.

Madeira has several unusual kinds of local transportation. Oxen draw sleighs over the iceless steep streets and roads. Basket sleds for fast, downhill travel provide thrills. Visitors to remote places can also travel in hammocks carried on poles by two persons.

History. The Romans called the Madeiras the *Purpuriarae*, or "Purple" islands. The Portuguese first sailed to the island of Madeira in 1419. They gave it that name

Camera Press, Pix

The Harbor of Funchal, Madeira, presents a picturesque sight, with its old fortress and array of small boats. An ocean liner and freighters are anchored in the distance. The town is the main seaport and capital of the island group.

—meaning *wood*—because it was heavily forested. They cleared much of the land by burning trees, the ashes from which gave the soil increased fertility. Funchal was founded in 1421. Porto Santo also was settled about that time. The Spaniards seized and held the islands from 1580 to 1640. The British occupied them twice in the early 1800's.   CHARLES EDWARD NOWELL

MADEIRA RIVER, or RIO MADEIRA, is the largest branch of the Amazon River and an important trade waterway of South America. Madeira is Portuguese for *wood* or *timber*. The river was named for the great amount of driftwood that floats on its waters.

The Madeira begins where several large streams meet on the boundary between Brazil and Bolivia. It flows northeast for about 2,000 miles (3,200 kilometers) before emptying into the Amazon River about 100 miles (160 kilometers) east of Manaus (see BRAZIL [physical map]).

The Madeira's mouth is nearly 2 miles (3 kilometers) wide. Ships can sail upstream about 700 miles (1,100 kilometers) to a series of rapids. Twenty of these rapids extend for 230 miles (370 kilometers), with a drop of 475 feet (145 meters). A railroad runs on the riverbanks around the rapids. Rubber and other products come to the region by way of the river and the railroad.

One branch of the Madeira is the Rio Teodoro, once called Rio Duvida. This stream is 1,000 miles (1,600 kilometers) long. Theodore Roosevelt explored the Rio Teodoro in 1914.   MARGUERITE UTTLEY

See also RIVER (chart: Longest Rivers).

MADERO, FRANCISCO INDALECIO. See MEXICO (The Revolution of 1910).

MADINAT ASH SHAB, *mah DEE naht ashsh shahb* (pop. 20,000), is a city in Yemen (Aden). It lies in the southwestern part of the country, about 14 miles (23 kilometers) northwest of Aden.

Madinat ash Shab was founded in 1959. It became the capital of Yemen (Aden) in 1967, when the country gained independence. However, government offices were gradually moved to Aden during the late 1960's and early 1970's, and Aden replaced Madinat ash Shab as the capital.

MADISON, Ind. (pop. 13,081), is an Ohio River port and tobacco-auction center. It was once the largest city in Indiana. Madison is located in southeastern Indiana on the north bank of the Ohio River, 90 miles (145 kilometers) from Indianapolis. It is 46 miles (74 kilometers) from Louisville, Ky., and 88 miles (142 kilometers) from Cincinnati, Ohio (see INDIANA [political map]). Tobacco buyers from all parts of the United States attend auctions held in Madison.

Indiana's first railroad ran from Madison to Indianapolis, the state capital, in 1847. During the Civil War, Madison was a banking center. In 1862, James F. Lanier, a Madison banker, loaned about $1 million to the state administration of Governor Oliver P. Morton, and kept Indiana from bankruptcy.

Madison's well-kept old mansions give the city an atmosphere of the middle 1800's. Among these old homes are the *Shrewsbury Home* and the *Lanier Home*. Francis Costigan, a famous architect of that period, built both houses. Clifty Falls, a state park, is situated on the bluff above Madison. Hanover College is 7 miles (11 kilometers) outside the city.   PAUL E. MILLION, JR.

MADISON, Wis. (pop. 168,671; met. area pop. 290,272), is the capital and second largest city of the state. Only Milwaukee has more people. Madison is the home of the largest campus of the University of Wisconsin System. It also is a center of medicine and recreation. The city serves as the trade center of a rich agricultural region.

Downtown Madison lies between Lakes Mendota and Monona, and Lake Wingra is in the western part of the city. These lakes make Madison one of the nation's most beautiful state capitals. Madison is 76 miles (122 kilometers) west of Milwaukee. For location, see WISCONSIN (political map).

Two land investors, James D. Doty and Stevens T. Mason, founded Madison in 1836. They named it for James Madison, the fourth President of the United States. Doty and Mason chose the site because its lakes provided scenic beauty. The development of the University of Wisconsin, and the city's role as state capital, have helped Madison become one of the Midwest's fastest growing urban centers.

Description. Madison covers about 77 square miles (199 square kilometers), including about 25 square miles (65 square kilometers) of inland water. It is the county seat of Dane County. The Madison metropolitan area includes the county—1,233 square miles (3,193 square kilometers).

The dome of the white granite state Capitol towers 286 feet (87 meters) above the heart of downtown Madison (see WISCONSIN [picture: The State Capitol]). Federal, state, and municipal government buildings stand nearby. The University of Wisconsin campus lies about 1 mile (1.6 kilometers) west of the Capitol on the south shore of Lake Mendota.

Madison's public school system includes about 45 elementary schools and 4 high schools. The Madison Public Library consists of a main library and six branches. About 35,000 students attend the University of Wisconsin-Madison, one of the nation's largest universities. The city is also the home of Edgewood College. Madison also is a medical center, with a large Veterans Administration hospital, a state mental hospital, and about 10 other hospitals.

The city's cultural attractions include the State Historical Society of Wisconsin and the Madison Art Center. Symphony orchestras, country and western stars, and other performing groups appear in Madison regularly. The University of Wisconsin also operates the 1,200-acre (486-hectare) Arboretum and Wildlife Refuge in Madison. The city zoo is in Henry Vilas Park. Lakes in and near Madison provide boating, fishing, and swimming.

Economy of Madison depends heavily on government operations and on trade. Federal, state, and municipal government agencies—plus the University of Wisconsin—employ about a third of Dane County's workers. Another third hold jobs in retail and wholesale trade and in such services as finance, insurance, and research. The city has more than 100 research and testing laboratories. Many of these laboratories handle university projects.

About a tenth of the county's workers are employed in the more than 200 manufacturing plants in the area. Farming and cattle raising in the Madison area have helped make food processing the city's largest industry.

Downtown Madison, Wis., Lies on a Narrow Isthmus Between Lakes Monona, *foreground,* and Mendota, *background.*

Oscar Mayer and Company, one of the nation's biggest meat-packing firms, ranks as Madison's largest private employer. It has more than 4,000 workers in the city. Major products of Madison include batteries, dairy equipment, and hospital supplies.

Railroad freight lines and bus and trucking companies serve Madison. Airlines use nearby Madison Municipal Airport.

Government and History. Madison has a mayor-council form of government. The voters elect the mayor and the 22 members of the Common Council to two-year terms.

Winnebago Indians lived in what is now the Madison area before white settlers came. During the 1830's, the site was bought by James D. Doty, a former federal judge, and Stevens T. Mason, governor of the Michigan Territory. In 1836, the first legislature of the Wisconsin Territory made Madison the capital, even though the community did not yet actually exist. Madison's first white settlers, Eben and Rosaline Peck, arrived from nearby Blue Mounds in 1837. They erected a hotel for the workers who built the first Capitol.

Madison began functioning as the capital in 1838. It was incorporated as a village in 1846, with a population of 626. When Wisconsin gained statehood in 1848, Madison remained the capital. In 1856, Madison was incorporated as a city. By then, its population had reached about 7,000. Madison grew slowly during the late 1800's. By 1900, it had a population of 19,164.

Oscar Mayer and Company opened its meat-packing plant in the city in 1919 and helped make Madison a major food-processing center. During the 1920's, the city became the headquarters of the Progressive Party, led by the La Follette family of Madison. This party pioneered in social reform legislation.

During the 1960's, a rapid increase in employment by the federal, state, and municipal governments created a population boom in Madison. The government work force in the area rose by about 30,000, and the city's population jumped from 126,706 to 171,769 by 1970.   CLIFFORD C. BEHNKE

MADISON, DOLLEY PAYNE (1768-1849), a famous Washington hostess, was the wife of President James Madison. She is best known for her flight from Washington in August, 1814, when the British invaded the city during the War of 1812. She saved many state papers and a portrait of George Washington.

She and Madison were married in 1794 when he was a Congressman. While Madison served as secretary of state under President Thomas Jefferson, a widower, Mrs. Madison often helped Jefferson when he entertained guests. She also entertained frequently on her own. When Madison became President, official functions became more elaborate than Jefferson had permitted. Mrs. Madison was noted for her charm and tact. At her home, people of strongly differing views could meet at ease.

Mrs. Madison was born in Guilford County, North Carolina, the third child of Quaker parents. She did not spell her name "Dolly," as is done today. Tradition also says wrongly that her real name was "Dorothea." She spent her childhood in Scotchtown, Va. In 1783, the family moved to Philadelphia. Dolley and John Todd, Jr., a lawyer and a Quaker, were married in 1790. They had two sons. Todd and one of the sons died in 1793. When she married Madison in 1794, she was expelled from the Society of Friends because of her marriage to a non-Quaker. After Madison's two terms as President the couple retired to Montpelier, his Virginia plantation. In 1837, after his death, she returned to Washington to live.   ROBERT J. TAYLOR

See also MADISON, JAMES (picture).

27

JAMES MADISON

James Madison

Oil painting on canvas (about 1792) by Charles Willson Peale; Thomas Gilcrease Institute of American History and Art, Tulsa, Okla.

The United States Flag had 15 stars and 15 stripes when Madison took office, even though there were 17 states.

JOHN ADAMS
2nd President
1797—1801

JEFFERSON
3rd President
1801—1809

MONROE
5th President
1817—1825

J. Q. ADAMS
6th President
1825—1829

4TH PRESIDENT OF THE UNITED STATES 1809-1817

MADISON, JAMES (1751-1836), is called "the Father of the Constitution." He planned the system of checks and balances that regulate the legislative, executive, and judicial branches of the United States government. Madison served his country in many public offices during a period of 40 years. As Secretary of State and as President, he kept the United States out of the Napoleonic Wars. But, reluctantly, he led the country into the War of 1812. After the war, Madison's wise policies encouraged national growth.

Madison was a close friend of Thomas Jefferson, whom he followed in the presidency. Together, these two Virginians made an unexcelled team in constructive statesmanship. Madison displayed skill at solving difficult problems of government. Jefferson contributed a fine ability to phrase political truths. Their close agreement on political matters led them to join in organizing the Democratic-Republican party.

Physically small and frail, Madison did as much as any American toward building a strong federal government. At the Constitutional Convention, he worked to strengthen the national union of states. He spoke out fearlessly for nationalism when most Americans put states' rights ahead of the national interest. But Madison was by nature a mediator. He resisted Alexander Hamilton's tendency to strengthen the federal government at the expense of the states. He also softened Jefferson's views favoring states' rights. Most Americans today accept Madison's view on the relationship between the states and the federal government, rather than the extreme views of either Hamilton or Jefferson.

Streams of settlers surged westward during Madison's administration. The lack of imported goods during the War of 1812 encouraged industries to expand, and set the country on the path to becoming an industrial nation. The war also gave the American people their national anthem. Early one morning, as British shells burst about Fort McHenry in Baltimore harbor, Francis Scott Key wrote "The Star-Spangled Banner."

Early Life

James Madison was born in the home of his mother's parents on March 16, 1751 (March 5 by the calendar then in use). They lived at Port Conway, Va., about 12 miles (19 kilometers) from Fredericksburg. James was the eldest of 12 children. The families of his father, James Madison, and his mother, Nelly Conway Madison, had settled in Virginia during the 1600's. Many

--------- IMPORTANT DATES IN MADISON'S LIFE ---------

1751 (March 16) Born at Port Conway, Va.
1779 Elected to the Continental Congress.
1787 Served at the Constitutional Convention.
1789 Elected to the U.S. House of Representatives.
1794 (Sept. 15) Married Dolley Payne Todd.
1801 Appointed Secretary of State.
1808 Elected President of the United States.
1812 Recommended war with Great Britain.
　　　 Re-elected President.
1829 Served at the Virginia Constitutional Convention.
1836 (June 28) Died at Montpelier, his family estate.

28

slaves worked on the Madison plantation, Montpelier.

James was a frail and sickly child. He studied with private tutors, and attended the Donald Robertson School in King and Queen County. At the age of 18, he entered the College of New Jersey (now Princeton University). He took an active interest in politics, and was an early member of the American Whig Society. Madison studied very hard, sometimes sleeping only five hours a night. He completed the regular course at Princeton in two years, and was graduated in 1771.

Madison spent the next six months studying Hebrew, philosophy, and other subjects that showed his deep interest in religious questions. A weak speaking voice prevented him from taking up a career as a minister. He soon turned his attention to politics.

Political and Public Career

Entry into Politics. Madison entered politics in 1774, when he was elected to the Committee of Safety in Orange County, Virginia. Committees of this kind provided local government in the days when the British colonial government was crumbling. In 1776, Madison served on a committee that drafted a new Virginia constitution and the Virginia Declaration of Rights. Other colonies later copied these documents.

Madison served in Virginia's first legislative assembly in 1776, where he met Thomas Jefferson. The two men soon began a lifetime friendship. Madison was defeated for re-election in 1777. Late in life, he said he lost because he did not provide enough refreshments for the electors. In 1778, the Virginia Assembly elected Madison to the Governor's Council, an advisory group. He held this post until December, 1779, when he was elected to the Continental Congress.

Madison took his seat in Congress in March, 1780. In those days, Congress had no power to raise taxes, and

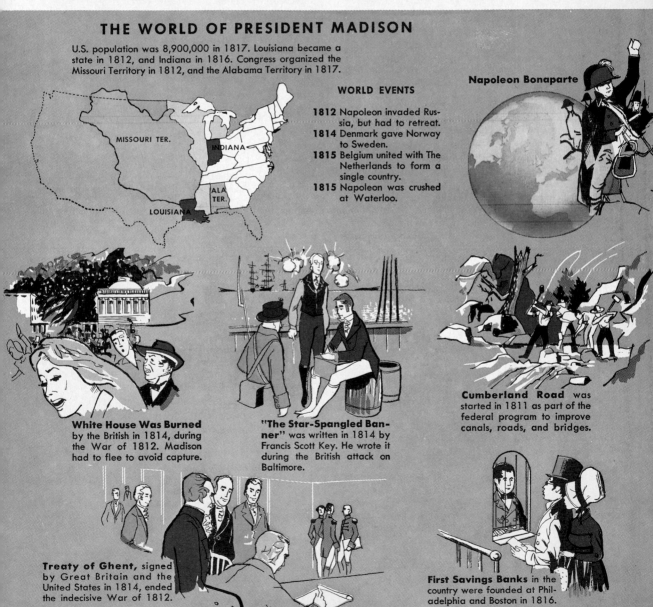

THE WORLD OF PRESIDENT MADISON

U.S. population was 8,900,000 in 1817. Louisiana became a state in 1812, and Indiana in 1816. Congress organized the Missouri Territory in 1812, and the Alabama Territory in 1817.

MISSOURI TER.

INDIANA

ALA. TER.

LOUISIANA

WORLD EVENTS

1812 Napoleon invaded Russia, but had to retreat.

1814 Denmark gave Norway to Sweden.

1815 Belgium united with The Netherlands to form a single country.

1815 Napoleon was crushed at Waterloo.

Napoleon Bonaparte

White House Was Burned by the British in 1814, during the War of 1812. Madison had to flee to avoid capture.

"The Star-Spangled Banner" was written in 1814 by Francis Scott Key. He wrote it during the British attack on Baltimore.

Cumberland Road was started in 1811 as part of the federal program to improve canals, roads, and bridges.

Treaty of Ghent, signed by Great Britain and the United States in 1814, ended the indecisive War of 1812.

First Savings Banks in the country were founded at Philadelphia and Boston in 1816.

found it difficult to pay national debts. Madison strongly favored increasing the powers of Congress in financial matters. He also advocated many other measures to stabilize and dignify the government.

Virginia Assemblyman. Madison returned to Virginia in 1783. By that time, Americans generally recognized him as the ablest member of Congress. He planned to study law, history, and the sciences. Jefferson sent books from France to further Madison's studies. These studies were partially interrupted when the people of Orange County elected him to the state assembly for three successive one-year terms.

In the assembly, Madison continued the struggle Jefferson had begun for separation of church and state in Virginia. His chief opponent was Patrick Henry, who favored state support for teachers of the Christian religion. In 1786, the assembly passed Virginia's Statute of Religious Freedom. Madison wrote to Jefferson that thus in Virginia "was extinguished forever the ambitious hope of making laws for the human mind."

Constitutional Convention. Madison represented Virginia at the Constitutional Convention of 1787. Although only 36 years old, he took a leading part. Madison fought for strong central government, and drafted the Virginia plan for the union. This plan, also called the Randolph plan, foreshadowed the constitution that the convention finally adopted (see CONSTITUTION OF THE UNITED STATES [The Compromises]).

Madison proved valuable to the convention in many ways. He had a deep knowledge of confederacies of the past. He was well acquainted with the Articles of Confederation, and fully understood the problems of federalism. He also wrote his famous *Notes on the Federal Convention*, the only full record of the debates.

Madison's part in the adoption of the Constitution did not end at the convention. He served as a member of the Virginia Ratifying Convention. At the same time, he joined Alexander Hamilton and John Jay of New York in writing *The Federalist*, a series of letters to newspapers. Scholars still consider these letters the most authoritative explanation of the American constitutional system. See FEDERALIST, THE.

Congressman. Madison's support of the Constitution displeased many Virginians who supported states' rights. They united in the Virginia legislature to defeat him in 1788 for a seat in the first United States Senate. Early the next year, Madison defeated James Monroe in an election for the U.S. House of Representatives.

Madison, one of the ablest members of the House, proposed resolutions for organizing the Departments of State, Treasury, and War. He also drafted much of the first tariff act. Most important, he was largely responsible for drafting the first 10 amendments to the Constitution, the Bill of Rights (see BILL OF RIGHTS).

At first, Madison supported many policies of the Federalist party. But he soon decided that Alexander Hamilton's financial plans favored Eastern merchants at the expense of Western and Southern farmers. Madison then turned against the Federalists. After Jefferson returned from France in 1789, he and Madison joined in organizing the Democratic-Republican party, the forerunner of today's Democratic party. During this period in Philadelphia, Madison met Dolley Payne

Portrait by Ezra Ames, 1818. The New-York Historical Society, N.Y.C.

Dolley Payne Madison, the President's wife, dazzled Washington with her stylish clothes and brilliant manner of entertaining. She served as official White House hostess for 16 years, assuming the duties of First Lady for the widowed Thomas Jefferson, and continuing during the eight years her husband was in office.

Todd, a young widow to whom he was married in 1794 (see MADISON, DOLLEY PAYNE).

By 1797, Madison had become weary of politics, and retired to his estate. In 1798, Congress passed the Alien and Sedition Acts (see ALIEN AND SEDITION ACTS). Madison was outraged. He drafted the Virginia Resolutions of 1798, proposing joint action by the states in declaring these laws unconstitutional. He was elected to the Virginia legislature in 1799 and 1800, and led the fight against what he considered Federalist efforts to undermine basic human rights.

Secretary of State. Thomas Jefferson became President in 1801, and appointed Madison Secretary of State. The purchase of Louisiana was the most important success in foreign relations (see LOUISIANA PURCHASE). War with the Barbary pirates between 1801 and 1805 caused excitement throughout the country. The peace treaty signed with Tripoli brought only brief satisfaction. The pirates soon began preying on American shipping again (see BARBARY STATES).

Madison and Jefferson failed to force Great Britain and France to respect the rights of Americans on the high seas. The British and French were fighting each other in the Napoleonic Wars, and each had blockaded the other's coast. American ships that tried to trade with either country were stopped by warships of the other. Many American seamen were seized and forced to serve on British or French warships. The Embargo Act of 1807 attempted to protect American ships by stopping all commerce with foreign countries. But the loss of trade brought widespread economic distress to the United States, and many Northern merchants evaded the embargo. In the end, the embargo hurt Americans more than it did the British or French.

The Embargo Act was repealed in 1809, just before Jefferson left office. In its place, Congress passed the Non-Intercourse Act, which opened trade with all countries except Great Britain and France. Congress hoped this law would force the British and French to recognize American commercial rights. See EMBARGO (The Embargo Act); NON-INTERCOURSE ACT.

Jefferson chose Madison to succeed him as President. Madison received 122 electoral votes to 47 for the Federalist candidate, former minister to France C. C. Pinckney. Madison's running mate, Vice-President George Clinton, polled 113 electoral votes.

Madison's Administration (1809-1817)

"Mr. Madison's War." Trade with Britain and France was still the government's greatest problem when Madison became President. British and French warships continued to stop American shipping, in spite of the Non-Intercourse Act. In 1810, Congress passed a bill that reopened trade with both Britain and France. This curious bill attempted to stop violations of American shipping by economic pressure. It provided that if Britain ended its attacks on American ships, the United States would stop trade with France—and vice versa. But this bait did not work. Napoleon blandly announced that he would revoke the French blockade against neutral trade with Great Britain. But, at the same time, he issued secret orders which maintained the French blockade against American shipping. Madison halted all trade with Great Britain, but the French continued to stop American ships.

Americans were angered by France's deceit. Reports that the British were stirring up the Western Indians also aroused feelings against the British. These reports seemed to be confirmed when Tecumseh, chief of the Shawnee tribe, tried to organize an Indian alliance to fight the Americans. Governor William Henry Harrison of the Indiana Territory shattered the Indian forces in the Battle of Tippecanoe on Nov. 7, 1811 (see HARRISON, WILLIAM HENRY [Entry into Politics]). But people throughout the West believed that the British as well as the Indians were their enemy.

Adding to the war feeling was a strongly nationalistic generation which had arisen in politics. This group included many persons who felt that a war would result in the annexation of Canada and Spanish Florida. Henry Clay of Kentucky, Felix Grundy of Tennessee, and John Calhoun of South Carolina acted as spokesmen in the House of Representatives for this group.

Madison knew that the United States was unprepared for war, and that New England merchants feared war would destroy trade. But he also knew that people outside New England wanted it, and that the nation could tolerate no more insults from Great Britain. He finally recommended war, and Congress approved it on June 18, 1812. The Federalists opposed the war, and called it "Mr. Madison's War."

A few months later, Madison was re-elected President by 128 electoral votes to 89 for Mayor DeWitt Clinton

——— VICE-PRESIDENTS AND CABINET ———

Vice-President	*George Clinton
	*Elbridge Gerry (1813)
Secretary of State	Robert Smith
	*James Monroe (1811)
Secretary of the Treasury	*Albert Gallatin
	George W. Campbell (1814)
	Alexander J. Dallas (1814)
	*William H. Crawford (1816)
Secretary of War	William Eustis
	John Armstrong (1813)
	*James Monroe (1814)
	*William H. Crawford (1815)
Attorney General	Caesar A. Rodney
	William Pinkney (1811)
	Richard Rush (1814)
Secretary of the Navy	Paul Hamilton
	William Jones (1813)
	B. W. Crowninshield (1814)

*Has a separate biography in WORLD BOOK.

Virginia State Chamber of Commerce

Montpelier, the family estate of James Madison, stands in Orange County, Virginia. Madison and his wife retired there after he left the presidency.

of New York City. Madison's running mate, Governor Elbridge Gerry of Massachusetts, won 131 votes to 86 for Jared Ingersoll, attorney general of Pennsylvania.

Progress of the War. American military forces had little success at the start of the war. The British Navy clamped on a blockade that the pitifully small U.S. Navy could not break. American land forces attacked Canada in 1812, but were defeated. The fight for Canada continued for two years, with no decisive victories on either side. In 1814, Napoleon was defeated in Europe. Great Britain then sent experienced troops to Canada, ending American hopes for conquest.

In the summer of 1814, General Winfield Scott fought the British to a standstill at Chippewa and Lundy's Lane in southern Ontario. British troops invaded Maryland and, on August 24, burned the Capitol and other public buildings in Washington. Dolley Madison fled the White House so late that British soldiers ate a hot meal she had prepared. Only heroic resistance at Fort McHenry kept the British from capturing Baltimore.

In September, 1814, American forces stopped an invasion down the west side of Lake Champlain. Early in 1815, Andrew Jackson won a stunning victory at New Orleans. The Treaty of Ghent was ratified in February, 1815. It settled none of the problems that had caused the war. But it did preserve American territorial integrity (see GHENT, TREATY OF; WAR OF 1812).

In 1814, before the end of the war, New England Federalists had held a secret meeting known as the *Hartford Convention*. None of the convention's activities was disloyal. But rumors sprang up that the members planned secession of the New England States. The Federalist party was branded as unpatriotic, and fell apart shortly after James Monroe was elected President in 1816. See HARTFORD CONVENTION.

The Growth of Nationalism. Albert Gallatin, Madison's first Secretary of the Treasury, believed that the War of 1812 had "renewed and reinstated the national feeling of character which the Revolution had given and which was daily lessening. The people . . . are more American; they feel and act more as a nation." The end of the war ushered in "the era of good feeling." With the disappearance of the Federalist party, political conflicts were submerged within the Democratic-Republican party. During the two years after the war, the country experienced great domestic growth. The settlement of the West was hastened by improved roads and canals, and a land system that made it easier to claim frontier property. The tariff of 1816 continued the protection of American industries. Madison received the credit for this prosperity.

Life in the White House. Mrs. Madison began an extravagant round of parties as soon as her husband took office. She served elaborate dinners, and delighted in surprising her guests with delicacies. She was the first person to serve ice cream in the White House. Washington Irving wrote of the presidential couple: "Mrs. Madison is a fine, portly, buxom dame who has a smile and a pleasant word for everybody . . . as to Jeemy Madison—ah! poor Jeemy!—he is but a withered little apple-John."

The British invasion of the capital, and the burning of the White House, ended social gaiety. The Madisons fled Washington. When they returned, they established a new residence in the Octagon House, a private home just west of the White House. In 1815, they moved to a house on the corner of Pennsylvania Avenue and 19th Street. Dolley Madison resumed her busy social life, but longed to reoccupy the White House. Reconstruction work proceeded slowly, however, and the Executive Mansion was not ready for occupancy until nine months after Madison left office in 1817.

Later Years

In retirement at Montpelier, Madison busied himself with the affairs of his estate. After Jefferson's death in 1826, he became *rector* (president) of the University of Virginia. He also served as a member of the Virginia Constitutional Convention of 1829. Madison died at Montpelier on June 28, 1836. His wife returned to Washington, where she lived until her death in 1849. The Madisons are buried in a family plot near Montpelier. They had no children, but they reared the son of Mrs. Madison by her first husband. An authoritative work on the life of Madison is *James Madison* by Irving Brant.   RALPH L. KETCHAM

Questions

Why is Madison called "the Father of the Constitution"?

What were some important principles that Madison supported in the Continental Congress?

Who called Madison "a withered little apple-John"?

What effect did Madison have on the relationship of church and state in Virginia?

How did Madison prove valuable in the first United States Congress?

How did the War of 1812 affect American nationalism?

How did Madison explain his defeat for re-election to Virginia's Assembly in 1777?

What was Madison's relationship to *The Federalist*?

What was his approach to federal-state relations?

How did Dolley Madison shine as First Lady?

Reading and Study Guide

For a *Reading and Study Guide on James Madison*, see the RESEARCH GUIDE/INDEX, Volume 22.

MADISON RIVER. See MONTANA (Rivers and Lakes; physical map).

MADISON SQUARE GARDEN is a famous indoor sports and entertainment arena in New York City. The Garden is one of seven facilities in the circular Madison Square Garden Center at 4 Pennsylvania Plaza, New York, N.Y., 10001. The 20,000-seat arena hosts a variety of events, including circuses, ice shows, political meetings, and sports contests. In addition to the main arena, the 5,000-seat Felt Forum provides space for smaller events. The center also has such facilities as an exposition rotunda, a motion-picture theater, a 48-lane bowling center, a hall of fame honoring outstanding Garden performers, and the National Art Museum of Sport.

The present Garden Center was completed in 1968.

The first of three earlier Gardens received its name in 1879. It occupied an abandoned railroad station at Madison Square. The next Garden was built in 1890 on the same site. In 1925, another Garden was built on a new site at Eighth Avenue and 50th Street.

Critically reviewed by MADISON SQUARE GARDEN

MADONNA AND CHILD are the Virgin Mary and the infant Jesus in works of art. They rank among the most important art subjects that the Christian religion has inspired. Madonna means *my lady* in Italian. But the term has come to mean *the Virgin Mary*. Painters and sculptors produced their greatest works on the Madonna during the Renaissance (see RENAISSANCE). Michelangelo's *Medici Madonna* is one of the finest sculptures

Madonna Enthroned with Saints by the Italian painter Giotto shows the Virgin Mary seated on a throne holding the Christ child. Saints and kneeling angels gaze at Mary and Jesus.

Tempera on wood panel, also called the *Ognissanti Madonna* (about 1300); Uffizi Gallery, Florence, Italy (SCALA)

of the Madonna. Terra-cotta figures of the Madonna by Luca della Robbia are well known (see DELLA ROBBIA [picture: *Madonna and Child Jesus*]). For other pictures of sculptures of the Madonna, see SCULPTURE (color picture: *The Virgin and Child*); IVORY (picture: Virgin and Child in Ivory).

Painters of the Madonna. Saint Luke painted the first Madonna picture, according to legend. But the Virgin Mary and Child became symbols of the accepted Christian faith only after the Council of Ephesus, in present-day Turkey, in A.D. 431. Then the number of Madonna pictures began to increase. The oldest ones are those found in the catacombs of the early Christians. Portraits of the Madonna in the Byzantine period served as models until the 1200's. Then the painters of the early Renaissance introduced a new style, with more background scenery. Giovanni Cimabue, the first of these painters, tried to put natural life into his paintings instead of copying stiff Byzantine figures.

The Madonna and Child developed as a popular subject for painters in the later Renaissance period. Raphael produced some of the greatest paintings of the Madonna. His painting *Sistine Madonna*, completed in 1515, hangs in the Dresden Gallery in Germany. It shows the Virgin Mary carrying Jesus in her arms. On one side, Pope Sixtus II kneels in prayer. Saint Barbara kneels on the other side. Below, two cherubs lean forward. Raphael originally painted this work as an altarpiece for the Church of San Sisto in Piacenza.

Other great painters who portrayed the Madonna included Alesso Baldovinetti, Giovanni Bellini, Leonardo da Vinci, Giorgione, Fra Filippo Lippi, Andrea del Sarto, and Titian.

Types of Madonna Paintings. Paintings of the Madonna are usually divided into five classes, according to the general styles of treatment:

(1) *Portrait of the Madonna*. In this class, the Madonna usually appears as a half-length figure against a background of solid gold leaf, or with cherubs. She wears a blue robe, starred or marked with gold, often draped over her head. The first paintings of the Madonna, in the Greek or Byzantine period, belong to this group. Many old churches in Italy contain examples of portraits of the Madonna (see FRA ANGELICO [picture: *Madonna of Humility*]). Baldovinetti's *Madonna*, in the Louvre, Paris, is an example from the late Renaissance.

(2) *The Madonna Enthroned*. The Madonna sits on some sort of throne or platform in this largest class of paintings. The treatment varies widely. Two examples are reproduced in color in the PAINTING article: *Enthroned Madonna and Child* by an unknown Byzantine artist and *Madonna of the Long Neck* by the Italian artist Parmigianino. See also BELLINI (picture: *Madonna with Saints*); LIPPI (picture: *Madonna and Child*).

(3) *The Madonna in Glory*. The Madonna and her attendants hover in the sky in paintings of this group. Heaven is suggested by a *halo* (circle of light), clouds, or cherubs, or by posing the figures in air just above the earth. The halo originally surrounded the entire figure, instead of only the head. It was generally oval in shape. Examples of this type include *The Sistine Madonna* by Raphael; and *Madonna of the Stars* by Fra Angelico, in the monastery of San Marco in Florence. El Greco's

The Virgin with Saint Inés and Saint Tecla, another example of this type of painting, appears in the article on MARY.

(4) *The Madonna in Pastoral Scenes*. Paintings in this class have a landscape background. Two well-known examples are reproduced in color in the PAINTING article: *Madonna of the Goldfinch* by Raphael and *Madonna of the Rocks* by Leonardo da Vinci. For other examples, see BOTTICELLI, SANDRO (picture: *Adoration of the Magi*); HALO (picture: *Madonna and Child*).

(5) *The Madonna in a Home Environment*. Only a small number of paintings come under this heading. The painters of northern Europe were fond of home life. So they painted the Madonna in settings that resemble their own homes. *Madonna* by Quentin Massys pictures a Flemish bedroom of the 1400's. In *Madonna of Chancellor Rolin*, Jan Van Eyck pictured the Madonna in Flemish scenery of the 1430's. Another work of this class is *In a Carpenter's Home* by Rembrandt.   THOMAS MUNRO

See also ENGRAVING (picture: A Renaissance Engraving).

MADONNA COLLEGE. See UNIVERSITIES AND COLLEGES (table).

MADONNA LILY. See LILY.

MADRAS, *muh DRAS* (pop. 2,469,449; met. area 3,169,930), is India's fourth largest city. Bombay, Delhi, and Calcutta are larger. Madras lies on the eastern coast, and is the capital of the state of Tamil Nadu (formerly Madras). For location, see INDIA (political map). Although Madras does not have a good harbor, the city carries on a large sea trade. Several canals and railroads center in Madras. Cotton, rice, coffee, hides, and skins are brought from the interior for shipment to other countries.

Madras' factories assemble automobiles, manufacture bicycles and cigarettes, and weave cotton cloth. Tanning hides for leather is also important. Madras is the site of Madras University, one of India's leading educational institutions. The Madras Institute of Technology is also located there.

Madras was founded in 1639, when an Indian rajah granted some land to a British subject. The first settlers built a fortified trading post, and a village soon grew up around it. Madras can claim an even earlier date of founding, for it now includes the old village of Saint Thomé, which the Portuguese established in 1504. The city received its municipal charter in 1687. French forces captured the city in 1746 during the War of the Austrian Succession. The French returned Madras to the British in 1749 as a result of the Treaty of Aix-la-Chapelle that ended the war.   ROBERT I. CRANE

MADRAS, *MAD ruhs*, is a shirting fabric that is characterized by a woven design on a plain ground. It is usually made with colored yarns, and in many patterns, such as stripes or small figure effects. Madras is generally preshrunk and *mercerized* (see MERCERIZING).

Madras gingham is lighter in weight than the average gingham. It is made of fancy-weave, vat-dyed yarns. Curtain madras, or *grenadine*, has an all-over design made by an extra *filling* (crosswise) yarn that forms a decorative design on the sheer background. This extra filling yarn is cut, so the trimmed ends are shaggy, outlining the design.   HAZEL B. STRAHAN

MADRASAH. See ISLAM (The Mosque); ISLAMIC ART (Madrasahs).

Madrid's Gran Vía, also called the Avenida de José Antonio, is the main street of the city's business district. Banks, hotels, restaurants, stores, and theaters line both sides of this busy avenue.

MADRID, *muh DRIHD* (pop. 3,201,234), is the capital and largest city of Spain. It stands on a plateau about 2,150 feet (655 meters) above sea level and is one of the highest capitals in Europe. Madrid became the capital largely because of its location near the exact geographic center of Spain. For location, see SPAIN (political map).

Spain had reached its height as a colonial power when King Philip II made Madrid the capital in the mid-1500's. The Spanish colonial empire began to decline during the 1600's, but Madrid remained an important center of government and culture. Since the mid-1900's, Madrid has also become one of Spain's leading industrial cities.

The City covers about 234 square miles (607 square kilometers). Madrid suffered severe damage during the Spanish Civil War (1936-1939), and much of the city has been reconstructed or restored from the wartime ruins.

A large, crescent-shaped plaza called the Puerta del Sol (Gate of the Sun) marks the center of downtown Madrid. One of the city's main streets, the Calle de Alcalá, extends eastward from the Puerta del Sol. The old section of Madrid lies southwest of the Puerta del Sol. Some of the buildings that line the narrow, winding streets of this area date from the 1500's and 1600's. Madrid's modern business district is north of the Calle de Alcalá. Banks, hotels, restaurants, stores, and theaters stand along the Gran Vía (also called the Avenida de José Antonio), the main street of the busi-

ness section. The Salamanca district, a residential area built chiefly during the late 1800's and the 1900's, occupies the near northeast part of the city. A huge park called the Retiro covers more than 350 acres (142 hectares) just southeast of the center of Madrid.

Nearly all of Madrid's famous buildings and monuments are in or near the old section and the central business district. The Royal Palace, built in the 1700's, stands at the western edge of the old section. The Spanish royal family lived in the palace until 1931, when King Alfonso XIII was forced to leave the country. Elaborate gardens border the palace, which is now a museum. Madrid also has a number of lovely old churches and impressive public squares with fountains and statues of famous Spaniards.

Since 1950, a rapid population growth has caused Madrid to expand in all directions. Today, residential areas and industrial suburbs surround the central city. Like other rapidly growing cities, Madrid has such problems as air pollution and crowded living conditions. Many of the city's trees have been cut down to widen streets and to provide parking space for the increasing number of automobiles.

The People of Madrid are called *Madrileños.* They speak Castilian Spanish, the official language of Spain. Most of the people live in apartments because they cannot afford the high cost of a house.

Most stores and offices in Madrid open at 9 A.M. and close at about 1 P.M., when Madrileños leave work to eat a leisurely lunch. The business places are open again

35

from 4 P.M. to about 7 P.M. Like other Spaniards, most Madrileños have dinner between 10 P.M. and midnight. They like to dine at Madrid's many fine restaurants, which feature beef, lamb, and seafood dishes. Sidewalk cafes throughout the city are favorite meeting places, where Madrileños chat with friends.

Large crowds attend the bullfights held at the Plaza de Toros. But soccer ranks as Madrid's most popular sport. The city's soccer stadium, one of the largest in the world, seats more than 100,000 spectators.

Education and Cultural Life. Madrid's educational institutions, museums, and libraries make the city the cultural center of Spain. The University of Madrid, the nation's largest university, occupies a section of Madrid called University City. The city also has a number of technical institutes.

Madrid is the home of one of the world's outstanding art museums, the Prado, also called the National Museum of Painting and Sculpture. The Prado houses a collection of more than 2,000 paintings by Spanish and foreign masters. Its exhibits of Spanish paintings include more than 30 works by El Greco and more than 100 by Francisco Goya. The museum also displays 50 paintings by Diego Velázquez, including *The Maids of Honor*, which appears in color in the PAINTING article.

Madrid has a number of other art museums, as well as many museums that feature exhibits on natural history and science. The city is also the home of Spain's National Library and the National Historical Archives.

Climate. Madrid has a dry climate, with hot summers and cool winters. It receives an average of less than 17 inches (43 centimeters) of rain a year. Temperatures average about 40° F. (4° C) in January and about 74° F. (23° C) in July. During August, which is usually the hottest month in Madrid, San Sebastian serves as the official seat of the Spanish government. San Sebastian lies on the country's cooler north coast.

Economy. From the mid-1500's to the mid-1900's, the economy of Madrid depended on the city's role as a government center. Most of the workers in Madrid had jobs related to politics or government administration. The city had almost no industry.

Since the mid-1900's, the Spanish government has encouraged large-scale industrial development in Madrid and its suburbs. Today, the city ranks second to Barcelona as a Spanish industrial center. Factories in the Madrid area manufacture automobiles, chemicals, clothing, leather goods, trucks, and other products.

Highways and railroads link Madrid to other Spanish cities. Barajas International Airport lies about 7 miles (11 kilometers) northeast of downtown Madrid.

History. In the A.D. 900's, the Moors, a Moslem people, built a fortress called Magerit on the site of what is now Madrid (see MOOR). Spanish Christians, under King Alfonso VI of León and Castile, gained control of the area in 1083.

Madrid remained a small, unimportant town until 1561, when Philip II made it the capital of Spain. Philip, who ruled a huge colonial empire, chose Madrid primarily because of its central location. During the late 1500's and early 1600's, Madrid grew rapidly and became one of the great cities of western Europe. Wealthy aristocrats and royal officials built homes there. But

Mort Rabinow, Stock, Boston

Modern Apartment Buildings in and near Madrid provide housing for many families. A rapid population growth since 1950 has caused Madrid and its suburbs to expand in all directions.

the rapid population growth also brought problems. Most Madrileños were poor and lived in shabby, crowded neighborhoods. Epidemics and a high crime rate made the city unsafe. During the 1700's, the government took steps that made Madrid cleaner and safer.

French forces under Napoleon I occupied Madrid from 1808 to 1813. On May 2, 1808, a group of Madrileños staged an unsuccessful revolt against the French. This uprising started a Spanish resistance movement that in time helped drive the French out of Spain.

Madrid, unlike many cities in a number of countries, failed to develop large industries during the 1800's. As a result, it did not attract large numbers of workers, and its rate of population growth dropped.

Madrid attracted worldwide attention during the Spanish Civil War, which began in 1936. The city was the scene of fierce fighting between the Loyalists, who supported the government, and the rebel forces of General Francisco Franco. The Loyalists moved the capital to Valencia in 1936 and to Barcelona in 1937. After the defeat of the Loyalists in 1939, Franco reestablished Madrid as the capital.

Since the mid-1900's, Madrid has again experienced rapid population growth. Government programs to develop industry and to build modern housing and office buildings in the city have helped contribute to Madrid's growth.   STANLEY G. PAYNE

See also SPAIN (pictures).

MADRIGAL, *MAD rih gul*, is a pastoral song, usually contemplative in nature, in which two or more voices sing separate melodies to a simple text. It usually has no instrumental accompaniment, and amounts to vocal chamber music, with one voice to a part.

Italian composers began writing madrigals in the late 1200's. The form reached its high point in the early 1600's in the works of Luca Marenzio, Carlo Gesualdo, and Claudio Monteverdi. Outside of Italy, it developed chiefly in England. It had a number of names, including *songs*, *canzonets*, and *ayres*. English madrigal composers of the 1500's included William Byrd, Thomas Morley, Thomas Weelkes, and John Wilbye. The madrigal was usually a secular song, but such composers as Orlando di Lasso and Giovanni Palestrina wrote sacred madrigals. Some German and Spanish composers composed madrigals. But the movement never gained the significance it did in Italy and England. RAYMOND KENDALL

See also MUSIC (The Renaissance).

MADROÑA, *muh DROH nyuh*, or MADRONE, is a small tree with white, urn-shaped flowers and leathery evergreen leaves. The rough, berrylike fruit has mealy flesh and hard seeds. It grows along the Pacific coast of the United States, from southern California to British Columbia, and in other countries. See also HEATH.

Scientific Classification. Madroña belongs to the heath family, *Ericaceae*. It is classified as genus *Arbutus*, species *A. menziesii*. GEORGE B. CUMMINS

MAECENAS. See VIRGIL (His Life); HORACE.

MAELSTROM, *MAYL struhm*, is a swift and dangerous current in the Arctic Ocean. This current sweeps back and forth between two islands of the Lofoten group off the northwestern coast of Norway. It has been a menace to sailors for hundreds of years. The Maelstrom becomes more dangerous when the wind blows against it between high and low tide. The waters then form immense whirlpools that destroy small ships.

Writers, including the Norwegian poet Peter Dass and the American author Edgar Allan Poe, have greatly exaggerated the Maelstrom's power. As a result, the word *maelstrom* has come to mean any kind of whirlpool or any turmoil of widespread influence. HENRY STOMMEL

See also WHIRLPOOL.

MAETERLINCK, *MAY tur lingk*, **MAURICE** (1862-1949), was a Belgian dramatist, poet, naturalist, and philosopher. Maeterlinck was born in Ghent. He became a lawyer but spent his life writing. He won the 1911 Nobel prize for literature.

Maeterlinck's contribution to drama was his ability to express a world beyond reality. His most famous play is *The Blue Bird* (1909). It is a symbolic story of a child who searches for happiness and finds it in his own home. Maeterlinck's short plays *The Intruder* (1890) and *The Blind* (1890) treat the commonplaceness of death and the need for love in symbolic terms. These plays have little physical action and Maeterlinck called them *static drama*. In *Pelleas and Melisande* (1892), Maeterlinck dramatized the medieval story of Paolo and Francesca. The play symbolizes the inescapable bond between two persons in love and the necessity of their death. Maeterlinck's other plays include *Monna Vanna* (1902) and *The Mayor of Stilmonde* (1919).

Maeterlinck's mystical philosophy is most evident in his essays *The Treasure of the Humble* (1896) and *Wisdom and Destiny* (1898). His ideas about the mystery of life and death also appear in several nature studies, notably *The Life of the Bees* (1901) and *The Life of the Ants* (1930). Both works were basic to further discoveries about the social systems under which ants and bees live. His dreamy and melancholy poetry was published in *Hot Houses* (1889) and *Twelve Songs* (1896). FREDERICK J. HUNTER

MAFEKING, *MAFF ee KING* (pop. 6,493), is a railroad center in Cape Province in northern South Africa. It is also a dairy center and cattle-raising area. Mafeking was the administrative capital of the British protectorate of Bechuanaland (now Botswana) until 1965, when Gaborone became the capital. For location, see SOUTH AFRICA (color map).

During the Boer War, a Boer army surrounded British troops under Colonel Robert Baden-Powell in Mafeking. The British held out for 217 days, until help arrived. Mafeking was founded in 1885. HIBBERD V. B. KLINE, JR.

See also BADEN-POWELL, LORD.

MAFFEI, PAOLO. See MAFFEI GALAXIES.

MAFFEI GALAXIES, *mah FAY ee*, often called *Maffei 1* and *Maffei 2*, are two large star systems. They probably belong to the group of galaxies that includes the earth's galaxy, the Milky Way. The Maffei galaxies are less than 12 million light-years from the earth. A light-year is the distance that light travels in a year. It equals about 6 trillion miles (9.5 trillion kilometers).

Each of the Maffei galaxies measures from 50,000 to 100,000 light-years in diameter. Maffei 1, the brighter of the two systems, may consist of as many as 100 billion stars. Maffei 2 has only about 10 billion stars. Astronomers classify Maffei 1 as an *elliptical galaxy* because of its oval shape. Maffei 2 resembles a flattened coil and is classified as a *spiral galaxy*.

The Maffei galaxies remained unknown until 1968 because they are hidden by dense clouds of cosmic dust and gas in the earth's galaxy. They were discovered that year by the Italian astronomer Paolo Maffei, for whom they were named. Maffei photographed the galaxies through a telescope by using film sensitive to *infrared rays*, the invisible heat rays given off by the galaxies. Infrared rays, unlike light rays, can penetrate dust clouds. In 1971, astronomers at several California observatories determined the approximate size and shape of the Maffei galaxies. FRANK D. DRAKE

MAFIA, *MAH fee ah*, is the name of a secret Sicilian terrorist society. *Mafia* comes from the Arabic word *maehfil*, meaning *union*. The Mafia began in the 1600's as an organization to combat corruption and tyranny in the Kingdom of the Two Sicilies. Later, lawless and criminal elements, who robbed, murdered, and waged bloody vendettas, gained control (see VENDETTA). The Mafia has been a power both in Italy and among Italians abroad. Its members, organized into cells of no more than five persons, are bound by an iron oath of fidelity. Authorities have had difficulty in gathering evidence against the Mafia. The society operates outside of the law, but some of its activities are legal. WILLIAM H. MAEHL

MAGARAC, *MAG uh rak*, **JOE,** is the mythical strong man of the steel mills. He was reputed to be a 7-foot (213-centimeter) giant, born in an ore mountain and made of steel. Joe Magarac made so many steel rails, by squeezing the hot steel through his fingers, that his mill was ordered shut down. In protest, he melted himself in boiling metal. His stubborn self-sacrifice made the name *Magarac*, Croatian and Serbian for *jackass*, one to be proud of rather than laughed at. B. A. BOTKIN

Magazines reach millions of people. Most readers buy them at newsstands or have them delivered at home. A large readership helps a magazine attract advertising, a major source of income.

MAGAZINE is a collection of articles or stories—or both—published at regular intervals. Most magazines also include illustrations.

Magazines provide a wide variety of information and entertainment. For example, some magazines in the United States cover such subjects as current events, literary criticism, or tips on how to repair appliances. Other magazines debate foreign policy and national defense or describe the latest developments in medicine. Many magazines seek to simply entertain their readers with such material as articles about TV shows or interviews with motion-picture stars. The United States has about 16,500 magazines, more than any other country.

Magazines, like newspapers, represent the work of many writers. But magazines differ from newspapers in form and content. Magazines are designed to be kept much longer than newspapers. For this reason, most magazines are smaller and are printed on better paper. Many have covers and a binding of staples or stitching. In content, magazines have less concern with daily, rapidly changing events than do newspapers.

Some periodicals that appear in newspaper form are really magazines. On the other hand, some weekly newspapers feature long, detailed articles like those found in many magazines.

The best writing is often found in magazines. Some magazines allow journalists to experiment with new forms of writing. For example, a kind of writing called the *New Journalism* first appeared in magazines. This writing, which started during the 1960's, used such fictional devices as storytelling and colorful description to discuss nonfictional events. It presented a highly personal style that differed from the objective, factual reporting of traditional journalism.

Kinds of Magazines

Magazines are usually classified by the audience they serve. These classifications include: (1) children's magazines, (2) hobby magazines, (3) intellectual magazines, (4) men's magazines, (5) women's magazines, and (6) trade and business magazines. Magazines can also be grouped by the interval at which they are published—that is, as weeklies, biweeklies, monthlies, and quarterlies. Most magazines are monthlies.

Children's Magazines are published for young people of various ages. Most of them feature stories, jokes, articles on a wide variety of subjects especially interesting to children, and instructions for making games or useful items.

Hobby Magazines appeal to hobbyists in all fields. Their audiences include collectors of coins, stamps, and other items; people interested in certain sports or games; home decorators; photography enthusiasts; and many other groups.

Intellectual Magazines provide a thoughtful analysis of current cultural and political events. These publications include *opinion magazines*, which discuss current events from a particular economic or political viewpoint. Many intellectual magazines publish fiction and poetry as well as articles.

Men's Magazines carry articles or stories on such subjects as adventure, entertainment, men's fashions, and sports. Some also have features and interviews about the arts and current affairs.

Women's Magazines include many of the monthlies with the largest number of readers. Publications called *service magazines* offer ideas on cooking, home decorating, and other homemaking skills. Some women's periodicals deal with child-raising, fashion trends, or romance. Others discuss the role of women in society and provide career information.

Trade and Business Magazines serve readers in a specific field or industry, such as agriculture or space technology. Their articles tell of new products and techniques that affect a particular industry. About half these magazines have *controlled circulations*—that is, the publishers obtain lists of people they want to reach, and deliver their magazines only to those persons.

Other Magazines include *newsmagazines*, which summarize the week's news. *Digests* reprint material, in condensed form, that has appeared in other magazines or in books. *Guide magazines* provide such information as listings of television shows or descriptions of various places of interest in a community. *Scholarly journals* publish the results of research for scientists or other experts in various fields.

A number of magazines publish material of interest to various ethnic, racial, or religious groups. Some magazines for Negroes, for example, feature news articles about blacks or offer specialized information for black businessmen.

How Magazines Are Produced

Magazines must meet regular publishing deadlines. A newspaper may have one or more deadlines a day, but a magazine's deadlines are weeks or months apart.

Planning a Magazine. Every issue of a magazine must be planned thoroughly before publication. Most monthlies, for example, are planned several months in advance. The editors and staff members first decide what major articles, stories, and other items will appear in the issue. They plan the illustrations, if any, at the same time. Regular columns and editorials must also be planned.

Making Assignments. The editors assign the articles to staff members or to free-lance writers. Each article has a deadline and a specified length. Photographs may be taken by staff or free-lance photographers or purchased from picture agencies. Special drawings may be used to illustrate certain kinds of articles. Magazines sometimes publish unassigned articles and photographs by free-lance journalists who offer material for sale.

Scheduling the Advertising. Ads are planned for an issue of a magazine while the writers work on their assignments. The editors and staff artists create a *layout*, which shows how the advertising and editorial material will be arranged on each page.

Editing and Assembling an Issue. After the articles have been written, one or more editors go over them to check their accuracy and readability. Members of the staff may write additional short articles or other items and choose letters from readers to be published. All the written material, called *copy*, is then set in type.

Photographs and other illustrations must be reduced or expanded in size if necessary. Then they have to be reproduced in some form—as engravings, for example—that can be used in making printing plates.

Proofreaders check proofs of the printed copy for errors. The editors examine proofs of the illustrations to be sure the color and size are accurate. Then they paste the text and illustration proofs on blank pages. This group of pages, called a *dummy*, shows how the printed magazine will look.

The magazine is printed according to the dummy. It may be printed by the *letterpress* process, which involves pressing lead type against paper. Another common method, *offset lithography*, reproduces the type and illustrations with photographic plates.

How Magazines Earn Income

Most magazines receive income from two sources: (1) advertising and (2) sales of the publication by subscriptions or by newsstand purchases.

Advertising ranks as by far the most important source of income for almost all magazines. An advertiser puts his message in magazines because they are read by certain groups. For example, a photography magazine attracts camera fans who may find its ads valuable in buying certain photographic equipment. An advertiser of such equipment can reach many potential customers by putting his ads in such a magazine. Some advertisers spend thousands of dollars for a single page of advertising space in a magazine.

Many publishers conduct surveys to find out what groups of people read their magazines. These surveys can identify reader groups by age, income, occupation, race, sex, and other characteristics. Advertisers study such surveys to decide which magazines are read by the people most likely to buy their products.

Sales. Readers get almost all magazines by subscription through the mail or buy them at newsstands. Magazines to be sold on newsstands are shipped by airplane, train, and truck to various points. Distribution companies then deliver them to newsstands.

Subscription and newsstand sales cannot cover the production costs of most magazine publishers. The actual selling of a magazine is also expensive. Attracting subscribers, for example, may involve an expensive promotional campaign that attracts only a small number of new subscriptions. In newsstand sales, the publisher gets paid only for the magazines actually sold.

History

The earliest magazines probably developed from newspapers or from bookseller catalogs. Such catalogs, which reviewed books on sale, first appeared during the 1600's in France and then in other countries. Pamphlets published at regular intervals appeared in England and America in the 1700's, primarily as literary publications. They included *The Tatler* and *The Spectator*, both published in England.

One of the first British magazines, *The Gentleman's Magazine*, was published from 1731 to 1914. Edward Cave, an English printer, started it as a collection of articles from various books and pamphlets. Later, it published original material. Samuel Johnson, the famous English writer and critic, contributed to this magazine.

The first magazine published in America, the *American Magazine, or A Monthly View*, was published in 1741

MAGAZINE

PRODUCING A MAGAZINE

Each issue of a magazine is planned weeks or even months in advance by a group of editors, *above*. The editors choose topics to be covered in the magazine. They then make assignments and set deadlines. These editors have assigned a writer and a photographer to prepare an article on Egypt, *below*.

The Writer interviews many Egyptians to create an accurate, timely article.

The Photographer takes dramatic pictures of the land and its people.

A Layout Artist arranges the text and pictures in an attractive way.

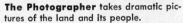

After Being Printed, the magazine pages are assembled and stapled together. The finished copies are then trimmed, addressed, and mailed.

Name	Publication Period	Circulation*
UNITED STATES		
TV Guide	Weekly	19,495,113
Reader's Digest	Monthly	17,931,180
National Geographic Magazine	Monthly	9,960,287
Family Circle	Monthly	8,369,237
Better Homes and Gardens	Monthly	8,056,355
Woman's Day	Monthly	8,002,758
McCall's Magazine	Monthly	6,503,187
Modern Maturity	Bimonthly	6,500,000
Ladies' Home Journal	Monthly	6,001,578
National Enquirer	Weekly	5,719,918
Good Housekeeping	Monthly	5,198,082
Penthouse	Monthly	4,510,824
Playboy	Monthly	4,479,169
Redbook Magazine	Monthly	4,431,266
Time	Weekly	4,311,084
Star	Weekly	3,008,948
Newsweek	Weekly	2,958,851
Cosmopolitan	Monthly	2,658,571
American Legion Magazine	Monthly	2,597,816
Pace	Bimonthly	2,400,000
Sports Illustrated	Weekly	2,336,344
People	Weekly	2,309,212
U.S. News & World Report	Weekly	2,100,796
Field and Stream	Monthly	2,042,764
CANADA		
Reader's Digest†	Monthly	1,576,240
Chatelaine†	Monthly	1,278,791
TV Guide Magazine	Weekly	1,084,194
Maclean's Magazine	Weekly	662,097
Family Circle	Monthly	532,152

*Figures are for national circulation only.
†Includes English and French editions.
Sources: '79 *Ayer Directory of Publications;* individual magazines.

in Philadelphia and lasted only three months. Mathew Carey, a Philadelphia journalist, started two early American magazines, *The Columbian* in 1786 and *The American Museum* in 1787.

In 1830, Louis A. Godey founded *Godey's Lady's Book,* the first American magazine for women. Sarah Josepha Hale edited the magazine, which helped shape the tastes of thousands of women. Among the first influential intellectual magazines was *The Dial,* published in the early 1840's by New England transcendentalists and edited by Margaret Fuller (see TRANSCENDENTALISM). Around the mid-1800's, a number of important magazines were started. Frank Leslie began *Leslie's Weekly,* one of the first magazines to feature many illustrations. *Atlantic Monthly,* launched in 1857, was first edited by the famous poet James Russell Lowell. During the Civil War (1861-1865), many readers turned to *Harper's Weekly* for its drawings of the battle front.

In the late 1800's and early 1900's, reformers who exposed conditions in business, industry, and politics wrote for *Everybody's Magazine* and *McClure's Magazine.* These writers, called *muckrakers,* included Ray Stannard Baker, Lincoln Steffens, and Ida M. Tarbell. *McClure's Magazine,* founded by S. S. McClure, became one of the first successful inexpensive magazines. Before this time, magazines had been published mainly for wealthy

people. *The Nation,* founded as a liberal weekly newspaper, later became a magazine. The *Ladies' Home Journal* worked for social causes under the editorship of Edward W. Bok. Important literary publications started during the early 1900's included *Vanity Fair* in 1914 and *The New Yorker* in 1925.

Leading magazine publishers of the 1900's have included Henry R. Luce, who founded *Life, Time, Sports Illustrated,* and other magazines. John H. Johnson started *Negro Digest* in 1942. He later founded several other magazines that were written chiefly for black readers.

Every year, many magazines are started and others die out. To last, a magazine must have an editorial content that remains useful to an audience. It also needs advertisers who want to reach that audience and believe they can do so most effectively by advertising in the magazine.

During the 1920's and 1930's, such *general magazines* as the *Saturday Evening Post* ranked as the major means of nationwide communication. These publications featured text and photographs on a wide range of subjects. But after the widespread growth of television in the late 1940's, advertisers began to promote their products on TV rather than in general magazines. Television enabled the advertisers to reach larger audiences than they could through magazines and to emphasize their message with motion. Since that time, the lack of advertising and an increase in overall costs have caused many general magazines to stop regular publication.

A magazine publisher once needed relatively little money to launch a publication. For example, two prominent American magazines, *The New Yorker* and *Time,* were started in the 1920's with little funds. But today, high costs—particularly those involving production and mailing—require a great deal of money to start and maintain a magazine. To cut expenses, many magazines reduced the number and size of their pages during the 1960's and early 1970's. Many magazines that were launched during those years aimed for a small, specialized audience rather than a large readership. For example, such periodicals as *New York* were started mainly for residents of a particular geographical area. Such specialization enabled publishers to cut the cost of production and postage and to attract advertisers who wanted to reach certain groups. Many publishers used statistical studies of the population to find possible subscribers. PETER P. JACOBI

Related Articles in WORLD BOOK include:

BIOGRAPHIES

Adams, Samuel H.	Johnson, John H.
Bok, Edward W.	Leslie, Frank
Buckley, William F., Jr.	Luce (Henry R.)
Church, William C.	Munsey, Frank A.
Curtis, Cyrus H. K.	Ross, Harold W.
Fuller, Margaret	Steffens, Lincoln
Godey, Louis A.	Steinem, Gloria
Grosvenor, Gilbert H.	Sullivan, Mark
Hale, Sarah J.	Tarbell, Ida M.

OTHER RELATED ARTICLES

Advertising	Commercial Art	Trade Publication
Audit Bureau of	Editorial	Writing
Circulations	Journalism	Yank

MAGAZINE

MAGAZINE is a military and naval term for a protected building or storage room for ammunition. The term comes from an Arabic word meaning *storehouse*. The ammunition supply chamber of a repeating rifle or machine gun is also called a magazine.

Shore magazines are usually concrete buildings shaped like beehives. They are half buried in the ground and are covered with earth. Some powder magazines are built in many compartments, each of which is covered with a light roof. If an explosion occurs, the damage will be confined to a small space and the force will move upward when the roof gives way.

On ships, magazines are placed as far as possible from the engines and firerooms, and far below the water line. They are made up of many watertight rooms with steel walls lined with asbestos. In the tropics, magazines are cooled by ventilators which pipe cool air from a refrigerator, while other pipes take away hot air.

All magazines are equipped with water pipes so they can be flooded in case of fire. No iron or steel tools are allowed inside a magazine, and the people who work in them must wear shoes without nails. These precautions are taken to avoid the danger of an explosion caused by sparks from metals. Ammunition is lifted out through openings.   Jack O'Connor

MAGAZINE MOUNTAIN. See Arkansas (Land).

MAGDALEN COLLEGE. See Oxford University (picture: The Tower of Magdalen College).

MAGDALEN ISLANDS, *MAG duh luhn* (pop. 13,515), is a group of tiny islands in the Gulf of St. Lawrence. The islands make up one of the counties of Quebec. They cover an area of 78 square miles (202 square kilometers). They lie about 50 miles (80 kilometers) northwest of Cape Breton and about 100 miles (160 kilometers) southwest of Newfoundland. Most islanders are French Canadians. They make their living by fishing in the surrounding waters, which are rich in lobster, cod, herring, and seal.

The islands contain large deposits of gypsum. The making of grindstones is a leading industry. The village of Cap-aux-Meules (pop. 1,305) is the islands' largest incorporated place.   Alfred Leroy Burt

MAGDALENE. See Mary Magdalene.

MAGDEBURG, *MAG duh boorg* (pop. 270,692), is a manufacturing city, inland port, and rail center in East Germany. It is located on the banks of the Elbe River. The city is commercially important because of its great machine shops, beet-sugar refining plants, and synthetic oil plant. Magdeburg was founded in the A.D. 800's.   James K. Pollock

MAGEE, SNAKE, is a legendary oil-well driller from West Virginia. Cable-tool drillers there were called "snakes" because they drilled formations only a snake could get through. The story of " 'Snake' Magee and the Rotary Boiler" described how a boiler blew up and hurled Magee 16 miles (26 kilometers). His tool-dresser said, "You were blown back so fast you arrived before you started. You can't sue for injuries because you ain't been to work yet this morning."   B. A. Botkin

MAGELLAN, *muh JEHL uhn,* **FERDINAND** (1480?-1521), was a Portuguese sea captain who commanded the first expedition that sailed around the world. His voyage provided the first positive proof that the earth is round. Magellan did not live to complete the voyage, but his imaginative planning and courageous leadership made the entire expedition possible. Many scholars consider it the greatest navigational feat in history.

Early Life

Magellan was born about 1480 in northern Portugal. His name in Portuguese was Fernão de Magalhães. His parents, who were members of the nobility, died when he was about 10 years old. At the age of 12, Magellan became a page to Queen Leonor at the royal court. Such a position commonly served as a means of education for sons of the Portuguese nobility.

At the court, Magellan learned about the voyages of such explorers as Christopher Columbus of Italy and Vasco da Gama of Portugal. He also learned the fundamentals of navigation. In 1496, Magellan was promoted to the rank of squire and became a clerk in the marine department. There, he helped outfit ships for trade along the west coast of Africa.

Magellan first went to sea in 1505, when he sailed to India with the fleet of Francisco de Almeida, Portugal's first viceroy to that country. In 1506, Magellan went on an expedition sent by Almeida to the east coast of Africa to strengthen Portuguese bases there. The next year, he returned to India, where he participated in trade and in several naval battles against Turkish fleets.

In 1509, Magellan sailed with a Portuguese fleet to Melaka, a commercial center in what is now Malaysia. The Malays at-

Ferdinand Magellan

tacked the Portuguese who went ashore, and Magellan helped rescue his comrades. In 1511, he took part in an expedition that conquered Melaka. After this victory, a Portuguese fleet sailed farther east to the Spice Islands (also called the Molucca Islands). Portugal claimed the islands at this time. Magellan's close personal friend Francisco Serrão went along on the voyage and wrote to Magellan, describing the route and the island of Ternate. Serrão's letters helped establish in Magellan's mind the location of the Spice Islands, which later became the destination of his great voyage.

Magellan returned to Portugal in 1513. He then joined a military expedition to Morocco, where he suffered a wound that made him limp for the rest of his life.

Voyage Around the World

Planning the Expedition. After returning to Portugal from Morocco, Magellan sought the support of King Manuel I for a voyage to the Spice Islands. The best maps available had convinced Magellan that he could reach the islands by sailing south of South America. He believed such a route would be shorter than the eastward voyage around the tip of Africa and across the Indian Ocean. But Manuel disliked Magellan and refused to support the proposed voyage.

Magellan then studied astronomy and navigation for about two years in Porto in northern Portugal. In Porto, he met Ruy Faleiro, an astronomer and geographer who strongly influenced his ideas. Magellan and Faleiro concluded from their studies that the Spice Islands lay in territory that had been awarded to Spain in 1494 (see LINE OF DEMARCATION). Therefore, Magellan decided to seek support for his plans from the king of Spain.

In 1517, Magellan went to Spain. There, he presented his proposal for visiting the Spice Islands as part of a westward circumnavigation of the earth. The next year, Magellan convinced Charles I of Spain to support such a voyage. The king promised Magellan a fifth of the profits from the voyage, plus a salary.

Preparations for the expedition took more than a year. The Spaniards became suspicious of Magellan during this period, partly because he recruited many Portuguese sailors. As a result, the king forced him to replace most of the Portuguese with Spanish crewmen.

The Voyage Begins. On Sept. 20, 1519, Magellan set sail from Sanlúcar de Barrameda in southern Spain. He commanded a total of 241 men and a fleet of five ships, the *Concepción, San Antonio, Santiago, Trinidad,* and *Victoria.* Dissatisfaction among the crewmen plagued the voyage from the beginning, and hostility among the Spaniards toward Magellan grew rapidly. About a month after the voyage began, the Spanish captain of the *San Antonio* challenged Magellan's authority, and Magellan had him arrested.

The fleet sailed across the Atlantic Ocean to the coast of Brazil. The ships followed the coast to the bay where Rio de Janeiro now stands. They remained there for two weeks and then sailed south in search of a passage to the Pacific Ocean. However, they could not find a passage before the end of summer in the Southern Hemisphere. In late March 1520, the fleet anchored for the winter at San Julián in what is now southern Argentina.

During the winter, a storm destroyed the *Santiago.* In addition, a mutiny broke out shortly after the men set up their winter quarters. Magellan and loyal crew members put down the mutiny and executed the leader. They also marooned two other mutineers when the fleet sailed again.

Magellan and his crew resumed their voyage on Oct. 18, 1520. Three days later, they discovered the passage to the Pacific—a passage known ever since as the Strait of Magellan. As the fleet sailed through the strait, the crew of the *San Antonio* mutinied and returned to Spain. On November 28, the three remaining ships sailed out of the strait and into the ocean. Magellan named the ocean the Pacific, which means *peaceful,* because it appeared calm compared with the stormy Atlantic.

Sailing Across the Pacific involved great hardship for Magellan and his crew. They were the first Europeans ever to sail across the Pacific, and it was far larger than anyone had imagined. They sailed for 98 days without seeing any land except two uninhabited islands. Their food gave out and their water supply became contaminated. They ate rats, ox hides, and sawdust to avoid starvation. Most of the crew suffered from scurvy, a disease caused by the lack of fresh fruits and vegetables. Nineteen men died before the fleet reached Guam on March 6, 1521.

Conflicts with the people of Guam and the nearby island of Rota prevented Magellan from fully resupplying his ships. But the crew seized enough food and water to continue on to the Philippines.

Magellan and his crew remained in the Philippines for several weeks, and close relations developed between them and the islanders. Magellan took special pride in converting many of the people to Christianity. Unfortunately, however, he involved himself in rivalries among the people. On April 27, 1521, Magellan was killed when he took part in a battle between rival Filipino groups on the island of Mactan.

The Voyage of Magellan 1519 to 1522 This map traces Magellan's search for a western passage to the Spice Islands. He became the first European to sail across the Pacific Ocean. Magellan was killed on the island of Mactan in 1521. One of his ships, commanded by Juan Sebastián del Cano, completed the voyage.

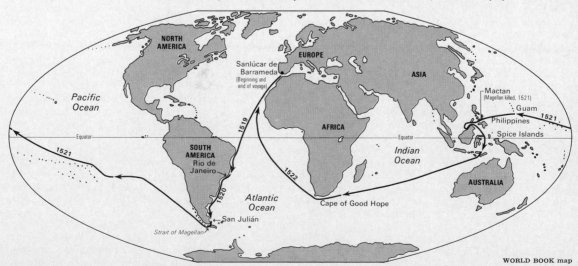

WORLD BOOK map

The Fatal Battle of Mactan (1595), an engraving by Theodore de Bry; Bibliothèque Nationale, Paris

Magellan Was Killed in Battle on the island of Mactan in the Philippines on April 27, 1521. The engraving above shows Magellan's forces fighting the people of Mactan.

The End of the Voyage. After the battle on Mactan, only about 110 of the original crew members remained —too few to man three ships. Therefore, the men abandoned the *Concepción*, and the two remaining vessels sailed southward to the Spice Islands. There, the ships were loaded with spices. The leaders of the fleet then decided that the two ships should make separate return voyages.

The *Trinidad*, under the command of Gonzalo Gómez de Espinosa, tried to sail eastward across the Pacific to the Isthmus of Panama. Bad weather and disease disrupted the voyage, and more than half the crew died. The survivors were forced to return to the Spice Islands, where the Portuguese imprisoned them.

The *Victoria*, commanded by Juan Sebastián del Cano, continued its westward voyage back to Spain. Like the *Trinidad*, the *Victoria* experienced great hardship, and many of the crew died of malnutrition and starvation. The *Victoria* finally reached Sanlúcar de Barrameda on Sept. 6, 1522, nearly three years after the voyage had begun. Only Del Cano and 17 other survivors returned with the ship.

Results of the Voyage. One of the crew members who returned with Del Cano was an Italian named Antonio Pigafetta. He had faithfully written down the events of the voyage, and his journal is the chief source of information about the expedition. According to Pigafetta, the voyage covered 14,460 leagues (50,610 miles or 81,449 kilometers). Pigafetta praised Magellan for his courage and navigational skill. However, nearly everyone else at the time gave Del Cano the credit for the voyage. The Portuguese considered Magellan a traitor, and the Spanish condemned Magellan because of reports of his harshness and errors in navigation.

Magellan failed to find a short route to the Spice Islands, but his voyage contributed greatly to knowledge about the earth. In addition, the discovery of the Strait of Magellan led to future European voyages to explore the vast Pacific. JOHN PARKER

See also EXPLORATION (Magellan's Globe Circling Expedition); WORLD, HISTORY OF (picture: Magellan's Ship).

44

MAGELLAN, STRAIT OF, is a narrow, rough waterway that separates the islands of Tierra del Fuego from the mainland of South America. The Strait of Magellan is almost at the southern end of the continent. In 1520, Ferdinand Magellan, the Portuguese explorer, led the first European expedition through the strait during the first voyage around the world.

The Strait of Magellan is located at the southern tip of South America. The strait experiences high winds and heavy rains throughout the year.

WORLD BOOK maps

The Strait of Magellan is 350 miles (563 kilometers) long and varies from 2 to 20 miles (3 to 32 kilometers) in width. Before the Panama Canal opened, the strait and Cape Horn were the shortest water routes from the Atlantic Ocean to the Pacific Ocean. ROBERT N. BURR

See also CAPE HORN; MAGELLAN, FERDINAND.

MAGELLANIC CLOUDS. See GALAXY.

MAGERØY. See NORTH CAPE.

MAGGIORE, LAKE. See LAKE MAGGIORE.

MAGGOT, *MAG ut,* is the larva, or young, of many kinds of flies. The maggot has a soft body which usually tapers toward the front. It looks somewhat like a worm or caterpillar. It has no legs and no distinct head. Maggots move by wriggling or flipping their bodies. They are usually white, but may be colored. Most maggots live buried in their food. Some are scavengers and live in dead or decaying matter. Others are parasites in animal and plant tissue. Still others prey on insects. See also FLY (The Life of a Fly); LARVA. E. GORTON LINSLEY

MAGI, *MAY jie,* were the priests of the ancient Medes and Persians. After the rise of Zoroaster, the Magi became the priests of the Zoroastrian religion (see ZOROASTRIANISM). The ancient Greeks and Hebrews knew them as astrologers, interpreters of dreams, and givers of omens. The Greek word "magic" originally meant the work of the Magi. Later, the Magi became corrupt. The "wise men from the East" who brought gifts to the baby Jesus are supposed to have been Magi (see BOTTICELLI, SANDRO [picture: *Adoration of the Magi*]). According to one tradition, the wise men were Melchior, Balthasar, and Gaspar. BRUCE M. METZGER

MAGIC is the supposed use of unnatural or super-human power by a human being. A person uses magic to try to control human actions or natural events. Magic often seems to achieve results, but the results actually have other causes. For example, a person might cast a magic spell to make an enemy sick. The enemy may learn about the spell, become frightened, and actually feel ill.

People throughout the world have practiced magic from the dawn of history. But beginning in the 1600's, science has provided an increasingly greater under-standing of the true causes of natural events. This increased scientific knowledge has reduced man's de-pendence on magic. But most people in primitive societies still believe in magic. Even in modern societies, many people still trust in such forms of magic as astrology and fortunetelling.

The word *magic* also refers to a type of entertainment in which the performer does tricks of so-called magic. In such entertainment, neither the magician nor his audience believes he has supernatural powers.

Elements of Magic

The practice of magic includes the use of special words, actions, and objects. Most magic also involves a person called a magician, who claims to have super-natural powers.

Magic Words. To work most magic, the magician sings or speaks special words in a certain order. These magic words are called *incantations* or *spells*. Some in-cantations form prayers to demons, spirits, or other supernatural forces. Many societies believe the magic will not work unless the magician recites the spells perfectly. Other magic words have no actual meaning, though they supposedly possess power when spoken by a magician.

Magic Actions accompany the words spoken in per-forming much magic. Many of these movements act out the desired effect of the magic. For example, a magician trying to make rain fall may sprinkle water on the ground. The magician's combined words and ac-tions form a ceremony called a *rite* or *ritual*.

Magic Objects include certain plants, stones, and other things with supposed supernatural powers. Any such object may be called a *fetish* (see FETISH). But this term often refers to an object—for example, a carving or a dried snake—honored by a tribe for its magic powers, Many tribes believe fetishes have magic power because spirits live in these objects.

Many people carry magic objects called *amulets*, *charms*, or *talismans* to protect themselves from harm (see AMULET). Many amulets and talismans are stones or rings engraved with magic symbols.

The Magician. In some societies, nearly everyone knows how to work some magic. In other societies, only experts practice magic. Magicians may be called *medicine men*, *shamans*, *sorcerers*, or *witch doctors* (see SHAMAN). In many societies, magicians must inherit their powers. In others, any person may become a magician by studying the magical arts.

Many societies believe a magician must observe cer-tain rules and *taboos* (forbidden actions) for his spells to work. For example, he may be required not to eat various foods or to avoid sexual activity for a certain period before the ceremony.

Kinds of Magic

Many anthropologists classify magic as *homeopathic* or *contagious*, according to its basic principle. The Scottish anthropologist Sir James G. Frazer first de-scribed these two types of magic in his famous book *The Golden Bough* (1890).

Some people divide magic into *black magic* and *white magic*. Black magic harms people, but white magic helps them. Witches usually practice black magic. But when a saint cures a sick person, he uses white magic.

Two Witch Doctors in Africa compare magical remedies. Many of the "medicines" that they use consist of such sub-stances as powdered animal horns and teeth.

Homeopathic Magic is based on the belief that like produces like. In this type of magic, also called *imitative magic*, a person acts out or imitates what he wants to happen. He often uses a model or miniature of whatever he wants to influence. For example, a fisherman may make a model of a fish and pretend he is netting it. He believes this ritual will assure him a good catch. In some European folk dances, the dancers leap high into the air to make their crops grow tall. People once believed that yellow flowers would cure *jaundice*, a yellowish discoloration of the body.

Many taboos come from homeopathic magic. People avoid certain harmless things because they resemble various harmful things. For example, Eskimo parents might warn their sons against playing a string game, such as *cat's cradle*, in which children loop string around their fingers. Playing such games might cause the children's fingers to become tangled in the harpoon lines they will use as adults.

Contagious Magic comes from the belief that after a person has had contact with certain things, they will continue to influence him. The most common examples of contagious magic involve parts of the body that have been removed, such as fingernails, hair, and teeth. A person's nails and hair supposedly can affect the rest of his body long after they have been cut off. A person can injure an enemy by damaging a lock of the victim's hair or a piece of his clothing. He can even cripple the enemy by placing a sharp object in that person's footprint.

People who believe in contagious magic fear that an enemy can gain power over them by obtaining parts of their body. Therefore, they carefully dispose of their nails, hair, teeth, and even their body wastes.

Witches and voodoo magicians often practice a type of homeopathic magic called *envoûtement*. The magician makes a doll or some other likeness of an enemy. He harms the enemy by sticking pins into the doll or injuring it in some other way. In some societies, the doll includes a lock of the enemy's hair or a piece of his clothing. This type of envoûtement is a combination of homeopathic and contagious magic.

Why People Believe in Magic

People turn to magic chiefly as a form of insurance—that is, they use it along with actions that actually bring results. For example, a hunter in a primitive tribe may use a hunting charm. But he also uses his hunting skills and his knowledge of animals. The charm may give him the extra confidence he needs to hunt even more successfully than he would without it. If he shoots a lot of game, he credits the charm for his success. Many events occur naturally without magic. Crops grow without it, and sick people get well without it. But if people use magic to bring a good harvest or to cure a patient, they may believe the magic was responsible.

People also tend to forget magic's failures and to be impressed by its apparent successes. They may consider magic successful if it appears to work only 10 per cent of the time. Even when magic fails, people often explain the failure without doubting the power of the magic. They may say that the magician made a mistake

in reciting the spell or that another magician cast a more powerful spell against him.

Many anthropologists believe that people have faith in magic because they feel a need to believe in it. People may turn to magic to reduce their fear and uncertainty if they feel they have no control over the outcome of a situation. For example, farmers use knowledge and skill when they plant their fields. But they know that weather, insects, or diseases might ruin the crops. So farmers in some societies may also plant a charm or perform a magic rite to ensure a good harvest.

History

Ancient Times. Man's use of magic goes back at least as far as 50,000 B.C. About that time, prehistoric men buried cave bears, probably as a magic rite. Scientists believe that much prehistoric art had magical purposes. Prehistoric hunters, for example, probably used cave paintings of animals in rites intended to help them hunt the animals.

Magic played an important role in the life of the ancient Egyptians, who used amulets, magic figures, and rites. The ancient Greeks and Romans consulted priests called *oracles*, who interpreted advice from the gods (see ORACLE). The Greeks and Romans also tried to tell the future from dreams.

According to one legend, the three wise men who visited the baby Jesus were astrologers who located Him by magic use of the stars (see MAGI). The Bible has many references to magic, sorcery, and witchcraft.

During the Middle Ages, nearly all Europeans believed in magic. Clergymen considered magic sinful, but they believed in its power. The so-called science of *alchemy* included much magic (see ALCHEMY). Alchemists hoped to discover the *philosopher's stone*, a magic substance that could change iron, lead, and other metals into gold. They also tried to find the *elixir of life*, a miraculous substance that could cure disease and lengthen life.

Many men joined a secret brotherhood called the *Rosicrucians*, an early version of the present-day Rosicrucian Order. The Rosicrucians studied magic lore and devoted themselves to curing the sick and helping people in other ways. The Masons, another secret group, also had elements of magic in their rituals.

From the 1500's to the 1700's, belief in magic continued widespread. Even highly educated people believed in its power. The Swiss physician Philippus Paracelsus, for example, experimented with alchemy and believed in the power of talismans. Sir Isaac Newton, the famous English astronomer and mathematician, studied alchemy. Most people believed in witchcraft, and thousands of persons were tried and executed as witches.

Many forms of magic tried to predict the future. People believed a person's character could be described or his future foretold in various ways. These methods included studying the palm of his hand, his facial features, or even the moles on his skin. Some people used *tarot cards*, a set of playing cards with special pictures, for fortunetelling.

After about 1600, advances in science gradually weakened people's belief in magic. But as late as the

Bettmann Archive

Tarot Cards are used in fortunetelling. The designs shown above are based on a set made in the 1300's for King Charles VI of France. The hanged-man card, *left,* frequently indicates spiritual growth. The temperance card, *right,* often stands for harmony.

1700's, the Italian magician Count Allesandro di Cagliostro won fame for his powers. Cagliostro traveled through Europe selling love potions and elixirs of life.

Magic Today still plays an important role in the life of many primitive tribes. Even among modern peoples, magic has many followers with an interest in such subjects as astrology, fortunetelling, and witchcraft. For example, many people who have faith in astrology read their daily horoscope in a newspaper.

Countless people believe in superstitions that involve forms of magic. Some persons carry a fetish, such as a rabbit's foot or a lucky penny. They believe these articles have magic power to bring good luck. Homeopathic magic appears in the superstition that a newborn baby must be carried upstairs before it is carried down.

This act supposedly guarantees that the child will rise in the world and have a successful life.

Magic also survives in much of today's advertising. The manufacturers of such products as gasolines and headache remedies boast of new, secret ingredients. Advertisements may claim that a mouthwash or a toothpaste will magically transform an unpopular person into a popular one. Many people buy these and other products for the magic qualities promised by such advertising. ALAN DUNDES

Related Articles in WORLD BOOK include:

Astrology	Genii	Palmistry
Augur	Hypnotism (History)	Psychical Research
Clairvoyance	Mesmer, Franz	Spiritualists
Divination	Mind Reading	Superstition
Evil Eye	Necromancy	Taboo
Exorcism	Occult	Voodoo
Fortunetelling	Omen	Witchcraft

MAGIC FLUTE. See MOZART, WOLFGANG A.; OPERA (Opera Repertoire).

MAGICIAN is an entertainer who performs tricks that seem impossible. Magicians pluck dollar bills out of the air and change one orange into three. They read people's thoughts and produce bowls of goldfish from a scarf. They make people float in the air—and even make them disappear.

Many people think a magician's hands move so quickly that the audience cannot follow the actions and see how tricks are performed. But the hand is not quicker than the eye. Most magicians avoid rapid hand movements because they know such motions confuse people and weaken the effect of the trick.

Magicians base most of their tricks on a technique called *misdirection.* They use carefully planned actions and words to distract the audience by centering its attention on the wrong place at the right time. Suppose that a magician wants to conceal a left-hand movement from the audience. He distracts the spectators by extending his right hand and following the motion with his eyes. The audience automatically looks in that same direction and thus does not see the left-hand movement of the magician. In addition, the spectators do not know that a magician uses various secret devices.

Gifford/Wallace, Inc.

A Magician suspends his assistant in the air with only a post under her head for support. Such tricks of magic, in which a person seems to float in the air, are called *levitation.*

The "Fantastic Suitcase" was an amazing illusion developed by Robert-Houdin, a famous French magician of the 1800's. Robert-Houdin pulled birds, cages, hats, and pans from a thin suitcase. He ended the trick by lifting out his young son.

Professional magicians perform on television, in theaters, and in night clubs. Many young people find magic a fascinating hobby, and some earn money by doing tricks at birthday parties and other gatherings. Young magicians can gain poise and self-confidence by performing before an audience. They also may develop mental alertness and skill in using their hands.

Kinds of Magic

Magic includes a number of types of tricks. The most common kinds of magic are (1) sleight of hand, (2)

Harry Houdini, an American magician, specialized in escaping from apparently impossible predicaments. In the water torture trick, *above*, Houdini freed himself from a box filled with water.

close-up magic, (3) illusions, (4) escape magic, and (5) mentalist magic.

Sleight of Hand, also called *legerdemain* and *prestidigitation*, requires especially skillful hand movements. The oldest known sleight-of-hand routine, which was performed in ancient Egypt and remains popular today, involves several small balls. The magician makes the balls appear, disappear, or change size while they are hidden under inverted cups or dishes. Gali Gali, a modern Egyptian magician, ended the trick by changing the balls into baby chicks. Paul Rosini, an American magician, turned the cups right side up and then poured out wine.

More varieties of sleight-of-hand tricks can be performed with a deck of cards than with any other objects. Cardini, a British magician, produced fans of cards at his fingertips. Then he made lighted cigarettes appear, followed by cigars and a pipe. Other magicians have used doves, handkerchiefs, clocks and watches, jewels, and lighted electric bulbs in sleight-of-hand feats.

Close-Up Magic is performed at a table with the spectators only a short distance away. In close-up magic, magicians work with a few small objects. For example, every time the American magician Albert Goshman lifted a saltshaker, a silver coin appeared beneath it. Johnny Paul, another American magician, borrowed a piece of paper currency from a spectator and put it at one end of the table. Then he made the money move across the table into his hand. Don Alan of the United States shuffled a deck of cards and placed the deck in a transparent glass. Selected cards then rose mysteriously from the glass.

Illusions. Magicians called *illusionists* perform large-scale tricks with the aid of human assistants, animals, and elaborate equipment. One of the most famous illusions is sawing a woman in half. Horace Goldin, an American magician, placed his assistant in a wooden box with her head, hands, and feet extending out through holes. He then sawed through the box in full view of the audience. After cutting the box in two, Goldin opened it and the assistant stepped out of the box unharmed.

The first great modern illusionist was Robert-Houdin, a French magician who performed in the mid-1800's. Robert-Houdin became known as the father of modern magic because he contributed so many new tricks. For example, he suspended his young son in the air horizontally, with the boy's arm resting on the top of an upright pole. Later, Adelaide Herrmann, a British illusionist, also performed this trick.

The three best-known American illusionists of the 1900's were probably Harry Blackstone, Harry Kellar, and Howard Thurston. Blackstone made a camel disappear. Kellar featured an illusion in which he made a cage containing a live canary disappear in full view of the audience. Thurston fired a pistol, and an automobile on the stage immediately vanished.

Escape Magic. Some magicians specialize in making apparently impossible escapes from various predicaments. The most famous escape performer was Harry Houdini, an American, who freed himself from police handcuffs, leg irons, and locked jail cells. He also let

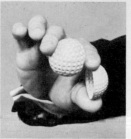

One Ball Changes into Two in this sleight-of-hand trick. The magician uses a rubber ball and a metal shell that fits over it, as shown in the first photo above. The spectators believe they see one actual ball. The next two photos show the magician secretly separating the shell from the ball. The magician then displays the shell and the ball as if they were really two balls.

himself be handcuffed and placed in a crate that was nailed shut and lowered into a river. Houdini escaped in a few seconds. See HOUDINI, HARRY.

Mentalist Magic. Some magicians, called *mentalists*, perform mind-reading tricks and predict future events. Mentalists call out the names of strangers in an audience and duplicate designs sealed in envelopes by spectators. They also write the correct total of numbers selected later by volunteers. During a television broadcast, Dunninger, a famous American mentalist, seemingly read the mind of a stranger in a submerged submarine.

Becoming a Magician

People enjoy magic because of its mystery. If they know how a trick is done, it loses its appeal—and so magicians seldom reveal the secrets of their tricks. But basic methods can be learned from books on magic. Some of these books can be obtained from general bookstores or public libraries. Others are sold by stores that specialize in equipment for magicians. One introduction to magic is *The Amateur Magician's Handbook* (3rd rev. ed., 1972) by Henry Hay.

Two organizations—the Society of American Magicians (S.A.M.) and the International Brotherhood of Magicians (I.B.M.)—have clubs in many cities of the United States and Canada. The S.A.M. has headquarters at 66 Marked Tree Road, Needham, Mass. 02192. The headquarters of the I.B.M. are at 114 N. Detroit Street, Kenton, Ohio 43326. Each group publishes a monthly magazine and holds an annual convention. At the convention, magicians give lectures and demonstrate new tricks, and dealers in magicians' supplies display new equipment.   MILBOURNE CHRISTOPHER

MAGINOT LINE, *MAZH uh noh,* is a fortified line of defense along the eastern border of France. It was constructed after World War I. Forts stand above ground, flanked by pillboxes and barbed-wire entanglements. Underground chambers provide space for communications systems, hospitals, storerooms, garages, and living quarters for the officers and men, as shown in the picture *below.* In June, 1940, the Germans invaded France through Belgium, passing north of the Maginot Line. In three weeks, they swept past and then behind the line, and captured it from the rear. The line was overhauled in the 1950's for possible use in case of atomic war. See also SIEGFRIED LINE.   THEODORE ROPP

MAGLOIRE, PAUL E. See HAITI (Recent Developments).

MAGMA. See IGNEOUS ROCK; ROCK (Igneous Rock); VOLCANO.

Wide World

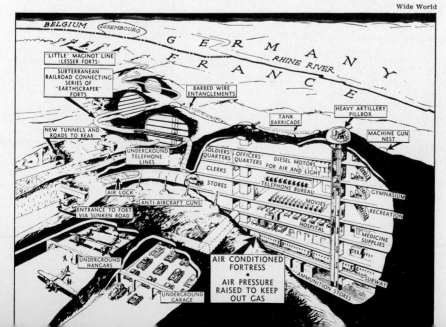

The Maginot Line was designed to protect France from a German attack. It included huge underground fortresses, complete with garages and hangars. This drawing was made shortly before World War II.

Derek Gilby

The Magna Carta Memorial at Runnymede stands in a meadow southwest of London, England. King John approved historic Magna Carta on this site in 1215. The granite shaft inside the circular stone structure bears the inscription, "To Commemorate Magna Carta—Symbol of Freedom Under Law." Members of the American Bar Association contributed the funds to build the monument. The organization dedicated the memorial in 1957.

MAGNA CARTA, *MAG nuh KAHR tuh*, is a document that marked a decisive step forward in the development of constitutional government in England. In later centuries, much of the rest of the world also benefited from it, because many other democratic countries followed English law in creating their own governments. These countries include the United States and Canada.

The Latin words *Magna Carta* mean *Great Charter*. In the charter, King John was forced to grant many rights to the English aristocracy. The ordinary Englishman gained little. English barons forced the king to approve the charter in June, 1215. The historic action took place at Runnymede, a meadow alongside the River Thames southwest of London. A monument now stands there.

It is an error to say that Magna Carta guaranteed individual liberties to all men. In later centuries, it became a model for those who demanded democratic government and individual rights for all. In its own time, however, the greatest value of Magna Carta was that it placed the king under the law, and decisively checked royal power.

Bryce Lyon, the contributor of this article, is Barnaby C. and Mary Critchfield Keeney Professor of History at Brown University and the author of A Constitutional and Legal History of Medieval England.

Reasons for the Charter. Normans from northern France conquered England in A.D. 1066. Able kings then ruled the country for more than a hundred years. They respected feudal law and tried to govern justly. But there was no real control over the kings' power. When John became king in 1199, he abused his power. He demanded more military service from the feudal class than did the kings before him. He sold royal positions to the highest bidders. He increased taxes without obtaining the consent of the barons, which was contrary to feudal custom. John's courts decided cases according to his wishes, not according to the law. Persons who lost cases had to pay crushing penalties.

In 1213, a group of barons and church leaders met at St. Albans, near London. They called for a halt to the king's injustices, and drew up a list of rights they wanted John to grant them. The king twice refused. After the second time, the barons raised an army to force the king to meet their demands. John saw that he could not defeat the army, and so he agreed to the articles on June 15, 1215. Four days later, the articles were *engrossed* (written out in legal form) as a royal charter. Copies of the charter were made for distribution throughout the kingdom.

Promises in the Charter. Magna Carta contained 63 articles, most of which pledged the king to uphold feudal law. These articles chiefly benefited the barons and other members of the feudal class. Some granted the church freedom from royal interference. A few articles guaranteed the rights of the rising middle class in the towns. Ordinary freemen and peasants were hardly mentioned in the charter, even though they made up by far the biggest part of England's population.

Some articles that in 1215 applied only to the feudal class later became important to all the people. For example, the charter stated that the king must seek the advice and consent of the barons in all matters important to the kingdom. It also said that no special taxes could be raised without the consent of the barons. Later, such articles were used to support the argument that no law should be made or tax raised without the consent of England's *Parliament* (the lawmaking body that represents all the people).

Still other articles became foundations for modern justice. One article says that no freeman shall be imprisoned, deprived of property, sent out of the country, or destroyed, except by the lawful judgment of his *peers* (equals) or by the law of the land. The idea of due process of law, including trial by jury, developed from this article. In John's time, however, there was no such thing as trial by jury in criminal cases.

The charter contained several articles designed to make the king keep his promises. A council of barons was formed to make certain that John did so. If John violated the charter and ignored the warnings of the council, it had the right to raise an army and force him to live by the charter's provisions.

The Charter After 1215. Magna Carta did not end the struggle between John and the barons. Neither side intended to abide by the charter completely. War broke out immediately, and John died in the midst of it in 1216. But in the years that followed, other English kings agreed to the terms of the charter. It came to be

Mansell

An Original Copy of Magna Carta,
above, is preserved in the British Library
in London. It is one of several copies of the
charter that were sent to various cathedrals
and castles throughout England in 1215.
Altogether, four copies still survive—two in
the British Library, one in the cathedral at
Salisbury, and one in the Lincoln Cathedral.
No one knows which of the four, if any, was
the "original" document. Like other medieval charters, Magna Carta was written
in Latin on parchment. An enlargement of
a portion of the charter is shown at *right.*
Royal charters were sealed rather than
signed. The Seal of King John, *above,*
authenticated Magna Carta.

recognized as part of the fundamental law of England.

Magna Carta was largely forgotten during the 1500's. But members of Parliament brought it to life again during the 1600's. They used it to rally support in their struggle against the despotic rule of the Stuart kings. Members of Parliament came to view the charter as a constitutional check on royal power. They cited it as a legal support for the argument that there could be no laws or taxation without the consent of Parliament. These members of Parliament used the charter to demand guarantees of trial by jury, safeguards against unfair imprisonment, and other rights.

In the 1700's, Sir William Blackstone, a famous lawyer, set down these ideals as legal rights of the people in his famous *Commentaries on the Laws of England* (see BLACKSTONE, SIR WILLIAM). Also in the 1700's, colonists carried these English ideals on legal and political rights to America. The ideals eventually became part of the framework of the Constitution of the United States.

Four originals of the 1215 charter remain. Two are in the British Library in London, one in Salisbury Cathedral, and one in Lincoln Cathedral. The one in Lincoln Cathedral is considered to be in the best condition. For many years, the document was commonly known as *Magna Charta*. But in 1946, the British government officially adopted the Latin spelling, *Magna Carta*.　　　　　　　　　　　　　　BRYCE LYON

See also FEUDALISM; JOHN (king).

MAGNA CARTA OF LABOR. See LEO (XIII).

MAGNA CUM LAUDE. See DEGREE, COLLEGE (The Bachelor's Degree).

MAGNALIUM. See ALLOY (Alloys for Strength and Lightness).

MAGNEL, man *YEHL*, **GUSTAVE PAUL ROBERT** (1889-1955), a Belgian professor and civil engineer, pioneered in the development of prestressed concrete. Prestressed concrete structures are stronger than structures made of reinforced concrete. He developed principles for the design and analysis of reinforced concrete structures. He was also noted as a consulting engineer on many engineering projects. Magnel wrote *Design and Analysis of Reinforced Concrete, Strength of Materials, Prestressed Concrete,* and *Analysis of the Vierendeel Trusses.* He also wrote more than a hundred technical papers.

He was born in Esschen, Belgium, and was graduated from the University of Ghent. He became a professor there in 1927.　　　　　　　　　ROBERT W. ABBETT

MAGNESIA, mag *NEE shuh*, or MAGNESIUM OXIDE (chemical formula, MgO), is a white, tasteless, earthy substance. It is used as an antacid and a mild cathartic. It is an alkali that does not release carbon dioxide. This property makes it a good antidote against poisoning by acids where an accumulation of gas might rupture the stomach. Manufacturers use magnesia in refining metals from their ores, in making crucibles and insulating material, and in making special cements. Milk of magnesia is a mixture of water and magnesia. Doctors prescribe it as an antacid and a laxative. They also use magnesia medically as a dusting powder. Manufacturers make large quantities of magnesia from magnesium chloride.　　　　　　　　AUSTIN SMITH

MAGNESIUM, mag *NEE shee uhm* (chemical symbol Mg), is the lightest metal that people use to build things. This grayish-white element has a specific gravity of 1.74. This means that it weighs only 1.74 times as much as an equal volume of water. Steel is $4\frac{1}{2}$ times heavier than magnesium. Even aluminum weighs $1\frac{1}{2}$ times as much as magnesium.

Magnesium also ranks as the third most abundant *structural* (building) metal in the earth's crust. Only aluminum and iron are more plentiful. But seawater is a more important source of magnesium than is the earth. The oceans hold 0.13 per cent magnesium chloride, a compound of magnesium.

Plants and the bodies of animals also contain certain amounts of magnesium. The element plays an important role in the life processes. In the human body, for example, magnesium activates large protein molecules called *enzymes*, which speed up vital chemical reactions. Such foods as beans, liver, nuts, and whole grain cereals are rich in magnesium.

Magnesium has an atomic number of 12, and an atomic weight of 24.312. It melts at 648.8° C ($\pm$0.5° C) and boils at 1090° C. See ELEMENT, CHEMICAL (tables).

Uses of Magnesium. Pure magnesium does not have enough strength for general structural uses. However, *alloys* (mixtures) of magnesium and other metals have been developed to meet specific needs (see ALLOY [Alloys for Strength and Lightness]). Magnesium alloys are made by adding small amounts of aluminum, lithium, manganese, silver, thorium, zinc, zirconium, and the rare earths (see RARE EARTH). Manufacturers use magnesium alloys in building airplanes, guided missiles, electronic equipment, trucks, portable tools, furniture, ladders, and other equipment where light weight is important. Magnesium is also used widely in baseball catchers' masks, snowshoes, skis, boats, horseshoes, and in the wheels and bodies of racing cars. Other uses of magnesium alloys include automobile parts, cameras, hospital equipment, and motion-picture and television equipment. Magnesium's *damping capacity* (the ability to absorb vibration) has opened many new uses for the metal.

Magnesium has a great many non-structural uses. For example, magnesium is alloyed with aluminum to produce most of the usable forms of aluminum. Magnesium plays an important part in the chemical reactions used to produce such important metals as titanium, beryllium, uranium, and zirconium. Magnesium is also used to protect pipelines, underground storage tanks, and the hulls of ships from corrosion. In the home, the ability of magnesium to protect other metals keeps rust and corrosion from water heaters and oil tanks. Magnesium also finds a place in home medicine chests in such compounds as milk of magnesia and Epsom salts.

Producing Magnesium. Because magnesium is so plentiful in seawater, it is available to most of the countries of the world. Even nations that do not border on the oceans can produce magnesium because the metal is so common in the earth's crust. It usually occurs in combination with other elements in such mineral rocks as dolomite, magnesite, brucite, and olivine. These rocks are available in many places. The only limit to the production of magnesium is the availability of a low-cost source of power to produce the metal from seawater or rocks.

The United States produces about 75,000 short tons (68,000 metric tons) of magnesium a year. Russia produces about 35,000 short tons (31,800 metric tons) a year. Most U.S. production comes from plants in Texas using the water of the Gulf of Mexico. Two other U.S. plants, one in Alabama and the other in Connecticut, produce magnesium by another process. Other magnesium-producing nations include Canada, France, Great Britain, Italy, Japan, Norway, and Poland.

Manufacturers use two chief processes to produce magnesium. These processes use either electrolytic cells or thermal reduction. The electrolytic process uses seawater, and the thermal-reduction process uses dolomite, magnesite, and other rocks.

Electrolytic Cells produce most of the magnesium in the United States. In this process, seawater is mixed with lime (calcium hydroxide). From this mixture, the magnesium in the seawater *precipitates* (separates) as magnesium hydroxide. This is filtered out of the mixture. Hydrochloric acid is added to the magnesium hydroxide to form magnesium chloride. Workers feed the magnesium chloride into an electrolytic cell, after removing the water. In this cell, an electric current breaks the magnesium chloride into magnesium metal and chlorine gas. See ELECTROLYSIS.

Thermal Reduction produces magnesium by the direct reduction of one of the mineral rock sources of the metal (see REDUCTION). Reducing agents, such as ferrosilicon, are used to break down the rock. The reducing agents cause vapors of magnesium to form at temperatures above the boiling point of the metal. The workers distill these vapors to form solid magnesium crystals (see DISTILLATION). They melt the crystals and pour the molten metal into forms as *ingots* (blocks) of pure magnesium metal.

History of Magnesium. The British chemist Sir Humphry Davy first produced magnesium metal in 1808. In 1833, the British physicist and chemist Michael Faraday produced magnesium by the electrolysis of magnesium chloride. The German scientist Robert Bunsen developed an electrolytic cell for the production of magnesium in 1852. Bunsen's cell was the basis for the cell used by German manufacturers in the late 1800's and early 1900's. By 1909, the Germans were producing magnesium on a commercial scale. American production of magnesium began in 1915 when World War I cut off imports from Germany.

Until the 1930's, manufacturers found few uses for magnesium and few changes were made in production processes. New uses were found during World War I, but these were largely military uses in incendiary bombs, signal flares, and tracer bullets.

Interest in magnesium grew during the 1930's. By the start of World War II in 1939, the need for a lightweight metal for airplane construction and other uses resulted in a number of applications. The Germans pioneered in using magnesium in aircraft parts as well as other military uses.

Since World War II, scientists and engineers have developed new applications of magnesium as a result of a need for a lightweight metal that can be handled easily. Magnesium can now be made in a variety of shapes for specific uses.   JERRY SINGLETON

See also EPSOM SALT; MAGNESIA.

Dow Chemical Co.

Magnesium Hydroxide settles to the bottom of huge tanks containing seawater mixed with lime. The hydroxide is pumped off and used to finish the magnesium extraction process.

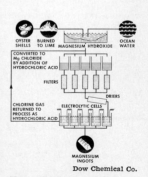

Dow Chemical Co.

Electrolysis of seawater produces magnesium, *above.* The pure metal weighs less than ¼ as much as steel.

Ward's Natural Science Est.

Man First Discovered Magnetism in a loadstone, *above,* which can pick up a few paper clips or other small iron or steel objects. Today a powerful electromagnet, *right,* can lift many large, heavy bars of iron or steel.

Interlake Steel Corp.

MAGNET AND MAGNETISM. Magnetism is a force that acts between certain objects called magnets. We often think of magnets as toys that pick up nails or other bits of iron and steel. But magnetism is an important force in nature. The earth itself acts as if its center contained a large magnet. Surrounding the earth is a *magnetic field* where magnetism can be found. Magnetic fields lie around every magnet. Fields a million times stronger than the earth's field are inside tiny pieces of matter called atoms. A field a million times weaker than the earth's field surrounds our Galaxy.

Every day, we use magnets and magnetism in many ways. Magnets in telephones, television sets, and radios help change electrical impulses into sounds. Compasses made with magnets help navigators guide ships safely. Without magnetism, we could not produce large amounts of electricity. Nor could we use electricity to do all the jobs that it does.

Anyone who has played with a bar magnet knows that it will pick up and hold more objects on its ends than on its middle. The areas at the ends where the magnetism is strongest are called the *poles* of the magnet. Every magnet has at least two poles. If a bar magnet is broken in the middle, new poles will appear at the broken ends.

If we hold a bar magnet by a string tied around its center, one end will point toward the north. The other end will point toward the south. If we turn the magnet

Henry H. Kolm, the contributor of this article, is one of the founders of the Francis Bitter National Magnet Laboratory at the Massachusetts Institute of Technology.

around, it will swing back to the north. The poles are named by the direction they point. The north and south poles of the magnet point as they do because the earth's magnetic poles attract them. The magnetic poles of the earth are near the North and South geographic poles.

The poles on opposite ends of a magnet act differently toward each other. We can see how the poles of a magnet act by experimenting with two bar magnets on a table. If the north pole of one magnet comes close to the north pole of another magnet, the two poles *repel* (push away from) each other. Two south poles also repel each other. But a north and a south pole attract each other and stick together. Two like magnetic poles always repel each other, and two unlike poles always attract each other.

Making and Using Magnets

How Magnets Are Made. The best-known magnets are pieces of metal that attract some other kinds of metal. These magnets keep their magnetism permanently and are called *permanent magnets*. Most permanent magnets are made of steel or mixtures of iron, nickel, cobalt, and other substances. These materials are called *magnetically hard* because they can be magnetized only in strong fields.

A permanent magnet can be made from hard magnetic substances in several ways. Moving another permanent magnet in one direction across the steel or other material will magnetize it. An electric current flowing through a coil of wire will also magnetize the steel.

Hammering or tapping a substance while it is in a magnetic field will help magnetize it. In fact, magnetic substances can be magnetized slightly by hammering them in the weak magnetic field of the earth.

When a permanent magnet picks up an object, such as an iron nail, the nail becomes a *temporary magnet*. The nail can pick up other bits of metal and will be attracted or repelled by the poles of another magnet. But the nail will keep its magnetism only so long as it is near a permanent magnet. If the permanent magnet is taken away, the nail no longer acts like a magnet. Materials such as the iron in the nail are called *magnetically soft* because they can be magnetized in weak fields.

Some magnets are made from certain metals after the metals have combined with the element oxygen. These magnets, known as *ceramic magnets* or *ferrites*, can be either hard or soft.

Many common magnetic materials are mixtures of hard and soft substances. They can be magnetized easily, and they keep some permanent magnetization.

A coil of wire acts just like a permanent magnet when an electric current flows through it. One end of the coil becomes the north pole and the other end becomes the south pole of the *electromagnet*. But if the flow of current changes direction, the poles will also switch places. An electromagnet will remain magnetized only so long as electricity flows through it.

Sometimes, a magnetically soft material, such as iron, is put in the center of the coil. The iron makes the field of the electromagnet stronger.

How Magnets of Different Shapes Are Used. Magnets are made in many shapes and have their poles in different places. Each of these magnets has special uses. For example, permanent bar magnets are used in magnetic compasses. The compass needle is a bar magnet that points toward the earth's north magnetic pole. Some doors have bar magnets fastened near them to hold them shut.

A permanent bar magnet can be bent into a horseshoe, bringing the poles closer together and making a stronger magnetic field between them. Horseshoe magnets are used when a strong magnetic field is needed in a small space. The electronic tubes in radar sets need powerful horseshoe magnets to work properly. Horseshoe magnets also are used in some small electric motors.

Circular magnets look like small doughnuts. They do not have poles. Instead, the magnetism moves around the inside of the magnet in one direction or the other. Many electronic computers use large quantities of circular magnets to store numbers or other information. These magnets, sometimes called *cores*, are made of hard magnetic materials. They are connected to the computer by wires that run through their centers.

Magnets shaped like disks have one pole around the edge and the other pole in the center. They are used in radio and television loudspeakers.

Magnets shaped into long, round cylinders look like round bar magnets. Cylindrical magnets have some special uses, such as holding magnetic substances in place on a machine.

Electromagnets are used if magnetism is not needed all the time. For example, an electromagnet on the hook of a crane will pick up scrap iron to be loaded on a railroad car when electricity flows through the magnet. When the iron is hanging over the car, the electricity is turned off and the iron falls into the car.

Electromagnets have many uses in the home, indus-

MAGNETS OF DIFFERENT SHAPES

Bar Magnets placed near doors are used as magnetic latches to keep the doors closed.

WORLD BOOK photo

Horseshoe Magnets create magnetic fields for small motors like those used in slot cars.

WORLD BOOK photo

Circular Magnets in electronic computers "remember" numbers and instructions.

WORLD BOOK photo

Disk Magnets in radio speakers help create sounds from electric impulses.

Zenith Radio Corp.
WORLD BOOK photo

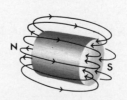

Cylindrical Magnets in some machines hold in place the object being worked on.

MAGNET AND MAGNETISM

try, and scientific research. They not only can be turned on and off, but they also make stronger magnetic fields than permanent magnets can. Electric door bells and electric motors used in home appliances contain electromagnets. Larger electric motors used in industry also have electromagnets. Magnetic vibrators use electromagnets to make vibrations so rapid that they cannot be heard. Such vibrators can wash dirt out of watches and other delicate mechanisms, and cut hard substances such as silicon and germanium. They can even drive pipes into the ground. Scientists have built especially powerful electromagnets to help them study the effects of strong fields on various substances.

How Magnets Work

What Causes Magnetism? Although the most common magnets are made from magnetic materials, magnetism can be produced without any magnetic substances at all. A coil of wire can make a magnetic field exactly like the field around a permanent magnet. But the coil will be a magnet only so long as electric current flows through it. This fact gave scientists the first clue to the discovery that magnetism is caused by moving electric charges. They found that a bar magnet contains moving electric current just as a coil electromagnet does. But the current is a permanent part of the bar magnet.

To understand how electricity can be present in a bar magnet, we must know about the tiny particles, called *atoms*, that make up all things. Every atom has a central core called a *nucleus*. Moving around the nucleus, like planets around the sun, are even smaller particles called *electrons*. The electrons carry an electric charge, and their motion makes an electric current. As happens with a coil of wire, electric current produces a magnetic field. In most atoms, the electrons spin in

A WORLD BOOK SCIENCE PROJECT
EXPERIMENTING WITH MAGNETISM

The purpose of this project is to demonstrate magnetic fields from permanent magnets and the magnetic effects of an electric current. The materials needed for the project are shown below. They can be purchased at most hardware or hobby stores.

MATERIALS NEEDED

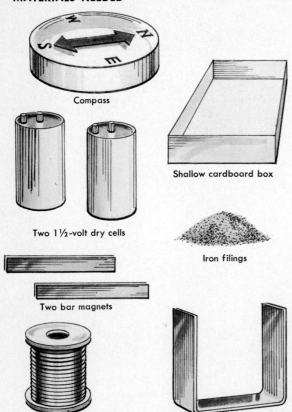

Compass

Shallow cardboard box

Two 1½-volt dry cells

Iron filings

Two bar magnets

10 feet of insulated wire

Bent steel bar, 1/16-inch thick

MAPPING MAGNETIC FIELDS

To Map the Field of a Bar Magnet, place the magnet under a sheet of white paper. Sprinkle iron filings on the paper, and tap the paper gently. The filings will line up as shown.

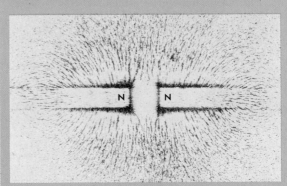

The Field Between Two Magnetic Poles curves outward from the gap between the poles if they are alike, *above.* If opposite poles are used, the field extends across the gap from one pole to the other, *below.*

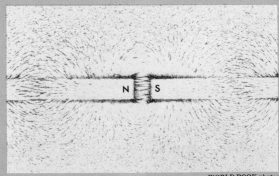

WORLD BOOK photos

Other Experiments include mapping the field when one of the magnets is turned to a different position, or when several magnets are placed under the paper. You can also study the effect of placing a steel coat hanger, coins, or other metal objects in contact with one or more magnets.

different directions and their magnetic fields cancel each other. But in atoms of magnetic elements, such as iron and nickel, the fields do not cancel each other. These magnetic atoms are sometimes called atomic *dipoles*. Materials which contain many atomic dipoles can be magnetized. These materials are called *ferromagnetic* because atomic magnets were first discovered in iron, and *ferrum* is the Latin word for iron.

To understand how ferromagnetic materials become magnetized, we can look at what happens to a piece of steel that moves into a magnetic field. The steel contains small bunches of atomic dipoles, called *magnetic domains*, that are already magnetized. But the magnetic domains cancel each other because they point in different directions and the steel is not a magnet. As the magnetic field around the steel becomes stronger, the domains in line with the magnetic field grow larger.

As the domains in line with the field grow larger, the steel becomes magnetized more strongly until it is completely magnetized. If the direction of the magnetic field is reversed, the domains will turn around and line up in the opposite direction. The north and south poles of the magnet will also turn around.

The steel becomes demagnetized if the domains move out of line. The domains will shift, for example, if the steel is heated or hit. If the magnet is not in a magnetic field, the domains may shift out of line. This explains why heating or hitting a substance can help magnetize or demagnetize it.

Ferromagnetic materials are magnetically hard or soft, depending on how their atomic dipoles behave. The dipoles in hard materials behave as though they were sticky. It takes a strong magnetic field to line them up, but they will remain lined up when the field is gone. The dipoles in soft materials act slippery and even a weak field will line them up temporarily.

MAGNETISM AND ELECTRICITY

To See the Magnetic Effects of Electricity, wrap about 10 turns of wire around a small box, *below*. Then strip the insulation from the ends of the wire.

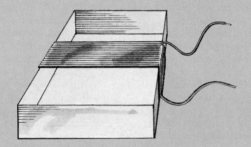

To Observe the Magnetism, place a compass inside the box, *below*, and turn the box so that the compass needle lines up with the wire. Connect the wire to the terminals of a dry cell, and see how the compass needle moves.

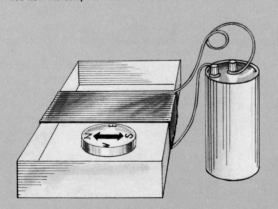

To Experiment Further, try switching the wires from one terminal to the other to see how the compass needle changes direction. By switching the wires at the proper rate, you may be able to make the needle spin completely around. You can also try changing the number of turns of wire to see the effect this has on the compass.

EXPERIMENTING WITH AN ELECTROMAGNET

To Make an Electromagnet, wind two layers of wire around a flat iron bar that is bent into the shape shown below. Strip the insulation from the ends of the wire.

To Use the Electromagnet, connect the wire to two dry cells, *below*. When you hold the compass between the poles of the electromagnet, the needle will point to the poles. The electromagnet will pick up iron objects when the current is on.

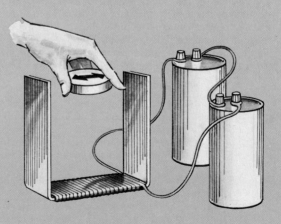

Electromagnet Experiments. Try mapping the field of your magnet. You can also change the number of turns of wire and the number of dry cells to increase the lifting power of the magnet. The more turns of wire you add, or the more dry cells you connect, the stronger your magnet will be.

MAGNET AND MAGNETISM

Most materials cannot be picked up by an ordinary magnet and are not ferromagnetic. Their action in even a strong magnetic field cannot be discovered except with sensitive instruments. Some elements, such as sodium and oxygen, have magnetic atoms that do not form magnetic domains. Scientists call these elements *paramagnetic* substances. They are only slightly attracted to strong magnets. Other materials, such as glass and water, move away from a magnetic field. These materials are called *diamagnetic* substances.

The Nature of Magnetic Fields. We can examine the magnetic field surrounding a magnet by using another magnet, such as a compass needle. As we move the compass around the magnet, the needle will stay in line with the direction of the field. The field can be thought of as a bunch of imaginary lines pointing in the direction shown by the compass. These imaginary lines, called *flux lines*, curve from the north pole to the south pole of the magnet. We can think of flux lines as closed loops, with part of the loop inside the magnet, and part forming the field outside.

The magnetic field is strongest at the poles, where the flux lines are close together. There are fewer lines farther away from the poles, showing that the field becomes weaker in those areas. If we measured the strength of the field, we would find that it is one-fourth as strong 2 centimeters away from a pole as it is 1 centimeter away from the pole.

In addition to applying force on magnetic poles, a magnetic field also applies force on electric charges. But to apply the force, either the field or the charge must be moving. Magnetic fields change the direction of moving charges. Such charges may be beams of electrons in television picture tubes. Moving magnetic fields, for example, cause electricity to flow in transformers. See ELECTROMAGNETISM.

Measuring Magnetic Fields. The strength of a magnetic field is usually measured in units of *gauss*. The earth's magnetic field at the surface is about $\frac{1}{2}$ gauss. The field near the poles of a toy horseshoe magnet is likely to be several hundred gauss. The most powerful permanent magnet can produce a field of about 1,000 gauss. An electromagnet using a soft iron center can make a maximum field of about 30,000 gauss. Fields above 250,000 gauss have been made with electromagnets that are *pulsed* (turned on for only an instant).

The Study of Magnetism

Early Discoveries. Human beings have known about magnets at least since the beginning of written history. But they did not learn much about how magnets work or how to use them until several hundred years ago. The first known magnets were hard black stones called *loadstones*. No one knows when or by whom these stones were discovered, but the ancient Greeks knew of the loadstone's power to attract iron.

Throughout the Middle Ages, many people believed that loadstones had medical powers. During this period, it was discovered that a loadstone would point to the north. In 1269, Petrus Peregrinus de Maricourt of France traced the lines of force on a loadstone and discovered its two poles. In 1600, William Gilbert, an English physician, discovered the earth's magnetism

and also explained the action of a loadstone compass.

Real progress in understanding magnetism came after the relationship between electricity and magnetism was discovered. Hans Christian Oersted of Denmark found in 1820 that electric current moves a compass needle. He established the connection between electricity and magnetism. Michael Faraday, a British scientist, then found that moving a magnet near a wire produces an electric current. Another British scientist, James Clerk Maxwell, expressed the relationship between electricity and magnetism in a mathematical theory.

The magnetic properties of materials were first explained by the French scientist André Ampère. He realized that many tiny electric currents within a permanent magnetic substance have exactly the same effect as one large flow of current around an electromagnet. The first actual electromagnet was built in 1825 by William Sturgeon, an English electrician.

Current Research. Magnetism is a valuable research tool because it can penetrate matter and interact with the nuclei and electrons that make up atoms. Scientists generate strong magnetic fields to make electrons in *semiconductors* (partial conductors of electricity) produce infrared rays. Nuclear physicists use magnetic fields to change the direction of high energy particles.

Magnetism itself is the object of much current research, and its mysteries are far from solved. For example, scientists do not know what produces the enormous electric currents deep within the earth that appear to be responsible for the earth's magnetic field. The deepest mystery of all is the question of why no one has ever found a single magnetic pole. Some of the world's leading physicists have searched for such a *monopole*. In 1975, a team of American physicists claimed that they had discovered a monopole among high-energy particles from space called *cosmic rays*. But this claim has not been accepted by most scientists.   HENRY H. KOLM

Related Articles in WORLD BOOK include:

Compass	Electricity	Hall Effect
Cosmic	(Electricity and	Loadstone
Rays	Magnetism)	Magnetic Equator
Electric	Electromagnet	Magnetohydro-
Generator	Electromagnetism	dynamics
Electric Motor	Gauss	Permalloy

MAGNETIC AMPLIFIER, also called a *saturable reactor*, is a device used to control large amounts of electric power. It is used where currents are too large, or other conditions are too severe, for transistor or vacuum tube amplifiers. For example, magnetic amplifiers are often used to control the speed of large motors or the brightness of airport runway lights.

A magnetic amplifier consists of two coils of wire—a *main coil* and a *control coil*—wound around an iron core. An alternating current flows through the main coil and creates a changing magnetic field around the core. This changing field limits the amount of current that can flow. But if another current is passed through the control coil, the core becomes *saturated* (completely magnetized). The saturation cancels the limiting effect of the changing field, and enables much more current to flow through the main coil.   HENRY H. KOLM

MAGNETIC COMPASS. See COMPASS.

MAGNETIC DECLINATION. See COMPASS.

MAGNETIC EQUATOR is an imaginary line that circles the earth close to the geographic equator. Scientists believe that the earth is like a huge magnet with magnetic North and South poles. The magnetic equator marks the place on the earth's surface where the magnetic attraction of the North and South magnetic poles is equal. The magnetic poles lie close to the geographic North and South poles. The north magnetic pole is near Bathurst Island, in northern Canada. The south magnetic pole is in Wilkes Land, in the Antarctic. Scientists often call the magnetic equator the *aclinic line*. At all points along the line, a magnetic needle will remain horizontal with no dip to either side.

See also DIPPING NEEDLE.

MAGNETIC FIELD. See MAGNET AND MAGNETISM.

MAGNETIC POLE. See EARTH (The Earth's Magnetism); NORTH POLE; SOUTH POLE.

MAGNETIC STORM is a strong fluctuation in the earth's magnetic field. Such a storm is caused by high-energy particles and intense radiation given off by the sun as a result of solar activity. The overall level of magnetic storm activity varies with the recurring 11-year *solar activity cycle* (see SUN [The Sun's Stormy Activity]). It also varies with the 27-day period of the sun's rotation.

Many magnetic storms are associated with *coronal holes*, which are regions of low density in the sun's corona. A continuous flow of charged particles from the sun called the *solar wind* emerges chiefly from the coronal holes. High-speed streams of the solar wind appear as the sun's activity increases. When the rapidly moving particles of these streams strike the earth's magnetic field, some of the particles are trapped by the field. The interaction of these particles with the earth's magnetic field produces a magnetic storm.

The solar wind is separated into large regions of either positive or negative magnetic polarity. A magnetic storm occurs when a boundary between such regions of opposite polarity is swept past the earth by the sun's rotation. The passage of these boundaries is the solar phenomenon most closely linked to magnetic storms.

Scientists believe many *solar flares*, which are eruptions on the sun's surface, also cause magnetic storms. Such storms start abruptly, unlike those associated with the solar wind, which begin gradually. Solar flares emit high-energy electrons and protons as well as radiation in the form of gamma rays and X rays. The electrons and protons are trapped by the earth's magnetic field. The gamma rays and X rays affect the field by causing changes in the ionosphere and in the *Van Allen belts*, which are doughnut-shaped regions of charged particles that surround the earth.

Magnetic storms demonstrate how solar activity directly affects the earth. They cause disturbances in the ionosphere, which interfere with short-wave radio reception. Scientists detect magnetic storms by means of such interference. In addition, abrupt changes in the earth's magnetic field resulting from magnetic storms can cause surges in power transmission lines. Magnetic storms are also accompanied by auroras.

The increased magnetic field of the sun not only causes magnetic storms but also shields the earth from high-energy cosmic rays produced by exploding stars called *supernovae*. The resulting decrease in these cosmic rays bombarding the earth is known as the *Forbush effect*.   JAY M. PASACHOFF

See also AURORA BOREALIS; SOLAR WIND; SUNSPOTS.

MAGNETIC TAPE. See TAPE RECORDER; COMPUTER (Input Equipment).

MAGNETITE. See IRON AND STEEL (Kinds of Iron Ore); LOADSTONE; MINERAL (color picture).

MAGNETO, *mag NEE toh*, is a device that generates electric current. It operates on the principle that an electric current is generated in a conductor moving through a magnetic field. One essential part of the machine is a powerful horseshoe magnet. Another is a coil of fine wire which revolves between the two poles in front of the magnet. An alternating current is set up in the coil as it moves through the magnetic field.

A reciprocating gasoline engine used in an airplane has two magnetos which supply electric current to the spark plugs. The current ignites the mixture of fuel and air in the cylinders.   H. S. STILLWELL

See also ELECTRIC GENERATOR; ELECTROMAGNETISM; IGNITION.

MAGNETOHYDRODYNAMICS, *mag NEE toh HY droh dy NAM iks*, is the study of electric and magnetic effects in fluids that conduct electricity. These fluids include liquid metals and *ionized* (electrically charged) gases. Magnetohydrodynamics is abbreviated *MHD*.

One branch of magnetohydrodynamics is the study of electric and magnetic effects around the earth and on the sun. These effects include sunspots, magnetic storms in the earth's magnetic field, and *auroras* (northern and southern lights) in the upper atmosphere. Scientific theories about these effects are based on a physical law that describes the motion of an electrically charged particle in a magnetic field. This law says that the particle's path is governed by the strength of the field and by the particle's speed, direction, and charge.

A second branch of magnetohydrodynamics is the study of a method for generating electricity. This branch is based on a physical law that describes the voltage generated along an electrical conductor as it moves through a magnetic field. The law says that the voltage depends on the strength of the magnetic field and on the length, speed, and direction of motion of the conductor through the field. In magnetohydrodynamics, this law is used in designing generators that produce electricity from a high-speed stream of ionized gas called a *plasma*. The plasma is shot through a strong magnetic field where it produces a voltage between two electrodes. In theory, this kind of generator is more efficient than an ordinary electric generator. But many technical difficulties must be overcome before MHD generators can be widely used.   WILLIAM W. SEIFERT

See also AURORA BOREALIS; MAGNETIC STORM; PLASMA (in physics); SUNSPOT.

MAGNETOMETER, *MAG nuh TAHM uh tuhr*, is a device that measures the strength of a magnetic field. The simplest magnetometers measure the magnetic field near an electric motor or the poles of a magnet. These magnetometers have a tiny coil of wire. When the coil is moved through a magnetic field, an electric voltage is produced in the coil. This voltage indicates the strength of the field.

Other magnetometers can measure weaker magnetic fields. Airplanes tow such magnetometers through the air to measure the slight irregularities in the earth's magnetic field. These measurements help prospectors locate deposits of iron ore, petroleum, and other natural resources. Similar magnetic measurements of the ocean floor have led to important scientific discoveries about changes on the earth's surface.　　　HENRY H. KOLM

See also PETROLEUM (Geophysical Studies); CONTINENTAL DRIFT (Causes of Continental Drift).

MAGNETOSPHERE. See EARTH (The Earth's Magnetism).

MAGNETRON. See RADAR (Advances During World War II).

MAGNIFYING GLASS is a lens which makes close objects appear larger. Both sides of the lens are usually curved to form a double convex lens. The magnifying glass can give two kinds of images. A glass held close to a page in a book forms a *virtual image*. The light rays which produce this image *diverge* (spread out) as they pass through the lens and appear to originate on the same side of the lens as the page. The virtual image appears upright and larger than the object.

A *real image* is formed when light rays from an object pass through the lens and are focused on the other side. The real image appears inverted, or upside down. Its size depends on the distance of the object from the lens. The distance from the center of the lens to the point where parallel light rays are focused is called the *focal length*. If the object is more than twice the focal length away from the lens, the image will be smaller. If the object is less than twice the focal length away, the image will be larger.

The magnifying power of a lens depends on its focal length. The greater the curve of a lens, the shorter its focal length. It bends the rays more, and they meet at a smaller distance from the lens. The focal length of most magnifying glasses is about 10 inches (25 centimeters).

A magnifying glass held between a piece of paper and the sun can be used to start a fire. Heat from the many rays focusing at a common point (focus) on the paper will make the paper burn.　　　S. W. HARDING

See also LENS; MICROSCOPE.

MAGNITOGORSK, *mag NEE toh gawrsk* (pop. 369,-000), is the principal steel center of Russia. The city also makes mining machinery. It lies in the Ural Mountains, about 800 miles (1,300 kilometers) east of Moscow. For location, see RUSSIA (political map). The city received its name from its rich deposits of magnetite, a type of iron ore. When the city was founded in 1931, coal had to be transported from the Kuznetsk Basin in Siberia. Coal was later discovered in Karaganda, closer to Magnitogorsk.　　　THEODORE SHABAD

MAGNITUDE is the scale used by astronomers to measure the brightness of luminous objects in space. The brighter a star or planet, the lower its magnitude number. The magnitude system is based on the work of the ancient Greek astronomer Hipparchus. About 150 B.C., Hipparchus classified the stars according to brightness. He called the brightest stars first magnitude; the next brightest, second magnitude; and so on down to the faintest stars. He called such stars sixth magnitude.

Later astronomers found that first magnitude stars were about 100 times as bright as sixth magnitude stars. They adopted a system that made a star of any magnitude about $2\frac{1}{2}$ times as bright as a star of the next

brightest magnitude. This scale has been extended to zero and negative magnitudes because some stars and planets are brighter than first magnitude ones. For example, the sun has a magnitude of −27.

The word *magnitude* generally refers to *apparent magnitude*, or the brightness of a star as seen from the earth. To compare actual brightness, astronomers use *absolute magnitude*, which shows how bright stars would appear if they all were the same distance—32.6 light years—from the earth. At that distance, the sun would be a fifth magnitude star.　　　ERIC D. CARLSON

See also SIRIUS; STAR (Measuring Brightness).

MAGNOLIA, *mag NOII lih uh,* is the name of a group of trees and shrubs that grow in North America and Asia. Eight of the 35 kinds grow wild in the eastern United States. Magnolias have large, snowy-white or colored flowers, conelike fruits, and large leaves.

Southern magnolia is popular because of its large whitish flowers. This evergreen is native from North Carolina to Texas. It is the state tree and flower of Mississippi and the state flower of Louisiana. *Sweet bay*, also called *swamp magnolia*, has smaller flowers. Its leaves are green on top and whitish underneath.

The leaves of the *umbrella tree* and the *big-leaf magnolia* tend to stretch out from the ends of the branches like the ribs of an open umbrella. Big-leaf magnolia has the largest flowers of any native tree in the United States. They measure about 10 inches (25 centimeters) across the six creamy-white petals. It also has the biggest undivided leaves, with blades 15 to 30 inches (38 to 76 centimeters) long and up to 10 inches (25 centimeters) wide.

Magnolia lumber is used mainly for furniture. The *cucumber tree*, which gets its name from the shape of its fruits, has wood similar to that of the tulip tree.

Scientific Classification. Magnolias belong to the magnolia family, *Magnoliaceae*. The southern magnolia is genus *Magnolia*, species *M. grandiflora*. The sweet bay magnolia is *M. virginiana;* the umbrella tree is *M. tripetala;* the big-leaf is *M. macrophylla;* and the cucumber tree is *M. acuminata*.　　　ELBERT L. LITTLE, JR.

See also BAY TREE; TULIP TREE.

Gottfried Hampfler, *The Flower Grower*
Sweet-Smelling Magnolia Blossoms often grace gardens in the southern United States. This beautiful blossom extends its large, snowy petals over rich, dark-green leaves.

Schünemann, Bavaria

The Magpie is a noisy, aggressive cousin of the crow, and has the crow's thievish habits. It can imitate various bird calls.

MAGNOLIA STATE. See MISSISSIPPI.

MAGOG. See GOG AND MAGOG.

MAGPIE is a bird that belongs to the same family as the crows and the jays. The black-billed magpie lives in western North America from Mexico to Alaska. The yellow-billed magpie lives only in California. Other kinds of magpies live in Europe and Asia.

The black-billed magpie is black, with white feathers on the underparts and wing tops. Its long tail narrows at the tip. Its bill is heavy and black.

Magpies eat almost all kinds of food, including the eggs and young of other birds. Their bulky nests are domed over and have an opening in the side. A magpie usually places its nest in thorny bushes for added protection. The female lays 5 to 10 grayish-white eggs spotted with brown and tan. The maximum life span of the magpie is about 12 years.

These birds usually travel in groups, and are noisy and quarrelsome. Magpies delight in imitating the calls of other birds. People can tame these birds and teach them to speak simple syllables. Superstitious people consider it a bad omen if a magpie comes to live near the home.

Scientific Classification. Magpies are in the crow family, *Corvidae*. The black-billed magpie is genus *Pica*, species *P. pica*. The yellow-billed is *P. nuttalli*.   GEORGE J. WALLACE

MAGRITTE, *mah GREET*, **RENÉ** (1898-1967), was a Belgian surrealist painter. Magritte painted in a precise, realistic style. But his pictures portray a strange dream world of solid objects floating in the air, birds and human beings made of stone, or small objects enlarged to fill an entire room. Many of Magritte's paintings include mysterious men in bowler hats. His work *Golconda* shows a pattern of these men suspended in air.

Magritte was born in Lessines, near Ath, and studied art in Brussels. His early works show the influence of cubism. Magritte's surrealist period began in 1922 after he saw a reproduction of a painting by the modern Italian artist Giorgio de Chirico (see CHIRICO, GIORGIO DE).

See also SURREALISM.   WILLARD E. MISFELDT

MAGSAYSAY, *mahg sy sy*, **RAMÓN R.** (1907-1957), became the third president of the Philippines on Dec. 30, 1953. He served as president until his death in a plane crash. During World War II, he commanded guerrillas in their fight against the Japanese in western Luzon. He helped prepare the way for the U.S. invasion of the Philippines in 1944.

He became secretary of national defense in 1951, and reformed the army. He ended the revolt by Hukbalahaps (Communist guerrillas) with a combination of armed attacks and land awards to the Huks (see PHILIPPINES [The 1950's]). His success led to his election as president. Magsaysay was born in Zambales province, the son of a farmer.   GEORGE E. TAYLOR

MAGUARI. See STORK.

MAGUEY, *MAG way*, is the name given to several kinds of agave plants which grow in Mexico. The name is usually used for the *pulque agave*. Mexicans often drink the juice of this plant. They use it to make *pulque* (a fermented drink) and *tequila* (a distilled liquor).

H. Armstrong Roberts

The Maguey, or Pulque Agave, grows in dry places in southern Mexico. People make beverages from the juice of its leaves.

57

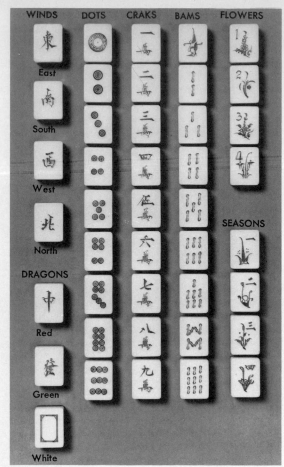

WINDS	DOTS	CRAKS	BAMS	FLOWERS

East

South

West

North

DRAGONS

SEASONS

Red

Green

White

WORLD BOOK photo

A Mah Jongg Set has four tiles of each wind, dragon, dot, crak, ai.d bam. Some sets include flower and season tiles.

The plant's leaves are green with gray spines, and may grow 9 feet (3 meters) long and 1 foot (30 centimeters) wide. The greenish flowers grow on stalks 20 feet (6 meters) high. People often eat parts of the stems and flowers. See also CENTURY PLANT.

Scientific Classification. The maguey is in the agave family, *Agavaceae.* The pulque agave is genus *Agave,* species *A. atrovirens.* HAROLD NORMAN MOLDENKE

MAGYARS, *MAG yahrz,* are a group of about 15 million persons who are usually called Hungarians. They are traditionally considered to be descendants of the early Magyars, a people who founded Hungary in the late 800's. More than 10 million Magyars live in Hungary today, and they make up about 95 per cent of the nation's population. About 3½ million Magyars inhabit neighboring countries, and about 1½ million live in the United States and other Western nations. The Magyar language belongs to the Finno-Ugric group of languages, which also includes Estonian and Finnish.

From about 3000 B.C. to A.D. 500, the early Magyars lived between the Volga River and the Ural Mountains in what is now an area of Russia. By the late 800's, they had moved southwest to settle in what became Hungary. From then until the mid-900's, the Magyars raided many neighboring peoples. During the 1000's, the Magyars

adopted Christianity and founded a powerful kingdom.

In 1526, the Magyars were conquered by the Ottoman Turks. The Austrian Hapsburgs took control of Hungary in the late 1600's. Many Magyars became inhabitants of neighboring countries under the Treaty of Trianon, part of the peace settlement following World War I (1914-1918). STEVEN BELA VARDY

See also HUNGARY (People; History); CZECHOSLOVAKIA (History).

MAH JONGG, *MAH ZHONG,* also spelled *mah-jongg* or *mah-jong,* is a game that has been played in China since about 500 B.C. It is now played in many parts of the world.

Mah jongg is similar to many card games. But small, rectangular tiles engraved with Chinese drawings and symbols are used instead of playing cards. The "deck" consists of 136 standard tiles and several additional tiles. In the Orient, players use eight additional tiles. In the United States, the number of additional tiles varies from year to year, as determined by the National Mah Jongg League in New York City.

Four persons usually play mah jongg, but two, three, five, or six can also play. Players try to form winning combinations of tiles by drawing from a pile of tiles, exchanging tiles with other players, and by discarding tiles. A rulebook lists point values for the winning combinations. Usually, each player begins the game with chips equaling 5,000 points. Losers give chips to the winner equal to the value of the winning hand. Play may continue for a set number of rounds or until one player wins a certain number of points. LILLIAN FRANKEL

MAHABHARATA, *muh HAH BAH ruh tuh,* is one of the outstanding sacred writings of Hinduism and one of the two great epic poems of India. The other is the *Ramayana.*

According to Hindu tradition, the wise man Vyasa dictated the *Mahabharata* to Ganesh, the god of wisdom. Actually, the *Mahabharata* is a collection of writings by several authors who lived at various times. Parts of it may be more than 2,500 years old. The *Mahabharata* was written in Sanskrit, a language of ancient India.

The word *Mahabharata* means *Great King Bharata.* The epic tells the story of the descendants of King Bharata, two families who lived in northern India, perhaps about 1200 B.C. The Pandava brothers lose their kingdom to their Kaurava cousins and engage in a mighty struggle to win it back. Many lives are lost in the conflict. The story illustrates the futility of war. Some of the heroes are taken from history, and some represent human ideals and gods.

The main story of the *Mahabharata* is often interrupted by other stories and discussions of religion and other subjects. The part called the *Bhagavad-Gita* is an important writing of Hinduism. CHARLES S. J. WHITE

See also BHAGAVAD-GITA; RAMAYANA; HINDUISM; MYTHOLOGY (Hindu Mythology).

MAHAN, *mah HAN,* **ALFRED THAYER** (1840-1914), an American admiral, wrote many books on naval strategy and the influence of sea power on a nation's affairs. He became one of the world's great authorities on sea power. His books influenced the naval policies of many nations. His great work, *The Influence of Sea Power upon History, 1660-1783,* which he wrote in 1890, influenced President Theodore Roosevelt in his naval building program. It is also believed to have caused

Kaiser Wilhelm II of Germany to build a powerful German navy.

Mahan was born at West Point, N.Y. His father was a professor at the United States Military Academy and had written notable books on military engineering. Mahan studied at Columbia University and at the United States Naval Academy. He was graduated in 1859, and served in the South Atlantic and Gulf of Mexico squadrons during the Civil War.

He spent interesting years in travel and historical study before he wrote his first book, *Gulf and Inland Waters*. It was published in 1883. Mahan served as president of the Naval War College in Newport, R.I., in 1886 and in 1892. While there, he wrote *The Influence of Sea Power upon History*. He retired from the Navy in 1896 after 37 years of active service. But he returned to serve on the Naval Board during the Spanish-American War.

Admiral Mahan's importance in history is due to his thorough study of sea power. Mahan's studies convinced him that a country's strength on the sea is of great importance to its prosperity and its position in the world. He tried through his books to convince Americans of this fact and to obtain a powerful U.S. naval force.

His works include *The Influence of Sea Power upon the French Revolution and Empire, 1793-1812*, published in 1892; *Lessons of the War with Spain* (1899); *Types of Naval Officers* (1901); and *Armaments and Arbitration* (1912). He also wrote his autobiography, *From Sail to Steam* (1907), and biographies of Farragut (1894) and Nelson (1897). DONALD W. MITCHELL

MAHARAJAH. See RAJAH.

MAHATMA. See GANDHI, MOHANDAS KARAMCHAND.

MAHAVIRA. See JAINISM.

MAHAYANA. See BUDDHISM (Buddhist Schools); RELIGIOUS LIFE (Buddhism).

MAHICAN INDIANS. See MOHICAN INDIANS.

MAHLER, GUSTAV (1860-1911), was a Bohemian composer and one of the greatest conductors of his time. He is best known as the composer of nine symphonies. He failed to finish his 10th. Mahler tried to write music so varied and grandiose that the whole world was reflected in it. He used a larger orchestra than any composer before him, and added choruses and vocal soloists in several of the symphonies. His largest work, the *Symphony No. 8* (1907), is known as the "Symphony of a Thousand" because of the number of performers it requires. He also wrote *The Song of the Earth* (1908), an orchestral song cycle based on old Chinese poems.

Mahler was born in Kalischt, near Čáslav (in what is now Czechoslovakia). He began to study piano at the age of 6. He was already an accomplished pianist when he entered the Vienna Conservatory at 15. He became an opera conductor in 1880, and later became director of the Vienna Court Opera. His energy and competence soon made the Vienna Opera the finest in Europe. He came to the United States in 1907, and became the conductor of the New York Philharmonic Orchestra. He also conducted the Metropolitan Opera Company for three years. He was noted for his Mozart and Wagner productions. HOMER ULRICH

MAHOGANY is often called the finest cabinet wood of the world, because it has most of the qualities desired for furniture making. It is strong and hard enough to stand ordinary use as furniture, yet soft enough to be easily sawed, planed, and carved. Mahogany does not shrink, swell, or warp as much as many other equally hard woods. The wood has an attractive color and grain, and a high luster.

The color of mahogany varies from light tan to dark reddish-brown. The wood darkens when exposed to daylight. It usually has an interlocking pattern or grain. Sometimes mahogany has curly, wavy, raindrop, or speckled figures. When lumberers cut lengthwise through forks in the tree trunk, the wood shows a beautiful ostrich-plume effect. Workers often quartersaw or quarterslice mahogany into *veneer*, or thin sheets. They saw through the center of the log lengthwise so as to divide it into four sections. Then they cut planks alternately from each face of the quarter. The wood usually shows a ribbon or stripe figure when quartersawed. Fur-

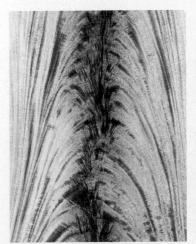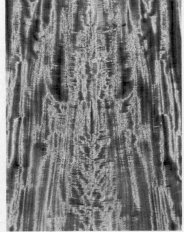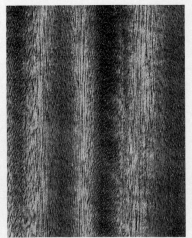

Mahogany Assoc., Inc.

Mahogany Wood Grains help beautify furniture. Popular types of the wood include African mahogany, *left*, Honduras mahogany, *center*, and Philippine mahogany, *right*. Philippine mahogany is the trade name for several kinds of hardwoods that are not true mahogany trees.

niture manufacturers glue the mahogany veneer to plain wood to make a beautiful surface finish.

Mahogany is one of the heavier woods. The long, clean tree trunk may reach a height of 60 to 80 feet (18 to 24 meters) before the first branch appears. The heaviest and finest mahogany comes from the West Indies, where the tree *Swietenia mahagoni* grows to a height of more than 100 feet (30 meters). This kind of mahogany is very scarce. Most mahogany comes from southern Mexico, northern South America, and Africa. In Mexico and South America, the wood comes from the *Swietenia macrophylla* tree. In Africa, it is found in trees of the genus *Khaya*. Wood from trees of the genus *Cedrela* looks like mahogany, but is softer, lighter, and more brittle than true mahogany.

The Cathedral of Santo Domingo in the Dominican Republic was the first building to use mahogany wood-work. The church was completed in 1540. People believe Sir Walter Raleigh used mahogany in 1595 to repair his ships in the West Indies. In the 1700's, Chippendale, Hepplewhite, and other furniture makers made mahogany furniture popular.   HARRY E. TROXELL

MAHOMET. See MUHAMMAD.

MAHOUT. See ELEPHANT (Training Elephants).

MAID MARIAN. See ROBIN HOOD.

MAID OF ORLÉANS. See JOAN OF ARC, SAINT.

MAIDENHAIR FERN is the name of a group of delicate, graceful ferns that grow on damp rocks and in woods of North America and southern Europe. It has beautiful *fronds* (leaves), which are divided into two parts. The maidenhair fern gets its name from its leaf-stalks, which are slender, shiny, and brown or black in color. The maidenhair has been used to make a cough medicine called *syrup of capillaire*.

Scientific Classification. The maidenhair fern is a member of the common fern family, *Polypodiaceae*. The common maidenhair fern is genus *Adiantum*, species *A. pedatum*.   ROLLA M. TRYON

MAIDENHAIR TREE. See GINKGO.

MAIDU INDIANS, *MY doo*, once lived in the Feather and American river valleys of what is now north-central California. These Indians formed one of the seed-gathering tribes (see INDIAN, AMERICAN [Indians of the California-Intermountain Region]).

The Maidu lived in small settlements that banded together to form village communities. Each village of 100 or more persons claimed the right to the territory surrounding it. No other tribe could gather food in that area. Acorns provided an important food for the Maidu. These bitter nuts contain poisonous tannic acid. The Maidu removed the poison by grinding the kernels into meal and pouring hot water over it to dissolve the acid. The Maidu also caught salmon and hunted rabbits, birds, and deer. Like the Pomo and other Indians of the area, the Maidu built sweat houses for steam baths (see POMO INDIANS). The men used them as ceremonial centers and meeting places.

Most Maidu today still live in California, working as farmers and woodcutters.   CHARLES E. DIBBLE

MAIL. See POST OFFICE.

MAIL-ORDER BUSINESS includes companies that sell their products through catalogs or circulars or by letter. These companies are often called *mail-order houses*.

Smaller mail-order houses usually offer their goods by mail only. Larger firms permit customers to order by mail, by telephone, and through sales offices where shoppers can make selections from catalogs and from samples of goods on display. Some mail-order companies also operate retail department stores.

The catalogs of larger mail-order houses offer a great variety of products—from safety pins to diamond rings. Some of the largest catalogs list as many as 135,000 separate items.

Before the establishment of mail-order houses, some retail stores sold certain types of goods by mail. In 1872, Montgomery Ward and Company of Chicago started the first mail-order house to sell general merchandise (see WARD, AARON MONTGOMERY). Today, it ranks as the second largest mail-order firm in the world. The world's largest mail-order house, Sears, Roebuck and Company, was founded in North Redwood, Minn., in 1886. Simpson-Sears is the largest mail-order house in Canada.

When the leading present-day mail-order firms were established, most of their customers lived on farms and in small towns. After World War I, the mail-order business began to decline. Improved roads and the increased use of automobiles made it easier for country people to travel to larger towns and cities to shop. This development led the larger firms to open retail stores.

In spite of a decreasing farm population, the mail-order business began to grow again after World War II. New firms selling specialized types of goods entered the business. Older firms developed new sales techniques. The mail-order industry recognized the importance of the rapidly growing city and suburban markets, and developed new methods of reaching customers there. These methods included telephone-order services, separate catalog-sales offices in towns and suburbs, and increased circulation of catalogs in city areas.

The modern mail-order catalog reflects the fact that city people as well as country people buy from these books. Although some larger catalogs offer farm equipment, they also offer clothes and other products that keep pace with the latest fashions.

MAILER, NORMAN (1923-   ), is an American author. Critics have often attacked his work, but Mailer's readers usually find his essays and novels fascinating and disturbing. Mailer has tried to analyze the myths and unconscious impulses that underlie human behavior. He often stresses sex and violence. But he uses these elements for serious artistic purposes, not merely to shock.

Mailer first achieved success with his war novel *The Naked and the Dead* (1948). In *Barbary Shore* (1951), he wrote about politics. *The Deer Park* (1955) describes the corruption of artistic and social values in Hollywood. *An American Dream* (1965) concerns events surrounding a man's murder of his wife. But it is really a surrealistic journey through the power structures and obsessions of modern urban

Pictorial Parade
Norman Mailer

America. Some of Mailer's best essays were collected in *Advertisements for Myself* (1959) and *Existential Errands* (1972). *The Armies of the Night* (1968), which describes his experiences and observations during a peace demonstration, shared the 1969 Pulitzer prize for general nonfiction. The book also received the 1969 National Book Award for arts and letters. *Miami and the Siege of Chicago* (1968) presents Mailer's reactions to the 1968 national political conventions. Mailer wrote his personal observations about the Apollo 11 mission to the moon in *Of a Fire on the Moon* (1971). *The Executioner's Song* (1979) is based on the life of Gary Gilmore, a convicted murderer who was executed in 1977. The book won the 1980 Pulitzer prize for fiction. Mailer was born in Long Branch, N.J.   EUGENE K. GARBER

MAILGRAM. See TELEGRAPH (Special Services).

MAILLOL, ARISTIDE (1861-1944), was a French sculptor. Like many sculptors of his generation, Maillol reacted against the emotionalism and irregular forms of Auguste Rodin, who had dominated French sculpture to that time. Maillol turned instead to a serene balanced style of broadly proportioned figures. Solid and clear forms were his primary aims. Maillol tried to return to what he believed to be the calm, harmonious spirit of early classical Greek sculpture. His *The Mediterranean* is reproduced in color in the SCULPTURE article.

Maillol was born in Banyuls. He began his career as a painter and designer of tapestries before turning to sculpture in the late 1890's. He dealt almost exclusively with the female figure, and his style changed little during his career. Maillol gave his subjects stationary poses and restful expressions.   MARCEL FRANCISCONO

MAIMONIDES, *my MAHN ih deez* (1135-1204), was a Jewish philosopher. His principal philosophical work, *Guide for the Perplexed*, completed in 1190, tried to harmonize Judaism with the teachings of Aristotle. The work influenced Christian theologians like Saint Thom-as Aquinas because of its use of Aristotle's doctrines.

Maimonides was a rabbi. His full name was Moses ben Maimon. Persecution forced him to leave his home in Córdoba, Spain, in 1148. After years of wandering, he settled in Egypt. He wrote many works on law, logic, astronomy, and medicine.   W. T. JONES

MAIN, in sewerage systems, is the large pipe that is used to collect sewage from smaller pipes connected to buildings. In water or gas systems, a main is the pipe that delivers the water or gas to smaller pipes linked to buildings. See also SEWAGE; WATER.   RAY K. LINSLEY

MAIN RIVER is the largest eastern branch of the Rhine River in Germany. The Main rises in the highlands of Bavaria and winds westward for 307 miles (494 kilometers). It empties into the Rhine near the city of Mainz. For location, see GERMANY (physical map). A canal has been dug in the river bed between Mainz and Frankfurt for river traffic. The Ludwigs Canal connects the Main River with the Danube River near the city of Regensburg.   JAMES K. POLLOCK

MAINE. The sinking of the United States battleship *Maine* helped cause the Spanish-American War. The *Maine* arrived in Havana, Cuba, on Jan. 25, 1898, to protect American lives and property in case of riots. On Feb. 15, 1898, it blew up, killing about 260 of the crew. A naval court of inquiry concluded that a submarine mine had caused the explosion. The United States accused Spain in this matter because Havana was then a Spanish port. But Spain claimed that an explosion inside the ship caused the disaster.

The slogan "Remember the *Maine*" spread throughout the United States. It aroused patriotic sentiment in favor of war against Spain.   FRANK FREIDEL

See also SPANISH-AMERICAN WAR (American Intervention).

National Archives, Washington

The Sinking of the *Maine* in Havana Harbor on Feb. 15, 1898, angered the American people and helped spark the Spanish-American War. "Remember the *Maine*" became a popular patriotic slogan.

Clearing Up by Robert Eric Moore from the WORLD BOOK Collection

The Rocky Coast of Maine

MAINE forms the northeastern corner of the United States. West Quoddy Head, a small peninsula of Maine, is the country's easternmost piece of land. Nearby Eastport lies farther east than any other U.S. city. On a map, northern Maine looks like a giant wedge between the Canadian provinces of New Brunswick and Quebec. Augusta is the capital of Maine, and Portland is the largest city.

Maine, the largest New England state, is probably best known for its beautiful shore on the Atlantic Ocean. Along this famous "rock-bound" coast are lighthouses, sandy beaches, quiet fishing villages, thousands of offshore islands, and Acadia National Park—New England's only national park. Jagged rocks and cliffs, and thousands of bays and inlets, add to the rugged beauty of Maine's coast. Inland, the state has sparkling lakes, rushing rivers, green forests, and towering mountains.

Many cities and towns lie in the lowlands of southern Maine. But forests cover nearly 90 per cent of the state. Trees from the forests are the raw materials of a giant wood-processing industry—the backbone of Maine's economy. Mills in Maine make paper, pulp, toothpicks, and a variety of other products from trees. Maine leads the states in toothpick production, and ranks high in other wood products. Maine's nickname, the *Pine Tree State*, came from the tall pines that once made up most of the state's forests.

Maine is also an important farming and fishing state. It is a leader in growing potatoes and raising *broilers* (chickens 9 to 12 weeks old). The nation's largest lobster catch is trapped off the coast of Maine. More sardines are packed every year in Maine than in any other state.

Pioneering English colonists first settled in Maine in 1607, thirteen years before the Pilgrims landed at Plymouth Rock. Cold weather and lack of supplies forced the settlers back to England in 1608. English colonists made permanent settlements in Maine in the 1620's. Maine was a part of Massachusetts for the better part of 200 years. Then, on March 15, 1820, it became the 23rd state of the United States.

The name *Maine* probably means *mainland*. Early English explorers used the term *The Main* to distinguish the mainland from the offshore islands. New Englanders often refer to Maine as *Down East*. They call Maine's people *Down Easters* or *Down Easterners*. These terms probably came from the early New England use of the word *down* to mean *north*. Maine lies farther north than any other New England state. For the relationship of Maine to the other states in its region, see NEW ENGLAND.

62

MAINE

THE PINE TREE STATE

Ralph Crowell, Sanford
Traditional New England Church in Wiscasset

Ralph Crowell
Fishing for Trout in a Maine Stream

FACTS IN BRIEF

Capital: Augusta.

Government: *Congress*—U.S. senators, 2; U.S. representatives, 2. *Electoral Votes*—4. *State Legislature*—senators, 33; representatives, 151. *Counties*—16.

Area: 33,215 sq. mi. (86,026 km²), including 2,295 sq. mi. (5,944 km²) of inland water but excluding 1,102 sq. mi. (2,854 km²) of Atlantic coastal water; 39th in size among the states. *Greatest Distances*—north-south, 332 mi. (534 km); east-west, 207 mi. (333 km). *Coastline*—228 mi. (367 km).

Elevation: *Highest*—Mount Katahdin, 5,268 ft. (1,606 m) above sea level. *Lowest*—sea level along the coast.

Population: *Estimated 1975 Population*—1,059,000. *1970 Census*—993,663; 38th among the states; distribution, 51 per cent urban, 49 per cent rural; density, 30 persons per sq. mi. (12 persons per km²).

Chief Products: *Agriculture*—potatoes, eggs, broilers, milk. *Fishing Industry*—lobsters, clams. *Manufacturing*—paper products, leather products, lumber and wood products, food products, textiles, nonelectric machinery, electric and electronic equipment, transportation equipment. *Mining*—sand and gravel, zinc.

Statehood: March 15, 1820, the 23rd state.

State Abbreviations: Me. (traditional); ME (postal).

State Motto: *Dirigo* (*I direct* or *I guide*).

State Song: "State of Maine Song." Words and music by Roger Vinton Snow.

The contributors of this article are V. Paul Reynolds, Editor of the Editorial Page of the Bangor Daily News; *Joseph M. Trefethen, Professor Emeritus of Geology at the University of Maine at Portland; and Robert M. York, Maine State Historian and Dean of Graduate Studies at the University of Maine at Portland-Gorham.*

Maine (blue) ranks 39th in size among all the states, and is the largest of the New England States (gray).

Constitution. Maine is governed under its original constitution. The constitution was adopted in December 1819, about three months before Maine became a state. *Amendments* (changes) to the constitution may be proposed by a two-thirds vote in both houses of the state Legislature. To become law, these amendments need the approval of a majority of the state's voters in a regular election. Amendments also can be proposed by a constitutional convention. A two-thirds vote in both houses of the Legislature is needed to call a constitutional convention. Maine has never held such a convention.

Executive. The governor is the only Maine executive official elected by the people. The governor serves a four-year term and receives a $35,000 yearly salary plus a $15,000 annual expense account. The governor may serve any number of terms but may not serve more than two of the terms in succession. For a list of all the governors of the state, see the *History* section of this article.

Maine has no lieutenant governor. The Legislature elects the attorney general, secretary of state, and state treasurer to two-year terms. It elects the state auditor to a four-year term.

Legislature of Maine consists of a 33-member Senate and a 151-member House of Representatives. Each of the state's 33 senatorial districts elects one senator. Maine has 151 representative districts, each of which elects one representative. Legislative sessions begin on the first Wednesday after the first Tuesday in January each year. The sessions may last up to 50 days in even-numbered years and up to 100 days in odd-numbered years.

In 1969, Maine voters approved a constitutional amendment requiring the Senate to be *reapportioned* (redivided) to give equal representation based on population. The Legislature drew up a reapportionment plan

but the governor vetoed it. In February 1972, the state Supreme Judicial Court ordered a plan which required a 33-member Senate. The plan became effective in November 1972.

Courts. The Supreme Judicial Court is Maine's highest court of appeals for all civil and criminal cases. The court has a chief justice and six associate justices. The governor appoints the justices to seven-year terms. Maine's superior court handles all cases requiring trial by jury, and all cases appealed from lower courts. The governor appoints the 14 superior court justices to seven-year terms.

Each county has a probate court, whose judges are elected by the people to four-year terms. Maine's 13 district courts hear cases involving damages of less than $20,000. District court judges are appointed by the governor to seven-year terms.

Local Government. Maine's 22 cities have *home rule*. That is, they may adopt or revise charters without approval of the state Legislature. Most cities in the state have a mayor-council or city-manager government.

Maine has about 500 towns and *plantations* (small incorporated areas). A town in Maine is similar to a township in many other states. Several communities may exist in the same town. But the entire town is governed as a unit. The town meeting is the most common form of government in Maine towns. It allows citizens to take a direct part in government. Each year, town voters assemble to elect officials, approve budgets, and conduct other business. The chief town officials are called *selectmen*. Maine's plantations are governed in much the same way as towns. A board of assessors heads a plantation's government. Each of Maine's 16 counties has its own government.

Taxation provides about three-fourths of the state government's income. Almost all the rest comes from federal grants and other United States government programs. Sales taxes bring in the largest part of Maine's income. These taxes, ranked in order of importance, include a general sales tax, personal and corporation income taxes, and taxes on motor fuels, tobacco products, public utilities, alcoholic beverages, insurance, and horse racing. License fees are Maine's second most important kind of tax. The state also has a death and gift tax and a state property tax. The property tax is the chief source of income for Maine's public school districts.

Politics. Maine was a Democratic state before the 1850's. But most Maine voters became Republicans in the period shortly before the Civil War. They favored the Republican Party's antislavery and pro-Northern policies. For about a hundred years, until the 1950's, Maine voters almost always elected Republicans in state, congressional, and presidential elections. The Republicans are still a strong party in Maine. But the Democrats received almost as much support as the Republicans, and at times even greater support, during the 1960's and 1970's.

Maine has voted for more Republican presidential candidates than any other state except Vermont. Since 1856, only three Democrats—Woodrow Wilson in 1912,

Maine Dept. of Commerce and Industry

Governor's Mansion stands across the street from the Capitol. The residence is usually called Blaine House, because James G. Blaine, a leading political figure of the late 1800's, once owned it.

The State Seal

Symbols of Maine. On the seal, the farmer and the seaman represent two of Maine's chief occupations. The pine tree on the shield symbolizes Maine's many forests, and the moose represents its wildlife. The North Star above the shield stands for the state's northern location. The motto, *Dirigo*, means *I direct*. The seal was adopted in 1820. The state flag bears a reproduction of the seal on a field of blue. It was adopted in 1909.

The State Flag

Seal, flag, bird, and flower illustrations, courtesy of Eli Lilly and Company

Lyndon B. Johnson in 1964, and Hubert H. Humphrey in 1968—have won Maine's electoral votes. For years, Maine held its elections for Congress and governor in September. Its voters often chose candidates from the party that won November elections in other states. This led to the slogan, "As Maine goes, so goes the nation." In 1960, Maine began voting in November. For Maine's voting record in presidential elections, see ELECTORAL COLLEGE (table).

State Capitol is in Augusta. The original structure, designed by Charles Bulfinch, was completed in 1832. Portland was Maine's capital from 1820 until 1832, when Augusta became capital.
Maine Dept. of Economic Development

The State Bird
Chickadee

The State Flower
White Pine Cone
and Tassel

The State Tree
White Pine

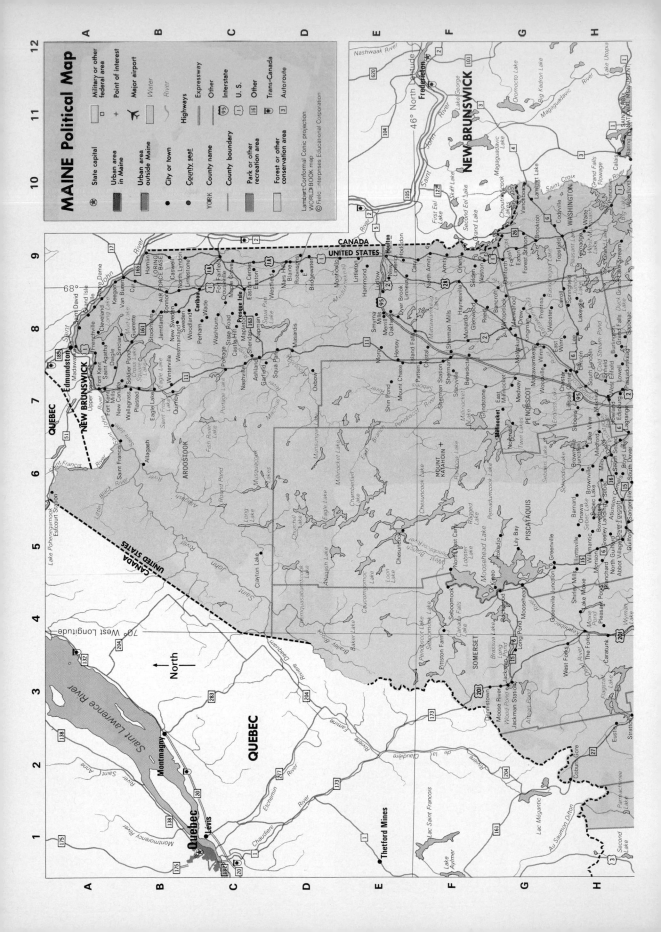

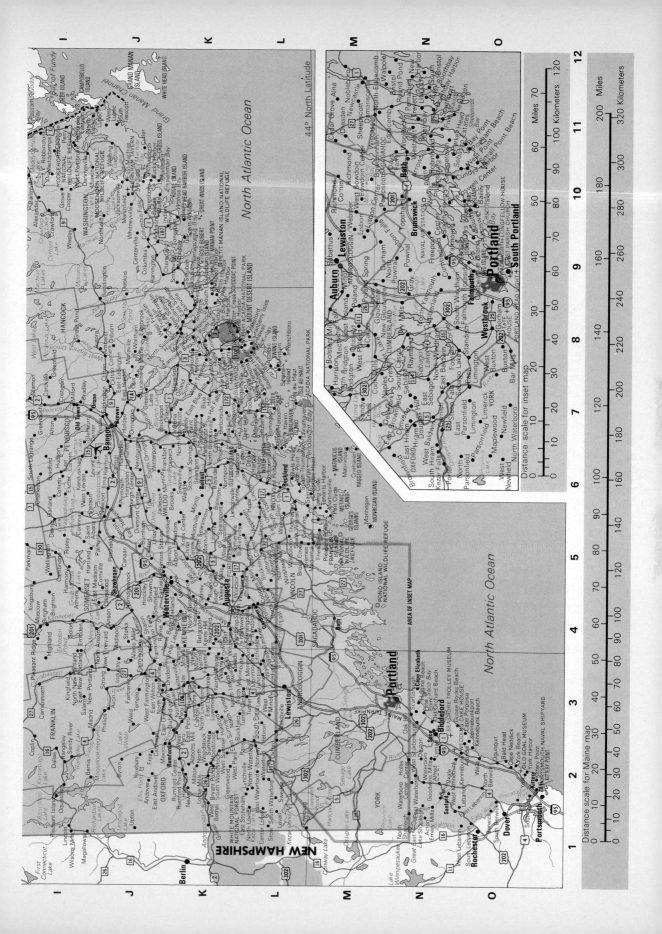

Atkinson
Corners .... H 6
Atlantic .... L 8
Auburn ...24,151.°M 8
Augusta ..21,945. K 7
Aurora .... 495. J 8
Bailey Island ...... N 10
Baileyville .2,167. O 7
Bald Head .... J 8
Baldwin* ...... 878. N 7
Bancroft .... 53. O 7
Bangor ...33,168. N 7
Bar Harbor .2,392. L 8
Bar Mills .... N 8
Barnard .... H 6
Baring .... 24. O 7
Bath ......9,679.°M 8
Bay Point .... N 8
Bayside .... K 7
Beals .... 663. K 8
Beddington ...... 32. J 8
Belfast ....5,957.°K 7
Belgrade ...1,302. K 7
Belgrade Lakes .... K 7
Belmont .... 349. K 7
Benedicta ...... 177. J 7
Benton .....1,729. K 7
Benton Station .... K 7
Bernard .... L 8
Berwick ....1,765. K 8
Bethel .....2,320. M 8
Biddeford .19,983. N 8
Bingham ....1,184 .. J 6
Birch Harbor ...... L 8
Blaine, see
  Mars Hill
  [-Blaine]
Blanchard ...... 56. H 5
Blue Hill ...1,367. K 7
Blue Hill Falls .... M 8
Bolsters Mills ...... N 7
Boothbay ...1,814. N 11
Boothbay
  Harbor ...2,320. N 11
Bowdoin* ...... 858. M 10
Bowdoin Center .... M 10
Bowdoinham 1,294. M 9
Bowerbank ...... 29. H 7
Boyd Lake .... H 7
Bradford .... 569. J 7
Bradley .....1,010. J 7
Bremen .... 454. M 8
Brewer .....9,300. J 7
Bridgewater .895. A 7
Bridgton ...1,779 .. M 7
Brighton .... 58. J 6
Bristol .....1,721. M 8
Broad Cove .... N 8
Brooklin .... 598. L 8
Brooks .... 751. K 7
Brooksville ..673. K 7
Brownfield ..... 478. N 7
Brownville .1,490. J 7
Brownville
  Junction .... H 6
Brunswick (16,195.) N 10
Brunswick
  Station* ..1,679 .. N 10

Criehaven .... M 7
Crouseville ..281. C 8
Crystal ....4,096. N 9
Cumberland .24,151.°M 8
Cumberland
  Center .... N 9
Cumberland
  Foreside .... N 9
Cundys Harbor .... O 7
Cushing .... 522. L 6
Cutler .... 588. O 2
Dallas .... 155. A 8
Damariscotta
  scotta* ..1,264.°M 12
  [-New-
  castle]
Danforth ....1,188. M 12
Dark Harbor 794. A 9
Days Ferry .... G 6
Dayton .... 546. N 2
Deblois .... 20. J 7
Dedham .... 663. J 7
Deer Isle ...1,211. K 8
Denmark ...... 522. G 7
Dennistown ...... 48. B 8
Dennysville .... 397. G 3
Derby .... H 6
Detroit .... 663. J 6
Dexter .....(3,725.) J 6
Dixfield ....1,535. G 5
Dixmont .... K 3
Dixmont Center .... J 6
Douglas Hill ...... N 7
Dover-
  Foxcroft .3,102. H 6
Dresden ....(4,178.) H 6
Drew .... 32. G 8
Dry Mills .... M 8
Dryden .... G 5
Durham .....1,264. M 8
Dyer Brook .... 165. E 9
Eagle Lake .... 908. B 7
East Baldwin ...... N 7
East Blue Hill ...... K 8
East Boothbay .... N 11
East Brownfield .... N 7
East Corinth ...... J 7
East Dixfield ...... G 5
East Eddington .... J 7
East Franklin ...... K 8
East Hiram .... N 7
East Holden ...... J 7
East Lebanon ...... O 2
East Limington .... N 7
East Livermore .... K 3
East Machias 1,057. J 9
East Madison ...... J 4
East Milli-
  nocket .....2,564. F 8
East Monmouth .... L 4
East New
  Portland .... J 4
East Newport .... J 6
East Orland ...... J 7
East Parsonfield .. O 2
East Peru .... L 8
East Pittston ...... L 5

Goose Rocks
  Beach .... O 3
Gorham .....3,337. O 3
Gouldsboro (7,839.) K 8
Grand Falls ...... 6. O 8
Grand Isle ..... 797. A 8
Grand Lake .... H 9
Gray ....2,939. N 8
Great Pond .... J 8
Greeley
  Landing .... H 6
Green Lake .... J 7
Greenbush .... 591. J 7
Greene .....1,772. L 3
Greenfield .... 117. J 7
Greenville 1,714. G 5
Greenville
  Junction .... G 5
Greenwood .... 610. G 4
Grindstone ...... 522. J 7
Grove .... 397. A 8
Guerette .... 278. B 8
Guilford ...1,216. H 6
Hall Quarry .... K 8
Hallowell ..2,814. L 4
Hamlin .... 357. A 9
Hammond ...... 73. E 9
Hampden ...2,207. J 7
Hampden
  Highlands .... J 7
Hancock ...1,070. K 8
Hancock
  Point .... K 8
Hanover .... 275. G 4
Harborside ...... 787. K 8
Harmony ..... 650. J 5
Harpswell* .2,552. N 10
Harpswell
  Center .... N 10
Harrington 1,045. K 9
Harrison ...1,414. M 7
Hartford .... 312. L 3
Hartland ...1,414. J 6
Haynesville .... 153. F 9
Hebron .... 553. M 3
Hermon ....2,376. J 7
Hersey .... 81. E 9
Higgins Beach .... O 3
Highland .... J 5
Hinckley .... J 5
Hiram .... 686. N 7
Hodgdon ...... 933. E 9
Holden .....1,841. J 7
Hollis* .....1,560. N 2
Hollis Center ...... N 2
Hope .... 500. L 6
Houlton ....6,760. E 9
Howland ...1,418. H 7
Hudson .... 482. J 7
Hulls Cove .... K 8
Indian Point ...... K 8
Indian River ...... K 10
Industry .... 347. J 5
Island Falls ..913. F 8
Isle au Haut .. 45. L 7
Islesboro .... 421. K 7
Islesford .... L 8
Jackman ...... 848. G 3
Jackman Station .. G 3

Livermore
  Falls .....(3,450.) K 3
Locke Mills .... K 2
Long Island ... 56. K 8
Long Pond .... G 4
Longcove .... M 6
Loring* ....
Lovell .... 607. N 7
Lowell .... 154. J 8
Lubec ......1,949. J 11
Lucerne in
  Maine .... J 7
Ludlow .... 259. E 9
Lyman .... 864. N 2
Lynchville .... L 2
Machias ....1,368. J 9
Machiasport 1,894. J 9
Madawaska 5,585. A 8
Madison ....4,278. J 4
Madrid .... 75. J 3
Magalloway .... 107. J 1
Manchester 1,331. K 4
Manset .... L 8
Maple Grove ...... A 8
Mapleton ...1,598. C 8
Maplewood .... O 6
Mariaville .... 108. J 7
Marion .... J 10
Marlboro .... K 8
Mars Hill 1,875. D 9
Marshfield .... 227. J 9
Martinsville ...... M 7
Masardis .... 317. D 7
Matinicus .... M 7
Matinicus
  Isle* .... 90. M 7
Mattawam-
  keag .... 326. H 7
Maxfield .... 24. H 7
McKinley .... L 8
Mechanic
  Falls ......2,193. L 3
Meddybemps .. 76. H 10
Medford .... 146. H 6
Medomak .... M 7
Medway ....1,491. H 7
Mercer .... 313. J 4
Merrill .... E 8
Mexico .....4,309. K 2
Milbridge ..1,154. K 9
Milford ....1,519. J 7
Millinocket 7,558. G 7
Milo ....2,572. H 7
Milton .... 33* K 2
Minturn .... L 8
Molunkus .... H 8
Monhegan ...... 44. N 11
Monmouth 2,062. L 4
Monroe .... 478. K 7
Monson .... 669. H 6
Monticello 1,072. E 9

North
  Woodstock ...... K 2
North Yar-
  mouth (3,595.) .. N 9
Northeast
  Harbor .... 57. K 8
Northfield .... 744. K 6
Northport ...2,430. K 7
Norway* ...(3,595.) L 2
Notre Dame ...... A 8
Oak Hill ...... 154. N 3
Oakfield .... 836. E 8
Oakland ....3,535. K 5
Ogunquit ...2,261. O 2
Olamon .... J 7
Old Orchard
  Beach .....5,273. N 3
Old Town ...9,057. J 7
Onawa .... G 6
Oquossoc .... H 2
Orient .... 83. F 9
Orland .....1,307. K 7
Orono ......9,989. J 7
Orrington 2,702. J 7
Orrs Island .... N 10
Osborn .... 33. J 8
Otis .... 123. J 8
Otisfield .... 589. M 3
Otter Creek ...... K 8
Owls Head 1,284. L 6
Oxbow .... 92. D 7
Oxford .....1,892. L 3
Palermo .... 645. K 5
Palmyra ....1,104. J 6
Paris ....3,739. L 3
Parker Head ...... N 11
Parkman ...... 457. J 5
Parsonfield .971. O 2
Passadum-
  keag .... 326. J 7
Patten .....1,068. F 8
Pejepscot .... N 10
Pemaquid .... M 7
Pembroke ..... 700. H 11
Penobscot .... 786. K 7
Perham .... 436. C 8
Perry .... 878. H 11
Phillips .... 979. J 4
Phippsburg 1,229. N 10
Pittsfield ...4,274. J 6
Pittston* ...1,617. L 4
Pittston Farm ...... G 4
Plantation
  Number 14* 29. J 10
Plantation
  Number 21* 83. J 10
Plantation
  Number 33* 43. J 8
Pleasant Island ... K 2
Pleasant Point .... H 11
Pleasant Pond .... H 4
Pleasant
  Ridge .... 116. J 4
Plymouth ...... 542. J 7
Poland .....2,015. M 3
Poland Spring .... M 9
Popham Beach .... N 10
Port Clyde .... M 6

Sedgwick ...... 578. K 7
Selden .... F 9
Shapleigh ..... 559. N 2
Shawmut .... J 5
Sheepscot .... M 11
Sheridan .... C 8
Sherman Mills 949. F 8
Sherman Station .. F 8
Shin Pond .... E 7
Shirley* .... 174. H 5
Shirley Mills ...... H 5
Sidney .....1,319. K 4
Sinclair .... B 8
Skowhegan 6,571.°J 5
Small Point
  Beach .... O 11
Smithfield ..... 527. J 4
Smithville .... K 8
Smyrna Mills .. 318. E 8
Smyrna Center .... E 8
Soldier Pond ...... A 8
Solon .... 712. J 5
Somerville .... 215. L 5
Sorrento .... 199. K 8
South Addison .... K 9
South
  Berwick ...1,863. O 2
South
  Bristol .... 664. N 11
South Casco ...... M 8
South China ...... K 5
South Dover ...... H 6
South Eliot .... O 2
South Freeport .... N 10
South
  Gouldsboro ...... K 8
South Harpswell .. O 10
South Hiram ...... N 7
South Hope ...... L 6
South Lagrange .. H 7
South Lebanon .... O 1
South Lincoln .... H 7
South
  Orrington .... J 7
South
  Paris .....2,315.°L 3
South
  Penobscot ...... K 7
South Port-
  land .....23,267. O 9
South Sebec ...... H 6
South
  Thomaston 831. L 6
South Warren .... L 6
South
  Waterford .... M 2
South
  Windham .... N 3
South
  Windsor .... L 5
South
  Woodstock ...... K 2
Southport .... 473. N 11
Southwest
  Harbor ....1,657.°L 8
Springfield .... 336. J 8
Springvale 2,914. O 2
Spruce Head ...... M 6
Squa Pan .... D 8
Stacyville ..... 547. F 7
Standish ...3,122. O 9
Starboard .... J 10
Starks .... 323. J 4
State Road .... K 8
Steep Falls .... N 7

Welchville ...... 360. L 3
Weld .... J 5
Wellington .... 232. J 4
Wells ......4,448. O 2
Wesley .... 110. J 8
West Appleton .... K 6
West Baldwin ...... N 7
West Bath ..... 836. N 8
West Bethel ...... K 2
West Bowdoin .... M 10
West Buxton ...... N 9
West
  Cumberland ...... N 9
West Enfield ...... H 7
West
  Farmington ...... J 3
West Forks .... 74. H 4
West Franklin .... K 8
West
  Gardiner 1,435. L 4
West
  Gouldsboro ...... K 8
West
  Kennebunk ...... O 2
West Lebanon .... O 1
West Levant ...... J 6
West Lubec .... J 11
West Minot .... L 3
West Mount
  Vernon .... K 4
West
  Newfield .... O 2
West Paris 1,171. K 2
West
  Pembroke .... H 11
West Peru .... K 3
West Point .... O 11
West Poland ...... M 3
West
  Rockport .... L 6
West Scarboro .... N 3
West Sullivan .... K 8
West Sumner ...... K 2
West Trenton ...... K 8
West Trescott .... J 10
Westbrook 14,444. N 9
Westfield ...... 517. D 9
Westmanland .. 52. B 8
Weston .... 162. G 9
Westport .... N 11
Whitefield 1,131. L 5
Whiting .... 269. J 10
Whitneyville .. 155. J 9
Willimantic .. 126. H 5
Wilsons Mills ...... J 1
Wilton .....2,225. J 3
Windham* .6,593. N 3
Windsor ...1,097. K 5
Winn .... 516. G 8
Winslow ...5,389. K 5
Winslows Mills .. L 6
Winter
  Harbor ....1,028. K 9
Winterport 1,963. J 7
Winterville .... 164. B 7
Winthrop ...4,335. K 4
Wiscasset .2,244. M 11
Woodland .... K 2
Woodstock .1,005. K 2
Woodville ...... 62. H 7
Woolwich ..1,710. N 11
Wytopitlock ...... H 8
Yarmouth ..2,421. N 9
York ....4,854. O 2
York Beach 2,912 O 2
York Harbor ...... O 2

▲Entire town (township), including rural area.
*Does not appear on map; key shows general location.
°County seat.

Source: Latest census figures (1970). Places without population figures are unincorporated areas and are not listed in census reports.

John C. Olson, *Portland Press-Herald*

Crowds of Shoppers stroll along Congress Street in downtown Portland. Portland is Maine's largest city.

Veteran Lobstermen mend their traps in Friendship. Almost every community on Maine's coast has at least a small fishing fleet.

Eric M. Sanford

The 1970 U.S. census reported that Maine had 993,663 persons. The state's population had increased 3 per cent over the 1960 census figure of 969,265. The U.S. Bureau of the Census estimated that by 1975 the state's population had reached about 1,059,000.

About 51 per cent of Maine's people live in urban areas. That is, they live in or near municipalities with 2,500 or more persons. Maine's largest cities, in order of size, are Portland, Lewiston, Bangor, Auburn, South Portland, and Augusta. See the articles on Maine cities listed in the *Related Articles* at the end of this article.

Maine has two Standard Metropolitan Statistical Areas (see METROPOLITAN AREA). These areas are (1) Lewiston-Auburn and (2) Portland. About a fourth of the state's people live in these two areas. For the populations of these areas, see the *Index* to the political map of Maine.

About 96 of every 100 persons in Maine were born in the United States. About three-fourths of those born in other countries came from Canada. Other groups came from Germany, Great Britain, Ireland, Italy, and Russia. Roman Catholics make up Maine's largest single religious group. But there are more Protestants than Catholics in the state. The largest Protestant groups include Baptists, Episcopalians, Methodists, and members of the United Church of Christ.

POPULATION

This map shows the *population density* of Maine, and how it varies in different parts of the state. Population density means the average number of persons who live in a given area.

Persons per sq. mi.	Persons per km²
More than 90	More than 35
30 to 90	12 to 35
15 to 30	6 to 12
Less than 15	Less than 6

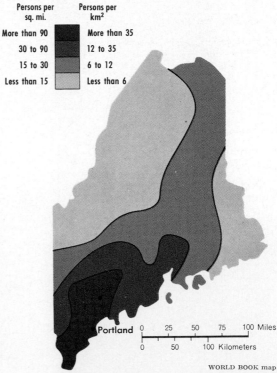

Portland

| 0 | 25 | 50 | 75 | 100 Miles |

| 0 | 50 | 100 Kilometers |

WORLD BOOK map

70

Schools. Colonial Maine offered little opportunity for formal education. Parents and local ministers often served as teachers. The first school in Maine may have been an Indian mission founded in 1696 by Sebastian Rasle, a Roman Catholic priest. Maine's first known school for white children opened in York in 1701. The state's first schoolhouse was built in Berwick in 1719. A school fund was provided by the Legislature in 1828. Schools began to receive tax support in 1868.

A commissioner of educational and cultural services and a nine-member board of education head Maine's public-school system. The governor appoints the members, subject to the approval of the Legislature, to five-year terms. The governor appoints the commissioner, subject to the approval of the Legislature, from a list of three persons nominated by the board. The commissioner serves four years. Children between the ages of 7 and 17 must attend school. For the number of students and teachers in Maine, see EDUCATION (table).

Libraries. One of Maine's earliest libraries was formed in 1751. This collection of books alternated between parish houses in Kittery and York. Maine now has about 250 public libraries.

Maine's biggest library is the State Library in Augusta. This library and the Maine Historical Library in Portland own large collections of books about Maine and its history. Maine's largest public libraries are the Bangor Public Library and the Portland Public Library.

Museums. The Maine State Museum in Augusta features exhibits on the state's history. The Bowdoin College Museum of Art has paintings and drawings by American, European, and Oriental artists. The Portland Museum of Art owns large collections of paintings and sculptures. The Robert Abbe Museum of Stone Age Antiquities features Indian items. Other museums include the Treat Gallery in Lewiston, the Brick Store Museum in Kennebunk, the William A. Farnsworth Library and Art Museum in Rockland, and the Bath Marine Museum in Bath. See also the *Places to Visit* section of this article.

UNIVERSITIES AND COLLEGES

Maine has 15 universities and colleges accredited by the New England Association of Schools and Colleges. For enrollments and further information, see UNIVERSITIES AND COLLEGES (table).

Name	Location	Founded
Atlantic, College of the	Bar Harbor	1969
Bangor Theological Seminary	Bangor	1814
Bates College	Lewiston	1855
Bowdoin College	Brunswick	1794
Colby College	Waterville	1813
Husson College	Bangor	1898
Maine, University of	*	*
Maine Maritime Academy	Castine	1941
Nasson College	Springvale	1912
New England, University of	Biddeford	1953
Portland School of Art	Portland	1882
St. Joseph's College	North Windham	1915
Thomas College	Waterville	1894
Unity College	Unity	1968
Westbrook College	Portland	1969

*For campuses and founding dates, see UNIVERSITIES AND COLLEGES (table).

University of Maine

The University of Maine has six four-year campus units. Stevens Hall on the Orono campus, above, houses the College of Arts and Sciences and the College of Business Administration.

MAINE / A Visitor's Guide

Maine's beautiful coastal area attracts thousands of vacationers yearly. Visitors enjoy the rugged beauty of Atlantic waters pounding against rocky shores, and the many lighthouses along the coast. Hundreds of sandy beaches, bays, coves, and inlets provide areas for swimming, fishing, and sailing. Inland, hunters stalk bears, deer, and many other game animals in the vast wilderness of the north. People who enjoy fishing can try their luck in 2,500 lakes and ponds and 5,000 rivers and streams. Skiers and climbers enjoy Maine's mountains. Maine's skiing season lasts from about mid-December to mid-April. In addition, the state has many historic sites, and picturesque landmarks such as small white churches.

Kabel Art Photo, Publix

Boothbay Harbor, a Resort Village on Maine's Atlantic Coast

PLACES TO VISIT

Following are brief descriptions of some of Maine's many interesting places to visit.

Black Mansion, in Ellsworth, is often called *Maine's Mount Vernon.* It resembles George Washington's Virginia home, *Mount Vernon.* Built about 1820, the Black Mansion has a low porch supported by five tall columns. Other features include fine china, silverware, furniture, and a winding staircase.

Burnham Tavern, in Machias, is the place where colonists met in 1775 to plot the capture of the British ship *Margaretta.* The capture was made during the first naval battle of the Revolutionary War. Burnham Tavern, built about 1770, still displays its original sign: "Drink for the thirsty, food for the hungry, lodging for the weary, and good keeping for horses."

First Parish Church is a Unitarian church in Portland. It was the site of Maine's only constitutional convention, in 1819. Many of Portland's wealthiest families worshiped in the church during the 1700's and 1800's.

Fort Western, in Augusta, dates from 1754. It was at this fort that Benedict Arnold and his men met before marching up Maine to attack Quebec in 1775.

Old Gaol Museum, in York, is the oldest public building in Maine. It was built in 1653, and served as a *gaol* (jail) until 1860. Old Gaol Museum now houses local history relics.

Penobscot Marine Museum, in Searsport, displays valuable paintings, ship models, old sailing charts, navigation instruments, fishing and whaling equipment, ships' logs, books, and other historical items.

Portland Head Light, near Portland, towers 101 feet (31 meters) over the surf. Built in 1791, it ranks among the oldest and most famous American lighthouses.

Seashore Trolley Museum, near Kennebunkport, is the largest U.S. museum that exhibits only electric railroad equipment.

Tate House is the oldest house in Portland. This three-story wooden structure was built in 1775. It includes quarters once used by slaves.

Wadsworth-Longfellow House, in Portland, ranks

72

Thunder Hole in Acadia National Park

David Corson, Shostal

Dearborn's Studio

Wedding Cake House in Kennebunk

Maine State Development Office

Portland Head Light in Portland Harbor

Greater Portland Chamber of Commerce

Wadsworth-Longfellow House in Portland

Dick Smith

Ox-Pulling Contest at the Fryeburg Fair

as Maine's most popular historic site. This three-story brick building was the boyhood home of Henry Wadsworth Longfellow, the famous poet.

Wedding Cake House, in Kennebunk, is a two-story, square house with elaborate outside decorations. According to legend, a sea captain was ordered to sea in an emergency, and his bride had no wedding cake. So he added the decorations to make the house look like a wedding cake.

National Park and Forest. Acadia National Park, in southeastern Maine, is the only national park in New England. See ACADIA NATIONAL PARK.

White Mountain National Forest lies chiefly in New Hampshire, but part of it extends into southwestern Maine. See NATIONAL FOREST (table).

State Parks and Memorials. Maine has 29 state parks and 18 state memorials. It has no state forest system. For information on the state parks and memorials, write to Director, Maine Bureau of Parks and Recreation, State House, Augusta, Me. 04333.

ANNUAL EVENTS

Many of Maine's most popular annual events are sports contests. The summer months feature boat races and other water-sports contests. Among the state's outstanding annual events is the Maine Seafoods Festival. This celebration is held in Rockland during the first weekend in August. Other annual events include:

January-June: Winter activities in Bethel, Carrabassett Valley, Greenville, Jackman, Kingfield, Locke Mills, Rangeley, and other places (January and February); Downeast Tennis Classic in Portland (early May).

July-December: Clam Festival in Yarmouth (July); Maine Broiler Festival in Belfast (July); Windjammer Days at Boothbay Harbor (July); Blueberry Festival in Union (August); Retired Skippers Race in Castine (August); Fairs in Bangor, Cumberland Center, Farmington, Fryeburg, Presque Isle, Skowhegan, Topsham, Union, and Windsor (various times during the summer and in early autumn); Maine State Fair in Lewiston (first week in September).

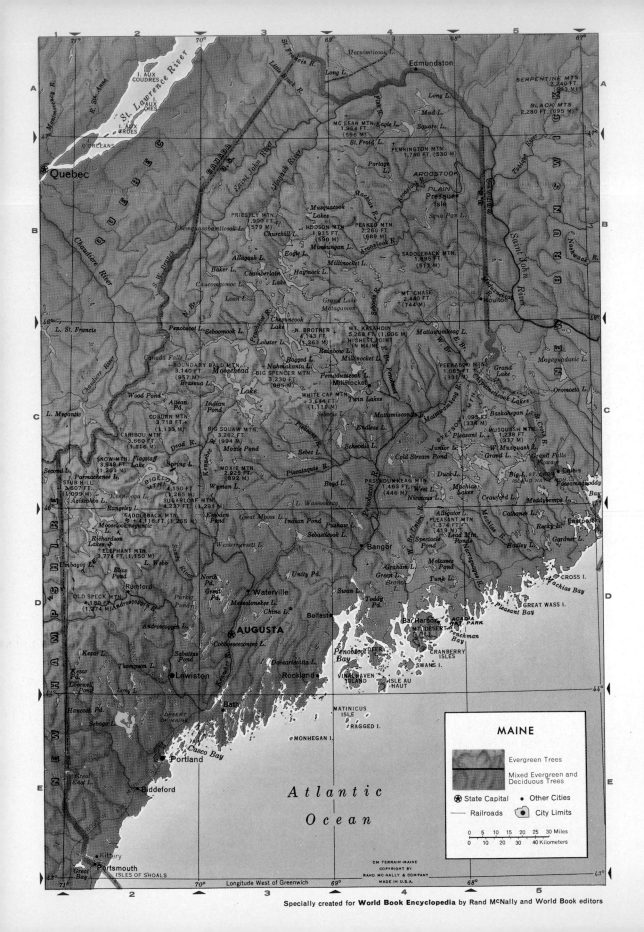

MAINE

Evergreen Trees

Mixed Evergreen and
Deciduous Trees

✪ State Capital   • Other Cities

— Railroads   ▣ City Limits

0 5 10 15 20 25 30 Miles
0   10   20   30   40 Kilometers

CM TERRAIN-MAINE
COPYRIGHT BY
RAND McNALLY & COMPANY
MADE IN U.S.A.

Specially created for **World Book Encyclopedia** by Rand McNally and World Book editors

MAINE/*The Land*

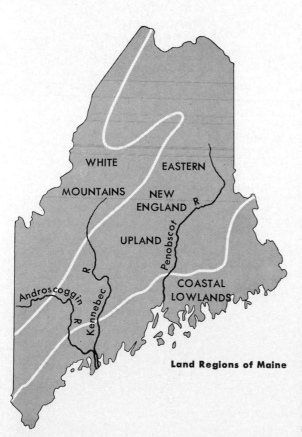

Land Regions of Maine

Land Regions. Maine has three natural land regions. They are, from southeast to northwest: (1) the Coastal Lowlands, (2) the Eastern New England Upland, and (3) the White Mountains Region.

The Coastal Lowlands cover southeastern Maine. They are part of a region of the same name that stretches along the entire New England coast. In Maine, the region extends from 10 to 40 miles (16 to 64 kilometers) inland from the Atlantic Ocean. Sandy beaches line the coast in the south. Old Orchard Beach, with 11 miles (18 kilometers) of hard-packed sand, is one of the longest and smoothest beaches on the Atlantic Coast. Salt marshes, crossed by tidal creeks, lie west of the beaches. In the northeast, the beaches shrink to small bays or strips of sand between high cliffs.

Most of the Coastal Lowlands lie near sea level. The land was once much higher. It was pushed down thousands of years ago, during the Ice Age, by the weight of ice and snow. The tops of sunken hills form more than 400 offshore islands from about 2 to 25 square miles (5 to 65 square kilometers) in area, and thousands of smaller islands. Mount Desert, Maine's largest island, covers about 100 square miles (260 square kilometers).

The Eastern New England Upland lies northwest of the Coastal Lowlands. The entire upland extends from the Canadian border to Connecticut. In Maine, the region is from 20 to 50 miles (32 to 80 kilometers) wide. The land rises from elevations near sea level in the east to about 2,000 feet (610 meters) in the west. The Aroostook Plateau lies in the northeasternmost part of the region. The plateau's deep fertile soil is good for agriculture. Farmers there grow the country's second largest potato crop. Many lakes dot the Eastern New England Upland south of the Aroostook Plateau. Swift streams also flow through this area. Most of them are fed by springs and by melted snow. Mountains cut through the center of the region.

Fields of Potatoes thrive in the deep fertile soil of Aroostook County. This area is part of Maine's Eastern New England Upland region, which extends from the Canadian border to Connecticut.

Fort Knox State Park, *above,* is near Bucksport in the Coastal Lowlands. The land in this region varies. Sandy beaches and high cliffs line the shore, and salt marshes lie inland.

The White Mountains Region covers northwestern Maine and part of New Hampshire and Vermont. In Maine, the region is about 5 miles (8 kilometers) wide in the north and 30 miles (48 kilometers) wide in the south. This region includes hundreds of lakes and most of Maine's highest mountains. The mountains are an extension of New Hampshire's White Mountains. A series of *eskers* (also called *kames, horsebacks,* or *hogbacks*) covers part of the White Mountains Region. These long, low gravel ridges vary from 1 to 150 miles (1.6 to 241 kilometers) long. The eskers were formed during the Ice Age by streams that flowed beneath the glaciers.

Coastline of Maine has many deep harbors and thousands of bays, coves, and inlets. Measured in a straight line, the coastline totals 228 miles (367 kilometers). But if all the area washed by water is measured, the coastline totals 3,478 miles (5,597 kilometers).

Mountains. Mount Katahdin, Maine's highest peak, rises 5,268 feet (1,606 meters) in the central part of the state. Nine other mountains are more than 4,000 feet (1,200 meters) high, and 97 others are over 3,000 feet (910 meters) high. Most of the mountains are forested and look green all year long. Cadillac Mountain towers 1,530 feet (466 meters) on Mount Desert Island. It is the highest point on the Atlantic coast between Labrador, Canada, and Rio de Janeiro, Brazil.

Rivers and Lakes. Maine has more than 5,000 rivers and streams. Two of the chief rivers, the Androscoggin and the Saco, begin in New Hampshire. They flow across southern Maine and empty into the Atlantic Ocean. Two other important rivers, the Kennebec and the Penobscot, rise in lakes of north-central Maine. They wind down the center of the state, and empty into coastal bays. The St. Croix River forms the southern part of the border between Maine and New Brunswick. In northern Maine, the Saint John River also is part of the border with New Brunswick. The Saint John is the longest river in the northern part of the state.

Many of Maine's more than 2,500 lakes and ponds gleam like blue gems among dark forests. Moosehead, the largest lake, covers about 120 square miles (311 square kilometers) in the west-central part of the state. Other large lakes in Maine include the Belgrades, the Grands, the Rangeley, and the Sebago.

Mount Katahdin, *below,* is the highest point in Maine. It rises 5,268 feet (1,606 meters) near the center of the state. Mount Katahdin is one of many tall rugged peaks that add beauty to Maine and help make it a favorite recreation center.

MAINE/Climate

Maine has cooler weather than most of the rest of the United States. Arctic air and coastal winds keep the state from being warmed by Gulf Stream air. This makes Maine winters colder than winters in many places that are as far north. Maine has few hot summer days.

Maine's temperature averages 24° F. (−4° C) in January and 67° F. (19° C) in July. The state's record low temperature, −48° F. (−44° C), was set in Van Buren on Jan. 19, 1925, and the record high, 105° F. (41° C), was set in North Bridgton on July 10, 1911.

Maine's yearly *precipitation* (rain, melted snow, and other forms of moisture) averages about 43 inches (109 centimeters). The annual snowfall varies from about 70 inches (180 centimeters) near the coast to about 100 inches (250 centimeters) in the interior.

Maine Dept. of Commerce and Industry

Heavy Winter Snow blankets Sugarloaf Mountain near Kingfield. Low temperatures keep the snow in ideal condition for skiing.

SEASONAL TEMPERATURES

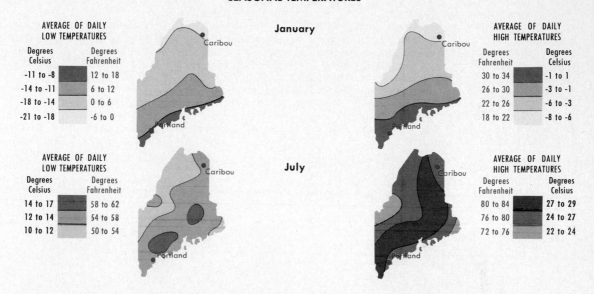

AVERAGE OF DAILY LOW TEMPERATURES — January

Degrees Celsius	Degrees Fahrenheit
-11 to -8	12 to 18
-14 to -11	6 to 12
-18 to -14	0 to 6
-21 to -18	-6 to 0

AVERAGE OF DAILY HIGH TEMPERATURES — January

Degrees Fahrenheit	Degrees Celsius
30 to 34	-1 to 1
26 to 30	-3 to -1
22 to 26	-6 to -3
18 to 22	-8 to -6

AVERAGE OF DAILY LOW TEMPERATURES — July

Degrees Celsius	Degrees Fahrenheit
14 to 17	58 to 62
12 to 14	54 to 58
10 to 12	50 to 54

AVERAGE OF DAILY HIGH TEMPERATURES — July

Degrees Fahrenheit	Degrees Celsius
80 to 84	27 to 29
76 to 80	24 to 27
72 to 76	22 to 24

AVERAGE YEARLY PRECIPITATION
(Rain, Melted Snow and Other Moisture)

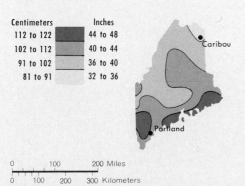

Centimeters	Inches
112 to 122	44 to 48
102 to 112	40 to 44
91 to 102	36 to 40
81 to 91	32 to 36

0   100   200 Miles
0   100   200   300 Kilometers

WORLD BOOK maps

AVERAGE MONTHLY WEATHER

	CARIBOU					PORTLAND				
	Temperatures				Days of Rain or Snow		Temperatures			Days of Rain or Snow
	F° High	Low	C° High	Low			F° High	Low	C° High	Low	
JAN.	18	-1	-8	-18	14	JAN.	31	11	-1	-12	12
FEB.	20	0	-7	-18	13	FEB.	32	11	0	-12	11
MAR.	31	13	-1	-11	12	MAR.	41	22	5	-6	11
APR.	43	26	6	-3	13	APR.	52	32	11	0	12
MAY	59	38	15	3	13	MAY	63	42	17	6	13
JUNE	69	48	21	9	14	JUNE	73	51	23	11	12
JULY	75	54	24	12	14	JULY	79	57	26	14	9
AUG.	72	51	22	11	12	AUG.	77	55	25	13	9
SEPT.	63	43	17	6	11	SEPT.	70	47	21	8	8
OCT.	51	33	11	1	11	OCT.	60	37	16	3	8
NOV.	36	22	2	-6	13	NOV.	47	28	8	-2	11
DEC.	22	7	-6	-14	14	DEC.	35	16	2	-9	11

Manufacturing is Maine's most important economic activity. The tourist industry ranks second, followed by agriculture. The southwest is Maine's chief manufacturing center. About 12 million tourists visit Maine annually and contribute about $1 billion to the state's economy. Farms thrive in southern Maine and in Aroostook County.

Natural Resources of Maine include forests, swift rivers and streams, fertile soils, and mineral deposits.

Soil in Maine ranges from sand in the coastal area to rich loams in the potato-growing districts of Aroostook County and other regions. Clay soils cover much of Maine's lowlands. These soils once supported many small farms. But most of the farms have been abandoned or made into tree farms. Gravelly soils are common at Maine's higher elevations. These soils once supported farms. But they are not well suited to crops, and have been largely abandoned since 1930.

Minerals. Central Maine has many granite and limestone deposits, but few of them are mined. Slate deposits lie near Brownville and Monson. Tourmaline, a gemstone that is Maine's state mineral, is found in southwestern Maine. Aroostook County has one of the country's largest reserves of low-grade manganese and iron ore. Other Maine minerals include brick clay, copper, mica, peat, sand and gravel, and zinc. Most mines are on the coast.

Forests cover about 18 million acres (7.3 million hectares) in Maine, or about 90 per cent of the total land area. The forests supply the raw material for many manufactured products of Maine. Private companies and individuals own nearly all of Maine's forest land. Until the late 1700's, the white pine tree was Maine's greatest resource. It was used mainly to make masts for ships. By the mid-1800's, the pines had been cut down throughout the state. Today, most of Maine's many pine trees are second-growth trees. Other valuable trees include the balsam fir, basswood, beech, hemlock, maple, oak, spruce, and white and yellow birch.

Plant Life. The speckled alder, a common shrub, thrives in Maine's swamps and pastures. Witch hazel borders much of the state's forest land. Chokeberries, shadbush, sumac, and thorn apples grow along country roads and farm fences, and in old cellar holes. Blueberry bushes carpet the ground in much of Hancock and Washington counties and in a few other areas.

Maine's most common wild flowers are the anemone, aster, bittersweet, black-eyed Susan, buttercup, goldenrod, harebell, hepatica, Indian pipe, orange and red hawkweed, white oxeye daisy, and wild bergamot. The delicate mayflower and the lady's-slipper are found scattered through many of Maine's wooded areas. Jack-in-the-pulpit, knotgrass, lavender, and wild lily of the valley grow along the coast and many lakeshores.

Animal Life. Bobcats and black bears are found in several areas of Maine, particularly in the northern and

FARM, MINERAL, AND FOREST PRODUCTS

This map shows where the state's leading farm, mineral, and forest products are produced. The major urban areas (shown on the map in red) are the state's important manufacturing centers.

WORLD BOOK map

Maine Dept. of Commerce and Industry

Lobsterman removes a day's catch from his traps near Deer Isle. Maine leads all the states in the amount of lobsters caught—about 18½ million pounds (8.4 million kilograms) annually.

A Papermaking Machine in a Bucksport plant makes paper used for catalogs and magazines. The production of paper and related products is Maine's leading manufacturing activity.

western woods and mountains. Other fur-bearing animals of the forests include beavers, foxes, lynxes, martens, minks, raccoons, and skunks.

Game animals are found in almost every part of Maine. They include rabbits, squirrels, and white-tailed deer. Deer are Maine's leading attraction for hunters. Moose live in isolated areas.

More than 320 kinds of birds live in Maine. The most common ones are buntings, chickadees, grackles, owls, sparrows, swallows, thrushes, and wrens. Ducks, gulls, loons, and other sea birds live on the coastal islands. In early spring and late fall, thousands of migratory ducks and geese congregate at Merrymeeting Bay, where the Androscoggin and Kennebec rivers meet.

Maine's most common game fishes in lakes and streams are brook trout, landlocked salmon, and small-mouth bass. Other fishes include bass, white and yellow perch, and pickerel. Every spring, thousands of alewives swim up the coastal rivers to lay their eggs. Then they return to the ocean. Atlantic salmon are found in the Dennys, Machias, and other rivers. Fishes in Maine's coastal waters include cod, flounder, hake, mackerel, pollack, striped bass, and tuna.

Manufacturing accounts for 82 per cent of the value of goods produced in Maine. Goods manufactured there have a *value added by manufacture* of about $2\frac{1}{3}$ billion a year. This figure represents the value created in products by Maine industries, not counting such manufacturing costs as materials, supplies, and fuel.

Paper Products, which include cardboard boxes, paper bags, and pulp, as well as paper, are Maine's leading manufactured products. These products have a value added of about $680 million yearly. The manufacture of paper ranks as Maine's most important industry. There are large paper and pulp mills in Augusta,

Production of Goods in Maine

Total value of goods produced in 1977—$2,875,723,000

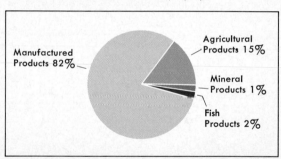

Manufactured Products 82%

Agricultural Products 15%

Mineral Products 1%

Fish Products 2%

Percentages are based on farm income, value added by manufacture, and value of fish and mineral production.

Sources: U.S. government publications, 1978-1979.

Employment in Maine

Total number of persons employed in 1978—418,300

		Number of Employees
Manufacturing	🚶🚶🚶🚶🚶🚶🚶🚶🚶🚶	110,700
Wholesale & Retail Trade	🚶🚶🚶🚶🚶🚶🚶🚶	89,300
Government	🚶🚶🚶🚶🚶🚶🚶	81,500
Mining & Community, Social, & Personal Services	🚶🚶🚶🚶🚶🚶	70,300
Construction	🚶🚶	19,100
Transportation & Public Utilities	🚶🚶	18,100
Finance, Insurance, & Real Estate	🚶🚶	15,800
Agriculture	🚶	13,500

Sources: *Employment and Earnings*, May 1979, U.S. Bureau of Labor Statistics; Maine Department of Manpower Affairs.

Brewer, Bucksport, East Millinocket, Hinckley, Jay, Lincoln, Madawaska, Millinocket, Rumford, Topsham, Waterville, Westbrook, and Woodland. The Great Northern Paper Company, with factories in Millinocket and East Millinocket, is one of the nation's largest producers of newsprint. Spruce and fir trees provide most of the wood used in the paper and pulp industries.

Leather Products in Maine have a value added of about $285 million a year. Leather products factories employ more workers than any other single industry. Footwear is made in Bangor, Belfast, Farmington, Gardiner, Livermore Falls, Norridgewock, North Jay, Old Town, Skowhegan, Wilton, and many other towns.

Lumber and Wood Products have a value added of about $270 million a year. Sawmills in Maine turn out about 1 billion board feet (2.4 million cubic meters) of lumber and about 358 million cubic feet (10 million cubic meters) of pulpwood a year. Maine's toothpick production, about 125 million a day, is the largest in the nation. Other wood products include boxes, canoes, clothespins, fencing, furniture, ice cream sticks, lobster traps, matches, skis, splints, toys, and wood flour. Many Maine fir trees are cut each year for Christmas trees.

Food Products in Maine have a value added of about $219 million a year. Maine is an important food canning and food freezing state. Blueberries, chicken, and French fried potatoes are the chief frozen foods processed in the state. Maine leads the states in the number of sardines packed each year. Maine factories also pack other fish and such shellfish as clams, lobsters, scallops, and shrimps. Other processed foods include apple juice, beans, cucumbers, pumpkins, and squash. The Aroostook County, Eastport-Lubec, and Portland areas are centers of Maine's food processing industry.

Textiles. Maine's textile industry has gradually declined since the 1920's. But the industry still plays an important part in the state's economy. Cotton mills are located in Augusta, Biddeford, and Lewiston. Woolen mills operate in the communities of Guilford, Kezar Falls, Lisbon, Oakland, Waterville, and Winthrop.

Other Industries. The production of nonelectric machinery, electric and electronic equipment, and transportation equipment is also important in Maine. Maine has many small, thriving boatyards that build fishing and sailing craft. Blue Hill, Camden, East Boothbay, Mount Desert, South Bristol, Southwest Harbor, and Thomaston are the leading boat-building areas. The Bath Iron Works in Bath is one of the nation's largest shipbuilders.

Agriculture. Farm products account for 15 per cent of the value of goods produced in Maine. Maine has a yearly farm income of about $425 million. The state's 7,600 farms average about 216 acres (87 hectares) in size. About 5,000 farms are full-time commercial farms, and the rest are worked only part time.

Livestock and Livestock Products account for about two-thirds of the income of Maine farmers. Eggs are the leading livestock product, earning about $99 million a year. Maine farmers raise about 76 million broiler chickens worth about $84 million yearly. Dairy products, chiefly milk, earn about $68 million annually. Maine farmers also raise beef cattle, hogs, lambs, sheep, and turkeys.

Potatoes, Maine's single most valuable farm product, earn about $115 million a year. Only Idaho, Washington, and Oregon grow more potatoes than Maine. Most of Maine's 2¾-billion-pound (1.2-billion-kilogram) annual potato crop comes from Aroostook County. Large amounts of potatoes also come from Cumberland, Oxford, and Penobscot counties.

Other Field Crops. Oats are an important field crop in Maine. Many farmers rotate oats and potatoes to keep soil fertile. Hay, which was once an important commercial product, is now raised chiefly as cattle feed. Many farmers also grow corn to feed cattle. Other crops include dry beans, peas, and sugar beets.

Fruits. Apples, Maine's most valuable fruit, are grown chiefly in Androscoggin, Cumberland, Franklin, Ken-

Penobscot Shoe Co., Old Town, Maine

Shoe Manufacturing ranks as a leading industrial activity of Maine. Leather products factories employ more workers than any other industry in the state. Many communities throughout Maine produce shoes and other kinds of footwear.

nebec, Oxford, and York counties. The chief varieties are Cortland, Delicious, McIntosh, and Northern Spies. Other Maine fruits include blueberries, pears, plums, raspberries, and strawberries.

Fishing Industry. Maine's annual fish catch is valued at about $62 million. Maine is a leading state in the value of fish and shellfish caught. Its yearly lobster catch, which totals about 18½ million pounds (8.4 million kilograms), is the largest of any state. The fish catch also brings in valuable amounts of bloodworms, clams, cod, flounder, ocean perch, pollock, and sea herring. Portland and Rockland are the most important fishing ports in Maine. Almost every community along the coast has at least a small fleet of fishing boats.

Mining brings in about $42 million a year. Sand and gravel are the state's most valuable minerals, earning about $16 million annually. The leading producers of sand and gravel include Aroostook, Cumberland, Kennebec, Penobscot, and Sagadahoc counties. Another of Maine's valuable minerals is zinc, which earns about $5 million a year.

Maine has over a hundred granite quarries, but only a few of them are worked today. The most important ones are in southern and coastal Maine. Other products mined in the state include limestone, clays, copper, lead, peat, and stone. Beryl and other gemstones are also mined in Maine. Many specimens of green and pink tourmaline have been collected in Androscoggin, Oxford, and Sagadahoc counties.

Electric Power. About 65 per cent of Maine's electricity comes from nuclear power plants. Hydroelectric power plants generate about 25 per cent of the electricity produced in the state. The majority of the hydroelectric plants are on the Androscoggin, Kennebec, Penobscot, and Saco rivers. The rest of the state's electricity comes from plants that burn oil.

Transportation. Maine began developing good roads during the early 1800's. Today, the state has about 22,-000 miles (35,400 kilometers) of roads and highways, most of which are surfaced. The Maine Turnpike runs about 100 miles (160 kilometers) between York and Augusta. U.S. Interstate Highway 95 extends the turnpike from Augusta to Houlton, near the Canadian border. U.S. Highway 1 follows the coast of Maine.

Maine's first railroad was built in 1836 to carry lumber between Bangor and Old Town. Railroads in the state now operate on about 1,800 miles (2,900 kilometers) of track. The Maine Central Railroad operates on about 750 miles (1,210 kilometers) of track, and the Bangor and Aroostook Railroad has about 535 miles (861 kilometers) of track. Neither of these freight railroads provides passenger service. The Canadian Pacific Railroad is the only passenger line that serves Maine. It links five Maine cities with Canadian cities.

Delta Air Lines provides Maine's chief air passenger and airmail service. Air Canada, the main Canadian airline, also serves Maine. Maine has about 50 public airports and about 110 private airports.

Large ocean-going vessels can dock at some Maine ports. Portland and Searsport have the state's busiest docks. Portland is 116 miles (187 kilometers) nearer to Europe than any other large U.S. port. The State Pier at Portland is 1,000 feet (300 meters) long. It has 1½ miles (2.4 kilometers) of track, and can hold as many as 110 freight cars. Ferries operate between both Portland and Bar Harbor, Me., and Yarmouth, N.S.

Communication. Maine has 8 daily newspapers and about 40 weeklies. The *Bangor Daily News* has the largest circulation of the dailies. The Gannett newspaper chain publishes the *Kennebec Journal* in Augusta, the *Central Maine Morning Sentinel* in Waterville, the *Portland Press Herald*, the *Portland Express*, and Maine's only Sunday paper, the *Maine Sunday Telegram* in Portland. The *Falmouth Gazette*, Maine's first paper, began in Falmouth (now Portland) in 1785.

Maine's first radio station, WABI, began operating in Bangor in 1924. The state's first television station, WABI-TV, started broadcasting in 1953, also from Bangor. Today, about 85 radio stations and 12 television stations operate in the state.

HISTORIC MAINE

Northern Boundary with Canada was fixed by treaty in 1842. Earlier border disputes, called the Aroostook War, centered around Fort Kent.

Maine Entered the Union in 1820 as a free state (without slaves). Its admission was part of the Missouri Compromise.

In 1775, Benedict Arnold led an American army through the Kennebec Valley into Canada to attack Quebec.

Invention of the Doughnut Hole in 1847 by Captain Hanson Gregory is still commemorated at Camden.

Massachusetts Bought Maine for about $6,000 in 1677 from the heirs of Ferdinando Gorges, who had received the land as a gift in 1622.

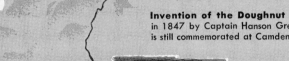

Shipbuilding became Maine's first industry. The first ship built by English colonists in America was launched on the Kennebec River in 1607.

Machias ●

An Early Sawmill was established near York in 1634. York (then called Gorgeana) became the nation's first incorporated English city in 1641.

★ AUGUSTA

Camden ●

The First Naval Battle of the Revolutionary War was fought off Machias in 1775, when patriots captured the British armed schooner *Margaretta*.

● Portland

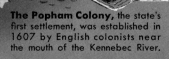

The Popham Colony, the state's first settlement, was established in 1607 by English colonists near the mouth of the Kennebec River.

● York
● Kittery

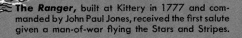

The *Ranger*, built at Kittery in 1777 and commanded by John Paul Jones, received the first salute given a man-of-war flying the Stars and Stripes.

Indian Days. Thousands of Indians lived in what is now Maine before white settlers came. The Indians belonged to the Abnaki and Etchemin tribes of the Algonkian Indian family. The Abnaki lived west of the Penobscot River, and the Etchemin lived east of the river. The Indians had villages, but often moved in search of food. Their enemy, the Iroquois, frequently raided their villages. Maine Indians lived in peace with the earliest white settlers.

Exploration and Settlements. Vikings, led by Leif Ericson, probably visited Maine about A.D. 1000. Many historians believe that John Cabot, an Italian sea captain in the service of England, reached Maine in 1498. France sent many explorers to Maine. These explorers and the dates they reached Maine included Giovanni da Verrazano (1524), Pierre du Guast, Sieur de Monts (1604), and Samuel de Champlain (1604). Champlain explored and named Mount Desert, the largest island along Maine's coast.

In 1605, Sir Ferdinando Gorges and Sir John Popham, two wealthy Englishmen, sent George Waymouth to explore the Maine coast. Waymouth's favorable reports about the area led Gorges and Popham to attempt a settlement in Maine. In 1607, they financed a group of colonists who established Popham Plantation, near the mouth of the Kennebec River. Cold weather and other hardships forced the settlers to return to England in 1608. While in Maine, the settlers built a boat called the *Virginia*. It was the first boat built by English colonists in America. The English made many permanent settlements in Maine during the early 1620's. Perhaps the first one was the settlement made near present-day Saco in 1623.

Ownership Disputes developed over Maine during the 1600's. In 1622, the Council for New England, an agency of the English government, gave Ferdinando Gorges and John Mason a large tract of land in present-

day Maine and New Hampshire. The land was divided between the two men in 1629, and Gorges received the Maine section. Gorges established Maine's first government in 1636. In 1641, he made the community of Gorgeana (now York) a city. It was the first chartered English city in what is now the United States.

After Gorges died in 1647, the people of Kittery, Wells, and York united under a new government. Between 1652 and 1658, they and the people of Casco Bay,

Fort Popham Memorial is a brick and granite fortification begun in 1861 but never completed. Troops were stationed there as late as World War I. The fort stands near Popham Beach, where the first English settlement in Maine was established in 1607.

Maine Dept. of Commerce and Industry

Maine Dept. of Commerce and Industry

Kennebunk, Saco, and Scarborough agreed to make Maine a part of the Massachusetts Bay Colony. In 1660, the heirs of Gorges disputed Massachusetts' ownership of Maine, and claimed Maine for themselves. In 1664, an English board of commissioners ordered Maine restored to the Gorges family. Massachusetts finally gained clear title to Maine in 1677, when it bought the area from the Gorges family for about $6,000.

French and Indian Wars were fought in Maine and the rest of New England off and on from 1689 to 1763. The French and their Indian allies battled to gain control of the area from the English colonists. William Pepperell of Maine led the capture of a French fort at Louisbourg, Nova Scotia, in 1745. The capture was one of the major events of the war. The wars ended with the Treaty of Paris in 1763. The treaty ended all French claims to Maine and most of the rest of North America.

The Revolutionary War. During the 1760's, Great Britain passed a series of laws that caused unrest in Maine and the rest of colonial America. Most of these laws either imposed severe taxes or restricted colonial trade. In 1774, a group of Maine patriots burned a supply of British tea stored at York. This event, called the *York Tea Party*, resembled the more famous Boston Tea Party of 1773.

The Revolutionary War (1775-1783) started at Lexington and Concord, Mass. Hundreds of Maine patriots joined the colonists' fight for independence. The war brought great hardships to Maine towns. In 1775, British troops burned the town of Falmouth (now Portland) to punish the townspeople for opposing the king's policies.

The first naval battle of the Revolutionary War was fought off Machias in June, 1775. In the battle, a group of Maine patriots captured the British ship *Margaretta*. Also in 1775, Benedict Arnold and his troops made a long march from Augusta to Quebec. They tried to capture Quebec from the British, but were pushed back. British troops occupied Castine in 1779. Colonial troops tried to recapture the town, but were badly defeated.

Maine's population increased greatly after the war. Massachusetts rewarded its soldiers with gifts of land in Maine, and sold Maine land to other persons.

In the early 1800's, Maine's economy depended on its pine forests. Wood from the forests was used to build ships and many other products. It was also traded for a variety of goods. The Embargo Act of 1807, which limited U.S. trade with other countries, hurt Maine's thriving shipping industry. But the slowdown in shipping forced Maine to seek new income by developing its manufacturing industries.

Statehood. In 1785, a movement began for the separation of Maine from Massachusetts and for Maine's admission to the Union. Many people in Maine protested heavy taxation, poor roads, the long distance to the capital city of Boston, and other conditions. But before the War of 1812, most voters wanted Maine to remain a part of Massachusetts. The separation movement grew much stronger after the war. Many of those who favored separation won election to the legislature. They swayed many voters to their side. The people voted for separation in 1819, and Maine entered the Union as the 23rd state on March 15, 1820. William King became the first state governor, and Portland was the first capital of Maine. Augusta became the capital in 1832.

Maine's admission to the Union became involved in the Missouri Compromise. The compromise called for Maine to enter the Union as a *free state* (a state without slaves) and Missouri to enter the Union as a slave state. This arrangement kept the number of slave and free states equal. See MISSOURI COMPROMISE.

Ever since 1783, the boundary between Maine and New Brunswick had been disputed. The argument led to the so-called Aroostook War of 1839. The U.S. government sent General Winfield Scott to Maine, and he reached a temporary agreement with Canadian officials. No fighting took place. The boundary was finally set by the Webster-Ashburton Treaty of 1842. See WEBSTER-ASHBURTON TREATY.

In 1846, Maine became the first state to pass a law prohibiting the manufacture and sale of alcoholic beverages. But the law did not provide for effective enforcement. In 1851, the state passed a new law that effectively banned the production and sale of alcoholic beverages. This law remained in force until 1934.

Antislavery feelings grew strong in Maine during the

Published by Nathaniel Currier, 1855, The Mariners Museum, Eldredge Collection, Newport News, Va.

early 1830's. The state's Baptists and Congregationalists opposed slavery especially strongly. About 72,000 Maine men served with the Union forces during the Civil War (1861-1865). Hannibal Hamlin, a former U.S. Senator and governor of Maine, served as Vice-President of the United States during the war under President Abraham Lincoln.

Industrial Development increased greatly after the Civil War. The textile and leather industries were among those that grew at record rates. Farming activity and rural populations decreased as industry grew. During the 1890's, Maine began developing hydroelectric power on its swift-running rivers. Businessmen competed for the best power sites, and the state legislature acted to protect the state's power interests. In 1909, the Maine legislature outlawed the sale of hydroelectric power outside the state. The legislature wanted to keep the power in Maine to attract new industries. The law remained in force until 1955.

The Early 1900's. In 1907, Maine adopted an initiative and referendum law (see INITIATIVE AND REFERENDUM). The state adopted a direct primary voting law in

THE GOVERNORS OF MAINE

	Party	Term		Party	Term
William King	Democratic	1820-1821	Daniel F. Davis	Republican	1880-1881
William D. Williamson	Democratic	1821	Harris M. Plaisted	Democratic	1881-1883
Benjamin Ames	Democratic	1821-1822	Frederick Robie	Republican	1883-1887
Albion K. Parris	Democratic	1822-1827	Joseph R. Bodwell	Republican	1887
Enoch Lincoln	Democratic	1827-1829	S. S. Marble	Republican	1887-1889
Nathan Cutler	Democratic	1829-1830	Edwin C. Burleigh	Republican	1889-1893
Joshua Hall	Democratic	1830	Henry B. Cleaves	Republican	1893-1897
Jonathan Hunton	National		Llewellyn Powers	Republican	1897-1901
	Republican	1830-1831	John Fremont Hill	Republican	1901-1905
Samuel E. Smith	Democratic	1831-1834	William T. Cobb	Republican	1905-1909
Robert Dunlap	Democratic	1834-1838	Bert M. Fernald	Republican	1909-1911
Edward Kent	Whig	1838-1839	Frederick W. Plaisted	Democratic	1911-1913
John Fairfield	Democratic	1839-1841	William T. Haines	Republican	1913-1915
Edward Kent	Whig	1841-1842	Oakley C. Curtis	Democratic	1915-1917
John Fairfield	Democratic	1842-1843	Carl E. Milliken	Republican	1917-1921
Edward Kavanagh	Democratic	1843-1844	Frederic H. Parkhurst	Republican	1921
Hugh J. Anderson	Democratic	1844-1847	Percival R. Baxter	Republican	1921-1925
John W. Dana	Democratic	1847-1850	Ralph O. Brewster	Republican	1925-1929
John Hubbard	Democratic	1850-1853	William Tudon Gardiner	Republican	1929-1933
William G. Crosby	Whig	1853-1855	Louis J. Brann	Democratic	1933-1937
Anson P. Morrill	Republican	1855-1856	Lewis O. Barrows	Republican	1937-1941
Samuel Wells	Democratic	1856-1857	Sumner Sewall	Republican	1941-1945
Hannibal Hamlin	Republican	1857	Horace A. Hildreth	Republican	1945-1949
Joseph H. Williams	Republican	1857-1858	Frederick G. Payne	Republican	1949-1952
Lot M. Morrill	Republican	1858-1861	Burton M. Cross	Republican	1952-1955
Israel Washburn, Jr.	Republican	1861-1863	Edmund S. Muskie	Democratic	1955-1959
Abner Coburn	Republican	1863-1864	Robert Haskell	Republican	1959
Samuel Cony	Republican	1864-1867	Clinton Clauson	Democratic	1959
Joshua L. Chamberlain	Republican	1867-1871	John Reed	Republican	1959-1967
Sidney Perham	Republican	1871-1874	Kenneth M. Curtis	Democratic	1967-1975
Nelson Dingley, Jr.	Republican	1874-1876	James B. Longley	None	1975-1979
Seldon Connor	Republican	1876-1879	Joseph E. Brennan	Democratic	1979-
Alonzo Garcelon	Democratic	1879-1880			

Satellite Station near Andover is part of a worldwide communications system. This system includes the *Telstar* and *Early Bird* satellites. The station sends and receives signals, and tracks satellites as they orbit the earth. An inflated dome 161 feet (49 meters) high, *background*, covers an antenna. The control building, *foreground*, houses computing and tracking equipment.

American Telephone and Telegraph Co.

1911. This law gives Maine voters a voice in choosing candidates for state elections.

The number of small farms in Maine continued to decrease during the 1920's. Many large farms were started, especially in Aroostook County. These farms specialized in potato growing and in dairy and poultry products. Industrial growth also continued during the 1920's. However, some Maine textile mills moved to the South because of lower labor costs there. The state made up its loss with a greatly expanded paper and pulp industry. The Great Depression of the 1930's slowed Maine's economy. But conditions improved as the depression eased in the late 1930's.

The Mid-1900's. Margaret Chase Smith, a Maine Republican, won fame during the 1940's. She became the first woman elected to both houses of the U.S. Congress. Mrs. Smith served in the House of Representatives from 1940 to 1949 and in the Senate from 1949 to 1973.

During World War II (1939-1945), Maine mills and factories produced military shoes and uniforms. Shipyards in Bath and South Portland built cargo and combat vessels. After the war, the state legislature passed laws to encourage industry to come to Maine. These laws included reduced tax rates for new businesses. The highway system in the state was expanded, and many motels were built for Maine's growing tourist trade.

During the 1950's, Maine's economy was helped by the construction of Air Force bases in the state. Small-scale farming all but ended in Maine, and some of the state's oldest textile mills closed. Many small electronics companies were established during this period.

The state Department of Economic Development, established in 1955, and various community development groups helped bring new industries to Maine during the 1960's. Paper and pulp companies expanded, and Maine's food-processing industry also grew. Improved skiing facilities attracted thousands of winter tourists to the state.

Politically, most Maine voters remained Republicans. But the Democratic Party gained strength during the 1950's and 1960's. In 1955, Edmund S. Muskie became Maine's first Democratic governor since 1937. In 1958, he became the first Democrat ever elected to the United States Senate by Maine voters. In 1964, the Democrats won control of the state legislature. President Lyndon B. Johnson won Maine's electoral votes in 1964—the first time Maine voted for a Democratic presidential candidate in more than 50 years.

In 1966, the Republicans regained control of the state legislature. Muskie was the Democratic vice-presidential candidate in 1968. Maine supported him and presidential candidate Hubert H. Humphrey. In 1969, the Maine legislature approved state personal and corporate income taxes for the first time.

Maine Today is working to attract more people to live in the state and to bring in additional industries. Several developments indicate improvement for Maine's economy during the 1970's. Small farms in the state continue to decrease in number, but agriculture in general remains vital to Maine's economy. More plants are being built to process Maine potatoes, and the future of the state's broiler-chicken industry continues bright.

Paper and pulp manufacturing, the foundation of Maine's economy, is still expanding. Shoe and textile production contributes greatly to the economy, but both industries have been hurt by imported shoes and fabrics. An increase in the number of shrimp caught off the coast has boosted Maine's fishing industry, and tourism has become an important year-round operation in the state.

In 1974, James B. Longley became the first person to be elected governor of Maine without the endorsement of a major party. He received about 40 per cent of the votes, and his Democratic and Republican rivals split the rest.

V. PAUL REYNOLDS, JOSEPH M. TREFETHEN, and ROBERT M. YORK

Related Articles in WORLD BOOK include:

BIOGRAPHIES

Blaine, James G.	King (William)
Coffin, Robert P. T.	Longfellow, Henry W.
Fessenden, William Pitt	Muskie, Edmund S.
Gilbreth (family)	Reed, Thomas B.
Hamlin, Hannibal	Sewall, Arthur
Jewett, Sarah Orne	Smith, Margaret Chase

CITIES

Augusta	Bar Harbor	Lewiston	Presque Isle
Bangor	Bath	Portland	

HISTORY

Acadia	Missouri Compromise
Colonial Life in America	Webster-Ashburton Treaty
French and Indian Wars	

PHYSICAL FEATURES

Aroostook River	Passamaquoddy Bay
Kennebec River	Penobscot River
Mount Desert Island	Saint John River

OTHER RELATED ARTICLES

Acadia National Park	Portsmouth Naval Shipyard
Leather (graph)	Potato (graph)
New England	Saint Croix Island
Paper (graph)	National Monument

Outline

I. **Government**
  A. Constitution
  B. Executive
  C. Legislature
  D. Courts
  E. Local Government
  F. Taxation
  G. Politics

II. **People**

III. **Education**
  A. Schools
  B. Libraries
  C. Museums

IV. **A Visitor's Guide**
  A. Places to Visit
  B. Annual Events

V. **The Land**
  A. Land Regions
  B. Coastline
  C. Mountains
  D. Rivers and Lakes

VI. **Climate**

VII. **Economy**
  A. Natural Resources
  B. Manufacturing
  C. Agriculture
  D. Fishing Industry
  E. Mining
  F. Electric Power
  G. Transportation
  H. Communication

VIII. **History**

Questions

What caused the Aroostook War?
What is Maine's most popular historic site?
What was Maine's first industry?
What is the legend of Wedding Cake House?
When did the English first try to settle in Maine?
What is Maine's most important economic activity?
What is Maine's largest island?
In what way was Maine involved in the Missouri Compromise?
To what state did Maine belong before it joined the Union?
What man from Maine served as Vice-President of the United States?

Books for Young Readers

ANNIXTER, PAUL. *Swiftwater.* Farrar, 1950. Fiction.

BAILEY, BERNADINE. *Picture Book of Maine.* Rev. ed. Whitman, 1967.
CARPENTER, ALLAN. *Maine.* Rev. ed. Childrens Press, 1979.
CLIFFORD, HAROLD B. *Maine and Her People.* 4th ed. Bond Wheelwright, 1976.
FIELD, RACHEL. *Calico Bush.* Macmillan, 1931. Fiction.
FREEMAN, MELVILLE C., and PERRY, E. H. *The Story of Maine for Young Readers.* 2nd ed. Bond Wheelwright, 1976.
JEWETT, SARAH ORNE. *A White Heron: A Story of Maine.* Harper, 1963. Fiction. Reprint of a story written in 1886 which was originally published in author's *The Country of the Pointed Firs, and Other Stories.*
RICH, LOUISE D. *Three of a Kind.* Watts, 1970. Fiction.

Books for Older Readers

BANKS, RONALD F., ed. *A History of Maine: A Collection of Readings on the History of Maine, 1600-1970.* Kendall/Hunt, 1969.
BERCHEN, WILLIAM. *Maine.* Houghton, 1973.
CLARK, CHARLES E. *Maine: A Bicentennial History.* Norton, 1977.
FRANKLIN, LYNN. *Profiles of Maine.* Maine Antique Digest, 1976.
ISAACSON, DORRIS A., ed. *Maine: A Guide 'Down East.'* 2nd ed. Rockland, Maine Courier-Gazette, 1970. A rev. ed. in the Amer. Guide Series; it is also published by the Maine State Museum.
MAINE HISTORICAL SOCIETY. *The Maine Bicentennial Atlas: An Historical Survey.* The Society, 1976.
RICH, LOUISE D. *State O' Maine.* Harper, 1964. *The Coast of Maine: An Informal History and Guide.* Rev. ed. 1975.
SALTONSTALL, RICHARD. *Maine Pilgrimage: The Search for an American Way of Life.* Little, Brown, 1974.

MAINE, UNIVERSITY OF, is a coeducational, state-supported system of higher education. Its full name is the University of Maine System. It has campuses in Augusta, Farmington, Fort Kent, Machias, Orono, Portland-Gorham, and Presque Isle, Me. The Augusta campus grants associate's degrees. The Farmington, Fort Kent, Machias, and Presque Isle campuses offer bachelor's degrees. The Portland-Gorham campus, which is called the University of Southern Maine, grants bachelor's, master's, and professional degrees. It has a college of liberal arts, and schools of business and economics, education, law, and nursing. The Orono campus has colleges of arts and sciences, business administration, education, life sciences and agriculture, and technology. It offers bachelor's, master's, and doctor's degrees.

All the campuses of the university became the University of Maine System in 1968. For enrollment, see UNIVERSITIES AND COLLEGES (table).

Critically reviewed by the UNIVERSITY OF MAINE SYSTEM

MAINLAND is the name of two islands. See ORKNEY ISLANDS; SHETLAND ISLANDS.

MAINSPRING. See CLOCK (Mechanical Clocks); WATCH (Dial Watches; History).

MAINTENON, *man t'NAWN,* **MARQUISE DE** (1635-1719), FRANÇOISE D'AUBIGNÉ, became the second wife of Louis XIV of France in 1683. She had great influence over the king and in France until the death of Louis in 1715.

Madame de Maintenon was born in Niort, France. She married Paul Scarron, a crippled poet who was much older than she, in 1652. After he died in 1660, she became the governess of Louis XIV's children by his mistress, Madame de Montespan.

Louis grew to love and respect the governess more than the mistress. Six months after the death of the queen in 1683, he secretly married her. She was never officially recognized as the king's wife.

After her marriage to the king, Madame de Maintenon founded a school for girls at St. Cyr, where she retired after the king's death.　　　　RICHARD M. BRACE

See also LOUIS (XIV).

MAINZ, *mynts* (pop. 176,700), is the capital of Rhineland-Palatinate, a West German state. Mainz lies on the rising ground along the left bank of the Rhine River. For location, see GERMANY (political map).

Mainz was founded on the site of a Roman camp and is one of the oldest German cities. Mainz has chemical and cement factories, flour mills, and motor and locomotive plants. The city has been the seat of Johannes Gutenberg University since 1946.　　　JAMES K. POLLOCK

MAIPU, or MAIPO. See MOUNTAIN (table).

MAIR, CHARLES (1838-1927), was a Canadian journalist and poet. He was a reporter for *The Gazette* of Montreal, and helped found the "Canada First" movement which tried to stir up national feeling after the Dominion of Canada was formed. Rebels held him prisoner during the first Riel Rebellion (see CANADA, HISTORY OF [The Struggle for Unity]). He wrote *Dreamland and Other Poems* (1868), *Tecumseh, a Drama* (1886), and *Through the Mackenzie Basin* (1908). He was born in Lanark, Ont., and attended Queen's University, Kingston, Ont. He died in British Columbia.　　DESMOND PACEY

MAISONNEUVE, SIEUR DE. See MONTREAL (History).

MAITLAND, FREDERIC WILLIAM (1850-1906), an English historian, pioneered in the study of early English legal history. His scholarship produced much of what is known today about the history of Anglo-Saxon law. Maitland was able to sift through masses of contradictory and confusing evidence and find the truth. His important works include *History of the English Law* (1895), which he wrote with Frederick Pollack, and *Domesday Book and Beyond* (1897).

Maitland was born in London, and attended Eton school and Cambridge University. He studied law at Lincoln's Inn, one of the four famous "Inns of Court" in London, where lawyers lived and studied. He practiced law for several years, then became a professor of English law at Cambridge in 1888.　ROLAND N. STROMBERG

MAIZE, *mayz*, is common corn. It is sometimes called *Indian corn*. Field corn, or dent corn, is one kind of maize that is more widely grown than any of the other types. It is used for silage or for grain. The grain contains much starch and little sugar. Maize is widely used to feed livestock, and is of great importance in industry. Other types of maize, such as sweet corn and popcorn, are used primarily as food for man. In Great Britain and most other parts of the English-speaking world, *maize* is used to mean all forms of corn. See also CORN.

Scientific Classification. Maize is in the grass family, *Gramineae*. It is genus *Zea*, species *Z. mays*.　GUY W. MCKEE

MAJESTY. It was once believed that emperors, kings, and queens were too far above ordinary people to be spoken of or addressed simply by name. Instead of addressing a ruler simply as "King Charles," a person

said "Your Most Gracious Majesty." In this way, he could feel that he was speaking, not to the king as a person, but to the king's *majesty*, which meant his royal power or dignity.

The word *majesty* comes from the Latin *majestas*, meaning *greatness* or *grandeur*. In the Middle Ages, this title was given to the rulers who followed the Roman emperors. Later, it was applied to kings, and a distinction was made between *imperial* majesty and *royal*, or *kingly*, majesty.

Henry VIII was the first English ruler to claim the title of majesty. But the word *majesty* was not generally used until the time of the Stuart kings. Before that time, English kings were spoken of as "His Grace" or "His Highness." The king of Spain had the title "His Catholic Majesty." The king of France was called "His Most Christian Majesty."　　　　MARION F. LANSING

MAJLIS. See IRAN (Government).

MAJOLICA, *muh JAHL ih kuh*, or MAIOLICA, *muh YAHL ik kuh*, is a type of white-glazed pottery. The name probably comes from the Spanish island of Majorca in the Mediterranean Sea, a shipping point for Moorish lusterware that was exported to Italy. The word *majolica* was first used in the middle 1500's, and referred to a variety of white earthenware pottery decorated with bright colors. It now refers to wares more properly called *faïence*. They differ from earlier majolica in style, design, and technique (see FAÏENCE).

Examples of majolica include vases, jars, pitchers, plates, bowls, bottles, and flasks. The best majolica came from northeastern Italy. The earliest signed piece was dated 1489, but the art of majolica was lost by 1570. Since that time, craftsmen have been unable to reproduce the beauty of the old ware.　EUGENE F. BUNKER, JR.

See also POTTERY.

MAJOR. See RANK IN ARMED SERVICES.

MAJOR, in education. See CURRICULUM.

MAJOR AXIS. See ELLIPSE.

MAJOR GENERAL. See RANK IN ARMED SERVICES.

MAJOR LEAGUE. See BASEBALL.

MAJORCA, *muh JAWR kuh*, or MALLORCA, *may YAWR kuh* (pop. 460,030), is the largest island of the Balearic group. It lies a little more than 100 miles (160 kilometers) off the eastern coast of Spain and is a Spanish possession. The island has an area of about 1,400 square miles (3,626 square kilometers). Palma is the only large city. For location, see SPAIN (color map).

Farming is the chief occupation on Majorca. Products include almonds, figs, olives, oranges, and wine. The island also has limestone and marble quarries and some manufacturing.　　　RUPERT CLAUDE MARTIN

See also BALEARIC ISLANDS; MAJOLICA.

MAJORITY RULE is government by the larger number of citizens in a political unit. Under majority rule, the majority chooses officials and determines policies for the entire population. The candidate who receives the greatest number of votes wins an election. Here the term *majority* differs from the term *plurality*. A candidate with a majority receives more than half the votes cast. A candidate with a plurality receives more votes than any other candidate, but does not necessarily have a majority of the votes.

See also DEMOCRACY (Majority Rule and Minority Rights).

MAKALU, MOUNT. See MOUNT MAKALU.

MAKARIOS, ARCHBISHOP (1913-1977), a Greek Orthodox clergyman, became the first president of Cyprus in 1959. In July 1974, Cypriot troops led by Greek officers overthrew him, and he was forced to flee the country. He returned to Cyprus in December 1974 and served as president again until his death in 1977. While he was out of office, Turkish troops took over a large part of northeastern Cyprus. See CYPRUS (History).

Wide World

Archbishop Makarios

Makarios was elected bishop of Kitium in 1948. In 1950, he was elected archbishop and *ethnarch* (national leader) of the Greek Cypriots. He led the Greek Cypriot movement for independence from Britain and for *enosis* (union with Greece) during the 1950's. Britain exiled him to the Seychelles Islands in 1956, but freed him in 1957. Makarios was elected president after Britain agreed to independence for Cyprus.

Archbishop Makarios was born in Pano Panayia, Cyprus. His real name was Michael Mouskos. He entered a monastery at age 13. He later studied at the National University of Athens in Greece. He also studied theology in the United States.　　FRANCIS NOEL-BAKER

MAKEMIE, *muh KEHM ih,* or *muh KAYM ih,* **FRANCIS** (1658?-1708), a minister and a businessman, founded the first Presbyterian presbytery in America in Philadelphia in 1706. He was born near Rathmelton, County Donegal, Ireland. Makemie chose to be a minister, although Presbyterians were being persecuted in his homeland at the time. He became an ordained minister to the American Colonies. He traveled widely in America and also went to the West Indies. But he did his most important ministerial work on the eastern shore of Maryland and Virginia, where he founded a number of churches. He was prosecuted in New York colony in 1707 for preaching without a license, but won acquittal. This was an important victory for religious toleration in America.　　LEFFERTS A. LOETSCHER

MAKEUP. See THEATER (Makeup Techniques); COSMETICS.

MAKO SHARK. See SHARK (Kinds of Sharks; picture).

MALABO (pop. 40,000) is the capital and largest city of Equatorial Guinea. The city lies on Fernando Po, an island in the Gulf of Guinea. For location, see EQUATORIAL GUINEA (map).

Malabo is an important seaport. It handles such exports as bananas, cabinet woods, cacao, cinchona bark, coffee, kola nuts, and palm oil. Most of the city's people work for import-export companies. An airport lies near Malabo.

British businessmen and colonists founded the city in 1827. The British called it Clarencetown or Port Clarence. Spain took control of the city in 1844 and named it Santa Isabel. Malabo received its present name in 1973 after Equatorial Guinea had gained independence from Spain.　　IMMANUEL WALLERSTEIN

MALACCA. See MELAKA.

MALAGASY REPUBLIC

MALACCA, STRAIT OF, is a channel between the Malay Peninsula and the island of Sumatra. The strait connects the China Sea and the Indian Ocean. It is about 500 miles (800 kilometers) long and from 25 to 100 miles (40 to 160 kilometers) wide. The city of Singapore lies on Singapore Island at the southeastern end of the strait. See INDONESIA (map).

MALACHI, *MAL uh ky,* is the name given to the author and to the title of the last book of the Old Testament. The name means *my messenger.* Malachi is probably not the real name of the writer, but a title taken from chapter 3, verse 1, of the book itself. The book was probably written about 470 or 460 B.C. The people of Jerusalem were discouraged and were losing their religious faith. Malachi, a prophet, took up their questions and criticisms one by one, and answered that the fault lay with the people. They and their priests had grown careless in religion. If they would correct this, God was ready to bless them. Malachi spoke, too, about the return of Elijah, and the coming Day of the Lord, a day of triumph of good over evil.　　WALTER G. WILLIAMS

MALACHITE, *MAL uh kyt,* is a beautiful green copper ore. It consists of copper oxide, carbon dioxide, and water, and its chemical formula is $2CuO \cdot CO_2 \cdot H_2O$. Malachite is formed in layers that vary in color from apple green to dark gray-green (see MINERAL [picture]). It is used chiefly as an ornamental stone. Fine pieces of malachite are mined in the Ural Mountains of Russia and in Cornwall, England. Other sources of the ore include Africa, Australia, and Arizona.

In ancient times, people made bracelets of malachite because they thought it provided protection against disease, lightning, and witchcraft. Some scholars believe malachite is the stone that the Hebrews called *soham.* This stone was one of the sacred jewels in the high priest's breastplate.　　ROBERT H. CARPENTER

MALADJUSTMENT sometimes results when a person is unable to adapt to conditions in which he or she must live. The term means *bad adjustment.* In maladjustment, this failure may have damaged the person's own ability to act effectively, so it may not help merely to move somewhere else. The symptoms of the damage may be constant gloom, worry, and irritability. If these conditions become very serious, the person may need a psychiatrist's help to make a readjustment.

Many psychiatrists believe the real causes of maladjustment go back to training in early childhood. In later life, an especially important time for making adjustments is puberty.　　WILLIAM C. BEAVER

MÁLAGA, *MAL uh guh* or *MAH lah GAH* (pop. 411,-131), is a seaport and a manufacturing and resort center in Spain. It lies 65 miles (105 kilometers) northeast of Gibraltar, and is the capital of Málaga province. For location, see SPAIN (physical map).

Malaga wine is made in the city from Malaga grapes grown nearby. Exports include olives, olive oil, wine, raisins, lead, almonds, lemons, grapes, and esparto grass, used to make baskets and shoes. Factories produce cotton and linen goods, pottery, soap, chemicals, iron products, and sugar.

Málaga Cathedral was begun in the 1500's. The Phoenicians founded Málaga.　　STANLEY G. PAYNE

MALAGASY REPUBLIC. See MADAGASCAR.

MALAMUD, BERNARD (1914-   ), an American author, has written chiefly about Jews in the United States. His works often mix realism with supernaturalism, and humor with morality and sympathy for those who suffer. Malamud's novel *The Assistant* (1957) tells of a young man who robs a poor Jewish grocer. The young man returns to work for the grocer, and eventually saves the grocer from suicide and becomes a Jew himself. *The Fixer* (1966) is the story of an insignificant Jew in Czarist Russia who becomes, through persecution, a sort of hero. Malamud's other novels include *The Natural* (1952), *A New Life* (1961), and *The Tenants* (1971). His short stories have been published in *The Magic Barrel* (1954), *Idiots First* (1963), *Pictures of Fidelman* (1969), and *Rembrandt's Hat* (1973). Malamud was born in New York City.   PHILIP YOUNG

MALAMUTE. See ALASKAN MALAMUTE.

MALAR. See FACE.

MALARIA, *muh LAIR ee uh,* is a serious infectious disease of man. It occurs most often in tropical and subtropical countries. But it also occurs in temperate regions during summer months. The word *malaria* comes from two Italian words that mean *bad air*. People gave the disease this name because of its association with the musty, bad-smelling air of swamps.

Malaria ranks as a leading cause of death in many tropical regions of the world. About 1 million persons die of it every year. Malaria was common in the southern states before World War II. It has been wiped out in the United States, although many persons catch it while traveling in other parts of the world.

Cause. Malaria is caused by one-celled animals, called *protozoans*, of the genus *Plasmodium*. These animals are parasites. They spend part of their lives in the red blood cells of human beings, and part in female *Anopheles* mosquitoes. These mosquitoes carry and spread the malaria parasites. When an *Anopheles* mosquito bites a person who has malaria, it sucks up the blood cells that contain the parasites. The parasites de-velop and multiply in the mosquito's stomach, then move into its salivary glands or mouth parts. When the mosquito bites another person, it injects saliva containing the malaria parasites into the victim. The parasites enter the person's red blood cells. There they grow and burst the blood cells, causing anemia (see ANEMIA).

Symptoms. A person who has malaria suffers intense attacks of chills, fever, sweats, and great weakness. There are three kinds of malaria. The *falciparum*, or *estivo-autumnal*, type ranks as the most dangerous. In this type, fever and chills occur at irregular intervals. In the second type, *quartan* malaria, fever occurs about every 72 hours. In the most common type, *vivax*, or *tertian*, malaria, the fever often occurs every other day. Although vivax malaria is relatively mild, it causes much chronic illness. Persons with this type of malaria often have *relapses* (recurrent periods of fever).

Treatment. Doctors treat malaria with drugs that destroy the parasites. For centuries doctors used quinine to prevent and treat this disease. But during World War II, the supply of quinine from the East Indies was cut off. Scientists then developed new compounds that were even more effective than quinine. Among these were Atabrine, chloroquine, and primaquine. Some malaria parasites found recently cannot be checked with these drugs, and doctors are again using quinine.

Control and Prevention. Malaria may be controlled and prevented by destroying the *Anopheles* mosquitoes and their breeding places. This can be done by draining swamps and by spraying breeding places with oil or chemicals that destroy the larvae. But extensive drainage projects are impractical in many parts of the world. Therefore, scientists developed a highly effective control method based on killing infected mosquitoes. This method, now used throughout the world, depends on the use of insecticides and makes use of the habits of the mosquitoes as well. Many of these mosquitoes bite only when they are indoors at night. Immediately after biting, they usually seek rest on a nearby surface. People spray the walls and ceilings of rooms with insecticides such as DDT and dieldrin, which remain active a long time. When a mosquito rests on these surfaces, the insecticide destroys it. In some areas, mosquitoes have become resistant to commonly used insecticides.

Malaria in Animals. Malaria parasites also infect birds, lizards, and monkeys. The *Culex* mosquito carries the parasites that infect birds. Scientists have used these animals to learn about malaria in humans.

History. Many years ago, the Indians of Peru used the bark of the cinchona tree to treat malaria. But the study of the cause of malaria involved the work of many scientists. In 1880, the French scientist Charles Laveran discovered the protozoa that caused malaria. In 1898, Sir Ronald Ross, an English scientist, showed that certain mosquitoes infect birds with malaria. Soon afterward, Giovanni Grassi of Italy worked out the lifecycle of the human malaria parasite.   THOMAS H. WELLER

Related Articles in WORLD BOOK include:

Atabrine	Laveran,	Quinine
Cinchona	Charles L. A.	Ross, Sir Ronald
Insecticide	Mosquito	

MALASPINA GLACIER. See ALASKA (Glaciers); GLACIER (Famous Glaciers).

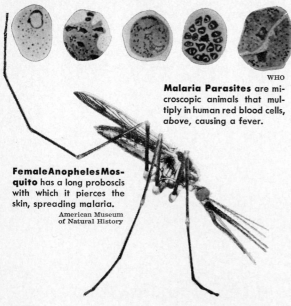

WHO

Malaria Parasites are microscopic animals that multiply in human red blood cells, above, causing a fever.

Female Anopheles Mosquito has a long proboscis with which it pierces the skin, spreading malaria.
American Museum of Natural History

Malawi

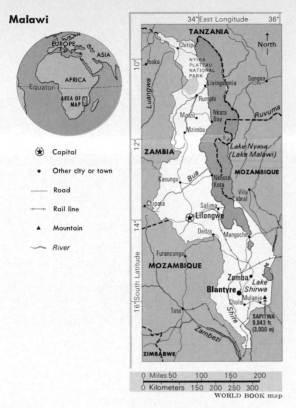

34°East Longitude 36°

TANZANIA

Chitipa

Isoka

NYIKA PLATEAU NATIONAL PARK

Livingstonia

Songea

Luangwa

Rumphi

Mzuzu

Nkata Bay

Ruvuma

Mzimba

ZAMBIA

Lake Nyasa (Lake Malawi)

Bua

Kasungu

MOZAMBIQUE

Nkhota Kota

Chipata

Vila Cabral

Salima

★ Lilongwe

Dedza

Mangoche

Furancungo

MOZAMBIQUE

Zomba

Lake Shirwa

Blantyre

Mulanje ▲

Tete

Cholo

Shire

SAPITWA 9,843 ft. (3,000 m)

Zambezi

ZIMBABWE

★ Capital
• Other city or town
— Road
┼─┼ Rail line
▲ Mountain
〜 River

| 0 Miles 50 | 100 | 150 | 200 |
| 0 Kilometers | 150 200 250 | 300 |

WORLD BOOK map

MALAWI, *muh LAH wee*, is a small scenic country in the eastern part of southern Africa. It is a country about 520 miles (837 kilometers) long and from 50 to 100 miles (80 to 160 kilometers) wide, an area slightly larger than the state of Pennsylvania. Malawi lies on the western shore of Lake Nyasa, called Lake Malawi in that country.

Malawi is a farming country, but only about one-third of the land is suitable for agriculture. Mountains, forests, and rough pastures cover most of the country. Most of the people grow only enough food to feed their families. Malawi has little industry, and thousands of the men go to neighboring countries to work. Most of them work in mines in South Africa, Zambia, and Zimbabwe. They send their earnings back to their families in Malawi.

The country takes its name from the Malawi group of people who settled there in the 1500's. Once the British protectorate of Nyasaland, it became independent in 1964. Lilongwe is the capital of Malawi, and Blantyre is the nation's largest city.

Government. Malawi is a republic, with a president as its head of state and chief executive. A Cabinet assists the president. The president appoints the members of the Cabinet. Under the constitution, the people elect the president to a five-year term. However, in

W. E. F. Ward, the contributor of this article, is the author of several books on Africa, and is former deputy educational adviser in the British Colonial Office.

1970, a constitutional amendment made Hastings Kamuzu Banda president for life. The people elect 60 of the 78 members of Malawi's parliament to five-year terms. The president appoints the remaining 18 members. The Malawi Congress Party is the country's only political party.

People. Most of Malawi's 6,268,000 persons are black Africans who live in small villages. In these rural areas, the people live in round or oblong houses that have mud walls and thatched roofs. Most of the people belong to Bantu tribes. The leading tribes are the Chewa (Cewa), Ngura, Nyanja, Yao, and Ngoni (Angoni). About 9,000 Europeans and about 14,000 Asians and persons of mixed origin also live in Malawi.

In most Western cultures, the father is the head of the family and descent is determined through him. But most Malawi tribes determine descent through the mother. Today, thousands of men go to neighboring countries to work for periods ranging from nine months to two years. While they are gone, the women farm to raise food for their families. *Maize* (corn) is their main food crop. The people grow sorghum and millet where the climate is unsuitable for maize.

By custom, the land belongs to the family. An individual can cultivate part of the land but cannot sell it or pass it down to his or her children. The land always remains the property of the entire family.

Chichewa and English are Malawi's official languages. Nyanja and Yao are the most popular languages in central and southern Malawi. Most of the people in northern Malawi speak Tumbuka.

Many of the Malawi tribes practice tribal religions. About 700,000 of the people are Christians, and about 500,000 are Muslims.

About 400,000 children attend primary schools, and about 4,500 attend the country's 17 secondary schools. Malawi relies heavily on Great Britain and the United States for the money and teachers to operate its schools. The government opened Malawi's first university at Zomba in 1965.

Land. Malawi is a land of great scenic beauty. Grassland and *savanna* (areas of coarse grass and trees) cover much of the land. The African Rift Valley runs the length of Malawi from north to south. Lake Nyasa fills most of the valley. It is 1,550 feet (472 meters) above sea level. The Shire River flows out of the southern end

---

FACTS IN BRIEF

Capital: Lilongwe.

Official Languages: Chichewa and English.

Form of Government: Republic.

Area: 45,747 sq. mi. (118,484 km²).

Population: *Estimated 1981 Population*—6,268,000; distribution, 91 per cent rural, 9 per cent urban; density, 137 persons per sq. mi. (53 persons per km²). *1977 Census*—5,571,567. *Estimated 1986 Population*—7,337,000.

Chief Products: *Agriculture*—coffee, cotton, hides and skins, peanuts, tea, tobacco, tung oil. *Manufacturing and Processing*—bricks, cement, cotton goods, furniture, soap.

Flag: The flag has black, red and green horizontal stripes, with a red rising sun on the black stripe. See FLAG (color picture: Flags of Africa).

Money: *Basic Unit*—kwacha. See MONEY (table).

79

of the lake to the Zambezi River. West of the lake, the land rises steeply to a plateau about 4,000 feet (1,200 meters) above sea level. Malawi's highest mountain, Sapitwa (9,843 feet, or 3,000 meters), rises on a plateau southeast of the Shire River.

The lowlands in the Shire Valley and along the lake have a hot, humid, tropical climate. The temperature in this area averages from 74° to 78° F. (23° to 26° C). The plateaus are much cooler, averaging about 58° F. (14° C) in higher areas and about 65° F. (18° C) in lower areas. The northern parts of the country average about 70 inches (180 centimeters) of rainfall a year. The southwestern parts get an average of only 30 inches (76 centimeters) a year.

Economy. Malawi is a poor country. It has no important mineral deposits. Its economy is based on agriculture, but only about a third of the land is suitable for farming. The most important export crop is tea, which is grown on estates in the highlands that are owned by Europeans. Important crops grown by Africans include tobacco, cotton, and peanuts. Many farmers raise livestock. Fishing on Lake Nyasa has also become an important industry. Malawi's few manufacturing industries produce such goods as soap, cotton goods, fishing nets, furniture, and bricks. Valuable hardwood forests cover the northwest part of the country, but they are too difficult for workmen to reach.

Malawi has nearly 6,000 miles (9,700 kilometers) of roads, but only about 500 miles (800 kilometers) are paved. A main road runs the length of the country, and Malawi has roads linking it with Tanzania, Zambia, and Zimbabwe. A railroad running down the Shire Valley connects Malawi with the Mozambique port of Beira on the Indian Ocean. An international airport near Blantyre provides air service to eastern and southern Africa.

History. The Malawi group of Bantu people entered what is now Malawi from the north in the 1500's. In the 1830's, two other Bantu tribes, the Ngoni and Yao, invaded the area. The Yao were slave-traders who sold slaves to the Arabs along the eastern coast of Africa.

The British missionary David Livingstone reached the area in 1859. He found it torn by tribal wars, and saw the suffering the slave-traders caused. Livingstone called for "commerce and Christianity" to bring peace to the area. In 1875, the Free Church of Scotland set up a mission that later became an important religious center. Scottish businessmen formed the African Lakes Corporation three years later to introduce lawful business instead of the slave trade. In 1889, the British made treaties with the tribal chiefs on the western shore of Lake Nyasa. Two years later, Britain proclaimed the territory as the Protectorate of Nyasaland.

In 1953, the British made the protectorate part of a federation with Northern and Southern Rhodesia, the Federation of Rhodesia and Nyasaland. The Africans living there opposed the creation of the federation, and protested strongly against it. After a British government study, the federation was dissolved in 1963. Hastings Kamuzu Banda, a physician educated in the United States, then became prime minister of a self-governing protectorate. In July, 1964, the protectorate became the independent nation of Malawi, a constitutional monarchy that recognized Queen Elizabeth II as queen of Malawi. In 1966, Malawi adopted a new constitution and became a republic, with Banda serving as president of the country. A constitutional amendment passed in 1970 made Banda president for life.   w. e. f. ward

See also Banda, Hastings K.; Lilongwe.

MALAY ARCHIPELAGO, also called the East Indian Archipelago or Malaysia, is in a part of the Pacific Ocean that contains the largest group of islands in the world. The equator runs through the middle of the group. The archipelago lies between southeastern Asia and Australia, and includes the Philippines, Indonesia (including the Moluccas and Lesser Sunda Islands), New Guinea, and smaller groups. The archipelago covers 1,108,099 square miles (2,869,963 square kilometers). For location, see the maps with Indonesia; Pacific Islands.

The islands have much fine, fertile soil. Oranges, mangoes, guavas, rice, corn, sugar, coffee, cacao, coconuts, sago, breadfruit, and yams flourish. Exports include *gutta-percha* (a substance similar to rubber), cam-

S. T. Darke, Three Lions

Mealtime in Malawi. Children dry fish before cooking them at a village near Nkhota Kota. Malawi fishermen use mosquito netting to catch thousands of these fish in Lake Nyasa.

phor, and other forest products. Several of the Malayan islands also contain deposits of gold, manganese, chromium, iron, sulfur, oil, tin, and phosphate rock.

Naturalists and other scientists have discovered much valuable scientific material in the islands. Their most famous find was the fossil bones of the Java man. Scientists believe he lived about 1½ million years ago (see JAVA MAN). About 205 million people live on the islands of the Malay Archipelago. Most of them belong to the Malaysian or Papuan racial groups. JOHN F. CADY

See also EAST INDIES.

MALAYA, *muh LAY uh,* is a region in Southeast Asia that covers the southern end of the Malay Peninsula. The region is occupied by West Malaysia, a part of the Federation of Malaysia. Malaya's location between the Bay of Bengal and the South China Sea makes the region an important trade and shipping center.

Malaya covers 50,806 square miles (131,588 square kilometers), almost three-fourths of the Malay Peninsula. Thick rain forests occupy most of the land. Mountains cross Malaya from north to south. Malaya's highest mountain, Gunong Tahan, rises 7,186 feet (2,190 meters) in the north-central part of the region.

Malaya has a population of about 10,600,000. About half the people are Malays (see MALAYS). Chinese and Indians make up most of the rest of the population.

During the late 1700's, Great Britain began to establish trading posts on the Malay Peninsula and nearby islands. The British gained control of Malaya during the 1800's and early 1900's. In 1948, the Federation of Malaya was established under British protection. Malaya gained independence in 1957. In 1963, it united with Sabah (formerly North Borneo), Sarawak, and Singapore to form the Federation of Malaysia. Singapore left the federation in 1965.   NORTON GINSBURG

See also MALAYSIA.

MALAYS, *MAY layz,* are a group of peoples of Southeast Asia. Most of them live in Indonesia, Malaysia, and the Philippines. The Malays belong to the Asian geographical race, which also includes the Chinese and Japanese.

The Malays spread out over the area several thousand years ago, and displaced such earlier populations as the Negritos, who still live in isolated places in the region. Rice and fish are the main staples of the Malays. The Malays have formed several new nations, including the Philippines, the Republic of Indonesia, and Malaysia. The term *Malay* may be applied to many of their languages.   FELIX M. KEESING

See also RACES, HUMAN (table: Geographical Races).

MALAYSIA, *muh LAY zhuh,* a country in Southeast Asia, is the world's leading producer of natural rubber and tin. The country's official name is the FEDERATION OF MALAYSIA. The federation was formed in 1963, when Malaya, Sabah (formerly North Borneo), Sarawak, and Singapore united. Singapore left the federation in 1965 after disagreements with the Malaysian government.

Malaysia covers the southern part of the Malay Peninsula and most of the northern part of the island of Borneo. The country consists of two regions, West Malaysia and East Malaysia. The region on the Malay Peninsula is West Malaysia, and the region on Borneo is East Malaysia. More than four-fifths of the people live in West Malaysia. West Malaysia and East Malaysia are separated by about 400 miles (644 kilometers)

James H. Pickerell

Kuala Lumpur is the capital and largest city of Malaysia. The city, like the country as a whole, has a variety of population groups, including Chinese, Indians, and Malays.

of the South China Sea. Malaysia covers an area slightly larger than New Mexico.

Most of the Malaysian people are Malays or Chinese (see MALAYS). Cultural differences between these two groups have caused political and social problems in Malaysia. About half the people live in rural areas.

Malaysia consists of 13 states and the federal territory of Kuala Lumpur. Eleven of the states once formed Malaya. They are Johor, Kedah, Kelantan, Melaka, Negeri Sembilan, Pahang, Perak, Perlis, Pulau Pinang, Selangor, and Terengganu. These states and the federal territory make up West Malaysia. The other states are Sabah and Sarawak, which make up East Malaysia.

───────── **FACTS IN BRIEF** ─────────

Capital: Kuala Lumpur.

Official Languages: English, Malay.

Form of Government: Constitutional monarchy (federation: 13 states, 1 federal territory).

Area: 127,316 sq. mi. (329,749 km²). *West Malaysia*—50,806 sq. mi. (131,588 km²). *East Malaysia*—76,510 sq. mi. (198,161 km²).

Elevation: *Highest*—Mount Kinabalu, 13,455 ft. (4,101 m) above sea level. *Lowest*—sea level, along the coast.

Population: *Estimated 1981 Population*—14,072,000; distribution, 51 per cent urban, 49 per cent rural; density, 111 persons per sq. mi. (43 per km²). *1970 Census*—10,413,524. *Estimated 1986 Population*—16,155,000.

Chief Products: *Agriculture*—copra, palm oil, pineapples, rice, rubber, timber. *Mining*—bauxite, iron, tin.

National Anthem: "Negara Ku" ("My Country").

Flag: A yellow crescent and star lie on a blue background in the upper left corner. The yellow is the color of royalty, and the blue stands for the unity of the Malaysian people. The crescent represents Islam. The star's 14 points and the flag's 14 red and white stripes symbolize Malaysia's 14 original states. See FLAG (picture: Flags of Asia and the Pacific).

Money: *Basic Unit*—ringgit (sometimes called Malaysian dollar). See MONEY (table: Exchange Rates).

Kuala Lumpur, the capital and largest city of Malaysia, forms the federal territory.

Government. The 13 states of Malaysia are united under the federal government, but each state has some independence. Nine of the states have princes called *rulers*. Every five years, the nine rulers elect a king from their number.

The king has few governing powers. The prime minister is the nation's chief executive. Malaysia has a Parliament made up of a Senate and a House of Representatives. The Senate's 58 members serve six-year terms. Each state legislature elects two senators, and the king appoints the others on the advice of the prime minister. The people elect the 144 members of the House of Representatives to five-year terms. All Malaysians who are 21 or older may vote. The National Front, a coalition of political parties controlled by Malays, is Malaysia's most powerful political group.

People. Malays, Chinese, and Indians form the largest groups in West Malaysia. In East Malaysia, a people called *Dyaks* make up the largest group in Sarawak (see DYAKS). The *Kadazans*, a people related to the Dyaks, form the largest group in Sabah.

About 45 per cent of the Malaysian people are Malays. Chinese make up about 35 per cent of the population. Most of the Malays are farmers who grow rice and other food for their own use. The majority of Malays are Muslims. Their religion, Islam, is Malaysia's official religion. Malays make up the most powerful group in Malaysian politics, but Chinese control much of the nation's economy. Many of the Chinese are bankers or merchants. Chinese own large shares of Malaysia's major industries. Most of the Chinese live in cities.

Indians make up about 10 per cent of Malaysia's population. Together, the Dyaks and Kadazans also make up about 10 per cent. Most of the Indians are Hindus. Many of them work on plantations. Most

Dyaks and Kadazans fish, hunt, and raise food for their own use. They practice local traditional religions.

The chief languages are Chinese, English, Malay, and Tamil, an Indian language. About three-fourths of the people can read and write. Most Malaysian children go to elementary school, but only about a third of these attend high school. About 8,000 students attend the University of Malaya in Kuala Lumpur.

Land and Climate. Low, swampy plains cover much of the East and West Malaysian coasts. The inland areas are mountainous and covered with forests. Mount Kinabalu, the highest peak, rises 13,455 feet (4,101 meters) in Sabah. Major rivers include the Kinabatangan in Sabah and the Rajang in Sarawak.

Malaysia has a tropical climate. Coastal temperatures stay between 70° and 90° F. (21° and 32° C). Mountain temperatures vary between 55° and 80° F. (13° and 27° C). About 100 inches (250 centimeters) of rain falls yearly in West Malaysia, and about 150 inches (381 centimeters) falls annually in East Malaysia.

Economy. About half the workers of Malaysia are employed in agriculture. Major farm products include coconut oil, *copra* (dried coconut), palm oil, pepper, pineapples, rice, and rubber. Malaysia produces almost half the world's natural rubber and almost a third of its tin. Malaysia also produces *bauxite* (the ore from which aluminum is made), iron ore, and timber. Less than 10 per cent of the work force have jobs in industry. Most of these industrial laborers work in plants that process such raw materials as rubber and tin.

Malaysia has about 10,000 miles (16,000 kilometers) of paved roads and about 1,300 miles (2,090 kilometers) of railroads. Georgetown and Port Swettenham are the nation's busiest ports. Georgetown, Kota Kinabalu, and Kuala Lumpur have international airports.

History. By A.D. 100, Malays lived in scattered settlements on the Malay Peninsula. The peninsula be-

Malaysia

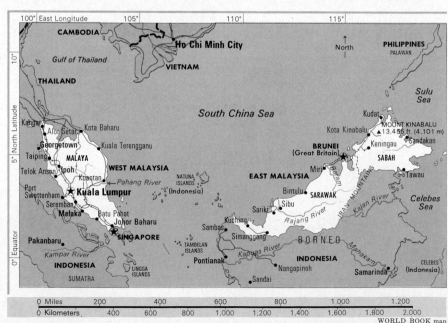

★ Capital

• Other City or Town

— Road

⊢— Rail Line

▲ MOUNTAIN

〰 River

WORLD BOOK map

came a crossroads in the trade between China and India. Indian traders brought Buddhism and Hinduism to the Malays. From the 800's to the 1400's, Buddhist and Hindu Malay kingdoms struggled for control of the peninsula. In the early 1400's, the prince of Melaka, a kingdom on the southwest coast, became a Muslim. As Melaka gained control over the surrounding area, Islam spread among the Malays.

The Portuguese captured Melaka in 1511, but they lost it to the Dutch in 1641. During the late 1700's, the British began to set up trading posts on the peninsula and nearby islands. In 1826, the British formed a colony made up of Melaka, the island of Pinang, and the island of Singapore. It was called the Colony of the Straits Settlements. During the 1800's and early 1900's, the British gained control of Sabah, Sarawak, and nine Malay states on the peninsula.

Japan conquered all Southeast Asia during World War II (1939-1945) but finally was defeated by the Allies. In 1948, the nine peninsula states, plus Melaka and Pinang, united to form the Federation of Malaya, under British protection. Singapore became a separate British colony. Malaya gained independence in 1957. Malaya, Sabah, Sarawak, and Singapore united in 1963 and formed the Federation of Malaysia. Disagreements soon arose between Singapore and the rest of Malaysia, and Singapore left the federation in 1965.

The Federation of Malaysia developed one of the strongest economies in Southeast Asia. Even so, the new nation faced many problems. Cultural differences led to friction, and sometimes violence, between the country's Malays and its Chinese. Malaysian Communists and other rebels engaged in guerrilla warfare against the government. Malaysia, like most other countries, experienced a severe *recession* (economic slump) in the early 1970's.

Abdul Rahman served as Malaysia's first prime min-

ister. Abdul Razak succeeded him in 1970. Under Abdul Razak's leadership, Malaysia took steps to close the economic gap between its poor people—chiefly Malays—and its wealthy Chinese. Abdul Razak died in 1976. Hussein Onn succeeded him.   NORTON GINSBURG

Related Articles in WORLD BOOK include:

Clothing (picture:	Malaya	Sarawak
Traditional	Melaka	Singapore
Costumes)	Rubber	(History)
Georgetown	(graph)	Straits
Kuala Lumpur	Sabah	Settlements
Kuching	Sandakan	Tin (graph)
Malacca, Strait of		

MALCOLM X (1925-1965) was a leader of a movement to unite black people throughout the world. He was assassinated in New York City on Feb. 21, 1965.

Frank Castoral, Photo Researchers
Malcolm X

His followers interpreted his death as a sacrifice for the "black revolution," and he quickly became a hero of that movement.

In 1946, Malcolm X was sentenced to prison in Massachusetts for burglary. While in prison, he adopted the beliefs of the Black Muslims, members of a religious movement which at that time believed in separation of the races. After his release from prison in 1952, Malcolm X became a leading spokesman for the Black Muslims. In 1964, following a disagreement with the leader of the Black Muslims, Malcolm X formed a rival group, the Organization of Afro-American Unity (OAAU). Malcolm was killed before the OAAU was firmly established. Three men, including two Black Muslims, were sentenced to life in prison for Malcolm's murder.

Malcolm X was born Malcolm Little in Omaha, Nebr. *The Autobiography of Malcolm X* was published in 1965.   C. ERIC LINCOLN

See also BLACK MUSLIMS.

MALDIVES, *mal DEEVZ,* is the smallest independent country in Asia and one of the smallest in the world. It consists of about 2,000 small coral islands that form a chain 475 miles (764 kilometers) long and 80 miles (129 kilometers) wide in the Indian Ocean. The northern tip of the Maldives is about 370 miles (595 kilometers) south of India. These green tropical islands cover a total land area of only 115 square miles (298 square kilometers), slightly greater than the area of Milwaukee, Wis. Milwaukee has about five times as many people.

The Maldivian people live a simple life that has changed very little for hundreds of years. Most of the men go out to sea daily to catch bonito and tuna.

Great Britain governed the Maldives as a protectorate for 78 years. The islands became independent in 1965. The country's official name in Divehi, the official language, is DIVEHI RAAJJE (REPUBLIC OF MALDIVES). Male, the capital, has 15,000 people.

Government. The Maldives is a republic. The president, who is head of the government, is elected to a

Harrison Forman
Workers in a Malaysian Tin Factory prepare bars of tin for export. Malaysia ranks as the world's leading producer of tin, and the valuable metal is one of the country's chief exports.

Maldives

⊛ **Capital**

▒ Shallow Water

▲ Highest Known Elevation

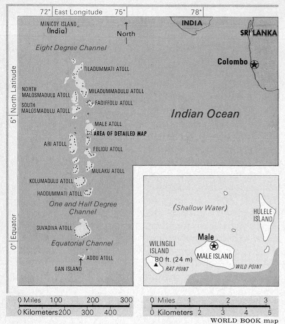

WORLD BOOK map

fish. They cook and smoke them over a fire. Most of the fish are exported to Sri Lanka. The people eat some of the fish. Their diet also includes coconuts, papayas, pineapples, pomegranates, and yams.

Land. The 2,000 small islands are grouped together in about 12 clusters called *atolls*. Barrier reefs around the atolls help to protect the islands from the sea.

None of the islands covers more than 5 square miles (13 square kilometers), and most are smaller than that. Most are like little platforms about 6 feet (1.8 meters) above sea level. An 80-foot (24-meter) elevation on Wilingili Island is the highest point. The islands have clear lagoons and white sand beaches. The land is covered with grass and low-growing tropical plants. Coconut palms and fruit trees grow on the islands.

The climate is hot and humid. Daytime temperatures average about 80° F. (27° C). The northern islands receive at least 100 inches (250 centimeters) of rain a year, and those in the south receive almost 150 inches (381 centimeters). Two *monsoons* (seasonal winds) blow over the islands each year and bring most of the rain.

Economy of the Maldives is based on the government-controlled fishing industry. The sale of dried fish in Sri Lanka is one of the chief sources of the government's income.

The people raise breadfruit, coconuts, papaya, pineapples, pomegranates, and yams. Women use the coconut husk fibers, called *coir*, to make yarn and ropes. The women also collect cowrie shells from the shores and weave reed mats. The men make lacquer ware. Dried fish is the Maldives' chief export. Other exports include coir yarn, *copra* (dried coconut meat), cowrie shells, and fish meal. Rice, sugar, and wheat flour are the major imports. Sri Lanka is the country's chief trading partner.

FACTS IN BRIEF

Capital: Male.

Official Language: Divehi.

Form of Government: Republic.

Head of State: President.

Legislature: The *Majlis* has 54 members who serve five-year terms. The president appoints 8 members; voters elect 46.

Local Government: An elected committee governs each atoll. Each inhabited island has a government-appointed *kateeb* (headman).

Political Divisions: 19 districts.

Total Land Area: 115 sq. mi. (298 km²). *Greatest Distances* —north-south, 550 mi. (885 km); east-west, 100 mi. (161 km).

Elevation: *Highest*—80 ft. (24 m) above sea level, on Wilingili Island. *Lowest*—sea level.

Population: *Estimated 1981 Population*—150,000; distribution, 86 per cent rural, 14 per cent urban; density, 1,303 persons per sq. mi. (503 persons per km²). *1974 Census*—128,697. *Estimated 1986 Population*—169,000.

Chief Products: *Agriculture*—breadfruit, coconuts, papaya, pineapples, pomegranates, yams. *Fishing*—bonito, tuna. *Handicrafts*—coir yarn, cowrie shells, lacquer ware, woven mats.

Flag: The flag has a white crescent on a dark green rectangle with a red border. The colors and the crescent on the flag stand for Islam. It was adopted in 1965. See FLAG (color picture: Flags of Asia and the Pacific).

Money: *Basic Unit*—rupee.

four-year term by the *Majlis* (legislature). A nine-member Cabinet assists the president. The 54 members of the Majlis serve five-year terms. The people elect 46 members, and the president appoints 8. An elected committee handles local government on each *atoll* (cluster of islands). The government appoints a *kateeb* (headman) for each island. A chief justice appointed by the president administers the laws. Law in the Maldives is based on the Sunni Muslims' code of law.

People. Most Maldivians are descendants of Sinhalese people who came from Sri Lanka. Some Maldivians are descendants of people from southern India and Arab traders and sailors. Almost all Maldivians belong to the Sunni Muslim sect.

Maldivians are small, slight, quiet people. They live on only about 210 of the country's islands. Most of them have just enough food for their families. They *barter* (trade) for other things they need.

Maldivian men go to sea every day in thousands of boats to catch fish. They build their boats of coconut or other timber that grows there. Most of the boats are 36 feet (11 meters) long and 8 or 9 feet (2.4 or 2.7 meters) wide at the widest point. Each boat can hold about a dozen fishermen. The fishermen sail 15 or 20 miles (24 or 32 kilometers) out from the islands, throw live bait fish into the water, and use rods and reels to haul in big fish.

When the boats return home, the women prepare the

Wide World

A Maldivian Fisherman Heads for Home with his share of the day's catch. Fish is a leading food and also the chief export.

Sailboats are the most common form of transportation in the Maldives. Steamships sail regularly between Male and Sri Lanka.

History. Little is known about the Maldives before they came under Portuguese rule during the 1500's. From 1656 to 1796, the Dutch ruled the islands from Sri Lanka.

In 1887, the Maldives officially became a British protectorate. As a protectorate, the Maldives had internal self-government, and Britain handled foreign affairs. In the 1950's, a dispute between the Maldivians and the British over an air base on Gan Island led to the *secession* (withdrawal) of three southern atolls. The Maldivian government accused Britain of backing the rebellion. It crushed the rebellion in 1960.

In 1960, Britain and the Maldives signed an agreement that gave Britain free use of the Gan Island base. The Maldivians received the right to conduct most of their foreign affairs. Britain promised the islands about $2 million for economic development.

On July 26, 1965, Britain and the Maldives signed a new agreement that gave the islands complete independence. The Maldives became a republic in November 1968. In 1976, Britain withdrew from the Gan Island air base. ROBERT I. CRANE

See also COLOMBO PLAN; MALE.

MALE, *MAH lay* (pop. 15,000), is the capital and leading town of the Maldives. It is located on Male Island, which is part of Male Atoll (see MALDIVES [map]). Male Island is about 1 mile (1.6 kilometers) long and ½ mile (0.8 kilometer) wide. An airfield on Hulele Island serves Male. ROBERT I. CRANE

MALEMUTE. See ALASKAN MALAMUTE.

MALENKOV, MAL un KAWF, or muh lyun KAWF, **GEORGI MAXIMILIANOVICH** (1902-), became premier of Russia after the death of Joseph Stalin in March, 1953. Nikita S. Khrushchev forced him to resign as premier in February, 1955, and Malenkov became deputy premier under Premier Nikolai Bulganin. In June, 1957, Malenkov tried to unseat Khrushchev as first secretary of the Soviet Communist Party. He failed, and lost his high political posts. He was sent to Kazakhstan to manage a power plant. He was expelled from the party in 1964. Malenkov was born in Orenburg. He became Stalin's private secretary in 1925. He became a member of the Politburo in 1946, and second secretary of the Presidium in 1952. ALBERT PARRY

MALETSUNYANE FALLS, MAH lay tsoon YAH nay, is a waterfall in south-central Lesotho, about 20 miles (32 kilometers) from the mouth of the Maletsunyane River. Its 630-foot (192-meter) drop makes it one of the highest in Africa.

MALHERBE, mal EHRB, **FRANÇOIS DE** (1555-1628), was a French poet who became a haughty critic of French poetic language and style. He ridiculed the French poets of the 1500's, mercilessly attacking their flowery vocabularies and elaborate sentence structures. Some scholars believe he smothered French lyric poetry by setting rigid rules that dominated poets until the romantic period of the early 1800's. But he gave the language simplicity, clarity, force, and dignity.

Malherbe insisted that poetry be understandable, even to the poorest people of Paris. But he sternly avoided expressing personal feelings. Instead, he wrote about love and death, the great moral truths, and patriotic subjects of his day. His poetry consists of *Odes* and *Stanzas* (1600-1628). He was born in Caen. JOEL A. HUNT

MALI, *MAH lee*, is a big country in western Africa. Most of it is flat or rolling grassland, but the northern part is desert. Mali covers a larger area than New Mexico, Oklahoma, and Texas combined. But it has only about half as many people as Texas.

Mali is an agricultural country. It lacks the mineral wealth and other resources needed for economic development. About 86 per cent of Mali's people live in rural areas. They include wandering Arab and Moorish herdsmen and black farmers.

From 1895 to 1959, France ruled Mali as the French Sudan. Mali merged with Senegal in 1959 to form the Federation of Mali, but the federation broke up in 1960. Mali then became a republic on Sept. 22, 1960. Its name in French, the official language, is RÉPUBLIQUE DU MALI (REPUBLIC OF MALI). Bamako, a city of about 170,000, is the country's capital and largest city.

Government. Mali's 1960 constitution established the country as a republic, with a strong central government headed by an elected president. In 1968, military officers overthrew the government, dissolved all political organizations, and jailed President Modibo Keita and other important government officials. The military leaders set up a Military Committee of National Liberation to govern Mali. The president of the committee serves as the country's head of state and head of government. The Council of Ministers (Cabinet) carries out the policies established by the committee.

Mali

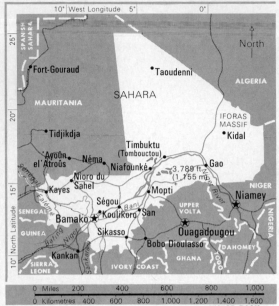

Capital
Other City or Town
Road
Rail Line
Highest Known Elevation
River

WORLD BOOK map

Mali is divided into 6 regions, 42 *cercles* (districts), and 224 *arrondissements* (wards). The central government appoints local officials.

People. Mali's population is made up of three major groups—the white ethnic groups, the Fulani, and the Negroes. There are about 500,000 members of the white groups, which include the Tuareg, Moors, and Arabs. Most whites are wandering Muslim herders who live in the desert. They have a diet of millet, dates, and camel milk and live in camel-hair tents. Their loosely organized societies are coordinated by *marabouts* (holy men) and are divided into *castes* (social classes).

The 700,000 Fulani live in the Niger Valley between the northern whites and the southern Negroes. Some Fulani are wandering Muslim cattle-raisers. They wear long white or brown robes and large cone-shaped straw hats. The herdsmen live in low huts made of straw mats or tree branches. Some of them wear only an animal skin tied around the waist. Some Fulani have mixed with the Negroes. They are settled farmers, and many are *animists* (people who believe that all objects have souls). They live in mud brick houses.

More than half the people are settled Negro farmers who live in southern Mali. Most Negroes belong to the Bambara, Malinke, and Sarakole ethnic groups (see MALINKE). Most Bambara, the largest group, are animists. Some are woodworkers and others make cotton clothes. The Malinke include both animists and Muslims. The Sarakole are mainly farmers, cattle-

raisers, and merchants. The Negroes live in neat villages of circular, sun-dried mud brick huts. Their diet consists of corn, yams, manioc, peanuts, and rice.

Other important Negro groups in Mali include the Songhai, the Bozo, and the Dogons.

About 95 per cent of Mali's adults cannot read and write. Only about 10 per cent of the school-age children attend primary, secondary, and technical schools.

Land. The southern half of Mali is a flat or rolling plateau covered with grass and trees. Highlands rise in the south and in the east. The highest point, in the southeast, is 3,789 feet (1,155 meters) above sea level. The northern half of Mali lies in the Sahara.

Most people live in the valleys of the Sénégal and Niger rivers and their tributaries. The Sénégal and its tributaries flow through southwestern Mali toward the northwest. The Niger River system flows northeast and then makes a great loop to the southeast. Mali's most fertile area is the lowland region that lies along the Niger between Bamako and Timbuktu.

Mali's annual temperature averages about 86° F. (30° C) along the Sénégal and Niger rivers. Northern Mali is hotter. The average annual rainfall varies from 40 to 60 inches (100 to 150 centimeters) in the south to less than 10 inches (25 centimeters) in the north. Mali has three seasons. It is cool and dry from November to February; hot and dry from March to May; and cool and rainy from June to October.

Economy. Mali's economy is based chiefly on farming and livestock-raising. Mali produces more than enough food for its people and exports some agricultural products. But Mali's natural resources are limited and it has few industries. Mali receives economic aid from France, the United States, China, and other countries.

The main crops include cotton, millet, peanuts, rice, shea nuts, and sorghum. Shea nuts provide an oil that is used for making butter, cooking oil, and soap. Nomadic peoples raise millions of cattle, goats, and sheep, and also raise camels, donkeys, and horses.

Exports include peanuts, hides and skins, live animals, meat, and wool. About 8,000 short tons (7,300 metric tons) of fish are exported annually. Imports include automobiles and machinery. Most trade is with France and neighboring African countries.

FACTS IN BRIEF

Capital: Bamako.

Official Language: French.

Form of Government: Republic. *Head of State*—President.

Area: 478,767 sq. mi. (1,240,000 km²). *Greatest Distances*—east-west, 1,150 mi. (1,851 km); north-south, 1,000 mi. (1,609 km). *Coastline*—none.

Population: *Estimated 1981 Population*—6,541,000; distribution, 86 per cent rural, 14 per cent urban; density, 13 persons per sq. mi. (5 per km²). *1976 Census*—6,035,-272. *Estimated 1986 Population*—7,222,000.

Chief Products: *Agriculture*—cotton, livestock, millet, peanuts, rice, shea nuts, sorghum. *Fishing*—fresh and dried fish. *Mining*—gold, iron, salt.

Flag: The flag has three vertical stripes of green, gold, and red which symbolize devotion to republicanism and the Declaration of the Rights of Man. See FLAG (color picture: Flags of Africa).

Money: *Basic Unit*—franc. See MONEY (table: Exchange Rates).

84b

Ségou, in Southern Mali, has a central market place where cotton and other important crops are sold.

Mali's chief industries process agricultural products such as cotton, rice, and peanuts. Mali also produces some gold, salt, and iron.

The country has about 8,000 miles (13,000 kilometers) of roads, but many are impassable during the rainy season. A railroad runs 800 miles (1,300 kilometers) from Koulikoro to Dakar, Senegal. Air-Mali, the country's airline, operates within Mali and also has flights to other African countries and to Europe.

History. Areas in what is now Mali were part of powerful Negro empires from about the A.D. 300's to the 1500's. These empires—Ghana, Mali, and Songhai— were important trading centers.

The Ghana Empire lasted from about the 300's to the 1200's. It lay in what are now western Mali and southeastern Mauritania. See GHANA EMPIRE.

The Mali Empire flourished from about 1240 to 1500. It covered a large part of West Africa, including most of what is now Mali. The former city of Mali, northeast of Ségou, Mali, was its capital. See MALI EMPIRE.

The Songhai Empire probably began in the mid-800's. It reached its peak in the mid-1400's and included parts of what are now Mali, Niger, and Upper Volta. The city of Gao, Mali, was its capital. Moroccan invaders overran Songhai in 1591. But they could not control the huge empire, and many small kingdoms later ruled the area. See SONGHAI EMPIRE; GAO.

France entered what is now Mali in the mid-1800's. In Mali, it met one of the strongest movements that resisted colonial rule in Africa. From the 1850's to the 1890's, El Hadj Omar, a Tukulor conqueror, and Samory, a Malinke marabout, fought the French. But France crushed the resistance in 1895 and made the area a French colony which they called the Sudan.

The colony became a territory in the French Union in 1946. In 1958, it became the Sudan Republic, a self-governing republic within the French Community. In 1959, it joined Senegal to form the Federation of Mali. The federation became an independent political unit within the French Community in June, 1960, but it broke up in August, 1960. On Sept. 22, 1960, the Sudan Republic became the Republic of Mali. Modibo Keita became its first president.

Keita tried to develop the country's economy. But Mali seems to lack the resources for agricultural and industrial development. In 1962, Mali tried to achieve economic freedom from France by setting up its own currency. This led Mali into debt. In 1968, the military overthrew Keita. Moussa Traore, a military officer, took control of Mali as head of a military committee. During the early 1970's, Mali's economy suffered as a result of a severe drought that sharply reduced the production of crops and livestock.   CLEMENT HENRY MOORE

See also BAMAKO; SENEGAL; TIMBUKTU.

MALI EMPIRE was a Negro empire that flourished in West Africa from about 1240 to 1500. At its height, the Mali Empire controlled most of what is now Gambia, Guinea, Mali, and Senegal, and parts of Mauritania, Niger, and Upper Volta.

Between 1235 and 1240, Sundiata, the king of Kangaba, conquered the nearby lands of the Sosso. He

THE MALI EMPIRE IN 1337

This map shows the Mali Empire, in dark gray, at the height of its power in 1337. Mali controlled an area in West Africa including most of what are now the countries of Gambia, Guinea, Senegal, and Mali. The present boundaries are shown as white lines. The Tuareg and Songhai tribes conquered most of Mali by 1500.

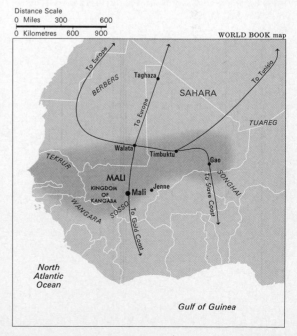

Distance Scale

WORLD BOOK map

built a new city, Mali, to be the capital of his empire (see SUNDIATA KEITA). Later, under Mansa Musa, who ruled from 1312 to 1337, the empire spread eastward to Gao. Mansa Musa brought the empire to the peak of its political power and cultural achievement. Timbuktu became a famous center of learning, especially in law and the study of Islam, the Muslim religion.

The cities of the Mali Empire were centers for the caravan trade from beyond the Sahara. The people were successful farmers and herders. Members of the governing classes were Muslims, but most of the people continued to worship tribal gods.

Control of the vast empire required skill and power that Mansa Musa's successors lacked. After about 1400, Songhai and other states conquered Mali's outlying areas. Tuareg raiders captured southern Sahara market towns. By 1500, the Songhai Empire controlled most of the Mali Empire.   LEO SPITZER

See also TIMBUKTU; GAO; JENNE; WALATA; MANSA MUSA.

MALIBRAN, MAH LEE BRAHN, **MARIA FELICITA** (1808-1836), was a French-Spanish mezzo-contralto. She became noted for the peculiar tone and unusual range of her voice, and for her fiery temperament. At the age of 5, she played in Paer's opera *Agnese* in Naples, Italy. She created a sensation at her debut in Paris in 1824. She was born in Paris.   SCOTT GOLDTHWAITE

MALICE is ill will toward another person. In law, a crime is said to be malicious if it is committed for the sole purpose of injuring someone. Malice usually involves harming a person or damaging property. *Malicious mischief* is damage to property without cause.

MALIGNANCY is the tendency of a disease to be severe and possibly cause death. It most frequently refers to a *malignant tumor,* or cancer, in contrast to a *benign* (mild) tumor (see CANCER; TUMOR). Benign tumors remain in one part of the body and grow slowly. Malignant tumors spread to many parts of the body and grow rapidly. They are made up of actively dividing cells that vary in size and shape. The cells have little resemblance to the cells from which they originate. These features make the tumor malignant. Many people say *malignancy* when they mean *cancer.*   J. F. A. McMANUS

MALINKE, mah LING kee, is the name of a group of West African people. The Malinke are descendants of the founders of the powerful Mali Empire. Most of the 1½ million Malinke live in Mali, but many live in Gambia, Guinea-Bissau, the Ivory Coast, and Senegal. The Malinke are also known as the *Mandingo.*

The Malinke speak a language that belongs to the *Mande* language group. This group has many *dialects* (local forms of speech). Malinke who speak different dialects may not be able to communicate with one another.

During the 1200's, Mande-speaking people lived in independent states in Africa. The largest and most famous Malinke state, the Mali Empire, flourished from about 1240 to 1500. Its leaders converted to Islam, the religion of the Muslims, but few of the Malinke people became Muslims. Today, many Malinke still practice tribal religions. Most of the rural people are farmers or cattle herders, though many city dwellers are traders or artists.   LEO SPITZER

MALINOWSKI, MAH lee NAWF ski, **BRONISLAW** (1884-1942), was a British anthropologist. He became known for his intensive study of the culture of the peoples of the Trobriand Islands in the southwest Pacific, and for his contributions to theories on human culture. Malinowski was born in Poland, and studied at Jagiellonian University and the University of London. He taught at the University of London for many years, and at Yale University from 1939 until his death. He wrote *Argonauts of the Western Pacific, Sexual Life of Savages in North West Melanesia,* and *Coral Gardens and Their Magic.*   DAVID B. STOUT

See also MYTHOLOGY (How Myths Began).

MALL. See SHOPPING CENTER.

MALL is a broad, parklike thoroughfare. In Washington, D.C., the National Mall stretches between the Capitol and the Lincoln Memorial (see WASHINGTON, D.C., with map). In London, the Mall leads from Buckingham Palace to Trafalgar Square (see LONDON [Central London; map]).

MALLARD, MAL erd, is a wild duck which lives in Europe, northern Asia, and throughout North America. It is about 2 feet (61 centimeters) long, and has curly upper tail feathers. The male mallard is beautifully colored during the breeding season and in the winter. It is grayish-brown on the back, and purplish-chestnut colored underneath. Its head and neck are glossy green, shaded with Prussian blue and purple. Glossy black feathers cover the lower back, rump, and tail. Two white and two black bars mark each of the side wings. A white band circles the neck. The bill is greenish-yellow and the feet are orange-red.

The female mallard is a tawny and dusky-brown color. She lays from 6 to 15 olive-colored eggs. The nest is made of grass or weeds and lined with down.

Scientific Classification. The mallard belongs to the surface duck family, *Anatidae.* It is a member of genus *Anas,* and is species *A. platyrhynchos.*   JOSEPH J. HICKEY

See also BIRD (color picture: Wild Ducks and Wild Geese); DUCK (Domestic Ducks).

MALLARMÉ, mah lahr MAY, **STÉPHANE** (1842-1898), was a French poet and critic born in Paris. He is best known for his dream poem *L'Après-midi d'un faune* (*The Afternoon of a Faun,* 1865). Except for weekly meetings with a group of European poets and artists in Paris, Mallarmé lived detached from society. He considered society hostile to the values of the poet.

Recognized by the younger generation as a master of poetic theory, Mallarmé became the mentor of a literary movement known as *symbolism* (see SYMBOLISM). According to him, the poet must suggest, not describe, the natural object. He must deliberately make his poetic image ambiguous, so that reality is presented in an atmosphere of mystery. Mallarmé's other works include esoteric sonnets; a metaphysical prose poem, *Igitur;* and *L'Hérodiade,* a long poem about Salome. His last poem, "Un Coup de dés jamais n'abolira le hasard" (1897) expresses the confrontation between the chaos of the universe (*le hasard*) and man's desire to shape his own destiny (*le coup de dés*).   ANNA BALAKIAN

See FRENCH LITERATURE (Poetry Reborn).

MALLEABILITY, MAL ee ah BIL ih tih. When metals can be hammered or rolled into thin sheets, they are said to be *malleable.* Gold, for example, is one of the most malleable of metals. It can be hammered into gold leaves so thin that they are almost transparent. The other common metals in the order of their malleability are silver, copper, aluminum, tin, zinc, and lead. Cast iron is stiff and brittle and has practically no malleability. Its stiffness is caused by the carbon atoms which are united with the iron. Cast iron can be made slightly malleable by heating it for a long time with some substance which will remove some of the carbon atoms. Cast iron which has been treated in this way is called *malleable iron* and has many uses in industry. Any metal becomes more malleable when it is heated and usually when it is purified. Another property similar to malleability is *ductility*. This means that metal can be drawn out into wire. See also DUCTILITY. LOUIS MARICK

MALLEIN TEST. See GLANDERS.

MALLEUS. See EAR (The Middle Ear).

MALLOPHAGA. See INSECT (table).

MALLORCA. See MAJORCA.

MALLORY, STEPHEN RUSSELL (1813?-1873), was an American lawyer and political leader who served as secretary of the Confederate Navy. He was born in the West Indies. His father was a Connecticut shipbuilder, but was living in Trinidad when Stephen was born. The family settled in Key West, Fla., in 1820.

Mallory was appointed inspector of customs in Key West in 1833, and studied law while holding that position. After he was admitted to the bar, President Polk appointed him collector of customs in Key West. In 1850, Mallory was elected to the United States Senate from Florida.

Florida seceded from the Union in 1861, and Mallory resigned from the Senate. President Jefferson Davis appointed him secretary of the Confederate Navy, which was then almost nonexistent. Mallory had to organize the Navy and direct it. He also had to build the ships and equip them from what little material he found available.

Mallory attacked his task with great ability. He succeeded in building a small but efficient Navy, and showed much foresight in ordering ironclads built instead of the older type of wooden warships. His naval experts developed deadly torpedoes and underwater devices which kept the Union Navy out of the great rivers of Virginia until late in the war.

After the fall of Richmond, Mallory fled south with President Davis and was captured in Georgia. He was held prisoner for nearly a year, but was pardoned by President Andrew Johnson in 1867. RICHARD N. CURRENT

MALLOW, *MAL oh,* is the popular name of a large family of plants. The mallow family includes about 1,000 kinds of herbs, shrubs, and trees that grow in tropical and temperate regions of the world. The plants of this family have fibrous stems and sticky sap. Many well-known flowers, such as the hibiscus, hollyhock, and marsh mallow, belong to the mallow family. The cotton plant and okra are also members.

Scientific Classification. The mallows make up the mallow family, *Malvaceae.* ROBERT W. HOSHAW

Related Articles in WORLD BOOK include:

Cotton	Hollyhock
Flower (color picture: Flowers	Indian Mallow
That Grow in Wet Places)	Marsh Mallow
Flowering Maple	Okra
Hibiscus	Rose of Sharon

MALMAISON. See JOSEPHINE.

MALMÖ, *MAHL muh* (pop. 263,829; met. area 449,-296), is the third largest city in Sweden. It lies at the southern tip of Sweden, 16 miles (26 kilometers) from Copenhagen, Denmark (see SWEDEN [political map]). The city exports food and other products to European ports. Eight railroad lines connect it with other cities of Sweden. Malmö has a modern airport. Its beautiful town hall dates from 1546. JAMES J. ROBBINS

MALNUTRITION, *mal noo TRISH uhn,* is an unhealthy condition caused by poor intake, absorption, or use of nutrients by the body. Symptoms of malnutrition include cramps, diarrhea, weakness, and weight loss. *Primary malnutrition* results when the body does not get enough food or the right kinds of food. *Secondary malnutrition* occurs when, because of disease, the body cannot use nutrients even though they are present in the food.

There are a number of types of malnutrition, depending on the nutrient or nutrients missing. *Protein-calorie malnutrition* occurs when the diet is low in both proteins and calories. This condition is called *marasmus* if the diet is particularly low in calories. It is called *kwashiorkor* if the diet is especially low in proteins.

Malnutrition caused by a low intake of vitamins may lead to *vitamin deficiencies.* Various diseases result from deficiencies of different vitamins (see VITAMIN). Malnutrition may also be due to *mineral deficiencies.* For example, lack of iron or copper can cause an abnormal condition of the blood called *anemia.*

Social and economic conditions as well as natural conditions such as flooding and drought may produce malnutrition. Poverty, war, disease, and ignorance concerning a balanced diet also cause countless cases of malnutrition. JEAN MAYER

Related Articles in WORLD BOOK include:

Anemia	Nutrition
Beriberi	Pellagra
Diet	Rickets
Food	Scurvy
Goiter	

MALOCCLUSION. See DENTISTRY (Orthodontics); TEETH (Malocclusion).

MALONE COLLEGE. See UNIVERSITIES AND COLLEGES (table).

MALORY, SIR THOMAS (? -1471?), was the author of the book *Le Morte Darthur.* This title is French for *The Death of Arthur.* In *Le Morte Darthur,* Malory described the life of King Arthur of Britain and the careers of many knights of the Round Table. The book provides the fullest version of the legends about Arthur and his court ever written in English.

Malory described the circumstances of Arthur's birth, his rise to the British throne, his reign as king, and his death. *Le Morte Darthur* includes an account of the knights' quest for the Holy Grail, the cup or dish used by Jesus Christ at the Last Supper. An important theme in the book is the love of Sir Lancelot, one of the greatest knights of the Round Table, for Queen Guenevere, Arthur's wife. *Le Morte Darthur* also relates the love story of Sir Tristram and Isolt, the wife of Tristram's uncle, King Mark.

Scholars disagree on the identity of the author of *Le Morte Darthur.* Records from the 1400's show that several Englishmen named Thomas Malory lived at this time. A knight of Warwickshire, who was imprisoned for a series of crimes, is most commonly identified as the author.

Malory translated and adapted much of his work from earlier French and English writings about Arthur. He completed *Le Morte Darthur* about 1469. William Caxton, the first English printer, published the first edition of the book in 1485. A manuscript copy of Malory's work was found at Winchester College in England in 1934. The most accurate and complete modern editions of *Le Morte Darthur* are based on the Winchester manuscript.

Malory's book has influenced the work of many artists and writers, including the English poets Edmund Spenser and Lord Tennyson.   ROBERT W. ACKERMAN

See also ARTHUR, KING; ROUND TABLE.

MALPEQUE BAY. See PRINCE EDWARD ISLAND (Places to Visit; picture).

MALPIGHI, *mahl PEE gee,* **MARCELLO** (1628-1694), an Italian anatomist, has been called the first histologist (see HISTOLOGY). He discovered the capillary blood vessels that carry the blood between the arteries and veins. He was the first to describe the red blood corpuscles, and one of the first to use the microscope in medicine. Malpighi's book, *Anatomical Treatise on the Structures of the Viscera,* appeared in 1666. His descriptions of the minute structure of the lungs, spleen, and kidneys are considered to be among the classics of medicine.

Malpighi was born near Bologna, Italy. He studied at the University of Bologna. At 28, he became a professor of medicine at the University of Pisa. He returned to Bologna in 1659, and stayed there more than 30 years teaching, writing, and doing research. He served as personal physician to Pope Innocent XII from 1691 until his death.   CAROLINE A. CHANDLER

MALPIGHIAN TUBE. See INSECT (Digestive System; diagram).

MALPRACTICE SUIT is a lawsuit in which a professional person is accused of injuring a patient or client through negligence or error. Most malpractice suits involve physicians. A smaller number involve lawyers and other professional men and women.

The number of malpractice suits against doctors increased greatly in the United States during the late 1960's and the early 1970's. Most of the suits were filed against surgeons and other specialists who perform medical procedures that involve great risks to patients.

The increased number of suits and the large amounts of money awarded in successful suits drove up the cost of malpractice insurance for physicians. Some insurance companies dropped all malpractice coverage. Doctors in several cities went on strike in protest.

The higher cost of malpractice insurance contributed to the rising cost of medical care in the 1970's. Physicians passed on the cost to patients by increasing their fees. They also began to order expensive laboratory tests and X rays to protect themselves in case they were later sued. Many surgeons became hesitant to perform risky operations.

Physicians and many state legislatures proposed various solutions to the problem. One proposal involved the creation of panels of doctors, lawyers, and judges to review malpractice cases before the suits go to court. Other suggestions included a legal limit on the amount of money awarded in malpractice suits and a limit on the fee of the trial lawyers.

Malpractice suits against lawyers also increased during the 1970's. Many clients sued attorneys who lost a case. Most malpractice suits resulted from a technical mistake, such as failing to file a suit on time. Others involved lawyers who failed to complete the legal work on a case.   THOMAS G. ROADY, JR.

MALRAUX, *mal ROH,* **ANDRÉ** (1901-1976), was a French author who combined intellectual achievement with political activity. Malraux was born in Paris. From 1923 to 1927, he traveled in the Far East as a student of archaeology, Oriental languages, and art. While there, he became involved in local revolutionary struggles for freedom. In the 1930's, Malraux participated in the struggles against Naziism in Germany, and Fascism in Spain. During World War II, he fought with the French resistance forces against the Germans. He served as France's first secretary of cultural affairs, from 1958 to 1969.

Raymond Depardon,
Gamma /Liaison

André Malraux

Malraux's novels reflect his involvement in battles for freedom. However, his books are not autobiographical. Even in his autobiography, *Anti-Memoirs* (1967), he did not write about himself so much as about some of the great political figures of his day. Malraux's fiction explores humanity's devotion to ideals. He wanted art "to give men a consciousness of their own hidden greatness." His style is simple, concise, and fact-filled. But it may burst into poetic imagery and suggests our solitude and everpresent sense of death. His best novels include *The Royal Way* (1930), *Man's Fate* (1933), *Days of Wrath* (1935), and *Man's Hope* (1937).

Malraux also wrote *The Voices of Silence* (1951) and other important works on art that compare works of different periods and civilizations.   EDITH KERN

MALT is a food product which results when barley and certain other grains are specially treated. Beermakers use most of the malt made. It is also used in distilling, baking, and making other foods and drugs.

In the malting process, manufacturers steep grain in water for 24 to 96 hours. They then spread it on large, ventilated floors and allow it to sprout and grow for 5 to 10 days. Temperature and moisture are carefully controlled during this time. Next, large *kilns* (ovens) dry the grain for 2 or 3 days. The drying is started at low temperatures and gradually increased to 180° F. (82° C). Finally, the malt is aged for 4 to 8 weeks before manufacturers use it.

During the malting process, certain chemical changes take place in the grain. The insoluble starch changes into a sugar called *maltose*. Malting also releases certain *enzymes*. The enzymes are *diastase*, which has the power to convert starch into sugar, and *peptase*, which can change certain proteins.   H. F. PEROT

See also BREWING; MALTOSE.

MALTA is an independent island country in the Mediterranean Sea, about 60 miles (97 kilometers) south of Sicily. It consists of the islands of Malta, Comino, Cominotto, Filfla, and Gozo. It is one of the most densely populated countries in the world, with 2,753 persons per square mile (1,063 persons per square kilometer).

Terrace farming over much of Malta makes the countryside look much like giant steps. The balmy climate attracts many visitors. Tourists also come to Malta to view some of the world's finest examples of Baroque and Renaissance art and architecture.

Malta was once a British crown colony. In 1964, Malta became an independent country. Valletta, on the island of Malta, is the capital and chief port of the country. See VALLETTA.

Government. Malta is a republic. The president is head of state and is appointed by parliament to a five-year term. The prime minister is usually the leader of the majority party in parliament. The prime minister is assisted by a Cabinet. The 65 members of the House of Representatives are elected by the people to five-year terms.

People. Malta has a population of about 336,000. The Maltese have the medium height, regular features, black hair, and dark eyes of most Mediterranean peoples. Most of them speak Maltese, a West Arabic dialect with some Italian words. Both English and Maltese are official languages. Maltese is used in the courts. The country has both Maltese and English newspapers. Roman Catholicism is the state religion of Malta.

Land. Malta covers a total area of 122 square miles (316 square kilometers). Malta island covers 95 square miles (246 square kilometers). Gozo covers 26 square miles (67 square kilometers). Cominotto and Filfla are tiny and uninhabited.

Malta has a mild climate. Winters are moist and mild, and frost is unusual. Summers are hot and dry, but the heat is moderated by sea breezes. Temperatures average 66° F. (19° C). Malta gets about 21 inches (53 centimeters) of rainfall a year. Northwest winds sometimes reach hurricane force in autumn and winter.

Economy. Most of the people work at the dockyards and in the building industry. Malta is becoming more dependent upon tourists. The one-time British naval dockyards are now used for commercial shipbuilding and repair. A few light industries have been set up.

--------------------- FACTS IN BRIEF ---------------------

Capital: Valletta.

Official Languages: Maltese and English.

Form of Government: Republic.

Area: 122 sq. mi. (316 km²).

Population: *Estimated 1981 Population*—336,000; distribution, 92 per cent urban, 8 per cent rural; density, 2,753 persons per sq. mi. (1,063 persons per km²). *1967 Census*—315,765. *Estimated 1986 Population*—341,000.

Chief Products: *Agriculture*—barley, grapes, onions, potatoes, wheat. *Manufacturing and Processing*—beverages, processed food, shipbuilding and repair.

Flag: A silver replica of the George Cross, a British medal awarded to Malta for bravery in World War II, appears on a red and white field. See FLAG (picture: Flags of Europe).

Money: *Basic Unit*—Maltese pound.

Malta

⊛ NATIONAL CAPITAL
• OTHER CITY OR TOWN
— ROAD

WORLD BOOK map

Maltese farmers raise citrus fruits, barley, grapes, onions, potatoes, and wheat. However, crops are small because of the rocky soil. Malta must import most of its food. The country has no minerals or natural resources, except salt and limestone.

Malta imports more goods than it exports. It carries on nearly half of its trade with Great Britain. Italy is its second most important trade partner.

The country has about 600 miles (970 kilometers) of road. There is ferry service between Malta and Gozo. British airlines maintain local and international service.

Malta has compulsory elementary education for all children from 6 to 14 years old. There are about 120 Roman Catholic primary and secondary schools operated by the government. The country also has about 80 private schools. Instruction is in both English and Maltese. The Royal University of Malta is in Msida, near Valletta.

History. Malta is a region of great historical interest. Through the years, it has had much military importance because of its strategic location and natural harbors.

Remains of late Stone Age and Bronze Age people have been found in limestone caverns on the islands. Rough stone buildings from early ages have also been discovered in Malta. The Phoenicians colonized Malta in about 1000 B.C. Temples, tombs, and other relics of the Phoenicians still stand. Greek, Carthaginian, Roman, and Arab conquerors followed the Phoenicians into Malta. According to tradition, Saint Paul the Apostle was shipwrecked near Malta about A.D. 60 and converted the inhabitants to Christianity.

Malta passed to the Norman kings of Sicily around 1090. About 1520, the Holy Roman Emperor Charles V inherited the area when he received the crown of Spain. In 1530, Charles V gave Malta to the Knights of the Order of Saint John of Jerusalem. The Knights are sometimes called the Hospitallers. The Knights of Saint John wore the Maltese cross as their badge (see CROSS). They had fought against the Muslims since the time of the First Crusade in the 1090's. In 1565, the Turks laid siege to Malta with great naval and military forces. Though heavily outnumbered, the Knights held out against the Turks for months, and finally defeated them. The town of Valletta was named after Jean de la Vallette, the Grand Master who led the Knights' defense against the Turks.

The French under Napoleon Bonaparte took Malta from the Knights of Saint John in 1798. British forces drove out the French in 1800. The people of Malta offered control of the colony to Great Britain. Britain's control was not completely recognized, however, until peace was made with France in 1815, after the Napoleonic Wars. Great Britain developed its Mediterranean military headquarters on Malta.

During World War I, Malta served as a strategic naval base for Allied forces. Great Britain granted Malta a measure of self-government in 1921. However, political crises in Malta caused Britain to revoke the Maltese political power. Malta's constitution was suspended in 1930 because of a dispute between the state and Roman Catholic authorities. They disagreed about the role of the church in state affairs. The constitution was re-established in 1932, then withdrawn a year later. This time the pro-Italian sympathies of the Maltese ministry led Britain to suspend the constitution. Full authority was reinvested in the governor in 1936.

During World War II, Malta controlled the vital sea lanes between Italy and Africa. The natural rocks and deep inlets of the colony concealed anchorages and submarine bases. Many underground passages provided bomb shelters. Fighter planes based on Malta defended convoys of ships. The colony suffered heavy bomb damage. In 1942, King George VI of England awarded the George Cross to Malta in recognition of the courage and endurance of the Maltese people during the war. In 1953, the North Atlantic Treaty Organization (NATO) established its Mediterranean military headquarters on Malta.

The constitution of 1947 gave the colony increased partial self-government. The Maltese Labour Party gained control of the assembly and proposed political integration with Great Britain. In a 1956 referendum, the people voted for integration. A bill was prepared in the British Parliament, providing for local government in Malta and giving it three members in Britain's House of Commons. No further progress was made, because the Maltese wanted guarantees of employment in the dockyards. An independence movement began to grow in Malta in 1958. A constitution approved in 1962 provided that the colony become a state with internal self-government. The new legislative assembly favored full independence. Great Britain agreed to grant full independence, effective in May, 1964. But disagreement among Malta's political factions delayed the action until September, 1964.

Malta's political parties could not agree on whether to become a republic or a constitutional monarchy after independence. Some factions did not even want independence from Great Britain. But the Nationalist Party defeated the Labour Party on these measures and Malta became an independent constitutional monarchy on Sept. 21, 1964. Dr. Borg Oliver, leader of the Nationalists, became prime minister. In 1971, the Labour Party won a majority in parliament. Party leader Dom Mintoff became prime minister.

In 1974, Malta's parliament amended the constitution to change the form of government to a republic. Mintoff remained as prime minister, and Sir Anthony Mamo, the former governor general, became Malta's first president. The Labour Party kept its majority in parliament in the 1976 elections.

In 1979, an agreement between Great Britain and Malta that permitted Britain's use of military facilities on Malta expired. Britain and NATO then withdrew their military forces from Malta.   FRANCIS H. HERRICK

Valletta, The Capital of Malta, is also the country's most important port. The city has been Malta's capital since 1571.

MALTA, KNIGHTS OF. See KNIGHTS OF SAINT JOHN.

MALTA FEVER. See UNDULANT FEVER.

MALTESE was probably the world's first lap dog. It developed on the Mediterranean island of Malta more than 2,000 years ago. Ladies in Greek and Roman noble families were fond of these little dogs. They carried them in the long sleeves of their robes, and waited on them like babies. The Maltese grew to be one of the gentlest of all toy dogs. It usually weighs from 4 to 6 pounds (2 to 3 kilograms). Its black eyes have dark rims that make the eyes look large. Its white coat falls from a part down its back, and sometimes grows so long it trails on the ground. JOSEPHINE Z. RINE

See also DOG (picture: Toy Dogs).

MALTESE. See CAT (Breed Colors).

MALTESE CROSS. See CROSS (picture); KNIGHTS OF SAINT JOHN.

MALTHUS, *MAL thus,* **THOMAS ROBERT** (1766-1834), was an English economist. He is best known for his *Essay on the Principle of Population,* published in 1798. Malthus' main idea in this book is that population tends to increase more rapidly than food supplies. He believed that wars and disease would have to kill off the extra population, unless people decided to limit the number of their children.

Malthus' *Essay* suggested to Charles Darwin the relationship between progress and the survival of the fittest. This was a basic idea in Darwin's theory of evolution (see DARWIN [Charles R.]). Malthus' prediction failed to come true in the 1800's. Improved methods of agriculture provided enough food for most people. But rapid population growth in the 1900's, especially in underdeveloped countries, led to renewed interest in Malthus' theories. Many conservationists warned that food production could not keep pace with population indefinitely. The *neo-Malthusians* urged the use of birth control, though Malthus himself had rejected that solution.

Malthus was born on Feb. 17, 1766, in Surrey. He decided to be a clergyman, and was graduated from Cambridge University. About 1796, he took a parish in Surrey. He became a professor of history and political economy in the college of the East India Company in 1805, and held this post until his death. H. W. SPIEGEL

See also POPULATION (Effects).

MALTOSE, *MAWL tohs,* is the chemical term for malt sugar. The formation of maltose in the body is the first step in the digestion of starchy foods. The enzyme *ptyalin* in saliva changes starch into maltose. Other enzymes in the body split the maltose into glucose (see GLUCOSE). Commercially, the enzyme *diastase* in malt changes starch into maltose. Fermentation changes maltose into alcohol. This is recovered by distillation. Maltose is used for sweetening some foods. See also BREWING; DIGESTION; MALT. W. NORTON JONES, JR.

MAMBA, *MAHM bah,* is the name of three of the most dreaded snakes of Central and South Africa. They are closely related to the cobras, but do not have a hood.

The mambas are slender and look somewhat like whips. They are usually about 6 to 8 feet (1.8 to 2.4 meters) long, but may be as long as 14 feet (4.3 meters). Mambas glide very rapidly in trees as well as on the ground. They produce a poison as powerful as that of the African cobras and vipers. The black mamba is green when young and dark brown when

New York Zoological Society
The Mamba of Africa Is a Graceful But Deadly Snake.

adult. The green mamba is green throughout life.

Scientific Classification. The mambas belong to the terrestrial poisonous snake family, *Elapidae*. They make up the genus *Dendroaspis*. The black mamba is genus *Dendroaspis*, species *D. polylepis*. The green mamba is *D. angusticeps*. CLIFFORD H. POPE

MAMELUKE, *MAM uh lyook.* The Mamelukes were Turkish and Circassian prisoners of Genghis Khan. They were sold as slaves to the Sultan of Egypt. The Egyptians trained them as soldiers, and eventually promoted them to high government posts. In A.D. 1250, the Mamelukes seized control of Egypt, and ruled it for more than 250 years. See EGYPT (History; picture).

The Mameluke sultans overran Asia Minor, Syria, and the island of Cyprus. Selim I of Turkey finally defeated them in 1517 and conquered Egypt. But even under Turkish rule, the Mamelukes remained powerful. They organized cavalry squadrons and attacked Napoleon I when he invaded Egypt in 1798. After the French defeated the Mamelukes in the Battle of the Pyramids, some of them joined the French Army.

Egypt's Viceroy Muhammad Ali ordered the massacre of all Mamelukes in 1811. A few escaped, fled to Nubia, and tried to organize an army of Negroes. They failed, and the Mamelukes disappeared. A. E. R. BOAK

Mameluke Warriors serving under Napoleon I during the French invasion of Spain massacred many Spaniards on May 2, 1808.

The Charge of the Mamelukes (The 2nd of May, 1808) by Francisco Goya, 1814, The Prado, Madrid

The Flying Lemur of Southeast Asia glides from tree to tree by spreading the folds of skin that connect its neck, legs, and tail. The animal does not really fly, but it can travel nearly 100 yards (91 meters) through the air.

The Zebra is a beautiful African mammal that looks like a striped horse. The black-and-white stripes help hide the zebra in tall grass. The kind of zebra shown here, Grevy's zebra, is in danger of dying out because of illegal hunting.

Among Alaskan Fur Seals, the males and females live together only during the summer mating season. The rest of the year, the males make their home in the Gulf of Alaska, while the females live as far south as the coast of California.

The Star-Nosed Mole has 22 pink, fleshy "feelers" at the end of its snout. The mole uses these growths to find the insects and worms it feeds on. This mammal lives in damp or muddy soil in various parts of eastern North America.

MAMMAL

MAMMAL is a *vertebrate* (backboned animal) that feeds its young on the mother's milk. There are about 4,000 kinds of mammals, and many of them are among the most familiar of all animals. Cats and dogs are mammals. So are such farm animals as cattle, goats, hogs, and horses. Mammals also include such fascinating animals as anteaters, apes, giraffes, hippopotamuses, and kangaroos. And people, too, are mammals.

Mammals live almost everywhere. Such mammals as

monkeys and elephants dwell in tropical regions. Arctic foxes, polar bears, and many other mammals make their home near the North Pole. Such mammals as camels and kangaroo rats live in deserts. Certain others, including seals and whales, dwell in the oceans. One group of mammals, the bats, can fly.

The largest animal that has ever lived, the blue whale, is a mammal. It measures up to 100 feet (30 meters) long and weighs more than 100 short tons (91 metric tons). The smallest mammal is a kind of shrew that measures less than 3 inches (8 centimeters) long and weighs only $\frac{1}{14}$ ounce (2 grams).

Some mammals live a long time. Elephants, for example, live about 60 years, and some human beings reach the age of 100 years or more. On the other hand, many mice and shrews live less than a year.

Richard G. Van Gelder, the contributor of this article, is Curator of Mammalogy at the American Museum of Natural History and the author of Biology of Mammals.

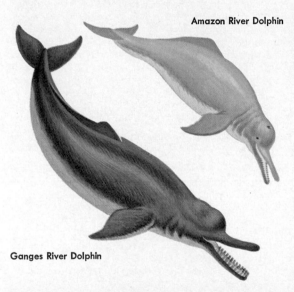

Amazon River Dolphin

The Sloth spends most of its life in the treetops. This South American mammal moves very slowly along the underside of branches, hanging upside down by its long claws.

Ganges River Dolphin

Dolphins are mammals that live in water. Most kinds of dolphins live in the ocean. However, the Amazon River dolphin and the Ganges River dolphin dwell in freshwater.

Interesting Facts About Mammals

The Largest Mammal—and the largest animal that has ever lived—is the blue whale. It measures up to 100 feet (30 meters) long when fully grown.

The Smallest Mammals are certain kinds of shrews that grow less than 3 inches (8 centimeters) long and weigh no more than a penny. Shrews live in many parts of the world.

Shrew

The Potto, a small African tree dweller, has one of the strongest grips of all mammals. A potto can grasp a branch so tightly with its hands and feet that the animal may remain clinging to the branch even after it has died.

Potto

The Rhinoceros has horns that look like closely packed hairs. Actually, they consist of many fibers of *keratin,* the horny substance that makes up the nails of people. African rhinos have two horns. Indian rhinos have one.

African Rhinoceros

A Young Marmoset rides on its father's back. Most male mammals have little to do with raising their offspring. But among these South American monkeys, the father and mother share the job of carrying and protecting their babies.

Marmosets

The Hyrax is a small mammal that looks much like a guinea pig. But scientists believe that its nearest relatives are actually elephants. Hyraxes, which are also known as conies, live in Africa and the Middle East.

Hyrax

WORLD BOOK illustrations by James Teason

Mammals differ from all or most other kinds of animals in five major ways. (1) Mammals nurse their babies—that is, they feed them on the mother's milk. No other animals do this. (2) Most mammals give their young more protection and training than do other animals. (3) Only mammals have hair. All mammals have hair at some time in their life, though in certain whales it is present only before birth. (4) Mammals are *warmblooded*—that is, their body temperature remains about the same all the time, even though the temperature of their surroundings may change. Birds are also warmblooded, but nearly all other animals are not. (5) Mammals have a larger, more well-developed brain than do other animals. Some mammals, such as chimpanzees, dolphins, and especially human beings, are highly intelligent.

This article provides general information about mammals. Several hundred separate WORLD BOOK articles give details on specific kinds of mammals. Readers can find these articles by consulting the general articles listed in the *Related Articles* at the end of this article. In addition, the article ANIMAL has much information on mammals, such as the table *Names of Animals and Their Young.*

The Importance of Mammals

How People Use Mammals. Since the earliest times, human beings have hunted other mammals. Prehistoric people ate the flesh of wild mammals, used their skins for clothing, and made tools and ornaments from their bones, teeth, horns, and hoofs.

About 10,000 years ago, people learned they could

domesticate (tame and raise) certain useful mammals. Hunters bred dogs, one of the first domestic animals, to track and bring down game animals. People later domesticated the wild ancestors of today's cattle, goats, hogs, and sheep. Since then, these mammals have provided meat and other products. Horses and oxen have long been used to carry people or their goods. Camels, elephants, goats, llamas, reindeer, and even dogs have also been used in this way.

Some mammals, especially cats, dogs, hamsters, and rabbits, are popular pets. Certain mammals are used in scientific research. For example, new drugs are tested on domestic mice and rats and on dogs, guinea pigs, and monkeys.

Although domestic mammals provide many products, people still hunt wild mammals. They hunt such mammals as antelopes, deer, rabbits, and squirrels for their flesh or hides. Whales are killed for their meat and oil, and seals for their skins. Beavers, muskrats, otters, and other wild mammals that have thick coats are trapped for their fur. Elephants, hippopotamuses, and walruses are sometimes killed for their tusks, which consist of ivory.

Wild mammals are also a source of enjoyment. Many people travel to national parks to delight in viewing bears, deer, moose, and other mammals in their natural homes. Other people visit zoos, where they can see interesting mammals from many countries. Even in the largest cities, people can still find some wild mammals to enjoy, such as the friendly gray squirrel.

Mammals in the Balance of Nature. Mammals are important not only to people but also to the whole system of life on the earth. Many mammals help plants grow. For example, animals that eat plants leave seeds in their *droppings* (body wastes). Many of these seeds sprout into plants. Similarly, many of the nuts that squirrels bury for a food supply grow into trees. Gophers, moles, prairie dogs, and other burrowing mammals dig up the soil. This activity enables air, moisture, and sunlight to break down the soil, which can then be used by growing plants.

Flesh-eating mammals also help maintain the balance of nature by feeding on plant-eating animals. If such flesh-eaters as coyotes, mongooses, and weasels did not control the number of plant-eaters, certain species of plants in an area could be drastically reduced or even wiped out. Other mammals help keep the insect population under control. For example, aardvarks, giant anteaters, and pangolins eat millions of ants and termites at each meal. Every night, bats eat great numbers of insects. *Scavenger* mammals, such as hyenas and jackals, clean up the remains of large animals that have been killed or that died naturally.

Even the wastes and dead bodies of mammals are important to the balance of nature. Mammal droppings are a valuable fertilizer. The bones of dead mammals break down into chemicals that are needed by animals and plants. For additional information, see the article BALANCE OF NATURE.

The Bodies of Mammals

Mammals have many ways of life, and each species has a body adapted to its particular way of life. How-ever, all mammals share some basic body characteristics. These characteristics include certain features of their (1) skin and hair, (2) skeleton, and (3) internal organ systems.

Skin and Hair cover the body of mammals. Skin consists of an inner layer, the *dermis*, and an outer layer, the *epidermis*. The dermis contains the arteries and veins that supply the skin with blood. The epidermis, which has no blood vessels, protects the dermis. It also produces special skin structures, including hair, horns, claws, nails, and hoofs.

The skin of mammals has a rich supply of glands. *Mammary glands* produce the milk that female mammals use to nurse their young. *Sebaceous glands* give off oil that lubricates the hair and skin. *Sweat glands* eliminate small amounts of liquid wastes, but their main purpose is to help mammals cool off. As sweat evaporates from the skin, it cools the surface. Many mammals, such as dogs and skunks, also have *scent glands*. Dogs use their scent glands for communication and identification. Skunks spray a bad-smelling odor from their scent glands as a means of self-defense.

Many mammals have two coats of hair. The *underhair* consists of soft, fine hairs that provide a thick, warm coat. The outer *guard hair* consists of longer, slightly stiffened hairs that give shape to a mammal's coat and protect the underhair. Many mammals have long, stiff hairs about the mouth or other parts of the head. These hairs, called *vibrissae* or *tactile hairs*, serve as highly sensitive touch organs. The whiskers of cats and mice are examples of such hairs.

Hair serves many purposes. The hair color of many mammals blends with the animals' surroundings and so helps them hide from their enemies or prey. Some mammals have specialized guard hairs, such as the quills on a porcupine, that provide protection from enemies. But the main purpose of hair is to keep the animal warm. Dolphins and whales, which lack body hair, have a thick layer of fat that provides warmth. Other mammals with little hair, such as elephants and rhinoceroses, live in warm climates. See SKIN; HAIR.

Skeleton of mammals provides a framework for the body and protects vital organs. In addition, the muscles that enable a mammal to move about are attached to the skeleton. The skeleton of all adult mammals—whether blue whales or shrews—consists of more than 200 bones. Some of these bones are *fused* (united) and so form a single structure. The skeleton has two main parts. They are (1) the axial skeleton and (2) the appendicular skeleton.

The Axial Skeleton consists of three regions. These regions are the skull, the vertebral column, and the thoracic basket.

The skull houses the brain in a bony box called the *cranium*. The skull also includes the jaws and teeth and areas for the organs of hearing, sight, and smell. Some mammals have bony growths from the skull, such as the antlers on deer.

The vertebral column, or spine, consists of five kinds of *vertebrae* (backbones): *cervical*, in the neck; *thoracic*, in the chest; *lumbar*, in the lower back; *sacral*, in the hip; and *caudal*, in the tail. All mammals, except manatees and sloths, have seven cervical vertebrae. The number of each of the other kinds of vertebrae varies with the species of mammal.

The thoracic basket is made up of the ribs, which are attached to the thoracic vertebrae. Most of the ribs also are joined to the breastbone. The thoracic basket forms a bony cage that protects the heart, lungs, and other vital organs.

The Appendicular Skeleton is made up of the limbs and their supports. The forelimbs are attached to the axial skeleton by the shoulder girdle, which consists of a broad shoulder blade and, in most species, a narrow collarbone. The hindlimbs are attached to the sacral vertebrae by a hip girdle consisting of three bones. In many mammals, the three bones of the hip girdle are fused to one another and to the sacral vertebrae.

A single bone forms the upper portion of each limb. In most mammals, the lower part of each limb has two bones. These bones are fused in some mammals. The wrist, palm, ankle, and sole consist of several small bones. The number of these depends on how many fingers or toes the mammal has. See SKELETON.

Internal Organ Systems are groups of organs that serve a particular function. The major systems of mammals include (1) the circulatory system, (2) the digestive system, (3) the nervous system, and (4) the respiratory system.

The Circulatory System consists of the heart and blood vessels. Mammals have an extremely efficient four-chambered heart, which pumps blood to all parts of the body. The blood, in turn, carries food and oxygen to the body tissues, where they are burned to release energy. The red blood cells of mammals can carry more oxygen than can the cells of all other animals except birds. The high efficiency of the circulatory system is associated with warm-bloodedness. Mammals must burn large amounts of food to maintain a high body temperature. See HEART; BLOOD.

The Digestive System absorbs nourishing substances from food. The system consists basically of a long tube that is formed by the mouth, the esophagus, the stomach, and the intestines. The digestive system of mammals varies according to the kind of food an animal eats. Mammals that eat flesh, which is easy to digest, have a fairly simple stomach and short intestines. Most mammals that eat plants, however, have a complicated stomach and long intestines. For example, such mammals as cows and sheep have a four-chambered stomach. Each chamber helps break down the coarse grasses that the animals eat. See DIGESTION; RUMINANT.

The Nervous System regulates most body activities. It consists mainly of the brain and spinal cord and their associated nerves. Most kinds of mammals have a larger brain than do other animals of similar size. In addition, mammalian brains have an extremely well-developed

Some Major Characteristics of Mammals

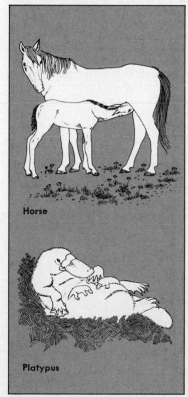

Horse

Platypus

Alpaca

Porcupine

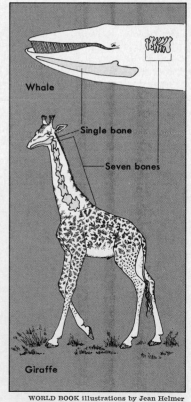

Whale

Single bone

Seven bones

Giraffe

WORLD BOOK illustrations by Jean Helmer

Mammals Nurse Their Young. A colt, like most baby mammals, sucks milk from his mother's nipples. Baby platypuses lap milk from their mother's abdomen.

Mammals Have Hair. In the alpaca and most other mammals, a thick coat of hair provides warmth. The porcupine's quills are special hairs used for self-defense.

Mammals Have Similar Skeletons. Only one bone forms each side of the lower jaw in mammals. Almost all mammals have seven backbones in the neck.

The Anatomy of a Mammal

Although mammals differ greatly in size and shape, they all share a number of physical characteristics. These characteristics include the same basic skeletal and internal organ systems. The diagrams below show the skeleton and internal organs of a male dog.

WORLD BOOK diagrams by Jean Helmer

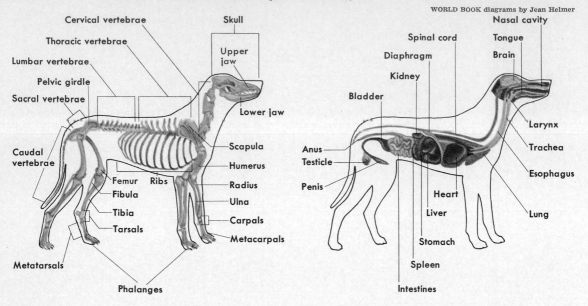

Cervical vertebrae — Skull — Upper jaw — Thoracic vertebrae — Lumbar vertebrae — Pelvic girdle — Sacral vertebrae — Lower jaw — Scapula — Humerus — Radius — Ulna — Carpals — Metacarpals — Caudal vertebrae — Femur — Ribs — Fibula — Tibia — Tarsals — Metatarsals — Phalanges

Nasal cavity — Tongue — Brain — Spinal cord — Diaphragm — Kidney — Bladder — Larynx — Trachea — Esophagus — Anus — Testicle — Penis — Heart — Liver — Lung — Stomach — Spleen — Intestines

cerebral cortex. This part of the brain serves as the center for learning and gives mammals superior intelligence. See BRAIN; NERVOUS SYSTEM.

The Respiratory System enables mammals to breathe. It is made up of two lungs and various tubes that lead to the nostrils. A muscular sheet called the *diaphragm* divides the chest cavity from the abdominal cavity and aids in breathing. Only mammals have a muscular diaphragm. In most mammals, the nostrils are at the end of the snout or nose. Dolphins and whales have their nostrils, called *blowholes*, at the top of the head. Dolphins and some whales have one nostril. Other whales have two. See LUNG; RESPIRATION.

Other Organ Systems of mammals include the endocrine, excretory, and reproductive systems. The endocrine system consists of glands that produce *hormones*, substances which help regulate body functions. The excretory system eliminates wastes from the body by means of the kidneys. For information on these two systems, see the articles HORMONE and KIDNEY. For a discussion of the mammalian reproductive system, see the section of this article titled *How Mammals Reproduce*.

The Senses and Intelligence of Mammals

Senses. Mammals rely on various senses to inform them of happenings in their environment. The major senses of mammals are (1) smell, (2) taste, (3) hearing, (4) sight, and (5) touch. However, the senses are not equally developed in each species of mammal. In fact, some species do not have all the senses.

Smell is the most important sense among the majority of mammals. Most species have large nasal cavities lined with nerves that are sensitive to odors. These animals rely heavily on smell to find food and to detect the presence of enemies. In many species, the members communicate with one another through the odors produced by various skin glands and body wastes. For example, a dog urinates on trees and other objects to tell other dogs it has been there. A few species of mammals, especially human beings, apes, and monkeys, have a poorly developed sense of smell. Dolphins and whales seem to lack the sense entirely. See SMELL.

Taste helps mammals identify foods and so decide what foods to eat. This sense is located mainly in *taste buds* on the tongue. However, much of the sense of taste is strongly affected by the odor of food. See TASTE.

Hearing is well developed in most mammals. The majority of species have an outer ear, which collects sound waves and channels them into the middle and inner ear. Only mammals have an outer ear. See the article EAR for a description of the human ear, which is typical of the ears of most mammals.

Some mammals use their sense of hearing to find food and avoid obstacles in the dark. Bats, for example, produce short, high-pitched sounds that bounce off surrounding objects. Bats can use these sounds and their echoes to detect insects and even thin wires. Dolphins and whales also use this system, called *echolocation*, to find food and avoid objects underwater. However, most of the sounds they make are pitched much lower than are the sounds made by bats. Other echolocating mammals include sea lions, seals, and shrews.

Sight is the most important sense among the *higher primates* (apes, monkeys, and people). The structure and function of the eye is similar in all mammals (see EYE). However, the eyes of the higher primates have more *cones* than do those of most other mammals. These structures give apes, monkeys, and people sharp daytime vision and the ability to tell colors apart. A few other mammals that are active during the day have some color vision, but most mammals are color blind. Many species of mammals that are active at night have large eyes with a reflector at the rear. This reflector, called the *tapetum lucidum*, helps the animal see in the dark. It produces the *eyeshine* a person sees when light strikes the eyes of a cat or a deer at night.

Touch. Most mammals have a good sense of touch. *Tactile nerves*—that is, nerves which respond to touch—are found all over a mammal's body. But some areas have an especially large number of these nerves and are therefore very sensitive to touch. The whiskers of such mammals as cats, dogs, and mice have many tactile nerves at their base. These whiskers help the animals feel their way in the dark. Moles and pocket gophers have a highly sensitive tail, which aids them when backing up in their dark, narrow tunnels. The fingers of primates also have many tactile nerves as do the paws of raccoons.

Intelligence is related to the ability to learn. Through learning, an animal stores information in its memory and then later uses this information to act in appropriate ways. Mammals, with their highly developed cerebral cortex, are able to learn more than other kinds of animals.

Intelligence is hard to measure, even in human beings. But chimpanzees, dogs, and dolphins can learn much when trained by people. These species are among the most intelligent mammals. The amount of the surface area of the brain, especially of the cerebral cortex, generally indicates an animal's learning ability. In the more intelligent mammals, the cerebral cortex is fairly large and has many folds, which further increase its surface area. Human beings have the most highly developed cerebral cortex.

What Mammals Eat

Most mammals are *herbivorous*—that is, they eat plants. Plant food is generally tough and so tends to wear teeth down. Herbivorous mammals have special teeth that help counteract such wear. Many plant-eating mammals, including cattle, elephants, and horses, have high-crowned teeth that wear down slowly. The front teeth of beavers, rats, and other rodents grow continuously and thus never wear down.

Some mammals are *carnivorous*. They eat animal flesh. Many of them are speedy animals that catch, hold, and stab their prey with long, pointed *canine teeth.* Such mammals, which include leopards, lions, and

wolves, do not thoroughly chew their food. They swallow chunks of it whole. Dolphins, seals, and other fish-eating mammals also use their teeth to grasp prey, which they swallow whole. Some carnivorous mammals commonly feed on the remains of dead animals, instead of hunting and killing fresh prey. Hyenas are especially adapted to such a diet and have extremely powerful jaws that can crush even large bones.

Various mammals eat insects. Many of these *insectivorous* mammals, such as bats and shrews, have teeth that can crush and slice off the hard outer parts of insects. This action exposes the softer flesh and juices, which the mammals feed on. Other insect-eaters, such as aardvarks, anteaters, echidnas, numbats, and pangolins, have weak teeth or none at all. These mammals eat ants and termites, which they lick up with their long, sticky tongues and swallow without chewing.

Some mammals eat both plants and animals. These *omnivorous* mammals have teeth that can grind up plants and tear off flesh. They include bears, hogs, opossums, and human beings. Some omnivorous mammals change their diet with the seasons. For example, spotted skunks feed mostly on fruits, seeds, and insects in summer. In winter, they eat mainly mice and rats.

How Mammals Move

On Land. Most mammals live on the ground. The majority of these *terrestrial* animals move about on four legs. They walk by lifting one foot at a time—first one forefoot, then the opposite hindfoot, next the other forefoot, and then the opposite hindfoot. At faster speeds, most four-legged mammals *trot,* lifting one forefoot and the opposite hindfoot at the same time. A few species, such as camels, elephants, and giraffes, pace rather than trot. *Pacing* involves lifting both feet on one side of the body at the same time. At their fastest speed, most terrestrial mammals *gallop.* While galloping, the animal usually has only one foot on the ground at a time. At some point during the gallop, all four feet are in the air.

The Teeth of Mammals Mammals have three basic types of teeth: (1) *incisors* (front teeth), (2) *canines* (side teeth), and (3) *premolars* and *molars* (cheek teeth). The number and shape of these teeth vary according to diet.

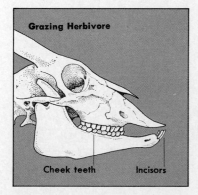

Grazing Herbivore

Cheek teeth   Incisors

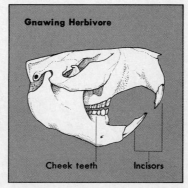

Gnawing Herbivore

Cheek teeth   Incisors

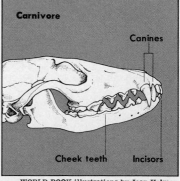

Carnivore

Canines

Cheek teeth   Incisors

WORLD BOOK illustrations by Jean Helmer

Sheep Teeth. A sheep snips off grass by pressing its lower incisors against a pad on its upper jaw. It uses the cheek teeth for grinding and has no canine teeth.

Beaver Teeth. A beaver uses its huge incisors to gnaw the bark off plants. Like sheep, beavers use the cheek teeth for grinding and have no canine teeth.

Red Fox Teeth. A red fox has small incisors but large, pointed canine teeth, which it uses to stab and hold prey. The cheek teeth are used for crushing.

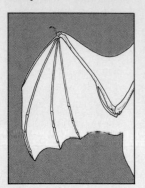  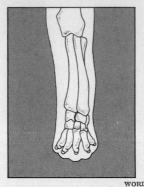 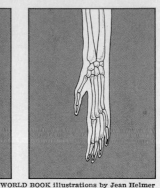

WORLD BOOK illustrations by Jean Helmer

A Bat's Forelimb is adapted for flying. The bones of the hand and forearm provide the framework of the bat's wing.

A Walrus' Forelimb forms a paddle-shaped flipper, which the animal uses to pull itself through the water.

An Elephant's Forelimb provides a sturdy, pillarlike support to carry the enormous body over the ground.

A Gibbon's Forelimb is adapted for swinging through trees. The animal has powerful arms and flexible fingers.

Jerboas, kangaroos, and kangaroo rats are terrestrial mammals that move by hopping. These animals have powerful hind legs. They also have a long tail that is used for balance.

In Trees. Many mammals that live in forested areas spend most of their time in the trees. These *arboreal* animals have a number of special body features that help them move through the trees. Monkeys, for example, can use their hands and feet to grasp tree branches. Many monkeys of Central and South America also have a *prehensile* (grasping) tail, which they can wrap around branches for support. Other arboreal mammals with a prehensile tail include kinkajous, opossums, and phalangers. Some species of anteaters, pangolins, and South American porcupines also have such a tail. Squirrels and tree shrews have sharp, curved claws that aid them in climbing trees. The claws of tree sloths are so long and curved that the animals cannot walk erect on the ground. These mammals spend most of their life hanging upside down from branches.

In Water. Dolphins, porpoises, manatees, and whales are mammals that live their entire life in water. They have a streamlined body and a powerful tail, which they move up and down to propel themselves through the water. Their forelimbs are paddlelike flippers, used for balance and steering. They have no hindlimbs.

Many other mammals spend much, but not all, of their time in water. Some of these animals, such as capybaras, hippopotamuses, and walruses, swim by moving their forelimbs and their hindlimbs. Other species use mainly their forelimbs. Such swimmers include platypuses, polar bears, and fur seals and sea lions. Still other mammals use only their hindlimbs to swim. These animals include beavers and hair seals.

In the Air. Bats are the only mammals that can fly. Their wings consist of thin skin stretched over the bones of the forelimbs. Bats fly by beating their wings forward and downward, then upward and backward.

The so-called flying lemurs, flying phalangers, and flying squirrels cannot actually fly. These mammals have a fold of skin between the forelimb and hindlimb on each side of the body. By stretching out these "wings," the animals can glide from tree to tree.

Underground. Pocket gophers, moles, and certain other mammals spend almost all their life underground. Most of these *fossorial* mammals have strong claws and powerful forelimbs. Many of them have poor vision, and some are blind. The forelimbs of moles are turned so that the broad palms face backward and the elbows point upward. Strong chest muscles attached to the forelimbs enable moles to "swim" through the soil, much as a person swims when doing the breaststroke.

How Mammals Reproduce

All mammals reproduce sexually. In sexual reproduction, a *sperm* (male sex cell) unites with an *egg* (female sex cell) in a process called *fertilization*. The fertilized egg develops into a new individual. In all species of mammals, the eggs are fertilized inside the female's body. Male mammals have a special organ, the penis, which releases sperm into the female during *copulation* (sexual intercourse). See REPRODUCTION.

Mating occurs among most mammals only during the period when the female is in *estrus*, or *heat*. At this time, the female is sexually excited and will permit copulation. See ESTROUS CYCLE.

The time of the estrous period varies with different species. Among many mammals, especially those that live in regions where the climate is constant the year around, the females may come into heat at any time. Such *polyestrous* (many-estrous) mammals include baboons, elephants, and giraffes. Among species that live in regions with distinct seasons, all the females may come into heat at a particular time of year. This *breeding*, or *rutting*, season is so timed that the offspring will be born when environmental conditions are best for their survival. Some seasonal breeders have one heat period a year. Such *monestrous* (one-estrous) species include certain bats, bears, and deer. Other species, such as cottontail rabbits, have several heat periods during their breeding season. These mammals are *seasonally polyestrous*.

Most smaller mammals are *promiscuous* in their mating behavior. No lasting bond forms between the mates. They remain together only long enough to copulate. Some other species are *polygamous*. The males of such

92f

species, which include American elks and fur seals, gather a *harem* (group of females) just before and during the mating season. The male tries to mate with each member of his harem. The association between the male and the harem ends after the breeding season. Among many kinds of mammals, the males and females remain together for some time after mating. However, only a few mammals seem to take one mate for life. Zoologists believe that such *monogamous* species include beavers, wolves, and a tiny antelope called a dik-dik.

Reproduction. Mammals can be divided into three groups according to the way in which new individuals develop from the fertilized eggs. These groups are

(1) placentals, (2) marsupials, and (3) monotremes.

Placentals give birth to fairly well-developed offspring. The vast majority of mammals are placentals. After fertilization occurs, a placental mammal begins to develop in the *uterus*, a hollow organ in the mother's abdomen. Another organ, called the *placenta*, attaches the developing mammal to the uterus wall. The developing mammal receives nourishment from the mother through the placenta.

The time during which the unborn young develops in the uterus is called the *gestation period*. Among placen-

How Mammals Reproduce

All mammals reproduce sexually. A new individual begins to form after a *sperm* (male sex cell) unites with an *egg* (female sex cell). This union is called *fertilization*. Mammals can be divided into three groups according to the way in which the fertilized egg develops into a new individual. These groups are (1) placentals, (2) marsupials, and (3) monotremes.

Norman Myers, Bruce Coleman Inc.

Placentals give birth to fairly well-developed offspring, such as the newborn zebra shown above. A young placental mammal develops inside its mother, receiving nourishment from her through an organ called the *placenta*. Placentals make up the vast majority of mammals.

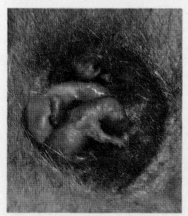  

Leonard Lee Rue III, Bruce Coleman Inc.   Warren Garst, Tom Stack & Assoc.   WORLD BOOK diagram by Jean Helmer

Marsupials give birth to poorly developed young, such as these baby opossums. Young marsupials complete their development attached to the mother's nipples.

Monotremes, such as the platypus, *left,* lay eggs rather than bear their young alive. The female platypus digs a long tunnel in the bank of a stream, *right.* There she lays one to three eggs that have a leathery shell. The only other monotreme is the echidna, or spiny anteater. Platypuses and echidnas live in Australia and on nearby islands.

92g

George Schaller, Bruce Coleman Inc.

A Lion Cub sucks nourishing milk from its mother's nipple. All baby mammals feed on mother's milk. Among many species, the young continue to nurse long after they can eat some solid foods.

Joe Branney, Tom Stack & Assoc.

A Mother Brown Bear shows her cubs how to catch fish. Many young mammals learn how to obtain food by watching and imitating the behavior of their parents and other adults.

H. Albrecht, Bruce Coleman Inc.

Young Wild Dogs romp together in a make-believe fight. This kind of play serves as an important learning experience. It helps the puppies develop the skills they will need for hunting.

tal mammals, the gestation period ranges from about 16 days in golden hamsters to about 650 days in elephants. Most species with a short gestation period give birth to young that are generally helpless and may be blind and hairless. Most species with a long gestation period bear young that are alert soon after birth. The newborns may also be fully haired, and some can even walk or run almost immediately.

Marsupials give birth to very tiny, poorly developed offspring. Directly after birth, the young attach themselves to the mother's nipples. The babies remain attached until they develop more completely. The nipples of most female marsupials are in a pouch, called the *marsupium*, on the stomach. Marsupials are often known as *pouched mammals*. However, not all female marsupials have a pouch. Certain South American species, for example, lack this feature.

There are about 240 species of marsupials. Almost all of them live in Australia and nearby islands. Australian marsupials include kangaroos, koala bears, and wombats. Several kinds of opossums, which are marsupials, live in Central and South America. One species lives in the United States and Canada.

Monotremes, unlike all other kinds of mammals, do not give birth to live young. Instead, they lay eggs that have a leathery shell. After an incubation period, the eggs hatch. The only monotremes are the echidnas and the platypus. They live in Australia, New Guinea, and Tasmania.

Care of the Young. All baby mammals feed on milk from their mother's mammary glands. Baby placentals and marsupials suck the milk from the mother's nipples. Female monotremes do not have nipples. The milk is released through pores on the mother's abdomen, and the young lap it up. The nursing period lasts only a few weeks in mice, hares, and many other species. But among some mammals, such as elephants and rhinoceroses, the young may nurse several years before they are *weaned*—that is, taken off the mother's milk. In most species, the young can eat solid food long before they are weaned.

Young mammals must learn many of the skills they need to survive. Much of this learning occurs during the nursing period, when the young are taught how to obtain food and how to avoid dangers. Among most kinds of mammals, the mother alone raises the young. However, the males of some species help care for their offspring. For example, male mice of certain species aid in nest building. Male coyotes and African wild dogs bring back food for the mother and puppies. Male lions help protect the mother and cubs from attacks by hyenas and other lions.

Among many smaller mammals, such as mice and shrews, the young leave the parental nest or den as soon as they are weaned. But among cheetahs, elephants, wolves, and numerous other species, the young remain with their parents long after the nursing period ends.

Ways of Life

Group Life. Many mammals live in *social groups* of several individuals. The simplest social group consists of an adult male and female and their offspring. Beavers and certain species of monkeys form such family groups. A larger social group, such as a wolf pack, may have a number of adult and young animals of both sexes. Zebra herds, which consist of an adult male and several females and their young, make up another kind of social group.

Among many social species, the group members are ranked according to a *dominance hierarchy*. The *dominant* (controlling) members of the group get first choice of food and mates. They may establish their dominance at first by winning fights. Thereafter, they keep their position mostly by threats. See DOMINANCE.

Group life offers several advantages. Coyotes, lions, wolves, and other *predators* (hunters) that live in groups cooperate in surrounding and bringing down prey. However, prey species can also profit from group life. If one deer senses danger, for example, it can warn the entire herd by flashing the white underside of its tail. Among some prey species, such as baboons and musk oxen, the group assembles into a defensive formation for protection against predators.

Some mammals spend most of their life alone. Such *solitary* mammals include leopards, tigers, and most other cats except lions. However, even solitary mammals spend some time with members of their species. For example, adult males and females get together to mate, and a mother remains with her young at least until they are weaned.

Solitary mammals have several advantages over social species. They do not have to share available food and shelter. In addition, a solitary predator can hunt its prey more silently than can a group. Among prey species, a solitary animal attracts less attention than a group does, and it can hide more easily.

Territoriality is a form of behavior in which an animal or group of animals claims and defends a particular area. Other members of the species are kept out of the territory. Many species of mammals establish territories only during the breeding season. For example, a male fur seal claims a territory before mating. He drives all other males from his territory, while he tries to herd as many females as possible into the area. Other mammals, such as gibbons and howler monkeys, claim a territory to help ensure the group of an adequate food supply.

Mammals mark the boundaries of their territories in various ways. For example, hyenas leave solid body wastes and scents produced by special glands to indicate their territorial borders. Wolf packs mark their territories with urine. Such markers serve as No Trespassing signs to other members of the species.

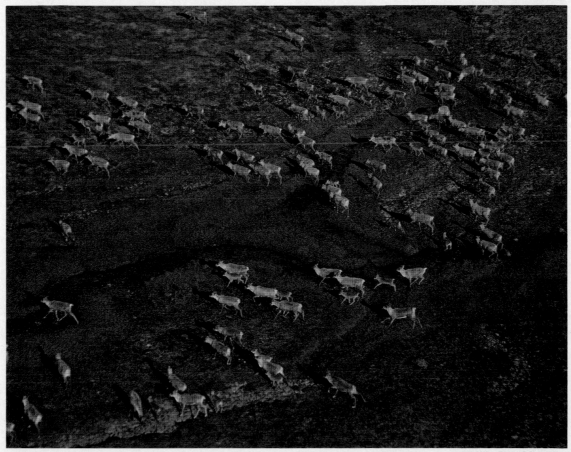

Rod Allin, Bruce Coleman Inc.

Barren Ground Caribou are *social mammals*—that is, they live in groups. Caribou herds may include hundreds of members. The herds spend the summer in the Arctic tundra. As autumn approaches, the animals migrate southward to evergreen forests, where they can obtain food during the winter.

R. T. W. from Carl E. Östman

Vervets, like all other species of monkeys, are social mammals. Vervets generally form bands of no more than 20 members. These monkeys are common throughout much of Africa.

K. W. Fink, Bruce Coleman Inc.

A Male Sea Lion, center, claims a territory during the mating season. He keeps all other males out of his territory but tries to gather as many females as possible into the area.

Mammals usually defend their territories by threats rather than by actually fighting. A group of howler monkeys, for instance, keeps other howlers out of its territory by shouting at them.

Many mammals are not territorial. But most species, including those that do not claim a territory, have a *home range.* A mammal wanders over its home range during the daily activities of feeding, drinking, and seeking shelter. Unlike a territory, a home range is not defended against members of the same species. See TERRITORIALITY.

Migration. Many kinds of mammals make seasonal migrations to obtain a better food supply, to avoid harsh weather, or to do both. For example, various species of North American bats migrate southward each autumn because the insects that they feed on become scarce during the cold northern winter. Great herds of wildebeests and zebras in central Africa migrate in search of green grass during the yearly dry season. American elks of Canada and the Western United States spend the summer on high mountain slopes. In winter, they live in the valleys below, where the snow is not as deep.

Some mammals migrate to an area to give birth or to mate. Every fall, for example, gray whales swim from their Arctic feeding grounds to the warmer waters off the northwest coast of Mexico. These waters provide little or no food for the whales. The animals make the journey to give birth because newborn whales could not survive in the cold Arctic waters. See MIGRATION (Migration of Animals).

Hibernation. Some kinds of mammals hibernate to avoid winter food shortages. During hibernation, an animal goes into *torpor,* a type of sleep from which it cannot be awakened quickly. The body temperature of a torpid mammal drops to nearly that of the surrounding air. The animal's heartbeat and breathing slow down greatly. While in this condition, the animal does not eat food. It lives off the fat in its body. Some hibernating mammals pass in and out of torpor all during the winter.

Mammals that hibernate include certain kinds of bats; echidnas; and chipmunks, woodchucks, and some other rodents. Most of these animals become extremely fat before they go into hibernation. They usually spend the winter in a den or some other protected place where the temperature is not likely to fall below freezing.

Bears, skunks, and certain other mammals may also den up during the coldest part of the winter. But these animals do not go into a deep torpor and thus are not true hibernators. Their body temperature drops only slightly, and they can be awakened quickly.

A few kinds of mammals, mostly rodents, become torpid during the hottest, driest part of the summer. This summer torpor is called *estivation.* See HIBERNATION.

Methods of Attack and Defense. Mammals that hunt rely mainly on their sharp teeth to catch and kill prey. Most of these predators also have sharp claws, which they use to grab and hold their victims. Solitary predators generally stalk their prey by slinking and hiding, and many of these hunters have coats that blend with their surroundings. After a predator has sneaked up on its prey, it makes a final dash at high speed to catch the animal before it can escape. Group hunters, such as African hunting dogs and wolves, usually take turns in the chase until they have worn the prey out.

Most mammals try to escape predators by fleeing. Many hoofed mammals, such as deer and impalas, can run swiftly for long distances. Gophers, prairie dogs, and many other small mammals rush into a burrow or other hiding place. On the other hand, fawns and rabbits sometimes escape hunters by remaining absolutely still. This defense works because many predators are "sight hunters" and are attracted mainly by movement. The American opossum takes this defense one step further. It "plays dead" by going completely limp. Many predators lose interest in the apparently dead animal.

Some mammals have special features that help protect them from enemies. The bony shell of armadillos and the scales of pangolins serve as protection against sharp-clawed predators. The thick skin of elephants and rhinoceroses serves the same purpose. Echidnas, hedgehogs, and porcupines have sharp, stiff quills that stop most attackers. Skunks and their relatives spray a foul-smelling liquid when threatened. An animal that has been sprayed by a skunk will probably not want to threaten it again. The skunk's bold black-and-white markings make it easy for predators to remember to

Mammals have various means of capturing prey and of defending themselves against their enemies. The most important means include speed, concealment, and special protective body structures.

Jack Couffer, Bruce Coleman Inc.

A Lion Chases a Waterbuck. In this contest, both mammals rely on speed—the lion to attack, and the waterbuck to escape. In most instances, a healthy adult waterbuck will escape.

George Schaller, Bruce Coleman Inc.

A Tiger's Striped Coat provides almost total concealment in tall grass, enabling the animal to sneak up on its prey.

Leonard Lee Rue III, FPG

An Armadillo's Bony Shell protects the animal like a suit of armor. When attacked, the armadillo curls up into a tight ball.

avoid the animal. Most prey species, however, have protective coloration that blends with their surroundings. The coat of some species changes seasonally to match the color of the terrain. For example, the coat of Arctic hares is brownish in summer. In winter, the coat turns white and so helps hide the animals against the snow.

The Evolution of Mammals

The Ancestors of Mammals. Mammals *evolved* (developed gradually) from a group of reptiles called the *synapsids*. These reptiles arose during the Pennsylvanian Period (310 million to 275 million years ago). By the middle of the Permian Period (275 million to 225 million years ago), a branch of the synapsids called the *therapsids* had appeared. Over tens of millions of years, the therapsids developed many features that would later be associated with mammals. The therapsids are often referred to as the *mammallike reptiles*. One group of therapsids, the *cynodonts*, developed especially mammallike teeth, skulls, and limbs. Most scientists believe that the first mammals evolved from the cynodonts.

The First Mammals probably split off from the cynodonts late in the Triassic Period (225 million to 180 million years ago). Numerous fossils from this period might be either early mammals or cynodonts. Scientists cannot be sure because many characteristics of mammals—such as hair, mammary glands, and warm-bloodedness—are not preserved in the fossil record.

By the start of the Jurassic Period (180 million to 130 million years ago), mammals had definitely evolved. They were tiny, shrewlike animals that probably ate insects and worms. Mammals remained fairly small throughout the Jurassic Period and the following Cretaceous Period (130 million to 65 million years ago). Dinosaurs ruled the land during these periods. However, many primitive groups of mammals developed in Jurassic times. Most scientists believe that one of these early groups led directly to modern monotremes, though the fossil record of egg-laying mammals is extremely incomplete. Many other early groups died out in the Cretaceous Period. But one group, the *pantotheres*, probably gave rise to marsupials and placentals by the middle of the period.

A Classification of Mammals

Mammals make up the class Mammalia, one of the seven classes of vertebrates. Zoologists divide the class into various orders of related species. The classification used here recognizes 18 orders of living mammals. The orders are listed according to their probable evolutionary development.

WORLD BOOK illustrations by Jean Helmer

Order Monotremata—monotremes. Primitive mammals that lay eggs. Mammary glands lack nipples. Teeth present only in young; adults have horny beak. Order consists of five species of echidnas and one species of platypus.

Echidna

Order Marsupialia—marsupials. Varied group of mammals whose young are poorly developed at birth. They complete development attached to the mother's nipples, which are in a pouch in most species. Order consists of 242 species, including kangaroos, koalas, opossums, and wombats.

Kangaroo

Order Insectivora—moles, shrews. Small mammals with teeth adapted for crushing insects. Most have pointed snout and five-toed feet. Order consists of about 400 species, including elephant shrews, hedgehogs, moles, and shrews.

Hedgehog

Order Dermoptera—flying lemurs. Tree-dwelling Asian mammals with flaps of skin adapted for gliding. Order consists of two species of flying lemurs, or colugos.

Flying Lemur

Order Chiroptera—bats. Only mammals that are capable of true flight, having forelimbs adapted as wings. Order consists of about 875 species of bats.

Bat

Order Primates—primates. Most species are tree dwellers. Hands have five fingers, and feet five toes. Many species have thumbs and big toes capable of grasping. Order consists of 166 species, including apes, human beings, lemurs, and monkeys.

Baboon

Order Edentata—edentates. Mammals that lack teeth or have only molars. Forelimbs adapted for digging or for clinging to branches. Order consists of 31 species of anteaters, armadillos, and sloths.

Armadillo

Order Pholidota—pangolins. Toothless mammals covered with horny scales. A few hairs grow between scales. Order consists of eight species of pangolins.

Pangolin

Order Lagomorpha—lagomorphs. Small mammals with two pairs of upper incisors, no canine teeth, and molars without roots. Tail short or absent. Order consists of 63 species of hares, pikas, and rabbits.

Hare

Order Rodentia—rodents. Small, gnawing mammals with one pair of chisel-like upper incisors; no canines. Order consists of 1,687 species, including beavers, gophers, mice, porcupines, rats, and squirrels.

Squirrel

Order Cetacea—cetaceans. Aquatic mammals with streamlined bodies, paddlelike forelimbs, no hindlimbs, horizontally flattened tail, and nostrils on top of head. Order consists of 84 species of dolphins, porpoises, and whales.

Dolphin

Order Carnivora—carnivores. Most are meat-eaters and have claws and large canine teeth. Order consists of 284 species, including bears, cats, raccoons, seals, walruses, weasels, and wolves. Seals and walruses sometimes put in separate order.

Wolf

Order Tubulidentata—aardvark. Burrowing, insect-eating mammal with long, piglike snout and long, sticky tongue. Order consists of only one species.

Aardvark

Order Proboscidea—elephants. Large, thick-skinned mammals. Nose and upper lip form trunk; upper incisors enlarged as tusks. Order consists of two species, African elephant and Asian elephant.

Elephant

Order Hyracoidea—hyraxes. Small mammals with hooflike claws and short tail. Order consists of 11 species of hyraxes.

Hyrax

Order Sirenia—sea cows. Aquatic mammals with paddlelike forelimbs, no hindlimbs, and flattened muzzle. Order consists of four species of dugongs and manatees.

Manatee

Order Perissodactyla—odd-toed ungulates. Hoofed mammals with one or three toes on each foot. Axis of limb passes through middle toe. Order consists of 16 species, including horses, rhinoceroses, and tapirs.

Tapir

Order Artiodactyla—even-toed ungulates. Hoofed mammals with two or four toes on each foot. Axis of limb passes between middle of toes. Order consists of 171 species, including antelopes, bison, camels, deer, giraffes, goats, hippopotamuses, hogs, peccaries, pronghorns, and sheep.

Deer

94

The Age of Mammals began with the extinction of the dinosaurs at the end of Cretaceous times. During the Cenozoic Era (65 million years ago to the present), mammals became the dominant land animals. By the end of the Eocene Epoch (55 million to 40 million years ago), all the modern *orders* (main groups) of mammals had developed. The modern families of mammals appeared during the Oligocene Epoch (40 million to 26 million years ago).

Mammals reached their greatest variety during the Miocene Epoch (26 million to 14 million years ago). The number of mammalian species began to decline during the Pliocene Epoch (14 million to 1¾ million years ago). The Pleistocene Epoch, which began about 1¾ million years ago, brought enormous changes in climate. Several waves of glaciers advanced over much of North America, Europe, and Asia. Many mammals —including ground sloths, mammoths, saber-toothed cats, and woolly rhinoceroses—died out. Most of these extinctions were probably due to the changes in climate. But some might have been caused by a group of new, terribly skillful predators—human beings.

The Future of Mammals. Although extinctions are a normal part of evolution, human beings have caused an increasingly rapid decline in the number of wild mammals. In the past few hundred years, human hunters have exterminated such mammals as the blaubok, or bluebuck, of Africa; the zebralike quagga; and Steller's sea cow. Human beings have also reduced the population of orang-utans, rhinoceroses, tigers, and many other mammals to a size so low that these species might not survive.

Most large wild mammals are now few in number and confined to parks, some of which provide little protection or insufficient living space. Other large mammals, such as whales, are still hunted. Every year, people turn more and more wild lands into farms and so increasingly deprive mammals of living space. The survival of most wild mammals will depend on the establishment and careful management of large nature preserves and parks. RICHARD G. VAN GELDER

Related Articles in WORLD BOOK include:

MAMMALS

See the following general articles and their lists of *Related Articles:*

Outline

Questions

How do monotremes differ from all other mammals?

What are some of the purposes of hair?

Which is the most important sense among the majority of mammals?

How does the diet differ among herbivorous, carnivorous, and omnivorous mammals?

What are *domestic* mammals? What are some of the ways people use such mammals?

When did the first mammals probably appear? From which group of animals did they evolve?

What are some of the advantages of group life?

What is the *cerebral cortex*? Why is it important to mammals?

How does a *territory* differ from a *home range*?

What are some of the special body features of *arboreal* mammals?

MAMMARY GLANDS are glands in the breasts of all mammals, both male and female. They produce milk. They are one of the major features that distinguish mammals from other kinds of animals (see MAMMAL).

In males, the mammary glands remain undeveloped. In females, they enlarge and develop. The gland itself consists of many *lobules* (sacks) that secrete milk. Many *ducts* (tubes) are connected to these lobules. The ducts combine and form several main ducts that empty the milk into the nipple. Milk is released through the nipple. See also LACTATION. THEODORE B. SCHWARTZ

MAMMOTH, *MAM uhth*, was a prehistoric animal closely related to present-day elephants. Mammoths were huge, lumbering beasts. Some measured more than 14 feet (4.3 meters) high at the shoulders. Mammoths had trunks and tusks. Many had tusks 13 feet (4 meters) long. The tusks curved down from the animal's upper jaw, then curved up and crossed in front of the trunk. Certain mammoths, called *woolly* or *hairy* mammoths, had long hair on their bodies, which helped protect them from the severe cold of the Ice Age.

Mammoths rank among the most common fossils. The bodies of mammoths have been found perfectly preserved in ice in Siberia. Alaskan miners often wash petrified mammoth bones and teeth out of gravel when they pan for gold. Fossils of these enormous beasts have also been found in New York and Texas.

The oldest known mammoth bones date from 4 mil-

Painting by Charles R. Knight, from the Field Museum of Natural History

The Hairy Mammoth was a relative of the modern elephant. Mammoths lived in the frozen regions of North America, Europe, and Asia, but died out many thousands of years ago.

lion years ago in India. Mammoths spread to other continents and reached North America about 500,000 years later, during the Ice Age. Prehistoric people hunted them for food. Pictures of mammoths drawn by cave dwellers can be seen on the walls of caves in southern France. Mammoths died out about 10,000 years ago.

Scientific Classification. Mammoths belong to the elephant family, *Elephantidae*. They make up the genus *Mammuthus*.   SAMUEL PAUL WELLES

See also FOSSIL (Whole Animals and Plants); MASTODON; PREHISTORIC ANIMAL (picture).

MAMMOTH CAVE NATIONAL PARK surrounds Mammoth Cave, part of the world's longest known cave system. The park lies in central Kentucky, about 100 miles (160 kilometers) south of Louisville. Two rivers, the Green and the Nolin, flow through the park. Mammoth Cave National Park was established in 1941. It attracts about 1¾ million visitors annually. For area, see NATIONAL PARK SYSTEM (table: National Parks).

Mammoth Cave is often called one of the wonders of the Western Hemisphere. The cave is located in a ridge that consists mainly of limestone. Through millions of years, mildly acidic water trickled through cracks in the limestone and wore it away, forming the cave. Visitors can be guided through 12 miles (19 kilometers) of corridors on five levels in the cave. The lowest level lies 360 feet (110 meters) below the surface of the earth. Many rocks in the cave have interesting colors and shapes. These rocks resemble flowers, trees, and waterfalls.

The cave contains several lakes, rivers, and waterfalls. The largest river, Echo River, varies in width from 20 to 60 feet (6 to 18 meters) and in depth from 5 to 25 feet (1.5 to 8 meters). Strange eyeless fish live in Echo River (see BLINDFISH). These colorless creatures are about 3 inches (8 centimeters) long. Other blind creatures living in Mammoth Cave include beetles and crayfish. Several species of bats live in parts of the cave that are not visited frequently by people.

Historians believe that the first white people to see Mammoth Cave were local settlers who came to the area during the late 1700's. A deed filed in 1798 describes a large cave that probably was Mammoth Cave. But moccasins, simple tools, torches, and the remains of mummies found in the cave indicate that it was known to prehistoric Indians. Saltpeter, used to make gunpowder, was mined in the cave during the War of 1812. Mammoth Cave contained the only large supply of saltpeter that was known in the United States at that time. After the war ended, miners stopped working in the cave. It became a public showplace in 1816.

Another famous cave, Floyd Collins Crystal Cave, lies within the national park. Collins, a cave explorer, discovered Crystal Cave in 1917. Crystal Cave forms part of the Flint Ridge cave system, one of three cave systems in the park. The other two are the Joppa Ridge and the Mammoth Cave systems. In September, 1972, explorers discovered a connection between Mammoth Cave and the Flint Ridge cave system. The combined Mammoth-Flint Ridge cave system is the longest known cave system in the world. It has about 200 miles (320 kilometers) of explored passages.   STEVEN Q. SMITH

MAN. See HUMAN BEING.

MAN, ISLE OF. The Isle of Man lies in the Irish Sea, halfway between England and Ireland, and 20 miles

National Park Service

Mammoth Cave, in central Kentucky, has many unusual rock formations that may be seen by visitors on guided tours.

WORLD BOOK maps

The Isle of Man, which lies in the Irish Sea, belongs to Great Britain.

(32 kilometers) south of Scotland. The island is a summer resort for the people of the British Isles. Scholars believe that its name comes from a Celtic word that means *hilly land*. A breed of cats, usually without tails, called *Manx*, originated on the island (see CAT).

The island has an area of 227 square miles (588 square kilometers). Farms, rolling moorlands, and low mountains cover the island. It has a coastline of 50 miles (80 kilometers). The coast in many places is rocky and beautiful. A low mountain chain runs the length of the island. Its highest peak is Snaefell, 2,034 feet (620 meters) above sea level.

The Isle of Man has a population of about 65,000. The people are Celtic and are called *Manx* or *Manxmen*. In some parts of the island, the people speak English and Manx, their own Celtic language. The chief industries include the tourist trade, farming, cattle raising, and fishing. Douglas, the capital of the Isle of Man, lies beside a beautiful bay on the east coast. The Court of Tynwald, the island's 1,000-year-old parliament, is the oldest parliament in the British Commonwealth. The ruins of Rushen Castle, built in A.D. 947, stand near Castletown, the ancient capital.

The Isle of Man has been ruled by Ireland, Wales, Norway, Scotland, and England. In 1765, Great Britain bought the island. The Isle of Man still has its own representative assembly and courts. The British Crown appoints the governor.   FREDERICK G. MARCHAM

MAN AND SUPERMAN. See SHAW, GEORGE B.

MAN FRIDAY. See ROBINSON CRUSOE.

MAN O' WAR. See HORSE RACING (History).

MAN-OF-WAR BIRD. See FRIGATE BIRD.

MAN WITHOUT A COUNTRY, THE. See HALE, EDWARD EVERETT.

MANA. See MYTHOLOGY (Mythology of the Pacific Islands).

MANACLES. See HANDCUFFS.

MANAGEMENT means directing businesses, government agencies, foundations, and many other organizations and activities. The central idea of management is to make every action or decision help achieve a carefully chosen goal. The word *management* is also used to mean the group of persons called *executives*, who perform management activities.

The need for management has increased as modern business becomes more complex. In earlier days, an individual might operate a small business or farm without planning the exact way to do it. But today, some businesses employ thousands of workers, use millions of dollars worth of equipment, and sell products throughout the world. It has become important to make decisions in the light of carefully chosen goals.

Management in Business became a separate function with the development of joint-stock companies in the 1500's (see JOINT-STOCK COMPANY). Before that time, the proprietors or partners who owned a business also managed it. The discovery of ocean-trade routes to all parts of the world created new opportunities for trade. They also created a need for large amounts of money to finance this trade. But the amounts needed were more than single individuals could supply or were willing to risk. The joint-stock company could bring together individuals with money to assist in the financing of trade even if they knew little or nothing about the business. The stock owners could hire managers with skill and experience. The managers often had little or no ownership in the businesses they managed.

The need for large *capital* (amounts of money) to operate a business brought about the separation of management from ownership. This need for capital has continued ever since. Managements today usually have relatively little share in the ownership of the companies they operate. The term *management* has become a general term used in contrast to stockholders and labor.

Industrial Management is the aspect of business management which has been most important in the United States in the 1900's. The invention and improvement of machines has made it especially important to plan the entire process of production carefully. Modern machines are efficient, but they are also expensive. A company must decide exactly what is to be made and how the work is to be done. Materials must be available in a smooth flow as they are needed. The work must be planned through every step, from the raw material to the finished product. In present-day industry every step depends on the previous steps, and an interruption at any point can halt the entire production process.

Personnel Management. One or more persons who become ill, angry, or emotionally upset can interrupt production just as quickly and completely as a serious fire or accident that puts machines out of operation. As industries and businesses have become larger, managements of companies have had to pay more attention to *personnel* (employee) problems. A friendly spirit between workers in various departments and between workers and management helps as much as mechanical efficiency to make a business a success. In fact, wise management strives to link the human and the technical aspects of its activities. Good morale among employees is a vital goal.

Market Management becomes necessary when a firm grows so large that it has only a few competitors of similar size. It would not be possible for a single executive or small firm to think of *managing* the market in which it sells its products. The market controls the company, not the other way around. But large businesses produce and sell a great portion of the total of their type of product. They must plan the marketing of their products as carefully as they plan production. Because they are large, they can do this. Such companies can set carefully planned prices, confident that no competitor is likely to undercut them. They can plan a system to distribute the product that will keep the goods moving steadily from the factory to the consumer. They make sure that no interruption occurs anywhere in their production and distribution systems.

Financial Management depends on and measures the success of other management processes. Financial management must obtain the capital required to support the production and distribution of a company's goods. If the firm produces and distributes its products successfully, it should yield a profit. In turn, if it has a record of profitable operation, it becomes an attractive place for investors to put their capital. In this way, a company finds it easier to obtain capital. Financial management provides the capital with which a business can begin. It also tests its operation continuously to ensure that all uses of capital in the business help make a profit.

MANAGEMENT AND BUDGET, OFFICE OF

The Importance of Management. In addition to the branches of business management already mentioned, the terms *land management, water management, natural resource management* and the like are frequently used. In fact, wherever complex problems appear that can be controlled by human beings, the skills of management are called into play. The growth of management in business has been greater than in other fields, however. Business executives with skill and experience in management can often shift from firm to firm, wherever their skills are needed, even between different kinds of businesses. This kind of mobility has served to make business managers a professional management class that has become one of the most influential in our society. The management class makes decisions that can determine the prosperity of entire nations. ROBERT D. PATTON

Related Articles in WORLD BOOK include:

Centralization	Industrial Revolution	Manufacturing
Corporation	Industry	Partnership
Industrial	Joint-Stock Company	Stock, Capital
Relations	Labor Movement	

MANAGEMENT AND BUDGET, OFFICE OF (OMB),

is a United States government agency that assists the President in preparing the federal budget and evaluating government programs and organization. The OMB was created in 1970 as part of the Executive Office of the President. It replaced the Bureau of the Budget, which since 1921 had assisted the President in determining federal expenditures.

In addition to formulating the budget, the OMB has the overall responsibility of evaluating and coordinating various federal programs. For example, the office determines the performance and objectives of each program and recommends to the President how much money the government should spend. The OMB also works to increase cooperation between government agencies by providing a formal information network within the executive branch. Other functions of the OMB include improving the financial management of government agencies, improving government organization and administrative management, and developing programs to recruit and train career government personnel. The OMB issues *The Budget of the United States Government, The Budget in Brief*, and other publications.

Critically reviewed by the OFFICE OF MANAGEMENT AND BUDGET

MANAGUA, *mah NAH gwah* (pop. 677,680), is the capital, largest city, and chief commercial center of Nicaragua. It lies on the southern shore of Lake Managua in western Nicaragua. For location, see NICARAGUA (map).

Managua was severely damaged in 1972 by an earthquake that killed about 10,000 persons and destroyed almost the entire downtown area. Today, the city consists of several suburban developments with no central business district. The former downtown section consists of empty fields, except for a few large concrete buildings that survived the earthquake. These structures include the National Palace, the Presidential Palace, and a sports stadium. The Metropolitan Cathedral was badly damaged, but efforts have been made to save this majestic structure.

Since the earthquake, new business and residential areas have been built on the outskirts of Managua.

David Mangurian

Managua was badly damaged by an earthquake in 1972. Only a few buildings in the city's downtown section survived. The rest of the area is now vacant, as shown above.

These areas include shopping centers with stores, restaurants, and motion-picture theaters. The buildings were specially constructed to withstand severe earthquakes. In addition, large villages of housing units were built for the thousands of families left homeless after the 1972 earthquake.

The economy of Managua is based mainly on trade. The city is Nicaragua's chief trading center for coffee, cotton, and other farm crops. Managua is also an important industrial center. Its chief products include beer, cement, matches, textiles, and shoes. The city lies on the Inter-American Highway, the country's major north-south route.

Managua was built in the 1850's on the site of an Indian community. It was established as the capital to settle disputes between Nicaragua's two chief political parties. Previously, the capital had alternated between León, which was controlled by the Liberal Party, and Granada, the headquarters of the Conservative Party.

In 1931, an earthquake badly damaged much of Managua, but the city was quickly rebuilt. Since the 1972 earthquake, plans have been made to establish parks and erect government buildings in the demolished area. Managua is a rapidly growing city. Its population has more than tripled since 1960. NATHAN A. HAVERSTOCK

MANAMA, *mah NAH muh* (pop. 94,697), is the capital, largest city, and chief port of Bahrain, an island nation in the Persian Gulf (see BAHRAIN). Manama lies on the northern tip of the country's main island, also called Bahrain.

Historians believe that Manama was founded in the 1300's. It became an important port, largely because of its excellent location along major trade routes. Today, the city is a major commercial center in the Persian Gulf region. It has numerous warehouses and stores, as well as modern hotels and government offices.

In 1961, the government of Bahrain opened a new

Field Museum of Natural History

The Manatee lives in rivers or coastal bays. The animal is helpless on land because it has no hind legs.

harbor for Manama. This harbor is suitable for modern ocean vessels. Also in the 1960's, Manama began to develop light industries. These industries include the construction and repair of ships.   ROBERT GERAN LANDEN

MANASSAS, BATTLES OF. See CIVIL WAR (First Bull Run; Second Bull Run; table: Major Battles).

MANATEE, *MAN uh TEE,* sometimes called SEA COW, is a large water mammal. It belongs to the same group of mammals—the order *Sirenia*—as the dugong. There are three species of manatees. The West Indian manatee lives in the Caribbean Sea and along the northeastern coast of South America. It is also found in the coastal waters of the Southeastern United States, particularly in the bays and rivers of Florida. The Amazon manatee dwells in the Amazon and Orinoco river systems. The African manatee lives in the rivers and coastal waters of western Africa. The West Indian and Amazon manatees have been hunted for their flesh, hide, and oil, and both are endangered species.

The manatee feeds on water plants in fresh or salt water. Its upper lip is divided into halves, which close like pliers on the plants. A manatee can consume more than 100 pounds (45 kilograms) of water plants in a day. In Guyana, in South America, manatees have been used to keep waterways free of weeds.

A manatee grows about 14 feet (4 meters) long and weighs about 1,500 pounds (680 kilograms). It has light to dark gray skin, with short, bristlelike hairs scattered over its body. Its front legs are paddle shaped, and its tail is rounded. It has no hind legs.

Scientific Classification. Manatees make up the genus *Trichechus* in the family Trichechidae. The West Indian manatee is *T. manatus;* the Amazon manatee, *T. inunguis;* the African manatee, *T. senegalensis.*   KARL W. KENYON

See also DUGONG; SEA COW; SIRENIA.

MANAUS, *muh NOWS* (pop. 388,811), is a major inland city of Brazil, and the capital of the state of Amazonas. Manaus lies on the Negro River, 10 miles (16 kilometers) from the junction of the Negro and Amazon rivers (see BRAZIL [political map]). It is 1,000 miles (1,600 kilometers) from the mouth of the Amazon, but can be reached by ocean liners. It is the trading center for the area around the Amazon Basin. It trades in products of the Amazon forests, including hardwoods, Brazil nuts, and rubber.   MANOEL CARDOZO

MANCHESTER (pop. 530,580; met. area pop. 2,389,260) is the fourth largest city in England. It is the center of one of the greatest manufacturing districts in the world. The only larger English cities are London, Birmingham, and Liverpool.

Manchester is situated in Lancashire, on the Irwell River. It lies 32 miles (51 kilometers) northeast of Liverpool. The city of Salford, on the west bank of the Irwell, is connected with Manchester by 16 bridges. The two cities are almost like one municipality. For location, see GREAT BRITAIN (political map).

Industry and Trade. Manchester has long been known as a world center of cotton manufacture, but it has more than 700 other industries. Great engineering works have been established in Manchester, as well as factories which produce automobiles and rubber goods.

Many mills and workshops stand outside the city itself. As a result, an ever-widening circle of dense population has grown up around the center of the city. This outer area distributes the numerous and varied products that the city sends to every part of the world. Manchester exports chemicals, dyes, oil, and cotton goods.

Manchester lies more than 30 miles (48 kilometers) from the Irish Sea. But the Manchester Ship Canal has made the city a great seaport. Other canals lead from the city in all directions. It is also a leading railroad center. In 1830, the first passenger railroad in England was built between Manchester and Liverpool.

Buildings and Public Works. A fine town hall of Gothic design stands in Manchester. The clock tower, 286 feet (87 meters) high, contains a chime of 21 bells. Manchester has excellent libraries, including the John Rylands Library. The Victoria University of Manchester is well known among scholars. During World War II, German planes bombed Manchester. But the city has rebuilt most of its industries and buildings.

The Manchester Ship Canal was opened in 1894. It made the inland town of Manchester a great seaport. It is 36 miles (58 kilometers) long, 121 feet (37 meters) wide, and 28 to 30 feet (8.5 to 9.1 meters) deep. It connects directly with all the barge canals of the kingdom. Seagoing vessels can pass through it and into the heart of Manchester. The canal was built at a cost of $75 million.   FREDERICK G. MARCHAM

MANCHESTER, N.H. (pop. 87,754; met. area pop. 132,512), is the largest city and chief manufacturing center of New Hampshire. Manchester lies in the south-central part of the state, about 17 miles (27 kilometers) south of Concord, the capital. The city covers about 40 square miles (104 square kilometers) along both banks of the Merrimack River. The Uncanoonuc Mountains curve around the western part of the city (see NEW HAMPSHIRE [political map]).

Most of the people of Manchester are foreign-born or the descendants of foreign-born. Nearly half of the population are French Americans from Canada.

The city is the home of the Manchester Institute of Arts and Sciences, the Currier Gallery of Art, the Association Canado-Americaine, and the Carpenter Memorial Library. Notre Dame and St. Anselm's colleges are also in the city. The residence of General John Stark, a figure of the Revolutionary War, is in Manchester.

Manchester was once known as the home of the largest cotton mills in the world. The mills failed in the 1930's. Today, the city's chief products include boots and shoes and cotton and woolen goods. Manchester is an insurance center and distributing point. The city is served by a freight railroad and several bus lines. No railroad passenger trains stop there.

The first white settlement there was started in 1722. Manchester was first called Harrytown, and then Derryfield. It received its present name in 1810. Manchester became a city in 1846. It has a mayor-council form of government.   J. DUANE SQUIRES

MANCHESTER TERRIER is a breed of dog that originated in Manchester, England, during the 1800's. Dog breeders produced the Manchester terrier to compete in rat-killing matches. In these matches, people bet on how many rats a dog could kill in a given period of time. By mating the black-and-tan terrier, an excellent ratcatcher, with the swift whippet, the breeders hoped to produce a superior ratter. Today, Manchesters are popular house pets. They are extremely loyal to their owners and make excellent watchdogs.

Manchester terriers have a smooth, black coat. They have a tan mark over each eye, on each cheek, and on the chest. The mark on the chest is shaped like the letter *V*. The Manchester's ears are set high on its long, narrow head. The dog has an arched back and a short, whiplike tail.

The Manchester terrier has two varieties—the standard and the toy. The standard Manchester stands 14 to 16 inches (36 to 41 centimeters) high at the shoulder and weighs 12 to 22 pounds (5.4 to 10 kilograms). The standard's ears droop naturally. Some owners have the ears cropped to make them stand straight up. The toy Manchester weighs 5 to 12 pounds (2.3 to 5.4 kilograms). The toy's ears, unlike those of the standard, are naturally erect. The toy Manchester was bred from the standard.   JOAN McDONALD BREARLEY

See also DOG (picture: Terriers).

MANCHINEEL, *man chih NEEL,* is a tree that grows on sandy beaches in Florida and in many parts of tropical America. It stands from 10 to 50 feet (3 to 15 meters) high. The manchineel has smooth, pale brown bark, and long, drooping branches. The egg-shaped leaves are about 3 inches (8 centimeters) long. They have jagged edges. The manchineel has small purple flowers. Its fruit resembles a crab apple.

The milky sap and yellowish-green fruits of the manchineel are extremely poisonous. Even dew or rainwater that drips from the leaves can cause blisters on the skin. Sap or smoke from burning wood that comes into contact with the eye can cause temporary blindness.

Scientific Classification. Manchineel is in the spurge family, *Euphorbiaceae.* It is genus *Hippomane,* species *H. mancinella.*

MANCHU, *MAN choo.* The Manchus were a people who conquered China in the 1600's. Most Manchus

lived in Manchuria, in northeast China. They were related to a Tungusic people whom the Chinese called *Nüchên* or *Juchen.* The Tungus lived in Manchuria as early as the 200's B.C. In A.D. 1644, the Manchus set up a dynasty in China that became known as the *Ch'ing (Pure)* dynasty. The dynasty prospered in the 1700's, but declined rapidly in the 1800's. It ended in 1912, when the Chinese overthrew their Manchu rulers.

The Manchu rulers forbade marriage between their people and the Chinese people until the early 1900's. Since that time, many Manchus and Chinese have intermarried, and most of the Manchus have adopted Chinese names.   THEODORE H. E. CHEN

See also MANCHURIA (History); CHINA (History).

MANCHURIA, *man CHOOR ee uh,* is a region in northeastern China known for its rich natural resources, especially coal and iron. Much of China's heavy industry centers around the Manchurian cities of Ch'angch'un, Harbin, and Shen-yang. The region also has fertile soil and produces much of China's food.

Manchuria consists of the Chinese provinces of Heilungkiang, Kirin, and Liaoning. The region covers 474,907 square miles (1,230,000 square kilometers). Most of Manchuria's people are of Chinese ancestry, but some are Manchus, the original people of the region.

Manchu rulers controlled all China for more than

Manchuria

This map shows the northeastern part of China, called Manchuria. China, Japan, and Russia fought for this region for many years. Today, Manchuria is important for its heavy industry.

⊛ National capital   • Other city or town

★ Provincial capital   ——— International Boundary

——— Provincial boundary

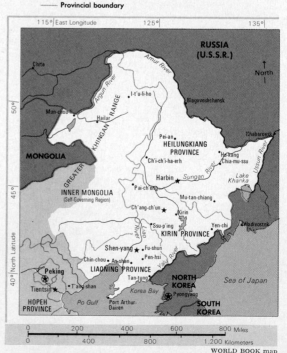

WORLD BOOK map

Marc Riboud, Magnum

Manchurian Steelworkers in An-shan help produce steel that is used to make heavy machinery and other industrial products. Manchuria is China's most important industrial region.

leased land on the Liaotung Peninsula and built a naval base at Port Arthur and a port at Dairen.

In the Russo-Japanese War (1904-1905), Japan defeated Russia and took control of the Liaotung Peninsula. In 1931, the Japanese conquered the rest of Manchuria. They made the region a puppet state called *Manchukuo*. During World War II (1939-1945), Manchuria was an important industrial base for Japan.

During the last days of World War II, Russia declared war on Japan and occupied Manchuria. Before returning Manchuria to China in 1946, the Russians helped the Chinese Communists seize power there. The Chinese Communists conquered all China in 1949.

During the 1960's, China claimed some Russian territory beyond Manchuria. In 1969, China and Russia clashed over control of an island in the Ussuri River. The fighting stopped after the two nations agreed to discuss their differences.   RICHARD H. SOLOMON

Related Articles in WORLD BOOK include:

Ch'ang-ch'un	Harbin	Russo-Japanese
China	Japan (The Rise	War
Cold War (The	of Militarism)	Shen-yang
Great Blocs Split)	Manchu	Yalu River
Dairen	Port Arthur	

250 years, until 1912. In the early and mid-1900's, Japan and Russia fought for control of Manchuria. The region has been part of Communist China since 1949.

People. Manchuria has a population of about 91 million. About 90 per cent of the people are descendants of Chinese who migrated to Manchuria around 1900. Most of China's 2,400,000 Manchus live in the region, and Manchuria also has about 1,000,000 Koreans and 200,000 Mongols. Large numbers of these peoples have been absorbed into Chinese society through intermarriage and public education. Today, almost all the people of Manchuria speak Mandarin, the official language of China. They follow Chinese customs and live as do the people of any other part of China.

Land and Climate. A broad central plain makes up most of Manchuria. Forested mountains border the plain on the east, north, and west. In the south, the Liaotung Peninsula extends into the Yellow Sea. The Amur and Ussuri rivers separate Manchuria from Russia on the northeast. Korea lies across the Yalu River to the southeast. Manchuria has long, bitterly cold winters and short, hot summers.

Economy. Manchuria has rich deposits of coal and iron, both used in making steel. Its factories make such steel products as machinery, railroad equipment, tools, and trucks. They also produce cement, chemicals, electrical equipment, and paper. Grains, especially sorghums and soybeans, make up much of Manchuria's agricultural production. The region's farmers also grow cotton, sugar beets, and tobacco.

History. In early times, Manchu warriors on horseback frequently invaded and conquered parts of China. The Manchus conquered northern China in 1644, and gradually extended their control to the whole country. The Manchus ruled until 1912. Chinese rulers since 1912 have looked upon Manchuria as part of China.

Russia expanded across Asia during the 1800's and seized land from China. In 1860, Russia and China signed an agreement giving Russia all the territory north of the Amur River and east of the Ussuri River. In 1896, China agreed to permit Russia to build the Chinese Eastern Railway across Manchuria to the Russian port of Vladivostok. Two years later, Russia

MANDALAY, *MAN duh LAY* (pop. 417,266), is Burma's second largest city and chief inland river port. It lies 350 miles (563 kilometers) north of Rangoon on the Irrawaddy River. For location, see BURMA (map).

Mandalay is best known for its old pagodas, temples, and monasteries. The chief industry is silk weaving. Silk is sold in the city's *bazaars* (market places).

The Burmese founded Mandalay in 1857. It was the capital of Burma from 1860 to 1885, when the British captured the city. The British moved the capital to Rangoon. About 85 per cent of Mandalay was destroyed during World War II. The Burmese rebuilt parts of it after the war.   JOHN F. CADY

MANDAMUS, *man DAY mus*, is a court order which requires a person, lower court, government official, or an officer of a corporation to do a legal duty. On many occasions, a public official may be required to perform an act, such as to make a commission or sign a paper. If the official refuses to do the act, a *writ of mandamus* may be sought, and a court may order the official to perform the act.

Mandamus can be obtained only where the law says the official must do the act, but not where the law says the official may decide whether to do it or not. In such a case, a court will not compel the official to decide in favor of the person seeking the writ of mandamus. But the court may compel the official to decide one way or the other. A court may not issue a writ of mandamus if it believes that some other remedy is available to handle the situation, such as a suit for money damages against the official.   ERWIN N. GRISWOLD

See also INJUNCTION; WRIT.

MANDAN INDIANS are a tribe that has lived in western North Dakota, along the Missouri River, for more than 500 years. The Mandan were originally village dwellers and lived in large, earth-covered lodges. They hunted and also cultivated fields of beans, corn, squash, sunflowers, and tobacco. The early Mandan exchanged their crops for goods that other tribes brought to their villages. During the 1700's, the Mandan began to trade with European explorers and traders. They exchanged European products for goods from Indian tribes farther west.

In 1837, a smallpox epidemic nearly wiped out the Mandan. The survivors found refuge in the nearby villages of the Arikara and the Hidatsa tribes. From the 1840's to the 1860's, the three tribes settled in villages on what is now the Fort Berthold Reservation in North Dakota.

In the late 1800's, the United States government began to divide the reservation into small parcels of land, which were assigned to each eligible Arikara, Hidatsa, and Mandan. The three tribes then left their villages and moved to their assigned lands. In the late 1940's, the government took about a fourth of the reservation to build Garrison Dam, a huge hydroelectric project. Indian families who lived on land taken by the government had to settle elsewhere on the reservation. Today, about 400 Mandan live there. Most of them are farmers or ranchers.   BEATRICE MEDICINE

See also INDIAN, AMERICAN (pictures: A Mandan Chief; The Scalps of Enemy Warriors).

MANDARIN, *MAN duh rin.* English-speaking people used the name *mandarin* for any high military or civil official of the Chinese Empire. The Chinese term is *kwan,* which means *a public official.* The dialect of North China, which is the language these officials spoke, is also called *Mandarin.* Today it is the national language of China. See CHINESE LANGUAGE.

A Chinese became a mandarin by taking promotional examinations. He showed his rank by the color of the buttons on his cap. Governors and generals had red coral buttons. Lieutenant governors and judges wore blue ones. Lower officers had other colors.

Each mandarin had an official robe. The military man's robe had beasts embroidered on it. The civil official had decorative birds on his robe. Judges wore plainer robes.

To ensure the honesty of a mandarin, he was never assigned to the province from which he came. He could neither marry nor acquire property in the province to which he was sent. And he could not serve over three years in one province.   THEODORE H. E. CHEN

MANDATED TERRITORY. After World War I, certain colonies and territories were taken from the defeated nations and placed under the administration of one or more of the victorious nations. These regions were called *mandated territories.* The League of Nations supervised the administration of these territories. The League expected the governing countries to improve conditions for the people in the mandated territories, and to prepare the people for self-government.

The mandated territories included areas once controlled by Germany and Turkey. Great Britain received mandates for Iraq, Palestine (including Jordan), and Tanganyika. France received Syria (including Lebanon). Both countries were given parts of the Cameroons and Togoland. Belgium received Ruanda-Urundi. Japan was given former German islands in the North Pacific Ocean. Australia received German islands in the South Pacific, including the northeastern section of New Guinea and Nauru. New Zealand received West-

Museum of Fine Arts, Boston

Chinese Mandarins served as important government officials. This mandarin was an imperial high commissioner during the Ch'ing dynasty. The bird on the gown indicates he was a civil official.

ern Samoa, and the Union of South Africa (now South Africa) obtained German South West Africa.

The League appointed a commission to supervise the mandate system. The commission had no power to govern, but usually persuaded the nations with mandates to improve education, public health, and the economy in the mandated regions. However, the governing nations often failed to train the people to govern themselves.

The mandate system came to an end in 1947. By that time, several of the mandated territories, including Iraq, Syria, Lebanon, and Jordan, had become independent countries. The remaining mandated territories, with the exception of South West Africa, were placed under the stronger United Nations trusteeship system. The same countries continued to administer the territories, but they were under the control of the UN Trusteeship Council and General Assembly (see TRUST TERRITORY). South Africa resisted UN attempts to bring South West Africa into the trusteeship system.   ELTON ATWATER

MANDIBLE, *MAN duh b'l,* or lower jawbone, is shaped like a horseshoe. A person can feel the entire bone from chin to temple. The *corpus* (body) of the mandible runs backwards from the chin to the *angle,* at which point it turns upward to form the *ramus.* The ramus makes a joint at the temple. This joint allows the mouth to open and close. In adults, the body of the mandible contains eight teeth on each side. The chewing muscles attach to the ramus, and most of the tongue muscles attach to the corpus.   IRVIN STEIN

See also HEAD (picture).

MANDINGO. See MALINKE.

WORLD BOOK photo, courtesy Chicago Symphony Orchestra

The Mandolin has been popular for hundreds of years, particularly among southern Europeans and Latin Americans.

MANDOLIN, *MAN doh lin*, is a musical instrument with strings. It was probably copied from the lute, a much older instrument (see LUTE). The mandolin is shaped like a pear cut in half lengthwise. It has four or five double strings of wire, a fretted neck, and a flat headpiece with tuning screws. The player produces a tone with a rather stiff *plectrum* (pick), which he holds between his right thumb and forefinger. Musical sounds can be sustained by *trilling* (shaking the strings rapidly). The four-stringed mandolin in common use is tuned in fifths, like the violin. It is often used to accompany informal singing.   CHARLES B. RIGHTER

MANDRAKE is the name of two similar plants that belong to the nightshade family. Mandrakes grow wild in southern Europe and Asia. The stem of the mandrake cannot be seen, and the leaves seem to grow directly from the roots. The roots are large and shaped like a carrot. The white, bluish, or purple flowers of the mandrake grow on stalks among the leaves.

People have long had superstitious beliefs about the mandrake. According to one superstition, the mandrake shrieks when it is pulled out of the soil. Many persons also believe that it brings good luck to a household when it is properly consulted. The root of the mandrake was once used as a narcotic and anesthetic, and in so-called *love potions*. The mandrake was also described as growing best under a gallows.

People in the United States and Canada often use the name *mandrake* for the *May apple*, which belongs to the barberry family (see MAY APPLE).

Scientific Classification. Mandrakes belong to the nightshade family, *Solanaceae*. They make up the genus *Mandragora*. The species of mandrakes include *M. autumnalis*, and *M. officinarum*.   JULIAN A. STEYERMARK

MANDRILL is a large, colorful monkey that lives in the forests of Cameroon and other parts of western Africa. It resembles a baboon, having long arms, small piglike eyes, large canine teeth, and a muzzle similar to that of a dog. The male mandrill is strikingly colored.

Its cheeks are blue, its long flat nose is red, and its rump is red and blue.

Like most other monkeys, mandrills live in groups. They usually move about on the ground, roaming through the forests eating fruits and other vegetation, and perhaps insects.

Scientific Classification. The mandrill belongs to the Old World monkey family, *Cercopithecidae*. It is genus *Mandrillus*, species *M. sphinx*.   GEORGE B. SCHALLER

MANED WOLF. See Fox (South American "Foxes").

MANES. See MANICHAEISM.

MANET, *ma NAY*, **EDOUARD** (1832-1883), was a French painter who helped break tradition by using his subject matter primarily for visual effect, rather than for telling a story. Since Manet's time, painting has been dominated by this concern with the importance of the picture itself, not its storytelling function.

Manet is often identified with the impressionist style of painting, and he and the impressionist artists influenced each other. However, Manet refused to exhibit his works in impressionist shows. The public considered impressionism revolutionary and treated it hostilely. Manet preferred to seek popular success by exhibiting in conservative shows sponsored by the government.

Manet was born in Paris. From 1850 to 1856, he studied with the skillful but traditional artist Thomas Couture. Couture taught Manet to love technique for its own sake. From Couture, Manet learned how to use outline expressively, how to obtain a lively effect with broken brushstrokes, and how to achieve strong lighting with a minimum of tones. Manet wanted to use this technical knowledge to portray modern life in a spontaneous way. But Couture and other conservative French painters preferred sentimental storytelling.

In 1863, Manet shocked the people of Paris with his painting *Luncheon on the Grass*. This picture shows a female nude at a picnic with two men in modern cloth-

George H. Harrison from Grant Heilman

The Male Mandrill has vivid coloring that helps make it one of the most unusual looking monkeys. The colors become even more brilliant when this west African monkey is excited.

Edouard Manet completed *Bar at the Folies Bergère, left,* in 1882. The painting shows the firm modeling and bright, vivid colors that are typical of much of his work. The portrait of Manet, *above,* was painted by his friend Henri Fantin-Latour in 1867.

ing. Many people felt that the painting was indecent. It is reproduced in color in the PAINTING article. In 1865, Manet's *Olympia,* a painting of a female nude, created an even greater scandal. The public objected to the nude's bold pose and to the picture's severe lighting contrasts and flat silhouetted forms.

During the 1860's, Manet also painted scenes from modern history, though Biblical and ancient historical scenes were popular at the time. One painting shows the execution of Emperor Maximilian of Mexico in 1867. Another of Manet's modern historical scenes, *Combat of the Kearsarge and the Alabama* (1864), shows a naval battle of the American Civil War. It is reproduced in the ALABAMA (ship) article.

Manet's last great painting was *Bar at the Folies Bergère* (1882). This work is remarkable for its dazzling color and rich textures. ALBERT BOIME

See also IMPRESSIONISM.

MANGANESE, *MANG guh nees* (chemical symbol, Mn), is one of the most important metals used in industry. Its chief use is to strengthen steel and to remove impurities from it. Steelmakers have found few substitutes for it. But the United States does not mine enough manganese for its steel industry. The United States imports about 98 per cent of the manganese it uses. Johann Gahn discovered the element in 1774.

Uses. Pure manganese metal is seldom used commercially. It is usually used in ores, compounds, or alloys. About 95 per cent of the manganese used in the United States goes into the production of steel.

To produce 1 short ton (0.9 metric ton) of steel, steelmakers need about 13 pounds (6 kilograms) of manganese. They may add the manganese to the steel in scrap steel; in *ferromanganese,* an alloy of iron containing a high percentage of manganese; or in *spiegeleisen,* an alloy of iron containing a lower percentage of manganese. Manganese removes harmful oxygen and sulfur from the molten steel. It takes up the oxygen or sulfur and forms *manganous oxide* or *manganous sulfide.* These

compounds do not dissolve easily in molten iron. They separate from the iron and become part of the slag, which is poured off. Manganese that remains in the steel increases its strength. *Manganese steel* is an especially hard alloy used in making mining machinery and such heavy-duty machinery as rock crushers.

Manganese oxide is used in dry-cell batteries to prevent *polarization* (the formation of hydrogen, which does not conduct electricity) on the carbon electrode. In the past, manufacturers used manganese oxide in making glass. Iron impurities in the sand that was used to make glass gave it a yellowish color. Manganese oxide eliminated this color. But, after a few years of exposure to the sun, glass containing manganese turned purple. For this reason, glass manufacturers now use selenium in place of manganese.

Manganese sulfate is an important ingredient in the fertilizers used in parts of the United States. It is hard to grow citrus fruits in Texas and Florida unless manganese is added to the soil. If such crops as tomatoes, beans, potatoes, and corn are grown in soils containing large amounts of lime, they will not mature fully unless treated with fertilizers containing manganese.

Potassium permanganate is an important chemical. It is used as an oxidizing agent in various industrial processes (see OXIDATION). It also has value in quantitative analysis, because it changes color when the concentration of hydroxide ions in a solution changes (see CHEMISTRY [Branches of Chemistry]).

Manganese dioxide is used in manufacturing *hydroquinone,* a chemical used as a photographic developer. It is also used to *bond* (hold) enamels to steel. Manganese dioxide and certain manganese salts are used to make paint and varnish dry faster. Manganese salts produce attractive colors in bricks, pottery, and tiles. Other uses for manganese compounds include weldingrod coatings, pigments, and insecticides.

Chemistry. Pure manganese is a silver-gray metal with a pinkish tinge. It is relatively soft, compared with iron. Manganese is unstable, and reacts easily with other chemicals to form many compounds. If placed in cold water, manganese will react with the water and release hydrogen gas from it. The atomic weight of manganese is 54.9380, and its atomic number is 25. See ELEMENT, CHEMICAL (tables).

Manganese can be prepared from its oxides by reduction with carbon or aluminum. It can also be reduced by electrolysis or by an electric furnace. See ELECTRIC FURNACE; ELECTROLYSIS; REDUCTION.

Sources. Geologists estimate that manganese ranks as the 11th most abundant element in the earth's crust. But it is rare compared with other elements such as iron, oxygen, magnesium, and silicon, which total 93 per cent of the earth. Meteorites probably have about twice as large a percentage of manganese as does the earth.

Manganese does not exist naturally in its pure state, because it reacts so easily with other elements. More than a hundred different manganese minerals are known. Of these, the three most abundant in ores are the black oxides, *pyrolusite* and *psilomelane*, and the pink carbonate, *rhodochrosite*.

The most important known manganese ores lie in rocks in Russia. The *residual* deposits in India, Africa, and China rank next in importance. Residual deposits have been enriched by the *leaching* (washing and dissolving away) of impurities near the surface.

Mining and Metallurgy. The black oxides are usually mined from shallow pits or open cuts, and from shallow underground mines. Most of the pink carbonate is mined from veins, usually along with other minerals.

Manganese ore may be improved in grade by several methods, including hand sorting and simple "gravity" methods using water for washing. The pink carbonate ore is usually concentrated by the flotation process, using soap reagents (see FLOTATION PROCESS). This process is followed by *sintering* (heating fine particles of ore at high temperatures) so that they form lumps.

Leading Manganese-Mining Countries

Tons of manganese mined in 1977

Russia	9,370,000 short tons (8,500,000 metric tons)
South Africa	5,564,000 short tons (5,047,600 metric tons)
Gabon	2,040,000 short tons (1,851,000 metric tons)
India	1,955,000 short tons (1,773,500 metric tons)
Australia	1,529,000 short tons (1,387,100 metric tons)
China	1,100,000 short tons (998,000 metric tons)
Brazil	990,000 short tons (898,000 metric tons)

Source: *Minerals Yearbook, 1977*, U.S. Bureau of Mines.

Production. The chief manganese-producing countries include Russia, South Africa, Gabon, and India. Australia, Brazil, China, and Mexico also produce manganese. Brazil became the leader in manganese production in the Western Hemisphere with the opening of its Amapa deposit in 1957.

The small amount of manganese produced in the United States has come mainly from Minnesota, New Mexico, and South Carolina. At times, the government has encouraged production by giving subsidies and by setting up protective tariffs (see TARIFF [Kinds of Tariffs]). High-grade ore reserves in the United States are limited. But Arizona, Maine, and Minnesota have reserves of low-grade material that could be made

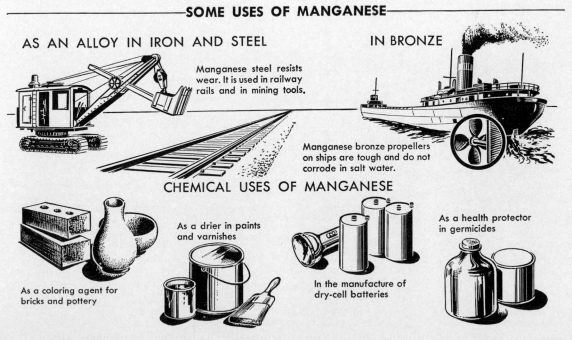

SOME USES OF MANGANESE

AS AN ALLOY IN IRON AND STEEL

Manganese steel resists wear. It is used in railway rails and in mining tools.

IN BRONZE

Manganese bronze propellers on ships are tough and do not corrode in salt water.

CHEMICAL USES OF MANGANESE

As a coloring agent for bricks and pottery

As a drier in paints and varnishes

In the manufacture of dry-cell batteries

As a health protector in germicides

available in times of extreme need. Manganese found at the bottom of the sea may be important in the future. Because of the limited reserves in the United States and the importance of the metal in wartime, the United States has kept stockpiles of manganese ores since the 1940's.   HARRISON ASHLEY SCHMITT

See also ALLOY (Alloys of Iron); IRON AND STEEL (Methods of Making Steel).

MANGE, *maynj,* is a skin disease that affects dogs, horses, sheep, and cattle. It is much like the itch in human beings. Mange usually attacks dirty, neglected animals which live in groups or herds, or in crowded shelters.

Mange is caused by tiny mites that burrow into the skin and live there. Different kinds, or species, of mites attack different kinds of animals. They produce soreness, swelling, and itching. Tiny pimples and sores form on the skin, and the hair or wool falls out in patches. The sores and breaks in the skin become worse as a result of the animal's continuous scratching.

Mange can be treated by dipping or hand rubbing the skin with sulfur, lime, and arsenic mixtures. In most cases, a veterinarian should be consulted. Mange can be prevented by general cleanliness and by washing and brushing the animal.   D. W. BRUNER

See also MITE.

MANGEL-WURZEL. See BEET.

MANGO, *MANG goh,* is the fruit of an evergreen tree that grows in tropical regions throughout the world. It originally grew wild in southeastern Asia. Settlers brought it to America in the 1700's.

The mango tree is attractive. It is thick and dark green, and may grow 40 to 50 feet (12 to 15 meters) tall. The tree has slender, pointed leaves that are about 1 foot (30 centimeters) long. Tiny pink flowers grow in clusters at the ends of small branches.

The fruit of the mango tree is usually about the size of an apple, but it may weigh as much as 3 pounds (1.4

Clusters of Mangoes hang from an evergreen mango tree. Residents of the tropics like to roast mango seeds and eat them.
J. Horace McFarland

kilograms). It consists of a soft, juicy, yellow or orange pulp covered by a skin that may be yellow, red, or green. A thick husk surrounds the large flat seed of the mango. Many tough fibers grow into the pulp. The fruits, or mangoes, are usually shaped like a kidney, but they may be round or egg-shaped. There are about 500 varieties. Finer, grafted varieties of the mango have no fibers, and the fruit can be eaten with a spoon. The mango has a delicious, spicy flavor.

The fiberless Indonesian and Philippine varieties of mango have become popular in southern Florida. In 1900, the U.S. Department of Agriculture brought these varieties to the United States. Small amounts of the fruit have been sent to northern markets. Frost easily destroys the mango tree. Grafted trees bear fruit after 2 or 3 years. Seedlings need a year or two longer.

Scientific Classification. The mango belongs to the cashew family, *Anacardiaceae.* It is in the genus *Mangifera,* and is species *M. indica.*   JULIAN C. CRANE

MANGOSTEEN, *MANG goh steen,* is a tree that grows in Indonesia. It is about 30 feet (9 meters) tall. The shining green leaves are leathery, thick, and about 8 inches (20 centimeters) long. The pinkish flowers of the mangosteen measure almost 2 inches (5 centimeters) across. The reddish-purple edible fruit is shaped like a tangerine, with thick, juicy, white flesh. They are about $2\frac{1}{2}$ inches (6 centimeters) across. Cold weather kills the mangosteen. A few of these plants grow in gardens in the southernmost parts of the United States.

Ewing Galloway

The Fruit of the Mangosteen tastes much like an orange. The fruit has a reddish-purple rind.

Scientific Classification. Mangosteens belong to the garcinia family, *Guttiferae.* They are classified as genus *Garcinia,* species *G. mangostana.*   JULIAN C. CRANE

MANGROVE, *MANG grohv,* is a tropical tree that grows in salty ocean water. As the mangrove develops, it sends down roots from its branches. At last, hundreds of roots support its leafy crown above the water. The roots look like stilts. In hot regions, large thickets or forests on stilts, grow in shallow water. Mangroves flourish along bays, lagoons, and river mouths.

Mangrove thickets form the chief plant growth along long stretches of coast in the tropics. The thickets grow only in places by quiet ocean water. The thousands of stiltlike roots catch silt, which piles up in the quiet water. At the mouths of streams, the roots slow down the current and help settle the silt. In this way, the mangroves aid in building up dry land. At last, the plant

Nature Magazine

Mangroves Grow in Shallow Salt Water near seacoasts of tropical countries. Their spreading roots catch and hold particles of dirt and sand. This action helps build up shorelines.

stands in mud above the reach of the tide. But it kills itself in forming land, for its roots need to be washed in ocean water, at least during high tide.

The seed often germinates while the mangrove fruit is on the tree. It sends down a root up to 1 foot (30 centimeters) long. When the fruit falls, the heavy root holds it upright as it floats on the water. Sometimes, the root tip strikes mud and begins to form a new tree.

The red mangrove grows along the coasts from Florida to northern South America. It grows about 25 feet (8 meters) high and has a round top, with thick, oval leaves. People use the wood for wharf piles and fuel. They use the bark for tanning hides and making dyes.

Scientific Classification. The mangrove belongs to the mangrove family, *Rhizophoraceae*. The red mangrove is genus *Rhizophora*, species *R. mangle.*   K. A. ARMSON

MANHATTAN COLLEGE. See UNIVERSITIES AND COLLEGES (table).

MANHATTAN ISLAND (pop. 1,539,233) is one of the commercial, financial, and cultural centers of the world. It has an area of 31 square miles (80 square kilometers), including 8 square miles (22 square kilometers) of inland water, and forms the borough of Manhattan, New York City's smallest borough. The East River is its eastern border, with Upper New York Bay on the south, the Hudson River on the west, and the Harlem River and Spuyten Duyvil Creek on the north. Bridges and tunnels connect the island with the other boroughs and with New Jersey (see NEW YORK CITY [map]).

Manhattan Island has many famous landmarks and tourist attractions. They include Broadway, Chinatown,

the Empire State Building, Greenwich Village, Rockefeller Center, Times Square, the United Nations headquarters, Wall Street, and many churches, colleges, museums, skyscrapers, and theaters. Most of New York City's municipal buildings stand on Manhattan Island.

Peter Minuit, governor of the Dutch West India Company, bought the island in 1626 from the Manhattan Indians. He paid for it with beads, cloth, and trinkets worth $24. About 200 people lived in the settlement, then called New Amsterdam. WILLIAM E. YOUNG

See also MINUIT, PETER; NEW YORK CITY (Manhattan).

MANHATTAN PROJECT was created by the United States government in 1942 to produce the first atomic bomb. The official agency that produced the bomb was the Corps of Engineers' Manhattan Engineer District, commanded by Major (later Lieutenant) General Leslie R. Groves. He directed industrial and research activities at such sites as Oak Ridge, Tenn., and Los Alamos, N.Mex.   RALPH E. LAPP

See also ATOMIC BOMB.

MANHATTAN SCHOOL OF MUSIC. See UNIVERSITIES AND COLLEGES (table).

MANHATTANVILLE COLLEGE. See UNIVERSITIES AND COLLEGES (table).

MANIA. See MENTAL ILLNESS (Manic-Depressive Psychosis).

MANIC-DEPRESSIVE. See MENTAL ILLNESS.

MANICHAEISM, *MAN uh* KEE *ihz uhm*, is a religious system based on the doctrines of Manes, a Persian born about A.D. 215. Manes combined the Christian theory of salvation and the Zoroastrian concept of *dualism*, or the belief that two opposing principles govern the universe (see ZOROASTRIANISM). According to this system, the world originated as a mixture of light and darkness, which represent good and evil. Manichaeans believe that the soul, which arose from the Kingdom of Light, wants to escape from the body, which represents the Kingdom of Darkness. They believe that the soul can attain release only through wisdom, not through the renunciation of material or sensual things. They also believe that a savior will provide the wisdom necessary for release. Manichaeism was suppressed in Persia, but was important in other countries through the 900's.

MANICURE. See NAIL (picture: Care of the Nails).

MANIFEST is a detailed list of the goods a vessel is carrying. It also tells who owns the goods. The ship's captain certifies that the manifest is correct. The port collector uses it in figuring the *duty* (tax) on goods.

MANIFEST DESTINY was a term used to describe the belief in the 1840's in the inevitable territorial expansion of the United States. Persons who believed in manifest destiny maintained that the United States, because of its economic and political superiority, and its rapidly growing population, should rule all North America. The phrase was first used in 1845 by John L. O'Sullivan in an article on the annexation of Texas. The spirit of manifest destiny was revived at the end of the 1800's, during and after the Spanish-American War (see SPANISH-AMERICAN WAR). See also UNITED STATES, HISTORY OF THE (Expansion).   RAY ALLEN BILLINGTON

MANIFOLD, INTAKE. See CARBURETOR; GASOLINE ENGINE (Fuel System).

MANILA

MANILA (pop. 1,455,272; met. area pop. 4,904,262) is the capital and largest city of the Philippines. It is also the country's leading port and chief cultural, social, and commercial city. Spanish invaders of the Philippines founded the city nearly 400 years ago. Manila now serves as the world's greatest market for abacá, a kind of hemp. Manila is also a center for the cigar, coconut oil, and sugar industries. The city's beautiful setting and architectural landmarks earned it the name of the *Pearl of the Orient*.

Location and Size. Manila stretches along the east shore of Manila Bay on the island of Luzon. A crescent of mountains surrounds the city on the north, east, and south. The Pasig River flows down from the mountains and divides the city into two sections. Manila covers a total area of about 15 square miles (38 square kilometers). It is the center of a large metropolitan area that covers 242 square miles (628 square kilometers). For location, see PHILIPPINES (color map).

Description. Intramuros, or the Walled City, stands on the south bank of the Pasig River. Spaniards began construction of Intramuros in 1571, and completed it in 1739. They built high city walls and surrounded them with a wide moat to protect themselves from attacks by unfriendly Filipinos. The walls and some of the churches, convents, monasteries, and public buildings still stand in this old Spanish colonial town, despite heavy bombing during World War II. Outstanding among the old buildings is St. Augustine Church, built in 1599 by Spaniards and Filipinos.

The Luneta, one of Manila's favorite parks, looks across Manila Bay from just outside Intramuros. The Philippine Armed Forces Band gives concerts every Sunday in the park. A statue of Dr. José Rizal stands on the spot in the park where this national hero was executed by the Spanish on Dec. 30, 1896. Roxas Boulevard (formerly Dewey Boulevard) runs south along Manila Bay from the Luneta. This picturesque drive passes the mansions of wealthy Manilans and lovely hotels, apartment buildings, restaurants, and night clubs. The United States Embassy and the headquarters of the Philippine Navy also lie along the boulevard.

The modern business district of Manila lies on the north bank of the Pasig River. Six bridges connect the two parts of the city. The Escolta and the Avenida Rizal, Manila's fashionable shopping streets, run through this newer section. A large Chinatown lies next to the Escolta. Many tourists travel to Quiapo, just north of the river, to visit its colorful market and lively restaurants, shopping centers, and movie houses. Thousands of people go to the Quiapo Church every Friday to worship before the shrine of the miraculous image of the Black Nazarene. Tondo, in the northwestern corner of the city, presents a sharp contrast to the modern buildings elsewhere in the newer business district. Many of the people in Tondo live in primitive thatched huts.

Important buildings in Manila include the Malacañang Palace, home of the Philippine president, and the José Rizal Memorial Stadium. Outstanding government buildings are the Legislative Building, the City Hall, the Post Office, and the Agricultural and Finance department buildings. Japanese bombings during World War II destroyed the Manila Cathedral, originally built in 1654, but it was rebuilt in 1958.

Industry and Trade. Industries in Manila turn out a variety of textiles, and clothing and accessory manufacturers produce hats, leather goods, pearl buttons, and shoes. Handmade items include embroidered goods and rattan furniture. Processing plants produce beer, coconut oil, soap, sugar, and tobacco products. The city also has an automobile assembly plant. Other products include building materials, cosmetics, drugs, glassware, ink, machinery, matches, nails, paints, pencils, radio equipment, and rope and twine.

Manila ranks as one of the leading trade centers of East Asia. Nearly half of the abacá sold in the city goes to the United States to make rope and twine. The United States also purchases about half of Manila's copra exports. Other leading exports include copal, dried fish, fruits, kapok, lumber, ramie fiber, and sugar, and chromite, iron, and manganese ores.

Transportation and Communication. Manila's superb harbor and location make it an important port on most of the Pacific and Far East trade routes. Four large piers in the harbor can handle up to 12 large ships at one time. Manila also has an international airport. Two railways, the Manila Railroad Company and the Philippine Railway Company, also serve the city.

Manila has six radio stations, including one in suburban Quezon City and the government-owned station,

Chas. W. Miller

The Manila Post Office, center, stands on the south bank of the Pasig River, just across from the main business district. The muddy river cuts through the heart of the city and forms an essential part of the harbor on Manila Bay.

The Luneta Is One of Several Spacious Parks That Add to the Beauty of Manila.

DZFM. The city also has one television station. Publishers print several periodicals in English, including 7 daily newspapers and 7 weekly magazines. The city also has 7 newspapers printed in Spanish, 2 dailies and 10 weeklies in Tagalog, and 7 Chinese dailies.

Education. Manila has 12 universities. The University of Santo Tomás, founded in 1611, is older than Harvard. The University of the Philippines stands in Quezon City. Dozens of colleges also operate in Manila. The National Museum and Santo Tomás Museum have an interesting variety of collections. The city also has 14 public libraries. The Manila Symphony Orchestra, the Filipino Youth Symphony, the Army Band, and college orchestras play concert music. Ballet and opera groups are active.

Government. The entire Manila metropolitan area is governed by *Metro-Manila*. A five-member commission heads this areawide governmental unit. Metro-Manila is divided into hundreds of smaller units called *barangays*. The *sangguniang* (an assembly of barangay chairmen) and other barangay officials advise the Metro-Manila commission on legislative matters. Manila's judicial system includes a municipal court with eight branches.

History. Before the coming of Europeans, the Manila area belonged to the monarchies ruled by Rajah Soliman and Rajah Lakandula. Miguel López de Legazpi, a Spanish conquistador, founded Manila in 1571. The Ayuntamiento in Intramuros was built in 1735 to house the city council and the mayor's office. This building became the seat of the national government when the United States took possession of the Philippines. An earthquake destroyed a large part of the city in 1863. Spain surrendered Manila to the United States in 1898, during the Spanish-American War. The American administration of the city installed a modern water supply system, electric lighting, and made several other improvements.

Japanese forces seized Manila on Jan. 2, 1942, just four weeks after the beginning of World War II in the Pacific. American forces began the liberation of the city on Feb. 3, 1945, and a bitter three-week battle followed. Among the first places liberated were the Santo Tomás internment camp and the Bilibid Prison, where the Japanese had kept American prisoners. Few buildings remained standing in Manila when the Japanese finally surrendered the city on February 24. But the Filipinos began rebuilding almost immediately.

Manila became the national capital of the Philippines when independence was proclaimed on July 4, 1946. But in 1948, Philippine President Elpidio Quirino signed an act that recognized Quezon City as the official capital of the country. But Manila continued to serve as the seat of the Philippine government, pending the completion of new government buildings in Quezon City. In 1975, the Philippine government established Metro-Manila, a single governmental unit for the entire Manila metropolitan area. Imelda Romualdez Marcos, the wife of Philippine President Ferdinand E. Marcos, became the head of the new government unit. In 1976, the Philippine government made Manila the country's official capital again.   Russell H. Fifield

See also World War II (The War in Asia and the Pacific).

MANILA BAY is the entrance to the city of Manila on Luzon in the Philippines. The bay faces southwesterly towards the South China Sea. For location, see Philippines (color map). Manila Bay is about 40 miles (64 kilometers) long and 35 miles (56 kilometers) wide. Its waters are deep enough for large ships. There are two excellent harbors at Cavite and Manila.

The rocky, fortified island of Corregidor is at the mouth of Manila Bay. Some of the most bitter fighting of World War II took place on Corregidor. It was attacked by the Japanese during the first days of the war. During the Spanish-American War, an American fleet under Commodore George Dewey destroyed a Spanish fleet in a battle at Manila Bay.   F. G. Walton Smith

See also Bataan Peninsula; Corregidor; Spanish-American War.

MANILA BAY, BATTLE OF. See Spanish-American War.

MANILA HEMP. See Abacá.

MANIOC. See Tapioca.

Atikameg Lake in Clearwater Provincial Park

Manitoba Dept. of Economic Development

Ice Fishing on a Frozen Lake in Manitoba
Manitoba Dept. of Economic Development

MANITOBA

——————— FACTS IN BRIEF ———————

Capital: Winnipeg.

Government: *Parliament*—senators, 4; members of the House of Commons, 12. *Provincial Legislature*—members of the Legislative Assembly, 57. *Voting Age*—18.

Area: 251,000 sq. mi. (650,087 km²), including 39,225 sq. mi. (101,592 km²) of inland water; 6th in size among the provinces. *Greatest Distances*—north-south, 761 mi. (1,225 km); east-west, 493 mi. (793 km). *Coastline* (Hudson Bay)—570 mi. (917 km).

Elevation: *Highest*—Baldy Mountain, 2,729 ft. (832 m) above sea level. *Lowest*—sea level, along Hudson Bay.

Population: *1976 Census*—1,021,506; 5th among the provinces; distribution, 70 per cent urban, 30 per cent rural; density, 4 persons per sq. mi. (2 per km²).

Chief Products: *Agriculture*—wheat, beef cattle, hay, barley. *Fishing Industry*—yellow pickerel, whitefish. *Forest Products*—pulpwood, logs and bolts. *Fur Industry*—mink, muskrat. *Manufacturing*—food products, fabricated metal products, nonelectric machinery, transportation equipment, printed materials. *Mining*—nickel, copper, zinc, petroleum.

Entered the Dominion: July 15, 1870, the fifth province.

The contributors of this article are Peter McLintock, Editor of the Winnipeg Free Press; *W. L. Morton, Vanier Professor of History at Trent University and author of* Manitoba: A History; *and Thomas R. Weir, Professor and Head of the Department of Geography at the University of Manitoba.*

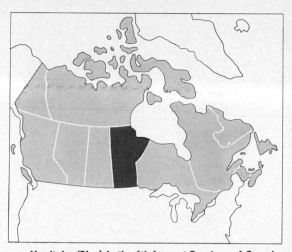

Manitoba (Blue) Is the 6th Largest Province of Canada.

Sawmill Near Cedar Lake in Western Manitoba

Charles R. Meyer, Photo Researchers

MANITOBA, MAN uh TOH buh, is one of Canada's three Prairie Provinces. It lies midway between the Atlantic and Pacific oceans. Winnipeg, Manitoba's capital and largest city, is the main transportation center linking eastern and western Canada.

About half the people of Manitoba live in Winnipeg, the province's major industrial center. Busy food-processing plants and other factories there help make manufacturing the chief source of income in Manitoba. St. Boniface, a district of Winnipeg, has the largest stockyard in Canada. The area also has clothing factories, petroleum refineries, and plants that produce transportation equipment.

Winnipeg lies in rolling plains that cover the southern section of Manitoba. This fertile region has the province's richest farmlands. In summer, vast fields of wheat and other grains wave in the sun. Large numbers of beef cattle graze in fenced pastures. Other important farm products include hay, hogs, milk, and poultry.

A vast, rocky region lies across the northern two-thirds of Manitoba. This thinly populated region has great deposits of copper, gold, nickel, and zinc. Thompson has one of the few facilities in the western world for all stages of nickel production, from mining to processing. The thriving town was carved out of the wilderness after prospectors discovered vast deposits of nickel. Manitoba ranks among the leading North American producers of nickel and zinc. Thick forests stretch across the southern half of the region. Balsam fir, spruce, and other trees there provide wood for Manitoba's furniture factories and paper mills.

Manitoba's many rivers and lakes cover almost a sixth of the province and help make it a popular vacationland. Tourists enjoy boating and swimming in the clear, sparkling waters. Fishermen come from many parts of North America to cast for bass, pike, and trout. In the rugged forests of Manitoba, hunters track caribou, elk, moose, and smaller game. In the marshes and prairies, they shoot ducks, geese, and partridges.

Beavers and other fur-bearing animals made the Manitoba region important during the late 1600's. English fur traders entered the rich fur country from Hudson Bay in the northeast. French-Canadian traders came westward from Quebec during the early 1700's. The adventurous fur traders paddled their birchbark canoes up Manitoba's rivers and traveled through unexplored forests and plains. They traded with the Indians of the region and built forts and trading posts in the wilderness. Irish and Scottish farmers began breaking up the plains in the early 1800's. Vast wheat fields were created in the fertile Red River Valley. Manitoba began exporting wheat, and the grain became famous for its high quality.

The word *Manitoba* probably came from the Algonkian language of the Indians. The tribes thought the *Manito* (great spirit) made the echoing sounds that came from a strait of Lake Manitoba. These sounds were actually made by waves dashing against limestone ledges on the shore. The Indians called this narrow part of the lake *Manito waba* (great spirit's strait). Manitoba has the nickname of the *Keystone Province*. The nickname came from Manitoba's location in the center, or keystone, of the "arch" formed by the 10 Canadian provinces.

For the relationship of Manitoba to the other Canadian provinces, see the articles on CANADA; CANADA, GOVERNMENT OF; CANADA, HISTORY OF; PRAIRIE PROVINCES.

Lieutenant Governor of Manitoba represents Queen Elizabeth in the province. He or she is appointed by the governor general in council of Canada. The lieutenant governor's position is largely honorary, like that of the governor general.

Premier of Manitoba is the actual head of the provincial government. The province, like the other provinces and Canada itself, has a *parliamentary* form of government. The premier is a member of the legislative assembly, where he or she is the leader of the majority party. The voters elect the premier as they do the other members of the assembly. The premier receives a salary of $16,600 a year, plus allowances for serving as a member of the assembly. For a list of Manitoba's premiers, see the *History* section of this article.

The premier presides over the executive council, or cabinet. The council also includes ministers chosen by the premier from among party members in the legislative assembly. Each minister directs one or more branches of the provincial government. The executive council, like the premier, resigns if it loses the support of a majority of the assembly.

Legislative Assembly is a one-house legislature that makes the provincial laws. It has 57 members elected from 57 electoral districts. Their terms may last up to five years. However, the lieutenant governor, on the advice of the premier, may call for an election before the end of the five-year period. If he or she does so, all members of the assembly must run again for office.

Courts. The highest court in Manitoba is the court of appeal. It is made up of the chief justice of Manitoba and four *puisne* (associate) judges. The court of queen's bench hears all major civil and criminal cases. Although Manitoba has no counties, it is divided into 16 county court districts. Each district has one county judge, except that which includes Winnipeg. This district, because of its large population, has five judges.

The governor general in council appoints all Manitoba's higher-court judges. They serve until the age of 75. Minor court officials, such as provincial judges, are appointed by provincial authorities.

Local Government. Manitoba has about 185 incorporated cities, towns, villages, and rural municipalities. Each is governed by a council headed by a mayor or a reeve. All these officials are elected to three-year terms. The number of council members ranges from 4 to 50, depending on the area's population. The province also has about 20 local government districts in thinly settled areas. These districts are governed by resident administrators appointed by the provincial government.

The five cities of Manitoba received their charters under special acts of the legislative assembly. The towns, villages, and rural municipalities were incorporated under the province's municipal act. They are supervised by the department of municipal affairs.

In 1971, the Manitoba legislature passed a law that combined Winnipeg and 11 of its suburbs into one municipality, the city of Winnipeg. The suburbs included St. Boniface and St. James-Assiniboia. As a result of the law, which took effect Jan. 1, 1972, Winnipeg became Canada's third largest city. The legislature also eliminated the Metropolitan Corporation of Greater Winnipeg, a regional authority that had administered services for Winnipeg and its suburbs.

The Legislative Building's Grand Staircase is flanked by buffaloes. Manitoba has a single-house legislature called the general assembly.

Manitoba Dept. of Economic Development

Manitoba Dept. of Economic Development

Government House stands east of the Legislative Building in Winnipeg. The mansion is the home of the lieutenant governor of Manitoba. He serves as Queen Elizabeth's official representative in the province.

Symbols of Manitoba. On the coat of arms, the buffalo symbolizes the importance of the Red River buffalo in Manitoba's history, and the position of Manitoba as a Prairie Province. The cross of St. George represents Manitoba's bond with Great Britain. The coat of arms was adopted in 1870. The provincial flag, adopted in 1965, bears Manitoba's coat of arms and the British Union flag.

Taxation provides about 60 per cent of the provincial government's income. About 30 per cent of the tax money comes from federal-provincial tax-sharing arrangements. The rest comes from provincial taxes, such as those on corporate and personal incomes, gasoline, and general sales.

Manitoba gets nearly all the rest of its income from federal grants and provincial fees and licenses. Other income is chiefly from the sale of liquor, which is government controlled.

Politics. The major political parties of Manitoba are the Progressive Conservative, Liberal, and New Democratic parties. The Progressive Conservative Party was formerly named the Conservative Party, and today members are usually simply called Conservatives. In 1932, the Liberals joined the provincial government headed by a farmers' organization called the Progressives. They were called the Liberal Progressives until 1961. The New Democratic Party, a socialist party, controlled the provincial government from 1969 until 1977, when the Progressive Conservatives won power. A Manitoba citizen must be at least 18 years old to vote.

The Provincial Flag

**The Provincial
Coat of Arms**

The Floral Emblem
Pasqueflower

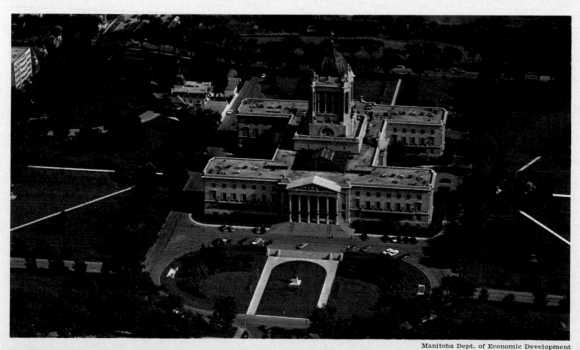

Manitoba Dept. of Economic Development

The Manitoba Legislative Building in Winnipeg stands in a landscaped park on the Assiniboine River. Winnipeg became the provincial capital in 1870. Manitoba has had no other capitals.

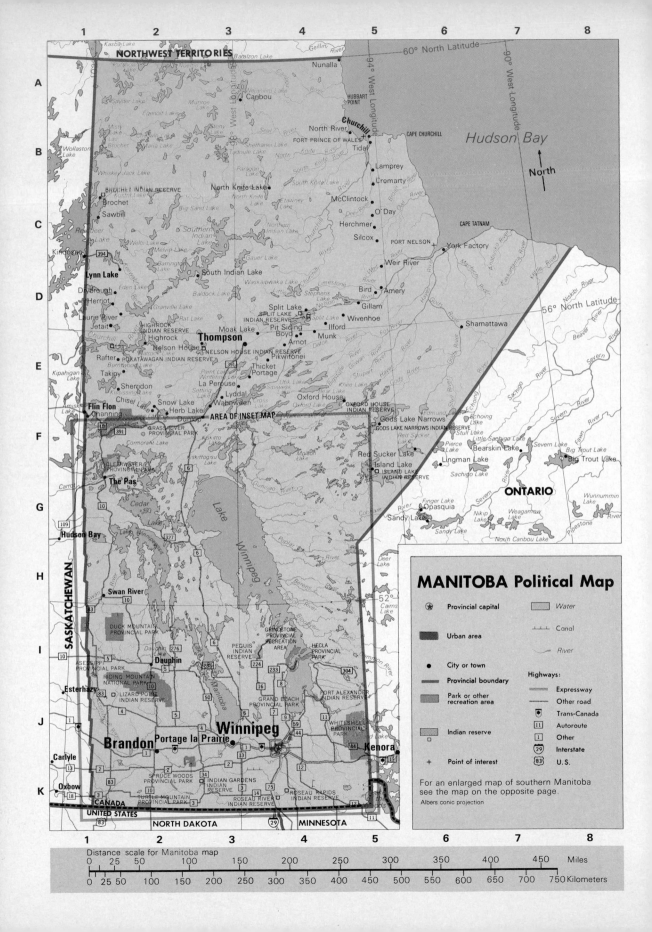

MANITOBA Political Map

Legend:

- ⊛ Provincial capital
- ▨ Water
- ▮ Urban area
- +++ Canal
- ∿ River
- ● City or town
- ▬ Provincial boundary
- ▨ Park or other recreation area
- □ Indian reserve
- + Point of interest

Highways:
- ═══ Expressway
- ─── Other road
- 🛡 Trans-Canada
- 11 Autoroute
- 1 Other
- 29 Interstate
- 83 U.S.

For an enlarged map of southern Manitoba see the map on the opposite page.
Albers conic projection

Distance scale for Manitoba map

0 25 50 100 150 200 250 300 350 400 450 Miles

0 25 50 100 150 200 250 300 350 400 450 500 550 600 650 700 750 Kilometers

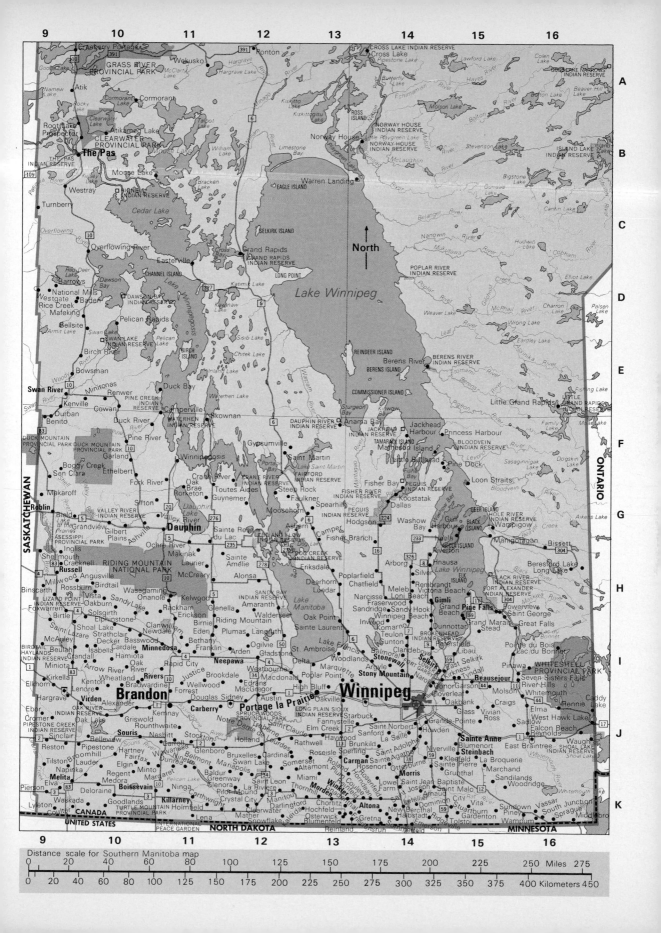

MANITOBA MAP INDEX

Population

1,021,506	..Census..	1976
988,247	....“....	1971
963,066	....“....	1966
921,686	....“....	1961
776,541	....“....	1951
729,744	....“....	1941
700,139	....“....	1931
610,118	....“....	1921
461,394	....“....	1911
255,211	....“....	1901
152,506	....“....	1891
62,260	....“....	1881
25,228	....“....	1871

Metropolitan Area

Winnipeg 578,217

Cities, Towns, and Villages

Akudlik (Camp 20)* ..71..B 10
Alexander ....280..J 10
Alonsa ......140..H 12
Altamont ......113..K 12
Altbergthal* ...27..K 3
Altona .....2,480..K 14
Amaranth ....248..H 12
Angusville ....153..H 9
Anola* ......133..J 15
Arborg ....861..H 14
Arden ....160..I 11
Argyle ....25..I 14
Arnaud ....78..K 14
Ashern ....642..G 13
Ashville ....39..G 10
Austin ....421..I 12
Baden ....21..D 9
Bagot* ....47..J 13
Bakers Narrows* ....35..F 1
Baldur ....378..K 11
Balmoral ......118..I 14
Barrows ......219..D 9
Basswood ......82..I 11
Beaconia* .....22..K 5
Beausejour ..2,422..I 15
Bellsite ....74..D 9
Belmont ....317..J 11
Benito ....507..F 9
Berens River ....E 14
Bethany ....46..I 11
Beulah ....31..I 9
Bield ....22..G 9
Big Black River* ......51..G 4
Big Eddy* .....94..B 10
Binscarth ....430..H 9
Birch River ...617..E 9
Bird ....36..D 5
Birds Hill* ...631..I 14
Birnie ....56..I 11
Birtle ....821..H 9
Bissett ....114..G 16
Blumenfeld ....116..K 13
Blumenort ....379..J 15
Blumenort* .....140..K 13
Boggy Creek ....F 9
Boissevain ..1,584..K 10
Bowsman ......483..E 9
Bradwardine ...37..I 10
Brandon ...34,901..J 2
Broad Valley* 54..I 3
Brookdale .....78..I 11
Brunkild ......101..J 14
Bruxelles ......41..J 12
Camp Morton* .39..J 4
Camper ......19..G 13
Camperville ...530..F 11
Carberry ....1,423..J 11
Cardale ....49..I 10
Cardinal ....25..J 12
Carlowrie* ....35..K 4
Carman ....2,272..J 13
Carrick* ....39..K 4
Carroll ....33..J 11
Cartwright* ..361..K 11
Chater* ....36..J 2
Chatfield ......32..H 14
Chortitz ......202..K 13
Churchill ....1,687..B 5
Clandeboye ....152..I 14
Clanwilliam ...118..I 11
Clearwater ......81..K 12
Clearwater Lake* ....62..C 4
Cloverleaf ....31..I 15
Comeau* ......43..J 3
Cormorant .....378..A 10
Cowan ....94..F 10
Cranberry Portage ....861..A 9
Crandall ....52..I 10
Crane River ..252..G 12
Cromer ....48..J 9
Cross Lake ....A 13
Crystal City ..513..K 12
Cypress River* 255..J 12
Darlingford ..158..K 13
Dauphin ....9,109..I 2
Dawson Bay* ..45..H 2
Decker ....43..I 10
Deerhorn ......21..H 13
Deloraine ...1,019..K 10
Delta ....49..I 13
Domain* ....39..K 4
Dominion City 385..K 14
Douglas ....164..J 11
Dropmore* .....16..I 1
Duck Bay ....535..E 11
Dufresne* .....30..K 4
Dufrost* ......41..K 14
Dugald* ......328..J 14
Dunnottar ....219..I 14
Dunrea ....122..J 11
Durban ....77..F 9
East Braintree .23..J 16
East Selkirk ..901..I 15
Easterville ....565..D 11
Eden ....106..I 11
Edrans ....20..I 12
Elgin ....163..J 10
Elie* ....372..J 13
Elkhorn ......527..I 9
Elm Creek ....296..J 13
Elma ....100..J 16
Elphinstone ..237..H 10
Elva ....29..K 9
Emerson ......756..K 14
Erickson ......558..H 11
Eriksdale .....303..H 13
Ethelbert ......493..F 10
Evergreen Place* ....95..I 3
Fairfax ....19..J 10
Falcon Lake* .149..J 16
Fannystelle ...125..J 13
Fisher Bay ....16..G 14
Fisher Branch 529..G 14
Flin Flon† ..8,152..F 1
Fork River .....90..G 11
Forrest ....72..I 11
Fort Churchill* .201..B 5
Foxwarren ....178..H 9
Franklin ....34..I 11
Fraserwood ....74..H 14
Friedensfeld* ..54..K 3
Friedensruh ....86..K 13
Gardenton ......61..K 15
Garland* ....69..I 2
Garson ....290..I 15
Gilbert Plains 847..G 10
Gillam ......2,365..D 5
Gimli ....1,659..H 14
Giroux* ....66..J 15
Gladstone .....976..I 12
Glass ....25..J 14
Glenboro ....720..J 12
Glenella ....164..H 12
Glenlea* ....97..K 4
Glenora ....48..K 12
Gnadenthal ...121..K 13
Gods River* ..198..F 5
Gonor ....I 14
Goodlands ......83..K 10
Gordon* ....28..J 4
Grahamdale* ...21..I 3
Grand Marais .220..H 15
Grand Rapids .503..C 12
Grande Pointe 154..J 14
Grandview ..1,013..G 10
Granville Lake* ....92..D 2
Graysville* ....38..K 3
Great Falls ..267..I 16
Gretna ....510..K 14
Griswold ....94..J 10
Grosse Isle* ...148..J 4
Grunthal ....537..K 14
Gull Lake* .....23..J 4
Gunton ....100..I 14
Gypsumville ..114..F 12
Halbstadt ......39..K 14
Hamiota ....765..I 10
Harding* ....25..J 1
Hargrave ....36..J 9
Harrowby* .....16..I 1
Hartney ....484..J 10
Haskett* ....41..K 3
Haywood ....152..J 13
Hazelridge* .....51..I 15
Herb Lake ......17..F 2
Herchmer ....41..C 5
High Bluff ....141..I 13
Hilbre* ....31..I 3
Hillcrest Trailer Park ....51..J 4
Hillridge* ......251..J 3
Hochfeld ....197..K 13
Hodgson ....111..G 14
Holland ....405..J 12
Holmfield ......35..K 11
Homewood* ....36..K 3
Horndean ....95..K 13
Hybord* ....105..G 2
Île des Chênes* ....689..J 14
Ilford ....199..D 4
Inglis ....255..H 9
Interprovincial Pipe Line* ..24..J 2
Inwood ....171..H 14
Jenpeg Camp* .29..F 3
Jenpeg Townsite* ...336..A 13
Justice ....28..I 11
Kaleida ....16..K 13
Kane* ....15..K 3
Kelwood ......249..H 11
Kemnay ....64..J 10
Kenton ....176..I 10
Kenville ....125..F 9
Killarney ...2,348..K 11
Kleefeld ......173..J 14
Kola* ....65..J 1
Komarno ....55..H 14
Kronstal* ....38..K 3
La Broquerie .565..J 15
La Rochelle* ..75..K 4
Lac du Bonnet 971..I 15
Ladywood* ....15..J 3
Lake Francis ..38..I 13
Landmark* ...465..J 14
Langruth .....147..I 12
La Rivière ....218..K 12
La Salle .....190..J 14
Lauder ....69..J 10
Laurier ....229..H 11
Lavenham* .....33..J 2
Lena ....27..K 11
Lenore ....49..I 10
Letellier ....181..K 14
Libau ....87..I 15
Limestone .....72..D 5
Little Grand Rapids ....F 16
Lockport* ......275..I 14
Long Spruce* .376..D 5
Loni Beach ....157..H 14
Loon Straits ...21..G 15
Lorette* ....755..K 4
Lowe Farm ...286..K 14
Lundar ....688..H 13
Lyleton ....72..K 9
Lynn Lake ..2,568..D 1
Macdonald ......55..I 13
MacGregor ...789..I 12
Mafeking ....276..D 10
Makaroff ....25..G 9
Makinak ....23..G 11
Manibridge* ..232..C 4
Manigotagan ..172..G 15
Manitou ....883..K 12
Manson* ....20..I 1
Marchand ......112..J 15
Margaret ....32..J 11
Mariapolis ....177..K 12
Marquette ......56..I 13
Mather ....83..K 12
Matheson Island .....116..F 14
McAuley ....134..I 9
McClintock ....20..C 5
McCreary ....614..H 11
McMunn* ....22..J 5
McTavish* ......31..K 3
Medora ....84..K 10
Meleb ....38..H 14
Melita ....1,169..K 9
Miami ....375..K 13
Middlebro ....93..K 16
Middlechurch* 348..J 4
Miniota ....206..I 9
Minitonas ....605..E 10
Minnedosa ..2,718..I 11
Minto ....90..J 11
Missi Falls* ...47..C 3
Mitchell* ......278..J 15
Moorepark* ....31..J 2
Moose Lake ...514..B 11
Moosehorn ....183..G 13
Morden .....3,886..K 13
Morris ....1,572..K 14
Mulvihill* ......17..I 3
Myrtle* ....24..K 3
Napinka ....151..K 10
Narol ....I 14
National Mills .32..D 9
Navin* ....92..J 4
Neelin* ....24..K 2
Neepawa ....3,508..I 11
Nelson House ..61..E 3
Nesbitt ....40..J 11
Neubergthal* .118..K 3
Neuenburg* ....62..K 4
Neuhorst* ....64..K 13
New Bergthal ..118..K 14
New Bothwell* 207..J 14
Newdale ....217..I 10
Newton Siding* 46..J 3
Ninette ....307..K 11
Ninga ....92..K 11
Niverville ...1,251..J 14
North Knife Lake ....C 4
Norway House ......B 13
Notre Dame de Lourdes .651..J 12
Nutimik Lake* 23..J 4
Oak Bluff* .....34..K 4
Oak Brae ......18..G 11
Oak Lake ....367..J 10
Oak Point ....201..H 13
Oak River .....221..I 10
Oakbank .....468..J 14
Oakburn ......290..H 10
Oakville ....398..J 13
Ochre River ..298..G 11
Old Altona* ....88..K 13
Onanole ....334..H 11
Oozewekwun* .887..J 2
Osterwick .....150..K 13
Otterburne ....161..J 14
Overflowing River ....17..C 10
Paint Lake Service Camp* 19..F 3
Pas, The ....6,602..G 1
Pas Airport, The* ....89..G 1
Paungassi* ...222..H 4
Pelican Bay* ..28..J 4
Pelican Rapids 226..D 10
Petersfield ...181..I 14
Pierson ......221..K 9
Pikwitonei ...202..E 4
Pilot Mound ..730..K 12
Pinawa .....2,174..I 16
Pine Creek Settlement* .42..H 2
Pine Dock .....90..F 14
Pine Falls ....945..H 15
Pine Ridge* ...57..J 4
Pine Ridge Valley Trailer Camp* .....305..J 4
Pine River ....398..F 10
Piney ....122..K 16
Pipestone .....158..J 9
Pit Siding* ....29..C 4
Plum Coulee ..477..K 13
Plumas ....289..I 12
Pointe du Bois ....164..I 16
Poplar Point ..250..I 13
Poplarfield .....70..H 13
Portage la Prairie ..12,555..J 3
Powerview .....668..H 15
Prawda* ....44..K 5
Princess Harbour .....47..F 14
Prospector .....35..B 9
Rapid City ....412..I 11
Rathwell ....149..J 12
Red Deer Lake* 56..G 1
Red Sucker Lake ....345..F 6
Reinfeld .....138..K 13
Reinland .....120..K 13
Rennie ....128..J 16
Renwer ....27..E 10
Reston ....539..J 9
Richer* ....307..J 15
Ridgeville .....35..K 14
Ridgeway Trailer Court* ......19..G 13
Riding Mountain ...193..H 11
River Hills ...110..I 16
Rivercrest* ...458..J 4
Rivers .....1,185..I 10
Riverton ......685..H 14
Roblin ....1,971..G 9
Roland ....302..K 13
Rorketon .....248..G 11
Rosa* ....16..K 4
Roseau River* .52..K 4
Rosebank* .....34..K 3
Roseisle ....39..J 13
Rosenfeld .....270..K 14
Rosengart* .....67..K 13
Rosenhoff* ......66..K 4
Rosenort ....108..J 14
Rosenort* ......76..K 13
Ross ....J 15
Rossburn ....652..H 10
Rossendale* ....24..J 2
Rosser* ....76..I 14
Russell ....1,524..H 9
Ruttan Lake Mining Camp* ....42..D 2
St. Adolphe ..617..J 14
St. Ambroise .314..I 13
St. Claude ....612..J 13
St. Eustache* .344..I 13
St. Francois Xavier* ....141..J 3
St. George .....540..H 15
St. Jean Baptiste ....562..K 14
St. Joseph ......50..K 14
St. Laurent ...163..I 13
St. Lazare ....476..H 9
St. Leon ......153..K 12
St. Malo ....731..K 14
St. Martin .....42..F 12
St. Pierre* ....906..J 14
Ste. Agathe ...317..J 14
Ste. Amelie ......33..H 11
Ste. Anne ...1,174..J 15
Ste. Genevieve* 113..K 4
Ste. Rose du Lac ...1,038..G 11
San Clara .....120..F 9
Sandilands ......87..K 15
Sandy Hook ....H 14
Sandy Lake ...351..H 10
Sanford ......347..J 14
Sarto* ....27..K 4
Schanzenfeld* 174..K 13
Schoenwiese* ..57..K 13
Selkirk .....9,862..I 14
Seven Sisters Falls ....58..I 16
Seymourville* ..62..J 5
Shellmouth ....36..H 9
Sherridon .....107..E 1
Sherritt Gordon Mines* .....202..F 2
Shoal Lake ...865..I 10
Shortdale* .....35..I 1
Sidney ....134..J 12
Sifton ....207..G 11
Silver ....33..H 14
Silverton Station* .....38..J 1
Sinclair ....31..J 9
Snow Lake ..1,585..F 2
Snowflake ......32..K 12
Solsgirth ....20..H 10
Somerset ....625..K 12
Sommerfeld ...107..K 14
Souris ......1,712..J 10
South Bay* ...60..D 3
South Beach* .30..G 13
South Indian Lake ....668..D 3
South Junction .48..K 16
Sperling ....128..J 13
Sprague ....85..K 16
Springstein* ..138..J 14
Starbuck ....263..J 14
Stead ....30..I 15
Steep Rock ....117..G 12
Steinbach ...5,979..J 15
Stockton ......50..J 11
Stonewall ...1,826..I 13
Stonewall Trailer Court* .....132..J 4
Stony Mountain .1,334..I 14
Strathclair ...396..I 10
Stuartburn .....60..K 15
Sundown .....102..K 15
Swan Lake ...338..J 12
Swan River .3,742..H 1
Teulon ....873..I 14
Thalberg* ......24..J 4
Thicket Portage ....255..E 3
Thompson .17,291..E 3
Thornhill ......43..K 13
Tilston ....54..J 9
Tolstoi ....77..K 15
Toutes Aides ...34..G 11
Treesbank* ....26..J 2
Treherne ......706..J 12
Tyndall ....411..I 15
Umpherville Settlement* .195..C 4
Upper Seven Sisters* ....101..J 4
Valley River ...30..G 11
Valleyview Trailer Court* .....475..G 1
Vassar ....134..K 16
Victoria Beach 50..H 15
Virden .....2,936..J 10
Vista ....48..H 10
Vita ....213..K 15
Vogar* ....128..H 12
Wabowden ....847..F 3
Waldersee ....21..H 12
Wampum ....25..K 16
Wanless* ......250..F 1
Warren* ....302..I 14
Warren Landing 36..B 13
Wasagaming ...100..H 11
Waskada ......257..K 10
Wawanesa ....487..J 11
Wellwood ....79..I 11
Westbourne ....88..I 12
Westgate ......33..D 9
West Hawk Lake ....88..J 16
Westview* ....38..I 2
Wheatland .....43..I 10
White House Plain Trailer Court* 193..K 4
Whitemouth ..314..I 16
Winkler ....3,749..K 13
Winnipeg .560,874..J 4
Winnipeg Beach ....582..H 14
Winnipegosis .893..F 11
Woodlands ...149..I 13
Woodlands Trailer Court* 51..J 3
Woodridge .....175..K 15
Wytonville* ....38..K 2
York Landing* 198..D 4

*Does not appear on map; key shows general location.
†City on Manitoba-Saskatchewan border; total population 8,560.

Source: Latest available census figures (1976). Places without population figures are populated unincorporated areas reported in the 1976 census without population figures.

MANITOBA/*People*

The 1976 Canadian census reported that Manitoba had 1,021,506 persons. The population had increased 3 per cent over the 1971 figure of 988,247.

About two-thirds of the people of Manitoba live in cities and towns. About 57 per cent—578,217 persons—live in the metropolitan area of Winnipeg. Winnipeg has the province's only Census Metropolitan Area as defined by Statistics Canada.

Besides Winnipeg, Manitoba has three cities with populations of more than 12,000. They are, in order of size, Brandon, Thompson, and Portage la Prairie. See the separate articles on the cities and towns listed in the *Related Articles* at the end of this article.

About 85 out of 100 Manitobans were born in Can-

POPULATION

This map shows the *population density* of Manitoba, and how it varies within the province. Population density means the average number of persons who live in a given area.

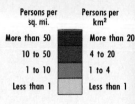

Persons per sq. mi.		Persons per km²
More than 50	▨	More than 20
10 to 50	▦	4 to 20
1 to 10	▥	1 to 4
Less than 1	☐	Less than 1

0   100   200 Miles
0   100   200   300 Kilometers

WORLD BOOK map

J. Coleman Fletcher, Miller Services

Downtown Winnipeg is the chief commercial center of Manitoba. About half the province's people live in the city.

ada. The province also has large numbers of persons born in Germany, Great Britain, Poland, and Russia. About 40 per cent of the people have English, Irish, or Scottish ancestors. Some descendants of French settlers live in towns where French is still a major language. The St. Boniface district of Winnipeg is the major center of French-Canadian culture in the province.

Manitoba has about 62,000 *métis* (persons of mixed white and Indian ancestry). About 41,000 Indians and 130 Eskimos live in the province. Southwestern Manitoba has more than a hundred Indian reservations. Most of the Eskimos live near Churchill.

The United Church of Canada has the largest church membership in Manitoba. Other large religious groups are Roman Catholics, members of the Anglican Church of Canada, and Lutherans.

MANITOBA/*Education*

Schools. The first school in the Manitoba region was a log cabin built in 1818 in St. Boniface, now a district of Winnipeg. Roman Catholic priests established the school for children of French-Canadian settlers. Other missionaries opened Roman Catholic or Protestant schools after new settlements developed in the region.

In 1871, the church-supported educational system was ended. The province created a board of education to direct the schools and provide them with public funds. Roman Catholic board members managed the Roman Catholic schools, and Protestant members supervised theirs. In 1890, the province abolished the board of education and its double school system. The provincial Department of Education was created to head a single education system. In 1908, the cabinet office of minister of education was established in Manitoba.

A Manitoba law of 1965 requires children between the ages of 7 and 16 to attend school. The province has about 755 public schools. For information on the number of students and teachers in Manitoba, see EDUCATION (table). Brandon University is in Brandon, and the University of Manitoba and the University of Winnipeg are in Winnipeg. Each of these universities has a separate article in WORLD BOOK. For enrollments, see CANADA (table: Universities and Colleges).

Libraries and Museums. Three of the most important libraries in the province are the University of Manitoba Library, the Legislative Library, and the Centennial Library, all in Winnipeg. Students of early Manitoban history use a special library of the Hudson's Bay Company that is operated by the Provincial Archives. The Museum of Man and Nature and the St. Boniface Historical Museum, both in Winnipeg, attract thousands of visitors yearly.

The Annual World Championship Dog Derby in The Pas

MANITOBA / A Visitor's Guide

Visitors to Manitoba can see many reminders of the province's colorful history. Forts and trading posts of the early fur-trading days are popular attractions. The Basilica of St. Boniface, in Winnipeg, stands on the site of the first Roman Catholic church in western Canada. It is perhaps the most beautiful cathedral in the region. Many people who helped make Manitoba history are buried in the churchyard. They include Louis Riel, who led two uprisings of the métis.

Lake Winnipeg and many other beautiful lakes of Manitoba have popular summer resorts that offer boating and swimming. The province also has fine golf courses. People come from most parts of North America to fish for bass, pike, and trout in the province's lakes and rivers. Hunters seek ducks, elk, geese, and moose in the forests and swamps. Many visitors attend performances by the Royal Winnipeg Ballet or Winnipeg Symphony Orchestra, or other cultural events.

PLACES TO VISIT

Following are brief descriptions of some of Manitoba's many interesting places to visit.

Agricultural Museum, in Austin, has one of Canada's largest collections of steam engines, as well as gasoline tractors and other antique farm equipment. It also includes a reconstructed pioneer village.

Fort Prince of Wales, near Churchill, overlooks Hudson Bay. It has the massive remains of the northernmost fortress in North America. The stone structure was built by the Hudson's Bay Company between 1733 and 1770. It became a national historic park in 1940.

International Peace Garden lies partly in Manitoba and partly in North Dakota. It honors the long friendship between Canada and the United States. A *cairn* (memorial made of stones) consisting of rocks from both countries marks the international boundary.

Lower Fort Garry, 20 miles (32 kilometers) north of Winnipeg, is the only stone fur-trading fort in Canada still standing complete. It was built during the 1830's

by the Hudson's Bay Company on the Red River. The area became a national historic park in 1951.

Norway House, built in 1826, stands at the northern end of Lake Winnipeg. This old Hudson's Bay Company post has many articles from fur-trading days.

Red River Valley, near Winnipeg, was the site of the first Manitoba colony. Historic old houses and early stone churches dot the prairies and grain fields in the valley.

The Pas is a historic northern crossroads town northwest of Cedar Lake. Its name came from the Cree Indian word *opas* (narrows).

National and Provincial Parks. Riding Mountain National Park, Manitoba's only national park, lies west of Lake Winnipeg. For its area and chief features, see CANADA (National Parks).

Manitoba has 12 provincial parks. For information on these parks, write to Manitoba Government Travel, 304-200 Vaughan St., Winnipeg, Man. R3C IT5.

Fishermen Cast for Trout in a Rushing Manitoba Stream

ANNUAL EVENTS

Manitoba's outstanding annual event is probably the World Championship Dog Derby, a dog sled race over snow. The event is part of the famous Trappers' Festival, held in The Pas each February. Other annual events in Manitoba include the following.

February-April: Canadian Power Toboggan Championships in Beausejour (February); Bonspiel in Winnipeg (February); Manitoba Royal Winter Fair in Brandon (March or April).

June-July: Altona Sunflower Festival (July); Manitoba Stampede in Morris (July); Provincial Exhibition in Brandon (July); Selkirk Highland Gathering (July); Threshermen's Reunion in Austin (July).

August: Icelandic Celebration in Gimli; National Ukrainian Festival of Canada in Dauphin.

Lower Fort Garry on the Red River North of Winnipeg
Photos, Malak, Miller Services

The Royal Winnipeg Ballet Performs Throughout Canada
Manitoba Dept. of Industry and Commerce

Land Regions. Manitoba has four main land regions. They are, from northeast to southwest: (1) the Hudson Bay Lowland, (2) the Canadian Shield, (3) the Manitoba Lowland, and (4) the Saskatchewan Plain.

The Hudson Bay Lowland is a wet plain bordering the southern part of Hudson Bay. In Manitoba, this almost treeless flatland extends about 100 miles (160 kilometers) into the interior. Few persons live there.

The Canadian Shield is a vast, horseshoe-shaped region that covers almost half of Canada and part of the United States. The rough shield, made up of granites and other rocks, covers nearly two-thirds of Manitoba. It has many lakes, streams, and forests, and deposits of copper, nickel, and other minerals. See CANADIAN SHIELD.

The Manitoba Lowland forms part of the Western Interior Plains, the Canadian section of the North American Great Plains. It is a flat area of forests, lakes, limestone rock, and swamps. The forests have great stands of timber, and the lakes are rich in fish.

The Saskatchewan Plain also forms part of the Western Interior Plains. This region is a rolling plain broken by low hills. Its rich, well-drained soils make it the main farming region of Manitoba.

Mountains. The Duck, Porcupine, and Riding mountain ranges form the Manitoba Escarpment. It rises between the two plains regions. The highest point in Manitoba is 2,729-foot (832-meter) Baldy Mountain, in the Duck Mountain range near the Saskatchewan border. The Turtle and Pembina hills of North Dakota extend into the southern part of Manitoba.

Land Regions of Manitoba

George Hunter, Photri

Wheat and Other Crops grow near the village of Wellwood in the Saskatchewan Plain area of Manitoba.

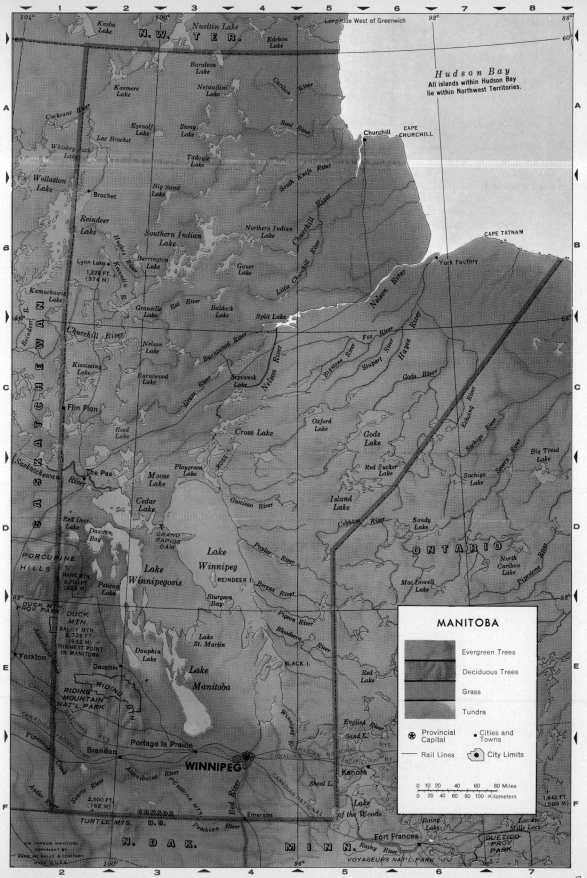

MANITOBA

Evergreen Trees

Deciduous Trees

Grass

Tundra

⊗ Provincial Capital
• Cities and Towns
— Rail Lines
◉ City Limits

0 10 20 40 60 80 Miles
0 20 40 60 80 Kilometers

MANITOBA

Rivers and Lakes cover almost a sixth of Manitoba, or 39,225 square miles (101,592 square kilometers). The rivers form a great waterway system that drains western Canada from as far west as the Rocky Mountains. The Red, Saskatchewan, and Winnipeg rivers flow into Lake Winnipeg. Important branches of the Red River are the Assiniboine and Pembina rivers. The Nelson River flows northeast out of Lake Winnipeg across the Canadian Shield, and empties into Hudson Bay. The Churchill and Hayes rivers also drain the northern part of the province.

Three lakes are so large that they are often called the *Great Lakes of Manitoba*. Lake Winnipeg, which covers 9,398 square miles (24,341 square kilometers), is the largest body of water entirely within any province or state. Lake Winnipegosis covers 2,103 square miles (5,447 square kilometers), and Lake Manitoba spreads over 1,817 square miles (4,706 square kilometers). Other lakes include Dauphin, Gods, Island, Reindeer, Southern Indian, and Tadoule. Cedar, Cross, and Moose lakes were enlarged and joined together during construction of the Grand Rapids hydroelectric project on the Saskatchewan River. The resulting reservoir, completed in 1965, covers 2,000 square miles (5,200 square kilometers). The three sections kept their names.

Mines at Flin Flon, *right,* produce most of Manitoba's zinc and copper. The area lies in the Canadian Shield. This rocky region has many lakes and streams, forests, and mineral deposits.

Rich Farmland Surrounds a Village near Portage la Prairie in southern Manitoba. This area lies in the Manitoba Lowland, an important agricultural region.

Photographic Survey Corp., from Photo Researchers

George Leavens, Photo Researchers

Churchill is one of the few towns in the Hudson Bay Lowland of Manitoba. This region's heavy clay soil is not good for farming.

George Hunter, Publix

MANITOBA /Climate

Manitoba has long, bitterly cold winters and warm summers. In general, the temperature decreases from the southwestern part of the province to the northeastern section. The average January temperature is 0° F. (−18° C) in the south and −17° F. (−27° C) in the north. The lowest recorded temperature in Manitoba, −63° F. (−53° C), occurred in Norway House on Jan. 9, 1899. Manitoba's average July temperatures range from 68° F. (20° C) in the south to 55° F. (13° C) in the north. The highest temperature was 112° F. (44° C), recorded in Treesbank, near Wawanesa, on July 11, 1936, and in Emerson on July 12, 1936. Manitoba's *precipitation* (rain, melted snow, and other forms of moisture) averages 17 inches (43 centimeters) a year. About 50 inches (130 centimeters) of snow falls a year.

Manitoba Dept. of Industry and Commerce

Warm Summer Sunshine brightens the southern Manitoba countryside. Winter will bring bitter cold and deep snow to the area.

SEASONAL TEMPERATURES

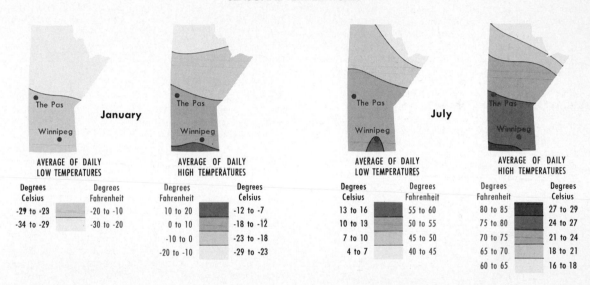

January

AVERAGE OF DAILY LOW TEMPERATURES

Degrees Celsius	Degrees Fahrenheit
-29 to -23	-20 to -10
-34 to -29	-30 to -20

AVERAGE OF DAILY HIGH TEMPERATURES

Degrees Fahrenheit	Degrees Celsius
10 to 20	-12 to -7
0 to 10	-18 to -12
-10 to 0	-23 to -18
-20 to -10	-29 to -23

July

AVERAGE OF DAILY LOW TEMPERATURES

Degrees Celsius	Degrees Fahrenheit
13 to 16	55 to 60
10 to 13	50 to 55
7 to 10	45 to 50
4 to 7	40 to 45

AVERAGE OF DAILY HIGH TEMPERATURES

Degrees Fahrenheit	Degrees Celsius
80 to 85	27 to 29
75 to 80	24 to 27
70 to 75	21 to 24
65 to 70	18 to 21
60 to 65	16 to 18

AVERAGE YEARLY PRECIPITATION
(Rain, Melted Snow and Other Moisture)

Centimeters	Inches
51 to 64	20 to 25
38 to 51	15 to 20
25 to 38	10 to 15

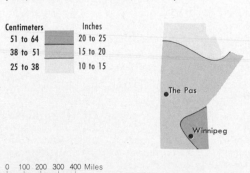

```
0   100 200 300 400 Miles
0    200    400    600 Kilometers
```

WORLD BOOK maps

AVERAGE MONTHLY WEATHER

	THE PAS					WINNIPEG				
	Temperatures				Days of Rain or Snow	Temperatures				Days of Rain or Snow
	F° High	F° Low	C° High	C° Low		F° High	F° Low	C° High	C° Low	
JAN.	3	-16	-16	-27	7	JAN. 9	-8	-13	-22	12
FEB.	10	-12	-12	-24	7	FEB. 14	-5	-10	-21	10
MAR.	25	1	-4	-17	7	MAR. 28	9	-2	-13	9
APR.	44	21	7	-6	7	APR. 48	28	9	-2	9
MAY	60	36	16	2	7	MAY 64	41	18	5	10
JUNE	69	46	21	8	11	JUNE 73	51	23	11	12
JULY	76	53	24	12	11	JULY 80	57	27	14	10
AUG.	73	50	23	10	10	AUG. 78	54	26	12	9
SEPT.	61	40	16	4	10	SEPT. 66	45	19	7	9
OCT.	47	29	8	-2	9	OCT. 52	34	11	1	8
NOV.	25	9	-4	-13	9	NOV. 30	16	-1	-9	11
DEC.	9	-8	-13	-22	8	DEC. 15	1	-9	-17	11

For many years, the economy of Manitoba was based chiefly on agriculture. Many new industries developed during the 1940's, and industrial production increased rapidly. Since the 1950's, manufacturing has been Manitoba's chief source of income.

All values given here are in Canadian dollars. For their value in U.S. money, see MONEY (table).

Natural Resources of Manitoba include fertile soils, rich minerals, valuable forests, and much wildlife.

Soil. The deep, fertile soils of the southern plains are perhaps the province's chief natural resource. Some were deposited by glaciers or by ancient glacial lakes. The soils of the Manitoba Lowland vary from fertile clays to bog and peat. Fertile clay covers vast areas of the Canadian Shield north of Lake Winnipeg. The soils of the Hudson Bay Lowland contain clay.

Minerals. The Canadian Shield has large deposits of chromium, cobalt, copper, nickel, zinc, and other minerals. Great deposits of gypsum lie in the Manitoba Lowland. The uplands have salt deposits. The southwest yields bentonite, limestone, petroleum, and potash.

Plant Life. Manitoba has about 51,000 square miles (132,000 square kilometers) of forests that produce some lumber. About half of Manitoba's timber production is used to make pulp for paper. The most common trees are the aspen, black spruce, jack pine, and white spruce. Others include ash, birch, maple, oak, and tamarack.

Animal Life. Caribou, elk, and moose live in the northern forests. Deer thrive there and in most parts of southern Manitoba. Fur-bearing animals of the forests include the beaver, fox, lynx, mink, and muskrat. Other animals in Manitoba include the bear, coyote, ermine, otter, raccoon, and squirrel.

Thousands of ducks and geese fly north in spring to breed in Manitoba's lakes and ponds. Grouse, partridges, prairie chickens, ptarmigans, and other game birds live in the province. Fish there include bass, pickerel, pike, sauger, sturgeon, trout, and whitefish.

Manufacturing. Goods manufactured in Manitoba have a *value added by manufacture* of about $1 billion yearly. This figure represents the value created in products by Manitoba's industries, not counting such costs as materials, supplies, and fuels.

Food processing is the major industry. It accounts for about a fifth of all manufacturing. The industry has an annual value added by manufacture of about $245 million. Meat packing is the most important activity. The St. Boniface area of Winnipeg has the largest stockyard in Canada. Large flour mills operate in Steinbach, Virden, and Winnipeg.

The manufacture of fabricated metal products is Manitoba's second-ranking industry. It has a value added by manufacture of about $135 million. Winnipeg is the chief center of this industry.

Other leading industries in Manitoba produce nonelectric machinery, transportation equipment, printed materials, clothing, paper products, primary metals, and clay, glass, and stone products. Winnipeg is a printing and publishing center, and also makes transportation equipment. Brandon, the center of Manitoba's chemical industry, is a major producer of fertilizers and pharmaceutical products. Copper and zinc are processed in Flin Flon, Fox Lake, and Ruttan Lake. Factories in the province account for about a fifth of Canada's clothing exports. The clothing industry is centered in Winnipeg.

Agriculture provides an annual income of about $910 million. The province has about 32,000 farms. They total about 19 million acres (7,690,000 hectares) and average about 593 acres (240 hectares) in size.

Wheat is Manitoba's most valuable farm product. Manitoba No. 1 Hard is the grade name for the finest wheat in many of the world's grain markets. Canada's major grain market is in Winnipeg.

The raising of beef cattle is Manitoba's second most valuable agricultural activity. Beef cattle are raised in many parts of Manitoba. Dairying is important in the Red River Valley and other parts of the Manitoba Lowland. Farmers also raise hogs and poultry.

Manitoba ranks among the leading provinces and states in the production of barley and rye. Farmers grow flaxseed, mustard seed, rapeseed, and sunflower—all for their oil. Other important crops include hay, oats, sugar beets, and potatoes.

Fur farming is another important agricultural industry. Southern Manitoba has about 40 fur farms. Almost all the fur farmers raise minks. About four-fifths

Production of Goods in Manitoba

Total value of goods produced in 1976—$2,596,504,000

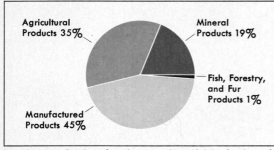

Agricultural Products 35%

Mineral Products 19%

Fish, Forestry, and Fur Products 1%

Manufactured Products 45%

Percentages are based on farm income, value added by forestry and manufacture, and value of fish, fur, and mineral production. Fish, forestry, and fur products are each less than 1 per cent.

Sources: Canadian government publications, 1978.

Employment in Manitoba

Total number of persons employed in 1977—433,000

Economic Activities		Number of Employees
Community, Business, & Personal Services	🧍🧍🧍🧍🧍🧍🧍🧍🧍	121,000
Wholesale & Retail Trade	🧍🧍🧍🧍🧍🧍	77,000
Manufacturing	🧍🧍🧍🧍	55,000
Transportation, Communication, & Utilities	🧍🧍🧍🧍	50,000
Agriculture	🧍🧍🧍	42,000
Government	🧍🧍🧍	33,000
Construction	🧍🧍	24,000
Finance, Insurance, & Real Estate	🧍🧍	23,000
Mining	🧍	6,000
Fishing & Forestry	🧍	2,000

Source: *The Labor Force*, December 1977, Statistics Canada.

of Manitoba's fur production comes from trapping. Muskrat pelts earn the most income of fur brought in by trappers. The provincial government leases the trapping areas, mostly to Indians and métis. In Canada, the Winnipeg fur market ranks second only to that of Montreal.

Mining production in Manitoba has an annual value of about $490 million. Nickel is the most valuable mineral, followed by copper, zinc, and petroleum, in that order. A huge nickel deposit was found in the Mystery Lake-Moak Lake area of north-central Manitoba in 1956. The discovery led to the development of the important mining center of Thompson. Manitoba ranks among the leading provinces and states in zinc production. Mines at Flin Flon and in the Lynn Lake area produce copper, nickel, and zinc.

In 1951, large oil fields were discovered near Virden. Today, Manitoba's oil wells produce about 4 million barrels of oil annually. Other important minerals include clay, cobalt, gold, peat, silver, and stone. Quarries of granite, limestone, and marble provide building materials.

Forestry. Timber cut in Manitoba has an annual value of about $15 million. Lumberjacks cut balsam fir, spruce, and other trees in the southern half of the province. These trees provide wood for the furniture, lumber, and paper industries of Manitoba.

Fishing Industry. Manitoba's annual fish catch is valued at about $8 million. It brings in about 25 million pounds (11,300,000 kilograms) of fish. Much of the catch is shipped to the United States. Whitefish and pickerel account for about 75 per cent of the total value of the catch. The catch also includes perch, pike, sauger, and trout. Northern lakes provide about a fourth of the catch. Lake Winnipeg provides about a third, and lakes Manitoba and Winnipegosis supply the rest.

Electric Power. The production of hydroelectric energy has been important in Manitoba since the 1920's. Hydroelectric power plants generate about 95 per cent of Manitoba's electricity. Six hydroelectric plants on the Winnipeg River, one on the Saskatchewan River, four on the Nelson River, and two on the Laurie River supply power to Manitoba, neighboring provinces, and parts of the United States. Some power plants in Manitoba operate on steam.

Transportation. Six major airlines serve Manitoba. Two of them connect Winnipeg and European cities by an Arctic route. Four of the airlines link Winnipeg and a number of cities in the United States. Smaller airlines connect Churchill, The Pas, Thompson, and Winnipeg.

The province has about 5,400 miles (8,690 kilometers) of railroad tracks. Canada's two main railways enter Winnipeg and branch out in Manitoba. One branch line connects Churchill, The Pas, and Thompson. Two U.S. railroads have terminals in Winnipeg.

About 52,000 miles (83,700 kilometers) of roads, most of them in southern Manitoba, serve the province. The most important one is the cross-country Trans-Canada Highway, which crosses Manitoba through Winnipeg and Brandon. Other major roads link Flin Flon and Winnipeg with North Dakota, and Winnipeg

with Grand Rapids. In winter, bulldozers pack the snow to make roads in northern Manitoba.

Rivers and lakes provide many waterways throughout the province. A cruise ship operates between Winnipeg and Selkirk on the Red River, and to several ports on Lake Winnipeg. Barges also serve these lake ports. Churchill, on Hudson Bay, is Manitoba's chief seaport. Trains carry great quantities of wheat yearly to Churchill for export to Great Britain and other European countries.

Communication. The first newspaper published in Manitoba, *The Nor' Wester*, was issued in 1859 in Fort Garry (now Winnipeg). Today, the province has eight daily newspapers, the largest of which are the *Free Press* and *Tribune*, both of Winnipeg. Weekly newspapers are published in about 60 cities and towns. The *Free Press Weekly*, printed in Winnipeg, has the largest circulation of these papers. A French-language weekly, *La Liberté*, is published in the St. Boniface district of Winnipeg.

The first radio station in Manitoba, CKY, began broadcasting from Winnipeg in 1922. The first television station, CBWT, began operating there in 1954. A French-language radio station broadcasts from the St. Boniface area. Manitoba has about 25 radio stations and 6 major TV stations.

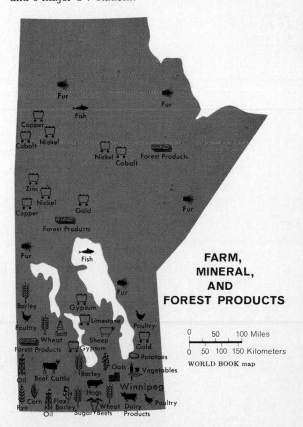

FARM, MINERAL, AND FOREST PRODUCTS

0   50   100 Miles
0 50 100 150 Kilometers
WORLD BOOK map

This map shows where the province's leading farm, mineral, and forest products are produced. The major urban area (shown in red) is the province's most important manufacturing center.

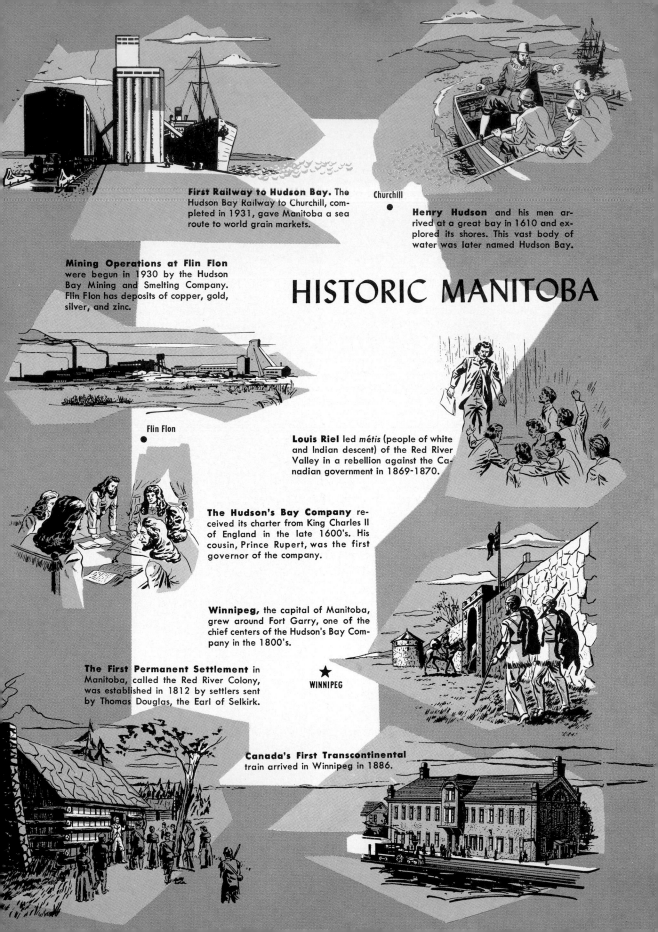

First Railway to Hudson Bay. The Hudson Bay Railway to Churchill, completed in 1931, gave Manitoba a sea route to world grain markets.

Henry Hudson and his men arrived at a great bay in 1610 and explored its shores. This vast body of water was later named Hudson Bay.

Mining Operations at Flin Flon were begun in 1930 by the Hudson Bay Mining and Smelting Company. Flin Flon has deposits of copper, gold, silver, and zinc.

HISTORIC MANITOBA

Louis Riel led *métis* (people of white and Indian descent) of the Red River Valley in a rebellion against the Canadian government in 1869-1870.

The Hudson's Bay Company received its charter from King Charles II of England in the late 1600's. His cousin, Prince Rupert, was the first governor of the company.

Winnipeg, the capital of Manitoba, grew around Fort Garry, one of the chief centers of the Hudson's Bay Company in the 1800's.

The First Permanent Settlement in Manitoba, called the Red River Colony, was established in 1812 by settlers sent by Thomas Douglas, the Earl of Selkirk.

★ WINNIPEG

Canada's First Transcontinental train arrived in Winnipeg in 1886.

Churchill •

Flin Flon •

Indian Days. Five Indian tribes lived in the Manitoba region when the first explorers and fur traders arrived. The Chipewyan Indians hunted caribou across the northern section. The Woods Cree, who were wandering hunters of beavers and moose, lived in the central forests. The Plains Cree fished and trapped animals in the prairies and wooded lowlands. The Assiniboin lived on the southwestern plains. These allies of the Cree were buffalo hunters. The Chippewa, who also hunted buffalo, lived in the southeastern section of the plains.

Exploration. Sir Thomas Button, an English explorer, was the first white man in the Manitoba region. He sailed down the west coast of Hudson Bay in 1612. Button spent the winter at the mouth of the Nelson River, and claimed the land for England. Two English seamen, Luke Foxe and Thomas James, explored Hudson Bay and its west coast in 1631.

In 1670, King Charles II of England granted trading rights in the region to the Hudson's Bay Company of London. The region was called Rupert's Land. By 1690, English fur traders had fought many battles with their French-Canadian rivals, who were pushing westward into the Hudson Bay region. The company sent Henry Kelsey on an expedition to find new sources of fur. Kelsey left the company's outpost in York Factory and traveled among the Indians of central and southern Manitoba from 1690 to 1692. He persuaded many of them to bring furs north to the company trading posts. See HUDSON'S BAY COMPANY; RUPERT'S LAND.

In 1731, Pierre Gaultier de Varennes, Sieur de la Vérendrye, left Montreal in search of an overland route to the Pacific Ocean. He and his men were French-Canadian fur traders. They built a series of forts between the Lake Superior area and the lower Saskatchewan River. These outposts included Fort Rouge, which La Vérendrye built on the site of present-day Winnipeg in 1738. The fur trade that he established cut heavily into that of the Hudson's Bay Company.

In 1763, the British defeated the French in the French and Indian War. France gave up its Canadian lands to Great Britain, and French exploration and trade in the Manitoba region stopped. In 1783, the North West Company was established in Montreal to compete with the Hudson's Bay Company. This competition forced the Hudson's Bay Company to build posts to defend its trade. See NORTH WEST COMPANY.

The Red River Colony. While the two fur companies competed for trade, plans were being made for the Manitoba region's first farming settlement. In 1811, Thomas Douglas, fifth Earl of Selkirk, obtained a land grant from the Hudson's Bay Company. It involved more than 100,000 square miles (260,000 square kilometers) along the Red River. Selkirk sent several groups of Scottish Highlanders and Irishmen there. The first settlers arrived in 1812. See SELKIRK, EARL OF.

The early colonists suffered great hardships. Frosts, floods, and grasshoppers ruined many of their crops. At first, the settlers depended almost entirely on buffaloes and other game animals for food. Farm equipment, livestock, and supplies were brought from the United States, and production gradually increased.

IMPORTANT DATES IN MANITOBA

1612 Sir Thomas Button of England, the first white man in Manitoba, explored the west coast of Hudson Bay.

1690-1692 Henry Kelsey of the Hudson's Bay Company explored inland from Hudson Bay to what is now southern Manitoba.

1738 Pierre Gaultier de Varennes, Sieur de la Vérendrye, a French-Canadian fur trader, arrived at the site of present-day Winnipeg.

1812 Settlers sent by the Earl of Selkirk established the Red River colony.

1869-1870 The métis resisted union with Canada by revolting in the Red River Rebellion.

1870 Manitoba became Canada's fifth province.

1876 Manitoba farmers began exporting wheat.

1878 The first railroad in Manitoba connected Winnipeg and St. Paul, Minn.

1912 The Canadian government extended Manitoba's northern boundary to Hudson Bay.

1954 The province completed rural electrification.

1960 Nickel mining operations began in Thompson.

1963 The first laboratories in the Whiteshell Nuclear Research Establishment went into operation.

1969 The voters of Manitoba elected the first socialist government in Canada outside Saskatchewan.

1972 Winnipeg and its suburbs merged into one city, making Winnipeg Canada's third largest city.

The Red River colony lay in the heart of the North West Company's area of operations. As the colony expanded, it interfered with the fur trade. The company became increasingly hostile. Company trappers in the region were *métis* (people of mixed white and Indian ancestry). The North West Company turned them against the settlers. The métis tried to force the farmers to leave by burning their homes and destroying their crops. The violence reached a climax in 1816. The métis massacred Robert Semple, the colonial governor, and about 20 men in the Battle of Seven Oaks, near present-day Winnipeg. Peace was restored after the North West Company combined with the Hudson's Bay Company in 1821.

The Red River Rebellion. The Dominion of Canada was created in 1867. Almost immediately, it sought to acquire Rupert's Land, including the Manitoba region, from the Hudson's Bay Company. Under pressure from the British government, the company agreed in 1869 to give up its rights in almost all of Rupert's Land for $1,500,000. Great Britain began making plans to unite this vast region with Canada. However, the métis of the Red River Valley opposed the union and rebelled later in 1869. The métis held no legal title to their lands. They feared they would lose the lands to British-Canadian settlers who would pour in after union with Canada.

Louis Riel, the leader of the métis, used buffalo hunters as soldiers. They turned back federal surveyors and William McDougall, whom Canada had sent to govern the territory. The métis captured Fort Garry, in present-day Winnipeg, and set up their own government. In 1870, the Canadian government granted the métis a bill of rights in the Manitoba Act. This act made Manitoba Canada's fifth province on July 15, 1870. The province covered the southeastern section of what is now Manitoba. Winnipeg became the capital, and Alfred Boyd was the first premier. See RED RIVER REBELLION.

Growth as a Province. The expected land rush of settlers into Manitoba began after 1870. Between 1871 and 1881, the population more than doubled—from 25,228 to 62,260. In 1876, Manitoba began to export wheat. Farmers in the Red River Valley filled wooden carts with wheat, loaded them onto steamboats, and shipped them up the Red River. The wheat went to Minnesota and then to Toronto, Ont. Wheat soon replaced fur as Manitoba's most valuable product.

In 1878, the first railroad in the province connected Winnipeg and St. Paul, Minn. Another line linked Winnipeg with cities in eastern Canada in 1881, and the wheat-producing region with Lake Superior in 1882. Huge quantities of Manitoba grain were shipped to Canadian and European markets through ports on the Great Lakes.

During the 1890's, thousands of settlers came to Manitoba from European countries. Winnipeg grew rapidly. By 1901, the population of the province had increased to more than 10 times that of 1871. The Canadian government extended the provincial boundary west to what is now Saskatchewan in 1881, and east to Ontario in 1884. In 1912, the northern boundary was extended to Hudson Bay. This extension gave Manitoba its present size and shape.

Industrial Developments. Great agricultural expansion took place in Manitoba from 1900 to 1913. Manitoba remained almost entirely a farming province until the 1920's. But even before 1913, when the great land boom ended, Manitoba was beginning to build industrial plants. Most of these early factories were in Winnipeg. After 1912, St. Boniface began to develop stockyards and meat-packing plants.

Manitoba's boundary extension to Hudson Bay in 1912 opened up lands for mineral development. In 1915, prospectors discovered huge deposits of copper and zinc on the site of Flin Flon. The town developed rapidly after mining operations became fully developed in 1930. Extensive mining of gold, nickel, and silver also began during the 1930's, particularly in areas around northern Lake Winnipeg.

During the early 1900's, Winnipeg became the manufacturing and transportation center of western Canada. In Winnipeg, railroads exchanged the products of eastern and western Canada. Livestock, lumber, minerals, and wheat were shipped east for export to European markets.

Cheap power and plentiful water encouraged the growth of many industries during the 1920's and 1930's. A pulp and paper plant opened in Pine Falls in 1927. Fur-processing and clothing trades developed rapidly in Winnipeg during the 1930's.

Political Developments. The Conservative Party, led by Sir Rodmond P. Roblin, controlled the provincial government from 1900 until 1915. This government did much to develop Manitoba's economy, and got its boundaries extended in 1912. A Liberal government, headed by T. C. Norris, replaced it. The Liberal administration passed many progressive and social-reform laws. These laws included giving women the right to vote, setting minimum wages, enforcing school attendance until the age of 14, and providing money for needy mothers.

In 1922, a group of organized farmers called the United Farmers of Manitoba, or Progressives, defeated the Liberal government. This group was actually a citizens' movement, and not really a political party. The members opposed political parties, and elected independent candidates. They formed a government under John Bracken, principal of the Manitoba Agricultural College. The Liberals and the Progressives combined in 1932 to form the Liberal Progressive Party.

During the 1930's, two new political parties appeared in Manitoba. The Co-operative Commonwealth Federation, later called the New Democratic Party, was made up of farmers and factory workers. The other was the Social Credit Party. Its members believed that governments should pay all citizens a dividend based on economic production.

The Mid-1900's. World War II (1939-1945) created a great demand for Manitoba cattle, metals, wheat, and wood. Many industries built new plants in the province during the war, and manufacturing continued to grow rapidly in the late 1940's. By 1950, for the first time in Manitoba's history, manufacturing outranked agriculture as the province's main source of income.

After World War II, Manitoba needed fewer farmworkers because of the increased use of machines and new farming methods. Thousands of Manitobans moved from rural areas to cities and found jobs in factories.

Geologists discovered important mineral deposits in Manitoba during the 1940's and 1950's. Copper, nickel, and zinc ores were found in a northwestern area in 1945. Oil companies developed rich oil fields near Virden in the early 1950's. In 1956, prospectors found huge nickel deposits in the Moak Lake-Mystery Lake area. The International Nickel Company built a giant nickel complex at Thompson, and nickel mining began there in 1960. Thompson became one of the largest centers of nickel production in the world. In the late 1960's, International Nickel began a $100-million expansion of its facilities in Manitoba.

THE PREMIERS OF MANITOBA

	Party	Term
1. Alfred Boyd	None	1870-1871
2. Marc A. Girard	Conservative	1871-1872
3. Henry J. H. Clarke	None	1872-1874
4. Marc A. Girard	Conservative	1874
5. Robert A. Davis	None	1874-1878
6. John Norquay	Conservative	1878-1887
7. David H. Harrison	Conservative	1887-1888
8. Thomas Greenway	Liberal	1888-1900
9. Hugh J. MacDonald	Conservative	1900
10. Rodmond P. Roblin	Conservative	1900-1915
11. Tobias C. Norris	Liberal	1915-1922
12. John Bracken	Liberal Progressive	1922-1943
13. Stuart S. Garson	Liberal Progressive	1943-1948
14. Douglas L. Campbell	Liberal Progressive	1948-1958
15. Duff Roblin	Progressive Conservative	1958-1967
16. Walter Weir	Progressive Conservative	1967-1969
17. Edward R. Schreyer	New Democratic	1969-1977
18. Sterling R. Lyon	Progressive Conservative	1977-

The province continued to develop its rich sources of electric power in the 1950's and 1960's. By 1954, all rural areas had electricity. In 1963, the first laboratories began operating at the Whiteshell Nuclear Research Establishment near Winnipeg. A nuclear reactor went into operation there in 1965.

During the 1960's, several chemical companies built large facilities in Brandon. Many companies in various fields expanded, particularly those in the aerospace, electronics, farm machinery, and wood processing industries. Huge shipments of Manitoba wheat were exported to many countries, including China and Russia. Also during the 1960's, the provincial and federal governments built a $63-million flood control system on the Red River.

Premiers of the Liberal Progressive Party governed Manitoba during the 1940's and most of the 1950's. The Progressive Conservatives won power in 1958 and held it until 1969. That year, Manitoba voters elected the first socialist government ever to hold office in Canada outside Saskatchewan. The government was headed by Edward R. Schreyer of the New Democratic Party.

Manitoba Today. The industrial expansion that began in Manitoba during the 1940's is still going on. But it presents challenges to the province. Rapidly growing urban areas face the need for more schools, increased public services, and expanded highways. Differences in income between urban and rural Manitobans continue to widen. Living standards in northern Manitoba are far below those of more developed areas in the province.

In 1972, Winnipeg and 11 of its suburbs merged into an enlarged city of Winnipeg, making it Canada's third largest city. The merger was designed to improve government services affecting the entire Winnipeg area.

In 1977, the Progressive Conservative Party regained control of the provincial government. Conservative leader Sterling R. Lyon headed the new government.

PETER McLINTOCK, W. L. MORTON, and THOMAS R. WEIR

MANITOBA / Study Aids

Related Articles in WORLD BOOK include:

BIOGRAPHIES

Bowell, Sir Mackenzie
Riel, Louis
Roy, Gabrielle
Schreyer, Edward R.
Selkirk, Earl of

Stefansson, Vilhjalmur
Strathcona and Mount Royal, Baron of
Woodsworth, James S.

CITIES AND TOWNS

Brandon
Churchill

Flin Flon
Portage la Prairie

Thompson
Winnipeg

PHYSICAL FEATURES

Canadian Shield
Churchill River
Hudson Bay
Lake Agassiz
Lake Manitoba

Lake Winnipeg
Lake Winnipegosis
Nelson River
Red River of the North

Saskatchewan River
Winnipeg River

OTHER RELATED ARTICLES

Athabaska
Barley (graph)
Flax (graph)
Hudson's Bay Company

Prairie Farm Rehabilitation Act
Red River Rebellion
Rye (graph)

Outline

I. Government
  A. Lieutenant Governor
  B. Premier
  C. Legislative Assembly
  D. Courts
  E. Local Government
  F. Taxation
  G. Politics

II. People

III. Education
  A. Schools
  B. Libraries and Museums

IV. A Visitor's Guide
  A. Places to Visit
  B. Annual Events

V. The Land
  A. Land Regions
  B. Mountains
  C. Rivers and Lakes

VI. Climate

VII. Economy
  A. Natural Resources
  B. Manufacturing
  C. Agriculture
  D. Mining
  E. Forestry
  F. Fishing Industry
  G. Electric Power
  H. Transportation
  I. Communication

VIII. History

Questions

What is Manitoba's largest city?
Why is Manitoba called the *Keystone Province?*
How much of Manitoba do rivers and lakes cover?
Who were the *métis?* Why did they rebel in 1869?
What is the province's most important crop?
Why did the English and French Canadians fight each other during the region's early days?
Where do Manitoba's Indians and Eskimos live?
Where is Manitoba's nickel-producing center?
Which land region covers two-thirds of the province?

Books for Young Readers

CAMPBELL, MARIA. *Riel's Peoples How the Métis Lived.* Douglas & McIntyre (North Vancouver), 1978.

CHAFE, JAMES W. *Extraordinary Tales from Manitoba's History.* McClelland (Toronto), 1973.

CHALMERS, J. W. *Red River Adventure: The Story of the Selkirk Settlers.* Macmillan (Toronto), 1956.

DAWES, DENISE. *Manitoba Past and Present.* Peguis (Winnipeg), 1971.

GRISDALE, ALEX. *Wild Drums: Indian Legends of Manitoba.* Peguis (Winnipeg), 1972.

KNIGHT, LOWRY. *Manitoba: A People and a Province.* Fitzhenry & Whiteside (Don Mills, Ont.), 1977.

KURELEK, WILLIAM. *A Prairie Boy's Winter.* Tundra (Montreal); Houghton (Boston), 1973. *A Prairie Boy's Summer.* 1975.

Books for Older Readers

ARTIBISE, ALAN F. J. *Winnipeg: An Illustrated History.* Lorimer (Toronto), 1977.

HOCKING, ANTHONY. *Manitoba.* McGraw (Scarborough, Ont.), 1979.

JACKSON, JAMES A. *The Centennial History of Manitoba.* Manitoba Historical Society (Winnipeg), 1970.

MORTON, WILLIAM L. *Manitoba: A History.* 2nd ed. Univ. of Toronto Press, 1967.

ROSS, ALEXANDER. *The Red River Settlement.* Hurtig (Edmonton), 1971; Tuttle (Rutland, Vt.), 1972. Reprint of an early history first published in 1856.

WILSON, KEITH. *Manitoba: Profile of a Province.* Peguis (Winnipeg), 1975.

MANITOBA, LAKE. See LAKE MANITOBA.

MANITOBA, UNIVERSITY OF, is a coeducational, government-supported school in Winnipeg, Man. It is the only institution in the province that offers courses in almost all fields. It grants degrees in agriculture, architecture, arts, commerce, dentistry, education, engineering, environmental studies, fine arts, home economics, interior design, law, medicine, music, nursing, occupational therapy, pharmacy, physical education, physiotherapy, science, and social work. It also gives diplomas in agriculture, anesthesiology, art, dental hygiene, occupational therapy, physiotherapy, psychiatry, radiology, and surgery. The university has a graduate school and a summer school. It was founded in 1877. For enrollment, see CANADA (table: Universities and Colleges). Critically reviewed by the UNIVERSITY OF MANITOBA

MANITOULIN ISLANDS, MAN ih TOO lihn (pop. 11,372), in Lake Huron, are famed for their resorts. The islands lie northwest of Georgian Bay and are separated from the northern shore of Lake Huron by the North Channel. They are formed by the northern section of the Niagara Escarpment, a series of cliffs. There are three large islands and many smaller ones with a total area of 1,389 square miles (3,597 square kilometers). Most of the islands are in Ontario. They include Manitoulin Island (1,068 square miles, or 2,766 square kilometers), which is the world's largest inland island, and Cockburn Island (68 square miles, or 176 square kilometers). Drummond Island, in Michigan, covers 176 square miles (456 square kilometers). *Manitoulin* is an Indian name for *sacred isles.* JOHN BRIAN BIRD

MANN, mahn, is the family name of three German authors. All three of them left Germany in 1933 when the Nazis took power, and eventually moved to the United States.

Thomas Mann (1875-1955) won the 1929 Nobel prize for literature. His writings combine wisdom, humor, and philosophical thought. His intellectual scope, keen psychological insight, and critical awareness of cultural and political conditions made him one of the foremost humanistic writers of his time. His writing has a tone of gentle irony, which creates an atmosphere of artistic detachment and tolerance. He often wrote in a highly stylized, stilted manner as a *parody* (mock imitation) of earlier writers, especially Goethe.

A superb literary craftsman, Mann maintained a balance in his writings between the traditional realism of the 1800's and experimentation with style and structure. He was a critical, yet sympathetic, analyst of European middle class values and attitudes. The central theme in his writings is a dualism between spirit and life. Mann expressed *spirit* as intellectual refinement and creativity, and *life* as naive and unquestioning vitality. He often presented this dualism through the conflict between the attitudes of the artist and the middle class.

Mann's first novel, *Buddenbrooks* (1901), made him famous. It describes the physical decline and accompanying intellectual refinement of a merchant family similar to Mann's. Variations on this theme appear in two shorter works, *Tristan* (1903) and *Tonio Kröger* (1903). The short novel *Death in Venice* (1912) portrays a writer's moral collapse through an uncontrollable and humiliating passion for a young boy.

Mann published the novel *The Magic Mountain* in 1924, after working on it for 12 years. In the book, patients of a tuberculosis sanitarium represent the conflicting attitudes and political beliefs of European society before World War I. Mann's longest work is *Joseph and His Brothers* (1933-1943). In this four-novel series, Mann expands on the Biblical story of Joseph by analyzing it from the standpoint of both psychology and mythology.

Doctor Faustus (1947) is Mann's most despairing novel. In it, a German composer rejects love and moral responsibility in favor of artistic creativity. His story symbolically parallels the rise of Nazism. *Confessions of Felix Krull, Confidence Man* (1954) is a delightful novel about a rogue's adventures in middle class society.

Mann's brilliant essays deal with politics, literature, music, and philosophy. Collections include *Order of the Day* (1942) and *Essays of Three Decades* (1947). *Last Essays* was published in 1959, after his death.

Mann was born into a wealthy family in Lübeck. He lived in Switzerland from 1933 to 1938, when he moved to the United States. He became a U.S. citizen in 1944. He returned to Switzerland in 1952 and died there.

Heinrich Mann (1871-1950) was Thomas Mann's brother. Most of his novels are passionate criticisms of the middle class and political and social conditions in Germany. They express a violent opposition to nationalism, militarism, and capitalism, and they call for a democratic and humanistic socialism. The Nazis banned Mann's books. Mann's masterpieces are *Professor Unrat* (1905, translated in English as *The Blue Angel*), *The Little Town* (1909), and *The Patrioteer* (1918). Mann was born in Lübeck and died in California.

Klaus Mann (1906-1949) was Thomas Mann's son. He moved to the United States in 1936 and became a citizen in 1943. Out of despair over the political and cultural decline of Europe, he committed suicide. His writings include *Symphonie Pathétique* (1935), a novel about the composer Peter Tchaikovsky; and *The Turning Point* (1942), an autobiography. With his sister Erika Mann, he wrote *Escape to Life* (1939) and *The Other Germany* (1940). He was born in Munich. WERNER HOFFMEISTER

MANN, HORACE (1796-1859), played a leading part in establishing the elementary school system of the United States. He aroused public interest in educational problems. He summed up his great desire to serve humanity in his last public statement: "Be ashamed to die until you have won some victory for humanity."

Mann gave up his law practice in 1837 to become the secretary of the newly established Massachusetts State Board of Education. He fought so well for educational reforms that nearly every one of the states profited. He has been called the *Father of the Common Schools.*

Mann strengthened education in his own state through a series of laws that improved the financial support and public control of schools. He founded the first state normal school in the United States in 1839 in Lexington, Mass. This improved the quality of public school teachers. His study of European educational methods in 1843 was the subject of one of his famous 12 annual reports. These influential reports covered almost every phase of the problems facing the educational system in the United States.

Mann resigned from the State Board of Education in 1848 to take a seat in the U.S. House of Representatives as an antislavery Whig. Mann was defeated as a Free Soil Party candidate for governor of Massachusetts. He served as president of Antioch College in Yellow Springs, Ohio, from 1853 until his death.

Mann was born on May 4, 1796, in Franklin, Mass., and graduated from Brown University. He began his public career as a member of the Massachusetts state legislature in 1827. He was elected to New York University's Hall of Fame when it was established in 1900 to honor great Americans. Claude A. Eggertsen

MANNA, *MAN uh,* was the food given to the Israelites during their 40 years of wandering in the wilderness (Exod. 16 and Num. 11). It looked like small, round flakes of a yellowish-white color, and tasted like wafers made with honey. Manna rained from heaven each morning. It was gathered early, because it melted in the sun. The daily portion of each person was an *omer* (about 6 pints, or 2.8 liters). The people gathered up just enough food for each day. The manna spoiled and was unfit to eat if more was gathered. But twice the usual amount was said to fall on the sixth day. Each person then took two omers, because the Sabbath was a day of worship and rest. This manna stayed fresh two days. The fall stopped when the Israelites crossed into Canaan, the Promised Land. Some historians say manna was a gluey sugar from the tamarisk shrub. Cyrus H. Gordon

MANNED SPACECRAFT CENTER. See Lyndon B. Johnson Space Center.

MANNERHEIM, CARL GUSTAV EMIL VON (1867-1951), a Finnish military and political leader, helped found the Republic of Finland in 1919. He had a fortified line built across the Karelian Isthmus called the *Mannerheim Line.* He directed the Finnish defense against Russian invaders in the famous "Winter War" of 1939-1940, and in fighting that lasted from 1941 to 1944. He was president of Finland from 1944 to 1946.

Mannerheim was born in Villnäs, near Turku, Finland, which was then under Russian control. He served in the Russian Army in the Russo-Japanese War (1904-1905) and in World War I. An anti-Communist, he left Russia after the Communist revolution of 1917.

Mannerheim took command of the Finnish Army in January 1918, after Finland declared its independence from Russia. In December 1918, he became *regent* (temporary ruler) of Finland, and toured Europe seeking recognition for his country and food for his people. In 1919, Mannerheim ran unsuccessfully for president. He then retired from public life until the 1930's, when he took over command of Finnish defenses. Alfred Erich Senn

MANNERHEIM LINE. See Mannerheim, Carl von.

MANNERISM is a term that refers to a style of European art that flourished from about 1520 to 1600. The mannerist style appears most fully and typically in central Italian art. But some mannerist traits can be found in all European art of the time, including architecture and the late works of the Renaissance artists Raphael and Michelangelo.

Mannerist artists tended to consider artistic invention and imagination more important than faithful reproduction of nature. Space in many mannerist paintings appears illogical or unmeasurable, with abrupt and disturbing contrasts between figures close to the viewer and those far in the distance. Most mannerist paintings stress surface patterns. Strongly three-dimensional forms

Detail of *The Feast in the House of Simon* (about 1610 to 1614), an oil painting; The Art Institute of Chicago, Joseph Winterbotham Collection

A Mannerist Painting shows the use of distorted space and elongated figures that gives the style a strong dramatic quality. El Greco, the leading mannerist artist, painted this picture.

compressed within these patterns create an effect of confinement or of a struggle between a figure and its setting. Many figures are distorted in proportion and have contorted poses. The most striking mannerist was the Spanish painter El Greco (see Greco, El). Marcel Franciscono

See also Painting (Mannerism [with picture]); Sculpture (Michelangelo); Cellini, Benvenuto; Tintoretto.

MANNERS AND CUSTOMS. See Custom; Etiquette.

MANNHEIM, *MAN hime* (pop. 330,900), is an important river port in West Germany. It lies near the point where the Rhine and Neckar rivers meet (see Germany [political map]). Mannheim's large docks make up one of Europe's largest inland harbors. Its factories produce precision instruments, motors, and farm machinery. Much coal and iron is traded there.

Mannheim began as a small fishing village. It was fortified and chartered in 1606-1607. The great German poet and playwright Friedrich von Schiller wrote plays for the city's National Theater. James K. Pollock

MANNING, TIMOTHY CARDINAL (1909-   ), archbishop of Los Angeles, was appointed a cardinal of the Roman Catholic Church by Pope Paul VI in 1973. Manning was born in County Cork, Ireland. He studied for the priesthood in Ireland and in California and was ordained a priest in Los Angeles in 1934. Manning became a United States citizen in 1944. In 1946, he was ordained a bishop and became auxiliary bishop of Los Angeles. In 1967, he was named the first bishop of Fresno, Calif. Manning became archbishop of Los Angeles in 1970. John A. Hardon

MANOLETE, *MAH noh LEH tay* (1917-1947), won fame as a Spanish *matador* (bullfighter). He was a national hero, and hundreds of paintings, statues, and monuments honor him. He was awarded *La Cruz de la Beneficencia*, Spain's highest civilian decoration. Manolete was born Manuel Laureano Rodríguez y Sánchez in Córdoba, Spain, the son of a matador. He began his career in 1938 and by 1946 received the highest fees ever paid a matador to that time. On the eve of Manolete's retirement, he was gored to death by a bull in Linares, Spain.

MANOMETER, *muh NAHM uh tuhr,* is an instrument used to measure the pressure of a gas or vapor. There are several types of manometers. The simplest kind consists of a U-shaped tube with both ends open. The tube contains a liquid, often mercury, which fills the bottom of the U and rises a short distance in each of the arms. The person using this type connects one of the arms to the gas whose pressure is to be measured. The other arm remains open to the atmosphere. In this way, the liquid is exposed to the pressure of the gas in one arm and atmospheric pressure in the other.

If the pressure of the gas is greater than that of the atmosphere, the liquid rises in the arm of the tube exposed to the air. The user measures the difference between the heights of the liquid in the two arms to determine the pressure of this amount of liquid. The sum of this pressure and of the atmospheric pressure is the pressure of the gas. Gas pressure is often measured in units of the height of the liquid in the manometer. For example, gas pressure is often expressed as centimeters of mercury, where normal atmospheric pressure is 76 centimeters.

In some manometers, the air is removed from one arm of the tube and that end is sealed. This eliminates difficulties caused by changes in atmospheric pressure. The difference between the levels of the liquid in the arms shows the pressure of the gas. This manometer is often called a *vacuum gauge* or *pressure gauge.* Some manometers work on the principle of a spring attached to an indicator. The indicator moves in front of a graduated scale that gives direct pressure readings. Doctors use a type of manometer, called the *sphygmomanometer,* to measure blood pressure.   CLARENCE E. BENNETT

See also BAROMETER; GAUGE.

MANON. See MASSENET, JULES.

MANON LESCAUT. See FRENCH LITERATURE (The Great Novelists); PUCCINI, GIACOMO.

MANOR. See MANORIALISM.

MANORIALISM was the economic system of Europe from the end of the Roman Empire to the 1200's. The name comes from *manerium,* the Latin word for *manor,* meaning a large estate controlled by a lord and worked by *peasants.* Manors covered most of Europe. They supplied food, clothing, shelter, and nearly everything else needed by the lords and peasants.

Most manors were made up of the lord's land and small plots of land held by the peasants. The lord lived in a manor house, which was usually surrounded by a garden, an orchard, and farm buildings. The peasants' huts were clustered nearby. Most manors also included a church, a mill for grinding grain into flour, and a press for making wine.

The peasants depended on the lord for protection from enemies, for justice, and for what little government there was. The peasants farmed both the lord's land and their own. They were *bound to the soil.* This means that they were part of the property, and they remained on the land if a new lord acquired it. Unlike slaves, they could not be sold apart from the land. Peasants rarely traveled far from the manor.

The manorial system began to decline when trade and industry revived. This revival brought back an economic system based on payment with money for goods and services. Manorialism ended first in western Europe. It remained as late as the 1800's in some parts of central and eastern Europe. Large family estates in Great Britain and other parts of Europe still exist as reminders of manorialism.   BRYCE LYON

See also FEUDALISM; MIDDLE AGES; SERF; VILLEIN.

MANPOWER. See LABOR FORCE.

MANSA MUSA (? -1337) was the ruler of the Mali Empire in Africa from 1312 to 1337. He was a grandson of Sundiata Keita, an earlier Mali ruler. Mansa Musa greatly expanded the empire and made it the political and cultural leader of West Africa. He brought the trading cities of Gao and Timbuktu under his rule and made Timbuktu a great center of learning.

Mansa Musa spread Islam, the Muslim religion, throughout the empire. In 1324, he traveled to Mecca, the holy city of the Muslims. Mansa Musa's party supposedly included thousands of his people and hundreds of camels bearing gold and gifts. He brought back many learned people, including an architect who designed *mosques* (Muslim houses of worship) for Gao and Timbuktu. After Mansa Musa died, his son, Mansa Maghan I, became ruler of the empire.   LEO SPITZER

MANSFIELD, KATHERINE (1888-1923), a British author, wrote symbolic short stories about everyday human experiences and inner feelings. Many of her stories are studies of childhood, based on her early years in Wellington, New Zealand. Mansfield often used herself and her brother as models for the main characters. Her stories were published in *In a German Pension* (1911), *Prelude* (1918), *Bliss* (1920), and *The Garden Party* (1927). Her *Journal* (1927) gives a fascinating picture of her mind and the development of her writing.

Katherine Mansfield was born Kathleen Mansfield Beauchamp in Wellington. She began her literary career after moving to England in 1908. She suffered from tuberculosis, and spent much of her life in hospitals and sanitariums.   JOHN ESPEY

Bettmann Archive

Katherine Mansfield

MANSFIELD, MIKE (1903-   ), a Montana Democrat, served as majority leader of the United States Senate from 1961 to 1977, longer than any other person. He served as a member of the United States House of Representatives for 10 years before he was elected to the Senate in 1952. In 1977, President Jimmy Carter appointed him United States ambassador to Japan. Mansfield also carried out foreign assignments for Presidents Dwight D. Eisenhower, John F. Kennedy, and Lyndon B. Johnson.

Michael Joseph Mansfield was born in New York City and was raised in Montana. At the age of 14, he dropped out of eighth grade and joined the U.S. Navy. He served as a seaman during World War I, spent the next year as a private in the U.S. Army, and was in the U.S. Marine Corps from 1920 to 1922. Mansfield worked as a miner and mining engineer from 1922 to 1930. Although he never went to high school, he graduated from Montana State University in 1933 and earned a master's degree there in 1934. Mansfield taught Latin-American and Far Eastern history at Montana State until he entered Congress in 1943. Mansfield served in the U.S. Senate from 1953 to 1977.　　WILLIAM J. EATON

United Press Int.
Mike Mansfield

MANSFIELD, RICHARD (1854?-1907), was one of the best-known actors in the United States during the 1890's. He excelled in both romantic and tragic character roles. He was especially good in portrayals of evil old men. His great stage successes included *Beau Brummell, Cyrano de Bergerac, The Scarlet Letter,* and *Dr. Jekyll and Mr. Hyde.* Mansfield also was a skilled dancer and singing comedian. He was probably born in Berlin, Germany.　　CLIFFORD EUGENE HAMAR

MANSHIP, PAUL (1885-1966), was an American sculptor. His works appear in public buildings throughout the United States. He worked in stone and metals. Many of his sculptures recall the traditions of European art. One of his best-known works, *Prometheus,* is in Rockefeller Center in New York City. Manship was born in St. Paul, Minn. He studied under Solon Borglum in New York City.　　WILLIAM L. MACDONALD

MANSLAUGHTER is the legal term for the wrongful unplanned killing of another person. It is different from *murder* in that it is not done with malice.

The law recognizes two kinds of manslaughter, *voluntary* and *involuntary.* Voluntary manslaughter, also called *nonnegligent manslaughter,* is a killing done in the heat of the moment, without previous plan. A person who kills someone in a violent quarrel without first planning to do so is guilty of voluntary manslaughter. Involuntary manslaughter, also called *manslaughter by negligence,* is done as the result of criminal carelessness, or while the offender is engaged in some wrongful act. If a reckless driver kills someone, the driver is guilty of involuntary manslaughter.

Punishment for manslaughter varies in different states and countries. The usual penalty in the United States is imprisonment of from 1 to 14 years. This is less severe than are the penalties for murder.　　FRED E. INBAU

See also HOMICIDE; MURDER; MALICE.

MANSON, SIR PATRICK (1844-1922), a Scottish physician, was called the *father of tropical medicine.* He demonstrated in 1877 that the parasite *Filaria* caused the disease elephantiasis. Later he showed that mosquitoes carried the parasite (see FILARIA). In 1900, he confirmed that malaria was transmitted to human beings in this way. He also contributed to our knowledge of other tropical diseases, including leprosy and beriberi.

Manson was born in Aberdeenshire (now Grampian Region), Scotland. He began his career in China, where he worked for 24 years. He helped establish the London School of Tropical Medicine.　　HENRY J. L. MARRIOTT

MANTEGNA, *mahn TEH nyah,* **ANDREA** (1431-1506), was a leading painter of the Italian Renaissance. He painted sculpicturelike figures that are sharply outlined and precisely detailed. The surfaces of his works are glossy and smooth. Mantegna used perspective for dramatic effects, with many figures appearing as if seen from below. He was also a famous engraver. Mantegna's engravings influenced many other painters, including the famous German artist Albrecht Dürer.

Mantegna was born in Isola di Carturo, Italy, near

The Risen Christ Between Saint Andrew and Saint Longinus (about 1500); Rijksprentenkabinet, Rijksmuseum, Amsterdam, The Netherlands

An Engraving by Mantegna shows the sculpturelike figures and precise details that are typical of the artist's style.

Padua. He received his early art training in Padua and soon earned a reputation as a painter. In 1459 or 1460, Mantegna entered the service of the ruling Gonzaga family in Mantua. He spent the rest of his life there and painted the Gonzagas in superb frescoes. One of these frescoes, *Family and Court of Ludovico Gonzaga II,* is reproduced in the PAINTING article. Mantegna also painted several portraits and altarpieces.　　ROBERT F. REIFF

See also CAESAR, JULIUS (picture); ENGRAVING (picture: A Renaissance Engraving); JESUS CHRIST (picture: Jesus Was Arrested).

MANTID is an insect that is sometimes called *praying mantis* because it often lifts its front legs as if it were praying. It takes this position when hunting. Mantids usually live in warm countries, but the common European mantid can live in the northern United States.

The many kinds of mantids are among the greediest of all insects. They feed not only on other kinds of in-

Ralph Buchsbaum

The Praying Mantis Often Looks As If It Were Praying.

sects, but on other mantids as well. A female mantid does not hesitate to devour her own mate if she is hungry. These insects prefer to eat their prey alive.

A full-grown, large mantid varies from 2 to 5 inches (5 to 13 centimeters) in length, depending on the kind. It easily escapes notice. In form and color it closely resembles the plants on which it stays. The first segment of the body behind the head, the prothorax, is long and thin, and held almost erect. The rest of the body is thicker, but long and slender. The wings are short and broad. The armlike forelegs have sharp hooks that hold the victim.

Female mantids lay their eggs in masses. They glue the eggs to trees and shrubs with a sticky substance from their bodies. The eggs remain there during the winter, and the young hatch in spring. Mantids help human beings by eating harmful insects.

Scientific Classification. The mantid belongs to the order *Orthoptera*. It makes up the praying mantis family, *Mantidae*. Some scientists consider the mantid to be a separate order, *Mantodea*. URL LANHAM

See also ANIMAL (Hiding; picture).

MANTISSA. See LOGARITHMS (Common Logarithms).

MANTLE is a membrane or a tissue. See SHELL; CLAM; OYSTER; SCALLOP; MOLLUSK.

MANTLE. See EARTH (Inside the Earth); CONTINENTAL DRIFT (Causes of Continental Drift).

MANTLE, MICKEY (1931-   ), ranks among the leading home run hitters in baseball history. Mantle hit 536 home runs in regular season play. He spent his entire major-league career with the New York Yankees —from 1951 through 1968. He mainly played center field and was a switch hitter.

Mantle led the American League in home runs four times and was named the league's most valuable player three times. He hit 18 World Series home runs, a record. Unlike most sluggers, Mantle had great speed. How-

ever, leg injuries reduced his baserunning effectiveness during the 1960's. Mantle struck out more times than any other batter and ranks third in the number of career walks. Mickey Charles Mantle was born in Spavinaw, Okla. He was elected to the National Baseball Hall of Fame in 1974. JOSEPH P. SPOHN

MANTRAYANA. See BUDDHISM (Buddhist Schools).

MANU, in Hindu mythology, was the man who systematized the religious and social laws of Hinduism. These ancient laws are called the *Manu Smriti* (*Code of Manu*). They still influence the religious and social life of India, where Hinduism is the chief religion. The *Manu Smriti* has three main parts: (1) *varna*, (2) *ashrama*, and (3) *dharma*.

Varna sets forth the basis of *caste*, the strict Hindu class system. Hinduism has four major *varnas* (castes). See HINDUISM (Caste).

Ashrama describes the four ideal stages of a Hindu man's life. First, he studies Hindu scriptures called the *Vedas*, and the duties of his caste. Second, he marries. Third, after he fulfills his family obligations, he retires with his wife to a forest to meditate. Finally, in old age, the husband and wife separate and wander as beggars called *sannyasis*, preparing for death.

Dharma describes the four goals of life. They are (1) *dharma*—fulfilling one's religious obligation in society, (2) *kama*—enjoying sex and other physical pleasures, (3) *artha*—achieving worldly success through one's occupation, and (4) *moksha*—gaining spiritual release from worldly existence. CHARLES S. J. WHITE

MANUA ISLANDS. See AMERICAN SAMOA.

MANUAL TRAINING. See INDUSTRIAL ARTS.

MANUEL II. See PORTUGAL (The First Portuguese Republic).

MANUEL, DON JUAN. See SPANISH LITERATURE (The Middle Ages).

MANUELITO, *mahn yoo ayl EE toh,* (1818?-1893) was a leader of the Navajo Indians. He played an important part in the Navajos' fight to prevent white settlers from taking over their land.

In 1860, following conflicts between the Navajos and the settlers, Manuelito helped lead an attack on Fort Defiance in what is now Arizona. The next year, he and other Navajo leaders signed a peace treaty with the United States. But fighting soon broke out again. In 1863 and 1864, U.S. Army troops led by the frontiersman Kit Carson captured thousands of Navajos. The Army did not capture Manuelito, but he surrendered in 1866.

In 1868, the government established a reservation for the Navajos in what became parts of Arizona, New Mexico, and Utah. Manuelito headed the first

Smithsonian Institution, National Anthropological Archives, Washington, D.C.

Manuelito

Navajo police force, which was founded in 1872 to protect the reservation. He was probably born in Bear's Ears, near what is now Moab, Utah. RUTH W. ROESSEL

MANUFACTURERS, NATIONAL ASSOCIATION OF. See NATIONAL ASSOCIATION OF MANUFACTURERS.

Chrysler Corporation

Manufacturing Provides Jobs for Millions of People in the United States and Canada, two of the leading manufacturing countries. U.S. plants produce about a third of the world's cars.

MANUFACTURING is the industry that makes automobiles, books, clothing, furniture, paper, pencils, and thousands of other products. The word *manufacture* comes from the Latin words *manus* (hand) and *facere* (to make). But, today, manufacturing means the making of articles by machinery as well as by hand.

Manufacturing plants have great importance to the welfare of their communities. When a factory hires 100 workers, for example, it also creates about 175 jobs outside the factory. These include jobs for waitresses, store clerks, and other persons who provide the factory employees with the goods and services they need.

Until the early 1900's, the world's greatest manufacturing centers were in western Europe. The United States became the leading manufacturing nation during World War I, when its industries expanded to make war materials. Since then, the United States has ranked as the world's greatest producer of manufactured goods.

Manufacturing is the chief industry in the United States and Canada. It earns about one-fourth of the income of the United States and about a third of Canada's income. It employs about a fourth of the workers of the two nations.

Kinds of Manufacturing

Manufactured items may be divided into heavy or light, and durable or nondurable goods. A *durable* product lasts for a long time. A *nondurable* product is used up quickly. For example, a locomotive is a heavy durable product. A sweater is a light durable product. A loaf of bread is a light nondurable item.

All manufactured products are either consumer goods or producer goods. Retail stores, such as groceries or drugstores, sell *consumer goods* to millions of buyers. These products include radios, rugs, food, and thousands of other items. *Producer goods* are products that are used to make other products. They include springs, bearings, printing presses, and many other items.

Manufacturing Around the World

Manufacturing industries are usually located in regions that have abundant natural resources, good transportation, mild climates, and large populations. North America, Europe, and Asia rank as leaders in all these categories and the three regions produce more than 90 per cent of the world's manufactured goods.

In the United States, about 321,000 companies make about a fourth of the world's manufactured goods, ranging from airplanes to zippers. About $367 billion has been invested in these firms. U.S. manufacturing firms employ about 20 million persons, and pay about $211 billion annually in wages, salaries, and stock dividends (see STOCK, CAPITAL). Manufacturing accounts for about $26 of every $100 earned in the United States.

Most big U.S. manufacturers are near large cities, chiefly in the northeastern quarter of the country. The 15 major manufacturing regions, in order of importance, are Chicago, Los Angeles-Long Beach, New York City, Detroit, Philadelphia, Houston, Pittsburgh, Cleveland, Newark, St. Louis, Boston, Rochester, Dallas-Fort Worth, Milwaukee, and San Francisco-Oakland. See UNITED STATES (Manufacturing).

Tire Factory in Romania is part of that country's effort to shift its economy from agriculture to heavy industry. The "Danubiana" tire factory, *above*, is located near Bucharest.

Adding Machine Factory in Italy is part of one of the country's major industries, the manufacture of business machines.

Shipyards in Gdynia, Poland, and those in neighboring Gdańsk form one of the busiest shipbuilding centers in the world.

Cotton Mill in Brazil helps make textiles one of the most important manufactured products on the South American continent.

In Canada. Canada ranks among the leading manufacturing countries. Its major manufacturing industry produces wood pulp and paper. Other important industries smelt and refine metals, and produce petroleum products, food products, and transportation equipment. About half of Canada's manufactured goods comes from Ontario and about a fourth from Quebec. The nation has about 28,000 factories that employ about 1,914,000 persons. They produce goods with a value added by manufacture of about $47 billion a year. See CANADA (Manufacturing).

In Europe. Western Europe and Russia rank after the United States as the world's main manufacturing regions. The major manufacturing nations of western Europe are France, Great Britain, Italy, The Netherlands, Spain, Sweden, and West Germany. The governments of some European countries, such as Great Britain and Italy, own many of the factories. In Russia and other Communist nations, the government owns all the factories. See EUROPE (Manufacturing and Processing); EUROPEAN COMMUNITY.

In Asia, large-scale manufacturing is mostly centered in China, India, Japan, and Russia. Most countries produce only a few goods which workers make by hand. But Asia leads the world in the production of silk. See ASIA (Industry).

In Africa, there is almost no manufacturing. Most of the land is dry or tropical. The continent has poor transportation and includes vast areas with sparse populations. Africa has about a third of the world's potential water power. But most of the sites for power plants are in regions where it would be difficult to develop industries. Less than 1 per cent of Africa's available water power is used. See AFRICA (Manufacturing).

In Latin America, manufacturing is still largely in the handicraft stage. Latin Americans make furniture, pottery, silverware, textiles, and tinware by hand for tourists. Argentina, Brazil, and Chile produce textiles, shoes, and wine. Argentina and Uruguay have important meat-packing industries. Argentina and Brazil manufacture automobiles. See the Manufacturing sections of CENTRAL AMERICA; SOUTH AMERICA.

The Main Steps in Manufacturing

Design. Manufacturers of consumer goods often change the styles of their products. The new designs attract the public's interest and frequently include improvements on the old styles. Manufacturers also spend much time and money designing attractive packages for their products.

Manufacturers must design products that will be easy to use, and that will not be too expensive to produce or to ship from place to place. Sometimes, after a company designs a new product, it builds and tests a *prototype* (sample of the product) before selling the item to customers.

Raw Materials used in manufacturing come from farms, forests, fisheries, mines, and quarries. Some manufacturers, such as those that make food products, buy most of their raw materials from nearby areas. Others may require raw materials that must be shipped from the other side of the world. For example, Ohio manufacturers make the most tires in the world. But most of the natural rubber the factories use comes from Asia.

Making Products involves one or more of three processes: (1) synthetic, (2) analytic, and (3) conditioning.

Manufacturers who use the *synthetic* process mix ingredients or assemble ready-made parts. A paint manufacturer mixes chemicals to produce paint, and an

All photos Chris-Craft

The Steps in Manufacturing are the same for nearly all types of products. First, the manufacturer designs the product, *above left.* Then, the manufacturer buys the raw materials needed to make it. Workers at the factory use the raw materials to produce the finished product, *above right and below left.* After the product is completed, a salesperson sells it to customers.

100 Leading U.S. Manufacturers

Manufacturer	Sales*	Assets*	Employees	Manufacturer	Sales*	Assets*	Employees
1. General Motors	63,221	30,598	839,000	51. Cities Service	4,661	4,005	18,100
2. Exxon	60,335	41,531	130,000	52. Marathon Oil	4,509	3,758	13,354
3. Ford Motor	42,784	22,101	506,531	53. Georgia-Pacific	4,403	3,344	40,000
4. Mobil	34,736	22,611	207,700	54. Armco	4,357	3,096	52,140
5. Texaco	28,608	20,249	67,841	55. Greyhound	4,351	1,725	50,912
6. Standard Oil of California	23,232	16,761	37,575	56. Coca-Cola	4,338	2,583	36,100
7. International Business Machines	21,076	20,771	325,517	57. Colgate-Palmolive	4,312	2,385	56,600
8. General Electric	19,654	15,036	401,000	58. Gulf & Western Industries	4,312	4,508	106,000
9. Gulf Oil	18,069	15,036	58,300	59. W. R. Grace	4,310	3,268	66,800
10. Chrysler	16,341	6,981	157,958	60. PepsiCo	4,300	2,419	95,000
11. International Tel. & Tel.	15,261	14,035	379,000	61. Deere	4,155	3,887	59,208
12. Standard Oil (Ind.)	14,961	14,109	47,011	62. International Paper	4,150	4,099	51,306
13. Atlantic Richfield	12,298	12,060	50,716	63. McDonnell Douglas	4,130	3,098	70,547
14. Shell Oil	11,063	10,453	34,974	64. Ralston Purina	4,058	1,898	70,000
15. U.S. Steel	11,050	10,536	166,848	65. Aluminum Co. of America	4,052	4,167	46,000
16. E. I. du Pont de Nemours	10,584	8,070	132,140	66. American Can	3,981	2,478	52,900
17. Western Electric	9,522	6,134	161,000	67. Continental Group	3,944	2,997	56,532
18. Conoco Inc.	9,455	7,445	42,780	68. Borden	3,803	2,166	39,600
19. Tenneco	8,762	10,134	104,000	69. Weyerhaeuser	3,799	4,464	46,040
20. Procter & Gamble	8,100	4,984	55,600	70. TRW	3,787	2,327	93,353
21. Union Carbide	7,870	7,866	113,371	71. National Steel	3,750	3,130	38,170
22. Goodyear Tire & Rubber	7,489	5,231	154,013	72. Litton Industries	3,651	2,279	90,400
23. Sun	7,428	5,498	33,721	73. Sperry Rand	3,649	3,287	88,275
24. Caterpillar Tractor	7,219	5,031	84,004	74. Champion International	3,632	2,856	42,975
25. Eastman Kodak	7,013	6,801	124,800	75. Bendix	3,626	2,037	76,000
26. Phillips Petroleum	6,998	6,935	30,008	76. Signal Companies	3,572	2,424	49,500
27. Dow Chemical	6,888	8,789	53,500	77. Honeywell	3,548	2,826	86,328
28. International Harvester	6,664	4,316	95,450	78. Consolidated Foods	3,536	1,663	80,900
29. Westinghouse Electric	6,663	6,318	141,776	79. Getty Oil	3,515	4,718	14,156
30. RCA	6,601	4,873	118,000	80. Johnson & Johnson	3,497	2,382	67,000
31. Beatrice Foods	6,314	2,560	84,000	81. Lockheed	3,496	1,692	61,337
32. United Technologies	6,265	4,074	152,213	82. Republic Steel	3,479	2,585	41,394
33. Occidental Petroleum	6,253	4,609	33,161	83. American Brands	3,293	2,897	54,520
34. Bethlehem Steel	6,185	4,933	94,500	84. Allied Chemical	3,268	3,228	31,979
35. Union Oil of California	5,955	5,525	16,297	85. Inland Steel	3,248	2,598	36,062
36. Xerox	5,902	5,578	104,736	86. General Mills	3,243	1,613	66,574
37. Rockwell International	5,833	3,536	114,208	87. CBS	3,242	1,780	38,000
38. Esmark	5,827	2,116	45,000	88. Raytheon	3,239	2,061	63,600
39. Kraft	5,670	2,301	46,881	89. Textron	3,231	1,988	70,000
40. Boeing	5,463	3,573	81,200	90. CPC International	3,222	1,861	42,000
41. General Foods	5,376	2,433	49,000	91. Farmland Industries	3,216	1,585	10,000
42. LTV	5,261	3,720	47,400	92. General Dynamics	3,205	1,779	77,100
43. Standard Oil (Ohio)	5,198	8,326	24,145	93. Owens-Illinois	3,112	2,600	64,588
44. Ashland Oil	5,167	2,886	32,000	94. American Home Products	3,063	1,862	49,619
45. Monsanto	5,019	5,036	62,851	95. Dresser Industries	3,054	2,355	55,100
46. Philip Morris	4,969	5,608	60,000	96. Iowa Beef Processors	2,968	355	9,396
47. R. J. Reynolds Industries	4,952	4,616	37,346	97. FMC	2,913	2,249	45,854
48. Firestone Tire & Rubber	4,878	3,486	112,000	98. Warner-Lambert	2,878	2,667	58,000
49. Amerada Hess	4,701	3,435	7,562	99. Reynolds Metals	2,829	2,709	36,200
50. Minnesota Mining & Mfg.	4,662	4,088	85,000	100. PPG Industries	2,794	2,335	37,400

*In millions of dollars.

Source: ''The Fortune Directory,'' Fortune, May 1979, © 1979, Time Inc.

25 Leading Manufacturers Outside the U.S.

Manufacturer	Sales*	Assets*	Employees	Manufacturer	Sales*	Assets*	Employees
1. Royal Dutch/Shell Group	39,680	36,022	155,000	14. Bayer	9,220	10,104	170,400
2. National Iranian Oil	22,315	9,212	66,024	15. BASF (Badische Anilin- & Soda-Fabrik)	9,116	7,323	113,798
3. British Petroleum	20,941	17,253	81,000	16. Nippon Steel	8,911	12,799	82,563
4. Unilever	15,965	9,067	327,000	17. Daimler-Benz	8,633	4,479	138,042
5. Philips' Glöeilampen-fabrieken	12,703	13,765	383,900	18. Peugeot-Citroën	8,524	6,206	184,500
6. Française des Pétroles	10,875	9,884	44,510	19. Nestlé	8,392	7,443	140,009
7. Siemens	10,641	11,198	319,000	20. Thyssen	8,325	5,723	134,271
8. Volkswagenwerk	10,410	7,420	191,891	21. Petrobrás (Petróleo Brasileiro)	8,284	9,040	57,813
9. ENI (Ente Nazionale Idrocarburi)	10,368	15,470	103,349	22. Hitachi	8,222	9,287	141,225
10. Hoechst	10,042	9,872	180,907	23. Imperial Chemical Industries	8,139	9,058	154,000
11. Renault	10,018	7,528	243,456	24. Mitsubishi Heavy Industries	8,090	10,505	105,200
12. Petróleos de Venezuela	9,628	6,303	25,225	25. Elf-Aquitaine	7,755	10,758	37,000
13. Toyota Motor	9,601	6,167	60,202				

*In millions of dollars.

Source: ''The Fortune Directory,'' Fortune, August 14, 1978, © 1978, Time Inc.

automobile company assembles parts to make a car.

In the *analytic* process, the manufacturer breaks down a raw material. Oil refineries break crude oil down into gasoline, oil, and other parts. A hog goes through an analytic process at a packing house and comes out as ham, bacon, and other pork products.

The *conditioning* process changes the form of raw materials. Carloads of ore from mines become ingots (bricks) or sheets of metal. Rocks from quarries are made into various grades of gravel.

Besides making the product, a manufacturer must have a system of *quality control*. Specially trained workers check the raw materials and examine the finished products. They make sure that the products meet the standards of the company. Careful *production control* is also essential. Experts make sure that the right materials in the right amounts go to the proper place in the factory at the proper time.

Distribution and Sales account for a large part of the prices we pay for products. For example, 1 gallon (3.8 liters) of paint costs much more than the chemicals and labor needed to make it. The final price includes the costs of advertising, packaging, shipping, storage, commissions to salesmen, office work, and taxes. In addition to these costs, the price must give a fair profit to the manufacturer, the wholesalers, and the retailers.

How Science Helps Manufacturing

Engineers and scientists continually experiment and search for new materials that will improve manufactured items. As a result of research since the early 1800's, manufacturers use hundreds of kinds of plastics. Plastics products have replaced less sturdy, less attractive, and more expensive materials. See PLASTICS.

Research not only develops new products, but also finds new uses for old ones. In addition, it leads to lower prices as manufacturers discover more efficient ways to make products. For example, until automobile companies developed the assembly-line method of manufacturing in the early 1900's, only the wealthiest families could afford cars (see ASSEMBLY LINE).

Widespread industrial research began after World War I, when research became more and more important as a part of manufacturing. Today, companies in the United States pay about $23¾ billion a year for research. About 359,000 scientists and engineers do research work in some 5,200 company laboratories and 725 gov-

Leading Manufactured Products in the U.S.

Value added by manufacture in 1977

Nonelectric Machinery	$67,406,000,000
Transportation Equipment	$64,166,400,000
Chemicals	$56,522,500,000
Food Products	$56,232,800,000
Electric and Electronic Equipment	$49,708,300,000
Fabricated Metal Products	$44,943,000,000
Primary Metals	$37,298,200,000
Printed Materials	$31,543,600,000
Paper Products	$21,699,400,000
Rubber and Plastics Products	$19,834,300,000

Source: U.S. Bureau of the Census.

Leading Manufacturing Countries

Value added by manufacture in 1977

United States	$586,023,100,000
Russia	$300,318,300,000
Japan	$181,091,600,000
West Germany	$163,873,400,000
France	$106,726,100,000
Great Britain	$66,978,400,000
Italy	$58,902,000,000
Canada	$46,776,161,000
Brazil	$45,996,900,000
Poland	$34,882,000,000

Sources: U.S. Bureau of the Census; Statistical Office of the UN; Statistics Canada.

Leading Manufacturing States and Provinces

Value added by manufacture in 1977

California	$55,452,000,000
New York	$44,677,000,000
Ohio	$43,294,000,000
Illinois	$40,277,000,000
Michigan	$37,480,000,000
Pennsylvania	$35,985,000,000
Texas	$32,923,000,000
Ontario	$24,274,000,000
New Jersey	$23,197,000,000
Indiana	$22,594,000,000

Sources: U.S. Bureau of the Census; Statistics Canada.

ernment, university, and independent laboratories. See RESEARCH.

How Governments Help Manufacturing

Thousands of government laws and regulations protect a manufacturer's property in noncommunist nations. The government also provides legal, orderly ways to buy and sell property and to establish companies. Government helps keep money stable so that the value of a dollar does not change greatly from day to day and from one area to another. The government permits manufacturers the right to patent an invention. Patents grant businesses exclusive rights to new products or methods that the manufacturers develop (see PATENT).

Governments furnish businesses with statistics that help them plan their sales and purchases. They give manufacturers loans at low rates of interest, and sometimes give them *subsidies*, or outright grants (see SUBSIDY). Governments protect home industries by levying tariffs on goods imported from other countries (see TARIFF). Many nations encourage manufacturers to build factories by not levying taxes on their profits for a certain number of years.   FRANK F. GROSECLOSE

Related Articles. See the section on Manufacturing in each state, province, and country article. See also articles on specific products such as AUTOMOBILE. Other related articles in WORLD BOOK include:

Aviation	Industrial	Printing
Careers	Revolution	Publishing
Ceramics	Industry	Technology
Chemical Industry	Machine	Textile
Clothing	Mass	Transportation
Factory	Production	Value Added
Food	Metal	by Manufacture
Forest Products	Plastics	

MANURE, *muh NOOR* or *muh NYOOR,* is any substance applied to the soil to make it more fertile. In the United States, the word *manure* usually applies to animal *excrement* (waste). In Europe, the word is used for almost any type of fertilizer, including both animal manure and green crops that are plowed under and decay in the soil.

Most animal manure in the United States is from the wastes of cattle and chickens. Horses, pigs, and sheep also provide manure. Animal manure is a valuable source of the *organic* (carbon-containing) matter that plants need for growth. However, it contains only a small amount of other necessary plant foods such as nitrogen, phosphoric acid, and potash. Animal manure should be used in combination with commercial fertilizer and green manure to provide a well-balanced supply of plant food.

Green manure crops provide a large amount of organic matter. They also provide other necessary plant foods as they decay in the soil. These crops are usually grown between the growing seasons of *cash crops* (the crops the farmer sells), or during the winter and early spring. Most farmers use grasses and *legumes* (plants with pods, such as beans and peas) for green manure.

All forms of manure and organic matter improve the soil because they absorb plant food and improve the soil's texture and condition. They also may increase the size and quality of the crop.   WILLIAM RAYMOND KAYS

See also FERTILIZER.

MANUS ISLAND. See ADMIRALTY ISLANDS.

MANUSCRIPT generally means a handwritten or typewritten version of a book, article, or other work prepared by a writer for a publisher or typesetter. The word *manuscript* may also mean any material written by hand before the invention of printing. This second definition is the subject of this article.

Handwritten manuscripts were the chief records of history for about 4,500 years, until printing came into general use during the 1400's. Most manuscripts can be identified with certain periods of history by the materials on which they are written. In ancient times, for example, such materials as papyrus, parchment, and wax tablets were used for manuscripts. During the Middle Ages, manuscripts were written on parchment and, later, on paper.

Ancient manuscripts tell much about life thousands of years ago. From these manuscripts, scholars have learned about the business transactions, customs, family affairs, government activities, and religious beliefs of ancient peoples. Many manuscripts of the Middle Ages are valuable works of art because of their beautiful decorations.

Manuscripts of the Ancient Near East

Papyrus Manuscripts. Papyrus was the chief writing material of ancient times and was used as early as 3000 B.C. It was used in ancient Egypt, Greece, Rome, and other lands surrounding the Mediterranean Sea.

Papyrus was made from a tall, reedlike plant called *papyrus,* which grew along the Nile River of Egypt. Strips of papyrus were pressed together into sheets about the size of a sheet of typing paper. The first papyrus books were made by pasting the sheets together to form rolls. Most rolls measured about 20 feet (6 meters) long, but many were longer. Some existing rolls are more than 100 feet (30 meters) long. By the A.D. 200's, many papyrus manuscripts were made of sheets that had been laced together to form a book. Any book made in this way is called a *codex.*

Papyrus decays in damp climates because it is plant material. For this reason, almost all existing papyrus manuscripts are from Egypt and surrounding areas, which have a dry climate. Most of these manuscripts date from 332 B.C. to A.D. 641.

Parchment Manuscripts. Parchment was also a widely used writing material in ancient times. Parchment is made from the skin of goats, sheep, or other animals. After the hair has been removed, the skins are stretched and scraped and then rubbed smooth with chalk. *Vellum* is high-quality parchment made from the skin of calves, kids, lambs, or other young animals. Ancient peoples often scraped the text off a leaf of vellum and wrote on it again. Such vellum manuscripts are called *palimpsests.*

Wax Tablets. In ancient Greece, Rome, and what is now Turkey, people also wrote on wax tablets with a sharp, pointed instrument called a *stylus.* On the end opposite the point, the stylus had a flat or rounded surface, which was used to erase the writing by smoothing the wax. Sometimes, several wax tablets were laced together to form a codex.

Other Manuscripts. The people of ancient Palestine and Syria wrote on pieces of leather. They also used

The Book of Kells is an illuminated manuscript of the four Gospels created in Kells, Ireland, in the 700's or 800's.

rolls of leather, which they made by sewing leather strips together. Some manuscripts were written on thin sheets of copper that could be rolled up. For more than 3,000 years, many peoples in Mesopotamia wrote on clay tablets. Thousands of these tablets still exist.

Manuscripts of the Ancient Far East

Paper Manuscripts. The Chinese invented paper about A.D. 100. Their first books written on paper took the form of rolls. Later, they made books by folding long strips of paper into accordionlike pleats.

Before the Chinese invented paper, they wrote on bones, tortoise shells, and silk. They also wrote on bamboo strips that measured about ¼ inch (6 millimeters) wide and 6 to 9 inches (15 to 23 centimeters) long. They wrote on the strips in column form from top to bottom. Then they tied the strips together with string in much the same way that modern bamboo screens and window shades are made.

Palm Leaf Manuscripts. In ancient India and some surrounding lands, the people made books of strips cut from palm leaves. Generally, they used strips about 3 inches (8 centimeters) wide and 2 feet (61 centimeters) or more long. They made holes in the strips and then strung them together, forming the books. The people of India also wrote on birch bark.

European Manuscripts of the Middle Ages

Vellum began to replace papyrus as the chief writing material about the A.D. 300's and was used for manu-

scripts throughout the Middle Ages. Monks produced most of the books written during the Middle Ages. They worked in a special place in the monasteries called the *scriptorium*. Their work was highly specialized. One group of monks prepared the vellum, and a second group did the writing. A third group decorated the manuscripts. Finally, a fourth group of monks put the finished manuscripts in the monastery library, sold them, or traded them to other monasteries.

Many manuscripts of the Middle Ages were beautifully decorated in various colors. Often, gold or silver leaf was used on the initial letters and the decoration. Such manuscripts were called *illuminated*, because they looked as if they had been lit up. Today, we use the term *illuminated* to refer to any decorated manuscript, whether or not it has gold or silver.

Distinctive styles of illumination developed in different parts of Europe. There were, for example, Anglo-Irish, Byzantine, English, French, and Irish styles of illumination. All these styles used six basic forms of decoration: (1) animals, (2) branches with leaves or berries, (3) geometric designs, (4) ornamental letters, (5) *plaits* (braids), and (6) scrollwork.

Most books produced during the Middle Ages were Bibles, parts of the Bible, or other religious books. Nonreligious books included *bestiaries* (books about beasts), romances, and the works of ancient Greek and Roman authors.

Illustrated Manuscripts

One of the oldest illustrated manuscripts in existence is an Egyptian papyrus roll dating from about 1350 B.C. This manuscript is a copy of the *Book of the Dead*. The Egyptians placed copies of the book, which contained

Aztec Manuscript of the mid-1500's shows property records of a Mexican village. It is made of fiber from the maguey plant.

prayers and hymns, in their tombs. For a picture of a *Book of the Dead*, see HIEROGLYPHIC.

Illustrated papyrus rolls were also fairly common in ancient Greece and Rome. In some of these manuscripts, the illustrations ran along the length of the roll and pictured what was being described in the text.

After the codex form came into use, books had illustrations across the width of the page, with text above and below the pictures. Few full-page illustrations appeared in manuscripts before the 1100's, except for portraits of saints and the apostles. These portraits, which were copied from Byzantine manuscripts, appeared in manuscripts of the 600's and 700's.

By the 1000's, the custom had developed of beginning some sections of a manuscript with a small picture called a *miniature*. Some miniatures were painted within the large initial letter that began a manuscript section. Such letters are called *historiated* initials.

Manuscript Collections

Many great libraries have valuable collections of illuminated manuscripts of the Middle Ages. These libraries include the Bibliothèque Nationale in Paris; the Henry E. Huntington Memorial Library in San Marino, Calif.; the Pierpont Morgan Library in New York City; the British Library in London; and the Vatican Library in Vatican City.

Many countries also have special buildings, called *archives*, in which they keep valuable records and important historical documents. Notable archives include the Archive Nationale in Paris; the National Archives in Washington, D.C.; and the Public Record Office in London.   D. W. DAVIES

Related Articles in WORLD BOOK include:

Bible	England (picture:	Paleography
Book (History)	The Battle of Crécy)	Paper
Book of Kells	Europe (History [pictures])	Papyrus
Calligraphy	Library (History)	Parchment
City (pictures:	Limbourg, Pol de	Scribe
Trade Fairs,	Middle Ages (pictures)	Scroll
Cities in	Painting (Medieval	Stylus
Flanders)	Painting)	Writing

MANX. See CAT (Breeds of Cats); MAN, ISLE OF.

MANZANITA, *MAN zuh NEE tuh*, is a shrub of the heath family. It grows from British Columbia to Cali-

Bright Red Berries and Brilliant Green Leaves make the manzanita a popular evergreen shrub for ornamental use.

"Dick" Whittington

fornia. It is about 20 feet (6 meters) tall, and has attractive evergreen leaves. The leaves have smooth edges. White fuzz covers their under surface. The small, bell-shaped flowers of the manzanita are pink or white. The fruit is red and fleshy. The kind known as bearberry (*Arctostaphylos uva-ursi*) is a hardy creeping evergreen common in sandy soils. The leaves are often used in medicine for their action on the kidneys and bladder.

Scientific Classification. The manzanita belongs to the heath family, *Ericaceae*. It is genus *Arctostaphylos*, species *A. tomentosa*.   GEORGE B. CUMMINS

See also HEATH.

MANZONI, ALESSANDRO (1785-1873), ranks as one of Italy's greatest novelists because of his only novel, *The Betrothed*. This work, published in 1827 and revised in 1840, set the standard for modern Italian prose style. *The Betrothed* is a long historical story set in Lombardy during the 1600's, when the province was ruled by Spain. It describes the adventures of two simple, young silk weavers, Renzo and Lucia, whose marriage is prevented by a local tyrant, Don Rodrigo.

Manzoni was born in Milan. At the age of 16, he began writing poetry, classical in style and patriotic in inspiration and content. Manzoni was born a Roman Catholic, but paid little attention to his faith until 1810. He then underwent a crisis that led him back to Catholicism. That crisis deeply influenced all his works. In addition to *The Betrothed*, he wrote five religious *Sacred Hymns* (1812-1822), an ode to Napoleon, and two historical plays.   SERGIO PACIFICI

See also ITALIAN LITERATURE (In the 1800's).

MANZÙ, GIACOMO. See SCULPTURE (Modern International; color picture: Modeling in Clay).

MAO TSE-TUNG, *MAH oh DZUH DOONG* (1893-1976), led the long strug-

Eastfoto

Mao Tse-tung

gle that made China a Communist nation in 1949. He then became the ruler of China and one of the most powerful persons in the world. Mao controlled all of China's artistic, intellectual, military, industrial, and agricultural planning and policies.

Mao's round face with the mole on the chin became familiar throughout the world. Pictures of him appeared everywhere in China. Young and old learned his slogans and studied his writings. His writings, particularly on guerrilla warfare and the role of peasants in Communist revolutions, were influential outside of China. Mao also wrote poetry.

His Life. Mao was born to a peasant family in Shaoshan, a village in Hunan province. He was still a student when the revolution of 1911-1912 overthrew the Manchu government and made China a republic. While employed as a library worker at the National University in Peking in 1918, Mao became attracted to Communism. In 1921, Mao and 11 others founded the Chinese Communist Party in Shanghai.

The Communists joined forces with Sun Yat-sen's *Kuomintang* (Nationalist Party) in the effort to unite

China. But distrust between the Communists and Chiang Kai-shek, who became Nationalist leader after Sun's death in 1925, soon led to open warfare between the two groups. Mao and other Communist leaders led small bands to Kiangsi province in 1928. By 1931, Kiangsi province had become Chiang's chief target. He launched a series of "extermination campaigns" that nearly wiped the Communists out. In 1934, Mao led the Communists to Shensi province, in what is called *The Long March.* The 6,000-mile (9,700-kilometer) march lasted more than a year, and welded the survivors into a tightly-knit group under Mao's leadership.

Japan had invaded Manchuria in 1931, and launched full-scale war against China in 1937. The Communists and Nationalists joined in an uneasy alliance until World War II ended in 1945. As the Nationalist armies were driven inland during the war, Mao organized guerrilla warfare to spread Communism. By 1945, the Communists controlled areas populated by nearly 100 million Chinese.

In 1946, fighting between Communists and Nationalists began in Manchuria. The Communists gained control of China by October, 1949, and the Nationalists withdrew to Taiwan.

His Leadership. Mao formed the Chinese into a tightly controlled society more quickly than most observers thought possible. After taking power, he made an alliance with the Russians, who helped strengthen the Chinese army when Chinese forces aided North Korea during the Korean War (1950-1953).

After the Korean War, Mao began a series of programs to expand China's agricultural and industrial production. In 1958, a crash program called the *Great Leap Forward* failed. Russia refused to give China atomic help in the mid-1950's and Mao began independent atomic research which led to Chinese nuclear explosions in the 1960's.

In 1959, Mao gave up his title of chairman of the People's Republic. But he kept control of the country and of the Communist Party. By the 1960's, disputes between China and Russia had expanded into a struggle for leadership of the Communist world. Mao considered himself the true interpreter of Marx, Lenin, and Stalin. Mao believed that poor nations would inevitably revolt against richer nations. Mao also accused the Russian Communist Party of being too soft toward the United States.

In the mid-1960's, China suffered a series of diplomatic defeats, and Mao launched a campaign against so-called *revisionists* (those favoring changes), to maintain revolutionary enthusiasm. Young *Red Guards* publicly disgraced many officials. In the early 1970's, China improved its relations with the United States and other Western nations. Mao died in September 1976, after a long illness.   MARIUS B. JANSEN

See also CHINA (History); CHIANG CH'ING.

MAORIS, *MAH oh rihz,* were the original inhabitants of New Zealand. They belong to the Polynesian race. About 250,000 Maoris live in New Zealand. The Maoris make up more than 8 per cent of New Zealand's population.

Most Maoris are tall and have broad faces; brown eyes; and black, wavy hair. Through the years, many Maoris have intermarried with people of European ancestry. As a result, large numbers of New Zealanders of mixed parentage resemble Maoris. These New Zealanders are also called Maoris.

The original Maoris lived in isolated villages. They fished and hunted. Later, they also became farmers. The Maoris were skilled woodcarvers, and they decorated war canoes and communal houses with complicated designs. Their religion was based on *taboos* (prohibitions on certain objects, persons, and places).

During World War II (1939-1945), educational and job opportunities drew many Maoris into various cities. Today, Maoris hold positions in government, industry, and professional fields. They live in much the same way as New Zealanders of European ancestry.

The Maoris have pride in their cultural heritage, and many old customs remain part of their way of life. For example, they enjoy eating fermented corn custard and performing dances called *action songs.* The Maoris hold large gatherings known as *hui* at social centers called *marae.* These gatherings celebrate such ceremonial events as funerals, weddings, and the opening of new buildings. Some hui last two or three days and attract from 500 to 1,000 persons. Although most Maoris speak English, they generally use only their own language, called Maori, at these gatherings. Less than half the people speak Maori in their homes.   ALAN HOWARD

See also NEW ZEALAND; MYTHOLOGY (Mythology of the Pacific Islands).

A Maori Woman in Traditional Dress wears a feather cloak. Her chin is tattooed. The building behind her has woodwork carved in the traditional Maori style of lines and spirals.

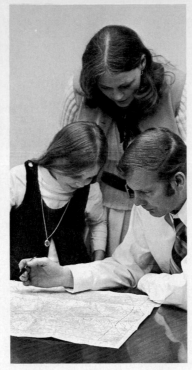

Maps Have Many Uses. A student may draw a map of the route he takes between his home and school. A family plans a vacation trip with the help of a road map. A policeman uses a detailed city map to pinpoint the site of a crime so officers can be sent to the scene quickly.

MAP

MAP is a graphic portrayal of a part or all of the earth. Maps have lines, words, symbols, and colors that show the distribution and arrangement of features upon the earth's surface. Maps may also show objects in space, such as stars and planets. Each feature is drawn in a reduced size so it can be shown on paper or on a globe. In some ways, a map is like an architect's drawing of a building. But there is a much greater reduction in size of the area shown on a map. One inch on a map, for example, may show a distance of 100 miles on the surface of the earth.

Almost everyone uses a map at one time or another. Maps help us travel from place to place and to understand the world around us. They help us plan vacation trips and follow news events in all parts of the world. Businessmen use maps to find good places to sell their products. Armed forces use maps to plan attack and defense strategy. Special kinds of maps serve different uses. One type of map may show the number of people in every country in the world. Another kind may indicate the amount of rain that falls in different lands. Still another may show the different types of trees that grow in various parts of the world.

Types of Maps

There are many different kinds of maps, but every map may be classed as one of two types: a *general reference map*, or a *special* or *thematic map*.

General Reference Maps show general information, such as continents, countries, rivers, cities, and other features. A *transportation map* is a type of general reference map. It usually shows features of the earth's surface that the traveler will easily recognize, such as roads and towns, as he goes from one place to another.

The most familiar transportation map is the automobile *road map*. Transportation maps are also especially designed for soldiers, hunters, prospectors, and hikers. Maps used by airplane pilots and ship captains are usually called *charts* (see CHART).

The traveler uses his map to find out where he is and to show him where he wants to go. The map helps him decide what direction he should take, which route to follow, how far he must travel, and how long it will take him to reach his destination.

Students and other persons use general reference maps of a slightly different kind in school, at home, in business, or in government when they want information about a specific region or about the world as a whole. These are the general reference maps found in textbooks, in encyclopedias, and in books of maps called *atlases* (see ATLAS). These maps may be used to show many things besides the location of a place. For example, a map can answer such questions about a city as: Does it lie inland or on the coast? Is it on a river that appears large enough to be navigable? How does it compare in size and population with nearby cities?

Although most maps are flat, a general reference map can be mounted on a ball called a *globe*. There are two kinds of globes. A *terrestrial* globe shows continents, oceans, and other surface features of the earth. It presents a more nearly perfect portrayal of the earth than any other kind of map. A *celestial* globe shows the stars and planets. See GLOBE.

Although globes are good maps of the world for many purposes, they have several disadvantages. One is that only about half of the earth's surface can be seen at a time. Another is that most globes are too small to give much information about any one country or region. Some globes are so big and heavy that they are awkward to move.

Special Maps, or thematic maps, show or emphasize some particular feature, such as rainfall, the distribution of people, or particular kinds of crops. There are as many kinds of special maps as there are features whose location is to be shown. People use special maps to learn how different parts of the earth vary in many ways. THE WORLD BOOK ENCYCLOPEDIA includes many useful special maps.

Maps on which different colors indicate various countries are called *political maps*. The relative size and arrangement of countries are easier to remember when shown by colors.

Maps that emphasize in some way the roughness of the earth's surface are called *physical maps*. Sometimes color indicates elevation above sea level. Shading is often used to suggest mountains and hills as they would appear from an airplane. Colors may also be used to show differences in rainfall or temperature. Frequently, the darker color indicates a heavier concentration of the subject. On other special maps, colors or symbols may show the distribution of vegetation or where various languages are spoken.

Map Language

The amount of information a person learns from a map depends on his ability to read it. For example, if a motorist goes on a long trip, he must know how to read a road map in order to know what highways to follow.

Scale. A map must be *drawn to scale* in order to be accurate. The scale of a map shows how much of the actual earth's surface is represented by a given measurement on a map. The scale must be shown so that the map reader can use the distances and areas shown on the map in measuring or figuring out the real distances and areas on the earth's surface. A *large-scale* map covers only a small region and shows most of the details of an area, such as roads and small rivers. A *small-scale* map leaves out many details and covers a much larger area, such as the world.

Scale can be expressed in three different ways. But all three ways do not always appear on every map.

Graphic Scale. On many maps, scale is shown graphically by means of a straight line on which distances have been marked off. Each mark usually represents a certain number of miles or kilometers on the earth's surface.

Words and Figures. The scale of a map is often expressed as so many units on the map equaling so many units on the ground. This scale might appear as 1 inch = 15 statute miles. In other words, 1 inch on the map equals 15 miles when measured on the surface of the earth.

Representative Fraction (R.F.). The most common method of expressing scale is to write a representative

fraction. For example, a scale might be written as 1:62,500 or $\frac{1}{62,500}$. This means that one unit of measurement on the map represents 62,500 of the same units on the surface of the earth. The advantage of this method is that the scale is expressed by the fraction regardless of what measurement system is used. On an American map, for example, 1 inch may equal 62,500 inches. On a German version of the same map, 1 centimeter might equal 62,500 centimeters. Both measurements would be accurate.

Symbols. Using many symbols on a map makes it possible to put a large amount of information on a single map. A map usually has a *legend* that explains what

© Rand McNally & Co.

General Reference Maps show elevations and political features. The map above shows high areas in orange, and low areas in green.

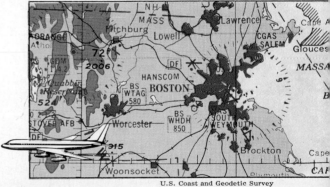

U.S. Coast and Geodetic Survey

Aeronautical Charts provide information for fliers. They show airports, compass directions, and radio station frequencies.

U.S. Geological Survey Maps show the exact locations of features on the earth. Surveyors rely on these maps for facts.

U.S. Geological Survey

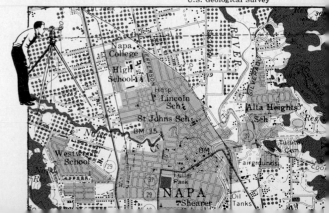

MAP

each symbol means. Some of these symbols represent *man-made*, or *cultural*, features of the landscape, such as highways, railroads, farms, dams, and cities. Others represent *natural* features, such as mountains, lakes, and plains. The symbols may be lines, dots, circles, squares, triangles, words, letters, colors, or combinations of these. The symbol often looks like or suggests the feature it represents. For example, some maps use a tree symbol for a forest or an orchard. Sometimes, however, there is little resemblance between the symbol and the feature represented by it. For example, a circle or a dot usually indicates a town or a city. Lines that pass through points of equal value are called *isolines*. For example, a 10-centimeter rainfall line connects places that have 10 centimeters of rainfall annually. The area on one side of the line has more rainfall than this amount, and the area on the other side has less. Other maps have isolines called *contours*, which link points of equal elevation.

Color. Most maps are printed in color, and the different colors used on a map are part of the map language. On political maps, color can be used to indicate different cities or countries or other types of political information. On physical maps, color can tell the map reader the elevation of various places. The map maker can use a standard series of colors called *layer tints* to show altitude. White may show land below sea level, and green shows land less than 1,000 feet above sea level. Yellow can represent the land between 1,000 and 2,000 feet. Tan can mark the land between 2,000 and 5,000 feet above sea level. Orange may be used for land between 5,000 and 10,000 feet, and dark brown for land more than 10,000 feet above sea level.

Map makers can use color to tell the map reader what the surface of the land is like, to show differences in temperature or rainfall among areas, and to indicate where different crops are grown.

On most general reference maps drawn in color, map makers use blue for rivers and bodies of water. Contours are usually shown in brown, and man-made features in black or red.

Geographic Grids. A network of accurately spaced north-south and east-west lines is necessary on every map for finding and describing locations. The entire system of these *grid lines* (called *meridians* and *parallels*) is worked out from the North and South poles. All grid lines are circles or parts of circles. Grid lines are shown in degrees because circles may be divided into degrees.

Meridians. By drawing a line from pole to pole through any place on the equator, we have a meridian, or north-south line. Each meridian is a half circle, because it runs halfway around the globe from pole to pole. By international agreement, the meridian passing through the original site of the observatory at Greenwich, a borough of London, England, is called the *prime meridian* (see GREENWICH MERIDIAN). The prime meridian is labeled 0°. All other meridians are numbered in degrees east and west of the prime meridian up to 180°. See INTERNATIONAL DATE LINE; MERIDIAN.

Parallels are lines drawn around a globe, with all points along each line an equal distance from a pole. The *equator* is the parallel drawn with all points along the line an equal distance from either pole. All the lines parallel the equator and are true east-west lines. Using the equator as 0°, parallels are numbered north and south to the poles. The distance from the equator to a pole is one-fourth of a circle, or 90°.

Longitude and Latitude. The distance in degrees of any place east or west of the prime meridian is known as its longitude. Longitude is marked by meridians, and is usually labeled along the top and bottom margins of a map. On the political map of MARYLAND in this volume, the meridians run from about 75° to 79½° west longitude. See LONGITUDE.

Distance in degrees north and south of the equator is called latitude. Latitude is marked by parallels and is usually labeled along the side margins of a map. Parallels on the MARYLAND color map run from about 38° to 39¾° north latitude. See LATITUDE.

How to Read a Map

What Maps Tell Us. There are several ways by which the surface features of the earth, such as mountains, plains, valleys, and deserts, are shown on physical maps.

A pictorial way of showing the earth's surface is the *terrain map*. WORLD BOOK uses this method on the physical maps with state, province, country, and continent articles. Shades of various colors suggest the color of the ground and vegetation as the map reader would see them from high in the air. For example, if the ground is barren or exposed rock or sand, the color is light gray or yellow. A lush growth of tall evergreens is shown by a deep blue-green. These maps also give elevations of principal terrain features so the map user may make comparisons.

Each of the state and province articles is also accompanied by a general reference political map. These maps give place-name references and locations. They indicate principal highways, and show rivers, lakes, and reservoirs. The legend with each map explains special features. Red lines outline the states and separate the counties. The size of type used in printing the name of a city gives the reader an idea of the city's population. The larger the type, the more important the city.

Special maps with each state and province article provide information on the average yearly rainfall, average daily temperatures for January and July, population density, and farm, mineral, and forest products.

How to Find Places on Maps. The location of a place can be given by longitude and latitude. A place at 77° west longitude could be anywhere along the meridian that extends from pole to pole, about one-fifth of the way around the world west from the prime meridian. But, if this place is also known to be at 39° north latitude, it can easily be located, because there is only one place along the meridian where it could be. A look at the MARYLAND map will show this location to be just north of Washington, D.C.

North, south, east, and west are usually indicated on maps by the initials N., S., E., and W. Thus, 77° west longitude is usually written 77° W., and 39° north latitude is written 39° N.

The *index* of a map provides an even easier way to find places. The index is an alphabetical list of cities and physical features represented on the map. After each place name, the index has two symbols—a letter and a number—which can be used to locate the place on the map.

How to Figure Distances on a Map. To find the distance between two cities, such as Chicago and Montreal, lay a slip of paper on the map so that the edge of the paper touches the two cities. Mark the paper as shown in the top picture. Then place the paper along the distance scale shown on the map, with the left-hand mark at 0. Mark the paper at 400 miles on the distance scale, *above left*. Then move the 400-mile mark to 0. The mark that represents Montreal is at 350 miles on the scale, *above right*. Thus, Chicago and Montreal lie 400 plus 350, or 750, miles apart. Distances in kilometers can be found by using this procedure with the metric portion of the distance scale.

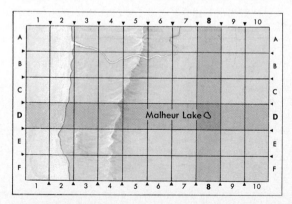
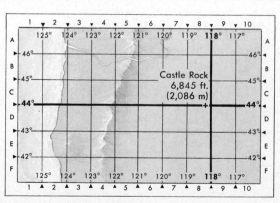

Location Symbols are often used to find a place on a map. Malheur Lake, in Oregon, lies between the two D's and the two 8's on the map at the left. An index to the map would show this location with the symbol D8. Latitude and longitude can also be used. On the map at the right, Castle Rock, Ore., is near 118° W. and at 44° N.

Large cities can be located easily by just looking at a map. But smaller towns, such as Frederick on the MARY-LAND map, are harder to find. The index to the MARY-LAND map shows the letter "C" and a number "8" after the name Frederick. Map makers letter and number maps to make them easier to read. Letters run along the side margins of a map, and numbers run along the top and bottom margins. The "C 8" after Frederick indicates that the town lies in the area "C 8." To find the area, the map reader looks along the side of the map to find the letter "C" and along the top or bottom to find the number "8." He then locates the imaginary position where "C" and "8" meet on the map, and looks for Frederick nearby.

137

HOW TO READ MAPS

Terrain Maps show what the surface of the earth might look like from a rocket flying high above the atmosphere. The use of shading in the map at the right suggests that the mountains rise above the surface of the land. Such maps may also show the kinds of trees and plants in a region by the use of different colors. Some of the many symbols used to indicate important physical features on terrain maps are explained in the white oval areas, *right*.

Political Maps make no attempt to show what the land actually looks like. Instead, they give detailed information about country, state, and county boundaries; cities and towns; and roads and highways. Oceans, rivers, and lakes are the main physical features on most political maps. Other useful information includes forest areas, Indian reservations, and various points of interest.

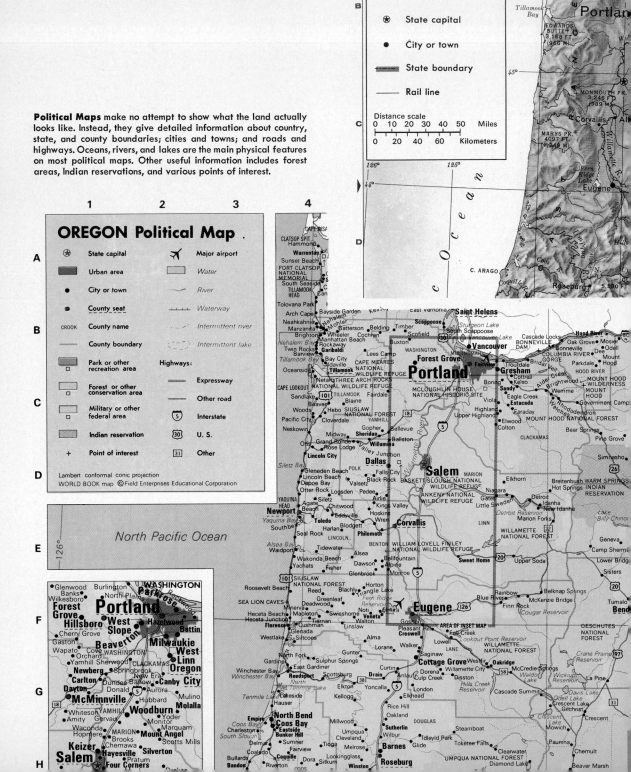

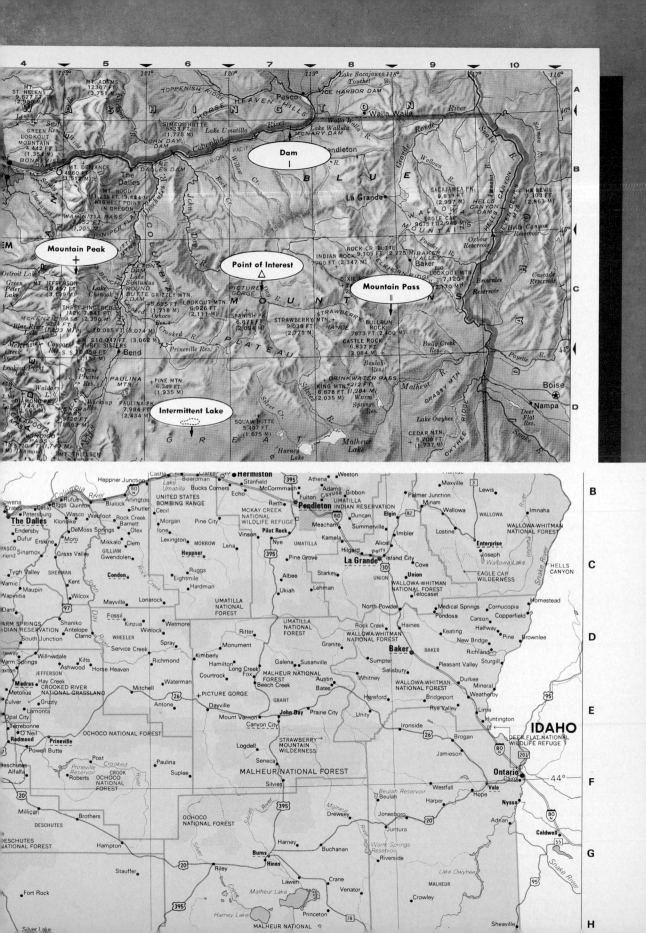

Lines of Latitude, or *parallels,* run around a globe from east to west so that all points along their path are an equal distance from the poles. You would be cutting along parallels of latitude on an orange if you sliced the fruit at right angles to its pith.

Lines of Longitude, or *meridians,* run from north to south on a globe from pole to pole. They cross the parallels of latitude at right angles. You could cut along the meridians of an orange by slicing wedges from the fruit that were parallel to its pith.

Map Projections

Any drawing on a flat surface that shows a globe's network of meridians and parallels is called a *projection.* This term comes from the fact that one way to transfer lines and points from a globe to a flat map is to use a transparent globe with a light inside it. The light projects the lines on the globe onto a large sheet of paper, where they can be copied. In actual practice, a map maker works out a pattern of meridians and parallels mathematically. It is not possible to make a flat map of the round earth that shows all distances, directions, shapes, and areas as accurately as a globe does. Every flat map has some distortion, or error.

Many different map projections have been developed throughout the years, but only a few are in common usage. A map should be drawn on a projection that comes closest to showing accurately the features that are required for some specific purpose. For example, a map that compares the sizes of two countries should show areas accurately. A square inch on one part of the map should equal the same number of square miles as a square inch on another part. A map used by a ship captain should show compass directions accurately by straight lines.

How to Find Distortions on Maps. Since all flat maps have some distortion, a way to find the inaccuracies is useful. This can be done by comparing meridians and parallels and the rectangles made by them on a map with those on a globe. The following grid facts can be seen on a globe:

(1) All meridians are equal in length and meet at the poles.

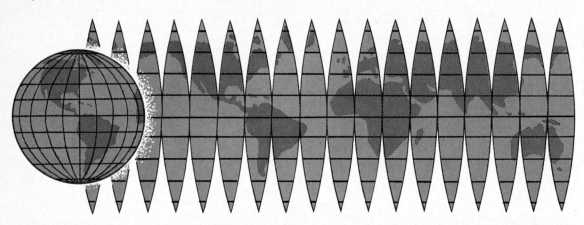

Maps on Flat Surfaces attempt to show the world as it appears on a globe, with as little distortion as possible. An accurate map can be made by cutting a globe apart along the meridians and flattening it. But its many parts make such a map hard to read.

Accurate Maps can be made in ways that are less difficult to read. A nearly flat map results from cutting a globe as shown, *left,* and opening it as far as possible, *center.* The map can then be flattened by stretching the parts that are still curved, *right.*

(2) All latitude lines are parallel.

(3) The length of parallels around the globe decreases from the equator to the poles.

(4) Distances along meridians between any two parallels are equal.

(5) All meridians and parallels meet at right angles, or 90°.

If the grid of a map projection disagrees with one or more of these five facts, the distortion on the map can be found. For example, the meridians on the Mercator projection shown on this page do not converge to meet at the poles, and the parallels do not decrease in length toward the poles. Therefore, the scale increases and areas are exaggerated away from the equator.

Although most projections are systematic arrangements of meridians and parallels according to a mathematical formula, it is easier to visualize their general form and characteristics if the earth's surface is considered to be projected upon a plane, a cylinder, or a cone. The projections described below are grouped in this order.

Azimuthal Projections. The azimuthal group of projections is developed by projecting the surface of a globe on a flat surface that touches the globe at a single point. The point of the projection is called an *eye point*, and may be on the globe itself, inside it, or some distance from it.

Gnomonic Projection is perhaps the best-known azimuthal projection. The grid is set up by projecting the surface of the globe from an eye point that is at the center of the globe. Distortion of shape, areas, and scale are very great in this projection. The gnomonic projection has only one true quality, but it is important for long-distance airplane flights. A straight line between two places on a gnomonic projection represents the *great-circle route* or the shortest distance between these two points (see GREAT-CIRCLE ROUTE). From this, a navigator can determine the latitude and longitude of places that lie along his course. Then he can transfer these positions to a Mercator chart of the same area. Straight lines drawn between these positions on the Mercator chart give him the directions for each part of his flight, so that the route will follow a great circle as closely as possible.

Cylindrical Projections. The cylindrical group of projections is worked out as if a cylinder, or tube, were rolled around a globe along the equator. The parallels and meridians are usually straight lines at right angles to each other.

Mercator Projection, a type of cylindrical projection, is drawn so that the distances between parallels, which are the same on a globe, become greater and greater as the parallels approach the poles. This distortion makes up for the fact that the distances between meridians remain the same from the equator to the poles on this type of map. The Mercator projection makes areas in high latitudes seem much larger than they are. But it is ideal for navigation charts. Shapes of features, such as islands and harbors, are accurate, and any compass course between two points on the map can be shown as a straight line.

Miller Cylindrical Projection is a modification of the Mercator projection. East-west distances are fairly accurate between 45°N. and 45°S. latitudes. The exaggeration of areas in high latitudes is not nearly so great

KINDS OF MAP DISTORTION

A Globe presents a picture of the earth with practically no distortions. If you imagined a man's face printed on the surface of the globe, the face would look completely natural.

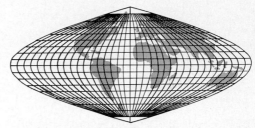

A Sinusoidal Projection does not have lines of longitude of equal length. It squeezes shapes near the top and bottom, and bends them at the left and right, as the faces below indicate.

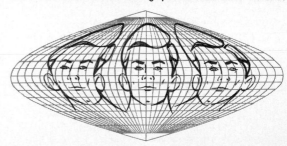

A Mercator Projection does not show lines of longitude converging at the poles. As a result, areas near the poles appear larger than they are, as the face below indicates.

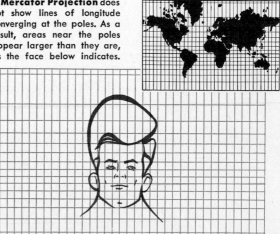

HOW CONTOUR MAPS ARE MADE

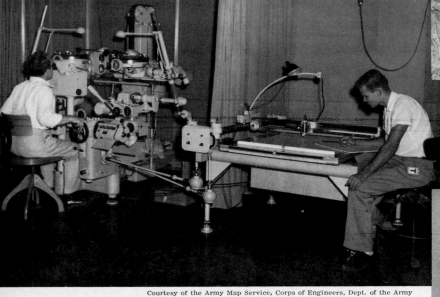

An Aerial Photograph, *above,* shows such features as hills and a river.

Even a Cow can be shown by means of a contour map.

Courtesy of the Army Map Service, Corps of Engineers, Dept. of the Army

The Stereoplanigraph, *above,* draws contour maps from aerial photographs. The operator, *left,* follows the contours on the photograph through eyepieces. The machine traces the contours on paper on the table, *right.*

as in the Mercator projection. For this reason, the Miller projection is useful for a map of the world because it does not greatly distort the parts of the world where most of the people live.

Conic Projections. The conic group of projections is made as if a cone were laid over the globe and touched it along some line of latitude. The parallels, which are arcs of concentric circles, are spaced evenly along the meridians, which are straight lines. As on the globe, the meridians come closer and closer together as they approach the pole. The group is well adapted for middle-latitude areas. The simple conic projection, although neither equal-area nor conformal, is fairly accurate for small areas. It is often used for maps in atlases.

Lambert Conformal Conic Projection is an accurate conic projection for large areas with greater east-west than north-south dimensions. The cone is thought of as cutting through the surface of the globe so that east-west distances are true along two parallels. These are known as the *standard parallels.* North-south and east-west distances are slightly under scale between the two standard parallels, and slightly over scale beyond them. The term *conformal* means that the map shows true shapes accurately. Distances, directions, and areas are shown from 90 to 98 per cent accurately. The small errors of azimuth or direction, and the closeness with which a straight line follows a great circle, make this type of projection useful in air navigation. The International Civil Aviation Organization has adopted it for its series of aeronautical charts covering the world. For an example of this type of map, see the physical map with MASSACHUSETTS.

Polyconic Projection may be thought of as a projection of strips of the earth's surface upon a series of touch-

ing cones. In practice, however, this principle is modified. A vertical straight line marks a central meridian that is divided to space the parallels truly. Each parallel is divided truly, and the curved lines that connect the division points form the meridians. Distortion is small near the central meridian. For this reason, the projection is excellent for showing areas of small east-west direction. For an example of this type of map, see the physical map with ALASKA.

Other Types of Projections. There are other projections, purely conventional in design, which cannot be related to these three general groups. They include the sinusoidal projection, the oval-shaped homolographic projection, and the interrupted homolosine projection, which is a combination of the sinusoidal and homolographic projections. For an example of a sinusoidal projection map, see the terrain map with SOUTH AMERICA.

How Maps Are Made

Many skilled scientists and technicians must work together to make a map. The information shown by a map is the result of scientific observation and the study of some part of the earth's surface. Many maps are made from other maps by selecting facts to be shown and by simplifying and reducing the scale. In general, a map goes through the following steps as it is made.

Observation. Various experts observe, plot, survey, photograph, and describe facts about the earth. The surveyor works out the exact location of places by measuring distances, directions, and elevations. In this way, places on the earth's surface are related to other parts of the earth to provide the correct space relations between places on maps. Surveyors use precision in-

The Contour Map, *above,* shows the results produced by the stereoplanigraph.

The Lines on the map, *below,* indicate the outline and the contours of a cow.

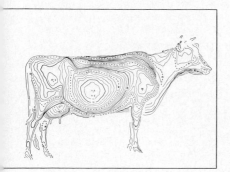

The Pantograph Router, *above,* makes a three-dimensional model of the features shown on a contour map. The operator traces the lines on the map, and a cutting blade forms the model.

Plastic Relief Maps can be made from the model produced by the router. A die is made from the model and placed on a forming machine. The machine uses pressure and heat to form maps.

struments to make these measurements. Aerial photography helps them with much of their work. Other specialists, including the explorer, the geographer, the geologist, the geodesist, the photogrammetrist, and the meteorologist, may carry on additional observations.

Organization. Any new information is added to the facts that are already known about the area to be mapped. The results are organized, simplified, and generalized so they can be translated into the language of maps. This is the work of another group of scientists, chosen according to the kind of facts to be presented and the purpose of the map. These men might be geographers, geologists, climatologists, sociologists, historians, or military strategists.

Planning. All the facts to be shown on the map are gathered together and analyzed. A *cartographer,* or map maker, plans the map. Sometimes a cartographic editor and a cartographic designer share the job.

Drafting. The map is put on paper as an original drawing or as a series of drawings by a cartographic artist or draftsman. Usually, this drawing is larger than the final map. The draftsman puts into symbols the facts and ideas of the scientists and cartographers to make the map easy to read, accurate, and pleasing to the eye.

Reproduction. If a large number of persons are to use a map, many copies must be made. The map drawing must be put on a material from which it can be printed directly, or from which printing plates can be made.

The Map Industry. Each year, hundreds of thousands of new maps are made. Government agencies make many of these maps. Governments need maps of various scales and types to help them carry out their duties. Many special maps are needed for military purposes. In the United States, they are made by various armed

forces agencies. The United States Geological Survey prepares large-scale topographic maps of areas within the United States. The National Ocean Survey gathers information about the earth and sea and publishes it in tables and maps useful to water and air navigators. Commercial map companies make maps chiefly on smaller scales and for special needs, such as road maps. These firms include Rand McNally & Company and the General Drafting Company, Inc. Firms that publish maps, globes, and charts chiefly for schools include A. J. Nystrom & Company, Denoyer-Geppert Company, and C. S. Hammond, Inc. Private organizations, such as the American Geographical Society and the National Geographic Society, also publish maps.

History

Old maps can tell us a great deal about where people traveled in ancient times. Men have made and used maps ever since people first moved about the earth exploring other territories, trading, or conquering other peoples. By comparing old maps, we can learn the extent of knowledge that various peoples had of the world throughout the ages. We usually think of maps in connection with reading and writing. But peoples who do not have written languages have often used maplike aids when traveling from place to place. The Eskimos scratched such maps on scraps of wood or ivory. Polynesians of the Pacific Islands made charts of rattan to indicate prevailing winds and ocean currents.

Ancient Maps. The oldest known map was made about 2300 B.C. It is a small clay tablet from Babylonia that probably shows a man's estate in a mountain-lined valley. The Egyptians made maps as early as 1300 B.C. One of the few remaining ancient Egyptian maps shows

The Oldest Map Known is a clay tablet found in Iraq. Made about 2300 B.C., it probably shows a man's estate in a valley.

the route from the Nile Valley to the gold mines of Nubia, part of ancient Ethiopia.

The Greeks made maps of the inhabited world in the early 300's B.C. They became one of the first peoples to realize that the earth is round. They designed the first projection and developed a longitude and latitude system. No ancient Greek maps exist today. The Romans used maps for taxing land and to assist in military campaigns. They were excellent surveyors, and were among the first to make road maps. But few of their maps have been preserved.

The most famous ancient maps were made by Claudius Ptolemy, a scholar who lived in Alexandria, Egypt, around A.D. 150. A map of the world as known at that time, and 26 regional maps of Europe, Africa, and Asia,

formed part of his eight-book *Geographia*. Only a few scholars knew about Ptolemy's maps until the late 1400's, when they were printed in an atlas.

Map Making in Europe. The *portolano*, or sailor's chart, came into common use during the 1300's and 1400's. It was developed as an aid to navigation along the coasts of the Mediterranean Sea. Maps of this type were drawn on sheepskin. They showed the outline of coasts and harbors, and located shipping ports. The oldest examples of portolano charts date from about 1300. But their fine workmanship indicates they were probably patterned after even earlier maps.

Christopher Columbus was a map maker. As a navigator, he used portolano charts. But, as a student of geography, he was also familiar with the maps of scholars. Only one map made by Columbus himself is known to exist today. This map shows the northwest coast of Hispaniola. The Naval Museum in Madrid, Spain, has a large, hand-drawn map showing the first explorations of Columbus. It was made by one of Columbus' pilots, Juan de la Cosa, and is dated 1500. The explorations of America and the voyages of the Portuguese around Africa led to great progress in map making during the 1500's. See COLUMBUS, CHRISTOPHER (map).

The growth of knowledge about the world can be traced in maps that were drawn to record discoveries. Almost every voyage of exploration had a chart maker who drew sketch maps of coast lines, harbors, and islands. He also drew a general map of each expedition from the sketch maps and the ship's log. Then scholars and cartographers added these latest discoveries to their atlas and globes.

Famous Map Makers. Martin Behaim (1459?-1507), a German merchant-navigator, made the oldest existing globe in 1492. The first map to use the name *America* was made in 1507 by a German map maker, Martin Waldseemüller (1470?-1518). This was a large world

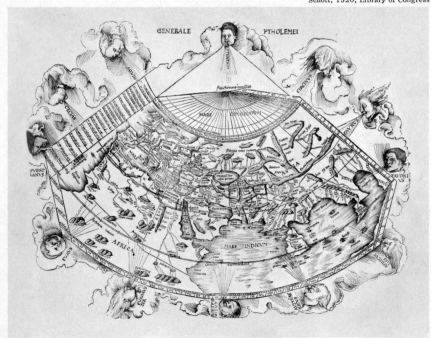

Until the 1500's, maps were based on the writings of Ptolemy, a Greek geographer and astronomer who lived about A.D. 150. An unknown cartographer created the map at the left in 1520. Although it is not accurate, the map shows the earth as being round.

map printed in 12 sheets and measuring about $4\frac{1}{2}$ by 8 feet (1.4 by 2.4 meters). Each sheet was separate, printed from a woodcut, and measured about 18 by 24 inches (46 by 61 centimeters).

One of the greatest map makers of the 1500's was Gerhard Kremer, who used the Latinized name of Mercator (1512-1594). This Flemish geographer not only produced some of the best maps and globes of his time, but also developed a map projection of great value to sailors (see MERCATOR, GERHARDUS). Another Flemish map maker, Abraham Ortelius (1527-1598), produced the first modern atlas in 1570. The German mathematician Johann Lambert (1728-1777) made contributions to the mathematical projection of maps.

Early Map Making in America. The first map made after English settlers came to Jamestown was a map of Virginia by the famous adventurer, John Smith (1580-1631). It was published in England in 1612. Smith also made the first English map of New England.

There were no professional map makers in the American Colonies, but skilled amateurs drew many maps of the area. Lewis Evans (c. 1700-1756) of Philadelphia produced *A General Map of the Middle British Colonies in America* in 1755. It measured about 26 by 20 inches (66 by 51 centimeters), and is considered the best map produced by a colonist before the Revolutionary War. *A Map of the British and French Dominions in America* was produced in England in 1755 by John Mitchell (? - 1768). It measured about 76 by 53 inches (193 by 135 centimeters). A copy of this map was used at the peace conference of 1783 to mark the boundary of the newly established United States of America.

As the pioneers moved westward, travelers and scholars made newer and better maps. Meriwether Lewis and William Clark used an English map of North America made by Aaron Arrowsmith (1750-1823) to guide them across the continent. Upon their return, they drew their own map. Other explorers, including Zebulon Pike, Jedediah Smith, and John C. Frémont, provided additional information about the West. Their information was put on maps used in the immigration to Oregon during the 1800's and the Gold Rush to California in 1849. Later, the government sent army engineers into the West to make railroad and geographical surveys. The maps that illustrated the reports of these surveys became the foundation of the first accurate and fairly complete maps of the United States, dating from about 1875. Four years later, the United States Geological Survey was organized and began making large-scale, detailed topographical maps.

Map Making in the 1900's. Road maps for automobile travel came into wide use about 1910 (see ROAD MAP [History]). Some oil companies give away road maps at gasoline service stations. These maps are up to date because new editions with added information are printed every year.

Air travel made many new kinds of maps and charts necessary for pilots and passengers. It also permitted map makers to acquire more accurate information about the earth. In addition, the airplane contributed to the development of *photogrammetry*, the science of making maps from air photographs. The use of vertical and oblique air photographs increased the speed with which maps can be made. The entire United States has been photographed, and air photos are used in making nearly all large-scale, detailed maps. The United States Air Force has special target maps for bombing, with concentric circles around the targets. For night flying, charts are printed on fluorescent paper which makes the map glow under ultraviolet light.

Other developments in technology have also affected map making. For example, map makers use computers in many ways. Computers sort and arrange data for mapping and then draw the map on film, paper, or a television screen. Another technique of map making uses scientific devices called *remote sensors*, which gather mappable data about the environment. Remote sensing devices include radar and *infrared* (heat radiation) instruments that collect data about the earth from airplanes and artificial satellites. GEORGE F. JENKS

Related Articles. See the color and black-and-white maps with the state, province, country, and continent articles. See also the following articles:

Outline

I. **Types of Maps**
    A. General Reference Maps
    B. Special Maps

II. **Map Language**
    A. Scale   C. Color
    B. Symbols   D. Geographic Grids

III. **How to Read a Map**
    A. What Maps Tell Us
    B. How to Find Places on Maps

IV. **Map Projections**
    A. How to Find Distortions on Maps
    B. Azimuthal Projections
    C. Cylindrical Projections
    D. Conic Projections
    E. Other Types of Projections

V. **How Maps Are Made**

VI. **History**

Questions

What two general kinds of features do symbols represent on a map?

What is a geographic grid? Why is it useful in map reading?

What is the prime meridian? How are other meridians numbered from the prime meridian?

Why is the globe the best kind of map for many purposes?

For what main purposes did the Romans use maps?

What does the scale on a map show? What are the three most common ways of showing scale?

What is meant by latitude? Longitude?

What is a map projection? What are the main types of map projections?

What are some kinds of general maps? Special maps?

Why is it valuable to know about distortion on a map?

Grant Heilman

E. R. Degginger

The Sugar Maple ranks as one of the most valuable trees of North America. Its sweet sap is used in making maple syrup, and its hard wood makes excellent lumber.

The Silver Maple is named for the silvery-white underside of its leaves.

MAPLE. The maple is a handsome tree from which we get maple sugar and a valuable wood. More than a hundred species of the maple family are known. They grow throughout the north temperate regions of the world. Thirteen species are native to the United States.

All maples which grow in the open have full, rounded tops. They furnish much of the welcome shade along our streets. Most people also find pleasure in their beautiful leaves and strange winged fruits. All maple leaves

Jerome Wexler, APF

E. R. Degginger

The Norway Maple, *above,* one of the largest European maples, grows as high as 100 feet (30 meters). It was introduced into North America, where it has become a popular shade tree. In spring, the tree has bright-yellow blossoms, *left.*

grow opposite each other, in pairs. They are broad and flat, with veins and lobes like fingers. There are from three to seven lobes. One species, the *box elder,* has a true compound leaf, made up of separate leaflets. See Box Elder.

The fruits of these trees are called *key fruits,* or *keys.* Each has a thin flat wing. Usually two seeds grow together with the wings on each side of the seeds. Often a pair of seeds looks like the propeller of an airplane. Maple-tree seeds supply food for squirrels, birds, and chipmunks.

The Sugar Maple. The *sugar, rock,* or *hard maple* is the most important of the maples. It grows from Newfoundland to the Great Lakes, south to Georgia, and west to Manitoba and Texas. It may reach a height of 135 feet (41 meters). Its trunk may be 5 feet (1.5 meters) across. The sugar maple has gray bark and dark-green leaves. In autumn the leaves turn to beautiful yellow, orange, and red. The maple leaf is the national emblem of Canada, and appears on the Canadian flag.

The delicious golden-brown maple syrup comes from the sugary sap of the hard maple. Manufacturing syrup and sugar from maple sap is an important business, especially in New York, Ohio, Ontario, Pennsylvania, Quebec, and Vermont. See Maple Syrup.

The hard maple also outranks all other maples as a lumber tree. Its wood is heavy, hard, and strong and takes a fine polish. The color is a light reddish-brown. From colonial times, it has had so many uses that it is hard to count them all. Furniture makers have used maple since furniture was first made in America. Hard maple is widely used for floors. Other maple products are saddles, shoe lasts, wooden kitchenware and novelties, boxes, crates, and parts of many musical instruments. Hard maple is much used as a fuel. Veneer, railroad ties, and pulpwood are also cut from this tree. The pioneers used its ashes to make soap.

Bird's-Eye Maple. The wood in a small percentage of hard maple trees shows a beautiful spotted design.

146

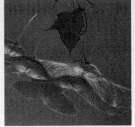

Charles E. Mohr, NAS   Jerome Wexler, NAS

The Fruit of Maple Trees, called *keys,* consists of a pair of winged seeds, *left.* The wind carries the keys away from the tree, and the seeds take root and start to grow, *right.*

Each spot is about ⅛ inch (3 millimeters) across, and looks a little like a bird's eye. These spots are caused by numerous indented places, more or less close together, in the annual rings of growth. Special methods of sawing are necessary to bring out the design. A method called *plain sawing,* or *tangent sawing,* gives bird's-eye lumber. Veneer is cut by slicing round and round the tree, cutting in the same direction as the growth rings. The saw pares off a thin layer from the surface as the log turns. Smoothing the surface by planing and polishing brings out the full richness of the design.

The bird's-eye design is seldom found in any other kind of wood. It is not known exactly what causes the indented places in the rings. They are not due to buds growing underneath the bark, as many people think. Most bird's-eye veneer comes from the northern peninsula of Michigan.

Curly and Wavy Grained Maple are other woods with special patterns. The fibers take either an irregular, curly course, or are arranged in regular waves. These growths produce beautiful effects of light and shade. The cause of curly and wavy grain also is unknown. Unlike bird's-eye grain, they appear in many other kinds of wood besides maple. They are found in both hardwoods and softwoods.

Figured maple with twisted wood fibers is highly prized both as lumber and veneer. It is used for bedroom furniture, desks, wall paneling, fancy gunstocks, and violin backs. The design preferred for violins is a fine wavy grain that has been given the name "fiddleback" figure. The figure has the same name when it appears in other woods that are not used for violins, such as mahogany.

Other American Maples include the *silver maple,* which is grown in many places. This is a hardy tree that grows quickly. It has beautiful shimmering silver and green leaves, but light, brittle wood. The *big-leaf,* or *Oregon maple* is one of the few valuable hardwoods of the Pacific coast. The *red, scarlet,* or *swamp maple* is a valuable ornamental and lumber tree. Its red or scarlet flowers appear in the spring before the leaves. The leaves turn to a beautiful scarlet in early fall. The *striped maple* and the *mountain maple* are two smaller trees usually found together in the northern woods.

In Canada, the government has furnished many trees for planting as protection against wind and snow. Of all the trees furnished, 30 per cent are maples.

Foreign Maples. The *sycamore maple* is an important hardwood tree in Europe. The branches of this tree spread wide, and its thick leaves look like those of the sycamore. It is planted in America to some extent. The *Norway maple* is a large tree with thick leaves and a milky sap. It resembles the sugar maple tree, and produces a vast amount of fruit, which covers the ground around the tree. The tree's green leaves turn to pale yellow in autumn. The Norway maple is popular in England and the United States. A variety of Norway maple, the *Schwedler maple,* has bright red leaves when young. The leaves turn dark green in summer. The Schwedler maple is a popular ornamental tree. *Japanese maples* also find wide use as ornamental trees. They seldom grow above 20 feet (6 meters) high. Their feathery leaves have delicate shades of red and green in the spring. These leaves have beautiful tints in autumn.

Insect Enemies. Several harmful insects attack the maple. Some bore into the bark while others eat the leaves. Maples are often damaged by tent caterpillars, sugar-maple borers, plant lice, scales, and galls. Various washes are good cures for scales.

Scientific Classification. The maple family is *Aceraceae.* The sugar, or rock, maple is genus *Acer,* species *A. saccharum.* The silver maple is *A. saccharinum.* The big-leaf, or Oregon, is *A. macrophyllum.* The striped maple is *A. pensylvanicum.* The mountain maple is *A. spicatum.* The red maple is *A. rubrum.* The sycamore maple is *A. pseudoplatanus.* The Norway maple is *A. platanoides.* The Japanese maple is *A. palmatum.*   THEODORE W. BRETZ

See also BOX ELDER; MAPLE SYRUP; TREE (Familiar Broadleaf and Needleleaf Trees of North America [picture]).

SOME KINDS OF MAPLE LEAVES

Maple leaves can be identified by their handlike appearance. They have a broad, flat shape, with three to seven lobes that resemble fingers. The maple leaf is the Canadian national symbol.

Werner Schulz   Walter Chandoha   E. R. Degginger   C. G. Maxwell, NAS

Norway Maple   **Sugar Maple**   **Silver Maple**   **Japanese Maple**

MAPLE, FLOWERING. See FLOWERING MAPLE.

MAPLE LEAF FOREVER is a song which has been popularly used as the Canadian unofficial hymn. The words and music were written in 1867 by Alexander Muir, a public schoolteacher in Toronto. He was born in Scotland, and was brought to Canada when he was 3 years old. The maple leaf was made the official emblem of Canada in 1860.   RAYMOND KENDALL

MAPLE SYRUP is a sweet, thick liquid obtained from the sap of certain maple trees. The *sugar maple* tree ranks as the chief source of this delicious food product. New York and Vermont lead the states of the United States in maple syrup production. But the Canadian province of Quebec produces more maple syrup than all the states together.

Some people pour pure maple syrup on pancakes, waffles, and other foods. But the "maple" syrups that most people use contain only a small amount of actual maple syrup. Most of these products are a combination of maple syrup, cane sugar syrup, and corn syrup. Maple syrup producers use some syrup to make maple sugar, maple butter and cream, and soft maple candy.

Maple sap is a colorless, watery solution that contains sugar and various acids and salts. Standards set by the U.S. government require that maple syrup consist of at least $65\frac{1}{2}$ per cent of these solids. It takes from 35 to 45 gallons (132 to 170 liters) of sap to make 1 gallon (3.8 liters) of maple syrup.

The typical maple flavors and *amber* (golden brown) colors develop during processing. Syrup is often classified by color, ranging from the palest amber, called *light amber* or *Fancy*, to the darkest amber, called *Commercial*. All maple syrups have the same food value, but they differ in flavor. In general, the lighter the syrup, the more delicate the taste.

Production. Syrup producers begin to collect sap from maple trees in late winter or early spring. The nights are cold during the *sapping* season, which lasts only a few weeks, but the days are warmer. This daily rise and fall in temperature starts the sap flowing.

Syrup producers use one of two methods to collect the sap from the trees. In the older method, a producer

Leading Maple Syrup Producing States and Provinces

Maple syrup produced in 1979

Quebec	🍁🍁🍁🍁🍁🍁🍁🍁🍁🍁🍁🍁🍁🍁🍁🍁🍁🍁🍁🍁 2,578,000 gallons (9,758,800 liters)
Vermont	🍁🍁🍁🍁 465,000 gallons (1,760,000 liters)
New York	🍁🍁🍁 315,000 gallons (1,192,000 liters)
Ontario	🍁🍁 217,000 gallons (821,400 liters)
Wisconsin	🍁 92,000 gallons (348,000 liters)
Ohio	🍁 90,000 gallons (340,000 liters)

Includes maple syrup later made into maple sugar and maple taffy.
Sources: U.S. Department of Agriculture; Statistics Canada.

drills one or more holes into a tree and drives a metal spout into each hole. The sap runs through the spout into a bucket that hangs from the spout. After all the buckets are filled, the producer empties their contents into a large bucket, which is taken by sled or wagon to a building called a *sugarhouse*.

In the more modern method, a producer inserts plastic spouts into holes drilled in the trees. The sap runs through tubes connected to the spouts and into a pipeline system that carries the sap to the sugarhouse. A properly managed pipeline system yields more sap than the bucket method, and it requires less time and labor.

After the sap reaches the sugarhouse, it is boiled in a long, shallow pan called an *evaporator*. The color and flavor develop during this process, and most of the water in the sap evaporates. Pure maple syrup remains. Some producers let part of the sap boil beyond the syrup stage until it becomes maple sugar. Then they hold *sugaring off* gatherings at which people sample both products.

History. Indians who lived near the Great Lakes and the St. Lawrence River produced maple sugar and syrup long before white explorers came to North Amer-

Ivan Massar, Black Star

James W. Marvin

Maple Syrup comes from the sap of certain maple trees, chiefly the sugar maple. Syrup producers collect the sap in buckets, *left*, or use a system of plastic pipelines, *above*. The pipelines run into a *sugarhouse*, where the syrup is made.

Constantine Manos, Magnum

In the Sugarhouse, the maple sap is boiled. This process turns the sap into thick syrup, which is collected in buckets, *above.*

ica. Early French and English explorers wrote of the "sweet water" that the Indians drew from trees and heated to make the maple products.

During the 1700's and 1800's, maple sugar ranked as an important food item. People in maple sugar-producing areas traded it for various foods and services. Gradually, white cane sugar became less expensive than maple sugar. By the late 1800's, cane sugar had replaced maple sugar for most purposes. At about that time, food manufacturers developed the blend of maple syrup and other syrups that became "maple" syrup.

Today, some food companies use artificial maple flavorings in certain foods. But these flavorings taste somewhat different from real maple syrup.   JAMES W. MARVIN

See also MAPLE (The Sugar Maple).

MAPUTO (pop. 354,684; met. area pop. 750,000), is the capital and largest city of Mozambique. It has an excellent harbor and is the chief port of Mozambique and several nearby countries. It lies on Delagoa Bay in southern Mozambique (see MOZAMBIQUE [map]).

The Portuguese founded the city about 1780 and named it Lourenço Marques. The city became the major white settlement in Mozambique, but most of the whites left in 1975 after Mozambique gained independence from Portugal. In 1976, the city's name was changed to Maputo.

The main sections of Maputo have wide, tree-lined streets and large beaches. The fortress of Nossa Senhora da Conceição, built in 1871, is a famous landmark. The city's major industries include cement-making, food processing, and tourism.   LEWIS HENRY GANN

MAQUIS, *MAH kees,* were French patriots who formed a secret army to fight German occupation forces in France during World War II. *Maquis* is a French word for the tough, scrubby vegetation of the Mediterranean Coast. People from all classes joined the Maquis to support the Free French, and to escape from being forced into German labor camps. The Maquis conducted intelligence and small-scale operations, blowing up trains, and sabotaging military production. Members lived in hiding in the mountains of southern and eastern France. The Allies parachuted supplies to them. When the war ended, the French government publicly thanked the Maquis for their services.   STEFAN T. POSSONY

MARA. See CAVY.

Jen and Des Bartlett, Bruce Coleman Inc.

Marabou Storks have a long, wedge-shaped bill and a nearly bald head. They eat small prey and frequently feed on the remains of large, dead animals. Marabous live in Africa and Asia.

MARABOU, *MAR uh boo,* is a stork that has beautiful white feathers. Manufacturers once used marabou feathers to make scarves, and to trim hats and gowns. Marabous live in Africa and Asia. The best-known marabou lives in Africa. It is a large bird with slate-gray wings, a white underside, and an almost bare head and neck. The male has a large pouch beneath its bill. Marabous eat birds, small mammals, and lizards, and are also useful as scavengers.

Scientific Classification. Marabous belong to the stork family, *Ciconiidae.* The African marabou is genus *Leptoptilus,* species *L. crumeniferus.*   GEORGE E. HUDSON

MARACAIBO, *MAR uh KY boh* (pop. 845,000), is Venezuela's chief coffee-exporting port and second largest city. The discovery of petroleum in 1912 made Maracaibo one of the world's great oil cities, and a thriving metropolis. Maracaibo lies on the west shore of the narrows that connect the Gulf of Venezuela with Lake Maracaibo (see VENEZUELA [political map]). The city has a good harbor. A bridge 5½ miles (8.9 kilometers) long across the lake connects Maracaibo with the mainland. The University of Zulia is located there. Maracaibo was founded in 1529.

MARACAIBO, LAKE. See LAKE MARACAIBO.

MARACAS. See VENEZUELA (Recreation).

MARAJÓ, *MAH rah ZHOH,* is a large island that belongs to Brazil. It covers 15,444 square miles (40,000 square kilometers) between the estuaries of the Amazon and Pará rivers in northeastern South America. For location, see BRAZIL (physical map). About 160,000 people live on the island.

Marajó is a plain just above sea level. Most of it is flooded during the six-month rainy season. During the dry season, the vast grasslands that cover most of the island make good pasture. Forests fringe the shores and banks of waterways. Some rubber trees are scattered through these forests. Wandering herders and rubber hunters visit Marajó in the dry season.   H. F. RAUP

MARAÑÓN RIVER. See AMAZON RIVER.

MARASCHINO CHERRIES, *MAR uh SKEE noh,* are preserved cherries used to decorate and add flavor to desserts and beverages. The cherries received their name because they were originally preserved in *maraschino,* a liqueur distilled from the fermented juice of the marasca cherry. Today, the cherries are artificially colored, flavored, and preserved. Several varieties of cherries are used. They are picked before they have fully ripened, and are pitted by a machine.   RICHARD A. HAVENS

MARAT, *mah RAH,* **JEAN PAUL** (1743-1793), was one of the most radical leaders of the French Revolution. He helped increase the violence of the period by demanding death for all opponents of the Revolution.

Marat was born in Boudry, Switzerland, near Neuchâtel. He became a physician and a writer. During the 1770's and 1780's, Marat wrote books on electricity, heat, light, and physiology, as well as on law and political theory. The French Academy of Sciences rejected Marat's chief ideas, and Marat believed that officials of the academy had cooperated to keep him from winning the recognition he deserved.

Portrait by Joseph Boze, Musee Carnavalet, Paris (Bulloz)
Jean Paul Marat

Marat strongly supported the French Revolution, which began in 1789. He believed it would improve conditions for the common people, especially the poor. To spread his views, Marat founded a newspaper called *L'Ami du Peuple* (The Friend of the People). The newspaper violently criticized those who opposed the Revolution.

In August 1792, the Legislative Assembly, France's national legislature, imprisoned King Louis XVI and many of his followers. Marat called for death for those who continued to support the king. Indirectly, he contributed to the violent mood of the public that led to the massacres in Paris in September. That month, bands of revolutionaries broke into the city's prisons and killed over 1,000 prisoners, including priests and aristocratic supporters of the king.

Later in September, Marat was elected to the National Convention, a body that was writing a new constitution for France. He joined a group called the *Jacobins,* who demanded the king's execution. Marat soon became the main target of moderate members of the convention, known as *Girondists.* They accused Marat of plotting against them and brought him to trial. He was acquitted and, in turn, called for the expulsion of Girondist leaders from the convention. They were expelled and then arrested in June 1793. The next month, Marat was stabbed to death in his home by Charlotte Corday, a young aristocrat who supported the Girondists (see CORDAY, CHARLOTTE).   ISSER WOLOCH

See also FRENCH REVOLUTION.

MARATHON, *MAIR uh thahn,* is a plain in Greece on which one of the decisive battles of history was fought. The plain is about 25 miles (40 kilometers) northeast of Athens. There the Athenians and their allies, the Plataeans, defeated the army of King Darius of Persia in 490 B.C.

Darius controlled Asia Minor, which included Greek cities in Ionia (western Asia Minor). The Ionians revolted against Persia in 499 B.C., and the other Greeks came to their aid. Darius decided to punish the Greeks for aiding the Ionians. He gathered a powerful army and a great fleet and sent them to Greece under two generals, Datis and Artaphernes. The Persians captured the island of Euboea and set up a base there. From this point the Persian army landed on the mainland of Greece and the fleet anchored near the Persian camp. The Greeks watched the Persians from the surrounding hills. After a few days, part of the Persian force, including the cavalry, set sail for the Bay of Phalerum. This force planned to attack Athens from the southwest. The main Persian force of about 20,000 men remained facing the Greeks on the plain of Marathon.

The Greeks had a force of 10,000 Athenians and 1,000 Plataeans. They sent Pheidippides, their swiftest runner, to bring help from Sparta—about 150 miles (241 kilometers) away. But the Spartan army was delayed because of religious observances and did not arrive until after the battle. The Athenian general Miltiades attacked the Persians with a running charge. The Persian bowmen fired a great shower of arrows, but the speed and heavy armor of the Greeks enabled them to reach the Persians with small losses. When the two armies came to grips, the superior weapons and bodily strength of the Greeks were decisive. The Greeks drove the Persians to their ships. The Persians lost 6,400 men, but the Athenians lost only 192. The Greek dead were buried under a mound of earth which may still be seen on the battlefield at Marathon.

As the fleet sailed away, Miltiades feared that the ships would attack Athens by sea. He was afraid that the city might surrender without knowing of the victory at Marathon. According to legend, he sent Pheidippides to carry news of the victory to Athens. Pheidippides, weary from his record journey to Sparta and back, raced the 25 miles (40 kilometers) to Athens. He reached the city and gasped out, "Rejoice, we conquer," then fell to the ground, dead.

The word *marathon* is now often used to refer to a foot race of 26 miles 385 yards (42.2 kilometers). This foot race is one of the sporting events at Olympic Games today (see OLYMPIC GAMES). *Marathon* also refers to any other long-distance race.   RICHARD NELSON FRYE

MARBLE, *MAHR buhl,* is any limestone that is hard enough to take polish. It is used for buildings, interiors, and statues. The finest marble is white, and is called statuary marble. All marble is composed of crystals of the minerals *calcite* or *dolomite,* which when pure are perfectly white. Colored marbles result from the presence of other minerals or small amounts of staining matter mixed with the calcite or dolomite. Black, gray, pink, reddish, greenish, and many kinds of mottled and banded marbles are used in the designs of buildings and in monuments. The color of red marble is due to tiny particles of hematite between calcite or dolomite crystals. *Serpentine* marbles are principally green and

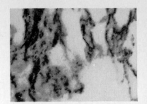

Pavanazzo Marble

Moore & Co., Carthage Marble Corp.

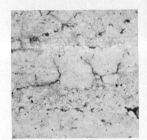

Travertine Marble

Marble Walls give a striking, elegant look to the interior of buildings. Marble is also often used for table tops, *left.*

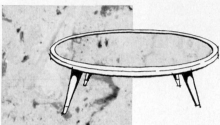

Italian Pearl Beige Marble

Florentine Gray Marble

yellowish-green silicates. *Fossiliferous* marbles are limestones which are full of fossil shells. On polished surfaces of such marbles, the cross sections of the shells can be seen through the rock.

Its Qualities. Marble, in the geological sense, is limestone that has been *metamorphosed* (changed) through the action of heat far below the earth's surface. Ordinary limestone is made up of fragments of shells or irregular grains of calcium carbonate. But in marble the limestone has been changed to a mass of crystals grown firmly together. Metamorphism has made marble more uniform in hardness and grain throughout, so that it can be carved better than ordinary limestone. Metamorphism has also made marble harder, and has freed it from small cavities and pores. As a result, marble takes a higher polish, and sculptors and architects prefer to work with it.

Ancient peoples made their finest buildings of either granite or marble. The Egyptians worked chiefly with granite. The Greeks were skillful in carving and design, and found marble more suited to their needs. Their temples and arcades at Athens and Corinth stand as monuments to their skill and the materials used. The ancient Greeks used Pentelic marble from Mount Pentelicus, north of Athens, for their finest work. The Parthenon, which stands on the Acropolis at Athens, is built of Pentelic marble. The Romans copied the forms of Greek sculpture and architecture, and also used marble with great skill.

The most famous quarries for any stone are the marble quarries at Carrara, Italy. Stone from them was used in Rome at the time of the Emperor Augustus. The finest varieties were discovered much later and were made famous by the great sculptor Michelangelo.

In the United States, marble has been used for memorials since colonial days. Marble headstones for soldiers who fell in the Revolutionary War have lasted longer than most other kinds. This stone has been a favorite in architecture from the time of the Erie Customhouse, erected in 1836, to the impressive building of the Supreme Court of the United States in Washington, D.C., completed in 1935.

Today, marble and granite are used less as building stone. Steel, aluminum, concrete, and artificial stone replace marble and granite in many large present-day buildings. White marble has lost much of its popularity, but colored or textured varieties are still in considerable demand.

The largest American marble quarry is in Vermont. This state has often led in marble production. Other important marble producing states are Alabama, Georgia, Montana, and Tennessee. One of the largest blocks of marble ever quarried came from Vermont. It weighed 93 short tons (84 metric tons). It was used for *The Covered Wagon,* a carving on the Oregon Capitol in Salem, Ore. (see OREGON [picture]).   ERNEST E. WAHLSTROM

Related Articles in WORLD BOOK include:

Building Stone	Limestone	Quarrying
Carbonate	Metamorphism	Sculpture
Dolomite	Onyx	Vermont (picture)

MARBLE, ALICE. See TENNIS (tables).
MARBLE BONES. See OSTEOSCLEROSIS.

MARBLES

MARBLES is a children's game played with little balls of many colors. It is a very old game. Egyptian and Roman children played with marbles before Christ was born. In the United States, the neighborhood marbles game is a sign of spring. The game is so popular that many cities and states have marble tournaments.

How to Play Marbles. Most American children play a game called *ringer*. Two to six children can play. A circle 10 feet (3 meters) across is marked on the ground. When two or more are playing, 13 marbles are placed on a cross marked at the center of the ring. Two lines, each about 9 inches (23 centimeters) long, form the cross. One marble is placed at the center and three each on the four parts of the cross. Each marble lies about 3 inches (8 centimeters) from the next one. Each player uses a larger marble, the shooter, to knock, or "shoot," the small marbles out of the ring. Some boys and girls call their shooters *taws*, *glassies*, or *monnies*. The marbles in the ring, or object marbles, are called *mibs*, *miggs*, *ducks*, *commies*, or *hoodles*. The player who shoots the most marbles out of the ring wins the game.

Players start the first game by *lagging* for turns. They toss or shoot their shooters from a *pitch line* drawn outside the circle, with its center touching the circle. On

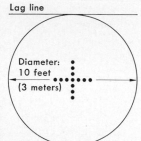

Lag line

Diameter: 10 feet (3 meters)

Pitch line

Marble Players often play a game called *ringer, left.* The game is played in a ring 10 feet (3 meters) in diameter, *above.* The player who shoots the most marbles out of the ring wins the game. Most marbles are made of colored glass, but they differ in color and design, *below.*

IMMY   MOONSTONE   RAINBOW   MARINE   CAT'S EYE

GENUINE CARNELIAN   FIRST AMERICAN   JAPANESE CAT'S EYE   SCRAP GLASS   PEPPERMINT STRIPE

TERMS USED WHEN TALKING ABOUT MARBLES

Bowling occurs when a player rolls a shot on the ground.

Edgers are marbles near the edge of the ring.

For Fair means playing for the fun of the game. After each game, the marbles are returned to their owners.

For Keeps occurs when each player keeps the marbles that he shoots out of the ring.

Histing occurs when a player raises his hand from the ground when shooting.

Hit occurs when a player knocks a marble out of the ring on a shot.

Hunching occurs when a player moves his hand forward across the ring line when shooting from the ring line, or when his hand advances from the spot where the shooter stopped, when shooting inside the ring.

Knuckling Down is a position in which one knuckle must touch the ground until the shooter has left the hand.

Lofting, a difficult shot, occurs when a player shoots in an arc through the air to hit a marble.

Marbles are the object marbles only. They can also be called *mibs*, *miggs*, *ducks*, *commies*, or *hoodles*.

Miss occurs when a player fails to knock a marble from the ring on a shot.

Roundsters, or *circling*, is the act of selecting the best location outside the ring for knuckling down.

Shooter is the attacking marble. It also can be called a *taw*, a *glassy*, or a *monny*.

Shot is the act of snapping the shooter at a marble by a quick extension of the thumb.

the opposite side of the circle, also with its center touching the circle, is a *lag line*. The player whose shooter comes closest to the lag line plays first, and others follow in order of the nearness of their shooters to the line. In the games that follow, the winner of the game before plays first, and all other players lag for their shooting turn.

All shots except the lag are made in a position called *knuckling down*. One knuckle of the hand must touch the ground until the shooter marble has left the hand. *Histing* (raising the hand from the ground) and *hunching* (moving the hand forward) are forbidden. The player holds the shooter between his forefinger and thumb, and shoots it out with his thumb.

A player starts his turn from any spot outside of the ring. If he knocks an object marble out of the ring, he may shoot again from the spot where the shooter has come to rest. If the shooter also leaves the ring, the player takes *roundsters*. That is, he may shoot from any position on, or outside of, the ring line. In case the shooter slips from the player's hand and does not move more than 10 inches (25 centimeters), the player calls "slips." He may then shoot again. Each player's turn continues until he misses the marbles with his shooter. He then picks up his shooter and waits for his next turn. He starts every new turn by taking roundsters.

The player who first shoots seven marbles out of the ring wins. When the seventh marble is shot from the ring, the shooter marble must also leave the ring. If it does not, the object marble is put back on the cross lines for the next player. Histing, hunching, smoothing the ground, or removing pebbles and other obstacles are penalized by loss of one shot.

Any player who changes shooters during the game must leave the game. Any player who walks across the ring must give up one of the marbles he has won. A player who talks with a coach during play gives up all the marbles he has won up to that point. Marbles given up are put back on the cross lines. In case of a tie score, the winners play another game. Some players like to play marbles *for keeps*. Each keeps the marbles he shoots from the ring. But often the game is played *for fair*, and the marbles are returned to their owner.

Composition of Marbles. The ordinary marble is made of glass. A pigment is often inserted to color the marbles. Most of these marbles come from West Virginia, where a plant in Clarksburg manufactures millions every year. *Aggies*, marbles made of agate, a fine-grained variety of quartz, are made in Idar-Oberstein, Germany. Germany also supplies marbles made from limestone. At one time, many marbles in the United States were made of painted and glazed clay. Many people collect marbles.   CARL A. TROESTER, JR.

MARBURY V. MADISON marked the first time the U.S. Supreme Court declared a federal law unconstitutional. This 1803 case is one of the most important decisions in history. It established the supremacy of the Constitution over laws passed by Congress and the right of the court to review the constitutionality of legislation.

In 1801, President John Adams appointed William Marbury justice of the peace in the District of Columbia. But Adams' term ended before Marbury took office, and James Madison, the new secretary of state, withheld the appointment. Marbury asked the Supreme Court, under Section 13 of the Judiciary Act of 1789, to force Madison to grant the appointment. But the court refused to rule on the appointment because Section 13 gave the Supreme Court powers not provided by the Constitution and, therefore, the court declared Section 13 unconstitutional.   STANLEY I. KUTLER

See also JEFFERSON, THOMAS (The Courts).

MARCEL. See HAIRDRESSING.

MARCEL, GABRIEL (1889-1973), was a French philosopher. He was an unsystematic thinker who presented his philosophy for the most part in three philosophical diaries: *Metaphysical Journals* (1927), *Being and Having* (1935), and *Presence and Immortality* (1959). His philosophy consists of reflections on concrete human experiences such as love and fidelity. He believed that human experience can be understood only by directly participating in it. Therefore, he attempted not merely to observe, but to relive these experiences in the course of his reflections. Marcel's other works include *Homo Viator* (1944), an analysis of hope; and *Man Against Society* (1951), an examination of the effects of a technological society on the human personality.

Marcel was born in Paris. He became a Roman Catholic at 39. He is often classified as a Christian existentialist (see EXISTENTIALISM).   IVAN SOLL

MARCELLUS is the name of two popes of the Roman Catholic Church whose reigns were brief.

Saint Marcellus I governed the church in 308 and 309. Little is known about his life, except that he divided the parishes of Rome into seven regions, each with its own burial places.

Marcellus II (1501-1555) governed the church until he died, 22 days after his election. As a cardinal, he served as one of the reform leaders in the court of Pope Paul III, who ruled from 1534 to 1549. He was one of Paul's three legates to the first session of the Council of Trent in 1545. Marcellus pledged himself to reconvene the Council of Trent to finish its work of reform and definition of doctrine, but he died before this could be done.   THOMAS P. NEILL AND FULTON J. SHEEN

MARCH is a highly rhythmic piece of music first used by military bands to accompany marching. The march usually has one dominant tune repeated over and over with other tunes coming in between. The tempo of military marches varies with the occasion. In the U.S. Army, soldiers march about 120 steps a minute. This march is called *quick time*. A *double-time* march is about 180 steps a minute. In the British Army, soldiers march about 75 steps a minute to a slow march, and about 108 steps a minute to a quick march. People often call a quick march *quickstep*.

One of the most famous composers of march music was John Philip Sousa. His works include "The Stars and Stripes Forever," "The Washington Post," and "Semper Fidelis." Sir Edward Elgar wrote the well-known *Pomp and Circumstance*, a set of five military marches.

Composers have used the march as an art form in operas and oratorios. Famous marches occur in Verdi's opera *Aïda* and Mozart's *The Marriage of Figaro*. The march from Handel's *Scipio* became the parade march of the British Grenadier Guards.

See also BAND; ELGAR, SIR EDWARD; SOUSA, JOHN P.

MARCH

MARCH is the third month of the year. It was the first month on the ancient Roman calendar, and was called *Martius*. When Julius Caesar revised the calendar, he established January 1 as the beginning of the year. March then became the third month. March has always had 31 days. Its name honors Mars, the Roman god of war.

March brings in spring and ends the winter. Spring in the northern half of the world begins with the *vernal equinox*, which occurs on March 20 or 21. On this day, the center of the sun is directly over the equator. March can be both wintry and springlike. Blustery, windy days occur as frequently as mild, sunny days.

In the Northern Hemisphere, many animals and plants awaken, or come to life again, during March. Sap flows in the trees, and green buds begin to appear. The first pussy willows and wild flowers can be found in the woods. Most frogs lay their eggs. Hibernating animals, such as bears, chipmunks, and woodchucks, leave their winter sleeping places. Wild geese and ducks begin their northward flights. In March, people begin to look for the first robin as a sign that spring has really come. Early songbirds appear.

Special Days. March has no national holidays, but there are several important state and religious holidays. Nebraskans celebrate the admission of their state to the Union on March 1. Texas celebrates March 2 as the anniversary of its independence from Mexico. On March 4, the people of Pennsylvania commemorate the anniversary of Penn's Charter. The Irish celebrate March 17 as the feast day of St. Patrick. In Maryland, March 25 is set apart for a celebration of the arrival of the first Maryland colonists in 1634. The Jewish festival of Purim usually occurs in March. It is held on the day corresponding to the 14th day of Adar on the Hebrew calendar.

IMPORTANT MARCH EVENTS

1 Ohio became the 17th state, 1803.
—William Dean Howells, American novelist, born 1837.
—Augustus Saint-Gaudens, American sculptor, born 1848.
—Nebraska became the 37th state, 1867.
2 De Witt Clinton, American statesman, born 1769.
—Sam Houston, American political leader, born 1793.
—Bedřich Smetana, Bohemian composer, born 1824.
—Carl Schurz, American political leader, born 1829.
—Texas declared its independence from Mexico, 1836.
—Pope Pius XII born 1876.
—Kurt Weill, German composer, born 1900.
3 Missouri Compromise passed, 1820.
—George Pullman, American inventor and businessman, born 1831.
—Florida became the 27th state, 1845.
—Inventor Alexander Graham Bell born 1847.
—Russia signed the Treaty of Brest-Litovsk, 1918.
4 William Penn received grant of Pennsylvania, 1681.
—The new United States Constitution went into effect, 1789. This date was used as Inauguration Day until 1937.
—Vermont became the 14th state, 1791.
—Knute Rockne, American football coach, born 1888.
5 Gerhardus Mercator, Flemish geographer, born 1512.
—British soldiers fired on a mob in the Boston Massacre, 1770.
—James Ives, American painter and lithographer, born 1824.
—Howard Pyle, American author and illustrator, born 1853.
—Heitor Villa-Lobos, Brazilian composer, born 1887.
—The Hall of Fame was founded, 1900.
—Joseph Stalin, Russian dictator, died 1953.
6 Michelangelo, the most famous artist of the Italian Renaissance, born 1475.
—Elizabeth Barrett Browning, English poet, born 1806.
—Philip H. Sheridan, Union cavalry general, born 1831.
—Santa Anna captured the Alamo, 1836.
—Ring Lardner, American humorist, born 1885.
7 Sir John Herschel, English astronomer, born 1792.
—Luther Burbank, American horticulturist, born 1849.
—Tomáš Masaryk, Czechoslovak statesman, born 1850.
—Maurice Ravel, French composer, born 1875.
—Alexander Graham Bell patented the telephone, 1876.
8 Jurist Oliver Wendell Holmes, Jr., born 1841.
—Frederick Goudy, American type designer, born 1865.
9 Amerigo Vespucci, Italian explorer, born 1454.
—Leland Stanford, American business leader, born 1824.

9 The *Merrimack* fought the *Monitor*, 1862.
—Ulysses S. Grant commissioned as commander-in-chief of the Union armies, 1864.
—Samuel Barber, American composer, born 1910.
10 Barry Fitzgerald, Irish-born actor, born 1888.
—Arthur Honegger, French composer, born 1892.
12 Canadian politician William Mackenzie born 1795.
—Sir John J. C. Abbott, prime minister of Canada, born 1821.
—Clement Studebaker, American manufacturer, born 1831.
—Adolph S. Ochs, American newspaper publisher, born 1858.
—Gabriele d'Annunzio, Italian poet, born 1863.
—Juliette Low founded the Girl Scout movement in America, 1912.
—First transatlantic radio broadcast, 1925.
—President Harry S. Truman announced the Truman Doctrine, 1947.
13 Joseph Priestley, English chemist, born 1733.
—Johann Wyss, Swiss author, born 1781.
14 Eli Whitney patented the cotton gin, 1794.
—Johann Strauss, Austrian composer, born 1804.
—Paul Ehrlich, German biochemist, born 1854.
—Albert Einstein, German-born scientist, born 1879.
15 Julius Caesar assassinated, 44 B.C.
—Andrew Jackson, seventh President of the United States, born in Waxhaw settlement, Lancaster County, S.C., 1767.
—Maine became the 23rd state, 1820.
—American Legion founded, 1919.
16 James Madison, fourth President of the United States, born at Port Conway, King George County, Va., 1751.
—Georg S. Ohm, German physicist, born 1787.
—United States Military Academy founded at West Point, N.Y., 1802.
16-17 Ferdinand Magellan reached the Philippines, 1521.

JACKSON   MADISON   CLEVELAND

Popular Beliefs. There are many superstitions about March. We often hear that "March comes in like a lion and goes out like a lamb." This means that the first day of March is often stormy, and the last day is mild and warm. Another saying is, "April borrowed from March three days, and they were ill." This refers to the first three days of April, which are generally rough and blustery like March. A third saying calls the first three days of March "blind days" because they are "unlucky." If rain falls on these days, farmers supposedly will have poor harvests. Some farmers are so superstitious about the three "unlucky" days that they will not plant seed until March 4.

March Symbols. The flower for March is the violet. The birthstones are the bloodstone (a variety of chalcedony) and the aquamarine. GRACE HUMPHREY

Related Articles in WORLD BOOK include:

Aquamarine	Chalcedony	Mars	St. Patrick's	Spring
Calendar	Equinox	Purim	Day	Violet

Quotations

The stormy March has come at last,
With wind, and cloud, and changing skies;
I hear the rushing of the blast
That through the snowy valley flies.
William Cullen Bryant

I wonder if the sap is stirring yet,
If wintry birds are dreaming of a mate,
If frozen snowdrops feel as yet the sun,
And crocus fires are kindling one by one.
Christina Rossetti

And the Spring arose on the garden fair,
Like the Spirit of Love felt everywhere;
And each flower and herb on Earth's dark breast
Rose from the dreams of its wintry rest.
Percy B. Shelley

The year's at the spring
And day's at the morn; . . .
God's in His heaven—
All's right with the world!
Robert Browning

—————— IMPORTANT MARCH EVENTS ——————

17 St. Patrick's Day.
—British evacuated Boston, 1776.
—Chief Justice Roger B. Taney born 1777.
—Jim Bridger, American frontier scout, born 1804.
—Kate Greenaway, English illustrator, born 1846.
—Bobby Jones, American golf champion, born 1902.

18 John C. Calhoun, American statesman, born 1782.
—Grover Cleveland, 22nd and 24th President of the United States, born in Caldwell, N.J., 1837.
—Nicholas Rimsky-Korsakov, Russian composer, born 1844.
—Rudolf Diesel, German inventor, born 1858.
—British statesman Neville Chamberlain born 1869.

19 Missionary and explorer David Livingstone born 1813.
—Political leader William Jennings Bryan born 1860.
—Ballet producer Sergei Diaghilev born 1872.
—Joseph Stilwell, American general, born 1883.

20 Henrik Ibsen, Norwegian poet and dramatist, born 1828.
—Charles W. Eliot, American educator, born 1834.
—Lauritz Melchior, Danish tenor, born 1890.

21 Johann Sebastian Bach, German composer, born 1685.
—Benito Juárez, Mexican political leader, born 1806.
—Modest Mussorgsky, Russian composer, born 1839.

22 Anton Van Dyck, Flemish painter, born 1599.
—Randolph Caldecott, English illustrator, born 1846.
—Robert Millikan, American physicist, born 1868.
—Arthur Vandenberg, U.S. political leader, born 1884.

23 Patrick Henry declared "Give me liberty, or give me death!" 1775.
—Roger Martin du Gard, French novelist and Nobel prize-winner for literature, born 1881.

24 William Morris, English poet and artist, born 1834.
—Andrew Mellon, American financier, born 1855.
—George Sisler, American baseball player, born 1893.

25 Lord Baltimore's colonists landed in Maryland, 1634.
—British Parliament abolished slave trade, 1807.
—Arturo Toscanini, Italian conductor, born 1867.
—Gutzon Borglum, American sculptor, born 1871.

25 Béla Bartók, Hungarian composer, born 1881.
26 A. E. Housman, English poet, born 1859.
—Robert Frost, American poet, born 1874.
—James Conant, American chemist and educator, born 1893.
—Tennessee Williams, American playwright, born 1911.
27 Louis XVII of France born 1785.
—Lithographer Nathaniel Currier born 1813.
—Wilhelm Roentgen, German physicist who discovered X rays, born 1845.
—Alaska hit by earthquake, 1964.
28 Pierre Laplace, French astronomer and mathematician, born 1749.
—Aristide Briand, French statesman, born 1862.
29 John Tyler, 10th President of the United States, born at Greenway Estate, Charles City County, Va., 1790.
—Parliament passed the British North America Act, 1867.
—Cy Young, American baseball player, born 1867.

TYLER

30 Francisco Goya, Spanish painter, born 1746.
—Treaty of Paris ended the Crimean War, 1856.
—United States purchased Alaska from Russia, 1867.
—Amendment 15 to the U.S. Constitution, stating that a person cannot be denied the ballot because of race or color, proclaimed, 1870.
—Jo Davidson, American sculptor, born 1883.
—Albert Einstein announced revised Unified Field Theory, 1953.
31 René Descartes, French philosopher-scientist, born 1596.
—Joseph Haydn, Austrian composer, born 1732.
—Edward FitzGerald, English translator of the *Rubáiyát* of Omar Khayyám, born 1809.
—Commodore Matthew C. Perry made the first treaty between the United States and Japan, 1854.
—Jack Johnson, American boxer, born 1878.
—United States took possession of the Virgin Islands by purchase from Denmark, 1917.
—Daylight Saving Time went into effect in the United States, 1918.
—Civilian Conservation Corps created, 1933.
—Newfoundland became the 10th province of Canada, 1949.

MARCH, PEYTON CONWAY (1864-1955), was chief of staff of the United States Army during World War I. He directed the operations that landed about 2 million American troops in France. March has been called the father of the modern U.S. Army. He combined the Regular Army, the National Guard, and the National Army divisions into a single force. He also reorganized the War Department, and built a small, well-organized army around a core of professional soldiers. March believed that a small corps of trained officers could build a large, powerful army in time of emergency.

March was born in Easton, Pa. He graduated from the United States Military Academy (West Point) in 1888, and fought in the Spanish-American War. March retired from active service in the Army in 1921. He wrote an account of his World War I experiences, *The Nation at War* (1932).　　　　MAURICE MATLOFF

MARCH HARE. See HARE.

MARCH OF DIMES BIRTH DEFECTS FOUNDATION is a health organization financed by funds gathered in the annual March of Dimes. It works to improve infant and maternal health care and to prevent birth defects by supporting research, treatment, and professional and public education. It also supports the Salk Institute for Biological Studies. The organization was founded by President Franklin D. Roosevelt in 1938 as the National Foundation for Infantile Paralysis. It financed the research that produced the Salk and Sabin vaccines, which help prevent poliomyelitis. In 1958, it changed its name to the National Foundation-March of Dimes. It adopted its present name in 1979. Headquarters are at 1275 Mamaroneck Avenue, White Plains, N.Y. 10605.

Critically reviewed by the MARCH OF DIMES BIRTH DEFECTS FOUNDATION

MARCIANO, ROCKY (1923-1969), was the world heavyweight boxing champion from 1952 to 1956. He retired in 1956 after winning all of his 49 professional fights. Marciano won the title on Sept. 23, 1952, by knocking out Jersey Joe Walcott in the 13th round in Philadelphia. Eight months later, in his first title defense, Marciano knocked out Walcott in the first round. Marciano then successfully defended his title five more times. Marciano is generally considered one of the hardest punchers in boxing history. His victories include 43 knockouts, with 11 coming in the first round. In 1951, he ended the comeback of former world champion Joe Louis by knocking him out in the 8th round.

Marciano was born Rocco Marchegiano in Brockton, Mass. He turned professional in 1948.　　HERMAN WEISKOPF

MARCO POLO. See POLO, MARCO.

MARCONI, *mahr KOH nee,* **GUGLIELMO** (1874-1937), an Italian inventor and electrical engineer, won recognition for his work in developing *wireless telegraphy*, or radio. This led to present-day radio broadcasting. He produced a practical wireless telegraph system in 1895 from basic discoveries that had previously been made in wireless telegraphy (see RADIO [History]). He produced the first transatlantic wireless signal in history on Dec. 12, 1901, and patented the horizontal directional aerial in 1905. He shared the 1909 Nobel prize in physics with Karl Ferdinand Braun for their development of wireless telegraphy. Braun, working independently of Marconi, developed a cathode-ray tube. Marconi invented the beam system of wireless for long-distance communication.

Early Life. Marconi was born on April 25, 1874, in Bologna, Italy. His father was a wealthy Italian, his mother Irish. He grew up as a delicate and studious child. He read widely as a boy, in the excellent scientific library in the Marconi home, and became interested in the study of electromagnetic waves. He was educated by tutors, and later studied at the University of Bologna.

First Experiments. In 1894, Marconi set up apparatus at his father's estate. With this apparatus, he sent and received signals by electrical waves over a longer distance than had ever been done before. But the Italian government took no interest in the early stages of his work. Marconi went to England in 1896 to seek capital for a wireless telegraph company. He applied for and received from the British government the first wireless patent, the famous No. 7777. The patent was based in part on the theory that the distance of communication increases rapidly as the height of aerials is increased.

Marconi formed the first wireless company in 1897. The company installed wireless sets in lighthouses along the English coast. In March, 1899, Marconi sent the

Guglielmo Marconi centered his life around wireless telegraphy. He outfitted his yacht, the *Elettra*, with a complete wireless laboratory. He experimented in this "floating laboratory," sending and receiving messages while crossing the Atlantic.

first wireless telegraph message across the English Channel, a distance of 85 miles (137 kilometers).

The value of the wireless for emergencies at sea was shown on April 28, 1899. Heavy seas had pounded the Goodwin Sands lightship off the English coast, and parts of the deckhouses had been swept away. The vessel communicated with a nearby station by wireless, and help arrived at the ship in time to prevent loss of life.

The First Transatlantic Signal. Marconi decided to try to send signals across the Atlantic in 1901. He built a sending station at Poldhu, Cornwall, England. He sailed to Newfoundland and set up receiving equipment at St. John's. The first signal sent, the letter "S," came through as scheduled, though exceedingly faint, on Dec. 12, 1901. See KITE (Other Uses).

Marconi showed the next year that wireless signals can be received over greater distances at night than in the day. While aboard the steamship *Philadelphia* bound for the United States, Marconi received signals sent from a distance of 2,099 miles (3,378 kilometers).

Marconi lost his right eye in an automobile accident in 1912. But he continued to work. He volunteered for active service when Italy entered World War I, and became commander of the Italian wireless service. He began experimenting with very short waves while he was in the wireless service. Marconi's work brought him honors from governments throughout the world. The Italian government made him a senator of the kingdom of Italy for life in 1909. He received the hereditary title of *marchese* (marquess) in 1929.   W. RUPERT MACLAURIN

MARCOS, FERDINAND EDRALIN (1917-   ), became president of the Philippines in 1965. In 1969, he became the first president to be re-elected. In 1973, the Philippines adopted a new constitution that gave Marcos broad powers as both president and prime minister for an unlimited term. In 1978, Marcos took the title of prime minister while remaining as president.

Marcos was born in Sarrat. While a law student at the University of the Philippines, Marcos was accused, tried, and convicted of murdering a man who had defeated his father in a local election. But he was acquitted by the Supreme Court. During World War II, Marcos fought with Filipino-American forces. The United States awarded him the Distinguished Service Cross and the Silver Star. Marcos served in the Philippine House of Representatives from 1949 to 1959. He was elected to the Senate in 1959 and later became president of the Senate.   JEAN GROSSHOLTZ

See also PHILIPPINES (Recent Developments; picture).

MARCUS AURELIUS, *aw REE lih us* (A.D. 121-180), was a Roman emperor devoted to Stoic philosophy. He defended the empire against the first heavy barbarian attacks from outside. He is perhaps the best known of all the Roman emperors because of his *Meditations*, a diary of philosophical reflections. The *Meditations* contain Marcus' own rules for living and for accepting the difficulties of life. They are considered among the most readable of all Stoic writings.

Marcus was born in Rome to a noble family. He was adopted by Antoninus Pius, who later became emperor. Marcus succeeded Antoninus in 161. Marcus' soldiers won victories in Parthia, but they brought a plague back to Rome that spread across the empire. At the height of the plague, barbarian tribes overran the northern frontiers. Marcus spent most of his later years fighting barbarians along the Danube and Rhine rivers. He died in Vienna.   RAMSAY MACMULLEN

MARCY, WILLIAM L. See JACKSON, ANDREW (The Spoils System); PIERCE, FRANKLIN (table: Vice-President and Cabinet); POLK, JAMES KNOX (table: Vice-President and Cabinet).

MARDI GRAS, *MAHR dee GRAH*, is a gay, colorful celebration held on Shrove Tuesday, the day before Lent begins. The date of Mardi Gras depends on the date of Easter. The celebration takes place at the end of a long carnival season that begins on January 6, or Twelfth Night. It is celebrated in many Roman Catholic countries and other communities. *Mardi Gras* is a French term meaning *fat Tuesday*. The term arose from the custom of parading a fat ox through the streets of Paris on Shrove Tuesday.

French colonists introduced Mardi Gras into America in 1766. The custom became popular in New Orleans, La., and spread throughout the Southern States. Mardi Gras is a legal holiday in Alabama, Florida, and in eight *parishes* (counties) of Louisiana. The New Orleans celebration is the most famous. But Biloxi, Miss., and Mobile, Ala., also celebrate Mardi Gras.

Mardi Gras in New Orleans attracts tourists from everywhere. Street parades begin about two weeks before Mardi Gras Day. Societies called *krewes* organize and pay for the parades and other festivities. The best-known krewes are Comus, the oldest, founded in 1857, and Rex, founded in 1872. During the carnival season, the krewes give balls and private parties. Their members parade in the streets in masks and fancy dress. A parade of beautiful floats and marching bands climaxes the carnival on Tuesday, Mardi Gras Day. Each year, the festivities carry out a specific theme.

Rex, King of Carnival, reigns for the day. He is the only one who parades unmasked. When his parade passes the reviewing stand, the King and Queen of Carnival exchange toasts in front of it. After the parade, the krewes hold fancy-dress balls. Rex and Comus, god of mirth, preside over the two grandest balls.

The Mardi Gras celebration goes back to an ancient Roman custom of merrymaking before a period of fast. In Germany it is called *Fastnacht*, and in England it is called *Pancake Day*.   ELIZABETH HOUGH SECHRIST

See also LOUISIANA (picture); SHROVE TUESDAY.

MARDONIUS. See XERXES (I).

MARDUK, *MAHR dook*, was the chief god of the ancient Babylonians. He was originally a god of only the city of Babylon. But when the Dynasty of Babylon came to power in Mesopotamia in about 2000 B.C., Marduk became the most important god of the area. The largest Babylonian temple honored him. Marduk's temple and its buildings covered more than 60 acres (24 hectares). His worshipers called him the "great lord, the lord of heaven and earth." His power was said to lie in his wisdom, which he used to support good people and to punish the wicked.   I. J. GELB

MARE. See HORSE (Life History).

MARE ISLAND lies at the east end of San Pablo Bay, 25 miles (40 kilometers) northeast of San Francisco, Calif. Ferry service connects it with the city of Vallejo, across a strait ½ mile (0.8 kilometer) wide. The Mare Island Naval Shipyard covers most of the island.

MARE ISLAND NAVAL SHIPYARD

MARE ISLAND NAVAL SHIPYARD is the largest and oldest U.S. naval yard on the West Coast. It is in Vallejo, Calif., about 25 miles (40 kilometers) northeast of San Francisco. The 3,315-acre (1,342-hectare) shipyard is part of the 12th Naval District. The shipyard repairs, overhauls, and converts ships of all types, and has the capacity to build new ships. During World War II, it built or repaired 1,598 ships.

The shipyard was established in 1854 as the home port of the 12 ships which at that time made up the entire Pacific Fleet of the U.S. Navy.   JOHN A. OUDINE

MARENGO, BATTLE OF, was the most important battle of Napoleon's second Italian campaign. Although outnumbered, his forces decisively defeated the Austrians at Marengo, near Alessandria, on the Lombardy Plains, on June 14, 1800.

At first, the battle went against the French. Baron Michael von Melas, the Austrian general, felt so sure of victory that he sent a courier to Vienna with news of the triumph. But Napoleon fought stubbornly.

Two generals helped Napoleon save the day for France. Louis Desaix, who was killed during the fighting, brought 5,000 reinforcements. François Étienne Kellermann led a brilliant cavalry charge that proved to be a decisive point in the battle.

Napoleon's troops suffered heavy losses, about 3,500 dead and the same number wounded. Austrian losses totaled about 3,000 prisoners and 7,000 dead or wounded.

The victory gave France undisputed control of Milan, Genoa, and Piedmont. It also made Napoleon a popular hero in France.   ROBERT B. HOLTMAN

See also NAPOLEON I (Wars Against Austria).

MARGARINE, or OLEOMARGARINE, is a butterlike food product made from vegetable oils or animal fats, or both. Many people cook with margarine and use it on bread and other foods. Some bakeries also use it.

In the United States, people use more than twice as much margarine as butter. Margarine usually costs less than butter, and it can be processed so that it has the same food value. Margarine also contains much less of a fatty substance called *cholesterol*. Many doctors warn that too much cholesterol in the blood can lead to a heart attack. As a result, large numbers of people eat margarine and other low-cholesterol foods.

How Margarine Is Made. The U.S. government requires that margarine contain at least 80 per cent fat. The fat must be *emulsified* (evenly distributed) in milk, water, or a type of milk made from soybeans. Manufacturers add *preservatives* to prevent decay. Most margarine also contains butterlike flavoring, salt, vitamins A and D, and yellow coloring.

One or more vegetable oils provide the fat content of most margarine. Soybean oil is by far the most commonly used oil. But processors also may use corn, cottonseed, palm, peanut, and safflower oils. Some margarine is produced with animal fats.

To make margarine, manufacturers emulsify melted oils with milk or water and chill the resulting substance until it hardens. In modern margarine plants, machines produce the product and then shape, wrap, and package it in one continuous operation.

Most household margarine is made in sticks or is packaged in small tubs. Manufacturers also make large blocks of hard margarine for commercial bakeries, and fluid household margarine in plastic squeeze bottles.

History. Hippolyte Mege-Mouries, a French chemist, developed margarine in the late 1860's as a substitute for butter. He called it *oleomargarine* because its chief ingredients were beef fat, called *oleo*, and *margaric acid*. The product was introduced into the United States in the early 1870's. Almost immediately, U.S. dairymen protested that margarine would ruin the butter market. As a result, Congress put a tax on margarine in 1886 to discourage its sale. By the 1930's, many states had banned the sale of yellow-colored margarine. Such margarine was more popular than the natural white variety.

People continued to buy margarine despite the restrictions, and criticism of the federal tax became widespread. Congress ended the tax in 1950. By 1967, all state bans on colored margarine had also ended. Largely because of such actions, margarine sales more than doubled from 1950 to 1970.   THEODORE J. WEISS

MARGAY, *MAHR gay*, is a wildcat that lives in Central and South America from northern Mexico to Bolivia and Brazil. Its reddish or grayish fur is thickly marked with black spots and streaks. Its tail is longer than the head and body. The margay is 2½ to 4 feet (76 to 122 centimeters) long and weighs 10 to 20 pounds

Holisher

The Margay of South America looks much like a domestic cat. This playful-looking margay is still a kitten, but it will soon reach an adult weight of 10 to 20 pounds (4.5 to 9 kilograms).

(4.5 to 9 kilograms). It closely resembles the *ocelot* (tiger cat) but is smaller, more slender, and has a longer tail. The name of the margay may have come from an Indian term for "little ocelot" or "small cat." Zoologists know little about its habits. See also OCELOT.

Scientific Classification. The margay belongs to the cat family, *Felidae*. It is classified as genus *Felis*, species *F. wiedii*.   ERNEST S. BOOTH

MARGHERITA PEAK. See ZAIRE (Land and Climate; map).

MARGIN in a stock exchange refers to funds that speculators deposit with their brokers to protect the brokers against loss. The deposit safeguards the brokers, in case speculators lose money after they have bought stocks. It must cover the difference between the selling price of the stocks and the amount the brokers can borrow from a bank, plus an amount to cover possible losses that might result from stocks quickly changing prices. In the United States, the Federal Reserve System sets the amount of margin required.

MARGINAL LAND. See RENT.

MARGRETE. See DENMARK (A Great Power).

MARGRETHE II, *mahr GRAYT ah* (1940-   ), is queen of Denmark. She succeeded her father, Frederik IX, upon his death in 1972.

Margrethe was born in Copenhagen. Her full name is Margrethe Alexandrine Torhildur Ingrid. In 1953, changes in the Danish constitution made Margrethe next in line for the throne. Until then, only males could rule Denmark. In preparation for her reign, Margrethe attended universities in Denmark, England, and France. She presided over the Danish Cabinet at formal functions when her father was ill.

Steen Jacobsen, Nordisk Pressefoto
Margrethe II

During the 1960's, Margrethe traveled to Africa, the Far East, and the Middle East in connection with her interest in archaeology. In 1967, she married Henri de Laborde de Monpezat, a French count, who became Prince Henrik of Denmark. Margrethe and Henrik have two sons, Frederik, the crown prince, and Joachim.   RAYMOND E. LINDGREN

MARIA. See MOON (The Moon's Surface; Age and History); MARS.

MARIA THERESA (1717-1780) was Holy Roman empress, queen of Hungary and Bohemia, and archduchess of Austria. She was an important figure in the affairs of Europe for 40 troubled years in the 1700's. She ranked as a wise and able ruler. With the aid of her brilliant foreign minister, Prince Kaunitz, she managed foreign affairs skillfully. Her economic reforms promoted the prosperity of her empire. She had 16 children. One daughter, the beautiful and tragic Marie Antoinette, was queen of France (see MARIE ANTOINETTE).

Maria Theresa was born in Vienna. Her father, Emperor Charles VI, was the last male Hapsburg heir. He issued a decree called a Pragmatic Sanction in 1713. By its terms, he made his daughter heir to his territories. The rulers of the principal states of Europe agreed to it, and promised not to attack Maria Theresa's lands (see PRAGMATIC SANCTION).

Charles VI died in 1740. Prussia, Spain, Bavaria, and France immediately attacked in the War of the Austrian Succession. They all claimed parts of Maria Theresa's territories in spite of their earlier promises. Maria Theresa fled to Pressburg, where she made a dramatic appeal to her Hungarian subjects. They rallied loyally to her defense. The war ended in 1748 with the Treaty of Aix-la-Chapelle. By this treaty, Maria Theresa lost the rich province of Silesia to Frederick II of Prussia (see FREDERICK [II] of

Maria Theresa of Austria, portrait by Martin Van Mytens, Brooks Memorial Art Gallery, Memphis, Tenn.
Maria Theresa of Austria

Prussia). The powers of Europe recognized her rights to her other possessions. Her husband, Francis Stephen, Duke of Lorraine, became Emperor as Francis I (see FRANCIS [I], Holy Roman Emperor). But Maria Theresa kept control over most state affairs (see SUCCESSION WARS).

In 1756, while the queen was planning to avenge the loss of Silesia, Frederick II suddenly attacked again. The Seven Years' War followed. After much bloodshed, Maria Theresa was forced to give up all claims to Silesia (see SEVEN YEARS' WAR). Her husband died in 1765, and her eldest son succeeded him as Joseph II. Maria Theresa, however, allowed her son only limited powers at first. In 1772 she joined with Russia and Prussia in the first partition of Poland, taking Galicia and Ludomeria. Then she took Bucovina from Turkey in 1775. She died in Vienna.   ROBERT G. L. WAITE

MARIANA ISLANDS, *MAIR ee AN uh,* are formed by the summits of 15 volcanic mountains in the Pacific. They are the southern part of a submerged mountain range that extends 1,565 miles (2,519 kilometers) from Guam almost to Japan. The Marianas have an area of 396 square miles (1,026 square kilometers) and a population of 121,335. About 107,000 of the people live on Guam. The islands' coastline is 220 miles (354 kilometers) long. For location, see PACIFIC ISLANDS (map).

The 10 northern Marianas are rugged islands. Some of them have volcanoes that erupt periodically. Pagan, Agrihan, and Anatahan are the largest islands in this group. The limestone or reef rock terraces on volcanic slopes in the five southern Marianas show that they are older than the northern group. Guam is the largest of the southern islands. Other important islands are Rota, Saipan, and Tinian. Farmers raise food crops and make *copra* (the dried meat of coconuts). Natural resources include phosphate and manganese ore.

The Portuguese explorer Ferdinand Magellan led the first European expedition to Guam and Rota. His party arrived at the islands in 1521. His sailors called them the *Islas de los Ladrones,* or *Islands of Thieves,* because the islanders helped themselves to articles on the ships after furnishing supplies of food and water. The islands received their present name from Spanish Jesuits who arrived in 1668. Spain governed the islands from 1668 to 1898. After the Spanish-American War, the United States kept Guam as a naval base. Spain sold the rest of the islands to Germany. Japan occupied Guam in 1941, but American armed forces recaptured the island in July, 1944, and built naval air bases on several of the islands. The Mariana Islands, except for Guam, are governed by the United States as part of the United Nations Trust Territory of the Pacific Islands. In 1976, the United States Congress approved an agreement to form the Commonwealth of the Northern Mariana Islands. The commonwealth, expected to be established in 1981, will consist of all the Marianas except Guam.   EDWIN H. BRYAN, JR.

Related Articles in WORLD BOOK include:

Chamorro	Pacific Islands,	Rota	World War II
Guam	Territory of the	Saipan	(Island
	Pagan	Tinian	Hopping)

Trust

MARIANA TRENCH. See PACIFIC OCEAN; DEEP.

MARIE ADELAIDE. See LUXEMBOURG (History).

MARIE ANTOINETTE

MARIE ANTOINETTE, AN twah NET (1755-1793), was the beautiful queen of France who died on the guillotine during the French Revolution. Her frivolity and plotting helped undermine the monarchy and start the revolution.

The young queen was lively, witty, and extravagant. The stiff formalities of court life bored her, so she amused herself with such pleasures as fancy balls, theatricals, horse races, and gambling. Marie lacked a good education and cared very little for serious affairs. She did not hesitate to urge the dismissal of the able ministers of France whose efforts to reduce royal spending threatened her pleasures. Louis XVI gave her the château called the Petit Trianon, where the queen and her friends amused themselves (see VERSAILLES).

Marie became very unpopular, and was blamed for the corruption of the French court. She lavished money on court favorites, and paid no attention to France's financial crisis. False and vicious stories were told about her. It was even rumored that she was a spy for Austria. The haughty attitude people associated with her name is illustrated by a story. She once supposedly asked an official why the Parisians were angry. "Because they have no bread," was the reply. "Then let them eat cake," said the queen. The suffering people of Paris readily believed this false story.

Her Early Life. Marie was born in Vienna. She was the youngest and favorite daughter of Emperor Francis I and Maria Theresa, rulers of the Holy Roman Empire. From childhood, Marie was brought up in the hope that she might one day be queen of France.

Marie Antoinette and Her Children in the Petit Trianon Park (detail) by Ulrich Wertmüller. Nationalmuseum, Stockholm

Marie Antoinette was a teen-ager when she became queen of France in 1774. She was executed less than 20 years later.

She married the French *dauphin* (crown prince) in 1770 at the age of 15. Four years later, he became King Louis XVI, and Marie became queen of France.

The Revolution. Tragedy struck Marie twice in 1789. Her eldest son died, and the French Revolution started. Her weak-willed husband gradually lost control of the nation, but Marie faced danger courageously. She tried to stiffen King Louis' will, but only made people angrier by her stubborn opposition to the revolutionary changes.

The king, partly on her advice, assembled troops around Versailles twice in 1789. Both times violence followed, and royal authority became weaker. The second time, early in October, 1789, a hungry and desperate Parisian mob that included many women marched to Versailles, and forced the royal family to move to the Tuileries palace in Paris. From then on, Louis and Marie were virtual prisoners in Paris.

The rulers might have been able to rally the nation in support of a constitutional monarchy like that of England, had they followed the advice of moderate statesmen like the Comte de Mirabeau (see MIRABEAU, COMTE DE). Instead, Marie Antoinette plotted for military aid from the rulers of Europe, especially from her brother, Leopold II of Austria. She refused to make any concessions at all to the revolutionists.

Downfall of the Monarchy. Finally, Marie influenced Louis to flee from Paris on the night of June 20, 1791. The royal family set out in disguise by carriage for the eastern frontier of France. But an alert patriot recognized the king from his picture on French paper money. The king and queen were halted at Varennes, and returned under guard to Paris. The flight made the people distrust their rulers even more. But Louis promised to accept a new constitution that limited his powers.

Marie now worked to get aid from abroad, and, when war with Austria and Prussia came in 1792, she passed military secrets on to the enemy. The people suspected such treason. On Aug. 10, 1792, they threw their rulers into prison. The king was suspended from office, and the monarchy was ended. Louis XVI died on the guillotine on Jan. 21, 1793. After bravely enduring terrible sufferings, Marie Antoinette, called Widow Capet by the revolutionists, was brought to trial on a charge of treason. She was executed on the guillotine on Oct. 16, 1793.   RAYMOND O. ROCKWOOD

See also FRENCH REVOLUTION; LOUIS (XVI); MARIA THERESA; SWISS GUARDS.

MARIE DE L'INCARNATION. See CANADIAN LITERATURE (Before 1760).

MARIE LOUISE (1791-1847) was the second wife of Napoleon Bonaparte and the daughter of Emperor Francis I of Austria. She married Napoleon in 1810 after his divorce from Josephine. Napoleon and Marie Louise had a son in 1811 who became known as Napoleon II (see NAPOLEON II).

Marie Louise was not permitted to go with Napoleon when he was exiled. She and her son lived at Schönbrunn, near Vienna. She received the Italian duchies of Parma, Piacenza, and Guastalla in 1816, and governed them until her death. Marie Louise was married twice after the death of Napoleon. She was born in Vienna, Austria.   VERNON J. PURYEAR

See also JOSEPHINE; NAPOLEON I.

MARIETTA, Ohio (pop. 16,861), the oldest town in Ohio, is a major manufacturing and trading center. The city lies on the north bank of the Ohio River at the mouth of the Muskingum River. Marietta and Parkersburg, W. Va., form a metropolitan area with a population of 148,132. For location, see OHIO (political map).

Marietta serves as a market for farm products of the Muskingum Valley. The chief manufactures include furniture, paints, safes, gasoline, lubricating oils, concrete products, alloys, phenol, and polystyrene.

Pioneers led by General Rufus Putnam founded Marietta in 1788. The city was named for Queen Marie Antoinette of France. Marietta has a mayor-council form of government, and is the seat of Washington County.   JAMES H. RODABAUGH

See also PUTNAM, RUFUS.

MARIGOLD is a hardy annual flower grown in Europe and America. Most marigolds stand 1 to 2 feet (30 to 61 centimeters) high and have deeply cut leaves on long stalks.

The attractive flowers are usually yellow or orange, sometimes reddish or brown. They have an odor which some people do not like. But scientists have developed some odorless marigolds. The *Aztec* and *French marigolds* originally grew wild in Mexico, but the French transplanted them. Marigolds can be raised from seed. They should be planted about 1 foot (30 centimeters) apart. They usually bloom late in summer. The marsh marigold belongs to the crowfoot family.

Scientific Classification. Marigolds belong to the composite family, *Compositae*. The pot marigold is genus *Calendula*, species *C. officinalis*. The Aztec marigold is *Tagetes erecta*; the French, *T. patula*.   ALFRED C. HOTTES

See also FLOWER (color pictures: Flowers that Grow in Wet Places, Fall Garden Flowers).

Pinney, Monkmeyer   J. C. Allen
Marigolds Vary in Shape and Color.

MARIHUANA. See MARIJUANA.

MARIJUANA, *MAIR uh WAH nuh,* or MARIHUANA, is a drug made from the dried leaves and flowering stalks of the hemp plant. People smoke marijuana in cigarettes and pipes and mix it with food and drinks. Marijuana causes various changes in the way a person feels and thinks. In the United States, Canada, and many other countries, laws prohibit the use, sale, or possession of the drug.

Some people confuse marijuana and hashish. Both drugs are made from hemp, but hashish is much stronger than marijuana. Marijuana has several nicknames, including "grass," "pot," and "mary jane."

Effects. Marijuana can produce a variety of reactions. It may make a person feel relaxed and free from care and cause him to giggle and laugh for no clear reason.

Marijuana may also bring on a dreamy state in which the user's thoughts flow together and his mood may shift suddenly from happiness to depression and fearful tension.

A person's reactions to marijuana depend on many things, including his mood when he takes the drug. For example, if a user takes marijuana in a secure setting among friends, he may experience a pleasant feeling. But if the user is tense, or depressed by his surroundings, the drug may cause fear and further depression. A high dosage of marijuana can cause anxiety reactions or even more severe mental disturbances, particularly if the person has never used the drug before.

Marijuana can also cause a person to lose his sense of time and space. Minutes may seem like hours, and nearby objects may seem far away. The drug may reduce memory, judgment, and coordination. It usually increases the appetite, but it may upset the stomach. The effects last from 2 to 5 hours if the drug is smoked and up to 12 hours if it is eaten or drunk.

Some people believe marijuana improves their ability to play and write music or to paint, study, or work. But scientists have found no proof of these beliefs. Marijuana may increase a person's willingness to accept new ideas without judging whether they are true or false. As a result, some marijuana users believe the drug gives them new understanding about life.

Regular use of marijuana does not cause *addiction* (physical dependence), which can result from the use of alcohol, heroin, or other drugs. However, some people who regularly use marijuana develop a strong desire for the drug's effects. Scientists have found no proof that marijuana leads to use of stronger drugs or causes users to lose interest in life.

In 1971, the U.S. National Institute of Mental Health reported that marijuana in the strength and amount taken by most American users does not seem to harm the body. But the institute warned that it needs more information—especially about long-term effects of the drug—before making a final judgment.

History. Chinese people used marijuana as early as the 2700's B.C. People in India have long used it for

Bureau of Narcotics and Dangerous Drugs
Most Marijuana Cigarettes, unlike cigarettes made of tobacco, are closed at both ends to avoid spilling the finely ground drug. Many of them are hand-wrapped and contain seeds.

Water color (1922); the Phillips Collection, Washington, D.C.

John Marin became famous for his vivid water-color paintings. Many of his works show dramatic scenes from nature. Marin's *Maine Islands, left,* reflects the blend of abstract and realistic elements that are typical of his style.

pleasure, in ceremonies, and as medicine. Today, the drug is used in most parts of the world.

Some Americans began to use marijuana in the 1920's. Many people believed—with insufficient evidence—that use of marijuana led to crime and violence. In 1937, the United States government outlawed the use, sale, or possession of marijuana, except for approved research. But during the 1960's, many young Americans of all social groups began smoking the drug. Most marijuana in the United States is smuggled from Colombia and Mexico.

In 1972, the National Commission on Marijuana and Drug Abuse, a U.S. government advisory group, called for the abolition of laws that forbid the possession or use of marijuana in private. The commission also recommended that growing or selling marijuana for profit should remain a crime. In 1973, Oregon became the first state to remove criminal penalties for the private possession or use of marijuana. Under the revised Oregon law, convictions for such offenses result only in a fine, rather than a jail term. By the late 1970's, 10 other states had enacted similar laws.   DONALD J. WOLK

See also DRUG ABUSE; HASHISH; HEMP.

MARIMBA, *muh RIM buh,* is a percussion instrument similar to the xylophone. It is larger, and has a deeper and richer tone. The marimba consists of wooden bars of different lengths with tuned resonators underneath, mounted on a large, tablelike frame. The marimba has a range of from four to seven octaves. A player hits the wooden bars with mallets.

The marimba is popular in Mexico, and in Central and South America. It originated in South Africa as an adaptation of the xylophone.   CHARLES B. RIGHTER

See also XYLOPHONE; GUATEMALA (Recreation).

MARÍN, DON FRANCISCO DE PAULA. See HAWAII (The Kingdom of Hawaii).

MARIN, JOHN (1870-1953), was one of the first American artists to paint in a modern style. He combined realistic images with elements of an abstract style called *cubism* (see CUBISM). Marin's paintings include bold, angular lines; clear, vivid colors; and overlapping planes. Many of his seascapes and landscapes express the powerful forces of change in nature. The active forms he used in his representation of objects give his work a sense of movement and energy.

Marin was born in Rutherford, N.J. He lived in Europe from 1905 to 1911. During this period, his work showed the influence of James A. M. Whistler, an American painter of the late 1800's. Marin first exhibited his paintings in Paris in 1908. His work was shown in the United States for the first time in 1909, at the gallery of Alfred Stieglitz in New York City. Stieglitz, a photographer and art promoter, was the nation's chief spokesman for modern art. He became Marin's most active supporter.

Marin returned to the United States in 1911 and began to develop the personal style that most clearly

Marimba Tones come from the tubes below the wooden bars that the musician strikes with mallets.

J. C. Deagan, Inc.

identifies his work. Most of Marin's paintings portray scenes of his immediate surroundings, such as the seacoast of Maine. One of his Maine seascapes, the water color *Off Stonington* (1921), appears in the PAINTING article. Marin traveled to other parts of the country to find new subjects. He painted his impression of New York City in *Lower Manhattan* (1922). *Storm Over Taos* (1930) reflects some of the beauty he saw in New Mexico.   ANN LEE MORGAN

MARIN COUNTY CIVIC CENTER. See WRIGHT, FRANK LLOYD (Later Career; picture).

MARINA is a dock or basin for small boats. Some marinas have repair, service, and supply shops; fueling stations; and restaurants and clubhouses, as well as slips and moorings for craft.

See also BOATING (picture).

MARINA FALL, or PRINCESS MARINA FALL, is a horseshoe-shaped waterfall on the Kuribrong River in west-central Guyana. Marina Fall has a sheer drop of 300 feet (91 meters) and a total fall of 500 feet (150 meters). For location, see GUYANA (map).

MARINE is a sea-soldier. Marines serve as assault landing forces. They keep units as national forces in readiness, prepared for instant expeditionary service. Marines are specially recruited, trained, and organized for service at sea and in land and air operations. Nearly all the world's major maritime nations, including the United States, maintain marine forces or some type of naval infantry. For information on the marines of the United States, see MARINE CORPS, UNITED STATES.

Marines of Other Lands. The British Royal Marines force operates as part of the Naval Service. Its motto is *Per Mare, Per Terram*, or "By Sea and by Land." The 8,000-man Royal Marines operate ships and landing craft, provide forces for amphibious raids, and furnish bands for the Naval Service. The two main commands of the Royal Marines are the commando forces and the training group.

The 5,000-man Royal Netherlands *Korps Mariniers* serves at sea and as expeditionary forces in the Dutch colonies. Its motto is *Qua Patet Orbis*, or "Throughout the Wide World."

Other countries that also have marines or naval infantry include Argentina, Brazil, Cambodia, Chile, Colombia, Dominican Republic, France, Indonesia, Iran, Mexico, the Philippines, Poland, Romania, Russia, South Korea, Spain, Taiwan, Thailand, Venezuela, and Yugoslavia.

MARINE BAND, UNITED STATES

History. The first marines were the *epibatae*, or "heavily armed sea-soldiers," of the Greek navies in the 500's B.C. Later, Roman warships carried *milites classiarii*, or "soldiers of the fleet." Both the Greeks and Romans used their marines to fight at sea, while sailors maneuvered the ships.

During the Middle Ages, nations did not maintain organized navies and marine forces. But it was common practice to put ordinary soldiers aboard ship whenever fighting was expected. In the 1600's, both Great Britain and The Netherlands realized the need for regular troops aboard men-of-war. The British formed a corps of marines in 1664, and the Dutch did so in 1665. When the American colonies revolted in 1775, the Continental Congress authorized the first marines.

The oldest role of marines is service aboard warships. In some countries, marines only perform guard duty at naval bases, or man sea coast defenses. France's *Infanterie coloniale*, or "colonial infantry," wears an anchor for its badge as a symbol that the regiment originated as a marine service.   ROBERT DEBS HEINL, JR.

See also NAVY.

MARINE ANIMAL. See MARINE BIOLOGY with its list of Related Articles.

MARINE BAND, UNITED STATES. See MARINE CORPS, UNITED STATES.

Royal Swedish Navy

Swedish Marines fire a mortar during a training mission on an island off the eastern coast of Sweden.

Sovfoto

Russian Marines receive orders from their commanding officer before beginning a combat training mission.

Photo Trends

British Royal Marines in training for Arctic warfare wear white uniforms that blend with the snow-covered land.

National Film Board of Canada

Marine Biologists Study Marine Life In Its Environment. These scientists may travel long distances to a lonely beach or stream, where they can study a particular fish community. They collect data on the fish and how they use light, water, and food.

MARINE BIOLOGY is the study of plants and animals that live in the sea. It deals with all forms of marine life, from huge whales to creatures so tiny they can be seen only under a microscope. Marine organisms live in all parts of the ocean, from shallow shore areas to the deepest points on the ocean floor. The scientists who study life in the sea try to classify all marine plants and animals, and try to discover how they develop and grow, how their bodies function, how they get food, and how they live in relation to other marine plants and animals. Marine biology has become increasingly important in recent years because it has helped human beings better understand their own basic life processes.

Many biologists who specialize in studying marine plants and animals never see them in their natural surroundings. They do most of their work in specially equipped laboratories. They are often called marine biologists. Some marine biologists study the environment of marine life, as well as the marine plants and animals. They are often called biological oceanographers.

John H. Ryther, the contributor of this article, is the Director of the Department of Biology at Woods Hole Oceanographic Institution, Woods Hole, Mass.

Marine Biologists use marine organisms in laboratory experiments that are designed to increase man's knowledge of human life processes. For example, much of man's knowledge of human reproduction and development has been developed through experiments with marine animals. Chemical substances that influence different animal *embryos* (developing young) were first discovered in experiments with marine organisms. The sea urchin is one of the animals most often used by biologists in these experiments. It produces many large eggs that make experiments and observations easier (see SEA URCHIN).

Marine biologists have used the squid's giant nerve fibers to do valuable research in discovering how nerves work. The squid's nerve fibers are larger and easier to handle and observe than those of most animals. The fibers are so large that scientists can place instruments inside different parts of the nerve. The instruments are then used to record the mechanical, chemical, and electrical responses of the nerves. These experiments may lead to greater understanding of how messages are sent from the brain to various points of action in the human body.

Marine biologists also use organisms from the sea to produce substances that are valuable to human beings.

Laboratory scientists have found substances in sponges, sea cucumbers, corals, and seaweed that can be used in treating such things as viral and bacterial infections, and cancer. Substances from certain subtropical sponges can be used to treat skin infections, food and blood poisoning, and pneumonia caused by *staphylococcal* bacteria (see STAPHYLOCOCCUS).

Some marine biologists have found that the poisons from certain kinds of shellfish and puffers are 200,000 times more powerful as anesthetics than drugs that are now being used for this purpose. They have found that the saliva of the octopus contains a substance that can be used as a powerful heart stimulant. The octopus also uses its saliva to paralyze crabs and then eat them. Scientists specializing in the study of marine life believe that many of these substances will eventually be refined for use as commercial drugs.

Most of the experiments with marine organisms are carried out at marine laboratories. Among the oldest and most famous of these are the Stazione Zoologica in Naples, Italy; the Laboratory of the Marine Biological Association of the United Kingdom in Plymouth, England; and the Marine Biological Laboratory at Woods Hole, Mass.

Biological Oceanographers try to find out how marine organisms live in relationship to one another and to their environment. They watch how organisms live in the sea, and try to trace how they *evolved* (gradually developed), adapted, and spread. They try to find out how the body organs of marine creatures can work deep in the sea at pressures as high as 15,000 pounds per square inch (1,060 kilograms per square centimeter). They want to learn how organisms living on the sea floor can locate their mates and find their food, despite the fact that they live in constant darkness, where there are no seasons or temperature changes.

Some marine oceanographers go down into the sea to observe and conduct experiments in the natural environment of marine organisms. Ocean-going vessels with deep-sea nets and dredges are used to capture organisms for study. Scientists often record environmental conditions, such as water temperature and the salt and oxygen content in given ocean areas, on special mechanical equipment that can be fastened to a *buoy* (floating marker). Deep-sea cameras are used to map the sea floor and to locate certain organisms. Scientists also now use special underwater cameras to make detailed photographic records of marine life at great depths. Special sound devices are used to record the vertical movements of fish. Among the leading U.S. organizations equipped for such studies are the Woods Hole (Mass.) Oceanographic Institution, the Scripps Institution of Oceanography in La Jolla, Calif., the Lamont Geological Observatory in New York City, and the Institute of Marine Science, in Miami, Fla.

Many marine oceanographers use scuba diving equipment to make underwater studies, especially in clear tropical waters along coral reefs. To observe deep sea life, they use special equipment, such as research submarines. Some of them, such as the bathyscaph called the *Trieste*, can withstand the great pressures found at the deepest parts of the ocean. The *Trieste*, built by the Swiss scientists Auguste and Jacques Pic-

card, made a record dive of 35,800 feet (10,910 meters) in the deepest known spot in the ocean in the Mariana Trench of the Pacific Ocean off Guam, in 1960. Scientists can stay submerged for longer periods of time in vessels such as this. See BATHYSCAPH (picture); OCEAN (Discovering the Secrets of the Deep).

The French undersea explorer Jacques-Yves Cousteau pioneered in using undersea stations where observers can live for relatively long periods to study sea life (see COUSTEAU, JACQUES-YVES). The U.S. Navy, in its Man-in-the-Sea program conducted off the California coast, and scientists at the Oceanic Institute in Hawaii have also used this method.   JOHN H. RYTHER

Related Articles. See OCEAN (Life in the Ocean; color pictures). See also the following articles:

ANIMAL LIFE

Animal (Animals of the Ocean)	Echinoderm	Seal
	Fish	Sponge
Coelenterate	Mollusk	Turtle
Crustacean	Puffer	Walrus
Dolphin	Sea Cow	Whale
Dugong	Sea Horse	

PLANT LIFE

Algae	Diatom	Irish Moss	Kelp	Seaweed

OTHER RELATED ARTICLES

Diving, Underwater	Plankton	Sargasso Sea

Marine Biologists Also Use Laboratories to study marine life. Scientists examine the sucking disks on the arm of a dead squid. Later they may cut the body apart for further study.

Frederick A. Aldrich

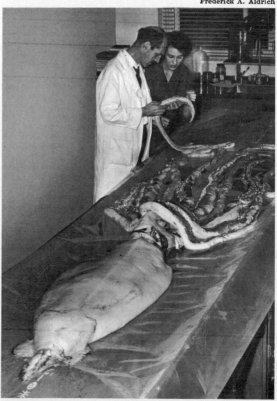

Photos courtesy of the U.S. Marine Corps.

The Marine Corps War Memorial in Arlington, Va., *above*, honors all marines who have died in action since 1775, the year the corps was founded. The memorial portrays the raising of the U.S. flag on Iwo Jima during World War II. The Marine Corps emblem is shown at the right.

MARINE CORPS, UNITED STATES, is the branch of the armed services that is especially trained and organized for amphibious assault operations. Marine assault troops, supported by air units, attack and seize enemy beachheads and bases. As the nation's amphibious force, marines in many strategic parts of the world stand alert to speed to any trouble spot. A well-known military saying is "The marines have landed, and the situation is well in hand." Marines have been the first to fight in almost every major war of the United States. Since 1775, these "soldiers of the sea" have grown from two battalions of sharpshooters into a combat organization of highly mobile ground divisions and air wings. Marines have made more than 300 landings on foreign shores, and have served from the polar regions to the tropics.

During the 1970's, the Marine Corps had a strength of about 185,000 men and about 3,600 women. It is a separate branch of the armed forces within the Department of the Navy in the Department of Defense. Marines are often called *leathernecks*, because in the early days they wore leather bands around their throats. The *WM's*, or women marines, have the same ranks as male marines.

The motto of the corps, adopted in 1868, is *Semper*

Fidelis (Always Faithful). The Marine emblem was also adopted that same year. "The Marines' Hymn," written in the 1800's, begins with the stirring words "From the halls of Montezuma to the shores of Tripoli." John Philip Sousa wrote the corps' march, "Semper Fidelis," while serving as leader of the Marine band. The band is called "The President's Own," because it plays for state affairs in the White House. The official colors of the corps are scarlet and gold.

Why We Have a Marine Corps

Every great maritime nation such as the United States must be able to defend its interests on land and sea, and protect the lives and property of its citizens in other regions. During war and other emergencies, the United States must be ready to send well-trained, disciplined forces to accomplish these goals.

The Marine Corps maintains fleet marine forces of combined air and ground units to seize and defend advance bases, and for land operations that are carried out as part of a naval campaign. It develops the tactics, techniques, and equipment for the amphibious landing operations. The corps provides detachments for service aboard warships and for the protection of naval bases and stations. It guards U.S. embassies, legations, and

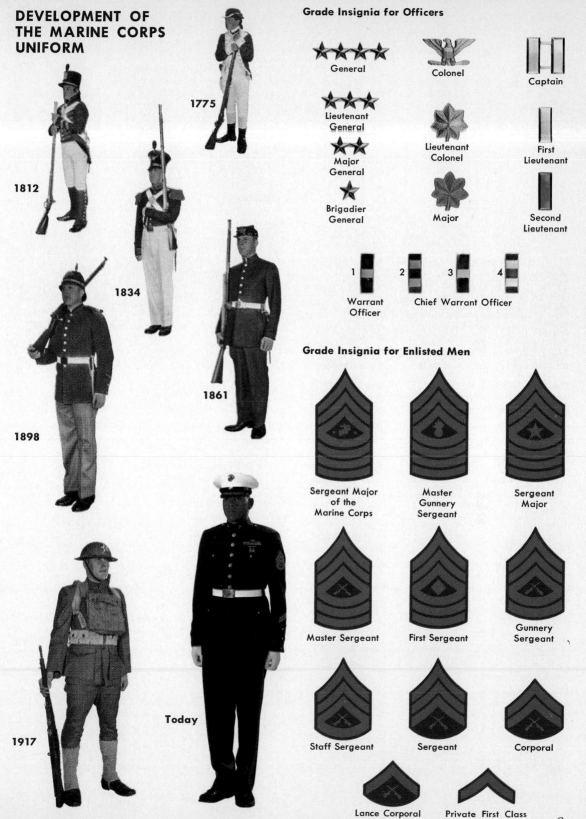

DEVELOPMENT OF THE MARINE CORPS UNIFORM

1775

1812

1834

1861

1898

1917

Today

Grade Insignia for Officers

General

Colonel

Captain

Lieutenant General

Lieutenant Colonel

First Lieutenant

Major General

Second Lieutenant

Brigadier General

Major

1 Warrant Officer

2 Chief Warrant Officer

3

4

Grade Insignia for Enlisted Men

Sergeant Major of the Marine Corps

Master Gunnery Sergeant

Sergeant Major

Master Sergeant

First Sergeant

Gunnery Sergeant

Staff Sergeant

Sergeant

Corporal

Lance Corporal

Private First Class

consulates in other countries, and performs such other duties as the President may direct.

Life in the Marine Corps

Training a Marine. Recruits receive basic training in *boot camp.* Recruits are called *boots* because in early days they wore leather leggings that looked like boots.

Male recruits receive 11 weeks of basic training at one of two recruit depots—in Parris Island, S.C., or in San Diego, Calif. They undergo physical conditioning and learn how to shoot, drill, obey orders, and follow the traditions of the corps. Women receive eight weeks of basic training in Parris Island, S.C. They are trained in most of the same disciplines as men. However, their fitness program differs and they do not learn to shoot.

Training an Officer. Marine Corps officers come from four main sources: (1) the U.S. Naval Academy, (2) the U.S. Military Academy, (3) civilian universities, and (4) the enlisted ranks of the corps. Each officer receives six or more months of initial training at the Marine Corps Basic School in Quantico, Va. Much of this training is in field tactics, about a third of which is night training. Women graduates of the U.S. Naval Academy or the U.S. Military Academy are also eligible for commissions in the Marine Corps. After receiving their commissions, women marines attend an officers' indoctrination course at Quantico.

A Typical Day. Because of the wide variety of marine duties, there is no completely typical day. Nevertheless, the following routine would be familiar to any marine in peacetime. At 6 A.M. the "field music" (bugler) sounds reveille. The marine rises, washes, makes the bunk, and has setting-up drill. Breakfast is followed by police call, when quarters and outside areas are *policed* (cleaned). At 8 A.M. comes morning colors, when the flag is hoisted while the band plays the National Anthem. After colors, troop inspection and guard mounting take place. All marines are inspected and drilled, and the guard is relieved. Drills and instructions go on until recall at about 11 A.M. Dinner is served at 11:30 A.M. At 1 P.M. drill call sounds again, and afternoon training lasts until the day's work is finished. Liberty call then announces that eligible marines may "go ashore," or leave the post if they wish. Supper is served at 5 P.M., and evenings are free unless night training is planned. Taps sounds at 10 P.M.

Careers in the Marine Corps. Young men between the ages of 17 and 28 may enlist in the corps for three, four, or six years. Women between the ages of 18 and 28 may enlist. Men may serve in a wide variety of job fields. Women can serve in all military job fields except the air, armor, artillery, and infantry crews.

Marines who re-enlist may, if qualified, rise to jobs as senior noncommissioned officers. The most capable marines can win appointments to the U.S. Naval Academy, receive direct commissions as officers, or be chosen as warrant officers. Marines may retire with pay after 20 years' service. For ranks and pay in the Marine Corps, see RANK IN ARMED SERVICES.

Weapons and Equipment

Marine Ground Weapons. The M16 rifle is the basic infantry weapon of the corps. Marines also use grenades, pistols, submachine guns, and machine guns.

Artillery provides support for Marine infantry. Marine artillery includes mortars, rocket launchers, guns, and howitzers. Armored units have tanks with heavy guns and flame throwers. Antiaircraft units have *Hawk* guided missiles. Special marine teams ashore use radio to direct gunfire and missile support from warships.

Marine Aviation provides close air support for fleet marine and other troops. It reinforces naval aviation. It attacks enemy forces so close to marine land operations that detailed coordination between air and ground units is required. The Marines have aviators with ground units at the front lines to control and direct air support. They fly the same kinds of aircraft as the Navy (see NAVY, UNITED STATES [Ships and Weapons of the Navy]). The Marines also operate assault helicopters to land men from naval helicopter carriers.

Organization of the Marine Corps

Headquarters of the Marine Corps is in Washington, D.C. The corps is one of the two naval services. It is a partner, but not literally a part, of the Navy. A commandant, appointed by the President, heads the corps. The commandant usually serves four years, and has the rank of general. The commandant serves as a member of the Joint Chiefs of Staff and is responsible directly

---

MAJOR MARINE CORPS POSTS

Name	Location
Albany Marine Corps Logistics Base	Albany, Ga.
Barstow Marine Corps Logistics Base	Barstow, Calif.
Beaufort Marine Corps Air Station	Beaufort, S.C.
Camp Elmore	Norfolk, Va.
Camp Garcia	Vieques, Puerto Rico
*Camp H. M. Smith	Oahu, Hawaii
*Camp Lejeune	Camp Lejeune, N.C.
*Camp Pendleton	Camp Pendleton, Calif.
Camp Smedley D. Butler	Okinawa, Japan
*Cherry Point Marine Corps Air Station	Cherry Point, N.C.
*El Toro Marine Corps Air Station	Santa Ana, Calif.
Futenma Marine Corps Air Station	Okinawa, Japan
Headquarters Battalion, Headquarters U.S. Marine Corps	Arlington, Va.
Iwakuni Marine Corps Air Station	Iwakuni, Japan
Kaneohe Bay Marine Corps Air Station	Oahu, Hawaii
Kansas City Marine Corps Finance Center	Kansas City, Mo.
Marine Barracks	District of Columbia
New River Marine Corps Air Station	Jacksonville, N.C.
*Parris Island Marine Corps Recruit Depot	Parris Island, S.C.
Quantico Marine Corps Air Facility	Quantico, Va.
Quantico Marine Corps Base	Quantico, Va.
*Quantico Marine Corps Development and Education Command	Quantico, Va.
*San Diego Marine Corps Recruit Depot	San Diego, Calif.
Tustin Marine Corps Air Station	Tustin, Calif.
Twentynine Palms Marine Corps Air-Ground Combat Center	Twentynine Palms, Calif.
Yuma Marine Corps Air Station	Yuma, Ariz.

*Has a separate article in THE WORLD BOOK ENCYCLOPEDIA.

to the secretary of the navy. The principal assistants of the commandant include the assistant commandant, the chief of staff, the deputy and assistant chiefs of staff, and the directors of headquarters divisions.

Operating Forces account for almost two-thirds of the entire Marine Corps. They consist of (1) the fleet marine forces, (2) marines aboard ships, and (3) security forces. The fleet marine forces make up the corps' combat strength and form parts of the Atlantic and Pacific fleets. They consist of three Marine divisions, three Marine aircraft wings, and various support units. The combat units operate as air-ground teams. One division and wing team is based on the East Coast of the United

active duty at any time. The standby and retired reserves can be activated only after Congress has declared a war or national emergency.

History

The Revolutionary War. The Continental Congress established a marine corps on Nov. 10, 1775, to fight in the Revolutionary War. Marines also served with the Continental Army in the battles of Trenton, Assunpink, Morristown, and Brandywine. After the Revolutionary War, no marine corps as such existed. Con-

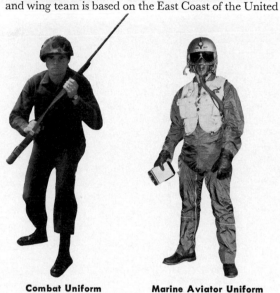

Combat Uniform

Marine Aviator Uniform

Utility Uniform

Winter Uniforms

States, another is on the West Coast, and the third is in the Far East and Hawaii. The teams are kept combat ready at all times.

Marines serve on many warships. They provide internal security aboard the vessels and serve as the ships' landing forces. Marine airplane and helicopter squadrons may fly from carriers.

Security forces include marines who guard American embassies and other important government installations and naval bases around the world.

The Supporting Establishment provides administrative, supply, training, and recruiting support for the operating forces. The Marine schools combine the corps' education and military development activities. The corps' two recruit depots handle basic training. The Marine supply centers provide logistic support.

Reserves. The Marine Corps Reserve consists of (1) the ready reserve, (2) the standby reserve, and (3) the retired reserve. Most members of the ready reserve enlist for six years but spend only the first six months on active duty. They train as organized combat units one weekend a month and serve for two weeks each year at a Marine base. Standby reservists are Marines who have served on active duty for at least two years. They do not serve in organized units for the remainder of their six-year obligation. The retired reserve is made up of retired enlisted Marines who have served 20 years on active duty. The ready reserve units can be called to

gress re-created the corps as a military service in 1798.

The Shores of Tripoli. Marines took part in the hard-fought naval battles that United States ships fought against France in 1797. In 1805, marines led the

— IMPORTANT DATES IN MARINE CORPS HISTORY —

1775 The Continental Congress authorized the formation of two battalions of marines.

1776 Marines made their first landing, on the Bahama Islands during the Revolutionary War.

1798 Congress re-created the Marine Corps as a separate military service.

1805 Marines stormed the Barbary pirates' stronghold at Derna on the shores of Tripoli.

1834 Congress placed the Marine Corps directly under the Secretary of the Navy.

1847 Marines occupied "the halls of Montezuma" in Mexico City during the Mexican War.

1913 The Marine Corps established its aviation section.

1918 Marines fought one of their greatest battles at Belleau Wood in France during World War I.

1942 Marines invaded Guadalcanal Island in the first United States offensive of World War II.

1945 Marines seized Iwo Jima Island in the western Pacific in the largest all-marine battle.

1950 Marines stormed ashore at Inchon, Korea, in the first major landing of the Korean War.

1952 The marine commandant became a member of the Joint Chiefs of Staff.

1965-1971 The Third Amphibious Force, the largest field command in Marine Corps history, served in Vietnam.

storming of the Barbary pirates' stronghold at Derna, Tripoli. Their action helped end the pirate menace in the Mediterranean Sea.

The War of 1812 saw marines in all major American naval victories. Captain John Gamble showed such ability that he was given command of a captured British warship. He became the only marine officer ever to command a naval ship. Marines helped Andrew Jackson's army administer the worst defeat of the war to the British in the defense of New Orleans in 1815.

The Creek and Seminole Wars. In 1836, the army was assigned to move the Creek and Seminole Indians of Georgia and Florida to new reservations. When the tribes refused to move, marine commandant Archibald Henderson personally led marines to reinforce the army. He was promoted to brigadier general for gallantry at the Battle of Hatchee-Lustee in Florida in 1837. Henderson became the corps' first general officer.

The Halls of Montezuma. During the Mexican War, from 1846 to 1848, marines made many landings on both coasts of Mexico. Marines were the first to enter the city gates of Mexico City. They raised the American flag over the National Palace, which later became known as "the halls of Montezuma."

The Civil War. When John Brown and his followers captured the army arsenal at Harpers Ferry, Va., in 1859, marines from Washington were the only troops available. They captured Brown and occupied the arsenal. In the Civil War itself, marines fought in many land and naval battles.

In the Far East. During the late 1800's and early 1900's, marines landed 17 times in China to protect American interests. They defended the besieged legations in Peking during the Boxer Rebellion in 1900, and also fought at Tientsin in the Peking relief force.

The Spanish-American War. Marines were the first American troops to land in Cuba. A battalion seized Guantánamo Bay in 1898. Marines were also the first American forces to land in the Philippines. They occupied Guam, and took part in the seizure of Puerto Rico. A Marine brigade served with the Army during the Philippine insurrection from 1899 to 1903.

In Central America. Marines landed in Panama six times between 1885 and 1903 to protect American lives and property, and to keep the Isthmus of Panama open. They also fought in two campaigns to stabilize Nicaragua, in 1912 and again from 1926 to 1933. Marine brigades exercised American protectorates over Haiti and Santo Domingo in the early 1900's.

World War I. Marines arrived in France in June, 1917, with the first troops of the American Expeditionary Force. They dismayed the Germans with long-range rifle fire and fierce assaults at Soissons, Saint Mihiel, Blanc Mont Ridge, and the Meuse-Argonne.

World War II. In August, 1942, the Marines invaded Guadalcanal in the Solomon Islands and launched the first American offensive of the war. Marines under Lieutenant General Holland M. Smith led the amphibious landings of the island-hopping drive westward through the Central Pacific. The conquest of Iwo Jima during February and March of 1945, was the largest all-marine battle in history (see IWO JIMA; WASHINGTON, D.C. [color picture]). Strength of the corps reached nearly 500,000 during World War II.

The Korean War. In August, 1950, marines arrived in Korea to help rescue the crumbling Pusan perimeter. They later made the amphibious landing at Inchon. After Chinese Communist troops entered the war, marines smashed seven enemy divisions in their winter march south from the Chosin Reservoir.

The Marines in Action

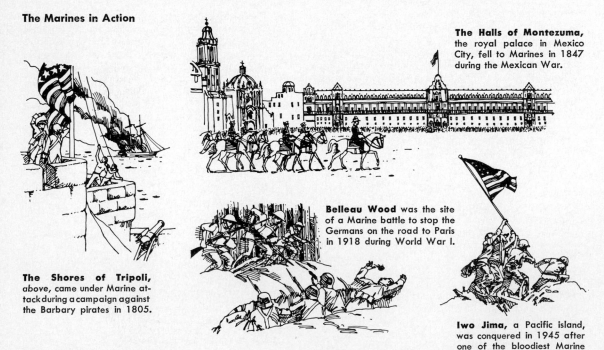

The Halls of Montezuma, the royal palace in Mexico City, fell to Marines in 1847 during the Mexican War.

Belleau Wood was the site of a Marine battle to stop the Germans on the road to Paris in 1918 during World War I.

The Shores of Tripoli, above, came under Marine attack during a campaign against the Barbary pirates in 1805.

Iwo Jima, a Pacific island, was conquered in 1945 after one of the bloodiest Marine battles in history.

WORLD BOOK illustrations by Tak Murakami

Recent Developments. During the Suez crisis in 1956, a Marine battalion covered the evacuation of American citizens from the trouble zone. In 1958, a reinforced Marine regiment landed in Lebanon and helped prevent the Lebanese government from being overthrown. The corps also completed reorganizing the combat structure of its fleet marine forces. In 1965, Marine units landed in the Dominican Republic to end the fighting there. Also in 1965, marines landed in South Vietnam. A total of about 450,000 marines served in the Vietnam War from 1965 to 1973.   T. P. Goggin

Related Articles. See the table *Major Marine Corps Posts* with this article. See also Navy, Department of the; Navy, United States. Additional related articles in World Book include:

History

Civil War	Spanish-American War
Korean War	Vietnam War
Mexican War	War of 1812
Revolutionary War	World War I
in America	World War II

Other Related Articles

Air Force, United States	Military Training
Decorations and Medals	Rank in Armed
Flag (picture: Flags of	Services
the Armed Forces)	Recruiting
Marine	Regiment
Military Discharge	Uniform
Military School	War Aces

Outline

I. **Why We Have a Marine Corps**
II. **Life in the Marine Corps**
  A. Training a Marine
  B. Training an Officer
  C. A Typical Day
  D. Careers in the Marine Corps

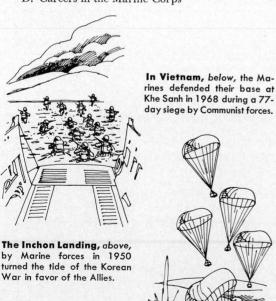

In Vietnam, *below,* the Marines defended their base at Khe Sanh in 1968 during a 77-day siege by Communist forces.

The Inchon Landing, *above,* by Marine forces in 1950 turned the tide of the Korean War in favor of the Allies.

WORLD BOOK illustrations by Tak Murakami

III. **Weapons of the Marine Corps**
  A. Marine Ground Weapons   B. Marine Aviation
IV. **Organization of the Marine Corps**
  A. Headquarters   C. The Supporting
  B. Operating Forces   Establishment
                           D. Reserves

V. **History**

Questions

What is the Marine Corps motto? What does it mean?
Why are marines often called *leathernecks?*
What are Marine operating forces? Support forces?
What are the duties of marines aboard warships?
What are some Marine ground weapons?
What is the chief purpose of the Marine Corps?
What is "boot camp"? The fleet marine force?
Why is Marine aviation important to Marine ground units?
When did the corps establish its aviation section?
Where did marines make their first landing?

MARINE CORPS WAR MEMORIAL. See Washington, D.C. (Marine Corps War Memorial; picture); Marine Corps, United States (picture); Iwo Jima (picture).

MARINE ENGINEERING. See Engineering (table).

MARINE INSURANCE. See Insurance (Marine).

MARINE PLANT. See Marine Biology with its list of Related Articles.

MARINER SPACE PROBE. See Space Travel (Space Probes); Venus (planet); Mars.

MARINER'S COMPASS. See Compass.

MARINUS is the name of two popes of the Roman Catholic Church. Some historians later listed them as Martin II and Martin III.

Marinus I (Martin II) was pope from 882 to 884. He was the first bishop elected to the papacy. He thought highly of the English and freed the Anglo-Saxon center in Rome from taxes. He was born in Tuscany.

Marinus II (Martin III) was pope from 942 to 946. He was not a brilliant pope, but he worked gently for church reforms.   Gustave Weigel and Fulton J. Sheen

MARION, FRANCIS (1732?-1795), was an American general whose shrewd, daring raids won him the nickname the *Swamp Fox* in the Revolutionary War. He and his soldiers darted out of the marshes to attack the British, then vanished before they could strike back.

Marion became a member of the South Carolina Provincial Congress in 1775, and voted for war. Soon after, he became captain of a volunteer group and fought in many engagements. He sprained his ankle in 1780, and was forced to leave Charleston before the town surrendered. This fortunate accident saved Marion from capture, and he later commanded the forces in the northern part of the state.

He had the only American troops left in South Carolina after the British defeated General Horatio Gates and General Thomas Sumter. His forces were too small to fight the British in open battle. So Marion organized them into a guerrilla band. The soldiers provided their own food and horses. Blacksmiths made the soldiers' swords from saw blades. Their bullets were melted pewter plates, and ammunition was so scarce in many of the battles that each soldier had only three rounds.

Marion had a secret hideout on Snow Island in the Pee Dee River, and the British had great difficulty finding it. From there he and his soldiers made quick raids on British communications and supply depots and rescued captured Americans. The British cavalry officer, Banastre Tarleton, spent much time and energy pursuing Marion, but he could never catch him. After the war, Marion served in the South Carolina Senate several times. He died on his plantation at Pond Bluff.

Marion was born in Berkeley County, South Carolina. He spent his youth on his parents' farm near Georgetown, S.C. He had his first taste of war as a lieutenant of colonial militia, when he fought against the Cherokee Indians in 1761. WILLIAM O. STEELE

MARIONETTE. See PUPPET (Marionettes).

MARIOTTE'S LAW. See GAS (Gas Laws).

MARIPOSA GROVE. See YOSEMITE NATIONAL PARK.

MARIPOSA LILY is a group of hardy, spring-blooming flowers of the lily family. The beautiful flowers are sometimes called *fairy lantern*, *globe tulip*, or *butterfly lily*. Native to the western United States, mariposa lilies have narrow leaves shaped like large blades of grass. The cup-shaped flowers grow singly or in small clusters, and resemble tulips. Colors range from white to purple to deep yellow or orange. Mariposa lilies grow well in sandy, porous soil, but need a lot of water. They grow from underground bulbs. Bulbs should be dried out in summer for fall planting. Mariposa lilies make excellent flowers for woodland or rock gardens.

Scientific Classification. Mariposa lilies belong to the lily family, *Liliaceae*. The white mariposa is genus *Calochortus*, species *C. albus*. ROBERT W. SCHERY

See also SEGO LILY.

J. Horace McFarland

The Mariposa Lily has three beautiful petals. Six pollen stalks surround its *pistil* (center part). The flowers vary in color.

MARIS, ROGER (1934-   ), hit more home runs in one season than any other major-league baseball player. He set a record in 1961 when he hit his 61st homer on the last day of the season. His team, the New York Yankees, played a 162-game schedule that year. In 1927, Babe Ruth, also a Yankee star, hit 60 home runs during a 154-game schedule. Both totals are considered records. See BASEBALL (Recent Developments).

Maris, an outfielder, batted left handed and threw right handed. He started his major-league career with the Cleveland Indians in 1957 and was traded to the

Kansas City Athletics in 1958. In 1960, his first year with the Yankees, he hit 39 home runs. Maris was voted the American League's most valuable player in 1960 and 1961. In 1966, he was traded to the St. Louis Cardinals. He retired from baseball following the 1968 season. Roger Eugene Maris was born in Hibbing, Minn., and grew up in Fargo, N. Dak. BILL GLEASON

UPI

Roger Maris

MARISOL (1930-   ) is an American sculptor known for her witty, life-size wooden figures. Marisol constructs her figures with crudely carved wooden blocks, on which she usually draws or paints realistic facial features and other details. Marisol often attaches everyday objects as well as plaster casts of her own face, hands, or feet to her sculptures. These additions make the figures seem alive. Many of her works consist of groupings of several physically independent figures. These characteristics may be seen in her sculpture *The Family*, which appears in the SCULPTURE article.

Marisol's combinations of drawing, sculpture, and ordinary objects show the influence of the American artists Jasper Johns and Robert Rauschenberg. Her work has often been associated with the pop art movement, but, unlike the pop artists, she rarely uses commercial objects or designs. Marisol Escobar was born in Paris of Venezuelan parents. She emigrated to the United States in 1950. JONATHAN FINEBERG

MARITAIN, MA *rih* TAN, **JACQUES** (1882-1973), a French educator and philosopher, helped lead the revival of *Thomistic* (scholastic) philosophy in the 1900's (see SCHOLASTICISM). He lectured on scholasticism in Europe and America, and taught at such universities as Toronto, Chicago, Columbia, and Notre Dame. His books include *An Introduction to Philosophy* (1937), *Degrees of Knowledge* (1938), *Man and the State* (1951), and *Creative Intuition* (1955). Maritain was awarded the French Grand Prize for Letters in 1963. He was born in Paris. THOMAS P. NEILL and FULTON J. SHEEN

MARITIME ACADEMIES. See SHIP (Careers in the U.S. Merchant Marine).

MARITIME ADMINISTRATION is an agency of the United States Department of Commerce that promotes a strong and efficient U.S. merchant marine. The agency administers programs to assure that the merchant marine is capable of meeting the nation's waterborne shipping demands in times of peace and of providing support to the armed forces in times of national emergency. See MERCHANT MARINE.

The administration awards subsidies to U.S. firms to help build and operate merchant ships used in foreign trade. These payments help the companies compete with foreign firms that have lower costs. The agency also insures mortgages and loans made by private lending institutions for building or reconstructing ships.

The agency develops new ship designs and conducts research to improve the efficiency and safety of shipping operations. It also operates the U.S. Merchant

Marine Academy in Kings Point, N.Y. The agency was established in 1950.

Critically reviewed by the MARITIME ADMINISTRATION

MARITIME COLLEGE is a professional school primarily for men at Fort Schuyler, N.Y. It is a member college of the State University of New York. The oldest maritime school in the United States, it was established in 1847 as the New York Nautical School. Courses lead to bachelor's degrees, and prepare students for the maritime industry. For the enrollment of Maritime College, see UNIVERSITIES AND COLLEGES (table [New York, State University of]).

MARITIME COMMISSION, FEDERAL. See FEDERAL MARITIME COMMISSION.

MARITIME LAW regulates commerce and navigation on the high seas or other navigable waters, including inland lakes and rivers. It involves all vessels, from huge passenger liners to small pleasure boats, and covers such matters as contracts, insurance, property damage, and personal injuries. Maritime law is sometimes referred to as *admiralty law*, because at one time it was administered under the jurisdiction of admirals.

Although a general maritime law has developed internationally, it operates in any nation according to the laws and usages of that country. Each nation bases its own maritime law on the general law, with whatever modifications and qualifications it thinks are necessary and proper. Maritime law, in general, does not have any legal force of its own. There is no international court to enforce maritime decisions. But all nations that have vessels on the sea set up national maritime courts. These courts consider maritime cases in much the same way that civil courts hear other kinds of complaints. Federal district courts administer maritime law in the United States. Admiralty courts handle maritime law cases in Great Britain.   WARREN ADAMS JACKMAN

See also FLOTSAM, JETSAM, AND LAGAN; SALVAGE; INTER-GOVERNMENTAL MARITIME CONSULTATIVE ORGANIZATION.

MARITIME PROVINCES. See ATLANTIC PROVINCES.

MARIUS, GAIUS (157-86 B.C.), was a Roman general and statesman. He was not of noble ancestry, but he worked his way into political leadership. He served seven times as one of the two *consuls* (chief government officials) of Rome, between 107 and 86 B.C. He opposed Rome's aristocratic *oligarchy* (rule by few).

As a general, Marius reorganized Rome's infantry legions, improved training methods, and opened military service to men of the lowest social classes. A strong professional army developed. The troops, if treated well, often became more loyal to their generals than to the state, so successful military command became a means to political power.

Marius was born near Arpinum, in central Italy. He won his greatest military victories against the Numidians in North Africa, and the Cimbri and Teutone tribes in northern Italy.   HENRY C. BOREN

MARIVAUX, *mar ih voh*, PIERRE (1688-1763), was a French playwright and novelist. His works deal chiefly with the rising middle class, which was slowly replacing the nobility as the ruling social force in France.

Marivaux is best known for his comedies. His originality lies in his basing his comedies on the problem of love as seen by women. His heroines are elegant, intellectual, and cunning, and their speech is delicate and refined. His comedies include *The Double Inconstancy* (1723), *The Game of Love and Chance* (1730), and *The False Confessions* (1737). Marivaux also wrote two unfinished novels, *The Life of Marianne* (1731-1741) and *The Successful Peasant* (1735-1736). These books were among the first French novels to give a realistic picture of the middle class. Marivaux was born Pierre Carlet de Chamblain de Marivaux in Paris.   JULES BRODY

MARJORAM, *MAHR joh rum*, is the popular name of a group of herbaceous plants which belong to the mint family. These plants grow wild in the Mediterranean region and in Asia. Several kinds are cultivated in North America. Marjoram is also called *oregano*.

The marjoram plant stands 1 to 2 feet (30 to 61 centimeters) tall and bears small whitish or purplish flowers. *Sweet marjoram* is grown in American gardens. Its leaves, stems, and flowers can be used to flavor stews, soups, and dressings. Manufacturers use oil

J. Horace McFarland
Marjoram

of sweet marjoram in making toilet soaps. *Common marjoram* also grows in the United States. It is used to season foods. It has purple flowers which grow in clusters. Marjoram is used in commercial oils such as salad oils.

Scientific Classification. Marjoram belongs to the mint family, *Labiatae*. Sweet marjoram is classified as genus *Majorana*, species *M. hortensis*. Common marjoram is *Origanum vulgare*.   HAROLD NORMAN MOLDENKE

MARK is the monetary unit of Germany. After World War I, it became almost valueless, but in 1924 it was stabilized and called the *reichsmark*. It is now called the *Deutsche mark*. See also MONEY (table: Exchange Rates).

MARK, GOSPEL OF. See GOSPELS; MARK, SAINT.

MARK, SAINT, according to tradition, was the author of the second Gospel in the New Testament. This book is supposed to report Peter's teachings as Mark remembered them (see GOSPELS). Mark was brought up in Jerusalem. His mother, Mary, lived there, and her home was a gathering place for Christians.

Mark went with Saint Paul and Barnabas, Paul's friend, on their first missionary journey. But there was a quarrel, and Mark returned to Jerusalem. Later he sailed for Cyprus with Barnabas. For 10 years no one heard from him. Then he suddenly joined Paul at Rome.

He probably worked with both Paul and Peter for the rest of his life. Another tradition tells that he founded the church at Alexandria.   FREDERICK C. GRANT

MARK ANTONY. See ANTONY, MARK.

MARK TWAIN. See TWAIN, MARK.

MARKET ECONOMY. See FREE ENTERPRISE SYSTEM.

MARKET RESEARCH is the process of gathering and analyzing information to help business firms and other organizations make marketing decisions. Business executives use market research to help them identify *markets* (potential customers) for their products and decide what marketing methods to use. Government officials use such research to develop regulations regarding

MARKETING

advertising, other sales practices, and product safety.

Market research services are provided by several kinds of companies, including advertising agencies, management consultants, and specialized market research organizations. In addition, many large business companies have their own market research department.

Market researchers handle a wide range of assignments. They estimate the demand for new products and services, describe the characteristics of probable customers, and measure potential sales. They determine how prices influence demand, and they test the effectiveness of current and proposed advertising. Market researchers also assess a company's sales personnel and analyze the public "image" of a company and its products.

A market research study begins with a statement of the problem that the client wants to solve. This statement leads to a detailed definition of the information to be gathered. There are two types of market research information, *secondary data* and *primary data*. Secondary data are statistics and other information that are already available from such sources as government agencies and universities. To save time and money, market researchers use secondary sources as much as they can. Primary data are data that must be obtained through research. The chief techniques for gathering such data include mail questionnaires, personal interviews, telephone interviews, and direct observation in stores. The researchers carefully select the individuals to be questioned. They design and test research materials, such as questionnaires or guides for interviewers. Finally, they collect the data, analyze the information, and report the results of their study. The computer is an important tool in analyzing market research data.

Market research can reduce the risk involved in many business decisions, but some risk always remains. Expenditures for market research must be carefully controlled so that the costs do not exceed the probable benefits from reduced risk.   FREDERICK E. WEBSTER, JR.

See also ADVERTISING (Research); MARKETING; PUBLIC OPINION POLL.

MARKETING is the process by which sellers find buyers and by which goods and services move from producers to consumers. Everyday life involves many marketing activities. For example, advertising and selling are part of the marketing process. Other marketing activities include financing by banks and deliveries to stores and homes. Marketing is so important to industry that about half the cost of goods and services results from the marketing process. More people work in marketing than in production.

Consumers in the United States, Canada, and most other non-Communist countries can choose from a huge variety of products and services. Therefore, a company must have an effective marketing program to make its products and services attractive to customers. In a large firm, executives called *marketing managers* direct marketing. But every business, regardless of size, engages in five major marketing activities: (1) market research, (2) product development, (3) distribution, (4) pricing, and (5) promotion.

Market Research is the study of the probable users of a product or service. Such potential customers are called a *market*. There are many sources of market information. For example, government statistics about population and income indicate the size of a market and its purchasing power. See MARKET RESEARCH.

Product Development includes determining the various goods to be offered, as well as developing the products themselves. Manufacturers continually meet the demands of the public by adding new products, changing existing ones, and dropping others.

Distribution is the movement of goods and services from producer to consumer. A manufacturer must establish a system that keeps products moving steadily from the factory to the customer. Such a system is called a *marketing channel* or a *channel of distribution*.

Many types of companies take part in distribution. They include *wholesalers*, who sell large quantities of goods to *retailers*. The retailers, in turn, sell small numbers of products to consumers. Independent dealers called *jobbers* buy goods from manufacturers in large quantities and sell them to retail dealers in small quantities. Other firms provide such services as financing, transportation, and storage.

Pricing. When setting the price of a product, most manufacturers start with their *unit production cost*, the expense of making one unit of the item. They add a percentage of this cost to provide a profit for themselves. Every company in the marketing channel then sells the product for more than it cost. Each of these firms adds an amount that covers its expenses and enables it to make a profit. The amount added to the cost at each stage is called a *markup*. The final selling price of an item equals its production cost plus the total of the markups. See PRICE; PROFIT.

Some people believe a large part of the money spent on marketing is wasted. They especially criticize a practice called *planned obsolescence*. This practice involves the manufacture of products that probably will break down after a certain amount of use or will become outdated in a relatively short time. However, most economists believe the marketing process actually benefits consumers. For example, market research helps industry offer what customers need and want. Marketing also provides consumers with shopping information and makes products available in convenient quantities at nearby locations.

Promotion includes advertising and personal selling. Companies engage in a variety of promotional activities to inform customers about products and services and to persuade them to buy. See the articles on ADVERTISING and SALESMANSHIP for more information about this phase of marketing.   FREDERICK E. WEBSTER, JR.

Related Articles in WORLD BOOK include:

Careers (Marketing and Distribution)
Consumption
Cooperative (Marketing Cooperatives)
Farm and Farming (Marketing Farm Products)
Food (Marketing)
Livestock (Marketing Livestock)
Management (Market Management)
Packaging
Retailing
Trade

MARKHAM, *MAHR kum,* **EDWIN** (1852-1940), an American poet and lecturer, won recognition with his poem "The Man with the Hoe" (1899). He also wrote the books of poems *Lincoln and Other Poems* (1901) and *New Poems* (1932); and a sermon entitled "The Social Conscience" (1897). Markham was born in Oregon

City, Ore., but his mother took him to California when he was 5. He graduated from Christian College in Santa Rosa, Calif. For several years, he worked as a schoolteacher and superintendent of schools in California communities. He lived near New York City after 1899.   PETER VIERECK

MARKHOR. See GOAT (picture: Wild Goats).

MARKKA, *MAHRK kah,* is the monetary unit of Finland. The coin has been made of gold, silver, and various alloys. The markka is equal to 100 pennia. For its value in dollars, see MONEY (table: Exchange Rates).

MARKLE FOUNDATION, JOHN AND MARY R. See FOUNDATIONS.

MARKOVA, DAME ALICIA (1910-   ), is considered the first great English ballerina. At 14, she joined the Sergei Diaghilev ballet company and became a soloist. After that company disbanded in 1929, she spent almost a decade with Sadler's Wells (now the Royal) Ballet and then with the Markova-Dolin Ballet. Her greatest role was the title character in *Giselle.*

In 1938, Alicia Markova joined the Ballet Russe de Monte Carlo, the leading international company. By this time, her movements were perfect and her pure, soaring style was flawless at any speed. During World War II, she danced with the Ballet Theatre. She retired in 1963 and became director of the Metropolitan Opera Ballet. She received the title *Dame Commander of the British Empire* in 1963.   P. W. MANCHESTER

See also DOLIN, ANTON (picture).

MARKS AND MARKING. See GRADING.

MARL is a type of rock that consists of almost equal amounts of calcium carbonate and clay. It is a *sedimentary rock,* a layered rock formed by the accumulation of other rocks and mineral fragments. Most marl forms at the edges of freshwater lakes.

People use marl in various ways, depending on the impurities present in the rock. *Greensand marl* has a large amount of phosphorus and potash, and farmers have used this type of marl as a fertilizer. *Shell marl* contains many fossil shells and is often used as a decorative stone. Cement companies use marl in their manufacturing process.   WALTER E. REED and BARRIE WALL

MARLBOROUGH, *MAWL buh ruh,* **DUKE OF** (1650-1722), JOHN CHURCHILL, was one of England's greatest generals. He won a series of brilliant victories at Blenheim, Ramillies, Oudenarde, and Malplaquet in his campaigns in the War of the Spanish Succession (see BLENHEIM, BATTLE OF; SUCCESSION WARS [The War of the Spanish Succession]).

His character and motives have been criticized, but his military genius has never been questioned. He had a winning personality, and was a successful diplomat. He was an ancestor of Sir Winston Churchill, who wrote a biography of him.

Marlborough deserted King James II to support William of Orange when the English Parliament invited William to accept the English throne in 1688

The Duke of Marlborough
Detail from portrait by Sir Godfrey Kneller, reproduced by kind permission of His Grace, The Duke of Marlborough

(see JAMES [II]; WILLIAM [III] of England). William made him earl of Marlborough, and gave him commands in the army. Marlborough's position became stronger when William died and Princess Anne came to the throne as Queen Anne (see ANNE). Marlborough's wife, Sarah Jennings (1660-1744), was the queen's closest friend. Anne made him commander of all the armed forces at home and in Europe. In the War of the Spanish Succession, Marlborough, who was then a duke, won a series of victories.

At the peak of his success, Marlborough lost his influence at home. His political enemies had turned the queen against him and his wife. He was removed from his command, and retired from public life. His final downfall was not due to lack of ability. It was the fault of his wife, who was domineering and ill tempered. England generously rewarded him for his services. He received an estate in Oxfordshire, and Blenheim Palace was built for him there in 1705.

Marlborough was born in Devonshire. He served in the war against The Netherlands, under the French Marshal Turenne, the greatest military leader of that day. He won rapid promotion.   W. M. SOUTHGATE

MARLIN, *MAHR lin,* or SPEARFISH, is the name of a group of large game fishes that live in the ocean. They are related to the swordfishes and sailfishes. Most marlins weigh from 50 to 400 pounds (23 to 180 kilograms), but some weigh much more. The marlin has a pointed spear that may measure 2 feet (61 centimeters) long. The marlin's *dorsal* (back) fin looks like a sickle, and its tail is crescent shaped. *White marlins* live in the Atlantic Ocean and *striped marlins* live in the Pacific. *Blue marlins* live in both the Atlantic and Pacific. Marlins often leap high in the air. See also FISH (pictures: Fish of Coastal Waters and the Open Ocean); SAILFISH; SWORDFISH.

Scientific Classification. Marlins belong to the family *Istiophoridae.* The blue marlin is genus *Makaira,* species *M. nigricans.* The white marlin is *Tetrapturus albidus,* and the striped marlin is *T. audax.*   LEONARD P. SCHULTZ

The Marlin Is a Strong, Exciting Game Fish.
California Dept. of Fish and Game

MARLOWE, CHRISTOPHER (1564-1593), was the first great Elizabethan writer of tragedy. His most famous work, *The Tragical History of Doctor Faustus* (about 1588), is an imaginative view of a legendary scholar's fall to damnation through lust for forbidden knowledge, power, and sensual pleasure. Never before in English literature had a writer so powerfully shown the soul's conflict with the laws defining the place of human beings in a universal order. See FAUST.

Marlowe was born in Canterbury and studied at Cambridge. Evidently at some time during his university years, he did secret service work for the government. The few years before his death in a tavern fight have left evidence of his duels and reports of his unconventional, skeptical political and religious thought.

Marlowe established his theatrical reputation with *Tamburlaine* (Parts I and II, c. 1587). In "high astounding" poetry and spectacle, Marlowe wrote about an awe-inspiring conqueror, Tamburlaine. These plays reflect the widespread fascination in Marlowe's time with the reach and limits of the human will's desire for dominion. In *Tamburlaine*, Marlowe influenced later drama with his concentration on a heroic figure and his development of *blank verse* (unrhymed poetry) into a flexible poetic form for tragedy. But artificial and crude elements make Tamburlaine less attractive than his more mature plays—*The Jew of Malta* (c. 1589), *Edward II* (c. 1592), and *Doctor Faustus*. Marlowe's nondramatic poetry includes the unfinished work *Hero and Leander* and the pastoral lyric "The Passionate Shepherd to His Love." LAWRENCE J. ROSS

MARMARA, *MAHR muhr uh,* **SEA OF,** is part of the trade waterway that connects the Black Sea with the Mediterranean Sea. The Sea of Marmara was once called *Propontis*. The Bosporus, a strait, connects it with the Black Sea on the east. Another strait, the Dardanelles, connects it with the Aegean Sea, an arm of the

Location of the Sea of Marmara

Mediterranean, on the west. The Sea of Marmara is about 140 miles (225 kilometers) long and 40 miles (64 kilometers) across at its widest point. It covers about 4,300 square miles (11,100 square kilometers). See also BOSPORUS; DARDANELLES. JOHN D. ISAACS

MARMOSET is one of the world's smallest monkeys. Different species vary in size, but most measure less than 1 foot (30 centimeters) long, not including the tail, and weigh less than 1 pound (0.5 kilogram). Most marmosets have tails that are longer than their bodies. Thick, soft hair covers the entire animal. Some marmosets have tufts of hair on top of their ears, and some have beards or mustaches. The hair on the head of a *golden marmoset* looks somewhat like a lion's mane.

Marmosets, many of which are also known as *tamarins*, live in the tropical forests of Panama and South America. They eat insects, spiders, and fruit. Marmosets travel in family groups, scampering from tree to tree like squirrels. These monkeys move about only during the

San Diego Zoo

Golden Marmosets have soft, golden hair. They use their long, clawed fingers to pluck insects out of cracks in branches.

day. At night they sleep in holes in trees. Males carry the young on their back. Marmosets are shy. When startled, they flee quickly with shrill cries. Some species, including the golden marmoset and Goeldi's marmoset, have become endangered due to destruction of their forest homes and capture for the pet trade.

Scientific Classification. Marmosets make up the marmoset family, Callithricidae. The family has five genera. The golden marmoset is genus *Leontideus*, species *L. rosalia*. JOHN H. KAUFMANN and ARLEEN KAUFMANN

MARMOT, *MAHR muht,* is the largest member of the squirrel family. Marmots live in burrows, and are common in Europe, western North America, and in much of Asia. They are rodents. The woodchuck is a kind of marmot that lives in open areas (see WOODCHUCK). North American marmots are from 1 to 2 feet (30 to 61 centimeters) long. They have short legs, small ears, and furry tails up to 9 inches (23 centimeters) long. Most marmots have gray fur on their backs and yellowish-orange fur on their bellies. Marmots eat plants. They grow fat in autumn and sleep through winter. Female marmots give birth to four or five young in May. Marmots live in *colonies* (groups) on mountain slopes.

Scientific Classification. Marmots belong to the squirrel family, Sciuridae. The common marmot is genus *Marmota*, species *M. flaviventris*. DANIEL BRANT

MARNE, BATTLES OF THE. See WORLD WAR I (The March Through Belgium; The Last Campaigns).

MARNE RIVER, *mahrn,* is the largest branch of the Seine River in France. The Marne rises in eastern France and winds north and west for 310 miles (500 kilometers). It empties into the Seine River 4 miles (6 kilometers) above Paris. The Marne's rapid current provides water power for flour mills. Large barges can navigate the Marne. It is connected to the east by a canal that runs through Nancy to Strasbourg on the Rhine River. ROBERT E. DICKINSON

MAROT, *ma ROH,* **CLEMENT** (1496-1544), was a French poet who served in the households of King Francis I and Marguerite de Navarre. Marot composed light, elegant, witty verse that pleased the gay, wealthy members of court society. But his poetry also reveals, with great artistry and devotion to truth, the social and intellectual realities of the time. Shortly before his death, he published a significant translation of the Psalms. Some critics consider Marot an unimportant court poet. Others, especially present-day critics, call him a genuine moralist who wrote with delicacy and discretion.

Marot was born in Cahors. He died in Italy, exiled from Roman Catholic France because of his Protestant beliefs. JOEL A. HUNT

MARQUAND, *mahr QUAHND,* **JOHN PHILLIPS** (1893-1960), an American novelist, pictured the decayed aristocratic society in Boston with gentle but effective satire. He won a Pulitzer prize in 1938 for *The Late George Apley.* This, and *Wickford Point* (1939), *H. M. Pulham, Esq.* (1941), and *Point of No Return* (1949) are usually considered his best works. They show how the inheritors of wealth conform to old customs without understanding the duties of a new age.

Marie S. Newberry
John P. Marquand

He also wrote *Repent in Haste* (1945); *Melville Goodwin, USA* (1951); *Sincerely, Willis Wayde* (1955); and *Stopover: Tokyo* (1957). *Thirty Years* (1954) contains essays and reports on his own observations. Marquand won his first success with romantic novels and with serialized detective stories about Mr. Moto, a secret agent.

Marquand was born in Wilmington, Del. He was graduated from Harvard University, and became a reporter on the Boston *Transcript.* HARRY R. WARFEL

MARQUE AND REPRISAL, *mahrk, rih PRY zuhl.* Governments at war once granted written *commissions* (licenses) to private owners of ships, giving them the authority to wage war against enemy shipping. These commissions were called *letters of marque and reprisal.* Vessels sailing under such commissions were known as *privateers.* See also PRIVATEER.

MARQUESAS ISLANDS, *mahr KAY zuhz,* are a group of 11 volcanic islands which lie about 740 miles (1,190 kilometers) northeast of Tahiti, in the south Pacific Ocean. They belong to France. The islands cover an area of 492 square miles (1,274 square kilometers), and have a population of about 5,600. The capital is Atuona, on Hiva Oa. The people are governed from Papeete in Tahiti. For location, see PACIFIC ISLANDS (map).

The Land. The Marquesas, in order of size, are Nuku Hiva (the largest), Hiva Oa, Ua Pu, Fatu Hiva, Ua Huka, Tahuata, Eiao, Hatutu, Motane, Fatu Huku, and Motu Iti. All are fertile and mountainous. The highest point, on Hiva Oa, is 4,130 feet (1,259 meters) above sea level. There are sheltered harbors in deep bays. The Marquesas have a healthful climate with variable rainfall. The chief crops include breadfruit, taro, bananas, sweet potatoes, and coconuts. The chief export is *copra,* the dried meat of coconuts.

The People. The Marquesas were once populated by at least 100,000 Polynesians, a brown-skinned people famous for their long and daring voyages in the Pacific Ocean. They are related to the Tahitians, but have a civilization of their own. The first explorers found them generous and hospitable. The Polynesians built houses on platforms made of stone blocks, and were clever at carving wood, shell, and bone. After contact with Europeans, diseases killed most of the Polynesians.

History. In 1595, Álvaro de Mendaña of Spain became the first European to reach the Marquesas. Captain James Cook, Joseph Ingraham, and others explored the islands. The Marquesas are famous in art and literature. Paul Gauguin, the French painter, lived, painted, died, and was buried on Hiva Oa. Herman Melville, the American novelist, described the islands in his novel *Typee.* It is a fictional tale of the actual adventures of Melville as a young man. EDWIN H. BRYAN, JR.

See also PACIFIC ISLANDS.

MARQUESS, *MAHR kwihs,* is a degree of nobility in the British peerage. A marquess, also spelled *marquis,* ranks higher than an earl or a baron, and second only

Polynesians on the Marquesas Islands at one time decorated their bodies with elaborate tattoos, *left.* A drawing made in the late 1700's, *below,* shows the outrigger canoes they used.
American Museum of Natural History, New York

to a duke. The name *marquess* once meant the ruler of an outlying province. A marquess's wife is a marchioness.

MARQUETTE, JACQUES (1637-1675), was a French explorer and Roman Catholic missionary in North America. He accompanied the French-Canadian explorer Louis Jolliet on an expedition down the Mississippi River. They were probably the first whites to explore the upper Mississippi and parts of Illinois and Wisconsin.

Early Life. Marquette was born in Laon, France, and attended schools run by Jesuit priests. He joined the Jesuit order in 1656 and spent the next 10 years studying and teaching in France. In 1666, he was sent as a missionary to New France, the French province in the region that is now Canada.

In New France, Marquette spent two years learning Indian languages. In 1668, he established a mission among the Ottawa Indians at Sault Sainte Marie in what is now Ontario. He went to the St. Esprit mission on Lake Superior in 1669 and worked among the Huron and Ottawa Indians. In 1671, he moved with them to the St. Ignace mission on northern Lake Michigan.

The Indians often talked about a great river called the Mississippi, a word that meant *big river* in their language. At that time, little was known about the geography of North America. Marquette and others thought the river might flow into the Pacific Ocean.

Exploration and Discovery. Governor Comte de Frontenac of New France believed the Mississippi might provide an easy route to the Far East for traders. In 1673, he sent Louis Jolliet to find the river and trace its course. Marquette knew some Indian languages, and so he was chosen to go with Jolliet.

In May 1673, Marquette, Jolliet, and five other men set out in two canoes from St. Ignace. They paddled south on Lake Michigan, into the Fox River, and up through what is now Wisconsin. The expedition traveled overland from the Fox River to the Wisconsin

River. At the mouth of the Wisconsin, they saw the Mississippi.

The explorers paddled down the Mississippi and realized that it flowed south. They decided it probably flowed into the Gulf of Mexico, rather than into the Pacific Ocean. Along the way, they met many friendly Indians. But when the men reached the mouth of the Arkansas River, they encountered hostile Indians. A friendly Indian told Marquette that whites lived farther south on the river. The explorers realized these people must be Spaniards who had settled along the Gulf of Mexico. Marquette and Jolliet feared that the Indians and Spaniards would attack them. Having learned the course of the river, they turned back.

The expedition traveled up the Mississippi to the Illinois River and from there to the Kankakee River. They journeyed overland from the Kankakee to the Chicago River and on to Lake Michigan. Their journey had taken about five months.

Final Journey. In 1674, Marquette set out from near present-day Green Bay, Wis., to establish a mission among the Kaskaskia Indians in the area of Ottawa, Ill. However, he became ill and spent the winter in a hut on the Chicago River. He reached his destination in the spring of 1675, but his health became worse. He started out to St. Ignace for medical aid but died on the way.   DAVID P. HARDCASTLE

See also ILLINOIS (French and Indian Control); JOLLIET, LOUIS.

MARQUETTE UNIVERSITY is a coeducational school conducted by the Society of Jesus in Milwaukee, Wis. The university admits students of all faiths. The courses offered lead to degrees in liberal arts, business administration, journalism, engineering, nursing, speech, dentistry, law, and other fields. The university has a graduate school and a summer school.

Marquette was chartered in 1864 and opened in 1881. It became a university in 1907. For enrollment, see UNIVERSITIES AND COLLEGES (table).

Critically reviewed by MARQUETTE UNIVERSITY

MARQUIS. See MARQUESS.

MARQUIS, DON (1878-1937), was a noted American writer and newspaper columnist. His daily columns, "The Sun Dial" in the New York *Sun* and "The Lantern" in the *New York Herald Tribune*, became highly popular. He introduced *archy*, the cockroach, and *mehitabel*, the cat. Marquis published *archy and mehitabel* in 1927. He wrote humorous books, including *Love Sonnets of a Cave Man* (1928). His *The Old Soak* (1921) was made into a play in 1922. His serious books include *The Dark Hours* (1924) and *Out of the Sea* (1927). Donald Perry Marquis was born in Walnut, Ill.   EDWIN H. CADY

MARRAKECH, *muh RAH kehsh* (pop. 332,741), is the third largest city in Morocco and one of its traditional capitals. It lies in southwestern Morocco (see MOROCCO [map]). The city is noted for its *mosques* (Muslim houses of worship), parks, gardens, and pink clay buildings. Its chief industries include food processing, flour milling, and leather and textile manufacturing.

Marrakech was once the capital of a vast Berber empire. The city was founded by the Berber ruler Yusuf ibn-Tashfin in 1062, and reached the height of its prosperity in the 1400's. Its importance declined when a succession of Arab rulers replaced the Berbers in Morocco.   KEITH G. MATHER

WORLD BOOK map

Jacques Marquette was one of the first whites to explore the upper Mississippi River and nearby areas. In 1673, he made a historic trip down the river with the explorer Louis Jolliet.

Hal McKusick, DPI

The Bride and Groom exchange marriage vows at a wedding ceremony. The groom, *above*, has put a ring on the ring finger of the bride's left hand. The bride may also give him a ring.

MARRIAGE is the relationship between a man and a woman who have made a legal agreement to live together. When a man and woman marry, they become husband and wife. Marriage is also an important religious ceremony in many of the world's religions.

Most couples decide to marry because they love each other and want to spend the rest of their lives together. A man and woman who marry hope to share a special sexual relationship and a permanent romantic attraction. But each hopes the other will always be a close friend as well. Each also expects the other to help with many problems and to share certain responsibilities. These responsibilities include earning a living, budgeting money, paying bills, preparing meals, and taking care of a home.

Most couples who marry plan to have children and to raise them together. A husband and wife are legally responsible for the care and protection of their children. Marriage thus serves as the basis of family life (see FAMILY).

In the United States, more than 2 million persons marry each year. About 93 per cent of all Americans marry at least once by the time they are 40 years old. This percentage is one of the greatest of any nation in the world.

Many people choose never to marry. Some of these men and women may not find a mate with whom they want to share their life. Others may not want the responsibilities required of a successful marriage. Still

The contributors of this article are Carlfred B. Broderick, Professor of Sociology at the University of Southern California; and Harvey T. Pulliam-Krager, Assistant Professor of Sociology at California State University at Los Angeles.

other men and women prefer to stay unmarried because they enjoy their independence.

Many married couples find they are not happy as husband and wife. Some marriages fail because the man and woman married when they were young and inexperienced in many ways. People who marry before they are 18 years old are much more likely to have unsuccessful marriages than if they had waited until they were older. A man and woman also have less of a chance of achieving a happy marriage if they marry primarily because the woman is pregnant. And if a man and woman differ in age, race, religion, or background, their chances of a successful marriage drop significantly.

In the United States, about a third of all marriages end in divorce. Most divorced men and women remarry, and many have a successful marriage with another partner. See DIVORCE.

Dating and Courtship. In India and many other countries, most marriages are arranged by parents' deciding whom their children will marry. But in Western countries, including the United States and Canada, nearly everyone makes his or her own decision about whom and when to marry.

Before people marry, they date members of the opposite sex. A man and woman who date each other spend a lot of time together learning to know the other person. After they have dated over a period of time, they may find that they love each other and decide to become engaged. In many cases, the man gives the woman an engagement ring as a token of their agreement to marry. The use of a ring as an engagement token comes from the ancient custom of using a ring to seal an important agreement.

The age at which people start to date varies widely.

Brent M. Jones

Raising a Family is one of the many rewards of marriage, but it is also a serious responsibility for the parents. The family shown above are enjoying a meal together at a restaurant.

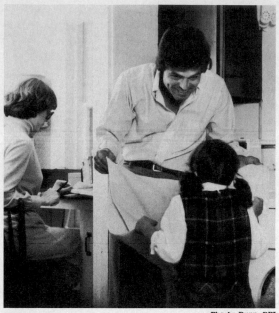

Phoebe Dunn, DPI

Many Married Couples share tasks that once were handled by either the husband or wife. The woman above is working on the family budget while her husband and daughter fold laundry.

Some states permit a couple to marry even if the bride or groom cannot be present at the wedding ceremony. However, someone must serve as a *proxy* (substitute) for the absent person. This type of marriage is called *marriage by proxy.*

In nearly all states, a couple must have a marriage license to marry. Most states require both the man and woman to have a blood test before they can obtain a license. This test shows whether a person has syphilis, a venereal disease (see VENEREAL DISEASE). In some states, a couple must also have a medical examination before they can obtain a marriage license.

Most states require a waiting period between the day a couple apply for a license and the day they marry. This period, which averages from three to five days, gives both persons time to make sure they want to marry. The waiting period developed from a Roman Catholic custom that required a couple to announce their engagement publicly on each of the three Sundays before the wedding. During the time between the first announcement and the wedding, anyone who believed

Marital Status of the U.S. Population

Per cent of persons 14 years old and over

Year	Married	Single	Widowed	Divorced
1890	53.5	39.1	7.1	0.3
1900	54.1	37.9	7.6	0.4
1910	55.8	36.4	7.3	0.5
1920	58.3	33.3	7.7	0.7
1930	59.0	32.2	7.6	1.2
1940	59.6	31.2	7.8	1.4
1950	67.0	22.8	8.3	1.9
1960	67.3	22.0	8.4	2.3
1965	65.8	23.5	8.1	2.6
1970	64.1	25.0	8.0	2.9
1975	62.5	26.0	7.4	4.1
1977	61.3	26.6	7.2	4.9
1978	60.5	27.1	7.2	5.2

But generally, the younger they are when they begin to date, the younger they are when they marry.

Most men and women date and marry people they live near, or with whom they work or go to school. Most people also date and marry those whom they consider attractive and who, in turn, regard them as attractive. In addition, people tend to date and marry individuals who are like themselves in certain ways. For example, people of the same nationality, race, and religion tend to marry each other. A man and woman are also more likely to marry if they have similar social and educational backgrounds and are about the same age.

Laws Concerning Marriage. A man and woman must follow certain laws when they marry. The United States and Canada have basically the same laws concerning marriage. Neither nation has federal marriage laws, but each state and province has its own regulations.

In all except three states, both the man and woman must be at least 18 years old to marry without parental consent. Nebraska and Wyoming require a couple to be at least 19, and Mississippi has a minimum age of 21. Most states allow people to marry as young as 16 with parental consent. A judge's permission is required in some states if a person under 16 wants to marry.

According to law, both the man and woman must freely consent to marry. If a person is forced or tricked into marrying against his or her will, a judge will *annul* (cancel) the marriage.

State laws prohibit close relatives from marrying each other. Laws also forbid a person to marry if he or she is married to someone else. A person who marries a second time while a first marriage is still in effect commits the crime of *bigamy.*

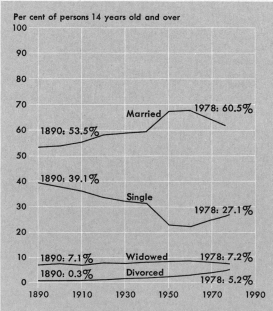

Per cent of persons 14 years old and over

Married — 1890: 53.5% — 1978: 60.5%
Single — 1890: 39.1% — 1978: 27.1%
Widowed — 1890: 7.1% — 1978: 7.2%
Divorced — 1890: 0.3% — 1978: 5.2%

Source: U.S. Bureau of the Census.

that the couple should not marry was expected to say so. Today, some couples announce their engagement at church services or through church bulletins. Such announcements are called *banns*.

If an unmarried couple live together as husband and wife, a court may declare them married after a certain period of time. The time period varies among the states that permit such *common-law marriages*, but it is usually several years. A couple is not required to have a license or wedding ceremony for a common-law marriage.

Most states have laws forbidding persons of the same sex to marry. However, many homosexual couples establish long-term relationships that are similar to marriage and consider themselves married.

Wedding Ceremonies and Customs. Most wedding ceremonies involve two requirements. First, the man and woman must say that they want to become husband and wife. Second, the ceremony must have witnesses, including the official who marries the couple. If the couple has a religious ceremony, it is conducted by a member of the clergy, such as a minister, priest, or rabbi. If a couple is married in a *civil* (nonreligious) ceremony, a judge or some other authorized official performs it. During the days of long sea voyages, the captain of a ship was authorized to conduct a marriage ceremony while the ship was at sea.

Many couples prefer a traditional religious ceremony, though some people depart from custom. Some even write their own wedding service. A traditional marriage ceremony begins with the bridesmaids and ushers walking slowly down a center aisle to the altar. They stand on each side of the altar throughout the ceremony. The groom enters and waits for the bride at the altar. The bride then walks down the aisle with her father, another male relative, or a family friend. She wears a white dress and veil and carries a bouquet. At the altar, the bride and groom exchange marriage vows and accept each other as husband and wife. The groom puts a wedding ring on the ring finger of the bride's left hand, and the bride may also give the groom a ring. After the ceremony, the bride and groom kiss and then leave down the main aisle.

People of many backgrounds follow the traditional wedding ceremony, but certain religious groups add their own features to it. For example, different Protestant groups have their own versions of the ceremony. Many Roman Catholic weddings take place during a a mass, and the bride and groom receive Holy Communion. Marriage is a *sacrament* (important religious ceremony) in the Roman Catholic and Eastern Orthodox churches (see SACRAMENT).

Most Jewish weddings are held under a special canopy that represents the couple's future home. At the end of the ceremony, an empty glass or other breakable object is placed on the floor and the groom breaks it with his foot. This act symbolizes the destruction of the ancient Jewish temple in Jerusalem and reminds the couple that a marriage can also break if it is not protected.

A Quaker man and woman marry at a public gathering where they declare their commitment to each other. Quakers believe that God makes a couple husband and wife, and so a minister or other official is not required to be present.

Many wedding customs have been popular since an-

Leon Kofod

Some Societies Permit *Polygamy*, the practice of having more than one wife or husband. This photograph shows a man of the African nation of Liberia with two of his wives.

cient times. For example, Roman brides probably wore veils more than 2,000 years ago. Bridal veils became popular in Great Britain and the New World during the late 1700's. The custom of giving a wedding ring may also date back to the ancient Romans. The roundness of the ring probably represents eternity, and the presentation of wedding rings symbolizes that the man and woman are united forever. Wearing the wedding ring on the ring finger of the left hand is another old custom. People once thought that a vein or nerve ran directly from this finger to the heart. An old superstition says that a bride can ensure good luck by wearing "something old, something new, something borrowed, and something blue." Another superstition is that it is bad luck for a bride and groom to see each other before the ceremony on their wedding day.

After many weddings, the guests throw rice at the bride and groom as a wish for children and good fortune. Rice was once a symbol of fertility, happiness, and long life. The bride may toss her bouquet to the unmarried female guests. The woman who catches the flowers will supposedly be the next to marry. This custom probably started in France in the 1300's. The bride may also throw her garter to the unmarried men, and the man who catches it will supposedly be the next male to marry.

Marriage Problems. A man and woman expect certain things of each other even before they marry. After marriage, some husbands and wives cannot satisfy their partner's expectations. They may become disappointed and unhappy with each other and have problems with their marriage.

A couple may argue about almost anything, such as how to spend their money or how to discipline the children. If they do not work out their differences, they may find it difficult to be friends, romantic partners, or good parents.

Couples with marriage problems should seek help from a trained marriage counselor. Only a few states require marriage counselors to be licensed. A couple can obtain names of qualified counselors in their area from the American Association of Marriage and Family Counselors, 225 Yale Avenue, Claremont, Calif. 91711.

Changing Attitudes About Marriage. Almost every society has certain traditional ideas about marriage. For example, most societies expect men and women to marry. Most cultures also have traditions about the role and duties of a husband and wife. Traditionally, the husband is expected to earn a living and the wife is expected to keep house and raise children.

Many Americans disregard traditional marriage patterns. For example, a large number of married couples share responsibilities that traditionally are handled by either the husband or the wife. An increasing number of married women have paying jobs and help support their families. In 1940, about 15 per cent of all married women earned money. In 1975, about 45 per cent held a full- or part-time job. More and more husbands share responsibilities traditionally handled by women. Such responsibilities include cooking, doing housework, and caring for the children.

On the average, men and women remain single longer than they once did. In 1950, men married at an average age of 23, and women married at an average age of 20. In the late 1970's, men averaged almost 24 when they married, and women married at the average age of 22.

An increasing number of people choose not to marry. If a man and woman wish to avoid marriage, they may decide to live together with no formal obligations to each other. This arrangement is more common among young adults, but some couples of all ages live together without marrying.

Marriage in Other Cultures. In most countries, one man marries one woman and they stay married unless one of them dies or they are divorced. This system of marriage is called *monogamy*. Some societies permit *polygamy*, in which a man has more than one wife, or a woman has more than one husband. The marriage of a man to more than one woman is called *polygyny* and is practiced by many African and Middle Eastern peoples. Islamic law permits a man to have as many as four wives. Some societies practice *polyandry*, the marriage of a woman to more than one man.

In certain cultures, marriage involves a gift from the family of the bride or groom to the other's family. In many societies, for example, the bride's family gives money or property to the groom or his family. Such a gift is called a *dowry*. In some cases, the dowry is given to the bride so that she and her husband may benefit from it. In other cultures, the groom and his family present gifts to the family of the bride. This offering is called a *bride price*.

Some societies require a person to marry someone who belongs to his or her own tribe or group. This custom is called *endogamy*. In other places, an individual must follow the rules of *exogamy* and marry a person from another tribe or village. The most common rule of exogamy requires a man or woman to marry someone outside his or her own family. Each culture has its own rules about which family members a person is forbidden to marry. However, most societies forbid *incest*, which is marriage or sexual relations between certain close relatives. In nearly all cultures, such relatives include a parent and child or a brother and sister.

CARLFRED B. BRODERICK and HARVEY T. PULLIAM-KRAGER

Related Articles in WORLD BOOK include:

Annulment	Greece (People)
Banns of Marriage	Gretna Green
Bigamy	Indian, American (Marriage)
Breach of Promise	Poland (picture: Weddings)
Culture (pictures)	Polygamy
Divorce	Proxy
Dower	Sex
Eugenics	Wedding Anniversary
Family	

See also *Marriage and Divorce* in the RESEARCH GUIDE/INDEX, Volume 22, for a *Reading and Study Guide*.

MARRIAGE OF FIGARO, THE. See OPERA (*Marriage of Figaro, The*).

MARRIC, J. J. See CREASEY, JOHN.

MARROW. See BONE (Structure of the Bones).

MARRYAT, FREDERICK (1792-1848), was an English author whose novels about life at sea were widely read during the 1800's. The novels have declined in popularity, but they remain fine examples of adventure stories.

Marryat was born in London. As a boy he tried to run away to sea several times. When Marryat was 14 years old, his father allowed him to join the navy. Marryat's 23 years of sea adventures in the British navy provided material for his writing. *The Naval Officer, or Scenes and Adventures in the Life of Frank Mildmay* (1829), for example, is largely an autobiographical novel. Marryat's other sea novels include *The King's Own* (1830), *The Pirate and the Three Cutters* (1836), and *Mr. Midshipman Easy* (1836). His children's stories include *Masterman Ready* (1841-1842). JAMES DOUGLAS MERRITT

MARS was the god of war in Roman mythology. The ancient Romans gave Mars special importance because they considered him the father of Romulus and Remus, the legendary founders of Rome.

Originally, Mars was a god of farmland and fertility. The month of March, the beginning of the Roman growing season, was named for him. Since ancient times, the area enclosed by a bend in the Tiber River in Rome has been called the Field of Mars. The early Romans dedicated this section of land to Mars because of its fertility.

Mars became the god of war after the Romans came into contact with Greek culture. They gave him many characteristics of the Greek god of war, Ares. In time, the Romans associated Mars principally with war. Before going into battle, Roman troops offered sacrifices to him. After a victory, they gave Mars a share of their spoils. The word *martial*, which means *warlike*, is based on his name. The planet Mars is named for him.

Artists show Mars in armor and wearing a crested helmet. Editorial cartoonists still use this image of Mars as a symbol for war. The wolf and the woodpecker were associated with Mars. His love affair with Venus, the Roman goddess of love, became a popular subject for poets and painters. PAUL PASCAL

See also ARES; MYTHOLOGY (Roman Mythology).

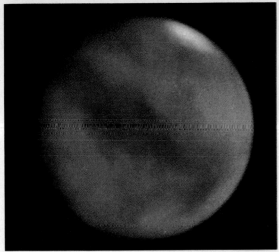

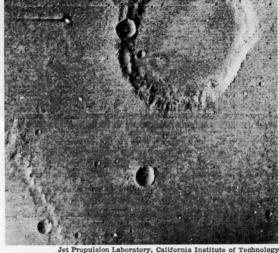

Hale Observatories   Jet Propulsion Laboratory, California Institute of Technology

Mars' Surface Features, including light areas, dark areas, and polar cap, are visible in this photograph taken from the earth, *left.* The earth's atmosphere makes the picture blurred. Craters on Mars were photographed by the U.S. *Mariner VI* space probe in 1969, *right.* This picture was taken 2,300 miles (3,700 kilometers) from Mars. The large crater is about 24 miles (39 kilometers) across.

MARS is the only planet whose surface can be seen in detail from the earth. It is reddish in color, and was named Mars after the bloody red god of war of the ancient Romans.

Mars is the fourth closest planet to the sun, and the next planet beyond the earth. Its mean distance from the sun is about 141,500,000 miles (227,700,000 kilometers), compared with about 93,000,000 miles (150,000,000 kilometers) for the earth. At its closest approach to the earth, Mars is 35,000,000 miles (56,000,000 kilometers) away. Venus is the only planet that comes closer.

The diameter of Mars is about 4,200 miles (6,760 kilometers), a little over half that of the earth. Pluto and Mercury are the only planets smaller than Mars.

Orbit. Mars travels around the sun in an *elliptical* (oval-shaped) orbit. Its distance from the sun varies from about 155 million miles (250 million kilometers) at its farthest point, to about 128 million miles (206 million kilometers) at its closest point. Mars takes about 687 earth-days to go around the sun, compared with about 365 days, or 1 year, for the earth.

Rotation. As Mars orbits the sun, it spins on its *axis,* an imaginary line through its center. Mars' axis is not *perpendicular* (at an angle of 90°) to its path around the sun. The axis tilts at an angle of about 25° from the perpendicular position. For an illustration of the tilt of an axis, see PLANET (The Axes of the Planets). Mars rotates once every 24 hours and 37 minutes. The earth rotates once every 23 hours and 56 minutes.

Surface. The surface conditions on Mars are more like the earth's than are those of any other planet. But the plants and animals of the earth could not live on Mars. The temperature on Mars averages about

The contributor of this article is Hyron Spinrad, Professor of Astronomy at the University of California in Berkeley.

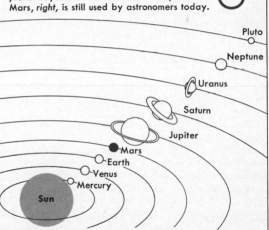

MARS AT A GLANCE
Mars, shown in blue in the diagram, is the next planet beyond the earth. The ancient symbol for Mars, *right,* is still used by astronomers today.

Distance from Sun: *Shortest*—128,000,000 miles (206,000,000 kilometers); *Greatest*—155,000,000 miles (250,000,000 kilometers); *Mean*—141,500,000 miles (227,700,000 kilometers).

Distance from Earth: *Shortest*—35,000,000 miles (56,000,000 kilometers); *Greatest*—248,000,000 miles (399,000,000 kilometers).

Diameter: 4,200 miles (6,760 kilometers).

Length of Year: About 1 earth-year and 10½ months.

Rotation Period: 24 hours and 37 minutes.

Average Temperature: −80°F. (−62°C).

Atmosphere: Carbon dioxide, nitrogen, argon, oxygen, and water vapor.

Number of Satellites: 2.

The Windblown Plains of Mars are covered by sand dunes and jagged rocks. They resemble the deserts of southwestern North America. This closeup photograph of Mars' surface was taken in 1976 by the U.S. *Viking I* space probe. A part of the probe's equipment appears in the center.

Jet Propulsion Laboratory

—80° F. (—62° C). The planet seems to have had large amounts of surface water millions of years ago, but almost none today. However, scientists think that water may be frozen in the planet's large polar caps or beneath its surface. The atmosphere surrounding Mars contains only a trace of oxygen. In spite of the scarcity of liquid water and oxygen, many scientists believe some form of life may exist on Mars.

As seen from the earth through a telescope, the surface of Mars has three outstanding features—bright areas, dark areas, and polar caps. At least part of the planet's surface is covered by craters, caused by meteors crashing into it. Photographs sent back by unmanned space probes show that Mars also has canyons, deep gorges, and surface features that resemble dry river beds. Such features seem to support the view of some scientists that large quantities of water once flowed on the planet's surface.

Bright Areas of Mars are reddish rust-brown in color and cover about two-thirds of the planet's surface. They are dry, desertlike regions that are covered by dust, sand, and rocks. Much of the surface material seems to contain a brick-colored mineral called *limonite*, which is found in various deserts on the earth.

Dark Areas of Mars cover about one-third of the planet's surface. They form irregular patterns, and generally appear greenish or bluish gray in color. These dark regions are called *maria* (seas), even though they do not have any measurable amounts of water.

Astronomers once thought the bright areas of Mars were higher than the maria. But after bouncing radar beams off the surface of the planet, some astronomers think the dark areas are higher. The difference in height between the two regions probably averages about 5 miles (8 kilometers). The slopes from high to low ground are probably gradual rather than steep.

The color and size of Mars' dark areas vary throughout the planet's year. Parts of the maria become lighter in color or disappear during the Martian fall and winter. They become darker and larger during the Martian spring and summer. Many astronomers think the variation is caused by blowing sand and dust that covers and uncovers parts of Mars' surface.

A series of lines running between Mars' dark areas was discovered in 1877 by Giovanni V. Schiaparelli, an Italian astronomer. Schiaparelli called these lines "channels," but when the word was translated from Italian into English, it became "canals." As a result, some scientists thought the lines might be man-made waterways. Astronomers now know the canals on Mars are not man-made, and do not carry water. The canals change color during the Martian seasons.

Polar Caps of Mars cover small areas located at the planet's north and south poles. The polar caps appear white from the earth, and they may contain large amounts of frozen water. Like the maria on the planet, each polar cap grows and shrinks with the Martian seasons. A cap appears to evaporate and become smaller when it is tilted toward the sun, and then freeze and get larger when it is tilted away from the sun. The evaporating polar caps may provide some of the water va-

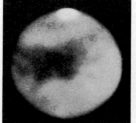

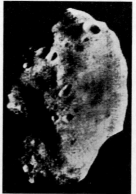

Seasons on Mars cause changes in the planet's surface features. During a Martian winter, the polar cap is large and the dark areas are small, *left*. During a Martian summer, the polar cap shrinks and the dark areas become larger, *right*.

Lowell Observatory

NASA   Lowell Observatory

Mars Has Two Satellites, Phobos and Deimos. Phobos, *left*, was photographed by the *Mariner IX* space probe. Viewed through a telescope, *right*, Phobos appears as a bright spot to the left of Mars. Deimos is fainter and farther away, to the right.

por that is present in the atmosphere of the planet.

Atmosphere of Mars is thinner and contains fewer gases than that surrounding the earth. It consists chiefly of carbon dioxide, with small amounts of nitrogen, argon, and oxygen. The planet's atmosphere also contains extremely small traces of water vapor. The *atmospheric pressure* (force exerted by the weight of the gases) on Mars is less than 0.15 pound per square inch (0.01 kilogram per square centimeter)—about one-hundredth the atmospheric pressure on the earth.

Three general types of clouds can be seen in the Martian atmosphere. Pink clouds of dust often cover large areas of the planet. Thin blue clouds appear to be made up of ice crystals. Thicker white clouds, thought to consist of water vapor, occasionally move across the planet.

Temperature. The tilt of Mars' axis causes the sun to heat the planet's northern and southern halves unequally, resulting in seasons and temperature changes. The seasons on Mars last about twice as long as those on the earth, because Mars takes almost twice as long to go around the sun as the earth does.

Temperatures on Mars are generally lower than those on the earth, because Mars is farther from the sun than

the earth is. The average temperature for the entire planet is about −80° F. (−62° C). There is a wide variation between daytime and nighttime temperatures. The average daytime temperature is about −10° F. (−23° C). But in areas near Mars' equator, daytime temperatures may rise as high as 70° F. (21° C). Astronomers estimate the average nighttime temperature on Mars to be about −150° F. (−101° C).

Density and Mass. Mars is about four-fifths as *dense* as the earth (see DENSITY). The *mass* of Mars is only about a tenth that of the earth (see MASS). Because of the planet's smaller mass, its force of gravity is about three-eighths as strong as the earth's. A 100-pound object on the earth would weigh about 38 pounds on Mars.

Satellites. Two small *satellites* (moons) travel around Mars. The closer and larger one, named Phobos, is about 5,800 miles (9,330 kilometers) from the center of Mars. Its diameter is about 14 miles (23 kilometers) at its equator and 11 miles (18 kilometers) from pole to pole. It travels around Mars once about every 7½ hours. Deimos, the smaller satellite, is about 14,600 miles (23,-500 kilometers) from Mars' center, and circles the planet once about every 30 hours. Deimos has a diameter of about 6 miles (10 kilometers). An American astrono-

MARS

The first detailed map of Mars, below, was prepared from wide-angle photographs taken by the Mariner IX spacecraft. This map shows volcanic craters and peaks, windblown plains, and a giant canyon. The canyon extends 2,500 miles (4,020 kilometers) across the planet.

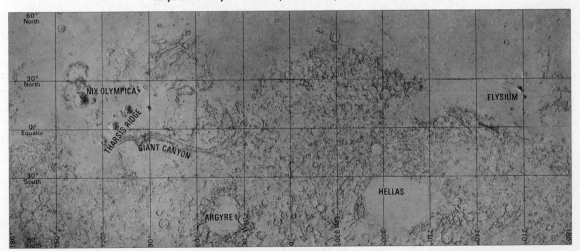

NORTH AND SOUTH POLAR REGIONS

Polar caps, which appear white from the earth, cover small areas at the north and south poles of Mars, right. The polar caps remain frozen the year around, though their size varies with the seasons on Mars.

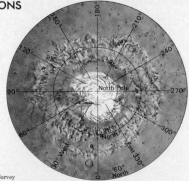
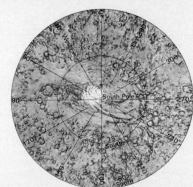

mer, Asaph Hall, discovered both satellites in 1877.

Flights to Mars. The unmanned U.S. spacecraft *Mariner IV* flew as close as 6,118 miles (9,846 kilometers) to Mars in 1965. *Mariner VI* and *Mariner VII* flew within about 2,000 miles (3,200 kilometers) of Mars in 1969. In 1971 and 1972, *Mariner IX* orbited Mars at a distance of about 1,000 miles (1,600 kilometers). It photographed both Martian satellites, a dust storm on the planet, and many surface details. A Russian probe, *Mars 3*, also orbited the planet in 1971. It released a capsule that made the first soft landing on Mars. But the capsule transmitted information for only 20 seconds before it unexpectedly fell silent.

Photographs sent to the earth from *Mariner IV* and *Mariner IX* revealed meteor craters on Mars' surface. Astronomers had never seen craters in observations from the earth. *Mariner IV* instruments showed that Mars has no measurable magnetic field.

On July 20, 1976, the U.S. *Viking I* space probe landed on Mars in a desertlike region near the planet's equator. A second unmanned U.S. craft, *Viking II*, landed farther north on September 3 of the same year. Both probes transmitted high-quality, closeup photographs of the planet's surface features. Their instruments also analyzed Mars' atmosphere and soil to seek signs of life. In spite of these experiments, scientists still have not been able to determine whether life exists on the planet. HYRON SPINRAD

See also ASTRONOMY; PLANET; SOLAR SYSTEM; SPACE TRAVEL (Reaching the Planets and Stars).

MARS 3. See MARS (Flights to Mars).

MARSEILLAISE, *MAHR seh LAYZ*, is the national hymn of France. A young captain of the engineers named Claude Joseph Rouget de Lisle (1760-1836) wrote it during the French Revolution. It is believed that he composed both the words and the music in one night. Some historians believe he took the music from an old Protestant hymn and the words from war slogans. Others say he wrote the song in 1792 at a banquet the mayor of Strasbourg gave for 600 army volunteers. It aroused such enthusiasm that 400 more men joined the company.

Some of the best known lines are the following:

Allons enfants de la patrie,
Le jour de gloire est arrivé.

Aux armes citoyens! Formez vos bataillons.
Marchons, marchons, qu'un sang impur
Abreuve nos sillons.

The song was first heard in Paris when the Marseille battalion sang it as they marched to storm the Tuileries. After that, it was called "Song of the Marseillais," and finally "The Marseillaise." The composer died in 1836 in Choisy-le-Roi. A monument to his memory has been built there. In 1875, France adopted the song as its national hymn. RAYMOND KENDALL

MARSEILLE, *mahr SAY* (pop. 908,600; met. area pop. 1,070,912), is the second largest city in France and the country's main seaport. Paris is the only larger French city. Marseille, the nation's oldest city, lies in southeast France on the Mediterranean Sea. For location, see FRANCE (political map).

The City has the shape of a half-circle. It extends inland from an old port that is too small for modern ships. This port, called Old Harbor, is filled with pleasure boats and surrounded by restaurants and cafes. It is the city's major tourist attraction. The Canèbiere, a main street lined with modern shops, extends inland from Old Harbor. It also attracts tourists.

A huge, modern port—which is one of the world's busiest—extends about 5 miles (8 kilometers) west of Old Harbor. Trading ships from many parts of the world dock at the port. Crew members of the ships visit the city and give it a busy, international flavor.

Marseille has many beautiful churches. Notre-Dame-de-la-Garde, one of the churches, has a large image of the Virgin Mary on its tall steeple. The image can be seen far out at sea.

Economy of Marseille is based on trade and manufacturing. The city's port handles about a third of the traffic of all French seaports. About 4,500 ships use the port annually. Industries in the Marseille area process chemicals, food, and petroleum from many parts of the world. The city's chief manufactured products include bricks, candles, engines, medicines, soap, and tiles. Marseille has an airport, and highways and trains connect the city with other major European cities, particularly Paris.

History. Marseille was founded about 600 B.C. by Greek adventurers from Asia Minor, who called it *Massalia*. Marseille was an independent city until the first century before the birth of Christ. It then came under Roman domination and fell into decline. In the Middle Ages, the city regained its importance during the Crusades, a series of Christian military expeditions to recapture the Holy Land from the Muslims. Many soldiers and supplies were sent through the port to the Holy Land.

Provence, the region where Marseille is located, became part of France in 1481. Bloody struggles took place in Marseille in the late 1700's during the French Revolution. The opening of the Suez Canal in 1869 provided a water route between the Mediterranean Sea and Indian Ocean. The canal greatly increased the importance of Marseille as a shipping center. J. A. LAPONCE

For the monthly weather in Marseille, see FRANCE (Climate). See also MARSEILLAISE.

MARSH is a wet area where such nonwoody plants as cattails, grasses, rushes, and sedges grow. A wet area in which trees and bushes grow is called a *swamp* or a *bog* (see SWAMP). Marshes are found in places where the shape of the land and the nature of the soil combine to produce permanently moist ground. Even deserts may have marshes in low places and near springs. Marshes provide food or shelter for many kinds of animals, including muskrats, raccoons, frogs, turtles, and ducks.

Most marshes are covered by fresh water or by salt water. An *estuarine* marsh is washed by a tide of salt water part of the time and by fresh water the rest of the time. Estuarine marshes lie along coasts at places where fresh water flows into the sea—at river mouths, for example. The mixture of salt and fresh water provides a rich supply of food that supports an especially large variety of animal and plant life. Today, pollution endangers many estuarine marshes. CLAIR L. KUCERA

MARSH, REGINALD (1898-1954), was an American artist famous for his vigorous and realistic pictures of American city life. He excelled in portraying crowds on skid row and the waterfront, and in burlesque houses. Some of his scenes are grim in feeling, but full of vitality.

Marsh worked in various painting media and also made drawings. Some of his best works are drawings.

Marsh was born in Paris of American parents. He grew up in New Jersey and graduated from Yale University. He worked as a book and magazine illustrator and as a graphic artist for the New York *Daily News*. He taught at the Art Students League in New York from the early 1930's until his death. GEORGE EHRLICH

MARSH GAS. See METHANE.

MARSH HAWK is the only harrier hawk that lives in North America. The marsh hawk is one of the best-known birds of prey in North America. It visits almost every part of the continent at some time during the year.

Most male marsh hawks are about 19 inches (48 centimeters) long with a wingspread of 40 to 45 inches (102 to 114 centimeters). Females are 2 to 3 inches (5 to

Allen Cruickshank

The Marsh Hawk is a friend to the North American farmer. This valuable bird kills rats, mice, snakes, and other harmful pests.

8 centimeters) longer. The male is light-gray and white. The female is brown and tan. Both have a white patch above the base of the tail. They eat mice, poultry, game birds, and snakes.

Scientific Classification. The marsh hawk belongs to the Old World vulture family, *Accipitridae*. It is genus *Circus*, species *C. cyaneus*.

OLIN SEWALL PETTINGILL, JR.

See also HAWK.

MARSH MALLOW is a plant that grows in meadows and marshes of eastern Europe. It is now grown in the United States. It has woody stalks, which grow 2 to 4 feet (61 to 120 centimeters) high, and large leaves. Downy hair covers both stalks and leaves. The plant has pink flowers. Its root is white and shaped

J. Horace McFarland

Marsh Mallow Flower

like a carrot. During famines, people have eaten the roots. The root once was used as an ingredient in the candy called marshmallow.

Scientific Classification. The marsh mallow belongs to the mallow family, *Malvaceae*. It is genus *Althaea*, species *A. officinalis*. HAROLD NORMAN MOLDENKE

MARSH MARIGOLD. See COWSLIP.

MARSHAL is the highest title in the armies of many countries. *Marshal* is also the title of a police officer in many small towns or villages.

In England, the word *marshal* was used to mean *commander of the army* as early as the 1100's. Under the early Frankish kings, the marshal was first a master of horse and later a commander of cavalry. The title grew in dignity and honor until *Maréchal de France* (Marshal of France) became one of the highest honors that could be conferred upon a person. The countries of Europe have given the title *marshal* to top-ranking military commanders. Joseph Stalin, former dictator of Russia, used the title *Marshal* during World War II. The British Army uses the title *field marshal*, and the head of the air forces is called an *air marshal*. The *provost marshal* is the highest military police officer.

In the United States, officers of the federal court are called *United States marshals*. They open and close sessions of district courts and courts of appeals, and may serve the processes of the courts in their districts. *Deputy United States marshals* can make arrests for violation of federal laws. A United States marshal is assigned to each federal court district.

Temporary police are sometimes called marshals, and in some towns the head of the fire department is called the *fire marshal*. ERWIN N. GRISWOLD

MARSHALL, ALFRED (1842-1924), was a British educator and the most influential economist of his day. Marshall combined two different theories about what determines the value or price of a good. "Classical" theorists had said price was determined mainly by the cost of producing the good, and theorists of the late 1800's had stressed the *utility* (usefulness) of the good and the consumer demand for it. In *Principles of Economics* (1890), Marshall concluded that all of these factors helped to determine price.

Marshall also believed that a self-regulating economy, free of major government interference and based on free competition and private enterprise, would lead to better social conditions, a fair distribution of income, and full employment. Marshall's emphasis on consumer welfare led to the development of *welfare economics*. This branch of economics judges economic systems according to how well they contribute to consumer satisfaction and human well-being.

Marshall was born in London. In 1883, he began teaching economics at Oxford University. He taught at Cambridge University from 1885 to 1908. At Cambridge, Marshall helped train a generation of economists who made the "Cambridge school" the most important of its time. DANIEL R. FUSFELD

MARSHALL, GEORGE CATLETT (1880-1959), an American soldier and statesman, served as chief of staff of the United States Army during World War II (1939-1945). He also served as secretary of state from 1947 to 1949 and as secretary of defense from 1950 to 1951.

MARSHALL, GEORGE CATLETT

Marshall was the first professional soldier to become secretary of state. In 1947, while serving in that post, he proposed the European Recovery Program, also called the Marshall Plan. Under this plan, the United States spent billions of dollars to rebuild wartorn western Europe. The Marshall Plan is credited with helping check the spread of Communism in Europe. Marshall's role in European reconstruction earned him the 1953 Nobel peace prize.

U.S. Army

George C. Marshall

His Early Life. Marshall was born on Dec. 31, 1880, in Uniontown, Pa. He was the youngest of four children. His father owned coal and coke properties. The senior Marshall was extremely proud of his distant cousin John Marshall, the former chief justice of the Supreme Court (see MARSHALL, JOHN).

Marshall graduated from the Virginia Military Institute in Lexington, Va., in 1901. He was not an outstanding student, but he ranked in the upper half of his class. He received an army commission as a second lieutenant of infantry in 1902. Marshall married Elizabeth Carter Coles in 1902. She died in 1927, and Marshall was married to Katherine Tupper Brown in 1930.

His Early Career. Marshall began his army career with duty in the Philippines in 1902. He returned home in 1903, and attended the Army School of the Line and the Army Staff College at Fort Leavenworth, Kans. He was graduated first in his class from the School of the Line. Marshall said later of this achievement, "Ambition had set in." He also served at various military posts in the United States.

Assigned to the Philippines again in 1913, he showed great ability for planning and tactics in mock battles. In 1916, he returned to the United States and was promoted to captain. When the United States entered World War I in 1917, Marshall sailed for France with the first field units to go overseas. He served for a year as training officer and then as chief of operations of the First Division. He was transferred to the First Army in 1918, and served as chief of operations in the closing months of the war.

Marshall helped plan the First Army's attack on St. Mihiel. He directed the movement of more than 400,000 men and 2,700 guns from St. Mihiel to the Meuse-Argonne front for the final American battle of the war. This transfer, made at night in less than two weeks, completely surprised the Germans. General John J. Pershing, commander of the U.S. forces, hailed it as one of the great accomplishments of the war.

Marshall served as senior aide to Pershing from 1919 to 1924. From 1924 to 1927, he served in China as executive officer of the 15th Infantry Regiment.

From 1927 until 1932, Marshall was assistant commandant in charge of training at the Infantry School, Fort Benning, Ga. He did much to raise the level of instruction there. He later helped organize and administer Civilian Conservation Corps (CCC) camps.

World War II. Marshall was made a brigadier general in 1936. In 1938, he became chief of the war plans division of the War Department and then deputy chief of staff of the army. On Sept. 1, 1939, the day World War II began in Europe, Marshall became chief of staff of the U.S. Army, which then totaled less than 200,000 men, including the Army Air Corps. He also became a four-star general.

Marshall introduced mass maneuvers in which soldiers gained experience under combatlike conditions. He organized the army into units especially trained to take part in desert, mountain, and jungle warfare.

Marshall helped make the U.S. Army the greatest fighting force in history by 1945. He remained in Washington, D.C., throughout the war. His work there was so important that he could not be spared to serve as a battle leader. He was responsible for building, arming, and supplying a force of 8,250,000 soldiers and airmen. He was a leader in planning the overall war strategy, and the directing force behind the movements of U.S. armies. Under his command, General Dwight D. Eisenhower and General Douglas MacArthur led American forces to victory in Europe and the Pacific.

On Dec. 16, 1944, Marshall became a General of the Army. In November, 1945, a few months after the war ended, he retired as chief of staff. After he retired, President Harry S. Truman appointed him special representative to China. He spent the next year in China trying to end the civil war between the Chinese Nationalists and the Communists.

Statesman. Marshall returned to the United States in January, 1947, to assume the post of secretary of state in President Truman's Cabinet. As secretary, he urged Congress to pass the European Recovery Program. Under the plan, the United States sent about $13 billion in aid to European countries. Marshall also worked to secure aid for Greece and Turkey and to supply food to West Berlin when the Communists blockaded that city. These programs and the Marshall Plan did much to check Communist influence in Europe (see MARSHALL PLAN). Marshall also began negotiations that led to the North Atlantic Treaty Organization (NATO). In 1949, he resigned his Cabinet post because of poor health.

Marshall served as president of the American Red Cross in 1949 and 1950. When the Korean War began in 1950, Truman asked Marshall to head the Department of Defense. An act of Congress set aside the rule that the secretary of defense must be a civilian. Marshall helped strengthen NATO and build up the United Nations fighting forces in Korea. He resigned as secretary of defense in September, 1951.

Marshall died on Oct. 16, 1959, and was buried at Arlington National Cemetery. In 1964, the George C. Marshall Research Library, containing his papers and souvenirs, opened in Lexington, Va.   FORREST C. POGUE

MARSHALL, JAMES WILSON (1810-1885), discovered gold in California on Jan. 24, 1848. He found small pieces of gold while he was building a sawmill for John Sutter 48 miles (77 kilometers) north of Sutter's Fort. News of the discovery started the great gold rush of 1849. In spite of his important discovery, Marshall died a poor and bitter man. The first persons who came to the gold site paid a small fee, but later arrivals refused to pay. The claims of Marshall and Sutter were swept aside. Marshall was born in Hunterdon County, New Jersey.　　　　　　　　　　HOWARD R. LAMAR

MARSHALL, JOHN (1755-1835), is known as the *great chief justice*. When Marshall became chief justice of the United States in 1801, the Supreme Court of the United States was so poorly respected that it was difficult to get able people to serve as justices. Many felt that it would never settle important questions. But 34 years later, when Marshall's term as chief justice ended with his death, the court had become a vigorous and equal third branch of government. The structure of the government had been made clear through his decisions. Later court interpretations have rested heavily upon the strong principles he created.

Marshall's service as chief justice featured a continuous argument between the Supreme Court and the Democratic-Republicans, led by Thomas Jefferson, James Madison, and, later, Andrew Jackson. Jefferson and his followers believed in a weak judiciary and "states' rights." Marshall opposed these beliefs. His decisions established a powerful Supreme Court and a strong national government, with the right to override the states whenever national and state interests clashed. The Democratic-Republicans often threatened to impeach Marshall and to make constitutional changes that would take away the Court's power. But the clarity and persuasiveness of Marshall's decisions always kept those who opposed him on the defensive, and so they were unable to carry out their plans.

Early Life. John Marshall was born on Sept. 24, 1755, in Germantown, Va. His father was a colonel in the Revolutionary War. Marshall grew up on his father's farm and had little formal schooling. He was a tall, awkward boy, but he had great strength and agility. When the Revolutionary War broke out, he joined the

patriot army and fought in several battles. By 1777, he had risen to the rank of captain. He served in Virginia, New Jersey, New York, and Pennsylvania, and was at Valley Forge during the winter of 1777-1778. During the war years, he saw much of his country for the first time. Later, he said that he had gone into the army a Virginian and had come out an American.

Marshall became a lawyer in 1781, after studying law on his own and attending some lectures at William and Mary College. He joined the Federalist party, and served in the Virginia legislature. In 1788 he became a delegate to the state convention that adopted the new federal Constitution. He and James Madison wanted it adopted, and led the debate in favor of ratification. Marshall's reputation as a lawyer grew rapidly. President Washington offered him the position of attorney general. He declined, but in 1797 agreed to go to Paris with Charles Cotesworth Pinckney and Elbridge Gerry to try to settle various questions growing out of French interference with American trade (see XYZ AFFAIR). Marshall was elected to the U.S. House of Representatives as a Federalist on his return. In 1800, President John Adams appointed him secretary of state.

The Chief Justice. Marshall, appointed by President Adams, began his great career as the fourth chief justice on Feb. 4, 1801. At that time the present relationship among the executive, legislative, and judicial branches of the government had not been established. Nor was the relationship between the national government and the states well defined. It fell to Marshall, as chief justice, to solve these problems.

In the famous case of *Marbury v. Madison* (1803), Marshall established the power of the Supreme Court to declare laws unconstitutional. This doctrine, which we know today as the power of "judicial review," is now accepted without question. But, if it had not been established, over strong opposition, the Constitution might have become the same kind of weak charter as the Articles of Confederation.

His Decisions. Marshall believed in a strong federal government to enable the United States to act effectively as a nation. A series of his decisions made this principle vital. In *McCulloch v. Maryland* (1819), Marshall upheld the power of Congress to create the United States Bank. In doing so, he laid down the principle of broad interpretation of the federal powers. In this case, also, he firmly established the doctrine that federal power must prevail over state power in case of conflict. In cases defining the national power over interstate commerce, Marshall's broad interpretation set out principles which are as applicable in the most recent cases as they were in his time.

The force and persuasiveness of Marshall's constitutional interpretations became most apparent after 1811. From that time until Marshall's death in 1835, most of the justices of the Court were appointed by Presidents who strongly opposed him. The new justices also opposed Marshall, but they soon found themselves agreeing with his important opinions.　　JERRE S. WILLIAMS

See also SUPREME COURT OF THE UNITED STATES; LIBERTY BELL.

MARSHALL, PETER (1902-1949), was a Presbyterian minister who served as chaplain of the United States

Detail of portrait by Richard N. Brooke, U.S. Capitol, House Wing (Library of Congress)

John Marshall, the fourth chief justice of the United States, established the Supreme Court's power to review legislative acts.

Senate from January, 1947, until his death. His prayers as chaplain of the Senate were in striking language, and parts of them were widely quoted. His wife, Catherine Marshall, wrote a biography of him, *A Man Called Peter* (1951). It was later made into a motion picture.

Marshall was born in Coatbridge, Scotland. His father died when he was 4, and he struggled against poverty through childhood. He came to the United States in 1927, and was graduated from the Columbia Seminary in Decatur, Ga., in 1931. He served three pastorates, the last being the New York Avenue Presbyterian Church in Washington, D.C. He preached there the last 12 years of his life.   LEFFERTS A. LOETSCHER

MARSHALL, THOMAS RILEY (1854-1925), served as Vice-President of the United States from 1913 to 1921, under President Woodrow Wilson. He made the famous remark: "What this country needs is a good five-cent cigar." He was the first Vice-President in nearly 100 years to serve two terms with the same President. He was also the first Vice-President to preside at a Cabinet meeting in the absence of the President. Marshall refused to listen to those who urged him to declare himself President after President Wilson became seriously ill in 1919.

Marshall was born in North Manchester, Ind., and was graduated from Wabash College. He practiced law, and served as governor of Indiana from 1909 to 1913. Marshall sought the Democratic presidential nomination in 1912. However, he was nominated for the vice-presidency instead.   IRVING G. WILLIAMS

See also VICE-PRESIDENT OF THE UNITED STATES (picture).

MARSHALL, THURGOOD (1908-   ), became the first Negro to serve as an associate justice of the Supreme Court of the United States. He was nominated by President Lyndon B. Johnson in 1967. Marshall served as chief counsel for the National Association for the Advancement of Colored People (NAACP) from 1938 to 1961. He presented the legal argument that resulted in the 1954 Supreme Court decision that racial segregation in public schools is unconstitutional. In 1961, he was appointed to the U.S. Court of Appeals. In 1965, he was appointed solicitor general of the United States.

Marshall was born in Baltimore. He graduated from Lincoln University, and studied law at Howard University. He began practicing law in 1933. Marshall won the Spingarn Medal in 1946.   CARL T. ROWAN

See also SUPREME COURT OF THE U.S. (picture).

MARSHALL FORD DAM is an irrigation, power, and flood-control dam on the Colorado River in Texas. It is also known as Mansfield Dam. The dam is 278 feet (85 meters) high and 5,093 feet (1,552 meters) long. Its reservoir can hold 2,200,200 acre-feet (2,713,910,000 cubic meters) of water.

MARSHALL ISLANDS are a group of 34 low-lying coral atolls and islands in the central Pacific Ocean. They are located east of the Caroline Islands and northwest of the Gilbert Islands, which are part of the nation of Kiribati. They lie in the part of the Pacific called Micronesia, meaning *small islands*.

The Land and Its Resources. The Marshall Islands have an area of about 70 square miles (181 square kilometers) and a coastline of 75 miles (121 kilometers).

Wide World

Marshall Islands Villagers are noted for their expert handicraft work. Women on the tiny island of Rong Rong gather near their thatched-roof huts for a "weaving bee."

They lie in two parallel chains about 130 miles (209 kilometers) apart. Each chain extends about 650 miles (1,050 kilometers) in a curve from northwest to southeast. The eastern group is called the *Radak* or *Sunrise Chain;* the western group, the *Ralik* or *Sunset Chain.* About 1,150 islets lie along the reefs that form the atolls.

The climate is tropical, but ocean breezes cool the air. Rainfall is light on the northern islands, but heavier on those to the south. Only a few kinds of plants, such as coconut palms and breadfruit trees, can grow in the coral sand. *Copra* (dried coconut meat) is the chief product. Fish are plentiful among the reefs.

The People are called Micronesians. They are noted for their handicraft, and their sailing and fishing skills. Many Micronesians died of diseases brought to the islands by Europeans in the early 1900's. The islands' population is about 29,500.

History. The first white man to visit the Marshall Islands was probably Alvaro de Saavedra, a Spanish navigator who sailed the Pacific in 1529. The islands were named for John Marshall, a British sea captain who explored them in 1788. Germany gained possession of the islands in 1886 and bought them from Spain along with the Mariana and Caroline islands in 1899. Japanese forces occupied the Marshalls during World War I. After the war, Japan was allowed to rule the islands under a mandate of the League of Nations. But in 1933 Japan left the League. The Japanese declared themselves the owners of the Marshalls. They closed the islands to Europeans and built war bases on them.

Early in 1944, American forces landed on Kwajalein and Enewetak, in the eastern Marshalls, and, later, took possession of all the islands. The United States governs the islands as part of the United Nations Trust Territory of the Pacific Islands.   EDWIN H. BRYAN, JR.

See also ENEWETAK; KWAJALEIN; WORLD WAR II (Island Hopping).

MARSHALL PLAN encouraged European nations to work together for economic recovery after World

War II. The United States agreed to send aid to Europe if the countries would meet to decide what they needed. The official name of the plan was the European Recovery Program. It is called the Marshall Plan because Secretary of State George C. Marshall first suggested it.

The Marshall Plan began in April, 1948, when Congress established the Economic Cooperation Administration (ECA) to administer foreign aid. Seventeen nations formed the Organization for European Economic Cooperation (OEEC) to assist the ECA and develop cooperation among its members. The United States sent about $13 billion in food, machinery, and other products to Europe. Aid ended in 1951.

In 1961, the Organization for Economic Cooperation and Development (OECD) succeeded the OEEC. Twenty nations, including the United States and Canada, formed the OECD to promote the economic growth of member nations and to aid underdeveloped areas.   EDWARD McNALL BURNS

See also EUROPE (History); FOREIGN AID; MARSHALL, GEORGE C.; TRUMAN, HARRY S. (The Marshall Plan).

MARSHALL UNIVERSITY. See UNIVERSITIES AND COLLEGES (table).

MARSILIUS OF PADUA (1275?-1343?), an Italian political theorist, defended the claims of the Holy Roman Empire against those of the papacy. He held that the clergy should be concerned only with the soul's salvation and not with the affairs of this world. Unlike most medieval thinkers, Marsilius emphasized will rather than reason in his definition of law. "A law is useless," he said, "unless it is obeyed." Marsilius was born in Padua, Italy.   W. T. JONES

MARSTON, JOHN (1576-1634), was an English playwright. Two of his plays reflect the pessimism of their time, when the glories of the Elizabethan Age were becoming clouded by the uncertainties of life in the 1600's. *Antonio's Revenge* (1600) is a sensational drama of revenge about the assassination of a tyrant. With *Hamlet*, it is among the first examples of the great flowering of tragedy in English drama. *The Malcontent* (1604) is a far-from-joyous comedy of intrigue, bitter in its satire but intended to correct, not to condemn.

Marston was educated at Oxford. His talent for satire led to a running quarrel with Ben Jonson. He was briefly imprisoned in 1608 for critical comments about King James I. Later, Marston studied theology and in 1616 became rector of a country parish. ALAN S. DOWNER

MARSTON MOOR, BATTLE OF. See CHARLES (I) of England.

MARSUPIAL, *mahr SOO pee uhl*, is a mammal whose young are born in an extremely immature state. Newborn marsupials complete their development attached to their mother's nipples. In almost all species, the nipples are located in a pouch called the *marsupium*. There are about 240 species of marsupials. Almost all marsupials live in Australia, New Guinea, or the islands of Australasia. Marsupials of these regions include the bandicoot, cuscus, kangaroo, koala, native cat, Tasmanian devil, Tasmanian tiger, and wombat. Opossums are also marsupials. Many species of opossums live in South America and Central America. The Virginia opossum is the only marsupial that lives in the United States.

Kangaroos are the biggest marsupials. Some grow to be more than 7 feet (2.1 meters) tall. The smallest

marsupials are the so-called marsupial "mice," several tiny marsupials that are about as big as house mice.

Some marsupials eat only insects, some eat only meats, and some eat only plants. Other marsupials eat any kind of food they can find.

Marsupials are very small at birth. A newborn opossum, for example, is no larger than a kidney bean. Marsupials are not developed enough at birth to live outside the mother's pouch. After birth, they crawl from the birth canal along the mother's fur and into the pouch. Once inside the pouch, they attach themselves to the nipples of the *mammary* (milk) glands. To get enough food to stay alive, the young remain attached to the nipples continuously until they are developed enough to leave the pouch. Therefore, when there are more offspring than there are nipples, the extra offspring die. The young marsupials may stay in the pouch for several months. For some time after they leave the pouch, they stay near the mother. They sometimes return to the pouch when frightened.

The number of marsupials in the world has decreased during the 1900's. People have brought dogs, foxes, and other animals to areas where marsupials live. These animals prey upon marsupials and compete with them for food. Farmers kill many marsupials because marsupials eat crops. The opossum population has increased, however, because these animals will eat almost any kind of food and have a high reproduction rate.

Scientific Classification. Marsupials make up the order *Marsupialia* in the class *Mammalia* and the phylum *Chordata*. To learn where the order fits into the whole animal kingdom, see ANIMAL (table: A Classification of the Animal Kingdom).   WILLIAM V. MAYER

For pictures and more detailed information on specific marsupials, see BANDICOOT; CUSCUS; KANGAROO; KOALA; NATIVE CAT; OPOSSUM; POSSUM; TASMANIAN DEVIL; TASMANIAN TIGER; WOMBAT; AUSTRALIA (Native Animals; map).

MARTEL, CHARLES. See CHARLES MARTEL.

MARTEN, *MAHR ten*, is a slim, fur-covered mammal that looks somewhat like a weasel. It lives in forest areas of Asia, Europe, and northern North America.

One of the best-known American martens is the *pine marten* or *American sable*. It is fairly common only in the northern Rockies and in the Far North from Quebec to Alaska. This marten has thick, soft, brown hair and grayish-brown fur. It is about 2 feet (61 centimeters) long, including its tail. Martens weigh 2 to 3 pounds (0.9 to 1.4 kilograms). The pine marten eats mice, rabbits, squirrels, and birds. It lives in hollow trees and in rock formations. The female gives birth to two or three young in April, about nine months after mating.

From November to March, the pine marten's coat is thick and soft. During this season, marten trappers in Canada and the United States kill about 30,000 animals for use of the fur in coats, hats, and muffs.

The *fisher*, or *pekan*, is a large *species* (kind) related to the pine marten. A male fisher weighs about 15 pounds (7 kilograms). It has dark brown or grayish-brown fur. Now rare, the fisher lives in nearly the same areas as the marten. The fisher lives on the ground or in trees. It eats rodents, including porcupines.

Well-known European martens include the *stone mar-*

ten, which has a white throat and chest, and the *baum marten*, which has yellowish fur on its throat and chest.

Scientific Classification. Martens are in the weasel family, *Mustelidae*. The pine marten is genus *Martes*, species *M. americana*. The fisher is *M. pennanti*; the stone, *M. foina;* and the baum, *M. martes*. E. LENDELL COCKRUM

See also FUR; SABLE.

MARTHA was a friend of Jesus and the sister of Mary and Lazarus of Bethany. Jesus often stayed at their home. Martha busied herself about the house to provide comfort for Jesus. But Mary preferred to sit and listen to His teachings. For this reason, in later times, Martha became the symbol of the active life and Mary became the symbol of the thoughtful life. The Gospels of Luke and John mention Martha. FREDERICK C. GRANT

MARTHA'S VINEYARD, an island 4 miles (6 kilometers) off the southeastern coast of Massachusetts, is a popular summer resort. Vineyard Sound separates it from the mainland. The island covers about 100 square miles (260 square kilometers). For location, see MASSACHUSETTS (physical map). Its attractions include a mild climate, beaches, fishing, and yachting. About 6,000 people live on the island. However, over 40,000 tourists visit the island in the summer. Explorer Bartholomew Gosnold named the island for his daughter and for the grapevines he found when he visited there in 1602. WILLIAM J. REID

See also MASSACHUSETTS (color picture).

MARTÍ, *mahr TEE,* **JOSÉ JULIÁN** (1853-1895), was a Cuban patriot, author, and journalist. He dedicated his life to Cuba's struggle for independence from Spain, and became known to his people as the *Apostle*. Martí was jailed and exiled many times for his revolutionary writings and activities. He emerged from each setback with greater strength and appeal. He was finally ambushed and killed during a battle with the Spaniards.

Martí's books of verse, including *Ismaelillo* (1882) and *Simple Verses* (1891), show him to be a sensitive, sincere poet. His journalism set new standards of brilliance in Latin America.

Martí was born in Havana. He lived in exile in the United States from 1881 to 1895 and wrote many articles about life in the United States. He founded the Cuban Revolutionary party in 1892. MARSHALL R. NASON

See also CUBA (picture: The José Martí Monument).

MARTIAL, *MAHR shul* (A.D. 40?-104?), was an ancient Roman writer. He became famous for developing the *epigram* into its modern form—a sharp, stinging poem or saying (see EPIGRAM). Martial wrote more than 1,500 short verses and epigrams. They contain witty and sometimes obscene comments about the vices of ancient Roman society. Martial described his own work with the words, "My page smells of man." He also wrote several serious pieces, including one on the death of a slave girl named Erotion, whom he loved.

Martial's full name was Marcus Valerius Martialis. He was born in Bilbilis, Spain, near Calatayud. He came to Rome in A.D. 64 and soon became known for his witty verse. HERBERT MUSURILLO

MARTIAL LAW is a temporary form of government under which a country's armed forces control an area of that country. It may become necessary in an emergency, such as an invasion, a natural disaster, a political or economic crisis, or a riot. The military governs under martial law only while the civilian government of an area cannot function. When that government can resume control, martial law ends.

In wartime, the President of the United States may declare martial law in zones of military operations. A military officer takes complete command. He may substitute military law and proceedings for civil laws and courts.

In peacetime, the police of a city or state may not be able to control an emergency situation. The governor or the President may declare martial law and send troops into the area. Martial law does not exist if the local government remains in power but uses military help.

The U.S. Constitution does not specifically provide for martial law. But it implies the power by giving the federal government the right to protect a state from invasion or internal violence. FREDERICK C. LOUGH

MARTIN is the name for several birds in the swallow family. The *purple martin* is the best-known martin in North America. It is about 8 inches (20 centimeters) long. The male is a dark purplish-blue color. The birds

188

The Purple Martin has unusually long, pointed wings and a short, forked tail. This makes its flight easy and graceful.

Field Museum of Natural History

Martins require very little room in which to build a nest. This birdhouse is divided into 18 separate martin "apartments."

Allan Cruickshank

migrate to Central and South America in the winter. They have been seen in summer as far north as the Saskatchewan Valley in Canada.

Purple martins usually build their nests in large birdhouses which people make especially for them. They nest in *colonies* (large groups). They may build their nests in trees in regions where few people live. Martins will return to the same birdhouse year after year. The martin lays from 3 to 8 white eggs.

Martins help people by eating ants, flies, beetles, and other winged insect pests. In New England, English sparrows and starlings have driven most of the martins from their homes.

Scientific Classification. Martins belong to the swallow family, *Hirundinidae*. The purple martin is genus *Progne*, species *P. subis*. HERBERT FRIEDMANN

See also BIRD (picture: Other Kinds of Birdhouses; color picture: Birds' Eggs).

MARTIN, ARCHER JOHN PORTER (1910-   ), is a noted English biochemist. With Richard L. M. Synge, he was awarded the 1952 Nobel prize in chemistry. Martin and Synge did important work in *partition chromatography*, a method of chemical analysis. Their work led to the use of this technique in separating car-

bohydrates, amino acids, and other compounds important in biochemistry. Martin was born in London, and studied at Cambridge and Leeds universities. Later, he became head of the physical chemistry division at the National Institute for Medical Research located in London. HENRY M. LEICESTER

MARTIN, JOSEPH WILLIAM, JR. (1884-1968), a Republican from Massachusetts, served in the United States House of Representatives from 1925 to 1967. He was Speaker of the House from 1947 to 1949 and from 1953 to 1955. Martin served as the Republican leader in the House for 20 years—from 1939 until Charles A. Halleck of Indiana replaced him in 1959. A skillful leader, Martin was noted for keeping in touch with the voters in his district. He was permanent chairman of the Republican national conventions of 1940, 1944, 1948, 1952, and 1956.

Wide World

Joseph W. Martin, Jr.

Martin was born in North Attleboro, Mass. He started work as a newspaper reporter. He became a newspaper publisher in 1908 when he bought the North Attleboro *Evening Chronicle*. He went into politics in 1912. RICHARD L. WATSON, JR.

MARTIN, SAINT. See MARTINMAS.

MARTIN DU GARD, *mahr TAN dyoo GAHR*, **ROGER** (1881-1958), ranked among the most skillful French novelists. He received the 1937 Nobel prize for literature. His novel *Jean Barois* (1913) is perhaps the best literary presentation of the intellectual agonies that the unjust treatment of Captain Alfred Dreyfus caused in thoughtful French people (see DREYFUS, ALFRED). He published the 10-volume saga-novel *The World of the Thibaults* between 1922 and 1940. Martin du Gard was born in Neuilly-sur-Seine, and graduated from the École des Chartes. HENRI PEYRE

MARTINELLI, *MAHR tih NEL ee*, **GIOVANNI** (1885-1969), sang as a leading tenor with the New York Metropolitan Opera Company in more than 50 operas. He was a dynamic actor. Much of his success resulted from his belief that an opera singer must also have dramatic ability. Martinelli made his debut at the Metropolitan in 1913 in *La Bohème*. A special concert at the Metropolitan in 1938 celebrated his 25th year with that institution.

Martinelli was born in Montagnana, Italy, and played the clarinet in an Italian regimental band. He studied voice in Rome, and made his concert debut in Rossini's *Stabat Mater* in Milan in 1910. He sang at Covent Garden in London. in 1912. DANIEL A. HARRIS

United Press Int.

Giovanni Martinelli

189

MARTINGALE. See HARNESS.

MARTINI, *mahr TEE nee,* **SIMONE** (about 1285-1344), was an Italian painter. He was born in Siena, a leading art center of the 1300's. Simone's colorful, decorative, yet realistic style ranks as the outstanding example of the Sienese school of painting.

Scholars know nothing of Simone's life until 1315. That year, he painted *The Virgin in Majesty,* a *fresco* (wall painting) in the Siena city hall. This fresco honors the Virgin Mary, the patron saint of Siena. Perhaps Simone's greatest work is the *Annunciation* (1333), a dramatic, richly colored altarpiece painted for the Siena cathedral.

From about 1340 until his death, Simone worked in Avignon, France, which was the home of the popes at that time. He painted many works for the Palace of the Popes there. These paintings helped shape the naturalistic style of such Flemish masters of the 1400's as Robert Campin and Jan van Eyck.   SAMUEL Y. EDGERTON, JR.

See also JESUS CHRIST (picture).

MARTINIQUE, *MAHR t'n EEK,* is a French island in the West Indies. The oval-shaped island covers 425 square miles (1,102 square kilometers). It is about 40 miles (64 kilometers) long and 16 miles (26 kilometers) wide. Its capital is Fort-de-France. For location, see WEST INDIES (map).

Martinique has many volcanic mountains. The highest and most famous of these is Mont Pelée (4,583 feet, or 1,397 meters). This volcano suddenly erupted in 1902, and destroyed the entire city of Saint-Pierre. About 38,000 people died, and only one man escaped.

Martinque has a population of 381,000. Many of the people are blacks. Others are a mixture of both Latin and black ancestry. The island's chief crop is sugar cane. Pineapples, bananas, tobacco, and cotton also grow there. Rum distilling is the only important industry.

Christopher Columbus reached Martinique in 1502, on his fourth voyage. The French began to colonize it in 1635. They made Fort-de-France the capital. The Empress Josephine, first wife of Napoleon I, was born at Trois-Ilets in Martinique. The French government made Martinique an overseas *department* (state) in 1946. The island sends three deputies to the French National Assembly. In 1958, Martinique chose to remain in the French Community as an overseas department. It has its own local government.   W. L. BURN

See also FORT-DE-FRANCE; MONT PELÉE.

MARTINMAS is a feast day celebrated in the Roman Catholic Church on November 11. It honors Saint Martin (316?-397?), a bishop of Tours, France (then called Gaul), and a patron saint of the French. Martinmas falls at the end of the harvest season, and people throughout Europe celebrate it with feasts and new wine. In Belgium and other countries, children receive apples and nuts on this day. They also parade through the streets carrying lanterns and singing special songs. People in the British Isles usually eat goose dinners on Martinmas. In parts of Great Britain, Martinmas also marks the ending of one of the legal quarters into which the year is divided.

MARTYR is a person who defends a principle, even though it means sacrificing many things, perhaps even his or her life. Almost every religious movement has had such dedicated persons. Stephen was the first Christian martyr. He was stoned to death because he protested against the wickedness of his fellow citizens (Acts 7:59-60). Many early Christians became martyrs because the Romans persecuted them for not worshiping official Roman gods. Many social and political movements have created martyrs. The word *martyr* comes from the Greek, and means *witness.* See also ROMAN CATHOLIC CHURCH (The First 300 Years).   FLOYD H. ROSS

Martinique Market Places overflow with bananas and other tropical fruits. Women do most of the buying and selling.

MARVEL-OF-PERU. See Four-O'Clock.

MARVELL, ANDREW (1621-1678), was perhaps the finest of the English nonreligious poets who were influenced by John Donne and Ben Jonson in the mid-1600's. Marvell's best poems are a series of lyrics written about 1650, including such classics as "The Garden" and "To His Coy Mistress," with its witty opening:

> Had we but world enough, and time,
> This coyness, lady, were no crime,

and its grand ending:

> Let us roll all our strength, and all
> Our sweetness, up into one ball;
> And tear our pleasures with rough strife,
> Through the iron gates of life.
> Thus, though we cannot make our sun
> Stand still, yet we will make him run.

Marvell was born in Winestead. During the Puritan revolution, he supported Oliver Cromwell. He assisted John Milton when Milton was a high government official. Marvell served in Parliament from 1659 to his death. During his later years, he wrote political satire against the king and court. RICHARD S. SYLVESTER

See also METAPHYSICAL POETS.

MARX, KARL (1818-1883), was a German philosopher, social scientist, and professional revolutionary. Few writers have had such a great and lasting influence on the world. Marx was the chief founder of two of the most powerful mass movements in history —democratic socialism and revolutionary communism. See COMMUNISM; SOCIALISM.

Marx was sometimes ignored or misunderstood, even by his followers. Yet many of the social sciences—especially sociology—have been influenced by his theories. Many important social scientists of the late 1800's and the 1900's can be fully understood only by realizing how much they were reacting to Marx's beliefs.

The Life of Marx

Karl Heinrich Marx was born and raised in Trier, in what was then Prussia. His father was a lawyer. Marx showed intellectual promise in school and went to the University of Bonn in 1835 to study law. The next year, he transferred to the University of Berlin. There he became much more interested in philosophy, a highly political subject in Prussia, where citizens were not permitted to participate directly in public affairs. Marx joined a group of radical leftist students and professors whose philosophic views implied strong criticism of the severe way in which Prussia was governed.

In 1841, Marx obtained his doctorate in philosophy from the university in Jena. He tried to get a teaching position but failed because of his opposition to the Prussian government. He became a free-lance journalist and helped create and manage several radical journals. After his marriage in 1843, he and his wife moved to Paris. There they met Friedrich Engels, a young German radical, who became Marx's best friend and worked with him on several articles and books. Marx lived in Brussels, Belgium, from 1845 to 1848, when he returned to Germany. He edited the *Neue Rheinische Zeitung*, which was published in Cologne during the German revolution of 1848. This journal made Marx known throughout Germany as a spokesman for radical democratic reform. See GERMANY (History [The Revolution of 1848]).

Brown Bros.
Karl Marx

After the collapse of the 1848 revolution, Marx fled from Prussia. He spent the rest of his life as a political exile in London.

Marx led a hand-to-mouth existence because he was too proud—or too much a professional revolutionary—to work for a living. He did write occasional articles for newspapers. His most regular job of this kind was that of political reporter for the *New York Tribune*. But generally, Marx, his wife, and their six children survived only because Engels sent them money regularly. In 1864, Marx founded *The International Workingmen's Association*, an organization dedicated to improving the life of the working classes and preparing for a socialist revolution (see INTERNATIONAL, THE).

Marx suffered from frequent illnesses, many of which may have been psychological. Even when physically healthy, he suffered from long periods of apathy and depression and could not work. Marx was learned and sophisticated, but he was often opinionated and arrogant. He had many admirers but few friends. Except for Engels, he lost most of his friends—and many of them became his enemies. He broke all contact with his mother and was cool to his sisters. But with his wife and children, Marx was relaxed, witty, and playful.

Marx's Writings

Most of Marx's writings have been preserved. They include not only his books, but also most of his correspondence and the notes of his speeches.

Philosophic Essays. Some of Marx's philosophic essays were published during his lifetime, but others were not discovered until the 1900's. Marx wrote some of them alone and some with Engels. The essays range from one of about 15 sentences to a 700-page book, *The German Ideology* (1845-1846), which was written with Engels.

Marx wrote his essays between 1842 and 1847. They spell out the philosophic foundations of his radicalism. The chief themes in the essays include Marx's bitter view that economic forces were increasingly oppressing human beings and his belief that political action is a necessary part of philosophy. The essays also show the influence of the philosophy of history developed by the German philosopher Georg Wilhelm Friedrich Hegel (see HEGEL, GEORG WILHELM FRIEDRICH).

The Communist Manifesto was a pamphlet written jointly with Engels on the eve of the German revolution of 1848. Its full title is the *Manifesto of the Communist Party*. The manifesto is a brief but forceful presentation of the authors' political and historical theories. It is the only work they produced that can be considered a systematic statement of the theories that became known as *Marxism*. The *Communist Manifesto* considers history to be a series of conflicts between classes. It predicts that the ruling middle class will be overthrown by the working class. The result of this revolution, according to

Marx and Engels, will be a classless society in which the chief means of production are publicly owned.

Das Kapital (Capital) was Marx's major work. He spent about 30 years writing it. The first volume appeared in 1867. Engels edited the second and third volumes from Marx's manuscripts. Both of these volumes were published after Marx's death. The fourth volume exists only as a mass of scattered notes.

In *Das Kapital*, Marx described the free enterprise system as he saw it. He considered it the most efficient, dynamic economic system ever devised. But he also regarded it as afflicted with flaws that would destroy it through increasingly severe periods of inflation and depression. The most serious flaw in the free enterprise system, according to Marx, is that it accumulates more and more wealth but becomes less and less capable of using this wealth wisely. As a result, Marx saw the accumulation of riches being accompanied by the rapid spread of human misery. See FREE ENTERPRISE SYSTEM.

Other Writings. Marx and Engels also wrote what today might be called political columns. They discussed all sorts of events in and influences on national and international affairs—personalities, overthrowing of governments, cabinet changes, parliamentary debates, wars, and workers' uprisings.

Marx also wrote about the practical problems of leading an international revolutionary movement. The major source of these comments is his correspondence with Engels and other friends.

Marx's Theories

Marx's doctrine is sometimes called *dialectical materialism*, and part of it is referred to as *historical materialism*. These terms were taken from Hegel's philosophy of history. Marx never used them, but Engels did and so have most later Marxists. The concepts of dialectical and historical materialism are difficult and obscure and may be unnecessary for an understanding of Marx's theories. See MATERIALISM.

Marx's writings cover more than 40 years. His interests shifted and he often changed his mind. But his philosophy remained surprisingly consistent—and very complex. Aside from the brief *Communist Manifesto*, he never presented his ideas systematically.

Production and Society. The basis of Marxism is the conviction that socialism is inevitable. Marx believed that the free enterprise system, or capitalism, was doomed and that socialism was the only alternative.

Marx discussed capitalism within a broad historical perspective that covered the history of the human race. He believed that the individual, not God, is the highest being. People have made themselves what they are by their own labor. They use their intelligence and creative talent to dominate the world by a process called *production*. Through production, people make the goods they need to live. The means of production include natural resources, factories, machinery, and labor.

The process of production, according to Marx, is a collective effort, not an individual one. Organized societies are the chief creative agents in human history, and historical progress requires increasingly developed societies for production. Such societies are achieved by continual refinement of production methods and of the

division of labor. By the division of labor, Marx meant that each person specializes in one job, resulting in the development of two classes of people—the rulers and the workers. The ruling class owns the means of production. The working class consists of the nonowners, who are *exploited* (treated unfairly) by the owners.

The Class Struggle. Marx believed there was a strain in all societies because the social organization never kept pace with the development of the means of production. An even greater strain developed from the division of people into two classes.

According to Marx, all history is a struggle between the ruling and working classes, and all societies have been torn by this conflict. Past societies tried to keep the exploited class under control by using elaborate political organizations, laws, customs, traditions, ideologies, religions, and rituals. Marx argued that personality, beliefs, and activities are shaped by these institutions. By recognizing these forces, he reasoned, people will be able to overcome them through revolutionary action.

Marx believed that private ownership of the chief means of production was the heart of the class system. For people to be truly free, he declared, the means of production must be publicly owned—by the community as a whole. With the resulting general economic and social equality, all people would have an opportunity to follow their own desires and to use their leisure time creatively. Unfair institutions and customs would disappear. All these events, said Marx, will take place when the *proletariat* (working class) revolts against the *bourgeoisie* (owners of the means of production).

Political Strategy. It is not clear what strategy Marx might have proposed to achieve the revolution he favored. An idea of this strategy can come only from his speeches, articles, letters, and political activities. As a guideline for practical politics, Marxism is vague. Marx's followers have quarreled bitterly among themselves over different interpretations and policies.

Marx Today

Today, Marx is studied as both a revolutionary and an economist. His importance as a pioneer in the social sciences is being recognized increasingly. Marx has often been attacked because he rebelled against all established societies, because he was an arrogant writer who scorned his critics, and because of his radical views.

As the founding father of the Communist movement, Marx is regarded in most Communist countries as one of the greatest thinkers of all time. In those countries, many people believe that Marx's writings are the source of all important truths in social science as well as philosophy. They believe that a person cannot be an intelligent student of society, history, economics, philosophy, and numerous other fields without first studying Marx or his principal disciples.

Scholars in the Western world were slow to recognize the importance of Marx. For many years, few Americans bothered to study his writings. But today, in a variety of fields, it has become essential to have some knowledge of Marx. One of these fields is economics. Although his methods of analyzing capitalism are considered old-fashioned, many scholars recognize the brilliance of this analysis. Many people consider his criticism of capitalism and his view of what humanity has made of the world as timely today as they were 100 years ago. Even

Marx's analysis of the business cycle is studied as one of the many explanations of inflation and depression.

In sociology, Marx's work is also regarded with increasing respect. Without his contributions, sociology would not have developed into what it is today. Marx did pioneering work in many areas with which sociology deals. He wrote on social classes, on the relationship between the economy and the state, and on the principles that underlie a political or economic system.

Many people still turn to Marx for an explanation of current social, economic, and political evils. But most of them are unlikely to agree with his view of the ease and speed with which the working class will overthrow the class system and establish a Communist classless society.   ALFRED G. MEYER

See also ENGELS, FRIEDRICH; LENIN, V. I. For a *Reading and Study Guide*, see *Marx, Karl*, in the RESEARCH GUIDE/INDEX, Volume 22.

MARX BROTHERS were three American brothers who became famous for their zany antics in motion pictures. The brothers were Groucho (Julius, 1890-1977), Chico (Leonard, 1886-1961), and Harpo (Adolph, later changed to Arthur, 1888-1964). Groucho became known for his insults, long cigar, and bushy mustache and eyebrows. Chico spoke in an Italian accent and played the piano. Harpo, who never spoke in the films, played the harp.

The Marx brothers as a team made 13 movies, many of which ridiculed parts of society. The brothers' first two films, *The Cocoanuts* (1929) and *Animal Crackers* (1930), were based on Broadway shows in which they had starred. Their other movies include *Monkey Business* (1931), *Horse Feathers* (1932), *Duck Soup* (1933), *A Night at the Opera* (1935), and *A Day at the Races* (1937).

The Marx brothers were born in New York City and began their career when they were children. With two other brothers, they starred in vaudeville and several Broadway shows before making movies. Zeppo (Herbert) played romantic roles in their films until he left the team in the mid-1930's. Gummo (Milton) appeared on the stage but made no movies.   ROGER EBERT

MARXISM. See MARX, KARL.

MARY was the mother of Jesus. She is also known as the Virgin Mary, the Blessed Virgin Mary, or the Blessed Virgin. Mary's family lived in Nazareth. She gave birth to Jesus in a stable at Bethlehem. She had gone there with her husband, Joseph, to have their names put down as members of the House of David. This was how the census was taken at that time.

The sufferings of Jesus brought great sorrow into Mary's life. At the Crucifixion, He asked His beloved disciple, John, to take care of her. Little is known about her later life. It is believed that she died in Jerusalem about A.D. 63. She is venerated by the Roman Catholic, Anglican, and Eastern Orthodox churches as the Mother of God.

National Gallery of Art, Washington, D.C., Widener Collection
The Virgin with Saint Inés and Saint Tecla, painted by El Greco, shows a contrast between the Virgin Mary's flowing dark robe and the faintly flushed skin of the Child Jesus.

United Press Int.
The Marx Brothers starred in *Horse Feathers*, a zany 1932 motion picture comedy. They were Chico, *left*, holding an apple; Groucho, smoking the cigar; and Harpo, *far right*.

The story of Mary has always been a favorite subject of artists and musicians. Many great paintings and songs have been based on the incidents and traditions of her life.   FREDERICK C. GRANT and FULTON J. SHEEN

Related Articles in WORLD BOOK include:

Anne, Saint	Christmas	Jesus Christ
Annunciation	Fátima	Joseph
Assumption	Immaculate	Madonna and Child
Ave Maria	Conception	

MARY was the name of three queens of England.

Mary I (1516-1558) was the daughter of Henry VIII and Catherine of Aragon. She became queen in 1553, after Edward VI, her brother, died. An attempt to set her aside in favor of Lady Jane Grey, "the nine-day queen," failed. See CATHERINE OF ARAGON; EDWARD (VI) of England; HENRY (VIII) of England.

Mary was a devout Roman Catholic and tried to bring England back to the Roman Catholic Church. She repealed all the religious laws of Edward VI. She revived certain severe laws against heresy or disbelief in church doctrine. She became known as "Bloody Mary" because of the persecutions she caused. More than 300 persons were burned at the stake during her brief reign. Among them were Thomas Cranmer, Nicholas Ridley, and Hugh Latimer, all high-ranking Protestant clergymen. See CRANMER, THOMAS; LATIMER, HUGH; RIDLEY, NICHOLAS.

Mary married Philip II of Spain. Their marriage was unpopular, because many English people looked upon Spain as their greatest enemy. Philip persuaded Mary to join Spain in a war against France. But France was victorious, and the war ended in 1558. Mary died soon after, deserted by her husband and saddened at the thought that she would be succeeded by her Protestant sister, Elizabeth (see ELIZABETH I). See PHILIP (II) of Spain.

Mary II (1662-1694) was the older of the two Protestant daughters of James II. She married William of Orange, the chief executive of the Dutch Republic. During the Glorious Revolution of 1688, Parliament offered the throne to William and Mary as joint rulers. William accepted on the understanding that he would be responsible for the administration of affairs. Mary died from smallpox in 1694. William served as king until his death in 1702. See JAMES (II) of England; STUART, HOUSE OF; WILLIAM (III) of England.

Mary of Teck (1867-1953) was the queen *consort* (wife) of King George V. Mary endeared herself to the British by her homely virtues. In place of the gay court of Edward VII, she and her husband lived conservatively. Through their efforts, the monarchy regained the prestige it had enjoyed under Queen Victoria. After the death of George V in 1936, Mary retired to Marlborough House in London. Her eldest son became king as Edward VIII. After his abdication, her second son became George VI. Upon his death her granddaughter became Queen Elizabeth II (see ELIZABETH II). During these years Queen Mary took an active part in public affairs. Her plain dress and old-fashioned hats were famous throughout the British Empire. See also GEORGE (V, VI) of England; EDWARD (VII, VIII).   W. M. SOUTHGATE

MARY, QUEEN OF SCOTS (1542-1587), was the only child of King James V of Scotland and Mary of Guise. The princess was only a week old when her father died, but she was immediately proclaimed queen of Scotland. The life story of this beautiful woman who was beheaded by her cousin Elizabeth I is one of the great tragedies of history.

Mary was sent to France at the age of 6 to be educated. She married the French *dauphin* (crown prince) at the age of 15. He became king soon after their marriage, but died in 1560 (see FRANCIS [II] of France).

Her Reign. Mary returned to Scotland in 1561. She found Scotland becoming a Protestant country, and she was a Roman Catholic. She did not oppose the spread of the Protestant faith at first. But, in 1565, she married her cousin, Henry Stuart, who was known as Lord Darnley. This young Catholic nobleman's rise to power caused the powerful Protestant lords to revolt. The rebellion was quickly put down. But the queen soon discovered that she had married a weak and worthless husband, and she came to hate him.

An Italian musician, David Rizzio (1533?-1566), was Mary's private secretary, and became one of her favorites. Scottish tongues began to wag about the relationship between Rizzio and the queen. A band of men led by two Scottish earls burst into Mary's private supper room in March, 1566. They dragged Rizzio from the table, and stabbed him to death. Darnley, Mary's husband, was one of the leaders in the murder, but Mary fled with him to Dunbar. Mary gave birth to a son two months later. He later became King James I of England (see JAMES [I]).

Mary still hated her husband. Before long she began

Mary I of England by Master John, National Portrait Gallery, London

Queen Mary I of England became known as "Bloody Mary" because of the bitter persecutions she caused the Protestants in her attempt to bring England back to the Roman Catholic faith.

to show marked attention to James Hepburn, Earl of Bothwell (see BOTHWELL, EARL OF). Early in 1567, the house in which Darnley was living was blown up by a charge of gunpowder, and he was found dead. All Scotland believed that Bothwell had planned the crime. Three months later, Mary married Bothwell.

Her Death. This marriage was Mary's fatal mistake. She was forced to abdicate in favor of her son in 1567, and she became a prisoner on an island in Loch Leven. Mary escaped from the island in 1568, and raised a small army. But almost all Scotland was against her. Her forces were defeated, and she fled to England for protection. Mary was the center of plots against her cousin, Queen Elizabeth I, because she had a claim to the English throne and wanted to bring England back to the Roman Catholic faith (see ELIZABETH I). Mary lived almost as a prisoner in the house of the Earl of Shrewsbury.

When plots against her became increasingly serious, Elizabeth moved Mary to a prison. Mary became involved in a plot to kill Elizabeth in 1586. She maintained her innocence. The court found her guilty, and she was beheaded on Feb. 8, 1587.   W. M. SOUTHGATE

MARY, VIRGIN. See MARY.

MARY MAGDALENE, *MAG duh leen*, was a faithful follower of Jesus. She was called Magdalene because she was born in the village of Magdala. Luke gives her name at the head of a list of women of Galilee (Luke 8: 2). Mary Magdalene was known as the one out of whom Jesus "had cast seven demons." She followed Jesus the rest of His life, and stood at the cross when He was crucified. She was the first person to see Him after He arose from the tomb (John 20).   FREDERICK C. GRANT

See also JESUS CHRIST (The Resurrection).

MARY OF BETHANY was the sister of Martha and Lazarus. Jesus often visited their home. Mary sat at His feet and listened to His teaching (Luke 10: 39). When Martha complained that she was not helping with a meal, Jesus said, "Only one thing is needful; Mary has chosen the better part, which shall not be taken from her."   FREDERICK C. GRANT

See also LAZARUS; MARTHA.

MARY OF BURGUNDY. See MAXIMILIAN I.

MARY OF GUISE. See MARY, QUEEN OF SCOTS; KNOX, JOHN.

MARY OF TECK. See MARY (Mary of Teck).

MARY WASHINGTON COLLEGE. See UNIVERSITIES AND COLLEGES (table).

MARYCREST COLLEGE is a coeducational liberal arts college in Davenport, Iowa. The Roman Catholic Sisters of Humility of Mary conduct it. Marycrest College began as a division of St. Ambrose College. In 1954, Marycrest became an independent school. For enrollment, see UNIVERSITIES AND COLLEGES (table).

MARYE'S HEIGHTS. See CIVIL WAR (Fredericksburg).

MARYGROVE COLLEGE. See UNIVERSITIES AND COLLEGES (table).

MARYHILL CASTLE. See WASHINGTON (Places to Visit).

MARYKNOLL. See MISSIONARY (Organization).

A Principal Marriage (1600) by Georges Boba, Musée de Dijon, Dijon, France

Mary, Queen of Scots, Married Francis II, the Future King of France, When She Was 15 Years Old.

MARYLAND

The Old Line State

MARYLAND is an important industrial and shipping state. It lies in the northeastern corner of the Southern States. Chesapeake Bay, which cuts deep into Maryland, gives the state several excellent harbors. Baltimore, the state's largest city, is one of the greatest port cities in the world. Annapolis, the home of the United States Naval Academy, is the capital of Maryland.

Chesapeake Bay divides Maryland into two parts. The part of Maryland east of the bay is called the Eastern Shore. The part west of the bay is the Western Shore. The two parts join north of the bay in the northeastern corner of the state. The Eastern Shore shares the Delmarva Peninsula with parts of Delaware and Virginia. The Eastern Shore and part of the Western Shore are low and flat. But western Maryland has rolling plains, hills and valleys, mountains, and plateaus. Most parts of Maryland have good farmland. Forests cover nearly half the state.

The leading products of Maryland's industries include electrical machinery, food products, and primary metals. Most of the state's manufacturing is centered in the Baltimore area. The Bethlehem Steel Corporation plant outside Baltimore is one of the world's largest steel mills.

Tobacco farms cover much of southwestern Maryland. Vegetable farming thrives on the Eastern Shore. Most mines and orchards are in the west. Dairy farming prospers throughout the state. Maryland is the leading U.S. producer of oysters.

Maryland was named for Queen Henrietta Maria, the wife of King Charles I of England. In 1632, Charles chartered the Maryland region to Cecil Calvert, the second Lord Baltimore. Calvert, a Roman Catholic, believed in religious freedom, and welcomed settlers of all faiths to Maryland.

The Lords Baltimore ruled Maryland during most of the period it was an English colony. During the Revolutionary War, the Second Continental Congress met for about three months in the city of Baltimore. After the war, the Congress of the Confederation met for several months in the Maryland State House in Annapolis. In 1791, Maryland gave part of its land to the federal government for the District of Columbia.

Francis Scott Key wrote "The Star-Spangled Banner" while watching the British bombard Baltimore's Fort McHenry during the War of 1812. Maryland, although a southern state, remained loyal to the Union during the Civil War. Several Civil War battles were fought in Maryland, including the Battle of Antietam—one of the bloodiest of the war.

Maryland is nicknamed the *Old Line State* because its heroic "troops of the line" won praise from George Washington during the Revolutionary War. For Maryland's relationship to the other states in its region, see SOUTHERN STATES.

Maryland (blue) ranks 42nd in size among all the states, and 13th in size among the Southern States (gray).

The contributors of this article are George Beishlag, Professor of Geography at Towson State University; Aubrey C. Land, University Research Professor of History at the University of Georgia, and former Professor of History at the University of Maryland, College Park; and Fred Theroux, Editorial Writer of The News American *in Baltimore.*

The Star-Spangled Banner Flies Day and Night over Historic Fort McHenry in Baltimore Harbor.

FACTS IN BRIEF

Capital: Annapolis.

Government: *Congress*—U.S. senators, 2; U.S. representatives, 8. *Electoral Votes*—10. *State Legislature*—senators, 47; delegates, 141. *Counties*—23, and the independent city of Baltimore.

Area: 10,577 sq. mi. (27,394 km²), including 686 sq. mi. (1,777 km²) of inland water but excluding 1,726 sq. mi. (4,470 km²) of Chesapeake Bay; 42nd in size among the states. *Greatest Distances*—east-west, 198.6 mi. (319.6 km); north-south, 125.5 mi. (202 km). *Coastline* —31 mi. (49 km); including Chesapeake Bay, Potomac River, and other rivers, 3,190 mi. (5,134 km).

Elevation: *Highest*—Backbone Mountain, 3,360 ft. (1,024 m) above sea level, in the southwestern corner of the state. *Lowest*—sea level, along the ocean.

Population: *Estimated 1975 Population*—4,098,000. *1970 Census*—3,922,399; 18th among the states; distribu-tion, 77 per cent urban, 23 per cent rural; density, 371 persons per sq. mi. (143 persons per km²).

Chief Products: *Agriculture*—broilers, milk, corn, soybeans, beef cattle, tobacco. *Fishing Industry*—oysters, clams, crabs. *Manufacturing*—food products, electric and electronic equipment, primary metals, nonelectric machinery, chemicals, transportation equipment, printed materials, paper products, fabricated metal products, clothing. *Mining*—coal, stone, sand and gravel, clays.

Statehood: April 28, 1788, the 7th state.

State Abbreviations: Md. (traditional); MD (postal).

State Motto: *Fatti Maschii Parole Femine* (Manly deeds, womanly words), Italian motto of the Calvert family.

State Song: "Maryland, My Maryland," sung to the music of the German tune "O, Tannenbaum." Words by James Ryder Randall.

Constitution. Maryland has had the same constitution since 1867, shortly after the Civil War. Earlier constitutions were adopted in 1776, 1851, and 1864.

An *amendment* (change) in the constitution may be proposed by the state legislature or by a constitutional convention. Legislative amendments must be approved by three-fifths of the members of both houses of the legislature. All amendments must be approved by a majority of the voters who cast ballots on the amendment.

Executive. Maryland's governor serves a four-year term and receives a yearly salary of $60,000. The governor may be elected to an unlimited number of terms, but may not serve more than two terms in a row. For a list of Maryland's governors, see the *History* section of this article.

The people elect the lieutenant governor, the attorney general, and the comptroller to four-year terms. The governor appoints the secretary of state, the adjutant general, and members of the state boards. The state treasurer is elected by the legislature and serves a four-year term.

Legislature, called the *general assembly*, consists of a 47-member Senate and a 141-member House of Delegates. Each of the state's 47 legislative districts elects one senator and three delegates. All Maryland legislators serve four-year terms.

The legislature meets each year. Sessions begin on the second Wednesday in January and are limited to 90 days. However, regular sessions may be extended 30 days by a three-fifths vote of the members of each house. Special sessions may be called by the governor, or by the legislature if a majority of its members sign a petition requesting such a session.

Courts. Maryland's chief courts include the Court of Appeals, the Court of Special Appeals, and eight circuit courts. The Court of Appeals, the highest state court, handles appeals of civil cases and of criminal cases involving the death sentence. It has seven judges. The Court of Special Appeals hears appeals of criminal cases and of certain civil cases, such as automobile accidents. This court consists of 13 judges. The circuit courts hear general cases. The number of judges in each circuit varies from 4 to 21. The governor appoints all judges of the appeals courts and of the circuit courts to serve for at least one year. At the next general election, these judges may run for 15-year terms. The governor also appoints the chief judges who head each of these courts.

Maryland also has a district court system. It consists of 12 courts that hear minor civil and criminal cases and traffic cases. A chief judge heads the system. The number of associate judges in each district varies from 2 to 22. The governor appoints all district court judges to 10-year terms. The chief judge of the Court of Appeals appoints the chief judge of the District Court to a 10-year term. All District Court appointments require the approval of the state senate.

Local Government in Maryland is centered in the state's 23 counties. Incorporated cities function as independent units of government. But all other areas in a county come under the jurisdiction of the county government. Baltimore, which is not part of any county, is governed by a mayor, an 18-member city council, and a council president. Most other incorporated cities use the mayor-council or commissioner form of government.

County councils govern Anne Arundel, Baltimore, Harford, Howard, Montgomery, Prince Georges, and Wicomico counties. Members of these councils are elected to four-year terms. Voters in each of the other counties elect the members of a board of county commissioners to four-year terms. Elected county administrative officers include clerk of the circuit court, state's attorney, sheriff, register of wills, surveyor, and treasurer or financial director.

Cities and counties in Maryland may adopt *home rule* (self-government) to the extent that they may govern their own affairs without control by the state legislature. All the cities and five of the counties in Maryland have adopted home rule.

M. E. Warren

Governor's Mansion stands west of the Capitol and faces it. The residence was completed in 1869. The end chimneys, gables, and two wings were added in 1935.

The State Seal

Symbols of Maryland. The front of the seal shows Lord Baltimore, founder of Maryland, as a knight. A shield on the back of the seal bears the coats of arms of the Calvert and Crossland families. Lord Baltimore was related to both families and used the combined arms. The farmer beside the shield symbolizes Maryland. The fisherman represents Lord Baltimore's Avalon colony in Newfoundland. The seal was adopted in 1876. The flag, with an adaptation of Baltimore's arms, was adopted in 1904.

Seal illustration courtesy of Maryland
Department of Economic Development

Taxation. Sales and gross receipts taxes account for about 35 per cent of the state government's income. Individual state income taxes account for another 25 per cent. Other income includes a corporate income tax, estate and gift taxes, licenses, and property taxes. About 15 per cent of the state income comes from federal grants and other U.S. government programs.

Politics. In most state elections, the Republican Party's strength is limited to a few counties in southern and western Maryland. The rest of the state is strongly Democratic, with the greatest Democratic strength in the city of Baltimore. Only five Republicans have ever served as governor of Maryland. But in presidential elections since 1900, a nearly equal number of Democratic and Republican candidates have won the state's electoral votes. For Maryland's electoral votes and for the state's voting record in presidential elections, see ELECTORAL COLLEGE (table).

State Capitol is in Annapolis. The building, begun in 1772, is the nation's oldest statehouse in daily use. St. Marys City was the capital from 1634 until 1694, when Annapolis became the capital.

M. E. Warren

The State Flag

The State Bird
Baltimore Oriole

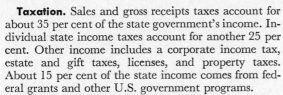

The State Flower
Black-Eyed Susan

Kevin L. Martin

The State Tree
White Oak (Wye Oak)

197

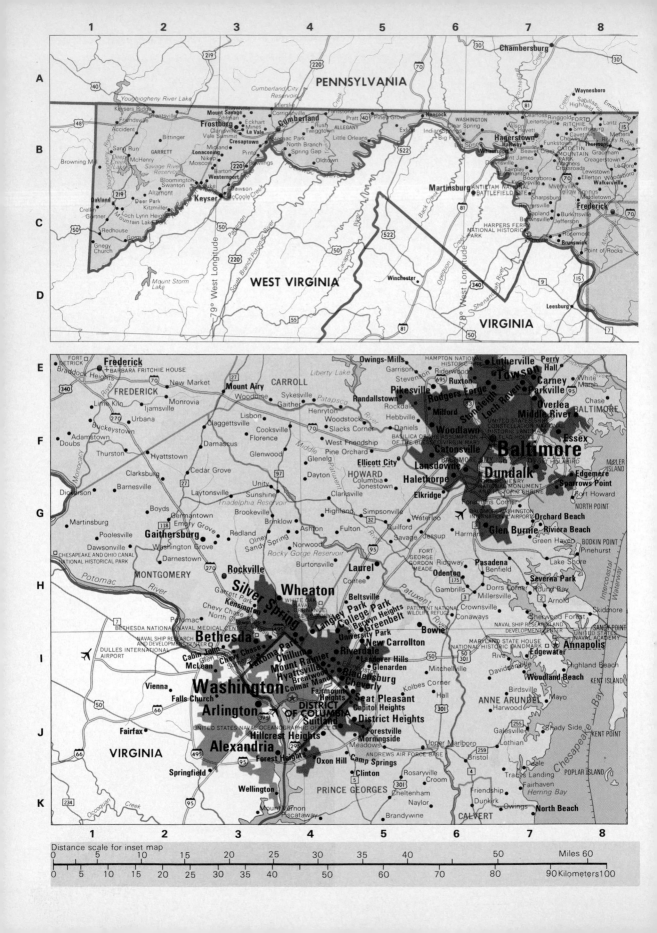

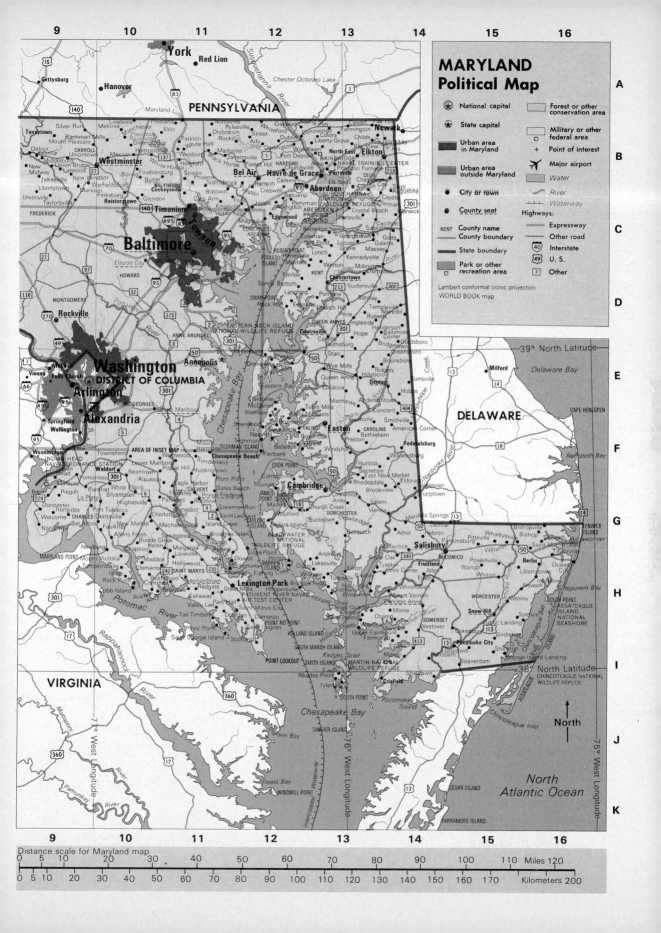

MARYLAND Political Map

Legend:

- ★ National capital
- ✪ State capital
- ▮ Urban area in Maryland
- ▮ Urban area outside Maryland
- ● City or town
- ● County seat
- KENT County name
- County boundary
- State boundary
- Park or other recreation area
- Forest or other conservation area
- Military or other federal area
- + Point of interest
- ✈ Major airport
- Water
- River
- Waterway

Highways:
- Expressway
- Other road
- 40 Interstate
- 49 U.S.
- 7 Other

Lambert conformal conic projection
WORLD BOOK map

Distance scale for Maryland map

0 5 10 20 30 40 50 60 70 80 90 100 110 Miles 120

0 5 10 20 30 40 50 60 70 80 90 100 110 120 130 140 150 160 170 Kilometers 200

PENNSYLVANIA

VIRGINIA

DELAWARE

North Atlantic Ocean

Chesapeake Bay

39° North Latitude

38° North Latitude

71° West Longitude

76° West Longitude

75° West Longitude

North

Population

4,098,000	Estimate..	1975
3,922,399	..Census..	1970
3,100,689	" ..	1960
2,343,001	" ..	1950
1,821,244	" ..	1940
1,631,526	" ..	1930
1,449,661	" ..	1920
1,295,346	" ..	1910
1,188,044	" ..	1900
1,042,390	" ..	1890
934,943	" ..	1880
780,894	" ..	1870
687,049	" ..	1860
583,034	" ..	1850
470,019	" ..	1840
447,040	" ..	1830
407,350	" ..	1820
380,546	" ..	1810
341,548	" ..	1800
319,728	" ..	1790

Metropolitan Area

Baltimore 2,071,016
Washington,
 D.C. 2,925,521
 (1,231,569 in Md.;
 937,284 in Va.;
 756,668 in D.C.)
Wilmington
 (Del.) 499,493
 (385,856 in Del.;
 60,346 in N.J.;
 53,291 in Md.)

Counties

Allegany ...84,044..B 4
Anne
 Arundel 298,042..E 11
Baltimore 620,409..B 11
Calvert ...20,682..G 11
Caroline ..19,781..F 13
Carroll ...69,006..B 9
Cecil .....53,291..B 13
Charles ...47,678..G 9
Dorchester .29,405..G 13
Frederick .84,927..C 8
Garrett ...21,476..B 2
Harford ..115,378..B 12
Howard ...62,394..D 10
Kent .....16,146..D 13
Mont-
 gomery .522,809..D 9
Prince
 Georges .661,719..F 10
Queen
 Annes ...18,422..D 13
St. Marys .47,388..H 11
Somerset ..18,924..H 14
Talbot ...23,682..F 13
Washing-
 ton ....103,829..B 6
Wicomico ..54,236..H 14
Worcester .24,442..H 15

Cities, Towns, and Villages

Abell ....H 11
Aberdeen ..12,375..B 13
Aberdeen Proving
 Ground ...7,403..C 13
Abingdon ....C 12
Accident ....237..B 2
Accokeek ....F 10
Adamstown ....F 1
Aikin ....B 13
Airey ....G 13
Allen ....H 14
Allens Fresh ....G 10
Allview* ...2,314..D 10
Andrews ...6,418..J 5
Annapolis .30,095.°E 11
Aquasco ....G 11
Arbutus* ..22,745..B 11
Arnold ....H 7
Ashton ....G 4
Aspen Hill* 16,823..D 9
Avenel-Hillan-
 dale* .....19,520..E 10
Avenue ....H 10
Bainbridge
 Center* ..5,257..B 13
Baldwin ....C 11
Baltimore 905,787°.C 11
Baltimore Highlands, see
 Lansdowne [-Balti-
 more Highlands]
Barclay .....187..D 14
Barnesville ..162..G 1
Barrelville .....B 3
Barstow ....G 11
Barton ......723..B 3
Bay View ....B 13
Beauvue ....H 11
Beaver Creek ....B 7
Bel Air ..6,307.°B 12
Bel Air
 North* ...2,771..B 12
Bel Air
 South* ...3,360..B 12

Bel Alton ....G 10
Belcamp ....C 12
Bellevue ....G 12
Beltsville ..8,912..H 5
Benedict ....G 11
Benfield ....H 6
Benson ....C 12
Berlin ....1,942..H 16
Berwyn
 Heights ..3,934..I 5
Bethesda .71,621..I 3
Bethlehem .....F 13
Betterton ....327..C 13
Big Pool ....B 6
Big Spring .....B 6
Birchwood
 City* ....13,514..E 10
Birdsville ......J 7
Bishop ....G 16
Bishops Head ...H 13
Bishopville .....G 16
Bittinger ....B 2
Bivalve ....H 13
Black Horse ....B 11
Bladensburg 7,488..I 4
Bloomington ....C 2
Boonsboro .1,410..B 7
Boonsboro ....E 14
Boring ....B 10
Bowie ....35,028..I 6
Bowling Green, see
 Potomac Park
 [-Bowling Green]
Boyds ....G 2
Bozman ....F 12
Braddock Heights .E 1
Brandywine .....K 5
Brentwood .3,426..I 4
Brinklow ....G 4
Brookeville .136..G 4
Brooklyn* .13,896..D 11
Brookview ...95..G 14
Broomes Island .G 11
Brownsville ....C 7
Brunswick .3,566..C 7
Bryantown .....G 10
Buckeystown ....F 1
Burkittsville .221..C 7
Burrsville .....E 14
Burtonsville ....H 4
Butler ....B 11
Cabin John .....I 3
California .....H 11
Callaway ....H 11
Calvert ....B 13
Calverton* ..6,543..D 10
Cambridge .11,595.°G 13
Camp
 Springs ..22,776..J 5
Cape St.
 Claire* ...2,689..E 12
Capitol
 Heights ..3,835..J 5
Carmody Hills-
 Pepper Mill
 Village* ..6,335..E 10
Catonsville .54,812..F 6
Cavetown ....B 8
Cecilton ....581..C 13
Cedar Grove .....G 2
Chapel Oaks-
 Cedar Heights
Centreville ..1,853.°E 13
Champ ....H 14
Chance ....H 13
Chapel Oaks-
 Cedar
 Heights* ..6,049..E 10
Chaptico ....H 10
Charlestown* ..721..B 13
Charlotte Hall ..G 10
Chase ....C 12
Cheltenham .....K 5
Cherry Hill ....B 13
Chesapeake
 Beach .....934..F 11
Chesapeake
 City .....1,031..B 14
Chester ....E 12
Chestertown .3,476.°D 13
Cheverly ..6,808..I 5
Chevy
 Chase ...16,424..I 3
Chevy
 Chase* ...2,265..E 9
Chevy Chase
 Section
 Four* ....2,266..E 9
Chevy Chase View .I 3
Chewsville .....B 7
Childs ....B 13
Chillum ..35,656..I 4
Church Creek 130..G 13
Church Hill ..247..D 13
Churchville ....B 12
Claggettsville ..F 3
Claiborne .....E 12
Clarksburg .....G 4
Clarksville .....G 4
Clarysville .....B 3
Clear Spring .499..B 6
Clements ....H 11
Clinton ....K 5
Cobb Island ....H 10
Cockeysville ....C 11
Cokesbury ......I 15

Coleman ....C 13
Colesville* .9,455..D 10
College
 Park ...26,156..I 4
Colmar
 Manor ...1,715..I 4
Colora ....B 13
Columbia ..8,815..G 5
Compton ....H 11
Concord ....F 14
Conowingo .....B 12
Contee ....H 5
Cooksville .....G 4
Coral Hills* 9,058..F 10
Cordova ....E 13
Cornersville ...G 12
Corriganville ...B 3
Cottage City* .993..E 10
Cove Point .....G 12
Crapo ....H 13
Crownsville .....H 7
Crumpton ....D 13
Cresaptown .1,731..B 3
Crisfield .3,078..I 14
Crocheron .....H 13
Crofton* ..4,478..E 11
Croom ....K 6
Crownsville .....H 7
Crumpton ....D 13
Cumberland 29,724.°B 4
Damascus .2,638..F 3
Dameron ....H 12
Dames Quarter ..H 13
Daniels ....F 5
Dares Beach ....G 11
Darlington .....B 12
Darnestown ....H 2
Davidsonville ...I 7
Dawson ....C 3
Dawsonville ....H 2
Dayton ....G 4
Deal Island ....H 13
Deale ....1,059..K 7
Deer Park ...310..C 2
Defense
 Heights* ..6,775..E 10
Delmar ...1,191..G 15
Denton ...1,561.°E 14
Dentsville .....G 10
Detour ....B 9
Dickerson ....G 1
District
 Heights ..7,659..J 5
Dominion ....E 12
Doncaster ....G 9
Dorrs Corner ...H 6
Dowell ....H 12
Downsville .....B 7
Drawbridge .....G 13
Drayden ....H 11
Dublin ....B 12
Dundalk ..85,377..F 7
Dunkirk ....K 6
Eagle Harbor .14..G 11
Earleville .....C 13
East New
 Market ....251..G 13
East Pines, see
 Riverdale Heights-
 East Pines
Easton ...6,809.°F 13
Eckhart Mines ..B 3
Eden ....H 14
Edesville ....D 12
Edgemere .10,352..G 8
Edgewater ....I 7
Edgewood ..8,551..C 12
Edmonston .1,441..I 4
Eldersburg-Flohr-
 ville* ....1,739..C 10
Eldorado ....99..G 14
Elk Mills ......B 14
Elkridge ....G 6
Elkton ...5,362.°B 14
Ellerslie ....B 4
Ellerton ....B 8
Ellicott
 City .....9,435.°C 10
Elliott ....H 13
Emmitsburg .1,532..B 9
Emory Grove ....G 3
Essex ....38,193..F 7
Ewell ....B 5
Exline ....B 3
Fair Hill ......B 13
Fairbank ....F 12
Fairhaven ....K 7
Fairlee ....D 12
Fairmount ......I 14
Fairmount
 Heights ..1,972..J 5
Fairplay ....B 7
Fairview ....B 7
Fallston ....C 12
Faulkner ....G 10
Federalsburg 1,917..F 14
Ferndale* .9,929..D 11
Finksburg .....C 10
Fishing Creek ..H 12
Flintstone .....B 4
Flohrville, see
 Eldersburg-
 Flohrville
Florence ....F 3
Forest
 Heights ..3,600..J 4
Forest Hill ....B 12
Forestville .16,188..J 5

Fork ....C 12
Fort Howard .....G 8
Fort Meade 16,699..H 5
Fort Ritchie 2,126..A 8
Fountain
 Head* ...2,029..A 7
Fowblesburg ....B 10
Frederick .23,641.°C 8
Freeland ....B 11
Friendship .....K 7
Friendsville .566..B 1
Frostburg .7,327..B 3
Fruitland .2,315..H 14
Fulton ....G 4
Funkstown .1,051..B 7
Gaither ....F 4
Gaithers-
 burg .....8,344..G 3
Galena ....361..C 13
Galestown ..123..G 14
Galesville .....J 7
Gambrills ....H 6
Gapland ....C 7
Garrett
 Park .....1,276..H 3
Garrison ....E 6
Georgetown .....C 13
Germantown .....G 2
Girdletree .....I 15
Glen Arm ....C 11
Glen Burnie 38,608..G 6
Glen Echo ...297..I 3
Glenarden .4,447..I 5
Glenelg ....F 4
Glenwood ....F 4
Glyndon ....C 10
Goldsboro ...231..E 14
Golts ....C 14
Good Luck* 10,584..E 10
Goodwill ......I 15
Gorman ....C 2
Gortner ....C 1
Graceham ....B 8
Grantsville .517..B 2
Grasonville .1,182..E 12
Great Mills ....H 11
Green Haven .....G 7
Greenbelt .18,199..I 5
Greenmount ....B 10
Greensboro .1,173..E 14
Guilford ....G 5
Hagerstown 35,862.°B 7
Halethorpe .....F 6
Halfway ...6,106..B 7
Hall ....J 6
Halpine* ..6,118..D 9
Hampstead ..961..B 10
Hancock ..1,832..B 6
Harmans ....G 6
Harmony ....J 7
Harwood ....J 7
Havre de
 Grace ....9,791..B 13
Hebbville ....F 6
Hebron ....705..G 14
Helen ....G 11
Henderson ...135..D 14
Herford ....B 11
Highfield ....B 8
Highland ....G 4
Highland
 Beach ....6..I 8
Hillandale, see Avenel-
 Hillandale
Hillcrest
 Heights ..24,037..J 4
Hillsboro ....177..E 13
Hobbs ....E 14
Hollywood ......H 11
Honga ....H 12
Hoopersville ...H 12
Hughesville ....G 10
Hurlock ...1,056..F 14
Huyett ....B 7
Hyattstown .....F 2
Hyattsville .14,998..I 4
Ijamsville ......F 2
Indian Head 1,350..F 9
Indian Head
 Plant* ...1,449..F 9
Indian Springs ..B 6
Ingleside ......D 13
Ironshire ......I 15
Ironsides ....G 9
Island Creek ...G 11
Issue ....H 10
Jarrettsville ...B 11
Jefferson ......C 8
Jessup ....G 6
Johnsville .....B 9
Jonestown ......C 12
Joppa ....C 12
Joppatowne* 9,092..C 12
Keedysville .431..C 7
Kemp Mill* 10,037..D 9
Kennedyville ...C 13
Kensington .2,322..H 3
Kentland* .9,649..E 10
Keymar ....B 9
Kingsville .....C 12
Kitzmiller ..443..C 2
Knoxville ....C 7
Lake Shore .....H 7
Lakesville .....H 13
Landover* .5,597..E 10
Landover
 Hills ....2,409..I 5

Langford ....D 13
Langley
 Park ...11,564..I 4
Lanham-Sea-
 brook* .13,244..E 10
Lansdowne-Baltimore High-
 lands ...17,770..F 6
Lantz ....A 7
La Plata ..1,561.°G 10
Laurel ...10,525..H 5
La Vale [-Narrows
 Park] ....3,971..B 3
Laytonsville .293..G 3
Le Gore ....B 9
Leitersburg ....B 7
Leonardtown 1,406.°H 11
Lewistown ......B 8
Lexington Park
 [-Patuxent
 River] ....9,136..H 11
Liberty Grove ..B 13
Libertytown ....C 9
Libertytown ....H 15
Lime Kiln ......F 1
Lineboro ....B 10
Linkwood ....G 13
Linthicum* .9,775..D 11
Linwood ....B 9
Lisbon ....F 3
Little Orleans ..B 5
Loch Lynn
 Heights ...507..C 1
Lonaconing .1,572..B 3
London-
 towne* ...3,864..E 11
Lothian ....J 7
Loveville ......H 11
Lower Marlboro .F 11
Luke ......424..C 3
Lusby ....G 11
Lutherville
 [-Tim-
 onium] ..24,055..E 7
Lynch ....C 13
Maddox ....H 10
Madison ....G 12
Madonna ....B 11
Magnolia ....C 12
Manchester .1,466..B 10
Manokin ....I 14
Marbury ....G 9
Mardela
 Springs ...356..G 14
Marston ....C 9
Martinsburg .....G 1
Marydel ....176..D 14
Maryland
 City* ....7,102..D 11
Maryland Line ..B 11
Massey ....C 14
Matthews ....F 13
Maugans-
 ville* ...1,069..A 7
Mayo .....2,154..J 7
McCoole ....C 3
McDaniel ....F 12
McHenry ....B 2
Mechanicsville ..G 10
Melrose ....B 10
Mexico ....B 10
Middle
 River ...19,935..F 8
Middleburg .....B 9
Middletown .1,262..C 8
Midland ....665..B 3
Milford ....F 6
Millersville ....H 6
Millington ...474..D 14
Mitchellville ...I 6
Monie ....H 14
Monrovia ....F 2
Montrose* .5,902..D 9
Morganza ....H 11
Morningside 1,665..J 5
Moscow ....B 3
Motters ....B 8
Mount Airy .1,825..C 8
Mount Harmony ..F 11
Mount Pleasant .B 10
Mount
 Rainier ..8,180..I 4
Mount
 Savage ...1,413..B 3
Mount Vernon ...H 14
Mountain Lake
 Park .....1,263..C 1
Myersville ...450..C 8
Nanjemoy ....G 9
Nanticoke ......H 13
Narrows Park, see La
 Vale [-Narrows Park]
Naylor ....K 6
Neavitt ....F 12
New Carroll-
 ton ....14,870..I 5
New Market ..339..C 2
New Midway .....B 9
New Windsor .788..B 9
Newark ....H 16
Newburg ....H 10
Newcomb ....F 12
Nikep ....B 3
Norrisville ....B 11
North Beach .761..K 7
North
 Brentwood* .758..I 4

North East .1,818..B 13
North
Potomac* 12,784..D 9
North Takoma
Park*....7,373..D 10
Norwood ....H 4
Oakland ....1,786.°C 11
Oakland* ..1,256..C 10
Oakwood ....B 12
Ocean
City .....1,493..H 16
Odenton ....5,989..H 6
Oldtown ....B 4
Olney ......2,138..G 3
Orchard
Beach ....G 7
Overlea ....13,124..F 7
Owings ....K 7
Owings-
Mills ....7,360..E 5
Oxford ......750..F 12
Oxon Hill ..11,974..K 4
Palmer
Park*.....8,172..E 10
Park Hall ....H 12
Parkton ....C 11
Parkville ..33,589..E 7
Parsonsburg ......G 15
Pasadena ....H 7
Patuxent ....G 11
Patuxent River, see
Lexington Park
[-Patuxent River]
Pepper Mill Village,
see Carmody Hills-
Pepper Mill Village
Perry Hall ..5,446..E 8
Perryman ....C 12
Perryville ..2,091..B 13
Phoenix ....B 11
Pikesville ..25,395..E 6
Pine Orchard ......F 5
Pinehurst ....H 8
Piney Grove ....B 5
Piney Point ....I 11
Pinto ....B 3
Piscataway ....K 4
Pisgah ....G 9
Pittsville ...477..G 15
Pleasant
Hills* ....1,754..B 12
Plum Point ....F 11
Pocomoke
City ......3,573..I 15

Point of Rocks ....C 8
Pomfret ....G 10
Pomona ....D 13
Pomonkey ....F 9
Poolesville ...349..G 1
Port Deposit .906..B 13
Port Herman ....C 13
Port Tobacco ......G 10
Potomac ....I 3
Potomac
Heights* ..1,983..F 9
Potomac Park
[-Bowling
Green] ....2,253..B 4
Potomac
Valley*...5,122..D 9
Powellville ....H 15
Preston .....509..F 13
Price ....D 18
Prince Frederick..°G 11
Princess Anne 975.°H 14
Principio Furnace ..B 13
Public Landing ....H 15
Pumphrey* .6,425..D 11
Pylesville ....B 12
Quantico ....G 14
Queen Anne ..292..E 13
Queenstown ...387..E 12
Randalls-
town ....33,683..F 5
Randolph* .13,215..D 9
Rawlings ....B 3
Redhouse ....C 1
Rehobeth ....I 14
Reisters-
town ....12,568..C 10
Rhodes Point ......I 13
Rhodesdale ....G 14
Ridgely .....822..E 13
Ringgold ....B 8
Rising Sun ...956..B 13
Rison ....G 9
Riva ....I 7
Riverdale ..5,724..I 4
Riverdale Heights-
East
Pines* ...8,941..E 10
Riviera
Beach ...7,464..G 7
Rock Hall .1,125..D 12
Rock Point ....H 10
Rockdale ....F 6
Rockville ..41,821.°D 9
Rocky Ridge ......B 9

Rodgers Forge .....E 7
Rohrersville ......C 7
Rosedale* .19,417..C 11
Rosemont ....250...C 7
Round Bay ....H 7
Royal Oak ....F 12
Ruxton ....E 6
Sabillasville .....B 8
St. George Island ..I 11
St. James ....B 7
St. Leonard ....G 11
St. Martin ....G 16
St. Marys City ....H 12
St. Michaels 1,456..F 12
Salem ....G 13
Salisbury ..15,252.°G 14
Sandgates ....G 11
Sandy Bottom ......D 12
Sandy Spring ......G 4
Sassafras ....C 14
Savage ....2,116..G 5
Scotland ....I 12
Seabrook, see
Lanham-Seabrook
Seat
Pleasant ..7,217..J 5
Secretary ....352..F 13
Selby-on-the-
Bay* .....2,450..E 11
Severna
Park ....16,358..H 7
Shady Side .1,562..J 7
Sharpsburg ...833..C 7
Sharptown ....660..G 14
Sherwood ....F 12
Sherwood Forest ...H 7
Showell ....G 16
Silver Hill,
see Suitland
[-Silver Hill]
Silver Run ....B 9
Silver
Spring ..77,411..I 4
Simpsonville ......G 5
Skidmore ....H 8
Smithsburg ...671..B 8
Smithville ....F 14
Snow Hill .2,201.°H 15
Solomons ....H 12
Somerset ..1,303..I 3
South
Gate* ....9,356..D 11
South Kensing-
ton* .....10,289..E 9

South
Laurel* ..13,345..D 10
Sparks ....B 11
Sparrows Point ....G 7
Spence ....H 15
Spring Gap ....B 4
Stevenson ....E 6
Stevensville ......E 12
Still Pond ....I 15
Stockton ....I 15
Stoneleigh ....E 7
Street ....B 12
Sudlersville ..417..D 14
Suitland [-Silver
Hill] ....30,355..J 4
Sunderland ....F 11
Sunnybrook ....B 11
Sunshine ....G 4
Swanton ....C 2
Sykesville ..1,399..F 4
Takoma
Park ....18,507..I 4
Tall Timbers ......H 11
Taneytown ..1,731..B 9
Taylors Island ....G 12
Taylorsville ......C 9
Taylorville ....H 16
Templeville ...102..D 14
Thomas ....G 12
Thurmont ..2,359..B 8
Tilghman ....F 12
Tilghmanton ....B 7
Timonium, see Luther-
ville [-Timonium]
Toddville ....H 13
Tompkinsville .....H 10
Towson ....77,768.°C 11
Tracys Landing ....K 7
Trappe ......426..F 13
Tunis Mills ....F 12
Tyaskin ....H 14
Tylerton ....I 13
Union Bridge .904..B 9
Uniontown ....B 9
Unionville ....C 9
Unity ....G 4
University
Park ....2,926..I 4
Upper Fairmount ..I 14
Upper Falls ....C 12
Upper
Marlboro ..646.°E 10
Urbana ....F 2
Vale Summit ....B 3

Valley Lee ....H 11
Vienna .....358..G 14
Waldorf ....7,368..F 10
Walker
Mill* ....7,103..E 10
Walkersville .1,269..C 8
Warfieldsburg .....B 10
Warwick ....C 14
Washington
Grove .....688..H 3
Waterloo ....G 5
Waterview ....H 13
Welcome ....G 9
Wenona ....I 13
West Friendship ...F 4
West
Laurel* ...4,478..D 10
Western-
port ......3,106..C 3
Westminster 7,207.°B 10
Westminster
South* ....2,242..B 10
Westover ....I 14
Westwood ....F 11
Whaleysville ......G 15
Wheaton ...66,280..H 4
White Hall ....B 11
White Marsh ....E 8
White
Oak ....19,769..H 4
White Plains ......G 10
Whiteford ....B 12
Whitehaven ....H 14
Willards .....494..G 15
Williamsburg ......F 14
Williamsport 2,270..B 7
Wilson ....B 7
Windyhill ....F 13
Wingate ....H 13
Wittman ....F 12
Woodbine ....F 4
Woodland Beach ...I 7
Woodlawn [-Wood-
moor] ....28,821..F 6
Woodlawn ....B 13
Woodmoor, see Wood-
lawn [-Woodmoor]
Woodsboro ....439..B 9
Woodstock ....F 5
Woolford ....G 12
Worton ....D 13
Wye Mills ....E 13
Yellow Springs ....C 8
Zihlman ....B 3

*Does not appear on the map; key shows general location.
°County seat.
†Independent city.

Source: Latest census figures (1970). Places without population figures are unincorporated areas and are not listed in census reports.

MARYLAND/People

POPULATION

This map shows the *population density* of Maryland, and how it varies in different parts of the state. Population density means the average number of persons who live in a given area.

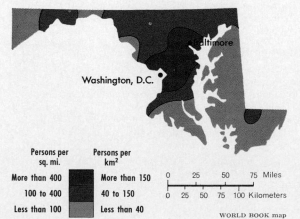

Persons per sq. mi.	Persons per km²
More than 400	More than 150
100 to 400	40 to 150
Less than 100	Less than 40

0   25   50   75 Miles
0   25   50   75   100 Kilometers

WORLD BOOK map

The 1970 U.S. census reported that Maryland had a population of 3,922,399. The population had increased 27 per cent over the 1960 figure of 3,100,689. The U.S. Bureau of the Census estimated that by 1975 the state's population had reached about 4,098,000.

More than five-sixths of the people of Maryland live in urban areas. That is, they live in or near cities and towns of 2,500 or more persons. About one-sixth of the people live in rural areas of the state. About 86 out of 100 persons in Maryland live in one of the state's three Standard Metropolitan Statistical Areas (see METROPOLITAN AREA). These areas are Baltimore and the Maryland portion of the Wilmington, Del., and the Washington, D.C., metropolitan areas. For the populations of these areas, see the *Index* to the political map of Maryland.

Baltimore is the state's largest city. Other large population centers, in order of population, are Dundalk, Towson, Silver Spring, Bethesda, and Wheaton. See the separate articles on the cities of Maryland listed in the *Related Articles.*

About 97 of every 100 persons living in Maryland were born in the United States. Roman Catholics make up the largest single religious group, followed by Methodists. Other large religious groups include Baptists, Episcopalians, Jews, Lutherans, and Presbyterians.

Schools.

Schools. Church leaders and private tutors taught children in the early days of the Maryland colony. Only the children of wealthy families received schooling. The colony first provided funds for public education in 1694. King William's School (now St. John's College) in Annapolis was the colony's first free school. It was founded as an academy in 1696. In 1826, Maryland provided for the establishment of public schools throughout the state. The state board of education and the office of superintendent of public instruction were created in 1865.

Today, the State Board of Education administers Maryland's public school system. The governor appoints the nine members of the board to five-year terms. The board appoints the state superintendent of schools to carry out its policies. A state law requires children between the ages of 6 and 16 to attend school. For the number of students and teachers in Maryland, see EDUCATION (table).

Libraries. In 1699, the Reverend Thomas Bray, an Episcopal minister, set up 30 *parish* (church district) libraries in the colony, with a central library in Annapolis. These were Maryland's first libraries. In 1882, Enoch Pratt, a Baltimore iron merchant, established the Enoch Pratt Free Library of Baltimore. Today, this library ranks as one of the outstanding libraries in the nation. The Enoch Pratt's main library, together with its branches and bookmobiles, has the largest collection of books in Maryland.

The Johns Hopkins University library in Baltimore has a large collection of medical books. The Maryland Historical Society, founded in 1844, has an outstanding collection of books and manuscripts dealing with the history of Maryland. The Maryland State Law Library, in Annapolis, has many rare books, maps, and newspapers. The University of Maryland has a large collection of current East Asian materials.

Museums. The Peale Museum, also called the Municipal Museum of the City of Baltimore, is one of the oldest museums in the United States. It opened in 1814 as the Baltimore Museum and Gallery of the Fine Arts. Rembrandt Peale, the founder, was the son of the famous painter, Charles Willson Peale. The museum displays many works including those of both Peales.

MARYLAND /A Visitor's Guide

Maryland's long shoreline offers opportunities for boating, fishing, and swimming. Visitors can hunt game birds and animals in the fields and forests, and along rivers. Old mansions and historic sites throughout the state appeal to sightseers. Visitors can still watch a form of old English jousting, in which galloping riders try to catch small rings on a spear.

PLACES TO VISIT

Barbara Fritchie House, in Frederick, is a reproduction of the home from which Barbara Fritchie supposedly defied Confederate forces. The building contains her clothing, spinning wheel, china, and Bible.

Basilica of the Assumption of the Blessed Virgin Mary, in Baltimore, was the first major Roman Catholic cathedral in the United States. It was designed by Benjamin Henry Latrobe, and completed in 1821.

Flag House, in Baltimore, was the home of Mary Pickersgill. In this brick building, built in 1793, she made the huge flag that inspired Francis Scott Key to write "The Star-Spangled Banner."

St. Marys City, a village near Leonardtown, became Maryland's first colonial settlement in 1634. A copy of the first Maryland state house stands in the village.

National Monuments and Historic Sites. Antietam National Battlefield Site, near Sharpsburg, was the site of one of the bloodiest Civil War battles. On Sept. 17, 1862, Union forces at Antietam turned back the first Confederate invasion of the North. The State House of Maryland in Annapolis was made a national historic landmark in 1960. It served as the U.S. Capitol in 1783 and 1784, and is the oldest state Capitol still in regular use by a legislature. Fort McHenry National Monument and Historic Shrine in Baltimore honors the defense of Baltimore against the British during the War of 1812. During that defense, on Sept. 13 and 14, 1814, Francis Scott Key was inspired to write "The Star-Spangled Banner."

Other sites in Maryland include Antietam National Cemetery in Sharpsburg, Chesapeake and Ohio Canal National Historical Park between Washington, D.C., and Cumberland, Md., Clara Barton National Historic Site in Glen Echo, Hampton National Historic Site in Towson near Baltimore, Monocacy National Battlefield near Frederick, and U.S. Frigate *Constellation* National Historic Landmark in Baltimore. Maryland shares Harpers Ferry National Historical Park with West Virginia.

State Parks and Forests. Maryland has 33 state parks and 9 state forests. For information on the state parks of Maryland, write to Director, Maryland State Park Service, Tawes Building, Annapolis, Md. 21404.

M. E. Warren

M. E. Warren

◄ State Jousting Championships in St. Margarets

Sailing in Chesapeake Bay ►

The Baltimore Museum of Art has exhibits of paintings, prints, and sculpture. Its collection of paintings by Henri Matisse is the largest in any public gallery.

The Maryland Historical Society in Baltimore owns the original manuscript of "The Star-Spangled Banner." The society's Noel Wyatt and Elizabeth Patterson Bonaparte collections include Empire furniture, miniatures, glass, jewelry, and lace. Other important museums include the Walters Art Gallery in Baltimore and the U.S. Naval Academy Museum in Annapolis.

UNIVERSITIES AND COLLEGES

Maryland has 27 universities and colleges accredited by the Middle States Association of Colleges and Schools. For enrollments and further information, see UNIVERSITIES AND COLLEGES (table).

Name	Location	Founded	Name	Location	Founded
Baltimore, University of	Baltimore	1925	Morgan State University	Baltimore	1867
Baltimore Hebrew College	Baltimore	1919	Mount St. Mary's College	Emmitsburg	1808
Bowie State College	Bowie	1867	Notre Dame of Maryland,		
Capitol Institute of Technology	Kensington	1964	College of	Baltimore	1895
Columbia Union College	Takoma Park	1904	Peabody Conservatory of Music	Baltimore	1857
Coppin State College	Baltimore	1900	St. John's College	Annapolis	1696
De Sales Hall School of Theology	Hyattsville	1949	St. Mary's College of Maryland	St. Marys City	1967
Frostburg State College	Frostburg	1902	St. Mary's Seminary and University	Baltimore	1791
Goucher College	Towson	1885	Salisbury State College	Salisbury	1925
Hood College	Frederick	1893	Towson State University	Baltimore	1866
Johns Hopkins University	Baltimore	1876	United States Naval Academy	Annapolis	1845
Loyola College	Baltimore	1852	Washington College	Chestertown	1782
Maryland, University of	*	*	Washington Theological Union	Silver Spring	1969
Maryland Institute, College of Art	Baltimore	1931	Western Maryland College	Westminster	1867

*For campuses and founding dates of the University of Maryland, see UNIVERSITIES AND COLLEGES (table).

ANNUAL EVENTS

One of Maryland's most famous annual events is the Preakness Stakes, a horse race run each May at the Pimlico race track in Baltimore. The Preakness, with the Kentucky Derby and the Belmont Stakes, makes up the famous *Triple Crown* of horse racing. Other annual events in Maryland include the following.

January-March: Governor's Open House in Annapolis (January 1); Winterfest in McHenry (March); Maryland Day in St. Mary's City (Sunday nearest March 25).

April-June: House and Garden Pilgrimages in various parts of the state (April-May); Maryland Kite Festival near Baltimore (April); Steeplechase Races in Baltimore County (April); Tobacco Auctions in southern Maryland (April-June); Revolutionary War Days in Charles County (May); June Week at the U.S. Naval Academy in Annapolis (first week in June); Flag Day Ceremonies at Flag House in Baltimore (June).

July-September: Miles River Yacht Club Regatta in St. Michaels (July); State Jousting Championships in different locations (August-October); National Hard Crab Derby in Crisfield (Labor Day weekend); Heritage Weekend in Annapolis (September); Defender's Day, statewide (September).

October-December: Autumn Glory Festival in Garrett County (October); Old Princess Anne Days in Princess Anne (October); Chesapeake Appreciation Festival near Annapolis (late October); International Horse Race in Laurel (November).

M. E. Warren

Graduation at U.S. Naval Academy in Annapolis

Antietam National Battlefield Site near Sharpsburg
Zehrt, FPG

Roche, FPG

Barbara Fritchie House in Frederick

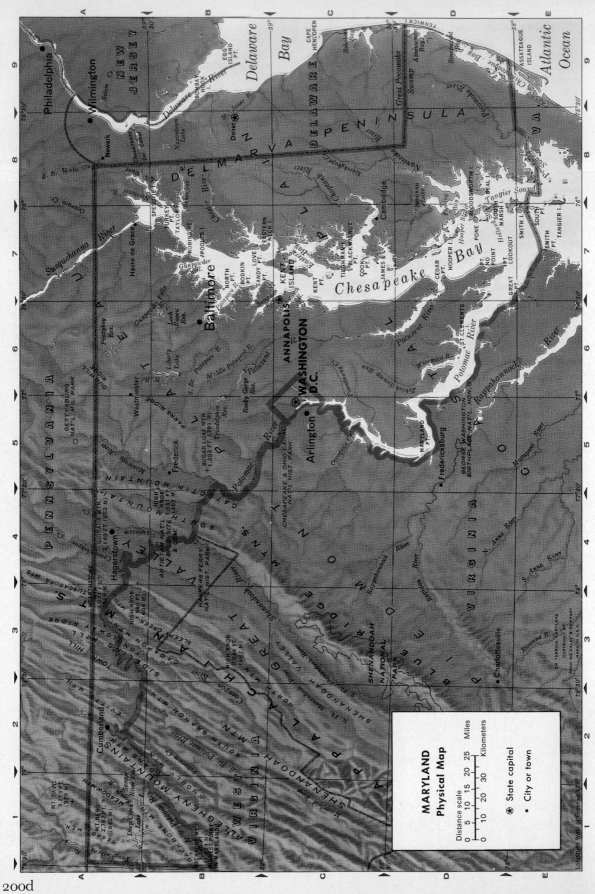

MARYLAND
Physical Map

Distance scale

Miles
0 5   10   15   20   25

Kilometers
0   10   20   30

⊛ State capital
• City or town

Specially created for **World Book Encyclopedia** by Rand McNally and World Book editors

200d

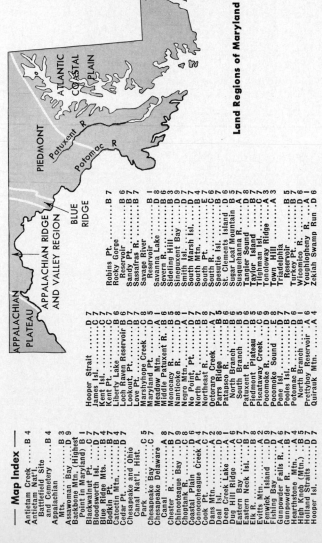

Land Regions of Maryland

MARYLAND/The Land

Land Regions. Chesapeake Bay divides most of Maryland into two parts. The area east of Chesapeake Bay is called the Eastern Shore. The area west of the bay is called the Western Shore. Maryland has five main land regions. They are, from east to west: (1) the Atlantic Coastal Plain, (2) the Piedmont, (3) the Blue Ridge, (4) the Appalachian Ridge and Valley, and (5) the Appalachian Plateau.

The *Atlantic Coastal Plain* stretches along the east coast of the United States from New Jersey to southern Florida. In Maryland, the coastal plain covers the entire Eastern Shore and part of the Western Shore. The plain touches a narrow tip of northeastern Maryland. It extends across southern Maryland from the southeastern corner of the state almost to Washington, D.C. The coastal plain is flat on the Eastern Shore, but it rises to about 400 feet (120 meters) on the Western Shore. The Eastern Shore has some marshy areas. The Pocomoke Swamp, which is 2 miles (3 kilometers) wide, extends from Pocomoke Sound to the Delaware border. The part of the Western Shore south of Baltimore is called Southern Maryland. Tobacco has been raised in Southern Maryland since colonial times.

The *Piedmont* extends from New Jersey to Alabama. In Maryland, the Piedmont is about 50 miles (80 kilometers) wide. It stretches from the northeastern to the central part of the state. Low, rolling hills and fertile valleys cover the region. The Piedmont rises to about 880 feet (268 meters) at Parrs Ridge, and to about 1,200 feet (366 meters) at Dug Hill Ridge on the Pennsylvania border. Both these ridges run in a southwesterly direction. They form the divide between streams flowing westward into the Potomac River and those flowing eastward into Chesapeake Bay. Frederick Valley, along the Monocacy River, is one of the richest dairy-farming areas in the United States.

The *Blue Ridge* region extends from southern Pennsylvania to northern Georgia. In Maryland, the region is a narrow, mountainous strip of land between the Piedmont and the Appalachian Ridge and Valley region. South Mountain and Catoctin Mountain form most of the Blue Ridge. Nearly all the region is over 1,000 feet (300 meters) above sea level. It rises to a height of over 2,000 feet (610 meters) near the Pennsylvania border. The Blue Ridge region was named for the blue haze that sometimes hangs over its forest-covered ridges.

The *Appalachian Ridge and Valley* is a land region that stretches southwestward from New Jersey to Alabama. The Maryland portion is a strip of land that separates Pennsylvania from West Virginia. At Hancock, Maryland measures less than 2 miles (3 kilometers) from its northern to its southern borders.

The Great Valley, known in Maryland as Hagerstown Valley, covers the eastern portion of the state's ridge and valley region. Much of this fertile valley is filled with orchards and farms. West of the valley, a series of ridges crosses the state from northeast to southwest. Some of the ridges rise to almost 2,000 feet (610 meters). Forests cover about two-thirds of the region.

The *Appalachian Plateau* extends from New York to Georgia. It covers a triangle-shaped area in the extreme western part of Maryland. The Allegheny Mountains cover most of the region. They make up part of the huge Appalachian range. Backbone Mountain, in the southwestern corner of the state, is the highest point in Maryland. It rises 3,360 feet (1,024 meters). Streams have cut deep valleys into the Appalachian Plateau. These valleys served as early trails to the West. Forests cover nearly three-fourths of the plateau region.

Coastline of Maryland measures only 31 miles (49 kilometers) along the Atlantic Ocean. But the many arms and inlets of Chesapeake Bay give Maryland a total coastline of 3,190 miles (5,134 kilometers). These arms and inlets provide excellent harbors. Islands in Chesapeake Bay include Bloodsworth, Deal, Hooper, Kent, Smith, South Marsh, Taylors, and Tilghman.

Blue Haze, *above,* hangs over the hills and valleys of the Blue Ridge region, a narrow strip of land in northern Maryland.

Fertile Farmland, *left,* makes Frederick County one of Maryland's finest agricultural areas. It is in the Piedmont region.

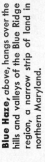

"The Narrows," *above,* lies near Cumberland. This area of Maryland is in the Appalachian Ridge and Valley region.

Hunters Watch for Ducks, *right,* on Chesapeake Bay in the Atlantic Coastal Plain.

Rivers and Lakes. Most of Maryland is drained by rivers that flow into Chesapeake Bay. Seven large rivers cross the Eastern Shore area. They are the Chester, Choptank, Elk, Nanticoke, Pocomoke, Sassafras, and Wicomico. The Susquehanna River flows into the state from Pennsylvania and empties into Chesapeake Bay. The Gunpowder, Patapsco, and Patuxent rivers all drain the Western Shore and flow into the bay.

The Potomac River forms Maryland's southern and southwestern boundary. South of Washington, D.C., the Potomac widens into an arm of Chesapeake Bay. Tributaries of the Potomac River drain a large part of western Maryland.

All Maryland lakes are man-made. The largest, Deep Creek Lake in the Allegheny Mountains, covers about 4,000 acres (1,600 hectares). This lake was formed by a dam built across a small tributary of the Youghiogheny River. The dam provides hydroelectric power.

Deep Creek Lake, in the Allegheny Mountains, is Maryland's largest lake. It lies in the Appalachian Plateau region.

M. E. Warren, Alpha

MARYLAND / Climate

Maryland has a humid climate, with hot summers and generally mild winters. Temperatures in the mountainous regions of the northwest are lower than those along the Atlantic coast and in the Chesapeake Bay region. January temperatures average 29° F. (−2° C) in Garrett County in the northwest, and 39° F. (4° C) along the coast. Average July temperatures range from 68° F. (20° C) in Garrett County to about 75° F. (24° C) in the Chesapeake Bay region. The state's record high temperature, 109° F. (43° C), occurred at Boettcherville on July 3, 1898, and at Cumberland and Frederick on July 10, 1936. Oakland recorded the lowest temperature, −40° F. (−40° C), on Jan. 13, 1912.

Maryland's *precipitation* (rain, melted snow, and other forms of moisture) averages about 44 inches (112 centimeters) a year. Rain falls fairly evenly throughout the state. Snow ranges from about 9 inches (23 centimeters) a year in the southeast to about 78 inches (198 centimeters) in the Appalachian Plateau.

SEASONAL TEMPERATURES

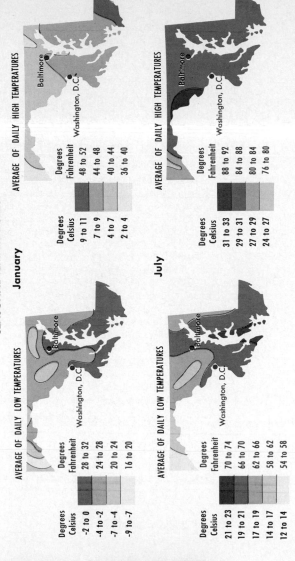

January

AVERAGE OF DAILY LOW TEMPERATURES

Degrees Celsius	Degrees Fahrenheit
-2 to 0	28 to 32
-4 to -2	24 to 28
-7 to -4	20 to 24
-9 to -7	16 to 20

AVERAGE OF DAILY HIGH TEMPERATURES

Degrees Celsius	Degrees Fahrenheit
9 to 11	48 to 52
7 to 9	44 to 48
4 to 7	40 to 44
2 to 4	36 to 40

July

AVERAGE OF DAILY LOW TEMPERATURES

Degrees Celsius	Degrees Fahrenheit
21 to 23	70 to 74
19 to 21	66 to 70
17 to 19	62 to 66
14 to 17	58 to 62
12 to 14	54 to 58

AVERAGE OF DAILY HIGH TEMPERATURES

Degrees Celsius	Degrees Fahrenheit
31 to 33	88 to 92
29 to 31	84 to 88
27 to 29	80 to 84
24 to 27	76 to 80

AVERAGE YEARLY PRECIPITATION
(Rain, Melted Snow and Other Moisture)

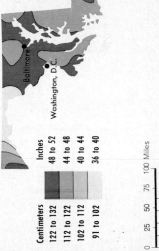

Centimeters	Inches
122 to 132	48 to 52
112 to 122	44 to 48
102 to 112	40 to 44
91 to 102	36 to 40

0 25 50 75 100 Miles
0 50 100 Kilometers

WORLD BOOK maps

AVERAGE MONTHLY WEATHER

BALTIMORE

	Temperatures F° High	Low	C° High	Low	Days of Rain or Snow
JAN.	43	26	6	-3	12
FEB.	44	26	7	-3	8
MAR.	53	33	12	1	13
APR.	63	42	17	6	11
MAY	73	53	23	12	11
JUNE	83	62	28	17	10
JULY	87	66	31	19	6
AUG.	85	64	29	18	10
SEPT.	78	58	26	14	8
OCT.	67	46	19	8	7
NOV.	55	36	13	2	9
DEC.	44	27	7	-3	9

WASHINGTON, D.C.

	Temperatures F° High	Low	C° High	Low	Days of Rain or Snow
JAN.	44	29	7	-2	11
FEB.	46	29	8	-2	10
MAR.	55	36	13	2	12
APR.	65	45	18	7	11
MAY	76	55	24	13	12
JUNE	84	64	29	18	11
JULY	87	68	31	20	11
AUG.	85	67	29	19	11
SEPT.	79	61	26	16	8
OCT.	68	49	20	9	8
NOV.	57	39	14	4	9
DEC.	46	31	8	-1	10

Baltimore is Maryland's major manufacturing center. Other manufacturing cities in the state include Cambridge, Cumberland, Frederick, Hagerstown, Salisbury, and Westminster. Most of the state has good farmland. Most mining takes place on the Western Shore. The state's tourist industries thrive along Chesapeake Bay; in the areas near Washington, D.C., and Baltimore; and at Maryland's many historic sites.

Natural Resources of Maryland include fertile soils, trees, waters filled with sea life, and many minerals.

Soil. Light, sandy loams and stiff, clay soils cover much of the Eastern Shore, although the northern part has heavier soils. The Western Shore south of Baltimore also has loam and clay soils. North-central Maryland has fertile, limestone soils. The valleys of western Maryland have a thin covering of soil. Orchards thrive there.

Forests cover about 2,700,000 acres (1,090,000 hectares), about 40 per cent of the state's land area. A belt of hardwood forest stretches across much of central Maryland. Over 150 kinds of trees grow in the state. Oaks are the most common. Others include the ash, beech, black locust, hickory, maple, and tupelo.

Plant Life. The black-eyed Susan, Maryland's state flower, grows on the Western Shore. The Western Shore also has many kinds of berries, including blackberries, dewberries, raspberries, and wild strawberries. Grasses and grasslike plants called *sedges* grow on the Eastern Shore. Azaleas, laurel, and rhododendrons grow along the edges of the woods.

Animal Life includes eastern cottontail rabbits, minks, opossums, raccoons, red and gray foxes, and white-tailed deer. The north-central part of the state has chipmunks, otters, squirrels, and woodchucks. Hunters find grouse, partridge, wild turkeys, and woodcocks in western Maryland, and wild ducks and geese along the coastal plain. Songbirds are plentiful. The Baltimore oriole is not common but was chosen as the state bird because it is orange and black, the colors of the Lords Baltimore, Maryland's first rulers.

Maryland's coastal waters have great quantities of bluefish, crabs, diamondback terrapins, menhaden, oysters, sea trout, shad, shrimps, and striped bass (called *rockfish* or *rock* in Maryland). Each spring, shad, croakers, alewives, and other fishes swim up Chesapeake Bay to lay their eggs in the larger rivers. Trout live in the cold rivers and streams of northern and western Maryland. Carp, catfish, and suckers are found in the waters of the Piedmont and the coastal plain.

Minerals. Sand and gravel deposits are found in many counties on Maryland's Western Shore. About 10 counties have valuable deposits of stone. Other minerals in the state include clays, coal, granite, limestone, natural gas, and talc.

Manufacturing, including processing, accounts for 89 per cent of the value of goods produced in Maryland. Manufactured goods have a *value added by manufacture* of about $7 billion a year. This figure represents the value created in products by Maryland's industries, not counting such costs as materials, supplies, and fuels. Maryland's chief manufactured products, in order of importance, are (1) food products, (2) electric and electronic equipment, and (3) primary metals.

Food Products have a value added of about $1 billion yearly. Factories in Baltimore process meats and manufacture spices, food concentrates, and other food products. Baltimore is the state's sugar refining center. Factories in Cambridge process, can, and freeze foods.

Electric and Electronic Equipment has an annual value added by manufacture of about $960 million. Chief products of the industry are radio and television equipment. Most of the electrical machinery is made in Baltimore.

Primary Metals industries manufacture products that have a value added of about $850 million a year. These industries smelt, refine, and roll such metals as aluminum, copper, and steel. Most primary metals plants are in the Baltimore area. The Bethlehem Steel Corporation plant in Sparrows Point is one of the largest steel mills in the world. Most metals are imported from outside the state.

Other Leading Industries. The production of non-electric machinery is the fourth-ranking industrial activity of Maryland. The Baltimore area is the chief production center of machine tools. Other leading industries in Maryland produce chemicals and transportation equipment. Large factories in the Baltimore area make such chemical products as paint and soap. The area also has major shipbuilding facilities. Other industries in the state produce clothing, fabricated metal products, paper products, and printed materials.

Production of Goods in Maryland

Total value of goods produced in 1977—$8,003,602,000

Manufactured Products 89%

Agricultural Products 8%

Fish and Mineral Products 3%

Percentages are based on farm income, value added by manufacture, and value of fish and mineral production. Fish products are less than 1 per cent.
Sources: U.S. government publications, 1978-1979.

Employment in Maryland

Total number of persons employed in 1978—1,622,600

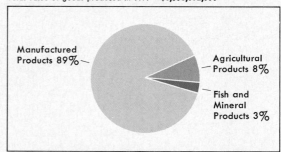

	Number of Employees
Government	383,000
Wholesale & Retail Trade	378,600
Mining & Community, Social, & Personal Services	317,300
Manufacturing	242,000
Construction	102,500
Finance, Insurance, & Real Estate	85,600
Transportation & Public Utilities	84,600
Agriculture	29,000

Sources: *Employment and Earnings*, May 1979, U.S. Bureau of Labor Statistics; *Farm Labor*, February 1979, U.S. Dept. of Agriculture.

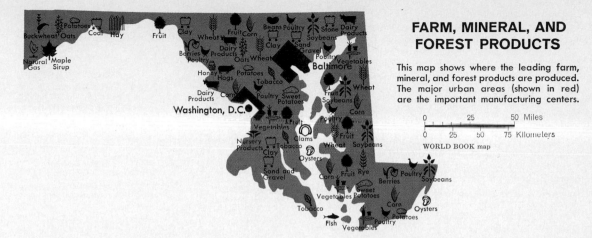

FARM, MINERAL, AND FOREST PRODUCTS

This map shows where the leading farm, mineral, and forest products are produced. The major urban areas (shown in red) are the important manufacturing centers.

WORLD BOOK map

Agriculture. Farm products in Maryland earn an annual income of about $668 million, or 8 per cent of the value of goods produced in the state. Farmland covers about 45 per cent of the state. Maryland's 16,400 farms average about 170 acres (69 hectares) in size.

Livestock and Livestock Products have an annual value of about $428 million. *Broilers* (chickens between 9 and 12 weeks old) are Maryland's leading farm product, earning about $186 million a year. Most of the state's broilers are raised in the central and southern parts of the Eastern Shore. Milk is the second leading farm product. It earns about $162 million yearly. Frederick County leads the state in milk production, followed by Washington, Carroll, Harford, and Montgomery counties. Other important livestock products include beef cattle, eggs, and hogs.

Crops in Maryland have an annual value of about $229 million. Corn is Maryland's leading cash crop, bringing in about $69 million a year. Corn is grown throughout the state. Soybeans are the state's second leading cash crop. Tobacco ranks third, and Maryland is a leading tobacco state. Other crops produced include apples, cucumbers, greenhouse and nursery products, hay, snap beans, tomatoes, and wheat.

Mining in Maryland has an annual value of about $196 million. Coal ranks as Maryland's most valuable mineral. Allegany and Garrett counties, in western Maryland, mine *bituminous* (soft) coal. Quarries in the northern and western regions produce most of the stone. Large quantities of sand and gravel come from pits on the Western Shore. Fire clay is produced in Harford County. Baltimore, Frederick, and Washington counties, all on the Western Shore, lead the state in limestone production. Natural gas comes from Garrett County. Other important minerals include gem stones, peat, and talc.

Fishing Industry. The annual fish catch in Maryland is valued at about $31 million. Maryland leads all states in the production of oysters, and ranks second only to Maine in soft-shell clam production. Valuable catches in Chesapeake Bay include bluefish, bullheads, catfish, clams, crabs, eels, menhaden, oysters, snapper turtles, striped bass, and white perch. Fish caught in Atlantic coastal waters include croakers, flounder, hard crabs, lobster, oysters, surf clams, and tuna.

Electric Power. Steam plants, operated on coal or oil, supply most of Maryland's electric power. A nuclear power plant operates at Calvert Cliffs, near Lusby.

Transportation. Early transportation in the Maryland region was provided by steamboats traveling over Chesapeake Bay and its tributaries. In 1828, construction began on the Baltimore and Ohio Railroad. This railroad was the first in the Western Hemisphere to carry both passengers and freight. The Chesapeake and Delaware Canal was completed in 1829, connecting Chesapeake Bay with the Delaware River. In the 1920's, motor trucks and buses replaced steamboat transportation in the Chesapeake Bay country.

Today, nearly all Maryland's 27,400 miles (44,100 kilometers) of roads and highways are surfaced. In 1963, the John F. Kennedy Expressway became the state's first modern tollway. It is part of a major nonstop highway that extends from Florida to Maine. Maryland has about 25 public airports and about 110 private airports. Baltimore-Washington International Airport, near Baltimore, is a major national and international terminal. It serves both Baltimore and Washington, D.C. Railroads operate on about 1,100 miles (1,800 kilometers) of track in Maryland. Seven railroads provide freight service, and passenger trains serve Baltimore and Washington, D.C. Baltimore also ranks as a leading U.S. seaport.

Communication. The *Maryland Gazette*, published in Annapolis from 1727 to 1734, was the first colonial newspaper south of Philadelphia, and one of the first in the colonies. In 1844, the first telegraph line in the United States opened between Baltimore and Washington, D.C. Maryland's oldest radio stations, WCAO and WFBR of Baltimore, began broadcasting in 1922. The state's first television station, WMAR-TV, was established in Baltimore in 1947.

Today, Maryland has about 80 newspapers, 13 of which are dailies, and about 150 periodicals. *The News American* and *The Sun*, both in Baltimore, are the largest dailies. The state has about 95 radio stations and 10 television stations.

Indian Days. Indians probably lived in the Maryland region hundreds of years before white people came. Early white explorers found Algonkian Indians and a few Susquehannock in the region. The Algonkian tribes included the Choptank, Nanticoke, Patuxent, Portobago, Wicomico, and others. Most of the Indians left the region during the early years of white settlement. But they gave their names to many of Maryland's rivers, towns, and counties.

Exploration and Settlement. The Spaniards became the first white people to visit the Maryland region when they explored Chesapeake Bay in the 1500's. In 1608, Captain John Smith of Virginia sailed northward up Chesapeake Bay into the Maryland region. Smith wrote a description of what he saw. In 1631, William Claiborne, also of Virginia, opened a trading post on Kent Island in the bay. Claiborne's was the first white settlement in the Maryland region.

In 1632, King Charles I of England granted the

—— IMPORTANT DATES IN MARYLAND ——

1608 Captain John Smith explored Chesapeake Bay.

1631 William Claiborne established a trading post on Kent Island.

1632 King Charles I of England granted the Maryland charter to Cecil Calvert, second Lord Baltimore.

1634 The first settlers arrived in Maryland.

1649 Maryland passed a religious toleration act.

1654 William Claiborne seized control of the colony.

1658 Lord Baltimore regained control.

1691 England assumed direct rule of the colony.

1715 The Lords Baltimore regained proprietorship of the colony.

1767 Mason and Dixon completed their survey of the Maryland-Pennsylvania boundary, begun in 1763.

1774 Marylanders burned the *Peggy Stewart* and its cargo of tea in protest against the Boston Port Bill.

1776 Maryland declared its independence.

1776-1777 The Second Continental Congress met in Baltimore.

1783 George Washington resigned his commission as commander in chief at Annapolis.

1788 Maryland became the seventh state on April 28.

1791 Maryland gave land for the District of Columbia.

1814 Francis Scott Key wrote "The Star-Spangled Banner" during the British bombardment of Fort McHenry.

1828 Construction of the Baltimore & Ohio Railroad began.

1850 The National (Cumberland) Road, west from Cumberland, was completed.

1862 Federal forces drove back the Confederates from Antietam Creek near Sharpsburg.

1864 A constitution abolishing slavery was adopted.

1919-1933 Maryland resisted the nation's prohibition laws and became known as the *Free State.*

1950 Baltimore's Friendship International Airport (now Baltimore-Washington International Airport) began operating.

1952 The Chesapeake Bay Bridge (now the William Preston Lane, Jr., Memorial Bridge) was opened to traffic.

1957 The Baltimore Harbor Tunnel opened.

1962-1966 Maryland reapportioned its legislative and congressional districts.

1972 Maryland voters approved a state lottery to raise money for the state government.

The Battle of Antietam, near Sharpsburg, in September, 1862, halted General Lee's first invasion of the North.

Religious Toleration Law was passed in 1649. Called the *Act Concerning Religion,* it gave equal rights to all Christians.

HISTORIC MARYLAND

Washington, D.C., occupies land Maryland gave the U.S. in 1791, after George Washington chose that site for the capital.

Maryland region to George Calvert, the first Lord Baltimore. But George Calvert died before the king signed the charter. King Charles then chartered the region to Calvert's son, Cecil, the second Lord Baltimore. The region was named *Maryland* in honor of Queen Henrietta Maria, the wife of Charles. Cecil Calvert sent colonists to Maryland on two ships, the *Ark* and the *Dove.* In 1634, the two ships anchored off St. Clements Island in the Potomac River. The colonists established St. Marys City near the southern tip of the Western Shore.

Colonial Days. Lord Baltimore appointed his brother, Leonard Calvert, as governor of the Maryland Colony. Lord Baltimore encouraged the colonists to suggest laws and to assist his brother in the colony's administration. Lord Baltimore was a Roman Catholic, and he wanted freedom of worship for those of his faith. But he also wanted persons of other faiths to settle in Maryland. He believed that religious restrictions would interfere with the colony's growth and development. In

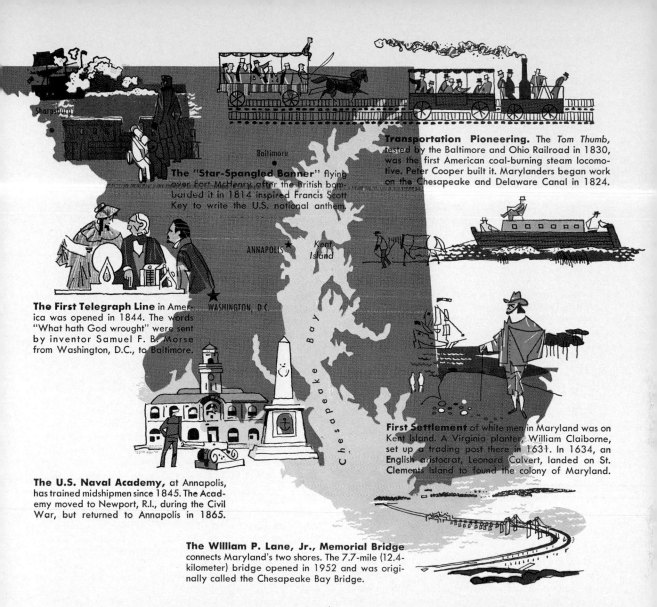

Transportation Pioneering. The *Tom Thumb*, tested by the Baltimore and Ohio Railroad in 1830, was the first American coal-burning steam locomotive. Peter Cooper built it. Marylanders began work on the Chesapeake and Delaware Canal in 1824.

The **"Star-Spangled Banner"** flying over Fort McHenry after the British bombarded it in 1814 inspired Francis Scott Key to write the U.S. national anthem.

The First Telegraph Line in America was opened in 1844. The words "What hath God wrought" were sent by inventor Samuel F. B. Morse from Washington, D.C., to Baltimore.

First Settlement of white men in Maryland was on Kent Island. A Virginia planter, William Claiborne, set up a trading post there in 1631. In 1634, an English aristocrat, Leonard Calvert, landed on St. Clements Island to found the colony of Maryland.

The U.S. Naval Academy, at Annapolis, has trained midshipmen since 1845. The Academy moved to Newport, R.I., during the Civil War, but returned to Annapolis in 1865.

The William P. Lane, Jr., Memorial Bridge connects Maryland's two shores. The 7.7-mile (12.4-kilometer) bridge opened in 1952 and was originally called the Chesapeake Bay Bridge.

1649, the colonial assembly approved Lord Baltimore's draft of a religious toleration law, granting religious freedom to all Christians. After the law was passed, a band of Puritans fled from Virginia and came to Maryland. Maryland became famous for its religious freedom.

William Claiborne's trading settlement on Kent Island was part of the Maryland Colony. But Claiborne refused to recognize Lord Baltimore's authority. In 1654, Claiborne led a group of Protestant settlers who overthrew Lord Baltimore's government. Claiborne controlled Maryland for four years.

On orders from the English government, Claiborne returned Maryland to Lord Baltimore in 1658. Lord Baltimore promised to uphold the religious freedoms established in 1649. But many Protestants in Maryland resented a Roman Catholic as owner of the colony. In 1689, the Protestant Association, a group led by John Coode, seized control of the colony. Coode demanded that England take over the government of Maryland.

As a result, royal governors appointed by the English crown began to rule the colony in 1691.

The Calvert family regained control of Maryland in 1715 under the fourth Lord Baltimore, a Protestant. Maryland remained in the hands of the Lords Baltimore until the Revolutionary War. Maryland prospered during the years before the Revolution. Tobacco farming in the colony became profitable. Many colonists grew wealthy and built beautiful mansions. Maryland's population grew rapidly. In the 1700's Maryland and Pennsylvania quarreled over the boundary line between them. In 1763, both colonies agreed to have Charles Mason and Jeremiah Dixon of England survey the land. The survey was completed in 1767, and the boundary became known as *Mason and Dixon's Line.*

The Revolutionary War. In the mid-1700's, Great Britain found itself deeply in debt. To help raise money, Britain placed severe taxes and trade restrictions on the American colonies. The people of Maryland, like those of the other colonies, opposed these measures.

200k

Marylanders resisted the Stamp Act of 1765 (see STAMP ACT). In 1774, colonists in Maryland protested the Boston Port Bill. This bill was a British attempt to punish the people of Boston for the Boston Tea Party (see BOSTON PORT BILL). Marylanders burned the British ship *Peggy Stewart* and its cargo of tea in Annapolis.

In 1774, delegates from Maryland attended the First Continental Congress in Philadelphia. They supported a policy forbidding the colonists to trade with Great Britain. The Revolutionary War began in Massachusetts in April, 1775. That May, the Second Continental Congress met in Philadelphia, and on July 2, 1776, Maryland delegates voted for independence. Maryland adopted its first constitution on Nov. 8, 1776. In December, 1776, the Continental Congress moved to Baltimore because the British threatened Philadelphia. The congress remained there until the following March. Thomas Johnson, Maryland's first governor under its constitution, took office on March 21, 1777.

Maryland troops fought throughout the Revolutionary War. Baltimore industries built ships and cannons for the colonial forces. But little fighting took place on Maryland soil. The British admiral Richard Howe sailed up Chesapeake Bay in 1777 and landed troops at the mouth of the Elk River. The troops moved into Pennsylvania that same year, and they defeated General George Washington in the Battle of Brandywine.

Statehood. During the war, the Continental Congress formed a government of the United States under the Articles of Confederation. Some of the states claimed western land that extended beyond their colonial boundaries. Maryland refused to sign the Articles of Confederation until the states promised to turn these western lands over to the United States government. Maryland signed the Articles on March 1, 1781. See ARTICLES OF CONFEDERATION; CONGRESS OF THE CONFEDERATION.

After the war, the Congress of the Confederation accepted Maryland's invitation and met in Annapolis from November, 1783, to June, 1784. George Washington resigned his commission as Commander in Chief of the Continental Army in the Maryland State House.

During the 1780's, Maryland and Virginia disagreed over navigation rights in Chesapeake Bay and on the Potomac River. The dispute led to a series of interstate conferences. These and other problems were finally taken up in 1787 by the state delegates to a constitutional convention in Philadelphia. The delegates drew up the United States Constitution. Maryland *ratified* (approved) the Constitution on April 28, 1788, and became the seventh state of the Union. In 1791, Maryland gave land to Congress for the District of Columbia, the new national capital.

The War of 1812 and Industrial Development. Several battles of the War of 1812 were fought in Maryland. In 1813, the British raided a number of Maryland towns and farmhouses along Chesapeake Bay. During the summer of 1814, a large British force under General Robert Ross sailed up the Patuxent River. Ross's troops defeated American forces in the Battle of Bladensburg on Aug. 24, 1814. The British moved on to Washington,

D.C., that same day. They burned the Capitol and other government buildings.

On Sept. 12, the British attacked Baltimore. British troops landed at North Point, southeast of Baltimore at the mouth of the Patapsco River. British ships sailed up the river and fired on Fort McHenry. But American forces defended the city and drove the British out of Maryland. The Battle of Baltimore inspired Francis Scott Key to write "The Star-Spangled Banner," which later became the national anthem of the United States. See STAR-SPANGLED BANNER.

During the early and middle 1800's, Baltimore grew into an important industrial city. It became a leading seaport, and one of the nation's shipbuilding centers. Goods were shipped between Baltimore and the West on the Baltimore and Ohio Railroad, on the Chesapeake and Ohio Canal, and on the Chesapeake and Delaware Canal. In 1830, Peter Cooper built the *Tom Thumb*, the first coal-burning American steam locomotive. The Baltimore and Ohio Railroad used the *Tom Thumb* between Baltimore and Ellicotts' Mills (now Ellicott City). The *De Rosset*, the first ocean-going iron steamship built in the United States, was completed in Baltimore in 1839. Maryland adopted a new constitution in 1851, its first since 1776.

The Civil War. Maryland was a slave state, but it also was one of the original 13 states of the Union. When the Civil War began in 1861, Marylanders were divided in their loyalties between the Union and the Confederacy. After Virginia joined the Confederacy, the fate of Washington, D.C., depended on whether Maryland remained in the Union. If Maryland joined the Confederacy, Washington, D.C., would be surrounded by Confederate territory. Union forces rushed across Maryland to defend the nation's capital. Maryland finally decided to stay in the Union, but many Marylanders joined the Confederate armies.

Several Civil War battles were fought on Maryland soil. In 1862, General Robert E. Lee's Confederate troops invaded Maryland. Union forces fought them in the Battle of Antietam, near Sharpsburg, on September 17. That day, more than 12,000 Union soldiers and 10,000 Confederates were killed or wounded. Lee withdrew to Virginia the next day. In June, 1863, Lee led his troops across Maryland into Pennsylvania, where he was defeated in the Battle of Gettysburg. In 1864, Confederate General Jubal A. Early crossed the Potomac River into Maryland. He defeated a Union division in the Battle of Monocacy, near Frederick, on July 9. Early's forces advanced to within sight of Washington, D.C., before Union forces drove them back.

In 1864, Maryland adopted a constitution that abolished slavery. The new constitution also placed harsh penalties on Marylanders who had supported the Confederate cause. A less severe constitution was adopted in 1867, and is still in effect.

Maryland maintained its industrial and commercial development after the Civil War. Baltimore, already a great industrial city, became a well-known cultural center in the middle and late 1800's.

The Early 1900's. Maryland's industrial expansion continued into the 1900's. The state's factories and shipyards expanded greatly after the United States entered World War I in 1917. The U.S. Army established the Aberdeen Proving Ground, its first testing center, along the northwest shore of Chesapeake Bay in 1917.

In 1919, the U.S. Congress passed a law making it illegal to manufacture, sell, and transport alcoholic beverages. Marylanders were among the leading opponents of prohibition law, because they considered it a violation of their state's rights. As a result, Maryland became known as the *Free State*. This nickname is still sometimes used to honor Maryland's traditions of political and religious freedoms.

The Great Depression of the 1930's struck the industrial city of Baltimore particularly hard. Maryland passed social and welfare laws in cooperation with the federal government to ease hardships. In 1938, the state legislature approved the first state income tax law and a $15-million federal housing project.

The Mid-1900's. During World War II (1939-1945), manufacturing activity increased greatly in Maryland. Thousands of workers came to the state from the Appalachian mountain region and other parts of the South.

After the war, Maryland's industry and population continued to grow, and the state improved its transportation systems. Baltimore's Friendship International Airport (now Baltimore-Washington International Airport) opened in 1950. Between 1952 and 1963, the state completed Baltimore Harbor Tunnel, Chesapeake Bay Bridge (now William P. Lane, Jr., Memorial Bridge), John F. Kennedy Expressway, and an expressway connecting Baltimore and Washington.

The growth of Maryland's urban population created political problems. Until the 1960's, voters in thinly populated rural areas were electing most of the state's legislators. Between 1962 and 1966, Maryland *reapportioned* (redivided) its state legislative and United States congressional districts for more equal representation.

Maryland expanded its school system during the 1960's and 1970's. The University of Maryland, which has its main campus in College Park, opened branches in Baltimore, Catonsville, and Princess Anne. Several state teachers' colleges became general state colleges, and many two-year community colleges opened.

In 1967, Spiro T. Agnew became the fifth Republican governor in Maryland's history. In 1969, Agnew took office as Vice-President of the United States under President Richard M. Nixon. Nixon and Agnew won re-election in 1972. But Agnew resigned as Vice-President in 1973. He left the office when a federal grand jury investigated charges that he had participated in widespread graft as an officeholder in Maryland and as Vice-President (see AGNEW, SPIRO T.).

Maryland Today. Maryland's industrial growth and its location on Chesapeake Bay have tied the state economically to the northeastern industrial states. Many new cities, suburbs, and industrial communities have grown up between Baltimore and Washington. The state faced the challenge of providing these expanding areas with schools, water and power supplies, and other services. In 1972, Maryland voters approved a state lottery to raise money for the state government. Maryland is also seeking solutions to the problems of air and water pollution.

The population increase during and after World War II brought changes in housing and education that are still going on in Maryland. Thousands of the people who moved to Maryland from the South were blacks. As more and more blacks settled in Baltimore, increas-

ing numbers of white families moved to the city's suburbs. At this time, black children in Maryland attended segregated schools, as required by state law. But in 1954,

——— THE STATE GOVERNORS OF MARYLAND ———

	Party	Term
Thomas Johnson	None	1777-1779
Thomas Sim Lee	None	1779-1782
William Paca	None	1782-1785
William Smallwood	Unknown	1785-1788
John Eager Howard	Federalist	1788-1791
George Plater	Federalist	1791-1792
James Brice	Unknown	1792
Thomas Sim Lee	Federalist	1792-1794
John H. Stone	Federalist	1794-1797
John Henry	Federalist	1797-1798
Benjamin Ogle	Federalist	1798-1801
John Francis Mercer	Dem.-Rep.*	1801-1803
Robert Bowie	Dem.-Rep.	1803-1806
Robert Wright	Dem.-Rep.	1806-1809
James Butcher	Unknown	1809
Edward Lloyd	Dem.-Rep.	1809-1811
Robert Bowie	Dem.-Rep.	1811-1812
Levin Winder	Federalist	1812-1816
Charles Ridgely	Federalist	1816-1819
Charles Goldsborough	Federalist	1819
Samuel Sprigg	Dem.-Rep.	1819-1822
Samuel Stevens, Jr.	Dem.-Rep.	1822-1826
Joseph Kent	Democratic	1826-1829
Daniel Martin	Democratic	1829-1830
Thomas King Carroll	Democratic	1830-1831
Daniel Martin	Democratic	1831
George Howard	Democratic	1831-1833
James Thomas	Whig	1833-1836
Thomas W. Veazey	Whig	1836-1839
William Grason	Democratic	1839-1842
Francis Thomas	Democratic	1842-1845
Thomas G. Pratt	Democratic	1845-1848
Philip Francis Thomas	Democratic	1848-1851
Enoch Louis Lowe	Democratic	1851-1854
Thomas Watkins Ligon	Democratic	1854-1858
Thomas Holliday Hicks	Know-Nothing	1858-1862
Augustus W. Bradford	Union	1862-1866
Thomas Swann	Democratic	1866-1869
Oden Bowie	Democratic	1869-1872
William Pinkney Whyte	Democratic	1872-1874
James Black Groome	Democratic	1874-1876
John Lee Carroll	Democratic	1876-1880
William T. Hamilton	Democratic	1880-1884
Robert M. McLane	Democratic	1884-1885
Henry Lloyd	Democratic	1885-1888
Elihu E. Jackson	Democratic	1888-1892
Frank Brown	Democratic	1892-1896
Lloyd Lowndes	Republican	1896-1900
John Walter Smith	Democratic	1900-1904
Edwin Warfield	Democratic	1904-1908
Austin L. Crothers	Democratic	1908-1912
Phillips Lee Goldsborough	Republican	1912-1916
Emerson C. Harrington	Democratic	1916-1920
Albert C. Ritchie	Democratic	1920-1935
Harry W. Nice	Republican	1935-1939
Herbert R. O'Conor	Democratic	1939-1947
Wm. Preston Lane, Jr.	Democratic	1947-1951
Theodore R. McKeldin	Republican	1951-1959
J. Millard Tawes	Democratic	1959-1967
Spiro T. Agnew	Republican	1967-1969
Marvin Mandel†	Democratic	1969-1979
Harry R. Hughes	Democratic	1979-

*Democratic-Republican
†Lieutenant Governor Blair Lee III served as acting governor from June 4, 1977, to Jan. 15, 1979.

the Supreme Court of the United States ruled that compulsory segregation of public schools was unconstitutional. Baltimore desegregated its public schools almost immediately. School desegregation in the rest of the state has proceeded slowly but steadily.

Baltimore, like many cities, had racial violence after the assassination of civil rights leader Martin Luther King, Jr., in 1968. Since then, federal, state, and local agencies have increased their efforts to end racial dis-

crimination in education, employment, and housing.

In August 1977, a federal jury found Governor Marvin Mandel guilty of mail fraud and corruption. A panel of the 4th U.S. Circuit Court of Appeals overturned the conviction in January 1979. However, in July 1979, the full court upheld the conviction.

Today, Maryland is a national center for space research, development, and production. Basic planning for space projects is carried out at the National Aeronautics and Space Administration's Goddard Space Study Center in Greenbelt.

GEORGE BEISHLAG, AUBREY C. LAND, and FRED THEROUX

MARYLAND /Study Aids

Related Articles in WORLD BOOK include:

BIOGRAPHIES

Agnew, Spiro T.
Baltimore, Lord
Banneker, Benjamin
Carroll (family)
Chase, Samuel
Davis, David
Decatur, Stephen
Few, William
Hanson, John
Hopkins, Johns
Jenifer, Daniel of
 St. Thomas

Johnson, Thomas
Key, Francis Scott
McHenry, James
Mencken, H. L.
Paca, William
Ruth, Babe
Shehan, Lawrence J. Cardinal
Shriver, Sargent
Stoddert, Benjamin
Stone, Thomas
Taney, Roger B.

CITIES

Annapolis
Baltimore
Bethesda
Cambridge

Cumberland
Hagerstown
Salisbury

HISTORY

Civil War
Claiborne's Rebellion
Colonial Life in America
Mason and Dixon's Line

Revolutionary War in
 America
Star-Spangled Banner
War of 1812

PHYSICAL FEATURES

Allegheny Mountains
Appalachian Mountains
Chesapeake Bay

Delmarva Peninsula
Potomac River
Susquehanna River

PRODUCTS

For Maryland's rank among the states in production, see the following articles:

Chicken   Oyster   Tobacco

OTHER RELATED ARTICLES

Aberdeen Proving Ground
Andrews Air Force Base
Camp David
Fort George G. Meade
Fort McHenry National Monument and Historic Shrine

Maryland Day
National Naval Medical
 Center
Southern States

Outline

I. Government
    A. Constitution
    B. Executive
    C. Legislature
    D. Courts
II. People
III. Education
    A. Schools
IV. A Visitor's Guide
    A. Places to Visit

E. Local Government
F. Taxation
G. Politics

B. Libraries   C. Museums

B. Annual Events

V. The Land
    A. Land Regions   C. Rivers and Lakes
    B. Coastline
VI. Climate
VII. Economy
    A. Natural Resources   E. Fishing Industry
    B. Manufacturing   F. Electric Power
    C. Agriculture   G. Transportation
    D. Mining   H. Communication
VIII. History

Questions

For whom was Maryland named?

Why did Maryland delay signing the Articles of Confederation?

What important developments in transportation occurred in Maryland during the 1800's?

What two agricultural products earn the greatest income for Maryland farmers?

Why did the fate of Washington, D.C., depend on whether Maryland remained in the Union during the Civil War?

What are Maryland's two leading manufacturing industries? What is the leading manufacturing city?

What famous Marylander wrote "The Star-Spangled Banner"? Under what circumstances?

When and why did Maryland give land to the U.S. government?

By what name has the Maryland-Pennsylvania boundary become known? Why?

Why is Maryland called the *Old Line State?* The *Free State?*

Books for Young Readers

CARPENTER, ALLAN. *Maryland.* Childrens Press, 1966.
COOLIDGE, OLIVIA E. *Come By Here.* Houghton, 1970. Fiction.
GURNEY, GENE and CLARE. *The Colony of Maryland.* Watts, 1972.
HALL, MARJORY. *The Carved Wooden Ring.* Westminster, 1972. Fiction.
KAESSMANN, BETA, and others. *My Maryland: Her Story for Boys and Girls.* Rev. ed. Maryland Historical Society, 1971.
MASON, VAN WYCK. *The Maryland Colony.* Macmillan, 1969.

Books for Older Readers

CAREY, GEORGE G. *Maryland Folklore and Folklife.* Cornell Maritime Press, 1970.
EVITTS, WILLIAM J. *A Matter of Allegiances: Maryland from 1850 to 1861.* Johns Hopkins Univ. Press, 1974.
FINLAYSON, ANN. *Colonial Maryland.* Nelson, 1974.
PAPENFUSE, EDWARD C., and others, eds. *Maryland: A New Guide to the Old Line State.* Johns Hopkins Univ. Press, 1976. A rev. ed. in the Amer. Guide Series.
RADOFF, MORRIS L., ed. *The Old Line State: A History of Maryland.* Maryland Hall of Records Commission, 1971.
WALSH, RICHARD, and FOX, W. L., eds. *Maryland: A History, 1632-1974.* Maryland Historical Society, 1974.

MARYLAND, UNIVERSITY OF, is a coeducational state-supported system of higher education. It consists of five campuses, each with its own chancellor. A president heads the entire university. The main campus is in College Park, Md. The system was established in 1971. Courses lead to bachelor's, master's, and doctor's degrees.

University of Maryland, College Park has divisions of agriculture and life sciences, arts and humanities, behavioral and social sciences, human and community resources, and mathematical and physical sciences and engineering. The school was founded in 1856 as the Maryland State College of Agriculture. It became part of the University of Maryland in 1920.

University of Maryland at Baltimore is one of the nation's oldest and largest centers of graduate and professional education. The campus has schools of dentistry, law, medicine, nursing, pharmacy, and so-

University of Maryland

University of Maryland campus in College Park, Md., lies in a wooded area about 8 miles (13 kilometers) northeast of Washington, D.C. Buildings on the campus include the Memorial Chapel, *center,* and dormitories, *upper right.*

cial work and community planning. It was founded in 1807 and is the oldest campus of the university.

University of Maryland, Baltimore County, in Catonsville, includes divisions of education, graduate studies, humanities, mathematics, science, and social sciences. This campus opened in 1966.

University of Maryland, Eastern Shore, in Princess Anne, offers programs in liberal arts and sciences. It was founded as a private school in 1886 and became a division of the university in 1948.

University of Maryland, University College offers programs of adult continuing education at centers throughout the state and in about 20 foreign countries. University College was established in 1947 and has headquarters in College Park.

For enrollments, see UNIVERSITIES AND COLLEGES (table).   Critically reviewed by the UNIVERSITY OF MARYLAND

MARYLAND DAY is a holiday observed on March 25 in the state of Maryland. It commemorates the first

Roman Catholic Mass that colonists celebrated when they landed in 1634. The first action of the colonists after landing on the shores of St. Clements Island in the Potomac River was to celebrate the Feast of the Annunciation.

MASACCIO, *muh SAH chee OH* (1401-1428), an Italian painter, was one of the first great masters of the Italian Renaissance. He brought a new sense of naturalness to painting through the realistic treatment of sunlight, distant haze, and other elements of the earth's atmosphere. Masaccio portrayed figures in lifelike poses and also used perspective to give realism to his paintings. Masaccio's work was admired by many famous

The Holy Trinity with the Virgin and Saint John (1425), a fresco in the church of Santa Maria Novella, Florence, Italy; SCALA

A Painting by Masaccio shows his ability to create solid-looking forms through the use of perspective and light and shade.

203

MASADA

Italian artists, including Michelangelo and Raphael.

Masaccio was born in San Giovanni di Valdarno, Italy, near Florence. His real name was Tommaso Cassai, but he was nicknamed Masaccio—which means *simple Tom*—because of his absent-mindedness. He studied art in Florence and gained recognition as a master painter by the time he was 21. Masaccio's most important work is a series of frescoes in the church of Santa Maria del Carmine in Florence. One of these paintings, *The Tribute Money*, shows his advanced use of form and perspective. It is reproduced in color in the PAINTING article.   ROBERT F. REIFF

See also PAINTING (The Renaissance); RENAISSANCE (The 1400's).

MASADA was a historic Jewish fortress that stood on a huge rock in Judea (now southern Israel). The rock is also called *Masada*, the Hebrew word for *mountain fortress*. In A.D. 73, 960 Jewish patriots killed themselves at Masada rather than surrender to Roman troops. For many Israelis, this devotion to liberty is a national symbol called the "spirit of Masada."

The rock is about 20 miles (32 kilometers) southeast of Hebron. For location, see DEAD SEA (map). Masada has cliffs that rise 1,400 feet (427 meters). The top of the rock is flat and measures about 1,900 feet (579 meters) long and 650 feet (198 meters) wide.

The Jewish leader Jonathan established the fortress sometime during the Hasmonean Revolt (167-142 B.C.). During that period, the Jews successfully fought for their independence from the Syrians. In 63 B.C., the Romans gained control of Judea. Herod the Great, who was appointed king of Judea by the Romans in 40 B.C., reinforced the fortress and also built two palaces on the rock.

Jewish patriots called *Sicarii* captured Masada in A.D. 66, when the Roman governor Gessius Florus ruled Judea. In A.D. 73, just before the Romans recaptured the fortress, Eleazer Ben Jair, the leader of the Sicarii, persuaded the Jews to burn the camp and commit suicide. Only two women and five children survived. Byzantine monks settled briefly on Masada during the 400's and 500's.

From 1963 to 1965, an archaeological expedition headed by Yigael Yadin of Israel discovered various ruins of ancient Masada, including Herod's palaces. The expedition also found armor, Biblical and other scrolls, coins, ritual baths, and a synagogue.

Today, many tourists and Israeli citizens visit Masada. Israeli Army recruits go there to swear an oath that "Masada will not fall again."   ELLIS RIVKIN

MASAI. See KENYA (The People).

MASARYK, *MASS uh rick*, was the family name of two Czechoslovak statesmen, father and son.

Czechoslovak Embassy

Tomáš Masaryk

Tomáš Garrigue Masaryk (1850-1937) was a scholar and a statesman who, with his student Eduard Beneš, founded Czechoslovakia in 1918 (see BENEŠ, EDUARD). Masaryk became the first president of Czechoslovakia in 1918, and served until 1935.

He began his career in 1891 in the Austro-Hungarian parliament, where he fought for the rights of Slavic minority groups. When World War I broke out, he fled to Switzerland and then to England. In his absence, the Austro-Hungarian government in 1916 sentenced him to death for high treason.

Masaryk came to the United States in 1917 to seek support for his dream of an independent Czechoslovakia. He met with President Woodrow Wilson, and with Czechs, Slovaks, and Ruthenes who lived in America. He gained his objective when the Allied armies defeated Austria-Hungary in 1918. The Republic of Czechoslovakia was created from a part of Austria-Hungary.

Masaryk's 17-year term as president of the Czechoslovak republic was generally a time of peace and prosperity. But the Slovaks gradually became restless, because they thought he had not fulfilled a promise to grant them the right of self-government. Also, the German minority group turned increasingly to Nazi Germany for sympathy and help. Masaryk resigned in 1935 because of poor health. Beneš succeeded him.

Masaryk was born on an estate in Moravia, where his father served as a coachman to the Austrian emperor, Francis Joseph. He was educated at the universities of Vienna and Leipzig. He taught philosophy and sociology at Charles University in Prague.

Jan Garrigue Masaryk (1886-1948), the son of Tomáš, entered the Czechoslovak foreign service in 1919, and served as minister to London from 1925 to 1938. In 1940 he became foreign minister of the Czechoslovak government-in-exile. When the government returned to Czechoslovakia after World War II, Masaryk kept the post of foreign minister. He fought a losing battle from 1945 to 1948 against the increasing Communist domination of his country.

Zane Cohn

Masada, a huge rock in Israel, was the site of a historic Jewish fortress. Ruins of the fortress include this storeroom.

Masaryk died mysteriously in 1948. His body was found in a courtyard, three stories under his apartment window in Prague. It has never been determined whether he was murdered or killed himself in protest against the Communist seizure of the government in February, 1948. He was born in Prague.   R. V. BURKS

See also CZECHOSLOVAKIA (History).

MASBATE. See PHILIPPINES (The Islands).

MASCAGNI, *mah SCAH nyee,* **PIETRO** (1863-1945), was an Italian opera composer. He studied music in Leghorn, his birthplace, and at the Milan Conservatory. In 1888, Mascagni entered a one-act opera in a competition and won first prize. The opera, *Cavalleria Rusticana,* was a drama of raw passion in a Sicilian village. It was presented in Rome in 1890 and made Mascagni world famous as the leader of a realistic, boisterous operatic style called *verismo.* Another verismo success was Ruggiero Leoncavallo's two-act *Pagliacci* (1892). The two operas are usually performed together.

Mascagni never came close to repeating his first success. His only other opera that is still performed is *L'Amico Fritz* (1891). *Cavalleria Rusticana* remains popular because of its emotional melodies and the theatrical force of its *libretto* (words).   HERBERT WEINSTOCK

MASCONS. See MOON (Gravity).

MASCULINE GENDER. See GENDER.

MASEFIELD, JOHN (1878-1967), an English writer, in 1930 became the 16th poet laureate of England (see POET LAUREATE). His vigorous and sympathetic pictures of the poor and unfortunate made him "the poet of the people." Masefield's best-known long poems are "The Everlasting Mercy," "Dauber," "Reynard the Fox," and "The Widow in the Bye Street." They tell tales of love and tragedy among the people of Shropshire, and among the men of the sea.

Masefield wrote over a hundred works. He wrote an autobiography, *So Long to Learn* (1952) at 74. His best-known novels are *Captain Margaret* (1908), *Multitude and Solitude* (1909), *Sard Harker* (1924), and *Odtaa* (1926). His plays include *The Tragedy of Pompey the Great* (1909) and *End and Beginning* (1933). He also wrote the books of poetry *Salt-Water Ballads* (1902), *Ballads* (1903), *A Mainsail Haul* (1905), and *The Bluebells and Other Verse* (1961). His individual poems include "A Consecration," "On Growing Old," and "Sea Fever."

Masefield was born in or near Ledbury, in what is now the county of Hereford and Worcester, England. In 1961, Masefield received the Companions of Literature award for his distinctive contribution to English letters.   JOHN HOLMES

British Combine

John Masefield

MASER is an electronic device that generates and amplifies radio and light waves. Masers are used as atomic clocks (see ATOMIC CLOCK). They are also used to amplify weak radio signals, such as those from distant stars. *Lasers* (optical masers) produce an extremely narrow beam of light (see LASER). Scientists hope that laser beams may be used to transmit radio and television signals. The word *maser* stands for *Microwave Amplification by Stimulated Emission of Radiation.*

The essential part of a maser is a substance that has been put into an *excited* (high energy) state. In this state, the atoms of the substance are able to radiate energy of a particular frequency when *stimulated* (triggered) by a radio or light wave of the same frequency. The energy released by the atoms is added to the stimulating wave, amplifying it.

In the *ammonia maser,* heat is used to excite ammonia gas. In the *ruby maser,* radio waves are used to excite the chromium in a synthetic ruby placed in a magnetic field. Ruby masers are operated at temperatures of only a few degrees above absolute zero.

The first ammonia maser was built in the United States in 1953. Several years later, American and Russian scientists developed the ruby maser. The first continuously operating laser was produced in the United States in 1961.   JOHN ROBINSON PIERCE

MASERU, *MAZ uh roo* (pop. 17,000; met. area pop. 29,000), is the capital of Lesotho, a country in southern Africa. Maseru lies near the northwestern border of the country. A railroad links it with cities in South Africa. The city is the seat of government for the country, and has a hospital and technical training school where manual and local arts are taught. Most of the people are Africans, but a few Europeans live and work there. See also LESOTHO.   HIBBERD V. B. KLINE, JR.

MASH. See WHISKEY; BREWING.

MASK is a covering that disguises or protects the face. Most masks worn as a disguise have the features of a human being or an animal. In the United States, such masks are generally worn for fun at masquerades and on Halloween and other special occasions. Various kinds of protective masks serve different purposes. For example, a welder wears a steel mask with a special lens that protects his eyes from the intense light produced by welding.

Throughout history, people in almost every society have used masks as a disguise. By hiding the features of the face, masks prevent other people from making judgments about the wearer's personality and character. Most of these masks not only hide the identity of the wearer but supposedly also give him magic powers. Such masks represent gods or spirits. The custom of wearing masks probably began with animal heads worn by people. Such masks may have been used in hunting. They probably served as disguises and as magic symbols to make the hunt successful. However, masks may have developed from the practice of marking the face with colorful designs that had magic powers.

Some masks are made of paper or are carved from wood or stone. Others are made of cloth, grass, hide, leather, metal, or shell. Some masks have realistic human or animal features, but others give the wearer a grotesque appearance. Many masks represent the art forms of a society. The masks may involve highly developed craft skills and may be painted with symbolic designs and colors.

This article discusses masks worn for other purposes than to protect the face. Such masks may be divided into four groups according to their major use: (1) cere-

Marvin Newman, Woodfin Camp, Inc.

Colorful Masks are worn in many countries during *carnival*, a period of merrymaking just before Lent. Carnival celebrations include such festivities as masked balls, parades, and dancing in the streets. The drummers shown above are marching in a carnival procession in Basel, Switzerland.

Field Museum of Natural History (WORLD BOOK photo)

Some Masks Have Skirts that cover much of the wearer's body. The mask on the left was made by the Cubeo Indians of Colombia. The one on the right was made by the Senesi people of Papua New Guinea.

Field Museum of Natural History (WORLD BOOK photo)

Many Masks Have Grotesque Features. A demon mask from Sri Lanka, *left,* has fangs and bulging eyes. A Chinese theatrical mask, *right,* represents an official of hell in a religious play.

monial masks, (2) theatrical masks, (3) burial masks and death masks, and (4) festival masks. These categories overlap, however. Many burial masks, for example, serve ceremonial purposes.

Ceremonial Masks developed from the belief of many primitive societies that gods controlled the forces of nature. Dancers at various ceremonies wore masks that represented these gods. A mask made its wearer un-

recognizable, and so he seemed to almost lose his identity and become the spirit itself. When these ceremonial dancers wore such masks, the people believed that the gods were actually present. If people wore a mask that represented a certain spirit, the powers of that spirit supposedly remained for many generations. After the wearer of the mask died, another man took his place in wearing it.

Many Indian tribes of North America used masks in their ceremonies. Male members of the False Face Society of the Iroquois Indians wore wooden masks at ceremonies held to heal the sick. The False Face performers visited villages and were often escorted by male clowns called Shuck Faces, who wore masks made of braided corn husks. Adults welcomed the masked visitors, but most of the children became terrified.

The Indians of the northwest Pacific Coast used masks with a movable mouth and eyelids. They wore these masks in ceremonies honoring certain animals. Many of these masks actually consisted of two or three masks. The outer mask of a double mask—or the two outer masks of a triple mask—represented a bird or some other animal. The outer mask could be folded back, revealing a mask of a human face. Such masks are related to the belief that some human beings had the power to change into animals and back again. This belief was common among many societies.

Some peoples in New Guinea, West Africa, the Amazon region of South America, and the southwestern United States still use masks in spiritual ceremonies. For example, the Hopi Indians of Arizona have special ceremonies in which male dancers wear masks that represent their ancestors or certain gods. The people believe

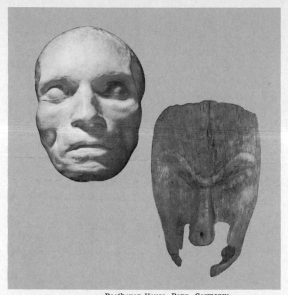

Beethoven House, Bonn, Germany;
Museum of the American Indian, New York City

Burial and Death Masks are important in many societies. The death mask of the German composer Ludwig van Beethoven, *left*, is a cast taken after he died. The Aleut, who live in Alaska, cover the faces of their dead with a wooden burial mask, *right*.

the ceremonies bring visits from these beings, who appear in the form of spirits called *Kachinas*. Kachinas produce rain, make corn grow, and sometimes whip young boys and girls who are about to be formally initiated into adulthood. The masks themselves are also called Kachinas.

Some primitive peoples wore grotesque masks when they went to war. They believed that the appearance of these masks, which represented their gods, would frighten the enemy.

Theatrical Masks. The ancient Greeks used masks in their classical drama, which developed from religious ceremonies of earlier times. Masked singers and dancers represented gods and mythological heroes. The masks also expressed anger, joy, love, and other emotions. These masks were needed to let the audience follow the action of the play. The theaters were so large that many people could not see the facial expressions of the actors. Also, simple amplifiers built into the masks helped carry an actor's voice a great distance.

Since ancient times, Chinese drama has used masks to help portray types of characters. The color of the mask plays an important part in the drama. For example, red represents a loyal person, and white represents a cruel one. A type of play called a *masque* developed from such theatrical uses of masks (see MASQUE). A type of Japanese play called *no* uses a large number of masks, each representing a different emotion.

Burial Masks and Death Masks have had an important role in many societies. The ancient Egyptians put a personalized mask over the face of every mummy, or they made the mask part of the mummy case. The mask supposedly identified the dead person so that the wandering soul could always find its body.

Some peoples still use masks in ceremonies relating

to death. In an annual mourning ceremony held on New Ireland, an island near Australia, dancers wear masks that represent certain dead persons. The spirits of the dead supposedly return during the ceremony.

The Aleut, who live on the Aleutian Islands of Alaska, put a mask on a person after he dies. They believe the mask protects the dead from the dangerous glances of spirits. Some Indian tribes of the Andes Mountains of South America also follow this custom.

In Western countries, death masks are sometimes used to preserve the features of the dead. A plaster cast is made of the face, and plaster likenesses are made from this mold. Famous death masks include those of Ludwig van Beethoven and Napoleon Bonaparte.

Festival Masks developed from masks used in religious ceremonies. Some North American Indian tribes still use such masks in harvest festivals. Processions and festivals in China, India, and other countries also include masked people. In the United States, people of all ages wear masks at Mardi Gras and other celebrations.   ALAN DUNDES

For pictures of masks, see AFRICA (The Arts); ARCHAEOLOGY; BOLIVIA; DRAMA (Greek Drama); EGYPT, ANCIENT; INDIAN, AMERICAN; SCULPTURE (African; Pacific Islands).

MASOCHISM. See MENTAL ILLNESS (table: Terms).

MASON (bricklayer). See BUILDING TRADE.

MASON (Freemason). See MASONRY.

MASON, CHARLES. See MASON AND DIXON'S LINE.

MASON, GEORGE (1725-1792), was a Virginia statesman during and after the Revolutionary War. He played an important part in the Constitutional Convention, although he refused to sign the final draft of the Constitution. He disliked the way public affairs were conducted, and refused many public offices that were offered to him. But his writings and his leadership made him an influential figure in the colonies.

Mason also helped extend the western borders of the United States. He was a sponsor of the George Rogers Clark expedition to the Northwest Territories. His paper, *Extracts from the Virginia Charters* (1773), formed a basis for American claims to all land south of the Great Lakes.

The Declaration of Rights. Perhaps Mason's most important work was his part in writing the Declaration of Rights as a member of the Virginia Convention of May, 1776. Thomas Jefferson drew on this document when he wrote the Declaration of Independence. It formed the basis for the Bill of Rights, which was added in the form of amendments to the original federal Constitution. It was popular in France during the French Revolution.

His Constitutional Views. He favored the proposed federal Constitution, but objected to the compromise arrangement made between the New England states and those of the extreme South on the tariff and slavery questions. He refused to sign the federal Constitution as it was finally adopted, because the Constitutional Convention refused to change or include certain clauses he favored. He worked hard during the last weeks of the convention, but was unsuccessful. Later years proved, however, that he was right on several points. During the convention, Mason had insisted that the

Constitution should include a Bill of Rights. It became obvious a few years later that Mason was correct. The first 10 amendments passed constitute the Bill of Rights. Mason also maintained that the judiciary section of the Constitution was weak. The 11th Amendment repaired this weakness.

Mason was one of the first Southerners to favor freeing the slaves. His greatest objection to the Constitution was that it compromised on the slavery question. He believed that slaves should be educated first and then set free, and that the process should be gradual.

Early Life. Mason was born in Fairfax County, Virginia, where his family had extensive landholdings. He later built Gunston Hall there. He studied law under the guidance of his guardian, John Mercer. He managed his plantation and took an active part in community affairs. Mason repeatedly refused public office. Finally, at the insistence of his neighbors, he agreed to become a member of the third Virginia Convention that met in Richmond in 1775. Mason wrote a large part of the Virginia Constitution.   ROBERT J. TAYLOR

MASON, JOHN. See NEW HAMPSHIRE (Settlement).

MASON, JOHN L. See CANNING (History).

MASON, JOHN YOUNG. See OSTEND MANIFESTO.

MASON, LOWELL (1792-1872), an American hymnwriter and music educator, wrote more than 1,650 religious compositions. He published many popular works, including hymn collections and books on music and music education. His best-known compositions include "Nearer My God to Thee" and "From Greenland's Icy Mountains." Mason was the first music teacher in American public schools, and became superintendent of music for Boston public schools in 1838. Mason founded the Boston Academy of Music with George J. Webb in 1833. Mason was born in Medfield, Mass.   ARTHUR L. RICH

MASON AND DIXON'S LINE is usually thought of as the line that divides the North and the South. Actually it is the east-west boundary line that separates Pennsylvania from Maryland and part of West Virginia, and the north-south boundary between Maryland and Delaware. Before the Civil War, the southern boundary of Pennsylvania was considered the dividing line between the slave and nonslave states.

In the 1700's, a boundary quarrel arose between Pennsylvania and Maryland. The two agreed to settle the dispute by having the land surveyed. In 1763, they called in two English astronomers, Charles Mason and Jeremiah Dixon. They completed their survey in 1767. The line was named after them.

The surveyors set up milestones to mark the boundary. Through the years souvenir hunters removed many stones and used them as doorsteps and curbstones. Authorities finally recovered many of them, however, and replaced nearly all of the stolen markers. Occasionally a dispute arose as to the exact location of the line. But surveys made in 1849 and in 1900 showed that there was no important error in the line Mason and Dixon decided upon. Another survey in the 1960's resulted in a slight shift of the line, which is now at 39° 43' 19.521″ north latitude.   RAY ALLEN BILLINGTON

MASON AND SLIDELL, *SLY d'l*, Confederate statesmen, are famous because of a Civil War event that

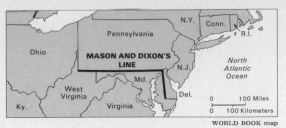

WORLD BOOK map

Location of Mason and Dixon's Line

nearly caused war between the United States and Great Britain (see TRENT AFFAIR).

James Murray Mason (1798-1871) drafted the Fugitive Slave Law that became part of the Compromise of 1850 (see COMPROMISE OF 1850). He served as a Democrat from Virginia in both houses of Congress, and was one of the leaders of the states' rights group. After the Trent Affair, he served as Confederate Commissioner to England, but failed to win England's recognition of the Confederacy. He lived in Canada until 1868. He was born in Fairfax County, Virginia.

John Slidell (1793-1871), a Louisiana Democrat, served in both houses of Congress. President James K. Polk sent him on a secret mission to Mexico in 1845. Mexico's refusal to confer with him was one cause of the Mexican War (see MEXICAN WAR). After the Trent Affair, he served as Confederate Commissioner to France. He was born in New York City.   FRANK E. VANDIVER

MASON CITY, Iowa (pop. 31,839), is an industrial and transportation center in a fertile agricultural region in north-central Iowa. Besides its farm crops and dairy and meat industries, the city is known especially for its portland cement, brick, and clay tile products. Six railroads serve Mason City. The town was settled as Shibboleth in 1854, and became Mason City in 1855. It is the seat of Cerro Gordo County. Mason City has a mayor-council government. For location, see IOWA (political map).   WILLIAM J. PETERSEN

MASONRY, or FREEMASONRY, is the name of one of the largest and oldest fraternal organizations in the world. Its full title is Free and Accepted Masons. It aims to promote brotherhood and to foster morality among its members. The Masons spend millions of dollars annually for hospitals; homes for widows, orphans, and the aged; relief for people in distress; and scholarships for students.

Masons try to promote "morality in which all men agree, that is, to be good men and true." Throughout its history, Masonry has brought together men of varied beliefs and opinions. It does not sponsor any particular denomination of faith. Men of any religion that professes belief in one God may join. But some faiths forbid their members to become Masons.

Masons call God the "Great Architect of the Universe." They base most of their symbols and rituals on the tools and practices of the building professions. At times, some Masons dress in elaborate, colorful costumes, and take part in dramatic rituals, many of which are secret to all except members.

The Lodges and Degrees of Masonry. Men who wish to become Masons must apply for membership. Most of these individuals apply through a friend who is already a member. After a man has been accepted by the

33rd Degree Mason

Master Mason

MASONIC EMBLEMS

32nd Degree Mason

Knights Templars

Painting by Stanley Massey Arthurs (Acacia Mutual Life Insurance Co., Washington, D.C.)

George Washington, wearing his regalia as a member of the Masons, laid the cornerstone of the United States Capitol in Washington, D.C., in 1793. The historic ceremony was under the auspices of the Grand Lodge of Maryland.

Masons, he joins a *Blue Lodge,* the basic organization of Masonry. Members of Blue Lodges may hold three degrees. When they join, they automatically receive the *Entered Apprentice* degree. Later, they may earn the second degree, called *Fellowcraft,* and the third degree, called *Master Mason.* Each degree in Masonry teaches moral lessons. To earn the degree, a Mason must learn the lessons and participate in a ceremony that illustrates them. After a Mason acquires the third degree in a Blue Lodge, he may receive further degrees in either or both of the two branches of advanced Masonry, the *Scottish Rite* and the *York Rite.*

If a Mason enters the Scottish Rite, he may advance through 29 degrees, designated both by names and numbers. The first degree in the Scottish Rite is the fourth degree in Masonry. The highest is the 33rd, an honorary degree that members receive in recognition of outstanding service to Masonry, the community, or the nation. Names of the 33 degrees vary from one area to another. Some of the names commonly used include *Knight of the Sun* for the 28th degree, *Grand Inspector Inquisitor Commander* for the 31st degree, and *Sovereign Grand Inspector General* for the 33rd degree.

If a Mason chooses to advance in the York Rite, the first four degrees he receives are called *Degrees of the Chapter.* They include *Mark Master, Past Master, Most Excellent Master,* and *Royal Arch.* The next three degrees make up the *Degrees of the Council.* They are *Royal Master, Select Master,* and *Super-Excellent Master.* In some states, members of the York Rite do not have to receive the Degrees of the Council in order to go on to higher degrees in the rite. The three highest degrees make up the *Orders of the Commandery* called *Knight of the Red*

Cross, Knight of Malta, and *Knight Templar,* which is the highest degree in the York Rite.

The names *Scottish Rite* and *York Rite* are symbols of early times in Masonry. The earliest traditions are associated with Scotland and the city of York, England.

Organization. In most countries, all the Blue Lodges come under the jurisdiction of one *National Grand Lodge,* at the head of which is a *Grand Master.* But in the United States and Canada, each state and province has a Grand Lodge and a Grand Master at the head of all the local Blue Lodges in the area. The Masons in the United States and Canada do not have a National Grand Lodge, but they do hold an annual conference for Grand Masters in North America each February in Washington, D.C. The conference has no administrative authority, but it gives the delegates an opportunity to discuss plans, problems, and other matters of interest to their state or province and local lodges.

The chapters, councils, and commanderies in the York Rite each come under the jurisdiction of a state *Grand Body.* Most state grand bodies adhere to the leadership of the general grand bodies, which have nationwide jurisdiction.

The Scottish Rite in the United States has two groups, called *jurisdictions.* Separate supreme councils govern each group. The Southern Jurisdiction includes the 35 states south of the Ohio or west of the Mississippi rivers (including Alaska and Hawaii) and all the territories of the United States. The Northern Jurisdiction covers the remaining 15 states. All other countries have only one Supreme Council to head the Scottish Rite.

More than a hundred fraternal organizations have a relationship with Masonry, but they do not form part of its basic structure. One of the best known is the *Order of the Eastern Star*, an organization for women relatives of Masons who have achieved at least the degree of Master Mason. The Masons and the Order of the Eastern Star also sponsor organizations for boys and girls. Boys may join the *Order of De Molay*. Girls may become members of *Job's Daughters* in some states and *Rainbow for Girls* in other states.

The Ancient Arabic Order of Nobles of the Mystic Shrine admits members who are at least 32nd-degree Masons in the Scottish Rite or Knights Templar in the York Rite. In some states, wives of Shrine members may belong to the *Daughters of the Nile*.

History. Many of the ideas and rituals of Masonry stem from the period of cathedral building from the 900's to the 1600's. At that time, *masons* (stoneworkers) formed associations called *guilds* in various European cities and towns. Freemasons were stoneworkers who traveled from community to community. They had organizations, sometimes referred to as *lodges*. With the decline of cathedral building in the 1600's, many of the masons' organizations became purely social societies. The groups began accepting members who had never been stoneworkers, and called these men *speculative masons*.

In 1717, four fraternal lodges, which may have been originally founded as masons' organizations, united under the Grand Lodge of England. The Masons of today consider the formation of the Grand Lodge of England to be the beginning of their organized society. The order spread quickly to other lands, and included such famous persons as Benjamin Franklin, Frederick the Great of Prussia, Wolfgang Amadeus Mozart, George Washington, and Voltaire.

British colonists brought the organization to North America. Some historians believe that it may have been a group of Masons who staged the Boston Tea Party in 1773 (see BOSTON TEA PARTY). After 1832, the Masons abandoned their political activities, and the organization assumed the social and fraternal character that it has today.

The Masons now emphasize the fact that they do not foster any religious, political, or economic creeds. As a result, they became one of the world's largest fraternal organizations during the 1900's. By the early 1970's, membership had grown to nearly 4 million in the United States. There were about $1\frac{1}{2}$ million Masons in the rest of the world. About 1 of every 16 adult American males is a Mason.   FRED W. McPEAKE

Related Articles in WORLD BOOK include:

De Molay, Order of	Knights Templars
Job's Daughters, Inter-	Rainbow for Girls
national Order of	Shrine

MASQAT. See MUSCAT.

MASQUE, *mask,* is a form of dramatic entertainment named after the masks worn by the performers. It originated in England, where it was first called *mummery.* It developed into a folk play. Italy adopted it later as a court spectacle including songs, dances, and scenery. From Italy it went to France, then back to England during the early 1500's. The performances were usually given at court, with nobles and ladies taking parts. Ben Jonson developed the literary form of the masque in

the 1600's. He also introduced the antimasque, using two sets of performers. Inigo Jones, architect and scene designer, used elaborate designs and staging methods for masques. The masques generally lacked story, action, crisis, or ending. The performers recited long, poetic speeches. John Milton's *Comus* is considered a masque.   CHARLES W. COOPER

See also JONSON, BEN; MILTON, JOHN (His Early Life and Works); DRAMA (picture: Masques).

MASQUERADE, *MAS kuh RAYD,* is the name of a party or dance at which fancy masks and costumes are worn. The word as a verb also means *to disguise* or *falsely pretend.*

MASS is often defined as the amount of matter in an object. However, scientists usually prefer to define mass as a measure of *inertia,* a property of all matter. Inertia is the tendency of a stationary object to remain motionless and of a moving object to continue moving at a constant speed and in the same direction. See INERTIA.

The greater an object's mass, the more difficult it is to speed it up or slow it down. For example, a railroad locomotive has a greater mass than an automobile. For this reason, it takes more force to stop a moving locomotive than it does an automobile.

Force, mass, and acceleration are related by Newton's *second law of motion* (see MOTION [Newton's Laws of Motion]). This law is represented by the equation $F=ma$, where F is force, m is mass, and a is acceleration. See ACCELERATION.

The unit of mass depends on the system of *mechanical units* used. Scientists prefer the Meter-Kilogram-Second (MKS) absolute system in which the unit of mass is the kilogram (1,000 grams). Engineers prefer the Foot-Pound-Second (FPS) gravitational system in which the unit of mass is the slug. A *slug* equals 14.594 kilograms.

Mass and Weight are not the same thing. Weight is the force on an object due to the pull of earth's gravity. A body weighs less, the farther it gets from the surface of the earth. But its mass remains constant, no matter where it is. For example, a crew in a spaceship would be "weightless" beyond the earth's gravitational field (see SPACE TRAVEL [Living in Space]).

Conservation of Mass. Scientists once thought that matter could not be created or destroyed. This was based on the *law of the conservation of mass* (or *matter*), which states that the mass of materials that take part in a chemical reaction is the same as the mass of the products. For example, burning a piece of coal produces carbon-dioxide gas, water vapor, and ash. The mass of these products is the same as the mass of the piece of coal. But nuclear reactions, such as those that take place in an atomic bomb or nuclear reactor, result in a loss of mass accompanied by a release of energy. Scientists now say that the *total* mass and energy in the universe does not change. However, the quantity of each does vary.

Mass and energy are related by Albert Einstein's famous equation $E=mc^2$. In this formula, E represents energy, m represents mass, and c is the velocity of light. See E = MC².   ROBERT LINDSAY

Related Articles in WORLD BOOK include:

Density	Gravitation	Matter
Energy	Lavoisier,	Weight
Force	Antoine L.	

MASS is the celebration of the Eucharist in the Roman Catholic Church. According to Catholic teaching each Mass is a true sacrifice, in which the risen Christ becomes bodily present on the altar as a Victim who is offered anew by the Church to God the Father as expiation for the sins of humanity. The Mass is understood by Catholics to be a renewal, in an unbloody manner, by the mandate of Christ, of the one universally effective sacrifice freely offered by Christ Himself in His Crucifixion, for the redemption of the world. The principal parts of the Mass are the Offertory, the Consecration, and the Communion. See COMMUNION.

The priest who performs the Mass is called the *celebrant*. He speaks or sings the Mass prayers, usually in the *vernacular* (language of the area). The people attending the Mass and the *altar boys* (celebrant's helpers) speak or sing the responses to the prayers. Before the 1960's, Latin was used in most Masses. The altar boys, and sometimes a choir, responded to the prayers.

Masses have different names, but are the same in essentials. Mass in which most of the prayers and responses are spoken is *Low Mass*. At *High Mass*, most of the prayers and responses are sung. A Mass for repose of souls of the dead is a *Requiem Mass*.   FULTON J. SHEEN

The Episcopal Church also celebrates Mass. It is sometimes called the Service of Holy Eucharist. Celebration of the Eucharist in the Eastern Orthodox Church is generally called *Liturgy*. The Lutheran Church has the Order of Service or Order of Worship. It is called Mass in some European countries. See LITURGY.

See also ROMAN CATHOLIC CHURCH (The Eucharist).

MASS MEDIA. See COMMUNICATION.

MASS NUMBER. See ATOM (Atomic Weight).

MASS PRODUCTION is the production of machinery and other articles in standard sizes in large numbers. Mass production makes it possible to manufacture things faster. It also means that a replacement can be obtained for any part of a machine that breaks down.

Mass production began in 1800, when the United States was building up its army. Until that time, gunsmiths started a second gun only after they had completed the first one. Thus, each gun was a little different.

In 1798, the government hired the inventor Eli Whitney to make 10,000 muskets in two years. By 1800, Whitney had delivered only 500. He was called to Washington to explain the delay.

Whitney opened a box in front of a board of experts. He placed 10 musket barrels, 10 stocks, 10 triggers, and so on, in separate piles. Then he assembled the pieces from each pile into a complete musket, showing that anyone could do this if the parts were properly made. Whitney had spent about two years developing *machine tools*, which made perfectly fitting parts. He could produce 10,000 muskets while a gunsmith made one.

In 1918, five engineering societies established what is now the American National Standards Institute, Inc. The institute studies and sets up standards of quality and methods of mass production in most U.S. industries. Its work has greatly increased the speed of production.

In the early 1900's, American automobile manufacturers originated the moving assembly line. After the automobile parts are made, the automobile frame is placed on a moving belt. Workers are stationed all along the belt in an assembly line. As the car moves slowly along the assembly line, each worker does a

special task. The task must be done in a certain length of time, and with exactness, because the work of the entire line is stopped if it is necessary to halt the moving belt. See ASSEMBLY LINE; CONVEYOR BELT.

Mass production led to the *division-of-labor* system, in which each worker is skilled in a single operation. Mass production enables industry to make more goods at less cost than by hand methods.   ROBERT D. PATTON

See also AIRPLANE (Building an Airplane); AUTOMOBILE (How the Auto Industry Grew); INDUSTRIAL REVOLUTION (diagram); MACHINE TOOL; WHITNEY, ELI.

MASS SPECTROSCOPY, *spehk TRAHS' kuh pee* or *SPEHK truh SKOH pee*, is a method of separating ionized atoms or molecules according to their mass (m) and electric charge (z). It involves the use of an instrument called a *mass spectrometer*. Mass spectroscopy provides an effective means of identifying elements, isotopes, and organic molecules. It also can be used to determine the chemical composition and structure of these and other more complex substances.

In a common type of mass spectrometer, electrons bombard a sample of a substance, forming ions. The ions are then introduced into a magnetic field. The field deflects the lighter ions more than the heavier ones, producing a pattern of ions called a *mass spectrum*. This pattern has peaks that correspond to each m/z value—that is, the ratio of the mass to the charge of each ion—in the sample. The mass spectrum is scanned by varying the intensity of the magnetic field, and each m/z value is recorded by an electrical detector.

Mass spectroscopy has many important uses in science and industry. For example, nuclear chemists use it to measure the amount of uranium-235 in the presence of uranium-238. These two uranium isotopes undergo almost identical chemical reactions, and so they are difficult to distinguish by ordinary chemical analysis (see URANIUM [Uranium Isotopes]). Manufacturers of electronic equipment rely on mass spectroscopy to detect small amounts of impurities in silicon, which is used in transistors and other semiconductor devices.

A mass spectrometer can be combined with a computer and with a separating device called a *gas chromatograph* to analyze mixtures that contain hundreds of components. These mixtures include body fluids, industrial chemicals, and pollutants.   FRED W. McLAFFERTY

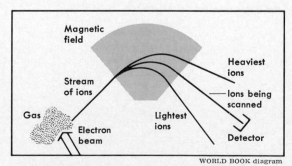

WORLD BOOK diagram

In a Mass Spectrometer, electrons bombard a gas sample to form ions. A magnetic field deflects the lighter ions more than the heavier ones. By varying the field's intensity, each of the deflected ions is exposed to a detector in rapid succession. The detector measures the mass and charge of the ions.

Fred Bond, Publix

Lexington Common, Where the Revolutionary War Began

Massachusetts Institute of Technology

Laboratory at the Massachusetts Institute of Technology

MASSACHUSETTS

THE BAY STATE

Massachusetts (blue) ranks 45th in size among all the states and 4th in size among the New England States (gray).

MASSACHUSETTS is the sixth smallest state, but it stands among the leaders in many fields. Only New Jersey, Hawaii, Connecticut, Delaware, and Rhode Island have smaller areas. Yet Massachusetts is an important manufacturing state. Boston, the capital and largest city of Massachusetts, is a major U.S. seaport and air terminal. The many great universities in and around Boston make the area one of the world's great educational, research, and cultural centers. A wealth of historic landmarks makes Massachusetts one of America's main tourist spots.

The land in Massachusetts is a series of hills and valleys. From sea level near the Atlantic Ocean, the state reaches a height of about 3,500 feet (1,100 meters) near its western border. The best farmland lies in the river valleys and near the coastline. Massachusetts produces more cranberries than any other state. Boston,

Fishing Boats in Gloucester

Sunny Day—Gloucester by Emile A. Gruppe from the WORLD BOOK Collection. Courtesy Findlay Galleries, Inc.

Gloucester, and New Bedford are important fishing ports. Boston and Gloucester are also centers for the canning and processing of fish.

The Norse explorer Leif Ericson may have visited the Massachusetts region about the year 1000. Ericson was one of the first Europeans to sail to North America. In 1620, the Pilgrims settled at what is now Plymouth. The Puritans arrived in 1630. Both these groups left England in search of religious freedom. The first newspaper, printing press, and library in the British colonies were established in Massachusetts. The first college in the colonies, Harvard, was founded at Cambridge in 1636. Boston Latin School, the first secondary school in the colonies, opened in 1635. The first public high school in the United States, Boston English High School, opened in 1821.

Many of the events that led up to the Revolutionary War took place in Massachusetts. These included the Boston Massacre in 1770 and the Boston Tea Party in 1773. On the night of April 18, 1775, Paul Revere made his famous ride to warn his fellow patriots that British troops were coming. On April 19, 1775, minutemen at Lexington and then at Concord fought the first battles of the Revolutionary War. On Feb. 6, 1788, Massachusetts became the sixth state to join the Union.

Three U.S. Presidents came from Massachusetts. John Adams, the second President, and his son, John Quincy Adams, the sixth President, were both born in Braintree (now Quincy). John F. Kennedy, the 35th President, was born in Brookline. Calvin Coolidge, the 30th President, grew up in Massachusetts.

Massachusetts gets its name from the Massachusett Indian tribe, which lived in the region when the Pilgrims arrived. The name probably means *near the great hill*, or *the place of the great hill*. Historians believe it refers to the Great Blue Hill south of Boston. Massachusetts is often called the *Bay State* because the Puritans founded their colony on Massachusetts Bay. Massachusetts is one of four states officially called *commonwealths*. The others are Kentucky, Pennsylvania, and Virginia.

For the relationship of Massachusetts to other states in its region, see NEW ENGLAND.

The contributors of this article are Benjamin W. Labaree, Director of the Munson Institute of American Maritime History and a former Professor of History at Williams College; Michael G. Mensoian, Professor of Geography and Chairman of the Department of Regional Studies at Boston State College; and Walter E. Salvi, Jr., News Editor of the Boston Herald *and the* Sunday Herald Advertiser.

Constitution. Massachusetts adopted its Constitution in 1780, during the Revolutionary War. The Massachusetts Constitution is the oldest state constitution still in use, though it has been *amended* (changed) more than 100 times.

The Constitution provides for two kinds of amendments. *Initiative amendments* are introduced to the legislature on petitions signed by a specified number of qualified voters. *Legislative amendments* are introduced by members of the legislature. Both types of amendments must be approved during joint sessions of the legislature. Initiative amendments must be approved by one-fourth of the legislators. Legislative amendments require approval by a majority of the legislature. All amendments must then be approved in a similar manner by the next legislative body. Finally, an amendment must be approved by a majority of the persons voting on the amendment in a general election. An initiative amendment must also receive approving votes equal to 30 per cent of the total number of ballots cast in the election.

A state law permits amendments to be proposed by a constitutional convention. Before a constitutional convention can meet, it must be approved by a majority of the legislators and by a majority of the voters of Massachusetts.

Executive. The governor and lieutenant governor of Massachusetts are elected to four-year terms. The other elected state officials are the secretary of the commonwealth, the treasurer and receiver general, the attorney general, and the state auditor. These officials also serve four-year terms.

The governor is assisted by an 11-member cabinet, made up of the appointed heads of the state's 11 executive departments. The governor is also aided by an executive group called the governor's council. The council consists of the lieutenant governor and one member elected from each of eight state districts. The governor has the power to appoint the heads of state departments and the members of state agencies. The governor receives a yearly salary of $60,000. Massachusetts has no official residence for its governor. For a list of Massachusetts' governors, see the *History* section of this article.

Legislature, called the *General Court*, consists of a 40-member senate and a 160-member house of representatives. Each of the 40 senatorial districts in Massachusetts elects one senator. Each of the state's representative districts also elects one representative. All members of the General Court serve two-year terms. Both houses meet every year beginning on the first Wednesday in January. They stay in session until all business is completed.

Courts. All judges in Massachusetts are appointed by the governor and may serve until the age of 70. The supreme judicial court is the state's highest court. It has a chief justice and six associate justices. The appeals court handles appeals of civil and criminal cases. It consists of a chief justice and five associate justices. The superior court is the main trial court in the state. This court has a chief justice and 45 associate justices. Other state courts include district, housing, juvenile, land, municipal, and probate courts. The district and municipal courts are the lowest courts in Massachusetts.

Local Government in Massachusetts is centered in 39 chartered cities and in 312 incorporated towns. Most cities have a mayor-council form of government. Some cities use the council-manager system. A *town* in Massachusetts is similar to a *township* in other states. It is a geographic division of a county rather than a single community. Several communities and rural areas may exist in the same town. But the entire town is governed as a unit.

Towns in Massachusetts are governed by annual town meetings. Voters gather once each year to discuss the town's business. They express their opinions, and make plans for the coming year. The voters choose officials called *selectmen* to carry out the town's business until the next annual meeting. Massachusetts cities and towns have *home rule* (self-government) to the extent that they may pass local laws without interference from the state government.

Counties serve mainly as judicial boundaries. The state's 14 counties are divided into districts. Each county has one or more district courts. Each county elects a register of deeds, a register of probate and insolvency, a district attorney, a sheriff, and clerks of court. All counties elect commissioners, and most elect treasurers.

Taxation. During the early 1970's, gross receipts and excise taxes accounted for about 24 per cent of

The Sacred Cod hangs over the rear of the chamber of the Massachusetts House of Representatives in Boston. The fish, carved from a solid block of pine, is about 5 feet (1.5 meters) long. It symbolizes the importance of the fishing industry in the state's early growth and development.

The State Flag

Symbols of Massachusetts. The state seal bears the coat of arms of the Commonwealth of Massachusetts. The Indian points an arrow downward, symbolizing peace. The star over his right shoulder represents Massachusetts as a state. The arm and sword above the shield stand for the state motto. The seal was adopted in 1898. The flag, adopted in 1908, bears the coat of arms.

Flag, bird, flower, and tree illustrations, courtesy of Eli Lilly and Company

the state government's income. A state income tax provided another 24 per cent. Other sources of income include license fees, estate and gift taxes, and taxes on corporate income, property, and document and stock transfers. U.S. government grants and programs provide about 27 per cent of Massachusetts' income. In 1975, the legislature passed a limited 5 per cent sales tax.

Politics. Massachusetts has elected about an equal number of Democrats and Republicans to the United States Senate. In 1967, Massachusetts Republican Edward Brooke became the first black U.S. senator since the post-Civil War period. More Republicans than Democrats have served as governor. In presidential elections since 1900, more Democrats than Republicans have won the state's electoral votes. For Massachusetts' electoral votes and voting record in presidential elections, see ELECTORAL COLLEGE (table).

The State Bird
Chickadee

The State House in Boston, with its golden dome and impressive columns, overlooks Boston Common. The building was constructed in 1798. Boston has been the capital of Massachusetts since 1630.

Arthur Griffin

The State Flower
Mayflower

The State Tree
American Elm

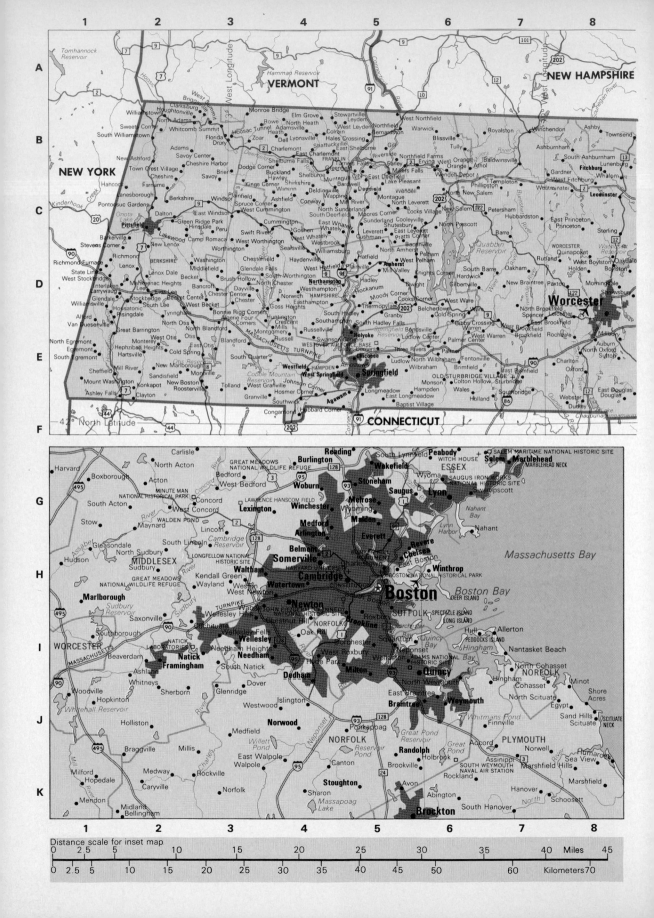

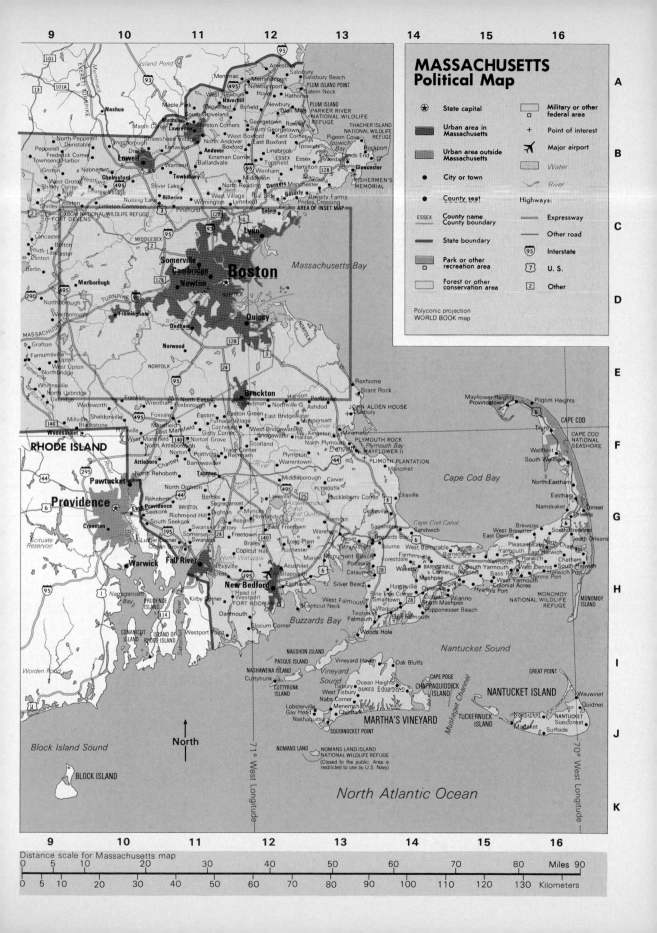

Population

5,828,000	Estimate..1975
5,689,170	..Census..1970
5,148,578	" ..1960
4,690,514	" ..1950
4,316,721	" ..1940
4,249,614	" ..1930
3,852,356	" ..1920
3,366,416	" ..1910
2,805,346	" ..1900
2,238,947	" ..1890
1,783,085	" ..1880
1,457,351	" ..1870
1,231,066	" ..1860
994,514	" ..1850
737,699	" ..1840
610,408	" ..1830
523,287	" ..1820
472,040	" ..1810
422,845	" ..1800
378,787	" ..1790

Metropolitan Areas

Boston 2,899,101
Brockton 150,416
Fall River 169,549
  (142,084 in Mass.;
  27,465 in R.I.)
Fitchburg-
  Leominster 97,164
Lawrence-
  Haverhill 258,564
  (221,208 in Mass.;
  37,356 in N.H.)
Lowell 218,268
  (212,860 in Mass.;
  5,408 in N.H.)
New Bedford ...161,288
Pittsfield 96,817
Providence-Warwick-
  Pawtucket
  (R.I.) 908,887
  (816,917 in R.I.;
  91,970 in Mass.)
Springfield-Chicopee-
  Holyoke 541,752
  (534,859 in Mass.;
  6,893 in Conn.)
Worcester 372,144

Counties

Barnstable .96,656..H14
Berkshire .149,402..D 2
Bristol ...444,301..G11
Dukes ......6,117..I 3
Essex ...637,887..B12
Franklin ..59,210..B 4
Hampden .459,050..E 4
Hampshire 123,981..D 4
Middle-
  sex ...1,398,397..C10
Nantucket ..3,774..J16
Norfolk ..604,854..E10
Plymouth .333,314..G13
Suffolk ..735,190..D11
Worcester .637,037..C 7

Cities and Towns

Abington ...12,334▲.K 6
Accord ....J 7
Acton ....14,770▲.G 2
Acushnet ...7,767▲.H12
Adams 11,256
  (11,772▲)..B 2
Agawam ...21,717▲.E 5
Alford ....302▲.D 1
Algerie
  Four Corners ...E 3
Amesbury ...10,088
  (11,388▲)..A12
Amherst ...17,926
  (26,331▲)..D 5
Andover ...23,695▲.B11
Arlington ..53,534▲.G 4
Ashburnham 1,013
  (3,484▲)..B 8
Ashby .....2,274▲.B 8
Ashdod E13
Ashfield ...1,274▲.C 4
Ashland ...8,882▲.I 2
Ashley Falls ....E 1
Assinippi .....K 7
Assonet G11
Athol 9,723
  (11,185▲)..B 6
Attleboro .32,907..F10
Auburn ...15,347▲.E 8
Avon ......5,295▲.K 5
Ayer 3,292
  (8,283▲)..C 9
Baldwins-
  ville ......1,739..B 7
Ballardvale B11
Bancroft ......D 3
Baptist Village ..F 5
Bardwell ......C 4
Barkerville ......C 2
Barnstable .1,202
  (19,842▲)..○H15
Barre 1,098
  (3,825▲)..C 7

Barrowsville ...F11
Bass River H16
Becket ....929▲.D 3
Becket Center ...D 3
Bedford ...13,513▲.G 3
Belchertown .2,636
  (5,936▲)..D 6
Bellingham .4,228
  (13,967▲)..K 1
Belmont ...28,285▲.H 4
Berkley ....2,027▲.G11
Berkshire ......C 2
Berlin .....2,099▲.D 9
Bernardston 1,659▲.B 5
Beverly ...38,348..C12
Beverly Farms ...C13
Billerica .31,648▲.C11
Blackstone .6,566▲.F 9
Blandford ...863▲.E 3
Bolton .....1,905▲.C 9
Bondsville .1,657..E 6
Bonnie Rigg
  Corners ....D 3
Boston ...641,071.○D11
Bourne 1,992
  (12,636▲)..G14
Boxborough 1,451▲.G 1
Boxford ...2,026
  (4,032▲)..B12
Boylston ...2,774▲.D 8
Braggville ......J 1
Braintree .35,050▲.J 6
Brant Rock E13
Brewster ...1,790▲.G16
Bridgewater .4,032
  (11,829▲)..F12
Brier ....B 3
Briggsville ......B 3
Brimfield ..1,907▲.E 6
Brockton ..89,040..E12
Brookfield .1,197
  (2,063▲)..E 7
Brookline .58,689▲.I 5
Brookville ......K 6
Brush Hollow ....D 3
Buckland ...1,892▲.B 4
Burlington .21,980▲.F 4
Buzzards
  Bay .....2,422..G13
Byfield A12
Cadys Corners ...E 5
Cambridge 100,361.○D11
Camp Romaca ....C 2
Canton ...17,100▲.K 4
Carlisle ...2,871▲.F 2
Carver ....2,420▲.G13
Caryville ......K 2
Cataumet H14
Cedarville G14
Centerville .2,876..H15
Charlemont ..897▲.B 4
Charlestown ......H 5
Charlton ...4,654▲.E 7
Chartley F11
Chatham ...1,652
  (4,554▲)..H16
Chelmsford .31,432▲.B10
Chelsea ...30,625..H 5
Cheshire ...1,021
  (3,006▲)..C 2
Cheshire Harbor ..B 2
Chester ....1,025▲.D 3
Chester Center ...D 3
Chesterfield ..704▲.D 4
Chestnut Hill ....I 4
Chicopee ..66,676..E 5
Chilmark .....340▲.J13
Clarksburg .1,987▲.B 3
Clayton ....F 2
Clicquot, see Millis
  [-Clicquot]
Clinton ...13,383▲.C 9
Cochesett F12
Cochituate ......I 3
Cohasset ...6,954▲.J 7
Cold Spring .....E 3
Cold Spring .....D 6
Colonial Acres ...H15
Colrain ....1,420▲.B 4
Colton Hollow ...E 6
Concord ..16,148▲.G 2
Congamond ......F 4
Conway ......998▲.C 4
Cooks Corner ....D 5
Copicut Hill H12
Cordaville* .1,457..D10
Cotuit H14
Craigville H15
Crescent Mills ...E 4
Cummington ..562▲.C 5
Cushman ....C 5
Cuttyhunk ......I 2
Dalton ....7,505▲.C 2
Danvers ..26,151▲.B12
Dartmouth .18,800▲.H12
Dayville ....D 3
Dedham ...26,938▲.○D11
Deerfield ..3,850▲.C 5
Dennis* ...6,454▲.G 6
Dennis Port 1,410..H16
Dighton ...4,667▲.G11
Dodge Corner ....B 4
Dorchester ......I 5
Douglas ...2,947▲.F 8
Dover 1,881
  (4,529▲)..J 3
Dracut ...18,214▲.B10

Drury ....B 3
Dudley ....8,087▲.F 8
Dunstable .1,292▲.B10
Duxbury ...2,477
  (7,636▲)..F13
Dwight ....D 5
East Boston .....H 5
East Boxford B12
East Braintree ...J 6
East Bridge-
  water ....8,347▲.F12
East Brimfield ...E 7
East
  Brookfield 1,392
  (1,800▲)..E 7
East Deerfield ...C 5
East Dennis G16
East Douglas 1,763..E 9
East
  Falmouth .2,971..H14
East Freetown ...G12
East Harwich H16
East Lee ....D 2
East Leverett ....C 5
East Long-
  meadow .13,029▲.F 5
East Mansfield ...F11
East Otis ......E 3
East Princeton ...C 8
East Shelburne ...B 4
East Walpole .....K 4
East Whately ....C 5
East Windsor ....C 3
Eastham ...2,043▲.G16
East-
  hampton .13,012▲.D 4
Easton ...12,157▲.F11
Easton Green F11
Edgartown .1,006
  (1,481▲).○I14
Egremont ..1,138▲.E 1
Egypt ....J 8
Ellisville G14
Elm Grove ......B 4
Erving ....1,260▲.B 6
Essex 1,626
  (2,670▲)..B13
Everett ...42,485..H 5
Fairhaven .16,332▲.H12
Fall River .96,898..H11
Falmouth ..5,806
  (15,942▲)..H13
Farley ....B 5
Farmersville H14
Farnums ......C 2
Farnumsville .....E 9
Finnville ......J 6
Fisherville .1,958..E 9
Fiskdale* ..1,612..E 7
Fitchburg .43,343.○B 8
Florida ......672▲.B 3
Forestdale H14
Forge Village B10
Fort Devens 12,019..C 9
Foxborough .4,090
  (14,218▲)..F11
Foxvale F11
Framing-
  ham ....64,048▲.D10
Franklin ...8,863
  (17,830▲)..E10
Frederick Corner ..B10
Freetown ..4,270▲.G11
Furnace Village ..F11
Gardner ..19,748..B 7
Gay Head ...118▲.J13
Georgetown .5,290▲.B12
Gibbs Crossing ...D 6
Gilbertville .1,247..D 6
Gill ......1,100▲.B 5
Ginty Corner F11
Gleasondale ......H 1
Glen Mills A12
Glendale ......D 1
Glendale Falls ...D 3
Glenridge ......J 3
Gloucester .27,941..B13
Goshen .....483▲.C 4
Gosnold* .....83▲.I 3
Goss Heights ....D 3
Grafton ...11,659▲.E 9
Granby 1,354
  (5,473▲)..D 5
Granville ..1,008▲.F 3
Great Bar-
  rington ...3,203
  (7,537▲)..E 1
Green Ridge Park ..E 1
Greenfield .14,642
  (18,116▲).○B 5
Grey Gables G13
Groton 1,314
  (5,109▲)..B 9
Groveland .5,382▲.A12
Hadley ....3,750▲.D 5
Hales Crossing ...B 5
Halifax ....3,537▲.F12
Hamilton ..6,373▲.B12
Hampden ..4,572▲.E 5
Hancock .....675▲.C 2
Hanover ..10,107▲.K 7
Hanson ....7,148▲.E12
Hardwick ..2,379▲.D 6
Hartsville ......E 2
Harvard ..12,494▲.G 1
Harwich ...3,842
  (5,892▲)..H16

Harwich Port H16
Hatchville H14
Hatfield ...1,380
  (2,825▲)..D 5
Hathorne A12
Haverhill .46,120..A11
Hawley .....224▲.C 3
Haydenville .....D 4
Heath ......383▲.B 4
Hephzibah Heights .E 2
Hicksville H12
Hillcrest H11
Hingham ..18,845▲.I 7
Hinsdale ...1,588▲.C 2
Hockanum ......D 5
Holbrook ..11,775▲.K 6
Holden ...12,564▲.D 8
Holland ......931▲.F 7
Holliston ..12,069▲.J 2
Holyoke ..50,112..E 5
Hoosac Tunnel .○B 3
Hopedale ..3,089
  (4,292▲)..K 1
Hopkinton .1,956
  (5,981▲)..J 1
Hosmer Corner ...E 4
Houghtonville ....B 2
Housatonic .1,344..D 1
Howe A12
Howlands G12
Hubbard Corner ..F 5
Hubbardston 1,437▲.C 7
Huckleberry Corner .G13
Hudson ...14,283
  (16,084▲)..H 1
Hull ......9,961▲.I 6
Humarock ......K 8
Huntington .1,593▲.D 3
Hyannis ...6,847..H15
Hyannis Port H15
Hyde Park ......I 5
Interlaken ......D 1
Ipswich ...5,022
  (10,750▲)..B12
Islington ......E 4
Johnson Corner ..E 4
Kendall Green ...H 3
Kent Corner B12
Kenwood B11
Kings Corner ....C 3
Kingston ...3,772
  (5,999▲)..F13
Kinsman Corner ..B12
Kirby Corner H11
Konkapot ......E 2
Lake Pleasant ...C 5
Lakeville ..1,432
  (4,376▲)..G12
Lakewood ......C 2
Lancaster ..6,095▲.C 9
Lanesbor-
  ough .....2,972▲.C 2
Larrywaug ......D 1
Lawrence .66,915.○B11
Lee 3,389
  (6,426▲)..D 2
Leicester ..3,173
  (9,140▲)..D 8
Lenox 2,208
  (5,804▲)..D 2
Lenox Dale ......D 2
Leominster .32,939..C 8
Leverett ...1,005▲.C 5
Lexington .31,886▲.G 4
Leyden .....376▲.B 5
Lincoln ....7,567▲.G 3
Linebrook B12
Littleton ..6,380▲.C 9
Littleton
  Common ...2,764..C10
Lobsterville J13
Locks Village ....C 5
Long-
  meadow ..15,630▲.E 5
Lowell ...94,239.○B10
Ludlow ...17,580▲.E 5
Ludlow Center ...E 5
Lunenburg .7,419▲.B 9
Luther Corner ...G11
Lynn .....90,294..C12
Lynnfield .10,826▲.C12
Lyonsville ......B 4
Madaket J15
Magnolia B13
Mahkeenac Heights .D 2
Malden ...56,127..G 5
Manchester .5,151▲.B13
Manomet F14
Mansfield ..4,778
  (9,939▲)..F11
Maple Park A11
Marblehead .21,295▲.F 7
Marion 1,262
  (3,466▲)..H13
Marlbor-
  ough ....27,936..D 9
Marsh Corner B11
Marshfield .2,562
  (15,223▲)..K 8
Marshfield
  Hills ....1,646..K 8
Marston Corners ..B11
Mashpee ..1,288▲.H14
Mattapoisett 2,188
  (4,500▲)..H13
Mayflower Heights .E15
Maynard ...9,710▲.G 2

Medfield ...9,821▲.J 3
Medford ..64,397..G 4
Medway ...3,716
  (7,938▲)..K 2
Melrose ..33,180..G 5
Mendon ....2,524▲.K 1
Menemsha J13
Merino
  Village* ..3,470..F 8
Merrimac ..4,245▲.A12
Merrimacport A12
Methuen ..35,456▲.B11
Middlebor-
  ough 6,259
  (13,607▲)..F12
Middlefield ..288▲.D 3
Middleton .4,044▲.B12
Midland ....K 1
Milford ...13,740
  (19,352▲)..K 1
Mill River ......C 4
Mill River ......E 2
Mill Valley ......K 1
Millbury ..11,987▲.E 8
Millers Falls 1,186..B 5
Millis* ....5,686▲.J 2
Millis
  [-Clicquot] 3,217..J 2
Millville ...1,197
  (1,764▲)..F 9
Milton ...27,190▲.I 5
Miramar F13
Monponsett F12
Monroe* .....216▲.B 3
Monson ...2,310
  (7,355▲)..E 6
Montague ..8,451▲.C 5
Montague City ...B 5
Monterey ....600▲.E 2
Montgomery ..446▲.E 4
Montville ......E 2
Monument Beach .H13
Moody Corner ....D 5
Moores Corner ...C 5
Morningdale ......D 8
Mount Wash-
  ington ......52▲.E 1
Myricks G12
Nabnasset B10
Nabs Corner J13
Nahant ....4,119▲.G 6
Namskaket G16
Nantasket Beach ..I 7
Nantucket ..2,461
  (3,774▲)..○J16
Nashaquitsa J13
Natick ...31,057▲.I 3
Needham .29,748▲.I 4
Needham Heights ..I 4
Neponset ....I 5
New Ashford ..183▲.B 2
New Bed-
  ford ...101,777.○H12
New Boston ......E 3
New Braintree 631▲.D 7
New Lenox ......C 2
New Marlbor-
  ough .....1,031▲.E 2
New Salem ...474▲.C 6
Newbury ...3,804▲.A12
Newbury-
  port ....15,807.○A12
Newton ...91,263..H 3
Norfolk ....4,656▲.K 2
North Acton .....F 2
North
  Adams ...19,195..B 2
North
  Amherst ..2,854..C 5
North
  Andover .16,284▲.B11
North Attle-
  borough .18,665▲.F10
North Blandford ..E 3
North Brook-
  field 2,677
  (3,967▲)..D 7
North Chatham ...H16
North Chester ....D 3
North Cohasset ...J 7
North
  Dighton ..1,264..G11
North Eastham ...G16
North Easton E11
North Egremont ..E 1
North Heath .....B 4
North Leverett ...C 5
North New Salem ..C 6
North Otis ......D 2
North Oxford 1,550..E 8
North
  Pembroke* 2,881..E13
North Pepperell ...B 9
North
  Plymouth .3,434..F13
North
  Reading ..11,264▲.B11
North
  Scituate ..5,507..J 7
North Sudbury ....H 2
North Sunderland ..C 5
North
  Uxbridge ..1,960..E 9
North Weymouth ..I 6
North Wilbraham ..E 5
North-
  ampton ..29,664.○D 5

Northbor-
ough ......9,218▲.D 9
North-
bridge ...3,321
(11,795▲)..E 9
Northfield ..1,191
(2,631▲)..B 5
Northfield Farms ..B 5
Northville ....E 12
Norton ...2,073
(9,487▲).F 11
Norton Grove ......F 11
Norwell ....7,796▲.J 7
Norwich ....D 4
Norwood ...30,815▲.I 6
Nutting Lake .....C 11
Oak Bluffs ..1,385▲.I 14
Oak Hill ....J 8
Oakdale ....D 8
Oakham ......730▲.D 7
Ocean Grove ......G 11
Ocean Heights ...I 14
Onset .....1,771..G 13
Orange ...3,847
(6,104▲)..B 6
Orleans ...3,055▲.G 16
Osterville .1,286..H 15
Otis ....820▲.E 3
Otis* ....5,596..G 13
Oxford ...6,109
(10,345▲)..E 8
Palmer ...3,649
(11,680▲)..E 6
Palmer Center ....E 6
Paxton ...3,731▲.D 8
Peabody ..48,080..F 6
Pelham ......937▲.D 6
Pembroke ..11,193▲.E 13
Pepperell ...1,076
(5,887▲)..B 9
Peru ......256▲.C 3
Petersham ..1,014▲.C 6
Phillipston ..872▲.C 7
Pigeon
Cove .....1,466..B 13
Pilgrim Heights ...E 16
Pine Tree Corner ..H 14
Pinehurst ...5,681..C 11
Pittsfield ..57,020.○C 2
Plainfield ....287▲.C 3
Plainville ....D 5
Plainville ...4,953▲.F 10
Pleasant Lake ..G 16
Plymouth ...6,940
(18,606▲).○F 13
Plympton ..1,224▲.F 13
Pocasset ....H 13
Ponkapoag ....J 5
Pontoosuc
Gardens ....C 2
Poponesset Beach ..H 14
Pratts Corner .....C 5
Prattville ....F 11
Prides Crossing ..C 12
Princeton ...1,681▲.C 8
Provincetown 2,836
(2,911▲)..E 15
Quidnet ....J 16
Quinapoxet ....D 8
Quincy ...87,966..D 12
Randolph ..27,035▲.J 5
Raynham ...2,526
(6,705▲)..F 11
Reading ...22,539▲.F 5
Rehoboth ..6,512▲.G 11
Revere ....43,159..H 5
Rexhame ....E 13

Rial Side ....C 12
Richmond ...1,461▲.D 1
Richmond
Furnace ....D 1
Richmond Hill ....G 11
Risingdale ....D 1
Riverdale ....B 13
Riverside ....B 5
Rochdale ...1,320..E 8
Rochester ..1,770▲.G 13
Rockland ..15,674▲.K 6
Rockport ..4,166
(5,636▲)..B 13
Rockville ....K 2
Roosterville ......E 3
Rowe ......277▲.B 3
Rowley ...1,325
(3,040▲)..B 12
Roxbury ....I 5
Royalston ....809▲.B 6
Russell ...1,382▲.E 4
Russellville ......E 4
Rutland ...1,751
(3,198▲)..D 8
Sagamore ..1,007..G 14
Salem ....40,556.○C 12
Salem Neck ....A 12
Salisbury ..2,439
(4,179▲)..A 12
Salisbury Beach ...A 12
Sand Hills, see
Shore Acres
[-Sand Hills]
Sandisfield ...547▲.E 2
Sandwich ..1,305
(5,239▲)..G 14
Saugus ...25,110▲.G 5
Savoy ......322▲.C 3
Savoy Center .....B 3
Saxonville ....I 2
Schoosett ....K 7
Sconticut Neck ...H 12
Scotland ....F 12
Sea View ....K 8
Searsville ....D 4
Seekonk ..11,116▲.G 10
Segreganset ......G 11
Sharon ...12,367▲.K 4
Shattuckville .....B 4
Shawsheen
Village ....B 11
Sheffield ..2,374▲.E 1
Shelburne ..1,836▲.B 4
Shelburne
Falls .....2,183..B 4
Sheldonville .....F 10
Sherborn ..3,309▲.J 2
Shirkshire ....C 4
Shirley ...1,718
(4,909▲)..C 9
Shore Acres [-Sand
Hills] ...2,949..J 8
Shrewsbury .19,196▲.D 9
Shutesbury ...489▲.C 5
Siasconset ....J 16
Silver Beach .....H 13
Silver Lake ......B 11
Slocum Corner ...I 12
Smalltown ....H 14
Somerset ..18,088▲.G 11
Somerville .88,779..D 11
South Acton ......D 2
South Ash-
burnham ..1,181..B 8
South Barre ......D 7

South Boston .....H 5
South Brewster ....G 16
South
Deerfield ..1,628..C 5
South Duxbury* .2,075..F 13
South Egremont ...D 1
South Georgetown ..B 12
South Groveland ..A 11
South
Hadley ...17,033▲.D 5
South Hadley Falls .E 5
South Hanover ....K 7
South Harwich ....H 16
South
Lancaster .2,679..C 9
South Lee ....D 2
South Lynnfield ...F 6
South Mashpee ...H 14
South Natick .....I 3
South Orleans ....G 16
South Quarter ....G 3
South Seekonk ...G 10
South Wellfleet ...F 16
South Williams-
town ....B 2
South
Worthington .....D 3
South
Yarmouth .5,380..H 15
South-
ampton ...3,069▲.E 4
Southborough ...5,798▲.I 1
Southbridge 14,261
(17,057▲)..E 7
Southwick ..1,263
(6,330▲)..F 4
Spencer ...5,895
(8,779▲)..D 7
Springfield 163,905.○E 5
Spruce Corner ....C 4
Squantum ....I 5
State Line ....D 1
Sterling ...4,247▲.C 8
Stevens Corner ...G 1
Stewartville ......B 4
Stockbridge ..1,147
(2,312▲)..D 2
Stoneham ..20,725▲.G 5
Stoughton ..23,459▲.K 5
Stow ......3,984▲.G 1
Sturbridge ..4,878▲.E 7
Sudbury ..13,506▲.H 2
Sunderland ..2,236▲.C 5
Surfside ....J 16
Sutton .....4,590▲.E 8
Swampscott 13,578▲.G 6
Swansea ..12,640▲.G 11
Swansea Factory ..G 11
Swanson Corners ..E 4
Sweets Corner ...B 2
Swift River ....C 4
Taunton ..43,756.○F 11
Teaticket ....H 14
Templeton ..5,863▲.C 7
Tewksbury .22,755▲.B 11
Thermopylae ......D 5
Three Rivers 3,366..E 6
Tisbury ...2,257▲.I 13
Tolland ....172▲.E 3
Tonset ....G 16
Topsfield ..5,225▲.B 12
Town Crest
Village ....B 2
Townsend ..1,329
(4,281▲)..B 9

Townsend Harbor ..B 9
Tracy Corner .....F 11
Tremont ....G 13
Truro .....1,234▲.F 16
Tully ....B 6
Turners
Falls .....5,168..B 5
Tyngs-
borough ...4,204▲.B 10
Tyringham ....234▲.D 2
Upton* ....3,484▲.E 9
Upton [-West
Upton] ...2,131..E 9
Uxbridge ..3,380
(8,253▲)..E 9
Van Duesenville ...D 1
Vineyard
Haven ....1,599..I 13
Waban ....H 8
Wadsworth ....E 10
Wakeby ....H 14
Wakefield .25,402▲.F 5
Wales .....852▲.E 6
Walpole ..18,149▲.K 3
Waltham ..61,582..H 3
Wamesit ....B 11
Wapping ....C 5
Waquoit ....H 14
Ware 6,509
(8,187▲)..D 6
Wareham* .11,492▲.G 13
Wareham
[-Wareham
Center] ...2,024..G 13
Warren ...1,688
(3,633▲)..E 6
Warrentown ......F 12
Warwick ....492▲.B 6
Washington ...406▲.D 2
Watertown .39,307▲.H 4
Watson ....C 4
Wauwinet ....J 16
Wayland ...1,752
(13,461▲)..H 2
Webster ..12,432
(14,917▲)..F 8
Wellesley ..28,051▲.I 3
Wellesley Fells ...I 3
Wellesley Hills ...I 3
Wellfleet ..1,743▲.F 16
Wendell ....405▲.C 6
Wendell Depot ....B 6
Wenham ...3,849▲.B 12
West Barnstable ..G 15
West Becket ......D 2
West Bedford .....G 3
West Boxford .....B 11
West
Boylston ...6,369▲.D 8
West Brewster ....G 16
West Bridge-
water 1,920
(7,152▲)..F 12
West Brook-
field 1,536
(2,653▲)..D 7
West
Concord ....G 2
West Cummington ..C 3
West Dennis .1,896..H 16
West Falmouth ...H 13
West Fitchburg ....C 8
West Granville ....F 4

West Groton ......B 9
West Hatfield .....D 4
West Leyden ......B 4
West Mansfield ...F 11
West
Medway* .2,269..K 2
West
Newbury ..2,254▲.A 12
West Newton ......H 4
West Northfield ...B 5
West Orange ......B 6
West Otis ....E 2
West Pelham ......D 5
West Roxbury ....I 4
West Spring-
field ....28,461▲.E 5
West Stock-
bridge ...1,354▲.D 1
West Summit ......B 1
West Tisbury .453▲.I 13
West Upton, see
Upton [-West Upton]
West Village .....C 11
West Ware ....E 6
West Warren 1,237..E 6
West Whately .....C 4
West
Yarmouth .3,699..H 15
Westborough 4,474
(12,594▲)..D 9
Westbrook ....C 5
Westfield .31,433..E 4
Westford ..10,368▲.B 10
Westhampton ..793▲.D 4
Westminster 4,273▲.C 8
Weston ...10,870▲.H 3
Westport ..9,791▲.H 12
Westport Point ...I 11
Westwood ..12,750▲.J 4
Weymouth ..54,610▲.J 6
Whalom ....C 8
Whately ...1,145▲.C 5
Whitcomb
Summit ....B 3
Whitinsville .5,210..E 9
Whitman ..13,059▲.E 12
Whitneys ....J 2
Wianno ....H 15
Wilbraham ..3,540
(11,984▲)..E 5
Williamsburg 2,342▲.D 4
Williams-
town 4,285
(8,454▲)..B 2
Williamsville .....D 1
Wilmington 17,102..C 11
Winchendon 3,997
(6,635▲)..B 7
Winchester .22,269▲.G 4
Windsor ....468▲.C 3
Winthrop ..20,335▲.H 6
Woburn ...37,406..G 4
Wollaston ....I 5
Woods Hole ......I 13
Woodville ....J 1
Worcester .176,572.○D 8
Worthington ..712▲.C 3
Wrentham ..1,723
(7,315▲)..E 10
Wyoma ....G 6
Wyoming ....G 5
Yarmouth ..12,033▲.H 15
Yarmouth Port ...H 15

*Does not appear on the map; key shows general location.
▲Entire town (township), including rural area.
○County seat.

Source: Latest census figures (1970). Places
without population figures are unincorporated
areas and are not listed in census reports.

Springfield is a transportation center of western New England. Downtown improvements completed in the 1970's include an office-hotel-store complex, *left center*, and Interstate 91, *foreground*.

Ellis Herwig, Stock, Boston

Customers Crowd a Boston Market to look for unusual foods. This market features foods common in Italy and eastern Europe.

The 1970 U.S. census reported that Massachusetts had a population of 5,689,170. The population had increased 11 per cent over the 1960 figure of 5,148,578. The U.S. Bureau of the Census estimated that by 1975 the state's population had reached about 5,828,000.

More than five-sixths of the people of Massachusetts live in urban areas. That is, they live in or near municipalities of 2,500 or more persons. About one-sixth of the people live in rural areas of the state. About 88 out of 100 persons in Massachusetts live in one of the 11 Standard Metropolitan Statistical Areas either entirely or partly in the state (see METROPOLITAN AREA). These areas are Boston, Brockton, Fitchburg-Leominster, Lowell, New Bedford, Pittsfield, and Worcester in Massachusetts; Fall River and Providence-Warwick-Pawtucket in Rhode Island and Massachusetts; Lawrence-Haverhill in Massachusetts and New Hampshire; and Springfield-Chicopee-Holyoke in Massachusetts and Connecticut. For the populations of these areas, see the *Index* to the political map of Massachusetts.

POPULATION

This map shows the *population density* of Massachusetts, and how it varies in different parts of the state. Population density is the average number of persons who live in a given area.

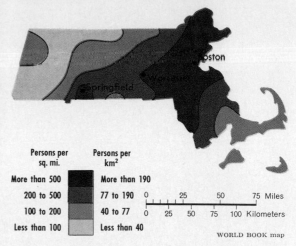

Persons per sq. mi.		Persons per km²
More than 500	▓	More than 190
200 to 500	▓	77 to 190
100 to 200	▓	40 to 77
Less than 100	▓	Less than 40

0   25   50   75 Miles
0 25 50 75 100 Kilometers

WORLD BOOK map

Boston is the state's largest city and the state capital. Other large cities, in order of population, are Worcester, Springfield, New Bedford, and Cambridge. See the separate articles on the cities of Massachusetts listed in the *Related Articles* at the end of this article.

About 91 out of 100 persons living in Massachusetts were born in the United States. The largest groups of persons born in other countries, in order of size, came from Canada, Italy, Great Britain, and Ireland.

More than half the people of Massachusetts belong to the Roman Catholic Church. The United Church of Christ has the second largest membership of all religious denominations in the state, and the Episcopal Church ranks third.

MASSACHUSETTS /Education

Schools. The Puritans of Boston built Massachusetts' first school in 1635. This school, the Boston Latin School, was the first secondary school in the American Colonies. In 1647, the Massachusetts Bay Colony ordered elementary schools set up in all towns of 50 or more families. This was the first time that any government in the world provided free public education at public expense. In 1852, Massachusetts became the first state to require its children to attend school.

The state department of education controls public education from kindergarten through secondary school. The department has a commissioner, a deputy commissioner, and a 12-member board of education. The board includes 11 members appointed by the governor and one student member elected by student representatives from the state's secondary schools. Children between the ages of 7 and 16 must attend school. For the number of students and teachers in Massachusetts, see EDUCATION (table).

Massachusetts has some of the nation's most highly regarded *prep schools* (private schools that prepare students for college). The state's universities and colleges rank among the world's outstanding educational institutions.

Libraries. The first library in the American Colonies was established in Massachusetts in 1638, when John Harvard gave his collection of books to Harvard College. It is now the world's largest university library, with over 9 million volumes. Today, nearly all the state's cities and towns have public libraries.

Several Boston libraries own outstanding collections. These include the Athenaeum, which has George Washington's collection of books; the Massachusetts Historical Society; and the state library, in the State House.

Other libraries with important collections include the Essex Institute in Salem and the American Antiquarian Society in Worcester. The Harvard library owns collections of rare books and old Indian manuscripts.

Amherst College

Amherst College was founded in Amherst in 1821. Converse Hall, *above,* once a library, houses offices of the college's officials.

Museums. The Museum of Fine Arts in Boston ranks as one of the world's great museums. It has the finest collection of Oriental art in the world. The Isabella Stewart Gardner Museum in Boston has many outstanding Renaissance paintings. Boston's famous Children's Museum is one of the oldest and largest museums for young people in the nation. The George Walter Vincent Smith Art Museum in Springfield and the Worcester Art Museum are among the nation's best-known smaller museums. The Addison Gallery of American Art of Phillips Academy in Andover owns one of the nation's most valuable collections of American paintings. The Sterling and Francine Clark Art Institute in Williamstown has a collection of paintings by French artists of the 1800's.

Other museums in Massachusetts include the Museum of Science in Boston, the Whaling Museum in New Bedford, the Peabody Museum of Salem, and the John Woodman Higgins Armory in Worcester.

UNIVERSITIES AND COLLEGES

Massachusetts has 67 universities and colleges accredited by the New England Association of Schools and Colleges. For enrollments and further information, see UNIVERSITIES AND COLLEGES (table).

Name	Location	Founded	Name	Location	Founded
American International College	Springfield	1885	Massachusetts Institute of Technology	Cambridge	1861
Amherst College	Amherst	1821	Massachusetts Maritime Academy	Buzzards Bay	1970
Andover Newton Theological School	Newton Centre	1807	Merrimack College	North Andover	1947
Anna Maria College	Paxton	1946	Mount Holyoke College	South Hadley	1837
Arthur D. Little Management Education Institute	Cambridge	1971	New England Conservatory of Music	Boston	1867
Assumption College	Worcester	1904	Nichols College	Dudley	1958
Atlantic Union College	South Lancaster	1882	North Adams State College	North Adams	1894
Babson College	Wellesley	1919	Northeastern University	Boston	1898
Bentley College	Waltham	1961	Our Lady of the Elms, College of	Chicopee	1928
Berklee College of Music	Boston	1962	Pine Manor College	Chestnut Hill	1911
Boston College	Chestnut Hill	1863	Regis College	Weston	1927
Boston Conservatory of Music	Boston	1867	St. Hyacinth College and Seminary	Granby	1957
Boston State College	Boston	1852	St. John's Seminary	Boston	1941
Boston University	Boston	1839	Salem State College	Salem	1854
Bradford College	Haverhill	1971	Simmons College	Boston	1899
Brandeis University	Waltham	1948	Simon's Rock Early College	Great Barrington	1964
Bridgewater State College	Bridgewater	1840	Smith College	Northampton	1871
Central New England College	Worcester	1888	Southeastern Massachusetts University	North Dartmouth	1949
Clark University	Worcester	1887	Springfield College	Springfield	1885
Curry College	Milton	1938	Stonehill College	North Easton	1948
Eastern Nazarene College	Quincy	1900	Suffolk University	Boston	1906
Emerson College	Boston	1880	Tufts University	Medford	1852
Emmanuel College	Boston	1919	Wellesley College	Wellesley	1870
Fitchburg State College	Fitchburg	1894	Wentworth Institute of Technology	Boston	1904
Framingham State College	Framingham	1839	Western New England College	Springfield	1919
Gordon College	Wenham	1889	Westfield State College	Westfield	1839
Hampshire College	Amherst	1965	Wheaton College	Norton	1834
Harvard University	Cambridge	1636	Wheelock College	Boston	1888
Hebrew College	Brookline	1921	Williams College	Williamstown	1793
Hellenic College	Brookline	1968	Worcester Polytechnic Institute	Worcester	1865
Holy Cross, College of the	Worcester	1843	Worcester State College	Worcester	1871
Lesley College	Cambridge	1909			
Lowell, University of	Lowell	1894			
Massachusetts, University of	*	*			
Massachusetts College of Art	Boston	1873			
Massachusetts College of Pharmacy	Boston	1936			

*For campuses and founding dates, see UNIVERSITIES AND COLLEGES (table).

MASSACHUSETTS/A Visitor's Guide

Skiing brings many visitors to the Berkshire Hills and to other parts of Massachusetts. The Atlantic Ocean and many lakes and rivers attract swimmers, fishing enthusiasts, and boaters. But Massachusetts offers perhaps its greatest rewards to the student of American history. Historic sites date back to the Pilgrims, to colonial witchcraft trials, and to the Revolutionary War.

Jack Zehrt, Publix
Saugus Iron Works National Historic Site in Saugus

Eric M. Sanford
Concert at Tanglewood Music Shed near Lenox

PLACES TO VISIT

Boston is a major cultural center and one of the nation's great historic cities. The city became known as the *Cradle of Liberty* when it led the American Colonies in their struggle for independence. Visitors can see many of Boston's historic shrines by strolling along the *Freedom Trail*. See BOSTON (Downtown Boston; illustration: Boston's Freedom Trail).

Bunker Hill Monument, on Breed's Hill in the Charlestown section of Boston, honors one of the early battles of the Revolutionary War. The 220-foot (67-meter) granite shaft was built between 1825 and 1842. A small museum has portraits, statues, and engravings of soldiers who fought in the Battle of Bunker Hill.

Cape Cod, a peninsula in southeastern Massachusetts, is a famous summer resort and vacation area. The peninsula faces Cape Cod Bay on the north, Nantucket Sound on the south, and the Atlantic Ocean on the east. Long sandy beaches stretch along the cape.

Constitution, or *Old Ironsides*, lies at anchor in the Charles River near the Charlestown section of Boston. This early U.S. Navy frigate became famous during the War of 1812. Oliver Wendell Holmes honored the ship with his famous poem "Old Ironsides."

Fishermen's Memorial, in Gloucester, is a statue that overlooks the city's harbor. The statue honors the many members of Gloucester fishing crews who lost their lives. Gloucester has been an important fishing port since colonial days.

Harvard University, in Cambridge, is one of the world's most famous universities. Harvard was founded in 1636. It is the oldest institute of higher learning in the United States. Harvard Yard, the center of the original college, still retains much of its early charm. The school has several libraries and museums.

John and Priscilla Alden House, in Duxbury, is probably the only house still standing that was occupied by Pilgrims who sailed on the *Mayflower*. It was built about 1653.

John Fitzgerald Kennedy Library, in Boston, has a collection of books, documents, and exhibits dealing with President Kennedy.

Old Sturbridge Village, in Sturbridge, is a re-creation of a typical New England town of the early 1800's.

Plimoth Plantation, in Plymouth, is a re-creation of the first Pilgrim village. *Mayflower II*, built the way the original *Mayflower* is thought to have looked, is maintained by the plantation.

Walden Pond, near Concord, is the small lake near which the writer Henry David Thoreau lived with nature for two years. Thoreau told of his beliefs, and described his experiences at the pond, in his book *Walden*.

Witch House, in Salem, was the home of Jonathan Corwin, a judge at the Salem witchcraft trials in the 1690's.

National Historical Parks, Seashores, and Historic Sites. Minute Man National Historical Park is located between Lexington and Concord. Cape Cod National Seashore includes beaches, marshes, and woodland areas on outer Cape Cod. Saugus Iron Works National Historic Site in Saugus is a reconstruction of the first successful ironworks in North America.

Massachusetts has several other national historic sites. For information on these areas, see the map and tables in the article on NATIONAL PARK SYSTEM.

State Parks and Forests. Massachusetts has 107 state parks, forests, and recreational areas. For information, write to Director, Division of Forests and Parks, 100 Cambridge Street, Boston, Mass. 02202.

Jack Zehrt. Publix

Bunker Hill Monument on Breed's Hill in Charlestown

Minuteman Statue in Lexington
Ewing Galloway

One of the outstanding yearly events in Massachusetts is the Berkshire Festival of the Boston Symphony Orchestra. Each July and August, musicians from many parts of the world give performances in the Tanglewood Music Shed near Lenox. Other annual events in Massachusetts include the following.

January-March: Winter Carnival in Northampton (February); Evacuation Day, when the British left Boston in 1776, in South Boston (March 17); Spring Flower Show in Revere (March).

April-June: Patriots' Day in Boston, Concord, and Lexington (third Monday in April); Boston Symphony Pops Concerts in Boston (May-June); Bunker Hill Day in Charlestown (June 17); Blessing of Fishing Fleets in Gloucester and Provincetown (late June).

July-September: Salt-Water Fishing Derbies in coastal towns (July-August); Sailing Regatta, all yacht clubs (weekends and special days); Esplanade Concerts in Boston (July); Jacob's Pillow Dance Festival in Becket (July-September); United States Tennis Association National Doubles Championship in Chestnut Hill (August); Fishermen's Memorial Service in Gloucester (August); Pilgrim Progress Processional in Plymouth (every Friday, August); Eastern States Exposition in West Springfield (September).

October-December: Scallop Festival in Buzzards Bay (October); Rowing Regatta on the Charles River in Boston and Cambridge (October); Pilgrim Thanksgiving Day in Plymouth (Thanksgiving Day); Boston Common Christmas Festival in Boston (begins the first day after Thanksgiving and ends the first week in January).

A Pilgrim House and the *Mayflower II* in Plymouth
Jack Zehrt, Publix

223

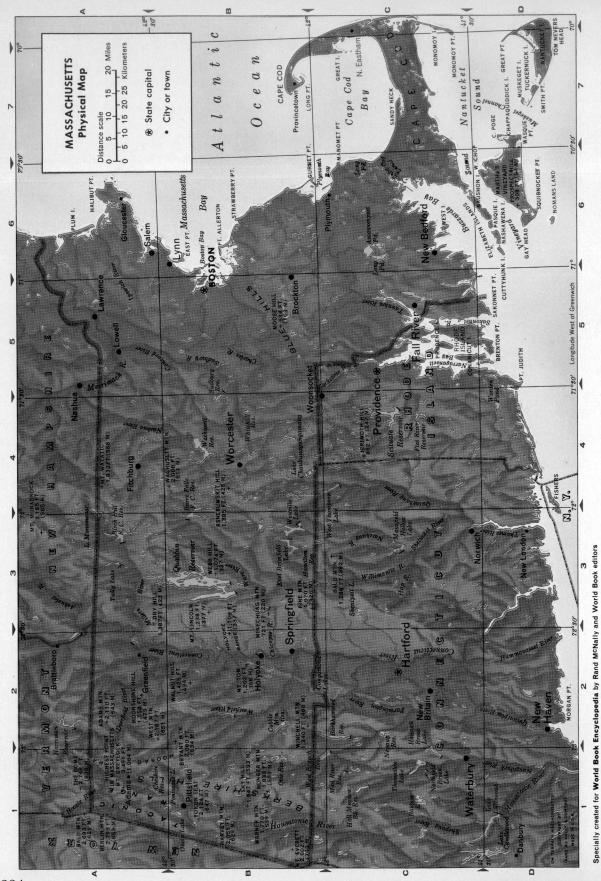

MASSACHUSETTS
Physical Map

Distance scale

0 5 10 15 20 Miles
0 5 10 15 20 25 Kilometers

⊛ State capital
• City or town

Atlantic Ocean

Massachusetts Bay

CAPE COD

Provincetown
LONG PT.
CAPE COD
Cape Cod Bay
MANOMET PT.
SANDY NECK
N. Eastham
GREAT I.
MONOMOY I.
MONOMOY PT.

Nantucket Sound

C. POGE
MARTHA'S VINEYARD
CHAPPAQUIDDICK I. GREAT PT.
MUSKEGET I.
TUCKERNUCK I.
NANTUCKET I.
SMITH PT.
TOM NEVERS HEAD

MONOMOY I.

CURTET PT.
Plymouth
Manomet

Buzzards Bay
WEST I.
New Bedford
ELIZABETH ISLANDS
CUTTYHUNK I. NASHAWENA I. PASQUE I. NAUSHON I. — W. CHOP
GAY HEAD
PROSPECT HILL
308 FT. (94 M)
SQUIBNOCKET PT.
NOMANS LAND
WASQUE PT.

NEW HAMPSHIRE

VERMONT

Halibut Pt.
PLUM I.
Gloucester
Salem
Lynn
EAST PT.
Boston Bay
BOSTON
PT. ALLERTON
STRAWBERRY PT.

Lawrence
Lowell
Nashua
Merrimack R.

Merrimack River
Concord River
Sudbury R.
Charles River

MOOSE HILL
534 FT.
Brockton
BLUE HILLS

Fitchburg
WACHUSETT MTN.
2,006 FT. (611 M)
Worcester
ASNEBUMSKIT HILL
1,395 FT. (425 M)
Woonsocket
Blackstone
Providence ⊛

RHODE ISLAND

Fall River
Taunton River
SAKONNET PT.
BRENTON PT.
PT. JUDITH

MT. MONADNOCK
3,165 FT. (965 M)
MT. WATATIC
1,832 FT. (558 M)

Greenfield
MOONSHINE HILL
1,558 FT. (475 M)
WEST HILL
2,137 FT. (651 M)
DRY HILL
1,387 FT. (423 M)
MT. LINCOLN
1,238 FT. (377 M)
WEBB HILL
1,074 FT. (327 M)

Springfield
Holyoke
MT. TOM
1,202 FT. (366 M)
MINECHOAG MTN.
721 FT. (220 M)
HOLYOKE RANGE
MT. HOLYOKE
955 FT. (291 M)

Hartford

CONNECTICUT

New Haven
New Britain
Waterbury
Danbury

Connecticut River
Housatonic River
Westfield River
Deerfield River

ADAMS MTN.
2,110 FT. (643 M)
HIGHEST POINT
MT. GREYLOCK
IN MASSACHUSETTS
Adams
3,491 FT. (1,064 M)
Pittsfield
YOKUN SEAT
2,124 FT. (647 M)
BRYANT MTN.
2,080 FT. (634 M)
HARVEY MTN.
2,065 FT. (629 M)
WARNER MTN.
1,719 FT. (524 M)
SKY HILL
1,947 FT. (593 M)
WINCHELL MTN.
1,340 FT. (408 M)

BALD MTN.
2,693 FT. (821 M)
BERLIN MTN.
2,798 FT. (853 M)
THE DOME
2,748 FT. (838 M)

EL EVERETT
2,602 FT. (793 M)

BALD MTN.
1,288 FT. (392 M)
PINE MTN.
1,070 FT. (326 M)

Brattleboro

Norwich
New London
Willimantic

Fishers I.
N.Y.

Longitude West of Greenwich

Specially created for **World Book Encyclopedia** by Rand McNally and World Book editors

224

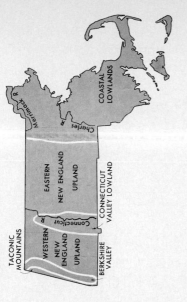

Land Regions of Massachusetts

TACONIC MOUNTAINS

WESTERN NEW ENGLAND UPLAND

BERKSHIRE VALLEY

CONNECTICUT VALLEY LOWLAND

EASTERN NEW ENGLAND UPLAND

COASTAL LOWLANDS

MASSACHUSETTS/The Land

Land Regions. Massachusetts has six main land regions. They are, from east to west: (1) the Coastal Lowlands, (2) the Eastern New England Upland, (3) the Connecticut Valley Lowland, (4) the Western New England Upland, (5) the Berkshire Valley, and (6) the Taconic Mountains.

The Coastal Lowlands are part of a large land region that extends over the entire New England coastline. The lowlands make up the eastern third of Massachusetts. They also include Nantucket Island, Martha's Vineyard, the Elizabeth Islands, and other smaller offshore islands. The region has many rounded hills, swamps, small lakes and ponds, and short shallow rivers. The lowlands are dotted with glacial deposits. These were left by glaciers thousands of years ago during the Ice Age. The Great Blue Hill, south of Boston, rises to a height of about 635 feet (194 meters). Several excellent harbors lie along the coast. They include Boston, Gloucester, and New Bedford.

The Eastern New England Upland makes up part of a land region that stretches from Maine to New Jersey. The upland is an extension of the White Mountains of New Hampshire. In Massachusetts it extends westward

from the Coastal Lowlands for 40 to 60 miles (64 to 97 kilometers). The upland region rises to a height of about 1,000 feet (300 meters), then gradually slopes downward toward the Connecticut Valley Lowland. Many streams cut through this region.

The Connecticut Valley Lowland is a long, sausage-shaped region. It extends from northern Massachusetts to southern Connecticut. In Massachusetts, the valley, which is 20 miles (32 kilometers) wide, is hemmed in by hills to the north, east, and west. The Connecticut River flows through the valley region. Rich soil and a mild climate provide good farming.

The Western New England Upland extends through Vermont, Massachusetts, and Connecticut. In Massachusetts, the region stretches 20 to 30 miles (32 to 48 kilometers) westward from the Connecticut Valley Lowland to the Berkshire Valley. The Berkshire Hills, a range that covers this region, is an extension of the Green Mountains of Vermont. In Massachusetts, the Western New England Upland region itself is often called the *Berkshire Hills.* The land rises from the Connecticut Valley to rugged, beautiful heights of over 2,000 feet (610 meters). Majestic Mount Greylock,

which rises 3,491 feet (1,064 meters), is the highest point in the state. Farms and towns lie on the region's slopes.

The Berkshire Valley is a narrow path of lower land that extends into northern Connecticut. In Massachusetts, it winds between the Berkshire Hills and the Taconic Mountains. This valley region is less than 10 miles (16 kilometers) wide. Its many green meadows are good for dairy farming.

The Taconic Mountains extend into Vermont. This region skirts the extreme western edge of Massachusetts. At its widest point, the region measures no more than 6 miles (10 kilometers) across. The Taconic Range slopes from northwestern Massachusetts to the southwestern corner of the state, where Mount Everett rises 2,602 feet (793 meters).

Coastline of Massachusetts measures 192 miles (309 kilometers). If the coastline of each bay and inlet were added to the total, the state's coastline would measure more than 1,500 miles (2,410 kilometers). Boston is the state's most important harbor. Other important harbors include Gloucester in the north, Quincy and Weymouth in Boston Bay, and New Bedford and Fall River in the south.

On a Tobacco Farm, *left*, near Hadley, workers harvest the leaves. Cigar tobacco is an important crop in the Connecticut Valley Lowlands region.

Quabbin Reservoir, *right*, near Ware, is a huge artificially created lake in the Eastern New England Upland region of central Massachusetts.

Massachusetts Metropolitan Dist. Comm.

Islands. The Elizabeth Islands, Martha's Vineyard, and Nantucket Island are the state's largest and most important islands. Together with Cape Cod, these islands form the boundaries of Nantucket Sound. Martha's Vineyard and Nantucket Island are important resort centers. A number of smaller islands also lie along the state's coast.

Rivers and Lakes. Massachusetts has 4,230 miles (6,808 kilometers) of rivers. The Connecticut River is the state's most important waterway. It flows southward and provides water for the most fertile Massachusetts farmlands. The Connecticut's chief tributaries include the Deerfield and Westfield rivers to the west, and the Chicopee and Millers rivers to the east. The far western part of the state has two important rivers—the Hoosic and the Housatonic. The Hoosic flows northward and westward into Vermont, and finally drains into the Hudson River. The scenic Housatonic River flows southward into Connecticut. The Blackstone River drains Massachusetts' eastern upland region and flows southeastward into Rhode Island.

The Merrimack River is the most important river in the Coastal Lowlands. It enters the state from New Hampshire. Then the Merrimack turns abruptly north-

eastward and flows almost parallel to the Massachusetts border until it empties into the Atlantic Ocean at Newburyport. The Nashua and Concord rivers are the Merrimack's main tributaries. The Charles, Mystic, and Neponset rivers all empty into Boston harbor. The Taunton River flows southward into Rhode Island's Mount Hope Bay.

Massachusetts has more than 1,300 lakes and ponds. More than a fourth of these lakes supply drinking water to nearby cities and towns. The state's two largest lakes—Quabbin and Wachusett—are artificially created reservoirs. Quabbin Reservoir, near Ware in the center of the state, is one of the nation's largest reservoirs of drinking water. It covers more than 39 square miles (101 square kilometers). Wachusett Reservoir, north of Worcester, covers $6\frac{1}{2}$ square miles (17 square kilometers). These reservoirs supply water to the Boston metropolitan area. Many of the state's lakes have Indian names. For example, Lake Chaubunagungamaug, also called Lake Webster, received its name from the Nipmuc Indians. The long form for this name is Chargoggagoggmanchauggagoggchaubunagungamaug. The name means "You fish your side of the lake. I fish my side. Nobody fishes the middle."

Eric M. Sanford

Martha's Vineyard, a famous resort area, has many beaches. The island is part of the Coastal Lowlands region of New England.

FPG

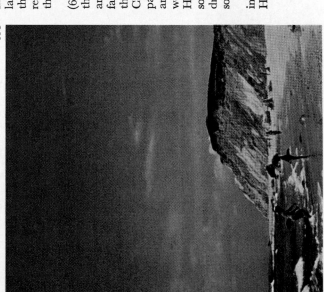

SEASONAL TEMPERATURES

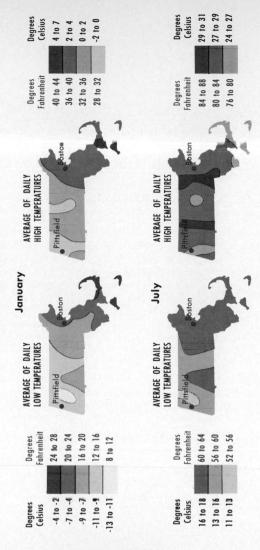

January

AVERAGE OF DAILY LOW TEMPERATURES

Degrees Celsius	Degrees Fahrenheit
-4 to -2	24 to 28
-7 to -4	20 to 24
-9 to -7	16 to 20
-11 to -9	12 to 16
-13 to -11	8 to 12

AVERAGE OF DAILY HIGH TEMPERATURES

Degrees Celsius	Degrees Fahrenheit
4 to 7	40 to 44
2 to 4	36 to 40
0 to 2	32 to 36
-2 to 0	28 to 32

July

AVERAGE OF DAILY LOW TEMPERATURES

Degrees Celsius	Degrees Fahrenheit
16 to 18	60 to 64
13 to 16	56 to 60
11 to 13	52 to 56

AVERAGE OF DAILY HIGH TEMPERATURES

Degrees Celsius	Degrees Fahrenheit
29 to 31	84 to 88
27 to 29	80 to 84
24 to 27	76 to 80

AVERAGE YEARLY PRECIPITATION
(Rain, Melted Snow and Other Moisture)

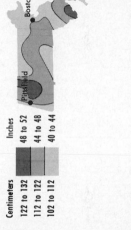

Centimeters	Inches
122 to 132	48 to 52
112 to 122	44 to 48
102 to 112	40 to 44

0   50   100 Miles
0   50   100   150 Kilometers

WORLD BOOK maps

AVERAGE MONTHLY WEATHER

BOSTON

	Temperatures F°		Temperatures C°		Days of Rain or Snow
	High	Low	High	Low	
JAN.	37	22	3	-6	12
FEB.	37	22	3	-6	10
MAR.	45	30	7	-1	12
APR.	55	39	13	4	11
MAY	66	49	19	9	11
JUNE	76	58	24	14	10
JULY	80	64	27	18	10
AUG.	79	64	26	18	10
SEPT.	73	56	23	13	9
OCT.	63	47	17	8	9
NOV.	52	37	11	3	10
DEC.	40	26	4	-3	11

PITTSFIELD

	Temperatures F°		Temperatures C°		Days of Rain or Snow
	High	Low	High	Low	
JAN.	30	13	-1	-11	14
FEB.	31	13	-1	-11	13
MAR.	40	22	4	-6	14
APR.	53	31	12	-1	14
MAY	66	43	19	6	14
JUNE	74	52	23	11	14
JULY	79	56	26	13	11
AUG.	78	54	26	12	11
SEPT.	70	47	21	8	12
OCT.	59	36	15	2	9
NOV.	46	28	8	-2	10
DEC.	33	16	1	-9	13

Winter Snow covers the Berkshire Valley near North Adams. The mountains get up to 75 inches (191 centimeters) of snow a year.

Eric M. Sanford

MASSACHUSETTS/Climate

Western Massachusetts is colder than the eastern part of the state. Boston, on the coast, has an average July temperature of 72° F. (22° C) and an average January temperature of 29° F. (−2° C). In the west, Pittsfield averages 68° F. (20° C) in July and 21° F. (−6° C) in January. Worcester, in the central portion of the state, has a July average of 70° F. (21° C) and a January average of 24° F. (−4° C). The highest temperature ever recorded in the state was 107° F. (42° C) at New Bedford and Chester on Aug. 2, 1975. The lowest recorded temperature, −34° F. (−37° C), occurred at Birch Hill Dam on Jan. 18, 1957.

The state's *precipitation* (rain, melted snow, and other forms of moisture) ranges from about 44 inches (112 centimeters) a year in the west to about 40 inches (100 centimeters) near the coast. From 55 to 75 inches (140 to 191 centimeters) of snow falls in the western mountains each year. The central part of the state averages about 49 inches (124 centimeters) a year and the coastal area about 42 inches (107 centimeters). Hurricanes occasionally lash the coastline. Destructive hurricanes hit the state in 1938 and 1944.

224c

Much of the state's manufacturing is centered in the industrial cities of the Coastal Lowlands. Springfield and Worcester in the central portion of the state are also important manufacturing centers. Massachusetts' huge tourist industry thrives around the Boston area, on Cape Cod, and in the Berkshires. Each year, about 7 million tourists visit Massachusetts. They spend about $1 billion. The state's most profitable farms lie along the river valleys, especially in the Connecticut Valley Lowland.

Natural Resources of Massachusetts include thick forests, hundreds of miles of rivers and streams and coastal waters filled with sea life.

Soil. Most of the river valleys have deep soils that are rich in peat. The Connecticut River Valley has the most fertile soil in the state. The marshy soils of the Coastal Lowlands, with underground peat deposits, are also quite rich. But much of the state's soil contains sand and gravel. Stones and boulders, deposited long ago by melting glaciers, are also common. These gravel and sandy acid soils are not very fertile. Farmers must treat them with large amounts of fertilizer.

Minerals. Most of the minerals found in Massachusetts are valuable building materials. Sand and gravel deposits lie throughout much of the state. The richest granite deposits are near West Chelmsford. Deposits of dolomitic marbles are found in Ashley Falls, Lee, and West Stockbridge.

Forests cover about 3 million acres (1.2 million hectares), or about three-fifths of the land area of Massachusetts. The most common softwood trees include the eastern white and red pines, the eastern hemlock, and the pitch pine. Common hardwoods include ash, beech, birch, maple, and oak trees. The 107 state forests, parks, and recreational reservations have about 230,000 acres (93,100 hectares) of woodland.

Plant Life. Every spring, blue and white violets blossom along the river valleys and in the lower portions of the upland regions. Marsh marigolds, skunk cabbages, and white hellebores also cover these regions in the springtime. Common shrubs and plants in the western hilly regions include azaleas, dogwoods, ferns, mountain laurels, rhododendrons, and viburnums. Mayflowers, Solomon's-seals, and trilliums are also common in the western regions. Rushes and sedges thrive along the Massachusetts seacoast and in the Coastal Lowlands.

Animal Life. Massachusetts' forests and woodlands are filled with foxes, muskrats, porcupines, rabbits, raccoons, and skunks. The tiny meadow mouse is the state's most common animal. Deer live throughout the state. Great numbers of beavers live in the streams of the Berkshire Hills, and the state permits limited trapping. Partridge, pheasant, and other game birds are found in the fields and forests. Many kinds of water, marsh, and shore birds, especially gulls and terns, nest along the seacoast. Bass, pickerel, sunfish, trout, and white and yellow perch swim in the lakes and ponds. Clams, fishes, lobsters, and oysters are found in the coastal waters. Massachusetts has many kinds of snakes. Poisonous copperheads and timber rattlesnakes live in the Berkshire and Blue hills.

Manufacturing accounts for 98 per cent of the value of goods produced in Massachusetts. Manufactured goods have a *value added by manufacturing* of about $17 billion a year. This figure represents the value created in products by Massachusetts' industries, not counting such costs as materials, supplies, and fuels. Massachusetts is an important manufacturing state. Its chief manufacturing industries, in order of importance, are (1) nonelectric machinery, (2) electric and electronic equipment, and (3) instruments.

Nonelectric Machinery has a value added of over $3 billion a year. The industry's leading products are office and computing machines. Boston is the center of this production. Textile machinery, printing trades machinery, and paper industries machinery are also important in Massachusetts. Plants in Lynn produce aircraft engines and steam generators. Worcester factories make boring, grinding, and textile machinery. Other factories throughout the state produce many types of metal products, and foundry and machine-shop products.

Electric and Electronic Equipment have a value added of about $2 billion yearly. Massachusetts factories produce appliances, electronic instruments, lamps, measuring instruments, radios, television sets and components, and turbines. Much of this industry is centered

Production of Goods in Massachusetts

Total value of goods produced in 1977—$17,300,206,000

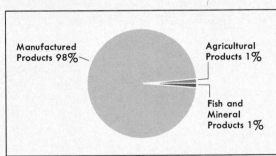

Manufactured Products 98%

Agricultural Products 1%

Fish and Mineral Products 1%

Percentages are based on farm income, value added by manufacture, and value of fish and mineral production. Fish and mineral products are each less than 1 per cent.

Sources: U.S. government publications, 1978-1979.

Employment in Massachusetts

Total number of persons employed in 1978—2,514,900

		Number of Employees
Manufacturing	🏃🏃🏃🏃🏃🏃🏃🏃🏃🏃	647,300
Mining & Community, Social, & Personal Services	🏃🏃🏃🏃🏃🏃🏃🏃🏃	566,900
Wholesale & Retail Trade	🏃🏃🏃🏃🏃🏃🏃🏃🏃	557,900
Government	🏃🏃🏃🏃🏃🏃	394,100
Finance, Insurance, & Real Estate	🏃🏃	142,500
Transportation & Public Utilities	🏃🏃	116,100
Construction	🏃	74,100
Agriculture	🏃	16,000

Sources: *Employment and Earnings*, May 1979, U.S. Bureau of Labor Statistics; Massachusetts Department of Food and Agriculture.

FARM, MINERAL, AND FOREST PRODUCTS

This map shows where the state's leading farm, mineral, and forest products are produced. The major urban areas (shown on the map in red) are the state's important manufacturing centers.

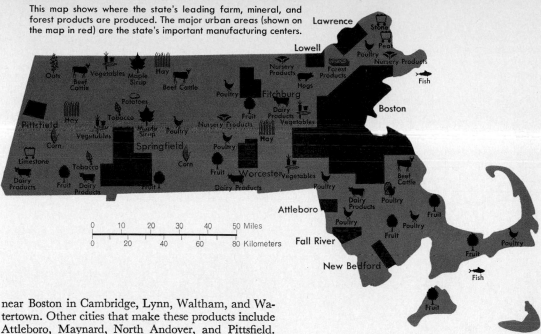

WORLD BOOK map

near Boston in Cambridge, Lynn, Waltham, and Watertown. Other cities that make these products include Attleboro, Maynard, North Andover, and Pittsfield. The Boston area is an important center for electronics research and development. Many electronics research laboratories stand along Route 128, which swings in an arc around Boston.

Instruments. The Boston area is a leading producer of measuring devices and other scientific instruments. These products have a value added of about $1½ billion annually.

Other Leading Industries. The fourth and fifth leading sources of manufacturing income in Massachusetts are the production of fabricated metal products and of printed materials. Factories in Boston and Cambridge make ducts, pipes, and aluminum windows. Boston also has plants that make metal tanks. Boston is a major center for printing and publishing.

Other important industries in the state include chemicals; clothing; food products; leather products; paper products; primary metals; rubber and plastics products; stone, clay, and glass products; textiles; toys and sporting goods; and transportation equipment.

Most of the state's textile mills and clothing factories are in the Coastal Lowlands. Boston and Cambridge are leaders in the state's candy industry, which supplies a nationwide market.

Agriculture in Massachusetts has a yearly gross income of about $217 million. The state's 5,200 farms average 125 acres (51 hectares) in size.

Milk is the leading source of farm income, earning about $66 million a year. Greenhouse and nursery products, such as flowers and ornamental shrubs, rank second among the state's farm products with a value of about $42 million each year. Dairying activities and nursery and greenhouse products supply about half of Massachusetts farm income. Eggs rank third, with an income of about $20 million yearly. Beef cattle, hogs, and turkeys are other Massachusetts livestock products.

Massachusetts farmers plant more acreage in hay than in any other crop. They use the hay to feed their dairy cattle. Truck gardeners near the towns and cities raise strawberries, tomatoes, and such fresh vegetables as asparagus and sweet corn. Cigar tobacco is an important product of the Connecticut Valley Lowland. Farmers in this region also raise cucumbers, potatoes, sweet corn, and other vegetables. Farmers grow fine apples in the Connecticut and Nashua river valleys. Massachusetts supplies about two-fifths of the cranberries in the United States.

Fishing Industry. Massachusetts ranks among the leading commercial fishing states. The state's annual fish catch is valued at about $114 million. New Bedford's catch is the most valuable in the state. It accounts for about half the scallops produced in the United States. Gloucester's fish catch is the second most valuable in Massachusetts. Gloucester's chief products include cod, flounder, haddock, ocean perch, and whiting. The fishing industry in Boston specializes in cod and haddock. Other valuable products of the Massachusetts fishing industry include anglerfish, clams, crabs, hake, herring, lobster, pollack, squid, swordfish, and tuna.

Mining in Massachusetts has a value of about $74 million a year. The state's most valuable mining products are stone, sand, and gravel. The most important types of stone in Massachusetts include basalt, granite, and limestone. Large stone quarries are in Berkshire, Hampden, Middlesex, and Norfolk counties. Other products mined in Massachusetts include clays, lime, and peat.

Electric Power. About 84 per cent of the state's electric power is produced by power plants that burn oil. Nuclear power plants in Massachusetts generate about 15 per cent of the electric power. New England's first nuclear power plant began operating in Rowe in 1960. Hydroelectric projects produce most of the rest of the state's power.

Transportation. Massachusetts has 31 public airports and 109 private airports. Logan International Airport in Boston is the state's busiest airport. Boston is served by about 20 airlines.

Railroads operate on about 1,500 miles (2,400 kilometers) of track in Massachusetts. Five railroads provide freight service, and passenger trains serve five cities.

Massachusetts has about 33,500 miles (53,910 kilometers) of roads and highways, nearly all of which are paved or surfaced. The Massachusetts Turnpike, a toll road, stretches westward from Boston to the New York state line. The Circumferential Highway swings in an arc around Boston and its suburbs, from Gloucester to Braintree.

Boston is the main seaport for Massachusetts and for much of New England. It handles about 25 million short tons (23 million metric tons) of cargo a year. Fall River, the second most important port in the state, handles mostly petroleum products.

Communication. In 1639, Stephen Daye set up the first printing press in the English colonies in Cambridge.

HISTORIC

MASSACHUSETTS

The Sewing Machine was invented by Elias Howe at Cambridge in 1845.

The Slavery Abolition Movement was promoted in New England by William Lloyd Garrison in the 1830's.

The Telephone was invented by Alexander Graham Bell in Boston in 1876.

John Adams   John Quincy Adams
both born in Braintree (now Quincy)

John F. Kennedy
born in Brookline

MASSACHUSETTS / History

Indian Days. Indians probably lived in the Massachusetts region more than 3,000 years ago. Early white explorers saw Algonkian Indians in the region about 1500. The Algonkian tribes included the Massachusett, Mohican, Nauset, Nipmuc, Pennacook, Pocomtuc, and Wampanoag. Disease killed many of these Indians in 1616 and 1617. By the time the Pilgrims arrived in 1620, the Indian population had dropped from about 30,000 to about 7,000.

Early Exploration. The first Europeans to reach Massachusetts were probably Vikings led by Leif Ericson in about the year 1000. Some French and Spanish fishermen may have visited the region during the 1400's. Historians believe that John Cabot sighted the Massachusetts coast in 1498, six years after Christopher Columbus' first voyage to America. In 1602, Bartholomew Gosnold of England landed on Cuttyhunk Island in the Elizabeth Islands. He gave Cape Cod its name. In 1605

and 1606, Samuel de Champlain of France drew maps of the New England shoreline. John Smith, an English sea captain, sailed along the Massachusetts coast in 1614. Smith's book, *A Description of New England*, guided the Pilgrims to Massachusetts.

The Pilgrims. In the early 1600's, a group of English Protestants separated from the Church of England. They wanted to worship God in their own way, but they were not permitted to do so. In 1620, more than a hundred of these people decided to make a *pilgrimage* (religious journey) to America. They hoped to find religious freedom there. On Sept. 16, 1620, these Pilgrims sailed from Plymouth, England, in the *Mayflower*. That November, the *Mayflower* anchored in what is now Provincetown harbor. Before leaving the ship, the Pilgrims drew up a plan of self-government, which they called the Mayflower Compact (see MAYFLOWER COMPACT). In December, the Pilgrims sailed across Cape

This was only 19 years after the Pilgrims landed in Massachusetts. In 1640, Daye printed *The Bay Psalm Book*, the first English-language book published in America.

The first two newspapers in the colonies were published in Boston. *Publick Occurrences Both Forreign and Domestick* was established in 1690. *The Boston News-Letter*, which was established in 1704, was the first successful newspaper in America.

Today, Massachusetts publishers issue about 230 newspapers. About 50 of them are dailies. The chief newspapers include *The Boston Globe*, the *Boston Herald American*, *The Christian Science Monitor* in Boston, *The Evening Gazette* in Worcester, *The Patriot Ledger* in

Quincy, the *Springfield Daily News*, the *Springfield Union*, *The Standard Times* in New Bedford, the *Sunday Herald Advertiser* in Boston, and the *Worcester Telegram*. About 280 periodicals also are issued by publishers in Massachusetts.

The state's oldest radio station, WGI, began broadcasting in Medford in 1920. The first television stations in Massachusetts, WBZ-TV and WNAC-TV, started in Boston in 1948. Today, Massachusetts has about 155 radio stations. There are also 13 television stations in the state.

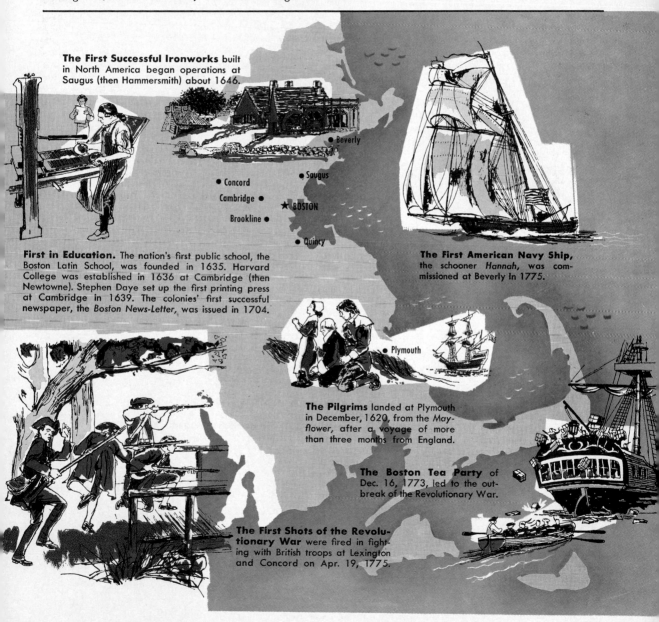

The First Successful Ironworks built in North America began operations at Saugus (then Hammersmith) about 1646.

First in Education. The nation's first public school, the Boston Latin School, was founded in 1635. Harvard College was established in 1636 at Cambridge (then Newtowne). Stephen Daye set up the first printing press at Cambridge in 1639. The colonies' first successful newspaper, the *Boston News-Letter*, was issued in 1704.

The First American Navy Ship, the schooner *Hannah*, was commissioned at Beverly in 1775.

The Pilgrims landed at Plymouth in December, 1620, from the *Mayflower*, after a voyage of more than three months from England.

The Boston Tea Party of Dec. 16, 1773, led to the outbreak of the Revolutionary War.

The First Shots of the Revolutionary War were fired in fighting with British troops at Lexington and Concord on Apr. 19, 1775.

Cod Bay and settled in Plymouth. See PILGRIM; MAY-
FLOWER.

The Pilgrims suffered great hardships during their
first winter in America. They had little food other than
the game they could hunt. Their houses were crude
bark shelters. About half the settlers died during the
winter of 1620-1621.

Early in 1621, the Pilgrims became friendly with
some Indians. The Indians taught them how to plant
corn and beans. By the time cold weather came again,
the settlers were living more comfortably. They had
enough food to last through the winter. The Pilgrims
celebrated the first New England Thanksgiving in 1621.
They gave thanks to God for delivering them from hunger and hardship (see THANKSGIVING DAY).

More settlers came to the Plymouth Colony during
the years that followed. Within 20 years after the Pilgrims landed, Plymouth Colony had eight towns and
about 2,500 persons.

The Puritans. In 1629, King Charles I of England
granted a charter to a group called the Puritans. The
charter gave the Puritans the right to settle and govern
an English colony in the Massachusetts Bay area. John
Winthrop, a London lawyer, led about 1,000 Puritans
to Massachusetts in 1630. They joined a settlement
that had been established in Salem about three years
earlier. In 1630, the Puritans left Salem and founded a
new settlement in the area of present-day Boston. The
Puritan colony prospered and grew. By 1640, the Massachusetts Bay Colony had about 10,000 settlers. See
PURITAN.

Colonial Days. The Massachusetts Bay Colony established political freedom and a representative form of
government. In 1641, the first code of laws of the colony
was set down in a document known as the Body of
Liberties. But the Puritans permitted no religion except
their own in the colony. Some religious groups were put
out of the colony, and others left on their own. These
Massachusetts settlers helped colonize other parts of
New England in their search for religious freedom. They
established settlements in Connecticut in 1635, Rhode
Island in 1636, New Hampshire in 1638, and Maine in
1652. Connecticut and Rhode Island soon became independent colonies. New Hampshire did not separate
from Massachusetts until 1680. Maine remained a part
of Massachusetts until 1820.

King Philip's War. Massasoit, chief of the Wampanoag tribe, had been a close friend of the Plymouth colonists. But his son, King Philip, who became chief in
1662, feared the white settlers. He believed that they
would wipe out the Indians and seize their lands.

In 1675, King Philip rose up against the colonists in
an attempt to protect his people and their homelands.
He planned to massacre all white settlers in New Eng-
land. The struggle became known as King Philip's War.
White and Indian settlements were burned and hun-
dreds of men, women, and children died on both sides.
An Indian serving with colonial troops killed King
Philip in 1676, but the struggle dragged on until 1678.
The Indian danger in eastern, central, and southern
Massachusetts ended. But a tenth of Massachusetts'
white male population had been wiped out.

Troubles with England. Although Massachusetts belonged to England, the colonists often resisted controls
from across the sea. England believed that its colonists
should trade only with the mother country. But many
Massachusetts colonists disagreed, and traded with
other countries. Attempts at stricter control had little
effect on some of the colonists. In 1684, King Charles II
canceled the Massachusetts charter. James II became
king of England in 1685.

In 1686, King James established a government in
Massachusetts and other northern colonies called the
Dominion of New England. The king made Sir Edmund
Andros governor of the dominion. King James was
overthrown in 1688. His daughter, Mary, and her husband, Prince William of Orange, became joint rulers of
England. When the Massachusetts colonists received
the news, they put Andros out of office and set up a
temporary government of their own. William and Mary
granted a new charter to Massachusetts in 1691. This
charter combined the Plymouth Colony with the Massachusetts Bay Colony and added the island of Martha's
Vineyard.

In 1692, Sir William Phips became Massachusetts'
first royal governor. One of his most important acts was
to end the persecution of persons believed to be witches
(see WITCHCRAFT).

The French and Indian Wars. In 1689, the first of the
four French and Indian Wars broke out. The English
colonists fought the French colonists and France's Indian allies. Between 1689 and 1713, settlers along
Massachusetts' northern and western borders fought off
continuous French and Indian attacks. In 1713, Great
Britain, France, and other European nations signed a
peace treaty at Utrecht, Holland. An era of prosperity
began in Massachusetts. Dozens of towns sprang up in
the central and western areas of the colony.

The French and Indian Wars broke out again in the
1740's. They finally ended in 1763 with victory for the
British.

Pre-Revolutionary Days. The colonial wars left
Britain in debt. To help pay for defense of the colonies,
the British placed severe taxes on the American colonies. The Massachusetts colonists ignored most of these
taxes. But the Stamp Act of 1765 led to bitter protests
(see STAMP ACT). The cry of "no taxation without representation" spread through the colony. An angry mob
destroyed the lieutenant governor's home. The presence
of British soldiers in Boston added to the bitterness between the colonists and the Crown. In 1770, British
soldiers killed several colonists while fighting a Boston
mob. This incident became known as the Boston Massacre. In 1773, angry colonists staged the Boston Tea
Party to protest a British tea tax. The colonists dumped
340 chests of British tea into Boston Harbor.

The British passed a series of measures to punish the
colonists. But these measures merely angered the colonists more and helped bring all the American colonies
together. On April 18, 1775, British troops marched
from Boston to seize supplies of gunpowder hidden by
the colonists at Concord. Paul Revere and others rode
across the Massachusetts countryside to warn their
fellow patriots that the British were coming. The next
morning, American minutemen at Lexington fought
the opening battle of the Revolutionary War (see
MINUTEMAN).

Halliday Historic Photo

Boston Harbor in 1768 is shown in an engraving by Paul Revere. British warships fill the harbor, and soldiers pour into the city.

The Revolutionary War began in Massachusetts. Much of the early fighting took place on Massachusetts soil. Massachusetts soldiers fought bravely at Lexington, Concord, and at Bunker Hill. On July 3, 1775, General George Washington took command of the Continental Army in Cambridge. In the spring of 1776, Washington drove the British out of Boston in the first major American victory of the war. Much of the fighting moved out of Massachusetts and into New York, New Jersey, and Pennsylvania in 1776. But Massachusetts continued to send men and supplies to the American forces. At sea, Massachusetts ships inflicted heavy damage on British merchant ships.

The effects of the Revolutionary War in Massachusetts were felt most by the farmers. Prices of farm products dropped after the war ended in 1783. Money became so scarce that many farmers could not pay their taxes or debts. The farmers, facing the danger of losing their farms and going to prison, grew restless. In September, 1786, Daniel Shays led a group of angry farmers to protest in front of the courthouse in Springfield. Fighting broke out between the farmers and government troops. The fighting, which became known as Shays' Rebellion, ended when the farmers surrendered in February, 1787.

Massachusetts farmers also opposed *ratification* (approval) of the United States Constitution. They felt that the Constitution was more favorable to trade and finance than to agriculture. On Feb. 6, 1788, Massachusetts ratified the Constitution and became the sixth state in the Union. Massachusetts ratified the Constitution only on the condition that a bill of rights be added. The Bill of Rights to the United States Constitution went into effect on Dec. 15, 1791.

Progress as a State. Massachusetts prospered during its early years as a state. In the early 1800's, France and Britain were at war. American shipowners who were willing to send their vessels into European waters could make huge profits. But both the British and the French tried to attack ships bound for their enemy's ports. President Thomas Jefferson feared that such an attack on an American ship might force the United States into the war. In 1807, he persuaded Congress to pass an embargo act, which stopped all American trade with other countries.

Hardships resulting from the embargo and the War of 1812 forced a new way of life upon the people of Massachusetts. Goods had to be manufactured at home rather than imported. In 1814, Francis Cabot Lowell built a textile factory in Waltham. It was one of the first factories in the United States. A number of other textile mills were soon operating in eastern Massachusetts. With the opening of New York's Erie Canal in 1825, crops could be brought to New England from the west. Farming in Massachusetts suffered. Many farmers left the state or went to work in factories.

The whaling industry flourished in New Bedford, Nantucket, and Boston until the early 1860's. It declined after kerosene replaced whale oil.

The *abolitionist* (antislavery) movement received wide support in Massachusetts. In 1831, William Lloyd

--------- **IMPORTANT DATES IN MASSACHUSETTS** ---------

1602 Bartholomew Gosnold, an English explorer, visited the Massachusetts region.

1620 The Pilgrims landed at Plymouth.

1630 The Puritans founded Boston.

1636 Harvard became the first college in the colonies.

1641 Massachusetts adopted its first code of law, the Body of Liberties.

1675-1678 Massachusetts colonists won King Philip's War against the Indians.

1689-1763 Massachusetts colonists helped the British win the French and Indian Wars.

1691 Plymouth and the Massachusetts Bay colonies were combined into one colony.

1764 The colonists began to resist enforcement of British tax laws.

1770 British soldiers killed several colonists in the Boston Massacre.

1773 Patriots dumped British tea into Boston Harbor during the Boston Tea Party.

1775 The American Revolutionary War began at Lexington and Concord.

1780 Massachusetts adopted its constitution.

1788 Massachusetts became the sixth state in the Union on February 6.

1797 John Adams of Massachusetts became President of the United States.

1807 The Embargo Act ruined Massachusetts shipping, and led to the rise of manufacturing.

1825 John Quincy Adams of Massachusetts became President of the United States.

1831 William Lloyd Garrison began publishing his antislavery newspaper *The Liberator* in Boston.

1912 A strike of textile workers at Lawrence led to improved conditions in the textile industry.

1919 Settlement of the Boston police strike brought national prominence to Governor Calvin Coolidge.

1938 A hurricane killed several hundred persons and caused millions of dollars in damages in Massachusetts.

1959 The U.S. Navy launched its first nuclear-powered surface ship, the cruiser *Long Beach*, at Quincy.

1961 John F. Kennedy of Massachusetts became President of the United States.

1971 Massachusetts began a major reorganization of its state government, including the consolidation of more than 150 smaller agencies into about 10 new departments.

Garrison of Boston began publishing his antislavery newspaper *The Liberator*. In 1832, abolitionists formed the New England Anti-Slavery Society in Boston. The society helped slaves escape to Canada. Some people in Massachusetts opposed the abolitionist movement. They objected to what they considered extremist tactics. They also feared that the Southern planters might cut off the cotton supply for the Massachusetts textile industry.

In 1850, Congress passed a series of acts which it hoped would settle the conflict between slave owners and those who opposed slavery. These acts were called the Compromise of 1850 (see COMPROMISE OF 1850). Senator Daniel Webster of Massachusetts defended the compromise as necessary to preserve the Union. But many persons in Massachusetts disagreed. Abraham Lincoln and the Republican Party carried the state in the 1860 presidential election.

Massachusetts gave strong support to the Union during the Civil War (1861-1865). The state furnished more than 125,000 men to the Union Army and about 20,000 men to the Navy. Massachusetts shipbuilders built and equipped many Union ships.

Industry in the state expanded after the war. The textile industry prospered, and the leather and metal products industries also grew rapidly. Thousands of immigrants poured into the state to meet the great demand for industrial labor.

George Zimberg

Boston's New Government Center, shown in this model, was built in Scollay Square in the 1960's and 1970's.

In 1876, the famous inventor Alexander Graham Bell developed the telephone in Boston. A telephone line between Boston and Providence, R.I., was installed in 1881.

The Early 1900's. Massachusetts' population swelled to about 2½ million by 1900. About 30 per cent of the state's people came to the United States from other countries. This huge number of people, with their variety of backgrounds, brought new problems into the state. Communities had to provide such services as water supply, sewage, housing, and police protection.

The State Governors of Massachusetts

	Party	Term		Party	Term
John Hancock	None	1780-1785	John D. Long	Republican	1880-1883
James Bowdoin	None	1785-1787	Benjamin F. Butler	Democratic	1883-1884
John Hancock	None	1787-1793	George D. Robinson	Republican	1884-1887
Samuel Adams	None	1793-1797	Oliver Ames	Republican	1887-1890
Increase Sumner	Federalist	1797-1800	John Q. A. Brackett	Republican	1890-1891
Caleb Strong	Federalist	1800-1807	William E. Russell	Democratic	1891-1894
James Sullivan	*Dem.-Rep.	1807-1809	Frederic T. Greenhalge	Republican	1894-1896
Levi Lincoln	Dem.-Rep.	1809	Roger Wolcott	Republican	1896-1900
Christopher Gore	Federalist	1809-1810	Winthrop M. Crane	Republican	1900-1903
Elbridge Gerry	Dem.-Rep.	1810-1812	John L. Bates	Republican	1903-1905
Caleb Strong	Federalist	1812-1816	William L. Douglas	Democratic	1905-1906
John Brooks	Federalist	1816-1823	Curtis Guild, Jr.	Republican	1906-1909
William Eustis	Dem.-Rep.	1823-1825	Eben S. Draper	Republican	1909-1911
Marcus Morton	Dem.-Rep.	1825	Eugene N. Foss	Democratic	1911-1914
Levi Lincoln	Dem.-Rep.	1825-1834	David I. Walsh	Democratic	1914-1916
John Davis	Whig	1834-1835	Samuel W. McCall	Republican	1916-1919
Samuel Armstrong	Whig	1835-1836	Calvin Coolidge	Republican	1919-1921
Edward Everett	Whig	1836-1840	Channing H. Cox	Republican	1921-1925
Marcus Morton	Democratic	1840-1841	Alvin T. Fuller	Republican	1925-1929
John Davis	Whig	1841-1843	Frank G. Allen	Republican	1929-1931
Marcus Morton	Democratic	1843-1844	Joseph B. Ely	Democratic	1931-1935
George N. Briggs	Whig	1844-1851	James M. Curley	Democratic	1935-1937
George S. Boutwell	Democratic	1851-1853	Charles F. Hurley	Democratic	1937-1939
John H. Clifford	Whig	1853-1854	Leverett Saltonstall	Republican	1939-1945
Emory Washburn	Whig	1854-1855	Maurice J. Tobin	Democratic	1945-1947
Henry J. Gardner	†American	1855-1858	Robert F. Bradford	Republican	1947-1949
Nathaniel P. Banks	Republican	1858-1861	Paul A. Dever	Democratic	1949-1953
John A. Andrew	Republican	1861-1866	Christian A. Herter	Republican	1953-1957
Alexander H. Bullock	Republican	1866-1869	Foster Furcolo	Democratic	1957-1961
William Claflin	Republican	1869-1872	John A. Volpe	Republican	1961-1963
William B. Washburn	Republican	1872-1874	Endicott Peabody	Democratic	1963-1965
Thomas Talbot	Republican	1874-1875	John A. Volpe	Republican	1965-1969
William Gaston	Democratic	1875-1876	Francis Sargent	Republican	1969-1975
Alexander H. Rice	Republican	1876-1879	Michael S. Dukakis	Democratic	1975-1979
Thomas Talbot	Republican	1879-1880	Edward J. King	Democratic	1979-

*Democratic-Republican   †Know-Nothing

Industrial workers became unhappy with wages and working conditions. A textile strike in Lawrence in 1912 brought nationwide attention to poor working conditions in the textile industry. Improvements followed the strike.

The United States entered World War I in 1917. The Yankee (26th) Division of Massachusetts was the first National Guard division to reach the battlefields of France. Prices climbed in Massachusetts during the war, and workers demanded higher wages to meet the increased cost of living. But often such demands were not met. In 1919, the mayor of Boston refused to let the city's policemen form a union. About three-fourths of the Boston police force went on strike. Governor Calvin Coolidge helped end the strike by sending the National Guard into Boston. Coolidge gained nationwide fame because of his action and was elected Vice-President of the United States in 1920. Three years later, Coolidge became President after President Warren G. Harding died.

Massachusetts' economy suffered during the 1920's because of competition from the textile and shoe industries in southern and western states. But other industries in Massachusetts continued to prosper. In 1929, the Great Depression hit the United States. Massachusetts carried on its own unemployment-relief program until the federal government organized nationwide programs. In 1938, a hurricane killed hundreds of persons in Massachusetts and caused great property damage.

The Mid-1900's. The state's economy soared during World War II (1939-1945). Massachusetts factories and shipyards produced huge quantities of war materials. The economy of the state continued to prosper after the war.

Many traditional Massachusetts industries, including the manufacture of shoes and textiles, declined greatly during the 1950's and 1960's. Between 1959 and 1963, the state's employment rate fell below the national average. Many industries in the state began to switch to space and rocket research or the production of electronics equipment. Hundreds of research laboratories developed in and around Boston, using the facilities and personnel of the many colleges and universities in the area.

The U.S. Navy launched its first nuclear surface ship, the cruiser *Long Beach*, at Quincy in 1959. In 1960, an atomic energy plant began operations in Rowe.

Like many other states, Massachusetts faced serious racial problems during the mid-1900's. In 1957, the state legislature prohibited segregation in public housing. New legislation in 1963 made it illegal in most private dwellings as well.

During the 1950's and 1960's, the Kennedy family of Brookline became powerful in state and national politics. John F. Kennedy served as President of the United States from 1961 until his assassination in 1963. When elected President, Kennedy was representing Massachusetts in the United States Senate. His brother, Robert F. Kennedy, served as United States attorney general from 1961 to 1964. Robert Kennedy was elected to the United States Senate from New York in 1964. He was assassinated in 1968 while campaigning in Los Angeles for the Democratic presidential nomination. The youngest Kennedy brother, Edward M. Kennedy, has served as a U.S. senator from Massachusetts since 1962.

Massachusetts Today faces several problems common to many states. These problems include air and water pollution, overcrowded cities, racial tension, and rising taxes. Many Massachusetts industries are moving from cities to suburban areas. These areas offer lower real estate taxes, more space, and better transportation facilities.

The high cost of Massachusetts' government and government services, especially its welfare program, contributes to the state's high tax rate. In 1969, the Massachusetts legislature approved a reorganization plan for the state government. This plan, designed to help reduce costs, went into effect in 1971. Under the reorganization plan, about 10 new state departments absorbed more than 150 smaller departments and agencies. The state uses profits from a lottery established in 1971 to help aid cities and towns.

Massachusetts' shoe and textile industries continue to decline. In addition, a decrease in defense spending by the federal government has cut into atomic energy and research in the state. But expansion in other areas promises to help steady the Massachusetts economy. The growth rate has increased in the computer industry and in such businesses as banking and insurance. The growth rate has also increased in the fields of education and medicine.　　　　　BENJAMIN W. LABAREE,
MICHAEL G. MENSOIAN, and WALTER E. SALVI, JR.

MASSACHUSETTS/Study Aids

Related Articles in WORLD BOOK include:

BIOGRAPHIES

MASSACHUSETTS

Lowell, James Russell
Mann, Horace
Martin, Joseph W., Jr.
Massasoit
Mather (family)
McCormack, John W.
O'Neill, Thomas P.
Otis, James
Paine, Robert T.
Parker, Theodore
Phillips, Wendell
Pickering, Timothy
Prescott, William
Randolph, Edward
Revere, Paul
Richardson, Elliot L.
Samoset

Sewall, Samuel
Shirley, William
Squanto
Standish, Miles
Sumner, Charles
Thoreau, Henry David
Volpe, John A.
Ward, Artemas
Warren, Joseph
Wheatley, Phillis
White, Peregrlne
Whittier, John G.
Williams, Roger
Wilson, Henry
Winslow, Edward
Winthrop (family)

CITIES AND TOWNS

Arlington
Boston
Brockton
Brookline
Cambridge
Chicopee
Concord
Fall River
Fitchburg

Gardner
Gloucester
Haverhill
Lynn
Medford
Nantucket
New Bedford
Newton
Northampton

Plymouth
Quincy
Revere
Salem
Somerville
Springfield
Weymouth
Worcester

HISTORY

Boston Massacre
Boston Tea Party
Brook Farm
Civil War
Colonial Life in America
Massachusetts Bay Colony
Mayflower
Mayflower Compact
Money (History of
   United States
   Currency; picture)

Pilgrim
Pine-Tree Shilling
Plymouth Colony
Plymouth Rock
Puritan
Revolutionary War in
   America
Shays' Rebellion
Witchcraft

PHYSICAL FEATURES

Berkshire Hills
Cape Cod
Cape Cod Canal
Connecticut River

Housatonic River
Martha's Vineyard
Merrimack River

OTHER RELATED ARTICLES

Hoosac Tunnel
Leather (graph)
New England

Publishing (graph)
Westover Air Force Base
Winsor Dam

Outline

I. **Government**
   A. Constitution
   B. Executive
   C. Legislature
   D. Courts
   E. Local Government
   F. Taxation
   G. Politics
II. **People**
III. **Education**
   A. Schools
   B. Libraries
   C. Museums
IV. **A Visitor's Guide**
   A. Places to Visit
   B. Annual Events
V. **The Land**
   A. Land Regions
   B. Coastline
   C. Islands
   D. Rivers and Lakes
VI. **Climate**

VII. **Economy**
   A. Natural Resources
   B. Manufacturing
   C. Agriculture
   D. Fishing Industry
   E. Mining
   F. Electric Power
   G. Transportation
   H. Communication
VIII. **History**

Questions

What nationwide holiday was first observed in Massachusetts? What was the occasion?

What distinction does the Massachusetts constitution have among all state constitutions?

What section of Massachusetts has the most fertile soil?

When and where was the first printing press in the British colonies set up?

What was Shays' Rebellion?

What great stride in education took place in the Massachusetts Bay Colony in 1647?

What mountain ranges extend into Massachusetts?

Why did Britain tax the American colonies after the French and Indian Wars? How did these taxes start a chain of events that led to the Revolutionary War?

Which three U.S. Presidents were born in Massachusetts?

How does local government operate in Massachusetts towns?

Books for Young Readers

BECK, BARBARA L. *The Pilgrims of Plymouth.* Watts, 1972.

CARPENTER, ALLAN. *Massachusetts.* Rev. ed. Childrens Press, 1978.

CLAPP, PATRICIA. *Constance: A Story of Early Plymouth.* Morrow, 1968. Fiction.

CRAWFORD, DEBORAH. *Four Women in a Violent Time: Anne Hutchinson, Mary Dyer, Lady Deborah Moody, and Penelope Stout.* Crown, 1970.

DAUGHERTY, JAMES H. *The Landing of the Pilgrims.* Random House, 1950.

DICKINSON, ALICE. *The Boston Massacre, March 5, 1770: A Colonial Street Fight Erupts into Violence.* Watts, 1968. *The Colony of Massachusetts.* 1975.

FORBES, ESTHER. *Johnny Tremain.* Houghton, 1943. Fiction. This Newbery medal winner tells of Revolutionary War days.

JACOBS, WILLIAM J. *William Bradford of Plymouth Colony.* Watts, 1974.

MARSHALL, CYRIL L. *The Mayflower Destiny.* Stackpole, 1975.

MORISON, SAMUEL E. *The Story of the Old Colony of New Plymouth (1620-1692).* Knopf, 1956.

PETRY, ANN. *Tituba of Salem Village.* Harper, 1964. Fiction.

SMITH, ROBERT. *The Massachusetts Colony.* Macmillan, 1969.

WOOD, JAMES PLAYSTED. *Colonial Massachusetts.* Nelson, 1969.

Books for Older Readers

BARBROOK, ALEC T. *God Save the Commonwealth: An Electoral History of Massachusetts.* Univ. of Massachusetts Press, 1973.

BROWN, RICHARD D. *Massachusetts: A Bicentennial History.* Norton, 1978.

FLEMING, THOMAS J. *One Small Candle: The Pilgrims' First Year in America.* Norton, 1964.

FORBES, ESTHER. *Paul Revere and the World He Lived In.* Houghton, 1942.

Massachusetts: A Guide to the Pilgrim State. 2nd ed. by Ray Bearse. Houghton, 1971.

MORISON, SAMUEL E. *Builders of the Bay Colony.* Rev. ed. Houghton, 1964.

WHITEHILL, WALTER M., and KOTKER, NORMAN. *Massachusetts: A Pictorial History.* Scribner, 1976.

WILLIAMS, SELMA R. *Kings, Commoners, and Colonists: Puritan Politics in Old New England, 1603-1660.* Atheneum, 1974.

MASSACHUSETTS, UNIVERSITY OF, is a state-supported coeducational university with campuses in Amherst and Boston, and a medical center in Worcester, Mass. The Amherst campus has colleges of arts and sciences and of food and natural resources; schools of business administration, education, engineering, health sciences, and physical education; a two-year school of agriculture; and a graduate school. It grants associate's, bachelor's, master's, and doctor's degrees. The Boston campus offers liberal arts programs leading to bachelor's and master's degrees.

The University of Massachusetts and Amherst, Hampshire, Mount Holyoke, and Smith colleges have set up cooperative programs. One program allows a student to take courses at any of the other schools if they are not offered at his or her own school. The schools also offer doctor's degrees jointly in several fields.

The University of Massachusetts was chartered in 1863 as Massachusetts Agricultural College. It took its present name in 1947. The Boston campus opened in 1965. For enrollment, see UNIVERSITIES AND COLLEGES (table).   Critically reviewed by the UNIVERSITY OF MASSACHUSETTS

MASSACHUSETTS BAY COLONY was one of the first settlements in New England. It was established in 1628 in Salem, Mass., by a small group of English Puritans. These Puritans wished to keep their religion pure, and free from what they felt were evils of the Church of England. John Endecott led the first group of settlers. In 1630, John Winthrop, who had become governor of the colony, led 1,000 more settlers to Boston.

The Puritans firmly believed that their simple way of carrying on a religious meeting and of organizing a congregation was the only correct one. They were unfriendly to newcomers to their settlements who proposed any form of worship that differed from their own. They also refused to obey trade laws passed by the English. As a result, in 1684, the Puritans lost the royal charter they had been given in 1629. In 1691, after they agreed to observe the king's rules, a new charter was issued. This charter included the Plymouth Colony as part of the Massachusetts Bay Colony. The colonists were governed under this charter until 1775, when the Revolutionary War began.

The colony's government expelled some settlers who disagreed with the religious beliefs of the founders. Many of those who left found new homes in Rhode Island or New Hampshire.

The colonists of the Massachusetts Bay Colony made many contributions to American life. Among the most important of these were a practical, local self-government and a love for learning.   MARSHALL SMELSER

See also ENDECOTT, JOHN; MASSACHUSETTS (History); PURITAN; WILLIAMS, ROGER; WINTHROP (family).

MASSACHUSETTS INSTITUTE OF TECHNOLOGY (M.I.T.) is a private coeducational university in Cambridge, Mass. It is famous for its scientific research activities and for combining education and research in all programs. The institute includes schools of architecture and planning, engineering, humanities and social science, management, and science. All these schools offer graduate programs. M.I.T. grants bachelor's, master's, and doctor's degrees.

M.I.T. has research centers in several broad fields, including cancer, communications sciences, earth and life sciences, energy, international and urban studies, and nuclear and space science. More than 70 laboratories at the institute conduct research in all fields represented at M.I.T. The institution has a wide sports program and sponsors activities in drama, music, publications, and other cultural areas.

M.I.T. was founded in Boston in 1861 and moved to Cambridge in 1916. The campus extends for more than a mile (1.6 kilometers) along the Charles River. For enrollment, see UNIVERSITIES AND COLLEGES (table).
          Critically reviewed by MASSACHUSETTS INSTITUTE OF TECHNOLOGY

MASSACRE OF SAINT BARTHOLOMEW'S DAY. See SAINT BARTHOLOMEW'S DAY, MASSACRE OF.

MASSAGE, *muh SAHZH,* is a type of medical treatment given by stroking, kneading, and striking certain muscular parts of the body. It is used to improve circulation, soothe the nerves, and stimulate the digestive organs. Massage also helps to increase the tone of muscles after a long illness. People who give massages should be well trained, and should have a knowledge of human anatomy. They must be able to use their hands skillfully in stroking motions on muscles. A man who gives a massage is called a *masseur,* and a woman, a *masseuse.*

Massage was a luxury to the ancient Greeks and Romans. The Chinese, Egyptians, Japanese, and Turks have used it for hundreds of years.   W. W. BAUER

MASSALIA. See MARSEILLE.

MASSANUTTEN. See VIRGINIA (Land Regions).

MASSASOIT, *MAS uh SOIT* (1580?-1661), was a chief of the Wampanoag tribe of Indians that lived in what is now southern Massachusetts and Rhode Island. He made a treaty with Governor John Carver of Plymouth Colony in the spring of 1621, shortly after the Pilgrims landed in America.

He agreed that his people would not harm the Pilgrims as long as he lived. In turn, the Pilgrims guaran-

Dallin

A Statue of Massasoit by the American sculptor Cyrus Dallin stands on a Pilgrim burial ground in Plymouth, Mass.

teed to protect the Indians and their rights. Massasoit kept the peace all his life.

As a reward for the Indians' friendship, Massasoit and a number of his braves are said to have been invited to join the feast in Plymouth Colony on the first Thanksgiving Day. Afterward, the chief solemnly told the English: "The Great Spirit surely must love his white children best."

When Massasoit died, he was succeeded by his elder son, Wamsutta, known as Alexander. Massasoit's younger son, Metacomet, known as King Philip, succeeded Alexander. E. ADAMSON HOEBEL

See also PHILIP, KING; PLYMOUTH COLONY (The First Year in the New Land).

MASSECUITE. See MOLASSES.

MASSENET, *mas NAY,* **JULES** (1842-1912), was a French composer best known for his operas. Massenet's operas are noted for their dramatic sense and graceful melodies. Perhaps the best known of his 25 operas is *Manon* (1884). The leading roles of Manon and her lover, Des Grieux, are still popular with singers. Massenet's other operas include *Werther* (1892), *Thaïs* (1894), and *Don Quichotte* (1910). He also wrote orchestral works, works for orchestra and voice, and more than 200 songs that rank among his best compositions.

Jules Émile Frédéric Massenet was born in Montaud, near St.-Étienne. While a student at the Paris Conservatory, he studied composition with the composer Ambroise Thomas. From 1878 to 1896, Massenet was a professor of composition at the conservatory. MILOŠ VELIMIROVIĆ

MASSEUR. See MASSAGE.

MASSEY, VINCENT (1887-1967), became the first Canadian-born governor general of Canada in 1952. He served in the post until 1959.

Massey had a long career in public service. During World War I, he served on the staff of the Military District No. 2 (Canada). He became secretary of the Government Repatriation Committee of Canada in 1918.

In 1926, Massey was appointed to the Canadian delegation that attended the Imperial Conference in London. At this conference, Canada won the right to name its own diplomatic representatives to the United States. Massey was minister to the United States from 1926 to 1930. From 1935 to 1946, he served as high commissioner for Canada in Great Britain.

Massey became noted for his great interest in education. In 1949, the Canadian government made him chairman of a royal commission to obtain information on the needs and desires of the people in relation to science, literature, and the arts. The commission made recommendations to strengthen the arts and sciences.

Massey was born in Toronto of a prominent industrial family. He studied at St. Andrew's College, and graduated from the University of Toronto. After

United Press Int.

Vincent Massey

receiving a postgraduate degree at Oxford University, he lectured at the University of Toronto from 1913 to 1915. Massey later served there as chancellor from 1947 to 1953. He was president of the Massey-Harris Company, manufacturers of farm implements, from 1921 to 1925. LUCIEN BRAULT

MASSINE, *mah SEEN,* **LEONIDE** (1896-1979), was a great Russian dancer and *choreographer* (dance composer). Massine invented a dance form called *symphonic ballet,* in which dances with no story were choreographed to well-known symphonies. His successful *Les Présages* to Tchaikovsky's *Fifth Symphony* in 1933 was the first of these ballets. It led to what has become a standard ballet form. Massine also choreographed and danced key roles in the ballets *The Three-Cornered Hat, Le Beau Danube,* and *Gaîté Parisienne.*

Massine was born in Moscow. He joined Sergei Diaghilev's Ballets Russes in 1913. Massine was director, dancer, and choreographer of Col. W. de Basil's Ballets Russes from 1932 to 1938. He served in the same capacity with the Ballet Russe de Monte Carlo from 1938 to 1941. P. W. MANCHESTER

MASSINGER, PHILIP (1583-1640), an English playwright, is best known for his comedy *A New Way to Pay Old Debts* (1621 or 1622). The play's chief character, the monstrous villain Sir Giles Overreach, so appealed to actors and audiences that the play was performed longer than any other non-Shakespearean play of the 1600's. The character of Sir Giles Overreach is based on the scandalous activities of a real nobleman, and the action is taken from Thomas Middleton's play *A Trick to Catch the Old One* (1608).

Massinger was born in Salisbury of a prominent family, and he was educated at Oxford. He wrote nearly 40 plays, some of them in collaboration with other playwrights. About 20 of his plays survive. From 1625 to his death, Massinger wrote one or two plays a year for The King's Men, the leading acting company of the day. ALAN S. DOWNER

MASSON, ANDRÉ. See PAINTING (Surrealism; picture); SURREALISM.

MAST. See SAILING (Spars); SHIP (History [with pictures]).

MASTABA. See PYRAMIDS (Egyptian Pyramids).

MASTECTOMY, *mas TEHK tuh mee,* is the surgical removal of a breast. In some cases, the tissues surrounding the breast are also taken out. Surgeons perform mastectomies to remove cancerous tumors and to prevent the cancer from spreading. There are two types of mastectomies: (1) radical and (2) simple.

A radical mastectomy involves more than the removal of the breast. It is performed if the physician suspects that the cancer may have spread beyond the breast to the *lymph nodes* of the underarm area (see LYMPHATIC SYSTEM). In a *conventional radical mastectomy,* the surgeon removes the breast; the underarm lymph nodes; and the pectoral muscles, which connect the breast to the ribs. A *modified radical mastectomy* involves the removal of the breast and most of the underarm lymph nodes, but leaves the pectoral muscles.

The conventional radical mastectomy was developed in 1894 by William S. Halsted, an American surgeon. It was the most common type of breast removal performed for cancer until the 1950's. Then, some surgeons began to use the modified radical, which results in less disfigurement. But many physicians questioned the effectiveness of the new procedure. By the late-1970's, studies indicated that the modified radical may be as effective as the conventional radical in cases where the cancer is detected at just one site in the breast. Early detection of breast cancer through self-examination and X rays has increased the number of cases in which a modified radical is performed.

A simple mastectomy consists of removing only the breast. This procedure is sometimes used in cases where the cancer appears to be confined to a single site. It also may be used to treat extremely early, microscopic breast tumors. In some cases, the surgeon may remove only the tumor and the breast tissue immediately surrounding it. This operation, called a *partial mastectomy* or a *lumpectomy*, causes the least disfigurement.

Physicians may prescribe anticancer drugs after a mastectomy in order to destroy any remaining cancer cells, especially if the cancer has spread to the underarm lymph nodes. After most lumpectomies, the remaining breast tissue is treated with radiation.

Most women who have had a mastectomy wear an artificial breast. In some cases, a plastic surgeon reconstructs the breast by implanting a material called *silicone gel* under the remaining tissue. TAPAS K. DAS GUPTA

See also CANCER.

MASTERS, EDGAR LEE (1869-1950), was an American author. He wrote novels, poetry, plays, biography, and history, but he became famous chiefly for one volume of poems, *Spoon River Anthology* (1915).

Masters modeled the *Anthology* on a collection of ancient Greek short poems and sayings called *The Greek Anthology*. Spoon River is an imaginary Midwestern village. Masters' work consists of more than 200 short poems in free verse. Each poem is spoken by a former resident of the village, now dead and buried in the Spoon River cemetery. Each of the dead persons seeks to interpret, from the grave, the meaning of life on earth.

Through the words of the dead, the village of Spoon River comes to life again, sometimes relating the histories of whole families. The community is seen as a place where life

Library of Congress
Edgar Lee Masters

was hard but where it could be good and satisfying. Among the best-known poems in the *Anthology* is one spoken by Petit, the Spoon River poet. Another poem is spoken by Ann Rutledge, a real-life girl whom young Abraham Lincoln supposedly loved.

Masters was born in Garnett, Kans., and grew up in Illinois. He studied law in his father's office in Lewistown, and was an attorney in Chicago from 1895 to 1920 when he devoted himself full-time to writing. Masters published his autobiography, *Across Spoon River*, in 1936. CLARK GRIFFITH

MASTERS AND JOHNSON, two American researchers, have made important contributions to the understanding of human sexual behavior. William Howell Masters (1915-   ), a physician, and his research associate, Virginia Eshelman Johnson (1925-   ), pioneered in the scientific study of sexual arousal and the treatment of sexual problems.

Masters began the sex research program at Washington University in St. Louis in 1954, and Johnson joined him in 1957. At that time, scientists knew little about the body's physiological responses to sexual stimulation. Masters and Johnson used motion pictures and special instruments to record such responses in men and women who volunteered to engage in sexual activity for the project.

Masters and Johnson wrote a summary of their findings called *Human Sexual Response* (1966). This book was written in technical language for physicians and other health scientists, but it became a best seller. The research of Masters and Johnson created great controversy. Their critics called them immoral and accused them of dehumanizing sex.

In 1964, Masters and Johnson established the Reproductive Biology Research Foundation (now called the Masters and Johnson Institute) in St. Louis. This clinic treats couples with sexual problems, trains other therapists, and conducts further research.

Masters and Johnson also wrote *Human Sexual Inadequacy* (1970), *The Pleasure Bond* (1975), and *Homosexuality in Perspective* (1979). Masters received his M.D. from the University of Rochester School of Medicine and Dentistry. Johnson began as a research assistant in the sex research project. Masters and Johnson were married in 1971. MARTIN WEISBERG

MASTERSINGER was one of a group of German poet-musicians who treated literary art as a sort of craft or trade. The name is from the German word *meistersinger*.

The tradition of the mastersingers began in the late Middle Ages when middle-class poets tried to revive the declining art of the *minnesingers*. The minnesingers were wandering poet-musicians, chiefly aristocrats (see MINNESINGER). Between the late 1200's and the late 1400's, the mastersingers developed rules for song composition and organized song schools modeled after medieval guilds. Members passed examinations for admission and promotion. Singing competitions were held and prizes were awarded.

Most mastersingers were businessmen and craftsmen. The most famous mastersinger was Hans Sachs, a Nuremberg shoemaker. The mastersingers reached their peak in the early 1500's, although the tradition continued into the 1800's.

In the early period, the *Tabulatur* (rule book) permitted composition only to prescribed melodies. But by the 1500's, original compositions were required to gain the title of *master*. Poetic themes were usually instructive stories. Mastersingers did not produce great literature, but achieved lasting fame through Richard Wagner's opera *Die Meistersinger*. JAMES F. POAG

MASTIC is a resin extracted from *Pistacia lentiscus*, a tree or small shrub that grows chiefly in southern Europe. Pharmacists use mastic as an ingredient in a mild cathartic. Mastic was once widely used as a protective dressing for wounds, and as a temporary protection for tooth cavities. It has also been used as a coating for tablets. Industry uses mastic for lacquers, varnishes, plasters, and tile cements, and also for calking.

Mastic resin has a pale yellowish color. It smells somewhat like balsam. K. L. KAUFMAN

See also CALKING; RESIN.

MASTICATION, MAS tuh KAY shun, is the first process in the digestion of food. The term is taken from a Latin word which means *to chew.* Mastication involves chewing or breaking the food into small pieces by grinding with the teeth. Mastication mixes the food with saliva, which reacts chemically with the food and also gives it a pasty texture. Saliva contains the enzyme *ptyalin,* which digests cooked starches into sugars. It also contains a slimy *mucus* that lubricates the food so it can be swallowed. Poor mastication causes overworking of digestive organs, and indigestion. ARTHUR C. GUYTON

See also DIGESTION; INDIGESTION.

MASTIFF, or OLD ENGLISH MASTIFF, is a breed of dog that was developed in England, perhaps about 55 B.C. It has a coat of short hair and an undercoat of dense hair. The coat is usually apricot, silver fawn (yellow brown), or dark fawn. Most mastiffs have a dark brown or black mouth, nose, and ears. They stand about 30 inches (76 centimeters) high at the shoulder, and weigh about 165 to 185 pounds (75 to 84 kilograms). See also DOG (picture: Working Dogs); GREAT DANE; BULLMASTIFF. OLGA DAKAN

MASTODON, MASS toh dahn, was an animal much like the elephant. It is now extinct. Mastodons first lived in North Africa about 40 million years ago. They spread to Asia, Europe, and the rest of Africa. Mastodons reached America about 15 million years ago, and lived there until at least 8,000 years ago.

There were about 100 different kinds of mastodons. They were stockier than and not as tall as elephants. Early mastodons had tusks in both jaws. Some of the later species lost the lower tusks. Others developed great, flat, lower tusks. These species are called *shovel-tuskers.* The mastodon's teeth were up to 3 inches (7.5 centimeters) wide and 6 inches (15 centimeters) long. Each tooth had four to six cross-rows of heavy enamel

Mastodon Americanus, painting by Charles R. Knight,
The American Museum of Natural History, New York

The Prehistoric Mastodon once roamed over North America. The animal was an ancient relative of present-day elephants.

cones which the mastodon used to grind plants it ate.

Scientific Classification. Mastodons belong to the mastodon family, *Mammutidae.* The American mastodon is genus *Mammut,* species *M. americanum.* The European mastodon is *M. angustidens.* SAMUEL PAUL WELLES

See also MAMMOTH; PREHISTORIC ANIMAL.

MASTOID, MASS toid, is one of the five parts of the temporal bone of the skull. It is located at the side of the skull, just behind the ear. The name *mastoid* means *nipple-shaped.* This describes the bottom of the mastoid, which extends downward, forming the *mastoid process.* The mastoid process may be felt as the hard area just behind and below the ear. Some people call it the *mastoid bone.*

The mastoid process is porous, like a sponge. The *pores,* or hollow spaces, are called the *mastoid cells.* They vary greatly in size and number in different individuals. The mastoid cells connect with a larger, irregularly shaped cavity called the *tympanic antrum,* or *cavity.* The tympanic antrum opens into the middle ear. The mucous membrane of the middle ear extends into the tympanic antrum and the mastoid cells. Infections of the middle ear spread through these connections and may infect the mastoid cells. Doctors call infection of the mastoid cells *mastoiditis.*

Mastoiditis may be serious, because the mastoid cells are close to the organs of hearing, to important nerves, to the covering of the brain, and to the jugular vein. A mastoid infection may spread to any of these.

Mastoiditis may result from blowing the nose the wrong way. If both nostrils are held closed when a person blows his or her nose, germs may be forced from the throat into the *Eustachian tubes.* These tubes connect the throat with the middle ear. Antibiotics have been effective in curing mastoiditis, but severe cases may require surgery (see ANTIBIOTIC). WILLIAM V. MAYER

See also EAR (The Middle Ear); HUMAN BODY (Trans-Vision three-dimensional color picture).

MASURIUM. See TECHNETIUM.

MAT. See PAPIER-MÂCHÉ; STEREOTYPING.

MATA HARI (1876-1917), a Dutch dancer, was executed by the French on charges of being a German spy during World War I. She began her stage career after an unhappy marriage to a Dutch colonial officer. She soon became popular throughout Europe, pretending to be a Javanese temple dancer. She apparently became associated with the German spy network when her strange dances lost their popularity. She was born Margaretha Gertrud Zelle at Leeuwarden, in The Netherlands. See also SPY. JOHN R. ELTING

MATADOR. See BULLFIGHTING.

MATANUSKA VALLEY is the site of a large-scale farming experiment carried on by the federal government in Alaska. The valley lies in south-central Alaska about 48 miles (77 kilometers) northeast of the city of Anchorage. High mountains to the north help to protect Matanuska from extreme climate. The soil is fertile. The government organized the new farming community in 1935. It established on farms about 200 families who had suffered from the economic depression in Michigan, Minnesota, and Wisconsin. Long, warm, summer days account for the high quality of vegetables grown in the area. Dairying and poultry raising also are important occupations. The Alaska Railroad and a modern highway carry produce out. LYMAN E. ALLEN

MATCH is a slender piece of cardboard or wood with a tip made of a chemical mixture that burns easily. Matches are used to produce fire. When the tip is rubbed against a rough or specially prepared surface, the chemicals burst into flame and ignite the match.

The United States ranks as the world's leading producer of matches. France, Russia, and Sweden also have large match industries. Matches, which were invented in the early 1800's, provided the first cheap, convenient method of producing fire.

Kinds of Matches

The matches we use today are of two chief types, the strike-anywhere match and the safety match.

Strike-Anywhere Matches will light when drawn across any rough surface. They are wooden matches with heads of two colors. In most cases, the heads are red and white. The white tip, called the *eye*, contains the firing substance. It is made chiefly of the chemical preparation, sesquisulfide of phosphorus. The rest of the bulblike head will not fire if struck, but will burn after the flaming eye sets it afire. It is larger around than the eye. This protects the matches from setting fire to each other by friction when they are packed into a box. When the match is lighted, the paraffin in which the matchstick had been dipped carries the flame from the head to the wood part.

Safety Matches can be lighted only by striking them across a special surface, usually on the side of the box in which they are contained. The head of the match is made of a substance containing chlorate of potash, and has a kindling temperature of approximately 360° F. (182° C). The striking surface is formed of a compound of red phosphorus and sand. *Book* matches are a type of safety match made of paper and bound into a folding paper cover. The striking surface is on the outside. The book should be closed before striking a match.

Matches Can Be Dangerous

Many disastrous fires and hundreds of deaths have been caused by the careless use of matches. All kinds of matches should be stored where children cannot reach them. Strike-anywhere matches should be placed out of the reach of mice. Rats or mice can set off matches by gnawing at the striking heads. A match should not be thrown away until the user is certain that the flame is out. Even then, it should be placed in a metal or other fireproof container.

How Matches Are Made

Wooden Matches are made by complex automatic machines that can manufacture and package more than a million matches an hour. First, a machine cuts *splints* (matchsticks) from thin strips of poplar wood. The splints are processed through an *anti-afterglow* solution, which prevents embers from forming after a match is blown out. Then the splints are dried and put into a matchmaking machine.

The matchmaking machine puts the splints into small holes in a belt of metal plates. As the belt fills up with splints, it dips them into a series of chemicals. The splints are first dipped into paraffin, which provides a base that carries the flame from the match head to the

Columbia Match Company

Combs of Matches are loaded into a booking machine, which cuts the combs to the proper size and staples them into matchbook covers. Workers then pack the matchbooks into boxes.

wood. The belt also passes the splints through a match-head solution, a chemical mixture that forms the bulbs and eyes of the matches. The heads may also receive a final chemical coating that protects them from moisture in the air. The finished matches are then punched from their plates, counted, and put into matchboxes in one automatic operation.

Book Matches are made by two machines from rolls of heavy paper called *paperboard* that has been treated with an anti-afterglow solution. The first machine, called a *match machine*, cuts the paperboard into *combs* (strips). Each comb is divided into from 60 to 120 smaller strips that eventually become matches. The machine dips the combs into paraffin and then dips the tips of the combs into the match-head solution.

Next, the combs are loaded into a *booking*, or *stitching*, machine. This machine cuts the combs into individual matchbook size and fits them into printed matchbook covers. Finally, the machine staples the combs and covers together to form the finished matchbooks, and workers pack the matchbooks into boxes.

Collecting Matchbook Covers

Collecting matchbook covers is an interesting and enjoyable hobby shared by thousands of persons. Match hobbyists collect covers from places they visit, trade covers with other collectors, and even buy rare or unusual covers from hobby shops or through advertisements in hobby magazines. Some match covers have become valuable because of their rarity. A single cover has sold for as much as $160.

Matchbook collectors often form clubs to help them trade covers and meet fellow hobbyists. The clubs hold meetings and conduct contests that award prizes to the best collections. Several clubs are organized on a nationwide basis. The largest of these is the Rathkamp Matchcover Society, 13321 Kenwood Avenue, Oak Park, Mich. 48237.

Because of the great variety of matchbook covers, collectors classify them in order to store or display them more easily. Collectors often specialize in certain kinds of covers, such as those from hotels, railroads, and gov-

A **Matchbook Collection** may include covers designed for any of many purposes, including advertising, decoration, the observance of a historic event, or simply as souvenirs.

WORLD BOOK photo

ernment organizations. Matchbook covers can also be classified by size. Most collectors prefer covers that have not been used. However, they often keep a used cover until they can find an unused one to replace it in their collections.

Collectors usually store covers in albums which they buy from hobby shops or make themselves. A matchbook album should have slots to hold the covers. A cover that is pasted in an album loses its value.

History

Early Fire-Making Devices were developed as scientists learned of chemical reactions that produced fire. In 1780, a group of French chemists invented the *phosphoric candle*, or *ethereal match*, a sealed glass tube containing a twist of paper. The paper was tipped with a form of phosphorus that burned upon exposure to oxygen. When a person broke the tube, air ignited the phosphorus. This and other early fire-producing devices were dangerous because of the poisonous fumes and extreme flammability of phosphorus.

The First Matches resembling those of today appeared in 1827, when John Walker, an English pharmacist, began to make and sell *congreves*. A congreve was a splint 3 inches (8 centimeters) long, tipped with antimony sulfide, chlorate of potash, gum arabic, and starch. A person lit one by drawing it through a fold of *glass paper*, a material somewhat like sandpaper. The match burst into flame with a series of small explosions that showered the user with sparks.

Charles Sauria, a French chemistry student, produced the first strike-anywhere match in the early 1830's. The match tip included phosphorus. Alonzo D. Phillips of Springfield, Mass., patented the first phosphorus matches in the United States in 1836. He made the matches by hand and sold them from door to door.

Neither Sauria nor Phillips knew that fumes from their phosphorus matches could cause a deadly disease called necrosis of the jaw, or *phossy jaw*. But after match factories began to operate during the mid-1800's, a number of workers who were exposed to phosphorus fumes died from the disease. As the match industry grew, the threat of widespread necrosis became alarming. In 1900, the Diamond Match Company purchased a French patent for matches with a striking head of sesquisulfide of phosphorus, a nonpoisonous compound. But the

French formula would not work in the United States because of the difference in climate.

In 1910, as a result of the spread of necrosis, the United States placed such a high tax on phosphorus matches that the match industry faced extinction. In 1911, William A. Fairburn, a young naval architect, solved the problem by adapting the French formula for sesquisulfide of phosphorus to the climate of the United States. The threat of necrosis ended.

The First Safety Matches were invented by Gustave E. Pasch, a Swedish chemist, in 1844. John Lundstrom, a Swedish manufacturer, began to produce them in large quantities in 1852.

The match industry centered in Sweden for many years. In the early 1900's, Ivar Kreuger, a Swedish promoter, formed the Swedish Match Company, a giant international match empire that owned factories, forests, and mines. The company operated match factories in about 40 countries and manufactured most of the world's matches. The stock market crash of 1929 weakened Kreuger's influence, and he committed suicide in 1932. However, the Swedish Match Company survived the crash and operated successfully under new management.

The Invention of Book Matches. Book matches were invented by Joshua Pusey, a Philadelphia patent lawyer, in 1892. Pusey made his matches in packages of 50. The striking surface was on the inside cover, dangerously near the heads of the matches. Because of this, book matches did not become popular until World War I (1914-1918). By that time, the Diamond Match Company had purchased Pusey's patent and made book matches safe and usable.

During World War II (1939-1945), when the United States Army had to fight the Japanese in areas where long rainy seasons prevailed, the match industry was called upon to produce a waterproof match. In 1943, Raymond D. Cady, a chemist with the Diamond Match Company, produced a formula which protected wooden matches so well that they would light after eight hours under water. This waterproof match is coated with a water- and heat-resistant substance. The substance does not interfere with the creation of enough friction to light the match.   BYRON A. JOHNSON

See also FAIRBURN, WILLIAM A.; FIRE (Methods of Starting Fires); SAFETY (Burns and Scalds).

236

MATCHLOCK. See HARQUEBUS.

MATE is the title of a merchant marine officer or naval petty officer. The word comes from the Old English *gemaca*, meaning *comrade* or *companion*. On merchant ships, the first mate is second in command. In the U.S. Navy, mates serve under warrant officers.

MATÉ, *MAH tay,* or PARAGUAY TEA, is a drink made from the dried leaves and shoots of a holly tree which grows in South America. People make the tea by pouring boiling water over the leaves and stems. Maté has a large amount of caffeine and produces a stimulating effect. The plant has three-cornered leaves 3 to 6 inches (8 to 15 centimeters) long. Its small flowers grow at the base of the leaf stems. Maté growing is a large industry in Paraguay, Argentina, and southern Brazil. Exporters ship large amounts to other countries in South America. Maté is sometimes called *yerba maté*.

Scientific Classification. The maté plant is a member of the family *Aquifoliaceae.* It is genus *Ilex*, species *I. paraguariensis.* JULIAN C. CRANE

A Maté Drinker of Uruguay draws the aromatic tea from a gourd container through a special straw called a *bombilla.*
Julien Bryan

MATERIALISM is a philosophy based on the ideas that matter is the only thing in the universe that has reality, and that matter is the basis of all that exists. The word comes from the Latin *materia*, which means *matter*. Materialists think that physical changes in the body and nervous system cause all mental processes. They justify this belief by pointing out that people can really know only what they see, hear, smell, taste, or touch. They deny the existence of mind or soul as distinct from matter, and insist that feelings, thoughts, and will have no independent existence.

This form of materialism was first expressed by two Greek philosophers, Democritus and Leucippus, in the 400's B.C. They stated that invisible material particles make up the physical world, and that similar particles make up the mind. Some later philosophers, including Epicurus and Lucretius, accepted this idea.

Materialism has always been a popular philosophy among scientists, because, if everything in the world is made of matter, then we can analyze and understand the world according to the laws which govern the way matter behaves. This idea is called *scientific materialism.* According to it, everything that exists now is the result of factors and conditions that existed before, and everything that will exist in the future must develop from some combination or change in the factors and conditions that exist now. This idea is often called *mechanism.* It was first fully stated by Baruch Spinoza.

A German philosopher, G. W. F. Hegel, explained this idea of the development of the universe, and gave it the name *dialectic.* Hegel was not a materialist, but his ideas influenced the development of a new philosophy, *dialectical materialism.* Karl Marx, Friedrich Engels, and V. I. Lenin developed it. In this system, the world develops along a dialectical path, with mechanical changes in what exists today producing what will exist tomorrow. The doctrine is materialist in its emphasis on the physical world and its denial of values based on the human mind or soul. Dialectical materialism is the philosophic basis for Communism, a political and economic movement. But the Communists have used dialectical materialism to suit their own purposes, and have not necessarily kept it logically coherent. See PHILOSOPHY (Philosophy and Government).

Except in its scientific or dialectical forms, materialism has not attracted as widespread popularity among philosophers as it has among scientists and lay people. Materialist philosophers of the past include Ludwig Büchner, Denis Diderot, Ernst Haeckel, Thomas Hobbes, and Julien de la Mettrie. H. M. KALLEN

Related Articles in WORLD BOOK include:

Communism	Epicurus	Marx, Karl H.
Democritus	Haeckel, Ernst H.	Mechanist
Diderot, Denis	Hobbes, Thomas	Philosophy

MATERIALS SCIENCE. See METALLURGY (Careers).

MATHEMATICAL ASSOCIATION OF AMERICA is a national organization of persons interested in mathematics. Its purpose is to assist in promoting the interests of mathematics in America. The association has about 19,000 members in 28 sections throughout the United States. It holds annual meetings and sponsors college and university programs. Its publications include *The American Mathematical Monthly, Mathematics Magazine,* books, and monographs. The association was founded in Columbus, Ohio, in 1915. Its headquarters are at 1225 Connecticut Avenue NW, Washington, D.C. 20036. Critically reviewed by the MATHEMATICAL ASSOCIATION OF AMERICA

MATHEMATICAL MODEL. See SYSTEMS ANALYSIS.

MATHEMATICAL SOCIETY, AMERICAN, is an association of mathematicians in the United States. Its purpose is to promote research and scholarship in pure and applied mathematics. The society has about 14,000 members. It publishes books and journals on mathematics, provides cataloging and indexing services, sponsors technical meetings, and cooperates with similar organizations in joint projects. The society was founded in New York City in 1888. Its headquarters are at 321 S. Main Street, Providence, R.I. 02904.

Critically reviewed by the AMERICAN MATHEMATICAL SOCIETY

MATHEMATICAL SYMBOL. See ALGEBRA (Symbols in Algebra); SET THEORY.

An Understanding of Mathematics begins by learning simple arithmetic principles in the early school years. A student studies advanced mathematics, including algebra, geometry, and calculus, in the later school years or at college.

MATHEMATICS is one of the most useful and fascinating divisions of human knowledge. It helps us in many important areas of study, and has the power to solve some of the deepest puzzles man must face.

Mathematics includes many different subjects. So the term *mathematics* is usually hard to define. But here is a definition that fits most of the mathematics we learn in school or college. *Mathematics is the study of quantities and relations through the use of numbers and symbols.* *Arithmetic*, for example, deals with quantities expressed by numbers. *Algebra* uses quantities and relations expressed by symbols. *Geometry* involves quantities associated with figures in space, such as length and area, and the relationships between figures in space. *Trigonometry* is concerned with the measurement of angles and with the relationships of angles. *Analytic geometry* applies algebra to geometric studies. *Calculus* works with pairs of associated quantities and the way one quantity changes in relation to the other. *New mathematics* refers to a way mathematical relationships are taught in many schools. For information on topics included in new mathematics, see NUMERATION SYSTEMS and SET THEORY.

The Importance of Mathematics

In Everyday Life. We use mathematics daily, even in such simple ways as telling time from a clock or counting the change returned by the grocer. A customer in a store uses mathematics whenever he buys something. A man and his wife use mathematics to make up a household budget or to figure out their income tax. And children use mathematics in many games and hobbies.

In Science. "Mathematics," wrote the English scientist Roger Bacon in 1267, "is the gate and key of the sciences." Most scientists depend on mathematics for exact descriptions and formulas of observations and experiments. Many scientific problems have become so complicated that only highly trained mathematicians working with giant electronic computers can supply the answers. The physical sciences, such as astronomy, chemistry, and physics, lean heavily on mathematics. And there is increasing use of mathematics in such social sciences as economics, psychology, and sociology.

In Industry. Almost all companies realize the tremendous value of mathematics in research and planning. Many major industrial firms employ trained mathematicians. Mathematics has great importance in all engineering projects. For example, the design of a superhighway requires extensive use of mathematics. The construction of a giant dam would be impossible without first filling reams of paper with mathematical formulas and calculations. The large number of courses an engineering student must take in mathematics shows the importance of mathematics in this field.

In Business, all transactions that involve buying and selling call for mathematics. Any business establishment, large or small, needs mathematics to keep its records. Bankers use mathematics to handle and invest money. Many companies employ *accountants* to keep their records and *statisticians* to analyze large groups of figures, such as the records of sales in a certain area. Insurance companies employ *actuaries* who specialize in computing the rates charged for insurance.

Kinds of Mathematics

Arithmetic is the first branch of mathematics learned in school, and almost everyone uses it daily. It includes the study of numbers and methods for *computing* (solving problems), with numbers. Arithmetic furnishes the basis for many other branches of mathematics. It includes four basic operations: addition, subtraction, multiplication, and division. See ADDITION; ARITHMETIC; DIVISION; MULTIPLICATION; SUBTRACTION.

Algebra, as learned in high school, forms one of the branches of mathematics used widely in business, industry, and science. It deals with numbers, but it differs from arithmetic because it is much more general than arithmetic. Arithmetic uses specific numbers. Algebra uses letters, such as x or y, to solve problems in which certain numbers are unknown. See ALGEBRA.

Algebra has produced a number of useful inventions in mathematics, such as *logarithms*. Logarithms are numbers developed by algebra that can be used to solve extremely long multiplications and divisions in arithmetic problems. Logarithms form the basis of the *slide rule*, a computing device frequently used by engineers. See LOGARITHMS; SLIDE RULE.

Geometry, as learned in high school, makes up one of the branches of mathematics most useful in building or measuring things. Architects, astronomers, construction engineers, navigators, physicists, and surveyors depend on geometry in their work. *Plane geometry* deals with figures, such as squares and circles, that lie on a *plane* (flat surface). *Solid geometry* deals with figures that have three dimensions, such as cubes, spheres, and pyramids. See GEOMETRY.

Trigonometry forms a branch of mathematics widely used by astronomers, navigators, and surveyors. The basic idea in trigonometry is computing the relations between the sides of a right triangle. These relations are called *trigonometric ratios*. *Plane trigonometry* deals with triangles on a plane. *Spherical trigonometry* deals with triangles on the surface of a sphere. See TRIGONOMETRY.

Analytic Geometry comes from the application of algebra to geometry. Using analytic geometry, a person can draw a curved line that represents an equation from algebra, such as $y=x^2$. Similarly, he can write an equation that is a mathematical description of a certain curved line. Engineers and physicists use analytic geometry in many ways. For example, designing an airplane calls for many equations that describe curves. See GEOMETRY (Analytic Geometry).

Calculus deals with changing quantities. It forms one of the most useful branches of advanced mathematics. Calculus has hundreds of practical applications in engineering, physics, and other branches of science. Suppose a gun fires a projectile into the air. The projectile's speed changes during the course of its flight. *Differential calculus* finds the rate at which the speed of the projectile changes. *Integral calculus* finds the speed of the projectile when the rate of change is known. These problems of changing quantities also relate to geometry. See CALCULUS.

Probability is the mathematical study of the likelihood of events. It has many important practical uses. Almost all scientific predictions use probability. Insurance companies use it to compute the rates they charge for insurance. The armed forces use probability to plan artillery fire and bombing. See PROBABILITY.

Statistics forms a branch of mathematics that analyzes large bodies of numbers. Scientists and other investigators often begin work on a problem by gathering facts. These facts usually come from measurements and counting of various kinds, and appear as collections of numbers. Statisticians analyze collections of numbers and show important trends. Using the study of probability, they can make predictions. See STATISTICS.

Non-Euclidean Geometry contributed much to the development of the theory of relativity, one of the outstanding advances in scientific thought (see RELATIVITY). It also helped explore the fundamental nature of mathematics itself. About 1830, János Bolyai of Hungary and Nikolai Lobachevsky of Russia, two mathematicians working independently of each other, produced new and sometimes strange systems of geometry. For example, in Lobachevsky's geometry, the angles of a triangle do not add up to 180°. But, as logical systems, these geometries are just as consistent and regular as the Euclidean geometry we learn in high school. See GEOMETRY (Non-Euclidean Geometry).

Pure and Applied Mathematics

Mathematics arose from attempts to solve practical problems, such as counting farm animals or measuring pieces of land. The ancient Greeks developed two kinds of mathematics, pure and applied.

Pure Mathematics includes systems of mathematics that need not have any practical applications. A storyteller can describe a mythical kingdom that never existed. In the same way, a mathematician can make up a system of mathematics, such as a system of geometry.

Applied Mathematics results from the use of pure mathematics in concrete situations. A pure mathematical system often has a number of separate practical applications. For example, we use geometry to build machines, design houses and furniture, and measure land. Behind almost every operation of applied mathematics lies a piece of pure mathematics.

Mathematics for Fun

Mathematics has a lighter side. It includes hundreds of entertaining puzzles, tricks, and problems. Perhaps this is one of the reasons why so many persons have followed careers in mathematics and so many others have made mathematics their hobby.

Which Salary Would You Choose? The president of a company interviews Jones and Smith, two young applicants for a job. The job requires a person with a sharp mind. "Which would you prefer," the president asks the men, "a starting salary of $8,000 a year with a $400 increase every year, or a starting salary of $4,000 every half year with a $100 increase every half year?" Jones says he prefers the first arrangement and Smith says he prefers the second. The president hires Smith. Why did he choose him?

Make a chart to show the salary arrangements by the year.

	JONES' CHOICE	SMITH'S CHOICE
First year	$8,000	$4,000 + $4,100 = $8,100
Second year	$8,400	$4,200 + $4,300 = $8,500
Third year	$8,800	$4,400 + $4,500 = $8,900
Fourth year	$9,200	$4,600 + $4,700 = $9,300

Contrary to Jones' impression, the second arrangement gives the higher salary.

A Little Pile of Paper. Suppose you take a huge sheet of thin paper, only $\frac{1}{1,000}$ inch (0.025 millimeter) thick.

Then you cut the sheet in half and put one piece on top of the other. Cut these two pieces in half and put the resulting four pieces together in a pile. Cut the pile of four pieces in half and put the resulting eight pieces in a pile. Suppose you cut the pile in half 50 times and each time pile up the resulting pieces.

Ask your friends how high they think the final pile of paper will be. Some persons suggest a foot, others suggest several feet or a meter, and occasionally someone guesses a kilometer or a mile. Usually, they show surprise when you tell them the pile is more than 17,-000,000 miles (27,000,000 kilometers) high!

But you can easily prove this. After the first cut, you have 2 pieces. After the second cut, you have 2×2, or 2^2 pieces. After the third cut, you have $2 \times 2 \times 2$, or 2^3 pieces. Clearly, after the fiftieth cut, the number of pieces is the product of fifty 2's, or 2^{50}. The number 2 multiplied by itself 50 times is about 1,126,000,-000,000,000. Because there are 1,000 sheets of paper to the inch, the pile is about 1,126,000,000,000 inches high. Divide this number by 12 to find the number of feet. Divide the number of feet by 5,280 to find the number of miles.

A Mind-Reading Trick. Many amusing "mind-reading" tricks have simple mathematical explanations. Suppose you ask a friend to think of a number and keep it secret. Then ask him—still keeping the number to himself—to multiply his number by 5, add 6, multiply by 4, add 9, and multiply by 5. Now ask him to tell you the result. When he does, you need only a moment's thought to tell him his original number.

Suppose your friend chooses 13. He multiplies by 5: $13 \times 5 = 65$. He adds 6: $65 + 6 = 71$. He multiplies by 4: $71 \times 4 = 284$. He adds 9: $284 + 9 = 293$. And he multiplies by 5: $293 \times 5 = 1,465$. He tells you the number 1,465. *Without telling him, subtract 165 from the number he tells you, divide by 100 (drop two zeros), and tell him his original number.* In the case of 1,465, subtract 165: $1,465 - 165 = 1,300$. Divide by 100: $1,300 \div 100 = 13$.

You can explain the trick by using n to represent the unknown number. Here are the steps. (1) n. (2) $5n$. (3) $5n+6$. (4) $4(5n+6) = 20n+24$. (5) $20n+24+9 = 20n+33$. (6) $5(20n+33) = 100n+165$. So $100n+165$ equals x, or the number your friend tells you. You solve $100n+165 = x$ by subtracting 165 from x and dividing it by 100. No matter what number your friend chooses, you can find it by following the rule given above.

Where Is My Missing Horse? After Mr. Klopstock's death, his estate consisted of 17 horses. His will provided that his friend Mr. Thom should be his executor. The terms of the will were these: one half of the horses should go to the widow, one third to the older son, and one ninth of the horses to the younger son. Mr. Thom found himself in great trouble. It seemed evident that Mr. Klopstock had miscalculated in drawing up his will. It would be impossible for any of the persons to receive a fraction

of a horse. Yet Mr. Thom solved the problem. How did he do it?

Mr. Thom found that the fractions $\frac{1}{2}$, $\frac{1}{3}$, and $\frac{1}{9}$ added together make $\frac{17}{18}$. In order to start with $\frac{18}{18}$, which equals one, he put his own horse into the corral with the other 17. Then he gave the widow $\frac{1}{2}$ of the horses, or 9. The elder son received $\frac{1}{3}$ of the horses, or 6. The younger son got $\frac{1}{9}$ of the horses, or 2. Then Mr. Thom rode away on his own horse and everybody was happy.

One Equals Two. A tricky problem in algebra seems to establish the fact that one equals two. Of course, such a conclusion seems impossible. The trick starts simply enough. Suppose that $b = a$. Here is what you can do:

(1) Multiply by a, then $ab = a^2$.
(2) Subtract b^2, then $ab - b^2 = a^2 - b^2$.
(3) Factor, then $b(a-b) = (a+b)(a-b)$.
(4) Divide by $(a-b)$, then $b = a+b$.
(5) Substitute a for b, then $a = a+a$.
(6) $a = 2a$.
(7) Divide by a, then $1 = 2$.

At first glance, all seems well. These processes appear to agree with principles in algebra. But there is an oversight in the application of these principles. It lies in the fact that $(a-b)$ in the third and fourth steps is equal to zero, because b equals a. For this reason, the conclusion reached is wrong. Division by zero is not permitted.

A Matter of Direction. From what point on the earth's surface can a man walk 12 miles due south, then walk 12 miles due east, then walk 12 miles due north, and find himself back at his starting point? The usual answer to this old riddle is the North Pole. But the earth actually has an infinite number of points from which such a walk could be taken.

In theory, the equator forms a circle around the middle of the earth. Going north or south from the equator, progressively smaller circles of latitude ring the earth until they reach the points of the North and South poles. Somewhere near the South Pole, there must be a circle of latitude whose circumference is exactly 12 miles long. And there must be a second circle of latitude exactly 12 miles north of the first circle. Suppose a man starts his walk at any point on this second circle. He walks 12 miles due south and finds himself on the first circle whose circumference is 12 miles. He walks 12 miles due east. That is, he walks around the 12-mile circle. Then he walks 12 miles due north to his starting point on the first circle!

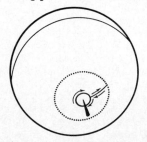

But other points can solve the problem. There must be circles of latitude north of the South Pole with circumferences of 6 miles, 4 miles, 3 miles, and so on. By starting at any point on a circle of latitude 12 miles north of any one of these circles, the man can take the required walk. For example, when he walks 12 miles due east on the 4-mile circle, he will walk around the circle three times before he starts his 12-mile journey north to his first circle.

An Extra Square. Suppose you mark off a square piece of cardboard into 64 little squares. The area of the cardboard is 8×8 little squares, or 64 little squares. Cut the cardboard into two triangles and two trapezoids, as shown in the accompanying picture.

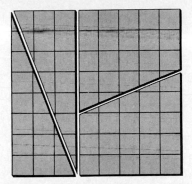

Now rearrange the two triangles and two trapezoids to form the rectangle shown in the picture.

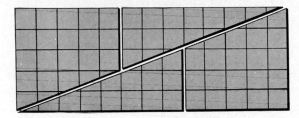

But this new rectangle has sides of 5 little squares and 13 little squares. It must have an area of 5×13 little squares, or 65 little squares. Where did the extra square come from?

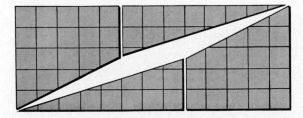

The answer to this problem is that the edges of the two triangles and two trapezoids do not really form a diagonal in the new rectangle. Instead, they form the flat parallelogram that is shown in exaggerated form in the bottom picture. The area of this parallelogram is exactly one little square.

A Strange Twist. You may find it difficult to predict the outcome of some experiments in geometry. Suppose you have a strip of paper about 3 centimeters wide and about 25 centimeters long, with a dotted line down the middle of its length. Mentally, paste the ends of the strip together to form a ring like a section of a cylinder. If, with a pair of scissors, you cut this ring along the dotted line, you will obtain two rings just like

the first ring, but only half as wide. Now imagine the unpasted strip of paper again. This time give the strip a half-twist (a twist of 180°) before mentally pasting the ends together. With the ends pasted and the strip in a half-twist, what will happen when you cut this new ring along the dotted line?

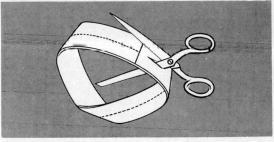

You should actually do this experiment at home with a strip of paper, paste, and a pair of scissors. When you discover what happens when you cut the ring with one half-twist, imagine what will happen with two, three, four, and five half-twists, or—in general—m half-twists on the strip.

In terms of geometry, if m, the number of half-twists, is even, the ring will be a surface with two sides and two edges. If you cut it along the line, it will become two rings, each with m half-twists, linked together $\frac{m}{2}$ times. If m, the number of half-twists, is odd, the ring will be a surface with only one side and one edge. If you cut it along the line, it will remain one ring with $2m+2$ half-twists. If m is greater than 1, the ring will be knotted. You may want to try cutting the twisted rings along two ruled lines, instead of one.

The ring with one half-twist takes its name—Möbius strip—from August Ferdinand Möbius (1790-1868), a German astronomer and mathematician. Möbius helped establish a study in geometry called *topology*. Topology deals with geometrical figures that are *deformed*, or pulled and twisted out of shape in various ways. See TOPOLOGY.

The Earth with a Pipeline Around It. Suppose that someone wants to lay a pipeline around the earth. Also suppose that the circumference of the earth is exactly 25,000 miles (40,200 kilometers). The manufacturer made the pipeline exactly 20 feet too long. Still, it was proposed to put it in position, supported above the surface of the earth by posts of equal length. How high above the surface of the earth would the pipeline be?

In a diagram, let R represent the radius of the earth, h the height of one of the posts, and C the circumference of the earth.

Now $2\pi R = C$.

The radius of the circle of pipeline is $R+h$.

Then $2\pi (R+h) = C+20$.

Substitute $2\pi R$ for C.

$2\pi R + 2\pi h = 2\pi R + 20$.

Subtract $2\pi R$ from each side, and $2\pi h = 20$.

Then $2 \times 3.1416 h = 20$.

And $h = \dfrac{20}{2 \times 3.1416}$

Finally, $h = 3.18$ feet.

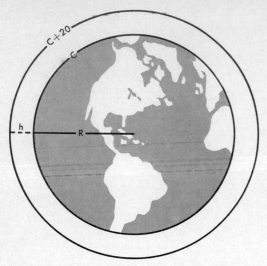

It may be hard to believe that adding only 20 feet to 25,000 miles would result in raising the pipeline more than 3 feet above the earth. But try adding the same number of feet to a much smaller circumference, such as 10 feet. The answer is the same, though you have used a different figure for the original circumference. In fact, the length of the original circumference makes no difference. The answer will always be found by dividing the added length by 2×3.1416.

History

Ancient Times. Before the time of recorded history, prehistoric people learned to count such things as the animals in their herds and flocks. They probably first used their fingers or pebbles to help keep track of small numbers. They learned to use the length of their hands and arms and other standards of measure. And they learned to use regular shapes when they molded pottery and chipped stone arrowheads.

By 3000 B.C., the peoples of ancient Babylonia, China, and Egypt had developed a practical system of mathematics. They used written symbols to stand for numbers, and knew the simple arithmetic operations. They used this knowledge in business and government. They also developed a practical geometry helpful in agriculture and engineering. For example, the ancient Egyptians knew how to survey their fields and to make the intricate measurements necessary to build huge pyramids. The Babylonians and Egyptians had even explored some of the fundamental ideas of algebra. But this early mathematics solved only practical problems. It was applied, rather than pure, mathematics.

The Greeks and the Romans. Between 600 and 300 B.C., the Greeks took the next great step in mathematics. They inherited a large part of their mathematical knowledge from the Babylonians and Egyptians. But they became the first people to separate mathematics from practical problems. For example, they separated geometry from practical applications and made it into an abstract exploration of space. They based this study of points, lines, and figures, such as triangles and circles, on logical reasoning rather than on facts found in nature. Thales of Miletus (c. 640-546 B.C.), a philosopher, helped begin this new viewpoint of geometry. The philosopher Pythagoras (c. 580- c. 500

B.C.) and his followers explored the nature of numbers. In geometry, the Pythagoreans developed the famous theorem that bears their name (see PYTHAGOREAN THEOREM). Thales, Pythagoras, and many other Greek mathematicians built up a large body of geometrical knowledge. Euclid (c. 300 B.C.), one of the foremost Greek mathematicians, organized geometry as a single logical system. His book, *The Elements*, remains one of the basic works in studying mathematics.

The Greeks also advanced other branches of mathematics. As early as 450 B.C., Greek mathematicians recognized *irrational numbers* such as the square root of 2. About 370 B.C., Eudoxus of Cnidus (c. 400-355 B.C.), a Greek astronomer and mathematician, formulated a surprisingly masterful definition of proportions. Archimedes (287?-212 B.C.), the leading mathematician of ancient times, devised processes that foreshadowed those of integral calculus. Archimedes made many other contributions to mathematics and physics. The Greek astronomer Ptolemy (c. A.D. 150) helped develop trigonometry. Diophantus (c. A.D. 275), a Greek mathematician, worked on numbers in equations. He earned the title of the father of algebra.

Although the Romans constructed many impressive buildings, they showed little interest in pure mathematics. Roman mathematics dealt largely with practical matters such as business and military science.

The Middle Ages. After the fall of Rome in A.D. 476, Europe saw no new developments in mathematics for

---

IMPORTANT DATES IN MATHEMATICS

c. 300 B.C. Euclid organized geometry as a single system of mathematics.
c. 225 B.C. Archimedes invented processes that foreshadowed those used in integral calculus.
c. A.D. 275 Diophantus helped found algebra.
c. 820 Al-Khowarizmi helped organize algebra as a branch of mathematics.
1614 John Napier published his invention of logarithms, an important mathematical aid.
1637 René Descartes published the first work on analytic geometry.
1640 Pierre Fermat founded the modern theory of numbers.
1654 Pierre Fermat and Blaise Pascal established the mathematical theory of probability.
c. 1675 Sir Isaac Newton and Baron von Leibniz, working independently, invented calculus.
1733 Leonhard Euler began a series of publications on calculus that started modern mathematical analysis.
c. 1830 János Bolyai and Nikolai Lobachevsky, working independently, invented non-Euclidean geometry systems.
1843 Sir William Hamilton invented a system of algebra that differed in many ways from traditional algebra.
1854 Georg Riemann invented a non-Euclidean geometry later used in the relativity theory.
1910-1913 Alfred North Whitehead and Bertrand Russell published *Principia Mathematica*, which tries to develop mathematics from logic.
1915 Albert Einstein announced his general theory of relativity.
1950 Einstein announced a major revision of his unified-field theory.
1970's Mathematical models became widely used to study systems and problems in business, industry, and science.

hundreds of years. But the Arabs preserved the mathematical tradition of the Greeks and Romans. One of the greatest discoveries in the history of mathematics appeared in Europe during the Middle Ages. Mathematicians in India developed zero and the decimal number system. After A.D. 700, the Arabs adopted these inventions from the Indians and used the new numbers in their mathematics. The Arabs also preserved and translated many of the great works of Greek mathematicians. They made important contributions of their own. For example, the mathematician Al-Khowarizmi (c. 820) organized and expanded algebra. The word *algebra* comes from an Arabic word in the title of one of his books on the subject. See ALGEBRA (History).

After 1100, Europeans began to borrow the mathematics of the Arab world. For example, European merchants started to use the decimal number system. Also, European scholars began to study Arab works on algebra and geometry. Leonardo Fibonacci (c. 1200), a leading European mathematician of the Middle Ages, contributed to algebra, arithmetic, and geometry.

The Renaissance, from the 1400's to the 1600's, produced many great advances in mathematics. The exploration of new lands and continents called for better mathematics for navigation. The growth of business demanded better mathematics for banking and finance. The invention of printing brought the appearance of hundreds of popular arithmetic textbooks. Many of the computation methods used today date from this period, such as the procedure for doing a long multiplication.

Interest also grew in pure mathematics. Michael Stifel (1487-1567), Nicolò Tartaglia (c. 1500-1557), Girolamo Cardano (1501-1576), and François Viète (1540-1603) pioneered in algebra. Viète introduced the use of letters to stand for unknown numbers. These men also helped develop trigonometry. Nicolaus Copernicus (1473-1543), the astronomer who defended the theory that the universe had the sun as its center, contributed to mathematics through his work in astronomy.

The 1600's brought many brilliant contributions to mathematics. John Napier (1550-1617), a Scottish mathematician, invented logarithms. Two Englishmen, Thomas Harriot (1560-1621) and William Oughtred (1574-1660), worked out new methods for algebra. The astronomers Galileo (1564-1642) and Johannes Kepler (1571-1630) expanded mathematical knowledge through their studies of the stars and planets. Gérard Desargues (1593-1662) helped expand geometry through his study of sections of cones. René Descartes (1596-1650) invented analytic geometry and aided many other branches of mathematics. Pierre de Fermat (1601-1665) founded the modern numbers theory. Blaise Pascal (1623-1662) and Fermat invented the mathematical theory of probability. Then, toward the end of this period, Sir Isaac Newton (1642-1727) and Baron von Leibniz (1646-1716) invented calculus. The invention of calculus marked the beginning of modern mathematics.

The 1700's saw wide applications of the new calculus. Abraham de Moivre (1667-1754) used calculus to contribute to the study of probability. Brook Taylor (1685-1731) helped develop differential calculus. Colin Maclaurin (1698-1746) also helped with calculus. But one of the greatest contributors to calculus was Leonhard Euler (1707-1783), a Swiss mathematician. Euler worked in almost every branch of mathematics. His contribu-

tions to calculus reached into so many fields that many mathematicians call him the founder of modern mathematical analysis. Count Lagrange (1736-1813) used calculus for the study of forces in physics. Gaspard Monge (1746-1818) applied calculus to geometry.

The 1800's brought further application of calculus throughout mathematics. The Marquis de Laplace (1749-1827) used calculus in physics, particularly in astronomy. Jean Baptiste Fourier (1768-1830) used it for the study of heat in physics. Adrien Marie Legendre (1752-1833) also worked with calculus and contributed to the theory of numbers. But the early work in calculus often rested on shaky theoretical foundations. As a result, many disturbing paradoxes appeared. The great achievements in mathematics in the 1800's included rebuilding the theoretical foundations of calculus and mathematical analysis. Four mathematicians—Baron Cauchy (1789-1857), Karl Friedrich Gauss (1777-1855) Georg Friedrich Riemann (1826-1866), and Karl Theodor Weierstrass (1815-1897)—helped carry out this important work.

Another outstanding advance of the 1800's was the invention of non-Euclidean geometry by János Bolyai (1802-1860) and Nikolai Lobachevsky (1793-1856). During the same period, Arthur Cayley (1821-1895) and Sir William Rowan Hamilton (1805-1865) invented new systems of algebra. These discoveries liberated geometry and algebra from their traditional molds and did much to shape present-day mathematics.

Recent Developments. The invention of new systems of algebra and geometry and the revision of the theoretical foundations of calculus had far-reaching effects on mathematics. In the 1900's, mathematicians began to explore the foundations of mathematics itself. Many philosophies of mathematics appeared, as well as attempts to give mathematics a basis in logic. Luitzen Brouwer (1881-1966), Georg Cantor (1845-1918), David Hilbert (1862-1943), Bertrand Russell (1872-1970), and Alfred North Whitehead (1861-1947) made important studies of the foundations of mathematics. The work of Albert Einstein (1879-1955) opened a whole new area for mathematical research.

New developments in science required a tremendous expansion of applied mathematics. Such fields as electronics, nuclear physics, and the exploration of space have used new inventions from pure mathematics to solve problems. For example, electronic computers use systems of mathematics designed by mathematicians. Also, mathematical models have been formulated to study many kinds of systems, including underground petroleum reserves and worldwide weather patterns. The models consist of mathematical equations that describe the relations between the parts or processes of a system. Computers are used to solve these equations.

Careers in Mathematics

Mathematics offers many career opportunities in business, government, industry, and teaching. Other professions, such as architecture, banking, and engineering, demand extensive training in mathematics.

Training. The amount of training needed for a career in mathematics depends on the career itself. A man or woman who wants to become a high-school mathe-

MATHEMATICS

matics teacher must earn at least a bachelor's degree in college. This degree must include the required courses in mathematics. At the same time, a student with this career in mind should take as much work as possible in both the physical and social sciences. For a teaching career in a college or university, a person must do graduate work. A doctor's degree in mathematics is an almost universal requirement.

People who want to become statisticians must have a strong college or university background in mathematics with emphasis on subjects allied to statistics, such as calculus. In addition, they should prepare themselves in the field in which they will use statistics.

Industry needs mathematicians at all levels of preparation, from the bachelor's to the doctor's degree. Persons with a bachelor's degree or limited training usually work at computing. Persons with a doctor's degree or more extensive training often serve industry as consultants. These consultants to industry are mathematicians with a flair for applied mathematics and the solution of industrial problems. Mathematics careers in government resemble those in industry. A mathematician's civil service rating depends on training and ability. The federal government employs mathematicians in the research laboratories and offices of such agencies as the Bureau of the Census, the Department of Defense, the Department of Energy, and the National Ocean Survey.

Actuaries usually work for insurance companies. An actuary must know statistics and general mathematics. In addition, an actuary must have a good background in economics and finance. Programmers, systems analysts, and other computer experts need a strong background in mathematics. HOWARD W. EVES

Related Articles in WORLD BOOK include:

AMERICAN MATHEMATICIANS

Banneker, Benjamin	Rittenhouse, David
Bowditch, Nathaniel	Steinmetz, Charles P.
Fisher, Irving	Von Neumann, John
Gibbs, Josiah W.	Wiener, Norbert
Peirce, Charles S.	

BRITISH MATHEMATICIANS

Napier, John	Russell, Bertrand A. W.
Newton, Sir Isaac	Whitehead, Alfred North

FRENCH MATHEMATICIANS

Cauchy, Augustin L.	Lagrange,	Legendre,
Châtelet, Marquise du	Joseph L.	Adrien M.
Descartes, René	Laplace,	Pascal,
Fermat, Pierre de	Marquis de	Blaise

GERMAN MATHEMATICIANS

Bessel, Friedrich W.	Hilbert, David
Clausius, Rudolf J. E.	Kepler, Johannes
Gauss, Karl F.	Leibniz, Gottfried W.

OTHER MATHEMATICIANS

Archimedes	Huygens, Christian
Bernoulli	Omar Khayyam
Eratosthenes	Ptolemy
Euclid	Pythagoras
Euler, Leonhard	Torricelli, Evangelista

APPLIED MATHEMATICS

Accounting	Budget	Engineering
Biomathematics	Discount	Insurance
Bookkeeping	Econometrics	Interest

Map	Navigation
Measurement	Surveying
Mechanical Drawing	Weights and Measures

BRANCHES OF MATHEMATICS

Algebra	Calculus	Probability	Topology
Arithmetic	Geometry	Statistics	Trigonometry

MATHEMATICAL MACHINES AND DEVICES

Abacus	Computer
Adding Machine	Slide Rule
Calculator	Vernier

OTHER RELATED ARTICLES

Chisanbop	Number	Progression
Determinant	and Numeral	Series
Game Theory	Numeration	Set Theory
Infinity	Systems	Square Root
Maya (Communication and Learning)	Permutations and Combinations	Systems Analysis

Outline

I. The Importance of Mathematics
   A. In Everyday Life   C. In Industry
   B. In Science   D. In Business

II. Kinds of Mathematics
   A. Arithmetic
   B. Algebra
   C. Geometry
   D. Trigonometry
   E. Analytic Geometry
   F. Calculus
   G. Probability
   H. Statistics
   I. Non-Euclidean Geometry

III. Pure and Applied Mathematics
IV. Mathematics for Fun
V. History
VI. Careers in Mathematics

Questions

How does mathematics help solve various problems in everyday life?

What invention has algebra produced to help solve long arithmetic problems?

How does analytic geometry combine two different kinds of mathematics?

What kinds of problems does calculus solve?

What are some contributions of non-Euclidean geometry to mathematics and science?

How does pure mathematics differ from applied mathematics?

In what ways did the Arabs help to contribute to mathematics?

How did the Renaissance stimulate mathematics?

What have been some main trends in mathematics in the 1900's?

Why is mathematics important in science?

MATHER was the name of a family of intellectual and religious leaders—grandfather, son, and grandson—in colonial America.

Richard Mather (1596-1669) was born in Lancashire, England. He was ordained a minister of the Church of England in 1620. But his Puritan beliefs antagonized church authorities, who suspended him from his ministry in 1633. In 1635, he came to the Massachusetts Bay Colony, where he helped establish the Congregational Church in America. From 1636 until his death, he was pastor of the parish in Dorchester, near Boston.

Mather helped compile *The Bay Psalm Book* (1640), the first book printed in the American Colonies (see BAY PSALM BOOK). He also helped write the *Cambridge Platform*, which set forth the principles of Congregational

Church discipline and government. The platform was adopted in 1648. About 1655, after his first wife died, Mather married the widow of John Cotton, the most prominent theologian of early colonial America.

Increase Mather (1639-1723), the son of Richard, was born in Dorchester. He graduated from Harvard College in 1656 and received his M.A. degree from Trinity College in Dublin, Ireland, in 1658. He returned to America in 1661 and married the daughter of John Cotton in 1662. In 1664, Mather joined the Second Church of Boston in the important post of teacher. He became president of Harvard in 1686.

During the late 1600's, many people opposed the strong governing powers of the Congregational Church. Some of these people, especially those in the Boston area, tried to liberalize the requirements for church membership. Mather was conservative in religious matters and strongly opposed the liberals. This opposition led to his removal as president of Harvard in 1701. For the rest of his life, Mather wrote pamphlets attacking people who he thought threatened established church practices.

Cotton Mather (1663-1728), the son of Increase, was born in Boston. He entered Harvard at the age of 12 and received his B.A. degree in 1678 and his M.A. in 1681. About 1680, he joined his father at the Second Church of Boston as an assistant. He remained there until his death.

Mather published nearly 500 books and pamphlets, many of which dealt with scientific subjects. In recognition of his scientific writings, he became the first American elected to the Royal Society, the famous British scientific academy. Both he and his father supported smallpox inoculation, though most colonists regarded it with suspicion.

Portrait c. 1727 by Peter Pelham, American Antiquarian Society, Worcester, Mass.

Cotton Mather

Mather's best-known book is *Magnalia Christi Americana* (1702). This book contains much information about the people and issues that were important in the early history of New England.

Many historians believe that Increase and Cotton Mather helped stir up the Salem witchcraft trials of the 1690's with their writings and sermons. The trials resulted in the execution of 20 persons as witches. Other historians believe that the Mathers' reputation for persecution during the trials has been greatly exaggerated. ROBERT L. FERM

MATHEWS, FORREST DAVID (1935-   ), served as secretary of the United States Department of Health, Education, and Welfare (HEW) from 1975 to 1977. He was appointed to the Cabinet post by President Gerald R. Ford. HEW spends about a third of the money collected by the federal government in taxes. Mathews supervised such HEW agencies as the Food and Drug Administration, the Office of Education, and the Social Security Administration.

Mathews was born in Grove Hill, Ala. He graduated from the University of Alabama in 1958 and earned an

M.A. degree in education there in 1959. Mathews received a Ph.D. degree in education from Columbia University in 1965.

From 1966 to 1968, Mathews served as an executive assistant to the president of the University of Alabama. He became executive vice-president of the university in 1968 and president a year later. He was one of the youngest persons ever to become president of a major U.S. university. Mathews returned to serve as the university's president in 1977. GUY HALVERSON

MATHEWSON, CHRISTY (1880-1925), was one of baseball's greatest right-handed pitchers. He won 373 games in the National League, 372 for the New York Giants and one for the Cincinnati Reds. He became the first pitcher in the 1900's to win 30 games a season for three consecutive years. Mathewson won 37 games in 1908, and pitched three shutouts in the 1905 World Series against Philadelphia. He became one of the first five players elected to the National Baseball Hall of Fame when it was established in 1936. Christopher Mathewson was born in Factoryville, Pa. ED FITZGERALD

See also BASEBALL (picture).

MATISSE, *mah TEESE,* **HENRI** (1869-1954), a French painter, was one of the most influential artists of the 1900's. He was the leader of the fauves, a group of painters who started the first important art movement of the era. Matisse was also a noted sculptor, book illustrator, and tapestry designer.

Matisse's favorite subjects included human figures, still lifes, and scenes of interiors. He believed that a painting was more important as an object of art than as a representation of reality. He made no attempt to create the illusion of realistic forms and space. Instead, he used intense color and lines to produce patterns and a sense of movement. Some critics believe that Matisse has no equal in the use of color among artists of the 1900's. His paintings feature unusual color combinations and elaborate patterns. Matisse's works, especially those of the 1920's, have a decorative quality similar to the art of the Near and Middle East.

Matisse was born in Le Cateau, near Cambrai. He entered law school in 1887 but began to paint in 1890 as a pastime while recovering from an operation. In 1891, Matisse moved to Paris to study art. In the early 1890's, he painted with dark colors. But he showed the influence of the bright colors of the im-

Collection of S. Max Becker, Jr., Glencoe, Ill.

© Gisele Freund, Photo Researchers

Henri Matisse was a famous French artist. The self-portrait on the left and the photograph on the right both date from 1949.

The Royal Museum of Fine Arts, Rump Collection, Copenhagen.

Portrait of Madame Matisse, painted in 1905, shows Matisse's emphasis on color, which is typical of the fauve movement.

pressionists in his painting *The Dinner Table* (1897).

In 1905, Matisse and the other fauve painters held an exhibition of their work. The brilliant colors and bold patterns of these paintings shocked the Paris art world. One of Matisse's fauve paintings, *Landscape at Collioure*, is reproduced in color in the PAINTING article. See also FAUVES.

From 1907 to about 1920, Matisse painted increasingly solid designs that reflected the influence of the French artist Paul Cézanne and of the cubists. Matisse also did his most important work as a sculptor during this period.

In his last years, Matisse created simple and abstract compositions made of cut paper. From 1948 to 1951, he designed and decorated the Chapel of the Rosary in Vence, France.   WILLARD E. MISFELDT

MATRIARCHAL FAMILY. See FAMILY (Traditional Families in Other Cultures).

MATTER is one of the two ways in which nature shows itself to human beings. Energy is the second way in which nature shows itself. All objects consist of matter. The objects may differ widely from one another. But they have one thing in common—they all occupy space. Therefore, scientists usually define matter as anything that occupies space. All matter has *inertia*. This means that it resists any change in its condition of rest or of motion. The quantity of matter in an object is called its *mass*, but scientists usually prefer to define mass as a measure of inertia. The earth's gravitational attraction for a given mass gives matter its *weight*. Gravity's pull on an object decreases as it moves away from the center of the earth. For this reason, objects that move from the earth into outer space "lose weight" even though their masses remain the same.

When we see people, animals, or machines working, feel heat from a fire, or see light from an electric bulb, we become aware of *energy*. All these processes involve energy. Scientists often define energy as the ability to do work, or to move matter. Heat is the variety of energy most familiar to us. All other kinds of energy may be changed into heat. See ENERGY.

Matter can be changed into energy and energy into matter. For example, matter changes into energy when radium and other radioactive elements disintegrate and when atomic bombs explode.

The Properties of Matter

All of us easily recognize many varieties of matter. Each variety possesses certain characteristics that are common to all samples of its special kind. We base our recognition of each variety of matter on knowledge of these special characteristics, or *properties*. These properties distinguish one kind of matter from other kinds. Matter has two main types of properties—physical and chemical.

Physical Properties. People recognize certain kinds of matter by sight, smell, touch, taste, or hearing. We can recognize gold and copper by color, sugar by taste, and gasoline by odor. These are examples of some of the physical properties of matter. Another physical property of matter is *density*, or the amount of mass for each unit of volume. Because of the difference in density, a block of cork weighs less than a block of all common woods the same size. *Solubility* (the ability of one kind of matter to dissolve in another) and *conductivity* (the ability of matter to conduct heat or electricity) are also physical properties.

Chemical Properties of matter describe how a substance acts when it undergoes chemical change. For example, a chemical property of iron is its ability to combine with oxygen in moist air to form iron oxide, or rust. Scientists call such changes in the composition of matter *chemical changes*. Some changes alter the value of physical properties, such as weight or density, but produce no change in the composition of the matter. Scientists call these *physical changes*. When water changes to steam it undergoes physical, but not chemical, change (see PHYSICAL CHANGE).

Materials and Substances. Any variety of matter recognized as a certain type or kind, such as wood or coal, is a *material*. If all samples of a given material have identical or similar properties, the material is a *substance*. For example, pure sand is a substance, but glass is a material because there are many kinds of glass. Many materials are mixtures of several varieties of matter. This means that substances in a mixture retain their individual chemical and physical properties. For example, salt and sand mixed together remain salt and sand. You can separate one from the other without changing its individual properties. Scientists usually separate the components of mixtures without changing their chemical properties. When they can obtain no further separation by physical means, pure, *homogeneous* (uniform) substances remain.

By using chemical processes, scientists may be able to separate a substance into two or more simpler kinds of matter with new properties. If so, they call the substance a *compound substance*, or a *chemical compound*. Substances that do not break down into simpler varieties of matter by chemical means are called *elementary substances*, or *chemical elements* (see ELEMENT, CHEMICAL).

Structure of Matter

All matter is made up of *atoms*. An atom is the smallest quantity of an element that can enter into chemical reaction to form a compound. The atoms of an elementary substance are all identical. When two or more elements combine to form a compound, the atoms of one substance combine with the atoms of the other substances. The atoms form larger particles called *molecules*. Water consists of molecules, each of which contains two atoms of hydrogen and one of oxygen. Atoms and molecules are extremely small. If the molecules in a single drop of water were counted at the rate of 10 million each second, a person would need about 5 million years to count them all.

Compounds may be *organic* or *inorganic*. Organic compounds contain the element carbon. They are called organic because most of the compounds found in living organisms (animals and plants) contain carbon. All other compounds are classed as inorganic. These classifications are not completely rigid. Organic molecules are among the largest molecules. They may contain thousands of atoms.

Molecules are bound together by electrical force. This force comes from the electrons in the atoms. Electrons in a molecule may be exchanged between atoms in what chemists call *ionic bonding*. Electrons may also be shared between atoms in what chemists call *covalent bonding* (see CHEMISTRY [Chemical Bonds]).

Conservation of Matter

Before the famous German-American scientist Albert Einstein developed his theory of relativity, scientists believed that matter was never created or destroyed (see RELATIVITY). Their idea was called the *conservation of matter*. But Einstein proved that mass and energy are interchangeable. For example, if a chemical change gives off energy as heat and light, then the substances that changed must have lost some mass. In all ordinary chemical reactions that take place in factories, homes, and laboratories, the amount of mass lost is far too

WORLD BOOK illustration

Matter exists in three forms—solids, such as rocks; liquids, such as water; and gases, such as air.

small to be measured. Measurable quantities of mass are changed into energy only in nuclear reactions that occur in atomic reactors or atomic bombs. Because of Einstein's work, scientists now state the conservation law this way: Mass-energy may not be created or destroyed, but each may be converted into the other.

States of Matter

Matter can ordinarily exist in three physical states—solid, liquid, and gas. For example, ice is solid water. When heated, it melts at a definite temperature to form liquid water. When heat causes the temperature of the water to rise to a certain point, the water boils, producing steam, a gas. Removal of heat reverses these processes. Experiments show that in spite of these changes, the chemical composition of water remains the same. A fourth state of matter, called plasma, exists under special conditions.

Solids. All solids have *form*. They also have *hardness* and *rigidity*, or the ability to oppose a change of shape. For example, stone does not change shape easily. Some solids, like salt or sulfur, are *brittle* and will shatter when struck. Others have great *tensile strength* and resist being pulled apart. Still others, particularly metals, have *malleability* (the ability to be beaten into thin sheets) and *ductility* (the ability to be drawn into wires). These properties depend on the particles that make up the substance and the forces acting among them. The atoms in almost all solids are arranged in regular patterns, called crystals. See SOLID.

Liquids have no shape of their own. But they have the ability to flow. They take the shape of any container in which they are placed. They fill it only when their volume equals that of the container. Iron and steel are rigid in their solid state. But manufacturers often melt them and pour them into molds. See LIQUID.

Gases. All gases, regardless of the composition of their molecules, have almost identical physical behavior. Compared with liquids or solids, they have low densities. They exert pressure equally in all directions. All are compressible. When heated, gases expand greatly or exert a greater pressure when confined in a vessel of fixed volume. See GAS.

Plasmas make up a fourth state of matter and cannot be seen by people in their everyday lives. Plasmas form in the interior of stars, in outer space, and in some laboratory experiments. Plasmas result when the atoms in a gas become *ionized* (electrically charged). Electrical forces between the gas atoms give the gas new physical properties. See PLASMA.   FRANCIS T. COLE

Related Articles in WORLD BOOK include:

Adhesion	Expansion	Liquid
Atom	Gas	Malleability
Cohesion	Gravitation	Molecule
Density	Inertia	Plasma
Elasticity	Lavoisier,	(in physics)
Element, Chemical	Antoine L.	Solid
Energy		Viscosity

MATTER WAVE. See QUANTUM MECHANICS (Understanding Quantum Mechanics).

MATTERHORN, *MAT uhr HAWRN*, is a famous mountain peak in the Pennine Alps. It rises 14,692 feet (4,478 meters) on the boundary between Valais, Switzerland, and the Piedmont region of Italy. It is about 40 miles

Conzett & Huber

The Matterhorn is one of the highest peaks in the Pennine Alps, on the boundary between Italy and Switzerland. The spectacular peak rises from a field of snow-packed glaciers.

(64 kilometers) east of Mont Blanc. For location, see SWITZERLAND (color map). The Matterhorn rises like a pyramid from the mountains around it. Snow always covers the upper slopes of this peak. Many experienced climbers have scaled its steep sides. The first person to make the dangerous climb to the top of the Matterhorn was Edward Whymper in 1865.   FRANKLIN CARL ERICKSON

See also ALPS; MOUNTAIN (picture chart; table); SWITZERLAND (picture).

MATTHEW, SAINT, was one of the apostles of Christ. In the Gospel of Mark, he is called *Levi*, the son of Alphaeus. If this Alphaeus is the same as the one mentioned in Matthew 10:3, he and James the Less may have been brothers (see JAMES [Saint James the Less]). He was a *publican* (professional tax collector). After becoming a disciple, Matthew gave a dinner in Jesus' honor. Many of his friends attended. It was at this dinner that Jesus rebuked the Pharisees.

Matthew is usually regarded as the author of the first Gospel. After Pentecost and the church's early years in Jerusalem, he preached in Syria, and perhaps in Ethiopia and Persia. Early writers said that he died a natural death, but, according to later stories, he was a martyr. His feast day is celebrated on September 21 except in the Eastern Orthodox Church, where it is November 16.   FULTON J. SHEEN and MERRILL C. TENNEY

MATTHIAS, *muh THIE us,* **SAINT,** was elected to take the place of Judas Iscariot as an apostle of Jesus

248

Christ. He was chosen by lot from the 120 disciples who had gathered in the upper room before the day of Pentecost. According to Acts 1:15-26, he was one of Jesus' original disciples and had been with Him since the baptism of John. He is not mentioned again in the New Testament, and nothing is known about the later career of Matthias.   FULTON J. SHEEN and MERRILL C. TENNEY

MATTHIAS CORVINUS. See HUNGARY (The Kingdom of Hungary).

MATTINGLY, THOMAS KENNETH, II (1936-   ), a United States astronaut, piloted the command module *Casper* on the Apollo 16 space flight in April, 1972. He remained in lunar orbit while his fellow astronauts, Charles M. Duke, Jr., and John W. Young, spent 71 hours on the moon. The mission was man's fifth moon landing and the first made in the moon's highlands. During the flight back to the earth, Mattingly took a 62-minute walk in space to retrieve films of the moon from cameras outside the command module.

Mattingly had been named command module pilot for the Apollo 13 mission in April, 1970. John L. Swigert, Jr., replaced him after physicians learned that Mattingly had been exposed to German measles.

Mattingly was born in Chicago. He earned a bachelor's degree in aeronautical engineering at Auburn University in 1958 and entered the Navy that same year. He became a Navy pilot in 1960. Mattingly was chosen to be an astronaut in 1966.   WILLIAM J. CROMIE

MATTRESS. See BED.

MATZAH, *MAHT suh,* is the Hebrew name for an unleavened bread. Jews eat matzahs during the Passover festival in memory of the flight of the ancient Hebrews from Egypt. The Bible says that the Hebrews baked matzahs because they had no time to bake leavened breads. People often use matzahs as tea biscuits or crackers.   LEONARD C. MISHKIN

MATZELIGER, JAN ERNST (1852-1889), invented a machine that revolutionized the shoe industry. He made the first shoe-lasting machine, which shaped and fastened the leather over the sole of a shoe. This process, previously done by hand, led to the mass production of shoes and greatly reduced their price.

Matzeliger, a Negro, was born in Paramaribo, Dutch Guiana (now Surinam). As a boy, he worked in a government machine shop there. In 1873, Matzeliger settled in Philadelphia and worked as a cobbler. In 1877, he took a job in a shoe factory in Lynn, Mass. Matzeliger completed his shoe-lasting machine in 1882 and patented it in 1883. He did not have enough money to produce and sell the machine himself, and so in 1885 he sold the patent to a company in Lynn that later became the United Shoe Machinery Company.

Matzeliger died of tuberculosis at the age of 37. He shared only partly in the great profits that resulted from his invention.   EDGAR ALLAN TOPPIN

MAU MAU, *mow mow,* was a secret movement that included Africans who wanted to end European colonial rule in Kenya. Most who took the oath of unity were Kikuyu people who lived in overcrowded areas. The movement began in the late 1940's. British forces started a drive to wipe out the movement after a series of murders and other terrorist attacks by the Mau Mau started in 1952. Jomo Kenyatta, who later became president of Kenya, was convicted of leading the movement and was held in a remote area until 1961. When the fighting ended in 1956, about 11,500 Kikuyu had been killed. About 2,000 other Africans, 95 Europeans, and 29 Asians lost their lives supporting the government. See also KENYA (History). CARL GUSTAF ROSBERG

MAUGHAM, *mawm,* **W. SOMERSET** (1874-1965), a fiction and drama writer, became one of the most popular British authors of the 1900's. His reputation stood far higher with the public than with critics.

Maugham usually wrote in a detached, ironic style, yet he often showed sympathy for his characters. His semiautobiographical novel *Of Human Bondage* (1915) established his position as a serious writer. Considered his finest work, it is a realistic story of a medical student's bondage to his lameness and his love for an unappreciative woman. *Cakes and Ale* (1930) is generally ranked next among Maugham's

Balkin, Pix
W. Somerset Maugham

novels. It is a comic satire about an English author (possibly Thomas Hardy, although Maugham denied it). Maugham based his novel *The Moon and Sixpence* (1919) on the life of the painter Paul Gauguin. Maugham's experiences in the British secret service during World War I provided the background for a group of related stories published as *Ashenden* (1928).

Maugham's short story collections include *The Trembling of a Leaf* (1921), *On a Chinese Screen* (1922), and *First Person Singular* (1931). *The Summing Up* (1938) and *A Writer's Notebook* (1949) are the direct, personal observations of a professional writer.

Maugham wrote many sophisticated plays, beginning with *Lady Frederick* (1907). His most popular comedies include *The Circle* (1921) and *The Constant Wife* (1927).

Maugham was born in Paris, the son of a British embassy official. His full name was William Somerset Maugham. He studied medicine at the request of his family, but he never practiced after completing his internship. HARRY T. MOORE

MAUI. See HAWAII (The Islands).

MAULDIN, BILL (1921-   ), became a noted soldier cartoonist during World War II, and won 1945 and 1959 Pulitzer prizes for his cartoons. Mauldin portrayed war and the combat infantrymen as they really were. His best-known book, *Up Front* (1945), is a collection of war cartoons and their stories. His other cartoon collections include *Sicily Sketchbook* (1943), *Mud, Mules, and Mountains* (1944), *Back Home* (1947), *Bill Mauldin in Korea* (1952), and *What's Got Your Back Up?* (1961). Born in Mountain Park, N. Mex., William Henry Mauldin was an editorial cartoonist for the *St. Louis Post-Dispatch* from 1958 to 1962 when he became editorial cartoonist for the *Chicago Sun-Times*. DICK SPENCER III

See also KENNEDY, JOHN F. (picture: The Nation's Sorrow).

MAUNA KEA, *MOU nah KAY ah,* is a volcano on the island of Hawaii. It is 13,796 feet (4,205 meters) high and ranks as the world's highest island peak. Measured from its underwater base, Mauna Kea is 33,476 feet (10,203 meters) tall, 4,448 feet (1,356 meters) higher

than Mount Everest. The name *Mauna Kea* means *white mountain.*

MAUNA LOA, *MOU nah LOH ah,* a volcanic mountain on the island of Hawaii, rises 13,677 feet (4,169 meters) above sea level in Hawaii Volcanoes National Park (see HAWAII [physical map]). At the top is Mokuaweoweo, a crater. Kilauea volcano lies on the southeastern slope.

Mauna Loa's longest eruption lasted 18 months in 1855-1856. Several eruptions have produced tremendous amounts of lava. Most of the lava comes from the sides of the mountain, and not from the peak crater. In 1926, lava destroyed a fishing village. Parts of other villages were buried in 1950. Lava flows have threatened the nearby city of Hilo. GORDON A. MACDONALD

See also KILAUEA; VOLCANO.

MAUNDY THURSDAY, or HOLY THURSDAY, comes three days before Easter. It commemorates two events of Christ's last week on earth: washing the feet of His disciples, and sharing the Last Supper with them. The name *Maundy* probably comes from the Latin *mandatum,* or *commandment.* It refers to Christ's words to the disciples (John 13: 34): "A new commandment I give unto you: that ye love one another."

Traditionally, the priest girded himself with a linen towel, took a vessel of water, and washed the feet of the faithful. In Austria, Portugal, Russia, and Spain, the emperor or king used to wash the feet of 12 poor persons on Maundy Thursday. In England, servants

Courtesy of Mr. and Mrs. Sidney Simon, New York, New York

"Beautiful view! Is there one for the enlisted men?"

Cartoonist Bill Mauldin accurately pictured the favorite gripes and the plight of the common soldier in World War II. This drawing lampooning officers became one of his most famous.

249

known as *yeomen of the laundry* washed the feet of the poor while the king or queen watched. James II was the last to perform the rite in full in the 1680's.

Roman Catholic bishops consecrate the oil used in the sacraments on Maundy Thursday. The altar is stripped for the rite of *Tenebrae* (darkness). In some cathedrals, the bishop washes the feet of 12 or 13 men or boys. Pope John XXIII revived the foot-bathing custom by a pope in 1961. Popes had not observed the rite since the reign of Pope Pius IX, who died in 1878.

Martin Luther and his followers condemned the practice of washing feet. A few Protestant groups still practice it. The ceremony is intended as a visible token of Christian brotherly love.   FLOYD H. ROSS

MAUPASSANT, GUY DE. See DE MAUPASSANT, GUY.

MAURER, *MOW rur,* **ION GHEORGHE** (1902-   ), became prime minister of Romania in 1961. He is also a member of the Presidium, the chief executive body of the Romanian Communist Party.

Maurer was born in Bucharest and earned a law degree at Bucharest University. During the 1930's, he served as defense attorney for Communists in various trials. Maurer joined the party in 1936. In 1945, he was named undersecretary for communications. From 1948 to 1955, Maurer was director of the Institute for Juridical Research of the Academy of Sciences. He became vice-president of the National Assembly in 1957 and minister for foreign affairs in 1958.   ALVIN Z. RUBINSTEIN

MAURETANIA. See MOROCCO (History); MOOR; ROMAN EMPIRE (map).

MAURI, or **MAURE.** See MOOR.

MAURIAC, *maw rih AK,* **FRANÇOIS** (1885-1970), a French author, won the 1952 Nobel prize for literature. Mauriac's novels are set among middle-class people in his native Bordeaux. The attitudes toward sin and love expressed in his fiction reflect his Roman Catholic faith. Mauriac's novels explore the mysteries of human existence, the nature of destiny, and human guilt before a judging though forgiving God. His stories are also noted for their psychology and the beauty of their language. His major novels include *Flesh and Blood* (1920), *A Kiss to the Leper* (1922), *Genitrix* (1923), *Thérèse Desqueyroux* (1927), and *The Knot of Vipers* (1932).

In 1934, Mauriac began to write essays on his view of life and literature for the newspaper *Le Figaro.* These essays have been republished periodically in collections called *Journals.* Mauriac also wrote several plays, including *Asmodée* (1938) and *Le Feu sur la terre* (1951). His poetry was collected in *Le Sang d'Atys* (1940). His biographies include two studies of Christ, *The Life of Jesus* (1936) and *The Son of Man* (1958).

Mauriac was elected to the French Academy in 1933. Claude Mauriac, his son, is also a well-known novelist.   EDITH KERN

MAURITANIA is a big country in western Africa. It covers a larger area than California, Oregon, and Washington combined, but it has only about half as many people as the San Francisco-Oakland metropolitan area. Mauritania stretches eastward from the Atlantic coast into the Sahara. Arabic-speaking people called Moors make up the majority of Mauritania's population. Black Africans form a large minority group.

Mauritania was once a colony in French West Africa.

Marc & Evelyne Bernheim, Rapho Guillumette

A Holy Man in Mauritania belongs to one of the highest castes (social classes) in this Islamic republic. The tablet he holds contains verses from the Koran, sacred book of the Islamic faith.

It became independent in 1960. Its name in French is RÉPUBLIQUE ISLAMIQUE DE MAURITANIE (ISLAMIC REPUBLIC OF MAURITANIA). The name comes from the fact that almost all the people are Muslims. Nouakchott, a town of about 135,000, is the capital and largest city.

Government. Military leaders have controlled the government of Mauritania since 1978. The top military leader serves as president. Two vice-presidents, both military officers, assist the president. One of the vice-presidents serves as premier. The premier heads a Cabinet, which carries out the operations of the government.

Mauritania is divided into seven regions and one district for purposes of local government. The capital makes up the district.

People. About 99 per cent of the people are Muslims, but the way of life differs among the various groups.

About one-fifth of the people are settled black farmers who live in neat villages along the Sénégal River. Their circular huts, which have walls made of sun-dried mudbrick, stand along narrow, twisting village pathways. Most of them speak the Tucolor language. The

Clement Henry Moore, the contributor of this article, is Associate Professor of Political Science at the University of Michigan.

─────── FACTS IN BRIEF ───────

Capital: Nouakchott.

Official Language: French. *National Language*—Arabic.

Area: 397,956 sq. mi. (1,030,700 km²). *Greatest Distances*—north-south, 800 mi. (1,287 km); east-west, 780 mi. (1,255 km). *Coastline*—414 mi. (666 km).

Population: *Estimated 1981 Population*—1,647,000; distribution, 90 per cent rural, 10 per cent urban; density, 5 persons per sq. mi. (2 per km²). *1976 Census*—1,481,000. *Estimated 1986 Population*—1,882,000.

Chief Products: *Agriculture*—dates, gum arabic, livestock (cattle, sheep, goats), millet. *Mining*—iron ore. *Fishing*—ocean and freshwater fish.

Flag: The flag is green and has a yellow star and crescent in the center. The green color and the star and crescent stand for Mauritania's ties to Islam and north Africa. The yellow stands for the country's ties to nations south of the Sahara. See FLAG (color picture: Flags of Africa).

Money: *Basic Unit*—ouguiya. See MONEY (table).

blacks were the first to gain a modern education, and many hold jobs in government and as teachers.

The majority of people are Moors, descendants of Arabs and Berbers. Most Moors speak Arabic. They lead a nomadic life, living in camel-hair tents and moving over the desert and other regions with their cattle in search of waterholes and sparse pastureland. The Moors are divided into two groups, the nomadic warrior tribes and the *marabout* (saintly) tribes.

Until the French came, the warriors were a nobility who kept black slaves. Other tribes served the warriors, whose chief occupation was fighting.

The peaceful marabout tribes have always raised livestock, such as cattle and sheep. Before French rule, leading marabout families were a learned class who studied religion and law and advised the warriors.

Mauritania has two chief languages. French is the official language, but most of the people speak Arabic. Arabic is called the national language. The Moors want to make Arabic the official language, but the blacks want to keep the two-language system. This dispute over language is the most dangerous threat to the country's unity.

There are few educated persons in Mauritania. Only 10 per cent of the children attend primary school. About 20 students complete high school each year. Those who want higher education study in France or Senegal.

Land. An imaginary line drawn between Nouakchott on the coast and Néma in the southeast divides Mauritania into two major land regions. The Sahara covers most of the area north of the Nouakchott-Néma line. It is broken only by rocky plateaus and a few oases.

The small part of the country south of the line receives enough rainfall to support farming and livestock-raising. It contains two fertile areas—a narrow plain along the Sénégal River and a *savanna* (grassland) in the southeast. Farmers raise millet, rice, and other crops on the plain. Herders raise livestock in the savanna area. Eighty per cent of the people live in the south.

Mauritania's climate is hot, but temperatures vary greatly. Desert temperatures may fall from over 100° F. (38° C) during the day to 45° F. (7° C) at night. The average monthly temperatures at Nouadhibou (formerly Port-Étienne) vary from a 91° F. (33° C) high in September to a 54° F. (12° C) low in January. There is little rain in the north. Southern Mauritania receives

more than 20 inches (51 centimeters) of rain a year.

Economy. Mauritania's economy is based on agriculture and 90 per cent of the people are farmers and livestock herders. The chief food crops include millet, dates, corn, red beans, and rice. Gum arabic, which is used to make mucilage, and livestock on the hoof are important exports. A rich fishing ground lies off the coast.

Large high-grade iron ore deposits near Fort-Gouraud are Mauritania's most important mineral resource. A French-operated company mines the deposits. The iron ore is exported chiefly to Great Britain, Germany, and Italy. Taxes on these exports make up almost one-third of the government's revenue.

Incomes in Mauritania are low and most workers make only enough to provide for their families. The government depends upon aid from other countries—chiefly France—to balance its budget. The government is trying to develop a meat-processing industry and to expand the fishing industry. But poor communications and transportation block economic development.

Mauritania's railroad, which is 420 miles (676 kilometers) long, links Fort-Gouraud and Akjoujt with Nouadhibou, the chief port. Mauritania has about 3,100 miles (4,990 kilometers) of dirt roads.

Mauritania

⊛ Capital

• Other City or Town

── Road

⊢→ Rail Line

+ Highest Known Elevation

∼ River

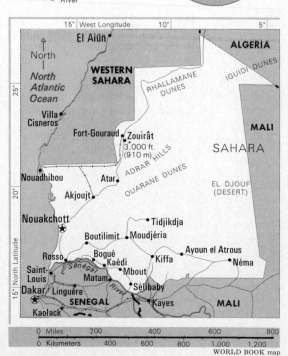

WORLD BOOK map

MAURITIUS

History. From the A.D. 300's to the 1500's, areas of what is now Mauritania were part of two great West African empires—Ghana and Mali. In the early 1900's, archaeologists identified a ruins in southeastern Mauritania as part of Kumbi Saleh, the capital of the Ghana Empire. See GHANA EMPIRE; MALI EMPIRE.

The Portuguese landed in Mauritania in the 1400's, but continuous European contact did not begin until the 1600's. Between the 1600's and the 1800's, France, Great Britain, and The Netherlands competed for the Mauritanian gum arabic trade.

France began to occupy Mauritania in 1902 and set up a protectorate there in 1903. Xavier Coppolani became the first governor. Modern Mauritania is largely the result of Coppolani's work in extending French rule over the country. It became a French colony in 1920.

After World War II, Mauritanian political leaders began to gain power. In 1946, Mauritania became a territory in the French Union. It became a self-governing republic in the French Community in 1958. Mokhtar Ould Daddah was elected prime minister in 1959. Supported by many Moorish leaders and the small group of educated black leaders, he favored independence and close ties with west African countries. On Nov. 28, 1960, Mauritania became fully independent. Morocco claimed that Mauritania was historically Moroccan territory and did not recognize its independence. Some of Ould Daddah's opponents fled to Morocco and worked to unite the two countries. But Morocco recognized Mauritania's independence in 1970.

In 1961, Mauritania adopted a constitution which set up a presidential system of government. Ould Daddah, elected the first president, merged Mauritania's four political parties into a single party, the Mauritanian People's Party. A 1965 constitutional amendment officially made Mauritania a one-party state. In the early 1970's, a severe drought caused widespread food shortages and losses of livestock in Mauritania.

In 1976, Spain gave up control of its overseas province of Spanish Sahara, and Mauritania and Morocco took over the administration of the province. This area—which borders Mauritania, Morocco, and Algeria—is now called Western Sahara. Mauritania claimed the southern part of the area, and Morocco claimed the northern part. But Algeria and an organization of people of Western Sahara called the Polisario Front opposed the claims. Fighting broke out between Polisario Front troops, and troops from Mauritania and Morocco. Algeria and, later, Libya, gave military aid to the Polisario Front.

In 1978, military leaders overthrew Ould Daddah and took control of the government. Military leaders have ruled the country since then. In 1979, Mauritania gave up its claim to Western Sahara and ended its role in the fighting. CLEMENT HENRY MOORE

See also FRENCH WEST AFRICA; NOUAKCHOTT.

MAURITIUS, *maw RIHSH uhs,* is an island nation in the Indian Ocean. It lies about 500 miles (800 kilometers) east of Madagascar and about 2,450 miles (3,943 kilometers) southwest of India. Population is one of the island's problems. Mauritius is about three-fifths as big as Rhode Island, but it has more people than that state.

Mauritius

- ⊛ Capital
- • Other City or Town
- — Road
- ▲ MOUNTAIN
- ⌒ River

WORLD BOOK map

Sugar cane fields cover about half of the island. Bare, black volcanic peaks tower over the sugar cane fields. Sugar is the island's chief product.

The Dutch claimed Mauritius in 1598. Later, France and then Great Britain ruled the island. Mauritius became independent in 1968. Port Louis, a city of about 141,100 persons, is the capital and leading port.

Government. Mauritius is a constitutional monarchy. A governor general, appointed by Great Britain, represents the Crown. But a premier, chosen by the majority party in the assembly, runs the government.

The 70-member Legislative Assembly passes laws for the country. Elections for the assembly are held at least once every five years. Adults cast three votes, and elect three assembly members from each of the island's 20 districts. To guarantee fair representation for minority groups, an electoral supervisory commission chooses eight more members from among unsuccessful candidates. They choose four members from minorities that do not have enough representatives in the assembly in proportion to their numbers in the population. They choose the other four on the basis of minority groups and political party. The people of Rodrigues elect two members to the Legislative Assembly.

--- **FACTS IN BRIEF** ---

Capital: Port Louis.
Official Language: English.
Form of Government: Constitutional monarchy.
Area: 790 sq. mi. (2,045 km²). *Greatest Length*—38 mi. (61 km). *Greatest Width*—29 mi. (47 km). *Coastline*—100 mi. (161 km).
Elevations: *Highest*—2,711 ft. (826 m). *Lowest*—sea level.
Population: *Estimated 1981 Population*—957,000; distribution, 54 per cent rural, 46 per cent urban; density, 1,212 persons per sq. mi. (468 per km²). *1972 Census*—851,335. *Estimated 1986 Population*—1,021,000.
Chief Product: *Agriculture*—sugar.
Flag: The flag's four horizontal stripes are red, blue, yellow, and green (top to bottom). Red stands for the struggle for freedom, blue for the Indian Ocean, yellow for the light of independence shining over the island, and green for agriculture. Adopted 1968. See FLAG (color picture: Flags of Africa).
Money: *Basic Unit*—rupee.

Throughout Mauritius, councils govern villages and towns. Their members are elected by adult voters.

People. The people of Mauritius are descendants of European settlers, African slaves, Chinese traders, and Indian laborers and traders. About 2 out of 3 persons are Indians, and about 3 out of 10 are persons of European and African or European and Indian ancestry called *Creoles.* The rest are Chinese or Europeans. Most Europeans are of French descent.

More than half of the people live in villages throughout the island. But most Europeans live in the towns. In the past, most villagers lived in houses that had mud walls and thatched roofs. But now many villagers are building houses with concrete and wood walls and corrugated iron roofs. Most men wear Western-style clothes. Indian women wear the colorful *sari* (a straight piece of cloth draped around the body).

English is the official language, but French may also be used in the Legislative Assembly. Most of the people speak *Creole,* a French dialect. Some Indians speak one or more of six Indian dialects, and the Chinese speak two Chinese dialects. Most Europeans speak French.

About half the people are Hindus, and about a third are Christians. Hindu temples, Muslim mosques, Buddhist pagodas, and Christian churches dot the island.

Primary education is free, but not compulsory. About 60 per cent of the people can read and write. Mauritius has an agricultural college, a teachers' training college, and a university college.

Land. Mauritius covers a total of 790 square miles (2,045 square kilometers). The country consists of the island of Mauritius, which has an area of 720 square miles (1,865 square kilometers), and several other islands. The other islands include Rodrigues, about 350 miles (563 kilometers) east of Mauritius; Agalega, two small islands about 580 miles (933 kilometers) north of Mauritius; and the Cargados Carajos Archipelago, about 250 miles (402 kilometers) north.

The island of Mauritius was formed by volcanoes that left the land covered with rocks and a thick layer of lava. A misty plateau in the center of the island rises 2,200 feet (671 meters) above sea level. This area may receive up to 200 inches (510 centimeters) of rain a year. In the north, the plateau slopes to the sea. But it drops sharply to the southern and western coasts. Dry regions that receive only about 35 inches (89 centimeters) of rain a year lie in the southwest. Coral reefs surround all but the southern part of the island.

Summer lasts from November to April, and the temperatures then average about 79° F. (26° C). Southeast winds bring rains to the plateau. Sometimes cyclones strike the island. Winter lasts from June to October. Temperatures then average about 72° F. (22° C).

Economy. More than a third of the nation's income comes from the sugar industry, and almost all its exports are sugar or sugar products. About two-thirds of all workers grow, harvest, or process sugar cane. About 90 per cent of the farmland is planted with sugar cane. Twenty-five large sugar estates own over half of the cane fields. The rest are cultivated by individual planters. Sugar is processed in factories on the island.

Farmers also raise tea in the wet uplands. About two-thirds of the tea crop is exported. Some tobacco is raised and made into cigarettes. People grow vegetables in small gardens or between the rows of sugar cane.

A few keep cattle, goats, or chickens. But almost all of the island's food, including rice, cattle, grain, meat, and wheat flour, must be imported. Mauritius has about 550 miles (885 kilometers) of paved roads. An airline owned partly by the government began operating between Mauritius and nearby Reunion in 1967.

History. Portuguese sailors were the first Europeans to visit Mauritius. In the 1500's, they stopped there for food and water. Mauritius was uninhabited until the Dutch claimed the island in 1598, and named it after Prince Maurice of Nassau. The Dutch brought slaves from the island of Madagascar to cut down the ebony forests, but they abandoned Mauritius in 1710.

In 1715, France took possession of the island, and renamed it Île de France. French colonists from the neighboring island of Bourbon (now Reunion) moved to Mauritius in 1722. They imported slaves, built a port, and planted coffee, fruit, spices, sugar, and vegetables. During the Anglo-French wars of the 1700's, the French launched attacks from the island against British shipping in the Indian Ocean and against British settlements in India. The British captured the island in 1810, made it a colony, and renamed it Mauritius.

In 1833, Britain ordered the abolition of slavery in its empire. More than 75,000 slaves were freed in Mauritius. Most of them refused to continue working on the sugar plantations. Planters then brought in nearly 450,-000 Indian laborers from 1835 to 1907.

In the 1950's, Mauritius began to achieve self-government. By 1962, the leader of the majority party in the assembly served as chief minister. Later, the chief minister (now called premier) and his cabinet were given partial control of the government. Mauritius became independent on March 12, 1968. BURTON BENEDICT

See also PORT LOUIS; DODO.

MAUROIS, *moh RWAH,* **ANDRÉ** (1885-1967), was the pen name of Émile Herzog, a French novelist and biographer. Maurois tried to attain in his life and writings the spirit of the French writer Michel de Montaigne —a skeptical detachment from life, mixed with humor. These qualities appear in his best works.

Maurois's place in literature probably rests with his biographies of English and French authors. His most notable works include the lives of Percy Shelley (*Ariel,* 1923), Benjamin Disraeli (*The Life of Disraeli,* 1927), Lord Byron (*Don Juan,* 1930), George Sand (*Lélia,* 1952), Victor Hugo (*Olympio,* 1954), and three generations of the Alexandre Dumas family (*The Titans,* 1957).

Maurois was born in Elbeuf. During World War I, he served as a French liaison officer with the British Army. His first works were two humorous novels based on his war experiences, *The Silence of Colonel Bramble* (1918) and *Les Discours du Docteur O'Grady* (1922). *Climats* (1928) established Maurois as a skillful novelist with an elegant style. He also wrote popular histories of France, England, and the United States. Maurois was elected to the French Academy in 1938. Maurois' *Memoirs: 1885-1967* was published in 1970.   EDITH KERN

MAURY, *MAW rih,* **MATTHEW FONTAINE** (1806-1873), was a United States naval officer and scientist who did much to improve ocean travel. He has been called the *Pathfinder of the Seas.* Maury spent years collecting information on winds and currents from ships'

records and from his own travels. His *Wind and Current Charts* formed the basis for all pilot charts that were issued by the U.S. government. He published works on navigation, naval reform, meteorology, and astronomy, including the *Physical Geography of the Sea and Its Meteorology*. In the 1850's, he aided in laying the Atlantic Cable (see CABLE [The Atlantic Telegraph Cable]).

Maury entered the Navy as a midshipman in 1825. He took charge of the Navy Department's Depot of Charts and Instruments in 1842. The Naval Observatory and the Hydrographic Office grew out of this office, and were developed according to his plans. He became a commander, effective in 1855.

During the Civil War, Maury joined the Confederate forces. He was in charge of all coast, harbor, and river defenses. The Confederacy sent him to England as a special envoy. While there, he invented an electric mine for harbor defense. He went to Mexico after the war and tried unsuccessfully to set up a colony of Virginians there. Later, he went to England, where he received honors and financial aid. When President Andrew Johnson pardoned Confederate leaders in 1868, Maury returned home. He became a professor of meteorology at the Virginia Military Institute in Lexington, Va.

Maury was born near Fredericksburg, Va. In 1930, he was elected to the Hall of Fame. RICHARD S. WEST, JR.

MAURYA EMPIRE, *MOW ree uh*, was the first empire of India to provide a uniform government for almost the entire country. The Maurya emperors ruled from about 321 to 185 B.C. During its early period, the empire provided efficient, stern government, resulting in prosperity but little freedom.

Chandragupta Maurya, who ruled from about 321 to 298 B.C., conquered much of North India and West Pakistan and part of Afghanistan. His son Bindusara held the throne from about 298 to 272 B.C., and Bindusara's son Asoka governed from about 272 to 232 B.C. Both expanded the empire far into South India. Asoka eventually gave up further conquest. The empire broke up into smaller units after Asoka's death.

During the Maurya Empire, public irrigation works helped farms produce good harvests. Craftworkers made cloth, gold, jewelry, and wood products. Many persons worked in farms, forests, mines, and workshops owned by the state. Many peasants and war prisoners worked as slaves to develop new agricultural lands. A system of royal inspectors, spies, and informers made sure that officials and citizens alike obeyed the emperor's will. The Maurya Empire traded with Ceylon, Greece, Malaya, Mesopotamia, and Persia. Broach, near the mouth of the Narbada River, was a seaport for commerce with the Persian Gulf states.

Pataliputra, the Maurya capital, stood at what is now Patna. It was surrounded by a wall with 570 watchtowers and 64 gates. The wooden palace of Chandragupta was in a park filled with flowering trees, fountains, and fish ponds. Asoka built a new palace of stone and also erected many stone monuments. J. F. RICHARDS

See also ASOKA; CHANDRAGUPTA MAURYA.

MAUSOLEUM. See TOMB.

MAUSOLEUM AT HALICARNASSUS. See SEVEN WONDERS OF THE WORLD.

MAUVE is a delicate pale purple or violet dye. In 1856, W. H. Perkin, an English chemist, discovered that the oxidation of *aniline* and *potassium dichromate* produces mauve dye (see OXIDATION). It is a mixture of derivatives of phenazine. It was the first synthetic coloring obtained from coal tar chemicals. FRED FORTESS

MAVE, QUEEN. See MYTHOLOGY (The Irish Cycles).

MAVERICK, SAMUEL AUGUSTUS (1803-1870), was a prominent Texas pioneer and statesman. He helped establish the Republic of Texas. His name has become part of the American language. In 1845, Maverick took a herd of 400 cattle in payment of a debt. He did not mark his cattle with a brand. They strayed, and neighboring ranchers called them *mavericks*. This came to be the name given to all unmarked cattle.

Maverick was born in South Carolina. He was graduated from Yale University and practiced law in Virginia and Alabama before going to Texas. THOMAS D. CLARK

MAVIS. See THRUSH (bird).

MAX PLANCK SOCIETY FOR THE ADVANCEMENT OF SCIENCE is the principal organization for scientific research in West Germany. The society distributes government funds for research in the natural and social sciences. It supports about 50 research institutes in a wide variety of fields and employs more than 4,000 scientists. The society also maintains libraries and training institutions. More than 20 winners of Nobel prizes have been members of the society.

The Max Planck Society, formerly called the Kaiser Wilhelm Society, was founded in 1911 by the German philosopher Adolph von Harnack. In 1948, the society changed its name to honor Max Planck, a German physicist who helped formulate the quantum theory. The society publishes a journal, *Die Naturwissenschaften* (*The Natural Sciences*). ROBERT H. MARCH

MAXILLAE. See FACE; INSECT (Mouth Parts).

MAXIM, *MACK sim*, was the family name of three famous American-born inventors.

Sir Hiram Stevens Maxim (1840-1916) invented the automatic gun that bears his name. The Maxim gun uses the force of recoil caused by the explosion of a cartridge to throw out the empty shell and ram home a new one. The invention of the Maxim gun changed many warfare methods.

Maxim was born near Sangerville, Me. He worked for a time in a machine shop and in a shipbuilding yard. He did early inventive work on gas-generating plants and electric lighting. He lost his rights to an important patent in a lawsuit with Thomas Edison. Maxim then moved to England, where he set up the Maxim Gun Company. The company later merged with the Vickers munitions company. Maxim experimented with internal-combustion engines for automobiles and airplanes. In 1894, he tested a steam-powered airplane that actually lifted itself off the ground. Maxim became a British citizen in 1900, and was knighted in 1901. See AIRPLANE (Powered Flight); MACHINE GUN.

Hudson Maxim (1853-1927), Sir Hiram Maxim's brother, invented *maximite*, an explosive one and a half times as powerful as dynamite. Maxim also invented a smokeless powder, a self-propelled torpedo, and a torpedo ram. He was born in Orneville, Me., and worked first as a book publisher. He later became interested in explosives, and worked briefly for his brother. He set up a company, but sold out to E. I. du Pont de Nemours

& Company and acted as an adviser to Du Pont.

Hiram Percy Maxim (1869-1936), son of Sir Hiram S. Maxim, invented a silencer for guns. Maxim also worked on mufflers to eliminate noises in gasoline engines, and developed several electrical appliances. His silencer was later used to quiet the roar of jet engines. He wrote the books *Life's Place in the Cosmos* (1933), and *Horseless Carriage Days* (1937). He was born in Brooklyn, N.Y.   CHARLES EDWARD CHAPEL

MAXIMILIAN, *MACK suh MIL ih un* (1832-1867), ruled as Emperor of Mexico from 1864 to 1867. He was a victim of a European nation's attempts to gain possessions and influence in North America.

Emperor Napoleon III of France used Maximilian to further his attempt to control Mexico. The French had landed in Mexico in 1862 to collect debts. They advanced inland and captured Mexico City. At this time, Napoleon III decided that he wanted to control Mexico. He offered the crown to Maximilian, then Archduke of Austria. Maximilian accepted on the basis of "proof" given by Napoleon and by Mexican exiles in France that the Mexican people wanted him. The United States was involved in the Civil War. It could not enforce the Monroe Doctrine, which forbade European intervention in the Americas.

Benito Juárez, president of Mexico, resisted the French (see JUÁREZ, BENITO PABLO). In 1865, Maximilian ordered that Juárez supporters be shot on sight. His advisers assured him that resistance had ended, and that this order would prevent further trouble.

Maximilian's empire was doomed when the Civil War in the United States ended. The United States could now enforce the Monroe Doctrine. Napoleon III was forced to withdraw his troops from Mexico, leaving Maximilian without support. Maximilian's wife Carlota (1840-1927) went to Europe to seek aid, but failed.

Maximilian left Mexico City in 1867 to fight Juárez. He and his soldiers marched to Querétaro, where General Gómez, a trusted aide, betrayed him. He was captured by troops of the Mexican Republic, and was executed by a firing squad on June 19, 1867.

Maximilian was born in Vienna. He was a brother of Austrian Emperor Francis Joseph. He trained with the Austrian navy and served briefly as its commander in chief. He married Carlota, daughter of King Leopold I of Belgium, in 1857.   DONALD E. WORCESTER

See also MEXICO (The French Invasion).

MAXIMILIAN I (1459-1519), reigned as Holy Roman Emperor from 1493 to 1519 (see HOLY ROMAN EMPIRE). He is noted for extending the power of the House of Hapsburg through wars and marriages (see HAPSBURG).

Maximilian, son of Emperor Frederick III, married Mary, daughter of Charles the Bold of Burgundy, in 1477. He fought Mary's war with Louis XI of France for possession of Burgundy and The Netherlands. He won the war, but the Netherland states, hostile to him, signed a treaty with Louis XI in 1482. The treaty forced Maximilian to give Burgundy back to Louis XI. Mary died the same year.

Maximilian became emperor in 1493. He married Bianca, daughter of the Duke of Milan, in 1494. He fought another long war with France for control of possessions in Italy, and lost. He was forced to grant Switzerland its independence after a war in 1499.

Maximilian arranged the marriage of his son, Philip,

Archduke of Austria, to Juana of Castile, daughter of Ferdinand and Isabella of Spain, in 1496. The marriage gave Spain to the Hapsburgs when Philip and Juana's son became king of Spain and, later, emperor as Charles V. Maximilian established claims on Hungary and Bohemia when his grandchildren married heirs of these countries. He was born in Wiener Neustadt, Austria.   FRANKLIN D. SCOTT

MAXIMITE. See MAXIM (Hudson).

MAXIXE DANCE. See DANCING (The 1900's).

MAXWELL is a unit of magnetic flux. It represents a single line of force. Flux density of 1 maxwell to a square centimeter is a *gauss* (see GAUSS).

MAXWELL, JAMES CLERK (1831-1879), a British scientist, was one of the greatest mathematicians and physicists of the 1800's. He is most famous for his studies of electricity in motion and the kinetic theory of gases (see GAS). He was an excellent experimental, as well as theoretical, physicist.

Maxwell used the experimental discoveries of Michael Faraday to arrive at exact mathematical descriptions of electric and magnetic fields (see FARADAY, MICHAEL). He assumed that these fields acted together to produce a new kind of energy called *radiant energy*. This led him to predict in 1864 the existence of electromagnetic waves that move through space with the speed of light. The discovery of these waves by Heinrich Hertz in 1887 led to the development of radio, television, and radar (see HERTZ, HEINRICH R.).

Maxwell's conclusion that light waves were electromagnetic and not mechanical in nature made the field of physical optics a subdivision of electricity. His findings provided the framework for later studies of the nature of X rays and ultraviolet rays. His work on the theory of gases in motion paved the way for great advances in thermodynamics. Using statistical methods, Maxwell could predict how many molecules of a gas had a particular speed at any given moment (see THERMODYNAMICS).

Maxwell was born in Edinburgh, Scotland, the son of wealthy parents. His mother died when he was nine. He was educated at the University of Edinburgh, which he entered at the age of 16, and at Trinity College, Cambridge. He was the pupil at Cambridge of William Hopkins, who was considered one of the ablest mathematics teachers of the time. Maxwell taught natural philosophy in 1856 at Marischal College which is located in Aberdeen, Scotland.

From 1860 to 1865, Maxwell served as professor of natural philosophy at King's College, London. He left retirement in 1871 to install the Cavendish Laboratory and to become the first teacher of experimental physics at Cambridge University. He was interested in theories of color and vision, and investigated the eye disorder known as color blindness.

Maxwell published many of the discoveries which Henry Cavendish, the physicist, had made about 60 years before (see CAVENDISH, HENRY). Maxwell's best-known work, *Treatise on Electricity and Magnetism*, was published in 1873. It is now recognized as the foundation of present-day electromagnetic theory (see ELECTROMAGNETISM).   SIDNEY ROSEN

MAXWELL AIR FORCE BASE. See AIR UNIVERSITY.

MAY

MAY is one of the most beautiful months of the year in the North Temperate Zone. The snow and ice have melted, and summer's intense heat has not yet begun. The first garden crops begin to sprout in May. The trees and grass are green, and wild plants are in bloom. Wild flowers that blossom in different parts of the United States include the jack-in-the-pulpit, anemone, hepatica, forsythia, dogwood, and blue, yellow, and white violets. Many birds have already built their nests, and mother birds are sitting on the eggs which will soon hatch.

May was the third month on the early Roman calendar, and March was the first. January and February were the 11th and 12th months. Julius Caesar changed the calendar to begin with January, making May the fifth month. May has always had 31 days.

There are several stories about how this month was named. The most widely accepted one is that it was named for Maia, the Roman goddess of spring and growth. But some scholars say that May is short for *majores*, the Latin word for *older men*. They believe that May was the month sacred to the *majores*, just as June was considered sacred to the *juniores* (young men).

May Customs. Even in ancient times, May 1 was a day for outdoor festivals. In Rome, May 1 fell at a time that was sacred to Flora, the goddess of flowers. The Romans celebrated the day with flower-decked parades. The English also observed many beautiful May-day customs. Maypoles were erected in village parks. On the morning of May 1, the village youths went to the woods and gathered "Mayflowers," or hawthorn blossoms, to trim the Maypole. The girls wore their prettiest dresses, each hoping that the people would elect her as May queen. The queen danced around the Maypole with her "subjects."

Special Days. In most states of the United States, the last Monday in May is observed as Memorial Day, or Decoration Day. It is a legal holiday in memory of those who died in the Civil War, Spanish-American War, World Wars I and II, the Korean War, and the Vietnam War. The graves of war heroes are decorated with flowers. Memorial Day was first observed in 1868.

Two special days in May have been designated by Presidential proclamations. Mother's Day, first observed in 1907, was recognized officially by Congress and the

---

IMPORTANT MAY EVENTS

1 Joseph Addison, English essayist, born 1672.
—The Act of Union joined England and Wales with Scotland to form Great Britain, 1707.
—Admiral Dewey won the Battle of Manila Bay, 1898.
—Empire State Building opened, 1931.

2 Leonardo da Vinci, Italian Renaissance artist and scientist, died 1519.
—Hudson's Bay Company chartered 1670.
—Catherine the Great of Russia born 1729.

3 Niccolò Machiavelli, author of *The Prince*, born 1469.
—First American medical school opened in Philadelphia, 1765.
—Jacob A. Riis, American newspaperman and social reformer, born 1849.

4 Rhode Island declared its independence, 1776.
—Horace Mann, American educator, born 1796.
—Thomas Huxley, English biologist, born 1825.
—Haymarket Riot took place in Chicago, 1886.

5 Christopher Columbus reached Jamaica, 1494.
—Karl Marx, author of *Das Kapital*, born 1818.
—Napoleon died on St. Helena, 1821.
—Mexicans defeated French at Puebla, 1862.
—Christopher Morley, American author, born 1890.

6 Robespierre, French statesman, born 1758.
—First postage stamp issued in England, 1840.
—Robert E. Peary, American explorer who reached the North Pole, born 1856.
—Psychoanalyst Sigmund Freud born 1856.
—Rabindranath Tagore, Hindu poet, born 1861.
—Works Progress Administration (WPA) set up, 1935.
—Airship *Hindenburg* blew up and burned, 1937.
—United States forces on Corregidor surrendered to Japanese, 1942.

7 Robert Browning, English poet, born 1812.
—Composer Johannes Brahms born 1833.
—Peter Ilich Tchaikovsky, Russian composer, born 1840.
—A German submarine sank the *Lusitania*, 1915.

8 Harry S. Truman, 33rd President of the United States, born in Lamar, Mo., 1884.
—First V-E Day celebrated, 1945.

Harry S. Truman

9 John Brown, American abolitionist, born 1800.
—Sir James Barrie, Scottish author, born 1860.
—Mother's Day became a public holiday, 1914.
—Admiral Richard E. Byrd flew to North Pole, 1926.

10 Ethan Allen captured Ticonderoga, 1775.
—Second Continental Congress met, 1775.
—Confederate General Stonewall Jackson died, 1863.
—First transcontinental railway completed in Promontory, Utah, 1869.
—Franco-Prussian War ended, 1871.

11 Robert Gray sailed into the mouth of the Columbia River, 1792.
—Ottmar Mergenthaler, Linotype inventor, born 1854.
—Minnesota admitted to the Union, 1858.
—Irving Berlin, American songwriter, born 1888.

12 King Gustavus I of Sweden born 1496.
—Edward Lear, English author of nonsense verse, born 1812.
—Florence Nightingale, English nurse, born 1820.
—Henry Cabot Lodge, U.S. political leader, born 1850.
—Lincoln Ellsworth, American explorer, born 1880.
—Roald Amundsen flew over the North Pole, 1926.

13 Austrian Empress Maria Theresa born 1717.
—Sir Arthur Sullivan, English composer, born 1842.
—United States declared war on Mexico, 1846.
—President Dwight D. Eisenhower signed a bill authorizing construction of the St. Lawrence Seaway, 1954.

14 Gabriel Fahrenheit, German physicist, born 1686.
—Robert Owen, social reformer, born 1771.
—Edward Jenner, a British physician, performed the first vaccination against smallpox, 1796.
—William Hickling Prescott, American historian, born 1796.
—Lewis and Clark began trip up Missouri River from a camp near St. Louis, 1804.
—Israel became an independent country as the last British troops left Palestine, 1948.

15 Élie Metchnikoff, Russian biologist, born 1845.
—Pierre Curie, codiscoverer of radium, born 1859.
—U.S. began first regular airmail service, 1918.

16 William Seward, American statesman who arranged the purchase of Alaska, born 1801.

17 Edward Jenner, English physician, born 1749.
—King Alfonso XIII of Spain born 1886.
—King George VI became the first reigning British monarch to visit Canada, 1939.

President in 1914. It is celebrated in honor of the nation's mothers on the second Sunday in May. The third Saturday of the month is Armed Forces Day, when the United States honors the men and women of the military services. In 1950, the Armed Forces Day celebration combined the Army, Navy, and Air Force tributes, which had been held at separate times.

The Kentucky Derby, the most famous horse race in the United States, takes place on the first Saturday in May at Churchill Downs, Louisville, Ky.

May Symbols. The hawthorn and the lily of the valley are considered the flowers for May. The birthstone is the emerald. GRACE HUMPHREY

Quotations

Here's to the day when it is May
And care as light as a feather,
When your little shoes and my big boots
Go tramping over the heather. *Bliss Carman*

'Twas as welcome to me as flowers in May.
James Howell

The maple puts her corals on in May.
James Russell Lowell

Then came fair May, the fairest maid on ground,
Deck'd all with dainties of the season's pride,
And throwing flowers out of her lap around.
Edmund Spenser

The voice of one who goes before to make
The paths of June more beautiful is thine,
Sweet May!
Helen Hunt Jackson

Hail, bounteous May, that doth inspire
Mirth, and youth, and warm desire;
Woods and groves are of thy dressing,
Hill and dale doth boast thy blessing.
John Milton

When May, with cowslip-braided locks,
Walks through the land in green attire.
Bayard Taylor

Related Articles in WORLD BOOK include:

Armed Forces Day	Hawthorn	May Day
Calendar	Kentucky Derby	Memorial Day
Emerald	Lily of the Valley	Mother's Day

IMPORTANT MAY EVENTS

18 Abraham Lincoln nominated for the Presidency for the first time, 1860.
—Czar Nicholas II of Russia born 1868.
—Bertrand Russell, British philosopher and mathematician, born 1872.
—Dame Margot Fonteyn, British ballerina, born 1919.
19 Johns Hopkins, American philanthropist, born 1795.
20 Honoré de Balzac, French novelist, born 1799.
—John Stuart Mill, English philosopher and writer, born 1806.
—Émile Berliner, American inventor, born 1851.
—Homestead Act signed by President Abraham Lincoln, 1862.
—Sigrid Undset, Norwegian novelist, born 1882.
—Amelia Earhart began the first solo flight by a woman across the Atlantic Ocean, 1932.
21 Albrecht Dürer, German engraver, born 1471.
—Alexander Pope, English poet, born 1688.
—First Democratic National Convention held, 1832.
—Glenn Curtiss, American aviator and inventor, born 1878.
—Clara Barton founded what became the American Red Cross, 1881.
—Charles Lindbergh finished first transatlantic solo flight, 1927.
22 Richard Wagner, German composer, born 1813.
—Sir Arthur Conan Doyle, British author and creator of Sherlock Holmes, born 1859.
—Laurence Olivier, British actor, born 1907.
23 Carolus Linnaeus, Swedish botanist, born 1707.
—South Carolina became the eighth state, 1788.
—Ambrose E. Burnside, Union general, born 1824.
24 First permanent English settlement in America established in Jamestown, Va., 1607.

—Queen Victoria of England born 1819.
—Jan Christiaan Smuts, South African statesman, born 1870.
—Brooklyn Bridge opened to traffic, 1883.

25 Constitutional Convention opened in Philadelphia with George Washington as president, 1787.
—Ralph Waldo Emerson, American essayist and poet, born 1803.
—Edward Bulwer-Lytton, English writer, born 1803.
26 Lord Beaverbrook, British publisher, born 1879.
27 Julia Ward Howe, American poet who wrote "The Battle Hymn of the Republic," born 1819.
—Jay Gould, American financier, born 1836.
—Isadora Duncan, American dancer, born 1878.
—Golden Gate Bridge opened at San Francisco, 1937.
28 William Pitt, English statesman, born 1759.
—Thomas Moore, Irish poet and composer, born 1779.
—Jean Louis Agassiz, American naturalist, born 1807.
—P. G. T. Beauregard, Confederate general, born 1818.
—Dionne quintuplets born 1934.
29 The Turks captured Constantinople, 1453.
—King Charles II of England born 1630.
—Monarchy restored to England, 1660.
—Patrick Henry, American statesman and orator, born 1736.
—Rhode Island ratified the Constitution, becoming the 13th state, 1790.
—Wisconsin became the 30th state, 1848.
—G. K. Chesterton, English author, born 1874.
—Bob Hope, American comedian, born 1903.
—John F. Kennedy, 35th President of the United States, born in Brookline, Mass., 1917.
30 Joan of Arc burned at the stake, 1431.
—Christopher Columbus began his third voyage, 1498.
—Kansas-Nebraska Bill became a law, 1854.
—Memorial Day first observed, 1868.
31 U.S. copyright law enacted, 1790.
—Walt Whitman, American poet, born 1819.
—Johnstown (Pa.) flood, 1889.
—Amendment 17 to the Constitution, providing direct election of senators, proclaimed, 1913.
—Battle of Jutland fought in the North Sea, 1916.

John F. Kennedy

MAY APPLE

MAY APPLE is an American plant that belongs to the barberry family. It grows wild in wooded areas of the eastern half of the United States. People often call the May apple *mandrake*.

The May apple grows in large groups or colonies. Its large leaves have 5 to 7 lobes. The leaves look somewhat like small umbrellas. They usually grow in pairs, on a stem about 1 foot (30 centimeters) high. A white flower grows on a short stalk in a fork of the stem. It is about 2 inches (5 centimeters) wide.

The May apple produces a small, round fruit about the size of a golf ball. Before it ripens, the fruit is green in color and has a bitter taste. If eaten, it can cause severe stomach pain. The ripe fruit is yellow and can be eaten. *Podophyllum resin*, a drug used to remove warts, comes from the root of the May apple.

Scientific Classification. The May apple belongs to the barberry family, *Berberidaceae*. It is genus *Podophyllum*, species *P. peltatum*.   GEORGE H. M. LAWRENCE

See also FLOWER (color picture: Flowers of the Woodland).

MAY BEETLE. See JUNE BUG.

MAY DAY (May 1) is celebrated as a spring festival in many countries. It marks the revival of life in early spring after winter. Some people believe that the celebrations on May Day began with the tree worship of the Druids (see DRUIDS). Others believe they go back to the spring festivals of ancient Egypt and India.

The English and other peoples whom the Romans conquered developed their May Day festivals from the Floralia. In their April festival of Floralia, the Romans gathered spring flowers to honor the goddess of springtime, Flora.

In medieval times, May Day became the favorite holiday of many English villages. People gathered spring flowers to decorate their homes and churches. They sang spring carols and received gifts in return. They chose a King and Queen of May. Villagers danced around a Maypole, holding the ends of ribbons that streamed from its top. They wove the ribbons around the Maypole until it was covered with bright colors.

Other European countries had their own May Day customs. In some, the day became a time for courting. In Italy, boys serenaded their sweethearts. In Switzerland, a May pine tree was placed under a girl's window. German boys secretly planted May trees in front of the windows of their sweethearts. In Czechoslovakia, boys at night placed Maypoles before their sweethearts' windows. But in France, May Day had religious importance. The French considered the month of May sacred to the Virgin Mary. They enshrined young girls as May queens in their churches. The May queens led processions in honor of the Virgin Mary.

The Puritans frowned on May Day. For this reason, the day has never been celebrated with the same enthusiasm in the United States as in Great Britain. But, in many American towns and cities, children celebrate the return of spring with dancing and singing. Children often gather spring flowers, place them in handmade paper May baskets, and hang them on the doorknobs of the homes of friends and neighbors on May Day morning. At May Day parties, children select May queens, dance around the Maypole, and sing May Day songs. These festivals often occur in parks or schools.

In 1889, a congress of world Socialist parties held in Paris voted to support the United States labor movement's demands for an eight-hour day. It chose May 1, 1890, as a day of demonstrations in favor of the eight-hour day. Afterward, May 1 became a holiday called Labor Day in many nations. It resembles the September holiday in the United States (see LABOR DAY). Government and labor organizations sponsor parades, speeches, and other celebrations to honor working people. The holiday is especially important in socialist and Communist countries.   ELIZABETH HOUGH SECHRIST

See also MAY (May Customs); RUSSIA (picture: Red Square in Moscow).

MAY FLY. See MAYFLY.

MAYA were an American Indian people who developed a magnificent civilization in Central America. The Maya civilization reached its period of greatest development about A.D. 300 and continued to flourish for almost 600 years. The Maya produced remarkable architecture, painting, pottery, and sculpture. They made outstanding advancements in astronomy and mathematics and developed an accurate yearly calendar. They also were one of the first peoples in the Western Hemisphere to develop an advanced form of writing.

The Maya lived in an area of about 120,000 square miles (311,000 square kilometers). Today, the territory of the Maya is divided among Mexico and several Central American countries. It consists of the Mexican states of Campeche, Yucatán, and Quintana Roo and part of the states of Tabasco and Chiapas. It also includes Belize, most of Guatemala, and parts of El Salvador and of Honduras. The heart of the Maya civilization was in the tropical rain forest of the lowlands of northern Guatemala. Many of the major Maya cities, such as Piedras Negras, Tikal, and Uaxactún, developed in this area.

The Land of the Maya included parts of present-day Mexico and of three Central American countries—El Salvador, Guatemala, and Honduras. This map shows the area inhabited by three chief Maya groups and the location of major Maya cities.

WORLD BOOK map

WORLD BOOK illustration by Alton S. Tobey

A Maya City Called Tikal lies in what is now Guatemala. This illustration is an artist's idea of how the city may have looked about A.D. 750. In the foreground, a priest prepares for a ceremony. In the background, other priests climb the stairway to the temple, 150 feet (45 meters) high.

By about A.D. 900, the Maya civilization had changed in several ways. For example, the people of the southern lowlands abandoned their cities and finally the entire area. Scholars are still trying to learn why the Maya society collapsed. They examine the remaining records of the Maya and look for clues among the ruins of Maya cities. Major changes also occurred in the northern lowlands, but the Maya continued to live there.

Today, descendants of the Maya live in Mexico and Central America. They speak Maya languages and carry on some of the religious customs of their ancestors.

Way of Life

Religion. The Maya worshiped many gods and goddesses. One Maya manuscript mentions more than 160 of them. For example, the Maya worshiped a corn god, a rain god known as *Chac*, a sun god called *Kinich Ahau*, and a moon goddess called *Ix Chel*. Each god or goddess influenced some part of Maya life. Ix Chel, for instance, was the goddess of medicine and weaving.

Religion played a central part in the daily life of the Maya. Each day in the Maya year had special religious importance, and religious festivals in honor of particular gods took place throughout the year. The Maya regarded their gods as both helpful and harmful. To obtain the help of the gods, the Maya fasted, prayed, offered sacrifices, and held many religious ceremonies. Deer, dogs, and turkeys were sacrificed to feed the gods. The Maya frequently offered their own blood,

which they spattered on pieces of bark paper. The Maya practiced some human sacrifice, such as throwing victims into deep wells or killing them at the funerals of great leaders.

In their cities, the Maya built tall pyramids of limestone with small temples on top. Priests climbed the stairs of the pyramids and performed ceremonies in the temples. Major religious festivals, such as those for the Maya New Year and for each of the Maya months, took place in the cities.

The Maya observed special ceremonies when burying their dead. Corpses were painted red and then were wrapped in straw mats with a few of their personal belongings. They were buried under the floor of the houses where they had lived. Maya rulers and other important persons were buried in their finest garments within the pyramids. Servants were killed and buried with them, along with jewelry and utensils, for use in the next world.

Family and Social Life. Entire Maya families, including parents, children, and grandparents, lived together. Everyone in a household helped with the work. The men and the older boys did most of the farmwork, such as clearing and weeding the fields and planting the crops. They also did most of the hunting and fishing. The women and the older girls made the family's clothes, prepared meals, raised the younger children, and supplied the house with firewood and water. The Maya had no schools. The children learned various skills by observing adults and helping them.

257

Religious festivals provided one of the favorite forms of recreation for the Maya. These festivals were held on special days throughout the year. Dancing and feasts took place at the festivals. The Maya also had a sacred game that resembled basketball and was played on specially designed courts. The players tried to hit a rubber ball through a stone ring with their elbows or hips.

Food, Clothing, and Shelter. Maya farmers raised chiefly beans, corn, and squash. Corn was the principal food of the Maya, and the women prepared it in a variety of ways. They made flat corn cakes, which today are called *tortillas*, as a type of bread. The Maya also used corn to make an alcoholic drink called *balche*, which they sweetened with honey and spiced with bark.

Other crops raised by the Maya included avocados, tomatoes, and chili peppers. The farmers cleared their fields by cutting down trees with stone axes. They burned the trees and brush and then used sticks to plant the seeds in the ashes. After the soil became worn out, the farmers shifted their fields to new locations.

Dogs were the only tame animals of the Maya, but the people raised turkeys and honeybees in their farmyards. The Maya hunted deer, rabbits, piglike animals called *peccaries*, and other wild animals. They fished and collected shellfish from the rivers and sea. The Maya also gathered fruits and vegetables from the countryside.

The clothing of the Maya kept them comfortable in the hot, tropical climate. Men wore a *loincloth*, a strip of cloth tied around their hips and passed between their legs. Women wore loose dresses that reached their ankles. The people wove these garments from cotton or other fibers. The people of the upper classes wore finer clothes decorated with embroidery and ornaments. They had splendid headdresses made of the brightly colored feathers of jungle birds. The wealthy also wore large amounts of jewelry, much of which was carved out of green jade and colorful shells.

Maya farmers lived in rural homesteads or small villages near their fields. They built their houses from poles lashed together and used palm leaves or grass to thatch the roofs. Maya cities served as centers for the surrounding countryside. The people gathered in these centers for such important events as markets and religious festivals. Scholars disagree about whether the cities had few or many permanent residents. Priests and other Maya leaders might have lived in the cities for short periods of time before important ceremonies and then returned to their permanent homes.

Trade and Transportation. The Maya took part in a trade network that linked a number of groups in Central America. The people of the Maya lowlands exported many items, including handicrafts, forest and sea products, and jaguar pelts. They imported jade, volcanic glass, and the feathers of a bird called the *quetzal* from the highlands of Guatemala, where other Maya-speaking peoples lived.

The Maya of Yucatán sent salt and finely decorated cottons to Honduras. In return, they received cacao beans, which they used in making chocolate. The Maya also transported goods as far as the Valley of Oaxaca in Mexico and the city of Teotihuacán, near what is now Mexico City. They carried most of their goods on their backs or on rivers in dugout canoes. The Maya did not have the wheel or any beasts of burden, such as horses or oxen.

Government. Historians know little about the government of the Maya. Each Maya city governed the area around it, and larger cities may have had control

Clay sculpture (A.D. 700 to 900), 5 in. (12.5 cm) high; Museo Nacional de Antropología e Historia, Mexico City (Bradley Smith)

A Maya Ballplayer wore thigh guards and a thick protective belt. The Maya ball game resembled basketball. The players hit a rubber ball through a stone ring with their elbows or hips.

Clay sculpture, 16 in. (40 cm) high; Museo Nacional de Antropología e Historia, Mexico City (Lee Boltin)

A Sculpture of the Maya Corn God has ears of corn in its headdress. Corn was the principal food of the Maya. They prayed to this god for plentiful harvests and offered sacrifices to him.

over several smaller cities. The rulers probably consisted of both chiefs and priests. One supreme chief, who had both religious and political powers, may have ruled each city. The Maya never united to form a central governmental unit. But in late Maya times, the rulers of such cities as Chichen Itzá and Mayapán controlled large parts of the population.

Communication and Learning. The Maya developed an advanced form of writing that consisted of many symbols. These symbols represented combinations of sounds or entire ideas and formed a kind of *hieroglyphic* writing (see HIEROGLYPHIC).

The Maya kept records on large stone monuments called *stelae*, as well as on some buildings and household utensils. They used the stelae to record important dates and to take note of great events in the lives of their rulers and the rulers' families. The Maya also made books of paper made from fig tree bark. Several books from the 1100's to the early 1500's have survived. They contain astronomical tables, information about religious ceremonies, and calendars that show lucky days for such activities as farming and hunting.

Other cultural advances by the Maya included the development of mathematics and astronomy. The Maya used a mathematical system based on the number 20, instead of 10 as in the decimal system. Dots and dashes represented numbers, and a special symbol represented zero. Mathematicians consider the zero one of the world's greatest inventions. Maya priests developed a knowledge of astronomy by observing the positions of the sun, moon, and stars. They made tables predicting eclipses and the orbit of the planet Venus.

The priests also used mathematics and astronomy to develop two kinds of calendars. One was a sacred almanac of 260 days. Each day was named with one of 20 day names and a number from 1 to 13. Each of the

Stone sculpture (A.D. 784) by an unknown Maya artist; Lee Boltin

A Maya Monument called a *stele* stands in Copán, a city in what is now Honduras. The Maya used such sculptures to record important dates and to note events in their rulers' lives.

20 day names had a god or goddess associated with it. The priests predicted good or bad luck by studying the combinations of gods or goddesses and numbers. The Maya also had a calendar of 365 days, based on the orbit of the earth around the sun. These days were divided into 18 months of 20 days each, plus 5 days at the end of the year. The Maya considered these last 5 days to be extremely unlucky. During that period they fasted, made many sacrifices, and avoided any unnecessary work.

The Maya used herbs and magic to treat illness. However, scholars know little about Maya knowledge of medicine.

Arts and Crafts. The Maya produced exceptional architecture, painting, pottery, and sculpture. Highly skilled architects built tall pyramids of limestone, with small temples on top. They constructed a type of arch by building the sides of two walls closer and closer together at the top. The gap between the walls was bridged by a row of flat stones. The Maya also built large, low buildings where chiefs and priests probably lived before important ceremonies. Many Maya buildings had flat ornaments called *roof combs*, which extended from the high point of the roof. The roof combs, like church steeples, gave buildings the appearance of great height.

Maya artists decorated walls with brightly colored murals that featured lifelike figures taking part in battles and festivals. The artists outlined the figures and then filled in the various parts in color. They rarely

Codex Tro-Cortesianus (late 1400's); Museo de America, Madrid, Spain (Ampliaciones y Reproducciones MAS)

Maya Writing used symbols that represented entire ideas or combinations of sounds. This section of a Maya manuscript came from an astrology book used by priests.

259

shaded the colors. A similar type of painting appears on Maya pottery.

The Maya made small sculptures of clay and carved huge ones from stone. Most of the small sculptures were figures of men and women. The large sculptures, some of which stood more than 30 feet (9 meters) high, were carved with figures of important persons in stiff poses.

History

Early Days. The heart of the Maya civilization developed in what is now the *department* (state) of El Petén, Guatemala. The first farmers may have settled in this area as early as 2500 B.C. in search of fertile land for crops. They lived in small villages and gathered food from the surrounding forest in addition to raising crops.

By 800 B.C., the Maya lowlands were completely settled. At that time, a group called the Olmec lived in the area west of the Maya. The Olmec were probably the Central American inventors of numbers and writing. They also had well-developed art. The Olmec civilization influenced the developing Maya culture. The Maya, like the Olmec, began to build pyramids and carve stone monuments. In addition, pictures of the Olmec jaguar god began to appear in Maya art. See OLMEC INDIANS.

The Classic Period of the Maya civilization lasted from about A.D. 300 to 900. During those years, the Maya founded their greatest cities and made their remarkable achievements in the arts and sciences. In addition, the Maya began the practice of erecting stelae to honor the most important events in the lives of their leaders.

During the first 300 years of the Classic Period, the Mexican city of Teotihuacán was the center of a large empire. The Teotihuacán civilization had a strong influence on Maya art and architecture. The collapse of Teotihuacán about 600 affected the Maya temporarily. For example, the Maya stopped construction work in their cities and halted the erection of stelae. After a brief period, however, the Maya civilization recovered and continued to grow for another 300 years.

Then, beginning in the 800's, the Maya stopped erecting stelae in city after city. They abandoned their major centers in the southern lowlands one by one and finally left the entire southern region. Scholars are still trying to discover the reasons for the collapse of the Maya society. Some experts believe it may have been caused by such factors as disease, crop failure, and the movement of other groups into the Maya area. However, many other historians think Maya farmers revolted against the government of the chiefs and priests for some reason and brought about the fall of the Maya society.

The Mexican Period. The Maya centers in northern Yucatán lasted about 100 years longer than those of the southern lowlands. Even after the Maya abandoned the northern centers, they continued to live in that area. About A.D. 950, Yucatán was invaded by the Toltec, a people from the central highlands of Mexico. The Toltec had established an empire in Mexico with the capital at Tula, north of what is now Mexico City. They took control of the old Maya city of Chichen Itzá and ruled the entire northern Maya population. The Toltec influenced the art and architecture of the Maya and introduced the worship of a feathered-serpent god named Kukulcán. Tula collapsed in the mid-1100's, and the Toltec rule of Yucatán ended in 1200. See TOLTEC INDIANS.

A new group of Maya leaders established a capital at Mayapán following the end of Toltec control. The Maya then restored their own culture and again erected stelae. However, some changes had occurred in their society. For example, business replaced religion as the dominant force in the Maya culture. Maya cities became prosperous commercial centers, and the people began to conduct an active sea trade.

About 1440, the leaders of some Maya cities revolted against the Mayapán rulers and defeated them. Yucatán was then divided into separate warring states. During

WORLD BOOK photo by Joya Hairs

The Ruins of Tikal in Guatemala are all that remain of the great Maya ceremonial center. This photograph shows the restored Temple of the Giant Jaguar, which rises 150 feet (45 meters) above the site. The temple stands on top of a pyramid consisting of nine terraces.

the early 1500's, Spanish conquerors invaded the Maya territory. By the mid-1500's, they had overcome almost all the remaining Maya.

The Maya Heritage. Today, many people of Mexico and Central America speak one of the nearly 20 languages and dialects that developed from the ancient Maya language. Some of these people live in the highlands of Mexico and Guatemala. Others inhabit the northern part of the Yucatán peninsula in Mexico. The Yucatecos of Yucatán are probably the most direct descendants of the Maya. Many descendants of the Maya farm the land as did their ancient ancestors and carry on some of the traditional religious customs.

The ruins of the Maya ceremonial centers are major tourist attractions. Such sites in Mexico include the ruins of Bonampak and Palenque in Chiapas, and Chichen Itzá in northern Yucatán. Many tourists also visit the ruins of Tikal in Guatemala and of Copán in Honduras. BARBARA VOORHIES

See also GUATEMALA; HONDURAS (picture: A Maya Ball Court); INDIAN, AMERICAN; MEXICO; RUBBER (picture: The Original Users of Rubber). For a *Reading and Study Guide*, see *Maya* in the RESEARCH GUIDE/INDEX, Volume 22.

MAYAGÜEZ. See FORD, GERALD R. (Foreign Affairs).

MAYAKOVSKY, VLADIMIR. See RUSSIAN LITERATURE (Post-Symbolism).

MAYALL TELESCOPE. See KITT PEAK NATIONAL OBSERVATORY.

MAYBACH, *MY bahk,* **WILHELM** (1846-1929), a German engineer, pioneered in building automobiles. He worked with his friend, Gottlieb Daimler, from the late 1860's until Daimler died in early 1900 (see DAIMLER, GOTTLIEB). They developed the first Mercedes automobile. Maybach left the Mercedes company in 1907. He invented the honeycomb radiator. Maybach was born in Heilbronn, Germany. SMITH HEMPSTONE OLIVER

MAYER, *MY er,* **JULIUS ROBERT VON** (1814-1878), was a German physician and physicist. He and James Joule shared credit for discovering the universal law of conservation of energy (see JOULE, JAMES). This principle, known as the first law of thermodynamics, states that the total energy of the universe remains the same, and cannot be increased or lessened.

Mayer published his article on heat and energy in 1842. Joule, an English physicist, reached the same conclusions while working independently. It has never been determined which scientist made the first discovery. Mayer was born at Heilbronn. R. T. ELLICKSON

See also HEAT (Heat and Energy).

MAYER, MARIA GOEPPERT (1906-1972), a German-born physicist, shared the 1963 Nobel prize in physics with J. Hans Jensen of Germany and Eugene Paul Wigner of the United States. Mayer and Jensen, working independently, prepared almost identical papers on the shell structure of atomic nuclei. They discovered that atomic nuclei possess shells similar to the electron shells of atoms. These shells contain varying numbers of protons and neutrons, which permits systematic arrangement of nuclei according to their properties. Maria Goeppert was born in Kattowitz, Germany (now Katowice, Poland). She married Joseph E. Mayer, an American chemist, in 1930, and moved to the United States. In 1960, they both joined the faculty of the University of California, San Diego. G. GAMOW

MAYFLOWER. See ARBUTUS.

MAYFLOWER was the ship that carried the first Pilgrims to America, in 1620. It was built around 1610 and probably looked like other ships of its time, which had three masts and two decks. It probably measured about 90 feet (27 meters) long and weighed about 180 short tons (163 metric tons). Its quarter-owner, Christopher Jones, served as master.

The *Mayflower* sailed from Plymouth, England, on Sept. 16, 1620, with 102 passengers. The ship reached the Cape Cod coast 66 days after it left England, and dropped anchor off what is now Provincetown Harbor on Nov. 21, 1620. It reached the present site of Plymouth, Mass., on December 26, five days after a small party had explored the site and decided to make Plymouth their new home.

The *Mayflower* left America on April 5, 1621.

Wide World

Mayflower II, built the way the original *Mayflower* is thought to have looked, made a 54-day voyage across the Atlantic Ocean in 1957. This was 12 days less than the Pilgrims' trip in 1620.

Historians are not certain what happened to the ship after it returned to England. Some believe it was dismantled after Jones died in 1622, although a ship called the *Mayflower* made trips to America after that. Others believe that William Russell bought the *Mayflower* for salvage, and used its hull as a barn roof. The barn stands in Jordans, a village outside London.

The *Mayflower II*, built the way the original *Mayflower* is thought to have looked, is kept in Plymouth, Mass. In 1957, it crossed the Atlantic in 54 days. The Britons who built the replica gave it to the American people as a symbol of friendship. MARSHALL SMELSER

See PLYMOUTH ROCK; PLYMOUTH COLONY; PILGRIM.

MAYFLOWER COMPACT was the first agreement for self-government ever put in force in America. On Nov. 21 (then Nov. 11), 1620, the ship *Mayflower* anchored off Cape Cod, Mass. The Pilgrim leaders persuaded 41 male adults aboard to sign the *Mayflower*

Compact, and set up a government in Plymouth Colony. The original compact has since disappeared. The version below follows the spelling and punctuation given in the history *Of Plimoth Plantation*, written by William Bradford, second governor of Plymouth colony.

"In ye name of God Amen. We whose names are underwritten, the loyall subjects of our dread soveraigne Lord King James, by ye grace of God, of Great Britaine, Franc, & Ireland king, defender of ye faith, &c. Haveing undertaken, for ye glorie of God, and advancemente of ye Christian faith and honour of our king & countrie, a voyage to plant ye first colonie in ye Northerne parts of Virginia, doe by these presents solemnly & mutualy in ye presence of God, and one of another, covenant, & combine ourselves togeather into a Civill body politick; for our better ordering, & preservation & furtherance of ye ends aforesaid; and by vertue hereof to enacte, constitute, and frame such just & equall Lawes, ordinances, Acts, constitutions, & offices, from time to time, as shall be thought most meete & convenient for ye generall good of ye colonie: unto which we promise all due submission and obedience. In witnes whereof we have hereunder subscribed our names at Cap-Codd ye -11- of November, in ye year of ye raigne of our soveraigne Lord King James of England, France, & Ireland ye eighteenth, and of Scotland ye fiftie fourth. Ano Dom. 1620."   MARSHALL SMELSER

See also PLYMOUTH COLONY.

MAYFLOWER DESCENDANTS, GENERAL SOCIETY OF, is an organization of persons descended from the Pilgrims. The general society has more than 13,000 adult members in 51 state societies. Members have proved their descent from 50 of the passengers who sailed to New England aboard the *Mayflower*. The organization was founded in 1897 to perpetuate the memory and promote the ideals of the Pilgrims. It publishes *The Mayflower Quarterly* and material about the Pilgrims and the Mayflower Compact. Headquarters are in Plymouth, Mass.   Critically reviewed by the
GENERAL SOCIETY OF MAYFLOWER DESCENDANTS

Robert C. Hermes, NAS

Mayflies have several life stages. This picture shows a *subimago, bottom;* a subimago shedding its skin, *top;* and an adult, *center.*

MAYFLY is a dainty insect with lacy wings and a slender tail that trails behind it in flight. Mayflies are often called *dayflies* because of their short lives. Adult mayflies live only a few hours or a few days. They do not eat, and usually have no mouth. They are not true flies. A true fly has two wings, and a mayfly has four wings. Mayflies are also called *shad flies* or *duns.* Imitation mayflies are frequently used as fishing lures.

A *nymph*, or young mayfly, hatches from eggs laid in streams and ponds. It breathes through gills and feeds on water plants. A nymph lives for a few months to two years in the water. It then leaves the water, sheds its skin, and becomes a winged *subimago*, or subadult. Mayflies are the only insects that go through this stage. After a few hours, the subimago sheds its

The Signing of the Compact by Percy Moran, Pilgrim Hall, Plymouth, Mass. (Pilgrim Society)

The First Written Agreement for Self-Government in America was signed on the ship *Mayflower,* before the new colonists built their settlement at Plymouth. The agreement, called the *Mayflower Compact,* promised "just and equal" laws.

skin and becomes a full-grown adult. Mayflies are most common in early spring, but may occur until late fall. The nymphs serve as a source of food for fish.

Scientific Classification. Mayflies make up the order *Ephemeroptera*. E. GORTON LINSLEY

MAYHEM, *MAY hem,* in law, is the offense of making a person less capable of self defense by maiming the body or by destroying or injuring one of its members. Such injuries call for legal distinctions, because not all injuries which result from assault are mayhem. Biting off a person's ear or nose was not mayhem under the old common law. But cutting off a finger or destroying an eye came under that law, because such an injury would make a person less capable of self defense.

Modern statutes now regard as mayhem any crime of violence which causes a permanent bodily injury. The person who inflicts the injury is subject to a civil suit as well as to criminal prosecution. The word is an old form of the word *maim*. FRED E. INBAU

MAYNOR, DOROTHY (1910-), is an American black soprano with an international reputation. Serge Koussevitzky heard her at the Berkshire Music Festival in 1939, and hired her as soloist with the Boston Symphony Orchestra. He called her singing "a musical revelation." In three months, she had appeared with four leading orchestras. Her performances include selections from works by the composers George Handel and Wolfgang Mozart, and from German *lieder* (songs) and Negro folk songs.

DeBellis, New York
Dorothy Maynor

Dorothy Maynor was born in Norfolk, Va., the daughter of a Methodist clergyman, and first sang in the choir of her father's church. MARTIAL SINGHER

MAYO, *MAY oh,* is the family name of four American surgeons who made the Mayo Clinic in Rochester, Minn., internationally famous (see MAYO CLINIC).

William Worrall Mayo (1819-1911) and his two sons started the Mayo Clinic in 1889 at St. Mary's Hospital in Rochester.

Mayo started practicing medicine in Minnesota in 1855. He became the leading physician and surgeon in the area. He was one of the first doctors in the West to use a microscope in diagnosis. In 1883, when a cyclone struck Rochester, Mayo was placed in charge of an emergency hospital. Sisters of the Order of St. Francis assisted him, and two years later the order started to build St. Mary's Hospital, with Mayo as its head. The hospital is still affiliated with Mayo Clinic.

Mayo took an active part in organizing the Minnesota Territory. He served in 1862 as an Army surgeon during a Sioux Indian outbreak. He became provost surgeon for southern Minnesota in 1863.

Mayo was born in Manchester, England, and studied at Owens College there. He came to the United States in 1845. He was graduated in medicine in 1854 from the University of Missouri.

William James Mayo (1861-1939), the older son of William Worrall Mayo, won fame for his surgical skill

in gallstone, cancer, and stomach operations. He and his brother, Charles, pioneered in the development of medical group practice through the Mayo Clinic. They also founded the Mayo Foundation and the Mayo Graduate School of Medicine. The brothers donated $1½ million in 1915 to establish the foundation and later contributed more. The school became one of the most important graduate medical centers in the world.

Mayo was graduated in medicine from the University of Michigan in 1883. He was president of the American Medical Association in 1906. He served during World War I in the Army Medical Corps and became a brigadier general in the medical reserve in 1921. He was born in Le Sueur, Minn.

Charles Horace Mayo (1865-1939), the younger son of William Worrall Mayo, was famous for reducing the death rate in goiter surgery. He was professor of surgery in the Mayo Graduate School of Medicine from 1915 to 1936. Mayo served as president of the American Medical Association in 1917, and as health officer of Rochester from 1912 to 1937. He also served in the armed forces during World War I and became a brigadier general in the medical reserve in 1921.

Mayo was graduated in medicine from Northwestern University in 1888. He was born in Rochester, Minn.

Charles William Mayo (1898-1968), the son of Charles Horace Mayo, became a member of the board of governors of the Mayo Clinic in 1933. He became a professor of surgery in the Mayo Graduate School of Medicine in 1947. He was an alternate delegate to the UN General Assembly in 1953. He also served as editor of *Postgraduate Medicine*. He retired from the Mayo Clinic in 1963. Mayo was born in Rochester, Minn., and was graduated from the University of Pennsylvania in 1926. NOAH D. FABRICANT

MAYO CLINIC, in Rochester, Minn., is one of the world's largest medical centers. Staff physicians care for clinic patients through an integrated group practice of medicine. A 12-member board of governors, which functions through several committees, administers the clinic. Board members and committee members are chosen from the clinic staff of about 500. About 650 younger physicians assist the staff as part of their residency training in medical and surgical specialties.

William Worrall Mayo and his sons, William James and Charles Horace Mayo, started the clinic in 1889 in Rochester (see MAYO [family]). They developed it to care for surgical patients, and gradually added physicians and surgeons to the staff. The name Mayo Clinic dates from about 1903. Just before World War I, the brothers turned the clinic into a general medical center. The clinic now registers about 225,000 patients a year. It has cared for about 3 million patients since its founding. Critically reviewed by the MAYO CLINIC

MAYO FOUNDATION is a nonprofit charitable organization that supports and conducts medical education and research. The foundation provides the main financial support for the Mayo Medical School and the Mayo Graduate School of Medicine in Rochester, Minn. These schools are associated with the University of Minnesota. Doctors from the Mayo Clinic make up the faculties of both schools, and the foundation and schools use clinic facilities (see MAYO CLINIC). The

Mayo Medical School awards the M.D. degree. The Mayo Graduate School of Medicine trains physicians and scientists in surgery, other fields of medicine, and related sciences.

The physician brothers William James Mayo and Charles Horace Mayo established the foundation in 1919. They believed income from the Mayo Clinic should be returned to people through education. The clinic gives its net earnings to the foundation. The Mayo Foundation has headquarters at 200 First Street SW, Rochester, Minn. 55901. Critically reviewed by the MAYO CLINIC

MAYOR is the head of a city government in the United States and many other countries. The people of England have used the title for hundreds of years. Colonists in America brought the name and office with them from England. In the United States, two kinds of mayors, called strong and weak, developed.

In cities that have a *strong mayor* government, the mayor takes a leading part in city administration. Such mayors enforce laws passed by the council, and can veto council rulings. They appoint lesser officials. They may name a managing director or chief administrative officer to supervise government operations. San Francisco was the first city to set up this kind of office.

In cities that have a *weak mayor* government, the mayor has little executive authority. The mayor is the head of the government, but the council has the final authority in directing the administration of the city.

More than half of the United States cities with a population of 5,000 or more operate under a mayor form of government. This includes 12 of the 15 largest cities. The average salary for mayors of cities with populations over 50,000 is about $16,000 a year.

In Austria, Belgium, Germany, and The Netherlands, the mayor is often called the *burgomaster*. The duties of a burgomaster are substantially those of a mayor in the United States. The position of mayor in Great Britain is largely honorary. In Canada, the mayor enforces ordinances, supervises lower officials, and presents proposals to the city council. H. F. ALDERFER

See also CITY GOVERNMENT; ADDRESS, FORMS OF (Mayors).

MAYPOLE. See MAY DAY; MAY (May Customs).

MAYS, BENJAMIN ELIJAH (1895-   ), is an American Baptist minister, educator, and public speaker. He was president of Morehouse College in Atlanta, Ga., from 1940 to 1967. Civil rights leader Martin Luther King, Jr., attended Morehouse. King's admiration for Mays influenced his decision to become a minister. Mays delivered a nationally televised speech at a memorial service for King, who was killed in 1968.

Mays was born in Epworth, near Greenwood, S.C. He earned a B.A. degree at Bates College in Maine and a Ph.D. degree at the University of Chicago. He became a minister in 1922. Mays was dean of the School of Religion at Howard University in Washington, D.C., from 1934 to 1940. He wrote *The Negro's God as Reflected in His Literature* (1938), and was coauthor of *The Negro's Church* (1933). Mays's autobiography, *Born to Rebel*, was published in 1971. EDGAR ALLAN TOPPIN

MAYS, WILLIE (1931-   ), became one of the most exciting players in baseball history. He electrified crowds with his sensational fielding, explosive hitting, and daring base running. During his major-league career, Mays hit 660 home runs. Only Henry Aaron and Babe Ruth hit more.

Mays played center field for the New York (later San Francisco) Giants during most of his major-league career. He was named the National League's Most Valuable Player in 1954 and 1965. He led the league in home runs four times and in stolen bases four times. Mays won the league batting championship in 1954 and had a career batting average of .302. During the 1954 World Series, Mays had a spectacular running, over-the-shoulder catch of a long fly hit by Vic Wertz of the Cleveland Indians. The catch ranks among the most memorable plays in series history.

Willie Howard Mays was born in Westfield, Ala.

New York National League
Baseball Club

Willie Mays

He joined the Giants in 1951. In 1972, he was traded to the New York Mets. He retired as a baseball player in 1973. Mays was elected to the National Baseball Hall of Fame in 1979. JOSEPH P. SPOHN

See also BASEBALL (picture).

MAYTAG, FREDERICK LOUIS (1857-1937), was an American businessman. He founded the Maytag Company, and built it into one of the world's largest washing machine manufacturers. Maytag was the first budget director for the state of Iowa, and served in the Iowa Senate for 10 years. He was born in Elgin, Ill.

MAZARIN, MAH ZAH RAN, **JULES CARDINAL** (1602-1661), was a French statesman, and a cardinal of the Roman Catholic Church. When Cardinal Richelieu, King Louis XIII's chief minister, died in 1642, Mazarin became chief minister of France. Anne of Austria, mother of the 4-year-old king, Louis XIV, ruled as her son's regent after Louis XIII died in 1643. She relied heavily on Mazarin's advice.

Mazarin sought to strengthen the French rulers at the expense of the aristocracy. Abroad, he employed diplomacy and the army to break out of the encirclement imposed upon France by the Spanish and Austrian Hapsburgs. This program helped the French rulers, but placed a tax burden upon the common people.

In serving his king, Mazarin never lost an opportunity to enrich himself. When he died a wealthy man, he was mourned by both the monarchy and the browbeaten aristocrats. The people disliked him because he taxed them heavily and thought little about their needs.

Mazarin was born in the south-central Italian district of Abruzzi. He served as a captain of infantry in the pope's army in the early campaigns of the Thirty Years' War. His skill in diplomacy resulted in a mission to France, where he attracted the notice of Cardinal Richelieu. Mazarin entered the service of France and became a French citizen. In 1641, Mazarin became a cardinal. RICHARD M. BRACE

See also LOUIS (XIV); LIBRARY (The 1600's).

MAZARIN BIBLE. See BOOK (Printed Books).

MAZATLÁN, MAH sah TLAHN (pop. 161,616), is western Mexico's trade and industry center, and the country's largest Pacific Ocean port. It stands at the foot of the Sierra Madre Mountains, near the mouth of the Gulf of California. For location, see Mexico (political map). Mazatlán is a popular winter resort. The city has a sugar refinery, cotton gins, textile mills, and frozen seafood packing houses. It was founded by Spaniards in the 1500's.   John A. Crow

MAZE. See Labyrinth.

MAZEPA, *muh ZEP uh,* **IVAN STEPANOVICH** (1632?-1709), also spelled *Mazeppa,* was a famous Cossack *hetman,* or chieftain (see Cossacks). Mazepa was born in western Russia and became a page at the court of King John Casimir of Poland. According to a story, Mazepa offended a nobleman there. He was strapped to a wild horse, and sent into the wilderness. The horse eventually reached a camp of Cossacks in the Ukraine. Mazepa grew up among them, and became their leader. Later, he fought without success for the independence of the Ukraine by aiding Charles XII of Sweden against Peter the Great of Russia. Byron's poem *Mazeppa* (1819) and Tchaikovsky's opera *Mazeppa* (1883) are based on his life story.   Arthur M. Selvi

MAZUROV, *muh ZOO rawf,* **KIRILL TROFIMOVICH** (1914-   ), was a member of the Politburo, the policy-making body of the Russian Communist Party, from 1965 to 1978. Mazurov also served as a first deputy chairman of the Soviet Council of Ministers. This council is the highest executive body of the Russian government.

Mazurov was born in what is now the village of Rudnya-Pribytovskaya, near Gomel', in Byelorussia. He worked with the Young Communist League from 1939 to 1947. He headed the Byelorussian Communist Party from 1956 to 1965, and served in the Presidium of the Supreme Soviet from 1958 to 1965. Walter C. Clemens, Jr.

MAZZINI, *maht TSEE nee,* **GIUSEPPE** (1805-1872), was an Italian patriot and republican leader who played an important part in uniting Italy in 1861. Mazzini spent many years in exile because he wanted to free the country from Austrian rule and unite it as a republic.

Mazzini began his political career in 1830 by joining the *Carbonari,* a group that wanted to unify Italy. He was a bold and active leader, and was exiled from Italy in 1830. Mazzini lived in exile for 18 years, first in Marseille, France, and later in Switzerland. During this time, he kept in contact with the liberal republicans in Italy.

In 1832, Mazzini organized a new society, called *Young Italy,* to work for Italian unity. One of his followers was Giuseppe Garibaldi, who later played an important role in unifying Italy.

Mazzini returned to Italy in 1848, when revolutions broke out in many European countries. He helped organize a republic at Rome, and became one of its leaders. But French troops attacked the new government and captured Rome. Mazzini again fled to Switzerland, and later to London.

Italy finally was united in 1861 under King Victor Emmanuel II of Sardinia, but only half of Mazzini's dream was realized. He wanted a republic, not a monarchy. He tried to organize a republican revolt in Palermo, Sicily, in 1870, but it failed. Mazzini was born in Genoa.   R. John Rath

See also Italy (History).

MBABANE, *'m bah BAHN* (pop. 17,800), is the administrative capital of Swaziland, a country in southern Africa. Mbabane lies in a mountainous region of Swaziland 200 miles (320 kilometers) east of Johannesburg, South Africa (see Swaziland [map]). Mbabane was founded as a mining camp. Tin mining and farming are major occupations. Most people living there belong to the Swazi group of the Bantu tribe. Hibberd V. B. Kline, Jr.

Mc. See Mac.

McADAM, JOHN LOUDON (1756-1836), a British engineer, originated the *macadam* type of road surface. He was the first person to recognize that dry soil supports the weight of traffic, and that pavement is useful only for forming a smooth surface and keeping the soil dry. His macadam pavements consist of crushed rock packed into thin layers. McAdam's paving methods spread to all nations. He was born in Ayr, Scotland. See also Roads and Highways (Paving). Robert W. Abbett

McADOO, WILLIAM GIBBS. See Hudson River Tunnels.

McAFEE, MILDRED HELEN (1900-   ), an American educator, commanded the WAVES during World War II. She received the Distinguished Service Medal in 1945 for her work as the first director of the WAVES, the women's reserve of the U.S. Navy. She was president of Wellesley College from 1936 to 1949.

Mildred McAfee was born in Parkville, Mo. She was graduated from Vassar College, and received her master's degree from the University of Chicago. In 1945, she married Douglas Horton, a clergyman. She retired in 1949. She was the first woman to become a member of the board of directors of Radio Corporation of America (RCA).   John S. Brubacher

McBRIDE, LLOYD (1916-   ), became president of the United Steelworkers of America (USWA), one of the largest labor unions in the United States, in 1977. He succeeded I. W. Abel, who retired.

McBride was born in Farmington, Mo. In 1930, at the age of 14, he went to work as a steelworker in St. Louis. The USWA was founded in 1936. McBride became president of a St. Louis local of the union in 1938, when he was only 22 years old. From 1965 to 1977, he served as director of a USWA district with headquarters in St. Louis.

As president of the USWA, McBride promised to uphold the union's no-strike agreement. This agreement prohibits the union from striking during its contract talks with steel companies.   James G. Scoville

McCARRAN, PATRICK ANTHONY (1876-1954), served as United States senator from Nevada from 1933 to 1954. McCarran sponsored the *Internal Security Act* (1950) and the *Immigration and Nationality Act* (1952), also known as the McCarran-Walter Act. The Internal Security Act established close controls over Communists. The Immigration and Nationality Act tightened controls over aliens and immigrants. Although a Democrat, McCarran often opposed the policies of Presidents Franklin D. Roosevelt and Harry S. Truman. McCarran was born in Reno, Nev. A statue of McCarran represents Nevada in Statuary Hall in the U.S. Capitol in Washington, D.C.   F. Jay Taylor

McCARRAN-WALTER ACT. See Immigration (Easing of Immigration Laws).

McCARTHY, EUGENE JOSEPH (1916-   ), served as a United States senator from Minnesota from 1959 to 1971. He was an unsuccessful candidate for the 1968 Democratic presidential nomination. As a candidate, he consolidated the widespread opposition among Americans to the Vietnam War. He attracted much student support, and won important primary elections in New Hampshire, Wisconsin, and Oregon.

McCarthy's success in the New Hampshire primary influenced Senator Robert F. Kennedy of New York to enter the Democratic race. It also helped persuade President Lyndon B. Johnson not to run for reelection. McCarthy lost in three states to Kennedy, and Vice-President Hubert H. Humphrey won the Democratic nomination. In 1976, McCarthy ran for the presidency as an independent candidate.

Eugene J. McCarthy

McCarthy was born in Watkins, Minn. He earned degrees from St. John's University and the University of Minnesota, and taught high school and college for 10 years. He was acting head of the sociology department at St. Thomas College in St. Paul, Minn., when he ran for the U.S. House of Representatives in 1948. He served in the House from 1949 to 1959, when he became a senator.   CHARLES BARTLETT

McCARTHY, JOSEPH RAYMOND (1908-1957), a Republican United States senator from Wisconsin, was one of the most controversial figures in American politics. He gained worldwide attention in the early 1950's by charging that Communists had infiltrated the government. McCarthy conducted several public investigations of Communist influence on U.S. foreign policy. Some persons praised him as a patriot, but others condemned him for publicly accusing people of disloyalty without sufficient evidence. His widely scattered charges gave rise to a new word, *McCarthyism*.

McCarthy was elected to the Senate in 1946. He attracted national attention in 1950 by accusing the Department of State of harboring Communists. President Harry S. Truman, a Democrat, and Secretary of State Dean Acheson denied McCarthy's charges. But most of McCarthy's fellow senators of both parties were aware of his widespread support and were anxious to avoid challenging him. So was General Dwight D. Eisenhower, both as Republican presidential candidate and soon after becoming President in 1953. McCarthy also accused the Eisenhower Administration of treason.

A number of circumstances caused many Americans to believe McCarthy's charges. These included the frustrations of the Korean War, the Chinese Communist conquest of mainland China, and the arrest and conviction of several Americans as Russian spies.

During nationally televised hearings in 1954, McCarthy accused the U.S. Army of "coddling Communists." The Army made countercharges of improper conduct by members of McCarthy's staff. As a re-

sult of the hearings, McCarthy lost the support of millions of people. The Senate condemned McCarthy in 1954 for "contemptuous" conduct toward a subcommittee that had investigated his finances in 1952, and for his abuse of a committee that recommended he be censured.

United Press Int.

Joseph R. McCarthy

McCarthy was born in Grand Chute, Wis., and graduated from Marquette University. He wrote two books, *America's Retreat from Victory: The Story of George Catlett Marshall* (1951) and *McCarthyism: The Fight for America* (1952). CHARLES BARTLETT

McCARTHY, MARY (1912-   ), is an American author. She has written novels, short stories, criticism, essays, travel books, and autobiography. In each form she has shown originality, especially in her combination of intellectual analysis and satirical wit.

Mary McCarthy was born in Seattle. She described her early years in *Memories of a Catholic Girlhood* (1957). Her novel *The Oasis* (1949) deals with an experiment in group living. Another novel, *The Groves of Academe* (1952), is a study of life at an experimental college. *The Stones of Florence* (1959) received high praise for its successful blend of history and art criticism.

Mary McCarthy's first novel to reach a wide audience was *The Group* (1963). Partly autobiographical, the novel relates the stories of several girls who graduate from Vassar College and enter the world of the 1930's. In this work, the author examines politics, suicide, psychiatry, and

Pix from Publix

Mary McCarthy

economics. *On the Contrary* (1961) is a collection of articles. A selection of her literary criticism appears in *The Writing on the Wall* (1970).   JOHN CROSSETT

McCARTNEY, PAUL. See BEATLES.

McCARTY, HENRY. See BILLY THE KID.

McCAULEY, MARY. See PITCHER, MOLLY.

McCLELLAN, GEORGE BRINTON (1826-1885), a Union Army commander, served for a time as the general in chief of all armies during the Civil War. He was a brilliant organizer of troops. Some authorities rank him as the greatest Northern general, while others contend that he was too cautious to lead an army. He was the Democratic candidate for President in 1864, but lost to Abraham Lincoln.

Military Career. At the outbreak of the Civil War, McClellan became a major general in command of Ohio volunteers. After clearing western Virginia of Confederate forces, he became a major general in the regular Army. In the summer of 1861, he took command of the Union Army in the East, which became known as the Army of the Potomac. He organized it into an efficient force. Later, he became general in chief of all armies. President Lincoln grew impatient because McClellan did not move against the Confederates. He relieved him as supreme general early in 1862. McClellan kept his position as Army commander.

McClellan finally advanced in the spring of 1862, moving against Richmond from the east in the Peninsular Campaign. After fighting at Yorktown, Williamsburg, and Fair Oaks, he drew close to Richmond. The Confederates under General Robert E. Lee then attacked him in the Battle of the Seven Days, and drove him back to Harrison's Landing on the James River. Washington authorities then transferred McClellan's army to northern Virginia, placing most of his troops temporarily under General John Pope's command. After Pope's defeat at the second Battle

Brown Bros.
George B. McClellan

of Bull Run, or Manassas, McClellan became commander of all troops in the Washington area. He led his army into Maryland to meet a Confederate invasion. He forced the enemy to retreat to Virginia in the Battle of Antietam, one of the war's bloodiest, in September 1862. Lincoln, displeased with McClellan's delay in following up his victory, replaced him with General Ambrose Burnside, and his military career ended.

Other Activities. McClellan was born in Philadelphia, Pa., and was graduated from the U.S. Military Academy in 1846, second in his class. He served as an engineer in the Mexican War. He went to Europe in 1855 as a member of a commission to study European military systems, and saw a part of the Crimean War. He also devised a cavalry saddle that was adopted by the Army. In 1857, McClellan resigned from the Army to become chief engineer of the Illinois Central (now Illinois Central Gulf) Railroad. Later, he became vice-president of that railroad, then served as president of the eastern division of the Ohio and Mississippi Railroad. McClellan was governor of New Jersey from 1878 to 1881. T. HARRY WILLIAMS

See also CIVIL WAR (The War in the East).

McCLOSKEY, JOHN CARDINAL (1810-1885), was the Roman Catholic archbishop of New York from 1864 until his death. He became the first American cardinal in 1875. He was well known as a preacher, and knew many European Catholic leaders. Persuasive rather than forceful, he was extremely influential during a period of tremendous growth in the numbers of Roman Catholics in the United States. Cardinal McCloskey was responsible for building the cathedral in Albany, N.Y., where he was bishop before he went to New York City, and the famous St. Patrick's Cathedral on Fifth Avenue in New York City. He was born in Brooklyn, N.Y. JOHN T. FARRELL and FULTON J. SHEEN

McCLOSKEY, ROBERT (1914-   ), is an American artist, and writer and illustrator of children's books. He won the Caldecott medal in 1942 for *Make Way for Ducklings*, and again in 1958 for *Time of Wonder*. He is the first person to win this award twice. McCloskey

received the Regina medal in 1974. He wrote about his boyhood experiences in his first book, *Lentil* (1940) and in *Homer Price* (1943). His summer home on a Maine island was the background for *Blueberries for Sal* (1948) and *One Morning in Maine* (1952). He was born in Hamilton, Ohio. RUTH HILL VIGUERS

McCLUNG, NELLIE (1873-1951), was a leading Canadian feminist and an author. She fought successfully for political and legal rights for Canadian women.

In 1912, McClung helped found the Winnipeg (Man.) Political Equality League, which campaigned for female *suffrage* (voting rights) in Canada. Manitoba was one of several provinces that in 1916 gave women the right to vote. Female suffrage became nationwide in 1918.

From 1921 to 1926, McClung represented Edmonton in the Alberta legislature. She was one of five women who began a court battle in 1927 to determine whether women were "persons" under the British North America Act, which serves as Canada's constitution. The Privy Council in England, the highest judicial authority in the British Empire, ruled in their favor in 1929. This ruling enabled women to serve in the Canadian Senate.

Public Archives Canada C 27674
Nellie McClung

McClung wrote several books about Canadian life and the women's movement. They included *In Times Like These* (1915) and *Purple Springs* (1921). Nellie Letitia McClung was born in Chatsworth, Ont. PATRICIA MONK

McCLURE, SIR ROBERT. See NORTHWEST PASSAGE.

McCLURE, SAMUEL SIDNEY (1857-1949), was an American editor and publisher. He founded the McClure Syndicate in New York City in 1884. This was one of the first newspaper syndicates. In 1893, McClure founded *McClure's Magazine*, one of the first successful inexpensive magazines. He was briefly connected with the S. S. McClure Newspaper Corporation, which was formed in 1915 when he bought the *New York Mail*.

McClure was born in Forcess, Ireland. His works include *My Autobiography*, *Obstacles to Peace*, and *The Achievements of Liberty*. JOHN ELDRIDGE DREWRY

McCOLLUM, ELMER VERNER (1879-1967), an American biochemist and educator, originated the letter system of naming vitamins. He and his associates presented evidence in 1915 that more than one vitamin existed. McCollum classified these substances as "fat-soluble A" and "water-soluble B" vitamins (see VITAMIN). He is also known for his work on the role of calcium and magnesium in the diet, and the effect of vitamin D on bone formation. He was coauthor of the book *The Newer Knowledge of Nutrition*. McCollum was born in Fort Scott, Kan. He was a professor of biochemistry at Johns Hopkins University. PAUL R. FREY

McCONNELL, JOSEPH, JR. See WAR ACES.

McCORMACK, JOHN (1884-1945), was perhaps the most famous of Irish tenors. His popularity as a concert artist was almost unrivaled. It enabled him to amass a fortune estimated at over $1 million. McCormack had a light, clear voice and perfect diction. He sang airs of the 1700's and Irish ballads equally well.

McCormack began his career at the age of 18 by winning a gold medal at the National Irish Festival in Dublin. After study in Italy, he won immediate success in Naples, London, New York, Boston, and Chicago. McCormack abandoned opera after 1913 in favor of concerts. He was born in Athlone, Ireland, but became a U.S. citizen in 1917.   SCOTT GOLDTHWAITE

McCORMACK, JOHN WILLIAM (1891-   ), a Democrat from Massachusetts, served as speaker of the United States House of Representatives from 1962 to 1971. Before his election as speaker, McCormack had been deputy to Sam Rayburn, the top House Democrat from 1940 until his death in 1961.

McCormack was born in Boston and attended public schools there. He served in the Massachusetts legislature from 1920 to 1926, and represented his South Boston district in the U.S. House of Representatives from 1928 to 1971. McCormack gained a reputation in Congress as a strong supporter of his party's legislative programs. In 1969, a group of liberal House Democrats tried to replace McCormack as speaker, but he was re-elected by a wide margin. McCormack retired from the House in January 1971, after more than 42 consecutive years of service.   CHARLES BARTLETT

McCORMICK, CYRUS HALL (1809-1884), invented a reaping machine that stands as the symbol of the mechanical revolution in agriculture. McCormick's machine was not a brilliant or even an original device. Other people had developed all its main features. But McCormick's reaper came at a time when the rich prairie wheatlands of the United States were ready for development if a practical way could be found to harvest huge crops.

The problem had two parts. (1) There were too few farmhands to do the harvesting, so a substitute for hand labor had to be found. (2) The great stretches of flat, stoneless prairie presented an ideal terrain for a mechanical reaper. McCormick saw the need for this machine and made the most of it. His drive and ability made him a millionaire before the age of 40.

He was born on a farm in Walnut Grove, Va. His

Chicago Historical Society

Cyrus Hall McCormick, *inset upper right,* gave a public demonstration of his first successful grain reaper in 1831, *above.*

father had tinkered unsuccessfully for years with a reaper. But Cyrus was determined to succeed. He built a reaper and first demonstrated it in 1831. He patented an improved model in 1834. At the age of 38, with $60 in his pocket, McCormick went to Chicago. There, he set up his own factory to manufacture reapers. Through years of court action and by purchasing others' patent rights, he established the superiority of his machines, and made his company the leader. In 1902, the McCormick holdings were merged into the present International Harvester Company.   RICHARD D. HUMPHREY

See also INTERNATIONAL HARVESTER COMPANY; REAPER.

McCORMICK, ROBERT RUTHERFORD (1880-1955), an American editor and publisher, made the *Chicago Tribune* one of the nation's most important newspapers. His grandfather, Joseph Medill, gave the *Tribune* its first fame (see MEDILL, JOSEPH). With his cousin, Joseph Medill Patterson, McCormick built an enterprise that included the *Tribune,* the New York *Daily News,* and the *Washington* (D.C.) *Times-Herald.* He took over sole control of the *Tribune* in 1925. A conservative Republican, McCormick fought the New Deal (see NEW DEAL). He was born in Chicago.   KENNETH N. STEWART

McCORMICK THEOLOGICAL SEMINARY is a coeducational graduate school of religion in Chicago. It grants bachelor's and master's degrees. The seminary was founded in 1830. It is controlled by the United Presbyterian Church in the U.S.A. The seminary has about 200 students.

McCOY, ELIJAH (1844?-1929), was an American engineer and inventor who developed the automatic lubricator. His invention, the *lubricator cup,* continuously supplies lubricants to moving parts of various machines.

Before McCoy's invention in the early 1870's, machines had to be shut down frequently for lubrication. The lubricator cup saves both time and money because it oils machine parts as they operate. Throughout his life, McCoy worked to design and improve lubricating systems for locomotives and other machines. The expression *the real McCoy,* meaning *the real thing,* may have come from machinery buyers who insisted that only McCoy lubricators be installed on new equipment.

McCoy was born in Colchester, Ont. His parents had been slaves who fled to Canada from Kentucky. McCoy was apprenticed to a mechanical engineer in Scotland and later worked as a fireman-oilman for several railroads in Michigan.   AARON E. KLEIN

McCRAE, *muh KRAY,* **JOHN** (1872-1918), was a Canadian physician, soldier, and poet. He contributed verses to Canadian periodicals before World War I. But he did not become famous until 1915 when he published "In Flanders Fields" in *Punch,* an English magazine. His poems were published after his death under the title *In Flanders Fields, and Other Poems* (1919). The second stanza of his famous poem is:

> We are the Dead. Short days ago
> We lived, felt dawn, saw sunset glow,
> Loved and were loved, and now we lie
> In Flanders fields.   Reprinted by permission of *Punch*

McCrae was born in Guelph, Ont., and was graduated from the University of Toronto. In 1900, he became a pathologist at McGill University and at Montreal General Hospital. As the chief medical officer at a hospital in Boulogne, France, in World War I, he witnessed the suffering and death he wrote about. He died of pneumonia before the end of the war. DESMOND PACEY

McCULLERS, CARSON (1917-1967), was an American novelist known for her stories of small-town life in the South. Many of her characters are lonely, disappointed people. Mrs. McCullers was particularly interested in adolescents who learn the meaning of loneliness while appearing to be part of a close family. *The Member of the Wedding* (1946), perhaps her most famous novel, portrays a 12-year-old girl experiencing the pains of growing up. Her other major themes include the search for individual identity, the nature of love, and the inevitability of death.

Wide World
Carson McCullers

Many characters in Mrs. McCullers' books are lonely because they are physically deformed. For example, two of the characters in her short novel *The Ballad of the Sad Café* (1951) are a dwarf and an abnormally large and powerful woman. Her other novels —*The Heart Is a Lonely Hunter* (1940), *Reflections in a Golden Eye* (1941), and *Clock Without Hands* (1961)— show the violence and pain that may accompany loneliness and lack of love. She also wrote two plays— an adaptation of *The Member of the Wedding* (1950) and *The Square Root of Wonderful* (1957). She was born in Columbus, Ga. JOHN B. VICKERY

McCULLOCH V. MARYLAND resulted in one of the most important decisions in the history of the U.S. Supreme Court. The court ruled in 1819 that Congress has implied powers in addition to those specified in the Constitution. The decision was based on a section of the Constitution called the "necessary and proper" clause. This clause gives Congress power "to make all laws which shall be necessary and proper" to carry out its other powers. The court also ruled that when federal and state powers conflict, federal powers prevail.

James McCulloch, cashier of the Baltimore branch of the Bank of the United States, refused to pay a Maryland state tax on the bank. The court first upheld the implied power of Congress to create a bank, because Congress needed a bank to exercise its specified powers. It then declared the tax unconstitutional because it interfered with an instrument of the federal government. In a famous opinion, Chief Justice John Marshall said that the American people "did not design to make their government dependent on the states." STANLEY I. KUTLER

McDERMOTT, GERALD (1941-   ), is an American illustrator of children's books. He won the 1975 Caldecott medal for his pictures for *Arrow to the Sun, A Pueblo Indian Tale* (1974). McDermott also wrote the text for the book. He adapted the story from an American Indian myth about an Indian boy's search for his father, the sun. McDermott also makes motion pictures for children. He based two of his children's books, *Anansi the Spider* (1972) and *The Magic Tree* (1973), on motion pictures that he had previously made. McDermott was born in Detroit. ZENA SUTHERLAND

McDIVITT, JAMES. See ASTRONAUT (table).

McDONALD, DAVID JOHN (1902-1979), was president of the United Steelworkers of America from 1952 to 1965. He played a leading part in the merger of the American Federation of Labor and the Congress of Industrial Organizations (AFL-CIO) in 1955. He became a vice-president of the AFL-CIO. He stressed the need to help steelworkers whose jobs are threatened by automation. McDonald was born in Pittsburgh. JACK BARBASH

McDOUGALL, WILLIAM. See RED RIVER REBELLION.

McDOWELL, EPHRAIM (1771-1830), a skilled American frontier surgeon, performed the first *ovariotomy* (removal of a tumor of the ovary). He performed the operation without anesthesia in Danville, Ky., in 1809. McDowell published an account of three similar cases in 1817, and performed eight of these operations in 17 years. McDowell was born in Rockbridge County, Virginia. Kentucky honors him with a statue in the U.S. Capitol in Washington, D.C. HENRY H. FERTIG

McDOWELL, IRVIN. See CIVIL WAR (The War in the East, 1861-1864).

McELROY, MARY ARTHUR. See ARTHUR, CHESTER ALAN (Life in the White House; picture).

McGILL, JAMES (1744-1813), a wealthy Canadian merchant, founded McGill University in Montreal, Quebec. He willed money and property to the institution, which was chartered in 1821 and opened in 1829. Born in Glasgow, Scotland, McGill settled in Montreal in 1770, and became a fur trader. He served in the first parliament of Lower Canada. GALEN SAYLOR

McGILL UNIVERSITY is a coeducational university in Montreal, Canada. It is supported chiefly by the province of Quebec. Most courses are conducted in English, though Montreal is primarily a French-speaking city.

The university offers programs in architecture, arts, computer science, dentistry, education, engineering, law, library science, management, medicine, music, nursing, physical and occupational therapy, religious studies, science, social work, and urban planning. It grants bachelor's, master's, and doctor's degrees. The divisions of agriculture and food science are on the Macdonald College campus in nearby Ste.-Anne-de-Bellevue.

The university operates a subarctic research laboratory in Schefferville, Que., and an institute for research in the natural sciences in Mont-St.-Hilaire, Que. The university also conducts research in Barbados on tropical animals, plants, geography, and geology.

James McGill, a Canadian merchant, willed money and land to establish the university. It was chartered in 1821 and opened in 1829. For enrollment, see CANADA (table: Universities). Critically reviewed by McGILL UNIVERSITY

McGILLICUDDY, CORNELIUS. See MACK, CONNIE.

McGILLIVRAY, ALEXANDER (1759-1793), became a powerful Creek Indian chief. His father was a wealthy Scot, and his mother was half Creek and half French. He served as a British agent during the Revolutionary War, and kept the southern Indian tribes loyal to England. After the war, McGillivray tried to unite these tribes. He tried unsuccessfully to force the United States to return lands to the Indians. He was born near what is now Montgomery, Ala. REMBERT W. PATRICK

McGILLIVRAY, WILLIAM (1764?-1825), served as director of the North West Company, in what is now

Canada, from 1804 to 1821. This company, a Canadian fur-trading organization, consisted of a group of Montreal fur-trading firms.

McGillivray was born in the county of Invernessshire in Scotland. He settled in Montreal in 1784 and went to work as a clerk for the North West Company. In 1786, McGillivray took charge of a trading post for the firm. He became a partner in the North West Company in 1790.

McGillivray helped develop the fur trade by sending traders into wilderness regions of western Canada. In 1821, he realized that the North West Company could not compete with the Hudson's Bay Company, a British fur-trading firm. He helped arrange the union of the two firms under the name of the Hudson's Bay Company. P. B. WAITE

McGINLEY, PHYLLIS (1905-1978), was an American poet who wrote light verse. Her collection *Times Three: Selected Verse from Three Decades* won the 1961 Pulitzer prize for poetry. With affection and humor, Phyllis McGinley praised the virtues of the ordinary life. She satirized the absurdities in life and defended femininity, morality, and domestic and suburban living in *Times Three* and in two books of witty essays, *The Province of the Heart* (1959) and *Sixpence in Her Shoe* (1964). She summed up her point of view by quoting a man who had failed as a philosopher because "cheerfulness was always breaking in." She wrote more than a dozen books for young people, including *The Horse Who Lived Upstairs* (1944) and *Sugar and Spice* (1960). *Saint-Watching* (1969) is an

Phyllis McGinley

analysis of the lives of several Christian saints.

Phyllis McGinley was born in Ontario, Ore. She lived in a suburb of New York City, which provided the setting for much of her writing. MONA VAN DUYN

McGOVERN, GEORGE STANLEY (1922-   ), was the Democratic presidential nominee in 1972. He lost to his Republican opponent, President Richard M. Nixon.

When McGovern ran for President, he was serving his second term as a U.S. senator. In 1962, he had been elected South Dakota's first Democratic senator since the 1930's. During the 1950's, he twice won election to the U.S. House of Representatives.

Early Life. McGovern was born on July 19, 1922, in Avon, S. Dak. He graduated from Dakota Wesleyan University and later taught history there. He earned a master's degree and a Ph.D. at Northwestern University. During

George S. McGovern

World War II (1939-1945), McGovern served as a bomber pilot and won the Distinguished Flying Cross. In 1943, he married Eleanor Faye Stegeberg (1921-   ) of Woonsocket, S. Dak. They had five children—Ann (1945-   ), Susan (1946-   ), Teresa (1949-   ), Steven (1952-   ), and Mary (1955-   ).

Career in Congress. McGovern was elected to the U.S. House of Representatives in 1956. He was re-elected in 1958 and ran unsuccessfully for the U.S. Senate two years later. In 1961, President John F. Kennedy named him director of the Food for Peace program. McGovern won election to the Senate in 1962 and was re-elected in 1968. In 1969, McGovern became chairman of a commission to recommend ways to reform the Democratic Party. In 1974, McGovern won re-election to a third term in the Senate.

Presidential Candidate. In 1972, the Democratic National Convention nominated McGovern for President and Senator Thomas F. Eagleton of Missouri for Vice-President. Twelve days after Eagleton's nomination, he revealed that he had been hospitalized three times in the 1960's for treatment of emotional exhaustion and depression. Eagleton's qualifications for the vice-presidency became the subject of a nationwide debate, and he resigned from the ticket at McGovern's request. He was replaced by Sargent Shriver, former director of the Peace Corps. See EAGLETON, THOMAS F.

In the election, McGovern and Shriver were defeated by Nixon and Vice-President Spiro T. Agnew. For the electoral vote by states, see ELECTORAL COLLEGE (table). DAVID S. BRODER

See also DEMOCRATIC PARTY; SHRIVER, SARGENT.

McGUFFEY, WILLIAM HOLMES (1800-1873), was an American educator and clergyman. From 1836 to 1857, he published illustrated reading books for the first six grades of elementary schools. More than 120 million copies of his *Eclectic Reader* were sold, and for many years nearly all American schoolchildren learned to read from it. The simple readers taught children to respect the U.S. governmental and economic system. They played an important part in forming the moral ideas and the literary tastes of the United States in the 1800's.

McGuffey was born on Sept. 23, 1800, in Washington County, Pennsylvania. He was graduated from Washington College, and became a Presbyterian minister in 1829. He taught at Miami University in Ohio from 1826 to 1836, and he was president of Ohio University from 1839 to 1845. After 1845, he taught at the University of Virginia. CLAUDE A. EGGERTSEN

McGUIGAN, *muh GWIG ahn,* **JAMES CHARLES CARDINAL** (1894-1974), was a Canadian cardinal of the Roman Catholic Church. He was ordained a priest in 1918. He was elevated to archbishop of Regina in 1930, and served as archbishop of Toronto from 1934 to 1971. He was made a cardinal in 1946.

Cardinal McGuigan was born in Hunter River, Prince Edward Island. He studied in Charlottetown at Prince of Wales College and St. Dunstan's University (now joined as the University of Prince Edward Island). He attended the Grand Seminary of Laval University, Quebec, and the Catholic University of America in Washington, D.C. WILLIAM R. WILLOUGHBY

McGUIRE AIR FORCE BASE, N.J., is the site of headquarters of the Twenty-first Air Force of the Military Airlift Command (MAC). The base is a departure point for MAC flights over the Atlantic Ocean and the Caribbean Sea. Fighter-interceptor aircraft and air defense missiles are also based there. The 5,000-acre (2,000-hectare) base lies beside Fort Dix, about 18 miles (29 kilometers) southeast of Trenton.

The base was established in 1942. In 1949, it was named for Major Thomas B. McGuire, Jr., a fighter pilot killed in World War II. McGuire was the second ranking Air Force ace of the war.   RICHARD M. SKINNER

McHENRY, FORT. See FORT McHENRY NATIONAL MONUMENT AND HISTORIC SHRINE.

McHENRY, JAMES (1753-1816), was an American soldier and statesman. He represented Maryland at the Constitutional Convention of 1787, and signed the U.S. Constitution. He was secretary of war from 1796 to 1800. During the Revolutionary War, he served as secretary to General George Washington, on Marquis de Lafayette's staff, and as a surgeon. Born in Ballymena, Ireland, he served in the Congress of the Confederation from 1783 to 1786.   KENNETH R. ROSSMAN

McINTOSH, CAROLINE CARMICHAEL. See FILLMORE, MILLARD (Later Years).

McINTYRE, JAMES FRANCIS CARDINAL (1886-1979), served as the Roman Catholic archbishop of Los Angeles from 1948 until he resigned in 1970. He was named a cardinal by Pope Pius XII in 1953. He left a promising business career in New York City in 1915, and was ordained six years later. He was an auxiliary bishop and coadjutor archbishop in New York City. In Los Angeles, he worked to make more educational facilities available to the growing numbers of Roman Catholics in the area. Cardinal McIntyre was born in New York City.   JOHN T. FARRELL and FULTON J. SHEEN

McKAY, ALEXANDER (? -1811), a Canadian fur trader and explorer, spent most of his life as a member of the North West Company. He accompanied Alexander Mackenzie on the first overland trip made by white people across North America (see MACKENZIE, SIR ALEXANDER). They reached the Pacific Coast in 1793.

McKay and others from the North West Company joined John Jacob Astor's Pacific Fur Company in 1810. They sailed to Oregon to build Astoria, their western headquarters. Shortly after their arrival, hostile Indians boarded their ship, *Tonquin*. The Indians killed McKay and all others on board.   HOWARD R. LAMAR

McKAY, CLAUDE (1890-1948), was a black poet and novelist. His poetry is noted for its lyricism and its powerful statements of black feelings. His four novels include *Home to Harlem* (1928), the story of a black soldier's return from France to the United States after World War I. McKay also wrote an autobiography, *A Long Way from Home* (1937), and *Harlem* (1940), a study of black life in New York City.

McKay was born in Jamaica. His first two works were collections of poetry published there—*Songs of Jamaica* (1911) and *Constab Ballads* (1912). McKay moved to the United States in 1912 and studied briefly at Tuskegee Institute and Kansas State University. He then lived in New York City, London, and Paris. McKay was associate editor of the socialist newspaper *The Liberator* for several years.   DEAN DONER

McKAY, DONALD (1810-1880), was a Canadian master craftsman who designed and built over 90 clipper ships. They were the fastest sailing vessels ever built, famed for grace and seaworthiness. McKay's beautiful *Flying Cloud*, 1,783 tons, was launched in 1851. It sailed around Cape Horn from New York to San Francisco in 89 days, and covered 374 nautical miles (693 kilometers) in one day. Both the speed of the cruise and the speed of the day's run set world records for sailing ships. McKay launched the *Great Republic*, the largest wooden sailing ship ever built, in 1853. McKay was born in Shelbourne County, Nova Scotia. See also SHIP (Clipper Ships).   V. E. CANGELOSI and R. E. WESTMEYER

McKEAN, THOMAS (1734-1817), was a Delaware signer of the Declaration of Independence. He served as a delegate to the Continental Congress and the Congress of the Confederation from 1774 to 1783, and was governor of Pennsylvania from 1799 to 1808. During his career as governor, he restrained radical politicians whose plans might have reduced the state to a condition of anarchy. McKean was born in New London, Pa. He studied law, and wrote most of the Delaware state constitution.   CLARENCE L. VER STEEG

McKINLEY, MOUNT. See MOUNT McKINLEY.

14   NEW SECOND READER.

LESSON II.

flew	trees	catch	ver'y	lit'tle
once	birds	think	po'ny	tall'er
been	knew	found	ta'ble	a-way'
come	grass	would	wi'ser	sum'mer
much	shone	school	stud'y	morn'ing

THE SCHOOL-BOY.

1. I once knew a boy. He was not a big boy.

2. If he had been a big boy, he would have been wi-ser.

3. But he was a lit-tle boy. He was not much tall-er than the ta-ble.

Newberry Library, Chicago

William H. McGuffey's *Eclectic Reader* was used in schools throughout the United States during the 1800's. Millions of copies were sold. A page from the reader is shown above.

WILLIAM McKINLEY

B. HARRISON
23rd President
1889 — 1893

CLEVELAND
24th President
1893 — 1897

T. ROOSEVELT
26th President
1901 — 1909

TAFT
27th President
1909 — 1913

Oil painting on canvas (1900) by William T.
Mathews; Corcoran Gallery of Art, Washington, D.C.

25TH PRESIDENT OF THE UNITED STATES 1897-1901

McKINLEY, WILLIAM (1843-1901), guided the United States into the path toward world leadership. During his term, American business flourished at home and abroad, and American soldiers and sailors won the Spanish-American War. This victory made the nation a world power. Guam, Hawaii, the Philippines, Puerto Rico, and American Samoa all came under the Stars and Stripes.

McKinley, a Republican, succeeded Grover Cleveland, and twice defeated William Jennings Bryan for the presidency. An assassin shot McKinley six months after the start of his second term, and Vice-President Theodore Roosevelt took office. McKinley was the third President to be assassinated, and the fifth to die in office.

His friends considered McKinley tactful and charming. Others sometimes regarded him as cold and pompous, perhaps because of his rigid bearing, piercing eyes, and his tight, thin lips. He went to church regularly and lavished great care and affection upon his invalid wife. He combined a stubborn dedication to the major goals of his administration with a politician's shrewd sense for compromise. This political flexibility was demonstrated by McKinley's changing attitudes toward tariffs and silver coinage in his later years.

The number of business trusts reached a new high under McKinley, and his administration did little to enforce the antitrust laws. Cries for change from farmers, labor leaders, and other reformers received scant notice from a people enjoying newly found economic prosperity and international prestige.

Electric lights and telephones added to the excitement of McKinley's day, along with snorting "horseless carriages." The people sang such hit tunes of the Gay 90's as "My Wild Irish Rose" and "Because." Lillian Russell reigned as the leading star of Broadway. The farm workers and immigrants who crowded into the sprawling tenement districts of big cities worked hard and long, often 85 hours a week.

Early Life

Childhood. William McKinley was born on Jan. 29, 1843, in Niles, Ohio, a rural town with a population of about 300. A country store occupied part of the first floor of the long, two-story family home. McKinley's father, also named William, and his mother, Nancy Allison McKinley, were of Scotch-Irish ancestry. His great-great-grandfather had sailed to America from Ireland in 1743 and settled in Pennsylvania. His grandfather, James McKinley, moved to Ohio about 1830 and set up an iron foundry.

Education. William, the seventh of nine children,

--- **IMPORTANT DATES IN McKINLEY'S LIFE** ---

1843 (Jan. 29) Born in Niles, Ohio.
1871 (Jan. 25) Married Ida Saxton.
1876 Elected to U.S. House of Representatives.
1891 Elected governor of Ohio.
1896 Elected President of the United States.
1900 Re-elected President of the United States.
1901 (Sept. 6) Shot by assassin in Buffalo, N.Y.
1901 (Sept. 14) Died in Buffalo from bullet wounds.

272

first attended school in Niles. When he was 9 years old, his parents decided that the school was not adequate. The family, except his father, moved to the town of Poland, near Youngstown. His father had to remain in Niles for a time because of his iron-manufacturing business.

William entered the Poland Seminary, a private school. He studied hard and recited his lessons easily. At the age of 10, he joined the Methodist Episcopal Church. He attended Sunday school regularly, and his mother hoped that he might become a bishop.

At 17, McKinley entered the junior class of Allegheny College in Meadville, Pa. Severe illness soon forced him to return home. He later taught briefly in a country school.

Bravery Under Fire. When the Civil War broke out in 1861, McKinley was the first man in his home town to volunteer. He became a commissary sergeant in a regiment commanded by another future President,

Rutherford B. Hayes. McKinley carried food and coffee to the regiment during the Battle of Antietam. His bravery under fire earned him a commission as second lieutenant. By the end of the war he had been promoted to brevet major.

After the war, McKinley decided to become a lawyer. He studied for about 18 months in the office of County Judge Charles E. Glidden in Youngstown. In 1866, he entered law school in Albany, N.Y. He was admitted to the bar in 1867, and began practicing law in Canton, Ohio.

Political and Public Activities

Entry into Politics. Early in life McKinley developed a strong interest in politics, and an ambition for high office. Many years later, he said: "I have never been in doubt since I was old enough to think intelligently

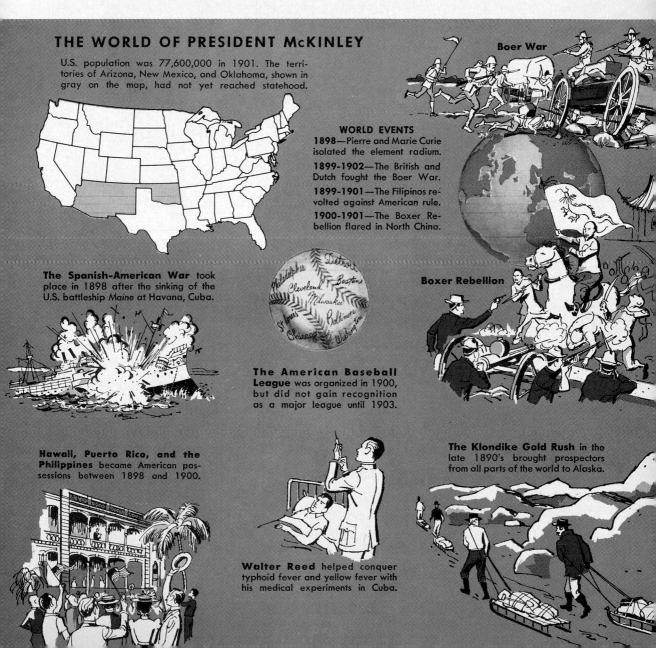

THE WORLD OF PRESIDENT McKINLEY

U.S. population was 77,600,000 in 1901. The territories of Arizona, New Mexico, and Oklahoma, shown in gray on the map, had not yet reached statehood.

Boer War

WORLD EVENTS

1898—Pierre and Marie Curie isolated the element radium.

1899-1902—The British and Dutch fought the Boer War.

1899-1901—The Filipinos revolted against American rule.

1900-1901—The Boxer Rebellion flared in North China.

The Spanish-American War took place in 1898 after the sinking of the U.S. battleship *Maine* at Havana, Cuba.

Boxer Rebellion

The American Baseball League was organized in 1900, but did not gain recognition as a major league until 1903.

Hawaii, Puerto Rico, and the Philippines became American possessions between 1898 and 1900.

Walter Reed helped conquer typhoid fever and yellow fever with his medical experiments in Cuba.

The Klondike Gold Rush in the late 1890's brought prospectors from all parts of the world to Alaska.

McKinley's Birthplace, *left*, a frame building, stood on South Main Street in Niles, Ohio. The house was later moved, and then destroyed by fire in 1937. Ida Saxton McKinley, *below*, the President's wife, was an invalid. She kept a diary during his last year in the White House.

that I would sometime be made President." In 1869, he won his first public office as prosecuting attorney of Stark County. This victory came as a personal tribute, because McKinley was a Republican and the county usually voted Democratic.

McKinley's Family. On Jan. 25, 1871, McKinley married Ida Saxton (June 8, 1847-May 26, 1907), whose grandfather had founded the first newspaper in Canton. At the time of her marriage, she was working as a cashier in her father's bank. The McKinleys had two daughters, but the younger one, Ida, died in 1873 when she was only 4 months old. Mrs. McKinley's mother also died that year. The other daughter, Katherine, died at the age of 4 in 1876. Overwhelmed by shock and grief, Mrs. McKinley remained an invalid the rest of her life. She later developed epilepsy. McKinley was devoted to his wife and constantly cared for all her needs. When he was governor of Ohio, he would turn before entering the state house in Columbus, then remove his hat and bow to his wife in their hotel room window across the street. He waved to her from a window at 3 o'clock every afternoon.

Congressman. McKinley was elected to the United States House of Representatives in 1876. He served until 1891, except for one break of 10 months. In May, 1884, the House voted to unseat McKinley, upholding the claim of Jonathan H. Wallace, a lawyer, that he had defeated McKinley in the election of 1882.

McKinley gained his greatest fame as a Congressman by vigorously supporting high tariffs to protect American industries from foreign competition. "Let England take care of herself," he cried, "let France look after her own interests, let Germany take care of her own people, but in God's name let Americans look after America." In 1890, he sponsored a tariff bill that raised duties to new highs.

In Congress, McKinley allied himself with men who favored an expansion of silver currency. He voted for bills providing for unlimited and, later, limited purchase and coinage of silver.

Governor. In 1890, McKinley lost his bid for an

eighth term in Congress. His tariff measure had proved unpopular, and he ran for office in a district that the Democratic-controlled state legislature had gerrymandered (see GERRYMANDER). The next year, McKinley rose from his defeat to win the governorship of Ohio. He improved the state's canals, roads, and public institutions. He established a state board of arbitration to settle labor disputes. His widening political fame brought him into contact with many men of national influence, including the Cleveland millionaire Marcus A. Hanna. In 1892, Hanna opened an unofficial McKinley-for-President headquarters at the Republican national convention in Minneapolis. McKinley received 182 votes, second only to the nominee, Benjamin Harrison. In 1893, McKinley won re-election as governor.

Crisis and Triumph. A personal financial crisis almost sidetracked McKinley's political career in 1893. He had cosigned notes totaling $100,000 to help a friend enter the manufacture of tin plate. The enterprise failed, and the banks came to McKinley for payment. Threatened with bankruptcy, McKinley appealed to Hanna for help. His wealthy political sponsor and a few other men raised enough money to pay off the entire debt, thus saving McKinley's future.

Hanna now set out to have McKinley nominated as the Republican candidate for President in 1896. He did his work so well that two thirds of the delegates arrived at the national convention with instructions to vote for McKinley. The convention also nominated a friend of Hanna, state Senator Garret A. Hobart of New Jersey, for Vice-President (see HOBART, GARRET A.).

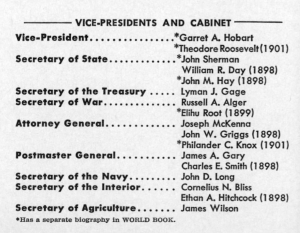

The Democrats nominated the great orator William Jennings Bryan for President, and chose Arthur Sewall, a wealthy Maine shipbuilder, as his running mate. They campaigned against McKinley and Hobart as symbols of the plutocracy, or "rule of the rich."

The Front-Porch Campaign. Hanna collected more than $3,500,000 in campaign funds, an astounding sum then. McKinley refused to leave his invalid wife for long campaign tours, so Hanna arranged to have thousands of visitors travel to Canton. McKinley stood on his front porch and gave brief, well-rehearsed talks keyed to the interests of the delegations.

McKinley expected to make high protective tariffs the chief issue of the campaign. But, at the Democratic national convention, Bryan delivered his famous "cross of gold" speech and raised the currency issue to first place in the campaign (see BRYAN [William Jennings]). As a Congressman, McKinley had favored the limited coinage of silver. He now took the opposite view. Business conditions favored a Republican sweep, and McKinley won by over 600,000 votes.

McKinley's Administration (1897-1901)

True to his campaign promise, McKinley persuaded Congress to pass a protective tariff in 1897 that sent rates higher than ever before. Congress also enacted another important bill, the Gold Standard Act of 1900 (see MONEY [The Rebirth of Paper Money]).

The Spanish-American War. A Cuban revolt against Spanish rule had been under way for two years when McKinley took office in 1897. Despite pressure for American support of the revolutionists, McKinley sought to maintain neutrality. Then, on Feb. 15, 1898, the battleship U.S.S. *Maine* blew up in Havana harbor. The exact cause of the explosion has never been discovered, but many Americans thought the ship had been sunk by the Spaniards. Public clamor for war

with Spain increased and soon reached fever pitch. Many members of Congress, the newspapers of William Randolph Hearst and some other publishers, and such expansion-minded men as Assistant Secretary of the Navy Theodore Roosevelt urged McKinley to declare war. For weeks McKinley pondered an answer. Roosevelt called him a "white-livered cur" who had "prepared two messages, one for war and one for peace, and doesn't know which one to send in." McKinley finally yielded to the demands for war. In his war message to Congress on April 11, McKinley declared: "In the name of humanity, in the name of civilization, in behalf of endangered American interests which give us the right and duty to speak and act, the war in Cuba must stop." See SPANISH-AMERICAN WAR.

America Enters World Affairs. The war with Spain lasted only 113 days. But it brought the nation into world politics, in both Europe and the Far East. In the peace treaty with Spain, the United States acquired Guam, the Philippines, and Puerto Rico. American expansion and influence soon extended to other areas. Pressured by American business interests, Congress annexed Hawaii in 1898. As the United States consolidated its Pacific possessions, the Filipinos revolted against American rule. McKinley finally concluded that "there was nothing left for us to do but to take them all, and educate the Filipinos, and uplift and civilize and Christianize them . . ."

In 1899, the United States issued the "Open-Door" notes asking for equality of trade in the vast and promising China market (see OPEN-DOOR POLICY). The next year, Tutuila and two of the smaller islands in the

Front-Porch Campaign. McKinley remained at home in Canton, Ohio, during his presidential campaigns and gave rehearsed speeches. He refused to leave his wife for tours about the country.
Culver

McKINLEY, WILLIAM

Samoan group came under United States control.

Life in the White House remained simple during McKinley's administration. Because of her illness, Mrs. McKinley did not take part in managing the White House. Her relatives and the President's nieces often served as official hostesses. McKinley reserved a private room on the second floor of the White House to greet his many visitors. Mrs. McKinley usually sat in a chair beside the President as he stood in the receiving line at receptions. The devoted couple often enjoyed long drives in their horse-drawn carriage.

At official dinners, McKinley seated his wife at his right so he could help her if necessary. In doing this, he ignored protocol which directed that the President's wife sit across the table from him.

"The Full Dinner Pail." The Republicans renominated McKinley by acclamation in 1900. For Vice-President, the delegates selected Theodore Roosevelt, who had returned as a hero from the Spanish-American War to be elected governor of New York.

The Democrats again nominated Bryan, and named Adlai E. Stevenson, Vice-President from 1893 to 1897, as his running mate. They campaigned for free silver and against imperialism.

But prosperity became the real issue of the campaign. The Republicans claimed that McKinley's re-election would give the people "four years more of the full dinner pail." The President won a sweeping victory.

Second Term. McKinley's second term also saw several events of international significance. The Supreme Court affirmed in the "Insular Cases" that the residents of the newly acquired dependencies did not have the rights of citizens and that Congress could impose tariffs on their trade. The United States had established civil government in Puerto Rico, and set up free trade with it. In June, 1901, Cuba added to its constitution an amendment that recognized the right of the United States to intervene in Cuban affairs under certain circumstances. In the Philippines, the appointment of William Howard Taft as civil governor paved the way for peace in the islands in 1902.

Assassination. McKinley delivered one of the most important speeches of his career at the Pan-American Exposition in Buffalo, N.Y., on Sept. 5, 1901. He expressed the hope that "by sensible trade relations which will not interrupt our home production, we shall extend the outlets for our increasing surplus . . . The period of exclusiveness is past." Such a position meant that McKinley had modified his high-tariff policy.

The next day, McKinley held a public reception in the exposition's Temple of Music. Hundreds of persons waited to shake his hand. Standing in the crowd was

---

McKINLEY'S SECOND ELECTION

Place of Nominating Convention . . Philadelphia

Ballot on Which Nominated 1st

Democratic Opponent . . . . William Jennings Bryan

Electoral Vote . . . . 292 (McKinley) to
155 (Bryan)

Popular Vote . . . . 7,218,491 (McKinley) to
6,356,734 (Bryan)

Age at Second Inauguration 58

276

---

an anarchist named Leon F. Czolgosz. As McKinley drew near, Czolgosz extended his left hand to grasp McKinley's outstretched hand. Czolgosz fired two bullets into the President's body with a revolver concealed by a handkerchief in his right hand. McKinley slumped forward, gasping, "Am I shot?" The crowd pounced on the assassin and began beating him. McKinley pointed to Czolgosz, imploring, "Let no one hurt him." He whispered to his secretary: "My wife—be careful, Cortelyou, how you tell her—oh, be careful." An ambulance rushed the wounded President to a hospital for emergency surgery. For a time, McKinley appeared to be recovering, but he died on September 14. Czolgosz, who had confessed a great urge to kill a "great ruler," was later electrocuted.

Roosevelt, who had been vacationing in the Adirondack Mountains, did not arrive in Buffalo until after McKinley had died. He then took the oath of office as President.

Mrs. McKinley, at the home of the president of the exposition, did not learn of the shooting until several hours later. She was so shocked that she never returned to the White House. Nor did she attend the burial rites. During her final years she lived in Canton. She died in 1907, and was buried there beside her husband at the McKinley Memorial.

An authoritative biography of McKinley is *In the Days of McKinley* by Margaret Leech.   Oscar Handlin

Related Articles in World Book include:

Bryan (William Jennings)
Cuba (History)
Hanna, Mark
Hobart, Garret A.
Ohio (Places to Visit)
Philippines (History)

President of the United States
Puerto Rico (History)
Roosevelt, Theodore
Spanish-American War
Tariff
Trust

Outline

I. Early Life
  A. Childhood
  B. Education
  C. Bravery Under Fire

II. Political and Public Activities
  A. Entry into Politics
  B. McKinley's Family
  C. Congressman
  D. Governor
  E. Crisis and Triumph
  F. The "Front Porch" Campaign

III. McKinley's Administration (1897-1901)
  A. The Spanish-American War
  B. America Enters World Affairs
  C. Life in the White House
  D. "The Full Dinner Pail"
  E. Second Term
  F. Assassination

Questions

Why was McKinley's election to his first public office a personal tribute?

Why did he seat Mrs. McKinley at his right at official dinners in defiance of diplomatic custom?

What were two of McKinley's achievements while he served as governor of Ohio?

What conditions favored his election in 1896?

What was McKinley's relationship to: (1) Marcus A. Hanna? (2) William Jennings Bryan? (3) Theodore Roosevelt?

When did he reverse his position on silver coinage?

Who assassinated McKinley? Where and when did the assassination occur?

In what ways did his administration encourage the expansion of American industry?

How did the world position of the United States change during McKinley's administration?

McKINLEY TARIFF ACT. See Harrison, Benjamin (Domestic Affairs).

McKINLY, JOHN. See Delaware (History).

McKISSICK, FLOYD BIXLER (1922-   ), a black American leader, became a spokesman for the doctrine of *Black Power* in the 1960's. This doctrine urged blacks to gain political and economic control of their communities. It also urged blacks to adopt their own values rather than those of white America. It rejected the idea of complete nonviolence, and called for blacks to meet violence with violence. See Black Americans (Black Power).

McKissick was born in Asheville, N.C. He earned a B.A. degree in 1951 and a law degree in 1952 at North Carolina College. He became a legal adviser to CORE (Congress of Racial Equality) in 1960, and served as its national chairman from 1963 to 1966. He was its national director from 1966 to 1968. After leaving CORE, he formed a company to promote black business projects. In 1974, the company began building Soul City, a new town near Henderson, N.C. The project was financed in part by federal funds and federally guaranteed bonds. In 1979, the government announced plans to end its support of Soul City.   C. Eric Lincoln

McKUEN, ROD (1933-   ), is a popular American poet and composer. Most of his poems and songs describe feelings of loneliness or love. McKuen often performs his works in concerts and on recordings. He has a hoarse voice that resulted from straining his vocal cords in 1961.

McKuen's best-known books of poetry include *Stanyan Street and Other Sorrows* (1966), *Lonesome Cities* (1968), and *In Someone's Shadow* (1969). He has written more than 1,000 songs, and many of the lyrics were published in *Listen to the Warm* (1967). He also has composed classical music and music for motion pictures. McKuen's book *Finding My Father* (1976) tells about his search for his father, who deserted the family shortly before McKuen's birth.

Rod Marvin McKuen was born in Oakland, Calif. He ran away from home when he was 11 years old. For several years, he wandered throughout the West doing odd jobs. His first book of poems, *And Autumn Came*, was published in 1954.   John S. Wilson

McLOUGHLIN, *muk LOF lin,* **JOHN** (1784-1857), is sometimes called the *father of Oregon.* He played a leading part in settling Oregon Territory. He was a partner in the North West Company, and had charge of Fort William. After the North West and Hudson's Bay companies merged, he directed their business in the Oregon country from 1824 to 1846. He developed trading posts and friendly relations with the Indians. He had to resign for helping new settlers at his company's expense. McLoughlin was born at La Rivière du Loup, Quebec. Oregon placed his statue in the United States Capitol in 1953.   Kenneth R. Rossman

McLUHAN, MARSHALL (1911-   ), is a Canadian professor and writer whose theories on mass communication have caused widespread debate. According to McLuhan, electronic communication—especially television—dominates the life of all Western peoples. It affects their ways of thinking as well as their institutions. McLuhan analyzed the effects of communications media on people and society in such works as *The Mechanical Bride* (1951), *The Gutenberg Galaxy* (1962), *Understanding Media* (1964), *The Medium Is the Massage* (1967), and *War and Peace in the Global Village* (1968).

McLuhan argued that each major period in human history takes its character from the medium of communication used most widely at the time. For example, he called the period from 1700 to the mid-1900's the *age of print.* During that time, printing was the principal means by which people acquired knowledge and shared it with others. McLuhan claimed that printing encouraged individualism, nationalism, democracy, the desire for privacy, specialization in work, and the separation of work and leisure.

According to McLuhan, the electronic age has replaced the age of print. Electronics speeds communication so greatly that people in all parts of the world become deeply involved in the lives of everyone else. As a result, said McLuhan, electronics leads to the end of individualism and nationalism and to the growth of new international communities. Electronics creates public participation and involvement and the need for general, rather than specialized, knowledge.

Herbert Marshall McLuhan was born in Edmonton, Alta. He received a Ph.D. from Cambridge University in England in 1942.   James W. Carey

McMAHON, *mak MAWN,* **WILLIAM** (1908-   ), served as prime minister of Australia in 1971 and 1972. He succeeded John G. Gorton after being elected to replace Gorton as leader of the Liberal Party.

McMahon was elected to Parliament in 1949. In 1951, he was appointed minister for the navy and air. He later served as minister for social services, minister for primary industry, minister for labour and national service, treasurer, and minister for foreign affairs.

McMahon was born in Sydney. He graduated from the University of Sydney and then practiced law. During World War II (1939-1945), he served in the Australian Army.   C. M. H. Clark

McMASTER UNIVERSITY is a provincially supported coeducational university in Hamilton, Ont. It has divisions of business, engineering, health sciences, humanities, science, and social sciences. The university grants bachelor's, master's, and doctor's degrees. It operates a nuclear reactor as part of an extensive research program. The Baptist Church controls McMaster Divinity College, which is affiliated with the university. McMaster University was founded in 1887. For enrollment, see Canada (table: Universities and Colleges).

Critically reviewed by McMaster University

McMATH TELESCOPE. See Kitt Peak National Observatory; Sun (Studying the Sun [pictures]).

McNAIR, ALEXANDER. See Missouri (Statehood).

McNAIR, LESLEY JAMES. See World War II (The Invasion of Europe).

McNAMARA, ROBERT STRANGE (1916-   ), was secretary of defense from 1961 to 1968. He served under Presidents John F. Kennedy and Lyndon B. Johnson. As secretary, McNamara became an important adviser to the Presidents in economic and foreign affairs as well as in military matters. He introduced systems of estimating military needs and costs 10 to 15 years into the future. In 1968, McNamara became president of the International Bank for Reconstruction and Development, often called the World Bank.

McNamara was born in San Francisco. He graduated from the University of California and the Harvard Business School, and taught at Harvard from 1940 to 1943. He was in the Army Air Forces in World War II, and then joined the Ford Motor Company. He became president of Ford shortly before he was named secretary of defense. F. JAY TAYLOR

McNARY, CHARLES LINZA (1874-1944), served as a United States senator from Oregon from 1917 until his death. He was the Republican candidate for Vice-President of the United States in 1940. He and presidential candidate Wendell L. Willkie were defeated by President Franklin D. Roosevelt and Henry A. Wallace. McNary served as Senate minority leader from 1932 until his death. McNary was born near Salem, Ore. He attended Stanford University. JESSE L. GILMORE

McNAUGHTON, *muk NAW t'n,* **ANDREW GEORGE LATTA** (1887-1966), was a noted Canadian soldier of World Wars I and II. He took command of the First Canadian Army at the outbreak of World War II in 1939. He helped plan the Canadian raid on Dieppe, France, in 1942. Ill health forced him to retire in 1944. He served as defense minister under Prime Minister Mackenzie King in 1944. He was chairman of the Canadian section of the Canada-United States Permanent Joint Board on Defense from 1945 to 1962.

McNaughton served as a gunnery officer in World War I, and became a brigadier general in 1918. He was credited with inventing the *rolling barrage,* an artillery attack made to protect advancing infantry.

McNaughton was the co-inventor of a cathode-ray direction finder used in airplanes (see CATHODE RAYS). He served as chairman of the Canadian National Research Council from 1935 to 1939. McNaughton was born in Moosomin, Sask. JEAN BRUCHÉSI

McPHERSON, AIMEE SEMPLE (1890-1944), an American evangelist, founded the International Church of the Foursquare Gospel. She also founded the Lighthouse of International Foursquare Evangelism Bible College. McPherson stressed salvation, divine healing, baptism by the Holy Spirit, and the Second Coming of Christ. She worked briefly as a missionary in Hong Kong until 1908. She built Angelus Temple in Los Angeles in 1922. McPherson was born in Salford, Ont., Canada. EARLE E. CAIRNS

McREYNOLDS, JAMES CLARK (1862-1946), was one of the "nine old men" of the Supreme Court of the United States during the 1930's. McReynolds served as an associate justice from 1914 to 1941. He consistently opposed President Franklin D. Roosevelt's New Deal measures. To offset this opposition, Roosevelt proposed in 1937 that when a justice reached 70 years of age, a younger justice be appointed to sit with him on the court. The proposal was never approved.

McReynolds was born in Elkton, Ky. He practiced law in Nashville, Tenn., and served from 1903 to 1907 as assistant attorney general under President Theodore Roosevelt. President Woodrow Wilson named him U.S. attorney general in 1913, and appointed him to the Supreme Court in 1914. DAVID A. SHANNON

MEAD, LAKE. See LAKE MEAD.

MEAD, MARGARET (1901-1978), was an American anthropologist. She became famous for her studies of the cultures of the Pacific Islands, Russia, and the United States. She also served in several important advisory posts for the United States government during and after World War II. From 1926 to 1969, she was a curator of anthropology at the American Museum of Natural History in New York City. She served as president of the American Association for the Advancement of Science in 1975. Mead wrote many books, including *Coming of Age in Samoa* (1928), *Growing Up in New Guinea* (1930), *Sex and Temperament in Three Primitive Societies* (1935), *Male and Female* (1948), *Culture and Commitment: A Study of the Generation Gap* (1970), and *Blackberry Winter* (1970), an autobiography.

Margaret Mead was born in Philadelphia. She was graduated from Barnard College, and received her Ph.D. degree from Columbia University. DAVID B. STOUT

See also ANTHROPOLOGY (picture: Margaret Mead).

MEADE, GEORGE GORDON (1815-1872), was a Union general in the Civil War. He commanded the victorious Union Army at the Battle of Gettysburg, from July 1 to 3, in 1863. This has been called the greatest engagement ever fought on American soil.

When the Civil War began, Meade became a brigadier general of Pennsylvania volunteers. He fought in most of the important battles in the East, including the battles of the Peninsula, the Seven Days, second Bull Run, Antietam, Fredericksburg, and Chancellorsville. He became a major general of volunteers after Antietam, and a corps commander after Fredericksburg. Late in June, 1863, he replaced General Joseph Hooker as commander of the Army of the Potomac. At Gettysburg, Meade defeated the Confederates in a defensive battle. When General Ulysses S. Grant became supreme Union commander in 1864, he kept Meade as commander of the Army of the Potomac.

Photograph by Mathew B. Brady, The National Archives, Washington, D.C.

George Meade

Meade was born in Cadiz, Spain, the son of an American naval agent. He was educated in the United States, and was graduated from the U.S. Military Academy. After serving in the Seminole War in Florida, he resigned from the Army to become a civil engineer. He returned to the Army in 1842 as a topographical engineer. He also served in the Mexican War. After the Civil War, Meade commanded various military departments. T. HARRY WILLIAMS

MEADOW LARK is a common North American bird that usually lives in grassy fields, meadows, and marshes. Meadow larks are found in many areas, particularly in the United States. They spend the summer as far north as southern Canada. In the winter, they live as far south as northern South America. There are two kinds of meadow larks, the *eastern* and the *western.*

Meadow larks are not true larks. Meadow larks belong to the same family as blackbirds and orioles. They are about the size of a robin, but have heavier bodies, shorter tails, and longer bills. The feathers of the back and wings are brownish, marked with black. The throat and under parts are bright yellow with a large black crescent on the breast. The white outer tail feathers can easily be seen when the bird flies.

The meadow lark's song is a clear, tuneful whistle. It is one of the first songs to be heard in the spring. The song of the western meadow lark is considered especially beautiful.

The meadow lark builds its nest on the ground, usually with a roof of grass so that the eggs cannot be seen and stolen. It lays three to seven white eggs, speckled with reddish brown. It eats some waste grain and helps the farmer by eating many harmful insects.

Scientific Classification. Meadow larks belong to the Icterid family, *Icteridae*. The eastern meadow lark is genus *Sturnella*, species *S. magna*. The western meadow lark is *S. neglecta*. GEORGE E. HUDSON

See also BIRD (table: State Birds; color pictures: Other Bird Favorites, Birds' Eggs).

MEADOW SAFFRON. See COLCHICUM.

MEADOWSWEET. See SPIRAEA.

MEAL. See DIET; FOOD; HOME ECONOMICS (Food and Nutrition); NUTRITION.

MEAN, in mathematics, is the sum of a series of numbers divided by the number of cases. Suppose five boys weigh 67, 62, 68, 69, and 64 pounds. The sum of their weights is 330 pounds. Divide this sum by 5, the number of boys, or cases: $330 \div 5 = 66$. The *mean* of this series of numbers is 66 and the *mean weight* of the boys is 66 pounds. This single weight of 66 pounds can be used to represent the differing weights of all five boys, even though none of them weighs exactly 66 pounds. The mean is often called the *arithmetic average* or *arithmetic mean*. See also AVERAGE; MEDIAN; MODE; STATISTICS (picture). ALBERT E. WAUGH

MEAN SOLAR DAY. See TIME (Measuring Time).

MEANY, GEORGE (1894-1980), served as the first president of the American Federation of Labor and Congress of Industrial Organizations (AFL-CIO). He held the office from 1955, when the AFL and CIO merged, until he retired in 1979. Before the merger, Meany had served as president of the AFL since 1952.

Meany made it one of his chief tasks to eliminate corruption in labor unions. He was influential in expelling the big and powerful Teamsters Union from the AFL-CIO in 1957, after its leaders were accused of unethical practices.

Meany played an important role in the AFL-CIO's international activities. He tried to strengthen anti-Communist forces in labor, and strongly supported U.S. policy on the Vietnam War (1957-1975). In 1963, he received the Presidential Medal of Freedom.

Meany was highly critical of President Richard M. Nixon's efforts to halt inflation. However, he

Wide World

George Meany

agreed in 1971 to serve on a Pay Board that Nixon set up to control wage increases. Several months later, Meany resigned from the Pay Board, accusing the Nixon Administration of favoring business over labor.

Meany was born in New York City. He became an apprentice plumber when he was 16 years old. Meany served as president of the New York State Federation of Labor from 1934 to 1939 and as secretary-treasurer of the AFL from 1940 to 1952. GERALD G. SOMERS

MEASLES is a disease that causes a pink rash all over the body. It is extremely *contagious* (easily spread from person to person). The disease occurs chiefly in children, but adults can catch it. Few people in the United States or Canada die of measles. But the disease kills many undernourished children in poor countries. The medical name for measles is *rubeola*. *German measles*, known medically as *rubella*, is a different disease with similar symptoms (see GERMAN MEASLES).

Before the 1960's, most children in the United States caught measles. In 1963—in a major medical advance—the American bacteriologist John F. Enders developed a measles vaccine. This vaccine has reduced the number of U.S. measles cases by more than 95 per cent.

Cause and Effects. A virus causes measles. People who have the disease spread the virus by coughing and sneezing. The first symptoms appear about 10 days after the virus enters a person's body. The patient's eyes, throat, and lungs become swollen and sore. A cough, fever, and runny nose develop. The fever may reach 105° F. (41° C). Small pink spots with gray-white centers develop inside the mouth, especially on the insides of the cheeks. They are called *Koplik's spots*. A person with symptoms of measles should call a physician.

Three to five days after the first symptoms appear, faint pink spots break out on the face near the hairline. The rash spreads all over the body within two or three days. About the time that it reaches the feet, the patient's fever drops and the runny nose and cough disappear. The rash begins to fade at the same time.

Some people who are weakened by measles suffer complications. Such complications include infections of the lungs and middle ear. The measles virus can harm the brain, but this rarely happens.

No drug exists to cure measles after it develops. Patients should be kept comfortable while the disease lasts. In most cases, a person has measles only once. The body produces *antibodies* (substances that fight infection) during the disease. These antibodies normally provide lifelong *immunity* (protection) from later attacks.

Prevention. In 1954, Enders and Thomas C. Peebles, an American physician, separated the measles virus from other substances and grew it in living cells in test tubes. Enders later developed a vaccine from the virus. Since 1963, millions of children have received an injection of the vaccine to prevent measles.

Measles vaccine contains live measles virus that has been weakened by a long period of growth in animal cells in a test tube. When injected into a person's body, the weakened virus produces a mild form of the condition that results in measles. In most people, the condition is so mild that no symptoms appear. But the body reacts to the weakened virus just as it would react to an ordinary virus. That is, it produces antibodies that fight the virus and later provide immunity to measles. Scientists do not know how long the immunity lasts, but it continues for many years—perhaps for life.

Before development of the vaccine, *gamma globulin treatment* was the most common method of trying to prevent measles. In this treatment, a doctor injects gamma globulin, a part of the blood. The gamma globulin

Time

WORLD BOOK photo

Temperature

Harold M. Lambert

Weight

WORLD BOOK photo

Length

WORLD BOOK photo

People Use Measuring Tools of various kinds daily. These tools include watches to tell the time, thermometers to give the temperature, scales to weigh objects, and rulers to measure length.

that is used comes from people who have had measles, and so it contains antibodies. The treatment was used for persons who had come in contact with the disease but had not yet developed any symptoms. It often prevented measles or made the disease less severe.

Physicians still use gamma globulin for persons who have come in contact with measles but have never received the vaccine. They use it instead of the vaccine because the vaccine cannot stop measles from developing in someone who has the virus.   THOMAS H. WELLER

See also DISEASE (table); ENDERS, JOHN F.

MEASURE. See WEIGHTS AND MEASURES.

MEASURE. See MUSIC (Rhythm; Notation).

MEASUREMENT is the process of finding out how many measuring units there are in something. These units include inches, meters, pounds, grams, and hours. Measurement ranks as one of our oldest skills.

Many of the questions people ask every day begin with "How many?" or "How much?" A person may ask a friend, "How many brothers and sisters do you have?" or, "How much do you weigh?" The answers to both questions use numbers. But the first question is answered by counting, and the second by measuring. Each child in a family is a whole person and must be counted, not measured. But a person's weight must be measured, and this is done by standing on a scale.

Almost everyone uses measurement daily. The food we eat, the clothes we wear, the work we do, and many of the games we play involve measurement. For example, shoppers buy meat by the pound and cloth by the yard. Many workers are paid by the hour. A football team must gain 10 yards for a first down. An athlete who runs 100 meters in the shortest time wins the race.

People also use measurement to help them understand one another and to work together easily. A boy could write to someone living far away and describe himself as tall and heavy. But he would do a better job of describing himself by saying he is 54 inches tall and weighs 85 pounds. In the same way, a carpenter building a house can order a door that measures 30 inches wide and know it will fit the doorway built for it.

This article discusses how measurements are made and how some important measurement units were developed. See the article on WEIGHTS AND MEASURES for tables of various weights and measurements.

How Measurements Are Made

Every measurement involves two things: (1) a number and (2) a unit. A number by itself is not a measurement. There would be no point in saying that a carton has a length of 6. No one would know whether the carton was 6 inches, 6 feet, or 6 meters long. But if someone described the carton as being 6 inches long, then the measurement would have meaning.

MAKING A MEASUREMENT

Many measurements are made by comparing the object to be measured with the scale of units on a measuring tool. But few objects can be measured in an even number of such units. Therefore, fractions of the unit must be used for accurate measurement. In the photograph at the near right, for example, the pencil measures between 6 and 7 inches long. Because it is closer to 7 inches on the ruler, we might say it is 7 inches long. But in the photo at the far right, we see that the pencil measures somewhat short of 7 inches. A more accurate measurement of its length is 6¾ inches.

WORLD BOOK photos

Systems of Measurement. There are two major systems of measurement: (1) the *customary* or *English* system and (2) the *metric* system. The measurement units in each system are related to one another.

The measurement units used most frequently in the United States and Canada belong to the customary system. This system of measurement started about the 1200's, though its units may be traced back even earlier. Most nations—and all scientists—use the metric system. The official name of this system is the *Système International d'Unités* (International System of Units). In 1975, the U.S. Congress passed the Metric Conversion Act, which called for a voluntary changeover to the metric system. See METRIC SYSTEM.

Measuring Tools. To make accurate measurements, we have invented such measuring tools as clocks, scales, tape measures, thermometers, and other devices. Measurement with tools involves comparing the object or event being measured with the units marked on the tool. For example, a ruler placed beside a pencil shows the number of inches and fractions of an inch equal to the length of the pencil.

Most measurements involve reading some kind of scale. No matter how many subdivisions the scale has, the object being measured is likely to fall between two of them. As a result, every measurement is an approximation. A measurement may come close, but it never matches the scale perfectly. Without a magnifying lens, for example, a ruler is accurate only to within a sixty-fourth of an inch. But simple measurements within a thousandth of an inch can be made with an instrument called a *micrometer caliper* (see MICROMETER).

Measuring tools include a wide variety of devices. Gauges and meters measure such items as gallons of gasoline or cubic feet of natural gas. A kilowatt-hour meter measures electricity. A speedometer measures the speed of an automobile or other vehicle, and an odometer records the distance traveled by the vehicle. Still other devices measure the volume of such substances as petroleum in barrels and grain in bushel baskets.

Measuring Size and Space

Measuring the size of objects or of space involves three related kinds of measurement: (1) length or distance, (2) area, and (3) volume. Length or distance is a measurement between two points, such as two towns or the two ends of a pencil. Area is the measurement of a surface, such as a floor or a cornfield. Volume is the measurement of the space taken up or enclosed by anything, such as a box or a room.

Length and Distance. Ancient peoples measured length by comparing the length of one thing, such as a stick, with the length of the thing they wanted to measure, such as an animal. Several ancient civilizations developed measurement systems based on units that were the length of certain parts of a man's body. A unit called the *cubit* was the length of a man's forearm from his elbow to the tip of his middle finger. Archaeologists have found the cubit cut on wooden rods and stone slabs made in Egypt as early as 3000 B.C.

Ancient peoples also based other units on body measurements. The Romans used the *uncia* for the width of a thumb. The English word *inch* comes from that word. Twelve uncia equaled a *foot*, which roughly equaled the length of a man's foot. Three feet equaled a *yard*, which was about the distance from a man's nose to the tip of the middle finger of his outstretched arm.

But measuring units based on men's measurements failed because not all men were the same size. As a result, measurements varied from man to man. Modern systems of measurement consist of units based on *measurement standards* that have a size agreed upon by users of the system. The customary and the metric systems both use the meter as the measurement standard for length. Scientists have defined the length of a meter as 1,650,763.73 wave lengths of light from energized atoms of krypton-86 (see KRYPTON). This distance equals about $39\frac{1}{3}$ inches. Therefore, such measurement tools as rulers, yardsticks, and meter sticks have the same sized measuring units throughout the world.

The common units for length in the customary system are, in order of increasing size: *inch*, *foot*, *yard*, and *mile*. The common metric length units are the *millimeter*, *centimeter*, *decimeter*, *meter*, and *kilometer*.

Area. Length alone cannot tell the size, or area, of a surface. A measurement of area must include both length and width. A room may be 4 meters long. But that measurement gives no idea of the size of the room because the room also has width. If the room has a width of 3 meters, multiplying 4 by 3 gives the area of the floor as 12 *square meters*. A square meter is the area covered by a square one meter long on each side.

An area does not have to be a square in order to measure it. Any area can be measured by finding out

WORLD BOOK photos

MEASURING AREA AND VOLUME

Area is the space covered by a surface, and volume is the total space that an object occupies or encloses. One way to measure an area is to divide it into squares, each of which equals one square unit of measurement, such as a square inch or square centimeter. In the photo at the near right, the boy shows that a square area contains 3 times 3 measuring squares, or 9 square units. In the same way, a volume can be divided into cubes, each of which equals one cubic unit of measurement. In the photo at the far right, the boy shows that a certain volume contains 3 times 3 times 3 measuring cubes, or 27 cubic units.

MEASUREMENT

how many square units fit into it. In the customary system, measurement units for area include *square inches*, *square feet*, *square yards*, and *square miles*. The metric system uses *square centimeters* in addition to square meters. Some units for area do not include the word *square*. For example, an *acre* equals 43,560 square feet.

Volume. The area covered by an object does not indicate its total size—that is, the volume of space it occupies. Many volume measurements are made with *cubic units*. One cubic unit has the same volume as a cube with edges equal to one unit of length. Thus, a cube with edges 1 foot long has a volume of 1 cubic foot.

Suppose an air-conditioning engineer wanted to find the volume of a 12-foot by 10-foot room with a ceiling 8 feet above the floor. The engineer could fill the room with 1-foot cubic boxes and then calculate the room's volume by counting the number of boxes. The area of the floor is 120 square feet, and so 120 boxes would be needed to cover it. Seven more layers of 120 boxes each would then fill the room. The engineer would use eight times 120 cubic-foot boxes, or 960 boxes, and so the volume of the room is 960 cubic feet.

One of the most important uses of volume measurement involves the *capacity* (amount of material) that a container can hold. Many products are sold by capacity measure. Milk, for example, is sold by the quart or gallon. Although these capacity measures do not use the word *cubic*, they are based on cubic measure. A gallon equals 231 cubic inches. Capacity measures differ for liquids and dry substances, such as grain or fruit. A *dry quart* contains 67.2 cubic inches, and a *liquid quart* contains 57.75 cubic inches or 32 fluid ounces of water. The basic unit of volume in the metric system is the *cubic decimeter*, commonly called the *liter*. A liter is slightly larger than a liquid quart.

Measuring Weight

Weight measurement has a number of important uses. Many common products are bought and sold by weight. Supermarkets sell most of their products, including butter, coffee, meat, and fresh fruit and vegetables, by weight. Many manufacturing processes, such as glassmaking, steelmaking, and the production of chemicals, require accurate weighing of the materials used.

The customary system has three systems for weight measurement: (1) *apothecaries'*, (2) *avoirdupois*, and (3) *troy*. These systems of weight can be confusing because they use the same names for many of their units. But the weights of the units and the number of smaller units differ. An avoirdupois pound contains 16 avoirdupois ounces, but the apothecaries' and troy pounds each contain 12 ounces. An avoirdupois ounce weighs slightly less than an apothecaries' or troy ounce.

People in the United States use the avoirdupois system for most weight measurement. They use troy weight to measure gems and precious metals. Apothecaries' weight was once widely used to measure drugs and medicine, but druggists now measure many prescriptions in metric units.

The weight of any object is the force of the earth's pull on the *mass* (quantity of matter) of the object. Thus, weight and mass are related. The metric system units for mass—the *gram* and the *kilogram*—also indicate the weight of an object and are often used for this purpose. For example, an object that weighs 1 pound at the earth's surface has a mass of 454 grams. A kilogram contains 1,000 grams.

The oldest known weights appear in records buried in ancient Egyptian graves about 4000 B.C. The oldest known records of weighing show stone weights that were used on balances to weigh gold. These records date from about 2500 B.C.

The measurement standard for all customary and metric units is a cylinder of platinum-iridium metal with a mass of exactly 1 kilogram. This cylinder is kept by the International Bureau of Weights and Measures in France and a copy is kept in Washington, D.C.

Measuring Time

When ancient peoples began to measure time, they based their measurement on (1) changes from day to night, (2) the time between full moons, and (3) the seasons. These three lengths of time became the basis for days, months, and years.

Later, people developed time units that were shorter than the day. The Babylonians used sundials to divide the time from sunrise to sunset into 12 parts, which came to be called hours. By the 1700's, clocks had be-

EARLY BASIC MEASUREMENTS

WORLD BOOK illustrations by Jim Conahan

The Cubit was one of the earliest units of length used by ancient peoples. It equaled the distance from a man's elbow to the tip of his middle finger.

A Shadow Clock told ancient Egyptians the number of hours before or after noon. The clock had to be turned around each day at noon.

A Balance compares the weight of one object with that of another. The ancient Egyptians developed the balance to weigh grain.

A Thermoscope was the first instrument to show temperature changes. Galileo and other Europeans experimented with such devices in the late 1500's.

282

come accurate enough to tell time in units that were shorter than an hour. The hour was divided into 60 minutes, and each minute was divided into 60 seconds.

Time units that are shorter than a second or longer than a year increase or decrease by units of 10. Seconds can be divided into tenths or hundredths. A period of 10 years is called a *decade*, and a 100-year period is a *century*.

The measurement standard for time is the atomic clock. Some of these clocks measure time so accurately that they will not gain or lose more than a second in over 300 years. An atomic clock measures time by counting the number of vibrations made by atoms of the element cesium. These atoms vibrate 9,192,631,770 times a second. The National Bureau of Standards in Washington, D.C., maintains highly accurate atomic clocks, and broadcasts time signals continuously by radio.

Measuring Temperature

Temperature measurement developed much later than other measurements. The Italian scientist Galileo developed one of the earliest thermometers in the late 1500's. His thermometer compared the temperature of one object with another. For this reason, it was not so useful as today's thermometers, which measure temperature on a fixed scale. The most common thermometers are glass tubes filled with mercury or colored alcohol.

There are two widely used temperature scales: (1) the *Fahrenheit* scale and (2) the *Celsius* scale. Both were developed during the early 1700's. People in the United States use the Fahrenheit scale for everyday temperature measurement. The Celsius scale is part of the metric system.

On the Fahrenheit scale, water freezes at 32° and boils at 212° under normal atmospheric pressure. On the Celsius scale, water freezes at 0° and boils at 100°. Because 100 degrees lie between those two temperatures, the Celsius scale is often called the *centigrade* scale. The word *centigrade* means *divided into 100 parts*. However, the scale was officially renamed the Celsius scale in 1948. There is no single measurement standard for temperature. Various temperatures are used to standardize thermometers. These temperatures include 0.01° C, at which water can exist as a liquid, a solid, and a gas at the same time.

Other Measurements

Measurement units for length, temperature, time, and mass are called *basic measurements*. These units can be combined into other measurement units called *derived measurements*. For example, area is measured by multiplying one length unit by another to form square units, which are a derived measurement.

Some derived measurements combine two or more different kinds of basic or derived measurements. The measurement of speed combines length units with time units. It tells the distance traveled in a certain time, using such units as *miles per hour* or *meters per second*. Another derived measurement, pressure, measures the force acting on a unit of area. Pressure units include *pounds per square inch* and *dynes per square centimeter*.

People in various fields use hundreds of other derived measurements. Scientists, for example, measure electricity with several derived units. The *volt* measures the force causing the flow of electric current, and the *ohm*

National Bureau of Standards

A Triple Point Cell, *above,* is used to establish one of the standards of measurement for temperature. Pure water exists as a liquid, a solid, and a gas—at the same time—only at 0.01° C. The cell shows when all three forms of water are present.

measures the resistance to the flow. Heating engineers measure heat energy in *British Thermal Units* (BTU) or in *calories*. Lighting engineers measure the amount of illumination on a surface in *foot candles*.

Indirect Measurement

Many objects can be measured by laying a measuring tool beside them and measuring them directly. But sometimes it is impractical or impossible to do this, and the measurement must be made indirectly. The amount of water in a swimming pool can be determined by finding the volume of the pool in cubic units. This indirect method is quicker and easier than dipping all the water out of the pool with a measured container.

Surveyors measure long distances on land indirectly by measuring angles and applying mathematical principles such as trigonometry (see SURVEYING; TRIGONOMETRY). Astronomers also must measure the distances to the moon and stars indirectly (see ASTRONOMY [Measuring Distances in Space]).

JOSEPH J. SNOBLE

Related Articles in WORLD BOOK include:

USES OF MEASUREMENT

Geodesy	Navigation	Testing
Instrument,	Pyrometry	Time
Scientific	Surveying	

MATHEMATICS OF MEASUREMENT

Area	Cube	Fraction
Arithmetic	Denominate Number	Geometry
Calculus	Distance	Mathematics

283

MEASUREMENT

Mensuration
Square

Trigonometry
Volume

SYSTEMS OF MEASUREMENT

Apothecaries' Weight
Avoirdupois
Calendar
Gregorian Calendar

Julian Calendar
Metric System
Troy Weight
Weights and Measures

MEASUREMENT OF MOTION AND FORCE

Acceleration
Ballistics
Dyne
Energy (Measuring Energy)
Falling Bodies, Law of
Force (Measuring Force)
Friction
Horsepower
Inertia
Kilogram-Meter

Knot
Momentum
Motion
Newton
Pascal
Power
Pressure
Torque
Velocity
Work

MEASUREMENT OF SPACE

Acre
Angstrom Unit
Area
Barrel
Bushel
Cable
Centimeter
Chain
Cube
Cubit
Distance
Ell

Fathom
Foot
Furlong
Gallon
Hogshead
Inch
Kilometer
League
Liter
Meter
Micron
Mile

Minim
Peck
Pint
Quadrilateral
Quart
Rhombus
Rod
Solid
Square Measure
Volume
Yard

MEASUREMENT OF TIME

Century
Day
Daylight Saving
Fourth Dimension
Horology

Hour
International
Date Line
Leap Year
Minute

Month
Olympiad
Standard Time
Week
Year

MEASUREMENT OF WEIGHT

Carat
Grain
Gram
Hundredweight

Kilogram
Ounce
Pennyweight

Pound
Scruple
Ton

OTHER MEASUREMENTS

Absolute Zero
British Thermal Unit
Calorie
Celsius Scale
Cord

Gauss
Gross
Light (Measuring Light)
Ohm's Law

MEASURING INSTRUMENTS AND DEVICES

Accelerometer
Altimeter
Ammeter
Anemometer
Atomic Clock
Balance
Barometer
Caliper
Chronometer
Clock
Divider
Electric Meter
Fathometer

Galvanometer
Hourglass
Hydrometer
Hygrometer
Light Meter
Manometer
Micrometer
Pedometer
Pendulum
Potentiometer
Quadrant
Radiosonde

Range Finder
Scale, Weighing
Sextant
Speedometer
Spirometer
Sundial
Tachometer
Theodolite
Thermometer
Voltmeter
Watch
Water Clock

OTHER RELATED ARTICLES

Kilo
International Bureau of
   Weights and Measures

National Bureau of
   Standards
Unit

284

Outline

I. **How Measurements Are Made**
   A. Systems of Measurement
   B. Measuring Tools
II. **Measuring Size and Space**
   A. Length and Distance
   B. Area
   C. Volume
III. **Measuring Weight**
IV. **Measuring Time**
V. **Measuring Temperature**
VI. **Other Measurements**
VII. **Indirect Measurement**

Questions

Why were measurement units based on parts of the human body replaced by other measurement standards?

How do you measure the area of a floor? The volume of a carton?

Why are all measurements really approximations, regardless of their accuracy?

Why does every measurement require both a number and a unit?

How do capacity units differ for dry and liquid materials?

What are the two main systems of measurement in use in the world today?

What are three common measuring tools?

What unit of measurement did the early Egyptians use to measure length? How was this unit determined?

What are *derived measurements?*

How does an atomic clock measure time?

MEASUREMENT, EDUCATIONAL. See TESTING.

MEASURING WORM is a green or brown caterpillar that crawls by looping its body. It humps the middle of its body, pulling the rear part close to the front part. Then it pushes the front part of its body forward to its full length and starts the process again. An old superstition says that if a measuring worm measures a person's length, the person will die.

The measuring worm is also called the *looper* or *inchworm.* The *omnivorous looper* is one of the best-known measuring worms in the United States. It can hold itself straight out from a branch so that it looks like a small twig. Some members of the measuring-worm family, such as the cankerworm, are serious pests (see CANKERWORM). If the worms become numerous, they may completely strip the leaves from the trees. Farmers use poison sprays to help control them. Similar kinds of measuring worms live in Europe and Asia.

The measuring worm becomes a delicate, butterfly-like moth. It develops in a cocoon or in a cell in the ground.

Scientific Classification. The measuring worm is the caterpillar of a moth in the measuring-worm moth and cankerworm moth family, Geometridae. The omnivorous looper is *Sabulodes caberata.*　　E. GORTON LINSLEY

Jerome Wexler, NAS

The Measuring Worm Crawls by Arching Its Body.

MEAT is animal flesh that is used as food. Meat consists mainly of the muscle, fat, and certain other tissues of animals. The most commonly eaten meats come from cattle (beef and veal), hogs (pork), sheep (lamb and mutton), fish, and such poultry as chickens, ducks, and turkeys. The white and dark meat of fish and poultry are considered separately from the red meat of cattle, hogs, and sheep. See FISHING INDUSTRY; POULTRY.

Americans eat about 37 billion pounds (17 billion kilograms) of red meat each year. People in the United States eat an average of about 155 pounds (70 kilograms) of red meat per person each year. About 95 pounds (43 kilograms) of this is beef; 54 pounds (24 kilograms), pork; 3 pounds (1.4 kilograms), veal; and 2 pounds (0.9 kilogram), lamb and mutton.

But in several other countries, the people eat more red meat than do Americans. Uruguayans average about 235 pounds (107 kilograms) per person a year. New Zealanders average 234 pounds (106 kilograms) a year; Australians, 210 pounds (95 kilograms); and Argentines, 198 pounds (90 kilograms).

Meat is necessary for a well-balanced diet. It is an energy food, and contains the five basic food elements that human beings need—proteins, minerals, vitamins, fats, and carbohydrates.

Food Value of Meat

Meat protein is well balanced and contains all the essential tissue-building elements called *amino acids* (see AMINO ACID). Nearly all meats contain the minerals iron and copper, which are needed for the blood. Liver is especially rich in iron and copper. Most meats also contain phosphorus, which aids in building strong bones and teeth.

Meat is an excellent source of vitamins. Nearly all of the vitamin B complex group are found in lean beef, lamb, pork, and veal. Thiamine (B_1) is important for the growth and working of the heart and nerves. Riboflavin (B_2) is needed for healthy skin and normal vision. Nicotinic acid (niacin) helps prevent a disease called *pellagra*, which leaves victims tired and nervous (see PELLAGRA). Pyridoxine (B_6) and vitamin B_{12} are also found in meat. Liver is rich in vitamin A, which is needed for normal vision and healthy skin. It also contains vitamin D, which builds bones and teeth, and vitamin C, which prevents a skin disease called *scurvy*.

The fat in meat is one of the best sources of body heat and energy. Some meats contain small amounts of carbohydrates in the form of glycogen (see GLYCOGEN). Carbohydrates supply energy and are necessary for normal body functioning.

Kinds of Meat

The meat of cattle, hogs, and sheep is known by several different names. Cattle meat, for example, is divided into two general classes—beef and veal.

Veal is the flesh of calves from 2 to 14 weeks old. Calves which are older are usually sold as calves or yearling beef. Veal is more tender than beef, and it contains a lower percentage of fat.

Beef is the flesh of full-grown cattle. In the United States, it is generally considered a tastier meat than veal. Good beef has white fat and bright cherry-red lean meat.

Swift & Company

A Worker Slices a Piece of Beef into T-Bone Steaks.

Lamb is the flesh of young sheep. The meat of a sheep becomes mutton when the animal is about a year old. Lamb has white fat and light-pink meat. Lamb has a much milder flavor than mutton.

Mutton has a darker color and a stronger flavor than lamb. The people of Great Britain and many other European countries prefer mutton to lamb.

Pork is the flesh of hogs. It is sold as pork no matter how old the hog is. All hogs have a high percentage of fat (from 20 per cent to 40 per cent). The eating quality of pork does not change much with the animal's age. Bacon, ham, pork chops, and spareribs are favorite pork meats.

Variety Meats. Various organs of animals are called variety meats. These meats may be sold as extra parts, fancy meats, or meat sundries. Variety meats are usually rich and full of flavor.

The variety meats from beef cattle include the heart, liver, kidney, *tripe* (first and second stomachs), brains, tongue, and *sweetbreads* (thymus glands). Lamb and mutton variety meats are the heart, liver, tongue, kidney, and brain.

More variety meats come from hogs than from any other farm animal. They include liver, heart, kidneys, brain, and tongue. In addition, feet, ears, lips, and snouts are sold as pork variety meats. These meats may be sold fresh, pickled, or canned. The intestines of hogs are sold as *chitterlings*, which are regarded as special delicacies in the southern United States.

How to Buy Meat

The shopper who knows how to buy meat properly can save money and provide the family with tastier

285

MEAT CARVING

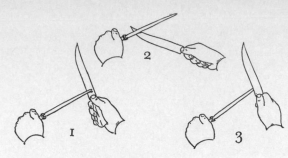

Diagrams prepared through the cooperation of the National Live Stock and Meat Board

Steel the Knife by passing the blade lightly over the steel. Work from heel to tip on one side of the blade, then from tip to heel on the other side.

PORK LOIN ROAST

Remove the Backbone before you bring the roast to the table. To cut between the backbone and the rib ends, place the roast so the ribs face you, and use them as a guide.

Slice the Roast with the fork inserted firmly in the top. Cut close to each rib. The size of the loin determines the number of boneless slices you can cut between the ribs.

ROAST LEG OF LAMB

Turn the Shank Bone to your right. Insert the fork firmly and carve two or three lengthwise slices from the thin side opposite the thick meaty cushion section of the roast.

Turn the Roast so that it rests on the surface just cut. Insert the fork at the left of the roast. Begin at the shank end, and slice down to the leg bone, making parallel slices.

Release All the Slices at the same time by running the knife along the leg bone.

286

TIPS TO THE CARVER

Carving will be easier if you remember a few helpful hints. A good knife needs sharpening only occasionally. But always steel it before using it. Always cut across the grain to avoid stringy-textured slices, except when carving steaks. To get neat slices, keep the blade at the same angle while cutting each slice.

TIPS TO THE HOSTESS

A few thoughtful precautions help the carver. Allow a large roast to stand for about 30 minutes after you take it from the oven. This makes it easier to cut. Give the carver enough room on the table and on the platter. If one platter is not big enough to hold the roast and the slices, use an additional one. Place glasses and dishes where they will not interfere with the carver.

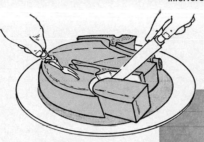

Hold the Roast firmly with the fork. Separate a section by running the knife between two muscles, then along the bone. You can remove the bone in the kitchen before carving.

Turn the Piece just separated so that the grain of the meat is parallel to the plate.

Carve the Slices across the grain. Cut and slice the other sections in the same way.

BLADE POT ROAST

Place the Roast on the platter with the small cut surface up and the ribs to your left. Insert the fork firmly between the top two ribs. Starting at the far outside edge, slice across the grain to the ribs.

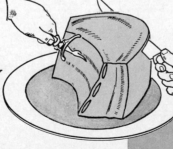

Release Each Slice by cutting carefully along the rib with the tip of the knife.

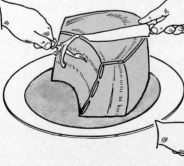

STANDING RIB ROAST

Lift the Slice on the blade of the knife after each cut. Place the slices to the side of the roast on the platter.

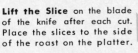

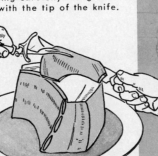

287

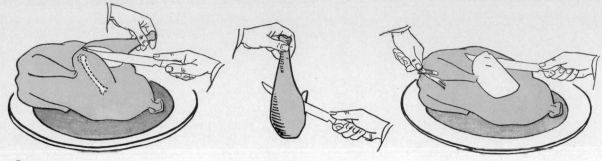

Remove the Drumstick by turning the turkey on its side with its breast-bone away from you. Hold the end of the drumstick, and pull it forward, as the knife cuts through the joint.

Carve the Drumstick into length-wise slices by standing it on its thick end and holding the thin end in your hand.

Carve the Thigh after the drumstick. Expose the thigh bone by slicing down to it. Remove the thigh bone by prying it loose with the tip of the knife. Then finish slicing the thigh meat.

ROAST TURKEY

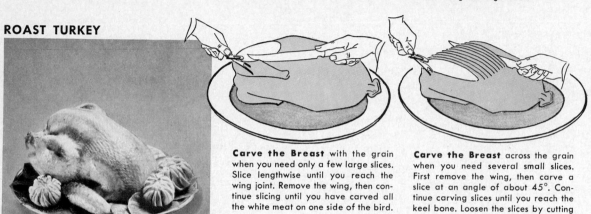

Carve the Breast with the grain when you need only a few large slices. Slice lengthwise until you reach the wing joint. Remove the wing, then continue slicing until you have carved all the white meat on one side of the bird.

Carve the Breast across the grain when you need several small slices. First remove the wing, then carve a slice at an angle of about 45°. Continue carving slices until you reach the keel bone. Loosen the slices by cutting along the bone under them.

Courtesy *Better Homes & Gardens* Magazine

OTHER CUTS

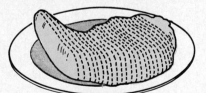

Beef Tongue should be cut in thin, even, parallel slices. Start carving from the large end and continue to the tip.

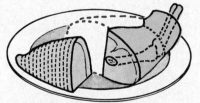

Half Ham contains a cushion section that you can easily remove and slice. Separate the other section from the shank and remove the bone. Then slice the meat.

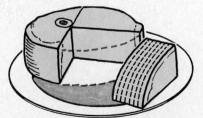

Center-Cut Ham Slice should be cut into three sections before you slice it. Carve across the grain. Make the slices any thickness you desire. Remove the bone before you slice the end section.

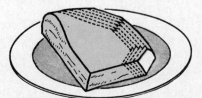

Beef Brisket often contains excess fat that you should trim off before you begin to carve. Place the round side of the brisket away from you. Take the slices from three sides in rotation.

288

BEEF CUTS	VEAL CUTS	LAMB AND MUTTON CUTS	PORK CUTS
Rump Roast	Rump Roast	Leg Roast	Butt Roast
Round Steak	Cutlets		Pork Steak
Hind Shank	Hind Shank		Fresh Ham Hocks
Porterhouse Steak	Loin End Chops	Loin Chops	Shoulder End Chops
Sirloin Steak	Loin Chops	Kidney Chops	Center Cut Chops
Club Steak			Rib Chops
T-Bone Steak			Ham End Chops
			Shoulder End Loin Roast
			Ham End Loin Roast
Flank Steak	Flank Steak	Rolled Breast	Sausage
Plate Boil	Rolled Veal Breast	Riblets	
Beef Short Ribs	Stew		
Brisket			
Rib Steak	Rib Chops	Rib Chops	Loin
Rolled Rib Roast	Rolled Rib Roast		
First Cut Rib Roast			
Center Cut Rib Roast			
Blade Rib Roast			
Chuck Arm Roast	Shoulder Arm Chops	Shoulder Roast	Boston Butt
Chuck Arm Steak	Shoulder Arm Roast	Shoulder Arm Chops	Sliced Shoulder
Chuck Blade Steak	Shoulder Blade Chops	Shoulder Blade Chops	Picnic Shoulder
Chuck Blade Roast	Shoulder Blade Roast		Skinned Shoulder
Boiling Beef	Stew	Shank in Stew	Pork Fore Shank
		or Rolled Breast	

meals. The smart buyer of meat knows the different cuts of meat which are sold. The wide variety of cuts which can be bought at retail shops are listed on the chart with this article.

Not all meat markets or butchers have all of these cuts. But all markets—both city and rural—have cuts which fall within certain price ranges. Supply and demand, as well as the quality of the meat, determine how much meat cuts cost. In general, chops and steaks are costly. The prime rib cut of beef is also expensive. Chuck, shoulder cuts, and shanks are less expensive, and a section of backbone called the *chine* is an excellent low-cost cut for boiling and roasting.

Steaks and chops are most popular because they are flavorful and easy to prepare. Less popular cuts are just as high in food value, however, and they cost much less. Lower grades of meat have less calorie value, but many yield more protein, minerals, and vitamins.

How to Cook Meat

There are two chief methods for cooking meat, dry heat and moist heat. *Dry-heat* methods, such as roasting, broiling, pan broiling, frying, and deep fat frying, are best for cooking tender cuts. These methods use as little water as possible, which helps meat keep its natural flavor. Cooks usually roast meat by placing it in an uncovered pan in an oven. Broiling means to cook by applying heat directly to the meat. Cooks place the meat under the gas flame or electric heating unit of an oven, or over hot coals. *Moist-heat* methods include braising, baking, simmering, and cooking in water. These methods are best for meats that are not very tender. Dry heat tends to harden the connective tissues of less tender meats, making them harder. Moist heat softens the tissues and makes the meat more tender.

How to Carve Meat

Meat must be carved, or cut in pieces, before it can be served. Except for steaks, all meats are cut across the grain to avoid giving a stringy texture to the slices. To cut neat and uniform slices of meat, the carver should hold the knife blade at the same angle for each slice. A meat platter or a carving board allows more room for cutting and makes carving easier. See the pictures with this article for a detailed discussion on how to carve various kinds of meat, including beef, pork, and poultry. JOHN C. AYRES

Related Articles in WORLD BOOK include:

KINDS OF MEAT

Beef	Ham	Mutton	Poultry
Fish	Lamb	Pork	Veal

OTHER RELATED ARTICLES

Amino Acid	Diet	Nutrition
Calorie	Food	Protein
Cooking	Meat Packing	Vitamin

MEAT EXTRACT is a concentrated paste made by boiling fresh, lean meat in vacuum kettles. The meat is boiled until the water takes on a brown color and the meat loses nearly all its color. Then the meat is removed, and the juice is boiled again until most of the liquid has evaporated, leaving the paste. Meat extract has a yellowish-brown color, and a pleasing, meaty odor and flavor.

Meat extract has little food value. It usually contains only about 7 per cent protein, and some minerals. The meat which is left over after boiling, even though flavorless, generally contains more food value than the extract. To add to the food value of extract, the boiled meat is sometimes ground or powdered and placed in the broth.

Meat extract has an appetizing flavor, stimulating to the appetite. It is often fed to sick persons or convalescents. It can be added to milk for persons who cannot digest milk alone. Meat extract often is used to flavor soups and sauces. JOHN C. AYRES

MEAT INSPECTION ACT. See ROOSEVELT, THEODORE (Domestic Problems).

Dressed Beef Carcasses are wrapped in heavy cloth before being put into a packing-house cooler. The cloth helps prevent shrinkage of the carcass. After cooling, the cloth is removed, leaving the carcass with a smooth, neat appearance.

Swift & Company

MEAT PACKING is the business of slaughtering cattle, hogs, and sheep, and preparing the meat for transportation and sale. The term *meat packing* comes from the once-common practice of packing highly salted meat in wooden barrels. The American colonists used this method to preserve meat for storage or for shipment overseas. Today, meat packers use refrigeration to preserve meat.

Meat packing is an important industry in many countries. The United States produces the most *red meat* (meat of cattle, hogs, and sheep). Russia, China, West Germany, France, and Brazil rank next in order of production.

In the United States alone, the meat-packing industry produces more than 36 billion pounds (16.3 billion kilograms) of meat annually. More than 120 million farm animals must be slaughtered yearly to produce this amount of meat. Raising and slaughtering these animals and processing the meat provide jobs for thousands of farmers, ranchers, butchers, and meat packers. The 6,000 meat-packing and processing plants in the United States employ about 230,000 workers. The industry pays out about $26 billion a year to the farmers and ranchers who raise livestock. It produces about $36 billion worth of meat and meat by-products.

Marketing of Livestock

Kinds of Markets. Each weekday, farmers and ranchers in the United States sell about 500,000 meat animals. More than two-thirds of the cattle, hogs, and sheep are sold directly to meat packers. This sales practice is called *direct marketing*. Some livestock owners sell their animals through large livestock trading centers called *terminal markets*. There are about 50 terminal markets in the United States. Stockyards at these markets provide pens, weight scales, and other facilities for handling and selling large numbers of livestock. Farmers and ranchers also sell animals through smaller markets called *auction markets* or *sale barns*. Auction markets operate throughout the farming areas of the

United States. Livestock owners ship their animals to packers or to market by train or truck.

Many meat packers operate slaughterhouses in terminal-market cities. But not all animals shipped to terminal markets are sold and processed in those areas. Some are shipped on to other markets and then sold. Others are bought and shipped on to meat-packing plants in other cities. The nation's largest terminal markets include those in Omaha, Neb.; Sioux Falls, S. Dak.; and South St. Paul, Minn.

Selling Livestock. In the direct-marketing process, livestock owners obtain bids from meat packers. The owners get bids by telephone or from a packing company buyer who visits their feedlot or farm. To make sure that the price is satisfactory, owners may listen to market reports on the radio or get price quotations from other meat packers. After a price has been agreed upon, the animals are shipped to the packer's slaughterhouse.

At terminal markets, livestock owners usually sell their animals through a *commission firm*. This firm acts as an agent for the owner. It sells the livestock to a meat packer or other buyer at the highest possible price. The commission firm receives a commission from the livestock owner for this service. The stockyard also charges the owner for the feed and facilities used by the animals.

Livestock buyers pay so much money per 100 pounds (45 kilograms), on the basis of live weight. Factors such as age, sex, weight, grade of the animal, and degree of fatness help buyers determine the price they pay. Expert livestock buyers can accurately estimate the meat yield of a live animal. Their estimate seldom varies more than 1 per cent from the actual meat yield after slaughtering and *dressing* (preparing meat for sale).

Packing Processes

Meat goes through more than 25 operations before it hangs dressed in packing-house coolers. Skilled workers perform these operations with great speed. Many pack-

Geo. A. Hormel & Co.

Meat Cutters use special knives to carve portions of hog carcasses into smaller wholesale or retail cuts.

ing plants slaughter and dress as many as 150 head of cattle or 600 to 1,200 hogs in an hour.

Slaughtering and Dressing. Workers use mechanical stunners to make the cattle unconscious, after which the animals are killed and dressed. The carcasses are suspended from an overhead rail for the dressing operation, in which the hide and *viscera* (internal organs) are removed. Workers cut the dressed carcasses into halves, wash them, and move them along the rail to refrigerated rooms. There the carcasses chill to about 35° F. (2° C) for 12 to 24 hours. Then workers may cut the halves into forequarters and hindquarters.

At wholesale or retail establishments, butchers divide the hindquarter cuts into flank, short loin, sirloin, and round. These cuts make up about half of a dressed beef carcass. The forequarter cuts, the other half, are divided into brisket, chuck, fore shank, rib, and short plate. A choice grade steer that weighs 1,000 pounds (450 kilograms) when alive will yield a carcass of about 600 pounds (270 kilograms).

Calves and lambs are made unconscious by an electric shock. Then workers slaughter and dress them in much the same way as cattle. Packers ship most calves and lambs to wholesalers and retailers as whole carcasses.

Hogs are made unconscious by electricity or gas before they are killed. The carcasses are then scalded and dehaired. The viscera are removed and the carcasses are washed before being cooled overnight in a hog-chill cooler at a temperature of about 35° F. (2° C). The next day, butchers cut the carcasses into wholesale cuts—hams, shoulders, loins, bellies, spareribs, and other cuts. These cuts are then sent to the shipping room to be graded by weight, boxed, and marked for shipment to markets or for further processing.

Lard makes up about 10 per cent of the weight of a dressed hog. Grinding and heating operations *render* (separate) the lard from the protein in the raw fat. The fat around the kidneys may be made into leaf lard, the best grade.

Curing and Smoking processes were once used to preserve meat. Today, meat is preserved by refrigeration. Curing and smoking produce the special flavor of bacon, ham, and other cuts.

Packers cure most meat by pumping a curing solution into the arteries of the meat, or by injecting the solution directly into the meat. The curing solution is made up largely of salt and water, but sugar may be included. Other ingredients are usually added to help develop the cherry-red color of cured meat and to preserve the flavor.

Smoking produces the distinctive smoked-meat flavor which consumers demand in certain meats. Modern smokehouses consist of air-conditioned, stainless-steel rooms. Controlled amounts of smoke from special hardwood sawdust are drawn into the rooms. The warm, fragrant smoke gives the meat a unique flavor and color.

Tenderizing. Consumers want tenderness, as well as flavor, in the meat they buy. Less-tender cuts of meat may be ground to tenderize them. For example, ground beef makes up about 30 per cent of all fresh beef consumed in the United States.

In recent years, chemical tenderizers that are enzymes taken from fruits such as pineapple, papaya, and figs, have been used by both packers and consumers. When meat is cooked, the heat activates these tenderizers. Consumers buy tenderizers in liquid or powder form.

Sausage Making. Packers make more than 200 varieties of sausage, but they use the same basic process to make most varieties. Meat is chopped or ground and mixed with seasonings and curing ingredients. Generally, this mixture is forced into *casings* (long tubes made from cellulose). The casings are tied or twisted at regular intervals to form sausage links. Then the sausage

Oscar Mayer & Co.

A Frankfurter Machine stuffs meat into long tubes and shapes the tubes into links at a rate of 36,000 links per hour.

A Hamburger Assembly Line forms ground beef into patties and packages them for retail sale. The worker at the left watches the process closely to make sure that each patty has the correct weight.

may be smoked, cooked, or dried, depending on the type of sausage being made.

Some sausages are ready to eat. Others require cooking. The most popular is the frankfurter, also called the hot dog or wiener.

By-Products

Modern production methods make it possible for meat packers to use much material that was once considered waste. In fact, packers are sometimes credited with using "every part of the pig but the squeal." Livestock producers would get less money for the animals they sell if meat packers depended only upon the sale of the carcass to make a profit.

Manufacturers divide by-products into two classes: (1) edible by-products or variety meats and (2) by-products, such as animal hides, that are not eaten.

The variety meats of cattle include the heart, liver, kidney, tongue, brains, *sweetbreads* (thymus glands), and *tripe* (first and second stomachs). In addition to variety meats, hogs yield edible by-products such as ears, feet, *chitterlings* (small intestines), and lard.

More than a hundred different articles are made as by-products of meat packing. Some of these are listed in a table that appears in this article.

U.S. Government Inspection

The Wholesome Meat Act of 1967 requires each state to provide inspection equal to federal standards for packers who sell in and have plants in that state. The U.S. Department of Agriculture must impose federal inspection standards on all plants in a state if that state's inspection standards do not equal federal standards. The law also requires that all meat produced in one state and sold in another must be inspected by the U.S. Department of Agriculture.

Animal By-Products

Blood

Adhesives	Plaster retardants
Animal feed	Plastics
Leather preparations	Textile sizing
Pharmaceuticals	

Bones, Horns, and Hoofs

Bone china	Ornaments and novelties
Bone meal	(such as combs, buttons,
Gelatin	and umbrella handles)
Glue	

Hair

Air filters	Felt padding	Rug pads
Brushes	Plastering materials	Upholstery

Hide

Athletic equipment	Furniture	Luggage
Belting	Gelatin	Shoes and soles
Chamois	Glue	Wallets and pocketbooks
Drumheads	Harnesses	Wearing apparel
Fertilizer	Jewelry	

Fats and Oils

Antifreeze	Leather dressing
Candies	Medicinal capsules
Candles	Nitroglycerin
Cellophane	Ointments
Chewing gum	Paints
Cosmetics	Plastics
Detergents	Shortenings
Food preservatives	Soap
Frozen desserts	Solvents
Illuminating and	Synthetic rubber
industrial oils	Tar
Insecticides	Weedkillers
Lard	

Organs, Glands, and Viscera (for medical use)

ACTH	Heparin	Progesterone
Adrenalin	Insulin	Rennet
(epinephrine)	Liver extract	Surgical sutures
Bile salts	Pepsin	Thyroid extract
Cortisone		

The inspection process extends through each stage of preparation of meat for sale. Labels used on federally inspected meat products must be approved, and they must give complete and accurate information.

The U.S. Department of Agriculture inspects about 90 per cent of all meat produced in the United States. It administers federal laws that control the slaughtering and dressing of animals, and the preparation of meat for sale. It also inspects meat and meat products brought into the United States, and inspects the wholesomeness of meat exported to other countries.

Government inspectors, many of them veterinarians, examine each animal to be certain it is produced under sanitary conditions. They make sure that meat products are wholesome and *unadulterated* (have no improper substances added). Inspectors check the construction, equipment, and sanitation in slaughtering and processing plants. They also inspect plants that make prepared meats such as luncheon meats; frozen meat pies and dinners; and canned and dehydrated soups.

History

Meat packing in the American Colonies began to develop as an industry during the 1640's. Packing houses packed pork in salt for shipment to plantations in the West Indies. The number of packing houses grew as communities developed that did not produce their own meat animals. In most cases, a packing house then served only one small community. When that community's farms failed to produce enough livestock, animals were herded in from other communities.

Before 1850, packing plants operated only during the winter. Many meat-packing plants were connected with icehouses. Workers cut ice from rivers and lakes in winter, and stored it in icehouses for use in warm weather. Meat packing became a year-round business after artificial refrigeration was developed.

However, until the industry developed refrigerated railway cars, packing plants had trouble keeping meat fresh during the time needed to ship it to big Eastern cities. By the 1880's, meat packers had perfected refrigerated railway cars. In the early 1900's, inventor Frederick McKinley Jones developed a refrigeration process that could be used in trucks.

Modern meat packing also began during this period when packers perfected assembly line production methods. In 1890, Congress passed a meat inspection law for meats to be exported. In 1906, a law was passed providing for federal inspection of meats shipped in interstate commerce.

Recent Developments. Since 1945, several hundred meat-packing plants have been built in towns and cities close to the farms and ranches where livestock are raised. Companies have lowered their transportation costs by building packing plants where livestock are raised. Many plants which make prepared foods have been built in and near big cities. These plants supply the processed meats that are sold in neighborhood supermarkets, butcher shops, and grocery stores.

Since the 1950's, the increased use of machinery has helped speed up meat-packing operations. Mechanical developments include continuous-process, frankfurter-making machines; semiautomatic slicing and weighing systems for packaged bacon; and mechanical knives and saws. Mechanically refrigerated trucks and railroad cars have eliminated the need for ice and salt to preserve meat that is shipped long distances. Most meat packers now use computers in their production operations.

Trends in new product development include more prepackaging of retail meat items containing recipes and detailed cooking instructions, and more precooked meat products. Many meat packers offer the consumer canned meats—hams, luncheon meats, sandwich spreads, and combination dishes that consumers can store easily and serve quickly. Nearly all meat is sold in prepackaged form. Much of the meat is boned, shaped, and ready for cooking. New methods of breeding and feeding have produced younger animals of the desired market weight and quality. As a result, meat is leaner and more tender.

LARRY L. BORCHERT

Related Articles in WORLD BOOK include:

Armour, Philip D.	Mutton
Bacon	Pork
Beef	Pure Food and
Cudahy, Michael	Drug Laws
Fat	Sausage
Food (The Food	Soybean (Uses of
Industry)	the Soybean)
Food Preservation	Suet
Ham	Sweetbread
Lamb	Swift (family)
Meat	Tripe
Meat Extract	Veal

MEATBIRD. See JAY.

MECCA, *MEHK uh* (pop. 250,000), is the holiest city of Islam, the religion of the Muslims. It lies in western Saudi Arabia in a dry, barren valley surrounded by desolate hills and mountains. For location, see SAUDI ARABIA (political map). The city is the birthplace of the Prophet Muhammad, the founder of Islam. It also is the site of the *Kaaba,* the shrine all Muslims face when they pray.

Only Muslims may enter Mecca, which Islam considers to be a sacred city. Islam requires every Muslim to make the *hajj* (a pilgrimage to Mecca) at least once if he or she is able to do so (see HAJJ).

The City. The Great Mosque, the center of worship for all Muslims, stands in the heart of Mecca. The outside of the mosque consists of an *arcade,* a series of arches supported by pillars. The arcade encloses a courtyard that measures about 600 by 800 feet (180 by 240 meters). The Kaaba, a cube-shaped stone building, is located in this open area. The Kaaba contains the Black Stone, which Muslims believe was sent from heaven by Allah (God).

In the 1950's, the Saudi government began a program to modernize Mecca. This program included the construction of tall, modern hotels for pilgrims. The government also added lighting and other facilities, built better roads, and increased the health and security services of the community. Modern houses replaced a large number of traditional dwellings. New suburbs were built, and many wealthy Meccans moved there. Mecca is the home of the Saudi Arabian Institute for Higher Education and of one of Saudi Arabia's royal palaces.

People. In the past, many Muslims who came to Mecca on the hajj settled there later. The city's popula-

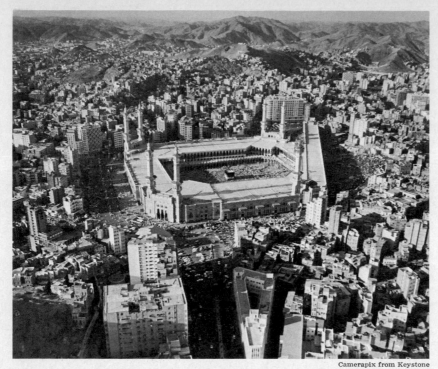

The Great Mosque in Mecca is the center of worship for all Muslims. The Kaaba, Islam's most sacred shrine, stands in the mosque's courtyard. More than a million Muslims make a pilgrimage to the Great Mosque annually.

Camerapix from Keystone

tion became a mixture of various nationalities. But since the 1930's, the government has strongly discouraged immigration to Mecca because it wants to preserve jobs in the area for people of Saudi Arabia.

Economy of Mecca depends on money spent by pilgrims. A hajj must be made between the 8th and 13th day of the last month of the Muslim year. About $1\frac{1}{4}$ million pilgrims crowd into Mecca within those few days. About half of them come from other countries. The city takes in more than $100 million during the annual great pilgrimage. The Saudi government spends almost $50 million yearly to provide health care, security, and other services for pilgrims.

Mecca has some minor industries. For example, a factory manufactures various products from clay. But the city no longer plays a major part in Saudi Arabia's economy, which has been based on oil exports since the late 1940's.

History. Mecca became a trading center about A.D. 400. The people of Mecca worshipped many gods, whose idols stood at the Kaaba. Muhammad was born in the city about 570.

The Meccans rejected Muhammad's religious teachings, and he and his disciples fled from the city in 622. Eight years later, Muhammad and his followers captured Mecca and destroyed the idols. They spared the Kaaba, which has remained as the Muslim shrine.

Mecca became the heart of the first Arab-Islamic empire. The city's political importance declined during the mid-600's, when Muslim conquests spread through distant lands. But Mecca kept its importance as the religious center of Islam.

A series of *sharifs* (descendants of Muhammad) ruled Mecca from 960 until 1924. That year, Abdal-Aziz ibn Saud, an Arab leader, conquered the city. Mecca became part of his kingdom, which he named Saudi

Arabia in 1932. Beginning in the 1950's, the government has worked to modernize Mecca and to ensure the comfort and safety of pilgrims to the city. MALCOLM C. PECK

See also HEGIRA; KAABA; MUHAMMAD; SAUDI ARABIA.

MECHANIC. See AUTOMOBILE (Servicing).

MECHANICAL ADVANTAGE. See MACHINE.

MECHANICAL DRAWING, or TECHNICAL DRAWING, is a drawing made with the aid of instruments. Drafters make such drawings to show exactly how to construct or use machines, buildings, or other objects. No ship, airplane, dam, engine, or any of the tools of industry could be made without mechanical drawings.

Mechanical drawings do not show objects as they appear in photographs, because photographs do not indicate true dimensions. Instead, a mechanical drawing shows as many views of an object as may be necessary to define its exact shape and size. The most common method is called *orthographic*, or right-angle, projection. This presents views of an object as seen from the front, side, and above. Another method, called *isometric* drawing, gives a distorted view of the front, top, and one side of an object.

Materials Needed. A simple set of instruments to make mechanical drawings consists of a drawing board, a scale, a T square, triangles, a compass, drafting tape, drawing pencils, an eraser, and drafting paper. Curves, inking pens, dividers, protractors, a ruler, and blueprinting or other copying machines may also be used. A device called a *drafting machine* is a combination of several drawing tools. Drafting can also be performed on a computerized drawing board.

Career Opportunities. Mechanical drawing is exacting work, and expert drafters are in great demand. Courses are taught in high schools, technical institutes, and colleges. Engineers who wish to concentrate on

WORLD BOOK photos

Mechanical Drawing requires skill and attention to detail. A drafter uses a variety of instruments to create a drawing that indicates the exact shape and size of an object.

A Drafting Machine, such as the one shown above, combines several drawing tools—a protractor, scale, T square, and triangle. The device helps a drafter work quickly and efficiently.

Mechanical Drawing

Drafters prepare mechanical drawings to provide technical information. Unlike a photograph or a perspective drawing, a mechanical drawing presents various views of an object to define its dimensions. Common drafting methods include *orthographic projection* and *isometric drawing*.

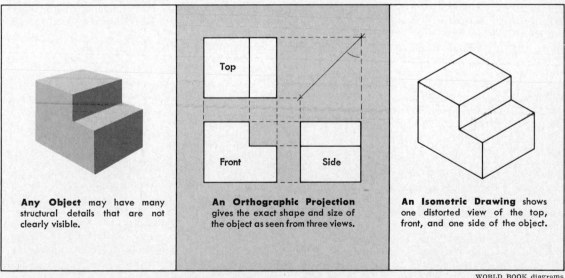

Any Object may have many structural details that are not clearly visible.

An Orthographic Projection gives the exact shape and size of the object as seen from three views.

An Isometric Drawing shows one distorted view of the top, front, and one side of the object.

WORLD BOOK diagrams

design must have a good background in drafting and be familiar with mathematics, physics, chemistry, mechanics, thermodynamics, and projection. A knowledge of such shop practices as patternmaking, molding, and welding is also important.   HARRY MUIR KURTZWORTH

See also BLUEPRINT; COMPUTER (picture: Computerized Drawing Board); PANTOGRAPH; PROTRACTOR; WORKING DRAWING.

MECHANICAL EFFICIENCY. See MACHINE.

MECHANICAL ENGINEERING. See ENGINEERING (Main Branches of Engineering).

MECHANICS is the science that studies the effects of forces on bodies or fluids at rest or in motion. Civil engineers use mechanics to determine stresses on bridges, dams, and other structures. Mechanics is also used to design rockets and airplanes. An important use of mechanics in physics is the study of the motion of atomic particles. Astronomers use the principles of mechanics to determine the motions of stars, planets, and other celestial bodies. Sir Isaac Newton first used the term to describe the science of building and using machines.

Solid mechanics includes *statics*, the study of bodies at rest or in equilibrium, and *dynamics* or *kinetics*, the study of motion or change of motion of moving bodies. *Kinematics* deals with pure motion, or motion apart from any cause. Scientists sometimes use the term *dynamics* to cover the whole field of mechanics.

Fluid mechanics includes *fluid dynamics* and *fluid statics*. Fluid dynamics is the study of fluids in motion. It includes *aerodynamics* (the study of gases in motion) and *hydrodynamics* (the study of liquids in motion). Fluid statics is the study of gases and liquids at rest. It includes *hydrostatics* (the study of liquids at rest). Hydrodynamics and hydrostatics together make up a branch of mechanics called *hydraulics*.

Related Articles in WORLD BOOK include:

Aerodynamics	Hydraulics	Machine
Dynamics	Kinematics	Statics

MECHANIC'S LIEN is a claim for materials or labor furnished by a contractor in the construction of a building. When filed with the proper public official, the lien must be paid before there is a clear title to the property involved. See also LIEN.

MECHANIST PHILOSOPHY, *MEHK uh nihst,* states that the universe behaves like a giant machine. Everything happens according to physical laws of cause and effect. Mechanists believe that no living thing has a choice in the way it behaves. They say that events of yesterday determine what happens today. Only the past and the present can control the future.

Mechanists admit that no one can predict exactly what will happen in the future. They think this is true because no one knows the present state of all the matter in the universe. Anyone who did, the mechanist believes, could predict the future accurately.

Mechanism is one of the two great philosophical theories of cause and effect in the universe. Opposed to the theory of mechanism is the theory of *teleology.* Anything that grows and develops can be explained in two ways. Mechanism explains it from behind, in terms of its origins. Teleology explains it from the front, in terms of the goal it is seeking. The word *teleology* comes from a Greek word meaning *end* or *purpose.* Teleologists believe that events may be determined not only by the past, but also by the future. They believe people can choose their goals. Greek philosophy is dominated by this idea that effort and growth are inspired by goals to be achieved. An ideal, purpose, or goal at work in the universe may direct the way in which events follow one another. The mechanist would say, "I passed the examination because I studied." The teleologist would say, "I studied because I knew there would be an examination and I intended to pass it."

The first great philosopher who made clear the full meanings of the teleological and mechanistic views was Baruch Spinoza (see SPINOZA, BARUCH).   H. M. KALLEN

MECKLENBURG is a farming region in northern East Germany. Before World War II, it consisted of huge estates held by powerful land owners called *Junkers.* Junkers played a major role in German history between the mid-1700's and mid-1900's (see JUNKER). Peasants lived and worked on the estates, but owned no property. The land owners controlled Mecklenburg's economy and ruled their estates. Peasants had few rights and often were at the mercy of cruel land owners.

In 1945, Mecklenburg became part of East Germany. The East German government destroyed the power of the land owners. The government also tried, with little success, to develop industry there.   THEODORE S. HAMEROW

MECKLENBURG DECLARATION OF INDEPENDENCE refers to a resolution supposedly passed on May 20, 1775, by a group of citizens living in Mecklenburg County, North Carolina. The citizens supposedly called the meeting to declare the county's independence from Great Britain. No written resolution or records from a meeting on May 20 have been found, and historians question that the meeting ever took place. In 1819, several men claimed that they attended such a meeting in Mecklenburg.

There is proof that Mecklenburg citizens met on May 31, 1775, to protest against unjust treatment of the colonies by Great Britain. Historians think that some of the people who attended this meeting mistakenly believed it to have taken place on May 20. But the state of North Carolina recognizes the Mecklenburg Declaration of Independence.   JOHN R. ALDEN

MECOPTERA is an order of slender insects with long legs. In some of these insects, the end of the abdomen curves upward much like a scorpion's tail. For this reason, they are commonly called scorpion flies. See also INSECT (table); SCORPION FLY.

MEDAL. See DECORATIONS AND MEDALS.

MEDAL OF FREEDOM, PRESIDENTIAL. See DECORATIONS AND MEDALS (Civilian Awards; table; picture).

MEDAL OF HONOR. See DECORATIONS AND MEDALS.

MEDAN, *may DAHN* (pop. 700,363), is a city on the island of Sumatra, Indonesia, 400 miles (640 kilometers) northwest of Singapore. Medan is a commercial center for a forested and agricultural area. Its products include rubber, tobacco, palm oil, tea, and fibers.

MEDAWAR, *MEHD uh wuh,* **SIR PETER BRIAN** (1915-   ), an English zoologist, shared the 1960 Nobel prize for physiology or medicine with Sir Macfarlane Burnet. In 1953, Medawar and his colleagues proved Burnet's idea on *acquired immunological tolerance.* This idea suggested that under certain conditions, tissues and organs can be transplanted from one animal to another and function properly even though the animals are not related. See BURNET, SIR MACFARLANE.

Medawar was born in Brazil and educated in England. He became professor of zoology at University College, London, in 1951.   IRWIN H. HERSKOWITZ

MEDEA was a woman in Greek mythology who had magical powers. She helped the hero Jason capture the Golden Fleece, the famous golden wool of a flying ram.

Medea was the daughter of Aites, the king of Kolchis. The Golden Fleece hung in a grove of trees there, guarded by a dragon that never slept. Medea fell in love with Jason when he and his companions, the Argonauts, came to Kolchis to capture the fleece. She put a spell on the dragon so Jason could take the fleece.

Medea and her brother, Apsyrtos, sailed from Kolchis with Jason and the Argonauts. When Aites tried to overtake them, Medea killed Apsyrtos and cut him into little pieces, which she threw into the water. The king stopped to recover the pieces of his son's body, and Jason and Medea escaped.

The expedition traveled to Iolkos, the Greek city where Jason had been born. There, Medea plotted against King Pelias, who had seized the throne of Iolkos from Jason's father. She told the king's daughters that she had a magic charm to make the king young again. However, Medea withheld the correct ingredients. The daughters tried the magic on the king, and he died. The king's son forced Jason and Medea to flee, and they settled in the city of Corinth.

Jason and Medea had two children and lived happily in Corinth for 10 years. But then Jason fell in love with Glauke, also called Creusa, the daughter of the king of Corinth. He left Medea and prepared to marry Glauke. In a jealous rage, Medea gave her rival a magic robe that burned Glauke to death when she put it on. Medea then killed the two sons she had by Jason and fled to Athens.

Medea lived with Aegeus, the king of Athens, and they had a son named Medus. When the king's first son, Theseus came to Athens, Medea feared he would replace Medus as the heir to the Athenian throne. She tried to poison Theseus, but Aegeus learned about the plot and banished Medea. Medea returned to Kolchis, where she lived the rest of her life.   C. SCOTT LITTLETON

See also ARGONAUTS; GOLDEN FLEECE; JASON.

MEDEIROS, HUMBERTO S. CARDINAL (1915-   ), archbishop of Boston, was appointed a cardinal of the Roman Catholic Church by Pope Paul VI in 1973. Medeiros was born on São Miguel Island in the Azores. He emigrated to the United States in 1931 and became a U.S. citizen in 1940. Medeiros was ordained a priest in 1946. In 1966, he was ordained a bishop and became bishop of Brownsville, Tex. He became known for his support of Mexican-American farmworkers who were campaigning for higher wages. Medeiros was named archbishop of Boston in 1970.   JOHN A. HARDON

MEDELLÍN, *MAY thay YEEN,* or *MAY duh LEEN* (pop. 1,064,741), is the second largest city in Colombia, and the country's chief commercial center. Medellín is high in the inland mountains. Nearby mines furnish coal for Medellín's factories. The city's markets sell coffee brought in from neighboring farms. The University of Antioquia and the National School of Mines are located in Medellín. For the location of Medellín, see COLOMBIA (color map).   E. TAYLOR PARKS

MEDFORD, Mass. (pop. 64,397), is the home of the famous Medford-built ships that sailed in the 1800's. Today, Medford is chiefly a residential area. It is located about 5 miles (8 kilometers) northwest of Boston on the Mystic River, and about 5 miles from the Atlantic Ocean. For the location of Medford, see MASSACHUSETTS (political map).

Medford factories make paper, furniture, mattresses, toys, paper boxes, and storage batteries. Tufts University in Medford includes Jackson College for women. The Barnum Museum at Tufts houses the zoological collection of showman P. T. Barnum.

Puritans settled Medford in 1630. It ranks as one of the oldest cities in the state, and a number of colonial buildings still stand there. In colonial days, shipbuilding and rum distilling became leading industries in the settlement. Both industries declined after the Civil War. Medford was incorporated as a town in 1864 and chartered as a city in 1892. It has a council-manager government.   WILLIAM J. REID

MEDIA, *MEE dee uh,* was an ancient country in what is now Northern Iran. It became the center of a large empire in the 500's B.C. Media was the homeland of the

Location of Media

Medes, a nomadic people. The Medes settled in Media in the 900's B.C., and then moved slowly southward.

Scholars have traced the recorded history of the Medes back to 836 B.C., when the Assyrians under King Shalmaneser III invaded Media. This was the first of many Assyrian invasions of Media. The Medes reached the peak of their power under Cyaxares, who reigned from 625 to 585 B.C. Cyaxares defeated Assyria and built an empire that included parts of what are now Turkey, Iran, Afghanistan, and Pakistan. Astyages, the son of Cyaxares and the last Median king, was defeated by Cyrus the Great of Persia about 550 B.C. Cyrus incorporated Median lands into the Persian Empire and made Media a Persian province.   JACOB J. FINKELSTEIN

See also CYRUS THE GREAT; NABOPOLASSAR.

MEDIA. See COMMUNICATION (Mass Communication); ADVERTISING (Ways of Advertising); MAGAZINE; NEWSPAPER; RADIO; TELEVISION.

MEDIAN, *MEE dee uhn,* is the middle value in a group of numbers arranged in order of size. Suppose five students receive test scores of 62, 84, 99, 77, and 88. To find the median of these scores, arrange them in order of size: 62, 77, 84, 88, and 99. The number in the middle is now 84. The *median* of this group is 84, and the *median score* is 84. The *arithmetic average* or *mean score* is 82. If the number of cases is even, there will be no number in the middle. Then, the median is the average of the two middlemost values.

If we learn that the median mark on a test is 84, we know that just as many students received marks above 84 as marks below 84. The median is always settled so that there are as many values larger than the median as there are values smaller.   ALBERT E. WAUGH

See also AVERAGE; MEAN; MODE; STATISTICS.

MEDIATION BOARD, NATIONAL. See NATIONAL MEDIATION BOARD.

MEDIC ALERT FOUNDATION is a nonprofit organization that issues identification emblems to persons with certain medical problems. The emblems are available to anyone who has diabetes, epilepsy, or any other problem that a doctor should know about before giving medical treatment. For example, people with a severe allergy may become seriously ill or die if they take certain drugs. Such persons might someday require emergency care while unconscious. If they wear a Medic Alert emblem that identifies their problem, the doctor will not give them the harmful drugs.

The metal emblems are available in the form of bracelets or necklaces. The symbol of the medical pro-

Medic Alert Foundation
Medic Alert Emblem

fession and the words *Medic Alert* appear on the front. The person's medical problem, serial number, and the foundation's telephone number are engraved on the back. The doctor can call the foundation collect for further information about the patient. Medic Alert Foundation headquarters are in Turlock, Calif.

Critically reviewed by the MEDIC ALERT FOUNDATION

MEDICAID is a federal-state program in the United States that provides medical care for many people who cannot pay for it. A state has considerable freedom to choose what medical services it provides. But to take part in the Medicaid program, a state must meet standards established by the federal government. One requirement is that a state's Medicaid plan provide medical care for all persons receiving public assistance. The state's plan may also include people called *medically indigent.* Such people can provide for their daily needs but cannot afford any large medical expenses.

The federal government pays a state from 50 to 83 per cent of the state's Medicaid costs. The percentage depends on the average income of people in the state. All states except Arizona have the program. Congress established Medicaid in 1965.   ROBERT J. MYERS

See also BLUE CROSS.

MEDICAL ASSOCIATION, AMERICAN. See AMERICAN MEDICAL ASSOCIATION.

MEDICAL CORPS is the name of the branch that handles health and medical matters in each of the United States armed services.

MEDICAL SCHOOL. See MEDICINE (Careers in Medicine; The Beginnings of Organized Medicine).

MEDICARE is a United States government health insurance program. It consists of hospital insurance and supplementary medical insurance. Nearly all persons 65 years old or older are eligible for Medicare. The program also provides health insurance for disabled persons of all ages who have been receiving social security benefits for at least two consecutive years and for certain persons with kidney disease. The law that established Medicare was passed in 1965. The program is managed by the Health Care Financing Administration, an agency of the United States Department of Health and Human Services.

Hospital Insurance helps pay the cost of hospital care, certain skilled nursing-home care after leaving the hospital, and post-hospital home health services. A person pays the first $180 of the hospital bill in each period or "spell of illness." Medicare then pays the rest of the patient's covered hospital expenses for 60 days, and all but $45 a day for 30 more days. Medicare also pays all covered expenses for the first 20 days of nursing home care and all but $20 a day for the next 80 days. Within each "spell of illness," a person may use the full 90 days of hospital and 100 days of nursing-home benefits. The patient is eligible again for these benefits anytime he or she has not been in a hospital or extended care facility for 60 days in a row. The patient also has a "lifetime reserve" of 60 hospital days. These can be used at any time, and cover all costs over $80 a day.

Hospital insurance is financed by a special tax paid by workers, their employers, and self-employed persons. The tax is collected with the regular Social Security contributions. The federal government pays the cost for uninsured persons who were 65 years old before 1968.

Medical Insurance helps pay the cost of physicians' services and certain other medical costs not covered by hospital insurance. The insured member pays the first $60 of covered medical expenses in a calendar year. Medical insurance then pays 80 per cent of the cost of covered services for the rest of the year. The program is financed by payments of $9.60 a month from members and by federal payments totaling about twice the members' contribution.

Critically reviewed by the HEALTH CARE FINANCING ADMINISTRATION

See also BLUE CROSS; BLUE SHIELD.

MEDICI, *MEHD ih chee,* was the name of a ruling family of Florence, Italy. Members of the family played important parts in the history of Italy and France from the 1400's to the 1700's. Their great wealth and influence as bankers first gave them control of Florence.

Except for brief periods, the Medici ruled Florence until 1737. Their cultural interests led them to become patrons of the arts, and Florence became an art center under their rule. Michelangelo and Raphael were among the great artists the Medici helped.

The Medici influence extended to Rome when three members of the family became popes. Leo X reigned from 1513 to 1521 and Clement VII from 1523 to 1534 (see LEO [X]; CLEMENT [VII]). Leo XI was pope for only 27 days in 1605.

Two women of the Medici family became queens of France. They adopted the French spelling of the name, *de Médicis.* Catherine de Médicis, the wife of Henry II and mother of three French kings, virtually ruled France from 1559 until her death in 1589 (see CATHERINE DE MÉDICIS). Marie de Médicis married Henry IV. After his death in 1610, Marie reigned until her son, Louis XIII, took over the throne. See RUBENS, PETER PAUL (picture).

Giovanni de' Medici (1360-1429) made a fortune in banking and commerce. Giovanni de' Medici is considered the first of the great Medici.

Cosimo de' Medici (1389-1464), the son of Giovanni, became the first Medici to win wide fame. He gave large sums of money to promote the arts. Cosimo wielded great influence in the city of Florence, and was called the *Father of his Country.*

Portrait by Giorgio Vasari, Uffizi, Florence (Alinari)

Lorenzo de' Medici

Lorenzo the Magnificent (1449-1492), the grandson of Cosimo, became the most famous Medici. Lorenzo made Florence the most powerful state in Italy, and worked to make it one of the world's beautiful cities. He built beautiful buildings and promoted the establishment of libraries.

While the people of Florence devoted themselves to luxury, Lorenzo took over the government. The Medici first lost power under Pietro de' Medici (1471-1503), the weak son of Lorenzo.   FRANKLIN D. SCOTT

See also FLORENCE (History); MICHELANGELO; PAWNBROKER (picture).

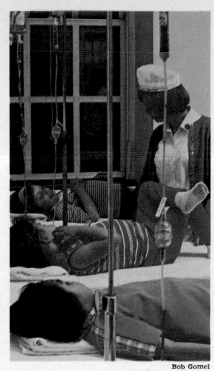

Bob Gomel   Paul Almasy, World Health Organization

Medical Care is provided by a variety of specially trained men and women. Doctors take charge of caring for patients. Nurses help doctors provide treatment. Other trained workers also assist in providing health care. The worker shown at the right is vaccinating members of a family in Afghanistan.

MEDICINE

MEDICINE is the science and art of healing. Medicine is a science because it is based on knowledge gained through careful study and experimentation. It is an art because it depends on how skillfully doctors and other medical workers apply this knowledge when dealing with patients.

Medicine seeks to save lives and relieve suffering. For this reason, it has long been one of the most respected professions. Many thousands of men and women in the medical profession spend their lives caring for the sick. When disaster strikes, hospital workers rush emergency aid to the injured. When epidemics threaten, doctors and nurses double their efforts to prevent the spread of disease. Other persons in the medical profession continually search for better ways of fighting disease.

Human beings have suffered from disease since they first appeared on the earth about 2½ million years ago. Throughout most of this time, they knew little about how the human body works or what causes disease. Treatment was based largely on superstition and guesswork. But medicine has made tremendous scientific

Louis Lasagna, the contributor of this article, is Professor of Pharmacology and Toxicology at the University of Rochester School of Medicine and Dentistry. He is also the author of The Doctors' Dilemmas. *Unless otherwise credited, the photographs in the article were taken for* WORLD BOOK *by Stephen Feldman, through the courtesy of Rush-Presbyterian-St. Luke's Medical Center, Chicago.*

progress in the last several hundred years. Today, it is possible to cure, control, or prevent hundreds of diseases, from measles and polio to tuberculosis and yellow fever. New drugs, machines, and surgical operations add years to the lives of many patients. Partly as a result of medical progress, people have a longer life expectancy than they had in the past. In 1900, most people in the United States did not live past the age of 50. Today, Americans live an average of about 71 years.

As medicine has become more scientific, it has also become more complicated. In the past, doctors cared for patients almost single-handedly. Patients received treatment at home for most kinds of illnesses. Very few patients went to hospitals. Today, most doctors no longer work by themselves. Instead, they head *medical teams* made up of nurses, laboratory workers, and many other skilled professionals. The care provided by such teams cannot generally be given at home. As a result, clinics and hospitals have become the chief centers for medical care in most countries.

Medical care is often considered part of the larger field of *health care*. In addition to medical care, health care includes the services provided by dentists, clinical psychologists, and other professionals in various fields of physical and mental health. This article deals chiefly with the kind of health care provided by physicians, including doctors of medicine (M.D.'s) and doctors of osteopathy (D.O.'s), and by people who assist physicians. Information about other kinds of health care can be found in separate WORLD BOOK articles, such as CLINICAL PSYCHOLOGY; DENTISTRY; OPTOMETRY; and PODIATRY.

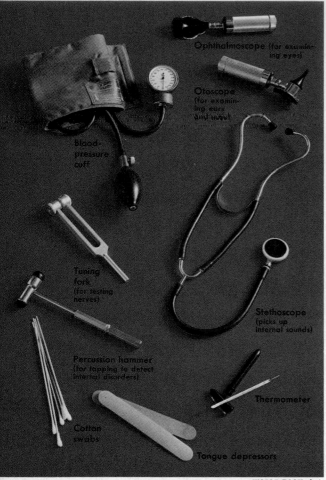

Ophthalmoscope (for examining eyes)

Otoscope (for examining ears and nose)

Blood-pressure cuff

Tuning fork (for testing nerves)

Stethoscope (picks up internal sounds)

Percussion hammer (for tapping to detect internal disorders)

Thermometer

Cotton swabs

Tongue depressors

WORLD BOOK photo

Some Basic Tools of Medicine. A doctor uses the equipment shown above in making physical examinations. Such examinations help the doctor judge the state of a patient's health.

WORLD BOOK photo

Many Electronic Devices help doctors fight illness. These doctors are watching X-ray pictures on closed-circuit television. The pictures, which show the movement of a dye injected into a patient's blood vessels, reveal any blockage in the vessels.

Medical care consists of three main elements: (1) the *diagnosis*, or identification, of disease or injury; (2) the *treatment* of disease or injury; and (3) the *prevention* of disease.

Diagnosis. Serious ailments require diagnosis by an expert, who, in most cases, is a doctor. Doctors use three main types of "clues" in making a diagnosis. The clues are provided by (1) the patient's *case history;* (2) the doctor's *physical examination* of the patient; and (3) the results of various *medical tests.*

Patients provide their own case history by telling the doctor about their general physical condition and past illnesses. Doctors use certain basic tools and techniques to perform a physical examination. For example, they use an instrument called a *stethoscope* to listen to a patient's heart and lungs. By pressing various parts of the body, they can check other internal organs for unusual hardness, softness, or changes in size or shape. Medical laboratories aid diagnosis by making chemical and microscopic tests on body fluids and tissues. A doctor may also order tests that use radioactive trace elements or X rays to detect disease (see RADIOACTIVITY [In Medicine]; X RAYS).

To make a final diagnosis, the doctor fits together all the clues from the patient's case history, physical examination, and medical tests. If the diagnosis is unusually complicated, the doctor may ask the opinion of other medical experts. The article DIAGNOSIS gives more information on how doctors identify disease.

Treatment. People can usually recover from minor illnesses and injuries without special treatment. In these cases, doctors may simply reassure their patients and allow the body to heal itself. But serious ailments generally require special treatment. In these cases, a doctor may prescribe drugs, surgery, or certain other kinds of treatment.

For thousands of years, drugs and surgery have provided two of the chief methods of treating disease. But modern science has helped make these methods much more effective than they used to be. Penicillin and other "wonder drugs" help cure many diseases that were once extremely difficult to treat. With the help of machines, surgeons can repair or replace organs that have been seriously damaged, including the heart and kidneys. Science has also helped develop entirely new methods of treatment. *Radiotherapy*, for example, makes use of X rays and radioactive rays to treat cancer.

Prevention. Doctors help prevent disease in various ways. For example, they give vaccinations to guard against such diseases as polio and measles. They may also order a special diet or drug to strengthen or aid a patient's natural defenses against illness. Doctors can prevent many diseases from becoming serious by diagnosing and treating them in their early stages. For this reason, doctors urge patients to have a physical examination at least once a year. They also urge eating a balanced diet and getting enough rest and exercise. See DISEASE (Preventing Disease).

Local governments help prevent disease by enforcing public health measures. For example, they make sure the community has pure drinking water and a system of garbage and sewage disposal. See PUBLIC HEALTH.

In industrially developed countries, most people can get high-quality medical care when they need it. These countries include Canada, Japan, the United States, and most Western European nations. Certain developing countries of Africa, Asia, and Latin America lack the facilities for high-quality medical care. Some of these countries have only 1 doctor for every 25,000 to 75,000 persons. Some developed countries, on the other hand, have 1 doctor for every 1,000 persons.

This section discusses how and where medical care is provided in the United States and Canada. It also describes efforts to improve the quality of medical care in various parts of the world.

How Medical Care Is Provided

In case of illness or injury, people first of all need someone to diagnose their condition and prescribe or give the necessary treatment. This kind of basic medical care is called *primary care*. It is provided by doctors and certain medical workers to whom people can go directly, without having to be referred by another doctor or medical worker. If a case is complicated or severe, the person who provides primary care refers the patient to a doctor or a hospital or other institution that provides *specialized care*.

The Role of the Doctor. Doctors have detailed knowledge of the human body and are specially trained in the diagnosis, treatment, and prevention of disease. For this reason, they make all major decisions regarding the care of patients.

The United States has about 335,000 doctors whose chief duty is to provide medical care. Canada has about 33,000 such doctors. Other doctors in both countries serve as medical researchers, teachers of medicine, or administrators of medical institutions. Doctors who provide medical care can be divided into two main groups: (1) *general practitioners* and (2) *specialists*.

General Practitioners provide primary care only. But they treat a wide variety of ailments. In many small

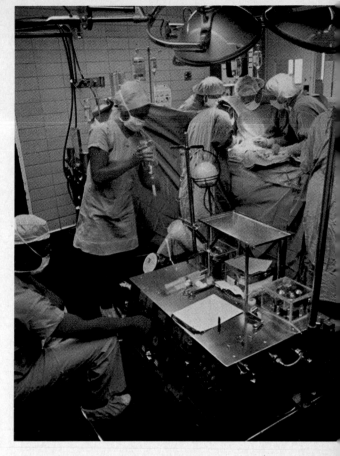

A Surgical Team, headed by a skilled surgeon, includes other doctors plus nurses and medical technicians. The team shown above is performing open-heart surgery. Most doctors depend on such teams of medical experts to help them care for patients.

Nurses with Special Training may relieve doctors of various routine duties, such as examining patients. Doctors who have such aid can give more time to duties that only a physician can perform.

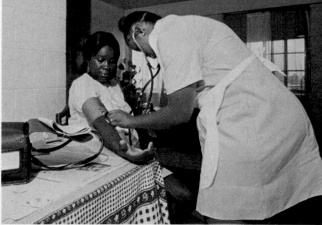

Mile Square Health Center; WORLD BOOK photo by Stephen Feldman

Home Care Workers provide certain medical services in the home, including periodic checkups of an expectant mother, *above*. Hospitals or community clinics employ most of these workers.

301

Merck & Co., Inc.

Skilled Technicians play a key role in modern medicine. Many help develop new drugs to fight disease, *left*. Some operate complex hospital equipment, such as the nuclear equipment used in cancer diagnosis, *center*. Others perform laboratory tests that aid in diagnosing disease, *right*.

towns, the only doctor is a general practitioner, who does everything from delivering babies to setting broken bones. General practitioners provide care for every member of the family, regardless of age, and so they are often called *family doctors*. About 20 per cent of all U.S. doctors and 50 per cent of all Canadian doctors are general practitioners.

Specialists. In the past, almost all doctors were general practitioners. But medical knowledge has increased so rapidly during the 1900's that no doctor can possibly keep up with all the important advances. As a result, more than 80 per cent of all U.S. doctors and about 50 per cent of all Canadian doctors today specialize in a particular field of medicine. *Dermatologists*, for example, specialize in diseases of the skin. *Pediatricians* specialize in children's diseases. Some specialists also provide primary care. They include *internists* who specialize in the diagnosis and nonsurgical treatment of diseases of adults; and pediatricians, who often provide primary care for children.

The growth of the medical specialties has led to a great improvement in the quality of medical care. Seriously ill patients, especially, receive much more effective treatment than ever before. But as more and more doctors become specialists, fewer doctors are available for primary care. To help remedy this situation, a new medical specialty called *family practice* was started in the late 1960's. *Family practitioners* are specially trained to provide primary care for the entire family. Their duties thus resemble those of the general practitioner. A table in the section *A Career as a Doctor* describes the major medical specialties.

The Role of Medical Workers. Doctors could not do their job without the help of many other skilled professionals. *Registered nurses*, for example, work closely with doctors in clinics, hospitals, and doctors' offices. *Pharmacists* fill prescriptions. Various kinds of *therapists* give special treatment as ordered by the doctor. Other skilled workers serve in clinics, medical laboratories, X-ray departments, and operating rooms. The section

Other Careers in Medicine discusses the jobs of various kinds of medical workers.

Where Medical Care Is Provided

In the Doctor's Office. Nearly 70 per cent of all U.S. and Canadian doctors who provide primary or specialized care have a private, or *office-based*, practice. They use their offices to examine patients and give certain kinds of treatment. Patients pay the doctor a fee for the services they receive. Most doctors in office-based practice are associated with a hospital where they send patients who need special care.

The majority of office-based doctors practice alone or in partnership with another doctor. The rest belong to a *group practice*. In group practice, three or more doctors share the same office area, equipment, and personnel. Group practice thus reduces each doctor's expenses. It also enables doctors to offer more services under the same roof. Such services include X-ray and laboratory tests and specialized treatment.

In Hospitals. The United States has about 7,000 hospitals, and Canada has about 1,400. More than 30 million patients are admitted to U.S. hospitals each year. Canadian hospitals admit over $3\frac{1}{2}$ million patients yearly. The hospitals range from small private institutions to huge community hospitals.

Hospitals offer services not available anywhere else. In most hospitals, patients receive round-the-clock care from a full-time staff of doctors, nurses, and other skilled workers. The largest, most modern hospitals have a variety of advanced equipment. Such equipment includes *heart-lung machines*, which may take over the work of a patient's heart and lungs during a complicated heart operation. The most modern hospitals also have *intensive care units*, which use television and other electronic devices to keep constant watch over seriously ill patients. The units are also equipped with oxygen masks and other lifesaving equipment. For more information about the various kinds of hospitals and the services they provide, see HOSPITAL.

In Clinics. Most clinics provide primary care for *outpatients*—that is, for patients who are not hospitalized. Some clinics are part of a hospital. The doctors and medical workers who staff such clinics are hospital employees or volunteers. Other clinics are run by doctors in group practice or by community organizations. Group practice clinics and some community clinics operate for a profit. But other community clinics are nonprofit organizations that offer free or inexpensive care for poor people. The doctors and medical workers who staff these clinics charge the patients a small fee or none at all. The U.S. government provides financial aid for some community clinics, which are called *neighborhood health centers.*

A number of clinics have both specialists and general practitioners on their staff. Some group practice clinics have specialists only. Many communities support certain types of specialized clinics, such as those that diagnose and treat venereal disease.

In Nursing Homes. Many nursing homes do not provide medical care on a regular basis. But many others have at least one professional nurse on the staff. Such homes are called *nursing care homes.* They accept patients who need round-the-clock care but do not need to be hospitalized. Doctors visit the patients as needed. Most nursing homes are privately owned.

In the Home. Some people need continuing medical attention but not the round-the-clock care given in hospitals and nursing care homes. Various public and private agencies and some hospitals sponsor home care programs for these people. The programs offer certain types of therapy and nursing care.

Few doctors make house calls today. But in some large cities, emergency medical services employ doctors who make house calls on request. Some specially trained medical workers also make house calls.

Improving the Quality of Medical Care

The Role of Medical Organizations. A number of national and international organizations work to improve the quality of medical care. These organizations encourage medical education and research, help standardize medical practice, and enforce codes of professional conduct. The American Medical Association (AMA) is the largest medical organization in the United States. It is composed of doctors of medicine. The American Osteopathic Association (AOA) is the chief medical organization for doctors of osteopathy. The National Medical Association has a membership made up largely of black physicians. The Canadian Medical Association is Canada's main medical organization.

The World Health Organization (WHO) is the chief international medical organization. About 130 countries belong to WHO. The organization promotes public health programs and the exchange of medical knowledge. It is especially dedicated to improving the quality of medical care in developing countries.

Most developing countries have a shortage of doctors and hospitals. Many people rely on such practices as the use of plant medicines or even treatment by witch doctors. Infectious diseases, such as malaria and tuberculosis, take a heavy toll. To help remedy this situation, medically advanced members of WHO help train medical personnel for the less advanced members. They also provide the less advanced members with badly needed medical supplies and equipment.

The Role of Medical Research. Progress in medicine depends largely on the work of medical research. Medi-

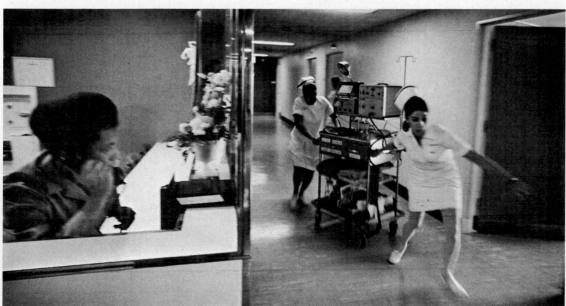

Luigi Pellettieri

A Modern Hospital provides many services that cannot be supplied anywhere else. These nurses are rushing emergency lifesaving equipment to the room of a heart-attack victim.

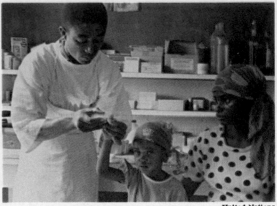

Brunei N. Borneo, DPI   United Nations

Providing Medical Care in Developing Countries requires overcoming great distances and a shortage of doctors. The medical team at the left reaches remote areas in Borneo by helicopter. A specially trained medical worker, *right,* tests for malaria in Cameroon.

cal researchers strive to increase our knowledge of (1) how the healthy body works; (2) how it is disturbed by disease; and (3) how disease can be prevented or cured. Some medical researchers are physicians. Others are scientists. Much medical research is done in laboratories. But physicians also carry on research by observing their patients.

Most medical discoveries provide only small clues to the solution of a difficult medical problem. As a result, the problem is solved only after years of work by many people. But researchers sometimes make dramatic discoveries. An outstanding example is the development of an effective polio vaccine by the American research scientist Jonas E. Salk in the early 1950's. For more information on medical research, see the articles RESEARCH (Biological Sciences and Medicine) and SCIENCE (In Medicine). See also the section of this article on *Current Problems in U.S. Medicine.*

MEDICINE/*Careers in Medicine*

A Career as a Doctor

Young men and women who choose a career as a doctor face a long, difficult, and expensive training period. This section discusses the training and licensing of doctors in the United States and Canada.

Premedical Education begins in college. Most medical schools accept only four-year college graduates. But some schools admit students after two or three years of college. The majority of premedical students take a liberal arts program, including courses in chemistry, higher mathematics, physics, and zoology.

Medical schools are crowded and can admit only a certain number of new students each year. Most schools accept only applicants whose past school records, test scores, and personal interviews indicate high potential.

Medical Education. Most medical schools are part of a university. In the United States, the tuition at private universities averages about $3,000 a year. At state universities, it averages about $1,000 for state residents and $2,000 for nonresidents. The annual tuition at all Canadian medical schools averages about $740.

Traditionally, a medical school offers a four-year course of study. The first two years consist largely of *preclinical training.* Students study such basic medical sciences as anatomy, biochemistry, microbiology, pathology, pharmacology, and physiology. The last two years consist largely of *clinical training*—that is, training by observing and caring for patients. Students ordinarily receive clinical training in a hospital associated with their medical school.

Since the early 1960's, many medical schools have made changes in the traditional course of study. For example, some schools are experimenting with a three-year program, which eliminates a year of preclinical or clinical training.

Students must pass all their courses to graduate from medical school. Upon graduation, a student receives either a Doctor of Medicine (M.D.) degree or a Doctor of Osteopathy (D.O.) degree, depending on whether the student graduated from a school approved by the AMA or by the AOA.

Internship and Residency. After graduating from medical school, almost every doctor serves at least a year as a hospital *intern.* Interns examine patients and prescribe treatment. But they work under the supervision of experienced doctors.

Most doctors specialize in a particular field of medicine after their internship. To prepare for a specialty, they must train for a year or more as a hospital *resident.* During residency, doctors work with the kinds of patients they will treat as specialists. A surgical resident, for example, works with surgical patients. Like interns, residents learn through experience. But they have more responsibility than interns have. Hospitals in the United States and Canada pay interns and residents an annual salary, which varies from hospital to hospital.

To become *certified* specialists, doctors must complete residency training and pass an examination given by their *specialty board*. A separate board governs each specialty field and certifies specialists.

Licensing. In the United States, every state requires doctors to obtain a license before they may practice medicine in the state. In each state, a state medical board sets licensing requirements and issues licenses. To obtain a license, a person must have an M.D. or a D.O. degree from an approved school and must pass a written examination approved by the state medical board. Most states also require completion of a one-year internship. To practice in another state, a doctor must obtain a license from that state. Every state grants licenses by *endorsement*, or *reciprocity*, to doctors from states whose licensing requirements and examination are the same as its own. In such cases, doctors do not have to take the licensing examination again. Each Canadian province has its own licensing requirements, which are similar to those in the United States.

Rewards and Responsibilities. Doctors rank among the highest paid professionals. The average income of U.S. and Canadian doctors is more than $40,000 a year. In addition to the financial rewards of practicing medicine, doctors also have the satisfaction of helping patients regain their health and lead a normal life.

Every state and province requires doctors to meet cer-

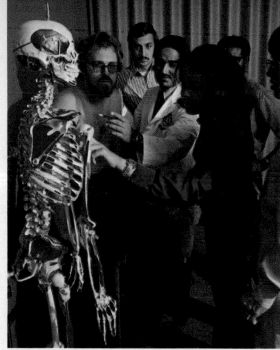

Rush Medical College; WORLD BOOK photo by Stephen Feldman

First-Year Medical Students study anatomy, above, and other basic medical sciences. Most medical schools require four years of study, but some schools offer a three-year program.

tain standards of professional conduct. Doctors who do not meet these standards are guilty of *malpractice* and are liable to lawsuits. Doctors also have their own *code*

MAJOR MEDICAL SPECIALTY FIELDS

Allergy and Immunology deals with disorders of the immune system, including allergies, autoimmune diseases, and immune deficiencies.

Anesthesiology is the study of anesthesia and anesthetics. *Anesthesiologists* give anesthetics during operations or supervise their administration.

Colon and Rectal Surgery is the surgical treatment of disorders of the lower digestive tract.

Dermatology is the diagnosis and treatment of skin diseases.

Emergency Medicine deals with the immediate recognition and treatment of acute injuries, illnesses, and emotional crises.

Family Practice is the supervision of the total health care of patients and their families, regardless of age.

General Surgery treats diseases by operations, except for those diseases treated by other surgical specialties.

Internal Medicine is the diagnosis and nonsurgical treatment of diseases of adults. Specialists are called *internists*. Some internists limit their practice to allergies; diseases of the heart and blood vessels; disorders of the digestive tract; or diseases of the lungs.

Neurological Surgery, or *neurosurgery,* is the surgical treatment of disorders of the nervous system.

Nuclear Medicine is the use of radioactive isotopes to diagnose and treat disease.

Obstetrics and Gynecology provide the special medical care required by women. *Obstetricians* provide care for women during pregnancy and during and immediately after childbirth. *Gynecologists* diagnose and treat diseases of the female reproductive organs.

Ophthalmology is the diagnosis, treatment, and prevention of eye diseases.

Orthopedic Surgery, or *orthopedics,* is the surgical treatment of bone and joint diseases and bone fractures.

Otolaryngology is the diagnosis and treatment of ear, nose, and throat diseases.

Pathology is the study of changes in the body that cause disease or are caused by disease.

Pediatrics is the diagnosis, treatment, and prevention of children's diseases.

Physical Medicine and Rehabilitation, or *physiatrics,* treats diseases and handicaps by such physical means as light, heat, and water therapy.

Plastic Surgery restores or rebuilds certain parts of the body that are imperfect or have been damaged.

Preventive Medicine deals with the relation between environment and health. Specialists may limit their practice to such fields as *public health* or *aviation medicine.*

Psychiatry and Neurology deal with the mind and nervous system. *Psychiatrists* treat mental disorders. *Neurologists* provide nonsurgical treatment of diseases of the nervous system.

Radiology is the use of X rays and radium to diagnose and treat disease.

Thoracic Surgery is the surgical treatment of diseases of the heart, the lungs, or the large blood vessels in the chest.

Urology deals with diseases of organs that pass urine and of the male reproductive organs.

of ethics, which concerns such matters as charging reasonable fees and respecting a patient's confidence. Doctors must also keep up with medical progress by reading medical journals and books, attending medical conferences, and consulting with other doctors.

Other Careers in Medicine

Careers in medicine, outside those requiring an M.D. or a D.O. degree, range from working in a laboratory to serving as a nurse or pharmacist. The articles NURSING and PHARMACY tell about a career as a nurse or pharmacist. This section deals mainly with other medical careers. Further information on these careers can be obtained from the American Medical Association, Department of Allied Medical Professions and Services, 535 N. Dearborn Street, Chicago, Ill. 60610.

Working with Patients. Some medical workers help care for patients by taking the place of physicians under certain conditions. Such workers are sometimes called *paramedical workers* or *paramedics*. Paramedics free doctors from routine medical duties and so enable them to spend more time on cases that only a doctor can handle. Two of the chief types of paramedics are *nurse practitioners* and *physician's assistants*.

Nurse Practitioners, or *nurse associates*, are registered nurses who have had additional medical training. This training enables them to take a case history, give a physical examination, make a diagnosis, and prescribe treatment. The nurse practitioner calls a doctor if a patient needs more than routine care. Some nurse practitioners are trained to assist specialists.

Physician's Assistants also provide certain types of routine medical care. But unlike a nurse practitioner, a physician's assistant does not have to be a registered nurse. Many physician's assistants receive their training in special programs conducted by university medical schools. Some physician's assistants work in doctors' offices. Others help provide medical care in hospitals. Many physician's assistants formerly served in a medical branch of the armed forces.

Many other kinds of medical workers also work with patients. *Medical assistants*, for example, take case histories and do clerical and laboratory work in the doctor's office. *Occupational therapists* teach useful activities to handicapped persons to help them overcome or lessen their handicap (see OCCUPATIONAL THERAPY). *Physical therapists* use such physical means as exercise, heat, or ultraviolet light to treat certain ailments (see PHYSICAL THERAPY).

Providing Technical Support. A number of important careers in medicine require special technical skills. Laboratory workers, for example, perform chemical and microscopic tests that may be needed for accurate diagnosis. *Medical technologists* perform the most difficult and highly specialized laboratory tests. They also supervise the work of *laboratory technicians* and *assistants*, who perform more routine laboratory tasks. *Radiologic technologists* prepare patients for X rays and operate the X-ray equipment under a doctor's supervision. *Nuclear medicine technologists* and *technicians* work with the nuclear equipment and materials used in diagnosis and treatment.

MEDICINE/*Financing Medical Care*

In the United States

Medical costs have risen sharply in the United States since the early 1960's. The greatest increase has been in the cost of hospital care. Most hospitals have granted large pay raises to their employees. Many hospitals have also installed expensive new equipment. To meet these expenses, hospitals raised their service charges by more than 150 per cent between 1960 and 1970.

There are three main methods of financing medical care in the United States. They are (1) private insurance; (2) government insurance and other government aid; and (3) direct personal payments.

Private Insurance. About 90 per cent of all Americans have some kind of private health insurance. An insured person pays a specified sum for the desired benefits. Almost all the benefits are for hospital and surgical care and doctors' fees. Most policies do not cover the cost of drugs, dental care, or most outpatient medical care. As a result, private insurance pays only about 28 per cent of all U.S. health care costs.

Two main types of organizations offer private health insurance: (1) insurance companies and (2) medical *prepayment* organizations. Insurance companies generally pay benefits to the insured person rather than to the provider of medical service. Prepayment organiza-

tions—and some insurance policies—pay benefits directly to the provider of medical care. The most common type of prepayment plan is like the one offered by the Blue Cross and Blue Shield organizations. Dues-paying members of these organizations may choose their doctor and hospital, but the services a member may receive are limited. For more information about the various kinds of private health insurance, see INSURANCE (Health Insurance).

Government Aid. The federal, state, and local governments pay about 40 per cent of all health care costs in the United States. The federal government pays by far the largest share. It supports Veterans Administration and Public Health Service hospitals. The National Institutes of Health, an agency of the U.S. Public Health Service, finances much of the medical research in the United States (see NATIONAL INSTITUTES OF HEALTH). Federal funds also help pay for hospital construction and help support medical schools.

The federal *Medicare* program is the largest public health care program in the United States. Medicare helps elderly people pay for extended hospital and nursing home care. Social security contributions support the program. People covered by Medicare may obtain additional government medical insurance at low cost to help pay doctors' fees and other medical expenses. The federal government cooperates with state governments to finance *Medicaid*, a health care plan for people of any age who cannot afford private health insurance. Each state decides what health services to include under its Medicaid plan. See MEDICARE; MEDICAID.

Direct Personal Payments. The majority of insurance policies do not cover the cost of drugs, dental work, eyeglasses, medical appliances, or most outpatient care. People ordinarily must pay these expenses themselves. About 30 per cent of all U.S. health care costs are paid in this way. Charitable organizations pay about 2 per cent of U.S. health care costs.

In Canada

Each Canadian province has its own program of public health insurance. In some provinces, the insurance is *compulsory* (required). In the rest, it is voluntary. But almost all Canadians are covered under the provincial programs. The programs pay all major health care expenses. Private insurance companies offer additional coverage for those who desire it.

The Canadian government shares the costs of public health insurance with the provinces. It pays about half the total costs, using general tax funds. The provinces finance their share of the costs in various ways. In most provinces, families or individuals covered by the plan must contribute a certain amount through regular payments or payroll deductions. The provinces contribute varying amounts from general tax funds, depending on how much is collected from individuals and families.

In Other Countries

In some countries, including China and Russia, medicine is completely *socialized*—that is, all medical facilities are publicly owned and all medical personnel are paid from public funds. Every citizen receives medical care free or at very low cost. In some other countries, medicine is largely socialized. Great Britain is the best-known example. In Britain, the central government owns most medical facilities, pays most medical personnel, and provides most medical care free or at low cost.

In many other countries, including most Western European countries, medicine is partly socialized. The central government does not own most medical facilities, nor does it pay most doctors, who are self-employed. But these countries have a national health insurance plan that provides free medical care or refunds almost all the money a patient spends for medical care. The plan is financed through the social security system in almost all the countries and is compulsory for workers covered by social security. Doctors who take part in the national plan must charge a set fee. But patients generally may choose their doctor and hospital.

EXPENDITURES FOR HEALTH CARE IN THE UNITED STATES — The graphs at the left show how health care costs have risen since 1940. The graphs at the right show how health care money is spent and where it comes from.

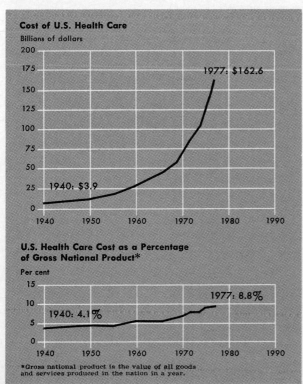

Cost of U.S. Health Care
Billions of dollars

1977: $162.6
1940: $3.9

U.S. Health Care Cost as a Percentage of Gross National Product*
Per cent

1977: 8.8%
1940: 4.1%

*Gross national product is the value of all goods and services produced in the nation in a year.

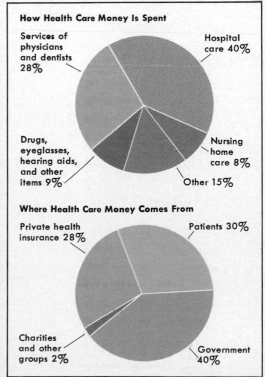

How Health Care Money Is Spent

Services of physicians and dentists 28%
Hospital care 40%
Drugs, eyeglasses, hearing aids, and other items 9%
Nursing home care 8%
Other 15%

Where Health Care Money Comes From

Private health insurance 28%
Patients 30%
Charities and other groups 2%
Government 40%

WORLD BOOK graphs

In prehistoric times, people believed that angry gods or evil spirits caused disease. To cure the sick, the gods had to be pacified or the evil spirits driven from the body. In time, this task became the job of the first "physicians"—the tribal priests who tried to pacify the gods or drive out the evil spirits.

The first-known surgical treatment was an operation called *trephining*. Trephining involved use of a stone instrument to cut a hole in a patient's skull. Scientists have found fossils of such skulls that date as far back as 10,000 years. Early man may have performed the operations to release spirits believed responsible for headaches, mental illness, or epilepsy. But trephining could have brought relief in some cases. Until the early 1900's, surgeons practiced trephining to relieve certain types of pressure on the brain.

Prehistoric man probably also discovered that many plants can be used as drugs. For example, the use of willow bark to relieve pain probably dates back thousands of years. Today, scientists know that willow bark contains *salicin*, a substance related to the *salicylates* used in making aspirin.

Ancient Times

The Middle East. By about 3000 B.C., the Egyptians had developed one of the world's first great civilizations and invented one of the first systems of writing. Shortly after 3000 B.C., they also began making important medical progress. Much of our knowledge of this progress comes from ancient Egyptian manuscripts.

The world's first physician known by name was the Egyptian Imhotep, who lived about 2700 B.C. The

Egyptians later worshiped him as the god of healing (see IMHOTEP). About 2500 B.C., Egyptian physicians began to specialize. Some physicians treated only diseases of the eyes or teeth. Others specialized in internal diseases. Egyptian surgeons produced a textbook that told how to treat dislocated or fractured bones and external abscesses, tumors, ulcers, and wounds.

Other ancient Middle Eastern civilizations also contributed to medical progress. The ancient Hebrews, for example, made progress in preventive medicine from about 1200 to 600 B.C. The Hebrews required strict isolation of persons with gonorrhea, leprosy, and other contagious diseases. They also prohibited the contamination of public wells and the eating of pork and other foods that might carry disease.

China and India. The ancient Chinese developed medical practices that have been handed down almost unchanged to the present day. This traditional medicine is based on the belief that two life forces, *Yin* and *Yang*, flow through the human body. Disease results when the two forces become out of balance. To restore the balance, the Chinese began the practice of *acupuncture*—inserting needles into parts of the body thought to control the flow of Yin and Yang. Chinese doctors still practice acupuncture. The technique has gained some popularity in Western countries, where it is occasionally used to treat certain disorders. But some experts question its value. See ACUPUNCTURE.

After about 800 B.C., Indian physicians became famous for their surgical skills. Indian surgeons successfully performed many kinds of operations, including amputations and plastic surgery.

HIGHLIGHTS IN MEDICAL HISTORY

┌ Prehistoric man practiced *trephining*— the first-known surgical treatment.

┌ Hippocrates showed that diseases have only natural, not supernatural, causes.

┌ The first university medical schools developed in Europe.

● c. 8000 B.C.   ● c. 2500 B.C.   ● 400's B.C.   ● A.D. 100's   ● 1100's

└ Egyptian physicians developed the first systematic methods of treating diseases.

└ Galen formulated the first medical theories based on scientific experimentations.

International College of Surgeons Museum, Chicago (WORLD BOOK photo)

Trephining involved cutting a hole in the skull, perhaps to release evil spirits. The ancient trephined skull and cutting tools shown above were found in Peru.

Plaster cast of a carving (about 350 B.C.) by an unknown Greek artist; Wellcome Historical Medical Museum, London

Ancient Greek Physicians, such as the one shown above examining a young patient, raised medicine to the level of a science. Hippocrates led this development.

Detail of a manuscript (about 1300); International College of Surgeons Museum, Chicago (WORLD BOOK photo)

During the Middle Ages, doctors had little scientific knowledge. The doctor above is using all his strength to bandage a fractured jaw as tightly as possible.

Greece and Rome. The civilization of ancient Greece was at its peak during the 400's B.C. Throughout this period, sick people flocked to temples dedicated to the Greek god of healing, Asclepius, seeking magical cures. But at the same time, the great Greek physician Hippocrates began showing that disease has only natural causes. He thus became the first physician known to consider medicine a science and art separate from the practice of religion. The *Hippocratic Oath*, one of the world's greatest expressions of medical ethics, reflects Hippocrates' high ideals. But the oath was probably composed from a number of sources rather than by Hippocrates himself. For the text of the oath, see the article HIPPOCRATES.

After 300 B.C., the city of Rome gradually conquered much of the civilized world, including Egypt and Greece. The Romans got most of their medical knowledge from Egypt and Greece. Their own medical achievements were largely in public health. The Romans built aqueducts that carried 300 million gallons (1.1 billion liters) of fresh water to Rome each day. They also built an excellent sewerage system in Rome.

The Greek physician Galen, who practiced medicine in Rome during the A.D. 100's, made the most important contributions to medicine in Roman times. Galen performed experiments on animals and used his findings to develop the first medical theories based on scientific experiments. For this reason, he is considered the founder of *experimental medicine*. But because his knowledge of anatomy was based largely on animal experiments, Galen developed many false notions about how the human body works. Galen wrote numerous

Detail of *The Plague* (mid-1600's); oil painting on canvas by Micco Spadaro; Museo della Certosa di S. Martino, Naples

Outbreaks of Bubonic Plague killed millions of people in Europe from the 1300's through the 1600's. The scene above shows plague victims being collected for burial in Naples in 1656.

Vesalius published the first scientific study of human anatomy.

Harvey started modern physiology with his book on blood circulation.

Jenner gave the first officially recognized vaccination, against smallpox.

1543   Mid-1500's   1628   1676   1796

Paré, the "father of modern surgery," introduced advanced surgical techniques.

Leeuwenhoek discovered bacteria, which helped lead to the germ theory of disease.

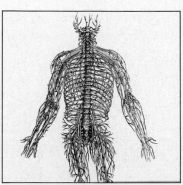

International College of Surgeons Museum, Chicago (WORLD BOOK photo)

The Scientific Study of Anatomy began with Andreas Vesalius' book *On the Fabric of the Human Body*. This illustration from the book shows the spinal nerves.

Wood engraving (1594) by an unknown artist; Bettmann Archive

Surgical Advances by Ambroise Paré included sewing through pieces of cloth glued to the patient's skin instead of stitching through the skin itself.

Detail of marble sculpture by Giulio Monteverde (1873); The Mansell Collection

Edward Jenner Vaccinates a Child. Jenner's discovery of a smallpox vaccine led to the development of vaccines to prevent many other diseases as well.

books describing his theories. These theories, many of which were wrong, guided doctors for hundreds of years.

The Middle Ages

During the Middle Ages, which lasted from about A.D. 400 to the 1500's, the Muslim Empire of Southwest and Central Asia contributed greatly to medicine. Rhazes, a Persian-born physician of the late 800's and early 900's, wrote the first accurate descriptions of measles and smallpox. Avicenna, an Arab physician of the late 900's and early 1000's, produced a vast medical encyclopedia called *Canon of Medicine*. It summed up the medical knowledge of the time and accurately described meningitis, tetanus, and many other diseases. The work became popular in Europe, where it influenced medical education for more than 600 years.

A series of epidemics swept across Europe during the Middle Ages. Outbreaks of leprosy began in the 500's and reached their peak in the 1200's. In the mid-1300's, a terrible outbreak of bubonic plague called the *Black Death* killed about a fourth of Europe's population. Throughout the medieval period, smallpox and other diseases attacked hundreds of thousands of people.

The chief medical advances in Europe during the Middle Ages were the founding of many hospitals and the first university medical schools. Christian religious groups established hundreds of charitable hospitals for victims of leprosy. In the 900's, a medical school was started in Salerno, Italy. It became the chief center of medical learning in Europe during the 1000's and 1100's. Other important medical schools developed in Europe after 1000. During the 1100's and 1200's, many of these schools became part of newly founded universi-

ties, such as the University of Bologna in Italy and the University of Paris in France.

The Renaissance

A new scientific spirit developed during the Renaissance, the great cultural movement that swept across Western Europe from about 1300 to the 1600's. Before this time, most societies had strictly limited the practice of *dissecting* (cutting up) human corpses for scientific study. But laws against dissection were relaxed during the Renaissance. As a result, the first truly scientific studies of the human body began.

During the late 1400's and early 1500's, the Italian artist Leonardo da Vinci performed many dissections to learn more about human anatomy. He recorded his findings in a series of more than 750 drawings. Andreas Vesalius, a physician and professor of medicine at the University of Padua in Italy, also performed many dissections. Vesalius used his findings to write the first scientific textbook on human anatomy, a work called *On the Fabric of the Human Body* (1543). This book gradually replaced the texts of Galen and Avicenna.

Other physicians also made outstanding contributions to medical science in the 1500's. A French army doctor named Ambroise Paré improved surgical techniques to such an extent that he is considered the father of modern surgery. For example, he opposed the common practice of *cauterizing* (burning) wounds with boiling oil to prevent infection. Instead, he developed the much more effective method of applying a mild ointment and then allowing the wound to heal naturally. Philippus Paracelsus, a Swiss physician, stressed the importance of chemistry in the preparation of drugs. He

Long and Morton introduced the use of ether, the first practical anesthetic.		Virchow pioneered in *pathology*, the scientific study of disease.		Lister introduced antiseptic methods to surgery.
1842-1846	Mid-1800's	1850's	Mid- to late 1800's	1865
	Nightingale founded the modern nursing profession.		Pasteur and Koch proved that certain bacteria cause certain diseases.	

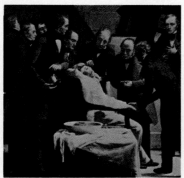

Detail of a mural (1893) by Robert Hinckley; Boston Medical Library

Ether Anesthesia was first demonstrated publicly at Massachusetts General Hospital in 1846. William Morton, *left*, administered the drug.

Staffordshire pottery figures (mid-1800's); Wellcome Historical Medical Museum, London

Florence Nightingale introduced modern nursing methods during the Crimean War (1853-1856). These pottery figures show her with a wounded British soldier.

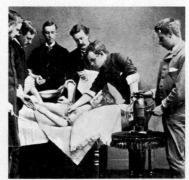

Detail of photograph taken about 1870 in Edinburgh, Scotland; Bettmann Archive

Antiseptic Surgery involved spraying surgical wounds with carbolic acid to prevent infection. Joseph Lister invented this procedure in 1865.

pointed out that in many drugs consisting of several ingredients, one ingredient made another useless.

Modern Times

The Beginnings of Modern Research. The English physician William Harvey performed many experiments in the early 1600's to learn how blood circulates through the body. Before Harvey, scientists had studied only parts of the process and invented theories to fill in the gaps. Harvey studied the entire problem. He performed dissections on both human beings and animals and made careful studies of the human pulsebeat and heartbeat. Harvey concluded that the heart pumps blood through the arteries to all parts of the body and that the blood returns to the heart through the veins.

Harvey described his findings in *An Anatomical Treatise on the Motion of the Heart and Blood in Animals* (1628). His discovery of how blood circulates marked a turning point in medical history. After Harvey, scientists realized that knowledge of how the body works depends on knowledge of the body's structure.

In the mid-1600's, a Dutch amateur scientist named Anton van Leeuwenhoek began using a microscope to study organisms invisible to the naked eye. Today, such organisms are called *microorganisms, microbes,* or *germs.* In 1676, Leeuwenhoek discovered certain microbes that later became known as *bacteria.* Leeuwenhoek did not understand the role of microbes in nature. But his research paved the way for the eventual discovery that certain microbes cause disease.

The Development of Immunology. Smallpox was one of the most feared and highly contagious diseases of the 1700's. It killed many people every year and scarred others for life. Doctors had known for hundreds of years that a person who recovered from smallpox developed lifelong *immunity* (resistance) to it. To provide this immunity, doctors sometimes inoculated people with matter from a smallpox sore, hoping they would develop only a mild case of the disease. But such inoculations were dangerous. Some people developed a severe case of smallpox instead of a mild one. Other inoculated persons spread the disease.

In 1796, an English physician named Edward Jenner discovered a safe method of making people immune to smallpox. He inoculated a young boy with matter from a cowpox sore. The boy developed cowpox, a relatively harmless disease related to smallpox. But when Jenner later injected the boy with matter from a smallpox sore, the boy did not come down with the disease. His bout with cowpox had helped his body build up an immunity to smallpox. Jenner's experiment was the first officially recorded vaccination. The success of the experiment led to the science of immunology—the prevention of disease by building up resistance to it.

Discovery of the First Anesthetic. For thousands of years, physicians tried to dull pain during surgery by administering alcoholic drinks, opium, and various other drugs. But no drug had proved really effective in reducing the pain and shock of operations. Then in the 1840's, two Americans—Crawford Long and William T. G. Morton—discovered that ether gas could safely be used to put patients to sleep during surgery. Long, a physician, and Morton, a dentist, made the discovery independently. With the discovery of an effective anesthetic, doctors could perform operations never possible before.

Roentgen discovered X rays, used in diagnosing diseases and treating cancer.

Freud developed the psychoanalytic method of treating mental illness.

| 1895 | 1898 | c. 1900 | Early 1900's |

The Curies discovered radium, used in treating cancer.

Eijkman and Hopkins demonstrated the existence of vitamins.

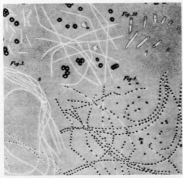

Detail of sketch by Robert Koch (1876); Aldus Archives

Anthrax Germs were the first microorganisms identified as a cause of illness. Robert Koch made the discovery and sketched the anthrax germs, *above.*

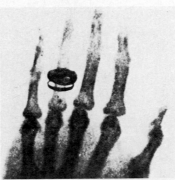

Wellcome Historical Medical Museum, London

An Early X-Ray Photograph by Wilhelm Roentgen shows his wife's left hand and wedding ring. Roentgen took the photograph the year he discovered X rays.

Detail of an illustration (1904) from *Vanity Fair* magazine; Wellcome Historical Medical Museum, London

Marie and Pierre Curie, the discoverers of radium, are shown at work in their laboratory. Radium has saved the life of countless cancer victims.

The Scientific Study of Disease, called *pathology*, developed during the 1800's. Rudolf Virchow, a German physician and scientist, led the development. Virchow believed that the only way to understand the nature of disease was by close examination of the affected body cells. He did important research in such diseases as leukemia, trichinosis, and tuberculosis. The development of improved microscopes in the early 1800's helped make his studies possible.

Scientists of the 1800's made dramatic progress in learning the causes of infectious disease. As early as the 1500's, scholars had suggested that tiny, invisible "seeds" caused some diseases. The bacteria discovered by Leeuwenhoek in the 1600's fitted this description. In the late 1800's, the research of Louis Pasteur and Robert Koch firmly established the *microbial*, or *germ*, *theory* of disease.

Pasteur, a brilliant French chemist, proved that microbes are living organisms and that certain kinds of microbes cause disease. He also proved that killing specific microbes stops the spread of specific diseases. Koch, a German physician, invented a method for determining which bacteria cause particular diseases. This method enabled him to identify the germ that causes *anthrax*, a severe disease of people and animals. The anthrax germ thus became the first germ definitely linked to a particular disease. Other research scientists followed the lead of these two pioneers. By the end of the 1800's, researchers had discovered the kinds of bacteria and other microbes responsible for such infectious diseases as bubonic plague, cholera, diphtheria, dysentery, gonorrhea, leprosy, malaria, pneumonia, tetanus, and tuberculosis.

Introduction of Antiseptic Surgery. Hospitals paid little attention to cleanliness before the mid-1800's. Operating rooms were often dirty, and surgeons operated in street clothes. Up to half of all surgical patients died of infections. In 1847, a Hungarian doctor, Ignaz Semmelweis, stressed the need for cleanliness in childbirth. But Semmelweis knew little about the germ theory of disease.

Pasteur's early work on bacteria convinced an English surgeon named Joseph Lister that germs caused many of the deaths of surgical patients. In 1865, Lister began using carbolic acid, a powerful disinfectant, to sterilize surgical wounds. But this method was later replaced by a more efficient technique known as *aseptic surgery*. This technique involved keeping germs away from surgical wounds in the first place instead of trying to kill germs already there. Surgeons began to wash thoroughly before an operation and to wear surgical gowns, gloves, and masks.

The Beginnings of Organized Medicine. During the 1800's and early 1900's, groups were founded in the United States and Canada to organize and reform the medical profession in the two countries. In 1847, U.S. doctors founded the AMA to help raise the nation's medical standards. Partly as a result of the AMA's efforts, the first state licensing boards were set up in the late 1800's. The Canadian Medical Association was founded in 1867 for much the same purpose. The National Medical Association was started in 1895 by black doctors who felt discriminated against by the AMA. Osteopathic physicians founded the AOA in 1897.

In 1910, the Carnegie Foundation for the Advancement of Teaching issued a report called *Medical Educa-*

Fleming discovered penicillin, the first antibiotic drug.

The development of new techniques and devices revolutionized heart surgery.

Scientists intensified investigation of viruses as a possible cause of cancer.

1928 — Early 1950's — 1954 — Early 1970's

Salk developed the first successful polio vaccine.

American surgeons transplanted a kidney—the first successful organ transplant.

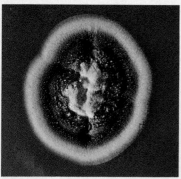

Abbott Laboratories

WORLD BOOK photo by Stephen Feldman, courtesy Rush-Presbyterian-St. Luke's Medical Center, Chicago

Medtronic, Inc.

Penicillium Mold, discovered by Alexander Fleming, is grown in laboratories to make the drug penicillin. This photograph shows the mold after four days' growth.

Cryosurgery, the use of extreme cold in surgery, was developed in the 1960's. The cold is applied by instruments like the one above, shown "gluing" a detached retina.

A Pacemaker implanted near the heart makes the organ beat steadily. An atomic pacemaker of the early 1970's, above, outlasts earlier battery-operated models.

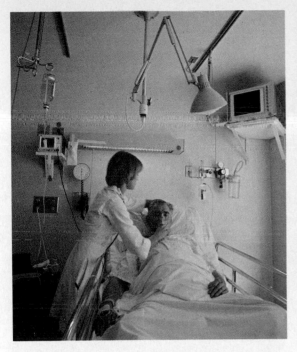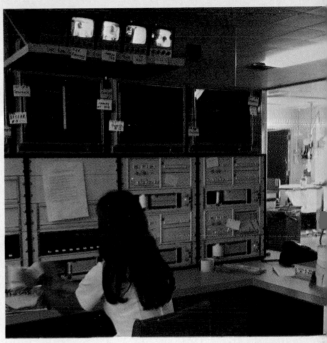

Engineering Advances led to the development of intensive care units in hospitals. Every room in such a unit, *left,* has lifesaving devices. Electronic devices record the patient's breathing and other body functions. This information appears on screens in the unit's monitoring station, *right.*

tion in the United States and Canada. The U.S. educator Abraham Flexner prepared the report for the foundation. Flexner's report stated that only 1 of the 155 medical schools in the United States and Canada at that time provided an acceptable medical education. The only school providing an acceptable education was the Johns Hopkins Medical School, founded in Baltimore in 1893. Flexner's report and the example of the Johns Hopkins school helped bring far-reaching reforms in U.S. and Canadian medical education.

The Medical Revolution. Advances in many fields of science and engineering have created a medical revolution in the 1900's. For example, the discovery of X rays by the German physicist Wilhelm Roentgen in 1895 enabled doctors to "see" inside the human body to diagnose illnesses and injuries. The discovery of radium by the French physicists Pierre and Marie Curie in 1898 provided a powerful weapon against cancer.

In the early 1900's, Christiaan Eijkman of The Netherlands, Frederick G. Hopkins of England, and a number of other physician-scientists showed the importance of vitamins. Their achievements helped conquer such nutritional diseases as beriberi, rickets, and scurvy. About 1910, the German physician and chemist Paul Ehrlich introduced a new method of attacking infectious disease. Ehrlich's method, called *chemotherapy,* involved searching for chemicals to destroy the microbes responsible for particular diseases.

Ehrlich's work greatly advanced drug research. In 1935, a German doctor, Gerhard Domagk, discovered the ability of sulfa drugs to cure infections in animals.

His discovery led to the development of sulfa drugs to treat diseases in human beings. In 1928, the English bacteriologist Sir Alexander Fleming discovered the germ-killing power of a mold called *Penicillium.* In the early 1940's, a group of English scientists headed by Howard Florey isolated penicillin, a product of this mold. Penicillin thus became the first antibiotic.

Since Domagk's and Fleming's discoveries, scientists have developed many other sulfa drugs and antibiotics. These drugs have helped control most infectious diseases. Other drugs have been developed to fight such disorders as diabetes and high blood pressure.

The development of new vaccines has helped control the spread of such infectious diseases as polio and measles. During the 1960's and 1970's, the World Health Organization conducted a vaccination program aimed at eliminating smallpox from the world.

Since 1901, many persons have received Nobel prizes in physiology or medicine. For a list of the winners and their achievements, see the article NOBEL PRIZES.

Much progress in modern medicine has resulted from engineering advances. Engineers have developed a variety of instruments and machines to aid doctors in the diagnosis, treatment, and prevention of diseases and disorders (see BIOMEDICAL ENGINEERING). Some of these devices have helped surgeons develop amazing new lifesaving techniques, especially in the fields of heart surgery and tissue transplants (see HEART [Treatment of Heart Problems]; TISSUE TRANSPLANT). Other advances have opened up whole new fields of medicine, such as *aviation medicine* and *industrial medicine.*

Financial Problems. Since the early 1960's, medical costs in the United States have risen rapidly. As a result, most people need some kind of health insurance. But some Americans do not have any health insurance, and many others are only partially covered. Various plans have been suggested to guarantee more complete health coverage for all Americans. One plan calls for employers to provide insurance that would protect all employees from large medical expenses. Under this plan, the government would provide increased health care benefits for the elderly, the poor, and the unemployed. Another plan calls for comprehensive national health insurance to cover all persons. Each of these plans would be financed largely through general tax revenues and through increased premiums on the health insurance now provided by employers.

One factor driving up the price of medical care has been the sharp rise in the cost of hospital services. In an effort to deal with this problem, the U.S. Department of Health, Education, and Welfare issued health planning guidelines in 1978. These guidelines were designed to hold down hospital costs by preventing the expensive duplication of hospital facilities, equipment, and services. However, such measures cannot eliminate cost increases resulting from inflation.

An increase in the number of malpractice suits during the 1970's also forced up the cost of medical care. As the price of malpractice insurance increased, doctors were forced to raise their fees. To protect themselves from malpractice charges, many physicians began to prescribe more cautious—and more costly—treatment.

Poor Distribution of Doctors. Most experts believe the United States has enough physicians, but that the supply is badly distributed. Many rural areas and inner cities do not have enough doctors, while many suburban areas have more than they need. To help remedy this situation, the federal government established the National Health Service Corps (NHSC) in 1970. Through NHSC, the government recruits physicians to work in areas that have a shortage of doctors. One NHSC program offers scholarships to medical students. In return for this financial aid, the students work for the corps after completing their education.

Legal and Ethical Questions. Modern medicine's ability to prolong life raises the question of when death actually occurs. In the past, people were considered legally dead when their heart and lung action stopped. But today, machines can keep a patient's heart and lungs working for days or even years after they can no longer function by themselves. As a result, many experts believe that people should be considered legally dead when their brain stops functioning. This new legal standard was accepted in several states during the 1970's.

Other ethical and legal questions raised by modern medicine include the practice of abortion and *euthanasia* (mercy killing). See ABORTION; EUTHANASIA.

Problems for Research. Medical research has yet to discover the exact cause of diseases of the heart and blood vessels and of cancer—the two chief causes of death from disease in the United States today. Knowledge of what causes these disorders would help scientists develop better ways of treating and preventing them. But research takes much time and money. In the 1970's, American scientists had increasing difficulty getting research funds.

LOUIS LASAGNA

MEDICINE/*Study Aids*

Related Articles in WORLD BOOK include:

CONTRIBUTORS TO MEDICAL PROGRESS

AMERICAN

Beadle, George W.	Menninger (family)
Beaumont, William	Minot, George
Blackwell, Elizabeth	Morgan, Thomas H.
Bloch, Konrad Emil	Morton, William T. G.
Crile, George W.	Mudd, Samuel A.
Cushing, Harvey	Murphy, John B.
DeBakey, Michael E.	Picotte, Susan La Flesche
Dooley, Thomas A., III	Reed, Walter
Drew, Charles R.	Robbins, Frederick C.
Enders, John F.	Rous, Francis P.
Goldberger, Joseph	Rush, Benjamin
Gorgas (William C.)	Sabin, Albert B.
Gorrie, John	Sabin, Florence R.
Hamilton, Alice	Salk, Jonas E.
Hench, Philip S.	Shaw, Anna H.
Holmes, Oliver W.	Smith, Theobald
Howe (Samuel G.)	Spock, Benjamin M.
Kendall, Edward C.	Stanley, Wendell
Landsteiner, Karl	Sumner, James B.
Lawless, Theodore K.	Tatum, Edward L.
Lazear, Jesse W.	Taussig, Helen B.
Loeb, Jacques	Theiler, Max
Long, Crawford W.	Thornton, Matthew
Mayo (family)	Trudeau, Edward L.
McCollum, Elmer V.	Waksman, Selman A.
McDowell, Ephraim	Walker, Mary E.

Warren, John C.	Williams, Daniel H.
Weller, Thomas H.	Wright, Sewall
White, Paul D.	

BRITISH

Addison, Thomas	Jenner, Sir William
Bright, Richard	Lister, Sir Joseph
Brown, Robert	MacLeod, John J.
Bruce, Sir David	Manson, Sir Patrick
Chain, Ernst B.	Martin, Archer J. P.
Fleming, Sir Alexander	Medawar, Sir Peter Brian
Florey, Lord	Pearson, Karl
Graves, Robert J.	Roget, Peter M.
Grenfell, Sir Wilfred	Ross, Sir Ronald
Harvey, William	Sloane, Sir Hans
Huxley (Julian S.)	Sydenham, Thomas
Jenner, Edward	

CANADIAN

Banting, Sir	Bethune, Norman	Osler, Sir William
Frederick G.	Black, Davidson	Selye, Hans
Best, Charles H.	McCrae, John	

FRENCH

Bernard, Claude	Laveran, Charles L. A.
Bichat, Marie F. X.	Lwoff, André
Carrel, Alexis	Monod, Jacques
Halpern, Bernard N.	Paré, Ambroise
Laënnec, René T. H.	Pasteur, Louis

GERMAN

Baer, Karl E. von
Cohn, Ferdinand J.
Domagk, Gerhard
Ehrlich, Paul
Fischer, Hans
Gall, Franz J.
Hahnemann, Samuel F.
Koch, Robert
Krebs, Sir Hans A.

Lynen, Feodor
Mayer, Julius R. von
Roentgen, Wilhelm K.
Schweitzer, Albert
Spemann, Hans
Virchow, Rudolf
Wassermann, August von
Weismann, August

ITALIAN

Galvani, Luigi
Golgi, Camillo
Malpighi, Marcello

Morgagni, Giovanni B.
Spallanzani, Lazzaro

OTHERS

Avicenna
Barnard, Christiaan N.
Burnet, Sir Macfarlane
Cori
Einthoven, Willem
Fibiger, Johannes A. G.
Finlay, Carlos J.
Freud, Sigmund
Galen
Gullstrand, Allvar
Hippocrates

Imhotep
Kitasato, Shibasaburo
Kocher, Emil T.
Mesmer, Franz
Metchnikoff, Élie
Ochoa, Severo
Paracelsus, Philippus A.
Pavlov, Ivan P.
Schick, Béla
Semmelweis, Ignaz P.
Vesalius, Andreas

DIAGNOSIS

Amniocentesis
Biopsy
Blood Count
Bronchoscope
Diagnosis
Electro-
cardiograph

Electro-
encephalograph
Fluoroscope
Gastroscope
Liquid Crystal
Manometer

Ophthalmoscope
Schick Test
Spirometer
Stethoscope
Thermography
X Rays

DISEASES

See DISEASE and MENTAL ILLNESS with their lists of *Related Articles.*

MEDICAL ORGANIZATIONS

American Medical
Association
Armed Forces Institute
of Pathology
Cancer Society,
American
Health Maintenance
Organization

Heart Association, American
Medic Alert Foundation
Menninger Foundation
National Medical Association
Public Health Service
World Health Organization
World Medical Association

PREVENTIVE MEDICINE

Antitoxin
Health

Immunity
Immunization

Inoculation
Mental Health

Sanitation

MEDICAL SCIENCES

Anatomy
Aviation Medicine
Bacteriology
Biochemistry
Dermatology
Embryology

Genetics
Geriatrics
Histology
Microbiology
Nutrition
Ophthalmology

Osteology
Pathology
Pediatrics
Pharmacology
Physiology
Psychiatry

TREATMENT

Blood Transfusion
Chemotherapy
Diathermy
Diet
Drug
First Aid
Gamma Ray
Hydrotherapy

Infrared Rays
Iron Lung
Irradiation
Massage
Occupational
Therapy
Oxygen Tent
Physical Therapy

Plasma
Plastic Surgery
Prosthetics
Psychoanalysis
Psychosomatic
Medicine
Psychotherapy
Serum

Sun Bath
Sun Lamp

Surgery
Tissue Transplant

Ultraviolet Rays

OTHER RELATED ARTICLES

Allopathy
Asclepius
Biofeedback
Biomedical
Engineering
Blood Bank
Bone Bank
Chiropractic
Dentistry
Eye Bank
Health Insurance,
National
Homeopathy

HOPE, Project
Hospital
Hygeia
Isotope (Uses of
Radioisotopes)
Malpractice Suit
Nobel Prizes
Nursing
Optometry
Osteopathy
Paramedic
Pharmacy

Placebo
Plastics
(In Medicine)
Podiatry
Pure Food and
Drug Laws
℞
Sanitarium
Trauma
Center
Veterinary
Medicine

Outline

I. **Elements of Medical Care**
   A. Diagnosis   B. Treatment   C. Prevention
II. **Providing Medical Care**
   A. How Medical Care Is Provided
   B. Where Medical Care Is Provided
   C. Improving the Quality of Medical Care
III. **Careers in Medicine**
   A. A Career as a Doctor
   B. Other Careers in Medicine
IV. **Financing Medical Care**
   A. In the United States   C. In Other Countries
   B. In Canada
V. **History**
VI. **Current Problems in U.S. Medicine**

Questions

What are the three main methods of paying for medical care in the United States?

Why is medicine both a science and an art?

What is primary care? Who provides it?

What are the three main elements of medical care?

Who proved that certain microbes cause disease?

What are *paramedical workers? Medical technologists?*

Who wrote the first scientific textbook on human anatomy?

What are the requirements for obtaining a license to practice medicine in each state of the United States?

What is the World Health Organization? What does it do?

Who was the first physician known to consider medicine a science and art separate from religion?

Books to Read

BEDESCHI, GIULIO. *The Science of Medicine.* Watts, 1975.

GARRISON, FIELDING H. *An Introduction to the History of Medicine with Medical Chronology, Suggestions for Study and Bibliographic Data.* Saunders, 1960. A reprint of the 4th ed., published in 1929.

GOLDSMITH, ILSE. *Why You Get Sick and How You Get Well.* Sterling, 1970. For young readers.

KRUZAS, ANTHONY T., ed. *Medical and Health Information Directory.* Gale, 1977.

MARKS, GEOFFREY J., and BEATTY, W. K. *The Story of Medicine in America.* Scribner, 1973.

MILLER, JONATHAN. *The Body in Question.* Random, 1979.

SOBEL, DAVID S., ed. *Ways of Health: Holistic Approaches to Ancient and Contemporary Medicine.* Harcourt, 1979.

STEVENS, ROSEMARY. *American Medicine and the Public Interest.* Yale, 1971.

Reading and Study Guide

See *Medicine* in the RESEARCH GUIDE/INDEX, Volume 22, for a *Reading and Study Guide.*

MEDICINE, PATENT. See PATENT MEDICINE.

Medicine Hat Chamber of Commerce

Medicine Hat, a trade center in southeastern Alberta, has large grain elevators along the rail lines.

MEDICINE HAT, Alberta (pop. 32,811), is a city on the South Saskatchewan River. It lies about 180 miles (290 kilometers) southeast of Calgary (see ALBERTA [political map]). The chinook belt of warm winds usually keeps Medicine Hat warmer than most other cities in the same latitude.

One of the largest known natural-gas fields in the world surrounds Medicine Hat and provides the basis for its industries. The city owns the gas field.

The city's name is the translation of the Blackfoot Indian word *saamis* (the headdress of a medicine man). A Blackfoot legend says a saamis was found there.

The city serves as a trading center for a large farming and ranching area. Its factories use gas for power, and this keeps Medicine Hat free from smoke. The chief products include flour, glass, linseed oil, cement, brick and tile, pottery, and machinery. Workers process slate, lignite coal, and clay found nearby. The city has a fertilizer plant, tire plant, and 16 greenhouses. One of these greenhouses, with 10 acres (4 hectares) under glass, ranks as the second largest in Canada.

Medicine Hat was founded in 1883 and chartered as a city in 1906. It has a mayor-council form of government. W. D. McDougall

MEDICINE MAN. See INDIAN, AMERICAN (Shamans); SHAMAN; ESKIMO (Religion).

MEDICINE ROCKS. See MONTANA (Places to Visit).

MÉDICIS, CATHERINE DE. See CATHERINE DE MÉDICIS.

MEDICO. See DOOLEY, THOMAS ANTHONY, III.

MEDIEVAL PERIOD. See MIDDLE AGES.

MEDILL, *muh DIHL,* **JOSEPH** (1823-1899), a crusading American editor and publisher, made the *Chicago Tribune* one of the world's most successful newspapers. He served as managing editor from 1855 to 1863, as editor in chief from 1863 to 1866, and as publisher from 1874 until his death. Many of his editorials concerned government reforms.

Medill worked hard to build the Republican Party. Some authorities believe he named the party. He helped sponsor Abraham Lincoln as a candidate for the presidency. Medill served at the Illinois Constitutional Convention of 1869, on the Civil Service Commission under President Ulysses S. Grant, and as mayor of Chicago from 1872 to 1874. He was born near Saint John, New Brunswick, Canada. JOHN TEBBEL

MEDINA, *muh DEE nuh* (pop. 90,000), is a city in western Saudi Arabia. It lies on a fertile plain about 270 miles (434 kilometers) north of Mecca. For location, see SAUDI ARABIA (political map). Medina and Mecca are the holiest cities in Islam, the Muslim religion, and only Muslims may enter them. The Holy Mosque of the Prophet Muhammad, who founded Islam, is in Medina. This Muslim house of worship holds Muhammad's tomb. Islam requires every Muslim to make at least one pilgrimage to Mecca if he or she can do so. Most pilgrims who visit Mecca also go to Medina.

Farmers grow fruits and vegetables in the area around Medina. Agriculture and money spent by pilgrims form the basis of Medina's economy. The city is the home of the Islamic University. Medina has kept much of its traditional appearance. But as it has expanded, the walls of the old city have disappeared. New suburbs have grown up, and wealthy residents live there.

No one knows when Medina was founded. It was originally called *Yathrib*, and farmers settled there before 200 B.C. Medina received its present name, which means *town* or *city*, about A.D. 600. Muhammad and his disciples found safety in Medina after they were forced to flee from Mecca in 622. Medina became the center of the Muslim community, but its political importance fell as the Islamic empire grew. MALCOLM C. PECK

See also HEGIRA; MUHAMMAD.

MEDINA, *muh DEE nuh,* **HAROLD RAYMOND** (1888-   ), an American judge, won international fame for his fair conduct of the trial of 11 American Communist party leaders in 1949. The Communist leaders were convicted of conspiring to teach and advocate the overthrow of the U.S. government by force. Medina urged the jury to be calm and patient, and cautioned that "justice does not flourish amidst emotional excitement and stress."

Judge Medina was born in Brooklyn, N.Y., and was graduated from Princeton University. He received his law degree from Columbia University in 1912, and taught there from 1915 to 1947. He practiced law in New York City until he was appointed a federal judge in 1947. He retired from that post in 1958. H. G. REUSCHLEIN

MEDINA SIDONIA, DUKE OF. See ARMADA (The Two Fleets).

MEDITATION. See TRANSCENDENTAL MEDITATION.

MEDITERRANEAN FRUIT FLY is an insect that destroys fruits and vegetables. It is an even greater pest than the corn borer, because it attacks more than 70 kinds of crops. The watermelon and pineapple are about the only fruits that this fruit fly does not destroy.

Scientists believe that the Mediterranean fruit fly first came from the Azores. Long ago it made its way to Africa, southern Europe, and Asia. Early in the 1900's, it appeared in Bra-

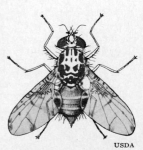

USDA
Mediterranean Fruit Fly

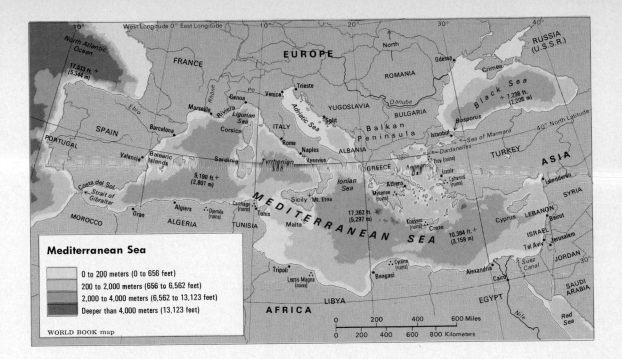

Mediterranean Sea

0 to 200 meters (0 to 656 feet)

200 to 2,000 meters (656 to 6,562 feet)

2,000 to 4,000 meters (6,562 to 13,123 feet)

Deeper than 4,000 meters (13,123 feet)

WORLD BOOK map

zil and Hawaii. In 1929, it was discovered in Florida. Congress provided $4¼ million to destroy the harmful insect. A strict quarantine was immediately ordered in the infested area. By July 25, 1930, all of these flies in the United States apparently had been destroyed. The fly invaded Florida again in 1956 and in 1962. It was destroyed by spraying infested areas.

This dangerous insect is about the size of a common house fly. A person can tell it from a house fly by its spotted wings, and the way it holds its wings at an angle with its body. The female fruit fly selects a ripe fruit while it is still on the tree and drills tiny holes into the skin or rind. Here the fly lays many tiny eggs. These eggs soon hatch into larvae. Then the larvae eat their way through the fruit, which soon drops to the ground. Larvae finish this stage of growth in three or four months. Then they burrow into the ground. When they come out, they are adult insects with wings.

The Mediterranean fruit fly thrives best in a warm climate, but sunlight kills the larvae. There are several insect parasites that destroy the eggs and larvae without doing other damage. These parasites alone cannot check the fruit fly. The only way to destroy the larvae completely is to boil the fruit for several hours, or burn it completely. If a person suspects that fruit is infested with larvae of the Mediterranean fruit fly, he should have it examined by an expert.

Scientific Classification. The Mediterranean fruit fly belongs to the family *Tephritidae*, or *Trypetidae*. It is genus *Ceratitis*, species *C. capitata*.   ROBERT L. USINGER

MEDITERRANEAN SEA, *MEHD uh tuh RAY nee uhn,* has been one of the world's chief trade routes since ancient times. Many early civilizations, including those of Egypt, Greece, Phoenicia, and Rome, developed along its shores. Today, the islands and coastal areas of the Mediterranean rank among the most popular tourist attractions in the world.

Location and Size. The Latin word *mediterranean* means *in the middle of land*, and land almost surrounds the Mediterranean Sea. Europe lies to the north, Asia to the east, and Africa to the south.

On the west, the Strait of Gibraltar connects the Mediterranean with the Atlantic Ocean. Another strait, the Dardanelles, links the Mediterranean on the east with the Sea of Marmara, the Bosporus, and the Black Sea. On the southeast, the Isthmus of Suez separates the Mediterranean and Red seas. The Suez Canal, a man-made waterway, crosses this thin strip of land. Ships sail through the canal between the Mediterranean and the Red Sea and Indian Ocean.

The Mediterranean covers about 969,100 square miles (2,510,000 square kilometers). The Black Sea, which many people consider part of the Mediterranean, has an area of about 196,100 square miles (507,900 square kilometers). Several other arms of the Mediterranean are also large enough to be called seas. They include the Adriatic, Aegean, Ionian, and Tyrrhenian seas.

The Mediterranean is more than three times as long as it is wide. It has a maximum length of about 2,200 miles (3,540 kilometers), between the Strait of Gibraltar and Iskenderun, Turkey. The widest part of the sea lies between Libya and Yugoslavia, a distance of about 600 miles (970 kilometers).

The Seabed. An underwater ridge between Sicily and Tunisia divides the Mediterranean into two basins. The eastern basin is deeper than the western one. The sea has an average depth of 4,926 feet (1,501 meters). It reaches its greatest depth—16,302 feet (5,093 meters)— in a depression called the Hellenic Trough that lies between Greece and Italy.

Earthquakes occur frequently throughout the Mediterranean region, especially in Greece and western Turkey. Volcanic action formed many of the islands in the Mediterranean. A few volcanoes in the region still erupt. They include Mount Etna, Stromboli, and Vesuvius.

Earth scientists explain the earthquakes and volcanic activity by the theory of *plate tectonics*. According to this theory, the earth's crust consists of about 20 rigid plates that are in slow, continuous motion. The two plates that carry the European and African continents are slowly drifting toward each other. Their motion squeezes and stretches the earth's crust in the Mediterranean region, causing earthquakes and volcanoes.

Coastline and Islands. Many bays and inlets indent the coastline of the Mediterranean. Several large peninsulas, including Italy and the Balkan Peninsula, jut out into the sea. Along most of the coast, rugged hills rise sharply from the water. Egypt and Libya have flatter coastal areas, with plains lying next to the sea.

Sicily, the largest island in the Mediterranean, covers 9,926 square miles (25,708 square kilometers). Other large islands include, in order of size, Sardinia, Cyprus, Corsica, and Crete.

Climate. The temperature at the surface of the Mediterranean averages about 61° F. (16° C). In summer, the surface temperature may reach 80° F. (27° C). Even in winter, it seldom drops below 40° F. (4° C). The water varies little in temperature in the middle depths and near the bottom. It stays between 55° and 59° F. (13° and 15° C) throughout the year.

The tremendous volume of warm water helps give the land surrounding it a warm, subtropical climate. Most Mediterranean countries have hot, dry summers and mild, rainy winters. These conditions provide what has become known as a "Mediterranean climate," even when they occur in other parts of the world. Two Mediterranean countries, Egypt and Libya, have tropical climates, hotter and drier than the typical Mediterranean type.

A hot wind known as the *sirocco* blows across the Mediterranean from Africa toward southern Europe. A cold, dry wind called the *mistral* blows the other way, from France out over the sea. See SIROCCO; MISTRAL.

The Water of the Mediterranean comes mostly from the Atlantic Ocean and the Black Sea. Several large rivers also empty into the Mediterranean. The largest include the Ebro of Spain, the Nile of Egypt, the Po of Italy, and the Rhône of France. The Nile has contributed less water since 1964, when the Aswan High Dam in Egypt began partly blocking its flow.

The warm, dry climate gives the sea a high rate of evaporation. As a result, the water of the Mediterranean is saltier than that of the Atlantic.

The Mediterranean has almost no tides. A strong current flows into the Mediterranean from the Black Sea. Another flows in from the Atlantic through the Strait of Gibraltar. In the days of sailing ships, this Atlantic current made it difficult for vessels to reach the ocean from the Mediterranean. Beneath the surface current, a deeper current of dense salty water flows from the Mediterranean to the Atlantic.

Economic Importance. The warm climate, beautiful scenery, and historical importance of the Mediterranean region attract millions of tourists yearly. The region includes such popular resort areas as the Greek islands, the French and Italian rivieras, and the Adriatic coast of Yugoslavia.

The Mediterranean has little large-scale commercial fishing, but it is an important source of food for the people of the region. The chief seafoods include anchovies, sardines, shrimp, and tuna. Other products from the Mediterranean include coral and sponges.

The Mediterranean serves as an important waterway that links Europe, the Middle East, and Asia. Ships use the Suez Canal as a route between the Mediterranean and Red seas.

Formation of the Mediterranean Sea can be explained by the theory of plate tectonics. Over 200 million years ago, the continents formed a single land mass called Pangaea. The Tethys Sea, a huge bay that developed into the Mediterranean, indented the east coast of Pangaea. Through the centuries, Pangaea broke up into continents that began to drift slowly toward their present location. As they drifted, Africa turned counterclockwise, and Eurasia turned clockwise. Their movement opened a waterway at the western end of the sea, linking it with the ocean. By about 65 million years ago, the rotation of these two continents had almost closed the eastern end of the Tethys Sea. The sea thus acquired its present shape.

Some earth scientists believe the Mediterranean dried up about a dozen times between $7\frac{1}{2}$ and $5\frac{1}{2}$ million years ago. During this period, the movement of the European and African continents repeatedly closed and reopened the Strait of Gibraltar. Each time it closed, the Mediterranean began to dry up. After about 1,000 years of evaporation, only a large desert remained. A few salty lakes, like Great Salt Lake in Utah, dotted this desert. When the strait reopened, water from the Atlantic rushed in, forming a huge waterfall. The waterfall carried about 1,000 times as much water as does Niagara Falls, and it refilled the Mediterranean in about 100 years.

In 1970, scientists found evidence that supported the desert theory. That year, geologists aboard a research vessel called the *Glomar Challenger* drilled cores of rock from the Mediterranean floor. The cores contained minerals, known as *evaporites*, that are formed by the evaporation of salty water.

Man and the Mediterranean. Many historians believe Western civilization was born in the Mediterranean region. Ancient cultures grew up on the banks of the sea, where conditions favored their development. The mild climate encouraged human settlement. The sea's calm waters and steady winds throughout most of the year made seafaring relatively easy. The sea also had natural harbors and many islands that sailors could use as ports.

Probably the first great civilization to develop in the Mediterranean region was that of ancient Egypt. By about 3100 B.C., the Egyptians had a unified national government and a system of writing. The first important European civilization, the Minoan culture, arose on the island of Crete about 3000 B.C. Another culture, the Helladic civilization, grew up on the Greek mainland. One Helladic city, Mycenae, became so powerful that some historians call the later Helladic civilization *Mycenaean*. By about 1500 B.C., Mycenaean ships controlled the Mediterranean. They traded with cities as far away as what are now Lebanon and Syria.

After about 1200 B.C., the Phoenicians began to win control of the Mediterranean. From their homes on the eastern shore, they sailed to all parts of the sea. Phoenician seamen even traveled through the Strait of Gibraltar into the Atlantic. Carthage, a colony founded by the Phoenicians, became another great sea power after about 600 B.C. By the A.D. 100's, the Roman Empire ruled all the lands that bordered the Mediterranean. The Romans called the Mediterranean *Mare Nostrum* (our sea).

For centuries, the Mediterranean served as the greatest water route in the world. From the 1100's to the 1400's, such Mediterranean trading centers as Barcelona, Constantinople, Genoa, and Venice linked Europe and Asia. The ships of these cities brought goods from India and China across the sea to Europe. The Portuguese explorer Vasco da Gama sailed around Africa in 1497, reaching India in 1498. Trading ships then began to use this easier, all-water route to the East. As a result, the importance of the Mediterranean as a trade route declined until the 1800's.

The opening of the Suez Canal in 1869 made the Mediterranean a part of the shortest water route between Europe and Asia. For nearly 100 years, the sea ranked as one of the world's busiest shipping lanes. The canal was closed during the Arab-Israeli War of 1967. It was reopened in 1975.

During the 1970's, water pollution became a serious problem in the Mediterranean. Garbage, industrial wastes, oil, pesticides, and sewage polluted the sea and threatened fishing and tourism in the region. Scientists fear that pollution could make the Mediterranean a dead sea—unable to support life—by the year 2000. In 1976, most of the nations with borders on the Mediterranean signed a treaty in which they agreed to work to reduce the pollution.   WARREN E. YASSO

Related Articles in WORLD BOOK include:

Adriatic Sea	Cyprus	Ionian Sea
Aegean Sea	Dardanelles	Marmara, Sea of
Atlantic Ocean	Europe (picture:	Sardinia
Black Sea	Rocky Islands)	Sicily
Bosporus	Gibraltar	Suez Canal
Corsica	Gibraltar,	Tyrrhenian Sea
Crete	Strait of	

MEDIUM. See ECTOPLASM; SPIRITUALISTS; MYTHOLOGY (African Mythology).

MEDIUM, in biology. See CULTURE (laboratory).

MEDLARS. See LIBRARY (United States Government Libraries).

MEDULLA OBLONGATA. See BRAIN (The Medulla Oblongata; color picture: The Parts of the Brain).

MEDULLARY CAVITY. See BONE (Structure).

MEDUSA. See JELLYFISH.

MEDUSA, *muh DOO suh*, was one of the three Gorgons, the daughters of the sea god Phorcus in Greek mythology (see GORGON). She was the only mortal Gorgon. Medusa had been beautiful in her youth, and was still proud of her hair. She boasted of her beauty to Athena, who became jealous and changed her into a hideous person. Medusa and her sisters had staring eyes, protruding fangs for teeth, and writhing snakes for hair. They were so ugly that anyone who saw them turned to stone.

Perseus killed Medusa by looking in his mirrorlike shield as he cut off her head (see PERSEUS). The winged horse Pegasus sprang from her beheaded body, and poisonous snakes arose from the blood that dripped from her head. Athena saved blood from Medusa's body and gave it to Asclepius, the god of healing (see ASCLEPIUS). The blood from Medusa's left side was a fatal poison, but that from her right side had the power to revive the dead.   O. M. PEARL

MEEKER, EZRA (1830-1928), was an American pioneer and author. In 1852, he took a five-month journey by ox-cart along the Oregon Trail from Iowa to Portland, Ore., with his wife and infant son. He returned to Iowa by the same route in 1906, painting inscriptions on landmarks along the way as part of a memorial observance. He made a similar trip by automobile in 1915. He spent much of his time after the age of 75 promoting the memory of the Oregon Trail. Meeker founded the Oregon Trail Association. His books include *Ox-Team Days on the Oregon Trail* (1922) and *Kate Mulhall* (1926). Meeker was born in Huntsville, Ohio.   JESSE L. GILMORE

MEERSCHAUM, *MEER shum*, is a soft, whitish fibrous or flaky clay. Manufacturers use it to make tobacco pipes. Meerschaum is also called *sepiolite*. It is so light that it will float in water. In German, the word *meerschaum* means *sea foam*. The mineral gets its name because it floats and has the look of foam. Large quantities of meerschaum are found in Asia Minor. Lumps of meerschaum are found in masses of other types of clay. Meerschaum is a compound of magnesium, silicon, oxygen, and water. It is a water-bearing magnesium silicate.

Many smokers prefer meerschaum tobacco pipes. The bowls of meerschaum pipes are white when new. With careful handling and use, the bowl slowly colors a rich brown. Meerschaum pipes break easily.   CECIL J. SCHNEER

Kaywoodie Pipes, Inc.

Meerschaum Miners use heavy iron picks to dig in clay for the whitish mineral used to make meerschaum pipe bowls.

MEETING. See PARLIAMENTARY PROCEDURE (Holding Meetings); CONVENTION.

MEGACYCLE. See MEGAHERTZ.

MEGAERA. See FURIES.

MEGAHERTZ, formerly called MEGACYCLE, is a unit used to measure the frequency of such waves as radio and television waves. It is 1 million *hertz* (cycles a second).

See also KILOHERTZ.

MEGALITHIC MONUMENTS

MEGALITHIC MONUMENTS, *MEHG uh LIHTH ihk,* are structures built of large stones by prehistoric people for burial or religious purposes. The word *megalith* means *large stone*. The stones may weigh from 25 to 100 short tons (23 to 91 metric tons) each. Megalithic monuments can be found in various parts of the world. The best-known ones are in western Europe and were built between 4000 and 1500 B.C.

Some megalithic structures served as tombs. Some of these tombs had passages. Other tombs, called *dolmens,* consisted of a small, simple chamber. Examples of such tombs have been discovered in southern Greece.

Single, erect stones are called *menhirs*. A monument composed of menhirs arranged in a circle and surrounded by a mound of earth and a ditch is called a *henge*. The most famous henge, Stonehenge, stands near Salisbury, England (see STONEHENGE). Menhirs were also arranged in parallel rows called *alignments*. Elaborate alignments near Carnac in northwestern France extend over 2 miles (3 kilometers). B. BENDER

MEGALOMANIA. See MENTAL ILLNESS (Paranoia).

MEGALOPOLIS is a region made up of two or more metropolitan areas. A metropolitan area consists of a central city with a population of at least 50,000 and its surrounding suburbs. Metropolitan areas form a megalopolis if they attract enough people and industry and then expand and begin to grow together.

The largest megalopolis in the United States is developing in the Northeast. It includes the metropolitan areas of Boston, New York City, Philadelphia, Baltimore, and Washington, D.C. It extends about 450 miles (724 kilometers) from southern New Hampshire into northern Virginia and about 100 miles (160 kilometers) inland. It covers more than 50,000 square miles (130,000 square kilometers) and has over 36 million persons. Other megalopolises developing in the United States include (1) the area from San Francisco, through Los Angeles, to San Diego and (2) the area from Milwaukee, through Chicago, to South Bend, Ind.

The French geographer Jean Gottmann introduced the term *megalopolis* in 1961 to describe the urban development in the Northeastern United States. The English use the term *conurbation* instead. A huge conurbation is developing in the area between London and the industrial Midlands of central England. Other developing megalopolises include the Tokyo-Yokohama-Osaka area in Japan and the Ruhr Industrial Basin in Germany, Holland, and Belgium. PHILIP M. HAUSER

See also METROPOLITAN AREA.

MÉGANTIC, LAKE. See CHAUDIÈRE RIVER.

MEGAPHONE is a hollow, cone-shaped device used to make a voice sound louder. A person using a megaphone speaks or shouts into the small opening at one end. The person's voice comes out at the much wider opposite end. The megaphone makes the voice sound louder because it points sound waves in one direction and keeps them from spreading out in all directions. Megaphones may be up to 2 feet (61 centimeters) long or more. Cheerleaders often use megaphones. A portable, battery-powered loudspeaker called a *bullhorn* is often used in place of a megaphone. PAUL J. SCHEIPS

MEGARA. See HERCULES.

MEGARON. See ARCHITECTURE (Mycenaean).

MEGE-MOURIES, HIPPOLYTE. See MARGARINE (History).

MEHARRY MEDICAL COLLEGE is one of the leading predominantly black medical schools in the United States. About half the nation's black physicians and dentists are graduates of this private coeducational school in Nashville, Tenn.

The college has schools of dentistry and medicine, a graduate school, a school of allied health professions, and a teaching hospital. It also operates several health centers and many community health care programs in Nashville and other areas. It grants master's and doctor's degrees. The college also offers certificates in such fields as dental hygiene, medical technology, nurse practitioner, and X-ray technology. In cooperation with nearby Fisk and Tennessee State universities, Meharry provides programs in health care administration and planning.

Meharry was founded in 1876 as the medical department of Central Tennessee College of Nashville. The department became an independent college in 1915. Meharry is supported by government grants and contributions from corporations, foundations, and individuals. For enrollment, see UNIVERSITIES AND COLLEGES (table). Critically reviewed by MEHARRY MEDICAL COLLEGE

MEHMET ALI. See MUHAMMAD ALI.

MEHTA, ZUBIN (1936-   ), is a symphony orchestra conductor. Mehta won fame for his conducting of such large-scale romantic compositions as the works of the French composer Hector Berlioz. His interpretations are forceful, though they have been criticized as lacking refinement and being too showy.

Mehta was born in Bombay, India. From 1954 to 1960, he studied conducting in Vienna, Austria, where he was particularly influenced by the work of Wilhelm Furtwängler and Herbert von Karajan. Mehta became musical director of the Montreal Symphony Orchestra in 1961 and took the same position with the Los Angeles Symphony in 1962. He held both of these directorships until 1967, when he resigned from the Montreal position. In 1978, Mehta left the Los Angeles Symphony to become music director of the New York Philharmonic. KEITH POLK

Megalopolis

The map below shows in light red the largest developing *megalopolis* (continuous metropolitan area) in the United States. Built-up areas are shown in dark red.

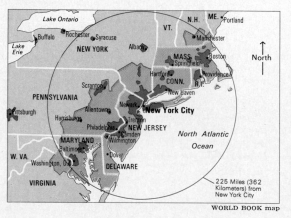

225 Miles (362 Kilometers) from New York City

WORLD BOOK map

ARTHUR MEIGHEN

Prime Minister of Canada
1920-1921
1926

BORDEN	MEIGHEN	KING	MEIGHEN	KING
1911-1920	1920-1921	1921-1926	1926	1926-1930

MEIGHEN, *MEE ahn*, **ARTHUR** (1874-1960), served as prime minister of Canada two times during the 1920's. He first took office as prime minister in July 1920, succeeding Sir Robert L. Borden. Meighen served as prime minister until December 1921. He held the office again from June to September in 1926. Meighen led the Conservative Party from 1921 to 1926 and in 1941 and 1942.

No other politician ever held so many top positions in the Canadian government as Meighen did. Besides prime minister, he served as Opposition leader in the Canadian House of Commons and as both Government and Opposition leader in the Canadian Senate. Meighen accomplished little as prime minister. But he became noted for his bitter and unsuccessful struggle for power with W. L. Mackenzie King, the leader of the Liberal Party. Meighen failed to lead the Conservatives to a parliamentary majority in the elections of 1921, 1925, and 1926. Each time, King became—or remained—prime minister.

Meighen, a lawyer, had a remarkable memory and a gift for eloquent expression. He especially liked to argue and became a skilled debater in Parliament. A newspaper paid tribute to Meighen's sharpness with words by calling him "The First Swordsman of Parliament." Meighen became one of Borden's chief aides during World War I (1914-1918). During this period, Meighen either developed or defended almost all the government's most controversial policies.

Many Canadians viewed Meighen as a brilliant, honest, and courageous statesman. But many others regarded him as quarrelsome and unwilling to compromise, and still others disliked his critical comments about King. Meighen himself felt that the public often misunderstood him.

Early Life

Arthur Meighen was born on June 16, 1874, on a farm near St. Mary's, Ont. He was the second of the six children of Joseph Meighen and Mary Bell Meighen. His parents placed a high value on education, and Arthur became a bright and eager student. He was a serious youth and made it clear to the family that he preferred to be called Arthur rather than Art. In 1896, he graduated from the University of Toronto with honors in mathematics.

Soon afterward, Meighen became a high-school teacher in Caledonia, Ont. But he did not like teaching and quit after a year. In 1898, Meighen moved to Winnipeg. He began to study law there as a clerk in a law firm. He was admitted to the bar in 1903 and established a law practice in Portage la Prairie, Man.

In June 1904, Meighen married Isabel Cox (1883-), a schoolteacher from Birtle, Man. They had two sons, Theodore and Maxwell, and a daughter, Lillian.

Entry Into Public Life

Meighen began his political career in 1908, when he won election to the Canadian House of Commons as a Conservative from Portage la Prairie. He was re-elected in 1911. In 1913, Meighen was appointed solicitor general after successfully helping end a bitter debate over a naval bill that Prime Minister Borden had introduced in the House of Commons. In 1917, Borden named Meighen secretary of state and minister of mines and, later that year, minister of the interior.

311

During World War I, Meighen either prepared or helped win parliamentary approval of several controversial measures. One such bill enabled the government to take control of some important railroads that had gone into debt. Another established a military draft. These bills made Meighen unpopular in Quebec, where Montreal business executives disliked the railroad takeover and French-speaking Canadians opposed the draft.

In October, 1917, Borden formed a government of Conservative and Liberal supporters of the draft. This administration became known as the Union Government. Two months later, Borden led the Unionists to victory in a general election. In 1920, he retired because of poor health. Borden's followers chose Meighen to succeed him as their leader and prime minister.

Prime Minister

First Term. When Meighen took office as prime minister on July 10, 1920, his government faced serious political problems. Many of its supporters in the West and in rural Ontario had begun to favor the new Progressive Party, organized by dissatisfied farmers. In addition, Meighen had no support in Quebec.

Meighen's most notable achievement as prime minister occurred at a conference of British Commonwealth leaders in London in 1921. The conference had been called to consider renewal of the Anglo-Japanese Alliance of 1902. Meighen was the only delegate who opposed renewal. He knew the United States disliked the treaty, and he believed Canada and Great Britain would be served best if it expired. Largely because of Meighen's arguments, the conference postponed a decision on renewal. This move helped lead to the Washington Naval Conference of 1921. At this conference, Britain, Japan, and the United States reached an agreement on arms limitation (see DISARMAMENT [History of Disarmament]).

By 1921, the wartime union of Conservatives and Liberals had fallen apart. Meighen led the Conservatives in the general election that year. But they suffered the worst defeat of any Canadian national party up to that time, winning only 50 of the 235 seats in the House of Commons. Meighen himself lost his seat from Portage la Prairie. W. L. Mackenzie King, the Liberal Party leader, replaced Meighen as prime minister on Dec. 29, 1921.

Opposition Leader. Meighen set out to rebuild the Conservative Party. In 1922, he won election to the House of Commons from Grenville, Ont., and became leader of the Opposition in the House. In the 1925 election, Meighen regained his seat from Portage la Prairie. The Conservatives emerged as the largest group in the House of Commons. But they fell seven seats short of a majority, and King remained prime minister.

In 1926, a scandal in the customs department disgraced the King administration. King asked Governor General Julian H. G. Byng to dissolve Parliament so a new election could be held. But Byng refused to do so, and King resigned. Byng believed that Meighen, as leader of the largest party in the House of Commons, should have a chance to form a government.

Second Term. On June 29, 1926, Meighen again became prime minister. But his government soon met defeat in the House of Commons on a motion charging that it had been formed illegally. Byng dissolved Parliament at Meighen's request. The Liberals won the election that followed, and King succeeded Meighen as prime minister on September 25.

Meighen, who had also lost his seat from Portage la Prairie, resigned as Conservative leader and retired from public service. By the end of 1926, he had become an investment banker in Toronto.

Later Years

Meighen began a political comeback in 1932, when Prime Minister Richard B. Bennett appointed him to the Canadian Senate. Bennett had succeeded Meighen as leader of the Conservative Party and had led the party to victory in the 1930 general election. Meighen became Government leader in the Senate, and then leader of the Opposition in the Senate after King led the Liberals back to power in 1935.

In 1941, the Conservative Party again elected Meighen as its leader. But his political career lasted only a short time longer. He sought election to the House of Commons from South York, near Toronto, but was defeated in February, 1942. In December, Meighen retired from politics a second time. He devoted the rest of his life chiefly to business activities. Meighen died on Aug. 5, 1960, in Toronto. ROGER GRAHAM

MEIGS, *megz,* **CORNELIA LYNDE** (1884-1973), an American author, wrote more than two dozen books for children. Most of them are based on incidents in American history. In 1934, she won the Newbery medal for *Invincible Louisa,* the life of Louisa May Alcott. Her other works include *Kingdom of the Winding Road* (1915), *Rain on the Roof* (1925), *The Trade Wind* (1927), and *As the Crow Flies* (1925). She was editor in chief and coauthor of *A Critical History of Children's Literature* (1953). She also wrote a play, *The Steadfast Princess,* that won a Drama League prize in 1916.

Cornelia Meigs was born in Rock Island, Ill. She spent her summers in New England. Some of her books relate the New England stories her parents and grandparents told her. She was graduated from Bryn Mawr College, and taught there 18 years. EVELYN RAY SICKELS

MEIJI. See MUTSUHITO.

MEIN KAMPF is a book by Adolf Hitler. The title is German for *My Struggle.* In the book, Hitler gave a fanciful account of his life and set down his political ideas. He described the alleged superiority of the German people, and said that the good of Germany ranked above all other values. The book stated Hitler's ideas on "race purity." These beliefs led to World War II and the slaughter of millions of Europeans. *Mein Kampf* was the "bible" for German Nazis and a guide for Nazi sympathizers in other countries. STEFAN T. POSSONY

See also HITLER, ADOLF (Mein Kampf).

MEIOSIS. See CELL (Cell Division; illustration).

MEIR, GOLDA (1898-1978), served as prime minister of Israel from 1969 to 1974. During her political career, she supported large-scale immigration to Israel and major housing and other construction programs. Her main problem as prime minister was the territorial conflict between Israel and several Arab nations (see MIDDLE EAST [History]). Meir followed a firm but open policy toward the Arabs.

In October 1973, war broke out for the fourth time

between Israel and the Arabs. Israel suffered heavy early losses, and Meir's government was severely criticized. As a result, she resigned in June 1974, even though she had led the Labor (Mapai) Party to victory in the December 1973 elections.

Golda Meir was born Golda Mabovitz in Kiev, in the Ukraine—a part of Russia. Her family moved to Milwaukee, Wis., in 1906, and she later taught school there. In 1921, she went to Palestine and joined a collective farm village. In 1948, Palestine was divided into the new nation of Israel and an Arab state. Meir served as Israel's minister of labor from 1949 to 1956 and as minister of foreign affairs from 1956 to 1966. She was secretary-general of the Labor Party from 1966 to 1969. She wrote an autobiography, *My Life* (1975). ELLIS RIVKIN

MEISTERSINGER. See MASTERSINGER.

MEITNER, *MYT nuhr,* **LISE** (1878-1968), was an Austrian physicist. Her discoveries in nuclear physics played a large part in developing nuclear energy. Otto Hahn and Fritz Strassmann, German physical chemists, split the uranium atom in 1938 when they bombarded uranium with neutrons and produced *barium* (see BARIUM). This discovery was not recognized officially until January, 1939, when Meitner and Otto Frisch announced their interpretation of the work of Hahn and Strassmann.

She developed a mathematical theory to explain the splitting of the uranium atom into two fragments. She calculated the energy released in nuclear fission. The Hahn-Strassmann experiment and the explanation of it by Meitner and Frisch were important events in the development of the atomic bomb and other uses of nuclear energy.

Meitner was born in 1878 in Vienna and started her studies in nuclear physics there. From 1908 to 1911, she served at the University of Berlin as assistant to Max Planck, originator of the quantum theory (see QUANTUM MECHANICS). She was a professor at the Kaiser Wilhelm Institute for Chemistry during World War I and won fame for her studies on radioactive radium, thorium, and actinium. In 1917, she and Hahn discovered radioactive *protactinium*, element 91 (see PROTACTINIUM). That same year, the element was discovered independently by the British scientists Frederick Soddy and John Cranston. Meitner became a professor of physics at the Catholic University of America in 1946. Later that year, she returned to Europe to become a member of the University of Stockholm staff. RALPH E. LAPP

See also ATOM (Splitting the Atom); NUCLEAR ENERGY (The First Artificially Created Fission Reaction).

MEKKA. See MECCA.

MEKNÈS, *mehk NEHS* (pop. 248,369), one of Morocco's four capitals, is a main trading center in northern Morocco. The city lies about 35 miles (56 kilometers) southwest of Fez (see MOROCCO [map]). It was founded in the 1100's, and became Morocco's capital when Sultan Ismail built a palace there in the 1670's.

Wide World

Golda Meir

MEKONG RIVER, *may kawng,* is the largest stream on the Indochinese peninsula. The Mekong is about 2,600 miles (4,180 kilometers) long. It flows southeastward from eastern Tibet, and forms part of the boundary between Thailand (Siam) and Laos. The river crosses Laos, Cambodia, and Vietnam before it empties into the China Sea near Ho Chi Minh City. In the region of the lower delta, the Mekong is known as the Sai Gon River. See THAILAND (map).

Ships can sail only about 350 miles (563 kilometers) up the Mekong. Farther inland, the river is interrupted by rapids and sand bars. J. E. SPENCER

See also RIVER (chart); ASIA (picture: Asia's Rivers).

MELAKA, or MALACCA, *muh LAK uh* (pop. 86,357), is the capital of the state of Melaka in Malaya. Melaka lies on the southwest coast of the Malay Peninsula, 125 miles (201 kilometers) northwest of Singapore. For location, see MALAYSIA (map). Melaka lies in an area that produces pepper, rice, and sage. During the 1400's, the city became the most important commercial port in Southeast Asia. The Portuguese captured it in 1511. The Dutch seized Melaka in 1641, and the British gained control of the city in 1824. Today, Melaka no longer ranks as a major Asian port. NORTON GINSBURG

MELAMINE. See PLASTICS (table: Kinds of Plastics).

MELANCHOLIA. See MENTAL ILLNESS (Manic-Depressive Psychosis).

MELANCHTHON, *muh LANGK thun,* **PHILIPP** (1497-1560), a German humanist and scholar, was Martin Luther's chief associate in starting and leading the Protestant Reformation. Melanchthon wrote the *Loci Communes* (*Commonplaces,* 1521), a widely read handbook that set down Lutheran doctrines in a systematic way for easy reference. He was also the chief author of the Augsburg Confession, which became the basic statement of faith of the Lutheran Church.

Melanchthon had a calmer personality than did Luther. He continually tried to find compromise solutions to issues that divided Protestants and Catholics, and Protestants from each other. Melanchthon declared that many such issues were unimportant and should not block Christian unity. But he also believed that the Roman Catholic Church had forsaken the true Christian tradition several hundred years after Christ. He especially opposed the power of the popes.

Melanchthon was born near Karlsruhe. Like Luther, he was a professor at the University of Wittenberg. He was a brilliant student of classical literature and of the works of the early church fathers. He has been called the founder of the German educational system because he established public schools where boys learned to read and write Greek, Latin, and German. RICHARD MARIUS

See also LUTHER, MARTIN; AUGSBURG CONFESSION; REFORMATION.

MELANESIA. See PACIFIC ISLANDS; RACES, HUMAN (table: Geographical Races).

MELANIN. See SKIN; HAIR (The Color of Hair).

MELATONIN. See PINEAL GLAND.

MELBA, DAME NELLIE (1861-1931), was a famous Australian coloratura soprano. Her real name was Helen Porter Mitchell. She adopted her stage name from Melbourne, Australia. Nellie Melba was born in Richmond, which is a suburb of Melbourne.

313

MELBOURNE

Nellie Melba first sang in public at the age of 6 in Melbourne. She made her operatic debut in 1887 in Brussels, Belgium, singing the role of Gilda in *Rigoletto*. She performed in Italy, Russia, Denmark, and England. Nellie Melba made her American debut in New York City in 1893. She was made Dame Commander in the Order of the British Empire in 1918. SCOTT GOLDTHWAITE

Radio Times Hulton Picture Library
Dame Nellie Melba

MELBOURNE (pop. 2,479,422) is the second largest city of Australia. Only Sydney has more people. Melbourne, the capital of the state of Victoria, lies on Port Phillip Bay on the southeastern coast (see AUSTRALIA [political map]). Melbourne is a busy seaport, Australia's chief financial city, and the commercial and industrial center of Victoria.

The City and its suburbs cover more than 2,300 square miles (5,960 square kilometers). Downtown Melbourne is on the northern shore of Port Phillip Bay. Important buildings include the State Library of Victoria and Parliament House, where the Victoria legislature meets. The Yarra River runs through Melbourne. Several parks surround the city. The Melbourne Cup, a famous horse race, takes place yearly at Flemington Racecourse.

The Melbourne area is the home of La Trobe, Melbourne, and Monash universities. The Victorian Arts Centre, scheduled for completion in the early 1980's, includes facilities for concerts and plays. The National Gallery of Victoria, an art museum, is part of the center.

The People. Most of Melbourne's residents are of British ancestry. About three-fourths of the people were born in Australia. Many people from England, Greece, Italy, and other European countries have settled in Melbourne since World War II ended in 1945. Melbourne also has about 2,700 persons who are descended from *Aborigines*, the first people who lived in Australia.

About 70 per cent of Melbourne's families own houses. Large suburbs of single-family homes extend east, north, and west of the city. Public transportation does not serve the entire area, and so many people drive to work. As a result, automobiles crowd the area's highways and pollute the air with exhaust fumes.

Economy. The value of Melbourne's manufactured products totals about 30 per cent of Australia's factory output and about 85 per cent of Victoria's. The chief products include automobiles, chemicals, food products, machinery, and textiles. The city's more than 10,000 factories employ about 400,000 workers. The home offices of many banking, insurance, and real estate companies are in Melbourne. The city is the headquarters of the Broken Hill Proprietary Company, Australia's largest corporation. This company mines ores and makes steel and steel products. Port Melbourne serves oceangoing vessels. The Melbourne area has an international airport at Tullamarine.

History. Aborigines lived in the Melbourne area before white settlers first arrived. John Batman, an Australian farmer, founded Melbourne in June, 1835. Batman represented a group of people from the nearby island of Tasmania who wanted land for sheep farms. He bought 600,000 acres (240,000 hectares) from the Aborigines and paid them with blankets, tomahawks, and other goods. In October, 1835, another group of settlers from Tasmania arrived. They were led by John Pascoe Fawkner. The governor of New South Wales later named the village in honor of William

Lillian N. Bolstad from Peter Arnold

Melbourne is an important center of Australian commerce and industry. The city and its suburbs form Australia's second largest metropolitan area. Beautiful parks and gardens line the Yarra River, which flows through the city.

Lamb, Viscount Melbourne, the British prime minister.

Melbourne was incorporated as a city in 1847. In 1851, part of New South Wales became a separate colony named Victoria, with Melbourne as its capital. That same year, miners discovered gold in Victoria, and a gold rush began. The city's population jumped from 23,000 in 1851 to 140,000 in 1861. It was Australia's largest city from 1856 until Sydney outgrew it in 1902. Melbourne also served as the capital of Australia from 1901 until 1927, when Canberra replaced it.

World War II (1939-1945) brought new industries and workers to the Melbourne area. The city grew steadily during the 1950's and 1960's. By the mid-1970's, it had about 2½ million people.　BARRY O. JONES

See also AUSTRALIA (pictures).

MELCHER, FREDERIC GERSHOM (1879-1963), won the Regina medal in 1962 for his contributions to children's literature. In 1919, he helped found Children's Book Week. He established the Newbery medal in 1921 for the outstanding children's book of the year, and the Caldecott medal in 1937 for the best-illustrated children's book of the year. Born in Malden, Mass., Melcher was co-editor of *Publishers' Weekly* for 40 years, and also served as board chairman of the R. R. Bowker Publishing Company. See also CALDECOTT MEDAL; LITERATURE FOR CHILDREN (Awards); NEWBERY MEDAL; REGINA MEDAL.

MELCHIOR. See MAGI.

MELCHIOR, *MEHL kee awr,* **LAURITZ LEBRECHT HOMMEL** (1890-1973), was a Danish operatic tenor. He won fame for his performances of roles in Richard Wagner's operas. He sang the role of Siegfried more than 100 times.

Melchior began his career as a boy soprano in Copenhagen, where he was born. He studied at the Royal Opera School there, and made his adult debut in 1913 as a baritone in *La Traviata.* He first appeared as a tenor in 1918.　DANIEL A. HARRIS

MELILOT. See CLOVER (Sweet Clover).

MELLETTE, ARTHUR CALVIN. See SOUTH DAKOTA (History).

MELLON, ANDREW WILLIAM (1855-1937), was an American financier. President Warren G. Harding appointed him secretary of the treasury in 1921. He served until 1932 under Presidents Harding, Calvin Coolidge, and Herbert Hoover. Mellon was often called the greatest secretary of the treasury after Alexander Hamilton. While he was in office, the government reduced its World War I debt by $9 billion, and Congress cut income-tax rates substantially.

Mellon was born in Pittsburgh of wealthy parents. In 1886, he joined his father's bank, Thomas Mellon and Sons, and became a shrewd judge of which new businesses and young business people deserved loans. Mellon served as an officer or director of many financial and industrial corporations. He became especially active in the development of the coal, coke, oil, and alumi-

Bettmann Archive
Andrew Mellon

num industries. By 1921, he had become one of the wealthiest men in America. Mellon served as ambassador to Great Britain in 1932 and 1933. In 1937, he gave his $25-million art collection to the U.S. government. He also donated $15 million for a museum to house it. This museum, the National Gallery of Art in Washington, D.C., opened in 1941 (see NATIONAL GALLERY OF ART).　DONALD L. KEMMERER

MELLON FOUNDATION, ANDREW W., is an organization that grants funds to institutions in the fields of higher education, cultural affairs, and the performing arts. It also provides funds for certain civic and social service programs. The foundation does not make grants to individuals or to strictly local organizations outside the New York City area. It ranks as one of the 10 wealthiest foundations in the United States. For assets, see FOUNDATIONS (table).

The foundation was established in 1969 in memory of Andrew W. Mellon, an American financier. Mellon's daughter and son, Ailsa Mellon Bruce and Paul Mellon, formed it by combining the Avalon Foundation and the Old Dominion Foundation. Ailsa had set up Avalon in 1940, and Paul established Old Dominion in 1941. The Andrew W. Mellon Foundation has headquarters at 140 East 62nd Street, New York, N.Y. 10021.　Critically reviewed by the ANDREW W. MELLON FOUNDATION

MELLON INSTITUTE. See CARNEGIE-MELLON UNIVERSITY.

MELLOPHONE is a wind instrument made of brass. It has three valves and is shaped like the French horn. The mellophone is less expensive and easier to play than the French horn. It is sometimes used as a substitute for the French horn in school and marching bands. Its curved tube is half the length of the French horn's tube. The two instruments play in the same pitch. But the mellophone cannot produce the rich tones of the French horn. See also FRENCH HORN.

MELODRAMA. See DRAMA (Forms of Drama; Romanticism).

MELODY. See MUSIC (Melody).

MELON. See DOLPHIN.

MELON is the name of the fruit of several plants that belong to the *cucurbit* family. Melon plants have trailing or climbing stems that fasten themselves with tendrils to the objects they climb over. *Tendrils* are modified leaves that look like small coils of wire. The fruits, or melons, are round or somewhat egg-shaped. They range from 1 inch (2.5 centimeters) to 1 foot (30 centimeters) or more across. The fruits vary from tan and yellow to light or dark green. The flesh may be green, white, yellow, pink, or red. See also CASABA; MUSKMELON; WATERMELON.

Scientific Classification. Melons belong to the gourd family, *Cucurbitaceae.*　ARTHUR J. PRATT

MELOS, *MEE lahs,* or MÍLOS, is a Greek island in the Aegean Sea. It lies about midway between Athens and Crete. For location, see GREECE (map). Melos is famous as the place where a remarkable statue of Venus was found in 1820. This statue is called the Aphrodite of Melos, or the Venus de Milo (see VENUS DE MILO).

Melos is about 13 miles (21 kilometers) long and up to 8 miles (13 kilometers) wide. It covers about 60 square miles (155 square kilometers) and has about

4,503 persons. In the Stone Age, Melos was famous for its *obsidian* (volcanic glass) which was used for cutting tools. The Athenians seized the island in 416 B.C., and massacred the men there. Thucydides, the Greek historian, wrote about this event. During World War I, the British used the harbor of Melos for their naval expedition against the Turks at Gallipoli.   JOHN H. KENT

MELPOMENE. See MUSES.

MELTING POINT is the temperature at which a substance changes from a solid to a liquid. The melting points of different substances vary considerably. For example, tungsten has an extremely high melting point, 3410° C, but solid hydrogen melts at the low temperature of −259° C.

The melting point of a material depends partly on whether it is a *pure substance* or a *mixture*. A pure substance is either a pure element, such as iron, or a simple compound, such as water. A mixture consists of two or more substances that are not chemically combined.

A pure substance melts at a definite temperature or within an extremely narrow temperature range. For example, when iron is heated, its temperature increases until the metal reaches its melting point of 1535° C. The iron remains at that temperature until all of the metal has melted.

Mixtures do not melt at a specific temperature. Simple mixtures, such as brass and steel, melt over a range of temperatures. For example, steel, which is a mixture of iron and other elements, has a melting point of 1400° C to 1500° C. Thus, the temperature of steel rises 100° during the melting process instead of remaining constant. Such complex mixtures as glass, tar, and wax do not melt over a specific temperature range. Instead, these substances gradually become softer and more fluid as their temperature increases.

Most simple mixtures have a different melting point than any of the pure substances that they contain. Brass, an alloy of copper and zinc, melts over a range of 900° C to 1000° C. However, the melting point of copper is 1083.4° C, and that of zinc is 419.58° C.

Chemists can determine the purity of a particular substance by finding its melting point. In most cases, a solid is a pure substance if it melts at a specific temperature or over a narrow temperature range. The solid is a mixture if it melts over a much broader temperature range.

The melting point of a substance is affected to some extent by atmospheric pressure. An increase in this pressure raises the melting point of most substances. But an increase in atmospheric pressure lowers the melting point of water and of the few other substances that expand when they freeze.

The liquid form of a pure substance freezes at the same temperature at which its solid form melts. Thus, the solid and liquid forms can exist together at the melting point without any temperature change in either. For example, if any proportions of ice and water are stirred together, the temperature of the substance will be 0° C. This temperature is the point at which ice melts and water freezes. If no heat is added or removed, the ice will melt at the same rate as the water freezes. Thus, the amounts of ice and water remain the same. However, if the ice water is heated, the ice will melt.

If the temperature is lowered below the melting point, the water will freeze.

The solid and liquid forms of a mixture can exist together over a range of temperatures. This range is determined by the type and amount of each of the pure substances in the mixture.

Some pure solids do not melt when heated. Instead, they change directly from a solid to a gas. Such substances as arsenic, dry ice, and iodine go through this process, which is called *sublimation*. They can be changed into liquid form only if kept under pressure in a closed container.   JOHN P. CHESICK

See also FREEZING POINT.

MELTING POT. See UNITED STATES (Population and Ancestry).

MELVILLE, HERMAN (1819-1891), ranks among America's major authors. He wrote *Moby Dick*, one of the great novels in literature, and his reputation rests largely on this book. But many of his other works are literary creations of a high order—blending fact, fiction, adventure, and subtle symbolism. Melville's wealth of personal experience in faraway places was remarkable even in the footloose and exploring world of the 1800's. Melville brought to his extraordinary adventures a vivid imagination, and a remarkable skill in handling the new American language.

Herman Melville by A. W. Twitchell. The Berkshire Athenaeum, Pittsfield, Mass.

Herman Melville

His Early Life. Melville was born in New York City. The family name was Melvill, and he added the "e" to the name. His father was a well-to-do merchant from New England, and his mother came from an old and socially prominent New York Dutch family. Melville lived his first 11 years in New York City. Then his father died after suffering a financial and mental breakdown in 1831 and the family moved to Albany, N.Y.

Young, inexperienced, and now poor, Melville tried a variety of jobs between 1832 and 1841. He was a clerk in his brother's hat store in Albany, worked in his uncle's bank, taught in a school near Pittsfield, Mass., and, in 1837, sailed to Liverpool, England, as a cabin boy on a merchant ship. He described this voyage in his novel *Redburn*. Melville returned to America and signed on the newly built whaling ship *Acushnet* for a trip in the Pacific Ocean. From this trip came the basic experiences recorded in several of his books, and above all, the whaling knowledge Melville later put into *Moby Dick*.

Melville sailed from New Bedford, Mass., on Jan. 3, 1841. He stayed on the *Acushnet* for 18 months, helping to catch and cut up whales. But when the *Acushnet* put in at Nukahiva in the Marquesas Islands, he and a shipmate *jumped* (deserted) ship. The two men headed inland until they accidentally came to the lovely valley of the Typees, a Polynesian tribe with a reputation as fierce cannibals. However, the natives turned out to be gentle and charming hosts. Melville described his experiences with these people in *Typee*.

Melville lived in the valley for about a month. He then joined another whaling ship, but he soon deserted it with other sailors in a semimutiny at Tahiti. After a few days in a local jail, Melville and a new friend began roaming the beautiful and unspoiled islands of Tahiti and Moorea. Melville described his life during these wanderings in the novel *Omoo*.

After short service on a third whaling ship, Melville landed at the Sandwich Islands, where he lived by doing odd jobs. On Aug. 17, 1844, he enlisted as a seaman on the frigate *United States*, flagship of the Navy's Pacific Squadron. He recounted his long voyage around Cape Horn to the United States in the novel *White-Jacket*.

Melville arrived in Boston Harbor in October, 1844. He was released from the Navy and headed home to Albany, his imagination overflowing with his adventures.

His Literary Career. Melville wrote about his experiences so attractively that he soon became one of the most popular writers of his time. The books that made his reputation were *Typee* (1846); *Omoo* (1847); *Mardi* (1849), a complex allegorical romance set in the South Seas; *Redburn* (1849); and *White-Jacket* (1850).

Melville then began *Moby Dick*, another "whaling voyage," as he called it, similar to his successful travel books. He had almost completed the book when he met Nathaniel Hawthorne. Hawthorne inspired him to radically revise the whaling documentary into a novel of both universal significance and literary complexity.

Moby Dick, or The Whale (1851), on one level, is the story of the hunt for Moby Dick, a fierce white whale actually known to sailors of Melville's time. Captain Ahab is the captain of the whaling ship *Pequod*. He has lost a leg in an earlier battle with Moby Dick, and is determined to catch the whale. The novel brilliantly describes the dangerous and often violent life on a whaling ship, and contains information on the whaling industry and a discussion of the nature of whales. On another level *Moby Dick* is a deeply symbolic story. The whale represents the mysterious and complex force of the universe, and Captain Ahab represents the heroic struggle against the limiting and crippling constrictions which confront an intelligent and non-passive person.

Curiously, Melville's popularity began to decline with the publication of his masterpiece. The novel, either ignored or misunderstood by critics and readers, damaged Melville's reputation as a writer. When Melville followed *Moby Dick* with the pessimistic and tragic novel *Pierre* (1853), his readers began to desert him, calling him either eccentric or mad. The public was ready to accept unusual and exciting adventures, but they did not want ironic, frightening exposures of the terrible double meanings in life.

Melville turned to writing short stories. Two of them, "Benito Cereno" and "Bartleby the Scrivener," rank as classics. Several of the stories were collected in *The Piazza Tales* (1856). But the haunting and disturbing question of the meaning of life that hovered over the stories also displeased the public. In 1855, Melville published *Israel Potter*, a novel set in the American Revolution. After *The Confidence-Man* (1856), a bitter satire on humanity, he gave up writing.

His Later Life. To make a living, Melville worked as deputy inspector of customs in the Port of New York from 1866 to 1885. For private pleasure he wrote poetry, which he published at his own and his uncle's expense.

He toured the Holy Land in 1856 and 1857. The trip resulted in a narrative poem *Clarel* (1876), which is 10,000 lines long. *Clarel* is one of Melville's least read works. The poem gives a powerful picture of a man's struggle to find his faith in a skeptical, materialistic world.

Melville began writing prose again after his retirement. At his death, he left the manuscript of *Billy Budd*. This short novel, published in 1924, is considered Melville's finest book after *Moby Dick*. It is a symbolic story about the clash between innocence and evil, and between social forms and individual liberty.

The 1920's marked the start of a Melville revival among critics and readers. By the 1940's, Americans at last recognized his genius. His reputation has since spread throughout the world.　　　HOWARD PATON VINCENT

MELVILLE, LAKE. See NEWFOUNDLAND (Rivers and Lakes).

MELVILLE ISLAND is one of a group of islands in the Arctic Ocean, north of Canada. It lies between Prince Patrick and Bathurst islands, and is one of the Parry Islands. The island covers about 16,300 square miles (42,220 square kilometers). It stretches nearly 200 miles (320 kilometers) from east to west, and about 130 miles (209 kilometers) at its widest north to south point. Frozen seas surround it most of the year. Sir William Parry of Great Britain became the first European to reach Melville in 1819, when he was searching for a northwest passage to Asia. The island is governed as part of the Northwest Territories of Canada. D. F. PUTNAM

See also CANADA (physical map).

MELVILLE PENINSULA is a wilderness region north of Hudson Bay in the Northwest Territories of Canada. It is about 250 miles (402 kilometers) long and about 140 miles (225 kilometers) wide at its widest point. Rae Isthmus connects it with the mainland. The straits of Fury and Hecla on the north separate it from Baffin Island. West of Melville is Committee Bay. East of it is Foxe Channel. D. F. PUTNAM

MEMBRANE is a thin sheet of tissues that covers surfaces or separates spaces in the body. There are three types of membranes—fibrous, serous, and mucous. These vary greatly in thickness and in the types of cells composing them.

Fibrous Membranes are tough and add strength to the parts they cover. They are made up entirely of fibrous connective tissue (see TISSUE [Connective Tissue]). The fibrous membrane that lines the inside of the skull is called *dura mater*. The *periosteum* is a fibrous membrane that covers the bones. The periosteum also serves as an attachment for muscles, and contains the blood vessels and nerves of the bones.

Serous Membranes line body cavities which do not open to the outside, such as the thorax and abdomen. They also cover the outside of the digestive organs and support them. The serous membranes secrete a watery fluid. This fluid keeps the membranes moist and prevents their sticking to each other or to the organs they touch. A serous membrane lines the *pericardium*, the sac around the heart (see HEART [Its Parts and Development]). Other serous membranes include the *pleura*, which lines the lung cavities, and the *peritoneum*, which lines the cavity of the abdomen (see PLEURA). Inflammation of the peritoneum is known as *peritonitis*. A serous membrane called the *synovial membrane* lines the cavities of the joints. It secretes a watery fluid that lubricates the joints and helps them move easily and smoothly. The largest of the synovial cavities is in the knee.

Mucous Membranes line organs and passages of the body that open to the outside. A clear, sticky fluid called *mucus* covers mucous membranes (see MUCUS). Glands just under the membranes produce the mucus. Mucous membranes form the lining of the mouth, throat, alimentary canal, reproductive system, nose, windpipe and lungs, the inner surfaces of the eyelids, and the Eustachian tube.   WILLIAM V. MAYER

MEMEL. See KLAIPĚDA.

MEMEL, TERRITORY OF, was made up of the town of Memel (now called Klaipěda) and a small strip of land on the coast of the Baltic Sea near Lithuania. Germany controlled the territory until the end of World War I. The Treaty of Versailles forced Germany to turn the territory over to the Allies. For the next three years, Memel remained under their control. In January, 1923, citizens of Lithuania seized Memel to get an outlet to the Baltic Sea. The Council of the League of Nations accepted the seizure, and Memel became part of Lithuania.

The president of Lithuania appointed a governor to rule the territory. The governor, in turn, appointed a council of five Memel citizens to assist him. A legislature of Memel citizens passed on the decisions of the council, but the governor could veto acts of the legislature. The legislature objected to the governor's power. But the Permanent Court of International Justice of the League of Nations ruled that he was within his rights.

Germany gained control of the territory in 1939. During World War II, Russian forces drove German troops out of Memel, and it became part of the Lithuanian Soviet Socialist Republic.   FRANCIS J. BOWMAN

MEMEL RIVER. See NEMAN RIVER.

MEMLING, HANS (1430?-1494), was a Flemish painter. His works are noted for their poetic beauty and technical perfection. He painted religious subjects, but is better known for the excellence of his portraits. Particularly famous are the small panels with which he decorated the Reliquary Shrine of St. Ursula in Bruges, Belgium. Memling was born in Seligenstadt, Germany, but spent most of his life in Bruges. Groups of his paintings hang in museums in Bruges.   JULIUS S. HELD

See also CLOTHING (picture: The Hennin).

MEMMINGER, CHRISTOPHER GUSTAVUS (1803-1888), an American statesman, served as secretary of the treasury for the Confederacy from 1861 to 1864. He tried unsuccessfully to reduce the amount of Confederate currency. When the credit of the Confederate government collapsed, many southerners blamed him and he resigned. Memminger was born in Württemberg, Germany. He came to Charleston, S.C., as a child.

MEMORABILIA OF SOCRATES. See XENOPHON.

MEMORIAL may take the form of a statue, monument, building, or park. Frequently, highways and streets, schools, churches, mountain peaks, and books are dedicated to the memory of heroes, public servants, or loved ones. Since ancient times, people have built memorials to preserve the memory of great persons or to commemorate important events and achievements. The

most common memorials are grave markers in cemeteries.   CHARLES L. WALLIS

Related Articles in WORLD BOOK include:

Arc de Triomphe	Monument
Christ of the Andes	National Park System
Jefferson Memorial	Sarcophagus
John F. Kennedy Center for the Performing Arts	Statue of Liberty
	Unknown Soldier
Lincoln Memorial	Washington Monument

MEMORIAL DAY, or DECORATION DAY, is a patriotic holiday in the United States. It is a day to honor Americans who gave their lives for their country. Originally, Memorial Day honored military personnel who died in the Civil War. It now also honors those who died in the Spanish-American War, World Wars I and II, the Korean War, and the Vietnam War.

Memorial Day is a legal holiday in most states. Most Northern States and some Southern States observe Memorial Day the last Monday in May. This date was made a federal holiday by a law that became effective in 1971. Most of the Southern States also have their own days for honoring the Confederate dead. Mississippi celebrates the last Monday in April as Confederate Memorial Day. Alabama celebrates on the fourth Monday in April. Georgia observes this holiday on April 26. North Carolina and South Carolina celebrate it on May 10. Virginia observes the holiday on the last Monday in May. Louisiana observes it on June 3, and Tennessee has a holiday called Confederate Decoration Day on that date. Texas celebrates Confederate Heroes Day on January 19.

Observance. On Memorial Day, people place flowers and flags on the graves of military personnel. Many organizations, including Boy Scouts, Girl Scouts, and fraternal groups, march in military parades and take part in special programs. These programs often include the reading of Abraham Lincoln's "Gettysburg Address." Memorials are often dedicated on this day. Military exercises and special programs are held at Gettysburg National Military Park and at the National Cemetery in Arlington, Va. To honor those who died at sea, some U.S. ports also organize ceremonies where tiny ships filled with flowers are set afloat on the water.

Since the end of World War I, Memorial Day has also been Poppy Day. Ex-servicemen sell small, red artificial poppies to help disabled veterans (see POPPY WEEK). In recent years, the custom has grown in most families to decorate the graves of loved ones on Memorial Day.

History. Several communities claim to have originated Memorial Day. But in 1966, the U.S. government proclaimed Waterloo, N.Y., the birthplace of the holiday. The people of Waterloo first observed Memorial Day on May 5, 1866, to honor soldiers who had died in the Civil War. Businesses were closed, and people decorated soldiers' graves and flew flags at half-mast.

Major General John A. Logan in 1868 named May 30 as a special day for honoring the graves of Union soldiers. Logan served as commander in chief of the Grand Army of the Republic, an organization of Union veterans of the Civil War. They had charge of Memorial Day celebrations in the Northern States for many years. The American Legion took over this duty after World War I.   ELIZABETH HOUGH SECHRIST

MEMORIAL UNIVERSITY OF NEWFOUNDLAND is a coeducational university supported by the province. The main campus is in St. John's and the Western Regional College is in Corner Brook. The university offers degree programs in arts, commerce, education, engineering, medicine, music, nursing, physical education, science, social work, and vocational education. The regional college offers two-year programs in arts and sciences. Queen's College, an Anglican divinity college on the St. John's campus, and Christian Brothers College, a Roman Catholic college at Mono Mills, Ont., are affiliated with the university.

Memorial University was founded in 1925. It became a degree-granting university in 1949. For its enrollment, see CANADA (table: Universities and Colleges).

Critically reviewed by MEMORIAL UNIVERSITY OF NEWFOUNDLAND

MEMORY. See COMPUTER (Memory).

MEMORY is the ability to keep a mental record of earlier experiences. Basically, memory is learning. Every person learns a great many things. For example, a person may learn to ride a bicycle. This is a *skill*. Or a person may learn the names of all the Presidents of the United States. This is a *verbal response*. A person also may learn to be afraid of snakes. This is an *emotional response*. Some skills, verbal responses, and emotional responses may be remembered throughout life. Others may be forgotten. Verbal responses are usually forgotten more easily than are skills or emotional responses.

Why We Forget

Psychologists are interested in the problems of memory. They want to find out why we forget things, and what we can do to remember better.

Look at the following list of grocery items: milk, butter, eggs, bread, steak, LETTUCE, peas, potatoes, apples, and pudding. With practice, you could learn this list of 10 items. In time, however, you will forget the list. An hour after first learning it, you might be able to remember about five of the items. A day or two later you might remember only one or two items. A week later you might not remember any of them.

The above example shows that time is one of the important factors in forgetting. Usually, a person forgets more and more as time goes on. Memory loss is greatest shortly after the original learning. After that, it is more gradual. There are some kinds of material that a person remembers better a little while after learning, rather than immediately after learning. For example, a person who spends five minutes memorizing a poem may find it can be recited better the next day than immediately after the five minutes of study. This improvement after a period of time is called *reminiscence*.

Some psychologists believe that time by itself does not produce loss of memory. They believe that the events that occur in time produce the failure to remember. A person will remember more items on a list eight hours later if learning them just before going to bed, than if learning them in the morning. Less forgetting occurs during sleep than during the day, probably because fewer events interfere with the recently learned material. Daily events, rather than the passage of time, interfere with the ability to remember learned material.

Some forms of activity interfere with remembering more than others do. Learning to ride a bicycle should have no effect on the number of items remembered on the grocery list. But learning another grocery list, with different items, would almost certainly interfere with remembering the first list accurately. This type of inter-

ference is called *retroactive inhibition*. In general, the more similar the second activity is to the first, the more it interferes with remembering the first activity.

The Process of Remembering

What Do We Remember? In a list of items, such as the grocery list, some of the items will be remembered better than others. One of the important things that determines whether an item is easily remembered or not is its position in the list. If the item is near the beginning of the list or near the end, it will be remembered fairly easily. If it is near the middle, it will not be easily remembered. For example, in the grocery list, milk and pudding should be fairly easy to remember. Psychologists call this the *serial position effect*.

The same difficulty in remembering material near the middle also occurs in material that is not in list form. For example, if a person hears a great many arguments during a debate, those arguments near the beginning and the end will be remembered best. Good public speakers know that in order to convince people of a point of view, they should place their best arguments at the beginning and at the end of their speeches.

In a list, any item that stands out in any way will be better remembered than the other items. On the grocery list, the word *LETTUCE* will be easier to remember because it is the only word written in capital letters. Anything that can be done to give emphasis to a word will help that word to be remembered.

People can remember words that mean something to them more easily than words that do not. Familiar words are easier to remember than unfamiliar words. A grocery list is much easier to remember than a list of *nonsense syllables*. Nonsense syllables are a series of letters that do not make up a word, and do not immediately suggest any word. Many nonsense syllables are made up of three letters: a consonant, a vowel, and another consonant. For example, *kud* would be a nonsense syllable. Psychologists use nonsense syllables to study memory.

How Much Do We Remember? Psychologists use three methods to determine how much a person remembers. These methods are: (1) recall, (2) recognition, and (3) relearning.

The most natural way to find out how much people remember of a grocery list is to ask them what they remember. This is called the method of *recall*. Another method, called *recognition*, is to ask them to separate items on the original list from items that were not on the list. Usually people will be able to recognize material that they cannot recall. However, they will not be able to recall material that they cannot recognize. Police often use the method of recognition to identify a suspect in a lineup. If a person selects the correct individual in the lineup, that person has recognized and remembered the suspect.

A third method of determining how much people remember is called the method of *relearning*. Here they are asked to relearn the original list. They will probably learn the list the second time faster than they did the first time. The difference in the time it takes to relearn the list is considered a measure of how much has been remembered. Sometimes people will not be able to recall the grocery list, and may not even be able to recognize it. Yet, they will be able to relearn the material more quickly than the first time. This shows that something was remembered even though the people were not aware of remembering.

How to Remember. If you really learn material well, you will remember well. Suppose you wanted to remember the grocery list of 10 items for a week or two. This might require *overlearning*. If you practice the list only until you are able to recall each item once, you may not remember the entire list for long. But if you continue to memorize the list long after you think you know it perfectly, you will remember the list much longer.

Recitation during the original learning process also helps the memory. While learning the list, you should repeat the items over and over to yourself.

You should try to remember the entire list as one *single unit*, rather than learn the first half one day and second half another day. This may be discouraging at first when you try to remember a very long list. But, in the long run, you learn it faster and remember it longer.

The longer the list is, the more items you will remember. You will remember more if you have learned more. But, you will remember most things that you have learned only if you have not learned too much.

Memorizing. Teachers and psychologists have differed widely in their opinions about the value of memorizing. But they generally agree there is little use memorizing things that have no particular meaning for the person who memorizes them. Children should not be encouraged to learn facts in the language of a textbook and repeat them word for word. It is much more important for them to understand the meaning of what they are learning, and to use facts to connect new knowledge with things learned previously. If they do this, children are more likely to remember what they learn.

Improving the Memory. A reliable memory is so important to success in life that people have spent much time inventing ways of improving the memory. The art of strengthening the memory by using certain formal or mechanical methods of remembering is called *mnemonics*. Mnemonics tries to make remembering easy by using various kinds of tricks or associations. For example, almost everyone remembers how many days there are in each month by repeating a jingle that begins:

> Thirty days hath September,
> April, June, and November,
> All the rest have thirty-one
> Excepting February alone . . .

But in order to remember a great many facts by using such devices, you also have to remember a great many devices. It may then become harder to remember the device than the thing you want to remember.

Loss of Memory. Sometimes people cannot remember the name of someone they know well. Or, perhaps they cannot remember something that was "on the tip of the tongue." Such failures to remember things that are well known may be *motivated*. This means that people may have wanted to forget the name because they disliked that individual. People may be unable to remember what they were about to say for some equally good reason.

Sometimes things that are forgotten remain in the unconscious mind, and reveal themselves in dreams or in some other way. People may feel uncomfortable in high places, or be afraid in the dark, without knowing why. The reason may be that as children they had unpleasant experiences, which they forgot later in life.

Some people suffer from the condition known as *amnesia*. These people have lost their memories, not their memory. They have forgotten, at least in their conscious mind, everything that happened before the emotional shock or accident that caused the amnesia. But they may be able to remember perfectly what happened just afterward, and their ability to memorize a set of historical dates or some other group of facts is usually as good as ever. See AMNESIA.

Individual Differences

Unusual Memories. One often hears of people who have miraculous memories. They never forget a face or a name. They can repeat whole books word for word, or they can play whole symphonies after having heard them once. Some persons who have excellent memories for detail may actually "see" the material when they remember it. This is known as *eidetic imagery*. Many persons with eidetic imagery can tell the exact position of a statement on a textbook page. They can glance at an object for only a second or two, and then give a complete description of it, based on their image.

People with eidetic imagery are often said to have a *photographic memory*. Actually, their memory is not photographic. If people had a true photographic memory, they would be able to glance at a page and then recite the words on the page from left to right or from bottom to top. People with eidetic imagery cannot do this. Eidetic imagery is rare in adults. But many children under 14 years of age can visualize objects with amazing clarity, and correctly answer detailed questions about them.

Normal Memories. Ordinary persons are likely to feel discouraged when they read about persons with extraordinary memories. Many people have trouble remembering the motion picture they saw last week or the errand they promised to do today. They may say to themselves, "I have no memory." But this is not true. Every person has a memory. People who had no memory would not be able to recognize their own parents, or even their own face in the mirror.

Some persons have excellent memories, and others have poor memories. However, certain general statements can be made about the memories of most persons. Memory tends to improve up to the time of maturity. After that, there may be a very gradual decline in the ability to remember things. Furthermore, the higher the person's intelligence, the better the person will be able to remember. RUSSELL M. CHURCH

See also LEARNING DISABILITIES.

MEMPHIS, *MEM fis*, was the first capital of ancient Egypt. According to tradition, Menes, who lived about 3100 B.C. and was the first king of Egypt, founded the city and made it his capital. Memphis stood near the site of present-day Cairo. During the Old Kingdom (2700-2200 B.C.), kings built pyramids at Giza and Ṣaqqārah near Memphis. The city was Egypt's capital until about 2200 B.C., and was an important religious and political center until about 330 B.C. Nothing remains of the ancient city itself. But cemeteries and the pyramids at Giza and Ṣaqqārah stand as reminders of the city's past glory.   BARBARA MERTZ

See also EGYPT, ANCIENT (map; History).

MEMPHIS is the largest city in Tennessee. It lies on a bluff on the east bank of the Mississippi River in the southwest corner of the state. Memphis serves as the commercial and industrial center of western Tennessee and parts of neighboring states.

Cotton and river trade accounted for much of the city's early growth. By 1900, Memphis was the world's largest market for cotton and hardwood lumber. It is still a leader in these activities. But industrial expansion since the end of World War II in 1945 has made Memphis one of the South's largest urban centers. The city has also become a center of higher education, medical care, motel development, and recorded music.

Memphis was named for the ancient Egyptian capital of Memphis, which lay on the Nile River. Settlers chose the site because the nearby Wolf River flowed into the Mississippi and provided an excellent harbor. The bluff site also furnished protection from floods.

The City covers 272 square miles (704 square kilometers) and is the county seat of Shelby County. The Memphis metropolitan area consists of Shelby and Tipton counties in Tennessee; Crittenden County, Arkansas; and DeSoto County, Mississippi. The metropolitan area totals 2,379 square miles (6,162 square kilometers).

The Mississippi River flows to the west of Memphis, and the Tennessee-Mississippi state line forms the southern boundary of the city. Memphis suburbs include Arlington, Bartlett, and Germantown, Tenn.; and West Memphis, Ark., which lies west of the river. Millington, another suburb, is the home of Naval Air Station Memphis. The Naval Air Technical Training Center at this air base trains more naval aircraft maintenance technicians than any other installation in the world.

Downtown Memphis extends east from the Mississippi to Third Street. It is bounded on the north by Poplar Avenue and on the south by Calhoun Avenue. The Memphis Civic Center stands on the north edge of the downtown area. The center consists of City Hall and county, state, and federal buildings. Nearby is the Memphis Municipal Auditorium. All these structures formed part of an urban renewal project that replaced large slum areas. A $27-million convention and exhibition center, connected to the auditorium, opened in 1974.

On the south edge of the business district is Beale Street, where the composer W. C. Handy worked as a

---

MEMPHIS

musician and wrote some of his music. Handy made this street famous in his song "Beale Street Blues."

The People. Almost all the people of Memphis were born in the United States. Blacks comprise about 40 per cent of the city's population. Other groups, in order of size, include those of Italian, German, Polish, and English descent.

Baptists make up the city's largest religious group. Memphis also has many Catholics, Episcopalians, and Methodists. It is often called the *City of Churches* because of its many beautiful houses of worship.

Poverty in the black community is a major problem in Memphis. Large numbers of blacks live in crowded, run-down dwellings in areas north and south of the downtown district. Many have little education and few work skills, and they cannot find jobs.

Like many other cities, Memphis has had racial problems. In 1968, the civil rights leader Martin Luther King, Jr., was assassinated in Memphis by James Earl Ray, a native of Illinois and an escaped convict. King had gone to Memphis to support a strike by city sanitation workers, most of whom were blacks. His death strained race relations in the city, but black and white leaders gradually eased the tension.

After King's death, the city made efforts to improve living conditions in the black community. Memphis worked with federal agencies to train blacks for jobs and to help blacks establish businesses. The Memphis Housing Authority rebuilt many old dwellings and constructed some low-rental dwellings. In addition, a project called the Greater Memphis Program gained wide support. This program aimed at creating jobs for the unemployed by attracting new industry to Memphis. The Memphis Area Chamber of Commerce sponsored the project.

The Economy. Memphis is the trade center of a region consisting of western Tennessee, eastern Arkansas, northern Mississippi, northwestern Alabama, western Kentucky, and southeastern Missouri.

The Memphis metropolitan area has about 870 manufacturing plants. They annually produce goods worth about $1 billion. About 15 per cent of the city's labor force is employed in manufacturing. The chief manufacturing industries, in order of size, make chemicals, food and food products, paper and related products, electrical equipment, nonelectrical machinery, and lumber and wood products. Memphis leads the world in the manufacture of hardwood flooring and ranks as a major center for the manufacture of cottonseed products.

The city serves as the world's largest market for cotton and hardwood lumber. Each year, members of the Memphis Cotton Exchange buy and sell about a third of the cotton produced in the United States. Memphis also is one of the South's largest livestock, meat-packing, and wholesale marketing centers.

Memphis ranks behind only St. Louis as the busiest inland port on the Mississippi River. Memphis handles over 11 million short tons (10 million metric tons) of freight yearly and ships goods to all parts of the world.

Memphis has 20 hospitals and is one of the South's great medical centers. Most of the hospitals, plus the University of Tennessee Center for the Health Sciences, are in the downtown Memphis Medical Cen-

---

──────────── **FACTS IN BRIEF** ────────────

Population: *1975 Estimate*—City, 661,319. *1970 Census*—City, 623,530; Metropolitan Area, 834,103.

Area: *City*—272 sq. mi. (704 km²). *Metropolitan Area*—2,379 sq. mi. (6,162 km²).

Altitude: 331 ft. (101 m) above sea level.

Climate: *Average Temperature*—January, 43° F. (6° C); July, 80° F. (27° C). *Average Annual Precipitation* (rainfall, melted snow, and other forms of moisture)—50 in. (127 cm).

Government: Mayor-council. *Terms*—4 years for the mayor and for the 13 council members.

Founded: 1819. Incorporated as a city in 1849.

Memphis is Tennessee's largest city and chief center of commerce, industry, and transportation. Downtown Memphis, *above*, stretches along the east bank of the Mississippi River.

ter. Three world-wide motel chains have headquarters in Memphis, including Holiday Inns, Inc., the world's largest. The city also is an important music recording center.

Four bridges span the Mississippi River at Memphis. About 75 truck lines and 8 railroads carry cargo to and from the city. The National Railroad Passenger Corporation (Amtrak) provides rail passenger service between Memphis and other cities. About 10 airlines use Memphis International Airport.

Memphis has about 20 radio stations and 4 television stations. It also has two daily newspapers, the *Memphis Press-Scimitar* and *The Commercial Appeal*.

Education. The Memphis public school system consists of about 110 elementary schools and more than 50 junior and senior high schools. These schools have a total enrollment of approximately 148,000 students, over half of whom are blacks. Memphis also has about 55 private and church-supported schools with an enrollment of about 14,000.

School integration is a major problem in Memphis. The city started to desegregate its public schools in 1961. But 10 years later, most of the black students still attended all-black schools. In 1973, the Memphis school system began busing some black students to all-white schools and some white students to all-black schools as ordered by a federal court.

Memphis State University, the city's largest institution of higher learning, has an enrollment of about 20,000. Other colleges and universities in Memphis include Christian Brothers College, Harding Graduate School of Religion, LeMoyne-Owen College, the Memphis Academy of Arts, Southern College of Optometry, Southwestern at Memphis, and the University of Tennessee Center for the Health Sciences.

Cultural Life. The Memphis Symphony Orchestra performs at the Memphis Municipal Auditorium. The auditorium also presents touring Broadway plays and performances of the Metropolitan Opera Association.

The Brooks Memorial Art Gallery has a collection of Italian Renaissance painting and sculpture, plus many other exhibits. The Memphis Academy of Arts and several smaller galleries also feature art work. The Memphis Pink Palace Museum has exhibits on the natural history of Memphis and the surrounding region. The Memphis Little Theatre offers a regular season of plays.

The Memphis Public Library consists of a main library and 17 branches. It owns about 980,000 volumes.

Recreation. Memphis has about 130 parks covering more than 6,000 acres (2,400 hectares). The largest, 590-acre (239-hectare) McKellar Park, features fishing, golfing, and other activities. Overton Park includes one of the South's largest zoos and an aquarium.

A Cotton Carnival held in Memphis each May dramatizes the city's position as the world's largest cotton market. This nine-day festival features events that tell the story of the city and its cotton trade. The Mid-South Fairgrounds includes the Coliseum. The Mid-South Fair, held the last week in September, features agricultural and commercial exhibits.

Symbols of Memphis. The red, white, and blue in the flag of Memphis, *left*, represent the United States and Tennessee, both of which use those colors in their flags. The flag includes the city seal. The steamboat on the seal, *right*, symbolizes commerce.

Government. Memphis has a mayor-council form of government. The voters elect a mayor and 13 council members to four-year terms. Seven of the council members are elected from districts, and six are chosen *at large* (from throughout the city). Property taxes provide most of the city's funds.

History. Chickasaw Indians lived in what is now the Memphis area long before white settlers first came there. Hernando de Soto, a Spanish explorer, arrived in the area in 1541 and became the first white person to see the Mississippi River.

In 1673, Louis Jolliet, a French-Canadian explorer, and Father Jacques Marquette, a French missionary, visited the area to trade with the Indians. In 1682, the French explorer Robert Cavelier, Sieur de la Salle, built Fort Prud'homme near what is now Memphis and claimed the area for France. By the 1700's, France, Great Britain, and Spain had claimed the Tennessee region. The United States gained control of the area in the late 1700's. In 1818, the U.S. government bought much of western Tennessee from the Chickasaws. General Andrew Jackson, Judge John Overton, and General James Winchester became owners of 5,000 acres (2,000 hectares) of the land. In 1819, the three men organized a settlement there and named it Memphis.

During the early 1800's, cotton planters established large plantations near Memphis and in nearby fertile areas. Slave traders brought hundreds of blacks from New Orleans to the Memphis market to be sold to the plantation owners. Memphis became the largest slave market in the central South. River trade also flourished. Memphis was incorporated as a city in 1849.

In 1860, Memphis had a population of 23,000 and ranked as the South's sixth largest city. After the Civil War began in 1861, Memphis became a military center for the Confederacy. The city fell to Union forces in 1862. River trade suffered greatly during the war, and many plantations were destroyed. After the war, Memphis began to rebuild. But in the 1870's, a series of yellow fever epidemics struck the city. About half the population fled. In 1878, the worst of the epidemics killed about 5,200 of the 19,600 persons who still lived in Memphis. The state legislature took away the city's charter in 1879.

By 1890, trade had increased and the population had climbed to 64,500. In 1892, a railroad bridge was completed across the Mississippi at Memphis. The bridge increased trade with the Southwest, and Memphis soon became the world's largest inland center for cotton and hardwood lumber. Memphis regained its charter in 1893. During the late 1800's, large numbers of freed slaves moved to Memphis from plantations and small towns. Many became laborers in the cotton and lumber mills. Industrial expansion helped Memphis continue its growth in the 1900's.

In 1909, E. H. Crump was elected mayor of Memphis. Crump became one of the most powerful political bosses in the nation's history. Until his death in 1954, Crump controlled almost all politics in Memphis and some state politics as well.

By 1960, the city's population had grown to 498,000. During the 1960's, a building boom brought many new factories and skyscrapers to Memphis. Memphis International Airport opened in 1963. The area of Memphis increased by about 70 per cent through annexation of suburbs. The city's population grew by about 25 per cent, largely as a result of this annexation.

Memphis began to integrate its public schools and

CITY OF MEMPHIS

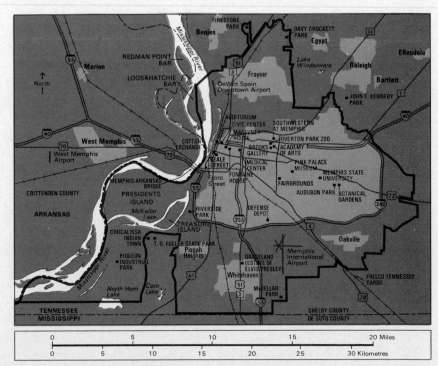

Memphis lies on the Mississippi River in southwestern Tennessee. It is the largest city in the state and an important shipping center. The map shows the main points of interest in the Memphis area.

——— City boundary

- - - - State boundary

▨ Built-up area

▨ Nonbuilt-up area

═══ Main road

——— Other road

┼┼┼ Rail line

• Point of interest

public facilities during the 1960's. Race relations became tense after James Earl Ray, a native Illinoisan, assassinated Martin Luther King, Jr., in Memphis in 1968. Efforts of black leaders and white leaders to improve conditions for the city's blacks eased the tension. Urban renewal projects eliminated many slum areas in the 1960's, and additional urban renewal took place during the 1970's. Civic improvements scheduled for completion in the early 1980's include the Beale Street renewal program.   EDGAR W. RAY

See also TENNESSEE (pictures).

MEMPHIS ACADEMY OF ARTS. See UNIVERSITIES AND COLLEGES (table).

MEMPHIS STATE UNIVERSITY. See UNIVERSITIES AND COLLEGES (table).

MEMPHREMAGOG. See LAKE MEMPHREMAGOG.

MENAGERIE. See CIRCUS (The Side Shows); ZOO (History).

MENANDER (342?-291? B.C.) was a Greek playwright who wrote over 100 comedies. We know his work only through fragments of his plays, adaptations of his plots by the Roman dramatists Terence and Plautus, and one whole play, *Dyscolos* (The Grouch), discovered in 1959.

Menander was born and lived in Athens during a troubled political period when powerful figures like Alexander the Great controlled political and military affairs. Writers then turned their attention to the experience of the individual in society. Menander's comedies dramatize humorous situations, especially in love affairs, in middle-class society. He is noted for his plot construction, characterization, clear style, and sympathetic view of humanity.   NORMAN T. PRATT

MENCIUS, *MEHN shee uhs* (390?-305? B.C.), was a major Chinese philosopher. He was one of the most influential figures in the development of the Chinese philosophy called Confucianism.

Mencius is best known for his belief that human nature is good. He also believed that the people of a nation were justified in deposing or even killing a bad ruler. Mencius defined a bad ruler as one who ignored the people's welfare and governed them unkindly. Many of Mencius' ideas appear in the *Meng-tzu*, a book that is probably a collection of his teachings.

Mencius was born in the state of Tsou, in what is now Shantung Province. His real name was Meng K'e. The name *Mencius* is the Latin form of *Meng-tzu*, a title that means *Master Meng*. Scholars know nothing about Mencius' early life except for information in some unreliable legends. Mencius served as political adviser for a number of Chinese rulers but later became tired of politics. He returned to Tsou, where he spent the rest of his life.   DAVID R. KNECHTGES

See also CONFUCIANISM (Early Confucianism).

MENCKEN, H. L. (1880-1956), was an American critic, editor, and journalist. He is best known for his attacks on American taste and culture and for his study of the American language. In witty and often savage language, Mencken criticized what he considered the shallowness and conceit of the American middle class. He also aided and called attention to new writers, including Sherwood Anderson, Theodore Dreiser, and Eugene O'Neill.

Mencken's *The American Language* (1919), made a sig-

nificant contribution to the study of language. In this work, which was revised and supplemented several times, Mencken examined the development of the English language in America. He praised the acceptance of new words and forms of expression as a reflection of the American style of life.

Henry Louis Mencken was born in Baltimore. He began his literary career in 1899 as a reporter for the *Baltimore Morning Herald*. From 1906 to 1941, he worked chiefly as a reporter, editor, and columnist for the *Baltimore Sun*.

In 1908, Mencken became drama critic of the magazine *Smart Set*. He and George Jean Nathan served as coeditors from 1914 to 1923. In 1924, he and Nathan founded *The American Mercury*, a magazine of humor and comments about American customs and politics. Both publications featured works by new writers and much of Mencken's criticism.

A. Aubrey Bodine

H. L. Mencken

Mencken's criticism and essays were collected in the six-volume *Prejudices*, published from 1919 to 1927. His other works include *The Philosophy of Friedrich Nietzsche* (1908) and a three-volume autobiography—*Happy Days, 1880-1892* (1940); *Newspaper Days, 1899-1906* (1941); and *Heathen Days, 1890-1936* (1943). DEAN DONER

MENDAÑA, ÁLVARO DE. See SOLOMON ISLANDS (country); MARQUESAS ISLANDS.

MENDEL, GREGOR JOHANN (1822-1884), an Austrian botanist and monk, formulated the basic laws of heredity. His experiments with the breeding of garden peas led to the development of the science of genetics.

His Life. Mendel was born in Heinzendorf, Austria (now Hynčice, Czechoslovakia, near Krnov). His parents were poor peasants. Mendel was an excellent student, and he decided to become a teacher. Many teachers at that time were priests. Therefore, in 1843, at the age of 21, Mendel entered the monastery of St. Thomas in Brünn, Austria (now Brno, Czechoslovakia). He became a priest in 1847.

The monastery was a scientific as well as a religious center, and Mendel was exposed to many scholars there. In 1851, the monastery sent him to study science and mathematics at the University of Vienna. He returned to the monastery in 1853 and taught biology and physics at a local high school for the next 14 years. Mendel's fame came from his research in the monastery garden during those years.

In 1868, Mendel was elected abbot of the monastery. From then on, his administrative responsibilities limited his opportunities for research.

His Work. In his experiments, Mendel studied the inheritance of seven pairs of traits in garden pea plants and in their seeds. These pairs included (1) rounded or wrinkled seeds and (2) tall or short plants.

Mendel bred and crossbred thousands of plants and observed the characteristics of each successive generation. Like all organisms that reproduce sexually, pea plants produce their offspring through the union of special sex cells called *gametes*. In pea plants, a male gamete, or sperm cell, combines with a female gamete, or egg cell, to form a seed.

Mendel concluded that plant traits are handed down through hereditary elements in the gametes. These elements are now called *genes*. He reasoned that each plant receives a pair of genes for each trait, one gene from each of its parents. Based on his experiments, he concluded that if a plant inherits two different genes for a trait, one gene will be *dominant* and the other will be *recessive*. The trait of the dominant gene will appear in the plant. For example, the gene for round seeds is dominant, and the gene for wrinkled seeds is recessive. A plant that inherits both these genes will have round seeds.

Mendel also concluded that the pairs of genes *segregate* (separate) in a random fashion when a plant's gametes are formed. Thus, a parent plant hands down only one gene of each pair to its offspring. In addition, Mendel believed that a plant inherits each of its traits independently of other traits. These two conclusions are known as Mendel's *Law of Segregation* and his *Law of Independent Assortment*. Since Mendel's time, scientists have discovered some exceptions to his conclusions, but his theories in general have been proved.

Brown Bros.

Gregor Mendel

Mendel's results were published in 1866, but they remained unnoticed for 34 years. Scientists discovered Mendel's neglected report in 1900 and soon recognized its importance. DANIEL L. HARTL

See also GENETICS (History); HEREDITY (Gregor Mendel).

MENDELEEV, *MEN duh LAY yef,* **DMITRI IVANOVICH** (1834-1907), a Russian chemist, introduced order into inorganic chemistry. He devised the periodic table that systematized the properties of the elements and permitted prediction of the existence of such new ones as gallium and germanium. The later synthesis of new elements has been based on his work.

Mendeleev was born in Tobolsk, Siberia, and was educated in St. Petersburg (now Leningrad). He taught there until 1890. Later, he worked out the standards for the Russian units of weights and measures. He wrote *Elements of Chemistry* (1868). HENRY M. LEICESTER

See also ELEMENT, CHEMICAL; MENDELEVIUM; CHEMISTRY (Development of Inorganic Chemistry; picture: Famous Chemists).

MENDELEVIUM, *MEHN duh LEE vee uhm* (chemical symbol, Md) is an artificially created radioactive element. Its atomic number is 101 and its most stable isotope has a mass number of 258. Mendelevium is chemically similar to thulium. It was discovered in 1955 by Albert Ghiorso, Bernard G. Harvey, Gregory R. Choppin, Stanley G. Thompson, and Glenn T. Seaborg. They named it in honor of the famous Russian chemist Dmitri Mendeleev. Mendelevium was first produced by bombarding einsteinium, element number 99, with helium ions. It has not been isolated in weighable amounts.

Mendelevium 256 has such a short life that half of any sample will decay in about one hour (see RADIOACTIVITY [Half-Life]). The decayed sample becomes an isotope of fermium, element 100, which also decays. See also ELEMENT, CHEMICAL; SEABORG, GLENN THEODORE; TRANSURANIUM ELEMENTS. GLENN T. SEABORG

MENDEL'S LAWS. See HEREDITY (Gregor Mendel); MENDEL, GREGOR.

MENDELSSOHN, *MEN d'l sun,* **ERIC** (1887-1953), a German architect, was famed for his free and imaginative approach to architectural problems. His work in Germany includes the Einstein tower in Potsdam (1920), a factory in Luckenwalde, and department stores in Breslau and Karl-Marx-Stadt. Fleeing persecution in Germany, he worked in England from 1933 to 1937. Then he lived in Palestine until 1941, and designed the government hospital in Haifa. He moved to the United States in 1941 and became an American citizen in 1947. His work in the United States includes the Maimonides Hospital in San Francisco and synagogues in St. Louis and Cleveland. WILLIAM T. ARNETT

MENDELSSOHN, FELIX (1809-1847), was a German composer, pianist, and conductor. He made his first public appearance as a pianist when he was 9. He wrote his first music when he was 10, and by the time he was a teen-ager he was a respected composer. Mendelssohn became probably the most famous composer of his time.

One of Mendelssohn's most significant achievements was his role in reviving interest in the music of Johann Sebastian Bach. In 1829, Mendelssohn organized and conducted a performance of Bach's "Passion According to St. Matthew." It was the first performance of that work since Bach's death, and it greatly contributed to renewed interest in Bach.

Perhaps more than any other conductor, Mendelssohn contributed to shaping audiences' taste for music. He had excellent musical taste and demanded excellence in performance. He deserves much of the credit for increasing the performances of works by Beethoven and Mozart. Mendelssohn also was the first conductor to organize concerts aimed at presenting composers representing particular periods in music history.

His Life. Mendelssohn was born in Hamburg on Feb. 3, 1809. His full name was Jakob Ludwig Felix Mendelssohn. He was the son of a wealthy banker and grandson of the German-Jewish philosopher Moses Mendelssohn. In 1812, the Mendelssohn family moved to Berlin. There Felix received private music lessons from the best teachers available, including Carl Zelter. Zelter was so impressed with his young pupil that he took Mendelssohn, then only 11 years old, to visit the famous German poet Goethe. The young Mendelssohn and the 72-year-old writer became close friends.

Portrait by Wilhelm Von Schadow. Dr. Felix Wach, Dresden, Germany (Historical Pictures Service, Chicago)

Felix Mendelssohn

323

During Mendelssohn's teen-age years, his home became the gathering place for the most respected intellectuals in Berlin. His family made an orchestra available so that Mendelssohn could try out the compositions flowing from his pen. At the age of 17, he wrote an orchestral overture, *A Midsummer Night's Dream* (1826), based on Shakespeare's play. Its lively and brilliant orchestration and catchy melodies established him as one of the leading composers of his day. Another 17 years passed before Mendelssohn wrote the incidental music, including the familiar "Wedding March," for the same play. But the two works are so similar in style that they sound as though they had both been composed at the same time.

In 1829, Mendelssohn made the first of 10 trips to England. There he achieved immediate fame as a composer, soloist, and conductor. Even today, Mendelssohn's works are admired and performed more in England than in any other country. In England, he wrote perhaps his greatest work, the oratorio *Elijah*, first performed in Birmingham in 1846. England also inspired his third symphony, *Scotch* (1842), and his famous overture *The Hebrides* (1830-1832), also known as *Fingal's Cave*.

In 1835, Mendelssohn became conductor of the orchestra of the *Gewandhaus* (Cloth Hall) in Leipzig. He held that post almost continuously until his death.

His Music has the basic elements of the "classical" period. His works contain smooth *progressions* (changes) in the harmony accompanying melodies that are easy to sing. Several of his works also show his skill in using *counterpoint* (the combination of several melodies at the same time). Mendelssohn was gifted in creating melody and in organizing the forms of his compositions so they would be clear and easily understood. This clarity can be found particularly in *Songs Without Words*, an eight-book collection of piano pieces.

Mendelssohn's compositions tend to be "classical" in form, but they are also filled with the emotion typical of the romantic spirit. During his lifetime, Mendelssohn was considered an experimenter and a champion of modern music. But later critics considered him as basically a conservative composer. Music historians do not agree on where to place Mendelssohn in the history of musical styles. He has been called both a "classical" and a "romantic" composer.

Mány of Mendelssohn's works contain elements of descriptive music, as in *A Midsummer Night's Dream*. This quality is not surprising, because Mendelssohn was also a talented painter. When he traveled, he always tried to find time for sketching and drawing.

Of Mendelssohn's large output of 200 musical compositions, audiences today most frequently hear only fragments of some of his best work. Among the Mendelssohn compositions still performed as complete works, the most popular are the fourth of his five symphonies (the *Italian*, 1833), and his concerto for violin in E minor (1844). MILOŠ VELIMIROVIĆ

MENDICANT ORDERS. See FRIAR.

MENEHUNE. See MYTHOLOGY (Mythology of the Pacific Islands).

MENELAUS, men uh LAY us, a King of Sparta, was the husband of Helen of Troy. Paris, a Trojan prince, persuaded Helen to elope with him to Troy. Menelaus and his brother, Agamemnon, gathered a huge army and attacked Troy. This started the Trojan War. After 10 years they took the city, and Menelaus recovered Helen. They wandered for eight years, but finally reached Sparta. Menelaus and Helen lived there peacefully for many years. JOSEPH FONTENROSE

See also AGAMEMNON; HELEN OF TROY; PARIS; TROJAN WAR; TROY.

MENELIK. See ETHIOPIA (History).

MENÉNDEZ DE AVILÉS, PEDRO. See FLORIDA (Exploration); GEORGIA (Exploration).

MENES. See EGYPT, ANCIENT (Early Days).

MENHADEN, men HAY d'n, or MOSSBUNKER, is a fish that lives in the Atlantic Ocean off the Americas from Nova Scotia to Brazil. Its name comes from an Indian word meaning *that which enriches the earth*. Early Indians often used these fish for fertilizing their crops. The fish has many local names, such as *pogy*, *bony fish*, *bunker*, *bugfish*, and *fatback*. The menhaden grows to be from 12 to 18 inches (30 to 46 centimeters) long and weighs from $\frac{3}{4}$ to 1 pound (0.3 to 0.5 kilogram).

Large schools of young menhaden appear along the east coast of the United States in the summer. They swim near the surface and make easy prey for fishing fleets as well as for sharks, tuna, and other flesh-eating fishes. Menhaden feed chiefly on tiny plants and animals in the sea, called *plankton* (see PLANKTON).

The Menhaden Swims Along the East Coast of America.

Menhaden can be eaten by humans, but only small quantities are sold for food. Menhaden yield a valuable oil, used in the manufacture of soap, linoleum, oilskin garments, paint and varnish, and in the tempering of steel. Ground menhaden meal serves as livestock feed and menhaden scrap is used for fertilizer. Menhaden meal is high in protein content. There are many menhaden-processing plants along the coasts of the Atlantic Ocean and Gulf of Mexico in the United States.

Scientific Classification. Menhaden belong to the herring family, *Clupeidae*. They are members of the genus *Brevoortia*, and are species *B. tyrannus*. LEONARD P. SCHULTZ

MENHIR. See MEGALITHIC MONUMENTS.

MENINGES. See BRAIN (How the Brain Is Protected); MENINGITIS.

MENINGITIS, MEN in JYE tis, is a disease of the *meninges* (coverings of the brain and spinal cord). It may be caused by a variety of microorganisms, or germs, that invade the human body. The bacteria that most commonly cause meningitis are meningococcus, tubercle bacillus, influenza bacillus, pneumococcus, streptococcus, and staphylococcus. Many kinds of viruses may also cause meningitis.

The disease is usually associated with infections that develop elsewhere in the body, as in the lungs. Germs travel from these infections to the meninges through the blood stream. If enough bacteria reach the meninges, and if the body's defense forces are weak enough, meningitis will occur.

Meningitis may also result when disease-producing germs invade any tissue in contact with the covering of the brain. Infections may spread from the nose, throat, sinuses, and ears. The microorganisms usually travel through the short, wide veins that meet the veins of the meninges. The microorganisms also may spread by traveling along the outer coverings of the nerves from the nose. They sometimes spread directly from infected bones, such as the sinuses and mastoid bones.

Symptoms. Meningitis frequently occurs in the course of some other illness. Meningitis usually starts with severe headaches, nausea, vomiting, and a rise in temperature. A spasm of the neck and back muscles pulls the head back. This spasm may be so severe that the patient cannot bend his head forward. The back may also be bowed backward. The patient may become delirious, and then fall into a coma.

Diagnosis. Doctors diagnose meningitis by examining the spinal fluid. They insert a needle between the vertebrae in the lower part of the back, and draw the fluid from the canal that contains the spinal cord. If they find pus, or an excess of white blood corpuscles, the diagnosis of meningitis is confirmed. The germ that causes the meningitis sometimes may be identified by staining the sediment of the spinal fluid, or by making cultures of the fluid or the patient's blood.

Treatment and Recovery. The development of sulfa drugs and a variety of antibiotics has increased the chances for recovery from meningitis. Most cases of influenzal meningitis can be cured. The length of time necessary for recovery depends on the severity of the infection. Many cases of pneumococcus meningitis, tuberculous meningitis, and influenzal meningitis in infants are still fatal. Persons who come in close contact with meningitis patients often receive sulfa drugs or antibiotics to protect them from the disease.

Epidemic Cerebrospinal Meningitis is the term often applied to meningitis caused by meningococcus bacteria. This microorganism causes more cases of meningitis than any other germ, but the cases seldom reach epidemic form. However, epidemics do occur, especially when many young people live together under conditions that favor the rapid spread of bacteria from person to person. An example of such conditions is when hundreds of new recruits live together in barracks during wartime.

This type of meningitis, commonly called *spinal meningitis*, usually is *primary*. This means that it reaches the brain directly from the nose and throat, without any infection developing there first. Sometimes the blood is heavily infected with meningococci. This most frequently happens in infants. In such instances, spots appear all over the body. Because of these spots, the disease was once called *spotted fever*.

Nonpurulent Meningitis is caused by microorganisms that do not form pus in the spinal fluid. The viruses of lymphocytic meningitis, mumps, infectious mononucleosis, or poliomyelitis are probably the chief causes of this type.   PAUL S. RHOADS

MENNINGER, *MEN ing ur*, is the family name of two noted American psychiatrists. With their father, Charles Frederick Menninger (1862-1953), they founded

the Menninger Clinic and the Menninger Foundation in Topeka, Kan. They pioneered in treating mental and physical disorders in a community clinic setting. The Menninger Clinic owes much of its renown to the zeal with which the family attacked problems in the treatment of mental disorders.

Karl Augustus Menninger (1893-   ) serves as chairman of the board of trustees of the Menninger Foundation. He has crusaded for the improvement of hospital facilities for psychiatric care and for greater individual and personal attention toward mental patients. His many writings, especially *The Human Mind* (1930), widely influenced public attitudes toward mental illness. His other works include *Man Against Himself* (1938), *Love Against Hate* (1942), *The Vital Balance* (1963, with others), *The Crime of Punishment* (1968), and *Whatever Became of Sin?* (1973).

Menninger was born in Topeka, Kan., and received his M.D. from Harvard University. He built an active medical practice, but devoted most of his time to the teaching and research program and the administration of the Menninger Foundation. The writings of Sigmund Freud interested Menninger, and his writings reflect many of Freud's concepts.

William Claire Menninger (1899-1966) became general secretary of the Menninger Foundation. He was chief consultant on psychiatry to the Surgeon General of the United States Army during World War II, and won the Distinguished Service Medal for this work. He also became a leader in the Boy Scout movement.

He was born in Topeka, and received his M.D. from Cornell University. Like his brother, he built an active medical practice, but spent most of his time working with the Menninger Foundation. His writings include *Psychiatry in a Troubled World* (1948) and *Psychiatry: Its Evolution and Present Status* (1948).   KENNETH E. CLARK

MENNINGER FOUNDATION, a nonprofit organization in Topeka, Kans., is one of the world's leading psychiatric centers. The foundation treats mentally ill patients, trains psychiatrists and other mental health personnel, conducts research, and develops programs in the social application of psychiatry.

The foundation includes the Menninger Clinic. The clinic has two psychiatric hospitals, one for adults and one for children; a department of neurology, neurosurgery, and internal medicine; and outpatient and aftercare programs.

The foundation's Menninger School of Psychiatry is one of the world's major training centers for psychiatrists. The Center for Applied Behavioral Sciences offers seminars and consultation services for leaders in business, government, and medicine. The Menninger Foundation also conducts research in many areas of human behavior.

Three physicians—Charles F. Menninger and two of his sons, Karl and William—established the Menninger Clinic in 1925. The foundation was set up in 1941. Its address is P.O. Box 829, Topeka, Kans. 66601.

Critically reviewed by the MENNINGER FOUNDATION

See also MENNINGER (family); KANSAS (picture).

MENNONITES, *MEN un ites*, belong to a Protestant group known for its emphasis on plain ways of dressing, living, and worshiping. There are many branches of

325

Mennonites. Those who live in rural areas dress and live much more simply than urban groups.

Mennonites base their beliefs on the Bible, especially the New Testament. Their *creed* (statement of beliefs) is the Sermon on the Mount (Matt. 5-7). Mennonites believe it forbids going to war, swearing oaths, or holding offices that require the use of force.

The first Mennonites belonged to a church organized in Zurich, Switzerland, in 1525. The members called themselves *Swiss Brethren*. They believed that church and state should be separate, and that Reformation leaders had not reformed the church enough. They also believed that baptism and church membership should be given only to those who voluntarily gave up sin. They baptized only persons who proved their goodness in their daily lives. They were nicknamed *Anabaptists*, meaning *rebaptizers* (see ANABAPTISTS). The name *Mennonite* came from Menno Simons, a Roman Catholic priest who led the Anabaptists in The Netherlands and northern Germany in the 1530's. The Mennonites later split into groups, including the Amish (see AMISH).

The Mennonites were persecuted in many countries. Dutch Mennonites moved to northern Germany and Prussia in the 1600's, and to the Russian Ukraine in the 1700's. In 1874, many moved from Russia to Canada and to Kansas, Nebraska, and nearby states. Swiss Mennonites settled in southern Germany and France, and moved to Pennsylvania in 1683 after William Penn offered them religious liberty. They are part of the group called *Pennsylvania Dutch* (see PENNSYLVANIA DUTCH).

There are about 400,000 Mennonites in the world, including about 320,000 members who live in North America.   JOHN A. HOSTETLER

MENOMINEE INDIANS, *muh NAHM uh nee*, are a tribe that has lived in the Wisconsin and Upper Michigan region for more than 5,000 years. The Menominee once occupied an area of about 9½ million acres (3.8 million hectares) of forests and lakes. They lived by hunting and gathering food. Wild rice grew in their territory, and the name *Menominee* means *wild rice people*. The Indians harvested rice from the water by canoe.

Treaties with the United States reduced Menominee lands to a reservation of 235,000 acres (95,000 hectares). Today, the economy of the reservation depends on a lumber operation, including a sawmill.

In 1953, the United States government adopted a policy of *termination*. This policy called for ending federal support and protection of certain reservation Indians as soon as possible. Termination was part of a national program to make Indians independent. Through this policy, the government abolished the Menominee reservation in 1961. Congress no longer recognized the Menominee as an Indian tribe. It also withdrew the protection and benefits that various treaties had guaranteed the Menominee. Termination brought economic hardship and threatened to destroy the tribe's culture.

The Menominee campaigned to have the Menominee termination reversed. In 1973, they regained their treaty rights and tribal status. The government re-established the Menominee reservation in 1975. ADA E. DEER

MENOPAUSE, or CLIMACTERIC, is the period in a woman's life when her menstrual cycle ends. Most women experience menopause sometime between the ages of 45 and 50. The length of menopause varies. In some women, the menstrual cycle ends abruptly. In others, it occurs less and less regularly during a period of several months or years before ceasing entirely.

Most scientists believe that menopause occurs only in human females. It is often called the *change of life* or simply the *change*. Menopause results from changes in the ovaries, the organs that produce the eggs and hormones necessary for reproduction. Ovarian activity decreases greatly during menopause and the completion of menopause marks the end of a woman's childbearing years. Some women fear that menopause will cause them to lose interest in sex. But many find that their enjoyment of sex increases after menopause, because they no longer worry about becoming pregnant.

Some women have various physical and emotional problems during menopause. The most common physical symptoms are sudden heat sensations called *hot flashes*. Others include cold shivers, dry skin, loss of memory, severe headaches, and weight gain. Emotional problems include anxiety, depression, and irritability. Some of these physical and emotional symptoms may result from the hormonal changes of menopause. But others result from aging or from problems that existed before menopause. Many of the symptoms can be relieved by treatment with sex hormones. These hormones must be prescribed by a physician. CHARLES R. BOTTICELLI

See also MENSTRUATION; WOMAN (Temperament and Emotions).

MENORAH. See B'NAI B'RITH (picture).

MENOTTI, *muh NAHT ee*, **GIAN CARLO** (1911-   ), an American composer, wrote some of the most popular operas of the mid-1900's. Unlike most composers, he also writes the *librettos* (words) for his operas and stages most of their premières. Menotti won the 1950 Pulitzer prize for music for *The Consul* (1950) and the 1955 prize for *The Saint of Bleecker Street* (1954).

Menotti's first performed opera, *Amelia Goes to the Ball*, was staged in 1938 at the Metropolitan Opera. In 1947, his tragedy *The Medium* and comedy *The Telephone* had a long run on Broadway. Menotti's next stage successes were *The Consul*, a tragedy about political refugees in Europe, and *The Saint of Bleecker Street*, which tells of life in New York City's Italian section. He wrote *Amahl and the Night Visitors*, perhaps his best-known opera, for television in 1951. Based on the story of the three wise men, it has been rerun many times on TV at Christmas. *Help! Help! The Globolinks!* (1969) is a comic opera about an invasion from outer space.

Menotti was born in Cadegliano, near Milan, Italy, and moved to the United States in 1928. In 1958, he founded the Festival of Two Worlds, an international festival of the arts that is held each summer in Spoleto, Italy.   GILBERT CHASE

MENSHEVIKS, *MEHN shuh vihks*, were members of a group in the Russian Social Democratic Labor Party. In 1903, the party split over a disagreement about membership. V. I. Lenin, a Russian revolutionary, became the leader of the *bolshinstvo* (majority), or Bolsheviks. His opponents became known as the *menshinstvo* (minority), or Mensheviks. The Bolsheviks favored party membership restricted to a small number of professional revolutionaries. The Mensheviks wanted fewer limitations on membership. See also BOLSHEVIK; LENIN, V. I.

MENSTRUATION, *MEHN stru AY shuhn,* is the loss of blood and cells that occurs about once a month in most women of child-bearing age. During each month, blood and cells build up in the lining of a woman's *uterus* (womb), a hollow, pear-shaped organ that holds a baby during pregnancy. The thickening of the lining prepares the uterus for pregnancy. If pregnancy does not occur, the lining breaks down. The blood and cells are discharged through the *vagina,* a canal that leads from the uterus to the outside of the body. The process of menstruation lasts from three to seven days, and this period of time is called the *menstrual period.*

Most girls have their first menstrual period between the ages of 10 and 16. A woman stops having menstrual periods during a time of life called *menopause,* which occurs between the ages of 45 and 50 in most women.

The Menstrual Cycle. Menstruation is part of the *menstrual cycle,* the process that prepares a woman for

pregnancy. In most women, this cycle repeats itself about every 28 days.

After every menstrual period, the pituitary gland releases an increased amount of chemical substances called *hormones* into the blood. These hormones affect two organs called the *ovaries,* which produce and store

PARTS OF THE FEMALE REPRODUCTIVE SYSTEM

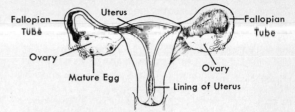

Fallopian Tube · Uterus · Fallopian Tube · Ovary · Mature Egg · Ovary · Lining of Uterus

The Four Phases of the Menstrual Cycle

Postmenstrual Phase. When menstrual bleeding stops, preparations for a new cycle begin at once. The pituitary gland gives off *FSH* (follicle-stimulating hormone). This hormone causes an egg to begin ripening within a *follicle* (tiny sac) in an ovary. Each ovary contains as many as 400,000 potential egg cells, but usually only one egg matures during any one menstrual cycle.

Intermenstrual Phase. The ovaries produce their own hormones. One of these, called *estrogen,* makes the cells lining the uterus divide rapidly to form a new lining. In this way, the uterus prepares to receive a fertilized egg. About 8 or 9 days after menstrual bleeding stops, the pituitary gland secretes a large amount of *LH* (luteinizing hormone). This hormone causes the ovary to release the mature egg, *right.* After the egg is released, the ovaries produce a hormone called *progesterone* that also helps build up the uterine lining.

Premenstrual Phase. The egg released by the ovary makes its way slowly down the *Fallopian tube* to the uterus. The journey takes about five days. If sperm are present, fertilization takes place in the Fallopian tube. This egg-sperm combination then settles into the lining of the uterus, which has become thick and spongy with many blood vessels and watery fluids, *right.* When this happens, the menstrual cycle usually stops until after the baby is born.

Menstrual Phase. If the egg does not become fertilized in the Fallopian tube, it dies in a day or two. It cannot attach itself to the uterine lining. Then the ovary stops making estrogen and progesterone. Without these hormones, the uterine lining breaks down and begins to shed, *right.* This shedding causes some bleeding. During this bleeding, or menstrual period, most of the lining and about 1½ ounces (44 milliliters) of blood are discharged from the body. After the bleeding ends, the menstrual cycle begins again.

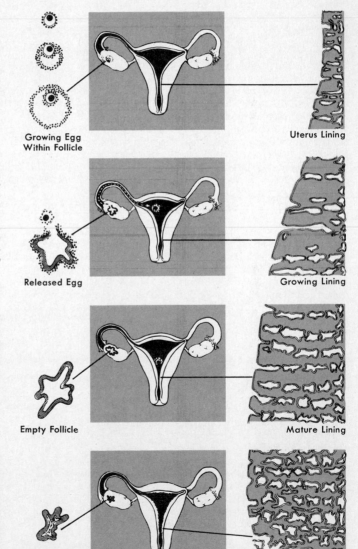

Growing Egg Within Follicle · Uterus Lining

Released Egg · Growing Lining

Empty Follicle · Mature Lining

Degenerating Follicle · Degenerating Lining

WORLD BOOK diagrams by Johns Hopkins University Art Department

eggs, the female sex cells. The hormones cause an egg in one ovary to mature. They also stimulate the ovaries to release hormones of their own. These ovarian hormones cause the lining of the uterus to thicken.

About midway through the menstrual cycle, the ovary releases the mature egg. The egg travels to the uterus through the *Fallopian tube*. Fertilization occurs if a *sperm* (male sex cell) unites with the egg in this tube. A fertilized egg attaches itself to the lining of the uterus and starts its nine-month development into a baby. Menstruation stops until the baby has been born. See REPRODUCTION (Human Reproduction).

If fertilization does not occur, the thick lining of the uterus is not needed. The lining breaks down and most of it passes out of the body through the vagina.

Effects of Menstruation. A few women have emotional tension or a mild backache shortly before the start of their menstrual period. Such discomforts result from changes in hormone levels. A substantial number of women experience abdominal cramps during menstruation. Medical researchers suspect that the cramps result from the overproduction by the uterus of powerful, hormonelike chemicals called *prostaglandins*.

Regular menstruation is a sign of good health. The loss of blood does not weaken a woman. Most women carry on their usual activities during menstruation. Some wear a pad called a *sanitary napkin* over the vaginal opening to absorb menstrual blood. Others insert a *tampon*, a roll of absorbent material, into the vagina.

Some women occasionally miss a menstrual period. A missed period might indicate pregnancy. Other causes of a missed period include emotional strain, sudden weight loss, or the presence of a tumor. If a woman frequently misses a period, she should consult her doctor. GRETAJO NORTHROP

See also ESTROUS CYCLE; MENOPAUSE.

MENSURATION, *MEN shuh RAY shuhn*, is the measurements of lines, surfaces, and solids. A line has one dimension—length. Length is measured in linear units, such as inches, feet, miles, or kilometers. A surface has two dimensions, length and width. The area of a surface is measured in square units, such as square inches. A solid has three dimensions, length, width, and thickness. The volume of a solid is measured in cubic units, such as cubic feet or cubic meters. PHILLIP S. JONES

For a more complete discussion, see MEASUREMENT.

MENTAL ABILITY TEST. See INTELLIGENCE QUOTIENT; TESTING.

MENTAL AGE. See INTELLIGENCE QUOTIENT.

MENTAL HEALTH includes the prevention of mental and emotional disorders, and the detection, treatment, and rehabilitation of the mentally ill. It also involves the promotion of mental well-being.

Prevention. In general, doctors can prevent mental illness in only a relatively few types of cases. These include mental illnesses resulting directly from brain injury, food deficiencies, and certain poisons. The basic causes of mental illness remain the object of scientific research involving both physical and psychological factors. Doctors believe that stress may bring on mental illness. Such stress may be pressures from relationships with other persons or from social conditions, or they may result from physical or chemical processes within the body.

Some mental illnesses may be prevented by avoiding pressures that become too great to handle.

Detection, Treatment, and Rehabilitation of persons suffering from mental illnesses require many services. These include the establishment and maintenance of child-guidance clinics in schools, community mental-health clinics to treat children and adults suffering from mental disorders, and full-treatment programs for the mentally ill in general hospitals and mental hospitals. Research into the causes, nature, and treatment of mental illness is also important.

Promotion of Mental Health deals with helping people to feel comfortable about themselves and others, and to meet the demands of life. These attitudes have their roots in a stable family life that provides children with good physical care and emotional satisfaction. Other elements contributing to mental health include communities as free as possible of social, moral, and physical dangers; schools that offer both knowledge and the opportunities for children to develop their full potentials and to learn to get along with others; warm friends; and steady, rewarding work.

The National Association for Mental Health was formed in 1950, and has about 1,000 state and local affiliates. They work for improved treatment and care for mental hospital patients, expanded community mental health services, special treatment services for mentally ill children, and rehabilitation services for discharged patients. The association also conducts a research program. It has headquarters at 1800 N. Kent Street, Rosslyn, Va. 22209.   PHILIP E. RYAN

See also BEERS, CLIFFORD; HEALTH (Elements of Mental Health); MENTAL ILLNESS; PSYCHIATRY; STRESS.

MENTAL ILLNESS means sickness of the mind. It may involve a mental breakdown so serious that the patient must have special care or enter a mental hospital. Or it may mean personality traits or quirks that lead to personal unhappiness. Mental illness can result in difficulty in getting along with others, and lack of ability to live a useful life.

Mentally ill persons are sick people, just as persons suffering from sore throats or heart disease are sick people. Like other sick persons, the mentally ill need specialized treatment.

Mental illness occurs in every country and among all peoples. No social or economic class of persons is free of it. About 20,000,000 persons in the United States suffer some form of mental illness, and about 679,000 patients enter mental hospitals every year. Mental patients occupy about one-fifth of the hospital beds in the United States.

At present we know little about preventing mental illness. Medical science knows neither specific causes of all kinds of mental illnesses nor specific ways of preventing them. Experts believe that early family life influences the development of some mental illnesses. A happy home life during the first years of life may do more than anything else to prevent many mental illnesses.

What Is Mental Illness?

Mental illness covers a wide range of conditions of the mind. Almost everyone has some minor disturbances of personality, character, and behavior. These include periods of depression, worry, and outbursts of unjustifiable anger. But these disturbances usually do not keep a person from living a generally satisfactory life. Doctors do not consider them illnesses unless they are severe or occur often. Sometimes, disturbances cause personal unhappiness, difficulties in personal relations, or behavior that breaks the rules of society. Then the condition may be considered a mental illness.

People in some countries accept as perfectly healthy persons whom we would call mentally ill. Mental illness appears in many forms, varying from culture to culture. Behavior can be judged *abnormal* (sick) only when it is considered in relation to the background in which the person lives. For example, our culture considers as abnormal a person who has an attitude of constant suspicion. But among the people of Dobu Island in Melanesia, the typical personality trait is a suspicious nature. Anthropological studies show that the social organization and religion of the Dobu Islanders are such that constant suspicion is the normal and expected attitude. According to the standards of our culture, such a mental state would probably be considered unhealthy. See CULTURE; BEHAVIOR.

Unhealthy Behavior. Mentally ill persons may be confused, unhappy, depressed, and uncertain about themselves. On the other hand, they may not know about their illness, because they explain their behavior by blaming other persons. Sometimes they withdraw into their own make-believe world, and become only dimly aware of what goes on around them. In the most serious stages of mental illness, people may cause physical harm to themselves or to others.

A break with reality is commonly called a *nervous breakdown*. This term has no meaning in medicine, and doctors do not use it. However, people often use the term to describe any unusual behavioral disturbance that takes place in a previously healthy person and that requires hospitalization or absence from everyday activities. The legal term *insanity* refers to any mental illness that requires a court to confine people in a mental institution, or to appoint a legal guardian for them.

Adaptation is the ability to adjust to the problems of life.

Amnesia is the inability to remember past experiences.

Anxiety is a condition of worry, tension, or uneasiness produced by some impending danger whose cause is largely unknown. This contrasts to fear of the known.

Conscious is the state of being freely aware, or knowing, as contrasted with *unconscious*, the state of not being aware.

Defense is a conscious or unconscious process of hiding one's feelings.

Delusion is a false belief that a person keeps, in spite of its being proved false.

Hallucination is the seeing, hearing, or otherwise sensing of something that does not really exist.

Inhibition is a blocking of thoughts or behavior.

Masochism refers to the condition of receiving pleasure from one's own pain and suffering.

Neurosis is a mild emotional disorder.

Phobia is a strong, unreasonable fear, such as fear of water or of height.

Psychosis is a severe behavioral disorder.

Rationalization is a person's attempt to make reasonable and logical any unreasonable thinking, feeling, or behavior.

Regression means a partial return to childish behavior, because of the inability to meet difficulties in life.

Repression is the act of keeping an idea or feeling out of the conscious mind.

Sadism refers to the condition of receiving pleasure from causing pain and suffering to others.

Sublimation is the replacement of childish tendencies with socially accepted behavior.

Even mentally healthy persons sometimes have moods of anxiety, depression, and discouragement, and are not always happy. At times, all normal people become worried, depressed, or angry. A doctor would probably suspect that a person who never showed any of these emotions was not entirely normal.

Causes of Mental Illness. Most cases of mental illness have several causes. These causes include chemical and metabolic disturbances in the brain. For example,

Patients in United States Mental Hospitals

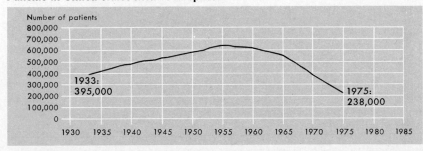

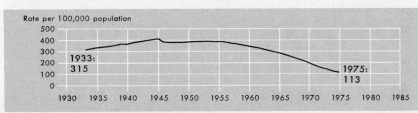

Year	Number of Patients	Rate per 100,000 Population
1933	395,000	315
1935	422,000	331
1940	479,000	364
1945	522,000	409
1950	580,000	386
1955	634,000	390
1960	611,000	343
1965	551,000	287
1970	391,000	194
1971	356,000	174
1972	324,000	157
1973	297,000	143
1974	263,000	125
1975	238,000	113

Source: National Institute of Mental Health.

329

disorders in body metabolism, such as too little sugar in the blood, may affect the way the mind functions (see METABOLISM). Chemical and metabolic disturbances, also called *biochemical imbalances*, may be inherited or they may develop at any time during life. They may also be caused by illness or injury. Biochemical imbalances present at birth cause many cases of mental retardation (see MENTAL RETARDATION). Psychological experiences also may damage a person's ability to deal with problems of living.

Accidental brain damage from injury to the head may occur during or after birth, and cause mental disorder. Hardening of the arteries, a disease of old age, may harm the nerve cells of the brain, because the blood does not flow properly to the brain. Sometimes the brain cells simply wear out, as in senility, and the mind does not function properly (see SENILITY). Poisons from body infections may harm the brain, or infection may occur in the brain itself. Some experts believe that imbalance of hormones may affect the mind.

Many psychiatrists believe that childhood experiences help cause mental illness. They believe that overprotection or frustration during the first year or two of life can make a person *maladjusted*, or unable to face later difficulties (see MALADJUSTMENT).

Anything that interferes with the normal development of the ability to face life can cause later trouble. Such trouble may not occur unless the person meets a particular crisis in later life. Depending on our past experiences and current problems, we all have weak spots. Anyone can reach a "breaking point" and become mentally ill.

The term *psychosomatic* is often used to describe illnesses in which emotional disturbances affect a person's physical health. Such conditions as asthma, ulcers, migraine headaches, and hay fever are often called psychosomatic illnesses. This term also refers to the relationship between mind and body. See PSYCHOSOMATIC MEDICINE.

Kinds of Mental Illnesses

Doctors classify mental illnesses into two general types: (1) organic and (2) functional. *Organic* mental illnesses result from defects that occur in the brain before birth, or when injury or illness cause damage to the brain. *Functional* mental illnesses involve no apparent physical change in the brain, yet the mind does not work properly. Most mental illness is functional.

Conditions such as drug addiction, alcoholism, delinquency, and criminality are symptoms of severe emotional illness. They may appear in any type of neurosis or psychosis.

Neurosis is a mild emotional disorder in which a person's thinking or behavior harms relationships with others or the person's own happiness. Neurotic persons frequently have *repressed* (hidden) ideas or conflicts. A neurosis reduces a person's ability to live happily, but he or she does not seriously lose a sense of reality.

Psychiatrists believe that neuroses usually result when childhood experiences lead to poor adjustment to the difficulties of later life. A child may develop a neurosis during the critical years of adolescence (see ADOLESCENCE). On the other hand, some persons may not suffer

neurotic disturbances until they meet a particular crisis in life. Still others, who suffer neuroses from early childhood, have severe changes in personality.

There are several common types of neuroses. Certain symptoms of all kinds of neuroses may appear in a neurotic person, or various mixtures of such symptoms may occur.

An *anxiety neurosis* involves mental and physical symptoms caused by the abnormal fear or dread of death, insanity, or other conditions that could destroy the individual. *Conversion hysteria* causes physical symptoms such as paralysis, numbness, or even convulsions (see HYSTERIA). *Depressive reactions* include "blue" and sad feelings, lack of decision, loss of appetite, and feelings of being inadequate to face life. *Hypochondria* is an overconcern for symptoms or diseases that do not exist (see HYPOCHONDRIA). Persons with *obsessive* and *compulsive neuroses* have repeated urges to perform certain acts. They spend much of their time thinking in the same manner, or performing the same acts over and over again. They may needlessly want to wash their hands dozens of times a day. Or, they may be excessively concerned about keeping things in order or scheduling their time. *Phobias* involve unreasonable fears about objects and situations, such as a fear of high places. The patients avoid the object of their phobia in order to lessen their worry (see PHOBIA). *Character neuroses* include passiveness, aggressiveness, moodiness, and elation. See NEUROSIS.

Personality Disorders occur in persons who have character traits such as extreme selfishness, that make it difficult for them to get along with others. Such disorders do not keep the person from enjoying the usual activities of life, as do the neuroses.

The *psychopathic personality* is the worst of these disorders. Doctors find it in persons who repeatedly perform selfish or antisocial acts, and apparently do not learn from their experience. The psychopathic personality may be a delinquent, a sexual pervert, a narcotics addict, or a criminal. This kind of disorder can rarely be treated successfully, because it is associated with conscience. Psychiatrists and psychologists believe that if conscience is not instilled in early childhood, it cannot be created later.

Manic-Depressive Psychosis is a major emotional illness. It involves periods of *mania* (elation) and *depression* (blueness). Several members of a family often suffer this condition.

In *melancholia* (depression appearing with or without manic attacks), a person may have difficulty sleeping and eating. He may lose weight, and even try to commit suicide. He usually feels worse in the early morning, but somewhat better at night, after the day's activities have been finished. Many depressed persons cry frequently.

In contrast, some people are only manic, and never become depressed. They talk excessively and move about a great deal. They seem to be happy, but many are sad inside. They act impulsively and are easily distracted.

Between attacks, manic-depressive persons return to their normal state without treatment. They may go through long periods with no attacks of mania or depression. Many doctors prescribe a drug called *lithium carbonate* to prevent or reduce the severity of such attacks. See PSYCHOSIS.

Schizophrenia means a "splitting" of the personality. The patient's intelligence may remain normal, but his emotions do not fit real-life situations. Schizophrenia does not mean that the patient has more than one personality.

Schizophrenic patients may be emotionally disturbed, aggressive, and destructive. They may return to childish behavior and be unable to care for themselves. Some withdraw into fantasy and hallucination. Most have serious difficulties in adjusting to reality. In general, doctors can rarely prevent or cure this disorder, but they can often help the patient. Schizophrenia occurs in several forms, and is the most frequent psychosis found among patients in mental hospitals.

In *catatonic schizophrenia*, a person may become completely inactive and immobile, and not seem to respond to reality. His muscles may become rigid and he may stay in one position for hours. Often he must be fed and his toilet needs cared for. On the other hand, he may become wildly excited and behave in violent and strange ways. When catatonic, such persons do not seem to know what is going on around them. However, they can hear, see, and understand. They remember their experiences during the course of their illnesses.

In *hebephrenic schizophrenia*, a person talks and acts in an irrational manner. He may behave childishly. These patients suffer rapid mental deterioration. Many must remain in mental hospitals throughout their lives.

The *paranoid schizophrenic* believes that other persons persecute him, and he behaves accordingly. He thinks that people talk about him and wish to harm him. He even suspects members of his own family. He may accuse others of poisoning him or of following him.

A person who suffers *simple schizophrenia* is emotionally dull, withdrawn, and isolated. He shows no strange symptoms, and often goes along for some time before his illness is detected. His emotions slowly diminish. This slow change led to the original term for schizophrenia, *dementia praecox*. This term was based on the belief that the disease began early in adolescence *(praecox)* and ended in loss of mental ability *(dementia)*. Doctors now know that schizophrenia may begin at any age and that it may never be associated with dementia.

Paranoia, a disorder that doctors often consider a type of schizophrenia, may also be present separately. Such persons show *megalomania*, or an exaggerated degree of self-love. They believe that other people act hostile and persecute them. However, unlike the paranoid schizophrenics, persons suffering from paranoia seem to be able to behave properly.

How Mental Illnesses Are Treated

Mental illness, like all illnesses, should be treated by physicians. Specialists in the diagnosis and treatment of mental disorders are called *psychiatrists*. A psychiatrist is trained as a medical doctor and has an M.D. degree. He must serve a three-year residency in a mental hospital as part of his training. See PSYCHIATRY.

Diagnosis. Psychiatrists use a number of methods to diagnose mental illnesses. The first step is a thorough medical examination to find any physical causes for the mental disturbance. Then the psychiatrist interviews the patient. The psychiatrist asks questions and encourages the patient to talk freely. The doctor also usually talks with members of the patient's family, his friends, and other associates. These talks help show how the person behaves in many situations. Sometimes the psychiatrist suggests a brain-wave test to detect any organic changes in the brain.

A *psychologist* often helps the psychiatrist diagnose cases. Psychologists test and measure a wide variety of behavior and mental reactions. For example, the psychiatrist may ask a psychologist to give the patient a Rorschach Ink-Blot Test. In this test, the patient tells the psychologist what he sees in a series of 10 standardized ink blots. The psychologist and psychiatrist are trained to interpret the patient's replies as expressions of his inner feelings. The psychologist, who usually holds a Ph.D. degree, is particularly concerned with conscious acts and learning processes. *Clinical psychologists* help people who have problems of adjustment. See CLINICAL PSYCHOLOGY.

Psychotherapy, the major type of treatment given by a psychiatrist, involves talks between the doctor and the patient. It gives the patient a chance to *ventilate*, or talk out, his deepest feelings toward persons who have played important parts in his life. Psychotherapy may enable a person to realize that relationships with people do not always cause discomfort.

The various forms of psychotherapy differ in goals, according to how the patient needs to be helped, and how much change the patient can make in his own personality. Psychotherapy may seek to give the patient confidence, or to help him understand the nature of his problems. Sometimes the psychiatrist tries to uncover unconscious reasons for the patient's feelings, in order to help him understand his actions.

Menninger Foundation

Play Therapy is often used in work with disturbed children. The child plays with toys or dolls and often acts out the emotional problems. The doctor interprets the child's play.

331

Physicians and psychologists often use a form of psychotherapy called *counseling*. They do not try to diagnose a person's problems or tell the person what to do. The doctor listens while the patient talks about personal problems. The doctor may offer advice, but often serves only as a sympathetic listener. The patient, simply by talking about the problems, may arrive at a decision or reach a conclusion. Many experts feel that counseling bolsters self-confidence and helps people meet personal problems. See PSYCHOTHERAPY.

Special psychological techniques for treatment of mental illness include psychodrama, play therapy, group therapy, family therapy, and hypnosis.

Psychodrama. Under the direction of a psychiatrist, a group of patients act out their problems. They may play the roles of themselves and of other persons in their lives. This acting-out frequently helps patients understand their disturbances.

Play Therapy is often used in work with children. The doctor gives the children dolls and toys to play with, and the youngsters generally use them to act out their family lives. By directing the actions and speech of the mother-doll and father-doll in relation to the child-doll, children reveal details of their own troubles. The doctor then interprets the child's play to the young patient. Children are often able to understand the importance of their play in terms of their illnesses.

Group Therapy involves groups of 8 to 10 persons, led by a psychiatrist. Mental patients seem to be helped by knowing that other people have similar problems. They often talk out their own problems better within a group than when alone with a doctor.

Family Therapy treats the patient and members of the patient's family as a group. Such treatment helps family members learn how to deal with one another better.

Hypnosis is often used to help patients bring hidden memories to the surface. Hypnosis usually does not work when it is used to command the patients to forget their symptoms. Injections of Pentothal Sodium, a hypnotic drug, also may help patients to remember what they consciously have forgotten. See HYPNOTISM.

Psychoanalysis is a technique developed by Sigmund Freud to uncover a patient's unconscious feelings. The patient lies down on a couch and tells the *psychoanalyst* whatever comes to mind. A psychoanalyst is a psychiatrist who has had additional training in psychoanalysis. Psychoanalysis requires three or four 45-minute sessions a week, and may last for several years. Psychiatrists find it useful in treating neuroses. See FREUD, SIGMUND; PSYCHOANALYSIS.

Drug Therapy. Physicians use two major types of drugs to combat mental illness: (1) tranquilizers and (2) antidepressants. Tranquilizers reduce anxiety and tension and even calm patients who have schizophrenia. Once anxiety is reduced, many patients can begin to deal with their problems, perhaps with the aid of psychotherapy. Some of the most widely used tranquilizers are chlorpromazine, hydroxyzine, and promazine. Another drug, lithium carbonate, is used to treat mania.

Antidepressants improve a depressed patient's mental outlook. Physicians use antidepressant drugs in combination with electric shock therapy and psychotherapy. Commonly used antidepressants include imapramine and phenelzine.

Drug therapy alone does not ordinarily cure mental illness. But it improves the psychological state of patients so that they can deal with their problems more effectively. The number of patients in mental institutions in the United States dropped by over 30 per cent between 1955 and 1970. One reason for the reduction was the introduction of drug therapy.

Electric Shock Treatment involves the application of an electric current to the patient's head. This causes a convulsion that lasts about 50 seconds, followed by a stupor that lasts about an hour. Psychiatrists use this treatment for depressions, melancholia, and sometimes mania. It occasionally produces amnesia for several weeks. Electric shock treatment shortens the period of depression, but does not prevent further attacks. Since the development of tranquilizers and antidepressants, physicians have used shock therapy less frequently.

WORLD BOOK photo

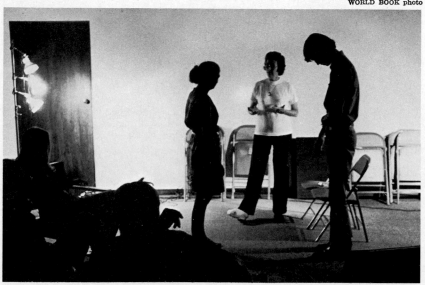

In a Psychodrama, patients portray themselves and other persons in their lives. Such role-playing helps some patients gain a better understanding of their problems.

Psychosurgery, a type of brain surgery, can help cure some kinds of mental illness that result from overproduction of chemicals or nerve impulses in a small area of the brain. Surgeons may reduce the symptoms of mental illness by destroying the overactive area or cutting connections between it and other parts of the brain. Surgeons formerly cut certain connections in the frontal lobes of the brain in an operation called a *lobotomy*. Such an operation reduced a patient's anxiety, but in some cases it also caused loss of memory, loss of interest in life, and even death. Few lobotomies have been performed since the 1950's.

In the 1960's, surgeons began to perform delicate operations on the *amygdala* and the *cingulum bundle*, tiny areas deep in the brain. Such surgery became possible as a result of the development of *stereotaxis*, a method of precisely locating areas deep in the brain. In stereotaxis, a surgeon drills a tiny hole in the patient's skull and then injects air or dye into the brain. The air or dye fills open spaces called *ventricles* and makes the location of the ventricles easily distinguishable by an X ray. The doctor then X-rays the patient's brain and calculates the location of any part by how distant it must lie from a ventricle. Surgery is performed by inserting into the brain a long needlelike device with an electrode at the tip. When the electrode reaches the desired part of the brain, the physician destroys that part with an electric current.

Hospitalization may be necessary for some patients. Unfortunately, after patients spend several years in an institution, their families may become unwilling to take them back, even if they are well enough to leave. This is one of the most serious difficulties in rehabilitating patients who have been in mental institutions.

Care at Home. Many types of mental illness can be treated while patients live at home. They may receive treatment from a psychiatrist, either at the doctor's office or at a psychiatric clinic. Patients living at home during treatment remain a part of their families and do not feel forgotten as often happens when they are placed in an institution for a long period of time.

History

Superstition and Folklore. Mental illness is as old as the history of humanity. Prehistoric people sometimes treated disturbances of the mind by drilling holes in the skull to let the "evil spirits" escape. Later, pagan priests and witch doctors performed rituals to drive out the "devils." People treated mental illness with magic, prayers, advice, and various home remedies. The people of ancient Greece believed that mental illness was caused by breathing diseased air.

During the Middle Ages, people still believed that mentally ill persons were possessed by devils. Beating, starvation, and other tortures were used in an attempt to drive the devils out of a sick person's body.

As late as the 1600's, the mentally ill were still tortured or put to death as witches, or chained in dungeons. The hospital of Saint Mary of Bethlehem in London became famous as *Bedlam*, where "mad" persons were publicly beaten and tortured for the entertainment of visitors. Today, the word *bedlam* has come to mean uproar and confusion.

Humane Treatment. During the late 1700's, Philippe Pinel, a French physician, and William Tuke, an Eng-

lish merchant, pioneered in improving the treatment of the mentally ill in France and England. Under their leadership, mental hospitals stopped chaining patients and began more humane treatment. By the early 1800's, physicians everywhere recognized mental illness as a form of illness, and it became the subject of medical research and treatment. During the late 1800's, Sigmund Freud developed his concepts of how unconscious forces can disrupt mental health. His theories became the basis for psychoanalytic treatment of the mentally ill. Alfred Adler and Carl Jung, students of Freud, developed their own modifications of his method.

Clifford W. Beers, once a mental patient, wrote a book in 1908 describing his experiences in two mental hospitals in Connecticut. This book, *A Mind That Found Itself*, spurred the growth of the mental-health movement in the United States. Beers helped establish the National Committee for Mental Hygiene, now the National Association for Mental Health, in 1909. This committee, composed of psychiatrists, psychologists, and public-spirited citizens, aimed to promote public understanding of the problems of mental illness. Ten years later, the movement had spread to become an international organization sponsoring work in the diagnosis, treatment, prevention, and cure of mental illness. See MENTAL HEALTH.

Research Programs. World War II brought additional emphasis on the treatment of mental illness. Physicians recognized that "battle fatigue," which afflicted thousands of fighting men, was the same thing as the "shellshock" of World War I. The symptoms included sleeplessness, battle dreams, anxiety, tremors, and loss of appetite. The doctors began investigating ways to combat and treat this form of mental illness. Today, medical units of the Army, Navy, and Air Force, along with the National Mental Health Institute of the United States Public Health Service, and various private foundations, support many programs of research in mental illness. The Veterans Administration also conducts a wide research program in its hospitals.

The development of tranquilizers and antidepressant drugs in the 1950's aided psychiatrists in treating many "hopeless" patients. The use of such drugs opened new channels for research and investigation.

Physicians no longer put special emphasis on any one aspect of human life as leading to mental illness. They recognize many factors that contribute to mental illness, and consider them all in treating patients. They realize that there are other factors which, when known, may lead to further improvements and progress in the treatment of mental illness.   ROY R. GRINKER, SR.

Related Articles in WORLD BOOK include:

KINDS OF MENTAL ILLNESS

Alcoholism	Delusion	Neurosis
Alexia	Depression	Phobia
Amnesia	Hallucination	Psychosis
Anxiety	Hypochondria	Pyromania
Autism	Hysteria	Regression
Catalepsy	Kleptomania	Schizophrenia

TREATMENT

Abnormal	Beers, Clifford	Hallucinogenic
Psychology	Chlorpromazine	Drug
Adler, Alfred	Freud, Sigmund	Hypnotism

MENTAL RETARDATION

Outline

I. **What Is Mental Illness?**
  A. Unhealthy Behavior   B. Causes of Mental Illness
II. **Kinds of Mental Illnesses**
  A. Neurosis
  B. Personality Disorders
  C. Manic-Depressive Psychosis
  D. Schizophrenia
  E. Paranoia
III. **How Mental Illnesses Are Treated**
  A. Diagnosis
  B. Psychotherapy
  C. Psychoanalysis
  D. Drug Therapy
  E. Electric Shock Treatment
  F. Psychosurgery
  G. Hospitalization
  H. Care at Home
IV. **History**

Questions

What does mental illness mean?
How do organic and functional mental illness differ?
What is the origin of the word *bedlam?*
What is a psychosomatic illness? Give an example.
Is it normal for people to be depressed, anxious, frustrated, and angry? When do such conditions indicate mental illness?
What is a nervous breakdown?
What is a psychopathic personality?
What is psychotherapy?
How did early man sometimes treat mental illness?
Who is considered to be the father of psychoanalysis?

Reading and Study Guide

See *Mental Illness* in the Research Guide/Index, Volume 22, for a *Reading and Study Guide.*

MENTAL RETARDATION is a condition of subnormal intellectual and social development. A mentally retarded person's intelligence ranks significantly below average, and the social functioning of such a person is less capable and independent than that of other people of the same age and cultural group. Perhaps 3 per cent of the people of the United States suffer some degree of retardation.

Many mildly retarded children are not recognized as retarded until they start school and fail to learn well. Most of these youngsters are not at all unusual in appearance. On the other hand, some seriously retarded youngsters are identified early in life because they are slow to sit up, walk, or talk, or because they have physical handicaps.

Physicians and social workers once advised parents of the retarded to place their child in a custodial institution. But today, experts believe that all but the most seriously retarded can benefit more by living in a community. In the 1970's, less than 4 per cent of the mentally retarded lived in institutions.

Caring for the retarded at home requires great patience and understanding. Many parents have difficulty adjusting to the fact that their child has below average mental ability. Counseling has helped many parents accept the situation and learn special techniques to help their child.

Degrees of Mental Retardation. Mental ability can be measured by IQ—that is, a person's score on an intelligence test (see Intelligence Quotient). People of average intelligence score from 90 to 109 on such a test. An IQ of below 70 signifies one of four degrees of mental retardation: (1) mild, (2) moderate, (3) severe, or (4) profound.

Mildly Retarded persons have IQ's of 55 to 69. They account for about 90 per cent of the mentally retarded in the United States. Some are placed in school classes for the *educable mentally retarded.* Others attend regular classes. By the time the mildly retarded reach their late teens, they may be able to do sixth-grade schoolwork. Many mildly retarded adults can support themselves as unskilled or semiskilled workers.

Moderately Retarded persons have IQ's of 40 to 54. They can make little or no progress in such subjects as reading, writing, and arithmetic. Most require special school classes for the *trainable mentally retarded.* They can learn to care for themselves and to perform useful tasks at home or in special workshops.

Severely Retarded persons have IQ's of 25 to 39. They require training in language, personal hygiene, and getting along with others. Severely retarded individuals must be cared for throughout life.

Profoundly Retarded persons have IQ's below 25 and never advance beyond the mental age of a baby or toddler. Many need constant care to survive, though they may learn to walk and to recognize familiar faces.

Causes. Mental retardation may result from many different factors. The normal development of a human being is so complex that almost anything that interferes with it may contribute to retardation.

Multiple Causes. Many mentally retarded individuals seem to be handicapped by a combination of factors, no one of which by itself could have produced the retardation. Most mildly retarded children, for example, come from families with little money, poor health, low educational achievement, poor nutrition, and other disadvantages. Some parents are too discouraged or too overworked to provide a good learning environment for their children. Furthermore, many different genes contribute to intelligence, and a child may inherit an unlucky combination of many genes.

Single Causes. In a small number of cases, a single cause accounts for most of the retardation. These causes have such overwhelming effects that normal development is impossible. Single causes may be *genetic* (inherited) or environmental.

Genetic conditions causing mental retardation include the presence of an extra chromosome or, more rarely, the absence of a necessary chromosome in the cells. *Chromosomes* are cellular structures that contain the heredity-controlling genes. The presence of an extra chromosome causes *Down's syndrome,* or *Mongolism* (see Down's Syndrome). Retardation may also result from the effects of a dominant gene or a pair of recessive genes that interfere with normal growth or metabolism (see HEREDITY [Genes]). *Phenylketonuria* (PKU), a condition in which a person cannot properly transform one kind of amino acid into a related amino acid, results from a pair of recessive genes. PKU causes brain damage if the diet is not controlled.

Environmental causes of mental retardation may occur before, during, or after birth. A child may be retarded if the mother contracts such a disease as *rubella* (German measles) or syphilis during pregnancy. The mental development of a child may also be affected by other factors concerning the mother's health during her youth or while she is pregnant. These factors include her nutrition, her age and general health, and her use of certain drugs. Events at birth can also cause retardation. They include premature birth, injury during delivery, and failure of the newborn to breathe properly. During childhood, retardation can result from such causes as brain infection, head injury, prolonged high fever, swallowing concentrated poisonous substances, or even breathing such substances from polluted air.

Prevention. Proper care of the mother before and during pregnancy can prevent many cases of mental retardation. Proper delivery and intensive care of sick or premature infants also help reduce the number of cases. Damage resulting from PKU and a few other disorders can be controlled after birth by means of a special diet or medication.

Physicians can identify through tests some couples for whom having children would involve a high risk of genetic damage. Many such couples decide not to risk having a defective child. Other tests can reveal certain kinds of genetic conditions in an unborn baby. The parents may then decide to discontinue the pregnancy. See GENETIC COUNSELING.

Retardation produced by multiple causes is more difficult to prevent. Many experts believe the number of such cases could be reduced most effectively by improving the health, education, and economic level of the poor.

Treatment. The mentally retarded cannot be "cured." But in most cases, a great deal can be done to help their intellectual and social development. Much of this treatment consists of appropriate education or training. In the United States, it is the legal right of every school-age child, no matter how seriously retarded, to have the opportunity to learn to function to the best of his or her ability. In some cases, training can begin in infancy. It may continue until the individual is well established in an adult role. Various forms of special treatment may be needed by a child who has emotional problems or physical handicaps.

As retarded children grow up, their education tends to center more and more on the skills they will need as adults. Many mildly retarded adults become good workers and good citizens. Mildly retarded adults who cannot hold a job and moderately to severely retarded adults may work in a *sheltered workshop*, a center that employs the handicapped. These men and women live with their families or in homes for the retarded in the community. Only the most severely retarded, who require intensive care, are likely to live permanently in residential facilities without doing any productive work. NANCY M. ROBINSON and HALBERT B. ROBINSON

MENTAL TELEPATHY. See TELEPATHY.

MENTHOL, *MEN thohl*, is an ingredient used widely in salves and cold or cough medicines. It has a pleasing odor, and gives the sensation of coolness because it is a *differential anesthetic*. Differential anesthetics anesthetize only certain sensations. Menthol partially anesthetizes most sensations except cold. It has little, if any, other medical effect. Some cigarettes use it to produce a cooling effect on the throat. But menthol does not reduce the dangers of smoking. It is a soft white solid found in oil of peppermint. It is also made synthetically. The chemical formula of menthol is $C_{10}H_{20}O$. SOLOMON GARB

MENTOR was the elderly friend and adviser of Odysseus, the hero of the *Odyssey*, an ancient Greek epic. Before Odysseus (Ulysses in Latin) went to fight in the Trojan War, he made Mentor the guardian of his son, Telemachus. In Mentor's shape, the goddess Athena helped Telemachus search for Odysseus. Today, the word *mentor* means a wise, faithful counselor.

MENUHIN, *MEHN yoo ihn*, **YEHUDI,** *yeh HOO dih* (1916-), is an American violinist who had spectacular success as a child prodigy. He promoted the works of contemporary composers and revived neglected, but valuable, music of the past. He took his first violin lessons at the age of 4. Three years later, he appeared as a soloist with the San Francisco Orchestra. At the age of 10, he played with the New York Symphony Orchestra. Menuhin won popular

RCA
Yehudi Menuhin

acclaim, and also the admiration of the greatest musicians. *Theme and Variations* (1972) is a collection of his essays and speeches on music and other subjects. *Unfinished Journey* (1977) is his autobiography. He was born in New York City. DOROTHY DELAY

MENZIES, *MEN zeez*, **SIR ROBERT GORDON** (1894-1978), was prime minister of Australia from 1939 to 1941, and from 1949 to 1966. He entered the Australian House of Representatives in 1934 as a member of the United Australia (now the Liberal) Party, and served as attorney general of the nation from 1934 to 1939. He was leader of the opposition to the Labor Party government from 1943 to 1948. Menzies was born in Jeparit, Victoria. He attended Grenville College, and graduated from Melbourne University. CHARLES LOCH MOWAT

MEPACRINE. See ATABRINE.

MEPHISTOPHELES, *MEF uh STAHF uh leez,* is the Devil in the medieval legend about a magician named Faust. Faust sold his soul to Mephistopheles in return for the Devil's services for 24 years. The name *Mephistopheles* may come from three Greek words meaning *not loving the light* or, possibly, from the Hebrew *mephiz* (destroyer) and *tophel* (liar).

In Johann Wolfgang von Goethe's great drama, *Faust*, Mephistopheles is a clever evil spirit who forever tempts man. But the Devil loses in the end, because the troubles he causes only help man to find wisdom and true faith. Mephistopheles also appears in Charles

335

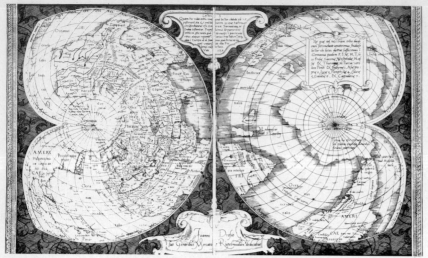

Gerhardus Mercator, *above,* worked out a basic system for mapmaking. His world map of 1538, *left,* shows many of the new lands discovered by explorers, including America.

The Mercator Map of America, 1538, by Gerhardus Mercator, The New York Public Library; Astor, Lenox, and Tilden Foundations; Newberry Library, Chicago.

François Gounod's opera *Faust* (1859), in Arrigo Boito's opera *Mefistofele* (1868), and in Christopher Marlowe's best-known play, *The Tragical History of Doctor Faustus* (written about 1588).　　　　　ARTHUR M. SELVI

See also DEVIL; FAUST; OPERA (Faust).

MER DE GLACE. See GLACIER (Famous Glaciers).

MERAK. See NORTH STAR (picture).

MERCANTILISM, *MUR kuhn tih LIHZ uhm,* or MERCANTILE SYSTEM, is a system by which a government regulates its agriculture, industry, and commerce to ensure that the country exports more goods than it imports. It brings into the government's treasury more money because more goods are sold than are bought.

Mercantilists believe that gold and money are the same as wealth. More exports than imports means increased wealth. Mercantilists favor government protection of industry against competition from industries of other countries. They also favor government subsidies to industries, and high tariffs on goods imported from other lands. The system was in use from the 1500's to the 1700's. After a period of free trade, it again came into use in the late 1800's. See also FREE TRADE.

MERCATOR, *mur KAY tuhr,* **GERHARDUS** (1512-1594), a Flemish geographer, became famous for his invention of the Mercator map projection. He was the most notable geographer of his time. He published an accurate map of Europe, and built globes that showed the earth and heavens. Mercator won lasting fame with his world map of 1569. He originated the term *atlas* for a collection of maps.

On his Mercator map, the *meridians* (lines of longitude) and the *parallels* (lines of latitude) appear as straight lines drawn at right angles to each other (see MAP [Cylindrical Projections]). Many navigators favor this projection, because a straight line drawn anywhere on the map shows a constant compass direction, and the shapes of very small areas are nearly perfect. But the Mercator map magnifies areas near the poles, and does not show areas in their true proportions.

Mercator was born Gerhard Kremer on March 5, 1512, in Rupelmonde, Flanders. He studied mathematics and surveying at the University of Louvain, and became a surveyor, mapmaker, and lecturer in geog-

raphy. Mercator surveyed and prepared a map of Flanders with such accuracy that he became the official geographer to Emperor Charles V. Later he became the official mapmaker for the Duke of Jülich and Cleves in Germany.　　　　　J. RUSSELL WHITAKER

MERCATOR PROJECTION. See MAP (Cylindrical Projections).

MERCENARY, *MUR suh NEHR ee,* is a person who serves for pay in the armed forces of a foreign country. Most men and women who become mercenaries do so to make money or because they love war and adventure.

In ancient times, Persia, Greece, and Rome used mercenaries. Mercenaries were most common from about 1100 to 1500, during the Middle Ages. At that time, many rulers hired trained professional soldiers to protect their states. Some rulers made money by hiring out their mercenary armies to other states. During the Revolutionary War in America (1775-1783), Great Britain hired German soldiers to fight the American colonists. Such military heroes as Casimir Pulaski of Poland and Baron von Steuben of Prussia—both of whom aided the colonists in the struggle for independence—are also technically considered mercenaries.

The rise of national armies largely ended the need for mercenaries. Today, a few countries use mercenaries instead of or as part of their military forces. Mercenary forces are used in some parts of Africa, Asia, and other developing areas.　　　　　JOHN E. JESSUP, JR.

See also ARMY (Armies in the Middle Ages); HESSIANS.

MERCERIZING, *MUR suh ryz ihng,* is a process of treating cotton fabric or yarns with a strong solution of sodium hydroxide. The treatment causes the fiber to become round, so that it resembles a rod, rather than the flattened, twisted ribbon of the cotton fiber that has not been treated.

Mercerization increases luster and strength, and enables dye to penetrate the cloth more easily. John Mercer of Lancashire, England, invented the mercerizing process in 1850.　　　　　HAZEL B. STRAHAN

MERCHANDISE MART is a major wholesale buying center and one of the largest buildings in the world. The Merchandise Mart stands on the north bank of the

Chicago River in downtown Chicago. The home office of THE WORLD BOOK ENCYCLOPEDIA and related publications is in the building.

Every year more than 500,000 visitors come to the Merchandise Mart from all parts of the world to purchase new goods to sell in retail stores. Over 3,200 manufacturers have permanent displays in the Mart. These displays include about 1,200,000 separate items of merchandise. Special "markets" or shows for buyers are held throughout the year. About 20,000 people work in the Mart and every day another 20,000 visit it on business.

The main structure of the Mart was originally 18 stories high, but another story has been added. The Mart's tower is 25 stories high. The building covers two city blocks. The Mart's total floor space equals almost 95 acres (38 hectares).

Marshall Field and Company built the Mart in 1930 at a cost of $32 million. In 1945, the Mart was purchased by Joseph P. Kennedy, former United States Ambassador to Great Britain and father of President John F. Kennedy. SARGENT SHRIVER

MERCHANDISING. See MARKETING.

MERCHANT. See RETAILING (Careers); TRADE (Early Trade).

MERCHANT MARINE is a fleet made up of a nation's commercial ships and the men and women who operate them. It includes both cargo and passenger ships.

The importance of a country's merchant marine is measured by its *gross tonnage*, rather than by the number of ships. Gross tonnage is the total space within the hull and enclosed deck space on a ship. Each 100 cubic feet of space in a ship equals one gross ton.

Technically, the tiny African country Liberia has the world's largest merchant marine. About 2,600 ships with about 80 million gross tons fly the Liberian flag. But few of these ships are actually Liberian vessels. Many ship owners from other countries register their vessels in Liberia because taxes are lower there. The United States has the eighth largest merchant marine, after Japan, Great Britain, Greece, Norway, Russia, and Panama. The United States has about 4,740 ships with about 15 million gross tons.

For a list of the leading merchant fleets of the world, see SHIP (table).

The United States Merchant Marine. The American Colonies had a large merchant fleet before the Revolutionary War. By 1800, America's merchant fleet ranked second in the world only to the British fleet. But much United States shipping was destroyed during the Civil War. Most of the remaining ships became obsolete when steel hulls and steam power were developed.

The United States Shipping Board was created in 1916. It improved the merchant marine by building and purchasing ships and regulating shipping. Since 1950, the Maritime Administration has assisted the merchant marine through programs designed to help U.S. shippers build and operate modern ships (see MARITIME ADMINISTRATION).

Careers in the Merchant Marine. One way to become an officer in the U.S. merchant marine is to gain admission to the U.S. Merchant Marine Academy in Kings Point, N.Y. Young persons can get information about the academy by writing to the Division of Maritime Academies, Maritime Administration, U.S. Department of Commerce, Washington, D.C. 20235. See UNITED STATES MERCHANT MARINE ACADEMY.

A person can also earn an officer's license by studying at a state nautical school. But few states have these schools (see SHIP [Careers in the U.S. Merchant Marine]). The courses generally require three or four years of study. Seamen can also earn an officer's license by spending three years at sea, working either on the deck or in the engine room to advance in unlicensed ratings. Then they must pass the licensed officer's examination. Young persons may obtain unlicensed positions aboard ship if they can get seamen's certificates from the Coast Guard. Wages are set by contracts between shipping companies and maritime unions.

Officers and seamen in the British merchant fleet receive their training by studying on training ships or enrolling in nautical schools for two or three years of study. Critically reviewed by the MARITIME ADMINISTRATION

MERCHANT MARINE ACADEMY. See UNITED STATES MERCHANT MARINE ACADEMY.

MERCHANT OF VENICE. See SHAKESPEARE, WILLIAM (Shakespeare's Plays).

MERCHANTS' GUILD. See GUILD.

MERCIA. See EGBERT; ANGLO-SAXONS.

MERCURIC OXIDE (chemical formula, HgO) is a compound of mercury and oxygen. It is a yellow or orange-red powder which dissolves in acids, but not in water. Its molecular weight is 216.6. When heated, mercuric oxide decomposes, or breaks down, giving off 7.4 per cent oxygen. It is considered a good oxidizing agent for this reason.

Mercuric oxide is used in the manufacture of mercury salts, pigments, paints, and pottery. It also is used in ointments for the treatment of parasitic skin diseases and eye diseases. GEORGE L. BUSH

MERCUROCHROME is the trade name for a weak antiseptic that is used in a water solution. The official name is *merbromin*. Mercurochrome is one of a group of antiseptics called *organic mercurials* that contain mercury. Mercurochrome is a coarse, green powder, but in a water solution it is a deep red. Mercurochrome's chemical formula is $C_{20}H_8O_6Na_2Br_2Hg$. Mercurochrome solutions normally do not burn or irritate when applied to wounds. SOLOMON GARB

See also ANTISEPTIC.

MERCUROUS CHLORIDE. See MERCURY (metal).

The Merchandise Mart, one of the world's largest buildings, covers two city blocks on the north bank of the Chicago River.
The Merchandise Mart

WORLD BOOK photo

Mercury is a silver-colored liquid at room temperature, *right*. Most mercury comes from the ore cinnabar, *left*.

MERCURY, a silver-colored metal, is one of the chemical elements. Unlike any other metal, mercury is a liquid at room temperature. It flows so easily and rapidly that it is sometimes called *quicksilver*. No one knows who discovered mercury, but the ancient Chinese, Egyptians, Greeks, Hindus, and Romans knew about the metal. It was named for the swift messenger of the gods in Roman mythology.

Mercury and mercury compounds have many uses. Mercury is used in some types of thermometers and barometers. Mercury compounds are used in agriculture and industry and in such common products as paint and paper. As a result, mercury has become widespread in the environment in some places. Many mercury compounds are extremely poisonous and can cause illness or death. After many people realized mercury's dangers, industries and government agencies began trying to reduce the amount of it reaching the environment.

Mercury has the chemical symbol Hg. Its atomic weight is 200.59 and its atomic number is 80. Mercury melts at $-37.97°$ F. ($-38.87°$ C) and boils at $673.84°$ F. ($356.58°$ C).

Uses. Mercury has many *properties* (qualities) that make it useful. For example, mercury expands and contracts evenly when heated or cooled. It also remains liquid over a wide range of temperatures. Mercury thermometers use these properties to tell temperature.

Mercury conducts electricity and is used in some electric switches and relays to make them operate silently and efficiently. Industrial chemical manufacturers use mercury in *electrolysis cells* to change substances with electricity. Mercury vapor, used in fluorescent lamps, gives off light when electricity passes through it.

Various *alloys* (mixtures of metals) containing mercury have many uses. Mercury alloys are called *amalgams*. They include silver amalgam, a mixture of silver and mercury that dentists use to fill cavities in teeth. Dental fillings that contain mercury are not a health hazard. Many dry cell batteries contain amalgams of zinc and cadmium to prevent impurities from shortening the life of the battery. See AMALGAM.

Sources. Most of the mercury used by people comes from an ore called *cinnabar*. To obtain pure mercury, refiners heat cinnabar in a flow of air. Oxygen in the air combines with sulfur in the ore, forming sulfur dioxide gas and leaving mercury behind.

Spain is one of the world's leading producers of mercury. Large deposits of cinnabar also occur in Chile, China, Czechoslovakia, Iran, Italy, Japan, Mexico, Peru, the Philippines, Russia, Turkey, the United States, and Yugoslavia. Alaska, California, and Nevada have the largest cinnabar deposits in the United States.

Compounds. Chemists divide mercury compounds into two groups. They call the first group *mercurous* or *mercury(I)* compounds. They call the second group *mercuric* or *mercury(II) compounds*.

Mercurous compounds include *mercurous chloride* (Hg_2Cl_2), also called *calomel*, and *mercurous sulfate* (Hg_2SO_4). Calomel is an antiseptic used to kill bacteria. Scientists use mercurous sulfate to speed up certain tests on organic compounds.

Mercuric compounds include *mercuric chloride* ($HgCl_2$), a powerful poison that surgeons once used to disinfect wounds. Mercuric chloride is also called *corrosive sublimate* or *bichloride of mercury*. Most ammunition uses *mercuric fulminate* ($Hg[OCN]_2$) to set off its explosive. Paint manufacturers use *mercuric sulfide* (HgS) in making a red pigment called *vermilion*. Mercury batteries contain *mercuric oxide* (HgO).

Several organic mercuric compounds have important medical uses. For example, some medicines called *diuretics*, which physicians use to treat kidney disease, contain these compounds. The antiseptic *Mercurochrome* is also a mercuric compound.

Mercury in the Environment is hazardous chiefly because its poisonous compounds have been found in plants and animals that people use for food. Scientists have discovered poisonous mercury compounds in such foods as eggs, fish, grain, and meat.

Among the most dangerous mercury compounds are those containing *methyl mercury*. They can damage brain cells. In the mid-1950's, more than 100 Japanese were poisoned by fish that contained large amounts of methyl mercury. The mercury came from industrial wastes that had been dumped into the bay where the fish were caught. In the early 1970's, some tuna and swordfish sold in U.S. stores were found to contain dangerous amounts of mercury. The government recalled the fish from the stores and warned the public.

Government and industry are working to keep mercury out of the environment. In the early 1970's, the U.S. and Canadian governments began to prohibit industries from dumping wastes containing mercury. Much mercury has been put into the environment in other ways. Mercury compounds were once used to prevent fungi from growing in lumber, paint, paper, and seeds, and to kill plant fungus diseases. Shipbuilders used paint containing mercury to prevent marine animals and plants from growing on the hulls of ships. In 1972, the U.S. government halted the use of mercury compounds for most of these purposes. STANLEY KIRSCHNER

Related Articles in WORLD BOOK include:

Atom	Environmental	Metallurgy
(picture)	Pollution (diagram:	(Amalgamation)
Barometer	How Mercury	Pump (Mercury
Bichloride of	Reaches Man)	Vacuum Pumps)
Mercury	Mercuric Oxide	Thermometer
Cinnabar	Mercurochrome	Vermilion

MERCURY is the smallest planet and the planet nearest the sun. It has a diameter of about 3,100 miles (4,990 kilometers), about two-fifths the earth's diameter. Mercury's mean distance from the sun is about 36,000,000 miles (57,900,000 kilometers), compared to 67,250,000 miles (108,230,000 kilometers) for Venus, the second closest planet to the sun.

Because of Mercury's size and nearness to the brightly shining sun, the planet is often hard to see from the earth without a telescope. At certain times of the year, Mercury can be seen low in the western sky just after sunset. At other times, it can be seen low in the eastern sky just before sunrise.

Orbit. Mercury travels around the sun in an *elliptical* (oval-shaped) orbit. It is about 29 million miles (46.7 million kilometers) from the sun at its closest point, and more than 43 million miles (69.2 million kilometers) at its farthest point. It is about 53 million miles (85.3 million kilometers) from the earth at its closest approach.

Mercury moves around the sun faster than any other planet because it is the closest planet to the sun. The ancient Romans named it Mercury in honor of the swift messenger of their gods. Mercury travels about 30 miles (48 kilometers) per second, and goes around the sun once every 88 earth-days. The earth goes around the sun once every 365 days, or one year.

Rotation. As Mercury moves around the sun, it rotates on its *axis*, an imaginary line that runs through its center. The planet rotates once about every 59 earth-days—a rotation slower than that of any other planet except Venus. A day on Mercury lasts about 180 earth-days because Mercury rotates so slowly. The earth rotates once a day.

Until 1965, astronomers believed that Mercury rotated once every 88 earth-days, the same time the planet takes to go around the sun. If Mercury did this, the sun would seem to stand still in Mercury's sky. One side of the planet would always face the sun, and the other side would always be dark. In 1965, astronomers bounced radar beams off Mercury. The signals returning from one side of the planet differed from those from the other side. Using these beams, the astronomers measured the movement of the opposite sides and found that Mercury rotates once in about 59 days.

Phases. When viewed through a telescope, Mercury can be seen going through "changes" in shape and size. These apparent changes are called *phases*, and resemble those of the moon. They result from different parts of Mercury's sunlit side being visible from the earth at different times.

As Mercury and the earth travel around the sun, Mercury can be seen near the other side of the sun about every 116 days. At this point, almost all its sunlit area is visible from the earth. It looks like a bright, round spot with almost no visible marks. As Mercury moves around the sun toward the earth, less and less of its sunlit area can be seen. After about 36 days, only half its surface is visible. After another 22 days, it nears the same side of the sun as the earth, and only a thin sunlit

The contributor of this article is Hyron Spinrad, Professor of Astronomy at the University of California in Berkeley.

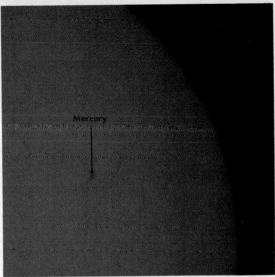

Russ Kinne, Photo Researchers

Mercury Appears as a Tiny Dot against the sun when it is directly between the sun and the earth. Mercury is so small and so near the sun that a telescope is needed to see it at this point.

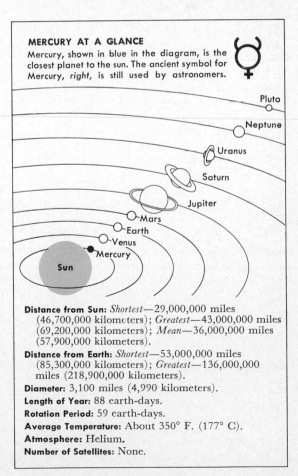

MERCURY AT A GLANCE
Mercury, shown in blue in the diagram, is the closest planet to the sun. The ancient symbol for Mercury, *right*, is still used by astronomers.

Pluto
Neptune
Uranus
Saturn
Jupiter
Mars
Earth
Venus
Mercury
Sun

Distance from Sun: *Shortest*—29,000,000 miles (46,700,000 kilometers); *Greatest*—43,000,000 miles (69,200,000 kilometers); *Mean*—36,000,000 miles (57,900,000 kilometers).

Distance from Earth: *Shortest*—53,000,000 miles (85,300,000 kilometers); *Greatest*—136,000,000 miles (218,900,000 kilometers).

Diameter: 3,100 miles (4,990 kilometers).

Length of Year: 88 earth-days.

Rotation Period: 59 earth-days.

Average Temperature: About 350° F. (177° C).

Atmosphere: Helium.

Number of Satellites: None.

NASA

The Planet Mercury was photographed in detail for the first time on March 29, 1974, by the U.S. probe *Mariner X*. The probe was about 130,000 miles (210,000 kilometers) from Mercury.

area is visible. The amount of sunlit area that can be seen increases gradually after Mercury passes in front of the sun and begins moving away from the earth.

When Mercury is on the same side of the sun as the earth is, its dark side faces the earth. The planet is usually not visible at this point, because Mercury and the earth orbit the sun at different angles. As a result, Mercury does not always pass directly between the earth and the sun. Sometimes Mercury is directly between the earth and the sun. When this occurs, every 3 to 13 years, the planet is in *transit* and can be seen as a black spot against the sun. Most transits occur in May and November. Astronomers can get valuable information about Mercury by observing the planet during transits.

Surface and Atmosphere. Mercury's surface appears to be much like that of the moon. It reflects about 6 per cent of the sunlight it receives, about the same as the moon's surface reflects. Like the moon, Mercury is covered by a thin layer of minerals called *silicates* in the form of tiny particles. It also has broad, flat plains; steep cliffs; and deep craters similar to those on the moon. Many astronomers believe the craters were formed by meteors crashing into the planet. Mercury does not have enough atmosphere to slow down approaching meteors and burn them up by friction.

Although Mercury may have a moonlike surface, its interior appears to resemble that of the earth. Many scientists think the interiors of both planets consist largely of iron and other heavy elements. The discovery of a magnetic field around Mercury led some scientists to believe that the planet has a large core of liquid iron, just as the earth does.

Mercury is dry, extremely hot, and almost airless. The sun's rays are about seven times as strong on Mercury as they are on the earth. The sun also appears about $2\frac{1}{2}$ times as large in Mercury's sky as in the earth's. Mercury does not have enough gases in its atmosphere to reduce the amount of heat and light it receives from the sun. The temperature on the planet is about 625° F. (329° C) during the day, and lower than 80° F. (27° C) at night. Because of the lack of atmosphere, Mercury's sky is black, and stars probably can be seen during the day.

Mercury is surrounded by an extremely small amount of helium and other gases. This envelope of gases is so thin that the greatest possible *atmospheric pressure* (force exerted by the weight of gases) on Mercury would be about 0.00000000003 pound per square inch (0.000-000000002 kilogram per square centimeter). The atmospheric pressure on the earth is about 14.7 pounds per square inch (1.03 kilograms per square centimeter).

The plant and animal life of the earth could not live on Mercury, because of the lack of oxygen and the intense heat. Astronomers do not know whether the planet has any form of life.

Density and Mass. Mercury's *density* is slightly less than the earth's (see DENSITY). That is, a portion of Mercury would weigh about the same as an equal portion of the earth. Mercury is smaller than the earth, and has much less *mass* (see MASS). Mercury's smaller mass makes its force of gravity only about a third as strong as that of the earth. An object that weighs 100 pounds (45 kilograms) on the earth would weigh only about 37 pounds (17 kilograms) on Mercury.

Flights to Mercury. The United States *Mariner X* became the first spacecraft to reach Mercury. The unmanned spacecraft flew to within 460 miles (740 kilometers) of Mercury on March 29, 1974. It swept past the planet again on Sept. 24, 1974, and on March 16, 1975. During those flights, the spacecraft photographed the surface of Mercury and made scientific measurements of the planet. It also detected Mercury's magnetic field.

Mariner X became the first spacecraft to study two planets. The probe photographed and made scientific measurements of Venus while traveling to Mercury. As the probe flew near Venus, the planet's gravity pulled on the spacecraft, causing it to move faster. Thus, *Mariner X* reached Mercury in less time and by using less fuel than if it had flown directly from the earth.

In the future, unmanned space probes may go into orbit around Mercury, crash into it, or land on it. The data returned by such probes will give astronomers a better picture of what the planet is like. The probes also may enable scientists to determine how Mercury was formed and if any life exists there.   HYRON SPINRAD

See also EVENING STAR; PLANET; SOLAR SYSTEM; SPACE TRAVEL.

MERCURY was the messenger of the gods and the god of roads and travel in Roman mythology. The ancient Romans also worshiped Mercury as the god of commerce, property, and wealth. The words *commerce*, *merchandise*, and *merchant* are related to his name. The Romans considered Mercury rather crafty and deceptive, and even as being a trickster or thief. Criminals regarded him as their protector. Mercury resembled the god Hermes in Greek mythology.

Mercury delivered his messages with miraculous speed because he wore winged sandals called *talaria*. He also wore a broad-brimmed winged hat called a *petasus* and carried a winged staff. The Greeks called the staff a *kerykeion*, from the Greek word for *messenger*. In Latin, the language of the Romans, the word was changed to *caduceus*. Mercury's caduceus had snakes curled around it to protect

The Louvre, Cossé Brissac collection, Paris (Alinari)

Mercury is a bronze statue by Giovanni Bologna of Italy.

him on his travels. In ancient times, most messengers and travelers wore a hat similar to Mercury's petasus. Messengers also carried a staff to identify themselves so they could travel without interference. Mercury later became associated with magic and science, and his caduceus has come to symbolize medicine.

Mercury was the son of Jupiter, the king of the gods, and Maia, a minor goddess. Artists portrayed him as a handsome young man, with an expression of alertness and intelligence. One of the planets was named for Mercury. PAUL PASCAL

See also ARGUS; HERMES.

MERCURY ARC. See ARC LIGHT.

MERCURY GLASS. See GLASSWARE.

MERCURY PROGRAM. See ASTRONAUT.

MERCURY VAPOR LAMP. See ELECTRIC LIGHT.

MERCY, SISTERS OF. See SISTERS OF MERCY.

MERCY COLLEGE. See UNIVERSITIES AND COLLEGES (table).

MERCY COLLEGE OF DETROIT. See UNIVERSITIES AND COLLEGES (table).

MERCY KILLING. See EUTHANASIA.

MERCY SEAT. See TABERNACLE.

MERCYHURST COLLEGE. See UNIVERSITIES AND COLLEGES (table).

MEREDITH, GEORGE (1828-1909), was an English novelist and poet. He wrote his novels in a subtle poetic prose, rich in metaphor. His best-known novel, *The Ordeal of Richard Feverel* (1859), is the story of the harm done a young man who is sheltered by his father and

educated at home. It is one of several Meredith novels in which a duel is fought over a woman. *The Egoist* (1879) and *Diana of the Crossways* (1885) show Meredith's support of the emancipation of women. The heroine exercises freedom of choice in love and marriage.

Meredith thought his poetry had more merit than his novels, and many scholars agree. His *Modern Love* (1862) is one of the finest poetic works of the Victorian Age. It is a long beautifully written sequence of 16-line sonnets inspired by his unhappy marriage to his first wife, who deserted him. Meredith was born in Portsmouth. He worked for many years as a journalist and literary critic. HARRY T. MOORE

See also ENGLISH LITERATURE (Later Victorian Literature).

MEREDITH, JAMES HOWARD (1933-), was the first black to attend the University of Mississippi. He tried to register at the school in the fall of 1962. He was accompanied by federal marshals, but police and other state officials repeatedly barred his entrance. A large protest group that gathered on the campus rioted against Meredith and the marshals. Two persons were killed. However, Meredith succeeded in registering, and federal troops were stationed on the campus to protect him until he graduated in 1963.

United Press Int.

James Meredith

In 1966, Meredith led a march in the South to encourage blacks to vote. A sniper shot him in Mississippi, but he recovered, and later completed the march.

Meredith was born in Kosciusko, Miss. He wrote the book *Three Years in Mississippi* (1966). C. ERIC LINCOLN

MEREDITH COLLEGE. See UNIVERSITIES AND COLLEGES (table).

MERGANSER, *muhr GAN suhr*, is the name of a group of ducks that eat fish. Mergansers grasp fish in their straight narrow bills which are hooked at the tips and notched at the edges. For this reason, people sometimes call them *sawbills* or *sheldrakes*. Mergansers live in many parts of the world. The *American, red-breasted,* and

The Merganser Is One of the Most Handsome Ducks, but has little commercial value because its meat has a fishy flavor.
Allan D. Cruickshank

hooded mergansers live in North America. They range from Mexico to Alaska and Greenland.

Mergansers have tufts of feathers on their heads. The male's feathers are black and white, and the female's are grayish-brown. The American merganser has a glossy greenish-black head and upper neck. The red-breasted merganser has a cinnamon-red breast. The hooded merganser has a large black-and-white head crest with two curving bands of black on the sides.

Scientific Classification. Mergansers belong to the water fowl family, *Anatidae*. The American merganser is genus *Mergus*, species *M. merganser*. The red-breasted merganser is species *M. serrator*. The hooded merganser is genus *Lophodytes*, species *L. cucullatus*.   LEON A. HAUSMAN

MERGENTHALER, *MUR guhn* THAW *luhr*, **OTTMAR** (1854-1899), invented the Linotype typesetting machine. Linotype machines set most of the newspapers and other material printed in the United States. Mergenthaler made a device with a keyboard that composed *matrices* (molds) for letters, and then cast an entire line of type at once. He demonstrated and patented the Linotype in 1884. It was first used in 1886. He was born in Württemberg, Germany, and came to the United States in 1872. See also LINOTYPE.   RICHARD D. HUMPHREY

MERGER is a combination of two or more business companies under one management. Usually one corporation buys all the capital stock of another corporation and dissolves the firm it has purchased. Some persons object to mergers on the grounds that they lead to monopolies. Those who favor mergers say they develop competition by making companies stronger, more efficient, and better able to supply things at reasonable prices. See also MONOPOLY AND COMPETITION.

MERICI, SAINT ANGELA. See URSULINES.

MÉRIDA, *MAY ree thah* (pop. 244,652), is the largest city on Mexico's Yucatán Peninsula. It stands in a region of henequen farms and cattle lands. It is connected by railroad with the nearby port of Progreso, and by roads with the ancient Mayan centers of Chichén Itzá and Uxmal. For location, see MEXICO (political map). Mérida has a beautiful cathedral and other buildings built by early Spanish settlers. Its museum contains handicraft of the Mayan Indians. The Spaniards founded Mérida in 1542.   JOHN A. CROW

MERIDEN, Conn. (pop. 55,959), is known as the *Silver City* because it leads the nation in the production of sterling and plated silverware. The city lies in the south-central part of the state (see CONNECTICUT [political map]). Peaks of the volcanic Hanging Hills rise as high as 1,000 feet (300 meters) west of the city. Factories of Meriden make electrical apparatus, tools, machinery, and plastics. The Meriden area was first settled in 1661. Meriden became a city in 1867. It has a mayor-council form of government.   ALBERT E. VAN DUSEN

MERIDIAN, *muh RIHD ee uhn*. If you look at a globe of the earth you will see a number of lines drawn from the north to south poles. Each line goes halfway around the globe and meets another line at both poles. These lines are called *meridians*. Two *meridians* that meet at the poles make a *meridian circle*. Meridian lines are used to measure longitude, which is the distance east or west of a line passing through Greenwich, England.

Geographers think of the whole world as being covered by meridians. Wherever you are, an imaginary line called a meridian passes through the place where you are standing. When the sun shines directly down on that line, it is noon *all along the meridian*.

In order to measure distance, everyone had to start counting meridians from the same place. Geographers who met at Washington, D.C., in 1884 decided that a line passing through the observatory at Greenwich, England, would be called the *prime meridian*. Distances on the map are measured east or west of this line. The *longitude* of a place is its distance east or west of the prime meridian. Pilots and sailors can tell where they are in the sky or on the sea if they know the degrees of longitude and latitude. Changes in time can be measured by degrees of longitude. Longitude is measured in degrees, minutes, and seconds. At the equator, a degree is about 69.20 miles (111.4 kilometers) wide. Distances to the north and south of the equator are measured in *latitude*.

See also GREENWICH MERIDIAN; INTERNATIONAL DATE LINE; LATITUDE; LONGITUDE; MAP (illustration: Lines of Longitude). STANDARD TIME.

MERIDIAN, Miss. (pop. 46,087), the third largest city in the state, is an industrial and trading center. Meridian lies in the eastern part of Mississippi. For location, see MISSISSIPPI (political map). For monthly weather, see MISSISSIPPI (Climate).

Leading industries include cotton, feed, grain, hosiery, and lumber mills; garment and mattress factories; railroad shops; and woodworking and box plants. It also is headquarters for the Mississippi Air National Guard.

Meridian was settled about 1854 where the tracks of the Mobile and Ohio, and Vicksburg and Montgomery railroads cross. It is the seat of Lauderdale County, and has a council-manager form of government.   CHARLOTTE CAPERS

MÉRIMÉE, *MAY ree MAY*, **PROSPER** (1803-1870), a French author, is best known for his *novelettes* (long short stories). One of them, "Carmen" (1845), was the source for Georges Bizet's famous opera of the same name. Set in Spain, Mérimée's "Carmen" tells of the love of Don José for Carmen, a gypsy girl. Don José's love leads him to army desertion, smuggling, and finally the murder of the unfaithful heroine. Mérimée's other novelettes include "Mateo Falcone" (1829) and "Colomba" (1840), tales of violence set in Corsica. "The Venus of Ille" (1837) is a fantastic tale in which the hero is apparently killed by a statue.

Mérimée was born in Paris. His first works were *Theatre of Clara Gazul* (1825), a group of plays; and *La Guzla* (1827), a book of ballads. He fooled the public by saying these works were translations. He wrote during the romantic age, and his work has elements of both romantic and classical literature. It is romantic in the violent passions it portrays, and in the strong personalities of its characters. It is classical in its unemotional presentation, formal style, and its attention to detail.   IRVING PUTTER

MERINO. See SHEEP (Fine-Wooled); WOOL (Sources of Wool; History).

MERIT BADGE. See BOY SCOUTS (Scouting).

MERIT SYSTEM. See CIVIL SERVICE.

MERLIN. See FALCON AND FALCONRY.

MERLIN. See ROUND TABLE; ARTHUR, KING.

MERMAID was a mythical creature that lived in the sea. According to popular belief, mermaids had bodies that were half human and half fish. They attracted mortal men by their beauty and their singing. They would sit and comb their golden hair. A magic cap lay beside them. They would slip the cap on the head of the man they wanted, and take him away with them. A human being could live in the sea by wearing the magic cap. There were also mermen, who captured mortal maidens.

Mermen and mermaids are often found in art and poetry. Certain sea animals such as the seal look a little like human beings from a distance. This similarity in appearance may explain the stories.   H. L. STOW

See also SIRENIA.

MERMAID TAVERN was one of the most famous of Elizabethan inns. It was located on Bread Street, Cheapside, in the heart of old London. The name of the tavern came from the painted sign of a mermaid hanging outside its door. Brilliant English literary men often met there, including William Shakespeare, Ben Jonson, Francis Beaumont, John Fletcher, John Selden, John Donne, and Robert Herrick.   KNOX WILSON

MERODACHBALADAN. See CHALDEA.

MEROË, *MEHR oh ee,* the capital of the ancient African state of Kush, was the site of an early advanced culture. From about 300 B.C. to about A.D. 200, Meroë flourished as a center of art and trade. The Meroite people developed characteristic architecture and art.

Meroë had good timber and pastureland and also one of the richest iron deposits in Africa. The Meroites used iron to make chariot fixtures and weapons. They sold some iron products to other countries.

Meroë became the capital of Kush about 300 B.C. after an Assyrian army destroyed Napata, the previous capital of the kingdom. King Ezana of Aksum, a nearby kingdom, conquered Meroë about A.D. 350. Meroë stood about 150 miles (241 kilometers) north of what is now Khartoum, Sudan.   LEO SPITZER

See also KUSH.

MERON, MOUNT. See ISRAEL (The Land).

MEROPE. See PLEIADES.

MEROVINGIAN, *MER oh VIN jih un,* was the name given to the line of the first Frankish kings who governed Gaul. These kings were the founders of the French state. The name Merovingian came from *Merovech,* the name of an early leader of the Franks.

Clovis I was the first powerful Merovingian king. At his death, in A.D. 511, the Merovingian kingdom included northern Gaul, Aquitaine, and some territory east of the Rhine River. His four sons divided up the kingdom. During their reign, the kingdom grew to include Burgundy, Provence, Thuringia, and Bavaria. But the kingdom was held together very loosely.

The Merovingian rulers finally became so weak that they were called the "do-nothing" kings. After the battle of Testry in A.D. 687, they were gradually pushed aside by the forerunners of the new royal line, the Carolingians.   FRANKLIN D. SCOTT

See also CHARLES MARTEL; CLOVIS; FRANK; PEPIN THE SHORT.

MERRILL-PALMER INSTITUTE is a specialized institution of higher education in Detroit, Mich. Its chief functions are instruction and research in the fields of human development and family life. College juniors and seniors attend the institute through a cooperative arrangement with more than 100 U.S. colleges and universities. Credits earned at the institute may be applied toward degrees at the participating schools. At the graduate level, the institute offers its own master's degree in child and family studies. The school also sponsors an interdisciplinary research program on the intellectual, physical, and social aspects of human development. The institute was founded in 1920.

Critically reviewed by the MERRILL-PALMER INSTITUTE

MERRILL'S MARAUDERS, sometimes called MERRILL'S RAIDERS, were about 3,000 United States infantrymen who fought under Brigadier General Frank Merrill during World War II. The Marauders were tough jungle fighters who won fame in the China-Burma-India theater. They went to India in October, 1943, after President Franklin D. Roosevelt called for volunteers for a "dangerous and hazardous" mission.

In March, 1944, after a 100-mile (160-kilometer) march, Merrill's Marauders surprised the enemy by blocking the only Japanese supply line in the Hukawng Valley.   CHARLES B. MACDONALD

MERRIMACK. See MONITOR AND MERRIMACK.

MERRIMACK RIVER is noted for its six waterfalls which furnish electric power for manufacturing centers in Massachusetts and New Hampshire. The river is formed where the Winnepesaukee and Pemigewasset streams meet at Franklin, N.H. It empties into the Atlantic Ocean at Newburyport, Mass. *Merrimack* is an Indian name meaning *swift water.* For location, see NEW HAMPSHIRE (physical map).

MERRY-GO-ROUND is an amusement ride that has been standard equipment of amusement parks and carnivals for many years. The merry-go-round consists of a revolving, circular platform. Brightly painted wooden horses and other animals are mounted to the platform on vertical metal poles. The animals go up and down as the merry-go-round whirls around. Merry-go-rounds are powered by a piston engine or electricity. The first merry-go-round was made in Europe, perhaps in France, in the late 1700's or early 1800's. It was called a *carrousel,* after an elaborate tournament-type entertainment first given at the court of France in the reign of Henry IV.

MERRY WIVES OF WINDSOR. See SHAKESPEARE, WILLIAM (Shakespeare's Plays).

MERSEY, RIVER, in northwest England, is one of the most important trade waterways in the world. The Mersey rises in the Pennine Hills, flows southwest to Runcorn, and enters the Irish Sea at Liverpool. The Mersey is about 70 miles (110 kilometers) long, and has a wide *estuary* (mouth).

A system of docks and basins extends along both banks of the estuary, and serves Liverpool and Birkenhead. A railway tunnel under the river connects the two manufacturing centers. An underwater tunnel for highway traffic was completed in 1934. Birkenhead has become the greatest cattle market in Great Britain. The Manchester Ship Canal connects Manchester with the river (see MANCHESTER).   JOHN W. WEBB

MERTHYR TYDFIL, *MUR ther TID vil* (pop. 53,680), is the center of the iron trade of south Wales. The city lies on the River Taff, on the northern rim of the coal district. Nearby iron and limestone deposits made it an early center for iron and steel manufacture.

New Mexico State Tourist Bureau

Rugged Bluffs Are Part of Red Rock Formations in the Colorful Broken Mesa Country Near Gallup, N. Mex.

MERTON, ROBERT KING (1910-   ), is an American sociologist. He became known for combining social theory and *quantitative* (statistical) research.

In his book *Science, Technology and Society in Seventeenth Century England* (1938), Merton discussed cultural, economic, and social forces that contributed to the development of modern science. He concluded that many Protestant reformers, including the English Puritans, indirectly helped bring modern science into being by encouraging people to study nature. In *Social Theory and Social Structure* (1949), Merton explored why individuals behave in ways that their society considers abnormal. He explained five different types of behavior, ranging from *conformity* to *rebellion*. According to Merton, a person who conforms accepts society's goals and its ways of achieving them. A person who rebels tries to change society with new goals and new ways of reaching them.

Merton was born in Philadelphia. He graduated from Temple University in 1931 and earned a Ph.D. degree from Harvard University in 1936. He joined the faculty of Columbia University in 1941.   ROBERT NISBET

MERTON, THOMAS (1915-1968), was an American poet and religious writer. He became a Roman Catholic and entered the Trappist monastery of Our Lady of Gethsemani in Kentucky in 1941. He later became a priest, and was known as Father M. Louis. Merton described his life in *The Seven Storey Mountain* (1948) and life in a Roman Catholic religious order in *The Sign of Jonas* (1953). He was born in France. HARRY R. WARFEL

MERV is an oasis in central Asia. It has been a center of life and industry for hundreds of years, although it lies in the midst of a great wasteland. The ancient Persians called the Merv "the cradle of the human race." The Merv covers about 2,000 square miles (5,200 square kilometers) in the vast plateau desert in the southeastern part of the Russian state, Turkmenistan (see RUSSIA [physical map]). Farming is the chief occupation. Some cotton and wool are produced. The ancient town of Merv is in ruins. The modern city, Mary, stands 25 miles (40 kilometers) west of the old site. It was founded by Russians in 1881.   ELDRED D. WILSON

MERWIN, W. S. (1927-   ), is an American poet and translator. He won the 1971 Pulitzer prize in poetry for his collection *The Carrier of Ladders* (1970).

Much of Merwin's poetry is intellectual and philosophical, dealing with such subjects as moral values and the nature of reality. Merwin explored human personal experience and family relationships in one of his best-known poems, "For the Anniversary of My Death." It appeared in a collection called *The Lice* (1967). Merwin wrote about nature and the animal world in two collections, *The Dancing Bears* (1954) and *Green with Beasts* (1956).

Merwin has won praise for his translations of European literature of the Middle Ages. His most important translations include *The Poem of the Cid* (1959) and *Spanish Ballads* (1960) from Spanish, and *The Song of Roland* (1963) from French. His prose works were collected in *The Miner's Pale Children* (1970) and *Houses and Travellers* (1977). William Stanley Merwin was born in New York City.   CLARK GRIFFITH

MESA, *MAY suh.* In the western and southwestern United States there are many flat-topped land forms that the early Spanish settlers called *mesas.* Mesa is Spanish for *table.* These mesas were once part of larger plateaus that were worn away by erosion over a long period of time. Mesas usually have steep sides. Grasses, desert bushes, or other plants cover the mesa tops. Two of the best-known mesas are the *Mesa Encantada,* or the Enchanted Mesa, of New Mexico and the *Mesa Verde,* or the Green Mesa, in Colorado. See also MESA VERDE NATIONAL PARK.   ELDRED D. WILSON

MESA VERDE NATIONAL PARK, *MAY suh VUR dee.* Hundreds of years ago Indians built high cliff dwellings of stone along the canyon walls of a huge plateau in southwestern Colorado. Some of the cliff dwellings are still standing. In 1906, the federal government set aside this region as a national park. The park was named Mesa Verde (Spanish for *green table*), because it is covered with forests of juniper and piñon pines. For area, see NATIONAL PARK SYSTEM (table: National Parks).

The Cliff Dwellers built their homes along overhanging walls of these canyons for protection against other tribes. Cliff Palace, the largest cliff house, contains more than 200 living rooms. About 400 people lived in Cliff Palace at one time. The structure is built much like a modern apartment building. It has sections which are two, three, and four stories high. Cliff Palace also has many underground rooms, known as *kivas,* where the Indians held religious ceremonies. Spruce Tree House, the second largest ruin in the park, has 100 living rooms. Scientists believe most of these homes were built in the 1100's. Cliff Palace was probably begun in 1066. Historians believe that the Cliff Dwellers left this region in the late 1200's because of a great drought.

Desert and mountain plants grow in the park, and there is a wide variety of animal life.　HERBERT E. KAHLER

See also COLORADO (color picture).

MESABI RANGE, *muh SAH bih,* is a chain of hills in northeastern Minnesota. The range was once one of the great iron-ore mining regions of the world. *Mesabi* is the Indian word for *hidden giant.* Most of the range lies in St. Louis County, which is bordered on the southeast by Lake Superior. The range itself is from 60 to 75 miles (97 to 121 kilometers) northwest of the lake.

The Mesabi range was first leased for mining in 1890 by Leonidas Merritt and his six brothers. By 1896, 20 mines were producing nearly 3 million short tons (2.7 million metric tons) of ore a year. The ore was so near the surface that *open-pit mining* was used. Power shovels scooped out the ore and transferred it to railway cars for shipment to Lake Superior ports.　WALLACE E. AKIN

See also MINNESOTA (Natural Resources).

MESCAL. See CENTURY PLANT.

MESCALINE is a powerful drug that distorts what a person sees and hears and intensifies the emotions. It is obtained from the top, or "button," of the peyote cactus, which grows in parts of Mexico and of the southwestern United States. Many Indian tribes have long used peyote buttons for religious ceremonies. The Native American Church, which has members from a number of tribes, uses the peyote as a sacrament. In the United States, federal law prohibits the possession or use of mescaline except by this church.

The effects of a 350-microgram capsule of mescaline last about 12 hours and resemble those of LSD (see LSD). Users may see beautiful color patterns or frightening visions of themselves and others as monsters. A mescaline experience may result in new insights, or it may cause extreme anxiety. A user's personality, the setting, and the dose all affect the experience.

The use of mescaline does not generally produce physical or psychological dependence. But regular users may become unproductive and disinterested in life. In most cases, these reactions end after a person stops taking the drug.　DONALD J. WOLK

MESETA. See SPAIN (introduction; The Meseta; picture).

MESHA. See MOABITE STONE.

MESHED, *meh SHEHD* (pop. 584,000), is Iran's third largest city and a leading religious center. It lies on a fertile plain in northeastern Iran, near Russia. Thousands of persons travel to Meshed each year to visit the gold-domed tomb of Imam Reza, a Muslim leader.

Meshed manufactures rugs, shawls, silk goods, porcelain, and jewelry. It also is a trading center for opium, timber, cotton textiles, and animal hides. Meshed was founded around Imam Reza's tomb and became a flourishing town in the 1300's.　RICHARD NELSON FRYE

See also ASIA (picture: Muslims).

MESMER, *MEHZ muhr,* **FRANZ,** or **FRIEDRICH ANTON** (1734-1815), an Austrian physician, pioneered in the practice of hypnotism. He developed a theory called "animal magnetism," later named *mesmerism.* Mesmer believed that a mysterious fluid penetrates all bodies. This fluid allows one person to have a powerful, "magnetic" influence over another person.

Mesmer was born at Iznang in Austria. He studied medicine in Vienna. He went to Paris to lecture and practice in 1778. Mesmer's sessions, or *séances,* in which he supposedly "magnetized" patients, created a sensation. But the medical profession considered him a fraud. His theories have been discarded, but hypnotism has been accepted as a subject for scientific study and as a possible means of treatment.　GEORGE ROSEN

See also HYPNOTISM (History).

MESODERM. See EMBRYO (Human Development).

MESOLITHIC PERIOD. See PREHISTORIC PEOPLE (How Prehistoric Hunters Lived; diagram); STONE AGE.

MESON, *MEHS ahn,* is an elementary nuclear particle. Mesons, pi-mesons particularly, are responsible for most forces acting between the protons and neutrons in the nuclei of atoms. Mesons are unstable, and spontaneously *decay,* or break down, into other particles (see RADIOACTIVITY [Half-Life]). Mesons exist in several forms, classed by their weights.

K-mesons may have a positive or a negative electrical charge, or they may be neutral. Charged K-mesons have a weight 966 times that of an electron. Neutral K-mesons have a weight 974 times that of an electron. K-mesons decay in a variety of ways, producing lighter-weight kinds of mesons and sometimes electrons and neutrinos. K-mesons belong to the class of particles called *strange particles.* They were discovered in 1947.

Pi-mesons, also called *pions,* exist in positive, negative, and neutral forms. Charged pi-mesons have a weight 273 times that of an electron. Neutral pi-mesons have a weight 264 times that of an electron. A charged pi-meson decays into a neutrino and a mu-meson, the lightest variety of meson. The neutral pi-meson decays into quanta of light or radiation. Pi-mesons were discovered in 1947.

Mu-mesons, also called *muons,* exist in positive and negative forms. They have a weight about 207 times that of an electron. They decay into electrons and neutrinos. Mu-mesons do not contribute to nuclear forces like other mesons. They resemble electrons and neutrinos and should logically be grouped with these particles. Mu-mesons were discovered in 1936. See LEPTON.

Physicists originally found mesons only among the particles produced by cosmic rays as they passed through matter. But various types of high-energy particle accelerators can produce mesons artificially. Physicists have recently found new types of mesons (or mesonlike states of matter), heavier than K-mesons and with extremely short lifetimes.　C. D. ANDERSON and HIDEKI YUKAWA

See also ANDERSON, CARL D.; YUKAWA, HIDEKI; ATOM (Inside the Atom; table: Some Known Atomic Particles).

MESOPAUSE. See MESOSPHERE.

MESOPOTAMIA. See ARGENTINA (Land Regions).

MESOPOTAMIA, *MEHS uh puh TAY mee uh,* was an area between the Tigris and Euphrates rivers now known as Iraq, eastern Syria, and southeastern Turkey. Several ancient civilizations grew there. In Greek, *Mesopotamia* means *between the rivers.* The mountains of Iran and Turkey rise east and north of the Mesopotamian region. The great Syrian desert lies to the west, and the Persian Gulf lies directly south of it. North of the city of Baghdad, the region is a fertile plateau that has cool temperatures and receives some rain. But the southern part, a plain of silt left behind by the rivers, is now being covered with sand and saturated with salt.

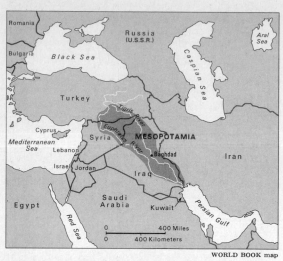

Location of Mesopotamia

WORLD BOOK map

Settlers from the north came into Mesopotamia before 4000 B.C. These settlers may have been related to early settlers of Turkey and Syria. But scholars have found no clear records to identify their language or race.

Sometime after 4000 B.C., the Sumerians invaded Mesopotamia. They probably came from the mountainous regions of present-day Iran and Turkey. They moved south to the Persian Gulf, building towns and draining much of the marshland around the gulf. By 2700 B.C., the Sumerians had a flourishing civilization in Mesopotamia. They developed a form of writing with wedge-shaped symbols called *cuneiform writing*, and used it to record their way of life (see CUNEIFORM).

While this great civilization was growing, Semitic peoples moved in from the west. The Semites adopted much of the Sumerian culture, but they spoke Akkadian, a language similar to Arabic and Hebrew. Semites made up nearly all the empires that controlled Mesopotamia between 2300 and 539 B.C. These included the Akkadian, Babylonian, Assyrian, and Neo-Babylonian (Chaldean) empires.

In 539 B.C., the Persians made Mesopotamia part of their empire. Alexander the Great conquered the Persians in 331 B.C. Later the Romans, Sassanids, Arabs, Mongols, and Turks ruled Mesopotamia. Iraq was created at the end of World War I, when the Ottoman Empire broke up.   JOHN WILLIAM SNYDER

Related Articles in WORLD BOOK include:

Assyria	Euphrates River	Persia, Ancient
Babylonia	Iraq	Sumer
Chaldea	Mitanni	Tigris River

MESOSPHERE is a layer of the earth's atmosphere. It lies between the *stratosphere* and the *thermosphere*, the uppermost layer of the atmosphere. The mesosphere begins at an altitude of about 30 miles (48 kilometers) and extends to about 50 miles (80 kilometers).

The temperature of the air in the mesosphere decreases as the altitude increases. At the base of the mesosphere, the temperature averages 28° F. (−3° C). The lowest temperature in the earth's atmosphere occurs at the top of the mesosphere, called the *mesopause*. There,

the air temperature averages −135° F. (−93° C).

Scientists believe the air in the mesosphere may mix, as it does in the *troposphere*, the lowest layer of the atmosphere. The temperature in both layers decreases with increasing altitude. One indication of air motion in the mesosphere comes from watching the trails of meteors passing through it. The zigzag trails of these meteors suggest that winds in the mesosphere undergo wide variations in both speed and direction.   FRANK SECHRIST

See also AIR (The Four Layers of Air; diagram).

MESOZOA. See ANIMAL (table: A Classification of the Animal Kingdom).

MESOZOIC ERA. See EARTH (The Mesozoic Era; table: Outline of Earth History).

MESQUITE, *mehs KEET*, is a thorny, low shrub which grows in dry climates. The shrub is common in the southwestern United States, Mexico, the West Indies, and parts of western South America. The mesquite also grows in the Hawaiian Islands, where it was brought by missionaries. The mesquite needs little water, and it

John Dominis, *Life*, © 1957 Time, Inc.

The Mesquite Tree casts a small patch of shade in hot, dry areas. Its roots may burrow 60 feet (18 meters) to obtain water.

will grow in deserts too hot and dry for other plants. Stories of desert life often mention the mesquite.

When the mesquite has plenty of water, it grows into a large tree. It may become 50 to 60 feet (15 to 18 meters) high with a trunk 3 feet (91 centimeters) across. People use the wood of the mesquite for fuel, to make fence posts, and to erect buildings. The seeds or beans serve as food for cattle and horses and were once an important food for the Indians of the Southwest. Two kinds of gum taken from the mesquite are used to make candies and Mexican dyes.

Scientific Classification. The mesquite belongs to the pea family, *Leguminosae*. The mesquite is genus *Prosopis*, species *P. juliflora*.   J. J. LEVISON

See also TREE (Familiar Broadleaf and Needleleaf Trees [picture]).

MESSAGE TO GARCIA. See GARCÍA Y ÍÑIGUEZ, CALIXTO; ROWAN, ANDREW SUMMERS.

MESSENGER. See MERCURY; POST OFFICE (History).

MESSENIA, *muh SEE nee uh*, is a *department* (political division) of Greece. It was also an important region in

WORLD BOOK map

Messenia Lies in Southwestern Greece.

ancient times. Messenia is located in the *Peloponnesus* (Greece's southern peninsula). It has an area of 1,155 square miles (2,991 square kilometers) and a population of about 173,100. Kalamai is the capital of the department. Messenia's farmland is the richest in Greece.

During the Late Bronze Age in Greece (1580-1100 B.C.), eastern Messenia was controlled by King Menelaus of Sparta, and western Messenia by King Nestor of Pylos (now Pilos). According to legend, both Nestor and Menelaus took part in the Greek invasions that destroyed the city of Troy about 1200 B.C. In the 1100's B.C., Dorian invaders from the north overran Messenia. Nestor's palace at Pylos was uncovered in 1939 by American archaeologist Carl Blegen. It is considered one of the great monuments of Bronze Age Greece.

In the late 700's B.C., Sparta conquered Messenia and enslaved the people. Messenians revolted unsuccessfully twice, and they stayed under Spartan rule. But in 371 B.C., Thebes defeated Sparta in the Battle of Leuctra and freed the Messenians. The Theban leader Epaminondas helped the Messenians build a new capital and fortress at Messene (now Messini). The walls of that fortress are still standing. Messenia remained independent under the protection of Macedonia and the Achaean League until the Romans conquered all of Greece in 146 B.C.

During the Middle Ages (A.D. 476 to about 1500), Slavs, Franks, Venetians, and Turks occupied Messenia. Frankish and Turkish castles still stand at Kalamai, Koroni, Methoni, and Pilos.   NORMAN A. DOENGES

MESSERSCHMITT, a German airplane. See AIRPLANE (pictures); JET PROPULSION (Development).

MESSIAEN, *mehs YAHN,* **OLIVIER** (1908-   ), is a French composer. He became known for using unusual musical ideas in his compositions. Messiaen has experimented with bird calls, electronic sounds, religious songs, and Oriental rhythms. His 10-movement symphony *Turangalila* (1949) features some of these techniques. He also composed *Quartet for the End of Time* (1941), *Twenty Glances at the Infant Jesus* (1944) for piano, and *Exotic Birds* (1955) for piano and orchestra.

Olivier Eugène Prosper Charles Messiaen was born in Avignon, France. In 1931, he became an organist at the Church of the Holy Trinity in Paris. He became a professor of harmony at the Paris Conservatory in 1942. Messiaen has taught and greatly influenced many modern composers, including Pierre Boulez of France and Karlheinz Stockhausen of Germany. He has also written extensively about composition, harmony, and rhythm.   JOSEPH BLOCH

MESSIAH, *muh SY uh,* is a Hebrew word meaning *the anointed one.* It has the same meaning as the Greek *Christos,* or *Christ.* The ancient Hebrews often called their high priests and kings *Messiahs* because they had been anointed with holy oil. Later, the prophets spoke of a king who would redeem Israel and bring about a period of peace and justice on earth. They believed that he would be a direct descendant of King David. The term *Messiah* came to refer to this ideal king.

Paul and the early Christians taught that Jesus was "Ho-Christos," the Messiah. In Christian literature, the term *Messianic prophecy* means all prophecy about the person, work, and kingdom of Jesus. The term *Messianic times* refers to the period when Jesus lived on earth and to the new era that He introduced. See JESUS CHRIST.

But the Jews did not accept Jesus as the Messiah the prophets had spoken of. They continued to look forward to the future coming of a Messiah. During the 1600's, Shabbetai Zebi, a Turkish Jew, claimed that he was the Messiah, and had come to revenge the suffering of the Jews. His revolutionary preachings gained him many followers throughout the world. He was finally forced to accept conversion to Islam in order to avoid being put to death. His messianic movement gradually died out. Jews refer to him as a *false Messiah.*

Today, most Orthodox Jews still speak of the coming of a personal Messiah. But many Conservative and Reform Jews look forward to a *Messianic Age* when peace and freedom will reign on earth. See JUDAISM.

MESSIAH, oratorio. See HANDEL, GEORGE F.

MESSIAH COLLEGE. See UNIVERSITIES AND COLLEGES (table).

MESSIER, CHARLES (1730-1817), was a French astronomer. He prepared the first catalog of *nonstellar* objects visible from the Northern Hemisphere. A nonstellar object appears as a fuzzy patch of light when seen through a small telescope. Messier began the catalog in the late 1750's and completed it in 1784. His listing, called the *Catalogue of Nebulae and of Star Clusters,* contains 103 nonstellar objects—galaxies, *nebulae* (clouds of dust and gas), and star clusters. Messier discovered most of these objects himself.

Messier did not originally intend to produce a catalog. He specialized in tracking comets and, while searching for them, saw hazy objects that did not change position. Messier concluded that these stellar objects were not comets. He recorded their position in the sky so that other astronomers would not confuse them with comets. Messier also discovered 21 comets.

Messier was born in Badonviller, France, near St.-Dié. He became chief astronomer of the Marine Observatory in Paris in 1759.   FRANK D. DRAKE

See also NEBULA.

MESSINA, *muh SEE nuh* (pop. 251,571), is the third largest city in Sicily, an Italian island in the Mediterranean Sea. It lies on the northeastern coast of the island, on the Strait of Messina (see ITALY [political map]). The city serves as a gateway to Sicily. Every day, thousands of workers commute by ferry across the less than 2 miles (3.2 kilometers) of water separating Messina and the Italian mainland. Messina, a market center, exports fruit, wine, and other products.

Historians believe that the Greeks founded Messina

during the 700's B.C. By 500 B.C., the city had become a well-known Greek colony. Since ancient times, Messina has been fought over by many nations. Earthquakes almost destroyed the city in 1783 and 1908. Messina suffered heavy damage from Allied air raids in 1943, during World War II.   EMILIANA P. NOETHER

MESSINA, STRAIT OF, is a stretch of water separating the island of Sicily from Italy. The strait is about 24 miles (39 kilometers) long. At one time, sailors would not attempt to cross its narrow northern end because of the jagged rocks and strong current. The strait serves as a travel route, but ships find it a dangerous crossing. Reggio di Calabria in Italy and Messina, Sicily, are ports on the strait. See also SCYLLA.   JOHN D. ISAACS

MESTIZO, *mehs TEE zoh,* is a Spanish word that comes from the Latin *mixtus,* meaning *mixed.* The word refers to a person whose parents belong to different races. A mestizo may be someone of mixed white and black or Malay ancestry. More commonly, the term is applied to a person of mixed white and American Indian parentage, especially in Latin America. Scholars estimate that there are more than 39 million mestizos in the Western Hemisphere, most of them in Central and South America.   DOUGLAS H. UBELAKER

See also MEXICAN AMERICANS (introduction; The Mexican American Heritage).

MESTROVIC, *MEHSH truh vihch,* **IVAN** (1883-1962), a Yugoslav-born sculptor, often used strong religious and patriotic themes in his work. These characteristics can be seen in his marble *Maiden of Kossovo* (1907), in low reliefs in wood executed during World War I, and in his marble *Pietà* (1942-1946). He executed the sculptural decoration of churches in Cavtat and Split.

Mestrovic was born at Vrpolje. He learned carving from a master mason in Split. During the World War I period, he gained a reputation as a Yugoslav patriot. He worked and taught in Yugoslavia until 1946, when he moved to the United States.   WILLIAM L. MACDONALD

METABOLIMETER. See METABOLISM.

METABOLISM, *muh TAB uh lihz uhm,* is the process by which all living things—people, animals, and plants—transform food into energy and living tissue. It can be thought of as the sum of two related chemical processes that take place inside the body. *Catabolism,* or destructive metabolism, is the breaking down of food substances to release energy and digest food. *Anabolism,* or constructive metabolism, is the *synthesis* (building up) of cells and tissues, and the repair of worn-out tissues.

Energy released during catabolism is used in three ways: (1) to make the reactions of anabolism work, (2) to heat the body, and (3) to enable the body's muscles and nerves to do their work. Materials used in the processes of metabolism are formed during digestion and put to work through respiration in the cells.

Digestion. Food consists of three main kinds of organic compounds: proteins, fats, and carbohydrates (starches and sugars). After food enters the body, it is broken down in the digestive tract. Enzymes in the digestive tract split the complex molecules of proteins, fats, and carbohydrates into smaller chemical units. For example, proteins are broken into amino acids and starches are split into sugars. These smaller units, or "food fuels," pass through the walls of the intestine into the blood stream. The blood carries them to all the tissues of the body. In the tissues, the cells may use these products of digestion as building blocks for new and growing tissue. Or they may burn the food fuels during the process of respiration. See DIGESTION.

Respiration is commonly understood to mean breathing. But breathing makes up only the first part of the whole process of respiration. During breathing, the lungs take in air. Oxygen in the air passes from the lungs into the blood stream, which carries it to the tissues. The second part of respiration is called *tissue respiration.* In this process, the cells use the oxygen to burn the food fuels. In addition to supplying energy for tissue building, tissue respiration also supplies the heat that human beings and warm-blooded animals need to maintain body temperature. See RESPIRATION.

In addition to proteins, carbohydrates, and fats, the body needs certain inorganic compounds, or minerals. These include calcium, iron, and salts. Water is also necessary. Certain complex compounds, called vitamins, are essential for metabolism. They are needed in very small amounts. People and animals depend mainly on plants as a source of vitamins. See VITAMIN.

Basal Metabolism. The rate of metabolism depends on various factors, including amount of food eaten, activity, and temperature. However, at rest, at room temperature, and several hours after a meal, metabolism settles down to a minimum constant rate. Doctors call this rate the *basal metabolism.* Normal persons of the same body size, age, and sex, have much the same *basal metabolic rate,* or rate at which the tissues burn food. The rate may be expressed as a plus or minus percentage of the normal rate. The basal metabolism provides a standard to compare metabolism under the varying conditions of health and disease.

The thyroid hormone, which is secreted into the blood by the thyroid gland, performs most of the regulation of the rate of metabolism. By measuring the basal metabolic rate, doctors can determine whether or not the thyroid is operating properly. A low rate indicates *hypothyroidism,* or too little thyroid hormone. A high rate indicates *hyperthyroidism,* or too much thyroid hormone.

To measure basal metabolism, physicians usually use a blood test called the *protein-bound iodine* (PBI) test. The PBI test measures the amount of iodine *bound* (connected) to protein molecules in a blood sample. Thyroid hormones contain iodine. These hormones, connected to proteins in the blood, contain the only protein-bound iodine that circulates in the blood. Great care must be taken in administering the PBI test, because extra iodine can enter the sample from a variety of sources.

In only a few cases, abnormal thyroid hormone levels do not indicate an abnormal metabolic rate. In these cases, physicians use an instrument called a *metabolimeter* to measure basal metabolism. A metabolimeter measures the amount of oxygen a person uses while resting. The amount of oxygen used indicates how quickly the body is using up food and producing heat and other forms of energy.   FRITZ LIPMANN

See also CELL (Metabolic Diseases); FOOD (How Our Bodies Use Food); KREBS CYCLE; POTASSIUM; SPIROMETER; STEROID; THYROID GLAND.

METACARPAL BONE. See HAND.

METACOMET. See PHILIP, KING.

METAL forms a large part of the earth on which we live. The earth's crust is said to be made up of about 8 per cent aluminum, 5 per cent iron, and 4 per cent calcium. Potassium, sodium, and magnesium also occur in large amounts. The core of the earth is much heavier than the crust, and scientists believe that it is made up mainly of nickel and iron. They also believe that more of the heavy metals, such as gold, lead, and mercury, lie in the core than near the surface.

What Metal Is. When chemists wish to learn whether an element is metallic or nonmetallic, they conduct what they call an *electrolysis* test. This test consists of dissolving the element in acid and running an electric current through the solution. If the element is metallic, the tiny atoms which make it up will show a positive charge. This means that when electricity is run through the solution, they will seek the point where the electricity enters the solution, or the *negative* pole.

Thus, chemists define metals as "those elements which, when in solution in a pure state, carry a positive charge and seek the negative pole in an electric cell." Only one nonmetallic element, hydrogen, is an exception to this definition.

Most metals have a silvery color. They are shiny, and usually heavier than water. Most of them conduct heat and electricity very well. Many of the most important metals can be hammered into thin sheets, and are described as *malleable*. They also can be drawn out into wires, and are called *ductile*.

A few metals, such as gold, copper, and strontium, are colored. Several others are not as heavy as water. Potassium, sodium, and lithium, for example, will float on water. Some metals are not malleable and ductile, but are so brittle that they break quickly when worked. Calcium is an example of such a metallic element.

Some substances such as boron and selenium are called *nonmetals*. Chemically, they are not metals, but they have one or more of the physical properties of metals.

Certain combinations, or *alloys*, of metals with other metals also are called metals. Among these are bronze, bell metal, gun metal, and type metal. Alloys and metals that do not contain iron are referred to as *nonferrous*.

Metals Through the Ages. Ancient man knew and used many native metals. Gold was used for ornaments, plates, and utensils as early as 3500 B.C. Gold objects showing a high degree of culture have been excavated at the ruins of the ancient city of Ur in Mesopotamia. Silver was used as early as 2400 B.C., and many ancients considered it to be more valuable than gold, because it was rarer in the native state. Native copper also was used at an early date in tools and utensils, because it was found near the surface of the ground in the native state and could be easily worked and shaped.

Since about 1000 B.C., iron and steel have been the chief metals for construction. Today, supplies of the best iron ore for steelmaking are being exhausted. The same is true for copper, lead, and zinc deposits. Metallurgists now substitute aluminum for steel in many cases. The supply of aluminum is almost unlimited.

Magnesium, another light, strong metal, has also become important. It is extracted from sea water and the common rock called *dolomite*. The atomic bomb is made from uranium, one of the important radioactive metals.

HARRISON ASHLEY SCHMITT

Related Articles in WORLD BOOK include:

Calcium Carbide, produced in electric furnaces, is used in acetylene and other compounds.

Jet Engines depend on parts made of titanium, a light, strong, heat-resistant metal.

Damascus Swords of the Middle Ages contained tungsten. It is still used to harden steel.

Union Carbide Corp.

Niobium is mined in western Africa. It must be separated from tin and tantalum ores.

METALS

Actinium	Gold	Promethium
Aluminum	Hafnium	Protactinium
Americium	Holmium	Radium
Antimony	Indium	Rhenium
Arsenic	Iridium	Rhodium
Barium	Iron	Rubidium
Berkelium	Lanthanum	Ruthenium
Beryllium	Lead	Samarium
Bismuth	Lithium	Scandium
Cadmium	Lutetium	Silver
Calcium	Magnesium	Sodium
Californium	Manganese	Strontium
Cerium	Mendelevium	Tantalum
Cesium	Mercury	Technetium
Chromium	Molybdenum	Terbium
Cobalt	Neodymium	Thallium
Copper	Neptunium	Thorium
Curium	Nickel	Thulium
Dysprosium	Niobium	Tin
Einsteinium	Nobelium	Titanium
Erbium	Osmium	Tungsten
Europium	Palladium	Uranium
Fermium	Platinum	Vanadium
Francium	Plutonium	Ytterbium
Gadolinium	Polonium	Yttrium
Gallium	Potassium	Zinc
Germanium	Praseodymium	Zirconium

OTHER RELATED ARTICLES

Alloy	Malleability
Assaying	Metallurgy
Corrosion	Mineral
Ductility	Mining
Element, Chemical	Rare Earth

Garrett Electronics

A Metal Detector is used to locate old coins, jewelry, and other objects buried underground. Many detectors can distinguish objects made of a valuable metal from those of iron or lead.

METAL DETECTOR is an instrument used to locate hidden or lost metal objects. It gives off signals in the presence of metal. Detectors are widely used by treasure hunters, who search outdoors for old coins, jewelry, and other valuable relics. Police use metal detectors in criminal investigations. Archaeologists and prospectors also use them.

Metal detectors vary in design and shape, but they all operate in basically the same way. A detector transmits radio waves by means of an antenna. A metal object absorbs some of these waves and reflects them back to the instrument. The detector's receiving circuit amplifies the reflected waves into a strong signal that tells the user of the object's presence.

All detectors can locate metals that lie buried underground or are hidden behind brick or stone walls. Many detectors have a feature called a "discriminating circuit," which distinguishes objects made of valuable metal from those of a nonvaluable material. Detectors are manufactured in many sizes. Most of these instruments are lightweight and portable.   ROY LAGAL

METAL FATIGUE. See FATIGUE, METAL.
METALLIC FIBER. See TEXTILE (table).
METALLOGRAPHY, MEHT *uh LAHG ruh fee*, is the study of the internal structure of metals and alloys. Metallographers determine how metals react under certain conditions, such as extreme heat. Industry depends on metallography in the creation and improvement of such metal products as missiles and rockets.

Metallographers study metal samples with X-rays and microscopes. Electron microscopes, which can magnify objects thousands of times, have brought great advancements in metallography.   C. N. J. WAGNER

350

METALLURGICAL ENGINEERING. See METALLURGY (Careers); ENGINEERING (table: Specialized Engineering Fields).

METALLURGY, *MET uh LUR jee*, is the science of separating metals from their ores and preparing them for use. All metal objects which we use are made possible by the work of metallurgy. Metals carry electricity to our homes and factories, and make up the framework of skyscrapers. Automobiles, trains, airplanes, and rockets are made of metal. So are many of the tools we use. Modern industry and manufacturing would be impossible without the use of metals.

The important science of metallurgy falls into two major divisions. One division is called *extractive*, or *recovery*, *metallurgy;* the other is *physical*, or *alloy*, *metallurgy*.

Extractive Metallurgy

Extractive metallurgy deals with taking metals from their ores and refining them to a pure state. It includes a wide variety of specialized commercial processes, such as mineral dressing, roasting, sintering, smelting, leaching, electrolysis, and amalgamation.

Mineral Dressing is a step in extractive metallurgy which occurs between the mining of the ore and extracting the metals from it. Mineral dressing removes as much of the waste materials as possible from the ore. This is usually done by grinding the ore so that the metals in it, along with certain nonmetallic materials, separate from the waste. Then the dirt and some of the other waste materials may be floated or washed away. In this *flotation process*, crushed ore is *agitated* (set in motion) in water with air or gas bubbles. Various chemicals or oils cause the mineral particles to stick to the bubbles. The minerals are then removed in a froth. The waste materials that occur along with mineral ore are called *gangue*. By the removal of the gangue, the amount of ore that must be handled during the actual process of metal extraction is reduced.

Roasting is a type of extractive metallurgy which removes sulfur and other impurities from the ore. When the ore is heated in air, the sulfur and certain other impurities combine with the oxygen of the air, and pass off as gases. The remaining solid material contains a *metallic oxide* (combination of metal and oxygen). This material must be further purified or reduced to yield the pure metal.

Sintering may occur when the temperature at which ores are roasted becomes very high. In this process, fine particles in contact with one another join together to form coarse lumps. The joining is caused by surface tension. It is the same force that causes small water drops to combine into larger drops. The sintering is sometimes accompanied by partial melting of the fine particles, but the particles often remain entirely solid throughout the process. The coarse lumps produced by sintering can be used more easily in later processes.

Smelting. After the ores have been subjected to such preliminary processes as dressing, roasting, or sintering, processors begin the actual work of extracting the metal. The usual method of metal extraction is by *smelting* (melting the ore in such a way as to remove impurities). In the case of iron, for example, the ore is placed in a huge, brick-lined furnace called a *blast furnace*, and subjected to high heat. Quantities of coke and limestone also are placed in the furnace. As the heat of the furnace is raised, the coke begins to burn and give off carbon monoxide. This gas takes oxygen from the iron, helping to purify the metal. Many of the other impurities of the ore melt and combine with the limestone to form a liquid collection of *refuse* (waste materials) which is lighter than the iron. This refuse rises to the top of the molten metal, and is taken from the furnace as slag. The slag is drawn off from holes in the side of the furnace at a height above the level of the molten iron. The molten iron is still not completely free of impurities. But all the iron has been taken from the ore. The metal must now be refined further to purify it.

Leaching. Some metals can be effectively separated from their ores by *hydrometallurgy* (leaching). This is a method of dissolving the metal out of the ore with a chemical solvent. The metal may then be recovered from the chemical solution by a process called *precipitation*. For example, gold is usually separated from its ore by treating the ore with a dilute alkaline solution of sodium cyanide. After the gold is dissolved in the sodium cyanide, it is placed in contact with metallic zinc. This causes all the gold to *precipitate* (separate) from the solution and gather on the metallic zinc.

Electrolysis. After the metal has been taken from its ore by leaching, it is sometimes recovered from the leaching solution by electrolysis. For example, copper is leached from some ores with sulfuric acid. Then it is placed in an electrolytic cell. There, electric current flows from a lead *anode* (positive pole) through the solution to a copper *cathode* (negative pole). The copper particles in the solution have a positive charge. These particles then seek their opposites, or the negatively charged copper cathode. Aluminum and magnesium also are recovered by electrolysis. This recovery is done at a high temperature from a solution of their molten salts.

Electrolysis is also used to purify the metal. Copper is one of the metals that can be refined by electrolysis. The impure metal is used as the anode. When electric current is passed through the solution, the atoms of pure copper on the anode give up electrons and pass into solution as positively charged particles. These particles pass through the solution toward the cathode. There, they acquire the necessary electrons to become neutral copper atoms on the cathode. Most impurities are left behind, and a plating of purified copper forms on the cathode.

Amalgamation is a method that is sometimes used to recover gold and silver from their ores. The finely ground particles of ore are carried by a solution over plates covered with mercury. The mercury attracts the metal and combines with it. The mercury forms an alloy, called an *amalgam*, with the gold or silver. Then the amalgam is heated. The heat causes the mercury to come to a boil and pass off as gas, leaving a metallic sponge of pure gold or silver.

Physical Metallurgy

Physical metallurgy is the branch of metallurgy which adapts metals to human use. It includes any operation used to convert a refined commercial metal into a useful finished product. This involves combining metals into alloys to get a metal with special properties. For example, physical metallurgy includes combining steel with nickel to make a chemically resistant, strong steel. It also includes the improvement of these properties by heat treatments, such as the tempering of steel and certain other metals to add strength. The forming of the metal into its final shape, and the surface treatment of the finished product also are classified as physical metallurgy. When blacksmiths heat and hammer a horseshoe, they are practicing metallurgy. The metal may be formed into its final shape by casting, rolling, forging, welding, pressing, extrusion, drawing, stamping, and other methods. Surface treatment may include heat treatment at the surface, and *carburizing* (combining with carbon). The application of a surface coating, such as in galvanizing, and the final surface cleaning are also considered parts of physical metallurgy.

History

Although we usually think of metallurgy as a modern science, it is one of the oldest. The people of prehistoric times knew something of physical metallurgy. The ancient Chinese and Egyptians found gold and silver in their pure state as grains and nuggets, and molded the metal into many different kinds of ornaments. The American Indians found large amounts of pure copper in the area near Lake Superior and molded the metal into weapons and implements.

Sometime before written history began, some of the ancient peoples discovered the simplest principles of smelting metals from their ores. Lead was probably the first metal ever to be separated from its ore by smelting, because it is very easy to reduce. But as long as 4,000 years ago, the Egyptians knew how to separate iron from its ore—and this metal is considered one of the hardest to reduce. By the time of the Assyrian civilization, smelting iron was a highly developed art. The ancient Assyrians even knew how to change iron into steel.

During the Middle Ages, when the alchemists were studying ways to make gold from other substances, great advances were made in metallurgy. The alchemists learned much about the behavior of metals and about various methods of using metals. They are credited with laying the foundations of the modern science of metallurgy. See METAL (Metals Through the Ages).

Careers in Metallurgy

The growing use of metals in industry has increased the importance of metallurgy as a career. *Metallurgists*, also called *metallurgical engineers*, can find jobs chiefly in the metal industry, especially in the manufacture of iron and steel. The mining industry also employs large numbers of metallurgists. Other openings can be found in other industries, in government, and in research. Metallurgists are usually classified into two groups. *Extractive* metallurgists are those who work on the extraction of metals from ores. *Physical* metallurgists are those concerned with the content and structure of metals and their alloys.

Since the mid-1940's, metallurgists have greatly increased their efforts to explain complex metallurgical behavior in terms of the basic laws of physics and chemistry. They also have extended the use of metallurgical research methods and skills to such nonmetallic

METAMORPHIC ROCK

materials as ceramics, semiconductors, plastics, organic solids, and glass. The name *materials science* has been given to this broadened field that deals with both metals and nonmetals.

People interested in metallurgy or materials science as a career should have an interest in science and the ability to do mechanical jobs. They should take as many high-school science and mathematics courses as possible. Most jobs require a bachelor of science degree in metallurgical engineering. Research positions usually require advanced degrees.　　　　WILLIAM W. MULLINS

Related Articles in WORLD BOOK include:

Alchemy	Iron and Steel
Alloy	Machine Tool
Amalgam	Metallography
Electrolysis	Powder Metallurgy
Flotation Process	Sintering
Flux	Slag
Forging	Solder
Ion Microscope	Zone Melting

METAMORPHIC ROCK is rock that has been changed by heat or by heat and pressure. This type of rock results from chemical and structural changes that occur in solid rock buried in the earth's crust. Metamorphic rock can be formed from the two other main kinds of rock, *igneous* and *sedimentary*. It also may be produced from other metamorphic rock.

Metamorphic rock is created by either of two processes, *contact metamorphism* or *regional metamorphism*. In contact metamorphism, rock is changed by heat produced by nearby *magma* (molten igneous rock). In regional metamorphism, both heat and pressure alter rock. The pressure is produced chiefly by movements in the earth's crust. These movements are often associated with the formation of mountains. During both types of metamorphism, some of the minerals in rock are broken down and form new minerals. This change in mineral composition is called *recrystallization*. When a rock recrystallizes, its texture may change, and the grains that make up the rock may become larger.

There are many kinds of metamorphic rock. Common varieties include *amphibolite*, which is metamorphosed basalt; *marble*, which is formed from limestone; and *slate*, which comes from shale.　　MARY EMMA WAGNER

See also METAMORPHISM; ROCK.

METAMORPHISM, *MET uh MAWR fiz'm*, is a general name for the changes in the form and composition of rocks. During metamorphism, rocks change chiefly because of the formation of new mineral crystals from the original minerals in the rocks. The number of kinds of changes that geologists can call *metamorphic* is almost unlimited.

Most geologists believe that metamorphism is caused either by heat or by a combination of heat and pressure. Some rocks are metamorphosed by the heat of hot igneous rocks, such as those formed from lava. This kind of change is called *contact*, or *local*, *metamorphism*. The heat and pressure from mountain-forming movements in the earth's crust often metamorphose very large bodies of rocks. This process is called *regional metamorphism*.　　ERNEST E. WAHLSTROM

See also METAMORPHIC ROCK; ROCK (Metamorphic Rock; table).

METAMORPHOSIS, *MET uh MAWR foh sis*, is a Greek word that means *to transform*. Biologists use the word to describe the rather abrupt changes, or transformations, which occur in the form and structure of many lower animals from the time of their birth until they reach the stage of maturity, or adulthood.

Many young animals, such as cats, dogs, and horses, look like their parents in form and structure. They differ chiefly in size from mature animals. But when such lower animals as the butterfly, the sea urchin, or the frog come from the egg, they appear to be different from the mature animal. In many of these young animals, striking changes in appearance and structure—that is, *metamorphosis*—must take place before they reach their adult condition.

The changes that occur in the life cycle of a butterfly or moth are among the most striking examples of metamorphosis. Because the butterfly passes through four separate stages of growth, scientists consider it an example of *complete metamorphosis*. The first stage is as an *embryo* that forms inside the egg (see EMBRYO).

The Larva. When the future butterfly is newly hatched, it is known as a *larva*. Scientists call the first stage of development after the creature comes out of the egg the *larval stage*. The larva of a butterfly or moth is a crawling, often fuzzy caterpillar. It may be brown, yellow, or green. It may be smooth, or hairy, or may have many long spines. In any case, the larva does not look at all like a beautiful, winged adult butterfly. The larva has a greater number of legs, and biting jaws instead of the long, slender, sucking tube of the butterfly. The larva has no wings. It eats a great deal and grows rapidly, *molting* (shedding its skin) several times. After about a

Complete Metamorphosis of a Butterfly

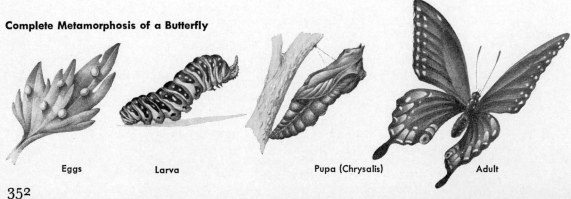

Eggs　　　　　Larva　　　　　Pupa (Chrysalis)　　　　　Adult

Metamorphosis of a Frog

Eggs   Tadpoles   Adult

month in the larval stage, it enters its third period of existence, called the *pupal* stage.

The Pupa. The third stage in a butterfly's life history is a very quiet one. The larva changes into an almost motionless, stiff object called a *chrysalis*. A chrysalis usually hangs from a twig or from the underside of a leaf. Most moth larvae spin a silk covering called a *cocoon*. Within this cocoon, the larva changes into a pupa. During the period when the moth or butterfly lies quietly in its covering, the wings, legs, and body of the mature insect develop. At the same time, other changes take place in the body of the insect.

The Adult, or Imago. The pupal period may last from two weeks to many months. When the end of the pupal period arrives, the case splits open, and the fully developed insect, or *imago*, emerges and expands its wings.

Other Examples. The grasshopper is an insect which passes through three stages of development, omitting the pupal period entirely. Scientists call its metamorphosis *incomplete*. The frog undergoes a wholly different type of metamorphosis. It comes out of the egg as a small, wriggling tadpole. The tadpole lives under water and breathes by means of gills. But as it grows larger, it develops lungs and pairs of forelegs and hind legs. Gradually, the tadpole loses its gills and tail by absorbing them into its body. Chemical substances which the tadpole secretes from ductless glands bring about all these *metamorphoses* (changes). When the tadpole is ready to leave its home in the water and live mostly on the land, the metamorphosis is finished. ALEXANDER B. KLOTS

Related Articles in WORLD BOOK include:

Butterfly   Fly (The Life of a Fly)   Larva   Nymph
Chrysalis   Insect (Growth   Molting   Pupa
Cocoon   and Development)   Moth

METAPHOR, *MEHT uh fawr,* a figure of speech, is an expression taken from one field of experience and used to say something in another field. For example, when we say, "He's a sly fox," we are using metaphor. That is, we are using the name of an animal to describe a man.

A metaphor suggests a comparison without using the word *like* or *as*. The statement "He is *like* a sly fox" or "He is sly *as* a fox" is a simile (see SIMILE).

Everyday speech is rich in metaphors. If we ask someone, "Did you *land* a job today?" the reply may be, "No, not a *bite*." These words from the special language of *fishing* are used to express thoughts about job-hunting. Common words, like *hunting*, actually develop new senses when they are repeatedly used as metaphors. For instance, we hardly realize that in the phrase "table leg," the word *leg* was originally a metaphor. And we may understand the meaning of "rocket fins" with-

out imagining the shape of a fish. But when told not to "make pigs of yourselves," we are probably aware of the unpleasant comparison the metaphor suggests.

Metaphors are important in the speech of politicians, scientists, and journalists. In 1946, Sir Winston Churchill used the now-famous phrase "iron curtain" to describe an international problem. Scientists speak of the "wave theory of light." And the phrase "priming the pump" is sometimes used to refer to government spending to stimulate a nation's business and industry. In each of these cases, the metaphor has been an important tool of thought.

Great works of literature are enriched by metaphor. Psalm 23 of the Bible is based on a metaphor. It begins with the words, "The Lord is my shepherd," and suggests the relation of God to humanity by considering the relation of a shepherd to sheep. The plays of Shakespeare contain brilliant metaphors, such as the passage in *As You Like It* beginning, "All the world's a stage." Poets often use surprising and beautiful metaphors, as in the line from Alfred Noyes' poem "The Highwayman," "The road was a ribbon of moonlight. . . ."

Mixed metaphors, using two or more unrelated metaphors in the same expression, are often unintentionally amusing. An example: "I smell a rat, but we shall nip it in the bud." CHARLES W. COOPER

METAPHYSICAL POETS is the name commonly given to a group of English poets of the 1600's. John Donne, the most important poet in the group, influenced the other members. Donne wrote on both religious and nonreligious topics. The group also included Richard Crashaw, George Herbert, and Henry Vaughan, who wrote mainly on religious subjects; and Lord Herbert of Cherbury, John Cleveland, Abraham Cowley, and Andrew Marvell, who wrote chiefly on nonreligious topics.

At its best, metaphysical poetry was truly *metaphysical*. That is, it explored the philosophical problems of the one and the many, unity and division, and the spirit and the flesh. The metaphysical poets often ignored traditional stanza forms. They used vividly colloquial language, irregular rhythms, clever but obscure or outlandish imagery, and, occasionally, extravagant diction.

Their diction and rhythms made the metaphysical poets unfashionable in the late 1600's and 1700's. Critic Samuel Johnson first used the term "metaphysical poets" in his *The Lives of the English Poets* (1779-1781). Johnson criticized the group for what he felt was an excessive use of learning. In the 1900's, the essays of T. S. Eliot helped stimulate interest in the metaphysical poets. Modern poets influenced by the group include

353

Eliot, Wallace Stevens, Hart Crane, Elinor Wylie, and Richard Eberhart. RICHARD S. SYLVESTER

See also COWLEY, ABRAHAM; DONNE, JOHN; HERBERT, GEORGE; MARVELL, ANDREW; VAUGHAN, HENRY.

METAPHYSICS, *MEHT uh FIHZ ihks,* is the name given to research about the eternal, universal nature of things. The natural scientist deals with the kinds of fundamental and basic properties that make up matter. The *metaphysician* (philosopher who deals with metaphysics) studies the basic kinds of things and properties that make up the entire *cosmos* (universe).

Branches of Metaphysics. Traditionally, metaphysics is subdivided into two branches. These are *ontology* and *cosmology.* Ontology deals with questions about the ultimate nature of things; whether a thing is one or many, or of what kind. Cosmology considers the type of organization of the world. If all things are determined, cosmology seeks to find out how, or by what method. If they are not, cosmology then tries to find out what causes the breakdown of determinism. Cosmology also seeks to discover whether things are arranged in some *hierarchy* (ascending order). If they are, it then tries to discover the *apex* (top) of that hierarchy, and how things ascend to various levels.

A person may realize that often things are not what they appear to be. He or she then begins to ask whether the things that we know are what they appear to be or whether they are *manifestations* (appearances) of something quite different. A person may ask such questions as these: "Are all things matter, or is there something else which appears to us as matter?" "Would the world appear different if we had other types of experience than taste, touch, smell, hearing, and seeing?" Answers to these questions may be classified as *qualitative* and *quantitative.* Qualitative ontology tries to answer the question, "What is the nature of reality?" Quantitative ontology seeks replies to "How many kinds of ultimate substances are there?"

Doctrines of Metaphysics. *Idealism* asserts that mind or spirit is in some sense basic to everything that exists. Most religions are based on idealistic ontologies. *Absolute idealism* asserts that there is only one universal spirit, of which all things are manifestations. *Supernaturalism,* a form of idealism, believes in the existence of something (God) beyond nature. *Naturalism,* opposed to supernaturalism, insists that there is only nature and that all things are to be explained in materialistic or scientific terms. *Materialism* affirms that matter is fundamental. Marxism is rooted in a materialistic ontology. *Dialectical materialism* says that the universe is composed of matter that develops through a series of conflicts to form the great variety of things in the world.

Monism holds that there is only one ultimate substance, out of which all things are constructed. Materialism and some forms of idealism are examples of monistic systems. *Dualism* maintains that there are two ultimate substances, usually mind and matter. *Pluralism* insists that there are many kinds of ultimate substances.

Many of these doctrines differ on the nature of change. Some cosmologies have maintained that change is unreal. Others have tried to describe the way in which things have changed and do change. *Dialectics* explains change as the result of conflict between opposites which then, so to speak, fuse into a new kind of thing that embraces both opposites. The greatest advocate of this type of explanation was the German philosopher Georg W. F. Hegel (see HEGEL, GEORG W. F.). *Evolution* explains change as the result of a development out of a given stage into something new. The cause may be either an internal drive or external compulsion. Henri Bergson, a French philosopher, advocated this doctrine (see BERGSON, HENRI). *Creation* explains change as the result of a creative act. This act may be either of God or of some principle of creativity inherent in the universe, such as love. Alfred North Whitehead, an English philosopher, advocated a similar view (see WHITEHEAD, ALFRED NORTH).

These questions metaphysicians raise cannot be answered by experimental observation in a laboratory. The laboratory method of solving questions assumes that nature is such that it can be observed in a laboratory. Metaphysics tries to justify its conclusions either by generalizing from the natural sciences or by *inferring,* or drawing conclusions, from the process of knowing to the nature of things known. Some metaphysicians have insisted that there is a process of knowing that reveals to us the structure of things in general (knowledge by acquaintance or intuition).

Opinions About Metaphysics. The progress of natural science and the diversity of answers to metaphysical questions have caused some philosophers to insist that these questions are meaningless because they cannot be answered. For example, we know of no way to answer the question, "Is reality mind or matter?" once and for all. Therefore, these philosophers consider it a meaningless question.

Other philosophers try to discover means of replying to metaphysical questions. They say that such questions are not really about the universe as it is, but about our methods of talking about the universe. Philosophers who take this position are called *linguistic analysts.* They do not affirm that there *are* particular things but that their words *assume* there are. These analysts claim that the function of metaphysics is to analyze the ways in which language is used. If people say that there are only particular things like *this* stone and *this* book, and that there are no general things like beauty and book, they mean that the words in their language are never general terms but singular terms. LOUIS O. KATTSOFF

See also ARISTOTLE (Metaphysics); IDEALISM; MATERIALISM.

METASTASIS. See CANCER (How Cancer Develops).

METATARSAL. See TRANSVERSE ARCH.

METAURUS, BATTLE OF. See ARMY (Famous Land Battles of History).

METAXAS, *MEH tah KSAHS,* **JOANNES** (1871-1941), was dictator of Greece from 1936 until his death. He became an army officer in 1890. He studied in a German military academy from 1899 to 1903, and became an admirer of German militarism. In 1934, he formed a Greek fascist-monarchist party. This group helped him become dictator in 1936. Metaxas admired the Italian dictator Benito Mussolini, but led Greece against the Italian invaders in 1940. Metaxas was born in Cephalonia. See also GREECE (History). ALBERT PARRY

METAZOAN is an animal made up of many different kinds of cells. Scientists classify these animals in the subkingdom *Metazoa.* This subkingdom includes all animals except the protozoans, which have only one cell (see PROTOZOAN). Sponges have many cells, but they differ so much from other many-celled animals that many scientists do not classify them as metazoans.

METCALFE, CHARLES THEOPHILUS (1785-1846), BARON METCALFE, a British statesman, served as Governor-General of Canada from 1843 to 1845. His dispute with the Canadian Cabinet over official appointments started a bitter struggle between the Reform and Conservative parties. The election of 1844 showed that a small majority favored his policy. But health soon forced him to resign. Metcalfe was born in Calcutta, India. He served in India from 1801 to 1836, and as Governor of Jamaica from 1839 to 1842. He attended Eton College in England.   JAMES L. GODFREY

METCHNIKOFF, *MECH nih kawf,* **ÉLIE** (1845-1916), was a great Russian biologist. He made important studies of the functions of *phagocytes.* These are white blood cells that attack disease germs. Doctors at first opposed his theory that inflammation at a wound is caused by a struggle between phagocytes and germs. But the theory was generally accepted before his death. Metchnikoff shared the 1908 Nobel prize for medicine. The biologist spent his $20,000 share of the Nobel prize on his studies.

His writings include *The Nature of Man, Lectures on the Comparative Pathology of Inflammation,* and *Immunity in Infective Diseases.* In *The Prolongation of Life,* he suggested that people should eat cultures of sour-milk bacteria to slow down the process of growing old.

Metchnikoff was born in Ivanovka in Kharkov province. He studied in Russia and Germany, and taught zoology at Odessa University. He joined the staff of the Pasteur Institute in Paris in 1892, and became its sub-director in 1895.   MORDECAI L. GABRIEL

METEOR, *MEE tee uhr,* is a bright streak of light seen briefly in the sky. Meteors are often called *shooting stars* or *falling stars* because they look like stars falling from the sky. Meteors result when chunks of metallic or stony matter called *meteoroids* enter the earth's atmosphere from space. Friction with the air makes the meteoroid so hot it glows and creates a trail of hot glowing gases. Meteoroids that reach the earth's surface before burning up are called *meteorites.*

Scientists estimate that as many as 200 million visible

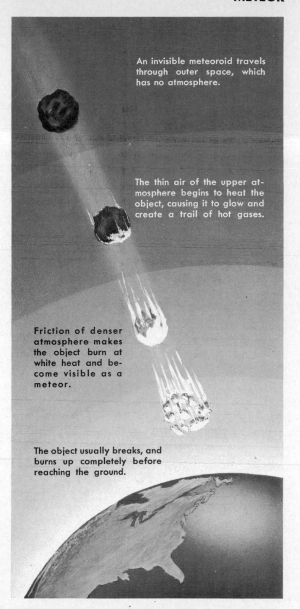

An invisible meteoroid travels through outer space, which has no atmosphere.

The thin air of the upper atmosphere begins to heat the object, causing it to glow and create a trail of hot gases.

Friction of denser atmosphere makes the object burn at white heat and become visible as a meteor.

The object usually breaks, and burns up completely before reaching the ground.

A Meteor Appears in the Sky whenever an object called a *meteoroid* hurtles into the earth's atmosphere from space.

Ernest Chilson, Flagstaff Chamber of Commerce

The Great Meteor Crater of Arizona lies between the towns of Flagstaff and Winslow. Scientists believe that a meteorite struck the earth about 50,000 years ago and dug a hole about 4,150 feet (1,265 meters) across and 570 feet (174 meters) deep.

meteors occur in the earth's atmosphere every day. These and invisible meteorites are estimated to add more than 1,000 short tons (910 metric tons) daily to the earth's weight. We first see most of these meteors when they are about 65 miles (105 kilometers) above the earth. Air friction heats them and the air around them to about 4000° F. (2200° C), and they burn out at altitudes of 30 to 50 miles (48 to 80 kilometers).

All known meteoroids belong to the solar system of which the earth is a part. They travel in a variety of orbits and velocities about the sun. The faster ones move at about 26 miles (42 kilometers) a second. The earth travels at about 18 miles (29 kilometers) a second. When

American Museum of Natural History, New York

The Willamette Meteorite is the largest meteorite ever found in the United States. It measures about 118 inches (300 centimeters) long and weighs about 15½ short tons (14 metric tons). Rust and atmospheric friction caused pits in one side. The meteorite was named after the Willamette Valley in Oregon, where it was found in 1902.

meteoroids meet the earth's atmosphere head-on, the combined velocity may reach about 44 miles (71 kilometers) a second. Those traveling in the same direction as the earth hit the atmosphere at much slower speeds. Meteors rarely blaze for more than a few seconds. But occasionally one leaves a shining trail that lasts as long as several minutes. Most of the meteors we see were originally no larger than a pinhead or a grain of sand.

Meteor Showers. The earth meets a number of swarms of meteoroids every year. When this happens, the sky seems filled with a shower of flying sparks. Some swarms of meteoroids have orbits similar to the orbits of comets. This shows that these swarms are fragments of comets.

--- IMPORTANT METEOR SHOWERS ---

Shower	Date
Quadrantid	January 3
Lyrid	April 21
Eta Aquarid	May 4
Delta Aquarid	July 29
Perseid	August 12
Orionid	October 22
Taurid, North	November 1
Taurid, South	November 16
Leonid	November 17
Geminid	December 12

The most brilliant meteoric shower took place on Nov. 13, 1833. The earth encounters this swarm, called the *Leonid* meteor shower, every November. It consists of a great ring of particles that revolves continually around the sun. Another brilliant Leonid meteor shower occurred in 1966. Written records indicate that the Leonid shower was seen as long ago as A.D. 902.

Astronomers name meteor showers after the constellations from which they appear to come. The table above lists some of the important annual showers and the dates of their greatest activity.

Meteorites sometimes explode into fragments with a noise that can be heard far away when they strike the earth or its atmosphere. In 1908, the famous Tunguska meteorite crashed into the earth in Siberia. People as far as 466 miles (750 kilometers) away saw this meteor in full daylight, and felt its blast at a distance of 50 miles (80 kilometers). The Tunguska meteorite had a

weight estimated at a few hundred tons. It scorched a 20-mile (32-kilometer) area and flattened forests like matchsticks. In 1947, a meteorite exploded into fragments over the Sikhote-Alin Mountains in eastern Siberia. It left more than 200 craters in the earth.

There are two kinds of meteorites, stony and iron. *Stony meteorites* are made up of many different stony minerals mixed with particles of iron. Some resemble minerals that come from volcanoes. *Iron meteorites* consist chiefly of iron combined with nickel. They also may have small amounts of cobalt, copper, phosphorus, carbon, and sulfur.

Scientists collect meteorites for study, because they are thought to be unchanged fragments of the material from which the moon and planets were made. The largest meteorite, at Hoba West in South West Africa, weighs about 66 short tons (60 metric tons). The Hayden Planetarium in New York City owns the Ahnighito, a 34-short-ton (31-metric-ton) nickel-iron meteorite that Arctic explorer Robert E. Peary brought to the United States from western Greenland in 1897.

In the 1950's, scientists discovered a 400-mile (640-kilometer) wide depression on the eastern shore of Hudson Bay in Canada, which may be the earth's largest meteorite crater. Canada also has four other craters found in the 1950's. These are a crater 7 to 8 miles (11 to 13 kilometers) wide at Deep Bay, Saskatchewan; the Chubb crater, 2 miles (3.2 kilometers) wide, on the Ungava Peninsula; and a 2-mile-wide crater at Brent and a crater 1½ miles (2.4 kilometers) wide at Holleford, both in Ontario. Southern Algeria has a crater that is 1¼ miles (2 kilometers) wide. The Meteor Crater between Flagstaff and Winslow in Arizona is about 4,150 feet (1,265 meters) wide and 570 feet (174 meters) deep. Its rim towers more than 150 feet (46 meters) above the surrounding ground level.   FRANK D. DRAKE

See also FIREBALL; LEONIDS; TEKTITE.

METEOROLOGICAL SATELLITE. See SPACE TRAVEL (Weather Satellites; table; pictures).

METEOROLOGICAL SOCIETY, AMERICAN, is an international organization that encourages the study of the atmospheric sciences. Its members include scientists and other persons interested in weather.

The society prepares educational films, and publishes books and papers on meteorological subjects. It provides career information and makes awards to college students. The society certifies consulting meteorologists. It was founded in 1919. Its headquarters are at 45 Beacon Street, Boston, Mass. 02108.

Critically reviewed by the AMERICAN METEOROLOGICAL SOCIETY

METEOROLOGY, MEE tee uh RAHL uh jee, is the study of the earth's atmosphere and the variations in atmospheric conditions that produce weather. Meteorologists measure wind, temperature, precipitation, air pressure, and other atmospheric conditions. They also measure chemical substances in the atmosphere, such as carbon dioxide and ozone, that affect the weather. By analyzing data about the atmosphere, meteorologists often can predict weather conditions.

Many meteorologists work as weather observers. They measure weather conditions and prepare weather maps used by forecasters. Other meteorologists, who are employed as forecasters, analyze weather maps and information from computers and other sources. They use such data to prepare detailed weather reports, make forecasts, and issue warnings of hazardous weather conditions. Forecasters also prepare special weather information. For example, they provide farmers with data about water-supply conditions. Some forecasters work for government agencies. Others work for private businesses, such as airlines, oil companies, and radio and television stations.

Large numbers of meteorologists conduct research. They work to develop better computer techniques to make forecasting more exact. They also work on the development of improved instruments to collect information about the weather. In addition, research meteorologists study ways to control the weather. For example, they experiment with cloud seeding to produce rain (see RAINMAKING).

How Meteorologists Study the Atmosphere. Meteorologists use a wide variety of scientific instruments to gather information about the atmosphere and the weather. These scientists make weather observations from land, in the air, and at sea. Meteorologists use such instruments as thermometers, barometers, and hygrometers to measure basic aspects of the weather. Balloons carrying these instruments measure conditions in the upper atmosphere (see BALLOON [Scientific Uses]). Radar devices determine the location, size, speed, and direction of storms.

Weather satellites, also called meteorological satellites, take pictures of the earth from great altitudes. Meteorologists use these pictures from the satellites to chart the movement of clouds. In addition, weather satellites measure air temperature and humidity and help detect storms that develop at sea. See SPACE TRAVEL (Weather Satellites).

Computers help meteorologists forecast the weather. These machines can predict certain elements of weather by solving complex sets of equations that describe the behavior of the atmosphere. Weather forecasting with computers is called *numerical forecasting*.

History. The word *meteorology* comes from *Meteorologica*, the title of a book by the ancient Greek philosopher Aristotle. In this book, Aristotle wrote about his weather observations.

Scientific observation of the weather began in 1593, when the Italian scientist Galileo invented a type of thermometer to measure air temperature. By the late 1700's, instruments had been invented to measure humidity, wind, air pressure and precipitation. During the 1800's, the use of weather maps enabled people to forecast the weather scientifically.

In the early 1900's, meteorologists began to explain the structure of the atmosphere. For example, the Norwegian meteorologist Vilhelm Bjerknes discovered that the atmosphere contains zones of rapidly changing con-

ditions called *fronts*. Shortly after World War II ended in 1945, the Swedish-American meteorologist Carl-Gustaf Rossby studied *jet streams*, which are atmospheric regions of extremely strong winds. The findings of such scientists greatly changed methods of forecasting the weather. The accuracy of forecasting improved after computers, weather satellites, and other modern instruments came into use.

Cooperation between nations further advanced the study of meteorology. In 1963, the United Nations (UN) approved the *World Weather Watch*, an observation system that maps the weather of many areas of the world. In 1967, the International Council of Scientific Unions (ICSU), an organization of scientists from many fields, established the Global Atmospheric Research Program (GARP). The First GARP Global Experiment was scheduled to begin gathering weather information from all parts of the world in 1978.　　　YOSHI KAZU SASAKI

See also WEATHER.

METER, also spelled *metre*, is the base unit of length in the metric system. Its symbol is *m*. A meter is equal to 39.37 inches. Scientists define the length of the meter as 1,650,763.73 wave lengths of the orange-red light from the isotope krypton-86, measured in a vacuum. The International Bureau of Weights and Measures adopted this measurement standard in 1960 in place of the platinum-iridium meter bar. See also CENTIMETER; METRIC SYSTEM; YARD.

METER, in poetry, is the number of feet in a line of verse. The word *meter* means *measure*. It can also refer to the *metrical pattern*—the foot, meter, and rhyme scheme—of a poem. See POETRY (Verse and Melody).

> Lives of great men all remind us
> We can make our lives sublime,
> And, departing, leave behind us
> Footprints on the sands of time.

When poetry like this is read aloud, the flow of word sounds is rhythmical. A definite pattern of rising and falling sounds becomes apparent. *Scanning* (marking accented syllables) may help to discover this pattern, as is shown in this example:

> Lives' of/great' men/all' re/mind' us
> We' can/make' our/lives' sub/lime'

The metrical pattern of a traditional poem is described in terms of the basic *foot* (rhythmic unit), the *meter* (verse length), and the line scheme. There are four or five different kinds of feet used in metrical patterns: the iamb (*de-DUMM*), anapest (*de-de-DUMM*), trochee (*DUMM-de*), dactyl (*DUMM-de-de*), and occasionally amphibrach (*de-DUMM-de*). The *meter* (verse length) is the number of feet to the line: monometer (a

The Meter Measure, *below*, Compares the Base Unit of Measure in the Metric System with a Yardstick, *above*.

357

line of only one foot), dimeter (a line of two feet), trimeter (three), tetrameter (four), pentameter (five), hexameter (six), heptameter (seven), and octameter (eight). The meter of this example is trochaic tetrameter (four *DUMM de* feet per line). The second and fourth lines lack a final syllable.

The *rhyme scheme* of a metrical pattern is the sequence or grouping of lines, often in stanzas that use rhyme. The stanza that appears in this article is a *quatrain* (four-line stanza) with *crossed rhymes* (alternate lines rhyme, *abab*).

But meter is not necessary to poetry. There are some non-metrical types of verse, such as free verse, that have no regular beat (see FREE VERSE). The rhythm of such poetry follows the meaning of the phrases and arrangement of the verses on the page.   CHARLES W. COOPER

See also POETRY (Metrical Patterns); BLANK VERSE; COUPLET.

METER, ELECTRIC. See ELECTRIC METER.

METHADONE is a drug used in experimental programs that help people overcome addiction to such narcotics as heroin, morphine, or opium. Most of these programs also include counseling to help addicts with psychological, social, and occupational problems.

Methadone itself can cause addiction with symptoms similar to those of heroin addiction. But if people already addicted to heroin, morphine, or opium take methadone, they no longer crave or even enjoy the other drugs. Methadone must be taken orally to produce those effects. If methadone doses are stopped, former drug cravings return. As a result, a former heroin addict may have to take methadone for life.

Lengthy methadone treatment has been criticized as a substitution of one addiction for another. But methadone therapy produces different effects than does addiction to heroin. A heroin user experiences *highs* (extremely happy feelings), dreamlike states, and sleepiness. Most heroin addicts cannot hold a job or maintain normal social relationships. But a former heroin addict who takes methadone in the prescribed manner has a clear mind and a feeling of well-being. In time, most addicts who are treated with methadone can lead normal lives. Long-term methadone therapy was developed in 1964 by two American physicians, Vincent Dole and Marie Nyswander, a husband-and-wife team.   DONALD J. WOLK

METHAMPHETAMINE is a powerful drug nicknamed "speed." It quickly produces feelings of joy, strength, and alertness. Methamphetamine gives a user the capacity to work and talk for long periods of time. Misuse of methamphetamine can be dangerous, and the drug can be obtained legally only with a doctor's prescription. Methamphetamine is one of the drugs called amphetamines. It has been sold under several brand names, including Methedrine.

Physicians sometimes prescribe methamphetamine pills for weight control. The pills have also been used to combat fatigue and to help people under tension improve their work.

Excess use of methamphetamine causes severe weight loss, pains in muscles and joints, excessive activity, and overconcentration on minor tasks. Some persons become suspicious and develop antisocial behavior.

Methamphetamine does not cause physical dependence. But in time, a user's body needs larger and larger doses to achieve the same effect. Users may become mentally dependent on the drug if, when they go without it, they find the world cold and demanding. Sudden withdrawal from the drug may cause deep depression and fatigue.   DONALD J. WOLK

See also AMPHETAMINE; DRUG ADDICTION.

METHANE is an important industrial compound that makes up a large part of natural gas. It is formed when plants decay in places where there is very little air. Methane is often called *marsh gas* because it is found around stagnant water and swamps. It is also the chief substance in *firedamp*, a gas that causes serious explosions in mines.

The chemical industry uses methane as a starting material for many other chemicals. Methane reacts at high temperatures with a limited amount of air to form acetylene and with ammonia to produce hydrogen cyanide. It also undergoes *partial combustion* (incomplete burning), producing hydrogen and carbon monoxide gases. This mixture serves as a source for commercial hydrogen, and for carbon monoxide used in making methyl alcohol (methanol).

Methane is a colorless, odorless, flammable gas. It is soluble in alcohol but only slightly soluble in water. Methane's chemical formula is CH_4, and it is the first member of the *paraffin* series of hydrocarbons. Mixtures of methane with air, oxygen, or chlorine are explosive.   LEWIS F. HATCH

See also ACETYLENE; DAMP; GAS (The Composition of Natural Gas); HYDROCARBON; METHANOL.

METHANOL is a useful industrial chemical. It is a colorless, flammable liquid with a mild odor. Methanol is also called *wood alcohol*, *wood spirit*, or *methyl alcohol*. Drinking or inhaling methanol can cause blindness or even death.

Many chemicals, including formaldehyde, are made from methanol. Formaldehyde is used in making adhesives and to preserve biological specimens. Methanol is widely used as a *solvent*, a chemical that dissolves other substances. Methanol can also be used as a motor fuel. Someday, it may replace gasoline because methanol can be made from coal. Coal is more plentiful than petroleum, from which gasoline is made. Scientists believe the world's supply of petroleum will become scarce by the early 2000's. However, methanol costs more to make than gasoline.

Methanol is made by the reaction of a mixture of hydrogen and carbon monoxide gases under high pressures. This mixture, called *synthesis gas*, can be produced from many kinds of waste products and from any fuel that contains carbon. Such fuels include coal, natural gas, oil, and wood. Synthesis gas is converted to methanol by a process called *contact catalysis* (see CATALYSIS). Most methanol in the United States is made from natural gas.

Methanol is the simplest member of the alcohol class of organic compounds. Its chemical formula is CH_3OH, and it boils at 64.7° C (148.5° F.).   MARTIN B. SHERWIN

METHODIST YOUTH FELLOWSHIP. See UNITED METHODIST YOUTH FELLOWSHIP.

METHODISTS belong to Protestant religious denominations that trace their beginnings back to John Wesley, a Church of England clergyman in the 1700's. In the United States, more than 15 denominations share the name *Methodist* and a common heritage in Wesley's teaching. The largest Methodist body is the United Methodist Church, formed in 1968 through a union of The Methodist Church and the Evangelical United Brethren Church. Other major denominations include the African Methodist Episcopal Church, the African Methodist Episcopal Zion Church, the Christian Methodist Episcopal Church, and the Free Methodist Church of North America.

There is no central organization of Methodist denominations in the United States, but many denominations are part of a World Methodist Council. However, this council has no legislative power and serves primarily as a *fraternal* (brotherly) association.

Doctrine. Methodist churches are *evangelical.* That is, they try to convince non-Methodists of the soundness of the Methodist approach to religion. All Methodists stress salvation through faith, and emphasize an orderly, active Christian life and God's forgiveness of personal sins. But Methodists emphasize that salvation comes through work as well as faith. They believe in a personal religious experience in which each individual gives proof of a belief in Jesus Christ as his or her personal savior. This experience may be sudden and highly emotional for some. For others, the experience may involve periods of study and prayer. But all Methodist denominations expect their members to declare their faith in Jesus Christ publicly. Each denomination strongly emphasizes the necessity of being a church member. Methodists accept the Bible as the supreme rule of faith and religious practice.

History. In the early 1700's, John Wesley began trying to find ways to reform the Church of England. He did not set out to found a new church.

The name *Methodists* first appeared in 1729 when Wesley was a tutor at Oxford University. While there, he and his brother Charles became leaders of a small group called the Holy Club. Other students noticed the strict, methodical way in which this group approached their religious life and began calling them *methodists.*

John Wesley tried unsuccessfully to find religious satisfaction by closely following the rules of the Church of England. A turning point in his life came in London in 1738, when he said his heart was "strangely warmed." Wesley said he discovered that inner peace comes by faith in God's mercy and grace, not through personal efforts alone.

Wesley became unwelcome in Anglican churches because of his evangelistic vigor in preaching and the strict discipline he urged on his followers. He and his followers then began to preach wherever people would gather to listen—on streets, in public squares, and in fields. Wesley believed that salvation is free to all people, not just to a select few, and that God's grace is equal to every need. Such a doctrine appealed to many persons in England at that time, especially to the poor and oppressed.

As the movement spread, Wesley established what he called the United Societies, in which he used many *lay* (unordained) preachers. Wesley trained, appointed, and supervised the preachers, and his doctrine spread mainly because of their devotion and enthusiasm. He organized them into a Methodist conference in 1744.

Wesley realized that this growing movement could not continue to work within the framework of the Church of England. Under his guidance, the United Societies developed as an independent church, although Wesley continued as an ordained Anglican clergyman. Wesley sent preachers to America. Philip Embury preached in New York City about 1766. Robert Strawbridge went to Maryland about the same time. Wesley later sent Francis Asbury and Thomas Coke, who became the first American Methodist bishops.

In 1784, about 60 ministers organized the Methodist Episcopal Church in Baltimore. The denomination grew quickly, as traveling preachers called *circuit riders* carried the Methodist religion to the frontier (see CIRCUIT RIDER). In 1828, a group insisting on more lay representation in church affairs separated and formed the Methodist Protestant Church. Like Methodism in England, this new church did not have bishops. In 1844, a group left the Methodist Episcopal Church to form the Methodist Episcopal Church, South. This division occurred over the issues of slavery and constitutional powers within the denomination. The Methodist Episcopal Church, the Methodist Protestant Church, and the Methodist Episcopal Church, South reunited in 1939 as The Methodist Church.

Methodists in Canada organized into the United Church of Canada in 1925. British Methodists, after periods of division, reunited in 1925. EARL KENNETH WOOD

Related Articles in WORLD BOOK include:

African Methodist Episcopal Church	Free Methodist Church
African Methodist Episcopal Zion Church	Oxnam, G. Bromley
	United Church of Canada
	United Methodist Church
Asbury, Francis	United Methodist Youth Fellowship
Camp Meeting	
Cartwright, Peter	Wesley
Delaware (Places to Visit [Houses of Worship])	Wesleyan Church
	Whitefield, George

METHUSELAH, *mee THOO zuh luh,* was the son of Enoch and the grandfather of Noah in the Old Testament. According to the Bible, he lived 969 years (Gen. 5:25-27). The expression "as old as Methuselah" describes a very old person. Babylonians believed that some of their heroes lived 36,000 years. JOHN BRIGHT

METHYL ALCOHOL. See METHANOL.

METHYL BENZENE. See TOLUENE.

METHYL MERCURY. See MERCURY (metal).

METIC. See GREECE, ANCIENT (The People).

MÉTIS. See MANITOBA (People; The Red River Colony); RED RIVER REBELLION; RIEL, LOUIS; SASKATCHEWAN REBELLION.

METONYMY, *muh TAHN uh mee.* We often use words figuratively, rather than literally. Some of these forms of expressions are called *metonymy.* When we "turn on the light," we actually flip a switch, closing an electric circuit and causing the light. But we give the name of the effect to the cause. When we "listen to records," we really hear music, but we name the cause to mean the effect. When we ask for "another cup," we really mean more coffee. The container symbolizes what it contains. These are common forms of metonymy.

In *synecdoche,* which is related to metonymy, we name the part for the whole. For instance, we use the name of an athletic team, but actually mean the school the team represents. CHARLES W. COOPER

METRE. See METER; METRIC SYSTEM.

Students Learn About the Metric System by Making Various Measurements with Metric Units.

METRIC SYSTEM

METRIC SYSTEM is a group of units used to make any kind of measurement, such as length, temperature, time, or weight. No other system of measurement ever used equals the metric system in simpleness. Scientists everywhere make measurements in metric units, and so do all other people in most countries.

In the mid-1970's, the United States and Canada began gradual changeovers to the metric system. All other major countries were already using the metric system. Through the years, the United States and Canada had used the *customary*, or *English*, system for most measurements. This system was developed in England from older units, beginning in about the 1200's.

A group of French scientists created the metric system in the 1790's. The system has been revised several times. The official name of the present version is *Système International d'Unités* (International System of Units), usually known simply as *SI*. The term *metric* comes from the base unit of length in the system, the *meter*, for which the international spelling is *metre*.

Using the Metric System

The scientists who created the metric system designed it to fit their needs. They made the system logical and exact. But a nonscientist needs to know only a few metric units to make everyday measurements.

Daniel V. De Simone, the contributor of this article, is Deputy Director of the Office of Technology Assessment, an agency of the United States Congress. He directed the U.S. Metric Study conducted by the government from 1968 to 1971.

The metric system may seem difficult to someone who has not used it. But much of this difficulty results from unfamiliarity with the units. It also comes from the need to convert measurements in the units of one system into the units of the other. After the metric system comes into widespread use in a country, the units become increasingly familiar. People no longer have to switch back and forth between two systems.

The metric system is simple to use for two reasons. First, it follows the decimal number system—that is, metric units increase or decrease in size by 10's. For example, a meter has 10 parts called *decimeters*. A decimeter has 10 parts called *centimeters*. Units in the customary system have no single number relationship between them. For example, feet and yards are related by 3's, but feet and inches are related by 12's.

Also, the metric system has only 7 base units that make up all its measurements. The customary system has more than 20 base units for just its common measurements. Customary units used for special purposes add many more base units to that system.

The Decimal Arrangement. The metric system is a decimal system just as are the money systems of the United States and Canada. In a decimal system, a unit is 10 times larger than the next smaller unit. For example, a meter equals 10 decimeters just as a dollar equals 10 dimes.

Most metric units have a prefix that tells the relationship of that unit to the base unit. These prefixes are the same no matter which base unit is used. This uniform system of names is another feature that simplifies metric measurement.

Greek prefixes are used to show multiples of a base unit. They make a base unit larger. For example, *hecto* means 100 times and *kilo* means 1,000 times. Latin prefixes are used to show the submultiples of the base unit. They make a base unit smaller. For example, *centi* means $\frac{1}{100}$ and *milli* means $\frac{1}{1,000}$. The table on page 361 shows all the prefixes, their symbols, and their relationship to the base unit.

An example will illustrate the basic simpleness of a decimal system. Suppose you want to measure the length and width of a room so you can draw a floor plan to scale. Using the customary system, you measure the room with a yardstick and get the length in units of yards, feet, and inches. To find the distance in just feet and inches, you multiply the number of yards by 3. Suppose the room measures 3 yards 1 foot 6 inches long. This measurement equals 10 feet 6 inches.

To prepare the scale drawing, you decide to let one inch of the drawing equal one foot of the room. The 10 feet in the room measurement equal 10 inches on the drawing. But the 6 inches must be divided by 12 to get the fraction of an inch needed to represent them on the drawing. Since $6 \div 12$ equals $\frac{1}{2}$, the correct scale distance for the drawing is $10\frac{1}{2}$ inches.

Using the metric system, you find the room measures 3 meters 2 decimeters long. This measurement can also be written as 3.2 meters. You let one decimeter of the drawing equal one meter of the room. Then, all you do to change the room measurement into the scale measurement is divide by 10. Moving the decimal point one place to the left divides a decimal number by 10. Therefore, the scale distance is 3.2 meters $\div$ 10, or .32 meters, which equals 3.2 decimeters.

Metric Measurement Units. Seven *base* (basic) units form the foundation of the metric system. Most everyday measurements involve only four of these units. (1) The *meter* is the base unit for length or distance. (2) The *kilogram* is the base unit for *mass*, the weight of an object when measured on the earth. (3) The *second* is the base unit for time. (4) The *kelvin* is the base unit for temperature. Most people, when measuring in metric units, use *Celsius* temperatures instead of kelvin temperatures. One kelvin equals one degree Celsius, but the two temperature scales begin at different points. See the section *Temperature Measurements* in this article.

The three other base units have specialized uses by scientists and engineers. (5) The *ampere* is the base unit for electrical measurements. (6) The *mole* is the base unit for measuring the amount of any substance involved in a chemical or other reaction. (7) The *candela* is the base unit for measuring light.

Every base unit is defined by a *measurement standard* that gives the exact value of the unit. For information on measurement standards, see the WORLD BOOK article on MEASUREMENT. The metric system also includes two supplementary units for measuring angles. These units are the *radian* and the *steradian* (see RADIAN).

All other units in the metric system consist of two or more base units. For example, the unit for speed, *meters per second*, combines the base units for length and time. Such combination units are called *derived units*.

Common Measurements

This section describes everyday measurements made by using the metric system. The examples give the approximate number of customary units in each metric unit. For the exact conversions between the two systems, see the WORLD BOOK article on WEIGHTS AND MEASURES. Other articles discuss the specialized metric units used by scientists and engineers. For example, see ENERGY for the metric units related to energy.

Length and Distance Measurements. The meter is used for such measurements as the length of a rope or of a piano or other large object. It also is used to measure the height of a mountain or the altitude of an airplane. A meter is slightly longer than a yard. Short lengths are measured in centimeters, or they may be measured in *millimeters*. A centimeter equals about $\frac{2}{5}$ of an inch. Books, pencils, and other small objects may be measured in centimeters. A millimeter equals about $\frac{1}{25}$ of an inch. Photographic film, small hardware, and tiny mechanical parts are measured in millimeters.

Long distances, such as those between cities, are measured in *kilometers*. A kilometer equals about $\frac{5}{8}$ of a mile. A short distance, such as that between two buildings on the same block, is measured in meters.

Surface Measurements tell how much area something covers. For example, the amount of carpeting needed to cover a floor is measured in square units. Most areas are measured in *square meters*. A square meter equals the surface covered by a square one meter long on each side. It is slightly larger than a square yard. Smaller areas may be measured in *square centimeters* or *square millimeters*.

Land is sometimes measured in units called *hectares*. A hectare equals 10,000 square meters, or about $2\frac{1}{2}$ acres. Large land areas, such as cities and countries, are measured in *square kilometers*. One square kilometer equals about 247 acres, or about $\frac{3}{8}$ of a square mile.

Volume and Capacity Measurements tell how much space something occupies or encloses. A volume measurement tells the size of a box, and a capacity measurement tells how much the box can hold. Volume and capacity are both measured in cubic units, such as *cubic meters* or *cubic decimeters*. The volume of a box with each side 1 meter long equals 1 cubic meter. A cubic meter contains 1,000 cubic decimeters and equals about $1\frac{1}{3}$ cubic yards.

Most capacity measurements for liquids are made in units called *liters*. A liter equals a cubic decimeter and is slightly larger than a liquid quart. Smaller units include the *deciliter* ($\frac{1}{10}$ of a liter) and the *milliliter* ($\frac{1}{1,000}$ of a liter). A milliliter equals a *cubic centimeter*.

Weight and Mass Measurements. The mass of an object is not really the same as its weight because its weight changes with altitude. However, the two measurements are equal at sea level on the earth. The kilogram is a unit of mass. But most people who use the metric system think of the kilogram as a unit of weight.

A kilogram equals about $2\frac{1}{5}$ avoirdupois pounds. The *gram* is used for small weight measurements. A gram equals $\frac{1}{1,000}$ of a kilogram. Manufacturers and shippers weigh bulk goods in *metric tons*. A metric ton equals 1,000 kilograms, or about $1\frac{1}{10}$ short tons in the customary system.

Time Measurements. The metric system measures time exactly as the customary system does for measurements longer than a second. For such measurements, the

THE METRIC SYSTEM AT A GLANCE

Length and Distance

Length and distance measurements in the metric system are based on the meter. All units for length and distance are decimal fractions or multiples of the meter. Commonly used units for such measurements include the millimeter, centimeter, meter, and kilometer.

One Millimeter
About the thickness of a paper match

One Centimeter
About the radius of a United States nickel

1 cm

One Meter
About the length of four volumes of WORLD BOOK placed top-to-bottom

One Kilometer
About the length of five city blocks

Surface or Area

Surface or area measurements in the metric system are also based on the meter. But area is measured in square units. Common units for these measurements include the square centimeter, square meter, hectare (10,000 square meters), and square kilometer.

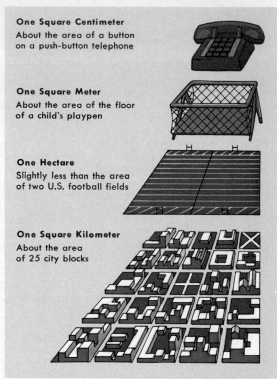

One Square Centimeter
About the area of a button on a push-button telephone

One Square Meter
About the area of the floor of a child's playpen

One Hectare
Slightly less than the area of two U.S. football fields

One Square Kilometer
About the area of 25 city blocks

WORLD BOOK illustrations by George Suyeoka

Volume and Capacity

Volume and capacity measurements in the metric system are based on the meter, but these measurements are made in cubic units. Common volume and capacity units include the cubic centimeter, liter (1,000 cubic centimeters), and cubic meter.

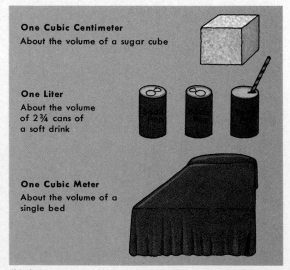

One Cubic Centimeter
About the volume of a sugar cube

One Liter
About the volume of 2¾ cans of a soft drink

One Cubic Meter
About the volume of a single bed

The illustrations on these pages will help show the size of the most common metric units. The metric conversion table will aid in the quick conversion of measurements into or out of the metric system.

Weight and Mass

Weight measurement in the metric system is based on mass, the amount of matter an object contains. The metric unit for mass—and thus weight—is the gram. Commonly used weight units include the gram, kilogram, and metric ton (1,000 kilograms).

One Gram
About the weight of a United States dollar bill

One Kilogram
About the weight of the U-V volume of WORLD BOOK

One Metric Ton
About the weight of a small automobile

Metric Conversion Table

WHEN YOU KNOW:	MULTIPLY BY:	TO FIND:*
Length and Distance		
inches (in.)	25	millimeters
feet (ft.)	30	centimeters
yards (yd.)	0.9	meters
miles (mi.)	1.6	kilometers
millimeters (mm)	0.04	inches
centimeters (cm)	0.4	inches
meters (m)	1.1	yards
kilometers (km)	0.6	miles
Surface or Area		
square inches (sq. in.)	6.5	square centimeters
square feet (sq. ft.)	0.09	square meters
square yards (sq. yd.)	0.8	square meters
square miles (sq. mi.)	2.6	square kilometers
acres	0.4	hectares
square centimeters (cm²)	0.16	square inches
square meters (m²)	1.2	square yards
square kilometers (km²)	0.4	square miles
hectares (ha)	2.5	acres
Volume and Capacity (Liquid)		
fluid ounces (fl. oz.)	30	milliliters
pints (pt.), U.S.	0.47	liters
pints (pt.), imperial	0.568	liters
quarts (qt.), U.S.	0.95	liters
quarts (qt.), imperial	1.137	liters
gallons (gal.), U.S.	3.8	liters
gallons (gal.), imperial	4.546	liters
milliliters (ml)	0.034	fluid ounces
liters (l)	2.1	pints, U.S.
liters (l)	1.76	pints, imperial
liters (l)	1.06	quarts, U.S.
liters (l)	0.88	quarts, imperial
liters (l)	0.26	gallons, U.S.
liters (l)	0.22	gallons, imperial
Weight and Mass		
ounces (oz.)	28	grams
pounds (lb.)	0.45	kilograms
short tons	0.9	metric tons
grams (g)	0.035	ounces
kilograms (kg)	2.2	pounds
metric tons (t)	1.1	short tons
Temperature		
degrees Fahrenheit (° F.)	5/9 (after subtracting 32)	degrees Celsius
degrees Celsius (° C)	9/5 (then add 32)	degrees Fahrenheit

*Answers are approximations.

Temperature

Everyday temperature measurements in the metric system are made on the Celsius scale. This scale was once called the centigrade scale. Water freezes at 0°C and boils at 100°C.

Water at 0°C (ice)   Water at 100°C (steam)

Metric Prefixes

These prefixes can be added to most metric units to increase or decrease their size. For example, a kilometer equals 1,000 meters. Centi, kilo, and milli are the most commonly used prefixes.

Prefix	Symbol	Increase or decrease in unit
exa (*EHK suh*)	E	1,000,000,000,000,000,000 (One quintillion)
peta (*PEH tuh*)	P	1,000,000,000,000,000 (One quadrillion)
tera (*TEHR uh*)	T	1,000,000,000,000 (One trillion)
giga (*JIHG uh*)	G	1,000,000,000 (One billion)
mega (*MEHG uh*)	M	1,000,000 (One million)
kilo (*KIHL uh*)	k	1,000 (One thousand)
hecto (*HEHK tuh*)	h	100 (One hundred)
deka (*DEHK uh*)	da	10 (Ten)
deci (*DEHS uh*)	d	0.1 (One-tenth)
centi (*SEHN tuh*)	c	0.01 (One-hundredth)
milli (*MIHL uh*)	m	0.001 (One-thousandth)
micro (*MY kroh*)	μ	0.000001 (One-millionth)
nano (*NAY nuh*)	n	0.000000001 (One-billionth)
pico (*PY koh*)	p	0.000000000001 (One-trillionth)
femto (*FEHM toh*)	f	0.000000000000001 (One-quadrillionth)
atto (*AT toh*)	a	0.000000000000000001 (One-quintillionth)

metric system does not follow the decimal system. For example, 60—not 100—seconds equal a minute, and 60 minutes equal an hour. Time measurements in both systems use a decimal arrangement for units longer than a year. Ten years equal a *decade*, 10 decades are a *century*, and 10 centuries are a *millennium*. For more information about time measurement, see TIME.

The metric system follows a decimal arrangement for time measurements shorter than a second. Scientists and others who work with electronic equipment, including computers and radar, use such measurements. For example, some electronic computers perform mathematical operations in *microseconds* and *nanoseconds*. A microsecond is $\frac{1}{1,000,000}$ of a second, and a nanosecond is $\frac{1}{1,000,000,000}$ of a second.

Temperature Measurements. Most people who use the metric system have thermometers marked in degrees Celsius (° C). Water freezes at 0° C and boils at 100° C. The normal body temperature of human beings is 37° C.

Celsius has been the official name of the metric scale for temperature since 1948. But many people still call this scale by its old name of *centigrade scale*. The word *centigrade* means *divided into 100 parts*. The Celsius scale has 100 degrees between the freezing and boiling temperatures of water.

Scientists do not know of any limit on how high a temperature may be. The temperature at the center of the sun is about 15,000,000° C, for example, but other stars may have an even higher temperature. On the other hand, nothing can have a temperature lower than −273.15° C. This temperature is called *absolute zero*. It forms the basis of the *kelvin scale* used by some scientists. One degree Celsius equals one kelvin. Because the kelvin scale begins at absolute zero, 0 K equals −273.15° C, and 273.15 K equals 0° C. See ABSOLUTE ZERO.

History

Before the development of the metric system, every nation used measurement units that had grown from local customs. For example, the English once used "three barleycorns, round and dry" as their standard for an inch. Grains of barley varied in size, of course—and so did the inch. As a result, no one could be sure that their measurements of the same thing would be equal.

During the 1600's, some people recognized the need for a single, accurate, worldwide measurement system. In 1670, Gabriel Mouton, the vicar of St. Paul's Church in Lyons, France, proposed a decimal measurement system. He based his unit of length on the length of one minute ($\frac{1}{21,600}$) of the earth's circumference. In 1671, Jean Picard, a French astronomer, proposed the length of a pendulum that swung once per second as the standard unit of length. Such a standard would have been more accurate than barleycorns because it was based on the physical laws of motion. In addition, a pendulum could have been duplicated easily to provide uniform measurement standards for everyone. Through the years, other people suggested various systems and standards of measurement.

The Creation of the Metric System. In 1790, the National Assembly of France asked the French Academy of Sciences to create a standard system of weights and measures. A commission appointed by the academy proposed a system that was both simple and scientific. This system became known as the metric system, and France officially adopted it in 1795. But the government did not require the French people to use the new units of measurement until 1840.

IMPORTANT DATES IN THE DEVELOPMENT OF THE METRIC SYSTEM

1670 Gabriel Mouton, a French clergyman, proposed a decimal system of measurement based on a fraction of the earth's circumference.

1671 Jean Picard, a French astronomer, proposed using the length of a pendulum swinging once each second as a standard unit of length.

1790 The National Assembly of France requested the French Academy of Sciences to develop a standard system of weights and measures. The system the academy developed became known as the metric system. Also in 1790, Thomas Jefferson, then U.S. secretary of state, recommended that the United States use a decimal system of measurement. Congress rejected the idea.

1795 France adopted the metric system but allowed people to continue using other measurement units.

1821 John Quincy Adams, then U.S. secretary of state, proposed conversion to the metric system. Congress again rejected the proposal.

1837 France passed a law that required all Frenchmen to begin using the metric system on Jan. 1, 1840.

1866 Congress legalized the use of the metric system in the United States but did not require that it be used.

1870-1875 An international conference on the metric system met to update the system and adopt new measurement standards for the kilogram and meter. Seventeen nations, including the United States, took part in the conference.

1875 The Treaty of the Meter was signed at the close of the 1870-1875 international conference. The treaty set up a permanent organization, the International Bureau of Weights and Measures, to change the metric system as necessary.

1889 New meter and kilogram standards based on those adopted by the 1870-1875 conference were made and sent to all countries that signed the Treaty of the Meter.

1893 The United States began defining all its measurement units as fractions of the standard meter and kilogram.

1890's Attempts were made in Congress to change U.S. measurements to metric, but none were successful. Many people, especially those in industry, opposed any change in the nation's measurement system.

1957 The United States Army and Marine Corps adopted the metric system as the basis for their weapons and equipment.

1960 A General Conference of Weights and Measures held by countries using the metric system adopted the present version of the system.

1965 Great Britain began a changeover to the metric system.

1968-1971 A congressional study explored the costs and benefits to the United States of converting to the metric system. The study recommended that the country make a planned conversion.

1970 Australia began a scheduled 10-year conversion to the metric system.

1975 Canada began a gradual changeover to the metric system.

1975 The United States Congress passed the Metric Conversion Act, which called for a voluntary changeover to the metric system.

In the original metric system, the unit of length equaled a fraction of the earth's circumference. This fraction was $\frac{1}{10,000,000}$ of the distance from the North Pole to the equator along the line of longitude near Dunkerque, France; and Barcelona, Spain. The French scientists named this unit of length the *metre*, from the Greek word *metron*, meaning *a measure*.

The units for capacity and mass came from the meter. The commission chose the cubic decimeter as the unit of fluid capacity and named it the liter. The scientists defined the unit for mass, the gram, as the mass of a cubic centimeter of water at the temperature where it weighs the most. That temperature is about 4° C (39° F.).

The original measurement standards of the metric units have been replaced by more accurate ones, and other units have been added to the system. Whenever necessary, an international group of scientists holds a General Conference of Weights and Measures to revise the system. The General Conference of 1960 named the system Système International d'Unités.

International Acceptance. Other nations began to convert to the metric system after 1840, when the French people were first required to use it. By 1850, Greece, The Netherlands, Spain, and parts of Italy had adopted the new units of measurement.

An international metric convention, held from 1870 to 1875, created measurement standards of greater accuracy for length and mass. Seventeen nations, including the United States, participated in this convention. In 1875, they signed the Treaty of the Meter, which established a permanent organization to change the metric system as necessary. This organization, called the International Bureau of Weights and Measures, has its headquarters near Paris.

By 1900, 35 nations had adopted the metric system. They included the major countries of continental Europe and South America. By the mid-1970's, almost every country in the world had either converted to the system or planned to do so. Canada and Australia had begun the process of converting to metric measurements. The United States remained as the only major country not to adopt the metric system.

The United States and the Metric System. In 1790, Secretary of State Thomas Jefferson recommended that the United States use a decimal measurement system. That same year, work leading to the metric system began in France. Congress rejected Jefferson's recommendation. In 1821, Secretary of State John Quincy Adams also proposed conversion to the metric system. But Congress again turned down such action. At that time, the United States traded mostly with England and Canada, neither of which was considering any change in its measurements. A conversion of U.S. measurements would have interfered with this trade.

The United States showed little interest in the metric system for more than 40 years following Adams' proposal. Meanwhile, the nation's industries developed machines and products based on customary units. Until the mid-1900's, many industries opposed conversion to metric measurements. They believed such a step would require costly changes in both their machines and their manufacturing methods. In 1866, Congress made the metric system legal in the United States. But it took no action toward requiring the use of metric measurements.

In 1893, the United States based the yard and the pound on fractions of the international metric standards for the meter and the kilogram. But during the next 70 years, only a few metric measurements began to come into daily use. In the 1950's, for example, pharmacists started to use metric units to fill prescriptions. In 1957, the U.S. Army and the Marine Corps began to measure in metric units. During the 1960's, because of the increasing number of foreign cars, many mechanics had to use tools based on the metric system. Also in the 1960's, the National Aeronautics and Space Administration (NASA) began to use metric units.

In 1965, Great Britain began a changeover to the metric system. Other members of the Commonwealth of Nations later decided to convert. These actions created new interest in the metric system in the United States. More and more people began to realize that, in time, the United States would be the only major country that used customary measurements.

In 1968, Congress authorized a three-year study of metric conversion. This study recommended a step-by-step conversion to the metric system during a period of 10 years. Such a planned conversion would help reduce the cost and problems of changing the nation's measurement system. In 1975, Congress passed a bill that established a policy of voluntary conversion to the metric system. This legislation created the U.S. Metric Board to develop and carry out a program of gradual conversion. The program is expected to promote the increased use of metric units of measurement by business and industry.

DANIEL V. DE SIMONE

Related Articles. See MEASUREMENT with its list of *Related Articles*. See also the following articles:

Absolute Zero	International Bureau	Mole
Ampere	of Weights and	National Bureau
Candela	Measures	of Standards
Celsius Scale	Kilogram	Time
Centimeter	Kilometer	Ton
Gram	Liter	Weights and
	Meter	Measures

Outline

I. **Using the Metric System**
  A. The Decimal Arrangement
  B. Metric Measurement Units

II. **Common Measurements**
  A. Length and Distance   D. Weight and Mass
     Measurements   Measurements
  B. Surface Measurements E. Time Measurements
  C. Volume and Capacity   F. Temperature
     Measurements   Measurements

III. **History**

Questions

Why is a decimal system of measurement easier to work with than a nondecimal system?

What are the seven basic metric units?

What do the letters *SI* stand for?

What is a *derived unit*?

What prefix is used to increase a unit by 1,000?

Where was the metric system developed? When?

Why did U.S. industry oppose the metric system?

Where does the term *metric* come from?

What was Gabriel Mouton's proposal for a decimal unit of length?

What did the Treaty of the Meter accomplish?

METROLINER. See ELECTRIC RAILROAD (History).

The Metronome beats exact time for musicians. The pendulum of this clockwork mechanism is upside down. A movable counterweight, attached to the upper part of the pendulum, is set according to a scale, right. The scale determines the number of beats that the pendulum makes each minute.

Ewing Galloway; Seth Thomas Clocks

METRONOME, *MEHT ruh nohm*, is an instrument that beats time for musicians. Dietrich Winkel of Amsterdam, a Dutch inventor, invented it. But the German Johann N. Mälzel patented it in 1816. The common type consists of a wooden box with a pendulum. A movable counterweight is attached to the pendulum. The mechanism ticks as the pendulum moves. The lower the counterweight is set, the faster the machine ticks. Most metronomes are wound by hand. Some operate by electricity.   CHARLES B. RIGHTER

METROPOLITAN is the title of an archbishop of the Eastern Orthodox Churches. Occasionally, Roman Catholic archbishops are called *metropolitans*. In A.D. 341, the Council of Antioch decreed that the bishop of the *metropolis* (capital city) of an ecclesiastical province should rank above the other bishops of the province. The bishops were to consult the metropolitan about all matters other than regular diocesan affairs. See also ARCHBISHOP.   R. PIERCE BEAVER

METROPOLITAN AREA includes a central city and the area that surrounds it. The cities, boroughs, villages, towns, or townships in the metropolitan area outside the central city are called *suburbs*. In the United States, a metropolitan area is officially called a *Standard Metropolitan Statistical Area* (SMSA). Two or more adjacent metropolitan areas may form a *Standard Consolidated Statistical Area* (SCSA). The United States has 13 SCSA's. Most metropolitan areas in the United States include at least one city with a population of 50,000 or more. A metropolitan area includes the entire county in which the city is located, and at least 75 per cent of the county's labor force must be nonagricultural. The term *greater* as applied to a city, such as Greater Paris, means a metropolitan area.

Metropolitan areas have developed in every country in the world. As cities grow, people move outside the city boundaries and form suburbs. Since the early 1900's, the most important population shift has been an almost steady flow of families from large cities to the surrounding suburbs. The development of modern transportation and paved roads and streets has been chiefly responsible for this mass movement.

Suburbanites, the people who live in the suburbs, view the city as the hub of their work and business activities. They also use its recreational, professional, commercial, and cultural facilities and services. As the workday begins, thousands of commuters speed toward the city by automobile or train on paths that resemble spokes on a wheel. People live far away, but travel the distance twice daily between work and home. A few people may commute from the city to work in the suburbs.

Industries and businesses often follow householders into the suburbs. They seek locations where parking is plentiful, where land is cheaper and available in larger plots, and where building restrictions may be less confining than in the cities. As this process of moving into the suburbs continues, another great metropolitan area may be established.

In the United States, about 150 million people, or about 75 of every 100 persons, live in the 277 standard metropolitan statistical areas. There are also 4 metropolitan areas in Puerto Rico. In Canada, over half of the people live in 23 metropolitan areas. About one-third of the people in England live in the country's six large *conurbations* (clusters of small cities and towns around a large central city). In France, one out of every six persons lives in metropolitan Paris.

Since the 1950's, many people have moved from cities to the suburbs of metropolitan areas. In metropolitan Chicago, more than 50 of every 100 persons live outside the city limits. About 60 of every 100 residents of Greater Los Angeles live in the suburbs.

Problems of Metropolitan Areas

Conflict in Authority. Most metropolitan areas have no centralized, metropolitan government to handle problems that affect the entire area. Government is almost completely decentralized. Each city, town, village, or other municipality usually has its own government. Little or no relationship exists between these governments and that of the central city. Some rural areas have no local government except that of the county in which they are located. The 277 standard metropolitan statistical areas of the United States have more than 24,800 local government units. These include over 500 counties, 4,000 townships, 6,100 municipalities, 8,700 special districts, and 5,200 school districts.

The process of government becomes scrambled with overlapping authority, and the results can only be unsatisfactory. Local government within the area remains fragmented. Many metropolitan areas straddle county and even state lines. Economic and social organizations, such as telephone companies, usually deal with the metropolitan area as a single unit. Some special districts and municipal authorities have been set up to provide centralized, but limited, administration and services to a metropolitan area.

People who live in a metropolitan area often have little feeling of political unity among themselves. Many able, civic-minded citizens who work in the city live in the suburbs. They have nothing to say about the government of the city. Yet this government may have a profound effect on their businesses, because it influences the entire metropolitan area. In this way, many cities lose the civic interests and moral resources that city workers contribute to their suburban communities.

Finances. The widespread movement from the city to the suburbs affects the financial position of both areas. A city finds its land values declining, its tax resources dropping, and blighted areas appearing. Industries may contribute to the development of the suburbs in which they are located. But they do not contribute to the maintenance of the central city.

A city often finds that it must provide services, such as health inspections, for the suburbs as well as for people within its own borders. It may impose taxes, because of the decline in the value of city land. Suburbanites usually resist such taxes.

Many suburbs have been built up almost overnight because of a growing need for housing. Some suburbs have only homes, and no taxable businesses and industries. They cannot raise enough money to provide the services needed by all new urban communities, especially with young families and small children. Such services include schools, police and fire protection, water and sewage systems, paved streets, building inspection, public-health services, recreational facilities, street and traffic lights, and zoning.

A large industry may be located in a region and be taxed by the government there. But its workers may live in the surrounding areas that do not receive any tax revenue from the industry. As a result, slums and blighted areas may appear quickly in suburbs that lack tax resources and means of financing their services.

Metropolitan Area Plans

Various plans have been devised in attempts to provide urban areas with the kinds of governments they need and deserve. But no agreement has been reached as to what the solution should be. The objectives of a

Metropolitan Area of Chicago

The Chicago Standard Metropolitan Statistical Area (SMSA) covers six Illinois counties. The map also shows five other SMSA's — Racine and Kenosha in Wisconsin, Gary-Hammond-East Chicago in Indiana, and Rockford and Kankakee in Illinois.

SMSA area

City of Chicago

SMSA boundary

State boundary

County boundary

★ County seat

• Other city or town

0   20 Miles
0   20 Kilometers

WORLD BOOK map

metropolitan plan include: (1) unity of government in the area, (2) supplying all the people with the services of government that an urban area needs, and (3) allowing these services to be provided locally rather than by state and national governments. Many authorities believe that long-range regional planning that considers the needs of both city and suburbs is essential.

Intergovernmental Cooperation. In the United States, many neighboring local units have agreed to work together. For example, they may agree to cooperate in such services as police and fire protection, public utilities, centralized purchasing, and regional planning. Authorities believe that these useful arrangements may answer the needs of the moment. But they do not permanently solve the problem of providing efficient and economical metropolitan government.

Annexation has long been used as one solution. Under this plan, the city *annexes* (absorbs) its outlying areas. In the past, cities usually grew to their present size by annexation. But people who live on the outskirts now generally oppose this method. They do not want to lose their governmental independence. They do not want to be merely small parts of a large city.

Extramural Jurisdiction. In some states, central cities have the power to exercise government control in areas outside municipal boundaries. For example, Alabama grants municipalities the right to exercise broad powers 3 miles (4.8 kilometers) outside their city limits. These powers include police and sanitary regulation. Municipalities also may levy business taxes and control subdivisions across city lines.

County Government in some states provides urban services for areas outside city limits. California has county governments that supply police and fire protection, health and welfare services, and other aid to such areas. But, in most states, counties lack the personnel or organization to handle these functions efficiently.

A metropolitan county government provides urban services for the entire county. For example, Dade County, which includes Greater Miami, Fla., operates under this plan. Its 13-member county commission hires a county manager. The commission carries out plans for serving and developing the entire county. Municipalities within the county handle only local affairs. Voters from Miami and from counties and districts in the metropolitan area elect members of the commission. Cities that reach 60,000 population elect other members.

City-county consolidation has been achieved in a number of cities, including Philadelphia, San Francisco, and New York City. It merges city and county functions under one government.

Special Districts or municipal authorities may consist of two or more local units in a metropolitan area. They have been set up to provide specific services of government, such as water supply and sewage disposal. Many districts or authorities must use the revenue from their services to pay for the construction, maintenance, and operation of the necessary facilities.

Districts and authorities have paved the way for more governmental unity. But they have also added to, rather than reduced, the complexity of local government. One of the largest and most successful municipal authorities

is the Port Authority of New York and New Jersey. It handles port development and transportation matters within a 20-mile (32-kilometer) radius of New York City, in both New York and New Jersey (see PORT AUTHORITY OF NEW YORK AND NEW JERSEY). Another authority, the Metropolitan Water District of Southern California, serves more than 10 million persons in over 120 cities, including Los Angeles. Pennsylvania has more than 1,000 municipal authorities to build and operate schools, waterworks, sewage disposal systems, parking facilities, and other utilities. Many authorities serve more than one local unit.

Metropolitan Federation merges all local governments in a metropolitan area into a new unit called *the federated city.* The local units retain their own identities and carry on the functions of local government that they are best fitted to handle. The federated city accepts specific functions for the entire region. It is then given the necessary taxing authority to finance them. London operates under a metropolitan federation.

The Municipality of Metropolitan Toronto merges the city with 5 suburban units of government. The federation controls water supply and distribution, sewage disposal, metropolitan road systems, land-use planning, police protection, welfare services, and public transportation. Member municipalities are responsible for such functions as fire protection and health services. The federation covers 241 square miles (624 square kilometers) and serves about $2\frac{1}{4}$ million persons. See TORONTO (Government; History).   H. F. ALDERFER

Related Articles in WORLD BOOK include:

City (Metropolitan	Community	State
Cities; table)	County	Government
City Government	Local	Suburb
City Planning	Government	Urban Renewal

METROPOLITAN LIFE INSURANCE COMPANY is one of the largest private business organizations in the world. It insures about one out of five persons in the United States and Canada. Metropolitan Life is a *mutual company* (operated exclusively for the benefit of its policyholders). Headquarters are in New York City. For assets and the amount of life insurance in force, see INSURANCE (table: 15 Largest).

Metropolitan Life sells both personal and group insurance. Its main business is in life insurance, but it also sells health insurance and annuities. It is one of the world's largest private owners and developers of real estate. It also ranks among the world's leading mortgage holders. The company carries on an extensive program of health and safety education.

Metropolitan Life was formed in 1868. It was one of the successors of the National Union Life and Limb Insurance Company. This earlier company had insured servicemen during the Civil War. Metropolitan Life gained much of its early success by selling small amounts of insurance to immigrants, laborers, and others with low incomes.   THE METROPOLITAN LIFE INSURANCE COMPANY

METROPOLITAN MUSEUM OF ART in New York City is the largest art museum in the United States. It includes more than a million works of art. The city of New York owns the building, but the collections belong to a corporation which runs the museum under a charter granted in 1870. The museum contains an auditorium which seats about 700 persons. Its store sells art books, color reproductions of art, silver, and jewelry. The public restaurant features a pool that has eight life-sized fountain sculptures in it.

The Collections of Ancient Art include Egyptian prehistoric pottery, wall paintings, sculpture, and jewelry. An original Egyptian tomb dated about 2460 B.C. also belongs to these collections. Articles from Greece and Rome include vases and stone sculptures, bronzes, gems, jewelry, glass, and wall paintings. Etruscan art includes terra-cotta work. Ceramics, ivories, metalwork, and sculpture represent art from Mesopotamia and ancient Persia.

The Collections of Eastern Art include oriental paintings, sculpture, pottery, lacquerware, and jade from India, Japan, and China. These collections also contain examples of Islamic art such as rugs and textiles, pottery, wood carvings, and glass.

The Collections of European Art include paintings from the 1200's to the present day. The museum also has examples of European sculpture, furniture, tapestries, textiles, pottery, glassware, metalwork, and other decorative arts from the Middle Ages and later periods. The museum also has collections of arms and armor, musical instruments, prints, and drawings.

American Art is represented by paintings from the Colonial period to the present time, and by sculptures. The museum also has American rooms with furniture and decorations dating from 1640 to the early 1800's.

The Junior Museum in the south wing of the museum is the center for children's activities. It has its own special exhibitions, library, auditorium, and studio. The Costume Institute collection has more than 15,000 articles of dress that cover 400 years of world history and five continents.

The Cloisters, located in Fort Tryon Park, is a branch of the museum devoted to medieval art. Its collections include tapestries, ivories, metalwork, sculpture, and stained glass. It features parts of monasteries and churches from France and Spain, and lovely outdoor gardens.　Critically reviewed by METROPOLITAN MUSEUM OF ART

METROPOLITAN OPERA ASSOCIATION is one of the most important opera companies in the world. The company performs at the Metropolitan Opera House in the Lincoln Center for the Performing Arts in New York City. The 14-story opera house, which opened in 1966, cost over 42\frac{1}{2}$ million and seats over 3,700 persons. It replaced the original Metropolitan Opera House, which opened in 1883. The first production in the old Metropolitan Opera House was Charles Gounod's *Faust*. During the 1932-1933 season, the company changed its name to the Metropolitan Opera Association. The "Met" broadcast its first performance in 1931, and televised its first complete opera, Giuseppe Verdi's *Otello*, in 1948.

Critically reviewed by the METROPOLITAN OPERA ASSOCIATION

See also THEATER (picture: Elevator Stages).

METROPOLITAN STATE COLLEGE. See UNIVERSITIES AND COLLEGES (table).

METTERNICH, *MET er nick,* **PRINCE VON** (1773-1859), an Austrian statesman and diplomat, dominated Europe from 1814 to 1848. That period is often called "The Age of Metternich." Metternich believed that democracy and nationalism would lead to disaster. He guided the efforts of Austria, Prussia, and Russia to crush nationalist revolts throughout Europe.

Metternich began his long diplomatic career in 1797.

Metropolitan Museum of Art, photograph by Mary Seth

Metropolitan Museum of Art in New York City attracts millions of visitors each year. The museum was opened at its present site on Fifth Avenue and 82nd Street in 1880. It now contains about 20 acres (8 hectares) of floor space.

He became Austrian ambassador to Prussia in 1803 and to France in 1806. As Austrian minister of foreign affairs (1809-1848), he helped establish the *Vienna System*, which controlled Europe after Napoleon's defeat in 1815. He lost office in the 1848 Revolution, and fled to England. He returned to Vienna in 1851, but never held office again.

His full name was Klemens Wenzel Nepomuk Lothar von Metternich. He was born in Koblenz. He married the granddaughter of Prince Wenzel Kaunitz, chancellor of Austria.　ROBERT G. L. WAITE

See also AUSTRIA (History); VIENNA, CONGRESS OF.

METZ, *mets* (pop. 107,537; met. area 166,354), is a manufacturing center about 175 miles (282 kilometers) northeast of Paris. The city serves as the capital of the department of Moselle. The factories of Metz produce munitions, muslin, hats, and hosiery.

The history of the city goes back to the Roman conquest, after which it was known as *Divodurum*, then *Mediomatrica*, and finally, *Metz*. The Huns plundered Metz in A.D. 451. It was part of the Holy Roman Empire from 962 until the French captured the city in 1552. But France did not get formal possession of Metz until 1648. The Germans captured Metz in 1870, and held it until the Treaty of Versailles returned the city to France after World War I. German troops captured Metz early in World War II. Allied forces freed the city in 1944.　EDWARD W. FOX

MEUSE RIVER, *muz,* rises in the Langre Plateau of eastern France, and flows north past Verdun through the Ardennes highlands. The river then flows northeast through Belgium past Namur and Liège. North of Liège, the river enters The Netherlands. Here, it makes a sweeping curve northwest and empties into the North Sea south of Rotterdam. The Meuse River is 575 miles (925 kilometers) long. In Belgium and The Netherlands, it is called the MAAS.

Several navigable canals join the Meuse along its course. Near Toul, France, it connects with the Marne-Rhine Canal. At Liège, the Meuse is linked with the Albert Canal, which goes to Antwerp. At Maastricht, the river meets the Juliana Canal.　ROBERT E. DICKINSON

367

El Pueblo De Los Angeles, Inc.

Mexican Americans in Los Angeles take part in *Las Posadas,* a Mexican tradition. This Christmastime ceremony represents the journey of Joseph and Mary to Bethlehem.

MEXICAN AMERICANS are Americans of Mexican descent. The approximately 6 million Mexican Americans make up the second largest minority group in the United States. The nation's more than 22 million Negroes form the largest minority. Mexican Americans live throughout the United States, but about 70 per cent of them live in California and Texas. Many Mexican Americans use Spanish as their main language, though most speak both English and Spanish.

Americans of Mexican descent generally use four terms to refer to themselves: Chicano, La Raza, mestizo, or Mexican American. The term *Chicano* is a short form of *Mexicano,* the Spanish word for *Mexican. La Raza* means *the people* or *one's people* in Spanish. Mexican Americans use this term to identify their cultural ties with other Spanish-speaking people. *Mestizo* is a Spanish word for people of mixed white and American Indian ancestry. *Mexican American* is the term most commonly used to distinguish members of this ethnic group from those of other U.S. ethnic groups.

Most Mexican Americans are mestizos by descent. They trace their heritage to Indian groups that built great civilizations in the region of Mexico long before Spanish explorers arrived during the 1500's. Some Mexican Americans have ancestors who lived in the West before it became part of the United States in the 1800's. Many more are descendants of people who moved from Mexico to the United States after 1900.

The ancestors of today's Mexican Americans had a strong influence on early American history. They helped establish Los Angeles and several other settlements that became major U.S. cities. They also taught important methods of farming, mining, and ranching to Americans who settled in the West. Between the late 1800's and the mid-1900's, most Mexican Americans worked on farms. Today, most of them live in cities.

Like most other minority groups, Mexican Americans suffer discrimination in education, housing, and jobs. Difficulty with the English language also has slowed

their progress in obtaining a good education and necessary job skills. But more and more Mexican Americans are overcoming the problem of prejudice and are slowly gaining positions of high responsibility in all areas of American life.

The Mexican-American Heritage

The Olmec Indians established the first major Mexican civilization. Their culture flourished along the southern Gulf Coast from about 1200 B.C. to 100 B.C. During the next 1,300 years, the Maya, Toltec, and Zapotec Indians built rich and powerful empires in the region of Mexico. See MAYA; OLMEC INDIANS; TOLTEC INDIANS; ZAPOTEC INDIANS.

The Aztecs ruled the last great Indian civilization of Mexico. They borrowed much of their culture from the earlier civilizations. Beginning about A.D. 1200, the Aztecs built large cities and developed well-organized governments. In 1521, an army led by the Spanish adventurer Hernando Cortes conquered the Aztec empire for Spain. See AZTEC.

During the next 300 years, Spain extended its rule over the region that now includes California and the southwestern United States. The Spaniards and Indians learned much from each other. The Indians introduced the Spaniards to new foods and medicines and helped them adapt to the desert and the climate. The Spaniards taught the Indians to ride horses and to raise cattle and sheep. Roman Catholic missionaries from Spain taught Christianity to the Indians, who often combined it with their own religions. Many Spanish men took Indian women as mates. Their descendants became the first mestizos of Mexico.

During the 1600's and 1700's, the Spaniards and Mexicans established many missions and other communities that later became important cities in the United States. In 1610, they founded Santa Fe in what is now New Mexico. Mexicans also helped establish Albuquerque, Los Angeles, San Antonio, and Tucson.

In the late 1700's and early 1800's, the Mexicans became increasingly displeased with Spanish rule. Miguel Hidalgo y Costilla, a Mexican priest, led a revolt against the Spaniards in 1810. This uprising was put down, but it started Mexico's struggle for independence. Mexico won its freedom from Spain in 1821.

During the 1820's, Mexico allowed many Americans to settle in what is now Texas. Dissatisfaction with Mexican rule led the Americans and some Mexican Texans to revolt in 1835. The next year, the Texans defeated Mexican forces in the Battle of San Jacinto and established the Republic of Texas. See TEXAS (History).

Mexico refused to recognize Texas' independence, and the conflict over Texas became a chief cause of the Mexican War (1846-1848). By the Treaty of Guadalupe Hidalgo, the United States gained most of the land that is now Arizona, California, Colorado, Nevada, New Mexico, Utah, and Wyoming. Mexico recognized Texas. See MEXICAN WAR; MEXICO (History).

The Meeting of Two Cultures

New Relationships. More than 75,000 Spanish-speaking persons lived in the areas that the United States acquired from Mexico during the mid-1800's. Most of these people became U.S. citizens. After the discovery of gold in California in 1848, settlers from the eastern United States poured into the West. They soon outnumbered the Mexican Americans in every area except New Mexico.

In California, Mexican Americans taught the newcomers important mining techniques. One such technique was how to use the gold-mining pan. Another was the use of mercury to separate silver from ore. Mexican Americans also showed their new countrymen how to tame wild horses, brand cattle, and irrigate the land.

Nevertheless, the two groups of Americans usually did not get along together. Racial and religious differences became chief sources of conflict. The newcomers were white, and most of them were Protestants. Most Mexican Americans were mestizos and Roman Catholics. The two groups also spoke different languages and had different customs. Many white newcomers regarded Mexican Americans as Mexicans and "foreigners."

Many Mexican Americans suffered as a result of laws dealing with the registration of property and the collection of property taxes. They spoke little or no English, and they did not understand the laws. Many did not see why they should register or pay taxes on land that their families had occupied for generations. Their land titles became worthless because they failed either to register the titles or to pay the new taxes. Other Mexican Americans had their land records burned or stolen. Many fought to keep their property, and thousands were murdered.

The courts offered little justice to Mexican Americans. Most courts prohibited the use of Spanish, which gave English-speaking Americans a great advantage. Gradually, most Mexican Americans became tenants or workers on land that belonged to English-speaking

Americans. The two groups lived apart in the towns and cities, and each had its own schools, stores, and places of entertainment. The Mexican Americans called their sections *barrios*, the Spanish word for *neighborhoods*.

The Growing Minority. The Mexican-American population began to grow rapidly during the early 1900's. Thousands of Mexicans fled the violence of the Mexican Revolution of 1910 and moved to the United States. Many were recruited by American railroads, mining companies, and farm owners. Others sought jobs that appeared after the United States entered World War I in 1917. Between 1910 and 1930, more than 600,000 Mexicans settled in the United States.

Throughout the early 1900's, Mexican Americans suffered discrimination in jobs and wages and lived in run-down housing. To fight these conditions, they organized labor unions and took part in strikes to obtain higher wages and better working conditions. Mexican Americans also formed civic groups to deal with their problems. In 1929, the major groups merged to form the League of United Latin American Citizens.

During the Great Depression of the 1930's, the number of people of Mexican descent in the United States declined. As a result of mass unemployment, thousands of Mexican immigrants were either deported or pressured to return to Mexico by U.S. government officials. A large number of these immigrants had lived in the United States for more than 10 years. Many of their children had been born there and were U.S. citizens.

Thousands of Mexicans came to the United States to work during World War II (1939-1945). Many were

MEXICAN AMERICANS IN THE UNITED STATES

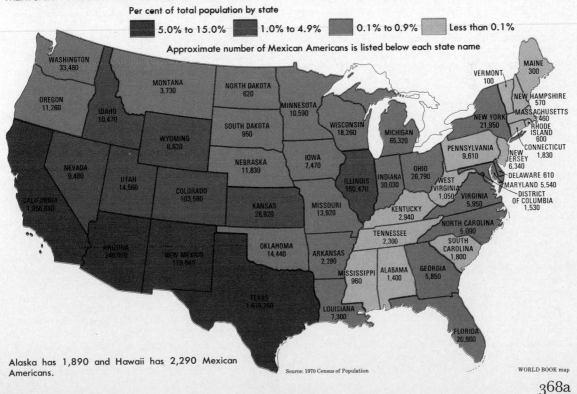

Per cent of total population by state

■ 5.0% to 15.0%   ■ 1.0% to 4.9%   ■ 0.1% to 0.9%   □ Less than 0.1%

Approximate number of Mexican Americans is listed below each state name

WASHINGTON 33,480
OREGON 11,260
MONTANA 3,730
NORTH DAKOTA 620
MINNESOTA 10,590
IDAHO 10,470
SOUTH DAKOTA 950
WISCONSIN 18,260
MICHIGAN 65,320
MAINE 300
VERMONT 100
NEW HAMPSHIRE 570
MASSACHUSETTS 3,460
RHODE ISLAND 600
NEW YORK 21,950
CONNECTICUT 1,830
WYOMING 6,620
NEBRASKA 11,830
IOWA 7,470
PENNSYLVANIA 9,610
NEW JERSEY 6,340
NEVADA 9,480
UTAH 14,560
COLORADO 103,580
ILLINOIS 160,470
INDIANA 30,030
OHIO 26,790
WEST VIRGINIA 1,050
DELAWARE 610
MARYLAND 5,540
DISTRICT OF COLUMBIA 1,530
CALIFORNIA 1,356,840
KANSAS 28,920
MISSOURI 13,920
KENTUCKY 2,940
VIRGINIA 5,950
ARIZONA 240,020
NEW MEXICO 119,040
OKLAHOMA 14,440
TENNESSEE 2,300
NORTH CAROLINA 5,090
SOUTH CAROLINA 1,800
ARKANSAS 2,280
MISSISSIPPI 960
ALABAMA 1,400
GEORGIA 5,850
TEXAS 1,619,250
LOUISIANA 7,300
FLORIDA 20,860

Alaska has 1,890 and Hawaii has 2,290 Mexican Americans.

Source: 1970 Census of Population

WORLD BOOK map

George Ballis, Black Star

Cesar Chavez, *center,* became a leading spokesman for Mexican-American farmworkers during the 1960's, when he led a strike against grape growers. The strike helped his union win acceptance.

braceros, farmworkers who had been issued temporary work permits by the federal government. Many others entered the United States illegally. These workers found jobs throughout the country.

Hundreds of thousands of Mexican Americans served in the U.S. armed forces during World War II. After the war, many Mexican-American veterans still faced discrimination. As a result, many of them helped form national organizations to deal with the urgent needs of Mexican Americans. These groups included the American G.I. Forum, the Community Services Organization, and the Mexican American Political Association.

Expanding Influence. During the 1960's, four Mexican Americans won election to Congress and became champions of civil rights. They were Senator Joseph Montoya of New Mexico and Representatives Eligio de la Garza and Henry B. Gonzales of Texas and Edward R. Roybal of California.

President Lyndon B. Johnson appointed several Mexican Americans to high government posts in the 1960's. For example, Vicente T. Ximenes became chairman of the President's Cabinet Committee on Mexican-American Affairs. Johnson made Hector P. García a member of the U.S. delegation to the United Nations and appointed Raul H. Castro U.S. ambassador to El Salvador. Other Mexican Americans who won distinction included civil rights leader Dolores Huerta, entertainer Vikki Carr, writer Tomas Rivera, golfer Lee Trevino, and playwright Luis Valdez.

Foods of Mexican origin also became increasingly popular in many parts of the United States during the 1960's. These foods included *chile con carne, enchiladas, tacos,* and *tamales.* See MEXICO (Food).

The Chicano Movement. In spite of the success of a growing number of Mexican Americans, many others became increasingly resentful about their unsolved problems. Such feelings found expression in the Chicano, or "brown power," movement. In Mexico, *Chicano* is a mocking slang expression for a clumsy person.

Mexican Americans used the term in jest during the 1950's when referring to one another. But in the 1960's, many young Mexican Americans gave the term a positive meaning that suggested racial and cultural pride.

One of the earliest Mexican-American spokesmen to reflect this new pride was Cesar Chavez, a labor union leader who began to organize California grape pickers in 1962. Another was Rodolfo Gonzales, who founded the Crusade for Justice in Denver in 1965. This group worked to provide social services and to develop job opportunities for Mexican Americans. In 1970, José Angel Gutiérrez helped establish La Raza Unida, a political party based in Texas. He later became president of the school board of Crystal City, Tex.

Mexican Americans Today

Most of the approximately 6 million Mexican Americans still live in the West. California has more Mexican Americans than any other state. About 80 per cent of all Mexican Americans live in cities. Los Angeles has a Chicano population of about 450,000, more than any other U.S. city.

Customs and Holidays. Most Mexican Americans observe several customs and holidays of Mexico in addition to those of the United States. For example, many Mexican Americans celebrate a Mexican Christmastime ceremony called *Las Posadas.* This celebration features a series of marches that symbolize the journey of Joseph and Mary to Bethlehem. Mexican-American children also enjoy breaking the *piñata,* a container filled with candy and gifts and hung above their heads.

Some Mexican Americans observe such Mexican holidays as *Cinco de Mayo* (May 5) and Guadalupe Day, on December 12. Cinco de Mayo honors a Mexican army's victory over an invading French force at Puebla, Mexico, in 1862. Guadalupe Day is Mexico's most important religious holiday. For more details on Mexican holidays, see MEXICO (Holidays).

Continuing Problems. Some Mexican Americans live in fine homes, in cities or suburbs. They have good-paying jobs in business, government, the professions, and all other occupations. But most Mexican Americans lack work skills and have low-paying and low-prestige jobs. They cannot afford good housing and live in crowded and generally run-down barrios. Many barrios lack health facilities and other city services that are well provided in higher-income neighborhoods.

Large numbers of Mexican Americans still work on farms. Most of these are migrant laborers. They move from one area to another, depending on where there are crops to be harvested. They generally receive low wages, and live under substandard conditions in unsanitary camps. Many states lack laws to protect migrant laborers against these conditions, and others that have such laws often fail to enforce them.

Mexican Americans have completed fewer years of school than most other ethnic groups in the United States. Largely because of this condition, they earn much less than most other U.S. ethnic groups. Many Mexican-American youths who enter school speak only Spanish. Many have difficulty understanding English, the language commonly used for instruction. This handicap greatly slows their progress. Many Mexican-American students also suffer from racial prejudice among teachers, a lack of Spanish-speaking teachers, and little attention to Mexican-American affairs. These conditions lead to a high rate of failure and cause many Mexican Americans to quit school. Racial prejudice makes it difficult even for educated Mexican Americans to find good jobs and housing.

Some Mexican Americans support the use of violence to draw public attention to their problems. Many others, however, reject such action as distasteful to the Mexican-American tradition of respectful conduct, hard work, and persistence. Even young Chicanos disagree among themselves about the goals of Mexican Americans and how to achieve these goals.

Recent Developments. During the early 1970's, La Raza Unida candidates won election to school and municipal agencies in several Western states. A number of school systems responded to Chicano pressures by hiring more Spanish-speaking teachers and adding Mexican-American studies. An increasing number of Mexican-American women became active in the movement to gain equal rights for women. Lupe Anguiano, a Mexican-American civil rights leader, played a leading role in this movement in the West.

Several Mexican Americans were appointed to high government positions during the 1970's. Romana A. Bañuelos served as treasurer of the United States from 1971 to 1974. Phillip V. Sanchez served as United States ambassador to Honduras from 1973 to 1976, when he was appointed ambassador to Colombia. In 1974, Jerry Apodaca was elected governor of New Mexico. Raul H. Castro served as governor of Arizona from 1975 to 1977, when he was appointed U.S. ambassador to Argentina.   DELUVINA HERNÁNDEZ

Related Articles in WORLD BOOK include:

American G.I. Forum
Baca, Elfego
Bañuelos, Romana Acosta
Castro, Raul Hector
Chavez, Cesar E.
Chicago (Ethnic Groups)
Cortina, Juan
  Nepomuceno
Cuauhtémoc
Gadsden Purchase
Galarza, Ernesto
Gamio, Manuel
Gonzales, Rodolfo

Guadalupe Hidalgo,
  Treaty of
Gutiérrez, José Ángel
Hidalgo y Costilla,
  Miguel
League of United Latin
  American Citizens
Los Angeles
Minority Group
San Antonio
Sánchez, George Isidore
Trevino, Lee

MEXICAN BEAN BEETLE. See BEAN BEETLE.

MEXICAN CESSION. See MEXICAN WAR (The Peace Treaty; map).

MEXICAN HAIRLESS is a dog that has no coat of hair. Its skin is bare, except for a little tuft of hair on its forehead and a slight fuzz along its tail. The rest of the skin is a spotted, pinkish color. A Mexican hairless dog weighs about 12 pounds (5 kilograms). It has a narrow head and a pointed nose. Its body is lightly built, with a rounded back and a long tail. The Mexican hairless probably originated in China in the 1300's. It was first imported into Mexico by sailors.   JOSEPHINE Z. RINE

MEXICAN ONYX. See ONYX.

MEXICAN WAR (1846-1848) was fought between the United States and Mexico over disagreements that had been accumulating for two decades. In the course of the war, United States forces invaded Mexico and occupied the capital, Mexico City. By the Treaty of Guadalupe Hidalgo, the United States acquired from Mexico the regions of California, Nevada, and Utah, most of Arizona and New Mexico, and parts of Colorado

and Wyoming. But many historians believe the war was an unnecessary attack on a weaker nation.

Causes of the War

Background of the War. In 1835, Texas revolted against the Mexican government, which then controlled the region. Texans established the Republic of Texas in 1836, but Mexico refused to recognize Texas' independence. The Mexican government warned the United States that if Texas were admitted to the Union, Mexico would declare war. James K. Polk was elected President of the United States in 1844. He had declared himself in favor of annexing Texas. In 1845, Texas was made a state. Mexico broke off relations with the United States, but did not declare war. The question of annexing Texas could thus have been settled by peaceful means. But other quarrels developed.

One of these disputes was the question of the boundary between Texas and Mexico. Texas claimed the Rio Grande as its southwestern border. Mexico said that Texas had never extended farther than the Nueces River. Also, Mexico owed U.S. citizens about $3 million to make up for lives and property lost in Mexico through revolution, theft, and confiscation since the 1820's. By the 1840's, many Americans demanded that the United States collect these debts by force.

Most important of all, feeling was growing in the United States that the country had a "manifest destiny" to expand westward into new lands (see MANIFEST DESTINY). The frontier movement had brought Americans into Mexican territory, especially California. Mexico was too weak to control or populate its northern territories. Both American and Mexican inhabitants were discontented with Mexican rule. California seemed almost ready to declare itself independent.

Events Leading Up to the War. In the fall of 1845, President Polk sent John Slidell to Mexico as American minister. Slidell was to offer to pay Mexico $25 million and cancel all claims for damages, if Mexico would accept the Rio Grande boundary and sell New Mexico

WORLD BOOK map

Campaigns of the Mexican War took place chiefly in Mexico and what are now California and Texas. The war ended soon after U.S. troops led by Maj. Gen. Winfield Scott occupied Mexico City.

and California to the United States. If Mexico refused to sell New Mexico and California, Slidell was to offer to cancel the claims on condition that Mexico agreed to the Rio Grande boundary.

A revolution was going on in Mexico when Slidell arrived. Both the old and new presidents were afraid their enemies would denounce them as cowards if they made concessions to the United States. They refused to see Slidell, who came home and told Polk that Mexico needed to be "chastised." Meanwhile, Polk had ordered Major General Zachary Taylor, who was stationed with 3,000 men on the Nueces River, to advance to the Rio Grande. Taylor reached the river in April 1846. A Mexican force crossed the river to meet him. On April 25, a small body of American cavalry was defeated by a larger body of Mexicans.

Polk had already decided to ask Congress to declare war on Mexico. The news of the battle gave him the chance to say that Mexico had "invaded our territory and shed American blood on American soil." In reality, Mexico had as good a claim as the United States to the soil where the blood was shed. But on May 13, 1846, Congress declared war on Mexico.

The War

The United States had two aims. The Americans wanted to occupy the territory that Mexico had been asked to sell. They also wished to invade Mexico in order to force the Mexicans to agree to peace.

The Occupation of New Mexico and California. In June 1846, Brigadier General Stephen W. Kearny set out with about 1,700 troops from Fort Leavenworth, Kans., to capture New Mexico. In August, the expedition entered the New Mexican town of Santa Fe and took control of New Mexico. The next month, Kearny pushed across the desert to California.

Meanwhile, in June 1846, a group of American settlers in California revolted against the Mexican government. This rebellion became known as the *Bear Flag Revolt* because of the portrayal of a grizzly bear on the settlers' flag. In July, U.S. naval forces under Commodore John D. Sloat captured the California town of Monterey and occupied the San Francisco area. On December 6, Kearny led about 100 troops in the bloody

The Mexican Cession was the land Mexico ceded (gave up) to the United States in the Mexican War. The cession covered what are now California, Nevada, Utah, and parts of four other states.

Battle of San Pasqual near San Diego. Reinforcements from San Diego helped save the small American army. In January 1847, U.S. troops under Kearny and Commodore Robert F. Stockton of the Navy won the Battle of San Gabriel near Los Angeles. This victory completed the American conquest of California.

Taylor's Campaign. Before war officially began, General Zachary Taylor had driven the Mexicans across the lower Rio Grande to Matamoros in the two battles of Palo Alto and Resaca de la Palma. On May 18, 1846, he crossed the river and occupied Matamoros. After waiting for new troops, he moved his army up the river and marched against the important city of Monterrey. Monterrey fell on September 24, after a hard-fought battle. Before the end of the year, Taylor had occupied Saltillo and Victoria, important towns of northeastern Mexico. But Mexico still refused to negotiate.

Polk and his advisers decided to land an army at Veracruz, on the east coast, and strike a blow at Mexico City. Many of Taylor's best troops were ordered to join Major General Winfield Scott, who was placed in charge of the new campaign. President Antonio Santa Anna of Mexico was in command of the Mexican Army. He learned of the American plans and immediately led a large army against Taylor at Buena Vista, in the mountains beyond Saltillo. The Mexicans were badly defeated. Taylor became a hero because of his victories, and was elected President of the United States in 1848.

Doniphan's Victories. In December 1846, Colonel Alexander W. Doniphan led about 850 troops south from Santa Fè to capture the Mexican city of Chihuahua. The Americans defeated a Mexican army at El Brazito on Christmas Day. Doniphan's army won the furious Battle of the Sacramento just outside Chihuahua on Feb. 27, 1847, and occupied the city on March 2.

Scott's Campaign. General Scott was at this time the officer of highest rank in the United States Army. With a force of about 10,000 men, he landed near Veracruz on March 9, 1847. Twenty days later he captured the city, and on April 8 he began his advance toward the Mexican capital. The American Army stormed a mountain pass at Cerro Gordo on April 17 and 18 and pushed on. Near Mexico City, American troops fought and won the battles of Contreras and Churubusco on August 19 and 20. The Mexican Army was superior in numbers but, again, was poorly equipped and poorly led.

After a two weeks' armistice, the Americans won a battle at Molino del Rey and stormed and captured the hilltop fortress of Chapultepec. On the following day the Americans marched into Mexico City.

The Peace Treaty. Despite all the American victories, Mexico refused to negotiate a peace treaty. In April 1847, Polk sent Nicholas P. Trist, Chief Clerk of the Department of State, to join Scott's army in Mexico and attempt to open diplomatic negotiations with Santa Anna. When the armistice of August failed, the President recalled Trist. But Santa Anna resigned shortly after Scott entered the Mexican capital. Mexico established a new government, and it was willing to accept the American demands. At the request of the Mexican leaders and General Scott, Trist agreed to remain in Mexico and negotiate a settlement.

The treaty was signed on Feb. 2, 1848, at the village of Guadalupe Hidalgo, near Mexico City. By this time, many people in the United States wanted to annex all Mexico. But the treaty required Mexico to give up only the territory Polk had originally asked for—the Rio Grande region, New Mexico, and California. The United States paid Mexico $15 million for this territory, known as the Mexican Cession. In 1853, the Gadsden Purchase gave an additional 29,640 square miles (76,767 square kilometers) to the United States (see GADSDEN PURCHASE).

Results of the War. The United States gained more than 525,000 square miles (1,360,000 square kilometers) of territory as a result of the Mexican War. But the war also revived the quarrels over slavery. Here was new territory. Was it to be slave or free? The Compromise of 1850 made California a free state and set up the principle of "popular sovereignty." That meant letting the people of a territory decide whether it would be slave or free. But popular sovereignty later led to bitter disagreement and became one of the underlying causes of war. So the Mexican War was an indirect cause of the Civil War. See COMPROMISE OF 1850; POPULAR SOVEREIGNTY.

The Mexican War gave training to many officers who later fought in the Civil War. Those who fought in the Mexican campaigns included Ulysses S. Grant, William T. Sherman, George B. McClellan, George Gordon Meade, Robert E. Lee, Thomas "Stonewall" Jackson, and Jefferson Davis.

Principal Battles

The chief battles of the Mexican War included:

Palo Alto, *PAL oh AL toh*, was one of the earliest battles of the war. Gen. Taylor's troops defeated Mexican forces under Gen. Mariano Arista on May 8, 1846, on a plain northeast of Brownsville, Tex.

Resaca de la Palma, *ray SAH kuh day lah PAHL muh.* A 2,300-man army under Taylor crushed Arista's 5,000 Mexican soldiers in Cameron County, near Brownsville, Tex., on May 9, 1846. Taylor's two victories allowed him to cross the Rio Grande and invade Mexico.

Buena Vista, *BWAY nah VEES tah.* Near the ranch of Buena Vista, Mexico, Taylor's 5,000-man force defended a narrow mountain pass against Santa Anna's army of from 16,000 to 20,000 men. Through this battle, fought on Feb. 22 and 23, 1847, the Americans established their hold on northeastern Mexico.

Cerro Gordo, *SEHR oh GAWR doh*, ranks among the most important battles the Americans fought on the march from Veracruz to Mexico City. A mountain pass near Jalapa, Cerro Gordo lies 60 miles (97 kilometers) northwest of Veracruz. General Scott's 9,000-man force attacked 13,000 Mexicans under Santa Anna, and forced them to flee. The battle, fought on April 17 and 18, 1847, cleared the way to Mexico City.

Churubusco, *CHOO roo VOOS koh.* In the small village of Churubusco, 6 miles (10 kilometers) south of Mexico City, Scott's invading army won another major victory on Aug. 20, 1847. Scott's soldiers stormed the fortified camp of Contreras, then attacked the Mexican force at Churubusco. The Mexicans finally fled, and sought refuge within the walls of the capital city. The Americans had about 9,000 men in the battle; the Mexicans, about 30,000.

Chapultepec, *chuh PUHL tuh PEHK*, was the last battle of the war before the capture of Mexico City. On Sept. 12, 1847, Scott's men attacked Chapultepec, a fortified hill guarding the city gates. The attacks continued the following day until the Mexicans retreated to Mexico City. On September 14, Scott's troops entered the Mexican capital.   NORMAN A. GRAEBNER

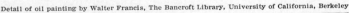

Related Articles in WORLD BOOK include:

Arista, Mariano
Davis, Jefferson
Frémont, John C.
Grant, Ulysses S.
   (Early Army Career)
Guadalupe Hidalgo,
   Treaty of
Jackson, Stonewall
Lee, Robert E.
   (The Mexican War)
McClellan, George B.

Mexico (War with Texas and the U.S.)
Polk, James K.
Santa Anna,
   Antonio L. de
Scott, Winfield
Sherman (William T.)
Taylor, Zachary
Texas (History)
Wilmot Proviso

Detail of oil painting by Walter Francis, The Bancroft Library, University of California, Berkeley

The Battle of San Pasqual was a short, bloody fight between United States and Mexican troops near San Diego, Calif., on Dec. 6, 1846. Brig. Gen. Stephen Watts Kearny led the U.S. forces.

WORLD BOOK photo by Henry Gill

Snow-Capped Mountains tower over what has been the heart of Mexico since the days of the Aztec Indians. The three peaks of Ixtacihuatl, an inactive volcano, rise southeast of Mexico City. Tough, green maguey plants, such as those shown above, grow throughout this dry region of Mexico.

MEXICO

MEXICO is the northernmost country of Latin America. It lies just south of the United States. The Rio Grande forms about two-thirds of the boundary between Mexico and the United States. Among all the countries of the Western Hemisphere, only the United States and Brazil have more people than Mexico. Mexico City is the capital and largest city of Mexico. It is also the largest city in the Western Hemisphere.

To understand Mexico, it is necessary to view the nation's long early history. Hundreds of years ago, the Indians of Mexico built large cities, developed a calendar, invented a counting system, and used a form of writing. The last Indian empire in Mexico—that of the Aztec—fell to Spanish invaders in 1521. For the next 300 years, Mexico was a Spanish colony. The Spaniards took Mexico's riches and kept the Indians poor and uneducated. But they also introduced many changes in farming, government, industry, and religion.

During the Spanish colonial period, a third group of people developed in Mexico. These people, who had both Indian and white ancestors, became known as *mestizos*. Today, the great majority of Mexicans are mestizos. Some of them think of the Spaniards as intruders and take great pride in their Indian ancestry. A number of government programs stress the Indian role in Mexican culture. In 1949, the government made an Indian the symbol of Mexican nationality. He was Cuauhtémoc, the last Aztec emperor, whose bravery

under torture by the Spanish made him a Mexican hero.

Few other countries have so wide a variety of landscapes and climates within such short distances of one another. Towering mountains and high, rolling plateaus cover more than two-thirds of Mexico. The climate, land formation, and plant life in these rugged highlands may vary greatly within a short distance. Mexico also has tropical forests, dry deserts, and fertile valleys.

Manufacturing, agriculture, mining, and tourism are all important to Mexico's economy. Leading manufactured products include cement, chemicals, clothing, and processed foods. Crops are grown on only about an eighth of Mexico's land. The rest of the land is too dry, mountainous, or otherwise unsuitable for crops. But Mexico is one of the world's leading producers of coffee, corn, cotton, oranges, and sugar cane. Mexico is rich in minerals. It is one of the world's leading silver producers. Petroleum production has long been important in Mexico. During the 1970's, vast, newly dis-

The contributors of this article are Homer Aschmann of the University of California, Riverside, author of The Central Desert of Baja California: Demography and Ecology; *Frank Brandenburg, author of* The Making of Modern Mexico; *Dwight S. Brothers of Harvard University, co-author of* Mexican Financial Development; *and Robert E. Quirk of Indiana University at Bloomington, author of* The Mexican Revolution, 1914-1915.

372

Salvador Femat, Piramide

The Basilica of Our Lady of Guadalupe, *above,* a famous shrine in Mexico City, features a contrast of old and new architecture. The building on the right dates from the 1700's. The modern structure on the left was built during the 1970's.

WORLD BOOK photo by Henry Gill

Oil Refineries in Mexico process large amounts of petroleum, one of the country's most valuable resources.

covered deposits of petroleum greatly increased the importance of Mexico's petroleum industry. Mexico also has large deposits of copper, gold, and sulfur. About a million tourists visit Mexico each year. The money they spend helps the nation's economy.

The Mexicans overthrew Spanish rule in 1821. But they believe their real revolution started in 1910, when they began a long struggle for social justice and economic progress. During this struggle, the government took over huge, privately owned farmlands and divided them among millions of landless farmers. It established a national school system to promote education, and has built many hospitals and housing projects. Since the 1940's, the government has especially encouraged the development of manufacturing and petroleum production. But all these changes have not kept up with Mexico's rapid population growth. More than a third of the people still live in poverty, and the government keeps expanding its programs to help them. As a result, many Mexicans believe their revolution is still going on.

─────────── FACTS IN BRIEF ───────────

Capital: Mexico City.

Official Language: Spanish.

Official Name: *Estados Unidos Mexicanos* (United Mexican States).

Form of Government: Republic—31 states, 1 federal district. *Head of State*—President (6-year term). *Congress*—Senate (64 members, 6-year terms); Chamber of Deputies (400 members, 3-year terms).

Area: 761,607 sq. mi. (1,972,552 km²), including 2,071 sq. mi. (5,364 km²) of outlying islands. *Greatest Distances*—north-south, 1,250 mi. (2,012 km); east-west, 1,900 mi. (3,060 km). *Coastline*—6,320 mi. (10,170 km).

Elevation: *Highest*—Orizaba (Citlaltépetl), 18,701 ft. (5,700 m) above sea level. *Lowest*—near Mexicali, 33 ft. (10 m) below sea level.

Population: *Estimated 1981 Population*—74,123,000; distribution, 64 per cent urban, 36 per cent rural; density, 98 persons per sq. mi. (38 per km²). *1970 Census*—48,381,547. *Estimated 1986 Population*—88,035,000.

Chief Products: *Agriculture*—alfalfa, beans, coffee, corn, cotton, fruits, henequen, livestock, rice, sugar cane, tobacco, vegetables, wheat. *Fishing*—abalones, oysters, sardines, shrimp, tuna. *Forestry*—chicle, ebony, mahogany, pine, rosewood. *Manufacturing*—cement, chemicals, clothing, fertilizers, iron and steel, handicraft articles, household appliances, processed foods, wood pulp and paper. *Mining*—coal, copper, fluorspar, gold, iron ore, lead, manganese, natural gas, petroleum, silver, sulfur, tin, zinc.

National Anthem: *Himno Nacional de México* (National Hymn of Mexico).

National Holiday: Independence Day, September 16.

Money: *Basic Unit*—peso. One hundred centavos equal one peso. For the value of the peso in dollars, see MONEY (table: Exchange Rates). See also PESO.

Mexico is a democratic republic with a president, a national legislature called the Congress, and a Supreme Court. There is no vice-president. If the president does not finish his term, the Congress chooses a temporary president to serve until a special or regular presidential election is held.

Constitution. The Mexican government is based on the constitution of 1917. The constitution, like that of the United States, provides for three branches of federal government—executive, legislative, and judicial. The constitution also establishes state governments with elected governors and legislatures.

The constitution of Mexico gives the federal government powers much greater than those of the U.S. government. These powers apply to economic matters, education, and state affairs. They provide for the goals of economic progress and social justice that were fought for in the Mexican Revolution of 1910 and afterward. The government has used its powers to break up privately owned farmlands and divide them among the poor, and to set up a national school system. The government has also taken over a number of industries, including railroads, telegraph operations, and the petroleum industry. It can suspend a state's constitutional powers, remove the governor from office, and appoint a temporary governor. This has happened many times to settle struggles for leadership, especially during the 1920's and 1930's.

Politics. Mexico has an "official" political party, the *Partido Revolucionario Institucional* (Institutional Revolutionary Party). It was established in 1929 as the *Partido Nacional Revolucionario* (National Revolutionary Party). The party is generally considered the official promoter of the economic and social goals of the Mexican Revolution. Its candidates have won all state and national elections by huge majorities.

Other Mexican political parties include the *Partido*

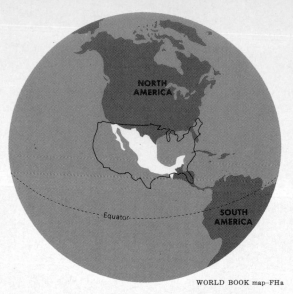

WORLD BOOK map-FHa

Mexico is about a fourth as large as the United States, not counting Alaska and Hawaii. It lies just south of the United States.

H. E. Harris & Co.

Mexico's Flag was adopted in 1821. The green stands for independence, white for religion, and red for union. The coat of arms is in the center.

Coat of Arms. A legend says the Aztec Indians built their capital Tenochtitlán (now Mexico City) where they saw the eagle shown in this symbol.

The National Palace, *right*, in Mexico City houses the office of the president of Mexico. It faces Constitution Plaza, called the *Zócalo*. The National Cathedral, *left*, also faces this public square.

WORLD BOOK photo by Henry Gill

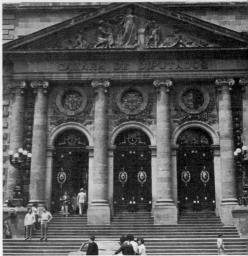

WORLD BOOK photo by Henry Gill

Dick Davis, Photo Researchers

The Palace of Justice, which houses Mexico's Supreme Court, has paintings by José Orozco telling of true and false justice.

The Chamber of Deputies Building houses Mexico's lower house of Congress.

de Acción Nacional (National Action Party), the *Partido Demócrata Mexicano* (Mexican Democratic Party), and the *Partido Socialista de los Trabajadores* (Workers' Socialist Party).

Married Mexican men and women who are at least 18 years old can vote in national, state, and local elec-

tions. Single persons must be at least 21 years old to vote in elections.

Armed Forces. Mexican men are required to serve a year in the army or the national guard after reaching the age of 18. The regular army, navy, and air force have a total of about 60,000 men.

MEXICAN GOVERNMENT IN BRIEF

Form: Republic.

Divisions: 31 States, 1 Federal District.

Head of State: President (can be elected to only one 6-year term).

Congress: Senate (64 members; 2 elected from each state and the Federal District; 6-year terms); Chamber of Deputies (400 members; elected from electoral districts; 3-year terms). Members of Congress cannot serve two terms in a row.

Courts: Highest court, Supreme Court of Justice (21 members appointed for life by the president). The Su-

preme Court appoints the judges of the 6 Federal Appeals Courts and the 44 District Courts to life terms. A Superior Court of Justice is the highest court in each state.

State Government: Governor (can be elected to only one 6-year term). Chamber of Deputies (7 to 15 members; cannot serve two terms in a row).

Local Government: Divisions, about 2,300 *municipios* (cities or townships). The local government divisions are governed by elected municipal presidents and councils (3-year terms).

STATES AND FEDERAL DISTRICT OF MEXICO

STATES

Map Key	Name	Area In sq. mi.	In km²	Population	Capital
E 5	Aguascalientes	2,158	5,589	447,639	Aguascalientes
B 1	Baja California Norte	27,071	70,113	1,320,310	Mexicali
D 2	Baja California Sur	28,447	73,677	187,970	La Paz
F 10	Campeche	21,666	56,114	349,456	Campeche
G 9	Chiapas	28,528	73,887	1,984,340	Tuxtla
B 4	Chihuahua	95,403	247,092	2,062,499	Chihuahua
C 6	Coahuila	58,522	151,571	1,363,588	Saltillo
F 5	Colima	2,106	5,455	332,015	Colima
D 5	Durango	46,196	119,648	1,149,134	Durango
E 6	Guanajuato	11,810	30,589	2,895,767	Guanajuato
G 7	Guerrero	24,631	63,794	2,074,772	Chilpancingo
F 7	Hidalgo	8,103	20,987	1,435,288	Pachuca
F 5	Jalisco	30,941	80,137	4,294,236	Guadalajara
F 7	México	8,286	21,461	6,684,229	Toluca
F 6	Michoacán	23,114	59,864	2,872,513	Morelia
F 7	Morelos	1,908	4,941	905,614	Cuernavaca
E 5	Nayarit	10,665	27,621	725,395	Tepic
D 7	Nuevo León	24,925	64,555	2,456,525	Monterrey
G 8	Oaxaca	36,820	95,364	2,377,720	Oaxaca
F 7	Puebla	13,096	33,919	3,133,474	Puebla
F 7	Querétaro	4,544	11,769	638,839	Querétaro
F 11	Quintana Roo	16,228	42,030	138,878	Chetumal
E 6	San Luis Potosí	24,266	62,848	1,560,601	San Luis Potosí
D 4	Sinaloa	22,429	58,092	1,786,681	Culiacán
B 3	Sonora	71,403	184,934	1,468,231	Hermosillo
G 9	Tabasco	9,522	24,661	1,101,335	Villahermosa
D 7	Tamaulipas	30,822	79,829	1,968,837	Ciudad Victoria
F 7	Tlaxcala	1,511	3,914	512,234	Tlaxcala
F 8	Veracruz	28,114	72,815	5,091,331	Jalapa
F 10	Yucatán	16,749	43,379	926,283	Mérida
E 6	Zacatecas	28,973	75,040	1,114,898	Zacatecas

FEDERAL DISTRICT

Map Key	Name	Area In sq. mi.	In km²	Population	Capital
F 7	Federal District	579	1,499	9,233,770	**Mexico City**

Source for population figures: 1977 official estimates. Each state has a separate article in WORLD BOOK.

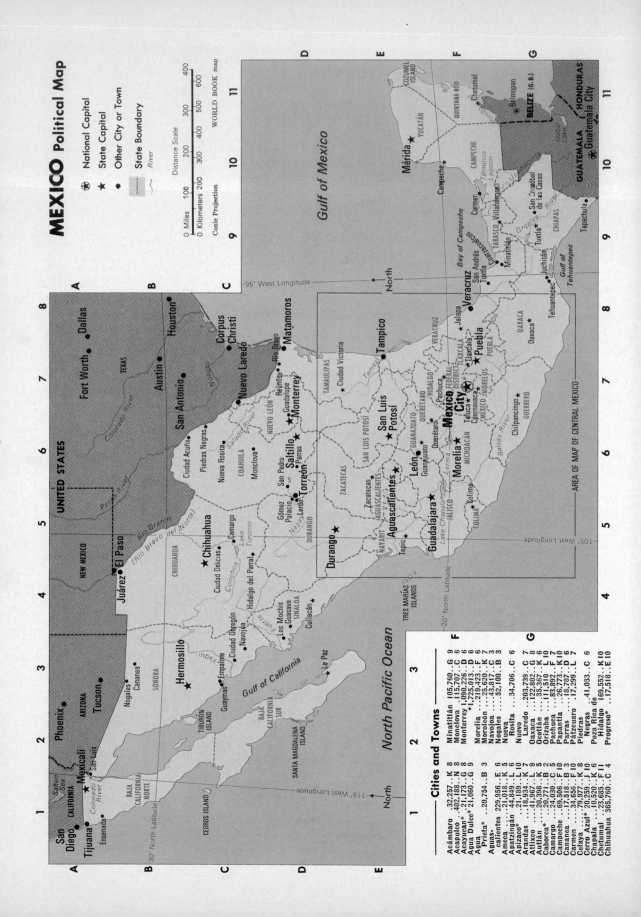

MEXICO Political Map

⊛	National Capital
★	State Capital
•	Other City or Town
	State Boundary
~	River

Distance Scale

WORLD BOOK map

0 Miles 100 200 300 400
0 Kilometers 200 400 600

Conic Projection

— Cities and Towns —

Acámbaro	.32,257.	K 8	Minatitlán	105,760.	G 9
Acapulco	.402,188.	N 8	Monclova	115,707.	C 6
Acayucan*	.21,173.	G 9	Monterrey	1,090,226.	D 6
Agua Dulce*	21,060.	G 9	Morelia	219,423.	K 7
Agua			Moroleón	25,620.	K 7
Prieta*	.20,754.	B 3	Navojoa	43,817.	C 3
Aguas-			Nogales	52,108.	B 3
calientes	229,956.	E 6	Nueva		
Amea	.21,018.	L 5	Rosita	34,706.	C 6
Apatzingán	44,849.	L 6	Nuevo		
Apizaco*	.21,189.	L 10	Laredo	203,739.	C 7
Arandas	.18,934.	K 7	Oaxaca	122,802.	G 8
Atlixco	.41,967.	L 9	Ocotlán	35,367.	K 6
Autlán	.20,398.	K 5	Orizaba	111,510.	L 10
Caborca*	.20,771.	B 2	Pachuca	83,892.	F 7
Camargo	.24,030.	C 5	Papantla	26,773.	K 10
Campeche	69,506.	F 10	Parras	18,707.	D 6
Cananea	.17,518.	B 3	Pátzcuaro	17,299.	L 7
Carmen	.34,656.	F 10	Piedras		
Celaya	.79,977.	K 8	Negras	41,033.	C 6
Cerro Azul*	20,529.	J 10	Poza Rica de		
Chapala	.23,685.	K 6	Hidalgo	169,552.	K 10
Chihuahua	365,760.	C 4	Progreso*	17,518.	E 10

North Pacific Ocean

Gulf of Mexico

Gulf of California

UNITED STATES

Phoenix

Tucson

El Paso

Juárez

Chihuahua

Hermosillo

La Paz

Durango

Guadalajara

Aguascalientes

León

Morelia

Mexico City

Toluca

Cuernavaca

Puebla

Tlaxcala

Jalapa

Veracruz

Oaxaca

San Luis Potosí

Torreón

Saltillo

Monterrey

Nuevo Laredo

Matamoros

Tampico

Mérida

Campeche

Chetumal

BELIZE (B.)

GUATEMALA

HONDURAS

Guatemala City

Belmopan

Dallas

Fort Worth

Austin

San Antonio

Corpus Christi

Houston

San Diego

Tijuana

Mexicali

CENTRAL MEXICO

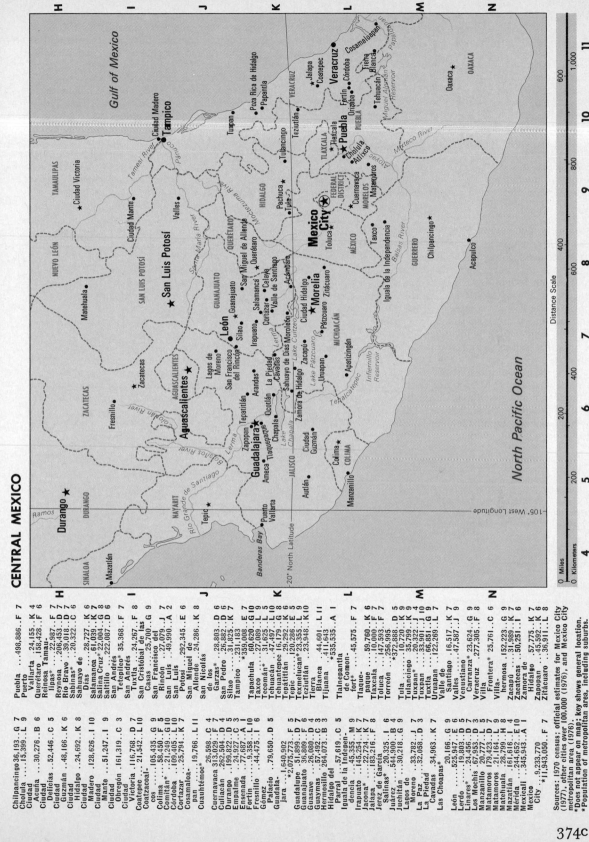

Gulf of Mexico

North Pacific Ocean

Distance Scale

Miles 0 — 200 — 400 — 600
Kilometers 0 — 200 — 400 — 600 — 800 — 1,000

-105° West Longitude

20° North Latitude

Chilpancino 36,193..G 7
Cholula ...15,399..L 9
Ciudad
  Acuña ....30,276..B 6
Ciudad
  Delicias ..52,446..C 5
Ciudad
  Guzmán ..48,166..K 6
Ciudad
  Hidalgo ..24,692..K 8
Ciudad
  Madero ..128,626..I 10
Ciudad
  Mante ...51,247..I 9
Ciudad
  Obregón .161,319..C 3
Ciudad
  Victoria .116,768..D 7
Coatepec ..21,542..L 9
Coatzacoal-
  cos .....105,435..G 9
Colima ....58,450..F 5
Comitán* ..21,249..G 10
Córdoba ...109,405..L 10
Cortazar ..25,794..K 7
Cosamaloa-
  pan .....19,766..L 11
Cuauhtémoc* 26,598..C 4
Cuernavaca 313,029..F 7
Culiacán ..262,304..D 4
Durango ..199,822..D 5
Empalme ...24,927..C 3
Ensenada ..77,687..A 1
Fortín ....44,475..L 10
Fresnillo ...9,358..I 6
Gómez
  Palacio ..79,650..D 5
Guada-
  lajara .*2,075,773..F 5
Guadalupe .31,899..D 6
Guanajuato .36,809..D 7
Guasave ...37,000..D 4
Hermosillo .264,073..B 3
Hidalgo del
  Parral ...57,619..C 5
Iguala de la Indepen-
  dencia ...45,355..M 9
Irapuato ..145,254..K 7
Jacona* ...22,724..K 7
Jalapa ....183,216..F 8
Jerez de García
  Salinas* .20,325..I 6
Juárez ....544,900..B 2
Juchitán ..30,218..G 9
Lagos de
  Moreno ...33,782..J 7
La Paz ....32,058..D 3
La Piedad
  Cavadas ..34,963..K 7
Las Choapas*

León .....20,166..G 6
Lerdo .....19,803..D 5
Linares* ..24,456..D 7
Los Mochis .67,953..D 3
Manzanillo .20,777..L 5
Matamoros .179,423..D 7
Matamoros .21,164..L 9
Matehuala .28,799..H 8
Mazatlán ..161,616..E 4
Mérida ....244,652..E 10
Mexicali ..345,943..A 1
Mexico
  City ...*9,233,770

Puebla ...498,886..F 7
Puerto
  Vallarta .24,155..K 4
Querétaro .158,428..F 6
Reinosa Tamau-
  linas ...22,987..F 7
Reynosa ..206,453..D 7
Río Bravo .39,018..D 7
Sabinas* ..20,322..C 6
Sabuayo de
  Díaz ....28,727..K 6
Salamanca .61,039..K 7
Salina Cruz* 22,004..I 9
Saltillo ..222,087..D 6
San Andrés
  Tepetilco* 35,368..F 7
San Andrés
  Tuxtla ...24,267..F 8
San Cristóbal de las
  Casas ...25,700..G 9
San Francisco del
  Rincón ..27,079..J 7
San Luis ..49,990..A 2
San Luis
  Potosí ..292,345..E 6
San Miguel de
  Allende ..24,286..K 8

Garzas* ...28,803..D 6
San Pedro .31,825..K 7
Silao .....231,183..K 7
Tampico ..231,183
Tapachula .359,008..E 10
Taxco ....27,089..L 9
Tecomán* ..60,620..L 5
Tehuacán ..31,625..L 10
Tehuantepec 16,179..G 9
Tepatitlán .29,292..K 6
Tepic ....120,286..E 5
Texmelucan* 23,355..L 9
Teziutlán ..23,948..K 10
Tierra
  Blanca ...44,601..L 11
Tijuana ...411,643..A 1
Tlalnepantla
  de Comon-
  fort* ....535,535..A I
Tlaque-
  paque ...45,575..F 7
Tlaxcala ..59,760..K 6
Toluca ...147,000..F 7
Torreón ...256,995..D 5
Tula .....310,820..F 7
Tulancingo .35,799..K 9
Tuxpan* ..20,322..J 4
Tuxpan ...33,901..J 10
Tuxtla ...66,851..L 9
Uruapan ..122,269..L 7
Valle de
  Santiago .16,517..K 7
Valles ....47,587..J 9
Venustiano
  Carranza* 23,624..G 9
Veracruz ..277,305..F 8
Villa
  Frontera* 25,761..C 6
Villa-
  hermosa .152,223..G 9
Zacapú ...31,989..K 7
Zacatecas .50,251..I 7
Zamora de
  Hidalgo ..57,775..K 7
Zapopan ...45,592..K 6
Zitácuaro .36,911..L 8

Sources: 1970 census; official estimates for Mexico City (1977), other cities over 100,000 (1976), and Mexico City metropolitan area (1976).
*Does not appear on map; key shows general location.
*Population of metropolitan area, including suburbs.

374c

Mexico has over 74 million people. This population is increasing about 3½ per cent a year, one of the greatest annual "population explosions" in the world. The growth rate is the result of Mexico's traditionally high birth rate and its sharply reduced death rate. Since the 1930's, improved living conditions and expanded health services have cut the death rate by more than half. Perhaps the government's chief problem is trying to provide housing, jobs, and schools for the rapidly increasing population.

The great majority of the Mexican people are *mestizos* (persons of mixed white and Indian ancestry). Their white ancestors were Spaniards who came to what is now Mexico during and after the Spanish conquest of 1519-1521. Their Indian ancestors were living in the region when the Spaniards arrived. Blacks and some Asians are also part of the racial mixture. The nation has some Indians and whites of unmixed ancestry. But most Mexicans think of themselves as mestizos. Being a mestizo is generally a matter of national pride.

Being an Indian in Mexico does not depend chiefly on ancestry. It is mostly a matter of way of life and point of view. For example, Mexicans are considered Indians if they speak an Indian language, wear Indian clothes, and live in a village where the people call themselves Indians. This is true even if they are actually mestizos.

Language. Almost all Mexicans speak Spanish, the official language of Mexico and nearly all other Latin-American countries. Many words that are used in the United States came from Mexico. They include *canyon, corral, desperado, lariat, lasso, patio, rodeo,* and *stampede.*

Most Mexican Indians speak Spanish in addition to their own ancient language. But more than a million speak only an Indian language. The major Indian languages include Maya, Mixtec, Náhuatl, Otomí, Tarascan, and Zapotec. See SPANISH LANGUAGE.

Religion. Nearly all of Mexico's people belong to the Roman Catholic Church. Mexico also has some Protestants, Jews, and other religious groups.

Roman Catholic missionaries and priests first arrived from Spain in the early 1500's. They baptized millions of Indians. But the rain, sun, and other forces of nature remained an important part of religion to the Indians. Today, millions of Indian villagers still combine ancient religious practices with Catholicism.

During the Spanish colonial period, the Roman Catholic Church was closely linked with the government as the official state church. The church became wealthy and powerful, and prohibited other religions. Beginning in the mid-1800's, the Mexican government greatly reduced the political and economic power of the church. Today, Mexican law provides freedom of worship, but it forbids any church to own land or to take part in political affairs.

The Virgin of Guadalupe is the patron saint of Mexico. According to Roman Catholic legend, she was seen twice by Juan Diego, a poor Indian, in December, 1531. She appeared as an Indian maiden on Tepeyac Hill in Mexico City. She asked Diego to tell Bishop Juan de Zumárraga to build a shrine in her honor on the hill. To prove her identity, she caused a picture of herself to appear on Diego's cloak. The bishop built the shrine and placed the cloak in it.

POPULATION

This map shows the population distribution of Mexico. Each dot represents 25,000 persons. The cities shown on the map are among the largest in Mexico.

Distance Scale
0 Miles   200   400
0 Kilometres   400   600

WORLD BOOK map–FHa

HISTORICAL POPULATION

1986	Estimate	88,035,000
1981	"	74,123,000
1970	Census	48,381,547
1960	"	35,970,823
1950	"	25,791,017
1940	"	19,653,552
1930	"	16,552,722
1921	"	14,334,780
1910	"	15,160,369
1900	"	13,607,259
1856	Estimate	7,661,520
1823	"	6,800,000
1521	"	9,120,000

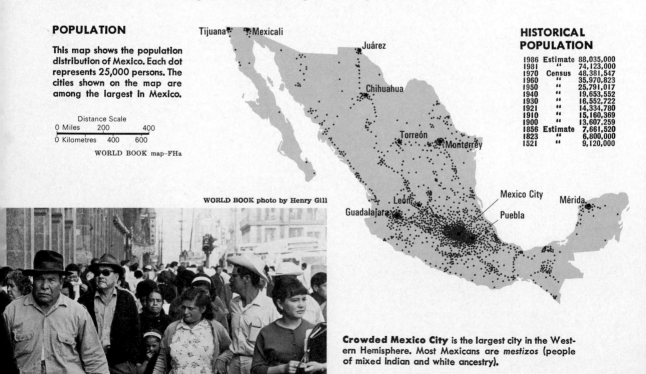

WORLD BOOK photo by Henry Gill

Crowded Mexico City is the largest city in the Western Hemisphere. Most Mexicans are *mestizos* (people of mixed Indian and white ancestry).

The way of life in Mexico includes many features from the nation's long Indian past and the Spanish colonial period. But Mexico has changed rapidly during the 1900's. In many ways, life in its larger cities is similar to that in the United States and Canada. Mexican villagers follow the older way of life more than the city people do. Even in the villages, however, government economic and educational programs are doing much to modernize the people's lives. These programs are bringing the Indian villagers into the general life of Mexico, and making them think of themselves as Mexicans rather than Indians. These Indians will probably be blended into the national life by about the year 2000.

City Life. About three-fifths of the people of Mexico live in cities and towns with populations of at least 2,-500. Forty-three Mexican cities have more than 100,-000 persons. Mexico City, the capital and largest city, has more than 9 million persons. Four other cities have populations of over 500,000. They are, in order of size, Guadalajara, Monterrey, Juárez, and León. See the separate articles on the cities of Mexico listed in the *Related Articles* at the end of this article.

Many Mexican cities and towns began as Indian communities. After the Spaniards arrived, they rebuilt the communities and made them more like Spanish towns. The main church and the chief public and government buildings were built around a *plaza* (public square). The plaza is still the center of city life. In the evenings and on Sunday afternoons, the people gather in the plaza to talk with friends or to listen to music.

Modern houses and apartment buildings in the new suburbs look like those in the United States and Canada. The older parts of the cities have rows of homes built in the Spanish colonial style. Most of these houses are made of stone or *adobe* (sun-dried clay) brick. Small balconies extend from some windows. A Spanish-style house also has a *patio* (courtyard), which is the center of family life. This gardenlike area may have a fountain,

flowers, vines, and pots of blooming plants. The poorest Mexicans live in slum shacks or rooms with almost no furniture. *Petates* (straw mats) serve as beds, and clay bowls may be the only dishes.

Village Life. Many Mexican farmers live in small villages near their fields. The village homes stand along dusty streets that are simple dirt roads or are paved with cobblestones. In most villages, a Roman Catholic church stands on one side of the plaza, the center of the community. On the other sides of most plazas are a few stores and government buildings.

Almost every village, and every city and town, has a market place. Going to market is one of the chief activities of the people in farm areas. Men, women, and children take along clothes, food, lace, pictures, toys, baskets, or whatever else they have to sell or trade. They either rent stalls in which to display their goods, or spread the merchandise on the ground. The people spend the day chatting with friends and doing a little business. Farmers often trade their goods instead of selling them, and much bargaining takes place.

The shape and style of village houses vary according to the climate. People on the dry central plateau build homes of adobe, brick, cement blocks, or stone, with flat roofs of red tile, sheet metal, or straw. Some of these houses have only one room, a hard-packed dirt floor, a door, and few or no windows. The kitchen may be simply a lean-to built of poles and cornstalks placed against an outside wall. If a house does not have a lean-to kitchen, the family may build a cooking fire on the floor. The smoke from the fire curls out through the door and windows.

In areas of heavy rainfall, many houses have walls built of poles coated with lime and clay. This mixture lasts longer in the rain than adobe does. The houses have sloping roofs to allow the water to run off easily. Some Indians in southern Mexico build round houses. In Yucatán, most village houses are rectangular with

Blindfolded Mexican Children take turns trying to break a *piñata*, a decorated container filled with candy and toys. The piñata, often shaped like an animal, is hung from a tree or ceiling at parties and before Christmas and Easter.

Ardean Miller, Alpha

Village Markets are social centers for Mexican families, as well as places to buy or trade food and other products.

WORLD BOOK photo by Henry Gill

Shoppers in Mexico's Big Cities look for bargain prices in large discount stores like those in the United States and Canada. The cities also have fashionable shops and traditional open-air markets.

Housing Projects are common in Mexico's rapidly growing big cities. Some projects in Mexico City include medical centers, nurseries, schools, shops, and theaters.

Mexican Craftworkers, such as these leatherworkers, are famous for their skill in creating beautiful objects of Indian, Spanish, or modern design. They sell many of their products to tourists.

Leisure Time in Mexico has greatly increased since the 1940's, when the nation's rapid industrial growth began. Large crowds attend art shows and other attractions in city parks.

rounded ends. The roofs are made of neatly trimmed palm leaves.

Many Indian villages are in the wilds of Yucatán and in rugged areas of central and southern Mexico. There, the Indians still follow their ancient customs and live much as their ancestors did before white people arrived. For example, some Maya Indians sacrifice turkeys to their gods in hope of getting rain.

Family Life. Mexican households consist of an average of five or six persons. In many homes, several generations of the same family live together. Most women, like those of other Latin-American countries, have few activities outside the home besides marketing. But many women in the cities have jobs, and the women in farm areas often help cultivate the fields. Mexican girls do not have so much individual freedom as girls in the United States. Farm boys work in the fields, and many city youths have part-time or full-time jobs.

Food. Thousands of years ago, the Indians of what is now Mexico discovered how to grow corn. It became their most important food. Today, corn is still the chief food of most Mexicans, especially in rural areas. Mexican housewives generally soften the corn in hot limewater, boil it, and then grind it into meal.

The main corn-meal food is the *tortilla,* a thin pancake shaped by hand or machine and cooked on an ungreased griddle. The tortilla is the bread of the poorer people. It can be eaten plain or as part of (1) the *taco,* a folded tortilla filled with chopped meat, chicken, or cheese, and then fried; (2) the *enchilada,* a rolled-up tortilla with a similar filling and covered with a hot sauce; or (3) the *tostada,* a tortilla fried in deep fat until it becomes crisp, and served flat with beans, cheese, lettuce, meat, and onions on top.

Many Mexicans eat *frijoles* (beans) that are boiled, mashed, and then fried and refried in lard. Poorer Mexicans may eat frijoles every day, often using a folded tortilla to spoon up the beans. Rice is also boiled and then fried. Other popular foods include *atole* (a thick, soupy corn-meal dish) and *tamales* (corn meal steamed in corn husks or banana leaves, and usually mixed with

Ancient Ways of Life are still followed in many of Mexico's Indian villages, but are slowly being replaced by modern customs. The Tarascan Indians, like their ancestors, use dugouts and butterfly nets to catch fish in Lake Pátzcuaro.

Mexican Farmers in many areas cultivate their fields with old-fashioned equipment, including wooden hoes and ox-drawn plows.

pork or chicken). Most Mexicans like their foods highly seasoned with hot, red chili pepper or other strong peppers. Turkey is a popular holiday dish. It is often served with *mole*, a sauce made of chocolate, chili, sesame seed, and spices.

The poorer families eat little meat because they cannot afford it. They may vary their basic diet of corn and beans with fruit, honey, onions, tomatoes, squash, or sweet potatoes. Favorite fruits include avocados, bananas, mangoes, oranges, and papayas. The fruit and leaves of the prickly pear, a type of cactus, are boiled, fried, or stewed. Richer Mexicans have a more balanced diet, and also eat tortillas and beans.

Popular beverages include water flavored with a variety of fruit juices, and cinnamon-flavored hot chocolate cooked with water and beaten into foam. Mexicans also drink coffee and milk. Alcoholic beverages include *mescal*, *pulque*, and *tequila*, which are made from the juice of the maguey plant, and beer and wine.

Clothing. Mexicans in the cities and larger towns wear clothing similar to that worn in the United States and Canada. The village people wear simple types of clothing that date back hundreds of years. Men generally wear plain cotton shirts and trousers, and leather sandals called *huaraches*. Wide-brimmed felt or straw hats called *sombreros* protect them from the hot sun. During cold or rainy weather, they may wear *ponchos* (blankets that have a slit in the center for the head and are draped over the shoulders). At night the men may wrap themselves in colorful *serapes*, which are blankets carried over one shoulder during the day. The village women wear blouses and long, full skirts, and usually go barefoot. They cover their heads with fringed shawls called *rebozos*. A mother may wrap her baby to her back with a rebozo.

Some of the villagers' clothing is homemade. Hand weaving was an ancient Indian art, and today the Indians are famous for their beautiful home-woven fabrics. Styles of weaving vary throughout Mexico, and an Indian's region can be identified by the colors and designs of his poncho or serape. For example, blankets with a striped rainbow pattern come from the Saltillo area.

Some Indians wear unusual clothing. Large capes made of straw are worn in Oaxaca state. On holidays, Indian women on the Isthmus of Tehuantepec wear a wide, lacy white headdress called a *huipil grande*. According to legend, this garment was copied from baby clothes that were washed ashore from a Spanish shipwreck. The Indian women thought the clothes were head shawls. In Yucatán, Maya women wear long, loose white dresses that are embroidered around the neck and bottom hem.

Mexicans sometimes wear national costumes on holidays and other special occasions. The men's national costumes include the dark-blue *charro* suit, made of doeskin or velvet. It has a *bolero* (short jacket) and tight riding pants with gold or silver buttons down the sides. A flowing red bow tie, spurred boots, and a fancy white sombrero complete the costume.

Probably the best-known women's costume is the *china poblana*. It is usually worn in the *jarabe tapatío*, or Mexican hat dance. A legend says the china poblana was named for a Chinese princess of the 1600's who was kidnapped by pirates and sold in the slave market. She was brought to Acapulco, where a kindly merchant of Puebla bought her. In Puebla, she dedicated her life to helping the poor. The princess adopted a costume that the local women later imitated. Today, it consists of a full red and green skirt decorated with beads and other ornaments, a gaily embroidered short-sleeved blouse, and a brightly colored sash. See CLOTHING (picture: Traditional Costumes).

Holidays. Mexicans celebrate their Independence Day, September 16, and other holidays with colorful *fiestas* (festivals). Every Mexican city, town, and village also holds a yearly fiesta to honor its local patron saint. Most fiestas begin before daylight with a shower of rockets, loud explosions of fireworks, and ringing of bells. During the fiestas, the people pray and burn candles to their saints in churches decorated with flowers and colored tissue paper. They dance, gamble, hold parades, and buy refreshments in the crowded

John Stage, Photo Researchers

Bullfighting is the most popular spectator sport in Mexico. Many small towns have bull rings where amateur bullfighters perform against young bulls. The major rings are in the big cities.

Corn Is Mexico's Chief Food. Many Mexican women soak boil, and grind the corn themselves, as the ancient Indians did. The corn meal is often flattened like a pancake to make *tortillas*.

John Stage, Photo Researchers

market places and public square. Fireworks are again set off at night.

In the smaller towns and villages, cockfights and amateur bullfights are also held during fiestas. In the larger towns and the cities, fiestas resemble carnivals or county fairs in the United States. Most of them include less religious worship than do the village fiestas. The people watch plays and professional bullfights, ride merry-go-rounds and Ferris wheels, and buy goods at merchants' booths.

Guadalupe Day is Mexico's most important religious holiday. It is celebrated on December 12, when the Virgin is believed to have made a sign of her appearance on Tepeyac Hill in Mexico City.

On the nine nights before Christmas, friends and neighbors gather and act out the journey of Mary and Joseph to Bethlehem. These nine ceremonies are called *posadas*. Each night after the posada, the children play the *piñata* game. Piñatas are containers made of earthenware or papier-mâché. Many are shaped like animals, and are filled with candy, fruit, and toys. A piñata is hung above the heads of the children. Then the youngsters are blindfolded and take turns trying to break the piñata with a stick. After it breaks, they scramble for the presents. On Twelfth Night, 12 days after Christmas, parents fill their children's shoes with presents. See CHRISTMAS (color picture: Christmas Is Children's Time). See also EASTER (In Mexico).

Sports popular in Mexico include baseball, soccer, swimming, and volleyball. Many amateur and professional baseball teams play throughout the country. Most Mexicans also enjoy watching bullfights. Mexico City has the largest bullfighting arena in the world. It seats about 50,000 persons. There are about 35 other major bullfighting arenas in Mexico.

Another popular sport is jai alai, which resembles handball. The players hit the ball against a wall with a basketlike racket. Jai alai is sometimes called the fastest game in the world because the ball travels so rapidly. Richer Mexicans also enjoy such sports as golf, horseback riding, polo, tennis, and yachting.

Farm Women and Girls of Teotihuacán do their laundry in a creek. Many Mexican families in dry regions use water from wells.

WORLD BOOK photo by Henry Gill

Throughout the Spanish colonial period, the Roman Catholic Church controlled education in what is now Mexico. During the 1800's, the newly independent government and the church struggled for power, and the government won control of the schools. Mexico's present constitution, adopted in 1917, prohibits religious groups and ministers from establishing schools or teaching in them. The government does permit churches to operate private schools. However, less than 15 per cent of the nation's elementary schools are private.

During the early 1900's, fewer than 25 per cent of Mexico's people could read or write. Since the Revolution of 1910, and especially since the early 1940's, the government has done much to promote free public education. It has built thousands of new schools and established teachers' colleges. The government spends increasing sums on education each year—more than a fifth of its national budget. Today, more than 75 per cent of the people can read and write.

Mexican law requires all children from the age of 6 through 14 to go to school. But there are not enough schools or trained teachers. More than a third of the youngsters do not attend school, especially in farm areas. There, less than 10 per cent of the schools go beyond the fourth grade. The population of Mexico increases about $3\frac{1}{2}$ per cent a year, and the school-expansion program simply cannot keep up.

Mexico's school system is managed by the national Ministry of Public Education. After kindergarten, a child has six years of elementary school. The relatively few students who plan to go to college study in high schools for five years. Others may attend three-year high schools, most of which stress job training. Courses of higher education at Mexico's many universities, specialized colleges, and technical institutes last from three to seven years. The oldest and largest Mexican university is the National Autonomous University of Mexico in Mexico City. It was founded in 1551 and has about 110,000 students. See MEXICO, NATIONAL AUTONOMOUS UNIVERSITY OF.

Hilda Bijour, Monkmeyer

Mexico's Village Schools generally have at least two grades, but some have only one. Less than a tenth go above fourth grade.

Marc & Evelyne Bernheim, Rapho Guillumette

The Boldly Modern Campus of the National Autonomous University of Mexico, in Mexico City, was built during the 1950's.

Research Institutes of Mexico have fine libraries for specialized study in various sciences and other fields. Most of these institutes are in Mexico City, the education center of Mexico.

Carl Frank

Reconstruction of *Presentation of a Prince* (Euramex Photographic)

WORLD BOOK photo by Henry Gill

Religious Art of the Spanish colonial period is represented by this highly decorated altar in the Church of Santa Prisca, built in Taxco during the 1750's.

MEXICO / *Arts*

The arts have been an important part of Mexican life since the days of the ancient Indian civilizations. The Maya and Toltec Indians built beautiful temples and painted *murals* (wall paintings) in them. The Aztec composed music and poetry. The Spaniards brought a love for beautiful buildings and for literature. They also built thousands of impressive churches. During the 1900's, Mexico has given the world many important architects, artists, composers, and writers.

Architecture of the ancient Indians was related chiefly to religion. The Indians built stone temples on flat-topped pyramids, and decorated them with murals and sculptured symbols. These symbols represented the feathered-serpent god Quetzalcoatl and the Indians' other gods. Many ancient structures still stand near Mexico City and at Chichén Itzá in Yucatán. See the Arts sections of the AZTEC and MAYA articles.

After the Spanish conquest, the earliest mission churches were designed in a simple style. The huge National Cathedral in Mexico City, begun in 1573, was designed in a more ornamental style. Churches built during the 1700's were even more highly decorated. During the 1900's, Félix Candela and other Mexican architects have combined ancient Indian designs with modern construction methods. Their work includes the beautiful buildings of the National Autonomous University of Mexico. Another example is the 44-story Latin-American Tower, one of the tallest buildings in Latin America, in Mexico City.

Painting. During the Spanish colonial period, many artists painted murals in churches or portraits of government officials. But Mexican painting is best known for the artists who did their work after the Mexican Revolution of 1910. Beginning in the 1920's, José

Gianni Tortoli, Photo Researchers

Ancient Pyramids and Temples attract visitors to Teotihuacán (House of the Gods) northeast of Mexico City. The huge Pyramid of the Sun, *rear*, is over 200 feet (61 meters) high.

Olle Stackman, Pix from Publix

The Story of the Mexican Revolution was told in murals by David Siqueiros and other well-known Mexican artists. Siqueiros is shown with part of his mural, *The March of Humanity*.

Victor Englebert

The Mexican Hat Dance is a popular Mexican dance. It is often performed by the Ballet Folklórico, a dance company that appears regularly in the Palace of Fine Arts in Mexico City.

WORLD BOOK photo by Henry Gill

Beautiful Silver Objects including candlesticks, jewelry, and tableware are produced by skilled silversmiths of Taxco. Silver shops line the city's streets and attract many tourists.

Orozco, Diego Rivera, and David Siqueiros painted the story of the revolution on the walls of public buildings. Important Mexican painters of later years include Rufino Tamayo and José Luis Cuevas. During the 1960's, many younger Mexican painters have turned from revolutionary themes and have followed the latest art influences from other countries.

Literature. Outstanding colonial writers included the dramatist Juan Ruiz de Alarcón and the poet Sor Juana Inés de la Cruz. In 1816, José Joaquín Fernández de Lizardi published *The Itching Parrot*, probably the first Latin-American novel. After 1910, revolutionary themes became important in novels by such writers as Mariano Azuela and Martín Luis Guzmán, and later by Carlos Fuentes and Agustín Yáñez. Leading Mexican poets of the 1900's include Amado Nervo, Octavio Paz, Carlos Pellicer, and Alfonso Reyes.

Music. The early Indians used drums, flutes, gourd rattles, and seashells as well as the human voice for music and dances. This ancient music is still played in some parts of Mexico. Much church music was written during the colonial period. In addition, popular Spanish music was combined with music styles of blacks and Indians. The *jarabe* style was prohibited by the Spaniards as "indecent and disgraceful." The *jarabe tapatío*, or Mexican hat dance, later became a popular Mexican dance.

Folk songs called *corridos* have long been popular in Mexico. They may tell of the Mexican Revolution, of a bandit or a sheriff, or of the struggle between church and state. During the 1900's, Mexican composers including Carlos Chávez and Silvestre Revueltas have used themes from these folk songs or from ancient Indian music.

374k

Mexico has six main land regions: (1) the Pacific Northwest, (2) the Plateau of Mexico, (3) the Gulf Coastal Plain, (4) the Southern Uplands, (5) the Chiapas Highlands, and (6) the Yucatán Peninsula. Within these regions are many smaller ones that differ greatly in altitude, climate, land formation, and plant and animal life.

The Pacific Northwest region of Mexico is generally dry. The Peninsula of Lower California, the region's westernmost section, consists largely of rolling or mountainous desert. During some years, the desert receives no rain at all. It has a few oases, where farmers in small settlements grow dates and grapes. The northwestern corner and southern end of the peninsula get enough rain for a little farming. The lowest point in Mexico is in the far northern area, near Mexicali. This area, 33 feet (10 meters) below sea level, is the southern end of the huge Imperial Valley of California.

The most valuable land of Mexico's Pacific Northwest lies along the mainland coastal strip. There, in fertile river valleys, is some of Mexico's richest farmland. The valleys are irrigated with the waters of the Colorado, Fuerte, Yaqui, and other rivers. Steep, narrow mountain ranges extend in a north-south direction in the state of Sonora, east of the coastal plain. The ranges lie parallel to each other and separate the upper river valleys. In these basins are cattle ranches, irrigated farmland, and copper and silver mines.

The Plateau of Mexico is the largest of Mexico's land regions. It has most of the Mexican people and the largest cities. The plateau is the most varied land region, and consists of five sections.

The Volcanic Axis, a series of volcanoes, extends across Mexico at the plateau's southern edge. Many of the volcanoes are active. The volcanic soils of this rugged zone are fertile and receive enough rain for agriculture. Corn, beans, and other crops have been grown on the slopes since the days of the ancient Indian civilizations. The highest point in Mexico is 18,-701-foot (5,700-meter) Orizaba (Citlaltépetl), the third tallest mountain in North America. Southeast of Mexi-

co City are the volcanoes Ixtacihuatl and Popocatépetl, both more than 17,000 feet (5,180 meters) high. To the west is Lake Chapala, Mexico's largest lake. It covers 417 square miles (1,080 square kilometers). See IXTACIHUATL; ORIZABA; POPOCATÉPETL.

The Bajío (Flat), which lies north of the Volcanic Axis on the plateau, is the heart of Mexico. It averages about 7,000 feet (2,100 meters) above sea level. The rainfall of this section is hardly enough to raise corn or beans, but wheat and barley grow well there. The Aztec capital of Tenochtitlán stood at the Bajío's southern edge, in the beautiful Valley of Mexico. Mexico City was built on the same site after the Spanish conquest, and became the capital during the colonial period. Today, it is also the country's leading center of culture, industry, and transportation. Several small lakes, including famous Lake Xochimilco, are in the Mexico City area (see LAKE XOCHIMILCO).

The Mesa del Norte (Northern Plateau) makes up more than half the Plateau of Mexico. It extends from the Bajío north to the United States. The mesa is highest in the south and west, with altitudes from 6,000 to 9,000 feet (1,800 to 2,700 meters). In the north and east, it is less than 4,000 feet (1,200 meters) high. Low mountains rise from 2,000 to 3,000 feet (610 to 910 meters) above its plains. This section receives little rainfall except in the higher mountains, where frost is a constant threat to farming. Only in such irrigated places as the Saltillo and Torreón areas is farming really successful.

The low mountains of the mesa have the richest silver mines in the world. The Spaniards began developing these mines during the 1500's. They also established huge dry ranches in the nearby dry hills and plains to supply the miners with beef, horses, and mules. In the Durango and Chihuahua areas, *vaqueros* (cowboys) developed skills at riding, roping cattle, and fighting Indians. American cowboys later copied these skills.

The Sierra Madre Occidental is a long mountain range that forms the western rim of the Plateau of Mexico. For hundreds of years, this range was a natural barrier

to transportation between the plateau and the west coast. Paved roads and a railroad were not built across it until the 1900's. The range includes some of Mexico's most rugged land. Short, steep streams flowing to the Pacific Ocean have cut canyons more than 1 mile (1.6 kilometers) deep through the mountains. The largest canyon is the spectacular Barranca del Cobre, cut by the Urique River. This deep, wide gorge is so wild that parts of it have not been explored on foot.

The Sierra Madre Oriental, the plateau's eastern rim, is actually a series of mountain ranges. In many places between the ranges, highways and railroads climb up to the plateau from the east coast. Monterrey, near large deposits of coal and iron ore, is the major center of the Mexican steel industry. See SIERRA MADRE.

The Gulf Coastal Plain. North of Tampico, the plain is largely covered by tangled forests of low, thorny bushes and trees. This section of the plain is generally dry, and farming is possible only along rivers and with the aid of irrigation. South of Tampico, the rainfall increases. The plant life gradually changes southward, and becomes a tropical rain forest in Ta-

LAND REGIONS OF MEXICO

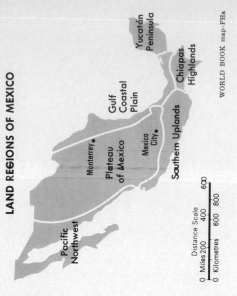

Pacific Northwest

Monterrey

Plateau of Mexico

Mexico City

Southern Uplands

Gulf Coastal Plain

Chiapas Highlands

Yucatán Peninsula

Distance Scale
0 Miles 200 400 600
0 Kilometres 600 800

WORLD BOOK map-FHa

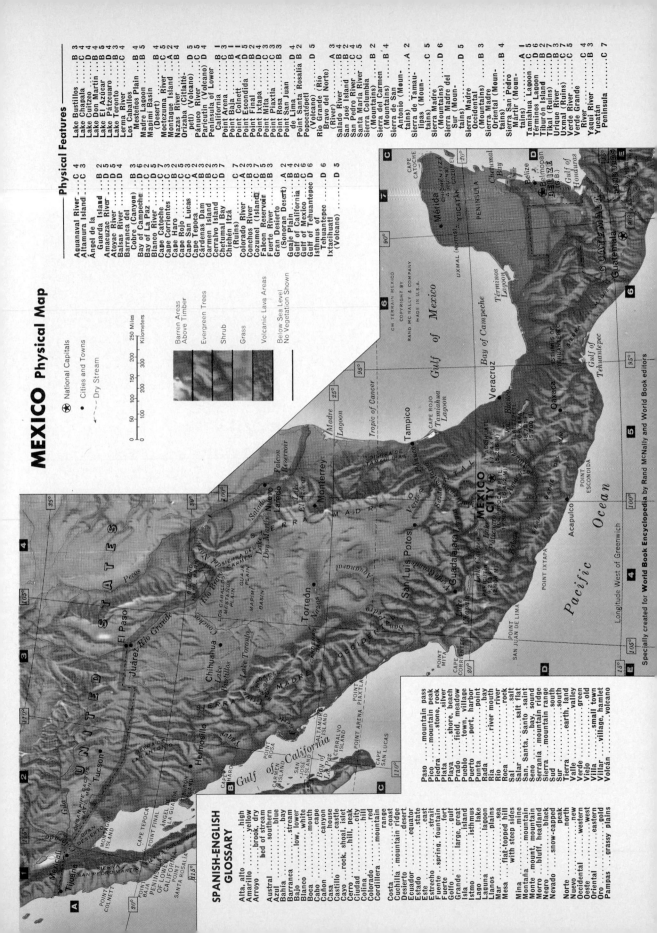

MEXICO Physical Map

⊛ National Capitals
• Cities and Towns
- - - Dry Stream

0 50 100 150 200 250 Miles
0 100 200 300 Kilometers

Barren Areas Above Timber
Evergreen Trees
Shrub
Grass
Volcanic Lava Areas
Below Sea Level No Vegetation Shown

Physical Features

Aguanaval River	C 4	Lake Bustillos	B 3
Altamura Island	C 3	Lake Chapala	C 3
Ángel de la Guarda Island	B 2	Lake Cuitzeo	D 4
Amacuzac River	D 5	Lake Don Martín	B 4
Atoyac River	D 4	Lake El Azúcar	B 5
Balsas River	D 5	Lake Pátzcuaro	D 3
Barranca del Cobre (Canyon)	B 3	Lerma River	C 4
Bay of Campeche	C 6	Los Caballos	B 5
Bay of La Paz	C 3	Mesteños Plain	B 5
Blanco River	D 5	Madre Lagoon	B 5
Cape Catoche	C 7	Mapimí Basin (Desert)	B 4
Cape Corrientes	D 4	Moctezuma River	C 5
Cape Haro	B 2	Montague Island	A 2
Cape Rojo	C 5	Nazas River	B 4
Cape San Lucas	C 3	Orizaba (Citlaltépetl) (Volcano)	D 5
Cape Tepoca	A 2	Parícutin (Volcano)	D 4
Cárdenas Dam	B 3	Peninsula of Lower California	B 1
Carmen Island	B 3	Point Arena	A 1
Cerralvo Island	C 3	Point Colnet	A 1
Chetumal Bay	D 7	Point Escondida	D 5
Chichén Itzá (Ruins)	C 7	Point Final	A 2
Colorado River	A 2	Point Ixtapa	D 4
Conchos River	B 3	Point Mita	C 3
Cozumel (Island)	C 7	Point Piaxtla	B 3
Falcon Reservoir	B 5	Point Rosa	B 3
Fuerte River	B 3	Point San Juan de Lima	D 4
Gran Desierto (Sonoran Desert)	A 2	Point Santa Rosalía	B 2
Guaje Plain	B 3	Popocatépetl (Volcano)	D 5
Gulf of California	B 2	Río Grande (Río Bravo del Norte) (River)	D 6
Gulf of Mexico	C 6		A 3
Gulf of Tehuantepec	D 6	Salado River	B 4
Isthmus of Tehuantepec	D 6	San José Island	C 3
Ixtacíhuatl (Volcano)	D 5	San Pedro River	C 5
		Santa María River	B 4
		Sierra Columbia	B 2
		Sierra del Carmen (Mountains)	B 4
		Sierra de San Antonio (Mountains)	A 2
		Sierra de Tamaulipas (Mountains)	C 5
		Sierra Madre (Mountains)	D 6
		Sierra Madre del Sur (Mountains)	D 5
		Sierra Madre Occidental (Mountains)	B 3
		Sierra Madre Oriental (Mountains)	B 4
		Sierra San Pedro Mártir (Mountains)	A 1
		Tamiahua Lagoon	D 6
		Términos Lagoon	D 7
		Tiburón Island	B 2
		Tikal (Ruins)	D 7
		Urique River	B 3
		Uxmal (Ruins)	C 7
		Verde River	C 5
		Verde Grande	C 4
		Yaqui River	B 3
		Yucatán Peninsula	C 7

SPANISH-ENGLISH GLOSSARY

Alta, alto ... high
Amarillo ... yellow
Arroyo ... brook, dry bed of stream
Austral ... southern
Azul ... blue
Bahía ... bay
Barranca ... stream
Bajo ... low, lower
Blanco ... white
Boca ... mouth
Cabo ... cape
Cañon ... canyon
Casa ... house
Castillo ... castle
Cayo ... rock, shoal, islet
Cerro ... rock, hill, peak
Ciudad ... city
Colina ... hill
Colorado ... red
Cordillera ... mountain range
Costa ... coast
Cuchilla ... mountain ridge
Desierto ... desert
Ecuador ... equator
Este ... east
Estado ... state
Estrecho ... strait
Fuente ... spring, fountain
Fuerte ... fort
Golfo ... gulf
Grande ... large, great
Isla ... island
Istmo ... isthmus
Lago ... lake
Laguna ... lagoon
Llanos ... plains
Mar ... sea
Mesa ... flat-topped hill with steep sides
Mina ... mine
Montaña ... mountain
Monte ... mount, mountain
Morro ... bluff, headland
Negro ... black
Nevado ... snow-capped peak
Norte ... north
Nuevo ... new
Occidental ... western
Oeste ... west
Oriental ... eastern
Oro ... gold
Pampas ... grassy plains
Paso ... mountain pass
Pico ... mountain peak
Piedra ... stone, rock
Plata ... silver
Playa ... shore, beach
Prado ... field, meadow
Pueblo ... town, village
Puerto ... port, harbor
Punta ... point
Ría ... river mouth
Río ... river
Roca ... rock
Sal ... salt
Salar ... salt flat
Santa, Santo ... saint
Seno ... bay, round
Serranía ... mountain range
Sierra ... mountain range
Sud ... south
Sur ... south
Tierra ... earth, land
Valle ... valley
Verde ... green
Viejo ... old
Villa ... small town
Villar ... village, hamlet
Volcán ... volcano

Longitude West of Greenwich

Specially created for World Book Encyclopedia by Rand McNally and World Book editors

MEXICO

basco. The southern section has some rich farmland.

Many of Mexico's longest rivers flow into the Gulf of Mexico from the coastal plain. They include the Rio Grande, which forms about 1,300 miles (2,090 kilometers) of Mexico's border with the United States. Large petroleum deposits lie beneath the plain and offshore. Huge sulfur deposits occur near the Gulf of Mexico in the Isthmus of Tehuantepec. The isthmus, which is 130 miles (209 kilometers) wide, is the narrowest part of Mexico. See GULF OF MEXICO; RIO GRANDE.

The Southern Uplands consist largely of steep ridges and deep gorges cut by mountain streams. The region includes a large, hot, dry valley just south of the Volcanic Axis. This valley is drained by the Balsas River. The Sierra Madre del Sur, a rugged mountain range, rises southwest of the valley along the Pacific Ocean. The famous beach resort of Acapulco is on this coast. A little farming takes place on the steep mountainsides. The Oaxaca Plateau makes up the eastern part of the Southern Uplands. Monte Albán, an ancient Indian religious center, was built there on a flattened mountaintop. Much of the gold of the Aztec empire probably came from the Oaxaca Plateau.

The Chiapas Highlands have great blocklike mountains that rise more than 9,000 feet (2,700 meters) above sea level. There are also many relatively flat surfaces at high altitudes. These tablelands are farmed by Indians who speak Maya and other ancient languages. Most of the region's modern farming development is taking place in deep, broad river valleys. With irrigation, farmers grow coffee, fruits, and other crops.

The Yucatán Peninsula is a low limestone plateau with no rivers. Limestone dissolves in water, and rainfall reaches the sea through underground channels dissolved out of the rock. Great pits have formed where the roofs of these channels have fallen in. The pits were the sacred wells of the ancient Maya Indians. The northwestern part of the region is dry bushland. There, leaves of agave plants provide a yellow fiber called henequen, which is used in making twine. To the south, the rainfall increases, and tropical rain forests cover the land. See YUCATÁN PENINSULA.

WORLD BOOK photo by Henry Gill

The Plateau of Mexico is the largest and most varied of the country's six main land regions. It has fertile uplands, snow-topped mountains, and dry plains.

Phil Stern, Globe Photos

The Pacific Northwest region of Mexico includes the Peninsula of Lower California. Much of the peninsula is a desert which receives no rain in some years.

476

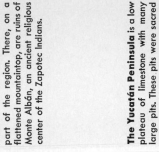

The Southern Uplands include the Oaxaca Plateau in the eastern part of the region. There, on a flattened mountaintop, are ruins of Monte Albán, an ancient religious center of the Zapotec Indians.

The Yucatán Peninsula is a low plateau of limestone with many large pits. These pits were sacred wells of the Maya Indians. Ruins of Chichén Itzá, a Maya city, stand near one of the pits.

Carver, Photo Researchers

WORLD BOOK photo by Henry Gill

Ian Graham, Photo Researchers

Bullaty-Lomeo from Nancy Palmer

The Gulf Coastal Plain is covered by tropical rain forests and some rich farmland in the south. Forests of low, thorny bushes and trees grow in the dry northern section.

The Chiapas Highlands rise more than 9,000 feet (2,700 meters) above sea level. They include many flatlands with Indian farm villages. Broad, deep valleys cut through the mountains.

The climate of Mexico varies sharply from region to region. These differences are especially great in tropical Mexico, south of the Tropic of Cancer. In the south, the wide variety in altitude results in three main temperature zones. The *tierra caliente* (hot land) includes regions up to 3,000 feet (910 meters) above sea level. It has long, hot summers, and mild winters with no frost. The *tierra templada* (temperate land), from 3,000 to 6,000 feet (910 to 1,800 meters), has temperatures that generally stay between 80° and 50° F. (27° and 10° C). Most crops can be grown there. The *tierra fria* (cold land) lies above 6,000 feet (1,800 meters). Frost is rare in this zone up to 8,000 feet (2,400 meters), but may occur at almost any time. The highest peaks are always covered with snow.

In tropical Mexico, most rain falls in summer, usually as short, heavy, afternoon showers. Toward the south, the rainy season begins earlier and lasts longer.

The northern half of Mexico is usually dry, and consists largely of deserts and semideserts. Only the mountainous sections receive enough rainfall for growing good crops without irrigation. Most of northern Mexico's rainfall also occurs during the summer. But northwestern Lower California receives most of its rainfall in win-

WORLD BOOK photo by Henry Gill

Sunny Acapulco, a popular winter resort on Mexico's Pacific coast, has an average January temperature of 78° F. (26° C).

ter. Above 2,000 feet (610 meters), summer days are hot and nights are cool. During the winter, days are warm and nights are cold. The coastal lowlands are hot, except on the cool Pacific coast of Lower California.

AVERAGE JANUARY TEMPERATURES

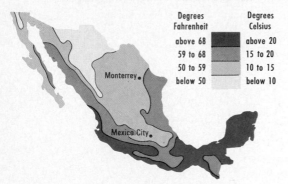

Degrees Fahrenheit	Degrees Celsius
above 68	above 20
59 to 68	15 to 20
50 to 59	10 to 15
below 50	below 10

AVERAGE JULY TEMPERATURES

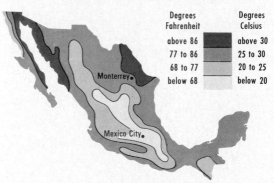

Degrees Fahrenheit	Degrees Celsius
above 86	above 30
77 to 86	25 to 30
68 to 77	20 to 25
below 68	below 20

AVERAGE YEARLY PRECIPITATION
(Rain, Melted Snow and Other Moisture)

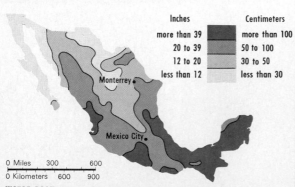

Inches	Centimeters
more than 39	more than 100
20 to 39	50 to 100
12 to 20	30 to 50
less than 12	less than 30

0 Miles   300   600
0 Kilometers   600   900

WORLD BOOK maps
Sources: Meteorological Office, London; *Atlas Geográfico General de México,* by Jorge L. Tamayo, published by Instituto Mexicano de Investigaciones Económicas.

AVERAGE MONTHLY WEATHER

	MEXICO CITY						MONTERREY				
	Temperatures F°		C°		Days of Rain or Snow		Temperatures F°		C°		Days of Rain or Snow
	High	Low	High	Low			High	Low	High	Low	
JAN.	66	42	19	6	4	JAN.	68	48	20	9	6
FEB.	69	43	21	6	5	FEB.	72	52	22	11	5
MAR.	75	47	24	8	9	MAR.	76	57	24	14	7
APR.	77	51	25	11	14	APR.	84	62	29	17	7
MAY	78	54	26	12	17	MAY	87	68	31	20	9
JUNE	76	55	24	13	21	JUNE	91	71	33	22	8
JULY	73	53	23	12	27	JULY	90	71	32	22	8
AUG.	73	54	23	12	27	AUG.	92	72	33	22	7
SEPT.	74	53	23	12	23	SEPT.	86	70	30	21	10
OCT.	70	50	21	10	13	OCT.	80	64	27	18	9
NOV.	68	46	20	8	6	NOV.	71	55	22	13	8
DEC.	66	43	19	6	4	DEC.	65	50	18	10	6

The economy of Mexico is growing much faster than those of most other Latin-American countries. Mexico's economic expansion is based on government policies and programs that developed after the Mexican Revolution of 1910. At that time, Mexico was mainly a land of huge estates owned by wealthy landlords. The government has broken up most of these holdings and distributed them among millions of landless Mexicans. Since the 1940's, the government has promoted industrialization. Today, manufacturing and petroleum production are Mexico's fastest-growing industries.

Mexico's economic expansion has made the nation a leader in the production of many products. For Mexico's rank in production, see the separate articles listed under Products in the *Related Articles* at the end of this article.

Natural Resources. Mexico has a wide variety of natural resources that support its rapidly expanding economy. They include rich farmland, rich mineral deposits, thick forests, and much plant and animal life. There are also many rivers for irrigating farmland and producing hydroelectric power. The warm climate, sandy beaches, and clear waters of the Pacific coast provide popular vacationlands for tourists.

Farmland. The various farming regions of Mexico vary greatly in altitude, rainfall, and temperature. As a result, many kinds of crops can be grown. However, most of the country is mountainous or receives little rainfall, and is naturally unsuited for growing crops. Crops are grown on only 12 per cent of the total land area.

The best farmlands are in the southern part of Mexico's central plateau. There, rich soils, enough rainfall, and a mild climate permit heavy cultivation. The northern part of the central plateau has little rainfall, and is used mainly for cattle grazing. Large irrigation projects there have developed some rich croplands. Fertile soils are found in the rainy, hot regions of the south and east, and in the eastern coastal plains. However, much work must be done to turn them into productive farmlands. This work includes clearing and draining the land, and controlling floods, insects, and plant diseases. The western coast has fertile soils, but much of it is mountainous and dry.

Minerals. During the 1500's, Mexico's gold and silver attracted European explorers to the region. There are rich mineral deposits throughout Mexico. Northwestern Mexico has the country's largest deposits of copper. Gold, lead, silver, and zinc are found in the central regions. The northeast has much coal. Petroleum is found chiefly along and near the east coast and in the Gulf of Mexico. The chief deposits of iron ore are in the southwest and the state of Durango. The Isthmus of Tehuantepec has enormous sulfur deposits.

Forests and Plant Life. Forests cover about a fifth of Mexico. The largest forests are in the northwestern and central mountains, and in the rainy south and southeast. The forests include ebony, mahogany, rosewood, walnut, and other valuable hardwoods used in making furniture. Large pine forests also grow in the mountains, and supply timber for Mexico's pulp and paper industry. Sapodilla trees in the south provide chicle, a gumlike, milky juice used in making chewing gum.

Mexico also has a great variety of flowers and cactus plants. The country's thousands of kinds of flowers include azaleas, chrysanthemums, geraniums, orchids, and poinsettias. The northern deserts have hundreds of kinds of cactus plants.

Animal Life. Bears, deer, and mountain lions live in Mexico's mountains. The northern deserts have coyotes, lizards, prairie dogs, and rattlesnakes. Mexico also has some alligators, jaguars, and opossums. Chihuahuas, the world's smallest dogs, originally came from Mexico.

Mexico has hundreds of kinds of birds, including the beautifully colored quetzals of the southern forests. Other birds include flamingoes, hummingbirds, herons, parrots, and pelicans.

Fish and shellfish are plentiful in the coastal waters, lakes, and rivers. Abalones, oysters, sardines, shrimp, and tuna are the most important commercial catches. Marlin, swordfish, and tarpon are among the fish caught in the seas off Mexico.

Manufacturing has expanded rapidly in Mexico since

Mexico's Gross Domestic Product

Total gross domestic product in 1975—$79,016,000,000

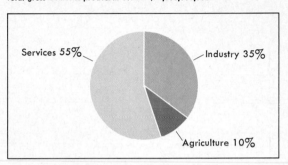

Services 55% Industry 35% Agriculture 10%

The gross domestic product (GDP) is the total value of goods and services produced by a country in a year, adjusted for net income sent or received from abroad. The GDP measures a nation's annual economic performance. It can also be used to compare the economic output and growth of countries.

Production and Workers by Economic Activities

Economic Activities	Per Cent of GDP Produced	Labor Force Number of Persons	Labor Force Per Cent of Total
Hotels, Restaurants, & Trade	31	1,654,181	10
Manufacturing	27	2,961,171	18
Agriculture, Forestry, & Fishing	10	6,783,288	41
Government	9	*	*
Construction	6	756,103	5
Housing	5	—	—
Other Services	5	3,712,352	22
Transportation & Communication	3	489,728	3
Banking, Insurance, & Real Estate	2	†	†
Mining	1	240,537	1
Utilities	1	*	*
Total	100	16,597,360	100

*Included in Other Services.
†Included in Hotels, Restaurants, & Trade.
Sources: Bank of Mexico; *Year Book of Labor Statistics, 1975*, ILO.

MEXICO

the 1940's. This expansion has led to related developments throughout the entire economy. For example, the production of raw materials for new factories has increased. Banking, marketing, and other services have expanded. Heavy government spending on construction has provided additional housing for the growing industrial centers. Power plants have been built for the new industries, as well as highways and railroads for carrying goods. Mexico's industrialization has been financed chiefly by the nation's businessmen, but the government and foreign investors have also contributed much.

Mexico City is the leading industrial center, followed by Monterrey and Guadalajara. Other expanding manufacturing centers include Puebla, Querétaro, Saltillo, San Luis Potosí, Toluca, and Veracruz. A government program is spreading industry still farther from the main centers, especially to northern cities.

Mexico's leading products include chemicals, clothing, and processed foods. The production of iron and steel is expanding rapidly. Until the 1960's, Mexican automobile factories merely assembled parts, most of which were imported. Today, Mexican plants are producing the parts in increasing quantities. Other important products include cement, fertilizers, household appliances, rubber, and wood pulp and paper.

Mexico has long been famous for the skill of its craftsmen who make various handicraft articles. These crafts-

FARM, MINERAL, AND FOREST PRODUCTS

This map shows where the leading farm, mineral, and forest products of Mexico are produced. It also shows crop, livestock, forest, and nonagricultural areas, and major manufacturing centers. Most farming and manufacturing activities are within 300 miles (480 kilometers) of Mexico City.

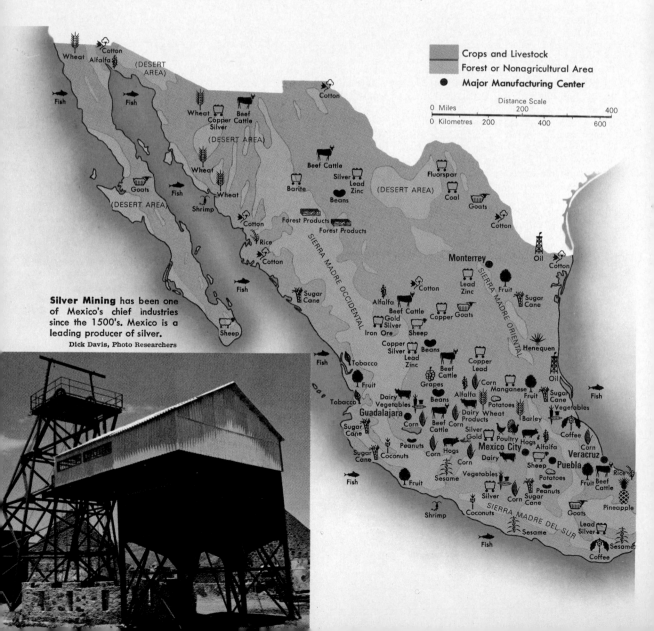

Silver Mining has been one of Mexico's chief industries since the 1500's. Mexico is a leading producer of silver.

Dick Davis, Photo Researchers

men follow beautiful old Indian or Spanish-colonial designs. Their products generally vary by area. The articles include silver jewelry from Taxco, glassware and pottery from Guadalajara and Puebla, and hand-woven baskets and blankets from Oaxaca and Toluca. Many of the products are sold to tourists, about a million of whom visit Mexico every year.

Agriculture. For hundreds of years, most Mexicans worked on huge haciendas. These estates were owned by wealthy Spaniards or by *creoles* (persons of Spanish ancestry born in the New World). A majority of the peasants were bound to the land for life in payment of debts. This system, called *peonage*, was declared illegal in 1917. Since then, the government has broken up most of the haciendas and distributed more than 130 million acres (52,600,000 hectares) of the land to the peasants. See PEONAGE.

The Mexican constitution of 1917 recognized the old system of *ejidos* (farmlands held in common by communities). On the ejidos, farmers either work on individual sections by themselves, or they work the land as a group and share in the crops. Mexico has about 18,000 ejidos, most of which are worked in individual sections. Farmers can pass their land on to their children, but they cannot sell or rent it.

The standard of living on most ejidos is low. The plots are small, and over half of them cover fewer than 5 acres (2 hectares). The ejidos consist mostly of poor cropland, forests, dry grazing land, or even land that is completely unproductive. They include about 45 per cent of Mexico's total cropland. The rest of the cropland consists of cooperatives, small family farms, or haciendas that the government has not broken up.

Since 1937, the government has promoted modern farming methods by means of educational programs, financial aid, and expansion of irrigation and transportation systems. As a result, production has greatly increased in many areas of Mexico. But ancient methods are still used in many other sections, especially on the ejidos.

More farmland in Mexico is used for corn, the people's basic food, than for any other crop. Other leading crops, in order of amount of farmland, include beans, wheat, cotton, sugar cane, and coffee. Also important are alfalfa, fruits, henequen, rice, tobacco, and vegetables.

Livestock is raised throughout Mexico. Beef cattle graze in the dry northern pasturelands. Dairy cattle are raised chiefly in central Mexico. Farmers also raise chickens, goats, hogs, horses, sheep, and turkeys.

Mining. A wide variety of valuable minerals are mined in Mexico. The country is one of the world's leading silver producers, mining about 38 million troy ounces (1.2 million kilograms) a year. Mexico pumps more than 354 million barrels of oil annually and production is growing rapidly. The petroleum industry is operated by a government agency. Mexico also produces much natural gas.

Mexico also mines large quantities of copper, gold, lead, sulfur, tin, and zinc. Other valuable minerals include antimony, bismuth, fluorspar, manganese, and mercury. Large iron ore and coal deposits support the nation's growing steel industry.

Electric Power. Mexico generates about 15 billion kilowatt-hours of electricity a year. The government handles almost all power production and distribution. Almost half the power is produced by hydroelectric plants, and steam or diesel stations produce most of the rest.

Foreign Trade of Mexico consists chiefly of exporting raw materials and partly processed goods, and importing manufactured products. Petroleum is the leading export. Other major mineral exports are copper, fluorspar, lead, sulfur, and zinc. The chief agricultural exports include coffee, cotton, henequen, shrimp, sugar, and tomatoes. The principal imports of Mexico include automobiles, machines and machinery, and industrial equipment.

In most years, the value of Mexico's imports is greater than that of its exports. The nation's industries are expanding steadily. But the new factories need much equipment and materials, and simply cannot supply the country's needs for industrial goods. To help pay for imports, Mexico depends on its large tourist income and on foreign loans and investments.

Automobile Production in Mexico has expanded rapidly since the 1960's. Mexico City is the center of the auto industry.

Chrysler Corporation

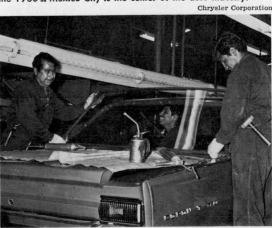

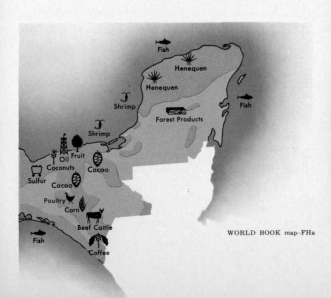

WORLD BOOK map-FHa

MEXICO

More than two-thirds of Mexico's trade is with the United States, but trade with Western European countries and Japan is increasing. Trade with other Latin-American countries is relatively unimportant. But Mexico is trying to increase it through the Latin American Free Trade Association, an economic union of Mexico and 10 other Latin-American nations.

Transportation in Mexico ranges from modern methods to ancient ones. Airlines, highways, and railroads connect all the major cities and towns. But some farmers still carry goods to market on their heads and backs, or by burros and oxcarts.

Mexico has over 20,000 miles (32,000 kilometers) of paved highways, including several that extend from the United States. There are also about 15,000 miles (24,000 kilometers) of unpaved, all-weather roads. The government is continually improving and extending the highway system. Mexicans own more than a million motor vehicles, including almost 700,000 automobiles. Many buses connect the cities and towns.

There are about 30 major airports in Mexico. Mexican and foreign airlines provide air service within Mexico and to all parts of the world. Mexico City is an important center of international air travel.

The government-owned national railway system includes almost all of the country's more than 15,000 miles (24,000 kilometers) of track. The system consists of almost 15 railroads.

Mexico has more than 30 seaports. The major ones include Coatzacoalcos, Tampico, and Veracruz on the Gulf of Mexico, and Ensenada and Mazatlán on the Pacific Ocean. The nation has a small merchant fleet.

Communication. The first book known to be published in the Western Hemisphere was a catechism printed in Mexico City in 1539. Today, books and magazines published in Mexico City are read widely throughout Mexico and all of Latin America. Mexico has about 200 newspapers with a total circulation of nearly 4½ million copies. About 20 daily newspapers in Mexico City account for almost half the total circulation. The largest newspapers include *Excélsior*, *La Prensa*, *Novedades*, and *Ovaciones* of Mexico City; *El Occidental* of Guadalajara; and *El Norte* of Monterrey.

Mexico has about 600 radio stations and about 25 television stations. Telephone and telegraph lines connect all parts of the country. Mexico's motion-picture industry produces about 65 films a year, more than any other Latin-American nation.

TRANSPORTATION

This map shows the major roads, rail lines, airports, and seaports of Mexico. Mexico's few inland waterways are also shown. Several branches of the Pan American Highway extend from the Mexican-U.S. border. They meet near Mexico City, and the highway continues south to Central America.

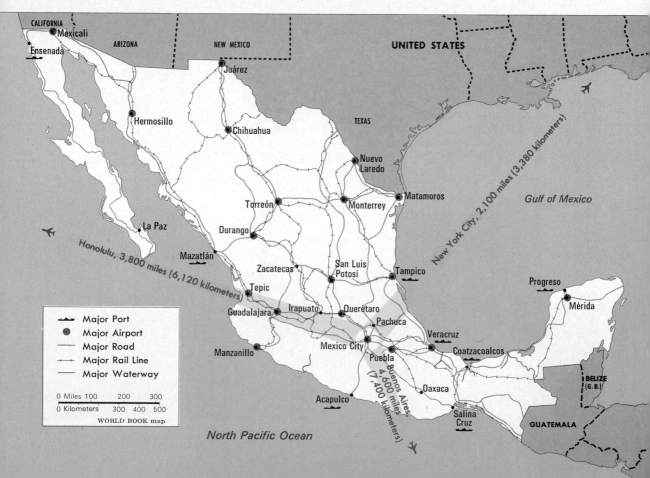

Ancient Times. The first people who lived in what is now Mexico probably arrived as early as 10,000 B.C. They were Indians of unknown tribes who migrated from the north. These Indians were hunters who lived in small, temporary communities. They followed the herds of buffalo, mammoths, mastodons, and other large animals that roamed the land. About 7500 B.C., the climate became drier. The herds could not find enough grass to eat and died off. The Indians then lived on small wild animals or the berries and seeds of wild plants.

Between 6500 and 1500 B.C., Indians in what is now the Puebla region discovered how to grow plants for food and became farmers. They grew corn, which became their most important food, and avocados, beans, peppers, squashes, and tomatoes. These Indians were among the first people to cultivate these vegetables. They also raised dogs and turkeys for food. As the wandering bands of hunters became groups of farmers, they established permanent settlements.

The Growth of Villages. By 1500 B.C., large farm villages stood along Lake Texcoco in the fertile south-central Valley of Mexico, and in the southern highlands and forests. The farmers used irrigation to improve their crops. The villages grew and new classes of people developed, including pottery makers, priests, and weavers. Trade in polished stones, pottery, and seashells was carried on with distant communities.

By 500 B.C., the villagers began to build flat-topped pyramids with temples on them. Some villages, including Cuicuilco near what is now Mexico City, became religious centers. Indians came from other communities to worship in the temples. Because these people were farmers, they worshiped gods that represented such natural forces as the rain and the sun. The villages grew into towns, from the Valley of Mexico to the Gulf and Pacific coasts, and south to what is now Guatemala.

The Olmec Indians of the southern Gulf Coast made the first great advance toward civilization in the Mexico region. Between 1200 B.C. and about 100 B.C., the Olmec developed a counting system and calendar. They also carved beautiful stone statues. See OLMEC INDIANS.

The Classic Period. Great Indian civilizations thrived between A.D. 300 and 900, the Classic Period of Mexico. Huge pyramids dedicated to the sun and the moon were built at Teotihuacán, near what is now Mexico City. In the religious centers of southern Mexico and northern Central America, the Maya Indians built beautiful homes, pyramids, and temples of limestone. They recorded important dates on tall, carved blocks of stone, and wrote in a kind of picture writing. In what is now the state of Oaxaca, the Zapotec Indians flattened a mountaintop and built their religious center of Monte Albán. See MAYA; ZAPOTEC INDIANS.

The reasons for the fall of these classic civilizations are not clear. The climate probably became even drier about A.D. 900, and not enough crops could be produced to feed the large population. Perhaps the city people attacked their neighbors to get more land. Or the farmers may have revolted against the priests who had been their rulers. In the north, wild Chichimec tribes attacked and destroyed many cities.

The Toltec and the Aztec. Many wars took place after the Classic Period. The fierce Toltec Indians established an empire during the 900's, with a capital at Tula, north of present-day Mexico City. The Toltec invaded the Yucatán Peninsula and rebuilt Chichén Itzá, an old Maya religious center. Toltec influence spread throughout the central and southern regions. This influence included the use of stone pillars to support roofs, the worship of the feathered-serpent god Quetzalcoatl, and human sacrifice in religion. See TOLTEC INDIANS.

The Aztec built the last and greatest Indian empire during the early 1400's, after invading tribes ended the Toltec power. The Aztec empire extended between the Pacific and Gulf coasts, and from the Isthmus of Tehuantepec north to the Pánuco River. The Aztec were skilled in medicine, and composed music and poetry. They were rich with gold, silver, and other treasure paid

---

IMPORTANT DATES IN MEXICO

c. 1500 B.C. Village life developed in the Valley of Mexico.

c. A.D. 300-900 Great Indian civilizations thrived during the Classic Period.

c. 900-1200 The Toltec empire controlled the Valley of Mexico.

c. 1325 The Aztec founded Tenochtitlán (now Mexico City).

1519-1521 Hernando Cortés conquered the Aztec empire for Spain.

1535 Antonio de Mendoza, the first Spanish viceroy, arrived in Mexico City to rule New Spain (now Mexico).

1810 Miguel Hidalgo y Costilla began the Mexican struggle for independence.

1821 Mexico won independence.

1824 Mexico became a republic.

1836 Texas won independence from Mexico.

1846-1848 The United States defeated Mexico in the Mexican War, and won much Mexican territory.

1855 A liberal government began a period of reform.

1863 French troops occupied Mexico City.

1864 Maximilian became emperor of Mexico.

1867 Liberal forces led by Benito Juárez regained power.

1876-1880 and **1884-1911** Porfirio Díaz ruled Mexico as dictator.

1910-1911 Francisco I. Madero led a revolution that overthrew Díaz.

1914 United States forces occupied Veracruz.

1917 A revolutionary constitution was adopted.

1920 The government began making revolutionary reforms.

1929 The National Revolutionary party was formed.

1934 The government began land distribution to farmers.

1938 Mexico took over foreign oil-company properties.

1942-1945 Mexico's industries expanded rapidly during World War II to supply the Allies with war goods.

1953 Women received the right to vote in all elections.

1963 Mexico and the United States settled the 99-year-old Chamizal border dispute.

1966 Work began on the Chamizal project to shift the course of the Rio Grande.

1968 The Summer Olympic Games were held in Mexico City.

1976 A major hurricane struck Baja California Sur, Mexico, killing 698 persons.

yearly by tribes they had conquered. Every year, thousands of prisoners of war were sacrificed to the Aztec gods. The Aztec capital, Tenochtitlán, founded about 1325, stood on an island in Lake Texcoco at the site of Mexico City. When the Spaniards arrived in 1519, Tenochtitlán had a population of about 100,000. No Spanish city of that time had so many people. See AZTEC.

The Spanish Conquest. The Spaniards began to occupy the West Indies during the 1490's, and discovered Mexico in 1517. That year, Diego Velázquez, the governor of Cuba, sent ships under Francisco Fernández de Córdoba to explore to the west and search for treasure. Córdoba found the Yucatán Peninsula and brought back reports of large cities. Velázquez sent Juan de Grijalva in 1518. Grijalva explored the Mexican coast from Yucatán to what is now Veracruz.

Reports of the strangers on the coast were carried to the Aztec emperor Montezuma II, or Moctezuma II, in Tenochtitlán. The tales of Spanish guns and horses—which the Indians had never seen before—and of men in armor made him fear that the Spaniards were gods.

A third expedition of about 650 Spaniards sailed from Cuba under Hernando Cortes, or Hernán Cortés, in February, 1519. Cortes' 11 ships followed Grijalva's route along the coast. At various points, Cortes defeated large Indian armies with his horses and cannons. He founded Veracruz, the first Spanish settlement in what is now Mexico.

Montezuma sent messengers with rich gifts for Cortes, but also ordered the Spaniards to leave the land. Instead, Cortes marched toward Tenochtitlán. He was joined by thousands of the Aztec's Indian enemies, who looked on him as the godlike destroyer of the cruel Aztec. Montezuma decided not to oppose the Spaniards because he feared Cortes was the god Quetzalcoatl. The invaders arrived in Tenochtitlán in November, 1519. They were far too few to control the great Aztec capital by themselves. Cortes soon seized Montezuma and held him as hostage for the safety of the Spaniards.

In June, 1520, the Aztec revolted. After a week of bitter fighting, they drove the Spaniards from Tenochtitlán. Cortes built a fleet of boats to cross Lake Texcoco,

From a book by Giovanni Battista Ramusio. Library of Congress

The Aztec Capital, Tenochtitlán (now Mexico City), stood on an island in Lake Texcoco. Raised roads connected it with the mainland. This map, published in 1556, is based on one believed to have been drawn by Hernando Cortes, conqueror of the Aztec.

and attacked the city in May, 1521. The Spaniards killed thousands of Aztec and destroyed Tenochtitlán almost completely. The city surrendered in August. Cortes then sent soldiers to take over the rest of the Aztec empire. See CORTES, HERNANDO.

Spanish Rule. King Charles I of Spain granted huge estates to Cortes and the other *conquistadores* (conquerors). In 1522, Charles named Cortes governor and captain-general of New Spain, which the colony was called. But Charles distrusted Cortes, and soon limited his power. In 1524, the king appointed a Council of the Indies to make laws for the Spanish-American colonies. In 1527, he established the first *audiencia* (court of judges) to govern New Spain. Antonio de Mendoza, a Spanish nobleman, arrived in 1535 to head the government as the first *viceroy* (king's representative).

The people had no elected legislature. Power was held by the *peninsulares* (persons born in Spain). Only they received high posts in the government of New Spain or in the Roman Catholic Church there. *Creoles* (persons of Spanish ancestry born in the New World) held only unimportant government or church posts. *Mestizos* (persons of mixed white and Indian ancestry) were free craftsmen, farmers, and laborers. Most Indians were forced to live and work on estates almost like serfs, or remained in their own villages. Negro slaves from Africa worked in mines or on estates.

AZTEC EMPIRE—1521

Aztec Empire   Present Boundary

Tenochtitlán

0 Miles   500   1,000
0 Kilometers   1,000   1,500

WORLD BOOK map

Spanish priests tried to turn the Indians to Roman Catholicism as early as the 1520's. The priests established missions in farm areas and built churches in the cities. Millions of Indians were baptized. But the forces of nature remained an important part of religion to them. Many Indians worshiped their old gods in private, and most continued ancient religious practices.

The Spaniards brought new kinds of animals and crops from Europe. Burros, for example, became a basic part of Indian life. But generally, the Indians still lived as they had for hundreds of years. They ate the same foods, lived in the same huts, and worked their fields in the same ancient ways.

Revolt Against the Spaniards. Most groups in New Spain opposed Spanish rule. The creoles were not allowed to hold power, and the mestizos and Indians were kept in ignorance and poverty. But for almost 300 years, until 1810, the people did not revolt.

By 1800, the creoles were ready for independence. The American Revolutionary War and the French Revolution provided examples of successful revolts against hated kings. New books from France preached freedom from harsh rule. The royal government became unbearable to the creoles. In addition, political confusion developed after the French invaded Spain in 1808.

Late on the night of Sept. 15, 1810, a creole priest named Miguel Hidalgo y Costilla launched the Mexican War of Independence. In the town of Dolores (now Dolores Hidalgo), he called Indians and mestizos to church. Hidalgo raised the *Grito de Dolores* (Cry of Dolores), in which he demanded independence from Spanish rule. Today, late on September 15, Mexico's president rings a bell and repeats the Grito de Dolores. Mexicans celebrate September 16 as Independence Day.

Hidalgo's untrained followers armed themselves with axes, clubs, and knives. They gained followers as they marched across estates and through such cities as Guanajuato and Guadalajara. The revolution spread into other regions, and Hidalgo soon controlled much of New Spain. Spanish troops captured Hidalgo in 1811 and executed him.

Hidalgo's struggle was continued by José María Morelos y Pavón, another priest. Morelos organized a trained army that was equipped with guns taken from the Spaniards. Morelos won many victories, and captured Acapulco in 1813. He then declared Mexico independent and organized a government.

Morelos' government outlined a liberal program of reform. It had three main goals: (1) establishing a republic in which all races had equal rights, (2) ending the special rights of the army and of the Roman Catholic Church, and (3) breaking up the large estates into small farms for the people.

Most creoles did not want Morelos' social and economic reforms, however. They turned against him and supported the viceroy. The Spanish forces began winning important victories in 1814, and Morelos was captured and shot the next year. The fight for independence was carried on by only a few small bands in the mountains. Most creoles and peninsulares united behind Ferdinand VII, the king of Spain.

Independence. In 1820, a liberal revolt swept Spain. Ferdinand was forced to accept a constitution that greatly limited his power. The liberal victory alarmed the conservatives in New Spain. They feared that social reforms in the colony would soon follow. To prevent such reforms, conservative leaders who had supported the viceroy decided secretly to bring about independence in their own way.

The conservatives persuaded the viceroy to send their military leader, Agustín de Iturbide, to crush the revolutionaries, now led by Vicente Guerrero. Instead, Iturbide and Guerrero agreed in February, 1821, to make Mexico independent. The new government was planned to grant equal rights to creoles and Spaniards. Liberals and conservatives both supported Iturbide, and his army increased by the thousands. Only a few Spanish forces remained loyal to Spain, and little fighting took place. Mexico became independent by the end of 1821.

The various Mexican groups had stayed united only because they opposed the Spanish government. The revolution broke apart soon after Spanish power had been driven from the country. Conservatives wanted a member of Spain's royal family to be king. Liberals called for a republic. A third group wanted Iturbide to take over. Iturbide seized power and was declared Emperor Agustín I in 1822. But he was a poor ruler, and most groups turned against him. A revolt led by General Antonio López de Santa Anna, a former officer in Iturbide's army, drove Iturbide from power in 1823.

A convention met in 1823 and began to write a constitution. The conservative delegates called for *centralism*, under which a strong central government would control the republic. But a majority of the delegates were liberals and favored *federalism*, which granted the states more power. A federalist constitution was completed in 1824, and Mexico became a republic. A two-house Congress was established. The newly created state legislatures elected Guadalupe Victoria, a former follower of Hidalgo and Morelos, to be Mexico's first president.

War with Texas and the United States. During the mid-1800's, struggles for power shook Mexico. Santa Anna switched his loyalty from one group to another, and became the leading political figure. He joined the liberals in 1832, and was elected president. After the Congress approved many liberal measures, the conserva-

Miguel Hidalgo y Costilla set off Mexico's War of Independence in 1810. Freedom from Spain was won in 1821.

From a mural by José Orozco. Guadalajara, Mexico (Ralph Mandol, DPI)

tives rebelled. Santa Anna then switched over to the conservatives and seized the powers of a dictator. He threw out the constitution, forced the liberals out of office, and established a centralist government.

Texas was then a part of Mexico, even though many persons from the United States lived there. In 1835, the Americans in Texas revolted against Santa Anna's government. In 1836, Santa Anna defeated a Texas force in the famous Battle of the Alamo at San Antonio. But later that year, the Texans crushed Santa Anna's troops at San Jacinto and captured him. To regain his freedom, Santa Anna signed a treaty recognizing Texan independence. The new republic of Texas included parts of present-day Colorado, Kansas, New Mexico, Oklahoma, and Wyoming. The Mexican government did not recognize Santa Anna's treaty, and removed him from office.

Texas wanted to be part of the United States, and joined the Union in 1845. But Mexico still claimed Texas, and border disputes developed. In April, 1846, American forces crossed the disputed region and were attacked by Mexican troops. The United States declared war on Mexico the next month.

American armies drove deep into Mexico and occupied much of the country. General Zachary Taylor fought Santa Anna in the Battle of Buena Vista in February, 1847, and both sides claimed victory. Taylor became a national hero in the United States, and was elected President the next year. In September, 1847, General Winfield Scott captured Mexico City after the bitter Battle of Chapultepec. In this battle, a number of young military students threw themselves

over a cliff to their deaths, rather than surrender. Today, the Monument to the Boy Heroes stands at the foot of Chapultepec Hill in their honor.

The Treaty of Guadalupe Hidalgo, signed in February, 1848, ended the Mexican War. Under the treaty, Mexico gave the United States the land that is now California, Nevada, and Utah; most of Arizona; and parts of Colorado, New Mexico, and Wyoming. Mexico also recognized Texas, down to the Rio Grande, as part of the United States. Mexico received $15 million from the United States. In the Gadsden Purchase of 1853, the United States paid Mexico $10 million for territory in what is now southern Arizona and New Mexico.

For fuller accounts of this period, see the separate articles on ALAMO; GADSDEN PURCHASE; GUADALUPE HIDALGO, TREATY OF; MEXICAN WAR; SAN JACINTO, BATTLE OF; SANTA ANNA, ANTONIO; TEXAS (The Texas Revolution).

Reform. The Mexican War exhausted the country's economy, and great political confusion developed. Santa Anna again seized power in 1853 and ruled as a dictator. But the liberals had been gaining strength since the war. In 1855, they revolted and drove Santa Anna from power.

Benito Juárez, a Zapotec Indian, and other men gave the liberal movement effective leadership. The liberals promoted the private ownership of land. After they took over in 1855, they passed laws to break up the large estates of the Roman Catholic Church and the lands of Indian villages. In 1857, a new constitution brought back the federal system of government.

The new reforms resulted in a conservative revolt in 1858. Juárez fled from Mexico City. The liberals declared him president, and he set up a government in Veracruz. During the civil war that followed—the War of the Reform—a conservative government operated in Mexico City. The Catholic bishops supported the con-

REPUBLIC OF MEXICO—1824

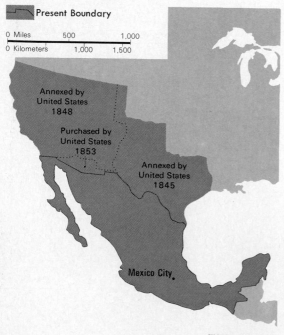

━━━ Present Boundary

0 Miles 500 1,000
0 Kilometers 1,000 1,500

Annexed by
United States
1848

Purchased by
United States
1853

Annexed by
United States
1845

Mexico City

WORLD BOOK map

U.S. Forces Captured Mexico City in September, 1847, during the Mexican War. They were led by General Winfield Scott.
From a lithograph by A. J. B. Bayot. Library of Congress

servatives because of the liberals' opposition to the church. In 1859, Juárez issued his Reform Laws in an attempt to end the church's political power in Mexico. The laws ordered the separation of church and state, and the takeover of all church property. The liberal armies defeated the conservatives late in 1860, and Juárez returned to Mexico City in 1861.

The French Invasion. The Mexican government had little money after the War of the Reform. Juárez stopped payments on the country's debts to France, Great Britain, and Spain. Troops of the three nations occupied Veracruz in 1862. The British and Spaniards soon left after they saw that the French were more interested in political power than in collecting debts. The French emperor, Napoleon III, took this opportunity to invade and conquer Mexico. French troops occupied Mexico City in 1863. Juárez escaped from the capital.

In 1864, Napoleon named Maximilian, brother of the Austrian emperor, to be emperor of Mexico. Maximilian was supported by Mexican conservatives. The United States opposed the French occupation of Mexico, but could do nothing because of its own Civil War. After the war ended in 1865, the United States put heavy pressure on France to remove its troops. In addition to this pressure, Napoleon needed his soldiers in Europe because he feared war would break out between France and Prussia. The French troops sailed from Veracruz in 1867. Juárez' forces then captured Maximilian and shot him. The conservative movement broke up. Juárez returned to Mexico City, and the country was united behind the liberals. After Juárez died in 1872, his Reform Laws were made part of the constitution.

The Dictatorship of Porfirio Díaz. After the election of 1876, a revolt overthrew the new government. The revolt was led by Porfirio Díaz, a mestizo general. He ignored the federal constitution and controlled all Mexico with his troops. His enemies were killed, jailed, or sent out of the country. Díaz had called for a policy of no re-election during his revolt, but served eight terms. Except from 1880 to 1884, Díaz held office until 1911. He allowed no effective opposition in his "elections."

Under Díaz, mines, oil wells, and railroads were built, and Mexico's economy improved. But industrial wages were kept low, and attempts to form labor unions were crushed. Indian communities lost their land to big landowners. Peasants were kept in debt and were prevented from leaving the estates. The great majority of Mexicans remained in poverty and ignorance. The benefits of Mexico's improved economy went chiefly to the big landowners, businessmen, and foreign investors.

The Revolution of 1910. Opposition to Díaz' rule began to grow after 1900. Francisco I. Madero, a liberal landowner, decided to run against him in 1910. During the campaign, Madero became widely popular. Díaz had him jailed until after the election, which Díaz won. Madero then fled to the United States.

In November, 1910, Madero issued a call for revolution. He had opposed violence, but he saw no other way to overthrow Díaz. Revolutionary bands developed throughout Mexico. They defeated federal troops, destroyed railroads, and attacked towns and estates. In May, 1911, members of Díaz' government agreed to force him from office, in hope of preventing further bloodshed. Díaz resigned and left Mexico, and Madero became president later that year.

Madero meant well, but he was a weak president. He could not handle the many groups that opposed him. Some of these groups wanted a dictatorship again. Others called for greater reforms than Madero put through. In 1913, General Victoriano Huerta seized power, and Madero was shot.

Many Mexicans supported Huerta's dictatorship, hoping for peace. But Madero's followers united behind Venustiano Carranza, a landowner, and the bitter fighting continued. President Woodrow Wilson of the United States refused to recognize Huerta's government, and openly sided with Carranza's revolutionaries. After some American sailors were arrested in Tampico in 1914, U.S. forces seized Veracruz. Wilson hoped to prevent the shipment of arms from the seaport to Huerta's army. Later in 1914, Carranza's forces occupied Mexico City, and Huerta was forced to leave the country. See WILSON, WOODROW (Crisis in Mexico).

The Constitution of 1917. The victorious revolutionary leaders soon began to struggle among themselves for power. Carranza's armies fought those of Francisco "Pancho" Villa and Emiliano Zapata. Villa and Zapata demanded more extreme reforms than Carranza planned. In 1915, the United States supported Carranza and halted the export of guns to his enemies. In revenge, Villa crossed the border in 1916 and raided Columbus, N.Mex. His men killed 16 Americans. President Wilson sent General John J. Pershing into Mexico, but Pershing's troops failed to capture Villa.

In 1916, Carranza's power was recognized throughout most of Mexico. He called a convention to prepare a new constitution. The constitution, adopted in 1917, combined Carranza's liberal policies with more extreme reforms. It gave the government control over education, farm and oil properties, and the Roman Catholic

"Pancho" Villa, a bandit chief, became a general in the Mexican Revolution of 1910. He controlled much of northern Mexico.
Bettmann Archive

Church. The constitution limited Mexico's president to one term, and it recognized labor unions.

Also in 1917, during World War I, Germany invited Mexico to join in declaring war on the United States. In return, Germany promised that Mexico would get back all the territory lost in the Mexican War. Carranza refused Germany's offer.

Carranza, like Madero, was a weak president and did little to carry out the new constitutional program. In 1920, he was killed during a revolt led by General Álvaro Obregón, who later became president.

Economic and Social Changes. Obregón distributed some land among the peasants, built many schools throughout the countryside, and supported a strong labor-union movement. Plutarco Elías Calles, who had fought Huerta and Villa, became president in 1924. Calles carried on the revolutionary program. He encouraged land reform and enforced constitutional controls over the Roman Catholic Church. The bishops protested by closing the churches from 1926 to 1929.

For several years after Calles' term ended in 1928, he remained the real power behind the presidency. In 1929, Calles formed the National Revolutionary Party. Until then, Mexican political parties had been temporary combinations of various groups organized by presidential candidates. The National Revolutionary Party stood for the goals of the Mexican Revolution. It included all important political groups and became a permanent party. It was reorganized as the Party of the Mexican Revolution in 1938, and as the Institutional Revolutionary Party in 1946. The party has won all state and national elections by large majorities.

By the 1930's, the push for reform had slowed down. Calles and many other old leaders were now wealthy landowners and opposed extreme changes. Younger politicians called for speeding up the revolutionary program. As a result, the National Revolutionary Party adopted a six-year plan of social and economic reform. General Lázaro Cárdenas was named to carry it out.

After Cárdenas became president in 1934, he ended Calles' power and gave Mexico strong leadership. He divided among the peasants more than twice as much land as all previous presidents combined had done. Cárdenas also promoted government controls over foreign-owned companies and strongly supported labor unions. In 1938, during a strike of oil workers, the government took over the properties of American and British oil companies. The companies and the British government protested angrily. But the United States government recognized Mexico's right to the properties as long as the companies received fair payment. During the 1940's, Mexico and the American and British companies agreed on payments that Mexico later made.

The Mid-1900's. Mexico entered a period of rapid economic growth in the 1940's. Manuel Ávila Camacho, who served as president from 1940 to 1946, did much to encourage industrial progress. World War II also contributed to the nation's industrial growth. Mexico entered the war on the side of the Allies in 1942. It sent an air force unit to the Philippines to fight the Japanese. But Mexico's contribution to the war effort was almost entirely economic. The country supplied raw materials and many laborers to the United States. It also manufactured war equipment in factories that the United States helped set up in Mexico. The value of Mexico's exports had nearly doubled by the end of the war in 1945.

The Mexican economy continued to improve after the war. Industry—as well as other economic activities—expanded during the late 1940's, the 1950's, and the 1960's. New factories produced such products as automobiles, cement, chemicals, clothing, electrical appliances, processed foods, and steel. The government expanded the country's highway, irrigation, and railroad systems. Many apartment buildings went up, especially in Mexico City. Agricultural exports from Mexico to the United States increased. A growing number of U.S. tourists to Mexico also helped the country's economy.

Miguel Alemán Valdés served as president of Mexico from 1946 to 1952. He was followed by Adolfo Ruiz Cortines, who served from 1952 to 1958; Adolfo López Mateos, from 1958 to 1964; and Gustavo Díaz Ordaz, from 1964 to 1970. Under these leaders, Mexico maintained close relations with the United States.

Mexico Today. In spite of Mexico's economic progress during the mid-1900's, large numbers of its people remain poor. Many Mexican farmers still lack modern agricultural equipment and irrigation systems, and wages for farm laborers are low. Each year, more and more Mexicans move from farms to cities in search of jobs. This movement of people has helped cause overcrowding and a shortage of jobs in the cities. Mexico's high rate of population growth has also contributed to overcrowding and unemployment.

In the 1970's, the worldwide problems of recession and inflation added to Mexico's economic problems. In Mexico—as elsewhere—economic production decreased and prices rose sharply. In 1976, Mexico's currency was devalued twice in an effort to stabilize the economy (see DEVALUATION).

President Luis Echeverría Álvarez, who held office from 1970 to 1976, increased government control over foreign businesses in Mexico. In foreign affairs, Echeverría took steps that strained Mexico's traditional friendship with the United States. For example, he improved Mexico's relations with the governments of Cuba and Chile in spite of U.S. opposition to those governments. Illegal immigration of Mexicans into the United States, plus drug smuggling from Mexico to the United States, caused additional problems between the two countries. Echeverría also worked to make Mexico a leader among the developing nations of the world.

José López Portillo became president in 1976. He reduced government controls over both foreign and domestic businesses to encourage more private investment in Mexico. Relations between Mexico and the United States improved somewhat after López Portillo became president.

During the 1970's, vast new deposits of petroleum were discovered in Mexico. The country's petroleum production, and its income from petroleum, increased sharply. The new income could help Mexico solve many of its economic problems.

HOMER ASCHMANN, FRANK BRANDENBURG, DWIGHT S. BROTHERS, and ROBERT E. QUIRK

Related Articles in WORLD BOOK include:

BIOGRAPHIES

Alemán Valdés, Miguel	Juárez, Benito P.
Avila Camacho, Manuel	López Portillo, José
Calles, Plutarco E.	Maximilian
Cárdenas, Lázaro	Montezuma
Carranza, Venustiano	Obregón, Álvaro
Chávez, Carlos	Orozco, José C.
Cortes, Hernando	Paz, Octavio
Cortina, Juan Nepomuceno	Rivera, Diego
Cuauhtémoc	Ruiz Cortines, Adolfo
Díaz, Porfirio	Santa Anna, Antonio
Díaz Ordaz, Gustavo	López de
Gamio, Manuel	Tamayo, Rufino
Hidalgo y Costilla, Miguel	Villa, Pancho
Iturbide, Agustín de	Zapata, Emiliano

CITIES

Acapulco	Monterrey	Tampico
Aguascalientes	Oaxaca	Taxco
Guadalajara	Orizaba	Tijuana
Juárez	Puebla	Torreón
Mexico City	San Luis Potosí	Veracruz

HISTORY

Alamo	Mexican War
Aztec	Olmec Indians
Guadalupe Hidalgo, Treaty of	San Jacinto, Battle of
Indian, American	Toltec Indians
Maya	Zapotec Indians

PHYSICAL FEATURES

Gulf of California	Orizaba	Sierra Madre
Gulf of Mexico	Parícutin	Vizcaíno Desert
Ixtacihuatl	Popocatépetl	Yucatán Peninsula
Lake Xochimilco	Rio Grande	

PRODUCTS

For Mexico's rank in production, see:

Banana	Chocolate	Corn	Lead	Silver
Cattle	Coffee	Horse	Orange	Sugar Cane

STATES

See the separate article on each state listed in the *Government* section of this article.

OTHER RELATED ARTICLES

Adobe	Enchilada	Latin America
Bullfighting	Guadalupe Day	Mexican Americans
Cactus	Henequen	Yaqui Indians

Outline

I. **Government**
II. **People**
   A. Language
   B. Religion
III. **Way of Life**
   A. City Life
   B. Village Life
   C. Family Life
   D. Food
   E. Clothing
   F. Holidays
   G. Sports
IV. **Education**
V. **Arts**
   A. Architecture
   B. Painting
   C. Literature
   D. Music
VI. **The Land**
   A. The Pacific Northwest
   B. The Plateau of Mexico
   C. The Gulf Coastal Plain
   D. The Southern Uplands
   E. The Chiapas Highlands
   F. The Yucatán Peninsula
VII. **Climate**
VIII. **Economy**
   A. Natural Resources
   B. Manufacturing
   C. Agriculture
   D. Mining
   E. Electric Power
   F. Foreign Trade
   G. Transportation
   H. Communication
IX. **History**

Questions

To which racial group do most Mexicans belong?
About how much of Mexico can support crops?
Why do Mexicans celebrate their Independence Day on September 16?
What are some words that came from Mexico and are used in the United States?
What is Mexico's "official" political party?
Who were the *peninsulares?* The *creoles?*
Why did United States forces seize Veracruz in 1914?
How does the voting age differ between married and single persons in Mexico?
What is Mexico's most important religious holiday?

Reading and Study Guide

See *Mexico* in the RESEARCH GUIDE/INDEX, Volume 22, for a *Reading and Study Guide.*

Books for Young Readers

CALDWELL, JOHN C. *Let's Visit Mexico.* Harper, 1965.
EPSTEIN, SAMUEL and WILLIAMS, BERYL. *The First Book of Mexico.* Rev. ed. Watts, 1967.
FRISKEY, MARGARET R. *Welcome to Mexico.* Childrens Press, 1975.
MARCUS, REBECCA B. and JUDITH. *Fiesta Time in Mexico.* Garrard, 1974.
TREVINO, ELIZABETH BORTON. *Here Is Mexico.* Farrar, 1970.
WEEKS, MORRIS, JR. *Hello, Mexico.* Norton, 1970.

Books for Older Readers

ALBA, VICTOR. *The Mexicans: The Making of a Nation.* Bobbs, 1967.
COY, HAROLD. *The Mexicans.* Little, Brown, 1970.
CROW, JOHN A. *Mexico Today.* Rev. ed. Harper, 1972.
FEHRENBACH, THEODORE R. *Fire and Blood: A History of Mexico.* Macmillan, 1973.
GORENSTEIN, SHIRLEY S. *Not Forever on Earth: Prehistory of Mexico.* Scribner, 1975.
MEYER, MICHAEL C., and SHERMAN, W. L. *The Course of Mexican History.* Oxford, 1979.
NEWLON, CLARKE. *The Men Who Made Mexico.* Dodd, 1973.
NOLEN, BARBARA, ed. *Mexico Is People: Land of Three Cultures.* Scribner, 1973.

MÉXICO, a state of Mexico, lies mainly within the beautiful Valley of Mexico. It borders the Federal District, which has the same boundaries as Mexico City (see MEXICO [political map]). México covers 8,286 square miles (21,461 square kilometers) and has 6,684,229 persons. Farmers grow barley, corn, wheat, alfalfa, and vegetables. Toluca is the capital.   CHARLES C. CUMBERLAND

MEXICO, NATIONAL AUTONOMOUS UNIVERSITY OF, is the largest university in Mexico. It was founded in 1551, in Mexico City, as the Royal and Pontifical University. The Roman Catholic Church operated it until the government closed it in 1867. It was reopened in 1910 as the National University of Mexico. The university became *autonomous* (free of government control) in 1929. A new campus was built in the early 1950's. The university has an enrollment of about 240,000. Courses are offered in law, philosophy, medicine, science, music, political and social science, commerce, engineering, architecture, and nursing. See also MEXICO (pictures).   P. A. McGINLEY

Marc & Evelyne Bernheim, Rapho Guillumette   W. R. Wilson

Colorful Mexico City has one of the most beautiful boulevards in the world, the Paseo de la Reforma, *left*. Skyscrapers rise over a statue of Christopher Columbus in a landscaped circle. The Plaza de Toros Monumental, the world's largest bullfight ring, *right*, is also in the city.

MEXICO CITY is the capital and largest city of Mexico. It is the second largest city in the world and the largest city in the Western Hemisphere. Mexico City has about as many people as Mexico's 23 next largest cities combined. The Mexico City metropolitan area is the country's commercial and industrial center, and much of Mexico's labor force lives there. The capital is also the center of Mexican culture, education, tourism, and transportation.

The Aztec Indians controlled a mighty empire from Tenochtitlán, which they built about 1325 where Mexico City now stands. During the early 1500's, Spanish invaders conquered the Aztec. The Spaniards built Mexico City on the ruins of Tenochtitlán, and made it the capital of their colony. Today, most of Mexico City's people have both Indian and Spanish ancestors.

Mexico City has many beautiful palaces that were built during the Spanish colonial period. They now house government offices, museums, or shops. The city also has new homes, industries, and skyscrapers of extremely modern styles. Many of the new buildings are constructed of concrete strengthened with steel, and are decorated with bright colors, stones, and tiles.

A large number of Spanish colonial homes still stand. Each has a gardenlike patio, which is the center of family life. The modern homes in the new districts look much like those in the United States and Canada. The poorest people live in slum shacks or rooms with almost no furniture. Their beds are *petates* (straw mats), and clay bowls may be their only dishes.

Mexico City has more than 350 neighborhood districts called *colonias*. Like Mexico's cities and towns, many colonias have their own *plazas* (public squares). The parklike plazas are centers of neighborhood life, and band concerts and local *fiestas* (festivals) are held there. Facing the plazas are churches, markets, restaurants, and theaters.

The soil under Mexico City is spongy, and about 85 per cent of it is water. Much of the city's water is pumped from the soil, which causes the ground to sink unevenly. Since the 1930's, parts of Mexico City have been sinking as much as 1 foot (30 centimeters) a year. New buildings and monuments have special foundations that prevent them from sinking. These supports also help prevent damage from the earthquakes that sometimes shake Mexico City.

Mexico City lies in the high, bowl-shaped Valley of Mexico. Mountains surround the valley, and there is no natural drainage through them. Canals carry rain water out of the valley, but especially heavy rains may cause floods. Rain falls briefly nearly every day in Mexico City from late May or early June until October. The

Robert E. Quirk, the contributor of this article, is Professor of History at Indiana University and the author of The Mexican Revolution, 1914-1915.

nearby bed of Lake Texcoco, which has been drained, becomes swampy during the rainy season. During the dry months, Mexico City is troubled by smog from automobiles and factories. Much dust also blows in from the dry lake bed. Although Mexico City is in the tropics, its high altitude gives it a mild climate. Nights are cool throughout the year.

Famous Landmarks. Constitution Plaza, called the *Zócalo*, is Mexico City's chief plaza. It covers the site of the old Aztec capital's main square, where the emperor's palace and the Great Temple once stood. Today, the City Hall, National Cathedral, National Palace, National Pawnshop, and Supreme Court of Justice all surround the Zócalo. The National Pawnshop, founded in 1775, offers loans on personal property at low rates of interest. Some Aztec ruins also are near the Zócalo.

The block-long National Palace was built during the 1600's as the Spanish governor's home. It now houses the offices of Mexico's president and other officials. Paintings by the famous Mexican artist Diego Rivera are on the walls, and Mexico's Liberty Bell hangs over the main entrance. Late each September 15, on the eve of Mexico's Independence Day, the president rings the bell in a public celebration.

The heart of Mexico City extends westward from the Zócalo along busy *avenidas* (avenues). It ends near the Paseo de la Reforma, one of the most beautiful boulevards in the world. Facing the Avenida Juárez stands the majestic Palace of Fine Arts. The palace has the National Theater, in which concerts, dance programs, operas, and plays are presented. It also includes art galleries and auditoriums. The palace is built almost entirely of marble. Its great weight has caused it to sink about 15 feet (5 meters) into the spongy soil underneath. Nearby rises the 44-story Latin-American Tower, one of the tallest buildings in Latin America. It "floats" on special supports topped by steel and concrete mats, which prevent sinking or earthquake damage.

The wide, tree-lined Paseo de la Reforma includes seven *glorietas* (landscaped circles in street intersections). A monument honoring a national hero or important event stands in each circle. At the Avenida de los Insurgentes, the main north-south road, the glorieta monument honors Cuauhtémoc, the last Aztec emperor. His bravery under Spanish torture made him one of Mexico's greatest heroes.

North of the downtown area is the Plaza of the Three Cultures. It has ruins of ancient Aztec temples and of a Spanish church built in 1524. Nearby, representing the third culture—that of today—is a huge government housing project of boldly modern architecture.

The Basilica of Our Lady of Guadalupe is Mexico's most famous religious shrine. It stands in northern Mexico City, at the foot of Tepeyac Hill. This church honors the Virgin of Guadalupe, Mexico's patron saint. According to Roman Catholic legend, she appeared on the hill to Juan Diego, a poor Indian, in December, 1531.

───── **FACTS IN BRIEF** ─────

Population: 9,233,770; met. area 11,943,050.
Area: 579 sq. mi. (1,500 km²); met. area 883 sq. mi. (2,287 km²).
Altitude: 7,575 ft. (2,309 m) above sea level.
Climate: *Average temperature*—December, 54° F. (12° C); May, 66° F. (19° C). *Average annual precipitation* (rainfall, melted snow, and other forms of moisture)—29 in. (74 cm). For the monthly weather in Mexico City, see MEXICO (Climate).
Government: *Chief executive*—head of the Department of the Federal District (appointed by the president).
Founded: About 1325 (as Tenochtitlan).

MEXICO CITY

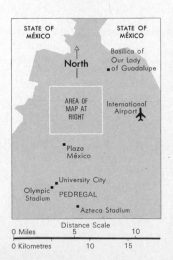

■ Mexico City and Federal District

INNER MEXICO CITY

+ Rail Line
  Major Street
  Park

Alameda Park.........13
Chamber of Deputies... 9
Chapultepec Hill.......18
City Hall.............. 5
Cuauhtémoc Monument..15
Independence Monument 16
Latin-American Tower...12
Los Pinos..............20
Medical Center........14
Museum of Modern Art..17
National Cathedral..... 7
National Museum
  of Anthropology......19
National Palace........ 3
National Pawnshop..... 8
National Polytechnic
  Institute............. 1
Palace of Fine Arts.....11
Plaza of the
  Three Cultures........ 2
Senate House.........10
Supreme Court
  of Justice........... 4
Zócalo
  (Constitution Plaza)... 6

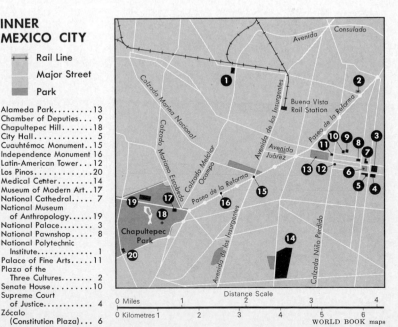

WORLD BOOK maps

The Plaza of the Three Cultures combines ruins of Indian and Spanish buildings near a modern housing project. The plaza honors the mixture of Indian and Spanish ancestry of Mexico's people.

Pilgrims from all parts of Mexico and from other countries come to worship at the shrine throughout the year. On Guadalupe Day, December 12, thousands of pilgrims pass through the church. The present Basilica of Our Lady of Guadalupe was completed in 1976. It replaced a basilica built during the 1700's. The old basilica—which stands next to the new one—had been sinking and was in danger of collapsing. Plans were made to repair and strengthen the old building and turn it into a museum.

Attractions north of Mexico City include handsome Spanish colonial churches in Acolman and Tepozotlán. Also to the north are ancient Indian pyramids and temples at San Juan Teotihuacán, Tenayuca, and Tula. Lake Xochimilco, in the southeast part of the capital, is famous for its "floating gardens."

Parks. Downtown Mexico City includes the Alameda, a park developed by a Spanish governor in the 1500's. He planted it with *álamos* (poplar trees), which gave the Alameda its name. During the colonial period, victims of the Spanish Inquisition were burned at the stake there (see INQUISITION). The Alameda is now the scene of holiday celebrations and concerts.

Chapultepec Park, the largest park in Mexico City, was first used by Aztec emperors. It is a popular family picnic area, with lakes for boating. It also includes flower gardens, fountains, a zoo, and an amusement area with rides and games. On Sundays, horsemen ride in the park. They often wear colorful national costumes.

In 1847, during Mexico's war with the United States, American troops captured Mexico City after the bitter Battle of Chapultepec. A number of young military students, who had defended Chapultepec Hill, threw themselves over a cliff rather than surrender. Today, the Monument to the Boy Heroes stands at the foot of the hill in their honor. Chapultepec Castle, on the hill, houses the National Museum of History. Also in the park are the National Museum of Anthropology, with many ancient and present-day Indian exhibits, and *Los Pinos* (The Pines), the home of Mexico's president.

Education. In Mexico, the law requires children between the ages of 6 and 14 to go to school. Much of Mexico offers no education beyond fourth grade, but Mexico City provides full educational opportunities.

The city has more than 2,000 elementary and high schools, as well as schools of higher learning.

Mexico's oldest and largest university is the National Autonomous University of Mexico. It was founded in 1551, and has about 110,000 students. In 1954, its new campus was completed in University City on the *Pedregal*, a plain in the southern part of the capital. Many of Mexico's leading architects and artists designed and decorated the colorful campus in a mixture of Indian, Spanish colonial, and modern styles (see MEXICO, NATIONAL AUTONOMOUS UNIVERSITY OF). Other schools of higher learning in Mexico City include the National Polytechnic Institute and schools devoted to such subjects as engineering and the fine arts.

Sports. Bullfighting is the national sport of Mexico, and Mexico City has two bullfighting rings. One of them, the Plaza de Toros Monumental, seats about 50,-000 persons and is the largest in the world. Baseball, football, and soccer are also popular. Soccer teams play in the Azteca Stadium, which holds 105,000 persons. An Olympic Stadium stands in a sports area built for the 1968 Summer Olympic Games.

Jai alai, a game similar to handball, attracts many Mexicans and tourists. The players hit the ball against a wall with a basketlike racket. The ball travels so fast that jai alai is sometimes called the fastest game in the world. Other popular sports in Mexico City include basketball, golf, horse racing, swimming, and tennis.

Manufacturing. Mexico City has about 25,000 factories. They account for about half the total value of all goods manufactured in Mexico. Important products include automobiles, chemicals, clothing, drugs, iron and steel, machinery, and textiles. Many foreign-owned factories assemble or finish products for sale in the Latin-American countries. About 3,000 Americans, most of them in commercial or industrial activities, live in the capital.

Much of the nation's labor force lives in Mexico City. Every year, great numbers of workers from other parts of Mexico come to the city in search of jobs. Most of the newcomers are unskilled laborers, and many cannot find work. Their families live in extreme poverty. The increasing population places great strain on Mexico City's food supplies. As a result, food prices

392

rise and cause the cost of living to go far higher than in the rest of Mexico.

Transportation. Almost all roads in Mexico lead to Mexico City. Highways connect the capital with other large Mexican cities and with the United States and Central America. Mexico City is also the center of Mexico's railroad network. The city's subway system began operating in 1970. Subway stations are decorated in traditional Indian, Mexican, and Spanish styles.

Mexico City is one of the main centers of international air travel in the Western Hemisphere. The huge Mexico City International Airport opened in 1952. It provides direct flights to almost 25 countries, including the United States, Canada, and nations in Central and South America, Europe, and the Far East. Flights also connect the capital with other large Mexican cities.

Communication. Mexico City has about 20 daily newspapers, and they account for almost half the total newspaper circulation in Mexico. The largest dailies include *El Universal, Excélsior, La Prensa, Novedades,* and *Ovaciones.* Several newspapers have a page printed in English. There are also English-language newspapers. Leading weekly magazines are *Tiempo* and *Siempre.*

The capital is Mexico's broadcasting center. Mexico City has about 30 radio stations, 5 commercial television stations, and an educational TV channel.

Government. Mexico City has the same boundaries as the Federal District, which is politically similar to the District of Columbia in the United States. Like Washington, D.C., Mexico City has no local legislature. It is governed by the head of the Department of the Federal District, who is appointed by the president of Mexico. Its laws are passed by the federal Congress. The people of Mexico City, unlike those of Washington, elect members of the Congress.

History. People have lived in what is now Mexico City for thousands of years. By 1500 B.C., several farm villages stood along Lake Texcoco. About 1325, the Aztec Indians founded their capital, Tenochtitlán, on an island in the lake. During the 1400's, they built an empire that controlled much of what is now Mexico.

Spanish invaders came to Tenochtitlán in 1519. Their leader, Hernando Cortes, or Hernán Cortés, destroyed the city almost completely in 1521. He built Mexico City on the ruins, and took over the rest of the Aztec empire for Spain. Mexico City became the capital of New Spain, which the Spaniards called their colony.

Thousands of people died in floods because Mexico City had no natural drainage. After 30,000 died in 1629, the Spaniards built a large canal to drain Lake Texcoco and to carry off rain water.

Mexico City remained under Spanish rule for 300 years, and was the largest city in the Western Hemisphere. In 1821, Mexico became independent after an army led by General Agustín de Iturbide took over Mexico City. A series of civil wars, fought for control of Mexico, began soon afterward and lasted until the 1920's. Mexico City was attacked many times. For the story of these struggles, see MEXICO (History).

Mexico City was captured by American troops in 1847, during Mexico's war with the United States. The Americans occupied the capital until the war ended in 1848. Mexico City fell again in 1863, to invading French troops. France named Maximilian, an Austrian archduke, emperor of Mexico in 1864. Maximilian

ruled until 1867, when Mexican forces overthrew him.

General Porfirio Díaz led a revolt and seized power in Mexico City in 1876. Díaz ruled as a dictator, and the capital became the center of tight, harsh control over all Mexico. The Mexican Revolution began in 1910, and Díaz resigned the next year.

Many factories were built in Mexico City during the 1940's, and the city expanded rapidly. The Lerma Waterworks were built during the 1950's to increase the capital's water supply.

President Lyndon B. Johnson of the United States visited Mexico City in 1966. He and President Gustavo Díaz Ordaz hailed the "firm friendship" of their countries. In 1968, the Summer Olympic Games were held in Mexico City.   ROBERT E. QUIRK

Related Articles in WORLD BOOK include:

Aztec	Ixtacihuatl	Mexico (country)
Cortes, Hernando	Juárez, Benito	Montezuma
Díaz, Porfirio	Lake Xochimilco	Orozco, José C.
Guadalupe Day	Maximilian	Popocatépetl
Iturbide, Agustín de	Mexican War	Rivera, Diego

MEYER, ALBERT GREGORY CARDINAL (1903-1965), a cardinal of the Roman Catholic Church, became archbishop of Chicago in 1958. Pope John XXIII named him a cardinal in December, 1959. Cardinal Meyer was born in Milwaukee. He studied at St. Francis Seminary in Milwaukee and at the North American College in Rome. He was ordained a priest in 1926, and was elevated to bishop of Superior, Wis., in 1946. In 1953, he became archbishop of the Milwaukee archdiocese.   THOMAS P. NEILL

MEYER, JULIUS LOTHAR (1830-1895), a German chemist, showed the relation between the atomic weights and properties of the elements. His work and that of the Russian chemist Dmitri Mendeleev led to the development of a periodic chart of the elements, which groups the elements according to their atomic weights and properties (see ELEMENT, CHEMICAL [Periodic Table]). Meyer also concluded that elements were composed of several kinds of smaller particles. This idea led other persons to study the structure of atoms. Meyer was born in Tübingen. See also CHEMISTRY (Development of Inorganic Chemistry).   K. L. KAUFMAN

MEYERBEER, GIACOMO (1791-1864), was one of the most popular opera composers of his day. He was born in Berlin, but achieved his greatest success while composing in Paris. The trend in French opera during the early 1800's was toward grand opera, which emphasized many performers on stage and impressive stage effects. These features replaced dramatic quality in many productions. Meyerbeer used this stress on the spectacular in his first Paris opera, *Robert le Diable* (1831), which gained him immediate fame. This work was followed by *Les Huguenots* (1836) and *Le Prophète* (1849). *L'Africaine,* perhaps his most interesting opera, was first performed in 1865, after his death.

Meyerbeer had an acute sense for building climaxes and for creating spectacular effects. Richard Wagner's early operas owe much to the influence of Meyerbeer's music.   MELOŠ VELIMIROVIĆ

MEYERHOF, OTTO. See NOBEL PRIZES (table: Nobel Prizes for Physiology or Medicine—1922).

MEZZO. See MUSIC (table: Terms Used in Music).

MEZZO-RILIEVO. See RELIEF (in art).

Downtown Miami lies on Biscayne Bay, about 3½ miles (5.6 kilometers) west of the Atlantic Ocean. Yachts dock at the city's Miamarina, *center*, and cruise ships anchor across the bay.

MIAMI, Fla. (pop. 334,859; met. area pop. 1,267,-792), is a world-famous resort city. Its recreational areas and warm weather attract about 12 million visitors yearly. Many retired people move to Miami from other parts of the United States because of the healthful climate of southeastern Florida. The city lies on Biscayne Bay at the mouth of the Miami River, about 3½ miles (5.6 kilometers) west of the Atlantic Ocean.

The first permanent white settlers of the Miami area built houses on Biscayne Bay. The community, which the settlers named for the Miami River, has grown rapidly as the result of industrial expansion and year-round tourism. Today, Miami ranks second only to Jacksonville as Florida's largest city.

The City. Miami, the county seat of Dade County, covers about 54 square miles (140 square kilometers) including 20 square miles (52 square kilometers) of inland water. The heart of downtown Miami is the intersection of Miami Avenue and Flagler Street. County government buildings stand nearby.

The Miami metropolitan area covers all of Dade County—2,408 square miles (6,237 square kilometers). This area includes Miami Beach, which lies 2½ miles (4 kilometers) from Miami across Biscayne Bay, and 25 other cities. The metropolitan areas of Miami and of Fort Lauderdale-Hollywood, Fla., form the Miami-Fort Lauderdale Standard Consolidated Statistical Area.

About 58 per cent of Miami's people were born in the United States. Cubans make up about a third of the population and they give the city a strong Latin culture. This culture has attracted many banks and companies that handle Latin-American trade. Other population groups in Miami include those of German, Italian, and Russian descent. About 15 per cent of the people are blacks. Baptists make up the largest religious group. The city also has many Jews, Methodists, and Roman Catholics.

Economy of the Miami metropolitan area depends mostly on tourism, which produces about $4 billion annually. Most tourist accommodations operate the year around, with lower rates during the summer. The city's temperature varies little, averaging 81° F. (27° C) in summer and 71° F. (22° C) in winter. For the monthly weather in Miami, see FLORIDA (Climate).

The Miami metropolitan area has about 3,000 manufacturing plants. The city ranks second only to New York City in the production of clothing. Other products include furniture, metal goods, printed materials, and transportation equipment.

About 110 U.S. and foreign airlines use Miami International Airport, one of the nation's busiest terminals. The airport serves as the main air gateway between the United States and Latin America. The Port of Miami handles passenger and cargo ships from many countries. Passenger trains also serve the city. Miami has 2 daily newspapers, the *Herald* and the *News*, and 10 television stations and about 35 radio stations.

Education and Cultural Life. The Dade County public school system operates about 170 elementary schools and 60 junior and senior high schools. About 140 private and church-supported schools serve the area. Institutions of higher learning in the area include Biscayne College, Florida International University, Florida Memorial College, Barry College, and the University of Miami. The university's Rosenstiel Institute of Marine and Atmospheric Sciences is an important center of ocean study. The Miami-Dade County Public Library system consists of a main library and 18 branches.

The city has an opera company, a symphony orches-

394

tra, and several art galleries and theaters. Other points of interest in the area include Crandon Park Zoo, Fairchild Tropical Garden, the Museum of Science and Natural History, the Seaquarium, and the Lowe and Vizcaya-Dade County art museums. Many visitors attend the annual Orange Bowl football game on New Year's Day. The Miami Dolphins of the National Football League play their home games in the Orange Bowl.

Government. Miami has a commission-manager form of government. The voters elect a mayor to a two-year term and four commissioners to four-year terms. The commission appoints a city manager to administer various government services.

Miami is also governed by a metropolitan county government called *Metro*. The nine-member Dade County Board of Commissioners heads Metro. The board administers pollution control, transportation, and other activities that affect the entire county. Metro, the first metropolitan government in the United States,

was created in 1957. Property taxes provide most of the city's and county's funds.

History. Tequesta Indians lived in what is now the Miami area long before white settlers first arrived. In 1895, Mrs. Julia D. Tuttle, a Florida pioneer, convinced railroad builder Henry M. Flagler that the area could become rich farmland. She sent him some flowers to show that the land had escaped a killing frost. In 1896, Flagler extended the Florida East Coast Railroad to the area in exchange for land. That same year, Miami was founded and received a city charter. About 1,500 persons lived there. The railroad helped Miami's population reach 5,000 by 1910 and 30,000 by 1920.

During the early 1920's, a great real estate boom centered in Miami. People made and lost fortunes with the construction of homes, hotels, and resorts. Just as the boom began to decline in 1926, a destructive hurri-

WORLD BOOK map

CITY OF MIAMI

Miami, an important tourist center, lies in southeastern Florida. The large map shows the city of Miami. The small map shows the Miami geographical area.

━━━━ City boundary
----- County boundary
═══ Main road
─── Other road
╂┼╂ Rail line
▪ Point of interest
▨ Built-up area
▨ Nonbuilt-up area
▨ Park

Miami Geographical Area

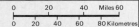

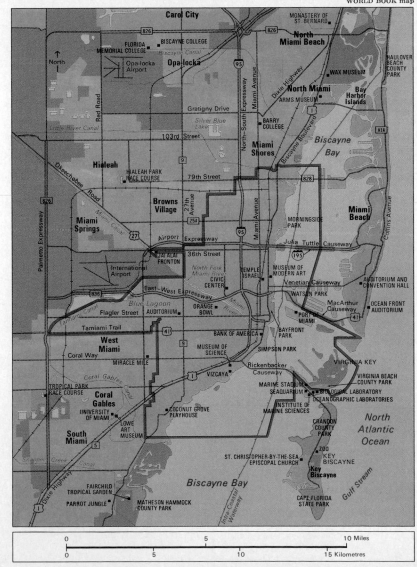

cane struck the city. Another severe storm hit in 1928. In spite of these setbacks, Miami's population climbed to 110,000 by 1930.

During World War II (1939-1945), Miami served as an important military training center. The armed services used most of the city's hotels as barracks. Many service personnel settled in Miami after the war. By 1950, the city had a population of 250,000.

Since 1959, when Fidel Castro became the dictator of Cuba, thousands of Cubans have fled to Miami, about 200 miles (320 kilometers) away. The first refugees included many business people and skilled workers. Many of the later refugees have been unskilled workers. An especially large number arrived in 1980.

Like many other large cities, Miami faces the problems of unemployment and housing shortages, which especially affect the black population. In 1980, racial tension erupted into violence after four white former Dade County policemen were found not guilty of killing a black Miami businessman. The verdict sparked rioting that led to 17 deaths and over $200 million in property damage.   JEANNE BELLAMY

MIAMI, UNIVERSITY OF, is a private coeducational university in Coral Gables, Fla. It has a college of arts and sciences; schools of business administration, continuing studies, education and allied professions, engineering and architecture, law, music, and nursing; and a full graduate program. The School of Medicine is in Miami. The Rosenstiel School of Marine and Atmospheric Science is on Virginia Key, about 10 miles (16 kilometers) from the Coral Gables campus. The Center for Advanced International Studies offers graduate programs in international and inter-American studies. The university was founded in 1925. For enrollment, see UNIVERSITIES AND COLLEGES (table).

Critically reviewed by the UNIVERSITY OF MIAMI

MIAMI BEACH, Fla. (pop. 87,072), is one of North America's most famous resort centers. It lies on an island

City of Miami Beach

"Hotel Row" in Miami Beach cuts through the center of the resort city. Miami Beach has over 30,000 hotel rooms and almost as many apartments to accommodate thousands of vacationers.

2½ miles (4 kilometers) across Biscayne Bay from the city of Miami. The island measures 10 miles (16 kilometers) from north to south and is 1 to 3 miles (1.6 to 5 kilometers) wide. Four causeways connect it with the mainland. For location, see MIAMI (map).

The city's major industry is the tourist trade. It can accommodate more than 200,000 visitors at one time. Miami Beach has more than 400 hotels and 2,100 apartment buildings. About 85 per cent of these hotels and apartment buildings remain open all year. The tropical climate, white sandy beaches, and recreational areas attract more than 2 million tourists to the city annually. A number of the city's resort hotels are among the most luxurious in the world. The city has many parks, fishing piers, playgrounds, beaches, recreation centers, and swimming pools. Tropical trees and shrubs line its modern boulevards, and gardens of brilliantly colored flowers border its green lawns.

Tequesta Indians lived in the Miami Beach area in the 1400's, and a Spanish mission was built in 1567. An attempt by a group of businessmen to start a coconut plantation failed in the 1880's. But John S. Collins, a member of the group, pioneered in developing the resort city. Other city founders include Carl G. Fisher, Thomas J. Pancoast, and John N. Lummus. In 1912, rock and sand were pumped from the bottom of Biscayne Bay and spread over mangrove roots and soft sand to create the modern city. Miami Beach was incorporated as a town in 1915. It was incorporated as a city in 1917. Miami Beach has a council-manager form of government.   KATHRYN ABBEY HANNA

See also FLORIDA (pictures).

MIAMI INDIANS, *my AM ee,* formed an important tribe in North America's eastern woodlands. They were closely related to the Illinois Indians, even though these two tribes frequently fought each other. Two groups of the Miami, the Piankashaw and the Wea, ranked as separate tribes.

The customs and Algonkian language of the Miami closely resembled the customs and language of the Illinois (see ILLINOIS INDIANS). According to early French explorers, the Miami were mild-mannered and polite. Miami chiefs had greater authority than other Algonkian leaders. The Miami raised corn and hunted buffalo.

When white explorers first encountered the Miami, they lived in the Green Bay area of Wisconsin. Gradually they split into various groups and moved southeast into Illinois and Michigan. Some groups also settled along the Wabash River in Indiana and on the Miami and Maumee rivers in the western part of Ohio.

The Miami played a prominent part in the Indian wars of the Ohio Valley in the 1790's. Under their most important leader, Little Turtle, they fought fiercely against U.S. forces led by Generals Josiah Harmar and Arthur St. Clair. General "Mad Anthony" Wayne defeated them at the Battle of Fallen Timbers in 1794 (see INDIAN WARS [Other Midwestern Conflicts]).

Soon after the War of 1812, the remaining Miami moved westward. They then settled in Oklahoma with groups of the Illinois Indians.   WAYNE C. TEMPLE

See also INDIAN, AMERICAN (Indians of the Eastern Woodlands); LITTLE TURTLE.

MIAMI RIVER, or GREAT MIAMI RIVER, flows through western Ohio (see OHIO [physical map]). It rises in Logan County and flows southwestward for about 160

miles (257 kilometers). It empties into the Ohio River at the southwestern corner of Ohio. Towns along the river include Dayton, Hamilton, Sidney, and Troy. The river is an important source of power for industries along its course. GEORGE MACINKO

MICA, *MY kuh,* is the name of a group of minerals that contain atoms of aluminum, oxygen, and silicon bonded together into flat sheets. Mica has perfect *cleavage*—that is, it splits cleanly into thin sheets or layers. These sheets are tough, flexible, and elastic. Mica may be colorless, black, brown, green, or violet.

The chief kinds of mica, in order of abundance, are (1) muscovite, (2) biotite, (3) phlogopite, and (4) lepidolite. They differ from one another according to the atoms of various substances that hold the aluminum-oxygen-silicon sheets together.

Muscovite contains aluminum and potassium, and it ranges in color from pale brown or green to colorless. Muscovite got its name because the Russians, or "Muscovites," once used it as window glass. Biotite contains iron, magnesium, and potassium and is black. Phlogopite has magnesium and potassium and is pale brown. Lepidolite contains aluminum and lithium and is pale violet.

Mica is found in *igneous* and *metamorphic* rocks (see ROCK [Igneous Rock; Metamorphic Rock]). These rocks glisten if they contain a large amount of mica.

Muscovite and phlogopite serve as insulators in electric appliances. They are also used in *capacitors* and *vacuum tubes* (see CAPACITOR; VACUUM TUBE). In ground form, muscovite and phlogopite also serve as a filler material and as a surface coating in the manufacture of paints, plastics, roofing materials, and wallboard. Lepidolite is a source of lithium, which is used in long-lasting dry cell batteries and in the manufacture of ceramic products. Biotite is transformed by weathering into *vermiculite*, used in construction materials (see VERMICULITE).

Mica is produced in the form of large sheets or in small pieces called *scrap mica* or *flake mica.* India is the leading producer of sheet mica, followed by Brazil and Madagascar. The use of sheet mica has declined since the 1940's because of the high cost of labor required to produce it. Its use also has fallen because synthetic materials have partially replaced natural sheet mica. In addition, the development of transistors and other devices has reduced the use of vacuum tubes, which contain sheet mica.

Scrap mica remains economical to use and is important in many industries. The United States is the largest producer of scrap mica. Most U.S. mica comes from North Carolina, followed by New Hampshire and South Dakota. MARIA LUISA CRAWFORD

MICA SCHIST, *MY kuh shihst,* is a type of rock formed mostly of quartz and mica. Schists will crack into many *laminations* (thin layers). The property of splitting in this way is called *foliation.* It is due to the internal structure of the schist.

MICAH was a Judean prophet in the late 700's B.C. The name *Micah* means *Who is like the Lord?* Micah criticized people because they concerned themselves more with beautiful ceremonials than with true religious conduct. He found fault with rich people for oppressing and cheating poor people. Micah also distinguished between "true" and "false" prophets, and said that sincer-

ity was the quality that distinguished a true prophet from a false one.

The book of Micah is the sixth of the minor prophets in the Old Testament. The first three chapters contain Micah's own words. The last four have been enlarged, and contain writings from much later periods. The most famous passages in the book are the summary of true religion (6:6-8), and the expectation of the Messiah from Bethlehem (5:2).

The name *Micah* is given to another Old Testament hero in chapters 17 and 18 of the Book of Judges. In the *Douay* (Roman Catholic) version, Micah is spelled as *Micheas.* WALTER G. WILLIAMS

MICE. See MOUSE.

MICELLE. See COLLOID.

MICHAEL. See ROMANOV.

MICHAEL, *MY kuhl* (1921-   ), served as king of Romania from 1927 to 1930 and from 1940 to 1947. His Romanian name was *Mihai.* He succeeded his grandfather, Ferdinand I. His father Carol II gave up his right to be king in 1925. But Carol took over the throne in 1930, and made Michael crown prince.

Michael regained the throne in 1940 when disorders forced Carol to abdicate and flee. But Michael was only a puppet, first, of the Romanian fascists and their German allies, later, of the invading Russians. He abdicated in December, 1947, and left Romania. He moved with his wife and children to Switzerland. He took a job with an aircraft company, teaching European fliers how to use American instruments. ALBERT PARRY

See also CAROL (II); ROMANIA (World War II; Communist Control).

MICHAEL, SAINT, is one of the seven archangels, or chief angels, named in the Old Testament. He appears with Gabriel as one of the four great angels. In Revelation 12:7, he is pictured as a military leader in the war between God and Satan. The feast of Saint Michael is on September 29 in the Roman Catholic and Anglican churches and on November 8 in the Greek Church. Milton makes Michael a prominent character in his epic *Paradise Lost.* FREDERICK C. GRANT and FULTON J. SHEEN

See also MICHAELMAS.

MICHAELMAS, *MIHK uhl muhs,* is a festival held on September 29 in the Roman Catholic and Anglican churches, and on November 8 in the Greek, Armenian, and Coptic churches. The feast honors Saint Michael the archangel (see MICHAEL, SAINT). It probably originated in the Roman Empire in the A.D. 400's. Michaelmas was particularly important during the Middle Ages when Saint Michael was the patron saint of knights and also one of the patron saints of the Roman Catholic Church.

In Great Britain and several other countries, Michaelmas is one of the four quarter days of the year when rents and bills come due. It is also the beginning of a quarterly court term and an academic term at Oxford and Cambridge. The people celebrate the day with meals of roast goose, a custom that started hundreds of years ago when people included a goose in their rent payments to landlords. An English proverb says, "If you eat goose on Michaelmas Day you will never want money all the year round." ELIZABETH HOUGH SECHRIST

MICHAELMAS DAISY. See ASTER.

Pietà (1498-1499), St. Peter's Church, Vatican City, Camera Clix

Michelangelo's *Pietà* was the most important work of his youth, and established his reputation as a sculptor. The marble statue shows the Virgin Mary cradling the dead Jesus after the Crucifixion.

MICHELANGELO (1475-1564) was one of the most famous artists in history and a great leader of the Italian Renaissance. Michelangelo was mainly interested in creating large marble statues, but his consistent creative energy also led him to become a great painter and architect, and an active poet. In addition, he was one of the most famous persons of his time.

Michelangelo is best known for his treatment of the human body in painting and sculpture. His figures convey a sense of grandeur and power, and arouse strong emotions in many spectators. Both in physical size and strength and in emotional intensity, these figures seem to go beyond real people. The figures have an emotional

---

Creighton Gilbert, the contributor of this article, is Jacob Gould Schurman Professor of the History of Art at Cornell University.

---

yet unsentimental quality and their physical strength gives more than the effect of mere bulk. Physical and spiritual strengths build on each other, producing a powerful product that seems to widen human experience. Michelangelo's work pressed toward the extremes of heroism and tragedy, but never seems false or artificial. See the picture of his statue of David with the DAVID article.

Early Life. Michelangelo was born on March 6, 1475. His full name was MICHELANGELO BUONARROTI. He came from a respectable Florence family, and was born in the village of Caprese, where his father was a government agent. After a brief classical education, he became an apprentice at the age of 12 to the most popular painter in Florence, Domenico Ghirlandajo.

But it was the work of the sculptor Donatello that had the strongest influence on Michelangelo. Before his apprenticeship was completed, Michelangelo stopped painting and began working as a sculptor under the guidance of a pupil of Donatello. Michelangelo attracted the support of the ruler of Florence, Lorenzo de' Medici, who invited the young artist to stay at his house. Michelangelo's earliest surviving sculpture is a small relief of a battle, completed when he was about 16. This work shows the obvious influence of a collection of fragments of ancient Roman marble sculpture belonging to Lorenzo. But the relief shows the force and movement that became typical of Michelangelo's style.

After the Medici family lost power in 1494, Michelangelo began traveling. He lived in Rome from 1496 to 1501. There he had his first marked success when he carved in marble a life-sized statue of the Roman wine god Bacchus. At 23, Michelangelo carved a version of the traditional Pietà subject, the dead Christ on the knees of the mourning Mary. Both figures are larger than life size. This statue, now in St. Peter's Church in Rome, established him as a leading sculptor. The work was plainer and less decorative than most statues of the time, and thus looked stronger and more solemn.

Michelangelo lived in Florence from 1501 to 1505. There he met Leonardo da Vinci. The new democratic government of Florence wanted to display the talents of the city's two outstanding artists. So it asked both Leonardo and Michelangelo to create large battle scenes for the walls of the city hall. Michelangelo's work, now lost, is known to us through his sketches and through copies by other artists. It displayed his expert ability to render human anatomy. On this project, Michelangelo learned from Leonardo how to show flowing and vibrant movement. Leonardo carried this manner of showing life and action farther than any previous artist. Amazingly, Michelangelo's ability to project solid forms did not decrease. The result was his fundamental style, showing figures that are both massive and full of intense vitality.

From about 1505 on, Michelangelo devoted nearly all his time to large projects. In his enthusiasm for creating grand and powerful works of art, he accepted projects that were far too large for him to complete. The first one was a tomb ordered by Pope Julius II that was to include 40 marble statues. The artist accepted the commission in 1505, but 40 years later, after changes and interruptions, he had completed only a few statues.

The Sistine Chapel. Julius II was a patron of the arts with a sweeping imagination equal to Michelangelo's. He gave the artist a more practical commission, painting the ceiling of the Sistine Chapel in the Vatican. This became Michelangelo's most famous work. The frescoes in the chapel show nine scenes from the Old Testament—three scenes each of God creating the world, the story of Adam and Eve, and Noah and the flood. These are surrounded by 12 larger than life size Old Testament prophets and classical prophetic women called *sibyls*. See pictures with ISAIAH; JEREMIAH; DAVID.

Michelangelo began the ceiling in 1508 and finished the first half in September, 1510. At first, he approached this task in a style resembling his earlier works. But soon he gained confidence, and developed new ways of showing tension and violence. After a pause, Michelangelo began the second half with scenes that are relaxed though powerful, such as *The Creation of Adam*, reproduced in color in the PAINTING article. Again he progressed to richer and more active compositions. But in the second half the mood is more restrained.

The Tomb of Julius II. Michelangelo finished the ceiling in 1512 and resumed work on the pope's tomb. He carved three famous figures that resemble the painted prophets and decorative figures on the Sistine ceiling. These figures are Moses and two prisoners, sometimes called *The Heroic Captive* and the *Dying Captive*. The figure of Moses in deep thought was later used as the centerpiece of the tomb. The statue is now located in the Church of St. Peter in Chains in Rome. The *Captives* did not fit into the final reduced design of the tomb. Its figures are interpreted as symbolizing either lands conquered by Julius II or elements of civilization hurt by his death. They fight their bonds with anxiety and muscular pressure, but the tension has declined in a way that suggests their coming defeat.

The Medici Chapel. Michelangelo spent the years from 1515 to 1534 working mainly for the Medici family, which had regained control of Florence. He designed and carved tombs for two Medici princes, and also designed the Medici Chapel, in which the tombs are placed. This project is more complete than any of his other large sculptural or architectural works.

Along with the statues of the two young princes, the tombs include the famous figures of Day and Night on one tomb and Dawn and Evening on the other. The figures recline on curving lids, conveying a sense of fate or individual tragedy. They make a great impact on spectators as an intensely significant observation about human destiny. Some read the parts of the monument from floor to ceiling as a symbol of the rising of the soul after its release from the body. Others see the four statues on the curved lids as a sign of the endless movement of time, in which life is only an incident. The tomb

The Crucifixion of Saint Peter was completed by Michelangelo when he was 75. This fresco and a companion work, *The Conversion of Saint Paul*, were commissioned by Pope Paul III.

Detail from The Vatican Museum

Duomo, Florence (Shostal)

Florentine Pietà, *above,* was intended for Michelangelo's own tomb. The bearded figure at the top of the group is an idealized self portrait of the sculptor when he was about 80 years old.

The Heroic Captive, *right,* shows the strength and emotional tension found in Michelangelo's sculpture. The 7-foot (2.1-meter) statue was completed in 1516 for the tomb of Pope Julius II.

Sistine Ceiling, *below,* was probably Michelangelo's greatest achievement as a painter. He completed this scene in 1511. The fresco shows God creating the sun, the moon, and plants.

The Vatican Museum

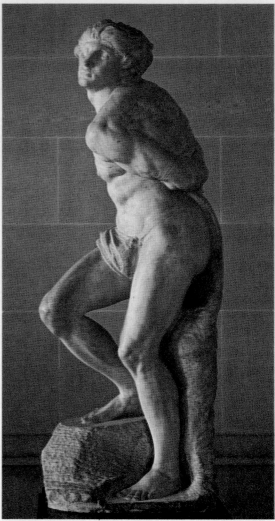

The Louvre, Paris

containing Dawn and Evening is reproduced in color in the SCULPTURE article.

Michelangelo also designed the architecture of the Medici Chapel. He planned the walls like a carved relief, with projections and hollows and long, narrow shapes to give an elongated effect. This approach, resembling carved architecture, is carried farther in the entrance hall and staircase to the Laurentian library in Florence, which he designed at the same time. It was his first architecture to come close to completion.

The Last Judgment. In 1534, the Medici officially became the ruling dukes of Florence. Michelangelo, who favored the republic, left the city and settled in Rome. He spent the next 10 years working for Pope Paul III. Most notable among his painting projects is the fresco *The Last Judgment* (1534-1541). The pope commissioned this work for the altar wall of the Sistine Chapel. In a single scene almost as large as his ceiling, Michelangelo showed the souls of mankind rising on one side and falling on the other. These figures move with a slow heaviness that suggests the fateful importance of their action. At the top, Christ controls them with a powerful gesture, like a puppet master. At the bottom, tombs open and the dead are rowed across a river in a scene based on Dante's *Divine Comedy*.

Later Years. The small amount of sculpture in Michelangelo's later years includes works to complete old commissions and two unfinished Pietà groups. He created both Pietàs for his own satisfaction and not for a patron. The Pietà now in the Cathedral of Florence was meant for his own tomb. It is designed as a massive pyramid, with Christ's body slumping down to the ground. In the Rondanini *Pietà*, now in Milan, the marble limbs are reduced to a ghostlike thinness. The bodies seem to lack substance, while the material of the stone is emphasized by the hacking chisel marks left on the unfinished surface. Because of this technique, many modern sculptors, including Henry Moore, admire this work above all others Michelangelo produced.

Michelangelo devoted much time after 1546 to architecture and poetry. In 1546, Pope Paul III appointed him supervising architect of St. Peter's Church, one of Julius II's unfinished projects. Michelangelo started the construction of its dome, still the largest of any church (see SAINT PETER'S CHURCH; ARCHITECTURE [Renaissance]). He also planned a square for the civic center of Rome and the buildings around it. The square, built after his death, avoids ordinary rectangles and focuses on key points leading to the Senate House.

In the works Michelangelo created after he was 70, he showed an ever wider range of interests and capacities, but less stress and violence. He still created works in complex patterns. But beginning with *The Last Judgment*, the Florentine *Pietà*, and the late buildings, he no longer emphasized complicated design. This applies also to his buildings, the interlocking of bodies in his paintings and sculpture, and the sentence structure of his poems. But his earlier work is more popular because it has a more immediate and exciting impact.

The Life of Michelangelo, by John Addington Symonds, is a good biography of the artist.   CREIGHTON GILBERT

See also *Michelangelo* in the RESEARCH GUIDE/INDEX, Volume 22, for a *Reading and Study Guide*.

MICHELET, *MEESH LEH,* **JULES** (1798-1874), a French historian, is best known for his 19-volume *History of France*. He was chief of the historical department of the archives of France, and professor of history and moral sciences at the College of France. He was liberal in his beliefs, and lost those posts when he refused to take an oath of loyalty to Napoleon III in 1851. Michelet was born in Paris.   FRANCIS J. BOWMAN

MICHELSON, *MI kul sun,* **ALBERT ABRAHAM** (1852-1931), an American physicist, spent over 50 years studying the problems of light. He received the 1907 Nobel prize in physics, the first American scientist to win that award. He worked for many years to determine the exact speed of light (see LIGHT [The Speed of Light]).

In 1880, Michelson developed a new kind of *interferometer*, a measuring instrument. He designed still another interferometer in 1920 and used it to make the first accurate measurement of a star's diameter (see INTERFEROMETER). The star measured was Betelgeuse (Alpha Orionis).

He worked with Edward Williams Morley, a chemist and physicist, to determine the relative motion of the earth and ether. Their findings furnished a basis for Einstein's work on the theory of relativity (see RELATIVITY [Special Theory]; ETHER).

Michelson also developed a standard unit of length. In analyzing the spectrum lines of various elements, he found that the red line of cadmium could be measured precisely. He suggested using the measurement as a standard unit of length. In 1925, the International Committee on Weights and Measures adopted his standard unit. Albert Michelson was born at Strelno, Germany, and came to the United States at the age of 2.   R. T. ELLICKSON

MICHENER, *MICH uh ner,* **JAMES ALBERT** (1907-), an American author, won the 1948 Pulitzer prize for fiction for his collection of stories, *Tales of the South Pacific* (1947). The book describes the life of U.S. servicemen among the people of the Solomon Islands during World War II. Joshua Logan, Richard Rodgers, and Oscar Hammerstein II based their musical comedy *South Pacific* (1949) on some of Michener's stories. The musical won the 1950 Pulitzer prize for drama.

Michener's other novels include *The Fires of Spring* (1949), *The Bridges at Toko-ri* (1953), *Sayonara* (1954), *Hawaii* (1960), *Caravans* (1963), *The Source* (1965), *The Drifters* (1971), and *Centennial* (1974). He has also written books on current events and Oriental art. Michener was born in New York City.   HARRY R. WARFEL

MICHENER, ROLAND (1900-), served as governor general of Canada from 1967 to 1974. He was Canada's *high commissioner* (ambassador) to India from 1964 until his appointment. He served as a Progressive Conservative in the Canadian House of Commons from 1953 to 1962, and was speaker from 1957 to 1962. He became a member of the Queen's Privy Council for Canada in 1962.

Daniel Roland Michener was born in Lacombe, Alberta. He graduated from the University of Alberta, and studied at Oxford University as a Rhodes Scholar. Michener served in the Ontario legislature from 1945 to 1948. The last two years of that term he was provincial secretary and registrar for Ontario.

Ford Motor Company Plant Near Detroit

MICHIGAN

THE WOLVERINE STATE

MICHIGAN is an important industrial, mining, farming, and tourist state in the Great Lakes region of the Midwest. It is one of the nation's leading manufacturing states. Michigan leads in the manufacture of automobiles. Detroit, Michigan's largest city, is called the *Automobile Capital of the World* and the *Motor City*. The Detroit area produces more cars and trucks than any other part of the nation. Flint, Pontiac, and Lansing, the state capital, also are important automaking centers. Michigan is a leading state in food processing and steel production.

Michigan touches four of the five Great Lakes—Erie, Huron, Michigan, and Superior. The state's 3,288-mile (5,292-kilometer) shoreline is longer than that of any other inland state. Michigan consists of two separate land areas, called the Upper Peninsula and the Lower Peninsula. The two peninsulas are connected by the

The contributors of this article are Willard M. J. Baird, author of This Is Our Michigan; *and Sidney Glazer, Professor of History at Wayne State University.*

Mackinac Bridge which spans 5 miles (8 kilometers) across the Straits of Mackinac.

Michigan is second only to Minnesota in iron ore production. It is also a leading state in both copper mining and salt production. Salt and other minerals are mined in the Lower Peninsula.

Most farming in Michigan takes place in the Lower Peninsula. The best farmland lies in the southern part of the state. The Lake Michigan shores of the Lower Peninsula are an excellent fruit-growing region. Michigan leads the nation in the production of cherries, and is a top producer of many other fruits. It is also the leading producer of dry beans.

Michigan is one of the leading tourist states. About 22 million persons visit the state each year. Both the Upper and Lower peninsulas offer resort and recreation facilities, and scenic beauty. In addition to the Great Lakes, Michigan has more than 11,000 smaller lakes. Forests cover more than half the state. Michigan offers excellent hunting and fishing opportunities for outdoor sport enthusiasts.

Capital: Lansing.

Government: *Congress*—U.S. senators, 2; U.S. representatives, 19. *Electoral Votes*—21. *State Legislature*—senators, 38; representatives, 110. *Counties*—83.

Area: 58,216 sq. mi. (150,779 km²), including 1,399 sq. mi. (3,623 km²) of inland water but excluding 38,575 sq. mi. (99,909 km²) of lakes Erie, Huron, Michigan, St. Clair, and Superior, 23rd in size among the states. *Greatest Distances in Upper Peninsula:* east-west, 334 mi. (538 km); north-south, 215 mi. (346 km). *Greatest Distances in Lower Peninsula:* north-south, 286 mi. (460 km); east-west, 200 mi. (322 km). *Shoreline*—3,288 mi. (5,292 km), including 1,056 mi. (1,699 km) of island shoreline.

Elevation: *Highest*—Mt. Curwood, 1,980 ft. (604 m) above sea level. *Lowest*—572 ft. (174 m) above sea level along Lake Erie.

Population: *Estimated 1975 Population*—9,157,000. *1970 Census*—8,875,083; 7th among the states; distribution, 74 per cent urban, 26 per cent rural; density, 152 persons per sq. mi. (59 persons per km²).

Chief Products: *Agriculture*—milk, corn, beef cattle, dry beans, hogs, soybeans, wheat, greenhouse and nursery products, eggs, cherries, apples. *Fishing Industry*—whitefish, chubs. *Manufacturing*—transportation equipment; nonelectric machinery; fabricated metal products; primary metals; food products; chemicals; electric and electronic equipment; printed materials; rubber and plastics products; clothing; paper products; stone, clay, and glass products; furniture and fixtures; instruments; lumber and wood products. *Mining*—petroleum, iron ore, natural gas, stone, sand and gravel, salt, copper.

State Abbreviations: Mich. (traditional); MI (postal).

Statehood: Jan. 26, 1837, the 26th state.

State Motto: *Si quaeris peninsulam amoenam, circumspice* (If you seek a pleasant peninsula, look about you).

State Song (unofficial): "Michigan, My Michigan." Words of 1863 version by Winifred Lee Brent. Words of more widely used version of 1902 by Douglas M. Malloch.

Alpha Photo Assoc.

Mackinac Bridge

K. Snyder, Alpha

Lake Michigan, for Which the State Is Named

French explorers of the early 1600's were the first white people to visit what is now the Michigan region. France controlled the region for nearly 150 years, but did little to develop it. Great Britain gained control of the Michigan region after defeating France in the French and Indian Wars (1689-1763). In 1787, after the Revolutionary War in America, Michigan became part of the Northwest Territory of the United States. In 1805, Congress established the Territory of Michigan. In 1837, Michigan became the 26th state of the Union.

Michigan is named for Lake Michigan. The Chippewa Indians called the lake *Michigama*, which means *great*, or *large*, *lake*. Michigan is nicknamed the *Wolverine State* because the early fur traders brought valuable wolverine pelts to trading posts in the region. The state is also known as the *Water Wonderland*, because of its many beautiful lakes and streams. Including its share of the Great Lakes, Michigan has more water than any other state. The Upper Peninsula is sometimes called the *Land of Hiawatha* because it is described in

Henry Wadsworth Longfellow's poem, *The Song of Hiawatha*.

For the relationship of Michigan to other states in its region, see MIDWESTERN STATES.

Michigan (blue) ranks 23rd in size among all the states and 7th in size among the Midwestern States (gray).

Constitution. Michigan's present Constitution went into effect in 1964. Earlier constitutions were adopted in 1835, 1850, and 1908.

Constitutional *amendments* (changes) may be proposed in three ways. *Initiative amendments* are introduced by petitions signed by a specified number of voters. *Legislative amendments* are introduced by members of the state Legislature. Legislative amendments must be approved by two-thirds of the members of both houses of the Legislature. Amendments can also be proposed by *constitutional conventions.* Beginning in 1978, and every 16 years thereafter, the voters will decide whether to call a constitutional convention. All proposed amendments must be approved by a majority of the voters who cast ballots on the amendment.

Executive. The Constitution of 1964 increased the governor's term of office from two years to four years. Michigan's governor may be re-elected any number of times. Also increased from two to four years were the terms of the lieutenant governor, secretary of state, and attorney general. The Constitution provided that the four-year terms begin with officials elected in 1966. Also, beginning in 1966, each party's candidates for governor and lieutenant governor began running for office as a team. Thus, voters cast a single vote for the governor and lieutenant governor together. The governor receives a yearly salary of $65,000. For a list of the state's governors, see the *History* section of this article.

The governor, with the consent of the state Senate, appoints various state officials who are not elected. These officials include the treasurer, members of boards and commissions, and department heads. Officials elected to eight-year terms include regents of the University of Michigan, trustees of Michigan State University, governors of Wayne State University, and members of the state board of education.

To run for governor, candidates of major political parties must be nominated by the people in a primary election. Candidates for other elective offices are nominated at party conventions. A *recall* law gives the people

the right to vote to remove from office any elected officials other than judges. A specified number of qualified voters must sign a petition to hold such a recall vote.

Legislature of Michigan consists of a 38-member Senate and a 110-member House of Representatives. The 1964 Constitution increased the terms of office of state senators from two to four years, beginning with the 1966 election. Representatives serve two-year terms. In 1964, and again in 1972, both legislative houses were redrawn according to population. This action was designed to give fairer representation to all persons in the state. Legislative sessions begin on the second Wednesday of every January, and last until all business has been completed. The governor may call special sessions.

Courts. Michigan's highest court is the state Supreme Court. This court has seven justices, elected to eight-year terms. The justices elect one of their members to serve as chief justice. The 1964 Constitution provided for a new 18-judge court of appeals, elected from three districts drawn according to population. Michigan has circuit courts in each of 52 districts. Circuit courts are the highest trial courts in the state. Each county has a probate court with from one to six judges. Many of the larger cities have municipal courts. All appeals, circuit, and probate court judges are elected to six-year terms. Other courts include common pleas and district courts.

Local Government. The county is Michigan's chief unit of local government. The state's 83 counties are divided into townships. Each county has a county board of commissioners as its legislative body. The board consists of representatives from each township and city in the county. Other county officers include the county clerk, county treasurer, prosecuting attorney, register of deeds, and sheriff.

The Constitution permits counties and cities to have *home rule* (self-government) to the extent that they may frame, adopt, and amend their own charters. However, these powers can be restricted by the Constitution and the Legislature. More than a hundred Michigan cities

State of Michigan

The Governor's Residence stands on landscaped grounds in southwestern Lansing. The ranch-style house was donated to the state by a Lansing businessman in 1969. Previous governors had lived in houses rented by the state.

The State Seal

The State Flag

Symbols of Michigan. On the seal, the sun rising over water and the man in a field appear on a shield supported by an elk and a moose. They represent Michigan's wealth, resources, and people. An eagle above the shield symbolizes the superior authority and jurisdiction of the U.S. government over state governments. The Latin word *Tuebor* means *I will defend.* The seal was adopted in 1835 and appears on the state flag. The flag was adopted in 1911.

have the city-manager form of government. Most of the other cities have the mayor-council form.

Taxation. Sales and income taxes account for more than 45 per cent of the state government's income. Other sources of income include estate and gift taxes, licenses, and property taxes. About 25 per cent of the state government's income comes from federal grants and programs.

Politics. The Republican party is strongest in rural areas of Michigan. Democratic strength lies in Detroit and other urban areas. Voting in state-wide elections has been fairly evenly divided since 1930. In the 1962 election, George W. Romney, a Republican, was elected governor. It was the first time in 14 years that a governor of Michigan had a state legislature controlled by his own political party. From 1964 to 1966, the Democrats controlled both houses of the state legislature for the first time in over 30 years. For Michigan's electoral votes and voting record in presidential elections, see ELECTORAL COLLEGE (table).

The State Capitol is in Lansing, Michigan's capital since 1847. Detroit was the state capital from 1837 to 1847.

John Penrod

The State Bird
Robin

The State Flower
Apple Blossom

The State Tree
White Pine

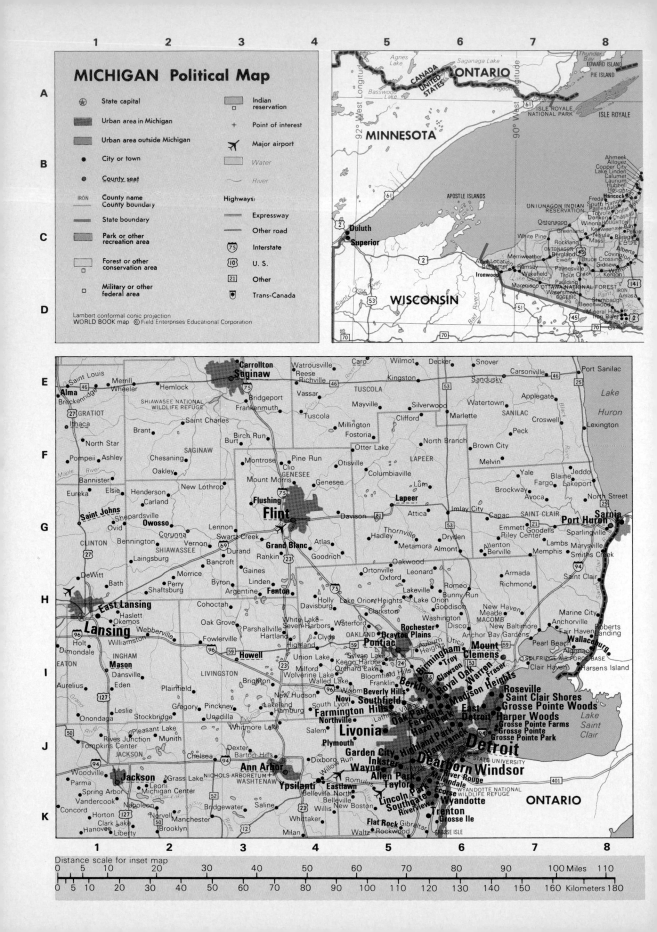

MICHIGAN Political Map

Legend:
- State capital
- Urban area in Michigan
- Urban area outside Michigan
- City or town
- County seat
- IRON — County name / County boundary
- State boundary
- Park or other recreation area
- Forest or other conservation area
- Military or other federal area
- Indian reservation
- Point of interest
- Major airport
- Water
- River

Highways:
- Expressway
- Other road
- 75 Interstate
- 10 U.S.
- 21 Other
- Trans-Canada

Lambert conformal conic projection
WORLD BOOK map © Field Enterprises Educational Corporation

Distance scale for inset map
0 5 10 20 30 40 50 60 70 80 90 100 Miles 110
0 5 10 20 30 40 50 60 70 80 90 100 110 120 130 140 150 160 Kilometers 180

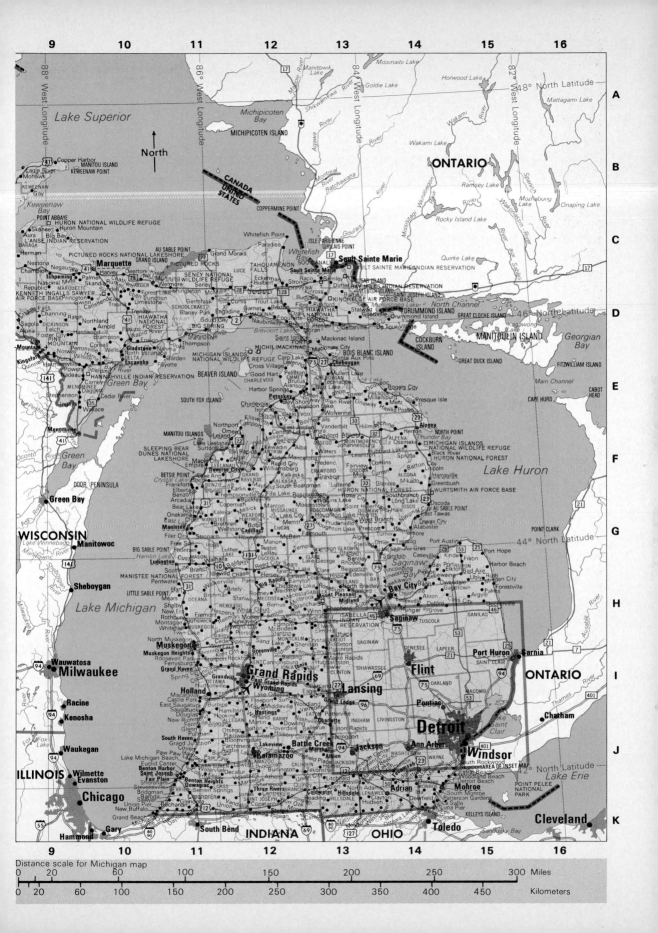

Population

9,157,000 Estimate..1975
8,875,083 ..Census..1970
7,823,194 ....."....1960
6,371,766 ....."....1950
5,256,106 ....."....1940
4,842,325 ....."....1930
3,668,412 ....."....1920
2,810,173 ....."....1910
2,420,982 ....."....1900
2,093,890 ....."....1890
1,636,937 ....."....1880
1,184,059 ....."....1870
749,113 ....."....1860
397,654 ....."....1850
212,267 ....."....1840
31,639 ....."....1830
8,896 ....."....1820
4,762 ....."....1810

Metropolitan Areas

Ann Arbor 234,103
Battle Creek 180,129
Bay City 117,339
Detroit 4,435,051
Flint 508,664
Grand Rapids ...539,225
Jackson 143,274
Kalamazoo-
Portage 257,723
Lansing-East
Lansing 424,271
Muskegon-Norton
Shores-Muskegon
Heights 175,410
Saginaw 219,743
Toledo (O.) 762,658
(643,486 in O.;
119,172 in Mich.)

Counties

Alcona .....7,113..F 14
Alger ....8,568..D 10
Allegan ....66,575..J 11
Alpena ....30,708..F 14
Antrim .....12,612..F 12
Arenac .....11,149..G 14
Baraga .....7,789..C 9
Barry .....38,166..J 12
Bay ......117,339..H 14
Benzie ......8,593..F 11
Berrien ...163,940..K 11
Branch ....37,906..K 12
Calhoun ..141,963..J 12
Cass ....43,312..K 11
Charlevoix .16,541..E 12
Cheboygan .16,573..E 13
Chippewa ..32,412..D 12
Clare ......16,695..G 13
Clinton ....48,492..I 13
Crawford ...6,482..F 13
Delta ......35,924..E 10
Dickinson ..23,753..D 9
Eaton .....68,892..J 13
Emmet .....18,331..E 12
Genesee ..445,589..I 14
Gladwin ...13,471..G 13
Gogebic ....20,676..D 7
Grand
Traverse .39,175..F 12
Gratiot ....39,246..I 13
Hillsdale ..37,171..K 13
Houghton ..34,652..C 8
Huron .....34,083..H 15
Ingham ...261,039..J 13
Ionia ......45,848..I 12
Iosco ......24,905..G 14
Iron ....13,813..D 8
Isabella ....44,594..H 13
Jackson ...143,274..J 13
Kalamazoo 201,550..J 12
Kalkaska ....5,272..F 12
Kent ......411,044..I 12
Keweenaw ..2,264..B 9
Lake ....5,661..G 11
Lapeer .....52,361..I 15
Leelanau ...10,872..F 11
Lenawee ...81,951..K 13
Livingston ..58,967..J 13
Luce ....6,789..C 12
Mackinac ...9,660..D 12
Macomb ..625,309..I 15
Manistee ...20,393..G 11
Marquette ..64,686..D 9
Mason .....22,612..G 11
Mecosta ....27,992..H 12
Menominee .24,587..E 9
Midland ...63,769..H 13
Missaukee ...7,126..G 12
Monroe ...119,215..K 14
Montcalm ..39,660..I 12
Montmorency 5,247..F 13
Muskegon .157,426..H 11
Newaygo ...27,992..H 12
Oakland ..907,871..I 14
Oceana .....17,984..H 11
Ogemaw ....11,903..G 13
Ontonagon .10,548..C 7
Osceola ....14,838..G 12
Oscoda .....4,726..F 13
Otsego .....10,422..F 13
Ottawa ...128,181..I 11
Presque Isle 12,836..E 13
Roscommon .9,892..G 13
Saginaw ..219,743..I 13
St. Clair .120,175..I 15
St. Joseph .47,392..K 12
Sanilac ....35,181..H 15
Schoolcraft ..8,226..D 11
Shiawassee .63,075..I 13
Tuscola ....48,603..H 14
Van Buren .56,173..J 11
Washtenaw 234,103..J 14
Wayne ..2,670,368..J 14
Wexford ...19,717..G 12

Cities, Towns, and Villages

Acme ....F 12
Addison* ....595..K 13
Adrian .....20,382..°K 14
Afton ....E 13
Ahmeek ......238..B 9
Akron ....525..H 14
Alanson ......362..E 13
Alba ....F 12
Albion ......12,112..J 13
Alden ....F 12
Algonac .....3,684..I 8
Allegan .....4,516.°J 12
Allen ....385..K 13
Allen Park .40,747..K 6
Allenton ....G 6
Allouez ....B 9
Alma ....9,611..E 1
Almont .....1,634..G 6
Alpena .....13,805.°F 14
Alpha ....282..D 9
Amasa ....D 9
Anchor Bay
Gardens ...2,272..I 7
Anchorville ....H 7
Ann Arbor 100,035.°J 14
Anvil Location ....D 7
Applegate .....301..E 7
Arcadia ....G 11
Argentine ....H 3
Argyle ....H 15
Armada ......1,352..H 7
Arnold ....D 10
Ashley ....521..F 1
Athens ....996..J 12
Atlanta ....°F 13
Atlas ....G 4
Attica ....G 6
Auburn ......1,919..H 14
Auburn Heights .....I 5
Au Gres ......564..G 14
Augusta* ....1,025..J 12
Aurelius ....I 1
Au Sable, see
Oscoda [-Au Sable]
Au Train ....D 10
Avoca ....G 7
Bach ....H 14
Bad Axe ...2,999.°H 15
Bailey ....I 12
Baldwin ....612.°H 11
Bancroft ....724..H 3
Bangor ......2,050..J 11
Bannister ....F 1
Baraga ......1,116..C 8
Bark River ....E 10
Baroda ....504..K 11
Barryton ....368..H 12
Barton City ....F 14
Barton Hills ..390..J 3
Bath ....H 1
Battle
Creek ....38,931..J 12
Bay City ...49,449.°H 14
Bay Port ....H 14
Bay Shore ....E 12
Bayport Park-
Lakeside* .2,101..I 14
Bear Lake ....376..G 11
Beaverton ......954..H 13
Beechwood* .2,714..I 11
Belding ......5,121..I 12
Bellaire ....897.°F 12
Belleville ....2,406..K 5
Bellevue ....1,297..J 13
Bennington ....G 2
Bentley ....G 13
Benton
Central* ..8,067..J 11
Benton
Harbor ...16,481..J 11
Benton
South* ....4,496..J 11
Benzonia .....412..F 11
Bergland ....C 7
Berkley .....21,879..I 6
Berrien
Springs ...1,951..K 11
Berville ....G 6
Bessemer ...2,805.°D 7
Beulah ....461.°F 11
Beverly
Hills .....13,598..I 5
Big Bay ....C 9
Big Rapids 11,995.°H 12
Bingham
Farms* .....566..J 14
Birch Run .....932..F 3
Birming-
ham .....26,170..I 5
Bitely ....H 11
Black River ....F 14
Blanchard ....H 12
Blaney Park ....D 11
Blissfield ...2,753..K 14
Bloomfield
Hills .....3,672..I 5
Bloomingdale .496..J 11
Boon ....G 12
Boyne City .2,969..F 12
Boyne Falls ..347..F 12
Brampton ....D 10
Brant ....F 2
Breckenridge 1,257..E 1
Breedsville* ...209..J 11
Brethren ....G 11
Brevort ....D 12
Bridgeport ....F 3
Bridgewater ....K 3
Bridgman ...1,621..K 11
Brighton ....2,457..I 3
Brimley ....D 13
Britton ....697..K 14
Brohman ....H 12
Bronson .....2,390..K 12
Brooklyn ....1,112..K 2
Brown City .1,142..F 6
Brownlee
Park* .....2,985..J 12
Bruce Crossing .....C 8
Brunswick ....H 11
Brutus ....E 13
Buchanan ...4,645..K 11
Buckley ......244..G 12
Bunny Run .1,391..H 6
Burlington ....314..J 12
Burnips ....I 12
Burr Oak .....873..K 12
Burt ....F 3
Burt Lake ....E 13
Burton* ...32,540..G 3
Byron ....655..H 3
Byron Center ....I 12
Cadillac ....9,990.°G 12
Caledonia* ....716..I 12
Calumet ....1,007..B 8
Camden ....405..K 13
Cannonsburg ....I 12
Capac ......1,279..G 6
Capehart, see
Selfridge-Capehart
Carleton .....1,503..J 14
Carlshend ....D 10
Carney ....E 10
Caro ....3,701.°E 5
Carp Lake ....E 13
Carrollton ...7,300..E 3
Carson City .1,217..I 13
Carsonville ....621..E 7
Caseville .....607..G 14
Casnovia* .....403..I 11
Caspian .....1,165..D 8
Cass City ...1,974..H 15
Cassopolis ...2,108.°K 11
Cedar ....F 12
Cedar
Springs ...1,807..I 12
Cedarville ....D 13
Cement City ...531..J 13
Center Line 10,379..I 6
Central Lake .741..F 12
Centreville ..1,044.°K 12
Champion ....D 9
Channing ....D 9
Charlevoix ..3,519.°E 12
Charlotte ...8,244.°J 13
Chase ....H 12
Chassell ....C 8
Chatham ....246..D 10
Cheboygan ..5,553.°E 13
Chelsea .....3,858..J 3
Chesaning ...2,876..F 2
Chippewa Lake .....H 12
Clair Haven .2,177..I 7
Clair Haven
West* ....1,367..I 15
Clare ....2,639..H 13
Clarkston ...1,034..H 5
Clarksville* ....346..I 12
Clawson ...17,617..I 6
Clayton ....505..K 13
Clifford ....472..F 6
Climax* ....594..J 12
Clinton ......1,677..J 14
Clio ....2,357..F 4
Cloverdale ....J 12
Clyde ....I 4
Cohoctah ....H 3
Coldwater ...9,155.°K 13
Coleman .....1,295..H 13
Coloma ......1,814..J 11
Colon* ......1,172..K 12
Columbiaville 935..F 5
Comins ....F 13
Comstock* ...5,003..J 12
Comstock
Park* ....5,766..I 12
Concord ....983..K 1
Constantine .1,733..K 12
Conway ....E 12
Cooks ....D 11
Coopersville .2,129..I 12
Copemish .....237..G 11
Copper City ...252..B 9
Cornell ....D 10
Corunna ....2,829.°G 2
Covert ....J 11
Covington ....C 8
Cross Village ....E 12
Croswell ....1,954..F 7
Crystal ....I 13
Crystal Falls 2,000.°D 9
Custer ....320..H 11
Cutlerville* ..6,267..I 12
Dafter ....D 13
Daggett ....366..E 9
Dansville .....486..I 2
Davisburg ....H 4
Davison ......5,259..G 4
Dearborn .104,199..J 6
Dearborn
Heights* .80,069..J 15
Decatur .....1,764..J 11
Decker ....E 6
Deckerville ...817..H 15
Deerfield ....834..K 13
Deford ....H 15
Delton ....J 12
De Tour ....494..D 14
Detroit ..1,513,601.°J 15
Detroit
Beach ....2,053..K 14
DeWitt ......1,829..H 1
Dexter ......1,729..J 3
Dimondale ....970..I 1
Disco ....H 6
Dixboro ....J 4
Dollar Bay ....C 8
Donken ....C 8
Dorr ....I 12
Douglas ....813..J 11
Dowagiac ....6,583..K 11
Dowling ....J 12
Drayton
Plains ...16,462..I 5
Drummond Island .D 14
Dryden ....654..G 6
Dundee .....2,472..K 14
Durand .....3,678..G 3
Eagle ....175..I 13
Eagle River ....°B 9
East
Detroit ..45,920..J 6
East Grand
Rapids ..12,565..I 12
East Jordan 2,041..F 12
East
Kingsford* 1,155..E 9
East Lake ....512..G 11
East
Lansing .47,540..H 1
East Saugatuck .....J 11
East Tawas .2,372..G 14
Eastport ....F 12
Eastwood* ...9,682..J 12
Eaton
Rapids ....4,494..J 13
Eau Claire* ..527..K 11
Eben Junction ......D 10
Eckerman ....D 12
Ecorse ......17,515..K 6
Eden ....I 1
Edenville ....H 13
Edmore .....1,149..H 12
Edwardsburg 1,107..K 11
Elberta ....542..F 11
Elk Rapids .1,249..F 12
Elkton ....973..H 14
Ellsworth .....362..F 12
Elm Hall ....H 13
Elmira ....F 13
Elsie ....988..G 1
Elwell ....H 13
Emmett ....297..G 7
Empire ....409..F 11
Engadine ....D 12
Epoufette ....D 12
Erie ....K 14
Escanaba ..15,368.°E 10
Essexville ...4,990..H 14
Estral Beach .419..J 15
Euclid Center ....J 11
Eureka ....G 1
Evart ....1,707..H 12
Ewen ....C 8
Fair Haven ....H 7
Fair Plain ..3,680..J 11
Fairgrove .....629..H 14
Fairview ....F 13
Falmouth ....G 12
Fargo ....G 7
Farmington* 10,329..J 5
Farmington
Hills ....48,694..J 5
Farwell ....777..H 13
Felch ....D 9
Fennville .....811..J 11
Fenton ......8,284..H 4
Fenwick ....I 12
Ferndale ..30,850..J 6
Ferrysburg ..2,196..I 11
Fife Lake ....274..G 12
Filer City ....G 11
Filion ....H 15
Flat Rock ...5,643..K 5
Flint .....193,317.°I 14
Flower Hills, see
Shorewood Hills-
Flower Hills
Flushing ......8,313..G 3
Forestville .....110..H 15
Foster City ....D 9
Fostoria ....F 5
Fountain .....156..G 11
Fowler ......1,020..I 13
Fowlerville .1,978..I 2
Franken-
muth .....2,834..E 4
Frankfort ...1,660..F 11
Franklin ....3,311..I 5
Fraser .....11,868..I 6
Freda ....C 8
Frederic ....F 13
Free Soil .....186..G 11
Freeland ....1,303..H 13
Freeport ......501..I 12
Fremont .....3,465..H 11
Frontier ....K 13
Fruitport ...1,409..I 11
Gaastra ....479..D 8
Gagetown .....408..H 14
Gaines ....408..H 3
Galesburg* ..1,355..J 12
Galien ....691..K 11
Garden ....336..E 11
Garden
City .....41,864..J 5
Gaylord .....3,012.°F 13
Genesee ....G 4
Germfask ....D 11
Gibraltar ...3,842..K 6
Gladstone ...5,237..E 10
Gladwin ....2,071.°G 13
Glendora ....K 11
Glenn ....J 11
Glennie ....F 14
Gobles* ....801..J 12
Good Hart ....E 12
Goodells ....G 7
Goodison ....H 6
Goodrich ....774..G 4
Gould City ....D 12
Grand Beach ..165..K 10
Grand
Blanc ....5,132..G 4
Grand
Haven ...11,844.°I 11
Grand Junction .....J 11
Grand Ledge 6,032..I 13
Grand Marais .....C 11
Grand
Rapids .197,649.°I 12
Grandville ..10,764..I 12
Grant ....772..H 12
Grass Lake ..1,061..K 2
Grawn ....F 12
Grayling .....2,143.°F 13
Greenbush ....F 14
Greenland ....C 8
Greenville ....7,493..I 12
Gregory ....J 2
Grosse Ile* ..8,306..K 6
Grosse
Pointe ....6,637..J 7
Grosse Pointe
Farms ...11,701..J 7
Grosse Pointe
Park ....15,641..J 7
Grosse Pointe
Shores* ...3,042..J 15
Grosse Pointe
Woods ...21,878..J 7
Gulliver ....D 11
Gwinn ....1,054..D 10
Hadley ....G 5
Hale ....G 14
Hamburg ....J 3
Hamilton ....J 11
Hamtramck 27,245..J 6
Hancock ....4,820..C 8
Hanover ....513..K 1
Harbor
Beach ....2,134..H 15
Harbor
Springs ...1,662..E 12
Hardwood ....D 9
Harper
Woods ...20,186..J 7
Harrietta ......132..G 12
Harrison .....1,460.°G 13
Harrisville ....541.°F 14
Harsens Island ......I 8
Hart ....2,139.°H 11
Hartford ....2,508..J 11
Hartland ....I 4
Harvey ....D 10
Haslett ....H 1
Hastings ....6,501.°J 12
Hawks ....E 14
Hazel Park .23,784..J 6
Hemlock ....E 2
Henderson ....G 2
Herman ....C 9
Hermansville ....E 9
Herron ....F 14
Hersey ....276..H 12
Hesperia ......877..H 11
Hessel ....D 13
Hickory Corners .....J 12
Higgins Lake ......G 13
Highland ....I 4
Highland
Park .....35,444..J 6
Hillman ....366..F 14
Hillsdale ....7,728.°K 13
Holland .....26,479..I 11
Holly ....4,355..H 4
Holt ....6,980..I 1
Homer ......1,617..J 13
Honor ....282..F 11
Hope ....H 13

Hopkins ......566..J 12
Horton ....K 1
Houghton ...6,067.°C 8
Houghton Lake ....G 13
Houghton Lake Heights ...1,252..G 13
Howard City 1,060..H 12
Howell ......5,224.°I 3
Hubbard Lake ....F 14
Hubbardston ..403..I 13
Hubbell .....1,251..B 9
Hudson ......2,618..K 13
Hudsonville .3,523..I 12
Hulbert ....D 12
Huntington Woods* ...8,536..I 6
Ida ....K 14
Idlewild ....H 12
Imlay City ..1,980..G 6
Indian River ....E 13
Ingalls ....E 9
Inkster ....38,595..J 5
Ionia ....6,361.°I 12
Iron Mountain ....8,702.°E 9
Iron River ..2,684..D 8
Ironwood ....8,711..D 7
Ishpeming ...8,245..D 9
Ithaca ......2,749.°I 13
Jackson ....45,484.°J 13
Jasper ....K 14
Jeddo ....F 8
Jenison* ...11,266..I 11
Johannesburg ......F 13
Jones ....K 12
Jonesville ...2,081..K 13
Kalamazoo .85,555.°J 12
Kaleva ....377..G 11
Kalkaska ....1,475.°F 12
Karlin ....G 12
Kawkawlin ....H 14
Keego Harbor ...3,092..I 5
Keeler ....J 11
Kent City .....686..I 12
Kenton ....D 8
Kentwood* .25,731..I 12
Kewadin ....F 12
Kincheloe* ..6,331..D 13
Kinde ....618..G 15
Kingsford ...5,276..E 9
Kingsley .....632..G 12
Kingston ....464..E 5
Kinross ....D 13
K I Sawyer* 8,224..D 10
Lachine ....F 14
Laingsburg .1,159..H 2
Lake ....H 12
Lake Angelus* 573..I 14
Lake Ann .....172..F 11
Lake City .....704.°G 12
Lake George ....G 12
Lake Leelanau .....F 12
Lake Linden .1,214..B 9
Lake Michigan Beach ....1,201..J 11
Lake Odessa 1,924..I 12
Lake Orion .2,921..H 5
Lake Orion Heights ...2,552..H 5
Lakeland ....J 3
Lakeport ....F 8
Lakeside, see Bayport Park-Lakeside
Lakeview ...1,118..H 12
Lakeview ..11,391..J 12
Lakeville ....H 6
Lakewood Club* ......590..H 11
Lamb ....G 7
Lambertville 5,711..K 14
L'Anse .....2,538.°C 9
Lansing ...131,403..I 13
Lapeer .....6,314.°G 5
Lapeer Heights* ..7,130..I 14
Lathrup Village ...4,676..J 5
Laurium ....2,868..B 8
Lawrence* ....790..J 11
Lawton ......1,358..J 12
Leland ....°F 12
Lennon ....624..G 3
Leonard ......378..H 6
Leoni ....K 2
LeRoy ....248..G 12
Leslie ....1,894..J 1
Level Park-Oak Park* .....3,080..J 12
Levering ....E 13
Lewiston ....F 13
Lexington .....834..F 8
Liberty ....K 1
Limestone ....D 10
Lincoln ......371..F 14
Lincoln Park ....52,984..K 6
Linden ......1,546..H 3
Linwood ....H 14
Litchfield ...1,167..J 13
Livonia ...110,109..J 5
Long Lake ....G 14
Lowell* .....3,068..I 12
Lucas ....G 12
Ludington ..9,021.°H 11
Lum ....G 6

Luna Pier ..1,418..K 14
Lupton ....G 14
Luther ....320..G 12
Luzerne ....F 13
Lyons* ....758..I 13
Mackinac Island ......517..D 13
Mackinaw City 810..E 13
Madison Heights ..38,599..I 6
Mancelona ..1,255..F 12
Manchester .1,650..K 3
Manistee ....7,723.°G 11
Manistique ..4,324.°D 11
Manitou Beach-Devils Lake 1,892..K 13
Manton .....1,107..G 12
Maple City ....F 11
Maple Rapids .683..I 13
Marcellus ...1,139..K 12
Marenisco ....D 7
Marine City .4,567..H 8
Marion ....891..G 12
Marlette ....1,706..E 6
Marne ....I 12
Marquette ..21,967.°C 10
Marshall ....7,253.°J 13
Martin ....502..J 12
Marysville ..5,610..G 8
Mason ......5,468.°I 1
Mass ....C 8
Mattawan* ..1,569..J 12
Maybee ....485..K 14
Mayfield ....F 12
Mayville ......872..E 5
McBain ....520..G 12
McBrides .....272..H 12
McMillan ....D 12
Meade ....H 7
Mears ....H 11
Mecosta ......396..H 12
Melvin ....202..F 7
Melvindale .13,862..J 6
Memphis ....1,121..G 7
Mendon* ......949..K 12
Menominee .10,748.°F 9
Merrill ....961..E 2
Merritt ....G 12
Merriweather ....C 7
Mesick ....376..G 12
Metamora ....468..G 5
Metz ....E 14
Michiana .....233..K 11
Michigan Center ....K 2
Middleton ....I 13
Middleville ..1,865..I 12
Midland ...35,176.°H 13
Mikado ....F 14
Milan ....3,997..K 4
Milford .....4,699..I 4
Millbrook ....H 12
Millersburg ...200..E 13
Millington ..1,099..F 4
Minden City ..327..H 15
Mineral Hills .234..D 8
Mio ....°F 13
Mohawk ....B 9
Moline ....I 12
Monroe ....23,894.°K 14
Montague ...2,396..H 11
Montgomery ..404..K 13
Montrose ....1,789..F 3
Moorestown ....G 12
Moran ....D 13
Morenci ....2,132..K 13
Morley ....481..H 12
Morrice ......734..H 2
Mount Clemens .20,476.°I 7
Mount Morris ....3,778..F 4
Mount Pleasant .20,524.°H 13
Muir ....617..I 13
Mullett Lake ....E 13
Mulliken .....454..I 13
Munger ....H 14
Munising ...3,677.°D 10
Munith ....J 2
Munson ....K 13
Muskegon ..44,631.°I 11
Muskegon Heights ..17,304..I 11
Nadeau ....E 10
Nahma ....E 10
Napoleon ....K 2
Nashville ...1,558..J 12
National City ......G 14
National Mine ......D 9
Naubinway ....D 12
Negaunee ...5,248..D 9
New Baltimore .....4,132..I 7
New Boston ....K 5
New Buffalo 2,784..K 11
New Era ......466..H 11
New Haven .1,855..H 7
New Hudson ....I 4
New Lothrop ..596..F 3
New Richmond ....J 11
Newaygo ....1,381..H 12
Newberry ...2,334.°D 12
Newport ....J 15
Niles ....12,988..K 11
Nisula ....C 8
North Adams .574..K 13
North Bradley ......H 13

North Branch .932..F 6
North Muskegon .4,243..I 11
North Star ....F 1
North Street ....G 8
Northland ....D 9
Northport ....594..F 12
Northville ...5,400..J 5
Norton Shores* ..22,271..I 11
Norvell ....K 2
Norway .....3,033..E 9
Novi ....9,668..I 5
Nunica ....I 11
Oak Grove ....H 3
Oak Park ..36,762..J 6
Oak Park, see Level Park-Oak Park
Oakley ....418..F 2
Oakwood ....H 5
Oden ....E 13
Okemos .....7,770..H 1
Old Mission ....F 12
Olivet ....1,629..J 13
Omena ....F 12
Omer ....366..G 14
Onaway .....1,262..E 13
Onekama ......638..G 11
Onondaga ....J 1
Onsted* ......555..K 13
Ontonagon ..2,432.°C 8
Orchard Lake .....1,487..I 5
Ortonville ....983..H 5
Oscoda [-Au Sable] ....3,475..G 14
Ossineke ....F 14
Otisville .....724..F 4
Otsego ......3,957..J 12
Ottawa Lake ....K 14
Otter Lake ....551..F 5
Ovid ....1,650..G 1
Owendale .....312..H 14
Owosso ....17,179..G 2
Oxford ......2,536..H 5
Painesdale ....C 8
Palmer ....D 9
Palms ....H 15
Paradise ....C 12
Parchment ..2,027..J 12
Paris ....H 12
Parma ....880..K 1
Parshallville ......I 4
Patterson Gardens ..2,169..K 14
Paulding ....D 8
Paw Paw ...3,160.°J 12
Paw Paw Lake .....3,726..J 11
Paynesville ....C 8
Pearl Beach 1,744..I 8
Peck ....580..F 7
Pelkie ....C 8
Pellston ......469..E 13
Pentwater ....993..H 11
Perkins ....D 10
Perrinton .....489..I 13
Perronville ....E 10
Perry ....1,531..H 2
Petersburg* .1,227..K 14
Petoskey ....6,342.°E 12
Pewamo* ......498..I 13
Pickford ....D 13
Pierson ....193..H 12
Pigeon .....1,174..H 14
Pinckney .....921..J 3
Pinconning .1,320..H 14
Pine Run ....F 4
Plainfield ....I 2
Plainwell ...3,195..J 12
Pleasant Lake ......J 2
Pleasant Ridge* ....3,989..J 15
Plymouth ..11,758..J 5
Pompeii ....F 1
Pontiac ....85,279.°I 14
Port Austin ...883..G 15
Port Hope .....377..G 15
Port Huron .35,794.°I 15
Port Sanilac ..493..E 8
Portage* ...33,590..J 12
Portland ....3,817..I 13
Posen ....339..E 14
Potterville ..1,280..J 13
Powers ....560..E 10
Prattville ....K 13
Prescott ......306..G 14
Presque Isle ....E 14
Princeton ....D 10
Prudenville ....G 13
Pullman ....J 11
Quakertown North* ....7,101..J 14
Quincy ....1,540..K 13
Quinnesec ....E 9
Raco ....D 13
Ralph ....D 9
Ramsay ......1,068..D 7
Rankin ....G 4
Rapid City ....F 12
Rapid River ....D 10
Ravenna .....1,048..I 11
Reading .....1,125..K 13
Reed City ...2,286.°H 12
Reeman ....H 11
Reese ....1,050..E 4
Remus ....H 12

Republic ....D 9
Rexton ....D 12
Rhodes ....H 13
Richland* .....728..J 12
Richmond ...3,234..H 7
Richville ....E 4
Ridgeway ....K 14
River Rouge ...15,947..J 6
Riverdale ....H 13
Riverview ..11,342..K 6
Roberts Landing ....I 8
Rochester ...7,054..I 6
Rockford ....2,428..I 12
Rockland ....C 8
Rockwood ...3,225..K 6
Rodney ....H 12
Rogers City ..4,275.°E 14
Romeo ....4,012..H 6
Romulus ...22,879..K 5
Roosevelt Park .....4,176..I 11
Roscommon ...810.°G 13
Rose City .....530..G 13
Rosebush ......439..H 13
Roseville ...60,529..I 6
Rothbury .....394..H 11
Royal Oak .86,238..I 6
Rudyard ....D 13
Ruth ....H 15
Saginaw ....91,849.°H 14
Sagola ....D 9
St. Charles ..2,046..F 2
St. Clair ...4,770..H 8
St. Clair Shores ..88,093..J 7
St. Helen ....G 13
St. Ignace ...2,892.°D 13
St. Johns ...6,672.°G 1
St. Joseph .11,042.°J 11
St. Louis ...4,101..E 1
Salem ....J 4
Saline ......6,050..K 4
Sand Lake .....380..I 12
Sandusky ...2,071.°E 7
Sanford ....818..H 13
Saranac* ....1,223..I 12
Saugatuck ..1,022..J 11
Sault Ste. Marie ..15,136.°C 13
Sawyer ....K 11
Schaffer ....E 10
Schoolcraft .1,277..J 12
Scottville ..1,202..H 11
Sears ....H 12
Sebewaing ..2,053..H 14
Selfridge Base* ....1,614..I 7
Selfridge-Capehart* .1,694..I 15
Seney ....D 11
Seven Harbors, see White Lake-Seven Harbors
Shaftsburg ....H 2
Shelby ......1,703..H 11
Shepardsville ......G 1
Shepherd ...1,416..H 13
Sheridan .....653..I 12
Sherwood ......400..K 12
Shingleton ....D 11
Shoreham .....666..K 11
Shorewood Hills-Flower Hills* .....1,629..K 10
Sidnaw ....C 8
Sidney ....I 12
Silverwood ....E 5
Six Lakes ....H 12
Skandia ....D 10
Skanee ....C 9
Smiths Creek ....G 8
Snover ....E 6
Somerset Center ....J 13
South Boardman .....F 12
South Haven 6,471..J 11
South Lyon ..2,675..J 4
South Monroe ...3,012..K 14
South Range ..898..C 8
South Rockwood .1,477..J 15
Southfield ..69,285..J 5
Southgate .33,909..K 6
Spalding ....E 10
Sparlingville 1,845..G 8
Sparta ......3,094..I 12
Spring Arbor 1,832..K 1
Spring Lake .3,034..I 11
Springfield ..3,994..J 12
Springfield Place .....4,831..J 12
Springport ....723..J 13
Spruce ....F 14
Stambaugh ..1,458..D 8
Standish ...1,184.°G 14
Stanton ....1,089.°I 12
Stanwood .....241..H 12
Stephenson ....800..E 9
Sterling ......507..G 14
Sterling Heights* .61,365..J 15
Stevensville .1,107..K 11
Stockbridge .1,190..J 2
Stony Point* 1,370..K 15
Stronach ....G 11
Strongs ....D 12
Sturgis .....9,295..K 12

Sunfield ......497..I 13
Sunrise Heights* ..1,626..J 12
Suttons Bay ..522..F 12
Swartz Creek .....4,928..G 3
Sylvan Lake .2,219..I 5
Tawas City ..1,666.°G 14
Taylor .....77,490..K 5
Tecumseh ...7,120..K 14
Tekonsha .....739..J 13
Temperance ....K 14
Temple ....G 12
Thompson ....D 11
Thompsonville .312..G 11
Thornville ....G 5
Three Oaks ..1,750..K 11
Three Rivers 7,355..K 12
Tipton ....K 14
Tolvola ....C 8
Topinabee ....E 13
Tower ....E 13
Traunik ....D 10
Traverse City .....18,048.°F 12
Trenary ....D 10
Trenton ....24,127..K 6
Trout Creek ....D 8
Trout Lake ....D 12
Troy ....39,419..I 6
Turner ....182..G 14
Tustin ....230..G 12
Twin Lake ....H 11
Twining ......198..G 14
Ubly ....899..H 15
Unadilla ....J 3
Union ....K 12
Union City ..1,740..J 12
Union Lake ....I 4
Union Pier ....K 11
Unionville .....647..H 14
Utica ....3,504..I 6
Vandalia ......427..K 11
Vanderbilt ...522..F 13
Vassar ......2,802..E 4
Vermontville ..857..J 13
Vernon ....818..G 3
Verona Park* 2,107..J 12
Vestaburg ....H 13
Vicksburg ...2,139..J 12
Vulcan ....E 9
Wakefield ...2,757..D 7
Waldron ....564..K 13
Walhalla ....H 11
Walker* ....13,349..I 12
Walkerville ..319..H 11
Wallace ....E 9
Walled Lake 3,759..I 5
Walloon Lake ....E 12
Waltz ....K 5
Warren ...179,260..I 6
Washington .1,563..H 6
Waterford ....H 5
Waters ....F 13
Watersmeet ....D 8
Watervliet ..2,059..J 11
Watrousville ....E 4
Watton ....C 8
Wayland ....2,054..J 12
Wayne ......21,054..J 5
Webberville .1,251..I 2
Weidman ....H 12
Wells ....1,085..E 10
Wellston ....G 11
West Branch 1,912.°G 13
Westland* .86,749..J 14
Weston ....K 14
Westphalia* ...806..I 13
Westwood* ..9,143..J 12
Wetmore ....D 11
Wheeler ....E 1
White Cloud 1,044.°H 12
White Lake-Seven Harbors ...4,504..H 4
White Pigeon 1,455..K 12
White Pine ..1,218..C 7
Whitefish Point ....C 12
Whitehall ...3,017..H 11
Whitmore Lake .....2,763..J 4
Whittaker ....K 4
Whittemore ...460..G 14
Williamsburg ....F 12
Williamston .2,600..I 2
Willis ....K 4
Willow Run ....K 4
Wilmot ....E 5
Wilson ....E 10
Winn ....H 13
Winona ....C 8
Wixom ......4,453..I 4
Wolf Lake ..2,258..I 11
Wolverine .....303..E 13
Wolverine Lake .....4,301..I 4
Woodhaven* .3,566..J 15
Woodland .....473..I 12
Woodland Beach ....2,249..K 15
Wurtsmith* ..6,932..F 14
Wyandotte .41,061..K 6
Wyoming ..56,560..I 12
Yale ....1,505..F 7
Ypsilanti ..29,538..K 4
Zeeland ....4,734..I 11
Zilwaukee* ..2,072..H 14

*Does not appear on the map; key shows general location.
°County seat.

Sources: Latest census figures (1970 and special censuses). Places without population figures are unincorporated areas and are not listed in census reports.

The 1970 United States census reported that Michigan had a population of 8,875,083. This figure was an increase of 13 per cent over the 1960 census figure of 7,823,194. The U.S. Bureau of the Census estimated that by 1975 the state's population had reached about 9,157,000.

Nearly three-fourths of Michigan's people live in urban areas. That is, they live in or near cities and towns of 2,500 or more persons. Slightly more than a fourth of the people live in rural areas. About 85 per cent

Factory Workers stream out of a factory in Dearborn, near Detroit, at the end of a day. Many Detroit area factories have thousands of employees and operate in two or even three shifts. Most of Michigan's people live in or near large industrial cities.

The Detroit News

of the people make their homes in one of the state's 12 Standard Metropolitan Statistical Areas (see METROPOLITAN AREA). These are Ann Arbor, Battle Creek, Bay City, Detroit, Flint, Grand Rapids, Jackson, Kalamazoo-Portage, Lansing-East Lansing, Muskegon-Norton Shores-Muskegon Heights, and Saginaw in Michigan, and Toledo in Ohio and Michigan. For the populations of these metropolitan areas, see the *Index* to the political map of Michigan. Most of the people live in the Lower Peninsula. Only about 300,000 persons, or about 3 of every 100, live in the Upper Peninsula.

Detroit is Michigan's largest city, and the fifth largest city in the United States. Other large cities in Michigan, in order of population, are Grand Rapids, Flint, Warren, Lansing, Livonia, Dearborn, Ann Arbor, Saginaw, and St. Clair Shores. All have populations of more than 80,000, and all are in the Lower Peninsula. The largest city in the Upper Peninsula of Michigan is Marquette. It has a population of more than 21,000 persons. See the separate articles on the cities of Michigan which are listed in the *Related Articles* at the end of this article.

About 95 out of 100 persons in Michigan were born in the United States. Of the more than 424,000 persons from other countries who live in the state, the largest group came from Canada. Other groups born outside the United States include, in order of size, those from Great Britain, Poland, Germany, Italy, Russia, The Netherlands, and Yugoslavia. About 10 per cent of Michigan's people are Negroes. Indians make up about 2 per cent of the population.

Roman Catholics make up the largest religious group in Michigan. Other large church groups in the state include Baptists, Episcopalians, Lutherans, Methodists, and Presbyterians. The House of David, a small but well-known religious organization, has its headquarters in Benton Harbor (see HOUSE OF DAVID).

POPULATION

This map shows the *population density* of Michigan, and how it varies in different parts of the state. Population density means the average number of persons who live in a given area.

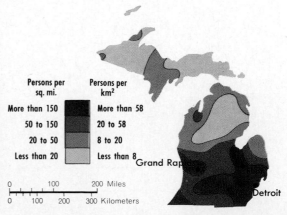

Persons per sq. mi.		Persons per km²
More than 150	▆	More than 58
50 to 150	▆	20 to 58
20 to 50	▆	8 to 20
Less than 20	▆	Less than 8

Grand Rapids

Detroit

```
0        100      200 Miles
0    100    200   300 Kilometers
```

WORLD BOOK map

Wayne State University

Wayne State University's McGregor Memorial Community Conference Center was designed by Minoru Yamasaki.

Schools. Roman Catholic missionaries who came to the Michigan region in the 1600's established schools for the Indians. In 1798, Father Gabriel Richard came to Detroit as pastor of Ste. Anne's Roman Catholic Church. He set up schools to provide regular classes and vocational training for Indian and white children.

In 1809, the territorial legislature passed Michigan's first school law. The law provided for school districts, school taxes, and the building of public schools. In 1827, the legislature provided for community schools maintained by townships. After Michigan entered the Union in 1837, the Legislature approved a state-wide system of public education, including a university. The Legislature also provided for the appointment of a superintendent of public instruction to administer the public school system. The Michigan superintendent was the first such administrator in the nation.

Eastern Michigan University, established in 1849, was the first state teachers college west of New York. Michigan State University, founded in 1855, was the first state school to offer agriculture courses for credit. In 1879, the University of Michigan became one of the first state universities to establish a *chair* (special teaching position) in education.

Today, Michigan has about 2,860 public elementary schools and about 1,100 public middle, junior, and senior high schools. The state board of education directs Michigan's public school system. It consists of eight members elected to the board by the voters. The board appoints the superintendent of public instruction. A state law requires children between the ages of 6 and 16 to attend school. For the number of students and teachers in Michigan, see EDUCATION (table).

Libraries. The state library was founded in Detroit in 1828, when many settlers were moving into the Michigan Territory. This library was later moved to Lansing. It now has over 1 million volumes. Michigan has 17 library cooperatives and 350 public libraries with 165 branches. Bookmobiles serve many rural communities. The state provides aid to local library systems.

Libraries of the University of Michigan at Ann Arbor have more than 4 million volumes. The William L. Clements Library at the university has a famous collection on early America. The Detroit Public Library has the Burton Historical Collection, containing reference works on Michigan and the Great Lakes area. Other large libraries are at Wayne State University and Michigan State University.

Museums. The Detroit Institute of Arts was established in 1885. Its collection of paintings and sculptures includes murals by the Mexican artist Diego Rivera. The Detroit Historical Museum has exhibits on the history of Detroit and Michigan.

Greenfield Village, in Dearborn, is a museum made up of a group of historical buildings. Its exhibits deal with American industrial history, and life in the 1700's and 1800's. The Grand Rapids Public Museum features natural history exhibits. The Michigan Historical Museum in Lansing displays pioneer items. The Kingman Museum of Natural History in Battle Creek exhibits wildlife, prehistoric mammals, and ancient relics. The Alfred P. Sloan, Jr., Museum in Flint has displays on

transportation. Mackinac Island has seven museums. One features the instruments of William Beaumont, a surgeon who made major discoveries about digestion.

UNIVERSITIES AND COLLEGES

Michigan has 42 universities and colleges accredited by the North Central Association of Colleges and Schools. For enrollments and further information, see UNIVERSITIES AND COLLEGES (table).

Name	Location	Founded
Adrian College	Adrian	1845
Albion College	Albion	1835
Alma College	Alma	1886
Andrews University	Berrien Springs	1874
Aquinas College	Grand Rapids	1922
Calvin College	Grand Rapids	1876
Center for Creative Studies	Detroit	1926
Central Michigan University	Mount Pleasant	1892
Concordia College	Ann Arbor	1963
Cranbrook Academy of Art	Bloomfield Hills	1942
Detroit, University of	Detroit	1877
Detroit Institute of Technology	Detroit	1891
Duns Scotus Seminary	Southfield	1930
Eastern Michigan University	Ypsilanti	1849
Ferris State College	Big Rapids	1884
General Motors Institute	Flint	1919
Grand Rapids Baptist College and Seminary	Grand Rapids	1941
Grand Valley State Colleges	Allendale	1960
Hillsdale College	Hillsdale	1844
Hope College	Holland	1851
Kalamazoo College	Kalamazoo	1833
Lake Superior State College	Sault Ste. Marie	1966
Lawrence Institute of Technology	Southfield	1932
Madonna College	Livonia	1947
Marygrove College	Detroit	1905
Mercy College of Detroit	Detroit	1941
Michigan, University of	*	*
Michigan State University	East Lansing	1855
Michigan Technological University	Houghton	1885
Nazareth College at Kalamazoo	Nazareth	1897
Northern Michigan University	Marquette	1899
Northwood Institute	Midland	1971
Oakland University	Rochester	1959
Olivet College	Olivet	1844
Sacred Heart Seminary College	Detroit	1919
Saginaw Valley State College	University Center	1964
Saint Mary's College	Orchard Lake	1885
Siena Heights College	Adrian	1919
Spring Arbor College	Spring Arbor	1873
Walsh College of Accountancy and Business Administration	Troy	1968
Wayne State University	Detroit	1868
Western Michigan University	Kalamazoo	1903

*For the campuses and founding dates of the University of Michigan, see UNIVERSITIES AND COLLEGES (table).

MICHIGAN / A Visitor's Guide

Michigan is a year-round playground for people who love sports and the outdoors. Thousands of lakes, rivers, and streams attract swimmers, water skiers, fishing enthusiasts, and boaters. Thick forests and scenic woodlands attract hunters and campers. In winter, many people travel to Michigan for skiing, skating, snowmobiling, tobogganing, iceboat racing, and ice fishing. International ski-flying competitions are held in Ironwood at Copper Peak, one of the world's largest artificially created ski-flying hills. Sightseers are drawn to the many beautiful waterfalls, and dunes, and to the rugged "Copper Country" of the western Upper Peninsula.

John Calkins, Shostal

Pictured Rocks near Munising

PLACES TO VISIT

Following are brief descriptions of some of Michigan's many interesting places to visit.

Arboretums of Michigan have some of the country's finest collections of plants, shrubs, and trees. *Leila Arboretum*, in Battle Creek, is a beautifully landscaped park that has rare plants and a wildlife museum. *Nichols Arboretum*, located in Ann Arbor, has a famous garden with a collection of about 140 kinds of hybrid lilacs.

Automobile Plants located in Dearborn, Detroit, Flint, Lansing, and Pontiac provide guided tours for visitors.

Big Spring, or *Kitchi-ti-ki-pi*, near Manistique, is a pool fed by more than 200 bubbling springs. It is 45 feet (14 meters) deep. The water is so clear that visitors can watch coins drift all the way to the bottom of the pool.

Detroit, the *Motor City*, produces more cars and trucks than any other city in the world. Detroit is the fifth largest city in the United States, and a leading port. Its famous Cultural Center includes libraries, museums, and Wayne State University. See DETROIT.

Fort Michilimackinac, in Mackinaw City, is a reconstruction of the fort built in the 1700's. Buildings include the home of British commander Robert Rogers, and Ste. Anne's Jesuit church.

Greenfield Village, in Dearborn, is a collection of historic buildings restored by Henry Ford. Greenfield Village includes buildings made famous by such persons as Abraham Lincoln, Thomas Edison, William H. McGuffey, and Stephen Foster. The Henry Ford Museum is next to the village. See GREENFIELD VILLAGE.

Kellogg Bird Sanctuary, on Gull Lake near Battle Creek, is a 100-acre (40-hectare) refuge for ducks, geese, pheasants, swans, and other wild birds.

Mackinac Island is a famous resort island in the Straits of Mackinac, between the Upper and Lower peninsulas. No automobiles are permitted on the island. See MACKINAC ISLAND.

Pictured Rocks, near Munising on Lake Superior, are beautifully colored cliffs carved into spectacular shapes by the action of waves.

Sleeping Bear Dune, near Empire, is a mound of sand that is shaped like a sleeping bear. It rises about 480 feet (146 meters). The sand is so fine that people ski on it in summer.

Soo Canals, at Sault Ste. Marie, permit ships to travel between Lake Huron and Lake Superior through huge locks. See SOO CANALS.

Tahquamenon Falls, near Newberry, are among the most beautiful sights of the Upper Peninsula. Henry Wadsworth Longfellow wrote about both the upper and lower falls of the Tahquamenon River in his poem *The Song of Hiawatha*.

United States Ski Hall of Fame, in Ishpeming, honors famous U.S. skiers, skiing events, and persons who have made outstanding contributions to the sport.

National Forests and Parks. Michigan has four national forests. The largest, Ottawa National Forest, lies in the western part of the Upper Peninsula. Hiawatha National Forest is in the central and eastern parts of the Upper Peninsula. Huron National Forest occupies much of the Au Sable River basin of the eastern Lower Peninsula. Manistee National Forest covers most of the Manistee River basin in the western Lower Peninsula. For the areas and other features of these forests, see NATIONAL FOREST (table).

Michigan's only national park, Isle Royale, is in northwestern Lake Superior, about 20 miles (32 kilometers) from the mainland of Minnesota. It includes Isle Royale and about 200 nearby small islands. The park has one of the largest remaining herds of great-antlered moose in the United States. Isle Royale National Park is about 48 miles (77 kilometers) from Michigan's Upper Peninsula. See ISLE ROYALE NATIONAL PARK.

State Parks and Forests. Michigan has over 70 state parks, 29 state forests, and more than 160 roadside parks and rest areas. Michigan's park system has over 13,000 prepared campsites, more than any other state. In addition, the state has over 70 organized winter-sport areas.

For information on the state parks and other attractions of Michigan, write to the Michigan Travel Bureau, P.O. Box 30226, Lansing, Mich. 48909.

WORLD BOOK photo by Holland Photography
Washing the Street for the Tulip Festival in Holland

Greenfield Village Store in Dearborn
Alpha Photo Assoc.

Tahquamenon Falls near Newberry
John Freeman, Publix

One of Michigan's most popular annual events is the week-long Tulip Festival, held each May in Holland. The people of the city dress in traditional Dutch costumes. The festival includes parades, dancing in wooden shoes, and traditional street washing. Other annual events in Michigan include the following.

January-March: International Sled Dog Races in Kalkaska (last weekend in January); I-500 Snowmobile Race in Sault Ste. Marie (early February).

April-June: Maple Syrup Festival in Shepherd and Vermontville (April); Blossomtime Festival in St. Joseph-Benton Harbor (May); Highland Festival and Games in Alma (May); Bavarian Festival in Frankenmuth (June); Muzzle Loaders Festival in Dearborn (June).

July-September: Seaway Festival in Muskegon (early July); National Cherry Festival, Traverse City (early July); International Freedom Festival in Detroit (July); Yacht Races to Mackinac Island from Chicago and Port Huron (July); Magic Get-Together in Colon (mid-August); Upper Peninsula State Fair in Escanaba (mid-August); State Fair in Detroit (late August); Mackinac Bridge Walk, from St. Ignace to Mackinaw City (Labor Day); Grape and Wine Festival in Paw Paw (late September).

October-December: Fall color tours, statewide (October); Red Flannel Days in Cedar Springs (October); Hunting season, parts of Upper and Lower peninsulas (October-November), statewide (November); Christmas at Greenfield Village in Dearborn (December).

National Music Camp in Interlochen
Publix Pictorial

International Bridge at Sault Ste. Marie
International Bridge Authority

Land Regions. Michigan has two main land regions: (1) the Superior Upland and (2) the Great Lakes Plains.

The Superior Upland extends along Lake Superior in Michigan, Wisconsin, and Minnesota. In Michigan, the Superior Upland covers the western half of the Upper Peninsula. Much of the region is a rugged plateau, rising from about 600 to 2,000 feet (180 to 610 meters) above sea level. Michigan's mountains are in this region. The Porcupine Mountains in extreme northwestern Michigan rise from the shores of Lake Superior. Mount Curwood is the highest point in the state, 1,980 feet (604 meters) above sea level. Forests cover many hills and mountains. The Superior Upland has some of the nation's richest iron and copper deposits.

The Great Lakes Plains stretch along the Great Lakes from Wisconsin to Ohio. In Michigan, the region covers the eastern Upper Peninsula and the entire Lower Peninsula. In the Upper Peninsula, parts of the Great Lakes Plains are lowlands covered by swamps. A short growing season and thin soils make many parts of the area unsuitable for farming. The Great Lakes Plains are part of a large midwestern land region called the *Interior Lowland*.

Much of the Lower Peninsula is fairly level, but some parts are rolling and hilly. The north-central Lower Peninsula rises 1,200 to 1,400 feet (366 to 427 meters) above sea level. Many high bluffs and sand dunes border Lake Michigan. The state's lowest point, 572 feet (174 meters) above sea level, is along the shore of Lake Erie. Parts of the northern Lower Peninsula have sandy wastes, covered with jack pine trees, scrub, and stumps. The southern half of the Lower Peninsula has good farmland.

Shoreline of Michigan is 3,288 miles (5,292 kilometers) long—more than that of any other inland state. This includes 1,056 miles (1,699 kilometers) of island shoreline. Four Great Lakes touch the state—Erie,

Land Regions of Michigan

A. M. Wettach

Sleek Dairy Cattle graze in a rich pasture near East Lansing. Michigan's best farmland lies in the southern Lower Peninsula. This area is part of the Great Lakes Plains region.

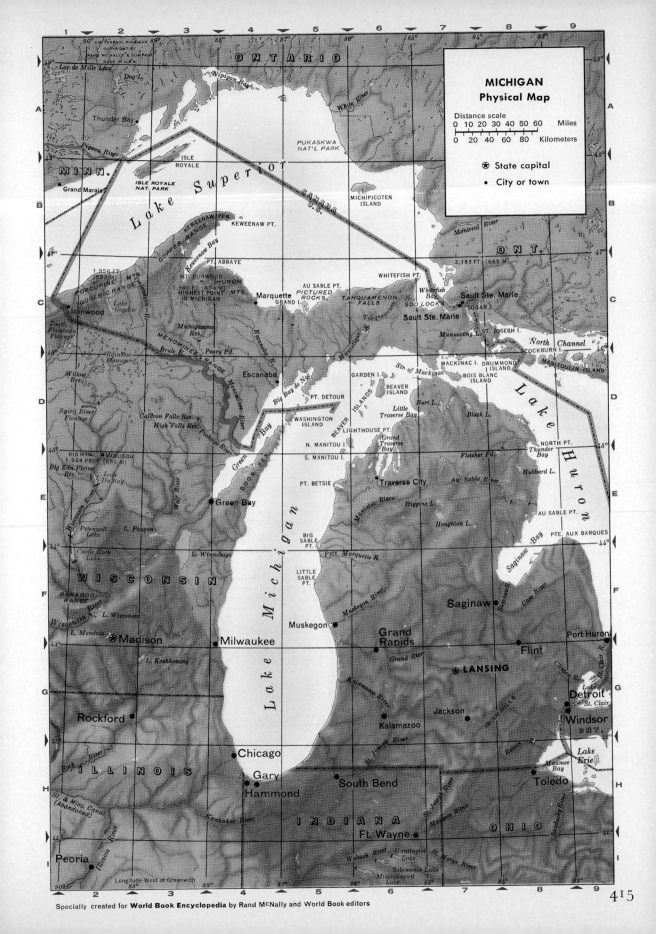

MICHIGAN
Physical Map

Distance scale
0 10 20 30 40 50 60   Miles
0 20 40 60 80   Kilometers

✳ State capital
• City or town

Huron, Michigan, and Superior. All of Michigan lies within 85 miles (137 kilometers) of these lakes.

Bays along the Lower Peninsula include Grand Traverse and Little Traverse on Lake Michigan, and Saginaw on Lake Huron. The Upper Peninsula has Whitefish and Keweenaw bays on Lake Superior, and Big Bay de Noc on Lake Michigan. Green Bay touches the southern tip of the Upper Peninsula.

Islands. Michigan's largest island, Isle Royale, covers about 210 square miles (544 square kilometers) in Lake Superior. The Beaver and Manitou islands are in Lake Michigan. Bois Blanc, Mackinac, and Round islands are in the Straits of Mackinac. Drummond Island, in Lake Huron, lies off the eastern tip of the Upper Peninsula. The small islands on the Detroit River include Belle Isle and Grosse Ile.

Rivers, Waterfalls, and Lakes. The chief rivers of the Upper Peninsula include the Escanaba, Manistique, Menominee, Ontonagon, Sturgeon, Tahquamenon, and Whitefish. Principal rivers in the Lower Peninsula are the Au Sable, Clinton, Grand, Huron, Kalamazoo, Manistee, Muskegon, Raisin, Saginaw, and St. Joseph. The Grand River, 260 miles (418 kilometers) long, is the longest in the state. The Detroit, St. Clair, and St. Marys rivers are important for commerce. The Detroit River connects Lakes Erie and St. Clair. Lakes Huron and St. Clair are joined by the St. Clair. The St. Marys River connects Lakes Huron and Superior. Other major rivers include the Cass and the Pere Marquette.

Michigan's Upper Peninsula has about 150 beautiful waterfalls. The best known falls are the Upper and Lower Tahquamenon Falls on the Tahquamenon River. Other important waterfalls include the Agate, Bond, Laughing Whitefish, Miners, and Munising— all in the Upper Peninsula.

Michigan has more than 11,000 inland lakes. The largest is 30-square-mile (78-square-kilometer) Houghton Lake in the north-central Lower Peninsula. Most of the larger lakes are in the Lower Peninsula. They include Black, Burt, Charlevoix, Crystal, Higgins, Mullet, and Torch lakes. Lake Gogebic is the largest lake in the Upper Peninsula.

Shostal

Lake of the Clouds is cradled in a valley in Porcupine Mountains State Park. This region has some of the highest elevations in the Middle West. It is part of Michigan's Superior Uplands region.

High Sand Dunes in Warren Dunes State Park near Bridgman spread over more than 2 miles (3.2 kilometers) of Lake Michigan's shore. The sand, moved by air currents, may cover trees.

Tad Stamm, Alpha

Mackinac Island, a famous resort area, lies in the Straits of Mackinac between Michigan's Upper and Lower peninsulas.

John Freeman, Publix

Michigan has a moist climate with cold winters and warm summers in the south and cool summers in the north. Winds from the Great Lakes bring much cloudiness. About 6 of every 10 days are partly cloudy in summer and about 7 of every 10 days in winter. Fall and winter are especially cloudy in the western Lower Peninsula and the eastern Upper Peninsula.

The Lower Peninsula is generally warmer than the Upper Peninsula. Average January temperatures range from 15° F. (−9° C) in the western Upper Peninsula to 26° F. (−3° C) in the southern Lower Peninsula. July temperatures average 65° F. (18° C) in the eastern Upper Peninsula and 73° F. (23° C) in the southern Lower Peninsula. Michigan's record low temperature, −51° F. (−46° C), occurred in Vanderbilt on Feb. 9, 1934. Mio recorded the highest temperature, 112° F. (44° C), on July 13, 1936. Air cooled by Lake Michigan in the spring usually prevents the budding of fruit trees until the danger of frosts has passed.

Michigan's yearly *precipitation* (rain, melted snow, and other forms of moisture) ranges from about 25 to

Michigan Tourist Council

Heavy Winter Snow blankets Michigan's Upper Peninsula, a winter sports center. Many ski tournaments are held at Iron Mountain, which has one of the highest artificial ski jumps in the world.

35 inches (64 to 89 centimeters). Annual snowfall varies from less than 30 inches (76 centimeters) in the southwestern Lower Peninsula to about 160 inches (406 centimeters) in the western Upper Peninsula. The state's record snowfall, 276½ inches (702.3 centimeters), occurred at Houghton during the winter of 1949-1950.

SEASONAL TEMPERATURES

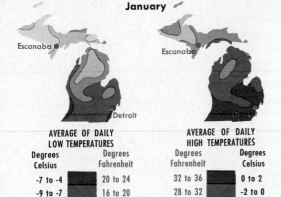

January

AVERAGE OF DAILY LOW TEMPERATURES

Degrees Celsius		Degrees Fahrenheit
-7 to -4		20 to 24
-9 to -7		16 to 20
-11 to -9		12 to 16
-13 to -11		8 to 12
-16 to -13		4 to 8

AVERAGE OF DAILY HIGH TEMPERATURES

Degrees Fahrenheit		Degrees Celsius
32 to 36		0 to 2
28 to 32		-2 to 0
24 to 28		-4 to -2
20 to 24		-7 to -4

July

AVERAGE OF DAILY LOW TEMPERATURES

Degrees Celsius		Degrees Fahrenheit
16 to 18		60 to 64
13 to 16		56 to 60
11 to 13		52 to 56
9 to 11		48 to 52

AVERAGE OF DAILY HIGH TEMPERATURES

Degrees Fahrenheit		Degrees Celsius
84 to 90		29 to 32
78 to 84		26 to 29
72 to 78		22 to 26
66 to 72		19 to 22

AVERAGE YEARLY PRECIPITATION
(Rain, Melted Snow and Other Moisture)

Centimeters		Inches
91 to 112		36 to 44
71 to 91		28 to 36
51 to 71		20 to 28

0   100   200   300 Miles
0   100 200 300 400 Kilometers

WORLD BOOK maps

AVERAGE MONTHLY WEATHER

	ESCANABA					DETROIT				
	Temperatures				Days of Rain or Snow		Temperatures			Days of Rain or Snow
	F° High	F° Low	C° High	C° Low			F° High	F° Low	C° High	C° Low
JAN.	25	10	-4	-12	12	JAN.	32	19	0	-7	13
FEB.	26	9	-3	-13	10	FEB.	34	19	1	-7	11
MAR.	34	18	1	-8	10	MAR.	44	27	7	-3	12
APR.	46	31	8	-1	10	APR.	57	36	14	2	13
MAY	58	42	14	6	11	MAY	70	47	21	8	11
JUNE	69	52	21	11	11	JUNE	80	58	27	14	10
JULY	75	58	24	14	11	JULY	84	63	29	17	9
AUG.	73	57	23	14	10	AUG.	81	61	27	16	9
SEPT.	65	50	18	10	12	SEPT.	74	55	23	13	8
OCT.	54	40	12	4	10	OCT.	62	43	17	6	7
NOV.	40	28	4	-2	11	NOV.	46	33	8	1	12
DEC.	29	16	-2	-9	11	DEC.	35	23	2	-5	11

The production of transportation equipment ranks as Michigan's most important industry. Detroit is the state's leading manufacturing center. Other important manufacturing cities include Battle Creek, Flint, Grand Rapids, Lansing, Livonia, Pontiac, Saginaw, and Warren. The southern Lower Peninsula has the state's best farmland. Most livestock and crops are raised there. Fruit growing thrives along the Lake Michigan shoreline of the Lower Peninsula. Michigan's valuable iron-ore and copper mines are in the western Upper Peninsula. Salt is mined around Detroit and in other parts of the Lower Peninsula.

Michigan is a leading tourist state. It ranks high among the states in the amount of money collected from the sale of hunting licenses. Each year, about 22 million persons visit the state. Natural attractions, and resort and recreation areas, can be found in many parts of both the Upper and Lower peninsulas.

Natural Resources of Michigan include fertile soils, rich mineral deposits, widespread forests, and plentiful plant and animal life.

Soil. The Upper Peninsula has soils that vary from fertile loams to areas of poor soils and infertile sands. The northern section of the Lower Peninsula has sandy and loamy soils similar to those of the Upper Peninsula. A variety of soils covers former glacial lake beds around Saginaw Bay and along the shoreline of eastern Michigan. These glacial soils range from rich, dark-brown or black loams and gray sands, to infertile soils that are shallow and poorly drained. The state's richest soils are in the southern half of the Lower Peninsula. These are mostly gray-brown forest soils.

Minerals. Michigan's Upper Peninsula has vast iron ore and copper deposits. Great stores of iron ore lie in the Marquette Range of the central Upper Peninsula. The Menominee Range in the southern Upper Peninsula, and the Gogebic Range in the western corner, also have enormous iron ore deposits. These iron deposits extend into Wisconsin, and are part of one of the greatest known iron ore regions in the world. The Keweenaw Peninsula, which forms the northernmost tip of Michigan, has been called the state's *treasure chest.* It is one of the few sources of *native* (pure) copper found in the world.

The Lower Peninsula has great deposits of salt. These deposits are so vast that they could probably supply the whole world with salt for a million years. The northern and southern parts of the Lower Peninsula have rich petroleum deposits. Reserves of coal are also found in the Lower Peninsula. Limestone and shale occur throughout the state. Gypsum deposits lie under part of the Lower Peninsula. Almost every county in Michigan has deposits of sand and gravel. Natural gas is found chiefly in the Lower Peninsula.

Forests cover about 19 million acres (7.7 million hectares), or over half of Michigan. About 12 million acres (4.9 million hectares) are privately owned. The rest are in state and national forests in the Upper Peninsula, and in the northern part of the Lower Peninsula.

Much of Michigan's forest land is covered by such hardwood trees as aspens, beeches, birches, maples, and oaks. Softwoods cover most of the remaining forest land.

Production of Goods in Michigan

Total value of goods produced in 1977—$40,708,999,000

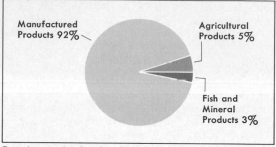

Manufactured Products 92%

Agricultural Products 5%

Fish and Mineral Products 3%

Percentages are based on farm income, value added by manufacture, and value of fish and mineral production. Fish products are less than 1 per cent.
Sources: U.S. government publications, 1978-1979.

Employment in Michigan

Total number of persons employed in 1978—3,630,600

	Number of Employees
Manufacturing	1,140,000
Wholesale & Retail Trade	712,500
Government	630,000
Community, Social, & Personal Services	598,500
Transportation & Public Utilities	150,800
Construction	144,600
Finance, Insurance, & Real Estate	144,600
Agriculture	96,000
Mining	13,600

Sources: *Employment and Earnings,* May 1979, U.S. Bureau of Labor Statistics; *Farm Labor,* February 1979, U.S. Department of Agriculture.

These include cedars, firs, hemlocks, pines, spruces, and other softwood trees. Michigan's state tree is the white pine. In order to keep a good supply of lumber in the state, Michigan foresters plant more trees each year than they cut down.

Plant Life. Bittersweet, clematis, grapes, moonseed, and several kinds of smilax grow wild in Michigan's thickest forests. Shrubs such as blackberry, currant, elder, gooseberry, raspberry, rose, and viburnum thrive in the more open forest areas. Ferns and mosses grow in the swamps, as do cranberries and lady's-slippers. Such flowers as the arbutus, mandrake, trillium, and violet bloom in early spring. Flowers that bloom later in the year include the daisy, iris, orange milkweed, rose, shooting star, and tiger lily. Other common flowers in the state include the aster, chicory, goldenrod, and sunflower.

Animal Life. Great numbers of fur and game animals make Michigan a paradise for hunters. Michigan probably has more deer than any other state except Texas. Other common fur and game animals in Michigan include badgers, black bears, bobcats, minks, muskrats, opossums, otters, rabbits, raccoons, red foxes, skunks, squirrels, and weasels. Hundreds of kinds of birds live in the state. The game birds most prized by hunters include ducks, grouse, and pheasants.

Many kinds of fish are found in Michigan's lakes, rivers, and streams. They include bass, crappie, perch, pike, and trout. Smelt runs occur each spring in streams that empty into parts of Lake Huron and Lake Michigan. Other fishes common in Michigan's waters include alewives, catfish, and chubs. Carp, lake herring, and whitefish are common in the Great Lakes.

Manufacturing accounts for 92 per cent of the value of goods produced in Michigan. Goods manufactured in the state have a *value added by manufacture* of about $37 billion a year. This figure represents the value created in products by Michigan's industries, not counting such manufacturing costs as materials, supplies, and fuels. Michigan ranks among the leading manufacturing states. Michigan's chief manufactured products are, in order of importance: (1) transportation equipment, (2) nonelectric machinery, (3) fabricated metal products, (4) primary metals, (5) food products, and (6) chemicals and related products.

Transportation Equipment has a value added of about $14 billion a year, or about one-third of the state's manufacturing income. Automobiles, buses, trucks, and other vehicles manufactured in Michigan may be seen in all parts of the world. The transportation equipment industries employ about a third of all the industrial workers in the state. Michigan's transportation industries rank high among the nation's users of rubber, plate glass, and upholstery leather.

Michigan is the leading manufacturer of automobiles among the states. Detroit is called the *Automobile Capital of the World* and the *Motor City*. Other important automobile-manufacturing cities in Michigan include Dearborn, Flint, Kalamazoo, Lansing, and Pontiac. Factories in Jackson and Muskegon produce airplane engines and parts.

Nonelectric Machinery has a value added of about $5 billion annually. Factories in Detroit account for about 58 per cent of this income. Michigan manufacturers produce large quantities of construction machines, engines, metalworking machines, office machines, refrigeration machinery, and turbines. Stoves and furnaces are manufactured in factories in Albion, Detroit, Dowagiac, and Holland.

Fabricated Metal Products have an annual value added of about $4½ billion. Products manufactured in Detroit account for about half this total. Flint and Grand Rapids are also important producers of fabricated metal products. These goods include cutlery, hand tools, hardware, and other products made from metals.

Primary Metals industries in Michigan turn out products that have a value added of about $3 billion yearly. Detroit accounts for more than half of this total. The primary metals industries smelt, refine, and roll metals. Michigan produces large quantities of

FARM, MINERAL, AND FOREST PRODUCTS

This map shows where the leading farm, mineral, and forest products are produced. The major urban areas (shown in red) are the important manufacturing centers.

A Copper Mine in White Pine contains some of Michigan's richest ore deposits. This area has supplied copper for thousands of years.

White Pine Copper Company

WORLD BOOK map

Automobile Workers install metal strips on cars as the vehicles move along an assembly line in a factory near Detroit. The Detroit area produces more automobiles than any other in the world.

foundry products. It ranks among the leading states in steel production. Detroit has the nation's largest forging plant.

Food Products rank high in the state, with a value added of about $2 billion yearly. Michigan is among the leading food processing states. Detroit is the state's largest processor of foods. Grand Rapids is also an important food processing center. Battle Creek, often called the *Cereal Center of the World*, produces more breakfast cereal than any other city in the world. Fremont has the largest baby foods plant in the United States. The state has important fruit and vegetable canneries and sugar refineries.

Chemicals and Related Products have a value added of about $1,989,000,000 yearly. The state's chief chemical plants are in Ludington, Marquette, Midland, Muskegon, and Wyandotte. Drug companies operate manufacturing plants in Ann Arbor, Detroit, and Kalamazoo.

Other Leading Industries. Industries that produce electric and electronic equipment, printed materials, and rubber and plastics products also rank among the leaders in Michigan. Other important industries in the state manufacture clothing; furniture and fixtures; scientific instruments; lumber and wood products; paper products; petroleum and coal products; stone, clay, and glass products; and textiles.

Michigan is among the leading states in the manufacture of sporting goods and athletic equipment. Muskegon has the nation's largest plant for making bowling

alley equipment. Alpena has the largest cement plant in the United States. Kalamazoo is the center of the state's paper manufacturing industry.

Agriculture. Farm products in Michigan have a yearly gross income of about $1¾ billion. Farmland covers about 30 per cent of the state's land area. Michigan's 63,000 farms average about 168 acres (68 hectares) in size.

Crops in Michigan have an annual value of about $983 million. Michigan stands among the nation's leaders in the production of many crops. The state's leading crops include apples, cherries, corn, dry beans, greenhouse and nursery products, potatoes, soybeans, sugar beets, and wheat.

The land along Lake Michigan in the Lower Peninsula is one of the most productive fruit-growing belts in North America. Michigan leads the nation in the production of cherries. It also ranks among the leaders in raising apples, blueberries, cantaloupes, grapes, peaches, pears, plums and prunes, and strawberries. Fruit tree blossoms attract many bees in spring, and honey is an important by-product of the fruit industry. Most of the grapes are grown in Berrien, St. Joseph, and Van Buren counties. Berrien County is the state's leading producer of fruit. Traverse City is famous for its cherries.

Much vegetable farming in Michigan takes place around Grand Rapids, Muskegon, and other industrial cities. Michigan is the leading producer of dry beans. Other important vegetables raised in the state include asparagus, carrots, celery, cucumbers, onions, potatoes, snap beans, sugar beets, sweet corn, and tomatoes. Most farmers in the state raise alfalfa, corn, and hay—usually as feed for livestock rather than as cash crops. Large quantities of celery are grown in Michigan's western counties.

Livestock and Livestock Products have an annual value of about $841 million. Milk, Michigan's leading farm product, earns about $452 million a year. Michigan ranks among the leading producers of milk. Cattle and calves rank second in importance among livestock and livestock products. Other such products include hogs and eggs. Most cattle, calves, and hogs are raised in the Lower Peninsula.

Dairying is also important throughout the Lower Peninsula. Zeeland is a center of baby chick hatcheries. Ottawa County has large turkey farms, and chicken, duck, geese, and turkey hatcheries.

Mining in Michigan has an annual value of about $1⅓ billion. Petroleum is Michigan's most valuable mineral. Petroleum production provides about $376 million yearly. The leading oil-producing counties are Calhoun, Grand Traverse, Hillsdale, Ingham, Kalkaska, Manis-

Workers Harvest Cherries in an orchard near Hartford. They use a machine that shakes the trunk of the tree and catches the falling cherries. Michigan leads the nation in the production of cherries.

tee, Otsego, and St. Clair. The state has about 3,770 oil-producing wells.

Iron ore ranks as Michigan's second most valuable mineral, with an annual value of about $315 million. In 1844, the earliest discoveries of iron ore deposits in the state were made near Ishpeming and Negaunee in the Upper Peninsula. Michigan was the leading producer of iron ore from about 1890 to 1900. Today, Minnesota mines more iron ore than Michigan does. But Michigan still supplies about 15 per cent of the nation's output. All of Michigan's iron mining takes place in the western Upper Peninsula—in Dickinson, Iron, and Marquette counties. Mining companies in the Upper Peninsula ship iron ore across the Great Lakes to steel mills in the eastern and midwestern United States.

The state's third most important mineral is natural gas. Natural gas production provides about $124 million yearly. The leading counties in the production of natural gas are Grand Traverse, Kalkaska, Manistee, and Otsego. Some gas fields are used to store gas piped in from Southwestern states.

Michigan is among the leaders in salt production. One of the world's largest salt mines is beneath the city of Detroit. Salt is also produced from natural brines in Gratiot County, and from artificial brines in Manistee, St. Clair, and Wayne counties. Most salts mined in Michigan are for industrial purposes, not as table salt. Michigan ranks second only to Arkansas among the states in the production of bromine. Michigan's bromine comes from the natural brines of the state's salt deposits. The state's drug and chemical industries also use some of the salt produced from Michigan brine wells.

Rogers City has the world's largest limestone quarry. Michigan is the leading producer of gypsum, peat, and magnesium compounds. The state is a major U.S. producer of iodine. It ranks among the leaders in the production of sand and gravel. Michigan is also a major producer of clay.

Indians were the first to mine copper in the Michigan region. They made tools and utensils from the copper of the Upper Peninsula. White settlers mined copper near Copper Harbor on Lake Superior, and later throughout the copper range of the Keweenaw Peninsula. Michigan led the United States in copper production from 1850 until 1887, when Montana became the leading U.S. producer. Production in Michigan gradually decreased during the early 1900's, when other states began to produce copper more cheaply than Michigan. A revival of copper mining in Michigan began in 1955 with the completion of the White Pines project near Ontonagon. Today, Michigan ranks among the leading copper-mining states.

Fishing Industry. Michigan has an annual fish catch valued at about $3¼ million. The most valuable fishes taken from the Great Lakes include catfish, chubs, lake herring, lake trout, whitefish, and yellow perch. Every spring, workers in the commercial fishing industry take smelts from the state's rivers and streams.

Electric Power. Michigan has about 150 generating plants. About 82 per cent of the state's power is produced by plants that use coal, oil, or gas. Nuclear power plants near Bridgman, Charlevoix, and South Haven produce 17 per cent of Michigan's power. Hydroelectric plants provide about 1 per cent.

Transportation. Indians and early pioneers in Michigan traveled in canoes along the waterways. The first roads followed Indian trails. The first highway in Michigan was built in the 1820's. It ran from Detroit across the Maumee River in what is now Ohio. The Erie and Kalamazoo Railroad was completed in 1836. Horses pulled the railroad's first trains. In 1837, the Erie and Kalamazoo started to operate what was probably the first steam locomotive west of the Allegheny Mountains. By the mid-1800's, stagecoach routes connected Detroit with Chicago. The state highway department was established in 1905. In 1908, Michigan became the first state to build a concrete highway—a stretch 1 mile (1.6 kilometers) long in Detroit. In 1957, the Mackinac Bridge was completed across the Straits of Mackinac. This was the first bridge to connect the Upper and Lower peninsulas. The International Bridge, across the St. Marys River at Sault Ste. Marie, was completed in 1962. It links Michigan with Ontario. This 2-mile (3-kilometer) bridge replaced ferry boats that once carried people across the river. Other links between Michigan and Ontario include a Detroit to Windsor bridge, a Detroit to Windsor tunnel, and a Port Huron to Sarnia bridge.

Today, Michigan has about 120,000 miles (193,000 kilometers) of roads, about 85 per cent of which are surfaced. Railroads operate on about 6,000 miles (9,700 kilometers) of track in the state. About 25 rail lines in Michigan provide freight service. Railroad passenger trains serve 10 Michigan cities, including Ann Arbor, Detroit, Flint, and Lansing. The state has about 420 airports.

Ships from Michigan ports carry huge cargoes of minerals and manufactured goods across the Great Lakes and through the Great Lakes-St. Lawrence Seaway system to other countries. The Soo Canals rank among the busiest ship canals in the Western Hemisphere, even though ice closes the canals from December to April. The canals handle about 90 million short tons (82 million metric tons) of cargo each year. Detroit, the state's largest port, handles about 25 million short tons (23 million metric tons) yearly. Other major ports are Calcite (near Rogers City), Escanaba, Grand Haven, Muskegon, Presque Isle, Saginaw, and Stoneport. Ferries from Frankfort and Ludington carry railroad and auto passengers across Lake Michigan to ports in the Upper Peninsula and Wisconsin.

Communication. Michigan's first regularly published newspaper, the *Detroit Gazette*, was established in 1817. Radio station WWJ in Detroit began broadcasting in 1920. WWJ and Pittsburgh's KDKA were the nation's first regular commercial radio stations. Michigan's first television station, WWJ-TV, began operating in Detroit in 1947.

Michigan has about 55 daily newspapers. Daily newspapers with the largest circulations include the *Detroit Free Press*, the *Detroit News*, the *Flint Journal*, and the *Grand Rapids Press*. Michigan publishers produce about 260 weekly and semiweekly newspapers, several foreign-language papers, and about 190 periodicals. The state has about 30 television stations and about 285 radio stations.

Indian Days. About 15,000 Indians lived in the Michigan region when white men first arrived. Most of the tribes belonged to the Algonkian language group. They included the Chippewa and Menominee tribes in the Upper Peninsula, and the Miami, Ottawa, and Potawatomi tribes in the Lower Peninsula. The Wyandot, who settled around what is now Detroit, belonged to the Iroquois language group. Only about 3,000 Indians lived in the forests of the Upper Peninsula.

French Exploration and Settlement. Étienne Brulé of France explored the Upper Peninsula around 1620. He was probably the first white man to visit the Michigan region. Brulé was sent to Michigan from Quebec by Governor Samuel de Champlain of New France (Canada). In 1634, Champlain sent another explorer, Jean Nicolet, to the region to search for a route to the Pacific Ocean. Nicolet sailed through the Straits of Mackinac and explored parts of the Upper Peninsula. In 1660, Father René Ménard, a Jesuit missionary, established a mission at Keweenaw Bay. In 1668, Father Jacques Marquette founded Michigan's first permanent settlement, at Sault Ste. Marie.

During the late 1600's, Father Marquette; Louis Joliet; Robert Cavelier, Sieur de la Salle; and other Frenchmen explored much of the region. They mapped many of the lakes and rivers. By 1700, the French had built forts, missions, and trading posts at several places in both the Upper and Lower peninsulas. In 1701, Antoine de la Mothe Cadillac founded Fort Pontchartrain, which grew into the city of Detroit.

The Michigan region made little progress under the French. Only a few settlers established farms in the region, mostly along the Detroit River. The main French interests were to convert the Indians to Christianity and to develop a profitable fur trade. They also hoped to use the region as a passage to the west.

British Control. During the late 1600's and the 1700's, France and Great Britain struggled to gain control of North America. British and French settlers fought a series of wars called the French and Indian Wars. The French were defeated in 1763. Britain won most of the French holdings in North America, including the Michigan region. See FRENCH AND INDIAN WARS.

In 1763, Indians massacred the British at Fort Michilimackinac in Mackinaw City. Indians also attacked a number of other forts, killing many of the settlers. Detroit stood under Indian attack for more than five months, but the warriors were finally turned away. In 1774, the British made Michigan a part of the province of Quebec. The British were more interested in fur trading than in settling the region.

During the Revolutionary War (1775-1783), the British sent raiding parties of Indians and whites from Detroit to attack American settlements. Spain and Britain were also at war during the American Revolution. In 1781, Spanish forces captured Fort St. Joseph in Niles, and held it for one day. The Revolutionary War ended in 1783, and the Michigan region came under the control of the United States. The British wanted to hold on to the valuable fur trade as long as possible. They did not surrender Detroit or Fort Mackinac to the United States until 1796.

Iron Ore was discovered at Negaunee in 1844. Michigan's first iron mining began there soon after. Remains of ancient Indian copper mines have been discovered on Isle Royale.

Negaunee •

Father Marquette

Territorial Period. In 1787, the Michigan region became part of the Northwest Territory—the first territory established by the United States government. In 1800, Congress created the Indiana Territory, which included part of Michigan. The Indiana Territory obtained the entire Michigan region in 1803. In 1805, Congress

——— **IMPORTANT DATES IN MICHIGAN** ———

1620? Étienne Brulé, a French explorer, visited what is now Michigan.

1668 Father Jacques Marquette founded Michigan's first permanent settlement at Sault Ste. Marie.

1701 Antoine Cadillac founded what is now Detroit.

1763 The British took possession of Michigan.

1783 The United States gained Michigan from the British after the Revolutionary War.

1787 Congress made Michigan part of the Northwest Territory.

1800 Michigan became part of the Indiana Territory.

1805 Congress created the Territory of Michigan, including the entire Lower Peninsula and the eastern Upper Peninsula.

1837 Michigan became the 26th state on January 26. Congress gave Michigan the entire Upper Peninsula.

1845 The state's iron mining industry began at Negaunee.

1854 The Republican Party was formally named at Jackson.

1855 The Soo Canal was completed.

1899 Ransom E. Olds established Michigan's first automobile factory in Detroit.

1914 The Ford Motor Company established a minimum daily wage of $5.

1935 Michigan workers formed the United Automobile Workers union.

1942-1945 Michigan's entire automobile industry converted to war production during World War II.

1957 The Straits of Mackinac Bridge was opened to traffic between Mackinaw City and St. Ignace.

1964 Michigan's new Constitution went into effect.

1967 Michigan's legislature adopted a state income tax.

1968 Michigan voters approved $435 million in bond issues to expand recreational areas and to fight water pollution.

HISTORIC MICHIGAN

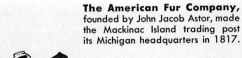

Sault Ste. Marie •

The Soo Canals at Sault Sainte Marie rank among the busiest ship canals in the Western Hemisphere. The first canal on the Michigan side was completed in 1855. Father Marquette founded Michigan's first permanent settlement there in 1668.

• Mackinac Island

The American Fur Company, founded by John Jacob Astor, made the Mackinac Island trading post its Michigan headquarters in 1817.

The Lumberman's Memorial, in Iosco County, honors Michigan's early lumbermen, who helped develop the Middle West. From 1870 to 1890, Michigan led the states in lumbering.

Thomas Alva Edison, the famous inventor, built his first electric battery at Fort Gratiot (Port Huron) in 1861.

The Republican Party formally adopted its name at Jackson in 1854. The party began as a series of antislavery meetings throughout the North earlier that year.

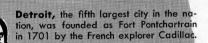

Detroit, the fifth largest city in the nation, was founded as Fort Pontchartrain in 1701 by the French explorer Cadillac.

Port Huron •

★ LANSING

• Detroit

Michigan's First Railroad, the Erie and Kalamazoo, was completed in 1836. The 35-mile (56-kilometer) line linked Adrian, Mich., with Toledo, Ohio.

• Jackson

• Adrian

Ford 1896

Henry Ford built his first workable automobile at Detroit in 1896. Three years later, Ransom E. Olds established Michigan's first automobile factory at Detroit.

Oldsmobile 1899

established the Territory of Michigan. It included the Lower Peninsula and eastern Upper Peninsula.

During the War of 1812, the British captured Detroit and Fort Mackinac. American forces regained Detroit in 1813. The British returned Fort Mackinac to the United States in 1814, after the war ended.

The Erie Canal was completed in 1825. It linked the Great Lakes with the Atlantic Ocean, and provided a transportation route between the eastern states and the western territories. Many settlers came to Michigan, especially from New York and New England.

In 1835, a convention drew up a state constitution. The people *ratified* (approved) the Constitution on Oct. 5, 1835, and elected 23-year-old Stevens T. Mason as their first state governor. But Congress delayed admitting Michigan to the Union because of a dispute between Michigan and Ohio. The dispute involved a strip of land near Toledo. Congress settled the question in 1836 by giving the 520-square-mile (1,347-square-kilometer) "Toledo Strip" to Ohio, and the entire Upper Peninsula to Michigan.

Progress as a State. Michigan became the 26th state of the Union on Jan. 26, 1837. The western Upper Peninsula soon proved to be a source of many valuable minerals. In 1842, the state obtained Isle Royale and the Keweenaw Peninsula in a treaty with the Indians. Iron-ore mining began near Negaunee in 1845. Large numbers of miners and prospectors soon came to the Upper Peninsula. By the late 1840's, mining was prospering in the state. But the miners needed some way to ship the ore from western Michigan to the iron and steel centers along the Great Lakes. This need was one of the chief reasons for the construction of the Soo Canal, which was completed in 1855 (see SOO CANALS).

The Republican Party was named in 1854 in Jackson. Delegates to a Michigan state convention met there on July 6, 1854. They were the first to formally adopt the name *Republican* (see REPUBLICAN PARTY).

Michigan soldiers fought in the Union army during the Civil War (1861-1865). General George A. Custer, a famous Union officer, led the Michigan cavalry. On May 10, 1865, the Fourth Michigan Cavalry captured Jefferson Davis, President of the Confederacy, near Irwinville, Ga.

After the Civil War, lumbering became an important industry in Michigan. The construction of sawmills aided the rapid development of manufacturing in the state. Michigan lumber was used in building many cities, towns, and farms of the Midwest. Michigan hardwood lumber helped develop the furniture industry, which started in Grand Rapids in the 1830's. By 1870, Michigan led the nation in lumber production.

Between 1870 and 1900, Michigan's population more than doubled. Agriculture developed as settlers poured into Michigan and cleared the land. Michigan took the lead among the states in the support of public education. Railroads and steamship lines promoted Michigan resorts, and the state's tourist industry began to develop.

The Early 1900's brought further industrial expansion. In 1899, Ransom E. Olds founded the Olds Motor Works in Detroit. By 1901, the factory was mass-producing Oldsmobiles. Henry Ford organized the Ford Motor Company in 1903. Detroit soon became the center of the nation's automobile industry. This new industry increased Michigan's population and its prosperity.

In 1914, Henry Ford announced that the Ford Motor Company would share its profits with its workers. Ford also established a minimum wage of $5 a day. At that time, most unskilled workers earned only $1 a day, and skilled workers earned $2.50.

After the United States entered World War I in 1917, Michigan factories built trucks, armored vehicles, airplane engines, and other military products. The improvement of Michigan's highways during the 1920's contributed to the growth of the automobile industry and related businesses. By the late 1920's, Michigan's tourist industry had become a leading source of income in the state.

Depression and Recovery. Michigan was hit hard by the Great Depression of the 1930's. Hundreds of thousands of workers lost their jobs. Federal measures to end the depression had important effects in Michigan. The state had more than a hundred Civilian Con-

Mass Production of Automobiles was begun by Oldsmobile in 1901. These workers pose with the parts for assembling the engines. The company made 425 cars in 1901. Today, Oldsmobile produces hundreds of thousands of automobiles each year.

Oldsmobile Div., General Motors

servation Corps (CCC) camps. In these camps, the government employed young men to work on conservation projects. The Works Progress Administration (WPA) employed about 500,000 persons in Michigan to work on public works projects. Before and during the depression, copper mining in other states became less costly than in Michigan. It cost more to mine copper in Michigan because the ore lies so deep in the earth. Michigan's copper mining decreased, and more unemployment resulted in the Upper Peninsula.

In 1935, workers in the automobile industry organized the United Automobile Workers union. In December, 1936, the union went on strike at the Fisher Body and Chevrolet plants in Flint. The strikers demanded a *closed shop* (an industry in which only union members can be hired). The union also called for *collective bargaining* (discussion of differences between company and union representatives). The Fisher and Chevrolet plant officials rejected the union's demands. The strikers then locked themselves inside the plants, and fought off police attempts to remove them. The union received collective bargaining rights on Feb. 11, 1937, and the strike ended. By 1941, the United Automobile Workers represented the workers of all the large automobile companies, and had won its chief demands. These included higher pay and recognition of the union as representative of the workers.

The Mid-1900's. During World War II (1939-1945), Michigan's entire automobile industry switched to manufacturing war materials. The production of airplanes, ships, tanks, and other military equipment brought prosperity back to the state.

Michigan's prosperity continued after the war. Millions of Americans bought new cars and other Michigan products. The state's mining industry began to recover. In 1955, a new copper mine opened near Ontonagon. Iron-mining companies in the Upper Peninsula developed new methods of recovering iron from nonmagnetic ore and new ways of processing ore for shipment to steel plants. In 1957, the Mackinac Bridge was completed, linking the Upper and Lower peninsulas.

The state faced financial problems during the late 1950's and early 1960's. A nationwide recession caused a slump in Michigan automobile sales and production. As a result, other business activities in the state also slowed down. Michigan's financial picture brightened as the nation began to prosper again during the 1960's, and purchases of automobiles and other Michigan products increased.

In 1961, Michigan voters authorized a constitutional convention to revise the outdated state constitution, adopted in 1908. The convention submitted a new constitution to the voters in 1962. They approved the constitution in 1963, and it went into effect in 1964. Also in 1964, both houses of the state legislature were *reapportioned* (redivided) to provide more equal representation based on population.

George W. Romney, a Michigan businessman, served as the state's governor from 1963 to 1969. Romney, a Republican, had played a leading role in the constitutional convention. As governor, he fought for passage of the new constitution. Romney's administration modernized the state tax structure. New taxes, including a state income tax adopted in 1967, enabled Michigan to increase spending for education, mental health facilities,

welfare programs, and other government services. From 1969 to 1973, Romney served as secretary of housing and urban development under President Richard M. Nixon.

In July, 1967, an eight-day riot broke out in a predominantly black section of Detroit. Rioters burned buildings and looted stores. Forty-three persons were killed, and about $45 million worth of property was damaged or destroyed.

Michigan Today faces increasing costs of education, mental health services, welfare programs, pollution control, and other government services. In 1972, Michigan established a state lottery to help raise money for these costs.

The manufacture of transportation equipment still provides the greatest income to the state, and Michigan continues to lead the nation in automobile production. But a nationwide recession contributed to another slump in the automobile industry during the mid-1970's, and unemployment in Michigan rose sharp-

--- **THE GOVERNORS OF MICHIGAN** ---

	Party	Term
Stevens T. Mason	Democratic	1837-1840
William Woodbridge	Whig	1840-1841
James W. Gordon	Whig	1841-1842
John S. Barry	Democratic	1842-1845
Alpheus Felch	Democratic	1846-1847
William L. Greenly	Democratic	1847
Epaphroditus Ransom	Democratic	1848-1849
John S. Barry	Democratic	1850
Robert McClelland	Democratic	1851-1853
Andrew Parsons	Democratic	1853-1854
Kinsley S. Bingham	Republican	1855-1858
Moses Wisner	Republican	1859-1860
Austin Blair	Republican	1861-1864
Henry H. Crapo	Republican	1865-1868
Henry P. Baldwin	Republican	1869-1872
John J. Bagley	Republican	1873-1876
Charles M. Croswell	Republican	1877-1880
David H. Jerome	Republican	1881-1882
Josiah W. Begole	Democratic and Greenback	1883-1884
Russell A. Alger	Republican	1885-1886
Cyrus G. Luce	Republican	1887-1890
Edwin B. Winans	Democratic	1891-1892
John T. Rich	Republican	1893-1896
Hazen S. Pingree	Republican	1897-1900
Aaron T. Bliss	Republican	1901-1904
Fred M. Warner	Republican	1905-1910
Chase S. Osborn	Republican	1911-1912
Woodbridge N. Ferris	Democratic	1913-1916
Albert E. Sleeper	Republican	1917-1920
Alexander J. Groesbeck	Republican	1921-1926
Fred W. Green	Republican	1927-1930
Wilber M. Brucker	Republican	1931-1932
William A. Comstock	Democratic	1933-1934
Frank D. Fitzgerald	Republican	1935-1936
Frank Murphy	Democratic	1937-1938
Frank D. Fitzgerald	Republican	1939
Luren D. Dickinson	Republican	1939-1940
Murray D. Van Wagoner	Democratic	1941-1942
Harry F. Kelly	Republican	1943-1946
Kim Sigler	Republican	1947-1948
G. Mennen Williams	Democratic	1949-1960
John B. Swainson	Democratic	1961-1962
George W. Romney	Republican	1963-1969
William G. Milliken	Republican	1969-

ly. Because of the state's dependence on the automobile industry, Michigan leaders are working to attract new industries, especially to the Upper Peninsula. They also hope to find new markets for Michigan products, both in the United States and in other countries.

In 1973, President Richard M. Nixon appointed Congressman Gerald R. Ford of Michigan to succeed Vice-President Spiro T. Agnew, who had resigned. Ford became the 38th President in 1974, when Nixon resigned because of his involvement in the Watergate political scandal.   WILLARD M. J. BAIRD and SIDNEY GLAZER

MICHIGAN/Study Aids

Related Articles in WORLD BOOK include:

BIOGRAPHIES

Cadillac, Antoine de la M.	Guest, Edgar A.
Cass, Lewis	Kellogg, W. K.
Chandler, Zachariah	Lindbergh, Charles A.
Chrysler, Walter P.	Marquette, Jacques
Coughlin, Charles E.	Milles, Carl W. E.
Couzens, James	Murphy, Frank
Dodge (family)	Olds, Ransom E.
Ford (family)	Pontiac
Ford, Gerald R.	Romney, George W.
Griffin, Robert P.	Vandenberg, Arthur H.

CITIES

Ann Arbor	Highland Park	Lincoln Park
Battle Creek	Holland	Muskegon
Dearborn	Jackson	Pontiac
Detroit	Kalamazoo	Saginaw
Flint	Lansing	Warren
Grand Rapids		

PHYSICAL FEATURES

Detroit River	Lake Saint Clair
Great Lakes	Lake Superior
Isle Royale National Park	Mackinac, Straits of
Lake Erie	Mackinac Island
Lake Huron	Manitoulin Islands
Lake Michigan	Saint Marys River

PRODUCTS AND INDUSTRY

For Michigan's rank among the states in production, see the following articles:

Apple	Cherry	Plum
Automobile	Gypsum	Salt
Bean	Manufacturing	Tomato
Cattle		

OTHER RELATED ARTICLES

Greenfield Village	Petoskey Stone
Midwestern States	Soo Canals
National Music Camp	War of 1812
Northwest Ordinance	

Outline

I. Government
   A. Constitution
   B. Executive
   C. Legislature
   D. Courts
   E. Local Government
   F. Taxation
   G. Politics
II. People

III. Education
   A. Schools
   B. Libraries
   C. Museums
IV. A Visitor's Guide
   A. Places to Visit
   B. Annual Events
V. The Land
   A. Land Regions
   B. Shoreline
   C. Islands
   D. Rivers, Waterfalls, and Lakes
VI. Climate
VII. Economy
   A. Natural Resources
   B. Manufacturing
   C. Agriculture
   D. Mining
   E. Fishing Industry
   F. Electric Power
   G. Transportation
   H. Communication
VIII. History

Questions

Why does Michigan have so many cloudy days?

Why did the Michigan region not prosper under French control?

Why did copper production in Michigan decrease in the early 1900's?

How did Michigan's lumber industry aid the growth of the state?

What Michigan canals rank among the busiest ship canals in the Western Hemisphere?

What territories of the United States did Michigan belong to before becoming a state?

What important event brought many settlers to Michigan in the 1820's?

How did Michigan obtain the Upper Peninsula?

What are two of the chief provisions of the Michigan Constitution adopted in 1963?

What city in Michigan is often called the *Cereal Center of the World*?

Books for Young Readers

BAILEY, BERNADINE. *Picture Book of Michigan.* Rev. ed. Whitman, 1967.

CARPENTER, ALLAN. *Michigan.* Childrens Press, 1964.

HOWARD, ELIZABETH. *Wilderness Venture.* Morrow, 1973. Fiction.

OLDENBURG, E. WILLIAM. *Potawatomi Indian Summer.* Eerdmans, 1975. Fiction.

ROBERTSON, KEITH. *In Search of a Sandhill Crane.* Viking, 1973. Fiction.

STONE, NANCY. *Whistle Up the Bay.* Eerdmans, 1966. Fiction. *The Wooden River.* 1973. Fiction.

Books for Older Readers

ANGELO, FRANK. *Yesterday's Michigan.* Seemann, 1976.

BALD, FREDERICK CLEVER. *Michigan in Four Centuries.* Rev. ed. Harper, 1961.

CARR, ROBERT W. *Government of Michigan under the 1964 Constitution.* Rev. ed. Univ. of Michigan Press, 1967.

CATTON, BRUCE. *Michigan: A Bicentennial History.* Norton, 1976.

DORR, JOHN A., and ESCHMAN, D. F. *Geology of Michigan.* Univ. of Michigan Press, 1970.

DUNBAR, WILLIS F. *Michigan: A History of the Wolverine State.* Eerdmans, 1965.

FITTING, JAMES E. *The Archaeology of Michigan: A Guide to the Prehistory of the Great Lakes Region.* 2nd ed. Cranbrook Institute, 1975.

KINIETZ, W. VERNON. *The Indians of the Western Great Lakes, 1615-1760.* Univ. of Michigan Press, 1965.

MAY, GEORGE S. *Pictorial History of Michigan.* 2 vols. Eerdmans, 1967-69.

MAY, GEORGE S., and BRINKS, H. J., eds. *A Michigan Reader: 11,000 B.C. to A.D. 1865.* Eerdmans, 1974.

WARNER, ROBERT M., and VANDER HILL, C. W., eds. *A Michigan Reader: 1865 to the Present.* Eerdmans, 1974.

MICHIGAN, LAKE. See LAKE MICHIGAN.

University of Michigan

The University of Michigan's Main Campus is in Ann Arbor The Harlan Hatcher General Library, *above*, is the central library of the Ann Arbor campus.

MICHIGAN, UNIVERSITY OF, is a state-supported coeducational institution. It was founded in Detroit in 1817, and its main campus has been in Ann Arbor since 1837. The university also has campuses in Dearborn and Flint. In 1837, the school became the first university to be controlled by regents elected by the voters.

The Ann Arbor campus has colleges of architecture and urban planning, art, business administration, dentistry, education, engineering, law, liberal arts, library science, medicine, music, natural resources, nursing, pharmacy, public health, social work, and graduate studies. The Dearborn and Flint campuses offer business administration, education, engineering, and liberal arts and science courses.

The university libraries contain nearly 5 million volumes. The William L. Clements Library of American History is noted for its collection of original documents relating to the Revolutionary War. The university also maintains several museums and research institutes. Its Phoenix Project undertakes research on peacetime uses of nuclear energy. For enrollment, see UNIVERSITIES AND COLLEGES (table).

Critically reviewed by the UNIVERSITY OF MICHIGAN

MICHIGAN STATE UNIVERSITY is a state-supported coeducational school in East Lansing, Mich. It ranks as one of the largest single-campus institutions of higher education in the United States.

Michigan State University has colleges of agriculture and natural resources, arts and letters, business, communication arts, education, engineering, human ecology, human medicine, natural science, osteopathic medicine, social science, urban development, and vet-

erinary medicine. It also has three liberal arts colleges —Lyman Briggs, James Madison, and Justin Morrill colleges—and a graduate school. Michigan State grants bachelor's, master's, and doctor's degrees.

The school was founded in 1855 as Michigan State College. It served as a model for the land-grant colleges and universities founded later in the United States. The university was the first state school to offer courses in agriculture for credit. The school took its present name in 1955. For enrollment, see UNIVERSITIES AND COLLEGES (table). CLIFTON R. WHARTON, JR.

MICHIGAN TECHNOLOGICAL UNIVERSITY is a state-supported coeducational school in Houghton, Mich. It grants bachelor's degrees in nine branches of engineering and in business administration, chemistry, forestry, geology, geophysics, mathematics, medical technology, and physics. It offers graduate degrees in civil, chemical, electrical, geological, mechanical, metallurgical, mining, and nuclear engineering, and in chemistry, engineering, mechanics, geology, geophysics, and physics. The university participates in the Argonne National Laboratory atomic energy program. The school was chartered in 1885. For enrollment, see UNIVERSITIES AND COLLEGES (table). THEODORE PEARCE

MICHOACÁN, MEE *choh ah* KAHN, is one of the most beautiful states in Mexico. The 23,114-square-mile (59,865-square-kilometer) state borders the Pacific Ocean in the southwest part of the country. For location, see MEXICO (political map). Mountainous Michoacán has won fame for its picturesque lakes such as Pátzcuaro, and for Parícutin and other volcanoes. Morelia is Michoacán's capital. The state has a population of 2,324,226. CHARLES C. CUMBERLAND

See also PARÍCUTIN; TARASCAN INDIANS; MORELIA.

MICKEY MOUSE. See DISNEY, WALT (with picture).

MICMAC INDIANS are a tribe of eastern Canada. They belong to the Algonkian language family. About 12,000 Micmac live on reservations in the provinces of New Brunswick, Nova Scotia, Prince Edward Island, and Quebec.

Large numbers of Micmac, especially young people, work in various cities but maintain close ties with family members on the reservation. Many of these young Indians share their wages with their families.

The Micmac once fished and gathered clams, mussels, and bird eggs from spring to fall. They hunted bears, moose, and small game during the winter. These Indians used birchbark canoes for summer travel, and wooden toboggans and snowshoes in winter. They lived in tepees that they covered with animal skins or birchbark. The Micmac made clothing from pelts and carved utensils from bark. The Micmac had many legends about a super being called *Glooscap*, who supposedly shaped much of their landscape.

A few related Micmac families usually camped together in bands. Many bands, such as the Bear River band and the Red Bank band, were named after the area where they once lived. A chief called a *sagamore* led each band. The sagamore provided his followers with canoes, hunting dogs, and weapons in exchange for fish, game, and pelts.

In the early 1500's, the Micmac traded with French, Portuguese, and Spanish fishermen who visited Canada yearly. When Jacques Cartier, a French explorer, came to Canada in 1534, the Indians traded their furs for beads and knives. The Micmac became allies of the French in an unsuccessful attempt to keep the British out of Canada.

During the early 1700's, the British took control of most of the land occupied by the Micmac. The Indians retreated to remote sections of their land as the British founded settlements along the Atlantic coast. The Micmac came under the authority of the Canadian government in 1867. JEANNE GUILLEMIN

See also PRINCE EDWARD ISLAND.

MICROBE. See MICROBIOLOGY; AIR (Particles).

MICROBIOLOGY is the study of microscopic organisms. These organisms include algae, bacteria, molds, protozoans, viruses, and yeasts. They are sometimes called *microbes*. Most cannot be seen without a microscope.

Many biologists specialize in the study of certain kinds of microorganisms. For example, *bacteriologists* work with bacteria, *mycologists* are concerned with fungi, and *virologists* study viruses.

Microorganisms. Nearly all microorganisms measure less than $\frac{4}{1000}$ inch (0.1 millimeter) across. Many microorganisms must be studied with microscopes that magnify objects at least 1,000 times. Most viruses are so tiny that they can be seen only with electron microscopes that magnify many thousands of times.

Viruses are called *acellular* microorganisms because they do not have true cell structures. All other microorganisms are *cellular*. They have cell membranes, cytoplasm, and a nuclear body. Bacteria are the smallest single-celled organisms. The smallest bacteria may be as small as $\frac{4}{10}$ of a *micron* (a micron is $\frac{1}{25,400}$ inch, or .001 millimeter). About 10,000 small viruses could be packed into a cell the size of one of these bacteria. Over a billion such cells could be packed into one of the largest *microbial* cells—the cells of a certain algae.

Fields of Microbiology. Many microbiologists study the relationships between microbes and man, animals, and plants. Medical microbiologists investigate the role of microorganisms in human and animal diseases and seek ways to prevent and cure these diseases. Dental microbiologists are concerned with the microorganisms found in the mouth, especially their role in tooth decay and other oral diseases. Agricultural microbiologists study plant diseases, the role of microorganisms in soil fertility, and spoilage of farm products by microorganisms. Industrial microbiologists use microorganisms to produce such products as alcoholic beverages, amino acids, antibiotics, citric acid, and vitamin C. General microbiologists study the basic features of microorganisms, including ecology, genetics, metabolism, physiology, and structure.

Microorganisms also play an important part in sewage treatment and pollution control. A rapidly growing new branch of microbiology is marine microbiology, which focuses on the vast number of microorganisms in the oceans. Some microorganisms are being grown and harvested experimentally for use as food. ROBERT E. MARQUIS

Related Articles in WORLD BOOK include:

Algae	Bacteriology	Mycology	Virus
Bacteria	Mold	Protozoan	Yeast

MICROBIOLOGY, INSTITUTE OF, is a part of Rutgers, The State University in New Brunswick, N.J. Scientists at the institute study the structure and function of bacteria, fungi, yeasts, protozoa, viruses, and other microorganisms. They also study the antibiotics, vitamins, and enzymes produced by microorganisms. The institute was founded in 1954 with royalties received from manufacturers of streptomycin. This antibiotic was first isolated by Selman A. Waksman and his associates at the New Jersey Agricultural Experiment Station in 1943. See also MICROBIOLOGY. SELMAN A. WAKSMAN

MICROCLINE. See FELDSPAR.

MICROCRYSTALLINE WAX is widely used in making special types of paper for packaging. Paper treated with microcrystalline waxes is strong enough to replace tin and steel in many types of containers. These waxes are extracted from the residual oils driven off during the process of refining petroleum (see PETROLEUM [Refining Petroleum]). Microcrystalline waxes were first used during the 1920's.

A popular wrapping material is made from a paper sheet coated with microcrystalline wax. This sheet is highly resistant to grease. It is pliable and self-sealing. Laminated paper—made of several sheets pressed together—and greaseproof paper, both made with microcrystalline waxes, have many uses in industry.

Microcrystalline waxes are used in rust compounds, in condenser coils for electrical systems, and for lining tank cars and concrete tanks used in shipping and storing wine and vinegar. They are also used in waterproofing rope, twine, and textiles. These waxes are flexible and adhesive, and resist moisture and chemical change. They come from a heavier part of petroleum than do the paraffin waxes. WILLIAM B. HARPER

MICROELECTRONICS. See ELECTRONICS (The Beginnings of Microelectronics; illustration: Devices Used in Microelectronics).

MICROENCAPSULATION is the process of enclosing a substance in a capsule so that the substance can be easily released. Such capsules are made of gelatin, plastic, starch, or other materials. Solids, liquids, and gases can be encapsulated.

Microencapsulation is used in making carbonless duplicator paper. This paper has a top sheet—coated on the underside with millions of capsules—and a bottom sheet. The capsules release a colorless dye when broken by the pressure of writing or typing. The dye reacts with a thin layer of white clay on the surface of the lower sheet, forming ink.

Microencapsulation is also used in making *timed-release* medicines. Such medicines are slowly released in the body so that their effect is extended for as long as 12 hours. KENNETH SCHUG

MICROFARAD. See FARAD.

MICROFILM is a small photographic film on which reduced images of printed and other material are photographed. Because the images are reduced, microfilm can store a large amount of material in a small space. For example, the contents of an entire book can be photographed, page-by-page, on a short strip of microfilm 35 millimeters (about $1\frac{3}{8}$ inches) wide. The strip can then be wound into a small roll and stored in a fraction of the space occupied by the book.

The microfilm copy of the book can be read easily by putting it through a projection machine to enlarge the image. Some projection machines will make an enlarged paper copy of the image on the film. This copy may be made the same size as the original page of the book. Most microfilm is black and white because color is more expensive and usually not necessary.

A microfilm strip which has been cut into short pieces and placed in a plastic card is called a *microfiche*. The microfiche measures about 4 by 6 inches (10 by 15 centimeters). Two or three of these cards can hold a book's contents.

Individual frames cut from a strip of microfilm can be inserted in punched cards used by high-speed business machines. Information on microfilm can then be found quickly by running the cards through a sorting machine.

Microfilm has many industrial, scientific, and educational uses. Two or three rolls can store four drawers of business records. A few small boxes of microfiche cards can store enough books to make a small library. Newspapers, libraries, and government offices use microfilm extensively. Copies of rare books and manuscripts are made for schools and libraries for much less than it would cost to print them. Architects and engineers can store large, detailed drawings on microfilm.

The process of making microfilm copies is called *microphotography*. This process has been known since the earliest days of photography. It became a large industry

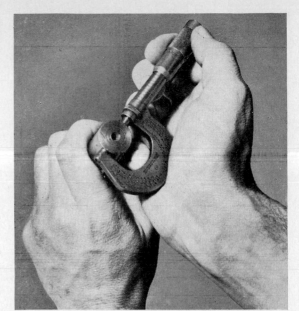

The Micrometer Caliper is used by mechanics to measure exceedingly small distances in doing precise work.

after the Library of Congress began to microfilm books about 1928. BEAUMONT NEWHALL

See also FILMSTRIP.

MICROMETEOROID. See SPACE TRAVEL (Protection Against the Dangers of Space).

MICROMETER, *my KRAHM uh tur,* is an instrument for measuring small dimensions. The simplest micrometer is a glass disk marked with squares. Each square measures $\frac{1}{100}$ inch (0.25 millimeter) along its sides. The size of the object is determined by the number of squares it covers. Surveyor's instruments have micrometers which measure distances by a screw with a very fine thread. The head of the screw rests against the scale. The surveyor takes measurements by turning the screw to raise it up and down along the scale.

Scientists use one kind of micrometer to measure the distances of stars on photographic plates. Measuring microscopes often have micrometers attached. One type of measuring instrument called a *micrometer caliper* has a micrometer screw attached. It can be closed on the object by turning the screw, which is scaled to show the measurements of how far it is turned. The micrometer caliper can measure accurately to $\frac{1}{10,000}$ inch or 0.0025 millimeter.

People sometimes use the term micrometer for the *micron*, one-millionth of a meter. HERMAN J. SHEA

See also CALIPER.

MICRON is a unit of measure in the metric system. It is a small measure, and comes from the Greek word *mikros*, meaning *small*. A micron is equal to $\frac{1}{1,000}$ of a millimeter, and is therefore $\frac{1}{1,000,000}$ of a meter, or .000039 inch. In chemistry, a micron is a particle that measures between .01 and .0001 millimeter in diameter. OLIVER J. LEE

MICRONESIA. See PACIFIC ISLANDS; RACES, HUMAN (table: Geographical Races).

MICROORGANISM. See MICROBIOLOGY; ANTIBIOTIC; FOOD PRESERVATION.

A Microfiche, *above,* can store many pages of information as tiny images on a plastic card. The cards are made by a photographic process, as are microfilms. A reading projector, *below,* enlarges the images on a viewing screen or copies them on paper.

MICROPHONE

MICROPHONE is a device that changes sound into electric energy. This energy instantly travels over wires or through the air to a loudspeaker or some other instrument that changes it back into sound. Microphones, often called "mikes," are also used in recording sound.

The first microphone was the telephone transmitter, which the American inventor Alexander Graham Bell developed in 1876. Today, microphones are used in public-address systems, in broadcasting radio and television shows, in recording the sound for motion pictures, and in making phonograph records and tape recordings. Citizens band (CB) radios and *ham* (amateur) radios also have mikes.

Microphones of various designs are used for different purposes. CB operators and some entertainers use mikes that are held in the hand. Other mikes are attached to stands. Still others have an arm called a *boom*, which holds the microphone above the head of a TV or movie performer. The boom and mike can follow the performer in any direction, but they stay out of view of the camera. *Lavalier microphones* are worn on a cord around the neck. Lapel mikes are fastened to the user's clothing.

Some microphones pick up sound from all directions, but others are sensitive to sound from only certain directions. An *omnidirectional microphone* picks up sound from all around. A *bidirectional microphone* is used for sound coming from the front or from behind, but not from the sides. A *unidirectional microphone* picks up sound from only one direction.

In some microphones, sound produces variations in an electric current. In others, sound generates a current. In all microphones, the current corresponds to the pattern of the sound waves.

Microphones may be classified according to how they change sound into electric energy. The five main types, in order of increasing complexity, are (1) carbon, (2) crystal and ceramic, (3) moving-coil, (4) ribbon, and (5) condenser. Moving-coil, ribbon, and condenser mikes can reproduce sound much more accurately than the other types and are used by the movie, recording, radio, and television industries.

Carbon Microphones have a small container called a *button*, which is filled with particles of carbon. An electric current from a generator or battery flows through the carbon. A metal disk called a *diaphragm* presses against the button and vibrates when struck by sound waves. The vibrations cause variations in the current running through the carbon. Carbon microphones are used chiefly in telephones.

Crystal and Ceramic Microphones contain substances called *piezoelectric crystals*. Pressure on these crystals makes them generate an electric current (see PIEZO-ELECTRICITY). The microphones may or may not have a diaphragm touching the crystals. An electric current is produced by pressure from sound waves that hit the diaphragm or strike the crystals directly. Crystal and ceramic mikes are used in ham radios, home tape recorders, and many public-address systems.

Moving-Coil Microphones, sometimes called *dynamic microphones*, have a wire coil attached to a diaphragm. The coil and diaphragm are suspended in a magnetic field. When sound waves hit the diaphragm, the coil moves across the field. This movement produces an electric current in the coil. Many CB radios have moving-coil microphones.

Ribbon Microphones have a metal ribbon suspended in a magnetic field. An electric current is generated when sound waves hit the ribbon and move it across the field.

Condenser Microphones, often called *capacitor microphones*, have two metal plates set slightly apart. The plates are electrically charged and serve as a *capacitor*, a device that stores a charge. The front plate is flexible and acts as a diaphragm. The back plate cannot move. Sound waves make the front plate vibrate, which causes variations in the electric current from the capacitor.

A condenser microphone must have a device called a *preamplifier*. The preamplifier reduces the strength of the current coming from the capacitor and thus prevents the sound from being distorted. In most condenser microphones, called *electret condensers*, the capacitor is permanently charged and a small battery in the microphone powers the preamplifier. Electret condensers are used in hearing aids.   STANLEY R. ALTEN

Related Articles in WORLD BOOK include:

Phonograph   Telephone
Public Address System   Television
Radio   Wiretapping

MICROPHOTOGRAPHY. See MICROFILM.

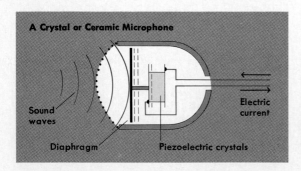

A Crystal or Ceramic Microphone

Sound waves — Electric current — Diaphragm — Piezoelectric crystals

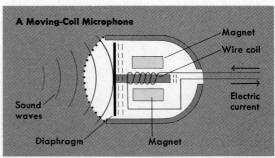

A Moving-Coil Microphone

Magnet — Wire coil — Sound waves — Electric current — Diaphragm — Magnet

WORLD BOOK diagrams by Arthur Grebetz

Microphones Change Sound into Electric Energy. Many microphones have a metal disk called a *diaphragm*, which vibrates when struck by sound waves. In a crystal or ceramic microphone, *left*, the diaphragm vibrates against substances called *piezoelectric crystals*, creating an electric current. In a moving-coil microphone, *right*, the vibrating diaphragm causes a wire coil to move across a magnetic field. This movement produces an electric current in the coil.

MICROSCOPE, *MY kruh skohp,* is an instrument that magnifies extremely small objects so they can be seen easily. It produces an image much larger than the original object. Scientists use the term *specimen* for any object studied with a microscope.

The microscope ranks as one of the most important tools of science. With it, researchers first saw the tiny germs that cause disease. The microscope reveals an entire world of organisms too small to be seen by the unaided eye. Physicians and other scientists use microscopes to examine such specimens as bacteria and blood cells. The details of nonliving things, such as crystals in metals, can also be seen with a microscope.

Biology students use microscopes to learn about algae, protozoa, and other one-celled plants and animals. The structure of these and all other organisms could not be studied without the microscope.

There are three basic kinds of microscopes: (1) *optical,* or *light;* (2) *electron;* and (3) *ion.* This article discusses optical microscopes. For information on the other types, see the WORLD BOOK articles on ELECTRON MICROSCOPE and ION MICROSCOPE.

How a Microscope Works. An optical microscope has one or more lenses that bend the light rays shining through the specimen (see LENS). The bent light rays join and form an enlarged image of the specimen.

The simplest optical microscope is a magnifying glass (see MAGNIFYING GLASS). The best magnifying glasses can magnify an object by 10 to 20 times. A magnifying glass cannot be used to magnify an object any further because the image becomes fuzzy. Scientists use a number and the abbreviation *X* to indicate (1) the image of an object magnified by a certain number of times or (2) a lens that magnifies by that number of times. For example, a 10X lens magnifies an object by 10 times. The

magnification of a microscope may also be expressed in units called *diameters.* A 10X magnification enlarges the image by 10 times the diameter of the object.

Greater magnification can be achieved by using a *compound* microscope. Such an instrument has two lenses, an *objective lens* and an *ocular,* or *eyepiece, lens.* The objective lens, often called simply the *objective,* produces a magnified image of the specimen, just as an ordinary magnifying glass does. The ocular lens, also called the *ocular,* then magnifies this image, producing an even larger image. Many microscopes have three standard objective lenses that magnify by 4X, 10X, and 40X. When these objective lenses are used with a 10X ocular lens, the compound microscope magnifies a specimen by 40X, 100X, or 400X. Some microscopes have *zoom* objective lenses that can smoothly increase the magnification of the specimen from 100X to 500X.

In addition to magnifying a specimen, a microscope must produce a clear image of the closely spaced parts of the object. The ability to provide such an image is called the *resolving power* of a microscope. The best optical microscopes cannot resolve parts of objects that are closer together than about 0.000008 of an inch (0.0002 of a millimeter). Anything smaller in the specimen—such as atoms, molecules, and viruses—cannot be seen with an optical microscope.

Parts of a Microscope. The microscopes used in most schools and colleges for teaching have three parts: (1) the *foot,* (2) the *tube,* and (3) the *body.* The foot is the base on which the instrument stands. The tube contains the lenses, and the body is the upright support that holds the tube.

The body, which is hinged to the foot so that it may be tilted, has a mirror at the lower end. The object lies on the *stage,* a platform attached above the mirror. The

PARTS OF A MICROSCOPE

The diagram at the left shows the external parts of a microscope. A person adjusts these parts to view a specimen. The cutaway diagram at the right shows the path that light follows when passing through the specimen and then through the lenses and tubes of the microscope.

WORLD BOOK diagram

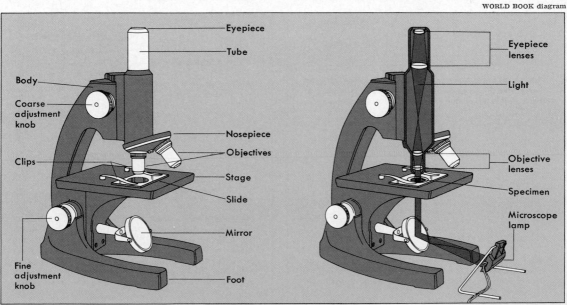

Eyepiece
Tube
Body
Coarse adjustment knob
Clips
Fine adjustment knob
Nosepiece
Objectives
Stage
Slide
Mirror
Foot

Eyepiece lenses
Light
Objective lenses
Specimen
Microscope lamp

THE MICROSCOPIC WORLD

The purpose of this project is to use a microscope to study the tiny animals and plants that live in water. The photographs with this project will help you identify the organisms you see. By using a camera that takes time exposures, you can take your own pictures through the microscope.

MATERIALS

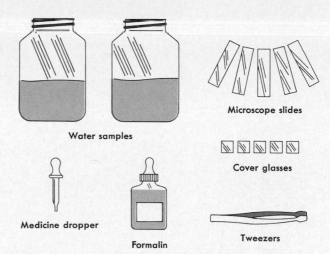

Camera

Water samples

Microscope slides

Cover glasses

Medicine dropper

Formalin

Tweezers

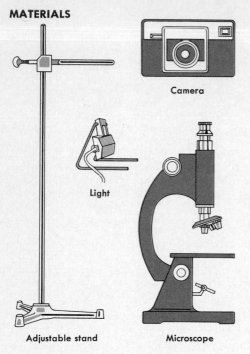

Light

Adjustable stand

Microscope

Materials for this project are shown above. The microscope should be able to magnify by at least 400X. With it, you will need microscope slides, cover glasses, and a microscope light. Water samples should come from a pond or slow-moving stream. If you want to take pictures, you will need a camera and stand, and formalin to kill the animals. CAUTION: Formalin is extremely irritating to the eyes and nose. Handle it with care and wash your hands after using it.

WORLD BOOK illustrations by Arthur Grebetz

PREPARING AND STUDYING THE SLIDES

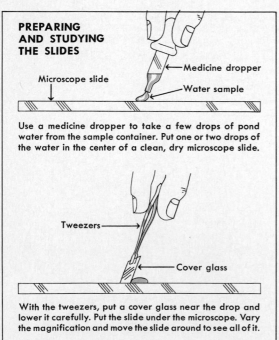

Medicine dropper

Microscope slide

Water sample

Use a medicine dropper to take a few drops of pond water from the sample container. Put one or two drops of the water in the center of a clean, dry microscope slide.

Tweezers

Cover glass

With the tweezers, put a cover glass near the drop and lower it carefully. Put the slide under the microscope. Vary the magnification and move the slide around to see all of it.

MOUNTING THE CAMERA

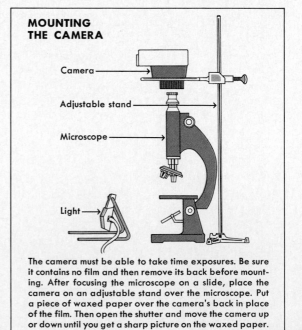

Camera

Adjustable stand

Microscope

Light

The camera must be able to take time exposures. Be sure it contains no film and then remove its back before mounting. After focusing the microscope on a slide, place the camera on an adjustable stand over the microscope. Put a piece of waxed paper over the camera's back in place of the film. Then open the shutter and move the camera up or down until you get a sharp picture on the waxed paper.

TAKING THE PICTURES

The animals on any slide you photograph must be killed with a drop of formalin or they will move and blur the picture. After you have focused the camera, close the shutter and load it with film. Be careful when moving the camera that you do not change its height over the microscope. Take the pictures on ordinary black-and-white film. Begin with a time exposure of 5 seconds at 100X magnification. Increase the exposure time if your pictures come out too dark, or decrease the exposure time if they are too light. Double the exposure time for each doubling of the magnification.

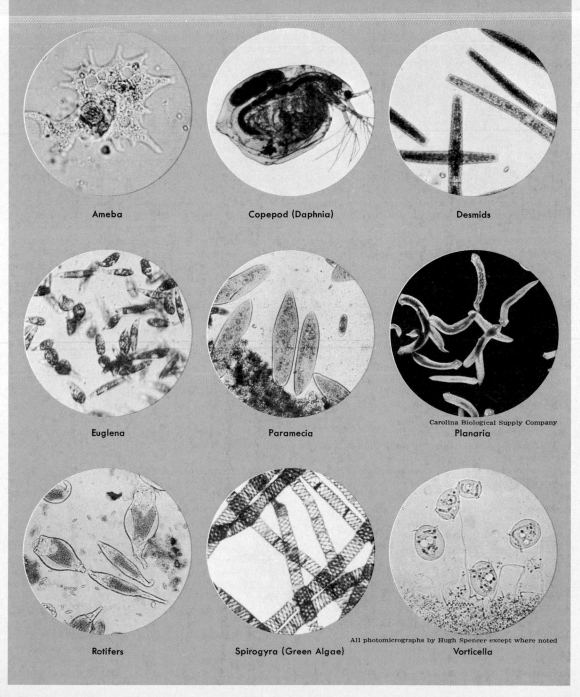

Ameba

Copepod (Daphnia)

Desmids

Euglena

Paramecia

Carolina Biological Supply Company
Planaria

Rotifers

Spirogyra (Green Algae)

All photomicrographs by Hugh Spencer except where noted
Vorticella

mirror reflects light through an opening in the stage to illuminate the object. The upper part of the body is a slide that holds the tube and permits the operator to move it up and down with a *coarse-adjustment* knob. This movement focuses the microscope. Most microscopes also have a *fine-adjustment* knob, which moves the tube a small distance for final focusing of a high-power lens.

The lower part of the tube contains the objective lens. In most microscopes, this lens is mounted on a revolving *nosepiece* that the operator can rotate to bring the desired lens into place. The upper end of the tube holds the ocular lens.

Using a Microscope. A microscope is an expensive instrument and can be damaged easily. When moving one, be sure to hold it with both hands and set it down gently on a firm surface.

To prepare a microscope for use, turn the nosepiece so that the objective with the lowest power is in viewing position. Lower the tube and lens by turning the coarse-adjustment knob until the lens is just above the opening in the stage. Next, look through the eyepiece and adjust the mirror so a bright circle of light appears in the eyepiece. The microscope is now ready for viewing a specimen. Most people keep both eyes open when looking into the eyepiece. They concentrate on what they see through the microscope and ignore anything seen with the other eye.

Most specimens viewed through a microscope are transparent, or have been made transparent, so that light can shine through them. Objects to be viewed are mounted on glass slides that measure 3 inches long and 1 inch wide (76 by 25 millimeters). The technique of preparing specimens for microscopic viewing is called *microtomy* (see MICROTOMY). See also the *Science Project* with this article.

To view a slide, place it on the stage with the specimen directly over the opening. Hold the slide in place with the clips on the stage. Look through the eyepiece and turn the coarse-adjustment knob to raise the lens up from the slide until the specimen comes into focus. Never lower the lens when a slide is on the stage. The lens could press against the slide, breaking both the slide and the lens.

After the specimen has been brought into focus, turn the nosepiece to an objective lens with higher power. This lens will reveal more details of the specimen. If necessary, focus the stronger objective with the fine-adjustment knob. A zoom microscope is changed to a higher power by turning a part of the zoom lens. Different parts of the specimen can be brought into view by moving the slide on the stage.

Advanced Microscopes have extra powerful lenses for greater magnification. Many such microscopes have a 100X objective lens, which provides a total magnification of 2,000X when used with a 20X ocular lens. This magnification is the practical limit for an optical microscope using ordinary light. However, some optical microscopes using only ultraviolet light can magnify as much as 3,000X. Many high-powered microscopes use *oil immersion* objective lenses. These lenses touch a drop of special oil placed between them and the slide. Immersion lenses produce a better image at high power than do lenses with air between the slide and the lens.

Microscopes used for scientific research have other features in addition to those found in basic microscopes. For example, a *mechanical stage* enables the user to accurately position a slide on the stage. Many advanced microscopes have a built-in lamp called a *substage illuminator* instead of a mirror. The illuminator gives the operator more control of the light reaching the specimen. A *substage condenser lens* focuses light from the illuminator or mirror on the specimen, providing better illumination.

Many research microscopes have a *binocular tube* that splits the light from the objective into two beams. An eyepiece in each beam allows the operator to view the specimen with both eyes. Some microscopes have *trinocular tubes* that split the light into three beams—one for each eye and one for a built-in camera. A *stereoscope* microscope gives a *stereoscopic* (three-dimensional) view of the specimen. Such a microscope has separate objective and ocular lenses for each eye.

Scientists use special microscopes to study the detailed parts of living cells or microbes. Ordinary microscopes cannot be used because most cells or microbes are killed by the staining needed to make some parts of the specimen visible. Many researchers use *phase contrast* and *dark-field* microscopes to study living things.

A phase contrast microscope changes the *phase* (relationship) between the light waves passing through the specimen and those not passing through it. This action makes some parts of the specimen appear brighter and other parts darker than normal. Thus, the parts of a transparent object that vary in thickness or have other optical properties can be seen.

A dark-field microscope prevents light from the illuminator from shining directly up the microscope tube. Instead, the microscope uses only the light *diffracted* (broken up) by the specimen. The specimen appears brightly lit against a black background. Various parts of the specimen diffract slightly different amounts of light, and so they appear brighter or darker than normal.

History of the Microscope. Engravers probably used glass globes filled with water as magnifying glasses at least 3,000 years ago. The Romans may have made magnifying glasses from rock crystal, but glass lenses of the type now used were not introduced until the late A.D. 1200's.

Historians generally credit a Dutch spectacle-maker, Zacharias Janssen, with discovering the principle of the compound microscope about 1590. In the mid-1600's, Anton Van Leeuwenhoek, a Dutch amateur scientist, made microscope lenses that could magnify up to 270X. He also built simple microscopes more powerful than the compound microscopes of his day. Leeuwenhoek was the first person to observe microscopic life and record his observations.

Few improvements in the microscope occurred until the early 1800's, when better glass-making methods produced lenses that provided undistorted images. C. A. Spencer, an optical instrument manufacturer of Canastota, N.Y., made the first American microscopes about 1838. German scientists demonstrated the first electron microscope in 1931. BRIAN J. THOMPSON

See also CELL (pictures); LEEUWENHOEK, ANTON VAN; ULTRAMICROSCOPE.

MICROTOME is a device used to cut materials very thin so that they can be seen in cross section under a microscope. It has a holder in which the specimen is clamped, a razor-sharp knife, a guide for the knife, and a turnscrew which regulates the thickness of the slice. See also MICROSCOPE; MICROTOMY.

WORLD BOOK photo

A Microtome cuts thin slices of human tissue for physicians to examine under a microscope. Wax holds the tissue together so the microtome can slice it thin enough for light to pass through.

MICROTOMY originally meant *microscopic cutting*. But it now means the art of preparing objects for examination with a microscope. Without preparation, few objects can be properly examined with a microscope (see MICROSCOPE). A piece of metal, for example, must be highly polished and etched before its structure can be seen. Rocks are sawed into slices thin enough to see through by the techniques of microtomy.

Scientists prepare biological materials either as smears, squashes, wholemounts, or sections. *Smears* are made by applying a thin layer of blood or other organic fluid to a microscopic slide. Technicians dry and stain the layer so the cells can be seen. Geneticists make *squashes* by crushing cells in order to see the number and shape of the chromosomes (see CHROMOSOME). *Wholemounts* are prepared from whole microscopic animals and plants that are killed in a *fixative* to keep their shape. They are then stained. Alcohol removes the water, and clove or cedar oil makes the objects transparent. Technicians next mount the objects in a drop of resin on a glass slide, which they cover with a glass *coverslip* about $\frac{1}{5,000}$ inch (.005 millimeter) thick.

Scientists study plant and animal tissues in *sections* about $\frac{1}{2,500}$ inch (.01 millimeter) thick. After being hardened and dried out, the tissues are soaked in wax and shaped into rectangular blocks. The wax supports the tissues so they can be sliced into sections on a *microtome* (see MICROTOME). The sections are then cemented to slides with egg white and the wax is dissolved. They are then stained and preserved under a coverslip. PETER GRAY

MICROWAVE is a short radio wave. It varies from .03937 inch to 1 foot (1 millimeter to 30 centimeters) in length. Microwaves travel in straight lines. Like light waves, they may be reflected and concentrated. But they pass easily through rain, smoke, and fog that block light waves. Thus they are well suited for long-distance communication and for control of navigation.

Microwaves first came to public notice through the applications of radar in World War II. In television, microwave transmission sends programs from pickup cameras in the field to the television transmitter. It is also used for linking stations in different cities. Microwaves transmit pictures and printed matter in a process called *Ultrafax* (see ULTRAFAX). Microwaves also cook food in microwave ovens. V. K. ZWORYKIN

See also RADAR; RADIO; RANGE (Microwave Ovens); TELEVISION; ULTRAHIGH FREQUENCY WAVE.

MICROWAVE OVEN. See RANGE (Microwave Ovens; picture).

MICRURGY is the study of microorganisms and cells under the microscope. Tiny instruments are used to separate, inject, and isolate the organisms and cells for detailed study.

MIDAS, *MY duhs*, was a character in Greek mythology. He was king of Phrygia, an ancient country in central Asia Minor. The god Dionysus gave Midas the power to turn everything he touched into gold, because he had helped Dionysus' teacher Silenus (see DIONYSUS).

At first, Midas' miraculous power pleased him. But soon it became a curse, because even his food turned to gold the moment he touched it. He prayed to Dionysus to help him, and the god told him to bathe in the river Pactolus. Midas washed himself, and the magic touch left him. But the sands of the river turned to gold.

Midas acted as judge at a musical contest between Apollo and Pan (see APOLLO; PAN). He awarded the prize to Pan, and Apollo angrily turned Midas' ears into those of an ass. Midas was ashamed and kept his ears covered. But he could not hide his ears from the slave who was his barber. The slave did not dare tell anyone, because he feared punishment. He dug a hole in the ground and whispered the truth into it. Reeds grew out of the soil and whispered the secret when the wind blew.

The expression *to have the Midas touch* is used to describe a person who makes money in everything he does. A *Midas* is a wealthy person. O. M. PEARL

Midas Bathed in a River to Lose His Golden Touch.

Midas at the Source of the Pactolus by Nicolas Poussin. Musee Fesch, Ajaccio, Corsica. Giraudon

"March" by the Limbourg brothers, from the Duc de Berry's *Très Riches Heures*,
an illuminated French manuscript of the 1400's. Musée Condé, Chantilly, France (Giraudon)

MIDDLE AGES

MIDDLE AGES were the period between ancient and modern times in western Europe. Before the Middle Ages, western Europe was part of the Roman Empire. After the Middle Ages, western Europe included the Holy Roman Empire, the kingdoms of England and France, and a number of smaller states. The Middle Ages are also known as the *medieval* period, from the Latin words *medium* (middle) and *aevum* (age). Sometimes the Middle Ages are incorrectly called the *Dark Ages*.

The history of the Middle Ages extends from the end of the Roman Empire to the 1500's. Historians today do not give exact dates for the end of the Roman Empire, because it ended over a period of several hundred years. This article uses the A.D. 400's as the starting date of the

Bryce Lyon, the contributor of this article, is Barnaby C. and Mary Critchfield Keeney Professor of History at Brown University and author of The Middle Ages in Western Europe.

Middle Ages. By that time, the Roman Empire was so weak that Germanic tribes were able to conquer it. The Germanic way of life gradually combined with the Roman way of life to form the civilization which we call *medieval*. Medieval civilization was greatly influenced by the Muslims in Spain and the Middle East, and by the Byzantine Empire in southeastern Europe.

This article tells about life in western Europe between the A.D. 400's and the 1500's. To understand how other civilizations influenced medieval civilization, see the WORLD BOOK articles on BYZANTINE EMPIRE; MUSLIMS; and ROMAN EMPIRE. See also WORLD, HISTORY OF.

THE BEGINNINGS

The Germanic Invasions. The Germanic peoples came from Scandinavia in northern Europe. They began moving into central Europe about 1000 B.C. By the A.D. 200's, they occupied regions in the Rhine and Danube river basins along the northern and north-

Illumination from *Roman Customs*, a French manuscript of the 1400's. Bibliothèque Nationale, Paris

Life in the Middle Ages centered around the control of land. Land was ruled by a powerful lord, defended by his knights, and farmed by his peasants. The peasants plowed the lord's fields, trimmed his grapevines, and did many other tasks. The lord's home, *left*, a mighty stone castle built for defense against his enemies, provided protection for the peasants. Lords, ladies, and knights feasted in the castle's huge banquet hall, entertained by wandering poets and singers, *above*.

eastern boundaries of the Roman Empire. Some Germans adopted the civilization of their Roman neighbors. They traded with Roman merchants, learned to farm the land, and accepted Christianity as their religion.

But most Germans were rough, ignorant people. The Romans called them *barbarians* (uncivilized people). The Germans lived in tribes, each governed by a chief. The few laws that these people had were based on tribal customs and superstition. The tribesmen were fierce in appearance—big, bearded, and clothed in animal skins or coarse linen. They fought with spears and shields, and were brave warriors. The Germans lived mainly by hunting and by a crude type of farming. They worshiped such Scandinavian gods as Odin and Thor. Few Germans could read or write.

During the A.D. 400's, the Germanic tribes began invading Roman territory. By then, the Roman Empire had lost much of its great power, and its armies could not defend the long frontier. The Visigoths invaded

Spain about A.D. 416. The Angles, Jutes, and Saxons began to settle in Britain about 450. The Franks established a kingdom in Gaul (now France) in the 480's. The Ostrogoths invaded Italy in 489. See ANGLE; FRANK; GOTH; JUTE; SAXON.

Barbarian Europe. The barbarian invasions divided the huge Roman Empire into many kingdoms. The barbarians were loyal only to their tribal chiefs or to their own families. Each group of tribesmen kept its own laws and customs. As a result, the strong central and local governments of the Romans disappeared.

In the Roman Empire, a strong system of laws protected the citizens and gave them the safety and security that comes from law and order. Barbarian superstitions replaced many Roman laws. For example, *trial by ordeal* became a common way of determining whether a person was guilty of a crime. The accused person plunged his arm into a pot of boiling water or picked up a red-hot iron bar with his bare hand. If his burns healed within three days, he was judged innocent. Otherwise, he was hanged. See also TRIAL BY COMBAT.

The barbarian invasions also destroyed most of the European trade that the Romans had established. Few persons used the great system of stone roads that had encouraged trade and communication among the prosperous cities of the Roman Empire. Without trade, money went out of use almost completely. The people were forced to make their living from the soil.

By the 800's, most of western Europe was divided into large estates of land called *manors*. A few wealthy landowners, called *landlords* or *lords*, ruled the manors, but most of the people were poor peasants who worked the land. Each village on a manor produced nearly everything needed by its people. This system of obtaining a living from the land was called *manorialism*. See MANORIALISM.

Towns lost their importance under manorial conditions. Most people who had lived in the towns went to the countryside and became peasants on the manors. Some towns were completely abandoned and gradually disappeared. The middle class, which had engaged in trade and industry, also disappeared.

Education and cultural activities were almost forgotten. Almost all state and city schools disappeared. Few persons could read or write Latin, the language of the well-educated. Even fewer were educated enough to preserve the little that remained of ancient Greek and Roman knowledge. The great skills of ancient literature, architecture, painting, and sculpture were forgotten.

The Christian Church was the main civilizing force of the early Middle Ages. It provided leadership for the people and saved western Europe from complete ignorance.

Little by little, the church made Christians of the barbarians. Although the people of Europe no longer honored one ruler, they gradually began to worship the same God. Men called *missionaries* traveled great distances to spread the Christian faith. They also helped civilize the barbarians by introducing Roman ideas of government and justice into their lives.

The popes, bishops, and other leaders of the church took over many functions of government after the Roman emperors lost power. The church collected taxes and maintained law courts to punish criminals. Church buildings also served as hospitals for the sick, and as inns for travelers.

Two church institutions—the *cathedral* and the *monastery*—became centers of learning in the early Middle Ages. Cathedrals were the churches of bishops. Monasteries were communities of men called *monks*, who gave up worldly life to serve God through prayer and work. The monks of some monasteries and the clergy of the cathedrals helped continue the reading and writing of Latin, and preserved many valuable ancient manuscripts. They also established most of the schools in Europe.

The Carolingian Empire united most of western Europe under one ruler in the late 700's. The *Carolingians* were a family of Frankish kings who ruled from the mid-700's to 987. The most important Frankish rulers were Charles Martel, his son Pepin the Short, and Pepin's son Charlemagne.

Charles Martel united the Frankish kingdom in the early 700's, when he captured lands held by powerful Frankish lords. Pepin the Short strengthened the Carolingians' control over the Frankish kingdom. In 768, Charlemagne became ruler of the kingdom. He then conquered much of western Europe, and united Europe for the first time since the end of the Roman Empire.

In creating their empire, the Frankish rulers depended on the assistance of loyal noblemen called *vassals*. A nobleman became a vassal when he pledged his loyalty to the king and promised to serve him. The king then became a *lord* to his vassal. Most vassals held important positions in the king's army, where they served as *knights*. Many vassals had their own knights, whose services they also pledged to the king.

The Carolingian kings rewarded their vassals by granting them estates called *fiefs*. A fief included the manors on the land, the buildings and villages of each manor, and the peasants who farmed the manors.

The early Middle Ages reached their highest point of achievement during the long rule of Charlemagne. He worked to protect the church from its enemies and to keep the people of Europe united under the church. Although Charlemagne never learned to write, he did improve education. He established a school in his palace at Aachen, and teachers from throughout Europe gathered there. They organized schools and libraries, and copied ancient manuscripts. These activities caused a new interest in learning called the *Carolingian Renaissance*. See CHARLEMAGNE.

Charlemagne's empire and the revival of learning did not last long after his death. His three grandsons fought each other for the title of emperor. In 843, the Treaty of Verdun divided the empire into three parts, one for each grandson. Soon after, the divided empire was attacked from outside by Magyars, Muslims, and Vikings. By the late 800's, the Carolingian Empire no longer existed.

FEUDAL EUROPE

Feudalism. After the end of Charlemagne's empire, Europe was again divided into many kingdoms. Most of the kings were weak and had little control over their kingdoms. As a result, hundreds of vassals—with such titles as *prince, baron, duke,* or *count*—became independent rulers of their own fiefs. These noblemen ruled their fiefs through a form of government called feudalism.

Under feudalism, the noblemen who controlled the land also had political, economic, judicial, and military power. Each nobleman collected taxes and fines, acted as judge in legal disputes, and maintained an army of knights within his own territory. He also supervised the farming of the manors on his fief. The fief-holders were the ruling class in Europe for more than 400 years.

A typical member of the ruling class under feudalism was a nobleman, a knight, a vassal, and a lord—all at the same time. He was a nobleman because he had been born into the noble class. He became a knight when he decided to spend his life as a professional warrior. He became a vassal when he promised to serve a king or other important person in return for a fief. Finally, he became a lord when he gave part of his own land to persons who promised to serve him.

Suppose that Sir John, a nobleman, was a vassal of William the Conqueror, king of England and duke of Normandy. When John pledged his loyalty to William, he also promised to supply the king with 10 knights. In return, William gave 20 manors to John as a fief. If the king called his army to battle, John had to go—and take nine other knights with him. If John did not have nine knights living in his household, he hired wandering knights. As payment, John gave each knight one manor as a fief. The knights then pledged their loyalty and service to John. In this way, they became John's vassals, and he became their lord.

A lord and a vassal had rights and duties toward each other. A lord promised his vassal protection and justice, and the vassal gave the lord various services, most of which were military. Feudal warfare was common in Europe. If a lord and his vassal performed their duties, there was peace and good government. But if either disregarded his duties, war broke out between them. The lords fought among themselves as well, because they often tried to seize each other's land. The church, which had its own princes and fiefs, was part of the feudal system, so it also suffered in the warfare. See FEUDALISM.

Feudal Government. During the 900's and 1000's, most of western Europe was divided into feudal states. A powerful lord ruled each state as if he were king. The kings themselves ruled only their own royal lands.

In France, the king ruled only the area called the *Île-de-France*, a narrow strip of land centered near Paris. The rest of France was divided into such feudal states as Aquitaine, Anjou, Brittany, Flanders, and Normandy. In some feudal states, no lord was powerful enough to establish a strong government. But in Anjou, Flanders, and Normandy, capable lords provided strong governments. The dukes of Normandy maintained tight control over the noblemen living there. No one could build a castle, collect taxes, regulate trade, or hold important court trials without the duke's permission. Only he could order an army into battle.

Under William the Conqueror, England became the strongest feudal state in Europe. William, who was duke of Normandy, invaded England in 1066. After defeating the Anglo-Saxon army, he became king of England. He then established the feudal system in England by making all landholders his vassals. See NORMAN CONQUEST; NORMANDY; WILLIAM (I, the Conqueror).

The strong governments in the feudal states of France and England provided some peace and security for the people. Strong feudal government allowed rulers in the 1100's and 1200's to establish strong central governments in France and England.

Feudalism did not provide strong government in Germany or Italy. For hundreds of years, powerful dukes fought the kings. Otto I, one of the most powerful German kings, won control over the dukes in the mid-900's. He then tried to create an empire similar to Charlemagne's. After conquering lands east of Germany, Otto invaded Italy. In 962, the pope crowned Otto *Holy Roman Emperor*. The Holy Roman Empire was small and weak, and included only Germany and northern Italy. In time, the German dukes tried to regain control of their kingdoms, and the empire was continually divided by warfare. Neither Germany nor Italy became united countries until the 1800's.

The Power of the Church became the single great force that bound Europe together during the feudal period. The church touched almost everyone's life in many important ways. The church baptized a person at his birth, performed the wedding ceremony at his marriage, and conducted the burial services at his death.

The church also became the largest landholder in western Europe during the Middle Ages. Many feudal lords gave fiefs to the church in return for services performed by the clergy. At first, feudal lords controlled the

Feudal States of Europe: 1096

Kingdom of France

Holy Roman Empire

This map shows the political divisions of Europe in 1096. France and the Holy Roman Empire were made up of many feudal states, each ruled by a lord. The kings ruled only their own royal lands. In France, the king ruled the Île-de-France, shown in yellow. England was a unified kingdom ruled by William II.

Data for map from *Mediaeval History*, by Bryce Lyon; Harper & Row, 1962.

WORLD BOOK map

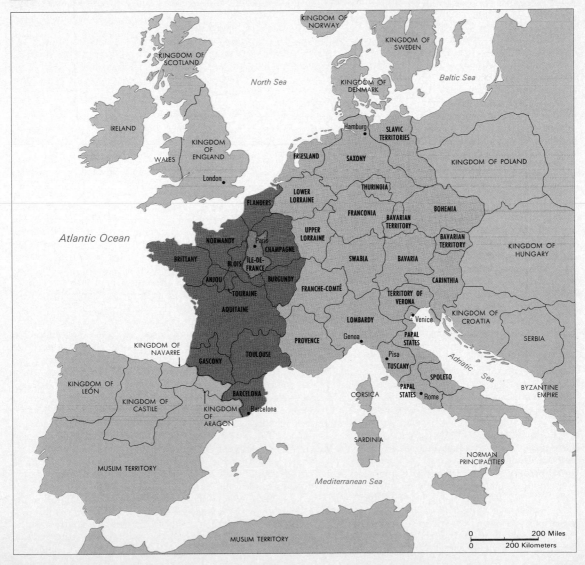

church, but it gradually won a large degree of freedom.

Although clergymen did not take a direct part in feudal warfare, they controlled the lords with their own types of weapons. One great power of the church was its threat of *excommunication*. To excommunicate a person meant to cut him off completely from the church and take away his hope of going to heaven. If a lord continued to rebel after being excommunicated, the church disciplined him with an *interdict*. This action closed all the churches on the lord's land. No one on the land could be married or buried with the church's blessing, and the church bells never rang. The people usually became so discontented that they rebelled, and the lord finally yielded to the church.

Life of the People. Europe during the 900's was poor, underdeveloped, and thinly populated. At least half the land could not be farmed because of thick forests or swamps. War, disease, famine, and a low birth rate kept Europe's population small. People lived an average of only 30 years. There was little travel or communication, and fewer than 20 per cent of the people went farther than 10 miles (16 kilometers) from their birthplace.

The people of western Europe consisted of three groups. The *lords* governed the large fiefs and did all the fighting. The *clergy* served the church. The *peasants* worked on the land to support themselves, the clergy, and the lords.

The Lords. A lord's life centered around fighting. He believed that the only honorable way to live was as a professional warrior. The lords and their knights, wearing heavy armor and riding huge war horses, fought with lances or heavy swords.

The behavior of all fighting men gradually came to be governed by a system called *chivalry*. Chivalry required that a man earn knighthood through a long and difficult training period. A knight was supposed to be courageous in battle, fight according to certain rules, keep his promises, and defend the church. Chivalry also included rules for gentlemanly conduct toward women. In times of peace, a lord and his knights entertained themselves by practicing for war. They took part in *jousts* (combat between two armed knights) and in *tournaments* (combat between two groups of knights). See KNIGHTS AND KNIGHTHOOD.

The lord lived in a manor house or a castle. Early castles were simple forts surrounded by fences of tree trunks. Later castles were mighty fortresses of stone. In the great hall of the castle, the lord and his knights ate, drank, and gambled at the firesides. They played dice, checkers, and chess.

The lord's wife, called a *lady*, was trained to sew, spin, and weave, and to rule the household servants. She had few rights. If she did not bear at least one son, the lord could end their marriage. Neither the lords nor their ladies thought education was necessary, and few could read or write.

The Clergy. Most bishops and other high-ranking clergymen were noblemen who devoted their lives to the church. They ruled large fiefs and lived much like other noblemen. Some of these clergymen were as wealthy and powerful as the greatest military lords.

Monks who lived in a monastery were required to live according to its rules. They had to spend a certain number of hours each day studying, praying, and taking part in religious services. Some monks who were outstanding scholars left the monastery and became advisers to kings or other rulers.

Many peasants who became clergymen served as priests in the peasant villages. Each village priest lived in a small cottage near his church. He gave advice and help to the peasants, settled disputes, and performed church ceremonies. The priests collected fees for baptisms, marriages, and burials. But most priests were as poor as the peasants they served.

The Peasants had few rights, and were almost completely at the mercy of their lords. With the help of his wife and children, a peasant farmed both the lord's fields and his own. He also performed whatever other tasks the lord demanded, such as cutting wood, storing grain, or repairing roads and bridges.

The peasant had to pay many kinds of rents and taxes. He had to bring his grain to the lord's mill to be ground, bake his bread in the lord's oven, and take his grapes to the lord's wine press. Each of these services meant another payment to the lord. Money was scarce, so the peasant usually paid in wheat, oats, eggs, or poultry from his own land.

The peasant lived in a crude hut and slept on a bag filled with straw. He ate black bread, eggs, poultry, and such vegetables as cabbage and turnips. Rarely could he afford meat. He could not hunt or fish because game on the manor belonged to the lord.

THE HIGH MIDDLE AGES

Medieval civilization reached its highest point of achievement between the 1000's and the late 1200's. This period is called the *High Middle Ages*.

During the 1000's, many capable lords provided strong governments and periods of peace and security under the feudal system. As a result, the people were able to devote themselves to new ideas and activities.

Economic Recovery. As government improved, so did economic conditions. Merchants again traveled the old land routes and waterways of Europe. Towns sprang up along the main trade routes. Most early towns developed near a fortified castle, church, or monastery where merchants could stop for protection. The merchants, and the craftsmen who made the goods sold by the merchants, gradually settled in the towns.

Europe's population began to increase during the 1000's, and many persons moved to the towns in search of jobs. At the same time, peasants began to leave the manors to seek a new life. Some became merchants and craftsmen. Others farmed the land outside the towns and supplied the townspeople with food. Medieval towns, which arose mainly because of the growth of trade, encouraged trade. The townspeople bought goods, and also produced goods for merchants to sell.

The peasants learned better ways of farming and produced more and more food for the growing population. Peasants began to use water power to run the grain mills and sawmills. They gained land for farming by clearing forests and draining swamps.

For the first time since the days of the Roman Empire, Europeans took notice of the world beyond their borders. Merchants traveled afar to trade with the peoples of the Byzantine Empire in southeastern Europe. The *crusades*, a series of holy wars against the Muslims, encouraged European trade with the Middle East (see CRUSADES). Italians in Genoa, Pisa, Venice, and other towns built great fleets of ships to carry the merchants' goods across the Mediterranean Sea to trade centers in Spain and northern Africa. The Italians brought back goods from these seaports. Many of the goods were exports from cities in India and China. Leaders in the towns of northern Germany created the Hanseatic League to organize trade in northern Europe.

Merchants exchanged their goods at great international trade fairs held in towns along the main European trade routes. Each fair was held at a different time of the year, and merchants traveled from one fair to another. The county of Champagne in northeastern France became the site of the first great European fairs. Its towns lay on the trade routes that linked Italy with northern Europe. Flemish merchants brought woolen cloth to the fairs. Italian merchants brought silks, spices, and perfumes from the Middle East, India, and China. Merchants from northern and eastern Europe brought furs, lumber, and stone. The merchants not only traded their goods, but also exchanged ideas about new methods of farming, new industries, and events in Europe and the rest of the world. See FAIRS AND EXPOSITIONS (Fairs of the Middle Ages).

Medieval Towns. Early towns were only small settlements outside the walls of a castle or a church. As the towns grew larger, walls were built around them. Soldiers on the walls kept a lookout for attacking armies.

The towns·were crowded because the walls limited the amount of land available. Houses stood crowded together. The people had to build upward because land was expensive, and many buildings were five or six stories high.

Streets were narrow, crooked, dark, and filthy. Until about 1200, they were not paved. The people threw all their garbage and rubbish into the streets, and disease spread quickly. During the 1200's, the people in some towns began to pave their streets with rough cobblestones. They also took some steps toward sanitation.

A citizen who went out at night took his servants along for protection against robbers. The servants carried lanterns and torches because no town had any street lighting. The wide use of lamps, torches, and candles made fire one of the great dangers for a medieval town. Wealthy citizens had stone and brick houses, but most houses were made of wood. A large fire was likely to wipe out a whole town. The city of Rouen, in France, burned to the ground six times between 1200 and 1225.

After the merchants and craftsmen settled in the towns, they set up organizations called *guilds*. A guild protected its members against unfair business practices, established prices and wages, and settled disputes between workers and employers.

Guilds played an important part in town government. When the first guilds were organized, the towns had few laws to protect merchants or craftsmen. Most laws were made and enforced by the lord who owned the land on which a town stood. As the townspeople gained power, they demanded the right to govern themselves. Often, a guild forced a lord to grant the people a charter giving them certain rights of self-government. The guilds led the fight for self-government, and so their members often ran the new town governments. See GUILD.

The Decline of Feudalism. Economic recovery brought many changes to the social and political organi-

A Medieval City Scene shows many small shops crowded together along a narrow cobblestone street. Shopkeepers and their families lived in the upper part of the wooden buildings. This scene includes a druggist, *right;* a tailor cutting cloth, *left;* and a barber shaving a customer, *background.*

Illumination from the French manuscript *Book of Government of Kings and of Princes* written by Gilles Romain in the 1500's. Bibliothèque de l'Arsenal, Paris (Bulloz)

Illumination from a French manuscript of the 1200's. The Pierpont
Morgan Library, New York

Building a Medieval Stone Wall required great engineering skill. In this illustration, workers cut stone into squares and carry it to a crane. A man provides power for the crane by walking on the steps of a large moving wheel. Another worker carries mortar up a ladder to the man who cements the pieces of stone together.

zation of Europe. Money came back into use with the growth of trade and industry, the rise of towns, and the crusades. The manorial system began to break down as people grew less dependent on the land. Many peasants ran away from the manors to the towns. Others bought their freedom with money they made by selling food to the townspeople. The lords of some towns encouraged new settlers to come. Many lords granted freedom to peasants who settled in their towns.

The feudal system, which was based on manorialism, began to break down, too. Ruling lords could pay for military and political service with money instead of fiefs. Their wealth provided better pay for the soldiers and officials they hired. In return, the lords received better service. They and their governments grew increasingly powerful.

During the 1100's and 1200's, great nation-states arose in England and France. Such powerful kings as Henry II of England and Louis IX of France forced feudal lords to accept their authority. These kings developed new and better forms of government. They also organized national armies to protect the people, and established royal laws and courts to provide justice throughout the land. See HENRY (II) of England; LOUIS (IX).

At the same time, small but well-organized governments took form in Flanders, and in Italian city-states including Florence, Genoa, Siena, and Venice.

Learning and the Arts during the high Middle Ages were devoted to glorifying God and strengthening the power of the church. From 1100 to 1300, almost all the great ideas and artistic achievements reflected the influence of the church.

Princes and laborers alike contributed money to build the magnificent stone cathedrals that rose above medieval towns. The stained glass windows and sculptured figures that decorated the cathedrals portrayed events in the life of Christ and other stories from the Bible. The cathedrals still standing in the French cities of Chartres, Reims, Amiens, and Paris are reminders of the faith of medieval people. See NOTRE DAME, CATHEDRAL OF; REIMS (picture).

Increasing contact with Arab and Byzantine civilizations brought back much learning that had been lost to Europe since the end of the Roman Empire. Scholars translated Greek and Arabic writings from these civilizations into Latin, and studied their meanings. More and more scholars became familiar with the writings of the Greek philosopher Aristotle. The scholars argued whether Aristotle's teachings opposed those of the church. A field of thought called *scholasticism* grew out of their discussions and writings (see SCHOLASTICISM). Among the great teachers and writers of this period were Peter Abelard, Albertus Magnus, and Thomas Aquinas (see ABELARD, PETER; ALBERTUS MAGNUS, SAINT; AQUINAS, SAINT THOMAS).

Students gathered at the cathedrals where the scholars lectured. Students and scholars formed organizations called *universities*, which were similar to the craftsmen's guilds. From the universities came men to serve the church and the new states, to practice law and medicine, to write literature, and to educate others.

THE LATE MIDDLE AGES

Between 1300 and 1500, medieval Europe gradually gave way to modern Europe. During this period, the Middle Ages overlapped the period in European history called the *Renaissance*. For a discussion of the great developments in art and learning during this period, see the WORLD BOOK article on RENAISSANCE.

A Halt in Progress. Although art and learning advanced, other areas of medieval civilization stood still or fell back. Europe had moved forward economically and socially almost without interruption during the high Middle Ages. The population had grown steadily, social conditions had improved, and industry and trade had expanded greatly. These developments ended in the 1300's. The population decreased, the people became discontented, and industry and trade shrank.

Wars and natural disasters played a large part in the halt of European progress. From 1337 to 1453, England and France fought the Hundred Years' War, which interrupted trade and exhausted the economies of both nations (see HUNDRED YEARS' WAR). In addition, the breakdown of feudalism and manorialism caused civil war throughout most of Europe. Peasants rose in bloody revolts to win freedom from lords. In the towns, workmen fought the rich merchants who kept them poor and powerless. To add to the miseries of the people, the *Black Death* killed about a fourth of Europe's population between 1347 and 1350. The Black Death, a form of bubonic plague, was one of the worst epidemic diseases (see BUBONIC PLAGUE). Severe droughts and floods also brought death, disease, and famine.

The Growth of Royal Power. By the 1300's, the breakdown of feudalism had seriously weakened the feudal lords. At the same time, economic recovery had enriched the kings. With the help of hired armies, they enforced their authority over the lords. Royal infantry—newly armed with longbows, spears called *pikes*, and guns—defeated armies of feudal knights. Meanwhile, the kings greatly increased their power by gaining the support of the middle classes in the towns. The townspeople agreed to support the kings by paying taxes in return for peace and good government. These developments gave birth to the nations of modern Europe.

Troubles in the Church. The power of the popes grew with that of the kings, and bitter disputes arose between the rulers of church and state. Churchmen took an increasing part in political affairs, and kings interfered in church affairs more and more. The popes sometimes surrendered their independence and gave in to the kings. This happened especially from 1309 to 1377, when the popes ruled the church from Avignon, France. After the popes returned to Rome, disputes over the election of popes divided the church. Two, and sometimes three, men claimed the title of pope. Such disputes hurt the influence of the church. They also caused criticism of church affairs and of church teaching. The religious unity of western Europe was weakened, leading to the Protestant Reformation of the 1500's. See CHRISTIANITY (Heresies and Schisms); POPE (The Troubles of the Papacy); REFORMATION.

The Growth of Humanism. During the late Middle Ages, scholars and artists were less concerned with religious thinking, and concentrated more on understanding people and the world. This new outlook was called *humanism*. The scholars and artists of ancient Greece and Rome had emphasized the study of humanity. Scholars and artists of the late Middle Ages rediscovered the ancient works and were inspired by them. Architects began to design nonreligious buildings, rather than cathedrals. Painters and sculptors began to glorify people and nature in their works. Scholars delighted in the study of pre-Christian authors of ancient times. More and more writers composed prose and poetry not in Latin but in the *vernacular* (native) languages, including French and Italian. This increasing use of the vernacular opened a new literary age, and gradually brought learning and literature to the common people.

The political, economic, and cultural changes of the late Middle Ages gradually changed Europe, and by the early 1500's it was no longer medieval. But the culture and institutions of the Middle Ages continued to influence modern European history.   BRYCE LYON

Related Articles. For a discussion of political developments in western Europe during the Middle Ages, see the History sections of the articles on AUSTRIA; BELGIUM; ENGLAND; FRANCE; GERMANY; ITALY; the NETHERLANDS; SPAIN; and SWITZERLAND. See also WORLD, HISTORY OF with a table of Major Events of the Middle Ages. Other related articles in WORLD BOOK include:

Outline

I. The Beginnings
  A. The Germanic Invasions
  B. Barbarian Europe
  C. The Christian Church
  D. The Carolingian Empire

II. Feudal Europe
  A. Feudalism
  B. Feudal Government
  C. The Power of the Church
  D. Life of the People

III. The High Middle Ages
  A. Economic Recovery
  B. Medieval Towns
  C. The Decline of Feudalism
  D. Learning and the Arts

IV. The Late Middle Ages
  A. A Halt in Progress
  B. The Growth of Royal Power
  C. Troubles in the Church
  D. The Growth of Humanism

Questions

How did the Germanic invasions of the A.D. 400's change European life?

What two church institutions preserved learning during the early Middle Ages?

What were Charlemagne's accomplishments?

What was *feudalism?* What did it accomplish for medieval Europe?

What were the three classes of medieval society during feudal times?

Why did towns develop during the high Middle Ages?

What was a *fief?* a *manor?* a *vassal?* a *guild?* the *Black Death?*

Why did economic and social progress come to a halt in the late medieval period?

What forces weakened the church in the late Middle Ages?

What was *humanism?* How did it affect medieval society?

MIDDLE AMERICA is a term geographers use for the area between the United States and South America. Middle America includes Mexico, Central America, and the West Indies. All the countries, except El Salvador, have coasts on the Caribbean Sea.

Related Articles in WORLD BOOK include:

MIDDLE ATLANTIC STATES

Tim Eagan, Woodfin Camp, Inc.

Towering Skyscrapers Form the Skyline of New York City, one of the cities that has helped make the Middle Atlantic States a leading center of commerce and industry in the United States.

MIDDLE ATLANTIC STATES are New York, New Jersey, and Pennsylvania. They give the United States one of its most important gateways to other parts of the world. Through their deep harbors come about a fourth of the goods shipped into the country. Their great cities rank among the most important trade centers of the world. Behind this threshold, the Middle Atlantic States are a heavily populated region of great industry. Nearly one of every five persons in the U.S. lives within its 102,745 square miles (266,108 square kilometers). About four-fifths of the almost 39 million people of the region live in urban areas.

The people of the Middle Atlantic States come from as many parts of the world as do the ships that dock at their busy ports. This has been true since colonial days, when such leaders as William Penn welcomed all newcomers to the region and encouraged them to live together in harmony. Successive waves of immigrants from various countries moved into the region and settled.

Of every 100 employed persons in the Middle Atlantic States, about 32 work in manufacturing. Clothing factories in New York make about a fifth of the clothes worn by Americans. Great steel mills in and near Pittsburgh manufacture a fifth of the nation's steel.

Only about 2 of every 100 persons in the Middle Atlantic States earn their living from agriculture. Many of these cultivate the rich truck farms of the New Jersey coastal plain that supply food for city markets.

The area is a center for publishing, higher education, and the cultural arts. Since the days of Benjamin Franklin, it has been the home of leading newspapers, magazines, and book publishing firms. Some of the nation's greatest universities are located here. New York City is a world leader in drama, opera, and music.

The Middle Atlantic region played a key role in the Revolutionary War. Philadelphia was the seat of the Continental Congress and the birthplace of the Declaration of Independence. Military campaigns swirled through the Middle Atlantic region. The battles at Princeton and Trenton were turning points of the war. General George Washington's troops spent their most rugged winters at Valley Forge and Morristown. General John Burgoyne surrendered to the colonists at Saratoga. After independence had been won, leaders from the Middle Atlantic region helped greatly in framing the U.S. Constitution at Philadelphia.

The Land and Its Resources

The Middle Atlantic States stretch westward between New England and the Southern States. New York and New Jersey face the Atlantic Ocean. Ocean-going ships steam up the Delaware River to reach the Pennsylvania ports of Chester and Philadelphia.

Land Regions. The landscape of the Middle Atlantic region has great variety. It includes a broad coastal

The Middle Atlantic States—New Jersey, New York, and Pennsylvania—lie between New England and the Southern States.

plain, mountainous ridges, deep valleys, and flat, fertile lowlands bordering the Great Lakes.

The Appalachian Plateau, made up of round-topped hills and ridges, extends southward from east-central New York, and covers most of northern and western Pennsylvania. Herds of dairy cattle graze on its hills. Miners take coal and stone from southwestern Pennsylvania.

The Appalachian Ridge and Valley Region is a land of wide, scenic valleys. It runs from east-central New York, through northwestern New Jersey, and into central Pennsylvania. Here, also, dairy cattle graze on the slopes, many of which are too steep for other farming.

The New England Upland Region is a narrow strip that rises in southeastern New York and extends through northern New Jersey to eastern Pennsylvania. Hard rock covers the region's flat-topped ridges. Its scenic landscape, cool air, and sparkling lakes make it a favorite summer resort.

The Piedmont begins in the southern tip of New York. It covers a wide area running diagonally through Pennsylvania. Rolling plains, rough uplands, and fertile valleys mark the region. Almost three-fourths of New Jersey's people live in the Piedmont. It includes the principal cities, factories, and highways of the state.

The Coastal Plain consists of gently rolling lowlands that front on the Atlantic Ocean. Most of southern New Jersey lies on this plain. White, sandy beaches stretch along the coast. Fisheries also operate there. Truck farms cover much of the plain's open land. The region also has large deposits of sand, clay, and gravel.

The Adirondack Mountains make up a circular region in northern New York. Its beautiful forests, rivers, and waterfalls make it a popular recreation area. Many people who live there work at lumbering and mining.

Natural Resources of the Middle Atlantic States include rich farm land, abundant woodlands, large mineral reserves, and plentiful water. All three states use water from the Delaware River.

Forests cover more than two-fifths of the region. During the late 1800's, lumbermen cut most of the virgin timber. Second-growth pine, hemlock, hickory, elm, oak, and maple trees now cover the mountain slopes.

Anthracite coal is found in north-central Pennsylvania. Oil fields in southwestern New York and northern Pennsylvania supply petroleum and natural gas. The nation's first commercially successful oil well was drilled near Titusville in northern Pennsylvania in 1859. The Middle Atlantic States have deposits of clay, granite, limestone, sand, slate, and talc. The portland cement industry is centered in Pennsylvania. The three-state region also provides garnet, gypsum, iron ore, kaolin, titanium, and zinc.

Climate of the Middle Atlantic region varies with the altitude and land surface. Extremes of temperature occur only for short periods at a time. The highest mountain area, the Adirondacks, has the coldest climate. January temperatures there have dropped as low as −50° F. (−46° C). Sometimes during January the mercury hits −10° F. (−23° C) in northern Pennsylvania. January temperatures in the three states average about 27° F. (−3° C). Ocean breezes usually hold the region's July temperatures to an average of about 74° F. (23° C). But coastal temperatures sometimes reach 100° F.

Three Lions

The Pennsylvania Dutch, noted as hard-working farmers, still maintain many traditional customs.

(38° C) in July. The region has an average annual rainfall of 42 inches (107 centimeters). Some sections of the mountains have more than 50 inches (130 centimeters) of rain a year, while the Great Lakes region averages barely 30 inches (76 centimeters).

Snowfall averages only about 14 inches (36 centimeters) annually at Cape May in New Jersey, but more than 50 inches (130 centimeters) in the Adirondacks. Occasional heavy snowstorms strike the great cities. Spring thaws sometimes cause severe floods.

Activities of the People

The Middle Atlantic region played a vital role in America's development because of its location and natural resources. In colonial days, it served as a bridge between Puritan New England and the more easy-going life of the South. As the nation grew, it became the natural center of commerce. As a result of the Industrial Revolution, many farmers became factory workers, and the coal and iron of the Middle Atlantic States provided raw materials for the new industries.

Grant Heilman

Rich Rolling Farmland covers about half of the Middle Atlantic States. Southeastern Pennsylvania and New Jersey have the richest soil.

WORLD BOOK photo by Three Lions

Giant Industrial Centers in the Middle Atlantic States make the region a manufacturing center.

Richard A. Peer

Fine Inland Waterways, such as the Saint Lawrence Seaway, open the area to world shipping.

The People. The character of the people helped to build the Middle Atlantic States into national leadership. During the early 1600's, the trade-and-commerce-minded Dutch settled in New Netherland. This area included parts of present-day New Jersey, Delaware, New York, and Pennsylvania. To cultivate their land, the Dutch brought farmers from Denmark, France, Germany, Ireland, and Norway. In 1664, the Dutch surrendered New Netherland to the English.

In Pennsylvania, William Penn created a new society based upon tolerance and concern for the welfare of others. He pioneered in the care of the poor, the sick, and the insane. His promise of religious freedom to everyone brought the first Mennonites from Holland and Germany to settle at Germantown in 1682. By the time of the Revolutionary War, the region had become established as a place where all people could find equal opportunity. Philadelphia was the largest city of the colonies and the leading center of government and culture.

As the young industries of the Middle Atlantic States began to grow, they attracted thousands of new im-migrants. Families of Italian and Slavic descent settled in the fast-expanding steel centers. Irish immigrants moved into the cities during the mid-1800's. Welshmen came to Pennsylvania in the 1840's. Many had had mining experience in the coal mines of Great Britain.

The industry and thrift of the Pennsylvania Dutch are apparent in their neat, prosperous farms. Their imaginative folk art and their delicious German cooking bring thousands of visitors each year to festivals at Hershey. These devout people live simply. Many Mennonites still drive to market in old-fashioned buggies. See MENNONITES; PENNSYLVANIA DUTCH.

Manufacturing and Processing industries grew upon a solid foundation of natural resources, strategic location, and a large and varied supply of labor. All three Middle Atlantic States stand among the 10 leading industrial states. The region earns about 18 times as much income in value of production from manufacturing and processing as it does from farming and mining.

Pennsylvania's factories and mills make durable goods, such as iron and steel, machinery, transportation

435

Great Steel Mills in the Middle Atlantic States supply much of the steel in the United States. Steel comes out of a hot strip mill, *foreground*, at speeds up to 2,300 feet (701 meters) a minute at U.S. Steel's Fairless Works, near Morrisville, Pa.

equipment, and metal products. New York and New Jersey manufacture mostly nondurable products, such as food and clothing. The region also ranks high in printing and publishing, chemical production, feed manufacturing, electrical equipment, and paper and paper products. Philadelphia is a shipbuilding center. Rochester leads the world in manufacturing photographic film, cameras, and optical goods.

Mining. The most important mineral deposits of the Middle Atlantic States are found in Pennsylvania. This state is the nation's only source of *anthracite* (hard coal), and ranks among the country's leading producers of *bituminous* (soft) coal. Great quantities of coal are needed to make iron and steel, and these rich fields keep Pennsylvania in front in its production. Pennsylvania's coal production has declined as other fuels have replaced coal for many purposes. This cutback in production has created hardships in mining areas, where people had come to depend upon the mines for their living.

The Middle Atlantic region also provides petroleum, as well as stone and clay products. In the 1850's, coal oil was widely used in lamps and lanterns. For more than 50 years, Pennsylvania led the states in the production of petroleum. Several other states now produce more petroleum, but Pennsylvania oil is still considered one of the best bases for lubricating oils.

Agriculture. Farms cover about a third of the Middle Atlantic region. About two-fifths of the farmland is used for raising crops, and part of the rest is woodland. The average farm covers 153 acres (62 hectares).

The area's best soils are in the limestone region of southeastern Pennsylvania and the clay-marl belt extending from southwest to northeast through central New Jersey. Because of its fertile soil, New Jersey is called *The Garden State.* Much of the soil in the region must be fertilized to produce profitably.

Dairying and poultry production are the most im-

portant farm activities. New York and Pennsylvania rank among the 10 leading producers of dairy cattle. Farmers in New York raise much hay for feed. The state ranks among the leading states in milk and cheese production. New York has many poultry farms, especially turkey farms. Pennsylvania ranks among the 10 leading egg-producing states.

Truck farming ranks next in importance after dairying and poultry raising. The flat coastal plain around Camden is one of the most intensive truck-gardening areas in the country. Farmers raise beans, celery, lettuce, onions, potatoes, sweet potatoes, and tomatoes.

Vineyards and orchards add color to the famous Finger Lakes region in New York and the Lake Erie area in northwestern Pennsylvania. New York wines are famous throughout the nation. Central Pennsylvania is noted for its apples and peaches.

Other Industries. New Jersey fishermen take crabs, lobsters, and oysters from the Atlantic waters and Delaware Bay. The development of fast transportation and the frozen-food industry enabled many of these sea delicacies to be shipped to such far-inland cities as St. Louis, Denver, and Salt Lake City.

The tourist industry provides the largest source of income for New Jersey. The broad beaches and resorts of this state attract throngs of vacationers and conventioners every year. Atlantic City is known throughout the world as a popular seaside resort.

Transportation. The great harbors of New York and the Delaware River are lined with ships from every part of the world. Sleek passenger liners dock at the Manhattan piers on the Hudson River. On the New Jersey side of the Hudson and in the Delaware River, freighters unload cargo from a number of countries.

Nature not only gave the Middle Atlantic region fine harbors, but also endowed it with a first-class system of inland waterways. Early settlers used the routes of the

436

Hudson, Delaware, Mohawk, and lesser rivers to explore the interior. Pioneers in Pennsylvania built the first Conestoga wagons in the early 1700's. These wagon bodies were shaped somewhat like a boat, so they could cross the rivers without being unloaded. The region developed as roads pushed through the mountains. The opening of the Pennsylvania Turnpike in 1940 marked the beginning of a new transportation era in America.

More than 23,000 miles (37,000 kilometers) of railroad track provide the region with its chief freight transportation system. Hundreds of airports, seaplane bases, and heliports meet the needs of the air age.

Regional Cooperation. Some of the industrial centers of the Middle Atlantic States overlap state boundaries. The Port of New York, for example, lies partly in New Jersey. The Delaware River harbor is in both Pennsylvania and New Jersey. About one of every six New Jerseyites works in either New York or Pennsylvania, and commutes to work.

Many mutual problems have resulted from this overlapping. Smoke from New Jersey factories can be a problem to New Yorkers. A too-narrow bridge across the Delaware River can be a traffic obstacle to people in Pennsylvania and New Jersey. An inadequately equipped airport can create a problem for the entire area.

As early as 1783, the Middle Atlantic States began to realize the need of working together to solve interstate problems. New Jersey and Pennsylvania ratified the Delaware River Compact that year. This agreement regulated the use of the river and the construction of dams across it. The compact has been changed from time to time to meet new needs.

In 1936, the Middle Atlantic States and Delaware created the Interstate Commission on the Delaware River Basin. This commission works to develop the natural resources of the basin, upon which all the states depend. The four states share the water supply of the basin according to careful agreement.

By means of interstate agencies, the Middle Atlantic States deal with common matters of sanitation, recreation, forestation, transportation, and commerce. The Port of New York Authority (now The Port Authority of New York and New Jersey) was established in 1921 to plan and develop the port facilities of the New York-New Jersey area. This authority built shipping piers, bridges, tunnels, truck and bus terminals, and airports (see PORT AUTHORITY OF NEW YORK AND NEW JERSEY). Pennsylvania and New Jersey created the Delaware River Port Authority in 1952. This authority also builds bridges and it operates a transit line between the cities of Philadelphia and Camden.   S. K. STEVENS

Related Articles. For additional information on the Middle Atlantic States, see the separate article on each state in this region with its list of Related Articles. Other related articles in WORLD BOOK include:

HISTORY AND GOVERNMENT

City Government
Civil War
Colonial Life in America
Local Government
Metropolitan Area
Revolutionary War in America

State Government
United States,
   Government of the
United States,
   History of the

PHYSICAL FEATURES

Adirondack Mountains   Allegheny Mountains

Allegheny River
Appalachian Mountains
Catskill Mountains
Delaware Bay

Delaware River
Delaware Water Gap
Hudson River
Piedmont Region

Outline

I. The Land and Its Resources
  A. Land Regions
  B. Natural Resources
  C. Climate

II. Activities of the People
  A. The People
  B. Manufacturing and Processing
  C. Mining
  D. Agriculture
  E. Other Industries
  F. Transportation
  G. Regional Cooperation

Questions

What percentage of the people of the Middle Atlantic States work in factories?

How did the location of the Middle Atlantic States influence the region's growth?

In what way did freedom of religion under William Penn help the region develop?

What are the most important mineral deposits of the region and where are they found?

What is the greatest source of income for New Jersey?

What are three reasons for the Middle Atlantic States' rise as a great manufacturing area?

What are three problems that have required cooperation among the states?

What reminders of early times might a visitor to the region see today?

MIDDLE CLASS is a group of people between the upper class and the lower class in a society. In the United States, most members of the middle class have a college education and an above-average standard of living. The term *middle class* first came into general use during the early 1800's in Europe. It referred to the *bourgeoisie* (business class), a group that developed between the aristocrats and the peasants.

Sociologists use the term *social stratification* to describe the process of dividing societies into classes. This process is based on many factors, chiefly a person's occupation. Other factors include income, power, reputation, and wealth.

The majority of middle-class people work for a living and do not inherit great wealth. Most middle-class occupations do not involve manual labor. Middle-class occupations include those of business owners and managers, clerks, lawyers, physicians, and teachers.

During the 1950's, 1960's, and early 1970's, the middle class ranked as the largest class in the United States. In 1974, more than half the nation's workers had middle-class—that is, nonmanual—occupations. Many values held by middle-class people became the principal values of society. These values included acting according to the moral standards of the community, achieving financial success, advancing in a job, and owning property. During the 1950's and early 1960's, many middle-class people were more concerned with achieving their goals than with changing conditions in society. But from the mid-1960's on, more members of this group, particularly the younger and better educated, became active in society. They objected to certain conditions, rather than simply accepting them. For example, many middle-class Americans supported peace movements and protested racial discrimination. SEYMOUR MARTIN LIPSET

See also SOCIAL CLASS.

A Pipeline on Das Island, part of the United Arab Emirates, carries petroleum that is pumped from the bottom of the Persian Gulf to oil tankers. Oil is the Middle East's most important natural resource.

Bo Dahlin, Carl Östman

MIDDLE EAST is a large region that covers parts of northeastern Africa, southwestern Asia, and southeastern Europe. Scholars disagree on which countries make up the Middle East. But many say the region consists of Bahrain, Cyprus, Egypt, Iran, Iraq, Israel, Jordan, Kuwait, Lebanon, Oman, Qatar, Saudi Arabia, Sudan, Syria, Turkey, United Arab Emirates, Yemen (Aden), and Yemen (Sana). These countries cover about 3,746,000 square miles (9,702,000 square kilometers) and have a population of about 196 million.

Most of the people of the Middle East are Arabs. Other peoples include black Africans, Armenians, Copts, Greeks, Iranians, Jews, Kurds, and Turks.

Much of the Middle East is desert. The people live crowded along the seacoasts, in river valleys, and in mountain valleys that have enough water for growing crops. Most of the people are farmers, and large numbers of them live in poverty. But huge deposits of oil have been discovered in many countries of the Middle East. The income from this valuable mineral has greatly improved the standard of living in many nations.

Two of the world's first great civilizations—those of ancient Egypt and of Babylonia—developed in the Middle East about 4000 B.C. The region also gave birth to three religions—Christianity, Islam, and Judaism.

Throughout its long history, the Middle East has been torn by conflicts among its own peoples and between its people and invaders. Since the mid-1900's, a major conflict between Arabs and Israelis has made the Middle East one of the world's chief trouble spots.

People

Most people of the Middle East belong to the Mediterranean branch of the European geographical race. As a group, they have darker skin and hair than other peoples of the European race, which also includes most European and American "whites." In southern Sudan, most of the people are members of the African geographical race. See RACES, HUMAN.

Arabs make up a majority of the population in all

Sydney N. Fisher, the contributor of this article, is the author of The Middle East: A History *and* The Military in the Middle East: Problems in Society and Government.

the Middle Eastern countries except Israel, Iran, Turkey, and Cyprus. The Arabs are united by a common culture and a common language, Arabic. Most people of Israel are Jews, and the Iranian ethnic group forms the majority in Iran. Turks account for a majority of the population in Turkey, and for a minority in Cyprus. Greeks rank as the largest group in Cyprus. The many minority groups of the Middle East include black Africans, Armenians, Copts, and Kurds.

Way of Life. Most Middle Eastern people live in villages and farm the nearby land. Many use the same kinds of tools that their ancestors did hundreds of years ago. Some of the people are nomads. They live in the desert and herd cattle, sheep, and goats. Many of the people who live in cities and towns are poor, unskilled workers. Others are business or professional people who lead comfortable lives.

Most people of the Middle East have strong ties with their families and with their villages or tribes. They also consider themselves part of both a language group and a religious group.

Religion and Language. Most Middle Eastern people, including most Arabs, Iranians, and Turks, are Muslims. Christians make up the second largest religious group. The churches include the Coptic, Greek Orthodox, and Maronite. Most Israelis practice Judaism.

Arabic is spoken in most Middle Eastern countries. Other languages include Armenian, Greek, Hebrew, Kurdish, Persian, and Turkish.

The Land

The Arabian Peninsula covers much of the central part of the Middle East. The peninsula is a desert plateau that begins at sea level along the Persian Gulf and gradually slopes upward to highlands along the Red Sea. In Yemen (Sana), these highlands reach about 12,000 feet (3,660 meters). The Syrian Desert covers much of Syria, Iraq, and Jordan. Another desert, the Sahara, covers large parts of Egypt and Sudan.

Mountains. In northeastern Turkey, the land rises more than 17,000 feet (5,180 meters). From this high point, four large mountain ranges spread out. These ranges are the Elburz and Zagros mountains of Iran

Middle East

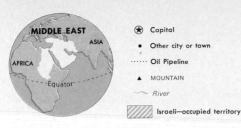

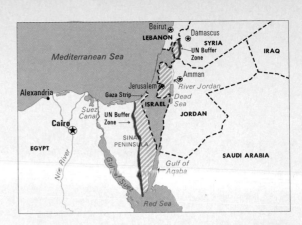

The map below shows the Middle East countries In white. Asia, Africa, and Europe come together in this region. The smaller map, *right*, shows Arab territory that Israel has occupied since the Arab-Israeli war of 1967.

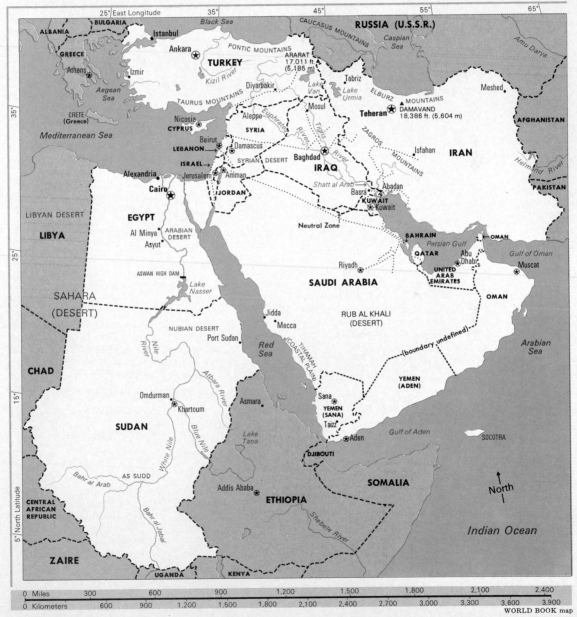

WORLD BOOK map

439

The Nile Valley in Egypt has rich soil and plentiful water for farming. Most of the people of the Middle East are farmers.

United Nations

and the Pontic and Taurus mountains of Turkey. A smaller chain of mountains extends into Lebanon.

Rivers. The Middle East has two great river systems —the Nile River system and the Tigris-Euphrates-Karun river system. The Nile River flows northward through Sudan and Egypt to the Mediterranean Sea. Almost all of Egypt's farmland lies along the Nile, and almost all the Egyptian people live in the Nile Valley or on the Nile Delta.

The Tigris and Euphrates rivers rise in Turkey. They meet in Iraq and form the Shatt al Arab. The Karun River rises in Iran and flows into the Shatt al Arab. The Shatt al Arab empties into the Persian Gulf.

Climate

The Middle East has a long, intensely hot summer and a mild winter. Temperatures vary with location. Summer temperatures may climb to 115° F. (46° C) or more in Egypt, Iran, Saudi Arabia, Sudan, and Turkey. Winter temperatures average from 40° F. (4° C) in the north to 50° F. (10° C) in the south. Temperatures in the northern mountains in Iran and Turkey often drop below 0° F. (−18° C) in winter.

The only parts of the Middle East that receive more than 10 inches (25 centimeters) of rain a year are some coastal regions and the mountain regions of Iran, Lebanon, Turkey, and Yemen (Sana). Most areas have rain only in winter. The heaviest rain, about 40 inches (100 centimeters) a year, falls along the Black, Caspian, and Mediterranean seas.

Economy

Agriculture has long ranked as the main economic activity in the Middle East. But since the mid-1900's, both the production of oil and manufacturing have grown in importance.

Agriculture. Wheat is the most important crop of the Middle East. Other cereal crops include barley, corn, millet, oats, and rice. Fruits, nuts, and vegetables are grown in many areas. These crops include apricots, beans, dates, figs, filberts, grapes, melons, olives, oranges and other citrus fruits, peaches, and pistachios. Other important crops are cotton, sugar beets, and tobacco. The people of the Middle East raise cattle for meat, leather, and dairy products. Sheep are raised for meat and wool.

Since the 1950's, agricultural production has grown because of improved equipment, scientific farming methods, better seeds, and increased irrigation. Many all-weather roads have been built, and trucks have been imported to carry farm products to markets.

Mining. The Middle East has more than half of the world's proved oil reserves. Iran and the Arab nations of Bahrain, Egypt, Iraq, Kuwait, Oman, Qatar, Saudi Arabia, Syria, and United Arab Emirates all are important oil-producing countries.

Most Middle Eastern oil is sold to European countries and Japan. Altogether, the oil-producing countries received about $80 billion a year for their oil during the late 1970's. They spend much of their oil income on construction of airports, factories, highways, hospitals, schools, and other improvements. In addition, much of the income is spent on arms and military training.

After the 1973 Arab-Israeli War, a number of Arab oil-exporting nations temporarily stopped oil shipments to the United States and The Netherlands. They also reduced shipments to other nations that supported Israel. The Arabs did this to win support for the Arab side in the Arab-Israeli conflict. Their action helped cause oil shortages in many countries. Other minerals produced in the Middle East include chrome, copper, gold, iron, manganese, and phosphates.

Manufacturing has increased since the 1950's, especially in Egypt, Iran, Israel, Kuwait, Saudi Arabia, and Turkey. The chief manufactured products include cement, chemicals, light industrial goods, processed foods, and textiles. Many factories have been built in large cities. But the increasing industrialization has worsened such problems as pollution and overcrowding.

History

People lived in parts of the Middle East as early as 25,000 B.C. About 4000 B.C., two of the world's earliest great civilizations—those of ancient Egypt and of Babylonia—developed in the region. The Egyptian civilization arose in the Nile Valley of Egypt (see EGYPT, ANCIENT). Babylonia developed on the fertile plain between the Tigris and Euphrates rivers of Iraq (see BABYLONIA). About 1900 B.C., a people called the Hittites came to power in Turkey. The three great civilizations balanced one another for 500 years. In the land between the three empires, many other peoples organized societies. These peoples included the Arameans, Hebrews, and Phoenicians. The Arameans developed a language that spread throughout the Middle East. The Hebrews firmly established a belief in one God. The Phoenicians may have developed an alphabet.

Beginning in the 800's B.C., all these civilizations

were destroyed by a series of invaders. The invaders included the Assyrians, Chaldeans, Medes, Persians, and finally Alexander the Great.

The Hellenistic Age. Alexander conquered the Middle East in 331 B.C. He introduced the Greek language and united the region into one empire. The next 300 years, called *the Hellenistic Age*, brought great achievements in scholarship, science, and the arts.

The Romans conquered most of the Middle East by 31 B.C. Roman armies, governors, and tax collectors controlled the people, and Latin became the language of the government. During the Roman rule, Jesus Christ was born in Bethlehem and died in Jerusalem.

Arab Rule. In the A.D. 600's, the followers of the Prophet Muhammad, called Muslims, swept out of the Arabian Peninsula and conquered what are now Egypt, Iran, Iraq, Israel, Jordan, Lebanon, and Syria. Many of the conquered people adopted the Arabic language and the Muslim religion. Many non-Arab Muslims in the conquered lands joined the army or entered government service. The Seljuk Turks from central Asia conquered much of the Arab empire in the 1000's. They were followed by the Ottoman Turks in the 1300's.

Under Ottoman rule, the Middle East declined in power. Meanwhile, strong states were developing in Europe. In 1869, French engineers completed the Suez Canal, which shortened the water route between Europe and the East. During the late 1800's, Great Britain gained influence in Egypt and in *sheikdoms* (kingdoms) on the Arabian Peninsula to protect its trade routes.

World War I. During World War I (1914-1918), the Arabs fought with the Europeans against the Turks to gain their independence. Turkey was defeated and, in 1923, it became a republic. But most Arab lands were divided into mandated territories by the League of Nations and placed under British and French rule (see MANDATED TERRITORY). The Arabs continued to demand independence. Many territories gained independence in the 1930's and 1940's. Britain withdrew from many sheikdoms in the 1960's. By late 1971, it had withdrawn completely from the Arabian Peninsula.

Palestine was one of the Arab territories mandated to Great Britain. In 1917, Britain issued the Balfour Declaration, which supported the creation of a Jewish homeland in Palestine—but without violating the civil or religious rights of the Arabs there. Many Jews moved to Palestine during the 1920's and 1930's. The Palestinian Arabs resented the growing Jewish immigration. They believed that Palestine was their homeland, and they wanted it to become an independent Arab state. The Arabs and the Jews fought each other, and both fought the British for control of Palestine.

In 1947, Britain asked the United Nations (UN) to help solve the conflict. The UN proposed that Palestine be divided into two states, one Arab and one Jewish. The Arabs, who made up the majority of the population, rejected the plan. They said the UN did not have the right to divide their land. The Jews accepted the plan. In May 1948, they established the state of Israel on land assigned to them by the UN. See PALESTINE.

The 1948 and 1956 Wars. After the creation of Israel, several Arab states joined the Palestinians in their fight against the Jewish state. The UN arranged a cease-fire late in 1948. When the war ended, Israel controlled 75 per cent of Palestine, about 2,000 square miles (5,200 square kilometers) more than the UN had assigned to it. Egypt and Jordan held the rest of Palestine.

About 700,000 Arabs who had been living in what became Israel fled or were driven from their homes. They became refugees in the Arab countries around Israel. During the early 1950's, the refugees sent raiding parties into Israel. Israel struck back at the Arab countries.

In 1954, Prime Minister Gamal Abdel Nasser of Egypt asked the Western nations for arms to defend his country. The West refused, and Nasser turned to Russia for aid. The United States then withdrew its offer to help Egypt build a dam across the Nile River near Aswan. Nasser reacted by seizing the Suez Canal from its British and French owners in July 1956. Egypt then built the Aswan High Dam with Russian help.

In October 1956, Great Britain, France, and Israel responded to the seizing of the canal by invading Egypt. Pressure from the United States, Russia, and other nations forced the invaders to withdraw. A UN peace-keeping force was stationed in Egypt along the Israeli border. Israel refused to permit the troops on its land.

The UN troops prevented raids across the Israeli-Egyptian border after the 1956 war. But raids continued back and forth along Israel's borders with Jordan and Syria.

The 1967 and 1973 Wars. In 1967, the Arabs believed that Israel planned a major attack on Syria. At Nasser's

Keystone

The Suez Canal provides a water route between the Mediterranean Sea and the Red Sea in the Middle East. The canal was blocked by sunken ships during the Arab-Israeli war of 1967 and remained closed until 1975.

demand, the UN troops were withdrawn from Egypt's border with Israel. Nasser then sent military forces into the Sinai Peninsula and closed the Straits of Tiran, the entrance to the Israeli port of Elat. Israel considered the closing of the straits to be an act of war. On June 5, 1967, Israeli planes wiped out the air forces of Egypt, Jordan, and Syria. Israeli forces then seized Egypt's Sinai Peninsula and Gaza Strip, all of Jordan west of the River Jordan, and the Golan Heights in Syria. The UN arranged a cease-fire on June 10, ending the war after six days of fighting. The war is sometimes called the *Six-Day War*.

After the war, no armistice was signed, and no solution was reached in the Arab-Israeli conflict. The Arabs wanted Israel to withdraw from the land it conquered in 1967, and Israel wanted the Arabs to recognize its right to exist. The Arabs said they would recognize Israel if it gave up the occupied land. But Israel refused to withdraw to its pre-1967 boundaries before negotiations. Russia rearmed Egypt and Syria, and the United States armed Israel. Palestinian Arabs formed guerrilla groups to fight Israel. The UN cease-fire was ignored by both the Arabs and the Israelis. In 1970, the United States arranged a temporary cease-fire. But minor clashes occurred occasionally during the early 1970's.

On Oct. 6, 1973, full-scale war broke out again. Egyptian troops crossed the Suez Canal, and major battles occurred in the Sinai Peninsula and in the Golan Heights. A series of cease-fires ended most of the fighting by November. In 1974, agreements were reached for separation of the Arab and Israeli forces. Also in 1974, Arab leaders agreed to give the Palestine Liberation Organization (PLO) the right to form an independent Palestinian state in certain Israeli-occupied territories in the event of a withdrawal. See PALESTINE LIBERATION ORGANIZATION; UNITED NATIONS (The Arab-Israeli Wars).

The Middle East Today remains one of the world's chief trouble spots because of the conflict between the Arabs and the Israelis. Many people—both in the Middle East and elsewhere—have called for a solution of the conflict to end the threat of further fighting. In 1977, President Anwar al-Sadat of Egypt and Israeli Prime Minister Menachem Begin started discussions of ways to end the conflict between their countries. In 1978, Sadat, Begin, and President Jimmy Carter held discussions in the United States at meetings arranged by Carter. The discussions resulted in a major agreement, which included plans for Israel's gradual withdrawal from the Sinai, the Gaza Strip, and Jordan west of the River Jordan. It also called for the creation of a peace treaty between Egypt and Israel. The treaty was signed in 1979. In 1975, Israel had withdrawn its troops from the far western part of the Sinai. In 1979, the Israelis pulled back to near the center of the peninsula. In spite of this progress, the Middle East remains a trouble spot. Many Arabs oppose the agreement and have criticized Sadat for negotiating independently from other Arab leaders.　　　SYDNEY N. FISHER

Related Articles in WORLD BOOK include:

COUNTRIES

Bahrain	Egypt	Iraq	Jordan
Cyprus	Iran	Israel	Kuwait
Lebanon	Saudi Arabia	Turkey	Yemen
Oman	Sudan	United Arab	(Aden)
Qatar	Syria	Emirates	Yemen (Sana)

OTHER RELATED ARTICLES

Ancient Civilization	Desert	Mediterranean Sea
Arabs	Islam	Petroleum

MIDDLE ENGLISH. See ENGLISH LANGUAGE (Development of English).

MIDDLE SCHOOL is a school designed for students in sixth, seventh, and eighth grade. Some middle schools include fifth grade. In a number of communities, students attend middle school rather than junior high school. Most middle schools offer subjects similar to those offered in grades 6, 7, and 8. Middle schools are sometimes called *intermediate schools*.

Middle schools try to meet the special needs of children of the sixth, seventh, and eighth grades. Most children of this age are entering *puberty*. This period of rapid growth marks the end of childhood and the start of physical and sexual maturity. Middle schools try to help students understand the physical and social changes of puberty. The schools provide guidance counselors to help students adjust to these changes.

Middle schools seek better ways to educate students. Many middle schools use a method of instruction called *individualized learning*, also called *individualized instruction*. This system enables each student to advance at his or her own speed and receive individual help from the teacher. The schools also use *team teaching*, in which several teachers share the responsibility for teaching a group of students.

Middle schools began in the United States about 1960 and their number has increased steadily. In the 1960's, many schools became overcrowded. To relieve the crowded conditions, some communities built middle schools. Such facilities as gyms and laboratories were designed to meet the needs of students in their preteens or early teens. Some of the first middle schools were in Centerville, Ohio; Mt. Kisco, N.Y.; and Upper St. Clair, Pa. In the mid-1970's, the United States had about 3,900 middle schools.　　　DONALD H. EICHHORN

See also JUNIOR HIGH SCHOOL.

MIDDLE STONE AGE. See PREHISTORIC PEOPLE (How Prehistoric Hunters Lived); STONE AGE.

MIDDLE WEST. See MIDWESTERN STATES.

MIDDLEMAN. See TRADE (The Use of Markets).

MIDDLETON, ARTHUR (1742-1787), was one of the South Carolina signers of the Declaration of Independence. He was also an American Revolutionary War leader. He served in the Colonial Legislature and in the First Provincial Congress of South Carolina. He became an opponent of the Tories, and served as a member of the first South Carolina Council of Safety (see TORY PARTY). He was a delegate to the Continental Congress in 1776 and 1777 and a delegate to the Congress of the Confederation in 1781. He was also elected in 1778, 1779, and 1780, but refused the election. The British captured him in 1780 at the siege of Charleston. He was born near Charleston, S.C.　　　ROBERT J. TAYLOR

MIDDLEWEIGHT. See BOXING (Weight Classes).

MIDGET. See DWARF.

MIDIANITES were a northern Arabian tribe. They were said to be descended from Midian, a son of Abraham. The Midianites lived east of the northern tip of the Red Sea. Moses lived with them after fleeing from

THE LAND OF THE MIDNIGHT SUN

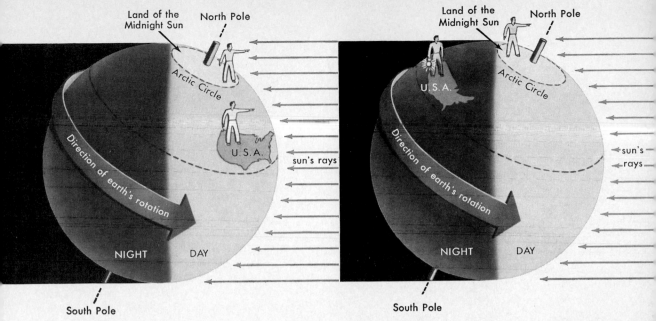

These diagrams show how the North Pole is tilted toward the sun about June 21. In the diagram on the left, both the United States and the Arctic regions are in daylight. In the diagram on the right, the earth's rotation has turned the United States away from the sun so that it Is in darkness, but the Arctic regions are still in daylight. All areas north of the Arctic Circle have the midnight sun at least one night in the year. At the North Pole, the sun does not set for six months of the year.

Egypt, and married a daughter of Jethro, a Midianite priest. In a later age, the Israelite hero, Gideon, defeated the Midianites at Jezreel. GLEASON L. ARCHER, JR.

MIDLAND EMPIRE. See BILLINGS.

MIDLAND LUTHERAN COLLEGE. See UNIVERSITIES AND COLLEGES (table).

MIDNIGHT SUN. The sun shines at midnight at certain times of the year in the polar regions. At the Arctic Circle, this occurs about June 21. Farther north, the periods of midnight sun last longer. For example, in northern Norway, the *Land of the Midnight Sun*, there is continuous daylight from May through July. At the North Pole, the sun does not set for six months, from about March 20 to about September 23. At the Antarctic Circle, 24 hours of sunlight occurs about December 21, and the South Pole has midnight sun from about September 23 to about March 20.

The midnight sun is caused by the tilting of the earth toward the sun. As the earth travels around the sun, first the South Pole, and then the North Pole, faces the sun. While one polar region faces the sun, it has continuous daylight. At the same time, the other polar region faces away from the sun and has continuous darkness.

See also ANTARCTIC CIRCLE; ARCTIC CIRCLE; DAY.

MIDSHIPMAN is a student at the United States Naval Academy in Annapolis, Md. Upon graduation, midshipmen receive commissions as ensigns in the Navy or as second lieutenants in the Marine Corps. Canadian naval cadets are also called midshipmen.

The term *midshipman* goes back to the 1600's, when the British Navy placed junior officers amidships to relay orders. In 1954, Great Britain substituted the rank of acting sublieutenant for that of midshipman. These men serve in a training program on shore. THEODORE ROPP

See also UNITED STATES NAVAL ACADEMY; CLOTHING (picture: Midshipmen).

MIDSUMMER NIGHT'S DREAM, A. See SHAKE-SPEARE, WILLIAM (Shakespeare's Plays).

MIDWAY, BATTLE OF. See WORLD WAR II (The Battle of Midway); MIDWAY ISLAND.

MIDWAY CHURCH. See GEORGIA (Places to Visit).

MIDWAY ISLAND lies 1,300 miles (2,090 kilometers) northwest of Honolulu in the Pacific Ocean. It is made up of two islands in an atoll 6 miles (10 kilometers) in diameter. It has an area of 2 square miles (5 square kilometers) and a total coastline of about 20 miles (32 kilometers). Midway has a population of about 2,200. The United States discovered Midway in 1859, and annexed it in 1867. United States companies built a cable relay station there in 1903, and an airport in 1935. The U.S. Navy Department controls the island.

The Battle of Midway was one of the most important naval battles in World War II. From June 4 to June 6, 1942, United States land- and carrier-based planes attacked a Japanese fleet approaching the islands. They sank four aircraft carriers and one heavy cruiser. The United States lost the destroyer *Hammann* and the aircraft carrier *Yorktown*.

The Battle of Midway was the first decisive U.S. naval victory over the Japanese in World War II. It crippled Japan's naval air power and ended Japan's attempt to seize Midway as a base from which to strike Hawaii. Many military experts believe it was the turning point in the Pacific campaign. EDWIN H. BRYAN, JR.

See also WORLD WAR II (The Battle of Midway).

443

MIDWESTERN STATES

Evergreen Trees
Deciduous Trees
Grass

⊛ Capitals
• Cities and Towns
— Rail Lines

0 20 40 60 80 100 120 140 Miles
0 40 80 120 160 Kilometers

Specially created for World Book Encyclopedia by Rand McNally and World Book editors

MIDWESTERN STATES

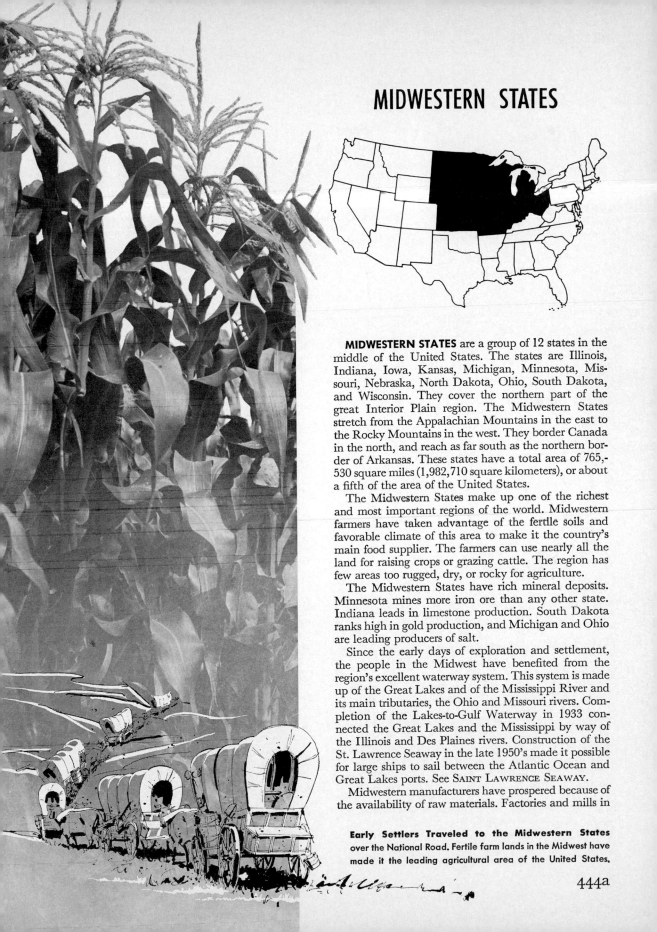

MIDWESTERN STATES are a group of 12 states in the middle of the United States. The states are Illinois, Indiana, Iowa, Kansas, Michigan, Minnesota, Missouri, Nebraska, North Dakota, Ohio, South Dakota, and Wisconsin. They cover the northern part of the great Interior Plain region. The Midwestern States stretch from the Appalachian Mountains in the east to the Rocky Mountains in the west. They border Canada in the north, and reach as far south as the northern border of Arkansas. These states have a total area of 765,-530 square miles (1,982,710 square kilometers), or about a fifth of the area of the United States.

The Midwestern States make up one of the richest and most important regions of the world. Midwestern farmers have taken advantage of the fertile soils and favorable climate of this area to make it the country's main food supplier. The farmers can use nearly all the land for raising crops or grazing cattle. The region has few areas too rugged, dry, or rocky for agriculture.

The Midwestern States have rich mineral deposits. Minnesota mines more iron ore than any other state. Indiana leads in limestone production. South Dakota ranks high in gold production, and Michigan and Ohio are leading producers of salt.

Since the early days of exploration and settlement, the people in the Midwest have benefited from the region's excellent waterway system. This system is made up of the Great Lakes and of the Mississippi River and its main tributaries, the Ohio and Missouri rivers. Completion of the Lakes-to-Gulf Waterway in 1933 connected the Great Lakes and the Mississippi by way of the Illinois and Des Plaines rivers. Construction of the St. Lawrence Seaway in the late 1950's made it possible for large ships to sail between the Atlantic Ocean and Great Lakes ports. See SAINT LAWRENCE SEAWAY.

Midwestern manufacturers have prospered because of the availability of raw materials. Factories and mills in

Early Settlers Traveled to the Midwestern States over the National Road. Fertile farm lands in the Midwest have made it the leading agricultural area of the United States.

444a

The Rich, Rolling Farmland of the Midwest produces much of the nation's food. Mid-western States are leaders in producing corn, wheat, vegetables, and dairy products.

Grant Heilman

the Midwest produce more food, iron and steel, fabricated metal products, machinery, transportation equipment, paper, and rubber products than those in any other region of the United States.

The combination of favorable geographic factors—good soil, comparatively mild climate, generally level land surface, and accessibility to the ocean—makes the Midwest different from the interior of any other continent. More people live in the Midwest than in any other area so far from the sea. The 59,242,000 Midwesterners make up more than one-fourth of the population of the United States.

The Land and Its Resources

The area covered by the 12 Midwestern States is basically a lowland whose eastern and western edges rise above the rest of the terrain. The elevation ranges from 230 feet (70 meters) above sea level near Cardwell, Mo., to 7,242 feet (2,207 meters) on Harney Peak, in the Black Hills of South Dakota. To the northeast, the Great Lakes form the world's largest group of fresh-water lakes.

Land Regions. The Midwest has five general land regions. The glaciers that moved over most of the Midwest during the Ice Age leveled the land and left few rugged areas. The flatness and vast expanse of the landscape awe visitors. They can look over the Midwestern farmlands stretching flat as far as the eye can see.

The Great Plains have a higher elevation than any other section of the Midwest. They form the western part of the region and extend through the western areas of North Dakota, South Dakota, Nebraska, and Kansas. The plains rise toward the west, and reach average elevations of 3,000 to 4,000 feet (910 to 1,200 meters) in all four states. The Great Plains are generally flat, broken occasionally by river valleys, canyons, and buttes. The region receives less rain and snow than other

parts of the Midwest. As a result, farmers are limited to crops requiring little moisture, such as wheat, or crops dependent on irrigation. Cattle graze on grasses that cover much of the land. See GREAT PLAINS.

The Ozark Plateau, an upland of lakes, hill farms, and scenic forests, rises in southern Missouri. Its elevation ranges from about 500 to 2,000 feet (150 to 610 meters). Vacationers enjoy the fishing and hunting, cool summers, and natural beauty. See OZARK MOUNTAINS.

The Superior Upland surrounds the southern and western parts of Lake Superior. This rugged area reaches its highest point (2,301 feet, or 701 meters) at Eagle Mountain in Minnesota. Iron deposits there supply the nation's iron and steel industry.

Great pine forests originally covered the land. During the 1800's, this area had many logging and lumbering camps. The lumbermen used the Great Lakes and south-flowing streams to ship the lumber to settlers in the prairies who needed wood. By the early 1900's, little remained of the great forests. Since then, foresters have controlled cutting and planted new trees, so that second-growth timber now covers much of the area. The upland has more than 6,000 square miles (15,000 square kilometers) of lakes that were gouged out by glaciers long ago. Campers, fishermen, and boating enthusiasts enjoy summer holidays there.

The Appalachian Plateau, an extension of the Appalachian Mountains, covers eastern Ohio. This hilly, eroded region has deposits of coal, oil, and other minerals. Farms lie chiefly in the valleys, and sheep and cattle graze on the hills. See APPALACHIAN MOUNTAINS.

The Interior Lowland makes up the remainder of the 12-state region. The rich soils of this prairie area are the food-producing heart of the nation, and one of the richest agricultural areas in the world. The lowland may be divided into three main parts: (1) the green fields of tall corn stretching from western Ohio to eastern Ne-

Midwestern Farm Life still includes such traditional community events as the farm auction sale, presided over by an auctioneer.

Great Industrial Centers have developed in Detroit, Chicago, and other Midwestern cities.

Beef Cattle and Other Livestock raised in the Midwest supply much of the nation's meat.

Scenic Recreation Areas can be found throughout the Midwest. The region has many lakes and rivers that attract campers, fishermen, and tourists.

braska; (2) golden, waving wheat fields that cover much of the western two-thirds of Kansas, western Minnesota, western Nebraska, and the eastern Dakotas; and (3) America's dairyland which extends through Wisconsin, northern Illinois, eastern Minnesota, northeastern Iowa, and southern Michigan.

Climate. The extreme western part of the Midwest is very dry. Farmers depend on irrigation to raise many crops. In the north, the winters are long and cold, and the summers short. North Dakota has an average January temperature of 9° F. (−13° C), but only receives about 30 inches (76 centimeters) of snow a year. In northern Minnesota, Wisconsin, and Michigan, heavy snows often blanket the countryside.

Summers are long and hot in the southern part of the Midwest. Winter temperatures generally average below freezing. The eastern section receives much more precipitation than the western part. Southern Illinois and Missouri are noted for long, hot summers. Temperatures in these regions in July average about 80° F. (27° C).

Water Conservation. The lack of water on the Great Plains affected settlers even before they began farming. Because of the dryness of the region, few trees grew and

the pioneers lacked firewood and lumber for building. As early as 1855, a Nebraska settler, J. Sterling Morton, began a tree-planting program. Today, Nebraska has the largest planted forests in the United States. The nation's tree-planting program gained new vigor after the dust storms of the 1930's. Farmers had plowed up so much land to produce crops that no trees or deep-root grasses were left to hold the soil down.

The Mississippi River system is the chief water source of the agricultural Middle West. In the west and north, tributaries such as the Platte in Nebraska carry little water. But widespread irrigation projects, begun on the Platte in the 1930's, have increased the productivity of large areas. In 1914, Ohio passed the first Conservancy Act in the United States. The act provided for the construction of dams and reservoirs to prevent flooding. In general, the Missouri River carries too little water in the north, but causes floods in its lower course. The federal Pick-Sloan Missouri Basin Program, begun in 1944, was designed to correct this condition (see MISSOURI RIVER).

Certain areas in the Midwest have a shortage of *ground water* (water stored in natural underground reservoirs). Cities and farms depend on ground water for farming and for home and industrial uses. Some sections, such as Kansas, southern Illinois, and the Dakotas, suffered from a shortage of ground water during the 1950's, because of a severe drought. The U.S. Department of Agriculture established a program to build small dams and channels that prevent water from small streams from pouring into rivers and being lost.

The heavily industrial Midwestern States surrounding the Great Lakes have no water shortage. Their problem comes from pollution, created by the intensive industrial use of water.

Work of the People

About three-fourths of all Midwesterners live in urban areas, and the rest live in rural areas. The rural population outnumbers urban dwellers in North and South Dakota. Most large Midwestern cities grew up along the Great Lakes or on the main river routes. Chicago, the region's largest city, sprawls on a plain along the shores of Lake Michigan. Milwaukee also lies along Lake Michigan. Detroit, the second largest Midwestern city, is on the banks of the Detroit River close to Lake Erie. Cleveland extends along the southern shore of Lake Erie. St. Louis lies along the Mississippi River. Water transportation plays a major part in the importance of these cities, but they also bustle with air, rail, and highway traffic. Indianapolis is the largest Midwestern city not on navigable water.

Manufacturing accounts for the greatest share of the value of goods produced in the Midwest. It accounts for about 75 per cent of the value of production. Agriculture contributes over 20 per cent, and mining earns the rest.

Agriculture. There are about 1,277,000 farms in the Midwest. Their average size ranges from 915 acres (370 hectares) in South Dakota to 145 acres (59 hectares) in Michigan. The four westernmost states have the largest and fewest farms, mainly because the people use much of the land for grazing cattle on large ranches, or for farming large wheat crops.

No agricultural region in the world is more mechanized than the Midwest. Farmers use power equipment to plow the land, to apply specially prepared liquid fertilizers, and to plant crops. Mechanized pickers harvest corn, and combines gather grains and beans. Special machinery cuts, bales, and chops hay and other forage. Power equipment unloads grain from trucks to elevators. Dairy farmers use machinery to milk cows.

Soon after World War I, prices dropped and farmers could not pay for the equipment and land they had bought on credit. The National Grange and especially the American Farm Bureau Federation helped obtain federal legislation to ease the farmers' problems.

Federal help came in 1933 with the establishment of the Agricultural Adjustment Administration. Congress passed the Hope-Aiken Act in 1948, and the Agricultural Act in 1954. These and other measures limit the amount of cropland and thus the amount of farm products on the market. The federal government pays farmers to let part of the land lie idle.

Since the 1920's, the Midwest has had the problem of farm surpluses, resulting from mechanization, gener-

ally abundant rainfall, and the increased size of farms. Except during World War II and the Korean War, farmers have produced more of some crops, such as wheat, than the market has demanded. The government buys the excess crops and puts them in sealed storage. This prevents the excess crops from flooding the market, and forcing prices down. Row upon row of cylindrical metal storage bins containing surplus food products stand in small towns throughout the Midwest.

Corn is worth about $12 billion a year for Midwestern farmers, and leads in value among agricultural products. Cattle and hogs follow, and dairy products rank fourth. Ten leading corn states lie in the Midwest. Farmers of Iowa, Illinois, and Indiana lead the nation in hog raising. Wisconsin and Minnesota, two states in the dairy belt, lead in dairy products. Kansas ranks first in wheat production, followed by North Dakota. In other agricultural products, North Dakota leads the states in barley and flaxseed. Iowa and Illinois lead in corn production. South Dakota leads in the production of rye. Iowa and Indiana rank among the top 10 states in egg production. Five of the top 10 beef-cattle states are in the Midwest.

The states bordering the Great Lakes produce large quantities of vegetables and fruits. Ohio, Indiana, Illinois, and Michigan rank among the leaders in tomatoes, and Minnesota and Wisconsin in green peas. Michigan and Wisconsin rank high in total vegetable production. Michigan orchards yield more cherries than those in any other state.

Manufacturing and Processing industries have developed chiefly in the five Midwestern States east of the Mississippi River—Illinois, Indiana, Michigan, Ohio, and Wisconsin. All these states, except Wisconsin, rank among the nation's top 10 industrial leaders in value added by manufacture. Only California and New York have a greater industrial output than Ohio.

In the Midwest, transportation equipment leads all other manufactured products in value. It is followed by machinery, processed foods, metal products, electrical machinery, and primary metals. Detroit is the automobile capital of the world. The leadership of Benjamin Goodrich and Harvey Firestone, who founded their companies in Akron, established Ohio as the leader in the nation in manufacturing tires and other rubber products.

The Midwest also pioneered in farm-machinery production. The first combine (harvester-thresher combination) was used in Michigan in 1837. Factories in Illinois, Indiana, and Minnesota now produce most of the nation's combines. John Deere made America's first steel plow in Grand Detour, Ill., in 1837. Cyrus McCormick built the nation's first reaper factory in Chicago in 1847. Chicago's International Harvester Company, one of the largest farm-implement manufacturers in the world, resulted from a merger in 1902 of a number of companies in Chicago, Milwaukee, and Springfield, Ill.

The Midwest's food industry processes, prepares, and packs countless products. Wheat comes to Minneapolis; Chicago; Kansas City, Mo.; Duluth; and Superior for milling. Plants in these and other cities turn corn, soybeans, and other grains into foods, beverages, and industrial products. Such Midwestern cities as Chicago; Kansas City, Mo.; and Omaha, Nebr., rank among the country's leading meat processers. This industry has grown out of the Midwest's abundant supply of cattle and hogs.

Furnaces and mills in Illinois, Indiana, Ohio, and Michigan produce about 50 per cent of the iron and steel made in the United States. Limestone for steel-making comes chiefly from Indiana, which leads the nation in the production of this mineral. Coal abounds in states bordering the Midwest, such as West Virginia, and can be imported cheaply.

Missouri is the nation's leading lead producer. The electrical machinery and automobile industries use large quantities of metal.

Pipelines bring oil from the Gulf Coast to great refineries that line the southern end of Lake Michigan. One of the world's largest oil refineries operates in Whiting, Ind.

Transportation. Farm products from the sprawling agricultural Midwest must travel great distances to reach far-off markets. For this reason, farmers throughout the years have sought ways to keep transportation rates low. They accomplished this mainly through legislation and cooperative movements.

The growth of railroads during the 1800's did much to speed settlement. But, as agriculture prospered, farmers found that they depended greatly on the railroads to bring in supplies, and especially to carry farm products to markets. The railroads took advantage of this dependence by charging rates that the farmers could not afford. In the 1870's, the National Grange fought the railroads by winning the passage of state laws regulating railroad rates. Cooperatives helped cut farmers' costs chiefly in two ways. By banding together, the farmers could afford to build storage facilities, such as grain elevators, previously supplied by railroads at high costs. By pooling their shipments, the farmers could obtain bulk rates for transporting their products.

In the early 1900's, many Midwestern States launched great highway-improvement programs. Trucking began to develop rapidly after World War I. Cooperatives took advantage of the expanded highways by forming their own trucking firms. In this way, they avoided paying railroad rates, especially on short hauls.

The population of Midwestern urban areas has been growing since the industrial expansion that followed the Civil War. Many persons moved to the cities in search of work. Others moved out of the crowded business and factory districts to the suburbs that now surround most metropolitan areas. To bring these people to work every day, and to take them home, cities have had to improve their transportation systems. JOHN H. GARLAND

Related Articles. For additional information on the Midwestern States, see the separate article on each state in this region with its list of Related Articles. Other Related Articles in WORLD BOOK include:

HISTORY AND GOVERNMENT

City Government	State Government
Colonial Life	United States,
in America	Government of the
Indian, American	United States,
Indian Wars	History of the
Local Government	Western Frontier Life
Northwest Territory	Westward Movement
Pioneer Life in America	

PHYSICAL FEATURES

Appalachian	Missouri River
Mountains	Ohio River
Detroit River	Ozark Mountains
Great Lakes	Platte River
Great Plains	Red River of the North
Mississippi River	Wabash River

Outline

I. **The Land and Its Resources**
   A. Land Regions
   B. Climate
   C. Water Conservation
II. **Work of the People**
   A. Agriculture
   B. Manufacturing and Processing
   C. Transportation

Questions

Why is the Midwest one of the world's best areas for farming?

What are the three main agricultural regions of the Midwest?

How is the terrain of the Midwest unusual in appearance?

What products manufactured in the Midwest have the greatest value?

Why is it sometimes said that Midwestern farmers produce too much?

Where do most of the Midwest's largest cities lie?

Why do the westernmost states of the area have the largest farms?

In what kind of machinery did Midwestern manufacturers pioneer?

Why do the Midwestern States surrounding the Great Lakes have water-pollution problems?

What four geographic factors make the Midwest different from the interior of any other continent?

What percentage of Midwesterners live in towns and cities?

How many Midwestern States are there? Name them.

MIDWIFE is a person who helps women give birth. Most midwives accept only patients who will probably have a normal delivery. Midwives also give care and advice during the patient's pregnancy and after she gives birth. They work chiefly in patients' homes, but also in hospitals and clinics.

Midwives must be able to recognize signs of difficulty during childbirth. If necessary, a physician is called, or the patient is moved to a hospital.

Two types of midwives practice in the United States. *Nurse-midwives* are registered nurses who have been certified by the American College of Nurse-Midwives. They have completed a midwife-training program that lasts from one to two years and includes classroom study and supervised work with patients. *Lay-midwives* have no formal training in midwifery.

Traditionally, most midwives have worked in rural areas that have relatively few doctors. During the 1970's, more and more city women began to use midwives, especially nurse-midwives.

Some states require one or both types of midwives to have a license. Other states, chiefly those with few doctors, require no licensing. LOIS KAZMIER HALSTEAD

MIDWIFE TOAD. Two small toads of central and southwestern Europe are called *midwife*, or *obstetrical*, toads because the male helps care for the eggs. They are about 2 inches (5 centimeters) long. The female lays

The Male Midwife Toad carries the fertilized eggs like a bunch of grapes attached to its hind legs until the tadpoles hatch.

from 20 to 60 eggs in two strings. The male fastens them to his legs and carries them until they hatch. He usually hides under a stone or in some other place while he carries the eggs. He comes out only after dark and bathes the eggs in a pond or stream. After three weeks he takes them into the water, where tadpoles hatch from the eggs.

Scientific Classification. The midwife toad belongs to the toad family, *Discoglossidae*. One of the toads is genus *Alytes*, species *A. obstetricans*. The classification of the other midwife toad is *A. cisternasi*.   W. Frank Blair

MIES VAN DER ROHE, *ME us vahn der ROH uh,* **LUDWIG** (1886-1969), a German architect, won fame for the clean, uncluttered design of his buildings of brick, steel, and glass. He built his first steel-framed building, an apartment house, in 1927 at an exposition he directed in Stuttgart, Germany. Two years later he directed the German exhibition at the international exposition in Barcelona, Spain. Here, Mies built his famed German Pavilion, with its marble walls reaching out beyond the building, its hovering roof slab, and its great expanse of glass. The sparse appearance of his buildings illustrates his motto, "Less is more."

Mies was born in Aachen, Germany. In 1930, he became director of the Bauhaus school in Dessau. That same year, he built his widely known Tugendhat house in Brno, Czechoslovakia. Two years later, he moved the Bauhaus to Berlin, where it remained until it was closed in 1933 (see BAUHAUS).

Mies came to the United States in 1938. That year, he became director of the school of architecture, planning, and design of the Armour Institute of Technology in Chicago. Armour merged with Lewis Institute in 1940 to form the Illinois Institute of Technology (IIT). Mies planned a new campus for IIT. He left the steel skeletons of the buildings exposed, and combined them with great expanses of glass and carefully arranged panels of brick. In his apartment buildings at the school, Mies exposed the reinforced concrete to view.

Mies retired from IIT in 1958. He was elected to the National Institute of Arts and Sciences in 1961.   WILLIAM T. ARNETT

See also ARCHITECTURE (Ludwig Mies van der Rohe); CHICAGO (Architecture); FURNITURE (The Bauhaus).

MIFFLIN, THOMAS (1744-1800), was an American soldier and politician. He became a member of the First Continental Congress in 1774. He served as an aide to General George Washington during the Revolu-

Ludwig Mies van der Rohe, *right,* pioneered in glass-and-steel architecture. Mies and Philip Johnson designed the 38-story, bronze-covered Seagram skyscraper in New York City, *above.* Associate architects were Kahn and Jacobs.

tionary War, and later as quartermaster general of the Continental Army. Mifflin also served in the Congress of the Confederation from 1782 to 1784. He represented Pennsylvania at the Constitutional Convention of 1787, and signed the United States Constitution. He served from 1788 to 1799 as the chief executive of Pennsylvania. He was born in Philadelphia of Quaker parents.   KENNETH R. ROSSMAN

MIGNONETTE, *MIN yun ET,* is an attractive garden plant of North America and Europe. Its name comes from a French word which means *little darling*. The mignonette has a low, bushy mass of smooth, soft-green leaves. The tiny flowers grow on tall spikes. They are yellowish-white with reddish pollen stalks inside, and have a delightful fragrance. Gardeners have produced larger-flowered mignonettes, but they are not so fragrant. Some of the cultivated varieties make excellent border

J. Horace McFarland
Mignonette

plants. The mignonette grows best in a cool temperature and a light soil. It is hardy and may be grown from seed plantings in May and July.

Scientific Classification. Mignonettes belong to the mignonette family, *Resedaceae*. They are genus *Reseda*, species *R. odorata*.   ALFRED C. HOTTES

MIGRAINE. See HEADACHE.

MIGRANT LABOR is a farm labor force that moves into a region temporarily to help harvest and process crops. Migrants usually harvest fruits and vegetables that must be picked as soon as they ripen. After migrants finish the work in one area, they seek jobs elsewhere. Few settle permanently in any community. In the 1970's, the United States had about 184,000 migrant workers. Most of them were American Indians, Mexican Americans, blacks, or Puerto Ricans.

Temporary farm workers generally receive low wages and often cannot find work. During the mid-1970's, migrant workers who were able to work all year earned about $5,900. But most migrants worked only part of the time and earned an average of about $2,600. Many migrants do not work in one place long enough to qualify for such government aid as food stamps and disability insurance. Many migrant families live in run-down, unsanitary housing. They often lack adequate food or medical care, and many suffer malnutrition or other health problems.

Many migrant workers have difficulty finding other kinds of work because they lack education. Only about a fifth of the migrant children go beyond sixth grade. Migrant youngsters tend to fall behind in their education because they change schools frequently. Some miss classes because they work to help support their family. Many schools sponsor summer sessions and other programs to promote the education of migrant children who temporarily live in the area. The federal Comprehensive Employment and Training Act of 1973 provided vocational training for adult migrants.

During the late 1960's, the California labor leader Cesar Chavez organized what is now the United Farm Workers of America (UFW). Many farm operators opposed the union, which seeks higher pay for migrants. They believed that increased labor costs would result in smaller profits and higher food prices. But by 1970, a number of growers had signed UFW contracts that provided wage increases.   GERALD G. SOMERS

See also CHAVEZ, CESAR ESTRADA; UNITED FARM WORKERS OF AMERICA.

MIGRATION is the movement of people or animals from one place to another. Throughout history,

entire groups of people and animals have at times left their homes and moved to new ones. People may migrate because they are forced to move, or merely because they want to move. Wars, famines, floods, and volcanic eruptions have all caused migrations.

The causes of animal migrations have remained basically the same for thousands of years. Animals cannot control their surroundings in the way that people can. Wild animals must move from area to area to find the physical conditions in which they can survive.

In prehistoric times, human beings often moved from one area to another much as the animals did. They seldom stayed anywhere for a long time, because the food supply usually ran out. As people learned to cultivate crops and domesticate animals, they could stay in one place longer than before. But when the soil no longer produced good crops, or when drought, floods, or fire ruined the crops, people had to migrate in search of food.

Human migration today is much different from migrations of animals and prehistoric people. Today, people usually move to improve their economic or social conditions, or because of political changes. Some migrations cause long-range changes in populations, because they bring together peoples that have different backgrounds.

Migration includes both *emigration* (the movement of people *out* of an area) and *immigration* (the movement

Van Bucher, Photo Researchers
Migrant Workers harvest crops in many parts of the United States. In a field near Salinas, Calif., *above*, migrants pick broccoli and toss it onto a moving belt. At the end of the belt, a worker packs the vegetables into boxes for shipment to processors.

Drawing by Rodney Thompson, from *Mankind Throughout the Ages* by Rugg and Krueger, published by Ginn & Co.

Forced Migrations were common among tribes living in Gaul during the 100's B.C. The Helvetians set fire to their homes and fled as conquering Roman soldiers approached their village.

of people *into* an area). *International migration* occurs between two countries, and *intercontinental migration* between two continents. When people move within one country, from one region, state, or province to another, the movement is called *internal migration*.

For an explanation of immigration and emigration, see the article on IMMIGRATION AND EMIGRATION.

Why People Migrate

Since earliest times, man has migrated for three chief reasons: (1) because he has used up or destroyed his natural resources, (2) because he seeks to improve or change some aspects of his way of life, or (3) because of wars, conquests, and invasions. These reasons are usually taken together and called *population pressure*.

Shortage of Resources. Early man often had to migrate because of the shortage of natural resources where he lived. The population grew so large that the land could not produce enough food to support everyone. People also had to migrate because they outgrew their water supply. This might happen because more and more persons used the water, or because of a drought. The Indians of Mesa Verde, in Colorado, left their cliff dwellings and migrated to new lands around A.D. 1300, partly because of a 20-year drought. The potato crop in Ireland failed in the 1840's. The famine that followed caused about a million persons to migrate from Ireland and settle in other countries, principally the United States.

Improvement of Life. In the late 1700's and early 1800's, individuals and families began moving from one country or region to another in search of better economic opportunities. Others moved for political or religious reasons. The western expansion across the United States was an internal migration. It resulted from people want-

ing free land and a chance to improve their way of life.

Floods, volcanic eruptions, and other natural disasters have wiped out homes and crops, causing people to migrate. Epidemics and plagues, particularly those of the Middle Ages, caused thousands to flee from their homes.

Wars and Conquests have caused people to migrate ever since tribes or nations first began attacking each other to gain power and riches. The victors have often forced the defeated peoples either to flee elsewhere or to become slaves. The resulting movement often stimulated other migrations. The peoples driven out by invading tribes had to force out their neighbors, or perish. Some invaders wandered into settled agricultural regions. Often they conquered these regions, adopted new ways of life, and became the rulers. When the region became overcrowded, new rulers would conquer or drive out the old ones. This type of migration occurred continuously for thousands of years, extending well into the era of written history.

Some peoples first began raiding their neighbors because of population pressure, but quickly found the attacks a profitable occupation. Drawn by the hope of wealth, they adopted raiding as a way of life.

History

Prehistoric Migrations were often caused by changes in climate. Men and animals moved southward through the ages to escape the great glaciers, or ice sheets, that gradually spread down over thousands of years from the North Pole. The people returned north after the glaciers melted. As many areas in northern Africa slowly dried up, hunters of the Stone Age followed the animals on which they lived into the fertile Nile Valley.

We do not know definitely how prehistoric man migrated over the earth's surface. One of the earliest known migrations took place when prehistoric men moved from North Africa to Europe. These migrants were of a type superior to the Neanderthal men of Europe, and seem to have replaced them. Most anthropologists and archaeologists believe that the Alpine people of eastern Europe migrated to central Europe in prehistoric times. But they disagree as to the size and importance of that migration. Nomads from the steppes (plains) of Russia seem to have migrated to central Europe at an early date.

Language similarities in the countries of Asia and Europe provide evidence that a people speaking an Indo-European tongue migrated widely over the world in early times. These people may have originated in the Caspian Sea region, but there is little evidence to confirm this theory.

Another great migration took place across the Bering Strait when people from Asia moved into the Americas. Anthropologists once thought this was a single migration that occurred about 20,000 years ago. Now they generally believe that the total migration took place over a long period, and that men came to America in several migrations (see ESKIMO [History]; INDIAN, AMERICAN). The most recent migration from Asia to America may have occurred not more than 1,000 years ago.

Invasions and Conquests. During the 200's B.C., a group of tribes pushed out of Mongolia. They drove some people westward toward the Ural Mountains, and others southeast into China. The Chinese called these people the *Hsiung-Nu*, and Europeans later gave them the name *Huns*. By the early A.D. 300's, the Huns had overrun most of northern China. After the Huns were driven west by fierce Mongolian tribes, they pushed into eastern Europe.

Other tribes fled from the Huns, and swept into Europe in what historians call *the barbarian invasion*. The Huns drove the Ostrogoths and Visigoths from southwestern Russia, and forced them to press into the Roman Empire. Other peoples, driven into what is now Germany, forced the Germanic nomads to fight their way south. One group, the Vandals and Suevians, made their way through Gaul and down into Spain. The Huns moved into what is now Hungary. Their migration ended after their chief, Attila, died in 453 (see ATTILA).

For hundreds of years, the military might of the Roman Empire prevented large migrations in northern Africa and the Middle East. But the slow decay of the empire gave the nomads of Arabia a chance to push forward in one of the greatest migrations in history. During the 600's and 700's, they occupied Arabia, Armenia, Egypt, Persia (now Iran), and Syria. The nomads swept along the entire length of North Africa, carrying the Berbers and other peoples with them. They moved north into Spain and Gaul. Their migrations into Asia forced other nomadic people northeast toward China. This set off another chain of Asiatic migrations that later reached into Europe.

Genghis Khan, a Mongol chief, led a great migration in the 1200's. He conquered Afghanistan, Persia, most of eastern Europe, Asia Minor, Mesopotamia, Syria, and northern China. The Mongols drove the Ottoman Turks from central Asia. The Turks slowly made their way across Asia Minor to the Balkan countries. They captured Constantinople (now Istanbul) in 1453, ending the Byzantine, or East Roman, Empire. See GENGHIS KHAN.

Seaborne Migrations. Important sea migrations include the movement of the Angles, Saxons, and Jutes into England beginning in the 450's. The most daring sea migrations were probably those of the Polynesians. They traveled great distances by canoe from their homes in southeast Asia to islands in the Pacific Ocean.

Large seaborne migrations from Europe began about 1500. The Portuguese, Spanish, French, Italians, and English ventured across the oceans in search of new land. They gradually settled the coast of America, which Christopher Columbus had reached in 1492. This set off a new migration that lasted almost 400 years. Adventurous explorers sailed the seven seas to find new trade routes and establish colonies (see EXPLORATION AND DISCOVERY). The major European colonial powers—England, France, Portugal, Spain, and The Netherlands—began to compete for new lands to conquer, develop, and colonize. The English set up the Virginia colony in 1607 and Plymouth Colony in 1620. Each of these colonies had about 100 settlers at the beginning. By 1700, migration and a high birth rate had increased the population of the English colonies in New England to about 275,000.

A Wave of Immigration. About 250,000 Europeans migrated to America between 1700 and 1820, and 750,000 persons arrived during the next 20 years. Most of them came from Europe. From 1840 to 1900, the United States admitted about 18 million newcomers. Thousands of Europeans also migrated to Australia, Africa, Canada, New Zealand, and South America.

As Europeans settled in America, they forced the Indians to migrate westward. The Spaniards brought horses to the Americas. With horses, the Indians could hunt buffalo on the great Western plains. Indian tribes began to find the plains a desirable place in which to hunt, fish, and live. They poured into the plains area in a vast migration that changed the population pattern of the United States. The Blackfeet migrated from the

Migration or Starvation, the choices that faced many peoples, usually led to migration. The Mandan Indians of North Dakota, shown in this lithograph from a painting by Karl Bodmer, set out for places where they could find more food during the winter.

Made to accompany *Travels in the Interior of North America* by Maximilian, Printz von Wied-Neuwied. London, 1843. Newberry Library, Ayer Collection, Chicago

North, the Sioux and Cheyenne from the East, the Comanche from the West, and the Pawnee from the South.

Migration in the 1900's. Heavy immigration continued from Europe to the United States and other countries until the early 1920's. Then many nations began to limit sharply the number of people who could immigrate. By 1930, almost all governments had placed restrictions on the number or types of people who could enter or leave their countries. These laws ended the relatively free movement of people as it had taken place in the past. During the 1930's, German Jews and other persons fleeing political and religious persecution sought refuge in other countries. Some escaped, but the great majority of oppressed people found no place in which to hide.

World War II (1939-1945) drove millions of persons from their homes in Europe and Asia. About 50 million people migrated from one country to another during the 10 years after the war, to seek political and economic security. About 20 million of them were displaced persons, refugees, expellees, and escapees. Five countries that came under Communist rule—Czechoslovakia, Hungary, Poland, Romania, and Yugoslavia—expelled more than 12 million Germans. More than 8 million of these migrants poured into West Germany. Millions of Czechs and Poles moved into lands formerly occupied by the expelled Germans. In the 1950's, almost 3 million people fled to West Germany from Russian-dominated East Germany. Mass transfers of populations also took place between Bulgaria and Turkey, and between Yugoslavia and Italy.

Large shifts of populations also took place in Asia during the 1900's. After the partition of India in 1947, about 17 million persons moved to new homes in a two-way movement of refugees between India and Pakistan. During the 1971 civil war between East Pakistan and West Pakistan, more than 9 million civilians fled to India to escape the fighting. Many of these refugees returned after the war ended and East Pakistan became the independent nation of Bangladesh.

Israel became an independent country in 1948. By the mid-1970's, more than 1½ million Jews had migrated to Israel, chiefly from eastern Europe, Asia, and Africa. The first Arab-Israeli war in 1948 forced about 700,000 Arabs living in Palestine to leave their homes. By the mid-1970's, more than 200,000 of these refugees still lived in camps along the Israeli border.

Huge migrations followed the defeat of the Chinese Nationalists in 1949. About 750,000 Chinese fled to Taiwan, and about the same number sought refuge in Hong Kong. Migrations also came as a result of the Korean and Vietnam wars. Over 700,000 persons migrated from North Korea to South Korea by 1952 as a result of the Korean War. During the Vietnam War (1957-1975), millions of Vietnamese fled from their homes in battle areas to safer areas of Vietnam. About 400,000 refugees left Cambodia, Laos, and Vietnam after the Communists took over those countries in 1975.

During the 1900's, millions of persons in the United States have moved from one state to another. The chief currents of this migration include movements (1) from Northern and Southern states to Western states, mainly California, (2) from the South to the North, (3) from rural areas to cities, and (4) from cities to suburbs.

During World War I (1914-1918), demands for military equipment created many new jobs in industry. Job opportunities drew thousands of blacks from the South to the manufacturing centers of the North. This was the beginning of a continuing black migration northward. In 1910, only about a tenth of all black Americans lived outside the South. Today, about half live outside the South.

During the depression years of the 1930's, many families moved out of the Dust Bowl region of the Southwest to seek jobs in California (see MIGRANT LABOR). During World War II, job opportunities drew thousands to Western and Eastern states.

Migration of Animals

Birds, fishes, insects, and other animals migrate regularly. Birds fly south for the winter and return north in the spring. Salmon swim from fresh water to salt water, and later return to their birthplaces to spawn and die. Caribou migrate from woodlands to tundra regions (see TUNDRA). Animals move about to find places with the most food. They seek regions with the best climate in which to breed and care for their young.

Most migrations take place between breeding grounds and regions where animals feed. For some animals, such as the lemming, the move is a one-way trip. Some scientists call this movement *emigration*, because these animals never return to their homes. For other animals, such as birds, the migration includes a return trip home. Birds move in *periodic* migrations, or at regular times during their lives. Lemmings move in *sporadic* migrations, once every 5 to 20 years. Painted lady butterflies breed in northern Africa during the winter, then fly north across the Mediterranean Sea to Europe, where they lay their eggs. The insects that hatch from these eggs fly south in the fall.

Scientists do not agree on the reasons that cause animals to migrate. Some believe that the increase in the number of animals causes overpopulation in one region. This threatens to wipe out the food supply, and the animals must move to other regions in search of food. We do not know how some birds and fishes find their way to the same spot to breed year after year. Many scientists believe that sunlight and the length of day have an effect on the migrations of animals.

Animals have also migrated with people across the oceans. Ships brought rabbits to Australia in 1788 and in 1859 and brought the first English sparrows to the United States in the middle 1800's.   ROBERT C. COOK

Related Articles in WORLD BOOK include:

MIGRATION OF ANIMALS. See MIGRATION (Migration of Animals); ANIMAL (Animal Travelers); BIRD (Bird Migration); INSECT (Hibernation and Migration).

MIGRATORY BIRD CONSERVATION COMMISSION considers and approves acquisitions of land for migratory bird refuges. The land is acquired by the United States Fish and Wildlife Service of the Department of the Interior. The commission makes an annual report to Congress. It consists of the secretary of the interior, who serves as chairman; the secretary of agriculture; the secretary of commerce; two senators; and two representatives. Congress created the agency in 1929.

Critically reviewed by MIGRATORY BIRD CONSERVATION COMMISSION

MIGRATORY BIRD LAWS AND TREATIES. See BIRD (Protective Laws).

MIHAILOVICH, *mee HY loh vich,* **DRAŽA** (1893?-1946), was a Yugoslav resistance leader during World War II. When the Germans invaded Yugoslavia in 1941, Mihailovich refused to surrender. He retreated to the mountains with a fighting patriot group called the *Chetniks.* The Yugoslav government-in-exile of King Peter II appointed Mihailovich its minister of war and the chief of staff of the Yugoslav Army in January 1942.

But the Chetniks were not the only resistance fighters in Yugoslavia. The Communist Partisans, led by Josip Broz Tito, formed a second group (see TITO, JOSIP BROZ). Russia insisted that the Allies aid Tito more than Mihailovich. Tito accused Mihailovich of collaborating with the Germans, and the Chetniks and Communist Partisans fought each other. Mihailovich's troops dwindled to almost nothing, and Tito's men captured him in March 1946. He was charged with treason. He denied collaborating with the Germans, but he was found guilty as charged and shot. Mihailovich was born near Belgrade.   ALBERT PARRY

MIKADO, *mih KAH doh,* was the ancient title of the Emperor of Japan. The term was also used by foreigners. The term *Mikado* comes from the Japanese words that mean *exalted gate.* This shows the reverence the Japanese people held for their ruler. After Chinese civilization came to Japan in the A.D. 500's, the Japanese came to call their emperor *Tenno,* which means *Heavenly Emperor.* The emperor is never referred to by his personal name. Recent emperors and their reigns are called by a name selected for them. The Emperor Hirohito is known as the *Showa Tenno* or *Showa Emperor.*

Many historians consider Japan's ruling dynasty the oldest in the world. Japanese legend assigns the date 660 B.C. to the reign of Jimmu, the first Mikado. According to tradition, he descended from the Sun Goddess. Japanese historians consider this date too early, but they trace the same family of emperors back through 124 reigns. See JAPAN (Early History).

William S. Gilbert and Arthur S. Sullivan wrote a popular operetta, *The Mikado.* See GILBERT AND SULLIVAN.   MARIUS B. JANSEN

MIKAN, GEORGE (1924-   ), became the most famous—and perhaps the best—basketball player of the 1940's and early 1950's. In 1950, sportswriters selected Mikan as the outstanding college or professional player of the first half of the 1900's. Mikan, who stood 6 feet 10 inches (208 centimeters) tall, used his height, strength, and great hook shot to become the first of basketball's high-scoring centers.

George Lawrence Mikan was born in Joliet, Ill. He played college basketball at DePaul University, where he won all-America honors in 1944, 1945, and 1946. Mikan starred with the Minneapolis Lakers professional team from 1947 to 1956. He led the Lakers to National Basketball Association (NBA) championships

in the 1948-1949, 1949-1950, 1951-1952, 1952-1953, and 1953-1954 seasons. Mikan scored a total of 11,764 points for the Lakers, an average of 22.6 points per game. Mikan led the league in scoring during the 1948-1949, 1949-1950, and 1950-1951 seasons.   NICK CURRAN

See also BASKETBALL (picture: Great Centers).

UPI
George Mikan

MIKI, TAKEO (1907-   ), served as prime minister of Japan from December 1974 to December 1976. Miki also headed Japan's Liberal-Democratic Party. He resigned from office after the 1976 elections, in which the Liberal-Democrats retained control of the *Diet* (parliament), but with a smaller margin of victory than in earlier elections. Before and during Miki's term in office, some Liberal-Democrats—though not Miki—had been accused of corruption. These charges contributed to the party's setback. See JAPAN (Recent Events).

Miki was born in Donari Town on Shikoku Island, Japan. He entered Meiji University in Tokyo in 1929. Miki went to the

Japan Consulate General
Takeo Miki

United States in 1932. While attending universities there, he held such jobs as lecturer and radio broadcaster for Japanese-American audiences. Miki returned to Japan in 1936 and graduated from Meiji University the next year.

In 1937, Miki became the youngest representative ever elected to the Diet up to that time. He won re-election to the Diet a record 16 times. Miki served as deputy prime minister from 1972 to 1974. Through the years, he also held nine Cabinet posts and various offices in his party.   LEWIS AUSTIN

MIKIMOTO, KOKICHI. See PEARL (Cultured Pearls).

MIKOYAN, *mee koh YAHN,* **ANASTAS** (1895-1978), was president of Russia in 1964 and 1965. He previously had served as the first vice-premier of Russia. He also served for many years as commissar of food supply and minister of trade. He first visited the United States in 1936 and introduced a few U.S. foods in Russia. He became supply chief of the Russian army during World War II.

Mikoyan was born in Russian Armenia, the son of a carpenter. Although he completed a theological course, he did not become a priest. He became a Communist in 1915, and took part in the Russian civil war of 1918-1920. He was a member of the party's Central Committee from 1922 to 1976, and of its Politburo from 1926 to 1966.   ALBERT PARRY

MILAM, BENJAMIN. See TEXAS (Texas Revolution).

MILAN

MILAN, *mih LAN* (pop. 1,738,487), is the second largest city in Italy. Only Rome is larger. Milan ranks as Italy's chief center of finance and manufacturing. The city's location in northern Italy, near a pass through the Alps, made it a center of trade as early as the A.D. 100's (see ITALY [political map]). Many tourists visit Milan to see the city's priceless works of art. Milan is the capital of Lombardy, one of the political regions of Italy. The city's name in Italian is MILANO.

The City covers 70 square miles (182 square kilometers). Much of Milan has a modern appearance, but the city also includes a number of beautiful ancient buildings.

Milan's large Gothic cathedral stands in the heart of the city, and the nearby area includes many cultural attractions. Music lovers from many parts of the world hear concerts at La Scala, one of the leading opera houses of Europe. The Ambrosian Library is a treasure house of rare books and ancient manuscripts. Masterpieces of Italian painting hang in the Brera Art Gallery, the Gallery of Modern Art, the Poldi Pezzoli Museum, and the Sforza Castle. The fortresslike castle once served as the home of Milan's rulers. Leonardo da Vinci painted *The Last Supper*, one of the most famous masterpieces in history, on a wall of the Monastery of Santa Maria delle Grazie. Visitors to Milan may see this painting, which appears in the JESUS CHRIST article.

Milan has two major universities, the Catholic University of the Sacred Heart and the University of Milan. The city also has several technical institutes.

The 36-story Pirelli Building, one of Italy's tallest business structures, stands in an area of modern office buildings in northern Milan. Industrial areas and residential suburbs extend from the city in all directions.

Like other modern cities, Milan has such problems as air pollution and traffic jams.

People of Milan are called Milanese. They have a reputation for ambition, energy, and skill in business. Many earn their living as management personnel with a business firm or as skilled workers. Almost all Milanese are Roman Catholics.

Many Milanese like to spend afternoons at a cafe, making business deals or simply chatting with friends. A favorite gathering place is the Galleria Vittorio Emanuele II, a large, glass-roofed building that includes restaurants and shops. The Galleria, often called the "living room of Milan," stands near the cathedral.

Economy. Many companies based in Milan operate banks, factories, and stores throughout Italy. Italian advertising and publishing are also centered in the city. The Milan area has thousands of small and medium-sized factories and several huge manufacturing plants. Leading products of Milan include chemicals, electrical appliances, textiles, tires, and transportation equipment. The city is a hub of major highways and railroad lines, and it has a large airport.

History. Around 400 B.C., the Celts, a people of western Europe, founded a town on the site of what is now Milan (see CELT). In 222 B.C., the Romans conquered the town, which they named Mediolanum. Mediolanum, later called Milan, became a Roman military base and also a center of trade between Rome and central Europe. By the A.D. 200's, it ranked as one of the largest cities of the Roman Empire. Barbaric tribes invaded Milan and other parts of Europe during the late 400's, and the empire fell in 476. The invasions ended trade, and Milan became a small town.

The city regained importance in the 1000's as European trade and commerce expanded. From 1277 to 1535, Milanese nobles governed the city. They hired

The Galleria in Milan is a large glass-roofed building that houses numerous restaurants and shops. The famous landmark is a popular meeting place of the people of Milan.

great artists who created beautiful buildings and works of art.

The Spanish Empire took over Milan in 1535, and Austria gained control of the city in 1714. French forces led by Napoleon conquered Milan in 1797, but Austria regained the city in 1815.

In 1859, Milan became part of the newly formed Kingdom of Italy. The city developed some of Italy's first modern industries during the late 1800's.

Benito Mussolini, who ruled Italy as dictator from 1922 to 1943, founded his Fascist movement in Milan in 1919. Allied bombings damaged large areas of Milan during World War II (1939-1945), but the people rebuilt their city.

The 1950's and 1960's brought great industrial growth to Milan. Thousands of people came from southern Italy to work in the city's factories. The resulting increase in population led to a severe housing shortage. During the 1960's and 1970's, the city helped finance the construction of hundreds of new apartment buildings to ease this shortage.　　　EMILIANA P. NOETHER

For the monthly weather in Milan, see ITALY (Climate). See also ITALY (picture: A Modern Skyscraper in an Ancient City); MILAN CATHEDRAL.

MILAN, EDICT OF. See CONSTANTINE I, THE GREAT.

MILAN CATHEDRAL in Milan, Italy, is the third largest church in Europe. It ranks after Saint Peter's at Rome and the cathedral at Seville, Spain. Its foundation was laid by Gian Visconti in 1385. From 1805 to 1813, it was completed by order of Napoleon I.

The Gothic cathedral is built of white Carrara marble, in the form of a Latin cross. It is 490 feet (149 meters) long and 180 feet (55 meters) wide. The tower rises 354 feet (108 meters) high. Over 2,000 statues cover the cathedral's outside walls. Marble spires, each bearing a life-size statue of a saint, Biblical character, or historical

Ted Spiegel, Black Star

Milan Cathedral in Italy is Europe's third largest church. Its roof is covered with 135 marble spires, each bearing a statue.

figure, rise from the roof. Many figures of Milan's history are buried in the cathedral.　　　BENJAMIN WEBB WHEELER

MILAN DECREE was a fundamental step in Napoleon's Continental System, a blockade against Great Britain. Napoleon issued it on Dec. 17, 1807, in retaliation against Britain. The British cabinet had ordered that neutral ships stop at British ports to have their cargoes examined, and to obtain licenses before going to ports under French control.

The Milan Decree provided that any ship that obeyed these instructions would be subject to capture. In 1806, Napoleon had issued the Berlin Decree, barring British ships from ports under French control. His aim now was to keep the British from using neutral ships to carry goods to these ports. Napoleon hoped that, by setting up an economic blockade of Europe, he could bring about Great Britain's downfall.

Although the Milan Decree increased the effectiveness of Napoleon's blockade, he could not adequately enforce it because the British had the most powerful navy afloat. But Napoleon did cause great distress to neutral powers. The decree led the United States to adopt severe acts to protect its commerce. Napoleon used these acts to his own advantage, and convinced the United States that he would withdraw his decree. In this way, he turned American anger against the British, and furnished a cause for the War of 1812 between the United States and Great Britain.　　　ROBERT B. HOLTMAN

See also CONTINENTAL SYSTEM; NAPOLEON I (Dominates Europe); WAR OF 1812 (Causes).

MILBURN, ROD. See OLYMPIC GAMES (table: Track and Field).

MILDEW is a fungus which attacks plants and some products made from plants and animals. Its name comes from a Middle English word, *mealdew*, which means *spoiled meal*. There are two main classes which damage useful plants: *powdery mildew* and *downy mildew*.

Powdery mildews attack green plants. There are about 50 different kinds of powdery mildews, and some of them can attack several different plants. About 1,500 different kinds of flowering plants may be infected by powdery mildew. These include such common plants as the gooseberry, pea, peach, rose, apple, cherry, and grape. The mildew fungus usually grows on the outside of the leaves. Sometimes it also forms flowerlike blotches on the stems and fruits. These blotches consist of many fungus threads that send out short branches with sucking organs into the stem or fruit. Copper sprays and sulfur dusts protect plants from powdery mildew.

Downy mildews produce yellow spots on the upper surfaces of the leaves or young fruits. The fungus grows from a single fertilized cell called a *spore*. When the mildew attacks the top of a leaf, small spores come out of the breathing pores on the bottom of the leaf. These spores produce even tinier spores which swim in the dewdrops on the surface of the leaf. The spores start new infections by sending tiny threads into the leaf.

Downy mildews attack many plants, including the grape, cucumber, cabbage, onion, and lettuce. One way to protect plants from downy mildew is to spray them with a Bordeaux mixture (see BORDEAUX MIXTURE). In 1845 and 1846, downy mildew almost destroyed the Irish potato crop, and a terrible famine followed.

Mildew is a serious problem in damp tropical countries because it attacks clothes unless they are kept dry. Even in temperate regions, clothing should not be allowed to remain wet long.

Mildew often attacks bookbindings in damp climates. Books kept in damp or poorly ventilated places also are subject to mildew. To protect books from mildew, keep the volumes in an enclosed bookcase along with a form of paraformaldehyde powder. The powder evaporates to form a protective atmosphere. If books must be stored in an open place, good air circulation will help prevent mildew. Once it has formed, dusting or wiping may remove it from the outside of the book. However, this will not stop mildew from continuing to grow.

Several chemical solutions will prevent mildew when applied to the bookbindings. Most of the solutions contain mercurials, such as mercuric chloride. They are highly poisonous and should be used with care.

Scientific Classification. Mildews belong to the fungi phylum, *Eumycophyta*. The powdery mildews are in the class *Ascomycetes* and the family *Erysiphaceae*. The downy mildews are in the class *Phycomycetes* and the family *Peronosporaceae*.   WILLIAM F. HANNA

See also FUNGI; FUNGICIDE; MOLD.

MILE is a unit of length. In the customary system of measurement used in the United States, the unit of length used to measure distances on land is called the *statute*, or *land, mile*. It is equal to 5,280 feet or 320 rods. The mile was first used by the Romans. It was about 5,000 feet long and contained 1,000 paces, each 5 feet in length. The term *mile* comes from *milia passuum*, the Latin words for *a thousand paces*. Around the year 1500, the 5,000 feet of the Roman mile was changed to the 5,280 feet of today, although many countries still kept their own length for the mile. The metric system measures land distances in *kilometers*. A kilometer equals 3,280.8 feet, or about $\frac{5}{8}$ of a mile. One mile equals 1.60934 kilometers.

Distances on the sea are measured in *nautical, geographical*, or *sea miles*. The nautical mile is obtained by dividing the circumference of the earth into 360 degrees and then dividing each degree into 60 minutes. One nautical mile equals one minute, or is $\frac{1}{21,600}$ of the

circumference of the earth. The *international nautical mile* used in the United States and other countries equals 6,076.11549 feet. This makes the international nautical mile equal to 1.150779 statute or land miles, or 1.852 kilometers.

A "knot" is a unit of speed, not of length. A ship traveling one nautical mile per hour is said to have a speed of *one knot*.   E. G. STRAUS

See also FURLONG; KILOMETER; KNOT; LEAGUE; WEIGHTS AND MEASURES.

MILES, NELSON APPLETON (1839-1925), a noted American soldier, fought in the Civil War, the Indian wars, and the Spanish-American War. He is an outstanding example of a citizen soldier, one who rose to the rank of lieutenant general in the United States Army without a formal military education.

Miles entered the army as a volunteer captain when the Civil War started. He fought in nearly every battle in the East. He was wounded several times, and won rapid promotion. At the age of 26, he became a major general of volunteers and commanded an Army corps.

He entered the regular Army in 1865. For the next 15 years, he directed campaigns against Indians in the West. In 1894, Miles commanded the troops that President Grover Cleveland sent to Chicago following the Pullman Strike disorders. In 1895, he became commanding general of the Army. Miles headed the expedition to Puerto Rico in 1898, during the Spanish-American War, and retired in 1903. He was born near Westminster, Mass.   T. HARRY WILLIAMS

MILETUS, *my LEE tus*, was one of the largest cities of ancient Greece. It stood on the western coast of Asia Minor in the district of Ionia (see GREECE, ANCIENT [color map]). Miletus' excellent harbor made the city an important trading center. In the 700's and 600's B.C., colonists from Miletus settled along the coast of the Hellespont (a channel now called the Dardanelles) and Black Sea. About 600 B.C., Thales founded the famous Milesian school of philosophy.

The city had a privileged position when the Persians took over the area in the mid-500's B.C. But in 499 B.C., the Milesian ruler Aristagoras led the Ionian Greeks in an unsuccessful revolt, and the Persians looted Miletus in 494 B.C. Miletus lost importance when its harbor silted up in the A.D. 400's.   DONALD W. BRADEEN

Roman Mile   5,000 Feet

Kilometer   3,280.8 Feet

Air or Sea (Nautical) Mile   6,076.1 Feet

Land or Statute Mile   5,280 Feet

Different Miles measure distances on land, on sea, and in the air. The ancient Roman mile was 5,000 feet. The metric system uses kilometers to measure distances. An air or sea mile equals $\frac{1}{60}$ of one degree of the distance around the earth. In the 1500's, Englishmen measured distances in 660-foot furlongs, so Queen Elizabeth I made the statute mile 8 furlongs, or 5,280 feet.

MILHAUD, *mee YOH,* **DARIUS** (1892-1974), was a French-born composer noted for his works for the stage. Milhaud wrote 15 operas, 13 ballets, and music for other ballets and for motion pictures. The French poet Paul Claudel wrote the *librettos* (words) for several of his works, including his famous opera, *Christophe Colomb* (1928). Milhaud's best-known ballet, *The Creation of the World* (1923), reflects his interest in jazz.

Milhaud was born in Aix-en-Provence in southern France, and this region inspired his *Suite Provençale* for orchestra (1936). Milhaud received his music training at the Paris Conservatory from 1910 to 1915. In 1917 and 1918, he served with the French Embassy in Rio de Janeiro, Brazil, and became acquainted with Brazilian popular music. Milhaud used this music in *Saudades do Brasil* (*Memories of Brazil*, 1920-1921), which he composed both for orchestra and for piano.

During the 1920's, Milhaud belonged to a group of young French composers called *Les Six.* He left France in 1940 during World War II. That year, he joined the faculty of the music department at Mills College in Oakland, Calif.   GILBERT CHASE

MILHOUS, KATHERINE (1894-1977), an American author and illustrator of children's books, received the Caldecott medal in 1951 for *The Egg Tree.* She was born in Philadelphia. Her books include *Lovina, Herodia, Appolonia's Valentine,* and *With Bells On.*   RUTH HILL VIGUERS

MILITARY ACADEMY, UNITED STATES. See UNITED STATES MILITARY ACADEMY.

MILITARY AIRCRAFT. See AIR FORCE; AIR FORCE, UNITED STATES; BOMBER; GUIDED MISSILE; HELICOPTER.

MILITARY AIRLIFT COMMAND (MAC) provides air transportation of thousands of tons of cargo and about $1\frac{1}{2}$ million U.S. armed forces military personnel each year. It also provides air weather services, rescue and recovery, and charting and photographic services. It is a major command of the U.S. Air Force.

MAC is the world's largest air transport service. Its worldwide routes stretch more than 100,000 miles (160,-000 kilometers). The 21st Air Force handles routes across the Atlantic and Caribbean. The 22nd Air Force flies routes in the United States and across the Pacific. In 1948, the Air Force and Navy air transport operations were merged to form the Military Air Transport Service (MATS). In 1966, MATS became MAC, and an Air Force responsibility. Headquarters are at Scott Air Force Base, near Belleville, Ill.   RICHARD M. SKINNER

MILITARY ATTACHÉ. See ATTACHÉ.

MILITARY DISCHARGE ends a person's period of service in the armed forces. Members of the Armed Forces of the United States receive one of five types of discharges: (1) honorable, (2) general, (3) undesirable, (4) bad conduct, and (5) dishonorable.

Honorable discharges are issued to all those whose military behavior has been proper and whose performance of duty has been "proficient and industrious." A person holding such a discharge is entitled to all benefits available to veterans.

General discharges are given to those whose military records do not entitle them to an honorable discharge. A general discharge may be issued if a person has been found guilty by a general court-martial. Veterans with general discharges are eligible for the same benefits as those holding honorable discharges.

Undesirable discharges are given to persons considered unfit for military service. They cancel many veteran benefits, and prohibit re-enlistment in any service.

Bad conduct discharges are given for reasons such as absence without leave, insubordination, and destruction of private property. They deprive the holder of all veteran benefits and certain citizenship rights.

Dishonorable discharges may be given for such reasons as theft, desertion, and destruction of government property. They cancel all veteran benefits and some citizenship rights.   CHARLES B. MACDONALD

MILITARY INSIGNIA. See INSIGNIA; also the color pictures in AIR FORCE, U.S.; ARMY, U.S.; MARINE CORPS, U.S.; NAVY, U.S.

MILITARY JUSTICE, UNIFORM CODE OF. See UNIFORM CODE OF MILITARY JUSTICE.

MILITARY LAW. See MARTIAL LAW.

MILITARY POLICE are the trained police maintained by a nation's armed forces. On military installations, these men and women have powers similar to those of civilian police. Military police enforce military laws and regulations, control traffic, prevent and investigate crime, apprehend military absentees, maintain custody of military prisoners, and provide physical security for military personnel and property. In combat situations, military police also maintain custody of prisoners of war. When necessary in combat, military police can be ordered to fight as infantry.

In the United States armed forces, police duties are carried out by Military Police (MP) for the Army and Marine Corps, the Shore Patrol for the Navy and Coast Guard, and the Security Police for the Air Force. The functions of the Shore Patrol are more limited than those of other military police (see SHORE PATROL).

Critically reviewed by the DEPARTMENT OF DEFENSE

MILITARY PREPAREDNESS. See NATIONAL DEFENSE.

MILITARY SCHOOL is an institution that educates and trains persons in military arts and sciences. All major countries operate military schools. Many U.S. military schools are privately operated.

Government Military Schools. In the United States, each branch of the armed forces has its own military schools. Courses in these schools for enlisted men and women range from the repair of guided missiles to food service. The armed forces maintain service academies, officer-candidate schools, and reserve officers training corps for persons learning to become officers. Service academies are the U.S. Air Force Academy at Colorado Springs, Colo.; the U.S. Coast Guard Academy at New London, Conn.; the U.S. Military Academy at West Point, N.Y.; and the U.S. Naval Academy at Annapolis, Md.

Military schools prepare officers for duties they may have to perform in peace or war. Courses at the first level cover specialized subjects. Schools at the next level stress command and staff work. They include the Air Command and Staff College and Air War College of Air University, Army War College, Command and General Staff College, Marine Corps Senior School, Naval Postgraduate School, and the Naval War College. Joint-service colleges operate at the highest level. They are the Armed Forces Staff College in Norfolk, Va., and the Industrial College of the Armed Forces and the National War College, both in Washington, D.C.

MILITARY SCIENCE

Private Military Schools and Colleges train boys of junior high school, high school, and college age. Students wear distinctive uniforms, and learn the fundamentals of military training, strategy, and tactics. Leading private military schools include Culver Military Academy in Culver, Ind.; Staunton Military Academy in Staunton, Va.; The Citadel in Charleston, S.C.; and Virginia Military Institute in Lexington, Va.

In Other Countries. Great Britain trains its officers at the Royal Military Academy in Sandhurst, the Army Staff College in Camberley, the Joint Services Staff College in Latimer, and the Imperial Defense College in London. Canada has the Royal Military College of Canada in Kingston, Ont., Royal Roads Military College near Victoria, B.C., and Collège militaire royal de Saint-Jean in St. Jean, Que. The chief French military school is Saint-Cyr, in Coëtquidan, Brittany. Russia has the Frunze Academy in Moscow.   CHARLES B. MACDONALD

Related Articles in WORLD BOOK include:

Air University	Quantico Marine Corps Develop-
Armed Forces Staff	ment and Education Command
College	Royal Military College of Canada
Army War College	United States Air Force Academy
Citadel, The	United States Coast Guard
National Defense	Academy
University	United States Military Academy
Naval War College	United States Naval Academy
	Virginia Military Institute

MILITARY SCIENCE is the study of scientific principles which control the conduct of war. It is also the application of those principles to battle conditions.

Related Articles in WORLD BOOK include:

Air Force	Marine Corps,
Air Force,	United States
United States	Military Training
Army	Navy
Army, United States	Navy, United States
Logistics	War

MILITARY SERVICE, COMPULSORY. See DRAFT, MILITARY.

MILITARY TANK. See TANK, MILITARY.

MILITARY TRAINING is training in the art and science of war. Modern military training is a great deal more complex than in ancient times. Battles then involved relatively simple formations, weapons, and equipment. Today, fighting troops must understand and be prepared to use mechanized equipment and intricate scientific instruments. They must be backed up by many more service troops than there are actual fighters. During World War II, nations trained both men and women in a variety of jobs. In some countries, such as Russia, women also engaged in combat.

All soldiers first learn to obey orders. Combat soldiers learn to handle various types of weapons: machine guns, bayonets, rifles, pistols, and grenades. They learn how to handle explosives. Soldiers assigned to a specialized branch of the army receive additional training for a particular job. They may learn to drive an automobile, to jump from an airplane, or build a bridge.

Training Schools. The Army, Navy, and Air Force maintain a system of schools or training stations for officers and enlisted personnel. In addition, each of these branches of the service has specialized schools for higher officer training. These include the Army War College, the Naval War College, and the Air Univer-

sity. The Armed Forces Staff College and the National Defense University are operated jointly by the services. The National Defense University includes the National War College and the Industrial College of the Armed Forces. The National War College teaches strategy and related subjects in politics, economics, and social problems. The Industrial College of the Armed Forces prepares officers for duties connected with *procurement* (purchase) and maintenance of supplies and equipment.

Military Training for Civilians. Many colleges and universities have Reserve Officers Training Corps units of the army, navy, and air force, which offer instruction for prospective officers. Students who successfully complete such training may be eligible for commissions in the regular army, navy, or air force. The army also conducts a junior branch of its ROTC in high schools and preparatory schools. The National Guard and Air National Guard are other volunteer organizations offering training to civilians. The individual states and territories conduct these groups.

Compulsory Military Training. From the days of the ancient Romans, many European countries have tried some form of enforced military service. France introduced a conscription law in 1792. Germany made the greatest progress in developing a military machine under nationwide conscription. It began its program after the Franco-Prussian War.

In the United States, the federal government first tried compulsory military training during the Civil War. Conscription laws providing for military training for male citizens were also in effect in the United States during World Wars I and II. The first U.S. peacetime draft law was enacted in 1940.   CHARLES B. MACDONALD

Related Articles in WORLD BOOK include:

Air Force, United States	National Defense
Army, United States	National Guard
Draft, Military	Navy, United States
Military School	Reserve Officers
Militia	Training Corps

MILITARY UNIFORM. See UNIFORM.

MILITIA, *muh LISH uh,* includes all able-bodied persons liable to be called into the armed forces in time of national emergency. The U.S. militia includes the Air Force Reserve, Air National Guard, Army National Guard, Marine Corps Reserve, and Naval Reserve.

Each of the 13 colonies in America required its citizens to enroll and train in the militia. Militiamen formed almost half of the Continental Army that fought in the American Revolutionary War. The United States Constitution gave Congress the right to call up the militia to "execute the laws of the Union."

The Militia Act of 1792 placed every "free able-bodied white male citizen" at the age of 18 in the militia. But it left the control and training of these units to each state. The act of 1903 made all male citizens subject to military service, and set up the National Guard as the organized militia (see NATIONAL GUARD).

The governments of ancient Egypt, Greece, and Rome all formed militias. The Spartans, for example, used the militia to organize their professional armies. Switzerland's militia system was set up in 1291. Militiamen in feudal England had to keep armor and weapons that were inspected twice a year.   CHARLES B. MACDONALD

See also DRAFT, MILITARY (History); PURITAN (picture); SWITZERLAND (Defense).

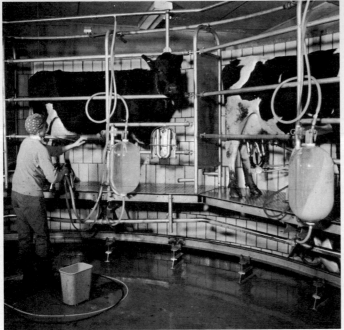

The Production of Milk begins at a dairy farm, where machines milk the cows, *left*. The raw milk then goes to a dairy plant for processing. Finally, the milk is packaged, and the containers are stored in a large refrigerated room, *right*, to await delivery to stores and homes.

MILK

MILK is the most nourishing of all foods and a favorite drink of people throughout the world. Milk has almost all the *nutrients* (nourishing substances) that people need for growth and good health. In addition, milk has most of these nutrients in large amounts and in such proportions that they can work as a team to help keep the body strong and healthy.

All female mammals produce milk to nourish their young. But when we think of milk, we generally think of the milk that comes from cows. Cows provide most of the milk used in the United States, Canada, and many other countries. In some parts of the world, however, other animals produce the main supply of milk. Goat milk is popular in parts of Europe, Latin America, Africa, and Asia. Camels provide milk in the desert lands of Arabia, central Asia, and northern Africa. Some South Americans drink llama milk. In Arctic regions, people get milk from reindeer. Sheep provide much of the milk in Greece, Iran, and Turkey. Water buffalo supply milk in Egypt, India, Pakistan, and many countries of Southeast Asia.

Butter, cheese, ice cream, yogurt, and several other foods are made from milk. Milk—or one of its products—is also an ingredient in many foods, such as cakes, casseroles, puddings, and sauces. Milk is also used in making numerous products besides food. For example,

Robert T. Marshall, the contributor of this article, is Professor of Food Science and Nutrition at the University of Missouri-Columbia and the coauthor of The Science of Providing Milk for Man.

manufacturers use *casein*, the main protein in milk, to make waterproof glues, various plastics, and paints.

This article discusses the food value of cow's milk. It then deals mainly with the United States milk industry.

Food Value of Milk

Cow's milk is about 87 per cent water and 13 per cent solids. The solids contain the nutrients in milk. This section discusses these nutrients and the importance of milk in the human diet.

Nutrients in Milk. The body needs five kinds of nutrients for energy, growth, and the replacement of worn-out tissue. These nutrients are (1) carbohydrates, (2) fats, (3) minerals, (4) proteins, and (5) vitamins. Milk has been called "the most nearly perfect food" because it is an outstanding source of these nutrients. But milk is not "the perfect food" because it lacks enough iron and does not provide all vitamins.

─── **INTERESTING FACTS ABOUT MILK** ───

Ancestors of Today's Dairy Cows were wild cattle that roamed the forests of northern Europe many thousands of years ago.

Average Yearly Milk Production per cow in the United States totals about 4,815 quarts (4,557 liters), almost twice as much as in 1940.

Daily Food for a Dairy Cow ranges from 40 to 60 pounds (18 to 27 kilograms) of feed. In addition, a cow requires 10 to 20 gallons (38 to 76 liters) of water a day.

First Dairy Cattle in America were brought to the Jamestown colony in Virginia in 1611.

Record Milk Production by a cow in one day is 195½ pounds (89 kilograms), enough to provide 100 persons with almost 1 quart (0.9 liter) each. A Holstein cow on an Indiana farm set the record in 1975.

MILK

Carbohydrates are a major source of energy for the body. The carbohydrate content of milk is mainly *lactose*, or *milk sugar*. In addition to providing energy, lactose helps the body absorb the minerals calcium and phosphorus in milk. Our bones and teeth consist largely of these minerals. Lactose also gives milk its sweet taste. See CARBOHYDRATE.

Fats, like carbohydrates, provide energy. They also supply certain fatty acids that the body must have. Fat gives milk its rich flavor. Milk fat also contains vitamins A, D, E, and K and several other substances. One of these substances, *carotene*, gives milk its golden tint. Milk fat appears as tiny *globules*. A drop of milk contains about 100 million such globules. See FAT.

Minerals help the body grow and remain healthy. Calcium and phosphorus are the most important minerals in milk. In fact, milk is the chief food source of calcium. Other minerals in milk include potassium, sodium, and sulfur and smaller amounts of aluminum, copper, iodine, iron, manganese, and zinc.

Proteins, like minerals, help the body grow and maintain itself. They also supply energy. The proteins in milk are *complete proteins*—that is, they contain all the *amino acids* (protein parts) needed for building blood and tissue. Only egg proteins and the proteins in some meats have a higher food value than milk proteins have. Casein makes up about four-fifths of the protein content of milk. It is found only in milk. See PROTEIN.

Vitamins are essential for growth, maintaining body tissue, and the prevention of such diseases as beriberi and rickets. Milk provides more vitamins—and in larger amounts—than do most other natural foods. Milk is an excellent source of vitamins A and B_2 and a good source of vitamin B_1. Other vitamins in milk include vitamins B_6, B_{12}, C, E, and K and niacin. Milk also has vitamin D, but the quantity is low. Most dairies add extra vitamin D to milk. See VITAMIN.

All milk—human and animal—contains the same nutrients. The amounts differ, however. Compared with cow's milk, for example, the milk from a water buffalo has 3 times as much fat and $1\frac{1}{2}$ times as much protein but only about three-fourths the sugar. Human milk has fewer proteins and minerals than cow's milk but about $1\frac{1}{2}$ times as much sugar.

The Composition of Cow's Milk

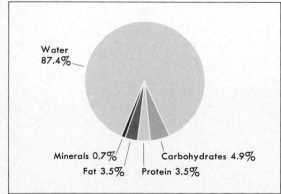

Water 87.4%

Minerals 0.7%
Fat 3.5%
Protein 3.5%
Carbohydrates 4.9%

Source: U.S. Agricultural Research Service.

In the United States, the federal government requires that *whole* milk sold as food meet certain standards. Whole milk is milk that has not had any of its natural nutrients removed. The government specifies that whole milk must contain at least 3.25 per cent milk fat and 8.25 per cent nonfat milk solids. Most cow's milk has about 3.5 per cent milk fat, 5 per cent lactose, 3.5 per cent protein, and 0.7 per cent minerals. The percentages differ somewhat between individual cows and breeds. The quality and composition of milk also depend on what a cow is fed and how the animal is cared for.

Milk in the Human Diet. Milk is an important part of most people's diet. It is the first food of newborn babies, whether they are breast-fed or bottle-fed. Because of its many nutrients, milk helps the body develop. Children who drink milk grow faster than other children who eat the same kinds of food but do not drink milk. Milk can also help people obtain the nutrients their diet might otherwise lack.

Doctors and nutrition experts disagree on exactly how much milk a person should drink. In general, they recommend that children and teen-agers drink at least three 8-ounce (240-milliliter) glasses a day. Adults should have at least one glass daily. Expectant mothers and mothers who are nursing their babies should drink three or four glasses a day.

Many people cannot drink the recommended amount of milk. For example, many adult members of the African and Asian races can digest only a small amount of milk because their bodies are low in *lactase*, the chemical substance that breaks down milk sugar. In the United States, a small percentage of the children under 2 years of age are allergic to milk. Finally, many doctors recommend that patients who have a large amount of *cholesterol* in their bloodstream avoid drinking whole milk because of its cholesterol content. Cholesterol is a fatty substance found in all animal tissues. However, a high level of cholesterol in the bloodstream may contribute to *arteriosclerosis*, a disease of the arteries that can cause heart attacks. Skim milk contains no cholesterol.

Milk from Farm to Table

Millions of Americans enjoy pure, fresh milk every day, especially at mealtimes. But few realize the many steps required—first at a dairy farm and then at a processing plant—to get this milk to the dining table.

At a Dairy Farm, milk is produced under highly sanitary conditions by special breeds of cows called *dairy cattle*. The milk is then marketed and transported to a local processing plant.

Production. Almost all U.S. dairy farmers use milking machines to milk their cows. The machines are faster and more sanitary than milking by hand. But some dairy farmers—especially those who have only a few cows—still do their milking by hand. See MILKING MACHINE.

The milk that cows produce is called *raw milk* until it has been pasteurized. Harmful bacteria grow rapidly in raw milk unless the milk is kept clean and cool. Dairy farmers therefore see that their cows and barns are clean, and they sanitize their milking equipment. Most farmers store raw milk in a refrigerated tank until it can be delivered to a processing plant. The tank is

460

connected to a milking machine by glass or stainless steel pipes. As a cow is milked, the milk flows into the tank and is cooled to less than 40° F. (4.4° C).

Local, state, and federal agencies have set standards of cleanliness for dairy farms and processing plants. To make sure these standards are met, local health inspectors check farms and plants, examine all dairy cows, and conduct laboratory tests of milk.

Almost all the fluid milk sold for table use in the United States is classified as *grade A*. Most communities have special rules regarding the sanitary conditions under which milk must be produced and processed to be classed as grade A. The rules are largely based on the Grade A Pasteurized Milk Ordinance, a set of recommendations developed by the U.S. Food and Drug Administration (FDA). Many states permit the sale of a *manufacturing grade* of milk. It costs somewhat less to produce and process than does grade-A milk. A manufacturing grade may have more bacteria and be produced and processed under less strict conditions. It is used chiefly in making such dairy products as butter, cheese, and ice cream.

Marketing. Most dairy farmers are members and joint owners of a dairy *cooperative*. A cooperative picks up the members' raw milk and sells it for them at the highest price to processing plants. Some cooperatives not only pick up the members' milk but also process it. See COOPERATIVE.

In the United States, the federal government sets minimum prices that farmers receive for their milk. The government keeps milk prices from falling below the minimum through a *price support program*. Under the program, the government buys dairy products when the farm price of milk falls below the minimum, or support, level. The supply available to consumers thus declines, and demand causes the price to rise again.

Transportation. A dairy cooperative operates large tank trucks to transport the milk of its members. At least every other day, a truck picks up milk from various dairy farms in an area and delivers it to a processing plant. The truck's tank is insulated to keep the milk cold, even in hot weather. At each farm, the milk haulers examine and take samples of the milk before pumping it into the tank. The samples are important because all the milk from the various farms becomes mixed in the tank. The samples from each farm go to the local health department and the milk processor to be tested for composition and quality.

At a Processing Plant. More than 40 per cent of the milk produced in the United States is processed into various kinds of fluid milk or cream. Most of the rest is made into such dairy products as butter, cheese, and ice cream. A small amount is used to make special types of dairy products, such as *acidophilus milk*. This milk is often used for treating intestinal disorders. The following discussion describes the processing of fresh fluid milk. To learn how some other dairy products are made, see the table *Kinds of Milk and Milk Products* on this page.

As soon as the tank truck arrives at a processing plant, laboratory technicians check the odor, taste, and appearance of the milk. They also measure the fat content, the number of bacteria, the amount of milk solids, and the acidity. Technicians further test the milk dur-

Kinds of Milk and Milk Products

There are many kinds of milk and milk products. They vary widely in flavor, texture, and use. This table briefly describes a few of these foods and the processes by which they are made.

Milk or Milk Product	Description	Manufacturing Process
*Butter	Churned milk fat.	Pasteurized cream mechanically churned, causing its milk fat to form into butter.
*Buttermilk, Cultured	Low-fat milk with tangy flavor.	Acid-producing bacteria added to pasteurized skim or low-fat milk; milk allowed to *ferment* (sour) until desired taste obtained.
*Cheese	Treated curd of milk.	Bacteria or other agent added to milk to form soft curd; liquid part of milk removed from curd; curd then made into different types of cheese.
Cream	Rich milk product containing at least 18 per cent milk fat.	Mechanically separated from nonhomogenized whole milk.
*Evaporated Milk	Whole milk with about 60 per cent of its water removed; requires no refrigeration until opened.	Pasteurized whole milk heated in a vacuum to remove proper percentage of water; milk then canned, sealed, and sterilized; may also be sterilized first, then canned and sealed.
*Ice Cream	Sweet, frozen dairy product.	Cream, concentrated milk, sugar, and flavoring mixed together and frozen; air whipped in to give proper texture.
Low-Fat Milk	Milk that has about 0.5 to 2 per cent milk fat.	Skim milk mixed with whole milk to obtain proper percentage of milk fat; mixture then pasteurized and homogenized.
Skim Milk	Milk that has about 0.1 per cent milk fat.	Mechanically separated from nonhomogenized whole milk.
Sour Cream	Smooth, firm, tangy cream with at least 18 per cent milk fat.	Acid-producing bacteria added to cream, causing it to sour; cream chilled after proper flavor reached; also made by adding acid and flavoring directly to cream.
*Yogurt	Thick, custardlike form of milk.	Nonfat dry milk mixed with partly skimmed milk; bacteria and flavoring added; mixture ferments, forming tangy curd; curd chilled after desired flavor obtained; fruit and sugar often added.

*Has a separate article in WORLD BOOK.

Hill Farm Dairy (WORLD BOOK photo)

Testing the Quality and Purity of Milk is a constant activity at a dairy plant. This technician is using a Milko-tester to check the fat content of a sample of whole milk.

ing and after processing. All this testing helps ensure the quality and purity of the milk. Milk is the most highly tested of all foods.

After the first tests, the milk is pumped into a large refrigerated storage tank. On its way to the tank, the milk passes through a *clarifier*. This machine removes any hair, dust, or similar matter that may be in the milk. After the milk is pumped from the storage tank, it goes through five basic steps. These steps, in order,

are (1) separation or standardization, (2) pasteurization, (3) homogenization, (4) fortification, and (5) packaging.

Separation or Standardization. Some of the milk that comes from the storage tank is separated. The rest is standardized. In separation, the cream, or fat, is mechanically *skimmed* (separated) from milk. Some of the cream is then either bottled or used to make butter or other dairy products. Some of the remaining *skim milk* is also either bottled or used to make such foods as cottage cheese or cultured buttermilk. The rest of the cream and skim milk is used to standardize the milk that has not been separated. See SEPARATOR.

In standardization, the fat content of milk is regulated by the addition of cream or skim milk. A device called a *Milko-tester* measures the fat content as the milk flows through a pipeline. If the content becomes lower than the desired level, cream is pumped in with the milk. If the fat content becomes higher, skim milk is pumped in. Standardization enables dairies to produce 2 per cent milk and other low-fat milks with a uniform fat content. It also ensures that the fat content of whole milk meets government requirements.

Pasteurization involves heating the milk to kill disease-causing bacteria. Almost all the milk sold in the United States is pasteurized. Most of it is pasteurized by the *high-temperature*, or *short-time*, method. This process requires milk to be heated to more than 161° F. (72° C) for at least 15 seconds and then immediately cooled. Some milk is pasteurized by the *low-temperature*, or *holding*, method. Such milk is heated to at least 145° F. (63° C) for 30 minutes or longer and then cooled. Other milk and such products as whipping cream are pasteurized by the *ultrahigh-temperature* method. This process requires a temperature of 280° F. (138° C) or higher for 2 or more seconds. The method

How a Dairy Processes Whole Milk

After raw milk arrives at a dairy, some of it is separated into skim milk and cream. The rest is processed into whole milk. The first step in the process is *standardization.* A Milko-tester indicates whether cream should be added to increase the fat content or skim milk to lower the fat content. After the proper fat content is reached, the milk is pasteurized, homogenized, and packaged as whole milk.

WORLD BOOK diagram by Lowell Stumpf

Raw Milk

Milko-tester checks fat content

Standardized Milk made by adding skim milk or cream

Skim Milk Storage Tank

Cream Storage Tank

Separator mechanically separates raw milk into skim milk and cream

Pasteurizer heats milk to kill harmful bacteria

Homogenizer breaks up fat globules

Packager fills and seals milk containers

Hill Farm Dairy (WORLD BOOK photo)

greatly increases the time a product may be stored before it spoils. See PASTEURIZATION.

Homogenization. Almost all the whole milk and low-fat milk sold in the United States is homogenized. Homogenization breaks up the fat globules in milk so the globules do not rise to the top. A machine called a *homogenizer* forces the milk through tiny openings under great pressure. The process increases the number of fat globules and gives every drop of milk the same amount of cream. Such milk tastes richer than non-homogenized milk. See HOMOGENIZATION.

Fortification improves the food value of milk by adding certain nutrients, especially vitamins and proteins. Most dairies add vitamin D because the quantity is low in milk. They fortify skim milk with vitamin A—as well as vitamin D—because skim milk loses much of its vitamin A content when the fat is removed. Dairies also increase the protein content of skim milk. A few dairies increase the amount of other vitamins and some of the minerals in milk.

Packaging is the final step in the processing of milk. The milk flows through stainless steel pipes to automatic packaging machines. The machines fill and seal the milk containers, most of which are paper cartons or plastic bottles. After the containers are sealed, they are put into cases and stored in a refrigerated room to await delivery. They are then loaded into refrigerated trucks and delivered to stores and homes. At one time, home delivery of milk was common in the United States. But today, almost all families buy their milk at a supermarket or other retail store.

The Milk Industry

Every state in the United States and every Canadian province produces milk. In the United States, the industry is concentrated in the *Dairy Belt*, which extends from New York to Minnesota. Wisconsin leads the states in milk production, followed by California and New York. Quebec and Ontario are the chief milk-producing provinces.

In the United States, milk producers receive about $9.9 billion a year for their products. The nation has about 5,000 dairy plants. About half the plants process fluid milk and employ almost 125,000 workers. The

rest of the plants make other milk products. Dairy plants produce approximately 25 billion quarts (24 billion liters) of milk yearly—enough to provide each American with $\frac{1}{3}$ quart (0.3 liter) a day. American consumers buy about $22 billion worth of milk and milk products a year. Canada has approximately 650 dairy plants. The plants produce about $2\frac{1}{2}$ billion quarts (2.3 billion liters) of milk annually.

History of the Milk Industry

No one knows when people first used animal milk for food. However, the people of ancient Babylon, Egypt,

Leading Milk-Producing States and Provinces

Milk production in 1977

Wisconsin
2,446,628,000 gallons (9,261,495,000 liters)

California
1,390,698,000 gallons (5,264,364,900 liters)

New York
1,189,302,000 gallons (4,501,998,100 liters)

Minnesota
1,102,674,000 gallons (4,174,075,400 liters)

Pennsylvania
905,930,000 gallons (3,429,318,000 liters)

Quebec
782,551,000 gallons (2,962,228,000 liters)

Ontario
697,773,000 gallons (2,641,358,000 liters)

Michigan
553,605,000 gallons (2,095,623,000 liters)

Ohio
528,837,000 gallons (2,001,866,000 liters)

Iowa
493,023,000 gallons (1,866,295,000 liters)

Sources: U.S. Department of Agriculture; Statistics Canada.

and India raised dairy cattle as early as 4000 B.C. At that time, the family cow was the chief source of milk. A family used as much milk as it needed and traded or sold the rest to neighbors. This practice is still common in some parts of the world.

In America, the family cow was especially common during colonial times. But by 1850, many U.S. farmers had begun to own several dairy cows and to supply milk to nearby homes. With the growth of cities, local laws prohibited keeping cows within city limits. Farmers outside the cities then began to increase the size of their herds and to establish dairy businesses.

As the dairy industry grew, several cities passed laws to control the sale of milk. Some of these laws made it illegal to add water to milk or to remove cream from it. Boston passed the first such law in 1856. However, none of the early laws set health standards for milk. Many dairies added chemical preservatives to milk. But after some of these chemicals were found to be harmful, laws prohibited their use. Gradually, cities and states began supervising the milk industry in order to protect the public health.

Several inventions and new processes helped speed the growth of the milk industry. In 1856, an American inventor named Gail Borden received a patent for the first successful milk-condensing process. About 1885, dairies first used glass jars and bottles, which workers filled by hand. The invention of a bottling machine in 1886 made filling the containers easier and faster.

In 1890, Stephen M. Babcock, an American agricultural chemist, developed a test to measure the fat content of milk (see BABCOCK, STEPHEN M.). Milk's market value depends on its fat content, which dairies still determine by the Babcock test. In the 1890's, a few dairy plants introduced pasteurization, a process invented by the French scientist Louis Pasteur. Homogenizers gradually came into use after 1900. Since the mid-1900's, many new milk-processing devices and methods have been developed. They have helped make possible today's large, modern dairy plants. ROBERT T. MARSHALL

Related Articles in WORLD BOOK include:

MILK AND MILK PRODUCTS

Butter	Cheese	Ice Cream
Buttermilk	Condensed Milk	Yogurt
Casein	Evaporated Milk	

MILK PRODUCTION

Dairying	Milking Machine
Dehydration	Pasteurization
Farm and Farming	Pure Food and Drug Laws
Homogenization	Separator

SOURCES OF MILK

Camel	Reindeer
Cattle (Dairy Cattle)	Sheep
Goat (Domestic Goats)	Water Buffalo
Llama	Yak

Outline

I. **Food Value of Milk**
   A. Nutrients in Milk
   B. Milk in the Human Diet
II. **Milk from Farm to Table**
   A. At a Dairy Farm
   B. At a Processing Plant
III. **The Milk Industry**
IV. **History of the Milk Industry**

Questions

What are some common food products made from milk?

What is a dairy *cooperative?* What is its purpose?

What are the three leading milk-producing states?

Why are some people able to digest only a small amount of milk?

What happens to milk during pasteurization? During homogenization?

What is *grade-A* milk? *Raw milk?*

What do laboratory technicians at processing plants test in milk?

Why is milk such a nourishing food?

What other animals besides cows supply milk for human use?

How do farmers help prevent the rapid growth of bacteria in raw milk?

MILK GLASS. See GLASSWARE (Milk Glass).

MILK RIVER. See MONTANA (Rivers).

MILK SNAKE. One type of king snake is called *milk snake* because farmers once believed that it took milk from cows. Today, scientists know that no snake is physically able to take milk from a cow. But any snake might drink milk it finds in a pail, mistaking it for water. Like other king snakes, the milk snake kills harmful rodents, such as rats and mice. It often comes into barnyards to hunt for rodents that nest there.

The milk snake may be 4 feet (1.2 meters) long, whereas other king snakes grow to be 6 feet (1.8 meters) in length. Milk snakes are gray with dark-bordered chestnut blotches on the back and sides. However, milk snakes found in the Western and Southern United States vary in size and color pattern. Some persons also call these snakes *house snakes.*

Scientific Classification. The milk snake is a member of the common snake family, *Colubridae.* It is genus *Lampropeltis,* species *L. doliata.* CLIFFORD H. POPE

See also KING SNAKE.

New York Zoological Society

The Milk Snake Is Valuable to Farmers because it eats the rats and mice that live in and around farm buildings.

MILK SUGAR. See SUGAR (Milk Sugar); MILK (Nutrients in Milk).

MILKING MACHINE is a device that milks cows. A motor-driven vacuum pump sucks the milk through rubber-lined cups that fit over the cow's teats. Hoses link the cups to the pump. The milk flows into a closed pail or through a pipeline to a tank. The action of the cups resembles the sucking of a calf. The pump creates alternately a vacuum and pressure in the cups. Part of the time the cups milk the cow, and part of the time they are idle or massage the teats. This permits blood to circulate in the teats to keep them healthy.

Most modern dairy farms use milking machines. The

machines provide a closed system from the cow to the milk container. This system keeps the milk cleaner than the milk from hand-milked cows. Milking machines lower the cost of producing milk by reducing the labor needed.

Anna Baldwin, a New Jersey farm woman, invented the first suction milking machine in 1878. But a Swedish engineer, Carl Gustaf de Laval (1845-1913), developed the first commercially successful machine. It grew out of a series of models he built, starting in 1894, and it went on the market in 1918.   A. D. LONGHOUSE

See also CATTLE (picture: A Milking Parlor); DAIRYING (The Milking Parlor of a Dairy Farm).

MILKING SHORTHORN. See CATTLE (Dual-Purpose Cattle; picture: Milking Shorthorn); FARM AND FARMING (picture: Machines Milk Cows).

MILKWEED. See BUTTERFLY (True Butterflies).

MILKWEED is the name of several plants which have tufts of silky hairs on the seeds, and stout stems filled with a milky juice. The *common milkweed* is one of the best-known milkweeds in North America. It grows along roadsides and in fields and waste places as far south as Georgia and Kansas.

The stems of the common milkweed stand about 4 feet (1.2 meters) high and bear large, hairy, pale-green leaves on short stalks. The purplish flowers grow in clusters at the tip of the stem. The flowers bloom from June to August and have a sweet odor that attracts insects. Each flower is shaped so that an insect has to walk through masses of pollen before it reaches the nectar. The insect then flies away with two bundles of pollen on its legs and thus brings about *cross-pollination* (see POLLEN AND POLLINATION).

In the autumn, large, rough seed pods take the place of the flower clusters of the milkweed. When the pods ripen and burst open, clouds of seeds are scattered by the wind. The milkweed can also reproduce itself from its creeping roots. In 1942, milkweed floss was collected as a wartime substitute for the kapok fiber used in life belts. The juice of the milkweed contains small amounts of a rubberlike substance. One of the most attractive milkweeds is the brilliant *butterfly weed*.

Scientific Classification. The milkweed is a member of the milkweed family, *Asclepiadaceae*. The common milkweed is classified as genus *Asclepias*, species *A. syriaca*. The butterfly weed is *A. tuberosa*.   EARL L. CORE

MILKY WAY is a glowing band of starlight coming from the billions of stars within our own *galaxy* (star system). The galaxy is shaped like a pancake. But at night, we see it as a milky-looking strip of stars because we are inside it. Actually, the stars fan out from the center in wide, curving arms that would give the galaxy a *spiral* (coil) shape if we could see it from above. Astronomers call the Milky Way a *spiral galaxy*.

Size of the Galaxy. The diameter of the galaxy is about 10 times greater than its thickness. It is so big that light, which travels 186,282 miles (299,792 kilometers) per second, takes about 100,000 years to travel from one end to the other. Our solar system is a tiny speck located about 30,000 light-years from the center of the galaxy. It is about midway between the upper and lower edges of the galaxy. See ASTRONOMY (illustration: The Milky Way).

On a dark, clear summer night, the Milky Way can be seen extending from the southern constellation Sagittarius, where it is brightest, to Cygnus, the great northern cross. During winter, it is dimmer and crosses the sky near Orion and Cassiopeia. The Milky Way has dark gaps in many places. These are formed by clouds of dust, called *nebulae*, that block out light from the stars behind them.

Composition of the Galaxy. The Milky Way contains clouds of dust and gas; planets; star clusters; and stars, each with its own distinctive pattern. For example, young stars and the open star clusters lie near the middle *plane* (imaginary flat surface) of the galaxy. The oldest stars and dense clusters, containing millions of stars, make a spherical halo near the center of the galaxy.

Gravity holds the Milky Way together, and all of its stars rotate around the center. However, not all stars rotate with the same speed. Their speed depends on their position in relation to the *mass* (matter) in the galaxy. Stars such as our sun, which are far from the center, rotate around the center much as the planets rotate around the sun. They move this way because, for them, most of the mass lies toward the center. Our sun moves in a circular path at a speed of 156 miles (250 kilometers) per second. Yet a complete trip around the center of the Milky Way takes the sun about 225 million years. The stars slightly closer to the center move faster, because they are attracted with greater force. However, the stars very close to the center move slower. For them, most of the mass lies toward the edges of the

J. Horace McFarland

Milkweed Flowers bloom along roadsides and in fields from June to August.

Lynwood M. Chace

The Milkweed Pod is rough-coated. When ripe, it bursts and scatters its seeds.

Lynwood M. Chace

The Pod Splits, showing the brown, overlapping seeds and their silky tufts.

Lynwood M. Chace

The Silky Floss carries the seeds away on the breeze as they pop out.

465

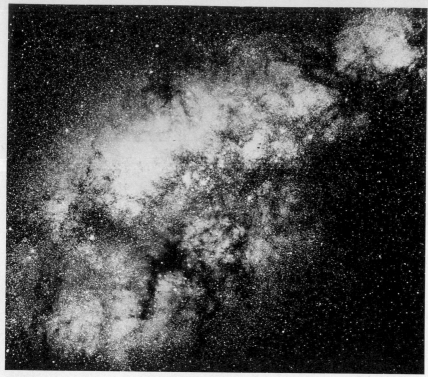

The Milky Way is made up of many billions of stars. It can be easily seen as a bright haze on a clear summer night.

Milky Way. A study of this motion reveals that the mass of the Milky Way is equal to 200 billion suns.

The Center of the Galaxy. Light from the center cannot reach us through the dust, but scientists know from studying radio waves and infrared rays that there is intense activity there. Astronomers have found that gas streams out from the center at 100 miles (160 kilometers) per second, but they do not know why this occurs. CHARLES A. WHITNEY

See also GALAXY; NEBULA; SOLAR SYSTEM; STAR.

MILL is a *money of account*, or coin term used in keeping accounts in the United States. A mill, which is not a coin, has the value of one-tenth of a cent.

MILL was the family name of three famous British writers—father and son and the son's wife. They won distinction in the fields of philosophy, history, psychology, and economics.

James Mill (1773-1836) established his reputation as a writer with the publication of *A History of British India* (1817). This work was partly responsible for changes in the Indian government. It also won him a job with the East India Company in 1819. He headed the company from 1830 until his death.

In 1808, Mill met Jeremy Bentham, a political economist called the *father of utilitarianism*. The utilitarians believed that the greatest happiness of the greatest number should be the sole purpose of all public action (see BENTHAM, JEREMY; UTILITARIANISM). Mill adopted the utilitarian philosophy and became Bentham's ardent disciple and the editor of *St. James's Chronicle*.

His writings helped clarify the philosophical and psychological basis of utilitarianism. *Analysis of the Phenomena of the Human Mind* (1829) is a study of psychology. He wrote *Elements of Political Economy*

(1821) as a textbook for his son, and it became the first textbook of English economics. *Fragment on Mackintosh* (1835) states his views of utility as the basis of morals.

Mill was born in Scotland and graduated from Edinburgh University, where he studied for the ministry. He became a Presbyterian minister in 1798 but left the ministry in 1802 to become a journalist.

John Stuart Mill (1806-1873) became the leader of the utilitarian movement. Mill was one of the most advanced thinkers of his time. He tried to help the English working people by promoting measures leading to a more equal division of profits. He favored a cooperative system of agriculture and increased rights for women. He served as editor of the *Westminster Review* from 1835 to 1840 and wrote many articles on economics.

His greatest contribution to philosophy and his chief work, *System of Logic* (1843), ranks with Aristotle's work in that field. Mill applied economic principles to social conditions in *Principles of Political Economy* (1848). His other works include *Utilitarianism* (1863), *On Liberty* (1859), *The Subjection of Women* (1869), and *Autobiography* (1873).

Mill was born in London and was educated completely by his father. He began to study Greek at the age of 3, and, at 14, had mastered Latin, classical literature, logic, political economy, history, and mathematics. He entered the East India Company as a clerk at 17. Like his father, he became director of the company. He retired after 33 years of service and was elected to Parliament in 1865.

Harriet Taylor Mill (1807-1858) was the wife of John Stuart Mill and helped him write many of his works. She called for increased rights for women and workers and greatly influenced Mill's writings in these areas.

Many of John Stuart Mill's writings probably originated from discussions with Harriet. She helped him write *Principles of Political Economy*. Some scholars also consider her the coauthor of *On Liberty*, *The Subjection of Women*, and *Autobiography*, all of which were published after her death. However, only the essay "Enfranchisement of Women" bears her name. It appears in her husband's *Discussions and Dissertations*, a four-volume work published from 1859 to 1875. In the introduction to *On Liberty*, he calls Harriet "the inspirer, and in part the author, of all that is best in my writings."

She was born Harriet Hardy in Walworth, near Durham, England. In 1826, she married John Taylor, a merchant. Harriet met John Stuart Mill about 1830, and they became close friends. Taylor died in 1849, and she married Mill in 1851.　　　　　H. W. SPIEGEL

MILLAIS, *mih LAY*, **SIR JOHN EVERETT** (1829-1896), an English painter, was a founder of the Pre-Raphaelite Brotherhood in 1848. The others were William Holman Hunt and Dante Gabriel Rossetti. This group believed that art should be simple and sincere as they considered it to be in the days before Raphael. Millais' Pre-Raphaelite paintings resembled colored photographs. He chose subjects from the Bible, history, legends, and poems. Millais painted *Christ in the House of His Parents* in this style. His other paintings include *Ophelia* and *The Eve of Saint Agnes*. He left the Pre-Raphaelite movement in 1859, and became a typical Victorian academic painter. He was born in Southampton.　　L. D. LONGMAN

See also CARLYLE, THOMAS (picture).

MILLAR, KENNETH. See MACDONALD, ROSS.

MILLAY, EDNA ST. VINCENT (1892-1950), was an American poet. Many of her poems have romantic themes. She wrote about love and death, about the self and the universe, and about the feelings of rebellious youth. In her treatment of these subjects, she combined sentimentality with wit and sophistication.

Millay was born in Rockland, Me., and graduated from Vassar College in 1917. She did some of her best work while very young. "Renascence," a poem about a personal religious experience, was written when she was only 19 years old. *A Few Figs from Thistles* (1920) was one of three works for which she won a Pulitzer prize in 1923. The other two works were *The Ballad of the Harp-Weaver* and eight sonnets.

Millay's later poetry became increasingly concerned with modern history. *Conversation at Midnight* (1937) deals with events that were leading to World War II. *The Murder of Lidice* (1942) tells about the de-

Culver
Edna St. Vincent Millay

struction of a Czechoslovak town by German troops during the war. Millay was fond of the sonnet form, and her many sonnets were published in 1941. A definitive collection of her poems appeared in 1956. She also wrote several plays, including the one-act poetic fantasy *Aria da Capo* (1919).　　CLARK GRIFFITH

MILLEDGEVILLE, Ga. (pop. 11,601), a distributing center for surrounding farms, lies 30 miles (48 kilometers) northeast of Macon (see GEORGIA [political map]).

Milledgeville was established in 1803, and was named for Governor John Milledge. It was the state capital from 1807 to 1868. Georgia's first state Capitol still stands there. Milledgeville is the home of Georgia College and Georgia Military College. The city's factories make textiles, brick, tile, medical supplies, and mobile homes. Milledgeville has a mayor-council form of government.　　　　　ALBERT B. SAYE

MILLEFIORI GLASS. See GLASSWARE.

MILLENNIUM, *muh LEHN ee um*, means any period of 1,000 years. But the term is usually used to refer to the period mentioned in the New Testament book of Revelation (20:1-6) as the time when holiness will prevail throughout the world (see REVELATION).

Some people have interpreted the passage in Revelation as meaning that Christ will reign on earth either before or after the 1,000-year period. These views are known as *premillennialism* and *postmillennialism*.

Because the book of Revelation frequently uses numbers symbolically, other people have interpreted this passage spiritually. They regard the millennium as the long period of time between Christ's first coming and His second coming. St. Augustine was the first to set forth this view, known as *amillennialism*. It is expressed in *The City of God*.　　　　　BRUCE M. METZGER

MILLEPEDE. See MILLIPEDE.

MILLER, ARTHUR (1915-　　), is a leading American playwright. His works record the conflict between the individual and the society which establishes the individual's moral code. Miller showed society's morality as valid in *All My Sons* (1947) and *A View from the Bridge* (1955). But in *Death of a Salesman* (1949), *The Crucible* (1953), *Incident at Vichy* (1964), and *The Price* (1968), he showed its morality as false. *Death of a Salesman*, which received a Pulitzer prize, is generally considered Miller's masterpiece. It tells of Willy Loman, a traveling salesman who chooses popularity and material success as his goals. Destroyed by his choice, Loman commits suicide in the end. The play typifies Miller's belief that the "common man" is the modern tragic hero.

Miller's work generally follows the Ibsen school of realistic drama. But much of the action in *Death of a Salesman* is seen through Loman's mind, thus establishing Miller's debt to expressionistic drama.

Miller was born in New York City. He was married to actress Marilyn Monroe from 1956 to 1961. His play *After the Fall* (1964) contains elements of this and other autobiographical episodes.　　MARDI VALGEMAE

MILLER, CINCINNATUS H. See MILLER, JOAQUIN.

MILLER, GLENN (1904-1944), was a popular American dance band leader, arranger, and trombonist. Miller's band featured a distinctive sound that he developed by blending a clarinet with four saxophones. The band played both smoothly danceable ballads and crisply driving swing numbers. It made many hit records, including "Moonlight Serenade," the band's theme song; "In the Mood"; "Little Brown Jug"; and "Sunrise Serenade." The band's vocalists—Tex Beneke, Ray Eberle, and Marion Hutton—became national favorites.

Miller was born in Clarinda, Iowa. From 1926 to 1936, he played trombone in several bands, including those of Tommy and Jimmy Dorsey, Red Nichols, Ray Noble, Ben Pollack, and Freddy Rich. Miller formed his first band in 1937. He achieved his greatest success from 1938 until he entered the United States Army Air Force in 1942. Miller disappeared during an air journey while in the service. NAT HENTOFF

MILLER, HENRY (1891-1980), became one of the most controversial American authors of his time. His emphasis on sex and his obscene language led to censorship trials and literary quarrels.

Miller's first important book, *Tropic of Cancer* (1934), was banned from publication in the United States until 1961. It was written in Paris, where Miller had exiled himself from an America he despised. As in all of Miller's work, the plot is not as important as the message. He believed that modern civilization is diseased. People, to be healthy again, must win freedom from society and glorify the self and the senses.

Tropic of Capricorn (1939) is even more poetic and has a stronger sense of prophecy. It mixes moments of mystic joy with descriptions of what Miller saw as the American cultural wasteland. Miller's basic position never changed, though his later subjects became more literary. He greatly influenced the "Beat" writers, including Jack Kerouac, Allen Ginsberg, and Lawrence Ferlinghetti. Miller was born and grew up in New York City. EUGENE K. GARBER

MILLER, JOAQUIN, *wah KEEN* (1839?-1913), was the pen name of the American poet Cincinnatus Hiner Miller. He once wrote an article in defense of the Mexican bandit Joaquin Murietta. When he published his first book, he took Joaquin as a pen name. Miller is perhaps best remembered today for the poem "Columbus."

He was born in Liberty, Ind., but spent much of his early life in the West. His family settled in Oregon in 1852. At the age of 15, Miller ran away from his Oregon home. He lived in various mining camps and with the Indians in California. An Indian tribe adopted him, and he was married to a chief's daughter. After she was killed in an accident, Miller returned to Oregon in about 1860 and became a lawyer. But he spent his time writing.

In 1871, he visited England, where he published his first notable collection, *Songs of the Sierras* (1871). He also wrote *Songs of the Sunlands* (1873), the autobiographical *Life Amongst the Modocs* (1873), and the play *The Danites of the Sierras* (1877). PETER VIERECK

MILLER, JOE (1684-1738), was a famous English comedian. He was a member of the Drury Lane Company from 1709 until his death. His acting in William Congreve's plays was largely responsible for their success. After Miller's death, John Mottley published a collection of coarse jokes and called it *Joe Miller's Jest Book* or *The Wit's Vade Mecum.* But Miller had told only three of the jokes. Miller was born either Joseph or Josias Miller. His birthplace is unknown.

MILLER, JOHN. See NORTH DAKOTA (History).

MILLER, LEWIS. See CHAUTAUQUA.

MILLER, WILLIAM. See ADVENTISTS.

MILLER, WILLIAM EDWARD (1914-   ), was the Republican nominee for Vice-President of the United States in the 1964 election. Senator Barry M. Gold-

water and Miller were defeated by a Democratic ticket headed by President Lyndon B. Johnson and Hubert H. Humphrey.

Miller, a New Yorker, served in the U.S. House of Representatives from 1951 to 1965 and was Republican national chairman from 1961 to 1964. He gained a reputation as a tough debater and campaigner, and a good organizer. Miller headed his party's congressional campaign committee in 1960. The Republicans gained 22 seats in the House, even though their presidential candidate, Richard M. Nixon, was defeated. Republican leaders gave Miller much credit for the victories. Miller also became known for his barbed comments about Democrats. Goldwater indicated this was one reason he chose Miller as his running mate.

Miller was born in Lockport, N.Y. He attended the University of Notre Dame and Albany Law School. He served in the Army during World War II, and later helped prosecute German war criminals at the Nuremberg trials. Miller entered politics when Governor Thomas E. Dewey of New York appointed him district attorney of Niagara County in 1948. ERIC SEVAREID

MILLERITES. See ADVENTISTS.

MILLER'S-THUMB. See SCULPIN.

MILLES, *MIL lus*, **CARL WILHELM EMIL** (1875-1955), was a Swedish-American sculptor. He became famous for creating fountains that combine graceful figures with splashing water. Examples are *Fountain of Faith*, in Falls Church, Va., and *Meeting of the Waters*, in St. Louis, Mo.

Milles was born near Uppsala, Sweden, and studied in Stockholm, Paris, Munich, and Rome. He came to the United States in 1929 and became a citizen in 1945. He taught for many years at the Cranbrook Academy of Art in Bloomfield Hills, Mich. The academy has a fine collection of his works. Many of his statues and fountains are beautifully displayed in a famous park, the Millesgården, in Stockholm. WILLIAM L. MACDONALD

See also SWEDEN (color picture: Statues).

MILLET, *MILL et*. Almost one-third of the world's people depend on millet for grain feeds and flours. Many kinds of grain and hay grasses are called millet. These grasses have many uses. In Canada and the United States, farmers grow various kinds of millet for hay, for enriching the soil, and for producing seed. In parts of Europe and Asia, millet is grown for human food. In India, farmers plant about 40 million acres (16 million hectares) with millet yearly to provide grain and flour. In Japan, about 35 million bushels (780 million kilograms) of millet seed are ground into flour each year.

Farmers in the United States usually grow *foxtail millet*. There are several varieties of foxtail millet, but all have thick, rounded flower heads at the top of slender stems. In *Hungarian millet*, a variety of foxtail millet, these spikes are purple. Foxtail millet grows chiefly in Kansas, Missouri, and Texas, and in neighboring states. It provides the best hay

J. Horace McFarland
Millet

when it is cut just after the flowers are in full bloom.

Broomcorn millet, which grows in Europe, is also raised in North and South Dakota, Montana, Wyoming, and Colorado. It has loose, bushy flower heads that look somewhat like small brush brooms. Farmers use varieties of broomcorn millet for seed rather than for hay.

Barnyard millet is a cultivated form of the weed called barnyard grass. Farmers grow it chiefly as hay.

Planting. The planting season for millet varies with the location. Millet may be planted as early as May and as late as August. Most varieties of millet are sensitive to cold. They should not be planted until the sun has thoroughly warmed the ground. Rich, loamy soils are best. The soil is prepared for millet as it is for other grasses. Insects and diseases do not usually attack millet. Hungarian millet may yield 2 to 3 short tons per acre (4.5 to 6.7 metric tons per hectare) within 50 to 80 days after seeding.

Feeding Value. A little millet hay makes satisfactory feed for farm animals, if it is not used continuously. Ripe millet seeds are a good food for poultry and birds. Crushed and ground millet seeds can be fed to livestock. But no millet hay or seed is fed to horses.

Scientific Classification. Millet belongs to the grass family, *Gramineae*. Foxtail millet is genus *Setaria*, species *S. italica*. Broomcorn millet is *Panicum miliaceum*, and barnyard millet, *Echinochloa frumentacea*.   WILLIAM R. VAN DERSAL

MILLET, *MEE LEH*, **JEAN FRANÇOIS** (1814-1875), a French painter, is famous today for a few paintings, such as *The Gleaners*, *The Man with the Hoe*, and *The Angelus* (see ANGELUS). He worked largely in dark, muddy colors. He painted figures of farmers and workers in the fields as symbols rather than as individuals. Millet is seen today by many as a traditionalist whose handling of his themes seems sentimental.

Millet was born near Cherbourg, in Normandy, of rural stock. He showed early talent. In 1836, the town council of Cherbourg gave Millet a small pension, and he went to Paris. He studied with Paul Delaroche, but Millet left Delaroche because he was temperamentally unable to learn by art school methods. Millet began to teach himself. He supported himself by painting signs and portraits and doing other work. After many exhibits, he was admitted to the French Academy in 1847.

In 1848, Millet moved to the village of Barbizon, where he became a leading figure in the group of landscape and nature painters living there. He painted at Barbizon the scenes from rural life for which he is famous. His paintings were then considered revolutionary. Millet was poor, but after his death, his paintings became valuable. By 1890, a collector had bought *The Angelus* for $150,000.   ROBERT GOLDWATER

MILLIGAN, EX PARTE. See EX PARTE MILLIGAN.

MILLIGRAM. See WEIGHTS AND MEASURES.

MILLIKAN, ROBERT ANDREWS (1868-1953), an American physicist, was one of the most illustrious U.S. scientists. He is noted for his measurement of the electrical charge carried by the electron, and for his contributions to cosmic-ray research.

Born at Morrison, Ill., Millikan studied at Oberlin College and received a master's degree in 1893. He entered Columbia University, where he became the only graduate student in physics, and obtained his Ph.D. degree. Millikan then went to the University of Chicago and its newly opened Ryerson Laboratory.

He remained until 1921. In 1909, he began a series of experiments to study the electrical charge carried by an electron. He found the charge by spraying tiny drops of oil into a specially built chamber. For this work he won the 1923 Nobel prize for physics.

Kourken

Robert A. Millikan

Millikan became director of the Norman Bridge Laboratory of Physics at the California Institute of Technology in 1921. He held this post until 1945. Under his guidance, the institute became famous for its brilliant contributions to science. Millikan conducted research in cosmic-ray phenomena and pioneered in measuring the intensity of cosmic rays by means of instrument-carrying balloons. He also developed techniques for investigating the nature of cosmic rays in deep lakes. His interest in cosmic-ray research led to the establishment of a research team that made many discoveries at the California Institute of Technology. Their major discovery was the *meson*, a basic atomic particle.

The challenge of education stimulated Millikan to write or collaborate in writing textbooks. They include *Electricity, Sound and Light* (1908), *Elementary Physics* (1936), and *Mechanics, Molecular Physics, Heat and Sound* (1937). Millikan was aware of the importance of science in the modern world, and for the general reader he wrote *Science and Life* (1923).   RALPH E. LAPP

See also COSMIC RAYS; ELECTRON; MESON.

MILLILITER. See METRIC SYSTEM.

MILLIMETER. See METRIC SYSTEM.

MILLINERY. See HAT (The Hat Industry).

MILLING. See CORN (Processing Corn); FLOUR (How White Flour Is Milled); RICE (As a Food).

MILLING, in industry. See COPPER (Milling); GOLD (The Milling Process); MACHINE TOOL (Milling).

MILLION is a thousand 1,000's. One million is written 1,000,000. An idea of the size of a million is given in these facts: 1 million minutes is 16,667 hours, or 694 days, or 1.9 years; 1 million hours is 41,667 days, or 114 years; and 1 million days is 2,740 years. As a power of 10, one million is written 10^6 (see POWER). See also DECIMAL NUMERAL SYSTEM (Larger Numbers).

MILLIPEDE, or MILLEPEDE, is a wormlike, many-legged animal. Millipedes have segmented bodies. Two

Cornelia Clarke

Most Millipedes Resemble Worms with Many Legs.

pairs of legs attach to each of their body segments, except to the first three or four segments and the last one or two segments. The word *millipede* means thousand-footed, but no millipede has as many as 1,000 feet. Some *species* (kinds) have up to 115 pairs of legs. The animals range from less than ⅛ inch (3 millimeters) to up to 9 inches (23 centimeters) long. They have round heads which bear a pair of short antennae. Millipedes usually feed on decaying plant life, but some species also attack crops growing in damp soil. They live in dark, damp places, under stones and rotting logs. Over 1,000 species of millipedes are found throughout the world except in the polar regions.

Scientific Classification. Millipedes are classified in the phylum *Arthropoda*. They make up the class *Diplopoda*. EDWARD A. CHAPIN

MILLS, ROBERT (1781-1855), was one of the first Americans trained as an architect and engineer. He studied with Thomas Jefferson. He designed the Washington Monument in Washington, D.C., which for many years was the tallest structure in the world (see WASHINGTON MONUMENT). He designed more than 50 important buildings, including the United States Post Office, Treasury, and Patent Office buildings in Washington, D.C. He also designed canals, churches, homes, and many courthouses. Mills was born in Charleston, S.C. HUGH MORRISON

MILLS, WILBUR DAIGH (1909-), a Democratic congressman from Arkansas, served as chairman of the powerful House Ways and Means Committee from 1958 to 1974. Mills played a central role in determining the taxes paid by Americans because this committee handles all federal tax legislation.

During the 1960's, Mills's control over tax bills brought him into frequent dispute with Presidents John F. Kennedy and Lyndon B. Johnson. Mills refused to support many of their proposals until he was certain of enough votes to pass them. But he helped win passage of the 1964 tax cut, the 1965 bill establishing Medicare, and the 1968 income tax surcharge bill.

Mills was born in Kensett, Ark. He graduated from Hendrix College and Harvard University law school. He served as county and probate judge of White County, Arkansas, from 1934 to 1938, and served in the House from 1939 to 1977. CHARLES BARTLETT

MILNE, *mihln,* **A. A.** (1882-1956), an English author, became famous for his children's stories and poems. Two of Milne's books, *Winnie-the-Pooh* (1926) and *The House at Pooh Corner* (1928), have become masterpieces of children's literature.

Milne based the characters in the Pooh stories on his son, Christopher Robin, and the young boy's stuffed animals. Milne's stories describe the adventures of Christopher Robin and his animal friends in a forest called the Hundred Acre Wood. Some of the well-known characters in the Pooh stories include Winnie-the-Pooh, a bear; Piglet, a small pig; and Eeyore, an old donkey (see LITERATURE FOR CHILDREN [picture: Classics of the 1900's]). In his autobiography, *It's Too Late Now* (1939), Milne told how the stuffed toys led to the creation of the Pooh characters.

In addition to the Pooh stories, Milne wrote two classic collections of children's poems, *When We Were Very Young* (1924) and *Now We Are Six* (1927). He wrote the children's play *Make-Believe* (1918) and adapted Kenneth Grahame's children's book *The Wind in the Willows* into a play, *Toad of Toad Hall* (1929).

Culver

A. A. Milne

Milne also created novels, short stories, and plays for adults. He wrote a famous detective novel, *The Red House Mystery* (1922), and a collection of short stories called *A Table Near the Band* (1950). His comic plays include *Mr. Pim Passes By* (1919), *The Truth About Blayds* (1921), and *The Dover Road* (1922).

Alan Alexander Milne was born in London and graduated from Cambridge University in 1903. From 1906 to 1914, he served as assistant editor of *Punch*, a humor magazine. Milne contributed many comic essays and poems to the magazine. JAMES DOUGLAS MERRITT

MILNES, *mihlnz,* **SHERRILL** (1935-), is an American operatic baritone known for his rich voice and great range. Milnes specializes in Italian operas, particularly those by Giuseppe Verdi, and has recorded many of the composer's operatic works. Milnes is probably best known for his portrayal of Iago in Verdi's *Otello.*

Milnes was born in Downers Grove, Ill. He made his professional debut in 1959 as an apprentice singer with the Santa Fe (N.M.) Opera. He first sang a major role in 1961 with the Baltimore Civic Opera. Milnes made his Metropolitan Opera debut in 1965 as Valentin in Charles Gounod's *Faust.* ELLEN PFEIFER

MILO. See SORGHUM (Grain Sorghums; picture).

MILSTEIN, *MIHL styn,* **NATHAN** (1904-), is one of the world's greatest violinists. He became known particularly for his interpretations of Bach violin sonatas. Milstein came to the United States in 1929 to make his American debut with the Philadelphia Orchestra. After that, his stature as an artist grew steadily. Milstein was born in Odessa, Russia. He studied in Russia under Peter Stoliarski who also developed the great Russian violinist David Oistrakh. He also studied with Leopold Auer in Russia, and Eugène Ysaÿe in Brussels, Belgium. DOROTHY DeLAY

MILTIADES, *mihl TY uh DEEZ* (540?-488? B.C.), was a famous general of ancient Athens. He defeated the Persians at the Battle of Marathon in 490 B.C., during the wars between Greece and Persia (see MARATHON).

Miltiades was a member of an aristocratic Athenian family. About 516 B.C., while securing trade routes for Athens, he made himself ruler of what is now the Gallipoli Peninsula in Turkey. He probably fought against Persian forces led by Darius. He lost his throne about 492 B.C. and was forced to flee to Athens.

Persians invaded Greece in 490 B.C., and the Athenians made Miltiades a general. Because of his experience in fighting the Persians, he convinced the other generals to attack the enemy at Marathon. After defeating the Persians and driving them from Greece, he commanded a fleet in the Aegean Sea. He died in Athens after being wounded in an accident at sea. RICHARD NELSON FRYE

MILTON, JOHN (1608-1674), an English poet and political writer, wrote one of the world's greatest epics, *Paradise Lost* (1667). He composed this famous epic and two other works, *Paradise Regained* (1671) and *Samson Agonistes* (1671), when he was totally blind.

Paradise Lost is a 12-book epic in blank verse based on the Bible story of the creation and of the fall of Satan and of Adam and Eve. *Paradise Regained*, a blank verse poem in four books, shows Christ overcoming Satan's temptations. *Samson Agonistes*, modeled after Greek tragedies, tells how Samson, betrayed by Dalila (Delilah) and blinded by the Philistines, finally defeats his captors. These three works established Milton as one of England's greatest poets.

Milton was a Puritan and a deeply religious man. He studied the Bible intensely and based many of his firmest beliefs directly on its words. He was a man of high moral character who expressed his literary creed by saying that the writer "ought himself to be a true poem." In a lofty and powerful style, Milton wrote about love, politics, and religion. His works fulfill his own definition of a good book. They pulse with "the precious lifeblood of a master spirit."

His Early Life and Works. Milton was born in London. He showed promise of unusual literary abilities while at Christ's College, Cambridge. There he wrote several poems in Latin, and an ode celebrating the birth of Christ, "On The Morning of Christ's Nativity" (1629). His early training pointed to a religious career. But Milton came to believe that "tyranny had invaded the church." He decided that he could not honestly become a clergyman under the doctrines of the Church of England. He chose to become a poet. While he was still a student, he wrote "L'Allegro" and "Il Penseroso" (1631?), two companion-poems noted for their charm and human interest. "L'Allegro" describes the pleasures of a mirthful man; "Il Penseroso" depicts the joys of a thoughtful, serious man. Milton graduated from Cambridge in 1632 and went to his father's country home, Horton, to study and write.

Milton wrote two major pieces at Horton, *Comus* (1634), and "Lycidas" (1637). *Comus*, a masque (dramatic presentation with music), concerns the nature of virtue. Milton wrote the words for the masque, and a friend, Henry Lawes, wrote the music. "Lycidas," a pastoral elegy, commemorates the death of a school friend, Edward King.

Milton left Horton in 1638 for a 15-month European tour. He heard while in Italy that a conflict was growing between the bishops of the Church of England and the Puritans. Milton returned to England to support the Puritan cause through a series of political writings.

Middle Years. Civil discord divided England from 1640 to 1660. King Charles I and the bishops clashed with Parliament over policies of church and state. Civil war broke out in 1642. The Puritans won. Charles was beheaded in 1649, and a Commonwealth government was established (see ENGLAND [The Civil War]).

During this period, Milton wrote a series of pamphlets supporting the Puritans. He believed that the Church of England was corrupt, and argued in *Of Reformation in England* (1641) that the bishops should be deprived of power. In 1649, he published *The Tenure of Kings and Magistrates*, which declared that the people had the right to choose and depose their rulers. Leaders of the

Yale University Art Gallery, George Heard Hamilton Collection, New Haven

Blindness Failed to Halt Milton's Work. He composed *Paradise Lost* and other poems while blind. According to legend, he dictated *Paradise Lost* to his daughters. This painting, *Milton Dictating Paradise Lost To His Daughters*, is by Eugène Delacroix.

Commonwealth government noticed the pamphlet and appointed Milton secretary for foreign tongues to the Council of State to translate dispatches to other countries into Latin. He also wrote tracts defending the Commonwealth as part of this job. He wrote, among other essays, "Defensio Pro Populo Anglicano" (1651), and "Eikonoklastes" (1649).

Milton had married Mary Powell, a 16-year-old girl, in 1643. Their marriage was unhappy. She left Milton after a month or two and did not return for two years. Milton wrote a series of pamphlets advocating divorce in certain cases. *The Doctrine and Discipline of Divorce* (1643) was the most notable. In 1644, Milton published his most famous prose work, *Areopagitica*, a defense of freedom of the press.

Milton's work and constant study strained his weak eyes, and he became blind in 1652. He wrote a sonnet on his blindness, "When I Consider How My Light Is Spent" (1655). His wife died in 1652, and he married Catharine Woodcock in 1656. She died 16 months later. He probably wrote the sonnet "Methought I Saw My Late Espoused Saint" (1658) about her.

Retirement. After the restoration of Charles II in 1660, the government executed several Puritans held responsible for the death of Charles I. Milton was arrested, but was not punished. He went into retirement, and married Elizabeth Minshull in 1663. He devoted the rest of his life to writing poetry. The three poems of his retirement were *Paradise Lost*, *Paradise Regained*, and *Samson Agonistes*. They present his mature views on man and his destiny, and stand as great monuments to England's most dedicated poet.   GEORGE F. SENSABAUGH

MILTON COLLEGE. See UNIVERSITIES AND COLLEGES (table).

Downtown Milwaukee borders Lake Michigan. Factories stand along the Menomonee River, *upper left*, which winds through the city. Apartment buildings, *lower right*, overlook the lakefront.

MILWAUKEE, *mihl WAW kee,* is the largest city in Wisconsin and one of the major industrial centers of the United States. The city ranks as a leading manufacturer of automobile parts and electrical equipment. Milwaukee is the nation's largest beer producer and is known as the *Beer Capital* of the United States. The city lies on the western shore of Lake Michigan, about 90 miles (140 kilometers) north of Chicago. The city's excellent harbor has made Milwaukee an important Great Lakes port.

Milwaukee's name comes from the Milwaukee River. Most historians say that the river's Algonquin Indian name, *Millioke,* means *good land.* Others translate the name as *great council place.* Milwaukee is often called the *Cream City* because of its many old cream-colored brick buildings.

Descendants of German immigrants make up a large part of Milwaukee's population. Business and street names, cultural events, and several famous restaurants in Milwaukee are reminders of the city's German heritage.

Solomon Juneau, a French-Canadian fur trader, settled in the Milwaukee area in 1818. He established a town on the east side of the Milwaukee River in 1833. The town later combined with neighboring villages and became Milwaukee.

Trade accounted for much of the city's early growth. During the 1860's, Milwaukee was a leading grain market. But by the late 1800's, manufacturing had become the city's chief source of income.

The Socialist Party played an important role in local politics during the 1900's. In 1910, Milwaukee became the first major city in the United States to elect a Socialist mayor.

Metropolitan Milwaukee

Milwaukee, the seat of Milwaukee County, covers 96 square miles (249 square kilometers), or about 40 per cent of the county. It extends about 10 miles (16 kilometers) along the shore of Lake Michigan. The city's metropolitan area occupies 1,489 square miles (3,856 square kilometers) and covers four counties—Milwaukee, Ozaukee, Washington, and Waukesha. More than a fourth of Wisconsin's people live in the Milwaukee metropolitan area.

The City. Milwaukee lies on a bluff overlooking a crescent-shaped bay. The Kinnickinnic, Menomonee, and Milwaukee rivers flow through the city to the bay.

The streets of Milwaukee run in a checkerboard pat-

FACTS IN BRIEF

Population: 669,022. *Metropolitan Area Population*—1,403,-884. *Consolidated Metropolitan Area Population*—1,574,-722.

Area: 96 sq. mi. (249 km²). *Metropolitan Area*—1,489 sq. mi. (3,856 km²). *Consolidated Metropolitan Area*—1,832 sq. mi. (4,745 km²).

Climate: *Average Temperature*—January, 22° F. (−6° C); July, 71° F. (22° C). *Average Annual Precipitation* (rainfall, melted snow, and other forms of moisture)—30 inches (76 centimeters). For the monthly weather in Milwaukee, see WISCONSIN (Climate).

Government: Mayor-council (four-year terms).

Founded: 1830's. Incorporated as a city, 1846.

tern. Many north-south streets have numbers instead of names. The Menomonee Valley, where many manufacturing companies are located, divides the city into the North Side and South Side. The main business district lies north of the valley, and older residential areas and industrial districts are to the south.

Downtown Milwaukee extends west for about 2 miles (3 kilometers) from the lakefront. Banks, department stores, office buildings, and motion-picture theaters line Wisconsin Avenue, the city's main street. Government buildings include City Hall on East Wells Street and the County Court House on North 9th Street. At the west end of downtown Milwaukee stand the Arena and the Auditorium. The Arena, which holds more than 10,000 persons, provides convention and sports facilities. Various exhibitions and stage shows are held in the adjoining Auditorium.

The Metropolitan Area. A network of freeways connects downtown Milwaukee and its suburbs. Wauwatosa and West Allis, the largest suburbs, lie west of the city. Other suburbs include Cudahy, Oak Creek, Shorewood, and Whitefish Bay. Large shopping centers, such as Bay Shore, Brookfield Square, and Southridge, serve the suburban communities. The metropolitan

Symbols of Milwaukee. The city flag, adopted in 1954, has a large gear to represent manufacturing. It also has symbols for Milwaukee's government, history, and shipping industry. Scenes on the city seal, *right*, stand for education and transportation.

areas of Milwaukee and of Racine, Wis., form the Milwaukee-Racine Standard Consolidated Statistical Area.

The People

About 90 per cent of Milwaukee's people were born in the United States. About 15 per cent of the people have German ancestry. Many of them live on the North Side. Blacks make up about 15 per cent of the population. Many blacks live in the inner city, close to the downtown area. Other groups include people of Irish,

CITY OF MILWAUKEE

Milwaukee lies on the western shore of Lake Michigan. The map at the right shows the city. The map below shows the metropolitan area of Milwaukee.

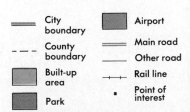

City boundary	Airport
County boundary	Main road
Built-up area	Other road
Park	Rail line
	Point of interest

Milwaukee Metropolitan Area

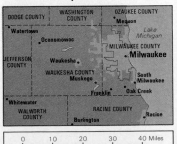

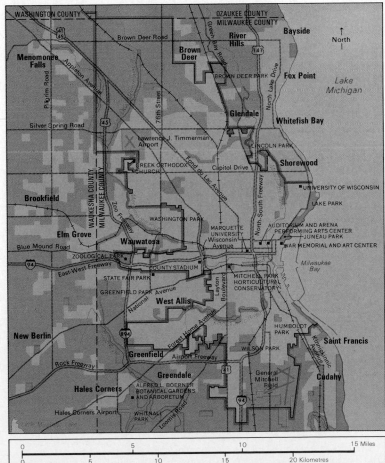

The Mitchell Park Conservatory, famous for its huge glass domes, features rare plants and flowers in natural settings.

Italian, Polish, Puerto Rican, or Scandinavian descent. Many Polish Americans live on the South Side.

Lutherans and Roman Catholics form the two largest religious groups in Milwaukee. Other major denominations include Baptists, Methodists, and Presbyterians.

Milwaukee has had some serious racial disturbances. In 1967, riots broke out in the black community. Civil rights groups have organized marches, picketings, and sit-ins to protest discrimination. Various groups work to aid minorities and improve race relations in the city. These groups include the Community Relations-Social Development Commission, which is financed by the federal government, and the Community Relations Commission of Milwaukee.

Economy

Industry. Milwaukee's 1,700 manufacturing plants employ about 35 per cent of the city's work force. The chief products include automobile parts, beer, electrical equipment, and farm and factory machinery. Other industries produce construction and mining equipment, food products, leather goods, and paper products. The city also has large meat-packing plants.

Transportation. Milwaukee's harbor handles more than 3½ million short tons (3.2 million metric tons) of cargo annually. Ships connect the city with about 100 overseas ports by way of the St. Lawrence Seaway. Ferry steamers carry passengers and their automobiles across Lake Michigan between Milwaukee and Michigan.

Passenger trains and five rail freight lines serve Milwaukee. An 80-mile (130-kilometer) expressway system, begun in the 1950's, was scheduled for completion in the mid-1980's. Milwaukee's main airport, Mitchell Field, averages about 700 take-offs and landings a day. About 70 truck lines also serve the area.

Communication. About 20 radio stations and 6 television stations, including 2 educational stations, serve Milwaukee. The Journal Company owns the city's two daily newspapers, the *Journal* and the *Sentinel*.

Education

The Milwaukee public school system includes about 170 elementary and secondary schools, with an enroll-

ment of more than 195,000 students. More than 25,000 students attend about 115 private and parochial schools.

The University of Wisconsin-Milwaukee, the city's largest university, has about 25,000 students, and more than 10,000 attend Marquette University. Alverno College, Cardinal Stritch College, and Mount Mary College are also in the area. Training for the Roman Catholic priesthood is provided at the undergraduate level by St. Francis De Sales College, a liberal arts college, and at the graduate level by the St. Francis Seminary School of Pastoral Ministry. Other institutions of higher learning include the Medical College of Wisconsin, the Milwaukee School of Engineering, and Milwaukee Area Technical College, one of the nation's largest vocational and adult education centers.

The Milwaukee public library system has over 2 million books. It operates a downtown building and about 15 branches.

Cultural Life

The Arts. The city's $12-million Performing Arts Center, which opened in 1969, serves the Milwaukee Symphony Orchestra, the Milwaukee Repertory Theater, a choral group, a ballet, and an opera company. The Skylight Theater also provides professional stage entertainment. Summer musicals and concerts at the Emil Blatz Temple of Music in Washington Park attract many Milwaukeeans.

Museums. The Milwaukee Art Center, in the city's lakefront War Memorial Center, displays American and European paintings and sculpture. The Milwaukee Public Museum contains many natural-history exhibits. It also has a model of a Milwaukee street as it looked in the early 1900's. The Milwaukee County Historical Center features exhibits of local history.

Recreation

Parks. The Milwaukee County Park System includes about 115 parks and parkways and covers more than 14,000 acres (5,700 hectares). The largest park, Whitnall Park, occupies about 1,200 acres (486 hectares). It features the beautiful Alfred Boerner Botanical Gardens, which have more than 1,000 species of flowers. A conservatory in Mitchell Park displays plants of desert, temperate, and tropical climates in their natural settings. The Milwaukee County Zoo has wide moats and glass-enclosed cages, rather than bars. Visitors may tour the zoo in a miniature train or rubber-tired zoomobile.

Sports. The Milwaukee Brewers of the American League play baseball in County Stadium. The Green Bay Packers of the National Football League play some of their games there. The Milwaukee Bucks of the National Basketball Association play in the Arena. The nation's top golfers compete in the Greater Milwaukee Open, held every July.

Annual Events and Places of Interest include:
Lakefront Festival of Arts, in late spring. Viewers can see thousands of paintings on the lawns surrounding the Milwaukee War Memorial Center.
Summerfest, a 10-day celebration in early July, features outdoor evening concerts, fireworks displays, a Fourth of July parade, and stage entertainment by various ethnic groups.
Greek Orthodox Church of the Annunciation in nearby Wauwatosa. Designed by the famous American architect

Frank Lloyd Wright, it features an unusual style of architecture.

Joan of Arc Chapel on the Marquette University campus. This chapel, built in France during the 1400's, was reconstructed on the campus in the 1960's.

Kilbourntown House in Estabrook Park was the home of Benjamin Church, a pioneer architect. Church built the house in 1844.

State Fair Park, in suburban West Allis, has facilities for rides, stage entertainment, and stock car races. About a million persons visit the park during the annual 10-day Wisconsin State Fair in August.

Villa Terrace, on the East Side, is an Italian-style home. It houses the Milwaukee Art Center's collection of decorative arts.

Government

Milwaukee has a mayor-council form of government. The voters elect the mayor to a four-year term. The mayor appoints major department heads and members of various boards and commissions. Most of the appointments are subject to approval by the council. The mayor has veto power over some council decisions and may also propose legislation. Milwaukee is divided into 19 districts called *wards*. The voters of each ward elect one representative, called an *alderman*, to the city council. The aldermen serve four-year terms. Property taxes provide nearly half the city's income. Other sources of income include state and federal aid.

The Milwaukee city government faces many problems, including decreasing revenue and air and water pollution. In an effort to solve these problems, Milwaukee leaders work chiefly with two groups. These groups are the Greater Milwaukee Committee, a voluntary organization of civic leaders, and the Southeastern Wisconsin Regional Planning Commission, which is both state and federally supported.

History

Early Development. The Fox, Mascouten, and Potawatomi Indians hunted in the Milwaukee area before the first white settlers came. In 1674, Father Jacques Marquette, a French missionary, stopped at the site. Later, other missionaries and fur traders began to visit the area. One of the traders, Jacques Vieau, opened a trading post there in 1795. Solomon Juneau, Vieau's clerk who later became his son-in-law, settled in the area in 1818. In 1833, Juneau founded a town on the east side of the Milwaukee River.

During the 1830's, many settlers came from the eastern United States. They included Byron Kilbourn of Connecticut and George H. Walker of Virginia. Kilbourn set up his own community on the west side of the Milwaukee River. Walker developed the area south of the Menomonee River. In the late 1830's, the settlements combined to form the Village of Milwaukee. Milwaukee received a city charter in 1846, and Juneau became the city's first mayor. By 1847, the population stood at about 12,000.

Beginning in the 1840's, many Europeans settled in Milwaukee. These immigrants included large numbers of Germans, Irish, and Poles. They played an important role in the cultural, economic, and political development of Milwaukee.

Economic Growth. During the 1850's and 1860's, Milwaukee flourished as a commercial center. Harbor improvements and the construction of roads and rail-

roads helped the city become a leading market for flour and wheat. After 1870, manufacturing became the city's chief economic activity. With the growth of such industries as meat packing and tanning, Milwaukee's population rose to more than 200,000 by 1890.

The 1900's. Industrialization provided a base for the Socialist movement of the late 1800's and 1900's. Milwaukee Socialists did little to promote socialism, which calls for public ownership of industry. Instead, they fought for labor and political reforms and higher social benefits. In 1910, Milwaukeeans elected Emil Seidel, a Socialist, as mayor. Milwaukee was the first major U.S. city to have a Socialist mayor. Seidel served until 1912. Since then, Milwaukee has had two other Socialist mayors—Daniel W. Hoan, from 1916 to 1940, and Frank P. Zeidler, from 1948 to 1960. The city council had a Socialist majority only under Seidel.

After World War II (1939-1945), Milwaukee began a redevelopment program. Projects in this program included construction of freeways and major changes in the downtown and lakefront areas. During the 1950's, the city modernized its harbor to receive ocean ships. The harbor improvements, followed by the opening of the St. Lawrence Seaway in 1959, made Milwaukee an important international port. The city's population grew to 741,324 by 1960.

Recent Developments. A nationwide trend toward suburban living developed during the 1950's. It brought a steady movement of middle-class Milwaukeeans to new residential areas outside the city. Although the population of the Milwaukee metropolitan area rose during the 1960's, the number of people living in the city decreased.

During the 1960's, Milwaukee cleared slum areas, built low-cost housing, and repaired hundreds of old buildings. In 1968, construction began on a $25-million urban renewal project northwest of the downtown area. This project, called Midtown, included industrial, recreational, and residential development of a 286-acre (116-hectare) area. The Midtown project was completed in 1976.   FREDERICK I. OLSON

MILWAUKEE DEEP. See DEEP.

MIMEOGRAPH. See DUPLICATOR.

MIMICRY, *MIHM ihk ree,* is the condition in which one living organism closely resembles, or mimics, its surroundings or another animal or plant. It is usually the result of similar color or construction. Mimicry may enable the organism to protect itself in its struggle for existence. For example, the monarch butterfly and the viceroy butterfly resemble each other in size, shape, and colors. The monarch is believed to be distasteful to birds, while the viceroy is not. But the viceroy often escapes being eaten because it resembles the monarch.

Another example of mimicry is the *Kallima,* or "dead leaf," butterfly of India, which brings its wings together over its back and places the "tails" of its wings against a twig when it rests. The Kallima escapes notice because the undersides of its wings resemble a dead leaf in color and texture.   C. BROOKE WORTH

See also ANIMAL (Animal Defenses; pictures: Animal Camouflage); BIRD (How Birds Protect Themselves; picture: Color Protects Them); BUTTERFLY (pictures: Kallima, The Monarch); PROTECTIVE COLORATION.

Gendreau

Leaves and Blossoms of the Mimosa have a featherlike appearance. The handsome tree is native to the tropics.

MIMOSA, *mih MOH suh,* is the name of a group of trees, shrubs, and herbs which have featherlike leaves. The mimosa grows chiefly in warm and tropical lands. The tree is similar to the acacia. The seed, or fruit, grows in flat pods. The small flowers may be white, pink, lavender, or purple. Mimosa grows throughout Asia, Africa, Mexico, and Australia. In the United States, it grows along the valley of the Rio Grande and in many states, including West Virginia, Virginia, Alabama, Kentucky, Louisiana, and Indiana.

Scientific Classification. The mimosas are members of the pea family, *Leguminosae.* They make up a genus called *Mimosa.*   J. J. LEVISON

MINARET, *MIN uh RET,* is a tower of the Moslem house of worship called a *mosque.* The minaret is one of the most typical features of Islamic architecture and one of the most beautiful. From the top of the minaret, a crier, or *muezzin,* calls the people to prayer. Minarets are built of brick and stone. Most of them are tall and

Four Minarets covered with intricate mosaics, and a low rounded dome with the same decoration, top the great mosque in Teheran. All mosques have at least one minaret.

Joseph Covello, Black Star

slender, but some are short and heavy. The minaret may be round, square, or many-sided. Some mosques possess only one minaret, but others have several.

The minaret may stand by itself, but it is usually a part of the mosque. An inside stairway leads to the top. In a few early minarets, this stairway wound around the outside. One or more balconies surround the minaret.

Minarets are found in Iraq, Iran, Syria, North Africa, Spain, Turkey, and India. Those built between the 1200's and 1500's are the finest. The oldest known minaret belongs to the mosque in Buṣrá ash Shām, Syria. It was built in the 600's.   KENNETH J. CONANT

See also MOSQUE.

MINAS BASIN. See BAY OF FUNDY.

MINCH, THE, is a broad strait which separates the island of Lewis with Harris, in the Hebrides, from the west coast of Scotland. Its average width is about 30 miles (48 kilometers). It is sometimes called North Minch to distinguish it from Little Minch, a narrow channel to the southwest.

MIND. Psychologists have held many views on the nature of the mind. Even today, they still disagree.

Early theories of mind held that man was made up of two different substances, *mind* and *matter.* Matter was something that could be seen and felt. Matter occupied space and had weight. Mind was a substance present in a person, but it took up no space and could not be weighed, seen, or touched. The mind was divided into several *faculties,* such as will, reason, and memory. Some people thought that the mind, like the muscles, developed through exercise, so that the way to strengthen the mind was to give the faculties work to do.

Some psychologists and philosophers who questioned the mind-substance idea offered the view that mind was the sum total of all a person's conscious states. This meant that the mind was simply a mass of thoughts, memories, feelings, and emotions. At any given moment, there would be only a few things in a person's consciousness, the things to which a person was giving attention; and there would be some other things of which he was aware without thinking about them, somewhat as we see things "out of the corner of our eye." Below this level of consciousness would be a whole vast mass made up of all the conscious states an individual had experienced since his birth. Whenever a new idea or impression made its way into a person's consciousness, all the earlier impressions that were like it or in some way related to it were supposed to rise up into consciousness and welcome the newcomer. In this way, the mind kept growing and rearranging itself.

The Nature of Mind. During the 1800's, psychologists began to try out some of these ideas on the nature of mind. For example, one man set himself the task of memorizing nonsense syllables over a period of time, and checking how long it took him each time he tried. He reached the conclusion that a person could memorize and memorize without in any way improving his memory. Other psychologists began to ask why it was, if mind and matter were separate substances, that drugs or illness or a blow on the head could so greatly disturb a person's mind. They wondered also why the mind seemed to fail as people grew very old.

Some of these psychologists went so far as to suggest that perhaps everything a person did could be explained in terms of the body, without using such ideas as mind or consciousness at all. These psychologists held that actual physical movements of the brain and central nervous system could account for all the events we speak of as "mental," if only we knew enough about them. The person who spoke of "mind" or "consciousness," according to this view, was simply an animal impelled through experiences and habits. This animal had built up certain associations in his nervous system, to make specific sounds on specific occasions.

This theory, sometimes called *extreme behaviorism*, made rapid headway among psychologists. However, its limitations soon became apparent. The modern psychologist, while still a behaviorist, has accepted many modifications of the original viewpoint.

Another view began to develop that perhaps mind, like matter, is just something that happens, and is not a separate, identifiable thing. For example, everyone knows that water is wet. But atoms of hydrogen and oxygen are not wet, and neither are the energy charges that make them up. We can say that wetness is a quality that comes into being when energy charges, organized in the form of hydrogen and oxygen atoms, are brought together to form water. If we break water down into its parts, the wetness is gone, and so is the water itself.

In the same way, mind is a quality that comes into being as people interact with the world around them. According to this theory, mind, like wetness, is something that emerges or comes into being when organisms reach a certain level of complexity in development.

Another theory states that mind is the foundation and the source of feeling, thinking, and willing. This foundation is distinct from the acts which it produces. The mind is the ultimate source of sensations, images, feelings, and thoughts. The thoughts are the mental activities. The *soul* is an even broader concept. It is the source of both mental and other life activities, such as breathing and walking.

Physical and Mental Relationship. Most people believe that a practical separation between mind and body is impossible. The mind can move the body, as when a man decides to flex his muscles. Almost any human reaction has both physical and mental sides, so that men smile with pleasure, frown in anger, or quiver with fear. Physicians tell us that mental states can actually produce heart disease, ulcer of the stomach, kidney trouble, and other diseases.

The body also affects the mind. Everyone can note for himself the difference in his mental state when he is hungry or well-fed, cold or warm, sick or well. It is known also that certain glands have a profound effect upon emotions, attitudes, and behavior. See BEHAVIOR.

The influence of the mind and the body on each other is difficult to explain. Some people explain it by discarding the mind. Others discard matter in order to explain it. A more common-sense view insists that they both exist and interact. According to the interaction theory, each human being is composed of both body and mind. However, the body and mind are incomplete until they form a unity called a *person*, or *ego*. Man is a single composite substance made up of two distinct principles. It is the *person* who thinks and remembers, not the mind, and not the body.

The discussion above deals with some of the many questions and problems involved in the nature of mind. The discussion shows that serious work is being done

on the subject. No one statement of the nature of mind is acceptable to all authorities.   FRANK J. KOBLER

Related Articles in WORLD BOOK include:

Emotion	Intuition	Subconscious	Thought and
Feeling	Memory	Suggestion	Judgment
Intelligence	Psychology		Will

MIND READING is a term loosely applied to various forms of *extrasensory perception* (*ESP*), especially *telepathy* and *clairvoyance*. Telepathy is an awareness of another person's thoughts, knowledge, or feelings without the aid of the senses of hearing, sight, smell, taste, or touch. Clairvoyance is an awareness of events, objects, or persons without the use of the known senses. The term *mind reading* may be considered a synonym for *telepathy*. But the term has little more than historical interest today because of changing ideas about the concept of the mind.

In the past, each person was considered to have a mind more or less independent of his body and behavior. It was also thought that one mind could "read" another mind without using the known senses. Today, scientists do not believe that the mind is independent of the rest of the body.   WILLIAM M. SMITH

See also EXTRASENSORY PERCEPTION; TELEPATHY; CLAIRVOYANCE; PARAPSYCHOLOGY.

MINDANAO. See PHILIPPINES (The Islands).

MINDORO. See PHILIPPINES (The Islands); SULU SEA.

MINDSZENTY, *mihnd ZEHN tih,* **JOSEPH CARDINAL** (1892-1975), a cardinal of the Roman Catholic Church, was a religious leader in Hungary. For many people, he became a symbol of resistance to Communism.

Pope Pius XII named Mindszenty bishop of Veszprém in 1944, and archbishop of Esztergom and primate of Hungary in 1945. The pope made him a cardinal in 1946. Mindszenty became a main target of the Communist-dominated secret police. In 1949, Mindszenty was convicted of treason by Hungary's Communist government and given a life sentence. He remained under house arrest until 1956, when Hungarian rebels freed him during their revolt. He took refuge in the United States Embassy in Budapest and lived there for 15 years. In 1971, Mindszenty left Hungary and went into exile in Rome. He did so at the request of Pope Paul VI, under an agreement between the Vatican and the Hungarian government. Mindszenty later settled in Vienna. In 1974, to improve relations between the church and the Hungarian government, the pope removed Mindszenty as primate of Hungary and archbishop of Esztergom.

Mindszenty was born Joseph Pehm in Csehimindszenty. His father was of German ancestry. Mindszenty was ordained a priest in 1915. During the Nazi occupation of Hungary, he changed his name to indicate his complete Hungarian nationality, using the name of his birthplace.   JOHN T. FARRELL and FULTON J. SHEEN

United Press Int.
Cardinal Mindszenty

475

MINE WARFARE

MINE WARFARE is the use of explosive devices called mines to kill enemy troops and destroy their ships, tanks, and other equipment. Some mines explode when a person steps on them. Others explode when run over by a tank or jeep. Mines may be designed to explode when moved or even touched. Naval mines are *detonated* (exploded) by the effects produced by a passing ship. Mines also may be exploded by remote control.

Mines can be positioned to prevent an enemy from entering an area. They can also be used to influence the course traveled by enemy troops or ships. By avoiding mined areas, enemy forces may be forced to take routes where they can be attacked more easily. Mines are inexpensive compared to many other weapons, and persons with little training can put them into place.

There are two chief kinds of mines, *land mines* and *naval mines*.

Land Mines

Land mines are planted in the ground. They may be laid out in planned patterns called *mine fields*. Mines may be planted by soldiers or fired into an area by artillery. They also may be dropped by helicopters.

There are five main types of land mines: (1) antipersonnel mines, (2) antitank mines, (3) chemical mines, (4) controlled mines, and (5) nuclear mines.

Antipersonnel Mines are used to kill or injure enemy soldiers. They have a sensitive *fuse* (triggering device) that is set off by the weight of even a small person. They also may be set off when someone walks into a wire or moves an object to which the mines are wired.

Some antipersonnel mines have small explosive charges and kill only a few persons a short distance away. Others can kill many people more than 200 yards (180 meters) away. Some antipersonnel mines fire an explosive charge that explodes in the air, spraying shrapnel over a large area (see SHRAPNEL).

Mines called *booby traps* are hidden in buildings or under dead soldiers. They may also be hidden in ordinary objects, such as appliances and briefcases, that are likely to be moved by enemy troops.

Antitank Mines destroy enemy tanks and other vehicles. These mines are larger than antipersonnel mines. Most types of antitank mines explode only when a weight of more than about 300 pounds (140 kilograms) moves over them. Soldiers can walk safely on antitank mines. But these mines destroy trucks and lightly armored vehicles and at least damage the metal tracks on which tanks move.

Chemical Mines release a poisonous gas when they are triggered. The gas kills or injures unprotected troops.

Controlled Mines are placed in position before a battle. They are exploded by remote control when enemy forces approach the mines.

Nuclear Mines contain small nuclear devices. These mines are used to blow up concrete bridges or to close off mountain passes. Such jobs would require many tons of conventional explosives. Nuclear mines are small enough to be carried by two persons or in a jeep.

Detecting Land Mines. Land mines can be detected by several methods. Soldiers may locate mines by crawling along the ground and carefully probing the area ahead with their bayonets. When a mine is found, it is

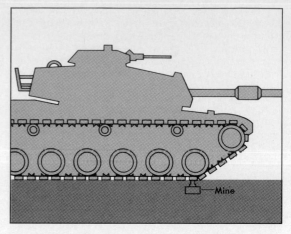

An Antitank Mine explodes when run over by a tank or other heavy vehicle, above. The mine, which is buried close to the surface, is triggered by the pressure of the vehicle.

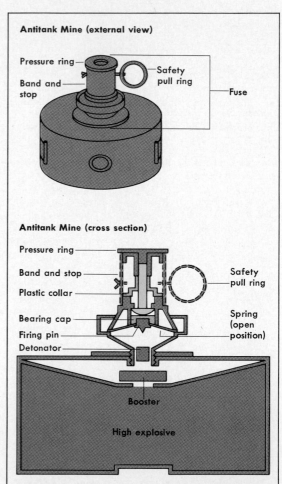

Antitank Mine (external view)

Pressure ring — Band and stop — Safety pull ring — Fuse

Antitank Mine (cross section)

Pressure ring — Band and stop — Plastic collar — Bearing cap — Firing pin — Detonator — Safety pull ring — Spring (open position) — Booster — High explosive

WORLD BOOK diagrams by Steven Liska

The Parts of an Antitank Mine are shown above. The mine is detonated when the pressure ring at the top is forced down into the mine. This action causes the firing pin to hit the detonator, which then sets off the booster. The booster then activates the high explosive, and the mine explodes.

cautiously dug out and the fuse is removed, or its position is marked so it can be bypassed. Individual soldiers use sensitive instruments called *mine detectors* to locate mines. Mines can be detected more rapidly by a mine-detecting device mounted on a jeep. The jeep stops automatically when the device detects a mine.

After mines have been detected, they may be marked and bypassed, exploded by artillery fire, or blown up by tanks fitted with special rollers or chain devices. The devices trigger the mines when passing over them. Devices called *snakes* are also used to clear mine fields. Snakes are long tubes packed with explosives. These devices are pushed into a mined area and are exploded. The blast sets off nearby mines and clears a path for troops and vehicles.

Naval Mines

Naval mines rest on or are anchored to the floor of a body of water. Some naval mines float freely, but such mines are dangerous to friendly ships as well as enemy vessels. Naval mines are laid by surface ships, including vessels called *minelayers*, and by aircraft and submarines. Some naval mines are self-propelled. They are launched from a submarine and travel a few miles before settling on the ocean floor. The CAPTOR mine of the United States Navy is anchored to the ocean bottom. The mine launches a torpedo after detecting the propeller noise of a passing submarine.

Kinds of Naval Mines. There are four chief kinds of naval mines: (1) acoustic mines, (2) contact mines, (3) magnetic mines, and (4) pressure mines.

Acoustic Mines are exploded by the sound of a ship's propellers.

Contact Mines are triggered when a ship touches them. They also may be exploded when a ship touches antennas that stick out from the mines.

Magnetic Mines are triggered by the magnetic field that surrounds a metal warship. To avoid setting off a magnetic mine, a ship may use a set of electrical cables called a *degaussing belt*, which reduces or neutralizes the magnetic field.

Pressure Mines explode when passing ships cause a change in the water pressure around the mines.

Detecting Naval Mines. Naval mines are difficult to detect and to *sweep* (remove or detonate). They may be fitted with counting devices that allow a certain number of ships to pass before the mines explode. The mines may also be fitted with timers that prevent them from firing for a certain number of hours or days.

Ships called *minesweepers* use sonar to locate mines, which are then swept (see MINESWEEPER). Minesweeping helicopters tow devices that sweep mines in shallow water.

Acoustic mines are blown up by noisemaking devices towed underwater. The anchor cables of contact mines are cut by instruments towed underwater by mine-sweepers. The mines then float to the surface and are exploded by gunfire. Some magnetic mines are triggered by electrical devices towed by ships. Pressure mines are cleared by having a small, specially equipped ship pass nearby to detonate them.

History

Land mines have been used in warfare for more than 200 years. The term *mine* came from the practice of

U.S. Navy

A Minesweeping Device towed by a helicopter, *above*, is called a *sled*. The magnetic field produced by the sled detonates magnetic mines that have been planted underwater.

digging tunnels under enemy positions, packing the tunnels with gunpowder, and exploding them. During the Civil War (1861-1865), Union soldiers mined a section of Confederate trenches at Petersburg, Va. The soldiers dug a tunnel more than 500 feet (150 meters) long, placed gunpowder in it, and blew a large crater in the Confederate defenses. In World War I (1914-1918), troops buried artillery shells that exploded when stepped on by a person or run over by a tank or truck. After World War I, mines with wood, metal, or plastic containers were developed. Land mines were widely used during World War II (1939-1945) and in almost all later wars.

The first naval mines—floating vessels that contained explosives—were used in the late 1500's. Early types of underwater mines, called *torpedoes*, were sealed wooden containers filled with gunpowder and equipped with a fuse. The fuse was set, and a diver swam under an enemy ship and attached the mine to the hull. During the Revolutionary War (1775-1783), David Bushnell, an American inventor, developed a submarine equipped with a mine-attaching device. During the Civil War, both the Confederate and Union navies used underwater mines. Naval mines were also used extensively in most later wars.   NORMAN POLMAR

MINE WORKERS OF AMERICA, UNITED. See UNITED MINE WORKERS OF AMERICA.

MINER. See MINING.

MINER, JACK (1865-1944), was a Canadian bird conservationist. He established a bird sanctuary on his farm near Kingsville, Ont., in 1904. Miner freed many birds after putting numbered metal anklets on them. He urged hunters to return the numbered bands from birds they shot. In this way, he learned where the migrating birds went. Friends established the Jack Miner Migratory Bird Foundation in 1931 to help him continue his work on the migrating habits of birds. Miner was born in Dover Centre, Ohio. His full name was John Thomas Miner.   LORUS J. MILNE and MARGERY MILNE

See also BIRD (Refuges and Sanctuaries); ONTARIO (Places to Visit).

Rocks Are Made of Minerals. A chunk of granite, *left*, contains bits of hornblende, feldspar, quartz, and mica. Alone, these minerals appear as shown, *right*.

Hornblende

Feldspar

Quartz

Mica

MINERAL

MINERAL is the most common solid material found on the earth. The earth's land and oceans all rest on a layer of rock made of minerals. All rocks found on the earth's surface also contain minerals. Even soil contains tiny pieces of minerals broken from rocks.

Minerals include such common substances as rock salt and pencil "lead," and such rare ones as gold, silver, and gems. There are about 2,000 kinds of minerals, but only about 100 of them are common. Most of the others are harder to find than gold.

Man digs minerals from the earth and uses them to make many products. He uses minerals to make cement and steel for building, fertilizers for farming, chemicals for manufacturing, and many other materials.

Scientists have given many minerals names that end in *ite*. Rock salt is the mineral halite, and pencil lead is graphite. Hematite is the world's most important source of iron. Other common minerals include gypsum, used in making wallboard, and talc, used in talcum powder and crayons.

Many persons use the term *mineral* for any substance taken from the earth. Such substances include coal, petroleum, natural gas, and sand—none of which is a mineral. Certain substances in food and water, such as calcium, iron, and phosphorus, also are called minerals. But mineralogists, the scientists who study minerals, do not consider any of them minerals.

Mineralogists use the term *mineral* to mean a sub-

stance that has all of the four following features. (1) A mineral is found in nature. A natural diamond is a mineral, but a man-made diamond is not. (2) A mineral is made up of substances that were never alive. Coal, petroleum, and natural gas are not minerals because they were formed from the remains of animals and plants. (3) A mineral has the same chemical makeup wherever it is found. Sand is not a mineral because samples from different places usually have different chemical makeups. (4) The atoms of a mineral are arranged in a regular pattern, and form solid units called *crystals*. The calcium and phosphorus found in milk are not minerals because they are dissolved in a liquid and are not crystals.

This article discusses only substances that mineralogists consider minerals. For information on coal, petroleum, and other mined products, see the articles listed in the *Related Articles* section of the MINING article. For information on other materials that are often called minerals, see the WORLD BOOK articles on FOOD (How Our Bodies Use Food) and OCEAN (The Ocean—A Liquid Mine).

William H. Dennen, the contributor of this article, is Professor of Geology at the University of Kentucky and author of Principles of Mineralogy. WORLD BOOK *photos by E. F. Hoppe, courtesy the Field Museum of Natural History, Chicago.*

Minerals vary greatly in appearance and feel. Some have glasslike surfaces that sparkle with color. Others look dull and feel greasy. The hardest minerals can scratch glass. The softest ones can be scratched by a fingernail. Four of the main characteristics of minerals are (1) luster, (2) cleavage, (3) hardness, and (4) color.

Luster of a mineral may be metallic or nonmetallic. Minerals with metallic luster shine like metal. Such minerals include galena, gold, and ilmenite. Minerals with nonmetallic luster vary in appearance. Quartz looks glassy, talc has a pearly surface, and varieties of cinnabar appear dull and claylike. The luster of a mineral also may differ from sample to sample. Some kinds of cinnabar, for example, have a metallic luster rather than a dull luster.

Cleavage is the splitting of a mineral into pieces that have flat surfaces. Minerals differ in the number of directions they split, and in the angles at which the flat surfaces meet. Mica splits in one direction and forms thin sheets. Halite has three cleavage directions, and it breaks into tiny cubes. A diamond may split in four directions, forming a pyramid. Other minerals, such as quartz, do not split cleanly, but break into pieces with irregular surfaces.

Hardness of minerals may be tested by scratching one mineral with another. The harder mineral scratches the softer one, and mineralogists use a scale of hardness based on this principle. Friedrich Mohs, a German mineralogist, invented the scale in 1822. The Mohs hardness scale lists 10 minerals from the softest to the hardest. These minerals are numbered from 1 to 10. The hardness of other minerals is found by determining whether they scratch, or are scratched by, the minerals in the Mohs scale. For example, galena scratches gypsum (number 2), but is scratched by calcite (number 3). Therefore, galena's hardness is $2\frac{1}{2}$—about halfway between that of gypsum and calcite. A person's fingernail has a hardness of about 2.

Color of some minerals depends on the substances that make up the crystals. The black of ilmenite, the red of cinnabar, and the green of serpentine all result from the chemical composition of these minerals. Other minerals get their color from chemical impurities. Pure quartz, for example, has colorless crystals. But tiny amounts of other substances in quartz crystals can give quartz a pink or green tint, or even make it black.

Other Identification Tests. Some minerals may be recognized by their *habit* (general appearance). Gold is found in the form of nuggets, and diamonds are found as crystals. Halite may have the form of grains, clumps of crystals, or large chunks. Mineralogists can also identify minerals by feeling, tasting, or smelling them. Talc and serpentine feel greasy. Epsomite and halite taste salty, and borax and melanterite taste sweet. Kaolinite has an earthy smell.

A *streak test* uses color to identify a mineral. The mineral is rubbed across a slightly rough, white porcelain plate. The rubbing grinds some of the mineral to powder and leaves a colored streak on the plate. But the streak is not always the same color as the sample. Hematite varies from reddish brown to black, but always leaves a red streak. Chalcopyrite, a yellow mineral, produces a green-black streak.

Many chemical tests can identify minerals. One of the simplest consists of pouring a warm, weak acid on the sample. If the acid fizzes, the sample belongs to a group of minerals called *carbonates*. Calcite, aragonite, and dolomite are examples of carbonates. These minerals contain carbon and oxygen, together with other chemicals. When attacked by acid, the minerals release carbon dioxide gas which forms bubbles in the acid. This test may be made at home, using vinegar for the acid. In the *flame test*, a bit of a mineral is ground into powder near the air holes at the base of a lighted Bunsen burner. Air carries the powder up into the flame. The powder gives the flame a color that identifies the mineral.

MOHS HARDNESS SCALE		
MINERAL	HARDNESS	COMMON TESTS
Talc	1	Scratched by a fingernail
Gypsum	2	
Calcite	3	Scratched by a copper coin
Fluorite	4	Scratched by a knife blade or window glass
Apatite	5	
Feldspar	6	
Quartz	7	Scratches a knife blade or window glass
Topaz	8	
Corundum	9	
Diamond	10	Scratches all common materials

Common Identification Tests. A mineral's hardness is tested by scratching it against minerals listed in the Mohs scale, *left*. A streak test of hematite, *center*, leaves a red streak. The tester rubs the mineral against rough porcelain and wipes the streak with his finger. *Right*, calcite cleaves into blocks, and mica into sheets.

Bornite Cu₅FeS₄. Copper-red with purple-blue tarnish. Hardness 3. Cleaves.

Chalcopyrite CuFeS₂. Yellow. Leaves a green-black streak. Hardness 3½-4. Does not cleave.

Copper Cu. Copper-red with brown tarnish. Hardness 2½-3. Does not cleave.

Galena PbS. Bright metallic lead-gray cubes. Hardness 2½. Cleaves to form cubes.

Gold Au. Yellow nuggets, grains, and flakes. Does not tarnish. Hardness 2½-3. Does not cleave.

Graphite C. Steel-gray. Feels greasy. Hardness 1-2. Cleaves into tablets and sheets.

Magnetite Fe₃O₄. Black. Attracted by magnet and may act as magnet. Hardness 5½-6½. Does not cleave.

Pyrite FeS₂. Pale yellow. Leaves green- to brown-black streak. Hardness 6-6½. Does not cleave.

Pyrrhotite FeS. Bronze-yellow. Weakly attracted to magnet. Hardness 3½-4½. Does not cleave.

Rutile TiO₂. Red to black with gem-like luster. May be transparent. Hardness 6-6½. Cleaves.

Silver Ag. Silver-white (above, as flecks in barite), tarnishing to black. Hardness 2½-3. Does not cleave.

Stibnite Sb₂S₃. Gray columns with black tarnish. Hardness 2. Cleaves in one direction.

COMMON MINERALS WITH NONMETALLIC LUSTER

Azurite $Cu_3(CO_3)_2(OH)_2$. Blue. Hardness $3\frac{1}{2}$-4. Cleaves irregularly.

Cinnabar HgS. Dark red, earthy to metallic luster. Hardness 2-$2\frac{1}{2}$. Earthy form does not cleave.

Fluorite CaF_2. Green or violet cubes. Hardness 4. Cleaves in four directions.

Gypsum $Ca(SO_4) \cdot 2H_2O$. Colorless, white, gray, or yellow to brown. Hardness 2. Cleaves into plates.

Malachite $Cu_2(CO_3)(OH)_2$. Bright green. Hardness $3\frac{1}{2}$-4. Cleaves irregularly.

Muscovite $KAl_2(AlSi_3O_{10})(OH)_2$. Colorless. Hardness $2\frac{1}{2}$-3. Cleaves to form tablets and sheets.

Orthoclase $K(AlSi_3O_8)$. White to pink. Leaves white streak. Hardness 6. Cleaves.

Quartz SiO_2. Clear or tinted glassy crystals. Hardness 7. Does not cleave.

Rhodochrosite $Mn(CO_3)$. Pink. Leaves white streak. Hardness $3\frac{1}{2}$-4. Polyhedral cleavage.

Sulfur S. Yellow. Melts and burns with a match. Hardness $1\frac{1}{2}$-$2\frac{1}{2}$. Cleaves irregularly.

Talc $Mg_3(Si_4O_{10})(OH)_2$. Pale green. Feels greasy. Hardness 1-$1\frac{1}{2}$. Cleaves into tablets and sheets.

Wulfenite $Pb(MoO_4)$. Orange-yellow square tablets. Hardness 3. Cleaves into tablets.

Mineral Crystals occur in many sizes. A giant crystal of beryl or feldspar may weigh several tons. Tiny crystals of kaolin may be too small to be studied even with a microscope. Regardless of their size, all crystals are basically the same. They are groups of atoms arranged in a regular pattern.

To imagine what it is like inside a crystal, you can think of "rooms" formed by the crystal's atoms. A room in a copper crystal is formed by 14 copper atoms. The room has an atom at each corner of the floor and ceiling, and an atom at the centers of the floor, the ceiling, and each of the four walls. A copper crystal consists of many of these rooms side by side and one on top of the other. The rooms share copper atoms where they meet. Mineralogists call such rooms *unit cells*.

Most minerals are composed of more than one kind of atom. Halite, for example, consists of sodium atoms and chlorine atoms. Other minerals may have as many as five kinds of atoms in complicated arrangements. Some unit cells have six walls instead of four, and others have slanted walls. Such differences in the shape of unit cells produce differences in the shape of mineral crystals.

Chemical Bonds are forces that hold atoms together in a crystal. These forces are electrical. They result when atoms exchange or share some of their electrons. Chemical bonds can hold two or more atoms together only in definite positions. The positions depend on the size of the atoms and on the number of bonding electrons. In turn, the shape of a unit cell depends on the positions the atoms take when they are bonded together.

Bonds between atoms are not all equally strong. Atoms may be held in some positions by powerful bonds, and in other positions by weak bonds. This variation in bonding explains why some crystals can be cleaved. Cleavage can take place when the weak bonds lie along a flat surface called a *cleavage plane*. When the crystal is cut along this plane, the weak bonds break and the crystal splits, exposing the flat surface.

How Minerals Grow. Almost all minerals grow in liquids. For example, some crystals grow in a liquid called *magma* deep inside the earth. This extremely hot substance contains all the kinds of atoms that make up the earth's minerals. When magma cools, some atoms become bonded together and form tiny crystals. The

---

HOW ATOMS ARE ARRANGED IN MINERALS

 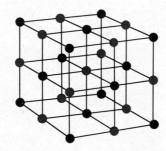 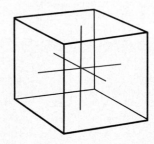

A Halite Crystal, *above left,* has four sides and is made up of billions of four-sided unit cells. Each cell, *center,* contains 14 sodium atoms (shown in black) and 13 chlorine atoms (blue). Halite belongs to the isometric crystal system—one of six systems into which all mineral crystals are grouped. A general diagram for the isometric system, *right,* includes three axes (imaginary lines) that show the directions followed by the edges of the crystal.

 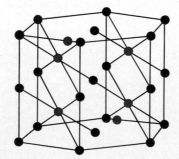 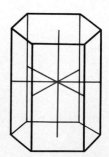

A Corundum Crystal, *above left,* has six sides. Its unit cell, *center,* is a six-sided "room" containing 21 oxygen atoms (black) and 6 aluminum atoms (blue). Corundum belongs to the hexagonal system, *right,* which has four axes.

crystals grow by adding layers of atoms to their flat outer surfaces. The new atoms must be the right size, and they must have the right number of bonding electrons to fit into the growing crystals.

The atoms of many chemicals are almost alike in size and electrical characteristics. Such atoms can take one another's place in a growing crystal. Some minerals have the same kind of crystal but differ in one of the atoms that make it up. For example, olivine has a basic crystal made of oxygen and silicon atoms. Either iron or magnesium atoms can fit into this crystal. As a result, there are two kinds of olivine—forsterite, which contains magnesium, and fayalite, which contains iron. Mineralogists use the term *isomorphic* for minerals that have the same form but different compositions.

Some mineral crystals are made of the same kinds of atoms but differ in the way the atoms are arranged. For example, quartz, coesite, and tridymite contain the same relative number of oxygen and silicon atoms, but their crystals have different forms. Mineralogists use the term *polymorphic* for minerals that have different forms but the same composition.

WHY SOME MINERALS CLEAVE

Graphite, *above*, consists of layers of carbon atoms. Weak bonds hold the layers together and form cleavage planes, *below*. The crystal splits into tablets along these planes.

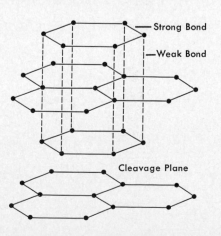

— Strong Bond

— Weak Bond

Cleavage Plane

Minerals were among the first substances to be used and described by man. Egyptian paintings of 5,000 years ago show that minerals were used in weapons and jewelry, and in religious ceremonies. Theophrastus, a Greek philosopher, wrote a short work on minerals about 300 B.C. Pliny the Elder of Rome wrote about metals, ores, stones, and gems about A.D. 77. Other early writings about minerals were done by German scientists. These writings include *De Mineralibus* (1262) by Albertus Magnus and *De Re Metallica* (1556) by Georgius Agricola.

Early Studies of crystals began in the 1600's. In 1665, Robert Hooke, an English scientist, showed that metal balls piled in different ways duplicated the shapes of alum crystals. In 1669, Nicolaus Steno, a Danish physician, found that the angles between the faces of quartz crystals were the same even though the crystals had different shapes. A French scientist, Romé de l'Isle, suggested in 1772 that Steno's discovery could be explained only if the crystals were composed of identical units stacked together in a regular way.

By the late 1700's, scientists had studied and described many minerals. But they had only guessed about the makeup of crystals and the reasons for their shape. About 1780, chemists began to develop correct ideas about the nature of chemical elements and other substances. These ideas helped scientists understand the chemical makeup of minerals, but did not remove the mystery about crystal shape and internal structure.

The 1900's. During the 1900's X-ray studies provided the key to the internal structure of minerals. The first X-ray experiment on minerals was performed in 1912 by the German scientist Max von Laue. At that time, scientists did not fully understand either X rays or crystals. Laue set up an experiment to investigate each at the same time. He believed that if X rays act like light rays, and if the atoms in a crystal have a regular arrangement, a beam of X rays sent through a crystal would be divided into several narrow beams. When Laue sent an X ray beam through a crystal of sphalerite, he found that the beam was divided. With the help of similar experiments, scientists finally learned how atoms are arranged to form crystals.

Mineralogists are still trying to answer many questions. They would like to know how billions of atoms can move relatively long distances to join a growing crystal in exactly the right places. For example, how do ice crystals form such perfect shapes as those shown in the SNOW article? Mineralogists also would like to know more about the "wrong" things that happen in a growing crystal. What controls the kind and the number of atoms that form impurities in a crystal? Why do such impurities affect a crystal's mechanical and electrical properties? The operation of electronic devices called *semiconductors* depends on the presence of impurities in crystals (see SEMICONDUCTOR).

New uses are constantly being found for such chemical elements as beryllium, indium, titanium, tantalum, and the rare earths. Mineralogists are trying to find minerals containing these elements. They are also developing methods for removing these elements from the minerals. WILLIAM H. DENNEN

MINERAL/Study Aids

Related Articles. For information on the minerals found in specific parts of the world, see the Economy section of the articles on each country, state, and province. See also the following articles:

MINERALS

Alabaster	Corundum	Hematite	Pyroxene
Amphibole	Cryolite	Hornblende	Quartz
Argentite	Diopside	Ilmenite	Rutile
Asbestos	Dolomite	Kyanite	Salt
Azurite	Emery	Limonite	Serpentine
Bauxite	Feldspar	Loadstone	Sillimanite
Beryl	Flint	Malachite	Talc
Calcite	Fluorite	Meerschaum	Trona
Carnotite	Galena	Mica	Vermiculite
Chalcocite	Glauconite	Molybdenite	Wolframite
Cinnabar	Graphite	Monazite	Zeolite
Columbite	Gypsum	Pyrite	

OTHER RELATED ARTICLES

See GEM; METAL; MINING; and ROCK with their lists of Related Articles. See also the following articles:

Alumina	Conservation (Mineral	Hardness
Ceramics	Conservation)	
Clay	Crystal and Crystallization	

Outline

I. Identifying Minerals
- A. Luster
- B. Cleavage
- C. Hardness
- D. Color
- E. Other Identification Tests

II. Inside Minerals
- A. Mineral Crystals
- B. Chemical Bonds
- C. How Minerals Grow

III. History of Mineralogy

Questions

Why does quartz have a variety of colors?
What is a unit cell?
What mineral has a salty taste? A sweet taste?
Why can some minerals be split into pieces with flat surfaces?
Why is a synthetic diamond not a mineral?
What did Max von Laue discover about minerals?
What holds together the atoms in a crystal?
How many kinds of minerals are there?
What kind of mineral is a carbonate? Why does acid fizz when poured on a carbonate?
How do minerals grow?

Reading and Study Guide

See *Rocks and Minerals* in the RESEARCH GUIDE/INDEX, Volume 22, for a *Reading and Study Guide*.

Books to Read

DINWIDDIE, DONAL, and MACFALL, R. P. *Popular Mechanics Complete Book of Rocks, Minerals, Gems, Fossils.* Hearst Books, 1978.

HAMMONS, LEE. *How to Identify Minerals.* Rev. ed. Arizona Maps & Books, 1979.

HURLBUT, CORNELIUS S., JR., and KLEIN, CORNELIS. *Manual of Mineralogy.* 19th ed. Wiley, 1977.

KERROD, ROBIN. *Rocks and Minerals.* Watts, 1977. For young readers.

KOHLAND, WILLIAM F. *Guide to Mineral Identification: A Laboratory and Field Manual.* Allegheny Press, 1977.

MASON, ANITA. *The World of Rocks and Minerals.* Larousse, 1976.

POUGH, FREDERICK H. *A Field Guide to Rocks and Minerals.* 4th ed. Houghton, 1976.

PRINZ, MARTIN, and others, eds. *Simon and Schuster's Guide to Rocks and Minerals.* Simon and Schuster, 1978.

SHEDENHELM, W. R. C. *The Young Rockhound's Handbook.* Putnam, 1978. For young readers.

MINERAL OIL is a clear, colorless, oily liquid with almost no taste or odor. It is also called *liquid paraffin*, *liquid petrolatum*, *white mineral oil*, and *white paraffin oil*. Mineral oil is used in medicinal and cosmetic preparations such as laxatives and hair tonics. It is also used as a *diluent* (dissolver) in the manufacture of plastics, and as a lubricant in industrial operations. Mineral oil is obtained when petroleum *fractions* (separated parts) are boiled at 600° to 750° F. (316° to 399° C). The fractions are refined to make pure mineral oil. See also PETROLATUM.   CLARENCE KARR, JR.

MINERAL WATER, or AERATED WATER, is spring water with a high content of mineral matter or of gas. (The term *aerated* means *charged with gas*.) The mineral matter includes salt, Epsom salt, lime, magnesia, iron, silica, boron, fluorine, and many others, including radioactive substances. The most common gases are carbonic acid and hydrogen sulfide.

In most cases, the water is rain water that has seeped underground through rocks, dissolving mineral matter on the way. Other springs may contain *magmatic* or *juvenile* water, which rises from deep in the earth after forming through a chemical process in rocks. Some of these springs are hot springs. Others have cooled to ordinary temperatures.

People have used mineral water since ancient times to cure such ailments as rheumatism, skin infections, and poor digestion. The temperature of the water, the location, the altitude, and the climate at the springs are all considered in the treatment.

There are many thousands of mineral springs in North America. About 800 of these have at one time or other had *spas* (resorts) where people used to come for the waters. Most of these resorts are in the Eastern and Midwestern states. Their popularity has declined since the turn of the century, and many have gone out of business. The best-known mineral springs today are at Saratoga Springs, N.Y.; Hot Springs, Ark.; and French Lick, Ind. Hot Springs has been made a national park (see HOT SPRINGS NATIONAL PARK).

The waters from some foreign springs are imported to the United States. Among these waters are the Apollinaris from Germany, Hunyadi-Janos from Hungary, and Vichy from France. Water taken from mineral springs is sold in sterilized glass bottles. RAY K. LINSLEY

See also BLACK FOREST.

MINERALOGY. See MINERAL.

MINERALS IN DIET. See NUTRITION.

MINERVA was one of the most important goddesses in ancient Roman mythology. She was the favorite child of Jupiter, the king of the gods. One myth tells of her being born out of Jupiter's forehead, fully grown and dressed in armor. Minerva resembled the Greek goddess Athena and like her was a virgin goddess.
Minerva had a variety

The Louvre, Paris (Giraudon)
Minerva was the Roman goddess of wisdom and warfare.

of functions. Originally, she represented skill in handicrafts, particularly those associated with women, such as spinning and weaving. Later, Minerva came to symbolize skill in a general sense. Still later, the Romans worshiped her as the goddess of wisdom. The owl has traditionally been considered wise because it was the bird of Minerva.

The Romans, who believed that warfare involved the higher mental powers, worshiped Minerva as the goddess of the intellectual aspect of war. Most artists showed her wearing armor and a helmet. Minerva carried a magic shield called the *aegis*.   PAUL PASCAL

See also ATHENA; AEGIS.

MINES, BUREAU OF, is an agency of the United States Department of the Interior. The bureau works to ensure efficient mining, processing, use, and recycling of mineral resources. It conducts research to improve mining methods, to promote mine safety, and to help assure adequate supplies of raw materials. The agency also works to reduce the harmful environmental effects of mining and to increase the efficiency of mines.

The bureau gathers statistics on the production and use of minerals throughout the world. This information is used to predict the supply and demand of raw materials. The Bureau of Mines was created in 1910.   Critically reviewed by the DEPARTMENT OF THE INTERIOR

MINESWEEPER is a ship that clears away naval mines. It uses sonar to locate the mines and tows special devices to *sweep* (remove or detonate) them. Most minesweepers are less than 200 feet (61 meters) long and are built of aluminum, fiberglass, or wood. Some navies also use helicopters to sweep mines. See also MINE WARFARE (Detecting Naval Mines).   NORMAN POLMAR

MING DYNASTY ruled China from A.D. 1368 to 1644, a period of Chinese rule between two foreign conquests. It was preceded by the Mongol Empire and followed by the Manchu dynasty. Ming rulers restored traditional institutions, such as the civil service, which the Mongols had temporarily suspended. Chinese authority extended into Mongolia, Korea, Southeast Asia, and the Ryukyu Islands. *Ming* means *bright* in Chinese, and the period was important especially in the arts. Ming architects built the imperial palace, which is in the area of Peking called the *Forbidden City*. Many buildings from this period are still standing. Artists produced beautiful porcelain, bronze, and lacquerware. Western traders came to China for the first time. Jesuit missionaries also came from Europe.   THEODORE H. E. CHEN

The Art Institute of Chicago

Ming Dynasty Pottery is highly valued by museums.

MING TREE is an imitation of the dwarf trees grown in Asia. Ming trees are made by gluing several gnarled branches or twigs together into the form of a windswept tree. Covering the branches with moss or lichens makes them look old and weathered. Ming trees can be placed in a low bowl along with a figurine and used as an ornament or table decoration.   GEORGE B. CUMMINS

MINIATURE PINSCHER is a toy dog of the terrier family. It comes from the Rhine Valley of Germany. The Germans sometimes call the dog a *reh pinscher* (deer terrier) because it looks like a small deer. It has a wedge-shaped head and bright black eyes. The dog may be red, or it may be black with a tan spot over each eye and stripes on its toes. It resembles the Doberman pinscher but weighs only 6 to 10 pounds (3 to 5 kilograms). See also DOG (color picture: Toy Dogs).   JOSEPHINE Z. RINE

MINIATURE SCHNAUZER, *SHNOW zuhr*, is a breed of dog that originated in Germany in the 1800's. Breeders developed the dog by mating the standard schnauzer with the affenpinscher. The high spirits and intelligence of the miniature schnauzer have helped make it one of the 10 most popular breeds in the United States. It is also a good watchdog and ratcatcher.

The dog's coloring may be salt and pepper, black and silver, black and tan, or all black. It has a shaggy beard and long, bushy eyebrows. Most owners have the dog's coat clipped short on top and the beard and eyebrows trimmed. The dog stands 12 to 14 inches (30 to 36 centimeters) tall at the shoulders and weighs about 15 pounds (7 kilograms).   JOAN McDONALD BREARLEY

See also DOG (picture: Terriers).

MINIBIKE. See MOTORCYCLE (Kinds).

MINIM is the smallest unit of fluid measure in the apothecaries' system of measurement. Druggists once used this system, but they now measure many prescriptions in metric units. One minim equals 0.0616 milliliter, or cubic centimeter. In the apothecaries' system, one minim is equal to one drop, and 60 drops equal to one fluid dram. The word *minim* comes from the Latin word *minimus*, meaning *smallest*.   E. G. STRAUS

MINIMUM WAGE is the smallest amount of money per hour that an employer may legally pay a worker. It may be established by law to cover all workers, or only those in certain industries. It is usually set so a person working a normal number of hours can support a family at acceptable standards. See WAGES AND HOURS.

A minimum wage is usually well below the average wage paid to factory workers. Self-employed persons usually are not covered by minimum wage laws. Employees of small businesses often are not covered.

Several U.S. states have minimum wage laws or boards that set minimum wages. Boards also set minimum wages for certain kinds of work done for the U.S. government. The U.S. Fair Labor Standards Act covers most workers in businesses engaged in interstate commerce. The original act, passed in 1938, set a minimum wage of 25 cents an hour and provided that the wage be raised to 40 cents by 1945. The minimum wage has since been increased by amendments to the Fair Labor Standards Act in 1949, 1955, 1961, 1966, 1974, and 1977. The 1977 amendment raised the minimum wage in stages from $2.65 an hour in 1978 to $3.35 an hour by 1981. About 56 million workers are covered by the federal minimum wage.

In Great Britain, wage boards set minimum wages for particular industries. In Great Britain and some other European countries, labor unions and employers set unofficial minimum wages by mutual agreement.

In an Open-Pit Copper Mine in Utah, electric power shovels dig the pit and railroad cars carry out the ore. The equipment moves to and from the pit over a continuous road formed by a series of connected, steplike ledges called *benches*.

MINING

MINING is the process of taking mineral substances from the earth. A mineral substance is almost any non-living thing that is found in the earth. These substances include metal compounds, coal, sand, oil, natural gas, and many other useful things.

Almost every substance that man gets from the earth is obtained by mining. Mining provides iron and copper for making airplanes, automobiles, and refrigerators. Mines also supply salt for food; gold, silver, and diamonds for jewelry; and coal for fuel. Men mine uranium for atomic energy, stone for buildings, phosphate to make plants grow, and gravel for highways.

Some minerals can be mined more cheaply than others because they are found at the surface of the earth. But some minerals lie buried far beneath the surface. They can be removed only by digging deep underground. Still other mineral elements are found in oceans, lakes, and rivers.

Man has mined the earth for thousands of years. About 6000 B.C., men dug pits and tunnels to obtain flint, a hard stone used to make tools and weapons. By 3000 B.C., men were mining tin and copper. These metals were combined to make bronze, a hard *alloy* (mixture of metals) that made better tools and weapons.

The ancient Romans probably were the first people to realize that mining could make a nation rich and powerful. Merchants traded valuable stones and metals and brought riches to the Roman Empire. The Romans took over the mines of every country they conquered.

The Roman Empire ended in the A.D. 400's. For about a thousand years, few advancements were made in mining. During the 1400's, coal, iron, and other minerals were mined in Europe, especially in Germany and France. Mining also began to develop in South America. The Inca Indians and other tribes of South America used metals to make tools, jewelry, and weapons.

Mining began in what is now the United States during the early 1700's. French explorers mined lead and zinc in the valley of the Mississippi River. In the mid-1800's, men began to dig up large amounts of coal in Pennsylvania. At about the same time, thousands of persons rushed to California hoping to find gold. In the West, the gold rush led to the discovery of copper, lead, silver, and other useful mineral substances.

J. Donald Forrester, the contributor of this article, is Dean Emeritus of the College of Mines of the University of Arizona, and Director Emeritus of the Arizona Bureau of Mines.

There are many methods of mining, but each is based on where and how a mineral deposit is found in the earth. Some mineral deposits lie at or near the earth's surface, and others are far underground. Some minerals are found as a compact mass, but others are widely scattered. Minerals also vary in hardness and in the ease with which the ore can be separated from the surrounding rocks. Certain mineral substances are liquids, or can be changed into liquids, and are obtained by various methods of pumping. For a discussion of the methods of mining a particular mineral, see the WORLD BOOK article on that mineral, such as GOLD.

Surface Mining Methods

Surface mining methods are used when deposits occur at or near the surface of the earth. These methods include placer mining, dredging, open-pit mining, strip mining, and quarrying.

Placer Mining is a way of obtaining gold, platinum, tin, and other so-called *heavy minerals* from gravel and sand deposits where nearby water supplies are plentiful. The mineral-bearing gravel and sand are shoveled into the upper end of a slanting wooden trough called a *riffle box*. In the box, they are washed by water. The valuable minerals are heavier than the sand and gravel, and settle in grooves on the bottom of the box. The noneconomic gravel and sand are washed away. The mineral-bearing gravel and sand may also be moved directly from a deposit into the riffle box by the force of water shooting out through a large nozzle called a *giant*. Placer mining done in this way is called *hydraulicking*. Sometimes a form of placer mining called *panning* is used to get gold and other minerals from streams.

Dredging is used especially where mineral-bearing sand and gravel layers are exceptionally thick. In dredging, a pond or lake must be formed so that a large, bargelike machine called a *dredge* can be floated. An endless chain of buckets is attached to a *boom* (long beam) at the front end of the dredge. The buckets dip into the water when one end of the boom is lowered. They dig up the mineral-bearing sand and gravel and move the material to a bin on the deck of the dredge. The material is taken from the bin and washed in much the same way as in placer mining. After the valuable minerals are collected, the sand and gravel are put on a conveyor belt and dumped back into the pond behind the dredge. By digging forward while at the same time disposing of the waste sand and gravel to the rear, the pond and the dredge move ahead as the deposit is mined.

When mining some kinds of loose gravel deposits, machines called *draglines* or *slacklines* are used. These machines have a scoop attached to a high boom. The scoop is pulled back and forth along the deposit to gather material, which is put into a separating bin.

Open-Pit Mining is used to dig valuable minerals from large deposits in hard rock. Often whole mountains are removed or large pits are dug by this method. When digging the mine, the miners make a series of connected, steplike ledges called *benches*. Each bench is lower than the one above. The benches form a road around the sides of the mine, so that the ore can be brought up from the pit by truck or railroad train.

A Mining Dredge digs for gold in Alaska. A revolving chain of buckets scoops up a mixture of gold and sand. The dredge separates the gold and sand, and dumps the sand into the pond.

Miners use explosives to break up great masses of ore-bearing hard rock. The men load the broken rock into large trucks or trains. By using electric power shovels, large amounts of a mineral can be collected cheaply by the open-pit method. Many copper, iron, diamond, phosphate, and gypsum mines are operated as open pits.

Strip Mining is used to obtain coal and other minerals that lie flat near the earth's surface. Huge power shovels remove the soil and rocks that cover the mineral deposit. The shovels transfer this material, called *overburden*, to piles of waste known as *spoil*. Smaller shovels remove the coal or ore.

Strip mining provides an economical method of obtaining vital minerals. But in many places, this process has left behind an ugly, unproductive area of pits and waste piles. Many states have laws that require mining companies to fill in strip mines after the mining has been completed. A number of firms also plant the mined area with grass or trees. In the United States, about 2 million acres (810,000 hectares) of land have been

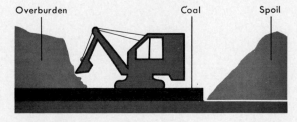

Strip Mining obtains coal or ore from near the earth's surface. Power shovels remove the rocks and soil that cover the valuable minerals and transfer this waste to piles called *spoil*.

strip mined. About a third of this land has been completely or partially reclaimed.

Quarrying is a method in which large blocks of rock are wedged loose or sawed out of a deposit that lies near the surface. Chains and pulleys are used to lift the blocks from the pit. Miners quarry such rock materials as marble, granite, sandstone, limestone, and slate.

Gravel and sand also are quarried. Power shovels dig into the gravel or sand deposit and load the material into trucks or trains. It is then taken to be washed or cleaned, or is hauled directly to a construction site.

Underground Mining Methods

Underground methods are used when the mineral deposit lies deep beneath the earth's surface. First the miners *drive* (dig) an opening to the mine. A vertical opening is called a *shaft*. A passage that is nearly horizontal, dug into the side of a hill or mountain, is called an *adit*. The miners usually make the opening by blasting with explosives. They may install timbers or other supports to prevent the passage from caving in. If the deposit is extremely hard, the miners must also use explosives to loosen the mineral-bearing mass.

The miners load the ore on trucks or small trains and remove it from the mine. Much of the machinery used in underground mines is operated by electric power or compressed air. Diesel-powered machinery must include devices that change carbon monoxide and other harmful gases in the exhaust into nonpoisonous gases. If poisonous exhaust gases accumulate in a mine, the miners may become sick or even die.

Shaft mines have elevators that take the miners to and from the mine and remove the ore. An elevator that carries miners is called a *cage*. Bucketlike elevator cars known as *skips* haul ore to the surface.

Underground mining is a hazardous occupation because of the danger of cave-ins, explosions, and other accidents. Serious lung diseases can also result from breathing air containing particles of minerals. The government and many states regulate mining practices to protect the health and safety of miners. Mining companies sponsor programs that promote safe working procedures. The number of U.S. mine accidents decreased greatly during the early 1970's, but more than 100 miners still were killed and many more injured every year. For more information on mining hazards and safety precautions, see COAL (Mine Safety Measures).

There are two main types of underground mining: (1) level and shaft mining and (2) room-and-pillar mining.

Level and Shaft Mining is used especially when a *vein* (mass of ore) extends downward into the earth. The miners dig a shaft that may reach a depth of 9,000 feet (2,700 meters) or more. They then remove the ore through a system of horizontal passages called *levels*. These passages are dug at different depths, usually 100 to 200 feet (30 to 61 meters) from each other. The levels are connected by a shaft, steeply sloping passages called *raises*, and openings called *stopes*, which have been formed by the removal of ore. The miners often remove the ore by working upward from one level to the next. The ore falls through the raises. It is then loaded into small train cars and carried to the shaft to be hoisted to the surface.

In level and shaft mining, the miners try to remove only the ore and leave most of the rock that surrounds it. Level and shaft mining generally costs more than other methods because of the time and expense involved in the construction of levels. Mine operators often use the process to mine unusually valuable deposits. Minerals mined by this method include copper, gold, lead, silver, and zinc.

For some deposits, a special type of level and shaft mining called *block caving* may be used. With this process, mining companies can obtain minerals that are scattered throughout a mass of rock. In block caving, the miners dig a shaft and levels to reach the ore. Then they cut a thin slice of rock from under the ore-bearing mass. Large blocks of rock cave in and break up as a result. The miners remove the broken rock from the mine and separate the crystals of ore from useless rock.

A **"Continuous Miner"** has rotating cutters. This 132-short-ton (120-metric-ton) machine can rip out 7½ short tons (6.8 metric tons) of potash a minute.

Westinghouse Air Brake Co.

MINING TERMS

Adit is a nearly horizontal passage from the earth's surface into a mine.

Crosscut is a horizontal mine passage whose direction is at a right or sharp angle to the directions of the veins or other geologic structures in a mine.

Drift is a horizontal mine passage that has been driven along or parallel to the course of a vein.

Footwall is the wall or zone of rock under an inclined vein. It is beneath the miner's feet as he excavates the ore.

Gangue is the worthless material mixed with the ore in a mineral deposit.

Hanging Wall is the wall or zone of rock above an inclined vein. It hangs above the miner as he excavates the ore.

Level is the group of drifts and crosscuts made at one depth in an underground mine. Miners usually develop several levels, each at a different depth.

Ore is a natural mass of minerals that can be mined at a profit. Most ores contain metal, but they also may be such nonmetallic substances as sulfur or fluorite.

Outcrop is the exposed surface of a mineral deposit.

Overburden is the soil or rock that covers a mineral deposit.

Quarry is an open or surface excavation from which building stone is usually obtained.

Raise is a passage driven upward from a lower level toward an upper level in an underground mine.

Shaft is a vertical passage from the earth's surface into a mine. It is shaped like an elevator shaft.

Stope is an underground excavation formed by the removal of ore between one level and the next in a mine.

Stripping is the process of removing the overburden from a mineral deposit.

Sump is an excavation made at the bottom of a shaft to collect water in order to remove it from a mine.

Tunnel is a horizontal underground passage that opens to the surface at both ends.

Vein is a mineral deposit with definite boundaries that separate it from the surrounding rock.

Winze is a passage that has been driven downward from a level in an underground mine.

AN UNDERGROUND MINE

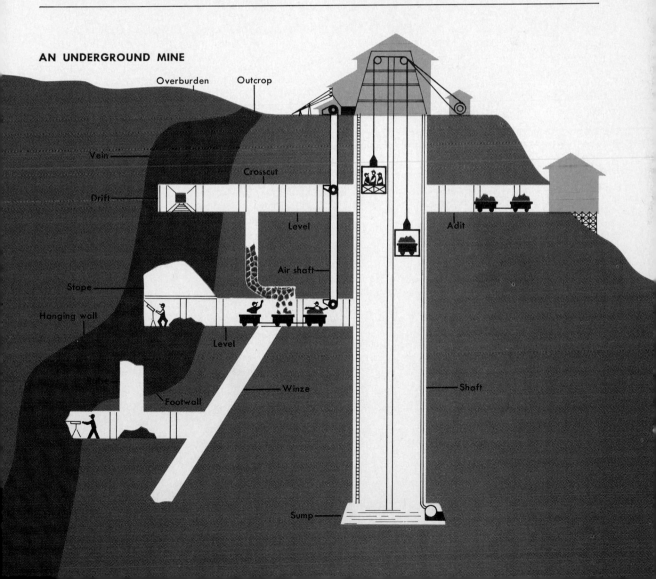

MINING

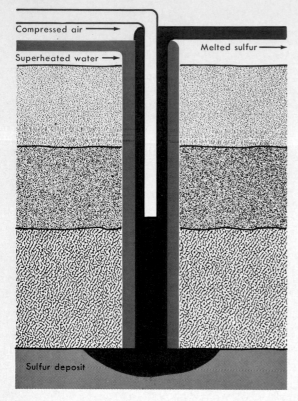

Compressed air →
Melted sulfur →
Superheated water →

Sulfur deposit

The Frasch Method of mining sulfur uses hot water that flows into a deposit through the outer of three pipes. The sulfur melts and begins to rise through the middle pipe. Compressed air from the inner pipe forces the sulfur through the middle pipe.

UNDERWATER MINING

This diagram shows equipment that pumps sulfur from beneath the ocean floor off the Louisiana coast. The Frasch process is used to mine sulfur deposits that lie as far as 2,500 feet (762 meters) below sea level. The mine's main units stand on platforms that are more than 60 feet (18 meters) above the water. The platforms rest on steel supports. Bridges connect the platforms and serve as a road for transporting equipment and workers. Each bridge extends 200 feet (61 meters). Workers live on this steel island in modern, air-conditioned quarters. They travel to and from the shore by helicopter.

Mine operators use block caving mostly to obtain copper ore, though other minerals are sometimes mined by this method.

Room-and-Pillar Mining is often used to obtain minerals from horizontal layers. The mine may be developed at a single depth. The miners dig an adit or a shaft to the mineral deposit. They divide the mine into "rooms" and leave pillars of ore to support the roof. Mining companies use this method to obtain such minerals as coal, lead, potash, salt, and zinc.

Pumping Methods

The waters of the ocean and of some lakes, including Great Salt Lake in Utah, contain huge amounts of mineral elements. They often are obtained by pumping the water into plants where it is treated. Pumps move large amounts of seawater through *precipitators* (separators) so that the minerals can be removed. Most of the magnesium used today is obtained by this method.

Pumping is sometimes used to get salt from beds beneath the earth's surface. Workers drill holes and circulate water underground to dissolve the salt and form a salt-water solution called *brine*. The brine is pumped to the surface and taken to a factory. There, the water is evaporated, and the salt forms a solid again. A somewhat similar method called *leaching* is used for some ores that contain copper (see COPPER [Leaching]).

The Frasch process, another pumping method, is often used in mining sulfur, which melts easily. The miners bore holes in a buried sulfur bed and inject superheated water. The sulfur melts and forms a liquid. The miners force the liquid sulfur to the surface by pumping compressed air into the holes. After the sulfur cools, it becomes a solid again and can be stored until needed.

Petroleum and natural gas also are pumped from the ground (see PETROLEUM; GAS [fuel]).

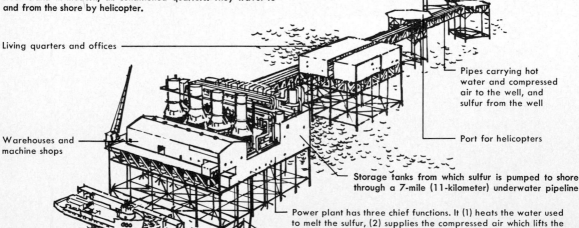

Machinery for drilling wells

Road for hauling equipment and supplies

Living quarters and offices

Pipes carrying hot water and compressed air to the well, and sulfur from the well

Port for helicopters

Warehouses and machine shops

Storage tanks from which sulfur is pumped to shore through a 7-mile (11-kilometer) underwater pipeline

Power plant has three chief functions. It (1) heats the water used to melt the sulfur, (2) supplies the compressed air which lifts the melted sulfur to the surface, and (3) provides electric power to run drilling machinery and other equipment.

MINING / The Mining Industry

In the mid-1970's, the annual value of mining production in the United States was about $62 billion. In Canada, the value of mineral production was about $13 billion a year. For the value of mining production in the individual states and provinces, see the Economy section of the WORLD BOOK articles on each state and province.

About 783,000 persons earn their living in the United States mining industry. The industry offers a wide variety of careers for professional, skilled, and semiskilled workers.

Management in the mining industry consists mainly of business people and engineers. These people manage mines, smelters, and refineries, and direct the search for new mineral deposits. They try to improve mining methods, and to develop new operating and engineering practices.

Many universities and colleges offer training for various specialized careers in mining industry engineering. The *geological engineer* or *exploration engineer* guides the search for mineral deposits and estimates their value. The *production engineer* decides on the best and cheapest method of removing minerals from the earth. The *beneficiation engineer* or *metallurgical engineer* directs the *beneficiation* (milling, smelting, and refining) of minerals so that the minerals can be sold or used by the company.

Some business firms own and operate their own mines to obtain minerals that are needed to manufacture their products. For example, many steel companies operate coal mines to get coke for making steel. Mines owned and operated in this way are called *captive mines*. The minerals they produce are used only by the company that owns the mine.

Jon Brenneis

Mining Exploration Teams of geologists, geophysicists, and other experts search for minerals. Mining companies use their reports on the probable size, shape, and value of deposits.

Leading Mining States and Provinces

Value of minerals produced in 1977

State/Province	Value
Texas	$19,635,000,000
Louisiana	$10,472,000,000
Alberta	$8,575,000,000
West Virginia	$3,719,000,000
California	$3,691,000,000
Kentucky	$3,534,000,000
Oklahoma	$3,510,000,000
Ontario	$2,976,000,000
Pennsylvania	$2,975,000,000
New Mexico	$2,906,000,000

Sources: U.S. Bureau of Mines; Statistics Canada.

Leading Mining Countries

Value of minerals produced in 1975

United States	$62,268,000,000
Russia	$59,846,300,000
Saudi Arabia	$19,367,500,000
China	$16,689,700,000
Iran	$14,319,700,000
Canada	$13,337,600,000
Venezuela	$10,898,100,000
West Germany	$10,524,500,000
Libya	$9,154,400,000
South Africa	$8,834,100,000

Sources: U.S. Bureau of Mines; Statistics Canada.

Bureau of Mines, USDI

Mining Engineers use scientific instruments to find the easiest and cheapest way of removing minerals from the earth.

Some mining engineers specialize in mine safety. The mining industry also employs salesmen, surveyors, and scientists, including chemists and physicists.

Among the workers in mines are men skilled in operating and maintaining various kinds of cranes, shovels, and machines. Other workers include mechanics, electricians, truck drivers, hoistmen, and laborers.

Many persons with mining experience work as federal or state mine inspectors. They help enforce laws that promote the health and safety of miners.

Further information on mining careers may be obtained by writing the American Institute of Mining, Metallurgical and Petroleum Engineers, 345 E. 47th St., New York, N.Y. 10017. J. DONALD FORRESTER

MINING / Study Aids

Related Articles. See also MINERAL and the Economy section of the various country, state, and province articles. Other related articles in WORLD BOOK include:

Alchemy	Iron and Steel	Salt
Assaying	Lead	Silver
Coal	Magnesium	Tin
Coke	Metal	United Mine Workers
Copper	Metallurgy	of America
Damp	Mines, Bureau of	Uranium
Diamond	Ore	Well
Engineering	Petroleum	Western Frontier Life
Gas (fuel)	Prospecting	(The Search for
Gem	Quarrying	Gold and Silver)
Gold	Safety Lamp	Zinc

Outline

I. **Kinds of Mining**
   A. Surface Mining Methods
   B. Underground Mining Methods
   C. Pumping Methods
II. **The Mining Industry**

Questions

What are captive mines?
What are the two chief types of underground mining?
What minerals are often obtained by open-pit mining?
What are some specialized positions for mining engineers?
When are draglines used in dredging?
How do miners obtain sulfur by the Frasch process?

What determines the method used to mine a mineral?
What is the difference between a shaft and an adit?
What is the overburden?
Why are selective methods of mining more expensive than other methods?

Reading and Study Guide

See *Mining* in the RESEARCH GUIDE/INDEX, Volume 22, for a *Reading and Study Guide.*

MINING ENGINEERING. See MINING (The Mining Industry); ENGINEERING (Main Branches; table).

MINISTER, in international relations, is a diplomatic agent who represents his country in a foreign land. He is appointed by the head of his country, and ranks below an ambassador. The President of the United States appoints ministers. Like all diplomatic agents in the United States, ministers get their credentials from the Secretary of State. Most countries tend to exchange ambassadors, rather than ministers.

In some countries, the name *minister* is also given to high administrative officers who make up the cabinet or executive body (see CABINET). PAYSON S. WILD

See also AMBASSADOR; DIPLOMACY (table); MINISTRY.

MINISTER is the general term for an ordained, professional officer of a Christian church. Specifically, it is the usual title of the pastor of a congregation in most Protestant churches. He conducts worship, administers the sacraments, preaches, and assumes responsibility for the pastoral care of the people. Orthodox, Roman Catholic, and Anglican churches have three "orders" of ministers: bishops, priests, and deacons. Protestant churches that stress the priesthood of all believers do not regard the minister as of a different "order" from the laity. He is considered to be the leader of a congregation of ministering disciples.

The word *minister* comes from Christ's description of Himself as one who "came not to be ministered unto, but to minister" (Matt. 20:28), and from His charge to the Apostles, "Whosoever will be great among you shall be your minister" (Mark 10:43). R. PIERCE BEAVER

MINISTER PLENIPOTENTIARY. See DIPLOMACY.

MINISTER RESIDENT. See DIPLOMACY.

MINISTRY, in government, is a body of executive officers who advise the head of a country or directly control a nation's affairs. Often, the members are members of parliament and heads of executive departments.

Ministries are part of the governmental setup of countries which have a parliamentary form of government. The ministry of Great Britain has furnished the model for all nations using the parliamentary system.

The British ministry consists of the prime minister and a number of other officers known as the *ministers.* The monarch appoints the prime minister. He usually selects the leader of the party in control of the House of Commons. He bases his selections of the other ministers on the recommendations of the prime minister. British ministers are members of Parliament and are divided into *cabinet ministers* and *ministers not in the cabinet.* Cabinet ministers vary from cabinet to cabinet. Major bills are introduced by ministers.

The British ministry represents the political party or parties that control the House of Commons. When it can no longer get parliamentary support, the ministry resigns. ROBERT G. NEUMANN

See also CABINET (The Cabinet System of Government); PRIME MINISTER.

MINK

The Mink is a small, swift, agile mammal. It is a member of the weasel family. Its beautiful fur is prized for making expensive coats.
Valleywood Mink Farm, Swanton, Ohio

Bethlehem Steel Co., Inc.

The White Mink has one of the most sought-after mink furs. Its color, extremely rare among minks, is known as a *mutation*.

Large Mink Ranches provide many of the mink pelts used to make coats. Mink ranchers try to improve the pelts by using selective breeding methods.

MacArthur Ranch, Janesville, Wis.

MINK is a small member of the weasel family. Its furs are made into costly coats for women. Minks live on wooded streams, lakes, and marshes of North America, from the Gulf of Mexico to the Arctic Circle, and in the northern parts of Europe and Asia. The mink is a swift and agile animal, at home on land or in the water. The male American mink is from 14 to 25 inches (36 to 64 centimeters) long, with a bushy tail extending another 9 inches (23 centimeters). It is about 5 inches (13 centimeters) high at the shoulders and sometimes weighs 2 pounds (0.9 kilogram). The female is much smaller, sometimes weighing only half as much as the male. The European mink is a little smaller. Wild mink fur varies from light brown or tan to a dark chocolate color, with a white patch on the chin and several spots of white on the throat and chest.

Minks have many of the land habits of the weasel, and the water habits of the otter. They like watercourses where food such as frogs, crayfish, and fish are plentiful. They also eat small mammals such as mice, and any birds they can catch on the ground. A litter of 4 to 10 young minks, called *kits*, is born in the spring in a den among rocks, under tree roots, or in a hollow log. The family stays together until late summer or fall, when the young scatter to find hunting ranges of their own.

The mink has a strong, acrid, unpleasant odor. Unlike the skunk, the mink cannot spray its scent at a distance, but the odor is stronger and, to many persons, more nauseating. As a rule, it is not noticeable except when the mink is in a rage. Like the other members of the weasel family, it can fight ferociously when it is cornered. Its chief enemies include the lynx, the bobcat, the fox, the great horned and snowy owls, and man. Trappers kill more minks than all the animals do.

The beautiful and costly mink furs never go out of fashion for coats, capes, jackets, neckpieces, stoles, and trimmings. The color of the fur often determines its value, and single pelts have sold for as much as $750 apiece. The value of a good dark-colored wild mink pelt is about $20. About 75 per cent of all the furs marketed come from mink ranches. These pelts bring $15 to $250 apiece. Minks in captivity have been bred to produce fur from white and pale silver to darkest brown. Such specially developed fur is called *mutation mink*.

Scientific Classification. Minks belong to the family *Mustelidae*. The North American mink is genus *Mustela*, species *M. vison*. The European mink is genus *Mustela*, species *M. lutreola*.   E. LENDELL COCKRUM

See also FUR.

MINKOWSKI, HERMANN. See FOURTH DIMENSION.

Forest J. Sorenson

Downtown Minneapolis lies on the west bank of the Mississippi River, which flows through the city. Rising above the downtown area is the 57-story tower of the IDS Center, a commercial-office complex completed in 1972. The tower ranks as the tallest building in Minnesota.

MINNEAPOLIS, MIHN *ee AP uh lihs,* is the largest city in Minnesota and a major Midwestern center of finance, industry, trade, and transportation. The city also is the home of the University of Minnesota, one of the nation's largest universities. Minneapolis lies in southeastern Minnesota, just west of St. Paul, its "twin city."

The name *Minneapolis* comes from the Indian word *minne,* meaning *water,* and the Greek word *polis,* which means *city.* Minneapolis got its name because of the 22 natural lakes that lie within the city limits. It has the nickname *City of Lakes.*

In the late 1840's, farmers and lumbermen settled

FACTS IN BRIEF

Population: 434,400. *Metropolitan Area Population*—1,965,-391.

Area: 59 sq. mi. (153 km²). *Metropolitan Area*—4,875 sq. mi. (12,626 km²).

Climate: *Average Temperature*—January, 14° F. (−10° C); July, 74° F. (23° C). *Average Annual Precipitation* (rainfall, melted snow, and other forms of moisture)—32 inches (81 centimeters). For the monthly weather in Minneapolis, see MINNESOTA (Climate).

Government: Mayor-council. *Terms*—2 years for the mayor and the 13 aldermen.

Founded: 1849. Incorporated as a city in 1866.

---

the area that is now Minneapolis. They chose the area because of its broad farmlands and hardwood forests. In addition, the nearby Falls of St. Anthony, on the Mississippi River, supplied water power for their flour mills and sawmills. In 1849, the lumbermen established a village called All Saints on the west side of the falls. The people of All Saints changed its name to Minneapolis in 1852.

From 1882 to 1930, Minneapolis led the world in flour production. After World War II ended in 1945, the city became an important producer of computers, electronic equipment, and farm machinery. Today, Minneapolis ranks as the nation's leading market center for farm equipment.

Metropolitan Minneapolis

The City covers 59 square miles (153 square kilometers), including 5 square miles (13 square kilometers) of inland water. The Mississippi River divides Minneapolis into two areas, the larger of which is west of the river. The city's grain-milling district occupies both banks of the river between the Third Avenue and Cedar Avenue bridges. Most of the huge University of Minnesota campus lies on the east bank, but part of the campus is on the west bank.

Downtown Minneapolis, on the west bank, faces the Falls of St. Anthony. Nicollet Avenue, the chief shopping street, features an eight-block-long shopping center called Nicollet Mall. The law permits cabs and buses—but not automobiles—to drive on Nicollet Mall.

The 57-story Investors Diversified Center stands near Nicollet Mall. When completed in 1972, the center was the tallest building between Chicago and San Francisco. The city's financial district is on Marquette Avenue, a block southeast of Nicollet Avenue. Hennepin Avenue, the main entertainment area in downtown Minneapolis, has many motion-picture theaters and nightclubs.

The Metropolitan Area covers about 4,875 square miles (12,626 square kilometers) and spreads over nine counties in Minnesota and one in Wisconsin. It takes in about 175 self-governing communities. Communities in the metropolitan area include St. Paul, Minnesota's capital and second largest city, and Bloomington, Minnesota's fourth largest city. The Minnesota part of the metropolitan area has more than 1,900,000 people—half the state's population. The Minneapolis and St. Paul business districts are connected by a part of University Avenue called The Midway.

The People

About 95 per cent of the people in Minneapolis were born in the United States. About a fourth of the city's population have Swedish ancestry. Other major groups include people of Canadian, German, or Norwegian descent. Negroes make up less than 5 per cent of the population.

Lutherans and Roman Catholics rank as the largest religious groups in Minneapolis. Other large religious groups include Methodists and Presbyterians.

Housing and other welfare services for elderly people have become a major problem in Minneapolis. Since 1950, the number of older residents in the city has been increasing, and many of them cannot afford private housing. During the 1970's, a federal construction program provided more than 6,000 apartments for old people.

Minneapolis started seven slum renewal projects dur-

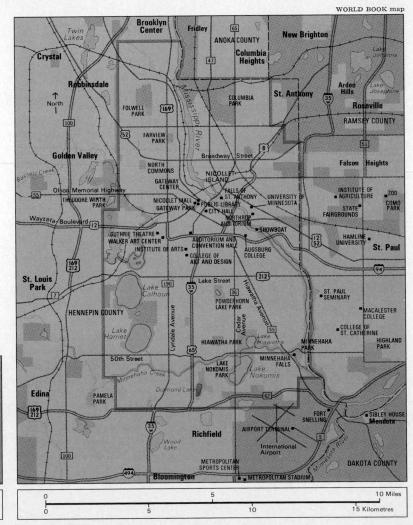

WORLD BOOK map

CITY OF MINNEAPOLIS

MINNESOTA
•Minneapolis

Minneapolis is an industrial city on the Mississippi River. The large map shows the city's major landmarks. The small map shows Minneapolis and its twin city, St. Paul.

City boundary
County boundary
Main road
Other road
Rail line
• Point of Interest
Built-up area
Nonbuilt-up area
Park

Minneapolis-St. Paul Area

Minnesota Department of Economic Development

The Nicollet Mall, *above, a landscaped shopping area in down-town Minneapolis, occupies eight blocks along Nicollet Avenue.*

ing the 1960's. These projects, costing a total of more than $85 million, were completed by 1975.

Economy

Industry and Commerce. About 3,000 manufacturing companies operate in the Minneapolis metropolitan area. They employ more than 215,000 workers and produce about $4\frac{1}{3}$ billion worth of goods annually. The city ranks as a major manufacturer of, in order of importance, machinery, food products, and fabricated metal products. Other important industries in the city include printing and publishing. Minneapolis is the headquarters of the Ninth Federal Reserve Bank District, which serves a six-state region.

Transportation. Eight commercial airlines use the Minneapolis-St. Paul International Airport. Passenger trains and six railroad freight lines serve the city. Twenty bridges in Minneapolis cross the Mississippi River. Several major highways, including two interstate routes, pass through the city. The Minneapolis-St. Paul area ranks among the nation's top trucking terminals. More than 40 trucking companies have their home office there.

Communication. Minneapolis has two daily newspapers, the *Minneapolis Tribune* and *The Minneapolis Star.* About 30 radio stations and 6 television stations broadcast in the area.

Education

The Minneapolis public school system includes about 90 elementary and high schools with a total of about 50,000 students. Blacks and Indians make up about 15 per cent of the enrollment. The city has a busing program to achieve racial balance in the public schools. About 12,000 students attend 36 parochial and private schools in Minneapolis.

494

The Twin Cities campus of the University of Minnesota has facilities in Minneapolis and St. Paul. With about 65,000 students, it is one of the nation's largest university campuses. Other institutions of higher learning in the city include Augsburg College, the Minneapolis College of Art and Design, and the Minneapolis Institute of Arts.

The Minneapolis Public Library has 15 branches and owns more than a million books. Libraries of the University of Minnesota have about $3\frac{1}{2}$ million volumes.

Cultural Life

The Arts. The Guthrie Theater Company, one of the best-known theater groups in the country, performs in The Guthrie Theater. The Minnesota Symphony Orchestra has its headquarters at Orchestra Hall in Nicollet Mall.

Museums. The Walker Art Center owns one of the country's finest collections of modern art. The Minneapolis Institute of Arts displays masterpieces dating from 2000 B.C. to modern times. The Science Museum and Planetarium of the Minneapolis Public Library features planetarium shows and science exhibits on subjects ranging from time and space to Egyptian mummies.

Recreation

Minneapolis has been called the *Vacation Capital* because it serves as the gateway to the lake region of northern Minnesota. The Minneapolis Aquatennial, held every July, features a canoe derby, costume balls, a torchlight parade, and water ballets. The annual Minnesota State Fair takes place in early fall at the State Fairgrounds in St. Paul. Its highlights include automobile races, carnival shows, and agricultural and industrial exhibits.

Parks. Minneapolis has about 150 public parks, which cover about 5,500 acres (2,230 hectares). Most of the parks line the shores of the Mississippi River or surround the many small lakes within the city. Theodore Wirth Park, the largest park, covers almost 740 acres (300 hectares) and has a wooded area for hiking. Minnehaha Park includes Minnehaha Falls, which is 53 feet (16 meters) high. The American poet Henry Wadsworth Longfellow made this falls famous in his poem *The Song of Hiawatha.* See MINNEHAHA FALLS.

Summer vacationers enjoy boating and swimming at Lake Minnetonka, which is 12 miles (19 kilometers) long and lies 12 miles southwest of the city. Many tourists visit Fort Snelling, the center of the first permanent white settlement in what is now the Minneapolis area.

Sports. The Minnesota Twins of the American League play baseball at Metropolitan Stadium in Bloomington. The Minnesota Vikings of the National Football League also play their home games there. The Minnesota North Stars of the National Hockey League meet opponents at the Metropolitan Sports Center in Bloomington.

Government. Minneapolis has a mayor-council form of government. The voters elect the mayor and 13 council members, called *aldermen,* to two-year terms. Property taxes provide the city's main source of income. But these taxes do not furnish enough money for all the projects desired by the city, and some programs have been reduced.

The state Pollution Control Department has a division in Minneapolis. This agency measures the quality of the city's air and water. It also works with polluters to help solve their problems.

In 1967, Minnesota established the Metropolitan Council of the Twin Cities Area. This governmental agency has the power to tax and to sell bonds. It deals with such areawide concerns as health, housing, land use, sewer construction, transportation, waste disposal, and water pollution. The council consists of 14 members and a chairperson, all appointed by the governor of Minnesota.

History

Early Days. Sioux Indians once farmed and hunted in what is now the Minneapolis area. In 1680, a Belgian explorer and missionary named Louis Hennepin became the first white person to visit the site (see HENNEPIN, LOUIS [picture]). From 1820 to 1822, American soldiers under Colonel Josiah Snelling built Fort St. Anthony there. The fort was renamed Fort Snelling in 1825. It served for more than 30 years as a trading center and a gateway to the northern wilderness and the western prairies.

During the 1840's, the great forests of the area attracted lumbermen from Maine. These men built sawmills near the Falls of St. Anthony. In 1849, the lumbermen founded the village of All Saints on the west side of the falls. They changed its name to Minneapolis in 1852. Grain millers built a large flour mill there in 1854 to take advantage of the area's rich wheat fields. Flour milling soon became the second major industry of Minneapolis.

The population of Minneapolis reached 2,564 in 1860. St. Paul, which was nine years older, had 10,401 people at that time. Minneapolis received a city charter in 1866. By 1870, it ranked as the state's principal lumbering center.

In the 1870's, a flour-sifting device called the *purifier* was perfected in Minneapolis. It enabled millers to produce high-quality flour from inexpensive spring wheat. Large flour mills helped the city grow. By 1880, Minneapolis had 46,887 people, compared with St. Paul's 41,473.

In 1882, Minneapolis became the world's leading flour-milling center. Both Minneapolis and St. Paul developed into important transportation centers about this time. But Minneapolis continued to grow faster than St. Paul because it had greater industrial development. By 1890, Minneapolis had a population of 164,738.

The 1900's. The increased use of steam-powered machinery during the late 1800's led to rapid growth of the city's lumber industry. From 1899 to 1905, Minneapolis led the world in lumber production. But by 1906, most of the nearby forests had been cut down, and the city's lumber trade declined sharply. The population of Minneapolis increased from 202,718 in 1900 to 301,408 in 1910.

By 1916, General Mills, Incorporated, The Pillsbury Company, and other local firms produced such huge quantities of flour that Minneapolis became known as *Mill City*. But a large increase in freight rates during the 1920's caused the grain companies to establish milling centers in other parts of the country. In 1930, Buffalo,

N.Y., replaced Minneapolis as the world's leading center of flour production. That year, Minneapolis had 464,356 people.

Recent Developments. Following World War II, Minneapolis became a leader in the manufacture of computers, electronic equipment, and farm machinery. By 1950, the downtown area had become old and shabby. People and industry began moving from the city to the suburbs during the 1950's. The population fell from 521,718 in 1950 to 482,872 in 1960. During the 1960's, the population of the Minneapolis metropolitan area increased, but the number of people living in the city continued to fall.

From 1961 to 1972, private investors spent about $300 million to redevelop the downtown area. Gateway Center, a $179-million renewal project begun in 1958, was largely completed in the mid-1970's. The center, featuring new apartment and office buildings, covers 18 blocks in the heart of the city.   JOHN R. FINNEGAN

See also MINNESOTA.

MINNEAPOLIS COLLEGE OF ART AND DESIGN. See UNIVERSITIES AND COLLEGES (table).

MINNEHAHA was an Indian maiden in Henry Wadsworth Longfellow's poem *The Song of Hiawatha*. She married Hiawatha.

See also SONG OF HIAWATHA.

MINNEHAHA FALLS is a beautiful waterfall in Minneapolis, Minn. It is 53 feet (16 meters) high. Water is sometimes pumped over the top to keep the falls going. A bronze statue of Hiawatha and his Indian bride stands at the top of the falls. Henry Wadsworth Longfellow made the falls famous in his poem *The Song of Hiawatha*.

See also MINNESOTA (color picture).

MINNESINGER, *MIN uh sing er,* was one of a group of German love poets who flourished from the 1100's to the 1300's. The minnesingers sang their poetry to music at court festivals.

Minne was an old German word meaning *love*. The minnesingers' expressions of love were regulated by the courtly society that placed much value on form. Courtly love, as many minnesingers portrayed it, was the hopeless love of a knight for a lady of high station. The knight's plea that the lady answer his love was often expressed in feudal terms such as a vassal might use in begging a favor from his lord. The lady usually remained unapproachable.

The doctrines and forms of courtly love developed in southern France and spread to Germany. In addition to ideas of the feudal system, several literary traditions influenced the minnesingers. These included Arabic poetry transmitted from Spain, classical literature such as Ovid's *The Art of Love*, and medieval Latin poetry. The homage paid to the Virgin Mary in the 1100's also contributed to the idealization of women so basic to much of courtly love poetry.

The leading minnesingers included Dietmar von Aist, Kürenberger, Heinrich von Veldeke, Friedrich von Hausen, Heinrich von Morungen, Reinmar von Hagenau, Walther von der Vogelweide, Neidhart von Reuental, Tannhäuser, and Ulrich von Lichtenstein.   JAMES F. POAG

See also TANNHÄUSER; WALTHER VON DER VOGELWEIDE.

St. Paul's Skyline Rises Beyond a Bend of the Mississippi River

MINNESOTA

The Gopher State

Camping on the Shores of Snowbank Lake
Minnesota Dept. of Economic Development

Minnesota (blue) ranks 12th in size among all the states, and is the largest of the Midwestern States (gray).

496

Minnesota Winter by Adolf Dehn from the WORLD BOOK Collection

Minnesota Farmland

MINNESOTA is one of the chief food-producing states in the United States. The state's wheat crops, flour mills, and dairy products give Minnesota one of its nicknames—the *Bread and Butter State*. But Minnesota is usually called the *Gopher State*, because many gophers live on its southern prairies.

About 1¼ million milk cows graze on the rich pastures of Minnesota's dairy farms. The farmers of this midwestern state also raise great numbers of beef cattle and hogs. Minnesota is a leading producer of barley, corn, flaxseed, hay, potatoes, soybeans, and sugar beets. All these farm products bring in an enormous income. But manufacturing is even more important to Minnesota's economy than agriculture.

One of Minnesota's most important industries is processing the products of its farms. Minnesota is a leading producer of milk, butter, and cheese. It is one of the top meat-packing, flour-producing, and vegetable-canning states.

Minnesota has rich deposits of iron ore, and about 55 per cent of all the iron ore mined in the United States comes from the state. Minnesota also has about 18 million acres (7.3 million hectares) of trees. These woodlands furnish raw materials for making pulp, paper, and other products.

Minnesota's scenic beauty, thousands of sparkling lakes, and deep pine woods make the state a vacation wonderland. Its plentiful game animals and fish attract people who enjoy hunting and fishing. In northern Minnesota, campers, canoeists, and hikers can explore vast wilderness areas.

The state's history is much the story of the development of its great natural resources. The fur-bearing animals of Minnesota's forests first attracted fur traders. Next, the fertile soil brought farmers, who poured into the region from the eastern states and from Europe. The thick forests of tall pines attracted lumberjacks from Maine, Michigan, and Wisconsin. Finally, miners came to Minnesota to dig the state's vast deposits of rich iron ore.

The name *Minnesota* comes from two Sioux Indian words meaning *sky-tinted waters.* St. Paul is the capital of Minnesota, and Minneapolis is the largest city. For the relationship of Minnesota to other states in its region, see the article on the MIDWESTERN STATES.

The contributors of this article are John R. Finnegan, Executive Editor of the St. Paul Dispatch-Pioneer Press; *Harold T. Hagg, author of* Exploring Minnesota; *and Philip L. Tideman, Professor of Geography at St. Cloud State University.*

FACTS IN BRIEF

Capital: St. Paul.

Government: *Congress*—U.S. senators, 2; U.S. representatives, 8. *Electoral Votes*—10. *State Legislature*—senators, 67; representatives, 134. *Counties*—87.

Area: 84,068 sq. mi. (217,735 km²), including 4,799 sq. mi. (12,378 km²) of inland water but excluding 2,212 sq. mi. (5,729 km²) of Lake Superior; 12th in size among the states. *Greatest Distances*—north-south, 411 mi. (661 km); east-west, 357 mi. (575 km). *Shoreline*—180 mi. (290 km).

Elevation: *Highest*—Eagle Mountain, 2,301 ft. (701 m) above sea level in Cook County. *Lowest*—602 ft. (183 m) above sea level along Lake Superior.

Population: *Estimated 1975 Population*—3,926,000. *1970 Census*—3,805,069; 19th among the states; distribution, 66 per cent urban, 34 per cent rural; density, 45 persons per sq. mi. (17 persons per km²).

Chief Products: *Agriculture*—milk, beef cattle, soybeans, corn, hogs, wheat, turkeys, sugar beets. *Fishing Industry*—catfish, walleye, carp. *Manufacturing*—nonelectric machinery; food products; fabricated metal products; electric and electronic equipment; paper products; printed materials; instruments; chemicals; lumber and wood products; stone, clay, and glass products. *Mining*—iron ore, sand and gravel, stone, lime.

Statehood: May 11, 1858; the 32nd state admitted to the Union.

State Abbreviations: Minn. (traditional); MN (postal).

State Motto: *L'Étoile du Nord* (The Star of the North).

State Song: "Hail! Minnesota." Words by Truman E. Rickard and Arthur E. Upson; music by Truman E. Rickard.

Constitution. Minnesota is still governed under its original constitution, adopted in 1858. The constitution may be *amended* (changed) in two ways. An amendment may be proposed in the legislature, where it must be approved by a majority of the lawmakers. Next, it must be approved by a majority of the voters in an election. The constitution may also be amended by a constitutional convention. A proposal to call such a convention must be approved by two-thirds of the legislature and by a majority of the voters in an election. Proposals made by a convention become law after they have been approved by three-fifths of the voters casting ballots on the proposals.

Executive. The governor of Minnesota holds office for a four-year term and can be re-elected any number of times. The governor receives a yearly salary of $62,000. For a list of all the governors of Minnesota, see the *History* section of this article.

The lieutenant governor, secretary of state, attorney general, treasurer, and auditor are also elected to four-year terms. The governor appoints the heads of most state departments, boards, and commissions. Their terms range from two to six years.

Legislature consists of a 67-member senate and a 134-member house of representatives. Each of the state's 67 senatorial districts elects one senator. Each of the 134 representative districts elects one representative. Senators serve four-year terms, and representatives serve two-year terms.

The legislature begins its regular session on the Tuesday after the first Monday in January in odd-numbered years. Minnesota's Constitution limits regular sessions to 120 legislative days over a two-year period. The governor may call special sessions of the legislature.

Courts. The state supreme court heads Minnesota's court system. The supreme court has a chief justice and eight associate justices. All are elected to six-year terms.

Minnesota has one district court. It is divided into 10 judicial districts. Each judicial district has three or more judges, who are elected to six-year terms. County courts operate in every county of the state except the two most heavily populated ones—Hennepin and Ramsey. The county courts deal with probate cases, family cases, and minor civil and criminal suits. Municipal courts handle minor civil and criminal cases in Hennepin and Ramsey counties. County and municipal court judges are elected to six-year terms.

Local Government. Minnesota has 87 counties. Each is governed by a board of commissioners, usually consisting of five members. The board's powers include borrowing money, collecting taxes, and determining how funds are to be spent. The members of the board are elected to four-year terms. Other county officials in Minnesota include the attorney, auditor, coroner, sheriff, and treasurer. These officials also serve four-year terms.

Minnesota has more than 850 cities. The state constitution allows cities to adopt *home rule* charters. This means that a city may choose the form of government best suited to its needs. About 100 cities operate under home rule charters. Most Minnesota cities use the mayor-council form of government. The rest use the commission or council-manager form.

Taxation. Taxes bring in about 70 per cent of the state government's income. Almost all the rest comes from federal grants and other U.S. government programs. Taxes on personal income provide about a third of the state's income. The state adopted a sales tax in 1967 to provide additional funds for municipalities and local school districts. Iron mining companies must pay a tax on all minerals they take from the ground.

Politics. Throughout most of its history, Minnesota has strongly favored Republicans for state offices and for President. About two-thirds of Minnesota's gover-

The Governor's Residence stands about 2½ miles (4 kilometers) from the State Capitol in St. Paul. The stone and red brick house was donated to the state by a St. Paul businessman in 1965. Previous governors had lived in houses rented by the state.

The State Seal

The State Flag

Symbols of Minnesota. On the seal, the Indian riding into the sunset and the farmer symbolize the white settlers' rise and the Indians' decline in pioneer Minnesota. The waterfall and the forest represent the state's natural features. The seal was adopted in 1858. The state flag, adopted in 1957, has a version of the seal and 19 stars. The stars symbolize Minnesota's entry into the Union as the 19th state after the original 13 states.

nors have been Republicans. Between 1860 and 1931, Minnesota had only three Democratic governors. For Minnesota's electoral votes and voting record in presidential elections, see ELECTORAL COLLEGE (table).

In 1920, a third party, the Farmer-Labor Party, was founded in Minnesota. The party soon became powerful. From 1931 to 1939, Minnesota's governors belonged to the Farmer-Labor Party. In 1944, the party joined with the Minnesota Democratic Party to form the Democratic-Farmer-Labor Party (DFL).

Hubert H. Humphrey, a DFL leader, served in the U.S. Senate from 1949 to 1964, and was Vice-President of the United States from 1965 to 1969. He was the Democratic nominee for President in 1968, but lost. Humphrey won reelection to the U.S. Senate in 1970 and 1976. During the 1970's, the DFL held the governorship under Wendell R. Anderson and Rudolph G. Perpich. The DFL won control of the state legislature for the first time in 1972.

In 1975, the Republican Party of Minnesota changed its name. The group is now known as the Independent-Republicans of Minnesota.

The State Bird
Common Loon

The State Flower
Pink and White Lady's-Slipper

The State Capitol stands on a hill overlooking St. Paul. The marble dome rises 220 feet (67 meters) above the ground. St. Paul became the capital in 1849. Minnesota had no other capitals.
Minnesota Dept. of Economic Development

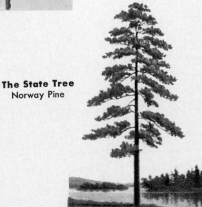

The State Tree
Norway Pine

499

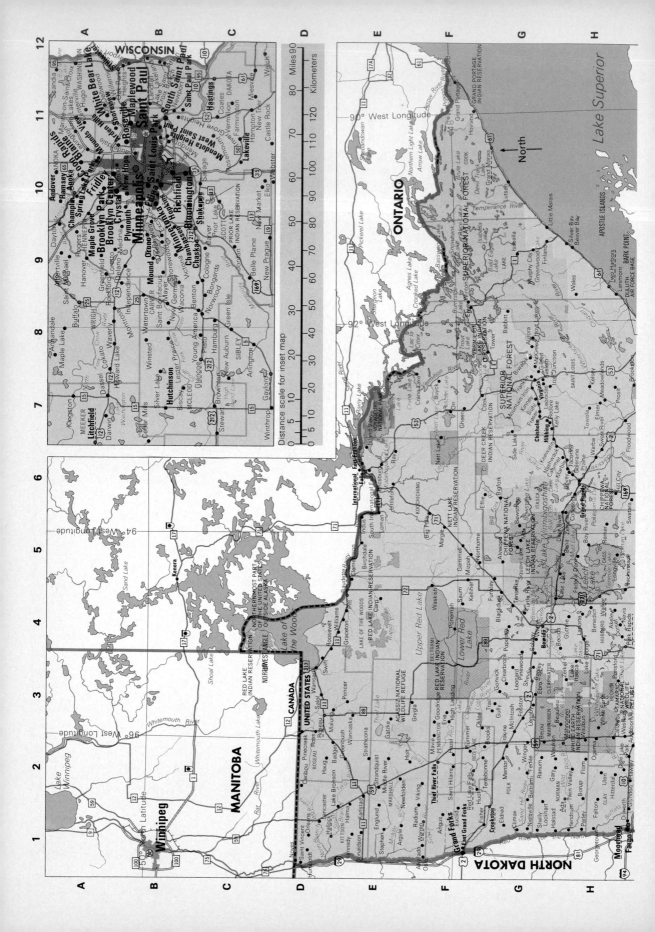

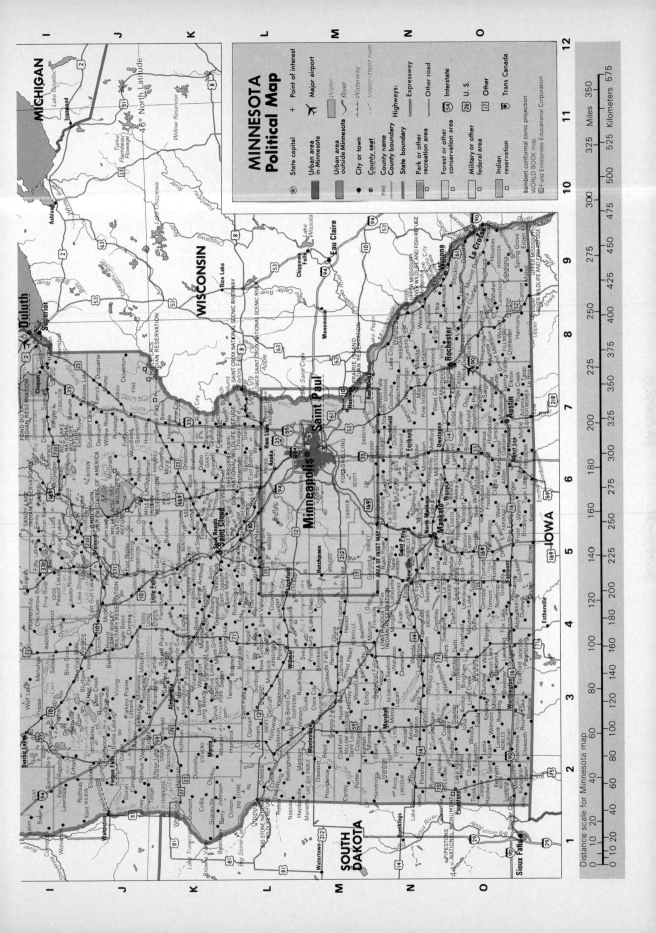

MINNESOTA
Political Map

✪	State capital
+	Point of interest
✈	Major airport
	Water
	River
	Waterway
	Intermittent river
⬛	Urban area in Minnesota
⬛	Urban area outside Minnesota
●	City or town
○ PINE	County seat
PINE	County name
	County boundary
	State boundary
⬛	Park or other recreation area
⬛	Forest or other conservation area
⬛	Military or other federal area
⬛	Indian reservation

Highways:
	Expressway
	Other road
54	Interstate
26	U.S.
17	Other
	Trans Canada

Lambert conformal conic projection
WORLD BOOK map
© Field Enterprises Educational Corporation

MICHIGAN

WISCONSIN

SOUTH DAKOTA

IOWA

Duluth
Superior
Minneapolis
Saint Paul
Saint Cloud
Rochester
Mankato
Austin
Winona
La Crosse
Eau Claire
Chippewa Falls
Rice Lake
Menomonie
Detroit Lakes
Fergus Falls
Little Falls
Brainerd
Alexandria
Willmar
Marshall
Montevideo
Worthington
Sioux Falls
Watertown
Estherville
Ashland
Ironwood

46° North Latitude
45°
44°

Distance scale for Minnesota map

| 0 10 20 | 40 | 60 | 80 | 100 | 120 | 140 | 160 | 180 | 200 | 225 | 250 | 275 | 300 | 325 | 350 Miles |
| 0 10 20 | 40 | 60 | 80 | 100 | 160 | 180 | 200 | 225 | 250 | 275 | 300 | 325 | 350 | 375 | 400 | 425 | 450 | 475 | 500 | 525 | 575 Kilometers |

Population

3,926,000 Estimate..1975
3,805,069 ..Census..1970
3,413,864 ....."...1960
2,982,483 ....."...1950
2,792,300 ....."...1940
2,563,953 ....."...1930
2,387,125 ....."...1920
2,075,708 ....."...1910
1,751,394 ....."...1900
1,310,283 ....."...1890
780,773 ....."...1880
439,706 ....."...1870
172,023 ....."...1860
6,077 ....."...1850

Metropolitan Areas

Duluth-Superior (Wis.) ....265,350 (220,693 in Minn.; 44,657 in Wis.)
Fargo (N. Dak.)-Moorhead......120,261 (73,653 in N. Dak.; 46,608 in Minn.)
Grand Forks (N. Dak.) .....95,537 (61,102 in N. Dak.; 34,435 in Minn.)
Minneapolis-St. Paul ....1,965,391 (1,931,037 in Minn.; 34,354 in Wis.)
Rochester 84,104
St. Cloud 134,585

Counties

Aitkin .....11,403..J 6
Anoka ....154,712..L 6
Becker ....24,372..H 3
Beltrami ...26,373..F 4
Benton .....20,841..K 5
Big Stone ...7,941..L 2
Blue Earth .52,322..O 5
Brown .....28,887..N 4
Carlton ....28,072..I 7
Carver .....28,331..M 6
Cass ....17,323..H 5
Chippewa ..15,109..L 3
Chisago ....17,492..K 7
Clay ....46,608..H 2
Clearwater ..8,013..G 3
Cook ....3,423..F 10
Cottonwood 14,887..O 3
Crow Wing .34,826..J 5
Dakota ...139,808..M 7
Dodge .....13,037..O 7
Douglas ....22,910..J 3
Faribault ..20,896..O 5
Fillmore ...21,916..O 8
Freeborn ...38,064..O 6
Goodhue ...34,804..N 7
Grant ....7,462..K 2
Hennepin .960,080..M 6
Houston ....17,556..O 9
Hubbard ...10,583..H 4
Isanti ......16,560..K 6
Itasca .....35,530..G 6
Jackson ....14,352..O 4
Kanabec ....9,775..K 6
Kandiyohi .30,548..L 4
Kittson .....6,853..E 1
Koochiching 17,131..F 6
Lac Qui Parle ....11,164..M 2
Lake ....13,351..G 9
Lake of the Woods .....4,196..E 4
Le Sueur ..21,332..N 6
Lincoln .....8,143..N 2
Lyon ....24,273..N 2
Mahnomen ..5,638..G 3
Marshall ...13,060..E 2
Martin .....24,316..O 4
McLeod ....27,662..M 5
Meeker ....18,387..L 4
Mille Lacs .15,703..J 6
Morrison ...26,949..J 5
Mower .....43,783..O 7
Murray ....12,508..O 3
Nicollet ...24,518..N 5
Nobles .....23,208..O 2
Norman ....10,008..H 2
Olmsted ....84,104..O 8
Otter Tail ..46,097..J 2
Pennington 13,266..F 2
Pine ....16,821..J 7
Pipestone ..12,791..O 2
Polk ....34,435..G 2
Pope ....11,107..K 3
Ramsey ..476,255..M 7
Red Lake ...5,388..F 2
Redwood ...20,024..N 3
Renville ...21,139..M 4
Rice ....41,582..N 6
Rock ....11,346..O 2
Roseau .....11,569..D 2
St. Louis .220,693..H 7
Scott ......32,423..M 6
Sherburne .18,344..L 6
Sibley .....15,845..M 5
Stearns ....95,400..K 4
Steele .....26,931..N 6
Stevens .....11,218..K 2
Swift ....13,177..L 3
Todd ....22,114..J 4
Traverse .....6,254..K 2
Wabasha ...17,224..N 8
Wadena ....12,412..I 4
Waseca ....16,663..O 6
Washington 83,003..L 7
Watonwan ..13,298..O 4
Wilkin ......9,389..J 2
Winona ....44,409..O 9
Wright .....38,933..L 5
Yellow Medicine ....14,523..M 2

Cities

Ada ....2,076.°H 2
Adams ....771..O 7
Adrian ......1,350..O 2
Afton ....1,993..B 12
Aitkin ......1,553.°I 6
Akeley ....468..H 4
Albany ......1,599..K 4
Albert Lea .19,418.°O 6
Alberta ....140..K 2
Albertville ....451..A 9
Alden ....713..O 6
Aldrich ....85..J 4
Alexandria ..6,973.°K 3
Alpha ....179..O 4
Altura ....334..O 8
Alvarado ......302..F 1
Amboy ....571..O 5
Andover ....8,000..A 10
Annandale ..1,234..A 8
Anoka .....13,295.°L 6
Apple Valley* ..15,315..M 6
Appleton ....1,789..L 2
Arco ....121..N 2
Arden Hills .5,149..A 11
Argyle ....739..E 1
Arlington ...1,823..C 8
Ashby ....415..J 2
Askov ....287..J 7
Atwater ......956..L 4
Audubon ......297..I 2
Aurora .....2,531..G 8
Austin .....26,210.°O 7
Avoca ....203..O 3
Avon ....725..K 5
Babbitt .....3,076..G 8
Backus ....257..I 5
Badger ....327..D 2
Bagley ......1,314.°G 3
Balaton ....649..N 2
Barnesville ..1,782..I 2
Barnum ....382..I 7
Barrett ....342..K 2
Barry ....52..K 1
Battle Lake ..772..J 3
Baudette ....1,440.°E 4
Baxter ......1,556..J 5
Bayport ....2,987..B 12
Beardsley .....366..K 1
Beaver Bay ...362..H 9
Beaver Creek .235..O 2
Becker ....365..L 5
Bejou ....157..G 2
Belgrade ......713..L 4
Belle Plaine 2,328..C 9
Bellechester ..199..N 7
Bellingham ....263..L 2
Beltrami ......171..G 2
Belview ....429..M 3
Bemidji ....11,490.°G 4
Bena ....169..H 5
Benson .....3,484.°L 3
Bertha ....512..J 4
Bethel ....311..L 6
Big Falls ....534..F 6
Big Lake ....1,015..L 6
Bigelow ....262..O 3
Bigfork ....399..G 6
Bingham Lake 214..O 4
Birchwood* ...926..L 7
Bird Island .1,309..M 4
Biscay ....105..B 7
Biwabik .....1,483..G 8
Blackduck .....595..G 4
Blaine .....20,625..A 10
Blomkest ......172..M 4
Blooming Prairie ....1,804..O 7
Bloomington 79,119..B 10
Blue Earth .3,965.°O 5
Bluffton ....195..I 3
Bock ....105..K 6
Borup ....128..H 2
Bovey ....858..H 6
Bowlus ....268..K 5
Boy River .....44..H 5
Boyd ....311..M 2
Braham ....744..K 6
Brainerd ...11,667.°J 5
Branch* ....880..K 7
Brandon ....414..K 3
Breckenridge 4,200.°J 1
Brewster ......563..O 3
Bricelyn ....470..O 6
Brook Park ...113..K 7
Brooklyn Center ...35,173..A 10
Brooklyn Park .....29,945..A 10
Brooks ....163..G 2
Brookston .....137..I 7
Brooten ....615..L 4
Browerville ...665..J 4
Browns Valley .....906..K 1
Brownsdale ....625..O 7
Brownsville ...417..O 9
Brownton ......688..C 7
Bruno ....130..J 7
Buckman ......158..K 5
Buffalo .....3,275.°L 5
Buffalo Lake .758..M 4
Buhl ....1,303..G 7
Burnsville* 19,940..M 6
Burtrum ....135..K 4
Butterfield ....619..O 4
Byron ....1,419..O 7
Caledonia ...2,619.°O 9
Callaway ......233..H 2
Calumet ....460..H 6
Cambridge ..2,720.°K 6
Campbell ......339..J 2
Canby ....2,147..M 2
Cannon Falls .....2,072..N 7
Canton ....391..O 8
Carlos ....278..K 3
Carlton ....884.°I 8
Carver ....669..C 9
Cass Lake ..1,317..H 4
Castle Rock ....D 11
Cedar Mills ...81..B 7
Center City ...324.°L 7
Centerville ....534..A 11
Ceylon ....487..O 4
Champlin ...6,298..A 10
Chandler ....319..O 2
Chanhassen .5,054..B 9
Chaska .....5,398.°B 9
Chatfield ...1,885..O 8
Chickamaw Beach ....87..I 5
Chisago City 1,068..L 7
Chisholm ....6,085..G 7
Chokio ....455..K 2
Circle Pines* 3,918..L 6
Clara City ..1,491..M 3
Claremont .....520..O 7
Clarissa ....599..J 4
Clarkfield ...1,084..M 3
Clarks Grove ..480..O 6
Clear Lake ...280..L 5
Clearbrook ....599..G 3
Clearwater ....282..L 5
Clements ......252..N 4
Cleveland .....492..N 5
Climax ....255..G 1
Clinton ....608..L 2
Clitherall ......131..J 3
Clontarf ....147..L 3
Cloquet .....8,699..I 8
Coates ....212..C 11
Cobden ....113..N 4
Cohasset ......536..H 6
Cokato .....1,735..A 8
Cold Spring .2,006..L 5
Coleraine ...1,086..H 6
Collegeville* ....K 5
Cologne ....518..C 9
Columbia Heights* .23,837..M 6
Comfrey ....525..N 4
Comstock ......135..I 1
Conger ....167..O 6
Cook ....687..F 7
Coon Rapids ..30,505..A 10
Corcoran* ..1,656..A 9
Correll ....95..L 2
Cosmos ....570..M 4
Cottage Grove* ...13,419..M 7
Cottonwood ....794..M 3
Courtland .....300..N 5
Crane Lake ....F 7
Cromwell ......181..I 7
Crookston ...8,312.°G 1
Crosby .....2,241..I 5
Cross Lake ...720..I 5
Crystal ....30,925..A 10
Currie ....368..O 3
Cuyuna ....82..I 5
Cyrus ....289..K 3
Dakota ....369..O 9
Dalton ....221..J 2
Danube ....497..M 4
Danvers ....136..L 3
Darfur ....179..O 4
Darwin ....361..A 7
Dassel ......1,058..A 7
Dawson .....1,699..M 2
Dayton ....517..A 10
Deephaven ..3,853..B 10
Deer Creek ...287..J 3
Deer River ....815..H 6
Deerwood .....448..J 5
De Graff ......195..L 3
Delano .....1,851..A 9
Delavan ....281..O 5
Delhi ....154..M 3
Dellwood ......524..A 11
Denham ....56..J 7
Dennison* .....203..N 7
Dent ....156..I 3
Detroit Lakes .....6,512.°I 3
Dexter ....252..O 7
Dilworth ....2,341..I 1
Dodge Center ....1,603..O 7
Donaldson ......69..E 1
Donnelly ......252..K 2
Doran ....101..J 2
Dover ....321..O 8
Dovray ....104..O 3
Duluth ...100,578.°I 8
Dumont ....204..K 2
Dundas ....460..N 6
Dundee ....138..O 3
Dunnell ....237..O 4
Eagan* ....10,398..M 7
Eagle Bend ..557..J 4
Eagle Lake ..1,010..N 5
East Bethel .2,586..L 6
East Grand Forks .....8,397..F 1
East Gull Lake 440..J 5
Easton ....352..O 5
Echo ....356..M 3
Eden Prairie* ..9,109..M 6
Eden Valley ..770..L 4
Edgerton ...1,119..O 2
Edina .....44,046..B 10
Effie ....165..G 6
Eitzen ....208..O 9
Elba ....158..O 8
Elbow Lake .1,484.°J 2
Elgin ....580..N 8
Elizabeth .....188..J 2
Elk River ...2,252.°L 6
Elko ....115..C 10
Elkton ....134..O 7
Ellendale .....569..O 6
Ellsworth ......588..O 2
Elmdale ....116..K 5
Elmore ....910..O 5
Elrosa ....203..K 4
Ely ....4,904..F 8
Elysian ....445..N 6
Emily ....386..I 5
Emmons ....412..O 6
Erhard ....148..I 2
Ericsburg ....E 6
Erskine ....571..G 2
Evan ....126..N 4
Evansville .....553..J 3
Eveleth .....4,721..G 7
Excelsior ...2,563..B 9
Eyota ....639..O 8
Fairfax .....1,432..N 4
Fairhaven ....L 5
Fairmont ..10,751.°O 5
Falcon Heights* ..5,641..M 6
Faribault ..16,595.°N 6
Farmington .3,464..C 11
Farwell ....102..K 3
Federal Dam .147..H 5
Felton ....232..H 2
Fergus Falls ....12,443.°J 2
Fertile ....955..G 2
Fifty Lakes ..143..I 5
Finland ....G 9
Finlayson .....192..J 7
Fisher ....383..G 1
Flensburg .....259..K 4
Floodwood .....650..H 7
Florence ....58..N 2
Foley ....1,271.°K 5
Forada ....158..K 3
Forest Lake 3,207..L 7
Foreston ......273..K 6
Fort Ripley ....54..J 5
Fosston .....1,684..G 3
Fountain ......347..O 8
Foxhome ......185..J 2
Franklin ....41..G 7
Franklin ....557..N 4
Fraser ....48..G 7
Frazee ......1,015..I 3
Freeborn ......296..O 6
Freeport ......593..K 4
Fridley ....29,233..A 10
Frost ....290..O 5
Fulda ......1,226..O 3
Funkley ....19..G 5
Garfield ....198..K 3
Garrison ....125..J 6
Garvin ....201..N 3
Gary ....265..G 2
Gaylord .....1,720.°N 5
Gem Lake* ...216..L 7
Geneva ....358..O 6
Genola ....97..K 5
Georgetown ...141..H 1
Ghent ....301..N 2
Gibbon ....877..N 4
Gilbert ......2,563..G 8
Gilman ....111..K 5
Glencoe .....4,217.°C 8
Glenville ......740..O 6
Glenwood ...2,584.°K 3
Glyndon ....674..I 1
Golden Hill ....O 8
Golden Valley* ..24,246..M 6
Gonvick ....344..G 3
Good Thunder 489..O 5
Goodhue ....539..N 7
Goodridge .....177..F 3
Goodview ...1,829..O 9
Graceville .....735..K 2
Granada ....381..O 5
Grand Marais ....1,301.°G 11
Grand Meadow ....869..O 7
Grand Rapids ...7,247.°H 6
Granite Falls 3,225.°M 3
Grasston ......132..K 7
Green Isle ....363..C 8
Greenbush .....787..E 2
Greenfield .....977..A 9
Greenwald .....244..K 4
Greenwood* ..587..L 5
Grey Eagle ...325..K 4
Grove City ...531..L 4
Grygla ....211..F 3
Gully ....96..G 3
Hackensack ...220..H 5
Hadley ....119..O 2
Hallock .....1,477.°D 1
Halma ....96..E 2
Halstad ....598..G 1
Ham Lake ..3,327..L 6
Hamburg ....405..C 8
Hammond ......179..N 8
Hampton ......369..C 11
Hancock ....806..L 3
Hanley Falls .265..M 3
Hanover ....365..A 9
Hanska ....442..N 5
Harding ....119..J 5
Hardwick ......274..O 2
Harmony ...1,130..O 8
Harris ....559..K 7
Hartland ....331..O 6
Hastings ...12,195.°M 7
Hatfield ....96..O 2
Hawley ......1,371..I 2
Hayfield ....939..O 7
Hayward ....261..O 6
Hazel Run ....115..M 3
Hector ......1,178..M 4
Heidelberg ......72..N 6
Henderson .....730..N 5
Hendricks .....712..N 2
Hendrum ....311..H 1
Henning ....850..J 3
Henriette ....56..K 7
Herman ....619..K 2
Heron Lake ..777..O 3
Hewitt ....198..J 4
Hibbing ....16,126..G 7
Hill City ......357..H 6
Hillman ....49..J 5
Hills ....571..O 2
Hilltop .....1,015..A 10
Hinckley ....885..J 7
Hitterdal ....201..H 2
Hoffman ....627..K 3
Hokah ....697..O 9
Holdingford ...551..K 5
Holland ....263..N 2
Hollandale ....287..O 6
Holloway ......146..L 2
Holt ....97..E 2
Homer ....O 9
Hopkins ....13,428..B 10
Houston .....1,090..O 9
Hovland ....F 11
Howard Lake 1,162..A 8
Hoyt Lakes .3,634..G 8
Hugo ....2,669..A 11
Humboldt ......112..D 1
Hutchinson .8,031..M 5
Ihlen ....132..O 2
Independence ....1,993..B 9
International Falls .....6,439.°E 6
Inver Grove Heights ..12,148..B 11
Iona ....260..O 3
Iron Junction .150..G 7
Ironton ....562..J 5
Isanti ....679..L 6
Island View ....44..E 6
Isle ....551..J 6
Ivanhoe ......738.°N 2
Jackson .....3,550.°O 4
Janesville ...1,557..O 6
Jasper ....754..O 2
Jeffers ....436..O 3
Jenkins ....148..I 5
Johnson ....53..K 2
Jordan ......1,836..C 9
Kandiyohi ....295..L 4
Karlstad ....727..E 2
Kasota ....732..N 5
Kasson .....1,883..O 7
Keewatin ...1,382..G 7
Kelliher ....289..F 5
Kellogg ....403..N 8
Kelly Lake ....G 7
Kennedy ....424..E 2
Kenneth ....89..O 2
Kensington ....308..K 3
Kent ....139..J 1
Kenyon .....1,575..N 7
Kerkhoven .....641..L 3
Kerrick ....114..J 7
Kettle River ..173..I 7
Kiester ....681..O 6
Kilkenny ......182..N 6
Kimball Prairie ....567..L 5
Kinbrae ....37..O 3
Kingston ....115..A 7
Kinney ....325..G 7
La Crescent .3,296..O 9
Lafayette ......498..N 5

Lake Benton ..759..N 2
Lake Bronson .325..D 2
Lake City ..3,887..N 8
Lake
  Crystal ..1,807..O 5
Lake Elmo* .4,798..M 7
Lake George ....H 4
Lake Henry ...92..L 4
Lake Lillian .316..M 4
Lake Park .658..I 2
Lake St. Croix
  Beach ..1,111..B 12
Lake Shore ..410..I 5
Lake Wilson .378..O 2
Lakefield ..1,820..O 3
Lakeland ..962..B 12
Lakeland
  Shores* ....72..M 7
Lakeville ..7,196..C 10
Lamberton ..962..N 3
Lancaster ..382..D 1
Landfall ..671..B 11
Lanesboro ..850..O 8
Lansing ......O 7
Laporte ...154..H 4
La Prairie ..413..H 6
La Salle ..132..O 4
Lastrup ...161..J 5
Lauderdale .2,571..B 11
Le Center .1,890..N 6
Lengby ...140..G 3
Leonard ...54..G 3
Leonidas ..157..G 7
Leota .....O 2
Le Roy ..870..O 8
Lester
  Prairie ..1,162..B 8
Le Sueur ..3,745..N 5
Lewiston ..1,000..O 9
Lewisville ..291..O 5
Lexington ..2,140..A 11
Lilydale ..664..B 11
Lindstrom ..1,260..L 7
Lino Lakes .3,692..A 11
Lismore ...323..O 2
Litchfield .5,262..L 5
Little
  Canada* ..5,977..M 7
Little Falls .7,467..K 5
Littlefork ..824..E 6
Long Beach ..219..K 3
Long Lake* ..1,506..M 5
Long
  Prairie ..2,416..K 4
Longville ..171..H 5
Lonsdale ..622..N 6
Loretto ..340..A 9
Louisburg ...75..L 2
Lowry ...257..K 3
Lucan ...254..N 3
Luverne ..4,703..O 2
Lyle ...522..O 7
Lynd ...267..N 2
Mabel ...888..O 9
Madelia ..2,316..O 5
Madison ..2,242..M 2
Madison Lake* .587..N 5
Magnolia ...203..O 2
Mahnomen .1,313..H 2
Mahtomedi* .3,799..M 7
Manchester ...89..O 6
Manhattan
  Beach ....46..I 5
Mankato ..30,895..N 5
Mantorville ..479..N 7
Maple Grove 10,039..A 9
Maple Lake ..1,124..A 8
Maple Plain* 1,169..M 5
Mapleton ..1,307..O 5
Mapleview ..328..O 7
Maplewood .25,186..A 11
Marble ...682..H 6
Marietta ...264..M 2
Marine-on-St.
  Croix ...513..A 12
Marshall ..9,886..N 3
Mayer ...325..B 8
Maynard ..455..M 3
Mazeppa ..498..N 7
McGrath ....70..J 6
McGregor ..331..I 6
McIntosh ..753..G 3
McKinley ..317..G 8
Meadowlands .128..H 7
Medford ..690..N 6
Medicine Lake* 446..M 6
Medina ..2,396..A 9
Meire Grove .171..K 4
Melrose ..2,273..K 4
Menahga ..835..I 4
Mendota ...327..B 11
Mendota
  Heights ..6,165..B 11
Mentor ...236..G 2
Merrifield .....J 5
Middle River .369..E 2
Miesville ...192..C 12
Milaca ..1,940..K 6
Milan ...427..L 2
Millerville ..109..J 3
Millville ..139..N 8
Milroy ...247..N 3
Miltona ...172..J 3
Minneapo-
  lis ..434,400..M 6
Minneiska ...80..N 9
Minneota ..1,320..N 2
Minnesota
  City ....301..O 9
Minnesota
  Lake ....738..O 5

Minnetonka 35,737..B 10
Minnetonka
  Beach* ....586..M 7
Minnetrista* 2,878..L 6
Mizpah ...118..F 5
Montevideo ..5,661..M 3
Montgomery .2,383..N 6
Monticello ..1,636..L 6
Montrose ...379..A 8
Moorhead ..29,687..I 1
Moose Lake .1,400..J 7
Mora ..2,582..K 6
Morgan ...972..N 4
Morris ..5,366..K 2
Morristown ..659..N 6
Morton ...591..N 4
Motley ...351..J 4
Mound ..7,572..B 9
Mounds
  View ...10,641..A 11
Mountain
  Iron ...1,698..G 7
Mountain
  Lake ...1,986..O 4
Murdock ...358..L 3
Myrtle ....83..O 7
Nashua ...114..J 2
Nashwauk ..1,341..G 6
Nassau ...126..L 2
Nelson ...175..K 3
Nerstrand ..231..N 7
Nevis ...308..H 4
New Auburn ..274..C 7
New
  Brighton* 19,507..M 7
New Germany .303..B 8
New Hope .23,180..B 10
New London ..736..L 4
New Market ..215..C 10
New Munich ..307..K 4
New Prague .2,680..D 9
New
  Richland ..1,113..O 6
New Trier ...153..C 11
New Ulm .13,051..N 5
New York
  Mills ....791..I 3
Newfolden ..390..E 2
Newport ..2,922..B 11
Nicollet ...618..N 5
Nielsville ...156..G 1
Nimrod ....64..I 4
Nisswa ..1,011..I 5
Norcross ...137..K 2
North
  Branch ..1,106..L 7
North
  Mankato ..8,071..N 5
North Oaks* 2,002..A 11
North Redwood 155..N 4
North St.
  Paul* ..11,950..M 7
Northfield .10,235..N 7
Northome ...351..F 5
Northrop ...188..O 5
Norwood ..1,058..C 8
Oak Park ....K 6
Oak Park
  Heights ..1,238..A 12
Oakdale* ..7,795..M 7
Oakland .....O 7
Odessa ...194..L 2
Odin ...166..O 4
Ogema ...236..H 2
Ogilvie ...384..K 6
Okabena ...237..O 3
Oklee ...536..F 3
Olivia ..2,553..M 4
Onamia ...670..J 6
Ormsby ...199..O 4
Orono ..6,787..B 9
Oronoco ...564..N 7
Orr ...315..F 7
Ortonville .2,665..L 2
Osakis ..1,306..K 4
Oslo ...417..F 1
Osseo* ..2,908..A 10
Ostrander ...216..O 8
Otter Tail ...180..J 3
Owatonna ..15,341..O 6
Palisade ...149..I 6
Park Rapids 2,772..H 4
Parkers
  Prairie ...882..J 3
Paynesville .1,920..L 5
Pease ...187..K 5
Pelican Lakes 233..I 5
Pelican
  Rapids ..1,835..I 2
Pemberton ..128..O 6
Pennock ...255..L 4
Pequot Lakes .499..I 5
Perham ..1,933..I 3
Perley ...149..H 1
Peterson ...269..O 9
Pierz ...893..K 5
Pillager ...184..I 5
Pine City ..2,143..K 7
Pine Island .1,640..N 7
Pine River ..803..I 5
Pine Springs* .204..M 7
Pipestone ..5,328..O 2
Plainview ..2,093..N 8
Plato ...303..C 8
Pleasant Lake .65..L 5
Plummer ...285..F 2
Plymouth .18,077..B 10
Porter ...207..M 2
Preston ..1,413..O 8
Princeton ..2,531..K 6

Prinsburg ....448..M 3
Prior Lake ..1,114..C 10
Proctor ..3,123..I 8
Quamba ...114..K 6
Racine ...197..O 8
Ramsey ..7,170..A 9
Randall ...536..J 5
Randolph ...350..N 7
Ranier ...255..E 6
Raymond ...589..M 3
Red Lake
  Falls ..1,740..F 2
Red Wing .12,834..N 7
Redwood
  Falls ..4,774..N 4
Regal ....44..L 4
Remer ...403..H 5
Renville ..1,438..M 3
Revere ...166..N 3
Rice ...448..K 5
Richfield .47,231..B 10
Richmond ...866..L 5
Richville ...102..I 3
Riverton ...103..J 5
Robbins-
  dale* ..16,845..L 6
Rochester ..53,766..O 8
Rock Creek* .815..J 7
Rockford ...730..A 9
Rockville ...302..L 5
Rogers ...544..A 9
Rollingstone ..450..O 9
Ronneby ....59..K 5
Roosevelt ...104..D 4
Roscoe ...195..L 4
Rose Creek ...504..O 7
Roseau ..2,552..D 3
Rosemount .4,034..C 11
Roseville ..34,438..B 11
Rothsay ...448..I 2
Round Lake ..506..O 3
Royalton ...534..K 5
Rush City .1,130..K 7
Rushford ..1,318..O 9
Rushford* ...601..O 9
Rushmore ...394..O 2
Russell ...398..N 2
Ruthton ...405..N 2
Rutledge ...123..J 7
Sabin ...333..I 1
Sacred Heart .707..M 3
St. Anthony ...66..K 4
St. Anthony* 9,239..M 6
St. Bonifacius .685..B 9
St. Charles ..1,942..O 8
St. Clair ...488..O 5
St. Cloud .40,715..K 5
St. Francis* ..897..L 6
St. Hilaire ...358..F 2
St. James ..4,027..O 4
St. Joseph ..1,786..K 5
St. Leo ...153..M 2
St. Louis
  Park .48,922..B 10
St. Martin ...188..L 4
St. Marys
  Point* ...319..M 7
St. Michael .1,021..A 9
St. Paul .309,714..M 7
St. Paul
  Park ..5,587..B 11
St. Peter ..8,339..N 5
St. Rosa ...93..K 4
St. Stephens .331..K 5
St. Vincent ..177..D 1
Sanborn ...505..N 4
Sandstone ..1,641..J 7
Sargeant ....85..O 7
Sartell ..2,665..K 5
Sauk Centre .3,750..K 4
Sauk Rapids 5,051..K 5
Savage ..3,611..C 10

Scandia ......A 12
Scanlon ..1,132..I 8
Seaforth ...132..N 3
Sebeka ...668..I 4
Sedan ....55..K 3
Shafer ...149..L 7
Shakopee ..7,727..C 10
Shelly ...260..G 1
Sherburn ..1,190..O 4
Shevlin ...185..G 3
Shoreview .10,995..A 11
Shorewood ..4,223..B 9
Silver Bay .3,504..H 9
Silver Lake ..694..B 7
Skyline ...400..N 5
Slayton ..2,351..O 3
Sleepy Eye .3,461..N 4
Sobieski ...189..K 5
Solway ....96..G 4
South Haven ..238..L 5
South International
  Falls ..2,116..E 6
South
  St. Paul .25,016..B 11
Spicer ...586..L 4
Spring Grove 1,290..O 9
Spring Hill ...90..K 4
Spring Lake
  Park ..6,417..A 10
Spring Park* 1,087..M 6
Spring
  Valley ..2,572..O 8
Springfield .2,530..N 4
Squaw Lake ..113..G 5
Stacy ...278..L 7
Staples ..2,755..J 4
Starbuck ..1,138..K 3
Steen ...191..O 2
Stephen ...904..E 1
Stewart ...666..C 7
Stewartville .2,802..O 8
Stillwater .10,191..A 12
Stockton ...346..O 9
Storden ...364..O 3
Strandquist ..138..E 2
Strathcona ...31..E 2
Sturgeon Lake 167..J 7
Sunburg ...144..L 3
Sunfish Lake* 269..M 7
Swanville ...300..K 4
Swatara .....H 6
Taconite ...352..H 6
Tamarack ...100..I 7
Taopi ....59..O 7
Taunton ...195..M 2
Taylors Falls .587..L 7
Tenney ....24..J 2
Tenstrike ...138..G 4
Thief River
  Falls ..8,929..F 2
Thomson ...159..I 8
Tintah ...167..J 2
Tonka Bay* 1,397..M 6
Tower ...699..G 8
Tracy ..2,516..N 3
Trail ....99..G 3
Trimont ...835..O 4
Trommald ....82..I 5
Trosky ...109..O 2
Truman ..1,137..O 5
Turtle River ..50..G 4
Twin Lakes ..230..O 6
Twin Valley ..868..H 2
Two Harbors 4,437..H 9
Tyler ..1,069..N 2
Ulen ...486..H 2
Underwood ..278..J 2
Upsala ...312..K 4
Urbank ...125..J 3
Utica ...240..O 8
Vadnais
  Heights* .3,411..M 7

Vergas ...281..I 3
Vermillion ..359..C 11
Verndale ...570..J 4
Vernon Center 347..O 5
Veseli .....N 6
Vesta ...330..N 3
Victoria ...850..B 9
Viking ...118..F 2
Villard ...221..K 3
Vining ...121..J 3
Virginia .12,463..G 7
Wabasha ..2,371..N 8
Wabasso ..893..N 3
Waconia ..2,445..B 9
Wahkon ...208..J 6
Waite Park .2,824..K 5
Waldorf ...285..O 6
Walker ..1,073..H 4
Walnut Grove .756..N 3
Walters ...152..O 6
Waltham ...189..O 7
Wanamingo ..574..N 7
Wanda ...124..N 3
Warba ...148..H 6
Warren ..1,999..F 1
Warroad ..1,086..D 2
Warsaw .....N 6
Waseca ..7,804..O 6
Watertown ..1,390..B 8
Waterville ..1,539..N 6
Watkins ...785..L 5
Watson ...228..M 3
Waubun ...345..H 2
Waverly ...573..A 8
Wayzata* .3,700..M 6
Webster .....N 6
Welcome ...694..O 4
Wells ..2,791..O 6
Wendell ...247..J 2
West Concord .718..N 7
West St.
  Paul ..18,799..B 11
West Union ...71..K 4
Westbrook ..990..O 3
Westport ....65..K 4
Whalan ...114..O 8
Wheaton ..2,029..K 2
White Bear
  Lake ..23,313..A 11
White Earth .....H 3
Wilder ...132..O 3
Willernie ...697..A 11
Williams ...264..D 4
Willmar .13,600..L 4
Willow River .331..J 7
Wilmont ...390..O 2
Wilton ...119..G 4
Windom ..3,952..O 4
Winger ...228..G 2
Winnebago .1,791..O 5
Winona ..26,438..O 9
Winsted ..1,266..B 8
Winthrop ..1,391..D 7
Winton ...193..F 8
Wolf Lake ...58..I 3
Wolverton ...171..I 1
Wood Lake ..418..M 3
Woodbury* ..6,184..M 7
Woodland* ...544..M 6
Woodstock ...217..O 2
Worthington 9,916..O 3
Wrenshall ...147..I 8
Wright ...132..I 7
Wykoff ...450..O 8
Wyoming ...695..L 7
Young
  America ...611..C 8
Zemple ....71..H 6
Zimmerman ..495..K 6
Zumbro Falls .203..N 8
Zumbrota ..1,929..N 7

Sources: Latest census figures (1970 and special censuses). Places without population figures are unincorporated areas and are not listed in census reports. *Does not appear on the map; key shows general location. °County seat.

National Park Service

Voyageurs National Park lies in northern Minnesota near the United States-Canadian border. Most travel in the park takes place on waterways.

503

The 1970 U.S. census reported that Minnesota had 3,805,069 persons. The state's population had increased 12 per cent over the 1960 census figure, 3,413,864. The U.S. Bureau of the Census estimated that by 1975 the state's population had reached 3,926,000.

About two-thirds of the people of Minnesota live in urban areas. About half live in the Minneapolis-St. Paul metropolitan area. Minnesota has six Standard Metropolitan Statistical Areas (see METROPOLITAN AREA). For the populations of these metropolitan areas, see the *Index* to the political map of Minnesota.

Minneapolis is the largest city in Minnesota. It adjoins St. Paul, Minnesota's capital and second largest city. The *Twin Cities*, as they are called, serve as the state's leading cultural, financial, and commercial center. Duluth, Minnesota's third largest city, is the westernmost port on the Great Lakes and an important industrial center. See the articles on Minnesota cities listed in the *Related Articles* at the end of this article.

About 97 of every 100 Minnesotans were born in the United States. The largest groups of Minnesotans who were born in other countries came from Denmark, Finland, Norway, and Sweden. Many also came from Austria, Canada, Germany, Great Britain, Poland, and Russia. Lutherans and Roman Catholics are the largest religious groups in Minnesota. Other large religious groups include Methodists, Presbyterians, and members of the United Church of Christ.

POPULATION

This map shows the *population density* of Minnesota, and how it varies in different parts of the state. Population density means the average number of persons who live in a given area.

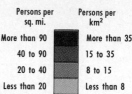

Persons per sq. mi.		Persons per km²
More than 90		More than 35
40 to 90		15 to 35
20 to 40		8 to 15
Less than 20		Less than 8

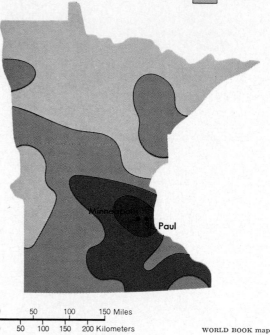

Minneapolis
St. Paul

| 0 | 50 | 100 | 150 Miles |
| 0 | 50 | 100 | 150 | 200 Kilometers |

WORLD BOOK map

Jerry Stransky, Webb AgPhotos

The Crystal Court Mall of the IDS Center in downtown Minneapolis attracts many shoppers. About half of Minnesota's people live in the Minneapolis-St. Paul metropolitan area.

Minnesota Dept. of Economic Development

Many Minnesota Indians, including this father and son, harvest wild rice. They gather the grain the same way their ancestors did. Minnesota has one of the largest Indian populations in the Midwest.

University of Minnesota

MINNESOTA / *Education*

Schools. The first teachers in Minnesota were missionaries who worked among the Indians. About 1820, the first school for white children was opened at Fort St. Anthony (later renamed Fort Snelling). Missionaries set up many Indian schools during the 1830's. In 1849, the territorial legislature passed a law providing for the establishment of public schools in Minnesota.

The state board of education directs the state department of education. The board has nine members. They are appointed to four-year terms by the governor with the approval of the state Senate. The board appoints its chief administrative officer, the commissioner of education, to a four-year term. Minnesota children are required to attend school between their 7th and 16th birthdays. For the number of students and teachers in Minnesota, see EDUCATION (table).

Libraries. Minnesota has about 150 public libraries. The largest public libraries in the state are those serving Minneapolis, St. Paul, and Hennepin County. The libraries of the Twin Cities Campus of the University of Minnesota have about $3\frac{1}{2}$ million volumes, the largest collection in the state. The Minnesota Historical Society library in St. Paul dates from 1849. It has one of the nation's largest collections of historical books about Minnesota and the Midwest. The University of Minnesota library owns the largest collection of books in the United States about Scandinavian countries. Other special collections include the State Law Library in St. Paul, the medical library of the Mayo Foundation in Rochester, and the James J. Hill Reference Library in St. Paul.

Museums. The Minneapolis Institute of Arts and the Walker Art Center, also in Minneapolis, have many outstanding works of art. The Minnesota Historical Society Museum in St. Paul features exhibits on the state's history. The American Swedish Institute in Minneapolis has glassware, antique furniture, and other items. The Science Museum of Minnesota in St. Paul

has exhibits on biology and other sciences. The University of Minnesota operates the James Ford Bell Museum of Natural History. The Lake Superior Museum of Transportation in Duluth features railroad cars. The Mayo Foundation sponsors the Mayo Medical Museum in Rochester.

———— UNIVERSITIES AND COLLEGES ————

Minnesota has 22 universities and colleges accredited by the North Central Association of Colleges and Schools. For enrollments and further information, see UNIVERSITIES AND COLLEGES (table).

Name	Location	Founded
Augsburg College	Minneapolis	1869
Bethel College and Seminary	St. Paul	1871
Carleton College	Northfield	1866
Concordia College	Moorhead	1891
Concordia College	St. Paul	1893
Gustavus Adolphus College	St. Peter	1862
Hamline University	St. Paul	1854
Macalester College	St. Paul	1885
Minneapolis College of Art and Design	Minneapolis	1886
Minnesota, University of	*	*
Minnesota State University System	*	*
Northwestern College	Roseville	1902
St. Benedict, College of	St. Joseph	1913
St. Catherine, College of	St. Paul	1905
St. John's University	Collegeville	1857
St. Mary's College	Winona	1912
St. Olaf College	Northfield	1874
St. Paul Seminary	St. Paul	1896
St. Scholastica, College of	Duluth	1912
St. Teresa, College of	Winona	1907
St. Thomas, College of	St. Paul	1885
United Theological Seminary of the Twin Cities	New Brighton	1960

*For campuses and founding dates, see UNIVERSITIES AND COLLEGES (table).

Minnesota is one of the nation's most popular playgrounds. Every year, about 5½ million residents and out-of-state visitors spend their vacations in Minnesota. Thousands of sparkling blue lakes attract swimmers, water skiers, and boaters. Fishermen find the cool northern waters filled with a great variety of game fish. The many animals challenge the hunter's skill. Wooded parks and deep forests are scattered throughout the state. Many campers pitch their tents under the tall pines, and sleep and cook outdoors.

PLACES TO VISIT

Following are brief descriptions of some of Minnesota's most interesting places to visit.

Fort Snelling is a restored military post near Minneapolis. It was built in the 1820's and features demonstrations dealing with military life of that period.

High Falls, on the Pigeon River along the Minnesota-Ontario border in Cook County, plunges over cliffs that are 133 feet (41 meters) high. Nearby are the remains of Fort Charlotte, an important trading post of the late 1700's.

Lumbertown, U.S.A., in Brainerd, is a reconstruction of a typical early logging town.

Mayo Clinic and Foundation, in Rochester, offers tours of the world-famous medical center.

Northwest Angle is the most northern part of the United States outside Alaska. A scenic boat trip runs from Warroad across Lake of the Woods to the angle.

Sibley House, in Mendota, is the oldest stone house in Minnesota. Henry H. Sibley, the state's first governor, built it in 1835. It has displays of pioneer furniture.

Statues of Paul Bunyan and Babe, in Bemidji, honor the legendary lumberman and his giant blue ox. Brainerd also has huge statues of Paul and his ox.

The Guthrie Theater, in Minneapolis, is a strikingly designed playhouse that opened in 1963. A permanent company of actors presents a series of plays every year.

National Parklands in Minnesota include two national monuments—Grand Portage and Pipestone. Grand Portage National Monument, on the northwestern shore of Lake Superior, marks the site of a historic canoe route and trading post. Indians once made peace pipes from the red pipestone found at Pipestone National Monument. Voyageurs National Park, in northern Minnesota, includes scenic lakes. The National Park Service manages several other national parklands in the state. For information on these areas, see the map and table in the WORLD BOOK article on NATIONAL PARK SYSTEM.

National Forests. Minnesota has two national forests. Superior National Forest lies in the northeast. Chippewa National Forest covers much of Itasca County and parts of Beltrami and Cass counties. For the features of each national forest, see NATIONAL FOREST (table).

State Parks and Forests. Minnesota has about 65 state parks and about 45 state forests. It began developing its state park system in the 1890's. For information on the state parks, write to Commissioner, Division of State Parks, Department of Natural Resources, Centennial Office Building, St. Paul, Minn. 55101.

Minnesota Dept. of Economic Development
High Falls on the Pigeon River

Minnesota Dept. of Economic Development
Sibley House in Mendota

Statues of Paul Bunyan and
Babe in Bemidji

Robert J. Kohl

Anthony Stack, Tom Stack & Associates

The Guthrie Theater in Minneapolis

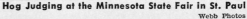

Hog Judging at the Minnesota State Fair in St. Paul
Webb Photos

Minnesota Dept. of Economic Development

Grand Portage National Monument

ANNUAL EVENTS

Minnesota's long, cold winters are ideal for winter carnivals and sports festivals. The St. Paul Winter Carnival begins the last week in January. The carnival features ice-skating races and ski-jumping contests. A snowmobile race is also held across the U.S.-Canadian border. The Minneapolis Aquatennial, held in July, features a canoe derby, costume balls, a torchlight parade, and water ballets. Minnesota holds its State Fair in St. Paul from late August through Labor Day. Other annual events in Minnesota include the following.

January-March: Snowmobile races in Park Rapids and Willmar (January); Sled Dog Races in Ely and Walker (January); Winter Carnival in Bemidji (January); Red River Valley Winter Show in Crookston (February); Ski Tur Derby in Cass Lake (March).

April-June: Inventors Congress in Redwood Falls (June); Fiesta Days in Montevideo (June); Svenskarnas Dag (Swedish) in Minneapolis (June); Water Ski Days in Lake City (June).

July-September: Agate Days in Moose Lake (July); Steamboat Days in Winona (July); Regatta in Walker (July); Pow Wow in Red Lake (July); Art Fair in Lutsen (July); Hiawatha Pageant in Pipestone (July-August); Northwest Water Carnival in Detroit Lakes (July); Lumberjack Days in Stillwater (August); Threshing Festival in Butterfield (August); Renaissance Festival in Shakopee (August-September, six consecutive weekends); Threshing Reunion in Rollag (August-September); Apple Festival in La Crescent (September); Marigold Days in Mantorville (September); King Turkey Day in Worthington (September).

October-December: Halloween festival in Anoka (October); Pumpkin Festival in Owatonna (October); Sled Dog Races in Walker (December); Victorian Christmas Fair in Minneapolis (November-December).

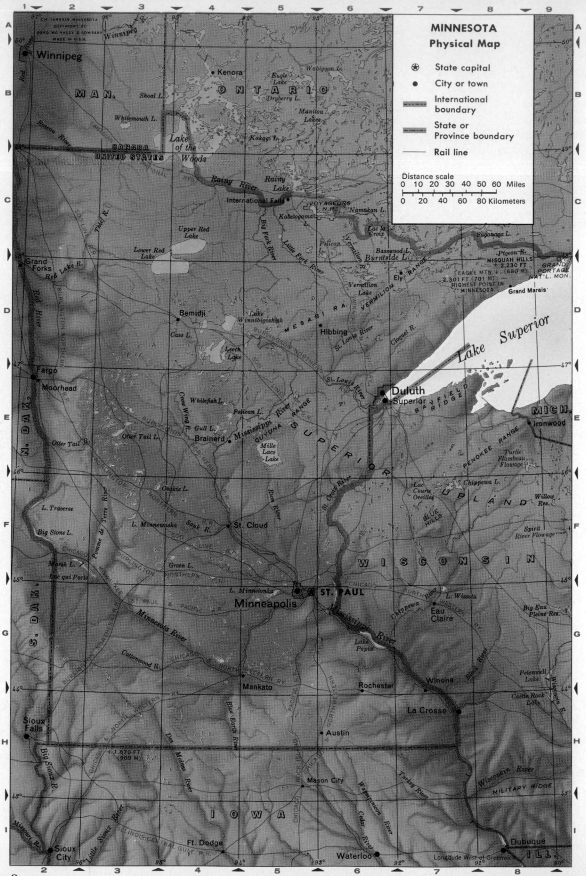

MINNESOTA
Physical Map

⊛ State capital
● City or town
International boundary
State or Province boundary
Rail line

Distance scale
0 10 20 30 40 50 60 Miles
0 20 40 60 80 Kilometers

Winnipeg

MAN.

ONTARIO

Kenora

Eagle Lake

Wabigoon L.

Shoal L.

Dryberry L.

Manitou Lakes

Whitemouth L.

Roseau River

CANADA
UNITED STATES

Lake of the Woods

Kakagi L.

Rainy River

Rainy Lake

International Falls

VOYAGEURS N.P.

Namakan L.

Kabetogama L.

Lac la Croix

Saganaga L.

Upper Red Lake

Big Fork River

Little Fork River

Pelican L.

Vermilion River

Basswood L.

Burntside L.

MISQUAH HILLS + 2,230 FT

Pigeon R.

GRAND PORTAGE NAT'L. MON.

Grand Forks

Red Lake R.

Lower Red Lake

Lake Winnibigoshish

MESABI RA.

Vermilion Lake

VERMILION

Ely

RANGE

EAGLE MTN. + 2,301 FT. (701 M) HIGHEST POINT IN MINNESOTA

(680 M)

Grand Marais

Bemidji

Cass L.

Hibbing

St. Louis River

Cloquet R.

Lake Superior

Fargo

Moorhead

Leech Lake

Whitefish L.

Pelican L.

Mississippi River

CUYUNA RANGE

St. Louis River

Duluth
Superior

BAYFIELD BRIDGED

MICH.

Ironwood

Otter Tail R.

Otter Tail L.

Crow Wing R.

Gull L.

Brainerd

SUPERIOR

PENOKEE RANGE

Turtle Flambeau Flowage

Mille Lacs Lake

Osakis L.

Rum River

Lac Courte Oreilles

Chippewa L.

Willow Res.

L. Traverse

L. Minnewaska

Sauk R.

St. Cloud

St. Croix River

BLUE HILLS

UPLAND

Spirit River Flowage

Big Stone L.

Pomme de Terre River

Green L.

WISCONSIN

Marsh L.

Lac qui Parle

L. Minnetonka

ST. PAUL

CHICAGO

L. Wissota

Big Eau Pleine Res.

Minneapolis

Mississippi River

Chippewa River

Eau Claire

Lake Pepin

Petenwell Lake

Minnesota River

Cottonwood R.

Mankato

Blue Earth River

Rochester

Winona

Black River

Castle Rock Lake

Wisconsin River

S. DAK.

N. DAK.

Sioux Falls

Big Sioux R.

+ 1,870 FT. (569 M)

Des Moines River

Austin

La Crosse

MILITARY RIDGE

Missouri R.

Sioux City

Little Sioux River

Ft. Dodge

Mason City

Cedar River

Waterloo

Turkey River

Wapsipinicon River

Wisconsin River

Dubuque

ILL.

IOWA

Longitude West of Greenwich

508

Specially created for **World Book Encyclopedia** by Rand McNally and World Book editors

During the Ice Age, which began about 1½ million years ago, a series of glaciers moved across Minnesota. Scientists believe the last glacier retreated from the region about 10,000 years ago. As the glaciers advanced south and west across Minnesota, they leveled most of the land. Only a small area in the southeast was untouched. The glaciers created gently rolling plains over most of the state. Thousands of low places formed by the glaciers filled with water. These places became lakes, swamps, or marshes.

Land Regions. Minnesota has four major land regions: (1) the Superior Upland, (2) the Young Drift Plains, (3) the Dissected Till Plains, and (4) the Driftless Area.

The Superior Upland is part of the southern tip of the Canadian Shield. The Canadian Shield is a vast area lying over old, hard rock. It covers about half of Canada (see CANADIAN SHIELD). The glaciers had less effect on the hard rock of the Superior Upland than on most other regions of the state. That is why this region includes the most rugged part of Minnesota. The area just north of Lake Superior is the roughest, most isolated part of the state. Eagle Mountain in Cook County is 2,301 feet (701 meters) high. It is Minnesota's highest point. The northeastern tip of the Superior Upland has an arrowhead shape, and is called the *Arrowhead Country.* Most of Minnesota's iron ore deposits are in the Superior Upland region.

The Young Drift Plains consist mainly of gently rolling farmlands. Glaciers smoothed the surface of this region, and deposited great amounts of fertile topsoil called *drift* as they melted. The region has some of the

Map Index

Basswood Lake	C 7	Mille Lacs Lake	E 5
Big Fork R.	C 5	Minnesota R.	G 3
Big Stone Lake	F 2	Misquah Hills	D 7
Blue Earth R.	H 4	Misquah Hills	D 8
Burntside Lake	D 6	Mississippi R.	G 6
Cass Lake	D 4	Namakan Lake	C 6
Cedar R.	I 6	Osakis Lake	F 3
Chippewa R.	G 7	Otter Tail Lake	E 3
Cloquet R.	D 7	Otter Tail R.	E 2
Cottonwood R.	G 3	Pelican Lake	C 6
Crow Wing R.	E 4	Pelican Lake	E 4
Cuyuna Range	E 5	Pigeon R.	C 9
Des Moines R.,		Pomme de Terre R.	F 3
West Fork	H 3	Rainy Lake	C 5
Eagle Mtn.		Rainy R.	C 4
(Highest Point		Red Lake R.	D 2
in Minnesota)	D 8	Red River of	
Green Lake	F 4	the North	D 2
Gull Lake	E 4	Roseau R.	B 2
Kabetogama Lake	C 6	Rum R.	F 5
Lac la Croix (Lake)	C 6	Saganaga Lake	C 8
Lac qui Parle (Lake)	F 2	St. Croix R.	F 6
Lake Minnetonka	G 3	St. Louis R.	D 6
Lake Minnewaska	F 3	St. Louis R.	E 6
Lake of the Woods	C 4	Sauk R.	F 4
Lake Pepin	G 8	Superior Upland	E 5
Lake Superior	D 8	Thief R.	C 2
Lake Traverse	F 2	Upper Red Lake	C 4
Leech Lake	D 4	Vermilion Lake	D 6
Little Fork R.	C 5	Vermilion Range	D 6
Lower Red Lake	C 3	Vermilion R.	C 6
Marsh Lake	F 2	Whitefish Lake	E 4
Mesabi Range	D 5	Winnibigoshish Lake	D 4

Land Regions of Minnesota

Duluth Harbor on Lake Superior is a St. Lawrence Seaway terminal. It joins the Superior, Wis., harbor to form one of the largest ports in the United States.

Norton and Peel

Minnehaha Falls in Minneapolis is in Minnesota's Young Drift Plains region.

National Park Service

An Indian Entertains Visitors at Pipestone National Monument. The red rock, called pipestone, is in the Dissected Till Plains.

Minnesota Dept. of Economic Development

You Can Walk Across the Mississippi River, *above,* where the river begins in the Superior Upland. This region includes the loneliest, most rugged parts of Minnesota. Apple orchards, *below,* thrive near La Crescent in the Driftless Area.

Norton and Peel

nation's richest farmland, and it is the most important farming area in Minnesota. Parts of the Drift Plains are sandy or stony, and not so well suited for crop farming. *Moraines* can be found in some places, especially in central Minnesota. These are deposits of stones and other earth materials pushed before or along the sides of the glaciers. The moraine areas are hilly and have many lakes. The northernmost tip of the Drift Plains was once part of the bed of Lake Agassiz, a huge lake that drained away at the end of the Ice Age (see LAKE AGASSIZ). Marshlands and wooded areas lie in parts of this northern section. But most of it is a level and almost treeless plain.

The Dissected Till Plains cover the southwestern corner of Minnesota. There, the glaciers left a thick deposit of *till*—a soil-forming material of sand, gravel, and clay. Streams have *dissected* (cut up) the region. The region's few level areas make excellent farmland.

The Driftless Area lies along the Mississippi River in the southeastern corner. Although glaciers never touched this region, the western part is almost flat. Swift-flowing streams have cut deep valleys into the eastern part, giving it a broken surface.

Lakes, Rivers, and Waterfalls. Minnesota has one of the greatest water areas of any state. Its thousands of inland lakes cover more than 4,750 square miles (12,300 square kilometers)—over a twentieth of the state's area. The number of lakes in Minnesota has been estimated as high as 22,000. There are more than 15,000 known lake basins in the state that cover 10 acres (4 hectares) or more. But opinions differ on how large a body of water must be to be properly called a lake.

The largest lake within the state, Red Lake, covers 430 square miles (1,110 square kilometers). Other big northern lakes include Cass Lake, Lake of the Woods, Leech Lake, Vermilion Lake, and Winnibigoshish Lake. Large lakes elsewhere include Big Stone Lake and Lake Traverse, in the west; and Mille Lacs Lake and Lake Minnetonka, near the center of the state.

Lake Itasca, in north-central Minnesota, is the source of the mighty Mississippi River. It flows out of the lake as a small, clear stream about 10 feet (3 meters) wide and less than 2 feet (61 centimeters) deep.

The Mississippi and its branches drain about 57 per cent of Minnesota. The Mississippi's chief branches include the Crow Wing, Minnesota, Rum, St. Croix, and Sauk rivers. The Rainy River and the Red River of the North drain the northern and northwestern areas of the state. The St. Louis and other rivers that empty into Lake Superior drain the land north of the lake.

One of Minnesota's most beautiful waterfalls is Minnehaha Falls, on Minnehaha Creek in Minneapolis. Henry Wadsworth Longfellow made this 53-foot (16-meter) falls famous in his poem *The Song of Hiawatha.* The 49-foot (15-meter) Falls of St. Anthony, on the Mississippi River in Minneapolis, was an important source of power in the early development of Minneapolis. The highest waterfall entirely within the state is 124-foot (38-meter) Cascade Falls, on the Cascade River in Cook County. Another famous waterfall is High Falls, along the Minnesota-Ontario border in Cook County. High Falls drops 133 feet (41 meters).

MINNESOTA / Climate

In July, Minnesota averages 68° F. (20° C) in the north and 74° F. (23° C) in the south. The record high, 114° F. (46° C), was set at Beardsley on July 29, 1917, and at Moorhead on July 6, 1936. January temperatures average 2° F. (−17° C) in the north and 15° F. (−9° C) in the south. The record low, −59° F. (−51° C), was set at Leech Lake Dam on Feb. 9, 1899, and at Pokegama Falls (now Pokegama Dam) on Feb. 16, 1903. Northwestern Minnesota has about 19 inches (48 centimeters) of *precipitation* (rain, melted snow, and other forms of moisture) yearly. The southeast receives about 32 inches (81 centimeters) of precipitation a year. Snowfall averages 20 inches (51 centimeters) annually in the southwest and 70 inches (180 centimeters) in the northeast.

St. Paul Winter Carnival Assn.

Ice Skaters race in St. Paul. Many Minnesota cities hold exciting sports carnivals during the long, severe winters.

SEASONAL TEMPERATURES

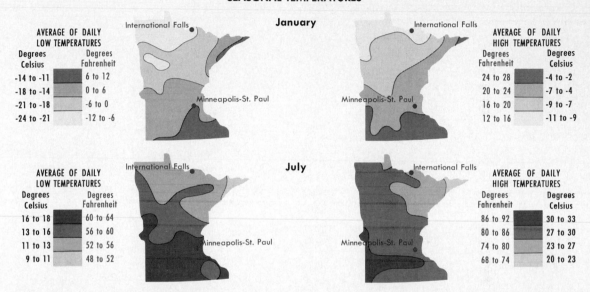

January

AVERAGE OF DAILY LOW TEMPERATURES

Degrees Celsius	Degrees Fahrenheit
-14 to -11	6 to 12
-18 to -14	0 to 6
-21 to -18	-6 to 0
-24 to -21	-12 to -6

AVERAGE OF DAILY HIGH TEMPERATURES

Degrees Fahrenheit	Degrees Celsius
24 to 28	-4 to -2
20 to 24	-7 to -4
16 to 20	-9 to -7
12 to 16	-11 to -9

July

AVERAGE OF DAILY LOW TEMPERATURES

Degrees Celsius	Degrees Fahrenheit
16 to 18	60 to 64
13 to 16	56 to 60
11 to 13	52 to 56
9 to 11	48 to 52

AVERAGE OF DAILY HIGH TEMPERATURES

Degrees Fahrenheit	Degrees Celsius
86 to 92	30 to 33
80 to 86	27 to 30
74 to 80	23 to 27
68 to 74	20 to 23

AVERAGE YEARLY PRECIPITATION
(Rain, Melted Snow and Other Moisture)

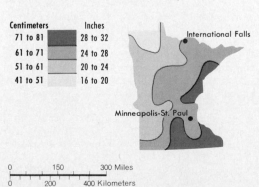

Centimeters	Inches
71 to 81	28 to 32
61 to 71	24 to 28
51 to 61	20 to 24
41 to 51	16 to 20

0   150   300 Miles
0   200   400 Kilometers

WORLD BOOK maps

AVERAGE MONTHLY WEATHER

	INTERNATIONAL FALLS					MINNEAPOLIS-ST. PAUL				
	Temperatures				Days of Rain or Snow	Temperatures				Days of Rain or Snow
	F°		C°			F°		C°		
	High	Low	High	Low		High	Low	High	Low	
JAN.	14	-8	-10	-22	12	23	6	-5	-14	8
FEB.	19	-5	-7	-21	11	27	9	-3	-13	7
MAR.	32	8	0	-13	11	39	23	4	-5	11
APR.	48	26	9	-3	10	56	36	13	2	9
MAY	63	38	17	3	12	69	48	21	9	11
JUNE	73	48	23	9	13	79	58	26	14	13
JULY	79	53	26	12	11	85	63	29	17	11
AUG.	75	51	24	11	12	82	61	28	16	10
SEPT.	65	42	18	6	12	73	52	23	11	9
OCT.	52	32	11	0	9	60	41	16	5	7
NOV.	32	16	0	-9	12	41	25	5	-4	8
DEC.	18	0	-8	-18	12	27	12	-3	-11	9

Natural Resources of Minnesota include fertile soil, important mineral deposits, thick evergreen forests, and a wealth of plant and animal life.

Soil is Minnesota's most important natural resource because it is the basis of the state's great farm economy. Minnesota has several types of soil. Most of them were formed from the drift deposited by the glaciers. The color and fertility of the soil indicate the direction from which the ice sheets came. Drift brought from the north was generally gray and more fertile. Drift from the northeast was reddish and less fertile. In some places, different kinds of drift were deposited in layers or mixed. In parts of southern Minnesota, the wind deposited a fine, silty material called *loess* on top of the drift. The loess formed a fertile, rock-free topsoil.

Minerals. The Mesabi Range, in Itasca and St. Louis counties, yields all of Minnesota's iron ore. Most of the ore mined in the Mesabi Range comes from a rock called *taconite* (see TACONITE). Ore from the Cuyuna Range, just north of Mille Lacs Lake, contains manganese, an important element in steelmaking.

Large deposits of granite are found near St. Cloud and along the upper Minnesota River. Quarries in the southern part of Minnesota produce limestone and sandstone. Sand and gravel are found throughout the state.

Forests cover about 35 per cent of Minnesota. Forests of jack, Norway, and white pine grow in various sections of the north. Other northern trees include the aspen, balsam fir, spruce, and white birch. Scattered groves of ash, black walnut, elm, maple, and oak trees grow in the south.

Other Plant Life in northern Minnesota includes blackberries, lilies of the valley, raspberries, rue anemones, wild geraniums, and wild roses. Blueberries, honeysuckles, sweet ferns, trailing arbutus, and wintergreen cover natural openings in the pine forests. Wild flowers in southern, western, and northwestern Minnesota include asters, bird's-foot violets, blazing stars, goldenrod, and prairie phlox.

Animal Life. White-tailed deer can be found over most of the state. Black bears and moose roam the woods and swamps of the north. Smaller animals found in various parts of Minnesota include beavers, bobcats, foxes, gophers, minks, muskrats, raccoons, and skunks. Quail and ring-necked pheasants feed in the grainfields. Ducks nest in the lakes and swamps during the summer. Fish in Minnesota waters include bass, northern pike, sunfish, trout, and walleye.

Manufacturing, including processing, accounts for about three-fifths of the value of all goods produced in Minnesota. Goods manufactured in the state have a *value added by manufacture* of about $9 billion yearly. This figure represents the value created in products by Minnesota's industries, not counting such costs as materials, supplies, and fuel. Minnesota's chief manufacturing industries, in order of importance, produce (1) nonelectric machinery, (2) food products, and (3) fabricated metal products.

Nonelectric Machinery manufactured in Minnesota has a value added of about $2 billion annually. The most important part of the nonelectric machinery industry is

Production of Goods in Minnesota

Total value of goods produced in 1977—$14,584,356,000

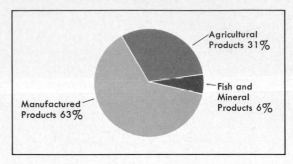

Agricultural Products 31%

Fish and Mineral Products 6%

Manufactured Products 63%

Percentages are based on farm income, value added by manufacture, and value of fish and mineral production. Fish products are less than 1 per cent.
Sources: U.S. government publications, 1978-1979.

Employment in Minnesota

Total number of persons employed in 1978—1,877,700

		Number of Employees
Wholesale & Retail Trade	👤👤👤👤👤👤👤👤👤	425,600
Manufacturing	👤👤👤👤👤👤👤👤	358,200
Community, Social, & Personal Services	👤👤👤👤👤👤👤	331,400
Government	👤👤👤👤👤👤	290,800
Agriculture	👤👤👤👤	195,000
Transportation & Public Utilities	👤👤	94,200
Finance, Insurance, & Real Estate	👤👤	86,400
Construction	👤👤	79,600
Mining	👤	16,500

Sources: *Employment and Earnings*, May 1979, U.S. Bureau of Labor Statistics; *Farm Labor*, February 1979, U.S. Department of Agriculture.

the production of office and computing machines. All sections of the state produce farm machinery. Factories in all parts of Minnesota also turn out machinery for construction, mining, printing, and paper manufacturing.

Food Products manufactured in Minnesota have a value added of about $1½ billion yearly. Meat packing is the most important food-processing activity, and Minnesota is one of the nation's leading meat-packing states. The largest plants are in Albert Lea, Austin, Duluth, and Winona. Large poultry-processing plants operate in southern Minnesota.

Minnesota ranks high among the states in milk, butter, and cheese production. The state's mills produce breakfast cereals, cake mixes, and wheat flour.

Minnesota is a top producer of canned vegetables. Most of the canning plants are in southern Minnesota. Sugar-beet refineries operate in the Red River Valley and along the Minnesota River. Minnesota is one of the leading processors of soybean oil in the United States. Large soybean-oil plants are located in Blooming Prairie, Dawson, Mankato, Minneapolis, St. Paul, and Savage. Minnesota also ranks high in the production of malt beverages.

Fabricated Metal Products manufactured in Minnesota have a value added of more than $916 million a year. The leading products of the industry include small arms and ammunition and structural metals. Minneapolis and St. Paul are the chief production centers of the industry.

Other Manufacturing Industries. Plants in Minneapolis and St. Paul produce chemicals and related products. They also produce electric and electronic equipment. Automobiles are assembled in St. Paul, and railroad equipment is manufactured in Brainerd, Fairmont, and St. Cloud. Printing and publishing and the production of paper products are also important to Minnesota's economy.

St. Paul has a large sandpaper factory. Other St. Paul plants produce *abrasives* (grinding and polishing materials), and a variety of adhesive tapes and industrial adhesives. Plants in several cities manufacture linseed oil and meal. Other products manufactured in Minnesota include carpets, cement, cosmetics, fur and knitted goods, furniture, glass, instruments, leather, lumber and wood products, and stone products.

Agriculture. Farm products account for about a third of the value of all goods produced in Minnesota. The state's yearly farm income totals about $4½ billion, making Minnesota one of the leading farming states. Minnesota has about 104,000 farms. They average about 291 acres (118 hectares) in size. Minnesota farms cover about 30 million acres (12 million hectares).

Thousands of Minnesota farmers sell their produce through farm cooperatives. Most of them are dairy cooperatives, but many handle grain and livestock. See COOPERATIVE.

Livestock and Livestock Products have an annual value of about $2 billion. Milk is Minnesota's most valuable farm product, earning about $817 million a year. Minnesota has about 1¼ million dairy cattle. The cows produce about 1 billion gallons (3.8 billion liters) of milk annually, making Minnesota one of the leading milk producing states. Most of Minnesota's milk is made into butter and cheese.

Beef cattle are the second most valuable source of farm income in the state. Minnesota leads the states in raising turkeys and ranks high in egg production. Minnesota farmers raise *broilers* (chickens between 9 and 12 weeks old), hogs, lambs, and sheep.

Crops in Minnesota have an annual value of about $2 billion. The state's most valuable crops are corn, soybeans, and wheat. Minnesota leads the states in the production of oats. The state's farmers feed much of the corn and oats to their cattle and hogs. Minnesota's annual hay crop ranks among the largest in the country. The state is also a leading producer of barley, flaxseed, potatoes, and sugar beets. Farmers in the Red River Valley grow potatoes, spring wheat, sugar beets, and sunflowers. Other crops include barley and rye.

FARM, MINERAL, AND FOREST PRODUCTS

This map shows where the state's leading farm, mineral, and forest products are produced. The major urban areas (shown on the map in red) are the state's important manufacturing centers.

WORLD BOOK map

Hull-Rust-Mahoning Mine, near Hibbing, is the world's largest open-pit iron mine. Minnesota's iron ore ranges produce about 55 per cent of the total mined in the United States. The state also produces large amounts of granite and limestone.

Gallagher's Studio

Apples are the most important fruit grown in Minnesota. Most of the apple orchards are in the southern part of the state. Other fruits include raspberries and strawberries. Minnesota raises a variety of vegetables for canning and freezing. It ranks among the leading states in the production of green peas and potatoes. Other vegetables include cabbages, carrots, dry beans, and onions.

Mining. The value of Minnesota's mineral output totals about $1 billion a year. About 55 per cent of the iron ore mined in the United States comes from Minnesota. The state produces about 35 million short tons (32 million metric tons) of ore yearly, including taconite. All the ore is mined by the *open-pit* method. The ore lies close to the surface and often can be uncovered by stripping away a thin layer of dirt. The world's largest open-pit iron mine, the Hull-Rust-Mahoning Mine, is near Hibbing. It is about 4 miles (6.4 kilometers) long, 2 miles (3.2 kilometers) wide, and 500 feet (152 meters) deep.

Minnesota began large-scale taconite mining in the 1950's. Taconite plants, which concentrate the low-grade ore, produce about 30 million short tons (27 million metric tons) of taconite pellets yearly.

Quarries in central Minnesota yield granite of unusually fine quality. Limestone is taken from extensive deposits in southern Minnesota. Clay comes from many areas, and is used in making bricks and tile. Sand and gravel are also produced throughout the state.

Fishing Industry. Minnesota's annual fish catch is valued at about $1½ million. The most valuable fishes taken from the Mississippi River include buffalo fish, carp, catfish, whitefish, and yellow perch. Lake herring, smelt, walleye, and yellow pike are the chief products of the Lake Superior catch. Minnesota's commercial fish catch from inland waters includes large amounts of buffalo fish, bullhead, and carp.

Electric Power. About 60 per cent of Minnesota's electric power is produced by plants that burn coal. Nuclear energy generates about 35 per cent of the state's electric power. Minnesota has two nuclear power plants at Prairie Island near Red Wing and one at Monticello. Several small hydroelectric plants are on the Minnesota, Mississippi, Rainy, St. Croix, and St. Louis rivers. The state also has some electric power stations that burn oil and gas.

Transportation. Minnesota's great network of rivers and lakes provided transportation for the explorers, fur traders, missionaries, and settlers who first entered the region. In the 1820's, the first steamboats sailed on the upper Mississippi. Railroad construction in the state progressed rapidly after 1865. Today, railroads operate on about 8,000 miles (13,000 kilometers) of track in the state. Twelve rail lines provide freight service, and passenger trains serve about 10 cities. The Twin Cities form the chief rail center of the Upper Mississippi Valley. Eight major airlines serve the Twin Cities. Minnesota has about 140 public airports and about 170 private airports.

About 129,000 miles (207,600 kilometers) of roads and highways cross the state. Nine-tenths of them are surfaced. The nation's largest bus system, Greyhound Bus Lines, had its start in Hibbing in 1914.

Barges bring coal, oil, and other products to Minnesota ports on the Minnesota, Mississippi, and St. Croix rivers. The barges return with grain and other products. Most of Minnesota's water traffic is on Lake Superior. The harbor at Duluth and Superior, Wis., is one of the busiest ports in the world. It handles about 35 million short tons (32 million metric tons) of cargo yearly. Iron ore makes up most of the outgoing cargo.

Communication. In 1849, James Madison Goodhue began publishing Minnesota's first newspaper, the *Minnesota Pioneer*, in St. Paul. Today, Minnesota has about 30 daily newspapers and about 370 weeklies. Daily newspapers with the largest circulations include the *Rochester Post-Bulletin*, the *Minneapolis Star*, the *Minneapolis Tribune*, the *St. Paul Dispatch*, and the *St. Paul Pioneer Press*. Minnesota also publishes about 180 magazines.

Minnesota's first licensed radio station was WLB (now KUOM), an educational station owned by the University of Minnesota. The station was licensed in Minneapolis in 1922. The first commercial radio station, WDGY, began broadcasting from Minneapolis in 1923. KSTP-TV, Minnesota's first television station, started broadcasting in Minneapolis in 1948. Minnesota now has about 190 radio stations and 18 television stations.

MINNESOTA/History

Indian Days. White people first entered the Minnesota region in the last half of the 1600's. They found Sioux Indians in the northern forests. The Sioux lived in dome-shaped wigwams. They raised crops, and were skilled hunters. By 1750, large numbers of Chippewa Indians were moving westward into Minnesota. They took over the northern forests, and forced the Sioux to move to the southwest. The Sioux became wanderers, and the two tribes remained enemies for many years. See INDIAN, AMERICAN (Table of Tribes).

Exploration. Two famous French fur traders, Pierre Esprit Radisson and Médard Chouart, Sieur des Groseilliers, were perhaps the first white men to set foot in Minnesota. They arrived in the area north of Lake Superior between 1659 and 1661. Another Frenchman,

Daniel Greysolon, Sieur Duluth (or Du Lhut), entered Minnesota about 1679. Duluth was an adventurer who hoped to blaze a trail to the Pacific Ocean. Duluth landed on the western shore of Lake Superior, and then pushed on into the interior of Minnesota. He claimed the entire region for King Louis XIV of France.

In 1680, Father Louis Hennepin, a Belgian missionary, set out from the Illinois region to explore the upper Mississippi. But Sioux Indians captured Hennepin and his two companions. The Indians took them into Minnesota. Although a captive, Hennepin saw much of the region. He became the first white man to visit the site of present-day Minneapolis, where he sighted and named the Falls of St. Anthony. Meanwhile, Duluth heard that Indians had captured three white men. He

HISTORIC MINNESOTA

Rich Iron Deposits were discovered in Minnesota in 1865 by geologist H. H. Eames. The first ore was mined from the Vermilion Range in 1884, and from the great Mesabi Range in 1892.

Lumberjacks began cutting timber on a commercial basis in the late 1830's in the Saint Croix Valley. Railroads created a lumbering boom that lasted from 1870 to 1910.

Lake Superior

Source of the Mississippi. Henry Schoolcraft discovered the source of the Mississippi River in 1832 at Lake Itasca.

Falls of Saint Anthony were sighted by Father Hennepin when he visited the region around Mille Lacs in 1680.

• Crosby

Duluth •

The First Flour Mill in Minnesota was built at the Falls of St. Anthony in 1823. Minneapolis was the state's leading flour center by the late 1800's.

Record Balloon Flight. Major David G. Simons set a new altitude record when he rose 101,516 feet (30,942 meters) in 1957 from a mining pit near Crosby, Minn. He remained aloft for 32 hours in a 400-foot (120-meter) balloon.

ST. PAUL
Minneapolis • ★

Early Minnesota Farmers. Five Swiss families settled on the military reservation at Fort Snelling in 1821. They may have been the first settlers in the state to devote themselves to farming.

Rochester •

The Mayo Clinic was established at Rochester, Minn., in 1889 by William W. Mayo and his two sons, William and Charles. It is one of the greatest medical research centers in the world.

Fort Snelling was built in the early 1820's as Fort Saint Anthony. It was later named for Colonel Josiah Snelling. Count Ferdinand von Zeppelin, a German army observer, made tests in balloon flying there in 1864.

Fort Snelling in southeastern Minnesota protected settlers and traders in the early 1800's. Canadian artist Paul Kane painted a view of the fort in *Fort Snelling, Sioux Scalp Dance,* above.

MINNESOTA

found the Indians and successfully demanded that they release the captives.

Struggle for Control. In 1762, France gave Spain all its land west of the Mississippi River, including western Minnesota. But the Spaniards did not try to explore or settle the region, and French trappers continued to collect furs there. In 1763, the French and Indian War ended. France lost this war with Great Britain over rival claims in North America. France gave Britain almost all its land east of the Mississippi, including eastern Minnesota. During the next 50 years, the North West Company and other British fur trading firms established posts in the region.

In 1783, the Revolutionary War ended. Great Britain gave its land south of the Great Lakes and east of the Mississippi to the United States. This vast area became part of the Northwest Territory, which Congress created in 1787. But British fur companies continued to trade in the region, and the United States did not gain full control until after the War of 1812.

The Louisiana Purchase. In 1800, Napoleon Bonaparte forced Spain to return the region west of the Mississippi River to France. France sold this region, called Louisiana, to the United States in 1803 (see LOUISIANA PURCHASE). Two years later, Zebulon M. Pike was sent to explore the upper Mississippi and the Minnesota wilderness.

In 1820, American soldiers under Colonel Josiah Snelling began building Fort St. Anthony in the southeastern part of Minnesota. It stood at the point where the Minnesota and Mississippi rivers meet. The fort was completed in 1822, and was renamed Fort Snelling in 1825. It became a center of industry and culture, as well as of military duty. Explorers used Fort Snelling as a base from which they set out for undiscovered parts of Minnesota. These explorers in-

――――――― IMPORTANT DATES IN MINNESOTA ―――――――

1659-1661 Pierre Esprit Radisson and Médard Chouart, Sieur des Groseilliers, possibly visited the Minnesota region.

1679? Daniel Greysolon, Sieur Duluth, explored the western shore of Lake Superior.

1680 Louis Hennepin sighted and named the Falls of St. Anthony.

1783 Great Britain granted the land east of the Mississippi River to the United States.

1803 The United States obtained the western Minnesota area through the Louisiana Purchase.

1820-1822 The U.S. Army built Fort St. Anthony.

1832 Henry R. Schoolcraft discovered Lake Itasca, the source of the Mississippi River.

1837 The Sioux and Chippewa Indians sold their claim to the St. Croix Valley.

1849 Congress created the Minnesota Territory.

1851 The Indians gave up their rights to large areas of land west of the Mississippi River.

1858 Minnesota became the 32nd state on May 11.

1862 Minnesota militiamen and U.S. troops put down a Sioux uprising.

1884 The first shipment of iron ore from the Vermilion Range left Minnesota.

1889 William W. Mayo and his two sons founded the Mayo Clinic in Rochester.

1892 The first ore was shipped from the Mesabi Range.

1944 The Farmer-Labor party joined the Minnesota Democratic party to form the Democratic-Farmer-Labor party.

1955 A large taconite-processing plant was opened at Silver Bay.

1964 Minnesota voters approved a constitutional amendment assuring taconite producers that taxes on taconite will not be raised at a higher rate than taxes on other businesses for 25 years.

cluded Lewis Cass, Stephen H. Long, and Henry R. Schoolcraft. In 1832, Schoolcraft discovered and named Lake Itasca, the source of the Mississippi River.

Lumbering began in the St. Croix Valley during the 1830's. In 1837, the Sioux and Chippewa Indians sold their claim to the logging area around the St. Croix River. A land boom followed. Towns sprang up as lumberers and settlers from New England flocked to the new land to cut timber and to build homes.

Territorial Days. Through the years, parts of Minnesota had belonged to the territories of Illinois, Indiana, Iowa, Michigan, Missouri, and Wisconsin, and to the territory and district of Louisiana. On March 3, 1849, Congress created the Minnesota Territory. Its southern, northern, and eastern boundaries were the same as those of the state today. The western boundary extended to the Missouri and White Earth rivers. Alexander Ramsey was appointed as the first territorial governor. About 4,000 white persons lived in Minnesota when it became a territory.

In 1851, the Sioux Indians, under pressure from the U.S. government, signed two treaties giving up their rights to a vast area west of the Mississippi River. Most of the land was in southern Minnesota. This new rich territory was opened to white settlement, and newcomers poured in.

Statehood. On May 11, 1858, Congress admitted Minnesota into the Union as the 32nd state. The people elected Henry H. Sibley as the first governor of their state. Sibley had been an agent of the American Fur Company, and had worked for the creation of the Minnesota Territory. Minnesota had a population of about 150,000 when it became a state.

The Civil War began in 1861. Minnesota became the first state to offer troops for the Union armies. In August 1862, when many Minnesota men were away fighting for the Union, the Sioux made a last effort to drive the whites from their old hunting grounds. The Indians swooped down on the frontier towns, killing hundreds of settlers and destroying much property. Federal troops in the state helped Minnesota militiamen put down the uprising.

Industrial Development occurred rapidly in Minnesota during the late 1800's. Railroads expanded across the state, and the old Sioux hunting grounds became wheat lands. Flour mills sprang up throughout the wheat region, but most were in the Minneapolis area. Minneapolis mills produced such huge quantities of flour that Minneapolis became known as the *Mill City*.

Minnesota waged a vigorous drive to attract newcomers. The railroads sent pamphlets to Europe, describing the opportunities in Minnesota. During the 1880's and 1890's, thousands of immigrants, especially Germans, Norwegians, and Swedes, settled in the state.

The outstanding event of the late 1800's was the development of rich iron ore resources. In 1884, the first ore was shipped from the Vermilion Range. In 1890, Leonidas Merritt and one of his six brothers discovered ore near Mountain Iron in the Mesabi Range. Two years later, the seven Merritt brothers shipped the first load of ore from the Mesabi Range. The Merritts became known as the *Seven Iron Men*.

In 1889, William W. Mayo and his two sons, William and Charles, established the Mayo Clinic in Rochester. The clinic's fame spread rapidly, and the Mayos turned it into a general medical center. The clinic became one of the world's leading medical research centers.

In 1894, a great forest fire swept across about 400 square miles (1,000 square kilometers) of eastern Minnesota. It wiped out the villages of Hinckley and Sandstone. More than 400 persons were killed, and property valued at over $1 million was destroyed.

The Early 1900's. In 1911, the first shipment of iron ore left the Cuyuna Range. A huge steel mill began operating in Duluth in 1916. After the United States entered World War I in 1917, there were heavy demands for Minnesota's products. Great crops of wheat and other grains were raised to feed the armed forces. Iron ore production totaled almost 90 million short tons (82 million metric tons) during 1917 and 1918.

In 1918, Minnesota was struck by another disastrous forest fire. Strong winds fanned a number of small fires into one huge fire that roared across large areas of Carlton and St. Louis counties in the northeast. The fire killed more than 400 persons and destroyed property valued at about $25 million.

During the 1890's and early 1900's, many Minnesota farmers joined cooperatives. They joined together to provide their own financial and storage services, and transportation for their products. The farmers felt that the railroads, banks, and grain companies charged too much for these services. During the 1920's, the new

The Governors of Minnesota

	Party	Term
Henry H. Sibley	Democratic	1858-1860
Alexander Ramsey	Republican	1860-1863
Henry A. Swift	Republican	1863-1864
Stephen Miller	Republican	1864-1866
William R. Marshall	Republican	1866-1870
Horace Austin	Republican	1870-1874
Cushman K. Davis	Republican	1874-1876
John S. Pillsbury	Republican	1876-1882
Lucius F. Hubbard	Republican	1882-1887
Andrew R. McGill	Republican	1887-1889
William R. Merriam	Republican	1889-1893
Knute Nelson	Republican	1893-1895
David M. Clough	Republican	1895-1899
John Lind	Democratic	1899-1901
Samuel R. Van Sant	Republican	1901-1905
John A. Johnson	Democratic	1905-1909
Adolph O. Eberhart	Republican	1909-1915
Winfield S. Hammond	Democratic	1915
Joseph A. A. Burnquist	Republican	1915-1921
Jacob A. O. Preus	Republican	1921-1925
Theodore Christianson	Republican	1925-1931
Floyd B. Olson	Farmer-Labor	1931-1936
Hjalmar Petersen	Farmer-Labor	1936-1937
Elmer A. Benson	Farmer-Labor	1937-1939
Harold E. Stassen	Republican	1939-1943
Edward J. Thye	Republican	1943-1947
Luther W. Youngdahl	Republican	1947-1951
C. Elmer Anderson	Republican	1951-1955
Orville L. Freeman	DFL*	1955-1961
Elmer L. Andersen	Republican	1961-1963
Karl F. Rolvaag	DFL*	1963-1967
Harold E. LeVander	Republican	1967-1971
Wendell R. Anderson	DFL*	1971-1976
Rudolph G. Perpich	DFL*	1976-1979
Albert H. Quie	I-R†	1979-

*Democratic-Farmer-Labor   †Independent-Republicans

Farmer-Labor Party supported the farmers. In 1931, Floyd B. Olson became the first Farmer-Labor governor.

The Great Depression of the 1930's hit Minnesota hard. Unemployment was widespread in the cities. About 70 per cent of the iron-range workers lost their jobs. Farm income fell sharply. The state government took many steps to fight the depression, and federal agencies were set up to provide employment and relief.

The Mid-1900's. Minnesota's economy recovered during World War II (1939-1945). The state's lumber and mining industries turned out huge amounts of raw materials for the armed forces. Until the early 1950's, Minnesota provided almost 60 per cent of the nation's iron ore. But the supply of high-grade ore suddenly dropped, as did the demand for the ore. The industry declined and several mines closed.

As a result of the mining slump, the state's iron industry began to develop low-grade taconite ore. Taconite contains about 30 per cent iron in the form of specks of iron oxide.

In 1964, Minnesota voters approved an amendment to the state constitution that boosted investment in the iron industry. The so-called taconite amendment guaranteed that taxes on taconite would not be raised at a higher rate than taxes on other products for 25 years. Previously, iron mining companies had been taxed at a higher rate, and producers had delayed plans to build taconite plants. After passage of the taconite amendment, producers invested more than $1 billion in taconite plants. But air and water pollution at these plants became a major concern (see TACONITE).

Many new industries began to operate in Minnesota during the 1950's and 1960's. The products of these industries include aerospace equipment, chemicals, computers, electronic equipment, heavy machinery, and processed foods.

In Minnesota, as in other states, the number of farms and farmworkers decreased. Large numbers of families moved from rural areas to cities. By 1950, the state's total urban population had grown larger than the rural population for the first time. In 1964, a federal court ordered Minnesota to *reapportion* (redivide) its legislative districts to give the city population equal representation in the state legislature.

The Farmer-Labor Party joined the state Democratic Party in 1944 to form the Democratic-Farmer-Labor Party (DFL). The DFL grew in strength in the 1950's.

Minnesota Today faces the continuing problems caused by the growth of its cities and the decline of rural areas. Several agencies have been set up to handle these problems. The Minnesota Municipal Commission reviews requests for the incorporation and expansion of communities. A metropolitan council is responsible for the Twin Cities area of Minneapolis-St. Paul.

Another problem is finding ways to develop Minnesota's many natural resources and, at the same time, preserve its natural beauty. Industrialists have increased efforts to develop the state's copper-nickel ore deposits and to expand logging operations. Environmentalists oppose these efforts. State officials are trying to find a balance between the two views.

The DFL made sharp gains during the early and mid-1970's. During that period, the governorship and both U.S. Senate seats were held by DFL members. In 1974, the party gained control of the Minnesota legislature for the first time. However, the Republicans, who changed their party's name to Independent-Republicans of Minnesota in 1975, regained many posts in the late 1970's. In 1978, Independent-Republicans were elected to the governorship and both U.S. Senate seats. Also, party members won the same number of seats in the state house of representatives as did members of the DFL.

JOHN R. FINNEGAN, HAROLD T. HAGG, and PHILIP L. TIDEMAN

MINNESOTA / Study Aids

Related Articles in WORLD BOOK include:

BIOGRAPHIES

Blackmun, Harry A.	Mayo (family)
Donnelly, Ignatius	McCarthy,
Duluth, Sieur	Eugene J.
Freeman, Orville L.	Mondale, Walter F.
Hench, Philip S.	Nier, Alfred O. C.
Hennepin, Louis	Pike, Zebulon M.
Hill, James J.	Pillsbury, John S.
Humphrey, Hubert H.	Radisson, Pierre E.
Kellogg, Frank B.	Rice, Henry M.
Kendall, Edward C.	Stassen, Harold E.
Lewis, Sinclair	Volstead, Andrew

CITIES

Bloomington	Minneapolis	Saint Cloud
Duluth	Northfield	Saint Paul
Hibbing	Rochester	Stillwater

HISTORY

Indian, American (Indians of the Plains)	Louisiana Purchase
	Northwest Territory

PHYSICAL FEATURES

Lake Agassiz	Minnehaha Falls	Rainy Lake
Lake of the Woods	Minnesota River	Red River of
Lake Superior	Mississippi River	the North
Mesabi Range		

PRODUCTS

For Minnesota's rank among the states in production, see the following articles:

Agriculture	Corn	Pea
Alfalfa	Hog	Potato
Barley	Honey	Rye
Butter	Iron and Steel	Soybean
Cattle	Milk	Turkey
Cheese	Oats	Vegetable

OTHER RELATED ARTICLES

Bunyan, Paul	Midwestern States
Farmer-Labor Party	Pipestone National
Grand Portage National	Monument
Monument	

Outline

I. Government
    A. Constitution   E. Local Government
    B. Executive   F. Taxation
    C. Legislature   G. Politics
    D. Courts
II. People
III. Education
    A. Schools   B. Libraries   C. Museums
IV. A Visitor's Guide
    A. Places to Visit   B. Annual Events

Questions

What two cities in Minnesota and Wisconsin make up one of the world's leading ports?

Why was Minnesota nicknamed the *Gopher State?* The *Bread and Butter State?*

The flags of which four nations have flown over Minnesota?

What is the state's chief manufacturing industry?

What are some of Minnesota's products?

Near what city is the largest open-pit iron mine in the world?

What political party was founded in Minnesota?

How much of the iron ore mined in the United States comes from Minnesota?

How many state constitutions has Minnesota had?

Why is taconite so important to Minnesota?

Books for Young Readers

BAILEY, BERNADINE. *Picture Book of Minnesota.* Rev. ed. Whitman, 1967.

CARPENTER, ALLAN. *Minnesota.* Rev. ed. Childrens Press, 1978.

CLARK, ANN N. *All This Wild Land.* Viking, 1976. Fiction.

FEARING, JERRY. *The Story of Minnesota.* 3rd ed. Minnesota Historical Society, 1977.

HOLBERT, SUE E., and HOLMQUIST, J. D. *A History Tour of 50 Twin City Landmarks.* Minnesota Historical Society, 1966.

POATGIETER, ALICE HERMINA, and DUNN, J. T., eds. *The Gopher Reader: Minnesota's Story in Words and Pictures.* 2 vols. Minnesota Historical Society, 1958-1975.

ROSENFELT, WILLARD E. *Minnesota: Its People and Culture.* Denison, 1973.

Books for Older Readers

ANDERSON, CHESTER G., ed. *Growing Up in Minnesota: Ten Writers Remember Their Childhoods.* Univ. of Minnesota Press, 1976.

BLEGEN, THEODORE C. *Minnesota: A History of the State.* 2nd ed. Univ. of Minnesota Press, 1975.

BRILL, CHARLES. *Indian and Free: A Contemporary Portrait of Life on a Chippewa Reservation.* Univ. of Minnesota Press, 1974.

FOLWELL, WILLIAM W. *A History of Minnesota.* 4 vols. Minnesota Historical Society, 1956-1969.

FRIDLEY, RUSSELL W. *Minnesota: A Students' Guide to Localized History.* Teachers College Press, 1966.

GILMAN, RHODA R., and HOLMQUIST, J. D., eds. *Selections from "Minnesota History": A Fiftieth Anniversary Anthology.* Minnesota Historical Society, 1965.

HEILBRON, BERTHA. *The Thirty-Second State: A Pictorial History of Minnesota.* 2nd ed. Minnesota Historical Society, 1966.

HOLMQUIST, JUNE D., and BROOKINS, J. A. *Minnesota's Major Historic Sites: A Guide.* 2nd ed. Minnesota Historical Society, 1972.

LASS, WILLIAM E. *Minnesota: A Bicentennial History.* Norton, 1977.

MITAU, G. THEODORE. *Politics in Minnesota.* Rev. ed. Univ. of Minnesota Press, 1970.

MOROSCO, BEATRICE. *The Restless Ones: A Family History.* Ross & Haines, 1963.

SCHWARTZ, GEORGE M., and THIEL, G. A. *Minnesota's Rocks and Waters: A Geological Story.* Rev. ed. Univ. of Minnesota Press, 1963.

MINNESOTA STATE UNIVERSITY SYSTEM

UPHAM, WARREN. *Minnesota Geographic Names: Their Origin and Historic Significance.* Rev. ed. Minnesota Historical Society, 1979.

MINNESOTA, UNIVERSITY OF, is a state-supported coeducational institution. Its main campus, the Twin Cities Campus, is in Minneapolis-St. Paul. The university also has campuses in Crookston, Duluth, Morris, and Waseca.

The Twin Cities Campus awards bachelor's, master's, and doctor's degrees. A special program allows some juniors and seniors to follow individual courses of study. The campus includes colleges of biological sciences, education, liberal arts, medical sciences, pharmacy, and veterinary medicine; a general college; an institute of technology; an institute of agriculture that includes a college of agriculture, forestry, and home economics; schools of business administration, dentistry, journalism, law, and social work; a continuing education and extension division; and a graduate school. The Mayo Graduate School of Medicine in Rochester is part of the graduate school.

The Duluth campus offers liberal arts courses leading to bachelor's and master's degrees. The Morris campus offers bachelor's degrees in arts and science. The campuses in Crookston and Waseca are two-year technical colleges offering programs in agriculture, business, and food management.

Other university facilities include the Hormel Institute in Austin, the Lake Itasca Forestry and Biological Station in Itasca State Park, the Forest Research Center in Cloquet, the Cedar Creek Natural History Area near Bethel, the Freshwater Biological Research Center in Navarre, and the Rosemount Research Center. The university also has an agricultural extension service and six agricultural experiment stations.

The University of Minnesota was chartered in 1851 as a preparatory school. It closed during the Civil War, and was reorganized as a four-year college in 1868. For enrollment, see UNIVERSITIES AND COLLEGES (table).

Critically reviewed by the UNIVERSITY OF MINNESOTA

See also MINNESOTA (picture: The Twin Cities Campus).

MINNESOTA RIVER. This large branch of the Mississippi River flows through a wide valley that was cut by the outlet of an ancient glacial lake (Lake Agassiz). The Minnesota rises in the Coteau des Prairies (*little hills of the prairie*), a group of hills in northeastern South Dakota. The river flows southeastward to Big Stone Lake on the boundary between South Dakota and Minnesota. It follows the lake southward to Ortonville. There it flows southeastward to Mankato, Minn. The river then turns sharply to the northeast and enters the Mississippi south of St. Paul, Minn.

The Minnesota River is 332 miles (534 kilometers) long. It drains an area of about 16,600 square miles (41,400 square kilometers). For location, see MINNESOTA (physical map).

Early explorers and fur traders sailed up the Minnesota River in their westward journeys. Today, the river is an important trade route.   WALLACE E. AKIN

See also LAKE AGASSIZ.

MINNESOTA STATE UNIVERSITY SYSTEM is a state-supported coeducational system of higher education.

MINNOW

The system consists of seven universities, each with its own president. A chancellor, who is appointed by a 10-member State University Board, heads the system, which has administrative headquarters in St. Paul.

Five of the system's universities include their location in their name. These schools are Bemidji State University (founded in 1919), Mankato State University (1868), Moorhead State University (1888), St. Cloud State University (1869), and Winona State University (1860). The other two schools are Metropolitan State University, established in 1971 in St. Paul, and Southwest State University, founded in 1963 in Marshall.

Each university in the system grants bachelor's degrees, and several also award master's degrees. Courses are offered in liberal arts, sciences, teacher education, and various professional fields. Several of the universities provide programs for students who cannot attend classes on campus. For enrollment, see UNIVERSITIES AND COLLEGES (table).   Critically reviewed by the
MINNESOTA STATE UNIVERSITY SYSTEM

MINNOW is a common name for fish in the carp and minnow family. This is the largest family of freshwater fishes, with over 1,000 species in North America, Europe, Asia, and Africa. Most American minnows are small, less than 6 inches (15 centimeters) long. But a few grow quite large. The *squawfish*, one of the largest minnows, reaches a length of 2 to 4 feet (61 to 120 centimeters). Minnows usually have only a few teeth, arranged in rows. The main row has about 4 or 5 teeth, and the other rows, if present, usually have fewer teeth. Minnows are difficult to classify because of their uniform size, form, and color.

Field Museum of Natural History

The Common Shiner is found in streams and lakes from the East Coast to the Rocky Mountains and as far south as Louisiana.

Minnows are used as forage fish. Forage fish furnish the food which allows game fish to reach a large size. Minnows are also used as live bait to catch larger fish. In many places, so many minnows have been caught for bait that there are few left, and some states have outlawed or limited the taking of minnows. Minnows are usually caught with nets. They are often raised in ponds and fish hatcheries. Some common minnows in North America are the *common shiner*, the *golden shiner*, and the *creek chub*.

Scientific Classification. The minnow belongs to the family *Cyprinidae*. The golden shiner is genus *Notemigonus*, species *N. crysoleucas*. The common shiner is genus *Notropis*, species *N. cornutus*, and the creek chub, genus *Semotilus*, species *S. atromaculatus*.   CARL L. HUBBS

See also CHUB.

MINOAN CIVILIZATION. See AEGEAN CIVILIZATION; ARCHITECTURE (Minoan Architecture); CRETE; PAINTING (Cretan Painting).

MINOR, in education. See CURRICULUM.

MINOR is a person who is under legal age. In the United States, the legal age was traditionally 21. However, the 26th Amendment to the U.S. Constitution, ratified in 1971, set the minimum voting age at 18. Since then, many states have lowered the legal age—known as the age of majority or adulthood—to 18. In 45 states, the legal age is now 18. In four others—Alabama, Alaska, Nebraska, and Wyoming—it is 19. The legal age is still 21 in Mississippi.

Under the law, minors have many privileges that are not given to adults. For example, they are not held responsible for a contract with an adult and can refuse to carry out their part of the bargain. They may even demand the return of money or property they have given to the adult under a contract. But minors are liable for the reasonable value of *necessaries*, such as food, clothing, lodging, medical care, and education. The law gives these privileges to minors because they are considered too inexperienced to be fully responsible for their actions. In some states, these privileges can be removed by a court action.

Minors may be held responsible for wrongdoing, such as damages they do to others, though age and inexperience may be taken into consideration.

At common law, infants under 7 years old were presumed to be incapable of committing a crime. Between the ages of 7 and 14, this presumption could be rebutted. For children over 14, the presumption was that they had criminal capacity. Punishment today varies with the minor's age and usually differs from that for adults. In most cities in the United States, there are special courts for minors (see JUVENILE COURT).   JOHN W. WADE

MINOR AXIS. See ELLIPSE.

MINOR LEAGUE. See BASEBALL (Minor Leagues).

MINORCA. See CHICKEN (Mediterranean Class).

MINORCA, or MENORCA, is the second largest island of the Balearic Islands, which lie off the eastern coast of Spain (see BALEARIC ISLANDS). Minorca has an area of 266 square miles (689 square kilometers) and a population of about 55,000. Some iron is mined there. Farm crops include cereals and hemp, and grapes, olives, and other fruits. Metalware, textiles, soap, wine, and sandals are manufactured on the island. Mahón is the chief city and port. For location, see SPAIN (political map).

Spain owns the island. England and France captured it several times. England ceded Minorca to Spain by the Treaty of Amiens in 1802.   WALTER C. LANGSAM

MINORITY BUSINESS ENTERPRISE, OFFICE OF, was an agency of the United States Department of Commerce. It coordinated federal programs designed to help members of minority groups become owners and managers of business companies.

The agency coordinated federal programs with those of many public and private state and local organizations. The organizations helped minority business people plan, establish, and operate businesses of their own. The agency provided funds for such organizations.

The agency also financed pilot projects conducted by public and private organizations that promote minority businesses. Such projects identified specific kinds of businesses, such as shipping firms, where minority-owned companies might expand. Other projects studied the problems of Mexican-American and Puerto Rican business people who speak little English. President Richard M. Nixon created the agency in 1969. In 1979, it was replaced by the Minority Business Development Agency.

MINORITY GROUP is composed of people in a society who differ in some ways from the dominant group, which exercises greater control in the society. For example, members of the minority group may look or speak differently or have a different cultural background than members of the dominant group. The dominant group generally discriminates against minorities. Thus, members of minority groups often do not have an equal chance in the economic, political, and social life of the society.

Social scientists often refer to minorities as racial or ethnic minorities. A *racial minority* is identified chiefly by one or more distinctive physical characteristics that are shared by members of the group. These may include skin color, type of hair, body structure, and shape of the head or nose. Blacks are a racial minority in the United States. An *ethnic minority* is identified chiefly by distinctive cultural practices. For example, its language or speaking accent, religion, or manner of living is different from that of the dominant group. The Amish people of the United States and Canada are an ethnic minority. Many Amish dress in plain styles that are different from the clothing worn by most Americans.

Some minority groups combine the characteristics of both racial and ethnic minorities. For example, most Chinese in California in the 1850's were distinguished from other Americans by their yellow-brown skin color and "inner" eyefolds as well as by their language, style of dress, food preferences, and other cultural characteristics.

The term *minority* literally means "less than half of the whole." Yet when used in relation to people, it does not refer to numerical size. A minority group is not always smaller in number than the dominant group. For example, blacks form a majority of the population in some parts of the South in the United States. But they are still a minority group, because many members of the dominant white group treat them as inferiors.

How a Group Becomes a Minority

A minority group usually develops when people leave their homeland and settle in another society. Members of the minority may move into or be brought within the territory of the dominant group either voluntarily or against their will. Or the dominant group may move in and take over the minority's territory. When these groups meet, the dominant group controls the minority because it has greater economic or military power, or some other superior strength.

When the minority group becomes enclosed in the territory of the dominant group, the process is generally called *incorporation*. Bringing black slaves to America from Africa from the early 1600's to the mid-1800's is an example of one type of incorporation. Immigration is another type. The United States has admitted many immigrants from Europe since the late 1700's, and many of these peoples become minority groups. Incorporation also occurs through *annexation* of adjoining

territory. After the Mexican War (1846-1848), for example, the United States gained many Spanish-speaking persons in areas that formerly belonged to Mexico.

The dominant group may move into the territory of the minority group. When one group sends some of its people to gain control over another territory and to use it as a source of wealth for the settlers' homeland, the process is called *colonialism*. The settlers retain close political, economic, and cultural ties with their homeland. Usually, the dominant group wants to use the colony for its natural resources, as a source of laborers, or as a trading partner. For example, countries such as Belgium, France, Great Britain, Portugal, and Spain set up colonies in Africa. In some cases, the dominant group breaks away from the mother country's political control. This happened when English settlers in North America revolted against Great Britain's political control. See COLONIALISM.

After establishing control over the minority, the dominant group may try to remove them from its territory. The dominant group may expel the minority, as white Americans did in the 1830's when they forced the Cherokee Indians to move from the Southeastern United States to reservations in what is now Oklahoma. Or the dominant group may attempt *annihilation* (complete destruction) of the minority. For example, American settlers gained control of North America by killing many of the native Indians. *Genocide* is a form of annihilation in which one organized group—usually a government—systematically kills members of another group. Between 1933 and 1945, the Nazis in Germany persecuted Jews on a regular basis. In the early 1940's, they murdered about 6 million European Jews.

Relationships Between Groups

The dominant and minority groups usually develop a manner of living together when incorporation or colonialism occur. The dominant group regulates these relationships, which usually lead to segregation, assimilation, or pluralism.

Segregation is the separation of groups of people by custom or by law. It is often a territorial separation. For example, Indian reservations and black ghettos physically set minorities apart in the United States. But a minority can be physically intermixed in a society and still be separated from the dominant group because of discrimination. See SEGREGATION.

Assimilation occurs when a dominant group absorbs members of a minority, and the minority no longer exists as a group. In assimilation, both groups want the minority to join the dominant group. The minority group generally alters its way of life to fit the culture of the dominant group. But the minority does not necessarily adopt the new way of life completely. It may keep some of its old customs, and modify some of the new customs while adopting them. Most Irish and Italian immigrants in the United States have assimilated in this way.

But assimilation has not been possible for all minorities. Usually, physical differences make assimilation difficult. As a result, most of the blacks in the United States have not been able to assimilate completely. Some minority groups, such as the Amish people, deliberately avoid assimilation. See Assimilation.

Pluralism is a compromise between the extremes of segregation and assimilation. Pluralism permits a minority group to retain some of its own cultural practices, if it also conforms to dominant group practices that are considered essential to the well-being of society. For example, the United States has followed a pluralistic policy in permitting religious freedom for many different groups.

Results of Minority Status

Minority group members generally recognize that they belong to a less-favored group, and this affects their behavior. A sense of isolation and common suffering is a strong social glue that binds them together. Common cultural and physical traits also help unify the group. Identification with the minority may continue even after a minority group member is assimilated into the dominant group. For instance, a person of Jewish descent may no longer practice the traditional Jewish religion, and may become a member of dominant group society in the United States. Yet the person may continue to think of himself or herself primarily as a Jew.

In responding to domination, minority group members must decide whether to attempt assimilation or to try to avoid contact with the dominant group. Assimilation is often the most common adjustment that members of minority groups make. But if they find assimilation impossible or if they do not want to assimilate, minorities may try to avoid the dominant group. They may try to achieve territorial separation from the dominant group. This may only mean that a minority chooses to live together in one section of a country or in one city neighborhood. But avoidance can involve more extreme separatism. An example of this approach is *Zionism*, a movement that began in the 1800's among Jews. It resulted in the establishment of the Jewish nation of Israel.

Minorities in the United States

The United States has become the home of many minority groups. These minorities include blacks, Jews, European immigrants, Spanish-speaking Americans, Orientals, and American Indians.

Blacks form the largest minority group in the United States. They make up about 11 per cent of the population. Blacks were brought to America as slaves beginning in the early 1600's, and most blacks remained slaves until after the Civil War (1861-1865). But even as they gradually gained legal freedom, most blacks could not assimilate into American life because of widespread discrimination. In the 1960's, some blacks reacted to their exclusion from society by starting *black nationalist* or *black power* movements. These movements called for separation and strengthening of black group identity. See Black Americans.

Jews have often fled to the United States to avoid persecution, only to meet continued discrimination. Today, there are about 6 million Jews in the United States. Most Jews have retained their religious beliefs and many traditional cultural practices. See Jews.

European Immigrants who came to the United States often became minority groups. Most of these minorities were eventually assimilated into American society. Be-

fore the 1880's, most Europeans who came to America were from northern and western Europe. Beginning in the 1880's, most immigrants came from southern and eastern Europe. Most European immigrants have come from Germany, Italy, Ireland, Great Britain, and Austria-Hungary. See Immigration and Emigration.

Spanish-Speaking Americans, also called *Hispanics* or *Hispanic Americans*, are primarily of Cuban, Mexican, and Puerto Rican ancestry. The United States has about 6 million Mexican Americans, who form the nation's second largest minority group.

Cubans began to migrate to the United States in large numbers during the 1960's, after Cuba came under Communist control. Most have settled in Miami.

Mexicans became incorporated into the United States when the nation acquired what are now large parts of the West and Southwest from Mexico. Since the Mexican War (1846-1848), many Mexicans have migrated to the United States. See Mexican Americans.

Puerto Ricans have migrated to the U.S. mainland in large numbers since World War II (1939-1945). Most have settled in New York City.

Orientals in the United States include Chinese and Japanese. There are about 700,000 Orientals in the United States today. See Oriental Exclusion Acts.

Chinese have often been discriminated against. They often live in city neighborhoods called *Chinatowns*. *Japanese* immigrants have often suffered the same injustices as the Chinese. During World War II, many Japanese were segregated in special camps.

American Indians were driven from their homes by European settlers and then were denied their rights for hundreds of years. Indians have been forced to live on reservations. They were not granted U.S. citizenship until 1924. About 792,000 Indians live in the United States. See Indian, American (Indians Today).

Minority Groups in Other Countries

Many nations have minority groups. European countries have often had minority nationality groups living within their boundaries. For example, before World War II, Germans lived in a part of Czechoslovakia called the Sudetenland. Religious minorities have also lived in Europe. Today, the Roman Catholics living in Northern Ireland are a minority, and Jews form a minority in many parts of Europe.

In South Africa, the dominant whites discriminate against blacks and other nonwhites, though nonwhites make up about four-fifths of the population. Whites follow a governmental policy of *apartheid* (apartness). Nonwhites are segregated from whites and face official discrimination in education, employment, politics, and many other ways. See South Africa.

There are 14 major and many smaller national minority groups living in Russia. During World War II, the Volga Germans, Chechen-Ingush, Crimean Tartars, and Kalmuks were expelled from their homelands, supposedly for disloyalty. Anti-Semitism has been practiced in Russia since the czars came to power. James W. Vander Zanden

Related Articles in World Book include:

Acculturation	Ethnic Group	Ghetto
Alienation	Genocide	Prejudice
Civil Rights,	Gentlemen's	Races, Human
Commission on	Agreement	Racism
Culture		

MINOS, *MY nahs,* a king of Crete in Greek legend, was the son of Zeus and Europa. He was famed as a lawmaker and as the ruler of a great empire. The great age of Crete is called Minoan, because of Minos' fame. Stories told about Minos by the Athenians show him as a cruel conqueror. They tell that Minos overcame Athens, and required the people of the city to send seven boys and seven girls each year as a sacrifice to the Minotaur (see MINOTAUR).

Other stories picture Minos as a wise ruler. He defeated the pirates who were attacking ships, and enacted just laws on the advice of his father, Zeus. Minos and his brother, Rhadamanthus, became judges in the Lower World after their death.   O. M. PEARL

MINOT, *MY nut,* **GEORGE** (1885-1950), an American physician, was one of the world's greatest authorities on blood diseases. In 1926, he announced the liver treatment for pernicious anemia patients. His research showed that when the patients were treated with a diet containing a large amount of liver, the anemia disappeared and the red blood count returned to normal. His discovery opened a new era for patients with anemia, a disease that had always been fatal.

Minot and his co-workers, G. H. Whipple and W. P. Murphy, received the 1934 Nobel prize in medicine for this research. He also received the 1929 Kuber Medal of the Association of American Physicians, the 1930 Cameron Prize of the University of Edinburgh, and the 1933 Medal of the Royal College of Physicians in London. Minot wrote many articles on the blood and its disorders. He also wrote about dietary deficiency. One of his works, written with William B. Castle, is *Pathological Physiology and Clinical Description of the Anemias* (1936).

Minot was born in Boston, Mass. He received his medical degree from Harvard University in 1912. He taught and did research work at Johns Hopkins University in 1914 and 1915. During World War I, he served as a contract surgeon for the United States Army. From 1928 to 1948, Minot was professor of medicine at Harvard Medical School, and director of Boston's Thorndike Memorial Laboratory.   NOAH D. FABRICANT

MINOTAUR, *MIN oh tawr,* was a mythical monster with the head of a bull and the body of a man. King Minos of Crete kept it in the Labyrinth, a mazelike building from which no one could escape (see LABYRINTH; MINOS). Minos sacrificed seven Athenian youths and seven Athenian maidens to it each year. Theseus of Athens finally killed the Minotaur, and escaped from the Labyrinth by following a thread given to him by Minos' daughter, Ariadne (see ARIADNE; THESEUS). He took Ariadne with him, but later deserted her.

The palace excavated at Knossos in Crete has so many passageways that it resembles the legendary Labyrinth (see KNOSSOS). Paintings and mosaics found there show bulls and bull-baiting games.   O. M. PEARL

MINSK (pop. 1,262,000; met. area pop. 1,276,000) is the capital of the Byelorussian Soviet Socialist Republic. It lies on the Svisloch River, about 470 miles (756 kilometers) southwest of Moscow on the railway route to Warsaw, Poland (see RUSSIA [political map]).

Factories in Minsk produce ball bearings, machine tools, peat-digging machines, radios, trucks, and tractors. Woodworkers in the city produce prefabricated houses and furniture.

Minsk is the home of the Byelorussian state university, medical and polytechnic schools, an academy of sciences, a state museum, and an opera and ballet theater. The city suffered heavy damage during the fighting in World War II.   THEODORE SHABAD

MINSTREL. The wandering poet musicians who flourished during the Middle Ages were known by various names in the different countries of Europe. They were called *troubadours* and *jongleurs* in France, and *minnesingers* in Germany. Other names for them were *skald* in Scandinavia and *bard* in Ireland. The early English minstrel was called a *scop.* But the name *min-*

Newberry Library, Chicago
Minstrels and Jugglers Entertain at a Royal Dinner during the Middle Ages. Many were highly skilled performers.

Theseus and the Minotaur (1848) by Antoine Louis Barye.
The Walters Art Gallery, Baltimore, Md.
The Minotaur in Greek mythology had a bull's head and a man's body. Theseus, a Greek hero, killed it on the island of Crete.

514a

strel was used for the later poet musicians of England.

Some minstrels belonged to the households of kings and nobles. Some traveled about and gave entertainments at the castles along their way. Sometimes they entertained the village folk. The minstrels often made up their own songs and stories as they entertained. But they also repeated ballads and folk tales of the time, thus helping to preserve them. The minstrels began to die out by the late 1400's. The printing press eventually replaced the storytellers.

Many songs and literary works tell about the deeds of the minstrels. Sir Walter Scott's novel *The Talisman*, tells of Blondel, the favorite minstrel of Richard the Lion-Hearted, king of England.   REGINALD FRENCH

Related Articles in WORLD BOOK include:

Bard	Minnesinger	Troubadour
Mastersinger	Skald	Trouvère

MINSTREL SHOW is one of the few purely American forms of entertainment. It was a kind of vaudeville show in which the performers blackened their faces with burnt cork to appear on the stage as blacks. They sat in a semicircle, with a band behind them. An *interlocutor* ("straight man") served as master of ceremonies. The star performers were the *end men*, who sat at each end of the row. Their stage names, Mr. Bones and Mr. Tambo, came from the ivory bones and the tambourine that they played. Minstrel shows featured comedy routines, sentimental songs, variety acts, and dancing. Performers often toured on floating theaters, or *showboats*.

Minstrel shows began in the 1840's, and enjoyed great popularity until about 1900. They probably originated in the dancing and singing of black slaves, but almost all the performers were whites. Famous troupes included the Virginia Minstrels and Christy's Minstrels. Stars such as Primrose and West, McIntyre and Heath, and Lew Dockstader delighted audiences from coast to coast. The entertainer Al Jolson began in show business as a member of Dockstader's troupe. Stephen C. Foster wrote many songs for minstrel shows, among them "My Old Kentucky Home" and "Old Black Joe."   GLENN HUGHES

MINT is a place where coins are made. In the United States and most other countries, only the federal government may *mint* (manufacture) coins. United States mints are supervised by the Bureau of the Mint, a division of the Department of the Treasury. Mints now operate in Denver and Philadelphia, and on a temporary basis in San Francisco. They make only coins. The Bureau of Engraving and Printing in Washington, D.C., makes paper money (see ENGRAVING AND PRINTING, BUREAU OF).

United States mints make dollars, half dollars, quarters, dimes, nickels, and cents. For a description of how United States coins are minted, see MONEY (Minting Coins).

Historians believe the world's first mint was founded during the 600's B.C. in Lydia, now a part of Turkey. Coins were used in commerce by ancient Mediterranean civilizations, including Greece and Rome. The use of coins gradually spread throughout Europe and Asia.

The first mint in the United States was established

Berry & Homer, Inc.

New Coins flow into a bin, *lower left*, after passing through a stamping press at the Philadelphia Mint. This press stamps designs on both sides of blank coins that are fed into it. The press also squeezes ridges on the rim of dimes, quarters, half dollars, and silver dollars.

in Boston in 1652. It produced coins under the authority of the General Court of the Massachusetts Bay Colony. The Articles of Confederation of 1781 gave both the U.S. Congress and the individual states authority to mint money and regulate its value. The first federal mint opened in Philadelphia in 1792, and is still in operation. Other federal mints have operated in Carson City, Nev.; Charlotte, N.C.; Dahlonega, Ga.; Denver; New Orleans; and San Francisco.

Coins were minted in England before the coming of the Romans in A.D. 43. The present British Royal Mint has operated in London since 1810. The Canadian mint was established in Ottawa in 1870 as a branch of the British Royal Mint. It became a part of the Canadian Department of Finance in 1931.   ARTHUR A. WICHMANN

See also BULLION.

MINT. Most people think of the pleasant flavor of peppermint when they hear the word *mint*. But, actually, mint is the name of a whole family of plants. Mint plants have square stems. Some plants have stems called *rootstocks* which take root along the ground. The leaves grow on the stems in twos, one on each side of the stem. Most mint plants have small, white, bluish, or pinkish two-lipped flowers. The flowers sometimes grow on spikes at the end of the stem, rather far above the pleasantly scented leaves.

Mint grows in all parts of the world. Both the leaf and the oil are used for flavoring in cooking and in

USDA

Mint

making perfume. Mint is also used in medicine. There are about 3,200 different kinds of mint. The best known members of the mint family are balm, horehound, catnip, hyssop, lavender, marjoram, peppermint, rosemary, sage, spearmint, and thyme.

Scientific Classification. Mint makes up the mint family, *Labiatae*.   HAROLD NORMAN MOLDENKE

Related Articles in WORLD BOOK include:

Balm	Horehound	Patchouli	Sage
Basil	Hyssop	Pennyroyal	Spearmint
Bergamot	Lavender	Peppermint	Thyme
Catnip	Marjoram	Rosemary	

MINTO, EARL OF (1845-1914), GILBERT JOHN ELLIOT-MURRAY-KYNYNMOND, served as Governor General of Canada from 1893 to 1904 and as Viceroy of India from 1905 to 1910. As Canada's governor general, he won permission from the British prime minister to send Canadian forces to fight in the Boer War of 1899 (see BOER WAR).

The Earl of Minto served as an attaché to the Turkish Army during the Russo-Turkish war in 1877. He became chief of staff during the Second Riel Rebellion of 1885.

He was born in London, the grandson of the first Earl of Minto. In 1891, he became head of the Minto estate at Hawick, Scotland.   LUCIEN BRAULT

MINUET, MIN yoo EHT, is a popular dance which originated in France about 200 years ago. The name *minuet* comes from the French word *menu*, meaning small, because of the dance's short, mincing, dainty steps. People danced the minuet in $\frac{3}{4}$ time, with a slow tempo. The minuet was introduced at the French court of Louis XIV about 1650, and reached its greatest popularity in the 1700's. In the 1800's, dancers walked the minuet as a *quadrille*. The minuet has come to represent dignity and gracefulness. It made a strong impact on the music of its time.   WALTER SORELL

MINUIT, MIN yoo it, **PETER** (1580-1638), was a Dutch colonial governor. He bought Manhattan Island from the Indians in 1626 for trinkets costing 60 Dutch *guilders*, or about $24 (see MANHATTAN ISLAND). This legalized the occupation of the island by the Dutch West India Company. Minuit made New Amsterdam, a settlement on the lower half of the island, the center of the company's activities. The community already was protected by water on three sides, but Minuit built Fort Amsterdam for further protection against the hostile Indians. New Amsterdam was the beginning of New York City.

The Dutch West India Company recalled Minuit in 1631 for granting too many privileges to the *patroons* (wealthy landowners). Later, the Swedish government asked him to lead its first expedition to America, and he returned to America in 1638. He built Fort Christina, named after the queen of Sweden, at what is now Wilmington, Del. Shortly after the establishment of the fort, he drowned at sea during a hurricane.

Minuit was born in Wesel, Germany, but moved to The Netherlands when he was a young man. In 1626, he became the governor and director-general of New Netherland, the Dutch colony in North America.   IAN C. C. GRAHAM

See also TREATY (picture).

MINUTE, in religion. See QUAKERS (Worship).

MINUTE, MIN it, is a unit used to measure both time and angles. In time, 60 minutes make up one hour.

Each minute is divided into 60 seconds. Because an hour is $\frac{1}{24}$ of a day, a minute is $\frac{1}{1,440}$ of a day. In measuring angles, 60 minutes make up one degree. A circle is divided into 360 degrees, so one minute is $\frac{1}{21,600}$ of a complete circle. Each minute of an angle is divided into 60 seconds.

The minute in time is an exact measurement, which means exactly so much time. The minute of an angle is an exact portion of a circle, and is independent of the size of the circle. But if the angle is denoted by a linear measurement along the circumference, the distance of a minute depends on the circle's diameter. For example, a minute on a baseball measures only a small fraction of an inch. On the earth's surface a minute is one nautical mile, about 6,076 feet, or 1,852 meters (see MILE).

The circle was first divided into 360 degrees by ancient civilizations, either the Babylonians, the Egyptians, or the Chaldeans. The Babylonians figured everything in units, 10's, and 60's instead of 10's and 100's, as we do. The degree was divided into 60 parts and each of these parts was divided into 60 parts.

The Romans called the first divisions of the degree the *partes minutae primae*, or "first small parts." The second division they called the *partes minutae secundae*, or "second small parts." These terms were finally shortened to *minute* and *second*.   DONALD H. MENZEL

See also DEGREE; HOUR; MEASUREMENT (Measuring Time).

MINUTE MAN NATIONAL HISTORICAL PARK. See NATIONAL PARK SYSTEM (table).

MINUTEMAN. In the years just before the Revolutionary War, volunteers were organized into military companies and trained to bear arms. These men were

Keith Martin, Concord

A Statue of a Minuteman in Concord, Mass., honors minutemen who fought during the Revolutionary War in America. The figure is the work of the American sculptor Daniel Chester French.

515

Keith Martin, Concord

"The Rude Bridge That Arched the Flood" stands in Concord, Mass. The original bridge has disappeared, but it has been duplicated as a memorial to the minutemen who fought there.

called *minutemen* because they were prepared to fight "at a minute's notice."

When the Massachusetts militia was reorganized in 1774, the Provincial Congress provided that one-third of all the new regiments were to be made up of minutemen. In 1775, several colonies trained military companies at the suggestion of the Continental Congress.

The most famous minutemen came from Massachusetts. Minutemen fought side by side with the militia at Lexington and Concord. The minutemen groups disappeared when regular armies were formed. JOHN R. ALDEN

MINUTES OF MEETING. See PARLIAMENTARY PROCEDURE (Minutes).

MIOCENE EPOCH. See EARTH (table: Outline of Earth History).

MIQUELON. See SAINT PIERRE AND MIQUELON.

MIRA, a giant red star, was the first star of variable brightness to be discovered. The German astronomer David Fabricius observed the changing brightness of the star in 1596. Its variation in brightness was the first indication that objects outside the solar system undergo any change. Because of this discovery, astronomers named the star *mira* (Latin for *wonderful*). Changes in Mira's size and temperature cause it to change from dim to bright and back to dim again every 11 months. At its brightest, Mira is about 300 times brighter than it is at its dimmest.

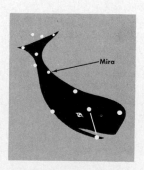

Mira appears in the whale-shaped constellation Cetus.

Mira is so big that if its center were where the center of the sun is, its surface would lie beyond the orbit of Mars. Mira is about 270 light-years from the earth. CHARLES A. WHITNEY

MIRABEAU, *MIR uh boh* or *MEE RAH BOH,* **COMTE DE** (1749-1791), HONORÉ GABRIEL VICTOR RIQUETI, was a French statesman, orator, and revolutionary leader. He was called "the tribune of the people."

Mirabeau was always in debt, and lived an unsavory private life. But his wonderful powers of oratory made him one of the leaders of France. He became the most powerful enemy of the royal court.

But, after the first weeks of the French Revolution, he tried to place his abilities at the king's service and to work with the government. He believed that France needed both the king and the assembly. He wanted a constitutional monarchy similar to that in England. But the king and the revolutionists were suspicious of him.

Mirabeau was born in Bignon. In 1767, he entered a military school in Paris. In the same year he became an officer in a cavalry regiment, but was imprisoned for misconduct. He was released on condition that he would join the Corsican expedition of 1769. He agreed and soon became a captain, but left the army in 1771. In 1774, Mirabeau was again in jail, this time for debt. From 1777 to 1780 he was imprisoned again, and left France on his release. He lived in The Netherlands and England, but returned to France in 1788. In 1789, he was elected to represent Aix in the States-General, the French Parliament. He was elected as a delegate of the Third Estate, the term used for the common people (see STATES-GENERAL).

Shortly afterward, the king's chamberlain ordered the deputies of the Third Estate to leave their place of assembly at Versailles. Mirabeau rose in his seat and thundered, "Go and tell your master that we are here by the will of the people and that we shall not budge save at the point of a bayonet." The deputies stayed.

In 1790, Mirabeau was elected president of the Jacobin Club, a powerful organization of French political leaders (see JACOBINS). In 1791, he became president of the National Assembly, a position where his influence might have done much good. But years of bad living habits had ruined his health. In three months Mirabeau died, with the prophetic words, "I carry with me the ruin of the monarchy." ANDRÉ MAUROIS

Bust of Mirabeau by Jean Antoine Houdon. Chateau de Versailles (Alinari from Art Reference Bureau)

Comte de Mirabeau

MIRACLE is an event of such supernatural or unusual character that the beholders believe that God or some unknown agent caused it. Miracles in the Bible were performed by God, sometimes through His spokesmen, such as the prophets in the Old Testament, and the apostles in the New Testament. Miracles in the Old Testament include the parting of the Red Sea and the fall of manna in the desert. The greatest miracle in the New Testament is the resurrection of Jesus Christ.

Other important miracles include Christ's healing of the sick and His feeding more than 5,000 persons with only a few loaves and fishes. The Roman Catholic Church accepts as miraculous certain events which have occurred since biblical times. These miraculous events include cures at Lourdes, France, and other shrines. See also CANONIZATION.   BERNARD RAMM

MIRACLE PLAY is a form of religious drama which was popular in the Middle Ages. It was based on the lives of the saints. At first, the plays were presented as a part of Roman Catholic Church services. But, like the mystery plays out of which they developed, they lost the approval of the church. The plays were driven from the church to the streets or public squares.

In England, trade guild members performed these plays on feast days. Miracle plays have been revived from time to time, but interest in this type of drama has become chiefly literary.   CHARLES W. COOPER

See DRAMA (Medieval Drama).

MIRAFLORES LOCKS. See PANAMA CANAL (The Pedro Miguel and Miraflores Locks).

MIRAGE, *mih RAHZH.* Sometimes when we drive in summer, we see something ahead of us on the highway that looks like a distant pool of water. Desert travelers often think they see a cool lake, only to discover nothing but wastes of sand when they draw near. Mirages are also seen at sea. The term *mirage* comes from a Latin word, *mirare,* meaning *to look at.*

All of these mirages are caused by hot air near the surface of the earth. The warm air *refracts* (bends) light rays from the sky toward our eyes. For example, sometimes when we are on a highway, we seem to see part of the sky on the road in front of us. Light rays from the sky strike the layers of hot air just above the pavement and are refracted along our line of vision. Sometimes, the resulting image of the sky includes part of a cloud, and what we see looks like a distant lake. Because mirages are actual light rays, they can be photographed.

Some mirages are very striking. Because the layers of hot air vary in position, the mirage lake we see may apparently have ripples, just like a real lake disturbed by the wind. Trees are sometimes seen upside down, just as they look when reflected in a pool of water. Light rays from the treetop coming at an angle downward are bent upward again along our line of vision. We actually "see" the top of the tree which lies beneath the horizon.

At sea, the dense layers of air next to the surface of the water often focus rays from a distant object into an upside-down image in the sky. Sometimes people at sea cannot see a distant ship because of hot air layers, but they do "see" the ship in the sky, upside down.

Mirages were known to the ancients, but they were not scientifically explained until the late 1700's. Gaspard Monge, who traveled with Napoleon's expedition to Egypt in 1798, saw the images and realized that they were caused by the bending of light waves in the atmosphere. Some scientists believe that *flying saucers* are mirages (see UNIDENTIFIED FLYING OBJECT). The Fata Morgana is a well-known mirage of a city that sometimes appears in the Strait of Messina off the coast of Sicily.   SAMUEL W. HARDING

MIRAMICHI RIVER, *MIHR uh mih SHEE,* is one of the greatest salmon streams in the world. It is the second largest waterway in New Brunswick, Canada, ranking

Mirage
Bending Light Rays Cause Mirages. Light rays bend when they pass through substances of different densities, such as air and water. This bending makes a pencil in a glass of water look broken.

David Linton

Layers of Cool and Warm Air Produce a Mirage. Light rays from an object, such as the distant rocks, *top,* bend as they pass from the cool, heavy air near the surface to the warm, light air above. This produces a mirage, *center,* that makes the rocks appear closer than they are. The diagram, *below,* shows how the light rays bend.

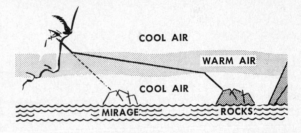

next to the Saint John River. The Miramichi forms where the Northwest Miramichi and the Southwest Miramichi meet and join in northeastern New Brunswick. The river flows northeastward for 135 miles (217 kilometers) and empties into the Gulf of Saint Lawrence through Miramichi Bay. Large ships can sail up to Newcastle, about 30 miles (48 kilometers) from the mouth of the river.   D. F. PUTNAM

MIRANDA, *mee RAHN dah,* **FRANCISCO DE** (1750-1816), a Venezuelan patriot, fought in the American, French, and Spanish-American revolutions. He took the lead in declaring Venezuela's independence from Spain in 1811 (see VENEZUELA [The Struggle for Independence]). Unsuccessful as a dictator, he surrendered his forces to the Royalists. His former subordinates, including Simón Bolívar, handed him over to the Spanish (see BOLÍVAR, SIMÓN). Miranda died in a Spanish dungeon. He was born in Caracas.   HARVEY L. JOHNSON

MIRANDA V. ARIZONA was a case in which the Supreme Court of the United States limited the power of police to question suspects. The court ruled in 1966 that nothing arrested persons say can be used against them in their trial unless they have been told they have certain rights. For example, suspects must be told they have the right to remain silent, and that anything they say can be held against them. They also must be told

Oil painting on canvas (1944); Yale University Art Gallery, Bequest of Kay Sage Tanguy

Joan Miró's *Women and Birds in the Night* shows the bright colors and simple forms that are typical of his style.

they can have a lawyer present during questioning, and, if they cannot afford one, the court will appoint one.

The court's decision reversed the conviction of Ernesto A. Miranda, a Phoenix warehouse worker, on charges of kidnaping and rape. Miranda had confessed to the charges, and his confession was used as evidence in his trial. However, he had not been told of his right to remain silent and had been denied the right to consult a lawyer.

The Supreme Court based its decision on the Fifth and Sixth amendments to the United States Constitution. The Fifth Amendment protects persons from being forced to testify against themselves. The Sixth Amendment guarantees a defendant's right to a lawyer.

Several later Supreme Court decisions limited the scope of the ruling in *Miranda v. Arizona*. In 1971, for example, the court ruled that a confession obtained in violation of the *Miranda* decision can be used at a trial to prove the defendant is lying.   STANLEY I. KUTLER

See also ESCOBEDO V. ILLINOIS.

MIRÓ, *mee ROH,* **JOAN,** *hwahn* (1893-   ), is a Spanish painter who won fame for his imaginative and extremely personal style. His highly abstract forms suggest people, animals, and other subjects. Many of his paintings contain a story or scene disguised by the apparent abstractness of the shapes and colors. Miró's painting *Landscape* appears in the PAINTING article.

Miró was born in Montroig, Spain, near Barcelona. In 1919, he went to Paris, where he helped establish the *surrealist* movement during the 1920's (see SURREALISM). He developed his characteristic style during the 1920's and early 1930's. Miró's mature work portrays

a world of fantasy, which he pictured in simple colors and abstract shapes that have no shading. Miró also gained recognition for works in other art forms, including ceramics, sculpture, and a type of printmaking called *lithography*.   JONATHAN FINEBERG

MIRROR. People use mirrors, or looking glasses, every day. Any smooth surface which reflects light rays rather than absorbs them is a mirror. Most mirrors are made of a pane of glass which is coated on the back so that the light cannot pass through, but is reflected. The amount of light reflected depends on the kind of material, the angle at which light strikes it, and how polished the surface is. The more mirrors are polished, the more light they will be able to reflect. But even the best mirrors never reflect all the light which falls upon them.

The angle at which light strikes the mirror from the object is called the *angle of incidence*. The angle at which light is reflected is called the *angle of reflection*. The angle of incidence is always equal to the angle of reflection. A perpendicular to the mirror which strikes the mirror at the point of reflection is called the *normal*.

When you stand close in front of a *plane* (flat) mirror, your image is the same size as yourself, and seems to be as far behind the mirror as you are in front of it. For example, if you are 3 feet from the mirror, your image seems 6 feet away. In a sense it is, because the light rays travel 6 feet before you see them—3 feet to the mirror, and 3 feet back to your eyes.

The image is always reversed. If you lift your right hand, your image seems to be raising its left hand.

If you want to see yourself full length in a mirror, the mirror must be at least half as tall as you are. This is because the angle of incidence must equal the angle of reflection. Suppose the top of the mirror is about on a line with the top of your head. Then the light rays which come from your feet and which are reflected back to your eyes by the mirror must strike the mirror at least half the distance between your feet and head. If you are 6 feet tall, the mirror must be at least 3 feet high.

A concave spherical mirror is shaped like the inside of an imaginary sphere. No matter how much or how little the mirror curves, it will fit the surface of some sphere. The center of this imaginary sphere is called the *center of curvature*. A line from the center of the mirror to this center of curvature is called the *principal axis* of the mirror. When parallel light rays strike the mirror, they are reflected so that they meet at a spot halfway between the mirror and its center of curvature.

WORLD BOOK illustration

A Mirror reflects light rays. The direction the light is reflected depends on the angle at which it falls on the mirror.

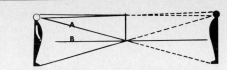

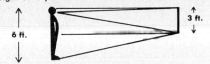

In a Plane Mirror, the image is at the mirror, but appears to be as far beyond it as the object is in front of it. In a mirror, *top,* the angle of incidence (A) equals the angle of reflection (B). Because of this, a mirror must be at least half the height of a person to reflect a full-length image, *below.*

In a Concave Mirror, *below,* such as those sometimes used for shaving, the position and size of the *image* (in gray) depend on the position of the *object* (in black) in relation to the mirror's *center of focus* (F) and *center of curvature* (C). The position of the object also determines whether the image is *real* (formed in front of the mirror), or *virtual* (appears formed behind the mirror).

Popular Science Monthly

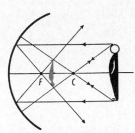

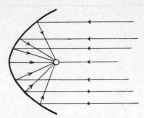

Object Beyond C produces a real, inverted, smaller image.

Object at C produces a real, inverted, equal-sized image.

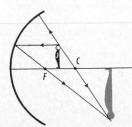

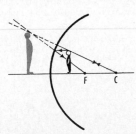

Object Between C and F produces a real, inverted image that is farther from the surface of the mirror than the original reflected object.

Object Between F and the Mirror produces an erect image, larger than the object. The image appears to be behind the mirror.

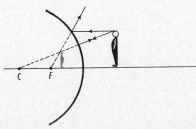

A Convex Mirror, as pictured in the diagram above, produces an upright image that is much smaller than the object. The image formed appears to be behind the mirror.

A Concave Mirror can be used in a solar cooker, *top.* Such a mirror, as shown in the diagram above, reflects the rays of the sun and focuses them on a single spot in the center of the cooker. This concentrated heat from the sun can cook food.

This point is called the *principal focus.* When the object is between the center of curvature and the principal focus, the image formed is larger than the object, and inverted. It appears beyond the center of curvature. The reflectors in automobile lights, bicycle lights, and in mouth mirrors used by dentists are concave mirrors.

Convex mirrors are just the opposite of concave mirrors. They curve toward the object instead of inward, away from it. They are parts of the outsides of imaginary spheres. The center of curvature and the principal focus are behind the mirror now. The reflected rays have to be extended behind the mirror in order to meet these points and form the image. The image is always behind the mirror, smaller than the object, and right side up. A polished ball will reflect such an image. Convex mirrors are often used to reflect a large field of vision smaller than it appears normally. Some automobile rear-view mirrors are convex for this reason.

County fairs, carnivals, and circus side shows use convex and concave mirrors for amusement. People stand before a convex mirror and see themselves stretched out grotesquely. Then they look in a concave mirror and see themselves short and round.　S. W. Harding

See also Aberration; Parabola; Reflection; Telescope.

MIRV. See Guided Missile (The Warhead; diagram).

MISCARRIAGE. See Pregnancy; Abortion.

MISDEMEANOR is any violation of the law which is less serious than a felony. Assault and battery, the theft of a small sum of money, and other such acts against public safety and welfare, are misdemeanors. So are most traffic offenses. Not all courts draw the same line between misdemeanors and felonies. A felony in one court may be a misdemeanor in another. Persons guilty of misdemeanors are usually fined or given a short jail sentence. See also FELONY. FRED E. INBAU

MISHNAH. See TALMUD.

MISKOLC, *MIHSH kawlts* (pop. 172,952), is the second largest city in Hungary. Only Budapest, the capital, is larger. Miskolc, a busy commercial center, lies on the Sajó River in the northeast industrial region of Hungary. For location, see HUNGARY (political map).

During the 1300's, Miskolc developed as a busy market town and center of the Hungarian wine trade. Handicrafts industries flourished there in the 1700's. Iron smelting and engineering industries developed during the 1800's and remain important. Other industries produce cement, furniture, paper, and textiles.

The city's Ottó Herman Museum features noted archaeological exhibits. The Technical University of Heavy Industry provides training in various fields of engineering. GEORGE BARANY

MISSAL, *MIS ul*, is the book containing the prayers and ceremonial directions of the complete yearly service, or *liturgy*, for the celebration of Mass in the Roman Catholic Church. The word comes from the Latin *missa*, meaning *mass*. All the separate books formerly used in the service were united into one volume to form the missal. In order to correct variations, the Council of Trent ordered its revision. Pope Pius V accomplished this in 1570.

The revised book was ordered to be used in every church which failed to show that its form of service had been in unbroken use for 200 years. Pope Clement VIII made further revisions in 1604, and Pope Urban VIII made others 30 years later. In 1884 and in 1898 Pope Leo XIII also revised the rules slightly. FULTON J. SHEEN

See also BREVIARY.

MISSILE, GUIDED. See GUIDED MISSILE.

MISSILE BOAT is a small, fast warship that carries guided missiles for attacking enemy ships. The navies of many countries use these boats to patrol and defend narrow seas and coastal waters.

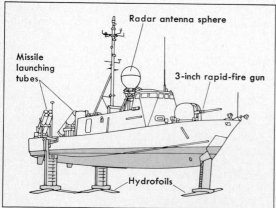

Radar antenna sphere

Missile launching tubes

3-inch rapid-fire gun

Hydrofoils

WORLD BOOK illustration by George Suyeoka

A Missile Boat of the U.S. Navy, above, skims over the water on hydrofoils. It can fire up to eight missiles at enemy ships.

Missile boats measure from about 83 to 200 feet (25 to 61 meters) long and can travel at speeds of 40 knots (nautical miles per hour) or faster. They carry from two to eight guided missiles. The missiles can be fired accurately to distances up to 60 miles (97 kilometers). Missile boats also have one or more guns for use against aircraft and small ships. The barrels of these guns range from 1 to 3 inches (25 to 76 millimeters) in caliber.

Missile boats have diesel or gas turbine engines. Missile boats of the United States Navy are *hydrofoils*. At high speeds, the hulls of such boats are raised above the water by wing-shaped structures below the surface. These hydrofoils are powered by diesel engines when their hulls are in the water, and by gas turbines when they are above the water.

The first missile boats were built by the Russian Navy and went to sea in 1958. In 1967, the Egyptian Navy used such boats to sink an Israeli destroyer. The Egyptian boats were in their own harbor when they fired three missiles at the destroyer, which was $12\frac{1}{2}$ miles (20.1 kilometers) off the coast. The United States and other nations began to develop missile boats following this and other sinkings by Russian-built craft. The first U.S. Navy missile boat, the *Pegasus*, was completed in 1976. NORMAN POLMAR

MISSION LIFE IN AMERICA. Missionaries often led the way in establishing contact between whites and Indians in what became the United States. The early missionaries arrived from Spain during the 1500's and from France and Great Britain in the 1600's. British and French mission work centered mainly in frontier churches and schools. The Spanish missions, on the other hand, were actually small settlements. There, the Indians not only took instruction in Christianity but also lived and worked. This article discusses the development, daily life, and heritage of the Spanish missions.

Members of the Franciscan order of the Roman Catholic Church founded most of the Spanish missions in what is now the United States. The missions spread across a vast region north of Spain's colonial empire in Latin America. This region, called the *Spanish Borderlands*, included all or much of present-day Arizona, California, Florida, Georgia, New Mexico, and Texas.

The Spanish government established and supported the missions. It did so chiefly to develop colonies and expand its empire. The government hoped the missionaries could convert the Indians to Roman Catholicism and persuade them to become loyal Spanish citizens. To achieve these goals, the priests taught the Indians much besides Catholicism—farming, stock raising, trades, principles of government, and duties of citizenship. Missions thrived in parts of the borderlands until the early 1800's, when Spain lost its American colonies to Mexico.

Development of the Missions

The Spanish province of Florida became the first center of missionary activity in the United States. The gray-robed Franciscans began to develop missions there during the 1570's. By 1634, about 35 missionaries directed more than 40 missions that had a total Indian population of about 30,000. This system lasted until 1763, when Britain won the region from Spain.

Spanish Missions in America thrived in parts of the South and West from the 1500's to the 1800's. They introduced Christianity to thousands of American Indians. This drawing, made in 1792, shows Mission San Carlos Borromeo de Carmelo, near what is now Carmel, Calif.

After the Franciscans opened their first Florida missions, they began their work in what is now New Mexico. By 1630, about 25 missions thrived there. That year, the Franciscan Alonso de Benavides reported to King Philip IV of Spain that 60,000 Pueblo Indians had become Christians. The Pueblo Revolt of 1680 closed the missions and drove the Spaniards from New Mexico (see INDIAN WARS [The Pueblo Revolt]). Some of the missions reopened after Spanish troops returned to the region in 1692.

Major Franciscan missionary activity in the Texas area began in 1690. But the missionaries achieved relatively little success in that area because some of the fiercest Indian tribes on the continent lived there. These Indians, including the Apaches and Comanches, regarded the Spaniards as invaders and attacked the missions frequently. Missions that survived the raids were in or near San Antonio or other large settlements. Missionary activity in Texas declined during the late 1700's.

A Jesuit missionary, Eusebio Francisco Kino, developed missionary work in what is now Arizona. He began to preach to Indians there in the 1690's. During the mid-1700's, the Franciscans took over the missions that Kino had founded in Arizona. See KINO, EUSEBIO FRANCISCO.

Mission life in America reached its fullest development in California. In 1769, the Franciscan Junípero Serra established the first California mission, San Diego de Alcalá, in present-day San Diego. He founded 8 additional California missions, and other Franciscans opened 12 more after his death in 1784. The California missions, some of which grew into major agricultural and manufacturing centers, came under the control of Mexico in 1821. The missions continued to prosper until 1834, when the Mexican government began to sell the rich mission land to private citizens. See INDIAN, AMERICAN (Indians of the California-Intermountain Region); SERRA, JUNÍPERO.

Life at the Missions

The Spanish missions fed, clothed, and often housed the Indians who entered them. In return, the Indians agreed to take instruction in Christianity, to observe Spanish customs, and to work for a certain mission.

Many missions included dining facilities, schools, storerooms, and workshops, as well as living quarters and a church. In most cases, these structures were built of adobe or stone blocks and stood around a square courtyard. All the missions had farms, and many operated ranches.

Christianity was the main subject taught in the mission schools. Indian children attended classes in Catholicism at least twice daily. The missionaries also taught Indian children and adults to read and write Spanish. In addition, many Indians received job training. The missionaries, or skilled workers whom they hired, taught the Indians such trades as blacksmithing, candle making, leatherworking, weaving, wine making, and woodworking.

Most of the mission Indians worked as farmers. Many did exceptionally well in this work, and others became expert ranchers or trades workers. The California Indians were highly productive, and their missions developed a thriving trade with ships from foreign countries. During the early 1830's, Indians of the California missions herded an annual total of about 400,000 cattle, 60,000 horses, and 320,000 goats, hogs, and sheep. They also harvested about 125,000 bushels of grain yearly during this period.

Some missions tried to introduce principles of European government to the Indians. The Indians in these mission communities elected a council that governed Indian affairs, and the missionaries worked closely with the council members. Many councils became so effective that they enabled one or two missionaries to control hundreds of Indians.

Activities in the missions followed a regular schedule. The day began with a religious service. The missionaries often combined these services with festivals and with ceremonies for births, deaths, and marriages.

After the morning service, the Indians ate breakfast and went to work. They had lunch at about noon and then worked several more hours. After dinner, they often danced, sang, or took part in other recreational activi-

WORLD BOOK photo by Zintgraff Photography

Mission San Jose was established in San Antonio, Tex., in 1720. Its many graceful carvings, which attract thousands of visitors yearly, are reminders of Spanish rule in America.

ties. During planting or harvesting periods, the Indians worked several extra hours each day and had little time for recreation.

Many Indians adjusted to the daily routine of mission life. But many others disliked following a schedule and resented the loss of their personal freedom. Large numbers of these Indians fled from the missions. Spanish soldiers stationed in or near the missions caught some of the runaways and returned them to the missions. Many soldiers caused problems for the missionaries by abusing Indian women. Some Indians rebelled against the missionaries or soldiers by burning buildings, destroying crops, or committing other violent acts.

The missionaries often tried to keep dissatisfied Indians at the missions by offering them gifts or special privileges. Some missions even gave the Indians a two-week vacation every five weeks.

Thousands of Christian Indians faced grave problems after the missions closed. Many did not want to resume tribal ways of life. But discrimination and a lack of education prevented even skilled Indians from getting a good job and receiving equal rights among whites.

A Visitor's Guide

A number of Spanish missions still exist. Some have been rebuilt or restored to preserve the heritage of mission life in America. A few missions continue to serve Indians. Following are brief descriptions of especially interesting missions to visit.

Nombre de Díos, in St. Augustine, Fla., is the oldest U.S. mission. It was established in 1565.

Nuestra Señora del Carmen, near El Paso, Tex., was founded in 1682 by Franciscan missionaries who fled from New Mexico during the Pueblo Revolt of 1680.

San Antonio de Valero, in San Antonio, Tex., is better known as the Alamo. It was the site of a famous battle in 1836, during the Texas Revolution.

San Esteban de Acoma, in Acoma, N. Mex., was founded by the Franciscan Juan Ramirez in 1629. It is on a *mesa* (tableland) 357 feet (109 meters) high.

San Jose, in San Antonio, Tex., was one of the most successful missions in the Southwest. The Franciscan Antonio Margil de Jesús founded it in 1720.

San Juan Capistrano, in San Juan Capistrano, Calif., was established by the Franciscan Junípero Serra in 1776. An earthquake destroyed part of it in 1812.

San Xavier del Bac, near Tucson, Ariz., is the only surviving mission in the state. The Jesuit Eusebio Francisco Kino founded it in 1700.

Santa Barbara, in Santa Barbara, Calif., was founded by the Franciscan Fermín Francisco de Lasuén in 1786. It became known as the Queen of the California Missions because of its architectural beauty.   ANNETTE PEEL

and MANUEL PATRICIO SERVÍN

See also the *History* and *Places to Visit* sections of the articles on ARIZONA; CALIFORNIA; NEW MEXICO; and TEXAS.

MISSIONARY is a person sent by a religious group to convert others to his or her faith. Many missionaries work to provide education, agricultural information, medical care, and other social services to the people they serve.

Various religions attract converts in many different ways. Buddhist organizations spread the teachings of Buddha throughout the world by sponsoring lectures and meditation sessions. Islamic missionaries conduct worship services and distribute religious literature to gain new believers. Some religions today, including Hinduism and Judaism, have no missionaries because they do not seek converts. Christianity carries on the most extensive program of missionary activities. This article discusses Christian missionaries.

Men and women may serve as *foreign missionaries* or *home missionaries*. Foreign missionaries leave their own countries and work in areas called *mission territories*. Major Christian mission territories include much of Africa, Asia, and Latin America, and many of the Pacific Islands. Home missionaries carry out assignments in their own lands.

There are more than 185,000 Christian missionaries, about 60 per cent of whom are women. Many missionaries are members of the clergy—ministers, nuns, priests, and religious brothers. But an increasingly large number of men and women, called *lay missionaries*, are not ordained and do not belong to religious orders.

Duties. Missionaries explain the teachings of their faith and try to inspire devotion to that religion. They lead worship services, preach sermons, and guide converts in the practice of their faith.

Many missionaries also use their skills to improve the quality of life among the people they serve. Today, missionaries provide the only education available in some rural areas of various developing countries. In addition, missionaries strive to wipe out sickness, hunger, and poverty. Some build and operate hospitals, train nurses, and bring medical care to isolated rural villages. Missionaries with technical skills may design and build housing, roads, and communications systems. Other missionary activities include caring for orphans, distributing food among the poor, and teaching more efficient farming methods.

The home missionary activity of several Christian

denominations places special emphasis on conversion. All Jehovah's Witnesses must work at least 10 hours each month spreading their faith to people on street corners and in private homes. Many young adult Mormons volunteer to spend two years spreading their beliefs as full-time missionaries without pay.

Other home missionaries express their faith chiefly through social work and other acts of charity. The Salvation Army ranks among the world's largest home mission organizations. It provides shelter and medical care for unwed mothers, nurseries for the children of working women, aid to convicts and their families, food for the poor, and other charitable services.

Organization. The Roman Catholic Church has over 135,000 missionaries, more than any other Christian denomination. More than half are Europeans. The various Protestant denominations have a total of more than 50,000 missionaries. Nearly two-thirds of them come from the United States.

Several Catholic religious orders devote most of their efforts to missionary activities. These groups include the Catholic Foreign Mission Society of America (Maryknoll) and the Congregation of the Missions (Vincentians). The Sacred Congregation for the Propagation of the Faith directs worldwide Catholic mission work. Protestant missionaries are recruited and financed by Protestant denominations, church-sponsored organizations, and independent agencies. The National Council of Churches and the World Council of Churches coordinate much Protestant missionary activity.

During the 1900's, Evangelical and Pentecostal churches have conducted active missionary campaigns in the United States and in Africa, Asia, and the Pacific. The Evangelical Foreign Missions Association and the Pentecostal Assemblies of the World coordinate much of this work.

History. Christian missionary work began soon after that religion was founded nearly 2,000 years ago. Christianity spread rapidly because of such enthusiastic missionary activity as that of Saint Peter and Saint Paul among the Jews and *gentiles* (non-Jews). By the 300's, Christianity had spread throughout the Roman Empire, including North Africa. In the 600's, and 700's, Islam became the main religion of North Africa and Spain, and by the 1500's had spread into southeastern Europe. During the Middle Ages, Christian missionaries converted the people of most European countries.

By the 1500's, Roman Catholic missionaries were sailing with European explorers and soldiers to little-known regions of Africa, Asia, and the Americas. The Dominican, Franciscan, and Jesuit orders established many missions throughout the world.

The Protestant foreign missionary movement began in the 1700's. William Carey and Robert Morrison, both of England, and other Protestant missionaries worked in the Far East and in Africa. In the United States, such preachers as Jonathan Edwards, Gilbert and William Tenent, and George Whitefield sought converts in the 1700's. During the late 1700's and early 1800's, revivalists from Baptist, Methodist, and other churches won converts and established congregations on the U.S. frontier. Revivalists of the 1800's and early 1900's gained converts in the growing cities. Today, revivalists use radio and television to seek converts.

Some people in mission lands resented foreign mis-

Cornell Capa, Magnum

A Protestant Missionary among the Auca Indians of Ecuador strives to learn the difficult language from an Auca woman.

sionary activity. This resentment came about partly because many missionaries persuaded the people among whom they worked to accept foreign rule. In addition, some missionaries considered ways of life in mission lands to be primitive and uncivilized. They sometimes insensitively imposed Western traditions and social values on native cultures. Some missionaries also supported governments that ignored the needs of the poor.

A strong sense of patriotic unity called *nationalism* swept through many developing countries after World War II ended in 1945. Many of these countries demanded and won independence from foreign rule. The leaders of some newly independent nations severely limited missionary activity, seized church-supported schools, and even deported or killed missionaries.

Today, foreign missionaries work in Africa, Asia, and Central and South America. Radio and television carry broadcasts of religious instruction to many regions. However, an increasing number of Christians in mission lands are being served by their own native clergy and lay people.   WILLIAM A. CLEBSCH

Related Articles in WORLD BOOK include:

Asbury, Francis	Judson, Adoniram
Bingham, (Hiram [1789-1869])	Las Casas, Bartolomé de
	Lee, Jason
Boniface, Saint	Marquette, Jacques
Brainerd, David	Mission Life in America
Brébeuf, Saint Jean de	Patrick, Saint
De Smet, Pierre J.	Salvation Army
Eliot, John	Schweitzer, Albert
Grenfell, Sir Wilfred T.	Serra, Junípero
Hennepin, Louis	Whitman, Marcus
Jogues, Saint Isaac	Whitman, Narcissa
Jones, Eli S.	Xavier, Saint Francis

MISSIONARY RIDGE, BATTLE OF. See CIVIL WAR (Chattanooga).

Ragsdale, FPG
Stanton Hall, a Mansion in Natchez

MISSISSIPPI THE MAGNOLIA STATE

Mississippi (blue) ranks 32nd in size among all the states, and 7th in size among the Southern States (gray).

MISSISSIPPI is a state of the Deep South that is going through a period of great change. It was once a land of farmers and quiet towns, but is becoming a state of factory workers and busy cities. Since the 1930's, the people of Mississippi have worked to build a modern economy based on industry as well as agriculture.

But tradition still plays an important part in Mississippi life. The people have great pride in their state's history, and Mississippi retains many reminders of the Old South. Stately *ante-bellum* (pre-Civil War) mansions bring back memories of Mississippi plantation life before the Civil War. Monuments throughout the state recall the heroic deeds of the Confederate soldiers who fought on the state's many battlefields.

Rich natural resources form the basis for Mississippi's industrial growth. The state is a leading producer of cotton and petroleum. These products supply much of

524

the raw material and fuel used by the rapidly growing manufacturing industries. Mississippi manufactures a wide variety of goods. They include, in order of importance, transportation equipment, lumber and wood products, electric and electronic equipment, food products, chemicals, and clothing.

Farmland and forest-covered hills spread over most of the state. Northwestern Mississippi is a major U.S. cotton-producing area. Many Mississippi farmlands are used to raise beef or dairy cattle. Other farmlands are used to grow crops. The state ranks as a leading producer of soybeans and sweet potatoes.

Mississippi takes its name from the mighty river that forms most of its western border. *Mississippi* means the *Great Water*, or the *Father of Waters*, in the language of the Indians who lived in the region in early times. Mississippi's nickname, the *Magnolia State*, comes from the beautiful magnolia trees that grow in most parts of the state. Mississippi gardens also have many colorful azaleas and camellias. They bloom for months each year because the climate is generally warm and moist.

The mild climate attracts many tourists to Mississippi, especially in winter. The Mississippi Gulf Coast is a popular winter vacationland. It has large, sunny beaches lined with fine hotels.

Jackson is the capital and largest city of Mississippi. For the relationship of Mississippi to other states in its region, see the article on SOUTHERN STATES.

The contributors of this article are Charlotte Capers, Director of the Information and Education Division at the Mississippi Department of Archives and History; T. M. Hederman, Jr., Editor in Chief of the Mississippi Publishers Corporation; and M. W. Myers, Professor of Geography at Mississippi State University. The photographs were taken for WORLD BOOK *by W. R. Wilson unless otherwise indicated.*

FACTS IN BRIEF

Capital: Jackson.

Government: *Congress*—U.S. senators, 2; U.S. representatives, 5. *Electoral Votes*—7. *State Legislature*—senators, 52; representatives, 122. *Counties*—82.

Area: 47,716 sq. mi. (123,584 km²), including 420 sq. mi. (1,088 km²) of inland water but excluding 556 sq. mi. (1,440 km²) of Gulf of Mexico coastal water; 32nd in size among the states. *Greatest Distances*—north-south, 352 mi. (566 km); east-west, 188 mi. (303 km). *Coastline*—44 mi. (71 km).

Elevation: *Highest*—Woodall Mountain, 806 ft. (246 m) above sea level in Tishomingo County. *Lowest*—sea level along the coast.

Population: *Estimated 1975 Population*—2,346,000. *1970 Census*—2,216,912; 29th among the states; distribution, 55 per cent rural, 45 per cent urban; density, 46 persons per sq. mi. (18 persons per km²).

Chief Products: *Agriculture*—soybeans, cotton, beef cattle, broilers, eggs, milk, cottonseed, rice. *Fishing Industry*—menhaden, shrimp. *Manufacturing*—transportation equipment; lumber and wood products; electric and electronic equipment; food products; chemicals; clothing; nonelectric machinery; paper products; fabricated metal products; furniture and fixtures; stone, clay, and glass products. *Mining*—petroleum, natural gas, sand and gravel, clays.

Statehood: Dec. 10, 1817, the 20th state.

State Abbreviations: Miss. (traditional); MS (postal).

State Motto: *Virtute et armis* (By valor and arms).

State Song: "Go Mis-sis-sip-pi" by Houston Davis.

Building Merchant Ships in Pascagoula Shipyards

Constitution. Mississippi adopted its present Constitution in 1890. The state had three earlier constitutions, adopted in 1817, 1832, and 1869. The Constitution of 1869 was written so that Mississippi could qualify to re-enter the Union after the Civil War. An *amendment* (change) to the Constitution must be approved by two-thirds of the members of each house of the state Legislature. Then the amendment must be approved by a majority of the people voting on the amendment in an election. The Constitution may also be amended by a constitutional convention called by a majority of each house.

Executive. The governor of Mississippi is elected to a four-year term. The governor receives a yearly salary of $43,000. Other executive officers elected to four-year terms include the lieutenant governor, secretary of state, treasurer, auditor, superintendent of public education, attorney general, and commissioners of agriculture and commerce, insurance, and land. The governor and treasurer may not serve two terms in a row. For a list of all the governors of Mississippi, see the *History* section of this article.

Legislature of Mississippi consists of a Senate of 52 members and a House of Representatives of 122 members. Mississippi state legislators are elected to four-year terms. Regular legislative sessions begin on the Tuesday after the first Monday in January each year. Most of the sessions last 90 days. The Legislature may extend the sessions by 30-day periods. Every fourth year, the regular sessions last 125 days. The governor may call special sessions of the legislature.

In the 1960's, Mississippi's legislative districts were *reapportioned* (redivided) to provide equal representation based on population. They were reapportioned again during the 1970's.

Courts in Mississippi are headed by the Supreme Court. The people elect the nine justices of the Supreme Court to eight-year terms. Three are elected from each of three districts that were set up for electing Supreme Court justices. The justice who has served the longest acts as chief justice. All other judges in the state are elected to four-year terms. Mississippi's chief trial courts are chancery and circuit courts. Chancery court judges handle civil cases. Circuit court judges handle both civil and criminal cases. Other courts include county, justice, and juvenile courts.

Local Government. The county is the chief unit of local government in Mississippi. The state has 82 counties, each with five districts. The people of each district elect one of the five members of a county board of supervisors, which administers the county. Most cities have the mayor-council form of government. The Legislature controls the county and city governments in the state.

Taxation provides about 70 per cent of the state government's income. Almost all the rest comes from federal grants and other U.S. government programs. The state receives about half of its tax revenue from a sales tax. Other large sources of income in Mississippi include highway use taxes, individual and corporation income taxes, and profit taxes on alcoholic beverages. Additional state government income comes from taxes on property, tobacco, and inheritances and gifts, and license fees.

Politics. The Democratic Party has controlled Mississippi politics throughout most of the state's history.

The Governor's Mansion in Jackson was completed in 1841 and became the official residence of Mississippi's governors the following year. The mansion and the landscaped grounds around it occupy an entire block along the city's main business street.

Mississippi Agricultural & Industrial Board

Inside the Governor's Mansion, graceful furniture and elaborate decorations reflect the dignity of the Old South. State guests are often entertained in this parlor.

The State Seal

The State Flag

Symbols of Mississippi. On the seal, the American eagle holds an olive branch, representing peace, and three arrows, symbolizing war. The seal was adopted in 1817. The flag, adopted in 1894, reflects Mississippi's ties to the United States and to the Confederacy. The red, white, and blue bars stand for the colors of the national flag. A replica of the Confederate Army's battle flag occupies the upper left portion.

Seal, flag, bird, and flower illustrations, courtesy of Eli Lilly and Company

Since 1876, all Mississippi governors, and most state and local officials, have been Democrats. Before the 1963 election, Republicans rarely nominated candidates for many state and local offices. As a result, nomination by the Democratic party in primary elections almost always meant election to office.

In presidential elections since 1876, Mississippi has cast its electoral votes for the Democratic candidate in every election except five. In 1948, Mississippi voted for the Dixiecrat party (see DIXIECRAT PARTY). In 1960, the state chose electors who voted for Senator Harry F. Byrd of Virginia rather than for the Democratic nominee, Senator John F. Kennedy of Massachusetts. In 1964, Senator Barry M. Goldwater of Arizona became the first Republican presidential candidate to win in Mississippi since 1872. In 1968, the state's electors voted for George C. Wallace, the nominee of the American Independent Party. In 1972, Republican Richard M. Nixon carried Mississippi. For Mississippi's electoral votes and voting record in presidential elections since 1820, see ELECTORAL COLLEGE (table).

The State Capitol is in Jackson, which became the capital in 1822. Earlier capitals were Natchez (1798-1802), Washington (1802-1817), Natchez (1817-1821), and Columbia (1821-1822).

Mississippi Agricultural & Industrial Board

The State Bird
Mockingbird

The State Flower
Magnolia

The State Tree
Magnolia

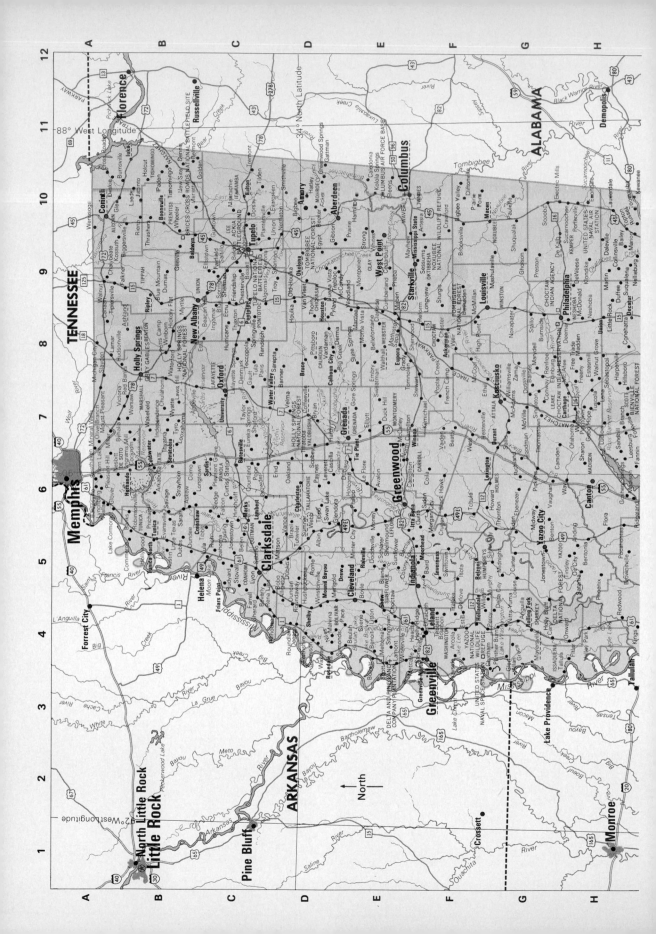

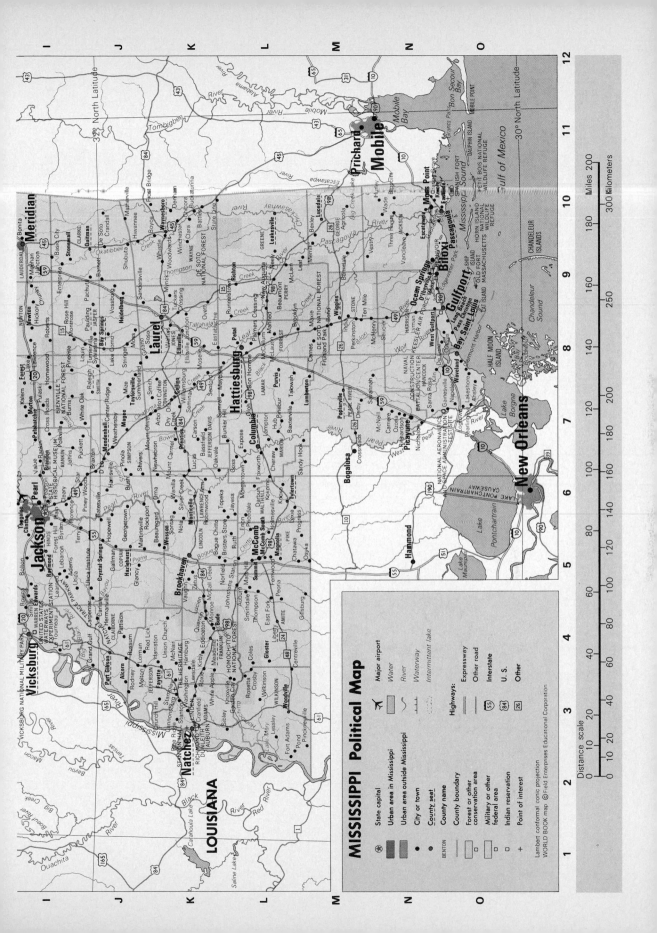

MISSISSIPPI Political Map

State capital	⊛
Urban area in Mississippi	
Urban area outside Mississippi	
City or town	●
County seat	○
County name	
BENTON	
County boundary	
Forest or other conservation area	
Military or other federal area	
Indian reservation	
Point of interest	+

Major airport	✈
Water	
River	
Waterway	
Intermittent lake	

Highways:

Expressway	
Other road	
Interstate	55
U. S.	84
Other	26

Lambert conformal conic projection
WORLD BOOK map ⓒ Field Enterprises Educational Corporation

Distance scale

Miles 200
Kilometers 300

LOUISIANA

Gulf of Mexico

Population

2,346,000	Estimate..1975
2,216,912	Census..1970
2,178,141	" "..1960
2,178,914	" "..1950
2,183,796	" "..1940
2,009,821	" "..1930
1,790,618	" "..1920
1,797,114	" "..1910
1,551,270	" "..1900
1,289,600	" "..1890
1,131,597	" "..1880
827,922	" "..1870
791,305	" "..1860
606,526	" "..1850
375,651	" "..1840
136,621	" "..1830
75,448	" "..1820
31,306	" "..1810
7,600	" "..1800

Metropolitan Area

Biloxi-Gulfport ..160,070
Jackson 258,906
Memphis (Tenn.) 834,103
 (750,112 in Tenn.;
 48,106 in Ark.;
 35,885 in Miss.)
Pascagoula-
 Moss Point 87,975

Counties

Adams ....37,293..K 3
Alcorn ....27,179..A 10
Amite ....13,763..L 4
Attala ....19,570..G 7
Benton ....7,505..B 8
Bolivar ....49,409..D 4
Calhoun ....14,623..D 8
Carroll ....9,397..F 6
Chickasaw ..16,805..D 9
Choctaw ....8,440..F 8
Claiborne ..10,086..J 4
Clarke ....15,049..J 9
Clay ....18,840..E 9
Coahoma ....40,447..C 5
Copiah ....24,764..J 5
Covington ..14,002..K 7
De Soto ....35,885..A 6
Forrest ....57,849..L 8
Franklin ....8,011..K 4
George ....12,459..M 10
Greene ....8,545..L 9
Grenada ....19,854..E 7
Hancock ....17,387..N 7
Harrison ..134,582..N 8
Hinds ....214,973..I 5
Holmes ....23,120..G 6
Humphreys ..14,601..F 5
Issaquena ....2,737..G 4
Itawamba ..16,847..C 10
Jackson ....87,975..N 10
Jasper ....15,994..J 8
Jefferson ....9,295..J 3
Jefferson
 Davis ....12,936..K 7
Jones ....56,357..K 8
Kemper ....10,233..H 9
Lafayette ..24,181..C 8
Lamar ....15,209..L 7
Lauderdale ..67,087..I 9
Lawrence ..11,137..K 6
Leake ....17,085..G 7
Lee ....46,148..C 9
Leflore ....42,111..E 5
Lincoln ....26,198..K 5
Lowndes ....49,700..F 10
Madison ....29,737..H 6
Marion ....22,871..L 7
Marshall ....24,027..B 7
Monroe ....34,043..D 10
Montgomery 12,918..E 7
Neshoba ....20,802..H 8
Newton ....18,983..I 8
Noxubee ....14,288..G 10
Oktibbeha ..28,752..F 9
Panola ....26,829..C 6
Pearl River 27,802..M 7
Perry ....9,065..L 9
Pike ....31,813..L 5
Pontotoc ..17,363..C 8
Prentiss ....20,133..B 10
Quitman ....15,888..C 5
Rankin ....43,933..I 6
Scott ....21,369..H 7
Sharkey ....8,937..G 4
Simpson ....19,947..J 6
Smith ....13,561..J 7
Stone ....8,101..M 9
Sunflower ..37,047..E 5
Tallahatchie 19,338..D 6
Tate ....18,544..B 6
Tippah ....15,852..B 9
Tishomingo ..14,940..B 10
Tunica ....11,854..B 5
Union ....19,096..B 9
Walthall ....12,500..L 6
Warren ....44,981..I 4
Washington 70,581..F 4
Wayne ....16,650..K 9
Webster ....10,047..E 8
Wilkinson ..11,099..L 3

Winston ...18,406..G 9
Yalobusha ..11,915..D 7
Yazoo ....27,314..H 5

Cities, Towns, and Villages

Abbeville ....B 7
Aberdeen ..6,507..D 10
Ackerman ..1,502..F 8
Agricola ....M 10
Alcorn ....J 3
Algoma ....C 9
Alligator ....280..D 5
Amory ....7,236..D 10
Anding ....H 5
Anguilla ....612..G 4
Ansley ....O 8
Arbo ....K 7
Arcola ....517..F 4
Arkabutla ....B 6
Arm ....K 6
Artesia ....444..F 10
Ashland ....348..B 8
Askew ....B 6
Auburn ....L 5
Austin ....B 5
Avalon ....E 6
Avon ....F 4
Bailey ....H 9
Baird ....F 5
Baldwyn ..2,366..B 10
Banks ....B 7
Banner ....D 8
Barnesville ....A 6
Barnett ....J 9
Bassfield ....354..K 7
Batesville ..3,796..C 6
Battles ....K 10
Baxterville ....L 7
Bay
 St. Louis ..6,752..O 8
Bay Springs 1,801..J 8
Beacon Hill ....C 9
Beatty ....F 7
Beaumont ..1,061..L 9
Beauregard ..199..K 5
Becker ....D 10
Belden ....C 9
Belen ....C 5
Bellefontaine ....E 8
Belmont ....968..B 11
Belzoni ....3,394..F 5
Benndale ....M 9
Benoit ....473..E 4
Benton ....G 6
Bentonia ....544..H 5
Berclair ....E 5
Bethenden ....F 9
Beulah ....443..E 4
Beverly ....M 10
Bexley ....M 10
Big Creek ....148..D 8
Bigbee ....D 10
Bigbee Valley ..F 10
Biggersville ....B 10
Bigpoint ....N 10
Biloxi ....46,497..N 9
Bissell ....C 9
Black Hawk ....F 6
Blaine ....E 5
Blue Mountain 677..B 9
Blue Springs ..125..C 9
Bobo ....D 5
Bogue Chitto ....K 5
Bolivar ....787..I 5
Bolton ....787..I 5
Bon Homme ....E 5
Bonita ....I 10
Booneville ..5,895..B 10
Bourbon ....F 4
Bovina ....I 4
Boyle ....861..E 5
Branch ....I 6
Brandon ....2,685..I 6
Braxton ....180..J 6
Brazil ....D 6
Bristers Store ....L 4
Brookhaven 10,700..K 5
Brooklyn ....M 8
Brooksville ....978..F 10
Brownsville ....H 5
Bruce ....2,033..D 8
Bryan ....D 7
Buckatunna ....K 10
Bude ....1,146..K 4
Buena Vista ....D 9
Bunker Hill ....L 7
Burns ....I 7
Burnside ....G 8
Burnsville ....784..A 10
Bush ....J 6
Byhalia ....702..A 7
Byram ....I 6
Caledonia ....245..E 10
Calhoun City 1,847..D 8
Camden ....H 7
Canaan ....D 8
Canton ....10,503..H 6
Carlisle ....J 4
Carnes ....M 8
Carpenter ....J 5
Carriere ....N 7
Carrollton ....295..F 6
Carson ....K 7
Carter ....G 5

Carthage ....3,031..H 7
Cary ....517..G 4
Cascilla ....D 6
Cedarbluff ....E 9
Center Ridge ....J 8
Centreville ..1,819..L 4
Chalybeate ....A 9
Charleston ..2,821..D 6
Chatawa ....M 5
Chatham ....G 4
Cheraw ....L 7
Chester ....F 8
Chesterville ....C 9
Chicora ....K 10
Choctaw ....E 4
Chulahoma ....B 7
Chunky ....280..I 8
Church Hill ....K 3
Clara ....J 9
Clarksdale ..21,673..C 5
Clarkson ....E 8
Cleary ....I 6
Clermont Harbor ....O 8
Cleveland ..14,043..E 5
Cliftonville ....F 10
Clinton ....12,100..I 5
Coahoma ....C 5
Cockrum ....B 7
Coffeeville ..1,024..D 7
Coila ....F 6
Coldwater ..1,450..B 6
Coles ....K 4
Collins ....2,245..K 7
Collinsville ....H 9
Colony Town ....F 5
Columbia ....7,587..L 7
Columbus ..25,795..E 10
Columbus
 Base ....4,074..E 10
Commerce ....B 5
Como ....1,003..B 6
Conehatta ....H 8
Conway ....G 7
Corinth ....11,581..A 10
Courtland ....316..C 6
Crandall ....J 10
Cranfield ....K 3
Crawford ....391..F 10
Crenshaw ..1,271..B 6
Crosby ....491..L 4
Cross Roads ....A 10
Crossroads ....M 7
Crowder ....815..C 6
Cruger ....415..F 6
Crystal
 Springs ...4,195..J 5
Cuevas ....O 8
Curtiss Station ....C 6
Daleville ....H 9
Darbun ....L 6
Darling ....C 6
Darlove ....F 4
Decatur ....1,311..H 8
Deemer ....H 8
Deeson ....D 4
De Kalb ....1,072..G 10
De Lisle ....O 8
Delta City ....G 4
Denham ....K 10
Denmark ....C 8
Dennis ....B 11
Derby ....M 7
Derma ....660..D 8
De Soto ....J 9
De Weese ....H 9
D'Iberville ..7,288..N 9
D'Lo ....485..J 6
Doddsville ....276..E 5
Dorsey ....C 10
Doskie ....G 7
Dossville ....G 7
Drew ....2,574..E 5
Dry Creek ....K 7
Dubard ....J 7
Dubbs ....B 5
Dublin ....D 5
Duck Hill ....809..E 7
Duffee ....I 9
Dumas ....B 9
Duncan ....599..D 4
Dundee ....D 5
Durant ....2,752..G 7
East Fork ....L 5
Eastabuchie ....K 8
Eastside ....O 10
Ebenezer ....G 6
Ecru ....417..C 9
Eddiceton ....K 4
Eden ....152..J 5
Edgewater Park ....N 9
Edinburg ....H 7
Edwards ....1,236..I 5
Egypt ....D 9
Electric Mills ....G 10
Elizabeth ....F 4
Elliott ....E 7
Ellistown ....C 9
Ellisville ....4,643..K 8
Ellisville Junction ..K 8
Enid ....80..D 6
Enon ....K 5
Enondale ....H 10
Enterprise ....458..I 9
Escatawpa ..1,579..N 10
Estesmill ....H 8
Estill ....F 4
Ethel ....560..F 8

Etta ....C 8
Eupora ....1,792..E 8
Eureka Springs ....C 7
Evansville ....B 5
Evergreen ....C 10
Expose ....C 9
Fairfield ....C 9
Falcon ....219..C 6
Falkner ....159..A 9
Fannin ....I 6
Farrell ....F 4
Fayette ....1,725..K 4
Fernwood ....L 5
Fitler ....H 4
Flora ....987..H 6
Florence ....404..I 6
Flowood* ....352..I 6
Forest ....4,085..I 8
Forest Hill ....H 6
Forkville ....H 7
Fort Adams ....L 2
Foxworth ....L 7
Free Trade ....H 8
Freeny ....H 8
French Camp .174..F 8
Friars Point 1,177..C 5
Friendship ....H 7
Frost Bridge ....K 10
Fruitland Park ....M 8
Fulton ....2,899..C 10
Gainesville ....O 7
Gallman ....75..J 5
Garden City ....L 3
Gatesville ....J 6
Gattman ....175..D 11
Gault ....C 7
Gautier ....2,087..N 10
Geeville ....B 9
Georgetown ....339..J 6
Gholson ....G 9
Gibson ....J 4
Gillsburg ....M 5
Gitano ....J 8
Glancy ....J 5
Glen ....A 10
Glen Allan ....G 4
Glendora ....201..D 6
Gloster ....1,401..L 4
Glover ....A 6
Golden ....339..B 11
Good Hope ....H 7
Goodman ....1,194..G 6
Gore Springs ....E 7
Goshen Springs ....I 6
Goss ....L 7
Grace ....G 4
Grady ....E 8
Grand Gulf ....J 4
Greenville ..42,099..F 4
Greenville
 North ....2,154..F 4
Greenwood ..22,400..E 6
Greenwood
 Springs ....D 10
Grenada ....9,944..E 7
Gulfport ....40,791..O 9
Gunnison ....545..D 4
Guntown ....304..C 9
Hamburg ....K 4
Hamilton ....E 10
Hardy ....D 7
Harperville ....H 8
Harriston ....K 4
Harrisville ....J 6
Hatley ....385..D 10
Hattiesburg 38,277..L 8
Hattiesburg
 South* ....2,491..L 8
Hazlehurst ..4,567..J 5
Heads ....E 4
Heidelberg ..1,112..J 9
Hermanville ....J 4
Hernando ....2,499..B 6
Hesterville ....G 7
Hickory ....570..I 9
Hickory
 Flat ....354..B 8
High Point ....F 8
Hillhouse ....D 4
Hillsboro ....H 7
Hinchcliff ....C 6
Hiwannee ....J 10
Holcomb ....E 6
Holcut ....B 10
Hollandale ..3,260..F 4
Holly Bluff ....G 5
Holly Ridge ....F 4
Holly
 Springs ....5,728..B 8
Hollywood ....B 5
Holmesville ....L 5
Homewood ....I 7
Hopewell ....L 7
Horn Lake ....241..A 6
Hot Coffee ....K 7
Houlka ....646..D 9
Houston ....2,720..D 9
Howard ....G 6
Hub ....L 7
Hudsonville ....A 7
Hurley ....N 10
Hurricane ....C 8
Hushpuckena ....D 4
Independence ....B 7
India ....M 8
Indianola ....8,947..F 5
Ingomar ....C 9

Ingrams Mill ....B 7
Inverness ..1,119..F 5
Isola ....458..F 5
Itta Bena ..2,489..E 5
Iuka ....2,389..B 11
Jacinto ....B 10
Jackson ..162,380..I 6
Jayess ....L 5
Johns ....I 7
Johnstons
 Station ....L 5
Jonestown ..1,110..L 5
Jonestown ....G 5
Kalem ....I 7
Kewanee ....I 10
Kilmichael ....543..F 7
Kiln ....N 8
Kings ....K 4
Kirby ....K 4
Klondike ....H 9
Knoxo ....L 6
Knoxville ....L 3
Kokomo ....L 6
Kolola Springs ....E 10
Kosciusko ....7,266..G 7
Kossuth ....227..A 9
Kreole ....N 10
Lafayette
 Springs ....C 8
Lake ....441..I 8
Lake Como ....J 8
Lake
 Cormorant ....A 6
Lakeshore ....O 8
Lamar ....A 8
Lambert ....1,511..C 5
Lamont ....E 4
Lampton ....L 7
Lauderdale ....I 10
Laurel ....24,145..K 8
Lawrence ....I 8
Laws Hill ....B 7
Leaf ....M 9
Leakesville ..1,090..L 10
Learned ....116..I 5
Lebanon ....I 5
Leedy ....B 10
Leesburg ....K 3
Le Flore ....E 6
Leland ....6,000..F 4
Lena ....233..H 7
Lessley ....I 3
Le Tourneau ....L 4
Leverett ....D 4
Lexie ....L 6
Lexington ..2,756..G 6
Liberty ....612..L 4
Little Rock ....H 8
Little Texas ....B 6
Litton ....E 4
Logtown ....O 8
Long Beach .7,113..O 8
Longtown ....B 6
Longview ....F 9
Looxahoma ....B 7
Lorman ....J 4
Louin ....382..J 8
Louise ....444..G 5
Louisville ..6,626..F 9
Lucas ....K 6
Lucedale ....2,083..M 10
Lucien ....O 8
Ludlow ....H 7
Lula ....445..C 5
Lumberton ..2,084..M 8
Lyman ....N 8
Lynchburg ....A 6
Lyon ....383..C 5
Maben ....862..E 8
Macon ....2,612..G 10
Madden ....H 8
Madison ....853..H 6
Magee ....2,973..J 7
Magnolia ....1,970..L 5
Mahned ....L 8
Malvina ....D 4
Mantachie ....534..C 10
Mantee ....142..E 8
Marietta ....204..B 10
Marion ....533..I 10
Marks ....2,609..C 6
Mars Hill ....A 8
Martin ....J 8
Martinsville ....I 6
Marydell ....G 8
Mashulaville ....G 9
Matherville ....J 10
Mathiston ....570..E 8
Mattson ....D 5
Maxie ....M 8
Maybank ....E 10
Mayersville ....G 4
Mayhew ....E 10
McAdams ....G 7
McAfee ....H 7
McCall Creek ....K 5
McCallum ....L 9
McCarley ....E 7
McComb ....11,969..L 5
McComb
 South ....1,085..L 5
McCondy ....D 9
McCool ....225..F 8
McDonald ....I 8
McHenry ....N 8
McLain ....632..L 9

Shoppers Stroll along one of the main streets in Jackson, the largest city in Mississippi. Jackson, the state capital, is a business and financial center.

McLaurin .... L 8	Ora .... K 7	Redwood .... H 4	Smiths .... I 5
McMillan .... F 8	Orange Grove .....N 10	Reform .... F 8	Smithville ....552..D 10
McNair .... K 4	Osyka ....628..M 5	Rena Lara ....D 4	Sontag .... K 6
McNeill .... N 7	Ovett .... K 9	Renfroe .... G 8	Soso ....272..J 8
McVille .... G 7	Oxford ..9,261..°C 9	Rich .... C 5	Southaven ..8,931..A 6
Meadville ....594..°K 4	Ozona .... N 7	Richardson .... N 7	Springville .... G 8
Melton .... J 4	Pace ....629..E 4	Richland .... G 6	Stallo .... G 8
Meltonia .... E 4	Pachuta ....271..J 9	Richton ..1,110..L 9	Stampley .... K 3
Mendenhall ..2,402..°J 7	Paden ....97..B 10	Ridgeland ..1,650..I 6	Stanton .... K 3
Meridian ..46,087..°I 10	Palmers Crossing ....K 9	Rienzi ....363..B 10	Star .... J 6
Meridian	Panther Burn ....G 4	Ripley ..3,482..°B 9	Starkville ..11,369..°E 9
Station* ..2,465..I 10	Paris .... C 8	Roberts .... I 8	State Line ....598..K 10
Merigold ....772..D 5	Pascagoula ..27,264..°O 10	Robinsonville ....B 5	Steens .... E 10
Merrill .... M 9	Pass	Robinwood ....K 6	Stewart .... F 8
Metcalfe .... F 4	Christian ..4,525..O 8	Rockport .... K 6	Stoneville .... F 4
Michigan City ....A 8	Pattison .... J 4	Rodney .... J 3	Stonewall ..1,161..I 9
Midnight .... G 5	Paulding .... °J 9	Rolling Fork 2,034.°G 4	Stovall .... C 5
Midway .... G 6	Paulette .... G 10	Rome ....171..D 5	Strayhorn .... B 6
Miller .... A 7	Paynes .... D 6	Rose Hill .... J 9	Stringer .... J 8
Mineral Wells ....A 7	Pearl ..12,165..I 6	Rosedale ..2,599..°D 4	Stringtown .... E 4
Minter City ....E 6	Pearlington .... O 7	Rosetta .... L 3	Strong .... E 10
Mississippi	Pearson .... I 6	Roundaway .... D 5	Sturgis ....321..F 9
State ....4,595..F 9	Pelahatchie ..1,306..I 7	Roundlake .... D 4	Sucarnoo-
Mize ....372..J 7	Peoria .... L 5	Roxie ....662..K 4	chee .... H 10
Money .... E 6	Percy .... G 4	Rudyard .... D 4	Summerland ....J 8
Monroe .... K 4	Perkinston .... M 8	Ruleville ..2,351..E 5	Summit ..1,640..L 5
Monte Vista ....E 8	Perthshire .... D 4	Runnelstown ....L 8	Sumner ....533..°D 6
Monticello ..1,790..°K 6	Petal ..6,986..L 8	Russell .... I 10	Sumrall ....955..K 7
Montpelier .... E 9	Pheba .... D 9	Russum .... J 4	Sunflower ....983..E 5
Montrose ....160..I 8	Philadelphia 6,274..°H 8	Ruth .... L 5	Suqualena .... H 9
Mooreville .... C 10	Philipp .... E 6	Sabino .... D 5	Swan Lake ....D 6
Moorhead ..2,284..F 5	Phoenix .... H 6	Sallis ....213..G 7	Sweatman .... E 7
Morgan City ..207..F 5	Picayune ..10,467..N 7	Saltillo ....836..C 9	Swiftown .... F 5
Morgantown ..2,008..L 6	Pickens ..1,012..G 6	Sandersville ..694..J 9	Sylvarena ....115..J 8
Morton ..2,672..I 7	Piggtown .... L 9	Sandhill .... H 7	Symonds .... D 4
Moselle .... K 8	Pinckneyville ....M 3	Sandy Hook ....M 7	Tallula .... H 4
Moss .... J 8	Pine Ridge ....K 3	Sanford .... K 8	Talowah .... L 8
Moss Point 19,321..N 10	Pinebur .... L 7	Santa Rosa ....N 7	Taylor ....92..C 7
Mound Bayou 2,134..D 4	Pineville .... J 6	Sapa .... E 8	Taylorsville ..1,299..J 8
Mount Carmel ....K 7	Piney Woods ....J 7	Sarah .... B 6	Tchula ..1,729..F 6
Mount Olive ..923..J 7	Pinola ....102..J 7	Sardis ..2,391..°C 6	Ten Mile .... M 8
Mount Pleasant ....A 7	Pittsboro ....188..°D 8	Sarepta .... C 8	Terry ....546..J 6
Murphy .... G 5	Plain .... G 9	Satartia ....95..H 5	Thaxton ....289..C 8
Myrick .... K 9	Plantersville ..910..C 9	Saucier .... N 8	Thomastown ....G 7
Myrtle ....308..B 8	Pleasant Grove ....C 8	Savage .... N 8	Thompson .... D 8
Napoleon .... O 7	Pleasant Hill ....A 7	Savannah .... N 8	Thorn .... D 8
Natchez ..19,704..°K 3	Pocahontas .... H 6	Schlater ....398..E 6	Thornton .... F 6
Neely .... L 9	Polkville ....166..I 7	Scobey .... D 7	Thrashers .... B 10
Nellieburg .... J 10	Pond .... D 6	Scooba ....626..G 10	Three Rivers ....N 10
Nesbitt .... A 6	Pontotoc ..3,453..°C 9	Scott .... E 4	Thyatira .... B 7
Neshoba .... H 8	Pope ....210..C 6	Sebastopol ....268..H 8	Tibbs .... C 5
Nettleton ..1,591..D 10	Poplar Creek ....F 7	Seminary ....269..K 8	Tie Plant .... E 7
New Albany ..6,426..°B 9	Poplarville ..2,312..°M 7	Senatobia ..4,657..°B 6	Tilden .... C 10
New Augusta ..511..°L 9	Port Gibson ..2,589..°J 4	Sessums .... F 9	Tillatoba ....102..D 7
Newhebron ....456..K 6	Porterville .... H 10	Shannon ....575..D 9	Tinsley .... H 5
Newton ..3,556..I 8	Potts Camp ....459..B 8	Sharon .... H 6	Tiplersville ....A 9
Nicholson .... D 4	Prairie ....82..E 9	Shaw ..2,513..E 4	Tippo .... E 6
Niles .... D 4	Prairie Point ....F 10	Shelby ..2,645..D 4	Tishomingo ....410..B 10
Nitta Yuma ....G 4	Prentiss ..1,789..°K 7	Shellmound .... E 5	Toccopola ....175..C 8
Nola .... K 6	Preston .... G 9	Sherard .... C 5	Tomnolen .... E 8
Norfield .... K 5	Pricedale .... L 6	Sherman ....468..C 9	Toomsuba .... H 10
North Carroll-	Prichard .... B 6	Sherwood .... E 8	Topeka .... K 6
ton ....611..F 6	Progress .... M 5	Shivers .... J 6	Topton .... H 10
Noxapater ....554..G 9	Puckett ....333..J 7	Shubuta ....602..J 9	Tougaloo .... I 6
Oakland ....493..D 6	Pulaski .... J 7	Shuford .... J 9	Tralake .... F 4
Oakvale ....166..K 6	Purvis ..2,062..°L 8	Shuqualak ....591..G 10	Trebloc .... D 9
Ocean	Pyland .... D 8	Sibley .... L 3	Tremont .... C 10
Springs ..9,580..N 9	Quentin .... K 4	Sidon ....348..F 6	Tribbett .... F 4
Ofahoma .... H 7	Quincy .... D 10	Silver City ....370..G 5	Troy .... D 9
Oil City .... H 5	Quitman ..2,702..°J 9	Silver Creek ..257..K 6	Tuckers Crossing ..K 9
Okolona ..3,002..°D 9	Quito .... F 6	Singleton .... G 7	Tula .... D 8
Old Houlka .... D 9	Raleigh ..1,018..°J 7	Skene .... E 4	Tunica ..1,685..°B 5
Olive	Randolph ....205..C 8	Slate Springs ..105..E 8	Tunica
Branch ..1,513..A 7	Rankin .... J 7	Slayden .... A 8	North ....1,325..B 5
Oloh .... L 7	Raymond ..1,620..°I 5	Sledge ....516..C 6	Tupelo ..20,471..°C 9
Oma .... K 6	Red Banks ....B 7	Smith .... K 7	Turnerville .... J 8
Onward .... H 4	Red Lick .... J 4	Smithdale .... L 4	Tuscola .... H 7

Tutwiler ..1,103..D 5
Tylertown ..1,736..°L 6
Tyro .... B 7
Union .... C 9
Union ..1,856..H 8
Union Church ....K 4
University .... C 7
Utica ..1,019..I 5
Utica
Institute .... J 5
Vaiden ....716..°F 7
Valley Park ....H 4
Value .... I 6
Vance .... D 5
Vancleave .... N 10
Van Vleet .... D 9
Vardaman ....777..D 8
Vaughan .... G 6
Vaughn .... K 5
Velma .... D 7
Verona ..1,877..C 9
Vestry .... N 9
Vicksburg ..25,478..°I 4
Victoria .... A 7
Vossburg .... J 9
Wade .... N 10
Wakefield .... B 7
Walls .... A 6
Walnut ....458..A 9
Walnut
Grove ....398..H 8
Walters .... K 8
Walthall ....161..°E 8
Wanilla .... K 6
Warsaw .... B 7
Washington ....K 3
Water
Valley ..3,285..°C 7
Waterford .... B 7
Waveland ..3,108..O 8
Waxhaw .... D 4
Way .... H 6
Waynesboro .4,671..°K 10
Wayside .... F 4
Weathersby ....85..J 7
Webb ....751..D 5
Weir ....573..F 8
Wenasoga .... A 10
Wesson ..1,253..K 5
West ....305..F 7
West Gulf-
port ..6,996..N 9
West Point .8,714..°E 10
Wheeler .... B 10
Whistle .... K 9
White Apple ....K 4
White Oak ....J 7
Whites .... E 10
Wiggins .... H 7
Wiggins ..2,995..M 8
Wilkinson .... L 3
Willet .... F 4
Williamsburg ....K 7
Williamsville ....G 7
Winborn .... B 8
Winchester .... K 10
Winona ..5,521..°E 7
Winstonville ....536..D 4
Winterville .... E 4
Woodland ....130..E 9
Woodville ..1,734..°L 3
Woodwards .... K 10
Wyatte .... B 7
Yazoo
City ..11,688..°G 5
Zama .... G 8
Zetus .... K 5

*Does not appear on the map; key shows general location.
°County seat.

Sources: Latest census figures (1970 and special censuses). Places without population figures are unincorporated areas and are not listed in census reports.

The 1970 U.S. census reported that Mississippi had 2,216,912 persons. This figure was an increase of 2 per cent over the state's 1960 census figure, 2,178,141. The U.S. Bureau of the Census estimated that by 1975 the state's population had reached about 2,346,000.

About 55 per cent of Mississippi's people live in rural areas. About 45 per cent live in urban areas. But Mississippi's urban population is growing as people move to the cities where manufacturing industries are being developed. Mississippi's urban population almost tripled between 1930 and 1970.

The largest city is Jackson, the state capital and center of Mississippi's business and financial activities. Jackson is the state's largest Standard Metropolitan Statistical Area (see METROPOLITAN AREA). The metropolitan area of Biloxi-Gulfport ranks second in population to Jackson. Expanding activity in shipbuilding and oil refining made the port city of Pascagoula one of the fastest growing cities of Mississippi during the 1960's. Mississippi has several large cities on the Mississippi River. These cities include Greenville, Natchez, and Vicksburg. See the separate articles on the cities of Mississippi listed in the *Related Articles* at the end of this article.

Almost all Mississippians were born in the United States. The 1970 census showed that 37 of every 100 persons in Mississippi are Negroes. This is a larger proportion of Negroes than in any other state.

More than half of all Mississippians who are church members are Baptists, and more than a fourth are Methodists. Other religious groups with large membership in Mississippi include Roman Catholics, Presbyterians, and Episcopalians.

WORLD BOOK photo by W. R. Wilson

Dockworkers at Gulfport unload fish meal from a merchant ship. Industries in the busy port cities of Gulfport and Pascagoula hire many workers. Pascagoula has large shipyards and oil refineries.

POPULATION

This map shows the *population density* of Mississippi, and how it varies in different parts of the state. Population density means the average number of persons who live in a given area.

Persons per sq. mi.		Persons per km²
More than 80		More than 30
40 to 80		15 to 30
Less than 40		Less than 15

Greenville

Ja...

Hattiesburg

Biloxi

```
0   25   50   75   100 Miles
0   50    100      150 Kilometers
```

WORLD BOOK map

Livestock Buyers bid for farm animals at an auction in Tupelo. Mississippi stockmen tend large herds of beef cattle and dairy cows. They also raise chickens, hogs, and sheep.

Terry Wood

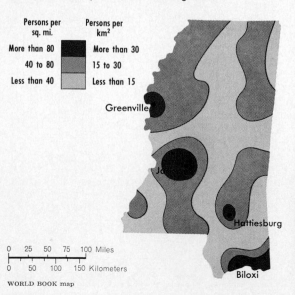

Schools. The Mississippi public school system was established by the Constitution of 1869. The state set up a board of education and provided that every child should receive free schooling for four months each year. At first, most Mississippians opposed public schools. The Civil War had caused hard times and the people had little money for school taxes. The opposition decreased as conditions improved, and by the 1890's the public school system had won general approval. In 1904, the state established a textbook commission, now called the state textbook purchasing board. The textbook purchasing board supplies books to all schoolchildren in both public and private schools. In 1908, Mississippi provided for the establishment of agricultural high schools.

The state's entire school system was reorganized during the 1950's and early 1960's. The aim was to improve the schools by a program of consolidation of small districts (see CONSOLIDATED SCHOOL). To meet the need for workers in new industry and business, Mississippi has also established a statewide network of vocational-technical training centers at both the high school and junior college levels.

Like other Southern states, Mississippi had separate schools for blacks and whites for many years. In 1954, the Supreme Court of the United States ruled that public school segregation on the basis of race is unconstitutional. The first racial integration in Mississippi public schools took place in 1964. Today, all the state's public school districts are integrated. Children from 7 through 13 years of age must attend school.

The state superintendent of public education directs Mississippi's elementary and secondary schools. The people elect the superintendent to a four-year term. Mississippi spends about 65 per cent of its tax revenue for public education. For the number of students and teachers in Mississippi, see EDUCATION (table).

Libraries. The Mississippi Library Commission, established in 1926, directs the state's public libraries. It also lends books to public and school libraries. County and regional libraries serve thousands of Mississippians, and bookmobiles bring library services to farming areas. In 1946, Mississippi's state department of education began a school-library program. Under this program, consultants help develop libraries in many of Mississippi's schools.

A library that was established in 1818 in Port Gibson is probably the first Mississippi library that served the public. The state library in Jackson was established in 1838.

Museums. Mississippi has one of the nation's finest historical museums, in the restored Old Capitol in Jackson. It is a division of the Department of Archives and History. Other historical museums include the Old Courthouse Museum in Vicksburg, and the Jefferson Davis Shrine at Beauvoir House near Biloxi. Art museums include the Jackson Municipal Art Gallery, the Mary Buie Museum in Oxford, and the Lauren Rogers Library and Museum of Art in Laurel. The Mississippi Museum of Natural Science in Jackson features many exhibits of natural history.

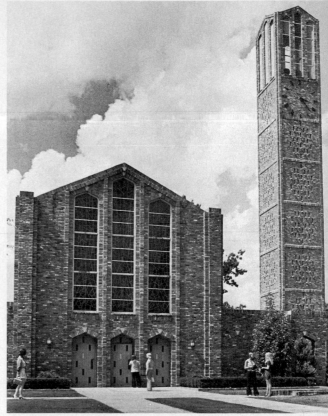

Mississippi State University

The Chapel of Memories stands on the former site of an old dormitory at Mississippi State University. It was built in memory of the many young men who had lived in the dormitory.

--------- **UNIVERSITIES AND COLLEGES** ---------

Mississippi has 16 universities and colleges accredited by the Southern Association of Colleges and Schools. For enrollments and further information, see UNIVERSITIES AND COLLEGES (table).

Name	Location	Founded
Alcorn State University	Lorman	1871
Belhaven College	Jackson	1894
Blue Mountain College	Blue Mountain	1873
Delta State University	Cleveland	1924
Jackson State University	Jackson	1877
Millsaps College	Jackson	1892
Mississippi, University of	University	1844
Mississippi College	Clinton	1826
Mississippi State University	Mississippi State	1878
Mississippi University for Women	Columbus	1884
Mississippi Valley State University	Itta Bena	1950
Reformed Theological Seminary	Jackson	1966
Rust College	Holly Springs	1866
Southern Mississippi, University of	Hattiesburg	1910
Tougaloo College	Tougaloo	1869
William Carey College	Hattiesburg	1906

MISSISSIPPI / A Visitor's Guide

The Gulf Coast of Mississippi is one of the nation's most popular winter resort regions. This vacationland has won fame for its large, sunny beaches and fine hotels. In other parts of the state, historic monuments and pleasant wooded areas are the chief attractions. Thousands of visitors also take tours of Mississippi's many old mansions and plantations. There, they can get some idea of what life was like in Mississippi before the Civil War. Pretty hostesses dressed in billowing hoop skirts serve as guides.

Excellent hunting and fishing in about 25 Wildlife Management areas attract many people to Mississippi. Hunters may shoot wild doves, ducks, geese, quail, turkeys, deer, rabbits, raccoons, and squirrels. Thousands of ponds and lakes have been stocked with fish. People can cast in fresh water for bass, bream, crappies, and other fishes. Or they may sit lazily on the banks of a Mississippi river or pond and wait for catfish to take their bait. Salt-water fishing enthusiasts fight big game fish in the waters off the Gulf Coast.

Fred L. Malone
Miss Mississippi Pageant in Vicksburg

Captured Cannon at Pascagoula's Old Spanish Fort

Beauvoir, Last Home of Jefferson Davis

PLACES TO VISIT

Following are brief descriptions of some of Mississippi's most interesting places to visit.

Capitols, in Jackson, offer many reminders of the state's rich history. The *Old Capitol,* now the State Historical Museum, was built chiefly by slave labor between 1833 and 1842. Here, Mississippi voted in January, 1861, to secede from the Union. The *New Capitol,* which was built in 1903, houses the state Legislature and the governor's offices.

Churches. St. Michael's Roman Catholic Church in Biloxi features stained glass windows and an ultra-modern wavy roof. The Church of the Holy Trinity in Vicksburg, completed in 1880, has a memorial honoring the Union and Confederate soldiers who fought in the siege of Vicksburg. St. Paul's Episcopal Church in Woodville dates from 1824, and the First Presbyterian Church in Port Gibson from 1829.

Delta and Pine Land Company Plantation covers 38,000 acres (15,400 hectares) near Scott. It is one of the largest cotton plantations in the world. The Fine Spinners and Doublers, Ltd., of Manchester, England, has owned it since 1911.

Elvis Presley Birthplace, at Tupelo in northeastern Mississippi, marks the site where the famous singer was born. The tiny house where Presley spent his early years is now part of Elvis Presley Park.

Florewood River Plantation, in the Delta near Greenwood, is a state park and museum. It has 22 buildings that show visitors what life was like on a cotton plantation before the Civil War.

Fort Massachusetts, on Ship Island, was a Union stronghold during the Civil War. Confederate troops captured the fort early in the war. They partly destroyed it when they evacuated the island in 1861. Union forces then rebuilt Fort Massachusetts and used it as a prison until the end of the Civil War. Another interesting fort is the Old Spanish Fort in Pascagoula, which dates from 1718.

Priest Blesses Fleet at the Biloxi Shrimp Festival

Azalea Festival in Mississippi

Petrified Forest, near Flora, contains giant stone trees dating back 30 million years. Facilities there include a nature trail, a geological museum, a rock and gem shop, and picnic areas.

Stately Old Homes in or near Natchez are reminders of the way of life of wealthy Mississippians before the Civil War. These mansions include *Auburn* (built in 1812), *D'Evereux* (1840), *Dunleith* (1847), *Edgewood* (1860), *Gloucester* (1804), *Linden* (1789), *Melrose* (1840), *Monteigne* (1853), *Richmond* (1786), *Rosalie* (1820), and *Stanton Hall* (1857). *Cedar Grove* (1858) and *McRaven* (1797) are in Vicksburg. Other homes include *Waverly* (1856) near Columbus, *Grey Gables* (1830) in Holly Springs, and *Hampton Hall* (1832) near Woodville.

Jefferson Davis spent his boyhood at *Rosemont* near Woodville. At Biloxi stands *Beauvoir*, Davis' last home. The building later became a home for Confederate veterans and their wives or widows. Beauvoir is now a shrine and a museum.

Vicksburg National Military Park honors the siege of Vicksburg, which lasted from May 18 to July 4, 1863. The siege, which ended in a Union victory, was a major turning point of the Civil War. Monuments for each state represented in the battle are located at the site of its troops' battle lines in the park. A visitor center at the Vicksburg National Military Park shows a short film about the siege.

National Forests. Mississippi has six national forests. The largest is De Soto in southeastern Mississippi. The others are Homochitto in the southwest; Bienville, Delta, and Tombigbee in central Mississippi; and Holly Springs in the north. For the area and chief features of each national forest in Mississippi, see NATIONAL FOREST (table).

State Parks. Mississippi has 24 state parks. For information on these state parks, write to Bureau of Recreation and Parks, Department of Natural Resources, 700 Robert E. Lee Building, Jackson, Miss. 39201.

ANNUAL EVENTS

The highlight of Mississippi's many annual events is the Shrimp Festival in Biloxi during the first week of June. It marks the opening of the shrimp-fishing season. The celebration includes colorful balls and parades, the crowning of a shrimp queen, and the blessing of the shrimp fleet.

Other annual events in Mississippi include the following.

January-March: Dixie National Livestock Show and Rodeo in Jackson (February); Mardi Gras festivities in various cities on the Mississippi Gulf Coast (February); McComb Azalea Festival (late March and early April).

April-June: Garden Pilgrimages in Carrollton, Columbus, Holly Springs, Natchez, and Oxford (April—some start in March); D'Iberville Landing and Historical Ball in Ocean Springs (April); Magnolia Open Golf Classic in Hattiesburg (April); World Catfish Festival in Belzoni (April); Flea Market in Canton (May); Jimmie Rodgers Day Celebration in Meridian (May).

July-September: Choctaw Indian Fair in Philadelphia (July); Miss Hospitality Pageant in Biloxi (July); Miss Mississippi Beauty Pageant in Vicksburg (July); Mississippi Deep Sea Fishing Rodeo in Gulfport (July); National Tobacco Spitting Contest in Raleigh (July); Neshoba County Fair in Philadelphia (August); Delta Blues Festival in Greenville (September); Pike County Fair in McComb (September).

October-December: Mississippi-Alabama State Fair in Meridian (October); Mississippi State Fair in Jackson (second week of October); Natchez Fall Pilgrimage (October); Gumbo Festival in Hancock County (November); Trees of Merrehope Festival in Meridian (December).

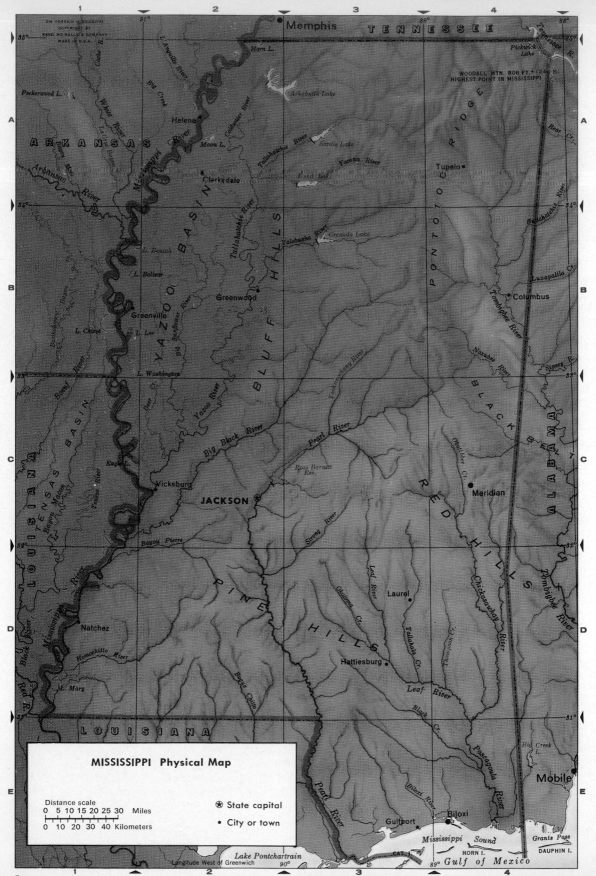

ON TERRAIN MISSISSIPPI
COPYRIGHT BY
RAND MC NALLY & COMPANY
MADE IN U.S.A.

91°

Memphis T E N N E S S E E

89°

88°

WOODALL MTN. 806 FT.+ (246 M)
HIGHEST POINT IN MISSISSIPPI

Horn L.

Pickwick
Lake

35°

Peckerwood L.

L. Anguilla River

Big Creek

Arkabutla Lake

Coldwater River

Tennessee R.

Bear Cr.

A

Helena

White River

La Grue Bayou

Mississippi River

Moon L.

Talla hatchie River

Sardis Lake

Yocona River

Tupelo

A

Arkansas River

Bayou Meto
River

Clarksdale

Enid Lake

34°

Buttahatchee River

34°

Cedar R.

P O N T O T O C   R I D G E

B

L. Beulah

Yalobusha River

Grenada Lake

Luxapalila Cr.

B

L. Bolivar

Greenwood

Columbus

Tombigbee River

Greenville

L. Chicot

Big Sunflower River

BLUFF HILLS

Noxubee River

Sipsey R.

L. Lee

33°

L. Washington

YAZOO   BASIN

Tombigbee River

33°

C

Deer Cr.

Yazoo River

Big Black River

Yockanookany River

Pearl River

Ross Barnett
Res.

Oktibbee Cr.

BLACK PRAIRIE

C

Eagle L.

Bayou Macon
River

Vicksburg

Bogue Chitto

JACKSON

Meridian

Tensas River

Steele Bayou

LOUISIANA   BASIN

Big Sunflower River

Bayou Pierre

Strong River

RED HILLS

D

Natchez

Okatoma Cr.

Leaf River

Laurel

Chickasawhay River

Tombigbee River

D

Homochitto River

Tallahala Cr.

Thompson Cr.

Black R.

Bogue Chitto

Hattiesburg

L. Mary

P I N E   H I L L S

Leaf River

Black Cr.

Red R.

Big Creek
L.

31°

L O U I S I A N A

31°

Passagoula River

Mobile

Pearl River

Biloxi River

Biloxi

Gulfport

Grants Pass

E

Mississippi Sound

CAT I.

HORN I.

DAUPHIN I.

E

Lake Pontchartrain

Longitude West of Greenwich

90°

89°

Gulf of Mexico

Specially created for **World Book Encyclopedia** by Rand McNally and World Book editors

Land Regions.

Land Regions. Mississippi has two main land regions: (1) the Mississippi Alluvial Plain, and (2) the East Gulf Coastal Plain.

The Mississippi Alluvial Plain covers the entire western edge of the state. It consists of fertile lowlands and forms part of the 35,000-square-mile (90,600-square-kilometer) *Alluvial Plain* of the Mississippi River. The region is quite narrow south of Vicksburg. North of the city, the plain spreads out and covers the area between the Mississippi River and the Yazoo, Tallahatchie, and Coldwater rivers. Floodwaters of the rivers have enriched the soil of the region with deposits of silt. The fertile soil of the Mississippi Alluvial Plain is famous for its large cotton and soybean crops. Most Mississippians call this region the *Delta.*

The East Gulf Coastal Plain extends over all the state east of the Alluvial Plain. Most of the region is made up of low, rolling, forested hills. The coastal plain also has prairies and lowlands. Yellowish-brown *loess* (soil blown by winds) covers the region in the west. Most Mississippians call these deposits the Cane, Bluff, or Loess Hills. The Tennessee River Hills rise in northeastern Mississippi. They include the highest point in the state, 806-foot (246-meter) Woodall Mountain. The Pine Hills, often called the Piney Woods, rise in the southeastern part of the region. They are covered largely with longleaf and slash-pine forests.

The main prairie is called the *Black Belt* or *Black Prairie* because its soil is largely black in color. This long, narrow prairie lies in the northeast. It stretches through 10 counties. Livestock graze there, and corn and hay grow well on the farmlands of the Black Belt. Small prairies also lie in central Mississippi, east of Jackson. Along the Mississippi Sound, lowlands stretch inland over the southern part of the region.

Coastline. Mississippi has a coastline of 44 miles (71 kilometers) along the Gulf of Mexico. With bays and coves, it has a total shoreline of 359 miles (578 kilo-

meters). The largest bays include Biloxi, St. Louis, and Pascagoula. The nation's longest sea wall protects about 25 miles (40 kilometers) of coastline between Biloxi and Point Henderson at Bay St. Louis. Other coastal towns include Gulfport, Pass Christian, and Ocean Springs. Deer Island is near the mouth of Biloxi Bay, and a chain

Land Regions of Mississippi

The Broad Mississippi River forms almost all of Mississippi's western border. Huge cotton crops grow in the Mississippi Alluvial Plain region that lies along the river. Powerful towboats push heavy barges past the cotton fields.

Mississippi's Famous Piney Woods Country forms part of the East Gulf Coastal Plain region. Pine trees in this area provide pine oil, rosin, and turpentine as well as lumber.

Vicksburg Harbor, *foreground,* provides a navigation channel of quiet water away from the Mississippi River, *background.* The construction of the harbor has created 245 acres (99 hectares) of industrial land.

of small islands lies off the coast. They include Cat, Horn, Ship, and Petit Bois islands. Mississippi Sound separates them from the mainland.

Rivers and Lakes. Mississippi has many rivers and lakes. The nation's most important river, the Mississippi, forms most of the state's western border. Its floodwaters, in earlier times, often deposited silt on the land, and helped make the land fertile. In some years, heavy floods damaged crops and homes. Today, wide *levees* (man-made walls) help protect many areas against damaging floods (see LEVEE; MISSISSIPPI RIVER).

The state has several main river basins. The rivers of the western and north-central basin drain into the Mississippi River. These rivers include the Big Black River and the Yazoo River with its large tributaries, the Coldwater, Sunflower, and Tallahatchie rivers. Rivers of the eastern basin drain into the Gulf of Mexico. They include the Pearl, Pascagoula, and Tombigbee. Many of Mississippi's lakes are man-made reservoirs. The Tennessee River, for example, flows through Pickwick Lake in the northeastern section of Mississippi. Other man-made lakes in the state include Arkabutla, Enid, Grenada, and Sardis reservoirs, all of which are in north-central Mississippi. All these lakes lie behind flood-control dams. In the early 1960's, the large Ross Barnett Reservoir was built on the Pearl River near Jackson. The Mississippi River has formed many *oxbow lakes*, mostly north of Vicksburg. These lakes form when a river changes its course to take short cuts (see OXBOW LAKE). Mississippi's oxbow lakes include Beulah, Lee, Moon, and Washington. Mississippi also has many slow-moving streams called *bayous*. Some bayous connect the lakes with the rivers in the Delta. Others link the inland waterways with the Gulf of Mexico.

MISSISSIPPI / *Climate*

Mississippi has a warm, moist climate, with long summers and short winters. In July, Mississippi temperatures average about 82° F. (28° C). Winds from the Gulf of Mexico, and frequent thundershowers, cool much of the state during the summers. Even in the interior part of the state, the temperature seldom goes above 100° F. (38° C). However, temperatures of 90° F. (32° C) or higher occur about 55 days a year on the Gulf Coast and more often in the interior. The highest temperature recorded in Mississippi was 115° F. (46° C) at Holly Springs on July 29, 1930.

January temperatures average 48° F. (9° C) in Mississippi. The lowest temperature was −19° F. (−28° C), recorded at Corinth on Jan. 30, 1966. Northern and central Mississippi occasionally have ice and snow. The Gulf Coast ordinarily has a frost-free season of 250 to 300 days. *Precipitation* (rain, melted snow, and other forms of moisture) ranges from about 50 inches (130

Warm, Sunny Weather all year around attracts many vacationers to the sandy beaches along Mississippi's Gulf Coast.

centimeters) a year in the northwest to about 65 inches (165 centimeters) in the southeast. Hurricanes sometimes sweep northward from the Gulf in late summer and fall.

SEASONAL TEMPERATURES

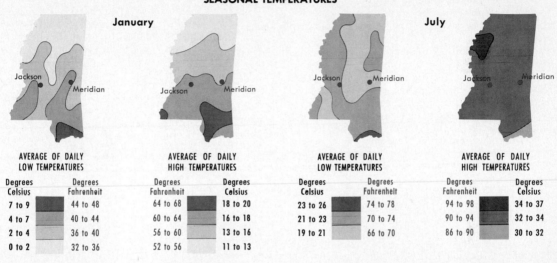

January

AVERAGE OF DAILY LOW TEMPERATURES

Degrees Celsius	Degrees Fahrenheit
7 to 9	44 to 48
4 to 7	40 to 44
2 to 4	36 to 40
0 to 2	32 to 36

AVERAGE OF DAILY HIGH TEMPERATURES

Degrees Fahrenheit	Degrees Celsius
64 to 68	18 to 20
60 to 64	16 to 18
56 to 60	13 to 16
52 to 56	11 to 13

July

AVERAGE OF DAILY LOW TEMPERATURES

Degrees Celsius	Degrees Fahrenheit
23 to 26	74 to 78
21 to 23	70 to 74
19 to 21	66 to 70

AVERAGE OF DAILY HIGH TEMPERATURES

Degrees Fahrenheit	Degrees Celsius
94 to 98	34 to 37
90 to 94	32 to 34
86 to 90	30 to 32

AVERAGE YEARLY PRECIPITATION
(Rain, Melted Snow and Other Moisture)

Centimeters	Inches
163 to 183	64 to 72
142 to 163	56 to 64
122 to 142	48 to 56

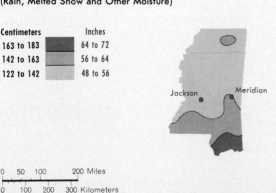

0   50   100   200 Miles

0   100   200   300 Kilometers

AVERAGE MONTHLY WEATHER

	JACKSON					MERIDIAN			
	Temperatures F°		C°		Days of Rain or Snow	Temperatures F°		C°		Days of Rain or Snow
	High	Low	High	Low		High	Low	High	Low	
JAN.	59	38	15	3	11	59	37	15	3	10
FEB.	62	40	17	4	11	62	39	17	4	10
MAR.	68	46	20	8	10	68	45	20	7	10
APR.	76	54	24	12	9	77	52	25	11	8
MAY	84	61	29	16	9	84	59	29	15	10
JUNE	91	68	33	20	9	91	67	33	19	10
JULY	94	71	34	22	11	92	70	33	21	12
AUG.	93	70	34	21	7	92	69	33	21	10
SEPT.	89	65	32	18	7	87	64	31	18	7
OCT.	80	53	27	12	5	78	51	26	11	5
NOV.	67	43	19	6	8	67	41	19	5	7
DEC.	59	39	15	4	10	60	37	16	3	10

The annual value of Mississippi's manufactured products is greater than that of its farm products. However, agriculture remains an important industry in the state. Many manufacturing industries, such as food processing and the clothing and textile industries, depend on the farms for their raw materials.

Natural Resources of Mississippi include rich soils, abundant water supplies, valuable mineral deposits, large forests, and a wide variety of wildlife.

Soil and Water are the state's most important natural resources. The Mississippi Alluvial Plain has some of the richest soil in the United States. Much of this fertile earth is largely silt deposited by floodwaters of the Mississippi River. Another fertile area of clay loam soils is in the Black Belt. These soils are gray or black in color. Sandy loam soil covers most of the East Gulf Coastal Plain. Mississippi has great supplies of surface water, and also many wells. Together, they furnish abundant fresh water for home and industrial use.

Minerals. Petroleum is the most valuable mineral resource of Mississippi. The state has reserves of about 215 million barrels of oil. The chief oil deposits are in southern Mississippi. The state has over 1 trillion cubic feet (28 billion cubic meters) of natural gas, chiefly in the south-central and southwestern counties.

Mississippi has many kinds of clays that are used by important industries. Such clays include bentonite, used to lubricate oil well drills, and fuller's earth, used in refining certain fats and oils. Other valuable Mississippi clays are ball clays, kaolin, and certain clays suitable for making brick and tile. Low-grade bauxite is found in an area that extends from Tippah County to Kemper County. Large deposits of sand and gravel are found in various places, and Tishomingo County has large deposits of sandstone. Other mineral resources of Mississippi include iron ore, lignite, limestone, and salt.

Forests cover more than half of Mississippi. They provide the raw materials for a huge output of products that make Mississippi a leading forest industry state. About 120 kinds of trees grow in Mississippi. The most important are the loblolly, longleaf, and slash pines of the Piney Woods area, and the shortleaf pine of northern and central Mississippi. Other trees include the ash, bald cypress, cottonwood, elm, hickory, oak, pecan, sweet gum, and tupelo. Mississippi conducts a widespread program of planting young trees to replace those that are cut down. Mississippi has over 4,700 tree farms —more than any other state.

Plant Life. The magnolia, an evergreen tree with fragrant white flowers, grows throughout the state. The magnolia is Mississippi's state flower. Many parts of the state also have azaleas, black-eyed Susans, camellias, crepe myrtle, dogwood, redbud, violets, Virginia creepers, and pink and white Cherokee roses.

Animal Life includes beavers, deer, foxes, opossums, rabbits, and squirrels. Among the state's game birds are wild doves, ducks, quail, and turkeys. The mockingbird is Mississippi's state bird. Fresh-water fish include bass, bream, catfish, and crappies. In the Gulf waters are crabs, oysters, shrimps, menhaden, mackerel, and speckled trout.

Production of Goods in Mississippi

Total value of goods produced in 1977—$7,898,340,000

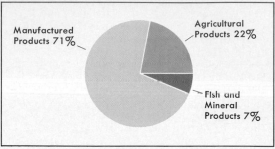

Manufactured Products 71%

Agricultural Products 22%

Fish and Mineral Products 7%

Percentages are based on farm income, value added by manufacture, and value of fish and mineral production. Fish products are less than 1 per cent.
Sources: U.S. government publications, 1978-1979.

Employment in Mississippi

Total number of persons employed in 1978—889,800

	Number of Employees
Manufacturing	235,800
Government	180,200
Wholesale & Retail Trade	159,300
Community, Social, & Personal Services	114,200
Agriculture	77,000
Construction	45,200
Transportation & Public Utilities	38,100
Finance, Insurance, & Real Estate	31,300
Mining	8,700

Sources: *Employment and Earnings*, May 1979, U.S. Bureau of Labor Statistics; *Farm Labor*, February 1979, U.S. Department of Agriculture.

Manufacturing accounts for 71 per cent of the value of all goods produced in Mississippi. Goods manufactured in the state have an annual *value added by manufacture* of about $5½ billion. This figure represents the value created in products by Mississippi's industries, not counting such costs as materials, supplies, and fuels. Mississippi's chief manufactured products, in order of importance, are (1) transportation equipment, (2) lumber and wood products, and (3) electric and electronic equipment.

Transportation Equipment manufactured in Mississippi has an annual value added of about $571 million. Shipbuilding is the most important activity of the industry. Large shipyards in Pascagoula build freighters, nuclear submarines, and tankers. Industries in the state also produce aerospace equipment, airplanes, and automobiles.

Lumber and Wood Products have a value added of about $514 million yearly. Mississippi is a leading state in wood production. About 23 million cubic yards (17.6 million cubic meters) of wood are taken from the state's forests each year. The lumber and wood products industry has about 1,100 plants. They include logging camps, sawmills, and factories that produce mobile homes, plywood, and wood containers. Large plants are located in Columbus, Greenville, Laurel, and Vicksburg.

FARM, MINERAL, AND FOREST PRODUCTS

This map shows where the state's leading farm, mineral, and forest products are produced. The major urban area (shown on the map in red) is the state's important manufacturing center.

John Deere

Harvesting Cotton. Many Mississippi farmers use machines to pick cotton. As the machines move through the rows of plants, barbed spindles pull the raw cotton fibers from the bolls.

WORLD BOOK map

Electric and Electronic Equipment has an annual value added of about $457 million. The state has about 70 plants that produce electric and electronic equipment. Chief products of this industry include generators, household appliances, lighting and wiring equipment, motors, switchboards, and transformers.

The production of food products is Mississippi's fourth-ranked industrial activity. Meatpacking plants are located in Jackson and the northeastern part of the state. Poultry processing plants are in the east-central part of the state, and seafood plants are located along the Gulf Coast in Harrison and Jackson counties. Other plants produce animal feed, bakery products, beverages, dairy products, and fats and oils.

The production of chemicals is also important to Mississippi's economy. The state's chief chemical products include agricultural chemicals, industrial chemicals, and plastics and synthetics. Large chemical plants are located in Hattiesburg, Pascagoula, and Yazoo City.

The clothing industry in Mississippi employs more people than any other industry in the state. Clothing plants are located throughout the state, but the largest ones are in the northeast. Chief clothing products include dresses, shirts, slacks, and work clothes.

Mississippi also produces nonelectric machinery, including construction machinery, farm and garden machinery, and refrigeration and service machinery. Most of the large companies that produce nonelectric machinery are located in the northern half of the state. Other important industries manufacture paper products; fabricated metal products; furniture and fixtures; stone, clay, and glass products; and textiles.

Agriculture. Mississippi's farm products provide an annual income of about $1¾ billion, or about 22 per cent of the value of goods produced in Mississippi. Mississippi has about 53,000 farms. These farms cover about half the state and average 274 acres (111 hectares) in size.

Soybeans are Mississippi's most valuable crop. Soybeans earn about $381 million a year, or about a fifth of the farm income in Mississippi. Most of the soybeans are raised on the Mississippi Alluvial Plain, and Mississippi ranks among the leading states in the production of soybeans. Cotton is also grown on the alluvial plain, one of the nation's leading cotton-growing regions. The production of cotton provides another fifth of Mississippi's farm income, or about $380 million yearly. Mississippi also ranks among the leading states in the production of rice and sweet potatoes. Field crops, such as corn and hay, are raised as livestock feed.

536e

Other grains that are grown in the state include oats, wheat, and grain sorghums. Other important agricultural products include cottonseed, forest products, greenhouse and nursery products, peanuts, and pecans.

Mississippi is an important livestock-raising state, largely because of its fine pastures and a long growing season for hay and other feed. Beef cattle graze in many parts of the state. Large herds of dairy cattle also are raised in many parts of Mississippi. They supply milk for Mississippi's dairies and cheese and ice cream plants. Livestock farmers also raise hogs and sheep. Mississippi ranks as a leading broiler-raising state. Most of the chickens raised in Mississippi are sold as *broilers* (chickens that are 9 to 12 weeks old). Other important poultry products include eggs and turkeys.

Mississippi truck farms and fruit farms produce a wide variety of products. Truck farmers grow cabbage, cowpeas, cucumbers, potatoes, and tomatoes. Mississippi fruits include apples, cantaloupes, peaches, pears, strawberries, and watermelons.

Mining accounts for 6 per cent, or about $499 million, of the value of goods produced in Mississippi each year. Mississippi ranks as a leading producer of petroleum. Petroleum and natural gas account for about $423 million, or about 85 per cent of the value of the state's mined products. Mississippi produces about 43 million barrels of petroleum each year from about 2,800 wells. The annual natural gas production is about 69 billion cubic feet (2 billion cubic meters).

Mississippi quarries produce about 12 million short tons (11 million metric tons) of sand and gravel a year. Clay production is about 1½ million short tons (1.4 million metric tons) annually. The most important clays include bentonite and fuller's earth, both used in refining certain oils. Mississippi leads the nation in the production of bentonite. Other minerals produced include natural gas liquids, stone, and sulfur.

Fishing Industry. Mississippi has an annual fish catch valued at about $26 million. Mississippi is a leading shrimp-fishing state, with a shrimp catch valued at about $4 million a year. Biloxi is Mississippi's chief shrimp-packing port. Pascagoula ranks as another center of the state's commercial fishing industry. The salt-water catch includes menhaden, oysters, and red snapper. The fresh-water catch in Mississippi includes buffalo fish, carp, and catfish.

Electric Power. Steam plants produce all the electricity generated in Mississippi. The chief plants are in Cleveland, Greenville, Gulfport, Hattiesburg, Jackson, Meridian, Natchez, and Vicksburg. Mississippi also buys some of its power from the Tennessee Valley Authority (TVA).

Transportation. The state has one of the finest highway systems in the South. There are about 66,000 miles (106,000 kilometers) of surfaced highways and about 1,600 miles (2,570 kilometers) of nonsurfaced roads. Mississippi has about 150 airports. The chief ones serve the Biloxi and Gulfport area, Columbus, Greenville, the Hattiesburg and Laurel area, Jackson, Meridian, and Tupelo. Three major airlines link Mississippi with cities in other states. Railroads operate on about 3,500 miles (5,630 kilometers) of track in Mississippi. About 10 railroads provide freight service, and passenger trains serve about 15 cities in the state.

Mississippi has two deep-water seaports, Gulfport and Pascagoula. Together, the dock facilities of these ports handle about 20 million short tons (18 million metric tons) of cargo every year. Nearby Biloxi ranks as another chief port. The Mississippi River connects Mississippi with many inland states. The state's leading river ports are Greenville, Natchez, and Vicksburg.

Communication. About 145 newspapers are published in Mississippi, including about 20 dailies. About 40 periodicals also are published. The state has about 185 radio stations and about 20 television stations.

Mississippi's earliest newspapers, all published in Natchez, were the *Mississippi Gazette* (established in 1799), the *Intelligencer* (1801), and the *Mississippi Herald* (1802). The oldest newspaper still published in Mississippi, the *Woodville Republican*, was founded in 1823. Dailies with the largest circulations include *The Daily Herald* of Biloxi, the *Clarion-Ledger* of Jackson, the *Jackson Daily News*, and the *Tupelo Journal*.

Alice Lusk, Mississippi Research and Development Center

Workers Sew Shirts in a factory in Lake, Miss. The manufacture of clothing is a leading industrial activity in the state. Mississippi farms supply much of the raw material used by the clothing industry.

Indian Days. Three powerful Indian tribes once ruled the Mississippi region. The Chickasaw lived in the north and east, the Choctaw in the central area, and the Natchez in the southwest. They held power over the Chakchiuma, Tunica, and Yazoo tribes that lived along the Yazoo River, and the Biloxi and Pascagoula tribes of the Gulf Coast. Between 25,000 and 30,000 Indians lived in the Mississippi region when the first white explorers arrived. See INDIAN, AMERICAN (Table of Tribes).

Exploration and Early Settlement. In 1540, the Spanish explorer Hernando de Soto became the first European to enter the Mississippi region. De Soto reached the Mississippi River in 1541 while searching for gold. The Spanish explorers found no treasure in the region and made no settlements there. In 1682, the French explorer Robert Cavelier, Sieur de la Salle, traveled down the Mississippi River from the Great Lakes to the Gulf of Mexico. Cavelier claimed the entire Mississippi Valley for France, and named it *Louisiana* for King Louis XIV. The region included present-day Mississippi.

In 1699, Pierre le Moyne, Sieur d'Iberville, established the first French settlement of the region at Old Biloxi (now Ocean Springs). In 1716, a second settlement was established by Jean Baptiste le Moyne, Sieur de Bienville, at Fort Rosalie (now Natchez). Three years later, in 1719, the first Negro slaves were brought to the region from West Africa. They worked in the rice and tobacco fields of the French colonists.

During the early 1700's, a scheme to develop the region was launched by John Law, a Scottish economist. Law's scheme failed and many people lost the money they had invested in his company. However, Law's venture brought much attention to Louisiana. As a result, thousands of settlers were attracted to the region (see MISSISSIPPI SCHEME). Old Biloxi, New Biloxi (now Biloxi), and Fort Louis de la Mobile (now Mobile, Ala.) served as capital of the region at various times during the early 1700's. In 1722, the French made New Orleans, in present-day Louisiana, the capital of the region. At that time, Louisiana made up a vast territory that extended from the Allegheny Mountains to the Rocky Mountains.

Many difficulties delayed development of the region. At first, the Indians fought the settlers. Later, the British battled the French for possession of the newly settled land. In 1730, the French put down an uprising of the Natchez Indians. But in 1736, British troops helped the Chickasaw Indians defeat the French colonists in the northeastern part of present-day Mississippi. That defeat stopped the French from gaining control of the Mississippi Valley. During the French and Indian War (1754-1763), the British and the Chickasaw blocked the French in the lower Mississippi Valley from joining the French forces in the Ohio Valley. The Treaty of Paris, signed after the war, gave the British all the land east of the Mississippi River. Thus, the Mississippi region came under British rule. The southern portion became part of the British province called West Florida. Nearly all of the remaining area became part of the Georgia colony.

The Port of Vicksburg in the 1800's was an important stop for Mississippi riverboats. The city is still a major river port.

Territorial Days. During the Revolutionary War (1775-1783), most of the settlers of West Florida remained loyal to Great Britain. But the Indians, trappers, and scouts of the rest of the Mississippi region supported the American colonies. In 1781, because the British were so busy with their war with the colonies, Spain was able to take over West Florida. Two years later, Great Britain granted West Florida to Spain. After the British lost the war, the Mississippi region north of about the 32nd parallel was made part of the United States. In 1795, the Spanish government accepted the 31st parallel as the U.S. border in a treaty signed in Madrid.

Congress organized the Mississippi Territory in 1798, with Natchez as the capital. Winthrop Sargent became the first governor of the new territory. It was bounded on the south by the 31st parallel, on the west by the Mississippi River, on the north by a line east from the mouth of the Yazoo River, and on the east by the Chattahoochee River. In 1803, the Louisiana Purchase made the Mississippi River part of the United States. Development of the territory was aided because the river allowed Mississippi trading ships to sail to the Gulf of Mexico.

In 1804, Congress extended the Mississippi Territory north to the border of Tennessee. More land was added in 1812. That year, the part of the West Florida Republic lying east of the Pearl River was incorporated into the Mississippi Territory. The republic had been formed in 1810 after American settlers took control of the region from Spain. The republic consisted of the land south of the 31st parallel between the Mississippi River and the Perdido River.

During the War of 1812, the Choctaw Indians under Chief Pushmataha remained friendly to the Americans. The Choctaw joined the Mississippi militia in helping General Andrew Jackson put down uprisings of the Creek Indians and in defeating a British army in the Battle of New Orleans.

Statehood. In 1817, Congress divided the Mississippi Territory into the state of Mississippi and the Alabama Territory. On Dec. 10, 1817, Mississippi was admitted to the Union as the 20th state. The first Mississippi state governor, David Holmes, had been territorial governor since 1809. Columbia, Natchez, and Washington served as the state capital at various times until Jackson became the capital in 1822.

In territorial days, Indian tribes had controlled almost two-thirds of Mississippi. The tribes gradually gave up their lands to the U.S. government. By 1832, most of the Indians had moved to the Indian Territory (now Oklahoma). The lands they left were opened for settlement. Many settlers came from the East to farm the fertile soil. Much of the soil was excellent for growing cotton. Cotton production had increased throughout the South after Eli Whitney invented the cotton gin in 1793.

After 1806, an improved type of cottonseed helped increase Mississippi's cotton production. The improved variety was developed from some seeds brought to Mississippi from Mexico. It was called Petit Gulf, the name of the Claiborne County area in which it was developed. The cotton producers used slave labor to operate large cotton plantations. Mississippi became one of the wealthiest states of the period.

During the 1850's, Mississippi farmers built many levees in the Delta region to control the floodwaters of the Mississippi and Yazoo rivers. In 1858, the legislature set up a board of levee commissioners. A large amount of the swampland in the state was drained and made suitable for farming.

The Civil War and Reconstruction. Most Mississippians did not favor *secession* (withdrawal) from the Union when South Carolina threatened to do so in 1832 (see NULLIFICATION). But their feelings changed during the next 29 years. The reasons for the change included violations of the Fugitive Slave Law, the struggle over slavery in Kansas, the founding of the Republican Party, and the economic differences between the North and the South. Mississippi became a strong defender of states' rights. See CIVIL WAR (Causes of the War).

On Jan. 9, 1861, a convention met in the Old Capitol in Jackson and adopted the Ordinance of Secession. Mississippi became the second state, after South Carolina, to secede from the Union. About five weeks later, Jefferson Davis of Mississippi became president of the Confederacy. He had been a soldier, planter, and a U.S. Senator. Davis also had served as Secretary of War under President Franklin Pierce.

More than 80,000 Mississippi troops served in the Confederate armies. Union and Confederate forces clashed in Mississippi, or on its borders, in many places. Important battles were fought at Corinth, Harrisburg (now Tupelo), Holly Springs, Iuka, Jackson, Meridian, and Port Gibson. In June, 1864, at Brice's Cross Roads, General Nathan Bedford Forrest of Mississippi defeated a larger Union cavalry force. Forrest supposedly explained his military successes by saying that he tried "to git thar fustest with the mostest men."

The Battle of Vicksburg ranks as the most important military action in Mississippi. The Confederate stronghold in Vicksburg fell to General Ulysses S. Grant's Union forces on July 4, 1863, after a 47-day defense. General Grant's capture of Vicksburg gave the Union control of the Mississippi River. The Union victories at Vicksburg and Gettysburg marked the turning point of the Civil War.

After the war, in 1867, the United States placed Mississippi under military rule during the Reconstruction period (see RECONSTRUCTION). Mississippi was readmitted to the Union in 1870, after adopting a new state constitution and ratifying amendments 14 and 15 to the United States Constitution. It took many years for Mississippi to recover from its war losses.

The Early 1900's were years of progress in agriculture, education, and industry. The lumber industry reached a high peak just before World War I began in 1914. New drainage projects in Mississippi opened large swampy areas to agriculture. County agricultural high schools were established in 1908. The state established an illiteracy commission in 1916 to start a special educational program for adults who could not read or write. In 1912, the Mississippi legislature passed laws regulating child labor.

After the United States entered World War I in 1917, Payne Field was established at West Point, Miss., as a training base for army pilots. Camp Shelby, near Hattiesburg, became one of the army's chief centers for preparing troops for overseas duty.

Legislative measures during the 1920's included the establishment of a state commission of education in 1924, and of a state library commission in 1926. The first milk condensery in the South opened at Starkville in 1926. Mississippi suffered greatly in the Mississippi River flood of 1927. About 100,000 persons fled from their flooded homes in the Delta. The damage to crops and property in Mississippi totaled over $204 million. The next year, Congress made the U.S. Army Corps of Engineers responsible for controlling floods on the Mississippi River.

Economic Development. During the Great Depression of the 1930's, Mississippi launched an important program of economic development. The program, called Balancing Agriculture With Industry (BAWI), was helped by special laws passed by the legislature in 1936. These laws freed new industries from paying certain taxes. The laws also allowed cities and counties to issue

---

IMPORTANT DATES IN MISSISSIPPI

1540 Hernando de Soto entered the Mississippi region.

1699 Pierre le Moyne, Sieur d'Iberville, established the first French colony at Old Biloxi.

1763 Mississippi became English territory after the French and Indian War.

1781 Spain occupied the Gulf Coast.

1798 The Mississippi Territory was organized.

1817 Mississippi became the 20th state on December 10.

1858 Mississippi started a swamp drainage program in the Delta.

1861 Mississippi seceded from the Union.

1863 Union forces captured Vicksburg in the Civil War.

1870 Mississippi was readmitted to the Union.

1936 Mississippi adopted special laws to encourage manufacturing.

1939 Petroleum was discovered at Tinsley.

1954 The Mississippi legislature passed a law banning required union membership.

1960 Mississippi passed laws that broadened the tax-free privilege of industrial properties.

1964 Atomic scientists set off the first nuclear test explosion east of the Mississippi River at Baxterville, Miss.

1969 Charles Evers became the first black mayor in Mississippi since Reconstruction. He was elected in Fayette.

HISTORIC MISSISSIPPI

Hernando de Soto, the Spanish explorer, was the first European to reach the Mississippi River. He came upon it at the northern border of Mississippi in 1541. He died one year later and was buried in the river near Natchez.

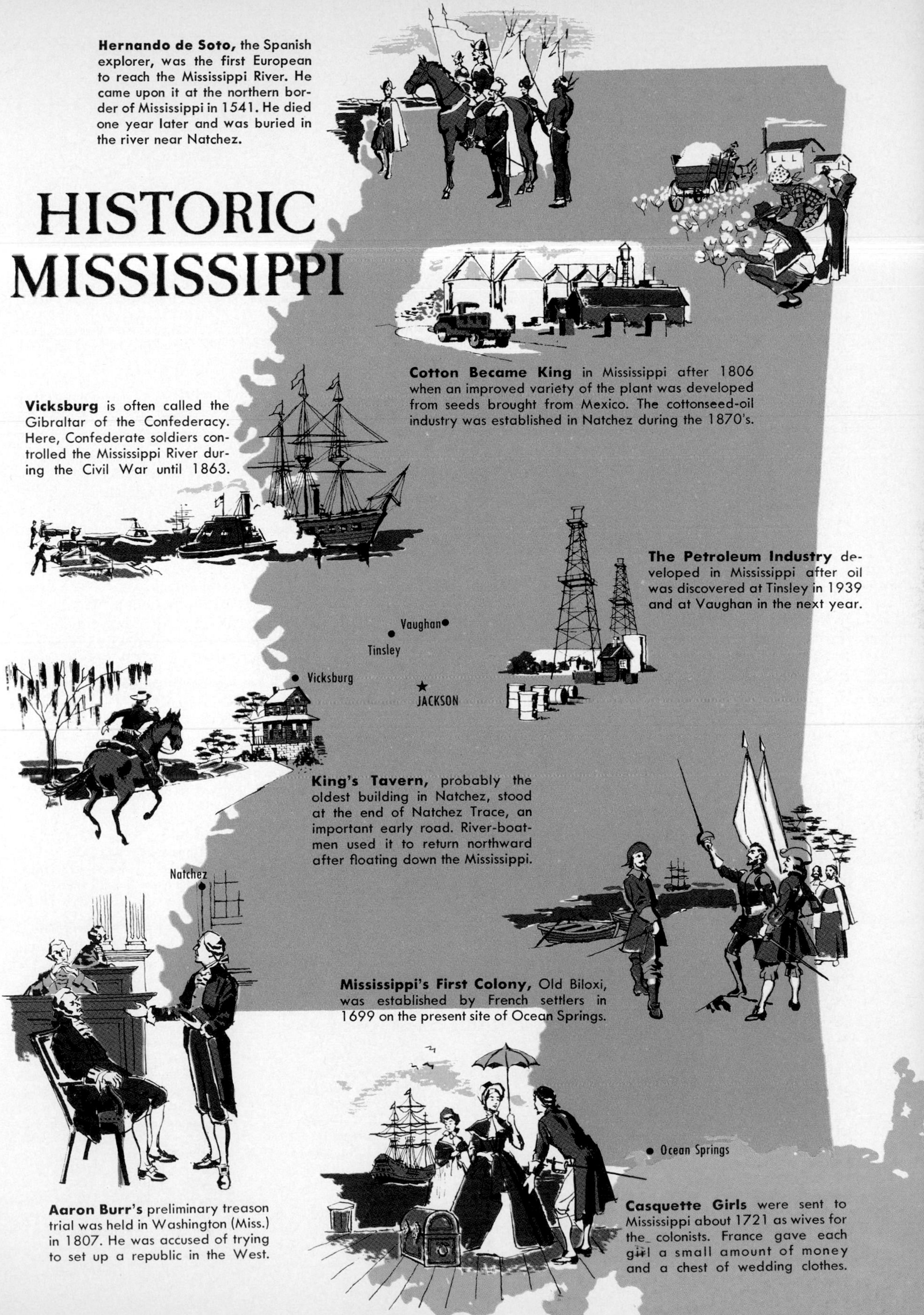

Cotton Became King in Mississippi after 1806 when an improved variety of the plant was developed from seeds brought from Mexico. The cottonseed-oil industry was established in Natchez during the 1870's.

Vicksburg is often called the Gibraltar of the Confederacy. Here, Confederate soldiers controlled the Mississippi River during the Civil War until 1863.

The Petroleum Industry developed in Mississippi after oil was discovered at Tinsley in 1939 and at Vaughan in the next year.

Vaughan
Tinsley
Vicksburg
JACKSON

King's Tavern, probably the oldest building in Natchez, stood at the end of Natchez Trace, an important early road. River-boatmen used it to return northward after floating down the Mississippi.

Natchez

Mississippi's First Colony, Old Biloxi, was established by French settlers in 1699 on the present site of Ocean Springs.

Ocean Springs

Aaron Burr's preliminary treason trial was held in Washington (Miss.) in 1807. He was accused of trying to set up a republic in the West.

Casquette Girls were sent to Mississippi about 1721 as wives for the colonists. France gave each girl a small amount of money and a chest of wedding clothes.

bonds and use the bond money to build factories for new industries. The BAWI program is administered by the state's Department of Economic Development. In developing the BAWI program, Mississippi became one of the first states to use national advertising to promote new industries. Mississippi's industrial development was strongly aided by the discovery of petroleum at Tinsley in 1939 and at Vaughan in 1940.

The Mid-1900's. During World War II (1939-1945), many war plants operated in Mississippi. The port of Pascagoula became an assembly center for ships sailing in convoys. After the war, the state's industrial development continued. In 1954, the legislature passed a right-to-work law. This law provided that no worker has to join a union if he or she does not want to do so. The law became part of the state's constitution in 1960.

During the 1960's, Mississippi worked to attract new industries. The legislature passed laws in 1960 broadening the tax-free position of industry. In 1963, a huge oil refinery was built in Pascagoula. In 1964, the state set up the Mississippi Research and Development Center. The center encourages new industries to move into the state and helps established companies expand. By 1966, more Mississippians worked in manufacturing than in agriculture. But Mississippi still had relatively little industry compared to many other states, and most of its workers earned low incomes. In 1968, the Ingalls shipyards began a $130-million expansion program in Pascagoula. In other coastal areas, the tourist industry boomed. During the 1960's, tourists spent about $200 million annually in the state.

Mississippi became active in the work of the Atomic Energy Commission (AEC) and the National Aeronautics and Space Administration (NASA). In 1964,

NASA

The Mississippi Test Facility, a testing ground for rockets, was built near Gulfport in the mid-1960's. Saturn rockets tested here launched the Apollo 11 astronauts to the moon.

AEC scientists set off a nuclear device near Baxterville. It was the first nuclear test explosion east of the Mississippi River. In 1965, NASA engineers began to test-fire engines of the Saturn V rocket near Gulfport. Saturn V rockets were used to launch U.S. spacecraft to the moon.

Like many other states, Mississippi has had racial problems. The state's constitution had provided for segregated schools. But in 1954, the Supreme Court of the United States ruled that compulsory segregation of public schools was unconstitutional. Efforts by civil rights groups to bring about integration were sometimes met with violence. In 1962, two persons were killed in riots that broke out when James Meredith enrolled as the first black student at the University of Mississippi. In 1963, Medgar Evers, Mississippi field secretary of the National Association for the Advancement of Colored People (NAACP), was shot and killed. In 1964, three civil rights workers were murdered near Philadelphia,

---

THE GOVERNORS OF MISSISSIPPI

	Party	Term		Party	Term
David Holmes	*Dem.-Rep.	1817-1820	Adelbert Ames	Republican	1874-1876
George Poindexter	Dem.-Rep.	1820-1822	John M. Stone	Democratic	1876-1882
Walter Leake	Dem.-Rep.	1822-1825	Robert Lowry	Democratic	1882-1890
Gerard C. Brandon	Dem.-Rep.	1825-1826	John M. Stone	Democratic	1890-1896
David Holmes	Dem.-Rep.	1826	Anselm J. McLaurin	Democratic	1896-1900
Gerard C. Brandon	Dem.-Rep.	1826-1832	Andrew H. Longino	Democratic	1900-1904
Abram M. Scott	Democratic	1832-1833	James K. Vardaman	Democratic	1904-1908
Charles Lynch	Democratic	1833	Edmond F. Noel	Democratic	1908-1912
Hiram G. Runnels	Democratic	1833-1835	Earl L. Brewer	Democratic	1912-1916
John A. Quitman	Whig	1835-1836	Theodore G. Bilbo	Democratic	1916-1920
Charles Lynch	Democratic	1836-1838	Lee M. Russell	Democratic	1920-1924
Alexander G. McNutt	Democratic	1838-1842	Henry L. Whitfield	Democratic	1924-1927
Tilghman M. Tucker	Democratic	1842-1844	Dennis Murphree	Democratic	1927-1928
Albert G. Brown	Democratic	1844-1848	Theodore G. Bilbo	Democratic	1928-1932
Joseph W. Matthews	Democratic	1848-1850	Martin Sennett Conner	Democratic	1932-1936
John A. Quitman	Democratic	1850-1851	Hugh L. White	Democratic	1936-1940
John I. Guion	Democratic	1851	Paul B. Johnson	Democratic	1940-1943
James Whitfield	Democratic	1851-1852	Dennis Murphree	Democratic	1943-1944
Henry S. Foote	†Union Dem.	1852-1854	Thomas L. Bailey	Democratic	1944-1946
John J. Pettus	Democratic	1854	Fielding L. Wright	Democratic	1946-1952
John J. McRae	Democratic	1854-1857	Hugh L. White	Democratic	1952-1956
William McWillie	Democratic	1857-1859	James P. Coleman	Democratic	1956-1960
John J. Pettus	Democratic	1859-1863	Ross R. Barnett	Democratic	1960-1964
Charles Clark	Democratic	1863-1865	Paul B. Johnson	Democratic	1964-1968
William L. Sharkey	**Whig-Dem.	1865	John Bell Williams	Democratic	1968-1972
Benjamin G. Humphreys	Whig	1865-1868	William Waller	Democratic	1972-1976
Adelbert Ames	‡U.S. Mil. Gov.	1868-1870	Cliff Finch	Democratic	1976-1980
James L. Alcorn	Republican	1870-1871	William F. Winter	Democratic	1980-
Ridgley C. Powers	Republican	1871-1874			

*Democratic-Republican; †Union Democratic; **Whig-Democratic; ‡United States Military Governor

Miss. Both white and black leaders in Mississippi spoke out against the violence.

In the fall of 1964, the first public schools in Mississippi began to desegregate. In 1969, the United States Supreme Court ordered an immediate end to all segregated public schools. As a result, a federal court in New Orleans ordered 33 Mississippi school districts to desegregate by December, 1969. Many white people then established segregated private schools and enrolled their children. Also in 1969, Charles Evers, brother of Medgar, was elected mayor of Fayette. He became the first black mayor in Mississippi since Reconstruction.

Mississippi Today has the lowest *per capita* (per person) income in the nation. Thousands of farmworkers in the Delta region are jobless because of increased use of machinery and the inability of many farm operators to pay minimum wages. Many high school and college graduates leave Mississippi to find jobs.

Mississippi faces the challenge of fully developing its economic program. Mississippi hopes to keep young people from leaving the state by attracting industries that require higher skills and pay higher wages. To attract such industries, many cities are working to improve transportation and other services and to increase cultural and educational opportunities.

CHARLOTTE CAPERS, T. M. HEDERMAN, JR., and M. W. MYERS

MISSISSIPPI / Study Aids

Related Articles in WORLD BOOK include:

BIOGRAPHIES

Bruce, Blanche K.	George, James Z.
Davis, Jefferson	Lamar, Lucius Q. C.
De Soto, Hernando	Revels, Hiram R.
Eastland, James O.	Welty, Eudora
Evers (family)	Williams, Tennessee
Faulkner, William	Wright, Richard

CITIES

Biloxi	Jackson	Meridian	Vicksburg
Greenville	Laurel	Natchez	

HISTORY

Civil War	Natchez Trace
Confederate States of America	Paris, Treaties of (1763, 1783)
Louisiana Purchase	Reconstruction
Mississippi Scheme	

PHYSICAL FEATURES

Gulf of Mexico	Tombigbee River
Mississippi River	Yazoo River

PRODUCTS

For Mississippi's rank among the states in production, see the following articles:

Chicken	Soybean	Sweet Potato
Cotton		

OTHER RELATED ARTICLES

Black Americans	Sardis Dam	Southern States

Outline

I. **Government**
   A. Constitution
   B. Executive
   C. Legislature
   D. Courts
   E. Local Government
   F. Taxation
   G. Politics

II. **People**

III. **Education**
   A. Schools
   B. Libraries
   C. Museums

IV. **A Visitor's Guide**
   A. Places to Visit
   B. Annual Events

V. **The Land**
   A. Land Regions
   B. Coastline
   C. Rivers and Lakes

VI. **Climate**

VII. **Economy**
   A. Natural Resources
   B. Manufacturing
   C. Agriculture
   D. Mining

   E. Fishing Industry
   F. Electric Power
   G. Transportation
   H. Communication

VIII. **History**

Questions

Where is Mississippi's chief cotton-producing area? Why is its soil so fertile?

What important social change was brought about by the growth of factories in Mississippi?

Why is Mississippi a leading winter vacationland? Where are the state's chief winter resorts?

What special event marks the opening of Mississippi's shrimp-fishing season?

How does Mississippi protect its valuable trees?

Why did the early Spanish explorers make no settlements in the Mississippi region?

Why does the Battle of Vicksburg rank as one of the most important battles of the Civil War?

How does Mississippi try to attract new industries?

How is Mississippi playing an important part in the U.S. space travel program?

Why did public opinion in Mississippi about secession change during the 29 years before the Civil War?

Books for Young Readers

BAILEY, BERNADINE. *Picture Book of Mississippi.* Rev. ed. Whitman, 1972.

CARPENTER, ALLAN. *Mississippi.* Childrens Press, 1968.

DeGRUMMOND, LENA Y., and DeLAUNE, L. D. *Jeff Davis: Confederate Boy.* Bobbs, 1960.

KELLEY, SALLY J. *Summer Growing Time.* Viking, 1971. Fiction.

MEREDITH, ROBERT K., and SMITH, E. B., eds. *Exploring the Great River: Early Voyages on the Mississippi from De Soto to La Salle.* Little, Brown, 1969.

TAYLOR, MILDRED D. *Song of the Trees.* Dial, 1975. *Roll of Thunder, Hear My Cry.* 1976. Both books are fiction, and the second won the Newbery medal.

Books for Older Readers

CROSS, RALPH D., and WALES, R. W., eds. *Atlas of Mississippi.* Univ. Press of Mississippi, 1974.

DANIELS, JONATHAN. *The Devil's Backbone: The Story of the Natchez Trace.* McGraw, 1962.

HAYNES, ROBERT V. *The Natchez District and the American Revolution.* Univ. Press of Mississippi, 1976.

LOEWEN, JAMES W., and SALLIS, CHARLES, eds. *Mississippi: Conflict & Change.* Pantheon, 1974.

McLEMORE, RICHARD A., ed. *A History of Mississippi.* 2 vols. Univ. Press of Mississippi, 1973.

NEWTON, CAROLYN S., and COGGIN, P. H. *Meet Mississippi.* Strode, 1976.

WELTY, EUDORA. *One Time, One Place: Mississippi in the Depression.* Random House, 1971.

The Lyceum Building at the University of Mississippi houses the school's administrative offices.

MISSISSIPPI, UNIVERSITY OF, is a state-supported coeducational school with campuses in University and Jackson, Miss. The main campus is in University, near Oxford. It has a college of liberal arts, a graduate school, and schools of business administration, education, engineering, law, and pharmacy. The University of Mississippi Medical Center in Jackson includes schools of dentistry, medicine, and nursing. The university grants bachelor's, master's, and doctor's degrees.

The university's library features the Deavours collection of Mississippiana, and the resource materials of such noted Mississippians as the authors William Faulkner and Stark Young. The university maintains Faulkner's home, Rowan Oak, near the main campus. The Museum of Classical Archaeology has important collections of the Egyptian, Greek, Near Eastern, and Roman civilizations. The Museum of Anthropology displays American artifacts. The university holds cooperative educational programs with Oak Ridge National Laboratory and Gulf Coast Research Laboratory.

The university was founded in 1844, and opened in 1848. For enrollment, see UNIVERSITIES AND COLLEGES (table). PORTER L. FORTUNE, JR.

MISSISSIPPI BUBBLE. See MISSISSIPPI SCHEME.

MISSISSIPPI COLLEGE is a coeducational liberal arts school in Clinton, Miss. It is controlled by the Mississippi Baptist Convention. It was founded in 1826 as Hampstead Academy and received its present name in 1830. Courses lead to A.B., B.S., and M.A. degrees. For enrollment, see UNIVERSITIES AND COLLEGES (table).

MISSISSIPPI RIVER is the chief river of North America and the longest river in the United States. It flows 2,348 miles (3,779 kilometers) from its source in northwestern Minnesota to its mouth in the Gulf of Mexico. The Mississippi and its tributaries drain almost all the plains that lie between the Appalachian Mountains and the Rocky Mountains. This drainage basin covers 1,247,300 square miles (3,230,490 square kilometers) and includes the nation's most productive agricultural and industrial regions.

The Mississippi is the nation's chief inland waterway. It carries agricultural goods, industrial products, and raw materials. Ships can travel the river for more than 1,800 miles (2,897 kilometers) from Minneapolis, Minn., to the Gulf of Mexico. The Mississippi ranges in depth from 9 feet (2.7 meters) to 100 feet (30 meters) during most of its course. The river reaches its widest point—about 4,500 feet (1,370 meters)—at Cairo, Ill.

The Mississippi, which is sometimes called "Old Man River," has played a vital role in the history of the United States. During the 1500's and 1600's, it provided a route for Spanish and French explorers. With the coming of steamboats in the 1800's, the Mississippi became a great transportation and trade route. The famous American author Mark Twain described the river vividly in his book *Life on the Mississippi* (1883).

The Course of the Mississippi. The Mississippi begins as a small, clear stream that rushes out of Lake Itasca in northwestern Minnesota. The river flows northward and then eastward, linking a series of lakes.

The Mississippi begins to curve southward near Grand Rapids, Minn. As it flows between Minneapolis and St. Paul, Minn., it is joined by the Minnesota River. Beginning with its junction with the St. Croix River, the Mississippi forms part of the boundary between Minnesota and Wisconsin. The river also makes up part of the boundaries of eight other states. Illinois, Kentucky, Tennessee, and Mississippi lie on the river to the east, and Iowa, Missouri, Arkansas, and part of Louisiana are on the western shore.

Two major tributaries, the Illinois River and the Missouri River, join the Mississippi above St. Louis. The muddy waters of the Missouri contrast with the clear waters of the Mississippi. Later, the waters mix and the Mississippi takes on the muddy color for which it is known in the South.

The Ohio River flows into the Mississippi at Cairo and doubles the volume of water of the Mississippi. This junction divides the upper Mississippi from the lower Mississippi. South of Cairo, the flood plain of the Mississippi forms a broad, fertile valley. The valley is more than 50 miles (80 kilometers) wide in some places. The river winds back and forth through this valley and forms broad loops. It sometimes changes its course and cuts off the loops, creating horseshoe-shaped lakes called *oxbow lakes*. Along its lower course, the Mississippi deposits small soil particles called *silt* along its banks. The silt builds up and forms embankments known as *natural levees*.

The Arkansas River joins the Mississippi about 50 miles (80 kilometers) north of Greenville, Miss. South of Natchez, Miss., the Red River enters the Mississippi flood plain, but most of its flow continues into the Atchafalaya River. About a fourth of the Mississippi's water also goes into the Atchafalaya.

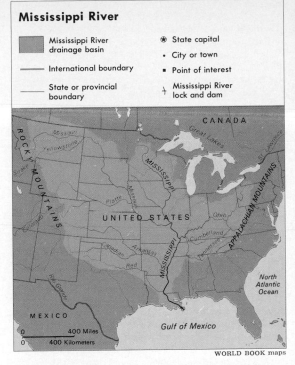

Mississippi River

▨	Mississippi River drainage basin	✦	State capital
—	International boundary	•	City or town
—	State or provincial boundary	■	Point of interest
		⌁	Mississippi River lock and dam

WORLD BOOK maps

As the Mississippi approaches the Gulf of Mexico, it deposits large amounts of silt to form a delta. The Mississippi Delta covers about 13,000 square miles (33,700 square kilometers). South of New Orleans, the river breaks up into several channels called *distributaries*, which enter the Gulf of Mexico. They include Main Pass, North Pass, South Pass, and Southwest Pass. The Mississippi River system empties over 640,000 cubic feet (18,100 cubic meters) of water per second into the gulf. This discharge totals about 133 cubic miles (554 cubic kilometers) of water per year.

Commerce. The Mississippi River carries about 40 per cent of the freight that is transported on the nation's inland waterways. More than 300 million short tons (270 million metric tons) of freight are transported on the Mississippi annually.

Most commercial freight on the Mississippi travels on large barges pushed by tugboats. Between Minneapolis and Cairo, the southbound freight consists mainly of agricultural products, such as corn, soybeans, and wheat. Coal and steel products from the Ohio River system are transported north. South of Cairo, goods from the Ohio double the Mississippi's traffic. Most of the cargo consists of southbound agricultural goods, coal, and steel products. At Baton Rouge, La., petrochemical products, aluminum, and petroleum are added to the barge traffic. Beginning at Baton Rouge, the Mississippi deepens and allows passage of ocean-going vessels. The greatest volume of traffic on the Mississippi moves between New Orleans and Southwest Pass.

Floods and Flood Control. From time to time, the Mississippi has caused serious floods. The floods result from heavy winter snows and spring rains in the upper reaches of the Missouri and Ohio river systems. The

Milt and Joan Mann

The Source of the Mississippi River is Lake Itasca in northwestern Minnesota. The Mississippi begins as a small, clear stream but it later reaches a width of about 4,500 feet (1,370 meters) at Cairo, Ill., and becomes increasingly muddy.

melting snow and the rain bring unusually large amounts of water into the Mississippi. The river then overflows into the surrounding flood plain. Especially destructive floods occurred in 1927, 1937, 1965, and 1973. See FLOOD.

Dams and levees have provided some protection against flooding by the Mississippi. A series of dams along the Missouri and Ohio rivers control the amount of water that enters the Mississippi. The Mississippi itself was dammed north of St. Louis. Along the lower course of the Mississippi, the natural levees have been heightened and new levees built to prevent flooding. Dredging of the river channel not only increases the amount of water the river can carry, but also aids navigation on the river. In addition, areas of land called *floodways* provide outlets for draining off water when the river reaches flood level.

Animal and Plant Life. The Mississippi River and its valley support many kinds of animals and plants. Such freshwater fishes as bass, sunfish, and trout live in the clear waters of the upper Mississippi. Carp, catfish, and buffalofish are found in the muddy waters of the lower Mississippi.

The most common animals in the Mississippi Valley are mink, muskrats, opossums, otters, and skunks. Large rodents called *nutrias* live in the swamps and marshlands of the delta area (see NUTRIA). This area also provides winter nesting grounds for ducks, geese, and other migratory birds. Pelicans, herons, and egrets live in the area throughout the year.

Forests of hardwood trees, such as basswood, hickory, maple, and oak, grow in the upper Mississippi Valley. South of Cairo, the forests consist mainly of bald cypress, gum, southern oak, and tupelo trees.

Pollution seriously threatens the wildlife of the Mississippi. Fertilizers and insecticides used on farms are washed into the river, and industries empty wastes into its waters. During the 1970's, steps were taken to prevent further pollution of the river. For example, federal regulations prohibited farmers from using certain insecticides and other harmful chemicals.

History. The Mississippi was formed about 2 million years ago at the beginning of the Pleistocene Ice Age. During this period, glaciers covered much of the Northern Hemisphere. Melting ice from the glaciers was carried to the Mississippi by the Missouri and Ohio rivers.

Various Indian tribes, including the Illinois, the Kickapoo, the Ojibway, and the Santee Dakota, lived in the upper Mississippi Valley. The name *Mississippi*, which means *big river*, came from these tribes. The lower valley was the home of such tribes as the Chickasaw, the Choctaw, the Natchez, and the Tunica.

The first European to travel on the Mississippi was

Robert H. Glaze, Artstreet

Along the Upper Course of the Mississippi, forests of hardwood trees and steep bluffs line the river's banks in many areas. The river often cuts off areas of land, creating islands.

Robert H. Glaze, Artstreet

The Port of New Orleans, on the Mississippi River, is the nation's second busiest, after that of New York City. Ships from all parts of the world dock at the wharves along the Mississippi.

U.S. Army Corps of Engineers

Southwest Pass, a *distributary* (channel) of the Mississippi flows into the Gulf of Mexico. The greatest volume of traffic on the Mississippi moves between New Orleans and Southwest Pass.

the Spanish explorer Hernando de Soto. He crossed the river in 1541 near what is now Memphis. During the early 1680's, the French explorer Sieur de la Salle traveled down the river and claimed the Mississippi Valley for France.

France lost all of its territories on the mainland of North America as a result of the French and Indian War (1754-1763). Great Britain gained the land east of the Mississippi, and Spain took over the land west of the river. After the Revolutionary War in America (1775-1783), the United States took control of the British territories. In 1800, France regained the land west of the Mississippi. The United States bought this land from France in the Louisiana Purchase of 1803.

After the entire Mississippi Valley became part of the United States, settlers and traders set out on the river in flatboats, keelboats, and rafts. The importance of the river as a transportation and trade route increased with the development of steamboats in the early 1800's. River cities, including St. Louis, Memphis, and New Orleans, served as supply centers for the westward movement.

During the Civil War (1861-1865), the Mississippi served as an invasion route for the Union forces. The capture of such river cities as New Orleans, Memphis, and Vicksburg, Miss., divided the Confederacy in half and assured victory for the North. After the war, railroads soon took over most of the river's former steamboat traffic. The completion of the Eads Bridge in 1874, connecting St. Louis and East St. Louis, Ill., provided a major rail crossing over the river. Many more bridges were built during the years that followed.

The importance of the Mississippi as a transportation route has increased greatly since the 1920's. No other means of transportation can move masses of heavy, bulky cargo as cheaply as the barges and tugboats on the mighty river.　　　　JOHN EDWIN COFFMAN

Related Articles in WORLD BOOK include:

De Soto, Hernando　　　　Levee
Inland Waterway　　　　　Louisiana
Jetty　　　　　　　　　　River (chart:
La Salle, Sieur de　　　　　　Longest Rivers)

MISSISSIPPI SCHEME was a wild financial project formulated in France in 1717. John Law, a Scottish economist, originated the scheme, which resulted in the organization of a concern known as The Mississippi Company. The French regent, Philip, Duke of Orléans, gave the company a *monopoly* (exclusive rights) to carry on far-reaching business operations in French-held Louisiana and Canada. At first, the scheme won widespread approval. Thousands of Frenchmen bought shares in Law's company without really knowing how their money was to be used. But when the stockholders discovered that the company actually did little to develop business enterprises in America, they became frightened, and began to sell their shares at greatly reduced prices. The result was a financial panic in 1720, known as the bursting of "The Mississippi Bubble." A few investors who sold their shares early at high prices made huge profits. But others suffered heavy losses, or were ruined financially. The scheme was a failure, but it helped advertise Louisiana and attracted thousands of settlers and slaves to the colony.　　OSCAR O. WINTHER

MISSISSIPPI STATE UNIVERSITY is a coeducational school in Mississippi State, Miss. It receives state and federal support. It has colleges of agriculture, arts and sciences, business and industry, education, engineering, and veterinary medicine; a school of forest resources and architecture; and a graduate school. Courses lead to bachelor's, master's, and doctor's degrees. The university includes an agricultural and forestry experiment station, an agricultural extension service, a boll weevil research laboratory, and a chemical regulatory laboratory. It is noted for its aerophysics laboratory and a seed technology laboratory. The school was founded in 1878, and took its present name in 1958. For enrollment, see UNIVERSITIES AND COLLEGES (table).

Critically reviewed by MISSISSIPPI STATE UNIVERSITY

MISSISSIPPI UNIVERSITY FOR WOMEN, in Columbus, Miss., is a school of arts and sciences. It is the oldest state supported college for women in the United States. Courses include the humanities, commerce, and medical technology. The school was founded in 1884. For enrollment, see UNIVERSITIES AND COLLEGES (table).

MISSISSIPPIAN PERIOD was the early part of the Carboniferous Period in the Paleozoic Era of geologic history. See EARTH (table: Outline of Earth History).

MISSOULA, *muh ZOO luh,* Mont. (pop. 29,497), is the state's third largest city and the agricultural trading center of five fertile valleys. It lies on the Pacific slope of the Rocky Mountains, 115 miles (185 kilometers) west of Helena (see MONTANA [political map]).

Missoula is the site of the University of Montana and the Montana Forest Tree Nursery. It also serves as the headquarters of Region One of the U.S. Forest Service. Nearby is a training center for *smoke jumpers,* members of the Forest Service who parachute into remote areas to fight forest fires.

The name *Missoula* comes from a Flathead Indian word, *Im-i-su-la* or *I-mi-sule-tiko,* meaning *by or near the cold, chilling waters.* Some think the word refers to Hell Gate Canyon, just east of Missoula, where Blackfeet Indians ambushed Flathead Indians.

Missoula was founded in 1860. It has a mayor-council form of government.　　　　DONALD H. WELSH

MISSOURI

The Show Me State

Cave Spring by Thomas Hart Benton from the WORLD BOOK Collection

Ozark Scene in Southern Missouri

MISSOURI, *muh ZOOR ee,* or *muh ZOOR uh,* is an important industrial and farming state of the Midwest. Its location and its two great rivers have made Missouri a center of water, land, and air transportation.

The mighty Mississippi River forms Missouri's eastern border. The wide Missouri River winds across the state from west to east. A wealth of food, manufactured products, and raw materials is shipped on these waterways—the nation's longest rivers. Kansas City and St. Louis rank among the chief U.S. air and rail terminals. They also are among the nation's top trucking centers. Twelve major commercial airlines serve the state. Railroad passenger trains and freight lines, and many national and interstate highways also crisscross Missouri.

Vast fields of golden grain and green grasses cover the state's rolling plains in the north and west. Swift streams tumble through the rugged, wooded plateau of southern Missouri. This scenic region, called the Ozarks, is a major playground of the Midwest.

Missouri's factories turn out airplanes, automobiles, railroad cars, trucks, and other vehicles. The state ranks high in shoe manufacturing and flour milling. Its plants also pack meat and process dairy products and other foods. Missouri is a leading state in corn, grain sorghum, and soybean production, and it is a major livestock center. Missouri produces more lead than any other state. It also has valuable deposits of clay, coal, iron, limestone, marble, and other minerals.

Missouri is sometimes called the *Mother of the West* because it once lay at the frontier of the United States. The state supplied many of the pioneers who settled the vast region between Missouri and the Pacific Ocean. St. Louis, St. Charles, Independence, St. Joseph, and Westport Landing (now Kansas City) served as jumping-off places for the westbound pioneers. The historic Santa Fe Trail led from Independence to the rich, faraway Southwest. Thousands of settlers also followed the Oregon Trail from Independence to the Pacific Northwest. Furs brought from the Northwest made St. Louis the fur capital of the world.

During the Civil War, Missourians were torn between their loyalties to the South and to the Union. After the war, manufacturing developed rapidly, and St. Louis and Kansas City grew into industrial giants. Agriculture also expanded, and Missouri became a great farming state.

Many outstanding Americans have lived in Missouri. They include Harry S. Truman, the nation's 33rd Presi-dent; Mark Twain, the creator of Tom Sawyer and Huckleberry Finn; Eugene Field, the beloved children's poet; General John J. Pershing, commander of U.S. forces in Europe during World War I; George Washington Carver, the great black scientist; Joseph Pulitzer, the famous journalist; General Omar N. Bradley, a brilliant commander in World War II; and Thomas Hart Benton and George Caleb Bingham, noted painters.

The state's name comes from the Missouri River. The word *Missouri* probably came from an Indian word meaning the *town of the large canoes*. Missouri's nickname is the *Show Me State*. This nickname is usually traced to a speech by Congressman Willard Duncan Vandiver of Missouri in 1899. Speaking in Philadelphia, Vandiver said: ". . . frothy eloquence neither convinces nor satisfies me. I am from Missouri. You have got to show me."

Jefferson City is Missouri's capital, and St. Louis is the largest city. For Missouri's relationship to other states in its region, see MIDWESTERN STATES.

FACTS IN BRIEF

Capital: Jefferson City.

Government: *Congress*—U.S. senators, 2; U.S. representatives, 10. *Electoral Votes*—12. *State Legislature*—senators, 34; representatives, 163. *Counties*—114, and the city of St. Louis.

Area: 69,686 sq. mi. (180,486 km²), including 691 sq. mi. (1,790 km²) of inland water; 19th in size among the states. *Greatest Distances*—north-south, 284 mi. (457 km); east-west, 308 mi. (496 km).

Elevation: *Highest*—Taum Sauk Mountain, 1,772 ft. (540 m) above sea level. *Lowest*—230 ft. (70 m) above sea level, along the St. Francis River near Cardwell.

Population: *Estimated 1975 Population*—4,763,000. *1970 Census*—4,677,399; 13th among the states; distribution, 70 per cent urban, 30 per cent rural; density, 67 persons per sq. mi. (26 per km²).

Chief Products: *Agriculture*—beef cattle, soybeans, hogs, milk. *Manufacturing*—transportation equipment, food products, chemicals, electric and electronic equipment, nonelectric machinery, fabricated metal products, printed materials. *Mining*—lead, stone.

Statehood: Aug. 10, 1821, the 24th state.

State Abbreviations: Mo. (traditional); MO (postal).

State Motto: *Salus populi suprema lex esto* (The welfare of the people shall be the supreme law).

State Song: "Missouri Waltz." Words by J. R. Shannon; music from an original melody obtained from John Valentine Eppel.

Missouri (blue) ranks 19th in size among all the states, and 6th in size among the Midwestern States (gray).

The contributors of this article are James E. Collier, author of Geography of the Northern Ozark Border Region in Missouri; *Lew Larkin, Former Editor of Missouri History for the* Kansas City Star; *and William E. Parrish, Dean of the College and Truman Professor of American History at Westminster College.*

Winter on the Missouri River near Jefferson City
Gerald R. Massie

Constitution of Missouri was adopted in 1945. The state had three earlier constitutions, adopted in 1820, 1865, and 1875. An amendment to the constitution may be proposed by a majority of the members of the state legislature. Or it may be proposed by a petition signed by 8 per cent of the voters in two-thirds of the state's congressional districts. To become part of the constitution, an amendment must be approved by a majority of the voters voting on the amendment. The constitution requires that the people vote every 20 years, starting in 1962, on whether to call a convention to amend the constitution.

Executive. The governor of Missouri is elected to a four-year term and is limited to two terms. The governor receives a yearly salary of $55,000. The governor appoints many of the key officials of state government agencies. For a list of all the governors of Missouri, see the *History* section of this article.

The other top state officials—the lieutenant governor, secretary of state, state treasurer, attorney general, and state auditor—are elected to four-year terms.

Legislature of Missouri is known as the General Assembly. It consists of a Senate of 34 members and a House of Representatives of 163 members. Missouri has 34 senatorial districts and 163 representative districts. Voters in each senatorial district elect one senator. Voters in each representative district elect one representative. Senators serve four-year terms, and representatives serve two-year terms.

In 1966, a commission *reapportioned* (redivided) the House of Representatives to provide equal representation on the basis of population. In 1971, both the House and Senate districts were redrawn.

The General Assembly meets every year on the first Wednesday after the first Monday in January. A regular session may last until May 15 in even-numbered years or until June 30 in odd-numbered years. But after April 30 (June 15 in odd-numbered years), the lawmakers cannot consider new bills. The governor may call special sessions, which are limited to 60 calendar days.

Courts in Missouri are headed by the state Supreme Court, composed of seven judges. The state court of appeals has three districts—the Western district in Kansas City, the Eastern district in St. Louis, and the Southern district in Springfield. The governor appoints the judges of the Supreme Court and the appeals courts for 12-year terms. They are selected from candidates proposed by nonpartisan commissions. Appointed judges must be approved by the voters in the next general election. When their terms expire, they must again be approved by the voters to remain in office. Every two years, the Supreme Court selects one member to serve as chief justice.

The state constitution also provides for circuit courts, associate circuit courts, and municipal courts. Circuit-court judges serve six-year terms, and the rest serve four-year terms. Judges of circuit and associate circuit courts in Jackson, Platte, Clay, and St. Louis counties—and in the city of St. Louis—are selected like the judges of the Supreme Court. The people elect all other judges.

Local Government. Voters in Missouri's 114 counties elect local officials. These officials generally include three judges of the county court, a sheriff, recorder of deeds, prosecuting attorney, collector of revenue, assessor, treasurer, coroner, public administrator, surveyor, and superintendent of public schools. The county court judges serve as the chief administrators of the county. They are responsible for health, welfare, and public works in the county, and set the county tax rate. The constitution provides that any county with more than 85,000 residents, or any city with over 10,000 persons, may organize its government in the way that best suits its people. Like most Missouri cities, St. Louis has a mayor-council form of government. But St. Louis is an independent city and is not part of any county. It is governed by a mayor, a 28-member Board of Aldermen, and the board president.

Walker, Missouri Division of Commerce

The Governor's Mansion stands east of the Missouri Capitol. The three-story residence was completed in 1871.

The State Seal

The State Flag

Symbols of Missouri. On the state seal, adopted in 1822, two grizzly bears represent the state. They hold shields of the United States and Missouri to show that the state supports itself and the Union. The helmet symbolizes enterprise and hardiness. The stars show that Missouri was the 24th state in the Union. The Roman numerals give the date that Missouri's first constitution was adopted. The seal appears on the flag, adopted in 1913.

Flower illustration, courtesy of Eli Lilly and Company

Taxation. Taxes and licenses bring in about two-thirds of Missouri's income. The federal government provides about one-third of the income. Missouri receives about half its income from a sales tax, individual and corporation income taxes, a gasoline tax, and vehicle licenses. Taxes are also collected on cigarettes, liquor, property, and other items.

Politics. Missouri voters tend to favor Democratic candidates, but the balloting between parties is usually close. In presidential elections since 1900, Missouri has voted for the winner every time except once—in 1956. For the state's voting record in presidential elections since 1820, see ELECTORAL COLLEGE (table).

St. Louis and Kansas City vote strongly Democratic, but the region around St. Louis is Republican. Northeastern Missouri, most of the counties along the Missouri River, and southeastern Missouri are Democratic. North-central and southwestern Missouri are Republican. About 30 counties switch back and forth between the two major parties. The party that wins these counties generally controls the state legislature. Missouri has had only six Republican governors since 1900.

The State Capitol, in Jefferson City, was completed in 1917. Jefferson City has been Missouri's capital since 1826. Former capitals were St. Louis (1820) and St. Charles (1821-1826).

Walker, Missouri Division of Commerce

The State Bird
Bluebird

The State Flower
Hawthorn

The State Tree
Flowering Dogwood

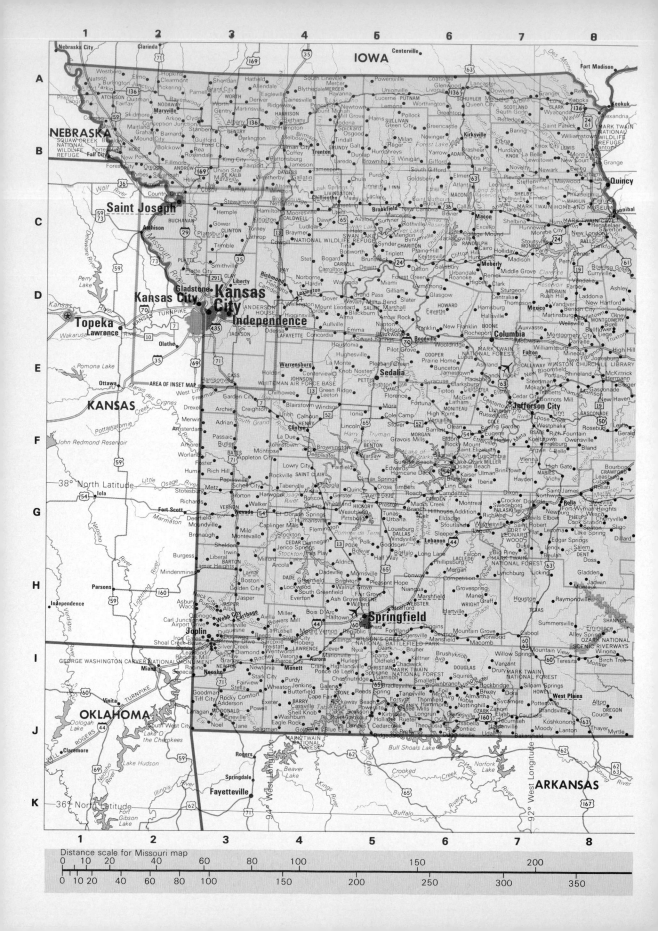

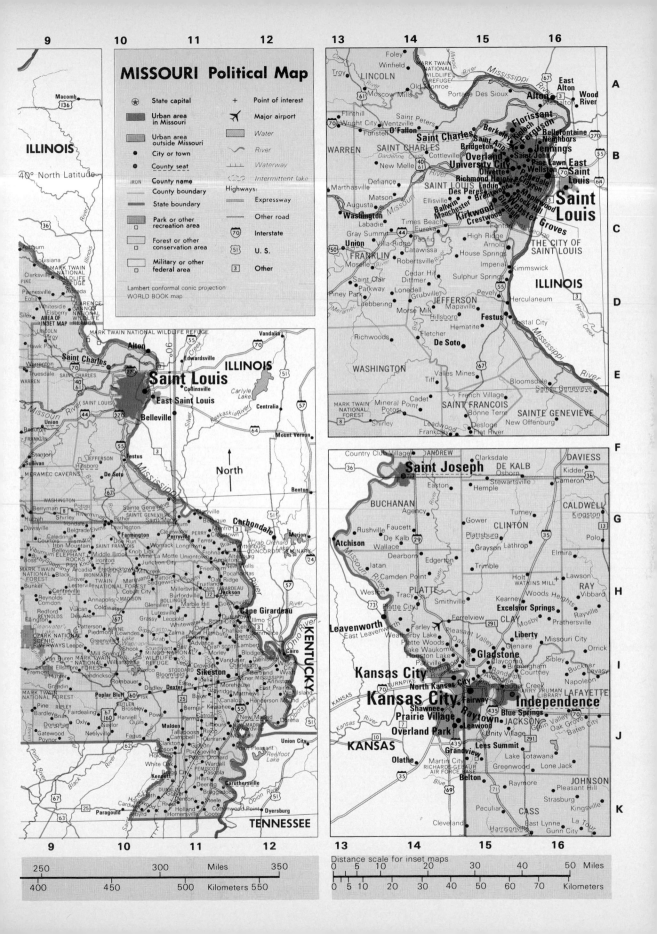

Population

4,763,000 .Estimate.1975
4,677,399 ..Census..1970
4,319,813 ....."....1960
3,954,653 ....."....1950
3,784,664 ....."....1940
3,629,367 ....."....1930
3,404,055 ....."....1920
3,293,335 ....."....1910
3,106,665 ....."....1900
2,679,185 ....."....1890
2,168,380 ....."....1880
1,721,295 ....."....1870
1,182,012 ....."....1860
682,044 ....."....1850
383,702 ....."....1840
140,455 ....."....1830
66,586 ....."....1820
10,783 ....."....1810

Metropolitan Areas

Columbia 80,935
Kansas City ..1,273,926
(867,008 in Mo.;
406,918 in Kans.)
St. Joseph 98,828
St. Louis 2,410,492
(1,827,236 in Mo.;
583,256 in Ill.)
Springfield 168,053

Counties

Adair .....22,472..B 6
Andrew ....11,913..B 2
Atchison ....9,240..A 1
Audrain ...25,362..D 7
Barry .....19,597..J 4
Barton ....10,431..H 3
Bates ......15,468..F 3
Benton .....9,695..F 5
Bollinger ...8,820..H 11
Boone .....80,935..D 7
Buchanan .86,915..C 2
Butler .....33,529..J 10
Caldwell ....8,351..C 4
Callaway ..25,991..E 7
Camden ...13,315..G 6
Cape
Girardeau 49,350..H 11
Carroll ....12,565..D 5
Carter ......3,878..I 9
Cass ....39,448..E 3
Cedar ....9,424..G 4
Chariton ...11,084..C 5
Christian ..15,124..I 5
Clark ....8,260..A 7
Clay ......123,702..D 3
Clinton ....12,462..C 3
Cole ....46,228..F 7
Cooper ....14,732..E 6
Crawford ..14,828..F 8
Dade ....6,850..H 4
Dallas .....10,054..G 5
Daviess .....8,420..B 4
De Kalb ....7,305..B 3
Dent ....11,457..H 8
Douglas .....9,268..I 6
Dunklin ....33,742..K 11
Franklin ...55,127..F 9
Gasconade ..11,878..F 8
Gentry ......8,060..B 3
Greene ...152,929..H 5
Grundy .....11,819..B 4
Harrison ...10,257..A 4
Henry ......18,451..F 4
Hickory .....4,481..G 5
Holt ....6,654..B 2
Howard .....10,561..D 6
Howell .....23,521..I 7
Iron ....9,529..H 10
Jackson ...654,178..E 3
Jasper .....79,852..H 3
Jefferson ..105,248..F 10
Johnson ...34,172..E 4
Knox ....5,692..B 7
Laclede ....19,944..H 6
Lafayette ..26,626..E 4
Lawrence ..24,585..I 4
Lewis ....10,993..B 8
Lincoln ....18,041..D 9
Linn ....15,125..B 5
Livingston .15,368..C 4
Macon ......15,432..C 6
Madison ....8,641..H 10
Maries ......6,851..F 7
Marion .....28,121..C 8
McDonald ..12,357..J 3
Mercer ......4,910..A 4
Miller ......15,026..F 7
Mississippi .16,647..I 12
Moniteau ..10,742..F 6
Monroe ......9,542..C 7
Montgomery 11,000..D 8
Morgan ....10,083..F 6
New Madrid 23,420..J 12
Newton .....32,981..I 3
Nodaway ..22,467..A 2
Oregon ......9,180..J 8
Osage ....10,994..F 7
Ozark ....6,226..J 6
Pemiscot ..26,373..K 11
Perry ....14,393..G 11
Pettis ......34,137..E 5
Phelps .....29,567..G 8
Pike ....16,928..D 9
Platte ......32,081..D 2
Polk ....15,415..G 5
Pulaski ....53,967..G 7
Putnam ......5,916..A 5
Ralls ....7,764..C 8
Randolph ..22,434..C 6
Ray ....17,599..D 4
Reynolds ....6,106..H 9
Ripley ....9,803..J 9
St. Charles 92,954..E 9
St. Clair ....7,667..F 4
St. Francois 36,875..G 10
St. Louis .951,671..E 10
Ste. Gene-
vieve ......12,867..G 10
Saline ......24,837..D 5
Schuyler .....4,665..A 6
Scotland .....5,499..A 7
Scott ....33,250..I 11
Shannon .....7,196..H 8
Shelby ....7,906..C 7
Stoddard ...25,771..I 11
Stone ....9,921..I 5
Sullivan .....7,572..B 5
Taney ....13,023..J 5
Texas ....18,320..H 7
Vernon .....19,065..G 3
Warren ....9,699..E 9
Washington 15,068..G 9
Wayne ....8,546..H 10
Webster ....15,562..H 6
Worth ....3,359..A 3
Wright ......13,667..H 6

Cities, Towns, and Villages

Adrian ....1,259..F 3
Advance ....903..I 11
Afton* .....24,264..E 10
Agency ....141..G 14
Airport Drive .300..H 3
Alba ....365..H 3
Albany ......1,804.°B 3
Aldrich ....66..H 4
Alexandria ....453..A 8
Allendale .....104..A 3
Alma ....380..D 4
Altamont ......225..B 4
Altenburg .....277..G 11
Alton ....715.°J 8
Amazonia ......326..B 2
Amity ....86..B 3
Amoret ....219..F 3
Amsterdam .....120..F 3
Anderson ....1,065..J 3
Annada ....109..D 9
Annapolis ......330..H 10
Anniston ....515..I 12
Appleton ....77..H 11
Appleton City 1,058..F 4
Arbela ....70..A 7
Arbyrd ....575..K 10
Arcadia ....627..H 10
Archie ....525..F 3
Arcola ....80..H 4
Argyle ....262..F 7
Arkoe ....49..B 2
Armstrong ......354..D 6
Arnold ....17,381..C 15
Arrow Rock ....81..D 6
Asbury ....201..H 3
Ash Grove ....934..H 4
Ashburn ....119..C 9
Ashland ....769..E 7
Atlanta ....377..B 6
Augusta ....259..C 14
Aullville ....108..D 4
Aurora ....5,359..I 4
Auxvasse ....808..D 7
Ava ....2,504.°I 6
Avilla ....119..H 3
Avondale ....512..I 15
Bagnell ....60..F 6
Baker ....72..I 11
Bakersfield ......210..J 7
Baldwin Park* 107..E 3
Ballwin ......10,656..C 15
Baring ....206..B 7
Barnard ....206..B 2
Barnett ....167..F 6
Bates City ......229..J 16
Battlefield* .....307..H 5
Bell City ....424..I 11
Bella Villa* 1,018..F 10
Belle ....1,133..F 8
Bellefontaine
Neighbors 14,084..B 16
Bellerive* ....437..E 10
Bellflower ....360..D 8
Bel-Nor* ......2,247..E 10
Bel-Ridge* ...5,346..E 10
Belton ....12,270..K 15
Benton ....640.°I 12
Benton City ....121..D 8
Berdell Hills* 449..E 10
Berger ....226..E 8
Berkeley ....19,743..B 15
Bernie ....1,641..J 11
Bertrand ....604..I 12
Bethany ......2,914.°B 4
Bethel ....143..B 7
Beverly Hills* 846..E 10
Bevier ....806..C 6
Bigelow ....84..B 1
Billings ....760..I 4
Birch Tree ......573..I 8
Birmingham ....266..I 15
Bismarck ....1,387..G 10
Black Jack* .4,145..B 15
Blackburn ......294..D 5
Blackwater .....249..D 5
Blairstown .....161..E 4
Bland ....621..F 8
Blodgett ....220..I 12
Bloomfield ..1,584.°I 11
Bloomsdale ....411..E 16
Blue Eye ....91..J 5
Blue Springs 6,779..J 16
Blue
Summit* .1,283..D 3
Blythedale ......213..A 4
Bogard ....294..C 5
Bolckow ....225..B 2
Bolivar ....4,769.°G 5
Bonne Terre .3,622..F 15
Boonville ...7,514.°D 6
Bosworth ....386..C 5
Bourbon ....955..F 9
Bowling
Green ....2,936.°C 8
Bradleyville ......92..I 6
Bragg City ....210..J 11
Brandsville ......145..J 8
Branson ......2,175..J 5
Brashear ....316..B 7
Braymer ....919..C 4
Breckenridge .598..C 4
Breckenridge
Hills* ....7,011..E 10
Brentwood .11,248..B 16
Bridgeton ..19,992..B 15
Bridgeton
Terrace* ....332..E 10
Brimson ....103..B 4
Bronaugh ....203..G 3
Brookfield ...5,491..C 5
Brookline* .....247..H 5
Brooklyn
Heights* ....128..H 3
Browning ....412..B 5
Browningtion .....95..F 4
Brumley ....87..F 6
Brunswick ..1,370..C 5
Bucklin ....654..C 6
Buckner ....1,695..I 16
Buell ....69..D 8
Buffalo ......1,915.°G 5
Bunceton ....437..E 6
Bunker ....447..H 9
Burgess ....69..H 3
Burlington
Junction ......634..A 2
Butler ....3,984.°F 3
Butterfield ......125..I 4
Cabool ....1,848..I 7
Cainesville ......454..A 4
Cairo ....248..C 6
Caledonia ....113..G 9
Calhoun ....360..F 4
California ...3,105.°E 6
Callao ....373..C 6
Calverton
Park* .....2,025..E 10
Camden ....286..D 4
Camden Point 227..H 14
Camdenton ..1,636.°G 6
Cameron ....3,960..F 16
Campbell ....1,979..J 11
Canalou ....358..I 11
Canton ....2,680..B 8
Cape
Girardeau 31,282..H 12
Cardwell ....859..K 10
Carl Junction 1,661..H 3
Carrollton ...4,847.°D 5
Carterville ...1,716..I 3
Carthage ...11,035.°H 3
Caruthers-
ville ....7,350.°K 11
Carytown* ....119..H 3
Cassville ....1,910.°J 4
Catron ....122..J 11
Cedar City ......454..E 7
Cedar Hill
Lakes* ....177..F 10
Center ....588..C 8
Centertown .....277..E 6
Centerview ......234..E 4
Centerville ......209.°H 9
Centralia .....3,623..D 7
Chaffee ....2,793..H 11
Chamois ....615..E 8
Charlack* ...1,872..E 10
Charleston ..5,131.°I 12
Cherryville ....47..G 8
Chilhowee ....297..E 4
Chillicothe ..9,519.°C 4
Chula ....244..B 5
Clarence .....1,050..C 7
Clark ....271..D 7
Clarksburg .....343..E 6
Clarksdale ......248..F 15
Clarkson
Valley* ......157..E 10
Clarksville ....668..D 9
Clarkton ......1,177..J 11
Claycomo ....1,841..I 15
Clayton ....16,100.°B 16
Clearmont ....226..A 2
Cleveland ....256..K 15
Clever ....430..I 5
Clifton Hill .....174..C 6
Climax Springs 104..F 5
Clinton ....7,504.°F 4
Clyde ....158..B 3
Cobalt City ....238..H 10
Coffey ....157..B 4
Cole Camp ..1,038..F 5
Collins ....150..G 4
Columbia ..58,812.°D 7
Commerce ....234..H 12
Conception
Junction .....237..B 3
Concord* ....21,217..E 10
Concordia ...1,854..D 4
Conway ....547..H 6
Cool Valley* 2,059..E 10
Cooter ....414..K 11
Corder ....476..D 4
Corning ....134..B 1
Cosby ....130..B 3
Cottonwood
Point ....80..K 11
Country Club
Hills* .....1,644..E 10
Country Club .943..C 2
Country Life
Acres* ....60..E 10
Cowgill ....232..C 4
Craig ....369..B 1
Crane ....1,003..I 4
Creighton ....294..F 4
Crestwood ..15,123..C 15
Creve Coeur* 8,967..E 10
Crocker ....814..G 7
Cross Timbers 204..G 5
Crosstown ....66..G 11
Crowder ....89..I 11
Crystal City 3,898..D 15
Crystal
Lake Park* .356..E 10
Cuba ....2,070..F 8
Curryville ....337..D 8
Dadeville ....149..H 4
Dalton ....135..D 5
Darlington ....164..B 3
Dearborn ....543..G 14
Deepwater ....565..F 4
Deerfield ....112..G 3
Deering ....138..K 11
De Kalb ....287..G 14
Dellwood* ....7,137..E 10
Delta ....462..H 11
Dennis Acres* .64..I 3
Denton ....89..K 11
Denver ....104..A 3
Des Arc ....222..H 10
Desloge ......2,818..F 15
De Soto ....5,984..F 10
Des Peres ....7,130..B 15
Dewitt ....135..D 5
Dexter ....6,024..I 11
Diamond ....608..I 3
Diehlstadt ....155..I 12
Diggins ....140..I 6
Dixon ....1,387..G 7
Doniphan ....1,850.°J 9
Doolittle ....509..G 7
Dover ....133..D 4
Downing ....406..A 7
Drexel ....723..F 3
Dudley ....248..I 11
Duenweg ....656..I 3
Duquesne ....738..I 3
Eagleville ....388..A 4
East Lynne ......255..K 16
East Prairie 3,275..I 12
Easton ....183..G 15
Edgar Springs 252..G 8
Edgerton ....477..H 15
Edina ....1,574.°B 7
Edmundson* 2,298..E 10
Eldon ....3,520..F 6
El Dorado
Springs ...3,300..G 4
Ellington ....1,094..H 9
Ellisville ......4,681..C 15
Ellsinore ....342..I 9
Elmer ....193..B 6
Elmira ....124..G 16
Elmo ....199..A 2
Elsberry .....1,398..D 9
Elvins ....1,660..G 10
Eminence ....520.°I 8
Emma ....224..D 5
Eolia ....321..D 9
Essex ....493..I 11
Esther ....1,040..G 10
Ethel ....162..B 6
Eugene ....163..F 7
Eureka ....2,384..C 14
Everton ....264..H 4
Ewing ....330..B 8
Excelsior
Springs ...9,411..H 16
Exeter ....434..J 4
Fair Grove ....431..H 5
Fair Play ....328..G 4
Fairfax ....835..A 1
Fairview ....263..I 3
Farber ....470..D 8
Farley ....174..I 14
Farmington .7,031.°G 10
Fayette ....3,520.°D 6
Fenton ....2,275..C 15
Ferguson ...28,759..B 16
Ferrelview ....140..H 15
Festus ....7,530..F 10
Fidelity* ....191..H 3
Fillmore ....251..B 2
Fisk ....503..I 10
Flat River ..4,550..F 15
Fleming* ....152..D 4
Flemington ......126..G 5
Flordell Hills* 989..E 10
Florissant .65,908..B 15
Foley ....224..A 14
Fordland ....399..I 6
Forest City ......365..B 2
Forsyth ....803.°J 5
Fort Leonard
Wood* ...33,799..G 7
Fortescue ....63..B 1
Foster ....170..F 3
Frankford ....472..C 8
Franklin ....252..D 6
Frederick-
town ....3,799.°H 10
Freeburg ....577..F 7
Freeman ....417..E 3
Freistatt ....115..I 4
Fremont ....107..I 9
Frohna ....225..G 11
Frontenac* ...3,920..E 10
Fulton ....12,248.°E 7
Gainesville ......627.°J 6
Galena ....391.°I 5
Gallatin ......1,833.°B 4
Galt ....261..B 5
Garden City .....633..E 3
Gasconade ....235..E 8
Gentry ....143..A 3
Gerald ....762..F 8
Gibbs ....112..B 6
Gibson ....75..J 11
Gideon ....1,112..J 11
Gilliam ....248..D 5
Gilman City .....376..B 4
Gladstone ..23,422..D 3
Glasgow ......1,336..D 6
Glen Echo
Park* ....268..E 10
Glenaire ....505..I 15
Glenallen ....134..H 11
Glendale .....6,981..B 15
Glenwood ....233..A 6
Gobler ....73..K 11
Golden City .....810..H 3
Goodman ....565..I 3
Gordonville .....125..H 11
Gower ....758..C 3
Graham ....213..B 2
Grain Valley ..709..J 16
Granby ....1,678..I 3
Grand Pass ......72..D 5
Grandin ....243..I 9
Grandview .17,456..J 15
Granger ....105..A 7
Grant City ..1,095.°A 3
Grantwood* .....994..E 10
Grayson ....62..G 15
Green City ......632..B 5
Green Ridge ....403..E 5
Greencastle .....235..B 6
Greendale* ......972..E 10
Greenfield ...1,172.°H 4
Greentop ....351..A 6
Greenville ....328.°I 10
Greenwood ......925..J 16
Guilford ....105..B 2
Gunn City ....71..K 16
Hale ....461..C 5
Half Way ....167..G 5
Hallsville ....790..D 7
Halltown ....106..H 4
Hamilton .....1,645..C 4
Hanley
Hills* .....2,801..E 10
Hannibal ..18,609..C 8
Hardin ....683..D 4
Harris ....174..A 5
Harrisburg ....150..D 6
Harrisonville 5,052.°E 3
Hartsburg ....120..E 7
Hartville ....524.°H 6
Harviell ....160..J 10
Harwood ....91..G 3
Hawk Point .....354..D 9
Hayti ....3,841..K 11
Hayti
Heights* ..1,232..K 11
Haywood City* 420..I 11
Hazelwood* 14,082..E 10
Henley ....64..F 7
Henrietta ....466..D 4
Herculaneum 2,439..D 15
Hermann ....2,658.°E 8
Hermitage ....284.°G 5
Higbee ....641..D 6
Higginsville .4,318..D 4
High Hill ....192..E 8
Highley
Heights* ....119..G 10
Hillhouse
Addition ....110..G 6
Hillsboro ....831.°F 10
Hillsdale* ....2,599..E 10
Hoberg ....64..I 4
Holcomb ....593..J 11
Holden ....2,089..E 4
Holland ....329..K 11
Holliday ....167..C 7

Hollister .....906..J 5
Hollywood .....86..K 10
Holt ....319..H 16
Holts Summit* ..2,318..E 7
Homestown* ..273..J 11
Hopkins ......656..A 2
Hornersville ..693..K 11
Houston ....2,178.°H 7
Houston Lake 338..I 15
Houstonia ....312..E 5
Howardville ..500..J 11
Hughesville ....92..E 5
Humansville ..825..G 4
Hume ....350..F 3
Humphreys ....140..B 5
Hunnewell ...304..C 7
Hunter ....129..I 9
Huntleigh* ....714..E 10
Huntsville ..1,442.°C 6
Hurdland ....225..B 7
Hurley ....148..I 5
Hurricane Deck 169..F 6
Iberia ....741..F 7
Illmo ......1,232..H 12
Independence ....111,630.°D 3
Ionia ....151..F 5
Iron Gates ...367..I 3
Irondale ......319..G 10
Ironton .....1,452.°H 10
Jackson ....5,896.°H 11
Jacksonville ..142..C 6
Jameson ......172..B 4
Jamesport ....614..B 4
Jamestown ...243..E 6
Jasper ....796..H 3
Jefferson City .....32,407.°E 7
Jennings ...19,379..B 16
Jerico Springs .188..G 4
Jonesburg .....479..E 8
Joplin .....39,256..I 3
Junction City .166..H 10
Kahoka .....2,207.°A 8
Kansas City ....507,330..D 3
Kearney ......984..H 16
Kelso ....401..H 12
Kennett ...10,090.°K 11
Keytesville ....730.°C 6
Kidder ....231..F 16
Kimberling City* ....633..I 5
Kimmswick ....268..D 15
King City ..1,023..B 3
Kingdom City* 53..E 7
Kingston .....291.°C 4
Kingsville ....284..K 16
Kinloch ....5,629..B 16
Kirksville ..15,560.°B 6
Kirkwood ..31,679..C 15
Knob Noster 2,264..E 4
Knox City ....284..B 7
Koshkonong ..216..J 8
La Belle .....848..B 7
Laclede ......430..C 5
Laddonia ......745..D 8
Ladue .....10,359..B 15
La Grange ..1,237..B 8
Lake Lotawana .1,786..J 16
Lake Ozark ...507..F 6
Lake Tapawingo* ......867..E 3
Lake Waukomis 1,105..I 15
Lake Winnebago* ....432..E 3
Lakeland* .....62..F 7
Lakeshire* ..1,186..E 10
Lakeside* ......124..F 6
Lamar ....3,760.°H 3
Lamar Heights .96..H 3
La Monte ....814..E 5
Lanagan .....374..J 3
Lancaster .....821.°A 6
La Plata ...1,377..B 6
Laredo ....383..B 5
Larussell ......97..I 4
Latham ....89..E 6
Lathrop ....1,268..C 3
La Tour ......83..K 16
Laurie* ......106..F 6
Lawson .....1,034..H 16
Leadington ...299..G 10
Leadwood ...1,397..F 15
Leasburg .....218..F 8
Leawood .....174..I 3
Lebanon ....8,616.°G 6
Lees Summit 16,230..J 16
Leeton ....425..E 4
Lemay* ....40,516..F 10
Leonard ......107..B 7
Leslie ....81..F 9
Levasy ....283..I 16
Lewis and Clark Village* ....150..C 2
Lewistown ....615..B 7
Lexington ...5,388.°D 4
Liberal ....644..H 3
Liberty ....13,704.°D 3
Licking ....1,002..H 7
Lilbourn ...1,152..J 11
Lincoln ....574..F 5
Linn ....1,289.°F 7
Linn Creek ....268..G 6
Linneus ......400.°B 5
Lithium ....56..G 11
Livonia ....119..A 6
Lock Springs ..85..B 4
Lockwood ....887..H 4
Lohman ....109..E 7
Lone Jack ....199..J 16
Longtown ....113..G 11
Louisburg ....152..G 5
Louisiana ...4,533..C 9
Lowry City ...520..F 4
Lucerne ......126..A 5
Ludlow ....175..C 4
Lupus ....68..E 6
Luray ....149..A 7
Lutesville ....626..H 11
Mackenzie* ....224..E 10
Macks Creek ..106..G 5
Macon ......5,301.°C 6
Madison .....540..C 7
Maitland .....319..B 2
Malden ......5,374..J 11
Malta Bend ..342..D 5
Manchester .5,031..C 15
Mansfield ..1,056..I 6
Maplewood 12,785..B 16
Marble Hill ..589.°H 11
Marceline ...2,622..C 5
Marionville .1,496..I 4
Marlborough* ....1,492..E 10
Marquand ....400..H 10
Marshall ..12,051.°D 5
Marshfield ..2,961.°H 6
Marston ......666..J 11
Marthasville .415..B 13
Martinsburg ..318..D 8
Mary Ridge* ..602..E 10
Maryland Heights* ..8,805..E 10
Maryville ...9,970.°A 2
Matthews .....538..I 12
Maysville ...1,045.°B 3
Mayview* .....330..D 4
McFall ....203..B 3
McKittrick ...101..E 8
Meadville ....409..C 5
Memphis ....2,081.°A 7
Mendon ......289..C 5
Mercer ....364..A 5
Merwin ....64..F 3
Meta ....387..F 7
Metz ....120..G 3
Mexico ....11,807.°D 7
Miami ....205..D 5
Middle Grove ..55..D 7
Middletown ...235..D 8
Midway* ......234..I 3
Milan ....1,794.°B 5
Mill Spring ..207..I 10
Miller ....676..H 4
Milo ....80..G 3
Mindenmines .279..H 3
Miner ....640..I 12
Mineral Point 369..E 14
Missouri City .375..I 16
Moberly ....12,988..C 6
Modena ....61..A 4
Mokane ....398..E 7
Moline Acres* ....3,722..E 10
Monett ......5,937..I 4
Monroe City 2,456..C 8
Montevallo ....54..G 3
Montgomery City ......2,187.°D 8
Monticello ....157.°B 8
Montrose .....531..F 4
Mooresville ...131..C 4
Morehouse ..1,332..I 11
Morley ....528..I 11
Morrison ......234..E 8
Morrisville ...256..H 5
Mosby ....337..H 16
Moscow Mills .399..A 13
Mound City .1,202..B 2
Moundville ...149..G 3
Mount Leonard ....139..D 5
Mount Moriah 165..A 4
Mount Vernon 2,600.°I 4
Mountain Grove ....3,377..I 7
Mountain View ....1,320..I 8
Napoleon .....263..I 16
Naylor ....586..J 10
Neck City ....114..H 3
Neelyville ....231..J 10
Nelson ....230..D 5
Neosho .....7,517.°I 3
Nevada ......9,736.°G 3
New Bloomfield .427..E 7
New Cambria .260..C 6
New Florence .635..E 8
New Franklin 1,122..D 6
New Hamburg 185..I 11
New Hampton 327..B 3
New Haven ..1,474..E 9
New London ..967.°C 8
New Madrid 2,719.°J 12
Newark ....114..B 7
Newburg ......806..G 7
Newtonia .....208..I 3
Newtown .....211..A 5
Niangua ......309..H 6
Nixa ....1,636..I 5
Noel ....924..J 3
Norborne .....950..D 4
Normandy* .6,236..E 10
North Kansas City ......5,046..I 15
North Lilbourn* ..334..J 11
North Wardell* ...157..K 11
Northmoor ...562..I 15
Northwoods* 6,407..E 10
Northwye .....138..G 8
Norwood .....294..I 6
Norwood Court* ......122..E 10
Novelty ....156..B 7
Novinger .....547..B 6
Oak Grove* ..340..F 9
Oak Grove ..2,025..J 16
Oak Ridge ....181..H 11
Oakland* ...1,609..E 10
Oakland Park* 156..I 3
Oaks ....162..I 15
Oakview ......494..I 15
Oakwood* .....201..D 3
Oakwood Manor* .....170..D 3
Oakwood Park* 266..D 3
Odessa ......2,839..D 4
O'Fallon ...7,018..B 14
Old Monroe ..330..A 14
Olean ....151..F 6
Olivette .....9,156..B 15
Olympian Village* ....399..F 10
Oran ....1,226..I 11
Oregon ....789.°B 2
Oronogo ......492..H 3
Orrick ....883..I 16
Osage Beach 1,091..F 6
Osborn ....338..F 16
Osceola ......874.°G 4
Osgood ....108..B 5
Otterville ....440..E 5
Overland ..24,819..B 15
Owensville ..2,416..F 8
Ozark ....2,384.°I 5
Pacific ......3,247..C 14
Pagedale ....5,044..B 16
Palmyra ....3,188.°C 8
Paris ....1,442.°C 7
Parkdale* .....836..F 10
Parkville ...1,253..I 14
Parkway ......233..D 13
Parma ....1,051..J 11
Parnell ....232..A 3
Pasadena Hills* ....1,337..E 10
Pasadena Park* ......760..E 10
Pascola ....180..J 11
Passaic ....56..F 3
Pattonsburg ..540..B 3
Peach Orchard 64..J 11
Peculiar ......705..K 15
Peerless Park* .51..E 10
Penermon* ...154..I 11
Perkins ....130..I 11
Perry ....839..C 8
Perryville ...5,149.°G 11
Pevely ....517..D 15
Phelps City ....76..A 1
Phillipsburg ..173..H 6
Pickering .....245..A 2
Piedmont ...1,906..I 10
Pierce City ..1,097..I 4
Pilot Grove ...701..E 6
Pilot Knob ....582..G 10
Pine Lawn .6,495..B 16
Pineville .....444.°J 3
Piney Park ....106..D 13
Platte City ..2,022.°D 2
Platte Woods .484..I 15
Plattsburg ..1,832.°C 3
Pleasant Hill 3,396..K 16
Pleasant Hope 265..H 5
Pleasant Valley ....1,535..I 15
Pocahontas ...127..H 11
Polo ....438..G 16
Poplar Bluff 16,653.°I 10
Portage Des Sioux ......509..A 15
Portageville .3,117..J 11
Potosi ....2,761.°G 9
Powersville ...125..A 5
Prairie Hill ...69..C 6
Prairie Home .231..E 6
Prathersville ..153..H 16
Preston ....132..G 5
Princeton ...1,328.°A 4
Purcell ....325..H 3
Purdin ....236..B 5
Purdy ....588..I 4
Puxico ....759..I 10
Queen City ...588..A 6
Quitman ....95..A 2
Qulin ....496..J 10
Ralls* ....89..C 8
Randolph* ....106..D 3
Ravenwood ....336..A 3
Raymondville .284..H 8
Raymore .....587..K 15
Raytown ...33,306..J 15
Rayville .....202..H 16
Rea ....54..B 2
Redings Mill .179..I 3
Reeds ....122..I 3
Reeds Spring .286..I 5
Reger ....75..B 5
Renick ....188..D 6
Rensselaer .....58..C 8
Republic ....2,411..I 5
Revere ....184..A 8
Rhineland ....190..E 8
Rich Hill ...1,661..F 3
Richards .....105..G 3
Richland ...1,783..G 6
Richmond ..4,948.°D 4
Richmond Heights ..13,802..B 15
Ridgeway .....469..A 4
Risco ....412..J 11
Ritchey ....101..I 3
Rivermines ...402..G 10
Riverside ...2,123..I 15
Riverview* ..3,741..E 10
Rives ....120..K 11
Rocheport ....307..D 6
Rock Hill ...6,815..C 16
Rockaway Beach ......195..J 5
Rock Port ..1,575.°A 1
Rockville .....203..F 4
Rocky Comfort 141..I 3
Rogersville ...574..I 5
Rolla ......13,571.°G 8
Roscoe ....137..G 4
Rosebud ......305..F 8
Rosendale .....245..B 2
Rothville ......131..C 5
Rush Hill .....151..D 8
Rushville ......300..G 13
Russellville ...557..E 6
Rutledge ......139..A 7
Saginaw ......224..I 3
St. Ann ...18,215..B 15
St. Charles 31,834.°E 10
St. Clair ...2,978..D 13
St. Elizabeth .287..F 7
St. George ..2,033..C 15
St. James ..2,929..G 8
St. John ...9,281..B 15
St. Joseph .78,230.°C 2
St. Louis .622,236†.E 10
St. Martins* ..431..F 7
St. Marys .....645..G 11
St. Peters ....486..B 14
St. Robert ..1,465..G 7
St. Thomas* ..195..F 7
Ste. Genevieve .....4,714.°G 11
Salem ......4,363.°G 8
Salisbury ...1,960..C 6
Sappington* 10,603..E 10
Sarcoxie ....1,175..I 3
Savannah ..3,324.°B 2
Schell City ...367..G 3
Schuermann Heights* ....290..E 10
Scott City ..2,464..H 12
Sedalia ....22,847.°E 5
Sedgewickville .92..H 11
Seligman ......424..J 4
Senath ......1,484..K 10
Seneca ......1,577..I 3
Seymour ....1,208..I 6
Shelbina ...2,060..C 7
Shelbyville ....601.°C 7
Sheldon ......498..G 3
Sheridan .....251..A 3
Shoal Creek Drive ......329..I 3
Shrewsbury* 5,896..E 10
Sibley ....279..I 16
Sikeston ...14,699..I 11
Silex ....306..D 9
Silver Creek ..410..I 3
Skidmore .....440..A 2
Slater ....2,576..D 5
Smithton .....402..E 5
Smithville ...1,785..D 3
South Gifford .64..B 6
South Gorin ..220..A 7
South Greenfield ......144..H 4
South Lineville 52..A 5
South West City ....453..J 3
Spanish Lake* ....15,647..E 10
Sparta ....380..I 5
Spickardsville 408..B 4
Springfield 120,096.°H 5
Stanberry ...1,479..B 3
Stark City ....122..I 3
Steele ......2,373..K 11
Steelville ...1,392.°G 8
Stella ....197..I 3
Stewartsville .634..C 3
Stockton ....1,063.°G 4
Stotts City ...203..I 4
Stoutland .....205..G 6
Stoutsville ....61..C 7
Stover ....849..F 5
Strafford* ....491..H 5
Strasburg .....181..K 16
Sturgeon ......787..D 7
Sugar Creek 4,755..I 15
Sullivan ....5,111..F 9
Summersville .435..H 8
Sumner ....178..C 5
Sunnyvale ....311..I 3
Sunrise Beach 126..F 6
Sunset Hills* 4,126..E 10
Sweet Springs 1,716..D 5
Sycamore Hills* ......821..E 10
Syracuse .....214..E 6
Tallapoosa ....205..J 11
Taneyville ....157..I 5
Taos* ....528..F 7
Tarkio ......2,517..A 1
Tarsney Lakes* 401..D 3
Thayer ......1,609..J 8
Theodosia ....132..J 6
Times Beach 1,265..C 15
Tina ....167..C 5
Tindall ....92..B 4
Tipton ......1,914..E 6
Town and Country* .2,645..E 10
Tracy ....252..H 14
Trenton ....6,731.°B 4
Trimble ......206..C 3
Triplett ......191..C 5
Troy ....2,538.°D 9
Truesdale ....262..E 9
Turney ....142..C 3
Tuscumbia ...256.°F 6
Union ......5,183.°F 9
Union Star ...417..B 3
Unionville ..2,075.°A 5
Unity ....242..J 15
University City .....47,527..B 15
Uplands Park* 695..E 10
Urbana ....369..G 5
Urich ....433..F 4
Valley Park* 3,662..E 10
Van Buren ...714.°I 9
Vandalia ...3,160..D 8
Vandiver .....102..D 7
Vanduser .....306..I 11
Velda* .....2,112..E 10
Velda Village Hills* .....1,205..E 10
Verona ....515..I 4
Versailles ..2,244.°F 6
Vibbard ....89..H 16
Viburnum ....520..G 9
Vienna ....505.°F 7
Vinita Park* ....2,905..E 10
Vinita Terrace* ....344..E 10
Waco ....108..H 3
Wakenda .....116..D 5
Walker ....227..G 3
Walnut Grove .442..H 4
Wardell ......275..J 11
Wardsville* ...460..F 7
Warrensburg ....13,125.°E 4
Warrenton ..2,057.°E 9
Warsaw ....1,423.°F 5
Warson Woods* ...2,544..E 10
Washburn .....257..J 4
Washington .8,499..C 13
Watson ....164..A 1
Waverly ......827..D 5
Wayland ......467..A 8
Waynesville .3,375.°G 7
Weatherby .....91..B 3
Weatherby Lake ......832..I 14
Weaubleau ...343..G 4
Webb City ..6,923..H 3
Webster Groves ...27,457..C 15
Wellington ....720..D 4
Wellston ...7,050..B 16
Wellsville ..1,565..D 8
Wentworth ....132..I 3
Wentzville ..3,223..B 14
West Line .....114..E 3
West Plains 6,893.°I 8
Westboro .....234..A 1
Weston .....1,267..H 14
Westphalia ....332..F 7
Westwood* ....311..E 10
Wheatland ....317..G 5
Wheaton ......360..I 4
Wheeling .....268..C 5
White Oak ....54..J 11
Whiteman* ..5,040..E 4
Whiteside .....125..D 9
Whitewater ...135..H 11
Wilbur Park* .692..E 10
Willard .....1,018..H 5
Williamsville .398..I 10
Willow Springs ...2,045..I 7
Wilson City ..295..I 12
Winchester* 2,329..E 10
Windsor ...2,734..E 4
Winfield .....620..A 14
Winona ....973..I 8
Winston ......189..B 3
Woods Heights ....362..H 16
Woodson Terrace* ..5,880..E 10
Wooldridge .....97..E 6
Worth ....113..A 3
Wright City ..943..B 13
Wyaconda ....356..A 7
Wyatt ....562..I 12
Zalma ....118..I 11

*Does not appear on the map; key shows general location.
†Independent city, not part of any county.

°County seat.
Sources: Latest census figures (1970 and special censuses).

The 1970 U.S. census reported that Missouri had 4,677,399 persons—an increase of 8 per cent over the 1960 figure, 4,319,813. The U.S. Bureau of the Census estimated that by 1975 the population was about 4,763,000.

Seven-tenths of the people live in urban areas. Most of them live in metropolitan areas. Missouri has five Standard Metropolitan Statistical Areas (see METROPOLITAN AREA). They are Columbia, Kansas City, St. Joseph, St. Louis, and Springfield. For their populations, see the *Index* to the political map of Missouri.

St. Louis and Kansas City, the state's largest cities, rank among the nation's chief transportation, grain, and livestock centers. See the articles on Missouri cities listed in the *Related Articles* at the end of this article.

Fewer than 2 out of 100 Missourians were born outside the United States. Most of the American-born whites have Czech, English, French, German, Irish, Italian, Polish, or Swiss ancestors. About 10 out of 100 Missourians are Negroes.

More than half of Missouri's church members are Protestants. The largest groups include the Baptists, Disciples of Christ, Episcopalians, Lutherans, Methodists, Presbyterians, and members of the United Church of Christ. About one out of six Missourians is a Roman Catholic.

Jack Zehrt, Publix

Competition Among Farmers is popular at local fairs. These Missouri farmers near St. Louis are watching a contest to determine which team of horses can pull the heaviest load.

POPULATION

This map shows the *population density* of Missouri, and how it varies in different parts of the state. Population density means the average number of persons who live in a given area.

	Persons per sq. mi.	Persons per km²
	More than 120	More than 46
	40 to 120	15 to 46
	20 to 40	8 to 15
	Less than 20	Less than 8

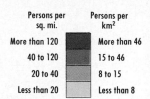

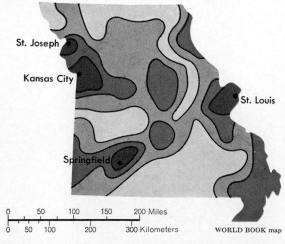

St. Joseph

Kansas City

St. Louis

Springfield

```
0      50     100    150    200 Miles
0    50   100      200      300 Kilometers
```

WORLD BOOK map

Tom Hollyman, Photo Researchers

Handicraft Skills are often passed down from generation to generation. A quilting bee provides a friendly social gathering for this group of Missouri women.

The William Rockhill Nelson Gallery of Art and Mary Atkins Museum of Fine Arts in Kansas City

MISSOURI /Education

Schools. Missouri's first school was a private elementary school established in St. Louis in 1774. In 1820, Missouri's first constitution included a provision for establishing a system of public education. The system did not start operating until 1839, however.

The state board of education supervises Missouri's public school system. The board has eight members appointed by the governor to eight-year terms. One term expires each year. The board appoints a commissioner of education, who serves as the chief administrative officer of the Department of Elementary and Secondary Education. All children between the ages of 7 and 16 must attend school. For the number of students and teachers in Missouri, see EDUCATION (table).

Libraries. Many of Missouri's public libraries grew out of public school libraries. Some started as *subscription libraries*, in which members contributed money and used the books free of charge. In 1865, the St. Louis public library was established. It was supported by

money from the school board and by fees and donations. In 1893, it became tax-supported. Today, Missouri has about 170 public libraries and about 70 college and university libraries. The library of the University of Missouri at Columbia is the largest in the state.

Museums. Missouri's largest art museums are the St. Louis Art Museum in St. Louis and the William Rockhill Nelson Gallery of Art and Mary Atkins Museum of Fine Arts in Kansas City. The St. Louis Art Museum has a collection from many countries and periods. The Nelson Gallery-Atkins Museum owns noted collections of Oriental and American art. The Capitol in Jefferson City houses a museum with collections of Missouri materials of historical, geological, scientific, and cultural interest. The Missouri Historical Society building in Forest Park in St. Louis displays trophies and gifts received by Charles A. Lindbergh, the aviator. The Harry S. Truman Library in Independence exhibits the souvenirs of the nation's 33rd President.

UNIVERSITIES AND COLLEGES

Missouri has 46 universities and colleges accredited by the North Central Association of Colleges and Schools. For enrollments and further information, see UNIVERSITIES AND COLLEGES (table).

Name	Location	Founded	Name	Location	Founded
Assemblies of God			Missouri Southern State College	Joplin	1967
Graduate School	Springfield	1972	Missouri Valley College	Marshall	1889
Avila College	Kansas City	1867	Missouri Western State College	St. Joseph	1969
Cardinal Glennon College	St. Louis	1818	Northeast Missouri State		
Central Methodist College	Fayette	1854	University	Kirksville	1914
Central Missouri State			Northwest Missouri State		
University	Warrensburg	1871	University	Maryville	1917
Columbia College	Columbia	1973	Ozarks, School of the	Point Lookout	1964
Conception Seminary College	Conception	1883	Park College	Parkville	1875
Concordia Seminary	Clayton	1839	Rockhurst College	Kansas City	1910
Covenant Theological Seminary	St. Louis	1956	St. Louis College		
Culver-Stockton College	Canton	1853	of Pharmacy	St. Louis	1932
Drury College	Springfield	1873	St. Louis University	St. Louis	1818
Eden Theological Seminary	Webster Groves	1850	St. Mary's Seminary College	Perryville	1834
Evangel College	Springfield	1955	St. Paul School of Theology	Kansas City	1958
Fontbonne College	St. Louis	1917	Southeast Missouri State		
Hannibal-LaGrange College	Hannibal	1858	University	Cape Girardeau	1873
Harris-Stowe College	St. Louis	1875	Southwest Baptist College	Bolivar	1966
Kansas City Art Institute	Kansas City	1962	Southwest Missouri State		
Kenrick Seminary	St. Louis	1893	University	Springfield	1908
Lincoln University	Jefferson City	1866	Stephens College	Columbia	1833
Lindenwood Colleges	St. Charles	1827	Tarkio College	Tarkio	1883
Maryville College	St. Louis	1846	Washington University	St. Louis	1853
Midwestern Baptist Theological			Webster College	St. Louis	1915
Seminary	Kansas City	1958	Westminster College	Fulton	1851
Missouri, University of	*	*	William Jewell College	Liberty	1849
Missouri Baptist College	St. Louis	1968	William Woods College	Fulton	1870

*For campuses and founding dates, see UNIVERSITIES AND COLLEGES (table).

MISSOURI / A Visitor's Guide

Missouri's mild climate and many attractions make the state a popular vacationland. Missouri has abundant wildlife, rugged hills, rushing streams, and peaceful woodlands to delight hunters, hikers, and photographers. People who like to fish can try their luck for bass, trout, and other fish in clear, spring-fed streams. Hunting for foxes and raccoons in the hills has long been a favorite sport. Visitors can take guided boat trips down rapid streams. The state's most unusual sights include great bubbling springs and deep caverns.

Missouri Division of Tourism
Meramec Caverns near Sullivan

Missouri Division of Commerce and Industrial Development
A Candlemaker in Silver Dollar City

Missouri Division of Tourism
Harry S. Truman Library in Independence

PLACES TO VISIT

Following are brief descriptions of some of Missouri's many interesting places to visit.

Climatron is a revolutionary greenhouse in the Missouri Botanical Garden in St. Louis. The great domed structure is completely air-conditioned and moisture-controlled. It displays a variety of plants.

Gateway Arch, in St. Louis, commemorates the city's role in the settlement of the West. The arch rises 630 feet (192 meters) and ranks as the tallest monument constructed in the United States. Small trains inside the arch carry visitors to an observation deck at the top.

Harry S. Truman Library, in Independence, opened in 1957. The building houses about 3½ million documents dealing with the history of U.S. foreign relations.

Lake of the Ozarks, in central Missouri, is one of the world's largest artificial lakes. It has a shoreline of more than 1,300 miles (2,090 kilometers). The lake and the areas around it form a popular resort and recreation center. See LAKE OF THE OZARKS.

Mark Twain Cave, near Hannibal, is a cave that the famous author Mark Twain learned about as a boy. In the novel *The Adventures of Tom Sawyer,* Tom and his friend Becky Thatcher get lost in this cave.

Mark Twain Home and Museum, in Hannibal, is the restored boyhood home of the writer. The museum has many objects connected with Mark Twain's life.

Meramec Caverns, near Sullivan, is a legendary hideout of the outlaw Jesse James. The first room of this huge cave is large enough to hold 300 automobiles.

Pony Express Stables, in St. Joseph, are preserved to help trace the heritage of the famed pony express. Express riders carried U.S. mail between St. Joseph and Sacramento, Calif., from April 1860 to October 1861.

Silver Dollar City, near Branson, is a reconstruction of an early American mining town. Craftworkers show how Conestoga wagons were built and demonstrate such crafts as candle dipping and glass blowing.

Winston Churchill Memorial and Library, in Fulton, was formerly the Church of St. Mary Aldermanbury. It was dismantled and moved from London after World War II, and rebuilt on the campus of Westminster College in Fulton. Winston Churchill delivered his famous "iron curtain" speech on the campus in 1946.

National Forest and Monument. Mark Twain National Forest, Missouri's only national forest, lies in the southern part of the state. For its area and chief features, see NATIONAL FOREST (table). George Washington Carver National Monument, near Diamond Grove, honors the famous Missouri-born black scientist. See GEORGE WASHINGTON CARVER NATIONAL MONUMENT.

State Forests and Parks. Missouri has 100 state forests. Indian Trail, the largest, covers 13,253 acres (5,363 hectares) in Dent County. Missouri has 37 state parks and 19 state historic sites that provide outdoor recreation and preserve the state's heritage. For information about Missouri's state parks, write to Director, Division of Parks and Historic Preservation, Box 176, Jefferson City, Mo. 65102.

Gateway Arch in St. Louis

--- **ANNUAL EVENTS** ---

Missouri's best-known annual event is perhaps its State Fair, held the third week in August in Sedalia. The fair attracts about 250,000 persons from Missouri and neighboring states. Other annual events in Missouri include the following.

January-March: Orchid Show at the Missouri Botanical Garden in St. Louis (February); National Intercollegiate Basketball Tournament in Kansas City (March).

April-June: Dogwood Festival in Camdenton (April); Maifest Celebration in Hermann (May); International Festival of St. Louis in St. Louis (May); Valley of Flowers Festival in Florissant (May); Festival of Mountain Folks' Music in Silver Dollar City near Branson (June); Ragtime Festival in St. Louis (June).

July-September: Kansas City Jazz Festival (July); National Tom Sawyer Fence Painting Contest in Hannibal (July); Bootheel Rodeo in Sikeston (August); Jour de Fete (Festival Day) in Ste. Genevieve (August); Ozark Empire Fair in Springfield (August); Cotton Carnival in Sikeston (September); Country Club Plaza Art Fair in Kansas City (September); National Crafts Festival in Silver Dollar City, near Branson (September-October).

October-December: Flaming Fall Revue in Ava (October); Veiled Prophet's Parade in St. Louis (October); American Royal Rodeo, Livestock and Horse Show in Kansas City (November); Future Farmers of America National Convention in Kansas City (November).

Mark Twain Museum and Home in Hannibal

The Winston Churchill Memorial and Library
Winston Churchill Memorial and Library in Fulton

Climatron at Missouri Botanical Garden in St. Louis

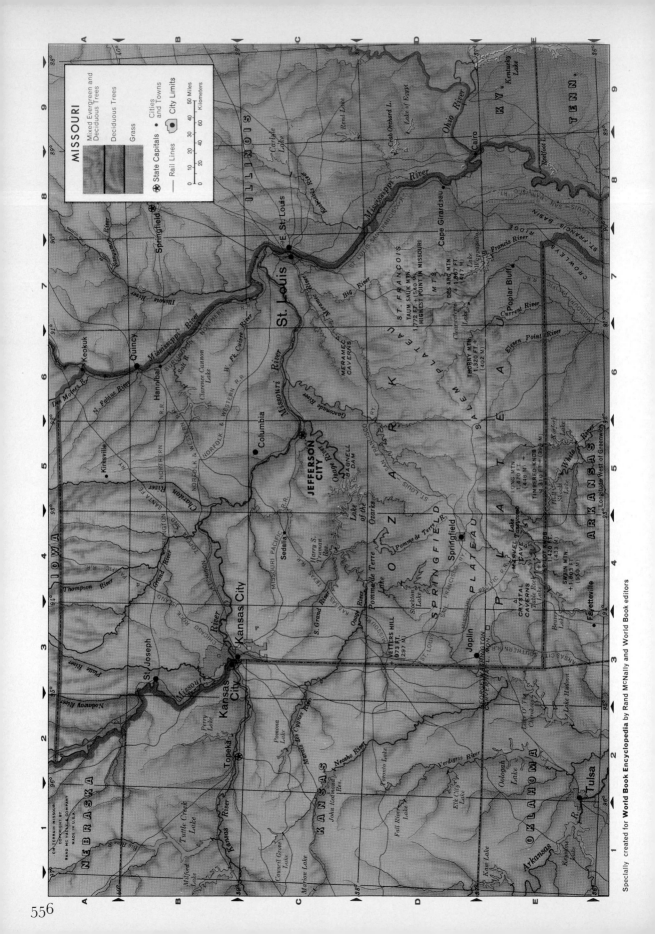

556

Specially created for **World Book Encyclopedia** by Rand McNally and World Book editors

Land Regions. Missouri has four main land regions. These are, from north to south: (1) the Dissected Till Plains, (2) the Osage Plains, (3) the Ozark Plateau (or Ozarks), and (4) the Mississippi Alluvial Plain.

The Dissected Till Plains lie north of the Missouri River. Glaciers once covered this region. The great ice sheets left a rich, deep deposit of soil-forming materials especially suited to the growing of corn. Many slow-moving streams drain the rolling surface of this region.

The Osage Plains lie in western Missouri. This is a region of flat prairie land, broken in places by low hills. Glacial ice never covered the region, and the soil is not so rich as that of the Dissected Till Plains. The chief crops are corn and other grains.

The Ozark Plateau is the state's largest land region. Forested hills and low mountains give it scenic beauty. The plateau rises from 500 to 1,700 feet (150 to 518 meters) or more above sea level. In the extreme southwestern corner of the state, a high, wooded tableland has soil especially good for gardening and raising strawberries. The river valleys are about the only level land in the Ozark region. The plateau is one of the nation's major tourist areas because of its many caves, large springs and lakes, and clear, fast-flowing streams.

The St. Francois Mountains rise in the southeast. This series of granite peaks, knobs, and domes covers about 70 square miles (180 square kilometers). The St. Francois Mountains do not form a continuous range. They rise more or less in groups, usually of two or three peaks. The mountains make up the highest and most rugged part of the state. One of the peaks, Taum Sauk (1,772 feet, or 540 meters), is the highest point in Missouri.

The Mississippi Alluvial Plain covers the southeastern corner of Missouri. This region was once a swampy wilderness. Much of the area has been cleared and drained, and the soil is unusually rich for farming. The southern part of the plain is known as the *Boot Heel* because of its shape.

Rivers and Lakes. Missouri owes much of its commercial and industrial importance to the two largest rivers in the United States—the Mississippi and the Missouri. These rivers and their branches provide water highways for transportation, water supplies for cities and industries, and hydroelectric power for homes and factories.

The Current River is one of Missouri's most beautiful rivers. It starts from Montauk Spring in the Ozarks, which has a daily flow of about 40 million gallons (150 million liters). The river's name comes from the swift flow of its cold, sparkling waters. Like the Black, James, St. Francis, and other rivers of the Ozark Plateau, the Current is noted for its game fish. Other rivers favored by fishermen include the Gasconade, Little Piney, Meramec, and White.

Lake of the Ozarks, Missouri's largest lake, is man-made. It provides a popular recreation area in the heart of the scenic Ozarks.

Land Regions of Missouri

DISSECTED TILL PLAINS

OSAGE
PLAINS

OZARK PLATEAU

MISSISSIPPI ALLUVIAL PLAIN

Missouri R.

Missouri R.

Osage R.

Mississippi R.

Mississippi R.

MISSOURI

Lake of the Ozarks, a man-made lake, is the largest lake in the state. It stretches through the heart of the Ozarks. The lake has a shoreline of more than 1,300 miles (2,090 kilometers), and covers about 60,000 acres (24,000 hectares). It is a popular recreation area. Other man-made lakes include Bull Shoals, Pomme de Terre, Table Rock, and Taneycomo.

Springs and Caves. About 10,000 springs bubble from the ground in the Ozark Plateau. More than a hundred springs have a daily water flow of over 1 million gallons (3.8 million liters) each. The largest is Big Spring, near Van Buren. It has an average flow of about 278 million gallons (1,052 million liters) of water a day. In addition to its fresh-water springs, Missouri has about 30 mineral springs.

More than 1,450 caves have been found in Missouri. Underground streams formed these caves beneath the Ozarks. One of the largest caves, Marvel Cave, is near Branson. An underground railroad winds through its 10 miles (16 kilometers) of passageways. Every year, about 20 marriages are performed in Bridal Cave, near Camdenton.

Big Spring, largest in the state, is near Van Buren. Many springs feed the clear lakes and swift rivers of Missouri's Ozark Plateau.

The Mighty Mississippi River forms the eastern border of the state. Old-time stern-wheel boats still carry crowds on sightseeing trips.

Rich Farmland covers the Mississippi Alluvial Plain. This region was once useless swampland.

Fields of Wheat, such as these near Clinton, spread across the Osage Plains region in western Missouri.

MISSOURI / Climate

Both winters and summers are milder in the mountain areas of Missouri than in the lower-lying plains. In July, average temperatures range from about 81° F. (27° C) in the Boot Heel section to about 79° F. (26° C) in the north and in areas of highest elevation. The state's record high temperature is 118° F. (48° C). It was set at Clinton on July 15, 1936; at Lamar on July 18, 1936; and at Union and Warsaw on July 14, 1954.

Average January temperatures vary from 29° F. (−2° C) in the north to about 38° F. (3° C) in the Boot Heel. Missouri's record low temperature of −40° F. (−40° C) was set at Warsaw on Feb. 13, 1905. The average yearly *precipitation* (rain, melted snow, and other forms of moisture) ranges from about 50 inches (130 centimeters) in the southeast to 30 inches (76 centimeters) in the northwest. Snowfall averages 8 to 12 inches (20 to 30 centimeters) a year in the southernmost counties and 18 to 22 inches (46 to 56 centimeters) north of the Missouri River. The growing season ranges from 225 days in the southeast to 170 days in the north.

Country Scene near Gray Summit shows the natural beauty made possible by Missouri's mild temperatures and ample rainfall.
John H. Gerard

SEASONAL TEMPERATURES

January

AVERAGE OF DAILY LOW TEMPERATURES

Degrees Fahrenheit	Degrees Celsius
28 to 32	-2 to 0
24 to 28	-4 to -2
20 to 24	-7 to -4
16 to 20	-9 to -7
12 to 16	-11 to -9

AVERAGE OF DAILY HIGH TEMPERATURES

Degrees Fahrenheit	Degrees Celsius
46 to 50	8 to 10
42 to 46	6 to 8
38 to 42	3 to 6
34 to 38	1 to 3

July

AVERAGE OF DAILY LOW TEMPERATURES

Degrees Fahrenheit	Degrees Celsius
68 to 72	20 to 22
64 to 68	18 to 20
60 to 64	16 to 18

AVERAGE OF DAILY HIGH TEMPERATURES

Degrees Fahrenheit	Degrees Celsius
92 to 94	33 to 34
90 to 92	32 to 33

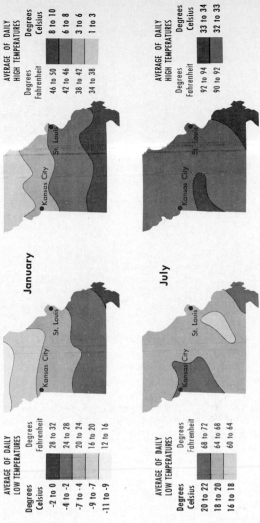

AVERAGE YEARLY PRECIPITATION
(Rain, Melted Snow and Other Moisture)

Inches	Centimeters
44 to 52	112 to 132
36 to 44	91 to 112
28 to 36	71 to 91

0   50   100   200 Miles
0   100   200   300 Kilometers

WORLD BOOK maps

AVERAGE MONTHLY WEATHER

KANSAS CITY

	Temperatures F° High	Low	C° High	Low	Days of Rain or Snow
JAN.	39	21	4	-6	7
FEB.	44	25	7	-4	7
MAR.	54	34	12	1	9
APR.	66	46	19	8	11
MAY	75	56	24	13	12
JUNE	85	66	29	19	11
JULY	91	71	33	22	8
AUG.	89	69	32	21	9
SEPT.	81	60	27	16	7
OCT.	70	49	21	9	7
NOV.	54	35	12	2	6
DEC.	42	25	6	-4	7

ST. LOUIS

	Temperatures F° High	Low	C° High	Low	Days of Rain or Snow
JAN.	41	26	5	-3	9
FEB.	45	29	7	-2	9
MAR.	54	37	12	3	11
APR.	66	47	19	8	12
MAY	75	57	24	14	12
JUNE	85	67	29	19	11
JULY	90	72	32	22	8
AUG.	88	70	31	21	8
SEPT.	80	62	27	17	7
OCT.	70	52	21	11	7
NOV.	54	38	12	3	8
DEC.	44	29	7	-2	9

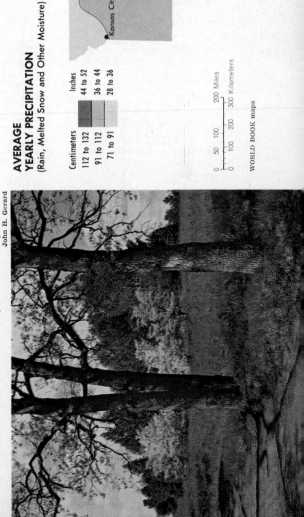

Natural Resources of Missouri include fertile soils, large mineral deposits, dense forests, and abundant plant and animal life.

Soil. The soils of the Dissected Till Plains are mainly glacial soils (clay mixed with sand and gravel) and *loess* (a brownish wind-blown dust). A band of rich loess, often more than 50 feet (15 meters) deep, lies along the Missouri River. The Osage Plains have soils of medium fertility, ranging from dark-brown loam to lighter-colored sandy or silt loams.

Brown limestone soils cover most of the southwestern part of the Ozarks. Elsewhere in the Ozarks, the soils are shallow and stony. The Mississippi River has deposited rich soils on the Mississippi Alluvial Plain. The state also has about 700,000 acres (280,000 hectares) of rich alluvial soil along the Missouri River.

Minerals. The state's most important metal is lead. Lead is mined in Iron, Reynolds, and Washington counties. Cadmium, copper, silver, sulfuric acid, and zinc are also recovered by processing the lead ore. Large fire clay deposits occur in east-central Missouri. An important barite reserve lies south of St. Louis. Limestone, Missouri's leading quarry product, is found in most of the state. Marble is quarried near St. Louis and in southwestern Missouri. Other quarry products include granite and sandstone.

Coal is found in about 50 counties stretching across the state from the southwest to the northeast. Missouri's coal reserves total about 12 billion short tons (11 billion metric tons). The state has several extensive deposits of iron ore in the eastern Ozarks. Missouri also has small amounts of oil and natural gas along its western border. Other minerals found in the state include cobalt, manganese, nickel, phosphate rock, sand and gravel, silica sand, and tungsten.

Forests. Commercially important forests cover about a third of the state, chiefly in the Ozarks. Missouri's forests are largely hardwoods. More than three-fourths of the commercially important forests are of various types of oak or hickory. The state also has large growths of ash, bald cypress, cottonwood, elm, maple, shortleaf pine, and sweet gum.

Other Plant Life. Plants that grow throughout Missouri include asters, dogwood, goldenrod, milkweed, roses, sweet Williams, verbenas, violets, and many kinds of mint and hawthorn. Mistletoe grows on many trees on the Mississippi Alluvial Plain. The Ozarks probably have more flowers than any region in the state.

Animal Life. White-tailed deer are the most numerous of Missouri's big-game animals. Other animals include beavers, cottontail rabbits, foxes, muskrats, opossums, raccoons, skunks, and squirrels. Bobwhite quail are Missouri's most plentiful game bird. Fish found in Missouri's lakes, rivers, and streams include bass, bluegills, catfish, crappies, jack salmon, and trout.

Manufacturing accounts for 78 per cent of the value of all goods produced in Missouri. Goods manufactured in the state have a *value added by manufacture* of about $13 billion a year. This figure represents the value created in products by Missouri's industries, not counting such costs as materials, supplies, and fuel. The state has more than 7,300 factories. About three-

Production of Goods in Missouri

Total value of goods produced in 1977—$16,517,948,000

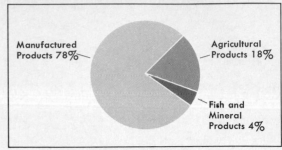

Percentages are based on farm income, value added by manufacture, and value of fish and mineral production. Fish products are less than 1 per cent.

Sources: U.S. government publications, 1978-1979.

Employment in Missouri

Total number of persons employed in 1978—2,084,900

		Number of Employees
Wholesale & Retail Trade	𝍖𝍖𝍖𝍖𝍖𝍖𝍖𝍖𝍖𝍖	461,400
Manufacturing	𝍖𝍖𝍖𝍖𝍖𝍖𝍖𝍖𝍖𝍖	452,800
Community, Social, & Personal Services	𝍖𝍖𝍖𝍖𝍖𝍖𝍖𝍖	349,700
Government	𝍖𝍖𝍖𝍖𝍖𝍖𝍖𝍖	336,700
Agriculture	𝍖𝍖𝍖𝍖	157,000
Transportation & Public Utilities	𝍖𝍖𝍖	135,000
Finance, Insurance, & Real Estate	𝍖𝍖𝍖	102,500
Construction	𝍖𝍖	82,200
Mining	𝍖	7,600

Sources: *Employment and Earnings,* May 1979, U.S. Bureau of Labor Statistics; *Farm Labor,* February 1979, U.S. Dept. of Agriculture.

fifths of the plants are in Kansas City and St. Louis.

Transportation Equipment from Missouri has a value added of about $3 billion a year. Factories in St. Louis and Kansas City produce airplanes, barges, railroad cars, truck and bus bodies, and truck trailers. Missouri ranks high in automobile production. There are large automobile assembly plants in St. Louis and Kansas City. Missouri is also a leading state in the aerospace industry. The Mercury capsules in which U.S. astronauts orbited the earth were made in St. Louis. St. Louis also manufactures the F-15 Eagle and F-18 Hornet supersonic fighter planes.

Food Products have a yearly value added of about $1½ billion. Slaughtering and meat-packing plants are centered in Kansas City, St. Louis, and St. Joseph. One of the nation's largest dairy-processing plants is in Springfield. It often handles about a million pounds of milk a day. Missouri ranks high among the states in the production of butter and cheese. St. Louis is a leading beer-brewing center. Kansas City, in the heart of the U.S. winter-wheat belt, has large flour mills. The nation's largest pancake-flour factory is in St. Joseph.

Chemicals and Related Products. Most of Missouri's chemical plants are in St. Louis and Kansas City. They turn out agricultural chemicals, drugs, insecticides, lubricants, medicines, paints, and many other products.

Chemicals produced in the state have an annual value added of about $1⅓ billion.

Other Important Industries in Missouri produce electric and electronic equipment, fabricated metal products, nonelectric machinery, primary metals, printed materials, and shoes. St. Louis and Kansas City have steel mills, and lead smelters are in Glover and Herculaneum. The city of Mexico has the nation's largest refractory brick factory. Festus-Crystal City is the site of one of the country's largest plate-glass factories.

Agriculture. Missouri is one of the nation's leading agricultural states. Its yearly farm income is about $3 billion. This amount is about a fifth of the value of all goods produced in the state. Missouri has about 117,000 farms. The average farm covers about 276 acres (112 hectares). Missouri has about 32 million acres (13 million hectares) in farmland. Farms located in the northern and southeastern parts of the state usually have a greater gross income than other farms in Missouri.

Livestock. The raising of beef cattle and hogs is profitable in Missouri because of the abundance of corn, small grains, and hay. Missouri farmers also raise dairy cattle. Sheep graze in the northeast and north-central parts of the state. Missouri produces about 1⅓ billion eggs a year. Its farmers raise about 22 million *broilers* (chickens between 9 and 12 weeks old), about 6 million other chickens, and about 10 million turkeys annually. They also raise ducks and geese.

Farmers throughout the state raise horses. Missouri was once famous for its mules, and the state was the nation's leading mule producer. Missouri mules did much of the work on farms before World War II. Since then, machinery has replaced them.

Field Crops. Soybeans rank as Missouri's leading crop. Corn ranks second. Soybeans are raised throughout northern and southeastern Missouri. More than half of the state's cropland is planted with soybeans. Farmers plant about a fourth of their cropland in corn. Corn is grown mainly in northern Missouri. Wheat and grain sorghum are the third and fourth most important crops. Cotton, greenhouse and nursery products, hay, oats, popcorn, rice, seed crops, and tobacco are also important crops.

Fruits and Vegetables. Farmers throughout the state grow apples. The biggest orchards are along the bluffs of the Mississippi and Missouri rivers and in the Ozark Plateau. Missouri stands high among the states in the production of watermelons, which are raised chiefly in the southeast. Other fruits include grapes, peaches, pears, raspberries, and strawberries. Most of the state's commercial vegetables grow in southeastern Missouri.

Mining accounts for 4 per cent, or about $715 million, of the value of goods produced in Missouri each year. Missouri ranks first in the nation in lead production. Miners take about 500,000 short tons (450,000 metric tons) of lead annually from mines in the state. About 2 million short tons (1.8 million metric tons) of clays and about 125,000 short tons (113,400 metric tons) of barite ore come from Missouri mines each year.

Quarries in the state produce about 50 million short tons (45 million metric tons) of limestone annually. Missouri's quarries lie throughout the state. Sand and gravel production totals about 15 million short tons (13.6 million metric tons) a year.

All of Missouri's coal comes from open-pit and strip mines. The leading coal-producing counties are Barton, Bates, Henry, Howard, Macon, Putnam, Randolph, and Vernon. Iron ore also ranks high in Missouri's mineral production. The ore comes from two large underground mines, one in Washington County and the other

FARM, MINERAL, AND FOREST PRODUCTS

This map shows where the leading farm, mineral, and forest products are produced. The major urban areas (shown in red) are the important manufacturing centers.

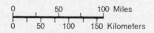

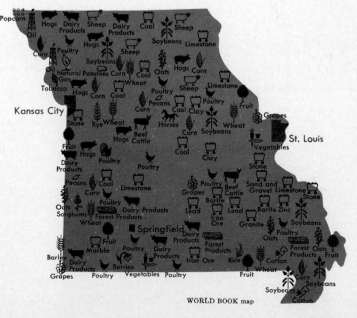

WORLD BOOK map

in Iron County. The mine in Washington County, the Pea Ridge Mine, is the nation's largest underground iron mine. The state also produces copper, natural gas, oil, phosphate rock, silver, and zinc.

Electric Power. Steam plants generate about 90 per cent of Missouri's electric power. A large hydroelectric power plant at Bagnell Dam in the Ozark Plateau generates electricity mainly for the St. Louis area.

The Taum Sauk Project near Lesterville is one of the largest pumped-storage hydroelectric plants in the United States. The plant stores and uses the same supply of water over and over again. The water is pumped from a lower reservoir to a higher one. When the water is released from the upper reservoir and flows to the lower one, its flow is used to generate electricity. The Taum Sauk Project, completed in 1963, has a capacity of about 400,000 kilowatts.

Transportation. Missouri's central location, its nearness to raw materials, and the great Mississippi and Missouri waterways have made Kansas City and St. Louis leading transportation centers in the nation.

Missouri has about 370 airports. Lambert-St. Louis International Airport in St. Louis and Kansas City International Airport are among the busiest airports in the country.

Railroads operate on about 7,000 miles (11,000 kilometers) of track in Missouri. About 20 rail lines provide freight service, and passenger trains serve about 10 cities in the state. St. Louis and Kansas City are among the most important U.S. railroad centers.

Missouri has about 117,000 miles (188,300 kilometers) of roads and highways. About 95 per cent of them are surfaced. The first land traffic in Missouri followed old Indian trails. In 1860 and 1861, St. Joseph was the eastern terminal of the pony express mail system. The famous Oregon and Santa Fe trails ran from Independence. Today, Kansas City and St. Louis rank among the nation's leading trucking centers.

Boats and barges can use the Mississippi River for 490 miles (789 kilometers) along the state's eastern border. St. Louis is the busiest inland port on the Mississippi River. River barges on the Missouri and Mississippi rivers carry much heavy freight.

Communication. Two famous Missouri journalists made newspaper history. They founded the state's leading papers and influenced journalism across the country. William Rockhill Nelson, founder of the *Kansas City Star*, fought for government reform. Joseph Pulitzer, who founded the *St. Louis Post-Dispatch*, established the Pulitzer prizes (see PULITZER PRIZES).

The first Missouri newspaper, the *Missouri Gazette*, began publication in St. Louis in 1808. Today, Missouri has more than 55 daily newspapers and about 255 weeklies. Newspapers with the largest daily circulations include the *Kansas City Star*, the *Kansas City Times*, the *St. Louis Globe-Democrat*, and the *St. Louis Post-Dispatch*. Missouri publishers also issue about 225 periodicals. Firms in St. Louis and Kansas City publish textbooks.

The first radio station in Missouri, WEW of St. Louis University, began broadcasting in 1921. The state's first TV station, KSD-TV, started in 1947 in St. Louis. There are now about 220 radio stations and about 25 TV stations.

MISSOURI/History

Indian Days. Indians known as Mound Builders lived in the Missouri region long before white men came there. The Indians built large earthwork mounds that still may be seen in various sections of the state (see MOUND BUILDERS). Many tribes of Indians lived in Missouri when the white man first arrived. The Missouri Indians dwelt in what is now east-central Missouri. The Osage, a tribe of unusually tall Indians, lived and hunted in the areas to the south and west. Other tribes included the Fox and the Sauk Indians, who lived in the north. See INDIAN, AMERICAN (Table of Tribes).

Exploration and Settlement. The daring French explorers Father Jacques Marquette and Louis Jolliet were probably the first white persons to see the mouth of the Missouri River. In 1673, they marked the spot where the Missouri joins the Mississippi. In 1682, another French explorer, Robert Cavelier, Sieur de la Salle, traveled down the Mississippi River and claimed the Mississippi Valley for France. La Salle named the region *Louisiana* in honor of King Louis XIV.

IMPORTANT DATES IN MISSOURI

1673 Father Jacques Marquette and Louis Jolliet probably became the first white persons to see the mouth of the Missouri River.

1682 Robert Cavelier, Sieur de la Salle, claimed the Mississippi Valley, including Missouri, for France. He named the region *Louisiana*.

c. 1735 Settlers from what is now Illinois established Missouri's first permanent white settlement, at Ste. Genevieve.

1762 France gave the Louisiana region to Spain.

1764 Pierre Laclède Liguest and René Auguste Chouteau established St. Louis.

1800 Spain returned the Louisiana region to France.

1803 France sold the Louisiana region to the U.S.

1812 Congress made Missouri a territory.

1815 Indian attacks on Missouri settlements ended when the Indians and United States government officials signed a peace treaty at Portage des Sioux.

1821 Missouri became the 24th state on August 10.

1837 Missouri gained its six northwestern counties as a result of the Platte Purchase.

1854 Border warfare began between antislavery Kansans and proslavery Missourians.

1861-1865 Missouri became a battleground during the Civil War.

1904 The Louisiana Purchase Centennial Exposition was held in St. Louis.

1931 Bagnell Dam on the Osage River was completed, forming the 60,000-acre (24,000-hectare) Lake of the Ozarks.

1945 Harry S. Truman of Independence became the 33rd President of the United States.

1965 The last section of the stainless steel Gateway Arch was put in place in St. Louis. The nation's tallest monument, it is 630 feet (192 meters) high.

HISTORIC MISSOURI

Harry S. Truman
born in Lamar

The Missouri Compromise, passed by Congress in 1820, brought Missouri into the Union the next year as a slave state.

The Dred Scott Decision was made by the Supreme Court of the United States in 1857. It prevented the Missouri slave, Dred Scott, from gaining his freedom, and was one of the events that led to the Civil War.

Mark Twain grew up in Hannibal

Hannibal •

St. Joseph •

The Pony Express linked St. Joseph, Mo., and Sacramento, Calif., in 1860. Riders covered the 1,966 miles (3,164 kilometers) in 8 to 9 days. The Pony Express operated for 18 months.

Independence

Lewis and Clark started their famous journey from near St. Louis to the Pacific Northwest in 1804. They gave the United States a strong claim to the great Oregon region.

St. Louis •

★
JEFFERSON CITY

St. Louis was founded in 1764 by Pierre Laclède Liguest, a French fur trader. The city's location near where the Mississippi and Missouri rivers meet has made it a great transportation center.

• Ste. Genevieve

• Lamar

Independence, where the Oregon and Santa Fe trails began, became the "Gateway to the West" for pioneers in the mid-1800's.

Ste. Genevieve was the first permanent settlement in the Missouri region. French settlers from what is now Illinois established it about 1735.

Jesse James, one of the nation's most dangerous bandits, terrorized Missouri for about 16 years following the Civil War. He was born near Centerville (now Kearney).

The Great Mississippi Steamboat Race, in 1870, ended with the victory of the *Robert E. Lee* over the *Natchez.* The historic three-day race between New Orleans and St. Louis was close until the *Natchez* got lost in fog near Cairo, Ill.

During the years that followed, French trappers and fur traders established trading posts along the river. French missionaries, eager to convert the Indians, founded a number of missions. Indian tales of gold and silver attracted other Frenchmen. These adventurers found lead and salt in what is now St. Francois County and remained to mine these minerals. About 1700, Jesuit missionaries established the first white settlement in Missouri, the Mission of St. Francis Xavier. They built it near the present site of St. Louis. The mission was abandoned in 1703 because of unhealthful swamps nearby. About 1735, settlers from what is now Illinois established Missouri's first permanent white settlement, at Ste. Genevieve. In 1764, Pierre Laclède Liguest and René Auguste Chouteau founded St. Louis.

By a secret treaty, signed in 1762, France gave up all its territory west of the Mississippi River to Spain. France and Spain had been allies in the Seven Years' War (see SEVEN YEARS' WAR). The Spaniards encouraged pioneers from the East to come to the region, and settlers poured into the Spanish land. One of the pioneers was Daniel Boone, the famous frontiersman. He moved to what is now St. Charles County in 1799, after the Spanish had granted him about 800 acres (320 hectares) of land. In 1800, the Spanish appointed Boone a *syndic*, or judge (see BOONE, DANIEL).

Napoleon Bonaparte, the ruler of France, forced Spain to return the territory west of the Mississippi to France in 1800. By that time, much of present-day Missouri had been explored and many communities had been established. Napoleon, badly in need of money to finance his wars in Europe, sold the Louisiana Territory to the United States in 1803 (see LOUISIANA PURCHASE). The northern part of the territory was called Upper Louisiana, and included the present state of Missouri. Upper Louisiana extended northward from the 33rd parallel to Canada, and westward to the Rocky Mountains. In 1812, Congress organized the Missouri Territory.

Territorial Days. The Missouri Territory began with a population of more than 20,000. The farming and mining industries were well established, and schools and churches had been built. So many settlers poured into the territory that the Indians became aroused by the loss of their ancient hunting grounds. For several years, the Indians led frequent, bloody raids on the frontier settlements.

In 1812, war broke out between the United States and Great Britain (see WAR OF 1812). The British gave weapons to the Indians and encouraged them to attack the Missouri pioneers. The settlers built forts and blockhouses for protection. Even after the war between the United States and Britain ended, the Indians continued to raid many settlements. The attacks ended in 1815, when the Indians and U.S. government officials signed a peace treaty at Portage des Sioux.

Statehood and Expansion. In 1818, Missouri asked Congress to be admitted into the Union. The territory had been settled mainly by Southerners who had brought Negro slaves with them. Missouri's application for admission as a slave state caused a nationwide dispute between slavery and antislavery sympathizers. This dispute was not settled until 1820, when Congress passed the Missouri Compromise. Under this legislation, Missouri entered the Union as a slave state on Aug. 10, 1821 (see MISSOURI COMPROMISE). A census taken in 1820 showed that the territory had 66,586 persons, including 10,222 slaves. Missourians elected Alexander McNair as the first governor of the state.

When Missouri entered the Union, it was the western frontier of the nation. The fur trade was the state's most important industry. In 1822, John Jacob Astor organized a St. Louis branch of the American Fur Company. Within the next 12 years, Astor ruined or bought out most other fur companies. He had a near monopoly on the fur trade west of the Mississippi River.

In 1836, Congress approved the purchase from the Indians of an area known as the Platte Country. By presidential proclamation, it became part of Missouri in 1837. This region extended the northern part of Missouri's western border to the Missouri River.

Since the 1820's, Missourians had been carrying on a regular trade with Mexicans over the Santa Fe Trail. This famous trail linked Independence, Mo., with Santa Fe in the Southwest. Tremendous wealth from the Southwest poured into Missouri, and Independence became a busy, thriving village. The great Oregon

The Santa Fe Trail and the Oregon Trail played important roles in the history of Missouri during the early 1800's. Both trails ran from Independence. This mural shows Independence as a village during the years when it was the starting point of the

Trail, which thousands of settlers followed to the Northwest, also began in Independence. See SANTA FE TRAIL; OREGON TRAIL.

The Civil War. In 1857, the Supreme Court of the United States issued the historic Dred Scott Decision. The court ruled that Scott, a Missouri slave, was merely property and did not have citizenship rights. The ruling greatly increased ill feeling between the North and the South (see DRED SCOTT DECISION). Meanwhile, many Missourians who lived near the western border of the state feared that the newly organized Kansas Territory would become a free state. As more and more antislavery families settled in Kansas, scattered warfare broke out between Missourians and Kansans (see BROWN, JOHN; KANSAS ["Bleeding Kansas"]). Kansas became a free state in 1861. Fighting between Kansans and Missourians continued into the Civil War.

Missouri became the center of national interest in 1861. The nation wondered whether Missouri would *secede* (withdraw) from the Union and join the Confederacy. Early in 1861, Governor Claiborne F. Jackson recommended that a state convention be called to determine the will of the people. The convention was held in February and March. Jackson and some members of the convention were strongly pro-South, but the convention voted to remain in the Union. Most Missourians wanted to stay neutral if war should come.

After the Civil War began in April, 1861, President Abraham Lincoln called for troops from Missouri. Governor Jackson refused Lincoln's call. Union soldiers and the Missouri state militia, which Jackson commanded as governor, clashed at Boonville on June 17, 1861. This battle was the first real fighting of the Civil War in Missouri. The Union troops, under General Nathaniel Lyon, routed the militiamen and gained control of northern Missouri. Jackson and his militiamen retreated to southwestern Missouri, where they reorganized. They then advanced to Wilson's Creek, near Springfield. There, in August, the militiamen and Confederate troops defeated the Union forces in a bloody battle.

On July 22, the state convention had met again. It voted to remove pro-Confederate state leaders from office. The convention replaced them with pro-Union men. Hamilton R. Gamble became governor. In September, 1861, Jackson called for the legislature to meet in Neosho in October. Not enough members attended to hold a legal session. But those present voted to secede from the Union and join the Confederacy.

The Confederate forces controlled a foothold in southwestern Missouri until March, 1862, when Union forces defeated them at Pea Ridge, Ark. In 1864, General Sterling Price tried to recapture Missouri for the South in a daring raid. He was defeated at Westport, which is a part of present-day Kansas City. Price's defeat marked the end of full-scale fighting in the state. Throughout the war, however, bands of both Union and Confederate guerrillas terrorized the countryside. They burned and looted towns and murdered innocent people.

After the war ended in 1865, Missouri adopted a new constitution. It included a clause that denied the right to vote to anyone who refused to swear that he had not sympathized with the South. This unpopular clause was repealed in 1870.

Progress as a State. Between 1850 and 1870, big changes took place in Missouri. St. Louis and Kansas City became important transportation centers. The frontier disappeared. Trade with Mexico over the Santa Fe Trail ended. The fur trade grew less important, although St. Louis remained one of the world's great fur markets. Tenant farmers replaced the relatively few slaves who worked the fields.

In 1875, Missouri adopted a new constitution. It reestablished the governor's term from two to four years. It also established a state railroad commission to regulate rates and shipping conditions.

For almost 20 years after the Civil War, many former Confederate guerrillas turned to crime. They held up banks, stagecoaches, and trains. In 1881, Governor Thomas T. Crittenden began a campaign to stop the outlaws. He offered a $5,000 reward for the arrest of Jesse James, one of the most notorious bandits. James was killed by one of his own gang in 1882.

The Louisiana Purchase Centennial Exposition was held in St. Louis in 1904. This world's fair attracted almost 20 million visitors from the United States and other countries. A popular exhibit featured automobiles. One of the automobiles had been driven all the way

trails. The Santa Fe Trail brought Missouri great wealth from Mexico and the Southwest. Thousands of settlers followed the Oregon Trail to the Northwest. The mural, painted by Thomas Hart Benton, is in the Harry S. Truman Library in Independence.

Independence And The Opening Of The West mural by Thomas Hart Benton, Harry S. Truman Library, Independence, Mo.

THE GOVERNORS OF MISSOURI

	Party	Term		Party	Term
1. Alexander McNair	*Dem.-Rep.	1820-1824	25. John S. Marmaduke	Democratic	1885-1887
2. Frederick Bates	*Dem.-Rep.	1824-1825	26. Albert P. Morehouse	Democratic	1887-1889
3. Abraham J. Williams	*Dem.-Rep.	1825-1826	27. David R. Francis	Democratic	1889-1893
4. John Miller	*Dem.-Rep.	1826-1832	28. William Joel Stone	Democratic	1893-1897
5. Daniel Dunklin	Democratic	1832-1836	29. Lon V. Stephens	Democratic	1897-1901
6. Lilburn W. Boggs	Democratic	1836-1840	30. Alexander M. Dockery	Democratic	1901-1905
7. Thomas Reynolds	Democratic	1840-1844	31. Joseph W. Folk	Democratic	1905-1909
8. Meredith M. Marmaduke	Democratic	1844	32. Herbert S. Hadley	Republican	1909-1913
9. John C. Edwards	Democratic	1844-1848	33. Elliott W. Major	Democratic	1913-1917
10. Austin A. King	Democratic	1848-1853	34. Frederick D. Gardner	Democratic	1917-1921
11. Sterling Price	Democratic	1853-1857	35. Arthur M. Hyde	Republican	1921-1925
12. Trusten Polk	Democratic	1857	36. Sam A. Baker	Republican	1925-1929
13. Hancock Lee Jackson	Democratic	1857	37. Henry S. Caulfield	Republican	1929-1933
14. Robert M. Stewart	Democratic	1857-1861	38. Guy B. Park	Democratic	1933-1937
15. Claiborne F. Jackson	Democratic	1861	39. Lloyd C. Stark	Democratic	1937-1941
16. Hamilton R. Gamble	Union	1861-1864	40. Forrest C. Donnell	Republican	1941-1945
17. Willard P. Hall	Union	1864-1865	41. Phil M. Donnelly	Democratic	1945-1949
18. Thomas C. Fletcher	Republican	1865-1869	42. Forrest Smith	Democratic	1949-1953
19. Joseph W. McClurg	Republican	1869-1871	43. Phil M. Donnelly	Democratic	1953-1957
20. B. Gratz Brown	†Lib. Rep.	1871-1873	44. James T. Blair, Jr.	Democratic	1957-1961
21. Silas Woodson	Democratic	1873-1875	45. John M. Dalton	Democratic	1961-1965
22. Charles H. Hardin	Democratic	1875-1877	46. Warren E. Hearnes	Democratic	1965-1973
23. John S. Phelps	Democratic	1877-1881	47. Christopher S. Bond	Republican	1973-1977
24. Thomas T. Crittenden	Democratic	1881-1885	48. Joseph P. Teasdale	Democratic	1977-

*Democratic-Republican   †Liberal Republican

from New York City to St. Louis under its own power.

In 1905, Governor Joseph W. Folk began one of the state's most progressive administrations. Missouri adopted statewide primary elections and began political, social, and industrial reforms. Laws were passed calling for the inspection of factory working conditions. Other laws regulated child labor and public utilities.

After the United States entered World War I in 1917, Missouri's mining, manufacturing, and agriculture expanded to supply the armed forces. General John J. Pershing, who was born in Linn County, became commander in chief of the U.S. forces in France. General Enoch H. Crowder, born in Grundy County, became the first director of the Selective Service System.

Bagnell Dam, an important source of electric power for the St. Louis area, was completed in 1931. The waters held back by the dam formed Missouri's great manmade lake, Lake of the Ozarks. Many Missourians lost their jobs during the Great Depression of the 1930's, and farmers suffered because of low prices. Under Governor Guy B. Park, the number of state government em-

Mill Creek Valley, below, a former slum in the heart of St. Louis, became an attractive residential area during the 1960's. This urban renewal project covers 465 acres (188 hectares).

Lewis Portnoy

ployees was cut and operating costs of government were reduced. The federal government set up several agencies in Missouri to provide employment and relief.

The Mid-1900's. During World War II (1939-1945), many new industries were developed in Missouri to provide supplies for the armed forces. In 1944, U.S. Senator Harry S. Truman of Independence was elected Vice-President. He became President after President Franklin D. Roosevelt died in 1945. Truman was elected to a full term as President in 1948.

New industrial plants boosted Missouri's economy during the 1950's. An electronics plant opened in Joplin, and factories in St. Louis and Neosho began producing parts for spacecraft. A uranium-processing plant went into operation in Weldon Spring.

During the 1960's, Missouri conducted a vigorous drive to attract more new industries. The state also encouraged tourism, which became a $500-million business annually. The mining industry in Missouri expanded during the 1960's with the discovery of iron ore deposits in Crawford, Dent, Franklin, Iron, and Washington counties.

By the early 1960's, most public schools in Missouri were desegregated. The state constitution had provided for segregated schools. But in 1954, the Supreme Court of the United States ruled that compulsory segregation of public schools was unconstitutional.

Missouri Today. Missouri faces serious problems in the 1970's. The state needs more money for education, health and welfare programs, and new highways. In 1969, the General Assembly increased personal and corporate income taxes. Missouri voters defeated the increases in a special election in 1970, but the legislature raised the taxes again later in the year.

Urban problems have become increasingly serious in Missouri. In St. Louis, for example, many middle-class families have moved to the suburbs. This population shift has drained the city of much financial support. To a lesser extent, this has also been happening in Kansas City. Inadequate transportation and an increase in crime have added to the problems of Missouri's cities.

In spite of its many problems, Missouri entered the 1970's relatively strong economically. The state's farms are continuing to produce large quantities of corn, cotton, livestock, soybeans, and wheat. Each year, Missouri spends increasingly more money for agricultural research. St. Louis, Kansas City, and many smaller cities annually report many new and expanded factories. The aerospace industry continues to thrive. Many firms, especially smaller companies, are relocating in smaller towns, where they can recruit workers from nearby farms. Iron ore reserves remain plentiful in Missouri. Tourism, which continues to grow, has become a billion-dollar industry.

JAMES E. COLLIER, LEW LARKIN, and WILLIAM E. PARRISH

MISSOURI/Study Aids

Related Articles in WORLD BOOK include:

BIOGRAPHIES

Ashley, William H.	Carver, George Washington
Atchison, David R.	Chouteau (family)
Benton, Thomas Hart (senator)	Eagleton, Thomas F.
	Field, Eugene
Benton, Thomas Hart (painter)	James, Jesse W.
	Nelson, William R.
Blair (Francis P., Jr.)	Pulitzer, Joseph
Bland, Richard P.	Robidoux (brothers)
Bradley, Omar N.	Truman, Harry S.
Brown, Benjamin Gratz	Twain, Mark

CITIES

Cape Girardeau	Independence	Saint Joseph
Columbia	Jefferson City	Saint Louis
Hannibal	Kansas City	Springfield

HISTORY

Civil War	Louisiana Purchase
Dred Scott Decision	Missouri Compromise
Latter Day Saints, Re-organized Church of	Pony Express
	Santa Fe Trail
Jesus Christ of	Western Frontier Life
Lewis and Clark Expedition	

PHYSICAL FEATURES

Lake of the Ozarks	Ozark Mountains
Mississippi River	White River
Missouri River	

PRODUCTS

For Missouri's rank among the states in production, see the following articles:

Automobile	Hog	Leather
Cattle	Horse	Soybean
Corn	Lead	Turkey

OTHER RELATED ARTICLES

Bagnell Dam	George Washington Carver
Clearwater Dam	National Monument
Eads Bridge	Midwestern States
Fort Leonard Wood	Osage Indians

Outline

I. Government
- A. Constitution
- B. Executive
- C. Legislature
- D. Courts
- E. Local Government
- F. Taxation
- G. Politics

II. People

III. Education
- A. Schools
- B. Libraries
- C. Museums

IV. A Visitor's Guide
- A. Places to Visit
- B. Annual Events

V. The Land
- A. Land Regions
- B. Rivers and Lakes
- C. Springs and Caves

VI. Climate

VII. Economy
- A. Natural Resources
- B. Manufacturing
- C. Agriculture
- D. Mining
- E. Electric Power
- F. Transportation
- G. Communication

VIII. History

Questions

From which Missouri city did the famous Santa Fe and Oregon trails run?

What is Missouri's leading crop?

Which political party has been the stronger in Missouri's history?

To what two rivers does Missouri owe much of its commercial and industrial importance?

Why is Missouri sometimes called the *Mother of the West?* Why was it nicknamed the *Show Me State?*

What are Missouri's chief manufactured products?

Missouri leads all states in producing what metal?

Why did Missouri become a transportation center?

What was the Missouri Compromise? The Dred Scott Decision?

Why did national interest focus on Missouri in 1861?

Books for Young Readers

BAILEY, BERNADINE. *Picture Book of Missouri.* Rev. ed. Whitman, 1966.

CARPENTER, ALLAN. *Missouri.* Childrens Press, 1966.

CLEMENTS, BRUCE. *I Tell a Lie Every So Often.* Farrar, 1974. Fiction.

HAYMAN, LEROY. *Harry S. Truman: A Biography.* Crowell, 1969.

KANE, HARNETT T. *Young Mark Twain and the Mississippi.* Random House, 1966.

KARSCH, ROBERT F., and SVOBODA, W. S. *The Missouri Citizen: History, Government, and Features of the State.* 3rd ed. State Publishing Co., St. Louis, 1970.

RABE, BERNIECE. *Naomi.* Nelson, 1975. Fiction.

Books for Older Readers

BENTON, THOMAS HART. *An Artist in America.* 3rd ed. Univ. of Missouri Press, 1968.

CHAPMAN, CARL H. and E. F. *Indians and Archaeology of Missouri.* Univ. of Missouri Press, 1964.

FOLEY, WILLIAM E. *A History of Missouri.* Vol. I: *1673 to 1820.* Univ. of Missouri Press, 1971.

KARSCH, ROBERT F. *The Government of Missouri.* 12th ed. Lucas Brothers, 1974.

McCANDLESS, PERRY. *A History of Missouri.* Vol. II: *1820 to 1860.* Univ. of Missouri Press, 1972.

McREYNOLDS, EDWIN C. *Missouri: A History of the Crossroads State.* Univ. of Oklahoma Press, 1962.

MOTT, FRANK L. ed. *Missouri Reader.* Univ. of Missouri Press, 1964.

NAGEL, PAUL C. *Missouri: A Bicentennial History.* Norton, 1977.

PARRISH, WILLIAM E. *A History of Missouri.* Vol. III: *1860 to 1875.* Univ. of Missouri Press, 1973.

MISSOURI, a ship. See WORLD WAR II (Victory in the Pacific; picture).

MISSOURI, UNIVERSITY OF

MISSOURI, UNIVERSITY OF, is a coeducational state university system with four campuses.

The University of Missouri-Columbia campus grants degrees in agriculture, arts and science, business and public administration, education, engineering, forestry-fisheries-wildlife, home economics, journalism, law, library and information science, medicine, nursing, public and community services, and veterinary medicine. Its school of journalism, founded in 1908, is the oldest in the world.

The University of Missouri-Kansas City campus grants degrees in administration, arts and sciences, dentistry, education, engineering, law, medicine, music, nursing, and pharmacy. It was founded as the privately controlled University of Kansas City in 1933. It became part of the University of Missouri in 1963.

The University of Missouri-Rolla campus offers degrees in arts and sciences, engineering, and mines and metallurgy. It was founded in 1870.

The University of Missouri-St. Louis campus grants degrees in arts and sciences, business administration, and education. It was founded as a junior college in 1960 and became a four-year campus of the University of Missouri in 1963.

Each campus also provides a graduate program. The university was founded in 1839 in Columbia. It is the oldest state university west of the Mississippi River. For enrollment, see UNIVERSITIES AND COLLEGES (table).

Critically reviewed by the UNIVERSITY OF MISSOURI

University of Missouri

A University of Missouri Landmark, these columns are all that remains of the old administration building on the Columbia campus. The building was destroyed by fire in 1892.

MISSOURI COMPROMISE. In 1818, the Territory of Missouri, which had been carved out of the middle of the Louisiana Purchase, applied for admission to the Union. Slavery was legal in the territory, and about 8,000 to 10,000 slaves already lived there. Most people expected Missouri to become a slave state.

When the question arose of admitting Missouri to the Union, there were exactly as many slave states as free states. Six of the original 13 states and five new states still permitted slavery, while seven of the original states and four new states had abolished it. This meant that the free states and the slave states each had 22 senators in the United States Senate. The admission of Missouri seemed certain to break this balance.

This balance had been temporarily upset a number of times, but it had always been easy to decide whether states east of the Mississippi River should be slave or free. Mason and Dixon's Line and the Ohio River formed a natural and well-understood boundary between the two sections. No such line had been drawn west of the Mississippi River. In addition, some parts of Missouri Territory lay to the north of the mouth of the Ohio River, while other parts of it lay to the south.

A heated debate broke out in Congress when Representative James Tallmadge of New York introduced an amendment to the bill enabling Missouri to become a state. Tallmadge, although a Democrat, proposed to prohibit the bringing of any more slaves into Missouri, and to grant freedom to the children of slaves born within the state after its admission. This proposal disturbed the South, which found cotton growing by means of slave labor increasingly profitable, and feared national legislation against slavery. Because the free states dominated the House of Representatives, the South felt it must keep the even balance in the Senate.

The Tallmadge amendment passed the House, but the Senate defeated it. During the next session of Congress, Maine applied for admission to the Union. Missouri and Maine could then be accepted without upsetting the Senate's balance between free and slave states, and the Missouri Compromise became possible.

The compromise, introduced into the Senate by Jesse B. Thomas of Illinois and adopted by Congress in March, 1820, admitted Maine as a free state and authorized Missouri to form a state constitution. A territory had to have an established constitution before it could become a state. The compromise also banned slavery from the Louisiana Purchase north of the southern boundary of Missouri, the line of 36° 30' north latitude, except in the state of Missouri.

The people of Missouri felt that it was their business to decide about slavery. So they wrote into their new constitution a clause which forbade any free blacks or mulattoes to enter the state.

Before Congress would admit Missouri, a second Missouri Compromise was necessary. This agreement, worked out in part by Henry Clay, required the Missouri legislature not to deny black citizens of the United States their constitutional rights. With this understanding, Missouri was admitted to the Union in 1821. Most newcomers to the state did not own slaves.

In 1848, Congress passed the Oregon Territory bill, which prohibited slavery in the area. President James K. Polk signed the bill on the grounds that the territory lay north of the Missouri Compromise line. Later proposals tried to extend the line by law across the continent to the Pacific Ocean. These efforts failed. The Missouri Compromise was repealed by the Kansas-Nebraska Act of 1854 (see KANSAS-NEBRASKA ACT). RAY ALLEN BILLINGTON

MISSOURI RIVER is the second longest river in the United States. Only the Mississippi is longer. The Missouri flows 2,315 miles (3,726 kilometers) from its headwaters in Montana to its mouth on the Mississippi. It drains an area of about 529,400 square miles (1,371,100 square kilometers). This drainage basin includes all or parts of 10 states and 2 Canadian provinces.

The Missouri has long been known for the large amount of mud in its water. Pioneers nicknamed the river the *Big Muddy*, and farmers have described it as "too thick to drink and too thin to plow." The river was named after the Missouri Indians, one of the tribes that lived near its mouth.

The Course of the Missouri. The headwaters of the Missouri are the Jefferson, Madison, and Gallatin rivers. They begin as small, rushing streams high in the Rocky Mountains of Montana and Wyoming. The headwaters merge and form the Missouri near Three Forks, Mont.

The Missouri flows north from Three Forks and cuts through a spectacular gorge called the Gates of the Mountains. Then it bends toward the northeast and plunges down a series of waterfalls known as the Great Falls of the Missouri. The city of Great Falls, Mont., at the foot of the waterfalls, is named for them. From Great Falls, the Missouri winds eastward across Montana. In North Dakota, the river makes a great bend toward the south. Then it flows southeast across South Dakota.

The Missouri forms part of the boundary between South Dakota and Nebraska. It turns south at Sioux City, Iowa, and flows between Iowa and Nebraska. The river also forms the Nebraska-Missouri boundary and part of the Missouri-Kansas boundary. At Kansas City, Mo., the river turns east again. It flows across Missouri and joins the Mississippi River about 20 miles (32 kilometers) north of downtown St. Louis. Every second, the Missouri empties an average of 76,300 cubic feet (2,161 cubic meters) of water into the Mississippi.

The Missouri, like most rivers, has an upper, middle, and lower part (see RIVER [The Course]). The upper Missouri is a clear, rapid-flowing stream in the mountains of western Montana. The middle Missouri begins just below Great Falls, where the river leaves the mountains and moves onto the Great Plains. It is slower and muddier than the upper part of the river. The lower Missouri is the slowest and muddiest part. It begins just downstream from Yankton, S. Dak., and extends to the Mississippi.

The Platte River is the longest branch of the Missouri. Other major tributaries include the James, Kansas, Milk, Osage, and Yellowstone rivers.

Navigation. The Missouri River was once used for commercial navigation along most of its course. Today, almost all traffic upstream from Sioux City is recreational, but commercial activity thrives on the lower Missouri. The commercial river traffic is extremely important to farmers of the western part of the Midwest. It carries their goods to market and brings them fertilizer and other agricultural supplies. The chief ports on the Missouri are Kansas City, Mo.; Omaha, Nebr.; and Sioux City.

Commercial traffic on the Missouri totals more than $3\frac{1}{4}$ million short tons (3.2 million metric tons) of freight yearly. Freight headed downstream consists mainly of such farm products as corn, sorghum, soybeans, and wheat. Upstream cargoes include benzine, cement, fertilizer, lime, paint, and phosphate. Most of the freight travels on barges pushed by powerful tugboats. A navigation channel at least 300 feet (91 meters) wide and 9 feet (2.7 meters) deep is maintained

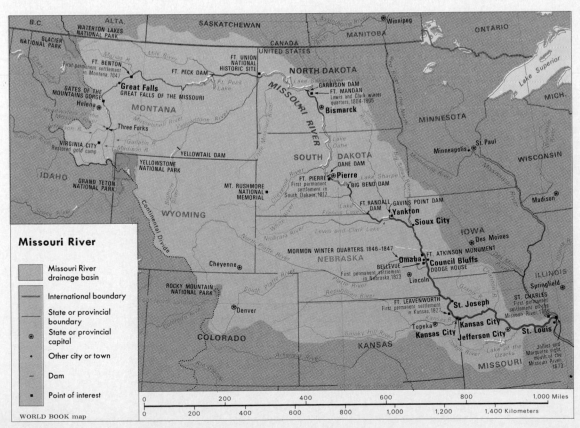

Missouri River

- Missouri River drainage basin
- International boundary
- State or provincial boundary
- ⊛ State or provincial capital
- • Other city or town
- – Dam
- ▪ Point of interest

WORLD BOOK map

Stuart S. White

The Gates of the Mountains, *above,* is a magnificent gorge cut by the Missouri River near Sieben, Mont. The American explorer Meriwether Lewis named the gorge in 1805 during his famous expedition with William Clark through the Pacific Northwest.

on the river between Sioux City and the Mississippi.

Dams and Reservoirs. A series of six huge dams form a nearly continual chain of long, winding reservoirs along the middle Missouri River. These dams, in order from north to south along the river, are Fort Peck, Garrison, Oahe, Big Bend, Fort Randall, and Gavins Point. About 60 smaller dams and reservoirs are on tributaries of the Missouri. See FORT PECK DAM; FORT RANDALL DAM; GARRISON DAM; OAHE DAM.

Flooding was once a serious problem on the Missouri. In spring, excess water from melting snow often caused the river to overflow, causing widespread damage. The six large dams on the middle Missouri have nearly eliminated this problem. The reservoirs of the dams store excess water in spring and gradually release it during the rest of the year, thus greatly reducing floods downstream.

The dams and their reservoirs also provide other services. Hydroelectric powerhouses at the dams generate electricity used by farms, homes, and industries throughout the middle Missouri Basin. Millions of visitors use the reservoirs annually for boating, fishing, swimming, and water skiing. Water from the reservoirs is also used to irrigate farmland and serve cities along the river.

Wildlife and Conservation. The Missouri and its valley provide a rich habitat for a wide variety of wildlife. Bears, deer, elk, moose, and other large animals live in the mountainous upper Missouri Valley. Smaller animals, such as beavers, foxes, muskrats, rabbits, skunks, and weasels, are common along the middle and lower parts of the river. Fishes of the cool, clear upper Missouri include graylings and rainbow trout. Bass, bullheads, catfish, carp, and perch inhabit the warmer, muddier waters below Great Falls.

The upper Missouri flows through forests of fir, hemlock, and spruce trees. The middle and lower sections of the river wind through grasslands. Forests of cottonwoods, hickories, oaks, poplars, and willows also lie along the middle and lower sections.

At one time, pollution threatened much of the wildlife along the Missouri. Pesticides and other chemicals used by farmers were washed into the river, and industries dumped wastes into it. These substances poisoned fish and other wildlife. Today, federal laws ban certain pesticides, and industrial discharges into the river are carefully controlled. As a result, the quality of the water is gradually improving.

History. The Missouri River was formed about 20 million years ago, during the late Tertiary Period. During the Pleistocene Ice Age, about 2 million years ago, the river marked the southern and western edge of many of the huge ice sheets that covered the land.

The Missouri River Basin was the home of several Indian tribes. The Wind River Shoshoni lived near the headwaters of the river, in western Montana. Several buffalo-hunting tribes occupied the Missouri Basin between eastern Montana and the Mississippi. They included the Arikara, the Assiniboin, the Dakotah (Sioux), the Kansa, the Missouri, and the Omaha. Many of these tribes spent much of their time on the grasslands away from the river. But the Missouri was a valuable water source, a favorite hunting ground, and an important transportation route for their canoes.

The first whites to see the Missouri River were the explorers Jacques Marquette of France and Louis Jolliet, a French Canadian. They reached the mouth of the Missouri in 1673 while exploring the Mississippi. The United States bought the Missouri River Basin from France in 1803 as part of the Louisiana Purchase. From 1804 to 1806, two Americans, Meriwether Lewis and William Clark, explored the territory drained by the Missouri. See LEWIS AND CLARK EXPEDITION.

During the early 1800's, the Missouri became one of the main transportation routes of the fur trade in the West. At first, keelboats hauled furs and supplies on the river. Steamboat traffic began on the Missouri in 1819, and steamers soon became the chief means of transportation. Many pioneers who traveled west in the mid-1800's went at least part of the way on a Missouri steamer. River traffic declined after railroads were built in the West during the late 1800's. But today, the lower Missouri is an important commercial waterway.

Major floods struck along the river in 1943, 1947, 1951, and 1952. But the six huge dams on the middle Missouri and the smaller dams on the tributaries have greatly reduced the threat of disastrous flooding. These dams make up the heart of the Missouri River Basin

Project. This program, authorized by Congress in 1944, is a flood control, electric power, and irrigation project. The program calls for construction of 137 dams and reservoirs on the Missouri and its tributaries. The entire project probably will not be completed until after the year 2000. JOHN EDWIN COFFMAN

See also MONTANA (picture: Headwaters of the Missouri River); RIVER (chart: Longest Rivers).

MIST. See FOG.

MISTLETOE, *MIHS uhl toh,* is a plant which grows as a parasite on the trunks and branches of various trees. It grows most often on apple trees, but may grow on other trees such as the lime, hawthorn, sycamore, poplar, locust, fir, and occasionally on oak.

Mistletoe is an evergreen with thickly clustered leaves. It has tiny yellow flowers which bloom in February and March. Birds eat the white, shiny fruits called berries. The berry seeds cling to the bills of birds and are scattered when birds sharpen their bills against the bark of trees. The berries may be poisonous to people.

J. Horace McFarland
American Mistletoe

Mistletoe is associated with many traditions and holidays, especially Christmas. Historians say the Druids, or ancient priests of the Celts, cut the mistletoe which grew on the sacred oak, and gave it to the people for charms. In Northern mythology, an arrow made of mistletoe killed Balder, son of the goddess Frigg. Early European peoples used mistletoe as a ceremonial plant. The custom of using mistletoe at Christmastime probably comes from this practice. In many countries, a person caught standing beneath mistletoe must forfeit a kiss.

Scientific Classification. Mistletoe belongs to the mistletoe family, *Loranthaceae.* American mistletoe is genus *Phoradendron,* species *P. flavescens.* European mistletoe is *Viscum album.* J. J. LEVISON

See also CHRISTMAS (Mistletoe); OKLAHOMA (color picture: The State Flower); PARASITE.

MISTRAL, *MIHS truhl,* is a swift, dry, cold northerly wind that blows down from the western Alps and the plateau of southern France and out over the Mediterranean. The cold heavy air from the high lands moves faster and faster as it approaches the warmer, lighter air over the sea in winter. This causes gusty, strong winds, as the cold air sinks to the level of the sea and the warm air rises above it. The mistral may cause extensive frost damage to plants. It is especially bad for the vineyards of southern France. The mistral often blows 100 days a year.

MISTRAL, FRÉDÉRIC (1830-1914), was a famous French poet who won the 1904 Nobel prize for literature. He wrote in modern Provençal, the language of southern France. Mistral led a movement of the 1800's called the *Felibrige.* This movement tried to revive the literary tradition and enrich the language of the medieval troubadours (see TROUBADOUR).

In 1859, Mistral published his masterpiece, *Mireille,* an epic describing the tragic love of a farmer's daughter

in the valley of the Rhône River. The poem's success did much to gain sympathy for the Provençal revival in literature. In addition to *Song of the Rhône* (1897) and other poems, Mistral compiled *Lou Tresor dóu Felibrige* (1878-1886), a dictionary of *langue d'oc,* the general term used for the dialects of southern France. He was born near Arles. LEROY C. BREUNIG

MISTRAL, *mees TRAHL,* **GABRIELA** (1889-1957), was the pen name of Lucila Godoy Alcayaga, a Chilean poet and educator. In 1945, she became the first Latin-American writer to win the Nobel prize for literature. A tragic love affair frustrated her hopes for love and motherhood, so she devoted herself to love of God and good causes. Her poems show compassion for the humble and the needy. Her best-known books of poetry include *Desolation* (1922), *Tenderness* (1924), *Felling of Trees* (1934), and *Winepress* (1954).

Mistral was born in Vicuña, Chile. She was a rural schoolteacher and later became a prominent educator in Chile. She served in the foreign service of Chile and at the League of Nations. Mistral later taught at Barnard College and Middlebury College in the United States. MARSHALL R. NASON

MITANNI, *mih TAWN ee,* was an ancient kingdom in northern Mesopotamia. The kingdom was located in what is now southeastern Turkey. The Mitannians used horses, and were skilled in the use of chariots in war. The neighboring Hittites learned how to use chariots in warfare from the Mitannians.

In the 1400's B.C., the Mitannians fought the Egyptians for control of Syria. But both kingdoms feared the rise of Hittite power. A Mitannian princess married into the Egyptian royal family as a sign of unity. About 1370 B.C., however, the Hittites defeated the Mitannians. Civil war further weakened them, and the kingdom was finally absorbed into the Assyrian Empire by about 1350 B.C. THOMAS W. AFRICA

MITCHEL, JOHN PURROY (1879-1918), was elected reform mayor of New York City in 1913. His election ended, for a time, control by Tammany Hall, a notorious political group. Mitchel reduced the city debt, fought dishonesty in the city's police department, and set up a relief fund and workshops for the unemployed. But many of his actions angered powerful interests, and he lost his bid for reelection in 1917.

Mitchel was born in Fordham, N.Y., and graduated from New York Law School. In 1906, as commissioner of accounts for the city, he exposed dishonest practices of two borough presidents, the fire department, and the licenses bureau. CHARLES B. FORCEY and LINDA R. FORCEY

MITCHEL AIR FORCE BASE, N.Y., served as a United States military post in all major wars from the Revolutionary War until 1961. The base lies about 25 miles (40 kilometers) east of New York City and covers 1,117 acres (452 hectares). It was named *Mitchel Field* in 1918 after Major John P. Mitchel, a World War I flier and former mayor of New York City. The first transcontinental air-mail flight took off from Mitchel Field in 1924. In 1929, famed American flier James H. Doolittle gave the first public demonstration of "blind flying" there.

MITCHELL, ARTHUR (1934-   ), was the first black American to dance with a major classical ballet com-

Martha Swope

Arthur Mitchell danced with Allegra Kent in George Balanchine's modern ballet *Agon* at the New York City Ballet, *above*.

Culver

General Billy Mitchell stands, *left*, during his court-martial. Later events proved that his air-power theories were correct.

pany. He performed with the New York City Ballet from 1955 to 1970.

Mitchell was born in New York City and attended the School of American Ballet. In 1955, he joined the New York City Ballet. His major roles included the part of Puck in *A Midsummer Night's Dream* and the *pas de deux* (dance for two persons) in *Agon*.

While with the New York City Ballet, Mitchell began to teach ballet to underprivileged children. In 1969, he formed the Dance Theatre of Harlem, a professional ballet company and dance school in the city's chief black community. Mitchell directs the company, teaches in the school, and composes dances. As a *choreographer* (composer of dances), Mitchell created such works as *Holberg Suite* (1970), *Rhythmetron* (1972), and *Manifestations* (1976).   DIANNE L. WOODRUFF

MITCHELL, BILLY (1879-1936), an Army general, became one of the most controversial figures in American military history. An early and vigorous advocate of air power, he was court-martialed for defiance of his superiors in 1925. He resigned from the Army rather than accept a five-year suspension. He was branded at first as an extremist and insurgent. But early in World War II, events confirmed many of Mitchell's predictions. In 1946, the United States Congress authorized the Medal of Honor for Mitchell.

Mitchell enlisted in the Army as a private at the start of the Spanish-American War in 1898. He remained in the Army and rose rapidly in the Signal Corps, which first controlled the development of aviation in the U.S. Army. Mitchell learned to fly in 1916, and became air adviser to General John Pershing in World War I. He was in Europe when the United States entered the war, and quickly got in touch with Allied air leaders. Major General Hugh M. Trenchard, head of the British Royal Flying Corps, greatly influenced Mitchell. Mitchell commanded several large air units in combat, including the largest concentration of Allied air power of World

War I, during the Battle of the Meuse-Argonne. He became a brigadier general by the end of the war.

After the war, Mitchell became assistant chief of the Air Service, and the leading advocate of an air force independent of the Army and the Navy. He found a natural resistance among leaders of the older services, and appealed to the public through books, magazine articles, newspaper interviews, and speeches. Because airplanes were then limited in size and range, many people thought his claims for air power were exaggerated. But he persuaded many others, especially after a 1921 experiment when he sank three former German ships—a destroyer, a cruiser, and a battleship—with aerial bombs. He repeated this success in later tests against three obsolete U.S. battleships. But Mitchell failed to achieve his goal, perhaps partly because he was frequently violent in argument and bitter in his condemnation of superiors who did not agree with him.

William Mitchell was born in Nice, France, of American parents. He wrote *Our Air Force* (1921), *Winged Defense* (1925), and *Skyways* (1930).   ALFRED GOLDBERG

MITCHELL, EDGAR DEAN (1930-   ), a United States astronaut, was the lunar module pilot on the Apollo 14 space flight. In February 1971, this flight made the third manned landing on the moon.

Mitchell was born in Hereford, Tex., on Sept. 17, 1930. He received a bachelor's degree from the Carnegie Institute of Technology (now Carnegie-Mellon University) in 1952 and from the U.S. Naval Postgraduate School in 1961. In 1964, Mitchell earned a doctor's degree in aeronautics and astronautics from the Massachusetts Institute of Technology.

Mitchell entered the U.S. Navy in 1952 and became an officer in 1953. The next year, he graduated first in his class from the Aerospace Research Pilot School. In 1964, he was assigned to the Navy Field Office of the Manned Orbiting Laboratory. In 1966, Mitchell was selected to be an astronaut. He retired from the Navy and the space program in 1972.   WILLIAM J. CROMIE

MITCHELL, JOHN (1870-1919), was president of the United Mine Workers of America from 1898 to 1908. At this time, many considered it the best-organized union in the United States. Mitchell became famous in the Pennsylvania hard coal strike of 1902. He united 150,000 immigrant miners, and won better wages and shorter hours for them. He was second in prestige to Samuel Gompers in the labor movement. Mitchell was born in Braidwood, Ill., and went to work in the mines at the age of 12. He wrote *Organized Labor* (1903).   JACK BARBASH

MITCHELL, JOHN NEWTON (1913-   ), served as attorney general of the United States from 1969 to 1972. He was one of President Richard M. Nixon's most influential advisers on both domestic and international problems. Mitchell was a central figure in the Watergate political scandal, and in 1975 he became the only attorney general ever convicted of a felony (see WATERGATE).

Mitchell resigned as attorney general in March 1972, to become director of the Committee for the Re-election of the President (CRP), a post he held for only four months. Two other CRP officials were among the seven men involved in the June 1972 burglary of Democratic Party head-quarters at the Watergate complex in Washington, D.C. In 1977, after he had been convicted of conspiracy, obstruction of justice, and perjury, Mitchell began serving a 2½- to 8-year prison term. His sentence was later reduced to 1 to 4 years, and he was paroled in 1979.

United Press Int.
John Mitchell

Mitchell was born in Detroit. He grew up in New York City and graduated from Fordham University and Fordham Law School. As a lawyer, Mitchell specialized in handling state and municipal bond issues and was considered an expert in public finance. Mitchell's New York City law firm merged with Nixon's in 1967. He served as Nixon's presidential campaign manager in 1968.   DAVID S. BRODER

MITCHELL, MARGARET (1900-1949), an American author, wrote *Gone with the Wind* (1936), one of the most popular novels of all time. It won the 1937 Pulitzer prize for fiction.

Gone with the Wind is a story of the South during the Civil War, written from the Southern point of view. The story begins just before the outbreak of the war in 1861. It describes the impact of the conflict on the South and ends during the postwar Reconstruction period. The main characters—the Southern belle Scarlett O'Hara and the dashing Rhett Butler—rank among the best-known figures in American fiction. The motion picture *Gone with the Wind* (1939) became one of the most popular films ever made (see MOTION PICTURE [picture]).

Mitchell was born in Atlanta, Ga., where much of the action of *Gone with the Wind* takes place. She wrote the book during a 10-year period. *Margaret Mitchell's "Gone with the Wind" Letters: 1936-1949* was published in 1976.   JOHN B. VICKERY

MITCHELL, MARIA (1818-1889), an American astronomer, became known for her studies of sunspots and of satellites of planets. She discovered a new comet in 1847. Although she was largely self-educated, she served as professor of astronomy at Vassar College from 1865 to 1888. She was elected to membership in several learned societies. In 1848, she became the first woman

member of the American Academy of Arts and Sciences. She later became a fellow of the society. She was elected to the Hall of Fame in 1905. Mitchell was born in Nantucket, Mass.   HELEN E. MARSHALL

MITCHELL, MOUNT. See MOUNT MITCHELL.

MITCHELL, WESLEY CLAIR (1874-1948), an American economist, devoted his life to a study of business cycles. He pioneered a new approach to the study of economics, insisting that economic theories should be based on detailed statistics rather than on general ideas or a few observations. He measured changes in prices, production, and other factors during periods of prosperity, crisis, depression, and revival. Mitchell believed that ups and downs in business activity occur in regular cycles in a modern, free enterprise economy.

Mitchell was born in Rushville, Ill. He taught economics at the University of California from 1902 to 1912 and at Columbia University from 1913 to 1944. Mitchell was a founder of the National Bureau of Economic Research and served as its director from 1920 to 1945. Mitchell's books include *Business Cycles: The Problem and Its Setting* (1927), and *The Backward Art of Spending Money* (1937).   DANIEL R. FUSFELD

MITE is the common name for small ticks. Scientists do not separate mites and ticks on the basis of structure, but most people call the smallest species mites and the larger ones ticks. These creatures are not insects, but are related to spiders and scorpions.

Some mites live on land, while others live in water. Some are too small to be seen easily with the naked eye and must be studied under a microscope. The male usually has a saclike body with a slight dividing line between its abdomen and thorax, and has four pairs of legs. The mouth has piercing and grasping organs. The digestive system begins in the sucking beak. The young larvae of most species hatch from eggs and have six legs. They shed their skins and change into nymphs with eight legs. After one or more other moltings, the nymphs change into adults.

More than half the different kinds of mites live at least part of their lives as parasites. They suck the blood of animals or the juice from plants, and eat cell tissues as well. Other mites eat feathers, cheese, flour, cereal, drugs, and other stored products. Several kinds of mites burrow into the skin of man and other mammals, espe-

P. S. Tice
Mites Annoy Man, Most Animals, and Some Plants.

cially horses, cattle, and sheep. They cause the skin to break out and itch, forming scabs and mange. The troublesome *chiggers*, or *red bugs*, which torment people in the woods are mites. Another kind which attacks man is a long wormlike mite which burrows into the hair follicles and the oil glands. All these mites except the last can be killed by sulfur preparations.

Several kinds of mites attack poultry. The best-known is the common *chicken mite*, which, like the bedbug, sucks the blood of its victims at night and hides in cracks during the day. Kerosene will kill it.

Sometimes a mite called the *red spider* destroys greenhouse plants. The *peartree blister mite* damages fruit trees. *Gall mites* form small lumps on leaves and twigs. Unlike other mites, they have only two pairs of legs. *Clover mites* attack plants and fruit trees. In the South, they spend the winter on clover plants. Other mites attack bulbs and roots of plants. A few species prey on plant lice, or aphids, and others on insects and grasshopper eggs, but the majority of mites do not help people.

Scientific Classification. Mites belong to the order *Acarina*. The itch mite of human beings is genus *Sarcoptes*, species *S. scabiei*. The skin mite of horses and cattle is *Psoroptes communis*. The chicken mite is *Dermanyssus gallinae*. The red spider is *Tetranychus bimaculatus*, or some closely related species.   EDWARD A. CHAPIN

See also CHIGGER; MANGE; PARASITE; TICK.

MITHRAS, *MITH ras*, was a god of the ancient Persians and the Aryans of India. The Aryans made him one of their 12 high gods. In the Zoroastrian religion of ancient Persia, he was an angel of light who fought on the side of the god Ahura Mazda against the forces of evil (see ZOROASTRIANISM). The Zoroastrian scriptures called Mithras "the Heavenly Light."

The Persians carried their belief in Mithras to Assyria and Asia Minor, where many people identified him with the sun. Mithraism took on the form of a mystery religion, with elaborate rites and ceremonies. It came into the ancient Roman world about 75 B.C., and ranked as a principal competitor of Christianity for 200 years.   CLIFTON E. OLMSTEAD

MITHRIDATES VI, *MITH rih DAY teez* (120?-63 B.C.), was king of Pontus, an area in what is now Turkey. One of Rome's most dangerous enemies, Mithridates opposed Roman expansion into Asia Minor.

He fought three wars against Rome. When Rome's Italian allies in central and southern Italy revolted in 90 B.C., Mithridates drove the Romans from Asia. He ordered every Roman citizen in Asia Minor killed—an estimated 80,000 were put to death.

When Rome attacked Mithridates' allies in Greece, he sent two armies there. But Sulla, a Roman general, defeated them, and Mithridates had to make peace in 84 B.C. The greatest war broke out in 75 B.C. when Rome took over Bithynia, a region adjoining Pontus. The Roman general Pompey drove Mithridates out of Asia Minor. Mithridates planned to continue the war from the Crimea in what is now southern Russia. But his son, Pharnaces, rebelled against him. Mithridates had himself killed by a bodyguard.   HENRY C. BOREN

See also PONTUS; SULLA, LUCIUS CORNELIUS.

MITNAGGEDIM. See HASIDISM.

MITOSIS. See CELL (Cell Division; illustration).

MITRAL VALVE. See HEART (Parts of the Heart).
MITRE, BARTOLOMÉ. See ARGENTINA (History).
MITROPOULOS, *mih TRAHP uh luhs*, **DIMITRI** (1896-1960), was a symphony orchestra and opera conductor. He became known for his performances of music by composers of the 1900's.

Mitropoulos was born in Athens, Greece. He received the most important part of his music education in Berlin as a student of Ferruccio Busoni, an Italian composer and pianist. After building a European reputation as a conductor, Mitropoulos made his United States debut in 1936 with the Boston Symphony Orchestra. From 1937 to 1949, he was chief conductor of the Minneapolis Symphony Orchestra. He became a U.S. citizen in 1946. In 1949, Mitropoulos became principal conductor of the New York Philharmonic Orchestra, a position he held until 1958. From 1954 until his death, he was also a conductor at the Metropolitan Opera. ROBERT C. MARSH

MITSCHER, *MICH er*, **MARC ANDREW** (1887-1947), an American naval officer, commanded the famous Task Force 58 in the South Pacific during World War II. From January to October, 1944, his force of aircraft carriers, battleships, cruisers, and destroyers sank or damaged 795 Japanese ships and destroyed 4,425 enemy planes.

Mitscher took command of the aircraft carrier *Hornet* in October, 1941. James Doolittle's bombers made the first air raid of the war on Japan from the decks of the *Hornet* on April 18, 1942. Several weeks later, Mitscher played an important role in the U.S. victory at the Battle of Midway. For several months during 1943, he commanded all air forces in the Solomon Islands.

Mitscher was born in Hillsboro, Wis. He graduated from the U.S. Naval Academy in 1910, and was one of the first U.S. Navy officers to adopt aviation as a career. He became a vice-admiral in 1944. After World War II, he became deputy chief of naval operations for air. He became an admiral in 1946 and took command of the Eighth Fleet.   DONALD W. MITCHELL

MIX, TOM (1880-1940), became one of America's most famous motion-picture cowboys. He entered the movies in 1910. His expert horsemanship and easygoing manner made him a star. He appeared in such Western motion pictures as *Riders of the Purple Sage*. Mix and his horse, Tony, were given a reception by the Lord Mayor of London in 1925.

Mix was born in Driftwood, Pa. He fought in the Spanish-American War at the age of 18, and in China during the Boxer Rebellion (1900). NARDI REEDER CAMPION

Culver

Tom Mix

MIXED NUMBERS are numbers made up of a whole number and a fraction. Thus, $6\frac{1}{2}$ years and $2\frac{1}{4}$ feet are mixed numbers. They must be reduced to their simplest forms for any calculation. See also FRACTION.

MIXTURE, in chemistry. See COMPOUND.

MIZAR. See BIG AND LITTLE DIPPERS.

MNEMONICS. See MEMORY (Improving the Memory).

MNEMOSYNE. See MUSES.

MOA, *MOH uh,* is any one of about 20 *species* (kinds) of extinct birds that once lived in New Zealand. Moas ranged in size from those as big as a large turkey to some that were 10 feet (3 meters) tall. Moas could not fly. They had small heads, long necks, stout legs, and no wings. They ate green plants and roots.

Moas existed until the 1600's, and one small kind may have survived until the mid-1800's. Maoris, the Polynesians who settled in New Zealand about 600 years ago, hunted moas for food. They may have been responsible for wiping out the bird.

Scientific Classification. Moas belong to the moa order, *Dinornithiformes,* and to the families *Dinornithidae* and *Anomalopteryginae.*   R. A. PAYNTER, JR.

MOABITE, *MO ub ite.* The Moabites lived in the land of Moab from the 1200's to the 500's B.C. The region of Moab lay east of the lower Jordan River and the Dead Sea. The Moabites were Semites, related to the Hebrews. The Moabites often fought against the Israelites, who lived to the west and to the north, and against the Edomites, who lived to the south.

MOABITE STONE. This ancient stone bears some of the earliest writing in Hebrew-Phoenician characters. The stone is of black basalt. It is about 3 feet 8 inches (112 centimeters) high and 2 feet 3 inches (68 centimeters) wide. F. A. Klein, a missionary, found it in 1868 at Diban, in ancient Moab. The writing on it was probably carved by a Moabite scribe sometime in the 800's B.C. It is a good example of the Hebrew-Phoenician characters used at the time.

When the French tried to buy the stone in Constantinople, the Arabs there became greedy. The Arabs broke the priceless, irreplaceable stone into many parts, hoping to get more money by selling the pieces. The French collected the larger pieces. An official of the French Embassy in Constantinople had also made a paper impression of the stone before it was broken.

The 34-line inscription tells of the deeds of Mesha, King of the Moabites, in his wars against the kings of Israel and against the Edomites. For a description of part of this conflict from the point of view of the people of Israel, see II Kings 3:4-27. The restored stone is in the Louvre, in Paris.   JOSEPH WARD SWAIN

MOAT. See CASTLE; ZOO.

MOBILE, *MOH beel,* is a contemporary type of sculpture. It is distinctive from other types of sculpture in that it achieves expression or meaning through movement. Traditional sculpture achieves its expression through the arrangement of solid forms. Mobiles are usually frail constructions of many rod-like projections loosely joined together. They are delicately balanced so they can swing freely in an infinite variety of moving arcs. The rods may end in *finials* (ending shapes) that recall the erosion effects of wind or water, or imaginative flight forms in space. Sculptors use many colors, textures, and materials for mobiles.

Most mobiles are suspended from above, so they can move freely overhead. Some are pivoted on a base. They are planned to present artistic interest not only in their actual shape, but also in the moving shadows they cast on walls and floor. Mobiles usually move as the result of natural currents of air, or the vibration of the earth. A few are designed for mechanical power.

A mobile's movement is of greater aesthetic value than its actual shape. The constantly swinging projections

The Moa was a large bird that looked somewhat like an ostrich. It lived in New Zealand, and was killed for food.

Amer. Mus. of Natural History

The Oriental Institute, The University of Chicago

The Moabite Stone bears a historical inscription which was carved with Hebrew-Phoenician writing in the 800's B.C.

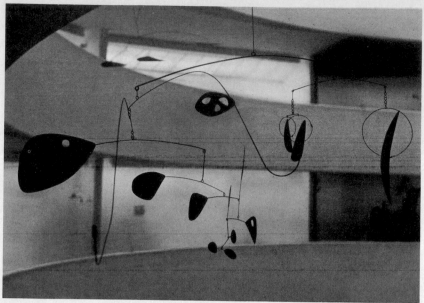

A Mobile is a type of sculpture that moves. Most mobiles consist of metal shapes suspended from wires attached to rods. The pieces may move through the action of air currents, or the sculptor may add a motor to move the mobile mechanically.

Mobile by Alexander Calder; the Solomon R. Guggenheim Museum, New York City

How To Make a Mobile

WORLD BOOK diagram

A Simple Mobile can be made by using pliers, two curved wires, and three birds cut out of cardboard.

To Begin the Mobile, attach a bird to each end of one wire. Tie a string to the wire and find the balance point.

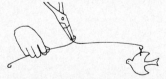

Form a Loop at the balance point by carefully twisting the wire with a pair of long-nosed pliers.

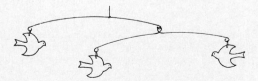

To Complete the Mobile, attach the remaining bird to one end of the second wire and the other end to the loop.

form arcs that cut shapes or volumes out of space. These volumes have no weight or substance, but they do remain fixed in our memory. The real design of a mobile is in this variety of space shapes, and in their abstract relationships with one another. Artists of many times and many places have created things that depend on movement for some part of their expression. But an American sculptor, Alexander Calder, was the first to create the true mobile, in which movement is the basic aesthetic purpose. Calder is regarded as the foremost creator of mobiles.

Wide acceptance of this new art form is obviously based on two significant facts. First, our art concepts have quite naturally grown to include the beauty of the machine in motion. Second, our minds have been freed to think and feel in terms of volumes of space that our eyes cannot see. BERNARD FRAZIER

See also CALDER, ALEXANDER; SCULPTURE (Form and Treatment; picture: *Red Petals*).

MOBILE, *moh BEEL* (pop. 190,026; met. area pop. 376,690), is Alabama's second largest city and its only seaport. Among Alabama cities, only Birmingham is larger. Mobile ranks as one of the busiest U.S. ports. It lies on the Mobile River where the river flows into Mobile Bay, 31 miles (50 kilometers) north of the Gulf of Mexico (see ALABAMA [political map]).

Mobile is one of the nation's oldest cities. A French-Canadian explorer founded it in 1702 as Fort Louis de la Mobile. He named the fort after the nearby Mabila Indians, who belonged to the Choctaw tribe. Mobile is called the *City of Six Flags* because six governments have controlled it. France, Great Britain, and Spain ruled during the 1700's. Then the United States, the Republic of Alabama, the Confederate States of America, and again the United States flew their flags there.

The City extends west of the Mobile River and covers 167 square miles (433 square kilometers). It is the seat of Mobile County. The Mobile metropolitan area spreads over all of Baldwin and Mobile counties, 2,947 square miles (7,633 square kilometers).

568

Mobile, a chief U.S. port, lies on the Mobile River. The 34-story First National Bank Building, *background,* towers over downtown Mobile. The Municipal Auditorium and Theater stands in the foreground.

The 34-story First National Bank Building is the tallest structure in downtown Mobile. The Municipal Auditorium and Theater occupies 12 acres (5 hectares) in the center of the city. The Brookley Aerospace and Industrial Complex in southeast Mobile is a former Air Force Base.

About 99 per cent of Mobile's people were born in the United States. Approximately a third are blacks. Baptists form the city's largest religious group, followed by Roman Catholics, Methodists, Episcopalians, and Presbyterians.

Mobile's public schools belong to the Mobile County school system, the largest school system in Alabama. The system has about 50 elementary schools, 15 junior high schools, and 15 senior high schools, with a total enrollment of 65,000 students. There are also many private and parochial schools in the city. Mobile is the home of Mobile College, Spring Hill College, and the University of South Alabama.

Mobile has 3 TV stations, 12 radio stations, and 2 daily newspapers—the *Press* and the *Register.* The Mobile Public Library has 10 branches.

Mobile sponsors a symphony orchestra and a small opera company. The Municipal Auditorium and Theater presents such events as the national Junior Miss Pageant, ballet, basketball games, circuses, and horse shows. The city celebrates Mardi Gras each year (see MARDI GRAS). The Historic Mobile Preservation Society and other groups maintain several homes as they were in the 1800's. Bellingrath Gardens, south of the city, displays flowers, shrubs, and trees from throughout the South. The battleship U.S.S. *Alabama,* which fought in World War II (1939-1945), is on exhibit in Mobile Bay. Several streets in Mobile and its suburbs form the 35-mile (56-kilometer) Azalea Trail, where thousands of azalea plants bloom every spring.

Economy of Mobile is based on manufacturing, state and federal government operations, and shipping. The city has about 200 factories. Its largest industry produces paper and wood pulp used for paper. Other products include aluminum, bakery goods, batteries, cement, chemicals, clothing, furniture, naval supplies, paint, rayon, refined oil, and seafood. The major government employers are Mobile General Hospital, the U.S. Corps of Engineers, and the U.S. Coast Guard.

Shipping activities in Mobile include shipbuilding and ship repairing. The Alabama State Docks, located in Mobile, can service more than 30 ships at a time. The Port of Mobile handles about 35 million short tons (32 million metric tons) of cargo annually.

Four railroads and 55 trucking companies provide freight service to Mobile. No railroad passenger trains stop there, but 4 bus lines and about 100 steamship firms serve the city. Three major airlines use Bates International Airport just outside Mobile. The Bankhead Tunnel, the first underwater tunnel in the South, carries automobile traffic under the Mobile River. Workers finished building the tunnel in 1940.

Government. Mobile has a commission form of government. Every four years, the voters elect a three-member commission made up of commissioners for finance, public safety, and public works. Each serves a 16-month term as mayor. Mobile gets most of its income from taxes on licenses, property, and sales.

History. Jean Baptiste Le Moyne, Sieur de Bienville, a French-Canadian explorer, founded Fort Louis de la Mobile in 1702. He established the fort as a trading post and a French outpost to control nearby Indians. In 1711, river floods forced the colony to move 27 miles (43 kilometers) south to the present site of Mobile.

France gave Mobile to Great Britain in 1763 after the French and Indian War (1754-1763). Spain captured Mobile in 1780, and the United States seized it in 1813. Mobile was incorporated as a city in 1819.

Mobile became an important seaport during the early 1800's as cotton production flourished in the South. Before the Civil War (1861-1865), Mobile was a cultural center. The Battle of Mobile Bay, won by Union forces under Rear Admiral David G. Farragut, closed Mobile's port in August, 1864. The city fell nine months later and was the last Southern stronghold to surrender.

The Civil War crippled cotton production in the South, and Mobile suffered economically. Exports of lumber and naval supplies and imports of general cargo gradually strengthened the city's economy. By the beginning of World War I (1914-1918), Mobile was again a thriving seaport. Between World War I and World War II, Mobile became a shipbuilding and railroad center. Construction of an Army Air Forces supply base in Mobile during World War II, and an expanding paper industry after the war, boosted the city to its greatest period of growth. Mobile's population increased from 78,720 in 1940 to 202,779 in 1960.

Mobile's economy suffered again during the 1960's, when the federal government gradually closed Brookley Air Force Base in the city. In 1964, Mobile began Task Force 200, a plan to encourage industrial development in the city. As part of the project, Mobile purchased the abandoned military base in 1969 and created the Brookley Aerospace and Industrial Complex. The city leases buildings and land in the complex to industry. From 1964 to 1969, Task Force 200 expanded Mobile's industrial employment by more than 16,000 jobs.

As in other cities both North and South, public school integration was a major problem in Mobile during the 1960's. Federal court orders forced Mobile to integrate some of its schools beginning in 1963. As the result of a 1968 ruling by a U.S. Court of Appeals, the city established widespread school integration in 1970. Many whites then set up private schools for their children.

Mobile rebuilt much of its downtown area during the 1960's. Housing projects and office buildings replaced hundreds of old structures. Wrecking crews cleared other areas to make way for an interstate highway system. Two more automobile tunnels under the Mobile River opened in 1975.   MAURICE WILSON CASTLE, JR.

See also ALABAMA (pictures; Climate; History); BIENVILLE, SIEUR DE; IBERVILLE, SIEUR D'.

MOBILE BAY, BATTLE OF. See CIVIL WAR (Mobile Bay).

MOBILE HOME is a type of movable house designed for year-around living. A mobile home has wheels and can be moved from one location to another by towing it with a small truck. Most mobile homes stand on concrete pads or permanent foundations in mobile home communities where their owners live. The mobile home is jacked up and placed on blocks or posts to keep the wheels off the concrete. A decorative wall around the bottom of the home gives it an attractive appearance. In these communities, the mobile homes are connected to electricity, gas, and water facilities.

Mobile homes range in size from about 29 to 70 feet (9 to 21 meters) long and about 8 to 14 feet (2.4 to 4.3 meters) wide. They have a living room, kitchen, one or more bedrooms and bathrooms, and closets and cabinets. All mobile homes are sold fully equipped with carpeting, draperies, furniture, kitchen appliances, lamps, and an electric, gas, or oil furnace. The owner can add such features as air conditioning, an automatic dishwasher, and a garbage disposal unit.

In the United States, more than 5 million persons live in mobile homes. A mobile home costs less than a regular home, and it needs few repairs. Its main disadvantage is its limited space. The space can be increased with a *doublewide* mobile home. This design consists of two mobile homes, each with a sidewall removed, fastened together at the parking site. The units can easily be separated and towed to a new location if the owner wants to move.   JOHN M. SCHEER

See also MOTOR HOME; TRAILER.

MOBILE RIVER is a short stream in southwestern Alabama. It offers transportation for cotton and other farm products of its valley. The Mobile was named for the Mobile, or Mabila, Indians who once lived along its banks. The Mobile River is formed where the Alabama and Tombigbee rivers meet in Clarke County. The Mobile flows southward for 38 miles (61 kilometers) before it empties into the Gulf of Mexico through Mobile Bay (see ALABAMA [physical map]). The port of Mobile lies at the river's mouth.   WALLACE E. AKIN

MÖBIUS, AUGUST FERDINAND. See MATHEMATICS (A Strange Twist).

MOBUTU SESE SEKO (1930-   ) became president of Congo (Kinshasa)—now Zaire—in 1965, after seizing control of the government. Mobutu had taken power in the country once before, in 1960.

Joseph Désiré Mobutu was born in a small village in what was then the colony called the Belgian Congo. He studied in Belgium and served in the colonial army. Trouble broke out among Congolese groups when the

James Annan

Mobile Homes are designed for comfortable year-around living. A typical community of mobile homes provides residents with such necessary facilities as electricity and water.

colony gained independence in 1960, and it threatened to destroy the nation. Mobutu headed a military government that restored order. He ruled for five months, and seized power again when trouble broke out in 1965. He adopted the African name Mobutu Sese Seko in 1972, shortly before the government ordered all Zairians to use African names.

MOBY DICK. See MELVILLE, HERMAN.

MOCCASIN, *MAHK uh suhn*, is an Algonkian Indian word for the slipperlike footwear worn by several tribes. Moccasins are made of animal skin, and may be decorated with beads or porcupine quills. They are soft, closely fitted, and have no heels. They may be ankle-length or extend to the hip. Hair is left on the skin of winter moccasins to serve as a lining. See also INDIAN, AMERICAN (picture: Woodland Indians).   LYNN FARNOL

MOCCASIN FLOWER. See LADY'S-SLIPPER.

MOCCASIN SNAKE. See WATER MOCCASIN.

MOCK ORANGE, sometimes called *syringa*, is a bush covered with clusters of small, single or double, white or creamy flowers. The flowers of some kinds of mock orange have purple spots at the base of their petals. In most plants, the flowers are fragrant, but some are odorless. Some types of mock orange have leaves with toothed edges. The bush generally does not grow very high, but some species reach 20 feet (6 meters).

Gardeners in the United States and Mexico grow many different kinds of mock orange. A few kinds also grow in Asia and Europe. Almost all types of this hardy plant bloom in June. Breeders have produced many hybrids of mock orange. The syringa is the state flower of Idaho (see IDAHO [color picture]).

Scientific Classification. Mock oranges belong to the saxifrage family, *Saxifragaceae*. They make up the genus *Philadelphus*.   J. J. LEVISON

MOCK-UP. See AIRPLANE (Design and Testing).

MOCKINGBIRD is an American bird famous for its ability to imitate the sounds of other birds. One naturalist reported a mockingbird in South Carolina that imitated the songs of 32 different kinds of birds in 10 minutes. The mockingbird's own song is one of the most versatile of all bird songs.

Mockingbirds live only in North, Central, and South America. In the United States, most mockingbirds live in the Southern States. However, some mockingbirds range as far north as Massachusetts and Michigan.

The bird has an ashy-white breast and an ash-gray coat. Its wings and tail are darker gray with white markings. Males and females have almost the same coloring, but the female has a little less white. The mockingbird grows from 9 to 11 inches (23 to 28 centimeters) long. It has a long slender body and tail.

The birds build their nests in thickets, low trees, and bushes. They lay from four to six pale greenish-blue or bluish-white eggs spotted with brown. Mockingbirds help people by eating insects and weed seeds. They often pick insects off the radiators of parked cars. This represents a recent change in food habits. They also eat wild fruits, and sometimes damage fruit crops.

Scientific Classification. The mockingbird belongs to the mockingbird family, *Mimidae*. It is classified as genus *Mimus*, species *M. polyglottos*.   GEORGE J. WALLACE

MODE, in grammar. See MOOD.

MODE, in mathematics, is that value in any group that occurs most frequently. Suppose a boy counts the eggs in 77 birds' nests. He finds that four nests have one egg each, 65 have two eggs each, five have three eggs, and three have four eggs. The nests that contain two eggs are by far the most common. Therefore, two is the *mode*, or *modal value*, in this group of numbers. The mode is a type of *average* that is often useful in the study of statistics. See also AVERAGE; MEAN; MEDIAN; STATISTICS (illustration).   ALBERT E. WAUGH

MODEL AIRPLANE. See AIRPLANE, MODEL.

MODEL AUTOMOBILE. See AUTOMOBILE, MODEL.

MODEL MAKING is one of the oldest crafts. In museums, we can see small models of boats, household articles, and tools made by ancient peoples more than 6,000 years ago. Today, many people make models as a hobby or a profession.

There are two kinds of models: copies and original forms. Making small-scale *copies* of such things as boats or airplanes is a fascinating and sometimes profitable hobby. These models require skill if they are carried out

Fred Stone

An Architect's Scale Model shows how this honeycomb-designed building will actually look when it is constructed.

Hal H. Harrison from Grant Heilman

A Mockingbird feeds its young insects and seeds. Mockingbirds can imitate the songs of many kinds of birds.

in great detail. But simple models can be made by almost anyone. Even small children can make models of houses and furniture from heavy paper, cardboard, or balsa wood. They can also use clay or *Plasticine*, an artificial modeling material.

Professional model makers are usually employed to make *original forms*, which show how something will work or look before it is actually made. Models of large objects, like buildings or bridges, are made to a small scale. Models of smaller articles, such as electric toasters, are usually made full size. Models of very small things, like coins, are made much larger than actual size. Model makers often use materials that are different from those used in the final structure or product. They may, for instance, paint wood in order to make it look like metal or use clear plastic instead of glass.

Architects use small-scale models of buildings to demonstrate their plans. Engineers construct models of dams, bridges, and other structures to exact scale, out of the materials they intend to use for the actual projects. Then they test the models and correct faults that may appear in their designs. Aviation engineers test small airplane models in wind tunnels, and shipbuilders try out miniature ships in specially constructed basins. Inventors use models to demonstrate ideas they wish to patent. Industrial designers and manufacturers make models of products ranging from fountain pens to steam shovels, before ordering the expensive tools necessary to produce them. RALPH R. KNOBLAUGH

MODEL PARLIAMENT was the parliament that met at Westminster in 1295. It is considered representative of early assemblies from which today's parliament gradually emerged. When Edward I of England ordered parliament to meet, he summoned not only churchmen and nobles, but also two knights elected from each county and two townsmen from each of many towns. Historians of the 1800's believed that the parliament of 1295 served as a model. But research indicates that knights and townsmen had been summoned before 1295, and some later parliaments included only nobles and churchmen. See also PARLIAMENT. BASIL D. HENNING

MODEL RAILROAD. See RAILROAD, MODEL.

MODEL ROCKET. See ROCKET, MODEL.

MODEL SHIP. See SHIP, MODEL.

MODEL T. See FORD (Henry Ford; picture).

MODELING. See SCULPTURE (The Sculptor at Work).

MODELING is a profession in which people display clothing and other products or illustrate various situations. Models of all ages—women, men, boys, and girls —pose for photographers and painters and work in fashion shows and various exhibits.

Kinds of Models. Different kinds of models specialize in a variety of assignments, but any model may work in more than one field. *Fashion models*, wearing the latest styles of clothing and accessories, pose for photographs that appear in magazines, newspapers, and catalogs. These models also display clothes in stores and fashion shows. *Commercial models* help sell many kinds of products in stores and wholesale showrooms and at exhibits and trade shows. They also appear in advertisements and television commercials.

Many publications hire *illustration models* to appear in pictures that accompany articles and stories. *Artist's*

models pose for art classes and individual artists. Clothing designers and patternmakers employ *fitter's models* for fitting clothes in every size in which the garments will be produced.

Physical Requirements for Modeling. A model's basic requirement is physical attractiveness. A woman need not be beautiful, nor a man handsome, to be a model. But a model must be attractive according to the ideal of the time. He or she also should be well groomed and graceful. A youthful appearance is necessary for most modeling, especially fashion modeling.

Size is vital in fashion work. Most fashion models are young women who wear a size 8 or 10 dress. A female model should be at least 5 feet 6 inches (168 centimeters) tall to display clothes to their best advantage. Most male models wear a size 40-regular suit and are at least 6 feet (183 centimeters) tall. A fitter's model must have the exact dimensions required for a standard size. Height is not as important for illustration models. Models who specialize in exhibiting such items as jewelry or shoes must have well-proportioned hands, legs, and feet.

A Model's Work. Modeling may seem glamorous and exciting, but it is difficult, demanding work. Models sometimes work for long periods under hot, bright lights. Advertisers plan ads far in advance, and so models may be required to pose in bathing suits in winter and in heavy coats during the summer.

A model must be able to follow directions. He or she also must have some acting ability in order to portray any mood desired by a client.

A model who is photographed earns an hourly fee for his or her time. For a fashion show, a model may work for a specific fee rather than at an hourly rate. Artist's models charge lower fees because artists operate on

David Puffer Photography and Sears-Men's Store (WORLD BOOK photo)

Models pose for a photographer, who positions them for a fashion advertisement. Although modeling may seem to be a glamorous occupation, it requires hard, tiring work and long hours.

smaller budgets and their work requires more time. The fees of models who perform in TV commercials are determined by contracts with the television and motion-picture actors' unions.

Models are photographed at a photographer's studio. Photographs also may be taken *on location* in other buildings, outdoors, or in another city or country.

Model Agencies represent models in dealing with clients. An agency accepts assignments for a model, sends bills to clients, and collects money owed the model. The agency receives a percentage of the model's earnings as a commission. Most successful models are registered with a licensed model agency.

A client arranges with an agency to hire a model for a certain length of time on a particular day. This arrangement is called a *booking*. The booking may be for appearing in a fashion show, making a TV commercial, or posing for a photographer or artist.

Careers. Modeling is a highly competitive field, and most models have only a short career because a youthful appearance is so important. A female model's career lasts an average of only one to three years.

Employers prefer models who have had training or actual experience in the field. A man or woman who wants to become a model can attend modeling and self-improvement classes. These classes teach poise, grooming, the use of makeup, and the selection of attractive clothing and accessories. Courses in dance, drama, and speech are also useful.

Most models are selected for a particular assignment on the basis of their *portfolio*. A model's portfolio consists of a series of photographs that show him or her in a variety of poses with different facial expressions. Female models also pose wearing a variety of hairstyles. After completing a job, a model may add the photographs from that assignment to the portfolio. Models also give potential clients a short series of photos called a *composite*. A composite includes a model's height and other physical characteristics and the name of the agency to contact.

In the United States, most modeling activity takes place in Atlanta, Chicago, Dallas, Los Angeles, and New York City. New York City is the center of most national advertising, and professional models find their best opportunities there. Some modeling jobs are available in certain small cities, but most of the assignments outside large metropolitan areas involve only part-time work.

Some successful models become identified with a single company or product. A few gain fame as celebrities and personally endorse certain products. Many people have used a modeling career as a stepping stone to some other interesting professions. These former models are employed in such fields as advertising, fashion merchandising, public relations, publishing, and retail buying. Models who make TV commercials gain experience that can be helpful for an acting or executive career in television or another field of entertainment.   RUTH TOLMAN

MODELMAKING. See MODEL MAKING.

MODERATE REPUBLICAN. See RECONSTRUCTION (The Radicals and The Moderates).

MODERATO. See MUSIC (Terms).

MODERATOR. See NUCLEAR ENERGY (How Nuclear Energy Is Produced); NUCLEAR REACTOR (The Core).

MODERN DANCE. See DANCING (Modern Dance; picture: A Performance of the Modern Dance *Imago*).

MODERNISM. See SPANISH LITERATURE (The 1900's [Poetry]); LATIN-AMERICAN LITERATURE (Modernism).

MODIGLIANI, *moh dee LYAH nee,* **AMEDEO** (1884-1920), was one of the greatest Italian artists of the 1900's. Nearly all his paintings and drawings are of a single figure—either a portrait or a reclining female nude. Modigliani's style emphasizes elongated bodies, long necks, and oval heads. Most of his subjects seem almost expressionless, but they suggest innocence and a hint of tragedy. His painting *Gypsy Woman with Baby* is reproduced in the PAINTING article.

Modigliani was a brilliant draftsman, and his creative

An oil portrait of Jean Cocteau (1917); Henry Pearlman collection, New York City

A Typical Modigliani Portrait shows a single figure with a long neck and little expression posed against a simple background.

use of lines is a major part of his style. His distorted figures reflect his interest in black African sculpture. His simple but elegant forms show the influence of his friend, the sculptor Constantin Brancusi (see BRANCUSI, CONSTANTIN).

Modigliani was born in Leghorn, Italy. He settled in Paris in 1906 and did most of his work there. He was a colorful and restless man who lived and died in extreme poverty. Overuse of alcohol and drugs helped cause his early death.   GREGORY BATTCOCK

MODOC INDIANS. See CAPTAIN JACK.

MODRED, SIR. See ARTHUR, KING; ROUND TABLE.

MOFFAT TUNNEL is one of the longest railroad tunnels in the world. It cuts through James Peak in Colorado for 6.23 miles (10.03 kilometers).

Moffat Tunnel has two separate *bores* (tubes). The

largest, 24 by 16 feet (7 by 5 meters), is used for trains. The other bore, 8 by 8 feet (2.4 by 2.4 meters), carries water from the Fraser River to Denver. Engineers bored through rock from each side of the Continental Divide, at an elevation of 9,200 feet (2,800 meters). The tunnel shortened the distance between Salt Lake City and Denver by 176 miles (283 kilometers). By using the tunnel, trains avoid snowstorms, snowslides, and steep grades. The tunnel was named for David H. Moffat, American banker and railroad builder. It was leased to the Denver & Salt Lake Railroad.   ARCHIBALD BLACK

See also COLORADO (color map: Historic Colorado).

MOGADISCIO, *MAHG uh DIHSH ee OH* (pop. 444,-882), is the capital and chief port of Somalia. For location, see SOMALIA (map). The city was once the capital of the Italian trusteeship of Somaliland. Most of its people are Africans, but some are Italians. See also SOMALIA (picture).

MOGOLLON is the name of prehistoric Indians who lived in southeastern Arizona and southwestern New Mexico from about 500 B.C. to A.D. 1200. Scientists believe they disappeared about A.D. 1250. They may have resembled present-day Zuñi and Hopi Indians. The early Mogollon lived in villages of pit-houses. Later, they built crude one-story pueblo villages. The Indians gathered wild berries and seeds and later hunted and farmed corn. They used crude stone tools. The Mogollon made tobacco pipes of stone or baked clay. They decorated their pottery with figures and geometric designs in red and brown or black and white.

MOGUL EMPIRE, or MUGHAL EMPIRE, ruled most of India in the 1500's and 1600's. Life in Mogul India set a standard of magnificence for its region of Asia, and the empire had peace, order, and stability. The centralized government of the empire provided a model for later rulers of India. A distinctive culture developed that blended Middle Eastern and Indian elements, and the Persian language became widely used.

Babar, a prince from what is now Afghanistan, founded the Mogul Empire in 1526. His grandson Akbar established its governmental structure. Akbar, who ruled from 1556 to 1605, controlled north and central India and Afghanistan. Jahangir, Akbar's son, ruled from 1605 to 1627 and was a patron of painting. His son Shah Jahan reigned from 1627 to 1658, during the height of the Mogul period. He encouraged architecture and built the famous Taj Mahal as a tomb for his wife. Shah Jahan's son Aurangzeb took the throne from his father in 1658 and imprisoned Shah Jahan.

The Mogul emperors were Muslims who ruled a largely Hindu nation. Under Akbar, Hindu warriors served as Mogul generals and governors, and other Hindus were administrators and clerks. Aurangzeb was not so tolerant of other religions. He imposed a tax on the Hindus and destroyed many of their temples. The Mahrattas, a Hindu warrior people of Central India, revolted and seriously weakened the empire.

The Mogul Empire began to break up shortly after Aurangzeb's death in 1707. Moguls continued to rule a small kingdom at Delhi until Great Britain took control of India in the 1800's.   J. F. RICHARDS

See also AKBAR; AURANGZEB; BABAR; INDIA (The Mogul Empire); SHAH JAHAN.

MOHAIR is the name given to the hair of the Angora goat. This animal is native to Asia Minor and also is raised in South Africa, California, and Texas. The name *mohair* is also applied to the lustrous, long-wearing fabrics which are produced from the hair of the Angora goat.

Mohair is smooth and resilient. It can be dyed to give brilliant permanent colors to decorative fabrics used to make draperies and clothing. Mohair is also used to make fabrics that must withstand rough wear, such as furniture upholstery. Mohair is sometimes incorrectly called alpaca, a fleece which is made from the hair of the alpaca (see ALPACA).   ERNEST R. KASWELL

See also GOAT (picture: Angora Goats).

MOHAMMAD. See MUHAMMAD.

MOHAMMAD REZA PAHLAVI, *moh ham AD reh ZAH pah lah VEE* (1919-1980), was the *shah* (king) of Iran from 1941 to 1979. He was overthrown in 1979 by a mass movement of Iranians led by Ayatollah Ruhollah Khomeini, a Muslim religious leader. As shah, Mohammad carried out many economic and social reforms, but he was a dictatorial ruler.

Mohammad was born in Teheran. He succeeded his father, Reza Shah Pahlavi, as shah. Reza had refused to cooperate with the Allies during World War II, and the Allies forced him to resign. After Mohammad became shah, he allowed the Allies to station troops in Iran and to send supplies through Iran to Russia.

At first, Mohammad did not take a great interest in affairs of state. In the mid-1940's, his authority was challenged by Iranian Communists and by nationalists led by Mohammad Mossadegh. In 1951, the nationalists forced the shah to appoint Mossadegh prime minister. Continuing opposition forced the shah to leave Iran in 1953. But, with American help, he soon returned and became Iran's most powerful leader.

In the 1960's, the shah began a program to distribute land to peasant farmers. In the 1960's and 1970's, he

Iranian Embassy

Mohammad Reza Pahlavi

used part of Iran's oil revenue to promote social and economic development. He expanded programs dealing with literacy and health care, and built many schools, airports, highways, railroads, dams, and irrigation facilities. He also bought much military equipment to increase Iran's power.

Although Iran had a parliament and a cabinet, the shah controlled the government. His vast power aroused much opposition, especially from students, intellectuals, religious leaders, and industrial workers. His critics accused him of denying freedom of speech and other rights and of using secret police and military force to silence opponents. They also claimed that his spending policies and government corruption were ruining Iran's economy. Many conservative Iranian Muslims claimed that some of his policies violated the teachings of Islam, the Muslim religion.

The shah was overthrown in February 1979, and then fled from Iran. While living in Mexico, he became ill.

In October 1979, the shah was admitted to a hospital in the United States. In November, Iranian revolutionaries took over the United States Embassy in Teheran and held a group of U.S. citizens who worked at the embassy as hostages. They said they would not release the hostages unless the U.S. government returned the shah to Iran for trial. The government refused to do so. The shah moved to Panama in December 1979 and to Egypt in March 1980. He died in Egypt in July 1980. See IRAN (Recent Developments).   Critically reviewed by MORROE BERGER

MOHAMMED. See MUHAMMAD.

MOHAMMEDANISM. See ISLAM; MUSLIMS.

MOHAWK INDIANS. See IROQUOIS INDIANS.

MOHAWK RIVER is the largest branch of the Hudson River. The east and west branches of the Mohawk meet in central New York. The river flows southeastward for 148 miles (238 kilometers) and enters the Hudson about 10 miles (16 kilometers) north of Albany.

The Mohawk River was named for the Mohawk Indians who lived in the region. A confederacy of Iroquois tribes also made its headquarters in the area. The Mohawk River valley has served as a highway from the Hudson Valley to the Great Lakes region since colonial days. The New York State Barge Canal and two railroads run parallel with the river. GEORGE MACINKO

MOHAWK TRAIL was a route westward along the Mohawk River from the Hudson River to the Great Lakes. The Iroquois Indian confederacy occupied the land it crossed. In pioneer days, thousands of settlers traveled westward along this route. Its importance declined after the building of the Erie Canal in 1825. The Penn Central Railroad and a modern highway now follow the course of the trail.   W. TURRENTINE JACKSON

See also TRAILS OF EARLY DAYS (map).

MOHENJO-DARO. See INDUS VALLEY CIVILIZATION.

MOHICAN INDIANS, *moh HEE kun,* is the name often given to two separate but related tribes of the eastern United States. One group, properly called the *Mahican,* lived along the Hudson River in New York state. The other, the *Mohegan,* settled in Connecticut. They broke off from the Pequot tribe, and formed one of the most powerful Indian groups in New England. Their chief Uncas remained friendly to the colonists, but the other Indians hated him and accused him of treachery (see UNCAS). Both groups lived like other tribes of the area (see INDIAN, AMERICAN [Eastern Woodlands]). After the coming of the white settlers, most Mahican moved westward to Wisconsin and lost their tribal identity. A few Mohegan, who have mixed with whites, still live in Mohegan, Conn.

James Fenimore Cooper's famous novel *The Last of the Mohicans* has given the Mohicans a prominent place in American literature.   WILLIAM H. GILBERT

See also INDIAN WARS (The Pequot War).

MOHL, HUGO VON (1805-1872), a German botanist, was the first to propose calling the living contents of plant cells *protoplasm.* Mohl helped develop the *Cell Theory.* According to this theory, all plants and animals are made up of cells. New cells are formed by the division of older cells, and the protoplasm carries on the work of the cells. Mohl was born in Stuttgart, Germany.   ROGERS MCVAUGH

MOHOROVIČIĆ DISCONTINUITY. See EARTH (The Earth's Crust).

MOHS, FRIEDRICH. See MINERAL (Hardness).

MOIRÉ, *mwah RAY,* is any cloth which has wavy designs on it, such as corded silk or rayon. The pattern is put on cloth with engraved rollers and heat. Moiré is a French word which means *watered.* The word moiré may also describe paper, rock, or metal which has a watered appearance. See also MOIRÉ PATTERN.

MOIRÉ PATTERN, *mwah RAY,* is a pattern of lines that results when two regular patterns overlap. For example, if an ordinary piece of window screen is folded over, wavy lines appear where the screen overlaps. These lines form a moiré pattern.

Two patterns consisting of straight, curved, or wavy lines, or even rows of dots, can create a moiré pattern. Moirés have produced interesting artistic designs. An

Edmund Scientific Co.

A Moiré Pattern of Wide Curving Lines results where two groups of narrow-lined circles overlap.

early application of them is in moiré cloth. Modern artists have used moirés in op art paintings.

In the 1960's, scientists discovered uses for moiré patterns. For example, when some crystals overlap, they produce moirés that can be seen with an electron microscope. From these patterns, scientists can discover how the atoms in the crystal are arranged.   GERALD OSTER

MOISTURE. See WEATHER (Moisture); HUMIDITY.

MOJAVE, *moh HAH vee,* in southeastern California, is a vast desert wasteland covering about 25,000 square miles (64,700 square kilometers). It lies between the Sierra Nevada and the Colorado River (see CALIFORNIA [physical map]). The Pacific Ocean once covered this region. Over a long period, high mountains rose and blocked the entry of water from the sea. Volcanic mountains erupted and covered the region with lava, mud, and ashes. Today, many small isolated mountain ranges and extinct volcanoes break up the great stretches of sandy soil. Dry lake beds in the region form the world's chief source of boron, a mineral that is used for jet-engine and rocket fuels.   GEORGE SHAFTEL

MOLAR. See TEETH (Permanent Teeth).

MOLASSES, *moh LASS ez,* is a thick, sweet, sticky syrup. It is yellowish or dark-brown. Molasses is used for cooking, candymaking, and as a livestock feed.

Most molasses is obtained as a by-product in the manufacture of sugar from sugar cane. Therefore, countries that grow sugar cane produce most of the world's molasses (see SUGAR CANE). In the United States, Louisiana is the center of molasses production.

How Molasses Is Made. Molasses is a liquid that is obtained from sugar crystals by changing cane juice to sugar. Molasses may be made by the open kettle method or by the vacuum pan method.

In the *open kettle method,* the cane juice is boiled in a large open pan. After it has been boiled several times, most of the water evaporates as steam. The syrup that remains receives additional boiling until it becomes a stiff mass of syrup and crystals called *massecuite.* The massecuite is placed in barrels that have tiny holes in the bottom. The molasses seeps through these holes, leaving sugar crystals inside the barrels.

Large sugar factories generally use the *vacuum pan method,* in which they boil the massecuite in large, covered vacuum pans. After the massecuite has been boiled several times, it is thoroughly stirred in a mixer. The mixture is then spun in rotating containers called *centrifugals.* The centrifugals have walls of fine copper mesh that permit the molasses to pass through but hold the sugar crystals.

Further boiling of the molasses produces varying grades. The molasses left after several boilings is called *blackstrap.* It is used chiefly to feed farm animals, for fertilizer, and to distill rum or alcohol.

Food Value. Molasses contains about 69.3 per cent carbohydrates, 25 per cent water, 2.4 per cent protein, and 3.2 per cent ash or mineral. One pound (0.5 kilogram) has a high energy value of 1,290 calories. RICHARD A. HAVENS

MOLASSES ACT was passed by the British Parliament in 1733. It taxed molasses and sugar coming into the North American colonies from parts of the West Indies not under British control. The purpose of the act was to limit this trade to British colonies. But most Americans ignored the act, and it was repealed in 1764.

MOLAY, JACQUES DE. See DE MOLAY, ORDER OF; KNIGHTS TEMPLARS.

MOLD is a hollow form. See CAST AND CASTING.

MOLD is a tiny, simple plant which belongs to the fungi group. It is closely related to the mildews, rusts, and mushrooms. Molds have no *chlorophyll,* or green coloring matter, and therefore cannot manufacture their own food. They must live on food made by other plants or animals, or on decaying matter. Some molds live as parasites on insects and certain fungi.

Common bread mold belongs to a group called the *black molds.* The group gets its name because all of these molds produce dark-colored spores. Common bread mold forms a cottony, soft, white growth on damp bread. A group of molds known as the *blue molds* also grow on bread. A green mold often grows on various kinds of cheeses. Other molds, called *water molds,* are often found in water and soil.

Molds develop from a tiny particle called the *spore.* When the spore settles on damp food, such as bread,

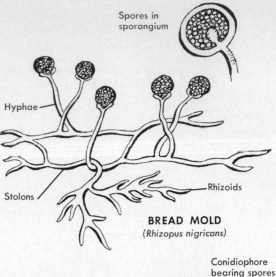

BREAD MOLD
(Rhizopus nigricans)

Spores in sporangium

Hyphae

Stolons

Rhizoids

MOLDS

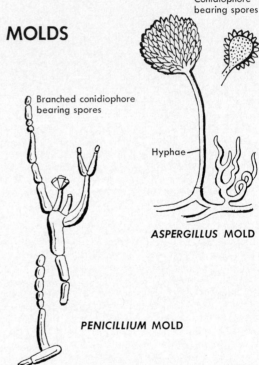

Conidiophore bearing spores

Branched conidiophore bearing spores

Hyphae

ASPERGILLUS MOLD

PENICILLIUM MOLD

it swells and begins to grow by producing tiny *hyphae* (threads). Some hyphae, called *rhizoids,* are like tiny roots. Others, called *stolons,* spread out on the surface.

As the plant body of the mold matures, many upright hyphae produce spore cases containing thousands of spores. Each spore case, called *sporangium,* is about the size of a pinhead. When the spore cases mature and break open, the spores are set free and are carried away by air currents. These spores in the air settle on damp foods and develop into new molds. In some molds, chains of spores are produced at the tips of certain hyphae, called *conidiophores.*

Moldy foods generally should be thrown away. But certain cheeses, such as Roquefort, owe their flavor to a mold which grows in them and ripens them.

Molds also are useful because they help to break up dead organisms and waste matter, and fertilize the soil. One mold produces the drug penicillin (see PENICILLIN).

Scientific Classification. Molds belong to the phylum *Eumycophyta*. They are in the classes *Phycomycetes* and *Ascomycetes*. WILLIAM F. HANNA

See also FUNGI; MILDEW; SLIME MOLD.

MOLDAVIA, *mohl DAY vih uh,* is a region in south-central Europe. Part of it makes up the Moldavian Soviet Socialist Republic in the southwest corner of Russia. The western part (Moldavia proper) is a district in northeastern Romania. The Prut River divides the two. See RUSSIA (political map).

The Moldavian Soviet Socialist Republic (MSSR) (pop. 3,948,000) covers 13,012 square miles (33,700 square kilometers). Farmers there raise cereals and tobacco. Kishinev is its capital. This part of Moldavia belonged to Romania from the end of World War I until 1940, when Russia made it part of the MSSR.

Romanian Moldavia (pop. 4,402,410) covers 17,788 square miles (46,070 square kilometers). Farmers raise sheep and cattle, and grow wheat, corn, barley, sugar beets, grapes, and sunflowers. Coal and manganese are mined. Iași and Galați are the chief cities. GEORGE KISH

See also BESSARABIA; ROMANIA; RUSSIA.

MOLE is a small, thick-bodied mammal that lives underground. The mole is a fast, tireless digger, and the shape of its body is well suited for burrowing. It has a narrow, pointed nose, a wedge-shaped head, and large forelegs. Its front paws, which turn outward, have long, broad nails. The forelegs work like shovels, scooping out the earth. The mole's hind legs are short and powerful. The animal is almost blind, with tiny eyes that are shaded by overhanging fur or skin. A mole does not have external ears, but it hears well.

A mole's home can be recognized by a mound of earth above it. This mound is considerably larger than the mound that the animal makes when digging for food. Moles eat mainly worms and insects and seldom eat plants. Their diggings often spoil gardens and fields, and farmers set traps in the animals' tunnels.

Mole fur has been used in making coats and jackets. Furriers prefer bluish-gray mole fur, but they also use black, brownish-black, and paler shades. Moleskin is lightweight, warm, soft, and thick. But it does not wear well and has lost popularity through the years.

The Common Mole of North America lives in the Eastern, Midwestern, and Southwestern regions of the United States. It is 5 to 8 inches (13 to 20 centimeters) long, including a tail about 1 inch (2.5 centimeters) long. It weighs from 1½ to 5 ounces (43 to 140 grams) and eats nearly its own weight in food every day. This mole lives almost its entire life underground. It tunnels near the surface when searching for food. Most common moles live in nests about 1 foot (30 centimeters) underground. Many nests are lined with leaves.

The Star-Nosed Mole has a fringe of fleshy feelers around its nose. It has dark, blackish-brown fur on its upper parts, shading to a paler color underneath. The animal's long, hairy tail thickens at the base. The star-nosed mole lives in southeastern Canada and in the Eastern United States as far south as Georgia. It likes to live near water and usually builds its home in the damp, muddy soil of a swamp or along the shore of a brook or pond. It is an expert swimmer. In the winter, the star-

Cy La Tour

The Mole searches for earthworms and other food by digging tunnels with its sharp claws and powerful legs. The mole is nearly blind, but it does not need keen vision in its underground tunnels.

nosed mole burrows deep into the soil to avoid frost. See MAMMAL (illustration: The Star-Nosed Mole).

The European Mole builds a home with many underground chambers. There is one central chamber that is connected to other smaller, round rooms. Passageways extend from these rooms in all directions. One passage, called the *bolt run,* serves as an exit in case of danger. The others lead to feeding grounds. In the central chamber is a nest in which three or four baby moles are born in early spring. The European mole is about the same size as the common mole of North America.

Moles also live in parts of Asia. The largest species of all moles is the Russian desman, which is about 14 inches (36 centimeters) long, including the tail. It lives in southeastern Europe and central western Asia. The smallest species are the shrew moles and longtailed moles of Asia and the Pacific Coast of North America. They are about 5 inches (13 centimeters) long, including their tails.

Scientific Classification. Moles belong to the order *Insectivora.* They are in the mole family, *Talpidae.* The common mole of the Eastern United States is genus *Scalopus,* species *S. aquaticus.* The star-nosed mole is *Condylura cristata.* The European mole is *Talpa europaea.* The Russian desman is *Desmana moschata.* FRANK B. GOLLEY

MOLE is a unit used in chemistry to measure amounts of chemicals that take part in chemical reactions. One mole of any substance contains 602,257,000,000,000,000,000,000 (602.257 billion trillion) atoms, molecules, ions, or radicals. This number is usually written 6.02257×10^{23}. It is called *Avogadro's number* in honor of the Italian physicist Amedeo Avogadro.

The mole is one of the basic units in the metric system of measurement. The weight in grams of one mole of any substance is the same as the substance's *formula weight* (the sum of the atomic weights of all the atoms represented in its chemical formula). For example, one mole of carbon (chemical symbol C) weighs 12 grams, because carbon's atomic weight is 12 and only one atom is represented in its formula. One mole of hydrogen (H_2) weighs two grams, because hydrogen's atomic weight is one and two atoms are represented in its formula. One mole of carbon can be combined with two moles of hydrogen to form one mole (16 grams) of methane (CH_4). KENNETH SCHUG

MOLE is a spot on the skin. A mole is a birthmark, even though it may appear long after a person is born. There are two main kinds of moles, *vascular moles* and *non-vascular moles*. Most vascular moles are made up of swollen blood vessels. They are blue or deep red in color. Non-vascular moles are solid knots of skin tissue or connective tissue. They are actually tumors, although they are seldom dangerous. A rare type of non-vascular mole, smooth and bluish-black in color, sometimes develops into a malignant tumor. The soft, hairy, brown mole is common, and quite harmless. A mass or tumor that occasionally forms in the *uterus* (womb) is also called a mole. See also TUMOR. W. B. YOUMANS

MOLE CRICKET is a large cricket which burrows in the ground like a mole. The most common kind of mole cricket is about $1\frac{1}{2}$ inches (4 centimeters) long, and is velvety brown. Its short front legs, like the mole's legs, are specially suited for burrowing. This insect has very short wings, but another kind of mole cricket has long wings and is able to fly. Mole crickets live throughout the tropical and temperate world.

Mole crickets live underground in burrows. They eat insect larvae, earthworms, and root and tuber crops, including potatoes. The *changa*, a mole cricket of Puerto Rico, is the worst insect pest of the sugar crop.

Scientific Classification. Mole crickets belong to the cricket family, *Gryllidae*. The American mole cricket is genus *Gryllotalpa*, species *G. borealis*. The changa is *Scapteriscus didactylus*. URL LANHAM

MOLECULAR BIOLOGY is the study of the structure and function of the large molecules essential to life. Among these molecules are proteins and nucleic acids. Proteins *catalyze* (speed up) chemical reactions that supply the energy for living cells. Nucleic acids carry

the *genetic code* (information) necessary for the development of all living cells.

Molecular biologists try to find out how these molecules are built and how they work. They use X rays, electron microscopes, and chemical methods that purify and break down molecules for their studies. They also study microorganisms.

The discovery of the structure of *deoxyribonucleic acid* (DNA) was one of the most important advances in molecular biology. This discovery made it possible to explain the laws of heredity on a chemical basis. DNA also determines the structure of proteins. Scientists working in molecular biology have unraveled the structure of *myoglobin* and *hemoglobin*, two proteins that store and transport oxygen. They also have discovered how muscles contract and how certain viruses are built up. See NUCLEIC ACID; PROTEIN.

Molecular biologists as well as other scientists want to learn how proteins are made in a cell, and how they work. They hope to discover how single germ cells can grow into complex organisms such as humans, animals, and plants. They also hope to find out how the brain works. M. F. PERUTZ

MOLECULE, *MAHL uh kyool*, is one of the basic units of matter. It is the smallest particle into which a substance can be divided and still have the *properties* (characteristics) of the original substance. If the substance were divided further, only *atoms* (individual particles) of chemical elements would remain. For example, a drop of water contains billions of water molecules. If the drop could be divided until only a single water molecule remained, that final drop would still have all the properties of water. But if the water molecule were divided, only atoms of the elements hydrogen and oxygen would remain.

Molecules are made up of atoms held together in certain patterns. Every atom consists of a positively charged *nucleus* (central core) surrounded by negatively charged electrons. In a molecule, there are an equal number of positive and negative charges.

Scientists use chemical formulas to show the composition of molecules. For example, a water molecule consists of two hydrogen atoms and one oxygen atom, and has the formula H_2O. The size of a molecule depends on the size and number of its atoms. Molecules are made up of from two to thousands of atoms. A molecule that consists of only two atoms, such as nitric oxide (NO), is called a *diatomic* molecule. A molecule made up of three atoms, such as water, is called a *triatomic* molecule.

Almost all gases, most common liquids, and many solids consist of molecules. But some substances are made up of different units called *ions* (atoms or groups of atoms with either a positive or a negative charge). These substances are called *ionic substances*.

Salts are examples of ionic substances. For example, sodium chloride, which is common table salt, consists of positive sodium ions and negative chloride ions. Electric forces among the ions hold the salt crystals together in a regular framework. Metals are also different from molecular substances. In addition to positive ions, metals consist of a large number of electrons that move about freely throughout the metal.

Molecules and Matter. Molecules are held together in a group by forces called *Van der Waals forces* (see VAN

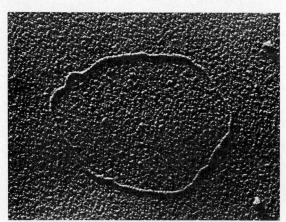

Humberto Fernandez-Moran, University of Chicago

A Molecule of DNA looks like a thin thread when magnified 120,000 times by an electron microscope. DNA molecules are among the largest molecules known to scientists. They are thousands or millions of times larger than most other molecules. DNA is a chemical found in all living cells.

DER WAALS, JOHANNES DIDERIK). These forces are usually weaker than those that hold the molecule itself together. The force between molecules depends on how far apart they are. When two molecules are widely separated, they attract each other. When they come very close together, they *repel* (push apart) each other.

In a solid, the molecules are so arranged that the forces which attract and repel are balanced. The molecules vibrate about these positions of balance, but they do not move to different parts of the solid. As the temperature of a solid is raised, the molecules vibrate more strongly. When the Van der Waals forces can no longer hold the molecules in place, the solid melts and becomes a liquid.

In a liquid, the molecules move about easily, but they still have some force on one another. These forces are strong enough to form a filmlike surface on a liquid and prevent it from flying apart.

In a gas, the molecules move about so fast that the attractive forces have little effect on them. When two molecules in a gas collide with each other, the repelling force sends them apart again. Therefore, gas molecules fill a container completely, because they move freely through all the space available.

Most substances can be changed into solids, liquids, or gases by either raising or lowering their temperatures. But some substances remain solid until they are heated to very high temperatures. Other substances are gases except when cooled to very low temperatures. The temperature at which these changes occur—and also other characteristics of a substance—depends on the size, shape, and weight of the molecules and on the strength of the Van der Waals forces between them.

Individual Molecules. Certain atoms within a molecule have strong attractive forces between them. These forces produce *bonds* between the atoms. The forces within a molecule determine its shape. The molecule takes the shape that forms the strongest bonds and the least amount of strain among its atoms. For example, an ammonia molecule has the shape of a *tetrahedron* (a pyramidlike figure with four faces). It consists of three hydrogen atoms attached to a nitrogen atom. Normal butane molecules have four carbon atoms arranged in a zigzag chain with ten hydrogen atoms attached. A benzene molecule has six carbon atoms in a ring with six hydrogen atoms attached. Many protein molecules form long spiral chains.

The weight of a molecule is indicated by its *molecular weight*. Molecular weight can be found by adding the *atomic weights* of all the atoms in a molecule. The molecular weight of carbon dioxide (CO_2) can be found by adding the atomic weight of carbon, which is 12, and the weights of the two oxygen atoms, which are about 16 each. Carbon dioxide has a molecular weight of about 44. A molecule's weight can also be measured with an instrument called a *mass spectrometer*.

The positive and negative charges in a molecule balance each other, but these charges are spread out unevenly in *polar* molecules. In a polar molecule, more positive charges collect at one end of the molecule and more negative charges collect at the other end. Some molecules are magnetic, because of the way the electrons move about within the molecule.

When two different kinds of molecules come near enough to each other, they may react and form one or more new molecules. Or two molecules of the same kind may combine and form one larger molecule. Molecules can also be broken down into smaller molecules.

DIAGRAMS OF SOME COMMON MOLECULES

Scientists study chemical compounds to learn how many atoms of each element are in the molecules and how these atoms are joined to each other. With this information, diagrams of molecules can be drawn with balls representing the individual atoms.

WORLD BOOK diagram

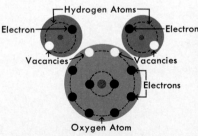

Hydrogen Atoms — Electron — Electron — Vacancies — Vacancies — Electrons — Oxygen Atom

A Molecule of Water forms when two atoms of hydrogen and one of oxygen, *above*, join together in sharing their electrons, *below*. The electrons fill the vacancies in all the atoms.

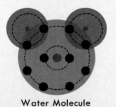

Water Molecule

A Carbon Dioxide Molecule has two oxygen atoms and a carbon atom.

An Ammonia Molecule has three hydrogen atoms and a nitrogen atom.

A Butane Molecule is a chain of carbon atoms with hydrogen atoms.

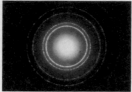

Film Studio, Education Development Center

Diffraction Patterns are produced on photographic film when X rays or electrons pass through molecules of various substances. X rays produced the pattern at the left, and electrons made the one at the right.

This can be done with ultraviolet light, fast-moving electrons, or nuclear radiation.

Studying Molecules. Scientists can study some molecules directly with an *electron microscope*. This method provides a picture of a molecule, but the picture is often too blurred to see fine details. Scientists also use several indirect methods to study molecules. For example, they study solids by *X-ray diffraction*. The way a solid deflects X rays tells them about the size, shape, and arrangement of the molecules in the solid. Scientists also use *neutron diffraction* and *electron diffraction* to study solids. They pass a beam of *neutrons* (uncharged particles) or *electrons* (negatively charged particles) through a solid, and observe how the beam is affected. Electron diffraction can also be used to study gases.

Scientists also learn about molecules by studying the way they absorb or give off light. Each kind of molecule has its own *spectrum* (band of colored light) when it absorbs or gives off light. By studying the spectrum of a substance, scientists can learn much about its molecules. For example, they can find the sizes and shapes of the molecules, the strength of the forces that hold the atoms together in the molecule, and the way the electrons move about in the molecules.   DAVID R. LIDE, JR.

Related Articles in WORLD BOOK include:

Atom	Ion and	Liquid
Bond (chemical)	Ionization	Liquid Crystal
Chemistry	Light (The Visible	Matter
Gas (matter)	Spectrum)	Solid

MOLESKIN. See MOLE.

MOLIÈRE, *mo LYAIR* (1622-1673), was the stage name of Jean Baptiste Poquelin, the greatest French writer of comedy. Molière's plays emphasize one broad principle: the comic contrast between how people see themselves and how others see them.

Molière experimented with many drama forms. During his short career, he wrote farce, high comedy, satire, and comedy-ballets. He wrote equally well in verse and prose. Molière was also a fine actor and director.

Molière was born in Paris, the son of a prosperous upholsterer. He earned a law degree, but he never practiced law. Instead, he

Molière in the Role of Caesar. Portrait by Nicolas Mignard, Comédie Française, Paris (National Photographic Service, Versailles)
Molière

and a group of friends founded the Illustre-Théâtre in 1643. From 1645 to 1647, the troupe toured France. In 1659, Molière staged *The Affected Young Ladies*, a one-act farce which he wrote. Its success attracted the attention of Louis XIV, who provided Molière with a permanent theater and asked him to write court entertainments.

Molière had no real philosophy, and his plays contain few ideas. But he had a knack for choosing controversial subjects that would attract public interest. In 1662, *The School for Wives*, his first masterpiece in verse, satirized the narrow education given to girls of the middle class. As a result, he was attacked by extremist religious groups. *Tartuffe, or The Imposter* (1664) was a satire on religious hypocrisy. It aroused such great church opposition that the play could not be performed for several years. Church opposition also forced *Don Juan* (1665) to close after a short run. Molière then satirized universal human failings in *The Misanthrope* (1666), *The Miser* (1668), *The Learned Ladies* (1672), and other plays.

Late in his career, Molière wrote a series of comedy-ballets in which the dramatic script was accompanied by interludes of song and dance, somewhat like today's musical comedies. The most important of these works are *George Dandin* (1668), *The Would-Be Gentleman* (1670), and *The Imaginary Invalid* (1673).   JULES BRODY

See also FRENCH LITERATURE (Drama); DRAMA (French Neoclassical Drama).

MOLINA, TIRSO DE. See TIRSO DE MOLINA.

MOLINE, Ill. (pop. 46,237), a leading farm implement manufacturing center, is known as the *Farm Implement Capital of the World*. Located on the Mississippi River, it is adjacent to Rock Island and East Moline, Illinois, and opposite Davenport, Iowa. The cities are linked by several bridges, and help form a metropolitan area of 362,638 persons. Moline lies 150 miles (241 kilometers) west of Chicago. For location, see ILLINOIS (political map).

The name of the city comes from the Spanish word *molino*, meaning *mill*, and was probably suggested by the water power of the Mississippi. Moline was laid out in 1843, four years before John Deere decided to locate his plow factory there. Moline has a mayor-council government.   PAUL M. ANGLE

MOLINO DEL REY, BATTLE OF. See MEXICAN WAR (Scott's Campaign).

MOLLOY COLLEGE. See UNIVERSITIES AND COLLEGES (table).

MOLLUSK is a soft-bodied animal without bones. Clams, octopuses, oysters, slugs, snails, and squids are mollusks. Most kinds of mollusks, including clams and oysters, have a hard armorlike shell that protects their soft bodies. Other kinds, such as cuttlefish and squids, have no outside shell. A special shell grows inside their bodies. This shell is called a *cuttlebone* in cuttlefish, or a *pen* in squids. A few kinds of mollusks, including octopuses and certain slugs, have no shell at all. For information about mollusk shells and how they are formed, see SHELL.

All mollusks have a skinlike organ called a *mantle*, which produces the substance that makes the shell. The edges of the mantle squeeze out liquid shell materials and add them to the shell as the mollusk grows. In mollusks with no outside shell, the mantle forms a tough wrapper around the body organs.

Gastropod (Pacific Islands Whelk)

Douglas Faulkner, Publix

Chiton (*Amphineura*)

Russ Kinne, Photo Researchers

Bivalve (Common Edible Scallop)

Walter Dawn

Tooth Shell (Scaphopod)

Ralph Buchsbaum

N. J. Berrill

Squid (Cephalopod)

Monoplacophoran (top and underside)

Henning Lemche

Mollusks live in most parts of the world. Some kinds live in the deepest parts of oceans. Others are found on the wooded slopes of high mountains. Still others live in hot, dry deserts. Wherever mollusks live, they must keep their bodies moist to stay alive. Most land mollusks live in damp places such as under leaves or in soil.

The Importance of Mollusks

Mollusks are used mainly for food. People in many parts of the world eat mollusks every day. Most Americans do not eat them nearly so often. The most popular kinds used as food in the United States are clams, oysters, and scallops.

Mollusk shells are made into many useful products, including pearl buttons, jewelry, and various souvenir items. Perhaps the best known mollusk products are the pearls made by oysters.

Some mollusks are harmful to people. Certain small, fresh-water snails of the tropics carry worms that cause a fatal disease. Shipworm clams drill into rope, boats, and wooden wharves, and cause millions of dollars worth of damage a year.

Kinds of Mollusks

Mollusks make up the largest group of water animals. There are about 100,000 known kinds of living mollusks, and scientists find about 1,000 new species every year. The fossils of about 100,000 other species of mollusks have also been found.

The mollusks make up a *phylum* (major division) of the animal kingdom. The scientific name of the phylum is *Mollusca*, a Latin word meaning *soft-bodied*. A table with this article shows the six *classes* (large groups) of mollusks. To learn where the phylum fits into the whole animal kingdom, see ANIMAL (table: *A Classification of the Animal Kingdom*).

The six classes of mollusks are (1) univalves or *Gastropoda*, (2) bivalves or *Pelecypoda*, (3) octopuses and squids or *Cephalopoda*, (4) tooth shells or *Scaphopoda*, (5) chitons or *Amphineura*, and (6) *Monoplacophora*.

Univalves or Gastropods (*Gastropoda*) are the largest class of mollusks. They include limpets, slugs, snails, and whelks. Most kinds of univalves have a single, coiled shell. The name *univalve* comes from Latin words meaning *one shell*. Some kinds, including garden slugs and the sea slugs called *nudibranchs*, have no shells.

The name *Gastropoda* comes from Greek words meaning *belly* and *foot*. Gastropods seem to crawl on their bellies, but actually they move about by means of a large, muscular foot. The foot spreads beneath the body, and the foot muscles move in a rippling motion that makes the animal move forward. Most sea snails and a few land snails have a lidlike part called an *operculum* at the back of the foot. When danger threatens, the snail draws back into its shell and the operculum closes the shell opening.

Certain kinds of univalves have two pairs of *tentacles* (feelers) on their heads. One pair helps the animals feel their way about. Some species have an eye on each of the other two tentacles. Others have no eyes at all. A univalve also has a ribbon of teeth. This ribbon, called a *radula*, works like a rough file and tears apart the animal's food. Most univalves that eat plants have thousands of weak teeth. A few kinds eat other mollusks, and have several dozen strong teeth.

Bivalves (*Pelecypoda*) form the second largest class of mollusks. They include clams, oysters, mussels, and scallops. All bivalves have two shells that are held together by hinges that look like small teeth. The shells of bivalves are usually open. When the animals are frightened, strong muscles pull the shells shut and hold them closed until danger has passed.

The word *Pelecypoda* comes from Greek words that mean *hatchet* and *foot*. Bivalves have a strong, muscular foot shaped like a hatchet. Many kinds of these animals move about by pushing the foot out and hooking it in the mud or sand. Then they pull themselves up to the foot. Some bivalves, such as the geoduck and razor clam, use the foot to dig holes. They push the foot downward into mud or sand. First the foot swells to enlarge the hole, and then it contracts and pulls the shell into the burrow. The Pholas clam can dig holes even in hard clay or soft rock.

Most kinds of bivalves have no head or teeth. They get oxygen and food through a muscular *siphon* (tube). The siphon can be stretched to reach food and water if the animal is buried in mud or sand.

Octopuses and Squids (*Cephalopoda*) are the most active mollusks. The argonaut, cuttlefish, and nautilus also belong to this group. All live in the ocean, and most of them swim about freely.

The word *Cephalopoda* comes from Greek words meaning *head* and *foot*. A cephalopod seems to be made up of a large head and long tentacles that look like arms or feet. Octopuses and squids have dome-shaped "heads" surrounded by tentacles. Octopuses have 8 tentacles, and squids have 10. The tentacles grow around hard, strong, beaklike jaws on the underside of the head. These powerful jaws tear the animal's prey, and are far more dangerous than the tentacles. The animal uses its tentacles to capture prey and pull it into the jaws. Octopuses and squids eat fish, other mollusks, and shellfish.

Tooth Shells (*Scaphopoda*) have slender, curving shells that resemble tusks. These mollusks are often called *tusk shells*. The word *Scaphopoda* comes from Greek words that mean *boat* and *foot*. A tooth shell has a pointed foot that looks somewhat like a small boat. All tooth shells live in the ocean, where they burrow in the mud or sand. The top of the shell sticks up into the water. Tooth shells have no head or eyes. They feed on one-celled plants and animals that are swept into the mouth by tentacles.

Chitons (*Amphineura*) have flat, oval bodies covered by eight shell plates. The plates are held together by a tough girdle. The name *Amphineura* comes from Greek words that mean *around* and *nerve*. This name refers to two nerve cords that go around the chiton's body. Chitons have a large, flat foot. They can use the foot to move about, but they usually cling firmly to rocks. They roll up into a ball when forced to let go of the rocks. Chitons have a small head and mouth, but no eyes or tentacles. Their long radula is crisscrossed with teeth, which they use to scrape seaweed from rocks for food.

Monoplacophora are extremely rare. They live in the deepest parts of the ocean, and most kinds are found only as fossils. The name *Monoplacophora* comes from Greek words meaning *single, shell,* and *bearer*. Monoplacophorans have one shell that is almost flat, like a limpet shell. These mollusks are unusual because they have several pairs of gills, six or more pairs of kidneys, and many nerve centers. Like other mollusks, they have a mantle. They also have a radula. Little is known about their habits.   R. TUCKER ABBOTT

Related Articles in WORLD BOOK include:

Abalone	Geoduck	Scallop
Argonaut	Limpet	Shell
Chiton	Mother-of-Pearl	Shipworm
Clam	Mussel	Slug
Cockle	Nautilus	Snail
Conch	Octopus	Squid
Cowrie	Oyster	Whelk
Cuttlefish	Periwinkle	

MOLLY MAGUIRES was a secret society that used its power to aid its members in labor disputes. It was founded in Ireland and branches were started in Pennsylvania in 1867. Its members terrorized the hard-coal region of Pennsylvania. They were finally suppressed in 1877.

MOLNÁR, *MAHL nahr,* or *MAWL nahr,* **FERENC** (1878-1952), a Hungarian dramatist, wrote clever comedies. His best-known play, *Liliom* (1909), is more serious than many of his other works. It is an understanding and forgiving character-study of an amusement park barker who fails in everything he tries to do. It was made into the American musical comedy *Carousel* in 1945. Other Molnár plays that became popular are *The Devil* (1907), *The Guardsman* (1910), *The Swan* (1920), and *The Play's the Thing* (1925). His works also include the famous children's novel *The Paul Street Boys* (1907).

Molnár was born in Budapest, the son of a well-known physician. He studied law, but decided to become a journalist. He won fame as a witty conversationalist and as the author of more than 40 plays. In 1940, he settled in the United States.   JOHN W. GASSNER

MOLOCH, *MOH lahk,* also spelled MOLECH, was an idol worshiped especially by the ancient Phoenicians and Amorites. From them, the idol-worshiping heretics of Israel borrowed the custom of sacrificing babies on the altar to Moloch, or else casting them on the lap of his image after it had been heated red-hot. The Bible forbids this worship (Lev. 18: 21; 20: 3-5). Kings Ahaz and Manasseh of Judah built altars to Moloch in the Valley of Hinnom (Gehenna in the New Testament), outside the walls of Jerusalem. King Josiah ended the practice (see GEHENNA).   GLEASON L. ARCHER, JR.

MOLOKAI. See HAWAII (The Islands).

MOLOTOV, *MAW loh tohv,* **VYACHESLAV MIKHAILOVICH** (1890-   ), became widely known during two terms as foreign minister of Russia. He was demoted in 1957 for his opposition to Nikita S. Khrushchev, first secretary of the Soviet Communist party. He was expelled from the Communist party's Presidium and sent into virtual exile as ambassador to Outer Mongolia. In 1960, he became Russia's delegate to the International Atomic Energy Agency. The Russian Communist party attacked him in 1961 and he returned to Moscow. In 1962, the Supreme Soviet (legislature) ordered his name removed from all Russian towns, buildings, and objects that had been named after him.

From 1939 to 1949 and from 1953 to 1956, Molotov served as commissar (later called minister) of foreign affairs. He helped create Russia's policy of hostility to the West, particularly to the United States. He attacked the North Atlantic Treaty Organization (NATO) as an agency that would lead to another war. He proposed a collective security treaty for European countries that would exclude the United States.

Molotov joined the Bolshevik party at the age of 16 (see BOLSHEVIKS). From 1906 to 1917, he helped plan the Bolshevik revolution. When the Bolshevik (now Communist) party seized power in Russia in 1917, Molotov received several important government positions. He served as premier of Russia from 1930 to 1941.

Molotov was born in the Kirov region of European Russia. His family name was Skriabin, but he changed it to Molotov, which means *of the hammer*. ALBERT PARRY

MOLTING is the process an animal goes through in shedding worn-out hair, skin or feathers, and growing a new body covering. It often takes place at a definite time of year known as the animal's *molting season*.

The process of molting varies with different animals. In insects, the outer covering of the *larva* (the newly hatched insect) is too firm to expand with the growing creature, and so must be renewed periodically. The old covering becomes detached by a fluid that appears beneath it, and then dries, hardens, splits, and finally drops away. A new covering is secreted by a special layer of cells. The caterpillars of several kinds of butterflies shed their skins as many as five times before they reach the chrysalis stage in their development. See METAMORPHOSIS.

Birds shed their feathers at least once a year. Some kinds of birds even shed their feathers three times a year.

John H. Gerard

A Molting Snake rubs its nose against a hard, rough object, such as a rock or tree trunk, until its skin breaks away. Then it slides out of the old skin, leaving it turned inside out. The process takes only a few minutes.

Each complete molt takes from four to six weeks. Birds have a very systematic way of molting. The feathers fall out, one after another, in a regular order. As they fall out, they are replaced in a correspondingly regular order with new feathers. Because the molting is regularly spaced in some birds, they are able to fly during molting periods. When a bird has two molting seasons, the first is to replace bedraggled winter plumage, and the second is to deck the bird out for the mating season. See BIRD (Feathers).

Many *mammals* (milk-giving animals) shed their hair once a year, usually in spring. Some animals replace body parts during molting. Deer shed their antlers and grow new ones. The lemming, an animal that looks like the guinea pig, and the ptarmigan, a grouselike bird, replace their claws. Scaly reptiles, such as snakes and lizards, and shellfish, such as lobsters and crabs, also undergo molts. They replace their outer coverings with new ones. L. B. AREY

See also CRUSTACEAN (Growth and Development).

MOLTKE, *MAWLT kuh,* **HELMUTH KARL VON** (1800-1891), was a Prussian military genius. He ranked next to Prince Otto von Bismarck as a builder of the German Empire.

Von Moltke was appointed to the Prussian general staff in 1832. He became chief of staff in 1858. As the Prussian chief of staff, Von Moltke prepared the military plans for the wars with Denmark in 1864, with Austria in 1866, and with France in 1870. His campaigns always succeeded. The great triumph of Von Moltke's career was the Prussian victory over France. His armies won decisively at Sedan on Sept. 2, 1870. Metz fell in October, and the Prussian armies entered Paris in triumph (see FRANCO-PRUSSIAN WAR).

Von Moltke was born in the duchy of Mecklenburg-Schwerin and grew up in the city of Lübeck. He was graduated from the Royal Military Academy in Copenhagen. ROBERT G. L. WAITE

MOLTO. See MUSIC (table: Terms Used in Music).

MOLUCCAS, *moh LUHK uhz,* or SPICE ISLANDS, are a large group of islands in the eastern part of Indonesia. They are valued for their spice plants. The chief islands in the group are Ambon, Ceram, and Halmahera. For a discussion of these islands, see INDONESIA. See also NETHERLANDS (The Netherlands Today).

MOLYBDENITE, *muh LIHB duh nyt,* is a bluish, lead-gray mineral. It is the chief source of molybdenum (see MOLYBDENUM). Molybdenite is a compound of molybdenum and sulfur, and occurs in granite, limestone, and other rocks. A low-grade deposit is considered practical for mining purposes, even if it contains less than 20 pounds of molybdenite per short ton of the ore. It is found in several states in the United States, and in Australia, Canada, Germany, and Norway.

MOLYBDENUM, *muh LIHB duh nuhm,* is a hard, silvery-white chemical element. Molybdenum is one of the strongest and most widely used *refractory metals* (heat resistant metals), because of its unusually high melting point of 2617° C. It also conducts heat and electricity easily. Molybdenum is mixed with steel and iron to produce strong *alloys*. Molybdenum steel is hard, strong, and resists *corrosion* (chemically wearing away).

Molybdenum is used in making parts for aircraft and

missiles and for making wire filaments in electronic tubes. It is also used as a protective coating on other metals. Molybdenum compounds have many industrial uses. Molybdenum disulfide is used as a lubricant in greases and oils. Molybdenum trioxide increases *adhesion* (sticking qualities) of enamels for coating metals. Some molybdenum chemicals are used as dyes.

Molybdenum is found in the minerals molybdenite and wulfenite. Canada and the United States are the leading producers. Carl Wilhelm Scheele of Sweden discovered molybdenum in 1778. Molybdenum has the chemical symbol Mo, the atomic number 42, and the atomic weight 95.94. It boils at 4612° C.   ALAN DAVISON

MOMBASA, *mahm BAH suh* (pop. 413,000), is an important seaport in Kenya, in eastern Africa. For location, see KENYA (map). Products shipped from Mombasa include animal hides and skins, coffee, cotton, gold, sugar, tea, and tin.

MOMENT, in physics, is the product of some quantity multiplied by a particular distance from a *fulcrum*, or axis. Moment of force is an example. A 100-pound person sitting 10 feet from the center of a seesaw produces a moment of 1,000 pound-feet. Engineers use the knowledge of moments to determine stresses in bridges and other structures.   CLARENCE E. BENNETT

See also LEVER (Law of Equilibrium).

MOMENTUM, *moh MEHN tuhm,* in physics, was called by Newton the quantity of motion of a moving body. When a baseball bat is swung, it has a momentum that depends on its mass and how fast it moves. The force exerted on the ball when the bat hits it depends on the rate of change in the bat's momentum.

To calculate the momentum of any moving object, multiply its *mass* (quantity of matter) by its *velocity* (speed and direction). An automobile that weighs 2,200

pounds has a mass of 1,000 kilograms. When driving north at 5 meters per second (about 11 miles per hour), it has a momentum of 5,000 (1,000 × 5) kilogram meters per second toward the north. An 11,000-pound truck has a mass of 5,000 kilograms. To have the same momentum as the car, the truck must drive north at only 1 meter per second (about 2 miles per hour).

An important law of physics states that momentum is conserved when two bodies act on each other without outside forces. If two objects collide, the total momentum of both objects after the collision equals their total momentum before collision. If the two objects have zero total initial momentum, their total final momentum also is zero. Thus, the momentum gained by one is equal and opposite to the momentum gained by the other. When a person dives off a still rowboat, the boat moves in a direction opposite to that of the dive. The boat's final momentum is equal and opposite to the person's final momentum, so that the total final momentum is zero, as it was before the dive.   LEON N. COOPER

See also FORCE; MASS; MOTION; VELOCITY.

MOMMSEN, THEODOR. See NOBEL PRIZES (table: Nobel Prizes for Literature—1902).

MONA LISA. See DA VINCI, LEONARDO (Return to Florence; picture).

MONACO, *MAHN uh koh,* is one of the smallest countries in the world. It has an area of only 0.58 square mile (1.49 square kilometers). Monaco lies on the

Momentum

When a person dives off a still boat, the boat moves in a direction opposite to the dive. The momentum gained by the boat is opposite and equal to the momentum gained by the diver.

BEFORE DIVING
Boat's Momentum = 0   Diver's Momentum = 0

AFTER DIVING
Boat's Momentum + Diver's Momentum = 0

Monaco

→← Rail Line
═ Tunnel
▦ Park
〰 Major Street

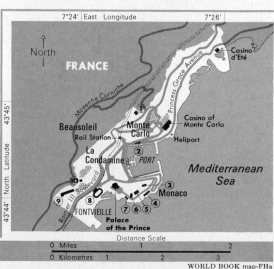

Cathedral of Monaco.......6	Monaco Hospital...........9
Government Palace........3	Museum of Fine Arts........1
International Hydro-	Museum of Prehistoric
graphic Office.........2	Anthropology..........10
Louis II Stadium...........8	National Council...........7
Marine Museum...........4	Town Hall.................5

WORLD BOOK map-FHa

French Riviera coast of the Mediterranean Sea. France borders it on three sides. Monaco is a popular tourist resort, with many fine hotels, clubs, flower gardens, and places of entertainment. One of its chief attractions is the famous Monte Carlo gambling casino.

Monaco is also known for automobile sports events. Drivers from all over the world compete each year in the Monte Carlo Rally. They drive more than 2,000 miles (3,200 kilometers) from starting points in many parts of Europe for the competition at Monte Carlo. In the Monaco Grand Prix, top racing drivers guide their cars on a 200-mile (322-kilometer) automobile race through the twisting streets of Monaco.

The towns of Monaco and Monte Carlo perch on terraced cliffs overlooking the Mediterranean. The town of Monaco is the capital of the country. Prince Rainier III and Princess Grace, the former American actress Grace Kelly, rule from a stately castle, part of which was built in the 1200's.

Monaco's official language is French. Its citizens are called *Monégasques*.

Government. Monaco is a *principality* (ruled by a prince). The prince represents Monaco in international affairs, such as the signing of treaties and agreements with other countries. Under the terms of a treaty with France in 1918, if Monaco's royal family has no male heirs, Monaco will come under French rule.

A minister of state, under the authority of the prince, heads the government. The minister is French, and is nominated by the French government. Three councilors who are responsible for finance, police and internal affairs, and public works assist the minister of state. The 18-member National Council is the legislative body of the principality. Monégasques elect National Council members to five-year terms. The council must approve changes in Monaco's constitution.

People. Only about a seventh of Monaco's people are Monégasque. More than half its residents are French, and most of the others are Americans, Belgians, British, and Italians. Most people in Monaco speak French. Most Monégasque citizens converse in a local dialect called Monégasque, which is based on French and Italian. Many wealthy people from other countries make Monaco their permanent home because the principality has no income tax. Since 1963, however, most French people living in Monaco have had to pay income tax at French rates.

The state religion is Roman Catholicism, but there is complete freedom of worship. Monaco's primary schools are run by the church. The principality also has a high school and a music academy.

Paul Popper, Ewing Galloway

The Harbor in Monaco lies at the foot of terraced Alpine cliffs. Glittering buildings cluster around the harbor's edge.

The Monaco government awards the Rainier III prize for literature each year to a writer in the French language. Monaco's libraries include the Princess Caroline Library, which specializes in children's literature. Monaco also has a marine museum, a prehistoric museum, a zoo, and botanical gardens. The marine museum houses a collection of rare exhibits, and also has one of the world's leading aquariums and a laboratory for marine research. The Grand Theater of Monte Carlo presents performances by some of the world's greatest singers and ballet dancers. Some of the world's leading conductors and soloists perform with Monaco's national orchestra.

Land. Monaco lies at the foot of Mt. Agel (3,600 feet, or 1,100 meters). In some places, the principality stretches only 200 yards (180 meters) inland from the Mediterranean.

Monaco has four distinct parts—the three towns and a small industrial area. Monaco, the old town and former fortress, stands on a rocky point 200 feet (61 meters) high. It is dominated by the royal palace.

Monte Carlo has the famous gambling casino, the opera house, hotels, shops, beaches, and swimming pools. The port area, La Condamine, lies between the town of Monaco and Monte Carlo. The industrial zone, called Fontvieille, lies west of the town of Monaco.

The country has a mild winter climate, with an average January temperature of 50° F. (10° C). Summer temperatures rarely exceed 90° F. (32° C). On the average, rain falls only 62 days a year.

Economy. Monaco's income comes mainly from the tourist trade. Each year, more than 600,000 tourists from all parts of the world visit the principality. A company called the Société des Bains de Mer owns the casino and most of the hotels, clubs, beaches, and other places of entertainment. Monaco's colorful postage stamps are popular with collectors, and are an important source of income.

Many foreign companies have their headquarters in Monaco because of the low taxation there. Factories in Fontvieille produce beer, candy, and chemicals.

FACTS IN BRIEF

Capital: Monaco.

Official Language: French.

Form of Government: Principality.

Area: 0.58 sq. mi. (1.49 km²).

Population: *Estimated 1981 Population*—26,000; distribution, 100 per cent urban; density, 45,195 persons per sq. mi. (17,450 persons per km²). *1968 Census*—23,035. *Estimated 1986 Population*—28,000.

Chief Products: Beer, candy, chemicals, dairy products.

Flag: The flag has two horizontal stripes, red and white. See FLAG (color picture: Flags of Europe).

Money: *Basic Unit*—French franc. See MONEY (table).

The principality has a local bus service. The main highway on the Riviera coast passes through Monaco, carrying motorists traveling between France and Italy. A railroad connecting France and Italy also runs through Monaco. The principality transmits its own radio and television programs. Its television transmitter stands on top of Mt. Agel, in French territory.

History. Monaco's museum contains much evidence, including remains and tools, of early peoples in the area. Phoenicians from the eastern Mediterranean probably settled in Monaco in about 700 B.C. In Greek and Roman times, Monaco was an important trading center, and its harbor sheltered ships from many lands.

The Genoese, from northern Italy, gained control of Monaco in the A.D. 1100's. They built the first fort there in 1215. In 1308, the Genoese granted governing rights over Monaco to the Grimaldi family of Genoa. The Grimaldi family became absolute rulers.

At various times from the 1400's to the 1600's, Monaco was occupied or controlled by France or Spain. France seized control of Monaco in 1793, during the French Revolution. But the Congress of Vienna restored control to the Grimaldi family in 1814. In 1866, Prince Charles III founded the town of Monte Carlo. In the early 1900's, Monte Carlo became a popular winter resort for the wealthy and famous of Europe.

The princes of Monaco ruled as absolute monarchs until 1911, when Prince Albert I approved a new constitution. Palace revolts and violence marked the early history of Monaco. Prince Jean II was murdered by his brother Lucien, who was later murdered by a relative. Prince Honoré I was drowned during a revolt.

Later rulers included Prince Albert, known as the *Scientist Prince*. He did much important marine research, and founded the famous Oceanographic Museum. Prince Louis II ruled from 1922 until 1949, except for the German occupation during World War II. His grandson Prince Rainier III succeeded him.

Rainier proclaimed a new constitution in 1962. The constitution provided votes for women, and abolished the death penalty. In 1963, under pressure from France, Monaco taxed business profits for the first time.

Rainier announced plans to build new hotels and reclaim land from the sea for new beaches and places of entertainment. After a long struggle with Aristotle Onassis, a wealthy Greek shipowner who controlled the Société des Bains de Mer company, Rainier enacted a law in 1966 giving the Monaco government greater control of the company. In 1967, Onassis sold his shares in the company to the government.　ANTHONY MANN

See also RAINIER III; KELLY, GRACE; MONTE CARLO; AUTOMOBILE RACING (picture).

MONAD. See LEIBNIZ, GOTTFRIED WILHELM.

MONADNOCK. See VERMONT (Land Regions); NEW HAMPSHIRE (Mountains).

MONARCH BUTTERFLY. See BUTTERFLY.

MONARCHY is a form of government in which one person who inherits, or is elected to, a throne holds executive power for life. These persons, or monarchs, have different titles, including *king*, *emperor*, or *sultan*, in various governments. The old idea of monarchy maintained that the power of the monarch was absolute. It sometimes held that the monarch was responsible only to God. This doctrine became known as "the divine right of kings" (see DIVINE RIGHT OF KINGS).

Revolutions, particularly in England and France, destroyed much of the power of monarchs. In the 1640's, the English Parliament raised an army, defeated King Charles I, and condemned him to death. In 1688, the English people feared James II would restore the Catholic faith, and forced him to give up his throne. The French Revolution of 1789 limited the power of Louis XVI, and in 1793 the revolutionists put him to death. As a result, *limited*, or *constitutional*, monarchy developed, in which a legislature, a constitution, or both, limit the power of a monarch. Norway, Denmark, and Sweden have limited monarchies. The British monarch has little power.　WILLIAM EBENSTEIN

Related Articles in WORLD BOOK include:

Coronation	Emperor	King	Queen
Czar	Kaiser	Majesty	Sultan

MONASTERY. See MONASTICISM; MONK; CLOISTER.

MONASTICISM, *muh NAS tuh sihz uhm,* is a special form of religious community life. People who practice monasticism separate themselves from ordinary ways of living so they can follow the teachings of their religion as completely as possible. Men who adopt a monastic life are called monks and live in a monastery. Monastic women are called nuns and live in a convent.

Monasticism has an important part in several major religions. The word comes from the Greek word *monos*, meaning *alone*. The first Christian monastics were called *ones who live alone* because they lived by themselves in the desert. Later, groups of them gathered together and formed communities that followed a life of prayer and self-discipline. Today, the members of monastic communities also follow this kind of life.

Christian Monasticism began in Egypt about A.D. 271, when Saint Anthony of Thebes went alone into the desert to lead a holy life. Others soon followed. In the

Religious News Service

Trappist Monks at a monastery in the United States pray as a member of the order is ordained. Monastics isolate themselves from the outside world to devote their lives to religion.

early 300's, Saint Pachomius, another desert holy man, gathered some of these religious hermits into monasteries.

Monasticism became especially influential in Europe during the early Middle Ages. At that time, Europe had thousands of monasteries that were great centers of learning. After about 1200, however, Christian monasticism began to be replaced by orders of wandering friars. It has never regained its former influence. See MIDDLE AGES (The Christian Church).

Life in a Christian monastic community involves work, prayer, and meditation. A monastery or convent may be in a rural area or in a city. It may consist of a small, walled-in group of huts or a huge complex that houses hundreds of people. But it is designed to isolate its people from the world outside.

Christian monasticism includes an extremely important element called the *rule*, a set of guidelines by which members of a monastic group live. Its essential purpose is to set specific times each day for study, work, prayer, and other activities. Eastern Orthodox monastic groups base their rule on the teachings of Saint Basil of Caesarea, who lived in the 300's. The Rule of Saint Benedict of Nursia, written in the 500's, is the model for most Roman Catholic groups.

In addition to following a rule, Christian monks and nuns take three vows—*poverty*, *chastity*, and *obedience*. The vow of poverty requires a person not to own any private possessions. The vow of chastity obligates a monk or nun to have no sexual relations. The vow of obedience requires a person to always follow the decisions of the leader of the monastic community.

There are several Christian monastic orders. Each of these groups of monasteries or convents follows the same rule and shares a common leadership. There are also many nonmonastic orders. The members of these groups dedicate their lives to preaching and service, rather than to prayer and meditation.

Non-Christian Monasticism. A number of non-Christian religions also have monastic communities. For example, monasticism in Buddhism began in the 500's B.C., about 800 years before Christian monasticism. Buddha, the founder of the religion, taught his followers to give up their family, work, and material things. Early Buddhist monks and nuns spent most of their time as wandering *mendicants* (holy beggars). Today, most Buddhist monastics live in monasteries or convents. Buddhist monks are the only preachers of their religion. They live by a highly detailed rule called the *Vinaya*, which guides everything they do. See BUDDHISM.

The monks and nuns of Jainism, an ancient religion of India, still live much as the first Buddhist monastics did. They are wandering mendicants who lead extremely strict lives and strive never to harm any living creature, not even an insect. See JAINISM.

Hinduism has had religious hermits since ancient times. But they were never well organized until about A.D. 800, when a great teacher named Sankara founded an order with four monasteries. Since then, about 10 large orders and many small ones have developed.

The Influence of Monasticism Today has declined almost everywhere. Perhaps the chief reason for this decline has been widespread *secularism* (doubt of the value of religion). Christian monastic groups have lost members who question the value of the traditional vows, especially the vow of chastity. In addition, Communist governments have persecuted Buddhist monastics in China, Tibet, and parts of Southeast Asia. Most Hindu monastic orders also have a dwindling membership.

On the other hand, there has been renewed interest in monasticism among some religious groups. The Ramakrishna Mission, a modern Hindu order involved in social work, has attracted a large following in India and in other parts of the world. Tibetan Buddhist exiles have founded successful monasteries in the United States. The Lutheran and Dutch Reformed churches and several other Protestant groups have also started monastic communities.   NANCY E. AUER FALK

Related Articles. See RELIGIOUS LIFE with its list of *Related Articles*. See also the following articles:

Cloister	Hermit	Roman Catholic Church
Convent	Library (The	(The Recognition
Essenes	Middle Ages)	of Christianity)
Fakir		

MONAZITE, *MON uh zite*, is a heavy, yellow-brown mineral. It is a compound of phosphates (phosphorus and oxygen) of the rare-earth metals and thorium. Its chemical formula is $(Th, Ce, La, Y)PO_4$. Monazite is one of the chief sources of thorium, a nuclear fuel used in some nuclear reactors. Monazite is also an important source for the rare-earth elements and compounds, used widely in glass and metal manufacturing.

Monazite occurs naturally in granite rocks and pegmatite veins. As these rocks weather and break up, the monazite settles in deposits in riverbeds and beach sand. Commercial supplies of monazite are taken from sand. The monazite is usually separated from other collected minerals by an electromagnetic process. The most important monazite deposits occur in India and Brazil. Other monazite deposits are found in the United States, Australia, Sri Lanka, Malaysia, Indonesia, Canada, and South Africa.   CECIL J. SCHNEER

MONCK, *mungk*, **BARON** (1819-1894), CHARLES STANLEY MONCK, a British statesman, was the first governor general of the Dominion of Canada. He served as governor general of British North America from 1861 to 1867 and of the Dominion of Canada from 1867 to 1868. He was influential in uniting Upper and Lower Canada. He was born in Tipperary County, Ireland, and was graduated from Trinity College, Dublin. He was elected to the English House of Commons in 1852, and also was lord of the treasury.   LUCIEN BRAULT

Oil portrait by an unknown artist, The Government House, Ottawa

Baron Monck

MONCTON, New Brunswick (pop. 55,934), is the transportation and distributing center for the Atlantic Provinces of Canada. It lies on a bend of the Petitcodiac River near the Bay of Fundy. Railroads and highways connect Moncton to Nova Scotia. A railway and ferry provide service to Prince Edward Island (see New Brunswick [political map]). Daily air flights link Moncton with other parts of Canada and with the United States. The city has several industries. For the monthly weather, see New Brunswick (Climate).

The famous *bore* (tidal wave) of the Petitcodiac River rushes past Moncton twice a day. It comes up from the Bay of Fundy with a roar that can be heard far away. The wall of water ranges up to 4 feet (122 centimeters) high. This makes it necessary for even large boats to be tied firmly. See Bore; Bay of Fundy.

Germans from Pennsylvania first settled Moncton in 1763. The town, then known as *The Bend*, became a shipbuilding center. The name was changed to Moncton in 1885, and a city charter was granted in 1890. During World War II, the city's airport was used to train British and Canadian air forces. Moncton has a mayor-council form of government. W. S. MacNutt

MONDALE, WALTER FREDERICK (1928-), served as Vice-President of the United States from 1977 to 1981 under President Jimmy Carter. Before Mondale's election as Vice-President, he was a U.S. senator from Minnesota. He had a reputation as a liberal who supported government action in many fields.

Early Life. Mondale was born on Jan. 5, 1928, in Ceylon, Minn. His father was a Methodist minister. Walter, the second youngest of seven children, acquired the nickname Fritz as a boy. He graduated from the University of Minnesota in 1951 and from the university's law school in 1956. He practiced law with a Minneapolis firm until 1960.

In 1955, Mondale married Joan Adams (1930-) of St. Paul, Minn. They had three children— Theodore (1957-), Eleanor Jane (1960-), and William (1962-).

Political Career. Mondale began his political career in May 1960, when Governor Orville L. Freeman of Minnesota appointed him attorney general of the state. Mondale had managed Freeman's third successful campaign for the governorship. Mondale was elected state attorney general in November 1960 and won reelection in 1962. In 1964, Governor Karl F. Rolvaag appointed Mondale to the United States Senate to replace Hubert H. Humphrey, who had been elected Vice-President of the United States. Mondale won election to a full term in 1966 and was reelected in 1972.

As a senator, Mondale became known for his liberal views on domestic issues. He voted for bills that favored civil rights, consumer protection, and education reform. Mondale played a leading role in winning congressional approval in 1974 of legislation to regulate political campaign spending and donations.

In 1973, Mondale began a campaign for the 1976 Democratic presidential nomination. However, he

Wide World

Walter F. Mondale

attracted little national attention and withdrew his candidacy in November 1974. At Carter's request, the 1976 Democratic National Convention nominated Mondale for Vice-President. In the election, Carter and Mondale defeated their Republican opponents, President Gerald R. Ford and Senator Robert J. Dole of Kansas.

As Vice-President, Mondale took on assignments in many fields. His duties included visiting foreign nations and advising Carter.

In the 1980 presidential election, Carter and Mondale again became the Democratic nominees. But they were defeated in their bid for a second term by their Republican opponents, former Governor Ronald Reagan of California and George Bush, former U.S. ambassador to the United Nations (UN). Guy Halverson

See also Carter, James E., Jr.; Vice-President of the United States (Growth of the Vice-Presidency).

MONDAY is the second day of the week. The word comes from the Anglo-Saxon *mōnandaeg*, which means the *moon's day*. In ancient times, each of the 7 days was dedicated to a god or goddess. Monday was sacred to the goddess of the moon. Monday comes after Sunday.

Black Monday is the name given to Easter Monday, April 14, 1360. On this day, many of the troops of King Edward III of England, who were fighting the French, died on their horses outside Paris because of the cold weather.

Blue Monday is a term used in the United States to indicate that it is a dismal day. It is the day the workweek begins, and in many parts of the country it is the traditional family washday. Grace Humphrey

See also Labor Day; Week.

MONDRIAN, *MAWN dree ahn*, **PIET** (1872-1944), was a Dutch painter known for his rigidly geometric style. He influenced modern architecture and commercial design as well as painting.

Mondrian used straight black lines in horizontal and vertical patterns against a white background. In many paintings, he used pure primary colors to fill in rectangles created by these lines. Mondrian's final paintings have brightly colored lines, rather than black ones. All his important works feature smooth surfaces with no sign of brushstrokes. Mondrian's *Lozenge Composition in a Square* is reproduced in the Painting article.

Mondrian called his style *neoplasticism*. It is also called *De Stijl* (*The Style*), after a magazine published from 1917 to 1928 by Mondrian and the Dutch painter Theo Van Doesburg. Mondrian published many of his theories of art in this magazine. He regarded neoplasticism as an attempt to unify the arts and give people an orderly environment of beauty.

Mondrian was born in Amersfoort. During the early 1900's, he developed his geometric style through several series of increasingly abstract paintings of buildings and trees. Mondrian lived in Paris from 1919 to 1938. He settled in New York City in 1940 to escape World War II in Europe. Willard E. Misfeldt

MONEL METAL, *moh NEL*, is an important alloy of nickel and copper. It contains about 67 per cent nickel and 28 per cent copper. The rest is made up of such elements as iron, manganese, or aluminum. Monel metal looks like nickel. It is about as hard as steel and can be forged and drawn into wire. It is easier to prepare than nickel, for some ores already contain nickel and copper in suitable proportions. The alloy is therefore cheaper than pure nickel. See ALLOY; COPPER; NICKEL.

Monel metal resists corrosion. It shows hardly any damage from steam, sea water, hot gas, air, or acids. This property makes it useful in sheet-metal work, in chemical plants, and on ships. It is used for pump fittings, propellers, and condenser tubes, and as a covering for sinks and soda fountains.　　WILLIAM W. MULLINS

MONERA, *muh NIHR uh,* is a group of primitive one-celled organisms. The group consists of bacteria and blue-green algae. These organisms, called *monerans,* live alone or in clusters called *colonies.* The individual organisms can be seen only with a microscope, but some colonies are visible with the unaided eye.

Most biologists believe monerans rank among the oldest types of organisms on the earth. Unlike all other living cells, monerans do not have a nucleus surrounded by a membrane. However, they do have a nuclear area that contains DNA, the chemical substance that controls heredity. Monerans also lack typical *organelles,* structures that perform various functions in other cells (see CELL [Inside a Living Cell]). For these reasons, many biologists classify Monera as a separate kingdom. Some classify monerans as part of either the protist or plant kingdom.

Monerans live throughout the world, even where no other life can survive. For example, blue-green algae live in the water of hot springs as well as in frozen wastelands. Free-living bacteria dwell throughout the soil and water, and parasitic species live within nearly all multicelled plants and animals.　　IRWIN RICHARD ISQUITH

See also ALGAE; BACTERIA; PROTISTA.

MONET, *maw NEH,* **CLAUDE** (1840-1926), a French painter, was a leader of the impressionist movement. He

MONETARY CONFERENCE, INTERNATIONAL

influenced art by trying to paint his personal, spontaneous response to outdoor scenes or events. Earlier artists had also painted outdoor studies rapidly—almost in shorthand. But they used such studies as "notes" for more elaborate pictures painted in the studio. Monet was the most important of the artists who first allowed their initial impressions of outdoor scenes to stand as complete works.

Monet was especially concerned with the effect of outdoor light and atmosphere. This concern can be seen in his *Old St. Lazare Station, Paris* (1877), reproduced in the PAINTING article, and in his *La Grenouillère* (1869).

Monet was born in Paris. In 1874, he exhibited a landscape called *Impression: Sunrise* (1872) in a show. This patchily textured work caused one critic to skeptically call the entire show *impressionist,* which gave the movement its name. The painting is reproduced in the article on FRANCE (Arts).

Monet's fascination with light led him to paint several series of pictures showing the effect of sunlight on a subject. For example, he painted views of a cathedral or of a haystack under changing atmospheric conditions and at different hours of the day.

In 1883, Monet settled in Giverny, near Vernon. There, at his country home, he painted garden scenes and a series of mural-sized pictures of water lilies. The swirling colors of the lilies influenced later abstract painters.　　ALBERT BOIME

MONETA, ERNESTO T. See NOBEL PRIZES (table: Nobel Prizes for Peace—1907).

MONETARY CONFERENCE, INTERNATIONAL. See BRETTON WOODS.

Monet's *Water Lilies* was one of a series the artist painted near the end of his life, when he was almost blind. The emphasis on light and color gives the picture an almost abstract quality.

Bills and Coins from Around the World look different and have different names because each nation has its own system of money. The money from nearly all countries consists of paper or of copper, nickel, and other metals that have little value by themselves.

Dollar (Canada)

500 yen (Japan)

5 francs (Belgium)

100 lire (Italy)

Pound (Great Britain)

Franc (Switzerland)

Dollar (United States)

5 riyals (Saudi Arabia)

Peso (Mexico)

Naira (Nigeria)

Deutsche mark (West Germany)

10 shekels (Israel)

Franc (France)

MONEY

MONEY is anything that people agree to accept in exchange for the things they sell or the work they do. Gold and silver were once the most common forms of money. But today, money consists mainly of paper bills; coins made of copper, nickel, and other metals; and checking account deposits.

Each country has its own system of money. The bills and coins look different and have different names. In the United States, for example, the basic unit of money is the U.S. dollar. Canada uses the Canadian dollar, France the franc, Great Britain the pound, Japan the yen, Mexico the peso, and West Germany the mark. The money in use in a country is called its *currency*.

The contributors of this article are Stanley Fischer, Professor of Economics at Massachusetts Institute of Technology; and Edward C. Rochette, Executive Vice-President of the American Numismatic Association. The photographs for this article were taken for WORLD BOOK *by James Simek, unless otherwise credited. Some rare examples of money were provided through the courtesy of Deak-Perera Chicago, Inc.; the Rare Coin Company of America, Inc.; and the Jeffery S. Zarit Company.*

Money has three main uses. First, and most important, money serves as a *medium of exchange*—that is, it is something which people will accept for their goods or services. Without a medium of exchange, people would have to trade their goods or services directly for other goods or services. If you wanted a bicycle, for example, you would have to find a bicycle owner willing to trade. Suppose the bicycle owner wanted skis in exchange for the bike and you did not own skis. You would then have to find something a ski owner or ski maker wanted and trade it for skis to give the bicycle owner. Such trading is called *barter*. Barter can take much time and make it difficult for people to get the things they want. A modern, industrialized country could not function without a medium of exchange.

A second use of money is that it serves as a *unit of account*. People state the price of goods and services in terms of money. In the United States, people use dollars to specify price, just as they use hours to express time and miles or kilometers to measure distance.

A third use of money is as a *store of wealth*. People can save money and then use it to make purchases in the future. Other stores of wealth include gold, jewels, paintings, real estate, and stocks and bonds.

Any object or substance that serves as a medium of

Christiana Dittmann, Rainbow

Barter at a Peruvian Market Place

Cowrie Shells (Africa, Asia, and Australia)

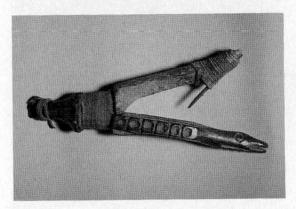

Fishhook (Northwest Coast of North America)

Trade Beads (Africa)

The Development of Money began as people came to accept certain goods as mediums of exchange. Before then, all people, like those at the upper left, used *barter* (the exchange of goods for other goods) to get what they wanted. The other pictures show former mediums of exchange.

exchange, a unit of account, and a store of wealth is money. To be convenient, however, money should have several qualities. It should come in pieces of standard value so that it does not have to be weighed or measured every time it is used. It should be easy to carry so that people can carry enough money to buy what they need. Finally, it should divide into units so that people can make small purchases and receive change.

In the past, people used beads, cocoa beans, salt, shells, stones, tobacco, and many other things as money. But above all, they used such metals as copper, gold, and silver. These metals made convenient, durable money.

Today, most money consists of paper. The paper itself is of little value, but it is accepted in exchange. People accept pieces of metal or paper in exchange for work or goods for only one reason: They know that others will take the same metal or paper in exchange for the things they want. The value of money therefore results from the fact that everyone will accept it as payment.

How Money Developed

Early people had no system of money as we know it. To get the things they wanted, people used the barter system of trading. Gradually, people learned that almost everyone would accept certain goods in exchange for any product or service. These goods included animal hides, cattle, cloth, salt, and articles of gold or silver. People began to use such merchandise as mediums of exchange, much as we use money.

Many people still use barter, especially in the developing countries of Africa, Asia, and Latin America. Millions of families in these countries live by farming and produce barely enough food to meet their own needs. As a result, they seldom acquire any money and must use barter to obtain the things they want. People in industrial countries also turn to barter if money becomes scarce or worthless. For example, barter became widespread in Germany after the country's defeat in World War II (1939-1945). German money became almost worthless, and people refused to take it. Instead, they bartered for most goods and services. They also used cigarettes, coffee, and sugar, which were in short supply, as mediums of exchange.

The First Coins may have been made during the 600's B.C. in Lydia, a country in what is now western Turkey. The coins were bean-shaped lumps of *electrum*, a natural mixture of gold and silver. The coins had a stamped design to show that the king of Lydia guaranteed them

589

to be of uniform size. The designs saved people the trouble of weighing each coin to determine its value. Traders accepted these coins instead of cattle, cloth, gold dust, or other goods as a medium of exchange. Other countries saw the advantages of the Lydian coins and began to make their own coins.

Many historians believe that coins were also invented independently in ancient China and in India. At first, the Chinese used knives, spades, and other metal tools as mediums of exchange. As early as 1100 B.C., they began to use miniature bronze tools instead of real ones. In time, the little tools developed into coins.

Coins today have many of the same features that they had in ancient times. For example, they have a government-approved design and a value stamped on them, like the coins of ancient Lydia.

The Development of Paper Money began in China, probably during the A.D. 600's. The Italian trader

Marco Polo traveled to China in the 1200's and was amazed to see the Chinese using paper money instead of coins. In a book about his travels, Polo wrote: "All his [the Chinese emperor's] subjects receive it [paper money] without hesitation because, wherever their business may call them, they can dispose of it again in the purchase of merchandise they may require."

In spite of Polo's description, Europeans could not understand how a piece of paper could be valuable. They did not adopt the use of paper money until the 1600's, when banks began to issue paper bills, called *bank notes*, to depositors and borrowers. The notes could be exchanged for gold or silver coins on deposit in the bank. Until the 1800's, most of the paper bills in circulation were notes issued by banks or private companies rather than by governments.

Some of the first paper currency in North America consisted of playing cards. This playing-card money was introduced in Canada in 1685. Canada was then a French colony. Money to pay the French soldiers sta-

The First Coins and Bills

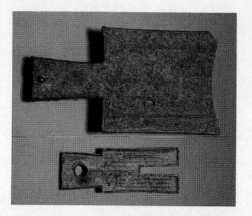

One of the First Coins was this bean-shaped gold *stater, above.* It was made in Lydia during the 500's B.C.

Miniature Tools, such as the spade and hoe at the right, were mediums of exchange in China as early as 1100 B.C.

An Ancient Greek Coin called a *tetradrachm* was issued during the 400's B.C. The front of the coin, *above left,* had a portrait of the goddess Athena. An owl was stamped on the back, *above right.*

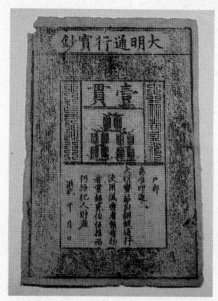

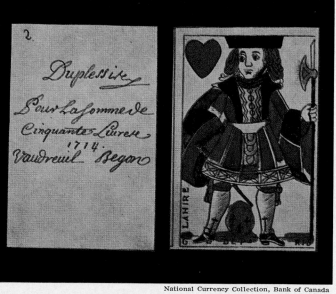

National Currency Collection, Bank of Canada

Paper Money was first used in China. This Chinese bill was printed on bark paper in the 1300's.

Playing-Card Money was used in Canada when it was a French colony during the 1600's and 1700's. The colonial governor signed the back of each card.

Money in the American Colonies

Money was scarce in the American Colonies. Paper currency was seldom used, and the British government permitted only the Massachusetts Bay Colony to mint coins. As a result, the colonists used any foreign coins they could get. Indian wampum and other goods also circulated in place of money.

The Oak-Tree Shilling was one of the first coins made in Massachusetts. The colony began to issue coins like the one above in 1652.

The Escudo was used throughout the Americas. The 8-escudo coin above was minted during the reign of King Ferdinand VI of Spain.

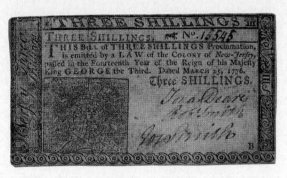

A 3-Shilling Note, *left,* was issued by the colony of New Jersey in 1776. A number of colonies issued their own paper currency.

Wampum, which consisted of beads made from shells, was used by the Indians to decorate garments and to keep records. The colonists, who had few coins, adopted wampum as money. Most wampum was made into necklaces or belts.

tioned there had to be shipped from France. Shipments were often delayed, however, and cash grew so scarce that the colonial government began to issue playing cards as currency. Each card was marked a certain value and signed by the governor. Such playing-card money circulated for more than 70 years.

History of United States Currency

In the American Colonies, money was scarce. Paper currency was seldom used. England did not furnish coins, and it forbade the colonies to make their own. The English government hoped to force the colonies to trade almost entirely with England. One way of doing so was by limiting the money supply. Without money, the colonists could not do business with traders in other countries who demanded payment in cash. But the colonists could buy products from English traders with *bills of exchange.* They received these documents from other English traders in exchange for their own goods.

The American colonists used a variety of goods in place of money. These goods included beaver pelts, grain, musket balls, and nails. Some colonists, especially in the tobacco-growing colonies of Maryland and Virginia, circulated receipts for tobacco stored in warehouses. Indian wampum, which consisted of beads made from shells, was mainly used for keeping records. But Indians and colonists also accepted it as money.

The colonists also used any foreign coins they could get. English shillings, Spanish dollars, and French and Dutch coins all circulated in the colonies. Probably the most common coins were large silver Spanish dollars called *pieces of eight.* To make change, a person could chop the coin into eight pie-shaped pieces called *bits.* Two bits were worth a quarter of a dollar, four bits a half dollar, and so on. We still use the expression *two bits* to mean a quarter of a dollar.

The Massachusetts Bay Colony became the first colony to make coins. In 1652, an English court granted the colony permission to do so. The colony produced several kinds of silver coins, including a *pine-tree shilling* and an *oak-tree shilling,* which were stamped with a tree design. England withdrew the permission to coin money soon after granting it, but Massachusetts continued to issue coins for 30 years. To hide its activities, the colony dated all coins 1652, no matter when they were made.

Massachusetts also became the first colony to produce paper money. In 1690, the colonial government issued notes called *bills of credit.* The bills were actually receipts for loans made by citizens to the government. Massachusetts used the bills to help finance the first French and Indian War, a war between English and French colonists for control of eastern North America.

The First United States Currency. During the mid-1700's, Great Britain tried to tighten its control over the American Colonies with new taxes, stricter trade regulations, and other laws. Friction between the Americans and the British mounted. In 1775, the Revolutionary War broke out between the two sides. The next year, colonial leaders meeting as the Second Continental Congress declared independence and founded the United States of America. To help finance the war for independence, each state and the Continental Congress began to issue paper money.

As war expenses mounted, the states and Congress printed more and more money. Congress itself issued about $240 million in notes called *continentals*. So many continentals were printed that by 1780 they were almost worthless. Americans began to describe any useless thing as "not worth a continental." The experience with continentals was so bad that the U.S. government did not issue paper currency again until the 1860's.

The United States won the Revolutionary War in 1783, but the struggle left the American monetary system in disorder. Most of the currencies circulated by the

states had little value. The Constitution of the United States, adopted in 1789, corrected this problem by giving Congress the sole power to coin money and regulate its value. The Coinage Act of 1792 set up the first national system of money in the United States. The act made the dollar the basic unit of money. It also put the nation on a system called the *bimetallic standard*, which meant that both gold and silver were legal money. The value of each metal in relation to the other was fixed by law. For years, 16 ounces (448 grams) of silver equaled 1 ounce (28 grams) of gold.

The Coinage Act of 1792 also established a national *mint* (agency to coin money) in Philadelphia. The mint produced $10 gold coins called *eagles*, silver dollars, and other coins.

Americans continued to use many foreign coins in addition to their new currency. A law passed in 1793 made these coins part of the U.S. monetary system. The

Money in the New Nation

Continental Currency was issued by the Continental Congress to help finance the Revolutionary War (1775-1783). So many of these notes were printed that they became almost worthless.

The Écu, a French coin, was one of many foreign coins that circulated in the United States after the nation won independence. A 1793 law made these coins part of the U.S. monetary system.

The Spanish Dollar, or piece of eight, was another foreign coin that circulated in the new nation. The coin shown at the far left and center was minted in Mexico in 1790. These dollars could be chopped into eight pieces, called *bits*, or into quarters, *near left*, called *two bits*.

A $10 Gold Piece called an *eagle* was issued by the U.S. Mint from 1795 to 1933. The eagle shown above dates from 1795. It has a liberty cap on the front and an eagle on the back.

Bank Notes were the most common paper money in the United States until the 1860's. Banks promised to exchange their notes for gold or silver. The State Bank of Illinois issued this note in 1840.

Later United States Money

U.S. currency of the 1800's and early 1900's included silver coins, gold pieces, and various types of paper money. Many bills, including gold and silver certificates, could be exchanged for gold or silver coins on demand. The use of these two metals as money is called the *bimetallic standard*.

Silver Dollar (1800)

U.S. Assay Office $50 Gold Piece (1851)

$20 Gold Double Eagle (1865)

Confederate $10 Bill (1861)

$5 Legal Tender Note (about 1862)

$50 Gold Certificate (about 1882)

$20 National Bank Note (about 1882)

$50 Silver Certificate (about 1891)

Andrew Jackson $10 Bill (about 1914)

value of a foreign coin depended on how much gold or silver it had. In 1857, Congress passed a law removing foreign coins from circulation.

The Rebirth of Paper Money. During the early 1800's, the only paper money in the United States consisted of hundreds of kinds of bank notes. Each bank promised to exchange its notes on demand for gold or silver coins. But numerous banks did not keep enough coins to redeem their notes. Many notes therefore were not worth their *face value*—that is, the value stated on them. As a result, people hesitated to accept bank notes.

The soundest bank notes of the early 1800's were issued by the two national banks chartered by the U.S. government. The First Bank of the United States was chartered by Congress from 1791 to 1811, and the Second Bank of the United States from 1816 to 1836. Both banks supported their notes with reserves of gold coins, and people considered the notes as good as gold.

Paper money as we know it today dates from the 1860's. To help pay the costs of the Civil War (1861-1865), the U.S. government issued about $430 million in paper money. The money could not be exchanged

for gold or silver. The bills were called *legal tender notes* or *United States notes*. But most people called them *greenbacks* because the backs were printed in green. The government declared that greenbacks were *legal tender*—that is, money people must accept in payment of debts. Nevertheless, the value of greenbacks depended on people's confidence in the government. That confidence rose and fell with the victories and defeats of the North in the Civil War. At one time, each greenback dollar was worth only 35 cents in gold coin. In the South, the Confederate States also issued paper money. It quickly became almost worthless.

In 1863 and 1864, Congress passed the National Bank Acts, which set up a system of privately owned banks chartered by the federal government. These national banks issued notes backed by U.S. government bonds. Congress also taxed state bank notes to discourage people from using them. As a result, national bank notes became the country's chief currency.

Some greenbacks also continued to circulate. The government announced that, beginning in 1879, it would pay gold coins for greenbacks. The U.S. Depart-

593

MONEY

ment of the Treasury gathered enough gold to redeem all the greenbacks likely to be brought in. But as soon as people knew that they could exchange their greenbacks for gold, they were not anxious to do so. The fact that the Treasury paid out only gold coins meant that the country was operating on an unofficial *gold standard*, rather than the bimetallic standard of the early 1800's.

Portrait on Bill:

William McKinley

Grover Cleveland

James Madison

Salmon P. Chase

Illustrations by U.S. Bureau of Engraving and Printing by special permission of the Chief, U.S. Secret Service, Dept. of the Treasury. Further reproduction in whole or in part is strictly prohibited.

Large U.S. Bills include Federal Reserve notes issued in denominations of $500, $1,000, $5,000, and $10,000, *above*. The government began withdrawing such bills from circulation in 1969.

The gold standard is a system in which a nation defines its basic monetary unit as worth a certain quantity of gold. The nation also agrees to redeem its money in gold on demand.

The new national banks system eliminated the confusion that had existed when hundreds of different bank notes were in circulation. But the system did not provide for the federal government to increase the supply of money when needed. Shortages of money contributed to a series of economic slumps during the late 1800's. Many people called for the government to provide more money by coining unlimited amounts of silver. Such a coinage policy was called *free silver*, and the argument over free silver became an important political issue. The dispute reached a climax during the presidential election of 1896. The Republican candidate, William McKinley, favored the gold standard. McKinley defeated William Jennings Bryan, the Democratic candidate, who supported free silver (see FREE SILVER). In 1900, Congress passed the Gold Standard Act, which officially put the nation on a gold standard. The United States went on and off the gold standard several times and finally abandoned it in 1971 (see GOLD STANDARD).

The United States suffered from repeated monetary difficulties until 1913, when Congress passed the Federal Reserve Act. This act created the Federal Reserve System, a central banking system that controls the nation's money supply.

United States Currency Today consists of coins and paper money. Under federal law, only the Department of the Treasury and the Federal Reserve System may issue U.S. currency. The Treasury issues all coins and a type of paper money known as *United States notes*. The Federal Reserve issues paper currency called *Federal Reserve notes*. All U.S. currency carries the nation's official motto, *In God We Trust*.

Coins come in six *denominations* (values): (1) penny, or 1 cent; (2) nickel, or 5 cents; (3) dime, or 10 cents; (4) quarter, or 25 cents; (5) half dollar, or 50 cents; and

United States Coins

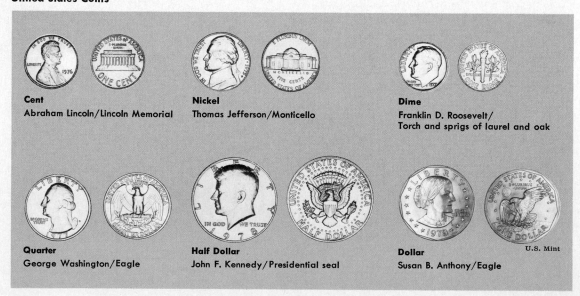

Cent
Abraham Lincoln/Lincoln Memorial

Nickel
Thomas Jefferson/Monticello

Dime
Franklin D. Roosevelt/
Torch and sprigs of laurel and oak

Quarter
George Washington/Eagle

Half Dollar
John F. Kennedy/Presidential seal

Dollar
Susan B. Anthony/Eagle

U.S. Mint

Federal Reserve Notes

Federal Reserve notes make up nearly all the paper money in the United States. The notes are issued by the 12 Federal Reserve Banks in the Federal Reserve System. The photographs on this page show the front and back of the seven bills now being issued: $1, $2, $5, $10, $20, $50, and $100.

George Washington

The Great Seal

Thomas Jefferson/Signing of the Declaration of Independence

Abraham Lincoln/Lincoln Memorial

Alexander Hamilton/U.S. Treasury

Andrew Jackson/The White House

Ulysses S. Grant/U.S. Capitol

Benjamin Franklin/Independence Hall

Illustrations by U.S. Bureau of Engraving and Printing by special permission of the Chief, U.S. Secret Service, Dept. of the Treasury. Further reproduction in whole or in part is strictly prohibited.

(6) $1. All coins are made of *alloys* (mixtures of metals). Pennies are an alloy of copper and zinc. Nickels are a mixture of copper and nickel. Dimes, quarters, half dollars, and dollars are made of three layers of metal sealed together. The core is pure copper, and the outer layers are an alloy of copper and nickel.

Dimes, quarters, half dollars, and dollars have ridges called *reeding* or *milling* around the edge. When coins were made of gold or silver, they were reeded to keep people from shaving slivers of valuable metal from the edge. Today, reeding helps blind people recognize certain denominations. For example, the reeding on a dime distinguishes it from a penny, which is about the same size but has a smooth edge.

Federal law requires that coins be dated with the year when they were made. Coins also must bear the word *Liberty* and the Latin motto *E Pluribus Unum*. The motto means *out of many, one* and refers to the creation of the United States from the original Thirteen Colonies.

Mints in Denver, Philadelphia, and San Francisco make all coins for general circulation. Coins made in Denver are marked with a small *D*. An *S* appears on

Chief Features of a Federal Reserve Note

Seal and letter of the Federal Reserve Bank that issued the note

Seal of the Department of the Treasury

Serial number

Serial number

Number of the Federal Reserve Bank that issued the note

Year when the note was designed

Printing plate identification numbers

595

most coins minted in San Francisco. Coins from the Philadelphia mint have no mint mark.

Paper Money. Federal Reserve notes make up nearly all the paper money issued in the United States today. About $100 billion of these notes were in circulation during the late 1970's. They come in seven denominations: $1, $2, $5, $10, $20, $50, and $100. The notes are issued by the 12 Federal Reserve Banks in the Federal Reserve System. Each note has a letter, number, and seal that identify the bank which issued it. In addition, each note bears the words *Federal Reserve note* and a green Treasury seal. Until 1969, Federal Reserve Banks also issued notes in four large denominations: $500, $1,000, $5,000, and $10,000.

The only other paper money issued in the United States today consists of United States notes. The Treasury issues them in the $100 denomination only. These notes, which are the descendants of Civil War greenbacks, carry the words *United States note* and a red Treasury seal. The Treasury keeps about $323

million in United States notes in circulation. All Federal Reserve and United States notes bear the printed signatures of the secretary of the treasury and the treasurer of the United States.

How Money Is Manufactured

Two bureaus of the U.S. Department of the Treasury manufacture currency. The Bureau of the Mint makes coins, and the Bureau of Engraving and Printing produces paper money.

Minting Coins. The production of a new coin begins with artists' proposed designs for the coin. After government officials select a design, an artist constructs a large clay model of the coin. Most models are about eight times the size of the finished coin. The artist does not add details because the clay is too soft. Instead, the artist makes a mold of the clay model and then makes a plaster cast from the mold. The plaster is hard enough to enable the artist to carve fine details. A machine called a *reducing lathe* traces the finished plaster model and carves the design, reduced to coin size, onto a soft piece of steel called a *hub.* The hub is heat-treated to

How Coins Are Made   The Bureau of the Mint makes all U.S. coins. Bars of metal are rolled into strips about the thickness of the finished coins. A machine punches coin-sized disks, called *blanks,* out of the metal strips. The blanks are fed into a *coining press,* which stamps a design on both sides of each blank.

Designing a New Coin starts with a number of sketches. After a design has been selected, an artist makes a large model of the coin.

Reducing the Design to Coin Size is done by a *reducing lathe.* This machine traces the model coin and carves it in miniature on a steel *hub.*

Cutting the Hub is done by a sharp tool on the other end of the reducing lathe. The hub is heat-treated to harden it and used to make a set of *coin-stamping dies.*

Screening the Blanks removes imperfect ones. The perfect blanks are fed into the coining press, which uses the coin-stamping dies to produce the design.

Inspecting the Newly Minted Coins helps find defective ones. Imperfect coins are melted down, and the metal is then used over again.

Bureau of the Mint, Philadelphia (WORLD BOOK photos)

Counting and Bagging the finished coins is done by machines. The mint ships the coins to Federal Reserve Banks for distribution to the public.

harden it. A special machine takes an impression of the hub to make a set of steel tools called *dies*, which will be used to stamp coins. The hub is stored and used to make new dies after the first ones wear out.

Bars of metal are heated and squeezed between heavy rollers into strips the thickness of a coin. A machine punches out smooth disks of metal, called *blanks*, from the strips. The blanks are the size of coins but have no design. The blanks are fed into an *upsetting machine*, which puts a raised rim around the edge of each one. Then, the blanks are fed into a *coining press*. The press uses the set of two stamping dies to impress the design on both sides of each blank in one operation. The press also reeds the edge of all coins but pennies and nickels.

The mint ships the finished coins to Federal Reserve Banks for distribution to commercial banks. The Reserve Banks also remove worn and damaged coins from circulation. The mint melts them and uses the metal to make new coins.

Printing Paper Money. The production of a new bill begins when artists sketch their designs for it. The secretary of the treasury must approve the final design. En-

gravers cut the design into a steel plate. A machine called a *transfer press* squeezes the engraving against a soft steel roller, making a raised design on the roller's surface. After the roller is heat-treated to harden it, another transfer press reproduces the design from the roller 32 times on a printing plate. Each plate prints a sheet of 32 bills. Separate plates print the front and back of the bills.

Many people believe that the paper used for money is made by a secret process. However, the government publishes a detailed description of the paper so that private companies can compete for the contract to manufacture it. A federal law forbids unauthorized persons to manufacture any paper similar to that used for money.

The Bureau of Engraving and Printing uses high-speed presses to print sheets of paper currency. The design is printed first. Then the seals, serial numbers, and signatures are added in a separate operation. The sheets are cut into stacks of bills. Imperfect bills are

How Paper Money Is Made   The Bureau of Engraving and Printing makes all U.S. paper currency. The bureau uses special paper and ink that have been manufactured to its specifications to produce long-lasting money. High-speed presses print sheets of 32 bills each. The sheets are then cut into separate bills.

Designing a New Bill begins with a number of artist's drawings. The United States secretary of the treasury must approve the final design for a new bill.

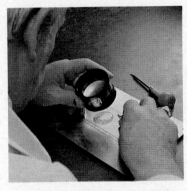

Making an Engraving. An engraver cuts the design for the bill into a steel plate. A machine called a *transfer press* copies the engraving 32 times on a printing plate.

Inspecting the Printing Plate ensures that it has no flaws. During printing, paper will be forced into the engraved lines of the plate to pick up ink.

Printing is done by fast presses that print thousands of sheets an hour. Separate plates print the front and back of the bills. Serial numbers are added in another step.

Inspecting the New Bills. The printed sheets are cut in half and examined. The inspectors mark any imperfect bills. Later, such bills are replaced.

Bureau of Engraving and Printing (WORLD BOOK photos)

Counting and Stacking are done by a machine that puts the bills in order of their serial numbers and bands them in stacks of 100 for delivery to banks.

replaced with new ones called *star notes*. Each star note has the same serial number as the bill it replaces, but a star after the number shows that it is a replacement bill. The bills are shipped to Reserve Banks, which distribute them to commercial banks.

Most $1 bills wear out after about 18 months in circulation. Larger denominations last for years because they are handled less often. Banks collect worn-out bills and ship them to Federal Reserve Banks for replacement. The Reserve Banks destroy worn-out money in shredding machines.

Money and the Economy

The quantity of money in a country affects the level of prices, the rate of economic growth, and therefore the amount of employment. If the money supply increases, people have extra money to buy things, and their demand for products grows. In response to the growing demand, manufacturers hire more workers to increase output. Earnings rise and spending increases, leading to further economic growth. However, if output cannot keep pace with demand, prices will increase. A continuing rise in prices is called *inflation*. Inflation may cause serious problems for people whose income does not keep pace with rising prices. If the money supply shrinks, on the other hand, people have less to spend. Goods and services remain unsold. Prices fall. Manufacturers cut back on production, and many businesses lay off workers.

The main economic goals of nearly all nations are to promote economic growth and high employment with a minimum increase in prices. A government's chief methods of promoting these goals are by its *monetary policy* and its *fiscal policy*. Monetary policy refers to how a government manages the nation's money supply. Fiscal policy refers to a government's taxing and spending programs. To stimulate the economy, for example, a government may increase the money supply, reduce taxes, or boost its own spending. The following discussion deals mainly with monetary policy. For information on fiscal policy, see ECONOMICS (Economic Stability).

The Value of Money is defined by economists as the quantity of goods and services that the money will buy. If prices go up or down, the value of money also changes. A major aim of any government's monetary policy is to keep prices stable and thus preserve the value of money, also called its *purchasing power*. Today, people worry most about inflation, which lowers the value of money. If prices double, for example, a dollar buys only half as much as before, and so the value of money has dropped one-half. You sometimes read or hear such a statement as "A dollar today is worth 42 cents." That statement means a dollar today buys only as much as 42 cents bought at an earlier time. The earlier time chosen for comparison is called the *base period*. Another way of describing the same price rise is to say that prices have risen 138 per cent since the base period. The *rate of inflation* is the rate at which prices in general are rising and the rate at which the value of money is falling.

Rapid, uncontrolled inflation can severely damage a country's economy. For example, prices in Germany increased 10 billion times from August 1922 to November 1923. Such severe inflation is called *hyperinflation*. The value of the German mark dropped so sharply and so rapidly that employers paid workers twice a day. Marks became so worthless that no one would take them, and people began to use barter instead of money. Employers paid workers by giving them some of the goods they produced. People spent so much time trading for the things they needed that production nearly came to a halt. The hyperinflation ended after the government introduced a new currency.

Inflation has many causes. But in most cases, prices cannot continue to rise for a long time without increases in the quantity of money. There never has been severe inflation without a large expansion in a nation's money supply.

Definitions of the Money Supply. The money supply includes more than just coins and paper money. In fact, checking account deposits are the most common form of money in the United States and many other countries. In the United States, about three-fourths of all payments are made by check. Checks are a safe and convenient medium of exchange. In addition, a canceled check provides written proof that payment was made.

Economists define the money supply in various ways, depending on which assets they include in their measurements. The definitions change as the banking system changes. Two major definitions of the U.S. money supply are called M-1 and M-2.

The most widely used definition of the money supply is M-1. M-1 consists of checking account deposits, also called *demand deposits*, and currency. In the late 1970's, individuals and organizations in the United States had about $300 billion in demand deposits and about $100 billion in currency. M-1 therefore totaled approximately $400 billion.

M-2 consists of M-1 plus money invested in savings accounts at commercial banks, at mutual savings banks, and at savings and loan associations. Such savings, called *time deposits*, are not immediately available to make purchases. The saver first has to withdraw the money, and the bank can require advance notice of withdrawal. However, most people can easily convert their savings to cash or checking deposits. M-2 amounted to about $900 billion in the late 1970's.

How the Money Supply Is Determined. The size of a nation's money supply is determined differently if the nation uses *commodity money* or *fiat money*. Commodity money typically consists of valuable metals, especially gold or silver. Fiat money is of little value itself. But it has value because people are willing to accept it. To increase the likelihood of people accepting its money, a government may make the currency legal tender. Then, the law requires people to accept the money at face value.

If a nation uses commodity money, the money supply is determined by the cost of producing the metal and the rate of production. During the late 1800's and early 1900's, the United States and many other countries were on the gold standard, which is a commodity money system. Each nation promised to redeem its currency for a specified amount of gold. For example, a U.S. dollar was officially valued at about 26 grains (1.7 grams) of gold. The amount of money countries could issue depended on how much gold was being mined in the world. A decline in gold output during the 1870's and 1880's slowed the growth of the money supply and caused prices to fall. The economic problems ended only after the discovery of new gold fields in South Africa and the invention of a more efficient method of extracting gold from the surrounding rocks.

The United States and most other countries today are on the fiat money system. Under this system, the money supply does not depend on the production of any commodity. Instead, the national government controls the money supply. The government does so through its *central bank*, which is a government agency in most countries. A nation's central bank issues currency, regulates the activities of the country's commercial banks, and performs other financial services for the government. The Federal Reserve System is the central bank of the United States. The central bank of Canada is the Bank of Canada. Other central banks include the Bank of England in Great Britain, the Banque de France in France, and the Deutsche Bundesbank in West Germany.

How the Federal Reserve System Adjusts the Money Supply

The Federal Reserve System, the central bank of the United States, regulates the nation's money supply. This chart shows how the Federal Reserve puts more money into circulation. To shrink the money supply, the Federal Reserve takes opposite actions.

WORLD BOOK diagram by David Cunningham

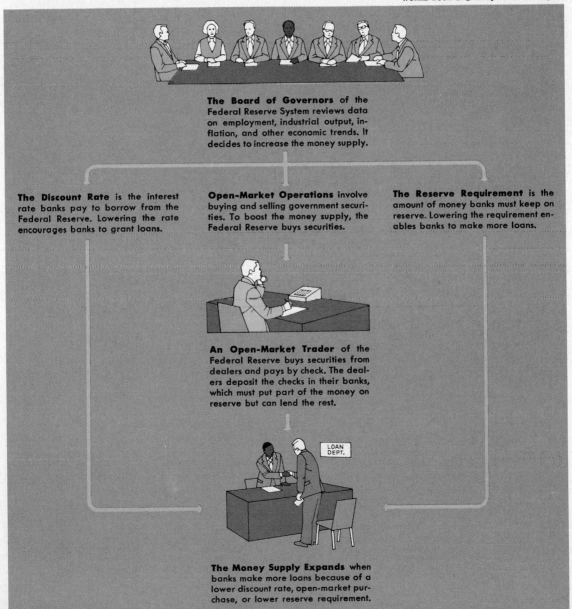

The Board of Governors of the Federal Reserve System reviews data on employment, industrial output, inflation, and other economic trends. It decides to increase the money supply.

The Discount Rate is the interest rate banks pay to borrow from the Federal Reserve. Lowering the rate encourages banks to grant loans.

Open-Market Operations involve buying and selling government securities. To boost the money supply, the Federal Reserve buys securities.

The Reserve Requirement is the amount of money banks must keep on reserve. Lowering the requirement enables banks to make more loans.

An Open-Market Trader of the Federal Reserve buys securities from dealers and pays by check. The dealers deposit the checks in their banks, which must put part of the money on reserve but can lend the rest.

LOAN DEPT.

The Money Supply Expands when banks make more loans because of a lower discount rate, open-market purchase, or lower reserve requirement.

598a

MONEY

The Role of the Federal Reserve System. The Federal Reserve System, often called simply the *Fed*, has 12 regional Federal Reserve Banks. Each bank is responsible for a Federal Reserve District. Most large commercial banks belong to the system. They use the Reserve Bank in their district much as people use a bank in their community. Each member bank must keep a certain sum of money either as currency in its vaults or as deposits at its Reserve Bank. This sum is a percentage of the member bank's own deposits and is called a *reserve requirement*. A bank may withdraw any excess deposits at the Reserve Bank to get currency when needed. It may also borrow from the Reserve Bank.

The Federal Reserve can control the money supply in several ways. It may raise or lower the *discount rate*, which is the interest rate that commercial banks pay to borrow from Reserve Banks. Or the Federal Reserve may raise or lower reserve requirements. Raising the discount rate or the reserve requirement reduces the ability of banks to make loans and thus shrinks the money supply. Lowering the discount rate or the reserve requirement has the opposite effect.

However, the Federal Reserve's chief means of adjusting the money supply is by buying and selling government securities. These activities are called *open-market operations*. If the Federal Reserve wants to increase the quantity of money, it makes an *open-market purchase*. It buys government securities from banks and other businesses and from individuals. The Federal Reserve pays for the securities with a check. The sellers now have more money than before, and so there is more money in the economy. When the sellers deposit the checks at their bank, the supply of money may increase further. Under Federal Reserve rules, a member that receives new funds must put a portion, from 3 to 22 per cent, on reserve in its district Reserve Bank. The bank then can lend or invest the rest. As a result, the quantity of money in the economy will rise by even more than the amount of the open-market purchase. To reduce the money supply, the Federal Reserve sells securities in an *open-market sale*.

The Federal Reserve's ability to control the money supply might make it seem easy to adjust the supply to promote the government's economic goals. For example, the Federal Reserve could expand the money supply whenever unemployment increased, thus creating more jobs. It could reduce the money supply whenever inflation occurred, thus holding prices down. But use of monetary policy to control the economy is far more difficult than it seems.

Monetary policy is often ineffective because changes in the money supply do not affect the economy immediately. If the effect of a change is long delayed, it may strike the economy at the wrong time. For example, the Federal Reserve might decide to increase the money supply in the hope of reducing joblessness within six months. But the drop in unemployment might not come for a year or more, and it might happen at a time when unemployment had already begun to fall for other reasons. Instead of reducing joblessness, the Federal Reserve's action might then only fuel inflation.

The Federal Reserve's task is also difficult because it is likely to increase unemployment when it tries to reduce inflation, and vice versa. If the Federal Reserve fights inflation by reducing the money supply, employers may cut back on production and more workers will lose their jobs. If the Federal Reserve boosts the money supply to create more jobs, price increases may follow. In such cases, the Federal Reserve may have difficulty deciding what to do. Some economists believe that the best way to fight inflation and unemployment is by a gradual, continuous increase in the money supply instead of frequent adjustments.

International Finance

Much trade takes place between nations. For example, Americans buy French cheese and Japanese automobiles, and the French and Japanese buy American airplanes and blue jeans. Most imported goods must be paid for in the currency of the selling country. An American automobile dealer who buys Japanese cars gets yen by buying them from a bank at the current *exchange rate*. An exchange rate is the price of one nation's currency expressed in terms of another country's currency. If the rate were 200 yen to the dollar, for example, the American would have to buy $6,000 in yen to pay for a Japanese automobile that cost 1.2 million yen.

Exchange rates are determined in foreign exchange markets. The rates vary from day to day in relation to international demand for various currencies. If Americans buy more Japanese products, for example, the U.S. demand for yen increases and the yen rises in price against the dollar. This system is known as *floating exchange rates* or *flexible exchange rates*.

Most countries do not allow the exchange rate for their currency to float freely, however. Each country has holdings of foreign currency. If the exchange rate

Money Brokers buy and sell foreign currency for immediate or future delivery. Their clients hope to profit—or to avoid losses—from changes in exchange rates.

Exchange Rates

An *exchange rate* is the price of one nation's currency in terms of another country's currency. Exchange rates vary from day to day, depending on the international demand for different currencies. This table shows the exchange rate in United States dollars for many world currencies on February 29, 1980.

Country	Monetary Unit	Price in U.S. Dollars	Units per U.S. Dollar
Afghanistan	Afghani	$ .0280	35.714
Albania	Lek	.2550	3.92
		.1429*	7.00*
Algeria	Dinar	.2725	3.6697
Angola	Kwanza	.0380	26.316
Argentina	Peso	.00064	1,562.5
Australia	Dollar	1.1050	.9050
Austria	Schilling	.0790	12.658
Bahamas	Dollar	1.0100	.9901
Bahrain	Dinar	2.6485	.37757
Bangladesh	Taka	.0685	14.599
Belgium	Franc	.0352	28.409
Benin	Franc	.004830	207.04
Bermuda	Dollar	1.01	.9901
Bolivia	Peso	.0520	19.23
Brazil	Cruzeiro	.0232	43.103
Bulgaria	Lev	1.1650	.86
		1.1364*	.88*
Burma	Kyat	.1575	6.3492
Burundi	Franc	.0114	87.719
Cameroon	Franc	.004830	207.04
Canada	Dollar	.8735	1.1448
Central African Rep	Franc	.004830	207.04
Chad	Franc	.004830	207.04
Chile	Peso	.0275	36.364
China	Yuan	.7000	1.43
		.6623*	1.51*
Colombia	Peso	.0250	40.00
Congo	Franc	.004830	207.04
Costa Rica	Colón	.1200	8.333
Cuba	Peso	1.3889*	0.72*
Czechoslovakia	Koruna	.1975	5.06
		.0958*	10.44*
Denmark	Krone	.1820	5.4945
Dominican Republic	Peso	1.00	1.00
Ecuador	Sucre	.0400	25.000
Egypt	Pound	1.45	.68966
El Salvador	Colón	.4025	2.4845
Ethiopia	Birr	.4900	2.0408
Finland	Markka	.2700	3.7037
France	Franc	.2415	4.1408
Germany, East	Mark	.4878	2.05
		.5747*	1.74*
Germany, West	Mark	.5642	1.7724
Ghana	Cedi	.3700	2.7027
Great Britain	Pound	2.2755	.43946
Greece	Drachma	.0275	36.364
Guatemala	Quetzal	1.00	1.00
Guinea	Syli	.0625	16.0
Guyana	Dollar	.4200	2.3810
Haiti	Gourde	.2010	4.9751
Honduras	Lempira	.5010	1.9960
Hong Kong	Dollar	.2055	4.866
Hungary	Forint	.0525	19.05
		.0492*	20.31*
India	Rupee	.1249	8.0064
Indonesia	Rupiah	.001650	606.1
Iran	Rial	.0142	70.475
Iraq	Dinar	3.41	.29326
Ireland	Pound	2.1350	.46838
Israel	Shekel	.2564	3.9
Italy	Lira	.001223	817.66
Ivory Coast	Franc	.004830	207.04
Jamaica	Dollar	.5800	1.7241
Japan	Yen	.003990	250.63
Jordan	Dinar	3.40	.29412
Kenya	Shilling	.1415	7.0671
Korea, South	Won	.0018	555.6
Kuwait	Dinar	$3.6600	.27322
Laos	Kip	.0017	600.0
Lebanon	Pound	.3125	3.200
Lesotho	Rand	1.2420	.80515
Liberia	Dollar	1.00	1.00
Libya	Dinar	3.42	.29240
Luxembourg	Franc	.0352	28.409
Madagascar	Franc	.004930	202.8
Malawi	Kwacha	1.2700	.78740
Malaysia	Ringgit	.4610	2.1692
Mali	Franc	.0025	400.0
Mauritania	Ouguiya	.0218	45.87
Mexico	Peso	.0455	21.978
Monaco	Franc	.2415	4.1408
Mongolia	Tughrik	.3448	2.90
Morocco	Dirham	.2750	3.6364
Mozambique	Escudo	.0350	28.571
Nepal	Rupee	.0865	11.561
Netherlands	Guilder	.5130	1.9493
New Zealand	Dollar	.9750	1.0256
Nicaragua	Córdoba	.1000	10.000
Niger	Franc	.004830	207.04
Nigeria	Naira	1.91	.52356
Norway	Krone	.2040	4.9020
Oman	Rial	2.8975	.34513
Pakistan	Rupee	.1030	9.709
Panama	Balboa	1.00	1.00
Papua New Guinea	Kina	1.4650	.6826
Paraguay	Guaraní	.0080	125.0
Peru	Sol	.0043	232.56
Philippines	Peso	.1375	7.2727
Poland	Zloty	.0350	28.57
		.0327*	30.56*
Portugal	Escudo	.0230	43.478
Romania	Leu	.2050	4.88
Russia	Ruble	1.58	.633
		1.5291*	0.654*
Rwanda	Franc	.0114	87.719
Saudi Arabia	Riyal	.2985	3.3501
Senegal	Franc	.004830	207.04
Sierra Leone	Leone	.9950	1.0050
Singapore	Dollar	.4640	2.1552
Somalia	Shilling	.1630	6.1350
South Africa	Rand	1.2420	.80515
Spain	Peseta	.0154	64.935
Sri Lanka	Rupee	.0685	14.599
Sudan	Pound	2.0175	.49566
Sweden	Krona	.2380	4.2017
Switzerland	Franc	.5920	1.689
Syria	Pound	.2625	3.810
Taiwan	Dollar	.0290	34.48
Tanzania	Shilling	.1240	8.0645
Thailand	Baht	.0515	19.417
Togo	Franc	.004830	207.04
Trinidad and Tobago	Dollar	.4300	2.3256
Tunisia	Dinar	2.58	.388
Turkey	Lira	.014286	69.999
Uganda	Shilling	.1349	7.4128
United Arab Emirates	Dirham	.2685	3.7244
United States	Dollar	1.00	1.00
Upper Volta	Franc	.004830	207.04
Uruguay	Peso	.1215	8.2305
Venezuela	Bolívar	.2335	4.283
Yemen (Sana)	Rial	.2275	4.3956
Yugoslavia	Dinar	.0565	17.699
Zaire	Zaire	.6650	1.5038
Zambia	Kwacha	1.3050	.76628
Zimbabwe	Dollar	1.75	.5714

*Preferential noncommercial rate for tourists and for remittances from non-Communist countries.

Sources: *Nominal New York Closing Quotations for Interbank Payments of Listed Currencies as of Close of Business, February 29, 1980,* Chase Manhattan Bank, New York City; *UN Monthly Bulletin of Statistics,* February 1980.

falls too far, the government will use some of its foreign holdings to buy enough of its own currency to stabilize the exchange rate.

The Balance of Payments is the difference between a nation's receipts of foreign currency and its expenditures of foreign currency. A nation's balance of payments affects its exchange rate. The world price of a country's currency tends to rise if the country's receipts exceed its expenditures. This condition is called a *balance-of-payments surplus*. A nation's currency will tend to decline on world markets if more money flows out of the country than comes in. This condition is called a *balance-of-payments deficit*.

The primary influences on the balance of payments are income levels and rates of inflation. Suppose income levels rise more quickly abroad than in the United States. People in other countries then will increase their imports of American goods. The United States will export more than it imports, creating a balance-of-payments surplus and causing the world price of U.S. dollars to increase. If inflation causes prices to rise more quickly in the United States than abroad, foreign goods become cheaper for Americans to buy and they import more. This situation creates a balance-of-payments deficit and causes the U.S. dollar to drop in price.

International Reserves. Each country has official holdings of foreign currency that it uses to stabilize exchange rates and to pay international debts. These holdings are called *international reserves*. The U.S. dollar plays a special role in international reserves, partly because the United States is one of the world's leading trading nations. Many countries keep nearly all their international reserves in U.S. dollars, and most countries are willing to accept payment in dollars. To some extent, the U.S. dollar thus functions as an international medium of exchange.

The International Monetary Fund (IMF) is an organization that works to improve financial dealings between countries. The IMF has introduced a type of international reserves called *Special Drawing Rights* (*SDR's*), which member countries can use to settle accounts among themselves. Unlike other reserves, SDR's exist only as entries on the account books of the IMF. Some economists think SDR's will become widely used as an international medium of exchange.

STANLEY FISCHER and EDWARD C. ROCHETTE

Related Articles. See BANKS AND BANKING and ECONOMICS. See also the following articles:

MODERN CURRENCIES

Bolívar	Dollar	Krone	Pound
Cent	Drachma	Lira	Quarter
Centavo	Escudo	Mark	Quetzal
Centime	Franc	Nickel	Rial
Córdoba	Guilder	Penny	Ruble
Crown	Half Dollar	Peseta	Rupee
Dime	Kopeck	Peso	Yen
Dinar	Krona	Piaster	Yuan

HISTORICAL CURRENCIES

Denarius	Florin	Napoleon	Real
Doubloon	Greenback	Piece	Shekel
Ducat	Groat	of Eight	Shilling
Eagle	Guinea	Pine-Tree	Sou
Farthing	Livre	Shilling	Talent

NEGOTIABLE INSTRUMENTS

Bill of Exchange	Money Order
Bill of Lading	Negotiable Instrument
Bond	Note
Check	Receipt
Draft	Savings Bond
Letter of Credit	Traveler's Check

GOVERNMENT AGENCIES

Engraving and Printing, Bureau of	Secret Service, United States
Federal Deposit Insurance Corporation	Treasury, Department of the
Federal Reserve System	

INTERNATIONAL FINANCE

Balance of Payments	Exchange Rate
Bretton Woods	International
Convertibility	Monetary Fund
Devaluation	Special Drawing
Eurodollar	Rights
European Monetary Agreement	

OTHER RELATED ARTICLES

Barter	Gresham's Law
Bullion	Indian, American (Money)
Coin Collecting	Inflation and Deflation
Colonial Life in America (Money)	Investment
Counterfeiting	Legal Tender
Depreciation	Mill
Depression	Mint
Free Silver	Silver (Uses of Silver)
Gold (Money)	Trade (The Use of Money)
Gold Standard	Wampum

Outline

I. How Money Developed
   A. The First Coins
   B. The Development of Paper Money
II. History of United States Currency
   A. The First United States Currency
   B. The Rebirth of Paper Money
   C. United States Currency Today
III. How Money Is Manufactured
   A. Minting Coins
   B. Printing Paper Money
IV. Money and the Economy
   A. The Value of Money
   B. Definitions of the Money Supply
   C. How the Money Supply Is Determined
   D. The Role of the Federal Reserve System
V. International Finance
   A. The Balance of Payments
   B. International Reserves

Questions

How did people obtain the things they needed before they used money?

What organization controls the supply of money in the United States?

What motto appears on all U.S. coins and paper money?

Where was the first paper money used?

What were some things that people in the past used as money?

Why do certain coins have ridges called *reeding* on the edge?

How does inflation affect the value of money?

Where are U.S. coins manufactured?

How did the expression *two bits*, meaning 25 cents, originate?

When did the U.S. government begin to issue *greenbacks*?

UNITED STATES OF AMERICA POSTAL MONEY ORDER

A U.S. Postal Money Order can be purchased at any United States post office. The post office fills in the amount of the money order. The purchaser adds his or her name and address and the name of the person who should receive payment.

U.S. Postal Service

MONEY ORDER is a document directing that a sum of money be paid to a certain person. Many banks and stores sell money orders, but most people buy them at a post office. A purchaser fills out a money order and mails it to the person named. The person receiving the order may cash it at any bank or post office. But the receiver must provide identification so that the money will not be given to the wrong person.

United States Postal Money Orders may be purchased at any post office in the United States. The highest amount of any single money order to be sent within the United States is $400. The limit for an international money order is $300. But there is no limit on the number of orders that a person may purchase at one time. Therefore, there is no limit to the amount of money that may be sent by money orders.

The rates on money orders sent within the United States are graduated as follows:

Amount of Money Order	Fee
Not more than $10.00	$0.55
$10.01 to $50.00	$0.80
$50.01 to $400.00	$1.10

International money orders may be sent to almost any part of the world. The fees for purchasing international money orders are listed in the table below.

Amount of International Money Order	Fee
Not more than $10.00	$0.90
$10.01 to $50.00	$1.10
$50.01 to $300.00	$1.40

A postal money order may be cashed at any time within 20 years from the date of issue. Money orders are cleared through Federal Reserve Banks. Orders may be endorsed once.

Canadian Postal Money Orders cannot exceed $200, but an unlimited number can be purchased. The fee is 25 cents for money orders issued in Canada for payment in Canada, Antigua, Bahamas, Barbados, Belize, Cayman Islands, Dominica, Fiji, Jamaica, St. Christopher (St. Kitts)-Nevis-Anguilla, St. Lucia, and the United States and its territories and possessions. The money order fee for Great Britain, Guyana, Ireland, Montserrat, St. Vincent, and Trinidad and Tobago is 50 cents. For all other countries, the fee is $1.00.

Critically reviewed by the CANADA POST OFFICE and the
U.S. POSTAL SERVICE

MONEYWORT. See LOOSESTRIFE.

Canada Post Office

CANADIAN POSTAL MONEY ORDER / MANDAT DE POSTE CANADIEN

A Canadian Postal Money Order is printed in both English and French. It has spaces for the sender's name and address and for the name of the person receiving the money.

MONGOL EMPIRE

The **Mongol Empire** covered most of Asia. It began under Genghis Khan during the early 1200's and pushed into eastern Europe for a period in the mid-1200's. The empire reached its greatest extent under Kublai Khan in the late 1200's. The Mongols controlled most of India from the 1500's to the 1700's. The original Mongol homeland makes up what is now Mongolia.

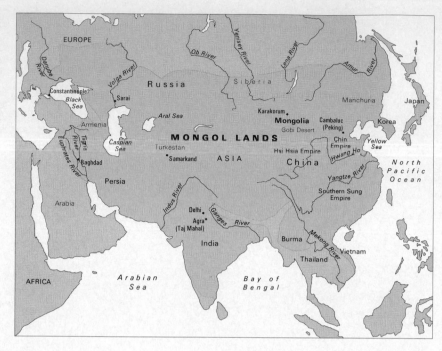

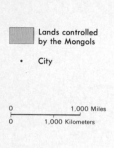
Lands controlled by the Mongols

• City

| 0 | 1,000 Miles |
| 0 | 1,000 Kilometers |

WORLD BOOK map

MONGOL EMPIRE was the biggest land empire in history. Its territory extended from the Yellow Sea in eastern Asia to the borders of eastern Europe. At various times it included China, Korea, Mongolia, Persia (now Iran), Turkestan, and Armenia. It also included parts of Burma, Vietnam, Thailand, and Russia.

The Mongols were the most savage conquerors of history. But their vast empire contributed to increased contacts between peoples. Migrations fostered these contacts and promoted trade. Roads were built to connect Russia and Persia with eastern Asia. Many Europeans came to China, and Chinese found their way into Russia and other parts of Europe. Printing and other Chinese inventions such as paper, gunpowder, and the compass may have been introduced to the West during Mongol times.

The Mongols originally consisted of loosely organized nomadic tribes in Mongolia, Manchuria, and Siberia. They lived in felt tents called *yurts*, and raised ponies, sheep, camels, oxen, and goats. They ate mainly meat and milk. Every Mongol was a soldier, and learned to ride and use a bow and arrow skillfully.

Early Empire

Genghis Khan. In the 1100's, Temujin, a Mongol chieftain who later became known as Genghis Khan, rose to power as *khan* (see KHAN). He began to unify and organize the scattered Mongol tribes into a superior fighting force. Genghis Khan was shrewd, ruthless, ambitious, and a strict disciplinarian. After he became the undisputed master of Mongolia, and "lord of all the peoples dwelling in felt tents," he set out on a spectacular career of conquest.

Genghis Khan aimed to train the best disciplined and most effective army of his time. As part of his military

strategy, he formed an officer corps from picked Mongols who were trained in military tactics. These men were then stationed with various tribes as a training force. The Mongol tribes specialized in the art of siege. They learned to use storming ladders, and sandbags to fill in moats. Besiegers approached fortress walls under the protection of gigantic shields. Each tribe prepared a siege train, which consisted of special arms and equipment.

Invasions. Genghis Khan wanted to conquer China to the south. As a skillful strategist, he decided to attack first Hsi Hsia, a state in northwest China. Hsi Hsia represented the Chinese military pattern, with Chinese-trained armies and Chinese-built fortresses. In this campaign, Genghis Khan could evaluate his armies, and train them for war against China.

The Mongols subdued Hsi Hsia, and then turned to North China. There a nomadic tribe called the Juchen had established the Chin dynasty. Genghis Khan chose spring for his assault on China, so that his horses would have food when crossing the Gobi Desert. Warriors carried everything they needed on the march, and each rider had a spare horse. The hordes drove herds of cattle for food in the desert. Genghis Khan conquered North China in 1215.

Before completing the conquest of China, Genghis Khan turned westward into central Asia and eastern Europe. His armies charged into the steppes of Russia and the Muslim lands, including Persia. They came within reach of Constantinople (now Istanbul), and destroyed much of Islamic-Arabic civilization.

All along their routes, the Mongol armies ruthlessly eliminated any resistance. They spread terror and destruction everywhere. When conquered territories resisted, the Mongols systematically slaughtered the pop-

600

ulation of entire cities. They laid waste to North China so completely that a horseman could ride long distances without stumbling over anything.

Genghis Khan died in 1227. The Mongols pushed into Europe under Ogotai, a son of Genghis Khan. In 1241, about 150,000 Mongol riders laid waste a large part of Hungary and Poland, and threatened the civilization of western Europe. Ogotai died in the midst of this campaign. His death forced the Mongol generals to break off their European campaign and return to Mongolia to elect a new khan.

Later Empire

Kublai Khan, a grandson of Genghis, completed the conquest of China after attacking the Sung dynasty in South China. Kublai Khan then founded the Yüan dynasty, which lasted from 1279 to 1368. He established the Mongol capital at Cambaluc, the site of present-day Peking. Successive attempts to extend the Mongol empire to Japan ended in failure. Mongol warriors were not successful fighters on the seas or in the tropical climate of Southeast Asia.

The Mongols under Kublai Khan had a reputation for some tolerance. Kublai permitted the existence of various religions. He enlisted the services of Muslims, Christians, Buddhists, and Taoists. He accepted Confucianism and Chinese political ideas, although he avoided having too many Chinese in high offices. In Persia and other Islamic lands, many Mongols adopted Muslim customs and the Muslim faith.

European Contacts. Marco Polo was one of the most famous Europeans to travel to the Orient at this time. His travel records contain much interesting information about the Mongols. His reports of beautiful Chinese cities and the riches of the country he called *Cathay* did much to arouse the interest of Europeans in exploring the possibilities of trade with the Orient. Many Europeans, including Christopher Columbus, then sought to go to the Orient by the sea route.

The Khan expressed a desire to have more mission-aries sent to China. Dominicans and Franciscans traveled to China and were welcomed by the Khan in Cambaluc. A Franciscan, John of Montecorvino, built a church in the capital and converted many people to Christianity.

Decline. The Mongol empire did not last long, because it was too big and had no unity of culture. Actually, it began to disintegrate shortly after it reached its peak of expansion in the late 1200's. The Mongols were dauntless fighters, but had little experience in administration. They relied upon other peoples to look after the affairs of their empire. They brought foreigners into China to avoid total reliance on the Chinese. The Mongols temporarily suspended the Chinese civil service system to allow these other peoples to assume positions.

Corrupt government and incompetent administration resulted in revolts in different parts of the empire. Even before the fall of the Yüan dynasty in China, the Mongols had lost control of many of their conquered lands. In some areas, they had never succeeded in firmly establishing their rule after their military conquests. Even at the peak of his power, Kublai Khan's authority did not extend to such distant places as Persia and Russia. The Mongols also lacked a firm hold in Southeast Asia.

Breakup. When Kublai Khan died, his empire broke up into several parts. These smaller empires were the Golden Horde on the steppes of southern Russia and the Balkans, the Mongolian-Chinese Chin Empire, and the realm of the Ilkhans in western Asia. A revolution in China in the 1300's resulted in the fall of the Yüan dynasty and restored Chinese rule in the form of the Ming dynasty.

The great Timur, or Tamerlane, a descendant of Genghis Khan, joined some of the Mongol empires together again and extended his rule over much of Asia in the late 1300's. A descendant of Tamerlane named Babar established a powerful Mongol state in India in 1526. Babar's realm was called *the Kingdom of the Great*

Medieval Tartar Huts and Waggons, drawing by Quinto Cenni. From *The Book of Sir Marco Polo* by Colonel Sir Henry Yule, London, published by John Murrey, 1903 (Newberry Library)

Mongols of the Middle Ages, *above,* often carried their tents on large wooden wagons when moving. A team of many oxen drew the wagon, and the driver stood in the entrance of the tent.

Mongols of Today, *left,* live in tents that closely resemble those of medieval times. A Mongol woman, dressed in warm clothing and heavy jewelry, stands in front of her felt-covered home.

601

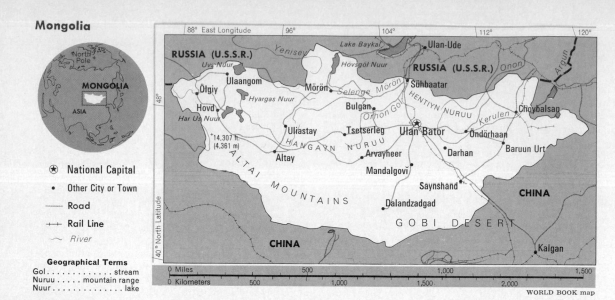

National Capital
Other City or Town
Road
Rail Line
River

Geographical Terms
Gol . . . . stream
Nuruu . . . . . mountain range
Nuur . . . . lake

WORLD BOOK map

Moguls. The term *Mogul* comes from the Persian word *mughul,* meaning *a Mongol.* A Mogul emperor, Shah Jahan, built the beautiful Taj Mahal in the early 1600's. The British destroyed the Mogul kingdom after it had begun to break up in the 1700's.   THEODORE H. E. CHEN

Related Articles. See the History sections of the various countries where Mongols ruled, such as CHINA (History). See also the following:

Genghis Khan   Mongolia   Shah Jahan
Kublai Khan   Polo, Marco   Tamerlane

MONGOLIA, *mahn GOH lee uh,* is a Communist country that lies between China and Russia in east-central Asia. Its official name is MONGOLIAN PEOPLE'S REPUBLIC. Mongolia is more than twice as large as Texas. However, a single Texas city—Houston—has almost as many people as all of Mongolia.

Mongolia is a rugged land. Plateaus and towering mountain ranges cover much of the country. The bleak Gobi Desert blankets much of southeastern Mongolia. Temperatures are usually very cold or very hot. Mongolia's little rainfall occurs in a few summer storms.

Raising livestock has long been the country's chief economic activity. Mongolians once wandered over the grassy plateaus where their animals grazed. Today, more than half of them work on cooperative livestock farms that were set up by the government.

Mongolia is the original home of an Asian people called *Mongols.* The Mongols built the largest land empire in history during the 1200's. They conquered an area from eastern Asia to eastern Europe. China ruled Mongolia from the 1680's to 1911. Mongolia was then called *Outer Mongolia.* A Mongol region to the south, called *Inner Mongolia,* is still part of China.

Government. Mongolia is a Communist country. Its constitution calls the country "a socialist state in the form of a people's democracy." There is only one political party, however, the Mongol People's Revolutionary Party (MPRP). The party is called the "guiding and directing force of society and the state." Only MPRP candidates and some non-party candidates may be put up for election to national and local councils.

The people elect the members of the Great National Khural, Mongolia's legislature, to three-year terms. The Khural elects a seven-member Presidium, Mongolia's real governing body. The Presidium makes the important decisions in domestic and foreign affairs. Its chairman is the head of state. The Khural also elects a Council of Ministers, which runs the government.

For administrative and judicial purposes, the country is divided into 18 provinces called *aimaks,* and two independent cities. These cities are Ulan Bator, Mongolia's capital, and Darhan, a new industrial area.

The People. Nearly all the people of Mongolia are Mongols. About 4 of every 100 persons belong to a group called *Kazakhs.* Some Chinese, Russians, and Tuvans also live in Mongolia. The official language of Mongolia is Mongolian. It is written in a special form of the Cyrillic alphabet, the alphabet Russians use. Many Mongolians believe in the form of Buddhism called *Lamaism.* The Communist government

─────────── **FACTS IN BRIEF** ───────────

Capital: Ulan Bator.

Official Language: Mongolian.

Form of Government: People's Democracy (Communist).

Area: 604,250 sq. mi. (1,565,000 km²). *Greatest Distances*—east-west, 1,500 mi. (2,414 km); north-south, 790 mi. (1,271 km).

Population: *Estimated 1981 Population*—1,721,000; distribution, 55 per cent rural, 45 per cent urban; density, 3 persons per sq. mi. (1 per km²). *1969 Census*—1,197,-600. *Estimated 1986 Population*—2,025,000.

Chief Products: *Agriculture*—camels, cattle, goats, grain, horses, meat, milk, potatoes, sheep, vegetables. *Manufacturing and Processing*—building materials, felt, processed foods, soap, textiles. *Mining*—coal, petroleum.

Flag: Vertical stripes of red, blue, and red, with gold symbols on the left stripe. Red stands for Communism and blue for the Mongols of the past. The flag was adopted in 1944. See FLAG (color picture: Flags of Asia and the Pacific).

Money: *Basic Unit*—tughrik, divided into 100 mongo. For the value of the tughrik, see MONEY (table).

tries to discourage religious practices among the people.

More than half the people live on livestock farms. The state has set up about 300 of these farms. The farms are like huge ranches with small towns in the center. The central buildings include houses, offices, shops, and medical posts for the people and animals. The state runs some farms for raising crops.

Few Mongolians still follow the traditional way of life of *nomadic* (wandering) herdsmen. Those who do, journey from place to place with their animals. They live in collapsible felt tents called *ger* or *yurts*, which help protect them from the intense heat and cold. The government is gradually settling the nomads on farms.

The Mongolian State University was founded in Ulan Bator in 1942. The country has teacher training colleges and technical schools where students study such subjects as agriculture, economics, and medicine.

Land. No part of Mongolia lies less than 1,700 feet (518 meters) above sea level. The Altai Mountains in the west rise to more than 14,000 feet (4,270 meters). A high plateau lies between the Altai Mountains and the mountains called Hangayn Nuruu in central Mongolia. This plateau has many lakes. Uvs Nuur, the largest, covers about 1,300 square miles (3,370 square kilometers). Dense forests cover the mountains called Hentiyn Nuruu, northeast of Ulan Bator. Eastern Mongolia is a lower plateau of grassland. It becomes less fertile as it nears the Gobi, a bleak desert area from southeastern Mongolia into Inner Mongolia.

Mongolia gets very hot and very cold. Temperatures ranging from −57° to 96° F. (−49° to 36° C) have been recorded in Ulan Bator. Snowfall and rainfall are usually light. Heavy rains may occur in July and August. Violent earthquakes sometimes shake Mongolia.

Economy. The state owns and operates most factories and the state farms in Mongolia. Livestock farms are cooperative property, owned by the members. Livestock-raising is the backbone of the economy. Herdsmen keep over 20 million animals, more than half of them sheep. Other animals include camels, cattle, goats, and horses. Cattle make up about 35 per cent of the country's exports, and wool about 40 per cent. Mongolia also exports dairy products, furs, hides, and meat.

The number of animals raised in the country has decreased during the 1950's and 1960's. During the same period, farmers have greatly increased their production of grains and other crops.

Mongolia has little industry. Building materials, processed foods, tent frames and felts, wool and woolen fabrics, furniture, glass and china, soap, and matches rank among the chief manufactured products. The government is trying to develop industry. Mongolia has deposits of coal, copper, gold, iron, and petroleum.

Mongolia's main railroad connects Ulan Bator with the Russian Trans-Siberian railroad in the north and with Chinese railroads in the south. The country has about 47,000 miles (75,600 kilometers) of roads. Most of these are dirt roads. Mongolia and Russia trade goods over Hövsgöl Nuur, a lake; and Selenge Mörön, a river. Air service links Ulan Bator with other countries and with provincial capitals in Mongolia.

Mongolia's leading daily newspaper is *Unen* (*Truth*). The country also has 9 other newspapers and 13 periodi-cals. There are 18 provincial newspapers in Mongolia.

History. Various groups of Mongol peoples were united under Genghis Khan in the early 1200's. Genghis Khan and his grandson Kublai Khan extended the Mongol Empire from Korea and China westward into Europe. The empire broke up in the late 1300's. See MONGOL EMPIRE.

Mongol princes reunited Mongolia briefly in the late 1500's, and converted the people to Lamaism. In the early 1600's, the Manchu rulers of Manchuria gained control of Inner Mongolia. The Manchus conquered China in 1644 and seized Outer Mongolia in the 1680's. Mongolia, like China, had little contact with the rest of the world during the 1700's and the 1800's. See MANCHU.

The Mongolians drove Chinese forces out of Outer Mongolia in 1911. They appointed a priest, called the *Living Buddha*, as king, and appealed to Russia for support. In 1913, China and Russia agreed to give Outer Mongolia control over its own affairs. Legally, Outer Mongolia remained Chinese territory. But, in fact, it came largely under the control of Russia.

Sovfoto

Ulan Bator, Mongolia's Capital, has many modern buildings and a central square that is larger than Moscow's Red Square. The theater, *left*, presents ballets, concerts, and operas.

Home on the Mongolian Plains for centuries has been the *ger* or *yurt*, a portable hut made of layers of felt covered with canvas or hide. The huts are also used in many towns.

Leavitt F. Morris

In 1920, during Russia's civil war, anti-Communist Russian troops occupied Outer Mongolia and ruled it through the Living Buddha. Mongolian and Russian Communists gained control of Outer Mongolia in 1921. They established the Mongolian People's Republic in 1924, after the Living Buddha died.

China did not recognize Mongolia's independence until 1946. Mongolia became a member of the United Nations in 1961. Mongolia supports Russia in the Russian-Chinese dispute for leadership of the Communist world. In 1966, Mongolia and Russia signed a new mutual-assistance pact. Many Soviet troops are in Mongolia for construction and defense.   CHARLES BAWDEN

Related Articles in WORLD BOOK include:

Altai Mountains	Gobi
China (History)	Horse (graph)
Clothing (picture:	Kublai Khan
Traditional Costumes)	Lamaists
Genghis Khan	Ulan Bator

MONGOLISM. See DOWN'S SYNDROME.

MONGOLOID. See RACES, HUMAN (How Races Are Classified).

MONGOOSE, *MAHNG goos,* is the name of several closely related small animals that live in Africa and southern Asia. They are related to the civet and the genet (see CIVET). The common mongoose is about 16 inches (41 centimeters) long and has stiff, yellowish-gray hair that is grizzled with brownish-black. It has a fierce disposition, but can be tamed.

The mongoose is known for its ability to kill mice, rats, and snakes. It is not immune to poison, but its swiftness allows it to seize and kill poisonous snakes such as the cobra. The mongoose has been introduced into Jamaica, Cuba, Puerto Rico, Hawaii, and other parts of the world to destroy hordes of rats. The mongoose also kills poultry, wild birds, and other beneficial small animals. It eats birds' eggs and young birds. The mongoose reproduces rapidly. Mongooses cannot be brought into the United States without a permit from the Bureau of Sport Fisheries and Wildlife. A permit is granted only if the animal will be used in a zoological exhibit or for educational, medical, or scientific purposes.

Scientific Classification. The mongoose belongs to the family *Viverridae.* There are about 16 genera. One, the Asiatic mongoose, is genus *Herpestes.*   E. LENDELL COCKRUM

MONITOR, *MAHN uh tuhr,* is the name of a group of about 30 kinds of lizards that live in the Solomon Islands, New Guinea, Australia, the East Indies, southern Asia, and Africa. In Australia, monitors are called *goannas.* Monitors have long heads and necks; short, powerful legs; and tails with whiplike ends. The different kinds are much alike and hard to tell apart. The body is usually black or brown with yellow bands, spots, or mottling. The deeply forked tongue looks like a snake's tongue. Monitors are usually at least 4 feet (1.2 meters) long. One, the *Komodo dragon,* is often 10 feet (3 meters) long (see KOMODO DRAGON).

When a monitor is cornered, it pretends to be ferocious. It stands high on its legs, puffs up its body, and swings its tail like a whip. The teeth can make deep wounds and the tail can lash with some force.

A monitor will eat almost any animal it can kill, such as other reptiles, birds, small mammals, large insects, and crustaceans. Many monitors like to live near water, and they are all good swimmers and divers. When they swim, they hold their legs against their sides, driving themselves forward by weaving their bodies and tails. Monitors lay eggs, and climb well. The two best-known species are the *Nile monitor* of Africa and the *water monitor,* which lives from India to northern Australia.

Scientific Classification. Monitors are in the monitor family, *Varanidae.* Nile monitor is genus *Varanus,* species *V. niloticus.* Water monitor is *V. salvator.*   CLIFFORD H. POPE

MONITOR. See TELEVISION (The Control Room).

MONITOR AND MERRIMACK fought a famous naval battle in the American Civil War. These two ships were called *ironclads,* because they had been covered with iron. The *Monitor* was built of iron as well as being ironclad. The battle focused worldwide attention on the importance of armor-plated ships. It was also one of the first sea battles in which the opposing ships were maneuvered entirely under steam power.

The *Merrimack,* or *Merrimac,* originally was a wooden frigate. Federal troops scuttled the ship when they

Peter Jackson, Bruce Coleman Ltd.

A Mongoose prepares to eat a snake it has killed. The mongoose can fight snakes successfully because of its ability to dodge and pounce with lightning speed.

evacuated the Navy yard at Portsmouth, Va., in 1861. Confederate forces raised it, and covered it with iron plates. They renamed it the *Virginia* although it is usually known by its original name. On Mar. 8, 1862, the *Virginia* (*Merrimack*) sank two Northern ships at Hampton Roads, Va. When it returned the next day, it found a Union ironclad waiting, the *Monitor*. John Ericsson, a Swedish-American inventor, had designed this "cheese box on a raft" for the Northern Navy (see ERICSSON, JOHN). The two ships battled for about four hours. The *Monitor* moved about more easily than the *Virginia* (*Merrimack*), but its shells had little effect on the Confederate ship. When the *Monitor* withdrew temporarily, the *Virginia* (*Merrimack*) returned to the James River. Within the year, both ships were lost. The *Virginia* (*Merrimack*) was destroyed to keep it from being captured by the Union, and the *Monitor* foundered while being towed at sea in a storm. In 1974, Duke University scientists announced that they had located the *Monitor* at the bottom of the Atlantic Ocean. They reported that the ship lay about 15 miles (24 kilometers) south of Cape Hatteras, off the coast of North Carolina. BERNARD BRODIE

See also CIVIL WAR (picture: The Battle of the Ironclads).

MONITORING STATION receives and measures signals from radio transmitters. These signals come from such sources as AM and FM radio stations, television stations, radios in airplanes and ships, and amateur radios. Some countries use monitoring stations as "listening posts" to obtain information from other countries.

In the United States, the Federal Communications Commission (FCC) operates monitoring stations. In Canada, the Department of Transport operates the stations. Both government agencies issue transmitter licenses and enforce operating regulations determined by national laws and international laws and treaties. These laws and treaties establish standards and procedures for equipping, installing, and operating radio stations. Monitoring stations measure radio transmissions often to make certain the stations are operating under these procedures and the terms of their licenses.

The FCC operates 19 monitoring stations in the United States. Canada has eight stations. Each country maintains many mobile monitoring vehicles. Long-range direction finders help locate sources of radio interference, unauthorized transmitters, and aircraft and ships in distress. See DIRECTION FINDER.

During World War II, the FCC operated as many as 102 monitoring stations, supported by automobiles with direction finders. This equipment was used to uncover radio transmitters operated by enemy agents.

Critically reviewed by the FEDERAL COMMUNICATIONS COMMISSION

MONIZ, *MOH neesh,* **ANTÔNIO CAETANO DE ABREU FREIRE EGAS** (1874-1955), shared the 1949 Nobel prize for physiology and medicine. Moniz introduced the *prefrontal leukotomy,* or *lobotomy,* operation as a therapeutic procedure in certain mental diseases. He and Almeida Lima operated on 29 patients with a hollow needle containing a steel-wire cutting loop. The tool cuts nerve fibers that connect parts of the brain.

Moniz was born in Avanca, near Estarreja, Portugal. He became professor of neurology in Lisbon in 1911. He held political posts from 1903 to 1919, including minister of foreign affairs. HENRY H. FERTIG

MONK, *mungk,* is a man who has taken religious vows and retired from worldly life to live with other monks. At first the term meant a person who lived entirely alone in order to devote himself to religion. Such persons were also called hermits, which is the name now reserved to them. The first group of Christian monks originated in northern Egypt early in the A.D. 300's. The members lived by themselves, but met at fixed times for worship. They studied the Scriptures, prayed, and thought of God.

Later, monks formed communities, with buildings known as *monasteries.* Many orders of monks now exist, especially in the Roman Catholic Church. All the monasteries of one order follow an identical rule of life. In any such order, the members take vows of poverty, chastity, and obedience. FULTON J. SHEEN

See also FRIAR; HERMIT; MONASTICISM; RELIGIOUS LIFE; TONSURE.

MONK, or **MONCK,** *mungk,* **GEORGE** (1608-1670), DUKE OF ALBEMARLE, was an English general and naval commander. He arranged the restoration of the Stuarts to the English throne in 1660.

Monk joined the army at the age of 17. He commanded Irish troops for the king in the English civil war of 1642-1649, which ended with the triumph of Parliament and Oliver Cromwell (see CROMWELL, OLIVER). The parliamentary troops defeated Monk in 1644, and imprisoned him in the Tower of London for two years. Cromwell then offered to free him if he would serve in the army of the Commonwealth of England. Monk did so, and was made a lieutenant general.

He served the Commonwealth as commander-in-chief of Scotland from 1651 to 1652 and from 1654 to 1659. He helped command the English Navy in 1652 and 1653, and defeated the Dutch in several naval battles.

After the death of Cromwell in 1658, Monk made possible the peaceful return of Charles II. The Presbyterian members who had been driven out of Parliament in 1648 were brought back. Their presence in Parliament made certain a majority in favor of restoring the Stuart king. Monk quietly shifted the armed forces throughout England in such a way that there would be no chance of an uprising (see RESTORATION).

Monk brought back Charles II in 1660. Charles rewarded Monk by making him duke of Albemarle, privy councilor, and lord lieutenant of Devon and Middlesex. Monk was born in Devonshire. W. M. SOUTHGATE

MONK, THELONIOUS (1917-   ), is an American composer and pianist. He became closely identified with the *bebop* movement in jazz in the early 1940's. Many of Monk's compositions, including "Round Midnight," "Blue Monk," and "Straight No Chaser," have become jazz standards. Monk's unique and unpredictable piano style helped establish him as one of the most adventurous individualists in jazz.

Monk was born in Rocky Mount, N.C., and grew up in New York City. Beginning in 1939, he played in the small groups that helped develop bebop in such Harlem jazz clubs as Minton's Play House and Monroe's Uptown House. He gained an international reputation in the late 1950's, after years of comparative obscurity. He usually leads a quartet, but occasionally forms an orchestra for concerts and recordings. LEONARD FEATHER

Francisco Erize, Bruce Coleman Ltd.; E. R. Degginger

Monkeys Live in Many Kinds of Environments. Spider monkeys, *left*, dwell in forests of Central and South America. They swing and run swiftly among the tree branches. Baboons, *right*, roam African *savannas* (grasslands with scattered trees). They feed on the ground and sleep in caves or trees.

MONKEY is one of many kinds of small, lively mammals that rank among the most intelligent animals. Scientists classify monkeys—together with man, apes, lemurs, and lorises—in the highest order of mammals, the *primates*. The intelligence of monkeys enables them to learn many tricks. Their liveliness makes them favorites in zoos. Because of the similarities between monkeys and man, scientists have used monkeys in research on human behavior and disease. For example, a blood substance called the *Rh factor* was discovered during experiments with the rhesus monkey (see RH FACTOR).

There are about 200 species of monkeys. Most of them live in tropical regions in Central and South America, Africa, and Asia. Some species live in forests and spend their entire life in the trees. Others live in *savannas* (grasslands with scattered trees) and spend most of their life on the ground. But even these monkeys sleep in trees—or on steep cliffs—for protection at night. All monkeys live together in various kinds of groups.

Monkeys vary greatly in size. The smallest species, the pygmy marmoset, measures only about 6 inches (15 centimeters) long, not including the tail. The mandrill, one of the largest species, may grow as long as 32 inches (81 centimeters), not including the tail.

Scientists classify monkeys into two major groups, New World monkeys and Old World monkeys. New World monkeys live in Central and South America, and Old World monkeys are found in Africa and Asia. The two groups differ in several ways. For example, New World monkeys have nostrils spaced widely apart. The

nostrils of Old World monkeys are close together. Most kinds of New World monkeys have 36 teeth. Old World monkeys have 32 teeth, as do human beings. Some species of New World monkeys can grasp objects with their tail, but no Old World monkey can.

New World monkeys have a remarkable variety of sizes, shapes, and colors. Scientists divide them into two main groups: (1) marmosets and tamarins; and (2) all other New World species, including capuchins, douroucoulis, howlers, spider monkeys, squirrel monkeys, woolly monkeys, and woolly spider monkeys. All New World monkeys are *arboreal*—that is, they live in trees.

Old World monkeys include baboons, colobus monkeys, guenons, langurs, and macaques. Some Old World monkeys, including colobus monkeys and langurs, are *leaf-eating monkeys* and live mainly in trees. Many other Old World monkeys live on the ground. Among the monkeys that live on the ground, the males may be twice as large as the females. See the *Related Articles* at the end of this article for a list of the mon-

WHERE MONKEYS LIVE

The black areas of the map below show the parts of the world in which monkeys live. Most species of monkeys live in the tropics.

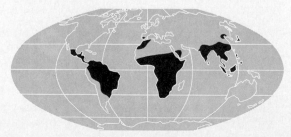

J. R. Napier, the contributor of this article, is Visiting Professor of Primate Biology at Birkbeck College of the University of London.

keys about which World Book has separate articles.

Many people believe that apes—chimpanzees, gibbons, gorillas, and orang-utans—are monkeys. But monkeys and apes differ in several ways. For example, apes are more intelligent than monkeys. Most monkeys have a tail, but none of the apes do. Monkeys are smaller than most species of apes.

Man has destroyed the living areas of several species of monkeys through various activities. Such activities have included logging, mining, and replacing forests and grasslands with cities and farms. As a result, some species are in danger of becoming extinct.

The Body of a Monkey

All monkeys, including those that live on the ground, are the descendants of monkeys that lived in trees. As a result, all monkeys have a body primarily suited for living in and moving through trees. For example, monkeys have long arms and legs that help them climb, leap, and run. They also can use their hands and feet to grasp objects—including the branches of trees. Most species have a long tail that helps them keep their balance. Some can use their tail to grasp branches while moving through the trees.

Head. Monkeys, unlike many other mammals, depend more on their eyes than their nose to gather information about their surroundings. They have large eyes that face forward. They can see in depth and distinguish colors. Their eyes help them judge distances and tell the size, shape, and ripeness of food.

Some large monkeys, including baboons and mandrills, have large, heavy jaws and eat grass and leaves. Smaller monkeys, such as marmosets and squirrel monkeys, have smaller, lighter jaws. They eat mostly fruit and insects.

Many kinds of Old World monkeys have cheek pouches much like those of hamsters and squirrels. The pouches enable the monkeys to store food temporarily. No New World monkey has these pouches.

Arms and Legs. Monkeys usually walk and run on all fours, either on tree branches or on the ground. Most species have legs that are slightly longer than their arms. Many kinds of monkeys can stand and even run on their legs, but only for a short period of time. For example, Japanese macaques sometimes walk or run on their legs while carrying food in their hands.

Hands and Feet. Old World monkeys have *opposable* thumbs—that is, the thumb can be placed opposite any of the other fingers. This enables a monkey to grasp a tree branch in much the same way that a person grips the handle of a hammer. Most kinds of New World monkeys have thumbs that are only partly opposable. Their thumbs also do not move so freely as those of Old World monkeys. Two kinds of New World monkeys—spider monkeys and woolly spider monkeys—have no thumbs. Among Old World monkeys, colobus monkeys have no thumbs.

The feet of most monkeys are larger and more powerful than their hands. All monkeys have five toes on each foot. The big toes look and function much like thumbs, giving the monkey an extra pair of grasping "hands."

Marmosets and tamarins have claws on their fingers and toes, except for their big toes, which have a nail. All other kinds of monkeys have flat or flattish nails on all their fingers and toes.

Tail. Most monkeys that live on the ground have a shorter tail than do most of those that live in trees. Arboreal monkeys may have a tail longer than their body. They use their tail for balancing on tree branches. They also use it as an *air brake*—that is, to slow themselves down when they leap from branch to branch.

Some New World monkeys, including howlers, spider monkeys, and woolly monkeys, can grasp objects with their tail. The tail of such monkeys has an area of bare skin at the end. This skin has many ridges, which enable the tail to grasp objects firmly. The tail of other monkeys is completely covered with hair.

The Life of a Monkey

No one knows exactly how long monkeys live in their natural environment. Monkeys in captivity live longer than most other kinds of mammals, except apes and human beings. Capuchins may live 40 years, and baboons and some macaques 30 years.

Food. Most kinds of monkeys eat almost anything they can find. Their food includes birds and birds' eggs, flowers, frogs, fruit, grass, insects, leaves, lizards, nuts, and roots. Baboons may catch and eat such animals as newborn antelope.

Leaves make up about 80 per cent of the food of the Old World leaf-eating monkeys. These monkeys have

THE SKELETON OF A GUENON MONKEY

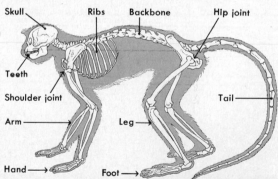

Skull · Ribs · Backbone · Hip joint · Teeth · Shoulder joint · Arm · Leg · Tail · Hand · Foot

WORLD BOOK illustrations by Marion Pahl

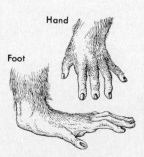

Hand · Foot

A Monkey's Hands and Feet both can grasp objects. The big toe of a monkey looks and moves like a thumb.

Shelly Grossman, Woodfin Camp, Inc.

A Monkey's Tail provides balance for running and jumping. A spider monkey, *above,* can swing by its tail.

Douc Langur
Pygathrix nemaeus
Found in Laos and Vietnam
and on the island of Hainan
Body length: 22 to 32 inches
(56 to 81 centimeters)*

De Brazza's Guenon
Cercopithecus neglectus
Found in central and eastern
African forests
Body length: 16 to 24 inches
(41 to 61 centimeters)*

Red Uakari
Cacajao rubicundus
Found in eastern Peru and
northwestern Brazil
Body length: 14 to 19 inches
(36 to 48 centimeters)*

Woolly Monkey
Lagothrix lagothricha
Found in the upper Amazon River
basin of South America
Body length: 15 to 23 inches
(38 to 58 centimeters)*

Douroucouli
Aotus trivirgatus
Found in forests of most of
South America and Panama
Body length: 10 to 19 inches
(25 to 48 centimeters)*

Patas Monkey
Erythrocebus patas
Found in African grasslands
from Tanzania northward
Body length: 23 to 29 inches
(58 to 74 centimeters)*

Red Colobus
Colobus badius
Found in tropical rain forests
of Africa
Body length: 18 to 24 inches
(46 to 61 centimeters)*

Proboscis Monkey
Nasalis larvatus
Found in Borneo
Body length: 21 to 30 inches
(53 to 76 centimeters)*

*not including the tail

WORLD BOOK illustrations by Helmut Diller

a special kind of stomach that is divided into compartments. They also have large salivary glands. Such specialized structures help leaf-eating monkeys digest their coarse food. Unlike other Old World monkeys, leaf-eating monkeys do not have cheek pouches.

Young. Most kinds of monkeys give birth to one baby at a time. Scientists do not know the length of pregnancy of many species of monkeys. The females of the other species carry their young inside their body for periods ranging from about 4½ months to about 8 months.

Most baby monkeys depend completely on their mother for food and security. They nurse on her milk for a few weeks to two years, depending on the species. A baby monkey hangs onto its mother almost from the moment of birth by grasping her fur. The mother carries the infant until it can travel safely on its own. At first, the infant clings to its mother's underside. Later, the young monkey rides on its mother's back. Among three kinds of New World monkeys—douroucoulis, marmosets, and titis—the father may carry the young on his back, giving them to the female for feeding.

Group Life. All species of monkeys live together in social groups. There are three kinds of monkey groups: (1) family groups, (2) multimale groups, and (3) one-male groups.

Family groups consist of an adult male, an adult female, and their young. At least three kinds of New World monkeys—douroucoulis, marmosets, and titis—live in family groups.

Multimale groups may consist of a number of adult males, about twice as many adult females, and their young. New World monkeys that live in such groups include capuchins, howlers, spider monkeys, and squirrel monkeys. Many Old World monkeys, including langurs, macaques, and most baboons, also live in multimale groups.

One-male groups consist of one adult male, several adult females, and their young. Young adult males and females may also belong to the group. Certain species of Old World monkeys live in such groups. They include geladas, Hamadryas baboons, and patas monkeys.

In general, monkeys that live in trees have a looser social organization than do monkeys that live on the ground. For example, most guenons and mangabeys live in trees and form one-male groups of which the male is the leader. But he does not have strong leadership, and he has little control over the actions of other members of his group. The females in the group may mate with other males. Members of his group may leave, and new members may join.

But monkeys that live on the ground, including most baboons, live in groups that are more tightly organized. A multimale baboon group is *closed*—that is, few members leave and few strangers join the group. Several dominant males control the group's movements, stop fights within the group, punish group members, and protect the group against enemies. The dominant males sometimes prevent other males in the group from mating with the females.

Scientists believe monkeys that live in trees have looser groups because these species are safer than those that live on the ground. The worst enemy of monkeys

R. C. Hermes, NAS   Lanceau, Agence de Presse Jacana

New World Monkeys and Old World Monkeys can be distinguished by their noses. The nostrils of New World monkeys, such as the woolly monkey, *left*, are widely spaced. Those of Old World monkeys, such as the mangabey, *right*, are close together.

that live in trees is a species of eagle that sometimes swoops down and catches young monkeys. On the other hand, monkeys that live on the ground have many enemies, including cheetahs, hyenas, jackals, leopards, and lions. These monkeys spend time in areas that have no nearby trees into which the monkeys can escape. As a result, monkeys that live on the ground must be tightly organized under strong leaders so they can defend themselves.

Monkeys that live on the ground defend themselves chiefly by threatening their enemies. If a cheetah approaches a group of baboons, for example, the leaders of the group gather together to face the danger. Each male baboon shows his long canine teeth and barks. If these actions do not frighten the cheetah away, the baboons may attack.

Communication. Monkeys communicate with one another in various ways. For example, a male rhesus monkey threatens members of its group by staring, opening its mouth and showing its teeth, bobbing its

E. R. Degginger

Vervets are among the commonest monkeys in Africa. Some may be found in city parks. They live in bands of from 6 to 20 members. Vervets feed and travel in the trees and on the ground.

Oxford Scientific Films from Bruce Coleman Inc.

Rhesus Monkeys, which are found in India, live in tightly organized groups. Like other ground-dwelling monkeys, they depend on group organization for defense.

head, and slapping the ground with its hands. *Social grooming* helps maintain friendly relations between baboons. In grooming, one baboon carefully cleans the fur of another. Both animals seem to find satisfaction in this activity. Baboons spend several hours a day in grooming.

Scientific Classification. Marmosets and tamarins make up the marmoset family, *Callitrichidae*. All the other New World monkeys belong to the New World monkey family, *Cebidae*. Old World monkeys make up the Old World monkey family, *Cercopithecidae*. Each family includes many genera and species. J. R. NAPIER

Related Articles in WORLD BOOK include:

Animal (Animals of the	Baboon	Marmoset
Tropical Forests; In-	Barbary Ape	Primate
telligence of Animals;	Capuchin	Spider Monkey
picture: Animals and	Howler	Squirrel Monkey
Their Young)	Macaque	Woolly Monkey
Ape	Mandrill	

MONKEY BREAD. See BAOBAB.

MONKEY FLOWER is the name given to a large group of herbs and small shrubs that have flowers with *two lips,* or two large petals growing one over the other. The petals often have spots that make the flower look more like a monkey's face. There are many different species, growing from 6 to 36 inches (15 to 91 centimeters) high. They grow in both South and North America, most of them along the Pacific Coast.

Monkey flowers can be grown in gardens, garden borders, and in greenhouses. They grow well in shady places and should be given plenty of water. Some of the shrubby kinds do not require much care.

Scientific Classification. The monkey flower belongs to the figwort family, *Scrophulariaceae*. It makes up the genus *Mimulus*. One kind of monkey flower is genus *Mimulus*, species *M. luteus*. J. J. LEVISON

MONKEYPOD TREE, or RAIN-TREE, is a beautiful shade tree that grows in tropical regions from southern Florida to Brazil. Its short, stout trunk bears spreading branches. The top of the tree may measure 100 feet (30 meters) across. The tree has pink and white flowers. Its leaves fold up at night and on cloudy days.

Scientific Classification. The monkeypod tree belongs to the pea family, *Leguminosae*. It is genus *Samanea*, species *S. saman*. ELBERT L. LITTLE, JR.

J. L. Kenner

The Monkeypod Tree is grown in tropical countries as a shade tree. Its wood makes attractive trays and bowls.

MONKSHOOD. See ACONITE (picture).

MONMOUTH, BATTLE OF. See NEW JERSEY (The Revolutionary War).

MONMOUTH, DUKE OF (1649-1685), JAMES SCOTT, was an Englishman who led an unsuccessful rebellion against King James II (see JAMES [II]). He was supposedly the son of Charles II and a Welsh woman named Lucy Walter, and was a pretender to the throne of England (see CHARLES [II] of England). There is some doubt about his real parentage, but Charles recognized him as his son.

Charles II became king in 1660 after Richard Cromwell fell from power. He called Monmouth back to England and made him Duke of Monmouth. In 1663, Monmouth married Anne, daughter of the Earl of Buccleuch.

The Duke of York ascended the throne as James II in 1685. Monmouth gathered an army in The Netherlands to invade England and demand the crown. He landed at Lyme, and issued a proclamation which declared James to be a usurper, tyrant, and murderer. But Monmouth was defeated at the Battle of Sedgemoor and taken to his uncle the king. Before a court headed by Lord Jeffreys, he begged for his life. But he was imprisoned in the Tower of London and executed. He was born in Rotterdam, The Netherlands. ANDRÉ MAUROIS

MONMOUTH COLLEGE. See UNIVERSITIES AND COLLEGES (table).

MONNET, *muhn NAY*, **JEAN** (1888-1979), a French statesman, led the movement to unify Western Europe in the 1950's and 1960's. He was called the *Architect of United Europe.* He proposed the European Coal and Steel Community in 1950 and became president of its executive branch in 1952. In 1955, he left the community and organized the Action Committee for a United States of Europe. Monnet helped create both the European Atomic Energy Community (Euratom), and the European Economic Community (Common Market) in 1957. See EUROPEAN COMMUNITY.

His career as an international financial adviser began during World War I when he directed Allied supply operations. From 1919 to 1923, he served as deputy secretary general of the League of Nations. He also helped to stabilize the economies of Algeria, Austria, China, Poland, and Romania after World War I. During World War II, Monnet served as a financial adviser to Great Britain and the United States. In 1947, he created the Monnet Plan, a five-year economic recovery plan for France.

In 1963, Monnet became one of the first Europeans to receive the Presidential Medal of Freedom, the highest civilian medal awarded by the United States. Monnet was born in Cognac.   LEONARD B. TENNYSON

MONOCLINIC SYSTEM. See CRYSTAL AND CRYSTALLIZATION (Classification of Crystals).

MONOCOTYLEDON, *MAHN uh KAHT uh LEE duhn,* is a type of flowering plant that has one *cotyledon* (seed leaf). The leaves of these plants have parallel veins. The flower parts usually grow in multiples of three. About 40,000 species of plants are monocotyledons, including bananas, pineapples, and corn. See also COTYLEDON.

MONOCYTE. See BLOOD (White Blood Cells; illustration).

MONOD, JACQUES (1910-1976), a French biochemist, shared the 1965 Nobel prize for physiology or medicine with François Jacob and André Lwoff. The scientists, all members of the Pasteur Institute in Paris, studied the cells of bacteria. They discovered in these cells a class of genes that controls the activity of other genes. Radiation and some chemicals can cause these controlling genes to function improperly. If this happens, the other genes may get out of control and damage the cells. Some scientists believe the discovery will aid research on cancer, a disease in which uncontrolled cell division takes place.

Monod was born in Paris. He became head of the Pasteur Institute's cellular biochemistry department in 1954 and director of the Institute in 1971. He was also a professor at the Faculté des Sciences in Paris from 1959 to 1967, and at the College de France from 1967 to 1972.   IRWIN H. HERSKOWITZ

MONOECIOUS PLANT. See BOTANY (table: Terms).

MONOFILAMENT. See PLASTICS (table: Terms).

MONOGAMY. See MARRIAGE (Marriage in Other Cultures).

MONOMER, *MAHN uh muhr.* Monomers are small molecules that can combine with each other to form larger molecules called *polymers.* Polymers are used in the manufacture of paint, plastics, synthetic rubber, and synthetic fibers. Heat, pressure, or chemical treatment may be used to cause monomers to combine. See also POLYMER; POLYMERIZATION.   DAVID R. LIDE, JR.

MONOMETER. See POETRY (table: Terms).

MONOMIAL. See ALGEBRA (table: Terms).

MONONGAHELA RIVER, *muh NAHN guh HEE luh,* provides river transportation between the rich soft coal fields of southwestern Pennsylvania and the steel factories at Pittsburgh. The river is formed where the Tygart and West Fork rivers meet in Marion County, W.Va. The Monongahela winds northeastward across the boundary of Pennsylvania to the mouth of the Cheat River. Here it flows northward until it unites with the Allegheny at Pittsburgh to form the Ohio River. The

Monongahela is 128 miles (206 kilometers) long. Boats can sail on all parts of the river in Pennsylvania. The name *Monongahela* comes from an Indian word that means *river with sliding banks.*   GEORGE MACINKO

MONONUCLEOSIS, also called INFECTIOUS MONONUCLEOSIS, is a mild infectious disease marked by a large increase in the number of abnormal *lymphocytes,* a type of white blood cell. The disease gets its name from these *mononuclear* (single nucleus) cells. Mononucleosis occurs most often in young adults, but it also strikes children and older people.

Mononucleosis is caused by the Epstein-Barr (EB) virus, one of the herpes viruses. Direct contact between people—kissing, for example—can spread the disease. The chief symptoms include chills, fever, sore throat, and fatigue. Mononucleosis is sometimes called *glandular fever* because swelling occurs in the lymph glands, especially those in the neck. Symptoms may also include enlargement of the spleen, inflammation of the mouth and gums, and skin rash. With some patients, the disease leads to jaundice and to enlargement of the liver.

Depending on the seriousness of the case, most doctors recommend mild to complete bed rest for a mononucleosis patient. The disease is not fatal, and most patients recover within three to six weeks.

A blood test called the Paul-Bunnell test can determine whether a person has mononucleosis. A sample of the *serum* (clear liquid) of the patient's blood is mixed with some sheep's blood. If the patient has mononucleosis, the sheep's blood cells will stick to one another.   STANLEY YACHNIN

MONOPHONY, *muh NAHF uh nee,* is music written for a single, unsupported voice or part. It can also mean such music with a simple accompaniment. Monophony is the oldest type of music, and the only form used in ancient Greek music and European folk music.

MONOPLACOPHORA. See MOLLUSK.

MONOPLANE. See AIRPLANE (Other Pioneer Planes and Fliers).

MONOPOLY, a game. See GAME (Games for Young People and Adults; picture).

MONOPOLY AND COMPETITION are terms used to describe selling conditions in a market or industry. *Competition* exists when many persons or companies try to sell the same kinds of goods to the same buyers. *Monopoly* exists when a single producer or seller controls the supply of a product for which there is no close substitute. Monopoly conditions also exist when a group of sellers acts together to set prices or other terms of sale of a product. The word comes from the Greek *monos,* meaning *single,* and *polein,* which means *to sell.*

Maintaining competition has always been a major issue in the United States. It came to a head in the late 1800's and early 1900's. John D. Rockefeller, J. P. Morgan, Jay Gould, and other "captains of industry" created giant business complexes that controlled entire industries. With their monopoly power, they regulated the supply of goods and set high prices for their products. The public outcry that resulted led to the passage of the Sherman Antitrust Act in 1890 and to its first vigorous enforcement in the "trust-busting" days of President Theodore Roosevelt.

MONOPOLY AND COMPETITION

Kinds of Monopoly and Competition. Monopoly and competition exist in many different forms and degrees. Markets and industries in the United States, for example, range from almost *pure monopoly* to almost *pure competition*.

Public utilities are almost *pure monopolies* of the one-seller type. Many of them sell a product or service for which the consumer cannot easily find a substitute. Public utilities provide essential public services, such as gas, water, electricity, telephone, and public transportation. They usually operate under government regulation or ownership. See PUBLIC UTILITY.

Pure, or *perfect*, *competition* occurs when the same kinds of goods or services are produced or sold by many firms. No producer or seller can control the price of the product, because no one controls a large part of the total supply. In the United States, the sale of some farm products comes closest to being pure competition.

A few large companies dominate in some U.S. industries. As few as three or four firms may make or sell three-fourths or more of an industry's products. This situation, where there are only a few competing producers, is called *oligopoly*. The term comes from the Greek *oligos* (few) and *polein* (to sell). Oligopolies develop most often in manufacturing industries that require such huge factories and expensive equipment that it is hard for new firms to enter the field.

Economists often divide oligopolies into two groups. The first includes industries whose products are made to a standardized size, shape, thickness, quality, or purity. Examples include certain grades of aluminum, steel, oil, and chemicals. A second type of oligopoly is called *differentiated oligopoly*, because producers differentiate their products from one another by emphasizing brand names. This type includes industries that produce cars, television sets, cigarettes, and soaps.

Monopolistic competition describes the case of many sellers—perhaps 20 or 30—selling differentiated products. Examples include clothing manufacturers, food packers, and retail merchants. Each seller has a limited form of monopoly, because his products differ in some ways from those of other sellers.

Effects of Limited Competition. Monopoly and oligopoly can adversely affect the quality and availability of what people buy. So long as customers feel they must have the product, a monopoly firm can sell a product of poor quality without losing sales. It can also charge high prices without fear of being undersold. In time, however, such practices may lead to the development of substitute products or even to the entry of new firms into the market.

Some economists believe a certain degree of monopoly may be desirable to encourage inventions and new ideas and practices in industry. They argue that monopoly and oligopoly firms can finance new projects better because they receive above normal profits and thus have money to put into new products. Others maintain there is little evidence that this is the only, or even the best, way to improve and change products.

History. In the late 1800's and early 1900's, a few U.S. industrialists merged and combined many small firms into extremely large corporations. They tried to monopolize many industries, including the railroad, steel, and petroleum industries. In some industries, large corporations combined under unified control. These combinations were called *trusts*. Some firms cut prices to force smaller firms out of business. Then they restricted production and raised prices. See TRUST.

The abuses of monopolies and trusts led to a series of federal laws. The Sherman Antitrust Act of 1890 prohibited great combinations that restricted interstate trade. But it was almost 20 years before the power of the act was felt. On the basis of this act, President Theodore Roosevelt's Administration filed antitrust suits against many monopolies. In the best-known of these suits, the courts ordered the Standard Oil trust broken up in 1911 (see STANDARD OIL COMPANY).

Two other federal laws were passed in 1914 to give support and clarification to the Sherman act. The Federal Trade Commission Act prohibited unfair methods of competition and unfair or deceptive marketing practices. The act established the Federal Trade Commission to investigate certain suspect business practices and to prevent business firms from destroying competition. The Clayton Antitrust Act prohibited such monopolistic practices as price discrimination and mergers that substantially reduce competition.

The latest important federal antitrust legislation was the Celler-Kefauver Act of 1950. This act tightened control over business mergers that might lessen competition or lead to monopoly. Most states also have laws that forbid monopolistic practices.

Federal and state governments have relied on two different methods in dealing with monopoly. The main effort has been to prohibit monopoly and monopolistic practices. These are the chief provisions of the federal antimonopoly laws. But in the public utility field, federal and state governments permit and even encourage monopolies. Certain features of public utilities would make competition in this field costly and inefficient. However, government commissions regulate the prices and activities of public utilities.

Critically reviewed by JOHN R. COLEMAN

See also CARTEL; CONGLOMERATE; FREE ENTERPRISE SYSTEM; MERGER.

MONORAIL RAILROAD is a railroad that has only one rail. Monorail cars run along a rail placed above or below them. Cars that run above the track have either a gyroscopic device to balance them, or guide wheels that grip the side of the rail to keep the cars from falling over (see GYROSCOPE). There are two types of suspended monorail systems. In the older type, the cars hang freely from wheels on a rail. The newer "split-rail" type suspends the cars from two rails spaced closely together and housed in one enclosure. The enclosure ensures quieter operation, and also keeps the track dry.

Monorail cars can be powered by electric motors, gas turbines, or gasoline engines. Rubber wheels cut noise considerably. Monorails are faster and cheaper to operate and maintain than two-rail elevated or subway lines. The smaller amount of friction in monorails allows greater speeds with less operating cost.

The first monorail system, built in Wuppertal, Germany, in 1901, still carries passengers. Many cities in the United States have studied the possibility of building monorail systems. They can be built quickly and can operate above a busy street. Ground supports require little space, because they have only one rail.

The first monorail train in the U.S. began operating at Houston, Tex., in 1956. Other monorails are located at Seattle, Wash.; Disneyland, in Anaheim, Calif.; Dallas, Tex.; Lake Arrowhead, Calif.; Pomona, Calif.; and New York City. Tokyo, Japan, built an 8.2-mile (13.2-kilometer) monorail system for use during the 1964 Olympic Games there.   CARLTON J. CORLISS

See also TRANSPORTATION (picture); WASHINGTON (picture).

MONOSODIUM GLUTAMATE. See WHEAT (Other Products).

MONOTHEISM. See RELIGION.

MONOTYPE is one of the two chief kinds of typesetting and type-casting devices. It casts and sets type one letter at a time in the proper sequence. It also spaces the letters in lines up to 10 inches (25 centimeters) wide, just as a compositor arranges letters into words by hand. The other machine is a *Linotype*. It casts and sets type in a *slug* (bar of metal) up to 7 inches (18 centimeters) wide (see LINOTYPE).

The Monotype sets type for fine books, catalogs, national magazines, dictionaries, technical books, and ordinary commercial printing. The Monotype machine is made up of two parts, the *keyboard* and the *casting machine*. They produce type in two separate operations.

The Keyboard resembles a large typewriter. Striking the keys *perforates* (punches holes) in a paper *controller ribbon* that controls the operation of the casting machine, which actually casts the type. The use of perforations in the controller paper is called *code control*, and is one of the earliest known applications of automation (see AUTOMATION). The keyboard provides 255 letters and characters used in printing. At the end of each word, the operator strikes a space bar. This space is important when the line is filled. When a line is nearly completed, the unused space at the end of the line is divided into equal parts. This leftover space is added to the spaces previously set between each word in the line. This operation is called *justifying the line*, and explains why the last character in a printed line falls exactly below the last character in the line above.

The Casting Machine casts type from molten metal (antimony, tin, and lead) and assembles each character and space in the proper sequence in the line. A frame that is called a *matrix case* holds 225 or 255 *matrices* (molds) that correspond to the characters on the keyboard. The perforated control paper "orders" a small device to pick up the proper matrix and carry it to the casting box. When the matrix is in place, molten metal pours over it to form the character. The type is then ejected from the casting machine.

One of the advantages of the Monotype is that errors can be corrected by changing single letters, since all letters and spaces are separate. An error in a Linotype slug can be corrected only by resetting and recasting the entire line.   DONALD H. NEALE

See also PRINTING (Setting the Type).

MONROE, La. (pop. 56,374; met. area pop. 115,387), is a commercial and industrial center for northeastern Louisiana. The city stands on the banks of the Ouachita River, about 200 miles (320 kilometers) northwest of Baton Rouge, and 25 miles (40 kilometers) south of the Arkansas state line (see LOUISIANA [political map]).

Large industrial plants in Monroe produce automobile headlights, chemicals, furniture, and paper. Two trunk-line railroads run into the city. Monroe is the home of Northeast Louisiana University.

Don Juan Filhiol built Fort Miro in 1790. In 1807, it became the seat of government for Ouachita Parish. The town changed its name to Monroe in 1819, and was incorporated as a city in 1900. Gas, discovered nearby in 1916, made power cheap, and attracted industries to Monroe. A modern Government Center opened in 1966 and a new Civic Center in 1967. Monroe has a commission form of government.

MONROE, HARRIET (1860-1936), founded *Poetry: A Magazine of Verse* in Chicago in 1912. She served as its editor until 1936. Monroe wrote poetry, but she became famous chiefly as an editor. Her magazine helped initiate and develop modern American poetry. Monroe was born in Chicago, and attended the Academy of the Visitation in Washington, D.C. She wrote an autobiography, *A Poet's Life*, which was published in 1938.   WILLIAM VAN O'CONNOR

How a Monotype Works

The Operator strikes the keys of the keyboard, *below*. This action punches holes in paper tape. Each pattern of holes represents a certain letter or some other character.

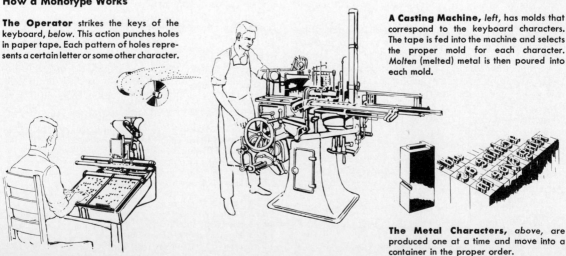

A Casting Machine, *left*, has molds that correspond to the keyboard characters. The tape is fed into the machine and selects the proper mold for each character. *Molten* (melted) metal is then poured into each mold.

The Metal Characters, *above*, are produced one at a time and move into a container in the proper order.

JAMES
MONROE

The United States Flag had 15 stars and 15 stripes when Monroe took office, even though there were 19 states.

JEFFERSON
3rd President
1801—1809

MADISON
4th President
1809—1817

J. Q. ADAMS
6th President
1825—1829

JACKSON
7th President
1829—1837

Oil painting on wood panel (1817) by Gilbert Stuart;
Pennsylvania Academy of the Fine Arts, Philadelphia

5TH PRESIDENT OF THE UNITED STATES 1817-1825

MONROE, JAMES (1758-1831), is best remembered for the Monroe Doctrine, which he proclaimed in 1823. This historic policy warned European countries not to interfere with the free nations of the Western Hemisphere.

Monroe became President after more than 40 years of public service. He had fought in the Revolutionary War. During the first years after independence, he had served in the Virginia Assembly and in the Congress of the Confederation. He later became a U.S. Senator; minister to France, Spain, and Great Britain; and governor of Virginia. During the War of 1812, he served as Secretary of State and Secretary of War at the same time.

In appearance and manner, Monroe resembled his fellow Virginian, George Washington. He was tall and rawboned, and had a military bearing. His gray-blue eyes invited confidence. Even John Quincy Adams, who criticized almost everyone, spoke well of Monroe.

At his inauguration, Monroe still wore his hair in the old-fashioned way, powdered and tied in a queue at the back. He favored suits of black broadcloth with knee breeches and buckles on the shoes. To the people, he represented the almost legendary heroism of the generation which led the country to freedom.

As President, Monroe presided quietly during a period known as "the era of good feeling." He looked forward to America's glorious future, the outlines of which emerged rapidly during his presidency. The fron-

tier was moving rapidly westward, and small cities sprang up west of the Mississippi River. Monroe sent General Andrew Jackson on a military expedition into Florida which resulted in the acquisition of Florida from Spain. Rapidly extending frontiers soon caused Americans to consider whether slavery should be permitted in the new territories. The Missouri Compromise "settled" this problem for nearly 30 years by setting definite limits to the extension of slavery in land lying within the Louisiana Purchase area.

Early Life

Boyhood. James Monroe was born in Westmoreland County, Virginia, on April 28, 1758. His father, Colonel Spence Monroe, came from a Scottish family that had settled in Virginia in the mid-1600's. The family

--- **IMPORTANT DATES IN MONROE'S LIFE** ---

1758 (April 28) Born in Westmoreland County, Virginia.
1783 Elected to the Congress of the Confederation.
1786 (Feb. 16) Married Elizabeth Kortright.
1790 Elected to the United States Senate.
1794 Named minister to France.
1799 Elected governor of Virginia.
1811 Appointed Secretary of State.
1814 Named Secretary of War.
1816 Elected President of the United States.
1820 Re-elected President.
1823 Proclaimed the Monroe Doctrine.
1831 (July 4) Died in New York City.

of his mother, Elizabeth Jones Monroe, came from Wales, and also had lived in Virginia for many years. James was the eldest of four boys and a girl.

James studied at home with a tutor until he was 12 years old. Then his father sent him to the school of Parson Archibald Campbell. The boy had to leave home early in the morning and tramp through the forest to reach Campbell's school. He often carried a rifle and shot game on the way. At the age of 16, James entered the College of William and Mary. But the stirring events of the Revolutionary War soon lured him into the army.

Soldier. Although only 18, Monroe was commissioned a lieutenant. He soon saw action, fighting at Harlem Heights and White Plains in the fall of 1776. His superior officers praised Monroe for gallantry in the Battle of Trenton, where he was wounded in the shoulder. During the next two years, he fought at Brandywine, Germantown, and Monmouth.

In 1778, Monroe was promoted to lieutenant colonel and sent to raise troops in Virginia. He failed in his mission, but it greatly influenced his future career. It

brought him into contact with Thomas Jefferson, then governor of the state. Monroe began to study law under Jefferson's guidance, and became a political disciple and lifelong friend of his teacher.

Political and Public Career

Monroe began his public career in 1782, when he won a seat in the Virginia Assembly. In 1783, he was elected to the Congress of the Confederation, where he served three years (see CONGRESS OF THE CONFEDERATION). Monroe did not favor a highly centralized government. But he supported moderate measures intended to let Congress establish tariffs. Monroe worked to give pioneers the right to travel on the Mississippi River. He also aided Jefferson in drafting laws for the development of the West. Two hurried trips to the western region had left Monroe unimpressed with its beauty or fertility. But he still believed that the West would be important in the future growth of the country.

State Politics. In 1786, Monroe settled down to the

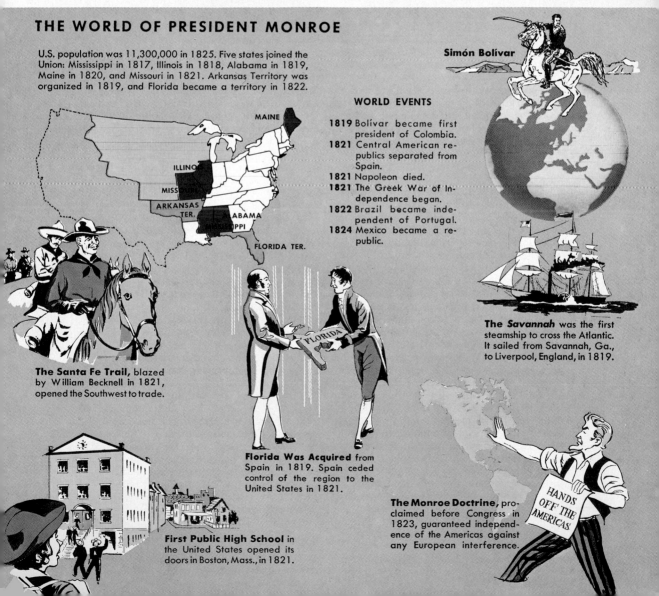

THE WORLD OF PRESIDENT MONROE

U.S. population was 11,300,000 in 1825. Five states joined the Union: Mississippi in 1817, Illinois in 1818, Alabama in 1819, Maine in 1820, and Missouri in 1821. Arkansas Territory was organized in 1819, and Florida became a territory in 1822.

Simón Bolívar

WORLD EVENTS

1819 Bolívar became first president of Colombia.
1821 Central American republics separated from Spain.
1821 Napoleon died.
1821 The Greek War of Independence began.
1822 Brazil became independent of Portugal.
1824 Mexico became a republic.

The *Savannah* was the first steamship to cross the Atlantic. It sailed from Savannah, Ga., to Liverpool, England, in 1819.

The Santa Fe Trail, blazed by William Becknell in 1821, opened the Southwest to trade.

Florida Was Acquired from Spain in 1819. Spain ceded control of the region to the United States in 1821.

First Public High School in the United States opened its doors in Boston, Mass., in 1821.

The Monroe Doctrine, proclaimed before Congress in 1823, guaranteed independence of the Americas against any European interference.

LIFE AND CAREER OF JAMES MONROE

Monroe's Birthplace, near Colonial Beach, Va., fell into ruin, and no one knows exactly what the building looked like.

Virginia Dept. of Conservation and Development

Monroe's Law Office in Fredericksburg, Va., has been preserved as a museum. It contains displays of many of Monroe's personal possessions.

An Army Officer. Monroe served in many Revolutionary War battles. His superior officers especially praised him for bravery at Trenton, where he was wounded.

James Monroe Memorial Foundation

practice of law in Fredericksburg, Va. But politics drew him like a magnet. He ran for the Virginia Assembly, and won easily. Monroe remained in the assembly four years.

In 1788, Monroe served in the convention called by Virginia to ratify the United States Constitution. His distrust of a strong federal government aligned him with Patrick Henry and George Mason, who opposed the Constitution. But Monroe offered only moderate opposition, and he gracefully accepted ratification.

Monroe's Family. In 1786, Monroe married 17-year-old Elizabeth Kortright (June 30, 1768-Sept. 23, 1830), the daughter of a New York City merchant. The couple had two daughters, Eliza and Maria, and a son, but the boy died at the age of 2. Monroe's admiration for Jefferson became so strong that in 1789 he moved to Charlottesville, Va. There he built Ash Lawn, not far from Jefferson's estate, Monticello.

U.S. Senator. Monroe ran against James Madison for the first United States House of Representatives, but lost. In 1790, the Virginia legislature elected him to fill a vacancy in the United States Senate. As a Senator, Monroe aligned himself with Madison and with Jefferson, then Secretary of State, in vigorous opposition to the Federalist program of Alexander Hamilton. Assisted by such leaders as Albert Gallatin and Aaron Burr, the three Virginians founded the Democratic-Republican party. This party developed into one of the two great parties which have formed the basis of American politics ever since (see DEMOCRATIC-REPUBLICAN PARTY).

Opposition to Washington. In 1794, President George Washington appointed Monroe minister to France. The President knew that Monroe opposed many administration policies, but he needed a diplomat who could improve relations with the French. He also knew that Monroe strongly admired France.

During talks in France, Monroe criticized the Jay Treaty between the United States and Britain as "the most shameful transaction I have ever known." Furious,

Washington recalled Monroe in 1796. See JAY TREATY.

Upon his return, Monroe became involved in a bitter personal dispute with Hamilton which nearly led to a duel. The quarrel resulted from the publication of materials that slandered Hamilton. Monroe was blamed, but denied responsibility. Hamilton eventually dropped his charges. The quarrel, and the humiliation of being recalled from France, made these years among the unhappiest in Monroe's life.

Diplomat Under Jefferson. In 1799, Monroe was elected governor of Virginia. In this post, he played an important part in preserving democratic processes during the tense years following passage of the Alien and Sedition Acts (see ALIEN AND SEDITION ACTS). Early in 1803, President Thomas Jefferson sent Monroe to Paris to help Robert R. Livingston negotiate the purchase of New Orleans. By the time Monroe reached France, Napoleon had offered the astonished Livingston the entire Louisiana Territory. Monroe urged Livingston to accept the offer without waiting to consult Jefferson, and the two men made arrangements for the treaty. See LOUISIANA PURCHASE.

Jefferson was pleased with Monroe's initiative, and sent him to Madrid to help Charles Pinckney purchase the Floridas from Spain. They failed, but Jefferson still had confidence in Monroe. The President named him minister to Great Britain. In 1806, Monroe helped conclude a trade treaty that was so unsatisfactory that Jefferson refused to submit it to the Senate.

Monroe felt his usefulness in London had ended, and returned home in 1807. He became a reluctant candidate for the nomination to succeed Jefferson as President. But Madison won the nomination and the presidency. Monroe served in the Virginia Assembly until he again was elected governor in 1811.

Secretary of State. Monroe resigned as governor after about three months to accept President Madison's appointment as Secretary of State. As his first task, he attempted to reach some understanding with the Brit-

Painting by Benjamin West; Photo courtesy James
Monroe Law Office Museum, Fredericksburg, Va.

Elizabeth Kortright Monroe closely observed European court life while her husband
was a diplomat. As First Lady, she introduced
more formal ways of White House entertaining.

Governor of Virginia. Monroe won
the governorship in 1799 and 1811.

Secretary of State. He headed
Madison's Cabinet for six years.

Virginia State Chamber of Commerce

Oak Hill, Monroe's retirement home, stands near Leesburg, Va. Thomas
Jefferson helped draw the plans for this cream-colored brick mansion.

ish over the impressment of American seamen. But he
soon concluded that war could not be avoided.

At the beginning of the War of 1812, Monroe was
eager to take command of the army. But Madison convinced him to stay in the Cabinet. Secretary of War
John Armstrong was forced to resign in 1814 because
of neglect of duty during the burning of Washington,
D.C. Madison asked Monroe to become Secretary of
War while continuing as Secretary of State. Monroe
held both offices for the rest of the war. After he took
over the War Department, American armies won several brilliant victories. These triumphs greatly increased
Monroe's popularity. See WAR OF 1812.

In 1816, while still Secretary of State, Monroe was
elected President of the United States. He received 183
electoral votes to 34 for Senator Rufus King of New
York, the Federalist candidate. Monroe's running mate
was Governor Daniel D. Tompkins of New York.

Monroe's Administration (1817-1825)

The years of Monroe's presidency are generally
known as "the era of good feeling." The Federalist
party had disappeared after the election of 1816, and
nearly everyone belonged to the Democratic-Republican party. The country prospered because of fast-grow-
ing industries and settlement of the West. A depression
in 1818-1819 caused only a temporary setback.

"The American System" provided the chief issue of
Monroe's first term. House Speaker Henry Clay of
Kentucky advanced this plan. The American System
proposed to strengthen nationalism in two ways: (1)
construction of new roads and canals to open the West,
and (2) enactment of a protective tariff to encourage
Northern manufacturers and develop home markets.

Monroe distrusted the American System, because he
doubted that the federal government had the power for
these activities. He studied the program during a 3½-
month tour of the North and West. But this trip did not
change his "settled conviction" that Congress did not
have the power to build roads and canals.

Clay continued his fight, and finally won Congress
over to his side. In 1822, Monroe vetoed a bill providing for federal administration of toll gates on the
Cumberland Road. He urged a constitutional amendment to give Congress the power to promote internal
improvements. In 1824, Monroe signed the Survey
Act, which planned improvements in the future.

Clay had more success in pushing through the protective tariff, the second part of his American System.
Congress had already raised tariff rates in 1816, and
it further increased the duty on iron in 1818. In 1824,
Congress raised tariff rates in general.

Life in the White House. The British had burned
the White House during the War of 1812, and the mansion had not been rebuilt when Monroe took office.
The new President maintained his residence on I Street,
near 20th Street, for nine months. On New Year's Day,
1818, President and Mrs. Monroe held a public reception marking the reopening of the White House.

Monroe had observed court etiquette during his trips
to Europe, and decided to adopt a strict social attitude
for the White House. Partly because of ill health, Mrs.
Monroe received only visitors to whom she had sent
invitations. She refused to pay calls, sending her elder
daughter, Mrs. Eliza Hay, in her place. Soon all Washington buzzed about the "snobbish" Mrs. Monroe.

As time passed, the public realized that Mrs. Monroe

--- VICE-PRESIDENT AND CABINET ---

Vice-President . . . . *Daniel D. Tompkins
Secretary of State . . . . *John Quincy Adams
Secretary of the Treasury . . . . . *William H. Crawford
Secretary of War . . . . *John C. Calhoun
Attorney General . . . . Richard Rush
                       William Wirt (1817)
Secretary of the Navy . . . . Benjamin W. Crowninshield
                       Smith Thompson (1819)
                       Samuel L. Southard (1823)

*Has a separate biography in WORLD BOOK.

had followed the President's wishes in establishing protocol. During Monroe's second term, her Wednesday receptions became popular. The visit of the Marquis de Lafayette on New Year's Day, 1825, added a touch of splendor to the last months of Monroe's term.

Beginnings of Sectionalism. In 1818, Missouri applied for admission to the Union as a slave state. The House of Representatives aroused anger in the South by passing a bill to admit Missouri with the provision that no more slaves could be brought into the state. The Senate defeated this provision, and Congress eventually agreed on a bill known as the Missouri Compromise. This law permitted slavery in Missouri, but banned it from the rest of the Louisiana Purchase region north of the southern boundary of Missouri. Monroe avoided interfering with these debates. But he made it known that he would not sign a bill placing any special restraints on Missouri's admission to the Union. See MISSOURI COMPROMISE.

War with the Seminole. Since the War of 1812, Americans in Georgia had been harassed by bands of Indians in Spanish Florida. In 1817, fighting broke out between the Seminole Indians and settlers in southern Georgia. President Monroe ordered Major General Andrew Jackson to raise a force of militia and put down the uprising. Jackson chased the Indians into the Everglades of Florida. Then he captured Pensacola, the Spanish capital of Florida.

Jackson's easy conquest convinced the Spanish that they could not defend Florida. In 1819, the Spanish agreed to give Florida to the United States in return for the cancellation of $5 million in American claims against Spain. See FLORIDA (History).

Diplomatic Achievements. Monroe's administration marked one of the most brilliant periods in American diplomacy. The Rush-Bagot Agreement, signed with Great Britain in 1817, prohibited fortifications on the Great Lakes. In 1818, Great Britain agreed to the 49th parallel as the boundary between the United States and Canada from Lake of the Woods on the Minnesota-Ontario border as far west as the Rocky Mountains. The British also consented to joint occupation of the Oregon region. American diplomats convinced Spain to give up its claims to Oregon in 1819, and the Russians agreed to a similar pact in 1824.

Re-Election. In the election of 1820, Monroe was unopposed for the presidency. Monroe received every vote cast in the electoral college but one. William Plumer, an elector from New Hampshire, cast his vote for John Quincy Adams.

The Monroe Doctrine. During the Napoleonic Wars, the Spaniards had become deeply involved in European affairs, and took little interest in their American colonies. Most of the colonies took advantage of this situation and declared independence from Spain. The Latin-American revolutions aroused great sympathy in the United States. As early as 1817, Henry Clay had begun a campaign for recognition of these new countries. In March, 1822, Monroe finally recommended that their independence be recognized. In December, 1823, the President proclaimed the historic Monroe Doctrine in a message to Congress. This doctrine has remained a basic American policy ever since.

The era of good feeling ended before Monroe finished his second term. Unlike the situation which followed the retirement of Jefferson and Madison, there was no single, outstanding figure who was the overwhelming choice to become the next President. Four candidates fought for the office. None won a majority of the votes, and the House of Representatives chose John Quincy Adams. See ADAMS, JOHN QUINCY (Election of 1824).

Later Years

Monroe retired to Oak Hill, his estate near Leesburg, Va. He served for five years as a regent of the University of Virginia. In 1829, he became presiding officer of the Virginia Constitutional Convention. His wife died on Sept. 23, 1830, and was buried at Oak Hill. Long public service had left Monroe a poor man, and he was too old to resume his law practice. Late in 1830, his financial distress forced him to move to New York City to live with his daughter and her husband. Monroe died there on July 4, 1831. In 1858, his remains were moved to Hollywood Cemetery in Richmond, Va. His law office in Fredericksburg has been preserved as a memorial. Authoritative books on the life of Monroe include *James Monroe: The Quest for National Identity* by Harry Ammon and *The Autobiography of James Monroe*, edited by Stuart Gerry Brown.   RALPH L. KETCHAM

Related Articles in WORLD BOOK include:

Adams, John Quincy
Clay, Henry
Hamilton,
  Alexander
Jackson, Andrew
Jay Treaty

Jefferson, Thomas
Louisiana Purchase
Madison, James
Missouri
  Compromise
Monroe Doctrine

President of
  the U.S.
Tariff
Tompkins,
  Daniel D.
War of 1812

Outline

I. **Early Life**
  A. Boyhood
  B. Soldier

II. **Political and Public Career**
  A. State Politics
  B. Monroe's Family
  C. U.S. Senator
  D. Opposition to Washington
  E. Diplomat Under Jefferson
  F. Secretary of State

III. **Monroe's Administration (1817-1825)**
  A. "The American System"
  B. Life in the White House
  C. Beginnings of Sectionalism
  D. War with the Seminole
  E. Diplomatic Achievements
  F. Re-Election
  G. The Monroe Doctrine

IV. **Later Years**

Questions

What two Cabinet posts did Monroe hold at once?

Why did Monroe oppose "the American System"?

What term is often used to describe the period of Monroe's administration? Why?

How did Monroe display initiative during negotiations for the purchase of Louisiana?

How did slavery become an issue during Monroe's administration?

How did Monroe meet Thomas Jefferson?

Why were Monroe and his wife unpopular during their early years in the White House?

How did Monroe arouse the hostility of George Washington while serving as minister to France?

What was the Monroe Doctrine?

In what ways did Monroe contribute to the founding of his country?

MONROE, MARILYN (1926-1962), was an American motion-picture actress. Her great beauty made her a world-famous sex symbol. But in spite of her success in films, Miss Monroe had a tragic life. She died at the age of 36 from an overdose of sleeping pills.

United Press Int.
Marilyn Monroe

Miss Monroe, whose real name was either Norma Jean Baker or Norma Jean Mortenson, was born in Los Angeles. She made her film debut in 1948 in *Dangerous Years*. Soon she won attention with small roles in *The Asphalt Jungle* (1950) and *All About Eve* (1950). Her most successful dramatic roles among her 30 films were in *Bus Stop* (1956) and *The Misfits* (1961). She appeared as a comedienne in *Gentlemen Prefer Blondes* (1953), *The Seven-Year Itch* (1954), and *Some Like It Hot* (1959). She was married to former baseball star Joe DiMaggio in 1954, and they were divorced that same year. Miss Monroe was married to playwright Arthur Miller from 1956 to 1961.   ALAN CASTY

MONROE DOCTRINE was set forth by President James Monroe in a message he delivered to the Congress of the United States on Dec. 2, 1823. It practically guaranteed all the independent nations of the Western Hemisphere against European interference "for the purpose of oppressing them, or controlling in any other manner their destiny." The Doctrine said also that the American continents were "henceforth not to be considered as subjects for future colonization by any European powers." This statement meant that the United States would not allow new colonies to be created nor permit existing colonies to extend their boundaries.

Origins. The Monroe Doctrine grew out of conditions in Europe as well as in America. The three leading absolute monarchies of Europe were Russia, Austria, and Prussia. They had pledged themselves to "put an end to the system of representative government, in whatever country it may exist in Europe." The United States feared that these three powers (sometimes inaccurately called "The Holy Alliance") might also try to suppress representative government in the Americas.

During and after the Napoleonic Wars, most of the Spanish colonies in America had taken advantage of unsettled conditions in Europe to break away from the mother country. As they won independence, these colonies formed themselves into republics with constitutions much like that of the United States. Only Brazil chose to keep its monarchy when it declared its independence from Portugal.

After Napoleon's downfall, the monarchy was restored in Spain, and it seemed quite possible that the Holy Alliance might try to restore Spain's colonies as well. The French monarchy, which had followed the policy of the Holy Alliance to the point of actually suppressing a democratic revolution in Spain, was also suspected of intending to help Spain regain its former American possessions. A rumor that France was on the point of doing this spread over Europe during 1823.

This threat disturbed not only the United States, but

Great Britain as well. As free republics, the Spanish-American nations traded with Great Britain. If they became colonies again, whether of Spain or of France, their trade with Great Britain would certainly be cut down. Great Britain had steadily opposed the doctrine of the Holy Alliance, and had few allies in Europe. George Canning, the British foreign minister, proposed to Richard Rush, the American minister in London, that Great Britain and the United States issue a joint warning against European aggression in the Americas.

President Monroe was at first inclined to accept the British offer. Ex-Presidents Jefferson and Madison strongly favored the idea. With Great Britain "on our side," Jefferson argued, "we need not fear the whole world." But Monroe's Secretary of State, John Quincy Adams, said that the United States should not "come in as a cock-boat in the wake of the British man-of-war." He urged that the United States alone make the kind of statement Canning had in mind. He said that the British would use their sea power to prevent European intervention in America whether they had an agreement with the United States or not. Thus the United States would have all the advantages of joint action without entering into what amounted to an alliance with Great Britain. Moreover, a strictly American declaration would clearly apply to Great Britain as well as to other European countries. Monroe finally decided to follow Adams' advice and proclaimed the Monroe Doctrine. He used practically the same words that Adams had used when he first proposed it to him.

Results. Until the late 1800's, Europe's respect for the rights of the smaller American nations rested less upon the Monroe Doctrine than upon fear of the British Navy. A possible exception to this rule occurred in the 1860's, shortly after the Civil War, while the wartime Army and Navy of the United States were still strong. Then the attitude of the American government forced Emperor Napoleon III to give up an attempt to set up a European kingdom in Mexico. It was not again until the 1880's, when the United States began to enlarge its new Navy of steel ships, that the United States had enough power to enforce the Monroe Doctrine.

From the point of view of trade, the Monroe Doctrine probably did the United States no good whatever. Europe continued to get the larger share of Latin-American trade, most of which went to Great Britain. Nor did the Doctrine improve relations between the United States and the Latin-American countries. The nations which the Doctrine was supposed to protect resented the way the United States assumed its own superiority over them. Besides, they feared "The Colossus of the North" far more than they feared any European nation. Until the 1890's, Great Britain and other countries generally ignored the Doctrine.

The Monroe Doctrine in Action. During the 1800's, the Doctrine was seldom invoked. President James Polk referred to it in 1845 during the dispute with Great Britain over Oregon. Secretary of State William Seward acted partly on the basis of the Doctrine when he denounced French intervention in Mexico in the 1860's. President Grover Cleveland used it when he threatened war with Great Britain in 1895 if the British would not arbitrate their dispute with Venezuela.

The Roosevelt Corollary. In the early 1900's, President Theodore Roosevelt gave new life and new meaning to the Monroe Doctrine. He pointed out that weakness or brutal wrongdoing on the part of any of the smaller American nations might tempt European countries to intervene. It seemed to Roosevelt that European nations might well feel justified in trying to protect the lives and property of their citizens or to collect debts justly owed to them. Roosevelt asserted that the Monroe Doctrine required the United States to prevent such justified intervention by doing the intervening itself. Under this "big stick" policy, the United States sent armed forces into the Dominican Republic in 1905, into Nicaragua in 1912, and into Haiti in 1915.

In general, President Woodrow Wilson continued Roosevelt's policy. But Wilson promised that the United States would "never again seek one additional foot of territory by conquest." He also showed restraint in dealing with the Mexican revolution that ran its course during his term in office. If he had wanted to, he could have used Roosevelt's interpretation of the Monroe Doctrine to justify a full-scale occupation of Mexico. Instead, he pursued a policy of "watchful waiting." See WILSON, WOODROW (Crisis in Mexico).

The "Good Neighbor Policy." After World War I, the United States worked to improve relations with the Latin-American countries. President Herbert Hoover made a good-will tour of South America before he took office.

President Franklin D. Roosevelt announced his Good Neighbor policy early in his Administration. He said that all the Americas should have a share in upholding the Monroe Doctrine. Thus the defense of the Western Hemisphere became a cooperative task.

During the Hoover and Roosevelt administrations, the United States gradually withdrew its forces from the smaller American states it had occupied, and gave up the special privileges it had claimed. By a series of reciprocal trade agreements, it steadily cut down the high tariff barriers that had done so much to keep the Americas apart. Conferences on inter-American affairs were held at Montevideo in 1933, at Buenos Aires in 1936, at Lima in 1938, and at Havana in 1940. Fear of aggression brought all the American republics closer together. They met again at Rio de Janeiro in 1942, at Mexico City in 1945, and at Petropolis, Brazil, in 1947. They set up the Organization of American States at a meeting in Bogotá, Colombia, in 1948.

Misunderstandings. Many persons in the United States have often confused the Monroe Doctrine with the doctrine of *isolation*, or staying out of world affairs, which was stated by George Washington in his Farewell Address in 1796. Monroe did indeed repeat in his message the country's policy of staying out of European affairs, but he used it simply to support his argument that the European nations in turn should stay out of American affairs. Isolationism is therefore no part of the Monroe Doctrine. It simply happened to be the policy of the United States government at the time when the Monroe Doctrine was announced.   JOHN DONALD HICKS

See also ADAMS, JOHN QUINCY (Secretary of State); MONROE, JAMES (The Monroe Doctrine); PAN-AMERICAN CONFERENCES; PAN AMERICAN UNION.

MONROVIA, *mun ROH vee uh* (pop. 208,629), is the capital and chief city of Liberia. It stands on the Atlantic Coast at the mouth of the Saint Paul River, and has a modern, well-developed harbor. Monrovia is the educational and cultural center of the country. The University of Liberia is in the city.

Black Star

Monrovia, the chief port and commercial center of Liberia, has one of the best-developed harbors on Africa's Atlantic coast.

Monrovia was named for James Monroe, President of the United States. The city was founded in 1822 by the American Colonization Society. This society bought the freedom of many American slaves, and helped them establish the Republic of Liberia.   ALAN P. MERRIAM

MONS, *mawns* or *mahnz* (pop. 61,732), is in western Belgium. Coal mined nearby furnishes power for many Mons factories. Important products include chemicals, cloth, and metal goods.

MONSANTO COMPANY. See CHEMICAL INDUSTRY (table).

MONSARRAT, *MAHN sahr raht,* **NICHOLAS** (1910-1979), was an English author. He won fame for his novel *The Cruel Sea* (1951), a story of naval combat in World War II. He also wrote *The Story of Esther Costello* (1953), *The Tribe That Lost Its Head* (1956), and *Richer Than All His Tribe* (1969). Monsarrat was born in Liverpool, England, graduated from Cambridge University, and moved to Canada in 1953.   HARRY T. MOORE

MONSIGNOR, *mawn SEE nyoor,* is a title given to certain clergymen who are dignitaries of the Roman Catholic Church. The word comes from the Italian *monsignore,* meaning *My Lord,* and it is abbreviated as Msgr. Cardinals are not addressed as Monsignor. But patriarchs, archbishops, bishops, and persons attached to the papal household are given this title. In the United States it is more common to address bishops and archbishops as "Your Excellency," though an archbishop may also be called "Your Grace."   FULTON J. SHEEN

MONSOON, *mahn SOON,* is a seasonal wind that blows over the northern part of the Indian Ocean and most of the surrounding land areas. The monsoon blows continually from the southwest from April to October. The wind blows from the northeast from November to March.

Monsoons are generated by the difference in the heating and cooling of air over land and sea. During the summer, radiant energy from the sun heats land surfaces far more than it does sea surfaces. The strongly heated air over the land rises and is replaced by a southwesterly wind carrying warm, moist air from the Indian Ocean. Water vapor in the rising air condenses and forms clouds and rain. This process releases large amounts of heat, which helps drive monsoons.

In winter, the land is cooled much more than the sea. The cool air over the land sinks and spreads out to the sea as a dry northeasterly wind.

The southwesterly monsoon brings extremely heavy rains to southern Asia, including Arabia, Pakistan, India, and Bangladesh. For example, the Indian city of Cherrapunji, near Shillong, receives an average of 240 inches (610 centimeters) of rain annually. The strength of the southwesterly monsoon—and the time in April that it begins—affects agriculture in southern Asia. Monsoons also blow over northern Australia, the eastern and northern coasts of Asia, and parts of Africa and North America.   FREDERICK SANDERS

See also ASIA (Climate).

MONT BLANC, *MAWN BLAHN*, or *MAHNT BLAHNGK*, is the highest mountain in the Alps and one of the most famous peaks in Europe. It is often called the *monarch of mountains*. Its name is French for *white mountain*.

Mont Blanc rises 15,771 feet (4,807 meters) on the border between France, Italy, and Switzerland. The base of the mountain is a huge mass of granite which extends into all three countries. Its highest peak is in southern France, in the province of Savoy. Mont Blanc is about 30 miles (48 kilometers) long and 10 miles (16 kilometers) wide. Thick woods and swift streams cover its lower slopes. But above 8,000 feet (2,400 meters), there is always a thick blanket of snow. It has huge glaciers. The most famous glacier is Mer de Glace (Sea of Ice). A scientific laboratory was built on Mont Blanc in 1893.

Jacques Balmat and Michel Paccard first climbed Mont Blanc in 1786. Today, it is easily climbed, and is a resort center. People can ride up 6,287 feet (1,916 meters) to Mer de Glace on a cog railway. For those who

Mont Blanc is frequently called the *monarch of mountains.* Its rugged slopes challenge climbers from all parts of the world.

Engelhard, Monkmeyer

MONTAIGNE, MICHEL EYQUEM DE

prefer to climb, there are shelters to aid them in their 50- to 60-hour journey. The world's highest aerial tramway goes up Aiguille du Midi, a lower peak of Mont Blanc. In 1965, the Mont Blanc tunnel, linking France and Italy, was opened for auto traffic.   EDWARD W. FOX

See also ALPS; MOUNTAIN (picture chart).

MONT CENIS TUNNEL, *MAWN suh NEE*, was the first tunnel to be cut through the Alps. It is a railroad tunnel through the mountain peak of Mont Cenis. It connects the Italian province of Turin with the French province of Savoy. The tunnel is 8.5 miles (13.7 kilometers) long and from 3,775 to 4,246 feet (1,150 to 1,294 meters) above sea level. Construction began of the Mont Cenis tunnel in 1857 and was finished in 1870. The power drill and the air compressor were tried out for the first time at Mont Cenis.   EDWARD W. FOX

MONT PELÉE, *MAWN puh LAY*, is an active volcano on the northern end of Martinique island in the French West Indies. It rises 4,583 feet (1,397 meters) above sea level.

The volcano erupted violently in 1902, after lying dormant since 1851. Floods of mud loosened by the eruption devastated the slopes of the mountain. A heap of lava 1,000 feet (300 meters) high formed in the crater. A slender spire of rock was thrust up another 1,000 feet from the crater. An avalanche of red-hot lava and clouds of hot gas swept down the mountain, destroying the city of Saint-Pierre and killing about 38,000 people. Only one man, a prisoner in the city's dungeon, escaped alive, although he was seriously injured. Milder eruptions occurred between 1929 and 1932. The French government now maintains a volcano observatory on Mont Pelée.   GORDON A. MACDONALD

MONT SAINT MICHEL, *MAWN SAN MEE SHEL*, is a large rock which juts from the waters of Mont Saint Michel Bay off the northwestern coast of France. At the top of the rock are an ancient abbey and town.

MONTAIGNE, *mahn TAYN*, **MICHEL EYQUEM DE** (1533-1592), a French writer, is considered by many the creator of the personal essay. Writers up to the present time have imitated his informal, conversational style. Montaigne's essays reveal his independent mind and sound judgment, his charm and wit, and his wealth of experience in life and literature. Montaigne first began publishing his essays in 1580, adding to them as life and experience gave him new insight and understanding. He wrote a total of 107 essays.

Montaigne was a practicing Roman Catholic. But the "Apology for Raymond Sebond" and other essays show so much skepticism that some critics have questioned whether he was really a Christian.

Montaigne was born in his family's castle near Bordeaux, into a family which had recently bought its way into the nobility. His mother was of Jewish origin. Montaigne studied law, and became a minor legal official in 1554. He retired in 1570 to devote himself to writing. In 1580 and 1581 he traveled widely in Switzerland, Germany, and Italy and from 1581 to 1585 he served as mayor of Bordeaux. The most important episode in Montaigne's life was his friendship with the French writer Étienne de La Boétie from 1558 to 1563, which he immortalized in his famous essay "Of Friendship."   ABRAHAM C. KELLER

Fred Bond, Publix

Grinnell Lake in Glacier National Park, Which Has 250 Lakes Within Its Boundaries

MONTANA  *THE TREASURE STATE*

Smelter Smokestack in Anaconda, One of the World's Largest, Is 585 Feet (178 Meters) High

Montana Highway Commission

MONTANA is the fourth largest state. Only Alaska, Texas, and California have larger areas. Western Montana is a land of tall, rugged mountains. There, miners dig deep into the earth to tap the state's vast deposits of copper, gold, and silver. Eastern Montana is a land of broad plains. There, herds of cattle graze on the prairie grasses, wheat grows in the fertile soil, and wells bring up petroleum from deep under the ground. Eastern Montana also has large coal deposits.

The name *Montana* comes from a Spanish word meaning *mountainous*. Early travelers, who saw the sun glistening on the lofty, snow-capped peaks, called the area the *Land of Shining Mountains*. These mountains contained a wealth of gold and silver, which gave the state another nickname, the *Treasure State*. Glacier National Park has mountain peaks so steep and remote that they have never been climbed.

Early Montana was Indian country. But gold was discovered there in 1862 and great numbers of eager prospectors rushed to the area. Mining camps sprang up overnight and wealth came to the territory. But the gold also brought problems. Outlaws spread terror in the mining camps until groups of citizens called *vigilantes* took the law into their own hands. The vigilantes hanged many of the outlaws and drove others away.

Montana was the scene of another struggle—the climax of the Indians' efforts to keep their land. The last stand of General George A. Custer and the final battles of the Nez Percé War were fought in Montana.

Montana Highway Commission

Strips of Wheat Form Patterns on Farms near Great Falls

The mountains, the battlefields, the old gold camps, and the vast, lonely distances still make a visitor feel close to the American frontier. In the capital, Helena (pronounced *HEHL uh nuh*), the main street is called Last Chance Gulch. The name comes from the gold camp that stood on that site. Even today, when a basement is dug for a building in Helena, the digging sometimes produces gold dust.

Billings is the largest city in Montana. For the relationship of Montana to the other states in its region, see the article on the ROCKY MOUNTAIN STATES.

The contributors of this article are Oscar Chaffee, State Editor of the Billings Gazette, *and Thomas A. Clinch, Head of the Department of History, Carroll College.*

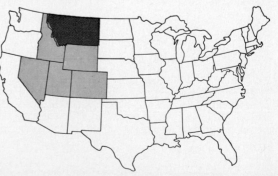

Montana (blue) ranks fourth in size among all the states, and is the largest of the Rocky Mountain States (gray).

Constitution of Montana went into effect in 1973. It replaced a Constitution that had been adopted in 1889 and amended about 30 times. Amendments may be proposed by (1) a two-thirds vote of the state legislature, (2) a petition signed by a certain number of voters, or (3) a constitutional convention. To be adopted, a proposed amendment must be approved by a majority of the citizens voting in an election.

A constitutional convention may be proposed by either a two-thirds vote of the legislature or a petition signed by a certain number of voters. Approval of proposals by a majority of the voters in an election is required to call a constitutional convention. The Montana Constitution requires that the people vote at least once every 20 years on whether to call a constitutional convention.

Executive. The governor of Montana serves a four-year term, and may be re-elected any number of times. The governor has powers of appointment involving key officials in about 20 executive departments and many state institutions. The governor also has strong veto powers over legislation. For example, the governor may veto individual items in an *appropriation* (money) bill, and sign the rest of the bill into law. The governor is paid $37,500 a year. For a list of the governors of Montana, see the *History* section of this article.

The lieutenant governor, attorney general, auditor, secretary of state, and superintendent of public instruction are elected to four-year terms. These officials may be re-elected any number of times.

Legislature consists of a 50-member Senate and a 100-member House of Representatives. Each of the 50 senatorial districts in Montana elects one senator, who serves a four-year term. Each of the 100 representative districts in the state elects one representative, who serves a two-year term.

Regular legislative sessions are held in odd-numbered years. These sessions generally begin on the first Monday in January and are limited to 90 legislative days. Special sessions may be called by either the governor or the legislature.

In 1965, Montana's legislative districts were *reapportioned* (redivided) to provide equal representation based on population. The districts were reapportioned again in 1971 and 1974.

Courts. The highest court of appeals in Montana is the state Supreme Court. It consists of four associate justices and one chief justice. All are elected by the voters to eight-year terms. The trial courts for major civil and criminal cases are the district courts. District judges are elected to six-year terms from each of 19 judicial districts. Municipal courts, police courts, and justice of the peace courts handle less serious cases.

Local Government. Fifty-three of the state's 56 counties elect three county commissioners to govern the county. The commissioners serve six-year terms. Elected chief executives administer two of the other counties, and a manager appointed by commissioners runs the remaining county. About 120 cities and towns operate with a mayor-council form of government. Several other cities, including Bozeman, Great Falls, and Helena, use the council-manager system.

Taxation. State taxes and fees provide about 65 per cent of the state government's income in Montana.

The Governor's Mansion Stands on a Hillside near the Capitol. The Building Was First Occupied in 1959.

Montana Highway Commission

The State Seal

The State Flag

Symbols of Montana. On the state seal, a plow, a pick, and a shovel rest on the soil to show Montana's agricultural opportunities and its mineral industries. The Great Falls of the Missouri River and the mountain scenery represent the natural beauty and resources of the state. The state motto appears on a ribbon. The seal was adopted in 1893. The state flag, adopted in 1905, bears an adaptation of the seal.

Flower illustration courtesy of Eli Lilly and Company

The State Bird
Western Meadow Lark

Much of the revenue comes from income taxes and a tax on coal production. The state government also taxes motor vehicles, property, and other items. Federal programs provide about a third of the state government's income.

Politics. In the early days, the Democratic Party dominated Montana politics. Many people voted Democratic because they came to Montana from the traditionally Democratic South. Montanans joked that part of the Confederate army never surrendered, it just retreated to Montana.

Since 1940, Montana voters have paid more attention to individual candidates than to parties. For example, they have repeatedly elected Democrats to the U.S. Senate, but have picked only three Democratic governors since 1940. Usually, the eastern congressional district elects a Republican to the House of Representatives, and the western district elects a Democrat. Montana has given its electoral votes about equally to Republican and Democratic presidential candidates. For the state's voting record in presidential elections, see ELECTORAL COLLEGE (table).

The State Flower
Bitterroot

State Capitol in Helena has a copper-covered dome 165 feet (50 meters) high. Helena has been the state capital since 1875. Earlier capitals were Bannack (1864-1865) and Virginia City (1865-1875).

Montana Highway Commission

The State Tree
Ponderosa Pine

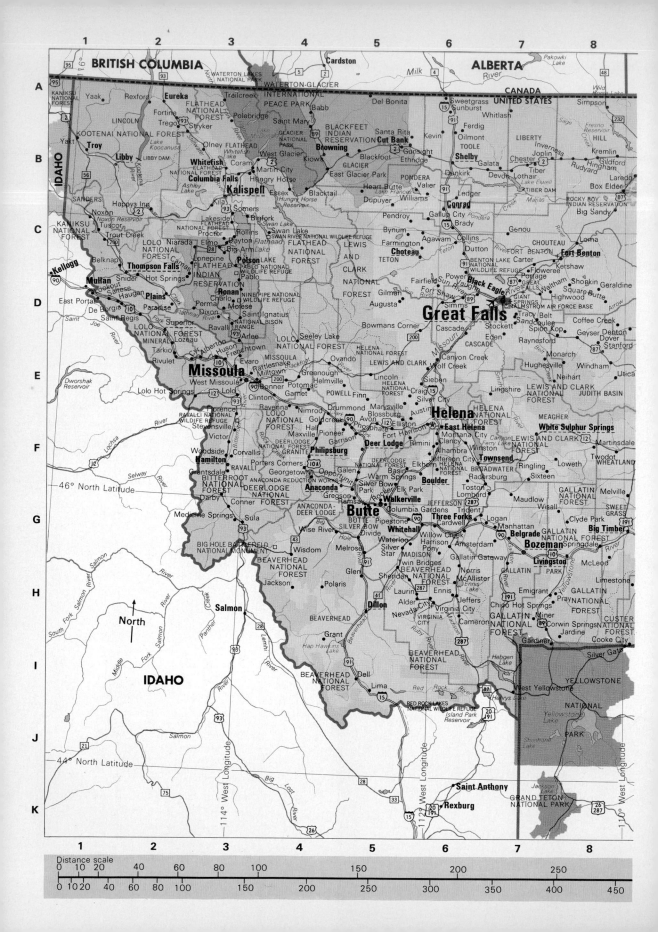

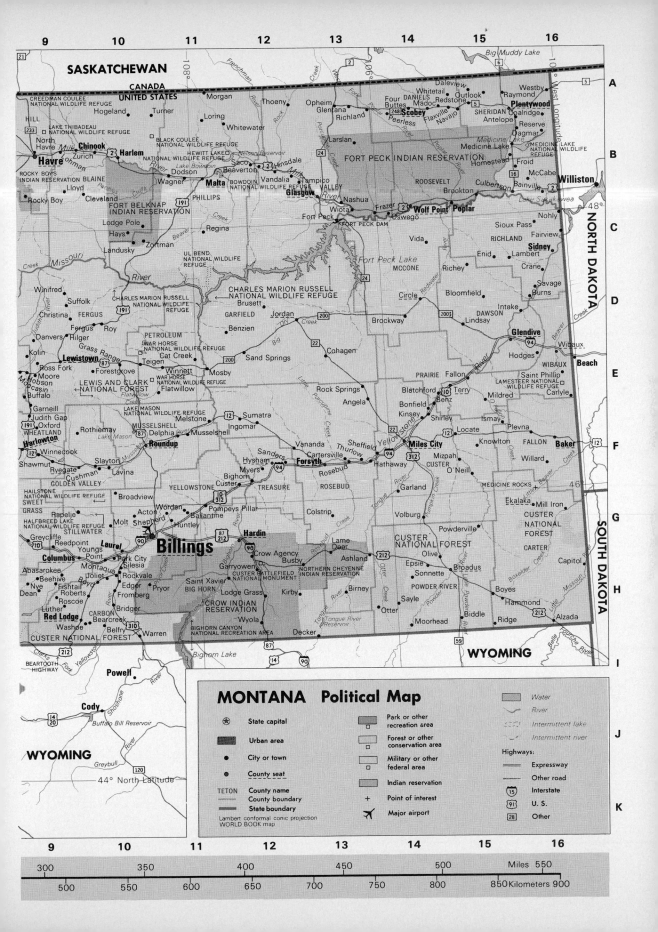

MONTANA MAP INDEX

Population

748,000	..Estimate.	1975
694,409	...Census.	1970
674,767	"	1960
591,024	"	1950
559,456	"	1940
537,606	"	1930
548,889	"	1920
376,053	"	1910
243,329	"	1900
142,924	"	1890
39,159	"	1880
20,595	"	1870

Metropolitan Areas

Billings 87,367
Great Falls 81,804

Counties

Anaconda-Deer Lodge†	.15,652	.G 4
Beaverhead	.8,187	.H 4
Big Horn	.10,057	.H 11
Blaine	.6,727	.B 10
Broadwater	.2,526	.F 7
Butte-Silver Bow**	.41,981	.G 5
Carbon	.7,080	.H 10
Carter	.1,956	.G 16
Cascade	.81,804	.E 6
Chouteau	.6,473	.C 7
Custer	.12,174	.F 14
Daniels	.3,083	.A 14
Dawson	.11,269	.D 15
Fallon	.4,050	.F 16
Fergus	.12,611	.D 10
Flathead	.39,460	.B 3
Gallatin	.32,505	.H 7
Garfield	.1,796	.D 12
Glacier	.10,783	.B 5
Golden Valley	.931	.F 9
Granite	.2,737	.F 4
Hill	.17,358	.A 9
Jefferson	.5,238	.G 6
Judith Basin	.2,667	.E 8
Lake	.14,445	.C 3
Lewis and Clark	.33,281	.E 5
Liberty	.2,359	.B 7
Lincoln	.18,063	.A 1
Madison	.5,014	.G 6
McCone	.2,875	.D 14
Meagher	.2,122	.F 7
Mineral	.2,958	.E 2
Missoula	.58,263	.E 4
Musselshell	.3,734	.F 10
Park	.11,197	.H 7
Petroleum	.675	.D 11
Phillips	.5,386	.C 11
Pondera	.6,611	.B 5
Powder River	.2,862	.H 14
Powell	.6,660	.E 4
Prairie	.1,752	.E 14

Ravalli	.14,409	.F 3
Richland	.9,837	.C 15
Roosevelt	.10,365	.B 14
Rosebud	.6,032	.G 13
Sanders	.7,093	.C 1
Sheridan	.5,779	.A 15
Stillwater	.4,632	.G 9
Sweet Grass	.2,980	.G 8
Teton	.6,116	.C 5
Toole	.5,839	.B 6
Treasure	.1,069	.G 12
Valley	.11,471	.B 13
Wheatland	.2,529	.F 9
Wibaux	.1,465	.E 16
Yellowstone	87,367	.G 11
Yellowstone National Park	64	.I 8

Cities and Towns

Abasarokee	...	.H 9
Acton	...	.G 10
Adler	...	.H 6
Agawam	...	.C 6
Alberton	.363	.E 3
Albion	...	.H 16
Alhambra	...	.F 6
Alzada	...	.H 16
Amsterdam	...	.G 7
Anaconda†	.15,652	.°G 4
Angela	...	.E 13
Antelope	...	.A 15
Archer	...	.A 15
Argenta	...	.H 5
Arlee	...	.D 3
Arrow Creek	...	.D 8
Ashland	...	.H 13
Augusta	...	.D 5
Austin	...	.E 5
Babb	...	.A 4
Bainville	.217	.B 16
Baker	.2,584	.°F 16
Ballantine	...	.G 11
Barber	...	.F 9
Basin	...	.F 5
Bearcreek	.31	.H 10
Bearmouth	...	.E 4
Beaverton	...	.B 12
Beehive	...	.H 9
Belfry	...	.H 10
Belgrade	.1,307	.G 7
Belknap	...	.C 1
Belmont	...	.F 10
Belt	.656	.D 7
Benchland	...	.E 8
Benz	...	.E 14
Benzien	...	.D 11
Biddle	...	.H 15
Big Arm	...	.C 3
Big Sandy	.827	.C 8
Big Timber	.1,592	.°G 8
Bigfork	...	.C 3
Bighorn	...	.F 12
Billings	.61,581	.°G 10
Birney	...	.H 13
Black Eagle	...	.D 7
Blackfoot	...	.B 5
Blacktail	...	.B 4

Blatchford	...	.E 14
Bloomfield	...	.D 15
Blossburg	...	.F 5
Bonfield	...	.E 14
Bonner	...	.E 3
Boulder	.1,342	.°F 6
Bowmans Corner	...	.D 6
Box Elder	...	.B 8
Boyd	...	.H 10
Boyes	...	.H 15
Bozeman	.18,670	.°G 7
Brady	...	.C 6
Bridger	.717	.H 10
Broadus	.799	.°H 15
Broadview	.123	.G 10
Brockton	.401	.C 15
Brockway	...	.D 14
Browning	.1,700	.B 5
Brusett	...	.D 12
Buffalo	...	.E 9
Burns	...	.D 10
Busby	...	.H 12
Butte**	.41,981	.°G 5
Bynum	...	.C 5
Camas	...	.D 2
Camas Prairie	...	.D 2
Cameron	...	.H 6
Canyon Creek	...	.E 6
Capitol	...	.H 16
Cardwell	...	.G 6
Carlyle	...	.E 16
Carter	...	.C 7
Cartersville	...	.F 13
Cascade	.714	.D 6
Cat Creek	...	.E 11
Centerville-Dublin Gulch*	.2,284	.G 5
Charlo	...	.D 3
Chester	.936	.°B 7
Chico Hot Springs	...	.H 7
Chinook	.1,813	.°B 9
Choteau	.1,586	.°C 6
Christina	...	.D 9
Circle	.964	.°D 14
Clancy	...	.F 6
Cleveland	...	.C 10
Clinton	...	.E 4
Clyde Park	.244	.G 8
Coalridge	...	.A 16
Coalwood	...	.G 14
Coffee Creek	...	.D 8
Cohagen	...	.E 13
Collins	...	.C 6
Colstrip	...	.G 13
Columbia Falls	.2,652	.B 3
Columbia Gardens	...	.G 5
Columbus	.1,173	.°G 9
Comanche	...	.G 10
Comertown	...	.A 16
Condon	...	.D 4
Conner	...	.G 3
Conrad	.2,770	.°C 6
Cooke City	...	.I 9
Coram	...	.B 3
Corvallis	...	.F 3
Corwin Springs	...	.H 7
Craig	...	.E 5

Crane	...	.D 16
Crow Agency	...	.G 12
Culbertson	.821	.B 15
Cushman	...	.F 10
Custer	...	.G 12
Cut Bank	.4,004	.°B 5
Cyr	...	.E 3
Dagmar	...	.B 16
Daleview	...	.A 15
Danvers	...	.D 9
Darby	.538	.G 3
Dayton	...	.C 3
De Borgia	...	.D 2
Dean	...	.H 9
Decker	...	.I 13
Deer Lodge	.4,306	.°F 5
Del Bonita	...	.A 5
Dell	...	.I 5
Delphia	...	.F 11
Denton	.398	.D 8
Devon	...	.B 7
Dillon	.4,548	.°H 5
Divide	...	.G 5
Dixon	...	.D 3
Dodson	.196	.B 11
Dooley	...	.A 16
Dover	...	.C 5
Drummond	.494	.E 4
Dunkirk	...	.B 6
Dupuyer	...	.C 5
Dutton	.415	.C 6
East Glacier Park	...	.B 4
East Helena	.1,651	.F 6
East Portal	...	.D 1
Eden	...	.D 7
Edger	...	.H 10
Ekalaka	.663	.°G 16
Elk Park	...	.G 5
Elkhorn	...	.F 6
Elliston	...	.F 5
Elmo	...	.C 3
Emigrant	...	.H 7
Enid	...	.C 15
Ennis	.501	.H 6
Epsie	...	.H 14
Essex	...	.B 4
Ethridge	...	.B 6
Eureka	.1,195	.A 2
Evaro	...	.E 3
Fairfield	.638	.D 6
Fairview	.956	.C 16
Fallon	...	.E 15
Farmington	...	.C 6
Ferdig	...	.B 6
Fergus	...	.D 10
Finn	...	.E 5
Fishtail	...	.H 9
Flatwillow	...	.E 11
Flaxville	.185	.A 15
Floral Park*	5,113	.G 5
Florence	...	.F 3
Floweree	...	.D 7
Forest Grove	...	.E 10
Forsyth	.2,449	.°F 13
Fort Benton	1,863	.°C 8
Fort Harrison	...	.F 6
Fort Logan	...	.E 7
Fort Peck	...	.C 13

Fort Shaw	...	.D 6
Fortine	...	.A 2
Four Buttes	...	.A 14
Four Corners	...	.B 6
Franklin	...	.F 9
Frazer	...	.C 14
Frenchtown	...	.E 3
Fresno	...	.B 8
Froid	.330	.B 15
Fromberg	.364	.H 10
Galata	...	.B 7
Galen	...	.F 5
Gallatin Gateway	...	.H 7
Gallup City	...	.C 6
Gardiner	...	.I 7
Garland	...	.E 8
Garneill	...	.E 9
Garnet	...	.E 4
Garrison	...	.F 5
Garryowen	...	.H 12
Genou	...	.C 7
Georgetown	...	.F 5
Geraldine	.370	.D 8
Geyser	...	.D 8
Gildford	...	.B 8
Gilman	...	.D 5
Glasgow	.4,700	.°C 13
Glen	...	.H 5
Glendive	.6,305	.°E 15
Glentana	...	.A 13
Goldcreek	...	.F 5
Grant	...	.I 4
Grantsdale	...	.F 3
Grass Range	.181	.E 10
Great Falls	.60,091	.°D 7
Greenough	...	.E 4
Gregson	...	.G 5
Greycliffe	...	.G 9
Gunsight	...	.B 5
Hall	...	.F 4
Hamilton	.2,499	.°F 3
Hammond	...	.H 15
Hanover	...	.E 9
Happys Inn	...	.C 2
Hardin	.2,733	.°G 12
Harlem	.1,094	.B 10
Harlowton	.1,375	.°F 9
Harrison	...	.G 6
Hathaway	...	.F 13
Haugan	...	.D 1
Havre	.10,558	.°B 9
Hays	...	.C 10
Heart Butte	...	.B 5
Heath	...	.E 9
Hedgeville	...	.E 9
Helena	.22,730	.°F 6
Helmville	...	.E 4
Heron	...	.C 1
Highwood	...	.D 7
Hilger	...	.D 9
Hill	...	.B 7
Hingham	.262	.B 8
Hinsdale	...	.B 12
Hobson	.192	.E 9
Hodges	...	.E 16
Hogeland	...	.A 10
Homestead	...	.B 15
Hot Springs	.664	.D 2

Hughesville ....E 8
Hungry Horse .....B 3
Huntley ....G 11
Huson ....E 3
Hysham ....373.°F 12
Ingomar ....F 12
Intake ....D 16
Inverness ....B 8
Ismay ....40..F 15
Jackson ....H 4
Jardine ....I 8
Jeffers ....H 6
Jefferson City ....F 6
Joliet ....412..H 10
Joplin ....B 7
Jordan .....529.°D 12
Judith Gap ..160..F 9
Kalispell ..10,506.°G 6
Kevin ....250..B 6
Kila ....C 3
Kinsey ....F 14
Kiowa ....B 4
Kirby ....H 12
Klein ....F 10
Knowlton ....F 15
Kolin ....E 9
Kremlin ....B 8
Lakeside ....C 3
Lambert ....C 15
Lame Deer ....G 13
Landusky ....C 10
Laredo ....B 9
Larslan ....B 13
Laurel .....4,454..G 10
Laurin ....H 6
Lavina .....169..F 10
Ledger ....C 6
Lennep ....F 8
Lewistown ..6,437.°E 9
Libby .....3,286.°B 1
Lima ....351..I 5
Limestone ....H 8
Lincoln ....E 5
Lindsay ....D 15
Lingshire ....E 7
Livingston ..6,883.°G 8
Lloyd ....B 9
Locate ....F 15
Lodge Grass ..806..H 12
Lodgepole ....C 10
Logan ....G 7
Lohman ....B 9
Lolo ....E 3
Lolo Hot Springs ..E 3
Loma ....C 8
Lombard ....G 7
Lonepine ....C 3
Lookout ....D 1
Loring ....A 11
Lothair ....B 7
Loweth ....F 8
Lozeau ....E 2
Luther ....H 9
Madoc ....A 14
Malmstrom* ..8,374..D 7
Malta .....2,195.°B 11
Manhattan ...816..G 7
Marsh ....E 15

Martin City ....B 3
Martinsdale ....F 8
Marysville ....E 5
Maudlow ....G 7
Maxville ....F 4
McAllister ....H 6
McCabe ....B 16
McLeod ....G 8
McQueen-East
  Butte* ..1,084..G 5
Medicine Lake 393..B 15
Medicine Springs ..G 3
Melrose ....G 5
Melstone ...227..F 11
Melville ....G 8
Menard ....G 7
Merino ....D 8
Mildred ....E 15
Miles City ..9,023.°F 14
Mill Iron ....G 16
Milltown ....E 3
Miner ....H 7
Missoula ..29,497.°E 3
Missoula
  South* ....4,886..E 3
Missoula
  West* .....9,148..E 3
Mizpah ....F 15
Moccasin ....E 9
Moiese ....D 3
Molt ....G 10
Monarch ....E 7
Montana City ......F 6
Montaqua ....H 10
Moore ......219..E 9
Moorhead ....H 14
Morgan ....A 11
Mosby ....E 11
Musselshell ....F 11
Myers ....F 15
Nashua .....513..C 13
Navajo ....A 15
Neihart .....109..E 7
Nevada City ....H 6
Niarada ....C 3
Nibbe ....G 11
Nimrod ....E 4
Nohly ....C 16
Norris ....H 6
North Havre 1,073..B 9
Noxon ....C 1
Nye ....H 9
Oilmont ....B 6
Olive ....H 14
Ollie ....E 16
Olney ....B 3
O'Neill ....F 15
Opheim .....306..A 13
Opportunity ....G 5
Oswego ....C 14
Otter ....H 14
Outlook .....153..A 15
Ovando ....E 4
Oxford ....F 9
Pablo ....D 3
Paradise ....D 2
Park City ....H 10
Peerless ....A 14

Pendroy ....C 5
Perma ....D 3
Philipsburg .1,128.°F 4
Phosphate ....F 5
Pioneer ....F 5
Pipestone ....G 5
Plains .....1,046..D 2
Plentywood ..2,381.°A 15
Plevna .....189..F 16
Polaris ....H 4
Polebridge ....A 3
Polson .....2,464.°C 3
Pompeys Pillar ....G 11
Pony ....G 6
Poplar .....1,389..C 15
Portage ....D 7
Porters Corners ...F 4
Potomac ....E 4
Powderville ....G 15
Power ....D 6
Pray ....H 8
Proctor ....C 3
Pryor ....H 10
Radersburg ....F 6
Ramsay ....G 5
Rapelje ....G 9
Rattlesnake* .1,492..E 3
Ravalli ....D 3
Ravenna ....E 4
Raymond ....A 15
Raynesford ....D 7
Red Lodge ..1,844.°H 9
Redstone ....A 15
Reedpoint ....G 9
Regina ....C 11
Reserve ....B 16
Rexford .....243..A 2
Richey .....389..D 15
Richland ....A 13
Ridge ....H 15
Rimini ....F 6
Ringling ....F 7
Rivulet ....E 2
Roberts ....H 10
Rock Springs ......E 13
Rocker ....G 5
Rockvale ....H 10
Rocky Boy ....C 9
Rollins ....C 3
Ronan .....1,347..D 3
Roscoe ....H 9
Rosebud ....F 13
Ross Fork ....F 9
Rothiemay ....F 9
Roundup ....2,116.°F 10
Roy ....D 10
Rudyard ....B 8
Ryegate .....261.°F 9
Saco ....356..B 12
St. Ignatius ..925..D 3
St. Mary ....B 5
St. Pauls ....C 10
St. Phillip ....E 16
St. Regis ....D 2
St. Xavier ....H 11
Saltese ....D 1
Sand Springs ......E 12
Sandcoulee ....D 7

Sanders ....F 12
Santa Rita ....B 5
Savage ....D 16
Savoy ....B 10
Scobey .....1,486.°A 14
Seeley Lake ....E 4
Shawmut ....F 9
Sheffield ....F 14
Shelby .....3,111.°B 6
Shepherd ....G 11
Sheridan ....636..H 5
Shirley ....F 14
Shonkin ....D 8
Sidney .....4,543.°C 16
Sieben ....E 6
Silesia ....H 10
Silver Bow
  Park .....5,524..G 5
Silver City ....E 6
Silver Gate ....I 8
Silver Star ....G 5
Simpson ....A 8
Sioux Pass ....C 16
Sixteen ....F 7
Slayton ....F 10
Snider ....D 2
Somers ....C 3
Sonnette ....H 14
Spion Kop ....E 6
Springdale ....G 8
Square Butte ......D 8
Stanford ....505.°E 8
Stevensville ..829..F 3
Stockett ....D 7
Stryker ....B 2
Suffolk ....D 9
Sula ....G 3
Sumatra ....F 12
Sun River ....D 6
Sunburst ....604..A 6
Superior ....993.°D 2
Swan Lake ....C 4
Sweetgrass ....A 6
Tampico ....B 12
Tarkio ....E 2
Terry ......870.°E 15
Thoeny ....A 12
Thompson
  Falls .....1,356.°D 2
Three Forks .1,188..G 6
Thurlow ....F 13
Tiber ....B 7
Toston ....F 6
Townsend ..1,371.°F 6
Trailcreek ....A 3
Trego ....B 2
Trident ....G 6

Troy ......1,046..B 1
Tuscor ....C 1
Twin
  Bridges ....613..H 5
Twodot ....F 8
Utica ....E 8
Valier .....651..B 6
Vananda ....F 12
Vandalia ....B 12
Van Norman ....D 13
Victor ....F 3
Vida ....C 14
Virginia
  City ....149.°H 6
Volburg ....G 14
Wagner ....B 11
Walkerville ..1,097..G 5
Waltham ....D 7
Warm Springs .....F 5
Warren ....I 10
Washoe ....H 9
Waterloo ....G 5
Webster ....F 16
West Glacier ......B 3
West Yellow-
  stone .....756..I 7
Westby .....287..A 16
White Pine ....C 1
White Sulphur
  Springs ..1,200.°F 7
Whitefish ..3,349..B 3
Whitehall ..1,035..G 6
Whitetail ....A 15
Whitewater ....B 11
Whitlash ....A 7
Wibaux .....644.°G 16
Willard ....F 16
Williams ....B 6
Willow Creek ......G 6
Windham ....E 8
Winifred .....190..D 9
Winnecook ....F 7
Winnett .....271.°E 11
Winston ....F 6
Wiota ....C 13
Wisall ....G 8
Wisdom ....G 4
Wise River ....G 4
Wolf Creek ....E 6
Wolf Point ..3,095.°C 14
Woodside ....F 3
Worden ....G 11
Wyola ....H 12
Yaak ....A 1
Yakt ....B 1
Youngs Point ......H 10
Zortman ....C 10

*Does not appear on map; key shows general location.
°County seat.
†City of Anaconda and Deer Lodge County were consolidated as Anaconda-Deer Lodge County on May 2, 1977.
**City of Butte and Silver Bow County were consolidated as Butte-Silver Bow County on May 2, 1977.
Sources: Latest census figures (1970 and special censuses). Places without population figures are unincorporated areas and are not listed in census reports.

MONTANA / People

The 1970 United States census reported that 694,409 persons lived in Montana. The population had increased 3 per cent over the 1960 figure of 674,767. Montana's 27,130 Indians, most of whom live on reservations, make up about 4 per cent of the state's population. The U.S. Bureau of the Census estimated that by 1975 the state's population had reached about 748,000.

About half the people live in cities and towns and about half live in farm areas. Billings and Great Falls are the only cities of more than 60,000 population, and they are the only Standard Metropolitan Statistical Areas (see METROPOLITAN AREA). For their populations, see the *Index* to the political map of Montana.

Most of Montana's cities began as mining towns, or as centers of trade for farm and ranch areas. For example, Butte grew from a mining camp. So did Helena, the state capital. Missoula developed as an agricultural trade center. See the separate articles on the cities of Montana listed in the *Related Articles* at the end of this article.

The majority of Montanans are Protestants, but Roman Catholics form the largest single religious group.

POPULATION

This map shows the *population density* of Montana, and how it varies in different parts of the state. Population density means the average number of persons who live in a given area.

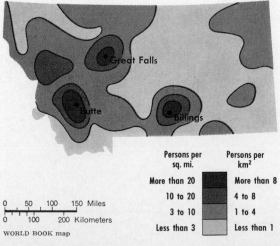

Persons per sq. mi.		Persons per km²
More than 20		More than 8
10 to 20		4 to 8
3 to 10		1 to 4
Less than 3		Less than 1

0   50   100   150 Miles
0   100   200 Kilometers

WORLD BOOK map

Schools. Montana's first schools were started in mining camps in the early 1860's. They had private teachers who charged tuition. The Roman Catholic Church organized a boarding school for Indians in the Flathead Valley in 1864. The legislature provided for free public schools in 1893, and for county high schools in 1897.

Today, the public schools are supervised by an elected superintendent of public instruction and a board of public education appointed by the governor. The superintendent serves a four-year term. Each county and most school districts have a superintendent of schools.

Libraries and Museums. The library at the University of Montana in Missoula owns an outstanding collection relating to the history of the Northwest. The library of the state historical society in Helena has a collection of early Montana newspapers. Montana has about 125 public libraries throughout the state.

The Montana Historical Society in Helena features exhibits on the development of the state. Many persons visit the museum to see its fine collection of paintings and sculpture by famous cowboy artist Charles M. Russell. Great Falls also has a Russell museum. The Montana College of Mineral Science and Technology at Butte has a museum of minerals. The World Museum of Mining is in Butte. Other museums are at Big Hole National Battlefield, Billings, Browning, Custer Battlefield National Monument, and Virginia City.

UNIVERSITIES AND COLLEGES

Montana has nine universities and colleges accredited by the Northwest Association of Schools and Colleges. For enrollments and further information, see UNIVERSITIES AND COLLEGES (table).

Name	Location	Founded
Carroll College	Helena	1909
Eastern Montana College	Billings	1925
Great Falls, College of	Great Falls	1932
Montana, University of	Missoula	1893
Montana College of Mineral Science and Technology	Butte	1893
Montana State University	Bozeman	1893
Northern Montana College	Havre	1929
Rocky Mountain College	Billings	1883
Western Montana College	Dillon	1893

Custer Hill at Custer Battlefield National Monument

Ernst Peterson, Publix

Few states equal Montana in attractions for outdoor recreation. People from all over the United States travel to Montana to catch trout and other fish or to hunt deer and other big game. Lovers of the outdoors also enjoy the state's national parks, national forests, dude ranches, ski lodges, summer resorts, and other attractions. Trips to old ghost towns and to the sites of Indian battles interest tourists who like history.

PLACES TO VISIT

Following are brief descriptions of some of Montana's most interesting places to visit.

Anaconda Reduction Works, at Anaconda, is one of the world's largest copper smelters. Its smokestack—585 feet (178 meters) high—is one of the world's largest.

Beartooth Highway leads from Red Lodge to Yellowstone Park. Motorists on this route see spectacular mountain views as they wind over the Beartooth Plateau, which is 11,000 feet (3,350 meters) high.

Flathead Lake Recreation Area, in northwestern Montana, offers boating, fishing, and swimming. It is one of the largest lakes west of the Mississippi River.

Giant Springs, near Great Falls, discharges 270,000 gallons (1,020,000 liters) of water a minute. This spring was sighted by Lewis and Clark in 1805.

Glacier National Park, in northwestern Montana, includes a large area of majestic mountain scenery. It has more than 50 glaciers that lie on the mountain slopes. Several of its rugged peaks have never been climbed. See GLACIER NATIONAL PARK.

Great Falls of the Missouri, near Great Falls, is the highest waterfall on the Missouri River. Its waters drop 400 feet (120 meters) in 8 miles (13 kilometers).

Medicine Rocks, near Ekalaka, lie in the badlands of eastern Montana. Wind and water carved these sandstone rocks into unusual shapes.

Virginia City, near Dillon, has been restored to look the way it did in 1865, when it was one of the nation's richest gold camps.

Yellowstone National Park lies mainly in northwestern Wyoming, but three of the five park entrances are in Montana. These are near Cooke City, Gardiner, and West Yellowstone. See YELLOWSTONE NATIONAL PARK.

Other National Parklands in Montana include the sites of two famous Indian battles. These sites, preserved by the federal government, are at the Custer Battlefield National Monument, south of Hardin; and Big Hole National Battlefield, near Hamilton. For more information about these and other areas in Montana that are managed by the National Park Service, see the WORLD BOOK article on NATIONAL PARK SYSTEM.

National Forests. Eleven national forests lie either entirely or partly in Montana. The largest of these are Beaverhead, Flathead, Gallatin, Kootenai, Lewis and Clark, and Lolo. The others are Bitterroot, Custer, Deerlodge, Helena, and Kaniksu. For the areas and features of all these forests, see NATIONAL FOREST (table).

State Parks and Forests. Montana has 43 state parks, monuments, and recreational areas. For further information write the Director, Fish, Wildlife, and Parks, Helena, Mont. 59601.

Ray Atkeson
Camping in Glacier National Park

Bill Browning, Montana Chamber of Commerce
North American Indian Days in Browning

Ray Atkeson
Old West Relics in Virginia City

Bob and Ira Spring
Grinnell Glacier Crevasse in Glacier National Park

ANNUAL EVENTS

Montana's "Cowboy and Indian" background is reflected in the rodeos and Indian ceremonies held throughout the state. Almost every Montana town has a rodeo. National riders compete for large prizes in some rodeos. In others, hometown cowboys show their skill. Rodeo owners buy wild horses in a May Bucking Horse Sale in Miles City. Indians on Montana's reservations perform colorful dances and ceremonies.

Winter events in Montana highlight skiing and snowmobile riding. The Western Snowmobile Association Roundup is a popular event held in March. The roundup features statewide races and rallies.

Other outstanding events in Montana include the following:

January-March: Central Montana Winter Carnival in Lewistown (January); Lions Winter Carnival in Red Lodge (January); Montana Winter Fair in Bozeman (January); Winter Carnival in Whitefish (February); Winter Carnival in Red Lodge (March).

April-June: Cherry Blossom Festival in Polson (May); Vigilante Parade in Helena (May); Whoop-up Days in Conrad (May).

July-September: Copper Cup Regatta in Polson (July); Flathead Lake Showboat in Polson (July); Jaycees Logger Days in Libby (July); Model T Races in Livingston (July); MonDak Old Fashioned Fourth of July in Sidney (July); North American Indian Days in Browning (July); Threshing Bee and Antique Show in Scobey (July); Yellowstone River Float, Livingston to Billings (July); Bitterroot Trail Ride in Hamilton (August); Eastern Montana Fair in Miles City (August); Festival of Nations in Butte (August); Festival of Nations in Red Lodge (August); Midland Empire Fair and Rodeo in Billings (August); Northwest Montana Fair in Glasgow (August); Northwest Montana Fair and Rodeo in Kalispell (August); State Fair and Rodeo in Great Falls (August); Western Montana Fair and Rodeo Meet in Missoula (August).

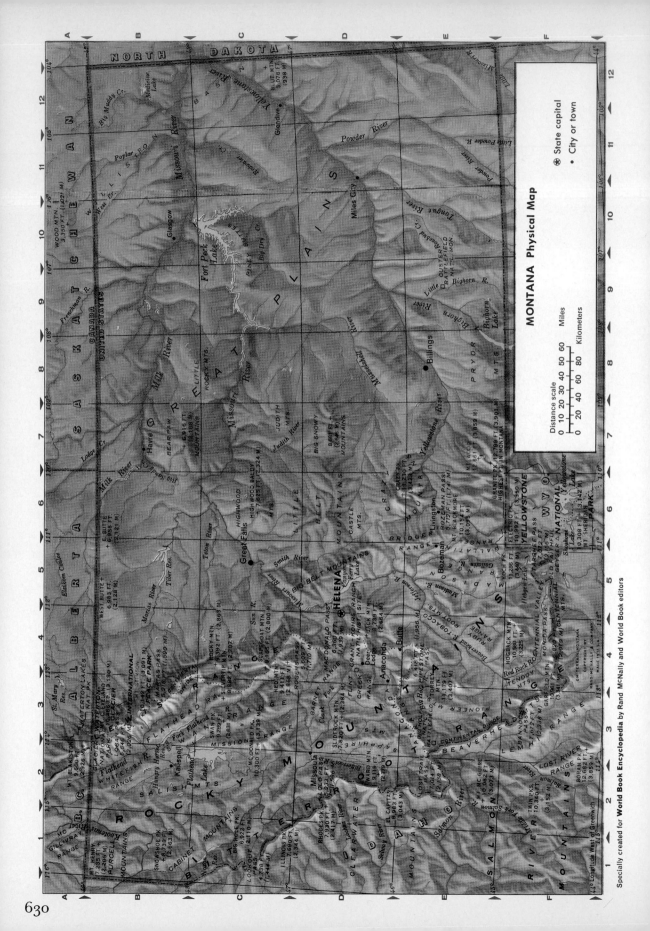

MONTANA Physical Map

Distance scale
Miles
Kilometers

0 10 20 30 40 50 60
0 20 40 60 80

⊛ State capital
• City or town

Specially created for World Book Encyclopedia by Rand McNally and World Book editors

MONTANA/The Land

Land Regions. Montana has two major land regions. They are (1) the Great Plains and (2) the Rocky Mountains.

The Great Plains of Montana are part of the vast Interior Plain of North America that stretches from Canada to Mexico. In Montana, this high, gently rolling land makes up the eastern three-fifths of the state. The land is broken by hills and wide river valleys. Here and there, groups of mountains rise sharply from the plains. These ranges include the Bear Paw, Big Snowy, Judith, and Little Rocky. In the southeast, wind and water have created a badland of gullies and colorful columns of red, yellow, brown, and white stone.

The Rocky Mountains cover the western two-fifths of Montana. This is a region of unusual beauty. The valleys have flat, grassy floors, and the mountains are forested with fir, pine, spruce, and other evergreens. In southwestern Montana, the valleys may stretch 30 to 40 miles (48 to 64 kilometers) from one mountain range to another. In the northwest, most valleys are narrow— from 1 to 5 miles (1.6 to 8 kilometers) wide. Snow covers the higher mountains four to six months each year. There are many permanent snowfields and a few active glaciers in the higher ranges. The glaciers that once covered this land carved the highest mountains into jagged peaks. They also left thousands of clear, cold lakes.

There are over 50 mountain ranges or groups in this area. The most important ranges include the Absaroka, Beartooth, Beaverhead, Big Belt, Bitterroot, Bridger, Cabinet, Crazy, Flathead, Gallatin, Little Belt, Madison, Mission, Swan, and Tobacco Root. The highest peaks rise in south-central Montana north of Yellowstone Park. Granite Peak in Park County is the highest mountain. It rises 12,799 feet (3,901 meters).

Faults in the earth's crust in this region create the danger of earthquakes. The worst quake period recorded was in 1935, when more than 1,200 shocks were felt in 80 days in the Helena area.

Rivers and Lakes. Montana is the only state drained by river systems which empty into the Gulf of Mexico, Hudson Bay, and the Pacific Ocean. The Missouri River system drains into the Gulf of Mexico by way of the Mississippi River. The Columbia drains into the Pacific Ocean. The Belly, St. Mary's, and Waterton rivers reach Hudson Bay through the Nelson-Saskatchewan river system.

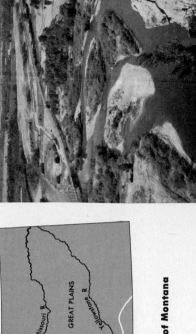

Headwaters of the Missouri River are in southwestern Montana near Three Forks. Three rivers join to form the Missouri: the Gallatin, *left,* the Madison, *center,* and the Jefferson, *right.*

Bill Browning, Montana Chamber of Commerce

Land Regions of Montana

Montana Highway Commission

Fort Peck Dam Spillway carries excess water from Fort Peck Lake to the Missouri River, *background*. Water flows down the spillway through these gates, *foreground*.

Montana's most important rivers are the Missouri and its branch, the Yellowstone. These rivers drain about six-sevenths of the state. The Missouri starts in western Montana, where the Jefferson, Madison, and Gallatin rivers meet near the town of Three Forks. The Missouri flows north past Helena, then through a deep scenic gorge called the Gates of the Mountains. It curves eastward. Fort Peck Dam, on the Missouri in northeastern Montana, is one of the largest U.S. earth-fill

dams. The Missouri leaves Montana at the North Dakota border. The main tributaries of the Missouri in Montana are the Marias, Milk, Sun, and Teton.

The Yellowstone flows north out of Yellowstone Park and then runs east and somewhat north. It joins the Missouri in North Dakota. The chief branches of the Yellowstone—the Bighorn, Clarks Fork, Powder, and Tongue rivers—flow into it from the south.

The *Continental Divide* winds through Montana. This height of land separates the waters running west into the Pacific from those that run east to the Atlantic.

The major rivers west of the divide are the Kootenai and the Clark Fork of the Columbia. The chief branches of the Clark Fork are the Bitterroot, Blackfoot, Flathead, and Thompson rivers. These western streams drain only about one-seventh of the land, but they carry as much water as the eastern Montana rivers.

Montana has only one large natural lake. This is Flathead Lake, which covers about 189 square miles (490 square kilometers) in the northwest. The largest man-made lake is Fort Peck Lake, on the Missouri River, which covers 383 square miles (992 square kilometers). Other large lakes include Canyon Ferry Lake, and Hungry Horse and Tiber reservoirs. Yellowtail Dam, which was completed in 1966, creates a lake 71 miles (114 kilometers) long in Montana and Wyoming.

In 1967, army engineers began building the Libby Dam on the Kootenai River in northwestern Montana. The dam will produce 840,000 kilowatts of hydroelectric power and provide flood control. It will create a lake that is 90 miles (145 kilometers) long and extends 42 miles (68 kilometers) into Canada. The $373-million project was made possible by the Columbia River Treaty between Canada and the United States. The power plant there began operation in 1975.

The Yellowstone River curves through lush farmlands of Paradise Valley near the Absaroka Mountains. Flat, fertile valleys stretch as far as 40 miles (64 kilometers) between mountain ranges in the Rocky Mountain region of southwestern Montana.

Ray Atkeson

MONTANA/Climate

Montana's climate varies considerably from one area to the other because the state is so large and has such great differences in elevation. The region west of the Continental Divide has cooler summers and warmer winters than the area east of the divide. In the west, the average January temperature is about 20° F. (−7° C). Eastern Montana's January average is around 14° F. (−10° C). July temperatures average 64° F. (18° C) in the west, and 71° F. (22° C) in the east. The state's record high temperature of 117° F. (47° C) was recorded at Glendive on July 20, 1893, and at Medicine Lake on July 5, 1937. Before Alaska became a state in 1959, Rogers Pass had the lowest temperature recorded in the United States, −70° F. (−57° C) on Jan. 20, 1954.

Most of Montana, except the western edge, has annual *precipitation* (rain, melted snow, and other forms of moisture) of 13 to 14 inches (33 to 36 centimeters). The western mountain areas receive more moisture than the plains. Heron, in the northwest, gets more than 34 inches (86 centimeters) a year. Snowfall in Montana ranges from as little as 15 inches (38 centimeters)

Bill Browning, Montana Chamber of Commerce

Heavy Snowfall in the mountains near Whitefish makes it possible for skiers to enjoy their sport during much of the year.

to as much as 300 inches (760 centimeters) annually.

In winter, a *chinook* wind sometimes blows down the eastern mountain slopes. This warm, dry wind melts the snow and exposes grazing land, allowing ranchers to graze cattle for part of the winter.

SEASONAL TEMPERATURES

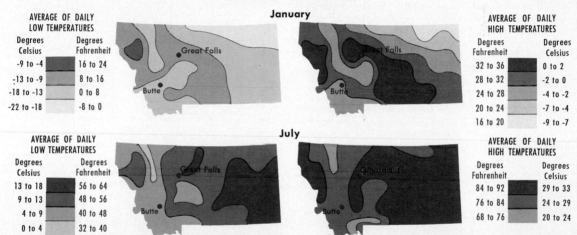

January

AVERAGE OF DAILY LOW TEMPERATURES

Degrees Celsius	Degrees Fahrenheit
-9 to -4	16 to 24
-13 to -9	8 to 16
-18 to -13	0 to 8
-22 to -18	-8 to 0

AVERAGE OF DAILY HIGH TEMPERATURES

Degrees Fahrenheit	Degrees Celsius
32 to 36	0 to 2
28 to 32	-2 to 0
24 to 28	-4 to -2
20 to 24	-7 to -4
16 to 20	-9 to -7

July

AVERAGE OF DAILY LOW TEMPERATURES

Degrees Celsius	Degrees Fahrenheit
13 to 18	56 to 64
9 to 13	48 to 56
4 to 9	40 to 48
0 to 4	32 to 40

AVERAGE OF DAILY HIGH TEMPERATURES

Degrees Fahrenheit	Degrees Celsius
84 to 92	29 to 33
76 to 84	24 to 29
68 to 76	20 to 24

AVERAGE YEARLY PRECIPITATION
(Rain, Melted Snow, and Other Moisture)

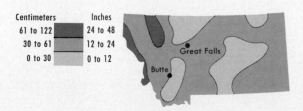

Centimeters	Inches
61 to 122	24 to 48
30 to 61	12 to 24
0 to 30	0 to 12

0   100   200 Miles

0 100 200 300 Kilometers

WORLD BOOK maps

AVERAGE MONTHLY WEATHER

	BUTTE					GREAT FALLS				
	F° High	F° Low	C° High	C° Low	Days of Rain or Snow		F° High	F° Low	C° High	C° Low	Days of Rain or Snow
JAN.	28	0	-2	-18	9	JAN.	32	14	0	-10	8
FEB.	33	5	1	-15	9	FEB.	35	15	2	-9	8
MAR.	40	14	4	-10	10	MAR.	43	22	6	-6	9
APR.	51	26	11	-3	9	APR.	56	33	13	1	8
MAY	61	33	16	1	11	MAY	66	42	19	6	11
JUNE	69	40	21	4	13	JUNE	73	49	23	9	13
JULY	80	45	27	7	10	JULY	84	55	29	13	8
AUG.	78	42	26	6	7	AUG.	81	53	27	12	7
SEPT.	66	34	19	1	7	SEPT.	69	44	21	7	7
OCT.	55	27	13	-3	7	OCT.	59	37	15	3	6
NOV.	41	16	5	-9	7	NOV.	45	26	7	-3	7
DEC.	31	6	-1	-14	8	DEC.	35	18	2	-8	6

Montana's land features divide it into two main economic regions. On the plains, agriculture and oil and coal production are important economic activities. In the mountains, metal mining and logging are the major activities. Both regions have manufacturing plants.

The U.S. government owns about 30 per cent of the land in Montana. Government agencies control grazing of sheep and cattle, cutting of trees, and mining in those areas. This makes the federal government an important factor in the economy of Montana.

Tourism also produces important income. The national parks alone attract about 2 million visitors a year.

Natural Resources. Montana is rich in natural resources. The state has swift-flowing streams, vast reserves of minerals, and large areas of cropland, grassland, and forestland.

Soil. The soils of the northern part of the state are a mixture of clay, sand, and gravel left by melting glaciers. Much of the soil of the southern part was formed from rocks of shallow seas that covered the area millions of years ago. Along the rivers and in the western valleys, silts deposited by water form the soils. In a few areas, fertile wind-blown dust lies in a thick layer. In southwestern Montana, ash from ancient volcanic eruptions has enriched the soil.

Minerals. Montana has huge deposits of three important minerals—coal, copper, and petroleum. Reserves of coal rank among the nation's largest. About $2\frac{1}{3}$ billion short tons (2.1 billion metric tons) of *bituminous* (soft) coal lie under Montana. In addition, there is about 200 times that much coal of lower quality. The reserves of copper around Butte are among the largest in the nation. Petroleum reserves total about 153 million barrels. Natural gas is found in many oil fields.

Beneath Butte Hill and Summit Valley, in the western mountains, lie huge ore reserves. In addition to copper, this ore contains gold, lead, silver, and zinc. Smaller quantities of metals lie in other western Montana areas. Other mineral reserves include bentonite, chromite, clay, fluorspar, gemstones, gypsum, limestone, manganese, phosphate rock, pumice, sand and gravel, talc, tungsten, uranium, and vermiculite.

Grasslands. About two-thirds of Montana, or about 61 million acres (24.7 million hectares), is used for grazing. The most important grasses are buffalo grass, blue grama, and western wheat grass.

Forests cover about 23 million acres (9.3 million hectares), or about one-fourth of Montana. About $8\frac{1}{2}$ million acres (3.4 million hectares) are not available for logging. Some forests are in national parks and other reserves. Others are too poor in quality or too far from transportation to be useful. About half of the $14\frac{1}{2}$ million acres (5.9 million hectares) of commercial timber is still virgin forest. Douglas fir is the most important tree for logging. Cedar, pine, and spruce also are important.

Wildlife. Montana has large numbers of big game animals. Deer are found both on the plains and in the mountains. Pronghorn antelope thrive on the plains. Bear, moose, mountain goats, mountain sheep, and elk live in the mountains. Small fur-bearing animals such as beaver, mink, and muskrat are also found there. Common game birds include wild ducks and geese, grouse,

Production of Goods in Montana

Total value of goods produced in 1977—$2,557,043,000

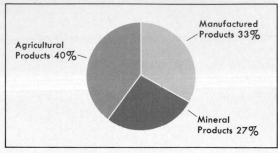

Agricultural Products 40%

Manufactured Products 33%

Mineral Products 27%

Percentages are based on farm income, value added by manufacture, and value of mineral production.

Sources: U.S. government publications, 1978-1979.

Employment in Montana

Total number of persons employed in 1978—310,400

	Number of Employees
Wholesale & Retail Trade	71,300
Government	71,200
Community, Social, & Personal Services	52,000
Agriculture	32,800
Manufacturing	26,200
Transportation & Public Utilities	21,600
Construction	16,300
Finance, Insurance, & Real Estate	12,100
Mining	6,900

Sources: *Employment and Earnings*, May 1979, U.S. Bureau of Labor Statistics; *Farm Labor*, February 1979, U.S. Department of Agriculture.

pheasants, and partridges. Montana's high, cold streams and lakes are famous for trout and grayling.

Agriculture. Farm products account for about $1 billion, or about 40 per cent of the value of goods produced in Montana each year. The state has about 21,500 farms that average about 2,884 acres (1,167 hectares). But many farms cover as much as 7,000 acres (2,800 hectares). Most of the farmland is used for grazing. Livestock products account for about half of the farm income. Montana supports about $2\frac{1}{2}$ million beef and dairy cattle—about 3 for each person in the state. Other leading livestock products include eggs, hogs, milk, sheep, and wool.

About 14 per cent of the farmland is planted in crops. Wheat, Montana's most valuable crop, has an annual value of about $306 million. Montana ranks among the leading states in wheat and barley production. Montana farmers also raise hay, potatoes, and sugar beets. About 1,800,000 acres (730,000 hectares) of Montana's farmland are irrigated. Sugar beets and hay are the chief irrigated crops. Farmers in irrigated areas also grow potatoes and other vegetables. The state's biggest fruit crop is sweet black cherries.

Manufacturing, including processing, provides a third of the annual value of Montana's products.

FARM, MINERAL, AND FOREST PRODUCTS

This map shows where the state's leading farm, mineral, and forest products are produced. The major urban areas (shown on the map in red) are the state's important manufacturing centers.

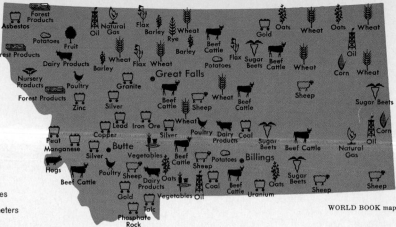

| 0 | 50 | 100 | 150 | 200 | Miles |
| 0 | 50 | 100 | 200 | 300 | Kilometers |

WORLD BOOK map

Goods manufactured there have a *value added by manufacture* of about $860 million a year. This figure represents the value created in products by industries, not counting such costs as materials, supplies, and fuel.

The manufacture of lumber and wood products is Montana's most important industry. Lumber and wood products have an annual value added of about $327 million. The state ranks as a leading producer of *softwood* logs. Softwood comes from cone-bearing trees such as pine. Most of the logs are sent to sawmills to be cut into lumber. Montana has about 100 sawmills that produce about $1\frac{1}{4}$ billion board feet (2.9 million cubic meters) of lumber a year. A mill at Missoula makes paper. Montana lumber also supplies plywood plants in Columbia Falls, Libby, and Missoula. Montana produces about 2 million Christmas trees a year. Eureka claims the title *Christmas Tree Capital of the World*.

Montana's second most important industry, the manufacture of food products, has a value added of about $104 million yearly. Sugar is refined in Billings and Sidney, and flour is milled in Billings and Great Falls. The state's largest meat-packing plants are in Billings and Missoula.

Other manufacturing includes refining and processing of mineral products. Anaconda, East Helena, and Great Falls lead in smelting and refining metals. Great Falls plants make copper and aluminum wire and cable, and a factory in Billings produces metal pipe. A plant in Columbia Falls produces aluminum from imported ore. Oil is refined in Billings, Cut Bank, Great Falls, Laurel, Mosby, and Wolf Point. Bricks are made in Lewistown and Billings. Cement plants operate in Gallatin County and in Lewis and Clark County. Printing and publishing are important in several areas of Montana.

Mining is carried on in most Montana counties. It provides about a fourth of the value of all goods produced in Montana, or about $685 million.

Petroleum, Montana's leading mineral product, has an annual value of about $280 million. It is found from the Rocky Mountains east to the North Dakota border. The Powder River and Williston basins, in eastern Montana, lead in petroleum production. Other producing areas include Carbon, Musselshell, Pondera, Rosebud, and Toole counties. Oil fields in northern Montana yield the most natural gas in the state. Oil fields in the Powder River area also yield natural gas.

Coal is Montana's second most valuable mineral. Coal production, chiefly from eastern Montana, has an annual value of about $157 million.

Butte Hill has yielded most of the metals produced in Montana. The metals output varies widely from year to year, depending on labor conditions and prices. Copper, the state's third most valuable mineral, provides about 90 per cent of the value of metal produced. The Butte ore that contains copper also contains gold, silver, and zinc. These large deposits make Montana a leader in the production of copper, gold, and silver. The state is also the leading producer of antimony, a metal that is mixed with other metals to harden them.

Montana leads the nation in production of vermiculite, an insulation material. Other materials produced in Montana include gypsum, used in wallboard; limestone, used in cement; and sand and gravel. Montana is one of the eight states that produce phosphate rock, which is used for fertilizer. It also produces clay and talc.

Electric Power. Montana is a leading state in hydroelectric power production. In the late 1960's, two new dams were added to power sources developed in the 1950's and early 1960's. A plant in Billings generates electricity by burning oils left from petroleum refining. Coal-burning power plants in Montana include those in Colstrip and Sidney.

Transportation. Montana has about 80,000 miles (130,000 kilometers) of roads, with about 60 per cent of them surfaced. The state has about 170 airports. Billings and Great Falls are the commercial aviation centers. Railroads operate on about 5,000 miles (8,000 kilometers) of track in Montana. Six railroads provide freight service, and passenger trains serve about 20 cities in the state. The Utah & Northern, the first railroad in Montana, entered the area in 1880.

Communication. Montana has about 85 newspapers, including about 10 dailies. The largest papers are the *Billings Gazette* and the *Great Falls Tribune*. The first important newspaper, the *Montana Post*, appeared at Virginia City in August, 1864. The first radio station, KFBB, began broadcasting at Great Falls in 1922. The first television stations, KXLF-TV and KOPR-TV, began operating in Butte in 1953. Today, the state has about 75 radio stations and 12 television stations.

632c

Indian Days. Before the white man arrived, two groups of Indian tribes lived in the region that is now Montana. The tribes that lived on the plains were the Arapaho, Assiniboin, Atsina, Blackfeet, Cheyenne, and Crow. The mountains in the west were the home of the Bannock, Kalispel, Kutenai, Salish, and Shoshoni tribes. Other nearby tribes such as the Sioux, Mandan, and Nez Percé hunted in the Montana region.

Exploration. French trappers probably came to the Montana area as early as the 1740's. The American explorers Meriwether Lewis and William Clark led their expedition across Montana to the Pacific Coast in 1805. They returned in 1806, and explored parts of Montana both going and coming. After 1807, fur traders became active there. In 1847, the American Fur Company built the first permanent settlement in Montana at Fort Benton on the Missouri River.

The United States got most of what is now Montana as part of the Louisiana Purchase (see LOUISIANA PURCHASE). The northwestern part was gained by treaty with England in 1846. At various times, parts of Montana were in the territories of Louisiana, Missouri, Nebraska, Dakota, Oregon, Washington, and Idaho.

The Gold Rush. In 1862, prospectors found gold in Grasshopper Creek in southwestern Montana. Other gold strikes followed and wild mining camps grew around the gold fields. These included Bannack, Diamond City, Virginia City, and others.

The mining camps had almost no effective law enforcement. Finally, the citizens took the law into their own hands. One famous incident involved the two biggest gold camps—Bannack and Virginia City. The settlers learned that their sheriff, Henry Plummer, was actually an outlaw leader. The men of the two towns formed a *vigilance committee* to rid themselves of the outlaws. These vigilantes hanged Plummer in January,

---

IMPORTANT DATES IN MONTANA

1803 Eastern Montana became U.S. territory through the Louisiana Purchase.

1805-1806 Lewis and Clark explored part of Montana on their journey to and from the Pacific Coast.

1846 The Oregon treaty with England made northwestern Montana part of the United States.

1862 Gold was discovered on Grasshopper Creek.

1864 Congress established the Montana Territory.

1876 The Sioux and Cheyenne Indians wiped out General Custer's troops at the Battle of the Little Bighorn.

1877 Chief Joseph and the Nez Percé Indians surrendered to federal troops after several battles.

1880 The Utah & Northern Railroad entered Montana.

1883 The Northern Pacific Railroad crossed Montana.

1889 Montana became the 41st state in the Union on Nov. 8.

1910 Congress established Glacier National Park.

1940 Fort Peck Dam was completed.

1951 The first oil wells in the Montana section of the Williston Basin started production.

1955 The Anaconda Aluminum Company dedicated a $65-million plant at Columbia Falls.

1966 Construction of Yellowtail Dam was completed.

1967 Construction began on the Libby Dam project.

1973 A new state constitution went into effect.

The Cattle Industry began in Montana in the 1850's when trader Richard Grant brought a herd of cattle to the region. He had bought them while he was traveling to Montana on the Oregon Trail.

Chief Joseph and his Nez Percé Indians surrendered to federal troops in 1877, after a chase of over 1,000 miles (1,600 kilometers). This ended Indian fighting in Montana.

HISTORIC MONTANA

1864. They adopted as their symbol the numbers 3-7-77. These numbers represented the dimensions of a grave—3 feet wide, 7 feet long, and 77 inches deep. Many outlaws were hanged or driven from Montana.

Many of the early prospectors came from the South, particularly from Confederate army units that broke up early in the Civil War (1861-1865). One of the major gold fields was called Confederate Gulch, because three Southerners found the first gold there.

During the boom years, gold dust was the principal money. For example, missionaries did not pass collection plates at their services. They passed a tin cup into which the miners put gold dust. Chinese laundrymen even found gold in their wash water after they washed the miners' clothing.

Sidney Edgerton, an Idaho official, saw the need for better government of the wild mining camps. At the time, Montana was part of the Idaho territory. Edgerton wrote Washington urging the creation of a new territory. Montana became a territory on May 26, 1864, and Edgerton served as its first governor.

The Cattle Industry began in Montana in the mid-1850's, when Richard Grant, a trader, brought the first herd to the area from Oregon. In 1866, Nelson Story, a cattleman, drove a thousand longhorn cattle from Texas to Montana. Story's herd started the Montana cattle industry in earnest. The coming of the

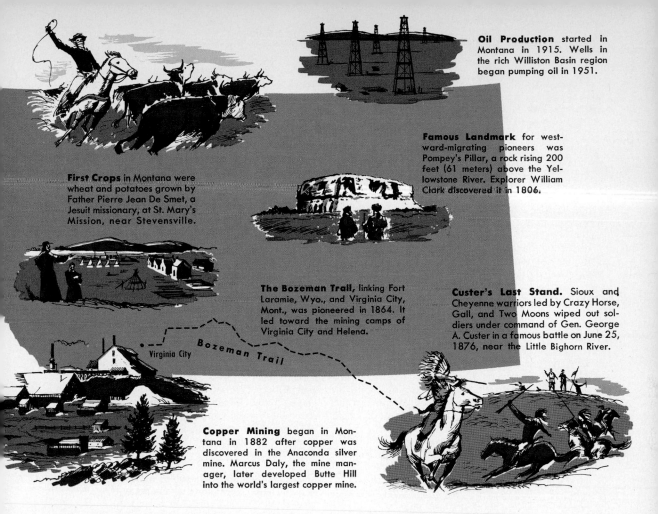

Oil Production started in Montana in 1915. Wells in the rich Williston Basin region began pumping oil in 1951.

Famous Landmark for westward-migrating pioneers was Pompey's Pillar, a rock rising 200 feet (61 meters) above the Yellowstone River. Explorer William Clark discovered it in 1806.

First Crops in Montana were wheat and potatoes grown by Father Pierre Jean De Smet, a Jesuit missionary, at St. Mary's Mission, near Stevensville.

The Bozeman Trail, linking Fort Laramie, Wyo., and Virginia City, Mont., was pioneered in 1864. It led toward the mining camps of Virginia City and Helena.

Custer's Last Stand. Sioux and Cheyenne warriors led by Crazy Horse, Gall, and Two Moons wiped out soldiers under command of Gen. George A. Custer in a famous battle on June 25, 1876, near the Little Bighorn River.

Virginia City

Bozeman Trail

Copper Mining began in Montana in 1882 after copper was discovered in the Anaconda silver mine. Marcus Daly, the mine manager, later developed Butte Hill into the world's largest copper mine.

Northern Pacific Railroad in 1883 opened the way to the eastern markets, and caused even more growth. But disaster struck the cattle industry in the bitterly cold winter of 1886-1887. Cattle died by the thousands in howling blizzards and frigid temperatures. Ranching continued after this, but on a smaller scale.

Indian Fighting. Two of the most famous Indian campaigns in American history were fought in Montana during the territorial days. On June 25, 1876, Sioux and Cheyenne Indians wiped out part of the 7th Cavalry Regiment under General George A. Custer. This famous battle, known as "Custer's Last Stand," was fought near the Little Bighorn River in southern Montana. The last serious Indian fighting in Montana started when the U.S. government tried to move the Nez Percé Indians from their lands in Oregon. Chief Joseph of the Nez Percé led his tribe toward Canada through Montana. The Indians and U.S. troops fought several small battles, and then a two-day battle at Big Hole in southwestern Montana. Troops under Colonel Nelson A. Miles captured Chief Joseph's Indians about 40 miles (64 kilometers) from the Canadian border. See INDIAN WARS (The Sioux Wars; The Nez Percé War).

Statehood. Between 1880 and 1890, the population of Montana grew from about 39,000 to nearly 143,000. The people of Montana first asked for statehood in 1884, but they had to wait five years. Finally, Montana

was admitted as the 41st state on Nov. 8, 1889. Joseph K. Toole of Helena became the first state governor.

Much of Montana's growth during the 1880's and 1890's came because of the mines at Butte. The earliest mines produced gold. Then silver was discovered in the rock ledges of Butte Hill. Later, the miners found rich veins of copper. Miners came to Butte from Ireland, England, and other areas of Europe. Smelters were built, and more men were hired to operate them. Butte Hill became known as the *Richest Hill on Earth*.

Marcus Daly and William A. Clark led the development of Butte copper, and controlled many of the richest mines. The two men became rivals in both business and politics. The great wealth produced by the mines gave both men great power. Daly built the town of Anaconda, and spent large sums of money in a campaign to make it the state capital. Clark opposed Daly's plan, and the voters picked Helena as the capital.

Clark wanted to be a U.S. Senator, but Daly opposed him. In the campaign of 1899, Clark was accused of bribery. He won, but resigned rather than face an investigation by a Senate committee. Two years later, Clark won his Senate seat in a second election. He was helped by F. Augustus Heinze, another mineowner. Heinze had arrived in Butte long after Daly and Clark became millionaires. But Heinze became wealthy through clever use of mining law and court suits.

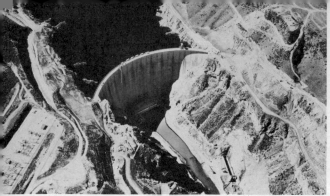

U.S. Bureau of Reclamation, Billings

Yellowtail Dam on the Bighorn River near Hardin was completed in 1966. Its reservoir is about 71 miles (114 kilometers) long.

First Daly, then the others sold their properties to a single corporation, which became the Anaconda Company. The company organized an electric power company, built a railroad, and constructed dams. It also controlled forests, banks, and newspapers. Anaconda became so important in the life of the state that Montanans referred to it simply as "The Company."

Progress as a State. During the early 1900's, Montana made increasing use of its natural resources. New dams harnessed the state's rivers, providing water for irrigation and electric power for industry. The extension of the railroads assisted the processing industries. New plants refined sugar, milled flour, and processed meat. In 1910, Congress created Glacier National Park, which became an attraction for the tourists.

Jeannette Rankin of Missoula was elected to the U.S. House of Representatives in 1916. She was the first woman to serve in Congress. She won fame in 1941 as the only member of Congress to vote against U.S. entry into World War II. Rankin said she did not believe in war and would not vote for it.

Depression Years. Montana suffered during the Great Depression of the 1930's. Demand for the state's metals dropped because of the nationwide lag in production. Drought contributed to the drop in farm income brought on by the depression.

However, state and federal programs continued to develop Montana's resources during the 1930's. The building of the giant Fort Peck Dam helped provide jobs. Completion of the dam in 1940 provided badly needed water for irrigation. Other projects included insect control, irrigation, rural electrification, and soil conservation. Construction of parks, recreation areas, and roads also continued under government direction. In 1940, Montana voters elected Republican Sam C. Ford of Helena as governor. He was only the third Republican governor in Montana history.

The Mid-1900's. Montana's economy boomed during World War II (1939-1945). The state's meat and grain were in great demand, and its copper and other metals were used to make war materials. After the war, lower prices for grain reduced agricultural income. Many Montanans moved from farming areas to towns and cities to find jobs. Some small farming towns were abandoned.

Montana's petroleum industry expanded rapidly in the early 1950's, when major oil fields were discovered in the Williston Basin along the Montana-North Dakota border. Wells in the new Montana fields began pumping oil in 1951. In 1955, the Anaconda Aluminum Company opened a $65-million plant in northwestern Montana, and aluminum products became important to the state's economy. During the 1960's, Anaconda spent more than $50 million to improve operations at the Butte mines and to make better use of the remaining ore there.

Tourism grew as an important source of income in Montana during the mid-1900's. The state developed more parks and historic sites, and private developers opened dude ranches, summer resorts, and skiing centers. Such ski areas as Big Mountain, near Whitefish, helped extend Montana's tourist season through the winter.

The state's irrigation and water conservation programs were also expanded. In 1966, Yellowtail Dam on the Bighorn River in southern Montana was completed. This dam provides water for electric power, irrigation, and recreation. Work began in 1967 on the $373-million Libby Dam project on the Kootenai River in northwestern Montana. The power plant there began operation in 1975.

Republicans held the governorship through most of the 1950's and 1960's. But in 1968, Republican Governor Tim M. Babcock was defeated in his bid for reelection by Forrest H. Anderson, a Democrat.

Montana Today is trying to attract new industries and to broaden its economy. Agriculture remains important to Montana's economy. But the increasing use of machines and improved farming methods has reduced the need for farmworkers.

In 1972, Montana voters approved a new state constitution. The constitution went into effect in 1973.

A major challenge facing Montana is to attract industries that would preserve the state's famed scenic beauty and outdoor sports activities. Citizens have formed a number of groups to help prevent pollution of natural resources and recreational areas. The state is working to help increase tourism by building more roads, boating facilities, and camping sites.

Demand for Montana's huge coal reserves increased sharply during the mid-1970's, when an energy shortage developed in the United States. This demand has led to large-scale coal-mining operations at Colstrip, Decker, and other sites in eastern Montana. Expansion of coal-burning electric power facilities at Colstrip is also under way. These developments have helped bring thousands of workers to the state.

OSCAR CHAFFEE and THOMAS A. CLINCH

THE GOVERNORS OF MONTANA	Party	Term
1. Joseph K. Toole	Democratic	1889-1893
2. John E. Rickards	Republican	1893-1897
3. Robert Burns Smith	Democratic	1897-1901
4. Joseph K. Toole	Democratic	1901-1908
5. Edwin L. Norris	Democratic	1908-1913
6. Sam V. Stewart	Democratic	1913-1921
7. Joseph M. Dixon	Republican	1921-1925
8. John E. Erickson	Democratic	1925-1933
9. Frank H. Cooney	Democratic	1933-1935
10. W. Elmer Holt	Democratic	1935-1937
11. Roy E. Ayers	Democratic	1937-1941
12. Sam C. Ford	Republican	1941-1949
13. John W. Bonner	Democratic	1949-1953
14. J. Hugo Aronson	Republican	1953-1961
15. Donald G. Nutter	Republican	1961-1962
16. Tim M. Babcock	Republican	1962-1969
17. Forrest H. Anderson	Democratic	1969-1973
18. Thomas L. Judge	Democratic	1973-

MONTANA/*Study Aids*

Related Articles in WORLD BOOK include:

BIOGRAPHIES

Custer, George A.
Daly, Marcus
Joseph, Chief
Mansfield, Mike

Rankin, Jeannette
Russell, Charles M.
Sitting Bull
Wheeler, Burton K.

CITIES

Billings
Butte

Great Falls
Helena

Missoula

HISTORY

Bozeman Trail
Lewis and Clark
  Expedition

Louisiana Purchase
Western Frontier Life
Westward Movement

NATIONAL PARKS AND MONUMENTS

Custer Battlefield National
  Monument
Glacier National Park

Yellowstone National
  Park

PHYSICAL FEATURES

Bitterroot Range
Kootenay River and
  District
Lewis and Clark Cavern

Missouri River
Rocky Mountains
Yellowstone River

PRODUCTS

For Montana's rank among the states in production, see the following articles:

Barley
Coal

Copper
Horse

Lumber
Sheep

Silver
Wheat

OTHER RELATED ARTICLES

Assiniboin Indians
Cheyenne Indians
Crow Indians
Fort Peck Dam

Gros Ventre Indians
Indian, American
Kutenai Indians
Rocky Mountain States

Outline

I. Government
  A. Constitution
  B. Executive
  C. Legislature
  D. Courts
  E. Local Government
  F. Taxation
  G. Politics

II. People

III. Education
  A. Schools
  B. Libraries and Museums

IV. A Visitor's Guide
  A. Places to Visit
  B. Annual Events

V. The Land
  A. Land Regions
  B. Rivers and Lakes

VI. Climate

VII. Economy
  A. Natural Resources
  B. Agriculture
  C. Manufacturing
  D. Mining
  E. Electric Power
  F. Transportation
  G. Communication

VIII. History

Questions

What three great river systems drain Montana?
What minerals are most important to Montana?
What Montana artist won fame for his paintings and sculptures of the West?
What two famous Indian battles were fought in Montana during territorial days?
What is Montana's most valuable farm product?
What did the symbol 3-7-77 mean in early Montana?
What expedition explored Montana in 1805-1806?
Why did early Montanans usually vote for Democrats?
Which two famous parks lie at least partly in Montana?
Why does Montana's climate vary so greatly?

Books for Young Readers

BEATTY, PATRICIA. *Something to Shout About.* Morrow, 1976. Fiction.
CARPENTER, ALLAN. *Montana.* Rev. ed. Childrens Press, 1979.
CORCORAN, BARBARA. *Sasha, My Friend.* Atheneum, 1969. *The Long Journey.* 1970. Both books are fiction.
HANSON, JUNE ANDREA. *Summer of the Stallion.* Macmillan, 1979. Fiction.
JOHNSON, DOROTHY M. *Montana.* Coward, 1971.
Montana: Two Lane Highway in a Four Lane World. Mountain Press, 1978.
RICHARD, ADRIENNE. *Pistol.* Little, Brown, 1969. Fiction.
WIER, ESTER. *The Loner.* McKay, 1963. Fiction.

Books for Older Readers

FARR, WILLIAM E., and TOOLE, K. R. *Montana: Images of the Past.* Pruett, 1978.
GUTHRIE, A. B., Jr. *The Big Sky.* Houghton, 1947. Fiction.
MALONE, MICHAEL P., and ROEDER, R. B. *Montana: A History of Two Centuries.* Univ. of Washington Press, 1976.
MONTANA HISTORICAL SOCIETY. *Not in Precious Metals Alone: A Manuscript History of Montana.* The Society, 1976.
SPENCE, CLARK C. *Territorial Politics and Government in Montana, 1864-89.* Univ. of Illinois Press, 1976. *Montana: A Bicentennial History.* Norton, 1978.
TOOLE, KENNETH ROSS. *Twentieth-Century Montana: A State of Extremes.* Univ. of Oklahoma Press, 1972. *The Rape of the Great Plains: Northwest America, Cattle and Coal.* Little, Brown, 1976.
WALKER, MILDRED. *Winter Wheat.* Harcourt, 1944. Fiction.

MONTANA, UNIVERSITY OF, is a coeducational state-supported school in Missoula, Mont. It includes the college of arts and sciences, and schools of fine arts, forestry, law, business administration, education, journalism, and pharmacy. The university awards bachelor's, master's, doctor of education, and doctor of philosophy degrees. It also has a biological station, and a 30,000-acre (12,000-hectare) forest experiment station. In addition, it operates a bureau of business and economic research, a wildlife research unit, a wood chemistry laboratory, and an immunological research institute. The university was chartered in 1893. For the enrollment of the University of Montana, see UNIVERSITIES AND COLLEGES (table).

Critically reviewed by the UNIVERSITY OF MONTANA

MONTANA COLLEGE OF MINERAL SCIENCE AND TECHNOLOGY. See UNIVERSITIES AND COLLEGES (table).

MONTANA STATE UNIVERSITY is a state-supported coeducational school in Bozeman, Mont. The university has colleges of agriculture, arts and architecture, education, engineering, and letters and sciences; and schools of business and nursing. Courses lead to bachelor's, master's, and doctor's degrees. The Engineering Experiment Station, the Montana Agricultural Experiment Station, and the Montana Cooperative Extension Service are connected with the university. Montana State University was founded in 1893. For enrollment, see UNIVERSITIES AND COLLEGES (table).

Critically reviewed by MONTANA STATE UNIVERSITY

MONTAUK PENINSULA

MONTAUK PENINSULA is a long strip of land at the eastern end of Long Island. Montauk Point, at the tip of the peninsula, forms the extreme eastern point of the state of New York. A United States lighthouse has stood on the point since the 1790's. Fishing is a major industry. See NEW YORK (map).   WILLIAM E. YOUNG

MONTCALM, *mahnt KAHM,* or *mawn KAHLM,* **MARQUIS DE** (1712-1759), LOUIS JOSEPH DE MONT-CALM-GOZON, a French general, was killed in one of the last great battles between the French and English in America. Montcalm was wounded on the Plains of Abraham in the battle for the city of Quebec. He died in the city a few hours later. The French-Canadians consider him a hero, although his army lost the battle to the English. The English commander, General James Wolfe, was killed in the action.

Montcalm defeated the British in the first part of the French and Indian War. He captured Oswego and Fort William Henry on Lake George, and successfully defended Ticonderoga. But lack of support from the French government handicapped him.

Detail of a portrait by an unknown artist. Marquis de Montcalm, Paris (Public Archives of Canada)

Marquis de Montcalm

As the war progressed, Montcalm realized that a decisive battle would be fought between the French and English at Quebec. He gathered his main forces to defend the city, and threw back the first English attack. But Wolfe appeared with his whole force on the Plains of Abraham on Sept. 13, 1759. Montcalm led the French attack, but his troops broke under the heavy fire of the English. Montcalm was wounded and died.

Montcalm was born in France, near Nîmes. He joined the French army at the age of 12, and became a captain at 17. He won distinction in the War of the Austrian Succession. By 1756, he had become commander of the French troops in America.   RAYMOND O. ROCKWOOD

See also FRENCH AND INDIAN WARS (The French and Indian War); QUEBEC, BATTLE OF; WOLFE, JAMES.

MONTE CARLO (pop. 9,948) is part of the principality of Monaco. It lies on the Riviera, 9 miles (14 kilometers) from Nice, France, and overlooks the Mediterranean Sea. The district near Monte Carlo is a popular resort area. Exports from the Monte Carlo region include olive oil, oranges, and perfumes.

Monte Carlo has been famous as a gambling center since the middle of the 1800's. Citizens of Monaco are forbidden to gamble at the club, but each year thousands of visitors come to play roulette, baccarat, and other games of chance.   GEORGE KISH

See also MONACO.

MONTE CASSINO, *MAHN tee kuh SEE noh,* is an abbey in Italy, located between Rome and Naples. Here St. Benedict founded the Roman Catholic Benedictine order (see BENEDICTINES). About A.D. 529, St. Benedict sought refuge from persecution inside the ruined city of Cassino. Later, St. Benedict and his followers built the monastery on a height above the town.

The Benedictine order at Monte Cassino reached the height of its influence from 1058 to 1087. Abbot Desiderius, who later became Pope Victor III, ruled it during that time. The monks of Monte Cassino produced manuscripts and paintings which became famous throughout the world. In 1071, a new abbey church was consecrated. It was named a cathedral in 1321.

In 1866, when Italy dissolved many of its monasteries, Monte Cassino became a national monument. Its buildings held a monastery, a school for laymen, and two seminaries. The abbey's library contained an excellent collection of manuscripts. During World War II, the Allied advance was held up at Cassino and the abbey was bombarded. But most of its treasures were saved. By 1952, the Italian government had rebuilt the buildings along their original lines. They put the masterpieces of the monastery on display for the public.   SHEPARD B. CLOUGH

MONTE CORNO. See APENNINES.

MONTE CRISTO, *MAHN tee KRIHS toh,* or *MOHN tay KREES toh,* is a small, barren island in the Mediterranean. The island covers 4 square miles (10 square kilometers). In ancient times it was known as *Oglasa.* It became famous through Alexandre Dumas' well-known novel, *The Count of Monte Cristo.* The novel tells how the hero discovered a treasure there.

Monte Cristo lies 27 miles (43 kilometers) south of the island of Elba. Most of the island is a mountain of granite, rising 2,000 feet (610 meters) above sea level.

Woodward, Black Star

Monte Carlo's famous casino plays host each year to thousands of vacationers. They take part in many gambling activities. Huge fortunes have been won and lost in the casino.

Benedictine monks once had a monastery on Monte Cristo. But the Benedictines abandoned it after Mediterranean pirates attacked them in 1553. More than 300 years later, the Italian government tried to establish a penal colony on Monte Cristo. It soon gave up the attempt. BENJAMIN WEBB WHEELER

MONTE ROSA, *MOHN tay ROH zah,* is a mountain with several peaks. One of these, 15,203-foot (4,634-meter) Dufourspitze, is one of the highest in the Pennine Alps. All of Monte Rosa's peaks are more than 10,000 feet (3,000 meters) above sea level. The mountain stands on the border between Italy and Switzerland. See also ALPS. FRANKLIN CARL ERICKSON

MONTENEGRO, *mahn tuh NEE groh,* is one of the six republics of Yugoslavia. It covers about 5,333 square miles (13,812 square kilometers) and has a population of about 565,000. Montenegro's name in the Serbo-Croatian language is *Crna Gora,* which means "black mountain." Titograd is the capital and largest city.

Montenegro lies in southern Yugoslavia, on the Adriatic Sea. For location, see YUGOSLAVIA (map). Mountains cover most of the land, and thick forests grow in the north. Farmers raise almonds, fruit, olives, and tobacco, but less than 5 per cent of the land is suitable for farming. Montenegro has large reserves of bauxite, coal, lead, and timber. Factory products include aluminum, cement, iron and steel, and paper.

Tourism provides a major source of income for Montenegro. Many tourists come to the seacoast to enjoy the warm climate and unpolluted beaches. People who fish, hike, and hunt are attracted to the mountains.

Montenegrins make up about two-thirds of the population, which also includes Albanians, Serbs, and members of other groups. Most Montenegrins speak Serbo-Croatian and use the Cyrillic alphabet. A majority of them belong to the Eastern Orthodox Church.

WORLD BOOK map

Location of Montenegro

Montenegro formed part of the medieval Serbian kingdom. After 1355, the kingdom began to collapse, and Montenegro became an independent state. Nobles ruled the country until 1516. Eastern Orthodox bishops then ruled until 1851. That year, Montenegro's ruler took the title of prince, and the position of bishop became a separate office. After World War I ended in 1918, Montenegro became part of Yugoslavia.

Before the 1960's, Montenegro's economic growth was held back by a poor transportation system. In the mid-1960's, construction began on a railroad between Bar, the major seaport of Montenegro, and Belgrade, the capital of Yugoslavia. Road-building projects were also started in the 1960's and 1970's. ALVIN Z. RUBINSTEIN

See also BALKANS.

MONTEREY, *MAHN tuh RAY,* Calif. (pop. 26,302), was California's capital under Spanish and Mexican rule, and under the Americans until 1850. The Presidio, founded by the Spanish in 1770, is today the home of the U.S. Army Language School. It was formerly the Capitol, and also marks the spot where Sebastián Vizcaíno, a Spanish explorer, landed in 1602. Monterey lies on the shores of the southern end of Monterey Bay (see CALIFORNIA [political map]). Tourists, conventions, and military bases provide much of the area's income. A colony of artists and writers is there. Monterey Institute of Foreign Studies and the Naval Postgraduate School are in Monterey. Fort Ord, an Army training center, is nearby. The Salinas-Seaside-Monterey metropolitan area has a population of 247,450. Monterey has a council-manager government. GEORGE SHAFTEL

MONTERREY, *MAHN teh REH ee,* or *MAHN tuh RAY* (pop. 858,107; met. area pop. 1,213,497), Mexico's third largest city, lies in a fertile valley near the Texas border (see MEXICO [political map]). The Pan American Highway links Monterrey with Laredo, Tex., 140 miles (225 kilometers) northeast. Many Mexicans who were born in the United States live in Monterrey. The city is known for its iron and steel foundries, and for its breweries. More than 500 factories produce textiles, cement, soap, plastics, and other products. A natural-gas pipeline between Texas and Monterrey aided the city's industrial growth. Monterrey has several old Spanish-style buildings and many modern structures. The nearby Technological Institute attracts many U.S. students. Spanish settlers founded Monterrey about 1560. It was incorporated as a city in 1596. JOHN A. CROW

MONTERREY, BATTLE OF. See MEXICAN WAR (Taylor's Campaign).

MONTES, ISMAEL. See BOLIVIA (Wars).

MONTESQUIEU, *mahn tuhs KYOO* (1689-1755), was a French philosopher. His major work, *The Spirit of the Laws* (1748), greatly influenced the writing of constitutions throughout the world, including the Constitution of the United States.

Montesquieu believed that laws underlie all things—human, natural, and divine. One of philosophy's major tasks was to discover these laws. It was difficult to study humanity because the laws governing human nature were complex. Yet Montesquieu believed that these laws could be discovered by *empirical* (experimental) methods of investigation (see EMPIRICISM). Knowledge of the laws would ease the ills of society and improve life.

According to Montesquieu, there were three basic types of government—monarchal, republican, and despotic. A monarchal government had limited power placed in a king or queen. A republican government was either an aristocracy or a democracy. In an aristocracy, only a few people had power. In a democracy, all the people had it. A despotic government was controlled by a tyrant, who had absolute authority. Montesquieu believed that legal systems should vary according to the basic type of government.

Montesquieu supported human freedom and opposed tyranny. He believed that political liberty involved separating the legislative, executive, and judicial powers of government. He believed that liberty and respect for properly constituted law could exist together.

Montesquieu, whose real name was Charles de Secondat, was born near Bordeaux. He inherited the title Baron de la Brède et de Montesquieu. He gained fame with his *Persian Letters* (1721), which ridiculed Parisian life and many French institutions. He also criticized the church and national governments of France. Montesquieu was admitted to the French Academy in 1727. He lived in England from 1729 to 1731 and came to admire the English political system.   STEPHEN A. ERICKSON

MONTESSORI, MAHN tuh SAWR ee, **MARIA** (1870-1952), an Italian educator, developed a special method of teaching young children that became known as the Montessori Method (see MONTESSORI METHOD). She believed that children should be free to find out things for themselves and to develop through individual activity. By her method, pupils were neither punished nor rewarded for things done in school.

Montessori was born in Ancona, Italy, and earned a medical degree from the University of Rome. She first taught mentally defective children, but in 1907 took charge of nursery schools in a Rome slum area. Later she traveled throughout the world, writing and lecturing about her teaching method.   GALEN SAYLOR

MONTESSORI METHOD is an educational system designed to help children learn how to learn by themselves. Montessori programs aim to develop positive learning attitudes and habits in children from about 3 to 6 years of age, an age when they are best able to form them. Many experts in education believe Montessori can help children become aware of their abilities and gain confidence in themselves while making use of their abilities.

Special teaching materials and learning tasks are used for developing awareness and confidence. These materials make use of children's desire to manipulate and discover insights on their own. They include three-dimensional geometric shapes and letters of the alphabet designed to be examined by a blindfolded child to improve the sense of touch. Devices such as a frame covered with cloth containing snaps, zippers, or buttons aim to teach the child how to perform everyday tasks without the help of adults. Counting devices provide experience in working with numbers. Other materials are designed to improve children's language skills and acquaint them with art, music, and science.

Supporters of Montessori programs believe that the materials, used under the guidance of specially trained teachers, help children develop a lasting curiosity and positive attitudes and habits toward learning. Montessori teachers must complete a year of training at a Montessori training center after receiving a bachelor's degree from a university or college.

Maria Montessori of Italy devised the Montessori Method in the early 1900's (see MONTESSORI, MARIA). Montessori schools were established in many parts of the world, but their number declined in the 1930's, largely because of inadequately prepared teachers.

In the 1950's, Nancy McCormick Rambusch revived the Montessori Method in the United States. She established the American Montessori Society, which sets standards for the more than 600 Montessori schools in the United States. The society's headquarters are at 175 5th Avenue, New York, N.Y. 10010.   URBAN H. FLEEGE

MONTEUX, mawn TUH, **PIERRE** (1875-1964), was a leading French conductor of the 1900's. He became known for a broad artistic viewpoint that led him to conduct works from many periods of music history.

Monteux was born in Paris. He first gained attention as a conductor in 1911 with the Diaghilev Ballets Russes. During his association with this ballet company, Monteux conducted several important premières, particularly the first performance of Igor Stravinsky's *The Rite of Spring* (1913).

In 1917, Monteux went to the United States to conduct at the Metropolitan Opera. From 1919 to 1924, he conducted the Boston Symphony Orchestra. He rebuilt the orchestra, which had declined at the close of World War I. Monteux conducted in Europe from 1924 to 1936. He then returned to the United States, where he conducted the San Francisco Symphony Orchestra from 1936 to 1952. From 1960 until his death, he served as principal conductor of the London Symphony Orchestra.   ROBERT C. MARSH

MONTEVERDI, mahn tuh VEHR dee, **CLAUDIO** (1567-1643), was an Italian composer. His works greatly influenced the change from the strict style of Renaissance music to the emotional style of the baroque movement (see BAROQUE). He is often considered the first important composer of opera, and his *Orfeo* (1607) the first modern opera. Only two of his other operas have survived in complete form— *The Return of Ulysses* (1641) and *The Coronation of Poppea* (1642), his masterpiece.

Monteverdi was a master of composing for orchestra. In writing for strings, he pioneered in using an agitated effect called *tremolo* and a plucking technique called *pizzicato*. He was also one of the great composers of religious music and madrigals (see MADRIGAL). Monteverdi's *Vespers* (1610) combined church chants with devices previously associated with *secular* (nonreligious) music using chords. These devices included *arias* (vocal solos) and *recitative* (speech recited to music).

Monteverdi was born in Cremona. From 1590 to 1612, he was employed as a musician and composer by the Duke of Mantua. From 1613 until his death, Monteverdi was choirmaster of the Cathedral of St. Mark in Venice. Beginning in 1637, he also served as composer for the first public opera house in Venice.   JAMES SYKES

MONTEVIDEO, MAHN tuh vuh DAY oh (pop. 1,229,-750), is the capital and largest city of Uruguay. According to an old legend, the city got its name from the cry of a Portuguese sailor when he first spotted the hill on which Montevideo now stands. The sailor shouted "Monte vide eu" (I see a mountain).

Location and Description. Montevideo stands on the eastern bank of the Río de la Plata (Silver River), 135 miles (217 kilometers) southeast of Buenos Aires, Argentina (see URUGUAY [map]). It has wide, tree-lined streets, well-planned business and residential sections, and attractive suburbs.

The oldest part of Montevideo, called Ciudad Vieja, or *Old City*, is on a small peninsula on the west side of the city. The Plaza Constitución, the original city square, lies in the heart of this section.

The Ciudad Nueva, or *New City*, lies east of the Ciudad Vieja. The University of the Republic and the government buildings stand in this section. Montevideo is often called the *City of Roses*. The city has many flower-filled squares and beautiful public parks, such as the Prado with its famous rose gardens, and Rodó Park, which completely surrounds a lake.

Industry and Trade. Montevideo's chief industry is meat packing. Cattle owners ship sheep and cattle to the city from farms and ranches on the rich Uruguayan

Plaza Independencia, in Montevideo, is often called the *Times Square of Montevideo.* The Palace of the President, *background,* is Uruguay's "White House." The statue of General Artigas, *right,* honors a hero of the fight to gain Uruguay's independence.

plains. Montevideo ships wool, meat, hides, and other agricultural products to all parts of the world. The city handles about three-fourths of all the goods exported from Uruguay. Companies of many countries, including the United States, have offices, factories, and packing houses in Montevideo.

Transportation in Uruguay centers in the capital. Roads, railroads, and airlines connect Montevideo with other cities in the country. Airliners and ships from many countries stop regularly at Montevideo.

Activities of the People. Montevideo has a number of museums, libraries, and theaters. The government radio station sponsors a symphony orchestra, and private organizations present ballets, concerts, and operas. The city is a center of intellectual life for Uruguay and for much of South America. The University of the Republic is one of South America's best universities.

History. Spanish settlers founded Montevideo in 1726. The city suffered many sieges and invasions during Uruguay's struggle for independence, and in the early years of the republic. Commerce and industry expanded rapidly in Montevideo during the late 1800's. By 1960, the population had grown 10 times as large as it was in 1879. John Tate Lanning

MONTEZUMA, *MAHN tee ZOO muh,* or Moctezuma, was the name of two Aztec rulers of Mexico (see Aztec).

Montezuma I (1390?-1464?) became emperor in 1440. He won fame as a military leader who expanded the boundaries of the Aztec Empire to the Gulf of Mexico. He started a vast public works program. He built a huge dike that kept the waters of Lake Texcoco from flooding his capital, Tenochtitlán (now Mexico City), and built an aqueduct to bring fresh water from the springs of Chapultepec to his capital.

Montezuma II (1480?-1520), the great-grandson of Montezuma I, was Emperor of Mexico when the Spaniards came. He ruled from 1502 to 1520. During his reign, he extended the Aztec domain as far south as Honduras. Like Montezuma I, he built many temples, water conduits, and hospitals. But his people disliked him for his appointments of favorites and his heavy taxation. The last New Fire Ceremony occurred in 1507 under his reign. It was a rite designed to insure the continuance of the world for another cycle.

He and his people believed that Hernando Cortés, the leader of the Spaniards, was Quetzalcoatl, the White God of the Aztec, who had sailed away many years before but promised to return. At first, Montezuma welcomed the Spaniards with gifts of golden ornaments. Later, he tried to keep them from entering Tenochtitlán, but it was too late. Cortés captured the city and the Emperor. The Indian people attacked the palace and Montezuma tried vainly to calm them. But he was stoned to death. Several American writers have used the dramatic meeting between Montezuma and Cortés as the theme of their books. William H. Gilbert

See also Cortés, Hernando.

MONTEZUMA CASTLE NATIONAL MONUMENT is in central Arizona. It contains a five-story cliff-dwelling ruin in a niche in the face of a cliff. The monument was established in 1906. It includes Montezuma Well. For area, see National Park System (table: National Monuments). For location, see Arizona (physical map).

A Keith Henderson illustration for William Prescott's *The Conquest of Mexico,* courtesy of Chatto and Windus

Montezuma II, Emperor of Mexico, rode in a magnificent litter to meet the conqueror of his country, Hernando Cortés.

MONTFORT, SIMON DE (1208?-1265), EARL OF LEICESTER, an English statesman and soldier, contributed to the growth of parliamentary government in England. He has been called "the father of the House of Commons." But his work was rather to advance and strengthen a parliamentary system already in existence.

Montfort was a favorite of King Henry III. But he lost favor because of his zeal for political reform. Henry III wanted to rule as he pleased, and Montfort led a rebellion aimed at limiting the king's power by law. King Henry and his son (later Edward I) took up arms, but Montfort captured them both at the battle of Lewes in 1264. Shortly after, Montfort assembled the parliament that won him fame.

Parliament had been only another name for the king's Great Council of barons and prelates, although some commoners had served in the past. Montfort wished to give all the people a voice in affairs. He called to this parliament of January, 1265, two representatives from each shire and two from each town and borough.

Montfort was killed a few months later in the battle of Evesham. His tomb became an English shrine. He was born in France, a son of the Earl of Leicester, and came to England when he was 21.   PAUL M. KENDALL

MONTGOLFIER, *mahnt GAHL fih er*, was the family name of two brothers, **Jacques Étienne** (1745-1799), and **Joseph Michel** (1740-1810). They invented the first balloons to carry men into the air. In June, 1783, they filled a balloon made of cloth and paper with hot air. On its first public trial, their balloon rose about 6,000 feet (1,800 meters). Five months later, Pilâtre de Rozier became the first man to fly, going up about 80 feet (24 meters) in a Montgolfier balloon. See AIRPLANE (Man's First Flights [picture]).

The Montgolfiers were born at Vidalon-lez-Annonay, France. They were directors of a paper factory in France. But they were poor businessmen, and had to be rescued from failure by pensions.   ROBERT E. SCHOFIELD

See also BALLOON (History).

MONTGOMERY, Ala. (pop. 133,386; met. area 225,-911), is the state capital and an agricultural center of the South. The city is known as the *Cradle of the Confederacy.* Southerners established the Confederate States of America there in 1861, and Montgomery was the first Confederate capital. Montgomery lies on three hills along the Alabama River in south central Alabama. For location, see ALABAMA (political map).

Two towns—East Alabama and New Philadelphia—united in 1819 and formed a single city. The people named it Montgomery in honor of Brigadier General Richard Montgomery, a Revolutionary War hero.

Description. Montgomery, the county seat of Montgomery County, covers about 50 square miles (130 square kilometers). Alabama State University, Huntingdon College, and campuses of Auburn University and Troy State University are in Montgomery.

Tourist attractions in the city include the State Capitol and the Montgomery Museum of Fine Arts. The First White House of the Confederacy is also in Montgomery. It was the home of Jefferson Davis, the President of the Confederacy. See ALABAMA (picture: State Capitol).

Government operations—on the federal, state, and local levels—and retail and wholesale trade have an important part in the city's economy. Government activities and trade each employ about 20 per cent of Montgomery's work force. Federal employers include nearby Gunter and Maxwell Air Force bases. Montgomery's chief industries include the manufacture of furniture, glass products, machinery, paper, and textiles.

Government and History. Montgomery has a mayor-council type of government. The mayor and the nine city council members are elected to four-year terms.

Alibamu and Creek Indians lived in what is now the Montgomery area before white settlers arrived. In 1817, a group led by Andrew Dexter of Massachusetts founded the town of New Philadelphia at the site of present-day Montgomery. That same year, a group headed by General John Scott of Georgia established Alabama Town nearby. In 1818, Scott's group moved its town nearer to New Philadelphia and renamed its settlement East Alabama. After the two towns united and formed Montgomery in 1819, the commerce and population of the area increased. Montgomery became the state capital in 1846. The city's population grew slowly but steadily during the late 1800's and early 1900's. It leveled off in the 1960's.

The civil rights leader Martin Luther King, Jr., lived in Montgomery and began his crusade there in 1955. In 1956, Montgomery became one of the first Southern cities to stop racial segregation on buses. See KING, MARTIN LUTHER, JR.

In the late 1960's and early 1970's, Montgomery set up four historical districts. Each district has homes and other buildings erected during different periods of the 1800's. In 1973, the United States Army Corps of Engineers completed a project that included construction of three dams on the Alabama River. The dams enabled barges to travel on the river for the first time. City leaders expected this development to help increase trade in Montgomery.   WILLIAM THOMAS JOHNSON, JR.

MONTGOMERY, BERNARD LAW (1887-1976), VISCOUNT MONTGOMERY OF ALAMEIN, was a British Army commander in World War II. His victories in North Africa and Europe made him the idol of Great Britain. Montgomery's appearance in his familiar beret in the victory parade in London in June, 1946, aroused a public demonstration greater than that given the king.

Montgomery was born in London. He became

Alabama Bureau of Publicity and Information
First White House of the Confederacy was in Montgomery, the capital of Alabama. Jefferson Davis lived here in 1861.

an infantry lieutenant in 1908. At the outbreak of World War II, Montgomery was a major general. He took command of the Third Division and led it for nine months in France. He was rescued with his men from the beach at Dunkerque in May, 1940 (see DUNKERQUE). Montgomery then commanded the defense zone of southeastern England. He prepared defenses in this region against an expected German invasion.

United Press Int.
Lord Montgomery

In 1942, Montgomery took command of the Eighth Army in North Africa. He swiftly developed his army into a smooth-working, hard-hitting combination of air, infantry, and armored forces. In the fall of 1942, Montgomery stopped an attack by Field Marshal Erwin Rommel's Afrika Korps. He began an advance at El Alamein that drove the Germans out of Africa.

After the African campaign, Montgomery helped plan the invasion of France. He was promoted to field marshal. During the final Allied drive against Germany in 1944, he commanded the British forces that landed in France. After the war, he became head of the British zone of occupation in Germany. He served as chief of the British Imperial General Staff from 1946 to 1948, and chairman of the commanders in chief of the Western European Union from 1948 to 1951. Montgomery served as Deputy Supreme Allied Commander of the North Atlantic Treaty Organization (NATO) from 1951 to 1958.　　　　　CHARLES LOCH MOWAT

MONTGOMERY, LUCY MAUD. See CANADIAN LITERATURE (After Confederation).

MONTGOMERY, RICHARD. See REVOLUTIONARY WAR IN AMERICA (Canada Invaded).

MONTGOMERY WARD AND CO. See MAIL-ORDER BUSINESS; WARD, AARON MONTGOMERY.

MONTH. The calendar year is divided into 12 parts, each of which is called a *month*. But the word *month* has other meanings. Several kinds of months are measured by the motion of the moon. At one point in the moon's regular path, it is closest to the earth. This point is called the *perigee*. The time the moon takes to revolve from one perigee to the next is an *anomalistic month*. This period averages 27 days, 13 hours, 18 minutes, and 33.1 seconds.

If the moon were looked at from a distant star it would seem to make a complete revolution around the earth in 27 days, 7 hours, 43 minutes, and 11.5 seconds. This period is a *sidereal month*. The *proper lunar month*, which is called the *synodical month*, is the period between one new moon and the next, an average of 29 days, 12 hours, 44 minutes, and 2.8 seconds.

The synodical month is one of three natural divisions of time. The other two are the rotation of the earth on its axis, or a day, and the revolution of the earth around the sun, or a year. Another astronomical month is the *solar month*, which is one twelfth of a solar year. The solar month is the time taken by the sun to pass through each of the 12 signs of the zodiac (see ZODIAC).

Our calendar months vary in length from 28 days to 31 days. The lengths of calendar months have been made by man, and have no relation to astronomy. At first the 12 months were 29 and 30 days alternately. Later, days were added to the months to make the year come out closer to a solar year, or the time required for the earth to go once around the sun.

In the Gregorian calendar which we use today, each day of the month is called by its number. June 1 is the "first of June," and so on. The ancient Greeks divided the month into 3 periods of 10 days, and the French Revolutionary calendar used months of equal length divided into 3 parts of 10 days each. The fifteenth day of the month was called the fifth day of the second decade.

The Roman system was even more complicated. The Roman calendar had three fixed days in each month, the *calends*, the *nones*, and the *ides*. The Romans counted backward from these fixed days. They would say something would happen, for example, three days before the nones. The calends were the first day of the month. The ides were at the middle, either the 13th or 15th of the month. The nones were the ninth day before the ides, counting both days. When the soothsayer told Julius Caesar to "beware the Ides of March," he meant a very definite day.　　　　　PAUL SOLLENBERGER

See also the articles in WORLD BOOK on each month of the year. See also CALENDAR; DAY; IDES.

MONTICELLO, *MAHN tuh CHELL oh,* is the home Thomas Jefferson designed and built on a hilltop in Albemarle County, Virginia. The name means *little mountain.* Jefferson said of the house, "All my wishes end where I hope my days will end, at Monticello."

Work on Monticello began in 1768. But the house was remodeled several times, and was not completed until 1809. Jefferson borrowed many ideas from classical European buildings. The columned portico idea came from the Temple of Vesta in Rome. The centralized plan came from Andrea Palladio's Villa Rotonda in Vicenza. The dome resembles the dome of the Hotel Salm in Paris. The house contains many things Jefferson invented, including a revolving desk, a dumb-waiter, and a calendar clock. Monticello belongs to the Thomas Jefferson Memorial Foundation.　　　SIBYL MOHOLY-NAGY

See also JEFFERSON, THOMAS (picture).

MONTMORENCY RIVER, *MAHNT moh REN sih,* is a short, swift stream in Quebec. It is named for François Xavier de Laval de Montmorency, first bishop of Quebec. The Montmorency rises in Snow Lake and flows southward for about 60 miles (97 kilometers). It empties into the Saint Lawrence River about 7 miles (11 kilometers) northeast of Quebec City. Montmorency Falls, which are about 150 feet (46 meters) wide and 274 feet (84 meters) high, lie at the mouth of the river. The Montmorency Falls furnish water power for nearby industry.　　　　　MURRAY G. BALLANTYNE

MONTPELIER, Vt. (pop. 8,609), the state capital, stands along the Winooski River in the central part of the state (see VERMONT [political map]). The life insurance and granite industries employ many of the city's people. Other industries include printing and the manufacture of plastics, machinery, and stone-finishing and sawmill equipment. Montpelier lies on an old Indian trade route. Founded in 1786, it became a city in 1894. It has a council-manager government. See also VERMONT (color picture: State Capitol).　　WALTER R. HARD, JR.

Montreal is Canada's largest city and chief transportation center. Downtown Montreal lies between Montreal Harbor, on the St. Lawrence River, and tree-covered Mount Royal, *background*.

MONTREAL

MONTREAL, Que., is the largest city in Canada and the largest French-speaking city in the world after Paris. About two-thirds of Montreal's people have French ancestors and speak the French language. The city ranks as one of the world's largest inland seaports and as Canada's chief transportation center. It is also a major center of Canadian business, industry, culture, and education.

Montreal is one of North America's most interesting cities. It lies on an island and is the only city on the continent built around a mountain. Montreal covers about a third of the Island of Montreal at the place where the St. Lawrence and Ottawa rivers meet in southern Quebec. A tree-covered mountain, Mount Royal, rises 763 feet (233 meters) in the city's center.

Montreal has some of Canada's tallest office buildings, largest department stores, and most luxurious hotels. Its downtown area includes the world's largest network of underground stores and restaurants. The city has a fascinating waterfront area called *Old Montreal*, where old stone buildings line narrow, cobblestone streets and impressive monuments stand in historic squares. Montreal also has outstanding museums and universities, and its *Place des Arts* (Square of the Arts) is one of North America's finest theater centers.

In 1535, Jacques Cartier of France became the first European explorer to reach the site that is now Mont-

Jean-Pierre Fournier, the contributor of this article, is a free-lance writer and former reporter for The Montreal Star.

real. Cartier climbed to the top of the mountain and named it *Mont Réal* (Mount Royal). The first permanent settlement on the site was established in 1642. That year, Paul de Chomedey, Sieur de Maisonneuve—a former French Army officer—brought a small group of Roman Catholic missionaries to the island from France. The settlement was first called *Ville-Marie* (Mary's City) in honor of the Virgin Mary. But by the early 1700's, it had become identified with the mountain, and was called *Montreal*.

Today, Montreal faces problems common to other large cities, including discrimination, poverty, slums, and unemployment. But these problems present an unusual challenge in Montreal. In almost all cities, minority groups suffer most from such problems. In Montreal, however, the problems mainly affect the majority group—the French Canadians. This situation has caused much unrest in Montreal and has led to riots and other kinds of violence.

―――――― FACTS IN BRIEF ――――――

Population: 1,080,546. *Metropolitan Area Population—* 2,802,485.

Area: 68 sq. mi. (176 km²). *Metropolitan Area—*1,032 sq. mi. (2,673 km²).

Altitude: 100 ft. (30 m) above sea level.

Climate: *Average Temperature—*January, 15° F. (−9° C); July, 70° F. (21° C). *Average Annual Precipitation* (rainfall, melted snow, and other forms of moisture)— 35 in. (89 cm). For information on the monthly weather in Montreal, see QUEBEC (Climate).

Government: Mayor-council. *Terms—*4 years for the mayor and the 52 council members.

Founded: 1642. Incorporated as a city in 1832.

Montreal lies on the triangular Island of Montreal. The island is about 32 miles (51 kilometers) long, and 10 miles (16 kilometers) wide at its widest point. The city of Montreal occupies 68 of the182 square miles (176 of the 471 square kilometers) that the island covers. The city lies on two separate parts of the island—one near the center and one in the northwest. The Montreal metropolitan area, called *Greater Montreal*, covers 1,032 square miles (2,673 square kilometers). It includes all of the Island of Montreal, nearby Jésus Island and several smaller islands, and parts of the Quebec mainland around the islands.

Montreal was built on a series of terraces that rise steeply from the bank of the St. Lawrence River west to Mount Royal. At shore level are port facilities and warehouses and wholesale trade establishments. Old Montreal lies on the lowest terraces, near the riverfront. Farther up are the towering office buildings and busy stores of downtown Montreal. Mount Royal, which most Montrealers call "the mountain," rises west of this area. Montreal's chief residential districts lie north, south, and west of Mount Royal. Many industrial plants line the St. Lawrence River and *Boulevard St.-Laurent* (St. Lawrence Boulevard).

Boulevard St.-Laurent, one of Montreal's chief east-west streets, runs through the center of the city. It divides Montreal into two sections. Montrealers call the sections the *East End* and the *West End*. Geographically, however, the sections are more nearly the northern and southern parts of the city.

Old Montreal borders the St. Lawrence River between Berri and McGill streets. Many of its old buildings stand side by side with tall, modern structures. Charming restaurants, historic houses, and small retail stores line the area's narrow streets. Several of these streets are paved with cobblestones.

Old Montreal has many reminders of Montreal's rich history. The city's oldest church, Notre-Dame-de-Bon-Secours, stands on *Rue St.-Paul* (St.-Paul Street) in the northern part of Old Montreal. This Roman Catholic stone church was built in 1771 on the foundations of an earlier building. The St. Sulpice Seminary, the oldest building in Montreal, is on *Rue Notre-Dame* (Notre-Dame Street) at the south end of Old Montreal. Ville-Marie's first priests opened it in 1685, and their followers have lived in the building ever since.

Two of Montreal's most historic *places* (squares) are near the seminary. Across Rue Notre-Dame is *Place d'Armes* (Parade Ground). The first clash between Ville-Marie's founders and the Iroquois Indians took place there in 1644. The Maisonneuve Monument in the square honors the city's founder. A few blocks east of the seminary, on Rue St.-Paul, is *Place Royale* (Royal Square). This square was the site of Fort Montreal, built by Ville-Marie's pioneers in 1642.

Important banks and insurance companies border Place d'Armes. Government buildings, including several courthouses and *Hôtel de Ville* (City Hall), line Rue Notre-Dame a few blocks north of Place d'Armes.

Downtown Montreal lies west of Old Montreal. It has some of Canada's tallest buildings, busiest department stores, and finest hotels.

Several downtown streets have special characteristics. Dorchester Boulevard, a wide north-south street that crosses the heart of downtown Montreal, is known for its soaring skyscrapers. The city's best-known one, the Royal Bank of Canada Building, rises 615 feet (187 meters) at Dorchester and University Street. It towers over Place Ville Marie, one of the city's chief office centers. The bank building is shaped like a cross. Its height and shape have made it a city landmark.

Rue Ste.-Catherine (St.-Catherine Street), a block west of Dorchester, is noted for its department stores, restaurants, and motion-picture theaters. Sherbrooke Street, two blocks west of Rue Ste.-Catherine, attracts many visitors because of its luxurious antique shops, art galleries, and hotels.

One of Montreal's liveliest sections lies beneath the downtown streets. This section is called the *underground city*. There, over 200 restaurants and stores and several motion-picture theaters border a network of passageways and squares. The network is the largest development of its kind in the world.

Metropolitan Area. Greater Montreal is Canada's second largest urban area. Only Toronto is larger. More than 2,800,000 persons, or about 12 per cent of Canada's people, live there. About 75 cities and towns make up the Montreal metropolitan area. Montreal is by far the largest of these communities. But about 60 per cent of the people in the metropolitan area live outside the city.

Laval, on Jésus Island, ranks as Montreal's largest suburb. It has a population of more than 246,000. Longueuil, with about 122,000 persons, is the largest suburb on the east shore of the St. Lawrence River. Westmount, an independent residential city on Mount Royal, lies entirely within Montreal's city limits.

Barbara K. Deans

Mountain Street, in downtown Montreal, has some of the city's most charming restaurants. Several of them feature French-style cooking and attract both residents and tourists.

About 85 per cent of Montreal's people were born in Canada. French Canadians are by far the largest group in the city. Montrealers of British ancestry form the second largest group. Signs throughout Montreal appear in both French and English. Since the end of World War II in 1945, hundreds of thousands of immigrants from Europe have settled in Montreal. Today, people of nearly all nationalities and races live in the city.

Roman Catholics make up about three-fourths of Montreal's population. Most of the Catholics are of French descent. The majority of English-speaking Montrealers are Protestants. Anglicans, Presbyterians, and members of the United Church of Canada form the city's largest Protestant denominations. Jews make up another large religious group in Montreal.

Ethnic Groups. About two-thirds of the city's people are of French descent. Approximately an eighth have British ancestors. Other large ethnic groups in Montreal include Chinese, Germans, Greeks, Italians, Poles, and Ukrainians.

Most of the French Montrealers rent apartments in the East End. Many of them are poor and live in crowded slums. People of British descent have a higher standard of living than any other ethnic group in Montreal. They make up the largest group in the West End. Most of the British Montrealers live in houses, which they own.

French is the chief language of about two-thirds of Montreal's people. English serves as the main language for most of the other Montrealers. About a third of all the people in Montreal speak both French and English.

Language difference ranks as a major cause of the economic problems of the French. Even though French-speaking people are by far the largest group in Montreal, English is the main language used in business in the city. This is so because English-speaking Quebecers or foreigners control most of Montreal's large businesses and industries and many of its smaller ones. An ability to speak English is required to get most well-paying jobs in the city. As a result, large numbers of French-speaking Montrealers must take low-paying jobs.

Housing. Montreal has more than 45,000 one- or two-family houses and over 300,000 apartments. Most of the houses are in the West End. A number of luxurious man-

Rus Arnold

Montreal's *Métro* Riders enter and leave the city's subway system through some of the world's most attractive stations. The *Place d'Armes* station, *above*, features colored windows. Other stations have decorated walls.

Paul Baich, Pictorial Parade

Shoppers and Office Workers relax or enjoy an outdoor lunch in the plaza of the *Place Ville Marie,* a popular downtown shopping center.

Gerry Souter, Van Cleve Photography

The Underground City, a shopping area beneath Montreal's downtown streets, features over 200 stores and restaurants. Escalators in major hotels serve the system, the largest development of its kind in the world.

MONTREAL

Montreal lies on the St. Lawrence River in southern Quebec. The top map shows the Montreal metropolitan area, which consists of more than 70 cities and towns. Many people who live in these communities commute daily to and from their jobs in Montreal. The city covers about a third of the Island of Montreal. The built-up area is shown in yellow. The map at the bottom shows the major points of interest in downtown Montreal.

QUEBEC

Montreal

City boundary
County boundary
Built-up area
Nonbuilt-up area
Park
Highway or street
Rail line
Subway (Métro)
Point of interest

WORLD BOOK maps

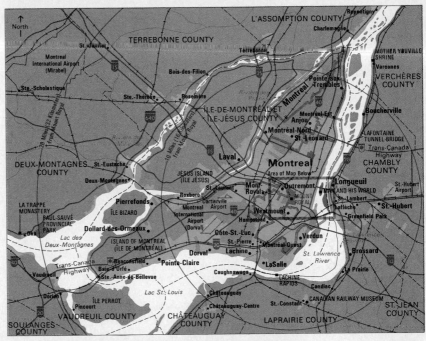

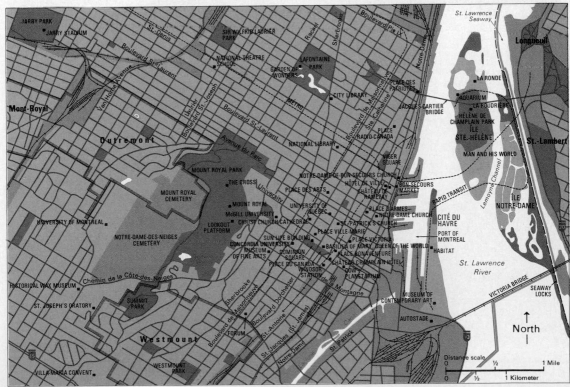

sions lie on the slopes of Mount Royal. Most of Montreal's apartments are in the East End. Rows of two- or three-story apartment buildings with outside staircases are a common sight there. Apartment buildings in this style, constructed chiefly during the 1920's and 1930's, were designed to preserve inside space.

Montreal is the site of one of the world's most unusual apartment developments. This development, called *Habitat*, stands on Cité du Havre, a strip of land that extends into the St. Lawrence River. Habitat consists of 158 apartments that look like a stack of concrete boxes. One apartment's roof serves as the terrace of another.

Montreal has many new houses and tall, modern apartment buildings. But the city also has a large number of old and run-down dwellings. The worst housing is in the East End. Slums spread across large areas in this section. During the 1960's, the city redeveloped 107 acres (43 hectares) in an area called *Little Burgundy*. The project included construction of 1,200 apartments at a cost of about $30 million (see CITY [picture: Urban Renewal]). However, Montreal officials estimate that more than 100,000 dwellings—housing about half the city's population—still require major repairs.

Montreal also suffers from a shortage of low-cost housing for large families. In the 1960's, nearly 10 times more dwellings were torn down than were rebuilt. Today, more than 85,000 apartments are overcrowded. In addition, Montreal offers the lowest proportion of low-cost housing of all major Canadian cities. It averages only 3 units of low-cost housing for every 1,000 persons. Toronto, Canada's second largest city, averages $8\frac{1}{2}$ units.

Education. Montreal has an unusual public school system. The system is organized on the basis of language and religion. Four kinds of schools exist within the system. They are (1) Roman Catholic schools that teach entirely in English, (2) Roman Catholic, French-language schools, (3) Protestant, English-language schools, and (4) Protestant, French-language schools. Most Jewish students attend either the Protestant schools or private Jewish schools. The system has about 500 schools. A Roman Catholic school board administers about 400 of them. A Protestant school board runs the rest. Montreal also has a number of nonreligious private schools.

Montreal is the home of two of Canada's most famous universities, the University of Montreal and McGill University. The University of Montreal is the largest university outside of France in which all courses are taught in French. McGill University, Canada's oldest English-language university, was founded in 1821. Other institutions of higher learning in Montreal include Concordia University, an English-language school; and the University of Quebec, which teaches in French.

The University of Montreal, McGill University, and Concordia University are privately owned. The province controls the University of Quebec.

The issue of language rights in schools has led to disputes in Montreal. Many French-speaking people believe that all the schools should teach only in French. Montrealers who prefer to educate their children in English-language schools oppose this view. They strongly support existing Canadian laws that guarantee them the right to choose the language of instruction for their children. Some protests involving language rights have led to riots.

Social Problems. Montreal, like other large cities, faces such problems as discrimination and poverty. In most cities, these problems largely affect minority groups. But in Montreal, nearly all the best jobs and housing belong to the English-speaking minority. The majority group—the French—suffers the most. This situation has created much social tension in the city.

In Montreal, as in other cities, lack of education and job training is a major cause of poverty. But in Montreal, language is also a barrier to a better way of life. As previously mentioned, an ability to speak English is a requirement for most well-paying jobs. Large numbers of French Canadians, including college graduates, have been refused jobs because they either spoke no English or failed to speak it well. Because of this problem, thousands of French-speaking Montrealers want to make French the language of business. Many of them also argue that the only way to solve the language problem and improve their living conditions is to make Quebec a separate nation. These people, called *separatists*, claim that the provincial government lacks the power to solve their problems and that the federal government lacks the desire to do so.

Montreal is the headquarters of the separatist movement. A few separatists have tried to publicize the movement by bombing English-owned stores and staging other terrorist acts in Montreal. But most of them hope to gain independence for Quebec by voter approval.

Barbara K. Deans

Balconies and Outdoor Staircases are a distinctive feature of many apartment buildings in Montreal's East End. Most French-speaking Montrealers live in this section of the city.

Montreal is Canada's chief transportation center. It ranks second only to Toronto among the top Canadian centers of finance, industry, and trade.

Montreal's location contributes much to the city's economic importance. Montreal lies on the St. Lawrence River at the entrance to the St. Lawrence Seaway. This location has helped make it one of the world's leading inland seaports. Waterways in the Montreal area also provide a large supply of low-cost hydroelectric power. This supply, about a fifth of the hydroelectric power produced in Quebec, has helped attract many industries to the city. In addition, Montreal lies in Quebec's most fertile and productive agricultural region. As a result, the city has become a major food-processing center.

Transportation. The St. Lawrence River links Montreal with the Atlantic Ocean, about 1,000 miles (1,600 kilometers) to the northeast. The St. Lawrence Seaway extends shipping services 1,300 miles (2,090 kilometers) inland. It makes Montreal a major stopover point for ships sailing between the Great Lakes and the Atlantic (see SAINT LAWRENCE SEAWAY).

Montreal Harbor stretches 15 miles (24 kilometers) along the west bank of the St. Lawrence River. It serves about 4,000 ocean-going or coastal and inland vessels and handles over 19 million short tons (17 million metric tons) of cargo yearly. Montreal is one of the largest grain ports in the world. Each year, between 100 million and 160 million bushels of grain are shipped from Montreal Harbor.

Montreal ranks as Canada's largest railroad center. CP Rail and the Canadian National Railways, the nation's two transcontinental rail lines, have their headquarters in the city. These railroads carry passengers and freight east to the Atlantic seaboard and west to the Pacific Coast. Several railways connect Montreal and a number of cities in the United States. In 1968, the Canadian National Railways began operating North America's first turbine-powered passenger train between Montreal and Toronto.

Major airlines use Montreal International Airport (Dorval), which lies just southwest of the city, and Montreal International Airport (Mirabel), northwest of Montreal. Air Canada, the nation's largest commercial airline, has its headquarters in the city.

More than 10 major highways serve Montreal. The Trans-Canada Highway, which runs from coast to coast, crosses downtown Montreal 100 feet (30 meters) underground. Nearly 20 railroad and highway bridges connect the Island of Montreal with Jésus Island and the east shore of the St. Lawrence River.

Montreal's subway, called the *Métro*, carries passengers between the downtown area and the outskirts of the city in less than 20 minutes. It can serve up to 60,000 riders an hour. The Métro, which opened in 1966, runs on rubber tires. As a result, it is one of the world's quietest subways. It was the first subway in the Western Hemisphere to use rubber tires. Buses also provide public transportation in Montreal.

Industry. Manufacturing is the leading source of employment in Greater Montreal. The more than 7,000 factories in the area employ about a fourth of its workers. These plants produce about $13 billion worth of goods yearly. They account for about two-thirds of Quebec's industrial production.

Greater Montreal's leading industries are petroleum refining and food processing. Refineries in Montreal produce about a third of Canada's gasoline. The area's chief food products are beer, canned goods, and sugar. Greater Montreal is also the nation's major center for the manufacture of clothing, tobacco products, and transportation equipment. The area also leads Quebec in the production of electrical machinery and fur products.

Trade and Finance. Companies in Greater Montreal play an important role in Canada's foreign trade. These companies handle about 20 per cent of the import business in the nation and about 10 per cent of its export business.

Montreal area companies also account for about 15 per cent of the wholesale and retail trade in Canada and about 65 per cent of such trade in Quebec. Wholesale companies, which sell goods to retail stores, employ more than 40,000 workers in Greater Montreal. Area retail stores employ about 50,000 workers. These stores include some of Canada's largest department stores. Place Bonaventure, in downtown Montreal, is one of the largest commercial buildings in the world. It has more than 3 million square feet (300,000 square meters) of space to display goods.

More than 40 per cent of Canada's financial companies are in Greater Montreal. Banks, credit organizations, savings firms, and other financial companies in the area employ over 60,000 persons. Loans by these companies contribute to the growth of business and industry throughout Canada.

The Bank of Montreal, founded in 1817, was the first bank in Canada. The Royal Bank of Canada, the country's largest bank, has its headquarters in Montreal. The Montreal Stock Exchange is the oldest stock market in Canada. The exchange opened in the city in 1874.

Communication. Four daily newspapers are published in Montreal. Three of the papers—*La Presse, Le Devoir,* and *Le Journal de Montréal*—are written in French. *The Gazette* is the only Montreal daily that is written in English. *La Presse* has the largest circulation of any of Quebec's daily newspapers. *The Gazette* was the first newspaper published in Montreal. It was founded in 1778.

Eleven radio stations broadcast from the city, six of them in French and five in English. Station CFCF of Montreal was Canada's first radio station. It began broadcasting in 1919.

Montreal has four television stations. Two of them broadcast in the French language and two in English. The French-language network of the Canadian Broadcasting Corporation (CBC) is based in Montreal. More French-language television programs are produced in Montreal than in any other city in the world except Paris. Television station CBFT, one of the first two Canadian stations, began broadcasting from Montreal in 1952. The other pioneer station was CBLT of Toronto.

642c

Beaver Lake in Mount Royal Park

Prazak, Miller Services

Barbara K. Deans

Ski Area on Mount Royal

Quebec Department of Tourism

The *Place des Arts*

Montreal is one of North America's leading cultural centers. It has outstanding dance, drama, and musical groups, and its art galleries, libraries, and museums rank among the finest in Canada. The city is also known for its many beautiful churches and well-planned parks. Montreal's sports attractions include professional baseball, football, and hockey.

Each year, about 4 million tourists visit Montreal. The city has about 11,000 hotel and motel rooms and 5,000 restaurants. Many restaurants specialize in French cooking. Visitors can also find restaurants featuring Chinese, Greek, Italian, or other kinds of cooking.

The Arts. The world-famous Montreal Symphony Orchestra makes its home in the city. Other internationally known Montreal groups include two dance companies—Les Feux-Follets and Les Grands Ballets Canadiens—and two French-language theater groups —Le Théâtre du Nouveau-Monde and Le Théâtre du Rideau-Vert. Montreal's International Theatre offers productions in five languages. This company performs at La Poudrière, a theater on *Île Ste.-Hélène* (St.-Helen's Island) in the St. Lawrence River.

Place des Arts at Rue Ste.-Catherine and St. Urbain Street is one of North America's finest centers for the performing arts. Many of Montreal's leading cultural groups entertain there. The center includes the Salle Wilfrid-Pelletier concert hall, which has a seating capacity of 3,000. A second structure houses the smaller Maisonneuve and Port-Royal theaters, which offer stage productions.

Libraries. Montreal's public library system is called the Montreal City Library. It consists of a main library and more than 25 branches. The system owns about 650,000 books written in French, 350,000 in English, and 10,000 in other languages. Other libraries in Mont-

Rus Arnold

Notre Dame Parish Church

real include the Fraser-Hickson Library, the Jewish Public Library, and the Quebec National Library.

Museums. The Montreal Museum of Fine Arts at Sherbrooke and Drummond streets displays paintings by leading Canadian and European artists. It also has collections of furniture, glass, lace, and silver from Canada and many works of art from Asia and South America. This museum is the oldest museum in Canada. It was founded in 1860.

The *Musée d'Art Contemporain* (Museum of Contemporary Art) stands at Cité du Havre. It exhibits modern works of art from Europe and North America. The Château de Ramezay, in Old Montreal, is a history museum. The building dates from 1705. It was once the home of Claude de Ramezay, second French governor of Montreal.

The Montreal Aquarium is on Île Ste.-Hélène. It has penguins, trained dolphins, and hundreds of varieties of fish from around the world. Dow Planetarium at *Rue St.-Jacques* (St. James Street) and Peel Street features programs on the space age.

Churches. Montreal is famous for its more than 300 churches. Several of them are noted for their Gothic architecture. Saint Patrick's Church, a Gothic structure in downtown Montreal, serves English-speaking Roman Catholics. Another Gothic structure, the Notre Dame Parish Church in Old Montreal, is attended by French-speaking Catholics. This church has two towers, one of which houses a huge bell. This bell, called *Le Gros Bourdon* (The Great Bell), weighs 12 short tons (11 metric tons). Notre Dame is also noted for its magnificently carved wooden interior.

Notre-Dame-de-Bon-Secours is another well-known church in Old Montreal. Some Montrealers call it *the Sailors' Church*. A statue of the Virgin Mary, on the roof

Hellmut Walter Schade

Notre-Dame-de-Bon-Secours Church

Ellefson, Miller Services

St. Joseph's Oratory

of the church, is said to perform miracles to help sailors.

The Cathedral-Basilica of Mary, Queen of the World, stands in the heart of the downtown area. The designers of this church patterned it after Saint Peter's Church in Vatican City. The church serves as the seat of the Catholic archdiocese of Montreal. The seat of the Anglican diocese, Christ Church Cathedral, is also in downtown Montreal. Saint Joseph's Oratory stands on the west slope of Mount Royal. Every year, more than 3 million persons visit this Roman Catholic shrine.

Parks. The Montreal park system includes about 400 parks and playgrounds. These recreation areas cover a total of more than 4,000 acres (1,600 hectares). Visitors can ride through Mount Royal Park, on Mount Royal, in horse-drawn carriages in summer or in sleighs during winter. During the summer, plays are performed at Mount Royal's Mountain Playhouse. The park includes Beaver Lake, a popular spot for ice-skating.

Montrealers also enjoy activities at Lafontaine and Maisonneuve parks. Lafontaine Park, at Sherbrooke and Amherst streets, has a lake for boating. Maisonneuve Park, at Sherbrooke and Pie IX Boulevard, includes the city's Botanical Gardens.

Sports. The Montreal Canadiens of the National Hockey League play in the Forum. The Montreal Alouettes face Canadian Football League opponents in Olympic Stadium. The stadium is also the home of the Montreal Expos of the National Baseball League.

Winter sports are a major attraction in the Montreal area. As many as 5,000 skiers may rush to Mount Royal after a snowfall. Skiing is also popular in the nearby Laurentian Mountains.

Other Places to Visit. Many of Montreal's most interesting places to visit are described in earlier sections of this article. For example, Old Montreal, discussed in *The City* section, has many attractions. Other popular places to visit in Montreal include lookout platforms on Mount Royal, an international exhibition called *Man and His World*, and the Métro.

Two lookout platforms on the mountain offer visitors magnificent views of the Montreal area. From an observation area on the west slope, visitors can gaze over Montreal's tree-lined streets, spired churches, towering office buildings, and old stone houses. An iron cross rises 100 feet (30 meters) near this platform. The cross, illuminated at night, is a memorial to Ville-Marie's survival of a flood in 1642. The other platform is on the south slope. It overlooks residential communities.

Man and His World spreads across Île Ste.-Hélène and nearby *Île Notre-Dame* (Notre-Dame Island). It is a continuation of Expo 67, a world's fair held in 1967 (see EXPO 67). The attraction is open daily in the summer and early fall, and it features exhibits from over 50 nations. La Ronde, a 135-acre (55-hectare) amusement park, lies near the exhibition area.

The Métro is one of the world's most attractive subways. Brightly colored mosaics and basket-weave designs decorate many of its ceramic walls. Because of these decorations, the Métro has been called "the largest underground art gallery in the world."

Olympic Park, built for the 1976 Summer Olympic Games, includes the circular Olympic Stadium, *center*. The stadium is the home of the Montreal Alouettes of the Canadian Football League, and the Montreal Expos of the National League play baseball there.

Organization. Montreal has a mayor-council form of government. The voters elect the mayor and the 52 members of the City Council to four-year terms.

The mayor acts as the administrative head of the city government. He supervises the various departments of the city's government. A seven-member executive committee prepares the city budget and proposes new *statutes* (laws). The committee consists of the mayor and six City Council members. The City Council appoints the councilmen and elects one of them chairman of the committee. The City Council passes the city's laws. It also appoints and dismisses directors of city departments and adopts the city budget.

Montreal gets some of its government services from an agency called the Montreal Urban Community Council. The council, created by the Quebec legislature in 1969, serves all the cities and towns on the Island of Montreal and nearby *Île Bizard* (Bizard Island). It administers such services as fire protection, law enforcement, long-range planning, public health, public transportation, sanitation, traffic control, and water supply. The council consists of the mayor and all the councilmen of Montreal and the mayor of each of the other communities.

Montreal has an annual budget of over $400 million. Only three other Canadian government budgets are larger—the federal government's and those of Ontario and Quebec provinces. Over half of Montreal's income comes from taxes on property. The rest of the city's funds come from taxes on sales, businesses, water, and amusements, and from aid given by the province.

Symbols of Montreal. The city flag and the coat of arms of Montreal include the national flowers of France (fleur-de-lis), England (rose), Scotland (thistle), and Ireland (shamrock). Immigrants from these countries played key roles in the city's growth.

Problems. Like most other big cities, Montreal has difficulty finding ways to pay for the rapidly rising costs of government services. Taxes do not provide enough money to meet these costs. The major problems faced by Montreal's government include building more low-cost housing and providing higher pay for city employees.

Montreal's public housing plans for the 1970's rely heavily on grants from the provincial and federal governments. These plans call for construction of 2,000 units of low-cost housing each year for five years at a total cost of about $150 million.

Some disputes over wage demands by city workers have led to strikes. During a one-day strike by policemen in October, 1969, a wave of bank robberies and looting broke out in Montreal. Threats of heavy fines and imprisonment ended the walkout.

MONTREAL/*History*

Algonquin, Huron, and Iroquois Indians lived in the Montreal region before Europeans arrived. The area's rivers and lakes offered the Indians a plentiful supply of fish and served as excellent transportation routes.

Exploration. In 1535, the French explorer Jacques Cartier sailed up the St. Lawrence River. The Lachine Rapids, south of what is now Montreal, prevented Cartier from going farther by ship. He then explored the Island of Montreal and found the Iroquois village of Hochelaga at the foot of Mount Royal. Several thousand Indians lived in the village. Another famous French explorer, Samuel de Champlain, visited the site of Montreal in 1603 and 1611.

French Settlement. In 1639, Jérôme Le Royer, Sieur de la Dauversière, a French tax collector, formed a company in Paris to establish a colony on the Island of Montreal. In 1641, the company sent a Roman Catholic missionary group to the island to convert the Indians to Christianity. The group, led by Paul de Chomedey, Sieur de Maisonneuve, arrived in 1642. The colonists built a fort at what is now Place Royale in Old Montreal and established the settlement of Ville-Marie.

Iroquois Indians attacked the colony, hoping to stop the profitable fur trade that the French had established with the Algonquins and Hurons. These two tribes were the chief rivals of the Iroquois. But despite the attacks, the colony prospered as a religious center and fur-trading post. The French and the Iroquois finally made peace in 1701.

By the early 1700's, Ville-Marie had become known as Montreal. It had a population of about 3,500 in 1710 and was the commercial heart of France's North American empire, called *New France*. Montreal's location on the St. Lawrence River made it an important center of trade. European goods passed through Montreal on the way to Canada's northwest. The St. Lawrence also linked Montreal to the rich supplies of furs southwest of the settlement. Montreal's location near the Ottawa River made it the gateway to the valuable forests of the Canadian northwest.

British Settlement. British troops under General Jeffery Amherst captured Montreal in 1760, during the French and Indian War (1754-1763). The battle marked the end of the fighting in this war and led to the collapse of New France. The Treaty of Paris, signed in 1763, officially ended the war and made Canada a British colony. Many English settlers then came to Montreal.

General Richard Montgomery's American forces occupied Montreal in November, 1775, during the Revolutionary War in America (1775-1783). Benjamin Franklin and other American diplomats tried to gain

Lithograph by J. Duncan, The Public Archives of Canada

Montreal's Waterfront District was the city's chief center of activity in the early 1800's, *above*. Today, the district is known as *Old Montreal* and has many historic sites.

French-Canadian support against the British. But their efforts failed, partly because most French Canadians regarded the war as just a quarrel between Britain and its colonies. In June, 1776, the arrival of British troops forced the American soldiers to withdraw, and Montreal became a British possession again.

During the late 1770's, fur traders in Montreal founded the North West Company as a rival to the Hudson's Bay Company fur trade. Montreal began to expand toward the north and the south on the Island of Montreal in the late 1700's. Many Englishmen established businesses in Montreal during this period. The English gradually gained control of the town's economy. A major cause of this development was that French life had traditionally centered around farming and retail trade. As a result, most French Canadians showed little interest in manufacturing. English- and French-speaking Montrealers settled in separate areas, establishing a pattern that still exists.

The Early 1800's. By 1800, Montreal's population had reached 9,000. Canada's first steamship, the *Accommodation*, sailed on the St. Lawrence River from Montreal to Quebec in 1809. In 1821, the Hudson's Bay Company bought the North West Company. The Hudson Bay area then became the chief market for furs, and Montreal declined as a fur-trading center.

The Lachine Canal, which crosses the southern edge of Montreal, opened in 1825. It provided a detour for small vessels around the Lachine Rapids and led to a sharp increase in trade and travel between Montreal and the Great Lakes. Shipping replaced fur trading as Montreal's chief industry, and Montreal grew in importance as a port. In 1832, Montreal was incorporated as a city. From 1844 until 1849, it served as the capital of the United Provinces of Canada. By 1850, the city's population had soared to about 50,000.

The Growing City. Montreal developed as a transportation center during the mid-1800's, when railways linked it to Boston, New York City, and Toronto. Investment by wealthy English-speaking businessmen helped Montreal become a major industrial center during this period. Many industries were built along the Lachine Canal. Thousands of French Canadians from Quebec and other Canadian cities came to Montreal to find jobs in the new factories. By 1871, about 107,000 persons lived in the city. About two-thirds of them were of French ancestry.

The Canadian Pacific Railway Company (now CP Rail), based in Montreal, completed Canada's first transcontinental railroad in 1885. The railroad attracted more industry and brought new prosperity to the city. By 1901, Montreal's population had risen to 267,730. The *annexation* (addition) of several neighboring communities helped it reach 467,986 by 1911.

The War Issue. During World War I (1914-1918), Canada fought on the side of the Allies, which included France, Great Britain, and the United States. Many of the French Canadians in Montreal supported the government's policy and volunteered for the war. Others opposed the policy because they felt the war did not concern Canada.

Canada's aid to the Allies in World War II (1939-1945) also caused unrest among many French Canadians. In 1940, Montreal Mayor Camillien Houde urged Montrealers to defy a Canadian government plan to count all the men in the country. Houde charged that the count, called the National Registration, would lead to a military draft for overseas service. Most French Canadians opposed such a draft, and Canadian government leaders had pledged not to establish one. Federal authorities arrested Houde and kept him in a prison camp until 1944.

The Changing City. By the early 1950's, Montreal's population had topped 1 million. During the late 1950's, the city entered a period of great economic growth. In 1958, a city development program enlarged Montreal Harbor. The opening of the St. Lawrence Seaway in 1959 attracted hundreds of industries.

In the 1960's, a construction boom in downtown Montreal gave the city a new skyline. Private developers tore down old, decaying structures throughout the area and replaced them with huge banks, hotels, and office buildings. The city's two tallest skyscrapers, the 49-story Royal Bank of Canada Building and the 47-story Place Victoria, were completed during this period. Other important downtown developments of the 1960's included Place Bonaventure, a trade mart; Place des Arts, a cultural center; and an underground shopping network.

The city built new highways and a new subway, the Métro, to help serve visitors attending Expo 67, an international exhibition held in Montreal in 1967. More than 50 million persons attended the exhibition.

The Separatist Movement. In 1960, the *Rassemblement pour l' Indépendence Nationale* (Assembly for National Independence) was founded in Montreal. Its chief aim was to bring about the separation of Quebec from the rest of Canada and make the province an independent nation.

The *Front de Libération du Québec* (Quebec Liberation Front), a terrorist organization known as the *FLQ*, joined the separatist movement in 1963. At first, the FLQ attacked armories and the English-Canadian area of Westmount. It soon became involved in labor disputes. Between 1963 and 1968, the FLQ claimed responsibility for hundreds of bombings and armed robberies in the Montreal area.

In October, 1970, members of the FLQ kidnapped British Trade Commissioner James R. Cross and Quebec Labor Minister Pierre Laporte in Montreal. Canadian Prime Minister Pierre E. Trudeau, a French Canadian born in Montreal, sent federal troops to Montreal and other Quebec cities to guard officials. The murder of Laporte later in the month increased tension in Montreal. The federal troops were withdrawn in January, 1971, after police arrested four FLQ members and charged them with the kidnapping and murder of Laporte. Cross's kidnappers had released him after government officials guaranteed their safe passage to Cuba.

Recent Developments. Montreal was the site of the 1976 Summer Olympic Games. Construction for the event included housing facilities for the athletes and a new, 50,000-seat sports stadium. Montreal officials began to rent the housing to the public in 1978. In 1976, the stadium became the home of the city's professional football team, the Montreal Alouettes. The city's professional baseball team, the Montreal Expos, began playing there in 1977.

In 1969, the Canadian government began acquiring land for the $400-million Montreal International Airport (Mirabel), just northwest of the city. The airport, which opened in 1975, covers about 138 square miles (357 square kilometers). It is the largest airport in the world in total area.

JEAN-PIERRE FOURNIER

MONTREAL/Study Aids

Related Articles in WORLD BOOK include:

BIOGRAPHIES

Amherst, Lord Jeffrey	Léger, Paul-Émile Cardinal
Bourassa, Henri	Papineau, Louis Joseph
Cartier, Jacques	Trudeau, Pierre Elliott
La Vérendrye, Sieur de	Vanier, Georges Philias

METROPOLITAN MONTREAL

Lachine	Montréal-Nord
Laval	Saint-Laurent
Longueuil	Westmount

HISTORY

French and Indian Wars	Paris, Treaties of
Hudson's Bay Company	Revolutionary War
North West Company	in America

OTHER RELATED ARTICLES

Ottawa River	Saint Lawrence River
Quebec (pictures)	Saint Lawrence Seaway

Outline

I. **The City**
   A. Old Montreal
   B. Downtown Montreal
   C. Metropolitan Area
II. **People**
   A. Ethnic Groups
   B. Housing
   C. Education
   D. Social Problems

III. **Economy**
   A. Transportation
   B. Industry
   C. Trade and Finance
   D. Communication
IV. **Cultural Life and Places to Visit**
   A. The Arts   E. Parks
   B. Libraries   F. Sports
   C. Museums   G. Other Places
   D. Churches   to Visit
V. **Government**
   A. Organization
   B. Problems
VI. **History**

Questions

How do major problems in Montreal differ from those in other cities?

Why did the Iroquois Indians attack Ville-Marie during the 1600's?

Why is Montreal's public school system unusual?

Who founded Montreal? When?

What are Montreal's two most important industries?

What governments in Canada have larger annual budgets than Montreal?

Why has the Métro been called the "world's largest underground art gallery"?

Why have Montrealers of French descent had difficulty getting jobs?

What is Montreal's *underground city?*

What are some of Montreal's housing problems?

University of Montreal

The University of Montreal, the largest French-language university outside France, stands on the slopes of Mount Royal.

MONTREAL, UNIVERSITY OF, is a private, coeducational university in Montreal, Que. All courses are conducted in French. They lead to bachelor's, master's, and doctor's degrees. The university has faculties of architecture, arts and science, business administration, dentistry, education, engineering, graduate studies, law, medicine, music, nursing, optometry, pharmacy, physical health and education, theology, and veterinary medicine. It also offers interdisciplinary studies. The faculty of continuing education conducts evening and summer courses. A large computing center serves all university departments. Research is conducted in all fields of study, especially in the medical, natural, physical, and social sciences.

The University of Montreal was founded in 1876 as the Montreal branch of Laval University. It separated from Laval in 1919, and was chartered as the University of Montreal in 1920. It was controlled by the Roman Catholic Church until a lay board of trustees was appointed in 1967. For enrollment, see CANADA (table: Universities and Colleges).

Critically reviewed by the UNIVERSITY OF MONTREAL

MONTRÉAL-NORD, Quebec (pop. 97,250), lies on Montreal Isle, and adjoins the northeast section of the city of Montreal (see QUEBEC [political map]). In English, the city's name is MONTREAL NORTH. It produces transportation equipment, wood products, and electrical appliances. Founded in 1915, Montréal-Nord became a city in 1959. It has a mayor-council form of government. HUBERT CHARBONNEAU

MONTRESOR, BENI (1926-   ), is a stage designer and illustrator of children's books. He won the Caldecott Medal for 1965 for his illustrations in *May I Bring a Friend?* (1964). He also wrote and illustrated *House of Flowers* (1962) and *Witches of Venice* (1963). He designed sets for theater, opera, ballet, and motion pictures. Montresor was born in Verona, Italy.

MONTS, *mawn,* **SIEUR DE** (1560?-1630?), PIERRE DU GUAST, a French explorer and colonizer, settled the region of Acadia in Canada. He was interested in the fur trade, discovery, and navigation. He was an intimate friend of King Henry IV of France, who made him a lieutenant general and governor of Acadia.

He sailed for America in March, 1604, with Jean de Biencourt de Poutrincourt and Samuel de Champlain. They explored the Bay of Fundy and settled at the mouth of the Saint Croix River. In 1605, they founded Port Royal, Nova Scotia. Sieur de Monts then returned to France, leaving Poutrincourt behind as governor.

Sieur de Monts later won permission to send Champlain to explore Canada. Champlain founded Quebec in 1608, and sailed to Canada again in 1610. Sieur de Monts was born in Saintonge, France. JEAN BRUCHÉSI

See also ACADIA; ANNAPOLIS ROYAL; CHAMPLAIN, SAMUEL DE; POUTRINCOURT, JEAN DE BIENCOURT DE.

MONTSERRAT, *MAHNT suh RAT,* is one of the Leeward Islands in the West Indies. It is a British dependency. It lies about 250 miles (402 kilometers) southeast of Puerto Rico (see WEST INDIES [map]). Montserrat has an area of 38 square miles (98 square kilometers) and a population of 12,000. It has three groups of mountains. The highest group is the Soufrière Hills, which rise about 3,000 feet (910 meters) in the southern part of the island. Sea-island cotton and tomatoes are the chief crops. The capital is Plymouth.

Christopher Columbus reached Montserrat in 1493 during his second voyage to the Western Hemisphere. He named it after a mountain in Spain. Irish settlers came to the island in 1632, and today many of the people speak with a *brogue* (Irish accent). The English and French fought for possession of Montserrat for about 150 years. Britain has controlled it since 1783.

MONTSERRAT, *MAHNT sur RAT,* is a mountain and a famous monastery near Barcelona in eastern Spain. The mountain's highest peak is 4,054 feet (1,236 meters) above sea level. Its name probably means *sawtoothed mountain,* referring to its jagged peaks.

The monastery of Montserrat, built in the 700's or 800's, is about 20 miles (32 kilometers) northwest of Barcelona. Many pilgrims visit the restored church to see the *Black Virgin,* patron saint of Catalonia. Christopher Columbus brought Indians to pay homage at this church. GEORGE KISH

MONUMENT is a structure, usually a building or statue, built in memory of a person or an event. *National monuments* are places of historic, scientific, or scenic interest set aside by the U.S. government as public property. They include such structures as historic forts and such natural features as canyons. For a list of national monuments that have separate articles in WORLD BOOK, see NATIONAL PARK SYSTEM (table). See also MEMORIAL and its Related Articles.

MONUMENT VALLEY. See UTAH (color picture; Places to Visit).

MONUMENT VALLEY NAVAJO TRIBAL PARK. See ARIZONA (Places to Visit).

MOOD is a person's state of mind or outlook on life. Everyone's mood may change from day to day, or, sometimes, from hour to hour. But in certain mental illnesses, usually called *manic-depressive psychoses,* the patient's mood is obviously disturbed (see PSYCHOSIS). Patients may be sad, or happy and excited, for no visible reason. Their mood changes often. Some psychiatrists believe that the basic trouble with such patients is a disturbance of their mood. They have suggested calling such illnesses *primary mood disturbances.* Psychoanalysts have shown that an apparently unexplainable mood can be caused by unconscious thoughts, wishes, or guilt feelings. If this is true, it is more correct to think of mood disturbances as a *secondary* cause of the symptoms of manic-depressive patients. CHARLES BRENNER

MOOD, or MODE, is a term applied to verb forms that distinguish among certain kinds of meaning. For example, the verb *is* in "He is my brother" is an *indicative*

mood form; that is, it states a fact. But the verb *were* in "if he were my brother" is a *subjunctive* mood form; that is, it expresses a condition contrary to fact.

Some languages have elaborate mood forms, but in English not many contrasts remain between the indicative and the subjunctive mood. For the verb *be*, the indicative forms of the present tense are *I am, you are, he is, we are,* and *they are*. The subjunctive forms are *I be, you be, he be, we be,* and *they be*. In the past tense, the indicative forms are *I was, you were, he was, we were,* and *they were,* and the subjunctive forms are *I were, you were, he were, we were,* and *they were*. Other verbs have a distinction at only one point: the third person singular of the present tense. For instance, *she calls* is indicative, but *she call* is subjunctive.

Subjunctive Uses. Although the subjunctive has limited forms and uses in English, it is useful as a way of expressing a wish, a request, urgency, or a condition contrary to fact:

I wish it *were* true. (wish)
She asked that we *be* admitted. (request)
It is necessary that he *stay*. (urgency)
If words *were* deeds, we would be finished. (condition contrary to fact)

Older English usage employed the present subjunctive frequently in clauses introduced by *if* and *though,* such as "If it *be* he, let him be admitted," and "Though she *call* repeatedly, I shall not answer."

Other older uses of the subjunctive survive in many expressions, most of which are blessings or prayerful wishes: *God bless you, Long live the king, Heaven forbid, Suffice it to say,* and *God be with you*.

Imperative Mood. The term *imperative mood* is commonly given to verbs that express commands or requests, such as "*Stop* the music," "*Leave* the room," and "*Give* this to your mother." In English, the imperative form is the *base* (simple) form of the verb. Imperative sentences usually have no subjects, and the omission of the subject is one of the chief signals that the sentence is a command or a request. But sometimes, imperative sentences do have subjects, as in "You do it, George."

Verb Phrases. The terms *mood* and *mode* are also applied sometimes to verb phrases like *might go, should stay,* and *may try*. Words like *may, might, should,* and *would* are often called *modal auxiliaries*. They express the same meanings conveyed by mood endings on the verb in such languages as Greek or Latin. In English, however, modern grammarians usually limit the term *mood* to the indicative, subjunctive, and imperative forms, omitting the modals.　　　　　WILLIAM F. IRMSCHER

MOODIE, SUSANNA (1803-1885), was a Canadian novelist and poet. She wrote *Roughing It in the Bush* (1852), a vivid account of pioneer life in Canada. She also wrote *Enthusiasm and Other Poems* (1830), *Life in the Clearings* (1853), *Mark Hurdlestone* (1853), *Flora Lindsay* (1854), *Matrimonial Speculations* (1854), *Geoffrey Moncton* (1856), and *Dorothy Chance* (1867). But these novels and poems were not equal to *Roughing It in the Bush*. She was born in Suffolk, England, and moved to Canada in 1832 with her husband, a British officer. DESMOND PACEY

MOODY, DWIGHT LYMAN (1837-1899), was an American evangelist. He founded the interdenominational Moody Memorial Church, the Moody Bible Institute, and the Moody Press in Chicago (see MOODY BIBLE INSTITUTE). He also established a pri-

vate high school for girls and another for boys near Northfield, Mass.

Moody was born in East Northfield, Mass. He left a job as a clerk in a Boston shoe store to become a shoe salesman in Chicago in 1856. He devoted all his time to Sunday school and YMCA activities after 1860. He conducted great evangelistic campaigns in the United States and Britain, appearing with Ira D. Sankey, a gospel singer and hymn writer.　　　　　EARLE E. CAIRNS

MOODY, HELEN WILLS. See WILLS, HELEN N.

MOODY, MARYON ELSPETH. See PEARSON, LESTER BOWLES (Education and War Service).

MOODY, PAUL. See LOWELL, FRANCIS CABOT.

MOODY, WILLIAM VAUGHN (1869-1910), was an American dramatist, poet, teacher, and literary historian. Critics hailed his play *The Great Divide* (1906) as a landmark in American drama because of its frank treatment of the collision between eastern puritanism and western frontier individualism. Moody planned a verse *trilogy* (three related plays) on the theme of "the unity of God and man." He completed *The Masque of Judgment* (1900) and *The Fire Bringer* (1904), but died before finishing the third play, *The Death of Eve*. He also wrote *The Faith Healer* (1909).

Moody's *Poems* (1901) contain the well-known lyrics "Gloucester Moors" and "The Quarry." While teaching at the University of Chicago, Moody wrote *History of English Literature* (1902) with Robert Morss Lovett. Moody was born in Spencer, Ind.　　　RICHARD MOODY

MOODY BIBLE INSTITUTE, in Chicago, is a school for training workers in various fields of Christian service. Dwight L. Moody, an evangelist, founded it in 1886. The institute offers a 3-year program on the college level. It also operates a radio network, publishes books and a monthly magazine, and produces films at the Moody Institute of Science in Whittier, Calif.

Critically reviewed by the MOODY BIBLE INSTITUTE

Moody Bible Institute offers college-level Christian service training. Its headquarters, *below,* are on LaSalle Street, Chicago.
Moody Bible Institute

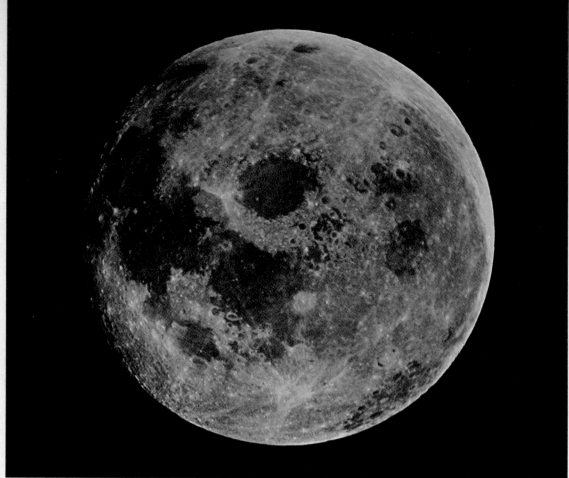

NASA

MOON

The Moon Was Photographed by the Apollo 11 Astronauts during their return trip to the earth. They had made man's first landing on the moon. The astronauts landed on the Sea of Tranquility, a large, dark-colored lava plain. The highland areas of the moon are lighter in color.

MOON is the earth's nearest neighbor in space. In 1969, this huge ball of gray rock became the first object in space to be visited by man.

The moon is the brightest object in the night sky, but it gives off no light of its own. When the moon "shines," it is *reflecting* (casting back) light from the sun. On some nights, the moon looks like a gleaming silver globe. On other nights, it appears as a thin slice of light. But the moon does not change its size or shape. It seems to change as different parts of it are lighted by the sun.

The moon travels around the earth once about every $29\frac{1}{2}$ days and is the earth's only natural satellite. The average distance between the centers of the earth and the moon is 238,857 miles (384,403 kilometers). A rocket journey from the earth to the moon and back takes about six days.

Because the moon is so near the earth, it seems much larger than the stars and about the same size as the sun. The moon measures about 2,160 miles (3,476 kilometers) across. This distance is about a fourth the di-

Eugene M. Shoemaker, the contributor of this article, is Professor of Geology at the California Institute of Technology and former chief investigator for the Apollo lunar geology experiments.

ameter of the earth and 400 times smaller than that of the sun. If the moon were seen next to the earth, it would look like a tennis ball next to a basketball.

The earth is not the only planet with a moon. For example, Jupiter has at least 13 satellites. The earth's moon is the fifth largest of the more than 30 natural satellites of the planets. For more information on natural satellites, see the separate planet articles.

The moon is a silent, lonely place with no life of any kind. Compared with the earth, it has changed little over billions of years. The moon has no air, no wind, and no water. On the moon, the sky is black—even during the day—and the stars are always visible. At night, the rocky surface becomes colder than any place on the earth. In the day, the rocks are too hot to touch.

Through the centuries, man has gazed at the moon, worshiped it, and studied it. Man's long-time dream of traveling to the moon became history on July 20, 1969, when astronaut Neil A. Armstrong of the United States set foot on it.

Space flights and moon landings have provided many facts about the moon. By exploring the moon, man may be able to solve mysteries about the earth, the sun, and the planets. For more information on exploring the moon, see the WORLD BOOK article on SPACE TRAVEL.

NASA   NASA

The Far Side of the Moon has a rugged surface. The large crater in the center of the photograph is International Astronomical Union Crater No. 308. It is about 50 miles (80 kilometers) wide. The lunar footprint at the right was made by Edwin E. Aldrin, Jr., an Apollo 11 astronaut.

─────────── THE MOON AT A GLANCE ───────────

Age: More than 4,500,000,000 (4½ billion) years.

Distance from the Earth: *Shortest*—221,456 miles (356,399 kilometers); *Greatest*—252,711 miles (406,699 kilometers); *Mean*—238,857 miles (384,403 kilometers).

Diameter: About 2,160 miles (3,476 kilometers).

Circumference: About 6,790 miles (10,927 kilometers).

Surface Area: About 14,650,000 square miles (37,943,000 square kilometers).

Rotation Period: 27 days, 7 hours, 43 minutes.

Revolution Period Around the Earth: 29 days, 12 hours, 44 minutes.

Average Speed Around the Earth: 2,300 miles (3,700 kilometers) per hour.

Length of Day and Night: About 14 earth-days each.

Temperature at Equator: *Sun at zenith over maria*, 260° F. (127° C); *Lunar night on maria*, −280° F. (−173° C).

Surface Gravity: About $\frac{1}{6}$ that of the earth.

Escape Velocity: 1½ miles (2.4 kilometers) per second.

Mass: $\frac{1}{81}$ that of the earth.

Volume: $\frac{1}{50}$ that of the earth.

Atmosphere: Little or none.

WORLD BOOK diagram

The Diameter of the Moon is 2,160 miles (3,476 kilometers), or about a fourth of the earth's diameter. If the moon were placed on top of the United States, it would extend almost from San Francisco to Cleveland.

646a

The Moon's Surface. When seen with the unaided eye from the earth, the moon looks like a smooth globe with dark and light patches of gray. Field glasses or a small telescope will bring into view the features first seen by Galileo, the Italian scientist of the 1600's.

The dark patches on the moon are broad, flat plains that Galileo may have thought were covered with water. He called them *maria* (singular, *mare*), a Latin word meaning *seas*. Today, we know the maria are lowlands of rock covered by a thin layer of rocky soil. Most of the light gray parts of the moon's surface are rough and mountainous. These areas are called *highlands*. The maria occur mainly on the near side of the moon, which faces the earth. The far side is nearly all highlands.

Most of the maria were formed from 3.3 to 3.8 billion years ago by great flows of *lava* (molten rock) that poured out and cooled on the moon's surface. The lava that formed the maria has filled in the low places on the moon. Some of the low places are giant craters. The lava filling these craters forms round maria.

Craters are the most numerous features of the moon's surface. The moon has craters within craters and even connected craters. Scientists estimate that the moon has half a million craters that are more than 1 mile (1.6 kilometers) wide. A total of about 30 thousand billion craters are at least 1 foot (30 centimeters) wide.

Most of the small craters are simple bowl-shaped pits with low rims. Most craters from 5 to 10 miles (8 to 16 kilometers) wide have high walls and level floors. Many craters wider than 15 miles (24 kilometers) have hilly floors or central peaks. Large craters are rimmed by mountains and have steep, terraced walls. The largest crater, the Imbrium Basin in the Sea of Rains, is about 700 miles (1,100 kilometers) wide. Its floor is covered by dark lava, which forms one eye of the familiar "man in the moon."

Certain craters on the moon are called *ray craters*. These craters are surrounded by light gray streaks known as *rays*. The rays look like splashes of bright material and extend out in many directions. Around Tycho, a crater 54 miles (87 kilometers) wide, a few rays are 10 to 15 miles (16 to 24 kilometers) wide and can be traced for nearly 1,000 miles (1,600 kilometers). Swarms of small *secondary craters* in the rays probably were formed by the impact of rocks thrown out of the ray craters. The rays probably are mixtures of broken rocks thrown from the ray craters and other rock fragments splashed out of the secondary craters. Scientists know that the ray craters were formed late in the history of the moon because their rays cross over maria, mountains, and other craters.

Billions of small craters on the moon have been formed by the bombardment of *meteoroids*, solid objects that travel through space. Many meteoroids also hit the earth's atmosphere each year. Most of them are melted or broken up high in the air, producing streaks of light called *meteors*. Only the largest meteoroids reach the earth's surface fast enough to dig a crater. The moon's lack of atmosphere means that even tiny meteoroids form craters. Erosion on the moon works so slowly that craters only 1 foot (30 centimeters) in diameter remain for millions of years.

NASA

Schmidt Crater, on the western edge of the Sea of Tranquility, is 7 miles (11 kilometers) wide. The moon has billions of craters. The largest is about 700 miles (1,100 kilometers) wide.

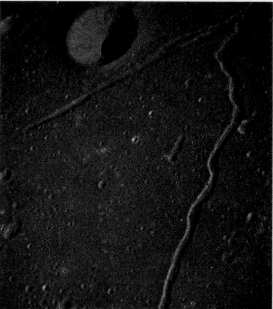

NASA

A Winding Rille, *right,* is one of several long, narrow valleys on the moon that probably were caused by flowing lava. Maskelyne G Crater, *top,* is about 4 miles (6 kilometers) wide.

Many large craters on the moon probably were formed when *comets* or *asteroids* hit the moon. These bodies also travel around the sun, but they are much larger than meteoroids. The moon's largest and oldest craters may have been created by the impact of *planetesimals*, solid objects that perhaps crashed together and formed the moon itself.

A few craters on the moon look like volcanic craters on the earth. Some of these craters are found on the tops of small mountains or in the centers of low, rounded hills. In other places, craters are lined up in a row just as volcanoes on the earth commonly are lined up. Many of the lunar craters that resemble volcanoes are found on the lava plains.

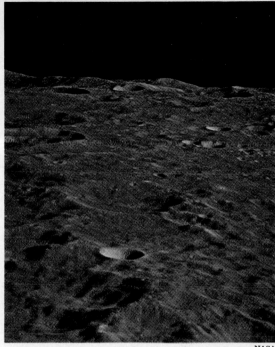

NASA

NASA

Rays of Bright Material spread from some craters across the moon's surface. This ray crater on the far side of the moon was photographed by the Apollo 13 astronauts.

The Surface of the Moon's Far Side has more craters and mountains than that of the side that always faces the earth. The far side has fewer "seas," and its craters appear smooth and worn.

NASA

NASA

NASA

A Basalt Rock returned by the Apollo 11 astronauts resembles lava rock from volcanoes on the earth. The holes were caused by gases escaping from the molten rock.

A Breccia Rock from the Apollo 12 mission consists of soil and rock pieces squeezed together. This sample is about 3½ centimeters, or 1⅜ inches, wide.

The Most Unusual Moon Rock is this lemon-sized Apollo 12 sample. It has high radioactivity and may be older than the lava flows that form the maria.

The mountainous areas of the moon are scattered with huge craters. All the major mountain ranges of the moon appear to be the broken rims of these huge craters. The rugged Apennine Mountains, near the Sea of Rains, rise about 20,000 feet (6,100 meters). The Leibnitz Mountains, near the moon's south pole, are at least 26,000 feet (7,920 meters) high. They are about as tall as the highest mountains on the earth.

The moon also has long, narrow valleys called *rilles*. Most rilles are straight and probably were formed when the moon's outer crust was cracked, and sections of the surface dropped down. *Sinuous rilles* are winding channels that look much like dry riverbeds. They probably were formed by the flow of lava on the maria.

What the Moon Is Made Of. Scientists have learned much about the composition of the moon by studying rocks and soil brought back by U.S. astronauts. But many questions will remain unanswered until samples can be taken from a number of places on the moon.

Moon soil collected by the first Apollo astronauts was dark gray to brownish gray in color. It consisted of tiny pieces of ground-up rock, bits of glass, and scattered chunks of rock. The soil was formed by repeated grinding and churning of the moon's surface as meteoroids hit it and craters were formed. Soil on the maria generally is from 5 to 20 feet (1.5 to 6 meters) deep. About half of it consists of bits of glass. A microscope shows that some soil grains are glass balls.

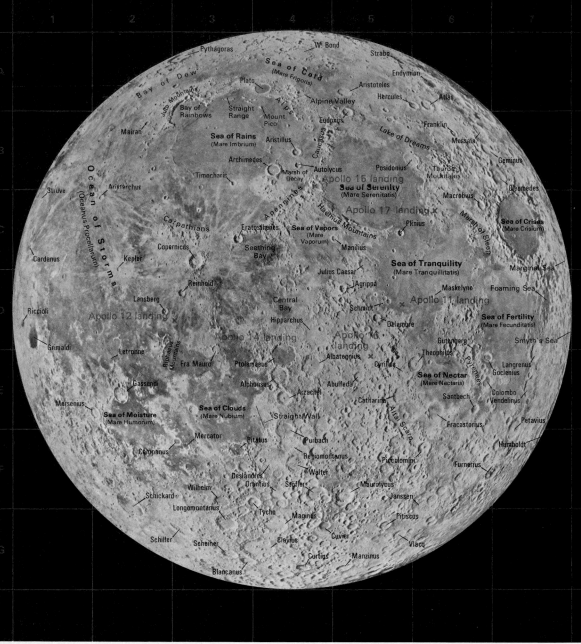

WORLD BOOK map based on U.S. Air Force photographic mosaic

Moon—Near Side

— Map Index —

Abulfeda, crater ....E 5
Agrippa, crater .....D 5
Aitken, crater ......E 11
Albategnius, crater .E 5
Alphonsus, crater ..E 3
Alpine Valley ......A 4
Alps, mountain
  range ....A 4
Altai Scarp,
  escarpment .....E 5
Anderson, crater ..C 11
Antoniadi, crater ..G 11
Apennines, mountain
  range ....C 4
Apollo, crater .....F 12
Apollo 11 landing ..D 5
Apollo 12 landing ..D 2
Apollo 14 landing ..D 3
Apollo 15 landing ..B 4
Apollo 16 landing ..E 5
Apollo 17 landing ..C 6
Archimedes, crater .B 3
Aristarchus, crater .B 2

Aristillus, crater ...B 4
Aristoteles, crater ..A 5
Arzachel, crater ....E 4
Atlas, crater ....A 6
Autolycus, crater ..B 4
Bay of Dew,
  lowland ....A 2
Bay of Rainbows,
  lowland ....A 3
Birkhoff, crater ...A 12
Blancanus, crater ..G 3
Boltzmann, crater .G 13
Campanus, crater ..F 2
Campbell, crater ..A 10
Cardanus, crater ..C 1
Carpathians,
  mountain range ..C 3
Catharina, crater ..E 5
Caucasus, mountain
  range ....B 4
Central Bay,
  lowland ....D 4
Chaplygin, crater ..D 9
Charlier, crater ..B 13
Chebyshev, crater .F 13
Clavius, crater ....G 4

Cleomedes, crater ..B 7
Cockcroft, crater ..B 12
Colombo, crater ....E 6
Compton, crater ....A 9
Copernicus, crater ..C 2
Cordilleras,
  mountain range ..E 14
Curtius, crater ....G 4
Cuvier, crater .....G 5
Cyrillus, crater ....E 5
Daedalus, crater ...D 11
Dante, crater .....C 11
Delambre, crater ..D 5
Deslandres, crater ..F 3
Doppler, crater ....E 12
Eastern Sea (Mare
  Orientale), low-
  land ....E 14
Endymion, crater ..A 5
Eratosthenes, crater C 3
Eudoxus, crater ...B 5
Fabry, crater ......B 9
Fermi, crater .....E 8
Fersman, crater ..C 14
Fitzgerald, crater ..B 12

Fleming, crater ....C 8
Foaming Sea,
  lowland ....D 7
Fowler, crater ....A 12
Fracastorius, crater E 6
Fra Mauro, crater .E 3
Franklin, crater ...B 6
Freundlich, crater .C 10
Furnerius, crater ..F 6
Gagarin, crater ....E 9
Galois, crater ....E 13
Gassendi, crater ...E 2
Geminus, crater ...B 7
Goclenius, crater ..E 7
Grimaldi, crater ...D 1
Gutenberg, crater ..D 6
Guyot, crater .....C 8
Haemus Mountains .C 5
Heaviside, crater ..E 10
Hercules, crater ...A 5
Hertzsprung, crater B 14
H. G. Wells, crater .B 9
Hilbert, crater ....E 8
Hipparchus, crater .D 4
Humboldt, crater ..F 7
Icarus, crater ....D 11

Janssen, crater .....F 5
Joule, crater ......B 13
Jules Verne, crater .F 9
Julius Caesar,
  crater ....C 5
Jura Mountains ...A 3
Kepler, crater ....E 10
Kekulé, crater ....C 13
Kepler, crater ....C 2
Korolev, crater ...D 12
Kovalevskaya,
  crater ....B 13
Lake of Dreams,
  lowland ....B 5
Landau, crater ...B 13
Langrenus, crater .E 7
Lansberg, crater ..D 2
Larmor, crater ...B 11
Letronne, crater ...E 2
Levi-Civita, crater .F 9
Leibnitz, crater ...F 11
Longomontanus,
  crater ....G 3
Mach, crater .....C 13
Macrobius, crater .C 6
Maginus, crater ...G 4

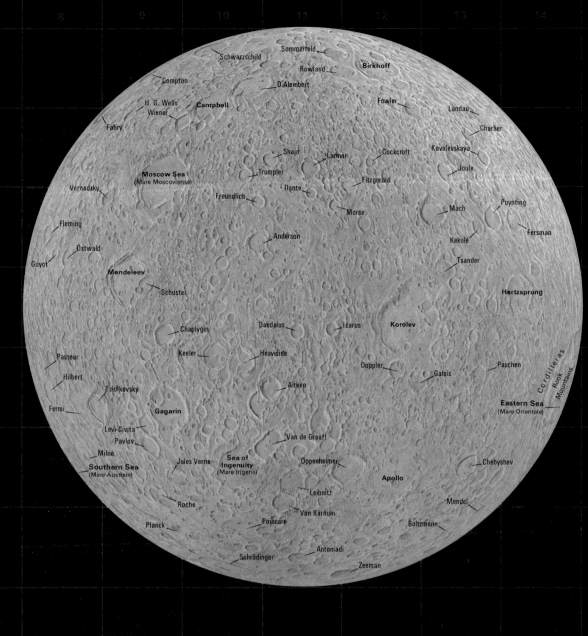

Moon—Far Side

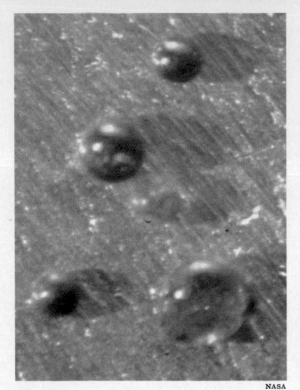

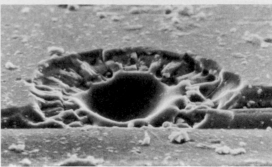

Microcraters on Some Moon Samples can be seen only with a microscope. This crater, magnified 1,700 times, was formed by the high-speed impact of cosmic dust on broken glass particles.

California Institute of Technology

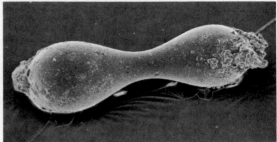

California Institute of Technology

Tiny Colored Glass Balls are found in much lunar soil. The spherules shown above are about the size of a period. These samples were brought back by the Apollo 11 astronauts.

NASA

A Dumbbell-Shaped Blob is one of the glassy objects that are found in the moon's soil. Such objects probably were formed when meteorites struck the moon, splattering molten droplets.

Nothing grows or lives in moon soil. The soil contains no plant or animal fossils. But some earth plants grow better when the soil is sprinkled with dust from the moon. Scientists are not yet sure why.

Moon rocks consist chiefly of minerals containing aluminum, calcium, iron, magnesium, oxygen, silicon, and titanium. Hydrogen, helium, and other gases are trapped in some of the rocks. Scientists believe some of these gases reached the moon as part of the *solar wind*, electrified gas that constantly streams from the sun. No new elements have been discovered in the moon samples. Scientists have found a few minerals not known to occur naturally on the earth, but these belong to well-known mineral families.

Two main types of rock have been collected by the astronauts. One type is *basalt*, a hardened lava and the most common volcanic rock on the earth. The lava rocks are mainly crystals of feldspar, pyroxene, and ilmenite. These minerals were formed at about 2200° F. (1200° C). They prove that part of the moon was extremely hot when the maria were formed. The second type of rock, called *breccia*, is made of soil and pieces of rock squeezed together when hit by falling objects.

The moon's outer crust seems stiff and strong, but much remains to be learned about its interior. On the Apollo 13 flight, mission controllers sent part of the giant Saturn rocket crashing into the moon. The resulting *seismic* (earthquakelike) vibrations lasted about four hours. These long-lasting vibrations had not been expected by scientists.

Gravity. Astronauts walk easily on the moon, even though they wear heavy equipment. They feel light because the force of gravity on the moon's surface is six times weaker than that on the surface of the earth. A boy or girl who weighs 60 pounds on the earth would weigh only 10 pounds on the moon. Gravity is weaker on the moon because the moon's *mass* (the amount of matter a body contains) is about 81 times smaller than the earth's mass. In 1968, scientists found that the force of gravity differs slightly from place to place on the moon. They believe the slight difference is caused by large concentrations of mass in many of the round maria. Scientists have used the term *mascons* to describe these areas, but the cause of mascons is not yet known.

Atmosphere and Weather. The moon has little or no atmosphere. If the moon ever did have a surrounding layer of gases, it would have leaked away into space because of the moon's weak gravity. The moon has no weather, no clouds, no rain, and no wind. There is no water on its surface. Astronauts on the moon must carry air with them to breathe. They must talk to each other by radio because there is no air to carry sound.

Temperature. The surface of the moon gets much hotter and colder than any place on the earth. At the moon's equator, noon temperatures on the maria are as high as 260° F. (127° C). Temperatures drop below −280° F. (−173° C) during the two-week lunar night. In some deep craters near the moon's poles, the temperature is always near −400° F. (−240° C). Space suits protect astronauts from the heat and cold.

646f

The Orbit of the Moon. Every $29\frac{1}{2}$ days, the moon makes a trip around the earth. It follows an *elliptical* (oval shaped) path called an *orbit*. One such trip around the earth is called a *revolution*. The moon moves at an average speed of about 2,300 miles (3,700 kilometers) per hour along its 1.4-million-mile (2.3-million-kilometer) orbit. The moon also travels with the earth as the earth circles the sun every $365\frac{1}{4}$ days, an earth year. The moon actually moves from west to east in the sky. But it seems to move from east to west as it rises and sets because the earth spins much faster than the moon revolves around the earth.

Because the moon's orbit is oval, the moon is not always the same distance from the earth. The point where the moon comes closest to the earth is 221,456 miles (356,399 kilometers) away. This point is called the moon's *perigee*. The moon's farthest point from the earth is 252,711 miles (406,699 kilometers) away. This point is the moon's *apogee*.

The gravitational pull of the earth keeps the moon in its orbit. If it were not for gravitational force, the moon would fly off into space. The natural tendency of any body is to travel in a straight line unless it is forced away from that line. For example, a ball on a string can be swung in a circle as long as the string does not break. If the string breaks, the ball simply flies off its circular

path in the direction it was moving when the string broke. The moon, unlike a ball on a string, moves in an elliptical orbit and its velocity and distance vary slightly from place to place along its orbit in a recurrent pattern. In this respect, the moon's motion is more like that of a ball on a long rubber band than of a ball on a string.

Scientists measure the moon's revolution around the earth in *synodic months* and *sidereal months*. A synodic month—about $29\frac{1}{2}$ days—is the period from one new moon to the next. It is the time the moon takes to revolve around the earth in relation to the sun. If the moon started on its orbit from a spot exactly between the earth and the sun, it would return to almost the same place in about $29\frac{1}{2}$ days. A synodic month equals a full day on the moon. This *lunar day* is divided into about two weeks of light and two weeks of darkness.

A sidereal month—about $27\frac{1}{3}$ days—is the time the moon takes to make one trip around the earth in relation to the stars. If the moon's revolution were to begin on a line with a certain star, it would return to the same position about $27\frac{1}{3}$ days later.

Rotation. The moon rotates completely on its *axis* (an imaginary line through its north and south poles) only once during each trip around the earth. The moon rotates from west to east, the same direction that it

HOW THE MOON GETS ITS LIGHT

The moon gives off no light of its own. It shines by reflecting sunlight. Like the earth, half of the moon is always lighted by the sun's direct rays, and the other half is always in shadow. At times during the month, only a small slice of the moon's side that faces the earth is in full sunshine. The moon appears as a thin, bright *crescent*. *Earthshine* (sunlight reflected by the earth), dimly lights the moon's "dark" side when it faces the earth. Because the moon is made up chiefly of dark gray rocks and dust, it reflects only 10 per cent of the light it receives.

WORLD BOOK diagram

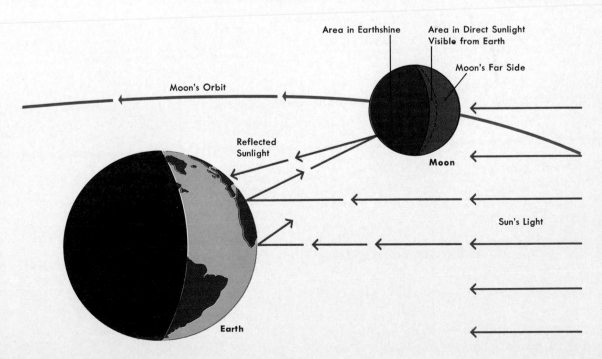

Area in Earthshine

Area in Direct Sunlight Visible from Earth

Moon's Far Side

Moon's Orbit

Reflected Sunlight

Moon

Sun's Light

Earth

travels around the earth. At its equator, the moon rotates at a speed of about 10 miles (16 kilometers) per hour. When you look up at the moon, you always see the same side. The moon is held in this position by gravitational forces. We know that the moon is rotating because we can see only one side of it. If the moon did not rotate, we would be able to see its entire surface.

Sometimes we can see a short distance around the *limb* (edge) of the moon. The moon seems to swing from side to side and nod up and down during each revolution. These apparent motions are called *librations*. They are caused by slight changes in the moon's speed of revolution and by a five-degree tilt of the moon's orbit to the orbit of the earth. At different times, the librations enable us to see a total of 59 per cent of the moon's surface from the earth. The other 41 per cent can never be seen from the earth. The moon's far side was a complete mystery until Oct. 7, 1959, when a Russian rocket orbited the moon and sent back a few pictures of one far side area to the earth. On Dec. 24, 1968, the Apollo 8 astronauts became the first men to see the far side.

The Phases of the Moon. During a synodic month, we can see the moon "change" from a slim crescent to a full circle and back again. These apparent changes in the moon's shape and size are actually different con-

ditions of lighting called *phases*. They are caused by changes in the amount of sunlight reflected by the moon toward the earth. The moon seems to change shape because we see different parts of its sunlit surface as it orbits the earth. Like the earth, half the moon is always lighted by the sun's rays except during eclipses. Sometimes the far side of the moon is in full sunlight even though it is out of view.

When the moon is between the sun and the earth, its sunlit side—the far side—is turned away from the earth. Astronomers call this darkened phase of the moon a *new moon*. In this phase, the side of the moon facing the earth is dimly lighted by *earthshine*, which is sunlight reflected from the earth to the moon.

A day after a new moon, a thin slice of light appears along the moon's eastern edge. The line between the sunlit part of the moon's face and its dark part is called the *terminator*. Each day, more and more of the moon's sunlit side is seen as the terminator moves from east to west. After about seven days, we can see half of a full moon. This half-circle shape is half of the moon's side that is exposed to sunlight and is the part that can be seen from the earth. This phase is called the *first quarter*. About seven days later, the moon has moved to a point where the earth is between the moon and the sun. We

WHY THE MOON HAS PHASES

The moon seems to change shape from day to day as it goes through *phases*. The moon changes from *new moon* to *full moon* and back again every 29½ days. The phases are caused by the moon's orbit around the earth as the earth and moon travel around the sun. Half of the moon is always in sunlight, but varying amounts of the lighted side are visible from the earth. As the moon and earth move along their orbits, more of the sunlit part is seen until it shines as a full moon. Then less and less of the sunlit part is seen until the dark new moon returns.

WORLD BOOK diagram

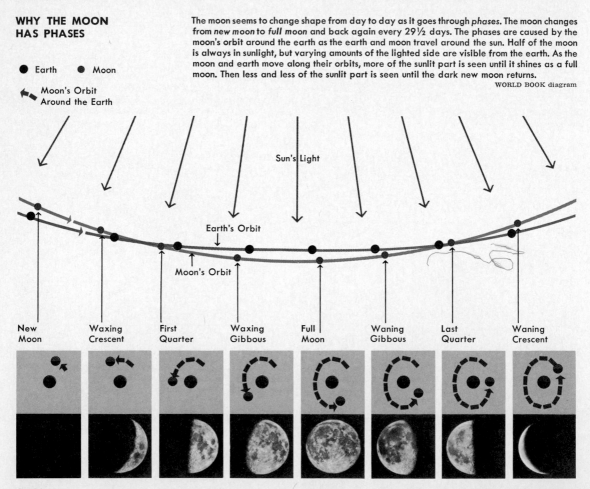

646h

can now see the entire sunlit side. This phase is called *full moon.* A full moon seems bright on a clear night. But a whole sky of full moons would be only about a fifth as bright as the sun.

About seven days after full moon, we again see half of a full moon. This phase is called the *last quarter,* or the third quarter. After another week, the moon returns to a point between the earth and the sun for the new moon phase. As the moon changes from new moon to full moon, it is said to be *waxing.* During the period from full moon back to new moon, the moon is *waning.* When the moon appears smaller than half of a full moon, it is called *crescent.* When the moon looks larger than half of a full moon, yet is not a full moon, it is called *gibbous.*

The moon rises and sets at different times. In the new moon phase, it rises above the horizon with the sun in the east and travels close to the sun across the sky. With each passing day, the moon rises an average of about 50 minutes later and drops about 12 degrees farther behind in relation to the sun. By the end of a week—at the first quarter phase—the moon rises at about noon and sets at about midnight. In another week—at full moon—it rises as the sun sets and sets as the sun rises. At last quarter, it rises at about midnight

and sets at about noon. A week later—back at new moon—the moon and the sun rise together in the east.

Eclipses. The earth and the moon both throw shadows into space. When a full moon passes through the earth's shadow, we see an *eclipse* of the moon. During a lunar eclipse, the moon is a dark reddish color. It is faintly lighted by red rays from the sun that have been *refracted* (bent) by the earth's atmosphere. During another kind of eclipse, the new moon passes directly between the earth and the sun. When part or all of the sun is hidden by the moon, we see a *solar eclipse* (an eclipse of the sun). Solar eclipses occur where the shadow of the moon passes across the earth. See ECLIPSE.

The Moon and Tides. Since ancient times, man has watched the rising and falling of the water level along the seashore. Just as the earth's gravity pulls on the moon, the moon's gravity pulls on the earth and its large bodies of water. The moon's gravity pulls up the water directly below the moon. On the other side of the earth, the moon pulls the solid body of the earth away from the water. As a result, two bulges called *high tides* are formed on the oceans and seas. As the earth turns, these tidal bulges travel from east to west. Every place along the seashore has two high tides and two low tides daily. See TIDE.

WHY WE SEE ONLY ONE SIDE OF THE MOON

When we look at the moon, we always see the same side. This is because the moon turns once on its axis in the same time that it circles the earth. Astronomers call the moon's motion *synchronous* rotation. The force of gravity always keeps the same side of the moon toward the earth. This diagram shows why one side of the moon can never be seen from the earth. As the moon turns, a moon landmark such as a crater, shown as a red dot, stays in about the same position during the month. Sometimes the landmark is hidden in the dark part of the moon facing the earth. But because it does not move to the side of the moon opposite the earth, we know that we are seeing only one side of the moon. If the moon did not turn in its journey around the earth, the landmark would gradually seem to move across the visible surface of the moon. It would disappear around the moon's western edge and return to view on the moon's eastern edge about 14 days later.

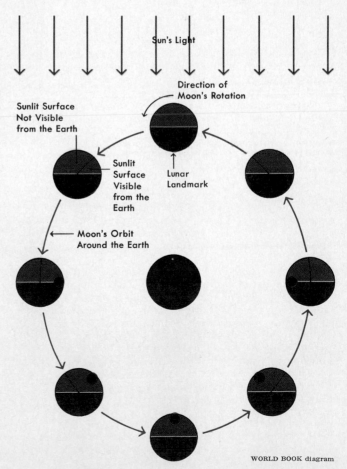

Sun's Light

Direction of Moon's Rotation

Sunlit Surface Not Visible from the Earth

Sunlit Surface Visible from the Earth

Lunar Landmark

← Moon's Orbit Around the Earth

WORLD BOOK diagram

Age and History. Scientists have learned that the moon is about 4.6 billion years old by studying lunar samples brought back by the Apollo astronauts. The moon's age is determined by measuring the amounts of radioactive atoms of certain elements in the lunar soil. Each of the radioactive atoms *decays* (changes into another element) at a known rate. How long this decay has been occurring can be figured by comparing the amount of radioactive atoms of an element with the amount of the atoms of the elements into which it has decayed. The earth and meteorites that have fallen on the earth are also about 4.6 billion years old. On the basis of this evidence, scientists believe that the entire solar system was formed at about that same time.

Most of the large craters in the highlands of the moon were formed when many large solid bodies from space struck the moon. Scientists believe this bombardment took place between 3.9 and 4.6 billion years ago. Also during this period, other solid bodies probably struck the earth and other planets. As time went on, fewer bodies were left in space and the number that struck the moon gradually decreased.

The maria formed when lava flowed out on the lunar surface between 3.3 and 3.8 billion years ago. The maria are smoother than the highlands because the lava covered the old craters on the lowlands.

Scientific Theories have been developed to explain how the moon was formed. But more scientific exploration is needed before the mystery can be solved.

The moon was once much closer to the earth than it is now. Early in its history, it may have been only about 10,000 miles (16,000 kilometers) from the earth. The earth also may have been spinning 10 times faster than it does today. The moon's orbit is still becoming larger as the earth spins more slowly. These changes are caused by friction from the tides, which slows the earth's rotation and forces the moon into a larger orbit.

In 1879, George H. Darwin, an English mathematician, suggested that the earth and the moon were once a single body. Shortly after the earth was formed, according to his theory, a huge bulge was produced on the earth by the attraction of the sun. The earth was spinning much more rapidly than it is today, and the bulge eventually broke away from the earth. Other scientists have pointed out that the material of the bulge probably would have become extremely hot and may have broken up into many pieces. Later, the pieces may have fallen together again to form the moon.

A second theory states that the moon was formed as a separate planet that followed its own orbit around the sun. Every few years, the moon came close to the earth because their orbits were similar. During one of these close passes, the moon was captured in the earth's gravitational field.

A third theory is that the earth and moon were formed close to each other from a disk of gas and dust around the sun. They were formed as a double-planet system, much like the systems of double stars that are common in our galaxy. The large craters created early in the moon's history may have been formed by the impact of smaller moons that were circling the earth, or by planetesimals that were orbiting the sun.

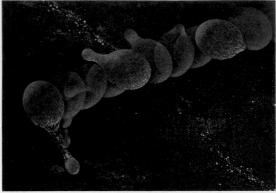

WORLD BOOK diagrams by Herbert Herrick

The "Escape" Theory of the moon's origin says that the earth and the moon were once a single body. The sun's gravity caused a bulge on one side of the fast-spinning earth. A lopsided dumbbell formed, and the small end broke away and became the moon.

The "Capture" Theory of the moon's formation says that the moon was once a planet that traveled around the sun. At some point along its orbit, the moon was captured by the earth's gravity and became a satellite of the earth.

A Third Moon Formation Theory says that the moon was formed at about the same time as the earth and in the same region of space. The two bodies were made from huge whirlpools of gas and dust that were left over when the sun was formed.

Measuring Time. Since ancient times, people have measured time by the phases of the moon. The American Indians recorded that a harvest or a hunt took place a certain number of "moons" ago. People in Muslim countries still use a calendar with 354 days, or 12 synodic lunar months. Jews use the lunar calendar to establish the dates of religious holidays. Christians observe Easter on a date that varies each year because it is related to the full moon. The words *month* and *Monday* come from Old English words related to *moon*.

Mythology. Early peoples thought the moon was a powerful god or goddess. The ancient Romans called their moon goddess Diana. She was the goddess of the hunt and the guardian of wild beasts and fertile fields. She used a moon crescent for a bow and moonbeams for arrows. The moon goddess of the ancient Greeks was Selene, and the early Egyptians honored the moon god Khonsu. The Babylonians knew the moon as Sin, sometimes called Nannar, the most powerful of the sky gods. Some American Indian tribes believed that the moon and the sun were brother and sister gods, with the moon being much more important than the sun. Today, some primitive peoples still worship the moon.

Legend and Folklore. Many peoples who did not think of the moon as sacred believed that it influenced all life on the earth. Early philosophers and priests taught that the moon was related to birth, growth, and death because it waxed and waned. Some people feared eclipses as signs of famine, war, or other disasters. According to one superstition, sleeping in moonlight could make a person insane. The word *lunatic*, which means *moonstruck*, comes from *luna*, a Latin word meaning *moon*. Even today, many people believe that the moon is related to changes in the weather. Others think that seeds grow especially well when planted during a waxing moon. The moon has an important place in *astrology*, a popular *pseudo* (false) science.

Legends of various lands told how the "man in the moon" had been imprisoned there for stealing or for breaking the Sabbath. Some people saw other figures in the moon's markings—Jack and Jill, a beautiful woman, or a cat, donkey, frog, or rabbit.

Many people once believed that some form of life existed on the moon. The ancient Greek writer Plutarch told of moon demons that lived in caves. Johannes Kepler, a German astronomer of the 1600's,

An Early Moon Map was drawn in 1645 by Johann Hevelius, a city official of Gdańsk, Poland. Hevelius, an amateur astronomer, charted about 250 lunar formations with a telescope.

Illustration by Johann Hevelius from *Selenographia*, Gdańsk, 1647. Courtesy the John Crerar Library, Chicago

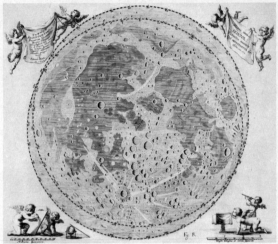

MILESTONES IN MOON STUDY

c. 2200 B.C. The Mesopotamians recorded lunar eclipses.

500's B.C. The Chaldeans predicted the dates of eclipses.

c. 459 B.C. Anaxagoras, a Greek philosopher, noted that the moon's light came from the sun and explained eclipses.

c. 335 B.C. Aristotle, a Greek philosopher, used lunar eclipses to prove that the earth was ball-shaped.

c. 280 B.C. Aristarchus, a Greek astronomer, found a way to measure the moon's distance from the earth.

c. 150 B.C. Hipparchus, a Greek astronomer, measured the period of the moon's revolution around the earth.

c. 74 B.C. Posidonius, a philosopher born in Syria, explained the effect of the moon and the sun on the earth's tides.

A.D. c. 150 Ptolemy, an astronomer in Egypt, discovered the irregularity of the moon's motion in its orbit. His largely incorrect writings became the chief astronomical authority for 14 centuries.

1543 Nicolaus Copernicus, a Polish astronomer, published a book reviving the idea that the earth was a moving planet. Present-day astronomy is based on his work.

c. 1588-1598 Tycho Brahe, a Danish astronomer, made observations leading to theories about the moon's motion.

c. 1600-1609 Johannes Kepler, a German astronomer, discovered the oval shaped orbits of the planets.

1609-1610 Galileo, an Italian scientist, made the first practical use of the telescope to study the moon.

c. 1645 Johann Hevelius, a Polish pioneer of moon mapping, charted more than 250 moon formations.

1687 Sir Isaac Newton explained the basis for the moon's motion and its tidal effect on the earth.

c. 1828 F. P. Gruithuisen, a German astronomer, suggested meteoroids as a cause of some lunar craters.

1850's William C. Bond and J. A. Whipple, of Harvard Observatory, took photographs of lunar features.

1920's Bernard Lyot, a French astronomer, concluded that a layer of dust covered the moon's surface.

1930 The American astronomers Edison Pettit and S. B. Nicholson obtained the first reliable lunar temperatures.

1946 The U.S. Army Signal Corps bounced radio waves from the moon's surface.

1959 Russia launched *Luna 2*, the first spaceship to hit the moon. Russia's *Luna 3* sent the first pictures of the moon's far side back to the earth.

1964-1965 U.S. spacecraft *Rangers VII, VIII,* and *IX* took the first close-up television pictures of the moon.

1966 Russia's *Luna 9* became the first spacecraft to make a soft landing on the moon.

1968 The Apollo 8 astronauts flew 10 orbits around the moon.

1969 The Apollo 11 and Apollo 12 astronauts landed on the moon. They collected samples, took photographs, set up scientific experiments, and explored the nearby area.

1970 Russia's *Luna 16* became the first unmanned spacecraft to return soil samples from the moon.

An Apollo 16 Astronaut Explores the Moon's Surface. Astronaut John W. Young collects moon rocks near the rim of a lunar crater. Young and astronaut Charles M. Duke, Jr., traveled to the crater from their landing site in a lunar rover, *background.*

wrote that lunar craters were built by moon creatures. In 1822, F. P. Gruithuisen, another German astronomer, told of discovering a "lunar city." In the 1920's, the American astronomer W. H. Pickering declared that swarms of insects might live on the moon. Many scientists hoped that certain chemicals might be found on the moon to give clues as to how life began on the earth.

Literature and Music. Many authors and poets have written about the moon and have described its beauty. In *A Midsummer Night's Dream*, the famous English playwright William Shakespeare compared the moon to "a silver bow new-bent in heaven." In "The Cloud," the English poet Percy Bysshe Shelley described the moon as "that orbèd maiden, with white fire laden, whom mortals call the moon. . . ."

Other writers have told of imaginary space flights to the moon. During the A.D. 100's, the Greek writer Lucian described a hero who was lifted to the moon after his ship got caught in a waterspout. In 1638, Francis Godwin, an English bishop, wrote a story about a man who flew to the moon in a raft pulled by trained swans. Later in the 1600's, the French author Cyrano de Bergerac wrote of a moon ship that used a form of rocket propulsion. The French novelist Jules Verne blasted his characters to the moon from a cannon 900 feet (270 meters) long in *From the Earth to the Moon*, published in 1865. In *The First Men in the Moon* (1901), the English writer H. G. Wells described an antigravity substance that sent travelers to the moon.

The moon has also been a favorite topic of musicians. One of the 14 piano sonatas written by Ludwig van Beethoven, the famous German composer, came to be known as the *Moonlight Sonata. Clair de lune*, meaning *moonlight*, is the title of musical works by at least three French composers, including Claude Debussy. Popular songs have included "Moonlight Bay," "Moonlight and Roses," "By the Light of the Silvery Moon," and "Moon River."

Moon Study. Some ancient peoples believed that the moon was a rotating bowl of fire. Others thought it was a mirror that reflected the earth's land and seas. In spite of such beliefs, early astronomers worked out many correct ideas about the moon's size, shape,

A Lunar Rover was first used on the moon by Apollo 15 astronauts in July, 1971. It carried James B. Irwin, *above,* and David R. Scott over 17 miles (27 kilometers) on the moon.

motion, and distance from the earth. In 1609, Galileo used a crude telescope for the first scientific study of the moon's surface.

Man's knowledge about the moon increased as *selenographers* (scientists who study moon geography) drew improved maps of the lunar surface. With the development of cameras and photography in the mid-1800's, the moon could be photographed in detail.

The space age, which began in 1957, opened a new chapter in man's study of the moon. On Sept. 12, 1959, Russia launched *Luna 2*, the first man-made object to reach the moon. Since that time, Russia and the United States have launched about 30 unmanned spacecraft that either landed on the moon or passed close enough to send back useful information. From 1966 to 1968, the United States landed five Surveyor spacecraft on the moon. These lunar probes took almost 90,000 detailed photographs and also sent back information on the moon's composition. During the same period, the United States launched five Lunar Orbiters that photographed 98 per cent of the moon's surface. These spacecraft paved the way to a manned landing by showing that the moon's surface would hold the weight of a spacecraft and by locating suitable landing sites. On July 20, 1969, Apollo 11 landed on the moon. Man's firsthand exploration and study of the moon had begun. In July, 1971, the Apollo 15 astronauts were the first to travel across the moon's surface in a powered vehicle called a *lunar rover*.

In December, 1972, Apollo 17 astronauts made the sixth and last manned landing in the Apollo program. In this program, a total of 12 men set foot on the moon. These astronauts explored lunar highlands, maria, craters, and rilles. They took thousands of photographs of the lunar landscape. Apollo astronauts gathered many samples of moon rocks and soil and provided scientists with enough material for years of study. The astronauts also set up various scientific experiments. For example, Apollo 17 astronauts placed instruments into holes they drilled into the moon's surface. These instruments measured the amount of heat escaping from the moon. Such measurements help scientists learn about the moon's early history.

Man's Future on the Moon. For years to come, scientific exploration will be man's main reason for traveling to the moon. Someday, a scientific base may be built there. For short periods, teams of astronaut-scientists could explore the surrounding area and conduct experiments at a temporary base. Later, these stations might be enlarged into permanent moon colonies where 50 to 100 people could live and work for months or even longer. Some scientists believe moon bases should be built underground for protection against the sun's radiation, extremes of heat and cold, and meteoroids.

Perhaps scientists will one day set up telescopes on the moon. The earth's atmosphere limits the study of faraway stars and galaxies. Astronomers on the moon would have a clearer view of the universe. Looking even farther into the future, some scientists think the moon could be used as a place to launch or refuel flights into deep space. Rockets could travel from the moon to the other planets on less power than is needed to travel to the planets from the earth. However, most scientists predict that earth-orbiting space stations will be better places than the moon to place telescopes and to launch deep space missions. Lunar exploration also may be carried out by unmanned surface vehicles sent to the moon but controlled from the earth. Russia's *Lunokhod 1* was the first such vehicle to explore the lunar surface. It landed on the moon on Nov. 17, 1970.

Today, the moon is a symbol of the peaceful exploration of space. No nation owns the moon. In 1967, more than 90 nations signed a treaty governing space exploration. This treaty declares that outer space, including the moon, cannot be claimed by any country or be used for military purposes.　　　EUGENE M. SHOEMAKER

MOON/Study Aids

Outline

I. What the Moon Is Like
 A. The Moon's Surface
 B. What the Moon Is Made Of
 C. Gravity
 D. Atmosphere and Weather
 E. Temperature

II. How the Moon Moves
 A. The Orbit of the Moon
 B. Rotation
 C. The Phases of the Moon
 D. Eclipses
 E. The Moon and Tides

III. How the Moon Was Formed
 A. Age and History　　B. Scientific Theories

IV. The Moon in History
 A. Measuring Time
 B. Mythology
 C. Legend and Folklore
 D. Literature and Music
 E. Moon Study
 F. Man's Future on the Moon

Questions

What causes the phases of the moon?

Why does an astronaut on the moon's surface weigh only $\frac{1}{6}$ of the amount he weighs on earth?

What are three theories of how the moon was formed?

What are *maria*? How were they probably formed?

Why does the same side of the moon always face the earth?

How much of the moon's surface can be seen from the earth?

What is a *synodic month*? A *sidereal month*?

When did the first man-made object reach the moon?

What makes the moon "shine"?

What is the moon's mean distance from the earth? What is meant by the moon's *perigee* and *apogee*?

Reading and Study Guide

See *Moon* in the RESEARCH GUIDE/INDEX, Volume 22, for a *Reading and Study Guide*.

MOON, MOUNTAINS OF THE. See RUWENZORI RANGE.

MOONEY, EDWARD CARDINAL (1882-1958), was named Roman Catholic Archbishop of Detroit in 1937. Pope Pius XII appointed him a cardinal in 1946. Cardinal Mooney was born in Mount Savage, Md. He studied at St. Charles College in Baltimore, St. Mary's Seminary in Cleveland, and the North American College in Rome, Italy. He served as Bishop of Rochester, N.Y., from 1933 to 1937. Cardinal Mooney's services on the executive board of the National Welfare Conference won him the unofficial title, "The dean of the American hierarchy." JOHN T. FARRELL and FULTON J. SHEEN

MOONEY, WILLIAM. See TAMMANY, SOCIETY OF.

MOONFLOWER is an attractive flower in the morning-glory family. It is a climbing vine that may grow 10 feet (3 meters) high. Its broad, heart-shaped leaves shut out sunlight and make an excellent screen for porches. The moonflower's pure white trumpet-shaped flowers may be 3 to 6 inches (8 to 15 centimeters) across. They are delicately scented, and close when exposed to strong sunlight. The moonflower grows quickly. The parts of the flower above ground die every year, but the roots remain alive. New parts grow from the roots each year.

W. Atlee Burpee
Moonflower

Scientific Classification. The moonflower is a member of the morning-glory family, *Convolvulaceae*. It is genus *Calonyction*, species *C. aculeatum*. H. D. HARRINGTON

MOONSTONE is a whitish variety of the mineral called *feldspar* (see FELDSPAR). Moonstone can be cut and used as a gem. It is a birthstone for June. Light will shine through it, but not so clearly as through glass. The stone also reflects light with a bluish to pearly-colored sheen which comes from inside the stone. Sri Lanka produces many moonstones. FREDERICK H. POUGH

See also BIRTHSTONE; GEM (color picture).

MOOR is a large area of open wasteland. A layer of peat that is usually wet covers some moors. The word is most often applied to the moors of Scotland and other parts of the British Isles, where heather grows in abundance. But there are also moors in northwest Europe and North America. Sphagnum moss grows on most moors, especially in North America. Many moors have special names. JOHN W. WEBB

See also PEAT.

MOOR. In ancient history, the Romans called the people of northwestern Africa *Mauri* and the region they lived in *Mauretania*. These peoples belonged to a larger group, the *Berbers* (see BERBERS). The Berbers became Muslims, and many of them adopted Arabic in addition to their own Berber language. They joined the Arabs in conquering Spain during the 700's. The so-called Moorish civilization of the Middle Ages was in large part Arabic. The Moors lost much of their land in Spain by the late 1200's. In 1492, Ferdinand and

Isabella of Spain drove out the last Moors. Most of the refugees settled in North Africa. Today, the term *Moor* may refer to all inhabitants of northwestern Africa who are Muslims and who speak Arabic. Or it can refer to Muslims of Spanish, Jewish, or Turkish descent who live in North Africa.

The term *Moor* in its French form *Maure* designates the nomads of the western Sahara in Africa. The term *Moor* also applies to the Arab-Sinhalese Muslims of Sri Lanka. In the form *Moro*, it refers to Muslims who live in the southern Philippines.

A common but incorrect belief that Moors are Negroes was spread by William Shakespeare's play *Othello*. Moors belong to the Mediterranean group of the Caucasoid (white) race. VERNON ROBERT DORJAHN

See also ALHAMBRA; ARAB; BOABDIL; FERDINAND V; GRANADA.

MOOR HEN. See GALLINULE.

MOORE, ANNE CARROLL. See REGINA MEDAL.

MOORE, CLEMENT CLARKE (1779-1863), an American scholar, is generally considered the author of the popular Christmas ballad "A Visit from St. Nicholas." The poem is also known by its first line, " 'Twas the Night Before Christmas." According to tradition, Moore wrote the poem in 1822 as a Christmas present for his children. It was first published anonymously in the *Troy* (N.Y.) *Sentinel* on Dec. 23, 1823. Some people have claimed that Henry Livingston, Jr., actually wrote the ballad. Livingston was a New York land surveyor who also composed poetry.

Moore was born in New York City. He was a Biblical scholar and taught Greek and Oriental literature in the Episcopal seminaries of New York City from 1821 to 1850. ROBERT J. MYERS

See also SANTA CLAUS (Appearance).

MOORE, DOUGLAS STUART (1893-1969), was an American composer, best known for his operas on American subjects. He won the 1951 Pulitzer prize for music for *Giants in the Earth*, based on Ole Rölvaag's novel about the hardships of Norwegian farmers in the Dakota Territory in the 1800's. Moore's most successful work, *The Ballad of Baby Doe* (1956), concerns a Colorado mining heiress. *The Devil and Daniel Webster*

The Surrender of Seville (1634) by Francisco Zurbarán, The Trustees of the Grosvenor Estates, London

Moors Surrendered Seville to Ferdinand III in 1248. The Moors lost much of their land in Spain by the late 1200's.

(1939) is based on Stephen Vincent Benét's short story set in New England. Moore's other compositions include the symphonic suite *Pageant of P. T. Barnum* (1926) and the symphonic poem *Moby Dick* (1928).

Moore was born in Cutchogue, N.Y. He became a professor of music at Columbia University in 1926 and was head of the Columbia music department from 1940 to 1962. He wrote *From Madrigal to Modern Music* (1942), an analysis of musical styles.   GILBERT CHASE

MOORE, GEORGE AUGUSTUS (1852-1933), was an Irish author. His novels show the influence of Honoré de Balzac's realism and Émile Zola's naturalism. *Confessions of a Young Man* (1888) is a clever portrayal of experimental painters in Paris. *Esther Waters* (1894) is a grim story of a servant girl's misfortunes. *Héloïse and Abelard* (1921), a fictional account of a famous medieval love story, ranks as Moore's fictional masterpiece. It is one of the few great imaginative reconstructions of life in the Middle Ages.

Moore was born in County Mayo. He worked to establish a native Irish drama and helped bring about the Irish Literary Revival. He described his efforts in *Hail and Farewell* (1911-1914), a memoir. *Avowals* (1919) and *Conversations in Ebury Street* (1924) are autobiographical works in the form of dialogues.   HARRY T. MOORE

MOORE, GERALD. See FISCHER-DIESKAU, DIETRICH.

MOORE, HENRY (1898-   ), is an English sculptor. His works resemble wood or stone objects that have been shaped by natural forces. Many are designed to stand permanently in natural outdoor surroundings.

Moore uses holes or openings in his work to emphasize its three-dimensional quality. The holes create a sense of mass or volume. Moore has associated the openings with the ". . . fascination of caves in hillsides and cliffs." A good example is Moore's elmwood *Reclining Figure*, which is reproduced in SCULPTURE (Looking at Sculpture).

Moore's bronze *Family Group* (1949) shows how he simplifies his human figures, treating the proportion freely. His figures are composed of flowing *convex* (curving outward) and *concave* (curving inward) forms that create rich contrasts of light and dark. A good example is his 1955 stone *Family Group*.

Moore was born into a coal-mining family in Castleford, near Leeds. He attended the Leeds School of Art and the Royal College of Art in London. As a young sculptor, he was inspired by Mexican and African carvings, and his own early work reflects the simple and monumental quality of primitive sculpture. Moore's early work aroused a mixed reaction among critics. He began to attract popular interest with his drawings of people in underground shelters during World War II. His best-known sculpture includes *King and Queen* (1953) and his *Reclining Figure* (1965) at Lincoln Center in New York City.   THEODORE E. KLITZKE

See also SCULPTURE (picture: Carving in Wood).

MOORE, SIR JOHN (1761-1809), was a British soldier. In 1808, he was sent to Spain with 10,000 men to reinforce the British position. Moore heard that Napoleon was marching with a superior force to crush him. Moore retreated, but the French forced him to fight at Coruna. He was killed just as his troops were winning. Moore was born in Glasgow, Scotland.

MOORE, MARIANNE (1887-1972), ranks with Emily Dickinson among America's finest woman poets. Al-

Wide World
Marianne Moore

though some of her verse is difficult to understand, Moore was a superb craftsman. She generally used poetic forms in which the controlling element is the number and arrangement of syllables rather than conventional patterns of meter or rhyme.

Moore's subjects—often birds, exotic animals, and other things in nature— may seem to limit her range, but she used them as symbols of honesty and steadfastness. These virtues mark her work, from *Poems* (1921) through *Complete Poems* (1967) and her critical prose collected in *Predilections* (1955). Her *Collected Poems* won the 1952 Pulitzer prize for poetry.

Marianne Moore was born in St. Louis, and became a teacher and a librarian. As the editor of *The Dial* magazine from 1925 to 1929, Moore played an important part in encouraging young writers and publishing their work.   ELMER W. BORKLUND

MOORE, STANFORD. See NOBEL PRIZES (table: Nobel Prizes for Chemistry—1972).

MOORE, THOMAS (1779-1852), an Irish poet, wrote the words for some of the best-loved songs in the English language. They include "Believe Me If All Those Endearing Young Charms," "The Last Rose of Summer," and "Oft in the Stilly Night." Moore wrote much light, serious, and satirical verse, and much prose. His works were as widely read in his day as the works of Lord Byron and Sir Walter Scott. But he is remembered today mostly for his verse set to music.

Moore was born in Dublin and was graduated from Trinity College there. He studied law for a time in London. His literary works include a translation of Anacreon's poems (1800); *Lalla Rookh* (1817), a romance; and a biography of Byron (1830).   GEORGE F. SENSABAUGH

MOORE COLLEGE OF ART. See UNIVERSITIES AND COLLEGES (table).

MOORER, THOMAS HINMAN (1912-   ), an admiral in the U.S. Navy, became chairman of the Joint Chiefs of Staff in 1970. He served in that position until 1974, when he retired from active duty in the Navy. Moorer was Chief of Naval Operations from 1967 until President Richard M. Nixon named him chairman of the Joint Chiefs.

Moorer was a Navy pilot during World War II (1939-1945). He became commander of the U.S. Seventh Fleet in 1962 and commander in chief of the U.S. Pacific Fleet in 1964. Moorer served as commander in chief of the U.S. Atlantic Fleet from 1965 to 1967. At the same time, he was Supreme Allied Commander in the Atlantic for the North Atlantic Treaty Organization.

Moorer was born in Mount Willing, Ala. He graduated from the U.S. Naval Academy.   DONALD W. MITCHELL

MOORES CREEK NATIONAL MILITARY PARK. See NATIONAL PARK SYSTEM (table: National Military Parks).

MOORISH ART. See ISLAMIC ART.

A Cow Moose and Her Calf Stroll Along the Shoreline of Waskesiu Lake in Saskatchewan, Canada.

MOOSE. The moose is the largest member of the deer family. It is larger than any deer that lived in past ages. The largest kind of moose live in Alaska. Sometimes they grow 7½ feet (2.3 meters) high at the shoulder and weigh from 1,500 to 1,800 pounds (680 to 816 kilograms).

Moose live in northern regions throughout the world. In Europe, they live from northern Scandinavia and northern Europe to Siberia. In North America, they live from Maine to Alaska and south through the Rocky Mountains to Wyoming. Outside of America, these animals are called *elk*, not moose. But the American elk is different. Its correct name is *wapiti*.

The moose has long legs, and high shoulders that look like a hump. The upper part of the moose's muzzle hangs 3 or 4 inches (8 or 10 centimeters) over its chin. The *bell*, an unusual growth of skin covered with hair, hangs underneath its throat. Its coat is brownish black on the upper parts. This dark color fades to a grayish or grayish brown on the belly and lower parts of the legs.

The bull moose has heavy, flattened antlers. The antlers on an unusually large moose spread 6 feet (1.8 meters) or more. Each antler has 6 to 12 short points which stick out like fingers from the palm of a huge hand. A moose sheds its antlers every year and grows a new pair. The antlers are full-grown by late August. The bull then strips off the dead skin, called "velvet," and polishes his great weapons against trees.

The mating season of the moose lasts from four to eight weeks in the fall. The bull wanders about at this time searching and calling for cows. The cows also call to bulls. A bull usually follows every sound to see if it was made by a cow or a rival bull. Hunters often try to lure the game within shooting range. They imitate the hoarse grunts of the bull or the love call of a cow by using a horn or calling through cupped hands.

Baby moose are born in late May or June. The mother carries them inside her body for about seven and one-half months before they are born. A cow may have one calf, twins, or, rarely, triplets. The calf is reddish-brown and has long legs. When the calf is about 10 days old, it can travel about with its mother. At this time, the bull moose stays by himself or with other males.

Moose like best to live in forest land that has willow swamps and lakes in it. There the animals spend the summer, and the cows care for their young.

Throughout this season, they often visit the water to get rid of flies and to feed on water plants. Moose are fine swimmers, and can cross lakes and rivers. They like to roll in mud holes and eat the salty earth or salt licks. In summer, they eat leaves and tender twigs as well as grass and herbs. Moose have such short necks and long legs they must straddle or get on their knees to eat low plants. They often push against and bend young trees to reach the tender leaves on top.

Moose remain strictly alone in summer. They stay together more in winter. Both males and females sometimes gather in small bands in swamps and woods. They find protection from the cold winds there. They browse on the twigs and shoots of trees. With their long legs, moose can walk easily in deep snow.

At one time, hunters killed nearly all the moose in the eastern United States, but today, a few of the animals live as far south as Massachusetts. Moose are protected by law in the United States and Canada.

Scientific Classification. Moose belong to the deer family, *Cervidae*. They are classified genus *Alces*, species *A. alces*.   VICTOR H. CAHALANE

See also ANIMAL (picture: Animals of the Temperate Forests); DEER; ELK.

MOOSE, LOYAL ORDER OF, is a fraternal order that has branches in the United States, Canada, and Great Britain. Each of the more than 1 million members is required to have unquestionable devotion to his country's flag and loyalty to democratic government. Members of the Moose take part in many civic and philanthropic endeavors.

The Loyal Order of Moose was founded in Louisville, Ky., in 1888. Headquarters are in Mooseheart, Ill., about 40 miles (64 kilometers) west of Chicago. Here the order maintains "Child City," a home for the dependent children of Moose members who died. It was founded in 1913 and includes more than 110 fireproof buildings. The home provides academic, vocational, and spiritual training.

Loyal Order of Moose Emblem

Moosehaven, "City of Contentment," lies on the St. Johns River, 14 miles (23 kilometers) from Jacksonville, Fla. This model home for the dependent aged of the Moose has 18 modern buildings, including a health care center.   Critically reviewed by the LOYAL ORDER OF MOOSE

MOOSE JAW, Saskatchewan (pop. 32,581), is a manufacturing center at the meeting point of Thunder Creek and the Moose Jaw River, about 400 miles (640 kilometers) west of Winnipeg. For location, see SASKATCHEWAN (political map). Farmers and ranchers of central Saskatchewan send their products to Moose Jaw's grain elevators and stockyards. Industries in the city manufacture asphalt, chemicals, clothing, food products, and windows.

The name Moose Jaw is believed to have come from the shape of a river that flows through the city. The town was chartered in 1884 and became a city in 1903. It has a mayor-council government.   F. C. CRONKITE

MOOSE RIVER drains many of the streams of northern Ontario into the Hudson Bay. The Mattagami and Missinaibi streams join to form the Moose River. It is only 75 miles (121 kilometers) long. But the streams that empty into it drain 42,100 square miles (109,000 square kilometers) of northeastern Ontario.

MOOSEHEAD LAKE. See MAINE (Rivers and Lakes).

MOOSEHEART, Ill. See MOOSE, LOYAL ORDER OF.

MOOT. See BOROUGH.

MOPED. See BICYCLE (Specialty Bicycles).

MORA, *MO ruh,* **JUAN RAFAEL** (1814-1860), served as president of Costa Rica from 1849 to 1859. He was called "National Hero" for defending Central America against an American adventurer, William Walker, in 1856 and 1857 (see WALKER, WILLIAM). Mora established public schools in Costa Rica and made elementary education compulsory. He encouraged the coffee industry, built public buildings, and gave Costa Rica its first national bank and its first street-lighting system.

Rebels drove Mora from Costa Rica in 1859. He returned in 1860, but was defeated in a revolt and was executed at Puntarenas. He was born in San José on Feb. 8, 1814.   DONALD E. WORCESTER

MORAINE, *moh RAYN,* is the earth and stones that a glacier carries along and deposits when the ice melts.

Moraine also means a line of such material on the surface of a glacier, or an uneven ridge of material deposited at the edge of the melting ice. A glacier in a mountain valley carries on each side a line of rock fragments which have rolled onto the ice from nearby slopes. Such a line is called a *lateral moraine.*

When two mountain glaciers unite, the lateral moraines between them merge into a *medial moraine* along the middle of the united glacier. A large ridge is built up when the ice melts from a mountain glacier, or in front of a continental ice sheet. This ridge has mounds and hollows and is called a *terminal moraine.* Some of the terminal moraines formed by the great ice sheets of the Ice Age are ranges of hills. Some of those built by the great mountain glaciers of the Ice Age are also hills. *Ground moraine* is the material deposited beneath the ice as the glacier melts.   ELDRED D. WILSON

See also GLACIER.

MORAL EDUCATION is instruction focused on questions of right and wrong. Moral education also includes the development of *values,* the standards by which people judge what is important, worthwhile, and good.

People receive moral education from many sources, including their church, family, friends, and teachers—and even television. Schools have always been involved in such education, either intentionally or unintentionally. For example, many stories for young readers include a moral lesson. During the 1970's, educators in the United States began to develop special teaching methods to help students deal with moral questions.

Methods of Moral Education

Schools use four chief methods in moral education: (1) inculcation, (2) values clarification, (3) moral development, and (4) value analysis.

Inculcation is an effort to teach children the values that educators believe lead to moral behavior. These values include fairness, honesty, justice, and respect for others. One way of teaching such standards is to provide appropriate praise and punishment. Another means is to have teachers reflect the desired values in their own behavior.

Values Clarification tries to help students understand the values they already have, not to teach them new ones. The learning procedures stress choosing thoughtfully from alternatives and acting on one's own convictions. Students also learn to respect their personal values and to declare them in discussions.

Moral Development helps students improve their ability to judge moral questions. This method is based on the theory that people progress from lower to higher stages of moral reasoning. According to the theory, young children's thinking about moral issues is based on their wish to avoid punishment or to satisfy their desires. Most adults reach a higher stage of development, where they obey moral laws to gain the approval of society. At the highest moral level, an individual might oppose the laws of society if they conflict with moral principles that are even higher.

Educators work to stimulate moral development by discussing difficult moral choices called *dilemmas.* One dilemma might be whether a physician should stop the treatment of a fatally ill patient who would rather die than continue to suffer unbearable pain. Classroom discussion focuses on exploring why a student favors a particular action, not on determining what action should be taken.

Value Analysis helps students apply techniques of logic and scientific investigation to matters involving values. Teachers stress the importance of exploring all alternatives, of gathering and evaluating the facts, and of making a logical decision.

Arguments About Moral Education

Some people oppose the teaching of moral education in schools. Many of these individuals feel that the family and church should provide such instruction. Others argue that moral education takes class time that should be used for such basic subjects as reading, writing, and mathematics.

Surveys indicate that most parents favor some form of moral education in schools. Supporters of such education argue that the family and church have not done a good job of teaching moral behavior. They believe schools should also teach young people the skills to solve problems of morality. DOUGLAS P. SUPERKA

MORAL RE-ARMAMENT (MRA) works to further democracy by stressing moral and spiritual values. It aims to change the motives of people and nations to form a basis for social, racial, and international understanding.

MRA was founded by Frank Buchman, an American evangelist whose *Oxford Group* started in the 1920's. In 1938, it became known as Moral Re-Armament. MRA became known in the 1960's for its "Up with People" musical demonstrations performed by youths in many countries. In 1968, "Up with People" separated from MRA to become an independent, nonprofit corporation. Moral Re-Armament headquarters are at 124 E. 40th Street, New York, N.Y. 10016.

MORAL VALUES. See ETHICS; MORAL EDUCATION; PHILOSOPHY (What Is Good and What Is Evil?).

MORALE is the general attitude or outlook of an individual or a group toward a specific situation. It influences, and is influenced by, such factors as courage, confidence, and determination. Morale may seriously affect both well-being and performance, and is closely related to what is called *esprit de corps*. When morale is "high," the spirit and confidence of an individual or a group are generally good, resulting in a high level of performance. When morale is "low," performance is usually correspondingly poor.

Business executives, military officers, college deans, athletics coaches, and other leaders have learned to analyze the morale in their groups. They recognize that the level of morale is a decisive factor in determining group or individual achievement. ALEXANDER A. SCHNEIDERS

See also ALIENATION.

MORALITY PLAY is a form of drama in which actors represent such qualities or conditions as virtue, vice, wealth, poverty, knowledge, or ignorance. People first produced morality plays in England in the 1400's. Like the miracle and mystery plays, they developed from religious pageants. Their purpose was to teach a lesson, or to show the eternal struggle between Good and Evil fighting to gain control of people. They moved slowly, and were usually dull and undramatic. The characters of Vice and the Devil came to be somewhat like a vaudeville team in a modern revue, and helped to make the morality plays entertaining to the audience. The clowns and fools of William Shakespeare's plays were a development of the comic characters in morality plays. Other actors represented such things as Bad Habits, Colic, Pill, and even Dinner, Supper, and Banquet.

Today, these plays are little more than a literary curiosity. *Everyman*, a favorite morality play in the 1500's, was printed in several editions. People still produce this dramatic allegory occasionally. *Everyman* is performed annually at the music and drama festival in Salzburg, Austria. CHARLES W. COOPER

See also MIRACLE PLAY.

MORATORIUM, MOHR *uh* TOH *ree um,* is a postponement of the time for payment of debts or financial obligations. It is accomplished by executive or legislative decree. A moratorium is often declared following a money panic, political or industrial upheaval, or national calamity, such as flood or earthquake. The moratorium delays legal action on debts. But it does not release the debtor from the obligation to pay. It merely postpones the day the debt is due.

The credit system is now widely used throughout the world, and moratorium has come to mean mostly the postponement of payment on commercial debts. Bills of exchange, drafts, and bank deposits are the kinds of things affected by a moratorium. Household and personal obligations are usually not included.

Moratoriums were used only on occasions of public disaster before World War I. The first war moratorium was decreed by England in 1914. The bills of exchange due in London were not met by payments because of the war. A one-year moratorium on intergovernmental debts was declared in 1931, to allow Germany to recover its financial stability. Franklin D. Roosevelt declared a moratorium in 1933, to save the financial system of the United States. L. T. FLATLEY

MORAVIA, moh RAY *vee uh,* is a geographic region of Czechoslovakia. It covers 10,076 square miles (26,097 square kilometers) and has a population of about 3,800,-000. Brno is the largest city of Moravia and the second largest of Czechoslovakia. Only Prague is larger. Moravia's name in the Czech language is *Morava*.

Moravia lies in the middle of Czechoslovakia, between Bohemia on the west and Slovakia on the east. Moravia slopes southwest from the Carpathian and Sudetes mountains to the Morava River. The Morava empties into the Danube River, which flows along the Czechoslovak-Austrian border.

Flat, fertile farmland makes up most of Moravia. The principal crops of the region include barley, corn, flax, oats, rye, sugar beets, and wheat. Many farmers also raise beef and dairy cattle.

Czechoslovakia's largest coal mines and an important industrial district are located around the city of Ostrava, in northern Moravia. The Ostrava area has large steelworks and other heavy industries. Moravian factories also produce chemicals, leather goods, machinery, shoes, textiles, and tractors.

Almost all the people of Moravia are Czechs, a Slavic people who speak the Czech language. Most Moravians belong to the Roman Catholic Church. Moravia has two universities and several technical schools.

After the A.D. 400's, Slavic tribes settled in Moravia.

During the 800's, these tribes united with other Slavic tribes and formed the Great Moravian Empire, which included a large part of central Europe. Beginning in the late 800's, the Magyars (Hungarians) invaded the Great Moravian Empire, and in time they destroyed it.

In the early 900's, Moravia became part of the territory ruled by the Duke of Bohemia. In 1526, Bohemia and Moravia came under the rule of the Hapsburg family of Austria (see HAPSBURG). The Hapsburgs ruled the Czechs for almost 400 years.

Moravia, a cultural region in central Czechoslovakia, has industrial cities, rich mineral deposits, and fertile farmland. Brno is the largest city.

WORLD BOOK map

In October, 1918, shortly before World War I ended, the independent republic of Czechoslovakia was established, with Moravia as one of its provinces. During World War II (1939-1945), German troops occupied Czechoslovakia. The Germans set up Moravia and Bohemia as a single protectorate within Germany. This protectorate was dissolved after Russian and United States forces drove the German troops from Czechoslovakia in 1945. In 1949, Czechoslovakia replaced its provinces, including Moravia, with smaller administrative units. VOJTECH MASTNY

MORAVIA, ALBERTO. See ITALIAN LITERATURE (The 1900's).

MORAVIAN CHURCH is a Protestant denomination that was formed after the death of religious reformer John Huss in Bohemia. In 1457, some supporters of the martyred Huss organized themselves as the *Unitas Fratrum* (Unity of Brethren). They stressed the sole authority of the Bible; simplicity in worship; receiving the Lord's Supper in faith without authoritative human explanation; and disciplined Christian living. In 1467, the group established its own ministry. Despite suppression, the Brethren flourished and were an important religious force by the time of Martin Luther. See BRETHREN; HUSS, JOHN.

The Brethren suffered great persecution during the Thirty Years' War (1618-1648). The group revived during the Pietist movement in Germany in the early 1700's. Pietists were Christians—mainly Lutherans—who wanted to return to the simple life of the early Christians. Beginning in 1722, refugees from Moravia under the leadership of Count von Zinzendorf reorganized the church. It then became known as the Moravian Church. The group built Herrnhut, a town on the count's estate in Saxony. Herrnhut became the base for missionary activity throughout the world, especially among developing countries. The church has always been noted for its missionary work.

Moravians first immigrated to America in 1735.

Bethlehem, Pa., is headquarters for the northern province of the church. Winston-Salem, N.C., is headquarters for the southern province. The church has three orders of the ministry—bishops, presbyters, and deacons. Provincial and district *synods* (conferences) of ministers and the laity administer the church.

Critically reviewed by the MORAVIAN CHURCH

MORAVIANTOWN, BATTLE OF. See WAR OF 1812 (Chief Battles of the War [Thames River]).

MORAY. See EEL.

MORAZÁN, MOH rah SAHN, **FRANCISCO** (1799-1842), a Central American soldier and statesman, was elected president of the United Provinces of Central America in 1830 and served for almost 10 years. He promoted trade and education.

The federation collapsed in 1839, and Morazán was elected president of El Salvador. He was forced into exile within a year. He was elected president of Costa Rica in 1842, but his enemies killed him. Morazán was born in Tegucigalpa, Honduras. He served as secretary general of Honduras in 1824 and as president of the Council of State in 1826. DONALD E. WORCESTER

MORDANT, MAWR dunt, is a chemical that combines with dyes to prevent them from dissolving easily. The dye alone might wash out, but the compound formed by the dye and the mordant will not, so the color is long lasting. Common mordants include salts of chromium, iron, aluminum, tin, or other metals. These are basic or metallic mordants, and are used with acid dyes. Tannic acid, lactic acid, and oleic acid are other common mordants. These are acid mordants, and combine with basic dyes. The compounds of basic mordants with dyes are called *lakes*. When alizarin, an acid dye, is mordanted with a basic aluminum salt, it colors cotton cloth a bright red, called *Turkey red*. FRED FORTESS

See also LAKE (dye).

MORDECAI. See ESTHER; HAMAN.

MORDVINOFF, MAWRD vihn awv, **NICOLAS** (1911-1973), an author, illustrator, and painter, won the Caldecott medal in 1952 for his illustrations in *Finders Keepers*, a children's book by William Lipkind. Mordvinoff was born in Petrograd (now Leningrad), Russia. He became a United States citizen in 1951.

MORE, SAINT THOMAS (1477?-1535), was a great English author, statesman, and scholar. He served as lord chancellor, the highest judicial official in England, from 1529 to 1532. But More resigned because he opposed King Henry VIII's plan to divorce his queen. He was beheaded in 1535 for refusing to accept the king as head of the English church. More has since become an example of the individual who places conscience above the claims of *secular* (nonreligious) authority. The Roman Catholic Church declared him a saint in 1935.

His Life. More was born in London, probably in 1477 but perhaps in 1478.

Detail of an oil portrait by Hans Holbein the Younger, the Frick Collection, New York

Saint Thomas More

He studied at Oxford University. More began his legal career in 1494, and became an undersheriff of London in 1510. By 1518 he had entered the service of King Henry VIII as royal councilor and ambassador. He was knighted and made undertreasurer in 1521, and was chancellor of the Duchy of Lancaster from 1525 to 1529.

More became lord chancellor after Cardinal Wolsey was dismissed late in 1529. At that time, Henry VIII was engaged in a bitter battle with the Roman Catholic Church. He wanted to divorce Catherine of Aragon so he could marry Anne Boleyn. More resigned his office because he could not support the king's policy against the pope. In April, 1534, More was imprisoned for refusing to swear to the Oath of Supremacy, the preamble to a law called the Act of Succession. The oath stated that Henry VIII ranked above all foreign rulers, including the pope. More was convicted of high treason on *perjured* (falsely sworn) evidence and was beheaded on July 6, 1535.

Character and Writings. More's personality combined intense concern for the problems of his day and spiritual detachment from worldly affairs. He was a devoted family man, and lived a plain, simple private life. He was famed for his merry wit. Yet to the people of his day, More was a contradictory figure—merriest when he seemed saddest and saddest when he appeared most happy. He was a patron of the arts. His friends included the humanist Erasmus and the artist Hans Holbein.

More's sympathetic philosophy is best reflected in *Utopia* (written in Latin in 1516). *Utopia* is an account of an ideal society, with justice and equality for all citizens. This masterpiece gave the word *utopia* to European languages. More also produced much English and Latin prose and poetry. His works include *History of King Richard III* (1513) and a long series of writings in which he defended the church against the attacks of Protestant reformers. He wrote his finest English work, *A Dialogue of Comfort Against Tribulation*, while in prison. RICHARD S. SYLVESTER

See also UTOPIA; RENAISSANCE (England).

MOREA. See PELOPONNESUS.

MOREELL, *moh REHL,* **BEN** (1892-1978), an American naval officer, founded the Seabees of the United States Navy. He commanded them during World War II (see SEABEES). Moreell served both as chief of the bureau of yards and docks and as chief of the civil engineer corps of the U.S. Navy from 1937 to 1946. He retired from the Navy as an admiral in 1946. In 1947, he became president and chairman of the board of Jones & Laughlin Steel Corporation. He retired in 1958. Moreell was born in Salt Lake City, Utah. ROBERT W. ABBETT

MORELIA, *moh RAYL yah* (pop. 219,423), is the capital of the Mexican state of Michoacán. It lies in central Mexico, about 130 miles (209 kilometers) northwest of Mexico City (see MEXICO [political map]). Its industries include flour mills, vegetable processing plants, and chemical factories. The city has a beautiful cathedral and an old stone aqueduct with 253 arches. Many of Morelia's buildings were built while Mexico was a Spanish colony. Morelia was founded as Valladolid in 1541. In 1828, the city was renamed for José María Morelos y Pavón, a leader in Mexico's fight for independence from Spain. ROBERT C. WEST

MORELOS, *moh RAY lohs,* with an area of 1,908 square miles (4,941 square kilometers), is the second smallest state in Mexico. It lies in central Mexico, just south of Mexico City. Its northern section has altitudes of over 10,000 feet (3,000 meters). Southern Morelos is lower and has many broad valleys. Cuernavaca is the capital and largest city (see CUERNAVACA). For location, see MEXICO (political map). The state has a population of 905,614. Crops include rice, corn, peanuts, and sugar cane. Morelos was founded in 1869. It was named for José María Morelos y Pavón, a Mexican hero. The revolt led by Emiliano Zapata in the early 1900's destroyed much property in the state. CHARLES C. CUMBERLAND

MORELOS Y PAVÓN, JOSÉ MARÍA. See MEXICO (Revolt Against the Spaniards).

MORES, *MAWR ayz,* is a general word used for the most important ideas and acts of people within a society. *Mores* is a Latin word meaning *customs*. Mores represent required behavior, and are formally expressed in the morals and laws of a people. For example, American criminal laws largely incorporate the mores of our society. Another source of American mores is the Ten Commandments.

Mores differ greatly from one culture to another. In King Solomon's time, a man was permitted to have many wives. In our society, he may legally have only one at a time. Mores also may change noticeably from time to time in the same society. JOHN F. CUBER

See also FOLKWAY.

MORGAGNI, *mohr GAHN yee,* **GIOVANNI BATTISTA** (1682-1771), an Italian anatomist and pathologist, became known as "the father of pathologic anatomy." He discovered and described many diseases of the heart and blood vessels. His great book, *On the Seats and Causes of Diseases* (1761), is a landmark in the history of pathology (see PATHOLOGY).

He was graduated from the University of Bologna. He became a professor of anatomy at the University of Padua in 1712. He lectured, studied, and wrote there about his post-mortem findings. He performed more than 600 autopsies himself. A statue of him stands in the Hall of Immortals of the International College of Surgeons in Chicago. Morgagni was born in Forlì, Italy, on Feb. 25, 1682. CAROLINE A. CHANDLER

MORGAN is the family name of three great American bankers.

Junius Spencer Morgan (1813-1890) founded the Morgan financial empire. As a young man, he made a fortune in the dry-goods business, and in 1854 became a member of the London banking firm of George Peabody and Company. The name later was changed to J. S. Morgan and Company, and the firm became a famous international banking house with headquarters in London. Morgan was born in what is now Holyoke, Mass.

John Pierpont Morgan (1837-1913), a son of Junius, became one of the greatest financiers in the

Brown Bros.
John Pierpont Morgan

United States. He joined his father's banking firm in 1856. Morgan was a member of the firm of Dabney, Morgan & Company from 1864 to 1871. In 1871, Morgan and the Drexel family of Philadelphia established the firm of Drexel, Morgan & Company. Morgan reorganized the firm under the name of J. P. Morgan & Company in 1895.

Morgan's firm became a leader in financing American business and in marketing bond issues of the United States government. It also sold bonds of the British government. Morgan helped organize the United States Steel Corporation in 1901. He was active in financing the International Harvester, American Telephone and Telegraph, and General Electric companies. Morgan and his associates served as directors of corporations, banks, railroads, public utility companies and insurance firms. In 1912, Morgan was investigated by a Congressional committee because of his great financial power, but nothing personally discreditable to him was revealed.

After the panic of 1893, Morgan helped reorganize many railroads, including the Northern Pacific, Erie, Southern, and the Philadelphia and Reading. In 1904, the Supreme Court of the United States dissolved the Northern Securities Company because it violated the Sherman Antitrust Act. Morgan and other financiers had created it to control key railroads in the West.

In 1895, Morgan's firm sold all of a $62 million government bond issue. The sale ended a gold shortage in the U.S. Treasury. During the panic of 1907, Morgan loaned money to banks to keep them from closing.

Morgan made many gifts to education and charity. He founded the Lying-in Hospital in New York City, and gave a large sum to the Harvard Medical School. Morgan was an ardent Episcopalian, and gave a substantial share of the funds to build the Cathedral of Saint John the Divine in New York City.

He was a great art collector and gave many valuable pictures, statues, and books to American libraries and museums. Some of his most famous collections were loaned to the Metropolitan Museum of Art in New York, which he helped found. Morgan was a famous yachtsman. He was active in defending the America's Cup in international yachting several times.

Morgan was born in Hartford, Conn. He was educated at the University of Göttingen in Germany.

John Pierpont Morgan, Jr. (1867-1943), was the son of John Pierpont Morgan. When his father died in 1913, Morgan took over many of the financial posts J. P. Morgan had held. Morgan succeeded his father as chairman of the board of United States Steel.

Morgan's firm became an official wartime purchasing agent for Great Britain in the United States in 1914. In this position, he placed contracts for the manufacture of food and munitions. The J. P. Morgan Company handled most of the postwar international loans, including many dealing with reparations. Morgan was appointed a member of the commission to revise the Dawes Plan in 1929 (see DAWES PLAN).

Like his father, Morgan made large gifts to education and the arts. In 1923, he dedicated his father's library as an institution of research. Under the terms of the gift, the library will be kept intact as a complete unit until March 31, 2013, a hundred years from the date of his father's death. In 1920, Morgan gave his house in London to the United States for use as the

Etching from Alexandre Olivier Exquemelin, *Bucaniers of America.* London, 1684. Courtesy of the Rare Book Division, The New York Public Library, Astor, Lenox and Tilden Foundations.

Sir Henry Morgan, a daring English pirate, was knighted by King Charles II for his attacks on the Spanish.

residence of the United States ambassador. Morgan was born at Irvington, N.Y., and was graduated from Harvard University. W. H. BAUGHN

MORGAN, DANIEL (1736-1802), served as an American officer in the Revolutionary War. He joined the Revolutionary forces in 1775 as a captain. He volunteered to go with Benedict Arnold on his expedition to Quebec, and was taken prisoner there. On his release in 1776, he became a colonel in charge of a Virginia regiment. He organized a corps of sharpshooters in 1777 that helped General Horatio Gates in his battles against General John Burgoyne. Morgan resigned from the army in 1779 because of poor health, but was recalled in 1780 and became a brigadier general. He commanded the American troops at the victory at Cowpens, S.C., in 1781. He received the thanks of Congress and a gold medal for his part in the battle.

After the war, he helped put down the Whiskey Rebellion in 1794 in western Pennsylvania (see WHISKEY REBELLION). He served as a Federalist from Virginia in the U.S. House of Representatives from 1797 to 1799. Morgan was probably born in Hunterdon County, New Jersey. JOHN R. ALDEN

MORGAN, EDWIN DENISON. See ARTHUR, CHESTER ALAN (Political Growth).

MORGAN, SIR HENRY (1635?-1688), the most famous English pirate, fought the Spanish fleet on the seas and robbed Spanish towns in the West Indies. He served for a time as lieutenant governor of Jamaica and commander in chief of English forces there.

Morgan's bold raids began in 1668. Thomas Modyford, the governor of Jamaica, issued Morgan a privateer's commission to cruise against the Spanish and collect information about a rumored attack on Jamaica.

His Attacks. Morgan attacked and captured the inland town of Puerto Principe (now Camagüey), Cuba. He then sailed to Portobelo, Panama, a town so well fortified that the French under his command deserted rather than risk the attack. Morgan took the city after a severe battle. He forced nuns and priests to place ladders against the city walls for his attacking force. Morgan's men looted the city. Governor Modyford disapproved of these attacks on Puerto Principe and Portobelo, because Morgan's orders were to attack ships, not towns. Morgan, however, celebrated his victories with a drinking party aboard his ship. The ship suddenly exploded, killing more than 300 men. But Morgan survived the explosion.

He looted Maracaibo, Venezuela, in 1669, and also captured three Spanish ships that had been sent specifically to take him. Morgan took a heavy ransom from Maracaibo and returned to Jamaica. Governor Modyford once again rebuked Morgan for the exploits, but made him commander of all the ships of war in Jamaica.

Attack on Panama. Morgan then commanded 1,400 men. In January, 1671, he attacked Panama City, Panama, and captured it in a remarkable battle. The Spaniards turned a herd of wild bulls against Morgan, but the bulls stampeded and helped rout the Spaniards. Morgan burned Panama City and took much of the city's treasures. Morgan shared some of the spoils with his men, but abandoned them and sailed away with the bulk of the loot.

His attack on Panama violated a peace treaty signed by Spain and England in 1670. England had agreed to end acts of piracy on Spanish towns in the West Indies if Spain would recognize England's rule over English West Indian colonies. Morgan was arrested for attacking Panama, and was sent to England for trial. King Charles II forgave him for his attack, and knighted him in 1674. Morgan then returned to Jamaica as lieutenant governor and commander in chief of the English forces there. He was dismissed in 1683, but served on the Jamaican council. He died in his bed in 1688.

Morgan was born in Wales and went to Jamaica as a boy.   WILLARD H. BONNER

MORGAN, JOHN HUNT (1825-1864), a Confederate general, led the daring Morgan Raiders during the Civil War. His troops, a group of volunteer cavalrymen, raided public property, burned bridges, took horses, and captured railroad supplies. They also caused severe losses among Union troops. Morgan never commanded more than 4,000 men, but it is said he captured as many as 15,000 soldiers.

In 1863, Morgan was ordered to invade Kentucky and draw General William S. Rosecrans' army from Tennessee. Morgan went farther than he was ordered. He broke through the federal lines in Kentucky and crossed the Ohio River into Indiana. A flood caused the river to rise, and Morgan could not return to Confederate territory. He was captured in

Historical Pictures Service
John Hunt Morgan

July, 1863, and was imprisoned in Columbus, Ohio.

Morgan escaped the next November and continued his raids. He was defeated in Kentucky, in June, 1864. He went to Greeneville, Tenn., where he was surrounded and shot by Union troops in September, 1864. Morgan was born in Huntsville, Ala. He spent his boyhood in Kentucky.   FRANK E. VANDIVER

MORGAN, JUSTIN (1748-1798), owned and gave his name to a horse, the original stallion of the breed of Morgan horses. The breed became famous for its strength, endurance, and speed (see HORSE [Saddle Horses; color picture]). When the horse was a colt, Morgan obtained it from a farmer in payment of a debt. This unusual stallion died at the age of 29.

Morgan was born in West Springfield, Mass. He moved to Randolph, Vt., in 1788, and became a schoolteacher, singing master, and town clerk. CHESTER B. BAKER

MORGAN, LEWIS HENRY (1818-1881), was an American anthropologist who studied the social organization of the Iroquois Indians. His writings on the stages of cultural development of peoples of the world were used widely for many years. Morgan's theory of evolution was that all races of people passed from savagery to barbarism to civilization in their development. His writings include *League of the Ho-dé-no-sau-nee* or *Iroquois* (1851), and *Ancient Society* (1877). He was also active in politics. He was born in Aurora, N.Y.   DAVID B. STOUT

MORGAN, THOMAS HUNT (1866-1945), an American geneticist, won the 1933 Nobel prize in physiology or medicine for his work on heredity described in *The Theory of the Gene* (1926). He showed through his experiments that certain characteristics are transmitted from generation to generation through genes (see HEREDITY [Genetics]).

Morgan studied the laws of heredity by using the fruit fly (*Drosophila melanogaster*) for experiments in breeding. His research clarified the physical basis for the linkage and recombination of hereditary traits. He was the first to explain sex-linked inheritance, that some traits pass to only one or the other sex. Morgan and his associates proved that genes are arranged on the chromosomes in a fixed linear order (see CHROMOSOME).

He began his experiments at Columbia University, where he was professor of biology from 1904 to 1928. He was director of the William G. Kerckhoff Biology Laboratory at the California Institute of Technology from 1928 to 1941. He wrote *Evolution and Genetics* (1925), *Experimental Embryology* (1927), and was co-author of *Mendelian Heredity* (1905). Morgan was born in Lexington, Ky. He studied at the University of Kentucky, McGill University, the University of Edinburgh, and received his Ph.D. from Johns Hopkins University. His many honors included membership in the Royal Society (1919).   MORDECAI L. GABRIEL

MORGAN HORSE. See HORSE (Saddle Horses; color picture); MORGAN, JUSTIN).

MORGANTOWN, W. Va. (pop. 29,431), is the home of West Virginia University. Manufacturing plants make brass plumbing fixtures, hand-blown glass, and textiles. Limestone quarries and two of the world's largest coal mines are located near the city. Morgantown lies on the banks of the Monongahela River, 72 miles (116 kilometers) south of Pittsburgh (see WEST VIRGINIA [political map]). Colonel Zackquill Morgan founded Morgantown about 1766. The city was known as Morgan's Town when it was chartered in 1785. It has a council-manager government. FESTUS PAUL SUMMERS

MORGARTEN, BATTLE OF. See SWITZERLAND (The Struggle for Freedom).

MORGENTHAU, *MAWR guhn thaw,* **HENRY, JR.** (1891-1967), served as United States secretary of the treasury from 1934 to 1945 under Presidents Franklin D. Roosevelt and Harry S. Truman. During World War II, he organized the Victory Bond campaign that raised more than $200 billion. He proved efficient in the treasury post, although he probably would have preferred the job of secretary of agriculture.

Morgenthau lived near Roosevelt's Hyde Park (N.Y.) estate, and they were close friends. When Roosevelt became governor of New York in 1929, he named Morgenthau head of his Agricultural Advisory Commission. Morgenthau served briefly in 1933 as chairman of the Federal Farm Board and then as governor of the Farm Credit Administration. He also served as undersecretary of the treasury before he was named secretary in 1934.

During World War II, he proposed the Morgenthau Plan for Germany. It would have eliminated most of Germany's heavy industries, and ended German military power. It was never adopted. Morgenthau took a leading part in the 1944 Bretton Woods (N.H.) international monetary conference. He was born in New York City. HARVEY WISH

MÖRIKE, *MUHR ih kuh,* **EDUARD** (1804-1875), was a German lyric poet. He overcame the vagueness that characterizes much romantic poetry. Some of his work suggests a pleasant, untroubled atmosphere. But Mörike's most admired poems are about single objects or moments in time, such as an old lamp in a summer house, or two lovers as they disappear around a corner.

Mörike also wrote prose. *Mozart on His Journey to Prague* (1855) is considered a masterpiece of short German prose. It is a charming story about Mozart, delicately clouded by an awareness of the young composer's approaching death. Mörike also wrote *Painter Nolten* (1832), a subtle psychological novel.

Mörike was born in Ludwigsburg. He became a Protestant minister in 1834. But he retired in 1843 to devote himself to writing. JEFFREY L. SAMMONS

MORÍNIGO, HIGINIO. See PARAGUAY (Recent Developments).

MORISON, SAMUEL ELIOT (1887-1976), was an American historian, teacher of history, and winner of two Pulitzer prizes. His *Admiral of the Ocean Sea,* a life of Columbus, won the prize in 1943, and his *John Paul Jones* received it in 1960. His other books include *History of United States Naval Operations in World War II* in 15 volumes (1947-1962), *The Intellectual Life of Colonial New England* (1960), *One Boy's Boston* (1962), *The Oxford History of the American People* (1965), *The European Discovery of America: The Northern Voyages* (1971), and *The European Discovery of America: The Southern Voyages* (1974).

Morison was born in Boston and was educated at Harvard University and in Paris. In 1915, he became a teacher of history at Harvard. He served in World War I (1914-1918) and World War II (1939-1945). Morison was elected to the American Academy of Arts and Letters in 1963. MERLE CURTI

United Press Int.
Christopher Morley

MORLEY, CHRISTOPHER (1890-1957), was a popular American literary journalist. His greatest success was as an essayist in such collections as *Shandygaff* (1918) and *Tales from a Rolltop Desk* (1921). His novels include *Parnassus on Wheels* (1917), *Where the Blue Begins* (1922), *Thunder on the Left* (1925), and *Kitty Foyle* (1939). He also wrote light verse, such as *Mandarin in Manhattan* (1933). He wrote one of the best literary columns of his time, first for the *New York Evening Post* and later for the *Saturday Review* (now *Saturday Review/World*). Morley was born in Haverford, Pa. ARTHUR MIZENER

MORLEY, EDWARD W. See MICHELSON, ALBERT A.

MORLEY, THOMAS (1557-1603?), was an English composer. He won fame for his light songs, which included canzonets, airs, and madrigals. Many of his *ballets,* a song form borrowed from Italy, are still sung today. "It Was a Lover and His Lass," with words from Shakespeare's *As You Like It,* is one of his best-known songs. Morley also composed some church music and music for the lute, viol, and flute. He was organist at Saint Paul's Cathedral and the Chapel Royal in London for many years. WARREN S. FREEMAN

MORMON CRICKET is not really a cricket but belongs to the family of katydids and long-horned grasshoppers. It can be very harmful to crops. It lives in the western United States and as far east as Kansas.

Mormon crickets are brown or black and grow about 2 inches (5 centimeters) long. They have small wings but cannot fly. In summer, the female lays its eggs one at a time in the ground. The young hatch the next spring and are full-grown by summer. Farmers use poisonous dusting powder and baits to kill them.

In 1848, a swarm of Mormon crickets threatened to ruin the crops of the Mormon settlers in Utah. But flocks of gulls suddenly appeared and ate the insects (see UTAH [picture: Mormons Gather]).

Scientific Classification. The Mormon cricket belongs to the katydid family, *Tettigoniidae.* It is genus *Anabrus,* species *A. simplex.* URL LANHAM

See also ORTHOPTERA.

The Mormon Cricket is very destructive to crops in the western United States. It has small wings but cannot fly.

USDA

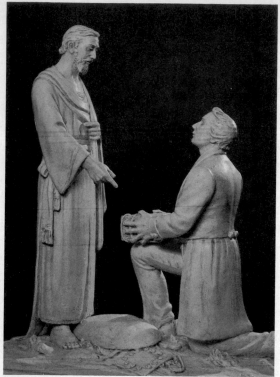

The Church of Jesus Christ of Latter-day Saints

Joseph Smith, *right,* the founder of the Mormon Church, said he received engraved golden plates from the angel Moroni. Smith translated them into the scriptures called the *Book of Mormon.*

MORMONS is the name commonly given to members of The Church of Jesus Christ of Latter-day Saints. They are so called because of their belief in the *Book of Mormon.* They claim that the Church as established by Christ did not survive in its original form, and was restored in modern times by divine means. Thus, they believe that their church is the true and complete church of Jesus Christ restored to earth. Mormons are more correctly called *Latter-day Saints,* using the word "saint" in its Biblical sense to designate any member of Christ's church.

The church has over 4 million members. Many Mormons live in the western United States, and church headquarters are in Salt Lake City, Utah. The church is also established in most other countries of the world.

Several other churches accept the *Book of Mormon,* but are not associated with the church described in this article. The largest of these is the Reorganized Church of Jesus Christ of Latter Day Saints, which has headquarters in Independence, Mo.

Church Doctrines

Mormon beliefs are based on ancient and modern revelations from God. Many of these revelations are recorded in scriptures. These scriptures include the Bible, the *Book of Mormon, Doctrine and Covenants,* and the *Pearl of Great Price.*

Mormons regard the Bible as the word of God, but they believe that it is not a complete record of all that

God said and did. The *Book of Mormon* is a history of early peoples of the Western Hemisphere. Mormons teach that the *Book of Mormon* was divinely inspired, and regard it as holy scripture. The *Book of Mormon* was translated by Joseph Smith from golden plates which he said he received from the angel Moroni. *Doctrine and Covenants* contains revelations made by God to Joseph Smith. The *Pearl of Great Price* contains writings of Smith and his translation of some ancient records.

Mormons believe in a unique concept of God. They teach that this concept was revealed by God through Joseph Smith and other prophets. Mormons believe that the Supreme Being is God the Father, who is a living, eternal being having a glorified body of flesh and bone. The human body is made in the image of God.

Mormons teach that God the Father created all people as spirit children before the earth was made. They regard Jesus Christ as the first spirit-child the Supreme Being created. They believe that Christ created the world under the direction of God the Father. This is why Mormons also refer to Christ as the Creator. Jesus Christ came down to earth and was born of the Virgin Mary. He was the only one of God's spirit-children begotten by the Father in the flesh. He is divine.

Jesus Christ died on the cross for the sins of all humanity and brought about the resurrection of all. He lives today as a resurrected, immortal being of flesh and bone.

God the Father and Jesus Christ are two separate beings. Together with the Holy Ghost, they form a Trinity, Godhead, or governing council in the heavens. The Holy Ghost is a third personage, but is a spirit without a body of flesh and bone.

Mormons claim that their doctrine is the one which Jesus and His apostles taught. They believe that the first principles and ordinances of the gospel are faith in Jesus Christ; repentance; baptism by immersion for the remission of sins; and the laying on of hands for the gift of the Holy Ghost. They believe that a person must be called of God by those who have the authority in order to preach the gospel and to administer its ordinances.

Mormons believe in life after death and in the physical resurrection of the body. The spirit, awaiting the resurrection of the body, continues in an intelligent existence. During this time, persons who did not know the gospel in life may accept it after death. Mormons believe, for this reason, that living persons can be baptized on behalf of the deceased. In this ceremony, a living Mormon acts as a representative of the dead person and is baptized for that person. Other rites are performed for the dead.

Since Mormons believe in life after death, they believe that family life continues after death. Marriages performed in a Mormon temple are for eternity, and not just for this life. Mormons believe in a final judgment in which all people will be judged according to their faith and works. Each person will be rewarded or punished according to merit.

Some Mormons practiced *polygamy* (the practice of a man having more than one wife at the same time) as a religious principle during the mid-1800's. But the church outlawed the practice in 1890 after the Supreme Court of the United States ruled it illegal.

They believe in upholding the civil law of the country

in which they are established. For example, they believe the Constitution of the United States is an inspired document. Mormons in the United States are urged by their religion to uphold its principles.

Church Organization

Mormons regard the organization plan of their church as divinely inspired. They have no professional clergy. However, all members in good standing, young and old, can participate in church government through several church organizations. A body called the General Authorities heads the church. This group consists of the president and two counselors; the Council of the Twelve Apostles; the Patriarch of the church; the First Quorum of the Seventy; and the three-member Presiding Bishopric.

Under the General Authorities are regional and local organizations called stakes and wards. Each *stake* (diocese) is governed by a president and two counselors, who are assisted by an advisory council of 12 men. A stake has between 2,000 and 10,000 members. A *ward* (congregation) is governed by a bishop and two counselors. Wards have an average of 500 to 600 members.

Worthy male members of the church may enter the priesthood, which is divided into two orders. The *Aaronic* (lesser) order is for young men 12 to 20 years old. The *Melchizedek* (higher) order is for men over 20. Each order is subdivided into *quorums* (groups). Mormons believe that the priesthood provides authority to act in God's name in governing the church and in performing religious ceremonies.

Several auxiliary organizations assist the priesthood. The Sunday School, the largest auxiliary organization, provides religious education for adults and children. The Women's Relief Society helps the sick and the poor, and directs women's activities. The Young Men and Young Women organizations provide programs for teen-agers and young adults. The Primary Association sponsors classwork and recreation for children under 12 years of age.

The church operates an extensive educational system. It provides weekday religious education for high school students in about 1,900 *seminaries* located near public high schools in 42 states and six foreign countries. The church conducts 66 weekday religious *institutes* for Mormon students near college campuses. It also maintains fully accredited colleges and universities in Utah, Idaho, and the Pacific Islands. Best known of these is Brigham Young University in Provo, Utah.

Mormons assist aged, handicapped, and unemployed members through a voluntary *welfare program*. Projects directed by the wards and stakes help the poor.

Voluntary contributions from members and income from church-operated businesses support the church. Most members contribute a *tithe* (one-tenth of their annual income) to the church. Thousands of young men and women work for 18 to 30 months in a world-wide missionary program without pay.

History

Revelations. During the early 1800's, Joseph Smith, the son of a New England farmer, received a series of divine revelations. According to Smith's account, God the Father and Jesus Christ appeared to him near Palmyra, N.Y., in 1820. They advised him not to join any existing church and to prepare for an important task. Smith said he was visited by an angel named Moroni three years later. Moroni told him about golden plates on which the history of early peoples of the Western Hemisphere was engraved in an ancient language. In 1827, Smith received the plates on Cumorah,

Mormon Pioneers Left Nauvoo, Ill., in 1846, on the way west to the valley of the Great Salt Lake in Utah. The Mormons had established the city of Nauvoo only seven years earlier. But it became a hotbed of anti-Mormon feeling. Many of the saints were killed and their homes and fields burned. After Joseph Smith's death, Brigham Young led the pioneers.

Mormon Temple in Utah, the magnificent six-spired granite structure of the Church of Latter-day Saints, dominates Temple Square In Salt Lake City. The domed Tabernacle, *left background,* is famous for its huge organ and choir.

a hill near Palmyra. His translation of the plates, called the *Book of Mormon,* was published in 1830.

Joseph Smith and his associates founded the church on April 6, 1830. The church grew rapidly, and had 1,000 members by the end of the first year.

Mormons in the Middle West. Mormon communities were established at Kirtland, Ohio, and Independence, Mo., during the early 1830's. Smith moved the church headquarters to Kirtland in 1831, and the town was the center of the church for almost 10 years. He instituted the basic organization and many of the present doctrines there. The first Mormon temple was completed there in 1836.

The 1830's were years of growth, but serious problems arose at the same time. Disputes among some church members themselves, the collapse of a Mormon bank in 1837, and conflict with non-Mormon neighbors broke up the Kirtland community. In 1838, Smith and his loyal followers moved to Missouri, and joined other Mormons there. But trouble again arose. The Missouri Mormons had been driven from Independence in 1834, and had settled in a town called Far West, in northern Missouri. In the fall of 1838, mobs attacked the Mormons in several of their settlements. In the "massacre at Haun's Mill," 20 Mormons, including some children, were killed. Joseph Smith and other leaders were

The Mormon Tabernacle in Salt Lake City, Utah, has a 375-member choir. The choir has won world-wide fame through concerts. The huge organ, begun in 1866, still contains some of the original pipes. Free weekday organ concerts attract thousands of visitors to the Tabernacle.

arrested on what Mormons believe were false charges. Ordered out of Missouri, about 15,000 Mormons fled to Illinois in 1838. Smith escaped from prison a few months later and rejoined his people in Illinois.

They founded the city of Nauvoo, which became one of the state's largest cities. The rapid growth of Nauvoo, and the important part Mormons played in state politics made non-Mormons suspicious and hostile again. One faction set up a newspaper to fight Smith, who had become a candidate for President of the United States. The paper was destroyed, and Smith was blamed for it. He, his brother Hyrum, and other leaders were arrested and jailed. On June 27, 1844, a mob attacked the jail. Smith and his brother were shot and killed.

The Mormons in Utah. Brigham Young became the next church leader. Mobs forced the Mormons out of Illinois in 1846. Joseph Smith had planned to move his people to the Great Basin in the Rocky Mountains. This plan was now put into effect by Young. In 1847, Young led the advance party of settlers into the Great Salt Lake valley. The population grew rapidly, and by 1849, the Mormons had set up a civil government. They applied for admission to the Union as the *State of Deseret*, but Congress created the Territory of Utah in 1850 instead, and appointed Young governor.

Trouble with non-Mormons began again. It was falsely reported in Washington, D.C., that the Mormons were rebelling. Anti-Mormon public opinion caused President James Buchanan to replace Young with a non-Mormon governor and to send troops to Utah in 1857. The trouble that followed has been called the Utah War or the Mormon War. It ended in 1858 when Young accepted the new governor and President Buchanan gave full pardon to all concerned.

The number of Utah settlements increased until the territory's population reached 140,000 in 1877. Congress continued to oppose the practice of polygamy, and the church outlawed the practice in 1890. A Mormon ambition was realized in 1896 when Utah was admitted to the Union as the 45th state.

Mormons Today have won a reputation as a temperate, industrious people who have made their churches monuments to thrift and faith. Their meeting houses are in many ways model community centers. They include facilities for worship, learning, and recreation. The great temple in Salt Lake City was built during the period from 1853 to 1893. There are 20 other temples in the world. The temples are devoted entirely to religious ceremonies, and are open only to worthy Mormons. All other Mormon meeting places, chapels, and recreation halls are open to the general public.

The promotion of music and the arts has long been important to the Latter-day Saints. The 375-voice Mormon Tabernacle Choir in Salt Lake City is famous for its broadcasts, telecasts, and concert tours. The choir, now more than a hundred years old, has been heard on U.S. radio networks since 1929.   Critically Reviewed by
THE CHURCH OF JESUS CHRIST OF LATTER-DAY SAINTS

Related Articles in WORLD BOOK include:

Cardston	Polygamy
Deseret	Smith, Joseph
Lamanites	Smith, Joseph F.
Latter Day Saints,	Trails of Early Days (map)
Reorganized Church of	Utah (History;
Jesus Christ of	pictures)
Lehi	Young, Brigham

W. Atlee Burpee

The Morning-Glory is full-blown when the sun rises, but the strong light often closes the blossoms before noon.

MORNING-GLORY is the name of a family made up mainly of climbing plants. The *garden morning-glory* is one of the best-known plants in this group. Others are the *bindweed, jalap, moonflower, scammony,* and *sweet potato.* The morning-glory grows rapidly and twines about nearby objects. It grows from 10 to 20 feet (3 to 6 meters) high and is widely used as a covering for posts, fences, and porches. The garden morning-glory has dark green leaves shaped like a heart. The flowers are shaped like a funnel and are of various shades and mixtures of purple, blue, red, pink, and white. The fragrant flowers open in the morning but close in the sunlight later in the day. The seeds may be soaked in water overnight to soften the seed covering and make sprouting easier. Japanese varieties have flowers 7 inches (18 centimeters) in diameter. Their flowers are mixtures of purple, rose, and violet. The morning-glory is the flower for September.

Scientific Classification. Morning-glories belong to the morning-glory family, *Convolvulaceae.* The garden morning-glory is classified as genus *Ipomoea,* species *I. purpurea.*   JULIAN A. STEYERMARK

Related Articles in WORLD BOOK include:

Bindweed	Jalap
Convolvulus	Moonflower
Dodder	Sweet Potato
Flower (picture: Garden Flowers)	

MORNING SICKNESS. See PREGNANCY.
MORNING STAR. See EVENING STAR.
MORNINGSIDE COLLEGE. See UNIVERSITIES AND COLLEGES (table).

MOROCCO is a kind of leather made from the skins of goats. It was first made by the Moors of southern Spain and Morocco. Genuine morocco is soft, elastic, and has fine grain and texture. Vegetable tanning is used to prepare morocco leather. The leather is then dyed and used for making bookbindings, upholstery, and fine shoes.

665

MOROCCO

Berber Horsemanship is a matter of great pride and importance because these people travel, herd livestock, and fight on horseback. In a mock battle, *left*, they show their skill as horsemen.

MOROCCO, *muh RAHK oh*, is a small, mountainous country in North Africa. It lies only 9 miles (14 kilometers) from Spain, across the Strait of Gibraltar. A strong power in Morocco could block the strait and halt any nation's ships entering the Mediterranean Sea from the Atlantic Ocean. Germany and France nearly went to war in the early 1900's over control of Morocco. Moroccans call their country EL MAGHREB-EL-AKSA in Arabic, which means *the Farthest West*. Rabat is the capital. Sometimes the government moves to Tangier in the summer. Casablanca is Morocco's largest city.

About 70 of every 100 Moroccans grow crops in the lowlands, or herd cattle, goats, and sheep in the highlands. Southeast of the mountains, the Sahara stretches along Morocco's border with Algeria and Western Sahara. Almost all Moroccans are Berbers, Arabs, or of mixed Berber and Arab descent. Their ancestors—who were called *Moors*—ruled Spain, Portugal, and much of North Africa from the 700's to the 1400's. France and Spain controlled what is now Morocco from 1912 until Morocco became independent in 1956.

The Land and Its Resources

The Land. The Atlas Mountains cover most of Morocco. The highest peak, Jebel Toubkal, rises 13,665 feet (4,165 meters) in the west-central region. Mountains in the north and west slope down to a narrow plain along the Atlantic and the Mediterranean. In the southeast, the mountains are lower near the Sahara.

Rivers and Lakes. Small rivers, including the Guir and Ziz, rush out of the Atlas Mountains and dry up in the desert. The Sebou, Tensift, Oum er Rbia and other rivers flow from the mountains to the Atlantic. The Moulouya River, 320 miles (515 kilometers) long, is the longest in Morocco. It flows from the Atlas range to the Mediterranean. Small lakes often dry up in summer and crops are planted in lake beds.

Natural Resources. The northwestern Atlas Mountains have large deposits of phosphates, Morocco's chief mineral resource. Morocco also has antimony, barium, coal, cobalt, copper, iron ore, lead, manganese, petroleum, and zinc deposits. Cedar, oak, olive, pine, and poplar trees cover the lower mountain slopes. Argan trees grow on the coastal plain.

Climate. Breezes from the Atlantic Ocean cool the coastal plain. Temperatures here average about 72° F. (22° C) in summer and 60° F. (16° C) in winter. From 13 to 16 inches (33 to 41 centimeters) of rain falls on the plain every year. The northwestern Atlas Mountains have cool weather with bitter, snowy winters. About 32 inches (81 centimeters) of rain a year falls there. Less than 8 inches (20 centimeters) falls on the desert, where the temperature averages 130° F. (54° C) in summer and about 62° F. (17° C) in winter.

Life of the People

Morocco has a population of about 20,368,000. About one-third of the people speak Berber. Two-thirds speak Arabic. Most of the Berbers live in the mountains

---
FACTS IN BRIEF

Capital: Rabat.

Official Language: Arabic.

Form of Government: Constitutional monarchy.

Area: 172,414 sq. mi. (446,550 km²). *Greatest Distances*—east-west, 760 mi. (1,223 km); north-south, 437 mi. (703 km). *Coastline*—Atlantic, 612 mi. (985 km); Mediterranean, 234 mi. (377 km).

Population: *Estimated 1981 Population*—20,368,000; distribution, 61 per cent rural, 39 per cent urban; density, 119 persons per sq. mi. (46 persons per km²). *1971 Census*—15,379,259. *Estimated 1986 Population*—23,612,000.

Chief Products: *Agriculture*—almonds, barley, beans, citrus fruits, corn, oats, olives, peas, wheat. *Manufacturing and Processing*—candles, cement and other building materials, foodstuffs, leather, soap, textiles. *Mining*—clay, lead, limestone, marble, phosphates.

Flag: The flag has a green star centered on a red field. See FLAG (color picture: Flags of Africa).

National Anthem: "Al Nachid Al Watani" ("The National Anthem").

National Holiday: Fête du Trône, March 3; Independence Day, November 18.

Money: *Basic Unit*—dirham. See MONEY (table).

(see BERBERS). Most of the Arabic-speaking people live in the lowlands. About 200,000 Europeans—most of them French and Spanish—live in or near cities. About 98 out of every 100 Moroccans are Muslims. Most of the Europeans living in Morocco are Roman Catholics.

Language. Arabic is Morocco's official language, but the Berber tribes speak various Berber dialects. French and Spanish are used in business and government.

Way of Life. In the average Moroccan family, the wife cares for the home and children, and the husband earns the living. Often, a grown son or other male relative lives with the family and helps the father.

Shelter. Most city people live in small adobe houses. Some of the houses were built hundreds of years ago. Many houses have no windows in order to keep out the heat. Many Berbers come to the cities looking for jobs. They are very poor and live in huts made of canvas, planks, and corrugated iron on the outskirts of the cities. In mountain towns, houses rise above each other on the steep slopes. The roof of one house may be level with the foundation of another.

Most Moroccan herdsmen live in tents made of wool or goat hair, mixed with braided or woven plant fibers. These tents stand in *douaouer* (circles). Farmers live in either *nouaïel* or *diour*. Nouaïel are round houses built of branches and roofed with straw. Adobe homes are called *diour*.

Food. Favorite Moroccan foods include lamb, chicken, fruits, and vegetables. The people enjoy *mechoui* (whole roasted lamb) and *pastilla* (salted pie containing lamb, eggs, pigeon, chicken, vegetables, and spices).

Clothing. Most Moroccans dress as their ancestors did. The men wear loose, wide trousers called *seraweel*. They also wear *kumsan* (cotton shirts that reach to their ankles). Kumsan are gathered at the waist with a wide sash. Large hooded cloaks called *djellabiat* serve as outer garments in cool weather. Men often wear turbans or tall, red, brimless hats called *tarabich*. Both men and women wear leather sandals.

Women wear linen shirts called *bloozat*, which have loose, short sleeves. Their loose trousers, also called *seraweel*, are tied at the waist with silk sashes. Outside the home, many Moroccan women follow the Muslim custom of covering their heads and their entire faces except their eyes with body-length cloaks called *haiak*.

Recreation. Moroccans enjoy hunting and trout fish-

Keith G. Mather, the contributor of this article, is a British expert on Africa and the Middle East. He has lived and traveled in Africa and has written extensively on African countries.

ing. Other favorite sports include basketball, boxing, field hockey, soccer, swimming, and volleyball.

City Life. Casablanca, Fez, Marrakech, Meknes, and Rabat are the only cities with more than 200,000 persons. Most large Moroccan cities have a modern section, a Jewish section called a *mellah*, and an Arab-Moorish section called a *medina*. The modern areas generally have tall apartment buildings, wide streets, and beautiful parks. In the medinas and mellahs, small, ancient adobe buildings are huddled together along winding streets. Many streets are so narrow that a man standing in the center can touch buildings on both sides. Merchants sell food, clothing, jewelry, and other items in the small crowded stalls of *souks* (open air markets). See also CASABLANCA; FEZ; MARRAKECH; RABAT.

Country Life. Most Moroccan farmhouses have two rooms, one for the father and one for the mother and children. Families sleep on mats on the floor, and eat their meals seated on the floor around a low table.

Work of the People

Agriculture. Farms near the coast and in the northwestern Atlas Mountains grow most of the country's agricultural products. Most farmers plant their crops by hand, and use horses to pull wooden plows. Wheat and barley are the main crops, but farmers also raise beans, corn, dates, grapes, nuts, oats, olives, peas, and citrus fruits. Farmers along the coast and herdsmen in the mountains raise cattle, goats, and sheep.

Fishing Industry. Fishing fleets catch anchovies, sardines, and tuna in the Atlantic and Mediterranean. The chief fisheries are in Agadir, Casablanca, and Safi.

Manufacturing and Processing. Morocco's main industries include food processing; leather tanning; the manufacture of leather goods, textiles, tiles, cement, and other building materials; and metal working. A chemical plant in Safi processes phosphates. Hydroelectric plants provide most of Morocco's power.

Skilled craftsmen pass their trades down from generation to generation. Their leather goods, woolen rugs, silver jewelry, brasswork, and pottery are world famous. See ISLAMIC ART.

Forest Products. Sawmills produce about 1,800,000 cubic feet (51,000 cubic meters) of timber a year from Morocco's cedar forests. Woodlands also supply more than 15,000 short tons (13,600 metric tons) of cork annually for domestic use and for export.

Trade. Morocco imports slightly more than it exports. The country imports machinery, petroleum, timber, textiles, and foods—coffee, dairy products, sugar, tea, and wheat. Morocco is the world's leading exporter of phosphates. The country's chief exports also include citrus fruits, cork, fish, tomatoes, vegetables, wine, and iron, lead, manganese, and zinc ores. Morocco trades mostly with France, West Germany, Spain, Britain, The Netherlands, and the United States.

Morocco is about one-eighteenth as large as the United States, not counting Alaska and Hawaii.

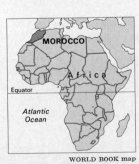

WORLD BOOK map
Location of Morocco

667

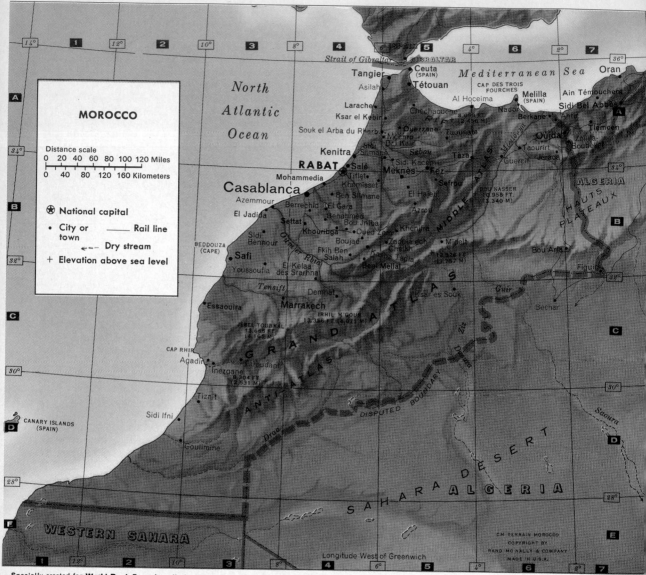

Specially created for **World Book Encyclopedia** by Rand McNally and World Book editors

Cities and Towns

Agadir	61,192..C 3
Ahfir	12,393..A 6
Al Hoceima	18,686..A 5
Asilah	14,074..A 4
Azemmour	17,182..B 3
Benahmed	10,460..B 4
Ben Slimane	17,302..B 4
Beni Mellal	53,826..B 4
Berkane	39,015..A 6
Berrechid	20,113..B 4
Bhalil*	6,633..B 5
Bou Arfa	15,924..B 6
Boujad	18,838..B 4
Bou Jniba	29,847..B 4
Casablanca	1,506,373..B 4
Ceuta (Spanish Possession)	67,187..A 5
Chechaouene	15,362..A 5
Demnat	7,140..C 4
El Gara	8,362..B 4
El Hajeb	12,601..B 5
El Jadida	55,501..B 3

El Kelaa des Srarhna	17,163..B 4
Erfoud*	5,400..C 5
Essaouira	30,061..C 3
Fez	325,327..A 5
Figuig	14,483..B 7
Fkih Ben Salah	26,918..B 4
Goulimine	16,544..D 2
Guercif	8,109..A 6
Ifni*	13,650..D 2
Ifrane*	6,016..B 5
Inezgane	11,495..C 3
Jerada	30,644..A 6
Kasba Tadla	15,776..B 4
Kenitra	139,206..A 4
Khemisset	21,811..A 4
Khenifra	25,526..B 5
Khouribga	73,667..B 4
Ksar el Kebir	48,262..A 5
Ksar es Souk	16,775..C 5
Larache	45,710..A 4
Marrakech	332,741..C 3
Martil*	5,410..A 5
Mechra Bel Ksiri	8,622..A 5

Meknès	248,369..B 5
Melilla (Spanish Possession)	64,942..A 6
Midelt	15,879..B 5
Mohammedia	70,392..B 4
Moulay Idriss*	8,189..A 5
Nador	32,490..A 6
Ouarzazate*	11,142..C 4
Oued Zem	33,323..B 4
Ouezzane	33,267..A 5
Oujda	175,532..A 7
Rabat	367,620..A 4
Safi	129,113..B 3
Salé	155,557..A 4
Sefrou	28,607..B 5
Segangane*	7,646..A 6
Settat	42,325..B 4
Sidi Bennour	37,068..B 3
Sidi Kacem	26,831..A 5
Sidi Slimane	20,398..A 5
Souk el Arba du Rharb	15,455..A 5

Tangier	187,894..A 5
Taounate	23,505..A 5
Taourirt	15,581..A 6
Tarfaya*	2,835..E 1
Taroudant	22,272..C 3
Taza	55,157..A 5
Tétouan	139,105..A 5
Tiflet	18,267..B 4
Tiznit	11,391..D 3
Youssoufia	22,435..B 3
Zaouia ech Cheikh	16,194..B 5

Physical Features

Anti-Atlas (Mountains)	D 3
Beddouza (Cape)	B 3
Bou Nasser (Mountain)	B 6
Cap des Trois Fourches (Cape)	A 6

Cap Rhir (Cape)	C 3
Daoura River	C 5
Draa River	D 4
Grand Atlas (Mountains)	C 4
Guir River	B 6
Hauts Plateaux (Plateau Region)	B 7
Irhil M Goun (Mountain)	C 4
Jebel Toubkal (Mountain)	C 4
Middle Atlas (Mountains)	B 5
Moulouya River	A 6
Oum er Rbia River	B 4
Rif (Mountainous Region)	A 5
Sebou River	A 5
Strait of Gibraltar	A 4
Tensift River	C 3
Ziz River	C 5

*Does not appear on map; key shows general location.
Source: 1971 census.

H. Armstrong Roberts

Moorish Archways pierce the walls that formerly protected the ancient city of Fez. All traffic had to pass through these gates.

Zoltan Glass, Pix

Modern Moroccan Apartments differ greatly from the windowless homes in which most Moroccans live in the cities and towns.

Tourism also provides some revenue for the country.

Transportation. Morocco has about 30,000 miles (48,-000 kilometers) of roads, but less than a third of this total is paved. Most travelers ride mules or horses. Over 1,000 miles (1,600 kilometers) of railroads link Morocco's large cities. Ships from many countries dock in Casablanca, Tangier, Safi, Kenitra, and Mohammedia. International flights provide service to airports in Casablanca, Rabat, Oujda, and Agadir.

Communication. Morocco has about 12 daily newspapers and about 35 weekly and monthly magazines. Extensive radio networks reach the entire country. Television is available in the cities.

Education

Only about a fifth of the people can read and write, but the number is increasing. In 1969, about 1,225,000 children attended primary schools, and 215,000 were in secondary schools. There are 23 teachers' colleges and more than 80 vocational training centers, including an engineering school. Morocco has two universities. About 9,500 students attend institutions of higher education. Arabic is gradually replacing French as the language used in schools.

Government

Morocco is a constitutional monarchy. The king is the head of state. He appoints a prime minister and other ministers to assist him. The king presides over the Council of Ministers (cabinet).

A Chamber of Representatives serves as Morocco's legislature. The chamber's 240 members are elected to six-year terms. Voters elect 160 of the members. The other 80 members of the chamber are elected by provincial assemblies and by representatives of agriculture, business, industry, and labor. The king has the power to dissolve the chamber.

Morocco is divided into 23 provinces and two *urban prefectures* (cities). There are two main political parties. The supreme court is the high court. There are also regional courts and three courts of appeal.

History

Early Years. In ancient times, the northern part of what is now Morocco formed part of the empire of Carthage. It became the Roman province of Mauretania after Rome conquered Carthage in 146 B.C. Berbers lived in the area then. When Roman power declined, Vandals crossed from Europe in 429 and invaded Morocco. Byzantine forces conquered the area 100 years later.

Arab armies swept westward across North Africa in the 600's. They conquered Morocco and introduced the Muslim religion. The Moroccan Berbers helped the Arabs conquer the Iberian Peninsula (now Spain and Portugal) in the 700's. The conquerors came to be known as Moors. Many more Arabs came to Morocco from the east in the 1000's.

The Moorish empire had great military power. It extended north into part of France. But it lacked unity until the Berber chieftain Yusuf Ibn-Tashfin unified it in the 1060's. Another Berber, Abd-el-Mumin, seized control in 1147. Within a hundred years, however, local princes regained power and lawlessness returned.

Spanish and Portuguese princes finally united against the Moors. By 1492, they had ended Moorish rule in the Iberian Peninsula, and within a few years, they conquered several cities along the Atlantic and Mediterranean coasts of Morocco. The Moors defeated them near Ksar el Kebir in northern Morocco, but Spain kept Ceuta and Melilla. In the late 1500's, the Moors turned back the Turks, who had conquered much of North Africa. But the local chiefs still fought among themselves, and the sultans who ruled the country were often overthrown.

The Pirate Era. Moroccan pirates provided one of the country's main sources of income from the 1300's to the

669

Fritz Henle, Photo Researchers

The Houses of Tétouan, Morocco, *above,* are crowded together along narrow, winding streets. Tétouan lies at the foot of the Rif mountains. It is a leading industrial center.

The Harbor at Tangier, *below,* lies at the western end of the Mediterranean, facing the Strait of Gibraltar. A Moroccan guide gazes across the bay from a rooftop in the Casbah.

George Danielle, Photo Researchers

1800's. The United States struck a blow against piracy in 1801 when it fought a war with Tripoli. Tripoli—now part of Libya—was a small North African state from which pirates attacked U.S. and European shipping. Sultan Moulay Souliman of Morocco came to Tripoli's aid in 1802 and declared war on the United States. But he called the war off before the United States even knew about his action (see BARBARY STATES). In 1814, Morocco abolished the practice of capturing and enslaving Christians. It outlawed piracy in 1817.

French and Spanish Control. In the early 1900's, the Moroccan sultans were weak and unable to keep order. European colonial powers then became interested in Morocco. France had already occupied Algeria. When fighting broke out in Morocco near the Algerian border, France moved to take over Morocco. But Germany objected. European powers met in 1906 and agreed to respect Moroccan independence and to maintain equal trading rights there (see ALGECIRAS CONFERENCE).

France sent troops to Morocco in 1907, and Spain sent troops in 1911. Again, Germany objected, but Great Britain backed France. In 1912, the sultan signed the Treaty of Fez, giving France control over Morocco's government and finances, and authority to keep an army there. France recognized three zones of Spanish influence: (1) the port of Ifni and its surrounding area; (2) a long strip of land along the Mediterranean coast; and (3) the area between the Draa River and the southern border. These zones were to be administered by a Spanish high commissioner in Tétouan. The rest of Morocco, except for Tangier, was administered by a French resident general in Rabat. But armed tribesmen fought against French and Spanish forces during the 1920's. France did not gain complete control of French Morocco until 1934. However, the French developed agriculture, industry, and mining, and built hydroelectric power stations, schools, and hospitals.

After France surrendered to Germany in World War II, the pro-German Vichy French government ruled French Morocco. But the Sultan and Moroccan nationalists supported the Allies. In 1942, Allied troops took French Morocco and made it a major Allied base.

Independence. After World War II, Moroccan nationalists tried to overthrow French and Spanish rule. Sultan Sidi Muhammad ben Youssef (King Muhammad V) also wanted independence for Morocco. He was forced into exile by the French in 1953 and replaced with Sidi Muhammad ben Moulay Arafa, who cooperated with the French. Moroccans greatly resented Ben Youssef's exile, and terrorism and killings flared anew.

France finally gave in to Moroccan pressure in 1955 and allowed Ben Youssef to return to Morocco and set up an independent monarchy. Ben Youssef promised to establish democratic government as soon as possible. France granted independence to French Morocco on Mar. 2, 1956. All of the northern Spanish zone except Ceuta and Melilla became part of independent Morocco.

The sultan became king of Morocco in 1957. He felt the new title was more in accord with his plan to establish a constitutional monarchy. In 1958, Spain turned over all of its southern holdings except Ifni to Morocco. It returned Ifni in 1969.

Recent Developments. In May, 1960, King Muhammad V assumed administrative control of the government. He appointed his son, Prince Moulay Hassan, as deputy premier. The king died on Feb. 26, 1961, and Moulay Hassan became King Hassan II.

In 1962, Morocco adopted its first constitution and became a constitutional monarchy with Islam as the state religion. King Hassan II appointed Ahmed Bahnini premier in 1963. He became the first premier in Moroccan history who was responsible to the legislature. But the government failed to put through the king's program of administrative and economic reforms.

Hassan proclaimed a state of emergency in 1965. He dismissed the cabinet, suspended the legislature, and took over the government's lawmaking and executive powers. He appointed a new government responsible to him. In 1970, voters approved a new constitution and elected a legislature, but Hassan suspended the legislature in 1972. A new legislature was elected in 1977.

In 1976, Spain ceded its overseas province of Spanish Sahara to Morocco and Mauritania. This area—which borders Morocco, Mauritania, and Algeria—is now called Western Sahara. Morocco claimed the northern part of the area, and Mauritania claimed the southern part. But Algeria and an organization called the Polisario Front, which consists of people who live in Western Sahara, opposed the claims. Fighting broke out between Polisario Front troops, and troops from Morocco and Mauritania. Algeria and, later, Libya, gave military aid to the Polisario Front. In 1979, Mauritania gave up its claim to Western Sahara and ended its role in the fighting. Morocco then claimed the area Mauritania had claimed. Fighting continued between Morocco and the Polisario Front.   KEITH G. MATHER

Related Articles in WORLD BOOK include:

Arab League	Fez	Muhammad V
Atlas Mountains	Hassan II	Olive (graph)
Casablanca	Larache	Rabat
Clothing (pictures)	Marrakech	Tangier

Outline

I. The Land and Its Resources
  A. The Land   C. Natural Resources
  B. Rivers and Lakes   D. Climate
II. Life of the People
  A. Language   C. City Life
  B. Way of Life   D. Country Life
III. Work of the People
  A. Agriculture   D. Forest Products
  B. Fishing Industry   E. Trade
  C. Manufacturing and F. Transportation
     Processing   G. Communication
IV. Education
V. Government
VI. History

Questions

Why did Morocco declare war on the United States in 1802?

What is unusual about Morocco's national capital?

Why is Morocco's location important?

How does the *mellah* differ from the *medina?*

How do most of the people earn their living?

What was unusual about the government of Tangier?

Who brought the Muslim religion to Morocco? When?

How was Morocco's government modernized?

MORONI (pop. 19,778) is the capital and largest city of Comoros, an island country southeast of the African mainland. It lies on the west coast of Grande Comore island. For location, see COMOROS (map).

Moroni is the nation's center of government, trade,

and tourism. Muslims from many countries visit the city's beautiful *mosque* (Muslim house of worship). The chief *lycée* (secondary school) of Comoros is located in Moroni. LEWIS HENRY GANN

MORPHEUS, *MAWR fyoos* or *MAWR fee us,* was the god of dreams in Greek mythology. He was one of the sons of Hypnos, the god of sleep. He took human form and appeared to people in their sleep. To be "in the arms of Morpheus" means to be asleep, and the drug morphine is named after him.

MORPHINE is a drug used to relieve severe pain and to treat several other medical problems. Some people use morphine because it makes them feel happier. In the United States, federal laws prohibit the use of this drug except when prescribed by a physician.

Anyone who uses morphine regularly may in time become addicted to it. If he stops his usual dose, he will feel ill for several days unless he takes medicine for this *withdrawal sickness.* Withdrawal sickness may include abdominal cramps, back pains, chills, diarrhea, nausea, vomiting, and weakness.

Morphine makes severe pain bearable and moderate pain disappear. The drug also stops coughing and diarrhea, checks bleeding, and may help bring sleep. Doctors give patients morphine only if other medicines would fail. Besides being addictive, it interferes with breathing and heart action and may cause vomiting.

Small doses of morphine leave the mind fairly clear. Larger doses cloud the mind and make the user feel extremely lazy. Most morphine users feel little hunger, anger, sadness, or worry, and their sex drive is greatly reduced. Most people with mental or social problems feel happy after using morphine, even though their problems have not really been solved.

Some morphine addicts can give up the drug fairly easily with medical help. But an addict with many problems—mental, physical, or social—may find morphine hard to give up. Personal counseling, controlled living situations, and such medicines as methadone may help addicts solve their problems and stop taking morphine (see DRUG ADDICTION; METHADONE).

Morphine is made from opium, and heroin is manufactured from morphine. These three drugs have similar effects. However, heroin is the strongest and opium is the least powerful. DONALD J. WOLK

See also HEROIN; OPIUM.

MORPHOLOGY, in grammar. See SYNTAX.

MORPHOLOGY, *mawr FAHL uh jee,* is the branch of biological science which deals with the form and structure of animals and plants. It covers the three main phases of animal and plant forms: (1) their development; (2) the history of an organism as a whole and of its separate parts; (3) the resemblances and differences between several forms of the same plant or animal. In the study of botany, morphology is sometimes called *structural botany.* In the study of animal structure, it is the foundation of anatomy. In geology, morphology is the study of the external form of rocks. The German writer Johann von Goethe made up the term *morphology* from the Greek words *morphe,* meaning *form,* and *logos,* meaning *doctrine.* WILLIAM C. BEAVER

MORRILL, JUSTIN SMITH (1810-1898), represented Vermont in the U.S. House of Representatives from

1855 to 1867, and in the U.S. Senate from 1867 to 1898. He proposed the Morrill Act of 1862, which established the Land-Grant Colleges and Universities (see LAND-GRANT COLLEGE OR UNIVERSITY). He introduced the Morrill Tariff Act in 1861. He helped found the Republican Party, and helped pass legislation that established the present Library of Congress. Morrill was born in Strafford, Vt. C. B. BAKER

MORRILL ACTS. See LAND-GRANT COLLEGE.

MORRILL TARIFF ACT OF 1861. See TARIFF (United States Tariffs).

MORRIS, ESTHER HOBART (1814-1902), led the fight for women's suffrage in Wyoming. Through her efforts, the territory of Wyoming passed a women's suffrage law in 1869 that became a model for later suffrage laws. When Wyoming became a state in 1890, it was the first state to permit women to vote.

Born Esther McQuigg in Tioga County, New York, she settled in the Wyoming territory in 1868. She became the first woman justice of the peace in the U.S. in 1870. A statue of her represents Wyoming in Statuary Hall in the U.S. Capitol in Washington, D.C. LOUIS FILLER

MORRIS, GOUVERNEUR (1752-1816), was an American statesman and diplomat. He headed the committee that wrote the final draft of the United States Constitution. Much of the credit for the wording in the Constitution belongs to him.

Morris was suspected of sympathies for England at the outbreak of the Revolutionary War, but he soon proved himself to be one of the most loyal American patriots. He spoke in favor of the power of the Continental Congress at the revolutionary congress of New York in 1775, and served as a leading member of the New York constitutional convention in 1776. He was a member of the Continental Congress from 1778 to 1779. Morris headed several committees, and acted as draftsman of important documents. He was one of General George Washington's most able supporters in Congress. He attracted the attention of Robert Morris, financial agent of Congress, and served as assistant superintendent of finance from 1781 to 1785. Morris was elected Pennsylvania delegate to the Constitutional Convention in 1787. At first he favored a strong, centralized government controlled by the wealthy.

In 1789, he went to Paris as a financial agent. From 1792 to 1794, he was minister to France. From 1800 to 1803 he was a U.S. senator from New York. Morris was also a key figure in promoting the Erie Canal project. He was born in Morrisania, N.Y. CLINTON ROSSITER

MORRIS, LEWIS (1726-1798), was a signer of the Declaration of Independence from New York. He served in the Continental Congress from 1775 to 1777, where he worked on committees supervising supplies of ammunition and military stores. Morris later served in the New York state legislature from 1777 to 1790. He was a major general of the New York state militia during the Revolutionary War. He was born in Morrisania, N.Y., and was a half brother of Gouverneur Morris (see MORRIS, GOUVERNEUR).

MORRIS, ROBERT (1734-1806), was a Pennsylvania signer of the Declaration of Independence. He made his greatest contribution to the new republic from 1781 to 1784, as American superintendent of finance. Morris represented Pennsylvania from 1789 to 1795 as a Federalist in the first United States Senate. He also was one of the best-known merchants in the United States.

Morris became prominent when he served in the Continental Congress from 1776 to 1778, and headed two of its most important committees. One committee obtained war materials, and the other instructed the country's diplomats in Europe.

Morris' political and business experience led to his appointment as finance superintendent. The nation's paper currency was almost worthless when he took office in 1781. Morris established the Bank of North America to help relieve the shortage of acceptable currency. He also issued notes, based on his own credit, that served as money.

Brown Bros.
Robert Morris

He was born in Liverpool, England. He came to America in 1747 with little money. As a result of his exceptional business and administrative ability, he built up a network of business connections in America and Europe that made him wealthy.

After leaving his government financial post in 1784, Morris became a land speculator. He lost his fortune in these operations, and was imprisoned for bankruptcy from 1798 to 1801. He spent his last years in poverty and obscurity. CLARENCE L. VER STEEG

See also PHILADELPHIA (The Revolutionary War Period); WASHINGTON, GEORGE (Recall to Duty).

MORRIS, WILLIAM (1834-1896), was an English poet, artist, and reformer. A man of many talents, he tried to make his vision of beauty an actual part of everyday life. In 1861, he helped found Morris & Company to produce home furnishings of good design and craftsmanship. Among these furnishings was the Morris chair. Morris practiced many crafts, such as wood engraving.

Morris developed a liking for the culture of the Middle Ages in his studies at Oxford. He believed that through arts and crafts he could find a way out of industrial ugliness back to the joys of creation men had experienced in the Middle Ages. All these interests came to focus in 1891, when Morris founded the Kelmscott Press. He designed three type faces, supervised the making of fine paper, and produced books. Morris was born in Walthamstow, England. RAY NASH

See also BOOK (Improvements in Books).

MORRIS BROWN COLLEGE. See UNIVERSITIES AND COLLEGES (table).

MORRIS DAM forms a water-supply reservoir for Pasadena, Calif. It lies on the San Gabriel River and is 328 feet (100 meters) high and 780 feet (238 meters) long. Engineers completed the dam in 1934.

MORRIS PLAN BANK was organized to lend money to people who owned no property. These people might otherwise have had to borrow from "loan sharks" or friends. Arthur J. Morris of Norfolk, Va., founded the first Morris Plan Bank in 1900. It was patterned after thousands of similar institutions in Europe.

Loans of the type that once were made by the Morris Plan Bank are now made by many commercial banks and by personal loan companies. Only a few Morris Plan Banks still operate. L. T. FLATLEY

See also LOAN COMPANY.

MORRISON, HERBERT STANLEY (1888-1965), BARON MORRISON OF LAMBETH, was one of the leaders of the British Labour Party. He began his career as an errand boy and a telephone operator, and rose to become foreign secretary of his country.

Morrison served during World War II as home secretary and minister of home security in the coalition government of 1940 to 1945. He was a powerful member of Prime Minister Winston Churchill's war Cabinet, even though he had been a conscientious objector in World War I. In Prime Minister Clement Attlee's Labour government of 1945-1951, Morrison served as lord president of the council, leader of the Labour majority in the House of Commons, and deputy prime minister. He served briefly as foreign secretary in 1951. He lost his government post when the Conservative Party came into power in 1951. He was made a peer in 1959. Morrison was born in Brixton, England. CHARLES LOCH MOWAT

MORRISTOWN (pop. 17,662), a city in north-central New Jersey, lies about 30 miles (48 kilometers) west of New York City (see NEW JERSEY [political map]). Many residents commute to their jobs in New York City on the Erie-Lackawanna Railroad. Morristown is headquarters for The Seeing Eye, Inc., which trains dogs to guide blind persons (see GUIDE DOG).

Morristown was an encampment for George Washington's armies for two winters during the Revolutionary War. The Jacob Ford Mansion, Washington's headquarters for seven months, is now a museum. Jockey Hollow, another section of Morristown, was the site of the crude huts where Washington's soldiers spent the winters. These historic places are preserved in Morristown National Historical Park. Morristown has a mayor-council government. The city is the seat of Morris County. RICHARD P. McCORMICK

MORRISTOWN NATIONAL HISTORICAL PARK. See NATIONAL PARK SYSTEM (table).

MORRO CASTLE. See HAVANA; SAN JUAN.

MORRO CASTLE DISASTER. See ASBURY PARK.

MORROW, DWIGHT WHITNEY (1873-1931), was an American lawyer, banker, and diplomat. He served brilliantly as United States ambassador to Mexico from 1927 to 1930 during the Mexican-American diplomatic crises (see COOLIDGE, CALVIN [Foreign Affairs]).

Morrow was born in Huntington, W.Va. After practicing law in New York City, he joined the banking firm of J. P. Morgan and Company in 1914. During World War I, his outstanding work on the Military Board of Supply earned him the Distinguished Service Medal. His daughter, Anne, married Charles A. Lindbergh (see LINDBERGH, ANNE MORROW). HARVEY WISH

MORROW, HONORÉ, AHN oh RAY, **WILLSIE** (1880?-1940), was an American historical novelist. She spent 10 years of research on the life of Abraham Lincoln before writing her novels about him. Her Lincoln trilogy, *Great Captain*, consists of *Forever Free* (1927), *With Malice Toward None* (1928), and *The Last Full Measure* (1930). She also wrote *Mary Todd Lincoln* (1928). Morrow was born in Ottumwa, Iowa. HARRY H. CLARK

MORS. See SOMNUS.

MORSE, SAMUEL F. B.

MORSE, SAMUEL FINLEY BREESE (1791-1872), developed the first successful electric telegraph in the United States, and invented the Morse code, still used occasionally to send telegrams (see TELEGRAPH). Morse also became one of the best early American portrait painters. He helped found the National Academy of Design, and became its first president in 1826.

Early Life. Morse was born on April 27, 1791, in Charlestown, Mass. He was the son of a minister and author. From early childhood Morse was talented in art, and studied to be an artist. His classmates at Yale College admired his clever art, and he was known there for his miniatures in ivory. He had such teachers at Yale as Jeremiah Day, a mathematician, and Benjamin Silliman, a chemist and physicist. He found their electrical and chemical experiments "amusing and instructive." But, when he was graduated in 1810, he wanted only to study art. His father opposed Morse's desire to become a professional artist. Finally, he consented to let Morse go to England to study art.

He went to London in 1811. He evidently arrived in a gay mood, and spent too much money on new clothes. He applied for admission to the Royal Academy of Arts. The academy would not accept him until he submitted some work. Morse was advised to do a small sketch of a statue in black and white chalk. He worked hard, but each time he submitted the sketch, he was told to "finish it." He learned he must "sacrifice painting to dress and visiting, or vice versa." After two years of study, Morse wrote, "I have had no new clothes for nearly a year. My best are threadbare, my shoes out at the toes, my stockings all want to see my mother."

Artistic Success. Hard work had its reward. Morse modeled a figure of Hercules in clay. A professor at the academy liked the statue so much, he advised Morse to enter it in competition for the gold medal of the Adelphi Society of Arts. One proud day in 1812, before an audience of English nobility, the Duke of Norfolk pinned the Adelphi gold medal on the young American.

Morse's painting, *The Dying Hercules*, was accepted in 1813 for the annual Royal Academy art exhibit. One British critic rated it among the nine best of a thousand paintings in the exhibit. Another painting, *The Judgment of Jupiter*, was accepted for the 1815 exhibit.

Morse came home from his London triumphs in 1815. But he went through many lean years before he became the well-known portrait painter. His portrait of Marquis de Lafayette (1825) is in the New York City Hall. The New York Public Library owns another Morse painting of Lafayette. Morse wanted to do more than paint portraits. He wanted to do vast historical pictures. The Capitol in Washington, D.C., was being built during this time. Morse heard that four huge paintings were to be in the rotunda of the Capitol. He went back to Europe in 1829 to prepare himself for this challenge. He stayed three years.

Morse and the Telegraph. Morse first became interested in the electric telegraph in 1832. He was on board the ship *Sully* on his way home from Europe. He learned during a dinner conversation at sea that men had found they could send electricity instantly over any known length of wire. From that moment on, he was on fire with the idea of an electric telegraph. He spent

Brown Bros.

Samuel F.B. Morse

the rest of the voyage making notes and drawing pictures. He said to the captain when he left the ship, "Well, captain, should you hear of the telegraph one of these days, as the wonder of the world, remember the discovery was made on the good ship *Sully*."

Morse arrived home almost penniless. He was counting on winning a commission to do a painting for the Capitol. The fee would support him while he worked on the telegraph. But John Quincy Adams, a member of the committee selecting artists, remarked that he did not think American artists were good enough. A fiery answer to Adams appeared in a New York paper. James Fenimore Cooper had written it, but people thought Morse had. Morse did not get a commission to do any of the paintings.

The Lean Years. Morse's brothers, Sidney and Richard, gave him a room on the top floor of their newspaper building. There Morse lived, cooking his own meals, and slaving over the telegraph. The new University of the City of New York offered him a position as teacher of painting and sculpturing. His salary evidently depended on fees from pupils, and every spare penny went into work on his invention. Leonard D. Gale, a professor, became interested and helped him.

There was plenty of work to do. Morse could not buy insulated wire on reels. He had to buy wire in pieces, solder the pieces together, then wrap the wire, bit by bit, with cotton thread. After he worked five years, he demonstrated the telegraph in 1837. He hoped the men who saw it would invest money to help him complete it. They found it interesting and amusing but would not invest in it.

The most valuable person watching the demonstration was Alfred Vail, a university student. Vail's father and brother owned an iron and brass works in Morristown, N.J. Vail offered to build a sturdier model of the telegraph. Morse made him a partner, with a one-fourth interest in the telegraph. In 1838, Morse took the new machine to Washington to obtain money from Congress to test the telegraph. Congress refused. Years of disappointment followed. Morse made a trip to England and France, but could find no support.

Morse prepared a dramatic demonstration of the telegraph in 1842. He waterproofed 2 miles (3.2 kilometers) of wire with pitch, tar, and rubber, and laid it under-

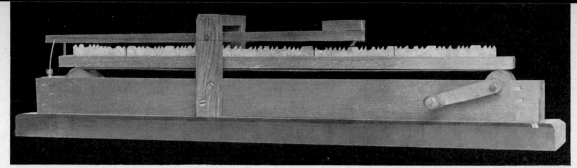

Morse Built a Notched Rod, or Port Rule, *above,* to operate the key of his telegraph sending device.

The First Public Telegraph Message, sent from Washington to Baltimore in 1844, was recorded on tape, *below.*

water from the Battery to Governors Island. The New York papers carried an announcement of the great demonstration. Unfortunately, a ship's anchor caught the wire. The sailors brought it up, and cut it. The crowds who had come to see the "wonder of the ages" went away later muttering about a hoax.

His Success. Morse made one more attempt in 1843 to interest Congress. The last night of the session, long after Morse had given up hope, Congress passed a bill appropriating $30,000 to test the telegraph. Morse strung the telegraph line from the United States Supreme Court room in the Capitol to Baltimore, Md. On May 24, 1844, Morse stood among a large group of spectators and tapped out on the telegraph

Samuel Morse First Won Recognition as a Painter. His portrait *Marquis de Lafayette, below,* shows his artistic skill.
Art Commission of the City of New York

his famous message, "What hath God wrought."

Morse and his telegraph were known within 12 years throughout North America and Europe. The English telegraph companies gave a banquet in his honor in 1856. W. F. Cooke, a rival inventor, in his tribute to Morse at the banquet said, "I was consulted only a few months ago on the subject of a telegraph for a country in which no telegraph at present exists. I recommended the system of Professor Morse. I believe that system to be one of the simplest in the world."

Credit for the invention of the telegraph also should be given to Morse's partners, Gale and Vail. Many others gave substantial help in developing it.

Morse won wealth and fame. Rulers of other countries decorated him. A group of European countries united to give him a cash award of 400,000 francs. Morse became an honorary member of societies in the United States and Europe. The telegraph operators of America gave him the unusual honor of unveiling a statue to him while he was still living. It was unveiled on June 10, 1871, in New York City's Central Park. Morse died the next year in New York City.   JEAN LEE LATHAM

MORSE, WAYNE LYMAN (1900-1974), served as United States senator from Oregon, first as a Republican, then as a Democrat. He was elected in 1944 and in 1950 as a Republican. Calling himself an "independent Republican," he withdrew from the Republican Party in 1952 and supported Democratic presidential candidate Adlai E. Stevenson. Morse became a Democrat in 1955, and was re-elected to the Senate as a Democrat in 1956 and 1962. He was defeated in bids for re-election in 1968 and 1972. Morse's major interests in the Senate included labor-management relations, Latin-American affairs, and international law. In the 1960's, Morse became one of the most outspoken critics of United States involvement in the Vietnam War.

Morse was born in Madison, Wis. He was graduated from the University of Wisconsin in 1923, and earned law degrees at the University of Minnesota and at Columbia University. Morse began teaching law at the University of Oregon in 1929. He was dean of the university's law school from 1931 to 1944.   JESSE L. GILMORE

675

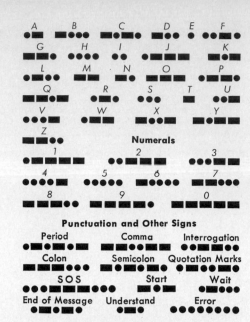

The Morse Code was once used to send telegraph messages in the United States and Canada.

The International Morse Code is now used chiefly to send messages by short-wave radio.

MORSE CODE is a system of dots, dashes, and spaces that telegraphers in the United States and Canada once used to send messages by wire. The code was named for Samuel Morse, who patented the telegraph in 1840. The letters that occur most frequently in our language are represented by the simplest symbols.

The dot is made by quickly pressing and releasing the key of the telegraph sender. This produces a rapid *click-clack* sound in the receiver at the other end. A short dash is twice as long as a dot. A long dash is equal to four dots. The space between the dots and dashes that make up a letter is the same length as a dot. The space between the letters of a word equals three dots. A space that is part of a letter combination equals two dots.

For years, all telegraph messages and most news were transmitted by Morse code. Now, most such messages are sent by automatic facsimile and printing telegraph machines. Radio and telegraph operators in other countries once used International Morse Code, also called International and Continental Code. But facsimile and printing methods of sending messages are now more widely used.   WESTERN UNION TELEGRAPH COMPANY

See also TELEGRAPH; TELETYPEWRITER.

MORTALITY RATE. See BIRTH AND DEATH RATES.

MORTAR. See BRICK (Mortar).

MORTAR is a short-range weapon that is used to reach nearby targets that are protected by hills or other obstacles. A mortar fires a shell on a high arc that enables it to clear obstacles. It has a higher angle of fire, shorter barrel, and lower muzzle *velocity* (speed) than a gun or a howitzer. Mortars are light, can be moved easily, and have great firepower. For example, the 81-millimeter mortar can fire a 12-pound (5-kilogram) shell about 2,500 yards (2,290 meters).

A mortar consists of a tube closed at the *breech* (bottom) end, that rests on a base plate. Two adjustable legs support the muzzle end. Soldiers fire the mortar by dropping the ammunition down the muzzle of the tube. When the ammunition reaches the bottom, it strikes the firing pin, which explodes the *primer*. Most mortar shells have fins to prevent them from tumbling in the air. Artillery mortars have *bore* diameters of 105 millimeters or larger. Infantry mortars have diameters less than 105 millimeters.

Before World War II, armies used heavy, stubby mortars. Large mortars were also used to defend coastlines. But howitzers have largely replaced these heavy mortars in present-day warfare. The lightweight and easily moved infantry mortar became an important weapon during World War II.   JOHN D. BILLINGSLEY

See also CIVIL WAR (picture); HOWITZER.

MORTARBOARD. See CAPS AND GOWNS.

MORTE DARTHUR. See MALORY, SIR THOMAS.

MORTGAGE is a loan agreement that enables a person to borrow money to buy a house or other property.

U.S. Army (WORLD BOOK photo)

The 81-mm Mortar has a maximum firing range of 10,500 feet (3,200 meters). It was used effectively in World War II.

The property is used as security for the loan. The lender may take possession of the property if the loan is not repaid on time. Almost all mortgages involve some kind of real estate.

A mortgage actually consists of two legal documents. One document, called a *note*, specifies the amount of the loan, the repayment terms, and other conditions of the agreement. The other document is the mortgage itself, which gives the lender legal claim to the property if the loan is not repaid. The term *mortgage* commonly refers to the entire loan agreement. The lender is called the *mortgagee*, and the borrower is the *mortgager*.

A person can obtain a mortgage from a bank, insurance company, mortgage company, savings and loan association, or other financial institutions. The interest rate and other terms vary from lender to lender. Most mortgage agreements require the mortgager to repay the loan in monthly installments over a period of 20 years or more. Part of each payment goes toward the unpaid balance of the loan, called the *principal*, and part toward the interest. As the borrower pays off the loan, more of each monthly payment goes toward the principal, and less toward the interest. The mortgager gradually increases the *equity*, which is the value of the property beyond the amount owed on it.

If the borrower misses a number of payments or violates any other condition of the agreement, the lender may *foreclose* the mortgage. Foreclosure is a legal procedure by which the lender takes over the mortgaged property. The lender then may sell the property, keep the amount owed, and give the borrower whatever is left. More than one mortgage may be placed on a property. If foreclosure occurs, the holder of the *second mortgage* gets nothing until the claims of the first have been fully met.

Two United States government agencies, the Federal Housing Administration (FHA) and the Veterans Administration (VA), guarantee some home mortgage loans against loss to the lender. Loans not protected by a government agency are called *conventional loans*.

Mortgage loans have traditionally been a popular investment for financial institutions because of the great safety of such loans. During periods of rapidly rising prices, however, lenders may hesitate to tie up their money in mortgages. Interest rates soar during these periods of *inflation*, but most mortgages pay interest at a fixed rate throughout their term. Thus, a lending institution that issues a 25-year mortgage at 8 per cent interest may lose an opportunity to lend the money later at 12 per cent. Inflation also drives down the purchasing power of money. As a result, the dollars that lenders get back have less buying power than the dollars they lent. During periods of inflation, many lending institutions charge an additional fee called *points* for granting a mortgage loan. Each point equals 1 per cent of the amount of the loan. For example, 3 points on a $60,000 mortgage total $1,800. The fee is regarded as prepaid interest and must be paid when the mortgage is signed.

To counteract the effects of inflation, lending institutions have developed *graduated-payment mortgages*, *variable-rate mortgages*, and other types of mortgages. In a graduated-payment mortgage, the borrower makes lower monthly payments for the first few years and higher payments later. In a variable-rate mortgage, the interest rate rises and falls in relation to current interest rates. MARK J. RIEDY

See also HOUSE (Financing a House).

MORTGAGE BOND. See BOND.

MORTICIAN. See FUNERAL DIRECTOR.

MORTON, JOHN (1724-1777), was a Pennsylvania signer of the Declaration of Independence. He served in the Continental Congress from 1774 to 1777. Morton began his political career in 1756 as a member of the Pennsylvania Assembly. He served in the assembly for nearly 20 years.

Morton also served as an associate judge of the Pennsylvania state Supreme Court. He served as one of four Pennsylvania delegates to the Stamp Act Congress in 1765 (see STAMP ACT). Morton was born in Ridley, Pa. ROBERT J. TAYLOR

MORTON, JULIUS STERLING (1832-1902), an American political leader and nature lover, established the first United States observance of Arbor Day (see ARBOR DAY). Morton was secretary of agriculture from 1893 to 1897 in President Grover Cleveland's Cabinet. He was secretary of the Nebraska territory from 1858 to 1861, and also served as acting governor for several months. He was born in Adams, N.Y., and received degrees from the University of Michigan and Union College. Nebraska placed a statue of Morton in the United States Capitol in 1937. ARTHUR A. EKIRCH, JR.

See also NEBRASKA (Places to Visit [Arbor Lodge]).

MORTON, LEVI PARSONS (1824-1920), served as Vice-President of the United States from 1889 to 1893, under President Benjamin Harrison. He also was minister to France from 1881 to 1885, and governor of New York in 1895 and 1896. Morton was a Republican. His political success started in 1879 when he was elected to a term in the House of Representatives from New York.

He entered the banking business during the Civil War, and became a prominent New York City banker. His company, through its London branch, was fiscal agent of the United

Culver

Levi Parsons Morton

States from 1873 to 1884. He taught school and owned a dry goods firm in New Hampshire before he became a banker. He was born in Shoreham, Vt. IRVING G. WILLIAMS

MORTON, OLIVER PERRY (1823-1877), served as governor of Indiana during the Civil War and as a Republican United States senator from 1867 until his death. He was elected lieutenant governor in 1860, and became governor in 1861 when Governor Henry Lane resigned to enter the Senate. As governor, Morton helped raise volunteer troops. He raised money through his own efforts to support troops when the Indiana legislature refused to grant him funds. While in the Senate, he served as an adviser to President Ulysses S. Grant. Morton was born in Wayne County, Indiana. Indiana placed a statue of Morton in the United States Capitol in 1900. W. B. HESSELTINE

677

MORTON, ROGERS CLARK BALLARD (1914-1979), held three Cabinet-level offices under Presidents Richard M. Nixon and Gerald R. Ford. Morton served as secretary of the interior from 1971 until 1975, when he became secretary of commerce. In 1976 and 1977, he was counselor to the President for domestic and economic matters, a post with Cabinet rank. From 1974 to 1976, Morton also served as head of the Energy Resources Council, which was formed to prepare a national energy policy.

As secretary of the interior, Morton worked to expand oil exploration in offshore areas of the United States. He encouraged the development of new energy sources. He also reorganized the Bureau of Indian Affairs to give more self-government to Indians living on federal reservations.

Morton was born in Louisville, Ky., and graduated from Yale University in 1937. He moved to Maryland in 1953 and represented that state as a Republican member of the U.S. House of Representatives from 1963 to 1971. Morton was chairman of the Republican National Committee from 1969 to 1971.　　GUY HALVERSON

MORTON, WILLIAM THOMAS GREEN (1819-1868), an American dentist, made the first public demonstration of ether in 1846. Crawford W. Long used ether during surgery in 1842, but he did not make his discovery public until 1848 (see LONG, CRAWFORD W.).

Morton first used ether in a tooth extraction at the suggestion of Charles T. Jackson of the Harvard Medical School. He used it again in 1846 in an operation performed by John C. Warren at Massachusetts General Hospital. Morton called his anesthesia *letheon*.

The method spread rapidly to England, France, and other countries. In 1852, the French Academy of Science awarded the Montyon prize of 5,000 francs jointly to Jackson and Morton. Both men claimed sole credit for the discovery, and Morton refused to share the prize with Jackson. A bitter quarrel and lawsuits followed, and Morton was ruined financially. Morton was born in Charlton, Mass. GEORGE ROSEN

See also ANESTHESIA; ETHER; MEDICINE (History [picture: Ether Anesthesia]).

MORTON ARBORETUM. See ARBORETUM; ILLINOIS (Places to Visit).

MOSAIC, *moh ZAY ihk,* is an art form in which small pieces of colored glass, stone, or other material are set into mortar. The pieces, called *tesserae* or *tessellae*, fit together to form a picture. Most mosaics decorate ceilings, floors, and interior walls, but some are used for such exterior surfaces as pavements and outside walls.

People in ancient Mesopotamia may have made mosaics as early as the 3000's B.C. However, the widespread use of mosaics began in the 300's B.C. in areas ruled by Greece. The Greeks later taught mosaic design to the Romans, who developed their own style of the art form during the A.D. 100's and 200's. The Romans spread mosaic art throughout the Roman Empire.

In the 500's, mosaics became the major decorative art form of the Byzantine Empire, which included parts of the eastern Mediterranean area. Mosaics of religious scenes decorated the walls and ceilings of many Byzantine churches. The finest Byzantine mosaics were made

Mosaics (1950's) designed by Juan O'Gorman;
Mexican Government Tourist Dept.

Modern Mexican Mosaics cover the 10-story library of the National Autonomous University near Mexico City. The mosaics trace Mexican history from prehistoric times to today.

Tree of Life (1964); collection of the New Jersey State Museum, Trenton, N.J.

A Modern American Mosaic designed by Ben Shahn uses quotations from the writings of an ancient Phoenician philosopher to express the artist's belief that all religions deserve respect.

The Good Shepherd (about A.D. 430) from the Mausoleum of Galla Placidia, Ravenna, Italy (Madeline Grimoldi)

from the 900's to the 1300's. With the decline of the Byzantine Empire in the 1400's, the use of mosaic art also declined. The art form never regained the importance that it had during the Byzantine era.

Through the centuries, peoples of various other cultures have created mosaic art. For example, Muslims in India and Persia made mosaics, as did the Aztec and Mayan Indians of Latin America. Architects in Mexico have used mosaics to decorate modern buildings. SLOBODAN ĆURČIĆ

See also BYZANTINE ART; INDIANA (Education [picture]); MEXICO (Arts [picture]); SHELL (picture: Shell Mosaic).

MOSAIC DISEASE is a plant disease caused by a virus. The leaves of affected plants become mottled with light and dark-

Grant Heilman
Mosaic Disease on Corn

green blotches. The disease usually stunts the growth of plants, and may cause flowers to become streaked and twisted. Plants attacked by the disease include beans, carnations, corn, orchids, potatoes, sweet peas, tobacco, and wheat, and weeds such as burweed and milkweed. Insects, such as aphids, often transmit the virus from diseased plants to healthy ones. Gardeners protect plants by using insecticides to control insects. There is no cure for a plant that has mosaic disease, and it should be removed and burned. Diseased plants should never be divided or used for cuttings because every part is infected. HENRY T. NORTHEN

MOSBY, *MOZE bih,* **JOHN SINGLETON** (1833-1916), was a famous Confederate ranger during the Civil War. He joined the Confederate cavalry in 1861, and served on "Jeb" Stuart's staff in 1862. He began his independent ranger activities in 1863. His raids on Union bases and camps were so effective that part of north-central Virginia soon became known as "Mosby's Confederacy." After the war, Mosby practiced law and held several public offices. He was born in Powhatan County, Virginia. FRANK E. VANDIVER

Weston Kemp

Red Square lies in the heart of Moscow. At one end stands famous St. Basil's Church, *left*, near Lenin's tomb, *center*. Spasskaya Tower, *right*, rises above a gate in the Kremlin walls.

MOSCOW, *MAHS koh* or *MAHS kow*, is the capital and largest city of Russia. It is the fourth largest city in the world, and ranks first in size among all European cities. Moscow also is the capital of the Russian Soviet Federated Socialist Republic. This state is the largest and most important of the 15 republics that make up Russia.

About a million *Muscovites* (people of Moscow) work in the city's many government offices. The Russian Communist Party, which controls the government, has its headquarters in Moscow. It influences Communists in many parts of the world. Many decisions made in Moscow affect millions of persons on all continents.

Moscow was once the home of Russia's czars, and the city has many old palaces and museums filled with art treasures. Today, Moscow is a huge industrial community. A Russian must have permission from the government to live in Moscow. This policy helps keep the residential sections from becoming too crowded.

Large new factories stand near huge apartment buildings in Moscow's main residential areas. The city's chief industry is the manufacture of automobiles, buses, and trucks. Moscow is also Russia's cultural center. Its ballet performances especially are world famous.

Moscow lies in the north-central part of European

Richard Antony French, the contributor of this article, is Senior Lecturer in the University College and School of Slavonic and East European Studies at the University of London.

Russia, about 400 miles (640 kilometers) southeast of Leningrad. The Moscow River flows through the city. Moscow is built in the shape of a huge wheel. Many wide boulevards extend from the center of the city like the spokes of a wheel. They cross circular boulevards, which form inner and outer rims of the wheel.

Famous Landmarks. At the center of the wheel stands the Kremlin. This old fortress is the center of the Russian government. Inside its walls, which extend 1½ miles (2.4 kilometers), are beautiful cathedrals and palaces, as well as government buildings. Some of the cathedrals date from the 1400's. Many czars are buried in the Cathedral of the Archangel. The Supreme Soviet, Russia's parliament, meets in the Grand Kremlin Palace. Russia's Communist Party meets in the Palace of Congresses. See KREMLIN.

Red Square lies just outside the Kremlin walls. This large plaza, nearly ¼ mile (0.4 kilometer) long, took its name in Russian from an old word meaning both *beautiful* and *red*. There, huge military and civilian parades celebrate the anniversary of the Russian Revolution and other special occasions. Some parades include hundreds of thousands of marchers and last several hours. Russian leaders watch the parades from atop the Lenin Mausoleum. Thousands of Russians line up daily at the tomb to view the preserved body of Lenin, the founder of Communist Russia.

Opposite the Kremlin on Red Square is GUM, Russia's largest department store. Saint Basil's Church is also on Red Square. This 400-year-old building is part of the State Historical Museum. It has eight onion-shaped domes. The Russia Hotel, one of the world's largest hotels, faces the Kremlin near Red Square.

Muscovites are proud of their subway system, called the *Metro*. The city has more than 70 subway stations, which look like palace halls and are the fanciest in the world. Each is designed differently. Many are beautifully decorated with chandeliers, marble panels, paintings, stained glass, and statues.

Sports and Recreation. Muscovites have many facilities for recreation. Luzhniki, a huge sports area, includes Lenin Stadium, which can seat about 103,000 persons. The stadium is used mostly for soccer, the people's favorite sport, and for track events. A soccer club called Dynamo has Moscow's second largest stadium.

Every year, about seven million persons go to Gorki Park, Moscow's most popular amusement center. It has an open-air theater, various exhibits, and facilities for such sports as boating, ice skating, and tennis. Many chess champions play at the Central Chess Club. In winter, the hills near Moscow attract skiers.

Music and Art. The Bolshoi Theater presents ballets that many persons consider Russia's highest artistic achievement. Young dancers from all parts of Russia are trained at the Bolshoi Theater's school. The Symphony Orchestra of the U.S.S.R. performs at the Tchaikovsky Conservatory. Moscow also has many famous drama theaters, such as the Maly and Moscow Art theaters.

The city has about 150 museums and art galleries. The State Historical Museum attracts many students of early Russian history. The Central Lenin Museum and the Museum of the Revolution have exhibits on the Russian Revolution. Dazzling treasures of the czars are displayed in the Armory Museum in the Kremlin.

Schools. Moscow State University is the largest university in Russia. It was established in 1755, and has more than 30,000 students. The science building, 37 stories high, is Moscow's tallest skyscraper. Moscow has more than a thousand elementary schools and high schools, and over 80 specialized institutes.

About 3,000 main and branch libraries operate throughout Moscow. The Lenin State Library, the largest library in Russia, has one of the largest collections of books and manuscripts in the world.

Economy. Moscow is the most important industrial city in Russia. Its factories produce a wide variety of products, but chiefly automobiles, buses, and trucks. Other important products include chemicals, electrical machinery, measuring instruments, steel, and textiles. About a million persons work in Moscow's factories.

Moscow is the transportation center of Russia. Highways and railways extend in all directions from the city to most parts of the country. Moscow also has three major airports, the largest of which is in Domodedovo, south of the city. The famous subway system, the Metro, has about 93 miles (150 kilometers) of track. More than 4¾ million passengers ride it daily. The Moscow Canal links the city to the great Volga River.

─────────── **FACTS IN BRIEF** ───────────

Population: 7,831,000; metropolitan area, 8,011,000.
Area: 339 sq. mi. (879 km²).
Altitude: 425 ft. (130 m) above sea level.
Climate: *Average temperature*—January, 14° F. (−10° C); July, 66° F. (19° C). *Average annual precipitation* (rainfall, melted snow, and other moisture)—24 in. (61 cm). For monthly weather, see RUSSIA (Climate).

Government: City Soviet of about 1,100 deputies, headed by a chairman (two-year terms).
Founded: 1147.

Moscow

Location of Moscow

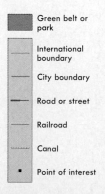

Green belt or park

International boundary

City boundary

Road or street

Railroad

Canal

Point of interest

Greater Moscow

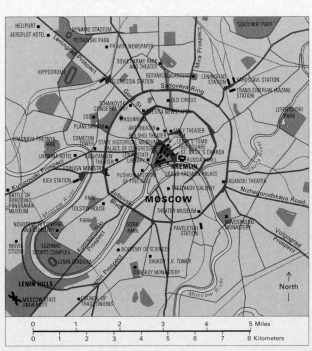

More than 1,400 magazines and about 30 newspapers are published in Moscow. Some of the newspapers are among the largest in the world. They include *Pravda* (Truth), published by the Communist Party, and *Izvestia* (News), the official government paper. Radio Moscow, operated by the government, broadcasts programs on four channels. The Central Television Studios, also government operated, transmit programs on two channels.

Government. Moscow is governed by a *City Soviet* (City Council), elected every two years. Before an election, the city is divided into districts of 6,000 persons each. More than a thousand districts are created in this way, and each district elects one deputy to the City Soviet. Every district has only one candidate. This person is nominated by the Communist Party or by such organizations as school groups, sports clubs, and trade unions. The candidate is elected unless most of the voters cross his or her name off the ballot.

The City Soviet elects one of its deputies as chairman. It also chooses an Executive Committee to govern Moscow between legislative sessions. All buildings and all public services such as education and transportation are managed by 30 city departments. The city government also supervises some industries. Moscow is divided into 30 wards. Each ward has its own elected soviet and executive committee.

History. Moscow was founded in 1147 by Yuri Dolgoruki, a prince of the region. The town lay on important land and water trade routes, and it grew and prospered. During the 1200's, Tartar invaders from Asia conquered Moscow and other Russian lands. The Russian princes were forced to recognize the Tartars as their rulers and pay them taxes.

During the 1300's, the Moscow princes collected taxes in their region for the Tartars. In exchange for increasing the taxes, the princes were granted more territory. The Moscow princes took land from rival princes with Tartar help. By the late 1400's, Moscow had become the most powerful Russian city. Moscow threw off Tartar control during the late 1400's under Ivan III, who was called Ivan the Great. His grandson, Ivan IV, later called Ivan the Terrible, was crowned czar of all Russia in 1547.

Moscow grew rapidly during the 1600's. The czars built palaces in the Kremlin, and nobles built mansions. New churches and monasteries arose, and industries developed. In 1703, Peter I, called Peter the Great, began building a new capital at St. Petersburg (now Leningrad). But Moscow remained an important center of culture, industry, and trade.

In the fall of 1812, invading French troops under Napoleon I entered Moscow without a struggle. Most of the people had abandoned the city. Soon afterward, a fire believed set by the Russians destroyed most of Moscow. After 35 days, the French troops left the city and began a disastrous retreat through the snow and cold.

In 1905 and in 1917, fierce revolutions against the czar took place in several Russian cities, including Moscow. In the 1917 revolution, the government fell to the Bolsheviks (later called Communists). They moved the capital back to Moscow in 1918.

Moscow grew rapidly during the 1930's. In World War II (1939-1945), German troops advanced almost to the city but never captured it. German air raids damaged Moscow, however. Since the 1950's, thousands of apartment buildings have been constructed in Moscow. Some are 25 stories high. In 1960, the Russian government more than doubled the city's area. A zone of forests and parks covering more than 600 square miles (1,600 square kilometers) was established around the city. This zone is called the *Green Belt*.

The 1980 Summer Olympic Games were held in Moscow. Moscow was the first Russian city ever to host the Olympics. A number of sports facilities, as well as housing for the athletes and hotels for visitors, were built in the city in preparation for the Olympics. See OLYMPIC GAMES (History).   RICHARD ANTONY FRENCH

See also LIBRARY (picture: Lenin State Library); RUSSIA (pictures).

MOSCOW ART THEATER became one of the most influential theaters of the 1900's. It presents plays by major Russian authors and has made several tours of Western countries. The theater is best known for its productions of plays by the Russian authors Anton Chekhov, Maxim Gorki, and Leo Tolstoy. One of the theater's founders, Konstantin Stanislavski, developed his *Method* style of acting there. The style stresses psychological realism in the interpretation and presentation of plays. The Method technique has had great impact on Western theater.

The Moscow Art Theater was founded in 1898 by Stanislavski and Vladimir Nemirovich-Danchenko. Its production in 1898 of Chekhov's *The Sea Gull* started his career as a successful playwright.

See also STANISLAVSKI, KONSTANTIN; DRAMA (picture: Realism and Naturalism).

MOSELEY, HENRY GWYN-JEFFREYS (1887-1915), was a British physicist noted for his research on X rays. About 1913, he discovered a systematic relationship between X-ray spectra and the atomic number of the elements emitting the X rays. This discovery allowed scientists to determine the atomic number of unknown elements and to arrange them in the proper places in the periodic table (see ELEMENT, CHEMICAL).

Moseley was born in Weymouth, England. He attended Oxford University. He did research there and at Manchester under Lord Rutherford, the physicist.

During World War I, Moseley was killed in the invasion of Gallipoli, in August, 1915. As a result of this loss, the British government assigned its scientists to noncombat duties during World War II.   RALPH E. LAPP

MOSELLE. See WINE (Where Wine Comes From).

MOSELLE RIVER, *moh ZEHL* or *MAW ZEHL*, a branch of the Rhine River, rises in the Vosges Mountains in eastern France. It flows northeastward for 314 miles (505 kilometers) and empties into the Rhine in Koblenz, West Germany. It is called the *Mosel* in Germany. Much of the Moselle is very shallow. A 170-mile (274-kilometer) canal finished in 1964 enables barges to go about 200 miles (320 kilometers) up the river. The famous Moselle wines are made along the river's banks. Major iron and steel works lie along the river in eastern France. The Moselle was the scene of bitter fighting during World Wars I and II. Twice in World War I the Germans followed the river for nearly its whole length during drives on Paris.   ROBERT E. DICKINSON

Moses Striking Water from the Rock (1581), an oil painting on canvas by Tintoretto; School of St. Rocco, Venice (SCALA)

Moses Strikes a Rock with a rod to provide water for the Israelites wandering in the desert. The Israelites had threatened to rebel against Moses' leadership unless they obtained water for themselves and their cattle. The story is told in the Book of Numbers, chapter 20.

MOSES was the principal leader and teacher of the Israelites and one of the most important characters in the Bible. He led his people out of slavery in Egypt to their homeland in Canaan, later called Palestine. At Mount Sinai, Moses declared the Ten Commandments as the law for his people. There, the Israelites were established as a nation under Moses' leadership.

Moses was a political organizer, a military chief, a diplomat, a lawmaker, and a judge as well as a religious leader. He kept the Israelite nation united during its years of wandering in the desert between Egypt and Canaan. The Bible pays tribute to Moses in the following passage: "And there arose not a prophet in Israel like unto Moses, whom the Lord knew face to face, in all the signs and the wonders, which the Lord sent him to do in the land of Egypt to Pharaoh . . . " (Deut. 34:10).

The first five books of the Bible—Genesis, Exodus, Leviticus, Numbers, and Deuteronomy—are called the "Five Books of Moses," or the *Pentateuch*. However, they do not mention Moses as the author. Biblical scholars believe the five books were passed orally from generation to generation until they were written down between about 1000 and 400 B.C.

Early Life. The story of Moses' life is in the books of Exodus, Leviticus, Numbers, and Deuteronomy. Moses was born in Egypt near the end of the 1300's B.C. He was the descendant of Hebrew slaves who had migrated from Canaan to Egypt hundreds of years earlier. The Egyptians had enslaved the Hebrews and forced them to build large cities and palaces.

The population of the Hebrews eventually grew so large that the Egyptian pharaoh feared they could not be controlled. Therefore, at about the time of Moses' birth, the pharaoh ordered all male Hebrew children killed. Moses' mother hid the baby in a basket in the rushes on the bank of the Nile River. The pharaoh's daughter found the infant and raised him with the help of Moses' own mother.

Moses was given an Egyptian name and received an Egyptian education, but he retained his Hebrew identity. As an adult, Moses saw an Egyptian beating a Hebrew. He killed the Egyptian and fled into the desert. While living there, he married Zipporah, the daughter of Jethro, a priest of the Midianite tribe. They had two sons, Gershom and Eliezer.

Moses settled in the land of Midian and lived as a shepherd. One day, according to the Bible, God spoke to him from a burning bush. He commanded Moses to return to Egypt and lead his people to the land that had been promised to Abraham, the ancestor of the Hebrews (see ABRAHAM). Moses argued that he was not capable of performing such a difficult task. But he accepted God's commandment to lead the Hebrews from Egypt.

The Exodus. Moses joined his older brother, Aaron, while returning to Egypt, and they met with the pharaoh. Moses told the pharaoh, "Let my people go" (Exod. 5:1), but the Egyptian ruler refused to do so. He punished the Hebrews by increasing their workload. According to the Bible, the Egyptians were then afflicted with nine terrible plagues. But after each one, the pharaoh continued to refuse to let the Hebrews leave. The 10th and final plague killed the pharaoh's oldest son and all other first-born Egyptian sons. However, the Hebrews remained unharmed.

The 10th plague caused the pharaoh and the Egyptian people great grief. The pharaoh finally agreed to let the Hebrews leave Egypt. Their flight from Egypt is called the *Exodus.* The pharaoh soon regretted losing so many slaves and sent his army to recapture them. According to the book of Exodus, when the Hebrews reached the Red (or Reed) Sea, God commanded Moses to lift up a rod and stretch his hand over the sea to divide the waters. The parting of the waters enabled his people to cross safely. The Egyptian soldiers followed the Hebrews into the sea but drowned when the waters flowed back into place.

The Covenant with God. Moses led the Hebrews across the Red Sea into the desert. They journeyed to Mount Sinai, where they entered into a *covenant* (agreement) with God. Under the terms of the covenant, the Hebrews became the new nation of Israel. The covenant provided that all the Israelites would live under God's eternal love and protection. In exchange, they would be ruled by God and obey His laws.

The basis of the covenant consisted of the Ten Commandments and laws found in the "Book of the Covenant," a set of God-given rules and guidelines. According to the Bible, Moses received the Ten Commandments and other laws from God on Mount Sinai. The Ten Commandments and the laws of the "Book of the Covenant" became part of what is known as the "Torah of Moses." These laws defined the Israelites' relationship with one another and with God. Moses established an administrative and legal system for the Israelites to help carry out the laws of the covenant.

While Moses was receiving the Ten Commandments, the Israelites became impatient. They wanted a god that they could see. They built a golden calf and began to worship it. The Israelites thought it represented the God who had led them out of Egypt.

After Moses came down from the mountain, he found his people dancing before the idol. He became so angry that he smashed the stone tablets on which the Ten Commandments had been inscribed. Many Israelites died soon afterward, and the people believed that the deaths were a punishment for their sin. According to tradition, Moses later received a new copy of the Ten Commandments.

Moses also organized the nation's official forms of worship. The Israelites' religious activities centered on a movable structure called the *Tabernacle.* The Tabernacle served as an official meeting place for God and the people, and it symbolized His relationship with the Israelites (see TABERNACLE). The people reestablished the old Hebrew holidays as national celebrations. The Exodus became a theme of the renewed festivals. The springtime holiday *Passover* celebrates the Israelites' escape from Egypt (see PASSOVER).

Journey to Canaan. The Israelites spent 40 years wandering in the desert between Egypt and Canaan. They lived under harsh conditions and often complained to Moses. The people also became impatient and frustrated, and they challenged Moses' authority as a religious and political leader. In addition, they questioned their faith in a God they could not see.

Moses often asked for God's help to care for his people. He frequently obtained food and water for them under God's direction. Throughout their wanderings in the desert, Moses served as an intermediary between God and the Israelites.

Hostile tribes attacked the Israelites several times while they wandered through the desert, but Moses always led his people to victory. He also foresaw the many difficulties that the Israelites would encounter after settling in Canaan.

When the Israelites reached Canaan, God allowed Moses to see the new land but not to enter it. According to the Bible, Moses did not cross the Jordan River into Canaan because he had not followed one of God's instructions (Num. 20:1-13). God had told Moses to obtain water for the Israelites by speaking to a rock. Water would then flow from the rock. But instead of speaking to the rock, Moses struck it. Joshua, an assistant of Moses, led the people into Canaan.

Moses died in God's favor at an advanced age. According to the book of Deuteronomy, God buried Moses on Mount Nebo in the desert.　　CAROL L. MEYERS

See also AARON; DEUTERONOMY; EXODUS; JEWS (History of the Jewish People); JOSHUA; PENTATEUCH.

Out for the Christmas Trees **by Grandma Moses** shows the innocence and charm of her paintings. She began to paint when she was 76, and painted 25 pictures in the year after her 100th birthday. She took her subjects from memories of her life on farms in northern New York and Virginia.

Grandma Moses, *left,* began painting when she was 76 years old. Her gaily colored pictures of the upstate New York countryside hang in many art museums today.

MOSES, GRANDMA (1860-1961), was an American primitive painter. She started painting when she was 76 years old and remained active until near her death. She never had an art lesson. Grandma Moses painted simple but realistic scenes of rural life. These colorful and lively pictures were based on memories of her own youth in the late 1800's. Critics have praised her work for its freshness, innocence, and humanity.

Grandma Moses was born ANNA MARY ROBERTSON in Washington County, New York. She was married to Thomas Moses in 1887. For many years, she embroidered pictures on canvas. She began to paint when arthritis made it difficult for her to hold embroidery needles. An art dealer first discovered her paintings in 1938, and she was represented in a show at the Museum of Modern Art in New York City in 1939. Her first one-man show was in 1940. Her autobiography, *My Life's History,* was published in 1952.   EDWIN L. FULWIDER

MOSHAV. See ISRAEL (Agriculture).

MOSHESH. See LESOTHO (History).

685

Kevin Martin

A Mosque is an Islamic house of worship. A slender *minaret* (tower) is the most prominent feature of the building. A man called a *muezzin* calls Muslims to prayer from a balcony on the minaret. The mosque shown at the left is part of the Islamic Center in Washington, D.C.

MOSLEMS. See MUSLIMS.

MOSQUE, *mahsk*, is a Muslim house of worship. The main features of a mosque include a *mihrab* (prayer niche pointing toward Mecca), a *mimbar* (pulpit) beside the niche, and a *minaret* (tower from which the people are called to prayer). Many mosques have pointed domes, several minarets, and open courts where worshipers gather and wash their faces and limbs before praying.

Early mosques were often little more than fenced-in yards. Later, they became elaborate. When the Muslims conquered a city, they sometimes converted churches into mosques. A mosque is part of the Islamic Center, Washington, D.C.   ALI HASSAN ABDEL-KADER

Related Articles in WORLD BOOK include:

Asia (picture:	Islam (The Mosque)	Mecca
Muslims)	Islamic Art (Mosques)	Minaret
Iran (picture)	Jerusalem (picture)	

MOSQUITIA. See MOSQUITO COAST.

MOSQUITO is an insect that spreads some of the worst diseases of man and animals. Certain kinds of mosquitoes carry the germs that cause such serious diseases as encephalitis, malaria, and yellow fever. When a mosquito "bites," or even touches any object, it may leave germs behind. Many kinds of mosquitoes do not spread diseases, but they have painful "bites." Many of the mosquitoes that cause disease live in the

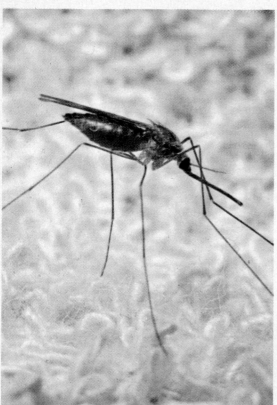

Edward S. Ross

An Anopheles Mosquito, its abdomen swollen with a victim's blood, may rest for more than 24 hours after feeding.

Ross E. Hutchins

A Culex Mosquito plunges its sharp, needlelike mouth parts through a person's skin and sucks his blood.

THE BODY OF A MOSQUITO

External

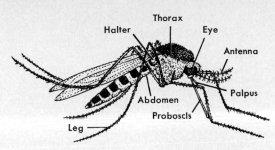

Internal

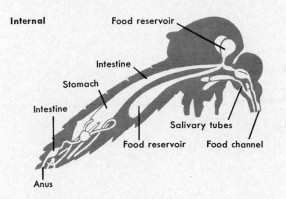

THE HEADS OF MOSQUITOES

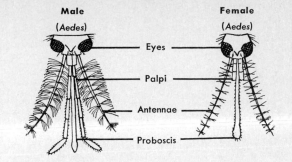

Male (Aedes)   **Female** (Aedes)

Eyes — Palpi — Antennae — Proboscis

HOW A MOSQUITO "BITES"

A mosquito stabs a victim's skin with sharp stylets hidden in the proboscis. As the insect pushes the stylets down, they curve and enter a blood vessel. The *labium* (lower lip) slides out of the way.

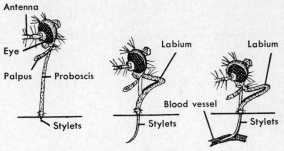

WORLD BOOK illustration by Tom Dolan

hot, damp, lands near the equator. But mosquitoes are found in all parts of the world, even in the Arctic.

There are more than 2,500 species of mosquitoes. About 150 species live in the United States. Biologists classify species of mosquitoes into about 100 groups, each called a *genus*. For example, the common house mosquito belongs to the genus *Culex*. Some other members of this genus carry encephalitis. Some mosquitoes in the genus *Anopheles* carry malaria, and some in the genus *Aedes* transmit yellow fever.

Man controls mosquitoes in many ways. Scientists have developed chemicals called *insecticides*, which kill insects. Small amounts of these chemicals kill mosquitoes when sprayed in homes, garages, and other buildings. Thick mists of insecticides may be sprayed into fields, forests, and gardens. Man also controls mosquitoes by destroying the places in which they grow. Mosquitoes lay their eggs in marshes, swamps, and other pools of quiet water. Engineers may build canals through marshes to drain off the water, and often fill small pools and swamps with soil. They also spread thin layers of oil or insecticides on top of the water.

Most kinds of mosquitoes are from $\frac{1}{8}$ to $\frac{1}{4}$ inch (3 to 6 millimeters) long. Among the smallest is a mosquito of Taiwan that measures about $\frac{1}{16}$ inch (1.6 millimeters) from the tip of one wing to the tip of the other. One of the largest is the American gallinipper. It grows about

Dale W. Jenkins, the contributor of this article, is former Assistant Director of Bioscience Programs at the National Aeronautics and Space Administration.

$\frac{5}{8}$ inch (16 millimeters) long and is about that long from wing tip to wing tip.

The hum of a mosquito is the sound of its wings beating. A mosquito's wings move about 1,000 times a second. A female's wings make a higher tone than a male's wings, and the sound helps males find mates.

Mosquitoes are *flies* (insects with two wings). The word *mosquito* is Spanish and means *little fly*.

The Body of a Mosquito

The mosquito's slender body has three parts: (1) the head, (2) the thorax, and (3) the abdomen. A thin, elastic shell covers the body. Fine hair and thin scales grow on the shell and on the wings. Most kinds of mosquitoes are black, brown, gray, or tan. Many species have white or light colored markings on their backs, legs, or wings. A few kinds are bright blue or green, and seem to shine with coppery or golden lights.

Head. The mosquito has a large, round head that is joined to the thorax by a short, thin neck. Two huge

--- **FACTS IN BRIEF** ---

Names: *Male,* none; *female,* none; *young,* wrigglers or tumblers; *group,* swarm.

Number of Eggs: 100 to 300 at a time, depending on species. As many as 1,000 a year for each female.

Length of Life: 30 days or more for female; 10 to 20 days for male.

Where Found: All parts of the world.

Scientific Classification: Mosquitoes belong to the fly order *Diptera.* They make up the family *Culicidae.*

compound eyes cover most of the head. These eyes, like those of most other kinds of insects, are made up of thousands of six-sided lenses. Each lens points in a slightly different direction and works independently. A mosquito cannot focus its eyes for sharp vision, but it quickly sees any movement. The eyes are always open, even when the insect sleeps.

A mosquito hears and smells with its two antennae, which grow near the center of its head between the eyes. A female mosquito's antennae are long and somewhat like threads. The male's antennae are also long, but have bushy hairs that give a feathery appearance.

The mouth of a mosquito looks somewhat like a funnel. The broadest part is nearest the head, and a tubelike part called the *proboscis* extends downward. A mosquito uses its proboscis to "bite," and as a straw to sip liquids, its only food. The males and females of many species sip plant juices.

How a Mosquito "Bites." Only female mosquitoes "bite," and only the females of a few species attack man and animals. They sip the victim's blood, which they need for the development of the eggs inside their bodies.

Mosquitoes do not really bite because they cannot open their jaws. When a mosquito "bites," it stabs through the victim's skin with six needlelike parts called *stylets*, which form the center of the proboscis. The stylets are covered and protected by the insect's lower lip, called the *labium*. As the stylets enter the skin, the labium bends and slides upward out of the way. Then saliva flows into the wound through channels formed by the stylets. The mosquito can easily sip the blood because the saliva keeps it from clotting. Most persons are allergic to the saliva, and an itchy welt called a "mosquito bite" forms on the skin. After the mosquito has sipped enough blood, it slowly pulls the stylets out of the wound, and the labium slips into place over them. Then the insect flies away.

The amount of blood taken varies greatly among individual mosquitoes. Some may sip as much as $1\frac{1}{2}$ times their own weight at a time.

Thorax. The mosquito's thorax is shaped somewhat like a triangle, with the broadest part above and the narrowest part underneath. Thin, flat scales of various colors form patterns on the upper part of the thorax of certain kinds of mosquitoes. These patterns help identify different species. One kind of mosquito that spreads yellow fever has a U-shaped pattern formed by white scales on a background of dark scales.

Strong muscles are attached to the inside shell wall of the thorax. These muscles move the mosquito's legs and wings. A mosquito has six long, slender legs, and each leg has five major joints. A pair of claws on each leg helps the insect cling to such flat surfaces as walls and ceilings. The mosquito uses all its legs when it walks, but usually stands on only four of them. Many kinds of mosquitoes rest on their four front legs. Some kinds hold their two hind legs almost straight out behind them, but others curve their legs over their backs. White scales form bands on the legs of some species.

Mosquitoes have two wings, unlike most other kinds of insects which have four wings. The wings are so thin that the veins show through. The veins not only carry blood to the wings, but also help stiffen and support

them. Thin scales cover the veins and the edges of the wings. The scales rub off like dust when anything touches them. Some species of mosquitoes may have scales of beautiful colors.

Instead of hind wings, which most other insects have, a mosquito has two thick, rodlike parts with knobs at the tips. These parts, called *halteres*, give the mosquito its sense of balance. The halteres vibrate at the same rate as the wings when the insect flies.

A mosquito lifts itself into the air as soon as it beats its wings. It does not have to run or jump to take off. In the air, the mosquito can dart quickly and easily in any direction. The halteres keep the insect in balance. A mosquito must beat its wings constantly while it is in the air. It does not glide during flight or when coming in for a landing as do butterflies, moths, and most other flying insects. A mosquito beats its wings until its feet touch a landing place.

Abdomen of a mosquito is long and slender, and looks somewhat like a tube. Some kinds of mosquitoes have an abdomen with a pointed end. Other kinds have an abdomen with a rounded end. The shape of the abdomen helps scientists identify the species.

A mosquito breathes through air holes called *spiracles* along the sides of its body. The abdomen has eight pairs of spiracles, and the thorax has two pairs. Air flows into the holes, and tubes carry the air from the spiracles to all parts of the mosquito's body.

The Life of a Mosquito

A mosquito's life is divided into four stages: (1) egg, (2) larva, (3) pupa, (4) adult. At each stage the mosquito's appearance changes completely, and the insect lives a different kind of life. In warm climates, some species develop from newly hatched eggs into adults in only a week. In the cold climate of the far north, mosquito eggs may remain frozen from autumn until late spring. They hatch in May or June, and take a month or more to grow into adults.

Egg. A female mosquito lays from 100 to 300 eggs at a time, depending on the species. One female may lay as many as 3,000 eggs during her lifetime. The eggs are laid through an opening called the *ovipositor* at the tip of the female's abdomen.

The females of most species of mosquitoes lay their eggs in water or near it, but each species has a favorite spot. Some like quiet swamps, and others prefer salt marshes. Still others lay their eggs in hidden pools that form in tin cans, garbage pails, fallen logs, or hollow tree stumps.

Among some species, the females drop their eggs one at a time. Frilly, transparent parts on the shell keep each egg afloat until it hatches. The females of other species arrange their eggs in groups that look somewhat like rafts. The female rests on the surface of the water while she lays her eggs, which are narrow at the top. With her hind legs, she carefully pushes the eggs, wide ends downward, into raftlike groups. Each group of eggs is held together by a sticky substance from the female's body. The eggs of most kinds of mosquitoes hatch in two or three days in warm weather.

All mosquito eggs must have moisture to hatch, but not all species lay their eggs in water. Certain mos-

THE LIFE CYCLE OF A CULEX MOSQUITO

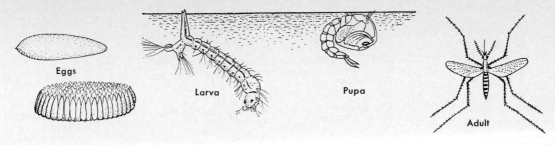

Eggs

Larva

Pupa

Adult

THE LIFE CYCLE OF AN ANOPHELES MOSQUITO

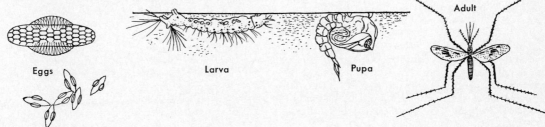

Adult

Eggs

Larva

Pupa

WORLD BOOK illustration by Tom Dolan

quitoes, called floodwater mosquitoes, drop their eggs in mud left by a flood. The eggs hatch after another flood takes place—perhaps years later. Another species, sometimes called pond mosquitoes, lays its eggs in hollow places left by ponds that have dried up. The eggs hatch after rains fill the ponds with water. The eggs of some kinds of pond mosquitoes do not hatch after the first rain. They must be soaked by a second or even a third rain before they hatch into larva.

Larva of a mosquito is often called a *wriggler* because it is so active. The wrigglers of most species move about by jerking their bodies through the water.

A wriggler looks somewhat like a worm or a caterpillar. A thin, skinlike shell covers its body. The wriggler has a broad head, with two short, bushy antennae on each side. It has two eyes behind the antennae, near the back of the head. Its mouth is on the underside of the head, near the front. Long hairs called *mouth brushes* grow around the jaws and sweep food into the wriggler's mouth. Unlike an adult mosquito, a wriggler can open its jaws and chew its food. The wriggler eats small plants and small animals that live in the water, including other wrigglers and one-celled animals called *protozoans*.

A wriggler breathes through a tubelike *siphon* (air tube) at the rear of its body. To get air, it pushes its siphon above the surface of the water.

The larvae of certain swamp mosquitoes do not have to come to the surface for air. They get air from the leaves, stems, and roots of various underwater plants. The larva of one kind of swamp mosquito has a breathing tube with two sharp tips. It uses one tip to hold itself to the plant, and moves the other tip back and forth in the plant tissue to get the oxygen stored there.

The larvae of many species of mosquitoes grow quickly. They *molt* (shed their skins and grow new ones) four times in 4 to 10 days. After the last molt, the larvae

change into pupae. The larvae of some species spend the winter at the bottom of ponds. They change into pupae early in spring.

Pupa. A mosquito pupa looks somewhat like a comma. The head and thorax are rolled into a ball, and the abdomen hangs down like a curved tail. A thin shell, like that of the larva, covers the pupa's body. The pupa breathes through trumpet-shaped tubes attached to the top of its thorax. The pupa sticks these tubes out of the water to get air. The pupa of certain swamp mosquitoes, whose larva gets air from underwater plants, pushes its tubes into the plant. After this pupa has changed into an adult, it pulls out the tubes or breaks them off and leaves them in the plant. The pupa then swims to the surface.

The pupae of most species of insects do not move, but almost all kinds of mosquito pupae can swim. These pupae are sometimes called *tumblers* because they roll and tumble in the water.

A mosquito pupa does not eat. It changes into an adult in two to four days. The pupal shell splits down the back, and the adult mosquito pushes its head and front legs out. The insect then pulls the rest of its body from the shell.

Adult. After the adult mosquito leaves the pupal shell, its wings dry quickly and it flies a short distance away. Most species of mosquitoes spend their whole lives within 1 mile (1.6 kilometers) of the place where they hatched. A few kinds may travel as far as 20 miles (32 kilometers) away to find food or mates.

A female mosquito attracts a mate by the high-pitched sound made by her wings. The males are deaf for the first 24 to 48 hours of their lives, until the hairs on their antennae are dry.

The females of some species must sip blood before they can lay eggs that will hatch. Each species of female prefers the blood of certain kinds of animals. Some feed

689

only on frogs, snakes, or other cold-blooded animals. Others prefer birds. Still others suck the blood of cows, horses, and man.

Some male mosquitoes may live only 10 to 20 days, but a female may live 30 days or more. The females of some species live through the winter in barns, garages, houses, caves, or in the bark of logs. Some species spend the winter as eggs or as larvae. They develop into adults in spring.   DALE W. JENKINS

Related Articles in WORLD BOOK include:

DDT	Finlay, Carlos Juan	Malaria
Dengue	Fly	Reed, Walter
Dragonfly	Gorgas, William C.	Sleeping Sickness
Elephantiasis	Insecticide	Yellow Fever

MOSQUITO BOAT. See PT BOAT.

MOSQUITO COAST, or MOSQUITIA, is a strip of land that lies along the east coast of Nicaragua and the northeast coast of Honduras. It has an area of over 32,500 square miles (84,175 square kilometers) and extends for about 200 miles (320 kilometers) from the San Juan River in Nicaragua to the Aguan River in Honduras. The southern part makes up the department of Zelaya in Nicaragua. The northern part lies in the departments of Gracias a Dios and Colón in Honduras. The Mosquito Coast received its name from the Mosquito Indians.   ROLLIN S. ATWOOD

See also HONDURAS; NICARAGUA.

MOSQUITO HAWK. See NIGHTHAWK.

MOSQUITO NETTING, or MOSQUITO BAR, is a rough, stiff cotton gauze made with a leno weave (see GAUZE). The best quality netting has 14 meshes per inch (6 per centimeter) while the poorer netting has 12 per inch (5 per centimeter). Mosquito netting is used to screen windows, beds, and baby carriages.

MOSS is made up of soft green plants growing so close together that they often form pads, or cushions. Sometimes they resemble groves of minute ferns or small trees. The mosses, together with the liverworts, are called *bryophytes* (see BRYOPHYTE; LIVERWORT).

One group of mosses grows in shallow fresh water. Another grows on land, on such places as damp banks, rocks, and trees. Mosses can live in damp climates at many different temperatures and heights. Some mosses also grow in dry, warm places. Mosses, lichens, and liverworts may have been the first plants to live on land.

A single moss plant has tiny leaves growing around a stem. The rootlets look like hairs and grow from the bottom of the stem. They are called *rhizoids*.

Devereux Butcher

The Sphagnum is one of the abundant members of the moss group. These mosses have considerable commercial use.

Devereux Butcher

Apple Moss gets its name from its round, applelike spore capsules. It grows in damp cavities or on shady banks.

Hugh Spencer

Haircap Moss develops these leafy shoots, which look like the tips of branches on some varieties of evergreen trees.

Devereux Butcher

Capsules with Spores on their straight stalks look like tiny spears. This is young cord moss, a common species.

Devereux Butcher

Aulacomnium grows in the woods where the soil is very rich. The beanlike pods on the long stalks contain the moss spores.

Growth of New Plants. New plants are usually formed in two stages—*sexual* and *asexual*. In the sexual stage, the moss plant is called a *gametophyte*. The plant produces male *sperm* and female *ova*, which join to form a new growth. Sperm and ova are formed in different organs that grow from the top of the moss stem or a branch. Male sex organs are called *antheridia*, and female organs are called *archegonia*. The antheridia burst when they become ripe and damp enough, and sperm are released. Some of the sperm may reach an archegonium, where a sperm may unite with an ovum. The fertilized ovum then grows into a plant called a *sporophyte*. The sporophyte consists of a long, erect stalk called a *seta*, with a podlike container called a *capsule* at the end.

The second, or *asexual*, stage in the growth of the new plant takes place in the sporophyte. Certain cells divide and form *spores*, which serve as tiny seeds (see SPORE). Most moss capsules have a mouth covered by a lid. When the spores ripen, the lid falls off. A set of "teeth" around the mouth controls the scattering of the spores. These teeth are *hygroscopic*, which means that they take water from the air. They move as they become moistened or dried.

A spore may sprout into a branching, threadlike growth called a *protonema*. Buds from the protonema then grow into gametophytes.

Many spores are scattered far and wide, and often sprout wherever it is warm and damp enough. In the hot sun some mosses curl their leaves. The curl is caused by cells that change in shape as they dry. The curled mosses look brown and dead, but showers and cooler weather make them fresh and green again. Some mosses quickly show the moisture changes in the air. They turn a different shade of green with every change.

How Mosses Help People. Mosses are soil makers. Their small rootlets, working slowly, break off tiny bits of rock. In time, they can break stone into a dust as fine as if it had been mashed with a hammer. The leaves gather dust particles from the air. These particles, with the dead tissue of the plant, make the soil deeper.

Many mosses hold the rain as it falls on the ground, instead of letting it run off. They keep the ground damp, and make it a good place for other plants to grow. They also help prevent floods by holding the water in the soil.

Peat beds are swampy places where peat moss (sphagnum) grows. The moss on the surface grows over layers of dead moss. The dead deposits have partly decayed through the ages and have changed to peat. People use peat as a fuel. They also grind it and mix it with the soil as a fertilizer. Peat helps the soil hold more moisture. Peat bogs lie in Ireland, Germany, Sweden, and Holland, and in parts of the United States. See PEAT MOSS.

Sphagnum moss makes an excellent packing material. It is especially useful for wrapping live plants that must be shipped. The moss has a spongy texture.

In Lapland, mothers line babies' cradles with moss, because it is soft and warm. It is also mixed with reindeer hair for stuffing mattresses. Some birds line their nests with moss. Frontiersmen used it to fill the cracks between the logs of their cabins.

Other Plants. Certain plants called moss are not true mosses. The Spanish moss which hangs from trees in the South is a flowering plant that belongs to the pineapple family (see SPANISH MOSS). Farmers of Ireland use the seaweed called Irish moss for food and medicine (see IRISH MOSS). The Icelanders and Laplanders make bread from Iceland moss, a lichen (see LICHEN). People in middle Asia eat cup moss, another lichen.

Scientific Classification. Mosses are in the phylum *Bryophyta*. They form the class *Musci*.   ROLLA M. TRYON

See also PLANT (pictures: Liverworts and Mosses).

MOSSADEGH, MOHAMMAD. See IRAN (The Nationalist Movement).

MÖSSBAUER, *MUHS bow uhr,* **RUDOLF LUDWIG** (1929-   ), a German physicist, shared the 1961 Nobel prize in physics for research into gamma rays. He discovered the "Mössbauer Effect," a method of producing gamma rays with a precise, predictable wave length. This enables physicists to use gamma radiation to make precise measurements. The "Mössbauer Effect" was later used to confirm some predictions made by Albert Einstein in his relativity theory.

Mössbauer was born in Munich and received his Ph.D. from the technical institute there. In 1972, he became director of the Institute Max von Laue-Paul Langevin in Grenoble, France.

MOSSBUNKER. See MENHADEN.

MOSUL, *moh SOOL* or AL MAWṢIL (pop. 293,100), is Iraq's third largest city and an important commercial center. It lies on the west bank of the Tigris River in the northern part of the country (see IRAQ [map]).

Mosul has long been a trading center where farmers buy and sell grain, fruit, and sheep. Ancient craftsmen made the city famous. "Mosul bronze" and *muslin,* a fine cotton cloth, took their names from Mosul. Oil, produced in the nearby hills, has given Mosul new importance since the 1930's.

The city has many Arabs and Kurds and some Turkomans. Iraq's largest Christian community lives there and in nearby villages. The Great Mosque, a Moslem house of worship that once was a Christian church, is Mosul's most impressive building.   MAJID KHADDURI

MOSZKOWSKI, *mawsh KAWF skee,* **MORITZ** (1854-1925), was a Polish-German pianist and composer. He

Motels serve millions of guests yearly. Many motels are near busy interchanges of major highways and provide convenient lodging for automobile travelers. Others are on the outskirts of a town or near airports. All motels provide free parking facilities, and many have restaurants.

became known for his piano pieces, the most popular being the *Spanish Dances*. His works include the opera *Boabdil, the Last Moorish King;* the ballet *Laurin;* the symphony *Joan of Arc;* and orchestral suites.

Moszkowski was born in Breslau, Germany (now Wrocław, Poland), and studied in Dresden and Berlin. He made his concert debut in 1873. He often toured as a pianist. He appeared in London in 1886 to play at the Philharmonic concerts, and returned there many times in later years both as pianist and conductor. Moszkowski lived in Berlin until 1897, and then he retired to Paris.   ROBERT U. NELSON

MOTEL is an establishment that provides overnight lodging, chiefly for automobile travelers. Most motels are located near busy interchanges of major highways, on the outskirts of towns, or near airports. All motels provide free parking facilities from which guests can easily reach their rooms. Some motels have restaurants and swimming pools.

The word *motel* comes from a combination of the words *motor* and *hotel*. Motels are also called *motor hotels, motor inns,* or *motor lodges.* The United States has more than 27,000 motels, and Canada has about 4,000.

The number of rooms in a motel ranges from about 20 to 80. Many large motels are in the downtown areas of cities. Most of them provide the same services and charge the same rates as commercial hotels (see HOTEL [Commercial Hotels]). On the other hand, most roadside motels offer fewer dining and other services, and they charge lower rates than the majority of hotels. The casual atmosphere of these motels, plus their convenient location on or near highways, appeals to large numbers of motorists.

Most motels do not require reservations because many automobile travelers cannot be sure where they will spend the night. Almost all roadside motels have large signs that tell whether vacant rooms are available.

Motorists can see these signs and do not have to leave their cars to find out if a motel has any vacancies.

Roadside motels use highway billboards to advertise their location and the services they provide. These billboards are located at various points for several miles along the major highways leading to a motel.

The first motels, called *tourist cabins,* were established during the early 1900's, when people began to travel by automobile. Tourist cabins originated in the Western United States, where people could not travel the long distances between towns in one day. These establishments also served fishermen, hunters, and other vacationers in remote areas.

The motel industry grew rapidly during the mid-1900's. People began to travel longer distances by car and needed places to stay along the way. The establishment of *motel chains,* which consist of two or more motels owned by one person or company, also stimulated motel development.

Through the years, several major motel chains have expanded by means of *franchises.* Under this system, an individual or a company buys a franchise—that is, the right to own and operate a motel in the chain. The purchaser runs the motel in the same manner and under the same name as the other motels in the chain. The franchise owner pays the chain a percentage of the motel's income. In return, the owner has the advantage of operating a motel with a well-known name and reputation.

During the 1970's, several companies established chains of *budget motels.* The rates at these motels may be as low as half of those charged by other motels. Budget motels have small rooms and provide fewer services than more expensive motels. They do not have restaurants, and many have no television sets or swimming pools. Some budget motels in areas with cool climates do not provide air conditioning. ROBERT A. BECK

Frank Lane

MOTH

The Hawk Moth looks like a hummingbird as it hovers in front of a flower. It sips the flower's nectar through its long tubelike proboscis.

MOTH. One of the most familiar sights of summer is a group of moths fluttering around a streetlight. These soft, winged insects live almost everywhere. Moths have been found in hot deserts and on cold mountaintops, and in every country from the equator to near the Poles. North America has from 10,000 to 15,000 different *species* (kinds) of moths.

Moths are close relatives of butterflies. In fact, there is no sure, simple way to tell moths and butterflies apart. Generally, moths fly at night and butterflies fly during the day. But many moths fly by day, visiting flowers and sucking nectar as do butterflies. Most moths are colored less brightly than butterflies. But many moths have bright colors, and many butterflies are plain and dull. When a moth rests, it folds its wings back flat over its body. A butterfly usually holds its wings up over its back, or spread out at an angle. Most moths have *antennae* (feelers) that look like tapering hairs. Butterflies have knobs at the tips of their antennae. See BUTTERFLY (picture, How to Tell Butterflies from Moths).

Some moths are helpful and many are harmful to man. The valuable silkworm moth spins the silk used to make beautiful cloth. Many moths pollinate flowers as they go from blossom to blossom searching for nectar. The clothes moth is the best known harmful moth. But the most harmful moths are the ones that destroy trees, food crops, and other plants.

Life Cycle of the Moth

Moths, like butterflies, have a complicated life history. The *eggs* laid by the female moth hatch into tiny *larvae*, or *caterpillars*. The caterpillar turns into a *pupa*. The pupa changes into an *adult* moth which spreads its wings and flies away. The entire process of changes is called *metamorphosis* (see METAMORPHOSIS).

Egg. The female moth generally lays its eggs on plants. But moths also lay their eggs on other things that the larva can eat.

Larva (Caterpillar). After the larva hatches, it usually eats its eggshell. Then it begins to eat the plant or other material on which it is living. The larva is the only stage that causes damage.

As the caterpillar grows, it goes through several steps. At the end of each step, the caterpillar sheds the hard skin that covers its head and body. It immediately swells out much larger and grows another hard skin. After another period of feeding, the caterpillar again sheds its skin and increases in size. This shedding of the skin is called *molting*. The caterpillars of various kinds of moths molt from four to a dozen or more times.

Head of a Moth Caterpillar includes a mouth, 12 tiny eyes, and 2 short *antennae*. The caterpillar chews its food with strong, biting jaws called *mandibles*. It uses the antennae to feel its way along. The eyes are arranged in a curved row on each side of the head, just above the mouth. A caterpillar has a good sense of taste, but sees only enough to tell light from dark.

A short projection called the *spinneret* sticks out below the mouth. The caterpillar squeezes out an almost continuous stream of liquid silk through the spinneret. The silk quickly hardens to a slender thread that gives the caterpillar a foothold wherever it goes. Some caterpillars swing from the silk thread to escape danger as spiders do.

Body of a Moth Caterpillar is divided into 12 *segments* (parts). The first three body segments behind the head form the *thorax*. Each segment of the thorax has a pair of short, sharp-tipped, jointed legs. These are true legs that change into the legs of the adult moth. The rest of the body is the *abdomen*. The abdomen has five pairs of false legs called *prolegs*. Each of these fleshy, leglike organs has a curved row of tiny hooks at its tip. Caterpillars breathe through openings called *spiracles*.

Pupa. After a moth caterpillar molts for the last time, it becomes a *pupa*. From the outside, a pupa looks dead. But inside, the pupa is very much alive. It is changing from a caterpillar to an adult moth. In some species of moths, this dramatic change takes place in less than a week. In other species, it may take several months, or even a year or more.

693

Before changing into pupae, many moth larvae spin around themselves silken cases called *cocoons*. (Only a few species of butterflies spin cocoons.) The silk in the cocoon of the silkworm moth is the kind used to make silk thread and cloth. The cocoon protects the larva from its enemies and the weather. As the larva changes into a pupa, a hard *pupal shell* develops. Thousands of species of moths do not spin cocoons. Their pupae rest in the earth or in rotting wood. See COCOON; SILK (Raising Silkworms).

Adult. To come out of its cocoon, an adult moth first cracks the pupal shell. The moth cracks the shell by expanding its body with air and contracting its muscles. Then the moth comes out of the cocoon. Some moths have body parts that serve as "cutters" to open the cocoon. Other moths produce a liquid that dissolves the cocoon. Some moths build cocoons with "escape hatches" through which the adult comes out.

The Adult Moth

Adult moths range in size from those with wings

Thorax is the front section of an adult moth's body. It supports the three pairs of slender legs and the two pairs of wings. The wings of most adult moths are thickly covered with tiny, flat scales that overlap like shingles on a roof. The scales usually are of varying colors. The arrangement of the scales gives most moths distinctive wing patterns. The scales rub off as a fine, powdery dust.

Most adult moths have a special part called the *frenulum*. (No butterflies have a frenulum.) During flight, a frenulum links the front and back wings on each side. It keeps the wings working together.

Abdomen. The rear section of the adult moth's body has most of the spiracles through which it breathes. The abdomen also includes the reproductive organs.

How Moths Live

Adult moths usually sleep during the day and come out at night to search for food. Although moths see well in the dark, they find flowers chiefly by using their sharp sense of smell. Moths drink water, the sap from trees, and other liquids in addition to nectar.

Enemies of moths include spiders, birds, frogs, toads,

Alexander B. Klots

The Proboscis, a hollow tube, coils under the moth's face when not in use. The moth straightens it out to sip nectar from deep inside flowers.

Richard L. Cassell

The Antennae of some moths look like feathery rabbit ears. They "smell" odors that help the moth find a mate.

Alexander B. Klots

The Frenulum, a bristle at the base of the front of the hind wing, locks into the front wing and holds the wings together.

$\frac{1}{10}$ inch (2.5 millimeters) long to giants with 12-inch (30-centimeter) wingspreads. Like other insects, an adult moth has three main sections: (1) the head, (2) the thorax, and (3) the abdomen. The body of a moth is covered with scales and hairs.

Head. The head of a moth includes the insect's most important sense organs. On each side is a large *compound eye*, which is made up of thousands of separate eyes. Adult moths have keen vision. They also have a good sense of smell which they use to find flowers and other sources of food. Male moths locate females chiefly by smell. The two antennae are the chief organs of smell. The antennae may also serve as organs of touch and perhaps hearing. Beneath the head are two pairs of jutting organs called the *palpi*. They serve as organs of taste, and perhaps smell.

Most adult moths cannot bite or chew. Instead of true jaws, an adult moth has a long, tubeshaped *proboscis* (a tube extending from the mouth). To get food, it thrusts the proboscis into flowers or liquids, and sucks up the food.

lizards, and other insects. Few moths are able to fight their enemies. They can only fly away or hide. Some moths taste bad or are even poisonous to certain other animals. Most of these moths have bright colors that warn their enemies. Other moths have colors that blend with their surroundings and make them hard to see.

Insect enemies of moths, such as wasps and flies, lay their eggs inside the moth caterpillar's body. The eggs develop into larvae, which feed on the caterpillar and kill it. Caterpillars depend chiefly on their color for protection. Most of them are brown, green, or some other plain color. But some have bold, bright colors and patterns. These colorations help disguise a caterpillar by making it look like something else.

Harmful Caterpillars

Farm and Forest Pests. One of the most destructive moth caterpillars is the *tent* caterpillar. Its pupae live in a silken, tentlike nest on tree branches which they strip for food. Many kinds of *tussock* moths have larvae that attack trees. These include the caterpillars of

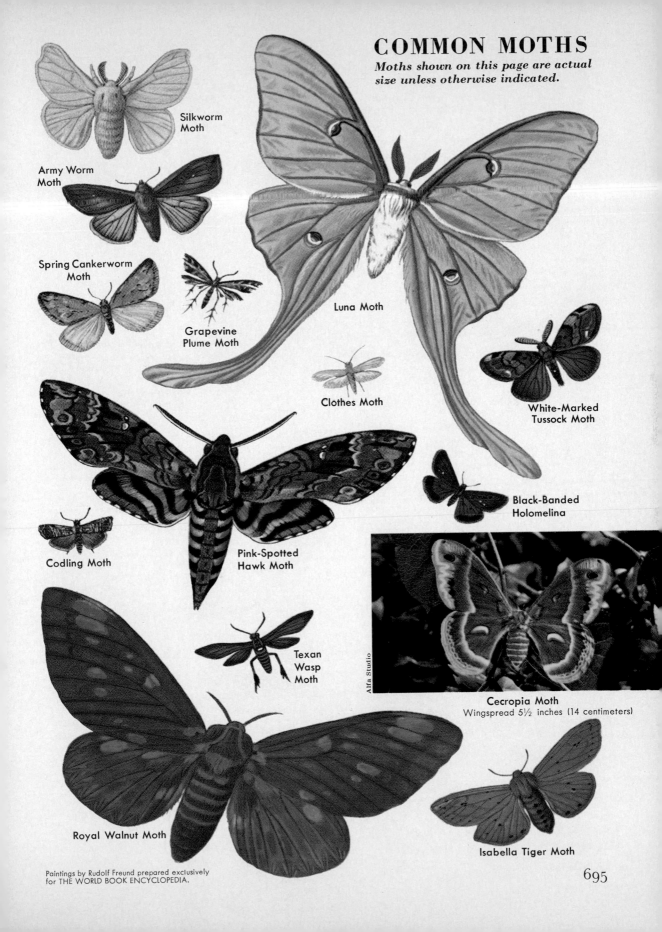

COMMON MOTHS
Moths shown on this page are actual size unless otherwise indicated.

Silkworm Moth

Army Worm Moth

Spring Cankerworm Moth

Grapevine Plume Moth

Luna Moth

Clothes Moth

White-Marked Tussock Moth

Codling Moth

Pink-Spotted Hawk Moth

Black-Banded Holomelina

Texan Wasp Moth

Alfa Studio

Cecropia Moth
Wingspread 5½ inches (14 centimeters)

Royal Walnut Moth

Isabella Tiger Moth

Paintings by Rudolf Freund prepared exclusively for THE WORLD BOOK ENCYCLOPEDIA.

695

MOTHS OF MANY LANDS

Imma grammozona
New Guinea

Chrysocale principalis
Mexico

Euchromia formosa
Madagascar

Napata splendida
Bolivia

Josia oribia
Mexico

The Giant Hercules Moth of Australia and New Guinea is probably the world's largest moth. It has a wingspan of 10 inches (25 centimeters) and could cover a robin from bill to tail.

A Nepticulid Moth of the Eastern United States is one of the smallest moths. It has a wingspread of about 1/8 inch (3 millimeters). It is shown twice life size.

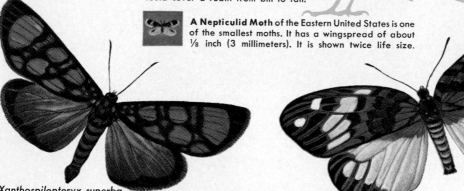

Xanthospilopteryx superba
Africa

Erasmia pulchella
Bhutan

COMMON MOTH CATERPILLARS
(Not to scale)

Clothes Moth

Pink Bollworm

Tent Caterpillar

Spring Cankerworm

Codling Moth

Tussock Moth

Peach Moth

Corn Earworm

Isabella Tiger Moth

Silkworm

Army Worm

European Corn Borer

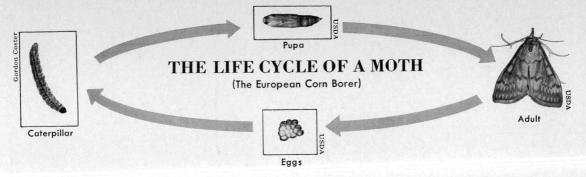

THE LIFE CYCLE OF A MOTH
(The European Corn Borer)

Gordon Coster

Caterpillar

Pupa · USDA

Eggs · USDA

Adult · USDA

the *gypsy* moth and the *brown-tail* moth. Caterpillars of *bagworm* moths feed on tree leaves. These insects received their name because the caterpillars make a "bag" of silk, leaves, and twigs. The caterpillars live in their bags and carry them about.

Moth caterpillars that attack crops include the *army worm*, the *corn borer*, the *corn earworm*, and the *cutworms*. The *codling* moth, the *peach* moth, and other moths have caterpillars that bore into apples, peaches, and other fruits. The caterpillar of the *pink bollworm* moth attacks cotton fields throughout the world.

Some moth caterpillars protect themselves with chemicals. Puss moth caterpillars can squirt acid at attackers. The caterpillars of slug moths and io moths have poisonous *spines* (needlelike growths) that cause a painful rash to develop on the skin of persons who handle them.

Clothes Moths damage clothing, rugs and carpets, upholstery, furs, and other household items. These moths all belong to the family *Tineidae*. The females lay their eggs on woolen and silk fabrics, and on furs. The caterpillars feed on these materials, causing serious damage. The adults do no harm.

Getting rid of clothes moths can be difficult. It does no good to kill a flying clothes moth, because the eggs have already been laid. The simplest way to prevent moth damage is to buy garments that have been moth-proofed by treating them with a special chemical. Dry cleaning or laundering, especially before storage, removes larvae or eggs. Woolen garments should always be stored in tightly sealed containers. Putting moth balls or moth flakes in a garment bag provides clothing with extra protection. Spraying with an insecticide or fumigation are also good ways to kill moth larvae.

Kinds of Moths

Both moths and butterflies belong to the order *Lepidoptera*. Some of the largest families of moths are described below. The scientific name of each family is given in parenthesis.

Giant Silkworm Moths (*Saturniidae*) include most of the largest moths. (The commercial *Chinese silkworm* belongs to another family, *Bombycidae*.) Among the giant silkworm moths are the moths with the largest wing area, the *Atlas* and *Hercules* of Asia. Also in the family are two large North American moths, the familiar *Cecropia* and *Polyphemus*. They have wings up to 6 inches (15 centimeters) from tip to tip. In addition, the group of giant silkworm moths includes the pale green, long-tailed *luna*.

Midget Moths (*Nepticulidae*) are tiny moths with wing spans of less than ⅛ inch (3 millimeters).

Owlet Moths (*Noctuidae*) are the most common moths in North America. *Cutworms*, *army worms*, and *bollworms* belong to this family.

Prominents (*Notodontidae*) are brown or gray moths that are found almost everywhere in the world.

Slug Caterpillar Moths (*Eucleidae*) are favorites with collectors. The caterpillars have varied shapes and colors, and many adults have striking colors.

Collecting Moths

The best place to collect moths is near a light, especially a fluorescent one. Moths are strongly attracted by the ultraviolet light produced by fluorescent lamps. Adult moths seldom live long in captivity. Many kinds never eat or drink after being captured. They usually batter themselves to death. Females kept in dark containers sometimes lay eggs from which caterpillars hatch. Caterpillars can also be collected and raised on foliage.   ALEXANDER B. KLOTS

Related Articles. The article on BUTTERFLY has much information that applies to moths. See also:

Army Worm   Cutworm   Measuring Worm
Brown-Tail Moth   Death's-Head Moth   Metamorphosis
Caterpillar   Gypsy Moth   Peach Moth
Codling Moth   Hawk Moth   Pink Bollworm
Corn Borer   Insect (pictures)   Tent Caterpillar
Corn Earworm   Leaf Miner   Tussock Moth

MOTH BALL is a small white or gray ball about the size of a marble, which is used to protect fabrics and furs from moths. The balls are stored with the fabrics. Moth balls are usually made of naphthalene.

MOTHER is the title often given to any source or origin, as it is the name of a female parent. For example, people may speak of the land of their birth as their *motherland* or *mother country*. They may call the language of their parents their *mother tongue*. Roman Catholics and many other Christians use the title *Mother of God* for the Virgin Mary. The woman in charge of a convent is called *Mother* or *Mother Superior*.

In other languages, the word for mother is similar. In Latin, the term is *mater*, in French *mère*, in German *Mutter*, in Greek *mētēr*, and in Russian *mat'*.

Early peoples in ancient civilizations compared nature's creative powers with those of a mother, because a mother is the source of life. In many places, they worshiped a great mother goddess. The Assyrians called their goddess *Ishtar*. The Greeks worshiped *Demeter*, and the Romans *Ceres*. Other names for the mother goddess were *Cybele* and *Rhea*.

697

Whistler's Mother is one of the world's most famous paintings. James Whistler, an American artist, painted it in Paris in 1871 to honor his mother.

In the United States, the second Sunday in May of each year honors motherhood (see MOTHER'S DAY).

MOTHER CAREY'S CHICKEN is the name sailors have given to the various kinds of birds called petrels (see PETREL). The name Mother Carey is a changed form of the Latin words *Mater cara*, which means *tender mother* or *dear mother*. This refers to the Virgin Mary, the Mother of Jesus. The sailors believe that the petrels are under her special care, and so they call them Mother Carey's chickens.

MOTHER GOOSE is the mythical little old lady who was supposed to have told the nursery stories and rhymes that children know and love so well. But whether or not she was a real person remains a mystery. In an old graveyard in Boston, Mass., there are several tombstones bearing the name of *Goose*. Some people claim that one of them marks the grave of Mother Goose. Her real name was supposed to have been Elizabeth Vergoose. Her son-in-law, a printer named Thomas Fleet, was supposed to have published in 1719 the songs and rhymes she sang to her grandchildren. No copy of this book has ever been found, however, and most scholars doubt the truth of this story.

Mother Goose probably was not a real person. The name "Mother Goose" is the direct translation from the French *Mère l'Oye*. In 1697, a Frenchman, Charles Perrault, published the first book in which this name was used. It was called *Stories and Tales of Past Times with Morals; or, Tales of Mother Goose*. It contains eight tales, but no rhymes. Among the tales were "Sleeping Beauty," "Cinderella," and "Puss in Boots." Perrault did not invent these stories. They were already quite popular in his day, and he only collected them. Some believe that these stories go back to the 700's and "Goose-Footed Bertha," the mother of the great military leader Charlemagne.

In 1729, Robert Sambers translated Perrault's tales into English. Then, about 1760, John Newbery, the first English publisher of children's books, brought out *Mother Goose's Melody*, a tiny book illustrated with woodcuts. The book contained 52 rhymes, including "Ding Dong, Bell," "Little Tom Tucker," and "Margery Daw," as well as 15 songs from Shakespeare's plays. This collection became extremely popular, and before long copies and imitations of Newbery's edition flooded the London bookstalls. Isaiah Thomas, a publisher in Worcester, Mass., republished Newbery's book in 1785.

Old King Cole. Newbery's edition was the first to associate rhymes as well as stories with Mother Goose. Many of these rhymes existed hundreds of years before they were called Mother Goose rhymes. Some of them are just jingles with no real meaning. Others seem to tell about real people and historical events. One tells about King Cole, who was supposed to have been a very popular king of Britain in the A.D. 200's. He seems to have loved music, and his daughter was supposedly a skilled musician. The king would have long been forgotten but for the rhyme:

> Old King Cole was a merry old soul,
> And a merry old soul was he;
> He called for his pipe, and he called for his
>   bowl,
> And he called for his fiddlers three.

It is quite possible that court jesters made up many of these rhymes. Others may have been made up by members of the nobility or by common people.

Little Jack Horner. According to legend, the Bishop of Glastonbury, England, had sent his steward, Jack Horner, to King Henry VIII with the title deeds of 12 estates. For safety, the deeds were hidden in a Christmas pie. On his way to the king, Jack Horner lifted the pie crust, pulled out a "plum," that is, the deed of an estate, and kept it. The rhyme goes:

> Little Jack Horner
> Sat in a corner
> Eating his Christmas pie.
> He put in his thumb,
> And pulled out a plum,
> And said, "What a brave boy am I."

To this day the Horner family owns the estate from that deed at Mells Park, England.

Hey Diddle Diddle. Queen Elizabeth I had a reputation for teasing her ministers the way a cat plays with mice. She loved to dance to the tune of a fiddle. One of her advisers was nicknamed "Moon," and another was known as the Queen's "Lap-Dog." She never ate without having one of her ladies in waiting, called "Spoon," taste her soup first. A gentleman of the court who carried in the food was called "Dish." When the "Dish" and the "Spoon" eloped, this jingle was invented:

> Hey diddle, diddle,
> The cat and the fiddle,
> The cow jumped over the moon;
> The little dog laughed
> To see such sport,
> And the dish ran away with the spoon.

Many collections of Mother Goose rhymes have been published over the years in England and the United States. ARTHUR M. SELVI

See also LITERATURE FOR CHILDREN with its Books to Read section; NURSERY RHYME; NEWBERY, JOHN; PERRAULT, CHARLES.

MOTHER OF CANADA. See SAINT LAWRENCE RIVER.

MOTHER-OF-PEARL. Certain sea animals, such as the pearl oyster, the abalone, and the nacre, line their shells with a layer of material in glowing color. This layer is called *mother-of-pearl*. It varies in color from pale grayish-blue and pink to purple and green. Shells containing mother-of-pearl are found off the coasts of tropical countries, particularly around the South Sea Islands, around the Philippine Islands, Australia, Panama, and Lower California. The finest mother-of-pearl is found in shells from Australia and Sri Lanka. Those from Panama are called *bullock shells* in commerce, and are small and thick.

Mollusks in many inland waters also produce mother-of-pearl. The shells of fresh-water clams in the Mississippi and other rivers are used in making buttons. The chief uses for mother-of-pearl are in pocketknife handles, buttons, and beads. WILLIAM J. CLENCH

See also PEARL (Mother-of-Pearl).

MOTHER OF PRESIDENTS. See OHIO; VIRGINIA.

MOTHER OF STATES. See VIRGINIA.

MOTHER OF THE WEST. See MISSOURI.

MOTHER'S DAY is set apart every year in honor of motherhood. On the second Sunday in May, many families and churches make a special point of honoring mothers. Many people follow the custom of wearing a carnation on Mother's Day. A colored carnation means that a person's mother is living. A white carnation indicates that a person's mother is dead.

A day for honoring mothers was observed many years ago in England. It was called *Mothering Sunday*, and came in mid-Lent. The Yugoslavs and people in some other countries have long observed similar days.

Julia Ward Howe made the first known suggestion for a Mother's Day in the United States in 1872. She suggested that people observe a Mother's Day on June 2 as a day dedicated to peace. For several years, she held an annual Mother's Day meeting in Boston. Mary Towles Sasseen, a Kentucky schoolteacher, started conducting Mother's Day celebrations in 1887. Frank E. Hering of South Bend, Ind., launched a campaign for the observance of Mother's Day in 1904.

Three years later, Anna Jarvis of Grafton, W.Va., and Philadelphia, began a campaign for a nationwide observance of Mother's Day. She chose the second Sunday in May, and began the custom of wearing a carnation. On May 10, 1908, churches in Grafton and Philadelphia held Mother's Day celebrations. The service at Andrews Methodist Episcopal Church in Grafton honored the memory of Anna Jarvis' own mother, Mrs. Anna Reeves Jarvis.

At the General Conference of the Methodist Episcopal Church in Minneapolis, Minn., in 1912, a delegate from Andrews Church introduced a resolution recognizing Anna Jarvis as the founder of Mother's Day. It suggested that the second Sunday in May be observed as Mother's Day.

United Press Int.
Anna Jarvis

Mother's Day received national recognition on May 9, 1914. On that day, President Woodrow Wilson signed a joint resolution of Congress recommending that Congress and the executive departments of the government observe Mother's Day. The following year, the President was authorized to proclaim Mother's Day as an annual national observance. ELIZABETH HOUGH SECHRIST

MOTHERS' PENSION. See AID TO FAMILIES WITH DEPENDENT CHILDREN.

MOTHERWELL, ROBERT (1915-   ), an American painter, is a leading member of the abstract expressionist school. He is known for several series of paintings.

Motherwell began his most famous series, *Elegies to the Spanish Republic*, in 1948 and continued it through the 1970's. This group of more than 100 paintings deals with his impressions of the Spanish Civil War (1936-1939). Motherwell used colors and shapes that suggest characteristics of Spain's landscape. In the mid-1950's, he created the *Je t'aime* series, which features broad, freely applied strokes. Each painting in this group includes the French words *je t'aime*, which mean "I love you." During the 1940's and 1950's, Motherwell also produced a number of collages. In the early 1960's, he painted a series called *Beside the Sea*. These works have simple shapes and sharp color combinations that represent the sea and splashing waves.

Motherwell was born in Aberdeen, Wash. He has written many essays on art and edited a series of books by modern artists. GREGORY BATTCOCK

See also ABSTRACT EXPRESSIONISM.

MOTION. See PARLIAMENTARY PROCEDURE (Motions).

MOTION

MOTION occurs when an object changes its position in space. But motion is a relative rather than an absolute term. An object may be in motion in regard to another object, and yet two moving objects can be stationary in regard to each other. For example, we may go for an automobile ride and pass a man standing by the side of the road. We will be in motion as far as the man by the side of the road is concerned. We will be at rest in regard to the friend on the seat next to us.

Actually, of course, everything on earth is in motion in regard to any fixed point in space. We may think we are sitting at rest in a chair, but because of the earth's rotation we are moving very rapidly. Furthermore, we are moving with the earth as it moves on its path around the sun. The sun itself is dragging the earth with it toward a point in distant space.

If we are driving a car and pass another car on the road going in the same or the opposite direction, the apparent motion of the other car is its motion *relative* to the motion of our car.

Scientists speak of two important kinds of motion. One is called *rectilinear* motion. This is motion in a straight line. When objects are moving freely without constraint, they normally move in a straight line. Motion along a curved path is called *curvilinear* motion.

Velocity and Acceleration. Usually, when we discuss how fast an object moves we use the term *speed*. Scientists, however, are more precise and use the term *velocity*. When we say that an object is moving with a constant velocity, we mean that it is moving in a straight line at a constant speed. The velocity of an object changes if either its direction or its speed changes. If an automobile goes around a curve and the speedometer does not change, its speed does not change. But its velocity changes because of a change of direction. Velocity may be expressed in any units of measurement we are using, as long as the units tell us how far an object travels during a certain interval of time. For example, we may speak of velocity in terms of miles per hour, feet per second, or centimeters per second. When the velocity of a moving object is constant, the motion is said to be uniform.

When the velocity of an object increases, it is accelerating. Acceleration is how much the velocity has increased during a certain period of time. The acceleration of an automobile traveling along a straight road is usually expressed in miles per hour per second. If a car starts off at a speed of 2 miles an hour for the first second, and travels 4 miles an hour the second second, and 6 miles an hour the third second, we say its acceleration is uniform at 2 miles per hour. Its velocity has increased two miles per hour each second.

If the velocity of an object is decreased, this is called *negative acceleration* or *deceleration*. This occurs in an automobile when the brakes are put on. An automobile may move ten feet, eight feet, six feet, four feet, and two feet in succeeding seconds. In the case of this particular automobile, the deceleration is *uniform*. Both acceleration and deceleration can be *variable* as well as uniform.

Certain simple laws regarding velocity may be determined by rolling a ball down an inclined plane. If a ball is allowed to roll down such a plane, it will roll down at a uniformly accelerated motion. The distance the ball will roll in any length of time is directly proportionate to the square of the number of seconds it rolls. The uniform acceleration of a ball started at rest will be twice the distance the ball travels during the first second.

We can find the final velocity of the ball at any given moment if we multiply the acceleration by the time. In cases where the acceleration is constant, the distance the ball will travel in any given number of seconds equals one half the acceleration times the square of the number of seconds it has traveled. A ball started from rest with an acceleration of 1 meter per second will travel 8 meters in four seconds.

The formula for finding the final velocity of an object started from rest, is $v = at$, which means the final velocity equals the acceleration times the time. The formula for finding the distance the ball travels is $S = \frac{1}{2}at^2$. In this formula, the distance is S, the acceleration is a, and t^2 represents the square of the time spent. To find the distance traveled in any given second, we can use the formula $S = \frac{1}{2}a(2t - 1)$. In other words, at any given second the ball will travel a space equal to one half of the acceleration times twice the time minus one.

The preceding formulas apply the same way to motion that is uniformly retarded. They also apply to bodies which are falling in the air. However, for freely falling bodies, in such formulas we substitute g, which equals 980 centimeters per second per second, or 32.16 feet per second per second, for the acceleration.

Momentum of a moving object is its mass times its velocity. The momentum is the impact produced when a moving object strikes an object at rest. A very heavy object moving slowly has a large momentum, as does a very light object moving at a great speed. The impact of both of these when they strike against an object is very great. The momentum of an automobile in motion is important to every driver or pedestrian. Whenever an object has momentum, it also has *kinetic energy*, which is called the energy of motion. The kinetic energy of an object is one half of its mass multiplied by its velocity squared. This energy is given up when one object strikes another, or is responsible for what is referred to as *impact*. For example, the impact of an automobile at 60 miles an hour is nine times as large as at 20 miles an hour.

One way to increase the momentum of a moving body is to increase its velocity. A simple way of increasing its velocity is to have a force act upon it for the longest possible time. A good tennis player or golfer knows that follow-through is important in striking the ball. In following through, the club or racket acts upon the ball for the longest possible time and therefore the ball travels faster.

Newton's Laws of Motion. The great scientist Sir Isaac Newton announced three laws that govern the actions of motion. These laws, however, do not take into effect such extraneous things as air resistance or other friction. They refer only to ideal motion, removed from any friction.

Newton's first law states that any body moving uniformly in a straight line or in a state of rest will remain in uniform motion in a straight line or in state of rest unless it is acted upon by some outside force. The property of matter that tends to keep it in motion when in motion, or at rest when at rest is called its *inertia*. Both

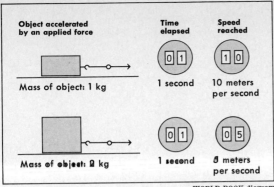

The Acceleration of an Object depends on the mass of the object and the force applied to it. A 1-kilogram object, *top*, will accelerate twice as fast as a 2-kilogram object, *bottom*, if the same amount of force is applied over a given period of time.

acceleration and deceleration require overcoming the inertia of an object.

Newton's second law of motion tells what happens when a force is applied to a moving body. The change which any force makes in the motion of an object depends upon the size of the force, and the mass of the object. The greater the force, the greater the acceleration; the greater the mass of the object, the smaller the acceleration. The motion or the change of motion takes place in the direction in which a force acts.

Suppose we try to discover the path taken by a moving bullet. We can calculate easily enough the direction and velocity of the bullet as it leaves the muzzle of the gun. But the bullet is also being acted upon by the gravity of the earth. If we fired a bullet horizontally from a gun, at the end of one second, no matter how far the bullet traveled, it would have dropped just as much as a freely falling body, which falls 16.08 feet (490 centimeters) during the first second after it is dropped. That is why the rear sights of rifles are adjusted so that the rifle is actually aimed higher at different targets. This takes care of the drop of the bullet as it moves from the gun.

The effects of two or more forces acting upon the path of a body are calculated by means of *vectors*. A vector is a quantity that tells how large a force is (its *magnitude*) and the direction in which it acts. Forces acting upon a single point are called *concurrent forces*. Suppose a rowboat is being pulled forward parallel to the shore of a lake by a boy walking along the shore. At the same time, another boy in the rowboat uses an oar to push the boat away from the shore, out into the lake. The boat then has two kinds of motion, one along the shore and the other out into the lake. Suppose the boy on the bank exerts a force of 10 pounds while the boy in the boat exerts 15 pounds of force. We can represent these forces by lines drawn in scale at right angles from the point where the boat started. If we construct a parallelogram from these lines, we can determine the resultant path of the boat by drawing a diagonal of the parallelogram, beginning at the point where the boat started. This diagonal also represents the magnitude of the combined forces.

Newton's third law of motion states that for every action there is an equal and opposite reaction. This is the principle behind the jet propulsion engine (see JET PROPULSION). There are many other examples of this law. We are all familiar with rotating lawn sprinklers that spin when water squirts from their nozzles. Such sprinklers have two or four arms. As the water emerges from the nozzles, the arms are pushed around in the opposite direction, and the water sprays over the lawn.

When you shoot a rifle, there is a kick or recoil. The explosion of the powder in the rifle occurs in all directions, but the bullet is permitted to escape out of the barrel of the rifle. In the meantime, the exploding powder shoves the rifle back against your shoulder.

Suppose you have a line of heavy bowling balls strung from the ceiling, so that each ball just touches the next ball as it hangs down. Take two balls from one end of the line and allow them to strike the others. Two balls will fly outward from the other end of the line. If you use one ball, one ball will be moved.

There are other examples of this reaction. Drop a baseball off the edge of a table. The ball will immediately fall to the earth. But at the same time that the ball is falling to earth, the earth is moving toward the ball. Of course, this action of the earth is very small, too minute even to be measured.

Friction. Much of what has previously been discussed about motion refers to ideal motion. Motion as we see it about us, however, is always affected by a factor called friction. Friction is really the resistance to motion. One of the most common things that causes friction is the air. Automobiles and airplanes are streamlined in order to reduce some of this resistance in the air.

However, friction is also a help, because unless friction existed between our feet and the earth, we would not be able to walk. We could not nail two boards together if it were not for friction, because only friction holds the nail in place. When we apply the brakes while driving an automobile, friction stops the car.

One way by which we reduce friction is by use of lubricating oil. Friction between liquid substances is much less than that between solid substances. There are many ways of combating friction. Some metals develop less friction when sliding over each other than the ordinary metals do. These are called antifriction metals and are used in many machines. Furthermore, the smoother the two surfaces that are to move against each other, the less friction there will be between them. Friction may be greatly reduced by the use of wheels, ball bearings, roller bearings, and lubricants. Because of these, one man can push an automobile, and six men can push a locomotive. Casters on a bed reduce the friction that would exist if we had to push the bed across the floor on its legs. *E. A. FESSENDEN*

Related Articles in WORLD BOOK include:

MOTION, PERPETUAL. See PERPETUAL MOTION MACHINE.

George C. Scott in *Patton*

Charlie Chaplin in *Easy Street*

Ginger Rogers
and Fred Astaire in *Swing Time*

Snow White and the Seven Dwarfs

Boris Karloff in *Frankenstein*

MOTION PICTURE

MOTION PICTURE is one of the most popular forms of art and entertainment throughout the world. Every week, millions of people go to the movies. Many millions more watch movies on television. In addition, TV networks use motion-picture techniques to film many programs that appear on television each week.

Motion pictures are a major source of information as well as of entertainment. Movies can take us back into history. They can re-create the lives of great men and women. Motion pictures can introduce us to new ideas and help us explore serious social issues. Students learn from educational films in school. Industries use movies to train employees and to advertise their products. Governments use films to inform and influence their own citizens and people in other countries.

The motion picture is a major art form, as are, for example, painting and writing. Artists express themselves by using paint, and writers by using words. Filmmakers express their ideas through a motion-picture camera. By using the camera in different ways, the filmmaker can express different points of view. Even the most realistic-looking movie shows only the filmmaker's version of reality. The filmmaker can point the camera up at a man and make him appear a hero on the screen, or point the camera down and make the same man seem insignificant.

We can enjoy many forms of art and entertainment by ourselves. For example, we can enjoy reading a poem or looking at a painting by ourselves. But we usually enjoy a motion picture most when we watch it with others. An exciting scene increases in suspense when we feel the tension sweeping through the audience. We usually enjoy a movie less if we see it in a nearly empty theater or on television.

In some ways, movies resemble stage plays. Both use performers, settings, and dialogue. However, playwrights usually must confine the performers to a single setting until a scene or act ends. They must use dialogue as the main tool to tell their story. In a play, the characters must describe events that happened elsewhere

Arthur Knight, the contributor of this article, is Professor of Cinema at the University of Southern California and the author of The Liveliest Art, *a history of motion pictures.*

Clark Gable and Vivien Leigh
in *Gone with the Wind*

John Barrymore
and Greta Garbo in *Grand Hotel*

and openly discuss their innermost thoughts. To keep the audience informed, the characters must explain actions already known to other characters.

Unlike playwrights, filmmakers can *show* rather than *tell* their story. In movies, action is more important than words. Filmmakers can change the setting as often as they wish. For example, they may film parts of a picture in a desert, on a mountain, and in a large city. Filmmakers can also film scenes from several different angles. Later, through a technique called *editing*, they can select the angle that most effectively expresses a dramatic point. Through editing, filmmakers can also show events happening at the same time in different places.

The motion picture is an art form that has become a gigantic industry. A movie may cost up to several million dollars to make and require the skills of many hundreds of workers. Highly technical devices, including cameras, sound-recording equipment, and projectors, are needed to film and show movies. In fact, motion pictures could not exist without many of the scientific and technical discoveries made during the 1900's. For this reason, motion pictures have been called the art form of the 20th century.

Motion pictures have become perhaps the most democratic of the arts. Most art forms can appeal to a small, specialized audience and still survive. But most movies cost so much money to make that they must attract large audiences to show a profit. As a result, most filmmakers attempt to please as many people as possible, regardless of their economic, educational, or social background. Few motion pictures can succeed without broad public support.

The movies have a brief history, compared with such art forms as music and painting. The beginning of the movies dates back only to the late 1800's. By the early 1900's, filmmakers had already developed distinctive artistic theories and techniques. However, movies received little scholarly attention until the 1960's. Today, the motion picture is recognized as a major art form. Thousands of books have been printed about films. Many universities and colleges offer degrees in motion pictures, and many more offer courses.

King Kong

John Wayne in *Red River*

2001: A Space Odyssey

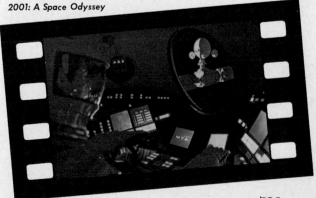

CREDITS (clockwise from lower left-hand corner): Bettmann Archive; © Walt Disney Productions; RKO Radio Pictures; © 1969 Twentieth Century-Fox Film Corp.; Culver Pictures; © 1939 Selznick International Pictures, Inc., renewed 1967 Metro-Goldwyn-Mayer Inc.; Metro-Goldwyn-Mayer Inc.; Herman G. Weinberg Collection; United Artists; © 1968 Metro-Goldwyn-Mayer Inc.

Laurence Olivier, *right*, in a scene from *Hamlet* (1948), directed by Olivier; Universal Studios

A Filmed Version of *Hamlet* has given many people their first opportunity to see this great tragedy by William Shakespeare. Movies of books and plays help students understand literature.

Most people consider motion pictures important mainly as a form of entertainment. But movies are also widely used in education. TV stations, government agencies, and businesses use films to provide information or to influence people's attitudes. The making of home movies has also become a popular hobby.

Entertainment. Most people go to the movies to relax or to escape from their cares for a few hours. They may want to lose themselves in a romantic story, laugh at a popular comedian, or see a part of the world they could never afford to visit in real life. Nearly all the most popular films in motion-picture history have emphasized pure entertainment. They include the historical romance *Gone with the Wind* (1939); the musicals *Mary Poppins* (1964) and *The Sound of Music* (1965); the thrillers *The Exorcist* (1973) and *Jaws* (1975); and films based on disasters, such as *The Poseidon Adventure* (1972) and *Earthquake* (1974).

Most television stations broadcast many hours of motion pictures a day. Nearly all movies on TV were originally shown in theaters and then sold to television. However, some movies are made especially for TV.

Filmmakers may try to educate as well as entertain their audience. For example, *I Am a Fugitive from a Chain Gang* (1932) shows the brutality of chain gangs.

Political corruption is the theme of *Mr. Smith Goes to Washington* (1939) and *All the King's Men* (1949). *Paths of Glory* (1957) and *Catch-22* (1970) attack war as senseless. *Pinky* (1949) and *In the Heat of the Night* (1967) deal with racial prejudice.

People disagree over whether motion pictures reflect or help create our society. For example, some people believe that violence in films encourages viewers to behave violently in real life. But others say violence is part of life and movies only mirror that fact.

Education. Motion pictures made especially for educational purposes have become important teaching aids. Teachers use such films in teaching geography, history, mathematics, and the physical and social sciences. Movies in the physical sciences use slow motion, cartoons, and other special techniques to demonstrate processes that otherwise could not be seen or studied thoroughly. For example, a film can slow down the formation of crystals so a class can study this process.

Teachers also use motion pictures made originally to be shown in theaters. Such movies as *Abe Lincoln in Illinois* (1940) and *The Howards of Virginia* (1940) help in teaching American history. An English film about juvenile delinquency, *The Loneliness of the Long Distance Runner* (1962), has become a standard teaching aid in the social sciences. Many great novels and plays have been filmed. Such movies help students understand and appreciate literature.

Some elementary schools, junior high schools, and high schools have courses in making motion pictures. In making movies, students learn to express themselves, as they do in painting, writing, or any other art.

Hospitals and medical schools film operations so students can watch doctors at work. Athletic teams take movies of their games and later examine the films to learn what mistakes the players made. Athletes also study movies to learn how to improve their skills.

Most educational films in the United States are made by schools and commercial firms. City, county, and state educational agencies, as well as colleges and universities, make these films available through film libraries. Some state university film libraries have as many as 7,000 films. In Canada, the National Film Board, a federal government agency, produces educational films. Many films produced by the board have won international awards.

Information. Television stations use motion pictures to inform as well as to entertain their viewers. TV networks and stations may cancel entertainment programs to present films of special interest at the moment. On

Scene from *The Living Desert* (1953); © Walt Disney Productions

A Documentary Film presents factual information in a dramatic way. This scene, from a documentary about desert animals, shows a kangaroo rat trying to escape from a rattlesnake.

the death of a world leader, for example, they may show films that trace the person's career. TV networks and stations also make and broadcast many *documentary films*—nonfiction movies that present factual information in a dramatic way. These documentaries deal with a variety of subjects, such as pollution, the popularity of football, and the history of presidential elections.

For many years, movie theaters showed newsreels in addition to feature films. But movie newsreels ended with the rapid development of TV in the 1950's. The newsreels could not be changed often enough to compete with the up-to-the-minute news coverage on TV.

Several U.S. government agencies have long created motion pictures dealing with problems and achievements in their fields. During the 1930's, under President Franklin D. Roosevelt, the federal government sponsored a number of documentaries on national problems. For example, *The Plow That Broke the Plains* (1936) described the great drought in the Dust Bowl of the Southwest. *The River* (1937) stressed the need to control flooding and to bring electricity to the Tennessee Valley. Both films were factual yet poetic statements about major problems of the day.

During World War II (1939-1945), the government used motion pictures to help soldiers understand why the United States was at war. All the warring nations used motion pictures for propaganda purposes. While the Germans and Japanese occupied countries in Europe and Asia, they showed propaganda films praising their way of life and attacking the United States and its allies. After these countries were liberated, the Americans showed films sympathetically describing life in the United States. Today, the International Communication Agency (ICA), a federal agency, produces motion pictures describing the American way of life for viewers in other countries.

Many states produce films to attract tourists or new industry. Such films show a state's beauty or recreational facilities or its industrial resources.

Today, nearly every major industrial firm has its own motion-picture unit or a film company that regularly makes movies for it. Many firms make films as part of their public relations programs. These films may tell the history of the company or explain how its products make life easier and more pleasant. Companies distribute such films free to schools and various adult groups. Businesses also use movies to train salespeople and to teach personnel how to use equipment.

A familiar industrial film is the television commercial. To produce a one-minute commercial, a company may spend tens of thousands of dollars, more than the cost of some full-length feature films.

Movies as a Hobby. Millions of people enjoy taking their own motion pictures at family gatherings and on vacation trips. Home movies began to develop as a hobby in the 1920's, following the invention of low-cost film that could be used in small cameras. The popularity of home movies has increased steadily over the years with the continual improvement in cameras and projectors and the development of low-cost color and sound film. For more detailed information, see PHOTOGRAPHY (Making Home Movies).

A Sound Stage bustles with activity before filming begins. Technicians ready the lights, camera, and sound-recording equipment in preparation for the director's call for "Action!"

From about 1915 to the late 1940's, large movie studios in and near Hollywood, Calif., made nearly all American motion pictures. Procedures in moviemaking varied little from one studio to another. Each studio had its own story department, which read literary works published in all parts of the world. If the department found a story that it believed would make a good motion picture, it recommended the story to a group of producers. If one of the producers liked the story, he or she took it to the studio's vice-president in charge of production. Finally, if the vice-president approved the story, it was turned over to one or more writers employed by the studio.

The studio writers were responsible for creating an acceptable movie script from the story. After the script gained studio approval, another department prepared a budget breakdown. This breakdown estimated how much the story would cost to film. If the studio decided the cost was reasonable, it assigned a director to the project. The producer, director, and heads of appropriate departments then selected the cast, designers, composer, and other key personnel. As far as possible, everyone working on the film was selected from people on the studio payroll. The studio used outsiders only

Unless otherwise credited, the photographs in this section were taken for WORLD BOOK *at Universal Studios by John Hamilton, Globe Photos.*

when everyone else was busy, a specialist was needed, or a role required a certain performer.

The studio production system began to decline during the late 1940's with the rise of independent producers. By the late 1940's, television had captured a large share of the moviegoing audience. Studios reduced the number of pictures they made and released many of their producers, directors, stars, writers, and other personnel. Many of these producers—as well as some leading directors, stars, and writers—then became independent producers and established their own film companies. Independent producers would find their own story and hire key personnel to work on the picture. Producers would then take their project to the various studios until they found one willing to provide money for the picture. Instead of being a salaried employee of a studio, the independent producer became a partner who would receive a major share of the film's profits if there were any.

Major studios still produce some movies, but the trend has increasingly been toward independent production. This section of the article describes chiefly how a movie is made by an independent producer. But the key personnel and many of the steps involved in moviemaking also apply to motion pictures produced by major studios.

The People Who Make a Motion Picture

Making a motion picture requires the skills of people in hundreds of different occupations. Many of these people—for example, carpenters, electricians, and painters—perform about the same work they would do anywhere else. But others perform jobs that are special to motion pictures. The most important of these people include: (1) the producer, (2) the director, (3) the writer, (4) the cinematographer (5) the actors and actresses, (6) the costume and set designers, (7) the editor, and (8) the composer.

The Producer is the only person involved in the production of a motion picture from its beginning until its release to the theaters. Producers find the story to be filmed and help prepare the budget. They hire the director and writer and work with them in developing the script. Producers help select the actors and actresses and approve the design of the costumes and sets. During the making of the movie, they supervise the work of the director, editor, and composer. Finally, they help create publicity campaigns to stir public interest in the motion picture when it is released.

The Director is probably the single most important person involved in the actual making of a motion picture. With the producer and other personnel, the director determines the final script, selects the cast, and arranges the work schedules. He or she also participates in approving the costumes and sets. Most important, the director supervises the filming of the motion picture. He or she guides the performances of the actors and actresses and decides how each scene should be interpreted and photographed. The director usually has many assistants, but retains the basic responsibility for the quality of the picture. Some directors also serve as producers.

Designing Sets and Costumes is one of the first steps in making a movie. The designers, *left,* examine a selection of sketches for a film's sets and *props* (furnishings). In a studio costume workshop, *right,* seamstresses finish costumes designed for several different films.

The Writer prepares the motion-picture script, also called the *scenario* or *screenplay.* The script may be an original story developed by the writer or an adaptation of a novel or a stage play. Many writers work only in the movies. If the film is to be based on a current novel or play, however, the producer may hire its author to adapt the work for the screen.

The Cinematographer operates the cameras during the filming of a picture. Good cinematographers must be able to use the various kinds of motion-picture cameras and lenses. They must also know how to use light and color effectively. In addition, the cinematographer must have a knowledge of composition so that the arrangement of the people and objects in each shot will produce the desired effect.

An inventive cinematographer is invaluable to a director. The cinematographer can suggest the best camera angles to express various ideas. For example, if a scene calls for men dragging a heavy load up a hill, the cinematographer can emphasize the feeling of strain by shooting the scene from below and at an angle. The cinematographer can also create special effects and visual tricks. By rocking the camera, for example, he or she can create the impression of an earthquake.

The Actors and Actresses in motion pictures range from *extras,* who appear on the screen as part of a crowd, to internationally famous stars. Some movie performers have built careers around a particular kind of role, such as that of a brutal gangster, a witty butler, or a bad-tempered old woman.

A Makeup Artist applies cosmetics to an actress before a day's shooting begins. The makeup will help make her coloring look natural under the bright lights needed for filming.

Set Decorators obtain and arrange props. These decorators are arranging props for a banquet scene. Most studios have prop departments that make and store an enormous variety of objects.

Preparing to Shoot a Scene on a sound stage, *left,* the director explains the action to actor Anthony Quinn. The cinematographer lines up the angle from which he will film the scene. The script supervisor records the director's instructions on the script, *above.* The script contains the dialogue, a description of the action, and the camera angles for each scene.

Many actors and actresses work both in movies and on the stage. However, movie acting differs greatly from stage acting. On the stage, performers complete their entire role during the course of a performance lasting from two to three hours. For a motion picture lasting the same length of time, the performer's scenes may take weeks to film. The movie actor or actress may also have to play scenes out of the natural order of the story. The same scene may be shot repeatedly until the director is satisfied. Thus, movie performers must keep control of their part to make the development of their character understandable.

Cracking the Clapstick is the final step before the director calls for the action to begin. The slate shows the number of the shot to be filmed. The clapstick assistant brings the bar down sharply, announces the number of the shot, and filming starts.

The Designers. A costume designer creates the clothing worn by the performers in a movie. A set designer called an *art director* plans the scenery. If the movie takes place during a particular period of history, the designers must do research to learn what people wore and how buildings and furnishings looked at that time. The costume designer then prepares sketches of the clothing to be worn in the film, and the set designer makes blueprints and sometimes models of the sets. After these designs are approved by the producer and director, the costumes and sets are made. Both the costumes and the sets are designed so the performers can move about freely. The sets are also designed so the cameras can easily photograph all the action.

The Editor, or *cutter,* works with the director in selecting the most effective shots taken of the various scenes of a motion picture. The editor must then assemble these shots—which number in the hundreds—into an understandable story.

The Composer writes the background music for a motion picture. Composers try to suit their music to the mood and action of the various scenes. Many composers conduct their own music when it is recorded for the film. Music from the film may also be recorded for release on phonograph records and tapes. Recordings of the entire score or of individual songs from a film can provide an important source of income for the movie and help advertise it.

Steps in Making a Motion Picture

Finding a Property is the first step in making a motion picture. A *property* is the story on which a motion picture can be based. Some properties are original stories. That is, they have never appeared in any other

Shooting a Scene. The cinematographer is filming the action from a movable perch above the set. A technician guides a microphone to pick up the dialogue as the actors move about. The dialogue is recorded on magnetic tape and later transferred onto the sound track.

form. However, most properties come from such sources as novels, plays, and musical comedies. Producers may pay an author hundreds of thousands of dollars for the right to make a movie out of his or her best-selling book or popular play.

Many properties come from literary classics. For example, several of William Shakespeare's plays and many of Charles Dickens' novels have been adapted for motion pictures. *Dr. Jekyll and Mr. Hyde*, Robert Louis Stevenson's famous horror story, has been filmed many times in many countries.

The success of a particular picture often leads producers to make similar movies. For example, if a picture about motorcycle gangs attracts large audiences, other producers may rush to make additional motorcycle movies.

Financing the Motion Picture. Most major motion pictures cost millions of dollars to make. But most independent producers do not have that much money to make a major movie, and so they ask the studios for financing.

In a typical case, a team of independent producers find a property they want to film. They then hire a director, writer, performers, and other key personnel. The producer then presents the project to a studio. If the studio likes the project, it will agree to finance it. Many factors determine whether a studio will back a film. The property may be desirable, such as a best-selling novel.

Special Effects are used to produce illusions. This scene calls for soldiers to blast a double door open with machine-gun fire. To achieve this effect, small explosives are taped to the sides of the doors not being filmed, *left*. At the proper moment, the charges are set off to give the illusion that bullets are shattering the wood, *center*. The photo, *right*, shows the damaged door as it will appear in the movie.

Filming on Location, *left,* can provide a movie with realistic settings that might be difficult, as well as more costly, to create at a studio. But on-location filming also has disadvantages. For example, personnel and equipment must be transported to the location. In isolated areas, trees may have to be cleared and roads built.

The Back Lot, *below,* consists of permanent outdoor sets erected on the grounds of a studio. The sets are full-sized reproductions of houses, other buildings, and streets. Most of the structures consist only of realistic fronts supported by wooden braces. Studios often use the same sets over and over in different films.

John Hamilton, Globe Photos

Universal Studios

The director may have a record of making profitable pictures, or the performers may be especially popular with the public.

Most studios offer an independent producer a *step deal.* A step deal gives the studio the right to withdraw financing at any point up to the time filming is ready to begin. For example, the studio may pull out of a project if it does not like the script.

Preparing the Script. After the money has been promised to make a picture, the script is written. Writing the script can take many months. The writer may prepare many versions before one finally meets with general approval. The scriptwriter usually works closely with the producer and director. Some directors write their own scripts.

Writing for motion pictures is a highly specialized craft. Scriptwriters not only provide dialogue for the characters, but they may also indicate various camera shots to help tell the story, explain an idea, or establish a mood. Writers may create long scenes that have no dialogue, such as scenes of a battle or a chase. But their script still must describe in detail the action that makes up such scenes.

Budgeting. After the script has been approved, it is turned over to the studio production department for budgeting. The production department estimates the cost of the sets and of the use of studio facilities. It also estimates how much the filming to be done outside the studio will cost. Such filming is called *location shooting.* The production department also estimates the salaries needed to pay the many people involved in the production of the movie. If the studio finds the total estimated cost of the picture acceptable, it completes arrangements with the independent producer to finance the project.

Casting a Motion Picture. The critical or financial success of a motion picture often depends largely on the actors and actresses. Casting thus requires much care. If performers appear in roles unsuited to them, the movie may be ruined, no matter how good the script and the directing.

When casting a movie, the producer and director must decide whether to use stars. Some pictures are built around a star. A producer may even wait until a certain star is available before beginning the project. Some producers feel that star names increase a picture's chances of making money. A star's popularity at the box office may also help a producer get studio financing for the picture.

In some cases, a producer may prefer not to use stars in a picture. The picture may not have a role big enough for a star, or the producer may believe that the presence of a star would distract the audience from the story. A producer may also feel that an unfamiliar actor or actress will help make a role more believable. If a picture is being made on a small budget, a producer may decide that a star would be too expensive.

Filming a Motion Picture begins after the script has been approved, the casting completed, the sets and costumes designed, and the locations selected. Filming usually takes several months. To save time and money, a director does not necessarily shoot the scenes of a picture in the order they will appear on the screen. For example, he or she may begin shooting scenes from the middle or the end of the film. All the scenes involving the stars may be shot at one time and all the scenes at a particular location another time. The director thus must have a clear idea of the emotional and narrative flow of the picture.

In many movies, all or most of the shooting takes place in studio buildings called *sound stages*. These large, windowless buildings resemble airplane hangars. These are called sound stages because both pictures and dialogue are recorded in them. A network of electric cables crosses the floor of a sound stage. These cables supply power for the lights and other equipment. The floor is also cluttered with partitions, machinery, and wires. The cameras are mounted on large vehicles called *dollies*. Microphones and dozens of powerful lights hang down just out of range of the cameras.

Many movies are filmed partly or entirely on location. In shooting a picture on location, the cast and other personnel may travel to several parts of the world. Skilled workers can build studio sets that resemble African jungles or the streets of Rome. But many producers feel that filming on location makes a movie more realistic. In addition, filming on location is sometimes less costly than creating the setting at a studio.

But shooting on location also has disadvantages. The cast, camera crew, technicians, and equipment must be transported to the location. Generators must be brought to provide power for lights and other electrical equipment. The personnel must be housed and fed. In some areas, trees and bushes must be cleared and roads built so trucks can carry personnel and equipment. Each day, the film that has been shot must be flown or driven to a laboratory to be developed. The next day, the developed film must be returned so the results can be viewed and the scenes reshot if necessary.

Editing a Motion Picture. The film shot each day during the filming of a movie is called that day's *rushes*. After a day's shooting, the editor and director review the preceding day's developed rushes and select the most effective shots. After all the shooting is completed, the editor assembles the selected shots into what is called a *rough cut*. The editor then edits the rough cut into the final film. It often takes as long to edit a movie as it does to film it.

In editing a motion picture, editors must keep many things in mind. They must blend the individual shots into a logical progression that tells the story clearly. Editors must also be able to sense when a shot has made its point and the audience can move to the next point. Editing also involves a sensitivity to rhythm and tempo. For example, abrupt changes in shots create visual excitement that would be suitable for a gunfight but might destroy a romantic scene.

Composing the Music. Most composers prefer to be hired for a film as early as possible to absorb its mood and style. In addition, they can then suggest sequences where music could effectively replace dialogue or where music and action could be effectively combined. But in most cases, the composer is hired after nearly all the principal photography has been completed. As a result, the composer can only add musical accents to scenes already filmed.

Before the editing is completed, the composer sketches various themes, and submits them to the producer and director for approval. With them, the composer also

The Film Editor, *left,* operates a machine called the Moviola. Two reels of film, like those at his left, run through the machine. The dark film has the pictures, and the light film carries the dialogue. The editor examines the film on the Moviola screen, *above,* and selects the shots he wants. He then organizes these shots so they tell the film's story.

Recording Sound Effects for a western film requires the creation of many different sounds. For example, the seated man is rubbing a leather purse to produce the sound of a saddle while bouncing on a wagon seat to make the noise of a buckboard.

selects places in the film where music could be particularly effective, as in romantic scenes or during action passages. In addition, the composer can write music to bridge awkward or abrupt shifts from one sequence of scenes to the next.

Generally, a composer can write a motion picture score in three to six weeks. But if music runs throughout the film, it may take considerably longer. The composer writes the final score against a detailed, shot-by-shot—almost second-by-second—breakdown of the film. On the written score, the composer notes where dialogue begins and ends, where significant action occurs, and where screams or other important sounds

must be heard. A composer may write a magnificent score, but it will be a failure if the music drowns the dialogue or does not accent the film's visual high points.

When the score is ready to be recorded for the film, the studio's music department contacts the musicians' union, which supplies the necessary musicians. The music is then recorded. As the conductor leads the orchestra, he or she watches the film so that the music matches the action.

Dubbing. When we watch a motion picture, we hear the dialogue, music, and other sounds in the movie as they come through loudspeakers. All these sounds have been recorded along one side of the motion-picture film called the *sound track*. But this sound track is really a composite of dozens of separate sound tracks. For each different kind of sound in a movie, a separate track, or recording, is made. There are individual tracks for dialogue, for music, and for all special sounds, such as boat whistles, crowd noises, or forest fires. All these separate sound tracks are blended together through a complicated process called *dubbing* to make the composite sound track we hear in a movie.

Dubbing requires that the various sounds be balanced delicately against one another. For example, a scene may show two men whispering on a boat in a fog. The sounds would include their voices, the put-put of the boat's motor, the lapping of the water against the boat, and the moan of a distant foghorn. These sounds must be mixed so that none overpowers the others.

Dubbing takes place in a small projection room after editing is nearly completed. The producer, director, and at least three technicians called *mixers* participate in the dubbing sessions. The technicians sit behind a *sound console* and face the viewing screen. The console is a long desk with controls to *fade in* (switch on) and *fade out* (switch off) each sound and to regulate its volume. Each technician is responsible for certain sounds. He or she has a specially prepared script that tells at precisely

Recording the Music for a movie takes place in a special studio, *left*. The conductor leads the orchestra as he follows the film's action on the screen. In a control room, *above*, a technician supervises the recording of the music on magnetic tape. The composer, at his right, offers suggestions.

At a Dubbing Session, technicians called *mixers* blend the individual sound tracks for the dialogue, music, and sound effects onto a master tape. The mixers watch the screen action as they operate controls on their *sound console* to switch on and balance the various sounds.

what moment, as the film runs through the projector, each of the sounds must be faded in and out. All the sounds for each shot are thus blended onto a *master tape*. The tape is played back immediately after each shot. If the sounds are not perfectly balanced, the tape is erased and the dubbing repeated until the director, producer, and technicians are satisfied. This procedure continues until the master tape for the entire film is completed. The master tape is then used to produce the composite sound track.

The Sneak Preview. Before releasing their films to the theaters, many producers show them at *sneak previews*. At a preview, the new movie is shown in addition to the advertised feature. Preview audiences are asked to fill out cards that reveal their reactions to the film. These reactions influence the final editing of the movie. Preview audiences may complain that some scenes are boring or that they do not understand certain scenes. To overcome such criticisms, the film may be re-edited in many places. To tighten up the action, minor cuts may be made or entire scenes dropped. Previously discarded scenes may be restored to clarify points in the story that the audience may find confusing. After the movie has been tested in previews, the final editing is completed.

Publicity and Advertising can play an important part in making a movie a financial success. Publicity for a new picture begins with the announcement that a property has been acquired and continues through nearly every phase of production. At first, the studio publicity department handles the publicity campaign. It sends many stories to newspapers and radio and television stations on casting and other items that might be of interest.

As a film nears completion, the studio exploitation department takes over the publicity campaign. The exploitation department tries to stimulate the maximum amount of public interest in a picture just before its release. The department may recommend that an album of the film's music be issued. It may also arrange for the picture's stars, director, or producer to appear on TV interview shows. If the film is based on a book, the book may be reissued in paperback, with advertising for the film on the cover. Sometimes, a studio will employ an author outside the movie industry to write a novel based on an original screenplay. The novel is then published at the same time that the motion picture is released.

Meanwhile, the producer works closely with the studio advertising department on developing newspaper and, perhaps, television ads for the film. These ads try to capture the public's imagination and make people want to see the picture.

Releasing a Motion Picture. After the final editing has been completed and the advertising campaign approved, a motion picture is ready for release to the theaters. Most films open on a *first-run* basis in downtown theaters in major U.S. cities. Generally after a picture no longer attracts enough customers at a first-run theater, it is shown at *second-run* neighborhood theaters. The picture is also exhibited in smaller towns and, usually, in many other countries. The film may finally appear on television.

Unless a motion picture is remarkably popular, it will be exhibited on a large scale in the United States for only a few months. During this brief time, public response largely determines whether the picture makes a profit.

The Storyboard on the wall, *left,* is a series of drawings that portrays the action and gives the dialogue for an animated movie. The music for the film, *above,* is carefully timed so it matches each sequence of action on the storyboard.

The Background Artist paints the backgrounds used in animation. The backgrounds must give the illusion of space so the characters appear to be moving in and around the settings.

The Animator draws the characters. He must create a series of drawings for each movement made by a character. He must also match each character's actions to the dialogue and sound effects.

Animation is the technique of making motion-picture cartoons from a series of drawings. A feature-length animated movie may require a million separate drawings and take three years to complete.

The first step in making an animated movie is finding a story. Many animated films are made for children and are based on fairy tales and children's books. After a story has been selected, an artist-writer prepares a *storyboard,* which serves as the film's script. The storyboard resembles a giant comic strip. It consists of rough sketches that portray the action of the story, with the dialogue printed with each sketch.

After the director and other key personnel approve the storyboard, the music and dialogue are recorded.

The photographs in this section were taken for WORLD BOOK *at Bill Melendez Productions in Los Angeles by John Hamilton, Globe Photos.*

The composer carefully follows the storyboard to make sure the music matches each sequence of the action.

Layout artists then work with the director to determine what settings will be drawn, how each character will act and look, and how the story can best be broken into scenes. After these decisions have been made, the layout artists prepare drawings to guide two other groups of artists—*background artists* and *animators.*

The background artists draw all the backgrounds for the film. Backgrounds include everything that will appear on the screen except the characters. The animators make separate drawings of the characters. They work from a *timing chart,* which indicates the number of *frames* (separate pictures) needed to express each word of the recorded dialogue. The animators must create the exact number of drawings required by the dialogue. In one episode, for example, a character may answer the phone by saying "Hello." The timing chart shows

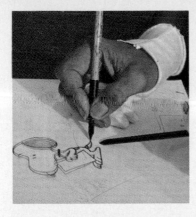

The Animator's Drawings are traced in ink onto sheets of transparent celluloid called *cels, above.* Other artists then paint on the reverse side of the cels all the colors needed for each character's clothes, hair, and skin, *right.*

The Completed Cels are assembled over the proper backgrounds. The cels shown above are from a movie about the characters in the comic strip "Peanuts." At the left, a technician places a cel of Charlie Brown over a background showing the inside of a library. At the right, she adds a cel of Snoopy.

that the word "Hello" requires eight frames. The animators thus must make eight drawings in which the character's mouth moves in sequence to form the word. They must also include all the character's body movements.

After the animators complete their drawings, another group of artists traces them onto sheets of transparent celluloid called *cels.* The cels are then sent to the painting department, where the proper colors are applied to the reverse side of the cels.

Technicians collect the completed cels and sort them into scenes. The cels and backgrounds are then sent to the camera department, where the cels are photographed frame by frame over the proper background. An *exposure sheet* tells the camera operator what cels and background are needed for each frame. After the photography is completed, the sound track is added. Prints of the film are then made, and the picture is released.

Cels and Backgrounds Are Photographed one frame at a time with a special camera. The *exposure sheet* at the cameraman's left tells him what background and cels he needs for each frame.

A 35-MILLIMETER MOTION-PICTURE CAMERA

A soundproof cover called a *blimp* prevents noise made by the camera from reaching the microphone. The blimp houses two reels. The *supply reel* holds the unexposed film. As the film moves through the camera, it is exposed by light entering through the lens. The exposed film winds onto the *take-up reel*. Controls on the camera are used to focus the lens and change the camera's position.

Mitchell Camera Corp.

- Blimp
- Lens
- Eyepiece for seeing through lens
- MITCHELL
- Wheels to control horizontal and vertical camera movement
- Knobs for focusing

When we watch a motion picture, we are actually seeing many thousands of separate still pictures. In each picture, the position of the subject is slightly different. Each picture is flashed on the screen for a fraction of a second, but we do not see the separate pictures. Instead, we see smooth, continuous movement because of a condition of the eye called *persistence of vision*. For example, when the eye sees an object under a bright light, the visual image of that object will persist for one-tenth of a second after the light has been turned off. In this way, each picture on the motion-picture screen is presented to the eye before the preceding image has faded out.

The Camera used to take movies operates much like a still camera. In both cameras, light from objects enters through a lens and exposes the film. But a movie camera takes pictures at a much faster rate.

The movie camera performs a number of precise operations to produce the series of pictures, or frames, that appear on the exposed film. As the camera photographs a subject, it repeatedly stops and starts the film and opens and closes the shutter. The shutter regulates the length of time that the light strikes the film. When

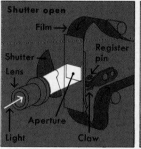

Shutter open — Film — Register pin — Shutter — Lens — Aperture — Light — Claw

Shutter closed — Shutter

The Shutter controls the length of time that light strikes the film. When the shutter is open, light travels through the lens and an opening called the *aperture* onto the unexposed film. The register pin holds the film motionless until one frame has been exposed. The shutter closes, and the pin then withdraws. A claw is next inserted into the sprocket holes. It pulls the film to the next frame. This cycle is repeated 24 times a second.

PHOTOGRAPHING A SOUND TRACK ON FILM

The sound track is photographed on film by a beam of light, shown in white. The beam shines from a recording lamp through a lens, which shapes it into a wedge. The wedge of light shines on a mirror vibrating from electrical impulses produced by the master tape recording of the sound track. As the mirror vibrates, it moves the wedge up and down across a slit in another lens. This action exposes a pattern of light on the film. The pattern is converted into sound when the film is run through a projector.

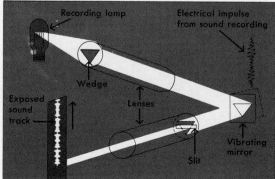

Recording lamp — Electrical impulse from sound recording — Wedge — Exposed sound track — Lenses — Vibrating mirror — Slit

WORLD BOOK diagrams by Mas Nakagawa

A 35-MILLIMETER COMPOSITE PRINT

The composite print carries both the sound track and the pictures. A narrow black band separates each frame. When the movie is projected on the screen at the proper speed, the bands are not seen and the action appears continuous. The composite print shown here has two identical sound tracks side by side. The use of two tracks improves the quality of sound reproduction.

- Frame
- Sound track
- Sprocket hole

Universal Studios

A 35-MILLIMETER PROJECTOR

The projector shines a beam of light from the lamphouse through the film as it moves through the projection unit. The soundhead helps convert the sound track into amplified sound.

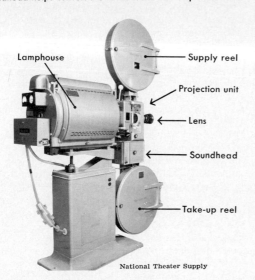

National Theater Supply

- Lamphouse
- Supply reel
- Projection unit
- Lens
- Soundhead
- Take-up reel

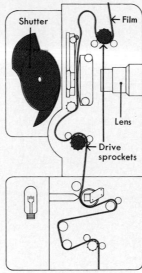

Shutter — Film — Lens — Drive sprockets

The Movement of Film through the projector is controlled by drive sprockets. Teeth in the sprockets fit into the film's sprocket holes and pull the film through the projector. As the film moves past the shutter, it is stopped and started repeatedly. This is called *intermittent movement*. After passing through the projection unit, the film runs through the soundhead without interruption. This is called *continuous movement*. The loops of film near the sprockets help maintain an even flow of film from intermittent movement to continuous movement.

HOW LIGHT TRAVELS THROUGH A PROJECTOR

In the lamphouse, a device called an *arc light* shines an intense light onto a metal reflector. This light is concentrated into a beam. A revolving shutter controls the passage of the beam through the projection unit. When a frame of film is in position between the aperture and the lens, the shutter opens. The beam shines through the film and projects the picture onto the screen. The shutter then closes and cuts off the beam while the film advances to the next frame.

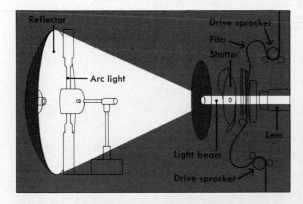

Reflector — Drive sprocket — Film — Shutter — Arc light — Lens — Light beam — Drive sprocket

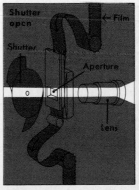

Shutter open — Film — Shutter — Aperture — Lens

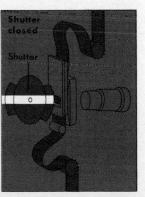

Shutter closed — Shutter

SOUND REPRODUCTION IN A THEATER

Light from an exciter lamp is concentrated into a beam. The beam shines through the sound track and strikes a photoelectric cell. The photoelectric cell converts the beam into electric impulses. These impulses are strengthened by an amplifier. Finally, the strengthened impulses are changed into sound waves in a speaker behind the screen.

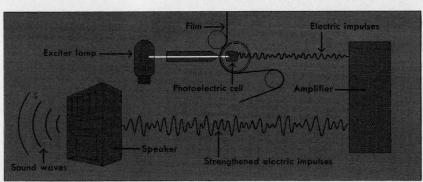

Film — Electric impulses — Exciter lamp — Photoelectric cell — Amplifier — Speaker — Sound waves — Strengthened electric impulses

the shutter is open, the film is motionless and light passes through the lens and exposes a frame. The shutter then closes, and a device called a *claw* is inserted into small, evenly spaced *sprocket holes* along each edge of the film. Using the holes, the claw pulls the film forward to the next frame. The shutter opens, and light passing through the lens exposes the motionless frame. This cycle is repeated 24 times a second.

Film for motion pictures is a flexible strip of Celluloid coated with chemicals that are sensitive to light. Both black-and-white and color film can be used in a standard motion-picture camera. Motion-picture film is made in several standard widths, which are expressed in millimeters. Film widths for movies shown in theaters are either 35 millimeters (about $1\frac{3}{8}$ inches) or 70 millimeters (about $2\frac{3}{4}$ inches). Most film for use in schools is 16 millimeters (about $\frac{5}{8}$ of an inch). Most home movies are 8 millimeters (a little more than $\frac{1}{4}$ inch).

Sound in a motion picture is recorded on a narrow band along one side of the film called the *sound track*. During the production of a movie, the dialogue, music, and sound effects are first recorded on separate magnetic tapes. These tapes are carefully blended onto a composite master tape through a process called *dubbing*. To learn about the process, see the section of this article *How a Motion Picture Is Made* (*Dubbing*). This master tape is then recorded on the exposed film, making a complete sound and picture print. As the film passes through the projector, the sound track is converted into the sounds we hear in the theater. Many

newer or larger theaters today use prints with the sound printed on separate magnetic strips that replace the conventional sound tracks. Sometimes the sound is printed on a magnetic stripe just to the left of the image. These techniques provide finer sound quality and are better suited to the stereophonic sound systems used in such theaters.

The Projector flashes the exposed frames of film onto the screen. Inside the projector, drive sprockets pull the film past a powerful beam of light.

The projector, like the camera, stops and starts the film 24 times each second. Each time the projector stops the film, a revolving shutter opens and a frame is flashed on the screen. While the film moves to the next frame, the shutter revolves and shuts out the light from the beam. The viewer's persistence of vision fills in the periods of darkness, making the action appear continuous. In reality, the screen is dark for a longer period of time than it is lit. If the images were projected continuously rather than as separate frames, the viewer would see the motion picture as a blur on the screen.

The Screen used in movie theaters has a highly reflective surface that gives a clear picture with bright colors. The screen may be covered with tiny beads of glass or painted with titanium dioxide or a mixture of white lead and white zinc. The speakers are placed behind the screen so that the sound seems to come from the picture itself. There are 20 to 40 holes per square inch (3 to 6 per square centimeter) of the screen to allow the sound to project through.

MOTION PICTURE / The Motion-Picture Industry

Movies are a billion-dollar industry in the United States. Americans pay almost $2 billion yearly to see movies. The payroll for workers in the industry totals over 1\frac{1}{2}$ billion a year. Motion-picture theater buildings in the nation are valued at more than 2\frac{1}{2}$ billion.

The motion-picture industry is divided into three branches—production, distribution, and exhibition. This section deals with distribution and exhibition. It also discusses attempts by government and private organizations to censor movies and the industry's attempts at self-regulation. The section ends with a discussion of motion-picture festivals and awards. For information on motion-picture production, see the section *How a Motion Picture Is Made*.

Distribution and Exhibition. From about 1915 to the late 1940's, the Hollywood studios controlled the three major branches of the American motion-picture industry. The studios not only made the movies, but they also distributed them to the theaters, most of which they owned. In the late 1940's, the Supreme Court of the United States ruled that studio control over production, distribution, and exhibition of movies had resulted in a monopoly. The Supreme Court ordered the motion-picture studios to give up their role as exhibitors. By early 1953, most of the studios had sold their movie theaters.

During the late 1940's, the studios also began to cut their production of new films, partly because of competition from television. The studios discovered that,

in most cases, they could earn more money distributing movies made by independent producers than by making and distributing their own pictures. Today, studios receive much of their income from distribution activities. In addition to the studios, there are many distributing companies that rent films to theaters.

The distributor charges the film's producer a fee of 30 to 50 per cent of all the money the film takes in. A new producer may have to pay a larger fee to attract a distributor than does an established producer with a record of profitable films. Distributors also charge for making the copies of the film sent to the theaters. In addition, they charge for advertising and publicizing the film. The costs of copying the film, advertising, and publicity come out of the first money the film takes in. The producer receives money only after these costs and the distribution fees have been deducted. The distributor can thus make a profit on a picture, while the film's producer may earn nothing.

Theater owners place bids with distributors for the films they want to exhibit. The decrease in the number of films produced has forced exhibitors to bid higher and higher against one another for the right to rent desirable films. To recover the ever-increasing cost of rentals, exhibitors have raised ticket prices. The higher prices have helped make the public very selective in its moviegoing. As a result of the high prices and competition from TV, movie attendance has dropped sharply. In the United States, about 90 million persons attended the movies weekly during the late 1940's. By the mid-1970's, the figure had dropped to less than 20 million persons a week.

Censorship and Self-Regulation. During the first half of the 1900's, several state and local governments had censorship boards that reviewed all movies before they could be shown in their areas. Some civic and religious groups also had censorship boards that advised members whether they believed a movie to be offensive. The censors were concerned largely with what they considered an objectionable emphasis on sex. The government boards could ban a picture from being shown in their city or state. Attacks by private censorship groups could affect a film's chance of succeeding at the box office.

Censorship remained an important factor in the American movie industry until the 1950's. Beginning in 1952, the Supreme Court made a series of decisions that eliminated the legal reasons that permitted local and state boards to function. In 1965, the last strong state censorship board—that of New York State—went out of existence. Some private censorship groups still exist, but they have less influence than earlier groups had.

The movie industry's efforts to regulate itself date back to 1922, when the studios established the Motion Picture Producers and Distributors of America. This organization reviewed scripts before filming began, attempting to catch and delete material it felt might be considered offensive.

In 1945, the organization became the Motion Pic-

ACADEMY AWARD WINNERS*

BEST PICTURE

1927-28	*Wings*	1946	*The Best Years of Our Lives*	1964	*My Fair Lady*
1928-29	*The Broadway Melody*	1947	*Gentleman's Agreement*	1965	*The Sound of Music*
1929-30	*All Quiet on the Western Front*	1948	*Hamlet*	1966	*A Man for All Seasons*
1930-31	*Cimarron*	1949	*All the King's Men*	1967	*In the Heat of the Night*
1931-32	*Grand Hotel*	1950	*All About Eve*	1968	*Oliver!*
1932-33	*Cavalcade*	1951	*An American in Paris*	1969	*Midnight Cowboy*
1934	*It Happened One Night*	1952	*The Greatest Show on Earth*	1970	*Patton*
1935	*Mutiny on the Bounty*	1953	*From Here to Eternity*	1971	*The French Connection*
1936	*The Great Ziegfeld*	1954	*On the Waterfront*	1972	*The Godfather*
1937	*The Life of Emile Zola*	1955	*Marty*	1973	*The Sting*
1938	*You Can't Take It with You*	1956	*Around the World in 80 Days*	1974	*The Godfather, Part II*
1939	*Gone with the Wind*	1957	*The Bridge on the River Kwai*	1975	*One Flew Over the Cuckoo's Nest*
1940	*Rebecca*	1958	*Gigi*		
1941	*How Green Was My Valley*	1959	*Ben-Hur*	1976	*Rocky*
1942	*Mrs. Miniver*	1960	*The Apartment*	1977	*Annie Hall*
1943	*Casablanca*	1961	*West Side Story*	1978	*The Deer Hunter*
1944	*Going My Way*	1962	*Lawrence of Arabia*	1979	*Kramer vs. Kramer*
1945	*The Lost Weekend*	1963	*Tom Jones*		

BEST DIRECTOR

1927-28	Frank Borzage (*Seventh Heaven*), Lewis Milestone (*Two Arabian Knights*)	1954	Elia Kazan (*On the Waterfront*)
1928-29	Frank Lloyd (*The Divine Lady*)	1955	Delbert Mann (*Marty*)
1929-30	Lewis Milestone (*All Quiet on the Western Front*)	1956	George Stevens (*Giant*)
1930-31	Norman Taurog (*Skippy*)	1957	David Lean (*The Bridge on the River Kwai*)
1931-32	Frank Borzage (*Bad Girl*)	1958	Vincente Minnelli (*Gigi*)
1932-33	Frank Lloyd (*Cavalcade*)	1959	William Wyler (*Ben-Hur*)
1934	Frank Capra (*It Happened One Night*)	1960	Billy Wilder (*The Apartment*)
1935	John Ford (*The Informer*)	1961	Robert Wise and Jerome Robbins (*West Side Story*)
1936	Frank Capra (*Mr. Deeds Goes to Town*)		
1937	Leo McCarey (*The Awful Truth*)	1962	David Lean (*Lawrence of Arabia*)
1938	Frank Capra (*You Can't Take It with You*)	1963	Tony Richardson (*Tom Jones*)
1939	Victor Fleming (*Gone with the Wind*)	1964	George Cukor (*My Fair Lady*)
1940	John Ford (*The Grapes of Wrath*)	1965	Robert Wise (*The Sound of Music*)
1941	John Ford (*How Green Was My Valley*)	1966	Fred Zinnemann (*A Man for All Seasons*)
1942	William Wyler (*Mrs. Miniver*)	1967	Mike Nichols (*The Graduate*)
1943	Michael Curtiz (*Casablanca*)	1968	Sir Carol Reed (*Oliver!*)
1944	Leo McCarey (*Going My Way*)	1969	John Schlesinger (*Midnight Cowboy*)
1945	Billy Wilder (*The Lost Weekend*)	1970	Franklin J. Schaffner (*Patton*)
1946	William Wyler (*The Best Years of Our Lives*)	1971	William Friedkin (*The French Connection*)
1947	Elia Kazan (*Gentleman's Agreement*)	1972	Bob Fosse (*Cabaret*)
1948	John Huston (*The Treasure of Sierra Madre*)	1973	George Roy Hill (*The Sting*)
1949	Joseph L. Mankiewicz (*A Letter to Three Wives*)	1974	Francis Ford Coppola (*The Godfather, Part II*)
1950	Joseph L. Mankiewicz (*All About Eve*)	1975	Milos Forman (*One Flew Over the Cuckoo's Nest*)
1951	George Stevens (*A Place in the Sun*)	1976	John Avildsen (*Rocky*)
1952	John Ford (*The Quiet Man*)	1977	Woody Allen (*Annie Hall*)
1953	Fred Zinnemann (*From Here to Eternity*)	1978	Michael Cimino (*The Deer Hunter*)
		1979	Robert Benton (*Kramer vs. Kramer*)

*Academy Awards are presented each spring for outstanding achievements in filmmaking during the preceding year.

ture Association of America. In 1968, the association adopted a classification system. Instead of reviewing scripts before production, the association rates the completed film as to its suitability for various age groups. The association classifies films into four categories: *G*—general, all ages admitted; *PG*—general, all ages admitted, but parental guidance suggested; *R*—restricted, persons under the age of 17 must be accompanied by a parent or guardian; *X*—no one under the age of 17 admitted (the age may vary in some parts of the country).

Festivals and Awards. The first film festival opened in Venice, Italy, in 1932. Today, more than 100 festivals are held every year throughout the world. The best-known festivals include those in Cannes, France; London; Los Angeles; Moscow; New York City; and San Sebastián, Spain. Many festivals show new feature pictures and award prizes for the best pictures and the best performances. Some festivals specialize in a particular

BEST ACTOR

1927-28	Emil Jannings (*The Way of All Flesh, The Last Command*)
1928-29	Warner Baxter (*In Old Arizona*)
1929-30	George Arliss (*Disraeli*)
1930-31	Lionel Barrymore (*A Free Soul*)
1931-32	Fredric March (*Dr. Jekyll and Mr. Hyde*), Wallace Beery (*The Champ*)
1932-33	Charles Laughton (*The Private Life of Henry VIII*)
1934	Clark Gable (*It Happened One Night*)
1935	Victor McLaglen (*The Informer*)
1936	Paul Muni (*The Story of Louis Pasteur*)
1937	Spencer Tracy (*Captains Courageous*)
1938	Spencer Tracy (*Boys Town*)
1939	Robert Donat (*Goodbye, Mr. Chips*)
1940	James Stewart (*The Philadelphia Story*)
1941	Gary Cooper (*Sergeant York*)
1942	James Cagney (*Yankee Doodle Dandy*)
1943	Paul Lukas (*Watch on the Rhine*)
1944	Bing Crosby (*Going My Way*)
1945	Ray Milland (*The Lost Weekend*)
1946	Fredric March (*The Best Years of Our Lives*)
1947	Ronald Colman (*A Double Life*)
1948	Laurence Olivier (*Hamlet*)
1949	Broderick Crawford (*All the King's Men*)
1950	José Ferrer (*Cyrano de Bergerac*)
1951	Humphrey Bogart (*The African Queen*)
1952	Gary Cooper (*High Noon*)
1953	William Holden (*Stalag 17*)
1954	Marlon Brando (*On the Waterfront*)
1955	Ernest Borgnine (*Marty*)
1956	Yul Brynner (*The King and I*)
1957	Alec Guinness (*The Bridge on the River Kwai*)
1958	David Niven (*Separate Tables*)
1959	Charlton Heston (*Ben-Hur*)
1960	Burt Lancaster (*Elmer Gantry*)
1961	Maximilian Schell (*Judgment at Nuremberg*)
1962	Gregory Peck (*To Kill a Mockingbird*)
1963	Sidney Poitier (*Lilies of the Field*)
1964	Rex Harrison (*My Fair Lady*)
1965	Lee Marvin (*Cat Ballou*)
1966	Paul Scofield (*A Man for All Seasons*)
1967	Rod Steiger (*In the Heat of the Night*)
1968	Cliff Robertson (*Charly*)
1969	John Wayne (*True Grit*)
1970	George C. Scott (*Patton*)
1971	Gene Hackman (*The French Connection*)
1972	Marlon Brando (*The Godfather*)
1973	Jack Lemmon (*Save the Tiger*)
1974	Art Carney (*Harry and Tonto*)
1975	Jack Nicholson (*One Flew Over the Cuckoo's Nest*)
1976	Peter Finch (*Network*)
1977	Richard Dreyfuss (*The Goodbye Girl*)
1978	Jon Voight (*Coming Home*)
1979	Dustin Hoffman (*Kramer vs. Kramer*)

BEST ACTRESS

1927-28	Janet Gaynor (*Seventh Heaven, Street Angel, Sunrise*)
1928-29	Mary Pickford (*Coquette*)
1929-30	Norma Shearer (*The Divorcee*)
1930-31	Marie Dressler (*Min and Bill*)
1931-32	Helen Hayes (*The Sin of Madelon Claudet*)
1932-33	Katharine Hepburn (*Morning Glory*)
1934	Claudette Colbert (*It Happened One Night*)
1935	Bette Davis (*Dangerous*)
1936	Luise Rainer (*The Great Ziegfeld*)
1937	Luise Rainer (*The Good Earth*)
1938	Bette Davis (*Jezebel*)
1939	Vivien Leigh (*Gone with the Wind*)
1940	Ginger Rogers (*Kitty Foyle*)
1941	Joan Fontaine (*Suspicion*)
1942	Greer Garson (*Mrs. Miniver*)
1943	Jennifer Jones (*The Song of Bernadette*)
1944	Ingrid Bergman (*Gaslight*)
1945	Joan Crawford (*Mildred Pierce*)
1946	Olivia de Havilland (*To Each His Own*)
1947	Loretta Young (*The Farmer's Daughter*)
1948	Jane Wyman (*Johnny Belinda*)
1949	Olivia de Havilland (*The Heiress*)
1950	Judy Holliday (*Born Yesterday*)
1951	Vivien Leigh (*A Streetcar Named Desire*)
1952	Shirley Booth (*Come Back, Little Sheba*)
1953	Audrey Hepburn (*Roman Holiday*)
1954	Grace Kelly (*The Country Girl*)
1955	Anna Magnani (*The Rose Tattoo*)
1956	Ingrid Bergman (*Anastasia*)
1957	Joanne Woodward (*The Three Faces of Eve*)
1958	Susan Hayward (*I Want to Live!*)
1959	Simone Signoret (*Room at the Top*)
1960	Elizabeth Taylor (*Butterfield 8*)
1961	Sophia Loren (*Two Women*)
1962	Anne Bancroft (*The Miracle Worker*)
1963	Patricia Neal (*Hud*)
1964	Julie Andrews (*Mary Poppins*)
1965	Julie Christie (*Darling*)
1966	Elizabeth Taylor (*Who's Afraid of Virginia Woolf?*)
1967	Katharine Hepburn (*Guess Who's Coming to Dinner*)
1968	Katharine Hepburn (*The Lion in Winter*), Barbra Streisand (*Funny Girl*)
1969	Maggie Smith (*The Prime of Miss Jean Brodie*)
1970	Glenda Jackson (*Women in Love*)
1971	Jane Fonda (*Klute*)
1972	Liza Minnelli (*Cabaret*)
1973	Glenda Jackson (*A Touch of Class*)
1974	Ellen Burstyn (*Alice Doesn't Live Here Anymore*)
1975	Louise Fletcher (*One Flew Over the Cuckoo's Nest*)
1976	Faye Dunaway (*Network*)
1977	Diane Keaton (*Annie Hall*)
1978	Jane Fonda (*Coming Home*)
1979	Sally Field (*Norma Rae*)

kind of film, such as documentaries and science fiction.

Many cities hold film festivals primarily to attract tourists. But the festivals also serve as a kind of international fair for distributors looking for profitable new films. In addition, the festivals give critics and film students an opportunity to learn what is happening in motion pictures around the world. The London and New York City festivals are especially popular with critics and students. Both festivals are held in autumn. They show the best motion pictures that appeared at other festivals earlier in the year.

The best-known film awards are made each spring by the Academy of Motion Picture Arts and Sciences. These awards, called the *Academy Awards* or *Oscars*, are presented for outstanding achievements in filmmaking during the preceding year.

The Academy Awards are given annually by the Academy of Motion Picture Arts and Sciences for outstanding achievement in filmmaking. Winners receive a statue called an Oscar, *right*. The statue was named in 1931 by an academy librarian who said it reminded her of her Uncle Oscar. The figure is made of bronze and covered with gold plate. It stands 10 inches (25 centimeters) high and weighs 7 pounds (3.2 kilograms).

© Academy of Motion Picture Arts and Sciences ®

--- BEST SUPPORTING ACTOR ---

1927-28	No Award
1928-29	No Award
1929-30	No Award
1930-31	No Award
1931-32	No Award
1932-33	No Award
1934	No Award
1935	No Award
1936	Walter Brennan (*Come and Get It*)
1937	Joseph Schildkraut (*The Life of Émile Zola*)
1938	Walter Brennan (*Kentucky*)
1939	Thomas Mitchell (*Stagecoach*)
1940	Walter Brennan (*The Westerner*)
1941	Donald Crisp (*How Green Was My Valley*)
1942	Van Heflin (*Johnny Eager*)
1943	Charles Coburn (*The More the Merrier*)
1944	Barry Fitzgerald (*Going My Way*)
1945	James Dunn (*A Tree Grows in Brooklyn*)
1946	Harold Russell (*The Best Years of Our Lives*)
1947	Edmund Gwenn (*Miracle on 34th Street*)
1948	Walter Huston (*The Treasure of Sierra Madre*)
1949	Dean Jagger (*Twelve O'Clock High*)
1950	George Sanders (*All About Eve*)
1951	Karl Malden (*A Streetcar Named Desire*)
1952	Anthony Quinn (*Viva Zapata!*)
1953	Frank Sinatra (*From Here to Eternity*)
1954	Edmond O'Brien (*The Barefoot Contessa*)
1955	Jack Lemmon (*Mister Roberts*)
1956	Anthony Quinn (*Lust for Life*)
1957	Red Buttons (*Sayonara*)
1958	Burl Ives (*The Big Country*)
1959	Hugh Griffith (*Ben-Hur*)
1960	Peter Ustinov (*Spartacus*)
1961	George Chakiris (*West Side Story*)
1962	Ed Begley (*Sweet Bird of Youth*)
1963	Melvyn Douglas (*Hud*)
1964	Peter Ustinov (*Topkapi*)
1965	Martin Balsam (*A Thousand Clowns*)
1966	Walter Matthau (*The Fortune Cookie*)
1967	George Kennedy (*Cool Hand Luke*)
1968	Jack Albertson (*The Subject Was Roses*)
1969	Gig Young (*They Shoot Horses, Don't They?*)
1970	John Mills (*Ryan's Daughter*)
1971	Ben Johnson (*The Last Picture Show*)
1972	Joel Grey (*Cabaret*)
1973	John Houseman (*The Paper Chase*)
1974	Robert De Niro (*The Godfather, Part II*)
1975	George Burns (*The Sunshine Boys*)
1976	Jason Robards (*All the President's Men*)
1977	Jason Robards (*Julia*)
1978	Christopher Walken (*The Deer Hunter*)
1979	Melvyn Douglas (*Being There*)

--- BEST SUPPORTING ACTRESS ---

1927-28	No Award
1928-29	No Award
1929-30	No Award
1930-31	No Award
1931-32	No Award
1932-33	No Award
1934	No Award
1935	No Award
1936	Gale Sondergaard (*Anthony Adverse*)
1937	Alice Brady (*In Old Chicago*)
1938	Fay Bainter (*Jezebel*)
1939	Hattie McDaniel (*Gone with the Wind*)
1940	Jane Darwell (*The Grapes of Wrath*)
1941	Mary Astor (*The Great Lie*)
1942	Teresa Wright (*Mrs. Miniver*)
1943	Katina Paxinou (*For Whom the Bell Tolls*)
1944	Ethel Barrymore (*None But the Lonely Heart*)
1945	Anne Revere (*National Velvet*)
1946	Anne Baxter (*The Razor's Edge*)
1947	Celeste Holm (*Gentleman's Agreement*)
1948	Claire Trevor (*Key Largo*)
1949	Mercedes McCambridge (*All the King's Men*)
1950	Josephine Hull (*Harvey*)
1951	Kim Hunter (*A Streetcar Named Desire*)
1952	Gloria Grahame (*The Bad and the Beautiful*)
1953	Donna Reed (*From Here to Eternity*)
1954	Eva Marie Saint (*On the Waterfront*)
1955	Jo Van Fleet (*East of Eden*)
1956	Dorothy Malone (*Written on the Wind*)
1957	Miyoshi Umeki (*Sayonara*)
1958	Wendy Hiller (*Separate Tables*)
1959	Shelley Winters (*The Diary of Anne Frank*)
1960	Shirley Jones (*Elmer Gantry*)
1961	Rita Moreno (*West Side Story*)
1962	Patty Duke (*The Miracle Worker*)
1963	Margaret Rutherford (*The V.I.P.'s*)
1964	Lila Kedrova (*Zorba the Greek*)
1965	Shelley Winters (*A Patch of Blue*)
1966	Sandy Dennis (*Who's Afraid of Virginia Woolf?*)
1967	Estelle Parsons (*Bonnie and Clyde*)
1968	Ruth Gordon (*Rosemary's Baby*)
1969	Goldie Hawn (*Cactus Flower*)
1970	Helen Hayes (*Airport*)
1971	Cloris Leachman (*The Last Picture Show*)
1972	Eileen Heckart (*Butterflies Are Free*)
1973	Tatum O'Neal (*Paper Moon*)
1974	Ingrid Bergman (*Murder on the Orient Express*)
1975	Lee Grant (*Shampoo*)
1976	Beatrice Straight (*Network*)
1977	Vanessa Redgrave (*Julia*)
1978	Maggie Smith (*California Suite*)
1979	Meryl Streep (*Kramer vs. Kramer*)

The First Successful Photographs of Motion were pictures of a horse. Eadweard Muybridge, a San Francisco photographer, took the pictures in the 1870's using 24 still cameras.

The idea of portraying things in motion has interested people since earliest times. In paintings in Altamira Cave in Spain, prehistoric artists tried to show animals running by painting them with many legs. Ancient Egyptian and Greek bas-reliefs portray figures in the act of moving.

About 65 B.C., the Roman poet Lucretius discovered the principle of the persistence of vision. About 200 years later, the astronomer Ptolemy of Alexandria experimentally proved the principle.

During the 1800's, many people experimented with devices that would make pictures appear to move. In 1832, Joseph Antoine Ferdinand Plateau, a Belgian scientist, developed the *phenakistoscope*, the first device that gave pictures the illusion of movement. Plateau placed two disks on a rod. He painted pictures of an object or a person along the edge of one disk. Each picture slightly advanced the subject's position. Slots were cut in the other disk. When both disks were rotated at the same speed, the pictures seemed to move as they appeared in the slots.

The first successful photography of motion took place in 1877 and 1878, when Eadweard Muybridge, a San Francisco photographer, made instantaneous photos of a running horse. Muybridge set up 24 cameras in a row, with strings stretched across a race track to the shutter of each camera. When the horse ran by, it broke each string in succession, tripping the shutters.

The Invention of Motion Pictures. During the late 1800's, inventors in France, Great Britain, and the United States tried to find ways to make and project motion pictures. These experimenters included Thomas Armat, Thomas A. Edison, Charles F. Jenkins, and Woodville Latham of the United States; William Friese-

Greene and Robert W. Paul of Great Britain; and the brothers Louis and Auguste Lumière and Étienne Jules Marey of France. After many failures, success came to several pioneers at about the same time. No one knows who first produced and projected movies.

In 1887, Edison began work on a device to make pictures appear to move. He succeeded in 1889, after Hannibal W. Goodwin, an American clergyman, had developed a transparent Celluloid film base that was tough but flexible. This base could hold a coating, or *film*, of chemicals sensitive to light. A series of pictures could be photographed on the film and moved rapidly through a camera. Previously, most photographs were taken on glass plates that had to be changed after each exposure. George Eastman, a pioneer in making photographic equipment, manufactured the film.

Using the Eastman film, Edison or his assistant William Kennedy Laurie Dickson invented the *kinetoscope*. Historians are not sure which man invented the device. The kinetoscope was a cabinet in which 50 feet (15 meters) of film revolved on spools. A person looked through a peephole in the cabinet to watch the pictures move.

In 1894, the Kinetoscope Parlor was opened in New York City. The parlor had two rows of coin-operated kinetoscopes. The kinetoscope also appeared in London and Paris in 1894. In spite of the kinetoscope's success, Edison believed that moving pictures were only of passing interest. However, other inventors in the United States and Europe disagreed. Using the principles of the kinetoscope, they developed improved cameras and projection equipment.

Motion pictures were projected on a screen publicly for the first time on Dec. 28, 1895. In a Paris café, the Lumière brothers showed some simple scenes, including that of a train arriving at a station. Movies were soon being shown in all the major cities of Europe.

Edison finally recognized that motion pictures had commercial possibilities and adapted a projector invented by Armat. Using this device, which he called the *projecting kinetoscope*, Edison presented the first public exhibition of motion pictures projected on a screen in the United States. The exhibition took place at Koster and Bial's Music Hall in New York City on April 23, 1896. The program included a few scenes from a prize fight, a performance by a dancer, and scenes of waves rolling onto a beach.

Early Motion Pictures. Pioneer filmmakers recognized that movies gave them an opportunity to record people and objects in vivid motion. They photographed crowds, horses, parades, waterfalls, and almost anything else that moved. By 1900, motion pictures had become a popular attraction in amusement arcades, music halls, traveling fairs, wax museums, and vaudeville theaters in many countries.

Filmmakers throughout the world adopted 35 millimeters as the standard size for movie film. Thus, a movie made in one country could be used in projectors in all other countries. Language differences presented no problem either. Until the late 1920's, movies were silent. That is, no sound came from the motion picture. The filmmakers inserted *titles*—printed dialogue and descriptions of action—into the film at appropriate places between scenes. To convert a film into another language, translated titles were inserted in place of the original titles.

At first, movies flourished simply because they were a novelty. The sense of reality particularly impressed audiences. When the screen showed ocean waves breaking on the shore, women raised their skirts to keep them dry. But audiences soon recognized that the motion picture's sense of realism was merely an illusion. They became bored, attendance declined, and the motion picture faced extinction.

The Movies Tell Stories. One development saved movies from extinction—they began to tell stories. As early as 1899, a French magician named Georges Méliès arranged short filmed scenes into a storytelling sequence. Méliès filmed hundreds of charming fairy tales and science fiction stories. He wrote and directed his films, acted in them, and designed the settings. Méliès thus became the film industry's first artist.

Edwin S. Porter, an American director, made the first movies using modern film techniques to tell a story. His most important film was *The Great Train Robbery* (1903), an 11-minute movie describing a train robbery and the pursuit and capture of the robbers.

Porter was perhaps the first director to recognize that a motion picture need not be filmed in the strict sequence of the action. The story of *The Great Train Robbery* switches back and forth between a number of settings, and so Porter realized it was impractical to shoot the story in sequence. Instead, he filmed all the scenes for each setting at one time and later edited the individual shots into an understandable story. Porter also created suspense by alternating scenes of the robbers escaping with scenes of a posse being formed to catch them. Porter's pioneer work in filming and editing set the standard for directors for several years.

The Nickelodeon. *The Great Train Robbery* was a tremendous hit at music halls, vaudeville houses, and wherever else it was shown. The film's success led to the establishment of *nickelodeons*—the first motion-picture theaters. Most nickelodeons were stores converted into primitive theaters by the addition of chairs. The nickelodeons charged 5 cents and showed a variety of films accompanied by piano music. Audiences consisted mainly of laborers, many of them immigrants who could not read and write.

By 1907, there were about 5,000 nickelodeons throughout the United States. The sudden growth of the nickelodeon increased the demand for motion pictures. Many studios were formed to produce movies to satisfy this demand.

Bettmann Archive

The First Important Movie was *The Great Train Robbery,* above, directed by Edwin S. Porter in 1903. It described a train robbery and the pursuit and capture of the bandits. Porter was the first director to use modern film techniques to tell a story.

Bettmann Archive

The First Movie Theaters were called *nickelodeons.* Most nickelodeons were stores converted into theaters by adding chairs. They charged 5 cents. They showed silent movies, while a pianist played music that suited the action on the screen.

718e

Culver Pictures

The Birth of a Nation, directed by D. W. Griffith, was the first motion-picture epic. The film dealt with the American Civil War and the period that followed. The movie was particularly famous for its spectacular battle scenes. A cameraman can be seen at the lower left.

The Birth of Hollywood. During the first years of the 1900's, most movies were made in New York City and in Fort Lee, N.J. But filmmakers soon realized that the Los Angeles area had a climate and a variety of natural scenery especially well suited to making movies. In 1907, the first movie was made in Los Angeles. In 1911, the Nestor Company built the first studio in a district of Los Angeles called Hollywood. Within a few years, more studios were built and Hollywood became the motion-picture capital of the world.

D. W. Griffith. Many film historians credit D. W. Griffith, an American director, with single-handedly creating the art of motion pictures. Between 1908 and 1913, Griffith directed hundreds of short films. In these films, Griffith developed basic filmmaking techniques still used today.

Before Griffith's time, directors always kept the camera in a fixed position when filming in the studio. The camera was placed about 12 feet (4 meters) from the performing area and at a right angle to it. In that way, the camera could photograph all the action and there was never any need to rearrange the lighting. But Griffith cared more about making his films dramatic than about the cost of rearranging the lights. He moved the camera closer and closer to the actors until, finally, the entire screen might be filled with a close-up of a face, a hand, or a pistol. Griffith did not invent the close-up, but he was the first filmmaker to demonstrate how it could be used dramatically and expressively.

Griffith also introduced the use of additional camera angles. Until his time, all the action in a scene had been taken in a single shot from a single camera position. Griffith moved his camera around the playing area to maintain the center of attention as it shifted from one part of the scene to another. By photographing a single scene from several viewpoints, Griffith could mingle long shots with close-ups. This technique provided visual variety and permitted him to emphasize whatever was important in the scene.

The breaking up of scenes into several shots also led Griffith to improve editing techniques. Griffith discovered he could create tensions within a scene through the rhythm of his editing. For example, many short scenes in succession would create a feeling of great excitement. Griffith also learned that, through editing, he could flash backward in time or show what a character was dreaming or thinking.

In two masterpieces, *The Birth of a Nation* (1915) and *Intolerance* (1916), Griffith proved that the motion picture was a major art form. *The Birth of a Nation* was the screen's first epic. It attempted to re-create episodes in the American Civil War and the Reconstruction period that followed in the South. The action is seen through the eyes of two families—one Northern and one Southern. *Intolerance* was an even more ambitious film that wove together stories from four periods in history.

The Rise of Stars. The first motion-picture performers were not identified by name on the screen. In fact, some performers preferred to remain unknown because movie acting was considered degrading compared with acting on the stage. But starting in 1910, a few of the more popular personalities were identified by name. In 1912, the famous stage star Sarah Bernhardt appeared in the motion picture *Queen Elizabeth*. Movie acting then quickly became respectable.

The American public soon singled out certain performers as special favorites. These performers were the first movie stars. The earliest stars included the cowboy actor Bronco Billy Anderson and the comedian John Bunny. Later stars of the silent films included Theda Bara, Charlie Chaplin, Douglas Fairbanks, William S. Hart, Buster Keaton, Mary Pickford, and Rudolph Valentino.

Mack Sennett and Silent Comedy. Mack Sennett, a Canadian, entered motion pictures in 1909 as a writer and actor at the Biograph Studio in New York City. By 1912, he had opened the Keystone Studio in Glendale, a Los Angeles suburb. In a short time, Sennett began producing a flood of wildly creative comedies. Nearly every major comic performer in American silent films worked at Keystone. They included Fatty Arbuckle, Charlie Chaplin, Charley Chase, Marie Dressler, Harry Langdon, Harold Lloyd, Mabel Normand, and Gloria Swanson. Many of Sennett's films featured a group of oddly dressed policemen called the Keystone Cops.

In his comedies, Sennett made brilliant use of trick photography and an editing technique that placed special emphasis on precise timing. He would edit a scene so that a speeding train would just miss hitting an automobile by a split second. Sennett sometimes reversed the film so that the characters seemed to be moving backward. He also speeded up or slowed down the film to achieve comic effects. Sennett even combined animated cartoon characters with live actors. Keystone comedies raced along at such a swift pace that the audience had little opportunity to notice that the action defied the laws of logic and gravity.

Movies Become Big Business. By 1912, motion pictures had begun to move out of nickelodeons and into real theaters, many of which had been used for stage plays. Movies became longer and more expensive to make. Filmmakers tried to attract a new audience—the middle class, which had avoided movies as unworthy of their attention. Movie companies began to film popular novels and plays, and they hired the biggest names in the theater to star in them.

During World War I (1914-1918), motion-picture production almost stopped in Europe because of shortages of materials and power. But the European people demanded movies as never before to escape for a few hours from the burdens of war. They especially liked the cheerful, glamorous movies made in the United States. American studios moved into the rich European market, using the profits to make pictures that were bigger, better, and even more glamorous.

The ever-increasing demand for movies led the American motion-picture industry to adopt more efficient methods of production. Thomas H. Ince, owner of Thomas H. Ince Pictures, is credited with introducing mass-production methods to filmmaking. At first, Ince directed all the pictures produced by his studio. But by 1915, studio production had grown to the point

where it became physically impossible for Ince to direct every film personally. To guide his movies through production, Ince appointed a group of supervisors called *producers*. Each producer was responsible directly to Ince, and each had control over a certain number of pictures.

Ince planned the production of each film systematically. He allowed a certain number of days for shooting on location and a certain number of days for shooting on the studio stages. Ince would have up to 10 or more pictures in various states of production at one time and so could rotate his movies through the studio facilities. In this way, he made full use of all his facilities all the time. Ince's "factory system" dominated Hollywood filmmaking until the 1950's.

By the mid-1920's, most of the major Hollywood studios had been established. They included Columbia, Fox, Metro-Goldwyn-Mayer, Paramount, United Artists, Universal, and Warner Brothers. The heads of the major studios approved of Ince's system. The studio heads were business executives, not artists. They cared chiefly about making profitable films, building chains of theaters to show their films, and further penetrating the worldwide market. The Ince system served them well in making money. But the system also restricted the creativity of the directors, who had to meet strict shooting schedules and thus could not experiment with new ideas. For this reason, much of the development of motion pictures as an art form during the 1920's took place not in the United States but in Europe.

New Techniques in Photography. Many of the most impressive motion pictures of the 1920's came from Germany. The German filmmakers became especially noted for their brilliant photographic techniques.

Almost all German movies of the 1920's were filmed entirely in huge, magnificently equipped studios in

Louise Fazenda, *left*, and Charlie Murray, *right*, in a scene from a 1917 Keystone comedy; Keystone Studio

Silent Comedies directed by Mack Sennett emphasized improbable and violent situations. Nearly all the important silent comedy stars worked for Sennett at his Keystone Studio.

what is now East Berlin. All the sets—even if the script called for a modern street or a fortress on a rocky cliff—were built on gigantic stages. These elaborate studio facilities gave directors complete control over their pictures. They could select their camera angles, place their lights, and arrange their performers without worrying about bad weather or other matters that often disrupt filming on location.

German directors preferred dark, moody backgrounds with the dramatic elements in a scene, such as an actor's face or hands, sharply lighted. The directors carefully arranged the performers and objects in each shot to achieve striking visual effects.

German directors introduced the *subjective* use of the camera—perhaps their greatest contribution to the art of motion pictures. Until about 1919, directors used the camera as a disinterested observer that looked at a scene or a character from the outside. However, the German directors wanted to express the inner emotional states of their characters and discovered they could do so by the imaginative use of the camera. As early as 1919, director Robert Wiene used unusual camera angles in *The Cabinet of Dr. Caligari* to suggest the world as seen by a madman. But the movie that revolutionized motion pictures through the creative use of the camera was *The Last Laugh* (1924), directed by F. W. Murnau.

The camera work in *The Last Laugh* is so expressive that the story is told entirely without titles. The film opens with a shot of the busy lobby of the Hotel Atlantic as seen from a descending elevator. The elevator gate opens, and the camera *dollies* (moves) across the lobby to the revolving doors of the entrance. Outside the doors is an elderly doorman, played by the great German actor Emil Jannings.

The doorman, proudly strutting in his glamorous uniform, greets the arriving and departing guests. The camera takes a closer shot and looks up at the doorman's majestic figure. A few moments later, a taxi arrives with a large trunk on its roof. The doorman looks for a porter, finds none, and struggles to take down the trunk himself. This shot is taken from above, diminishing the figure of the doorman while emphasizing the weight of the trunk. The doorman, exhausted by his struggle, leaves his post to rest. The hotel manager sees him resting and transfers him to the humiliating position of washroom attendant.

Most of the remainder of the film shows how the man reacts in horror and shame to his loss of status at the hotel. During one famous scene, at a wedding party, he becomes drunk and collapses in a chair. The room is shown spinning around, reflecting the confusion and dizziness in the man's mind.

New Techniques in Editing. While German directors were developing more expressive use of the camera, Russian filmmakers were pioneering in new editing techniques. In their experimental editing, the Russians arranged different shots into different sequences and cut shots to different lengths. Their experiments led to a new kind of editing called *montage*.

About 1922, the Russian filmmaker Lev Kuleshov demonstrated the effectiveness of montage. He inserted a close-up shot of the expressionless face of an actor at various points in a film. He placed the close-up among shots of a bowl of soup, a dead woman, and a child with a teddy bear. Kuleshov then showed the film to an audience. The viewers believed the actor showed hunger at seeing the bowl of soup, grief at seeing the dead woman, and delight at seeing the child with the teddy bear. The demonstration proved that a director could suggest an emotion or an idea by arranging shots in a certain order.

The greatest Russian film director, teacher, and theorist was Sergei Eisenstein. His first film, *Strike* (1924), was so effective that the Russian government invited him to make a picture celebrating the 20th

Emil Jannings in a scene from *The Last Laugh* (1924); Bettmann Archive

The Creative Use of the Camera by German filmmakers in the 1920's revolutionized the art of motion pictures. In *The Last Laugh,* director F. W. Murnau used expressive photography to capture a doorman's feeling of humiliation when he is transferred to the job of washroom attendant.

anniversary of an unsuccessful revolution in Russia in 1905. Eisenstein made *Potemkin* (1925), a motion picture based on a mutiny among the crew of the Russian battleship *Potemkin*. The film focused worldwide attention on Russian movies for the first time.

Potemkin shows Eisenstein's effective use of montage. In one shot, for example, soldiers fire their rifles. In the next shot, a woman clutches her stomach in agony. The viewer believes he has seen the troops shooting the woman, though this act is not shown.

Eisenstein also used editing to create powerful visual effects. In *Potemkin*, he built a sequence starting with the figure of a lone woman mourning at the corpse of a murdered sailor. A sequence of shots gradually added more people until, at the end, it seems as if the entire city has come to mourn.

The Movies Talk. A few motion pictures used sound before 1900. But these films depended on a mechanical hookup with a phonograph, and it was difficult to adjust the sound to the action on the screen. In the mid-1920's, Bell Telephone Laboratories developed a system that successfully coordinated sound on records with the projector. In 1926, Warner Brothers used the system, called Vitaphone, in *Don Juan*, a silent film with music and sound effects on record. In 1927, Warner produced *The Jazz Singer* starring Al Jolson. The picture was basically a silent film with a few songs by Jolson. But in one sequence, the actor spoke a few lines. *The Jazz Singer* revolutionized motion pictures and ended the era of silent films.

Meanwhile, a sound system called Movietone had been developed. In this system, sound was photographed directly on the film. The sound-on-film system was far superior to the sound-on-record method and was soon used for all talking pictures.

By 1929, the public demanded only sound movies. Theater owners rushed to install sound equipment. Public enthusiasm for sound pictures became so great that U.S. movie attendance increased from 60 million persons in 1927 to 110 million in 1929.

The first years of sound were actually a setback in the artistic development of motion pictures. Silent films were at the peak of their achievement in the late 1920's. When sound first became popular, several great European silent films were being shown in U.S. theaters. But the public ignored them, preferring talkies. In contrast to the brilliance of many silent films, the first talkies were clumsy, stiff, and self-conscious.

Many silent film stars had voices unsuited to sound films. For example, some had thick foreign accents, and others had voices that were too high-pitched. The careers of such stars ended almost immediately with talkies. But some other silent film stars, such as Greta Garbo and the comedy team of Stan Laurel and Oliver Hardy, successfully adjusted to sound.

Movies in the 1930's. During the early 1930's, Hollywood's most notable successes were musicals, gangster films, and newspaper movies. The musicals included *42nd Street* (1933) and *Gold Diggers of 1933* (1933). Among the most popular gangster movies were *Little Caesar* (1930), *The Public Enemy* (1931), and *Scarface* (1932). *The Front Page* (1931) was one of the best of the fast-paced and wisecracking newspaper movies.

During the early 1930's, Hollywood also produced several popular horror movies. *Dracula* (1931) was about a vampire. *Frankenstein* (1931) dealt with a monster created in a laboratory. *The Mummy* (1932) described how a mummy came back to life after lying for thousands of years in a tomb. The success of these movies led to many later films based on the same characters.

Sound-recording methods improved greatly during the 1930's. In addition, creative directors throughout the world used sound in imaginative ways. For example, the French director René Clair deliberately used the wrong sounds for certain scenes in *Le Million* (1931). In a scene of a fight for a jacket backstage at the Paris Opera, the action is accompanied by the cheers, shouts, and whistles of a crowd at a soccer match.

After about 1933, musical scores became increasingly important. The 1935 American film *The Informer* had an almost operatic score composed by Max Steiner. After the unexpected success of this picture, a full musical accompaniment became a status symbol in movies.

By the mid-1930's, sound movies had developed a new group of outstanding stars. The leading actors included Wallace Beery, James Cagney, Gary Cooper, W. C. Fields, Clark Gable, Cary Grant, Charles Laughton, Fredric March, the Marx brothers, and Spencer Tracy. Some of the most popular actresses were Joan Crawford, Bette Davis, Marlene Dietrich, Greta Garbo, Jean Harlow, Katharine Hepburn, and Mae West.

Most of the important directors of the 1930's had begun their careers in silent films. In England, Alfred Hitchcock became internationally famous for directing such thrillers as *The 39 Steps* (1935) and *The Lady Vanishes* (1938). Jean Renoir became one of France's leading directors with two dramas of social criticism—*Grand Illusion* (1937) and *The Rules of the Game* (1939).

Edward G. Robinson, *right*, in a scene from *Little Caesar* (1930), directed by Mervyn Le Roy; Bettmann Archive

Gangster Movies were among the most popular of the early sound films. *Little Caesar*, which portrayed the rise and fall of a mobster, became the most imitated gangster picture.

Hollywood Musicals of the 1930's became noted for their elaborate staging. Dance director Busby Berkeley staged this spectacular World War I musical number in *Gold Diggers of 1933*.

Scene from *Gold Diggers of 1933* (1933), directed by Mervyn Le Roy; the John Springer Collection, Bettmann Archive

John Ford of the United States directed many outstanding adventure and western films, including *The Lost Patrol* (1934) and *Stagecoach* (1939). Ernst Lubitsch began his directing career in Germany but settled in the United States in 1923. He won fame for such sophisticated and witty comedies as *Trouble in Paradise* (1932) and *Ninotchka* (1939).

The 1930's closed triumphantly with *Gone with the Wind* (1939), directed by Victor Fleming and starring Clark Gable and Vivien Leigh. The 220-minute Civil War drama was one of the longest films up to that time. It has been rereleased many times and has become one of the biggest money-makers in film history.

Orson Welles. Late in 1939, RKO studios invited Orson Welles, a 24-year-old American director and actor, to come to Hollywood to make a motion picture of his own choosing. Welles had won a reputation as a "boy wonder" for his work both in radio and on the stage. His experience gave him special understanding of the possibilities of sound and dialogue in movies. Welles directed two landmark motion pictures—*Citizen Kane* (1941) and *The Magnificent Ambersons* (1942). The second film is only partly Welles's work because RKO took the movie out of his hands before completion. Just as *The Birth of a Nation* and *Intolerance* stood as signposts to the future of silent films, so did Welles's two pictures show the way for later sound motion pictures.

Welles produced, directed, and starred in *Citizen Kane*. The film is the story of Charles Foster Kane, a powerful American newspaper publisher who closely resembles William Randolph Hearst, then one of the most powerful men in the United States. In the film, Welles used many experimental photographic techniques, such as startling camera angles and dramatic

lighting that cast deep shadows over much of the screen. The camera continually stressed the most important character, gesture, or incident in a scene. To achieve the effects Welles wanted, Gregg Toland, the cinematogra-

Orson Welles and Ruth Warrick in a scene from *Citizen Kane* (1941); Culver Pictures

Orson Welles produced, directed, and starred in *Citizen Kane*. Welles experimented with many photographic effects in the film. He used this striking angle, for example, to stress the coldness between the main character, Charles Foster Kane, and his wife.

pher, developed new camera lenses and lighting styles.

Welles revolutionized the use of the sound track in *Citizen Kane*. Earlier film scores served simply as an operatic or symphonic accompaniment to the movie. For *Citizen Kane*, composer Bernard Herrmann wrote a score to reflect the shifting moods of the story and to tie scenes together. From his radio experience, Welles introduced an off-screen narrator to describe portions of the action. He inserted a variety of off-screen voices to establish swiftly what an entire community was thinking about a topic. Welles cut away from one voice beginning a sentence to another completing it. He used the camera and sound track to compress time. For example, Welles condensed the long decline of Kane's marriage into three minutes of screen time by quickly showing a series of quarrels between Kane and his wife.

In *The Magnificent Ambersons*, Welles used dialogue realistically. He allowed his characters to interrupt one another or talk at the same time instead of permitting them to complete a sentence. In earlier sound movies, a character would complete a sentence or speech before the next character would begin talking.

Postwar American Movies. During World War II (1939-1945), the American motion-picture industry operated largely as it had before the war. However, great changes took place in the industry after the war ended. By the late 1940's, television had attracted a large portion of the moviegoing public. The studios reduced the number of pictures they made and released many of the directors, performers, producers, and writers they had under contract. Many of these people formed their own independent companies.

Many of the independent producers used their freedom from studio control to introduce serious themes into films. Stanley Kramer produced *Home of the Brave* (1949), a film about racial discrimination. Otto Preminger produced and directed *The Man with the Golden Arm* (1955), a drama about drug abuse. Such subjects might have frightened many studio heads, who believed movies should only entertain.

To lure the public from television, the movie studios developed such wide-screen processes as CinemaScope and Todd-AO and allowed their pictures to get bigger, more expensive, and more spectacular than ever. The studios produced such epics as *Ben-Hur* (1959), *Mutiny on the Bounty* (1962), and *Cleopatra* (1963). But motion pictures like these must take in enormous sums of money before they can even begin to show a profit. Many of the motion-picture spectacles were financial disasters. Some studios then turned to producing films that could not be seen on television. Such pictures stressed abnormal sexual behavior, nudity, and obscene language. The emphasis on sex and nudity continued into the 1970's. Films of the 1970's also placed a new emphasis on violence, notably in the works of such directors as Russ Meyer and Sam Peckinpah.

Movies about such disasters as airplane crashes, earthquakes, fires, or shipwrecks were popular during the early 1970's. The most successful "disaster" movies included *Airport* (1970), *The Poseidon Adventure* (1972), and *The Towering Inferno* (1974).

Postwar European Movies. European motion-picture production nearly ceased during World War II. How-

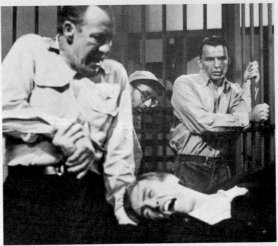

Scene from *The Man with the Golden Arm* (1955), directed by Otto Preminger; the John Springer Collection, Bettmann Archive

Postwar American Motion Pictures broke new ground in treating controversial subjects. *The Man with the Golden Arm*, starring Frank Sinatra, *right rear*, examined drug addiction.

ever, Europeans resumed making films as soon as the war ended. Many of these films introduced new styles and gifted directors to audiences in many countries.

Italy became the first country to capture worldwide attention for its films after the war. A group of talented Italian directors made a series of intensely realistic movies showing the miseries of war and the problems of returning to peacetime living. Their film style became known as *neorealism*. The neorealists worked against natural backgrounds whenever possible, both in the cities and in the countryside. They also preferred to use nonprofessional actors whenever possible.

The first neorealist film was *Open City* (1945), directed by Roberto Rossellini. In an almost documentary style, it shows the grimness of life in Rome under the German occupation. Director Vittorio De Sica used the streets of Milan to film *The Bicycle Thief* (1949), a moving story of a man and his son trying to find the stolen bicycle the man needs for his job. Neorealism served as a training school for later Italian directors who became famous. The most notable of these directors were Michelangelo Antonioni and Federico Fellini.

Both Antonioni and Fellini developed personal styles. Antonioni directed moody studies of characters apparently adrift without a sense of purpose in modern society. His best-known films include *L'Avventura* (1960) and *Blow-Up* (1966). Fellini gained acclaim in the 1950's for several realistic pictures, especially *La Strada* (1954) and *La Dolce Vita* (1959). He later turned to symbolic fantasies, as in *8½* (1963) and *Amarcord* (1974).

The political side of neorealism appears in the works of Bernardo Bertolucci and Lina Wertmuller. Bertolucci's best-known films include *The Conformist* (1970) and *1900* (1977). Wertmuller gained recognition for such films as *Love and Anarchy* (1973), *Swept Away* (1975), and *Seven Beauties* (1976).

France. The most important development in postwar French movies was the appearance of a group of

718k

Scene from *The Bicycle Thief* (1949), directed by Vittorio De Sica;
Culver Pictures

Italian Films gained international attention after World War II with such realistic movies as *The Bicycle Thief*. The film concerned a man and his son searching for a stolen bicycle.

based on Truffaut himself. Doinel appears in *The 400 Blows, Stolen Kisses* (1968), and *Bed and Board* (1970).

A number of French motion pictures showed a relaxed attitude toward sexual themes. The most popular of these movies in the United States included *A Man and a Woman* (1966) and *Cousin, Cousine* (1976).

England. Between 1945 and 1960, the English film industry was known largely for a series of light comedies and for the work of directors David Lean and Sir Carol Reed. Lean directed one of the greatest English postwar films, the romantic drama *Brief Encounter* (1945). Reed became known for several moody dramas, notably *Odd Man Out* (1947) and *The Third Man* (1949).

Beginning in 1959, English motion pictures were revolutionized by a series of films that realistically examined English working-class life. The film that started the trend was *Room at the Top* (1959), directed by Jack Clayton. Important movies that followed included *Saturday Night and Sunday Morning* (1960), directed by Karel Reisz and *The Loneliness of the Long Distance Runner* (1962), directed by Tony Richardson. A number of American-financed films of epic scope were made in England. They included *Lawrence of Arabia* (1962), *Tom Jones* (1963), and *Ryan's Daughter* (1970). During the 1970's, the English motion-picture industry declined sharply, producing few films.

Postwar Asian Movies. Since the late 1940's, Asian countries have produced more motion pictures yearly than have European countries and the United States combined. Hong Kong, India, Japan, South Korea, and Taiwan rank among the world's leading producers.

Few Asian films were shown in Western countries before the late 1940's. During the 1950's and 1960's, Asian motion pictures—particularly those produced in India and Japan—became popular in the West. However, in the 1970's, few Asian pictures were successful with Western audiences.

The film industry of India achieved international attention through the work of director Satyajit Ray. He became particularly noted for a series of three motion pictures describing the growth of a boy to manhood in modern India. The series, known as the *Apu Trilogy*, consists of *Pather Panchali* (1955), *The Unvanquished* (1957), and *The World of Apu* (1959). Western film critics and audiences especially admire Japanese movies dealing with the legends and history of Japan. The director

talented young directors who began what was called the *new wave* in filmmaking. Many of the directors who created the new wave had originally been film critics.

Most of the new wave films dealt with modern French life and centered on young people. Nearly all the films cost comparatively little money. But these movies had little else in common. Instead, each picture was marked by the individual style of its director. The major new wave directors and their first important films included Claude Chabrol (*The Cousins*, 1959); Jean-Luc Godard (*Breathless*, 1959); Louis Malle (*The Lovers*, 1958); François Truffaut (*The 400 Blows*, 1959); and Roger Vadim (*And God Created Woman*, 1956).

Godard and Truffaut gained the greatest international recognition during the 1960's. Godard aroused much debate because of his experiments in editing and photography and because of the Marxist philosophy in some of his pictures. His best-known films of the 1960's include *Weekend* (1967) and *La Chinoise* (1967). Truffaut became noted for his gentle, realistic motion pictures about a young man named Antoine Doinel, a character

Star Wars became the most profitable motion picture in history. This 1977 science-fiction movie describes the adventures of, *left to right*, Luke Skywalker, Han Solo, a hairy creature named Chewbacca, and Princess Leia. They fight the evil forces who terrorize their galaxy with a powerful weapon called the Death Star.

Akira Kurosawa earned international praise for his films *Rashomon* (1950) and *Seven Samurai* (1954). Other notable Japanese directors include Kenji Mizoguchi, Yasujiro Ozu, and Hiroshi Teshigahara.

Motion Pictures Today. The American motion-picture industry struggled desperately for economic survival during the late 1960's and early 1970's. About 80 per cent of all films produced lost money. Nearly every studio was in serious financial trouble, and unemployment in movie craft unions in Hollywood reached from 50 to 80 per cent.

A few motion pictures, however, made large profits during the late 1960's and the 1970's. They included *The Graduate* (1967), *Easy Rider* (1969), *Love Story* (1970), *M*A*S*H* (1970), *The Godfather* (1972), *The Sting* (1973), *Jaws* (1975), *Rocky* (1976), *Star Wars* (1977), *Saturday Night Fever* (1977), and *Grease* (1978). Most of these films were aimed at the increasingly important youth market. With the success of *Shaft* (1971), the studios also discovered the existence of a large black audience. The studios made many films in the early 1970's to appeal largely to this audience.

During the 1960's, historians, scholars, and educators began to take great interest in the history of motion pictures and in motion pictures as an art form. Before the 1960's, movies had received little serious scholarly attention. For many years, most information on motion pictures appeared in newspaper gossip columns and *fan magazines* and dealt largely with sensational or scandalous stories about the stars.

Since the early 1960's, thousands of hard-cover and paperback books have been published on motion pictures. These books trace the history of films, analyze the work of important directors and stars, and provide instructions on how to make movies. Publishers have issued collections of significant articles written years ago about films as well as reprints of historically important material, such as filmscripts. A selected list of important books on motion pictures appears on the next page.

Interest in film study grew enormously in American colleges and universities during the 1960's and early 1970's. In 1960, only about half a dozen universities offered degrees in motion pictures. By the late 1970's, over 300 institutions of higher learning were offering degree programs in film, television, or both. More than 1,000 other schools were providing at least one course.

During the 1960's and early 1970's, colleges and universities trained many young people in the art of directing films. These directors reject the traditional studio system of making movies. They prefer to shoot on location, using relatively inexpensive portable equipment available in 16 millimeters. They do not consider theaters important and exhibit their films at colleges and before film societies. Some critics believe the artistic survival of American motion pictures lies with these directors.

ARTHUR KNIGHT

MOTION PICTURE / Study Aids

Related Articles in WORLD BOOK include:

ACTORS AND ACTRESSES

DIRECTORS AND PRODUCERS

OTHER RELATED ARTICLES

Outline

I. **The Importance of Motion Pictures**
    A. Entertainment   C. Information
    B. Education   D. Movies as a Hobby
II. **How a Motion Picture Is Made**
    A. The People Who Make a Motion Picture
    B. Steps in Making a Motion Picture
III. **Animation**
IV. **How Motion Pictures Work**
    A. The Camera   C. Sound   E. The Screen
    B. Film   D. The Projector
V. **The Motion-Picture Industry**
    A. Distribution and Exhibition   C. Festivals and
    B. Censorship and Self-Regulation   Awards
VI. **The History of Motion Pictures**

Questions

How is sound recorded for motion pictures?
What contributions did Edwin S. Porter and D. W.

Griffith make to the development of motion pictures?
What is the purpose of *sneak previews?*
What is the editor's responsibility in filmmaking?
How do business and industry use motion pictures?
How did Thomas H. Ince change the course of the motion-picture industry?
What is meant by *dubbing* a motion picture?
Who is probably the single most important person involved in making a motion picture? Why?
How does movie acting differ from stage acting?
What movie ended the era of silent films?

Books to Read

GENERAL

BAZIN, ANDRE. *What Is Cinema?* 2 vols. Univ. of California Press, 1967-71.
BOBKER, LEE R. *Elements of Film.* 3rd ed. Harcourt, 1979.
EISENSTEIN, SERGEI M. *The Film Sense.* Rev. ed. Harcourt, 1947. *Film Form: Essays in Film Theory.* 1949.
HALLIWELL, LESLIE. *The Filmgoer's Companion.* 6th ed. Hill & Wang, 1977.
JACOBS, LEWIS, comp. *The Emergence of Film Art: The Evolution and Development of the Motion Picture as an Art, from 1900 to the Present.* 2nd ed. Norton, 1979.
JOWETT, GARTH. *Film: The Democratic Art.* Little, Brown, 1976.
MALTIN, LEONARD. *The Great Movie Comedians: From Charlie Chaplin to Woody Allen.* Crown, 1978.
MANCHEL, FRANK. *Film Study: A Resource Guide.* Fairleigh Dickinson, 1973.

MAKING MOTION PICTURES

GLIMCHER, SUMNER, and JOHNSON, W. E. *Movie Making: A Guide to Film Production.* Columbia Univ. Press, 1975.
GREGORY, MOLLIE. *Making Films Your Business.* Schocken, 1979.
ROBERTS, KENNETH H., and SHARPLES, WINSTON. *A Primer for Film-making: A Complete Guide to 16mm and 35mm Film Production.* Bobbs, 1971.
SCHIFF, LILLIAN. *Getting Started in Film-making.* Sterling, 1978. For young readers.
SMALLMAN, KIRK. *Creative Film-making.* Macmillan, 1969.

HISTORY AND CRITICISM

AGEE, JAMES. *Agee on Film.* 2 vols. Grosset, 1969.
ARMES, ROY. *A Critical History of the British Cinema.* Oxford, 1978.
BROWNLOW, KEVIN. *The Parade's Gone By. . . .* Univ. of California Press, 1968.
CRIPPS, THOMAS. *Slow Fade to Black: The Negro in American Film, 1900-1942.* Oxford, 1977.
DURGNAT, RAYMOND. *Films and Feelings.* MIT Press, 1971.
EVERSON, WILLIAM K. *American Silent Film.* Oxford, 1978.
KAEL, PAULINE. *I Lost It at the Movies.* Little, Brown, 1965. *Kiss Kiss Bang Bang.* 1968. *Going Steady.* Warner, 1970. *Deeper into Movies.* Little, Brown, 1973. *Reeling.* 1976. *When the Lights Go Down.* Holt, 1980.
KAUFFMANN, STANLEY. *Living Images: Film Comment and Criticism.* Harper, 1975.
KNIGHT, ARTHUR. *The Liveliest Art: A Panoramic History of the Movies.* Rev. ed. Macmillan, 1978.
MACGOWAN, KENNETH. *Behind the Screen: The History and Techniques of the Motion Picture.* Dell, 1965.
MANCHEL, FRANK. *When Movies Began to Speak.* Prentice-Hall, 1969.
RHODE, ERIC. *A History of the Cinema: From Its Origins to 1970.* Farrar, 1976.
SCHOEN, JULIET P. *Silents to Sound: A History of the Movies.* Scholastic Book Services, 1976. For young readers.
THURMAN, JUDITH, and DAVID, JONATHAN. *The Magic Lantern: How Movies Got to Move.* Atheneum, 1978. For young readers.

MOTION SICKNESS. See AIRSICKNESS; SEASICKNESS.

MOTIVATION is a word that is popularly used to explain why people behave as they do. In psychology and the other behavioral sciences, the word has a more limited use. Some scientists view motivation as the factor that determines behavior, as expressed in the phrase "All behavior is motivated." This usage expresses a general attitude or conviction, and is similar to the popular usage. However, when studying motivation, other scientists focus on two specific aspects of motivated behavior—the energization or arousal of behavior, and the direction of behavior.

Some scientists view motivation as the factor that energizes behavior. That is, motivation arouses an organism and causes it to act. According to this viewpoint, motivation provides the energy in behavior, but habits, abilities, skills, and structural features of organisms give direction or guidance to what they do. Other scientists, however, say that motivation serves some direction-giving function. Thus, in the behavioral sciences, motivation can mean energization or direction of behavior or both.

Energization is like arousal or activation, and means being "stirred up" or "ready for action." Energization can take place in several ways. An organism can be aroused by stimuli from outside or inside its body. If you touch a hot burner, pain from the external stimulus arouses behavior. A new or unexpected stimulus can arouse fear in some cases, and curiosity in other cases. Stomach contractions that produce hunger pangs are an internal stimulus. Thirst, which is often said to consist of dryness in the mouth and throat, is another internal stimulus.

Physiological conditions can make organisms sensitive to stimuli from the environment. For example, when hormones, the chemical secretions of the endocrine glands, reach a certain level in many species of birds, the birds begin nest-building activities.

After an organism has been aroused, its actions depend on the external or internal stimuli that call forth habits or other dispositions to respond in particular ways. An aroused organism with no habits or dispositions, or with no stimuli available to evoke habits or dispositions, acts aimlessly or restlessly. With such stimuli and habits present, the aroused organism acts purposefully and effectively.

Motivational conditions themselves may provide stimuli that direct behavior. For example, hunger or some other internal motive may direct an organism toward food. Or a motive state such as sex may make the organism sensitive to external stimuli, including a mate. But the directing function of the stimulation arising from motives differs from the arousal function of motives.

Kinds of Motives suggested by behavioral scientists usually include four groups: (1) homeostatic motives, (2) non-homeostatic motives, (3) learned motives, and (4) incentive-like motives.

Homeostatic Motives include hunger, thirst, respiration, and excretion. Just as a thermostat works to maintain a balanced temperature in a room, homeostatic motives work to keep the body in a balanced internal state. (The term *homeostasis* refers to the body's tendency to maintain such a balanced internal state.) Homeostatic motives are set in motion either by bodily deficits or by bodily excesses. When a person's body needs water, for example, bodily changes occur that make the individual thirsty and motivate him to seek something to drink.

Non-homeostatic Motives, like homeostatic ones, are biological in character, but they do not function homeostatically. Non-homeostatic motives include sex, such maternal activity as nest-building, and motives dealing with curiosity about the environment.

Learned Motives are acquired through reward and punishment in social situations, especially those of early childhood. These motives include anxiety, dependency, aggression, and a desire for social approval.

Incentive-like Motives include such incentives as money, prizes, status, and other goals. Through learning, we come to value these incentives so that the possibility of attaining them is motivating. Many homeostatic, non-homeostatic, and learned motives may also function through incentive-like processes. Food, for example, can arouse an animal because a hungry animal has learned that obtaining and eating food will reduce its hunger. In animals, also, a learned motive such as fear is usually associated with and aroused by a specific place where the animal experienced fear previously.

Theories of Motivation. Most general theories of motivation identify important sources of motives and describe their operation. Some theories stress sex and aggression, and others emphasize a variety of homeostatic, biological motives. Both groups of theories state that the organism seeks to remove a state of tension or arousal.

Still other theories emphasize such motives as curiosity, information-seeking, and interest in problem-solving. These theories indicate that organisms seek an intermediate level of arousal rather than the complete reduction of tension.

Some psychologists believe organisms tend to seek pleasure and avoid pain or unpleasantness. Other students of motivation say that realization of one's potentialities is the basic motivational factor.

In addition to general theories of motivation, there are theoretical descriptions of specific motivated behavior including sex, aggression, hunger, thirst, achievement, and dependency. A complete theory of motivation has not yet been formulated.   CHARLES N. COFER

See also DEVELOPMENTAL PSYCHOLOGY (Psychoanalytic Theory; Cognitive Theory); LEARNING (How We Learn; Efficient Learning); PERCEPTION (Factors Affecting Perception); PSYCHOLOGY.

MOTIVATION RESEARCH tries to learn how people choose things they buy. It also seeks to find out what people learn from advertising. Motivation researchers explore the feelings and points of view of consumers. They use knowledge from psychology, sociology, and other social sciences to interpret these emotions and attitudes. Motivation researchers interview people in a conversational way, and sometimes give them tests that must be analyzed by psychologists and sociologists. This type of research has shown that people do not shop with only price and quality in mind. They may buy something to impress others, or to keep up with their group. A person may also buy something to imitate someone he admires.   BURLEIGH B. GARDNER

See also ADVERTISING (Research).

MOTLEY, JOHN LOTHROP (1814-1877), an American historian and diplomat, won recognition chiefly for his

historical writings on The Netherlands. He wrote *The Rise of the Dutch Republic* (1856) and *History of the United Netherlands* (1860-1867). Motley was U.S. minister to Austria from 1861 to 1867, and minister to England from 1869 to 1870. He was elected to the Hall of Fame in 1910. Motley was born in Dorchester, Mass.   MERLE CURTI

MOTMOT is one of a group of South and Central American birds with oddly shaped tails. The tail feathers are long, and spread out at the tip like a tennis racket. The barbs on the bird's two middle tail feathers wear off. This gives the motmot's tail its unusual shape.

Motmots have handsome feathers colored blue, black, green, and cinnamon. They range from 6½ to 20 inches (17 to 51 centimeters) long. Motmots like to live alone, usually in gloomy forests. They sometimes build their nests in holes in trees. But some motmots build their nests in tunnels that they bore in river banks. The female lays three or four eggs. Motmots eat insects, reptiles, and fruit. The motmot has a *serrated* (saw-edged) bill.

The Beautiful Motmot is known for its oddly shaped tail.

Scientific Classification. Motmots belong to the motmot family, *Momotidae*.   GEORGE E. HUDSON

MOTON, *MOH tun*, **ROBERT RUSSA** (1867-1940), was an American Negro educator. He succeeded his close friend, Booker T. Washington, as president of Tuskegee Institute in 1915 (see TUSKEGEE INSTITUTE). Moton worked for racial good will. He served in 1930 as chairman of the Commission on Interracial Cooperation, and received the Spingarn Medal in 1932.

At the request of President Woodrow Wilson, Moton went to France in 1918 to study conditions affecting Negro soldiers in World War I. He served in 1930 as chairman of the U.S. Commission on Education in Haiti. Moton wrote several books, including *Racial Good Will* (1916), *What the Negro Thinks* (1929), and his autobiography, *Finding a Way Out* (1920). He was born in Amelia County, Virginia, a descendant of an African tribal chief. Moton was taught by his mother, who worked as a cook for a planter's family. He was graduated from Hampton Institute.   CLAUDE A. EGGERTSEN

MOTOR. See ENGINE; ELECTRIC MOTOR; ROCKET; STARTER, with picture.

MOTOR, ELECTRIC. See ELECTRIC MOTOR.

MOTOR CAR. See AUTOMOBILE.

MOTOR HOME is a vehicle that provides comfortable living quarters for people who are camping or traveling. Unlike a travel trailer, a motor home has its own engine and does not have to be pulled by a car. It can be driven and parked almost anywhere.

A motor home consists of one room, plus a bathroom

The Interior Arrangement of a Motor Home

Motor homes provide transportation and comfortable living quarters for camping trips and traveling. The interior of one of these vehicles includes areas for sleeping, cooking, and eating. The tables and couches can be converted into beds.

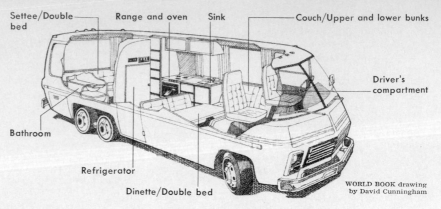

Settee/Double bed · Range and oven · Sink · Couch/Upper and lower bunks · Driver's compartment · Bathroom · Refrigerator · Dinette/Double bed

WORLD BOOK drawing
by David Cunningham

and areas for sleeping, cooking, and eating. In most motor homes, tables and couches can be converted into four to six beds. Motor homes have a heating unit, refrigerator, stove, and generator that operate on liquid petroleum gas. The generator provides electric current for lights and electric appliances. Motor homes also carry a water supply for the kitchen and bathroom. A tank holds waste water and sewage.

A motor home is not so large and well equipped as a mobile home, which is designed for permanent living. Most motor homes are about $7\frac{1}{2}$ feet (2 meters) wide and from 16 to 33 feet (5 to 10 meters) long.

In general, motor homes are more expensive to buy and operate than other recreation vehicles or automobiles. They range in price from $7,000 to more than $20,000. Some motor homes use large amounts of gasoline because they are so large and heavy.

Motor homes, like all motor vehicles, are required to meet federal safety standards. However, some experts believe the standards for motor homes are not satisfactory. For example, they are concerned because the roofs of motor homes do not have to meet the crush-resistance requirements of cars. During the mid-1970's, federal agencies worked to strengthen the laws governing motor homes, and manufacturers worked to improve efficiency and safety.

Motor homes came into wide use in the mid-1960's. By the mid-1970's, more than 350,000 families in the United States used these vehicles. Some motor homes served as traveling offices for country physicians or as showrooms for traveling salesmen.   F. M. RADIGAN

See also MOBILE HOME; TRAILER.

MOTOR SCOOTER. See MOTORCYCLE.

MOTORBOAT is a boat driven by any kind of engine except a steam engine. Motorboats range in size from 10-foot (3-meter) open runabouts to luxurious yachts 100 feet (30 meters) long. In addition to pleasure craft, they include diesel tugs, power barges, fishing trawlers, police launches, and patrol boats. Many types of motorboats are used by naval and coast guard services in all parts of the world. One of the most famous of these boats was the swift-striking PT (patrol torpedo) boat of the U.S. Navy in World War II (see PT BOAT).

Each year, thousands of vacationers enjoy motorboating in the inland or coastal waters of the United States and Canada. They use special trailers to carry smaller boats from their garages or back yards to lakes, bays, or oceans that may be far away. Boats as long as 25 feet (8 meters) can be carried behind family automobiles.

Thousands of boating enthusiasts build their own motorboats. Some of them, using only a set of plans, buy their own materials and assemble their boats from start to finish. But most home boatbuilders buy kits that have all the parts cut out and instructions supplied that tell how to assemble them. They build boats ranging from small, open runabouts to cabin cruisers that can sleep several persons.

There are two general types of motorboats: (1) outboard motorboats and (2) inboard motorboats. An *outboard* motorboat has one or more motors on the outside of the hull, usually at the *stern* (rear). An *inboard* motorboat has the motor inside the hull.

Outboard Motorboats are the most popular type of motorboat for sportsmen. They include small, open craft like rowboats, as well as *outboard cruisers* more than 20 feet (6 meters) long. These boats have cabins equipped with bunks, stoves, refrigerators, and radios. Outboard hulls may be made of wooden planks, fiber glass, aluminum, molded plywood, or sheet plywood. The most popular outboard motorboats measure from 10 to 18 feet (3 to 5.5 meters) long, and serve for cruising, fishing, and water skiing. Outboard motors are made of light aluminum alloys that do not rust in salt water. They range from about 10 to 100 horsepower (7 to 75 kilowatts). Some outboard motorboats are powered by two engines that run side by side at the stern.

Inboard Motorboats range from small launches to ocean-going yachts. Many vacationers enjoy speeding over lakes and towing water skiers with open inboard motorboats. These boats are generally from 17 to 25 feet (5 to 8 meters) long and have shiny paint or natural varnish finishes. They are particularly popular on freshwater lakes. Boatmen in coastal areas often use more rugged cabin boats for fishing in rough seas. Many of these boats, called *sea skiffs*, have hulls made with overlapping planks, like those of a clapboard house. This kind of construction, called *lapstrake* or *clinker planking*, makes the hull extremely sturdy.

A flat-bottomed inboard motorboat, called a *hydroplane*, has a light hull and a powerful motor designed especially for racing. It does not slice through the water like other motorboats. Instead, it lifts up and skims over the water's surface. Many small motorboats used for utility or cruising also have the shallow, hydroplane-type hull. But a narrower, deeper hull, called a *displacement* hull, is used on larger boats, including cabin cruisers, motor yachts, and work launches.

The engine of an inboard motorboat may be in the

back of the boat and connected to the propeller with gears. Or, it may be in the center of the boat and connected to the propeller by a long propeller shaft. Gears and clutches transmit the power from an inboard motor to the propeller so that the propeller does not turn as fast as the engine. In this way, both the engine and the propeller can turn at the most efficient speeds. Most inboard motors are cooled by water pumped in from the outside, run through the cooling system of the engine, then pumped out again. Other engines have separate, self-contained cooling systems, some air-cooled.

Boat engines, like those used in automobiles, use light materials, operate at high speeds, and often have cylinders aligned in a V shape. In fact, many inboard motorboats use converted automobile engines.

Development of the Motorboat. Historians are not sure who invented the first motorboat. Probably the first motorboat designed for pleasure use was developed by F. W. Ofeldt of the United States in 1885. This craft was powered by a 2-horsepower (1.5-kilowatt) engine which used naphtha for fuel. Gottlieb Daimler of Germany used a gasoline engine in a boat in 1887. A motorboat powered by an electric storage battery was exhibited at the Paris Exposition in 1889. But motorboating did not become practical or popular until the gasoline engine was perfected in the early 1900's.

The first motorboats had long, narrow hulls and large, heavy engines. Early motorboats seldom achieved speeds faster than 30 miles (48 kilometers) per hour. But inboard motorboats gradually exceeded 100 miles (160 kilometers) per hour. In 1939, Sir Malcolm Campbell of Great Britain set a record of 141.74 miles (228.11

kilometers) per hour, which lasted for many years. In 1952, Stanley Sayres of Seattle, Wash., set the record for propeller-driven inboard motorboats. His 3,000-horsepower (2,200-kilowatt) hydroplane sped 178.497 miles (287.263 kilometers) per hour. Donald Campbell, the son of Sir Malcolm Campbell, set records in 1957, 1958 and 1959 in a jet motorboat. In 1964, he smashed all previous records with a mark of 276.34 miles (444.73 kilometers) per hour (see CAMPBELL, DONALD). But jet engines cannot be used for most boating because of the danger of their exhausts to nearby persons and boats. The Gold Cup race is perhaps the leading national motorboat race. It was first run on the Hudson River in New York in 1904.

Outboard motorboats began to gain wide popularity in the 1940's. Before 1941, some 50-horsepower (37-kilowatt) racing motors had been built, but the average outboard motor in the United States had only 3.6 horsepower (2.7 kilowatts). Motor sizes expanded in the late 1940's, after light motors could be built of aluminum alloys. By the late 1950's, manufacturers were making outboard motors with as much as 70 horsepower (52 kilowatts). In 1960, Burt Ross, Jr., of Spokane, Wash., set an outboard-motorboat speed record of 115.547 miles (185.955 kilometers) per hour. In the early 1960's, manufacturers began producing jet turbine inboard boats, diesel outboard motors, and hydrofoils.

WILLIAM W. ROBINSON

See also BOATING; HYDROFOIL; HYDROPLANE; OUTBOARD MOTOR; YACHT.

Consolidated Shipbuilding Corp.

The First Motorboat Pleasure Craft appeared in the 1880's. The 21-foot (6.4-meter) launch was invented by F. W. Ofeldt. Its 2-horsepower (1.5-kilowatt) engine was propelled by naphtha.

A Powerful Speedboat, left, skims the water at 50 miles (80 kilometers) per hour. Racing models go much faster.

A Big Cabin Cruiser, below, is the "flagship" of the motorboat fleet. This ocean-going boat has sleeping space for 10.

Chris Craft

Chris Craft

Nicky Heath, Woodfin Camp, Inc.

Jack Zehrt   WORLD BOOK photo   Tom Nebbia, DPI

Motorcycles can be used for both recreation and transportation. For some riders, a motorcycle offers the fun of riding country trails. For others, such as policemen, it helps in performing a job. Many riders compete in races. Others use their "bikes" mainly to travel to and from work.

MOTORCYCLE is a two- or three-wheeled vehicle powered by a gasoline engine mounted midway between the wheels. A motorcycle has a much heavier frame than a bicycle, the vehicle from which it was developed. People in many parts of the world use motorcycles for transportation or ride them for recreation and sport. Many police departments use motorcycles for pursuit and traffic control because these vehicles can be maneuvered easily through traffic. Most motorcyclists call their machines "bikes," and some larger, specially built models are known as "choppers."

In the United States and Canada, motor vehicle laws affect the operation of motorcycles as well as of automobiles and other types of vehicles. Most of the states and provinces require cyclists to have a motorcycle operator's license, for which a person must pass a test. In some states and provinces, a motorcyclist needs only a regular driver's license. Many states and provinces require cyclists to wear safety helmets and goggles. Some U.S. and Canadian cities sponsor driving courses in motorcycle safety, and many high schools provide classroom instruction in motorcycle operation.

In the early 1970's, the United States had more than 5 million motorcycles. Many of the people of several European nations depend on motorcycles for transportation to their jobs or to school. These nations include France, Germany, Great Britain, and Italy. Japan ranks as the world's largest producer of the vehicles.

Kinds of Motorcycles. Manufacturers produce motorcycles in a variety of sizes, types, and weights. But there are two main kinds: (1) those designed primarily for use on streets and other paved surfaces, and (2) those intended chiefly for off-the-road riding. The first group consists of street and touring bikes, and also motor scooters. The second group includes trail bikes and such motorcyclelike vehicles as minibikes and minicycles.

Street Bikes are used on roads and highways for short trips and in-town riding. They weigh from 135 to 350 pounds (61 to 159 kilograms) and can reach speeds of 50 to 80 miles (80 to 130 kilometers) per hour.

Touring Bikes, used mainly for cross-country travel, can carry heavy loads. Most of these bikes weigh from 350 to 700 pounds (159 to 320 kilograms), but oversized models may weigh 800 pounds (360 kilograms) or more. Touring bikes can travel up to 100 mph (160 kph).

Motor Scooters have the engine mounted over or directly in front of the rear wheel. The driver sits with both feet on a floor board because a motor scooter does not have a bicycle-type frame.

Trail Bikes can travel rough country trails, climb hills, and cross streams. They weigh from 150 to 250 pounds (68 to 110 kilograms) and go as fast as 70 mph (110 kph).

Minibikes and Minicycles may be seen in country areas and on trails. They are not intended for use on paved streets or roads because most models do not meet minimum motor vehicle standards. Minicycles are sturdier than minibikes. They have motorcycle-type engines but weigh less and are more compact than most motorcycles.

The Parts of a Motorcycle. A motorcycle has four major parts: (1) the engine, (2) a transmission system, (3) wheels, and (4) brakes. A frame made of steel or chrome tubing holds these parts together.

Engine of a motorcycle has from one to four cylinders and operates on either a four-stroke or a two-stroke cycle (see GASOLINE ENGINE [Cycle]). A four-stroke engine has intake, compression, power, and exhaust strokes. It ignites on every fourth stroke. A two-stroke engine combines the exhaust and intake strokes. It ignites on every second stroke.

Transmission System. Most motorcycles have a four- or five-speed transmission. Racing models may have as many as eight speeds, and some small models have as few as three. Most motorcycles have chain drives, though some have shaft drives like those on automobiles.

Wheels. Motorcycles have steel- or aluminum-rimmed wheels, with tires similar to those on automobiles. Motorcycle tires have special treads that provide the extra traction needed for turns. The *front forks,* an extension of the frame, help hold the front wheel in place. They serve as a suspension system that cushions the rider against bumps. A *rear swing arm* allows the rear wheel to move up and down, providing additional comfort when riding over bumps.

Brakes. A motorcycle has front- and rear-wheel brakes, each of which works separately. The front brake supplies about 70 per cent of the vehicle's stopping power.

Operating a Motorcycle. The rider uses various hand and foot controls to operate a motorcycle. Most bikes have a kick starter, but some have an electric starter. A hand twist grip controls the throttle, which regulates the speed of the engine. A hand lever operates the clutch. When the rider squeezes the clutch lever, the engine can be run without the motorcycle moving. When this lever is released, the motorcycle moves forward. Another hand lever works the front brake, and a foot pedal controls the rear brake. Most bikes have a second pedal that shifts the gears, but some older touring models have a hand lever for shifting.

Motorcycling As a Sport enables cyclists to compete in various events. Most competition is governed by the American Motorcycle Association (AMA), which has headquarters in Worthington, Ohio. The association sponsors a number of annual races, including events at Daytona Beach, Fla.; Houston; and Ontario, Calif.

A point system, established by the AMA, determines a racing champion each year. Cyclists receive points for winning official national races or for finishing from

Bettmann Archive

The First Real Motorcycle was invented in 1885 by Gottlieb Daimler, a German engineer. He put an engine on a bicycle frame.

second to sixth in the events. The racer who earns the most points becomes Grand National Champion.

In 1978, Don Vesco of the United States set the world speed record for motorcycles. He sped across the Bonneville, Utah, salt flats at an average speed of 318.598 mph (512.734 kph).

History. The first real motorcycle was invented in 1885 by Gottlieb Daimler, a German engineer. He attached a four-stroke piston engine to a wooden bicycle frame. For the next few years, motorcycles remained largely experimental. During the early 1900's, with continual improvements, they developed into useful, dependable vehicles.

Today's motorcycles do not differ greatly in general appearance from the early models. But modern bikes have stronger frames, more powerful engines, and more dependable brakes. Larger, softer seats make riding more comfortable, and hydraulic springs help lessen road shocks.   JIM DAVIS

PARTS OF A MOTORCYCLE

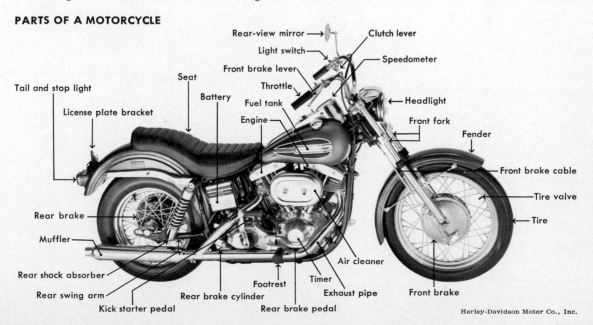

Rear-view mirror · Clutch lever · Light switch · Speedometer · Front brake lever · Throttle · Seat · Battery · Fuel tank · Headlight · Engine · Front fork · Tail and stop light · License plate bracket · Fender · Front brake cable · Tire valve · Tire · Rear brake · Muffler · Rear shock absorber · Rear swing arm · Kick starter pedal · Rear brake cylinder · Footrest · Timer · Exhaust pipe · Rear brake pedal · Air cleaner · Front brake

Harley-Davidson Motor Co., Inc.

MOTT, JOHN R. See Nobel Prizes (table: Nobel Prizes for Peace—1946).

MOTT, LUCRETIA COFFIN (1793-1880), was a leader of the abolitionist and women's rights movements in the United States. Mott helped establish two anti-slavery groups, and she and Elizabeth Cady Stanton, another reformer, organized the nation's first women's rights meeting.

Mott was born in Nantucket, Mass. Her family were Quakers, and she taught at a Quaker school near Poughkeepsie, N.Y., in 1808 and 1809. She moved to Philadelphia in 1809. Mott became a Quaker minister in 1821 and, like many other Quakers, was active in the abolitionist movement. She became known for her eloquent speeches against slavery. In 1833, Mott helped found the American Anti-Slavery Society and the Philadelphia Female Anti-Slavery Society. She helped organize the Anti-Slavery Convention of American Women in 1837.

In 1840, Mott went to London as a delegate to the World Anti-Slavery Convention. However, the men who controlled the meeting refused to seat her and the other women delegates. Mott met Stanton, who was attending the meeting with her husband. The two women were angered by the convention's action and pledged to work for women's rights.

Detail of a portrait by Joseph Kyle, from the collection of Mrs. Alan Valentine (R. E. Condit)
Lucretia Mott

In 1848, Mott and Stanton called a women's rights convention in Seneca Falls, N.Y., where the Stantons lived. The men and women at this meeting passed a "Declaration of Sentiments." This series of resolutions demanded more rights for women, including better educational and job opportunities and the right to vote.

After 1848, Mott began to speak widely for both abolition and women's rights. She also wrote a book, *Discourse on Woman* (1850). It discussed the economic, educational, and political restrictions on women in the United States and other Western nations. After slavery was abolished in the United States in 1865, Mott supported the movement to give blacks the right to vote. In 1864, she and other Quakers had founded Swarthmore College.　　　JUNE SOCHEN

See also STANTON, ELIZABETH CADY.

MOTT FOUNDATION, CHARLES STEWART, is an organization that donates money to educational and community development programs. It ranks as one of the wealthiest foundations in the United States. For assets, see FOUNDATIONS (table).

Charles S. Mott, a director of the General Motors Corporation, established the foundation in 1926. Most donations by the foundation finance community programs in Flint, Mich., where Mott lived. During the 1930's, the Mott Foundation helped the Flint board of education develop the concept of the community school. Such a school serves as a central point for meeting the educational, recreational, and welfare needs of all members of the community. Community education programs have since been adopted by thousands of U.S. schools. The Mott Foundation has headquarters at 510 Mott Foundation Building, Flint, Mich. 48502.

Critically reviewed by the CHARLES STEWART MOTT FOUNDATION

MOUFLON. See SHEEP (Wild Sheep).

MOULD. See MOLD (plant); CAST AND CASTING with its list of related articles.

MOULTING. See MOLTING.

MOULTON, FOREST RAY, helped develop geologic theories. See EARTH (How the Earth Began).

MOULTRIE, *MOO trih,* or *MOOL trih,* **WILLIAM** (1730-1805), was an American military leader in the Revolutionary War. Fort Moultrie in the Charleston (S.C.) harbor was named for him (see FORT MOULTRIE).

He entered the Continental Army at the start of the war, and became a brigadier general after his brave defense of Charleston harbor against the British fleet in 1776. He defeated the British again at Beaufort in 1779. Moultrie was captured when Charleston surrendered in 1780. He was set free in a prisoner exchange in 1782, became a major general, and served until the end of the war. Moultrie was governor of South Carolina from 1785 to 1787 and 1792 to 1794. His *Memoirs of the American Revolution* was published in two volumes in 1802. He was born in Charleston.　　　JOHN R. ALDEN

MOUND BIRD makes its home from the Nicobar Islands in the Indian Ocean eastward to the Philippines and Australia. It usually lives near the sea. Mound birds are dull-colored, and most are about the size of a chicken.

Mound birds lay 8 to 10 pinkish eggs in mounds of earth that they scrape together with their large feet. They mix leaves and other plant material with the earth. This material gives off heat as it decays. This heat and the heat of the sun hatch the eggs. The birds use the same mounds for many years, adding to them each season. Some mounds become more than 14 feet (4 meters) high and 70 feet (21 meters) around. The female places each egg in a hole $\frac{1}{2}$ to 5 inches (1.3 to 13 centimeters) deep which she digs in the top of the mound. The young birds hatch in six weeks.

Scientific Classification. Mound birds make up the megapode family, *Megapodiidae*.　　　RODOLPHE MEYER DE SCHAUENSEE

See also BIRD (Building the Nest).

CSIRO, Australia
Mound Birds heap earth and decaying plants over their eggs. The decaying material gives off heat, which hatches the eggs.

MOUND BUILDERS

A Sandstone Disk from a temple mound shows two rattlesnakes. The 8½-inch (22-centimeter) disk may have served as a palette.

Twin Burial Mounds stand at Fort Ancient State Memorial, near Lebanon, Ohio. Indians built the mounds in the A.D. 1100's or 1200s.

An Effigy Mound near Lake Koshkonong, Wisconsin, has the stylized shape of a turtle.

MOUND BUILDERS. Many mounds and earthworks made by early American Indians lie scattered throughout the central and eastern United States. Some are square, and others are round or oval. Effigy mounds have the shape of animals. Some mounds were burial places for the dead. Others, with flat tops, had lodges or temples on top. The valleys of the Mississippi and Ohio rivers contain an especially large number of mounds. Ohio and Illinois each have more than 10,000.

The Mound Builders were various groups of prehistoric American Indians who lived at different times and had various cultures. We do not know what these early Indians called themselves. Archaeologists, who study ancient times, have given the groups such names as Hopewell and Mississippian.

The Mound Builders used countless baskets of earth to make the mounds. This amount of labor indicates a well-developed social organization. The sharp flint axes and hatchets tell us that the Mound Builders could cut down trees and shape the wood. The arrowheads, knives, and sharp bone needles prove that they killed and skinned wild animals, ate their flesh, and used their pelts for clothing. Hoes and spades show that their owners knew how to farm. We know that corn ranked as one of their main crops. The Mound Builders also raised tobacco, and smoked it in beautiful stone pipes. Many mounds contain objects that come from faraway places, so we know that the Mound Builders traded a great deal. For example, Ohio mounds have contained black volcanic glass called *obsidian* and grizzly-bear teeth from the Rocky Mountains, copper from the

A Flat Pyramid Mound that stood at Aztalan village, near Lakemills, Wis., is shown in this artist's drawing. A stockade set with blockhouses surrounded the village.

Robert S. Peabody
Foundation for Archaeology

Stone Image of a Chief
came from Etowah Mounds,
Georgia. It measures 25 inches
(64 centimeters).

Objects Found in Mounds
help scientists learn how early
Indians lived. Mounds have
yielded pottery, tools, pipes,
stone sculptures, wood and shell
masks, and ornaments made
from shell, copper, and mica.

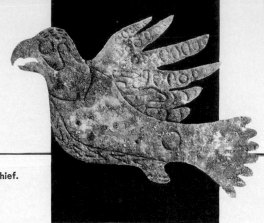

Ohio Historical Society

Copper Duck Hawk adorned a chief.

Thin Mica Hand was found in
a Hopewell grave mound in
south-central Ohio.
Ohio Historical Society

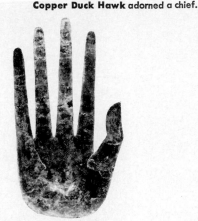

Ohio Historical Society

An Otter Holding a Fish
decorates a carved stone pipe.

Lake Superior region, mica from New England, and shells from the Gulf of Mexico.

Archaeologists have divided the mounds and their builders into two main groups: (1) burial mounds, and (2) temple mounds.

Burial Mounds. Indians of the Ohio River Valley began building large mounds of earth around A.D. 600. They used the mounds as tombs, sometimes burying as many as a thousand people in one mound. Many scholars believe that the Indians may have learned about building such mounds from Asian peoples. One of the best-known groups of burial mound Indians belonged to the *Hopewell* culture. They formed an alliance of tribes that stretched from Kansas to New York, and from the Gulf of Mexico to Wisconsin. Hopewell people lived by hunting, fishing, and farming. They built round lodges covered with skins or bark. The men wore simple breechcloths but painted their bodies with white and purple dye. Women wore wrap-around skirts. Both men and women liked jewelry of shells, copper, and mica. Hopewell Indians produced some of the finest arts and crafts of the eastern United States. Their carvings in wood and stone often represented realistic men and animals. Their work in copper probably excelled that of all other Indians north of the Rio Grande River.

Temple Mounds became widespread about the year 1000. Indians who built these mounds lived mainly along the Mississippi River and its branches, and their culture is often called *Mississippian*. Temple mound culture reached its peak in the area that now includes Arkansas, Kentucky, Tennessee, and the southeastern states. It also extended northward into Illinois, Wisconsin, and Minnesota. These Indians lived mainly by farming. They organized complicated village-states and religious cults. Their flat-topped mounds served as bases

for temples and chiefs' houses, and probably originated in Mexico. Mississippian peoples built square or rectangular houses and temples of poles covered with matting or thatch. Carvings and paintings decorated the temples, and a sacred fire burned inside. Mississippian Indians ranked among the best potters of eastern North America. Many Mississippian arts and crafts have curious decorations of crosses, spiders, snakes, weeping eyes, and other symbols. Scholars believe that these symbols represent a *Southern Death Cult*, which may have started in Mexico after the white men came.

Hernando de Soto saw temple mound peoples when his expedition traveled through southern North America in 1539-1542. Indians living in this way included the early Cherokee, Chickasaw, Creek, and Natchez. But, by the time white settlers arrived in greater numbers about 125 years later, the Indians had abandoned many of their old ways, and they no longer built such mounds.

Some Famous Mounds. One of the best-known effigy mounds is the *Great Serpent Mound*, near Hillsboro, Ohio. It has the shape of a serpent, and is more than 1,300 feet (396 meters) long. Temple mound sites include *Aztalan*, near Madison, Wis., a village with stockaded walls; and *Etowah Mounds*, near Cartersville, Ga. The *Cahokia Mounds*, near East St. Louis, Ill., include *Monk's Mound*, the largest earthwork in the world. See also the articles on the states where Mound Builders lived, such as OHIO (Places to Visit).   WAYNE C. TEMPLE

MOUND CITY GROUP NATIONAL MONUMENT, near Chillicothe, Ohio, contains a large group of prehistoric mounds. Historians believe the mounds were built by the Indian tribes who first inhabited the state. The monument covers 67.5 acres (27.32 hectares). It was established in 1923. See also MOUND BUILDERS.

MOUNT, in palmistry. See PALMISTRY.

MOUNT AETNA. See MOUNT ETNA.

MOUNT AGUNG. See VOLCANO (table).

MOUNT ALLISON UNIVERSITY is a coeducational university at Sackville, N.B. It is under the auspices of the United Church of Canada, but students of all faiths are admitted. The university grants bachelor's degrees and the master's degree in chemistry. It offers courses in arts, commerce, education, fine arts, music, sciences, and secretarial studies. It was chartered in 1858. For enrollment, see CANADA (table: Universities and Colleges).

Critically reviewed by MOUNT ALLISON UNIVERSITY

MOUNT ANGEL SEMINARY. See UNIVERSITIES AND COLLEGES (table).

MOUNT APO, *AH poh,* is a volcano on the island of Mindanao in the Philippines. It is nearly 10,000 feet (3,000 meters) tall, the highest mountain in the Philippines. Mount Apo forms part of a mountain ridge near Davao Gulf.

MOUNT ARARAT. See ARARAT.

MOUNT ASSINIBOINE, *uh SIN uh boin,* rises on the boundary between the Canadian provinces of British Columbia and Alberta. It forms part of the Continental Divide. The peak lies 20 miles (32 kilometers) south of Banff and stands 11,870 feet (3,618 meters) high. The mountain was first climbed in 1903. For location, see BRITISH COLUMBIA (physical map).

MOUNT ATHOS. See GREECE (Macedonia-Thrace); RELIGIOUS LIFE (The Eastern Orthodox Churches).

MOUNT BAKER. See WASHINGTON (Land Regions).

MOUNT CARMEL extends 13 miles (21 kilometers) in northwestern Israel from the Esdraelon Valley to the south coast of the Bay of Haifa. Mount Carmel rises 1,791 feet (546 meters) above sea level. For the location of Mount Carmel, see ISRAEL (map).

Mount Assiniboine is one of the highest peaks in the Canadian Rockies. It rises 11,870 feet (3,618 meters) above sea level.

Engelhard, Monkmeyer

MOUNT COOK is the highest peak (12,349 feet, or 3,764 meters) in New Zealand. It is in the Southern Alps in Tasman National Park, in the west-central part of New Zealand's South Island. The Maoris called it *Aorangi.* It was named Mount Cook for Captain James Cook, the English navigator who was the first European known to have seen it. See also NEW ZEALAND (picture: Majestic Mount Cook).

MOUNT DAMAVAND. See IRAN (Land Regions).

MOUNT DESERT ISLAND is an island off the coast of Maine (see MAINE [physical map]). Mount Desert has about 8,000 people. It covers 144 square miles (373 square kilometers). Cadillac Mountain, the highest peak, rises 1,530 feet (466 meters) above sea level. Acadia National Park, established on the island in 1919, was the first national park east of the Mississippi River. In 1604, French explorer Samuel de Champlain became the first European to reach Mount Desert. See also ACADIA NATIONAL PARK; CHAMPLAIN, SAMUEL DE; BAR HARBOR. ROBERT M. YORK

MOUNT ELBERT. See COLORADO (Land Regions).

MOUNT ELBRUS, the highest mountain in Europe, rises 18,481 feet (5,633 meters) in the Caucasus Mountains. Mount Elbrus lies about 150 miles (241 kilometers) from Tbilisi in the Georgian Soviet Socialist Republic in southwestern Russia. Over 20 glaciers, covering about 55 square miles (142 square kilometers), descend from the mountain. See also MOUNTAIN (table; picture chart). THEODORE SHABAD

MOUNT EREBUS. See ANTARCTICA (West Antarctica); MOUNTAIN (table; picture chart).

MOUNT ETNA is one of the most famous volcanoes in the world. It rises 11,122 feet (3,390 meters) on the eastern coast of the island of Sicily. Part of the mountain's base, which is about 100 miles (160 kilometers) around, lies on the Mediterranean Sea.

Mount Etna (sometimes spelled *Aetna*) makes a colorful picture with its snow-covered peaks, the forests growing on its slopes, and the orchards, vineyards, and orange groves about its base. The region around Etna is the most thickly populated area of Sicily. Nearby are the cities of Catania and Acireale, and 63 villages.

The first recorded eruption of Mount Etna occurred about 700 B.C. There have been more than 80 eruptions since then, some extremely violent. About 20,000 persons were killed in an earthquake that accompanied a 1669 eruption. Several towns were destroyed in 1950 and 1951 eruptions. Violent eruptions in 1960 ripped a hole in the mountain's east side. Eruptions also occurred in 1971, 1975, and 1979. GORDON A. MACDONALD

See also MOUNTAIN (picture chart); VOLCANO.

Wide World

Craters of Mount Etna in Sicily belch smoke after the violent eruption of 1928. Hot lava flowed from the craters, causing death and destruction in the densely populated areas nearby. Two towns were completely destroyed by lava.

MOUNT EVEREST
WORLD'S HIGHEST MOUNTAIN

Sir Edmund Hillary and Tenzing Norgay, a Nepalese tribesman, *right*, became the first men to climb Mount Everest, which rises 29,028 feet (8,848 meters). On May 29, 1953, after more than two months of climbing, they scaled the southeast ridge of the mountain and reached the summit. The snow-covered western face of the great peak, *below*, is seen from Mount Pumori.

MOUNT EVANS is a Rocky Mountain peak in north-central Colorado. It is the highest point (14,264 feet, or 4,348 meters) in the United States that can be reached by automobile.

MOUNT EVEREST is the highest mountain in the world. It rises about 5½ miles (8.9 kilometers) above sea level. The mountain is in the Himalaya range, on the frontiers of Tibet and Nepal, north of India (see NEPAL [map]). Surveyors disagree on the exact height of Mount Everest. A British government survey in the middle 1800's set the height at 29,002 feet (8,840 meters). The 1954 Indian government survey set the present official height at 29,028 feet (8,848 meters). But a widely used unofficial figure is 29,141 feet (8,882 meters). Mount Everest was named for Sir George Everest (1790-1866), a British surveyor-general of India. Tibetans call it *Chomolungma*. Nepalese call it *Sagarmatha*.

Many climbers have tried to scale Mount Everest since the British first saw it in the 1850's. Avalanches, crevasses, and strong winds have combined with extreme steepness and thin air to make the climb difficult. On May 29, 1953, Sir Edmund Hillary of New Zealand and Tenzing Norgay, a Nepalese Sherpa tribesman, became the first men to reach the top. They were members of a British expedition led by Sir John Hunt. It left Kathmandu, Nepal, on March 10, 1953, and approached the mountain from its south side—which had been called unclimbable. As the climbers advanced up the slopes, they set up a series of camps, each with fewer members. The last camp, one small tent at 27,900 feet (8,504 meters), was established by Hillary and Norgay, who reached the summit alone. See HILLARY, SIR EDMUND P.

In 1956, a Swiss expedition climbed Mount Everest twice. It also became the first group to scale Lhotse, the fourth highest peak in the world and one of the several summits of the Mount Everest massif.

In 1963, Norman G. Dyhrenfurth led a U.S. expedition that climbed Mount Everest. On May 1, James W. Whittaker, accompanied by Nepalese guide Nawang Gombu, became the first American to reach the top of the mountain. He climbed to the summit from the south. Thomas F. Hornbein and William F. Unsoeld, members of the same expedition, became the first persons to scale the difficult west ridge. They reached the top on May 22.

On September 24, 1975, Dougal Haston and Doug Scott became the first climbers to reach the top of Mount Everest by climbing the peak's southwest face. Haston and Scott were members of a British expedition.

Some Sherpa tribesmen claim a creature they call the *Yeti*, or *Abominable Snowman*, lives around Mount Everest. But climbers have not seen it. SIR EDMUND P. HILLARY

See also ABOMINABLE SNOWMAN; MOUNTAIN (picture chart); DYHRENFURTH, NORMAN G.; WHITTAKER, JAMES W.; ASIA (picture).

MOUNT FORAKER, *FOR uh ker*, is the sixth highest mountain in North America. It towers 17,400 feet (5,304 meters) in Mount McKinley National Park in south-central Alaska. Mount Foraker is part of the Alaska Range. It was first climbed in 1934. See also ALASKA RANGE; MOUNT MCKINLEY NATIONAL PARK.

MOUNT FUJI, *FOO jih*, or *FOO jee*, is the highest mountain in Japan (12,388 feet, or 3,776 meters). It lies on the island of Honshu, about 60 miles (97 kilometers) west of Tokyo. The Japanese call the mountain *Fujiyama* or *Fuji-san*. Fuji has long, symmetrical slopes. Its top often is hidden by clouds. Its crown of snow melts in summer. The Japanese have long considered it a sacred mountain, and more than 50,000 pilgrims climb to its summit every year. The top contains an inactive volcano crater. See also JAPAN (color picture); MOUNTAIN (picture chart); VOLCANO.   HUGH BORTON

MOUNT GODWIN AUSTEN, also called DAPSANG, or K2, is the world's second highest mountain. It is located in the Karakoram Range of the Himalaya in northern Kashmir. The peak, which reaches 28,250 feet (8,611 meters), is snow-covered and usually hidden in clouds. There are glaciers 30 and 40 miles (48 and 64 kilometers) long on its flanks. The mountain was named for Henry Haversham Godwin Austen (1834-1923), an Englishman who surveyed it in the late 1850's. He called it K2. See INDIA (color map).

An Italian expedition reached the top of the mountain for the first time in July, 1954. It was led by Ardito Desio. See also MOUNTAIN (picture chart).   J. E. SPENCER

MOUNT HAMILTON. See LICK OBSERVATORY.

MOUNT HERMON. See LEBANON (Land).

MOUNT HOLYOKE COLLEGE. See UNIVERSITIES AND COLLEGES (table); LYON, MARY.

H. Haga, Fuji Service & Trading

Mount Fuji rises 12,388 feet (3,776 meters) on the Japanese island of Honshu. It has been considered sacred since ancient times. Each summer, thousands of Japanese make a pilgrimage to the top.

MOUNT HOOD is an inactive volcano in the Cascade Mountain Range of northern Oregon. It rises about 30 miles (48 kilometers) south of the Columbia River. The mountain is 11,235 feet (3,424 meters) high. It has many glaciers. See also MOUNTAIN (picture chart).

MOUNT JEFFERSON. See OREGON (Land Regions).

MOUNT KAILAS. See HIMALAYA.

MOUNT KAMET. See HIMALAYA.

MOUNT KANCHENJUNGA, KAHN chen JOONG gah, or KINCHINJUNGA, KIN chin JANG gah, is the third highest mountain in the world. It rises 28,208 feet (8,598 meters). The mountain is part of the Himalaya, and stands about 100 miles (160 kilometers) east of Mount Everest, between Nepal and the Indian state of Sikkim. A British expedition climbed it for the first time in 1955. See also MOUNTAIN (picture chart).

MOUNT KATAHDIN. See MAINE (color picture).

MOUNT KATMAI. See ALASKA (Land Regions).

MOUNT KENNEDY. See CANADA (physical map).

MOUNT KENYA is an extinct volcanic cone in central Kenya, East Africa, 70 miles (110 kilometers) from Nairobi. It is 17,058 feet (5,199 meters) high, the second tallest mountain in Africa. Mount Kenya has glaciers on its slopes. Sir Halford Mackinder, an Englishman, first climbed it in 1899.

See also MOUNTAIN (picture chart).

MOUNT KILIMANJARO. See KILIMANJARO.

MOUNT KINABALU. See BORNEO (The Land).

MOUNT KOSCIUSKO, KAHZ ih US koh, is the highest peak in Australia. It rises 7,310 feet (2,228 meters). It is in the Snowy Mountains range of the Australian Alps, in southeastern New South Wales. Mount Kosciusko is 240 miles (390 kilometers) southwest of Sydney. See also MOUNTAIN (picture chart).

MOUNT LOGAN is the highest peak in Canada. It ranks also as the second highest peak in North America. It rises 19,520 feet (5,950 meters) and lies in the Saint Elias Range in the southwest corner of the Yukon Territory, near the Alaska boundary. The peak was named for Sir William E. Logan, director of the Canadian Geological Survey from 1842 to 1869. Until 1898, Mount Logan was believed to be the highest peak in North America. Then surveyors measured Mount McKinley in Alaska (see MOUNT McKINLEY). JOHN BRIAN BIRD

See also MOUNTAIN (picture chart); YUKON TERRITORY (map).

MOUNT LUCANIA, lyoo KAY nih uh, is the ninth highest mountain in North America. It rises 17,150 feet (5,227 meters) in the southwestern corner of Canada's Yukon Territory. It is one of the peaks of the Saint Elias Mountains. See also SAINT ELIAS MOUNTAINS.

MOUNT MAKALU, MUH kuh loo, is the fourth highest mountain in the world. Makalu stands in the Himalaya about 10 miles (16 kilometers) southeast of Mount Everest, near the border between Nepal and Tibet. Its highest peak, Makalu I, rises 27,824 feet (8,481 meters). Makalu II is 25,130 feet (7,660 meters) high. In 1955, French mountaineers led by Jean Franco became the first persons to climb to the top of Makalu. See also MOUNTAIN (picture chart). J. E. SPENCER

MOUNT MANSFIELD. See GREEN MOUNTAINS.

MOUNT MARCY. See ADIRONDACK MOUNTAINS.

MOUNT MAZAMA. See CRATER LAKE.

MOUNT McKINLEY, in central Alaska, is often called the *top of the continent* because it has the highest summit in North America. Mount McKinley has two ice-covered peaks, the South Peak (20,320 feet, or 6,194 meters), and the North Peak (19,470 feet, or 5,934 meters). The height of the South Peak was believed to be 20,269 feet (6,178 meters) for many years. But in 1956, after 10 years of surveys, the U.S. Geological Survey established the height as 20,320 feet (6,194 meters). The mountain is part of the Alaska Range. It was named for William McKinley, the twenty-fifth president of the United States. It is sometimes called by its Indian name, *Denali*, which means *The Great One* or *The High One*. The mountain is the chief scenic attraction of Mount McKinley National Park. Its north side is one of the world's greatest unbroken precipices.

In 1906, Dr. Frederick A. Cook, an American explorer, claimed to have been the first person to reach the summit. But in 1910 his claim was disputed (see COOK, FREDERICK ALBERT). That same year, a party of miners from Fairbanks, led by Peter Anderson and William Taylor, said they had reached the top. They claimed that they erected a flagpole that could be seen with binoculars from Fairbanks.

In 1913, Archdeacon Hudson Stuck, Harry P. Karstens, and two companions climbed to the summit of the South Peak, the first persons to attain that goal. From there, they sighted the miners' flagpole planted on the slightly lower North Peak. In 1932, Alfred D. Lindley, Harry J. Liek, Erling Strom, and Grant Pearson reached the top of the South Peak and two days later climbed the North Peak. This made them the first persons to ascend both peaks. JAMES J. CULLINANE

See also MOUNT McKINLEY NATIONAL PARK; MOUNTAIN (picture chart).

MOUNT McKINLEY NATIONAL PARK was established in February 1917, to protect the herds of wild animals that roam the finest game region in North America. The park is in south-central Alaska, about 120 miles (193 kilometers) southwest of Fairbanks and about 340 miles (547 kilometers) north of Seward. For area, see NATIONAL PARK SYSTEM (table: National Parks).

Mount McKinley, in the southwestern end of the park, is the chief attraction. It is the highest peak in North America, and towers to 20,320 feet (6,194 meters). Mount Foraker, near McKinley, rises 17,400 feet (5,304 meters). More than 300 other peaks of the Alaska Range rise along the park's southern border.

About 30 kinds of animals live in this rich game region. There are moose, caribou, mountain sheep, red and silver foxes, squirrels, and rabbits. More than 80 kinds of birds nest in the park. Birds found in Mount McKinley National Park include the Alaska jay, golden eagle, golden plover, jaeger, raven, robin, surfbird, wandering tattler, and white-crowned sparrow.

The park season lasts from June 1 to Sept. 15. The park may be reached by rail or highway. JAMES J. CULLINANE

See also ALASKA (picture); ALASKA RANGE; MOUNT McKINLEY; MOUNT FORAKER.

MOUNT MERON. See ISRAEL (The Land).

MOUNT MITCHELL, in western North Carolina, is the highest point east of the Mississippi River. It is 6,684 feet (2,037 meters) high and is located in Mount Mitchell State Park, 20 miles (32 kilometers) northeast of Asheville. The peak is part of the Black Mountains.

MOUNT NEBO, *NEE boh,* was the peak in the Mount Pisgah range from which Moses saw the Promised Land. According to the Bible (Deut. 34:5), he died there. Mount Nebo is probably Jabal an Naba, in present-day Jordan. A shrine to the Babylonian god Nebo may have stood on the mountain. See also MOUNT PISGAH.

MOUNT OF OLIVES is a low range of hills about ½ mile (0.8 kilometer) east of Jerusalem. It is also called MOUNT OLIVET. According to the Bible, Jesus went down from Olivet to make His triumphal entry into Jerusalem. Each night of His last week, He returned to Olivet (Luke 21:37) until the night of His betrayal. Acts 1 names Olivet as the place from which He rose into Heaven. The Church of the Ascension stands on Mount Olivet where the Ascension is supposed to have occurred. BRUCE M. METZGER and FULTON J. SHEEN

See also GETHSEMANE; JERUSALEM (Jerusalem at the Time of Jesus Christ); JESUS CHRIST (The Trial).

MOUNT OF THE HOLY CROSS is a peak in the Sawatch Mountains of west-central Colorado. It is 13,986 feet (4,263 meters) high. The peak is called Mount of the Holy Cross because two snow-filled crevasses once formed a large cross at the top of the moun-

tain. In 1929, the peak was established as a national monument. But one crevasse later crumbled away, and, by 1950, the cross no longer was apparent. The peak then was removed from the list of national monuments.

MOUNT OLYMPUS. See OLYMPUS.

MOUNT PALOMAR OBSERVATORY. See HALE OBSERVATORIES.

MOUNT PARNASSUS. See PARNASSUS.

MOUNT PISGAH, *PIHZ guh,* is a small mountain range in central Jordan. According to the Bible (Deut. 34:1), Moses saw the Promised Land from its highest peak, Mount Nebo. The mountain towers 2,631 feet (802 meters). The Pisgah range rises east of the River Jordan. The northern half of the Dead Sea lies southwest of the range. This range was part of the ancient kingdom of Moab in Palestine. Balak, a king of Moab, built his seven altars for the prophet Balaam on Mount Pisgah, offered sacrifices, and asked Balaam to curse the people of Israel. CHRISTINA PHELPS HARRIS

See also MOUNT NEBO.

MOUNT RAINIER, in Mount Rainier National Park, near Seattle, is the highest mountain in the state of

National Park Service

Majestic Mount Rainier, an inactive volcano, rises 14,410 feet (4,392 meters) high in Mount Rainier National Park in west-central Washington. Emmons Glacier covers the northeast slope.

MOUNT RAINIER NATIONAL PARK

Washington. Gassy fumes still rise from its great volcanic cone, but its deeply cut slopes show that the volcano was largely formed long ago. The peak is 14,410 feet (4,392 meters) above sea level. Automobile roads lead through fine cedar and fir forests to the mountain. Mountain torrents, patches of red heather, and white avalanche lilies line the routes. Indians of the Northwest called Rainier the *Mountain that was God*.

Hazard Stevens and P. B. Van Trump were the first to climb to the mountain's top. They climbed it by way of the Gibraltar Route in 1870. The climb to the top is a real test of endurance. Deep crevasses, ice caves, and steep cliffs make the shorter climbs exciting and colorful. With experienced guides, such climbing is not dangerous.

Paradise Valley, with hotel accommodations, perches at 5,400 feet (1,650 meters) on the slope near the timber line on Mount Rainier. Paradise Valley lies between the Nisqually and Paradise glaciers. Twenty-six glaciers feed the swift streams and tumbling waterfalls which roar through the glacial valleys. Wild flowers of every color border the glaciers. The Nisqually and the Cowlitz glaciers are the most often explored of the ice regions in the park. The Wonderland Trail encircles the mountain. Its 90-mile (140-kilometer) length can be covered in about a week to 10 days.   JAMES J. CULLINANE

See also SEATTLE (picture); WASHINGTON (picture); MOUNTAIN (picture chart).

MOUNT RAINIER NATIONAL PARK is in west-central Washington, near Seattle. The park was established in 1899 to preserve the natural beauty of majestic, ice-clad Mount Rainier. It covers 235,404 acres (95,265 hectares).

An old 14,410-foot (4,392-meter) volcanic cone, Mount Rainier bears a glacier system over 40 square miles (100 square kilometers) in extent. Twenty-six "rivers of ice" originate at or near its summit.

Covering the mountain's lower slopes are magnificent forests of Douglas fir, western hemlock, and western red cedar. Blacktail deer and mountain goats are among the animals that visitors may see in the national park.

To enjoy fully the park's spectacular scenery and interesting natural phenomena, visitors must hike or ride horseback. One park trail—the 90-mile (140-kilometer) Wonderland Trail—circles the peak and enters remote areas. Overnight shelters are provided for visitors. In winter, Paradise Valley, on the south side of Mount Rainier, is popular for skiing. It rises 1 mile (1.6 kilometers) high.   JAMES J. CULLINANE

See also FAIRY FALLS; MOUNT RAINIER.

MOUNT REVELSTOKE. See CANADA (National Parks).

MOUNT ROBSON is the highest point in the Canadian Rockies. It is 12,972 feet (3,954 meters) high, and rises on the east-central border of British Columbia. See BRITISH COLUMBIA (physical map). Mount Robson Provincial Park surrounds the snow-capped peak.

MOUNT ROGERS. See VIRGINIA (Land Regions); MOUNTAIN (picture chart: Mountains of the World).

MOUNT ROYAL. See MONTREAL.

MOUNT ROYAL PARK. See QUEBEC (Places to Visit); MONTREAL (Parks; picture: Beaver Lake).

MOUNT RUSHMORE NATIONAL MEMORIAL is a huge carving on a granite cliff called Mount Rushmore in the Black Hills of South Dakota. It shows the faces of four American Presidents: George Washington, Thomas Jefferson, Theodore Roosevelt, and Abraham Lincoln. The head of Washington is as high as a five-story building (about 60 feet, or 18 meters). This is to the scale of a man 465 feet (142 meters) tall.

Gutzon Borglum designed the memorial and supervised most of its work. Workmen used models that were one-twelfth actual size to obtain measurements for the figures. The models were lifted to the edge of the cliff to guide the workmen. The men cut the figures from Mount Rushmore's granite cliff with drills and dynamite.

South Dakota Dept. of Highways

Mount Rushmore is a national memorial to four great Americans. It has the largest figures of any statue in the world. The head of George Washington, *left*, is as high as a five-story building. The other heads, *left to right*, are Thomas Jefferson, Theodore Roosevelt, and Abraham Lincoln.

Work on the memorial began in 1927 and continued, with lapses, for over 14 years. Borglum died in 1941, before the memorial was completed, and his son Lincoln finished the work. Gilbert C. Fite described it in his book *Mount Rushmore*.

Mount Rushmore stands in the mountains 25 miles (40 kilometers) from Rapid City. It rises 5,725 feet (1,745 meters) above sea level, and more than 500 feet (150 meters) above the valley. Thus, the memorial stands taller than the Great Pyramid of Egypt (see PYRAMIDS). The memorial is part of the National Park System.   JAMES J. CULLINANE

See also BORGLUM, GUTZON; MOUNTAIN (picture chart: Mountains of the World); SOUTH DAKOTA (color picture).

MOUNT SAINT ELIAS. See SAINT ELIAS MOUNTAINS.

MOUNT SAINT HELENS is a volcano in the Cascade Mountains, 95 miles (153 kilometers) south of Seattle, Wash. The volcano erupted several times in 1980. More than 60 persons were reported dead or missing, and the eruptions also caused billions of dollars of damage to the surrounding area. Before the eruptions, Mount St. Helens had an elevation of 9,677 feet (2,950 meters) above sea level. But explosions blasted away more than 1,000 feet (300 meters) from the peak and created a huge crater. The eruptions were the first in the continental United States outside Alaska since 1921, when Lassen Peak in northern California last erupted.

Mount St. Helens has erupted many times in the past 4,500 years, but it was inactive from 1857 until 1980. Hot ash and rocks from the 1980 eruptions started forest fires and melted snow covering the upper slopes of the mountain. The resulting floods and mud slides washed away buildings, roads, and bridges. Explosions knocked down millions of trees. The eruptions also spread a thick

Roger Werths, *Longview Daily News* (Woodfin Camp, Inc.)
Mount St. Helens erupted in 1980, causing many deaths and enormous damage in southwestern Washington. The eruptions were the first in the continental United States outside Alaska since 1921.

layer of volcanic ash over a wide area, destroying crops and wildlife and blanketing cities. Geologists expected Mount St. Helens to erupt from time to time for several years.   FRANK PRESS

MOUNT SHASTA towers 14,162 feet (4,317 meters) above sea level in northern California. It rises almost 2 miles (3.2 kilometers) above the low mountains on which it rests. It is one of the southernmost of the great volcanoes in the Cascade Range between northern California and the Canadian border. For the location of the volcano, see CALIFORNIA (physical map). Successive lava flows over thousands of years made Mount Shasta. It is not considered an active volcano. But the mountain has a hot spring near its summit.

A second volcano called *Shastina* lies on the western slope of Mount Shasta, about 2,500 feet (762 meters) below the main peak. Shastina's crater is almost perfect, but the crater of Mount Shasta is badly scarred. Five small glaciers still exist on the mountain.   JOHN W. REITH

MOUNT SINAI. See SINAI.

MOUNT STEPHEN, BARON. See STEPHEN, GEORGE.

MOUNT TABOR, *TAY bur*, stands in northern Israel between Nazareth and Tiberias. The mountain rises 1,880 feet (573 meters) above the Plain of Esdraelon. It offers a beautiful view of the surrounding area. Walnut and oak trees once covered the slopes of Mount Tabor. Today, only a few trees grow on the mountain.

The Old Testament refers to Mount Tabor as the place where Barak fought Sisera (Judges 4). In 218 B.C., King Antiochus III of Syria founded a city at the summit of Mount Tabor. The early Christians believed the mountain was the scene of Christ's Transfiguration (see TRANSFIGURATION). The Crusaders built a church on the top of Mount Tabor. In 1212, the Arabs fortified the site, and called it Jabal al-Tor.   SYDNEY N. FISHER

See also DEBORAH.

MOUNT TAMBORA. See VOLCANO (table).

MOUNT VERNON was the home of George Washington. It lies in Fairfax County, Virginia, about 15 miles (24 kilometers) south of Washington, D.C. The tomb of George and Martha Washington is also at Mount Vernon. More than a million tourists visit this national shrine each year. The present estate covers about 500 acres (202 hectares).

Washington lived at Mount Vernon as a farmer before he was called upon in 1775 to take command of the Continental Army in the Revolutionary War. When the war ended, he came back to Mount Vernon to retire. But his service to his country was not finished. In 1789, he was elected as the first President of the United States. At the end of his second term, Washington returned to the estate to live in quiet and peace until his death two years later.

The Buildings. The mansion is a large, comfortable building with white pillars. It stands on a high bluff overlooking the Potomac River. There are 19 large rooms in the two-and-a-half story building. The attic has dormer windows. The mansion is built of wood, but the board siding on the outside is arranged to make it look like stone. The house has great dignity and beauty.

George Washington's father, Augustine, built the main section of the house during the 1730's. The elder

Mount Vernon, the estate of George Washington, covers about 500 acres (202 hectares) in Fairfax County, Virginia. It includes a mansion, *center rear,* and about 15 smaller buildings.

Washington's Bedroom is on the second floor of the south addition to the mansion. Washington died in this bed in 1799.

The Washington Dining Room at Mount Vernon was the scene of many formal dinner parties during the late 1700's.

The Mount Vernon Kitchen, a two-room building, stood near the mansion. The kitchen's west room is shown above.

The Ivy-Covered Tomb of George and Martha Washington is south of the house on the Mount Vernon estate.

Washington called the country estate the Little Hunting Creek Plantation. George Washington's elder half brother, Lawrence, inherited the property in 1743. He renamed it Mount Vernon in honor of Admiral Edward Vernon, his former commander in the British Navy. George Washington inherited Mount Vernon in 1761. He added the *piazza*, a two-story porch along the river side of the house, after returning from the Revolutionary War. See VIRGINIA (picture).

The inside of the house has been restored as nearly as possible to its original state. Many of the original furnishings have been returned. The beds upstairs are so high that persons used a stool or stepladder to get into them.

About 15 smaller buildings stand at the sides and behind the mansion. Some were living quarters for the servants and craftworkers. Others housed farm implements and animals. Nearly everything Washington's family needed was grown or made on the plantation, which at that time totaled 8,000 acres (3,200 hectares).

The Grounds and the Tomb. The grounds around the mansion add to the beauty of the estate. A wide, green lawn sweeps away from the east porch, and ends in a park at the foot of the hill. Flower gardens, and fruit and shade trees surround the buildings on the estate. Washington himself planted many of the trees which still flourish. The simple ivy-covered tomb where George and Martha Washington are buried stands at the foot of a hill, south of the house.

A National Shrine. By 1853, the estate was in a rundown condition because it could not be maintained as a self-supporting farm. Then a group of women formed the Mount Vernon Ladies' Association to save the grounds and buildings. These women aroused public interest in the project. Gifts of money from people in all parts of the country enabled them to buy the estate. They restored buildings which had fallen into ruin, and repaired the mansion. They recovered many of the original articles of furniture and decoration. John Augustine Washington, Jr., the last private owner of Mount Vernon, presented the key of the Bastille, which is exhibited in the central hall. Lafayette gave the key to Washington in 1790, during the French Revolution. Other valuable personal articles of the family were also placed in the house. Thus this lovely spot was saved to become a memorial. The Mount Vernon Ladies' Association of the Union now cares for the estate.

In 1931, the United States government completed the scenic Memorial Highway from Washington, D.C., to Mount Vernon. The road follows the banks of the Potomac River.　　　　　　　　　　CHARLES C. WALL

See also MOUNT VERNON LADIES' ASSOCIATION OF THE UNION; WASHINGTON, GEORGE.

MOUNT VERNON, N.Y. (pop. 72,778), is a suburb of New York City. It lies about 14 miles (23 kilometers) north of New York City's Grand Central Station. For location, see NEW YORK (political map). Its products include chemicals, clothing, decals, electrical equipment, paints, pharmaceuticals, wire from precious metals, and X-ray equipment.

The Mount Vernon area was first settled in 1664, and called *Hutchinson's*. Later, it was renamed Eastchester. In 1851, the Home Industrial Association of New York incorporated Mount Vernon as a community of homes for workers. It was chartered as a city in 1892. Old St.

MOUNT WILSON OBSERVATORY

Paul's Church, seized by Hessian troops as a barracks during the Revolutionary War, still stands in Mount Vernon.

John Peter Zenger, a New York newspaper editor, was arrested for his story of the election of an assemblyman. The election was held in Mount Vernon. His release helped to establish the American principle of freedom of the press. Mount Vernon has a mayor-council government.　　　　　　　WILLIAM E. YOUNG

MOUNT VERNON LADIES' ASSOCIATION OF THE UNION is a national organization that owns and cares for the estate of Mount Vernon, the home and burial place of George Washington. The association maintains the house and grounds as a national shrine. Everything is kept as nearly as possible the way it was when George Washington was alive.

The Mount Vernon Ladies' Association began for the sole purpose of preserving Mount Vernon for the people of the United States. When George Washington died, he left Mount Vernon to his nephew, Bushrod Washington. In 1853, John A. Washington, the great grandnephew of George Washington, offered to sell Mount Vernon to the United States government, or to the state of Virginia. Both Congress and the Virginia legislature refused to buy it. There was danger that the estate would be destroyed.

Ann Pamela Cunningham started the Mount Vernon Ladies' Association. She decided to raise $200,000 to buy Mount Vernon. She succeeded, and became the organization's first regent. Today, the association is made up of a regent and vice-regents. The regent is elected by the vice-regents. Each vice-regent represents a state that has taken part in the movement to preserve Mount Vernon. By the terms of its charter and title, the association has full ownership of Mount Vernon as long as the group exists and keeps its trust. Otherwise, the ownership of Mount Vernon will pass to the state of Virginia. The association maintains the estate with fees people pay for admission. The headquarters of the Mount Vernon Ladies' Association are in Mount Vernon, Va.　　Critically reviewed by the MOUNT VERNON LADIES'
　　　　　　　　　　　　　ASSOCIATION OF THE UNION

See also CUNNINGHAM, ANN PAMELA; MOUNT VERNON.

MOUNT VESUVIUS. See VESUVIUS.

MOUNT WASHINGTON is the highest peak in New Hampshire, and in the northeastern United States. It rises 6,288 feet (1,917 meters) in the Presidential Range of the White Mountains. It is the center of a summer and winter resort area. See also NEW HAMPSHIRE (color picture); WHITE MOUNTAINS.

MOUNT WASHINGTON COG RAILWAY. See NEW HAMPSHIRE (Places to Visit; color picture).

MOUNT WHITNEY, one of the highest mountains in the United States, rises 14,495 feet (4,418 meters). Snow-capped Mount Whitney lies in the southern part of the Sierra Nevada Range of California. Its cluster of granite pinnacles and domes rises sharply to more than 10,000 feet (3,000 meters) above the valley below. Mount Whitney was named for Josiah Dwight Whitney (1819-1896), state geologist of California. See also MOUNTAIN.　　　　　　　　　WALLACE E. AKIN

MOUNT WILSON OBSERVATORY. See HALE OBSERVATORIES.

MOUNTAIN

MOUNTAIN. The word *mountain* means different things to different persons. People who live in a vast, nearly level plain, such as the steppes of Russia, might call even a small hill a mountain. But those who live in an area similar to Colorado would not call a region mountainous unless it were very high and rugged.

By general agreement, geographers and geologists define a mountainous area as one that lies at least 2,000 feet (610 meters) above its surroundings. Its land surface consists of long slopes, deep canyons or valleys, and high, narrow ridges. The region also includes two or more zones of climate and plant life. See CLIMATE.

Mountains cover about a fifth of the land surface of the world. Some continents, such as Africa and Australia, have only a few mountains. Others, especially Asia, have vast areas that are high and rugged. *Submarine mountains* lie under water and help form the floors of seas and oceans. Some of them rise above the water to form groups of islands, such as the West Indies.

Most of the earth's surface has gradually been explored. As unexplored regions have become fewer, mountain climbers often defy death to be the first to scale a lofty peak.

Types of Mountains. Mountainous regions are created by movements of the earth's crust. These movements occur very slowly, but on a large scale. Different parts of the earth's crust react in different ways to these movements, and form four basic types of mountains.

In some places, the earth's crust folds into great waves, somewhat like the "upfolds" and "downfolds" of a washboard. An example of such *folded mountains* is the Jura range on the French-Swiss border.

In other places, the earth's crust breaks into huge blocks, some of which move upward and some downward. These are *faultblock mountains*, or *block mountains*, such as the Sierra Nevada in California.

The earth's crust may also change without folding or breaking into blocks. Instead, the top section of the crust rises into domes. The Black Hills of South Dakota are examples of these *dome mountains*.

In some places, the crust cracks and *lava* (molten rock) and rock ashes and gases move up through the cracks and pipelike vents. The lava and ashes pile up, layer on layer, building the land higher and higher. *Volcanic mountains* such as the Cascade Mountains of Washington and Oregon may result from such pile-ups. Individual volcanic peaks, such as Vesuvius in Italy, rise on top of these volcanic masses. Some volcanic masses build up from the bottom of the sea, creating such islands as the Hawaiian group. See VOLCANO.

How Mountains Are Measured. Surveyors usually measure the height of land surface, including mountains, by determining the distance of the land above sea level. When we say that the height, or altitude, of Pikes Peak in Colorado is 14,110 feet (4,301 meters), we mean that its *summit* (highest peak) rises 14,110 feet above the level of the sea. Actually, the mountain is far inland and its top rises only about 9,000 feet (2,700

FAMOUS MOUNTAINS OF THE WORLD

NAME	HEIGHT In feet	In meters	RANGE AND LOCATION	INTERESTING FACTS
Aconcagua	22,831	6,959	Andes in Argentina	Highest peak in the Western Hemisphere
Annapurna	26,504	8,078	Himalaya in Nepal	Eleventh highest peak in the world
Ararat	17,011	5,185	Armenian Plateau in Turkey	Noah's Ark supposed to have rested on Ararat after the Deluge
Cayambe	18,996	5,790	Andes in Ecuador	An extinct volcano with a square-topped crater
Chimborazo	20,561	6,267	Andes in Ecuador	For many years thought to be the highest mountain in the Western Hemisphere
Cho Oyu	26,750	8,153	Himalaya on Nepal-Tibet border	Seventh highest peak in the world (subpeak of Everest)
Communism Peak	24,590	7,495	Pamir-Alai in Russia	Highest peak in Russia
Cook	12,349	3,764	Southern Alps in New Zealand	Highest peak in New Zealand
Cotopaxi	19,347	5,897	Andes in Ecuador	Highest active volcano in the world
Dhaulagiri	26,810	8,172	Himalaya in Nepal	Fifth highest mountain in the world
Elbert	14,433	4,399	Sawatch in Colorado	Highest peak of Rocky Mountains
Elbrus, or Elbruz	18,481	5,633	Caucasus in Russia	Highest mountain of the Caucasus
Erebus	12,448	3,794	Ross Barrier on Ross Island	Active volcano in the Antarctic
Everest	29,028	8,848	Himalaya on Nepal-Tibet border	Highest mountain in the world
Fuji	12,388	3,776	On volcanic island in Japan	Considered sacred by many Japanese
Godwin Austen, or K2, or Dapsang	28,250	8,611	Karakoram in Kashmir	Second highest mountain in the world
Hood	11,235	3,427	Cascade in Oregon	Inactive volcano
Ixtacihuatl	17,343	5,286	Sierra Madre in Mexico	Aztec name for *white woman*
Jungfrau	13,642	4,158	Alps in Switzerland	Electric railroad partway up the mountain
Kanchenjunga, or Kinchinjunga	28,208	8,598	Himalaya on Nepal-India border	Third highest mountain in the world
Kenya	17,058	5,199	Isolated peak in Kenya	Near the equator
Kilimanjaro	19,340	5,895	Isolated peak in Tanzania	Highest mountain in Africa
Kosciusko	7,310	2,228	Australian Alps in New S. Wales	Highest peak in Australia
Lassen Peak	10,457	3,187	Cascade in California	One of the few active volcanoes in the United States
Lhotse I	27,890	8,501	Himalaya on Nepal-Tibet border	Fourth highest peak in the world (subpeak of Everest)

meters) above the surface of the nearby Great Plains.

A barometer is an instrument that records air pressure (see BAROMETER). The barometer and the barometric altimeter, an instrument based on the barometer, are used to measure heights. Altimeters give quick, accurate altitude readings. Most of our figures for mountain heights were obtained with altimeters.

For more accurate readings, surveyors use complicated instruments and techniques based on geometry and trigonometry. With these methods, they can measure a mountain without actually climbing it. They do need to see the peak, however.

None of these methods produce completely accurate measurements. Climatic and other conditions affect all instrument readings, and so the results tend to vary. For example, different surveys have reported the height of Mount Everest as 29,002, 29,141, and 29,028 feet. The last figure is the one most commonly accepted.

Scientists sometimes use the *geoidal method* to measure mountain heights. They first locate a mountain's position on the *geoid*, an imaginary reference surface produced by extending the mean sea level of the oceans under the continents. The scientists then calculate the distance between that point on the geoid and the earth's center to determine the height of the mountain.

People and Mountains. We have always been interested in mountains, either because we find them a barrier to travel and communication, or because they are useful or attractive. When mountains stand in our way, we seek ways to cross them or go around them.

In Europe, the Alps hinder land travel from Italy to countries in the north and west. The highways and railroads that cross the Alps include tunnels, trestles, and looping curves that follow the mountainsides.

Mountains have influenced history in many ways. Primitive people often stood in awe of mountains, because they believed that gods lived among the high peaks. The beginnings of modern religions, such as Judaism and Christianity, are connected with mountains. For example, Jehovah gave Moses the tablets bearing the Ten Commandments on Mount Sinai. Roman soldiers crucified Jesus Christ on Mount Calvary. Mountains have determined settlement patterns when great numbers of people migrated in search of new lands. The Appalachians limited settlement to the eastern seaboard of the United States for many years. Many conquering armies have been forced to retreat when they reached mountain areas. People familiar with the rugged terrain defeated the intruders who did not know how to do mountain fighting.

People who live in mountains or mountain valleys use the natural resources of their regions. The grass-covered slopes provide pastures for grazing animals. The thick mountain forests provide wood for fuel and lumber. Swift mountain streams turn turbines that generate electricity. Mines yield valuable minerals. Beautiful mountain scenery attracts vacationers for hiking, camping, hunting, and skiing.   ROBERT M. GLENDINNING

FAMOUS MOUNTAINS OF THE WORLD

NAME	HEIGHT In feet	In meters	RANGE AND LOCATION	INTERESTING FACTS
Lhotse II	27,504	8,383	Himalaya on Nepal-Tibet border	Sixth highest peak in the world (subpeak of Everest)
Logan	19,520	5,950	Saint Elias in Canada	Highest peak in Canada
Longs Peak	14,255	4,345	Rocky Mountains in Colorado	In Rocky Mountain National Park
Maipu, or Maipo	17,464	5,323	Andes on Chile-Argentina border	Active volcano
Makalu	27,824	8,481	Himalaya on Nepal-Tibet border	Fourth highest mountain in the world
Manaslu	26,658	8,125	Himalaya in Nepal	Tenth highest peak in the world
Matterhorn	14,692	4,478	Pennine Alps on Switzerland-Italy border	Favorite for daring mountain climbers
Mauna Kea	13,796	4,205	On volcanic island in Hawaii	Highest island peak in the world
Mauna Loa	13,677	4,169	On volcanic island in Hawaii	One of the world's most famous volcanic mountains
McKinley	20,320	6,194	Alaska Range in Alaska	Highest peak in North America
Mitchell	6,684	2,037	Appalachian in North Carolina	Highest peak in the Appalachians
Mont Blanc	15,771	4,807	Pennine Alps in France	Highest mountain in the Alps
Monte Rosa	15,203	4,634	Pennine Alps on Switzerland-Italy border	Iron, copper, and gold mined from its slopes
Nanga Parbat	26,650	8,123	Himalaya in Kashmir	Sixth highest mountain in the world
Orizaba	18,701	5,700	Mexican Plateau in Mexico	Highest peak in Mexico
Pikes Peak	14,110	4,301	Rampart in Colorado	Most famous of the Rocky Mountains
Popocatepetl	17,887	5,452	Mexican Plateau in Mexico	Aztec name for *Smoking Mountain;* volcano now inactive
Rainier	14,410	4,392	Cascade in Washington	Highest peak in Washington
Saint Elias	18,008	5,489	Saint Elias on Canada-Alaska border	Second highest peak in this range
Shasta	14,162	4,317	Cascade in California	Famous for its twin peaks
Tolima	17,110	5,215	Cordillera Occidental in Colombia	Active volcano
Vesuvius	4,190	1,277	Italy	Only active volcano on the mainland of Europe
Vinson Massif	16,864	5,140	Sentinel Mountains in Antarctica	Highest peak in Antarctica
Whitney	14,494	4,418	Sierra Nevada in California	Highest mountain in California

Sources: Rand McNally & Company; U.S. Geological Survey

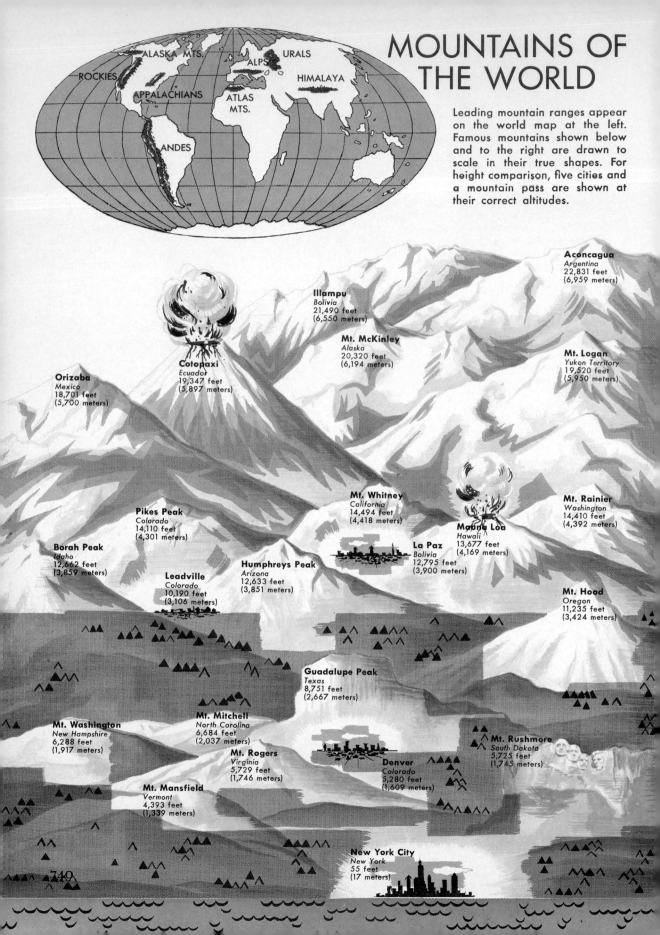

MOUNTAINS OF THE WORLD

Leading mountain ranges appear on the world map at the left. Famous mountains shown below and to the right are drawn to scale in their true shapes. For height comparison, five cities and a mountain pass are shown at their correct altitudes.

ALASKA MTS.
URALS
ALPS
ROCKIES
HIMALAYA
APPALACHIANS
ATLAS MTS.
ANDES

Aconcagua
Argentina
22,831 feet
(6,959 meters)

Illampu
Bolivia
21,490 feet
(6,550 meters)

Mt. McKinley
Alaska
20,320 feet
(6,194 meters)

Mt. Logan
Yukon Territory
19,520 feet
(5,950 meters)

Cotopaxi
Ecuador
19,347 feet
(5,897 meters)

Orizaba
Mexico
18,701 feet
(5,700 meters)

Mt. Whitney
California
14,494 feet
(4,418 meters)

Mt. Rainier
Washington
14,410 feet
(4,392 meters)

Pikes Peak
Colorado
14,110 feet
(4,301 meters)

Mauna Loa
Hawaii
13,677 feet
(4,169 meters)

La Paz
Bolivia
12,795 feet
(3,900 meters)

Borah Peak
Idaho
12,662 feet
(3,859 meters)

Humphreys Peak
Arizona
12,633 feet
(3,851 meters)

Leadville
Colorado
10,190 feet
(3,106 meters)

Mt. Hood
Oregon
11,235 feet
(3,424 meters)

Guadalupe Peak
Texas
8,751 feet
(2,667 meters)

Mt. Washington
New Hampshire
6,288 feet
(1,917 meters)

Mt. Mitchell
North Carolina
6,684 feet
(2,037 meters)

Mt. Rushmore
South Dakota
5,725 feet
(1,745 meters)

Mt. Rogers
Virginia
5,729 feet
(1,746 meters)

Denver
Colorado
5,280 feet
(1,609 meters)

Mt. Mansfield
Vermont
4,393 feet
(1,339 meters)

New York City
New York
55 feet
(17 meters)

30,000 feet
(9,144 meters)

25,000 feet
(7,620 meters)

20,000 feet
(6,096 meters)

15,000 feet
(4,572 meters)

10,000 feet
(3,048 meters)

5,000 feet
(1,524 meters)

Sea Level

Mt. Everest
Nepal-Tibet
29,028 feet
(8,848 meters)

Mt. Godwin Austen (K-2)
Kashmir
28,250 feet
(8,611 meters)

Kanchenjunga
Nepal-India
28,208 feet
(8,598 meters)

Mt. Makalu
Nepal-Tibet
27,824 feet
(8,481 meters)

Annapurna
Nepal
26,504 feet
(8,078 meters)

Lenin
Russia
23,406 feet
(7,134 meters)

Kilimanjaro
Tanzania
19,340 feet
(5,895 meters)

Mt. Elbrus
Russia
18,481 feet
(5,633 meters)

Mt. Damavand
Iran
18,386 feet
(5,604 meters)

Ararat
Turkey
17,011 feet
(5,185 meters)

Mt. Kenya
Kenya
17,058 feet
(5,199 meters)

Mont Blanc
France
15,771 feet
(4,807 meters)

Matterhorn
Switzerland
14,692 feet
(4,478 meters)

Jungfrau
Switzerland
13,642 feet
(4,158 meters)

Mt. Erebus
Antarctica
12,448 feet
(3,794 meters)

Mt. Fuji
Japan
12,388 feet
(3,776 meters)

Lhasa
Tibet
11,800 feet
(3,597 meters)

Mt. Etna
Sicily
11,122 feet
(3,390 meters)

Olympus
Greece
9,570 feet
(2,917 meters)

Great St. Bernard Pass
Switzerland and Italy
about 8,100 feet
(about 2,469 meters)

Parnassus
Greece
8,061 feet
(2,457 meters)

Mt. Kosciusko
Australia
7,310 feet
(2,228 meters)

Simla
India
7,186 feet
(2,190 meters)

Ben Nevis
Scotland
4,406 feet
(1,343 meters)

Vesuvius
Italy
4,190 feet
(1,277 meters)

Krakatoa
Indonesia
2,667 feet
(813 meters)

WORLD BOOK illustration

MOUNTAIN

Related Articles. See the various continent, country, state, and province articles where mountains are discussed, such as Asia (The Land); Argentina (Land Regions); Alabama (The Land). See Volcano with its list of *Related Articles*. See also the following articles:

AFRICA

Atlas Mountains
Kilimanjaro
Mount Kenya
Ruwenzori Range

ASIA

Altai Mountains
Annapurna
Ararat
Ghats
Himalaya
Hindu Kush
Khyber Pass
Krakatoa
Kunlun
   Mountains

Lebanon Mountains
Mount Apo
Mount Carmel
Mount Everest
Mount Fuji
Mount Godwin Austen
Mount Kanchenjunga
Mount Makalu
Mount Nebo
Mount of Olives

Mount Pisgah
Mount Tabor
Pamirs, The
Stanovoy
   Mountains
Tien Shan
Ural
   Mountains
Yablonovyy
   Mountains

AUSTRALIA AND NEW ZEALAND

Mount Cook
Mount Kosciusko
Owen-Stanley Mountains

CANADA

Canadian Shield
Coast Range
King Peak
Mount Assiniboine
Mount Logan

Mount Lucania
Mount Robson
Rocky Mountains
Saint Elias Mountains
Selkirk Mountains

EUROPE

Alps
Apennines
Ardennes
   Mountains
Ben Lomond
Ben Nevis
Black Forest
Carpathian
   Mountains
Caucasus
   Mountains

Dolomites
Harz Mountains
Hekla
Jungfrau
Jura
Matterhorn
Mont Blanc
Monte Rosa
Montserrat
Mount Elbrus
Mount Etna

Olympus
Parnassus
Pennine Chain
Pyrenees
Stromboli
Sudetes Mountains
Vesuvius

MEXICO

El Boquerón
Ixtacihuatl

Orizaba
Parícutin

Popocatepetl
Sierra Madre

SOUTH AMERICA

Aconcagua
Andes Mountains
Chimborazo
Cotopaxi

El Misti
Huascarán
Illampu

Ojos del Salado
Pichincha
Tupungato

UNITED STATES

Adirondack
   Mountains
Alaska Range
Allegheny
   Mountains
Aniakchak
Appalachian
   Mountains
Berkshire Hills
Bitterroot Range
Black Hills
Blue Ridge
   Mountains
Cascade Range
Catskill
   Mountains
Clingmans Dome

Coast Range
Cumberland
   Mountains
Diamond Head
Great Divide
Great Smoky
   Mountains
Green Mountains
Kilauea
Lassen Peak
Mauna Kea
Mauna Loa
Mesabi Range
Mount Evans
Mount Foraker
Mount Hood
Mount McKinley
Mount Mitchell

Mount of the
   Holy Cross
Mount Rainier
Mount Rushmore
Mount Shasta
Mount Washington
Mount Whitney
Olympic
   Mountains
Ozark Mountains
Pikes Peak
Rocky Mountains
Sierra Madre
Sierra Nevada
Stone Mountain
Teton Range
Wasatch Range
White Mountains

OTHER RELATED ARTICLES

Altitude
Animal
   (pictures: Animals
   of the Mountains)
Avalanche
Barometer
Cordillera

Crevasse
Divide
Erosion
Gap
Geology
Glacier

Hill
Hogback
Mountain Climbing
Mountain Pass
Plateau
Surveying

Outline

I. **Types of Mountains**
II. **How Mountains Are Measured**
III. **Man and Mountains**

Questions

What are the four main types of mountains? How are they formed?

What kind of mountain formations created the Hawaiian Islands?

How do geographers define a mountainous area?

About how much of the earth's surface is mountainous?

In what ways do people use mountainous regions?

What instruments do surveyors use to obtain most of the mountain heights we know?

MOUNTAIN ASH is the name for a group of trees and shrubs that grow in the Northern Hemisphere. They grow chiefly in high places. *American mountain ash* grows from Newfoundland south to northern Georgia. The leaves of the mountain ash are compound, made up of several separate leaflets. The white flowers grow in

The American Mountain Ash, *below,* grows to be about 30 feet (9 meters) tall. The tree is common in eastern North America. A sprig from a mountain ash, *right,* has clustered red berries and compound leaves like the leaves of roses.

U.S. Forest Service

Devereux Butcher

large, flattened clusters. The orange-to-red fruits are clusters of berrylike *pomes*.

Mountain ash is valuable as wildlife food and as an ornamental tree for lawns and gardens. The wood from the *European mountain ash*, or *rowan tree*, may be used for making tool handles. Superstitious people once believed the rowan tree would drive away evil spirits.

Scientific Classification. The mountain ash belongs to the rose family, *Rosaceae*. The American mountain ash is genus *Sorbus*, species *S. americana*. The rowan tree is *S. aucuparia*.   T. EWALD MAKI

See also TREE (Familiar Broadleaf and Needleleaf Trees [picture]).

MOUNTAIN AVENS is a small, hardy plant that grows wild in the northern and arctic regions. It is the floral emblem of Canada's Northwest Territories. The plant has small, saucer-shaped, yellow or white flowers. It grows on high ledges and rocky slopes in North America, Europe, and Asia.

Scientific Classification. The mountain avens belongs to the rose family, *Rosaceae*. It is genus *Dryas*. The yellow mountain avens of the Canadian Rockies is *D. tomentosa*.

MOUNTAIN BEAVER has lived on earth longer than any other rodent. Mountain beavers lived in North America at least 60 million years ago. Today, they live along the Pacific coast and in nearby mountains. Mountain beavers are also called *boomers*, *sewellels*, and *whistlers*, but these names are misleading. They are not related to beavers and do not make booming or whistling noises. *Sewellel* is an Indian word meaning *robe*.

Mountain beavers are about 1 foot (30 centimeters) long and look like large voles rather than like beavers (see VOLE). They have short, thick bodies, short legs, and small eyes and ears. Their fur is thick and short. Mountain beavers live in groups called *colonies*. They live in tunnels they dig in the banks of streams.

Scientific Classification. Mountain beavers are the only surviving members of the mountain beaver family, *Aplodontiidae*. They make up the genus *Aplodontia*, species *A. rufa*.   DANIEL BRANT

MOUNTAIN CLIMBING, or MOUNTAINEERING, is a difficult, adventurous sport. It requires special knowledge, skills, and equipment. Mountain climbers must be in good physical condition and have good judgment. Mountain climbing can be dangerous to an untrained person. Even many skilled climbers have lost their lives trying to conquer challenging peaks.

Making a Climb. A climb usually begins early in the day, perhaps before dawn. The climbers may plan to return before dusk, so they allow extra daylight time in case they meet unexpected delays. On low, easy mountains, climbers may go up more than 1 mile (1.6 kilometers) in vertical height in one day. On difficult peaks, they may advance much more slowly. Climbers slow down at high altitudes, because the air has less oxygen the higher one goes. This makes breathing difficult and tires climbers more quickly. Climbers sometimes use oxygen equipment at high altitudes.

Mountaineers must know how to use maps and compasses, because they often must find their way where there are no trails. They may travel through dense woods as they approach a mountain, and then cross steep slopes and rock slides above the tree line on the mountain. Climbers also may move up steep rock faces

George Burns, *The Saturday Evening Post*, © Curtis Publishing Co.
Mountain Climbers use ropes, ice axes, spiked boots, and snow glasses when scaling icy slopes or vertical rock faces.

and over snow fields and glaciers filled with crevasses.

In dangerous areas, climbers rope themselves together in groups of two, three, or occasionally more persons. Sometimes, only one climber may move at a time. The others brace themselves to tighten the rope and stop the fall if the climber should slip.

Climbing Equipment. Climbers carry packsacks loaded with first-aid supplies, food, and extra clothing for sudden changes in weather. If the climb requires more than one day, they also carry cooking gear, sleeping bags, and perhaps a tent. It is important for climbers to wear boots that help them avoid slipping. They may wear boots which have rubber soles with lugs, leather soles with nails, or a combination of these. Climbers may also strap *crampons* on their boots for climbing on ice or hard snow. Crampons are metal frames with 8 to 12 spikes. Climbers may also carry an *ice ax* to aid balance, to cut steps in snow and ice, and to stop themselves from falling. Ice axes have a 3-foot (91-centimeter) wooden shaft tipped on one end with a metal point. The other end has a metal head pointed on one side and adz-shaped on the other.

Climbing Areas. Most mountains in the United States can be climbed safely by parties of three or more persons over a weekend or a week's vacation. Every summer, professional and amateur climbers scale such famous American peaks as Mount Rainier and the Grand Teton. The leading climbing areas in the United States include the Rocky Mountains, the Cascade Range, and the Sierra Nevada Mountains. The larger cities near mountains have mountaineering clubs.

World interest in mountain climbing began in Europe in the 1800's, and the Alps have always been Europe's most popular climbing area. Almost none of the world's famous peaks were climbed until the 1800's. Other famed climbing areas include the Andes Mountains in South America, and the Himalaya (mountains) and the Karakoram Range in Asia. Large expeditions must be organized to climb the highest peaks in Asia. These mountains are far from roads, and an expedition must carry enough supplies to last several weeks.

Perhaps the best-known climb was the 1953 conquest of 29,028-foot (8,848-meter) Mount Everest, the world's highest peak. A British expedition, which included 10 climbers, set up camps on the slopes. Sir Edmund P. Hillary of New Zealand and Tenzing Norgay, a Sherpa guide, reached the summit.   PAUL W. WISEMAN

Critically reviewed by SIR EDMUND P. HILLARY

See also ALPS (Climbing the Alps); MOUNT EVEREST; HILLARY, SIR EDMUND.

MOUNTAIN GOAT. See CHAMOIS; IBEX; CASHMERE GOAT; ROCKY MOUNTAIN GOAT.

MOUNTAIN LAUREL is an evergreen plant that grows naturally in eastern North America. As a shrub, it stands 5 to 10 feet (1.5 to 3 meters) tall. As a tree, it reaches heights of 30 feet (9 meters) or more. Mountain laurel has pink or white flowers, which may have purple markings. Its glossy, dark leaves are oblong and pointed at the ends. The leaves and berries of the plant are poisonous. The plant is also called *kalmia*. Mountain laurels are often used in landscaping, and the plant has been introduced into western North America and Great Britain.

Scientific Classification. Mountain laurel is a member of the heath family, *Ericaceae*. It is genus *Kalmia*, species *K. latifolia*.

MOUNTAIN LION is a large wild animal of the cat family Mountain lions once lived throughout the forests of the United States and southern Canada. When settlers moved in, they drove this animal out. The number of mountain lions has been greatly reduced in both these countries, except in large national and state or provincial parks. Today, mountain lions live chiefly in western provinces and states from British Columbia and Alberta to California and New Mexico. Small numbers dwell in southeastern Canada and New England and southward through the Appalachian Mountains. They are also found in uninhabited areas of Florida and certain other parts of the South. Mountain lions are more common outside the United States and Canada. They live throughout much of Mexico, Central America, and southward to the tip of South America.

Early settlers gave the animal the name of *cougar*, or mountain lion. They thought it was a female lion. Other names for this animal are *catamount* and *puma*. Especially in the eastern states, it is known as *panther*, a name also given to several other kinds of cat (see PANTHER).

An adult mountain lion may be either a gray color or a reddish or yellowish color called *tawny*. Its hairs are fawn-gray tipped with reddish brown or grayish. This animal has no spots, and in this way it is different from the jaguar. The throat, the insides of the legs, and the belly are white, and the tip of the tail is black. Some mountain lions are solid black. A full-grown animal may be 5 feet (1.5 meters) long or more, not counting the tail, which is 2 to 3 feet (61 to 91 centimeters) long. The heaviest mountain lion on record weighed 227 pounds (103 kilograms). The body is slender, and the legs are long. The head is round and rather small.

Mountain lions have from one to five cubs at a time, generally two years apart. The average number is three. The cubs weigh about 1 pound (0.5 kilogram) at birth. They are covered with fur and are blind. They are lighter brown than their parents. The cubs have large brownish-black spots on the body and dark rings on the short tail. Adults care for their young until they are able to survive alone. Young lions need about two years to develop enough skill in hunting to find their own food. They may live to be 10 to 20 years old.

The cry of the mountain lion is wild and terrifying. It sounds like a woman screaming in pain. The animal also has a soft whistle call.

Maurice Hornocker

A Mountain Lion may reach a length of 5 feet (1.5 meters) or more, not counting its tail. Among the cats of North and South America, only the jaguar is larger. Mountain lions hunt and kill deer and elk, but they seldom attack people.

Warren Garst, Van Cleve Photography

Mountain Lion Cubs are covered with dark spots that disappear as the animals grow older. Cubs remain with their mother for up to two years.

The mountain lion usually hunts at night. It travels long distances after game in a single night. Its chief prey is deer, with elk the second choice. Occasionally it kills a bighorn. In case of need it will feed on small mammals—even skunks and porcupines. The mountain lion keeps under cover while stalking its prey. Then suddenly the lion leaps out upon the animal, breaking the animal's neck or dragging it down to the ground.

Ranchers regard mountain lions as pests. But the big cats seldom kill calves or other domestic animals. Biologists believe that mountain lions should be controlled but not killed off, because these big cats play an important part in the animal world. They feed mainly on old and diseased deer. Mountain lions are timid toward people and are very unlikely to attack them.

Scientific Classification. The mountain lion is a mammal that belongs to the cat family, *Felidae*. It is genus *Felis*, species *F. concolor*.   ERNEST S. BOOTH

MOUNTAIN MEN. See FUR TRADE (The 1800's); WESTWARD MOVEMENT (Exploration).

MOUNTAIN NESTOR. See KEA.

MOUNTAIN PASS is a passageway over a mountain barrier. Passes generally occur at low points on mountain watersheds, or in valleys between mountain ridges. The importance of a pass depends on the need for communication between the people living on each side.

Well-known passes include Donner (7,088 feet, or 2,160 meters) in California; Brenner (4,508 feet, or 1,374 meters) between Italy and Austria; and Khyber (3,370 feet, or 1,027 meters) between Pakistan and Afghanistan.   ROBERT M. GLENDINNING

MOUNTAIN STATE. See WEST VIRGINIA.

MOUNTAIN STATES. See ROCKY MOUNTAIN STATES.

MOUNTAIN TIME. See TIME (Time Zones; map).

MOUNTAINEERING. See MOUNTAIN CLIMBING.

MOUNTAINS OF THE MOON. See RUWENZORI RANGE.

MOUNTBATTEN, LOUIS (1900-1979), EARL MOUNTBATTEN OF BURMA, was a British naval leader. He became first sea lord of Great Britain in 1955, and received the rank of admiral of the fleet in 1956. He served as chief of the defense staff from 1959 to 1965, when he became governor of the Isle of Wight.

Mountbatten became a lieutenant in the British Navy in 1920. He later served as personal aide-de-camp to his cousin, the prince of Wales, later King Edward VIII. At the outbreak of World War II, he was a captain and the personal aide-de-camp to King George VI.

Mountbatten commanded the destroyer *Kelly*, which was sunk in the Battle of Crete in May, 1941. He was then given command of the aircraft carrier *Illustrious*, until he became chief of combined operations in March, 1942. In this position he helped plan commando raids against St. Nazaire and Dieppe in France. In 1943, he became supreme allied commander of the Southeast Asia Command.

After the war, Mountbatten became viceroy of India. In 1947, he supervised the creation of the dominions of Pakistan and India, and then stayed on as the first governor general of India. In 1948, Mountbatten resigned and returned to navy duty. He became a lord commissioner of the admiralty, fourth sea lord, and chief of supplies and transport in 1950. He served in the North Atlantic Treaty Organization (NATO)

Louis Mountbatten

from 1952 to 1954 as commander in chief of all allied forces in the Mediterranean except the U.S. Sixth Fleet.

Mountbatten was born in Windsor, England. He was the son of Prince Louis Alexander, a cousin of King George V of England. Mountbatten was educated at the Royal Naval Academy, Dartmouth. He entered the British Navy in 1913. He was the uncle of Prince Philip (see PHILIP, PRINCE).

Mountbatten was killed by a time bomb that blew up his yacht off the coast of Ireland. The Irish Republican Army (IRA) claimed responsibility for the bombing (see IRISH REPUBLICAN ARMY).   CHARLES LOCH MOWAT

MOUNTBATTEN-WINDSOR. See WINDSOR (family).

MOUNTED POLICE. See ROYAL CANADIAN MOUNTED POLICE.

MOURNING is the term which refers to outward signs of grief for the dead or some calamity. Almost every nation has special mourning customs and costumes. See FUNERAL CUSTOMS.

MOURNING DOVE is an American bird with a sad, cooing call. It breeds from southern Canada through Mexico, and winters as far south as Panama. The bird is about 12 inches (30 centimeters) long. It is grayish-brown, with a tinge of pink on its breast. The tail has a white border and black spots. This bird is a swift flier.

It places its nest, built loosely of twigs, in a tree or bush, or on the ground. The bird lays two white eggs. The young hatch in about two weeks, and there may be three or four families in a season. Very young birds put their beaks in the parents' throats and feed on partly digested food, mixed with a fluid that is called *pigeon's milk*. The mourning dove eats many weed seeds, as well as some insects.

Scientific Classification. The mourning dove belongs to the pigeon and dove family, *Columbidae*. It is genus *Zenaida*, species *Z. macroura*.   HERBERT FRIEDMANN

See also DOVE (picture); TURTLEDOVE.

Charles W. Schwartz

The Mourning Dove builds a flimsy nest of twigs. Inexperienced bird-watchers occasionally mistake the bird for the now-extinct passenger pigeon. The mourning dove is protected by federal law.

745

Cy La Tour

A House Mouse Stuffs Itself with Stolen Grain.

MOUSE is a small animal with soft fur, a pointed snout, round black eyes, rounded ears, and a thin tail. The word *mouse* is not the name of any one kind of animal or family of animals. Many kinds of *rodents* (gnawing animals) are called mice. They include small rats, small hamsters, gerbils, jerboas, lemmings, voles, harvest mice, deer mice, and grasshopper mice. All these animals have chisel-like front teeth that are useful for gnawing. A rodent's front teeth grow throughout the animal's life.

There are hundreds of kinds of mice, and they live in most parts of the world. They can be found in the mountains, in fields and woodlands, in swamps, near streams, and in deserts.

Probably the best known kind of mouse is the house mouse. It lives wherever people live, and often builds its nest in homes, garages, or barns. Some kinds of white house mice are raised as pets. Other kinds of house mice are used by scientists to learn about sickness, to test new drugs, and to study behavior.

House Mice

House mice probably lived in the homes of ancient man and stole his food, just as mice do today. The

Daniel Brant, the contributor of this article, is Professor of Biology at Humboldt State University.

word *mouse* comes from an old Sanskrit word meaning *thief*. Sanskrit is an ancient language of Asia, where scientists believe house mice originated. House mice spread from Asia throughout Europe. The ancestors of the house mice that now live in North and South America were brought there by English, French, and Spanish ships during the 1500's.

House mice always seem to be busy. Those that live in buildings may scamper about at any time of day or night. House mice that live in fields and forests usually come out only at night. All house mice climb well, and can often be heard running between the walls of houses.

——————— **FACTS IN BRIEF** ———————

Common Name	Scientific Name	Gestation Period	Number of Young	Where Found
*House Mouse	Mus musculus	18-21 days	4-7	Worldwide
American Harvest Mouse	Reithrodontomys fulvescens	21-24 days	1-7	North and South America
Grasshopper Mouse	Onychomys leucogaster	29-38 days	3-4	North America
Deer Mouse	Peromyscus maniculatus	21-27 days	1-9	North and South America

*The house mouse belongs to the family of Old World rats and mice, *Muridae*. The American harvest, grasshopper, and deer mice belong to the family of New World rats and mice, *Cricetidae*.

Body of a house mouse is $2\frac{1}{2}$ to $3\frac{1}{2}$ inches (6.4 to 8.9 centimeters) long without the tail. The tail is the same length or a little shorter. Most house mice weigh $\frac{1}{2}$ to 1 ounce (14 to 28 grams). Their size and weight, and the length of their tails, differ greatly among the many varieties and even among individual animals of the same variety.

The fur of most house mice is soft, but it may be stiff and wiry. It is grayish brown on the animal's back and sides, and yellowish white underneath. House mice raised as pets or for use in laboratories may have pure white fur, black or brown spots, or other combinations of colors. The house mouse's tail is covered by scaly skin or by short, fine hair.

A house mouse has a small head and a long, narrow snout. Several long, thin whiskers grow from the sides of the snout. These whiskers, like those of a cat, help the mouse feel its way in the dark. The animal has rounded ears, and its eyes look somewhat like round black beads. A mouse can hear well, but it has poor sight. Probably because house mice cannot see well, they may enter a lighted room even if people are there.

Like beavers, muskrats, rats, and other rodents, all mice have strong, sharp front teeth that grow throughout the animal's life. With these chisel-like teeth, mice can gnaw holes in wood, tear apart packages to get at food inside, and damage books, clothing, and furniture.

Food. A house mouse eats almost anything that human beings eat. It feasts on any grain, meat, or vegetable that it can find. Mice also eat such household items as glue, leather, paste, and soap. House mice that live out of doors eat insects, and the leaves, roots, seeds, and stems of plants. Mice always seem to be looking for something to eat, but they need little food. They damage much more food than they eat.

Homes. House mice live wherever they can find food and shelter. Any dark place that is warm and quiet makes an excellent home for mice. A mouse may build its nest in a warm corner of a barn, on a beam under the roof of a garage, or in a box stored in an attic or basement. The animal may tear strips of clothing or upholstery to get materials for its nest. It may line the nest with feathers or cotton stolen from pillows. House mice that live in fields or woodlands dig holes in the ground and build nests of grass inside. They may line the nests with feathers or pieces of fur.

Young. A female house mouse may give birth every 20 to 30 days. She carries her young in her body for 18 to 21 days before they are born. She has four to seven young at a time. Newborn mice have pink skin and no fur, and their eyes are closed. They are completely helpless. Soft fur covers their bodies by the time they are 10 days old. When they are 14 days old, their eyes open. Young mice stay near the nest for about three weeks after birth. Then they leave to build their own nests and start raising families. Most female house mice begin to have young when they are about 45 days old.

Enemies. Man is probably the worst enemy of the house mouse. People set traps and place poisons where mice can easily find them. Almost every meat-eating animal is an enemy of house mice. Cats and dogs hunt mice in houses and barns. Coyotes, foxes, snakes, and other animals capture them in forests and woodlands.

White-Footed Mouse and Her Young　　　　J. M. Conrader

Harvest Mouse　　　　Jane Burton, Photo Researchers

Grasshopper Mouse　　　　Cordell Andersen, NAS

Owls, hawks, and other large birds swoop down on them in fields and prairies. Rats and even other mice are also enemies. House mice may live as long as a year in a hidden corner of an attic or basement. But they have so many enemies that few wild mice survive more than two or three months. Some mice kept as pets or in laboratories may live six years.

House mice avoid their enemies by hiding. A mouse seldom wanders far from its nest. It spends most of its time within an area of about 200 feet (61 meters) in diameter. Wherever possible, the mouse moves along paths protected by furniture, boxes, or other objects. The mouse scampers as fast as it can across the open spaces between the objects. House mice do not like water and try to avoid it, but they can swim.

Some Other Kinds of Mice

American Harvest Mice look like house mice, but are smaller and have more hair on their tails. Most American harvest mice also have much larger ears. Harvest mice live near the Pacific Ocean, from southwestern Canada to Ecuador. They also live in the eastern United States south of the Potomac and Ohio rivers. Some kinds of harvest mice live in salt marshes or in tropical forests, but most species prefer open grassy regions.

Harvest mice build their nests in places where tall grass grows. They weave leaves of grass into ball-shaped nests that are 6 to 7 inches (15 to 18 centimeters) in diameter. The mice build their nests 6 to 12 inches (15 to 30 centimeters) above the ground in branches of bushes or on stems of grass. Harvest mice are excellent climbers and use the plant stems as ladders to reach their nests. They grasp the plant stems with their tails as they climb. Harvest mice also make nests in the ground.

These mice eat green plant sprouts, but they prefer seeds. They pick seeds off the ground, or they "harvest" seeds from plants by bending the plant stems to the ground where they bite off the seeds.

A female harvest mouse has one to seven young at a time. She carries the young mice in her body for 21 to 24 days before they are born. When the young are about 2 months old, they may start their own families.

Grasshopper Mice are about the same size as house mice, but they look fatter and have stubby tails. Their fur is brown or gray above and white underneath. They probably got their name because they eat grasshoppers.

THE SKELETON OF A MOUSE

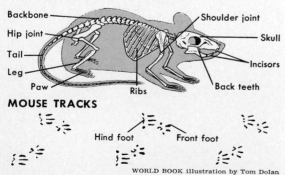

Backbone — Shoulder joint — Skull — Incisors — Back teeth — Ribs — Paw — Leg — Tail — Hip joint

MOUSE TRACKS

Hind foot   Front foot

WORLD BOOK illustration by Tom Dolan

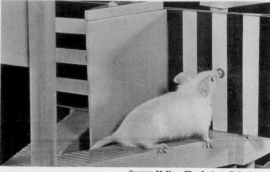

George McKay, The Jackson Laboratory

A Laboratory Mouse gets food when it presses a button on a wall with vertical stripes. The mouse has learned to avoid the wall with horizontal stripes because it gets no reward there. Scientists study mice to find out about their ability to learn.

These mice are found in the dry regions and deserts of the western and southwestern United States, and in northern Mexico. Grasshopper mice live wherever they can find shelter in the ground. They often use burrows abandoned by such rodents as gophers, ground squirrels, and deer mice.

The female grasshopper mouse carries her young inside her body for 29 to 38 days. Usually three or four young are born at a time. The young mice become adults when they are about three months old.

Grasshopper mice are most active at night, when they come out of their burrows to hunt. Unlike most other mice, grasshopper mice prefer to eat meat rather than plants. They eat any animal they can overpower, including insects, worms, and other grasshopper mice. Their favorite foods are grasshoppers and scorpions. Grasshopper mice hunt their prey much as cats do. They creep up to their victims and attack quickly.

Deer Mice, sometimes called *white-footed mice*, measure 6 to 8 inches (15 to 20 centimeters) long. Their tails are $2\frac{1}{2}$ to 4 inches (6 to 10 centimeters) long. The fur on their upper parts is gray, and the belly fur is white. The ears of these mice are large in relation to the size of their bodies.

There are more than 50 species of deer mice. They are found from northern Colombia throughout North America as far north as Alaska and Labrador. They live in every kind of region—mountains, plains, deserts, and swamps.

Deer mice build their nests in tunnels they dig, or in hollow logs, tree stumps, or cracks in rocks. The mice may go into houses to find soft materials such as cloth or cotton for their nests. They usually build several nests a year because they move out as soon as a nest gets soiled.

A female deer mouse gives birth to one to nine young at a time. She carries them in her body for 21 to 27 days before birth. The young live in the nest for three to six weeks, and then leave to build nests of their own.

Deer mice usually rest during the day and look for food at night. They eat berries, fruits, leaves, nuts, seeds, and insects. When excited, these mice thump their front feet rapidly on the ground, making a drumming noise.
DANIEL BRANT

See also RAT; RODENT; JUMPING MOUSE; VOLE.

MOUSE DEER. See Philippines (Natural Resources).

MOUSE TOWER (in German, Der Mäuseturm) is a tower on a small island in the Rhine River near Bingen, Germany. A famous legend tells about the tower and the cruel Bishop Hatto of Bingen who built it. According to the legend, the bishop fled there to escape a horde of mice. The mice came to avenge the deaths of peasants whom the cruel bishop had burned alive. The horde of mice attacked the tower and devoured the tyrant.

Experts have identified several historical characters with this story, including two Archbishop Hattos of Mainz. Robert Southey wrote a ballad about the tale, and it appears in a collection of folk tales gathered by Jakob and Wilhelm Grimm.

In reality, *Mäuseturm* appears to be a corruption of *mautturm*, meaning *toll tower*. The tower was probably built in the 1200's as a place for collecting tolls from boats on the Rhine.   Arthur M. Selvi

MOUSORGSKI, MODEST. See Mussorgsky, Modest.

MOUTH is the part of the body which is adapted for taking in food. The lips at the mouth opening help us drink and pick up our food. Inside, we have two rows of teeth, one above the other, to grind and crush food into pulp that can be digested. Salivary glands in the walls of the mouth give off saliva which mixes with our food as we chew it, and also helps digestion (see Saliva).

The entire mouth cavity is lined with mucous membrane. The top of the mouth (the roof) consists of a bony front part, called the *hard palate*, and a soft part in the rear, called the *soft palate*. The hard palate forms a partition between the mouth and the nose. The soft palate arches down at the back of the mouth to form a curtain between the mouth and the *pharynx*. The pharynx is the back part of the throat. It connects the mouth and the nose with both the *esophagus* (the tube that carries food to the stomach), and with the *trachea* (the windpipe that carries air to the lungs). A flexible bundle of muscles extends from the floor of the mouth to form the *tongue*. The tongue not only helps us to eat, swallow, and talk, but it contains almost all the sense organs of taste (see Taste).

Harmful germs enter the body through both the mouth and nose. Both these openings should be kept clean to help ward off disease. The mouth cavity is an excellent breeding place for germs because it is warm and moist all the time.

PARTS OF THE MOUTH

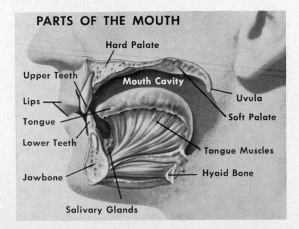

Hard Palate
Upper Teeth
Mouth Cavity
Lips
Tongue
Lower Teeth
Jawbone
Salivary Glands
Uvula
Soft Palate
Tongue Muscles
Hyoid Bone

The teeth should be scrubbed thoroughly at least twice a day, and the mouth should be rinsed out after every meal. The teeth should be brushed lengthwise as well as crosswise, to remove particles of food. Jagged teeth can infect the mouth through irritation and may even cause cancer. Diseased gums cause loss of teeth from periodontitis. Disease of the teeth may cause the body to become infected by bacteria. Trench mouth, or Vincent's infection, is a common infection of the mouth. Painful cankers may also attack the mucous membrane which lines the mouth.   Arthur C. Guyton

Related Articles in World Book include:

Canker	Dentistry	Periodontitis	Tongue
Cold Sore	Palate	Teeth	Trench Mouth

MOUTH ORGAN. See Harmonica.

MOUTHBREEDER. See Fish (picture: Mouthbreeding).

MOVABLE FEAST. See Feasts and Festivals.

MOVIE. See Motion Picture.

MOWAT, SIR OLIVER (1820-1903), a Canadian statesman, served as prime minister and attorney general of Ontario from 1872 to 1896. His term was one of the longest in British parliamentary history. During his administration, Mowat introduced the ballot in municipal and provincial elections and extended the voting franchise. He fought to obtain more political rights for the provinces. Before the provinces were united, he served as chancellor of Upper Canada (now Ontario). Mowat was knighted in 1892. He was lieutenant governor of Ontario from 1897 until his death. He was born in what is now Kingston, Ont.   William R. Willoughby

Historical Pictures Service
Sir Oliver Mowat

MOYNIHAN, DANIEL PATRICK (1927-   ), served as United States ambassador to the United Nations in 1975 and 1976. In that post, he became famous for his sharp criticism of opponents of U.S. policies. Moynihan, a Democrat, won election to the U.S. Senate from New York in 1976.

An authority on the problems of cities and of minority groups, Moynihan first became known for his books and articles on immigration, the antipoverty program, and black family life. From 1966 to 1969, he headed the Joint Center of Urban Studies at Harvard University and Massachusetts Institute of Technology. He served as counselor to the President under Richard M. Nixon in 1969 and 1970. Moynihan returned to Harvard in 1971 as professor of education and urban politics. He remained on the faculty until 1976. He served as ambassador to India from 1973 to 1975.

Moynihan was born in Tulsa, Okla., but grew up in New York City. He graduated from Tufts University and received a doctorate from Tufts's Fletcher School of International Law and Diplomacy. He was an assistant to Governor Averell Harriman of New York in the 1950's and served in the U.S. Department of Labor from 1961 to 1965.   David S. Broder

MOZAMBIQUE

MOZAMBIQUE, MOH zuhm BEEK, is a country on the southeast coast of Africa. It covers 302,330 square miles (783,030 square kilometers) and has a population of about 11 million. Mozambique is slightly larger than Texas and has about four-fifths as many people as that state.

About 90 per cent of the people of Mozambique live in rural areas. Most of the urban centers lie near the coast. Maputo is the capital, largest city, and chief port. Mozambique is noted for its many fine harbors, and its excellent port facilities are used by some neighboring countries. Mozambique was governed by Portugal from the early 1500's until 1975. The country became independent that year after a 10-year struggle against Portuguese rule.

Government of Mozambique is controlled by the nation's only political party, the Front for the Liberation of Mozambique. The party, known as Frelimo, bases its policies on the philosophy of Karl Marx and V. I. Lenin, two founders of Communism. The president of Frelimo is also the nation's president. The highest governmental power lies with the party's Central Committee, which is made up of 15 members appointed

───────────── FACTS IN BRIEF ─────────────

Official Name: *República Popular de Moçambique* (People's Republic of Mozambique).

Capital: Maputo.

Official Language: Portuguese.

Area: 302,330 sq. mi. (783,030 km²). *Coastline*—1,556 mi. (2,504 km). *Greatest Distances*—north-south, 1,100 mi. (1,770 km); east-west, 680 mi. (1,094 km).

Elevation: *Highest*—Mt. Binga, 7,992 ft. (2,436 m). *Lowest*—sea level.

Population: *Estimated 1981 Population*—10,600,000; distribution, 91 per cent rural, 9 per cent urban; density, 36 persons per sq. mi. (14 per km²). *1970 Census*—8,168,933. *Estimated 1986 Population*—11,876,000.

Chief Products: Cashews, coconuts, cotton, sugar.

Flag: The flag has four wedge-shaped diagonal stripes of green, red, black, and yellow, which are separated by white bands. In the upper left corner, a white cog wheel encloses a book, which has a gun and a hoe crossed over it. See FLAG (picture: Flags of Africa).

Money: *Basic Unit*—Escudo. See MONEY (table).

by Frelimo. The party also appoints the 210 members of the People's Assembly, Mozambique's legislative body. This group meets twice a year. Its Permanent Committee handles legislative matters between sessions.

People. Almost all Mozambicans are black Africans. Other groups, including Arabs, Europeans, and Pakistanis, make up less than 2 per cent of the population. Most of the blacks belong to groups that speak a Bantu language. Differences among the various languages limit communication among the groups. Few blacks can speak Portuguese, the country's official language. Some Mozambicans speak English when conducting business activities.

Mozambique

✹	Capital
•	Other city or town
———	Road
+—+—+	Rail line
▲	Mountain
〜	River

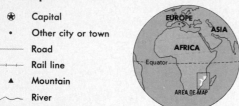

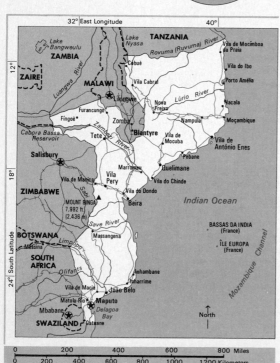

Jerry Frank, DPI

Maputo, the capital of Mozambique, is a leading African port. Ships from many countries carry cargo to and from the city. Maputo lies on Delagoa Bay, an inlet of the Indian Ocean.

Most Mozambicans are farmers, but their techniques are extremely primitive. Some farmers use the *slash and burn* method, which involves cutting and burning forest trees to clear an area for planting. Farmers in some areas of the country use more modern techniques.

About 75 per cent of the people practice traditional African religions. Many of this group are *animists*, who believe that everything in nature has a soul. Others worship the spirits of their ancestors. Most of the remaining 25 per cent are either Roman Catholics or Muslims.

Only about 15 per cent of Mozambique's population can read and write, but the government has begun programs to improve education. A university was established in Maputo in 1962.

Land and Climate. Almost half of Mozambique is covered by a flat plain that extends inland from the coast. The land rises steadily beyond the plain, and high plateaus and mountains run along much of the western border. Sand dunes and swamps line the coast. Grasslands, treeless plains, and tropical forests cover much of the country.

Many sizable rivers flow east through Mozambique into the Indian Ocean, and their basins have extremely fertile soil. Cashew trees and coconut palms grow throughout the country. Animal life in Mozambique includes crocodiles, lions, rhinoceroses, and zebras.

Mozambique has a basically tropical climate, but temperatures and rainfall vary considerably in different areas. Temperatures average 68° F. (20° C) in July and 80° F. (27° C) in January. About 80 per cent of the annual rainfall occurs from November to March. The rainfall ranges from about 16 to 48 inches (41 to 122 centimeters).

Economy of Mozambique is not well developed. The government, which owns all the farmland and the major industries, is working to increase agricultural production and industrial development.

Agriculture is Mozambique's major industry, but only about 5 per cent of the farmland is cultivated. The nation is a leading producer of cashews. Other important crops include coconuts, cotton, and sugar.

Mozambique's economy depends partly on payments by South Africa and Malawi for the use of railroads and port facilities. In addition, many Mozambicans work in South African mines.

Mozambique produces more than 300,000 short tons (270,000 metric tons) of coal yearly. Industrial development has been slow and has occurred mainly in the food-processing and oil-refining industries.

Mozambique has about 23,900 miles (38,460 kilometers) of roads and several railroads. An airport operates in Maputo. One television station, three radio stations, and four daily newspapers serve the nation.

History. People have lived in the area that is now Mozambique since the 4000's B.C. Bantu-speaking people settled there before A.D. 100, and Arabs lived in the area by the 800's. Portuguese explorers first visited Mozambique in 1497. They established a trading post there in 1505, and the country became a slave-trading center. However, most of Mozambique remained undeveloped until the late 1800's.

Through the years, Portuguese control of Mozambique was threatened by Arabs, Africans, and some European nations. In 1885, Africa was divided among various European powers, and Mozambique was rec-

Editorial Photocolor Archives

Outdoor Markets, where people buy food and other goods, serve as shopping centers in many parts of Mozambique. The market shown above is near Maputo.

Editorial Photocolor Archives

A Rural Village near Tete in northwestern Mozambique, consists of a cluster of huts with thatched roofs. The people of the village farm the land and graze livestock nearby.

ognized as a Portuguese colony. The colony was often called Portuguese East Africa. Borders similar to those of present-day Mozambique were established in 1891.

Towns and railroads were built in Mozambique during the late 1800's and early 1900's, and the Portuguese population rose. In the 1950's, many blacks became increasingly discontented with white Portuguese rule. Frelimo was established in 1961 as a guerrilla movement. It began military attacks against the Portuguese in 1964 and gained control of part of northern Mozambique. Fighting between Frelimo and Portuguese forces continued for 10 years.

Portugal agreed in 1974 to grant independence to its colonies, and Mozambique became an independent nation on June 25, 1975. Frelimo established a government that took control of all education, health and legal services, land, housing, and major industries. Most of the Portuguese left Mozambique at that time.

In 1976, Mozambique closed its border with Rhodesia (now Zimbabwe) to protest that country's white minority government. This action cost Mozambique much income from Rhodesian use of its railroads and ports. In addition, the government limited the number of Mozambican workers in South Africa, which has a white minority government.

Border fighting broke out between Mozambican and Rhodesian troops. Many black Rhodesians fled to Mozambique to use bases there in their fight against the Rhodesian government. In 1980, blacks gained control of Rhodesia's government, and the country's name was changed to Zimbabwe. The friction between Mozambique and that country ended. See ZIMBABWE (History).   L. H. GANN

See also MAPUTO.

MOZAMBIQUE CHANNEL separates Madagascar from Mozambique, a nation on the southeast coast of Africa (see MOZAMBIQUE [map]). The channel is more than 1,000 miles (1,600 kilometers) long and from 250 to 600 miles (402 to 970 kilometers) wide. It is an important shipping lane. Comoros, an island country, lies at the northern entrance. Important ports include Maputo, Beira, and Moçambique in Mozambique, and Majunga in Madagascar.   F. G. WALTON SMITH

MOZART, WOLFGANG AMADEUS (1756-1791), was one of the world's great composers. With Joseph Haydn, he was the leading composer of what historians of music call the *classical period*. Mozart died before his 36th birthday, but he still left over 600 works. Many consider his *Don Giovanni* the world's greatest opera.

His Life

Mozart was born on Jan. 27, 1756, in Salzburg, Austria, son of a respected musician. His father, Leopold, was the leader of the local orchestra, and also wrote the first important book about violin playing. At the age of 3, Wolfgang showed signs of remarkable musical talent. He learned to play the harpsichord, a keyboard instrument related to the piano, at the age of 4. He was composing music at 5. When he was 6, he played for the Austrian empress at her court in Vienna.

Before he was 14, Mozart had composed many works called *sonatas* for the harpsichord, piano, or the violin, as well as orchestral and other works. His father recog-

nized Wolfgang's amazing talent and devoted most of his time to his son's general and musical education. Wolfgang never attended school. Leopold took him on concert tours through much of Europe. Wolfgang composed, gave public performances, met many musicians, and played the organ in many churches. In 1769, like his father before him, he began working for the archbishop of Salzburg, who also ruled the province. The Mozarts often quarreled with the archbishop, partly because Wolfgang was often absent from Salzburg. The archbishop dismissed young Mozart in 1781.

Mozart was actually glad to leave Salzburg, a small town, and seek his fortune in Vienna, one of the music capitals of Europe. By this time people took less notice of him, because he was no longer a child prodigy. However, he was a brilliant performer and active as a composer. Mozart married in 1782. He did not have a regular job in Vienna and tried to earn a living by selling his compositions, giving public performances, and giving music lessons. None of these activities produced enough income to support his family. He even traveled to Germany for the coronation of a new emperor, but his concerts there did not attract as much attention as he hoped. He died in poverty on Dec. 5, 1791.

His Works

Operas. Mozart excelled in almost every kind of musical composition. Several of his 22 operas gained wide recognition soon after his death, and they still please audiences all over the world. *The Marriage of Figaro* (1786) and *Don Giovanni* (1787) are operas he composed with words in Italian. *The Magic Flute* (1791) has German words. Each of these contains *arias* (beautiful melodies for

Mozart composed the opera *The Magic Flute* the year he died. In this scene, Prince Tamino and Pamina, daughter of the Queen of the Night, prepare for initiation rites to prove themselves worthy of each other.

Unfinished portrait (1789) by Joseph Lange, Mozart Museum, Salzburg, from Art Reference Bureau; Fred Fehl

singers), *recitative* (rapidly sung dialogue), *ensembles* in which several people sing at the same time, and choruses. The orchestra provides an ever-changing expressive accompaniment. The drama ranges from slapstick and other forms of comedy to tragedy.

Symphonies. Mozart wrote over 40 symphonies, many of which are performed today. Some originally were *overtures* (orchestral introductions) for operas, and last only a few minutes. His later symphonies, which are the most popular today, are full-length orchestral compositions that last 20 to 30 minutes. Most consist of four *movements* (sections). His last and most famous symphony, Number 41 (1788), is nicknamed the *Jupiter*.

Church Music. Mozart composed a great amount of church music, most of it for performance at the Salzburg Cathedral. He wrote Masses and shorter pieces called *motets;* and he set psalms to music, especially for the vespers (afternoon or evening) service. The music is beautiful and varied. It includes choral and solo parts, usually with accompaniment by organ and orchestra. Mozart's best-known sacred work is the *Requiem* (Mass for the Dead), which he began in the last year of his life. While writing it, Mozart is said to have thought a great deal about his own death. Parts of the *Requiem* were composed during his final illness. He died before the work was finished.

Other Works. Mozart wrote other orchestral works, generally of a somewhat lighter nature, called *serenades.* Some were intended for outdoor performance. One has become well known under the title *Eine kleine Nachtmusik* (*A Little Night Music,* 1787). Mozart also wrote many compositions called *concertos* for a solo instrument such as violin or piano, with orchestral accompaniment. He often played the solo part.

Throughout his life Mozart composed *chamber music*— works for a small number of instruments in which only one musician plays each part. Mozart concentrated on string quartets (two violins, viola, and cello). He was influenced in this by Haydn, whose quartets he admired. He dedicated six quartets to Haydn.

Mozart's sonatas for piano and for violin and piano are outstanding. The piano was then still fairly new and was widely played by amateurs. More than any other composer, Mozart helped to make the instrument popular. His melodies for piano had a "singing," sustained quality, with gradual changes between soft and loud.

His Style. In spite of his hardships and disappointments as a composer, much of Mozart's music is cheerful and vigorous. He had a sense of humor, and liked puns and practical jokes. He composed many lighter works. These include the opera *Così Fan Tutte* (*All Women Are Like That,* 1790), much of his early instrumental music, and *canons* (rounds) with nonsense words.

Mozart also produced deeply serious music. His most profound works include the piano concerto in D minor, several string quartets, the string quintet in G minor, and his last three symphonies—E flat major, G minor, and the *Jupiter.* Larger works may contain both serious and light elements, as does *Don Giovanni.*

Mozart belonged to the Order of Freemasons and wrote several compositions for their meetings. Some scenes from his fairy-tale opera *The Magic Flute* were inspired by Masonic traditions and beliefs.

A catalog of Mozart's works was first prepared by Ludwig Köchel (1800-1877), a German music lover. To-day, Mozart's works are still identified by the numbers Köchel assigned to them.

Today Mozart's music is known and admired throughout the world. A famous music festival held each summer in Salzburg features his works.   REINHARD G. PAULY

See also *Mozart, Wolfgang Amadeus,* in the RESEARCH GUIDE/INDEX, Volume 22, for a *Reading and Study Guide.*

MRA. See MORAL RE-ARMAMENT.

MUCH ADO ABOUT NOTHING. See SHAKESPEARE, WILLIAM (Shakespeare's Plays).

MUCILAGE, *MYOO suh lihj,* is a thick, sticky substance which is usually made by dissolving gum in water, or in some other liquid. The purpose of mucilage is to cause two substances to *adhere* (stick together). Therefore, mucilage is classified as an *adhesive.* The exact ingredients of mucilage vary with the uses to which the adhesive is to be put. Gum arabic dissolved in hot water makes gum-arabic mucilage. When aluminum sulfate is added to the solution, the adhesive may be used to make paper stick to glass. Glycerin or sugar may be added to mucilage to keep it moist until it is used.

Dextrin is dissolved in cold water to make a mucilage which is used on the back of postage stamps. Glue and gelatin also are used to make mucilage, but these substances also need vinegar, glycerin, or acid in order to keep them in a fluid state.   CHARLES L. MANTELL

See also GLUE; GUM ARABIC.

MUCK, KARL (1859-1940), a German conductor, was principal conductor of the Boston Symphony Orchestra in 1906 and 1907, and again from 1912 to 1918. His second term in Boston ended when he was falsely accused of being a German spy, and was interned. In 1892, Muck was appointed *Kapellmeister* (conductor), and in 1908, musical director of the Berlin Royal Opera. From 1922 to 1933 he led the Hamburg Philharmonic Orchestra. He conducted outstanding performances of Wagner's *Parsifal* at the Bayreuth Festival from 1901 to 1932. He was born in Darmstadt.   DAVID EWEN

MUCKRAKING is a term applied to writings by American reformers of the early 1900's who exposed social and political evils. President Theodore Roosevelt in 1906 first used the word *muckraking* to condemn sensational and untruthful writers. The first muckraker was Josiah Flynt Willard. His series, *The World of Graft,* appeared in 1901 in *McClure's Magazine.* Later, articles by Lincoln Steffens, Ray Stannard Baker, Ida M. Tarbell, and Upton Sinclair dealt with city government, labor unions, and business.   LOUIS FILLER

See also AMERICAN LITERATURE (Social Critics).

MUCUS, *MYOO kuhs,* is a thick, clear, slimy fluid found in the nose, mouth, and other organs and passages that open to the outside of the body. It is made up mostly of a compound of protein and sugar. This fluid is produced by cells in the mucous membranes, and covers the surfaces of the membranes.

Mucus performs two principal duties. It provides lubrication for material which must pass over the membranes, such as food passing down the gullet, or food tube. It also catches foreign matter and keeps it from entering the body. The mucous membranes of the nose, sinuses, and *trachea* (windpipe) are covered with fine hairlike structures known as *cilia.* The motions of the cilia cause the mucus to carry bacteria and dust up the windpipe to the nose and throat where it can be swallowed or blown out. Infection of the mucous membrane is known as a "cold."　　　　　WILLIAM V. MAYER

See also COLD, COMMON; MEMBRANE; MOUTH; NOSE.

MUD DAUBER. See WASP (Solitary Wasps).

MUD HEN. See COOT.

MUD MOUNTAIN DAM, formerly called STEVENS DAM, is a large rock-fill dam on the White River in Washington, about 30 miles (48 kilometers) east of Tacoma. The dam is 425 feet (130 meters) high, and 700 feet (210 meters) long at the top. Its volume is 2,360,000 cubic yards (1,804,000 cubic meters). The reservoir holds 106,000 acre-feet (130,700,000 cubic meters) of water.　　　　　T. W. MERMEL

MUD PUDDLE CLUB. See BUTTERFLY (Assemblies).

MUD PUPPY is a rather large salamander which lives in American ponds and streams. Mud puppies may

New York Zoological Society

The Mud Puppy Looks Sluggish but it darts very quickly from the mud to catch and swallow its prey.

grow as much as 17 inches (43 centimeters) long, but an 8-inch (20-centimeter) animal may be full-grown. The mud puppy has a slimy body. It may be dark brown, gray-brown, or black, usually with darker spots. It has a powerful flat tail and four weak legs. It has deep purplish-red external gills behind its short, flat head. The mud puppy is also called the *water dog*.

Mud puppies live in the Great Lakes, the Mississippi River, and ponds and streams as far south as Georgia and as far west as Texas. Mud puppies usually stay in 2 to 8 feet (0.6 to 2.4 meters) of fresh water, especially among water plants. They attach their yellow eggs to some object lying under about 4 feet (1.2 meters) of sunny water. The young are about $\frac{3}{4}$ inch (19 millimeters) long when they hatch.

Mud puppies eat crayfish, fish eggs, and other water animals. They usually hunt during the hours of dawn or dusk. They may remain active throughout the year.

Scientific Classification. The mud puppy belongs to the family Proteidae. The most common mud puppy is classified as *Necturus maculosus*.　　　W. FRANK BLAIR

MUDD, SAMUEL ALEXANDER (1833-1883), was the doctor who set John Wilkes Booth's leg after President Abraham Lincoln's assassination. Mudd did not recognize Booth. A military court found him guilty as an accessory after the fact in the assassination. Sentenced to life imprisonment, Mudd saved many prisoners and guards in a yellow fever epidemic. He was freed in 1869, after nearly four years in prison. Mudd was born in Charles County, Maryland.　　　　　W. B. HESSELTINE

MUDFLOW. See VOLCANO (Rock Fragments).

MUELLER, PAUL (1899-1965), a Swiss chemist, won the 1948 Nobel prize for physiology or medicine for discovering the insect-killing properties of DDT. The drug first was produced in Austria in 1873, but Mueller discovered its value as an insect-killer in 1939 while searching for a plant contact insecticide. DDT was used widely during World War II. It suppressed typhus in Italy and Japan (see DDT). Mueller was born in Olten, Switzerland.　　　HENRY H. FERTIG

MUENCH, ALOISIUS J. CARDINAL (1889-1962), became a cardinal of the Roman Catholic Church in 1959. He became bishop of Fargo, N.Dak. in 1935 and the papal *nuncio* (ambassador) to West Germany in 1951. Cardinal Muench was born in Milwaukee, and was ordained a priest in 1913. He was elevated to archbishop in 1950.　　　　　THOMAS P. NEILL

MUEZZIN. See MINARET; ISLAM (Duties).

MUFFLER is a device that silences the noise of an engine. The mufflers on most automobiles look like long metal cans that are connected to the exhaust pipes. The heat and pressure inside the cylinders, where exhaust gases originate, are much greater than the heat and pressure of the outside air (see GASOLINE ENGINE). If the

How a Muffler Works

A muffler reduces the noise made by exhaust gases from a gasoline engine. The device passes the gases through perforated pipes called *louver tubes*. These tubes enable the gases to expand and cool so that the gases do not produce a loud noise when they reach the outside air. *Resonating chambers* also help deaden exhaust noise by absorbing some of the sound produced by the gases as they flow through the muffler.

Midas-International Corp. (WORLD BOOK diagram)

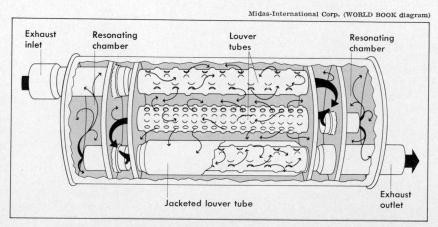

Exhaust inlet　Resonating chamber　Louver tubes　Resonating chamber　Jacketed louver tube　Exhaust outlet

exhaust gases went directly into the outside air, the sudden change would create a loud, sharp noise. Mufflers reduce the noise by forcing the exhaust gases through a series of *perforations* (small holes) before they reach the open air. The gases expand and cool as they pass through the perforations. OTTO A. UYEHARA

MUGWORT. See WORMWOOD.

MUGWUMPS were Republicans who refused to support their party's presidential candidate, James G. Blaine, in 1884. *Mugwump* is an Indian word meaning *chief*. The Mugwumps did not trust Blaine and believed he opposed government reform. They worked instead for the Democratic candidate, Grover Cleveland. The Mugwumps had considerable influence. In the election, Cleveland narrowly defeated Blaine. See also CLEVELAND, GROVER (Election of 1884). HAROLD W. BRADLEY

MUHAMMAD, *moo HAM uhd* (A.D. 570?-632), was the founder of the Islamic religion. He is called the *Prophet of Islam*. His followers are called *Muslims*. The name *Muhammad* means *Praised One*. There are several common spellings of the name, including *Mohammad*, *Mohammed*, and *Mahomet*.

Muslims believe Muhammad was the last messenger of God. They believe he completed the sacred teachings of such earlier prophets as Abraham, Moses, and Jesus. Muslims respect Muhammad, but they do not worship him.

Muhammad was one of the most influential men of all time. He felt himself called to be God's prophet. This belief gave him the strength to bring about many changes in Arabia. When Muhammad began to preach in the 600's, Arabia was a wild, lawless land. The fierce tribes of the deserts fought continual bloody wars.

In Mecca, a city in southwestern Arabia, there was poverty and suffering among the poor. Most of Muhammad's countrymen worshiped many gods, and prayed to idols and spirits.

Muhammad brought a new message to his people from God. He taught that there is only one God, and that this God requires men to make *Islam* (submission) to Him. Muhammad replaced the old loyalty to tribes with a new tie of equality and brotherhood among all Muslims. He also preached against the injustice of the wealthy classes in Mecca, and tried to help the poor.

During his lifetime, Muhammad led his countrymen to unite in a great religious movement. Within a hundred years after his death, Muslims carried his teachings into other parts of the Middle East, into North Africa, Europe, and Asia. Today, there are about 500 million Muslims throughout the world.

Early Life. Muhammad was born in Mecca, in southwestern Arabia. His father died before his birth, and his mother died when he was a child. His grandfather and later his uncle, Abu Talib, became his guardians. For a time, Muhammad lived with a desert tribe. He learned to tend sheep and camels. Later, he may have traveled with his uncle on caravan journeys through Arabia to Syria. Muhammad also probably attended assemblies and fairs in Mecca, where he may have heard men of different faiths express their ideas.

At the age of 25, Muhammad entered the service of Khadija, a wealthy widow. She was 15 years older than Muhammad, but he later married her. They had two sons and four daughters. The sons died young. One of the daughters, Fatima, married Ali, son of Abu Talib.

Many Muslims trace their descent from Muhammad through this couple (see FATIMITE DYNASTY).

His Religious Life. The most sacred shrine in Mecca was the Kaaba. It had a black stone, believed to be especially sacred, in one corner. When Muhammad was 35, a flood damaged the Kaaba. Because of his moral excellence, Muhammad was chosen to set the sacred stone back into place. See KAABA.

Later, when Muhammad was meditating alone in a cave on Mount Hira, a vision appeared to him. Muslims believe that the vision was of the angel Gabriel, who called Muhammad to be a prophet and proclaim God's message to his countrymen.

At first, Muhammad doubted that his vision had come from God. But his wife Khadija reassured him. She became his first disciple. For a time, no more revelations came, and Muhammad grew discouraged. Then Gabriel came once more, and told him, "Arise and warn, magnify thy Lord . . . wait patiently for Him."

At first, Muhammad may have told only relatives and friends of the revelations. But soon he began to preach publicly. Most of the people who heard Muhammad ridiculed him, but some believed. Abu Bakr, a rich merchant, became a disciple. Omar, one of the leaders of Mecca, persecuted Muhammad at first, but later accepted him as a prophet.

The Hegira. Muhammad continued to preach in Mecca until several calamities took place. First, both Khadija and Abu Talib died. Also the people of Mecca began to hate Muhammad for his claims and his attacks on their way of life.

Finally, in A.D. 622, Muhammad fled north to the nearby city of Medina, then called Yathrib. His emigration to Medina is called the *Hegira*. It is considered so important that the Muslim calendar begins with the year of the Hegira (see HEGIRA). The people of Medina welcomed Muhammad. His preaching and statesmanship soon won most of them as followers.

His Teachings. Muhammad was now the head of both a religion and a community, and he was able to make his religious message into law. He abolished the customs of worshiping idols and killing unwanted baby girls. He limited the practice of *polygyny* (marriage to more than one wife), and restricted divorce. He reformed inheritance laws, regulated slavery, and helped the poor. He also banned war and violence except for self-defense and for the cause of Islam.

Muhammad seems to have expected Jews and Christians to accept him as a prophet. At first he was friendly toward them. He chose Jerusalem as the direction to be faced in prayer, similar to the Jewish practice. He also set aside Friday as a Muslim day of congregational prayer, perhaps because the Jews began their Sabbath preparations then. But the Jews of Medina broke their alliance with Muhammad and conspired against him with his enemies in Mecca. Muhammad angrily drove them from the city and organized a purely Muslim society. To symbolize the independence of the new religion, he ordered Muslims to face Mecca, instead of Jerusalem, when praying.

The Meccans went to war against Muhammad and his followers. They attacked Medina several times, but they were always driven back. In 630, Muhammad entered Mecca in triumph. He offered forgiveness to the people there, most of whom accepted him as the Prophet of God. He destroyed the pagan idols in the Kaaba, prayed there, and proclaimed it a *mosque* (house of worship). Muhammad died two years later in Medina. His tomb is located in the Prophet's Mosque in Medina (see MEDINA).   CHARLES J. ADAMS

Critically reviewed by ALI HASSAN ABDEL KADER

See also ISLAM; MUSLIMS; KORAN; MECCA; FLAG (color picture: Historical Flags of the World).

MUHAMMAD II (1430?-1481), called THE CONQUEROR or THE GREAT, was the seventh ruler of the Ottoman Empire. He conquered Constantinople (now Istanbul) in 1453. This brought the Byzantine Empire to an end (see BYZANTINE EMPIRE). His armies also won Serbia, Bosnia, Albania, and other areas of southeast Europe, and the Crimea, Trebizond, and other Black Sea regions.

Muhammad became sultan in 1451 after the death of his father, Murad II. He reorganized the Ottoman government and established the Palace School for training government officials. He also built the Seraglio Palace in Constantinople (now Istanbul), a *mosque* (Muslim house of worship), several colleges, and many charitable institutions (see SERAGLIO).   SYDNEY N. FISHER

See also TURKEY (The Rise of the Ottoman Empire).

MUHAMMAD V (1844-1918) was the 35th sultan of the Ottoman Empire (Turkey). He had been kept a prisoner of the state until 1909 by his brother, the sultan Abdul-Hamid II. The revolutionary Young Turks deposed Abdul-Hamid in 1909 and placed Muhammad on the Ottoman throne. Throughout his nine-year reign, the Young Turks dominated Muhammad. They led the Ottoman Empire into the Balkan Wars and World War I. The empire lost much territory in these wars, and was greatly weakened (see TURKEY [The Young Turks]).   SYDNEY N. FISHER

MUHAMMAD V (1911-1961), SIDI MUHAMMAD BEN YOUSSEF, became king of Morocco in 1957. He had ruled as sultan since 1927, and maintained a staunch friendship with Western nations despite harsh treatment from the French government. The French seized him in 1953 and banished him to Corsica because of anti-French riots in Morocco. Affairs became so serious in 1955 that the French allowed him to return. Morocco gained its independence in 1956. In 1958, Muhammad V proposed that Morocco, Algeria, and Tunisia join together to form a federated Arab State of North Africa. His son Hassan II succeeded him as king. See also MOROCCO (Independence).   SYDNEY N. FISHER

MUHAMMAD, ELIJAH (1897-1975), was the head of the Black Muslim movement, a black organization that combines religious beliefs with strong social protest. He favored separation of blacks and whites, and formation of an all-black state or territory in the United States.

Wide World
Elijah Muhammad

He taught his followers to make themselves self-sufficient by establishing their own schools and businesses. He preached that blacks should be thrifty, clean, and hardworking, and should abstain from pork, drugs, tobacco, and alcoholic drinks.

Elijah Muhammad was born Elijah Poole in Sandersville, Ga., and moved to Detroit in the 1920's. He met W. D. Fard (or Farad), founder of the movement there, and changed his name to Elijah Muhammad. He became leader of the movement when Fard disappeared in 1934.   RICHARD BARDOLPH

See also BLACK MUSLIMS.

MUHAMMAD ALI, the boxer. See ALI, MUHAMMAD.

MUHAMMAD ALI, or MEHMET ALI (1769-1849), an Albanian soldier of fortune, made himself the master of the Turkish province of Egypt in 1805. He fought under the sultan of Turkey, leading a group of Balkan soldiers. His forces successfully put down the Greek rebellion of 1821. He was to acquire the Peloponnesus as a reward, but the navies of Great Britain, France, and Russia destroyed his fleet at the Battle of Navarino in 1827. In Egypt, Muhammad Ali introduced cotton and hemp farming, and developed irrigation. He was born in Kavala, Greece, then in the Turkish empire. See also EGYPT (History).   R. V. BURKS

MUHAMMAD ZAHIR (1914-   ) became *shah* (king) of Afghanistan in 1933. He ruled until 1973, when his brother-in-law, Lieutenant General Muhammad Daud Khan, overthrew the monarchy and proclaimed Afghanistan a republic.

Zahir Shah was born in Kabul, the capital of Afghanistan. He became shah after the death of his father, Nadir Shah, but other members of the royal family ran the country until the 1960's. In an effort to make Afghanistan more democratic, Zahir Shah forced Daud to retire from the post of prime minister in 1963. He then appointed a prime minister who was not a member of the royal family. In 1964, Zahir Shah gave Afghanistan a new constitution that guaranteed individual rights, limited the power of the royal family, and gave the people a greater voice in the government.

See also AFGHANISTAN (History).

MUHAMMADAN ART. See ISLAMIC ART.

MUHAMMADANISM. See ISLAM; MUSLIMS.

MUHLENBERG, *MYOO lun burg*, is the family name of four outstanding American religious leaders.

Henry Melchior Muhlenberg (1711-1787) helped found the Lutheran Church in the United States. He accepted an appointment as pastor to Lutherans in Pennsylvania in 1742. When he arrived from Germany in Philadelphia in 1742, he found weak and divided congregations. Within a month, Muhlenberg had gained control and began establishing the Lutheran Church. He was born in Einbeck, Hanover, Germany.

John Peter Gabriel Muhlenberg (1746-1807), the oldest son of Henry Melchior Muhlenberg, was an American Lutheran minister. He served churches in New Jersey from 1769 to 1771, then became a minister in Woodstock, Va., in 1771. There, on a Sunday in 1775, after conducting church service, Muhlenberg removed his robe to reveal a military uniform. He enrolled men in his parish into a regiment, and became its colonel. Muhlenberg commanded troops at the Revolutionary War battles of Brandywine, Germantown, Monmouth, and Yorktown, and rose to the rank of major general. He served as a Democratic-Republican representative from Pennsylvania in the United States Congress from 1789 to 1791, 1793 to 1795, and 1799 to 1801. He was born in Trappe, Pa. A statue of Muhlenberg represents Pennsylvania in the United States Capitol in Washington, D.C.

Frederick Augustus Conrad Muhlenberg (1750-1801), the second son of Henry Melchior Muhlenberg, was a Lutheran minister and American statesman. He served as a minister in Pennsylvania and New York from 1770 until 1779. He represented Pennsylvania in the first four U.S. Congresses, and served as speaker of the House of Representatives in the first (1789-1791) and third (1793-1795) Congresses. He was born in Trappe, Pa.

William Augustus Muhlenberg (1796-1877), grandson of Frederick Augustus Conrad Muhlenberg, was an Episcopal clergyman. In 1828, he established Flushing Institute, a boys' boarding school on Long Island. This was one of the first church-sponsored U.S. schools. Muhlenberg was born in Philadelphia.   F. A. Norwood

MUIR, *myoor,* **JOHN** (1838-1914), an explorer, naturalist, and writer, campaigned for forest conservation in the United States. His efforts influenced Congress to pass the Yosemite National Park Bill in 1890, establishing both Yosemite and Sequoia National Parks. He persuaded President Theodore Roosevelt to set aside 148 million acres (59,900,000 hectares) of forest reserves. A redwood forest near San Francisco was named Muir Woods in 1908 in his honor.

United Press Int.

John Muir

Muir tramped through many regions of the United States, Europe, Asia, Africa, and the Arctic. He spent six years in the area of Yosemite Valley and was the first person to explain the valley's glacial origin. In 1879, he discovered a glacier in Alaska which now bears his name. He called California "the grand side of the mountain," and owned a large fruit ranch there. In 1892, Muir founded the Sierra Club, which became a leading conservation organization (see SIERRA CLUB). Muir wrote *The Mountains of California* (1894), *Our National Parks* (1901), and *The Yosemite* (1912).

Muir was born in Dunbar, Scotland. His family moved to Wisconsin when he was 11. He grew up on a farm and developed a great love of nature. As a boy, he attracted attention with his inventions. He entered the University of Wisconsin at the age of 22. Muir supported himself by teaching and by doing farm work during the summer. His interests included botany.   CHESTER B. BAKER

MUIR WOODS NATIONAL MONUMENT, near San Francisco, Calif., has one of the state's most famous redwood groves. William Kent, a California statesman, donated it to the United States. The monument was established in 1908. For area, see NATIONAL PARK SYSTEM (table: National Monuments).

MUJIBUR RAHMAN, *MOO jee bur RAH mahn* (1920-1975), became the first prime minister of Bangladesh in January 1972. He resigned as prime minister in Jan-

uary 1975, and took office as president of Bangladesh. Military leaders of the country overthrew Mujib's government and killed him in August 1975.

Wide World

Mujibur Rahman

Mujib's rise to national leadership followed 25 years of political activity in East Pakistan (now Bangladesh). During that period, he was held as a political prisoner for a total of more than 10 years.

In 1970, Mujib became the unrivaled leader of the East Pakistanis. That year, the Awami League, the party headed by Mujib, won a majority of the seats in an assembly that was to write a new constitution for Pakistan. Mujib met with the West Pakistani leaders to discuss the proposed constitution. But the talks broke down, and civil war erupted between East and West Pakistan. The government imprisoned Mujib in West Pakistan. He was released after Bangladesh gained independence in December 1971. He returned home to a hero's welcome and to the tasks of building and leading a new nation.

Mujib was born in the village of Tungipara, 60 miles (97 kilometers) southwest of Dacca. He graduated from Islamia College in Calcutta and studied law for a short time at Dacca University.   STANLEY J. HEGINBOTHAM

See also BANGLADESH (History).

MUKDEN. See SHEN-YANG.

MUKDEN, BATTLE OF. See RUSSO-JAPANESE WAR (Last Battles).

MUKERJI, *MOO ker JEE,* **DHAN GOPAL** (1890-1936), is best known for his books which interpret India for children. His mother told him fables and old religious tales of India when he was a boy. In his stories, he used these and childhood memories of life in the jungle. In 1928, he won the Newbery medal for *Gay-Neck* (1927), the story of a carrier pigeon. Mukerji was born near Calcutta, the son of Brahmin parents. He attended the universities of Calcutta and Tokyo. He came to America in 1910 and was graduated from Stanford University in 1914.   EVELYN RAY SICKELS

MULATTO, *myoo LAT oh,* is a person of mixed white and black descent. The term *mulatto* is applied correctly to those who have one white and one black parent. Mulattoes are often called *half-breeds.* The child of a white person and a mulatto is a *quadroon.* Mulattoes vary in appearance. Some have dark skins and kinky hair and some do not. The word *creole* is often confused with *mulatto.* In the United States, a creole is a white Southerner of French or Spanish ancestry. See also CREOLE; MESTIZO.   VERNON ROBERT DORJAHN

MULBERRY is any one of a group of trees with small edible fruits resembling blackberries. The fruits have many tiny seeds. The oval or heart-shaped leaves are toothed and often divided into lobes. Mulberry trees have milky juice.

The *white mulberry* from China provides food for the silkworm, and has been grown since ancient times. After the silkworm eats the bright green leaves, it spins a cocoon of fine silky fibers. The silk industry then weaves these fibers into silken fabrics. The white mulberry has been planted in the United States, but the silkworm industry has never been successful in America. See SILK.

J. Horace McFarland
Mulberry

The *red mulberry* is a medium-sized tree that grows in the eastern half of the United States. It has large, dark green leaves. Birds and other wildlife eat the purplish fruits. Mulberry wood is used for fence posts, furniture, and the interiors of homes. The Indians made cloth from the fibrous bark. Europeans use the dark, juicy fruits of the *black mulberry* as dessert, and to make preserves and wine. *Paper mulberry* from eastern Asia has been planted for shade in the eastern part of the United States. Paper has been made from its bark.

Scientific Classification. Mulberries belong to the mulberry family, *Moraceae.* The white mulberry is genus *Morus,* species *M. alba.* The red mulberry is *M. rubra,* and the black is *M. nigra.*   ELBERT L. LITTLE, JR.

See also BANYAN TREE; BREADFRUIT; TREE (Familiar Broadleaf and Needleleaf Trees [picture]).

MULCH is any material that is spread over soil so that air can get through, but so that water in the soil cannot evaporate. Mulch may be made of manure, straw, hay, clover, chaff, alfalfa, corncobs, leaves, sawdust, wood chips, and many other substances. It is often applied about 2 to 3 inches (5 to 8 centimeters) thick. It helps keep water in the soil by reducing evaporation, and it also decays and enriches the soil. It also keeps down the number of weeds that would otherwise grow up to compete with plant crops. Mulch is valuable to home gardeners, but it often costs more than commercial fertilizers.   WILLIAM R. VAN DERSAL

MULDOON, ROBERT DAVID (1921-   ), became prime minister of New Zealand in 1975. Muldoon, the leader of the National Party since 1974, succeeded Wallace E. Rowling, head of the Labour Party. Muldoon is a conservative, and he believes New Zealand should work with other economically sound countries to stabilize international financial affairs.

Muldoon was born in Auckland, New Zealand, and graduated from Auckland University. He became an expert accountant and is a partner in an Auckland accounting firm.

Muldoon first won election to Parliament in 1960. He served as minister of finance from 1967 to 1972 and as deputy prime minister in 1972. Muldoon took office as prime minister after leading his party to a victory in the November 1975 election. In 1978,

New Zealand Embassy
Robert D. Muldoon

his party was again victorious, and he remained as prime minister.   DAVID BALLANTYNE

MULE, *myool,* is a domestic animal and beast of burden. It is the offspring of a *mare* (female horse) and a *jackass* (male donkey). The offspring of a male horse (stallion) and a female ass (jenny) is called a *hinny.* Mules are used in all parts of the world.

A mule looks somewhat like both its parents. Like the jackass, a mule has long ears, short mane, small feet, and a tail with a tuft of long hairs at the end. From the mother it gets a large, well-shaped body and strong muscles. She also gives it a horse's ease in getting used to harness. The father gives the mule a braying voice, sure-footedness, and endurance. Like the jackass, a mule saves its strength when it is forced to work hard and for a long time. A mule is less likely to suffer from overwork than a horse.

Mules resist disease well. It is sometimes said that they do not catch diseases, but experts have found that this is not true. Unfortunately, mules do not have offspring of their own, except in extremely rare cases. Animals which cannot have offspring are said to be *sterile.* All male mules and most female mules are sterile. A few female mules have produced young after they were bred to male asses or to stallions. These offspring are either three-fourths ass or three-fourths horse, depending upon the father.

Mules can remain strong under much harsh treatment and work, but they work better if they are treated with kindness. When owners take proper care of their mules, they will do as much work as horses, and will do it under harder conditions. The way mules can bear rough treatment makes them suitable for work in construction camps, mines, and military zones.

In the United States, over nine-tenths of all the mules work on farms and plantations. Most of them are used in the South.   E. LENDELL COCKRUM

See also DONKEY; GLANDERS.

MULE DEER is a beautiful deer that has large, furry ears similar to those of a mule. This grayish- to brownish-colored deer stands about 3 to 3½ feet (91 to 107 centimeters) high, and has large, branching antlers. The mule deer has a peculiar stiff-legged gait, but it can swiftly bound over the roughest trail. It lives from northern Mexico north to the southern parts of Alaska and Canada's Yukon Territory, and from northern Texas and eastern North Dakota west to the Pacific Coast. The mule deer eats grass during the spring, but lives on buds, leaves, and twigs of shrubs the rest of the year. It is also called the *blacktail,* but this name usually applies to the type of mule deer that lives in the forests near the northwestern Pacific Coast.

Scientific Classification. Mule deers belong to the deer family, *Cervidae.* They are classified as genus *Odocoileus,* species *O. hemionus.*   VICTOR H. CAHALANE

See also ANIMAL (picture: Animals of the Deserts).

MULHACÉN. See SPAIN (The Land).

MULLAH. See ISLAM (The Structure of Islam).

MULLEIN, *MUHL uhn,* or MULLEN, is the name of a group of woolly biennial plants that belong to the figwort family. There are over 100 kinds of mullein. Three grow in the United States and southern Canada. The *common mullein* grows in rocky pastures, along roadsides, and in waste places. A tall plant with a thick, woolly stem, it has thick, velvety leaves. Yellow flowers grow

A 20-Mule Team Once Hauled Shipments of Borax from a Mine and Refinery in Boron, Calif.

in clusters in the form of a spike at the top of the stalk. The *moth mullein* is smaller. It has smooth, lobed, and deeply-veined leaves.

Both the stem and leaves of the mullein irritate the skin when touched. The leaves of the mullein were formerly used to make a tea for treating coughs, nervous disorders, and inflammations.

The *white mullein* is a less common mullein which grows in the eastern United States. A thin, powdery down covers the plant. The mullein may be controlled by cutting the flower stalks before the seed forms or by spraying with a *herbicide* (chemical weed killer).

Scientific Classification. Mulleins belong to the figwort family, *Scrophulariaceae*. The common mullein is genus *Verbascum*, species *V. thapsus*. The white mullein is *V. lychnitis;* the moth, *V. blattaria*.   LOUIS PYENSON

MULLENS, PRISCILLA. See ALDEN.

MÜLLER, ERWIN W. See ION MICROSCOPE.

MÜLLER, FRIEDRICH MAX. See MYTHOLOGY (How Myths Began); RELIGION (The Origin of Religion).

MULLER, HERMANN JOSEPH (1890-1967), was an American geneticist. He received the 1946 Nobel prize for physiology or medicine for discovering that X rays can produce *mutations* (sudden changes in genes). Studying the breeding of fruit flies, Muller and geneticist Thomas Hunt Morgan made important discoveries in heredity while Muller was a student at Columbia University. Muller later made further experiments in producing mutations artificially in fruit flies. The results of these experiments, published in 1927, brought him the Nobel prize. Muller was born in New York City. He became a professor of zoology at Indiana University in 1945.   HENRY H. FERTIG

See also HEREDITY (Genetics).

MÜLLER, JOHANN. See TRIGONOMETRY.

MULLET, *MUHL iht.* Two different families of fish are called mullets. *Gray mullets* are bluish-silvery fish with stout bodies. They are from 1 to 2 feet (30 to 61 centimeters) long, and have blunt heads and small mouths. The teeth, if any, are very weak. Great numbers of these fish live close to the shore in nearly all temperate and tropical waters. Their flesh is wholesome and has a good flavor. The *common*, or *striped*, mullet is the largest and best of all the species. It weighs from 10 to 12 pounds (4.5 to 5.4 kilograms). Striped mullets are plentiful around the Florida Keys and on the Gulf Coast.

Surmullets, or *red mullets*, are small, brightly colored fish that live chiefly in warm seas. They have small mouths and weak teeth. Two long feelers called *barbels* hang like strings from the chin of the red mullet.

Scientific Classification. The gray mullets make up the mullet family, *Mugilidae*. The common mullet is genus *Mugil*, species *M. cephalus*. Red mullets belong to the goatfish family, *Mullidae*. The red mullet of Europe is genus *Mullus*, species *M. barbatus*.   LEONARD P. SCHULTZ

Common Mullein plants begin to grow in early spring, *left*. Their tall stems bloom with yellow flowers in the summer, *right*.

The Striped Mullet Thrives in Shallow Coastal Waters.

MULLIKEN, ROBERT SANDERSON (1896-   ), an American chemist, won the 1966 Nobel prize for chemistry. He received the award for his *molecular-orbital theory*, which he proposed in 1928. This theory explains how atoms combine to form a molecule.

The electrons of an atom orbit its nucleus in paths called *shells* (see ATOM [Electronic Structure]). Scientists once believed that the electrons in these shells continued to orbit the individual atomic nuclei after a molecule had been formed. Most scientists now accept Mulliken's theory that the electrons in the outermost shell orbit the entire molecule.

Mulliken's theory has been applied in such fields as biological and industrial research. For example, scientists have used it to study the structure of proteins, plastics, and other complex compounds.

Mulliken was born in Newburyport, Mass. He graduated from the Massachusetts Institute of Technology in 1917 and received a Ph.D. degree from the University of Chicago in 1921. Mulliken taught at the university from 1928 to 1961.   DANIEL J. KEVLES

MULOCK, SIR WILLIAM (1844-1944), the *Grand Old Man of Canada*, was a leader in law, politics, and education for more than 60 years. A Liberal, he represented York County in the House of Commons from 1882 to 1905. In 1896, Mulock became postmaster general. He introduced the two-cent postage rate from Canada to all parts of the British Empire. He served as Canada's first minister of labor, from 1900 to 1905. In 1905, he was appointed chief justice of the Exchequer Court of Ontario, and in 1923 he became chief justice of Ontario. He attended the University of Toronto, and served as chancellor of the university from 1924 to 1944. Mulock was born in Bondhead, in what is now Ontario.   JOHN T. SAYWELL

MULTAN, *mool TAHN* (pop. 538,949), ranks as one of the oldest cities of Pakistan. The city dates back to the 300's B.C. Multan is located near the left bank of the Chenab River, southwest of Lahore. The city is a manufacturing center for surgical instruments and steel furniture.   ROBERT I. CRANE

MULTIELECTRODE TUBE. See VACUUM TUBE (Kinds).

MULTILATERAL AID. See FOREIGN AID (Multilateral Aid Programs).

MULTINATIONAL CORPORATION is a business organization that produces and sells a product, or provides a service, in two or more countries. There are about 7,300 multinational corporations, also called MNC's or transnational corporations. About half of them operate in more than two nations. Some people use the term only for companies that operate in at least six countries and have annual sales of more than $100 million. This group includes about 200 U.S. companies, 80 European firms, and 20 Japanese corporations.

Multinational corporations account for about 15 per cent of the world's goods and services. Most of these firms are manufacturers. Typical examples of MNC's are General Motors Corporation of the United States, which produces automobiles and automobile parts; and Siemens Company of West Germany, which makes electrical equipment. A smaller number of MNC's are in such fields as banking, hotel management, mining, and petroleum production.

Operation. Most multinational corporations operate in fields that involve frequent technological change. Such fields include the production of computers, drugs, and electronic equipment. A typical firm in such fields has a large research organization in the country in which it has its headquarters. There, the firm develops new products and manufacturing processes. It then trains workers in its foreign plants to use these new skills. Some multinational corporations, instead of setting up plants of their own, grant foreign companies a license to use their methods and processes.

A multinational firm may have a few plants in one country that produce complete products to be sold in several countries. Or plants in many countries may each make parts of the finished products. This process, sometimes called *global integration*, provides economic benefits for a greater number of countries. It also gives the multinational corporation a larger area from which to choose the most economical locations for specialized plants. The corporation can then sell its products at lower prices than would otherwise be possible.

Development. Most MNC's have developed since World War II ended in 1945. Some companies establish plants abroad to meet the competition of firms in other countries making products at lower costs for labor and materials. Other firms want to avoid paying the tariffs placed on imported goods by other countries.

The economic role of multinational corporations has aroused debate both at home and abroad. In the United States, for example, some labor groups believe that U.S. MNC's have increased unemployment at home by establishing operations in other countries. Others argue that the firms have preserved more jobs for Americans by meeting competition from low foreign costs. Abroad, many people oppose U.S. multinational corporations because of their control over local economies and the profits they earn. Supporters of MNC's, however, emphasize the contributions the firms' technology and capital make to economic development.   JOHN FAYERWEATHER

MULTIPHASIC HEALTH TESTING LABORATORY. See BIOMEDICAL ENGINEERING (Biomedical Engineering in the Community).

MULTIPLE BIRTH is the birth of more than one baby at a time. Twins, triplets, quadruplets, and quintuplets are all examples of multiple birth. Human beings rarely have more than one child at a time. The smaller animals often have large litters. The opossum, for example, has up to 18 young in its litter. Dogs, cats, rabbits, and pigs all give birth to more than one offspring. Cows, horses, camels, and other large mammals usually have only one at a time.

Some scientists believe that the tendency to have more than one child at a time is hereditary. Twins, for example, seem to run in some families. Some twins come from two different eggs which merely happen to be fertilized and develop at the same time. Such twins are called *fraternal twins*. *Identical twins* are born from the cell mass originating from a single egg which has become divided. If the cell mass separates before it begins to take shape, the identical twins will be almost exactly alike in every respect. But the split may come after the cell mass has begun to take shape. The cell mass has already developed a right and left side. In that case, one twin may be left-handed, while the other is right-handed.

Multiple Births Occur Among Many Small Animals, Including Chihuahuas.

In the 1960's and 1970's, the use of *fertility drugs* caused an increase in the number of multiple births. Fertility drugs help some women who have previously been infertile to become pregnant. The drugs cause a woman's ovaries to release an egg about once a month. In some cases, the drugs cause the release of several eggs at the same time. If these eggs become fertilized, the woman may give birth to twins, triplets, or even more babies at one time. See REPRODUCTION (Human Reproduction).

If fertility drugs have not been used, human twins are born about once in every 96 births. The estimate for human triplets is one set in every 9,000 births, and for quadruplets one set in every 900,000 births. The odds in favor of quintuplets are only one set in about 85 million births.

Before the development of modern medicine, the children in multiple births had little chance to survive. The children often had less care and less food than they would have had if they had been born alone. Even twins suffered. Modern care and medical knowledge have increased the survival of multiple-birth children. The Dionne quintuplets, born near Callander, Ont., Canada, in 1934, were the first quintuplets known to live for more than a few hours after birth. Since the Dionnes, other sets of quintuplets have survived the period of infancy. The Rosenkowitz sextuplets, born in Cape Town, South Africa, in 1974, were believed to be the first recorded set of sextuplets to survive early infancy.   GEORGE W. BEADLE

See also QUADRUPLETS; QUINTUPLETS; TRIPLETS; TWINS.

MULTIPLE SCLEROSIS, *sklih ROH sihs,* sometimes called *MS,* is a disease of the nervous system. It may last for years and eventually can cause serious disabilities, including paralysis of the legs and partial loss of vision. MS afflicts more women than men, and it occurs chiefly in cool regions. Most victims begin to have symptoms of MS when they are from 20 to 45 years old. The disease cannot be cured.

Multiple sclerosis is characterized by the gradual destruction of *myelin,* the white matter of the brain and spinal cord. Many small hard areas called *plaques* appear scattered throughout the myelin and interfere with the normal function of nerve pathways. The word *sclerosis* comes from a Greek term that means *hard* and refers to the plaques.

The symptoms of MS vary, depending on the affected areas of the brain and spinal cord. In time, more and more plaques develop in the victim's myelin, causing new symptoms. Physicians diagnose multiple sclerosis chiefly from the symptoms. The disease cannot be diagnosed by laboratory tests.

The first symptoms appear suddenly. The victim may have double vision, an unsteady walk, loss of balance, and weakness in an arm or leg. Numbness or tingling may occur in the fingers, along with jerky movements of the arms, legs, or head. After several weeks, these symptoms become less severe and may disappear entirely. Periods of better health are followed by unpredictable symptoms that worsen progressively. About a third of the victims of multiple sclerosis become seriously handicapped, but few die from it.

Physicians do not know the cause of MS. Some researchers believe the disease is caused by a virus that infects people before they are 15 years old. The virus may produce an abnormal reaction in the body's immune system. Normally, the body protects itself from disease by producing substances called *antibodies,* which fight infection. However, sometimes the body has an *autoimmune reaction,* in which antibodies attack healthy tissues. In multiple sclerosis, antibodies may attack myelin.

During the 1970's, researchers discovered that certain *genes* are associated with MS. Genes are the tiny hereditary units that control each cell's activities. The genes associated with MS control the body's immune system. Some scientists think the genes react with an environmental factor, which has not been identified, to produce a condition that can lead to MS.   MILTON ALTER

MULTIPLEX STEREO. See HIGH FIDELITY (Development).

759

Students Develop Multiplication Skills by Working Problems.

MULTIPLICATION is a short way of adding or counting equal numbers. It is one of the four basic operations in arithmetic along with addition, subtraction, and division.

Suppose you want to know how much six gumballs will cost. The gumballs are 5¢ each. You can find the answer by addition: 5+5+5+5+5+5=30. Six gumballs will cost 30¢. But it is easier to learn that six 5's are always 30. Learning facts like this is the basis of multiplication.

Learning To Multiply

Many persons learn multiplication only by memorizing its facts and rules. Often they do not understand the methods that they are using. The best way for a person to learn multiplication is to find out how it works.

Writing Multiplication. The different operations in arithmetic are shown by special symbols. The symbol of multiplication is ×. The statement 6×5=30 means "six 5's are 30." People also read this as "5 multiplied by 6 is 30" or "6 times 5 is 30."

The number that is being multiplied, or added together a number of times, is called the *multiplicand*. The number that does the multiplying, or the number of multiplicands to be added, is called the *multiplier*. The result, or answer, is called the *product*. A multiplication problem is usually written like this:

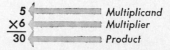

$$\begin{array}{r} 5 \\ \times 6 \\ \hline 30 \end{array}$$ Multiplicand / Multiplier / Product

You do not need to write the names every time, but it is important to keep the columns straight when multiplying larger numbers. An understanding of place value is important in learning multiplication. See DECIMAL NUMERAL SYSTEM (Learning the Decimal System).

Multiplication Facts. A statement such as 6×5=30 is a *multiplication fact*. It consists of a multiplier, a multiplicand, and a product. You should use addition to discover the multiplication facts. For example, 5+5+5+5+5+5=30. After discovering a multiplication fact, you should memorize it. By knowing the 100 multiplication facts, you can learn to multiply any numbers, large or small.

--- **MULTIPLICATION TERMS** ---

Annexing Zeros is a quick way of multiplying by 10, 100, 1,000, and so on. It means placing zeros at the end of the number being multiplied.

Carry, in multiplication, means to change a number from one place in the product to the next. A 10 in the 1's place is carried to the 10's place.

Multiplicand is the number that is multiplied. In 4×8=32, 8 is the multiplicand.

Multiplication Fact is a basic statement in multiplication, such as 6×3=18.

Multiplier is the number that does the multiplying. In 4×8=32, 4 is the multiplier.

Partial Product is the result of multiplying a number by one digit of the multiplier. It is used when the multiplier has two or more digits.

Product is the answer or result of multiplication. In 4×8=32, 32 is the product.

760

0	1	2	3	4	5	6	7	8	9
×0	×0	×0	×0	×0	×0	×0	×0	×0	×0
0	0	0	0	0	0	0	0	0	0

0	1	2	3	4	5	6	7	8	9
×1	×1	×1	×1	×1	×1	×1	×1	×1	×1
0	1	2	3	4	5	6	7	8	9

0	1	2	3	4	5	6	7	8	9
×2	×2	×2	×2	×2	×2	×2	×2	×2	×2
0	2	4	6	8	10	12	14	16	18

0	1	2	3	4	5	6	7	8	9
×3	×3	×3	×3	×3	×3	×3	×3	×3	×3
0	3	6	9	12	15	18	21	24	27

0	1	2	3	4	5	6	7	8	9
×4	×4	×4	×4	×4	×4	×4	×4	×4	×4
0	4	8	12	16	20	24	28	32	36

0	1	2	3	4	5	6	7	8	9
×5	×5	×5	×5	×5	×5	×5	×5	×5	×5
0	5	10	15	20	25	30	35	40	45

0	1	2	3	4	5	6	7	8	9
×6	×6	×6	×6	×6	×6	×6	×6	×6	×6
0	6	12	18	24	30	36	42	48	54

0	1	2	3	4	5	6	7	8	9
×7	×7	×7	×7	×7	×7	×7	×7	×7	×7
0	7	14	21	28	35	42	49	56	63

0	1	2	3	4	5	6	7	8	9
×8	×8	×8	×8	×8	×8	×8	×8	×8	×8
0	8	16	24	32	40	48	56	64	72

0	1	2	3	4	5	6	7	8	9
×9	×9	×9	×9	×9	×9	×9	×9	×9	×9
0	9	18	27	36	45	54	63	72	81

Most of the multiplication facts are easy to learn. If you play a game and make a score of 0 four times, your score is 0, because $4 \times 0 = 0$. Similarly, $5 \times 0 = 0$, $6 \times 0 = 0$ and $8 \times 0 = 0$. Zero multiplied by any number is zero. Any number multiplied by zero is also zero. You have now learned 19 of the multiplication facts!

If you make a score of 1 four times, your score is 4, because $4 \times 1 = 4$. Similarly, $5 \times 1 = 5$, $6 \times 1 = 6$, and $8 \times 1 = 8$. One multiplied by any number is that number. Any number multiplied by one is also that same number. You now know 17 more multiplication facts.

The two boxes of eggs shown below illustrate an important rule in multiplication.

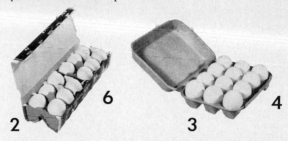

6   4   2   3

Each box contains 12 eggs. You can look at the box of eggs at the left in two ways. You might say that there are six rows of eggs with two eggs in each row. Or, you could say that there are two rows of eggs with six eggs in each row. You can also look at the box of eggs at the right in two ways. You might say that there are four rows of eggs with three eggs in each row. Or, you could say that there are three rows of eggs with four eggs in each row. The multiplication facts that show this are:

$$6 \times 2 = 12 \qquad 4 \times 3 = 12$$
$$2 \times 6 = 12 \qquad 3 \times 4 = 12$$

This example shows that *numbers can be multiplied in any order*. The products will always be the same. Knowing this rule cuts down the number of multiplication facts to be learned from 100 to 55.

Knowing the *squares* is helpful in learning the multiplication facts. A square is a number multiplied by itself. Here are the squares that help to learn the facts:

$$2 \times 2 = 4 \qquad 5 \times 5 = 25 \qquad 8 \times 8 = 64$$
$$3 \times 3 = 9 \qquad 6 \times 6 = 36 \qquad 9 \times 9 = 81$$
$$4 \times 4 = 16 \qquad 7 \times 7 = 49$$

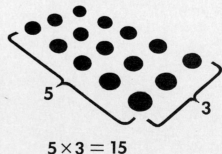

5   3

$$5 \times 3 = 15$$

Multiplication Facts Can Be Learned From Play. Toy soldiers on parade show a multiplication fact. The soldiers march forward in three straight lines. Five soldiers march in each line. How many soldiers are there all together? Adding the lines shows that there are $5+5+5$, or 15 soldiers all together. Three 5's, or 5×3, are always 15. And $5 \times 3 = 15$ is one of the 100 multiplication facts.

MULTIPLICATION

You can make pictures of the squares with dots. Here are the dot pictures of the squares of six and seven:

If you add a row of six dots to the first picture, you will have seven 6's. This shows that $36+6=42$ or $7\times6=42$. If you take away a row of dots from the second picture, you will have six 7's. This shows that $49-7=42$ or $6\times7=42$. Making dot pictures can help you learn the multiplication facts. For example, you can make a square containing four dots to show 2×2. Another square containing nine dots shows 3×3. A third square could show 4×4, and so on.

Learning the multiplication facts takes time and study. But knowing these facts is necessary to become skilled at multiplying. You can become even better at arithmetic if you learn the division facts as you learn the multiplication facts. The division facts are the opposite of the multiplication facts. See DIVISION (Division Facts).

Multiplying by One Digit

Any number from 0 to 9 is called a *digit*. The number 26 is a two-digit number. The number 514 is a three-digit number. A digit gets its value from the place it occupies in a number. The first place on the right is for 1's, the next to the left is for 10's, the next for 100's, and so on. For example, in the number 347, the 3 means three 100's, the 4 means four 10's, and the 7 means seven 1's. Depending on its place, the digit 2 may mean two 1's, (2), two 10's (20), two 100's (200), or two 1,000's (2,000). You combine the idea of place value with the multiplication facts to multiply large numbers.

Here is an example of the steps needed to work a multiplication problem using more than one multiplication fact. There are 32 students in a class. Each student uses one sheet of paper a day. How many sheets of paper will be needed for three days? We could solve the problem by using addition: $32+32+32=96$. The class will need 96 sheets of paper for three days. Multiplication is quicker and easier. The number 32 is three 10's and two 1's. The basic idea is to multiply first the 1's by 3 and then the 10's.

$$\begin{array}{r} 32 \\ \times 3 \\ \hline 96 \end{array}$$

First, you multiply the two 1's by 3. This is $3\times2=6$. You write the 6 in the 1's place in the product. Next, you multiply the three 10's by 3. This is $3\times30=90$. The 90 is nine 10's, and you write the 9 in the 10's place in the product. The answer is 96.

You multiply a larger number by one digit in much the same way:

$$\begin{array}{r} 302 \\ \times 4 \\ \hline 1208 \end{array}$$

First, you multiply the two 1's by 4. This is $4\times2=8$. You write the 8 in the 1's place in the product. Next, you multiply the 0 or "no" 10's by 4. This is $4\times0=0$. You write the 0 in the 10's place in the product. Then you multiply the three 100's. This is $4\times300=1,200$. You write the 12 in the 100's and 1,000's place in the product. The answer is 1,208.

When you multiply a large number by one digit, you must multiply each digit of the larger number—the 1's, 10's, 100's, and so on—one at a time. As you do the multiplication, you must write down the products of each of these multiplications—the 1's, 10's, 100's, and so on.

How To Carry in Multiplication

Students learn how to "carry" when they learn addition. When you add several numbers, there may be a 10 in the sum of the 1's column. You carry or add this 10 to the 10's column, usually by writing a small 1 above the 10's column. Carrying in multiplication is similar:

Addition	Multiplication
¹12	
12	
12	¹12
12	$\times 8$
12	96
12	
12	
12	
96	

When you add the eight 12's, the eight 2's total 16, or one 10 and six 1's. You write the six 1's in the 1's place in the sum. You add the 10 to the column of eight 10's by writing a 1 at the top of that column. Adding the 1's in the 10's column gives you nine 10's. You write nine 10's in the 10's place in the sum. To multiply 8×12, you multiply the 1's first. This is $8\times2=16$. You write the six 1's in the 1's place in the product. You write a 1 to be added to the product of 8×1 in the 10's place. This is $8\times1=8$ and $8+1=9$. You write the nine 10's in the 10's place in the product. *Be sure to multiply first. Then add the "carry number" to the product.*

Multiplying by Large Numbers

A multiplier that has more than one digit introduces a new idea in multiplication. This is the use of the *partial product*. You can learn this idea best from an example.

Jim wants to know how many cartons of milk his school used last month. It used 312 cartons each day for 23 days.

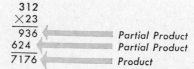

$$\begin{array}{r} 312 \\ \times 23 \\ \hline 936 \\ 624 \\ \hline 7176 \end{array}$$
Partial Product
Partial Product
Product

The multiplier, 23, has two digits. It has two 10's and three 1's. You must use these as separate parts. First, you multiply 312 by the three 1's. This is $3\times2=6$. You write the 6 in the 1's place in the product. Then, $3\times1=3$ and $3\times3=9$. You write the 3 and the 9 in the 10's and 100's places in the product. This product of 3×312 is a partial product. Next, you multiply 312 by the two 10's. You write the product of this multiplication below the first product. You start this new partial product one place to the left, in the 10's place, because 312 is now being multiplied by 10's, not by 1's. First, 2×2=4. This is four 10's. You write the 4 below the 10's place in the first product. Next, 2×1=2 and 2×3=6. You write the 2 and the 6 in the 100's and 1,000's places of the second partial product. Now, the two partial products must be added together. The first partial product is 3×312 or 936. The second partial product is 20×312 or 6,240. Thus, 936+6,240=7,176. The answer is that the school uses 7,176 cartons of milk in 23 days.

Multiplying by a three-digit multiplier is the same as by a two-digit multiplier. But there are three partial products instead of two. When you use the 100's part of the multiplier in this kind of problem, remember to write this product beginning in the 100's place.

```
    123
   ×234
    492  ◄──── First Partial Product
    369  ◄──── Second Partial Product
    246  ◄──── Third Partial Product
  28782  ◄──── Product
```

Notice that the partial product of 2×123 is started in the 100's column directly under the 2.

You do not write "carry numbers" when you are multiplying by larger numbers. You must carry in your mind. If you wrote in carry numbers, you could easily confuse them with the carry numbers from another part of the multiplier.

Multiplying by Zero

Zeros in combination with other digits represent 10's, 100's, 1,000's, and so on. When there are zeros in a multiplier, you can shorten the work of multiplication.

```
    14          14
   ×20         ×20
    00         280
   28
   280
```

In the example at the right, you can see that there will be no 1's in the 1's place. So you can write a 0 to show the 1's place, and write the product of the two 10's on the same line. This shortens the work.

You must be careful when you use this method with a three-digit multiplier that ends in zero. The difficulty comes in placing the second partial product:

```
    214
   ×320
   4280
   642
  68480
```

You begin the second partial product in the 100's place, because 3, the part of the multiplier being used, represents 100's. You should always check the place of the

MULTIPLICATION

multiplier when you write its partial product.

An easy way to multiply by 10, 100, 1,000, and other multiples of 10 is to *annex zeros*. This means to place zeros at the end of a number.

$$10 \times 2 = 20 \qquad 100 \times 2 = 200 \qquad 1,000 \times 2 = 2,000$$

Stated as a rule, this means that *to multiply by 10, annex a zero to the multiplicand. To multiply by 100, annex two zeros to the multiplicand, To multiply by 1,000, annex three zeros to the multiplicand.*

You can extend this method:

$$400 \times 12 = 4,800$$

You multiply 12 by 4, and annex two 0's.

When you multiply larger numbers, there may be a zero in the 10's place of the multiplier.

```
    423
   ×302
    846
  12690
 127746
```

In this case, you write a zero in the 10's place of the second partial product. This is to make sure you start the next partial product in the 100's place.

How To Check Multiplication

You should always check the answer in multiplication to be sure you have solved the problem correctly. You have seen that numbers can be multiplied in any order and the product remains the same. For example, 2×4=8 and 4×2=8. The best way to check a product is to change the places of the multiplier and multiplicand and do the multiplication again.

```
   15        12        342        153
  ×12       ×15       ×153       ×342
   30        60       1026        306
   15        12       1710        612
  180       180        342        459
                     52326      52326
```

The products are the same, but the partial products are different. If you make a mistake one way, you probably will not make it the other way. If your answers are different, you can locate your mistake.

When you multiply a large number by one digit, you can check it easily by dividing the product by the single digit. See DIVISION (Short Division).

```
   3425              3425
     ×5         5/17125
  17125
```

Multiplication Rules

These five rules will help you solve problems in multiplication.

1. Remember that multiplication is a short way of adding equal numbers. The multiplier tells you how many times a number is to be multiplied.

2. Learn the meaning of the multiplication facts and learn to recall the facts quickly. Remember that a number multiplied by zero is zero and that a number multi-

MULTIPLICATION

plied by one is the same number. Also remember that zero multiplied by any number is zero.

3. Remember the methods for multiplying by one or more digits. You multiply the 1's, 10's, 100's, and 1,000's of the multiplicand one after the other and write the result in the product. When the multiplier has two or more digits, you must use partial products.

4. Place value has great importance in multiplication. Always keep the columns straight, and start the product under the digit you are using in the multiplier.

5. Learn to check the answer after working a problem in multiplication. You can do this by changing the places of the multiplier and multiplicand, and doing the multiplication again.

Fun with Multiplication

Many of the games that can be played using the addition, subtraction, and division facts can be changed a little for the use of multiplication facts.

Product! is played by a group of children sitting in a circle. The leader selects a number, such as 5. The player next to the leader begins with 1, and the group counts around to the left. When the counting comes to a product of 5, the player calls "Product!" instead of the number. The counting goes like this: "1, 2, 3, 4, Product!, 6, 7, 8, 9, Product!", and so on. A player who forgets to say "Product!" is out, and the winner is the last player left in the game.

Finger Multiplying can be fun for one person. By using fingers, you can multiply 5, 6, 7, 8, or 9 by 5, 6, 7, 8, or 9.

Suppose you want to multiply 8×6. Close the fingers of both hands. Open 3 fingers on the left hand. The 5 closed on the right hand and the 3 open stand for 8. Now open 1 finger on the right hand. The 5 that were closed and the 1 now open on the right hand stand for 6. Now 3 fingers should be open on the left hand and 1 finger open on the right. This is the 10's digit of the answer. Add the fingers open: $3+1=4$. There are four 10's in the answer. The closed fingers give the 1's digit. There are 2 fingers closed on the left hand and 4 fingers

closed on the right hand. Multiply these to get the 1's digit. This is $2 \times 4 = 8$. Add the 10's and the 1's. Four 10's and eight 1's are 48. This shows that $8 \times 6 = 48$.

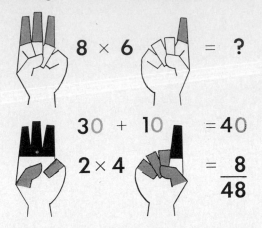

Another example is 9×7. Start with the fingers closed. Open 4 fingers on the left hand for 9 ($4+5=9$). Open 2 fingers on the right hand for 7 ($5+2=7$). Add the fingers open: $4+2=6$. This is the 10's digit. There is 1 finger closed on the left hand and 3 fingers closed on the right hand. Multiply these for the 1's digit. This is $1 \times 3 = 3$. Add the six 10's and the three 1's: $60+3=63$. This shows that $9 \times 7 = 63$. RICHARD MADDEN

Related Articles in WORLD BOOK include:

Outline

PRACTICE MULTIPLICATION EXAMPLES

1. 275 ×608	4. 840 ×364	7. 804 ×708	10. 307 ×400	13. 479 ×900	16. 358 ×679
2. 790 ×200	5. 300 ×705	8. 700 ×700	11. 906 ×368	14. 680 ×509	17. 478 ×297
3. 600 ×320	6. 500 ×457	9. 305 ×930	12. 947 ×350	15. 960 ×470	18. 689 ×698

19. How many stamps does Jim have in his stamp book? The book has 5 pages with 48 stamps on each page.

20. How much will 5 books cost at $2.25 each?

21. Pat rides her bicycle at a speed of 8 kilometers per hour for 3 hours. How far will she ride?

22. How far will Mr. Scott's automobile go on 10 gallons of gasoline? It goes 16 miles on 1 gallon.

23. Eggs cost 60¢ a dozen. How much will 6 dozen cost?

24. Four mothers plan to bring a dozen cookies each for a picnic. How many cookies will there be?

ANSWERS TO THE PRACTICE EXAMPLES

1. 167,200	5. 211,500	9. 283,650	13. 431,100	17. 141,966	21. 24 kilometers
2. 158,000	6. 228,500	10. 122,800	14. 346,120	18. 480,922	22. 160 miles
3. 192,000	7. 569,232	11. 333,408	15. 451,200	19. 240 stamps	23. $3.60
4. 305,760	8. 490,000	12. 331,450	16. 243,082	20. $11.25	24. 48 cookies

MULTNOMAH FALLS, *mult NOH muh,* occur on Multnomah Creek as it tumbles down from the Cascade Mountains. The creek empties into the Columbia River in northwest Oregon. The falls are about 620 feet (189 meters) high. See also WATERFALL (chart).

MUMFORD, LEWIS (1895-   ), is an American social critic, philosopher, and historian. Many of his books explore the relation between modern people and their environment. Several of his books deal with city planning. *The City in History* (1961) won the 1962 National Book Award for nonfiction. The book describes how human civilization is expressed in the development of cities.

Mumford wrote a four-volume philosophy of civilization called *The Renewal of Life.* The series included *Technics and Civilization* (1934), *The Culture of Cities* (1938), *The Condition of Man* (1944), and *The Conduct of Life* (1951). He also wrote several histories of architecture and studies of American culture. He was born in Flushing, N.Y. In 1975, Queen Elizabeth II of Great Britain knighted Mumford for his contributions to city planning in Great Britain.

MUMMERS' PARADE. See PENNSYLVANIA (Annual Events; picture).

MUMMY is an embalmed body that has been preserved for thousands of years. The ancient Egyptians believed that the dead lived on in the next world, and that their bodies had to be preserved forever as they were in life. They believed that the body would serve a person after it was projected into the next world. So they spent much effort in developing methods of embalming. Thousands of years later, archaeologists found the preserved bodies in tombs. Many museums have one

or more Egyptian mummies. The most famous are probably those of Ramses II and Tutankhamon, who were *pharaohs* (rulers) of Egypt.

Scientists now know what materials and processes the Egyptians used to mummify bodies. The process was simple when mummifying began, and gradually became more elaborate. Wealthy persons could afford a more expensive treatment than the poor. Ancient texts state that a complete treatment required 70 days. Embalmers removed the brain through a nostril. They removed the internal organs, except the heart and kidneys, through an incision such as a surgeon makes. They usually filled the empty abdomen with linen pads, and sometimes with sawdust. Then they placed the body in natron (sodium carbonate) until the tissues were dried out. Finally, they wrapped the body carefully in many layers of linen bandages and placed it in a coffin. Sometimes there were two or more coffins, one inside the other. The coffins were made of wood or stone, and were either rectangular or shaped like the wrapped mummy. The mummy in its coffin was then placed in a tomb, along with many objects of daily use. The ancient Egyptians believed that the dead would need this equipment in the next world.

The dry climate in some parts of the world, such as Peru, Mexico, and Egypt, preserves dead bodies almost as well as Egyptian embalming methods did. Such naturally preserved bodies are sometimes called mummies also.   GEORGE R. HUGHES

See also EMBALMING; PYRAMIDS; RAMSES II; TUTANKHAMON.

Ancient Mummies of Peru and Egypt show the burial customs of these lands. The Peruvian mummy, *left,* was buried in a sitting position. It was wrapped in cloth, with silver ornaments on the face. Dolls, cloth bags, and sticks wound with colored yarn surround the body. Egyptian mummies, *center and right,* were wrapped, and then stretched out full length in decorated coffins.

American Museum of Natural History

Mummy Case of a Woman Named Tinto, Field Museum of Natural History

Egyptian Funerary Customs XXII-XXIII Dynasty From Sheik Abd El Kurna
Mummy of Kharu-shery, The Metropolitan Museum of Art, New York

The Art Institute of Chicago,
The Kate S. Buckingham Fund

Edvard Munch's Lithograph *The Cry* illustrates the feeling of anguish and inner torment that appears in many of his works.

MUMPS is a contagious disease that causes painful swelling below and in front of the ears. Mumps is also called *parotitis* because it affects chiefly the *parotid* (salivary) glands in the cheeks. The swelling occurs in these glands. Mumps is caused by a virus in the saliva of an infected person.

Symptoms appear about 18 days after contact with the mumps virus. They include fever, headache, muscle ache, and sometimes vomiting. Then swelling begins in one or both parotid glands. The pain of the swollen glands may make it difficult for the patient to chew or swallow. Mumps may also attack the salivary glands under the jaw. The swelling lasts about a week.

Most cases of mumps are not serious. But the disease may also affect other parts of the body. The mumps virus may attack the central nervous system, causing extremely high fever, severe headache, and nausea. Mumps causes particularly painful swelling when it occurs in one or both testicles of an adult male. The virus also can infect the ovaries of a female. Mumps almost never makes a man or a woman *sterile* (unable to produce children).

About a third of the people who become infected with the mumps virus do not develop any symptoms. But they can still infect others. A person with mumps can transmit the disease as early as seven days before the swelling appears and up to nine days after.

No drug affects the mumps virus in a person who has the disease. But a mumps vaccine, which became available in the late 1960's, provides *immunity* (protection) from the disease. Most people who have had mumps on one or both sides of the body become immune to the disease for the rest of their life.

In 1934, mumps was first shown to be contagious. Two American medical researchers, Ernest Goodpasture and Claud Johnson, produced the disease in monkeys by injecting the animals with saliva taken from human mumps patients. THOMAS H. WELLER

MUNCH, *moongk,* **EDVARD** (1863-1944), was a Norwegian artist. His chief works show man as helpless, isolated, and tormented by emotions.

Munch painted many portraits, especially of young girls and women. He also painted scenes of figures in landscape settings and made lithographs and woodcuts. Most of his works vividly express an emotion, such as fear, jealousy, a terrifying sense of isolation, or sexual desire. These works rank among the early examples of expressionism, an art form that attempts to convey man's inner feelings (see EXPRESSIONISM).

Munch was born in Løten, near Oslo. He lived in Paris from 1889 to 1892 and was influenced by the French artist Paul Gauguin. From 1892 to 1908, Munch lived chiefly in Germany. His works had a strong influence on the German expressionists. After Munch returned to Norway in 1909, his art became more realistic, notably in a series of murals he painted for the University of Oslo. GREGORY BATTCOCK

MUNCHAUSEN, *MUHN* CHOW *zuhn,* **BARON,** was the name given to the narrator and central figure in an anonymous booklet of tall tales, *Baron Munchausen's Narrative of His Marvellous Travels and Campaigns in Russia*. It was first published in England in 1785. The booklet sold so widely that enlarged editions began to pour from the printing presses. These used extravagant boasts. The German translation appeared in 1786. The author is assumed to have been a German exile living in London named Rudolph Erich Raspe (1737-1794).

A real Baron Hieronymus Karl Friedrich Munchausen lived in Germany in the 1700's. Raspe may have known him. Although Munchausen may have told some good stories, he disapproved of the great lies the book attributed to him. Munchausen tried in vain to escape the swarm of visitors that the publication brought to him. He died in grief at being named the world's biggest boaster. His name is still used to describe an exaggerator or boaster. FRANK GOODWYN

MUNCIE, Ind. (pop. 80,177; met. area 129,219), is a major producer of glass fruit jars and other glass food containers. It lies on the West Fork of the White River 50 miles (80 kilometers) northeast of Indianapolis (see INDIANA [political map]). Muncie also produces automobile parts, meat products, and wire fencing. Muncie is the home of Ball State University.

Muncie was named for the Munsee Indians. The first white settlement was established about 1833. Muncie was chartered as a city in 1865. It has a mayor-council form of government. Muncie gained widespread attention when sociologists Robert S. and Helen M. Lynd studied social and economic conditions in the city. They reported their findings in *Middletown* (1929), and *Middletown in Transition* (1937). PAUL E. MILLION, JR.

MUNDELEIN, *MUHN duh lyn,* **GEORGE WILLIAM CARDINAL** (1872-1939), became Roman Catholic Archbishop of Chicago in 1915, and a cardinal of the Roman Catholic Church in 1924. As archbishop, he was faced with the problems of administering Church affairs in Chicago, the jurisdiction that probably had the greatest variety of nationalities as well as the most people. His declared objective was to make all of these Catholics aware of their need to become good American citizens.

He built a magnificent seminary for the education of priests at Mundelein, Ill. Cardinal Mundelein was born in New York City, and served in Brooklyn before going to Chicago. JOHN T. FARRELL and FULTON J. SHEEN

MUNG BEAN. See BEAN (Kinds of Beans).

MUNICH, *MYOO nik* (pop. 1,296,970), is West Germany's third largest city. It ranks next in population to Berlin and Hamburg. Munich lies 310 miles (499 kilometers) southwest of Berlin on the Bavarian plain. For location, see GERMANY (political map). It is the capital of Bavaria.

The German name for Munich is *München*, which means *Place of the Monks*. Tradition says that this name goes back to the 700's, when an outpost of the rich abbey of Tegernsee was stationed there.

Munich is well remembered today for its connection with the Nazi party, which was founded there in 1918. Munich was the scene of Adolf Hitler's "Beer Hall Putsch" of 1923. Hitler held a mass meeting in a beer hall and attempted a revolution to seize power (see HITLER, ADOLF [The Beer Hall Putsch]). In 1938, Great Britain, Italy, France, and Germany signed an agreement at Munich to hand Czechoslovakia's Sudetenland over to Germany (see MUNICH AGREEMENT).

Before the rise of the Nazi Party, Munich was as peaceful as a village and as rich in opportunities as a great metropolis. The Isar River rolled rapidly from a spring under blue glacier ice toward the Danube River. Along the banks of the Isar were many gardens with waterfalls, brooks, and miniature lakes.

Munich lies less than 100 miles (160 kilometers) from Brenner Pass in the Alps on the border between Austria and Italy. The location of Munich has made the city a meeting place of northern and southern Europe.

Industries. Munich has long been famous for the production of stained glass for church windows. The city also makes bells, chiefly for churches. Bells cast in the foundries of Munich have been sent to many lands.

Munich has been successful in the production of lithographing and engraving work. Other important manufactures include chinaware, delicate optical instruments, and mechanical-drawing tools. Beer is the city's most important export.

Important Buildings. The three most famous buildings in Munich are the Cathedral, the Palace, and the German Museum. But beautiful palaces, churches, and public buildings can be found throughout the city. The German Museum is one of the most famous museums in the world for exhibits in technology and science. The imposing State Library contains over a million books and more than 50,000 manuscripts. The National Theater, one of the largest theaters in Germany, was bombed and destroyed during World War II. It was completely restored after five years of labor. The $15 million building was reopened officially in 1963.

Three famous museums were almost destroyed by World War II bombings. They were the old Pinakothek, the new Pinakothek, and the Glyptothek. Some of the valuable paintings and sculptures in these museums were saved, reassembled, and exhibited after the war.

Ludwig-Maximilian University in Munich has about

25,000 students, and a library of over 700,000 volumes. Founded in 1471, the university was moved to Munich from Landshut in 1826.

History. Munich was founded in 1158 by Duke Henry the Lion. In 1181, the Emperor Frederick Barbarossa deposed Prince Henry and gave the city to a prince of the House of Wittelsbach. The Wittelsbachs ruled Munich and the surrounding country from that day to the end of World War I. From 1919 to the end of World War II, the history of Munich was the story of how the Nazi party grew and rose to power (see NAZISM). The Allies bombed much of the city during the war. After the war, Munich was the largest city in the United States zone of occupation. JAMES K. POLLOCK

MUNICH AGREEMENT forced Czechoslovakia to give up the Sudetenland, part of its territory, to Nazi Germany. As a result, Germany got a fifth of Czechoslovakia's land, 800,000 Czechs, over 3 million persons of German descent, and most of the country's industries. The agreement was drawn up in Munich, Germany, on Sept. 29, 1938, by Adolf Hitler of Germany, Neville Chamberlain of Great Britain, Édouard Daladier of France, and Benito Mussolini of Italy. It was signed the next day.

The Munich Agreement set up an international commission to mark off the new boundaries. People in some of the disputed areas were given the right to choose between the Czechoslovakian and German governments. When the commission drew the frontiers, more land passed into Germany's hands than the agreement provided. Germany soon took over all Czechoslovakia.

Britain and France believed that the Munich Agreement would keep Europe at peace. Neville Chamberlain, the Prime Minister of Britain, declared that the Munich Agreement had brought "peace for our time."

Bildagentur Mauritius from Van Cleve Photography

Munich, Germany, has many historic churches and palaces, as well as modern buildings erected since the end of World War II.

767

MUNICIPAL GOVERNMENT

Hitler said that the Sudetenland was "the last territorial claim I have to make in Europe." He had made it a point to "repatriate" all German-speaking people. There seemed to be some hope that Hitler's claims might end at this point. But German troops invaded Poland on Sept. 1, 1939, starting World War II.

The Munich Agreement was one of the worst of the tragic blunders that led up to the war. British and American cartoonists made Chamberlain, with his ever-present umbrella, the symbol of the Munich Agreement and of appeasement.　　　　　NORMAN D. PALMER

MUNICIPAL GOVERNMENT. See CITY GOVERNMENT.

MUNITIONS. See AMMUNITION; KRUPP.

MUÑOZ MARÍN, LUIS (1898-1980), served from 1949 until 1965 as the first elected governor of Puerto Rico. He was elected to Puerto Rico's Senate in 1964 and in 1968. Muñoz Marín founded the Popular Democratic Party, and was its leader until he resigned in 1968 (see PUERTO RICO [History]).

Muñoz Marín was born in San Juan, and educated in the United States. He was elected to the Puerto Rican legislature in 1932. Muñoz Marín won popularity for his support of social and economic reform. He promoted low-cost housing and land reform, and brought industries to the island. In 1952, he helped make Puerto Rico a commonwealth of the United States. JAIME BENÍTEZ

MUNRO, HECTOR HUGH (1870-1916), was a British writer who wrote under the pen name SAKI. Munro is best known for his witty short stories. Many of the stories satirize British society of the early 1900's. Munro's stories were published in *Reginald* (1904), *The Chronicles of Clovis* (1911), *Beasts and Super-Beasts* (1914), and *The Square Egg* (published in 1924, after his death). Munro also wrote two novels. *The Unbearable Bassing-*

ton (1912) is an entertaining satire on British society. In *When William Came* (1913), Munro predicted the coming of World War I and English reactions to it. *The Complete Works of Saki* was published in 1976.

Munro was born in Akyab (now Sittwe), Burma. He was taken to England when he was two years old, and became a well-known London journalist. Munro was killed in battle in France during World War I. JOHN ESPEY

MUNSEE INDIANS, *MUN see*, were a division of the Delaware Indian tribe. They lived around the headwaters of the Delaware River and along the western bank of the Hudson River. White settlers drove them from the Delaware River region about 1740, and the Munsee settled along the Susquehanna River. They later scattered throughout parts of the United States and Canada.

See also DELAWARE INDIANS.

MUNSELL COLOR SYSTEM. See COLOR (Color Systems; diagram).

MUNSEY, *MUN see*, **FRANK ANDREW** (1854-1925), was a pioneer publisher of low-priced magazines and newspapers. He had very little education or financial backing, but made a fortune of nearly $20 million. He started *Munsey's Magazine* in 1889. The magazine's circulation reached 650,000 by 1900. Munsey built a successful grocery chain and used his profits to buy 17 newspapers. He often bought competing newspapers and combined them into one publication. Munsey was born in Mercer, Me.　　　JOHN ELDRIDGE DREWRY

MUNTJAC. See DEER (Asian and European Deer).

MUNTZ METAL. See BRASS.

MUON. See MESON.

MURAL is a picture or design that decorates a wall. Most murals decorate walls inside buildings, but some are on ceilings or outside walls. An interior mural should harmonize with the style and scale of the room. The artist must plan the pattern so that the room's doors,

Fratelli Fabbri Editori, Milan, Italy

Biblical Scenes painted by the Italian artist Giotto cover the walls of the Scrovegni, or Arena, Chapel in Padua, Italy. These beautiful frescoes, which date from the early 1300's, rank among the masterpieces of Italian mural painting.

© 1976 Cityarts Workshop, Inc.

Exterior Murals were a popular American art form during the 1960's and 1970's. The mural shown above, called *Women Hold Up Half the World*, is on a building wall in New York City. It portrays some of the many roles played by women in modern society.

and architecture as well as gods and mythical heroes.

Giotto, a great Italian artist of the 1300's, painted many beautiful frescoes in churches. His works picture Biblical events dramatically and with a vivid natural quality. During the 1400's and 1500's, such famous Italian artists as Andrea Mantegna, Masaccio, Michelangelo, Piero della Francesca, and Raphael painted detailed, lifelike frescoes.

During the 1900's, such Mexican painters as José Clemente Orozco and Diego Rivera created murals showing scenes of Mexican history and legends. American artists, including Thomas Hart Benton, Philip Guston, Reginald Marsh, and Ben Shahn, decorated government buildings with murals of Americans at work and at home. During the 1960's, a number of American artists painted murals to express their views of a good community and to show their concern about such social problems as war, discrimination, and poverty.   REED KAY

There is a separate biography in WORLD BOOK for each painter mentioned in this article. See also LATIN AMERICA (picture); MEXICO (Art); MOSAIC; VATICAN CITY (picture).

MURANO. See GLASS (The Middle Ages).

MURASAKI SHIKIBU (A.D. 975?-1031?), or LADY MURASAKI, is the most famous writer of early Japanese literature. Her long novel *The Tale of Genji* is generally considered the greatest work of Japanese fiction.

The novel begins with the romantic adventures of Prince Genji, the "Shining Prince." He exemplifies courtliness and the unique Japanese sensitivity to nature. The tone grows somber as the book follows the next two generations of Genji's family. The themes of death, frustration in love, and a Buddhist sense of human impermanence dominate the story. Lady Murasaki flawlessly handled the large cast of characters in this complex novel. She portrayed the characters with a psychological realism that did not appear in Western literature until centuries later.

Lady Murasaki was one of several gifted writers who served as ladies-in-waiting to Japanese empresses during the 1000's. In addition to *The Tale of Genji*, she wrote poetry and a diary famous for its witty portrayal of her contemporaries.   MARK MORRIS

MURAT, *myoo RAH*, **JOACHIM** (1771?-1815), the most famous French cavalry commander under Napoleon I, ruled Naples as King Joachim I from 1808 to 1814. He served with Napoleon Bonaparte, and distinguished himself in Italy in 1796. Napoleon made him a general in 1799 for defeating the Turks in Egypt. Murat's cavalry attacks played an important part in Napoleon's victories at Austerlitz, Jena, and Friedland (see NEY, MICHEL).

He shared the misfortunes of the 1812 Russian campaign with Napoleon. Murat deserted Napoleon when he was defeated at Leipzig in 1813. But, when Napoleon escaped from his prison on the island of Elba in 1815, Murat tried to win all Italy for him. The Austrians, however, defeated him. After the Battle of Waterloo in 1815, Murat tried to recover his kingdom of Naples, but he was quickly captured, condemned, and executed.

Murat was born in Bastide, Lot, France. In 1800, he married Napoleon's sister Caroline.   VERNON J. PURYEAR

windows, and furniture do not break into the picture unpleasantly. Most murals are painted on a surface. Some are made of small pieces of glass, stone, or other material. These murals are called *mosaics*. This article discusses painted murals.

Most murals are painted directly on a plastered wall. In a technique called *fresco painting*, the artist paints while the plaster is still damp. An artist may also paint on dry plaster using a method known as *secco painting*. In some cases, the artist paints the picture on a canvas using oil paint or acrylic paint. The canvas is then cemented to the wall by a process called *marouflage*. See FRESCO; PAINTING (Materials and Techniques).

Artists have painted murals for many kinds of buildings. Prehistoric artists decorated caves with images of the animals that they hunted. Murals in ancient Egyptian tombs show people and possessions that were important to the owners of the tombs. Ancient Roman artists decorated homes with murals showing gardens

MURDER. When one person intentionally kills another without legal justification or excuse, the crime is called *murder*. The clearest example of this is a case where one person deliberately kills another because of hatred, envy, or greed. But there are also situations where a killing is considered murder even when no specific intent to kill exists. For example, a person who accidentally kills someone while committing a robbery is guilty of murder. The fact that the person is committing a serious crime indicates that he or she has a reckless disregard for human life and safety. This takes the place of actual intent to kill. The penalty for murder is a long prison sentence or death. However, many national, state, and provincial governments have abolished the death penalty.

A killing that has legal justification is called *justifiable homicide*. For example, a killing in self-defense or the killing of a person who was committing a robbery would be a justifiable homicide. The law regards a purely accidental killing as an *excusable homicide*. For example, if a pedestrian steps in front of a carefully driven automobile and is killed, the accident would be considered an excusable homicide.

When a person in a fit of anger intentionally kills another person after the victim has provoked the attack, the killing is called *voluntary manslaughter*. When a person's death results from reckless driving or other extreme negligence on the part of the killer, the offense is called *involuntary manslaughter*. The penalties in most cases of manslaughter are less severe than those for murder. FRED E. INBAU

See also CAPITAL PUNISHMENT; CRIME; HOMICIDE; MANSLAUGHTER.

MURDOCH, IRIS (1919-   ), is a British author of witty and complex novels. The meanings of her symbolic situations and dialogue are often difficult to understand. Murdoch lectured in philosophy at Oxford University from 1948 to 1962, and her interest in philosophic issues is apparent in all her works.

Jean Iris Murdoch was born in Dublin. Her first book was *Sartre, Romantic Rationalist* (1953), a study of the French philosopher Jean-Paul Sartre. In her first novel, *Under the Net* (1954), the leading character has a series of adventures during which he tries to discover some meaning in his life. Murdoch's other novels include *The Flight from the Enchanter* (1955), *The Sandcastle* (1957), *The Bell* (1958), *A Severed Head* (1961), *The Italian Girl* (1964), *The Red and the Green* (1965), *A Fairly Honourable Defeat* (1970), and *The Sacred and Profane Love Machine* (1974). JOHN ESPEY

MURDOCK, WILLIAM. See GAS (First Uses of Manufactured Gas).

MURFREESBORO, BATTLE OF. See CIVIL WAR (The War in the West; table: Major Battles).

MURIATIC ACID. See HYDROCHLORIC ACID.

MURILLO, BARTOLOMÉ ESTEBAN (1618-1682), was an important Spanish painter of the 1600's. He is considered the best interpreter of the gentle, optimistic side of Christianity. Murillo is known for the warmth and humanity of his religious paintings, especially those of the Holy Family and the Immaculate Conception.

Murillo's painting *The Immaculate Conception* is reproduced on the opposite page. It shows the delicate beauty and fine shadings of light and atmosphere that characterize his work. Like many of Murillo's paintings, this work has a gentleness that borders on sentimentality. The picture's complex spiraling composition and careful detail are typical of Murillo's work. Murillo also painted dignified and flattering portraits, and scenes of daily life, especially scenes showing children.

Murillo was born in Seville. His paintings before 1645 were influenced by the realism and dark coloring found in the work of the Spanish artists Jusepe de Ribera and Francisco Zurbarán. Later, influenced by Flemish and Venetian masters, Murillo became more concerned with problems of light, color, and atmosphere. In 1645, the Franciscan order in Seville gave Murillo his first important commission. Within 15 years, he was Spain's most important painter. MARILYN STOKSTAD

MURMANSK, *moor MAHNSK* (pop. 317,000), is Russia's chief port on the Arctic Ocean. It is the world's largest city north of the Arctic Circle. The warm Gulf Stream keeps the harbor free of ice the year round. Murmansk stands on the far-northern Kola Peninsula. For location, see RUSSIA (political map).

The city is a fishing and shipbuilding center. It has fish canneries, metal and woodworking factories, net and barrel factories, and refrigerating plants. Exporters ship fish, lumber, and minerals from the city. A polar research station is located there. A railroad links Murmansk with Leningrad. Murmansk was founded in 1915. THEODORE SHABAD

MURPHY, AUDIE (1924-1971), won fame as the most decorated United States soldier of World War II. He received 24 medals from the U.S. government, 3 from France, and 1 from Belgium. He later became a motion-picture actor.

Audie Leon Murphy was born in rural Kingston, Tex., near Greenville. He enlisted in the Army in 1942 and was appointed a second lieutenant in combat in 1944. Murphy served in North Africa and Europe. On Jan. 26, 1945, German forces attacked his unit near Colmar, France.

U.S. Army
Audie Murphy

Murphy jumped on a burning tank destroyer and used its machine gun to kill about 50 enemy troops. He received the Medal of Honor, the nation's highest military award.

Murphy began his motion-picture career about three years after being discharged from the Army in 1945. His films included *The Red Badge of Courage* (1951) and *To Hell and Back* (1955). Murphy died in an airplane crash. SAMUEL J. ZISKIND

MURPHY, EMILY GOWAN (1868-1933), was a Canadian social reformer and author. She helped win legal and political rights for Canadian women.

In the early 1900's, Murphy helped establish a court in Edmonton, Alta., that handled cases involving women. From 1916 to 1931, Murphy served as the court's first judge and as the first woman magistrate in the British Empire. During that period, she wrote a book about drug abuse, *The Black Candle* (1922), that

Murillo's Painting *The Immaculate Conception* is one of the best examples of the spiritual quality of much of his work. The picture also shows how Murillo sometimes emphasized sentimentality in his paintings. This picture was painted for the Seville Cathedral in Spain to honor the Roman Catholic doctrine of the Virgin Mary's freedom from the stain of original sin.

helped lead to the passage of drug laws in Canada.

In 1927, Murphy led a group of five women in a court battle to determine whether women were "persons" under the British North America Act, which serves as Canada's constitution. The Privy Council in England, the highest judicial authority in the British Empire, ruled in the women's favor in 1929. This ruling enabled women to serve in the Canadian Senate.

Murphy wrote several books under the pen name of "Janey Canuck." These books included *The Impressions of Janey Canuck Abroad* (1901) and *Janey Canuck in the West* (1910). Murphy was born in Cookstown, Ont. PATRICIA MONK

MURPHY, FRANK (1890-1949), of the United States, was a statesman and jurist noted for his liberal views. He served as a Detroit municipal court judge from 1922 to 1930 and as mayor of Detroit from 1930 to 1933. He was governor general of the Philippines from 1933 to 1935, U.S. high commissioner to the Philippines from 1935 to 1936, and governor of Michigan in 1937 and 1938. President Franklin D. Roosevelt made Murphy, a Democrat, U.S. attorney general in 1939. In 1940, the President appointed Murphy to the Supreme Court of the United States. Murphy was born in Harbor Beach, Mich. SIDNEY GLAZER

MURPHY, GEORGE LLOYD (1902-   ), a one-time motion picture and Broadway star, served as a United States senator from California from 1964 to 1971. As an actor, Murphy was probably best known for his dancing roles. In politics, he became identified with the conservative wing of the Republican Party.

Murphy was born in New Haven, Conn., and attended Yale University for two years. He started in show business as a dancer in the 1920's, and made his first motion picture in 1934. In 1952, he went into public relations and became increasingly active in politics. Murphy helped plan the 1956 and 1960 Republican National Conventions. CAROL L. THOMPSON

MURPHY, JOHN BENJAMIN (1857-1916), an American surgeon, was internationally famous as a teacher and a doctor. Dr. William Mayo once described him as "the surgical genius of our generation." Murphy's battle to establish appendicitis as a surgical disease contributed greatly to surgical progress. He developed new techniques in surgery of the blood vessels, joints, and tendons. He invented the "Murphy button" in 1892, a device that linked together the severed ends of intestines. It led to important advances in intestinal surgery.

From 1895 to 1916, he was chief surgeon at Mercy Hospital, Chicago. He was a professor of surgery at Rush Medical College and Northwestern University. He was born in Appleton, Wis. NOAH D. FABRICANT

MURPHY, WILLIAM P. See MINOT, GEORGE.

MURRAY, GILBERT (1866-1957), a British classical scholar, gained fame for his translations of Greek plays. He wrote poetry and plays of his own, and books on the Greek dramatists Aeschylus, Euripides, and Aristophanes. His works include *The Classical Tradition in Poetry* (1927) and *Hellenism and the Modern World* (1953). Murray was born in Sydney, Australia. He became a professor of Greek at Glasgow University, and later at Oxford. He was a leader in movements supporting the League of Nations. JOSEPH E. BAKER

MURRAY, JAMES (1719?-1794), was a British soldier who became the first British governor of Canada. He was born in Sussex, England, and went to America in 1757. He fought the French at Louisbourg in 1758.

Murray served as one of the three brigadiers under General James Wolfe in the successful battle against the French at Quebec. After the victory, Murray was left in command of the city. He later defended it against a French army led by General François de Lévis.

Detail of an oil portrait by an unknown artist; Public Archives of Canada

James Murray

Murray was made governor of Quebec in 1760. Three years later, when French rule was ended, he became governor of all Canada. He had to face many problems in the relations between the English and the Indians and also between the French Canadians and English officers and merchants. Some of the men working under him accused him of favoring the French. He was recalled to England in 1766, but was cleared of all charges. W. B. WILLCOX

MURRAY, SIR JOHN (1841-1914), was a British naturalist, oceanographer, and deep-sea explorer. He specialized in studying the ocean bottom. He was one of the naturalists on the expedition of H.M.S. *Challenger*, which made a scientific study of oceans and ocean bottoms from 1872 to 1876. Afterward, Murray edited the expedition's 50 volumes of scientific reports. He also wrote *The Depths of the Ocean* (1912) and *The Ocean* (1913), considered a classic in its field.

Murray was born in Cobourg, Ontario. He was graduated from the University of Edinburgh. He made a notable study of Scottish *lochs* (lakes). JOHN EDWARDS CASWELL

MURRAY, PHILIP (1886-1952), succeeded John L. Lewis as president of the Congress of Industrial Organizations (CIO) in 1940, and held that post until his death. He helped establish World War II government labor policies. He saw to it that the CIO unions kept their "no-strike" pledge during the war. He also served on the National Defense Mediation Board.

Murray rose to his CIO position after 36 years as a labor union organizer and leader. He advanced in the United Mine Workers to the post of vice-president, which he held from 1920 to 1942. Murray ended a long friendship with John L. Lewis soon after he succeeded him as president of the CIO.

When the CIO began organizing the steel industry in 1935, Murray became chairman of the organizing committee. He served as the first president of the United Steelworkers of America from 1942 to 1952. In the late 1940's, he led a successful fight to oust Communist-dominated unions from the CIO. He led the steelworkers in three national strikes after World War II. Pensions and union security were two of the major issues.

Murray was born in Blantyre, Scotland, the son of a coal miner. In 1902, he moved to the United States with his family, and began working in the mines at the age of 16. He got into an argument with a mine foreman soon after he started, and lost his job. The other miners went on strike in sympathy with Murray, but lost the strike. Murray served as a member of Woodrow Wilson's War Labor Board and on the National Bituminous Coal Production Committee during World War I. He was the co-author, with Morris L. Cooke, of *Organized Labor and Production* (1940).   JACK BARBASH

MURRAY RIVER is the largest waterway in Australia. It is also one of the most important sources of irrigation in the country. The Murray River system includes the Darling, Lachlan, and Murrumbidgee rivers, and drains an area larger than that of France and Spain combined. For location, see AUSTRALIA (physical map).

The Murray rises in the Australian Alps near the eastern boundary of Victoria. It flows northwestward and forms the boundary between Victoria and New South Wales. It then crosses eastern South Australia and empties into Encounter Bay, south of Adelaide. The Murray River is 1,600 miles (2,570 kilometers) long. With the Darling River, it forms a system 2,310 miles (3,718 kilometers) long.

A system of dams helps irrigate about 1½ million acres (610,000 hectares) of land. The dams were built under the Murray River Agreement made in 1915 by New South Wales, South Australia, and Victoria. The system, which includes the Hume Dam, permits ships to sail about 600 miles (960 kilometers) up the river. The Snowy Mountains Scheme includes 16 large dams and several small ones. It directs water into the Murray and Murrumbidgee rivers. It provides hydroelectric power for Victoria and New South Wales, and enough water to irrigate about 1,000 square miles (2,600 square kilometers).   C. M. H. CLARK

See also RIVER (chart: Longest Rivers).

MURRAY STATE UNIVERSITY. See UNIVERSITIES AND COLLEGES (table).

MURRE, *mur*, is the name of a group of sea birds in the auk family, related to the guillemot. Great colonies of murres live on rocky coasts of the North Atlantic and North Pacific. Thousands of the birds crowd the rock ledges during the breeding season. The female murre hatches a single egg, which it lays on the bare stone. The murre is from 16 to 17 inches (41 to 43 centimeters) long. It has short wings. The bird is brownish-black above, and white on the breast and throat.

The large eggs vary from white to blue and green. Black, brown, or lavender spots usually mark them. The eggs are pointed, and roll in a circle when moved.

Scientific Classification. Murres are members of the auk family, *Alcidae*. The common murre is genus *Uria*, species *U. aalge*.   ALEXANDER WETMORE

MURROW, EDWARD R. (1908-1965), was an American radio and television broadcaster. He won fame during World War II (1939-1945) for his on-the-scene radio broadcasts describing German bombing attacks on London. His listeners in America could hear the bombs exploding in the background.

Egbert Roscoe Murrow was born near Greensboro, N.C. He changed his first name to Edward while in college. Murrow became the European director of the Columbia Broadcasting System (CBS) in 1937. He turned to radio newscasting shortly before World War II.

Murrow narrated the television program, "See It Now," from 1951 to 1958. He started a new style of television newscasting with on-the-scene camera reporting that told about important issues in everyday

terms. In the most famous show of the series, Murrow attacked Joseph R. McCarthy. McCarthy was a U.S. senator whose investigations of Communist influence in the government had caused a national controversy (see McCARTHY, JOSEPH R.). From 1953 to 1959, Murrow narrated "Person to Person," a TV program that featured interviews with famous persons in their homes. He served as director of the U.S. Information Agency from 1961 to 1964.   ALEXANDER KENDRICK

Edward R. Murrow Foundation

Edward R. Murrow

MURRUMBIDGEE RIVER, *MUR um BIJ ee*, is an Australian stream that flows into the Murray River, north of the Victoria border. The stream rises in the Australian Alps and flows northwest for about 1,350 miles (2,173 kilometers) across the southern part of New South Wales. A system of dams, which was built under the Murray River Agreement in 1915, increased the importance of the river. See also AUSTRALIA (Rivers); MURRAY RIVER.   C. M. H. CLARK

MUSCAT, *MUS kat*, or MASQAT (pop. 9,973), is the capital of Oman, a country in Arabia. The city lies on Muscat Bay in the Gulf of Oman. Rugged mountains separate it from the peninsula's interior. Muscat is the country's administrative center. It is important because of its location at the entrance to the Persian Gulf. For location, see OMAN (map).   DOUGLAS D. CRARY

MUSCAT AND OMAN. See OMAN.

MUSCATEL. See WINE (The Six Main Classes of Wine).

Fish and Wildlife Service

A Fledgling Murre nestles between its mother's feet on a rocky nesting place where the sea birds gather.

MUSCLE is the tissue that makes it possible for a person or animal to move from place to place. Muscles make the heart beat, force blood to circulate, and push food through the digestive system.

The human body has more than 600 muscles. These muscles are usually grouped into two main types—*skeletal* and *smooth*. Skeletal muscles are attached to the skeleton, causing the bones to move. For example, several groups of skeletal muscles move the arm bones. Smooth muscles are found in the blood vessels, digestive system, and other internal organs. A third type of muscle, called *cardiac* (heart) muscle, resembles both skeletal and smooth muscles.

Skeletal Muscles make up a large part of the arms, legs, chest, abdomen, neck, and face. They vary greatly in size, depending on the type of job they do. For example, eye muscles are small and fairly weak, but thigh muscles are large and strong.

All muscles are made up of cells called *muscle fibers*. Skeletal muscle fibers differ in appearance from smooth muscle fibers. A fiber of skeletal muscle is long and slender. It may have many *nuclei* (structures that direct the fiber's activities). The fibers lie parallel to each other in bundles. Under a microscope, they show alternating light and dark bands called *striations*. For this reason, skeletal muscles are also called *striated muscles*.

Skeletal muscles are attached to bones in different ways. For example, the ends of most face muscles are attached directly to bones. But the ends of other skeletal muscles have white, tough, flexible cords of tissue, called *tendons*, that attach the muscles to bones.

To do its job, both ends of a skeletal muscle must be attached to the skeleton. The end of the muscle that normally does not move and is closest to the central part of the body is called the *origin*. The other end, called the *insertion*, is attached to the bone it moves. A *flexor* is a muscle that bends a joint and brings a limb closer to the body. An *extensor* muscle does the opposite. For example, flexor muscles of the upper arm bend the elbow, and extensors straighten the arm.

Skeletal muscles contract rapidly when a nerve *stimu-lates* them (causes them to react). Skeletal muscles usually move *voluntarily* (under conscious control), but they also may move *involuntarily* (without conscious control). For example, involuntary movement occurs when a person jerks his hand away from a hot object before he can think about doing so.

Skeletal muscles must be stimulated by a nerve or they will not operate. When a person suffers a nerve or spinal cord injury, paralysis may result.

Through exercise, a person can make his muscle fibers grow bigger, making an entire muscle larger. For example, the biceps of the upper arm can be enlarged by exercise. Too much exercise may *strain* (stretch or tear) the muscle fibers. That is why many persons may experience soreness after physical activities such as gardening or playing baseball or tennis.

Smooth Muscles differ from skeletal muscles in structure, location, and the way they contract. A smooth muscle fiber contains only one nucleus, and contracts more slowly and rhythmically than a skeletal muscle fiber. The walls of the stomach and intestines have sheets of smooth muscles arranged in circular and lengthwise patterns. These muscles contract slowly and rhythmically to move food along for digestion. The smooth muscles in blood vessels can relax to make the vessel openings wide, or contract to make them narrow.

Smooth muscles do not always have to be stimulated directly by a nerve to work. Certain body chemicals, called *hormones*, can make smooth muscles contract. For example, fear or excitement causes special nerve fibers to release hormones called *epinephrine* (adrenalin) and *norepinephrine* (noradrenalin). These hormones reduce the number of contractions of intestinal muscles until the movements finally stop. At the same time, they cause smooth muscles in the arteries of the intestines and skin to contract, reducing the flow of blood to those parts. As a result, more blood flows to the brain and skeletal muscles. Smooth muscles cannot be controlled voluntarily. Because of this, they sometimes are called *involuntary muscles*.

Cardiac Muscle (heart muscle) has striations like skeletal muscles, but it cannot be controlled voluntarily. A special regulator in the heart, called the *sinoatrial node* (*S-A node*), gives off rhythmic stimulations that cause heart muscle to contract, or beat. For further information on the heart, its parts, and how they work, see HEART.

How Muscles Work. Skeletal muscles must be stimulated by nerves. Smooth muscles are stimulated by a special set of nerves that belong to the *autonomic nervous system*, and by hormones (see NERVOUS SYSTEM). A person usually is unaware of the normal contractions of smooth and skeletal muscles. But when these contractions become severe or prolonged, a condition called *cramps* results.

Many scientific studies have been made to determine why muscles contract. According to the *sliding filament* theory, muscle cells are made up of long, parallel chains of protein molecules that can slide over each other. If the muscle cell is stimulated, the molecular chains slide over one another and the cell contracts.

Like all living cells, muscle fibers need energy to work. They get the energy from food. Special structures in the cell, called *enzymes*, break down the food to release the energy. The most important food sources for

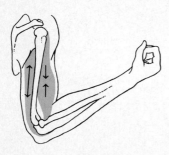
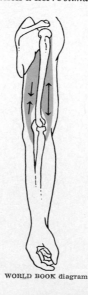

Most Muscles Work in Pairs. For example, when the biceps muscle in the front of the upper arm contracts, the triceps in the back of the arm relaxes, *above left*. The contraction of the biceps bends the arm toward the shoulder. When the triceps contracts, the biceps relaxes and the arm straightens, *above right*.

WORLD BOOK diagram

THE MUSCULAR SYSTEM

The External Skeletal Muscles

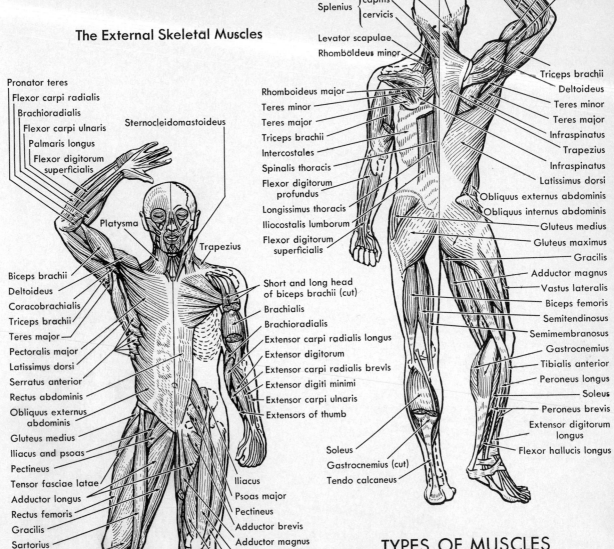

Pronator teres
Flexor carpi radialis
Brachioradialis
Flexor carpi ulnaris
Palmaris longus
Flexor digitorum superficialis

Sternocleidomastoideus

Platysma

Trapezius

Biceps brachii
Deltoideus
Coracobrachialis
Triceps brachii
Teres major
Pectoralis major
Latissimus dorsi
Serratus anterior
Rectus abdominis
Obliquus externus abdominis
Gluteus medius
Iliacus and psoas
Pectineus
Tensor fasciae latae
Adductor longus
Rectus femoris
Gracilis
Sartorius
Vastus medialis
Gastrocnemius
Soleus
Tibialis anterior
Flexor digitorum longus

Short and long head of biceps brachii (cut)
Brachialis
Brachioradialis
Extensor carpi radialis longus
Extensor digitorum
Extensor carpi radialis brevis
Extensor digiti minimi
Extensor carpi ulnaris
Extensors of thumb

Iliacus
Psoas major
Pectineus
Adductor brevis
Adductor magnus
Rectus femoris
Vastus lateralis
Vastus medialis
Tibialis anterior
Extensor digitorum longus
Extensor hallucis longus
Peroneus tertius

Venter occipitalis
Splenius
Splenius { capitis
cervicis
Levator scapulae
Rhomboideus minor

Rhomboideus major
Teres minor
Teres major
Triceps brachii
Intercostales
Spinalis thoracis
Flexor digitorum profundus
Longissimus thoracis
Iliocostalis lumborum
Flexor digitorum superficialis

Extensor carpi radialis brevis
Extensor carpi ulnaris
Extensor digitorum
Brachioradialis
Biceps brachii
Brachialis

Triceps brachii
Deltoideus
Teres minor
Teres major
Infraspinatus
Trapezius
Infraspinatus
Latissimus dorsi
Obliquus externus abdominis
Obliquus internus abdominis
Gluteus medius
Gluteus maximus
Gracilis
Adductor magnus
Vastus lateralis
Biceps femoris
Semitendinosus
Semimembranosus
Gastrocnemius
Tibialis anterior
Peroneus longus
Soleus
Peroneus brevis
Extensor digitorum longus
Flexor hallucis longus

Soleus
Gastrocnemius (cut)
Tendo calcaneus

TYPES OF MUSCLES

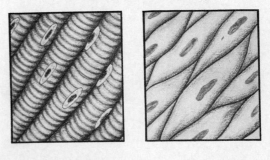

Skeletal   Smooth

energy are fats and *carbohydrates* (sugars and starches). Some of the energy escapes as heat, but the rest is captured to make a special "high energy" substance called *ATP* (adenosine triphosphate). This compound stores the energy and releases it when the fiber needs energy to do work.

All muscle fibers produce wastes, such as *lactic acid,* as they work. If a muscle works very hard, these wastes collect in the muscle. As a result, the fibers lose some of their ability to contract, and the muscle *fatigues* (becomes tired). Then the muscle must rest so that the body can remove the wastes.   GORDON FARRELL

Related Articles in WORLD BOOK include:

Convulsions	Human Body	Tendon
Cramp	(Trans-Vision)	Tetany
Diaphragm	Sphincter	Tongue

See also *Muscular System* in the RESEARCH GUIDE/INDEX, Volume 22, for a *Reading and Study Guide.*

MUSCLE SENSE, or CONSCIOUS PROPRIOCEPTION, is one of two senses that tells a person what position parts of his body are in. The other sense is sight. As a person walks down the street, he knows the position of his legs without looking at them. *Proprioceptors* (nerves) in the joints, muscles, and tendons of his legs are sensitive to pressure and tension. The proprioceptors send information about the state of the joints, muscles, and tendons to the brain. The brain combines the information, enabling the person to sense the position of his body and to influence movement. There are proprioceptors for most parts of the body.   W. B. YOUMANS

MUSCLE SHOALS is an area on the Tennessee River in northwestern Alabama. The Muscle Shoals rapids lie between the cities of Florence, Tuscumbia, and Sheffield. The town of Muscle Shoals lies east of the rapids. Congress created the Tennessee Valley Authority in 1933. The TVA controls two dams at Muscle Shoals. Wilson lies at the west end of the area, and Wheeler, about 15 miles (24 kilometers) east. The dams raise the water level above the rapids and form lakes that hold the season's rainfall. The dams have improved river navigation because the water in the lakes insures a more nearly uniform depth of water during wet and dry weather. Wilson and Wheeler provide hydroelectric power. Wheeler also controls floods.

Two nitrate plants were completed at Muscle Shoals in 1918, under the National Defense Act of 1916. They were built because it was feared World War I might cut off nitrate from Chile.   CHARLES G. SUMMERSELL

See also DAM; TENNESSEE VALLEY AUTHORITY.

MUSCOVITE. See MICA; MINERAL (color picture).

MUSCULAR DYSTROPHY, *DIS troh fee,* is any one of several serious muscle diseases that are *inherited* (passed on from parents to children). Muscular dystrophy causes muscles to become weak and waste away. It usually affects *skeletal muscles* (muscles that move bones), such as those of the arms and legs.

Muscular dystrophy is caused by *genes* that do not work normally. Genes are the tiny, basic units of heredity. They are located in cells, where they direct the development of living things. Scientists do not completely understand the changes produced in the muscles by the abnormal genes. As a result, no effective treatment has yet been developed for muscular dystrophy.

Doctors recognize various kinds of muscular dystrophy. The classifications are based on (1) the way the disease was inherited; (2) the age of the patient when the disease began; (3) the muscles most badly damaged; (4) the rate at which the disease develops; and (5) other disorders that develop during the disease.

Pseudohypertrophic muscular dystrophy is the most common kind in childhood. The word *pseudohypertrophic* means *false enlargement.* The name refers to the way the patient's calf muscles seem to get bigger. The muscles actually waste away, but they seem to grow because of the fat that collects in them. Pseudohypertrophic muscular dystrophy usually begins before the age of 5. It eventually affects most body muscles, including those that make the heart and lungs function. A patient usually is confined to a wheelchair by the age of 12 and dies before the age of 20. This form of muscular dystrophy is inherited as a *sex-linked recessive* disease. This means it usually develops only in the boys of a family. It is passed on by females, although females seldom develop it. It is the only one of the four main kinds of muscular dystrophy that is sex-linked.

Facio-scapulo-humeral muscular dystrophy first affects the face, shoulder, and upper arm muscles. Later, it affects almost all the muscles, but it does not progress as rapidly as the pseudohypertrophic type. It begins at about 13 or 14 years of age, but patients may be able to work for 30 or more years afterwards.

Limb-girdle muscular dystrophy first affects the muscles of the hips and shoulders. It also begins at about the age of 13 or 14, and develops at about the same rate as the facio-scapulo-humeral type.

Myotonic muscular dystrophy causes muscles to waste away and prevents them from relaxing normally. For example, after shaking hands, a patient may not be able to loosen his grip right away. Myotonic muscular dystrophy differs from the other forms in another way. That is, the patient may develop certain nonmuscular disorders—such as diabetes mellitus and cataracts—as the muscular disease gets worse. Patients with the myotonic form often do not become disabled until they are 30, 40, or even older.   VICTOR A. McKUSICK

MUSES were nine goddesses of the arts and sciences in Greek mythology. They were the daughters of Zeus, the king of the gods; and Mnemosyne, the goddess of memory. Each muse ruled over a certain art or science. Calliope was the Muse of epic poetry; Erato, love poetry; Euterpe, lyric poetry; Melpomene, tragedy; Thalia, comedy; Clio, history; Urania, astronomy; Polyhymnia, sacred song; and Terpsichore, dance.

The Muses lived on Mount Olympus with their leader, the god Apollo. Like him, the Muses remained young and beautiful forever. They could see into the future, which few other gods could do. They also had the ability to banish all grief and sorrow. The Muses had pleasing, melodic voices and often sang as a chorus. Early Greek writers and artists called on the Muses for inspiration before beginning to work. Any one or all of the Muses could be asked for assistance, even though each governed a special art or science.

Several words come from the Greek word *Mousa,* meaning *Muse.* They include *museum,* which originally meant *temple of the Muses;* and *music,* which meant *art of the Muses.*   C. SCOTT LITTLETON

See also MYTHOLOGY (picture: The Muses).

Museums preserve many interesting and beautiful objects from the past. The exhibit on the left traces the development of aircraft and railroad equipment. The dining room on the right, designed by architect Robert Adam for a London house of the 1760's, is displayed in its original form.

MUSEUM is an institution where artistic and educational materials are exhibited to the public. The materials that a museum has available for observation and study are called a *collection*. A museum's collection may include scientific specimens, works of art, and exhibits and information on history or technology. Museums also provide information for researchers, students, and other members of the community. Various members of a museum's staff prepare materials for display and care for them after they have been put on exhibition.

Most museums in the United States are owned and operated by an association established for that purpose. The association elects a board of directors that decides the overall policy of the museum. Some museums are operated by federal, state, and local governments or by colleges and universities.

Many museums are financed by private donations and government grants. Various associations and corporations also contribute to museums.

Kinds of Museums

There are three main kinds of museums: (1) art museums, (2) history museums, and (3) science and technology museums.

Art Museums preserve and exhibit paintings, sculpture, and other works of art. The collections of some art museums include works from many periods. Famous museums of this type include the Louvre in Paris and the Metropolitan Museum of Art in New York City.

Other museums specialize in art works of one period. The Museum of Modern Art in New York City displays works created since the late 1800's. The Isabella Stewart Gardner Museum in Boston exhibits paintings

Marjorie P. K. Weiser, the contributor of this article, is the coauthor of Museum Adventures *and* Museums, U.S.A.; A History and Guide.

by Italian artists of the Renaissance period, from about 1300 to 1600.

Some museums have collections of only one type of art. For example, the Museum of Navajo Ceremonial Arts in Santa Fe, N. Mex., features sand paintings and other materials used in rituals of the Navajo Indians.

Many art museums have special exhibits in addition to their regular collections. They borrow works of art from individuals or other museums for such special exhibits. The exhibits are usually displayed for several weeks.

History Museums illustrate the life and events of the past. The collections of such museums include documents, furniture, tools, and other materials.

Many city and state governments have historical societies that operate history museums. Most of these museums have exhibits on local history. The Chicago Historical Society features exhibits on Abraham Lincoln's early days in Illinois and the great Chicago fire of 1871.

Other types of history museums include *historic houses* and *historic villages*. Historic houses show how the people of a community lived during a certain period. Mount Vernon, George Washington's home near Arlington, Va., has been restored to its original condition and is open to the public.

Historic villages consist of groups of buildings that have been restored or reconstructed. Henry Ford, one of the first automobile manufacturers, established Greenfield Village near Dearborn, Mich. It includes the one-room schoolhouse he attended and many homes and shops from the 1600's through the 1800's.

Science and Technology Museums have exhibits on the natural sciences and technology. Some natural science museums are called *museums of natural history*. These museums exhibit displays of animals, fossils, plants, rocks, and other objects and organisms found in

Old Sturbridge Village, Sturbridge, Massachusetts

Historic Villages are reconstructions of towns from various periods in history. Old Sturbridge Village, *above*, in Massachusetts shows life in a New England community of the early 1800's.

nature. Most of them, including the National Museum of Natural History in Washington, D.C., have exhibits on ecology and the evolution of man. Many have special exhibits. The Field Museum of Natural History in Chicago, for example, has a reproduction of a forest from the Coal Age, about 300 million years ago.

Many of the exhibits in technology museums are sponsored by corporations and industries. These exhibits explain the operation of various types of machines and industrial methods. Visitors to the Museum of Science and Industry in Chicago can take a guided tour through a realistic reproduction of a coal mine.

The National Air and Space Museum at the Smithsonian Institution in Washington, D.C., has exhibits on the history and science of aviation and space travel. Exhibits include the Wright brothers' first airplane and the Mercury, Gemini, and Apollo spacecraft.

Other Types of Museums feature exhibits on only one subject. The Circus World Museum in Baraboo, Wis., has the world's largest collection of circus wagons. The Baseball Hall of Fame Museum in Cooperstown, N.Y., shows highlights of baseball history and displays the uniforms of famous players. Other specialized museums have exhibits on automobiles, clocks, and dolls.

Museums that display materials from several fields of study are called *general museums*. *Children's* or *junior museums* have exhibits designed to explain the arts and sciences to young people.

Some museums display reproductions or copies of objects. For example, wax museums have life-sized figures sculptured from wax or plastics. Most of these figures are realistic likenesses of important people in history. The figures are dressed in appropriate costumes and placed in lifelike settings. One display at the National Historical Wax Museum in Washington, D.C., shows Betsy Ross sewing the first United States flag.

Functions of Museums

Museums perform three main functions. These institutions (1) acquire new materials, (2) exhibit and care

for materials, and (3) provide various special services.

Acquisition of Materials. Every new object that a museum adds to its collection is called an *acquisition*. Many acquisitions are gifts from people who collect such items as paintings, precious stones, or sculpture.

Sometimes a museum buys a particular item that is needed to fill a gap in an exhibit. Museum employees may find new materials on archaeological expeditions or field trips. Museums also borrow materials or entire exhibits from other museums.

Acquisitions are received by the museum *registrar*, a staff member who records the description of each object. Every acquisition is photographed and given a number. Museum officials determine the value of each object and insure it for that amount.

Exhibition and Care of Materials. Various members of the museum staff prepare the materials for exhibition. The museum *curator* may conduct research to learn more about objects. Museum *conservators* clean, preserve, or restore objects before they are exhibited.

The curator decides how materials are displayed. For example, a new object may be added to an existing exhibit or become part of a special exhibit. It may be hung on a wall or placed in a case. *Designers* build cases and furniture for the displays. They also set up lights and electric wiring. *Preparators* create display backgrounds and prepare materials for exhibit. Every exhibit receives a label that gives visitors some information about it. Descriptions of all objects appear in the museum's catalog as well.

Museums also protect their exhibits from loss or damage. The doors and windows of many museum buildings have alarm systems in addition to locks. Museums keep all exhibit cases locked, and some cases may be connected to alarm systems. Some materials are displayed behind thick velvet ropes or on high platforms. Guards patrol the museum constantly. Museums may use special light bulbs and devices that control humidity and temperature to protect objects from environmental damage.

Special Services. Many museums have an *education department* that gives lectures and classes on the mu-

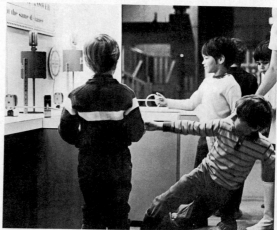

Ontario Science Centre, Toronto, Ontario, Canada

Most Museums offer demonstrations, lectures, and other educational services. The children shown above are working with various devices in an exhibit on weights and pulleys.

Old Sturbridge Village, Sturbridge, Massachusetts

Museum Conservators care for the objects in a museum's collection. This conservator is using a special technique to clean a painting while preparing it for exhibition.

Ashmolean Museum, Oxford, England

Many Art Museums Display Fabrics Called Tapestries, which consist of woven pictures and designs. The tapestry of the 1600's shown above illustrates a Biblical battle scene.

seum's collection. Most museums offer gallery talks, guided tours, and other programs for children and adults. Other activities provided by museums include art festivals, concerts, and hobby workshops. Many museums publish bulletins and pamphlets that describe current and future exhibits. Museums also furnish scholars with research materials and the use of special laboratories and libraries. Some museums serve as places where local artists can exhibit their work.

History

The word *museum* comes from the Greek word *mouseion*. In ancient Greece, the mouseion was the temple of the *Muses*, the goddesses of arts and sciences. In the 200's B.C., the word was used for a library and research area in Alexandria, Egypt.

Early Museums. Throughout history, churches have performed some of the functions of museums. Many worshippers enjoy viewing church furnishings and decorations, including paintings, sculpture, and other art.

During the A.D. 1400's and 1500's, European explorers brought back samples of animal and plant life from North and South America and the Far East. They also brought objects made by craftworkers of those regions. Many Europeans collected such materials and eventually needed an orderly way to display them. Some placed their collections in cabinets that lined the walls of long, narrow rooms called *galleries*. The collections themselves were called *cabinets*.

In the 1500's and 1600's, royal families hired famous artists and craftworkers to create luxurious art objects and furnishings. Today, the Uffizi Gallery in Florence, Italy, and other museums own these collections.

The first public museum, the *Ashmolean*, opened in 1683 at Oxford University in England. The museum featured a collection of *curiosities* (rare or strange ob-

jects) donated by Elias Ashmole, an English scholar.

Museums of the 1700's. In the mid-1700's, a Swedish botanist named Carolus Linnaeus developed a system of classifying plants and animals. For many years, as a result of his work, scientists concentrated more on putting organisms into various groups than on acquiring new knowledge. Collections of scientific specimens were used mainly for classification purposes.

During the late 1700's, scholars began to study and organize large and complex collections of all kinds. Valuable works of art were separated from objects of little artistic worth. At about this time, people began to use the word *museum* to describe a place where collections could be seen and studied.

The demand for public museums grew during the 1700's, a period when people began to believe that education should be available to everyone. In 1759, the British Museum in London opened with exhibits of manuscripts, plant specimens, and curiosities. These materials had once belonged to the collections of kings and noblemen. In 1750, the Palais de Luxembourg was opened on certain days for the public to view the French royal art collection. During the French Revolution (1789-1799), the government moved the royal collection to the Louvre, which became a public museum in 1793.

Early United States Museums. In 1773, the Charleston Library Society opened the first museum in the American Colonies. It featured objects related to the natural history of South Carolina. In the 1780's, Charles Willson Peale, a painter who studied natural history, opened a museum in his Philadelphia home. Peale's museum displayed animal and mineral specimens and portraits of Thomas Jefferson, George Washington, and other heroes of the American Revolution.

In 1866, George Peabody, a Massachusetts banker, gave large sums of money to Harvard and Yale universities for the establishment of science museums. Many colleges and universities then began to use donations from wealthy people to establish museums.

During the mid-1800's, the number of museums in the United States increased rapidly. More than 200 museums had been established during the nation's first 100 years. In 1876, the Centennial Exposition in Philadelphia included exhibits from various parts of the world. These exhibits influenced the construction of an increasing number of museums.

Museums Today. During the 1900's, more museums have been established than ever before. The United States and Canada had more than 5,000 museums in the 1970's.

Several developments have caused the growing public interest in museums. The education level of most people rose during the mid-1900's, and interest in cultural activities also increased. Additional leisure time has given more individuals an opportunity to visit museums. The museums themselves have offered increasingly informative and attractive exhibitions to interest larger numbers of people. Museums also began to offer more educational programs in the mid-1900's. Today, museums serve as community education centers.

Many museums had severe financial problems during the mid-1900's. Some began to charge admission fees, and others shortened their hours. A number sold duplicate or less desirable objects from their collections.

Careers

At one time, volunteers performed many functions in some museums. These institutions now rely on volunteers to perform some tasks, but many museums have enlarged their professional staffs.

Most of the museum jobs described in this article require a college degree. Museums hire men and women with training in such fields as art history, history, and library science. The staffs of many museums also include archaeologists, botanists, geologists, zoologists, and other scientists.

Few schools offer complete training programs for museum work. Some colleges and universities provide courses in museum management and techniques. Many museums offer on-the-job training.   MARJORIE P. K. WEISER

Related Articles in WORLD BOOK include:

MUSEUM OF MODERN ART in New York City is one of the world's leading museums devoted to the collection and exhibition of modern art. Its permanent collection includes thousands of paintings and works of sculpture from the 1880's to the present. The museum's collection covers the major modern art movements. For example, it includes examples of impressionism, post-

impressionism, cubism, surrealism, and abstract expressionism.

The museum collections also include prints, drawings, a representative selection of furniture and other manufactured objects, posters and typographical design, and architectural models and drawings. Every day the museum shows motion pictures from its library of commercial, documentary, educational, and experimental films. It also has a collection of photography from the 1840's to today.

The museum presents a number of exhibitions each year taken from public and private collections in the United States and other countries. It also organizes many shows that tour other museums and educational institutions throughout the world.

The museum also publishes several books each year. Its library has about 40,000 books, periodicals, and catalogs, and a large file of clippings for research and reference. The museum was founded in 1929 and is located at 11 West 53rd Street. It is supported by membership dues, private contributions, admissions, and the sale of books and services.

See also NEW YORK CITY (picture: Museum of Modern Art Sculpture Garden).

MUSEUM OF SCIENCE AND INDUSTRY is an educational institution in Chicago designed to acquaint the public with the basic principles of science, and the uses of science in industry. Its exhibits emphasize current developments in science and industry. They use some historical material to provide a suitable background.

The museum uses no uniform method of display. Each exhibit is designed individually. To make understanding easier, the exhibits emphasize audience participation. Visitors may push a button, or walk into a life-size display and become part of the exhibit. They may take a trip through a life-size coal mine, go aboard a full-sized submarine, and stroll down a 1910 street. They may also watch chicks hatch, see the latest developments in agriculture, and learn the fundamentals of nuclear energy.

The museum is located at 57th Street and Lake Michigan in Chicago's Jackson Park. It is housed in the Fine Arts Building of the World's Columbian Exposition of 1893. This outstanding example of classical architecture was reconstructed at a cost of $8 million to serve its present purpose. The building contains 600,000 square feet (56,000 square meters) of floor space. A small portion of the museum opened in 1933. The major areas opened in 1940. Julius Rosenwald founded the museum (see ROSENWALD, JULIUS).   D. M. MACMASTER

MUSHET, *MUSH et*, **ROBERT FORESTER** (1811-1891), was an English metallurgist. In 1870, he patented a special tungsten steel that had remarkable self-hardening qualities. It was especially suitable for machine tools, because it retained its cutting edge, even when red-hot from friction.

Mushet helped improve the Bessemer process of steelmaking when he discovered that the addition to the molten steel of an iron-manganese alloy called *spiegeleisen* would help recarburize it. This led to an improvement in the strength of the steel (see IRON AND STEEL [The Open-Hearth Furnace; History]).

Mushet was born in Coleford, England. Between 1858 and 1861, he took out about 20 patents on alloys of iron and steel.   RICHARD D. HUMPHREY

MUSHROOM. Mushrooms, or toadstools, which often grow from the ground like small umbrellas, are among the best-known of the plants called *fungi*. They grow in decaying vegetable matter, sometimes hidden under leaves or moss. The name *mushroom*, as well as the old-fashioned term *mushromp*, may come from the French word for moss.

Mushrooms and Toadstools. Botanists do not separate mushrooms and toadstools into two different groups. People generally give the name *mushroom* to the kinds that can be eaten, and *toadstool* to those that are poisonous. An edible kind may have poisonous relatives which belong to the same genus. Children usually think all mushrooms are toadstools, and avoid them all as poisonous. It is probably fortunate that they do. Children are not taught to recognize the different mushrooms, the way they are taught to recognize the common birds. Only a skilled person can tell which mushrooms are safe and which contain deadly poisons.

There are about 38,000 known species of mushrooms. Different mushrooms have many different shapes, from the ordinary umbrella to the less familiar coral, or branching, shape. They may also be shaped like shelves. Their colors range from pure white to pastel pinks and lavenders, from pale yellow to flaming orange and brilliant red, from dull gray to velvety brown.

Parts of the Mushroom

The main part of the mushroom plant is underground. It looks like a web of fine threads, sometimes packed close together like a mass of felt. This part of the plant is called the *mycelium*. The umbrella growth, which most people call a mushroom, is really a stalk that grows up from the mycelium. It may be compared with a fruit of other plants, for its work is to scatter the cells from which new mushroom plants grow. The umbrella is called a *sporophore*, which means the *part that bears the spores*.

In sporophores that are just beginning to grow, the top of the stalk forms a small knob, called a button. The button spreads out until it has the full umbrella shape. This wide top is the crown. If a person examines a full-grown mushroom, he will see many thin ridges on the underside of the crown. These thin growths are the *gills*, which bear the spores. They grow out all around the center stalk toward the edge of the crown.

The spores are cells that are specially suited for growing new mushroom plants. They are carried on tiny stalks that grow out from the surface of the gills. There may be millions of them on a single sporophore. Single spores are so small that they can be seen only through a microscope. A mass of spores sometimes looks like powder. Frequently, but not always, the mass has the same color as the gills. A mushroom crown laid with its gills down on a piece of paper will leave a spore print which shows a definite pattern. This print is made up of thousands of the spores.

The Life Story of the Mushroom

How the Mushroom Gets Its Food. Fungi have none of the green plant material called *chlorophyll*. Green plants with chlorophyll can use sunlight to prepare carbohydrates, a type of food they need. They manufacture it from water and carbon dioxide, one of the gases in the air. Mushrooms have no "leaf green" and

U.S.D.A.

The Deadly Destroying-Angel Mushroom grows in woods. It looks safe, but there is no known remedy for its fatal poison.

must use food that has already been prepared by some green plant. They may be found growing on old stumps or logs, decaying twigs or leaves, or even on rich soil. In this way they are able to get their food. Here and there is found a species which grows on the trunks or branches of living trees. Mushrooms which grow on living plants are called *parasites*.

The main part of the mushroom plant, the mycelium, lives entirely inside the material that gives it nourishment. When the mycelium grows in a log or tree it causes the wood to decay or rot. The decay makes more material for the mushroom to live on.

Mushrooms need a great deal of moisture. After a spell of wet weather in spring, summer, or fall many of these fungi spring up suddenly.

How a Mushroom Grows. The story of the common table mushroom will give a good idea of the way other mushrooms grow. This is the mushroom that is often raised for food. It is grown in a specially prepared mixture of well-fermented stable manure. The mixture, called a *compost*, is arranged on benches or in boxes. When the temperature is right, pieces of mushroom spawn are placed just below the surface of the compost, and about 1 foot (30 centimeters) apart.

The spawn is really the *mycelium*, the part of the mushroom plant that grows underground.

The mushroom spawn grows out like threads through the whole bed of compost. Meanwhile, a layer of soil about 1 inch (2.5 centimeters) deep has been placed over the compost. In seven or eight weeks, mushrooms begin to appear on the surface of the soil. They come up first in the so-called *pinhead* stage. The pinhead is really a little knot or head of new growth, shaped more or less like a ball. In a few days the pinhead has grown into a tiny button. If the air is dry, the pinhead may form below the surface of the soil. As it continues to grow, the button may then push up through the earth. These buttons seem to shoot up very quickly. Actually, it often takes a week for a pinhead to reach the "small button" stage of development. The button then will measure about $\frac{1}{2}$ inch (13 millimeters) across.

Chestnut

Rough-Stemmed

Beautiful-Stemmed

Granular

BOLETUS MUSHROOMS HAVE NO GILLS

Jack O'Lantern

Beefsteak

Little Helmet

Clitopilus

TREE-STUMP MUSHROOMS THRIVE ON DEAD WOOD

Common Field

Naucoria

Paneolus

Puffball

MUSHROOMS THAT GROW IN THE SUNLIGHT

Jar

Bird's Nest

Morel

Coral

MUSHROOMS WITH STRANGE AND UNUSUAL SHAPES

MUSHROOMS

Honey

Amanitopsis

Hygrophorus

Russula

BRIGHT-COLORED MUSHROOMS THAT GROW IN SHADY PLACES

Caesar's Amanita

Blushing Amanita

Fly Amanita

Destroying Angel

THE AMANITAS ARE DISTINCTIVE AND WIDESPREAD

Milky Blue

Violet Cortinarius

Masked Tricholoma

Spotted Cortinarius

RARE-COLORED BLUE AND PURPLE MUSHROOMS

Drawing Pad

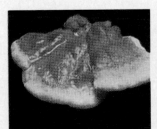

Sulfur Polypore

Zoned

Mahogany

THE SHELFLIKE BRACKETS GROW ON TREES

As the young button grows larger, the upper part, or cap, develops more rapidly. The gills grow underneath this cap, but are hidden by a curtain, or veil. As the cap grows wider and the stem grows longer, the veil covering the gills breaks away. Then the pink gills are easy to see. The broken veil remains attached to the stem and forms a ring called the *annulus*. The annulus stays on the stem for some time. The whole plant continues to grow larger, and soon looks like an open umbrella. When the mushroom is mature, the gills become brownish-black.

Different species and genera of mushrooms have very different kinds of veils and gill colors. In the genus *Amanita*, which contains several very poisonous species, there is sort of an envelope that covers the entire plant. This envelope breaks near the base as the mushroom expands, and leaves a kind of cup at the base of the stem. The envelope sometimes remains on the surface of the cap, where it breaks up into squares or large patches. In this case there is also an inner veil that forms a ring on the stem. Amanitas can be recognized by this ring. The table mushroom has no membrane covering it all over, so no cup will be formed at the base of the table mushroom's stem.

The gills of Amanita may be white or slightly colored. The gills of young common table mushrooms are pink, changing to brown or brown-black as they mature.

The spores growing in the gills may be carried off by the wind. They find their way to the ground or to leaves which later may be eaten by animals. When they sprout, they send off tiny threads. The threads can be seen by the naked eye only after they have grown and branched a great deal.

Fairy Rings. Sometimes a person sees circles of lighter grass growing on a lawn or meadow. These are the rings that the fairies are supposed to leave behind in the morning after they have danced at night.

In spite of this pretty story, the real cause of fairy rings is the growing habits of mushrooms. The mushroom spawn does not seem to be able to grow in the same place for a long time. The spot where it is growing spreads out, and the mushrooms grow in wider and wider rings. At first the grass above the spawn is thinner. But once the mushroom spawn has decayed, it fertilizes the soil and makes it richer. Then the grass in the circle is even thicker than that found in the rest of the lawn.

Kinds of Mushrooms

It would be impossible in this article to describe or even list all the kinds of mushrooms. Botanists have given each one a Latin name which tells what group it belongs to. Many also have familiar names.

Harmless Varieties. There are a thousand or more varieties of mushrooms that are good to eat. Many of these belong to the group called the *agarics*. Agaric mushrooms grow in pastures, lawns, and open fields.

The common table mushroom belongs to the agarics. It is the only mushroom cultivated on a large scale and sold on the market. In France it is called the *champignon*, from the French word *champ*, meaning *field*. This mushroom never grows very large. Its spores are brown, and it has no cup. Its gills are a delicate pink when the plant is young. As it grows older they turn to dark

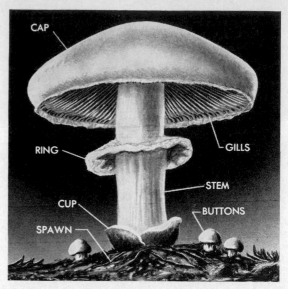

Parts of the Mushroom

brown. These are important points for the mushroom picker to remember. Wild common table mushrooms grow thickest in the fall or late summer.

The *horse mushroom* is another kind that is good to eat. It is similar to the common mushroom, but is very much larger and coarser.

The *parasol mushroom* is taller and more graceful. It looks like a small white or delicate tan umbrella on a slender handle.

The edible *Amanitopsis* should never be confused with its relative, the deadly poisonous *Amanita*, or death cup. The two plants look almost alike, but the dangerous one has a frill that the wholesome mushroom does not have.

The *oyster mushroom* grows in clusters on stumps or partly decayed trees. It has white gills and one-sided stalks.

One of the most delicious of the mushrooms is the *morel*. Its cups look like cone-shaped sponges, pitted like a honeycomb. The morel grows best among leaves or wood ashes.

The *chanterelle* or *little goblet*, is a dainty, reddish-yellow mushroom. It has this name because it is shaped like a cup.

The *coral mushroom* has a branching form of beautiful pink, lavender, or amber. This species is most common in Sweden. Another branching variety is the *golden Clavaria*, which is a beautiful honey color. It is also delicious to eat.

Fairy-ring mushrooms have a flavor like nuts. They are often dried and preserved for eating. Other familiar types are the *inkcap* or *shaggy mane*, the *bear's head*, and the *hedgehog* mushrooms. The inkcap first grows underneath the sod. When there is a warm rain, it pushes up overnight, and by the close of day has dripped away in an inky liquid.

Many tasty kinds of mushrooms are not so well-known. One of these is the *Jew's ear*. The Chinese are so fond of this type that they import it from the South Sea

Islands. Another is the *green Russula*, which looks like the trumpet of a gray-green morning-glory. The *golden Peziza* is shaped like a cup and lined with orange-red. Still others are the *trembling mushrooms*, a quivering mass like jelly, and the *liver fungus*, which is sometimes called *vegetable beefsteak*.

The familiar *puffballs* are also called *smoke balls* and *devil's-snuffboxes*. A puffball, if struck with a twig, gives off a tiny puff of "smoke." It is really scattering its dusty spores to the wind. Some puffballs grow to be more than 2 feet (61 centimeters) across.

One species harmful to timber is the curious *bracket mushroom*. It looks like a small shelf that grows partly around the tree trunk. Its colors are brown above and white below.

Poisonous Mushrooms. The most dreaded of the poisonous mushrooms are two members of the Amanita group, the *death cup* and the *fly Amanita*.

The death cup grows in the woods from June until fall. Its poison acts like the venom of a rattlesnake, as it separates the corpuscles in the blood from the serum. No antidote is known for the poison of the death cup. The only hope for anyone who has eaten it is to clean out his stomach promptly with a stomach pump. One variety is known as the *destroying angel*.

The death cup has often been mistaken for the common mushroom. A person can avoid this mistake if he observes carefully. The poisonous plant has white gills, white spores, and the fatal poison cup around its stem. The plant that is safe to eat has brown or brown-black gills, brown spores, and no cup. Many of the mistakes come from picking it in the button stage, for it does not show all these differences until it is larger.

The fly mushroom grows in the woods or along the roadside. It looks good enough to eat with its bright red, yellow, or orange cup. But it paralyzes the nerves which control the heart action.

History tells us that Czar Alexis of Russia died from eating the fly mushroom. Yet it is not quite so deadly as the death cup. When a person has eaten a fly mushroom, it is necessary to empty his stomach promptly and give him injections of atropine. The fly mushroom can be recognized by its scaly cap and stem, a deep frill at the top, white spores, and a bulblike base.

Satan's mushroom, the *emetic Russula*, and the *verdigris mushroom* are all poisonous to some people and not to others. A very unpleasant smelling mushroom is the *stinkhorn*, sometimes called the *fetid wood witch*. It often grows in backyards or under open stairways.

Doctors are able to recognize slightly different effects from the different kinds of poisonous mushrooms. But the symptoms are very similar in all cases of mushroom poisoning. There are always severe pains in the abdomen, followed by a bluish appearance of the skin. After these symptoms, the patient collapses. He is almost certain to die, unless a doctor can treat him promptly.

Mushrooms must be fresh when eaten. None should be eaten if it shows the least sign of decay, or if insects have been feeding on it. It is also dangerous to eat most that have a milky juice.

Some people believe any mushroom is poisonous if it has bright colors. This notion is not correct, for some of the most brilliant are also among the most wholesome. Another false notion is that only poisonous mushrooms will turn a silver spoon black when they are being cooked. Many safe kinds will also turn table silver black, after they have been cooked.

Mushrooms as a Food

Men have eaten mushrooms since very early times. The Greeks and Romans were fond of them. Today they are the chief food of the natives on Tierra del Fuego at the tip of South America, and of natives in some parts of Australia. More people in Europe than in America eat mushrooms.

In most countries, people consider mushrooms a table delicacy rather than a main food. These fungi are about 88 per cent water and almost half the rest is bulk that the body cannot digest. Food experts say that mushrooms are no more nourishing than cabbage.

Mushrooms can be eaten creamed, baked, fried, broiled, stewed, or served in salad. Stores sell many varieties at all seasons—fresh, dried, or canned.

Mushroom Culture. The business of raising mushrooms has become more and more popular around large cities. Growers find that it pays well. They can carry on a small business in cellars, caves, or old quarries. Almost any place where the temperature can be kept steady will do. Mushroom growing as an industry is something different. Today, a large plant must have specially designed mushroom houses, and standard methods of business. Still, it is not unusual for boys and girls to raise small crops for market. Many have earned money for their education this way. Many books on mushrooms tell how to grow the crops. The United States Department of Agriculture will also send helpful bulletins on the subject.

Scientific Classification. Mushrooms are fungi that belong to many different families of the division *Thallophyta* in the plant kingdom. These families belong to the class *Basidiomycetes*. The commonly cultivated field mushroom belongs to the family *Agaricaceae*. It is genus *Agaricus*, species *A. campestris*.   WILLIAM F. HANNA

See also FUNGI; PUFFBALL.

MUSIAL, STAN (1920-   ), ranks as one of the greatest baseball players of all time. Nicknamed *Stan the Man*, Musial was a star outfielder and first baseman for the St. Louis Cardinals between 1941 and 1963. He won seven National League batting titles, and had a .331 lifetime batting average. Musial played more games (3,026) and made more hits (3,630) than any other National League player. He became a Cardinal vice-president in 1963. President Lyndon B. Johnson named Musial director of the President's Council on Physical Fitness in 1964. Musial was elected to the National Baseball Hall of Fame in 1969. Stanley Frank Musial was born in Donora, Pa.   ED FITZGERALD

Wide World

Stan Musial

WORLD BOOK photo

The Chicago Symphony Orchestra and Chorus Perform the Music of Bach.

Ravi Shankar Plays the Music of India on a Sitar.
Capitol Records

Arthur Rubinstein and Quartet Play Chamber Music.
RCA Records

MUSIC

MUSIC is a basic social and cultural activity of mankind. Music has probably existed in some form from the earliest days of man. Man was born with a great musical instrument, his voice. He undoubtedly used his voice to express himself through music long before

Robert C. Marsh, the contributor of this article, is the music critic of The Chicago Sun-Times. *Halsey Stevens, one critical reviewer, is Composer-in-Residence and Professor of Music at the University of Southern California. James Sykes, the other critical reviewer, is a musician and a professor of music at Dartmouth College.*

he thought of making music with instruments. For thousands of years in man's early history, music existed only as simple and natural voice sounds. Then man began making music with a wide variety of musical instruments. Today, composers write their music down using special symbols, and performers can record their music permanently on records or tape.

Music takes many forms and reflects many different ways of life. But all types of music have one basic quality in common. That is, all music is a form of communication in which sounds are deliberately organized in some manner for an artistic purpose.

Ray Charles Plays the Blues.

The Carpenters Play Popular and Rock Music.

A musical performance is often called *re*-creative because it evolves from a previous creative work of art written down by the composer. Composers write music in a symbolic form called *notation*. Usually, notation provides only an outline of a performance, and the musicians, singers, and conductors must interpret the notes. Thus, a musical performance is really a partnership between composer and performer.

WORLD BOOK has separate articles on different types of music, including BALLET, FOLK MUSIC, JAZZ, and OPERA. A complete list of WORLD BOOK articles on music appears in the *Related Articles* section at the end of this article. This article deals primarily with what is commonly called *classical* music. Classical music may also be called *serious* music. But this term is inaccurate because jazz and folk music are serious forms of music, even though they are often performed in informal surroundings.

Enjoying Music

The way to enjoy music is to find music that interests you and listen to it. By listening repeatedly to music, you become familiar with the way composers and performers use music to communicate with an audience. If the music says nothing to you at first, try again, until you think you understand it. It is possible to enjoy music without understanding it fully. But the greatest enjoyment comes with the greatest understanding.

After listening to music, try to make some music yourself. You may want to play the piano, the violin, the clarinet, or some other instrument. If you cannot play, you can sing—either alone or with others. Even if you do not want anyone to hear the results, you may find pleasure in making music. You may discover that making music is a natural way to express yourself.

Understanding Music. It is easy to accept music as a quiet background sound that helps provide a pleasant atmosphere. But if you want to understand serious music, you must listen to it as an example of artistic communication. Music for listening must be loud enough for you to follow all that is being played or sung. Intelligent listening is an active process. When you listen to a familiar work of music, you can anticipate what comes next with the same pleasure you find in rereading a favorite story or poem. As you learn more about the music, you form ideas about how it should be performed. When you hear it again, you can judge whether the performance pleases or disappoints you.

If the music is unfamiliar, but in a musical style you know, you will find pleasure as it brings forth unexpected melodies and harmonies. You may also find a sense of challenge, because you may not fully understand the significance of some part of the music, and must wait for more than one hearing. If the style is also unfamiliar, you have an even greater challenge. You must learn not only what the composer is saying, but also how he says it. You will probably have to listen to the work several times before you fully understand its significance.

Only persons who know many styles of the musical language can enjoy the fullest pleasures of music. Instead of limiting yourself to the music you find familiar and enjoyable, give yourself a chance to explore new kinds as well. If you do not enjoy a piece of music the first time you hear it, go back to it later. You may be surprised at how much more you hear in it after a few months.

Judging Music. We appreciate music because it communicates something to us in which we find momentary or enduring satisfaction. We judge music by the success with which it communicates, and by the length of time in which we retain interest in what it has to say. If a specific work of music communicates nothing to us, then it means nothing to us—and what it means to others is unimportant. But if it is an acknowledged masterpiece, such as a Beethoven symphony, we owe it to ourselves to go back to it from time to time and try to understand it. We can study such music for years without exhausting the possibilities for discovery.

A person with limited musical experience can judge only his own responses. When he speaks, he is really talking only about himself. But a person who has learned many kinds of musical styles feels that he can talk about music itself. He thinks that if the music has any meaning, he will be able to grasp it.

Musical Instruments

Almost all the instruments that produce music can be grouped in three major classes: string, wind, and percussion. They make sounds in three different ways. Vibrating strings produce the musical tones in the first group. Wind blown into or through a tube produces the tones in the second group. Something struck produces the sounds in the third group. But, because of the way musical instruments are made, most experts divide them into six major groups: (1) stringed, (2) wood wind, (3) brass, (4) percussion, (5) keyboard, and (6) others.

Stringed Instruments are of four basic types—bowed, plucked, struck, and wind. In the first type, the string is *bowed* (rubbed with a bow) to produce sounds. The important bowed strings are the *violin* family, which includes the *violin, viola, cello* (or *violoncello*), and *bass* (or *double bass*). Other bowed strings include the older *viol* family.

In the second type of stringed instrument, the player *plucks* the strings to produce tones. He may use his fingers, as in playing a harp. Or he may use a *plectrum*, a small piece of ivory, wood, or metal. The most important plucked-string instrument in an orchestra is the *harp*. Other plucked strings, usually played by themselves rather than with an orchestra, include the *banjo, guitar, lute, lyre, mandolin, sitar, ukulele,* and *zither*. The *harpsichord* has plucked strings, but it is often classed with keyboard instruments.

In the third type, the string is *hammered* to produce a tone. Two older instruments, the *clavichord* and the *dulcimer,* or *cimbalom,* have hammered strings. The most important hammered-string instrument, the *piano,* is usually classed with keyboard instruments. In an orchestra, the piano may also be used for percussion.

In the fourth type of stringed instrument, the strings vibrate in the wind. The only instrument of this type is the *aeolian harp.* It is never used in orchestral music.

Wood-Wind Instruments are grouped together because at one time they were all made of wood. Today, they may be made of metal or plastic. Wood winds produce tones when the musician blows air into or through a tube, either directly or past a vibrating *reed.* He covers holes in the tube to play various tones. In the *flute* family, he blows across a hole in the tube. Two thin pieces of reed, vibrating together, produce the sound in the *bassoon, oboe,* and *English horn.* A single reed, vibrating against a slot in the mouthpiece, produces the sound in the *clarinet* and *saxophone* families.

Brass Instruments all have rather long *bores* (tubes) with mouthpieces at one end and flaring *bells* (openings) at the other. Many brass instruments have *valves* that serve to lengthen or shorten the tube, lowering or raising the pitch. The *horn* family has a narrow, conical bore, with a funnel-shaped mouthpiece and a large bell. The *trumpet* family has a narrow, cylindrical bore, a cup-shaped mouthpiece, and a moderate-sized bell. The *cornet* has a cup mouthpiece and a bore that is partly conical and partly cylindrical. The *bugle* has a cup mouthpiece, a wide, conical bore, and a moderate bell. The *trombone* family has a larger mouthpiece than the trumpets, and usually has a slide instead of valves to lengthen the bore. The *tuba* family has a wide, conical bore and a cup mouthpiece, as do the *flügelhorns.*

Percussion Instruments include two basic types: those that play definite pitches and those that produce indefinite pitches. *Kettledrums* or *timpani* can be tuned to specific pitches, and are grouped with *chimes, glockenspiels, marimbas, tubular bells,* and *xylophones.* Indefinite-pitch instruments include the *drum* family (except kettledrums) and *castanets, cymbals, gongs, tambourines, triangles,* and many others.

Keyboard Instruments include all instruments that have keyboards connected with a mechanism for producing tones. The *harpsichord* has plucked strings; the *piano,* hammered strings; the *celesta,* hammered metal bars; and the *organ,* pipes. Unlike other keyboard instruments, the organ can sustain a tone indefinitely. The *carillon* is often played from a keyboardlike console.

Other Instruments. Some reed instruments have *free reeds* that vibrate back and forth in a slot. They include the *accordion, concertina, harmonica,* and *harmonium.* *Bagpipes* have both double reeds (like the oboe) and single reeds (like the clarinet). The *flageolet,* the *ocarina,* and the *recorder* are flutes with a whistle mouthpiece.

Since the late 1800's, various new instruments have been invented. Some produce sound by electronic means. The *Theremin* and the *Ondes Martenot* are probably the most significant in the electronic group. Electric organs and pianos today substitute electronic tone generators for the more conventional pipes and strings. Electronic amplification has also been added to older instruments, chiefly the guitar and double bass. Other older instruments have undergone extensive technical improvements. Since 1945, composers have been able to use electronic tone generators to produce sounds without using regular orchestral instruments.

Instrumental Music

Music written for instruments is classified according to the number of performers who play it. One musician plays a solo, a small number play chamber music, and many—as many as a hundred—play orchestral music.

Instrumental Solos. Some instruments, such as the piano, violin, and harp, are excellent for solo performances. The musician can play more than one tone at a time, giving his music richness and depth. Other instruments, for example the flute and clarinet, can play only one tone at a time. However, composers have written important solo parts for them. These instruments are often accompanied by a piano, although the performance then technically becomes a duo.

Composers have written vast amounts of music for solo piano. This music ranges from simple pieces to the 32 complex piano sonatas by Beethoven. After a few

GROUPS OF INSTRUMENTS

Shown here and on the following three pages are 44 instruments, divided into the six major groups of instruments: stringed, woodwind, brass, percussion, keyboard, and other instruments.

STRINGED INSTRUMENTS

Lute

Violin

Banjo

Ukulele

Mandolin

Classical Guitar

Bass

Cello

Viola

Harp

WOODWIND INSTRUMENTS

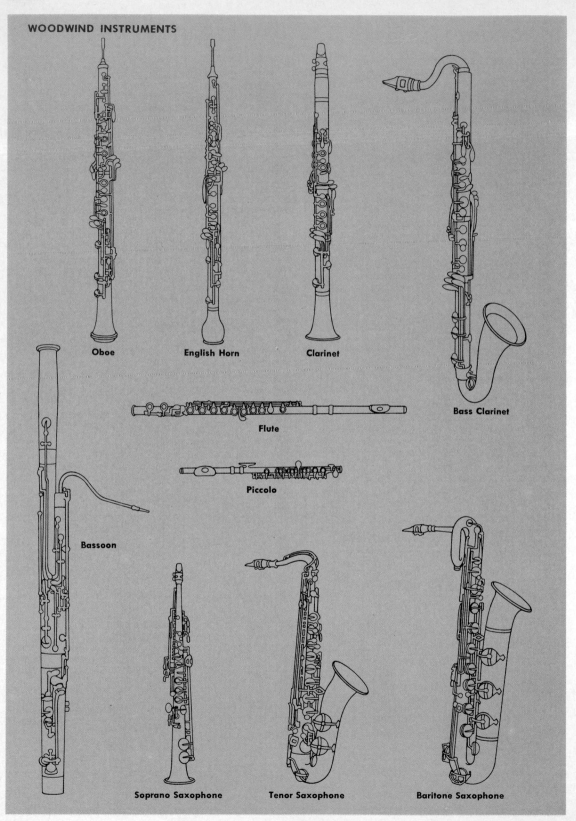

Oboe

English Horn

Clarinet

Bass Clarinet

Flute

Piccolo

Bassoon

Soprano Saxophone

Tenor Saxophone

Baritone Saxophone

BRASS INSTRUMENTS

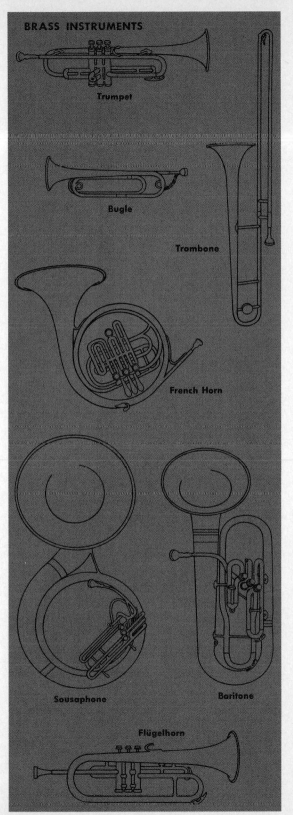

Trumpet

Bugle

Trombone

French Horn

Sousaphone

Baritone

Flügelhorn

PERCUSSION INSTRUMENTS

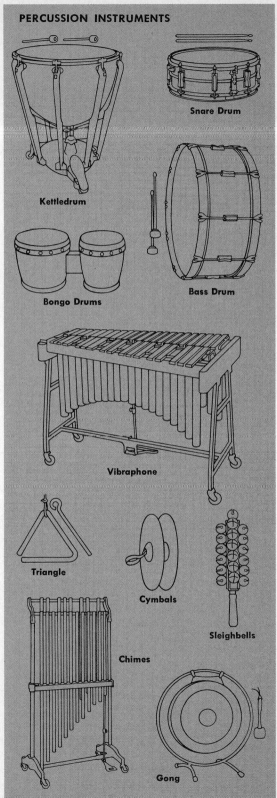

Snare Drum

Kettledrum

Bongo Drums

Bass Drum

Vibraphone

Triangle

Cymbals

Sleighbells

Chimes

Gong

KEYBOARD INSTRUMENTS

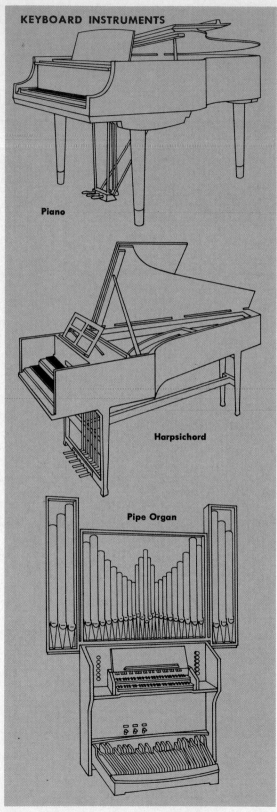

Piano

Harpsichord

Pipe Organ

OTHER INSTRUMENTS

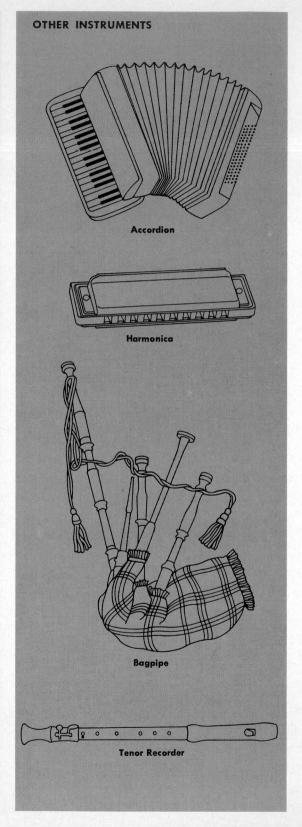

Accordion

Harmonica

Bagpipe

Tenor Recorder

lessons, almost anyone can play easy piano music. Concert pianists may spend years studying difficult music. Bach wrote the most famous works for violin and cello solo. The greatest composers have written little music for the solo harp, but skilled harpists can play much music that was written for piano.

Chamber Music is written for small combinations of instruments in a number of musical forms. It was originally played in *chambers* (private rooms), rather than in churches or public halls. Musicians played chamber music for the musical satisfaction it provided themselves and small groups of music lovers. It was not originally intended for public performance before large audiences.

The most important literature of chamber music is for a *string quartet*. This group has two violins, a viola, and a cello. In a *piano quartet*, the piano replaces one violin, although the term has also been used to mean a group of four pianos. The *duet sonata* has a piano and one other instrument such as a violin. The *string trio* consists of a violin, a viola, and a cello. The *piano trio* has a violin, a cello, and a piano. Mozart's *viola quintets* are written for two violins, two violas, and a cello. A *piano quintet* often has a piano and four members of the string quartet, but Schubert's "Trout" quintet uses a piano, a violin, a viola, a cello, and a double bass. A *wood-wind quintet* consists of flute, oboe, clarinet, bassoon, and French horn. The French horn is technically a brass instrument.

Sextets have six musicians, *septets* seven, and *octets* eight. Aaron Copland and a few other composers have produced *nonets* with nine players. There is also a great deal of musical literature which calls for groups of stringed, wind, and brass instruments ranging in size from 10 to 30 or more. Such a group is called a *chamber orchestra* today.

Orchestral Music, like chamber music, has been written in a variety of forms. It may be divided into two groups: works for soloist and orchestra, and works for orchestra alone.

Soloists and Orchestra together play several kinds of works. A vocal soloist sometimes sings with the orchestra in a *song cycle*, or in a work such as Brahms's *Alto Rhapsody*. An instrumental soloist performs with the orchestra in such works as Johannes Brahms's piano concerto in B♭ for piano and orchestra. In its early development, a *concerto* was understood as a "friendly rivalry" between two groups of performers. But it has come to mean an extended work in which the "rivalry" is expressed by a solo instrument and the orchestra, contrasting the individuality and resources of the two. Most concertos have three *movements* (sections) with a *cadenza* (a long passage for the soloist) near the end of the first movement. A *double* or *triple* concerto has two or three soloists. In a *concerto grosso*, a small group plays solo parts and is contrasted with a larger orchestra. See CONCERTO.

The Orchestra Alone plays many kinds of works, including overtures, suites, and symphonies. An *overture* may be a separate work, or it may be a short introductory work for a stage performance, such as an opera, a ballet, or a play. A *suite* is usually a group of short pieces, often in dance forms, as in Bach's four suites for orchestra, and Bartók's *Dance Suite*. A *symphonic poem*, also known as a *tone poem*, is a work for orchestra based on a nonmusical idea, such as a work of literature or a painting. The *symphony* is the most highly developed form of orchestral music. It is a work of large scope in which the composer expresses his most highly organized musical ideas. See SYMPHONY; SUITE.

Vocal Music

Singing Voices are grouped according to the ranges in which they sing and the color and quality of the voice itself. In terms of range, a *soprano* sings the highest woman's part. A *mezzo-soprano* sings a little below her, and a *contralto* or *alto* has the lowest woman's voice. A *tenor* sings the highest man's part, a *baritone* the middle range, and a *bass* the lowest part. In terms of *timbre* (tone color), a *coloratura* soprano has a light, sparkling, brilliant tone. The *lyric* soprano has a warmer, darker voice than the *coloratura*. The *dramatic soprano* makes an impact less by the high range of her voice than by the force with which she projects and the majesty of her tone. The highest male voices were once those of the *castrato* singers. Castrati were highly regarded in the 1600's and 1700's. The highest male voice heard today is the *countertenor*, whose range is approximately that of a contralto. The *Heldentenor* (heroic tenor) is a vocal type developed in the mid-1800's and characterized by robust brilliance. The *basso profundo* sings the lowest bass notes. A *basso cantante* or *bass-baritone* is a baritone with a well-developed lower range. A *basso buffo* sings comic roles.

Songs can be divided into two groups: those by composers whose names we know, and those of unknown origin. We know that "Sophisticated Lady" was written by Duke Ellington, and "The Erl King" by Schubert. But no one knows who composed the beautiful English folk song "Greensleeves." Songs can also be divided into *popular* and *art* songs. The few popular songs that last for many years usually have greater musical interest, or say something more, than the hundreds that fade away. Art songs are serious music, and the best ones may remain fresh for hundreds of years. The composer usually chooses a poem with some literary merit of its own, and sets it to music. He uses music to strengthen and amplify the meaning of the words. See FOLK MUSIC; POPULAR MUSIC.

Choral Music. The earliest choral music was sung in unison, with each person singing the same note. Choruses may have sung *a cappella* (without accompaniment) or with instruments playing the same melodies that were sung. In the Middle Ages, singers began combining two or more melodies, and by the 1500's and 1600's the practice of *part-singing* was highly developed. Instead of everyone singing the same notes, each voice or section had an individual part. Informal choral singing has long been a popular form of recreation. Amateur choral societies developed in Europe in the 1800's. At the same time, the barbershop quartet became popular in the United States (see BARBERSHOP QUARTET SINGING).

Opera was first written just before 1600. The first operas used simple *chords* (harmony). These chords allowed the solo voice to sing the words of the text clearly in a kind of simplified musical speech called *recitative*.

Operas combine music and stage action. A good opera is an exciting or moving stage performance and has music that emphasizes the dramatic or comic values of the story.

The cast of an opera may include a chorus of persons suitable to the story—villagers, soldiers, gypsies, or others. A soprano generally sings the part of the heroine. The leading male role is usually given to the tenor. Occasionally, when the composer is portraying a hero who is an older man or a man with flaws of character, the leading singer is a baritone. The most important female role, after the heroine, generally goes to a mezzo-soprano or a contralto, depending on the type of character to be portrayed. Contraltos make the best evil characters, just as baritones and basses are usually chosen for male roles of this type. But the baritone is often the hero's best friend, and the bass may be a king or other person of great dignity. A large orchestra usually accompanies the singers.

In *light opera* and *musical comedies*, the story almost always has a happy ending. The music is immediately appealing, and the purpose is as much to entertain as to transmit any artistic message. But these forms can comment effectively on the times. Sir Arthur Sullivan, Jacques Offenbach, Johann Strauss, Jr., Victor Herbert, Richard Rodgers, Frederick Loewe, and Leonard Bernstein won popularity and respect in these fields. See MUSICAL COMEDY; OPERA.

Oratorios use choruses, soloists, and instruments to tell a story in music without the theatrical action seen in an opera. Some, such as Handel's *Messiah*, are performed year after year. A well-known short oratorio is *Belshazzar's Feast* by Sir William Walton. An uncut performance of *Messiah* lasts more than three hours. The Walton oratorio lasts less than an hour. Most oratorios have religious subjects. They involve soloists (usually soprano, contralto, tenor, and bass), at least one chorus, often a supplementary chorus (such as one of children), and an orchestra. The narration in oratorio, as in certain types of opera, is done by the use of recitative. The oratorio form won wide popularity in the 1700's and 1800's. See ORATORIO.

The Elements of Music

Sound in Music usually has a definite *pitch* that we describe as "high" or "low." A musical sound, called a *tone*, is produced when something causes a series of vibrations that recur a certain number of times each second. For example, heavy wires that vibrate slowly, only 32.7 times a second, produce the lowest C on the piano. The thin wires that produce the highest C on the piano vibrate more than 4,000 times a second, or almost 130 times as fast as the lowest.

Musical tones also have other characteristics. For example, some tones are long and some short. We call this the *duration*. The same tone, played on different instruments, has different tone colors. This is the *quality* of the tone. Some tones are loud and others soft. We call this the *intensity* of the tone. A tone often has other tones that support and accompany it. They form its *harmony*. If a series of tones make up a tune, we may call it a *melody*. For other information on sound, see SOUND.

A *scale* is a series of tones arranged according to rising or falling pitch. The piano keyboard has a regular pattern of white and black keys. The distance from one key to the next, whether black or white, is always a half step. The half step above any white key is called its *sharp*, and the half step below any white key is called its *flat*. Composers use many kinds of scales. Most scales are based on the octave, except in Oriental music. An *octave* (named for the Latin word for eight) is the interval between two tones of the same name. The higher tone has twice as many vibrations per second as the lower, so the relationship is based as much on physics as on art.

In the illustrations on the opposite page we use the piano, an instrument which is tuned to *equal temperament*. This means that the intervals between tones have been made uniform. Each black key stands for two notes, such as $C\sharp$ or $D\flat$. Actually, these notes are not precisely the same. Equal temperament permits a keyboard instrument to be of practical size and still play in reasonably accurate tune in all keys. A stringed instrument without a fretted fingerboard, such as the violin, permits the player to produce $C\sharp$ and $D\flat$ as separate tones. A singer with a good ear can also make these distinctions. The notes from C to C on the piano comprise an octave. The octave may be divided into 12 equal parts, each of which is a half step. These 12 half steps make up the *chromatic scale*. You hear the chromatic scale when you play all the white and black keys from C to C on the piano.

Until about a hundred years ago, most western music was not based on the full chromatic scale, but on 7 tones taken from it. This seven-tone scale with its *octave* (eighth) tone is called the *diatonic* scale. The tones of the diatonic scale are not an equal distance apart. You hear the diatonic major scale when you play all the white keys from C to C on the piano, or when you sing *do-re-mi-fa-sol-la-ti-do*. The tones make up a specific pattern of whole steps and half steps, in this order: two whole steps; half step; three whole steps; half step.

Because of this pattern of whole steps and half steps, the seven tones of the diatonic major scale vary in importance. The strongest tone is the *tonic*, the first tone of the scale. The tonic serves as the central point for the organization of the other tones. The tonic also gives the scale its name. For example, in the D major scale, D is the tonic. Any of the 12 half steps within an octave may serve as the tonic in a diatonic major scale. This means that there are 12 different diatonic major scales. There are also 12 different diatonic minor scales, although most minor scales, as used by composers, are not completely diatonic in character. Different locations of the half steps are the chief distinction between major and minor scales.

Next to the tonic, the most important tones of the diatonic scale are the fifth, called the *dominant*, and the fourth, called the *subdominant*. In terms of melody, the seventh tone is important because it usually leads to the tonic. The seventh is called the *leading tone*.

Many composers of the last hundred years, and especially composers since the end of World War II, have preferred to use the chromatic rather than the diatonic scale.

Melody is a succession of musical tones—in its simplest form, a tune. We remember a beautiful song more for its melody than for its words. We can enjoy

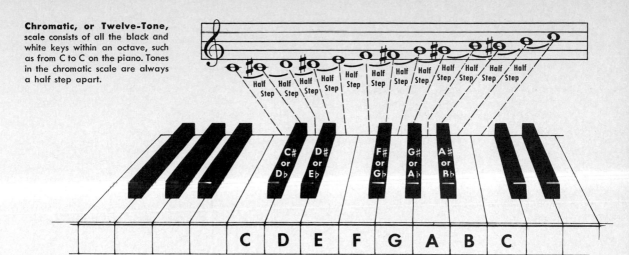

Chromatic, or Twelve-Tone, scale consists of all the black and white keys within an octave, such as from C to C on the piano. Tones in the chromatic scale are always a half step apart.

the flowing, attractive melodies in the symphonies of Brahms or Tchaikovsky long before we know much about the other elements of music. A melody consists of a series of tones played in a fixed pattern of pitches and rhythms. It may be repeated, expanded, or varied, according to the composer's wishes. But not all music has long, tuneful melodies. Composers often use a short series of notes, called a *motive*, as the basis for the development of their musical ideas. The first four notes of Beethoven's *Fifth Symphony* form such a motive. The theme of the first movement grows out of repetition and variation of this motive.

Harmony. The tones heard with a tone strengthen it and often help set its mood. Composers harmonize music in *chords*, which are groups of three or more related tones sounded at the same time. Chords are built on the scale and the physical properties of the tones themselves (see Harmonics). If you play C, E, G, and the C at the octave, you will hear the basic C major chord.

The chords and harmonies in a piece of music are usually based on the same scale. We can say that they are in the same *tonality* (sometimes called *key*). The name of the scale on which the work is based is drawn from the tone on which the scale starts (such as C or F),

and also from whether the chords are major or minor.

For the last 500 years, composers have usually used a harmonic system based on the tonic and dominant tones of the scale. After fixing the tonic tone and home key firmly in the listener's mind, the composer may *modulate* (shift) into the key in which the dominant of the "home" key becomes the new tonic. Modulation adds variety and may emphasize a contrasting section of his work. After the composer finishes the contrasting section, he usually returns to the "home" key.

Rhythm may be considered as everything that has to do with the duration of the musical sounds. Accent is an important factor in musical rhythm. The composer usually builds his music on a pattern of regularly recurring strong and weak accents. This pattern of accents permits the music to be divided into units of time called *measures* or *bars*. Weak accents help build the rhythm by creating anticipation for the strong ones. We can easily recognize the difference between a waltz rhythm of *ONE two three ONE two three* and a march rhythm of *ONE two ONE two*.

Tempo is the rate of speed at which music is played. It is related to, but not a part of, rhythm. A change in tempo can often change the meaning of music.

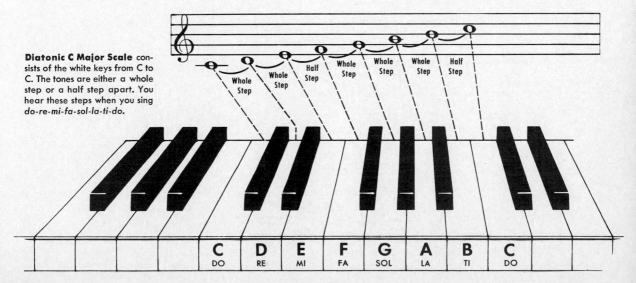

Diatonic C Major Scale consists of the white keys from C to C. The tones are either a whole step or a half step apart. You hear these steps when you sing *do-re-mi-fa-sol-la-ti-do*.

MUSIC

Tone Color is one of the most elusive qualities in music. Human voices may sing the same range of notes, yet produce widely different sounds. Different choices of chords give varying colors. Various instruments affect the tone color of the music they play. A melody may seem dark and mournful when played on the English horn. The same melody may sound bright and gay when played on the flute or violin. Tempo and rhythm are also factors in the effect a melody has on us.

In *orchestrating* his music, a composer takes advantage of differences in tone color. He may introduce the melody with one instrument, then have various other instruments play it, and finally have the entire orchestra play it. He may vary the groups that play the melody and its harmony. The strings are the foundation of the orchestra, and are often given the most important melodies. Wood winds have distinctive tones, and they, too, are given prominent melodies. Brass instruments provide rich sounds that may be massive, solemn, or brilliant. Percussion instruments emphasize the rhythmic elements. Special instruments, such as the saxophone or the mandolin, are sometimes introduced for special effects. Prokofiev, in his *Peter and the Wolf*, had instruments represent specific characters in the story —a flute for the bird, a bassoon for Peter's grandfather, an oboe for the duck, three horns for the wolf, and a string quartet for Peter himself.

The Language of Music

Notation. Music is written and printed in a picture language of its own called *notation*. Notation indicates (1) the pitch of the tones, (2) their place in a sequence of tones, (3) their *duration* (the length of time a tone is held), and (4) the composer's ideas about how they should be performed. *Notes* are written signs that represent *tones* (musical sounds). The notes appear on a *staff*, a set of five horizontal lines. The higher the composer places the note, the higher its pitch. The order in which he places it, from left to right, indicates its place in a sequence of notes. Notes are symbols in black and white. Different symbolic forms are used to show how long a time the sound is intended to last.

Medieval composers faced one of their main problems in finding a way to write music so that persons who had never heard a work could sing or play it. Guido d'Arezzo (995?-1050?), a monk, was probably the first to use parallel lines in the form of a staff and to name the notes of the scale (see GUIDO D'AREZZO). Churchmen now had a way to preserve religious music in writing. No one tried to preserve the secular music of the times.

A *clef* sign at the left end of a staff determines the position of notes on the staff. The *treble clef* is often called the *G clef* because its sign fixes the G above middle C on the second line from the bottom of the staff. The *bass clef*, often called the *F clef*, fixes the F below middle C on the second line from the top. Higher notes, such as those for the right end of the piano, appear in the treble clef. Lower notes appear in the bass clef. Music for the viola is written in the *alto C clef*, which fixes middle C on the third line. Music for the trombone, bassoon, and cello sometimes appears in the *tenor C clef*, where middle C is on the second line from the top.

A *key signature* appears at the right of the clef sign. By using sharp signs or flat signs, the composer indicates that certain notes should always be played sharp or flat. In this way, he shows the key of his work. Key signatures take from one to seven sharp or flat signs.

The composer may place an *accidental* in front of a certain note. *Accidentals* are the signs for sharp, flat, or

MUSICAL NOTES

The Treble Clef, *above*, is used for writing the notes above middle C.

The Bass Clef, *below*, is used for writing the notes below middle C.

The Grand Staff combines treble and bass, with middle C on a *ledger line*.

The Position of Each Note on a Staff Indicates Its Pitch.

natural that show a change from the key signature. Any note not marked sharp or flat is called *natural*. The natural sign cancels a sharp or flat. There are also double sharps and double flats.

A *time signature* appears at the right of the key signature. It is shown as a fraction, such as $\frac{4}{4}$, $\frac{3}{4}$, $\frac{5}{4}$, $\frac{12}{8}$, $\frac{6}{8}$, or $\frac{2}{2}$. The denominator shows what kind of note—quarter, eighth, or half—is the unit of measurement and receives one beat. The numerator shows how many beats there are to a measure. In a song marked $\frac{4}{4}$, the composer shows that four quarter notes should receive one beat each. One measure of $\frac{4}{4}$ may have a whole note worth four beats, or eight eighth notes worth half a beat each, or two quarter notes and a half note, or some other combination totaling four beats.

A given time unit may vary widely in its clock-time duration. If a beat of a quarter note lasts a long time, such as $1\frac{1}{2}$ seconds, the *tempo* (speed) is very slow. But if it lasts a short time, such as $\frac{1}{2}$ second, the tempo is fast.

Duration, or Time Values. The shape of a note indicates its duration, just as its position on the staff shows its pitch. Whole notes have open oval shapes. Half notes look like whole notes, but have *stems*. Quarter notes have solid oval shapes with stems. Eighth, sixteenth, thirty-second, and sixty-fourth notes have one, two, three, or four *flags* on their stems.

Rests indicate silence, or no sound. They have various shapes, and have the same time values as the notes they replace. In the orchestra, a musician may have many measures of rests in between the music he plays. *Bar lines* separate one measure from another. *Repeat signs* next to the bar lines at the beginning and end of a section show that the section is to be repeated.

Dynamics, or loudness and softness, are indicated by a set of abbreviations for Italian words. For example, *p* or *piano* means *soft*, *pp* or *pianissimo* means *very soft*,

and *f* or *forte* means *loud*. These and other terms appear in the list *Terms Used in Music* in this article.

Expression. When a composer wants a group of notes to be played smoothly as a unit, he marks them as a *phrase*. When he wants two tones of the same pitch to be played as a continuous sound, he *ties* them with a curved line over the notes. He may put abbreviations for dynamics next to certain notes, or he can mark volume changes with *crescendo* and *decrescendo* signs. Or he may write instructions for the musicians.

Scores contain music written for several instruments, or for instruments and voices. In a typical orchestral and vocal score, music for the wood-wind instruments appears at the top. Parts for the brass and percussion instruments are just below. Then comes the music for the soloists, either vocal or instrumental, followed by that for the chorus, if there is one. The music for strings appears at the bottom.

Each performer reads from a *part* that contains only the music he plays or sings. He follows the directions of the conductor. The performer keeps track of the bars during which he is silent, so he can make his entrances correctly. The conductor uses the full score. He must glance down the entire length of the page to read the notes for each part in any one measure, so he will know what each performer should be playing.

Names of Compositions. Musical works have various names, official and unofficial. The official name may identify the form of the work and indicate its home key, as in *Symphony No. 9 in D minor*. This name often includes an *opus* (work) *number* that tells where the composition comes in the composer's life work. He may have written other works between his eighth and ninth symphonies. For example, Beethoven's *Symphony*

NOTES							
	Whole	$\frac{1}{2}$	$\frac{1}{4}$	$\frac{1}{8}$	$\frac{1}{16}$	$\frac{1}{32}$	$\frac{1}{64}$
RESTS							
	Whole	$\frac{1}{2}$	$\frac{1}{4}$	$\frac{1}{8}$	$\frac{1}{16}$	$\frac{1}{32}$	$\frac{1}{64}$

Notes and Rests, above, have shapes that show how long they last. The notes and rests shown from *left to right* are whole, half, quarter, eighth, sixteenth, thirty-second, and sixty-fourth.

Note Equivalents, below. Two half notes or four quarter rests equal a whole note. A *dotted* note has one and a half times its value. That is, a dotted half note equals a half and a quarter.

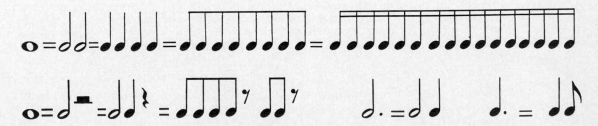

The Shape of Each Note or Rest Shows Its Time Value.

No. 8 in F major is opus 93, and his *Symphony No. 9 in D minor* is opus 125. Opus numbers usually indicate the order of publication, rather than of composition.

Some composers never use opus numbers. Others keep this added identification for the music they consider most important. Mozart wrote so much music that he never tried to keep track of it all. We identify his works by *Köchel numbers*, such as *K. 550*, which show their places in the catalog published by a music scholar, Ludwig von Köchel, in 1862. Some works are identified by their places in a famous edition of music issued by a well-known publisher. For many years, Haydn's last symphonies had such numbers as *B.&H. No. 13*, that showed their places in a set of scores issued by Breitkopf and Härtel, a famous publisher in Leipzig. We now use numbers and keys to identify his works, and *B.&H. No. 13* is called *Symphony No. 88 in G major*.

Unofficial names have come from composers and audiences alike. Tchaikovsky named his mournful sixth symphony *Pathétique*, meaning *pathetic*. Its official name is *Symphony No. 6 in B minor, op. 74*. Other works have unofficial names given them by the public. Beethoven's *Sonata in C sharp minor, op. 27, No. 2*, is commonly called the "Moonlight Sonata." Beethoven gave it an entirely different name, *sonata quasi una fantasia*, which means "sonata in the manner of a fantasy."

Some works have unofficial names taken from the persons to whom they were dedicated. Bach wrote six concertos for the ruler of Brandenburg, and we call them the *Brandenburg Concertos*. Other works are named for the places where they were composed (for example Mozart's "Linz" symphony, K. 425), or where they were first performed (such as Haydn's "Paris" symphonies, numbers 82 through 87). Still others are named for distinctive melodies or orchestrations, such as Haydn's "Drum Roll" symphony, number 103.

Many composers identify their works with titles that provide imaginative descriptions of what their music says, such as Debussy's *La Mer* (*The Sea*).

Musical Forms

The elements of music must take some form in order to be music, just as lines and colors must be arranged together to create a painting. Composers use various forms to organize these elements into works of art.

Song Form, usually a two-part song or three-part song, is one of the simplest types of musical form. A two-part form may be represented by A for the first theme and B for the second theme. Often a two-part song consists of two treatments of one theme, A, A'. More advanced is the three-part song (A-B-A) in which the first theme returns again to complete the form.

Sonata Form. The most important large form in serious music for the last 200 years has been the classical sonata form as written by Mozart and Beethoven. It originated in the 1700's and developed in the next century. We call a sonata for orchestra a *symphony*, a sonata for soloist and orchestra a *concerto*, and a sonata for a small instrumental group a *duet, trio, quartet,* or *quintet*. These works have more similarities as sonatas than they have differences in size or orchestration.

A sonata is usually divided into major sections called *movements*, somewhat like chapters in a book or acts in

a play. In most sonatas, the longest movement opens the work and sets its character. This movement involves the most complex musical writing. A slower, more lyric section may come next to provide contrast. Then comes a fast, short section in contrast to both the movements before it. The *finale* (last movement) usually returns to the feeling of the opening. It sums up the composer's ideas, sometimes quoting some of the themes heard earlier. Some sonatas have only one movement, and others may have five or six.

The first movement of most sonatas is usually written in *sonata form*. This means that the movement itself has four parts, played without pauses in between. The first part, called the *exposition*, states the main theme, or group of themes, in a *home tonality* (sometimes named in the title of the work). It also states a contrasting theme, or group of themes, in a different tonality. After fixing those themes in our minds, the composer introduces the second part of the movement, the *development*. Here he uses his themes or fragments of themes in many different ways and he often employs many changes of tonality. In this way, the music builds to a climax of expressive force. In the third section, the *recapitulation*, the composer restates the themes more or less as we first heard them. The fourth section, the *coda*, brings the movement to an end. The coda may be considered as part of the recapitulation, and the sonata form as having only three parts.

Variation Form consists of a series of different treatments of a theme. The theme itself is usually stated fully at the opening or close of the work. The composer may base his variations on the whole theme, or on only part of it, or even on part of its accompaniment. He usually changes key for some of his variations.

Canon and Fugue are *polyphonic* (many-voiced) forms in which one instrument or singer states a theme and the other performers then play or sing it in regular order. Such a repetition of a theme in succession in voice parts is called *imitation*. Imitation can be defined as the repetition of a melodic phrase or theme modified in some way but still resembling the original. In a *canon*, all the voices have the same theme throughout the work. *Rounds* follow the imitation form, as in the works "Row, Row, Row Your Boat" and "Frère Jacques." In a *fugue*, the composer may vary the different parts by imitating the theme with slight variations. He may also break off the theme entirely and introduce a second theme, or write a contrasting *episode* to give variety.

Free Form, as its name implies, gives the composer the greatest freedom of all. He may introduce two themes, the development of a third, then the third one itself. Or he may not use any conventional succession of themes. His problems in achieving unity become great, and he must make his harmonization and orchestration so unified that they give the sense of unity the form lacks. Debussy used free form in *Jeux* (*Games*).

History

Ancient Civilization. Many ancient works of art show musicians and their instruments. Unfortunately, we have little detailed knowledge of how men made or played these instruments. Only a few complete pieces of music from the ancient world still exist, almost all of them Greek.

Egypt. Early in Egyptian history, during the 4000's B.C., people clapped disks and sticks together, jingled metal rods, and sang songs. Later, in the great temples of the gods, priests trained choirs in singing ritual music. Court musicians sang and played several types of harps and wind and percussion instruments. Military bands used trumpets and drums.

Palestine. The people of Bible lands probably did not develop as much music as the Egyptians did. The Bible contains the words of many Hebrew songs and chants, such as the Psalms. It mentions harps, drums, trumpets, cymbals, and other instruments. The music in Solomon's temple at Jerusalem in the 900's B.C. probably included trumpets and choral singing to the accompaniment of stringed instruments.

China. The early Chinese believed that music had magic powers, as well as the power to please, because they thought it reflected the order in the universe. They were great systematizers, and set up an imperial bureau about 200 B.C. to establish an absolute system of pitch. Chinese music used a *pentatonic* (five-tone) scale. It had no half steps, and sounded somewhat like the five black keys of the piano. Chinese musicians played the zither, various flutes, and percussion instruments.

India. Musical traditions in India go back to the 1200's B.C. The people believed that music was directly related to the fundamental processes of human life. They developed religious music in ancient times, and worked out music theories by about 300 B.C. Musicians

Key Signatures tell what key the music is written in. If it has no flats or sharps, the music may be in the key of C major or its *relative minor*, A minor. Each major key has a relative minor.

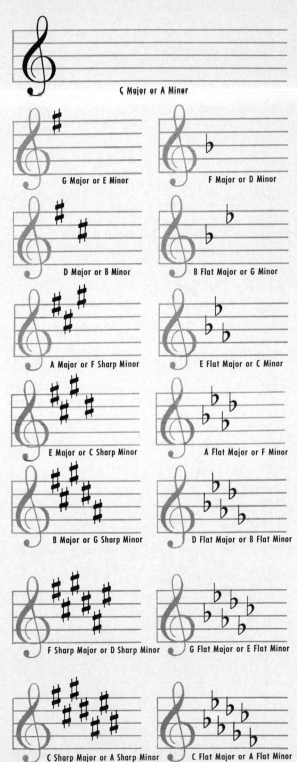

A Measure contains a set number of beats. Its *time signature* appears as a fraction, showing how many beats each measure has (four or three in the examples below) and what kind of note gets one beat (quarter notes in both examples illustrated below).

Accidentals are signs for sharp (♯), flat (♭), and natural (♮). They appear with the notes and make them higher or lower.

A and C, Both Natural   A and C Natural, B Flat

B Natural Instead of Flat   B Natural, Then Flat

played wind, stringed, and percussion instruments. Indian music was not based on a system of whole steps and half steps, like the diatonic scale. Instead of using specific notes, Indian composers followed a complicated set of formulas called *ragas*. Ragas permitted the choice between certain notes but required the omission of other notes. They set the emotional mood and even the philosophic meaning of the performance.

Greece. The Greeks used letters of the alphabet to represent musical tones. They grouped these tones in *tetrachords* (successions of four tones). The first and fourth tones have a relationship somewhat like that between C on the piano and the next F above. By combining these tetrachords in various ways, the Greeks created groups of tones called *modes*. Modes were the forerunners of more modern major and minor scales.

Greek thinkers worked out music theories more thoroughly than any other ancient people. In the 1800's and the first half of the 1900's, composers became interested in modes again. They felt that major and minor scales had lost their freshness.

Pythagoras, a Greek who lived in the 500's B.C., thought that music and mathematics provided keys to the secrets of the world. He believed that the planets produce different tones in harmony, so that the universe itself sings. This belief shows the importance of music in Greek worship, as well as in dance and drama. The Greeks wrote music for chorus and for instruments of the harp and wind families.

Rome. The Romans copied Greek music theory and performing techniques, but also invented such new instruments as the straight trumpet, which they called the *tuba*. They often used the *hydraulis*, or *hydraulus*, the first pipe organ, in the sports arena. Water pressure maintained an even flow of air for the pipes. Regardless

of legend, the emperor Nero could not have fiddled while Rome burned. The violin had not yet been invented, and he probably played a hydraulis or a lyre.

The Middle Ages. Chanting was part of Christian worship from early times. It gradually developed into a type of melody called *plain song*. St. Ambrose (A.D. 340?-397) helped work out a set of rules to maintain an appropriate style in singing hymns. Music that follows these rules is called *Ambrosian chant*. It was the first systematically composed form of plain song. Under Pope Gregory the Great, who died in 604, churchmen developed the *Gregorian chant*, which is more important today.

Plain song did not use the kind of musical scale we use today. It was built on a series of *modes* similar to those of Greek music. The diatonic scale of today fixes the pitches of certain notes and indicates the relationship between notes. Plain song did not always set the pitch of specific notes, but only set the relationships between notes. Plain song has no harmony or accompaniment. The music of antiquity and the early medieval period is often called *monophony*. It has a single melodic line which all performers played or sang. In the early Middle Ages, the people sang both religious and *secular* (nonreligious) music in the monophonic manner.

Later, they wanted to sing and play more interesting and complicated music than monophony. They put two or more melodies together, creating a type of music called *polyphony*, which means "many sounds." Early polyphony, sometimes called *organum*, appeared in Europe about 800. *Counterpoint* (polyphonic writing) developed in the next eight hundred years.

The Renaissance in music dates from the 1300's in southern Europe and from somewhat later in northern Europe. Composers wished to write music on secular themes without regard to the practices of the church. Composers were attracted to the possibilities of polyphonic writing, in which each voice could be assigned

THE HISTORY OF MUSIC

University Museum, University
of Pennsylvania, Philadelphia

In Babylonia, court musicians played ornate instruments. This lyre, probably made at Ur in the 2600's B.C., was covered with gold and shell.

In Egypt, musicians played reed pipes, and stringed instruments such as lyres, lutes, and harps. This wall painting was made in the 1400's B.C.

Musicians at a Banquet from the tomb of Djeserkara' sonb in Thebes, The Oriental Institute, Chicago

its own line of melody. Polyphonic writing provided technical opportunities for effects of great brilliance not previously possible. A secular form of composition, the *madrigal*, appeared in Italy during the 1300's. Composers wrote madrigals in their own language, rather than in Latin. Madrigal singing spread northward. Such Flemish composers as Guillaume Dufay (1400?-1474), Josquin des Prés (1445?-1521), and Orlando di Lasso (1532?-1594) wrote some works in this style. Most of their writing was religious, however.

In Italy, Giovanni Palestrina (1525?-1594) developed the most important systematic approach to polyphonic writing before Bach. During the Renaissance, English music reached heights it has never surpassed. Thomas Tallis (1505?-1585) was the first great English composer. He was closely rivaled by William Byrd (1543?-1623). Thomas Morley (1557-1603?), John Dowland (1563-1626), and Orlando Gibbons (1583-1625) set poetry of the period to music.

Baroque Music replaced the Renaissance style after 1600 and dominated European music until about 1750. Baroque music was elaborate and emotional. It was ideally suited to the treatment of dramatic subjects. The important new form was opera, closely followed by the oratorio, which also drew upon devices used in the theater.

Claudio Monteverdi (1567-1643) of Italy was the first major composer of opera. Jean Baptiste Lully (1632-1687), an Italian by birth, became the first master of operatic writing in France. Heinrich Schütz (1585-1672) wrote the first German opera and much sacred music. Alessandro Scarlatti (1659-1725) was the greatest Italian operatic composer of his era. His son Domenico (1685-1757) was one of a group of masters of secular instrumental music. Arcangelo Corelli (1653-1713) was another important figure in the group. Italian baroque music reached its height with the works of Antonio Vivaldi (1677?-1741). French composers who wrote in a similar style include François Couperin (1668-1733) and Jean Philippe Rameau (1683-1764). Henry Purcell (1659?-1695) was the major English composer in this period.

The Early 1700's: Bach. Johann Sebastian Bach (1685-1750) was the greatest member of the most important musical family in history. From the 1500's through the 1700's, more than 50 members of Bach's family gained recognition as musicians. Bach wrote music in nearly every form and style known in northern Europe during his lifetime. But, in his own time, he was most famous as the organist and choirmaster of various churches in Germany. Part of his job was to write music for religious services. He had little of it published and none was played more than a few times in public.

Bach gave methodical expression to the tonic-dominant system of harmony (explained in the *Harmony* section of this article). Musicians still study Bach's use of this harmony in such works as *The Well-Tempered Clavier*, a collection of 48 preludes and fugues that use all the major and minor keys. Other important composers of Bach's time include Dietrich Buxtehude (1637-1707) and Georg Philipp Telemann (1681-1767).

The Later 1700's: Classicism. Three composers dominated the music of the times. They were George Frideric Handel (1685-1759), Joseph Haydn (1732-1809), and Wolfgang Amadeus Mozart (1756-1791). As *classical* composers, they believed that music should be polished and gallant in manner. They wanted to express emotions only in a refined and elegant way. Their works sparkle with brilliance and gaiety and all three wrote huge amounts of music. Handel wrote over 40 operas and more than 20 oratorios. Haydn wrote more than 100 symphonies. As for Mozart, most people could not

Figurines de Tanagre, The Louvre, Paris
(Alinari from Art Reference Bureau)

In Greece, many people enjoyed playing such stringed instruments as the harp and the lyre. This statue was found in the ruins of Tanagra.

In China, palace musicians played instruments that resemble the lute, harp, xylophone, cymbals, and flute.

Palace Musicians (Sung Dynasty). The Art Institute of Chicago, Kate S. Buckingham Fund

even copy in 35 years the more than 600 works he wrote in that time. The public demanded this great output.

Haydn and Mozart, during their later years, wrote the first real symphonic masterworks. As a result, some persons think of them only in terms of their contributions to the symphony. But both composers also played an important part in developing the piano sonata, the string quartet, and other musical forms. Mozart also led in developing the opera. He surpassed his predecessor Christoph Willibald Gluck (1714-1787). Mozart produced works that have the universal quality of Shakespeare's greatest plays and that appear to speak directly to men of every era.

The Early 1800's: Romanticism. Classical composers felt the deepest emotions. But their musical works are composed in an artistic language that required a good deal of reserve. They emphasized elegance and form as tests of artistic discipline and taste. The romantics believed such conventions were artificial. They felt music should be fanciful and emotional, with the imagination providing the means, and sentiment sustaining the mood. Force of expression was intended to make up for any lack of polish in their work.

Ludwig van Beethoven (1770-1827) was a master of classical forms. But he departed from them whenever he felt it necessary to achieve his artistic goals. He was fundamentally a classicist, but wrote works that fully anticipated the romantic spirit. He specialized in piano music, string quartets, and orchestral works. The great German composer expected his works to be performed repeatedly and to live beyond his lifetime. Beethoven wrote only nine symphonies—less than a fourth as many as Mozart, and less than a tenth as many as Haydn. But Beethoven's symphonies are far more complex than any earlier ones.

An outstanding early romantic composer, Franz Schubert (1797-1828), wrote symphonies, piano music, string quartets, and more than 600 of the most beautiful songs ever composed. Another German romantic, Carl Maria von Weber (1786-1826), provided the first important example of national feeling in opera. In *Der Freischütz*, he began the practice of selecting story and music that reflected national character, instead of simply following classical models.

Felix Mendelssohn (1809-1847), also of Germany, won lasting fame for his instrumental music. His works include the *Overture* he wrote at the age of 17 for Shakespeare's *A Midsummer Night's Dream*. Mendelssohn was largely responsible for reviving interest in Bach's music. As a performer, he began the practice of stressing older music, rather than the latest works by living composers. Another German composer, Robert Schumann (1810-1856), composed four symphonies and much beautiful piano and vocal music. Frédéric Chopin (1810?-1849), born in Poland, spent most of his life in France. He wrote nothing for the orchestra alone, but his many works for the piano keep his name alive.

The Later 1800's: Nationalism. One of the outgrowths of romanticism was that many composers began searching for ways to express the feelings of their peoples in music. Musical nationalism developed in many ways in various countries. Some composers studied folk music, and used folk melodies in their works.

In France, nationalism took the form of a distinctive new tradition in opera and in dramatic symphonic works. Hector Berlioz (1803-1869) was the first composer to appreciate the tonal resources of the new instruments, such as the valve horn, that were developed during his lifetime. He also made new use of symphonic music to express vivid pictures, as in his *Fantastic Symphony* and *Harold in Italy*.

Giacomo Meyerbeer (1791-1864), although a German by birth, dominated French opera. His grandiose works are mostly forgotten, but we still enjoy those of his successors, including Ambroise Thomas (1811-1896), Charles Gounod (1818-1893), Léo Delibes (1836-1891), Jules Massenet (1842-1912), and Gustave Charpentier (1860-1956). Georges Bizet (1838-1875) wrote the ever-popular *Carmen*. Jacques Offenbach (1819-1880), also of German birth, created the French light opera.

In instrumental music, Belgian-born César Franck (1822-1890) wrote only one symphony, but influenced symphonic form. The same motifs dominate all three movements of his *cyclic* work. Vincent d'Indy (1851-1931) and Ernest Chausson (1855-1899) followed the cyclic form. Other French composers in the years after Berlioz included Camille Saint-Saëns (1835-1921), Gabriel Fauré (1845-1924), and Paul Dukas (1865-1935).

Franz Liszt (1811-1886), born in Hungary but active in both France and Germany, represents a tie between

Medieval Music was not usually written with notes, but with *neumes*, signs above the words that showed whether the melody should go up or down. This page was written in the A.D. 1000's.

The Newberry Library, Chicago

French and German music. His piano compositions and symphonic poems have never lost their popularity. His *Hungarian Rhapsodies* are based on Gypsy tunes rather than Hungarian folk tunes.

In Germany, Richard Wagner (1813-1883) dominated operatic music with his revolutionary music dramas. Anton Bruckner (1824-1896) wrote vast symphonies based on Wagner's principles. The last half of the 1800's saw sharp debates between Wagnerians and the followers of Johannes Brahms (1833-1897). Brahms rejected the influence of the theater, and tried to continue the tradition of Beethoven. His followers preferred "pure" or nondescriptive music to the scene-painting of Berlioz or the dramatizations of Wagner. The two groups often clashed at concerts, shouting boos and catcalls.

Gustav Mahler (1860-1911) was strongly influenced by Wagner, but developed a highly individual style in his symphonies and songs. Hugo Wolf (1860-1903) ranks with Schubert as a composer of music for voice. The Viennese style of waltz music and light opera began with Johann Strauss (1804-1849) and reached its height with his son Johann Jr., "the waltz king" (1825-1899).

In Italy, Gioacchino Rossini (1792-1868), Gaetano Donizetti (1797-1848), and Vincenzo Bellini (1801-1835) developed the opera. Italian opera reached its highest level in the works of Giuseppe Verdi (1813-1901). Giacomo Puccini (1858-1924) continued the tradition with emphasis on beautiful melodies. Other operatic composers included Ruggiero Leoncavallo (1858-1919) and Pietro Mascagni (1863-1945).

In Russia, serious music began with the operas of Mikhail Glinka (1804-1857). He was not a professional composer, and his most important followers also had other careers. Alexander Borodin (1833-1887) was a celebrated chemist, Modest Mussorgsky (1839-1881) was a government official, and Nicholas Rimsky-Korsakov (1844-1908) was a naval officer. These three joined Mily Balakirev (1837-1910) and César Cui (1835-1918) to form a group called *The Five*. Mussorgsky had the greatest musical ability of the group.

The most popular Russian composer was Peter Ilich Tchaikovsky (1840-1893). His last three symphonies remain the most widely admired Russian works in this form. Sergei Rachmaninoff (1873-1943) concentrated chiefly on piano works.

In the English-Speaking Countries, little music of international significance appeared during the 1800's. Sir Arthur Sullivan (1842-1900) began an English light-opera tradition in his famous partnership with Sir W. S. Gilbert, who wrote the words for Sullivan's music. Sir Edward Elgar (1857-1934) was the first important English symphonist, and Frederick Delius (1862-1934) developed an individual approach to the symphonic poem. Edward MacDowell (1861-1908), an American, wrote many beautiful piano works. Victor Herbert (1859-1924) began an American tradition of light opera.

In Other Parts of Europe. Nationalism flourished in the music of three Czech composers, Bedřich Smetana (1824-1884), Antonín Dvořák (1841-1904), and Leoš Janáček (1854-1928). Scandinavian composers included Edvard Grieg (1843-1907) of Norway, Carl Nielsen (1865-1931) of Denmark, and Jean Sibelius (1865-1957) of Finland.

The 1900's have seen four major developments in the history of music: (1) the continued growth of nationalism; (2) the appearance of major American and Latin-American composers; (3) the rise of international styles in music for the first time since the classical period of the 1700's; and (4) the search for new harmonic principles to replace tonic-dominant harmony.

Nationalism became a force in Spanish music with the works of Manuel de Falla (1876-1946). Russian composers, ruled by their Communist government, developed an officially anti-romantic outlook known as *socialist realism*, but it often showed strong romantic sympathies. Major exponents of this style included Sergei Prokofiev (1891-1953), Aram Khachaturian (1903-1978), Dimitri Kabalevsky (1904-   ), and Dimitri Shostakovich (1906-1975). In England, Ralph Vaughan Williams (1872-1958), Sir William Walton (1902-   ), and Benjamin Britten (1913-1976) usually followed fairly conservative practices.

Richard Strauss (1864-1949), the dominant figure in German music for more than 50 years, wrote for the theater or the concert hall with equal mastery. The Hungarian masters Béla Bartók (1881-1945) and Zoltán Kodály (1882-1967) discovered individual musical styles based upon Hungarian folk songs. Paul Hindemith (1895-1963) and Carl Orff (1895-   ) also developed strong personal styles in German music.

New American Composers began expressing vital new ideas in music during the 1900's. Charles Ives (1874-1954) wrote advanced and technically unorthodox music, and had to wait years before his major works were even performed. John Alden Carpenter (1876-1951), less extreme in his musical ideas, won earlier recognition. Many American composers studied in Paris with Nadia Boulanger (1887-1979), a great French music teacher. They included Walter Piston (1894-1976), Virgil Thomson (1896-   ), Roy Harris (1898-1979), and Aaron Copland (1900-   ). Three younger composers —Elliott Carter (1908-   ), Samuel Barber (1910-   ), and William Schuman (1910-   )—reveal more distinctively American influences. Howard Hanson (1896-   ) presented conservative musical ideas, and Roger Sessions (1896-   ) became an advanced harmonic innovator. Latin America produced such important composers as Carlos Chávez (1899-1978) of Mexico, Heitor Villa-Lobos (1887-1959) of Brazil, and Alberto Ginastera (1916-   ) of Argentina.

International Styles of the 1900's began with the "impressionism" developed in France by Claude Debussy (1862-1918). His works influenced Alexander Scriabin (1872-1915) in Russia and Charles Griffes (1884-1920) in America. Two Italian composers, Ottorino Respighi (1879-1936) and Ildebrando Pizzetti (1880-1968), also followed Debussy's example. In France, Maurice Ravel (1875-1937) won the widest acceptance in the years after Debussy, although some critics believe that Erik Satie (1866-1925) made more original contributions. Olivier Messiaen (1908-   ), a French composer, became noted for his rhythmic complexity and original harmonic style.

Melodic emphasis appeared in the works of a French group called *Les Six*, led by Arthur Honegger (1892-1955), Darius Milhaud (1892-1974), and Francis Poulenc (1899-1963). Czech-born Bohuslav Martinů (1890-1959) agreed with *Les Six* on the importance of melody. Ernest Bloch (1880-1959), born in Switzerland, also emphasized melodic content. Another Swiss composer, Frank Martin (1890-1974), combined melodic and rhythmic drive in his works.

Igor Stravinsky (1882-1971) led in developing many new musical styles. Born in Russia, he lived in France and Switzerland before settling in the United States. His musical development led him through nationalism and neoclassicism to composition in the 12-tone system which Arnold Schönberg had advocated in his most influential years. Stravinsky's early ballets, especially *The Rite of Spring* (which caused fist fights at its premiere in 1913), were quickly accepted as contemporary classics. In fact, the continued popularity of his early ballets sometimes obscured the merits of his later work. Another composer whose technique developed enormously through his lifetime was Edgard Varèse (1883-1965). Varèse was born in Paris but spent his most important years in the United States. He has been called the father of electronic music.

New Harmonic Principles appeared to Arnold Schönberg (1874-1951) to be the only way to keep music alive. The Austrian-born composer believed that musicians had exhausted the tonic-dominant system, and felt that music needed an entirely new harmonic structure. In Schönberg's *twelve-tone* technique, all 12 notes in the chromatic scale have equal value. There are no key signatures or scales. Instead, his works have *tone rows* in which all 12 tones are arranged in a predetermined order. All the melodies and harmonies are drawn from the tone row, which does not change within a composition. At first these innovations aroused storms of protest from audiences and from conservative composers and critics. Schönberg's most important disciples were two other Austrians, Anton Webern (1883-1945) and Alban Berg (1885-1935). Others experimented with various forms of *atonality* (writing in the chromatic scale without a conventional tonal center) and *polytonality* (writing in two or more keys at one time).

In the 1960's, nationalism apparently had ceased to function as a genuine force in serious music. The music world presented a situation similar to the 1600's, when international styles dominated the scene and composers of widely different backgrounds could share the same artistic viewpoint. In Communist countries, socialist realism was the official style. Other approaches to composition were condemned as lacking in emotional appeal. There were, however, signs of composition in styles other than socialist realism.

1650   1700

Ludwig Van Beethoven

Johann Sebastian Bach

Great Composers

This table includes the world's great composers of symphonies, operas, and concertos from 1650 to the present. Important Italian composers before 1650 included Claudio Monteverdi (1567-1643) and Giovanni Palestrina (1525?-1594).

Each composer has a separate biography in WORLD BOOK.

George Frideric Handel (1685-1759) German
Domenico Scarlatti (1685-1757) Italian
Johann Sebastian Bach (1685-1750) German
Jean Philippe Rameau (1683-1764) French
Antonio Vivaldi (1677?-1741) Italian
Alessandro Scarlatti (1659-1725) Italian
Henry Purcell (1659?-1695) English

1650   1700

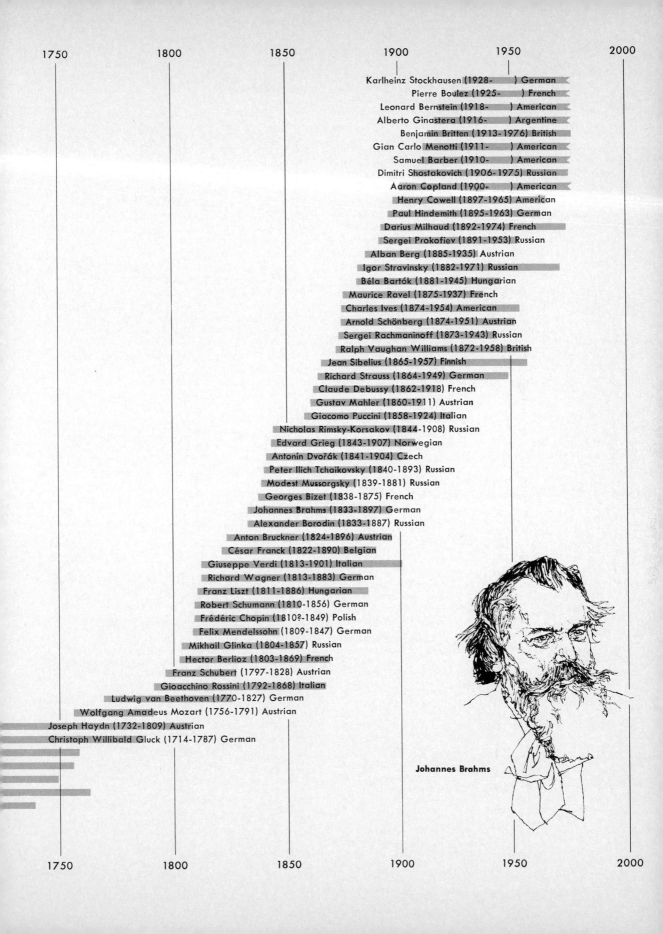

| 1750 | 1800 | 1850 | 1900 | 1950 | 2000 |

Karlheinz Stockhausen (1928-   ) German
Pierre Boulez (1925-   ) French
Leonard Bernstein (1918-   ) American
Alberto Ginastera (1916-   ) Argentine
Benjamin Britten (1913-1976) British
Gian Carlo Menotti (1911-   ) American
Samuel Barber (1910-   ) American
Dimitri Shostakovich (1906-1975) Russian
Aaron Copland (1900-   ) American
Henry Cowell (1897-1965) American
Paul Hindemith (1895-1963) German
Darius Milhaud (1892-1974) French
Sergei Prokofiev (1891-1953) Russian
Alban Berg (1885-1935) Austrian
Igor Stravinsky (1882-1971) Russian
Béla Bartók (1881-1945) Hungarian
Maurice Ravel (1875-1937) French
Charles Ives (1874-1954) American
Arnold Schönberg (1874-1951) Austrian
Sergei Rachmaninoff (1873-1943) Russian
Ralph Vaughan Williams (1872-1958) British
Jean Sibelius (1865-1957) Finnish
Richard Strauss (1864-1949) German
Claude Debussy (1862-1918) French
Gustav Mahler (1860-1911) Austrian
Giacomo Puccini (1858-1924) Italian
Nicholas Rimsky-Korsakov (1844-1908) Russian
Edvard Grieg (1843-1907) Norwegian
Antonín Dvořák (1841-1904) Czech
Peter Ilich Tchaikovsky (1840-1893) Russian
Modest Mussorgsky (1839-1881) Russian
Georges Bizet (1838-1875) French
Johannes Brahms (1833-1897) German
Alexander Borodin (1833-1887) Russian
Anton Bruckner (1824-1896) Austrian
César Franck (1822-1890) Belgian
Giuseppe Verdi (1813-1901) Italian
Richard Wagner (1813-1883) German
Franz Liszt (1811-1886) Hungarian
Robert Schumann (1810-1856) German
Frédéric Chopin (1810?-1849) Polish
Felix Mendelssohn (1809-1847) German
Mikhail Glinka (1804-1857) Russian
Hector Berlioz (1803-1869) French
Franz Schubert (1797-1828) Austrian
Gioacchino Rossini (1792-1868) Italian
Ludwig van Beethoven (1770-1827) German
Wolfgang Amadeus Mozart (1756-1791) Austrian
Joseph Haydn (1732-1809) Austrian
Christoph Willibald Gluck (1714-1787) German

Johannes Brahms

| 1750 | 1800 | 1850 | 1900 | 1950 | 2000 |

Some composers continued to write in diatonic or, more commonly, chromatic harmonies. They extended the limits of the tonic-dominant system of harmony without destroying it. Although frequently attacked by critics and other composers for their conservatism, these composers managed to retain a large portion of music audiences. The most fashionable and important international style was 12-tone music as defined by Schönberg and his disciples. Important figures in this style include Austrian-born Ernst Krenek (1900-   ), Luigi Dallapiccola (1904-1975) of Italy, Ben Weber (1916-1979) of the United States, and Pierre Boulez (1925-   ) of France. An American, Gunther Schuller (1925-   ), tried to combine jazz with the 12-tone technique. The German Karlheinz Stockhausen (1928-   ) was one of several composers to occasionally omit live performers in favor of purely electronic music.

The acceptance of the tape recorder after World War II made direct composition on tape possible. Composers used both natural sounds and electronically produced sounds in taped music. They altered the result in the laboratory, producing a synthesis of tones which cannot be performed except by tape playback. Electronic techniques have greatly extended the technical possibilities open to the composer and the range of musical expression.

Stockhausen and John Cage (1912-   ) of the United States became important figures in the development of *chance* or *aleatory* music. Unlike electronic music, aleatory music depends mainly upon live performance. But the composer does not specify all the pitches and rhythms of compositions. Performers introduce random elements, and no two performances of a given work are the same.

Careers in Music

Serious music is one of the most difficult professions in which to achieve a high level of success. Many fully qualified candidates compete keenly for almost every desirable position. The most successful concert artists and operatic celebrities may earn several thousand dollars for a single performance. But many excellent musicians receive less for a whole year's work.

People should have exceptional musical ability before they seriously consider a musical career. Mere interest and skill are not enough. To attain even minimum success, they need absolute dedication—the conviction that music is the most important thing in life. They should become musicians only if they cannot imagine themselves doing anything else.

Training for any career in music includes systematic groundwork in the principles of harmony and music theory. The would-be musician must know the music written for his instrument, and how to play the instru-

---

TERMS USED IN MUSIC

A cappella, *ah kah PEL uh,* is singing without accompaniment.

Accelerando, *ah chel er AHN doh,* means speeding up the tempo.

Accidentals, *ak sih DEN tulz,* are sharps, flats, and naturals not included in a key signature.

Adagio, *ah DAH joh,* means slow, but not as slow as largo.

Ad libitum, *ad LIHB ih tum,* allows the musician to play the written notes with great freedom.

Agitato, *ah jee TAH toh,* means restless or excited.

Allegretto, *al uh GRET oh,* means brisk and light, but not as fast as allegro.

Allegro, *uh LAY groh,* means fast and lively.

Andante, *ahn DAHN tay,* means smooth and flowing, at a moderate speed.

Andantino, *ahn dahn TEE noh,* means not quite andante. It usually means a little faster, but once meant a little slower.

Animato, *ah nee MAH toh,* means lively or animated.

Appassionata, *ah PAHS syo NAH tah,* means with great feeling.

Arpeggio, *ahr PEHJ oh,* is a series of tones played quickly, one right after another.

Brillante, *bree LAHN tay,* means bright or sparkling.

Cadenza, *kuh DEN zuh,* is a solo passage where the performer displays virtuosity.

*Canon is a strict form in which several voices sing or play the same tune one after another, overlapping, without variation.

Cantabile, *kahn TAH bee lay,* means songlike.

*Cantata, *kahn TAH tah,* is a fairly short work for one or more soloists and orchestra, often with chorus.

Chord is a group of related tones played together.

Clef is a sign that fixes the positions of certain notes on the lines and spaces of the staff.

Coda is the ending of a movement or other work.

Con brio, *kohn BREE oh,* means with liveliness and great spirit.

Con moto, *kohn MOH toh,* means with strong feeling of motion.

Crescendo, *kruh SHEN doh,* means growing louder.

Decrescendo, *day kruh SHEN doh,* means growing softer.

Diminuendo, *duh MIHN oo EHN doh,* means gradually growing softer.

Enharmonic keys are those that can be written in two different ways, but are played with exactly the same notes on a piano. Composers may write in F sharp major, rather than in G flat major, although the sound as played is identical.

Espressivo, *ehs press SEE voh,* means with expression.

*Fantasia, *fan TAY zhuh,* is a fantasy—a work in no specific form, or in a free form.

Fifth is an interval of five steps between tones.

Figured bass is a system of figures attached to a bass melody that continues throughout a composition. The figures, which the composer writes under the melody, indicate successive harmonies of the composition. Figured bass is usually played on a keyboard instrument with a cello reinforcing the bass melody. The practice of figured bass began with opera about 1600 and lasted into the 1700's. It is a central element in baroque music. It is also called *basso continuo* or *thoroughbass.*

Finale, *fuh NAH lee,* is the ending—the last act or scene of an opera or the last movement in a symphony, concerto, or other work.

Flat is the half step below a given tone, bearing the same letter name as that tone.

Forte, *FAWR tay,* means strong and loud.

Fortissimo, *fawr TISS ih moh,* means as loud as possible.

Glissando, *glih SAHN doh,* means sliding.

Grace note is a single note or part of a group used in a melody. It is printed in small type and subtracts its time value from the note which follows.

Interval is the difference in pitch between two tones, expressed in the steps of the scale.

*Key is the "home" center of a musical work.

Larghetto, *lahr GET oh,* means slower than adagio, but not as slow as largo.

Largo, *LAHR go,* means extremely slow.

Ledger line is a short line drawn above or below the

ment itself. Students should complete at least a general high school course, taking private music lessons at the same time. They should then study music in a college or conservatory, or with private teachers. While they study formally, they must also study and practice independently. They will soon discover that the greatest musicians are those who continue to learn.

Opportunities. Most persons who study music would like to become recognized performers or composers. But teaching music in public and private schools offers the largest number of career opportunities. Many composers earn their living by teaching, or by arranging or orchestrating the works of others. Musicians perform in symphony orchestras or dance bands, or in the small groups that play in theaters, on television or radio programs, or at public affairs. A few exceptionally talented musicians perform as soloists with orchestras or opera companies, or give solo concerts.

Several career fields combine musical talent with other interests. Concert management is a specialized field requiring a knowledge of both music and business. Music critics and historians must have the special abilities of both musicians and writers. The recording industry has openings for knowledgeable persons.

International cultural exchange programs and the role of the performing arts as an element in national prestige have grown in importance. Therefore, jobs have opened in arts programs with major foundations and with government information services. *Ethnomusicology*, which studies music as a key to understanding a society, is an important new field combining the arts and social studies. The field of serious jazz study is also gaining acceptance. The increase in community orchestras and choral groups provides additional opportunities for employment.

Before students can enter any of these careers, they must spend much time in preparation. But even a little success justifies a great deal of hardship and effort. Few successful professional musicians regret their choice of a way of life. ROBERT C. MARSH

Critically reviewed by HALSEY STEVENS and JAMES SYKES

Related Articles. See the Arts section of the articles on various countries, such as MEXICO (Arts). See also the following articles:

BIOGRAPHIES

For biographies of other persons relating to Music, see the lists of Related Articles at the end of HYMN; MUSICAL COMEDY; ORCHESTRA; ORGAN; PIANO; POPULAR MUSIC; SINGING; and VIOLIN. See also:

AMERICAN COMPOSERS

Barber, Samuel	Blitzstein, Marc
Berlin, Irving	Bloch, Ernest
Bernstein, Leonard	Cage, John
Billings, William	Carter, Elliott

TERMS USED IN MUSIC

---

staff. It is used for any note that is too high or too low to be drawn on the staff.

Legato, *lay GAH toh,* means graceful and smooth.

Maestoso, *mah es TOH zoh,* means majestic.

Major scale is one of the two basic modes of music. A major scale has two *tetrachords* (half scales), each rising two whole steps and then a half step. All major scales follow a set pattern which contains whole step and half step intervals as follows: two wholes, one half, three wholes, one half. On any of the *chromatic* half steps within a given octave, a major scale may be built, using this pattern.

Measure or **Bar** is a unit of musical time containing an indicated number of beats.

Mezzo, *MED zoh,* means medium. It modifies other terms, as in **mezzo forte** (fairly loud).

Minor scale is one of the two basic modes of music. There are three forms of minor scales starting on any given tone. They are *harmonic minor scale,* the most frequently used form of minor; *natural minor scale;* and *melodic minor scale.*

Moderato, *MAHD uh RAH toh,* means playing in moderate tempo.

Modulation, *mahd you LAY shun,* is moving from one key to another. This may involve a change in the key signature.

Molto, *MOHL toh,* means a great deal or very much. It modifies other terms, as in **molto allegro** (very fast).

Natural is a note that is neither sharp nor flat.

Non troppo, *nohn TROHP oh,* means not too much or not exaggerated.

Obbligato, *ahb luh GAH toh,* is an accompanying part.

Octave, *AHK tihv,* is an interval of eight notes.

Pianissimo, *pee uh NISS ih moh,* means as soft as possible.

Piano, *pee AH noh,* means soft.

Pitch is the highness or lowness of a tone, depending on the number of times that its sound waves vibrate in a second.

Più, *pyoo,* means more. It modifies other terms, as in **più presto** (faster than presto).

Pizzicato, *pit suh KAH toh,* means plucking the strings of a violin or other bowed instrument.

Poco, *POH koh,* means little.

Polyphony, *puh LIHF uh nee,* means having several voices sing or play several melodies at the same time.

Prestissimo, *press TIHS uh moh,* means fast as possible.

Presto, *PRESS toh,* means very fast.

Rallentando, *RAHL len TAHN doh,* means gradually slowing the tempo.

*****Round** is a short form in which several voices sing the same theme, overlapping, one after another.

Scale is a series of tones or steps leading from one tone to its octave.

*****Scherzo,** *SKEHR tso,* is a whimsical movement or work, often highly rhythmic.

Sforzando, *sfawr TSAHN doh,* means with a sudden, strong accent.

Sharp is the half step above a given tone, bearing the same letter name as that tone.

Song cycle is a group of poems set to music as a unit.

Sostenuto, *sahs tuh NOO toh,* means sustaining the tone.

Sotto voce, *soht toh* or *SAHT oh VOH chay,* means in a low, soft voice, almost a whisper.

Staccato, *stuh KAH toh,* means with clearly distinct tones, sharply separated from one another.

Staff consists of five horizontal lines and the spaces between them. Notes are written on the lines and spaces.

Tetrachord is a four-note half scale, rising two and a half steps. Differences in the location of the half steps are the chief difference between major and minor modes.

Third is an interval whose tones are written on adjacent lines or adjacent spaces of the staff, such as C-E or G♯-B.

Tremolo, *TREHM uh loh,* means quivering or trembling.

Triad is a chord made up of a *root* note and the notes a third and a fifth above it.

Vibrante, *vee BRAHN tay,* means pulsing or vigorous.

Vivace, *vee VAH chay,* means lively or played with great speed.

*Has an article in WORLD BOOK.

MUSIC

Copland, Aaron
Cowell, Henry
Dello Joio, Norman
Foster, Stephen C.
Friml, Rudolf
Gershwin, George
Gilmore, Patrick S.
Gould, Morton
Grofé, Ferde
Hanson, Howard H.
Harris, Roy

Ives, Charles E.
King, Karl
MacDowell, Edward A.
Menotti, Gian Carlo
Moore, Douglas S.
Piston, Walter
Schuman, William
Sessions, Roger
Sousa, John Philip
Thomson, Virgil
Varèse, Edgard

AUSTRIAN COMPOSERS

Berg, Alban
Bruckner, Anton
Czerny, Karl
Haydn, Joseph
Kreisler, Fritz
Mahler, Gustav

Mozart, Wolfgang Amadeus
Schönberg, Arnold
Schubert, Franz P.
Straus, Oscar
Strauss (family)
Webern, Anton

BRITISH COMPOSERS

Britten, Benjamin
Byrd, William
Delius, Frederick
Dowland, John
Elgar, Sir Edward W.
Gibbons, Orlando

Gilbert and Sullivan
Morley, Thomas
Purcell, Henry
Tallis, Thomas
Vaughan Williams, Ralph
Walton, Sir William

FRENCH COMPOSERS

Berlioz, Hector
Bizet, Georges
Boulez, Pierre
Couperin, François
Debussy, Claude
Delibes, Léo
D'Indy, Vincent
Dukas, Paul A.
Fauré, Gabriel U.
Franck, César A.
Gounod, Charles
Honegger, Arthur

Ibert, Jacques
Lully, Jean B.
Massenet, Jules
Messiaen, Olivier
Milhaud, Darius
Offenbach, Jacques
Poulenc, Francis
Rameau, Jean Philippe
Ravel, Maurice
Saint-Saëns, Camille
Satie, Erik

GERMAN COMPOSERS

Bach (family)
Beethoven, Ludwig van
Brahms, Johannes
Bruch, Max
Buxtehude, Dietrich
Gluck, Christoph W.
Handel, George F.
Henze, Hans Werner
Hindemith, Paul
Humperdinck, Engelbert

Mendelssohn, Felix
Meyerbeer, Giacomo
Schumann, Clara
Schumann, Robert
Stockhausen, Karlheinz
Strauss, Richard
Wagner, Richard
Weber, Carl Maria von
Weill, Kurt

ITALIAN COMPOSERS

Bellini, Vincenzo
Boccherini, Luigi
Boito, Arrigo
Cherubini, Luigi
Clementi, Muzio
Corelli, Arcangelo
Dallapiccola, Luigi
Donizetti, Gaetano
Leoncavallo, Ruggiero
Mascagni, Pietro
Monteverdi, Claudio

Paganini, Niccolò
Palestrina, Giovanni
Pergolesi, Giovanni B.
Puccini, Giacomo
Respighi, Ottorino
Rossini, Gioacchino A.
Scarlatti (family)
Tartini, Giuseppe
Verdi, Giuseppe
Vivaldi, Antonio

RUSSIAN COMPOSERS

Borodin, Alexander
Glinka, Mikhail I.
Khachaturian, Aram I.
Mussorgsky, Modest
Prokofiev, Sergei S.
Rachmaninoff, Sergei V.

Rimsky-Korsakov, Nicholas
Rubinstein, Anton G.
Scriabin, Alexander
Shostakovich, Dimitri
Stravinsky, Igor F.
Tchaikovsky, Peter I.

OTHER COMPOSERS

Albéniz, Isaac
Bartók, Béla
Chávez, Carlos
Chopin, Frédéric F.
Dvořák, Antonín
Falla, Manuel de
García, Manuel
Ginastera, Alberto
Grainger, Percy A.
Grieg, Edvard

Janáček, Leoš
Kodály, Zoltán
Lehár, Franz
Liszt, Franz
Nielsen, Carl A.
Paderewski, Ignace J.
Sibelius, Jean
Smetana, Bedřich
Villa-Lobos, Heitor
Wieniawski, Henri

KINDS OF MUSIC

Aleatory Music
Ballet
Chamber Music
Country and
  Western Music
Electronic Music

Folk Music
Hymn
Jazz
Musical Comedy
Opera

Operetta
Oratorio
Popular Music
Ragtime
Rock Music

ELEMENTS OF MUSIC

Counterpoint
Dynamics
Harmonics
Harmony

Key
Pitch
Rhythm

Sound
Tone
Treble

INSTRUMENTAL MUSICAL FORMS

Concerto
Étude
Fantasia
Fugue
March

Overture
Rondo
Round
Scherzo
Serenade

Sonata
Suite
Symphonic Poem
Symphony
Variations

MUSICAL INSTRUMENTS

Accordion
Bagpipe
Balalaika
Banjo
Bass
Bassoon
Bell
Bugle
Calliope
Castanets
Celesta
Cello
Chimes
Clarinet
Clavichord
Clavilux
Concertina
Cornet
Cymbal
Drum
Dulcimer
English Horn
Fife

Flageolet
Flügelhorn
Flute
French Horn
Glockenspiel
Gong
Guitar
Hand Organ
Harmonica
Harmonium
Harp
Harpsichord
Horn
Hornpipe
Jew's-Harp
Lute
Lyre
Mandolin
Marimba
Mellophone
Oboe
Ocarina
Orchestra Bells

Organ
Piano
Piccolo
Pipe
Recorder
Saxophone
Sitar
Spinet
Synthesizer
Tambourine
Theremin
Tom-Tom
Triangle
Trombone
Trumpet
Tuba
Ukulele
Viol
Viola
Violin
Virginal
Xylophone
Zither

VOCAL MUSIC

Ballad
Barbershop Quartet
  Singing
Barcarole
Bard
Calypso
Canon
Cantata
Carol

Chantey
Chorale
Lieder
Lullaby
Madrigal
Mastersinger
Minnesinger
Minstrel

Passion Music
Singing
Skald
Song
Spiritual
Troubadour
Trouvère
Voice

OTHER RELATED ARTICLES

American Society of Composers,
  Authors and Publishers
Band

Carillon
Cecilia, Saint
Folk Music

Outline

I. Enjoying Music
  A. Understanding Music   B. Judging Music

II. Musical Instruments
  A. Stringed Instruments   C. Brass Instruments
                  D. Percussion Instruments
  B. Wood-Wind Instruments   E. Keyboard Instruments
                  F. Other Instruments

III. Instrumental Music
  A. Instrumental Solos   C. Orchestral Music
  B. Chamber Music

IV. Vocal Music
  A. Singing Voices C. Choral Music E. Oratorios
  B. Songs   D. Opera

V. The Elements of Music
  A. Sound in Music C. Harmony E. Tempo
  B. Melody   D. Rhythm   F. Tone Color

VI. The Language of Music
  A. Notation   C. Names of Compositions
  B. Scores

VII. Musical Forms
  A. Song Form   D. Canon and Fugue
  B. Sonata Form   E. Free Form
  C. Variation Form

VIII. History

IX. Careers in Music

Questions

How can we learn to enjoy music? To judge it?

What career opportunities await music students?

What is the distance between tones in the chromatic scale? How does the diatonic scale differ?

What is the difference between a note and a tone?

How do *art* songs differ from *popular* songs?

Who is generally credited with devising the musical staff? Why was this development important?

How are a concerto and a symphony similar?

What is the basis for harmonic relationships?

Why did romantic composers disagree with the rules followed by classical composers?

How does a composer indicate the pitch of a tone?

Reading and Study Guide

See *Music* in the RESEARCH GUIDE/INDEX, Volume 22, for a *Reading and Study Guide*.

Books to Read

For books to read about opera, see the bibliography at the end of the OPERA article. For books on music for young readers, see LITERATURE FOR CHILDREN (Information Books/The Arts). See also the following books:

GENERAL BOOKS ON MUSIC

BRACE, GEOFFREY, and BURTON, IAN. *Listen! Music and Nature.* Cambridge, 1976. For young readers.

BROIDO, ARNOLD, and DAVIS, M. K. *Music Dictionary.* Doubleday, 1956. For young readers.

COPLAND, AARON. *What to Listen For in Music.* Rev. ed. McGraw, 1957.

DIAGRAM GROUP. *Musical Instruments of the World: An Illustrated Encyclopedia.* Paddington Press, 1976.

GROVE, GEORGE, ed. *The New Grove Dictionary of Music and Musicians.* Edited by Stanley Sadie. 20 vols. Grove's Dictionaries, 1979.

LLOYD, NORMAN. *The Golden Encyclopedia of Music.* Golden Press, 1968.

MARCUSE, SIBYL. *A Survey of Musical Instruments.* Harper, 1975.

ROBERTS, JOHN. *Black Music of Two Worlds.* Holt, 1972.

SCHOLES, PERCY A. *The Oxford Junior Companion to Music.* Oxford, 1954. For young readers.

THOMPSON, OSCAR, ed. *The International Cyclopedia of Music and Musicians.* 10th ed. Dodd, 1975.

CLASSICAL MUSIC

BERNSTEIN, LEONARD. *The Unanswered Question: Six Talks at Harvard.* Harvard, 1976.

BRINDLE, REGINALD SMITH. *The New Music: The Avant-Garde Since 1945.* Oxford, 1975.

GROUT, DONALD J. *A History of Western Music.* Rev. ed. Norton, 1973.

KUPFERBERG, HERBERT. *A Rainbow of Sound: The Instruments of the Orchestra and Their Music.* Scribner, 1973. For young readers.

THOMSON, VIRGIL. *American Music Since 1910.* Holt, 1971.

POPULAR MUSIC

BERGER, MELVIN. *The Story of Folk Music.* Phillips, 1976. For young readers.

FEATHER, LEONARD G. *The Encyclopedia of Jazz.* 2nd ed. Horizon, 1960.

FEATHER, LEONARD G., and GITLER, IRA. *The Encyclopedia of Jazz in the Seventies.* Horizon, 1976.

HAMM, CHARLES. *Yesterdays: Popular Songs in America.* Norton, 1979.

SHESTACK, MELVIN. *The Country Music Encyclopedia.* Harper, 1974.

STAMBLER, IRWIN. *Encyclopedia of Pop, Rock, and Soul.* St. Martin's, 1975.

MUSIC BOX is an instrument that plays tunes automatically. Steel pins protrude from a rotating cylinder driven by clockwork or a spring. The pins pluck metal teeth of various lengths, producing soft, high-pitched sounds of great delicacy. Several teeth may be tuned to the same note, so the box can repeat notes rapidly. Music boxes may be connected with clocks, and play certain tunes on the hour. Music-box movements are built into bracelets, toys, and other everyday objects.

Early music boxes had tiny flute pipes instead of teeth, and gave an organlike sound. Joseph Haydn wrote many charming pieces for the instrument. In the 1800's, some inventors developed music boxes that had as many as 400 teeth.   KARL GEIRINGER

MUSIC CLUBS, NATIONAL FEDERATION OF, is the largest music organization in the world. The federation is devoted to developing and maintaining high music standards in the United States and its possessions. It has about 600,000 members. Persons may join the federation as individuals or through music clubs, school clubs, choirs, choruses, conservatories, dance groups, or symphony orchestras.

The federation offers many awards and scholarships. Winners of the "Young Artist Auditions" receive $1,500 awards. The federation also sponsors "Cavalcade for Creative Youth," an annual contest for young composers, and it commissions works by American composers. It sponsors American Music Month and Parade of American Music in February and National Music Week in May. It publishes *Music Clubs Magazine* and *Junior Keynotes*. The federation was founded in 1898. The federation's headquarters are at 310 S. Michigan Avenue, Chicago, Ill. 60604.

Critically reviewed by the NATIONAL FEDERATION OF MUSIC CLUBS

MUSIC DRAMA. See MUSICAL COMEDY; OPERA; OPERETTA.

MUSICAL COMEDY

MUSICAL COMEDY is an entertainment written for the stage. It consists of a story, spoken in dialogue form, with songs, choruses, dances, and incidental music. *Musicals* are the unique contribution of the United States to world theater.

Nearly all well-known musical comedies originate on the Broadway stage in New York City, where they often play for several years to large audiences. The music is usually recorded and heard on radio and television by millions of people throughout the entire world. Many of our most popular and best-loved songs have originated in musical comedies.

Elements of Musical Comedy

The Story, called the *book*, is the most important thing in any musical comedy. It must be interesting and dramatic, and is usually amusing. The story must explain the characters and hold the interest of the audience throughout the *show*. It also connects the 20 or more musical numbers in the show. The story may be original. But most musicals are based on older well-known novels, plays, or motion pictures.

Music adds romantic color, humor, or drama to the story, particularly through the *lyrics*, or words, of the songs. Composers usually write original music, but may adapt classical or other music. For example, many of the musical themes for *Kismet* came from the music of Alexander Borodin.

Dancing provides variety, with colorful costumes and interesting patterns of steps, leaps, whirls, and general movement. Sometimes the dances merely entertain the audience. But they may also help tell the story with gestures and movements, as in Jerome Robbins' dances for *West Side Story* by Leonard Bernstein.

Staging a Musical Comedy

Writing. The writer, composer, and *lyricist*, or lyric writer, usually *collaborate*, or work together. Generally, the writer first works out a rough version of the story.

The composer and lyricist locate places in the story where they want to write songs. At this point, all three begin working together to make a whole show out of the separate elements.

After the composer gets an idea for a melody, the lyricist writes the words for the song. Both the composer and the lyricist make changes in order to accommodate one another.

Producing. When all the writing is completed, a producer or manager raises the money to put the musical on the stage. He or she tries to raise between $250,000 and $500,000 from various *angels*, or investors, who buy shares in the show. In return, they receive their investment and a certain percentage of the profits. The producer then selects a director to supervise the entire production. A scene-designer and a costume-designer prepare sketches from which the construction crew and costumers can work. In a musical, there may be 10 or 12 different stage sets, compared to one or two for a "straight" play. Elaborate production details may include revolving stages and many special effects. A conductor joins the staff to direct the singers and the orchestra, and a *choreographer*, or dance director, plans and rehearses the movements of dancers and singers. A press agent writes publicity and advertising.

The producers and directors hold many auditions to select the *principals*, or stars, and the supporting players, chorus, and dancers. They usually look for versatile performers who combine acting with singing and dancing. Usually they hear from 2,000 to 3,000 singers in order to select 12 to 16 men and women for the chorus. From about 1,000 dancers tested, they select 16 or 20. Rehearsals take place daily, for four or five weeks.

Performing. Some musical comedies play six to ten weeks in cities outside New York in order to change, cut, and improve the show. They also hold daytime rehearsals during these *out-of-town tryouts*.

Opening night on Broadway may make the difference between a *hit* and a failure. If the newspaper critics and the first-night audience like the musical, it will probably enjoy a long *run*. *Road companies* of the show

Zodiac

Fiddler on the Roof became one of the longest-running shows in Broadway history. This musical is a humorous and sentimental story of life in a Russian-Jewish village during the early 1900's.

Zodiac

Hair was the first well-known musical to emphasize rock music. Its youthful cast and high spirits made *Hair* especially popular with young audiences. The show pokes fun at current events, politicians, and traditional middle-class views about life. But *Hair* also satirizes the attitudes and conduct of many young people trying to rebel against society.

may play in American cities, while other companies perform abroad.

History

Beginnings. The first musical comedy is generally considered to be an English work, John Gay's *The Beggar's Opera*, written in 1728. But the musical-comedy form has had its widest development in the United States. It developed largely out of European operettas of the late 1800's and early 1900's. Operettas contained semiclassical music derived partly from grand opera and partly from folk songs. Most stories dealt with romantic, unrealistic situations. Perhaps the most famous European operetta was *The Merry Widow* (1905) by the Hungarian composer Franz Lehár. The most popular American operettas included *Naughty Marietta* (1910) by Victor Herbert, *The Firefly* (1912) by Rudolf Friml, and *The Student Prince* (1924) by Sigmund Romberg.

Modern Musicals. Beginning in the 1920's, American composers began to choose more realistic books and to write more varied and even serious music. Jerome Kern's *Show Boat* (1927) partly concerned racial discrimination. George and Ira Gershwin's *Of Thee I Sing* (1931) was a satire on American politics.

A trend toward collaboration began in the 1930's as composers and lyricists worked together to create musicals. The team of Richard Rodgers and Lorenz Hart wrote such notable musical comedies as *Pal Joey* (1940). After Hart died, Rodgers teamed with Oscar Hammerstein II to write some of the most popular musicals in theater history, including *Oklahoma!* (1943), *Carousel* (1945), *South Pacific* (1949), and *The King and I* (1951). Frederick Loewe and Alan Jay Lerner collaborated on *Brigadoon* (1947) and *My Fair Lady* (1956). Jerry Bock and Sheldon Harnick wrote *Fiddler on the Roof* (1964). Before this musical closed in 1972, it had become the longest running show in Broadway history.

In the late 1960's and the 1970's, many musicals reflected the influence of rock music. The most popular

was *Hair* (1967). Stephen Sondheim became the most important new composer and lyricist of the 1970's. Sondheim's major shows included *Company* (1970) and *A Little Night Music* (1973). Several musicals dealt with black themes, including *Raisin* (1973) and *The Wiz* (1975). *A Chorus Line* (1975) became the most popular musical of its time. The show concerns young dancers struggling to make a career in the theater. LEHMAN ENGEL

Related Articles in WORLD BOOK include:

Berlin, Irving	Operetta
Bernstein, Leonard	Porter, Cole
Gershwin, George	Robbins, Jerome
Hammerstein (Oscar II)	Rodgers, Richard
Herbert, Victor	Romberg, Sigmund
Kern, Jerome	Theater (Theater in the
Lehár, Franz	United States)

MUSICAL INSTRUMENT. See MUSIC (Musical Instruments).

MUSICAL NOTATION. See MUSIC (Notation).

MUSICIAN. See the Careers section in MUSIC.

MUSICIANS, AMERICAN FEDERATION OF, is a labor union affiliated with the American Federation of Labor and Congress of Industrial Organizations. It has local unions in the United States and Canada.

The Federation claims jurisdiction over nearly all workers in the field of music. These include instrumental performers, arrangers, copyists, orchestra librarians, conductors, and music machine operators.

The union was founded in 1896 in Indianapolis, Ind. It has headquarters at 1500 Broadway, New York, N.Y. 10036. For membership, see LABOR MOVEMENT (table). HERMAN D. KENIN

See also PETRILLO, JAMES CAESAR.

MUSK is an ingredient in many expensive perfumes. It is used to preserve the fragrance—and sometimes to add to the fragrance—of perfumes. Musk is formed as a liquid in a gland of the male musk deer, an animal that lives in the mountains of China and India. The gland lies under the skin of the deer's abdomen. When the gland is removed and dried, the musk forms into grains. The grains are extracted with alcohol to produce the perfume ingredient. PAUL Z. BEDOUKIAN

MUSK DEER is a small, clumsy-looking deer. It roams the mountainous forests of central, eastern, and northeastern Asia. It gets its name from a globe-shaped musk gland in the skin of the male's abdomen. Musk from this gland is used in making perfume. The musk in one gland weighs about 1 ounce (28 grams) when dried. Because of the value of musk, the deer has been hunted, trapped, and snared until it is nearly extinct.

The musk deer has no antlers. It stands from 20 to 24 inches (51 to 61 centimeters) tall at the shoulders, and about 2 inches (5 centimeters) higher at the rump. Its hind legs are longer and heavier than the front legs. The deer's coarse, brittle hair is yellowish-brown to dark brown. The male deer has a pair of long canine teeth it uses for fighting. The musk deer roams about alone instead of ranging in herds like other deer. It comes out only at night, to feed on lichens, grass, roots, and twigs of shrubs. Musk deer mate in January, and the doe bears a single spotted fawn the following June.

Scientific Classification. The musk deer belongs to the family Cervidae, and forms the subfamily Moschinae. It is classified as *Moschus moschiferus.* VICTOR H. CAHALANE

MUSK HOG. See PECCARY.

MUSK OX is a shaggy, slow, clumsy-looking animal that lives in the far north. Adult *bulls* (males) are about 7 to 8 feet (2.1 to 2.4 meters) long, 4 to 5 feet (1.2 to 1.5 meters) high, and weigh as much as 900 pounds (410 kilograms). The cows are smaller. Musk oxen are covered with long, shaggy, dark-brown hair—curly and matted over the humped shoulders and straight on the rest of the body. Musk oxen are agile even though their short, stocky legs make them look awkward. The animals have short tails and hoofs like those of cattle. The bull has massive, sharp-pointed horns that curve down, outward, and up. A pair of horns may measure 29 inches (74 centimeters) across.

Musk oxen feed on grass, willows, lichens, and other small plants. They once roamed in large numbers throughout the American arctic regions. But they have been almost wiped out by hunters. Musk oxen live in the Arctic coastal regions of Canada and Greenland. They have also been re-established in Alaska. Their soft, woolly underhair, called *qiviut*, is used to make light, warm clothing.

Scientific Classification. The musk ox belongs to the bovid family, *Bovidae*. The musk ox is genus *Ovibos*, species *O. moschatus*.   DONALD F. HOFFMEISTER

See also ANIMAL (picture: Animals of the Polar Regions).

MUSKEGON, *muhs KEE guhn*, Mich. (pop. 44,631), lies on the east shore of Lake Michigan, 110 miles (177 kilometers) northeast of Chicago. The city's location has made it a thriving industrial center. Muskegon, Muskegon Heights, and Norton Shores form a metropolitan area with a population of 175,410. For location, see MICHIGAN (political map).

Industries. Factories in Muskegon produce machinery, motors, billiard and bowling equipment, electric cranes, chemicals, gasoline pumps, knit goods, office and school furniture, paper, and wire products. The city also has metal refining and molding plants, oil refineries, and foundries that make gray iron, alloy iron, and steel, brass, and aluminum castings.

Transportation. The natural landlocked harbor, formed by the mouth of the Muskegon River, makes the city one of the state's largest ports in tonnage handled. In the late 1960's, it handled more than 3,765,000 short tons (3,415,600 metric tons) a year, 73,000 short tons (66,200 metric tons) of which was in foreign trade. Ferries carry railroad cars, automobiles, and passengers across Lake Michigan to Wisconsin.

Cultural Institutions. Muskegon is the home of an art gallery, donated by Charles H. Hackley. The city also has a community college, a museum, a manual training school, and a vocational school.

History. In 1812, Jean Baptiste Recollet set up a trading post on the site of Muskegon. The city derives its name from a Chippewa Indian word meaning *river with marshes*. Muskegon was once a center of the Michigan lumber industry. During the 1880's, it had 47 sawmills. The lumber industry declined after 1890 when supplies dwindled, and a number of mills burned. But the city industrialized rapidly and now has about 175 manufacturing plants. Muskegon was incorporated as a village in 1860 and received its city charter in 1869. It is the seat of Muskegon County. The city has a council-manager government.   WILLIS F. DUNBAR

MUSKELLUNGE, *MUS kuh lunj*, is the largest fish of the pike family. It may reach a length of 5½ feet (1.7 meters) and weigh about 70 pounds (32 kilograms). The muskellunge looks much like the common pike. But, unlike the common pike, the muskellunge has no scales on the lower half of its head. Muskellunges may be brown, gray, green, or silver. Most have dark bars or spots on their side, but some are plain.

The muskellunge lives in the lakes and quiet rivers of southern Canada. It is also found in the upper Mississippi Valley, the Great Lakes, and the St. Lawrence and Ohio rivers. Many people consider the muskellunge among the best of food fishes, equal to the black and striped bass.

The "muskie" is a prize among fishing enthusiasts. The tremendous size and strength of the muskellunge makes a stout line and a heavy hook necessary. For many years, the state of New York has hatched and stocked a kind of muskellunge known as *Chautauqua muskellunge*. This type reaches a length of 5 feet (1.5 meters). It is also called *salmon pike* or *white pickerel*. The Chautauqua muskellunge has white, delicious flesh.

Scientific Classification. The muskellunge belongs to the pike family, *Esocidae*. It is genus *Esox*, species *E. masquinongy*.   CARL L. HUBBS

See also FISH (picture: Fish of Temperate Fresh Waters).

MUSKET was the firearm that infantry soldiers used before the perfection of the rifle. The name was first used in Italy in the 1500's to describe heavy handguns. It may have come from the Italian word *moschetto*, meaning *young sparrow hawk*, or from the name of an Italian inventor, Moschetta of Feltro. Some people believe the musket originated in Russia and that the name comes from *Muscovy*, the early name for Russia.

Early muskets were 6 or 7 feet (1.8 to 2.1 meters) long and weighed 40 pounds (18 kilograms) or more. They fired either single round balls or round balls with smaller lead balls called *buckshot*. They were loaded from the muzzle. The first muskets were *matchlocks*, guns in which a cord match set off the powder charge. They were followed by flintlocks; *wheel locks*, in which a revolving wheel set off sparks; and *caplocks*, in which a paper held the explosive charge. Muskets were so inaccurate that it was difficult to hit a target more than 100 yards (91 meters) away. But muskets continued in military use long after the invention of the rifle. A soldier could slip a round musket ball easily down the barrel, but rifle bullets had to be pounded down.

Muskets were used extensively in the Revolutionary War and the Napoleonic wars. The soldiers stood in parallel lines and fired at each other.   JACK O'CONNOR

See also BLUNDERBUSS; FLINTLOCK; HARQUEBUS; POWDER HORN.

MUSKIE. See MUSKELLUNGE.

MUSKIE, EDMUND SIXTUS (1914-   ), became secretary of state in 1980 under President Jimmy Carter. Muskie, a former senator from Maine, was the Democratic candidate for Vice-President of the United States in 1968. Vice-President Hubert H. Humphrey and Muskie were defeated by their Republican opponents, Richard M. Nixon and Governor Spiro T. Agnew of Maryland.

In 1958, Muskie had become the first Democrat ever elected to the U.S. Senate by Maine voters. In 1954, he had been elected Maine's first Democratic governor since the 1930's.

Early Life. Muskie was born on March 28, 1914, in Rumford, Me. His father, a tailor, had come to the United States from Poland in 1903. He changed the family name from Marciszewski. Edmund's mother, who came from Buffalo, N.Y., recalled that he was a quiet boy who "wouldn't even play with other children, he was so bashful."

Leif Skoogfors, Liaison

Edmund S. Muskie

Edmund worked his way through Bates College in Lewiston, Me. He was elected to Phi Beta Kappa and graduated in 1936. He graduated from Cornell University Law School in 1939 and started to practice law in Waterville, Me. Muskie served as a naval officer during World War II.

Political Career. Muskie began his political career in 1946, when he was elected to the Maine House of Representatives. He was reelected in 1948 and 1950 and became minority leader of the few Democrats in the House.

Muskie not only was elected governor of a heavily Republican state in 1954, but he was reelected two years later. As governor, Muskie promoted economic and educational improvements and stepped up control of water pollution.

Muskie was elected to the U.S. Senate in 1958 and won reelection in 1964, 1970, and 1976. He campaigned for, but did not win, the 1972 Democratic presidential nomination. Muskie served as chairman of the powerful Senate Budget Committee from 1974 until 1980, when he became secretary of state. CARROLL KILPATRICK

See also HUMPHREY, HUBERT H.

MUSKMELON is the fruit of a plant that belongs to the gourd family. Muskmelons grow on vines that are sometimes nearly 7 feet (2.1 meters) long. Two or three melons grow on each vine. They are closely related to Persian melons and cucumbers. Muskmelons may vary in the size and color of the rind and flesh. The *honeydew* melon has a green, smooth rind and green flesh. The *cantaloupe* has a yellowish-brown rind and yellow-orange flesh. The seeds of all varieties attach to a netlike fiber in a central hollow of the melon. Ripe muskmelons have a distinctive, sweet flavor and an odor much like that of musk. The outer shell or rind of muskmelons is fairly hard. The thick inner layer of juicy pulp is the portion of the melon eaten.

Muskmelons can be grown only during the warm season. High quality muskmelons grow in nearly every state. In the United States, more than 90 per cent of the commercial crop grows in Arizona, California, and Texas. In late spring, farmers plant from 5 to 8 muskmelon seeds in hills that are spaced 5 feet (1.5 meters) apart each way. The plants spread their vines in all directions. As the fruits become mature, they take on a rich color and begin to separate from the stem. The cells that connect the fruit to the plant break down and pull away from the stems. A fruit that is partly separated from the stem is ripe, and it is ready to be harvested.

Until recently, people thought that muskmelons had little food value. But today, we know that the yellow pulp is a rich source of vitamins A and C. Melons have a fuel value of 185 calories per pound (408 calories per kilogram). They are made up of about 89.5 parts water, 9.3 parts carbohydrates, 0.6 parts ash, and 0.6 parts protein. Muskmelons are also a mild laxative.

Experts believe that muskmelons were grown first in India. But, by very early times, people in Asia and in Egypt also grew them. The ancient Romans and Greeks ate muskmelons. In America, muskmelons have been cultivated since colonial days.

Muskmelons were first grown commercially about 1890. At that time, the small hard-shelled type of melon, which we call cantaloupe, was brought to America from the town of Cantalupo, Italy. Unlike older types, this kind of muskmelon can be shipped across the country.

Scientific Classification. Muskmelons belong to the gourd family, *Cucurbitaceae*. The muskmelon is genus *Cucumis*, species *C. melo*. The cantaloupe is *C. melo*, variety *cantalupensis*. ARTHUR J. PRATT

See also MELON; GOURD.

Geo. W. Park Seed Co. Inc.   United Fresh Fruit, Vegetable Assn.

Muskmelons grow on long, leafy vines and have rinds that vary greatly in texture. Honeydew melons, *above left*, have a smooth rind, and cantaloupes, *above right*, have a coarse rind.

Leading Muskmelon-Growing States

Tons of muskmelons grown in 1976

California	410,200 short tons (372,130 metric tons)
Texas	86,000 short tons (78,020 metric tons)
Arizona	62,400 short tons (56,610 metric tons)
Indiana	11,700 short tons (10,610 metric tons)
Georgia	11,300 short tons (10,250 metric tons)
Michigan	7,500 short tons (6,800 metric tons)

Source: *Vegetables—Fresh Market, 1976 Annual Summary*, U.S. Department of Agriculture.

MUSKOGEE, *mus KOH gee*, Okla. (pop. 37,331), lies in rich farming country in the eastern part of the state (see OKLAHOMA [political map]). Its industry includes the manufacture of corrugated boxes, glassware, and steel products and the processing of poultry and other agricultural products. Many residents work in government institutions in the city. Since the early 1970's, the city has been an important port on the McClellan-Kerr Arkansas River Navigation System. It serves barges traveling between Tulsa and Mississippi River ports.

Muskogee is the home of Bacone College, a junior college; the Indian Capital Area Vocational Technical School; and the Oklahoma State School for the Blind. The city has a modern Civic Assembly Center. Cultural events are held in the Fine Arts Auditorium.

Muskogee developed in the 1870's. But long before that, the Creek Indians settled in the area. Their language, Muskogee, gave the town its name. Muskogee is the seat of Muskogee County. It has a council-manager form of government.   JOHN W. MORRIS

See also CREEK INDIANS; INLAND WATERWAY.

MUSKOKA LAKES, *mus KOH kuh*, are a group of scenic lakes in the rocky uplands of southern Ontario. The swift-flowing Muskoka River drains the Muskoka Lakes into Georgian Bay. The lakes lie from 125 to 150 miles (201 to 241 kilometers) north of Toronto. Lake Muskoka, the largest of the group, covers 54 square miles (140 square kilometers). Lake Joseph, Lake of Bays, Rosseau Lake, and hundreds of smaller lakes lie nearby. Many streams and waterfalls are in the area.

The lake district is one of the most famous summer-resort regions in North America. Well-known resort centers include Bala, Baysville, Bracebridge, Dorset, Gravenhurst, and Port Sydney. The area has forests of balsam fir, pine, and spruce. Birch and maple trees add color to the region each autumn.   D. F. PUTNAM

MUSKRAT is an animal that lives in swampy places near streams and rivers. Muskrats get their name from their unpleasant musklike odor. They live in many parts of North America, and in parts of Europe.

Muskrats are suited to life in the water. They use their scaly, flattened tails to steer in the water. The webbed toes on their hind feet help them swim. Muskrats grow about 1 foot (30 centimeters) long and have a 10-inch (25-centimeter) tail. Their light-brown fur is sold as "Hudson seal" after it has been dyed and the longer, coarser hairs have been removed. Muskrat meat is tasty and is sold as "marsh rabbit."

Most muskrats live in *burrows* (tunnels) that they dig in the banks of streams. They often damage dikes and levees as they dig. They also make houses by plastering water plants such as cattails and reeds together with mud. Muskrat houses usually have more than one underwater entrance. There may also be an entrance above water.

Muskrats eat a variety of foods. They eat green vegetation, berries, twigs, and corn and other farm crops. They even eat snails, the meat from *carcasses* (dead animals), and the plants that make up the insides of their own houses.

Muskrats increase rapidly after they move into a region. Female muskrats give birth to as many as three litters of three to eight young each year. As a result,

R. M. Cady, Courtesy Pennsylvania Game Commission

The Muskrat has a coat of long, shiny hair. Muskrat fur makes warm coats, and is often dyed to look like mink, seal, or sable.

Cross-Section of a Muskrat Burrow. The tunnel opens under water, so that the animals can swim in and out under the ice.

the muskrat population often increases rapidly and the animals may soon become overcrowded. Also, muskrats fight a great deal among themselves. Many of them travel as much as 20 miles (32 kilometers) to find peaceful homes away from other muskrats.

Muskrats are rodents. They are related to lemmings and voles, but are somewhat larger than these animals.

Scientific Classification. The muskrat belongs to the subfamily *Microtinae*, of the New World rat and mouse family, *Cricetidae*. The muskrat is genus *Ondatra*, species *O. zibethicus*.   DANIEL BRANT

See also FUR; TRAPPING.

MUSLIM LEAGUE. See INDIA (History).

MUSLIMS, or MOSLEMS, are people who practice the religion of Islam, preached by Muhammad in the A.D. 600's. *Muslim* is an Arabic word that means *one who submits* (to God). There are more than 500 million Muslims throughout the world today. They form the majority of the population in the Middle East, North Africa, and such southeast Asian nations as Bangladesh, Indonesia, Malaysia, and Pakistan. There are about 15,000 Muslims in the United States.

The first Muslims, the Arabs, began in the 600's to establish an empire that eventually stretched from the Atlantic Ocean to the borders of China. This empire absorbed many peoples and their cultures. The Muslims have been called the standardbearers of learning during the Middle Ages. They transmitted much of the knowledge of the ancient world, and helped lay the foundations for Western culture. Arab Muslims made such an impact on the Middle East that today much of the area is known as the *Arab world*. Arabic is its major language, and Islam its chief religion.

Early Period

Before Muhammad. Islam first began in Arabia. In ancient times, the pagan Arabs were organized into tribes which formed two distinct groups. By 100 B.C., the southern tribes had become powerful enough to establish several Arab kingdoms. One of the northern tribes, the Quraysh, later gained control of Mecca. This city lay on the main trade route from what is now Yemen (Sana) to Syria and Egypt. They built the city into a powerful commercial center.

At that time, the Arabs worshiped nature and idols. Their chief gods were al-Lat, al-Uzza, and Manat. The Kaaba, the most famous shrine in Arabia, stood in Mecca. The city attracted religious pilgrims, traders, and settlers from all Arabia and neighboring countries. Jews and Christians mixed freely with the Arabs. Many Arabs were converted to Judaism and Christianity.

The Prophet. Muhammad was born about A.D. 570, and grew up in Mecca. His family belonged to the Quraysh tribe. Muhammad was disturbed by the injustices of life in Mecca and because the people worshiped idols. When he was about 40, he experienced a vision in which he was called to be a prophet of God. Muhammad began to preach the punishment of evildoers. He urged the Arabs to worship the one God and to accept him as God's prophet.

The people of Mecca were frightened and angered by Muhammad's preachings, and began to oppose him. Muhammad went secretly to Medina (then called Yathrib), a town about 200 miles (320 kilometers) from Mecca. The people there had agreed to accept him as God's messenger and ruler. Muhammad's *Hegira*, or *Emigration*, took place in A.D. 622. Muslims count that year as the beginning of the Islamic Era. Muhammad began to attack caravans from Mecca. In 630, through diplomacy, he occupied the city. See MUHAMMAD.

The Spread of Islam

The First Caliphs. After Muhammad's death in 632, rulers later called *caliphs* led the Muslims (see CALIPH). The first four caliphs, called the *rightly guided*, and several famous Arab military leaders accomplished the first major expansion of the Muslim world. This expansion resulted from both political and religious motives, and gave the Arabs an important place in world history.

Muhammad gained control of most of Arabia when he took Mecca. But some tribes revolted after the prophet's death. Abu Bakr, the first caliph, subdued them and restored them to Islam. He also sent successful Arab forces into the Byzantine provinces of Syria and Palestine, and the Persian province of Iraq. These *holy wars* continued under the caliphs Omar, who ruled from 634 to 644, and Othman, who ruled from 644 to 656. The Muslims occupied the Persian capital of Ctesiphon. They also annexed the Byzantine provinces of Syria, Palestine, and Egypt, and part of North Africa. The Per-

Painting (1594) by an unknown Turkish artist; New York Public Library, Astor, Lennox and Tilden Foundations, Spencer Collection

Muhammad, *in white,* founded the Muslim religion. This painting shows him with Abu Bakr and Ali, two of his followers.

sians failed in their last attempt to regain their empire during the caliphate of Ali, who ruled from 656 to 661.

The Omayyad Caliphs, who ruled from 661 to 750, led the Arab Muslims to new victories. The caliphate was founded by the caliph Muawiya. He was a member of the aristocratic Meccan family of Umayyah, from which the caliphate takes its name. The Omayyads established their capital at Damascus in 661. They fought the Turkish tribes in Central Asia, sent an expedition into Sindh in India, and reached the borders of China. Under these caliphs, the Muslims also fought the Byzantines in Asia Minor and around the Mediterranean Sea. They twice laid siege to Constantinople (now Istanbul), but without success. The Muslims captured Cyprus, Rhodes, and Sicily, and completed the conquest of North Africa. Many Berbers were converted to Islam.

The Omayyads then turned to Europe, and invaded Spain in 711. A Muslim army crossed the Pyrenees Mountains and marched through southern France until Charles Martel turned it back in 732 near Tours. Many historians regard this battle as one of the most important ever fought, because it determined that Christianity, rather than Islam, would dominate Europe.

Gaining Converts. The caliphs did not conquer new lands solely to gain converts, but many conquered peoples embraced Islam. Unlike the Byzantine Christians, the Muslim conquerors granted a large measure of religious tolerance. All non-Muslims had to pay a special tax in return for not serving in the Muslim army. But many worked as officers and tax collectors in the civil administration and as doctors and tutors at the court. At first, only a few were converted to Islam. Gradually, the Muslims produced their own administrative and professional classes. Beginning about 750, conversion to

Islam increased until Islam became the predominant religion in most of the conquered lands.

Division of Islam. From the time of Muhammad's death in 632, several separate groups competed for leadership among the Muslims. In 750, two branches of Muhammad's family, the *Abbasids* and the *Shiites*, or *Alids*, overthrew the Omayyad caliphate. Dissatisfied Persians helped them. But a youthful Omayyad prince, Abd al-Rahman, escaped and made his way across North Africa to Spain. He subdued and pacified the rival Arab and Berber factions and established the Omayyad dynasty of Spain. The dynasty lasted from 756 to 1031. It had its capital at Córdoba.

In the East, the victors quarreled among themselves. The Abbasids outwitted the Shiites and established the Abbasid caliphate, also called the Caliphate of Baghdad. They ruled from 750 to 1258, and built the new capital city of Baghdad. Gradually, the Abbasid empire decayed, and independent dynasties sprang up. The Abbasid empire received its death blow when Baghdad fell to the Mongols in 1258. The Shiites, driven underground, agitated as a political and religious minority. One of their religious leaders, Ubaydullah, claimed descent from Fatima, the daughter of Muhammad. He founded the Fatimite dynasty, which lasted from 909 to 1171. This dynasty ruled North Africa, Egypt, Syria, Palestine, and the Hejaz. Cairo, Egypt, was its capital. See FATIMITE DYNASTY.

Muslim Influence in Europe

The Crusades. The Muslims threatened Christian Europe, and several wars resulted. The Christians of eastern and western Europe forgot their differences, and united in a series of wars called the *Crusades*. The Christians conquered Syria and Palestine, and captured Jerusalem in 1099. But a great Muslim general, Saladin, recaptured it for the Abbasids in 1187. The crusaders lost ground, and retreated from Acre (now 'Akko), their last stronghold in Syria, in 1291. See CRUSADES.

Muslim Learning. As a result of their conquests, Muslims came into contact with Greek science and philosophy, and with Persian history and literature. The Arabs became learned in these fields, and also developed a new science and literature of their own in Arabic. Muslim geographers explored many new areas. They also spread knowledge of other discoveries, including the Chinese inventions of paper and gunpowder, and the Hindu system of numerals (see ARABIC NUMERALS).

The Muslims not only honored learning, but also developed distinctive arts (see ISLAMIC ART). They also founded many academies and universities. The most famous were at Baghdad, Cairo, and Córdoba. Muslim scholars of many nations traveled freely throughout the Muslim world. European scholars traveled to Muslim countries, especially Spain, to study Islamic philosophy, mathematics, and medicine. They translated major Arabic works into Latin, the language of learning of the West. In this way, much of the knowledge of the classical world was preserved during the Middle Ages.

The Muslim Turks

Arabs dominated the early spread of Islam, and created the Muslim empire. An alien group, the Turks, invaded Muslim lands, and built their empire on the remains of the Abbasid empire.

The Seljuk Turks. Barbarian Turks of Central Asia challenged the Abbasid Caliphate of Baghdad in the 1000's. They were first led by Seljuk, and were named for him. The weak caliph had to receive them and honor their leader Tughril as *sultan*. The Seljuk Turks gained control of the Abbasid caliphs, but the Fatimites fought the Turkish invaders. The Seljuks became *Sunnite* Muslims and were among Islam's strongest supporters. After their last strong leader, Malikshah, died in 1092, they split into rival groups. See SELJUKS.

The Ottoman Turks. Various newly converted Turkish tribes served with the Seljuks. One group, the Ottoman Turks, took their name from their leader Othman. They seized Anatolia in the 1300's and established the Ottoman dynasty. This dynasty held power until 1922 and ruled the greatest Muslim state of modern times. The Ottoman Turks fought the Mongols and put an end to the Byzantine Empire when they seized Constantinople in 1453. Their empire expanded rapidly in Asia and Europe. They conquered the Mameluke dynasty in Egypt in the early 1500's. The Turkish sultans then assumed the title of *caliph*. They fought Christian Europe successfully until halted at Vienna in 1683.

Muslims Today

Colonialism. In 1700, three great Muslim empires existed: the Mogul empire in India, the Safavid empire in Persia, and the Ottoman empire in Turkey. The Mogul and Safavid empires came under the influence of European powers such as Great Britain and Russia and gradually disappeared. European expansion and economic control seriously weakened the Ottoman empire. By 1900, European colonial powers dominated most of the Muslim world. The French established themselves in North Africa, and the Dutch took Indonesia. Britain occupied Egypt and the Sudan, set up an empire in India, and ruled Malaya. In the 1900's, Italy seized territories in North Africa and the Levant.

European ideas also penetrated into Muslim countries and brought about many changes. Modern education and economic reform spread. The Muslim peoples wanted to be up to date, strong, and independent of their European masters.

Independence. Most Muslim peoples gained their independence in the 1900's. They form a highly important group of nations that stretches from the Atlantic Ocean to Indonesia. Some of the world's busiest trade and communications routes cross their territories. The chief problems of the newly independent Muslim countries have been to achieve stable governments and to feed their people. Some Muslim nations, such as Bangladesh, Egypt, and Pakistan, have too many people living on too little land. Other countries lack the moisture and fertile soil needed to produce food. None is truly industrialized yet. Old quarrels and conflicting interests keep the Muslim peoples from being united. But they are bound by religious and cultural ties and a determination to resist colonialism. CHARLES J. ADAMS

Critically reviewed by ALI H. ABDEL KADER

See articles on countries where Muslims live, such as EGYPT. See also ISLAM with its *Related Articles*.

MUSLIN, *MUZ lin*, is a closely woven white or unbleached cotton cloth. It is named for the city of Mosul, in Iraq, where it was first made. The British use the word *muslin* to mean sheer cotton fabrics, but in the United States, muslin means a firm cloth for everyday use. Wide muslin is called *sheeting*.

MUSSEL, *MUS'l*, is an animal that lives in water. Its body is covered with a protective shell made up of two similar pieces called *valves*. The valves are joined at one point by a hinge, and can be opened and closed somewhat like a lady's compact. The mussel's body lies inside the shell, and consists of various organs including the foot, gills, stomach, and heart. *Freshwater mussels* live in streams and lakes. *Sea mussels* live in ocean water.

Several kinds of sea mussels can be eaten. The common blue mussel, which is from 3 to 6 inches (8 to 15 centimeters) long, is a popular food in Europe. Its shell is bluish black on the outside and pearly-blue on the inside. The sea mussels use the *foot* to spin long, silky threads called a *byssus*. The byssus anchors the mussel to a rock, where it may spend the rest of its life.

Freshwater mussels are a valuable source of *mother-of-pearl*, which lines the inside of their shells. Mother-of-pearl is used to make pearl buttons.

Scientific Classification. Mussels are in the phylum Mollusca. Sea mussels belong to the family Mytilidae. The common mussel is *Mytilus edulis*. Freshwater mussels are in the family Unionidae. There are many genera, including *Anodonta* and *Elliptio*. R. TUCKER ABBOTT

See also BUTTON; MOTHER-OF-PEARL; PEARL; SHELL (color pictures); AQUACULTURE.

MUSSET, *myoo SAY*, **ALFRED DE** (1810-1857), was a French poet, dramatist, and novelist. He is remembered chiefly for his plays, *Comédies et Proverbes* (1840). He wrote these in a witty, poetic style, and they reveal a deep understanding of the inner motives of the characters. Musset believed that a writer should experience suffering to create good literature. He published his first book of poems, *Tales of Spain and Italy*, in 1829. He wrote his best poems in memory of his love for the famous woman writer George Sand (see SAND, GEORGE). Musset was born in Paris. He spent most of his adolescence among writers. WALLACE FOWLIE

MUSSOLINI, *MOOS soh LEE nee*, **BENITO** (1883-1945), founded Fascism and ruled as dictator of Italy for almost 21 years. He tried to build Italy into a great empire. Instead, he left it occupied by the armies of other nations.

As dictator, Mussolini took the title *Il Duce*, the leader. He reduced unemployment, and improved the railway service. But the price of his reforms was the enslavement of the Italian people. He kept control by such methods as murder, exile, and the prison camp. He was a strong man, who gloried in his strength. He wanted the men of Italy to be soldiers, and the women to be mothers of soldiers. He loved to hear the acclaiming shouts of "Duce! Duce!" from his people.

Mussolini was not a religious or a moral man. He abolished the Roman Catholic youth organizations, and fought church influence in state affairs. But in 1929 he improved relations with the Roman Catholic Church by signing an agreement with Pope Pius XI. This gave the pope temporal powers in Vatican City.

Early Life. Mussolini was born on July 29, 1883, in Dovia, Italy. His mother was the village schoolmistress, and his father, a blacksmith. After attending school at Predappio, Mussolini was sent at the age of 14 to a school at Faenza operated by the Salesian Friars. But he rebelled against the strict discipline of the school, and was expelled for bad conduct. He then went to a normal school at Forlì and earned a degree.

Mussolini taught in an elementary school for a short time. In 1902 he went to Switzerland, and earned his living as a workman. While there, he often got into trouble with the police for vagrancy and fighting. He returned to Italy in 1904 to perform his required military service. He then taught school in 1907 and 1908.

Mussolini went to Trent, Austria (now Trento, Italy), in 1909. He worked there for a socialist newspaper, and wrote several literary works. Again he got into trouble, this time for publicly supporting Italian claims to Trent, and was expelled from Austrian territory. Upon returning to Italy, he edited a socialist newspaper at Forlì. He became editor of *Avanti*, the leading socialist newspaper in Italy, in 1912.

Quarrels with Socialists. When World War I broke out, Mussolini aroused the anger of Socialist Party leaders because he urged that Italy enter the war immediately against Germany. As a result, he was expelled from the Socialist Party on Nov. 25, 1914.

Mussolini immediately founded his own newspaper, *Il Popolo d'Italia*. He wrote violent editorials trying to drive Italy into the war. When Italy did enter the war, he enlisted in the army and became a corporal. He served in the trenches from September 1915, until he was wounded in February 1917.

Fascist Dictator. In March 1919, Mussolini founded in Milan the first political group to be called fascist (see FASCISM). At first, its program was strongly nationalistic, intended to appeal to discontented war veterans. Mussolini urged the Italian people to rebuild the glories of ancient Rome. Later, he drafted a program to win property-owning Italians to his cause. By October 1922, his Fascist Party was powerful enough to force the weak King Victor Emmanuel III to call on Mussolini to head the government.

His Conquests. In 1935 and 1936, he invaded and conquered Ethiopia. There, with machine-gun fire, his

Cornelia Clarke

The Black, Ridged Shells of these freshwater mussels have a pearly lining which makes them valuable for the manufacture of pearl buttons. The shells are hinged at the back.

Benito Mussolini Loved Dramatic Poses. Clenched fist, jutting jaw, and theatrical actions were all part of his fiery speeches. Millions of Italians followed him blindly.

soldiers mowed down peaceful people who still used bows and arrows.

When the Spanish Civil War broke out in 1936, both Mussolini and Adolf Hitler decided to support the rebel leader, General Francisco Franco. They sent military forces to fight in Spain.

World War II. After Germany had almost completely conquered France in 1940, Mussolini entered World War II and invaded southern France. A few days later, France surrendered, but disaster after disaster followed elsewhere for the Italian armies. In Africa, Greece, and finally in Italy itself, Mussolini's armies met defeat. German forces kept Italy from total collapse for a time, but Mussolini had lost his cause. The Fascist Grand Council turned against him in July 1943, and he was overthrown and imprisoned. But German paratroopers rescued him. Mussolini then became the head of a puppet government in northern Italy.

His Death. In the spring of 1945, the German forces in northern Italy collapsed. With his mistress Clara Petacci and some followers, Mussolini fled north toward the border. The Italian underground discovered them at Lake Como, and shot Mussolini and Clara Petacci soon afterward. Their bodies were taken to Milan, and hung by the heels in front of a garage. Later, his body was hidden to prevent demonstrations by his followers. In August 1957, at the request of his widow, he was buried near Predappio.　　　　　　　　　　R. JOHN RATH

See also ITALY (History); WORLD WAR II (picture: War Leaders).

MUSSORGSKY, moo SAWRG skih, **MODEST** (1839-1881), was one of the greatest Russian composers in history. The powerful opera Boris Godunov (1874) ranks as his finest work. This opera, based on the life of a czar, reflects the interest in Russian themes that is found in most of Mussorgsky's music.

Mussorgsky was born in Karevo, near Pskov, and took piano lessons as a boy. His parents wanted him to have a military career and sent him to a cadet school in St. Petersburg (now Leningrad). Mussorgsky entered the army in 1856. The next year, he joined a group of young composers in St. Petersburg. These men later became

known as The Five. Mily Balakirev, the leader of the group, urged Russian musicians to stress their national heritage in their music.

In 1858, Mussorgsky left the army so he could devote himself to music. He had a somewhat disorganized method of composing and left many projects unfinished. They included the operas The Fair of Sorochinsk and Khovanshchina, which other composers completed. Mussorgsky was a fine pianist and composed many important works for the piano. His major piano compositions include Pictures at an Exhibition (1874). This work now is best known in an orchestration written by the French composer Maurice Ravel in 1922. Mussorgsky also had a gift for setting everyday Russian speech to music. He composed many series of songs, among them The Nursery (1868-1872) and Songs and Dances of Death (1875-1877).

Mussorgsky's harmonies were so daring that his friend Nicholas Rimsky-Korsakov revised much of Mussorgsky's work after his death. Today, most orchestras and opera companies perform Rimsky-Korsakov's versions of such works as Boris Godunov and the tone poem A Night on the Bald Mountain (1872).　　BORIS SCHWARZ

See also OPERA (The Opera Repertoire).

MUSTACHE. See BEARD.

MUSTAFA KEMAL PASHA. See ATATÜRK, KEMAL.

MUSTANG is the name of the small, hardy wild horse that once roamed the American Southwest. It descended from the Spanish horses brought to America by Hernando Cortés. Mustang perhaps came from the Spanish word mesteños, meaning strayed, or ownerless, horses.

See also COWBOY (His Horse).

MUSTANG. See AIR FORCE (picture: Fighting Planes of Three Wars).

MUSTARD is the name of a family of leafy, annual plants that grow in temperate regions, such as the United States and Canada. People use a powder made from the seeds of certain kinds of mustard plants in salad dressing, to flavor meat, and in preparing pickles and some kinds of fish.

Mustard has deep-green leaves that are large, thick, and rather jagged in shape. The leaves may be harvested while still tender, and eaten as potherb (greens). If the leaves are not harvested, the plant soon sends up a strong seed stalk and becomes unfit to eat.

Mustard is an easy crop to grow. Farmers sow the seeds for the spring crop about two weeks before the last frosts of spring. The seeds for fall crops should be sown about 50 days before the first autumn frosts. Popular varieties include black and white mustard. Both black and white mustard are annual plants.

Black Mustard grows to a height of 6 feet (1.8 meters) or more. Black mustard plants have bright yellow flowers, with smooth pods that lie close to the stem. Manufacturers use their dark brown seeds in commercial mustard products.

White Mustard grows only about 2 or 3 feet (61 to 91 centimeters) in height. It has stiff branching stems, hairy leaves, bristly pods, and small brilliant yellow flowers. The seeds of the white mustard plant are yellowish.

Mustard greens are an excellent source of vitamins A, B, and C. In addition, their bulk and fiber tend to have a mildly laxative effect. The oil which mustard seeds contain gives the substance its high flavor. It also makes mustard a valuable household remedy. Mixed with warm water, mustard can be used to cause vomit-

J. Horace McFarland

Lush Green Leaves of the Potherb Mustard Plant make an excellent summer vegetable that is high in vitamin content.

ing. It can also be used in a plaster to relieve pain.

Scientific Classification. Mustards belong to the mustard family, *Cruciferae*. The common white mustard is genus *Brassica*, species *B. hirta*. Black mustard is *B. nigra*. Most mustards used for greens are *B. juncea*. s. h. wittwer

MUSTARD GAS. See CHEMICAL-BIOLOGICAL-RADIOLOGICAL WARFARE.

MUTATION is a change in the hereditary material of an organism's cells. By altering this material, a mutation changes certain traits. Some mutations produce obvious changes. For example, the variety of grape called *Concord* is the result of a mutation. This mutation caused a wild grapevine to produce grapes that were bigger and sweeter than before. Mutations may be transmitted to future generations.

Hereditary material consists of *genes* and *chromosomes*. Genes, which are composed of a substance called *deoxyribonucleic acid* (DNA), determine the hereditary traits of an organism. The genes are lined up along the chromosomes, which are microscopic threadlike bodies.

A mutation can affect an individual gene or an entire chromosome. A gene mutation is caused by slight chemical changes in DNA. Sickle cell anemia is a blood disease caused by a gene mutation. The mutation causes a minor change in the DNA of a gene that controls the production of a person's red blood cells. A chromosome mutation occurs if the number or arrangement of chromosomes changes. Down's syndrome, also called Mongolism, is a mental and physical disorder caused by a chromosome mutation. The disorder occurs if a person is born with one extra chromosome.

Scientists do not know what causes most mutations, even though these changes occur at known rates. Some mutations are caused by such agents as ultraviolet light, X rays, and certain chemicals. Agents that cause mutations are called *mutagens*. The type of mutation that will be caused by a mutagen cannot be predicted.

An organism can pass a mutation on to its offspring only if the mutation affects cells that produce eggs or sperm. This type of mutation is called a *germinal mutation*. The other type of mutation, called a *somatic mutation*, occurs in other cells of the body.

A mutation may or may not have a visible effect on the organism that carries it. Most mutations that cause a visible change are harmful. However, some of these mutations enable an organism to both survive and reproduce better than other members of its species. Such beneficial mutations—if they are germinal—are the basis of evolution. If the mutant organism passes a beneficial trait on to its offspring, they also will have an advantage in survival and reproduction. After many generations, most members of the species will have the trait.

Breeders use mutations to produce new or improved species of crops and livestock. They do this by breeding certain plants and animals that have one or more favorable mutations.   DANIEL L. HARTL

Related Articles in WORLD BOOK include:

Breeding
Cell (Metabolic Diseases)
Cosmic Rays (Effects of Cosmic Rays)
De Vries, Hugo
Evolution (How Hereditary Characteristics Change)
Heredity
Mink (picture: The White Mink)
Races, Human (Mutations)
Radiation (How Radiation Can Change Living Things)
Sport

MUTINY is a revolt against authority. The term has been popularly confined to an unlawful attempt by a crew to take command of a naval ship. But it applies to any unlawful attempt by military personnel to seize or override military authority. Mutiny is one of the gravest military offenses. In 1842, Midshipman Philip Spencer, son of Secretary of War John C. Spencer, was hanged for mutiny, along with two seamen, on the U.S.S. *Somers*.   FREDERICK C. LOUGH

See also BLIGH, WILLIAM; SEPOY REBELLION.

MUTSUHITO, *moo tsoo hee toh* (1852-1912), reigned as emperor of Japan from 1867 to 1912. Japan developed from a feudal state into an industrial and military power during his reign. He introduced Western ideas into the Japanese way of life.

He began his reign in a period of confusion. Japan had been ruled by shoguns, or ruling lords, for hundreds of years (see SHOGUN). Japanese noblemen persuaded the shogun to resign in 1867, and restored the ruling power to Emperor Mutsuhito. He adopted as his title *Meiji* (enlightened rule). He is known as the *Meiji emperor* (see JAPAN [History; picture]).

Mutsuhito set out to equal the military and economic power of the West. His government sponsored industries, gave the farmers title to their land, instituted education for all his people, and developed up-to-date military forces. He introduced a strong, Prussian-style constitution. Japan defeated China in 1895, and Russia in 1905. Mutsuhito made an alliance with England in 1902, and added Korea to Japan's territory in 1910. These developments established Japan as a great power.

Mutsuhito was born in Kyoto, a year before Commodore Matthew Perry arrived in Japan. He was enshrined as a god after his death.   MARIUS B. JANSEN

See also TOKYO (Shrines and Temples; picture).

MUTTON is the flesh of grown sheep. The meat of young sheep is called *lamb*. The meat of a sheep becomes mutton when the animal is about a year old. Mutton is dark pink and has white fat. It is stronger in flavor and rougher in texture than lamb. Americans eat only about 2 pounds (0.9 kilogram) of lamb and mutton per person in a year. See also LAMB.   JOHN C. AYRES

MUTUAL BROADCASTING SYSTEM (MBS) is a radio network with outlets throughout the United States. The network has more than 600 affiliated stations from coast to coast. It provides news and sports programming to its stations, which are independently owned and operated. The network also covers such major events as space flights and national political conventions.

Four independent radio stations formed the network in 1934 as the Quality Group. They were WOR of New York City, WGN of Chicago, WLW of Cincinnati, and WXYZ of Detroit. Later in 1934, the network became the Mutual Broadcasting System. In 1936, MBS began to broadcast coast-to-coast. The Minnesota Mining and Manufacturing Company owned MBS from 1960 to 1966, when the Mutual Broadcasting Corporation was formed and it bought the network. MBS headquarters are in New York City.

Critically reviewed by the MUTUAL BROADCASTING SYSTEM

MUTUAL COMPANY is a business that is owned and operated by the users of the service it provides. Mutual companies include many insurance companies, banks, savings and loan associations, cooperatives, and credit unions. The government gives mutual companies special tax treatment because they do not seek *profit* in the usual sense. Instead, they pass on any *profits* to their members in the form of lower costs or insurance premiums, or higher interest paid on savings deposits.   LEONARD C. R. LANGER

MUTUAL FUND is a company that pools money from many investors and uses it to buy stocks and other securities. In exchange for their money, the investors receive shares of the mutual fund. The price of a share rises or falls, according to the market prices of securities owned by the fund.

A mutual fund has no fixed number of shares of stock. An investor may buy additional shares from the company at any time. For this reason, mutual funds are also called *open-end investment companies*. They differ from *publicly traded investment funds*, formerly called *closed-end investment companies*, which have a fixed number of shares that are sold on a stock exchange.

There are two chief kinds of mutual funds—*load funds* and *no-load funds*. Load funds authorize dealers to sell shares in the fund to investors. The price of a share equals the *net asset value* per share plus a *load*. The net asset value is a price determined by the stock market value of the securities in the fund. The load is a sales charge that includes a commission for the dealer. An investor in a no-load fund buys shares for their net asset value directly from the fund. There is no sales charge. If investors in any mutual fund want to sell their stock, they must sell it back to the fund. The fund must buy its shares back for their approximate net asset value.

Some mutual funds, called *growth funds*, invest mostly in common stocks of companies that have grown rapidly. Other funds, known as *income funds*, invest in preferred stocks and bonds that have consistently paid dividends or interest. Many mutual funds, called *balanced funds*, buy both stocks and bonds.

People buy shares of mutual funds largely because the funds employ professional investment managers. These experts select stocks or bonds that they believe are likely to yield the most profit for the investor. A mutual fund also enables people to own a number of securities. As a result, a mutual fund shareholder has less chance of losing money than a person who invests in only one security.   WILLIAM G. DEWALD

MUTUALISM. See SYMBIOSIS.

MVD, the Ministry of Internal Affairs, is one of two parts of Russia's police force. The other part is the KGB, the Committee of State Security. The MVD is responsible for conventional police protection and border police activities. The KGB is the secret police agency. Secret police have been a feature of Russian life under the czars and Communists. They have also been called Cheka, GPU, OGPU, and NKVD.

The MVD and the KGB were set up in 1946, when police powers in Russia were reorganized. The KGB was called the MGB, the Ministry of State Security, until 1954. In 1960, the MVD was abolished as a national organization. Some of its functions had been transferred to the KGB in 1956. New police agencies were created in each of Russia's 15 republics to handle other MVD functions. They were abolished in 1966 and replaced by a new national agency. The agency again became known as the MVD in 1968.   WILLIAM B. BALLIS

MWANAMUTAPA EMPIRE. See ZIMBABWE.

MYASTHENIA GRAVIS, *MY uhs THEE nee uh GRAV ihs*, is a disease characterized by progressive weakness of the skeletal muscles. This weakness increases with physical activity but can be partially relieved by rest. Myasthenia gravis afflicts all age groups and both sexes, but it occurs most frequently among women from 15 to 30 years old and among men from 40 to 70 years old. It is not contagious.

Myasthenia gravis affects primarily the skeletal muscles of the face, neck, arms, and legs (see MUSCLE). Symptoms may include a drooping eyelid, weakness of the arms and legs, and difficulty in breathing and chewing. Diagnosis can be difficult because the early symptoms are slight and may come and go.

Most researchers believe myasthenia gravis results from a defect at a *neuromuscular junction*, the point where a nerve impulse is transmitted to a muscle. Normally, a substance called *acetylcholine* is released from the nerve ending. This substance becomes attached to receptor molecules in the muscle, causing the muscle to contract. In myasthenia gravis, something interferes with the nerve-to-muscle connection. Many researchers suspect that myasthenia gravis is an *autoimmune disease*. In such diseases, the body's immune system, which normally attacks harmful bacteria and viruses, attacks the body's own tissues. The immune system appears to destroy the receptor molecules in the muscles of myasthenia gravis victims.

With medication, most victims of myasthenia gravis can live almost completely normal lives. Doctors treat the disease with drugs called *anticholinesterases*. The use of cortisone drugs may also be helpful. Removal of the thymus, a part of the immune system, may aid victims, particularly during the early stages of the illness. In certain advanced cases, physicians withdraw the victim's blood and cleanse it of the immune substances that may be attacking the muscle receptors. The purified blood is then transfused back into the patient's body.   GABRIEL GENKINS

MYCENAE, *my SEE nee*, was a city in ancient Greece, located 6 miles (10 kilometers) north of Argos in the southern peninsula. German archaeologist Heinrich Schliemann uncovered five royal graves at the site of Mycenae in 1876. This discovery started the study of the Bronze Age on the Greek mainland. These graves, known as the *Shaft Graves*, contained jewels, bronze weapons, and other objects made of bronze, gold, and silver.

Mycenae was the leading political and cultural center on mainland Greece from about 1450 to 1100 B.C., and its influence spread as far east as Cyprus. The Late Bronze Age on the Greek mainland from 1580 to 1100 B.C. is often called the *Mycenaean* period, because of Mycenae's prominence. The city became famous for its royal palace, walled fortress, and beehive-shaped tombs for kings. The tombs can still be seen at the site. Dorians sacked the city in the late 1100's B.C., and Mycenae never regained its power.   NORMAN A. DOENGES

See also ARCHITECTURE (Mycenaean); SHIP (Minoan and Mycenaean Ships).

MYCOLOGY, *my KAHL uh jee,* is the study of fungi. *Field mycologists* specialize in the fungi found in fields and woods. *Medical mycology* deals with the fungi that cause human and animal diseases. *Industrial mycology* concerns the activities of fungi in rotting or spoiling raw materials and manufactured goods, and the uses of fungi in industrial fermentations. See also FUNGI.

MYELITIS, *my uh LY tihs,* means inflammation of the spinal cord or of the bone marrow. It is a general term, and does not tell the cause or location of the inflammation or injury. Poliomyelitis is one form of myelitis (see POLIOMYELITIS). Other forms include multiple sclerosis and rabies (see MULTIPLE SCLEROSIS; RABIES). Symptoms of myelitis diseases often include backache and paralysis.   IRVIN STEIN

MYNA is the name of several kinds of birds in the starling family. Myna birds are native to India, Burma, and other parts of Asia. The common *house myna* is somewhat larger than a robin. Its colors range from rich wine-brown on the lower breast to deep black on the head, neck, and upper breast. It has a splash of white on the lower edge of its wings, and its bill and legs are a bright yellow. The myna feeds on plants, insects, and worms. It often builds its nest in crevices of buildings. The myna is a noisy bird that is common about yards and buildings. It is often seen among chickens or perched on the backs of cattle.

The *crested myna* has long feathers on its forehead that form a permanent bushy crest. It lives in cultivated fields and pastures. The crested myna is sometimes so fearless that a person may come quite close to one before it becomes alarmed. It has been brought to the Philippines, Japan, and British Columbia.

Talking mynas are sometimes kept as pets. Many imitate the human voice, and can talk, sing, and whistle.

Scientific Classification. Mynas are in the starling family, *Sturnidae*. The common house myna is classified as genus *Acridotheres*, species *A. tristis*. The crested myna is *A. cristatellus*. The talking myna is *Gracula religiosa*.   GEORGE E. HUDSON

Santa Catalina Island Co.
Myna Bird

MYOCARDIAL INFARCTION. See CORONARY THROMBOSIS.

MYOCARDITIS, *MY oh kahr DIE tis,* is an inflammation of the myocardium, the muscular part of the heart. *Acute bacterial myocarditis* is caused by bacterial infection. *Toxic myocarditis* is due to poisons or drugs which reach the heart through the blood system.

MYOGLOBIN. See KENDREW, SIR JOHN COWDERY; MOLECULAR BIOLOGY.

MYOMERE. See FISH (Skeleton and Muscles).

MYOPIA. See NEARSIGHTEDNESS.

MYRDAL, *MIHR dahl,* **GUNNAR** (1898-   ), is a Swedish sociologist and economist. He gained fame for his thorough studies of major world problems. His book *An American Dilemma: The Negro Problem and Modern Democracy* (1944) is considered an outstanding study of race relations in the United States. Myrdal's studies of the economic and social development of underdeveloped nations led him to write *Asian Drama: An Inquiry into the Poverty of Nations* (1968). This book tries to tell why so many people of southern Asia are poor, and what, if anything, can be done about it. Myrdal shared the 1974 Nobel prize in economics with Friedrich von Hayek of Austria.

Myrdal was born in Gustafs, near Sandviken, Sweden. His full name is Karl Gunnar Myrdal. He received a law degree and a doctor of laws in economics degree from the University of Stockholm. He was minister of commerce in the Swedish Cabinet from 1945 to 1947. He served as executive secretary of the United Nations Economic Commission for Europe from 1947 to 1957. In 1960, he became director of the Institute of International Economic Studies in Stockholm.

Myrdal's wife, Alva R. Myrdal, was the first woman in Sweden's history to serve as an ambassador. From 1956 to 1961, she was the Swedish ambassador to four nations at the same time—Burma, Ceylon (now Sri Lanka), India, and Nepal. She was a member of Sweden's parliament from 1962 to 1970 and served as minister of disarmament and church affairs in the Swedish Cabinet from 1967 to 1973. From 1962 to 1973, she headed Sweden's delegation to the United Nations Disarmament Conference in Geneva, Switzerland.   JAMES W. VANDER ZANDEN

MYRRH, *mur,* is a fragrant gum resin that is used in making perfume and incense. It comes from the trunks of certain small trees of the genus *Commiphora* that grow in eastern Africa and southern Arabia. Myrrh is sold to manufacturers in the form of *tears* (drops). The tears range in color from yellow to brown-red. Alcohol is added to the tears to dissolve the resin and leave the gum behind. The resin hardens, forming a hard, brown, resinlike substance that gives perfume and incense a spicy odor. When steam is passed through myrrh, a fragrant oil used in perfume and incense is produced.

Myrrh has been used in making incense and perfumes since ancient times. One of the Wise Men brought the infant Jesus a gift of myrrh (Matt. 2).   PAUL Z. BEDOUKIAN

MYRTLE, *MUR t'l,* is an attractive evergreen shrub or small tree. It grows wild in regions along the Mediterranean Sea and temperate regions of Asia. Some persons in the United States cultivate it as an ornamental plant. The myrtle has shining blue-green leaves and fragrant

J. Horace McFarland
Myrtle Blooms with Many Pretty Flat, White Flowers.

white flowers. The leaves, bark, and berries are also fragrant. Manufacturers use them in making perfume. The bark is used in tanning industries of southern Europe. Ancient Greeks thought myrtle was sacred to the goddess of love, Aphrodite. They used it in festivals.

The *common periwinkle* is often called *running myrtle*. It has creeping stems and attractive blue flowers.

Scientific Classification. Common myrtles belong to the myrtle family, *Myrtaceae*. They are classified as genus *Myrtus*, species *M. communis*. The common periwinkle is in the dogbane family, *Apocynaceae*. It is genus *Vinca*, species *V. minor*.   THEODORE W. BRETZ

See also BAYBERRY; GUAVA; PIMENTO.

MYRTLEWOOD. See LAUREL.

MYSTERIES were religious ceremonies held in ancient Greece. In these ceremonies, the Greeks worshiped certain gods and goddesses, especially Demeter, Dionysus, and Persephone. The ancient Romans also held ceremonies similar to the Greek mysteries.

The word *mystery* comes from a Greek word meaning *one who keeps quiet*, indicating an *initiate*, or person introduced to the secret rites of a mystery. The initiates were sworn to silence, and they often were put to death if they revealed the secrets of the mysteries. Because most of the initiates did keep silent, scholars know little about the initiations, which were a central part of the mysteries.

The *Eleusinian Mysteries* were the greatest of all Greek mysteries. They were connected with the worship of Demeter, Hades, and Persephone. These rites began in Athens, where the initiates first bathed in the sea. Then they marched to Eleusis in a religious procession. In the evening, certain ceremonies were spoken, revealed, and performed in the hall of mysteries at Eleusis. During the preliminary rites, initiates had to fast and partake of a sacred drink. The chief rites may have included a dramatic performance of the story of Hades and Persephone, a symbolic descent into the underworld, and a revelation of Demeter, the grain goddess. The initiates were promised happiness in the next world.

The followers of Orpheus conducted the *Orphic Mysteries*. Orpheus is supposed to have founded these rites in honor of Dionysus. Those who believed in the Orphic religion also claimed to know the secret of happiness after death.

Mystic cults in the Roman world included those of Cybele, Isis, and Mithras. These cults practiced magic rites, sacraments, purifications, and baptisms in their mysteries.   VAN JOHNSON

Related Articles in WORLD BOOK include:
Demeter	Mithras
Dionysus	Orpheus
Hades	Persephone
Isis	Rhea

MYSTERY PLAY. See ENGLISH LITERATURE (Early English Drama); MIRACLE PLAY; MORALITY PLAY.

MYSTERY STORY. See DETECTIVE STORY; LITERATURE FOR CHILDREN (Fiction).

MYSTIC SEAPORT, a reconstructed waterfront village, is a reminder of maritime life in the days of the great sailing ships. It lies on the Mystic River in Mystic, Conn. For location, see CONNECTICUT (political map).

Waterfront buildings and shops typical of the mid-1800's stand along Mystic Seaport's cobblestone streets. The *Australia*, the oldest American schooner afloat, and the *Charles W. Morgan*, New England's last wooden whaleship, are moored at the Seaport's docks. Sea Scouts and other youths learn sailing skills aboard these famous old sailing ships. Mystic Seaport also has one of the finest collections of clipper ship models in America. The Marine Historical Association established Mystic Seaport in 1929. Each year, hundreds of tourists visit the village.   ALBERT E. VAN DUSEN

See also CONNECTICUT (color picture).

MYSTICISM, *MIHS tuh sihz uhm*, is the belief that God or spiritual truths can be known through individual insight, rather than by reasoning or study. All the major religions include some form of mysticism.

A person who has mystical experiences is called a *mystic*. Most mystics find such experiences difficult to describe. Many say they have visions or hear inner voices that reveal a spiritual truth. Some mystics feel that their spirits fly out of their bodies or become possessed by a higher power. During these experiences, mystics may feel ecstasy or great peace.

Mystics differ in their practices and experiences, even within the same religion. However, most mystics share three basic goals: (1) knowledge of a spiritual reality that exists beyond the everyday world, (2) spiritual union with some higher power, and (3) freedom from selfish needs and worldly desires. To attain these goals, most mystics undergo some form of self-discipline. For example, they may isolate themselves from material comforts and other people. In addition, their discipline may involve extremes of mental and physical activity. Buddhist mystics may meditate for hours or even days without moving. Jews who belong to the Hasidic group often shout and twist their bodies while praying. Some members of the Islamic Sufi sect go into a trance as they perform a whirling dance.

Mysticism has played a prominent role in many religions. Devout Buddhists and Hindus may dedicate their lives to the mystical search for direct spiritual experience. Christian mystics have included several Roman Catholic saints and the Quakers. In Islam, Judaism, and other religions that emphasize the role of a supreme God, mystics may believe that their experiences result from divine actions. In religions in which many gods are worshiped, such as Hinduism and Taoism, mystics may attribute their insights to their own individual efforts.   NANCY E. AUER FALK

The Gods and Goddesses of Mythology appear in many forms. The ancient Greeks believed their goddess Athena, *left*, had a human shape. Hindus represent their god Ganesh, *center*, with the head of an elephant. The ancient Egyptians believed their god Anubis, *right*, had a jackal's head.

MYTHOLOGY

MYTHOLOGY. People have always tried to understand why certain things happen. For example, they have wanted to know why the sun rises and sets and what causes lightning. They have also wanted to know how the earth was created and how and where man first appeared.

Today, people have scientific answers and theories for many such questions about the world around them. But in earlier times—and in some parts of the world today—people lacked the knowledge to provide scientific answers. They therefore explained natural events in terms of stories about gods, goddesses, and heroes. For example, the Greeks had a story to explain the existence of evil and trouble. The Greeks believed that at one time the world's evils and troubles were trapped in a box. They escaped when the container was opened by Pandora, the first woman. Such stories are known as *myths*, and the study of myths is called *mythology*.

In early times, every society developed its own myths, which played an important part in the society's religious life. This religious significance has always separated myths from similar stories, such as folk tales and legends. The people of a society may tell folk tales and legends for amusement, without believing them. But

C. Scott Littleton, the contributor of this article, is Chairman of the Department of Sociology and Anthropology at Occidental College and the author of The New Comparative Mythology.

they usually consider their myths sacred and completely true.

Most myths concern *divinities* (divine beings). These divinities have *supernatural* powers—powers far greater than any human being has. But in spite of their supernatural powers, many gods and heroes of mythology have human characteristics. They are guided by such emotions as love and jealousy, and they experience birth and death. A number of mythological figures even look like human beings. In many cases, the human qualities of the gods reflect a society's ideals. Good gods have the qualities a society admires, and evil gods have the qualities it dislikes.

By studying myths, we can learn how different societies have answered basic questions about the world and man's place in it. We study myths to learn how a people developed a particular social system with its many customs and ways of life. By examining myths, we can better understand the feelings and values that bind members of society into one group. We can compare the myths of various cultures to discover how these cultures differ and how they resemble one another. We can also study myths to try to understand why people behave as they do.

For thousands of years, mythology has provided material for much of the world's great art. Famous myths and mythological characters have inspired masterpieces of architecture, literature, music, painting, and sculpture.

813

Most myths can be divided into two groups—*creation myths* and *explanatory myths*. Creation myths try to explain the origin of the world, the creation of man, and the birth of gods and goddesses. All early societies developed creation myths. Explanatory myths try to explain natural processes or events. The Norse, who lived in medieval Scandinavia, believed that the god Thor made thunder and lightning by throwing a hammer at his enemies. The ancient Greeks believed that the lightning bolt was a weapon used by the god Zeus. Many societies developed myths to explain the formation and characteristics of geographic features, such as rivers, lakes, and oceans.

Some explanatory myths deal with illness and death. Many ancient societies—as well as some primitive present-day societies—believed that a person dies because of some act by a mythical being. The people of the Trobriand Islands in the Pacific Ocean believed that men and women were immortal when the world was new. When a person began to age, he or she swam in a certain lagoon and shed his skin. The person quickly grew a new skin, renewing his youth. One day, a mother returned from the lagoon with her new skin. But her unexpected youthful appearance frightened her little daughter. To calm the child, the mother returned to the lagoon, found her old skin, and put it back on. From then on, according to this myth, death could not be avoided.

Some myths, through the actions of particular gods and heroes, stress proper behavior. The ancient Greeks strongly believed in moderation—that nothing be done in excess. They found this ideal in the behavior of Apollo, the god of purity, music, and poetry. Myths about national heroes also point up basic moral values. The story about young George Washington's confession that he had cut down his father's cherry tree has no basis in fact. Yet many people like to believe the story because it emphasizes the quality of honesty.

Mythical Beings fall into several groups. Many gods and goddesses resemble human beings, even though they have supernatural powers. These gods and goddesses were born, fell in love, fought with one another, and generally behaved like their human worshipers. These divinities are called *anthropomorphic*, from two Greek words meaning *in the shape of man*. Greek mythology has many anthropomorphic divinities, including Zeus, the most important Greek god.

Another group of mythical beings includes gods and goddesses who resemble animals. These characters are called *theriomorphic*, from two Greek words meaning *in the shape of an animal*. Many theriomorphic beings appear in Egyptian mythology. For example, the Egyptians sometimes represented their god Anubis as a jackal or a dog.

A third group of mythical beings has no specific name. These beings were neither completely human nor completely animal. An example is the famous sphinx of Egypt, which has a human head and a lion's body.

Human beings play an important part in mythology. Many myths deal with the relationships between mortals and divinities. Some mythical mortals have a divine father and a mortal mother. These human characters are called *heroes*, though they do not always act heroically in the modern sense. Most stories about heroes are called *epics* rather than myths, but the difference between the two is not always clear.

Mythical Places. Many myths describe places where demons, gods and goddesses, or the souls of the dead live. Most of these places are in the sky or on top of a high mountain. The people believed that the gods could see everything, and so they located them in a place higher than mortals could reach.

Mythical places exist in the mythologies of most peoples. Perhaps the most sacred place in Japanese mythology is Mount Fuji, the tallest mountain in Japan. The Greeks believed their gods lived on a mythical Mount Olympus that rose above the visible Mount Olympus in northern Greece.

The Greeks also believed in mythical places beneath the ground, such as Hades, where the souls of the dead lived. The Norse believed in Hel, an underground home for the souls of all dead persons, except those killed in battle. The souls of slain warriors went to Valhalla, a great hall in the sky. The Eskimos believe that their sea goddess, Sedna, lives in a world under the ocean.

Mythical Symbols. In their mythologies, people used many symbols to help explain the world. The Greeks symbolized the sun as the god Helios driving a flaming chariot across the sky. The Egyptians represented the sun as a boat.

Detail of a painting on papyrus (900's B.C.); Egyptian Museum, Cairo (Walter Sanders, *LIFE* Magazine © Time Inc.)

The Separation of the Earth from the Sky is described in many mythologies. According to Egyptian mythology, the god Shu, *standing center*, raised the sky goddess, Nut, away from her husband, the earth god, Geb, *lying down*. Nut's body thus formed the heavens.

Animals, human beings, and plants have all stood for ideas and events. Some peoples adopted the serpent as a symbol of health because they believed that by shedding its skin, the serpent became young and well again. The Greeks portrayed Asclepius, the god of healing, holding a staff with a serpent coiled around it. Today, the serpent and staff symbolize the medical profession. In Babylonian mythology, the hero Gilgamesh searched for a special herb that made anyone who ate it immortal. Plants can also have opposite meanings. In the Old Testament, Adam and Eve ate the forbidden fruit and lost their immortality.

Comparing Myths. We study the similar myths of various societies by comparing them to one another. We can compare these myths on the basis of their generic, genetic, or historical relationships.

Generic Relationships among myths are based on the way people react to common features in their environment. For example, the Maoris of New Zealand and the ancient Greeks both had myths that described how the earth became separated from the sky.

Genetic Relationships. A large society may develop a particular myth. Then, for some reason, the society breaks up into several separate societies, each of which develops its own version of the myth. These myths have a genetic relationship.

Myths about the Greek god Zeus and the ancient Indian god Indra have a genetic relationship. The two gods resemble each other in many ways. For example, each is a sky god, and each uses a lightning bolt as his chief weapon. These similarities can be explained by the fact that the ancient Greeks and the people of ancient India descended from a common culture, the Indo-European community. The Indo-Europeans lived several thousand years ago in the area east of the Volga River in what is now Russia. This culture worshiped a warrior god who ruled the sky. One group of Indo-Europeans migrated westward to what is now Greece. There, they developed a version of the sky god who became known as Zeus. Another group of Indo-Europeans, the Aryans, migrated southward into northern India. They developed the warlike sky god Indra.

Historical Relationships appear when similar myths develop among cultures that do not share a common origin. For instance, many ancient Near and Middle Eastern societies had a myth in which several generations of sons overthrew their fathers, who ruled as gods or kings. Variations of this myth appeared in Greece and Iran; among the Hittites, who lived in what is now Turkey; and among the Phoenicians, who lived in what is now Lebanon. Many scholars believe that all versions of the myth came from an earlier Babylonian myth dating from about 2000 B.C.

In the 700's B.C., the Greek poet Hesiod wrote a long poem called the *Theogony*. In this poem, Hesiod described the origin of the world and the history of the gods. The *Theogony* contains Greek myths that have generic, genetic, and historical relationships with myths of other cultures. For example, Hesiod describes how the earth became separated from the sky. This myth is generically related to a similar Maori myth. Zeus, a major figure in the *Theogony*, genetically resembles the Indian god Indra. Hesiod also wrote about successive generations of Greek gods being overthrown by their sons. This myth is historically related to similar myths in other cultures of the ancient Near and Middle East.

Oil painting on canvas by N. A. Abildgaard; Royal Museum of Fine Arts, Copenhagen, Denmark

The Creation of Life is the subject of many myths. According to a Teutonic myth, the giant Ymir and the cow Audhumla became the first living things. They were born out of melting ice. Audhumla's milk fed Ymir. As the cow licked the ice for its salt, she freed the body of Buri, the first man. Buri then created a son, Bor.

The Nile River plays an important part in Egyptian mythology. As the Nile flows northward through Egypt, it creates a narrow ribbon of fertile land in the midst of a great desert. The sharp contrast between the fertility along the Nile and the wasteland of the desert became a basic theme of Egyptian mythology. The creatures that live in the Nile or along its banks became linked with many gods and goddesses.

The Great Ennead. The earliest information we have about Egyptian mythology comes from *hieroglyphics* (picture writings) on the walls of tombs, such as the burial chambers in pyramids. These "pyramid texts" and other documents tell us that from about 3200 to 2250 B.C. the Egyptians believed in a family of nine gods. This family became known as the *Great Ennead*, from the Greek word *ennea*, meaning *nine*. The nine gods of the Great Ennead were Atum, Shu and Tefnut, Geb and Nut, Osiris, Isis, Nephthys, and Horus.

The term *Ennead* later came to include other deities as well. One of these was Nun, who symbolized a great ocean that existed before the creation of the earth and heavens. Another was the sun god, called Re or Ra. The Egyptians considered Re the ruler of the world and the first divine pharaoh.

The first god of the Great Ennead was Atum. He was sometimes identified with the setting sun. Atum also represented the source of all gods and all living things. Re created a pair of twins, Shu and his sister, Tefnut. Shu was god of the air, which existed between the sky and the earth. Tefnut was goddess of the dew. Shu and Tefnut married and also produced twins, Geb and his sister, Nut. Geb was the earth god and pharaoh of Egypt. Nut represented the heavens. Geb and Nut married, but Re opposed the match and ordered their father, Shu, to raise Nut away from Geb into the sky. Shu's action separated the heavens from the earth. Nut had speckles on her body, and the speckles became the stars.

The Osiris Myth. In spite of their separation, Geb and Nut had several children. These included three of the most important divinities in Egyptian mythology— Osiris, Isis, and Set.

IMPORTANT DIVINITIES IN EGYPTIAN MYTHOLOGY

The ancient Egyptians portrayed many of their gods and goddesses with human bodies and the heads of birds or other animals. The divinities held or wore objects symbolizing their power. For example, the god Osiris held a scepter and a whip, which represented the authority of gods and divine pharaohs.

WORLD BOOK illustrations by George Suyeoka

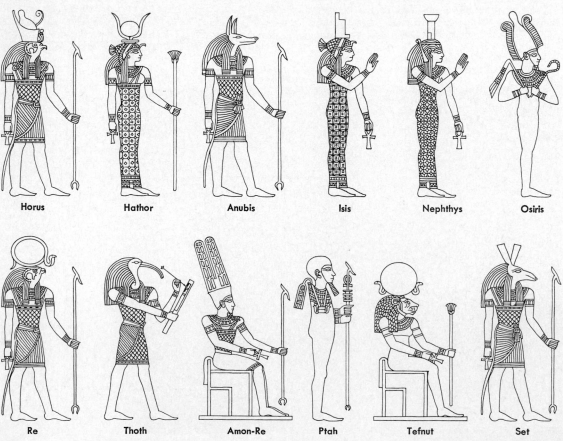

Horus   Hathor   Anubis   Isis   Nephthys   Osiris

Re   Thoth   Amon-Re   Ptah   Tefnut   Set

Originally, Osiris may have been god of vegetation, especially of the plants that grew on the rich land along the Nile. The goddess Isis may have represented female fertility. Set was god of the desert, where vegetation withers and dies from lack of water.

Geb retired to heaven. Osiris then became pharaoh and took Isis as his queen. Set grew jealous of Osiris' position and killed him. In some versions of this myth, Set cut Osiris' body into pieces, stuffed the pieces into a box, and set the box afloat on the Nile. Isis refused to accept her husband's death as final. She searched for Osiris' remains with the aid of her sister Nephthys and several other gods and goddesses. Isis finally found the remains of Osiris. With the help of other divinities, she put the body together, restoring Osiris to life. Osiris then became god of the afterlife.

Set had become pharaoh of Egypt after killing Osiris. But Horus, son of Osiris and Isis, then overthrew Set and became pharaoh. Thus, the forces of vegetation and creation—symbolized by Osiris, Isis, and Horus— triumphed over the evil forces of the desert, symbolized by Set. But more important, Osiris had cheated death. The Egyptians believed that if Osiris could triumph over death, so could human beings.

Other Egyptian Divinities included Hathor, Horus' wife; Anubis; Ptah; and Thoth. Hathor became the protector of everything feminine. Anubis escorted the dead to the entrance of the afterworld and helped restore Osiris to life. The Egyptians also believed that Anubis invented their elaborate funeral rituals and burial procedures. Ptah invented the arts. Thoth invented writing and magical rituals. He also helped bring Osiris back to life.

Many animals appear in Egyptian mythology. The hawk was sacred to Horus. The scarab, or dung beetle, symbolized Re (see SCARAB). The Egyptians considered both the cat and the crocodile as divine.

Between 1570 and 1090 B.C., various local divinities became well known throughout ancient Egypt. Some of them became as important as the gods and goddesses of the Ennead. The greatest of these gods was Amon. His *cult* (group of worshipers) originally centered in Thebes. In time, Amon became identified with Re, and was frequently known as Amon-Re. Amon-Re became perhaps the most important Egyptian divinity.

The Influence of Egyptian Mythology. The divinities of ancient Egypt and the myths about them had great influence on the mythologies of many later civilizations. Egyptian religious ideas may also have strongly affected the development of Judaism and Christianity.

During the 1300's B.C., the pharaoh Amenhotep IV chose Aton as the only god of Egypt. Aton had been a little-known god worshiped in Thebes. Amenhotep was so devoted to the worship of Aton that he changed his own name to Akhen*aton*. The Egyptians stopped worshiping Aton after Akhenaton died. However, some scholars believe the worship of this one divinity lingered among the Hebrews, who had settled in Egypt, and became an important part of the religion developed by the Hebrew leader Moses. These scholars have suggested that the Jewish and Christian belief in one God may come from the cult of Aton. See AKHENATON.

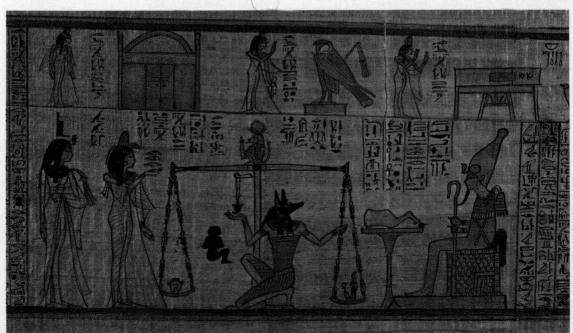

Detail of a papyrus scroll (about 1025 B.C.); Metropolitan Museum of Art, New York City, Museum Excavations and Rogers Fund, 1930

Osiris, Egyptian God of the Afterlife, judged the souls of the dead. In this scene, the jackal-headed god Anubis uses a balance scale to weigh a human heart, in the left pan, against objects representing truth and justice, in the right pan. Osiris, sitting at the right, makes the judgment.

The earliest record of Greek mythology comes from clay tablets dating back to the Mycenaean civilization, which reached its peak between 1450 and 1200 B.C. This civilization consisted of several city-states in Greece, including Mycenae. The clay tablets describe the chief Mycenaean god as Poseidon. He reappeared in later Greek mythology as a major figure. The god Zeus, who later became the chief god in Greek mythology, played a lesser part in Mycenaean myths.

During the 1100's B.C., the Dorians, who lived in northwestern Greece, conquered the Mycenaeans. The Dorian invasion ended the Mycenaean civilization, and what is often called the Dark Age of ancient Greece began. During this 400-year period, the Dorian and Mycenaean mythologies combined, helping form classical Greek mythology. See DORIANS.

The basic sources for classical Greek mythology are Hesiod's *Theogony* and Homer's *Iliad* and *Odyssey*, which date from about the 700's B.C. Hesiod and Homer rank among the greatest poets of ancient Greece. The *Theogony* and the *Iliad* and *Odyssey* contain most of the basic characters and themes of Greek mythology.

The Creation Myth. The *Theogony* includes the most important Greek myth—the myth that describes the origin and history of the gods. According to the *Theogony*, the universe began in a state of emptiness called *Chaos*. The divinity Gaea, or Earth, arose out of Chaos. She immediately gave birth to Uranus, who became king of the sky. Gaea mated with Uranus, producing children who were called the *Titans*.

Uranus feared his children and confined them within the huge body of Gaea. Gaea resented the imprisonment of her children. With Cronus, the youngest Titan, she plotted revenge. Using a sickle provided by Gaea, Cronus attacked Uranus and made him *impotent* (unable to breed children). Cronus then freed the Titans from inside Gaea. Because Uranus was impotent, Cronus became king of the sky. During his reign, the work of creating the world continued. Thousands of divinities were born, including the gods or goddesses of death, night, the rainbow, the rivers, and sleep.

Cronus married his sister Rhea, who bore him three daughters and three sons. But Cronus feared that he, like Uranus, would be deposed by his children. He therefore swallowed his first five children as soon as they were born. To save her sixth child, Zeus, Rhea tricked Cronus into swallowing a stone wrapped in baby clothes. Rhea then hid the infant on the island of Crete. After Zeus grew up, he returned to challenge his father. He tricked Cronus into drinking a substance that made him vomit his children. The children had grown into adults while inside their father. Zeus then led his brothers and sisters in a war against Cronus and the other Titans. Zeus and his followers won the war.

Detail of a painting (300's B.C.) on a Greek vase; the Louvre, Paris

The Greek Gods fought the giants after the gods had defeated the Titans. The giants were born from the blood of Uranus, father of the Titans. In this scene, Zeus, *center*, strikes at the giants with a thunderbolt. Hercules, *kneeling*, aims an arrow at a giant. Athena, *lower left*, attacks another giant with her spear.

The Building of the Trojan Horse (about 1760), an oil painting by Giovanni Domenico Tiepolo;
Wadsworth Atheneum, Hartford, Conn., Ella Gallup Sumner and Mary Catlin Sumner Collection

The Greeks Built the Trojan Horse, hid several soldiers inside, and left it outside the walls of
Troy. The Trojans believed the horse was a gift from the Greeks and pulled it into the city. After dark,
the soldiers sneaked out and opened the city gates for the Greek army.

They exiled the Titans in chains to Tartarus, a dark region deep within the earth. The victorious gods and goddesses chose Zeus as their ruler and agreed to live with him on Mount Olympus. The divinities who lived on Olympus became known as *Olympians*.

Greek Divinities can be divided into several groups. The earliest group was the Titans, led by Cronus. The most powerful group was the Olympians. Several ranks of divinities existed among the Olympians. The top rank consisted of six gods and six goddesses. The gods were Zeus, ruler of all divinities; Apollo, god of music, poetry, and purity; Ares, god of war; Hephaestus, blacksmith for the gods; Hermes, messenger for the gods; and Poseidon, god of earthquakes and the ocean. The goddesses were Athena, goddess of wisdom and war; Aphrodite, goddess of love; Artemis, twin sister of Apollo and goddess of hunting; Demeter, goddess of agriculture; Hera, sister and wife of Zeus; and Hestia, goddess of the hearth.

Three important gods became associated with the 12 Olympians. They were Hades, ruler of the underworld and brother of Zeus; Dionysus, god of wine and wild behavior; and Pan, god of the forest and pastures.

There were several groups of minor divinities in Greek mythology. Beautiful maidens called *nymphs* guarded various parts of nature. Nymphs called *dryads* lived in the forest, and nymphs called *nereids* lived in the sea. Three goddesses called *Fates* controlled the destiny of every man. The *Muses* were nine goddesses of various arts and sciences. All these divinities became the subjects of specific myths and folk tales.

Greek mythology also has a number of partly mortal, partly divine beings called *demigods*. Heracles (called Hercules by the Romans) probably ranked as the most important demigod. Heracles symbolized strength and physical endurance. Another demigod, Orpheus, became known for his beautiful singing.

Nearly all the Greek gods, goddesses, demigods, and other divinities became the subjects of specific cults. Many cults became associated with certain cities. The people of Delphi, famous for its *oracle* (prophet), especially worshiped Apollo (see DELPHI). The citizens of Athens looked to Athena as their protector. Ephesus became the center of the cult of Artemis. The Temple of Artemis in Ephesus is one of the Seven Wonders of the World (see SEVEN WONDERS OF THE WORLD).

Greek Heroes became almost as important as the divinities in Greek mythology. Heroes were largely or entirely mortal. They were born, grew old, and died. But they still associated with the divinities. Many heroes claimed gods as their ancestors.

Most Greek heroes and heroines can be divided into two main groups. The first group came before the outbreak of the Trojan War in 1194 B.C., and the second group fought in the war.

The most famous heroes before the Trojan War include Jason, Theseus, and Oedipus. Jason led a band of heroes called the Argonauts on a search for the fabulous Golden Fleece, the pure gold wool of a sacred ram. Theseus killed the Minotaur, a monster with the body of a man and the head of a bull. Oedipus, the king of Thebes, unknowingly killed his father and married his mother. Oedipus' story has been popular with artists and writers for more than 2,000 years.

819

Detail of a marble relief from a
Greek coffin; the Louvre, Paris

The Muses were nine Greek goddesses of the arts and sciences. They included Terpsichore (dance), holding a lyre; Urania (astronomy), with a globe; and Melpomene (tragedy), with a mask.

Painting (420 to 410 B.C.) on a Greek cup; courtesy of
the Museum of Fine Arts, Boston, Pierce Fund

The Centaurs, in Greek mythology, were part human and part horse. In one myth, pictured here, a centaur attempted to attack Deianira, the wife of Hercules. But Hercules rescued her.

The Trojan War was fought between Greece and the city of Troy. The war began after Helen, wife of the king of Sparta, fled to Troy with Paris, son of the Trojan king. The Greeks organized an army to attack Troy and bring Helen back to Greece. Our knowledge of the war comes chiefly from the *Iliad* and *Odyssey*.

The Greek heroes who participated in the Trojan War included Agamemnon, the commander in chief; Menelaus, Helen's husband; and Odysseus, the clever general who formed a plan that finally led to Troy's defeat. Achilles was the most famous Greek warrior, and the major Trojan heroes were Hector and Paris. The gods and goddesses participated in the war almost as much as the heroes. Nearly all the divinities sided with the Greeks. The major exception was the goddess of love, Aphrodite.

GREEK AND ROMAN DIVINITIES

Many gods and goddesses of Greek mythology held similar positions in Roman mythology. For example, each mythology had a goddess of love. The Greeks called her Aphrodite. The Romans called her Venus. The table below lists the most important Greek and Roman divinities.

Greek	Roman	Position
Aphrodite	Venus	Goddess of love
Apollo	Apollo	God of light, medicine, and poetry
Ares	Mars	God of war
Artemis	Diana	Goddess of hunting and childbirth
Asclepius	Aesculapius	God of healing
Athena	Minerva	Goddess of crafts, war, and wisdom
Cronus	Saturn	In Greek mythology, ruler of the Titans and father of Zeus; in Roman mythology, also the god of agriculture
Demeter	Ceres	Goddess of growing things
Dionysus	Bacchus	God of wine, fertility, and wild behavior
Eros	Cupid	God of love
Gaea	Terra	Symbol of the earth and mother and wife of Uranus
Hephaestus	Vulcan	Blacksmith for the gods and god of fire and metalworking
Hera	Juno	Protector of marriage and women. In Greek mythology, sister and wife of Zeus; in Roman mythology, wife of Jupiter
Hermes	Mercury	Messenger for the gods; god of commerce and science; and protector of travelers, thieves, and vagabonds
Hestia	Vesta	Goddess of the hearth
Hypnos	Somnus	God of sleep
Pluto, or Hades	Pluto	God of the underworld
Poseidon	Neptune	God of the sea. In Greek mythology, also god of earthquakes and horses
Rhea	Ops	Wife and sister of Cronus
Uranus	Uranus	Son and husband of Gaea and father of the Titans
Zeus	Jupiter	Ruler of the gods

To many people, Roman mythology largely seems a copy of Greek mythology. The Romans had come into contact with Greek culture during the 700's B.C., and afterward some of their divinities began to reflect the qualities of Greek gods and goddesses. But before that time, the Romans had developed their own mythology. In fact, many of the basic similarities between Roman and Greek mythology can be traced to the common Indo-European heritage shared by Rome and Greece.

Roman Divinities. Before the Romans came into contact with Greek culture, they worshiped three major gods—Jupiter, Mars, and Quirinus. These gods are known as the *archaic triad*, meaning *old group of three*. Jupiter ruled as god of the heavens and came to be identified with Zeus. Mars was god of war. He occupied a much more important place in Roman mythology than did Ares, the war god in Greek mythology. Quirinus apparently represented the common people. The Greeks had no similar god.

By the late 500's B.C., the Romans began to replace the archaic triad with the *Capitoline triad*—Jupiter, Juno, and Minerva. The triad's name came from the Capitoline Hill in Rome, on which stood the main temple of Jupiter. In the new triad, Jupiter remained the Romans' chief god. They identified Juno with the Greek goddess Hera and Minerva with Athena.

Between the 500's and 100's B.C., additional Roman mythological figures appeared, nearly all based on Greek divinities. These Roman divinities, with their Greek names in parentheses, included Bacchus (Dionysus), Ceres (Demeter), Diana (Artemis), Mercury (Hermes), Neptune (Poseidon), Pluto (Hades), Venus (Aphrodite), Vesta (Hestia), and Vulcan (Hephaestus).

In addition to Greek-inspired divinities, the Romans worshiped many native gods and goddesses. These included Faunus, a nature spirit; Februus, a god of the underworld; Pomona, goddess of fruits and trees; Terminus, god of boundaries; and Tiberinus, god of the Tiber River.

Romulus and Remus. In their mythology, the Romans—unlike the Greeks—tried to explain the founding and history of their nation. Thus, the Romans came to consider their divinities as historical persons. The best example of this historical emphasis is the story of Romulus and Remus, the mythical founders of Rome.

The ancient Romans believed that Romulus and Remus were twins born of a mortal mother and the war god, Mars. Soon after their birth, they were set afloat in a basket on the Tiber River. A she-wolf found the babies and cared for them. Finally, a shepherd discovered the twins and raised them to adulthood.

Romulus and Remus decided to build a city at the spot on the Tiber where the wolf had found them. In a quarrel, Romulus or one of Romulus' followers killed Remus. Romulus then founded Rome, supposedly in 753 B.C. The Romans believed that Romulus became the city's first king and established most of the Roman political institutions.

The Seven Kings. According to Roman mythology, Romulus was the first of seven kings who ruled Rome from its founding until the early 500's B.C. The kings after Romulus were Numa Pompilius, Tullus Hostilius, Ancus Marcius, Lucius Tarquinius Priscus, Servius Tullius, and Lucius Tarquinius Superbus. The seven kings became known for various achievements. For example, Numa started many of Rome's basic religious institutions. Tullus Hostilius was a warlike king who conquered the Albans, an Italian tribe that lived southeast of Rome.

There is little evidence that the seven early kings of Rome ever existed or that any of the events connected with their reigns ever took place. Some scholars believe these kings probably originated as divinities, whom the Romans converted into historical figures. The kings and the gods have many similarities. For example, Romulus resembles Jupiter because both were primarily rulers, not military leaders. Tullus Hostilius resembles Mars.

The Aeneid. During the 200's B.C., the Romans tried to relate the origins of their divinities to Greek myths. About the time of the birth of Christ, the Roman poet Virgil wrote an epic poem called the *Aeneid*. Virgil modeled the *Aeneid* on the *Iliad* and the *Odyssey* by Homer. Virgil tried to connect the origins of Rome to the events that followed the fiery destruction of Troy by the Greeks.

The *Aeneid* traces the wanderings of the Trojan hero Aeneas, who escaped unharmed from the burning city. He stopped for a time in the city of Carthage in northern Africa. There, he rejected the love of Dido, queen of Carthage. He then sailed for Italy and, in time, landed near the mouth of the Tiber River. After many adventures, Aeneas founded a town. Aeneas' son, Ascanius, later moved the town to Alba Longa, where Romulus and Remus were born. Virgil thus connected the founding of Rome with the Trojan War, a significant event in Greek mythology. See AENEID.

Relief on a Roman altar (A.D. 124); Museo Nazionale
Romano, Rome (photo by Raymond V. Schoder)

Romulus and Remus were the mythical founders of Rome. A wolf nursed the twins, *lower left*, after they were abandoned as babies. One of the shepherds, *above*, later found the boys.

The Celts were an ancient people of Indo-European origin. Most Celts lived in what is now southwestern Germany until about 500 B.C. They then began settling throughout western Europe, especially in the British Isles. See CELTS.

Most of our information on Celtic mythology is about mythical characters and events in the British Isles, particularly in Ireland. During the Middle Ages, Irish monks preserved many ancient Celtic myths in several collections of manuscripts. The most important collection is the *Lebor Gabala (Book of Conquests)*, which traces the mythical history of Ireland. Another important collection, the *Mabinogion*, comes from Wales. The first four stories in this collection are called the "Four Branches of the Mabinogi." These stories describe the mythical history of Britain. The Welsh myths show a much stronger Christian influence than do the Irish myths. The Welsh myths also tend to emphasize human characters. The Irish myths deal more with divinities.

The Irish Cycles. Much Irish Celtic mythology concerns three important *cycles* (series of related stories). They are (1) the mythological cycle, (2) the Ulster cycle, and (3) the Fenian cycle.

The Mythological Cycle, the oldest cycle, is preserved in the *Lebor Gabala*. The cycle describes the early settlement of Ireland through a succession of invasions by five supernatural races. The most important race was the Tuatha De Danann, or People of the Goddess Danu. The Tuatha was the fourth of the five invading races. They defeated the Firbolgs and the Fomoirans and were in turn defeated by the Sons of Mil, also called the Milesians. The Tuatha were the source of most of the divinities that the Irish people worshiped before they became Christians in the A.D. 400's.

The Ulster Cycle centers on the court of King Conchobar at Ulster, probably before the time of Christ. The stories deal with the adventures of Cuchulainn, a great Irish hero who can also be considered a demigod. In some ways, he resembled the Greek hero Achilles. But unlike Achilles and other Greek heroes, Cuchulainn had many supernatural powers. For example, he could spit fire in battle. He was also a magician and poet.

Many stories about Cuchulainn appear in the Ulster cycle. Probably the best known is the *Cooley Cattle Raid*. In this story, Queen Mave of Connaught ordered a raid on Ulster to capture a famous brown bull. Cuchulainn single-handedly fought off the invaders until the queen's forces finally captured the bull. However, the Ulster warriors led by King Conchobar came to Cuchulainn's aid and drove the invaders out of the country. Queen Mave plotted revenge against Cuchulainn and several years later used supernatural means to cause his death. See CUCHULAINN.

The Fenian Cycle, also called the *Ossianic cycle*, describes the deeds of the hero Finn MacCool, his son Ossian, and Finn's band of warriors known as the *Fianna*. Finn and the Fianna were famous for their great size and strength. In addition, Finn was known for his generosity and wisdom. Although divine beings and supernatural events play a part in these stories, the central characters are human. Some scholars believe the events in the

The Dream of Ossian (1811), an oil painting on canvas; Ingres Museum, Montauban, France (WORLD BOOK photo by Rességuié)

Ossian was a famous Celtic warrior and poet. The French artist Jean Auguste Dominique Ingres painted the aged Ossian dreaming of the many Celtic heroes he had glorified in his poetry.

Fenian cycle may reflect the political and social conditions in Ireland during the A.D. 200's.

The most famous story in the Fenian cycle is called "The Pursuit of Diarmuid and Grainne." In this story, Finn was to marry Grainne, the daughter of an Irish king. However, she fell in love with Diarmuid, Finn's friend and nephew, and persuaded Diarmuid to elope with her. Finn and his warriors pursued the lovers. Much of the story concerns the adventures of Diarmuid and Grainne as they fled Finn. Finally, Finn caught them and indirectly caused the death of Diarmuid. At first, Grainne hated Finn, but he courted her until she became his wife. See FINN MACCOOL.

Welsh Myths. Two races of divinities appear in Welsh mythology—the Children of Don and the Children of Llyr. Both races partly resemble the Tuatha De Danann in Irish mythology, possibly because many Irish Celts migrated to Britain and brought their mythology with them.

The most famous Welsh myths concern King Arthur and his knights. The mythical King Arthur was probably based on a powerful Celtic chief who lived in Wales during the A.D. 500's. Some stories about Arthur and his knights can be traced to such early Welsh literature as the "Four Branches of the Mabinogi." One of these stories tells of the knights' search for the Holy Grail, the cup Christ used at the Last Supper. Some scholars believe that the Christian myth of the Holy Grail originated in this story.

Teutonic mythology consists of the myths of Scandinavia and Germany. It is sometimes called *Norse* mythology, after the Norsemen who lived in Scandinavia during the Middle Ages. The basic written sources for Teutonic mythology consist of two works, called *Eddas*, composed in Iceland between about A.D. 1000 and the 1200's (see EDDA). Other information on Teutonic mythology comes from legends about specific families and heroes and from German literary and historical works of the Middle Ages.

The Creation of Life. According to the Eddas, two places existed before the creation of life—Muspellsheim, a land of fire, and Niflheim, a land of ice and mist. Between them lay Ginnungagap, a great emptiness where heat and ice met. Out of this emptiness came Ymir, a young giant and the first living thing. A second creature soon appeared, a cow named Audhumla. Ymir lived on Audhumla's milk. As Ymir matured, he gave birth to three beings. He bore them from his armpits and from one leg. The first divine family was thus born.

Meanwhile, a second giant, Buri, was frozen in the ice of Niflheim. Audhumla licked the ice off his body, freeing him. Buri created a son named Bor, who married the giantess Bestla. They had three sons—Odin, Ve, and Vili. The sons founded the first race of gods.

The Construction of the World. After Odin became an adult, he led his brothers in an attack on Ymir and killed him. Odin then became supreme ruler of the world. The gods defeated the giants in battle, but the surviving giants planned revenge on their conquerors.

Odin and his brothers constructed the world from Ymir's body. His blood became the oceans, his ribs the mountains, and his flesh the earth. The gods created the first man from an ash tree and the first woman from an elm tree. They also constructed Asgard, which became their heavenly home. Valhalla, a great hall in Asgard, was the home of warriors killed in battle.

Many divinities lived in Asgard. These divinities were called the *Aesir*, just as the leading Greek gods and goddesses were called the Olympians. The ruler of Asgard was Odin. Thor, Odin's oldest son, was god of thunder and lightning. Balder, another of Odin's sons, was god of goodness and harmony. Other divinities included Bragi, the god of poetry, and Loki, the evil son of a giant. The most important goddesses included Frigg, Odin's wife; Freyja, goddess of love and beauty; and Hel, goddess of the underworld.

A giant ash tree known as Yggdrasil supported all creation. In most accounts of Yggdrasil, the tree had three roots. One root reached into Niflheim. Another grew to Asgard. The third extended to Jotunheim, the land of the giants. Three sisters called Norns lived around the base of the tree. They controlled mankind's past, present, and future. A giant serpent called Nidhoggr lived near the root in Niflheim. The serpent was loyal to the race of giants defeated by Odin. It continually gnawed at the root to bring the tree down, and the gods with it.

Teutonic Heroes. Sigurd the Dragon Slayer probably ranks as the most important hero in Teutonic mythology. He appears in a Scandinavian version of German myths about a royal family called the Volsungs. Sigurd became the model for the mythical German hero Siegfried, who appears in the *Nibelungenlied*, a famous German epic of the Middle Ages. Other heroes in Teutonic mythology include Starkad, a mortal friend of Odin's, and the Danish warrior Hadding. See NIBELUNGENLIED.

The End of the World. Unlike many other major Western mythologies, Teutonic mythology includes an *eschatology* (an account of the end of the world). According to Teutonic mythology, there will be a great battle called *Ragnarok*. This battle will be fought between the giants, led by Loki, and the gods and goddesses living in Asgard. All the gods, goddesses, and giants in the battle will be killed, and the earth will be destroyed by fire. After the battle, Balder will be reborn. With several sons of dead gods, he will form a new race of divinities. The human race will also be re-created. During Ragnarok, a man and woman will take refuge in a forest and sleep through the battle. After the earth again becomes fertile, the couple will awake and begin the new race of mankind. The new world, cleansed of evil and treachery, will endure forever.

Plaster statue (1822) by George Christian Freund;
Ny Carlsberg Glyptotek, Copenhagen, Denmark

The Evil God Loki was the son of a giant and the enemy of the good Teutonic gods. One myth describes how Loki will lead the giants against the gods in the battle that will destroy the world.

About 1500 B.C., an Indo-European people called the Aryans swept out of central Asia and invaded the Indus Valley of northern India. They conquered the Dravidians, who had lived in the region at least 1,000 years. The Aryan and Dravidian religions gradually merged, creating Hinduism, the chief religion of India today. See HINDUISM; INDIA (History).

The Vedas. The earliest sources of Hindu mythology consist of four sacred books called the *Vedas*—the *Rig-Veda*, the *Yajur-Veda*, the *Sama-Veda*, and the *Atharva-Veda*. They were probably composed between 1200 and 600 B.C. Of the four, the *Rig-Veda* is the oldest and most important. According to the *Rig-Veda*, two gods—Mitra and Varuna—jointly ruled the universe. Next in rank, but first in importance among the gods, came the warrior god Indra. Then came a pair of twins—the Ashvins, or Horsemen—who were responsible for the physical well-being of the world. See VEDAS.

Brahman. A new group of gods gradually replaced the gods of the Vedas. The chief divinity was Brahman, the Supreme World-Spirit. Hindus believe that Brahman takes many forms. The three most important forms are Brahma, the Creator; Vishnu, the Preserver; and Shiva, the Destroyer. Hindus call these three divinities the *Trimurti*, which means *three forms* in the Sanskrit language of India.

Vishnu, the god of life, is perhaps the most popular Hindu divinity. Hindus believe that Vishnu has appeared in nine *avatars* (physical forms). These forms have been animal, human, and divine. In the future, Vishnu will take a 10th avatar—that of a winged white horse—and will destroy evil and sin in the world.

The Hindu Epics. Hindu mythology has many heroes and stories. The most important appear in two long epic poems, the *Mahabharata* and the *Ramayana*. The earlier of the two is the *Mahabharata*. Parts of it are more than 2,500 years old. According to Hindu mythology, Ganesh, god of wisdom, wrote down the *Mahabharata* as it was dictated by the ancient Hindu wise man Vyasa. The poem describes a conflict that occurred perhaps about 1200 B.C. between two groups of cousins—the Pandavas and the Kauravas—over who shall rule a kingdom. Much of the action centers on Arjuna, the most valiant warrior among the Pandavas.

Some time after the *Mahabharata* was written, a new section, the *Bhagavad-Gita* (*Song of God*), was added. In it, Arjuna, while preparing for battle, discusses the meaning of life and death with his charioteer. The charioteer is really the god Krishna, an avatar of Vishnu.

The *Ramayana*, composed perhaps in the 200's or 100's B.C., describes the adventures of Rama, an avatar of Vishnu. It tells of his search for Sita, his bride, who has been kidnaped by a demon, the king of Ceylon. The *Ramayana* became a major source of the art, drama, and literature of Indonesia, Malaysia, and Thailand as well as of India.

Painting on paper (about A.D. 1725 to 1750); Dr. and Mrs. J. LeRoy Davidson Collection, Los Angeles

The Warrior Arjuna and the God Krishna, disguised as a charioteer, discuss the meaning of life and death before an important battle. Their discussion makes up the *Bhagavad-Gita* (*Song of God*), a section of the *Mahabharata*, one of the great epic poems of Hindu mythology.

Many thousands of islands lie scattered throughout the Pacific Ocean. A rich tradition of myths and mythological figures flourished among the numerous cultures of the islands until the late 1800's, when many of the people became Christians. Some non-Christian cultures have retained their traditional mythologies. In addition, some Christians have kept parts of their native mythologies. See PACIFIC ISLANDS.

Creation Myths. Some cultures of the Pacific Islands believed that heaven and the earth always existed. These cultures therefore developed no myths about the creation of the world. Many cultures also assumed that the ocean, which plays such a vital part in Pacific Islands life, always existed.

Some island cultures believed that gods created the world. Other cultures thought the world developed slowly from a great emptiness. According to this myth, the earth and the sky first existed close together and then separated. Several versions of the myth explain how this separation occurred. For example, the Maoris of New Zealand have a myth in which the sky, Rangi, loved the earth, Papa. Rangi and Papa gave birth to many gods, who became crushed in the embrace of their parents. To survive, the gods separated the earth and the sky, so that life could exist between them.

Pacific Islands Divinities. Many similarities existed among the major divinities of the Pacific Islands cultures. Many islanders worshiped a god called Tangaroa. In the New Hebrides, he and another divinity ruled the world jointly. To some people in Tahiti, Tangaroa was a human being who became a divinity. For a picture of a statue of Tangaroa, see SCULPTURE (Pacific Islands).

The most famous demigod among the islands of Polynesia was Maui. According to some myths, Maui created the Hawaiian Islands by fishing them up from the ocean. One of the islands is named after him. The Polynesians also credited Maui with teaching man how to make fire and do other useful things.

The people of the Pacific Islands believed in the existence of little people similar to the dwarfs and elves of European folklore. The Hawaiians called these people the *menehune*. Pacific Islanders believed the menehune were responsible for events that could not be explained in any other way. For example, if a worker finished a job faster than expected, he credited the menehune for his unexplainable speed. If a wall was so old that nobody could remember who built it, the people decided the menehune must have put it up.

Mana and Taboo. The idea of *mana* was important in Pacific Islands mythology. The islanders considered mana an impersonal, supernatural force that flowed through objects, persons, and places. A man who succeeded at a difficult task had a large amount of mana. However, a warrior's defeat in battle showed he had lost his mana.

The islanders believed that certain animals, persons, and religious objects had so much mana that contact with them was dangerous for ordinary people. These mana-filled beings and objects were thus declared *taboo* (forbidden to touch). The islanders believed that if a person touched a taboo object, he would suffer injury or even death. See TABOO.

Wood sculpture with beaten bark cloth, 22½ inches
(57 centimeters) high; Museum of Man, Paris

The Fire Goddess Pele was worshiped in many parts of Polynesia. The Hawaiians believed she lived in the volcano Kilauea. When the goddess became angry, the volcano erupted.

Painted bark-cloth figure, 12 inches (30 centimeters) high seated;
Peabody Museum, Harvard University, Cambridge, Mass.

A Protective Figure from Easter Island represents the spirit of an ancestor. An islander places such a figure outside his home in the hope that the ancestor will protect the house from evil.

A wide variety of mythologies has developed among the many tribes that live in Africa south of the Sahara. Some of these mythologies are simple and primitive. Others are elaborate and complicated.

The majority of African tribes worship prominent features in nature, such as mountains, rivers, and the sun. Most of these tribes believe that almost everything in nature contains a spirit. Some spirits are friendly, but others are not. Spirits may live in animals, plants, or lifeless objects. Tribesmen pray or offer gifts to the spirits to gain their favor and obtain particular benefits.

Ancestor worship forms part of many African mythologies. Many Africans believe that, after death, the souls of their ancestors are reborn in living things or in objects. For example, the Zulus refuse to kill certain kinds of snakes because they believe the souls of their ancestors live in those snakes. See AFRICA (The Arts [picture: Baoule Ancestor Figure]).

Magic plays a major role in the tribal religions of Africa. Priests have great influence among many tribes because they are believed to have magical powers. Many Africans wear charms to protect themselves from harm.

According to several African mythologies, many divinities live in temporary homes on the earth called *fetishes* (see FETISH). Fetishes vary from simple stones to beautifully carved images. Some African tribes believe that fetishes protect them from evil spells and bring them good luck. For pictures of a fetish and other objects related to African mythology, see SCULPTURE (African).

The Ashantis make up the largest native group in Ghana, a small country in western Africa. In many ways, their mythology illustrates African mythology in general. Many Ashantis believe that a supreme god called Nyame created the universe. Nyame heads a large group of divinities, most of whom descended from him. Some of these divinities serve as protectors of specific villages or regions. Others represent geographic features. The Ashantis regard rivers as the most sacred geographic feature. They also associate many divinities with specific occupations and crafts, such as farming and metalworking.

Among the Ashanti divinities, only the earth goddess lacks a specific fetish. The Ashantis believe the earth itself is her fetish. A group of priests supervises the worship of fetishes. The Ashantis believe that their priests possess certain special powers. According to the Ashantis, the priests can persuade a fetish to speak through the lips of a human agent called a *medium*. A priest usually serves as the medium. For more information on African mythology, see AFRICA (Religions).

Wooden statue, 35½ inches (90 centimeters) high; Ifan Museum, Dakar, Senegal (Pictorial Parade)

Spirit Figures like this one of the Senufo tribe of Ivory Coast may represent an ancestor or a god. The Senufo believe such figures can help them understand the past and forecast the future.

Wooden statue, 31½ inches (80 centimeters) high; Musée Royale de l'Afrique Centrale, Tervuren, Belgium (Art Reference Bureau)

Fetish Figures like this one of the Songe tribe of Zaire are used to protect village property. Animal skin, beads, and other materials are added to increase a figure's powers.

At the time that Christopher Columbus landed in the New World, Indians lived throughout North and South America. The Indians had many different ways of life and many distinct mythologies. But all the mythologies shared several features. Most Indians believed in the supernatural, including a great variety of gods. The Indians created elaborate religious ceremonies through which they hoped to gain supernatural powers to aid them in searching for food or in fighting enemies. Indian mythologies have many heroes who gave man his first laws and established basic social institutions. Many mythologies describe the end of the world through some great disaster, such as a fire or flood. For more information on the religion of the Indians, see INDIAN, AMERICAN (Religion).

The Aztec Indians of central Mexico developed one of the most interesting Indian mythologies. The Aztec established a highly advanced civilization that lasted from the A.D. 1300's to 1521. In 1521, Spanish troops led by Hernando Cortes conquered the Aztec. Advanced cultures, such as those of the Toltec and Maya, had existed in Mexico before the Aztec came to power. The Aztec borrowed many of their divinities from these earlier Indian cultures. In addition, the Aztec conquered many neighboring Indian peoples. As these peoples became part of the Aztec empire, many of their divinities became part of Aztec mythology. The Aztec thus developed an extremely complicated mythology, composed of gods of earlier Indian civilizations, their own gods, and gods of conquered peoples.

The Aztec believed that the universe had passed through four ages called *suns* and that they were living in the fifth sun. The gods had ended each of the previous suns with a worldwide disaster and then created a new world. At the end of the first sun—the Sun of Precious Stones—floods destroyed the world. At the end of the second sun—the Sun of Fire—fire rained down from heaven and destroyed the earth. The third sun—the Sun of Darkness—ended with a terrible earthquake. The fourth sun—the Sun of the Wind—ended with a hurricane. Many Aztec interpreted the coming of the Spanish conquerers as the calamity that ended the fifth sun.

The chief Aztec divinity was probably the war god, Huitzilopochtli. The Aztec worshiped Tezcatlipoca, a sun god, under four forms, each identified with a specific color and direction. Almost every Indian civilization in Mexico worshiped the god Quetzalcoatl. The Aztec associated him with the arts. Tlaloc, the rain god, was probably the oldest god in Aztec mythology. His wife or sister, Chalchiuhtlicue, was goddess of running water. She protected newborn children, marriage, and innocent love. In contrast, Tlazolteotl was goddess of pleasure and guilty love. Farming formed the basis of the Aztec economy, and so the people worshiped many agricultural divinities. The most important was Tzinteotl, goddess of origins.

In Aztec mythology, souls of the dead lived in separate places, depending on how death occurred. For example, a place called Tonatiuhichan was reserved for warriors and victims of religious sacrifices. Other places were reserved for persons who had drowned or for women who had died in childbirth. Most souls passed to Mictlan, an underworld ruled by Mictlantecuhtli and his wife, Mictlanchihuatl. A statue of Xolotl, an Aztec god of death, is reproduced in the introduction to the SCULPTURE article.

Human sacrifice played an important role in Aztec religion. The Aztec held great ceremonies and festivals during which they offered human hearts to Huitzilopochtli and the other major divinities. The Aztec slashed open the chests of their sacrificial victims and tore out their hearts. Most of the victims were prisoners of war. The Aztec considered the victims as representatives of the gods themselves. During the period up to their deaths, some victims were dressed in rich clothing, given many servants, and treated with great honor. The Aztec believed that the souls of the sacrificial victims flew immediately to Tonatiuhichan and lived there forever in happiness.

Illustration from the *Codex Borbonicus;* library of the National Assembly, Palais Bourbon, Paris

The Aztec God Quetzalcoatl was a god of the wind and the protector of the arts. His portrait shows how the Aztec clothed their divinities in colorful and complicated religious symbols.

For at least 2,000 years, scholars have speculated about how myths began. Some believe myths began as historical events that became distorted with the passage of time. Others think myths resulted from man's attempt to explain natural occurrences that he could not understand. Scholars have also developed other theories of how myths began. None of these theories answers all the questions about myths, but each contributes to an understanding of the subject. The most important theories about the origins of myths were developed by Euhemerus, an ancient Greek, and four modern scholars—Friedrich Max Müller, Sir Edward Burnett Tylor, Bronislaw Malinowski, and Sir James George Frazer.

Euhemerus' Theory. Euhemerus, a Greek scholar who lived during the late 300's and early 200's B.C., developed one of the oldest known theories about the origin of myths. He was one of the first scholars to suggest that all myths are based on historical facts. Euhemerus believed that scholars had to strip away the supernatural elements in a myth to reach these facts. For example, he felt that Zeus was probably modeled on an early king of Crete who had such great power that he inspired many supernatural tales. Euhemerus' theory has one basic weakness. In most cases, modern scholars lack enough historical evidence to determine whether a mythical figure ever existed.

Müller's Theory. Friedrich Max Müller was a German-born British language scholar of the late 1800's. He suggested that all gods and mythical heroes were really representations of nature, especially the sun. To Müller, almost all major divinities and heroes were originally a symbol for the sun in one of its phases. For example, the birth of a hero stood for the dawn. The hero's triumph over obstacles represented the sun at noon, its highest point. The hero's decline and death expressed the sunset.

Müller decided that by the time such basic texts as the *Theogony* and the *Rig-Veda* appeared, the symbolic purpose of the gods and heroes had long been forgotten. Instead, people had come to believe in the divinities and heroes themselves. For example, the ancient Greeks believed that the sun god Helios drove his flaming chariot, the sun, across the sky every day. This belief began in an earlier attempt to express symbolically how each day the sun rose in the east and set in the west.

Today, few scholars take Müller's main theories seriously. However, he and his followers did influence most later theories about the origin of myths.

Tylor's Theory. Sir Edward Burnett Tylor was an English anthropologist of the 1800's. He believed that myths began through man's efforts to account for unexplainable occurrences in dreams. According to Tylor, man's first idea about the supernatural was his belief that he had a soul which lived in his body. While the body slept, the soul could wander freely and have many adventures. These adventures appeared to man in his dreams. Man then came to believe that animals had souls. Finally, he decided that everything in nature had a soul. Man could then explain, according to Tylor, such natural events as the eruption of a volcano. Gradually, man came to believe that the souls controlling natural occurrences could answer his prayers for protection or special favors. The idea that all things in nature have souls is called *animism* (see ANIMISM). Tylor considered animism the first step in the development of human thought—and the basis of myths.

Venus, Mother of Aeneas, Presenting Him with Arms Forged by Vulcan (1635), an oil painting on canvas by Nicolas Poussin; Art Gallery of Ontario, Toronto, gift of the Reuben Wells Leonard estate, 1948

The Trojan Warrior Aeneas receives weapons from his mother, Venus, to use in the Trojan War. Aeneas survived Troy's defeat by the Greeks and founded a colony in Italy. The ancient Romans traced their origin as a nation to Aeneas. According to the ancient Greek scholar Euhemerus, all myths are based on historical events, such as the Trojan War.

Malinowski's Theory. Bronislaw Malinowski was a Polish-born British anthropologist of the early 1900's. He disagreed with Tylor that myths began as prescientific attempts to explain dreams and natural occurrences. Instead, Malinowski emphasized the psychological conditions that lead man to create myths.

According to Malinowski, all people recognize that a frontier exists between what man can and cannot explain logically. Malinowski said man creates myths when he reaches this frontier. For example, early man lacked the scientific knowledge to explain thunder logically, and so he decided it was caused by a god using a hammer. Malinowski believed that man had to create such myths to relieve the tension brought on by his not knowing why something happens.

Frazer's Theory. Sir James George Frazer was a Scottish anthropologist of the late 1800's and early 1900's. He believed that myths began in the great cycle of nature—birth, growth, decay, death, and rebirth.

Frazer's theory developed from his attempt to explain an ancient Italian *ritual* (ceremony) conducted at Nemi, near Rome. At Nemi, there was a sacred grove of trees. In the middle of the grove grew a huge oak tree associated with the god Jupiter. A priest presided over the grove and the oak tree. Frazer's curiosity and interest were aroused by the way priests were re-placed. To become the priest, a man had to kill the current priest with a branch of mistletoe taken from the top of the oak. If the man succeeded, he proved that he had more vigor than the presiding priest and thus had earned the position.

Frazer's study of the Nemi ritual developed into one of the most ambitious anthropological works ever attempted, *The Golden Bough* (12 volumes, 1890-1915). In writing this work, Frazer made a broad study of ancient and primitive mythologies and religions. He concluded that the priests at Nemi were killed as a sacrifice. The ancient Italians believed that when a priest began to lose his vigor, so did Jupiter. As Jupiter became less vigorous, so did the world. For example, winters became longer and the land less fertile. To keep the world healthy, the priest, representing Jupiter, had to be killed and then reborn in the form of the more vigorous slayer.

Frazer wrote that societies throughout the world sacrificed symbols of their gods to keep these gods—and thus the world—from decaying and dying. According to Frazer, this theme of the dying and reborn god appears in almost every ancient mythology, either directly or symbolically. Frazer therefore concluded that myths originated from the natural cycle of birth, growth, decay, death, and—most important—rebirth.

MYTHOLOGY / What Mythology Tells Us About People

Many social scientists have developed theories telling how we can learn about people from the myths they tell. Some of these theories stress the role of myths in understanding society as a whole. Other theories emphasize the place of mythology in understanding why an individual acts the way he does.

Mythology and Society. During the late 1800's and early 1900's, the French sociologist Émile Durkheim developed several important theories on what he felt was the real meaning of myths. Durkheim believed that every society establishes certain social institutions and values, which are reflected in the society's religion. Therefore, according to Durkheim, most of a society's gods, heroes, and myths are really *collective representations* of the institutions and values of that society or of important parts within it. These representations determine how the individuals in the society think and act. By examining a society's myths, Durkheim believed, a sociologist can discover its social institutions and values.

Georges Dumézil, a modern French scholar, was influenced by Durkheim's ideas in the study of Indo-European mythology. According to Dumézil, the principal Indo-European divinities were collective representations of the *caste* (class) system common to several ancient Indo-European peoples. For example, in ancient India the gods Mitra and Varuna represented the Brahman, or priest, caste—the highest caste in Hindu society. The god Indra represented the warrior caste, which ranked below the Brahmans. The Ashvin twins represented a still lower caste—farmers and herdsmen. The relation between these divinities reveals what the Hindus considered proper conduct among the castes.

One ancient Indian myth tells that Indra killed a monster that threatened the peace and security of the gods. But the monster happened to be the chaplain of the gods and therefore a divine Brahman. As a result, Indra felt he had committed a great sin because he had killed a Brahman. This myth illustrates the ancient Indian belief that under no circumstances should a member of one caste harm a member of a higher caste.

Mythology and the Individual. During the early 1900's, the Swiss psychoanalyst Carl Jung developed an original and controversial theory about how myths reflect the attitudes and behavior of individuals. Jung suggested that everyone has a *personal* and a *collective* unconscious. An individual's personal unconscious is formed by his experiences in the world as filtered through his senses. An individual's collective unconscious is inherited and shared by all members of his race.

Jung believed that the collective unconscious is organized into basic patterns and symbols, which he called *archetypes*. Myths represent one kind of archetype. Other kinds include fairy tales, folk sagas, and works of art. Jung believed that all mythologies have certain features in common. These features include characters, such as gods and heroes, and themes, such as love or revenge. Other features include places, such as the home of the gods or the underworld, and plots, such as a battle between generations for control of a throne. Jung suggested that archetypes date back to the earliest days of mankind. By studying myths and other archetypes, Jung believed, scholars could trace the psychological development of particular races as well as of all mankind.   C. SCOTT LITTLETON

829

Related Articles in WORLD BOOK include:

EGYPTIAN MYTHOLOGY

Amon	Isis	Set
Anubis	Osiris	Sphinx
Hathor	Re	Thebes
Horus	Serapis	Thoth

GREEK MYTHOLOGY
GODS AND GODDESSES

Aeolus	Hades	Nereus
Aphrodite	Hebe	Pan
Apollo	Hecate	Persephone
Ares	Helios	Poseidon
Artemis	Hephaestus	Prometheus
Asclepius	Hera	Proteus
Athena	Hermes	Rhea
Atlas	Hestia	Satyr
Calliope	Hygeia	Selene
Cronus	Iris	Titans
Demeter	Morpheus	Triton
Dionysus	Muses	Uranus
Graces	Nemesis	Zeus

HEROES AND CHARACTERS FROM HOMER

See the separate articles HOMER; ILIAD; and ODYSSEY.
See also the following articles:

Achilles	Hector	Orestes
Agamemnon	Hecuba	Paris
Ajax	Helen of Troy	Penelope
Andromache	Iphigenia	Priam
Cassandra	Laocoön	Scylla
Circe	Lotus-Eater	Siren
Clytemnestra	Menelaus	Ulysses
Electra	Mentor	

OTHER HEROES AND CHARACTERS

Adonis	Daphne	Minos
Amazon	Deucalion	Narcissus
Andromeda	Endymion	Niobe
Antigone	Europa	Nymph
Arachne	Eurydice	Oedipus
Arethusa	Ganymede	Orion
Argonauts	Hercules	Orpheus
Ariadne	Hero and	Pandora
Cadmus	Leander	Perseus
Castor and	Hesperides	Phaëthon
Pollux	Io	Pygmalion
Cecrops	Jason	Sisyphus
Charon	Medea	Tantalus
Daedalus	Midas	Theseus
Damon and Pythias		

MONSTERS AND CREATURES

Argus	Giant	Medusa
Centaur	Gorgon	Minotaur
Cerberus	Griffin	Pegasus
Chimera	Harpy	Phoenix
Cyclops	Hydra	Unicorn

EVENTS, OBJECTS, AND PLACES

Aegis	Lethe
Ambrosia	Mysteries
Athenaeum	Nectar
Atlantis	Olympia
Cornucopia	Olympus
Delphi	Oracles
Elysian Fields	Parnassus
Epidaurus	Styx
Golden Fleece	Tartarus
Gordian Knot	Trojan War
Hellespont	Troy
Labyrinth	

ROMAN MYTHOLOGY

Aeneas	Lupercalia
Aeneid	Mars
Androcles	Mercury
Aurora	Minerva
Bacchus	Neptune
Ceres	Numa Pompilius
Cupid	Pluto
Diana	Psyche
Dido	Quirinus
Fates	Romulus and Remus
Faun	Saturn
Fortuna	Saturnalia
Furies	Servius Tullius
Genii	Sibyl
Janus	Somnus
Juno	Tarquinius
Jupiter	Venus
Lares and Penates	Vesta
Luna	Vulcan

CELTIC MYTHOLOGY

Arthur, King	Finn MacCool
Cuchulainn	Irish Literature (The Golden Age)

TEUTONIC MYTHOLOGY

Balder	Nibelungenlied	Skald
Brunhild	Niflheim	Snorri Sturluson
Edda	Norns	Tannhäuser
Elf	Odin	Thor
Frey	Saga	Valhalla
Freyja	Siegfried	Valkyrie
Loki	Sigurd	Volsunga Saga

HINDU MYTHOLOGY

Bhagavad-Gita	Manu	Thug
Brahman	Ramayana	Vedas
Juggernaut	Shiva	Vishnu
Mahabharata		

OTHER RELATED ARTICLES

Astarte	Malinowski, Bronislaw
Bulfinch (Thomas)	Marduk
Folklore	Moon (Mythology)
Frazer, Sir James G.	Pyramus and Thisbe
Gilgamesh, Epic of	Sun (Mythology and
Indian, American (Religion)	Sun Worship)
Lévi-Strauss, Claude	Tylor, Sir Edward B.

Outline

I. What Myths Are About
   A. Mythical Beings
   B. Mythical Places
   C. Mythical Symbols
   D. Comparing Myths
II. Egyptian Mythology
   A. The Great Ennead
   B. The Osiris Myth
   C. Other Egyptian Divinities
   D. The Influence of Egyptian Mythology
III. Greek Mythology
   A. The Creation Myth
   B. Greek Divinities
   C. Greek Heroes
IV. Roman Mythology
   A. Roman Divinities
   B. Romulus and Remus
   C. The Seven Kings
   D. The *Aeneid*
V. Celtic Mythology
   A. The Irish Cycles
   B. Welsh Myths
VI. Teutonic Mythology
   A. The Creation of Life

B. The Construction of the World
C. Teutonic Heroes
D. The End of the World
VII. Hindu Mythology
   A. The Vedas   C. The Hindu Epics
   B. Brahman
VIII. Mythology of the Pacific Islands
   A. Creation Myths   C. Mana and Taboo
   B. Pacific Islands Divinities
IX. African Mythology
X. American Indian Mythology
XI. How Myths Began
   A. Euhemerus' Theory
   B. Müller's Theory
   C. Tylor's Theory
   D. Malinowski's Theory
   E. Frazer's Theory
XII. What Mythology Tells Us About People
   A. Mythology and Society
   B. Mythology and the Individual

Questions

What is the difference between a *generic* and a *genetic* relationship among myths?

What is the function of a *fetish* in African mythology?

In Egyptian mythology, what was the *Great Ennead?*

What is the importance of the *Theogony* in Greek mythology?

How does a myth differ from a folk tale?

In Hindu mythology, what is the *Mahabharata?* The *Ramayana?* The *Bhagavad-Gita?*

What is the function of a *creation* myth? An *explanatory* myth?

What is the theory of *collective representation?*

In Pacific Islands mythology, what is *mana?* What is *taboo?*

What is the *mythological cycle* in Celtic mythology? The *Ulster cycle?*

Reading and Study Guide

See *Mythology* in the RESEARCH GUIDE/INDEX, Volume 22, for a *Reading and Study Guide.*

Books for Young Readers

BENSON, SALLY. *Stories of the Gods and Heroes.* Dial, 1940.
COLUM, PADRAIC. *The Children of Odin.* Macmillan, 1920. *The Golden Fleece and the Heroes Who Lived Before Achilles.* 1921.

COOLIDGE, OLIVIA E. *Greek Myths.* Houghton, 1949. *Legends of the North.* 1951.
D'AULAIRE, INGRI and EDGAR P. *D'Aulaires' Book of Greek Myths.* Doubleday, 1962. *Norse Gods and Giants.* 1967.
GATES, DORIS. *A Fair Wind for Troy.* Viking, 1976.
GRAVES, ROBERT. *Greek Gods and Heroes.* Doubleday, 1960.
HAWTHORNE, NATHANIEL. *A Wonder Book, and Tanglewood Tales.* Houghton, 1951. A reprinting of books first published in 1852 and 1853, respectively.
HOSFORD, DOROTHY G. *Thunder of the Gods.* Holt, 1952.
SEED, JENNY. *The Bushman's Dream: African Tales of the Creation.* Dutton, 1975.

Books for Older Readers

BULFINCH, THOMAS. *Bulfinch's Mythology: The Age of Fable; The Age of Chivalry; Legends of Charlemagne.* 2nd ed. Harper, 1970. A modern edition of books first published separately in 1855, 1858, and 1863.
CAMPBELL, JOSEPH. *The Masks of God: Primitive Mythology.* Viking, 1959. *The Masks of God: Oriental Mythology.* 1962. *The Masks of God: Occidental Mythology.* 1964. *The Masks of God: Creative Mythology.* 1968.
COOMARASWAMY, ANANDA K., and SISTER NIVEDITA. *Myths of the Hindus and Buddhists.* Dover, 1967. A reissue of a work originally published in 1913.
COURLANDER, HAROLD. *Tales of Yoruba Gods and Heroes.* Crown, 1973.
FRAZER, JAMES G. *The New Golden Bough.* Abridged ed. by Theodor H. Gaster. Phillips, 1959.
GRAVES, ROBERT. *The Greek Myths.* Rev. ed. 2 vols. Penguin, 1960.
HAMILTON, EDITH. *Mythology.* Little, Brown, 1942.
HENDRICKS, RHODA A., ed. *Classical Gods and Heroes: Myths as Told by the Ancient Authors.* Morrow, 1974.
Larousse World Mythology. Ed. by Pierre Grimal. Putnam, 1968.
MacCULLOCH, JOHN A., and other eds. *Mythology of All Races.* 13 vols. Cooper Square, no date. Reprint of 1932 ed.
ROSE, HERBERT J. *A Handbook of Greek Mythology.* Dutton, 1928.
TRIPP, EDWARD. *Crowell's Handbook of Classical Mythology.* Harper, 1970.
ZIMMERMAN, JOHN E. *Dictionary of Classical Mythology.* Harper, 1964.

MYXEDEMA. See GOITER.

MYXOMATOSIS. See RABBIT (Diseases).